City Crime Rankings
2013

Other titles in the State Fact Finder series

Crime State Rankings (now part of **State Stats**)
Education State Rankings (now part of **State Stats**)
Health Care State Rankings (now part of **State Stats**)
State Rankings

State Stats online database

What is *State Stats*? Drawing together the statistics from the *State Rankings* series of books by CQ Press and Morgan Quitno Press, *State Stats* is a new database from CQ Press that delivers a dynamic and engaging user experience that is unmatched in other resources. Featuring data from more than 80 different government and nongovernment sources and backed by a rich collection of more than 2,000 current and historical data series on popular topics of research interest, *State Stats* uniquely allows users to discover, view, and export key information measures for the 50 states and the District of Columbia.

Check it out online at http://library.cqpress.com/statestats.

State Stats makes research easy by providing in one place annual measures dating back more than 15 years. Data series are displayed in a clear and consistent format with detailed source information. Numerous topics are covered in categories including Agriculture; Crime and Law Enforcement, Defense; Demographics; Economics; Education; Employment and Labor; Geography, Energy, and the Environment; Health and Medicine; Social Welfare; Taxes and Government Finance; and Transportation.

The benefit of *State Stats* is in its ease of use and clean and concise presentation of data and trends. An intuitive interface lets users easily browse by state or by topic and then compare across states or across time. Users can then share, save, and export data. *State Stats* also features CQ Press's CiteNow!® function for generating source citations in APA, MLA, Chicago, or Bluebook styles.

Users can:

- Analyze data patterns by comparing across states, data series, and time
- Create and export custom visuals including line charts, scatterplots, and maps
- Generate tables and download data for statistical research
- Toggle user display between interactive visual and tabular data view
- Engage a moveable timeline to discover trends
- Explore interactive maps featuring zoom and hover functions

State Stats is cross-searchable with other CQ Press online products including *CQ Researcher* and the *CQ Press Political Reference Suite*. Ongoing updates to *State Stats* throughout the year ensure that users have the most current data available.

Working on an advanced data research project? The optional, advanced State Stats Data Cart allows for bulk data export across single-click download of complete data series and multiple series.

City Crime Rankings 2013

Crime in Metropolitan America

Kathleen O'Leary Morgan
and
Scott Morgan
with
Rachel Boba Santos

SAGE reference | **CQPRESS**

Los Angeles | London | New Delhi
Singapore | Washington DC

SAGE | CQPRESS

Los Angeles | London | New Delhi
Singapore | Washington DC

For information:

SAGE Publications, Inc.
2455 Teller Road
Thousand Oaks, California 91320
E-mail: order@sagepub.com

SAGE Publications Ltd.
1 Oliver's Yard
55 City Road
London, EC1Y 1SP
United Kingdom

SAGE Publications India Pvt. Ltd.
B 1/I 1 Mohan Cooperative Industrial Area
Mathura Road, New Delhi 110 044
India

SAGE Publications Asia-Pacific Pte. Ltd.
3 Church Street
#10-04 Samsung Hub
Singapore 049483

Publisher: Rolf A. Janke
Developmental Editor: John Martino
Production Editor: Tracy Buyan
Copy Editor: Pam Schroeder
Cover Designers: Silverander Communications, Michael Dubowe
Marketing Manager: Carmel Schrire

Copyright © 2013 by CQ Press, an imprint of SAGE.
CQ Press is a registered trademark of Congressional Quarterly Inc.

All rights reserved. No part of this book may be reproduced or utilized in any form or by any means, electronic or mechanical, including photocopying, recording, or by any information storage and retrieval system, without permission in writing from the publisher.

Printed in the United States of America.

SUSTAINABLE FORESTRY INITIATIVE
Certified Chain of Custody
Promoting Sustainable Forestry
www.sfiprogram.org
SFI-01268
SFI label applies to text stock

ISBN 978-1-4522-2520-3

13 14 15 16 17 10 9 8 7 6 5 4 3 2 1

Contents

Detailed Table of Contents — vi

Introduction and Methodology — viii

Distribution Analysis — xii

2012 Metropolitan Crime Rate Rankings — xx

2012 City Crime Rate Rankings — xxiv

Subject Rankings

Metropolitan Area Crime Statistics	1
City Crime Statistics	163
Metropolitan and City Populations	341

Appendix — **367**

Detailed Table of Contents

I. METROPOLITAN AREA CRIME STATISTICS

Crimes in 2011 2
Crime Rate in 2011 6
Percent Change in Crime Rate: 2010 to 2011 10
Percent Change in Crime Rate: 2007 to 2011 14
Violent Crimes in 2011 18
Violent Crime Rate in 2011 22
Percent Change in Violent Crime Rate: 2010 to 2011 26
Percent Change in Violent Crime Rate: 2007 to 2011 30
Murders in 2011 34
Murder Rate in 2011 38
Percent Change in Murder Rate: 2010 to 2011 42
Percent Change in Murder Rate: 2007 to 2011 46
Rapes in 2011 50
Rape Rate in 2011 54
Percent Change in Rape Rate: 2010 to 2011 58
Percent Change in Rape Rate: 2007 to 2011 62
Robberies in 2011 66
Robbery Rate in 2011 70
Percent Change in Robbery Rate: 2010 to 2011 74
Percent Change in Robbery Rate: 2007 to 2011 78
Aggravated Assaults in 2011 82
Aggravated Assault Rate in 2011 86
Percent Change in Aggravated Assault Rate:
   2010 to 2011 90
Percent Change in Aggravated Assault Rate:
   2007 to 2011 94
Property Crimes in 2011 98
Property Crime Rate in 2011 102
Percent Change in Property Crime Rate: 2010 to 2011 ... 106
Percent Change in Property Crime Rate: 2007 to 2011 ... 110
Burglaries in 2011 114
Burglary Rate in 2011 118
Percent Change in Burglary Rate: 2010 to 2011 122
Percent Change in Burglary Rate: 2007 to 2011 126
Larceny-Thefts in 2011 130
Larceny-Theft Rate in 2011 134
Percent Change in Larceny-Theft Rate: 2010 to 2011 ... 138
Percent Change in Larceny-Theft Rate: 2007 to 2011 ... 142

Motor Vehicle Thefts in 2011 146
Motor Vehicle Theft Rate in 2011 150
Percent Change in Motor Vehicle Theft Rate:
   2010 to 2011 154
Percent Change in Motor Vehicle Theft Rate:
   2007 to 2011 158

II. CITY CRIME STATISTICS (FOR CITIES LARGER THAN 75,000 POPULATION)

Crimes in 2011 164
Crime Rate in 2011 168
Percent Change in Crime Rate: 2010 to 2011 172
Percent Change in Crime Rate: 2007 to 2011 176
Violent Crimes in 2011 180
Violent Crime Rate in 2011 184
Percent Change in Violent Crime Rate: 2010 to 2011 ... 188
Percent Change in Violent Crime Rate: 2007 to 2011 ... 192
Murders in 2011 196
Murder Rate in 2011 200
Percent Change in Murder Rate: 2010 to 2011 204
Percent Change in Murder Rate: 2007 to 2011 208
Rapes in 2011 212
Rape Rate in 2011 216
Percent Change in Rape Rate: 2010 to 2011 220
Percent Change in Rape Rate: 2007 to 2011 224
Robberies in 2011 228
Robbery Rate in 2011 232
Percent Change in Robbery Rate: 2010 to 2011 236
Percent Change in Robbery Rate: 2007 to 2011 240
Aggravated Assaults in 2011 244
Aggravated Assault Rate in 2011 248
Percent Change in Aggravated Assault Rate:
   2010 to 2011 252
Percent Change in Aggravated Assault Rate:
   2007 to 2011 256
Property Crimes in 2011 260
Property Crime Rate in 2011 264
Percent Change in Property Crime Rate: 2010 to 2011 ... 268
Percent Change in Property Crime Rate: 2007 to 2011 ... 272

Burglaries in 2011 276
Burglary Rate in 2011 280
Percent Change in Burglary Rate: 2010 to 2011 284
Percent Change in Burglary Rate: 2007 to 2011 288
Larceny-Thefts in 2011 292
Larceny-Theft Rate in 2011 296
Percent Change in Larceny-Theft Rate: 2010 to 2011 300
Percent Change in Larceny-Theft Rate: 2007 to 2011 304
Motor Vehicle Thefts in 2011 308
Motor Vehicle Theft Rate in 2011 312
Percent Change in Motor Vehicle Theft Rate:
   2010 to 2011 316
Percent Change in Motor Vehicle Theft Rate:
   2007 to 2011 320
Police Officers in 2011 324
Rate of Police Officers in 2011 328
Percent Change in Rate of Police Officers: 2010 to 2011 . . 332
Percent Change in Rate of Police Officers:
   2007 to 2011 336

III. METROPOLITAN AND CITY POPULATIONS
Metropolitan Population in 2011 342
Metropolitan Population in 2010 346
Metropolitan Population in 2007 350
City Population in 2011 354
City Population in 2010 358
City Population in 2007 362

APPENDIX
Descriptions of Metropolitan Areas in 2011 368
County Index: 2011 375
National Crime Trends: 1992 to 2011 382
National, Metropolitan, and City Crime Statistics
   Summary: 2011 388

Introduction and Methodology

City Crime Rankings 2013 analyzes the latest (2011) FBI crime statistics for U.S. metropolitan areas and cities with populations of 75,000 or more. *City Crime Rankings* starts off by describing the data and methodology used in the rankings; it then provides a comparative analysis of cities and metropolitan areas, a distribution analysis of comparison scores and rates, and additional information and caveats regarding the analyzed data. The data and their limitations, the methodology, and the results of the comparative analysis of six types of reported crime are discussed. Also presented are charts illustrating the distribution of values for selected analyses along with the related statistics for the median, mean, standard deviation, minimum value, and maximum value. Lastly, the definitions of crimes based on the FBI's coding system are presented with supporting facts and caveats that provide context to the numbers presented in this volume.

The two main sections of the book, Metropolitan Area Crime Statistics and City Crime Statistics, report the statistics for 368 metropolitan areas and 437 cities with populations of 75,000 or more. Each section has 40 tables, presented in both alphabetical and rank order, that compare the actual numbers of reported crimes, crime rates, and percent changes over periods of one year (2010–2011) and five years (2007–2011). Each table spans four pages with the first two pages displaying the metro areas and cities in alphabetical order and the third and fourth pages displaying them in rank order. In addition, *City Crime Rankings* presents the actual numbers, rates, and percent change in police officers employed per capita by law enforcement agencies in each city.

To be included in this edition, cities must have reported crime data to the FBI for 2011. Metropolitan areas must have met two criteria: First, their central city or cities must have submitted 12 months of data in 2011, and second, at least 75% of all law enforcement agencies located in a specific metro area must have reported crime statistics for 2011. (The cities and metro areas not meeting these requirements were excluded from this edition of *City Crime Rankings* and are listed in the Missing Cities and Metro Areas section.)

The third section, the Metropolitan and City Population, presents population data for the cities and metro areas included in *City Crime Rankings*. It is followed by an appendix consisting of a listing of the counties and cities within each metropolitan area, a county index for 2011, and figures illustrating rates for each reported crime category for the past 20 years, with an examination of national trends and perspective of crime in the United States and a summary table of the 2011 national, metropolitan, and city crime statistics.

Purpose of This Book

The purpose of *City Crime Rankings* is to serve as a resource for researchers, city and law enforcement officials, and the community. The book provides the means by which individuals can compare local communities to other similar communities through contrast with the national level of reported crime—more specifically, crime rates per 100,000 for individual types of reported crime, for violent and property crime categories, and for overall crime.

In editions prior to the 2009 to 2010 edition, the terms *safest* and *dangerous* were used to describe the cities and metropolitan areas with the lowest and highest rankings in the comparative analysis, respectively. Even though the rankings are still provided, these terms are no longer used because perceptions of safety and danger are just that—perceptions. The data analyzed here are *reported crime* and *population*, which together constitute only two factors considered when determining safety or risk of crime victimization. Thus, the analyses in this book are purely descriptive. At no time do we attempt to explain why reported crime rates are higher or lower from one community to the next. These explanations—currently sought by criminologists and other social science researchers—are beyond the scope of this book.

Consequently, to enhance the usefulness of *City Crime Rankings,* a new section was introduced in the 2009 to 2010 edition and is continued subsequent editions. The Distribution Analysis section (see page xii) provides histograms of the comparison score and reported crime rate distributions as well as measures of central tendency such as median, mean, standard deviation, and minimum and maximum values for each distribution. Because the rank ordering of scores and crime rates does not illustrate the relative difference between metro areas' and cities' values, this analysis is provided, so the reader can better understand how the values are distributed and where a particular metro area's or city's ranking falls in comparison to others.

These statistics are used in a variety of ways, by a range of audiences, including the following:

- Law enforcement agencies use them to help identify crime problems for further study (Center for Problem-Oriented Policing, 2012).
- City governments compare their cities' crime levels to those of other jurisdictions to determine how their rates appear in relation to one another.
- The federal government uses this type of analysis to allocate grant funding (Bauer, 2004).
- The media publish these results to report and compare crime rates across cities and years.

In addition, it is important to examine the statistics of a city along with its metro area when using *City Crime Rankings*. Although a city's scores and rates are useful for understanding the crime levels within the boundaries of that city and for making comparisons to other law enforcement jurisdictions, criminals and opportunities for crime do not adhere to city boundaries but rather spill over to adjacent (i.e., metro) areas. In fact, crime rates and comparison scores tend to be lower in metro areas than in individual cities because many of the more populous cities are geographically small and include central business, retail, and industrial areas where residential population is low. These nonresidential areas contain more victims and targets (e.g., commuters, merchandise, vehicles) than do residential areas, so their crime rates appear higher when population is used as the denominator in the calculation of the crime rate. Researchers who study low-population areas within cities often use other denominators to determine rates, such as number of vehicles parked in lots for auto theft, number of businesses for commercial burglary, or square footage of retail establishments for shoplifting and theft (Santos, 2012).

However, these variables are not easily obtained for all U.S. cities. By expanding the geographic unit from city to metro area to include business, retail, industrial, and residential areas, using population of the entire area as a basis for determining rate is more practical. Thus, combining a major city with its suburbs provides an overall view of how crime is present in interrelated communities. For example, the city of West Palm Beach, FL, has a relatively low population, but it contains a large number of retail, commercial, and tourist locations and is the principal city in a much larger, more diverse metropolitan area. The table below presents the 2011 population, comparison scores, and rates for the city of West Palm Beach, FL, and the metro area of West Palm Beach, FL, Metropolitan Division (MD). As shown, there is a large difference between the city and its metro area for each variable. Thus, city statistics and metro-area statistics both serve useful purposes and should be considered together when examining a city situated within a metro area.

The Data and Their Limitations

The data featured in *City Crime Rankings* come from the FBI publication *Crime in the United States* (2012), which is available every fall (e.g., November 2012) and presents information for the previous year (e.g., 2011). This report is based on data collected through the Uniform Crime Reporting (UCR) Program, which began in 1930. The purpose of the UCR Program has been to develop reliable information about crime reported to law enforcement that can be used by law enforcement as well as by criminologists, sociologists, legislators, municipal planners, and the media for a variety of research and planning purposes. Although the program is voluntary, in 2011, more than 18,200 city, university and college, county, state, tribal, and federal law enforcement agencies provide information representing more than 99% of the population (FBI, 2012a).

Although law enforcement agencies collect common information on crimes reported to and discovered by them, each state has slightly different criminal laws, and each law enforcement agency has its own policies and procedures for recording activity. These differences make it very difficult to compare statistics across agencies. To classify criminal activity consistently, the UCR Program was created. The UCR Program provides national standards for the uniform classification of crimes and arrests (for further details, visit the FBI's Web site at http://www.fbi.gov/stats-services/crimestats). Notably, the UCR crime definitions are distinct and do not conform to federal or state laws.

There are well-documented criticisms of the UCR data that must be considered when using these data for any purpose. But while the nature of the data and their limitations should be understood, they should not preclude researchers, practitioners, and others from using the data to understand crime and guide policy decisions. The following is a brief discussion of the major issues and concerns surrounding UCR data.

While individual law enforcement agencies classify reported crimes based on the laws of their own states and jurisdictions, these agencies reclassify these crimes according to UCR definitions when reporting them and provide aggregate counts of (a) particular crimes (known as *Part I crimes:* murder, rape, robbery, aggravated assault, burglary, larceny–theft, motor vehicle theft, and arson) and (b) arrests for all crimes. Note that the FBI does not report the aggregate counts of *Part II crimes*—including simple assault, fraud, prostitution, and DUI—it reports only the arrests that occur. Thus, when statistics about reported violent and property crime are published in this or any other book or article, they are only based on the eight Part I crimes.

In addition, UCR reporting requires the use of a hierarchical coding system that means, if two crimes happen during one incident, only one is counted. For example, if one person is the victim of both rape and robbery, only the rape will be counted, or if a car is stolen out of a locked garage, it is considered a burglary, not a burglary and an auto theft. The UCR Program

	2011 Population	Comparison Score	Overall Crime Rate	Violent Crime Rate	Property Crime Rate
West Palm Beach, FL	101,281	101.01	6,074.2	759.3	5,314.9
West Palm Beach, FL, MD	1,338,125	11.77	3,913.8	492.1	3,421.7

has specific rules for coding that are not detailed here; however, the result is that the actual number of reported crimes might be underestimated in that the number of incidents is counted and not the number of unique crimes that occur.

The factor of actual versus reported crime is probably the most important one to consider when interpreting statistics based on UCR data. That is, the data provided to the FBI contain only those crimes reported or known to law enforcement as opposed to all crime that has actually occurred. We know from victimization surveys that not all crimes are reported to law enforcement (Bureau of Justice Statistics, 2012) and that different types of crimes are reported at different levels. The Bureau of Justice Statistics estimates from the National Crime Victimization Survey that violent crime is reported 40% to 50% of the time and that property crime is reported 30% to 40% of the time (Bureau of Justice Statistics, 2012). When UCR data are analyzed, we must recognize that the data do not represent the actual amount of crime. However, if the data are collected accurately and consistently, they can be used, with caution, to make comparisons across geographic areas and over time.

Additional criticisms of the UCR data include inaccuracy due to inputting errors and handling of missing data (Lynch & Jarvis, 2008; Maltz, 1999), pressure on some law enforcement agencies to "doctor" the numbers, and the use of aggregate numbers that mask other factors such as time of day, location, and circumstance of the crime (e.g., whether the crime is committed by a stranger or family member). Yet, the UCR data are the most comprehensive and consistently collected data on crime in the United States. In most cases, analysis of UCR data begins the conversation, and additional in-depth analysis of crime in local areas is required to really understand the nature and context of crime problems (Santos, 2012).

Methodology

As noted above, the crimes tracked by the UCR Program include the violent crimes of murder, rape, robbery, and aggravated assault and the property crimes of burglary, larceny-theft, motor vehicle theft, and arson. These crimes are also sometimes known as *Crime Index* offenses; the index is simply the total of the eight main offense categories. The FBI discontinued use of this measure in 2004 because its officials and advisory board of criminologists concluded that the index was no longer a true indicator of crime. The primary concern was that the Crime Index was inflated by a high number of larceny-thefts, which account for nearly 60% of reported crime, thereby diminishing the focus on more serious but less frequently reported offenses, such as murder and rape. The consensus of the FBI and its advisory groups was that the Crime Index no longer served its purpose and that a more meaningful index should be developed.

While the FBI considers how it will replace the Crime Index, *City Crime Rankings* continues to provide total crime numbers, rates, and trends for U.S. cities and metropolitan areas as a service to readers. We offer a cautionary note, however, that in 2011, larceny-theft comprised 60.0% of all reported crimes.

Our analyses are conducted on two geographic units: the city and the metropolitan statistical area (MSA) as provided by the FBI. The cities included in these analyses are those with populations of 75,000 or more. According to the FBI in 2011,

> each MSA contains a principal city or urbanized area with a population of at least 50,000 inhabitants. MSAs include the principal city; the county in which the city is located; and other adjacent counties that have, as defined by the OMB, a high degree of economic and social integration with the principal city and county as measured through commuting. In the UCR Program, counties within an MSA are considered metropolitan. In addition, MSAs may cross state boundaries. (FBI, 2012b)

The methodology used to produce the statistics presented in this book is fairly straightforward. In the first analysis, a score is calculated for each metropolitan area and city; this score is a summary of the percent differences of the reported crime rate from the national rate of six crime types (excluding larceny-theft and arson). Because this formula is unique to this book, it is described in detail below. The rest of the analyses are simple calculations of reported crime rates per 100,000 population and percent change for one year and five years. Lastly, all the analyses present a ranking that is a simple sort of the values computed for the analysis and numbered from highest to lowest. In case of a tie, the rankings are listed alphabetically. Parentheses indicate negative numbers and rates (except in the data distribution charts). Data reported as *NA* are not available or could not be calculated. The national totals and rates appearing at the top of each table are for the entire United States, including both metropolitan and nonmetropolitan areas. Specific totals for metropolitan areas and larger cities are provided in the Appendix.

Comparison Score Methodology

The methodology for determining the city and metro area comparison crime rate rankings involves a multistep process in which the reported crimes per 100,000 population rate are compared to the national reported crimes per 100,000 population rate and then indexed to create a summary score and ranking across six areas of reported violent and property crime. The methodology used for this edition of the book has been used for the past 13 editions and is described here in detail.

Reported crime rates per 100,000 population in 2011 across six crime categories—murder, rape, robbery, aggravated assault, burglary, and motor vehicle theft—were examined in this analysis. Larceny-theft was removed from this analysis because of the aforementioned concerns noted by the FBI and others. Cities with populations of 75,000 or more that reported data for the six categories of crime measured were included in the analysis. There is no population minimum for metropolitan areas. In all, 432 cities and 358 metro areas were included in the results.

The following are steps for the comparison score calculation and examples that illustrate the calculations:

1. The 100,000 residents of a city or metropolitan area is calculated from the reported crime and population data provided to the FBI by local law enforcement agencies for a particular type of crime. In the example that follows, the

Example: City A, Population 150,000

	Murder	Rape	Robbery	Aggravated Assault	Burglary	Motor Vehicle Theft
Reported Crime Count	11	31	126	375	957	175
City Rate per 100,000	7.33	20.67	84.00	250.00	638.00	116.67
National Rate	4.7	26.8	113.7	241.1	702.2	229.6
Percent Difference	55.96	(22.87)	(26.12)	3.69	(9.14)	(49.19)
Weighting Factor	0.1667	0.1667	0.1667	0.1667	0.1667	0.1667
Resulting Score	9.33	(3.81)	(4.35)	0.62	(1.52)	(8.20)

calculation for murder is 11 divided by 150,000 multiplied by 100,000, which results in a 7.33 per capita reported murder rate per 100,000 people for that year.

2. The percent difference between the metro area or city rate and the national rate for each of the six crimes is then computed. The use of percent difference for each crime separately eliminates weighting more frequent crimes more heavily (e.g., a city may have 1 murder and 1,500 burglaries). Negative numbers are displayed in parentheses here and throughout the analysis tables. The formula for this calculation is:

$$\frac{\text{Metro Area Rate or City Rate} - \text{National Rate}}{\text{National Rate}} \times 100$$

3. The number is then scaled to be one-sixth of the index to make it comparable to scores in the previous editions of this book. A number of years ago, each of the six crimes was weighted based on the results of a telephone survey that determined which crimes were of greatest concern to Americans. The polls indicated that most Americans believed crimes such as burglary are more likely to happen in their lives than more serious crimes such as murder. Thus, burglary received the highest weight, and murder received the lowest weight in the formula. In subsequent years, the polling was discontinued, and consequently, the weights were eliminated. However, equal weight is assigned to the crimes during this step in the analysis so that future scores will be more closely comparable to the scores with the weighted factors.

4. The final comparison score for each metro area and city is the sum of the individual scores for the six crimes. In this case, the sum is –7.93. The interpretation of these scores is that the higher a metro area or city score, the further above the national score; the lower the score, the further below the national score; and a score of 0 is equal to the national score.

5. The scores are then sorted from highest to lowest to produce the rankings. Note that the rankings do not indicate the actual difference between the scores, only their order. The 19th Annual America's Cities and Metropolitan Areas with the Highest and Lowest Crimes Rates tables on pages xx–xxvii provide the results of the metro area and city scores. The Metropolitan and Cities Comparison Scores Distribution Analysis for 2011 on pages xiii–xvi provides the results of the distribution of these scores.

This methodology results in a score for each metro area and city that compares its rate to the national rates, providing a means to gauge crime trends in communities.

References

Bauer, L. (2004). *Local law enforcement block grant program, 1996–2004.* Washington, DC: Bureau of Justice Statistics.

Bureau of Justice Statistics. (2012). *Percent of total crime reported to the police.* Retrieved November 8, 2012, from http://bjs.ojp.usdoj.gov

Center for Problem-Oriented Policing. (2012). Retrieved November 8, 2012, from www.popcenter.org

FBI. (2012a). *Crime in the United States.* Retrieved November 8, 2012, from http://www.fbi.gov/about-us/cjis/ucr/crime-in-the-u.s/2011/crime-in-the-u.s.-2011

FBI. (2012b). *Area Definitions.* Retrieved November 8, 2012, from http://www.fbi.gov/about-us/cjis/ucr/crime-in-the-u.s/2011/crime-in-the-u.s.-2011/area-definitions

Lynch, J. P., & Jarvis, J. P. (2008). Missing data and imputation in the Uniform Crime Reports and the effects on national estimates. *Journal of Contemporary Criminal Justice, 24,* 69–85.

Maltz, M. (1999). *Bridging gaps in police crime data.* Washington, DC: Bureau of Justice Statistics.

Santos, R. B. (2012). *Crime analysis with crime mapping.* Thousand Oaks, CA: Sage.

Distribution Analysis

This section presents charts depicting the distributions of the comparison scores as well as the individual and collective reported crime rates shown in *City Crime Rankings* to provide a mechanism of comparison beyond the rankings included in each analysis. The histograms in this section illustrate the distribution of values for the comparison score analyses as well as for the overall, violent, and property crime rate analyses. Along with each histogram, measures of central tendency, such as median, mean, standard deviation, and minimum and maximum values, are reported to provide further description of each distribution.

In each histogram (formatted as area charts for easier viewing), the values of the scores or rates are shown along the bottom (*x*-axis), and the frequency of cases (i.e., metro areas or cities) are shown along the left (*y*-axis). The values along the bottom are ranges for which the frequency of cases is totaled. These ranges and frequencies are different for each distribution, in this case, each histogram.

The median indicates the middle value of the distribution, meaning that 50% of the metro areas or cities have scores or rates above that value, and 50% have scores or rates below it. The mean is the average value of the distribution, and the standard deviation, described generally, is the measure of the spread of all the values from the mean. The minimum and maximum values are the lowest and highest values of the distribution, respectively.

These statistics are based on a normal curve, so one standard deviation above and below the mean contains 68% of the distribution, two standard deviations above and below the mean contain 95% of the distribution, and three standard deviations above and below the mean contain 99.7% of the distribution. The use of these statistics is purely descriptive, but it does help the reader assess the distribution as a whole as well as illustrate where an individual value sits in terms of all the other values. For example, if a score is two or three standard deviations above or below the mean, it may be considered an outlier because it falls with only 5% or 0.3% of the values, respectively.

For example, Figure 1 depicts the comparison scores for metro areas in 2011. The median is –5.4, the mean is –2.7, the standard deviation is 36.3, the minimum value is –84.2, and the maximum value is 182.2. These statistics are interpreted as follows:

- The lowest comparison score for metro areas is –84.2.
- The highest comparison score for metro areas is 182.2.
- The range of scores (maximum minus minimum) is 266.4.
- Fifty percent of the metro areas have comparison scores lower than –5.4, and 50% have scores higher than –5.4.
- The average comparison score for metro areas is –2.7, and the standard deviation is 36.3.
- 68% of the metro areas have scores between –39.0 and 33.6.
- 95% of the metro areas have scores between –75.3 and 69.9.
- 99.7% of the metro areas have scores between –111.6 and 106.2. (The fact that the lower end of this range [–111.6] is less than the minimum value of the distribution [–84.2] indicates the distribution is skewed.)

Assessing the score of 63.44 for the metropolitan area of Oakland-Fremont, California, for example, reveals that it is in the higher 50% of all the scores (above the median of –5.4) and falls between the first and second standard deviation above the mean with 95% of the other scores (between –75.3 and 69.9).

The remainder of this section presents a total of six charts and sets of statistics for both metropolitan areas and cities in the categories listed here:

1. Comparison Score
2. Overall Reported Crime
3. Reported Violent Crime
4. Reported Property Crime

A word of caution: These distribution analysis charts and statistics are provided to help the reader understand the nature of the values within each analysis, but the analyses are still based on data that must be interpreted within the constraints noted earlier. These charts are only descriptions of the data and do not provide predictions or explanations of why these values are different.

Missing Cities and Metropolitan Areas

To be included in the comparative analysis, cities and metro areas must report data for six crime categories: murder, rape robbery, aggravated assault, burglary, and motor vehicle theft. All metro areas and all cities with populations of 75,000 or more that reported crime data to the FBI were included. A number of

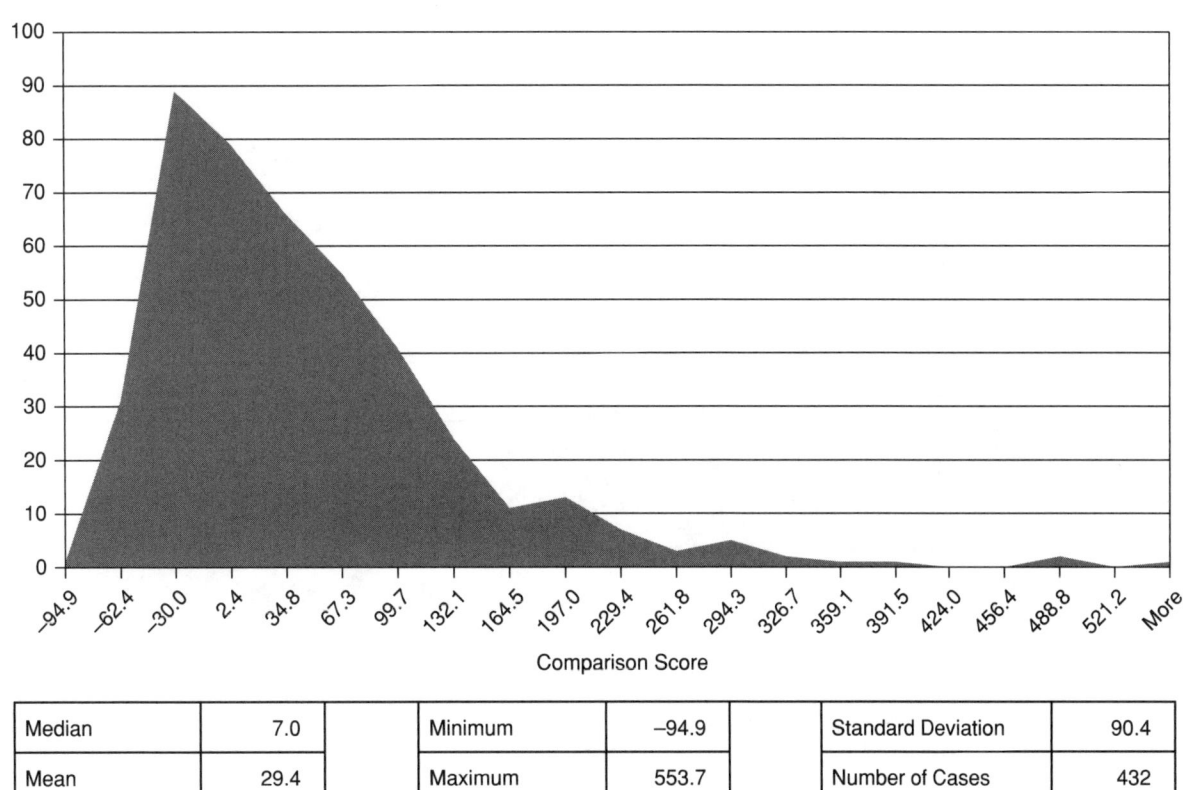

Figure 1 Metropolitan Areas Comparison Score Distribution Analysis for 2011

Frequency of MSAs

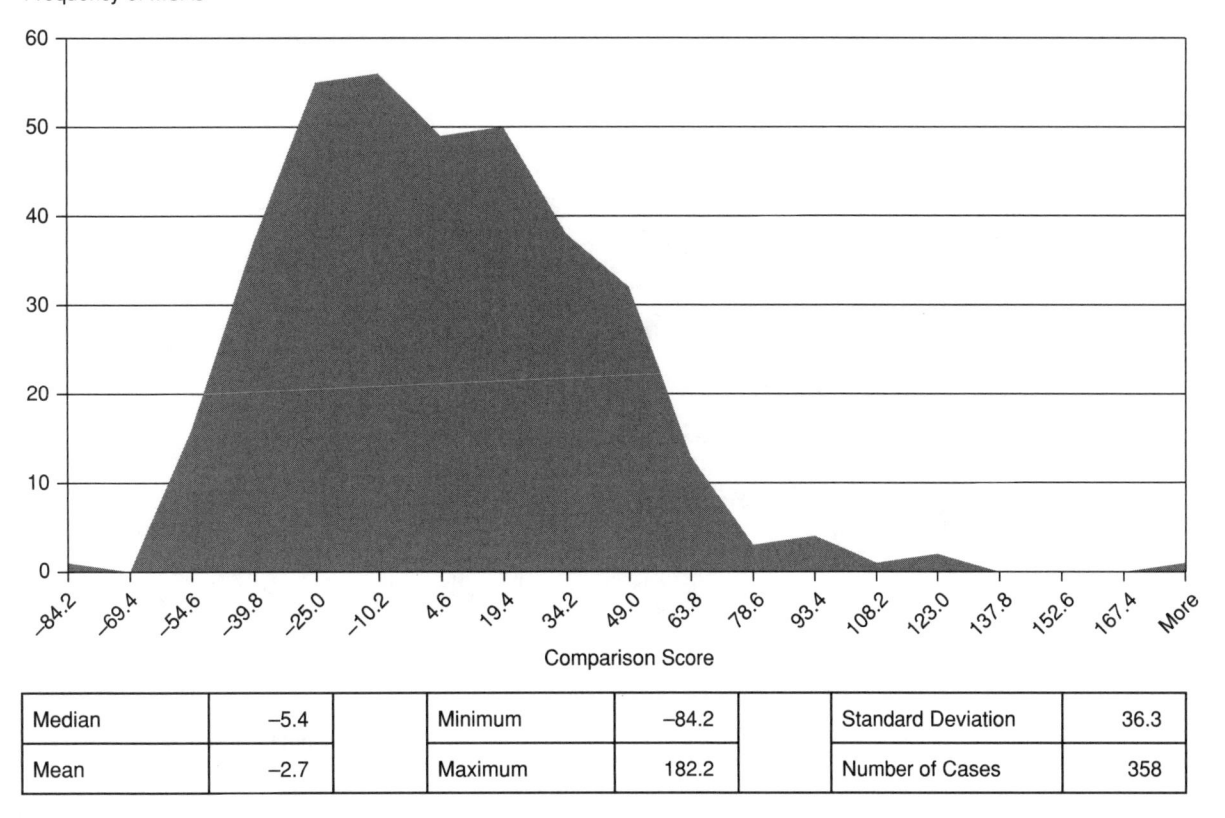

Median	−5.4	Minimum	−84.2	Standard Deviation	36.3
Mean	−2.7	Maximum	182.2	Number of Cases	358

Figure 2 Cities Comparison Score Distribution Analysis for 2011

Frequency of Cities

Median	7.0	Minimum	−94.9	Standard Deviation	90.4
Mean	29.4	Maximum	553.7	Number of Cases	432

Figure 3 Metropolitan Areas Overall Reported Crime Rate Distribution Analysis for 2011

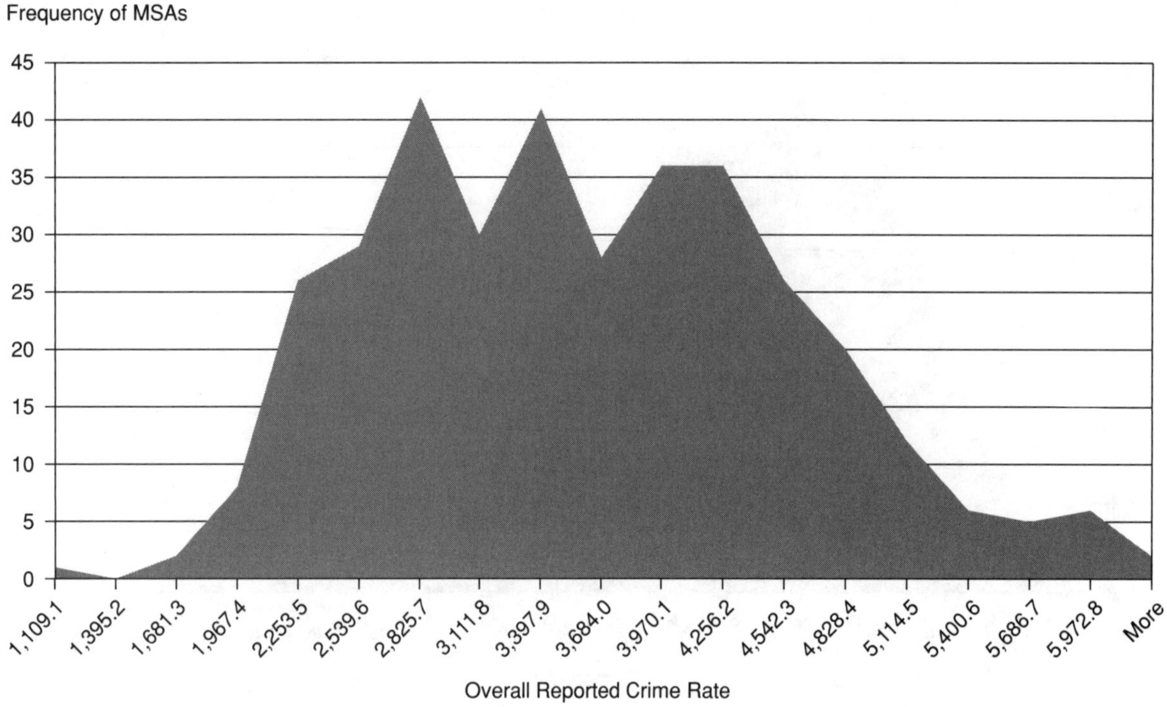

Median	3,397.5		Minimum	1,109.1		Standard Deviation	967.0
Mean	3,482.0		Maximum	6,258.9		Number of Cases	356

Figure 4 Cities Overall Reported Crime Rate Distribution Analysis for 2011

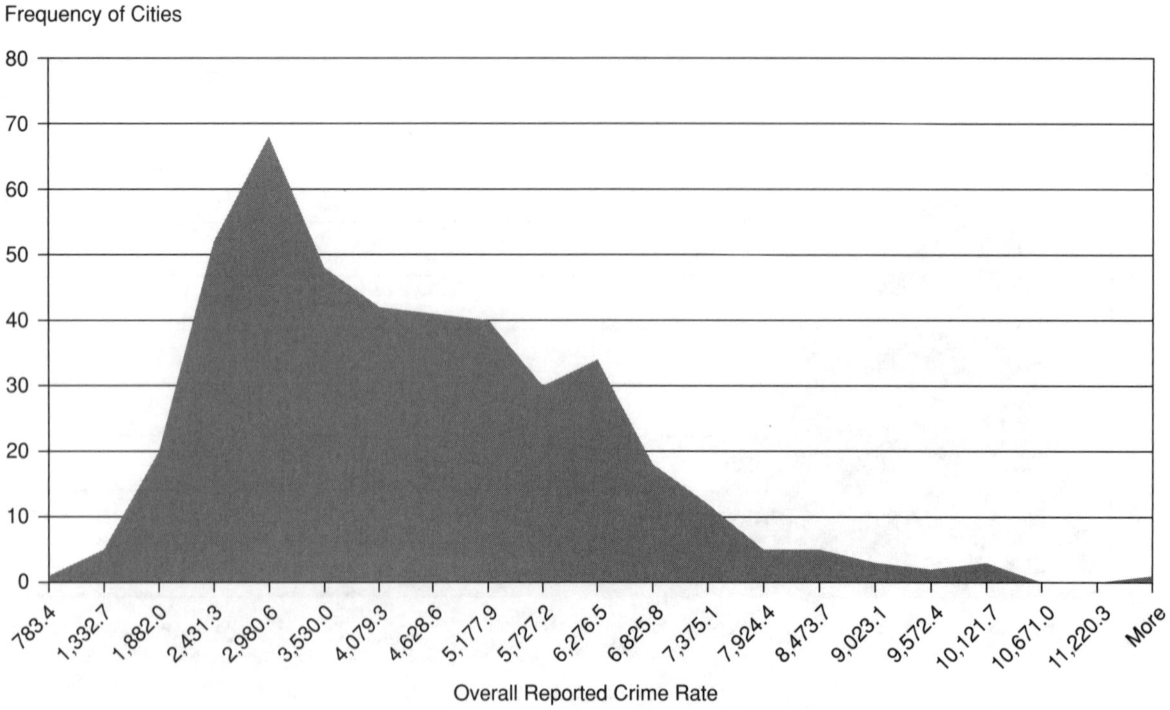

Median	3,766.5		Minimum	783.4		Standard Deviation	1,802.0
Mean	4,090.2		Maximum	11,769.6		Number of Cases	430

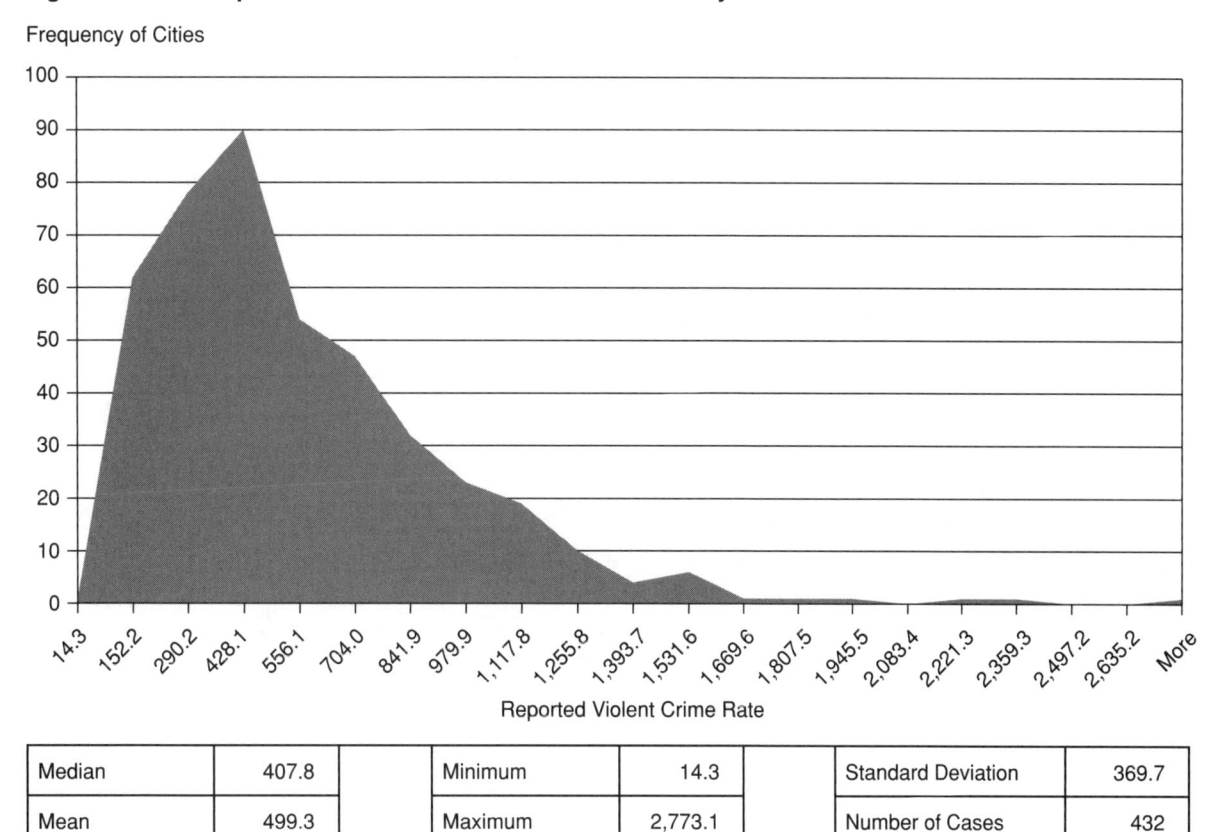

Figure 5 Metropolitan Areas Reported Violent Crime Rate Distribution Analysis for 2011

Frequency of MSAs

Reported Violent Crime Rate

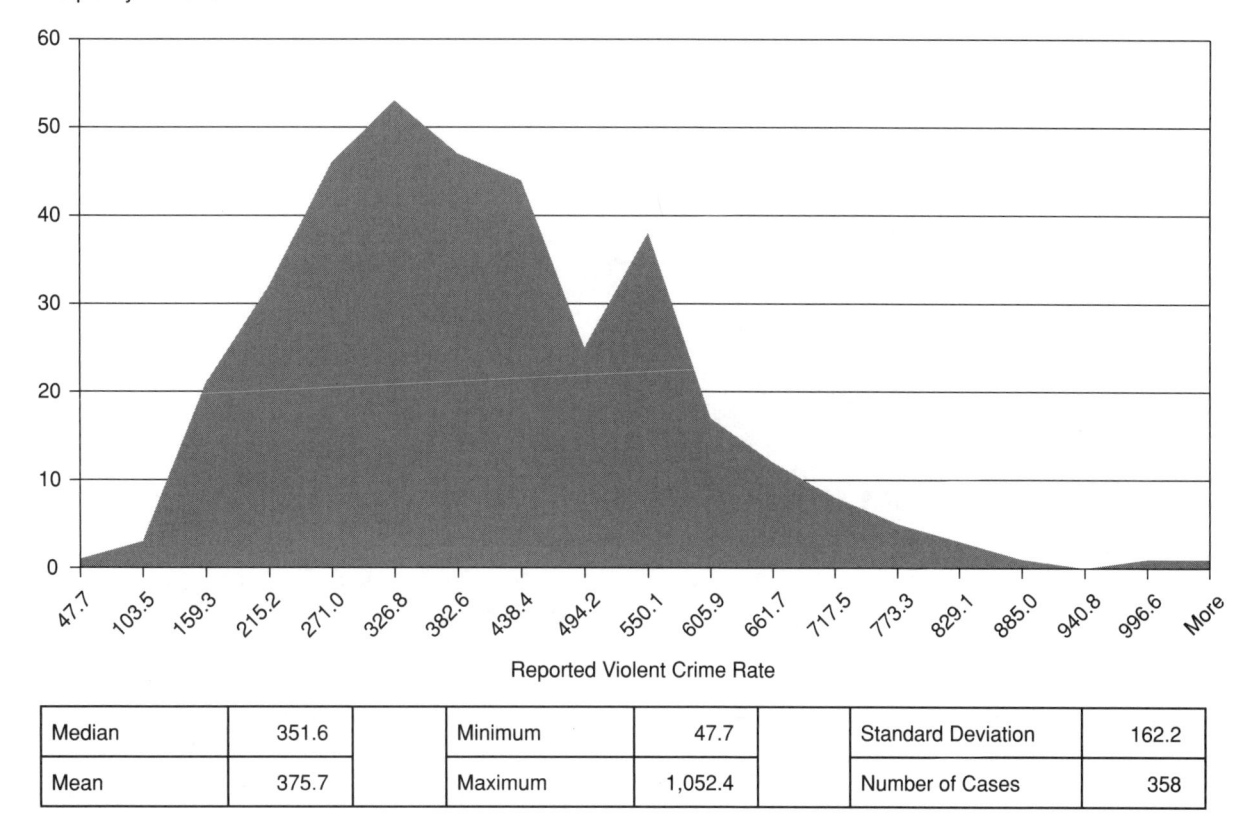

| Median | 351.6 | Minimum | 47.7 | Standard Deviation | 162.2 |
| Mean | 375.7 | Maximum | 1,052.4 | Number of Cases | 358 |

Figure 6 Cities Reported Violent Crime Rate Distribution Analysis for 2011

Frequency of Cities

Reported Violent Crime Rate

| Median | 407.8 | Minimum | 14.3 | Standard Deviation | 369.7 |
| Mean | 499.3 | Maximum | 2,773.1 | Number of Cases | 432 |

Figure 7 Metropolitan Areas Reported Property Crime Rate Distribution Analysis for 2011

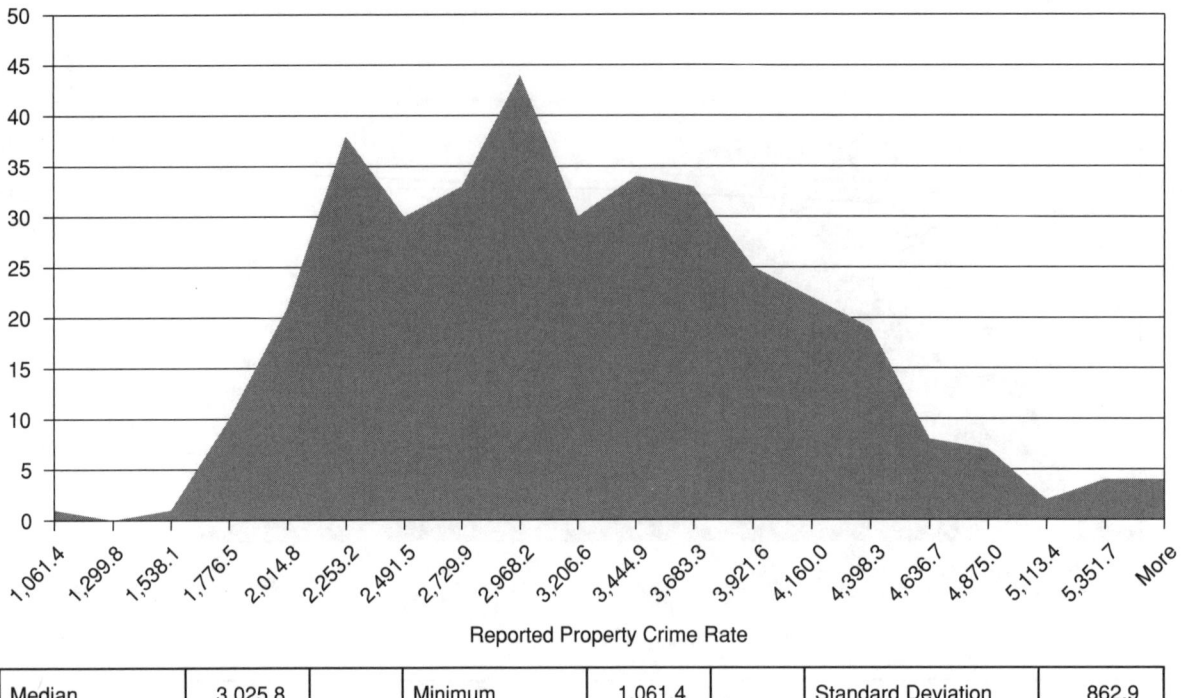

Frequency of MSAs

Reported Property Crime Rate

Median	3,025.8	Minimum	1,061.4	Standard Deviation	862.9
Mean	3,091.7	Maximum	5,590.1	Number of Cases	366

Figure 8 Cities Reported Property Crime Rate Distribution Analysis for 2011

Frequency of Cities

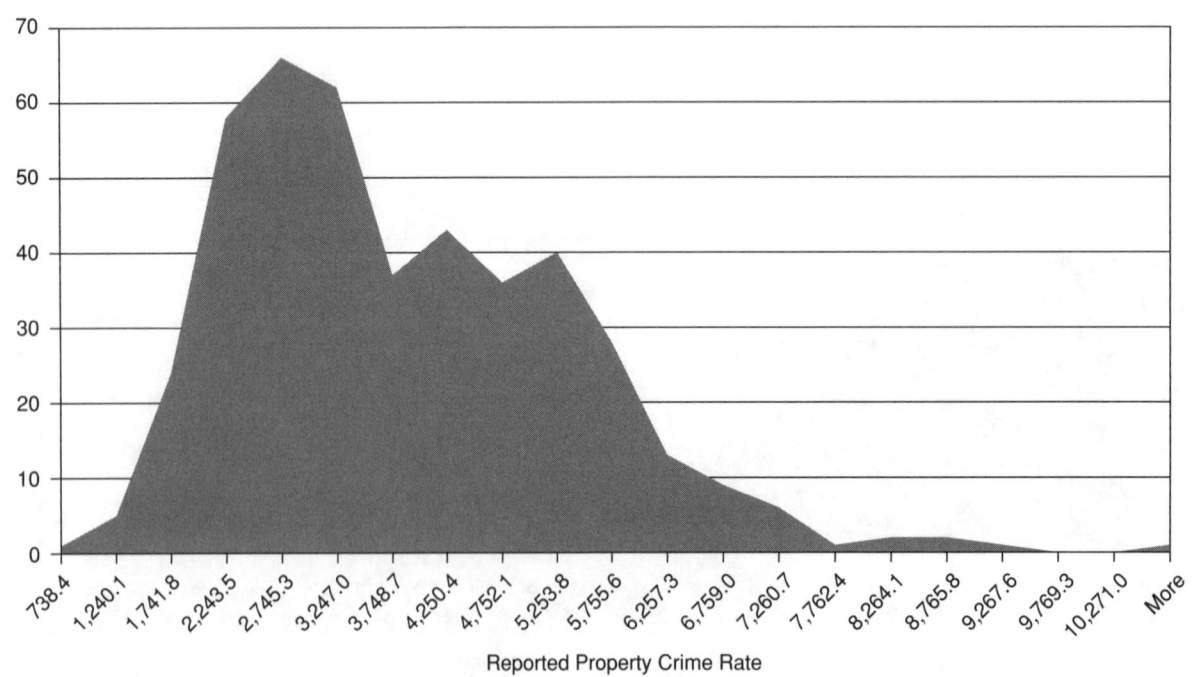

Reported Property Crime Rate

Median	3,272.4	Minimum	738.4	Standard Deviation	1,537.1
Mean	3,594.8	Maximum	10,772.7	Number of Cases	435

cities and metropolitan areas did not report complete crime information for 2011. This information is delineated below.

Missing Cities

The data collection method used by the city of Chicago, IL, and the state of Minnesota for the offense of forcible rape did not meet the FBI's UCR guidelines in 2011 (Minneapolis, MN, and St. Paul, MN, are exceptions). Given that the rape numbers were not available, the following cities are not included in the comparative analysis: Chicago, IL; Bloomington, MN; Brooklyn Park, MN; Duluth, MN; and Rochester, MN.

The FBI did not report crime data for 12 other cities with populations larger than 75,000. Crime statistics for these cities were unavailable for a number of reasons, ranging from general reporting difficulties and computer issues to changes in reporting systems. Below is a list of cities with populations greater than 75,000 (according to the U.S. Census Bureau) but for which no information was available in the FBI's 2010 Uniform Crime Report. These cities are Augusta, GA; Columbia, SC; Deltona, FL; Federal Way, WA; Greensboro, NC; Greenville, NC; Honolulu, HI; North Las Vegas, NV; Palm Coast, FL; Parma, OH; Providence, RI; and Waukegan, IL.

Missing Metropolitan Areas

For crime figures to be reported for a metropolitan area, 12 months of complete data must be submitted for 75% of agencies and for the principal city or cities within that area. A number of metropolitan areas are not included in the comparative analysis because of missing data for specific offenses. Forcible rape statistics were not available for the Chicago metropolitan area as well as all metropolitan areas in Minnesota.

Another group of metropolitan areas were not included in the comparative analysis because the FBI did not report data for them in its 2011 Crime in the United States report. These metropolitan areas are: Anderson, IN; Burlington-South Burlington, VT; Charleston-North Charleston-Summerville, SC; Coeur d'Alene, ID; Columbia, SC; Elkhart-Goshen, IN; Fayetteville-Springdale-Rogers, AR-MO; Greensboro-High Point, NC; Greenville, NC; Hattiesburg, MS; Honolulu, HI; Huntington-Ashland, WV-KY-OH; Ithaca, NY; Jackson, MI; Kalamazoo-Portage, MI; Lake Charles, LA; Lewiston, ID-WA; Morgantown, WV; Niles-Benton Harbor, MI; Parkersburg-Marietta-Vienna, WV-OH; Providence-New Bedford-Fall River, RI-MA; St. George, UT; Shreveport-Bossier City, LA; Steubenville-Weirton, OH-WV; Vineland-Millville-Bridgeton, NJ; Wheeling, WV-OH; Youngstown-Warren-Boardman, OH-PA.

An Overview of 2011 Crime

Crimes are reported by police agencies to the FBI as part of the UCR Program. More than 18,200 city, county, college and university, state, tribal, and federal law enforcement agencies participated in the program in 2011. Law enforcement agencies active in the program represented more than 99% of the total U.S. population in 2011.

Larcenies and thefts accounted for 60.0% of crimes, burglaries accounted for 21.2%, aggravated assaults for 7.3%, motor vehicle thefts for 7.0%, robberies for 3.5%, forcible rapes for 0.8%, and murders for 0.14%. The 2011 total crime rate of 3,295.0 crimes per 100,000 people is 1.7% lower than in 2010.

Violent Crime

Violent crimes include offenses of murder, forcible rape, robbery, and aggravated assault. A total of 1,203,564 such crimes were committed in 2011. Of these, 62.4% were aggravated assaults, 29.4% were robberies, 6.9% were forcible rapes, and 1.2% were murders. The 2011 national violent crime rate was 386.3 violent crimes per 100,000 population, a 4.5% decrease from 2010.

Five- and ten-year trends show the 2011 violent crime rate was 18.1% lower than it was in 2007 and 21.9% lower than in 2002. Actual numbers of violent crimes dropped 15.4% from 2007 levels and 15.5% lower than in 2002.

Among those violent crimes for which weapons information was available, firearms were involved in 67.7% of murders, 41.3% of robberies, and 21.2% of aggravated assaults.

Murder

Murder and nonnegligent manslaughter, as defined by the FBI, involve the willful (nonnegligent) killing of one human being by another. Down 0.7% from 2010, the national murder rate in 2011 was 4.7 murders per 100,000 population, or 14,612 murders total. Five-year trends show the 2011 murder rate was 14.7% lower than in 2007. A ten-year comparison of murder rates shows a drop of 10.0% from levels recorded in 2002.

Of those murders for which complete weapons data were available, 67.8% involved firearms. FBI data showed that 23.1% of murders were committed in conjunction with felonies or suspected felonies such as robberies, drug deals, and rapes. Among murders for which the relationship between the victim and offender was known, strangers committed slightly less than 21% of those murders in 2011. Approximately 89% of murder victims were male, 45.2% were white, and 45.2% were black.

Camden, NJ, had the highest murder rate in 2011 of any reporting city with more than 75,000 in population. The city's murder rate of 60.6 murders per 100,000 population was well above the national rate of 4.7 murders per 100,000 population.

Forcible Rape

The FBI defines forcible rape as the carnal knowledge of a female forcibly and against her will. While the definition includes assaults or attempts to commit rape by force or threat of force, it does not include statutory rape (without force) or other sex offenses. There is quite a bit of controversy surrounding this definition. Most states and the District of Columbia collect data for both male and female rapes; however, the UCR data reflects the narrower female-only definition. Sexual attacks on males are counted as aggravated assaults or sex offenses, depending on the circumstances and extent of injuries.

An estimated 52.7 of every 100,000 females in the United States were reported rape victims in 2011. Although the FBI's definition of rape is limited to female victims, the 2011 national rape rate of 26.8 per 100,000 applies to the entire U.S. population, both males and females. This national rape rate dropped 3.2% from levels recorded in 2010 and decreased 12.4% from 2007 levels.

A total of 83,425 rapes were reported to the FBI by law enforcement agencies in 2011. Of that total, 93.0% constituted rapes by force. The remainder included attempts or assaults to commit forcible rape.

Robbery

Robbery is the taking of or attempt to take anything by force or threat of force. The 354,396 robberies that occurred in 2011 represented a decrease of 4.0% from levels recorded in 2010. The national rate of 113.7 robberies per 100,000 population is lower as well, having decreased 4.7% from 2010.

The average dollar loss per robbery was $1,153. Banks lost an average of $4,704 per robbery. In addition, 43.8% of robberies occurred on streets or highways, 20.5% took place in commercial establishments, 17.0% were at residences, and 2.0% were at banks. The remaining robbery locations were termed *miscellaneous*.

Firearms of various types were used in 41.3% of robberies in 2011. Strong-arm tactics were used in 42.3% of robberies, knives or cutting instruments were used in 7.8%, and other dangerous weapons were involved in the remaining 8.7%.

Aggravated Assault

Aggravated assault is the unlawful attack by one person upon another for the purpose of inflicting severe bodily injury. This type of assault usually involves the use of a dangerous weapon. The FBI aggravated assault data includes attempts.

The 751,131 aggravated assaults that occurred in 2011 represent a 3.9% decrease from 2010 levels. The nation's 2011 rate of 241.1 aggravated assaults per 100,000 population is a 4.6% decrease from 2010. Aggravated assault rates fell 16.1% from 2007 levels and 22.1% from 2002 levels.

Assailants chose a variety of weapons with which to carry out their attacks in 2011. Slightly less than 27% were committed with "personal weapons" (e.g., hands or feet), 21.2% with firearms, 19.1% with knives, and 32.8% of assaults with "other" weapons.

Property Crime

Property crime includes the crimes of burglary, larceny-theft, motor vehicle theft, and arson. These offenses involve the taking of money or property, but there is no force or threat of force against the victims. While arson is considered a property crime, data for arson offenses are not included in this book. The vast majority of crimes committed in the United States are property crimes; in 2010, they accounted for approximately 87.9% of all crimes reported.

A total of 9,063,173 property crimes occurred in the United States in 2011. The national property crime rate measured 2,908.7 property crimes per 100,000 population. Property crime decreased from 2010 to 2011 in both number and rate: The number of property crimes fell 0.5% from 2010, while the rate decreased 1.3%. Five-year trends show that property crime rates decreased 11.2% from 2007. A ten-year comparison shows a decline of 19.9% from 2002.

Property crimes accounted for an estimated $15.6 billion in losses in 2011. Larceny-thefts accounted for 68.0% of all property crimes, burglaries for 24.1%, and motor vehicle thefts for 7.9%.

Burglary

Burglary is defined as the unlawful entry of a structure to commit a felony or theft. The use of force to gain entry is not required for an offense to be classified as burglary. The FBI tracks data for three types of burglaries: forcible entry, unlawful entry where no force is used, and attempted forcible entry. Burglary accounted for 23.8% of the estimated number of property crimes committed in 2011.

A total of 2,188,005 burglaries were reported in 2011, an increase of 0.9% from 2010. The year's burglary rate of 702.2 burglaries per 100,000 population is 0.2% higher than in 2010. Five- and ten-year trends show that burglary rates have decreased 3.3% since 2007 and 6.0% since 2002.

Burglaries of residential properties accounted for 74.5% of all burglary offenses. Burglary offenses cost victims an estimated $4.8 billion in lost property. The average dollar loss per burglary offense was $2,185.

Larceny-Theft

Larceny-theft is the unlawful taking of property from another person. It includes crimes such as shoplifting, pickpocketing, purse snatching, thefts from motor vehicles, thefts of motor vehicle parts and accessories, and bicycle thefts. No use of force, violence, or fraud is involved in these offenses. This category does not include embezzlement, "con" games, forgery, or worthless check writing.

A total of 6,159,795 thefts occurred in 2011, down 0.7% from 2010. This number represents 68.0% of property crimes reported for the year. The national rate of 1,976.9 larcenies and thefts per 100,000 population represents a 1.4% decrease from 2010 levels. Five and ten-year trends show that larceny-theft rates have decreased 9.5% since 2007 and are down 19.3% from 2002.

The average value of property stolen in 2011 was $987. Total losses from larceny-thefts measured more than $6.0 billion.

Motor Vehicle Theft

The motor vehicle theft category includes the stealing of automobiles, trucks, buses, motorcycles, motor scooters, snowmobiles, and so on. The definition does not include the taking of a motor vehicle for temporary use by those persons having lawful access to the vehicle.

A total of 715,373 motor vehicle thefts were committed in 2011. This represents a 3.3% decrease from 2010. The national rate of 229.6 vehicles stolen per 100,000 population represents a decrease of 4.0% from the prior year.

The total estimated value of these thefts was $4.3 billion, or an average of $6,089 per stolen vehicle. Automobiles were the most frequently stolen vehicle type, accounting for 73.9% of all those stolen.

Police Officers

Nationwide, a total of 698,460 sworn police officers were on the job in 2011, with an additional 303,524 civilian employees assisting. This equates to 2.4 full-time officers per 1,000 population.

Only police officers on each city's primary police force are reported in this volume. Many cities have a number of overlapping law enforcement agencies. For example, New York City has its Transit Police, Port Authority Police, and officials in other special law enforcement agencies. Those officers are not covered in *City Crime Rankings*.

Miscellaneous Notes Regarding City and Metro Crime Data

- Crime statistics for 2011 are not comparable to previous years' data for all cities in Alabama; Billings, MT; Buffalo, NY; Davenport, IA; Kansas City, MO; Lexington, KY; Pueblo, CO; Sterling Heights, MI; and Thornton, CO. Accordingly, one- and five-year crime rate trends are not available for these cities.

- Crime statistics for 2011 are not comparable to previous years' data for these metro areas: Anniston-Oxford, AL; Auburn, AL; Billings, MT; Birmingham-Hoover, AL; Columbus, GA-AL; Cumberland, MD-WV; Davenport, IA-IL; Decatur, AL; Detroit (greater), MI; Dothan, AL; Florence-Muscle Shoals, AL; Gadsden, AL; Great Falls, MT; Houston, TX; Huntsville, AL; Kansas City, MO-KS; Lexington-Fayette, KY; Missoula, MT; Montgomery, AL; Pueblo, CO; Tuscaloosa, AL; and Warren-Farmington Hills, MI. As a result, one- and five-year trends are not available for these metro areas.

- The population estimates reported in *City Crime Rankings 2013* are provided by the FBI. These estimates sometimes differ from those reported by the U.S. Census Bureau.

- Forcible rape data reported to the UCR Program by Minnesota (with the exception of Minneapolis and St. Paul) and the city of Chicago, IL, were not in accordance with national UCR guidelines. Therefore, these numbers are not available for Chicago as well as most cities and metro areas in Minnesota.

- Larceny-theft data were not reported for the cities or the metro areas of Toledo, OH, and Tucson, AZ, because they did not meet UCR guidelines. Thus, this information, as well as property crime statistics, is not available for these cities or metro areas.

- The Hamilton Township, NJ, data are for the township located in Mercer County.

- Honolulu, HI, has a combined city-county government. Therefore, the population and crime data provided in this book include areas outside the principal city of Honolulu.

- Charlotte, NC, crime and population data include Mecklenburg County.

- Indianapolis, IN, crime and population data include Marion County.

- Louisville, KY, data include offenses reported by the Louisville and Jefferson County Police Departments.

- Las Vegas, NV, has a metropolitan police department, and its crime and population numbers include areas outside of the principal city of Las Vegas.

- Savannah, GA, crime and population data include Chatham County.

- Toms River Township, NJ, was formerly known as Dover Township.

- The population shown for the city of Mobile, AL, includes 55,819 inhabitants from the jurisdiction of the Mobile County Sheriff's Department.

- *City Crime Rankings 2013* also provides rankings for Metropolitan Divisions (MDs). These are subdivisions of 11 large MSAs.

Alpha Order - Metro Area

2012 Metropolitan Crime Rate Rankings*

RANK	METROPOLITAN AREA	SCORE	RANK	METROPOLITAN AREA	SCORE	RANK	METROPOLITAN AREA	SCORE
112	Abilene, TX	(23.99)	204	Charleston, WV	1.23	263	Fort Lauderdale, FL M.D.	19.22
216	Akron, OH	5.02	211	Charlotte-Gastonia, NC-SC	4.11	184	Fort Smith, AR-OK	(4.26)
53	Albany-Schenectady-Troy, NY	(40.18)	37	Charlottesville, VA	(46.71)	136	Fort Wayne, IN	(18.58)
317	Albany, GA	43.13	252	Chattanooga, TN-GA	14.94	235	Fort Worth-Arlington, TX M.D.	9.38
327	Albuquerque, NM	46.40	83	Cheyenne, WY	(31.89)	342	Fresno, CA	56.92
299	Alexandria, LA	32.35	NA	Chicago (greater), IL-IN-WI**	NA	301	Gadsden, AL	32.55
49	Allentown, PA-NJ	(41.68)	NA	Chicago-Joilet-Naperville, IL M.D.**	NA	282	Gainesville, FL	22.96
67	Altoona, PA	(35.23)	171	Chico, CA	(8.73)	54	Gainesville, GA	(39.96)
283	Amarillo, TX	24.14	181	Cincinnati-Middletown, OH-KY-IN	(4.42)	277	Gary, IN M.D.	21.74
48	Ames, IA	(41.81)	209	Clarksville, TN-KY	2.90	93	Glens Falls, NY	(30.28)
340	Anchorage, AK	56.31	271	Cleveland-Elyria-Mentor, OH	21.02	258	Goldsboro, NC	17.76
345	Anderson, SC	60.74	242	Cleveland, TN	12.30	NA	Grand Forks, ND-MN**	NA
145	Ann Arbor, MI	(15.91)	115	College Station-Bryan, TX	(23.21)	154	Grand Junction, CO	(13.19)
335	Anniston-Oxford, AL	49.71	238	Colorado Springs, CO	11.33	152	Grand Rapids-Wyoming, MI	(13.78)
3	Appleton, WI	(65.68)	140	Columbia, MO	(17.77)	52	Great Falls, MT	(40.44)
94	Asheville, NC	(29.94)	328	Columbus, GA-AL	46.88	69	Greeley, CO	(34.92)
175	Athens-Clarke County, GA	(8.49)	72	Columbus, IN	(34.23)	10	Green Bay, WI	(60.22)
279	Atlanta, GA	22.25	294	Columbus, OH	30.27	289	Greenville, SC	26.20
262	Atlantic City, NJ	19.08	269	Corpus Christi, TX	20.96	236	Gulfport-Biloxi, MS	9.42
64	Auburn, AL	(35.87)	27	Corvallis, OR	(49.87)	61	Hagerstown-Martinsburg, MD-WV	(36.89)
316	Augusta, GA-SC	41.58	137	Crestview-Fort Walton Beach, FL	(18.49)	162	Hanford-Corcoran, CA	(10.71)
108	Austin-Round Rock, TX	(25.52)	159	Cumberland, MD-WV	(11.95)	118	Harrisburg-Carlisle, PA	(22.33)
323	Bakersfield, CA	44.52	234	Dallas (greater), TX	8.25	9	Harrisonburg, VA	(61.03)
319	Baltimore-Towson, MD	43.41	229	Dallas-Plano-Irving, TX M.D.	7.70	122	Hartford, CT	(21.91)
30	Bangor, ME	(48.15)	62	Dalton, GA	(36.63)	148	Hickory, NC	(15.19)
189	Barnstable Town, MA	(3.34)	341	Danville, IL	56.66	183	Hinesville, GA	(4.36)
315	Baton Rouge, LA	40.23	191	Danville, VA	(2.53)	33	Holland-Grand Haven, MI	(47.53)
322	Battle Creek, MI	43.83	167	Davenport, IA-IL	(9.91)	334	Hot Springs, AR	48.93
153	Bay City, MI	(13.47)	221	Dayton, OH	5.82	134	Houma, LA	(18.94)
303	Beaumont-Port Arthur, TX	34.23	106	Decatur, AL	(26.28)	300	Houston, TX	32.39
101	Bellingham, WA	(26.85)	292	Decatur, IL	28.71	255	Huntsville, AL	17.07
84	Bend, OR	(31.68)	230	Deltona-Daytona Beach, FL	7.75	63	Idaho Falls, ID	(36.45)
20	Bethesda-Frederick, MD M.D.	(52.50)	206	Denver-Aurora, CO	1.60	324	Indianapolis, IN	45.59
100	Billings, MT	(27.60)	110	Des Moines-West Des Moines, IA	(24.64)	42	Iowa City, IA	(44.09)
32	Binghamton, NY	(47.69)	339	Detroit (greater), MI	55.46	265	Jacksonville, FL	19.73
336	Birmingham-Hoover, AL	49.76	358	Detroit-Livonia-Dearborn, MI M.D.	182.19	124	Jacksonville, NC	(21.86)
75	Bismarck, ND	(33.41)	177	Dothan, AL	(7.62)	338	Jackson, MS	54.80
34	Blacksburg, VA	(47.33)	270	Dover, DE	21.01	349	Jackson, TN	66.93
117	Bloomington-Normal, IL	(22.38)	19	Dubuque, IA	(53.28)	71	Janesville, WI	(34.36)
66	Bloomington, IN	(35.36)	NA	Duluth, MN-WI**	NA	85	Jefferson City, MO	(31.43)
23	Boise City-Nampa, ID	(51.36)	284	Durham-Chapel Hill, NC	24.32	86	Johnson City, TN	(31.41)
118	Boston (greater), MA-NH	(22.33)	11	Eau Claire, WI	(59.06)	87	Johnstown, PA	(30.77)
222	Boston-Quincy, MA M.D.	5.98	8	Edison, NJ M.D.	(61.66)	244	Jonesboro, AR	13.32
41	Boulder, CO	(45.26)	185	El Centro, CA	(3.96)	165	Joplin, MO	(10.38)
57	Bowling Green, KY	(38.60)	127	El Paso, TX	(20.72)	200	Kankakee-Bradley, IL	(0.64)
172	Bremerton-Silverdale, WA	(8.57)	16	Elizabethtown, KY	(56.01)	302	Kansas City, MO-KS	34.11
130	Bridgeport-Stamford, CT	(19.81)	14	Elmira, NY	(57.80)	104	Kennewick-Pasco-Richland, WA	(26.49)
92	Brownsville-Harlingen, TX	(30.37)	128	Erie, PA	(20.57)	173	Killeen-Temple-Fort Hood, TX	(8.51)
274	Brunswick, GA	21.40	138	Eugene-Springfield, OR	(18.24)	147	Kingsport, TN-VA	(15.50)
195	Buffalo-Niagara Falls, NY	(1.39)	70	Evansville, IN-KY	(34.84)	18	Kingston, NY	(54.21)
163	Burlington, NC	(10.67)	278	Fairbanks, AK	21.99	237	Knoxville, TN	10.73
28	Cambridge-Newton, MA M.D.	(49.74)	NA	Fargo, ND-MN**	NA	143	Kokomo, IN	(16.30)
169	Camden, NJ M.D.	(9.60)	276	Farmington, NM	21.73	NA	La Crosse, WI-MN**	NA
178	Canton, OH	(6.20)	344	Fayetteville, NC	57.12	78	Lafayette, IN	(33.14)
176	Cape Coral-Fort Myers, FL	(8.12)	160	Flagstaff, AZ	(11.91)	210	Lafayette, LA	3.65
166	Cape Girardeau, MO-IL	(10.08)	356	Flint, MI	118.27	15	Lake Co.-Kenosha Co., IL-WI M.D.	(57.75)
82	Carson City, NV	(31.94)	46	Florence-Muscle Shoals, AL	(42.32)	132	Lake Havasu City-Kingman, AZ	(19.58)
58	Casper, WY	(37.97)	320	Florence, SC	43.48	186	Lakeland, FL	(3.81)
36	Cedar Rapids, IA	(46.74)	38	Fond du Lac, WI	(45.69)	21	Lancaster, PA	(52.13)
227	Champaign-Urbana, IL	7.60	35	Fort Collins-Loveland, CO	(46.85)	180	Lansing-East Lansing, MI	(4.61)

Note: All listings are for Metropolitan Statistical Areas (M.S.A.s) except for those ending with "M.D." Listings with "M.D." are Metropolitan Divisions which are smaller parts of eleven large M.S.A.s. See explanatory note at beginning of metropolitan area section.

Alpha Order - Metro Area (continued)

RANK	METROPOLITAN AREA	SCORE
218	Laredo, TX	5.43
174	Las Cruces, NM	(8.50)
329	Las Vegas-Paradise, NV	47.25
107	Lawrence, KS	(26.10)
346	Lawton, OK	62.07
13	Lebanon, PA	(58.10)
91	Lewiston-Auburn, ME	(30.40)
206	Lexington-Fayette, KY	1.60
273	Lima, OH	21.09
144	Lincoln, NE	(15.99)
351	Little Rock, AR	84.03
1	Logan, UT-ID	(84.15)
223	Longview, TX	6.32
268	Longview, WA	20.37
264	Los Angeles County, CA M.D.	19.39
215	Los Angeles (greater), CA	4.99
243	Louisville, KY-IN	12.33
307	Lubbock, TX	37.56
26	Lynchburg, VA	(49.93)
309	Macon, GA	38.31
257	Madera, CA	17.12
44	Madison, WI	(42.95)
65	Manchester-Nashua, NH	(35.85)
101	Manhattan, KS	(26.85)
NA	Mankato-North Mankato, MN**	NA
156	Mansfield, OH	(12.94)
168	McAllen-Edinburg-Mission, TX	(9.82)
120	Medford, OR	(22.32)
355	Memphis, TN-MS-AR	106.78
295	Merced, CA	30.50
310	Miami (greater), FL	38.74
348	Miami-Dade County, FL M.D.	66.56
103	Michigan City-La Porte, IN	(26.74)
95	Midland, TX	(29.90)
256	Milwaukee, WI	17.09
NA	Minneapolis-St. Paul, MN-WI**	NA
47	Missoula, MT	(42.00)
350	Mobile, AL	67.19
330	Modesto, CA	47.78
285	Monroe, LA	24.53
131	Monroe, MI	(19.68)
286	Montgomery, AL	24.72
120	Morristown, TN	(22.32)
164	Mount Vernon-Anacortes, WA	(10.47)
224	Muncie, IN	6.52
249	Muskegon-Norton Shores, MI	14.00
352	Myrtle Beach, SC	84.55
99	Napa, CA	(28.32)
55	Naples-Marco Island, FL	(39.06)
290	Nashville-Davidson, TN	26.90
7	Nassau-Suffolk, NY M.D.	(62.93)
205	New Haven-Milford, CT	1.34
353	New Orleans, LA	86.99
128	New York (greater), NY-NJ-PA	(20.57)
170	New York-W. Plains NY-NJ M.D.	(8.87)
254	Newark-Union, NJ-PA M.D.	15.88
220	North Port-Bradenton-Sarasota, FL	5.75
149	Norwich-New London, CT	(14.91)
347	Oakland-Fremont, CA M.D.	63.44
212	Ocala, FL	4.26
96	Ocean City, NJ	(28.97)
280	Odessa, TX	22.46
29	Ogden-Clearfield, UT	(49.10)

RANK	METROPOLITAN AREA	SCORE
331	Oklahoma City, OK	48.00
76	Olympia, WA	(33.24)
281	Omaha-Council Bluffs, NE-IA	22.60
297	Orlando, FL	30.94
6	Oshkosh-Neenah, WI	(64.10)
68	Owensboro, KY	(34.98)
24	Oxnard-Thousand Oaks, CA	(50.77)
219	Palm Bay-Melbourne, FL	5.45
45	Palm Coast, FL	(42.61)
287	Panama City-Lynn Haven, FL	25.45
208	Pascagoula, MS	1.94
133	Peabody, MA M.D.	(18.95)
261	Pensacola, FL	18.14
201	Peoria, IL	(0.02)
288	Philadelphia (greater) PA-NJ-MD-DE	25.84
311	Philadelphia, PA M.D.	38.79
241	Phoenix-Mesa-Scottsdale, AZ	12.27
357	Pine Bluff, AR	120.08
76	Pittsburgh, PA	(33.24)
187	Pittsfield, MA	(3.56)
39	Pocatello, ID	(45.68)
157	Port St. Lucie, FL	(12.80)
141	Portland-Vancouver, OR-WA	(17.45)
25	Portland, ME	(50.28)
31	Poughkeepsie, NY	(48.03)
139	Prescott, AZ	(18.18)
2	Provo-Orem, UT	(67.17)
314	Pueblo, CO	39.13
43	Punta Gorda, FL	(44.05)
97	Racine, WI	(28.56)
88	Raleigh-Cary, NC	(30.69)
275	Rapid City, SD	21.43
126	Reading, PA	(21.41)
308	Redding, CA	38.30
188	Reno-Sparks, NV	(3.38)
109	Richmond, VA	(25.11)
225	Riverside-San Bernardino, CA	6.63
89	Roanoke, VA	(30.55)
NA	Rochester, MN**	NA
111	Rochester, NY	(24.12)
333	Rockford, IL	48.61
12	Rockingham County, NH M.D.	(58.24)
304	Rocky Mount, NC	34.88
232	Rome, GA	8.07
246	Sacramento, CA	13.62
318	Saginaw, MI	43.32
79	Salem, OR	(32.70)
291	Salinas, CA	27.06
196	Salisbury, MD	(0.91)
198	Salt Lake City, UT	(0.78)
98	San Angelo, TX	(28.47)
251	San Antonio, TX	14.72
161	San Diego, CA	(11.04)
313	San Francisco (greater), CA	39.12
213	San Francisco-S. Mateo, CA M.D.	4.45
142	San Jose, CA	(16.59)
80	San Luis Obispo, CA	(32.16)
56	Sandusky, OH	(38.62)
50	Santa Ana-Anaheim, CA M.D.	(41.43)
123	Santa Barbara-Santa Maria, CA	(21.88)
225	Santa Cruz-Watsonville, CA	6.63
240	Santa Fe, NM	12.00
81	Santa Rosa-Petaluma, CA	(32.04)

RANK	METROPOLITAN AREA	SCORE
250	Savannah, GA	14.63
60	Scranton--Wilkes-Barre, PA	(36.93)
228	Seattle (greater), WA	7.67
203	Seattle-Bellevue-Everett, WA M.D.	0.91
113	Sebastian-Vero Beach, FL	(23.57)
4	Sheboygan, WI	(64.73)
105	Sherman-Denison, TX	(26.41)
90	Sioux City, IA-NE-SD	(30.44)
114	Sioux Falls, SD	(23.49)
244	South Bend-Mishawaka, IN-MI	13.32
248	Spartanburg, SC	13.99
260	Spokane, WA	18.11
332	Springfield, IL	48.31
231	Springfield, MA	7.91
202	Springfield, MO	0.07
197	Springfield, OH	(0.88)
5	State College, PA	(64.20)
354	Stockton, CA	89.39
NA	St. Cloud, MN**	NA
150	St. Joseph, MO-KS	(14.01)
267	St. Louis, MO-IL	20.33
337	Sumter, SC	54.17
73	Syracuse, NY	(33.89)
293	Tacoma, WA M.D.	29.27
312	Tallahassee, FL	38.91
192	Tampa-St Petersburg, FL	(1.77)
146	Terre Haute, IN	(15.64)
343	Texarkana, TX-Texarkana, AR	56.98
321	Toledo, OH	43.78
259	Topeka, KS	18.07
214	Trenton-Ewing, NJ	4.56
296	Tucson, AZ	30.82
326	Tulsa, OK	46.28
233	Tuscaloosa, AL	8.09
190	Tyler, TX	(2.91)
40	Utica-Rome, NY	(45.57)
194	Valdosta, GA	(1.66)
306	Vallejo-Fairfield, CA	36.81
247	Victoria, TX	13.77
179	Virginia Beach-Norfolk, VA-NC	(6.16)
298	Visalia-Porterville, CA	31.01
266	Waco, TX	20.27
158	Warner Robins, GA	(12.17)
59	Warren-Farmington Hills, MI M.D.	(37.75)
155	Washington (greater) DC-VA-MD-WV	(12.98)
192	Washington, DC-VA-MD-WV M.D.	(1.77)
135	Waterloo-Cedar Falls, IA	(18.63)
17	Wausau, WI	(55.15)
74	Wenatchee, WA	(33.67)
239	West Palm Beach, FL M.D.	11.77
151	Wichita Falls, TX	(13.90)
305	Wichita, KS	36.02
22	Williamsport, PA	(52.07)
253	Wilmington, DE-MD-NJ M.D.	15.52
199	Wilmington, NC	(0.65)
51	Winchester, VA-WV	(40.76)
271	Winston-Salem, NC	21.02
125	Worcester, MA	(21.56)
325	Yakima, WA	45.64
116	York-Hanover, PA	(23.07)
217	Yuba City, CA	5.05
182	Yuma, AZ	(4.41)

Source: CQ Press using reported data from the F.B.I. "Crime in the United States 2011"
*Includes murder, rape, robbery, aggravated assault, burglary, and motor vehicle theft. A negative score (in parentheses) indicates a composite crime number below the national rate, a positive number is above the national rate. **Not available.

Rank Order - Metro Area
2012 Metropolitan Crime Rate Rankings* (continued)

RANK	METROPOLITAN AREA	SCORE	RANK	METROPOLITAN AREA	SCORE	RANK	METROPOLITAN AREA	SCORE
1	Logan, UT-ID	(84.15)	61	Hagerstown-Martinsburg, MD-WV	(36.89)	120	Morristown, TN	(22.32)
2	Provo-Orem, UT	(67.17)	62	Dalton, GA	(36.63)	122	Hartford, CT	(21.91)
3	Appleton, WI	(65.68)	63	Idaho Falls, ID	(36.45)	123	Santa Barbara-Santa Maria, CA	(21.88)
4	Sheboygan, WI	(64.73)	64	Auburn, AL	(35.87)	124	Jacksonville, NC	(21.86)
5	State College, PA	(64.20)	65	Manchester-Nashua, NH	(35.85)	125	Worcester, MA	(21.56)
6	Oshkosh-Neenah, WI	(64.10)	66	Bloomington, IN	(35.36)	126	Reading, PA	(21.41)
7	Nassau-Suffolk, NY M.D.	(62.93)	67	Altoona, PA	(35.23)	127	El Paso, TX	(20.72)
8	Edison, NJ M.D.	(61.66)	68	Owensboro, KY	(34.98)	128	Erie, PA	(20.57)
9	Harrisonburg, VA	(61.03)	69	Greeley, CO	(34.92)	128	New York (greater), NY-NJ-PA	(20.57)
10	Green Bay, WI	(60.22)	70	Evansville, IN-KY	(34.84)	130	Bridgeport-Stamford, CT	(19.81)
11	Eau Claire, WI	(59.06)	71	Janesville, WI	(34.36)	131	Monroe, MI	(19.68)
12	Rockingham County, NH M.D.	(58.24)	72	Columbus, IN	(34.23)	132	Lake Havasu City-Kingman, AZ	(19.58)
13	Lebanon, PA	(58.10)	73	Syracuse, NY	(33.89)	133	Peabody, MA M.D.	(18.95)
14	Elmira, NY	(57.80)	74	Wenatchee, WA	(33.67)	134	Houma, LA	(18.94)
15	Lake Co.-Kenosha Co., IL-WI M.D.	(57.75)	75	Bismarck, ND	(33.41)	135	Waterloo-Cedar Falls, IA	(18.63)
16	Elizabethtown, KY	(56.01)	76	Olympia, WA	(33.24)	136	Fort Wayne, IN	(18.58)
17	Wausau, WI	(55.15)	76	Pittsburgh, PA	(33.24)	137	Crestview-Fort Walton Beach, FL	(18.49)
18	Kingston, NY	(54.21)	78	Lafayette, IN	(33.14)	138	Eugene-Springfield, OR	(18.24)
19	Dubuque, IA	(53.28)	79	Salem, OR	(32.70)	139	Prescott, AZ	(18.18)
20	Bethesda-Frederick, MD M.D.	(52.50)	80	San Luis Obispo, CA	(32.16)	140	Columbia, MO	(17.77)
21	Lancaster, PA	(52.13)	81	Santa Rosa-Petaluma, CA	(32.04)	141	Portland-Vancouver, OR-WA	(17.45)
22	Williamsport, PA	(52.07)	82	Carson City, NV	(31.94)	142	San Jose, CA	(16.59)
23	Boise City-Nampa, ID	(51.36)	83	Cheyenne, WY	(31.89)	143	Kokomo, IN	(16.30)
24	Oxnard-Thousand Oaks, CA	(50.77)	84	Bend, OR	(31.68)	144	Lincoln, NE	(15.99)
25	Portland, ME	(50.28)	85	Jefferson City, MO	(31.43)	145	Ann Arbor, MI	(15.91)
26	Lynchburg, VA	(49.93)	86	Johnson City, TN	(31.41)	146	Terre Haute, IN	(15.64)
27	Corvallis, OR	(49.87)	87	Johnstown, PA	(30.77)	147	Kingsport, TN-VA	(15.50)
28	Cambridge-Newton, MA M.D.	(49.74)	88	Raleigh-Cary, NC	(30.69)	148	Hickory, NC	(15.19)
29	Ogden-Clearfield, UT	(49.10)	89	Roanoke, VA	(30.55)	149	Norwich-New London, CT	(14.91)
30	Bangor, ME	(48.15)	90	Sioux City, IA-NE-SD	(30.44)	150	St. Joseph, MO-KS	(14.01)
31	Poughkeepsie, NY	(48.03)	91	Lewiston-Auburn, ME	(30.40)	151	Wichita Falls, TX	(13.90)
32	Binghamton, NY	(47.69)	92	Brownsville-Harlingen, TX	(30.37)	152	Grand Rapids-Wyoming, MI	(13.78)
33	Holland-Grand Haven, MI	(47.53)	93	Glens Falls, NY	(30.28)	153	Bay City, MI	(13.47)
34	Blacksburg, VA	(47.33)	94	Asheville, NC	(29.94)	154	Grand Junction, CO	(13.19)
35	Fort Collins-Loveland, CO	(46.85)	95	Midland, TX	(29.90)	155	Washington (greater) DC-VA-MD-WV	(12.98)
36	Cedar Rapids, IA	(46.74)	96	Ocean City, NJ	(28.97)	156	Mansfield, OH	(12.94)
37	Charlottesville, VA	(46.71)	97	Racine, WI	(28.56)	157	Port St. Lucie, FL	(12.80)
38	Fond du Lac, WI	(45.69)	98	San Angelo, TX	(28.47)	158	Warner Robins, GA	(12.17)
39	Pocatello, ID	(45.68)	99	Napa, CA	(28.32)	159	Cumberland, MD-WV	(11.95)
40	Utica-Rome, NY	(45.57)	100	Billings, MT	(27.60)	160	Flagstaff, AZ	(11.91)
41	Boulder, CO	(45.26)	101	Bellingham, WA	(26.85)	161	San Diego, CA	(11.04)
42	Iowa City, IA	(44.09)	101	Manhattan, KS	(26.85)	162	Hanford-Corcoran, CA	(10.71)
43	Punta Gorda, FL	(44.05)	103	Michigan City-La Porte, IN	(26.74)	163	Burlington, NC	(10.67)
44	Madison, WI	(42.95)	104	Kennewick-Pasco-Richland, WA	(26.49)	164	Mount Vernon-Anacortes, WA	(10.47)
45	Palm Coast, FL	(42.61)	105	Sherman-Denison, TX	(26.41)	165	Joplin, MO	(10.38)
46	Florence-Muscle Shoals, AL	(42.32)	106	Decatur, AL	(26.28)	166	Cape Girardeau, MO-IL	(10.08)
47	Missoula, MT	(42.00)	107	Lawrence, KS	(26.10)	167	Davenport, IA-IL	(9.91)
48	Ames, IA	(41.81)	108	Austin-Round Rock, TX	(25.52)	168	McAllen-Edinburg-Mission, TX	(9.82)
49	Allentown, PA-NJ	(41.68)	109	Richmond, VA	(25.11)	169	Camden, NJ M.D.	(9.60)
50	Santa Ana-Anaheim, CA M.D.	(41.43)	110	Des Moines-West Des Moines, IA	(24.64)	170	New York-W. Plains NY-NJ M.D.	(8.87)
51	Winchester, VA-WV	(40.76)	111	Rochester, NY	(24.12)	171	Chico, CA	(8.73)
52	Great Falls, MT	(40.44)	112	Abilene, TX	(23.99)	172	Bremerton-Silverdale, WA	(8.57)
53	Albany-Schenectady-Troy, NY	(40.18)	113	Sebastian-Vero Beach, FL	(23.57)	173	Killeen-Temple-Fort Hood, TX	(8.51)
54	Gainesville, GA	(39.96)	114	Sioux Falls, SD	(23.49)	174	Las Cruces, NM	(8.50)
55	Naples-Marco Island, FL	(39.06)	115	College Station-Bryan, TX	(23.21)	175	Athens-Clarke County, GA	(8.49)
56	Sandusky, OH	(38.62)	116	York-Hanover, PA	(23.07)	176	Cape Coral-Fort Myers, FL	(8.12)
57	Bowling Green, KY	(38.60)	117	Bloomington-Normal, IL	(22.38)	177	Dothan, AL	(7.62)
58	Casper, WY	(37.97)	118	Boston (greater), MA-NH	(22.33)	178	Canton, OH	(6.20)
59	Warren-Farmington Hills, MI M.D.	(37.75)	118	Harrisburg-Carlisle, PA	(22.33)	179	Virginia Beach-Norfolk, VA-NC	(6.16)
60	Scranton--Wilkes-Barre, PA	(36.93)	120	Medford, OR	(22.32)	180	Lansing-East Lansing, MI	(4.61)

Note: All listings are for Metropolitan Statistical Areas (M.S.A.s) except for those ending with "M.D." Listings with "M.D." are Metropolitan Divisions which are smaller parts of eleven large M.S.A.s. See explanatory note at beginning of metropolitan area section.

Rank Order - Metro Area (continued)

RANK	METROPOLITAN AREA	SCORE
181	Cincinnati-Middletown, OH-KY-IN	(4.42)
182	Yuma, AZ	(4.41)
183	Hinesville, GA	(4.36)
184	Fort Smith, AR-OK	(4.26)
185	El Centro, CA	(3.96)
186	Lakeland, FL	(3.81)
187	Pittsfield, MA	(3.56)
188	Reno-Sparks, NV	(3.38)
189	Barnstable Town, MA	(3.34)
190	Tyler, TX	(2.91)
191	Danville, VA	(2.53)
192	Tampa-St Petersburg, FL	(1.77)
192	Washington, DC-VA-MD-WV M.D.	(1.77)
194	Valdosta, GA	(1.66)
195	Buffalo-Niagara Falls, NY	(1.39)
196	Salisbury, MD	(0.91)
197	Springfield, OH	(0.88)
198	Salt Lake City, UT	(0.78)
199	Wilmington, NC	(0.65)
200	Kankakee-Bradley, IL	(0.64)
201	Peoria, IL	(0.02)
202	Springfield, MO	0.07
203	Seattle-Bellevue-Everett, WA M.D.	0.91
204	Charleston, WV	1.23
205	New Haven-Milford, CT	1.34
206	Denver-Aurora, CO	1.60
206	Lexington-Fayette, KY	1.60
208	Pascagoula, MS	1.94
209	Clarksville, TN-KY	2.90
210	Lafayette, LA	3.65
211	Charlotte-Gastonia, NC-SC	4.11
212	Ocala, FL	4.26
213	San Francisco-S. Mateo, CA M.D.	4.45
214	Trenton-Ewing, NJ	4.56
215	Los Angeles (greater), CA	4.99
216	Akron, OH	5.02
217	Yuba City, CA	5.05
218	Laredo, TX	5.43
219	Palm Bay-Melbourne, FL	5.45
220	North Port-Bradenton-Sarasota, FL	5.75
221	Dayton, OH	5.82
222	Boston-Quincy, MA M.D.	5.98
223	Longview, TX	6.32
224	Muncie, IN	6.52
225	Riverside-San Bernardino, CA	6.63
225	Santa Cruz-Watsonville, CA	6.63
227	Champaign-Urbana, IL	7.60
228	Seattle (greater), WA	7.67
229	Dallas-Plano-Irving, TX M.D.	7.70
230	Deltona-Daytona Beach, FL	7.75
231	Springfield, MA	7.91
232	Rome, GA	8.07
233	Tuscaloosa, AL	8.09
234	Dallas (greater), TX	8.25
235	Fort Worth-Arlington, TX M.D.	9.38
236	Gulfport-Biloxi, MS	9.42
237	Knoxville, TN	10.73
238	Colorado Springs, CO	11.33
239	West Palm Beach, FL M.D.	11.77
240	Santa Fe, NM	12.00
241	Phoenix-Mesa-Scottsdale, AZ	12.27
242	Cleveland, TN	12.30
243	Louisville, KY-IN	12.33

RANK	METROPOLITAN AREA	SCORE
244	Jonesboro, AR	13.32
244	South Bend-Mishawaka, IN-MI	13.32
246	Sacramento, CA	13.62
247	Victoria, TX	13.77
248	Spartanburg, SC	13.99
249	Muskegon-Norton Shores, MI	14.00
250	Savannah, GA	14.63
251	San Antonio, TX	14.72
252	Chattanooga, TN-GA	14.94
253	Wilmington, DE-MD-NJ M.D.	15.52
254	Newark-Union, NJ-PA M.D.	15.88
255	Huntsville, AL	17.07
256	Milwaukee, WI	17.09
257	Madera, CA	17.12
258	Goldsboro, NC	17.76
259	Topeka, KS	18.07
260	Spokane, WA	18.11
261	Pensacola, FL	18.14
262	Atlantic City, NJ	19.08
263	Fort Lauderdale, FL M.D.	19.22
264	Los Angeles County, CA M.D.	19.39
265	Jacksonville, FL	19.73
266	Waco, TX	20.27
267	St. Louis, MO-IL	20.33
268	Longview, WA	20.37
269	Corpus Christi, TX	20.96
270	Dover, DE	21.01
271	Cleveland-Elyria-Mentor, OH	21.02
271	Winston-Salem, NC	21.02
273	Lima, OH	21.09
274	Brunswick, GA	21.40
275	Rapid City, SD	21.43
276	Farmington, NM	21.73
277	Gary, IN M.D.	21.74
278	Fairbanks, AK	21.99
279	Atlanta, GA	22.25
280	Odessa, TX	22.46
281	Omaha-Council Bluffs, NE-IA	22.60
282	Gainesville, FL	22.96
283	Amarillo, TX	24.14
284	Durham-Chapel Hill, NC	24.32
285	Monroe, LA	24.53
286	Montgomery, AL	24.72
287	Panama City-Lynn Haven, FL	25.45
288	Philadelphia (greater) PA-NJ-MD-DE	25.84
289	Greenville, SC	26.20
290	Nashville-Davidson, TN	26.90
291	Salinas, CA	27.06
292	Decatur, IL	28.71
293	Tacoma, WA M.D.	29.27
294	Columbus, OH	30.27
295	Merced, CA	30.50
296	Tucson, AZ	30.82
297	Orlando, FL	30.94
298	Visalia-Porterville, CA	31.01
299	Alexandria, LA	32.35
300	Houston, TX	32.39
301	Gadsden, AL	32.55
302	Kansas City, MO-KS	34.11
303	Beaumont-Port Arthur, TX	34.23
304	Rocky Mount, NC	34.88
305	Wichita, KS	36.02
306	Vallejo-Fairfield, CA	36.81

RANK	METROPOLITAN AREA	SCORE
307	Lubbock, TX	37.56
308	Redding, CA	38.30
309	Macon, GA	38.31
310	Miami (greater), FL	38.74
311	Philadelphia, PA M.D.	38.79
312	Tallahassee, FL	38.91
313	San Francisco (greater), CA	39.12
314	Pueblo, CO	39.13
315	Baton Rouge, LA	40.23
316	Augusta, GA-SC	41.58
317	Albany, GA	43.13
318	Saginaw, MI	43.32
319	Baltimore-Towson, MD	43.41
320	Florence, SC	43.48
321	Toledo, OH	43.78
322	Battle Creek, MI	43.83
323	Bakersfield, CA	44.52
324	Indianapolis, IN	45.59
325	Yakima, WA	45.64
326	Tulsa, OK	46.28
327	Albuquerque, NM	46.40
328	Columbus, GA-AL	46.88
329	Las Vegas-Paradise, NV	47.25
330	Modesto, CA	47.78
331	Oklahoma City, OK	48.00
332	Springfield, IL	48.31
333	Rockford, IL	48.61
334	Hot Springs, AR	48.93
335	Anniston-Oxford, AL	49.71
336	Birmingham-Hoover, AL	49.76
337	Sumter, SC	54.17
338	Jackson, MS	54.80
339	Detroit (greater), MI	55.46
340	Anchorage, AK	56.31
341	Danville, IL	56.66
342	Fresno, CA	56.92
343	Texarkana, TX-Texarkana, AR	56.98
344	Fayetteville, NC	57.12
345	Anderson, SC	60.74
346	Lawton, OK	62.07
347	Oakland-Fremont, CA M.D.	63.44
348	Miami-Dade County, FL M.D.	66.56
349	Jackson, TN	66.93
350	Mobile, AL	67.19
351	Little Rock, AR	84.03
352	Myrtle Beach, SC	84.55
353	New Orleans, LA	86.99
354	Stockton, CA	89.39
355	Memphis, TN-MS-AR	106.78
356	Flint, MI	118.27
357	Pine Bluff, AR	120.08
358	Detroit-Livonia-Dearborn, MI M.D.	182.19
NA	Chicago (greater), IL-IN-WI**	NA
NA	Chicago-Joilet-Naperville, IL M.D.**	NA
NA	Duluth, MN-WI**	NA
NA	Fargo, ND-MN**	NA
NA	Grand Forks, ND-MN**	NA
NA	La Crosse, WI-MN**	NA
NA	Mankato-North Mankato, MN**	NA
NA	Minneapolis-St. Paul, MN-WI**	NA
NA	Rochester, MN**	NA
NA	St. Cloud, MN**	NA

Source: CQ Press using reported data from the F.B.I. "Crime in the United States 2011"
*Includes murder, rape, robbery, aggravated assault, burglary, and motor vehicle theft. A negative score (in parentheses) indicates a composite crime number below the national rate, a positive number is above the national rate. **Not available.

Alpha Order - City

2012 City Crime Rate Rankings*

RANK	CITY	SCORE
183	Abilene, TX	(4.94)
396	Akron, OH	162.89
375	Albany, GA	117.58
313	Albany, NY	60.60
336	Albuquerque, NM	77.88
66	Alexandria, VA	(48.58)
77	Alhambra, CA	(45.94)
321	Allentown, PA	66.23
18	Allen, TX	(72.10)
291	Amarillo, TX	47.56
9	Amherst, NY	(79.33)
200	Anaheim, CA	2.28
309	Anchorage, AK	58.22
80	Ann Arbor, MI	(45.35)
366	Antioch, CA	102.56
16	Arlington Heights, IL	(73.41)
267	Arlington, TX	35.15
59	Arvada, CO	(51.99)
269	Asheville, NC	36.64
221	Athens-Clarke, GA	7.70
421	Atlanta, GA	266.36
235	Aurora, CO	16.49
105	Aurora, IL	(35.85)
216	Austin, TX	6.87
220	Avondale, AZ	7.38
298	Bakersfield, CA	51.29
172	Baldwin Park, CA	(9.74)
420	Baltimore, MD	260.84
402	Baton Rouge, LA	170.58
370	Beaumont, TX	108.40
55	Beaverton, OR	(54.22)
51	Bellevue, WA	(54.82)
246	Bellflower, CA	21.48
145	Bellingham, WA	(20.11)
101	Bend, OR	(38.69)
254	Berkeley, CA	25.09
136	Bethlehem, PA	(23.47)
161	Billings, MT	(12.94)
425	Birmingham, AL	290.49
227	Bloomington, IL	11.31
167	Bloomington, IN	(11.20)
NA	Bloomington, MN**	NA
96	Boca Raton, FL	(41.65)
75	Boise, ID	(46.33)
333	Boston, MA	76.87
120	Boulder, CO	(31.26)
23	Brick Twnshp, NJ	(71.08)
404	Bridgeport, CT	171.94
381	Brockton, MA	128.58
50	Broken Arrow, OK	(54.93)
NA	Brooklyn Park, MN**	NA
93	Brownsville, TX	(42.39)
194	Bryan, TX	(0.14)
156	Buena Park, CA	(15.74)
405	Buffalo, NY	173.21
88	Burbank, CA	(44.64)
180	Cambridge, MA	(5.95)
432	Camden, NJ	553.67
33	Canton Twnshp, MI	(62.03)
54	Cape Coral, FL	(54.43)
78	Carlsbad, CA	(45.85)
4	Carmel, IN	(83.16)
102	Carrollton, TX	(37.99)
256	Carson, CA	26.82
13	Cary, NC	(74.68)
148	Cedar Rapids, IA	(19.08)
41	Centennial, CO	(60.10)
279	Champaign, IL	40.19
111	Chandler, AZ	(34.37)
212	Charleston, SC	4.71
283	Charlotte, NC	42.67
369	Chattanooga, TN	107.62

RANK	CITY	SCORE
97	Cheektowaga, NY	(41.50)
168	Chesapeake, VA	(10.80)
NA	Chicago, IL**	NA
222	Chico, CA	8.33
17	Chino Hills, CA	(72.32)
137	Chino, CA	(23.23)
132	Chula Vista, CA	(24.18)
213	Cicero, IL	5.32
413	Cincinnati, OH	207.36
192	Citrus Heights, CA	(0.54)
11	Clarkstown, NY	(78.15)
266	Clarksville, TN	34.30
282	Clearwater, FL	42.00
427	Cleveland, OH	308.74
117	Clifton, NJ	(32.68)
127	Clinton Twnshp, MI	(27.95)
197	Clovis, CA	1.85
108	College Station, TX	(35.17)
14	Colonie, NY	(74.49)
278	Colorado Springs, CO	40.10
195	Columbia, MO	0.67
324	Columbus, GA	69.59
387	Columbus, OH	134.32
406	Compton, CA	175.36
240	Concord, CA	17.58
65	Concord, NC	(48.89)
53	Coral Springs, FL	(54.48)
61	Corona, CA	(50.26)
264	Corpus Christi, TX	32.46
134	Costa Mesa, CA	(23.83)
90	Cranston, RI	(43.59)
371	Dallas, TX	113.83
72	Daly City, CA	(46.85)
106	Danbury, CT	(35.76)
285	Davenport, IA	44.65
166	Davie, FL	(11.25)
412	Dayton, OH	205.05
207	Dearborn, MI	4.04
308	Decatur, IL	58.06
209	Deerfield Beach, FL	4.49
128	Denton, TX	(27.54)
328	Denver, CO	73.37
284	Des Moines, IA	44.27
431	Detroit, MI	471.26
274	Downey, CA	39.03
NA	Duluth, MN**	NA
353	Durham, NC	89.93
190	Edinburg, TX	(1.84)
62	Edison Twnshp, NJ	(49.95)
24	Edmond, OK	(70.54)
241	El Cajon, CA	17.70
217	El Monte, CA	7.13
155	El Paso, TX	(15.75)
188	Elgin, IL	(2.09)
408	Elizabeth, NJ	178.22
114	Elk Grove, CA	(33.35)
273	Erie, PA	38.59
158	Escondido, CA	(15.31)
208	Eugene, OR	4.27
224	Evansville, IN	9.55
329	Everett, WA	73.42
198	Fairfield, CA	1.93
360	Fall River, MA	94.78
125	Fargo, ND	(29.13)
52	Farmington Hills, MI	(54.76)
351	Fayetteville, NC	86.08
1	Fishers, IN	(94.87)
430	Flint, MI	468.73
184	Fontana, CA	(4.82)
116	Fort Collins, CO	(32.72)
379	Fort Lauderdale, FL	124.97
317	Fort Smith, AR	64.36

RANK	CITY	SCORE
232	Fort Wayne, IN	12.18
305	Fort Worth, TX	57.10
95	Fremont, CA	(42.02)
346	Fresno, CA	82.46
30	Frisco, TX	(64.38)
115	Fullerton, CA	(33.09)
295	Gainesville, FL	50.72
104	Garden Grove, CA	(36.31)
165	Garland, TX	(11.98)
426	Gary, IN	296.14
25	Gilbert, AZ	(69.66)
315	Glendale, AZ	63.17
31	Glendale, CA	(62.80)
257	Grand Prairie, TX	27.29
293	Grand Rapids, MI	49.92
27	Greece, NY	(66.21)
173	Greeley, CO	(9.58)
149	Green Bay, WI	(18.96)
239	Gresham, OR	17.26
63	Hamilton Twnshp, NJ	(49.89)
367	Hammond, IN	106.70
157	Hampton, VA	(15.56)
411	Hartford, CT	201.40
318	Hawthorne, CA	64.48
297	Hayward, CA	50.80
288	Hemet, CA	46.08
98	Henderson, NV	(40.20)
205	Hesperia, CA	3.77
171	Hialeah, FL	(10.05)
247	High Point, NC	21.71
58	Hillsboro, OR	(52.00)
272	Hollywood, FL	37.75
28	Hoover, AL	(65.17)
377	Houston, TX	120.36
82	Huntington Beach, CA	(45.14)
344	Huntsville, AL	81.78
265	Independence, MO	32.73
399	Indianapolis, IN	165.18
277	Indio, CA	39.65
339	Inglewood, CA	79.82
10	Irvine, CA	(79.11)
140	Irving, TX	(22.87)
295	Jacksonville, FL	50.72
422	Jackson, MS	269.22
306	Jersey City, NJ	57.43
2	Johns Creek, GA	(88.42)
150	Joliet, IL	(17.82)
392	Kansas City, KS	151.88
414	Kansas City, MO	212.54
151	Kennewick, WA	(17.27)
141	Kenosha, WI	(21.83)
355	Kent, WA	90.90
325	Killeen, TX	69.87
372	Knoxville, TN	116.67
255	Lafayette, LA	26.26
21	Lake Forest, CA	(71.87)
271	Lakeland, FL	37.62
22	Lakewood Twnshp, NJ	(71.09)
133	Lakewood, CA	(23.97)
259	Lakewood, CO	28.39
215	Lancaster, CA	6.30
368	Lansing, MI	106.85
211	Laredo, TX	4.70
188	Largo, FL	(2.09)
196	Las Cruces, NM	1.15
322	Las Vegas, NV	68.30
144	Lawrence, KS	(20.42)
398	Lawrence, MA	165.12
361	Lawton, OK	95.85
68	League City, TX	(47.91)
38	Lee's Summit, MO	(61.06)
138	Lewisville, TX	(23.22)

xxiv 2012 City Crime Rate Rankings

Alpha Order - City (continued)

RANK	CITY	SCORE
242	Lexington, KY	18.34
181	Lincoln, NE	(5.80)
419	Little Rock, AR	246.15
122	Livermore, CA	(29.61)
70	Livonia, MI	(47.15)
289	Long Beach, CA	46.67
73	Longmont, CO	(46.79)
251	Longview, TX	23.75
268	Los Angeles, CA	35.36
311	Louisville, KY	59.16
260	Lowell, MA	28.64
292	Lubbock, TX	47.76
162	Lynchburg, VA	(12.71)
299	Lynn, MA	51.85
383	Macon, GA	129.57
163	Madison, WI	(12.40)
249	Manchester, NH	22.59
94	McAllen, TX	(42.27)
60	McKinney, TX	(51.64)
250	Medford, OR	22.67
300	Melbourne, FL	52.37
416	Memphis, TN	228.39
84	Menifee, CA	(44.89)
310	Merced, CA	58.81
42	Meridian, ID	(59.26)
186	Mesa, AZ	(2.57)
187	Mesquite, TX	(2.28)
376	Miami Beach, FL	119.87
393	Miami Gardens, FL	154.88
403	Miami, FL	171.13
123	Midland, TX	(29.60)
394	Milwaukee, WI	156.46
391	Minneapolis, MN	147.70
204	Miramar, FL	3.69
6	Mission Viejo, CA	(82.07)
92	Mission, TX	(42.88)
330	Mobile, AL	74.40
338	Modesto, CA	79.69
314	Montgomery, AL	60.99
243	Moreno Valley, CA	19.32
237	Murfreesboro, TN	17.08
37	Murrieta, CA	(61.16)
118	Nampa, ID	(31.97)
121	Napa, CA	(30.42)
8	Naperville, IL	(79.69)
109	Nashua, NH	(34.81)
373	Nashville, TN	117.40
365	New Bedford, MA	101.52
418	New Haven, CT	231.43
424	New Orleans, LA	284.16
76	New Rochelle, NY	(46.30)
210	New York, NY	4.59
423	Newark, NJ	281.79
43	Newport Beach, CA	(59.11)
245	Newport News, VA	20.88
5	Newton, MA	(82.39)
316	Norfolk, VA	64.04
142	Norman, OK	(21.53)
307	North Charleston, SC	57.57
225	Norwalk, CA	9.77
143	Norwalk, CT	(20.81)
428	Oakland, CA	348.76
177	Oceanside, CA	(6.88)
252	Odessa, TX	24.01
3	O'Fallon, MO	(84.18)
228	Ogden, UT	11.58
380	Oklahoma City, OK	127.25
110	Olathe, KS	(34.50)
347	Omaha, NE	83.10
203	Ontario, CA	2.99
44	Orange, CA	(59.02)
19	Orem, UT	(72.02)
389	Orlando, FL	145.81

RANK	CITY	SCORE
86	Overland Park, KS	(44.76)
129	Oxnard, CA	(27.08)
178	Palm Bay, FL	(6.50)
234	Palmdale, CA	15.10
174	Pasadena, CA	(8.78)
206	Pasadena, TX	3.83
390	Paterson, NJ	146.04
48	Pearland, TX	(55.42)
119	Pembroke Pines, FL	(31.88)
107	Peoria, AZ	(35.35)
350	Peoria, IL	83.85
409	Philadelphia, PA	182.00
326	Phoenix, AZ	71.85
334	Pittsburgh, PA	77.39
67	Plano, TX	(48.40)
169	Plantation, FL	(10.66)
320	Pomona, CA	66.07
349	Pompano Beach, FL	83.40
103	Port St. Lucie, FL	(37.06)
280	Portland, OR	40.57
342	Portsmouth, VA	80.65
64	Provo, UT	(49.66)
354	Pueblo, CO	90.57
154	Quincy, MA	(15.91)
258	Racine, WI	28.01
219	Raleigh, NC	7.37
7	Ramapo, NY	(81.40)
112	Rancho Cucamon., CA	(33.96)
382	Reading, PA	128.79
312	Redding, CA	59.92
113	Redwood City, CA	(33.72)
229	Reno, NV	11.67
248	Renton, WA	22.46
275	Rialto, CA	39.30
69	Richardson, TX	(47.64)
417	Richmond, CA	228.94
362	Richmond, VA	99.63
45	Rio Rancho, NM	(58.97)
230	Riverside, CA	11.94
287	Roanoke, VA	45.35
NA	Rochester, MN**	NA
386	Rochester, NY	131.94
397	Rockford, IL	163.77
81	Roseville, CA	(45.23)
26	Roswell, GA	(69.21)
47	Round Rock, TX	(55.96)
345	Sacramento, CA	82.44
146	Salem, OR	(19.80)
352	Salinas, CA	89.66
343	Salt Lake City, UT	81.17
124	San Angelo, TX	(29.35)
290	San Antonio, TX	47.54
388	San Bernardino, CA	138.88
201	San Diego, CA	2.76
302	San Francisco, CA	55.10
223	San Jose, CA	8.69
303	San Leandro, CA	56.72
83	San Mateo, CA	(45.00)
71	Sandy Springs, GA	(47.05)
74	Sandy, UT	(46.60)
199	Santa Ana, CA	2.11
135	Santa Barbara, CA	(23.80)
87	Santa Clara, CA	(44.65)
56	Santa Clarita, CA	(54.13)
262	Santa Maria, CA	29.25
159	Santa Monica, CA	(14.83)
153	Santa Rosa, CA	(16.47)
276	Savannah, GA	39.49
85	Scottsdale, AZ	(44.88)
193	Scranton, PA	(0.48)
286	Seattle, WA	44.89
337	Shreveport, LA	78.13
12	Simi Valley, CA	(75.14)

RANK	CITY	SCORE
179	Sioux City, IA	(6.05)
191	Sioux Falls, SD	(1.17)
130	Somerville, MA	(25.84)
378	South Bend, IN	122.69
357	South Gate, CA	91.67
233	Sparks, NV	15.05
176	Spokane Valley, WA	(7.10)
348	Spokane, WA	83.36
374	Springfield, IL	117.55
384	Springfield, MA	129.98
358	Springfield, MO	93.60
152	Stamford, CT	(17.06)
34	Sterling Heights, MI	(61.89)
410	Stockton, CA	191.94
244	St. Joseph, MO	20.84
429	St. Louis, MO	363.22
332	St. Paul, MN	76.68
363	St. Petersburg, FL	100.08
131	Suffolk, VA	(24.41)
20	Sugar Land, TX	(71.91)
49	Sunnyvale, CA	(55.32)
164	Sunrise, FL	(12.22)
29	Surprise, AZ	(64.64)
331	Syracuse, NY	75.42
385	Tacoma, WA	130.68
356	Tallahassee, FL	91.24
261	Tampa, FL	28.99
35	Temecula, CA	(61.36)
238	Tempe, AZ	17.12
175	Thornton, CO	(7.20)
15	Thousand Oaks, CA	(74.16)
400	Toledo, OH	166.08
32	Toms River Twnshp, NJ	(62.57)
341	Topeka, KS	80.60
57	Torrance, CA	(52.17)
79	Tracy, CA	(45.84)
415	Trenton, NJ	224.38
36	Troy, MI	(61.25)
335	Tucson, AZ	77.48
395	Tulsa, OK	159.34
263	Tuscaloosa, AL	32.35
40	Tustin, CA	(60.35)
226	Tyler, TX	10.96
214	Upper Darby Twnshp, PA	5.77
99	Vacaville, CA	(40.06)
407	Vallejo, CA	175.65
281	Vancouver, WA	40.87
126	Ventura, CA	(28.32)
294	Victorville, CA	50.48
91	Virginia Beach, VA	(43.12)
253	Visalia, CA	24.72
182	Vista, CA	(5.37)
304	Waco, TX	56.86
301	Warren, MI	54.65
46	Warwick, RI	(56.42)
401	Washington, DC	167.18
218	Waterbury, CT	7.23
160	West Covina, CA	(13.44)
89	West Jordan, UT	(44.05)
364	West Palm Beach, FL	101.01
270	West Valley, UT	37.59
236	Westland, MI	16.95
139	Westminster, CA	(23.11)
147	Westminster, CO	(19.74)
170	Whittier, CA	(10.50)
201	Wichita Falls, TX	2.76
340	Wichita, KS	80.24
323	Wilmington, NC	69.12
327	Winston-Salem, NC	73.03
39	Woodbridge Twnshp, NJ	(60.51)
319	Worcester, MA	65.65
359	Yakima, WA	93.65
185	Yonkers, NY	(4.52)
231	Yuma, AZ	11.99

Source: CQ Press using reported data from the F.B.I. "Crime in the United States 2011"
*Includes murder, rape, robbery, aggravated assault, burglary, and motor vehicle theft. A negative score (in parentheses) indicates a composite crime number below the national rate, a positive number is above the national rate. **Not available.

Rank Order - City

2012 City Crime Rate Rankings* (continued)

RANK	CITY	SCORE	RANK	CITY	SCORE	RANK	CITY	SCORE
1	Fishers, IN	(94.87)	73	Longmont, CO	(46.79)	145	Bellingham, WA	(20.11)
2	Johns Creek, GA	(88.42)	74	Sandy, UT	(46.60)	146	Salem, OR	(19.80)
3	O'Fallon, MO	(84.18)	75	Boise, ID	(46.33)	147	Westminster, CO	(19.74)
4	Carmel, IN	(83.16)	76	New Rochelle, NY	(46.30)	148	Cedar Rapids, IA	(19.08)
5	Newton, MA	(82.39)	77	Alhambra, CA	(45.94)	149	Green Bay, WI	(18.96)
6	Mission Viejo, CA	(82.07)	78	Carlsbad, CA	(45.85)	150	Joliet, IL	(17.82)
7	Ramapo, NY	(81.40)	79	Tracy, CA	(45.84)	151	Kennewick, WA	(17.27)
8	Naperville, IL	(79.69)	80	Ann Arbor, MI	(45.35)	152	Stamford, CT	(17.06)
9	Amherst, NY	(79.33)	81	Roseville, CA	(45.23)	153	Santa Rosa, CA	(16.47)
10	Irvine, CA	(79.11)	82	Huntington Beach, CA	(45.14)	154	Quincy, MA	(15.91)
11	Clarkstown, NY	(78.15)	83	San Mateo, CA	(45.00)	155	El Paso, TX	(15.75)
12	Simi Valley, CA	(75.14)	84	Menifee, CA	(44.89)	156	Buena Park, CA	(15.74)
13	Cary, NC	(74.68)	85	Scottsdale, AZ	(44.88)	157	Hampton, VA	(15.56)
14	Colonie, NY	(74.49)	86	Overland Park, KS	(44.76)	158	Escondido, CA	(15.31)
15	Thousand Oaks, CA	(74.16)	87	Santa Clara, CA	(44.65)	159	Santa Monica, CA	(14.83)
16	Arlington Heights, IL	(73.41)	88	Burbank, CA	(44.64)	160	West Covina, CA	(13.44)
17	Chino Hills, CA	(72.32)	89	West Jordan, UT	(44.05)	161	Billings, MT	(12.94)
18	Allen, TX	(72.10)	90	Cranston, RI	(43.59)	162	Lynchburg, VA	(12.71)
19	Orem, UT	(72.02)	91	Virginia Beach, VA	(43.12)	163	Madison, WI	(12.40)
20	Sugar Land, TX	(71.91)	92	Mission, TX	(42.88)	164	Sunrise, FL	(12.22)
21	Lake Forest, CA	(71.87)	93	Brownsville, TX	(42.39)	165	Garland, TX	(11.98)
22	Lakewood Twnshp, NJ	(71.09)	94	McAllen, TX	(42.27)	166	Davie, FL	(11.25)
23	Brick Twnshp, NJ	(71.08)	95	Fremont, CA	(42.02)	167	Bloomington, IN	(11.20)
24	Edmond, OK	(70.54)	96	Boca Raton, FL	(41.65)	168	Chesapeake, VA	(10.80)
25	Gilbert, AZ	(69.66)	97	Cheektowaga, NY	(41.50)	169	Plantation, FL	(10.66)
26	Roswell, GA	(69.21)	98	Henderson, NV	(40.20)	170	Whittier, CA	(10.50)
27	Greece, NY	(66.21)	99	Vacaville, CA	(40.06)	171	Hialeah, FL	(10.05)
28	Hoover, AL	(65.17)	100	San Marcos, CA	(39.59)	172	Baldwin Park, CA	(9.74)
29	Surprise, AZ	(64.64)	101	Bend, OR	(38.69)	173	Greeley, CO	(9.58)
30	Frisco, TX	(64.38)	102	Carrollton, TX	(37.99)	174	Pasadena, CA	(8.78)
31	Glendale, CA	(62.80)	103	Port St. Lucie, FL	(37.06)	175	Thornton, CO	(7.20)
32	Toms River Twnshp, NJ	(62.57)	104	Garden Grove, CA	(36.31)	176	Spokane Valley, WA	(7.10)
33	Canton Twnshp, MI	(62.03)	105	Aurora, IL	(35.85)	177	Oceanside, CA	(6.88)
34	Sterling Heights, MI	(61.89)	106	Danbury, CT	(35.76)	178	Palm Bay, FL	(6.50)
35	Temecula, CA	(61.36)	107	Peoria, AZ	(35.35)	179	Sioux City, IA	(6.05)
36	Troy, MI	(61.25)	108	College Station, TX	(35.17)	180	Cambridge, MA	(5.95)
37	Murrieta, CA	(61.16)	109	Nashua, NH	(34.81)	181	Lincoln, NE	(5.80)
38	Lee's Summit, MO	(61.06)	110	Olathe, KS	(34.50)	182	Vista, CA	(5.37)
39	Woodbridge Twnshp, NJ	(60.51)	111	Chandler, AZ	(34.37)	183	Abilene, TX	(4.94)
40	Tustin, CA	(60.35)	112	Rancho Cucamon., CA	(33.96)	184	Fontana, CA	(4.82)
41	Centennial, CO	(60.10)	113	Redwood City, CA	(33.72)	185	Yonkers, NY	(4.52)
42	Meridian, ID	(59.26)	114	Elk Grove, CA	(33.35)	186	Mesa, AZ	(2.57)
43	Newport Beach, CA	(59.11)	115	Fullerton, CA	(33.09)	187	Mesquite, TX	(2.28)
44	Orange, CA	(59.02)	116	Fort Collins, CO	(32.72)	188	Elgin, IL	(2.09)
45	Rio Rancho, NM	(58.97)	117	Clifton, NJ	(32.68)	188	Largo, FL	(2.09)
46	Warwick, RI	(56.42)	118	Nampa, ID	(31.97)	190	Edinburg, TX	(1.84)
47	Round Rock, TX	(55.96)	119	Pembroke Pines, FL	(31.88)	191	Sioux Falls, SD	(1.17)
48	Pearland, TX	(55.42)	120	Boulder, CO	(31.26)	192	Citrus Heights, CA	(0.54)
49	Sunnyvale, CA	(55.32)	121	Napa, CA	(30.42)	193	Scranton, PA	(0.48)
50	Broken Arrow, OK	(54.93)	122	Livermore, CA	(29.61)	194	Bryan, TX	(0.14)
51	Bellevue, WA	(54.82)	123	Midland, TX	(29.60)	195	Columbia, MO	0.67
52	Farmington Hills, MI	(54.76)	124	San Angelo, TX	(29.35)	196	Las Cruces, NM	1.15
53	Coral Springs, FL	(54.48)	125	Fargo, ND	(29.13)	197	Clovis, CA	1.85
54	Cape Coral, FL	(54.43)	126	Ventura, CA	(28.32)	198	Fairfield, CA	1.93
55	Beaverton, OR	(54.22)	127	Clinton Twnshp, MI	(27.95)	199	Santa Ana, CA	2.11
56	Santa Clarita, CA	(54.13)	128	Denton, TX	(27.54)	200	Anaheim, CA	2.28
57	Torrance, CA	(52.17)	129	Oxnard, CA	(27.08)	201	San Diego, CA	2.76
58	Hillsboro, OR	(52.00)	130	Somerville, MA	(25.84)	201	Wichita Falls, TX	2.76
59	Arvada, CO	(51.99)	131	Suffolk, VA	(24.41)	203	Ontario, CA	2.99
60	McKinney, TX	(51.64)	132	Chula Vista, CA	(24.18)	204	Miramar, FL	3.69
61	Corona, CA	(50.26)	133	Lakewood, CA	(23.97)	205	Hesperia, CA	3.77
62	Edison Twnshp, NJ	(49.95)	134	Costa Mesa, CA	(23.83)	206	Pasadena, TX	3.83
63	Hamilton Twnshp, NJ	(49.89)	135	Santa Barbara, CA	(23.80)	207	Dearborn, MI	4.04
64	Provo, UT	(49.66)	136	Bethlehem, PA	(23.47)	208	Eugene, OR	4.27
65	Concord, NC	(48.89)	137	Chino, CA	(23.23)	209	Deerfield Beach, FL	4.49
66	Alexandria, VA	(48.58)	138	Lewisville, TX	(23.22)	210	New York, NY	4.59
67	Plano, TX	(48.40)	139	Westminster, CA	(23.11)	211	Laredo, TX	4.70
68	League City, TX	(47.91)	140	Irving, TX	(22.87)	212	Charleston, SC	4.71
69	Richardson, TX	(47.64)	141	Kenosha, WI	(21.83)	213	Cicero, IL	5.32
70	Livonia, MI	(47.15)	142	Norman, OK	(21.53)	214	Upper Darby Twnshp, PA	5.77
71	Sandy Springs, GA	(47.05)	143	Norwalk, CT	(20.81)	215	Lancaster, CA	6.30
72	Daly City, CA	(46.85)	144	Lawrence, KS	(20.42)	216	Austin, TX	6.87

Rank Order - City (continued)

RANK	CITY	SCORE
217	El Monte, CA	7.13
218	Waterbury, CT	7.23
219	Raleigh, NC	7.37
220	Avondale, AZ	7.38
221	Athens-Clarke, GA	7.70
222	Chico, CA	8.33
223	San Jose, CA	8.69
224	Evansville, IN	9.55
225	Norwalk, CA	9.77
226	Tyler, TX	10.96
227	Bloomington, IL	11.31
228	Ogden, UT	11.58
229	Reno, NV	11.67
230	Riverside, CA	11.94
231	Yuma, AZ	11.99
232	Fort Wayne, IN	12.18
233	Sparks, NV	15.05
234	Palmdale, CA	15.10
235	Aurora, CO	16.49
236	Westland, MI	16.95
237	Murfreesboro, TN	17.08
238	Tempe, AZ	17.12
239	Gresham, OR	17.26
240	Concord, CA	17.58
241	El Cajon, CA	17.70
242	Lexington, KY	18.34
243	Moreno Valley, CA	19.32
244	St. Joseph, MO	20.84
245	Newport News, VA	20.88
246	Bellflower, CA	21.48
247	High Point, NC	21.71
248	Renton, WA	22.46
249	Manchester, NH	22.59
250	Medford, OR	22.67
251	Longview, TX	23.75
252	Odessa, TX	24.01
253	Visalia, CA	24.72
254	Berkeley, CA	25.09
255	Lafayette, LA	26.26
256	Carson, CA	26.82
257	Grand Prairie, TX	27.29
258	Racine, WI	28.01
259	Lakewood, CO	28.39
260	Lowell, MA	28.64
261	Tampa, FL	28.99
262	Santa Maria, CA	29.25
263	Tuscaloosa, AL	32.35
264	Corpus Christi, TX	32.46
265	Independence, MO	32.73
266	Clarksville, TN	34.30
267	Arlington, TX	35.15
268	Los Angeles, CA	35.36
269	Asheville, NC	36.64
270	West Valley, UT	37.59
271	Lakeland, FL	37.62
272	Hollywood, FL	37.75
273	Erie, PA	38.59
274	Downey, CA	39.03
275	Rialto, CA	39.30
276	Savannah, GA	39.49
277	Indio, CA	39.65
278	Colorado Springs, CO	40.10
279	Champaign, IL	40.19
280	Portland, OR	40.57
281	Vancouver, WA	40.87
282	Clearwater, FL	42.00
283	Charlotte, NC	42.67
284	Des Moines, IA	44.27
285	Davenport, IA	44.65
286	Seattle, WA	44.89
287	Roanoke, VA	45.35
288	Hemet, CA	46.08
289	Long Beach, CA	46.67
290	San Antonio, TX	47.54
291	Amarillo, TX	47.56
292	Lubbock, TX	47.76
293	Grand Rapids, MI	49.92
294	Victorville, CA	50.48
295	Gainesville, FL	50.72
295	Jacksonville, FL	50.72
297	Hayward, CA	50.80
298	Bakersfield, CA	51.29
299	Lynn, MA	51.85
300	Melbourne, FL	52.37
301	Warren, MI	54.65
302	San Francisco, CA	55.10
303	San Leandro, CA	56.72
304	Waco, TX	56.86
305	Fort Worth, TX	57.10
306	Jersey City, NJ	57.43
307	North Charleston, SC	57.57
308	Decatur, IL	58.06
309	Anchorage, AK	58.22
310	Merced, CA	58.81
311	Louisville, KY	59.16
312	Redding, CA	59.92
313	Albany, NY	60.60
314	Montgomery, AL	60.99
315	Glendale, AZ	63.17
316	Norfolk, VA	64.04
317	Fort Smith, AR	64.36
318	Hawthorne, CA	64.48
319	Worcester, MA	65.65
320	Pomona, CA	66.07
321	Allentown, PA	66.23
322	Las Vegas, NV	68.30
323	Wilmington, NC	69.12
324	Columbus, GA	69.59
325	Killeen, TX	69.87
326	Phoenix, AZ	71.85
327	Winston-Salem, NC	73.03
328	Denver, CO	73.37
329	Everett, WA	73.42
330	Mobile, AL	74.40
331	Syracuse, NY	75.42
332	St. Paul, MN	76.68
333	Boston, MA	76.87
334	Pittsburgh, PA	77.39
335	Tucson, AZ	77.48
336	Albuquerque, NM	77.88
337	Shreveport, LA	78.13
338	Modesto, CA	79.69
339	Inglewood, CA	79.82
340	Wichita, KS	80.24
341	Topeka, KS	80.60
342	Portsmouth, VA	80.65
343	Salt Lake City, UT	81.17
344	Huntsville, AL	81.78
345	Sacramento, CA	82.44
346	Fresno, CA	82.46
347	Omaha, NE	83.10
348	Spokane, WA	83.36
349	Pompano Beach, FL	83.40
350	Peoria, IL	83.85
351	Fayetteville, NC	86.08
352	Salinas, CA	89.66
353	Durham, NC	89.93
354	Pueblo, CO	90.57
355	Kent, WA	90.90
356	Tallahassee, FL	91.24
357	South Gate, CA	91.67
358	Springfield, MO	93.60
359	Yakima, WA	93.65
360	Fall River, MA	94.78
361	Lawton, OK	95.85
362	Richmond, VA	99.63
363	St. Petersburg, FL	100.08
364	West Palm Beach, FL	101.01
365	New Bedford, MA	101.52
366	Antioch, CA	102.56
367	Hammond, IN	106.70
368	Lansing, MI	106.85
369	Chattanooga, TN	107.62
370	Beaumont, TX	108.40
371	Dallas, TX	113.83
372	Knoxville, TN	116.67
373	Nashville, TN	117.40
374	Springfield, IL	117.55
375	Albany, GA	117.58
376	Miami Beach, FL	119.87
377	Houston, TX	120.36
378	South Bend, IN	122.69
379	Fort Lauderdale, FL	124.97
380	Oklahoma City, OK	127.25
381	Brockton, MA	128.58
382	Reading, PA	128.79
383	Macon, GA	129.57
384	Springfield, MA	129.98
385	Tacoma, WA	130.68
386	Rochester, NY	131.94
387	Columbus, OH	134.32
388	San Bernardino, CA	138.88
389	Orlando, FL	145.81
390	Paterson, NJ	146.04
391	Minneapolis, MN	147.70
392	Kansas City, KS	151.88
393	Miami Gardens, FL	154.88
394	Milwaukee, WI	156.46
395	Tulsa, OK	159.34
396	Akron, OH	162.89
397	Rockford, IL	163.77
398	Lawrence, MA	165.12
399	Indianapolis, IN	165.18
400	Toledo, OH	166.08
401	Washington, DC	167.18
402	Baton Rouge, LA	170.58
403	Miami, FL	171.13
404	Bridgeport, CT	171.94
405	Buffalo, NY	173.21
406	Compton, CA	175.36
407	Vallejo, CA	175.65
408	Elizabeth, NJ	178.22
409	Philadelphia, PA	182.00
410	Stockton, CA	191.94
411	Hartford, CT	201.40
412	Dayton, OH	205.05
413	Cincinnati, OH	207.36
414	Kansas City, MO	212.54
415	Trenton, NJ	224.38
416	Memphis, TN	228.39
417	Richmond, CA	228.94
418	New Haven, CT	231.43
419	Little Rock, AR	246.15
420	Baltimore, MD	260.84
421	Atlanta, GA	266.36
422	Jackson, MS	269.22
423	Newark, NJ	281.79
424	New Orleans, LA	284.16
425	Birmingham, AL	290.49
426	Gary, IN	296.14
427	Cleveland, OH	308.74
428	Oakland, CA	348.76
429	St. Louis, MO	363.22
430	Flint, MI	468.73
431	Detroit, MI	471.26
432	Camden, NJ	553.67
NA	Bloomington, MN**	NA
NA	Brooklyn Park, MN**	NA
NA	Chicago, IL**	NA
NA	Duluth, MN**	NA
NA	Rochester, MN**	NA

Source: CQ Press using reported data from the F.B.I. "Crime in the United States 2011"
*Includes murder, rape, robbery, aggravated assault, burglary, and motor vehicle theft. A negative score (in parentheses) indicates a composite crime number below the national rate, a positive number is above the national rate. **Not available.

I. Metropolitan Area Crime Statistics

Crimes in 2011 2	Percent Change in Aggravated Assault Rate:
Crime Rate in 2011 6	2010 to 2011 90
Percent Change in Crime Rate: 2010 to 2011 10	Percent Change in Aggravated Assault Rate:
Percent Change in Crime Rate: 2007 to 2011 14	2007 to 2011 94
Violent Crimes in 2011 18	Property Crimes in 2011 98
Violent Crime Rate in 2011 22	Property Crime Rate in 2011 102
Percent Change in Violent Crime Rate: 2010 to 2011 26	Percent Change in Property Crime Rate: 2010 to 2011 ... 106
Percent Change in Violent Crime Rate: 2007 to 2011 30	Percent Change in Property Crime Rate: 2007 to 2011 ... 110
Murders in 2011 34	Burglaries in 2011 114
Murder Rate in 2011 38	Burglary Rate in 2011 118
Percent Change in Murder Rate: 2010 to 2011 42	Percent Change in Burglary Rate: 2010 to 2011 122
Percent Change in Murder Rate: 2007 to 2011 46	Percent Change in Burglary Rate: 2007 to 2011 126
Rapes in 2011 50	Larceny-Thefts in 2011 130
Rape Rate in 2011 54	Larceny-Theft Rate in 2011 134
Percent Change in Rape Rate: 2010 to 2011 58	Percent Change in Larceny-Theft Rate: 2010 to 2011 138
Percent Change in Rape Rate: 2007 to 2011 62	Percent Change in Larceny-Theft Rate: 2007 to 2011 142
Robberies in 2011 66	Motor Vehicle Thefts in 2011 146
Robbery Rate in 2011 70	Motor Vehicle Theft Rate in 2011................... 150
Percent Change in Robbery Rate: 2010 to 2011 74	Percent Change in Motor Vehicle Theft Rate:
Percent Change in Robbery Rate: 2007 to 2011 78	2010 to 2011 154
Aggravated Assaults in 2011....................... 82	Percent Change in Motor Vehicle Theft Rate:
Aggravated Assault Rate in 2011 86	2007 to 2011 158

Please note the following for Tables 1 through 40 and 85 through 87:

- All listings are for Metropolitan Statistical Areas (M.S.A.s) except for those ending with "M.D."
- Listings with "M.D." are Metropolitan Divisions, which are smaller parts of eleven large M.S.A.s. These eleven M.S.A.s further divided into M.D.s are identified using "(greater)" following the metropolitan area name.
- For example, the "Dallas (greater)" M.S.A. includes the two M.D.s of Dallas-Plano-Irving and Fort Worth-Arlington. The data for the M.D.s are included in the data for the overall M.S.A.
- The name of a M.S.A. or M.D. is subject to change based on the changing proportional size of the largest cities included within it. Percent changes are calculated in this book if the MSA or M.D. has not substantially changed, despite the changes in name. In the tables in this book, some M.S.A. and M.D. names are abbreviated to preserve space.

Alpha Order - Metro Area

1. Crimes in 2011
National Total = 10,266,737 Crimes*

RANK	METROPOLITAN AREA	CRIMES
256	Abilene, TX	5,614
90	Akron, OH	25,439
92	Albany-Schenectady-Troy, NY	24,290
202	Albany, GA	7,799
64	Albuquerque, NM	42,273
200	Alexandria, LA	7,848
111	Allentown, PA-NJ	20,530
333	Altoona, PA	2,855
162	Amarillo, TX	11,633
342	Ames, IA	2,601
150	Anchorage, AK	12,722
169	Anderson, SC	10,802
189	Ann Arbor, MI	9,001
253	Anniston-Oxford, AL	5,696
300	Appleton, WI	4,160
160	Asheville, NC	11,836
198	Athens-Clarke County, GA	8,003
8	Atlanta, GA	211,017
171	Atlantic City, NJ	10,788
273	Auburn, AL	4,883
87	Augusta, GA-SC	26,578
44	Austin-Round Rock, TX	65,461
73	Bakersfield, CA	34,518
24	Baltimore-Towson, MD	100,930
283	Bangor, ME	4,439
215	Barnstable Town, MA	7,036
69	Baton Rouge, LA	37,746
237	Battle Creek, MI	6,080
345	Bay City, MI	2,408
121	Beaumont-Port Arthur, TX	17,542
221	Bellingham, WA	6,834
259	Bend, OR	5,442
91	Bethesda-Frederick, MD M.D.	24,790
241	Billings, MT	5,939
211	Binghamton, NY	7,196
57	Birmingham-Hoover, AL	52,343
331	Bismarck, ND	2,945
288	Blacksburg, VA	4,382
292	Bloomington-Normal, IL	4,243
251	Bloomington, IN	5,756
135	Boise City-Nampa, ID	13,984
20	Boston (greater), MA-NH	113,705
51	Boston-Quincy, MA M.D.	54,580
212	Boulder, CO	7,162
315	Bowling Green, KY	3,587
195	Bremerton-Silverdale, WA	8,287
113	Bridgeport-Stamford, CT	20,035
119	Brownsville-Harlingen, TX	18,272
248	Brunswick, GA	5,844
66	Buffalo-Niagara Falls, NY	38,607
227	Burlington, NC	6,647
78	Cambridge-Newton, MA M.D.	30,877
68	Camden, NJ M.D.	37,909
142	Canton, OH	13,733
114	Cape Coral-Fort Myers, FL	19,711
302	Cape Girardeau, MO-IL	4,011
355	Carson City, NV	1,423
340	Casper, WY	2,626
222	Cedar Rapids, IA	6,810
213	Champaign-Urbana, IL	7,133
179	Charleston, WV	10,256
41	Charlotte-Gastonia, NC-SC	68,777
285	Charlottesville, VA	4,419
97	Chattanooga, TN-GA	22,472
336	Cheyenne, WY	2,785
NA	Chicago (greater), IL-IN-WI**	NA
NA	Chicago-Joilet-Naperville, IL M.D.**	NA
240	Chico, CA	5,951
31	Cincinnati-Middletown, OH-KY-IN	80,978
188	Clarksville, TN-KY	9,055
40	Cleveland-Elyria-Mentor, OH	70,000
290	Cleveland, TN	4,288
194	College Station-Bryan, TX	8,301
104	Colorado Springs, CO	21,608
231	Columbia, MO	6,299
124	Columbus, GA-AL	16,972
321	Columbus, IN	3,339
30	Columbus, OH	83,464
107	Corpus Christi, TX	20,939
348	Corvallis, OR	2,326
238	Crestview-Fort Walton Beach, FL	6,033
318	Cumberland, MD-WV	3,361
6	Dallas (greater), TX	250,926
11	Dallas-Plano-Irving, TX M.D.	161,282
279	Dalton, GA	4,608
308	Danville, IL	3,791
329	Danville, VA	3,014
148	Davenport, IA-IL	12,814
77	Dayton, OH	31,400
289	Decatur, AL	4,294
306	Decatur, IL	3,941
109	Deltona-Daytona Beach, FL	20,806
32	Denver-Aurora, CO	79,922
115	Des Moines-West Des Moines, IA	19,301
14	Detroit (greater), MI	148,207
27	Detroit-Livonia-Dearborn, MI M.D.	93,957
271	Dothan, AL	4,989
218	Dover, DE	7,012
350	Dubuque, IA	2,057
NA	Duluth, MN-WI**	NA
103	Durham-Chapel Hill, NC	21,639
314	Eau Claire, WI	3,654
60	Edison, NJ M.D.	48,781
230	El Centro, CA	6,377
95	El Paso, TX	22,817
351	Elizabethtown, KY	1,992
349	Elmira, NY	2,278
196	Erie, PA	8,272
143	Eugene-Springfield, OR	13,640
167	Evansville, IN-KY	10,845
354	Fairbanks, AK	1,588
NA	Fargo, ND-MN**	NA
316	Farmington, NM	3,580
99	Fayetteville, NC	22,047
268	Flagstaff, AZ	5,150
112	Flint, MI	20,114
301	Florence-Muscle Shoals, AL	4,018
161	Florence, SC	11,726
353	Fond du Lac, WI	1,809
193	Fort Collins-Loveland, CO	8,319
33	Fort Lauderdale, FL M.D.	79,698
185	Fort Smith, AR-OK	9,680
151	Fort Wayne, IN	12,547
29	Fort Worth-Arlington, TX M.D.	89,644
61	Fresno, CA	45,939
269	Gadsden, AL	5,137
168	Gainesville, FL	10,807
277	Gainesville, GA	4,789
86	Gary, IN M.D.	27,009
347	Glens Falls, NY	2,342
252	Goldsboro, NC	5,737
NA	Grand Forks, ND-MN**	NA
281	Grand Junction, CO	4,512
110	Grand Rapids-Wyoming, MI	20,547
326	Great Falls, MT	3,151
235	Greeley, CO	6,155
243	Green Bay, WI	5,910
85	Greenville, SC	27,020
174	Gulfport-Biloxi, MS	10,570
226	Hagerstown-Martinsburg, MD-WV	6,695
304	Hanford-Corcoran, CA	3,978
140	Harrisburg-Carlisle, PA	13,802
352	Harrisonburg, VA	1,813
83	Hartford, CT	27,975
141	Hickory, NC	13,767
334	Hinesville, GA	2,821
264	Holland-Grand Haven, MI	5,243
250	Hot Springs, AR	5,805
205	Houma, LA	7,629
7	Houston, TX	250,630
125	Huntsville, AL	16,827
330	Idaho Falls, ID	2,973
35	Indianapolis, IN	76,859
324	Iowa City, IA	3,178
50	Jacksonville, FL	57,374
247	Jacksonville, NC	5,846
101	Jackson, MS	21,743
257	Jackson, TN	5,589
262	Janesville, WI	5,270
299	Jefferson City, MO	4,193
225	Johnson City, TN	6,715
319	Johnstown, PA	3,350
263	Jonesboro, AR	5,262
216	Joplin, MO	7,035
311	Kankakee-Bradley, IL	3,731
34	Kansas City, MO-KS	79,432
208	Kennewick-Pasco-Richland, WA	7,454
146	Killeen-Temple-Fort Hood, TX	13,045
165	Kingsport, TN-VA	11,355
309	Kingston, NY	3,770
80	Knoxville, TN	30,148
313	Kokomo, IN	3,681
NA	La Crosse, WI-MN**	NA
246	Lafayette, IN	5,859
152	Lafayette, LA	12,342
116	Lake Co.-Kenosha Co., IL-WI M.D.	19,052
220	Lake Havasu City-Kingman, AZ	6,872
96	Lakeland, FL	22,649
164	Lancaster, PA	11,532
149	Lansing-East Lansing, MI	12,801

Note: All listings are for Metropolitan Statistical Areas (M.S.A.s) except for those ending with "M.D." Listings with "M.D." are Metropolitan Divisions which are smaller parts of eleven large M.S.A.s. See explanatory note at beginning of metropolitan area section.

Alpha Order - Metro Area (continued)

RANK	METROPOLITAN AREA	CRIMES
156	Laredo, TX	12,087
206	Las Cruces, NM	7,578
43	Las Vegas-Paradise, NV	66,408
274	Lawrence, KS	4,878
224	Lawton, OK	6,765
338	Lebanon, PA	2,661
320	Lewiston-Auburn, ME	3,347
108	Lexington-Fayette, KY	20,928
282	Lima, OH	4,485
157	Lincoln, NE	11,915
65	Little Rock, AR	41,811
356	Logan, UT-ID	1,417
197	Longview, TX	8,209
310	Longview, WA	3,750
3	Los Angeles County, CA M.D.	274,252
2	Los Angeles (greater), CA	342,418
53	Louisville, KY-IN	54,203
130	Lubbock, TX	15,617
255	Lynchburg, VA	5,618
138	Macon, GA	13,900
280	Madera, CA	4,604
128	Madison, WI	16,018
177	Manchester-Nashua, NH	10,437
332	Manhattan, KS	2,930
NA	Mankato-North Mankato, MN**	NA
254	Mansfield, OH	5,689
74	McAllen-Edinburg-Mission, TX	33,632
207	Medford, OR	7,487
38	Memphis, TN-MS-AR	73,539
176	Merced, CA	10,541
4	Miami (greater), FL	270,178
16	Miami-Dade County, FL M.D.	138,109
294	Michigan City-La Porte, IN	4,232
297	Midland, TX	4,215
49	Milwaukee, WI	58,252
NA	Minneapolis-St. Paul, MN-WI**	NA
327	Missoula, MT	3,137
97	Mobile, AL	22,472
102	Modesto, CA	21,671
187	Monroe, LA	9,198
296	Monroe, MI	4,229
126	Montgomery, AL	16,496
266	Morristown, TN	5,178
258	Mount Vernon-Anacortes, WA	5,535
305	Muncie, IN	3,954
201	Muskegon-Norton Shores, MI	7,838
123	Myrtle Beach, SC	17,051
322	Napa, CA	3,251
214	Naples-Marco Island, FL	7,105
45	Nashville-Davidson, TN	63,683
59	Nassau-Suffolk, NY M.D.	50,345
84	New Haven-Milford, CT	27,664
62	New Orleans, LA	45,764
1	New York (greater), NY-NJ-PA	407,955
5	New York-W. Plains NY-NJ M.D.	255,788
54	Newark-Union, NJ-PA M.D.	53,041
81	North Port-Bradenton-Sarasota, FL	29,515
307	Norwich-New London, CT	3,843
26	Oakland-Fremont, CA M.D.	97,345
180	Ocala, FL	10,049
275	Ocean City, NJ	4,853
265	Odessa, TX	5,189
131	Ogden-Clearfield, UT	15,121

RANK	METROPOLITAN AREA	CRIMES
47	Oklahoma City, OK	60,789
204	Olympia, WA	7,710
75	Omaha-Council Bluffs, NE-IA	32,625
28	Orlando, FL	92,130
317	Oshkosh-Neenah, WI	3,516
323	Owensboro, KY	3,214
129	Oxnard-Thousand Oaks, CA	15,874
105	Palm Bay-Melbourne, FL	21,417
346	Palm Coast, FL	2,375
192	Panama City-Lynn Haven, FL	8,339
244	Pascagoula, MS	5,906
118	Peabody, MA M.D.	18,562
117	Pensacola, FL	18,717
155	Peoria, IL	12,127
9	Philadelphia (greater) PA-NJ-MD-DE	196,416
18	Philadelphia, PA M.D.	131,959
10	Phoenix-Mesa-Scottsdale, AZ	171,634
249	Pine Bluff, AR	5,836
55	Pittsburgh, PA	52,564
312	Pittsfield, MA	3,725
335	Pocatello, ID	2,803
144	Port St. Lucie, FL	13,544
36	Portland-Vancouver, OR-WA	76,506
137	Portland, ME	13,934
132	Poughkeepsie, NY	14,738
261	Prescott, AZ	5,393
153	Provo-Orem, UT	12,232
199	Pueblo, CO	7,997
284	Punta Gorda, FL	4,433
236	Racine, WI	6,107
76	Raleigh-Cary, NC	32,497
294	Rapid City, SD	4,232
178	Reading, PA	10,259
232	Redding, CA	6,256
154	Reno-Sparks, NV	12,132
71	Richmond, VA	34,766
17	Riverside-San Bernardino, CA	135,648
190	Roanoke, VA	8,825
NA	Rochester, MN**	NA
79	Rochester, NY	30,448
145	Rockford, IL	13,344
184	Rockingham County, NH M.D.	9,686
223	Rocky Mount, NC	6,792
298	Rome, GA	4,210
39	Sacramento, CA	70,573
228	Saginaw, MI	6,554
158	Salem, OR	11,886
159	Salinas, CA	11,844
278	Salisbury, MD	4,630
58	Salt Lake City, UT	50,767
291	San Angelo, TX	4,245
21	San Antonio, TX	110,817
37	San Diego, CA	76,111
12	San Francisco (greater), CA	157,398
48	San Francisco-S. Mateo, CA M.D.	60,053
63	San Jose, CA	44,644
219	San Luis Obispo, CA	6,876
343	Sandusky, OH	2,553
42	Santa Ana-Anaheim, CA M.D.	68,166
172	Santa Barbara-Santa Maria, CA	10,740
183	Santa Cruz-Watsonville, CA	9,913
242	Santa Fe, NM	5,930
182	Santa Rosa-Petaluma, CA	10,009

RANK	METROPOLITAN AREA	CRIMES
136	Savannah, GA	13,975
134	Scranton--Wilkes-Barre, PA	14,162
15	Seattle (greater), WA	143,682
22	Seattle-Bellevue-Everett, WA M.D.	108,972
287	Sebastian-Vero Beach, FL	4,409
344	Sheboygan, WI	2,551
293	Sherman-Denison, TX	4,241
276	Sioux City, IA-NE-SD	4,829
239	Sioux Falls, SD	6,010
147	South Bend-Mishawaka, IN-MI	12,989
163	Spartanburg, SC	11,602
89	Spokane, WA	26,235
175	Springfield, IL	10,545
94	Springfield, MA	23,687
100	Springfield, MO	21,973
234	Springfield, OH	6,166
339	State College, PA	2,641
70	Stockton, CA	34,836
NA	St. Cloud, MN**	NA
266	St. Joseph, MO-KS	5,178
23	St. Louis, MO-IL	102,357
286	Sumter, SC	4,416
120	Syracuse, NY	17,767
72	Tacoma, WA M.D.	34,710
127	Tallahassee, FL	16,199
25	Tampa-St Petersburg, FL	99,775
217	Terre Haute, IN	7,014
210	Texarkana, TX-Texarkana, AR	7,341
NA	Toledo, OH**	NA
170	Topeka, KS	10,796
186	Trenton-Ewing, NJ	9,614
NA	Tucson, AZ**	NA
67	Tulsa, OK	38,426
191	Tuscaloosa, AL	8,770
203	Tyler, TX	7,786
209	Utica-Rome, NY	7,409
272	Valdosta, GA	4,900
139	Vallejo-Fairfield, CA	13,889
270	Victoria, TX	5,132
46	Virginia Beach-Norfolk, VA-NC	61,498
122	Visalia-Porterville, CA	17,276
173	Waco, TX	10,674
229	Warner Robins, GA	6,417
52	Warren-Farmington Hills, MI M.D.	54,250
13	Washington (greater) DC-VA-MD-WV	153,760
19	Washington, DC-VA-MD-WV M.D.	128,970
303	Waterloo-Cedar Falls, IA	4,006
341	Wausau, WI	2,615
328	Wenatchee, WA	3,109
56	West Palm Beach, FL M.D.	52,371
233	Wichita Falls, TX	6,233
82	Wichita, KS	28,328
337	Williamsport, PA	2,772
88	Wilmington, DE-MD-NJ M.D.	26,548
133	Wilmington, NC	14,716
324	Winchester, VA-WV	3,178
93	Winston-Salem, NC	23,745
106	Worcester, MA	21,044
166	Yakima, WA	11,225
181	York-Hanover, PA	10,041
260	Yuba City, CA	5,400
245	Yuma, AZ	5,898

Source: CQ Press using reported data from the F.B.I. "Crime in the United States 2011"
*Includes murder, rape, robbery, aggravated assault, burglary, larceny-theft, and motor vehicle theft.
**Not available.

Rank Order - Metro Area

1. Crimes in 2011 (continued)
National Total = 10,266,737 Crimes*

RANK	METROPOLITAN AREA	CRIMES
1	New York (greater), NY-NJ-PA	407,955
2	Los Angeles (greater), CA	342,418
3	Los Angeles County, CA M.D.	274,252
4	Miami (greater), FL	270,178
5	New York-W. Plains NY-NJ M.D.	255,788
6	Dallas (greater), TX	250,926
7	Houston, TX	250,630
8	Atlanta, GA	211,017
9	Philadelphia (greater) PA-NJ-MD-DE	196,416
10	Phoenix-Mesa-Scottsdale, AZ	171,634
11	Dallas-Plano-Irving, TX M.D.	161,282
12	San Francisco (greater), CA	157,398
13	Washington (greater) DC-VA-MD-WV	153,760
14	Detroit (greater), MI	148,207
15	Seattle (greater), WA	143,682
16	Miami-Dade County, FL M.D.	138,109
17	Riverside-San Bernardino, CA	135,648
18	Philadelphia, PA M.D.	131,959
19	Washington, DC-VA-MD-WV M.D.	128,970
20	Boston (greater), MA-NH	113,705
21	San Antonio, TX	110,817
22	Seattle-Bellevue-Everett, WA M.D.	108,972
23	St. Louis, MO-IL	102,357
24	Baltimore-Towson, MD	100,930
25	Tampa-St Petersburg, FL	99,775
26	Oakland-Fremont, CA M.D.	97,345
27	Detroit-Livonia-Dearborn, MI M.D.	93,957
28	Orlando, FL	92,130
29	Fort Worth-Arlington, TX M.D.	89,644
30	Columbus, OH	83,464
31	Cincinnati-Middletown, OH-KY-IN	80,978
32	Denver-Aurora, CO	79,922
33	Fort Lauderdale, FL M.D.	79,698
34	Kansas City, MO-KS	79,432
35	Indianapolis, IN	76,859
36	Portland-Vancouver, OR-WA	76,506
37	San Diego, CA	76,111
38	Memphis, TN-MS-AR	73,539
39	Sacramento, CA	70,573
40	Cleveland-Elyria-Mentor, OH	70,000
41	Charlotte-Gastonia, NC-SC	68,777
42	Santa Ana-Anaheim, CA M.D.	68,166
43	Las Vegas-Paradise, NV	66,408
44	Austin-Round Rock, TX	65,461
45	Nashville-Davidson, TN	63,683
46	Virginia Beach-Norfolk, VA-NC	61,498
47	Oklahoma City, OK	60,789
48	San Francisco-S. Mateo, CA M.D.	60,053
49	Milwaukee, WI	58,252
50	Jacksonville, FL	57,374
51	Boston-Quincy, MA M.D.	54,580
52	Warren-Farmington Hills, MI M.D.	54,250
53	Louisville, KY-IN	54,203
54	Newark-Union, NJ-PA M.D.	53,041
55	Pittsburgh, PA	52,564
56	West Palm Beach, FL M.D.	52,371
57	Birmingham-Hoover, AL	52,343
58	Salt Lake City, UT	50,767
59	Nassau-Suffolk, NY M.D.	50,345
60	Edison, NJ M.D.	48,781
61	Fresno, CA	45,939
62	New Orleans, LA	45,764
63	San Jose, CA	44,644
64	Albuquerque, NM	42,273
65	Little Rock, AR	41,811
66	Buffalo-Niagara Falls, NY	38,607
67	Tulsa, OK	38,426
68	Camden, NJ M.D.	37,909
69	Baton Rouge, LA	37,746
70	Stockton, CA	34,836
71	Richmond, VA	34,766
72	Tacoma, WA M.D.	34,710
73	Bakersfield, CA	34,518
74	McAllen-Edinburg-Mission, TX	33,632
75	Omaha-Council Bluffs, NE-IA	32,625
76	Raleigh-Cary, NC	32,497
77	Dayton, OH	31,400
78	Cambridge-Newton, MA M.D.	30,877
79	Rochester, NY	30,448
80	Knoxville, TN	30,148
81	North Port-Bradenton-Sarasota, FL	29,515
82	Wichita, KS	28,328
83	Hartford, CT	27,975
84	New Haven-Milford, CT	27,664
85	Greenville, SC	27,020
86	Gary, IN M.D.	27,009
87	Augusta, GA-SC	26,578
88	Wilmington, DE-MD-NJ M.D.	26,548
89	Spokane, WA	26,235
90	Akron, OH	25,439
91	Bethesda-Frederick, MD M.D.	24,790
92	Albany-Schenectady-Troy, NY	24,290
93	Winston-Salem, NC	23,745
94	Springfield, MA	23,687
95	El Paso, TX	22,817
96	Lakeland, FL	22,649
97	Chattanooga, TN-GA	22,472
97	Mobile, AL	22,472
99	Fayetteville, NC	22,047
100	Springfield, MO	21,973
101	Jackson, MS	21,743
102	Modesto, CA	21,671
103	Durham-Chapel Hill, NC	21,639
104	Colorado Springs, CO	21,608
105	Palm Bay-Melbourne, FL	21,417
106	Worcester, MA	21,044
107	Corpus Christi, TX	20,939
108	Lexington-Fayette, KY	20,928
109	Deltona-Daytona Beach, FL	20,806
110	Grand Rapids-Wyoming, MI	20,547
111	Allentown, PA-NJ	20,530
112	Flint, MI	20,114
113	Bridgeport-Stamford, CT	20,035
114	Cape Coral-Fort Myers, FL	19,711
115	Des Moines-West Des Moines, IA	19,301
116	Lake Co.-Kenosha Co., IL-WI M.D.	19,052
117	Pensacola, FL	18,717
118	Peabody, MA M.D.	18,562
119	Brownsville-Harlingen, TX	18,272
120	Syracuse, NY	17,767
121	Beaumont-Port Arthur, TX	17,542
122	Visalia-Porterville, CA	17,276
123	Myrtle Beach, SC	17,051
124	Columbus, GA-AL	16,972
125	Huntsville, AL	16,827
126	Montgomery, AL	16,496
127	Tallahassee, FL	16,199
128	Madison, WI	16,018
129	Oxnard-Thousand Oaks, CA	15,874
130	Lubbock, TX	15,617
131	Ogden-Clearfield, UT	15,121
132	Poughkeepsie, NY	14,738
133	Wilmington, NC	14,716
134	Scranton--Wilkes-Barre, PA	14,162
135	Boise City-Nampa, ID	13,984
136	Savannah, GA	13,975
137	Portland, ME	13,934
138	Macon, GA	13,900
139	Vallejo-Fairfield, CA	13,889
140	Harrisburg-Carlisle, PA	13,802
141	Hickory, NC	13,767
142	Canton, OH	13,733
143	Eugene-Springfield, OR	13,640
144	Port St. Lucie, FL	13,544
145	Rockford, IL	13,344
146	Killeen-Temple-Fort Hood, TX	13,045
147	South Bend-Mishawaka, IN-MI	12,989
148	Davenport, IA-IL	12,814
149	Lansing-East Lansing, MI	12,801
150	Anchorage, AK	12,722
151	Fort Wayne, IN	12,547
152	Lafayette, LA	12,342
153	Provo-Orem, UT	12,232
154	Reno-Sparks, NV	12,132
155	Peoria, IL	12,127
156	Laredo, TX	12,087
157	Lincoln, NE	11,915
158	Salem, OR	11,886
159	Salinas, CA	11,844
160	Asheville, NC	11,836
161	Florence, SC	11,726
162	Amarillo, TX	11,633
163	Spartanburg, SC	11,602
164	Lancaster, PA	11,532
165	Kingsport, TN-VA	11,355
166	Yakima, WA	11,225
167	Evansville, IN-KY	10,845
168	Gainesville, FL	10,807
169	Anderson, SC	10,802
170	Topeka, KS	10,796
171	Atlantic City, NJ	10,788
172	Santa Barbara-Santa Maria, CA	10,740
173	Waco, TX	10,674
174	Gulfport-Biloxi, MS	10,570
175	Springfield, IL	10,545
176	Merced, CA	10,541
177	Manchester-Nashua, NH	10,437
178	Reading, PA	10,259
179	Charleston, WV	10,256
180	Ocala, FL	10,049

Note: All listings are for Metropolitan Statistical Areas (M.S.A.s) except for those ending with "M.D." Listings with "M.D." are Metropolitan Divisions which are smaller parts of eleven large M.S.A.s. See explanatory note at beginning of metropolitan area section.

Rank Order - Metro Area (continued)

RANK	METROPOLITAN AREA	CRIMES
181	York-Hanover, PA	10,041
182	Santa Rosa-Petaluma, CA	10,009
183	Santa Cruz-Watsonville, CA	9,913
184	Rockingham County, NH M.D.	9,686
185	Fort Smith, AR-OK	9,680
186	Trenton-Ewing, NJ	9,614
187	Monroe, LA	9,198
188	Clarksville, TN-KY	9,055
189	Ann Arbor, MI	9,001
190	Roanoke, VA	8,825
191	Tuscaloosa, AL	8,770
192	Panama City-Lynn Haven, FL	8,339
193	Fort Collins-Loveland, CO	8,319
194	College Station-Bryan, TX	8,301
195	Bremerton-Silverdale, WA	8,287
196	Erie, PA	8,272
197	Longview, TX	8,209
198	Athens-Clarke County, GA	8,003
199	Pueblo, CO	7,997
200	Alexandria, LA	7,848
201	Muskegon-Norton Shores, MI	7,838
202	Albany, GA	7,799
203	Tyler, TX	7,786
204	Olympia, WA	7,710
205	Houma, LA	7,629
206	Las Cruces, NM	7,578
207	Medford, OR	7,487
208	Kennewick-Pasco-Richland, WA	7,454
209	Utica-Rome, NY	7,409
210	Texarkana, TX-Texarkana, AR	7,341
211	Binghamton, NY	7,196
212	Boulder, CO	7,162
213	Champaign-Urbana, IL	7,133
214	Naples-Marco Island, FL	7,105
215	Barnstable Town, MA	7,036
216	Joplin, MO	7,035
217	Terre Haute, IN	7,014
218	Dover, DE	7,012
219	San Luis Obispo, CA	6,876
220	Lake Havasu City-Kingman, AZ	6,872
221	Bellingham, WA	6,834
222	Cedar Rapids, IA	6,810
223	Rocky Mount, NC	6,792
224	Lawton, OK	6,765
225	Johnson City, TN	6,715
226	Hagerstown-Martinsburg, MD-WV	6,695
227	Burlington, NC	6,647
228	Saginaw, MI	6,554
229	Warner Robins, GA	6,417
230	El Centro, CA	6,377
231	Columbia, MO	6,299
232	Redding, CA	6,256
233	Wichita Falls, TX	6,233
234	Springfield, OH	6,166
235	Greeley, CO	6,155
236	Racine, WI	6,107
237	Battle Creek, MI	6,080
238	Crestview-Fort Walton Beach, FL	6,033
239	Sioux Falls, SD	6,010
240	Chico, CA	5,951
241	Billings, MT	5,939
242	Santa Fe, NM	5,930
243	Green Bay, WI	5,910
244	Pascagoula, MS	5,906
245	Yuma, AZ	5,898
246	Lafayette, IN	5,859
247	Jacksonville, NC	5,846
248	Brunswick, GA	5,844
249	Pine Bluff, AR	5,836
250	Hot Springs, AR	5,805
251	Bloomington, IN	5,756
252	Goldsboro, NC	5,737
253	Anniston-Oxford, AL	5,696
254	Mansfield, OH	5,689
255	Lynchburg, VA	5,618
256	Abilene, TX	5,614
257	Jackson, TN	5,589
258	Mount Vernon-Anacortes, WA	5,535
259	Bend, OR	5,442
260	Yuba City, CA	5,400
261	Prescott, AZ	5,393
262	Janesville, WI	5,270
263	Jonesboro, AR	5,262
264	Holland-Grand Haven, MI	5,243
265	Odessa, TX	5,189
266	Morristown, TN	5,178
266	St. Joseph, MO-KS	5,178
268	Flagstaff, AZ	5,150
269	Gadsden, AL	5,137
270	Victoria, TX	5,132
271	Dothan, AL	4,989
272	Valdosta, GA	4,900
273	Auburn, AL	4,883
274	Lawrence, KS	4,878
275	Ocean City, NJ	4,853
276	Sioux City, IA-NE-SD	4,829
277	Gainesville, GA	4,789
278	Salisbury, MD	4,630
279	Dalton, GA	4,608
280	Madera, CA	4,604
281	Grand Junction, CO	4,512
282	Lima, OH	4,485
283	Bangor, ME	4,439
284	Punta Gorda, FL	4,433
285	Charlottesville, VA	4,419
286	Sumter, SC	4,416
287	Sebastian-Vero Beach, FL	4,409
288	Blacksburg, VA	4,382
289	Decatur, AL	4,294
290	Cleveland, TN	4,288
291	San Angelo, TX	4,245
292	Bloomington-Normal, IL	4,243
293	Sherman-Denison, TX	4,241
294	Michigan City-La Porte, IN	4,232
294	Rapid City, SD	4,232
296	Monroe, MI	4,229
297	Midland, TX	4,215
298	Rome, GA	4,210
299	Jefferson City, MO	4,193
300	Appleton, WI	4,160
301	Florence-Muscle Shoals, AL	4,018
302	Cape Girardeau, MO-IL	4,011
303	Waterloo-Cedar Falls, IA	4,006
304	Hanford-Corcoran, CA	3,978
305	Muncie, IN	3,954
306	Decatur, IL	3,941
307	Norwich-New London, CT	3,843
308	Danville, IL	3,791
309	Kingston, NY	3,770
310	Longview, WA	3,750
311	Kankakee-Bradley, IL	3,731
312	Pittsfield, MA	3,725
313	Kokomo, IN	3,681
314	Eau Claire, WI	3,654
315	Bowling Green, KY	3,587
316	Farmington, NM	3,580
317	Oshkosh-Neenah, WI	3,516
318	Cumberland, MD-WV	3,361
319	Johnstown, PA	3,350
320	Lewiston-Auburn, ME	3,347
321	Columbus, IN	3,339
322	Napa, CA	3,251
323	Owensboro, KY	3,214
324	Iowa City, IA	3,178
324	Winchester, VA-WV	3,178
326	Great Falls, MT	3,151
327	Missoula, MT	3,137
328	Wenatchee, WA	3,109
329	Danville, VA	3,014
330	Idaho Falls, ID	2,973
331	Bismarck, ND	2,945
332	Manhattan, KS	2,930
333	Altoona, PA	2,855
334	Hinesville, GA	2,821
335	Pocatello, ID	2,803
336	Cheyenne, WY	2,785
337	Williamsport, PA	2,772
338	Lebanon, PA	2,661
339	State College, PA	2,641
340	Casper, WY	2,626
341	Wausau, WI	2,615
342	Ames, IA	2,601
343	Sandusky, OH	2,553
344	Sheboygan, WI	2,551
345	Bay City, MI	2,408
346	Palm Coast, FL	2,375
347	Glens Falls, NY	2,342
348	Corvallis, OR	2,326
349	Elmira, NY	2,278
350	Dubuque, IA	2,057
351	Elizabethtown, KY	1,992
352	Harrisonburg, VA	1,813
353	Fond du Lac, WI	1,809
354	Fairbanks, AK	1,588
355	Carson City, NV	1,423
356	Logan, UT-ID	1,417
NA	Chicago (greater), IL-IN-WI**	NA
NA	Chicago-Joilet-Naperville, IL M.D.**	NA
NA	Duluth, MN-WI**	NA
NA	Fargo, ND-MN**	NA
NA	Grand Forks, ND-MN**	NA
NA	La Crosse, WI-MN**	NA
NA	Mankato-North Mankato, MN**	NA
NA	Minneapolis-St. Paul, MN-WI**	NA
NA	Rochester, MN**	NA
NA	St. Cloud, MN**	NA
NA	Toledo, OH**	NA
NA	Tucson, AZ**	NA

Source: CQ Press using reported data from the F.B.I. "Crime in the United States 2011"
*Includes murder, rape, robbery, aggravated assault, burglary, larceny-theft, and motor vehicle theft.
**Not available.

Alpha Order - Metro Area

2. Crime Rate in 2011
National Rate = 3,295.0 Crimes per 100,000 Population*

RANK	METROPOLITAN AREA	RATE	RANK	METROPOLITAN AREA	RATE	RANK	METROPOLITAN AREA	RATE
193	Abilene, TX	3,327.2	186	Charleston, WV	3,366.2	55	Fort Lauderdale, FL M.D.	4,497.9
160	Akron, OH	3,614.9	123	Charlotte-Gastonia, NC-SC	3,863.6	210	Fort Smith, AR-OK	3,214.4
259	Albany-Schenectady-Troy, NY	2,777.1	335	Charlottesville, VA	2,166.5	232	Fort Wayne, IN	2,998.9
29	Albany, GA	4,893.4	82	Chattanooga, TN-GA	4,212.0	93	Fort Worth-Arlington, TX M.D.	4,110.3
40	Albuquerque, NM	4,712.7	228	Cheyenne, WY	3,011.7	30	Fresno, CA	4,879.9
21	Alexandria, LA	5,052.5	NA	Chicago (greater), IL-IN-WI**	NA	28	Gadsden, AL	4,895.5
297	Allentown, PA-NJ	2,492.0	NA	Chicago-Joilet-Naperville, IL M.D.**	NA	107	Gainesville, FL	4,034.3
321	Altoona, PA	2,239.3	274	Chico, CA	2,673.6	280	Gainesville, GA	2,630.6
49	Amarillo, TX	4,559.5	130	Cincinnati-Middletown, OH-KY-IN	3,793.4	129	Gary, IN M.D.	3,795.0
239	Ames, IA	2,889.6	202	Clarksville, TN-KY	3,278.1	350	Glens Falls, NY	1,808.4
95	Anchorage, AK	4,091.2	185	Cleveland-Elyria-Mentor, OH	3,367.4	45	Goldsboro, NC	4,620.0
7	Anderson, SC	5,706.2	150	Cleveland, TN	3,670.2	NA	Grand Forks, ND-MN**	NA
285	Ann Arbor, MI	2,612.5	166	College Station-Bryan, TX	3,555.4	224	Grand Junction, CO	3,022.5
36	Anniston-Oxford, AL	4,780.8	198	Colorado Springs, CO	3,289.5	278	Grand Rapids-Wyoming, MI	2,656.1
349	Appleton, WI	1,835.4	155	Columbia, MO	3,632.4	126	Great Falls, MT	3,840.4
263	Asheville, NC	2,751.0	8	Columbus, GA-AL	5,689.5	308	Greeley, CO	2,392.8
94	Athens-Clarke County, GA	4,102.5	71	Columbus, IN	4,325.9	347	Green Bay, WI	1,921.5
116	Atlanta, GA	3,952.9	52	Columbus, OH	4,541.3	85	Greenville, SC	4,193.0
117	Atlantic City, NJ	3,916.3	35	Corpus Christi, TX	4,789.4	80	Gulfport-Biloxi, MS	4,232.0
170	Auburn, AL	3,465.0	273	Corvallis, OR	2,689.4	301	Hagerstown-Martinsburg, MD-WV	2,473.3
39	Augusta, GA-SC	4,713.1	197	Crestview-Fort Walton Beach, FL	3,291.6	288	Hanford-Corcoran, CA	2,570.1
137	Austin-Round Rock, TX	3,735.4	209	Cumberland, MD-WV	3,230.3	295	Harrisburg-Carlisle, PA	2,503.9
98	Bakersfield, CA	4,063.3	125	Dallas (greater), TX	3,856.9	355	Harrisonburg, VA	1,430.7
149	Baltimore-Towson, MD	3,688.7	139	Dallas-Plano-Irving, TX M.D.	3,729.2	264	Hartford, CT	2,736.8
241	Bangor, ME	2,884.3	212	Dalton, GA	3,197.8	144	Hickory, NC	3,719.5
208	Barnstable Town, MA	3,239.4	44	Danville, IL	4,630.4	165	Hinesville, GA	3,573.6
42	Baton Rouge, LA	4,661.0	253	Danville, VA	2,795.1	344	Holland-Grand Haven, MI	1,989.0
56	Battle Creek, MI	4,469.2	187	Davenport, IA-IL	3,361.5	2	Hot Springs, AR	6,000.0
323	Bay City, MI	2,236.0	140	Dayton, OH	3,728.7	157	Houma, LA	3,631.4
61	Beaumont-Port Arthur, TX	4,419.4	258	Decatur, AL	2,778.1	90	Houston, TX	4,127.7
189	Bellingham, WA	3,345.2	167	Decatur, IL	3,547.2	111	Huntsville, AL	4,010.2
175	Bend, OR	3,413.8	88	Deltona-Daytona Beach, FL	4,150.2	319	Idaho Falls, ID	2,254.2
343	Bethesda-Frederick, MD M.D.	2,037.7	221	Denver-Aurora, CO	3,088.5	68	Indianapolis, IN	4,354.1
143	Billings, MT	3,724.5	184	Des Moines-West Des Moines, IA	3,370.7	339	Iowa City, IA	2,071.9
244	Binghamton, NY	2,845.9	173	Detroit (greater), MI	3,452.3	83	Jacksonville, FL	4,206.5
46	Birmingham-Hoover, AL	4,617.9	18	Detroit-Livonia-Dearborn, MI M.D.	5,164.7	206	Jacksonville, NC	3,247.3
276	Bismarck, ND	2,662.4	177	Dothan, AL	3,409.2	109	Jackson, MS	4,018.3
277	Blacksburg, VA	2,657.3	76	Dover, DE	4,276.4	33	Jackson, TN	4,798.8
296	Bloomington-Normal, IL	2,494.7	332	Dubuque, IA	2,185.0	204	Janesville, WI	3,272.7
234	Bloomington, IN	2,971.6	NA	Duluth, MN-WI**	NA	255	Jefferson City, MO	2,788.8
320	Boise City-Nampa, ID	2,243.2	79	Durham-Chapel Hill, NC	4,236.7	188	Johnson City, TN	3,349.0
299	Boston (greater), MA-NH	2,483.7	318	Eau Claire, WI	2,257.7	313	Johnstown, PA	2,324.1
243	Boston-Quincy, MA M.D.	2,873.7	338	Edison, NJ M.D.	2,077.6	72	Jonesboro, AR	4,315.2
309	Boulder, CO	2,389.8	161	El Centro, CA	3,611.4	112	Joplin, MO	3,993.7
247	Bowling Green, KY	2,828.3	254	El Paso, TX	2,791.1	201	Kankakee-Bradley, IL	3,278.8
205	Bremerton-Silverdale, WA	3,248.9	354	Elizabethtown, KY	1,652.2	121	Kansas City, MO-KS	3,884.2
325	Bridgeport-Stamford, CT	2,223.6	289	Elmira, NY	2,553.0	238	Kennewick-Pasco-Richland, WA	2,896.8
62	Brownsville-Harlingen, TX	4,405.3	236	Erie, PA	2,939.0	215	Killeen-Temple-Fort Hood, TX	3,152.3
19	Brunswick, GA	5,133.2	127	Eugene-Springfield, OR	3,837.3	156	Kingsport, TN-VA	3,632.2
182	Buffalo-Niagara Falls, NY	3,384.7	231	Evansville, IN-KY	3,007.4	340	Kingston, NY	2,056.5
70	Burlington, NC	4,343.1	43	Fairbanks, AK	4,637.4	75	Knoxville, TN	4,280.4
342	Cambridge-Newton, MA M.D.	2,041.8	NA	Fargo, ND-MN**	NA	147	Kokomo, IN	3,711.0
225	Camden, NJ M.D.	3,021.0	268	Farmington, NM	2,722.5	NA	La Crosse, WI-MN**	NA
180	Canton, OH	3,393.2	3	Fayetteville, NC	5,942.1	240	Lafayette, IN	2,888.8
218	Cape Coral-Fort Myers, FL	3,142.7	131	Flagstaff, AZ	3,777.8	57	Lafayette, LA	4,467.8
87	Cape Girardeau, MO-IL	4,151.3	38	Flint, MI	4,727.5	333	Lake Co.-Kenosha Co., IL-WI M.D.	2,183.0
290	Carson City, NV	2,552.9	270	Florence-Muscle Shoals, AL	2,717.7	181	Lake Havasu City-Kingman, AZ	3,384.9
172	Casper, WY	3,452.7	9	Florence, SC	5,638.6	146	Lakeland, FL	3,711.1
281	Cedar Rapids, IA	2,626.3	351	Fond du Lac, WI	1,772.3	326	Lancaster, PA	2,213.0
222	Champaign-Urbana, IL	3,066.8	267	Fort Collins-Loveland, CO	2,728.9	260	Lansing-East Lansing, MI	2,760.7

Note: All listings are for Metropolitan Statistical Areas (M.S.A.s) except for those ending with "M.D." Listings with "M.D." are Metropolitan Divisions which are smaller parts of eleven large M.S.A.s. See explanatory note at beginning of metropolitan area section.

Alpha Order - Metro Area (continued)

RANK	METROPOLITAN AREA	RATE
37	Laredo, TX	4,729.4
164	Las Cruces, NM	3,581.7
183	Las Vegas-Paradise, NV	3,374.8
66	Lawrence, KS	4,373.7
14	Lawton, OK	5,393.6
345	Lebanon, PA	1,985.9
220	Lewiston-Auburn, ME	3,108.0
63	Lexington-Fayette, KY	4,402.5
81	Lima, OH	4,214.8
119	Lincoln, NE	3,908.4
4	Little Rock, AR	5,930.2
356	Logan, UT-ID	1,109.1
135	Longview, TX	3,750.4
162	Longview, WA	3,605.1
260	Los Angeles County, CA M.D.	2,760.7
279	Los Angeles (greater), CA	2,638.1
84	Louisville, KY-IN	4,195.4
15	Lubbock, TX	5,368.8
329	Lynchburg, VA	2,197.5
5	Macon, GA	5,906.1
226	Madera, CA	3,016.3
252	Madison, WI	2,804.9
287	Manchester-Nashua, NH	2,601.2
316	Manhattan, KS	2,291.0
NA	Mankato-North Mankato, MN**	NA
48	Mansfield, OH	4,567.0
78	McAllen-Edinburg-Mission, TX	4,251.4
152	Medford, OR	3,645.6
10	Memphis, TN-MS-AR	5,543.2
96	Merced, CA	4,073.0
34	Miami (greater), FL	4,790.0
12	Miami-Dade County, FL M.D.	5,457.9
132	Michigan City-La Porte, IN	3,777.4
227	Midland, TX	3,016.1
141	Milwaukee, WI	3,727.6
NA	Minneapolis-St. Paul, MN-WI**	NA
245	Missoula, MT	2,844.9
13	Mobile, AL	5,415.2
86	Modesto, CA	4,163.5
17	Monroe, LA	5,165.8
256	Monroe, MI	2,784.0
65	Montgomery, AL	4,383.3
134	Morristown, TN	3,756.6
41	Mount Vernon-Anacortes, WA	4,661.6
190	Muncie, IN	3,343.1
50	Muskegon-Norton Shores, MI	4,555.5
1	Myrtle Beach, SC	6,258.9
312	Napa, CA	2,354.3
334	Naples-Marco Island, FL	2,180.1
114	Nashville-Davidson, TN	3,969.6
352	Nassau-Suffolk, NY M.D.	1,769.2
175	New Haven-Milford, CT	3,413.8
122	New Orleans, LA	3,883.4
336	New York (greater), NY-NJ-PA	2,150.1
327	New York-W. Plains NY-NJ M.D.	2,200.1
303	Newark-Union, NJ-PA M.D.	2,461.5
89	North Port-Bradenton-Sarasota, FL	4,146.2
282	Norwich-New London, CT	2,622.1
133	Oakland-Fremont, CA M.D.	3,759.4
233	Ocala, FL	2,992.4
25	Ocean City, NJ	4,972.9
148	Odessa, TX	3,706.0
271	Ogden-Clearfield, UT	2,711.1

RANK	METROPOLITAN AREA	RATE
32	Oklahoma City, OK	4,800.1
230	Olympia, WA	3,009.1
136	Omaha-Council Bluffs, NE-IA	3,738.8
77	Orlando, FL	4,258.4
337	Oshkosh-Neenah, WI	2,096.3
257	Owensboro, KY	2,781.6
348	Oxnard-Thousand Oaks, CA	1,905.7
120	Palm Bay-Melbourne, FL	3,888.4
305	Palm Coast, FL	2,448.4
31	Panama City-Lynn Haven, FL	4,872.2
158	Pascagoula, MS	3,626.5
300	Peabody, MA M.D.	2,482.6
91	Pensacola, FL	4,112.6
213	Peoria, IL	3,188.6
105	Phoenix-Mesa-Scottsdale, AZ	4,036.3
6	Pine Bluff, AR	5,777.3
324	Pittsburgh, PA	2,223.7
250	Pittsfield, MA	2,821.5
223	Pocatello, ID	3,058.1
217	Port St. Lucie, FL	3,150.6
179	Portland-Vancouver, OR-WA	3,397.3
272	Portland, ME	2,710.7
331	Poughkeepsie, NY	2,188.8
292	Prescott, AZ	2,519.8
317	Provo-Orem, UT	2,277.9
26	Pueblo, CO	4,941.5
265	Punta Gorda, FL	2,733.7
219	Racine, WI	3,111.7
246	Raleigh-Cary, NC	2,838.6
196	Rapid City, SD	3,308.3
298	Reading, PA	2,485.5
169	Redding, CA	3,489.0
248	Reno-Sparks, NV	2,827.9
266	Richmond, VA	2,730.4
214	Riverside-San Bernardino, CA	3,173.4
249	Roanoke, VA	2,825.0
NA	Rochester, MN**	NA
242	Rochester, NY	2,875.0
128	Rockford, IL	3,807.4
314	Rockingham County, NH M.D.	2,312.2
64	Rocky Mount, NC	4,401.2
73	Rome, GA	4,314.2
207	Sacramento, CA	3,245.7
203	Saginaw, MI	3,276.7
229	Salem, OR	3,009.9
251	Salinas, CA	2,820.4
151	Salisbury, MD	3,663.3
60	Salt Lake City, UT	4,430.4
145	San Angelo, TX	3,718.0
20	San Antonio, TX	5,065.7
306	San Diego, CA	2,430.3
163	San Francisco (greater), CA	3,588.4
191	San Francisco-S. Mateo, CA M.D.	3,341.9
307	San Jose, CA	2,402.1
291	San Luis Obispo, CA	2,520.5
195	Sandusky, OH	3,309.8
322	Santa Ana-Anaheim, CA M.D.	2,238.2
294	Santa Barbara-Santa Maria, CA	2,504.3
138	Santa Cruz-Watsonville, CA	3,734.6
97	Santa Fe, NM	4,067.6
341	Santa Rosa-Petaluma, CA	2,044.5

RANK	METROPOLITAN AREA	RATE
115	Savannah, GA	3,968.1
293	Scranton--Wilkes-Barre, PA	2,504.7
92	Seattle (greater), WA	4,112.5
100	Seattle-Bellevue-Everett, WA M.D.	4,056.9
216	Sebastian-Vero Beach, FL	3,151.3
328	Sheboygan, WI	2,199.0
174	Sherman-Denison, TX	3,436.2
192	Sioux City, IA-NE-SD	3,341.2
286	Sioux Falls, SD	2,601.3
102	South Bend-Mishawaka, IN-MI	4,052.1
108	Spartanburg, SC	4,033.8
11	Spokane, WA	5,481.5
24	Springfield, IL	5,002.4
178	Springfield, MA	3,397.6
23	Springfield, MO	5,013.3
58	Springfield, OH	4,454.1
353	State College, PA	1,709.6
22	Stockton, CA	5,024.2
NA	St. Cloud, MN**	NA
103	St. Joseph, MO-KS	4,051.2
159	St. Louis, MO-IL	3,624.3
99	Sumter, SC	4,062.2
275	Syracuse, NY	2,669.5
74	Tacoma, WA M.D.	4,297.4
69	Tallahassee, FL	4,349.7
168	Tampa-St Petersburg, FL	3,536.7
104	Terre Haute, IN	4,047.2
16	Texarkana, TX-Texarkana, AR	5,307.8
NA	Toledo, OH**	NA
47	Topeka, KS	4,587.1
284	Trenton-Ewing, NJ	2,614.4
NA	Tucson, AZ**	NA
101	Tulsa, OK	4,055.5
113	Tuscaloosa, AL	3,977.0
153	Tyler, TX	3,636.2
302	Utica-Rome, NY	2,463.5
171	Valdosta, GA	3,464.7
194	Vallejo-Fairfield, CA	3,321.1
67	Victoria, TX	4,356.1
154	Virginia Beach-Norfolk, VA-NC	3,635.3
124	Visalia-Porterville, CA	3,861.6
59	Waco, TX	4,450.3
53	Warner Robins, GA	4,527.3
330	Warren-Farmington Hills, MI M.D.	2,192.9
269	Washington (greater) DC-VA-MD-WV	2,720.6
237	Washington, DC-VA-MD-WV M.D.	2,908.0
311	Waterloo-Cedar Falls, IA	2,374.7
346	Wausau, WI	1,942.1
262	Wenatchee, WA	2,760.6
118	West Palm Beach, FL M.D.	3,913.8
106	Wichita Falls, TX	4,034.6
54	Wichita, KS	4,517.9
310	Williamsport, PA	2,379.8
142	Wilmington, DE-MD-NJ M.D.	3,726.8
110	Wilmington, NC	4,010.8
304	Winchester, VA-WV	2,449.3
27	Winston-Salem, NC	4,908.3
283	Worcester, MA	2,619.3
51	Yakima, WA	4,543.7
315	York-Hanover, PA	2,301.1
211	Yuba City, CA	3,198.0
235	Yuma, AZ	2,970.9

Source: CQ Press using reported data from the F.B.I. "Crime in the United States 2011"
*Includes murder, rape, robbery, aggravated assault, burglary, larceny-theft, and motor vehicle theft.
**Not available.

Rank Order - Metro Area

2. Crime Rate in 2011 (continued)
National Rate = 3,295.0 Crimes per 100,000 Population*

RANK	METROPOLITAN AREA	RATE	RANK	METROPOLITAN AREA	RATE	RANK	METROPOLITAN AREA	RATE
1	Myrtle Beach, SC	6,258.9	61	Beaumont-Port Arthur, TX	4,419.4	121	Kansas City, MO-KS	3,884.2
2	Hot Springs, AR	6,000.0	62	Brownsville-Harlingen, TX	4,405.3	122	New Orleans, LA	3,883.4
3	Fayetteville, NC	5,942.1	63	Lexington-Fayette, KY	4,402.5	123	Charlotte-Gastonia, NC-SC	3,863.6
4	Little Rock, AR	5,930.2	64	Rocky Mount, NC	4,401.2	124	Visalia-Porterville, CA	3,861.6
5	Macon, GA	5,906.1	65	Montgomery, AL	4,383.3	125	Dallas (greater), TX	3,856.9
6	Pine Bluff, AR	5,777.3	66	Lawrence, KS	4,373.7	126	Great Falls, MT	3,840.4
7	Anderson, SC	5,706.2	67	Victoria, TX	4,356.1	127	Eugene-Springfield, OR	3,837.3
8	Columbus, GA-AL	5,689.5	68	Indianapolis, IN	4,354.1	128	Rockford, IL	3,807.4
9	Florence, SC	5,638.6	69	Tallahassee, FL	4,349.7	129	Gary, IN M.D.	3,795.0
10	Memphis, TN-MS-AR	5,543.2	70	Burlington, NC	4,343.1	130	Cincinnati-Middletown, OH-KY-IN	3,793.4
11	Spokane, WA	5,481.5	71	Columbus, IN	4,325.9	131	Flagstaff, AZ	3,777.8
12	Miami-Dade County, FL M.D.	5,457.9	72	Jonesboro, AR	4,315.2	132	Michigan City-La Porte, IN	3,777.4
13	Mobile, AL	5,415.2	73	Rome, GA	4,314.2	133	Oakland-Fremont, CA M.D.	3,759.4
14	Lawton, OK	5,393.6	74	Tacoma, WA M.D.	4,297.4	134	Morristown, TN	3,756.6
15	Lubbock, TX	5,368.8	75	Knoxville, TN	4,280.4	135	Longview, TX	3,750.4
16	Texarkana, TX-Texarkana, AR	5,307.8	76	Dover, DE	4,276.4	136	Omaha-Council Bluffs, NE-IA	3,738.8
17	Monroe, LA	5,165.8	77	Orlando, FL	4,258.4	137	Austin-Round Rock, TX	3,735.4
18	Detroit-Livonia-Dearborn, MI M.D.	5,164.7	78	McAllen-Edinburg-Mission, TX	4,251.4	138	Santa Cruz-Watsonville, CA	3,734.2
19	Brunswick, GA	5,133.2	79	Durham-Chapel Hill, NC	4,236.7	139	Dallas-Plano-Irving, TX M.D.	3,729.2
20	San Antonio, TX	5,065.7	80	Gulfport-Biloxi, MS	4,232.0	140	Dayton, OH	3,728.7
21	Alexandria, LA	5,052.5	81	Lima, OH	4,214.8	141	Milwaukee, WI	3,727.6
22	Stockton, CA	5,024.2	82	Chattanooga, TN-GA	4,212.0	142	Wilmington, DE-MD-NJ M.D.	3,726.8
23	Springfield, MO	5,013.3	83	Jacksonville, FL	4,206.5	143	Billings, MT	3,724.5
24	Springfield, IL	5,002.4	84	Louisville, KY-IN	4,195.4	144	Hickory, NC	3,719.5
25	Ocean City, NJ	4,972.9	85	Greenville, SC	4,193.0	145	San Angelo, TX	3,718.0
26	Pueblo, CO	4,941.5	86	Modesto, CA	4,163.5	146	Lakeland, FL	3,711.1
27	Winston-Salem, NC	4,908.3	87	Cape Girardeau, MO-IL	4,151.3	147	Kokomo, IN	3,711.0
28	Gadsden, AL	4,895.5	88	Deltona-Daytona Beach, FL	4,150.2	148	Odessa, TX	3,706.0
29	Albany, GA	4,893.4	89	North Port-Bradenton-Sarasota, FL	4,146.2	149	Baltimore-Towson, MD	3,688.7
30	Fresno, CA	4,879.9	90	Houston, TX	4,127.7	150	Cleveland, TN	3,670.2
31	Panama City-Lynn Haven, FL	4,872.2	91	Pensacola, FL	4,112.6	151	Salisbury, MD	3,663.3
32	Oklahoma City, OK	4,800.1	92	Seattle (greater), WA	4,112.5	152	Medford, OR	3,645.6
33	Jackson, TN	4,798.8	93	Fort Worth-Arlington, TX M.D.	4,110.3	153	Tyler, TX	3,636.2
34	Miami (greater), FL	4,790.0	94	Athens-Clarke County, GA	4,102.5	154	Virginia Beach-Norfolk, VA-NC	3,635.3
35	Corpus Christi, TX	4,789.4	95	Anchorage, AK	4,091.2	155	Columbia, MO	3,632.4
36	Anniston-Oxford, AL	4,780.8	96	Merced, CA	4,073.0	156	Kingsport, TN-VA	3,632.2
37	Laredo, TX	4,729.4	97	Santa Fe, NM	4,067.6	157	Houma, LA	3,631.4
38	Flint, MI	4,727.5	98	Bakersfield, CA	4,063.3	158	Pascagoula, MS	3,626.5
39	Augusta, GA-SC	4,713.1	99	Sumter, SC	4,062.2	159	St. Louis, MO-IL	3,624.3
40	Albuquerque, NM	4,712.7	100	Seattle-Bellevue-Everett, WA M.D.	4,056.9	160	Akron, OH	3,614.9
41	Mount Vernon-Anacortes, WA	4,661.6	101	Tulsa, OK	4,055.5	161	El Centro, CA	3,611.4
42	Baton Rouge, LA	4,661.0	102	South Bend-Mishawaka, IN-MI	4,052.1	162	Longview, WA	3,605.1
43	Fairbanks, AK	4,637.4	103	St. Joseph, MO-KS	4,051.2	163	San Francisco (greater), CA	3,588.4
44	Danville, IL	4,630.4	104	Terre Haute, IN	4,047.2	164	Las Cruces, NM	3,581.7
45	Goldsboro, NC	4,620.0	105	Phoenix-Mesa-Scottsdale, AZ	4,036.3	165	Hinesville, GA	3,573.6
46	Birmingham-Hoover, AL	4,617.9	106	Wichita Falls, TX	4,034.6	166	College Station-Bryan, TX	3,555.4
47	Topeka, KS	4,587.1	107	Gainesville, FL	4,034.3	167	Decatur, IL	3,547.2
48	Mansfield, OH	4,567.0	108	Spartanburg, SC	4,033.8	168	Tampa-St Petersburg, FL	3,536.7
49	Amarillo, TX	4,559.5	109	Jackson, MS	4,018.3	169	Redding, CA	3,489.0
50	Muskegon-Norton Shores, MI	4,555.5	110	Wilmington, NC	4,010.8	170	Auburn, AL	3,465.0
51	Yakima, WA	4,543.7	111	Huntsville, AL	4,010.2	171	Valdosta, GA	3,464.7
52	Columbus, OH	4,541.3	112	Joplin, MO	3,993.7	172	Casper, WY	3,452.7
53	Warner Robins, GA	4,527.3	113	Tuscaloosa, AL	3,977.0	173	Detroit (greater), MI	3,452.3
54	Wichita, KS	4,517.9	114	Nashville-Davidson, TN	3,969.6	174	Sherman-Denison, TX	3,436.2
55	Fort Lauderdale, FL M.D.	4,497.9	115	Savannah, GA	3,968.1	175	Bend, OR	3,413.8
56	Battle Creek, MI	4,469.2	116	Atlanta, GA	3,952.9	175	New Haven-Milford, CT	3,413.8
57	Lafayette, LA	4,467.8	117	Atlantic City, NJ	3,916.3	177	Dothan, AL	3,409.2
58	Springfield, OH	4,454.1	118	West Palm Beach, FL M.D.	3,913.8	178	Springfield, MA	3,397.6
59	Waco, TX	4,450.3	119	Lincoln, NE	3,908.4	179	Portland-Vancouver, OR-WA	3,397.3
60	Salt Lake City, UT	4,430.4	120	Palm Bay-Melbourne, FL	3,888.4	180	Canton, OH	3,393.2

Note: All listings are for Metropolitan Statistical Areas (M.S.A.s) except for those ending with "M.D." Listings with "M.D." are Metropolitan Divisions which are smaller parts of eleven large M.S.A.s. See explanatory note at beginning of metropolitan area section.

Rank Order* - Metro Area (continued)

RANK	METROPOLITAN AREA	RATE
181	Lake Havasu City-Kingman, AZ	3,384.9
182	Buffalo-Niagara Falls, NY	3,384.7
183	Las Vegas-Paradise, NV	3,374.8
184	Des Moines-West Des Moines, IA	3,370.7
185	Cleveland-Elyria-Mentor, OH	3,367.4
186	Charleston, WV	3,366.2
187	Davenport, IA-IL	3,361.5
188	Johnson City, TN	3,349.0
189	Bellingham, WA	3,345.2
190	Muncie, IN	3,343.1
191	San Francisco-S. Mateo, CA M.D.	3,341.9
192	Sioux City, IA-NE-SD	3,341.2
193	Abilene, TX	3,327.2
194	Vallejo-Fairfield, CA	3,321.1
195	Sandusky, OH	3,309.8
196	Rapid City, SD	3,308.3
197	Crestview-Fort Walton Beach, FL	3,291.6
198	Colorado Springs, CO	3,289.5
199	Philadelphia, PA M.D.	3,281.1
200	Philadelphia (greater) PA-NJ-MD-DE	3,279.6
201	Kankakee-Bradley, IL	3,278.8
202	Clarksville, TN-KY	3,278.1
203	Saginaw, MI	3,276.7
204	Janesville, WI	3,272.7
205	Bremerton-Silverdale, WA	3,248.9
206	Jacksonville, NC	3,247.3
207	Sacramento, CA	3,245.7
208	Barnstable Town, MA	3,239.4
209	Cumberland, MD-WV	3,230.3
210	Fort Smith, AR-OK	3,214.4
211	Yuba City, CA	3,198.0
212	Dalton, GA	3,197.8
213	Peoria, IL	3,188.6
214	Riverside-San Bernardino, CA	3,173.4
215	Killeen-Temple-Fort Hood, TX	3,152.3
216	Sebastian-Vero Beach, FL	3,151.3
217	Port St. Lucie, FL	3,150.6
218	Cape Coral-Fort Myers, FL	3,142.7
219	Racine, WI	3,111.7
220	Lewiston-Auburn, ME	3,108.0
221	Denver-Aurora, CO	3,088.5
222	Champaign-Urbana, IL	3,066.8
223	Pocatello, ID	3,058.1
224	Grand Junction, CO	3,022.5
225	Camden, NJ M.D.	3,021.0
226	Madera, CA	3,016.3
227	Midland, TX	3,016.1
228	Cheyenne, WY	3,011.7
229	Salem, OR	3,009.9
230	Olympia, WA	3,009.1
231	Evansville, IN-KY	3,007.4
232	Fort Wayne, IN	2,998.9
233	Ocala, FL	2,992.4
234	Bloomington, IN	2,971.6
235	Yuma, AZ	2,970.9
236	Erie, PA	2,939.0
237	Washington, DC-VA-MD-WV M.D.	2,908.0
238	Kennewick-Pasco-Richland, WA	2,896.8
239	Ames, IA	2,889.6
240	Lafayette, IN	2,888.8
241	Bangor, ME	2,884.3
242	Rochester, NY	2,875.0
243	Boston-Quincy, MA M.D.	2,873.7
244	Binghamton, NY	2,845.9
245	Missoula, MT	2,844.9
246	Raleigh-Cary, NC	2,838.6
247	Bowling Green, KY	2,828.3
248	Reno-Sparks, NV	2,827.9
249	Roanoke, VA	2,825.0
250	Pittsfield, MA	2,821.5
251	Salinas, CA	2,820.4
252	Madison, WI	2,804.9
253	Danville, VA	2,795.1
254	El Paso, TX	2,791.1
255	Jefferson City, MO	2,788.8
256	Monroe, MI	2,784.0
257	Owensboro, KY	2,781.6
258	Decatur, AL	2,778.1
259	Albany-Schenectady-Troy, NY	2,777.1
260	Lansing-East Lansing, MI	2,760.7
260	Los Angeles County, CA M.D.	2,760.7
262	Wenatchee, WA	2,760.6
263	Asheville, NC	2,751.0
264	Hartford, CT	2,736.8
265	Punta Gorda, FL	2,733.7
266	Richmond, VA	2,730.4
267	Fort Collins-Loveland, CO	2,728.9
268	Farmington, NM	2,722.5
269	Washington (greater) DC-VA-MD-WV	2,720.6
270	Florence-Muscle Shoals, AL	2,717.7
271	Ogden-Clearfield, UT	2,711.1
272	Portland, ME	2,710.7
273	Corvallis, OR	2,689.4
274	Chico, CA	2,673.6
275	Syracuse, NY	2,669.5
276	Bismarck, ND	2,662.4
277	Blacksburg, VA	2,657.3
278	Grand Rapids-Wyoming, MI	2,656.1
279	Los Angeles (greater), CA	2,638.1
280	Gainesville, GA	2,630.6
281	Cedar Rapids, IA	2,626.3
282	Norwich-New London, CT	2,622.1
283	Worcester, MA	2,619.3
284	Trenton-Ewing, NJ	2,614.4
285	Ann Arbor, MI	2,612.5
286	Sioux Falls, SD	2,601.3
287	Manchester-Nashua, NH	2,601.2
288	Hanford-Corcoran, CA	2,570.1
289	Elmira, NY	2,553.0
290	Carson City, NV	2,552.9
291	San Luis Obispo, CA	2,520.5
292	Prescott, AZ	2,519.8
293	Scranton--Wilkes-Barre, PA	2,504.7
294	Santa Barbara-Santa Maria, CA	2,504.3
295	Harrisburg-Carlisle, PA	2,503.9
296	Bloomington-Normal, IL	2,494.7
297	Allentown, PA-NJ	2,492.0
298	Reading, PA	2,485.5
299	Boston (greater), MA-NH	2,483.7
300	Peabody, MA M.D.	2,482.6
301	Hagerstown-Martinsburg, MD-WV	2,473.3
302	Utica-Rome, NY	2,463.5
303	Newark-Union, NJ-PA M.D.	2,461.5
304	Winchester, VA-WV	2,449.3
305	Palm Coast, FL	2,448.4
306	San Diego, CA	2,430.3
307	San Jose, CA	2,402.1
308	Greeley, CO	2,392.8
309	Boulder, CO	2,389.8
310	Williamsport, PA	2,379.8
311	Waterloo-Cedar Falls, IA	2,374.7
312	Napa, CA	2,354.3
313	Johnstown, PA	2,324.1
314	Rockingham County, NH M.D.	2,312.2
315	York-Hanover, PA	2,301.1
316	Manhattan, KS	2,291.0
317	Provo-Orem, UT	2,277.9
318	Eau Claire, WI	2,257.7
319	Idaho Falls, ID	2,254.2
320	Boise City-Nampa, ID	2,243.2
321	Altoona, PA	2,239.3
322	Santa Ana-Anaheim, CA M.D.	2,238.2
323	Bay City, MI	2,236.0
324	Pittsburgh, PA	2,223.7
325	Bridgeport-Stamford, CT	2,223.6
326	Lancaster, PA	2,213.0
327	New York-W. Plains NY-NJ M.D.	2,200.1
328	Sheboygan, WI	2,199.0
329	Lynchburg, VA	2,197.5
330	Warren-Farmington Hills, MI M.D.	2,192.9
331	Poughkeepsie, NY	2,188.8
332	Dubuque, IA	2,185.0
333	Lake Co.-Kenosha Co., IL-WI M.D.	2,183.0
334	Naples-Marco Island, FL	2,180.1
335	Charlottesville, VA	2,166.5
336	New York (greater), NY-NJ-PA	2,150.1
337	Oshkosh-Neenah, WI	2,096.3
338	Edison, NJ M.D.	2,077.6
339	Iowa City, IA	2,071.9
340	Kingston, NY	2,056.5
341	Santa Rosa-Petaluma, CA	2,044.5
342	Cambridge-Newton, MA M.D.	2,041.8
343	Bethesda-Frederick, MD M.D.	2,037.7
344	Holland-Grand Haven, MI	1,989.0
345	Lebanon, PA	1,985.9
346	Wausau, WI	1,942.1
347	Green Bay, WI	1,921.5
348	Oxnard-Thousand Oaks, CA	1,905.7
349	Appleton, WI	1,835.4
350	Glens Falls, NY	1,808.4
351	Fond du Lac, WI	1,772.3
352	Nassau-Suffolk, NY M.D.	1,769.2
353	State College, PA	1,709.6
354	Elizabethtown, KY	1,652.2
355	Harrisonburg, VA	1,430.7
356	Logan, UT-ID	1,109.1
NA	Chicago (greater), IL-IN-WI**	NA
NA	Chicago-Joilet-Naperville, IL M.D.**	NA
NA	Duluth, MN-WI**	NA
NA	Fargo, ND-MN**	NA
NA	Grand Forks, ND-MN**	NA
NA	La Crosse, WI-MN**	NA
NA	Mankato-North Mankato, MN**	NA
NA	Minneapolis-St. Paul, MN-WI**	NA
NA	Rochester, MN**	NA
NA	St. Cloud, MN**	NA
NA	Toledo, OH**	NA
NA	Tucson, AZ**	NA

Source: CQ Press using reported data from the F.B.I. "Crime in the United States 2011"
*Includes murder, rape, robbery, aggravated assault, burglary, larceny-theft, and motor vehicle theft.
**Not available.

Alpha Order - Metro Area

3. Percent Change in Crime Rate: 2010 to 2011
National Percent Change = 1.7% Decrease*

RANK	METROPOLITAN AREA	% CHANGE	RANK	METROPOLITAN AREA	% CHANGE	RANK	METROPOLITAN AREA	% CHANGE
313	Abilene, TX	(17.6)	NA	Charleston, WV**	NA	68	Fort Lauderdale, FL M.D.	4.0
73	Akron, OH	3.6	NA	Charlotte-Gastonia, NC-SC**	NA	238	Fort Smith, AR-OK	(6.3)
255	Albany-Schenectady-Troy, NY	(7.6)	299	Charlottesville, VA	(12.6)	77	Fort Wayne, IN	3.4
192	Albany, GA	(3.6)	165	Chattanooga, TN-GA	(2.4)	215	Fort Worth-Arlington, TX M.D.	(4.6)
81	Albuquerque, NM	3.2	248	Cheyenne, WY	(6.9)	100	Fresno, CA	1.9
185	Alexandria, LA	(3.4)	NA	Chicago (greater), IL-IN-WI**	NA	NA	Gadsden, AL**	NA
147	Allentown, PA-NJ	(1.4)	NA	Chicago-Joilet-Naperville, IL M.D.**	NA	198	Gainesville, FL	(3.9)
21	Altoona, PA	9.0	289	Chico, CA	(11.4)	105	Gainesville, GA	1.6
307	Amarillo, TX	(14.4)	70	Cincinnati-Middletown, OH-KY-IN	3.8	NA	Gary, IN M.D.**	NA
93	Ames, IA	2.2	50	Clarksville, TN-KY	5.9	42	Glens Falls, NY	6.7
226	Anchorage, AK	(5.3)	73	Cleveland-Elyria-Mentor, OH	3.6	261	Goldsboro, NC	(8.2)
24	Anderson, SC	7.8	18	Cleveland, TN	9.9	NA	Grand Forks, ND-MN**	NA
307	Ann Arbor, MI	(14.4)	287	College Station-Bryan, TX	(11.3)	45	Grand Junction, CO	6.3
NA	Anniston-Oxford, AL**	NA	285	Colorado Springs, CO	(11.0)	267	Grand Rapids-Wyoming, MI	(8.5)
314	Appleton, WI	(19.9)	35	Columbia, MO	7.0	NA	Great Falls, MT**	NA
86	Asheville, NC	2.5	NA	Columbus, GA-AL**	NA	172	Greeley, CO	(3.0)
169	Athens-Clarke County, GA	(2.8)	9	Columbus, IN	14.4	192	Green Bay, WI	(3.6)
97	Atlanta, GA	2.0	158	Columbus, OH	(1.9)	48	Greenville, SC	6.0
201	Atlantic City, NJ	(4.0)	270	Corpus Christi, TX	(8.9)	243	Gulfport-Biloxi, MS	(6.6)
NA	Auburn, AL**	NA	5	Corvallis, OR	16.4	30	Hagerstown-Martinsburg, MD-WV	7.4
279	Augusta, GA-SC	(9.9)	129	Crestview-Fort Walton Beach, FL	(0.2)	14	Hanford-Corcoran, CA	11.0
274	Austin-Round Rock, TX	(9.3)	NA	Cumberland, MD-WV**	NA	81	Harrisburg-Carlisle, PA	3.2
229	Bakersfield, CA	(5.6)	174	Dallas (greater), TX	(3.1)	238	Harrisonburg, VA	(6.3)
162	Baltimore-Towson, MD	(2.3)	162	Dallas-Plano-Irving, TX M.D.	(2.3)	184	Hartford, CT	(3.3)
270	Bangor, ME	(8.9)	177	Dalton, GA	(3.2)	20	Hickory, NC	9.6
222	Barnstable Town, MA	(4.9)	95	Danville, IL	2.1	254	Hinesville, GA	(7.5)
NA	Baton Rouge, LA**	NA	251	Danville, VA	(7.1)	97	Holland-Grand Haven, MI	2.0
106	Battle Creek, MI	1.5	NA	Davenport, IA-IL**	NA	153	Hot Springs, AR	(1.7)
315	Bay City, MI	(20.4)	106	Dayton, OH	1.5	229	Houma, LA	(5.6)
111	Beaumont-Port Arthur, TX	1.3	NA	Decatur, AL**	NA	NA	Houston, TX**	NA
189	Bellingham, WA	(3.5)	280	Decatur, IL	(10.1)	NA	Huntsville, AL**	NA
67	Bend, OR	4.1	150	Deltona-Daytona Beach, FL	(1.6)	110	Idaho Falls, ID	1.4
261	Bethesda-Frederick, MD M.D.	(8.2)	138	Denver-Aurora, CO	(0.6)	NA	Indianapolis, IN**	NA
NA	Billings, MT**	NA	30	Des Moines-West Des Moines, IA	7.4	36	Iowa City, IA	6.9
64	Binghamton, NY	4.3	NA	Detroit (greater), MI**	NA	169	Jacksonville, FL	(2.8)
NA	Birmingham-Hoover, AL**	NA	158	Detroit-Livonia-Dearborn, MI M.D.	(1.9)	NA	Jacksonville, NC**	NA
1	Bismarck, ND	32.9	NA	Dothan, AL**	NA	201	Jackson, MS	(4.0)
158	Blacksburg, VA	(1.9)	24	Dover, DE	7.8	280	Jackson, TN	(10.1)
282	Bloomington-Normal, IL	(10.4)	309	Dubuque, IA	(14.9)	86	Janesville, WI	2.5
269	Bloomington, IN	(8.8)	NA	Duluth, MN-WI**	NA	129	Jefferson City, MO	(0.2)
155	Boise City-Nampa, ID	(1.8)	123	Durham-Chapel Hill, NC	0.4	119	Johnson City, TN	0.6
211	Boston (greater), MA-NH	(4.3)	84	Eau Claire, WI	2.9	11	Johnstown, PA	12.1
185	Boston-Quincy, MA M.D.	(3.4)	70	Edison, NJ M.D.	3.8	13	Jonesboro, AR	11.3
196	Boulder, CO	(3.7)	211	El Centro, CA	(4.3)	162	Joplin, MO	(2.3)
213	Bowling Green, KY	(4.4)	301	El Paso, TX	(12.8)	NA	Kankakee-Bradley, IL**	NA
86	Bremerton-Silverdale, WA	2.5	286	Elizabethtown, KY	(11.2)	NA	Kansas City, MO-KS**	NA
26	Bridgeport-Stamford, CT	7.7	36	Elmira, NY	6.9	18	Kennewick-Pasco-Richland, WA	9.9
283	Brownsville-Harlingen, TX	(10.7)	42	Erie, PA	6.7	305	Killeen-Temple-Fort Hood, TX	(14.1)
299	Brunswick, GA	(12.6)	NA	Eugene-Springfield, OR**	NA	103	Kingsport, TN-VA	1.8
227	Buffalo-Niagara Falls, NY	(5.5)	NA	Evansville, IN-KY**	NA	205	Kingston, NY	(4.1)
86	Burlington, NC	2.5	205	Fairbanks, AK	(4.1)	115	Knoxville, TN	0.9
276	Cambridge-Newton, MA M.D.	(9.4)	NA	Fargo, ND-MN**	NA	12	Kokomo, IN	11.9
48	Camden, NJ M.D.	6.0	205	Farmington, NM	(4.1)	NA	La Crosse, WI-MN**	NA
3	Canton, OH	21.1	65	Fayetteville, NC	4.2	40	Lafayette, IN	6.8
90	Cape Coral-Fort Myers, FL	2.3	189	Flagstaff, AZ	(3.5)	246	Lafayette, LA	(6.7)
168	Cape Girardeau, MO-IL	(2.6)	61	Flint, MI	4.7	NA	Lake Co.-Kenosha Co., IL-WI M.D.**	NA
22	Carson City, NV	8.7	NA	Florence-Muscle Shoals, AL**	NA	NA	Lake Havasu City-Kingman, AZ**	NA
284	Casper, WY	(10.9)	90	Florence, SC	2.3	232	Lakeland, FL	(5.7)
198	Cedar Rapids, IA	(3.9)	255	Fond du Lac, WI	(7.6)	36	Lancaster, PA	6.9
NA	Champaign-Urbana, IL**	NA	177	Fort Collins-Loveland, CO	(3.2)	247	Lansing-East Lansing, MI	(6.8)

Note: All listings are for Metropolitan Statistical Areas (M.S.A.s) except for those ending with "M.D." Listings with "M.D." are Metropolitan Divisions which are smaller parts of eleven large M.S.A.s. See explanatory note at beginning of metropolitan area section.

Alpha Order - Metro Area (continued)

RANK	METROPOLITAN AREA	% CHANGE
296	Laredo, TX	(12.0)
45	Las Cruces, NM	6.3
266	Las Vegas-Paradise, NV	(8.4)
77	Lawrence, KS	3.4
233	Lawton, OK	(6.0)
26	Lebanon, PA	7.7
2	Lewiston-Auburn, ME	21.2
NA	Lexington-Fayette, KY**	NA
129	Lima, OH	(0.2)
177	Lincoln, NE	(3.2)
65	Little Rock, AR	4.2
242	Logan, UT-ID	(6.5)
295	Longview, TX	(11.9)
225	Longview, WA	(5.2)
198	Los Angeles County, CA M.D.	(3.9)
172	Los Angeles (greater), CA	(3.0)
32	Louisville, KY-IN	7.2
243	Lubbock, TX	(6.6)
205	Lynchburg, VA	(4.1)
106	Macon, GA	1.5
8	Madera, CA	14.9
158	Madison, WI	(1.9)
33	Manchester-Nashua, NH	7.1
217	Manhattan, KS	(4.7)
NA	Mankato-North Mankato, MN**	NA
54	Mansfield, OH	5.6
312	McAllen-Edinburg-Mission, TX	(16.9)
5	Medford, OR	16.4
150	Memphis, TN-MS-AR	(1.6)
62	Merced, CA	4.5
121	Miami (greater), FL	0.5
115	Miami-Dade County, FL M.D.	0.9
236	Michigan City-La Porte, IN	(6.1)
304	Midland, TX	(13.7)
167	Milwaukee, WI	(2.5)
NA	Minneapolis-St. Paul, MN-WI**	NA
NA	Missoula, MT**	NA
59	Mobile, AL	4.9
265	Modesto, CA	(8.3)
174	Monroe, LA	(3.1)
144	Monroe, MI	(1.2)
NA	Montgomery, AL**	NA
259	Morristown, TN	(8.0)
274	Mount Vernon-Anacortes, WA	(9.3)
5	Muncie, IN	16.4
153	Muskegon-Norton Shores, MI	(1.7)
135	Myrtle Beach, SC	(0.3)
260	Napa, CA	(8.1)
58	Naples-Marco Island, FL	5.0
150	Nashville-Davidson, TN	(1.6)
205	Nassau-Suffolk, NY M.D.	(4.1)
189	New Haven-Milford, CT	(3.5)
NA	New Orleans, LA**	NA
100	New York (greater), NY-NJ-PA	1.9
95	New York-W. Plains NY-NJ M.D.	2.1
60	Newark-Union, NJ-PA M.D.	4.8
147	North Port-Bradenton-Sarasota, FL	(1.4)
240	Norwich-New London, CT	(6.4)
129	Oakland-Fremont, CA M.D.	(0.2)
135	Ocala, FL	(0.3)
135	Ocean City, NJ	(0.3)
296	Odessa, TX	(12.0)
305	Ogden-Clearfield, UT	(14.1)

RANK	METROPOLITAN AREA	% CHANGE
NA	Oklahoma City, OK**	NA
298	Olympia, WA	(12.5)
28	Omaha-Council Bluffs, NE-IA	7.6
112	Orlando, FL	1.2
NA	Oshkosh-Neenah, WI**	NA
15	Owensboro, KY	10.7
303	Oxnard-Thousand Oaks, CA	(13.5)
73	Palm Bay-Melbourne, FL	3.6
201	Palm Coast, FL	(4.0)
196	Panama City-Lynn Haven, FL	(3.7)
129	Pascagoula, MS	(0.2)
177	Peabody, MA M.D.	(3.2)
44	Pensacola, FL	6.4
55	Peoria, IL	5.4
97	Philadelphia (greater) PA-NJ-MD-DE	2.0
85	Philadelphia, PA M.D.	2.6
77	Phoenix-Mesa-Scottsdale, AZ	3.4
36	Pine Bluff, AR	6.9
174	Pittsburgh, PA	(3.1)
215	Pittsfield, MA	(4.6)
90	Pocatello, ID	2.3
51	Port St. Lucie, FL	5.7
NA	Portland-Vancouver, OR-WA**	NA
68	Portland, ME	4.0
240	Poughkeepsie, NY	(6.4)
115	Prescott, AZ	0.9
63	Provo-Orem, UT	4.4
NA	Pueblo, CO**	NA
227	Punta Gorda, FL	(5.5)
47	Racine, WI	6.1
51	Raleigh-Cary, NC	5.7
106	Rapid City, SD	1.5
139	Reading, PA	(0.8)
93	Redding, CA	2.2
292	Reno-Sparks, NV	(11.6)
171	Richmond, VA	(2.9)
73	Riverside-San Bernardino, CA	3.6
217	Roanoke, VA	(4.7)
NA	Rochester, MN**	NA
267	Rochester, NY	(8.5)
261	Rockford, IL	(8.2)
28	Rockingham County, NH M.D.	7.6
72	Rocky Mount, NC	3.7
56	Rome, GA	5.3
277	Sacramento, CA	(9.5)
289	Saginaw, MI	(11.4)
118	Salem, OR	0.7
248	Salinas, CA	(6.9)
309	Salisbury, MD	(14.9)
258	Salt Lake City, UT	(7.9)
311	San Angelo, TX	(15.7)
289	San Antonio, TX	(11.4)
233	San Diego, CA	(6.0)
146	San Francisco (greater), CA	(1.3)
177	San Francisco-S. Mateo, CA M.D.	(3.2)
217	San Jose, CA	(4.7)
155	San Luis Obispo, CA	(1.8)
33	Sandusky, OH	7.1
121	Santa Ana-Anaheim, CA M.D.	0.5
177	Santa Barbara-Santa Maria, CA	(3.2)
129	Santa Cruz-Watsonville, CA	(0.2)
223	Santa Fe, NM	(5.0)
278	Santa Rosa-Petaluma, CA	(9.7)

RANK	METROPOLITAN AREA	% CHANGE
155	Savannah, GA	(1.8)
113	Scranton--Wilkes-Barre, PA	1.1
185	Seattle (greater), WA	(3.4)
185	Seattle-Bellevue-Everett, WA M.D.	(3.4)
257	Sebastian-Vero Beach, FL	(7.8)
NA	Sheboygan, WI**	NA
57	Sherman-Denison, TX	5.2
4	Sioux City, IA-NE-SD	16.6
124	Sioux Falls, SD	0.2
214	South Bend-Mishawaka, IN-MI	(4.5)
119	Spartanburg, SC	0.6
103	Spokane, WA	1.8
261	Springfield, IL	(8.2)
243	Springfield, MA	(6.6)
201	Springfield, MO	(4.0)
124	Springfield, OH	0.2
177	State College, PA	(3.2)
100	Stockton, CA	1.9
NA	St. Cloud, MN**	NA
40	St. Joseph, MO-KS	6.8
140	St. Louis, MO-IL	(0.9)
316	Sumter, SC	(25.4)
224	Syracuse, NY	(5.1)
192	Tacoma, WA M.D.	(3.6)
142	Tallahassee, FL	(1.1)
273	Tampa-St Petersburg, FL	(9.0)
NA	Terre Haute, IN**	NA
23	Texarkana, TX-Texarkana, AR	8.5
NA	Toledo, OH**	NA
141	Topeka, KS	(1.0)
77	Trenton-Ewing, NJ	3.4
NA	Tucson, AZ**	NA
124	Tulsa, OK	0.2
NA	Tuscaloosa, AL**	NA
293	Tyler, TX	(11.8)
248	Utica-Rome, NY	(6.9)
302	Valdosta, GA	(12.9)
237	Vallejo-Fairfield, CA	(6.2)
147	Victoria, TX	(1.4)
221	Virginia Beach-Norfolk, VA-NC	(4.8)
229	Visalia-Porterville, CA	(5.6)
205	Waco, TX	(4.1)
17	Warner Robins, GA	10.0
NA	Warren-Farmington Hills, MI M.D.**	NA
253	Washington (greater) DC-VA-MD-WV	(7.2)
251	Washington, DC-VA-MD-WV M.D.	(7.1)
293	Waterloo-Cedar Falls, IA	(11.8)
113	Wausau, WI	1.1
192	Wenatchee, WA	(3.6)
217	West Palm Beach, FL M.D.	(4.7)
287	Wichita Falls, TX	(11.3)
83	Wichita, KS	3.1
16	Williamsport, PA	10.3
233	Wilmington, DE-MD-NJ M.D.	(6.0)
165	Wilmington, NC	(2.4)
142	Winchester, VA-WV	(1.1)
51	Winston-Salem, NC	5.7
128	Worcester, MA	(0.1)
270	Yakima, WA	(8.9)
127	York-Hanover, PA	0.0
10	Yuba City, CA	12.5
144	Yuma, AZ	(1.2)

Source: CQ Press using reported data from the F.B.I. "Crime in the United States 2011"
*Includes murder, rape, robbery, aggravated assault, burglary, larceny-theft, and motor vehicle theft.
**Not available.

Rank Order - Metro Area

3. Percent Change in Crime Rate: 2010 to 2011 (continued)
National Percent Change = 1.7% Decrease*

RANK	METROPOLITAN AREA	% CHANGE	RANK	METROPOLITAN AREA	% CHANGE	RANK	METROPOLITAN AREA	% CHANGE
1	Bismarck, ND	32.9	61	Flint, MI	4.7	121	Miami (greater), FL	0.5
2	Lewiston-Auburn, ME	21.2	62	Merced, CA	4.5	121	Santa Ana-Anaheim, CA M.D.	0.5
3	Canton, OH	21.1	63	Provo-Orem, UT	4.4	123	Durham-Chapel Hill, NC	0.4
4	Sioux City, IA-NE-SD	16.6	64	Binghamton, NY	4.3	124	Sioux Falls, SD	0.2
5	Corvallis, OR	16.4	65	Fayetteville, NC	4.2	124	Springfield, OH	0.2
5	Medford, OR	16.4	65	Little Rock, AR	4.2	124	Tulsa, OK	0.2
5	Muncie, IN	16.4	67	Bend, OR	4.1	127	York-Hanover, PA	0.0
8	Madera, CA	14.9	68	Fort Lauderdale, FL M.D.	4.0	128	Worcester, MA	(0.1)
9	Columbus, IN	14.4	68	Portland, ME	4.0	129	Crestview-Fort Walton Beach, FL	(0.2)
10	Yuba City, CA	12.5	70	Cincinnati-Middletown, OH-KY-IN	3.8	129	Jefferson City, MO	(0.2)
11	Johnstown, PA	12.1	70	Edison, NJ M.D.	3.8	129	Lima, OH	(0.2)
12	Kokomo, IN	11.9	72	Rocky Mount, NC	3.7	129	Oakland-Fremont, CA M.D.	(0.2)
13	Jonesboro, AR	11.3	73	Akron, OH	3.6	129	Pascagoula, MS	(0.2)
14	Hanford-Corcoran, CA	11.0	73	Cleveland-Elyria-Mentor, OH	3.6	129	Santa Cruz-Watsonville, CA	(0.2)
15	Owensboro, KY	10.7	73	Palm Bay-Melbourne, FL	3.6	135	Myrtle Beach, SC	(0.3)
16	Williamsport, PA	10.3	73	Riverside-San Bernardino, CA	3.6	135	Ocala, FL	(0.3)
17	Warner Robins, GA	10.0	77	Fort Wayne, IN	3.4	135	Ocean City, NJ	(0.3)
18	Cleveland, TN	9.9	77	Lawrence, KS	3.4	138	Denver-Aurora, CO	(0.6)
18	Kennewick-Pasco-Richland, WA	9.9	77	Phoenix-Mesa-Scottsdale, AZ	3.4	139	Reading, PA	(0.8)
20	Hickory, NC	9.6	77	Trenton-Ewing, NJ	3.4	140	St. Louis, MO-IL	(0.9)
21	Altoona, PA	9.0	81	Albuquerque, NM	3.2	141	Topeka, KS	(1.0)
22	Carson City, NV	8.7	81	Harrisburg-Carlisle, PA	3.2	142	Tallahassee, FL	(1.1)
23	Texarkana, TX-Texarkana, AR	8.5	83	Wichita, KS	3.1	142	Winchester, VA-WV	(1.1)
24	Anderson, SC	7.8	84	Eau Claire, WI	2.9	144	Monroe, MI	(1.2)
24	Dover, DE	7.8	85	Philadelphia, PA M.D.	2.6	144	Yuma, AZ	(1.2)
26	Bridgeport-Stamford, CT	7.7	86	Asheville, NC	2.5	146	San Francisco (greater), CA	(1.3)
26	Lebanon, PA	7.7	86	Bremerton-Silverdale, WA	2.5	147	Allentown, PA-NJ	(1.4)
28	Omaha-Council Bluffs, NE-IA	7.6	86	Burlington, NC	2.5	147	North Port-Bradenton-Sarasota, FL	(1.4)
28	Rockingham County, NH M.D.	7.6	86	Janesville, WI	2.5	147	Victoria, TX	(1.4)
30	Des Moines-West Des Moines, IA	7.4	90	Cape Coral-Fort Myers, FL	2.3	150	Deltona-Daytona Beach, FL	(1.6)
30	Hagerstown-Martinsburg, MD-WV	7.4	90	Florence, SC	2.3	150	Memphis, TN-MS-AR	(1.6)
32	Louisville, KY-IN	7.2	90	Pocatello, ID	2.3	150	Nashville-Davidson, TN	(1.6)
33	Manchester-Nashua, NH	7.1	93	Ames, IA	2.2	153	Hot Springs, AR	(1.7)
33	Sandusky, OH	7.1	93	Redding, CA	2.2	153	Muskegon-Norton Shores, MI	(1.7)
35	Columbia, MO	7.0	95	Danville, IL	2.1	155	Boise City-Nampa, ID	(1.8)
36	Elmira, NY	6.9	95	New York-W. Plains NY-NJ M.D.	2.1	155	San Luis Obispo, CA	(1.8)
36	Iowa City, IA	6.9	97	Atlanta, GA	2.0	155	Savannah, GA	(1.8)
36	Lancaster, PA	6.9	97	Holland-Grand Haven, MI	2.0	158	Blacksburg, VA	(1.9)
36	Pine Bluff, AR	6.9	97	Philadelphia (greater) PA-NJ-MD-DE	2.0	158	Columbus, OH	(1.9)
40	Lafayette, IN	6.8	100	Fresno, CA	1.9	158	Detroit-Livonia-Dearborn, MI M.D.	(1.9)
40	St. Joseph, MO-KS	6.8	100	New York (greater), NY-NJ-PA	1.9	158	Madison, WI	(1.9)
42	Erie, PA	6.7	100	Stockton, CA	1.9	162	Baltimore-Towson, MD	(2.3)
42	Glens Falls, NY	6.7	103	Kingsport, TN-VA	1.8	162	Dallas-Plano-Irving, TX M.D.	(2.3)
44	Pensacola, FL	6.4	103	Spokane, WA	1.8	162	Joplin, MO	(2.3)
45	Grand Junction, CO	6.3	105	Gainesville, GA	1.6	165	Chattanooga, TN-GA	(2.4)
45	Las Cruces, NM	6.3	106	Battle Creek, MI	1.5	165	Wilmington, NC	(2.4)
47	Racine, WI	6.1	106	Dayton, OH	1.5	167	Milwaukee, WI	(2.5)
48	Camden, NJ M.D.	6.0	106	Macon, GA	1.5	168	Cape Girardeau, MO-IL	(2.6)
48	Greenville, SC	6.0	106	Rapid City, SD	1.5	169	Athens-Clarke County, GA	(2.8)
50	Clarksville, TN-KY	5.9	110	Idaho Falls, ID	1.4	169	Jacksonville, FL	(2.8)
51	Port St. Lucie, FL	5.7	111	Beaumont-Port Arthur, TX	1.3	171	Richmond, VA	(2.9)
51	Raleigh-Cary, NC	5.7	112	Orlando, FL	1.2	172	Greeley, CO	(3.0)
51	Winston-Salem, NC	5.7	113	Scranton--Wilkes-Barre, PA	1.1	172	Los Angeles (greater), CA	(3.0)
54	Mansfield, OH	5.6	113	Wausau, WI	1.1	174	Dallas (greater), TX	(3.1)
55	Peoria, IL	5.4	115	Knoxville, TN	0.9	174	Monroe, LA	(3.1)
56	Rome, GA	5.3	115	Miami-Dade County, FL M.D.	0.9	174	Pittsburgh, PA	(3.1)
57	Sherman-Denison, TX	5.2	115	Prescott, AZ	0.9	177	Dalton, GA	(3.2)
58	Naples-Marco Island, FL	5.0	118	Salem, OR	0.7	177	Fort Collins-Loveland, CO	(3.2)
59	Mobile, AL	4.9	119	Johnson City, TN	0.6	177	Lincoln, NE	(3.2)
60	Newark-Union, NJ-PA M.D.	4.8	119	Spartanburg, SC	0.6	177	Peabody, MA M.D.	(3.2)

Note: All listings are for Metropolitan Statistical Areas (M.S.A.s) except for those ending with "M.D." Listings with "M.D." are Metropolitan Divisions which are smaller parts of eleven large M.S.A.s. See explanatory note at beginning of metropolitan area section.

Rank Order - Metro Area (continued)

RANK	METROPOLITAN AREA	% CHANGE
177	San Francisco-S. Mateo, CA M.D.	(3.2)
177	Santa Barbara-Santa Maria, CA	(3.2)
177	State College, PA	(3.2)
184	Hartford, CT	(3.3)
185	Alexandria, LA	(3.4)
185	Boston-Quincy, MA M.D.	(3.4)
185	Seattle (greater), WA	(3.4)
185	Seattle-Bellevue-Everett, WA M.D.	(3.4)
189	Bellingham, WA	(3.5)
189	Flagstaff, AZ	(3.5)
189	New Haven-Milford, CT	(3.5)
192	Albany, GA	(3.6)
192	Green Bay, WI	(3.6)
192	Tacoma, WA M.D.	(3.6)
192	Wenatchee, WA	(3.6)
196	Boulder, CO	(3.7)
196	Panama City-Lynn Haven, FL	(3.7)
198	Cedar Rapids, IA	(3.9)
198	Gainesville, FL	(3.9)
198	Los Angeles County, CA M.D.	(3.9)
201	Atlantic City, NJ	(4.0)
201	Jackson, MS	(4.0)
201	Palm Coast, FL	(4.0)
201	Springfield, MO	(4.0)
205	Fairbanks, AK	(4.1)
205	Farmington, NM	(4.1)
205	Kingston, NY	(4.1)
205	Lynchburg, VA	(4.1)
205	Nassau-Suffolk, NY M.D.	(4.1)
205	Waco, TX	(4.1)
211	Boston (greater), MA-NH	(4.3)
211	El Centro, CA	(4.3)
213	Bowling Green, KY	(4.4)
214	South Bend-Mishawaka, IN-MI	(4.5)
215	Fort Worth-Arlington, TX M.D.	(4.6)
215	Pittsfield, MA	(4.6)
217	Manhattan, KS	(4.7)
217	Roanoke, VA	(4.7)
217	San Jose, CA	(4.7)
217	West Palm Beach, FL M.D.	(4.7)
221	Virginia Beach-Norfolk, VA-NC	(4.8)
222	Barnstable Town, MA	(4.9)
223	Santa Fe, NM	(5.0)
224	Syracuse, NY	(5.1)
225	Longview, WA	(5.2)
226	Anchorage, AK	(5.3)
227	Buffalo-Niagara Falls, NY	(5.5)
227	Punta Gorda, FL	(5.5)
229	Bakersfield, CA	(5.6)
229	Houma, LA	(5.6)
229	Visalia-Porterville, CA	(5.6)
232	Lakeland, FL	(5.7)
233	Lawton, OK	(6.0)
233	San Diego, CA	(6.0)
233	Wilmington, DE-MD-NJ M.D.	(6.0)
236	Michigan City-La Porte, IN	(6.1)
237	Vallejo-Fairfield, CA	(6.2)
238	Fort Smith, AR-OK	(6.3)
238	Harrisonburg, VA	(6.3)
240	Norwich-New London, CT	(6.4)
240	Poughkeepsie, NY	(6.4)
242	Logan, UT-ID	(6.5)
243	Gulfport-Biloxi, MS	(6.6)
243	Lubbock, TX	(6.6)
243	Springfield, MA	(6.6)
246	Lafayette, LA	(6.7)
247	Lansing-East Lansing, MI	(6.8)
248	Cheyenne, WY	(6.9)
248	Salinas, CA	(6.9)
248	Utica-Rome, NY	(6.9)
251	Danville, VA	(7.1)
251	Washington, DC-VA-MD-WV M.D.	(7.1)
253	Washington (greater) DC-VA-MD-WV	(7.2)
254	Hinesville, GA	(7.5)
255	Albany-Schenectady-Troy, NY	(7.6)
255	Fond du Lac, WI	(7.6)
257	Sebastian-Vero Beach, FL	(7.8)
258	Salt Lake City, UT	(7.9)
259	Morristown, TN	(8.0)
260	Napa, CA	(8.1)
261	Bethesda-Frederick, MD M.D.	(8.2)
261	Goldsboro, NC	(8.2)
261	Rockford, IL	(8.2)
261	Springfield, IL	(8.2)
265	Modesto, CA	(8.3)
266	Las Vegas-Paradise, NV	(8.4)
267	Grand Rapids-Wyoming, MI	(8.5)
267	Rochester, NY	(8.5)
269	Bloomington, IN	(8.8)
270	Bangor, ME	(8.9)
270	Corpus Christi, TX	(8.9)
270	Yakima, WA	(8.9)
273	Tampa-St Petersburg, FL	(9.0)
274	Austin-Round Rock, TX	(9.3)
274	Mount Vernon-Anacortes, WA	(9.3)
276	Cambridge-Newton, MA M.D.	(9.4)
277	Sacramento, CA	(9.5)
278	Santa Rosa-Petaluma, CA	(9.7)
279	Augusta, GA-SC	(9.9)
280	Decatur, IL	(10.1)
280	Jackson, TN	(10.1)
282	Bloomington-Normal, IL	(10.4)
283	Brownsville-Harlingen, TX	(10.7)
284	Casper, WY	(10.9)
285	Colorado Springs, CO	(11.0)
286	Elizabethtown, KY	(11.2)
287	College Station-Bryan, TX	(11.3)
287	Wichita Falls, TX	(11.3)
289	Chico, CA	(11.4)
289	Saginaw, MI	(11.4)
289	San Antonio, TX	(11.4)
292	Reno-Sparks, NV	(11.6)
293	Tyler, TX	(11.8)
293	Waterloo-Cedar Falls, IA	(11.8)
295	Longview, TX	(11.9)
296	Laredo, TX	(12.0)
296	Odessa, TX	(12.0)
298	Olympia, WA	(12.5)
299	Brunswick, GA	(12.6)
299	Charlottesville, VA	(12.6)
301	El Paso, TX	(12.8)
302	Valdosta, GA	(12.9)
303	Oxnard-Thousand Oaks, CA	(13.5)
304	Midland, TX	(13.7)
305	Killeen-Temple-Fort Hood, TX	(14.1)
305	Ogden-Clearfield, UT	(14.1)
307	Amarillo, TX	(14.4)
307	Ann Arbor, MI	(14.4)
309	Dubuque, IA	(14.9)
309	Salisbury, MD	(14.9)
311	San Angelo, TX	(15.7)
312	McAllen-Edinburg-Mission, TX	(16.9)
313	Abilene, TX	(17.6)
314	Appleton, WI	(19.9)
315	Bay City, MI	(20.4)
316	Sumter, SC	(25.4)
NA	Anniston-Oxford, AL**	NA
NA	Auburn, AL**	NA
NA	Baton Rouge, LA**	NA
NA	Billings, MT**	NA
NA	Birmingham-Hoover, AL**	NA
NA	Champaign-Urbana, IL**	NA
NA	Charleston, WV**	NA
NA	Charlotte-Gastonia, NC-SC**	NA
NA	Chicago (greater), IL-IN-WI**	NA
NA	Chicago-Joilet-Naperville, IL M.D.**	NA
NA	Columbus, GA-AL**	NA
NA	Cumberland, MD-WV**	NA
NA	Davenport, IA-IL**	NA
NA	Decatur, AL**	NA
NA	Detroit (greater), MI**	NA
NA	Dothan, AL**	NA
NA	Duluth, MN-WI**	NA
NA	Eugene-Springfield, OR**	NA
NA	Evansville, IN-KY**	NA
NA	Fargo, ND-MN**	NA
NA	Florence-Muscle Shoals, AL**	NA
NA	Gadsden, AL**	NA
NA	Gary, IN M.D.**	NA
NA	Grand Forks, ND-MN**	NA
NA	Great Falls, MT**	NA
NA	Houston, TX**	NA
NA	Huntsville, AL**	NA
NA	Indianapolis, IN**	NA
NA	Jacksonville, NC**	NA
NA	Kankakee-Bradley, IL**	NA
NA	Kansas City, MO-KS**	NA
NA	La Crosse, WI-MN**	NA
NA	Lake Co.-Kenosha Co., IL-WI M.D.**	NA
NA	Lake Havasu City-Kingman, AZ**	NA
NA	Lexington-Fayette, KY**	NA
NA	Mankato-North Mankato, MN**	NA
NA	Minneapolis-St. Paul, MN-WI**	NA
NA	Missoula, MT**	NA
NA	Montgomery, AL**	NA
NA	New Orleans, LA**	NA
NA	Oklahoma City, OK**	NA
NA	Oshkosh-Neenah, WI**	NA
NA	Portland-Vancouver, OR-WA**	NA
NA	Pueblo, CO**	NA
NA	Rochester, MN**	NA
NA	Sheboygan, WI**	NA
NA	St. Cloud, MN**	NA
NA	Terre Haute, IN**	NA
NA	Toledo, OH**	NA
NA	Tucson, AZ**	NA
NA	Tuscaloosa, AL**	NA
NA	Warren-Farmington Hills, MI M.D.**	NA

Source: CQ Press using reported data from the F.B.I. "Crime in the United States 2011"
*Includes murder, rape, robbery, aggravated assault, burglary, larceny-theft, and motor vehicle theft.
**Not available.

Alpha Order - Metro Area

4. Percent Change in Crime Rate: 2007 to 2011
National Percent Change = 12.1% Decrease*

RANK	METROPOLITAN AREA	% CHANGE	RANK	METROPOLITAN AREA	% CHANGE	RANK	METROPOLITAN AREA	% CHANGE
221	Abilene, TX	(18.1)	140	Charleston, WV	(10.3)	42	Fort Lauderdale, FL M.D.	1.1
55	Akron, OH	(1.5)	296	Charlotte-Gastonia, NC-SC	(35.5)	NA	Fort Smith, AR-OK**	NA
56	Albany-Schenectady-Troy, NY	(1.8)	278	Charlottesville, VA	(25.9)	117	Fort Wayne, IN	(8.6)
69	Albany, GA	(3.4)	219	Chattanooga, TN-GA	(17.6)	198	Fort Worth-Arlington, TX M.D.	(15.3)
NA	Albuquerque, NM**	NA	231	Cheyenne, WY	(19.4)	21	Fresno, CA	8.5
94	Alexandria, LA	(6.5)	NA	Chicago (greater), IL-IN-WI**	NA	NA	Gadsden, AL**	NA
107	Allentown, PA-NJ	(7.7)	NA	Chicago-Joilet-Naperville, IL M.D.**	NA	NA	Gainesville, FL**	NA
150	Altoona, PA	(11.4)	268	Chico, CA	(24.4)	152	Gainesville, GA	(11.6)
250	Amarillo, TX	(21.6)	40	Cincinnati-Middletown, OH-KY-IN	1.4	NA	Gary, IN M.D.**	NA
107	Ames, IA	(7.7)	221	Clarksville, TN-KY	(18.1)	145	Glens Falls, NY	(10.6)
200	Anchorage, AK	(15.4)	59	Cleveland-Elyria-Mentor, OH	(2.1)	162	Goldsboro, NC	(12.0)
56	Anderson, SC	(1.8)	149	Cleveland, TN	(11.3)	NA	Grand Forks, ND-MN**	NA
174	Ann Arbor, MI	(12.7)	230	College Station-Bryan, TX	(19.2)	128	Grand Junction, CO	(9.3)
NA	Anniston-Oxford, AL**	NA	165	Colorado Springs, CO	(12.3)	282	Grand Rapids-Wyoming, MI	(26.8)
293	Appleton, WI	(31.6)	32	Columbia, MO	2.5	NA	Great Falls, MT**	NA
178	Asheville, NC	(12.9)	NA	Columbus, GA-AL**	NA	237	Greeley, CO	(20.2)
131	Athens-Clarke County, GA	(9.7)	17	Columbus, IN	9.5	264	Green Bay, WI	(23.5)
NA	Atlanta, GA**	NA	137	Columbus, OH	(10.1)	119	Greenville, SC	(8.7)
92	Atlantic City, NJ	(6.2)	279	Corpus Christi, TX	(26.2)	NA	Gulfport-Biloxi, MS**	NA
NA	Auburn, AL**	NA	193	Corvallis, OR	(14.9)	NA	Hagerstown-Martinsburg, MD-WV**	NA
115	Augusta, GA-SC	(8.2)	104	Crestview-Fort Walton Beach, FL	(7.3)	60	Hanford-Corcoran, CA	(2.3)
208	Austin-Round Rock, TX	(16.4)	NA	Cumberland, MD-WV**	NA	25	Harrisburg-Carlisle, PA	6.9
163	Bakersfield, CA	(12.1)	232	Dallas (greater), TX	(19.8)	261	Harrisonburg, VA	(23.0)
182	Baltimore-Towson, MD	(13.4)	252	Dallas-Plano-Irving, TX M.D.	(22.2)	200	Hartford, CT	(15.4)
182	Bangor, ME	(13.4)	NA	Dalton, GA**	NA	64	Hickory, NC	(2.5)
26	Barnstable Town, MA	5.6	NA	Danville, IL**	NA	211	Hinesville, GA	(16.8)
125	Baton Rouge, LA	(9.0)	137	Danville, VA	(10.1)	NA	Holland-Grand Haven, MI**	NA
140	Battle Creek, MI	(10.3)	NA	Davenport, IA-IL**	NA	194	Hot Springs, AR	(15.0)
228	Bay City, MI	(19.0)	52	Dayton, OH	(0.9)	120	Houma, LA	(8.8)
81	Beaumont-Port Arthur, TX	(5.2)	NA	Decatur, AL**	NA	NA	Houston, TX**	NA
280	Bellingham, WA	(26.7)	NA	Decatur, IL**	NA	NA	Huntsville, AL**	NA
93	Bend, OR	(6.4)	65	Deltona-Daytona Beach, FL	(2.6)	262	Idaho Falls, ID	(23.2)
272	Bethesda-Frederick, MD M.D.	(24.8)	167	Denver-Aurora, CO	(12.4)	130	Indianapolis, IN	(9.6)
NA	Billings, MT**	NA	168	Des Moines-West Des Moines, IA	(12.5)	186	Iowa City, IA	(13.9)
15	Binghamton, NY	10.7	NA	Detroit (greater), MI**	NA	NA	Jacksonville, FL**	NA
NA	Birmingham-Hoover, AL**	NA	NA	Detroit-Livonia-Dearborn, MI M.D.**	NA	211	Jacksonville, NC	(16.8)
9	Bismarck, ND	15.4	NA	Dothan, AL**	NA	88	Jackson, MS	(6.0)
158	Blacksburg, VA	(11.8)	10	Dover, DE	14.4	237	Jackson, TN	(20.2)
NA	Bloomington-Normal, IL**	NA	275	Dubuque, IA	(25.4)	134	Janesville, WI	(9.9)
61	Bloomington, IN	(2.4)	NA	Duluth, MN-WI**	NA	88	Jefferson City, MO	(6.0)
226	Boise City-Nampa, ID	(18.5)	NA	Durham-Chapel Hill, NC**	NA	79	Johnson City, TN	(4.8)
100	Boston (greater), MA-NH	(6.9)	82	Eau Claire, WI	(5.3)	41	Johnstown, PA	1.3
156	Boston-Quincy, MA M.D.	(11.7)	36	Edison, NJ M.D.	1.8	147	Jonesboro, AR	(11.0)
NA	Boulder, CO**	NA	152	El Centro, CA	(11.6)	257	Joplin, MO	(22.7)
225	Bowling Green, KY	(18.3)	232	El Paso, TX	(19.8)	NA	Kankakee-Bradley, IL**	NA
23	Bremerton-Silverdale, WA	7.5	NA	Elizabethtown, KY**	NA	NA	Kansas City, MO-KS**	NA
72	Bridgeport-Stamford, CT	(3.6)	245	Elmira, NY	(20.5)	99	Kennewick-Pasco-Richland, WA	(6.8)
206	Brownsville-Harlingen, TX	(16.3)	6	Erie, PA	20.6	256	Killeen-Temple-Fort Hood, TX	(22.6)
77	Brunswick, GA	(4.6)	168	Eugene-Springfield, OR	(12.5)	147	Kingsport, TN-VA	(11.0)
70	Buffalo-Niagara Falls, NY	(3.5)	51	Evansville, IN-KY	(0.8)	19	Kingston, NY	8.8
31	Burlington, NC	3.3	NA	Fairbanks, AK**	NA	70	Knoxville, TN	(3.5)
134	Cambridge-Newton, MA M.D.	(9.9)	NA	Fargo, ND-MN**	NA	58	Kokomo, IN	(1.9)
28	Camden, NJ M.D.	4.3	111	Farmington, NM	(8.0)	NA	La Crosse, WI-MN**	NA
NA	Canton, OH**	NA	116	Fayetteville, NC	(8.5)	110	Lafayette, IN	(7.9)
284	Cape Coral-Fort Myers, FL	(28.9)	218	Flagstaff, AZ	(17.3)	163	Lafayette, LA	(12.1)
NA	Cape Girardeau, MO-IL**	NA	48	Flint, MI	(0.6)	NA	Lake Co.-Kenosha Co., IL-WI M.D.**	NA
20	Carson City, NV	8.7	NA	Florence-Muscle Shoals, AL**	NA	286	Lake Havasu City-Kingman, AZ	(29.4)
277	Casper, WY	(25.6)	180	Florence, SC	(13.1)	216	Lakeland, FL	(17.0)
234	Cedar Rapids, IA	(19.9)	196	Fond du Lac, WI	(15.1)	84	Lancaster, PA	(5.6)
NA	Champaign-Urbana, IL**	NA	131	Fort Collins-Loveland, CO	(9.7)	129	Lansing-East Lansing, MI	(9.4)

Note: All listings are for Metropolitan Statistical Areas (M.S.A.s) except for those ending with "M.D." Listings with "M.D." are Metropolitan Divisions which are smaller parts of eleven large M.S.A.s. See explanatory note at beginning of metropolitan area section.

Alpha Order - Metro Area (continued)

RANK	METROPOLITAN AREA	% CHANGE
283	Laredo, TX	(28.7)
29	Las Cruces, NM	4.2
294	Las Vegas-Paradise, NV	(32.7)
235	Lawrence, KS	(20.0)
54	Lawton, OK	(1.4)
36	Lebanon, PA	1.8
7	Lewiston-Auburn, ME	19.9
NA	Lexington-Fayette, KY**	NA
103	Lima, OH	(7.2)
235	Lincoln, NE	(20.0)
100	Little Rock, AR	(6.9)
246	Logan, UT-ID	(21.3)
291	Longview, TX	(31.0)
252	Longview, WA	(22.2)
211	Los Angeles County, CA M.D.	(16.8)
200	Los Angeles (greater), CA	(15.4)
35	Louisville, KY-IN	1.9
97	Lubbock, TX	(6.7)
61	Lynchburg, VA	(2.4)
27	Macon, GA	4.6
11	Madera, CA	14.2
158	Madison, WI	(11.8)
NA	Manchester-Nashua, NH**	NA
NA	Manhattan, KS**	NA
NA	Mankato-North Mankato, MN**	NA
44	Mansfield, OH	0.5
179	McAllen-Edinburg-Mission, TX	(13.0)
14	Medford, OR	11.5
241	Memphis, TN-MS-AR	(20.3)
87	Merced, CA	(5.8)
168	Miami (greater), FL	(12.5)
200	Miami-Dade County, FL M.D.	(15.4)
140	Michigan City-La Porte, IN	(10.3)
237	Midland, TX	(20.2)
228	Milwaukee, WI	(19.0)
NA	Minneapolis-St. Paul, MN-WI**	NA
NA	Missoula, MT**	NA
43	Mobile, AL	0.9
269	Modesto, CA	(24.7)
204	Monroe, LA	(15.6)
5	Monroe, MI	21.5
NA	Montgomery, AL**	NA
113	Morristown, TN	(8.1)
243	Mount Vernon-Anacortes, WA	(20.4)
74	Muncie, IN	(4.3)
104	Muskegon-Norton Shores, MI	(7.3)
237	Myrtle Beach, SC	(20.2)
269	Napa, CA	(24.7)
88	Naples-Marco Island, FL	(6.0)
152	Nashville-Davidson, TN	(11.6)
67	Nassau-Suffolk, NY M.D.	(3.1)
NA	New Haven-Milford, CT**	NA
280	New Orleans, LA	(26.7)
76	New York (greater), NY-NJ-PA	(4.4)
83	New York-W. Plains NY-NJ M.D.	(5.5)
78	Newark-Union, NJ-PA M.D.	(4.7)
NA	North Port-Bradenton-Sarasota, FL**	NA
NA	Norwich-New London, CT**	NA
241	Oakland-Fremont, CA M.D.	(20.3)
184	Ocala, FL	(13.6)
102	Ocean City, NJ	(7.1)
255	Odessa, TX	(22.3)
189	Ogden-Clearfield, UT	(14.5)
48	Oklahoma City, OK	(0.6)
117	Olympia, WA	(8.6)
180	Omaha-Council Bluffs, NE-IA	(13.1)
223	Orlando, FL	(18.2)
274	Oshkosh-Neenah, WI	(25.0)
NA	Owensboro, KY**	NA
247	Oxnard-Thousand Oaks, CA	(21.5)
96	Palm Bay-Melbourne, FL	(6.6)
243	Palm Coast, FL	(20.4)
33	Panama City-Lynn Haven, FL	2.3
188	Pascagoula, MS	(14.2)
36	Peabody, MA M.D.	1.8
39	Pensacola, FL	1.7
NA	Peoria, IL**	NA
97	Philadelphia (greater) PA-NJ-MD-DE	(6.7)
127	Philadelphia, PA M.D.	(9.2)
247	Phoenix-Mesa-Scottsdale, AZ	(21.5)
106	Pine Bluff, AR	(7.6)
174	Pittsburgh, PA	(12.7)
16	Pittsfield, MA	9.9
66	Pocatello, ID	(2.7)
177	Port St. Lucie, FL	(12.8)
152	Portland-Vancouver, OR-WA	(11.6)
30	Portland, ME	3.8
67	Poughkeepsie, NY	(3.1)
172	Prescott, AZ	(12.6)
174	Provo-Orem, UT	(12.7)
NA	Pueblo, CO**	NA
251	Punta Gorda, FL	(21.7)
146	Racine, WI	(10.8)
113	Raleigh-Cary, NC	(8.1)
13	Rapid City, SD	12.0
88	Reading, PA	(6.0)
3	Redding, CA	24.7
295	Reno-Sparks, NV	(33.2)
198	Richmond, VA	(15.3)
187	Riverside-San Bernardino, CA	(14.0)
151	Roanoke, VA	(11.5)
NA	Rochester, MN**	NA
86	Rochester, NY	(5.7)
NA	Rockford, IL**	NA
4	Rockingham County, NH M.D.	22.8
211	Rocky Mount, NC	(16.8)
61	Rome, GA	(2.4)
206	Sacramento, CA	(16.3)
285	Saginaw, MI	(29.3)
269	Salem, OR	(24.7)
290	Salinas, CA	(30.7)
266	Salisbury, MD	(23.9)
192	Salt Lake City, UT	(14.8)
273	San Angelo, TX	(24.9)
168	San Antonio, TX	(12.5)
292	San Diego, CA	(31.1)
223	San Francisco (greater), CA	(18.2)
189	San Francisco-S. Mateo, CA M.D.	(14.5)
211	San Jose, CA	(16.8)
133	San Luis Obispo, CA	(9.8)
156	Sandusky, OH	(11.7)
122	Santa Ana-Anaheim, CA M.D.	(8.9)
84	Santa Barbara-Santa Maria, CA	(5.6)
120	Santa Cruz-Watsonville, CA	(8.8)
NA	Santa Fe, NM**	NA
209	Santa Rosa-Petaluma, CA	(16.5)
NA	Savannah, GA**	NA
74	Scranton--Wilkes-Barre, PA	(4.3)
191	Seattle (greater), WA	(14.7)
185	Seattle-Bellevue-Everett, WA M.D.	(13.8)
111	Sebastian-Vero Beach, FL	(8.0)
289	Sheboygan, WI	(30.1)
45	Sherman-Denison, TX	0.0
2	Sioux City, IA-NE-SD	25.0
8	Sioux Falls, SD	19.6
165	South Bend-Mishawaka, IN-MI	(12.3)
267	Spartanburg, SC	(24.2)
1	Spokane, WA	29.1
NA	Springfield, IL**	NA
73	Springfield, MA	(4.0)
48	Springfield, MO	(0.6)
227	Springfield, OH	(18.9)
205	State College, PA	(16.1)
194	Stockton, CA	(15.0)
NA	St. Cloud, MN**	NA
80	St. Joseph, MO-KS	(5.0)
139	St. Louis, MO-IL	(10.2)
297	Sumter, SC	(36.4)
46	Syracuse, NY	(0.2)
217	Tacoma, WA M.D.	(17.2)
136	Tallahassee, FL	(10.0)
275	Tampa-St Petersburg, FL	(25.4)
NA	Terre Haute, IN**	NA
24	Texarkana, TX-Texarkana, AR	7.3
NA	Toledo, OH**	NA
122	Topeka, KS	(8.9)
34	Trenton-Ewing, NJ	2.2
NA	Tucson, AZ**	NA
126	Tulsa, OK	(9.1)
NA	Tuscaloosa, AL**	NA
160	Tyler, TX	(11.9)
144	Utica-Rome, NY	(10.5)
258	Valdosta, GA	(22.8)
262	Vallejo-Fairfield, CA	(23.2)
22	Victoria, TX	7.8
94	Virginia Beach-Norfolk, VA-NC	(6.5)
143	Visalia-Porterville, CA	(10.4)
258	Waco, TX	(22.8)
18	Warner Robins, GA	9.1
NA	Warren-Farmington Hills, MI M.D.**	NA
220	Washington (greater) DC-VA-MD-WV	(18.0)
210	Washington, DC-VA-MD-WV M.D.	(16.6)
288	Waterloo-Cedar Falls, IA	(30.0)
53	Wausau, WI	(1.3)
264	Wenatchee, WA	(23.5)
258	West Palm Beach, FL M.D.	(22.8)
287	Wichita Falls, TX	(29.6)
197	Wichita, KS	(15.2)
47	Williamsport, PA	(0.5)
122	Wilmington, DE-MD-NJ M.D.	(8.9)
NA	Wilmington, NC**	NA
172	Winchester, VA-WV	(12.6)
NA	Winston-Salem, NC**	NA
12	Worcester, MA	12.2
247	Yakima, WA	(21.5)
160	York-Hanover, PA	(11.9)
109	Yuba City, CA	(7.8)
252	Yuma, AZ	(22.2)

Source: CQ Press using reported data from the F.B.I. "Crime in the United States 2011"
*Includes murder, rape, robbery, aggravated assault, burglary, larceny-theft, and motor vehicle theft.
**Not available.

Rank Order - Metro Area

4. Percent Change in Crime Rate: 2007 to 2011 (continued)
National Percent Change = 12.1% Decrease*

RANK	METROPOLITAN AREA	% CHANGE	RANK	METROPOLITAN AREA	% CHANGE	RANK	METROPOLITAN AREA	% CHANGE
1	Spokane, WA	29.1	61	Bloomington, IN	(2.4)	120	Santa Cruz-Watsonville, CA	(8.8)
2	Sioux City, IA-NE-SD	25.0	61	Lynchburg, VA	(2.4)	122	Santa Ana-Anaheim, CA M.D.	(8.9)
3	Redding, CA	24.7	61	Rome, GA	(2.4)	122	Topeka, KS	(8.9)
4	Rockingham County, NH M.D.	22.8	64	Hickory, NC	(2.5)	122	Wilmington, DE-MD-NJ M.D.	(8.9)
5	Monroe, MI	21.5	65	Deltona-Daytona Beach, FL	(2.6)	125	Baton Rouge, LA	(9.0)
6	Erie, PA	20.6	66	Pocatello, ID	(2.7)	126	Tulsa, OK	(9.1)
7	Lewiston-Auburn, ME	19.9	67	Nassau-Suffolk, NY M.D.	(3.1)	127	Philadelphia, PA M.D.	(9.2)
8	Sioux Falls, SD	19.6	67	Poughkeepsie, NY	(3.1)	128	Grand Junction, CO	(9.3)
9	Bismarck, ND	15.4	69	Albany, GA	(3.4)	129	Lansing-East Lansing, MI	(9.4)
10	Dover, DE	14.4	70	Buffalo-Niagara Falls, NY	(3.5)	130	Indianapolis, IN	(9.6)
11	Madera, CA	14.2	70	Knoxville, TN	(3.5)	131	Athens-Clarke County, GA	(9.7)
12	Worcester, MA	12.2	72	Bridgeport-Stamford, CT	(3.6)	131	Fort Collins-Loveland, CO	(9.7)
13	Rapid City, SD	12.0	73	Springfield, MA	(4.0)	133	San Luis Obispo, CA	(9.8)
14	Medford, OR	11.5	74	Muncie, IN	(4.3)	134	Cambridge-Newton, MA M.D.	(9.9)
15	Binghamton, NY	10.7	74	Scranton--Wilkes-Barre, PA	(4.3)	134	Janesville, WI	(9.9)
16	Pittsfield, MA	9.9	76	New York (greater), NY-NJ-PA	(4.4)	136	Tallahassee, FL	(10.0)
17	Columbus, IN	9.5	77	Brunswick, GA	(4.6)	137	Columbus, OH	(10.1)
18	Warner Robins, GA	9.1	78	Newark-Union, NJ-PA M.D.	(4.7)	137	Danville, VA	(10.1)
19	Kingston, NY	8.8	79	Johnson City, TN	(4.8)	139	St. Louis, MO-IL	(10.2)
20	Carson City, NV	8.7	80	St. Joseph, MO-KS	(5.0)	140	Battle Creek, MI	(10.3)
21	Fresno, CA	8.5	81	Beaumont-Port Arthur, TX	(5.2)	140	Charleston, WV	(10.3)
22	Victoria, TX	7.8	82	Eau Claire, WI	(5.3)	140	Michigan City-La Porte, IN	(10.3)
23	Bremerton-Silverdale, WA	7.5	83	New York-W. Plains NY-NJ M.D.	(5.5)	143	Visalia-Porterville, CA	(10.4)
24	Texarkana, TX-Texarkana, AR	7.3	84	Lancaster, PA	(5.6)	144	Utica-Rome, NY	(10.5)
25	Harrisburg-Carlisle, PA	6.9	84	Santa Barbara-Santa Maria, CA	(5.6)	145	Glens Falls, NY	(10.6)
26	Barnstable Town, MA	5.6	86	Rochester, NY	(5.7)	146	Racine, WI	(10.8)
27	Macon, GA	4.6	87	Merced, CA	(5.8)	147	Jonesboro, AR	(11.0)
28	Camden, NJ M.D.	4.3	88	Jackson, MS	(6.0)	147	Kingsport, TN-VA	(11.0)
29	Las Cruces, NM	4.2	88	Jefferson City, MO	(6.0)	149	Cleveland, TN	(11.3)
30	Portland, ME	3.8	88	Naples-Marco Island, FL	(6.0)	150	Altoona, PA	(11.4)
31	Burlington, NC	3.3	88	Reading, PA	(6.0)	151	Roanoke, VA	(11.5)
32	Columbia, MO	2.5	92	Atlantic City, NJ	(6.2)	152	El Centro, CA	(11.6)
33	Panama City-Lynn Haven, FL	2.3	93	Bend, OR	(6.4)	152	Gainesville, GA	(11.6)
34	Trenton-Ewing, NJ	2.2	94	Alexandria, LA	(6.5)	152	Nashville-Davidson, TN	(11.6)
35	Louisville, KY-IN	1.9	94	Virginia Beach-Norfolk, VA-NC	(6.5)	152	Portland-Vancouver, OR-WA	(11.6)
36	Edison, NJ M.D.	1.8	96	Palm Bay-Melbourne, FL	(6.6)	156	Boston-Quincy, MA M.D.	(11.7)
36	Lebanon, PA	1.8	97	Lubbock, TX	(6.7)	156	Sandusky, OH	(11.7)
36	Peabody, MA M.D.	1.8	97	Philadelphia (greater) PA-NJ-MD-DE	(6.7)	158	Blacksburg, VA	(11.8)
39	Pensacola, FL	1.7	99	Kennewick-Pasco-Richland, WA	(6.8)	158	Madison, WI	(11.8)
40	Cincinnati-Middletown, OH-KY-IN	1.4	100	Boston (greater), MA-NH	(6.9)	160	Tyler, TX	(11.9)
41	Johnstown, PA	1.3	100	Little Rock, AR	(6.9)	160	York-Hanover, PA	(11.9)
42	Fort Lauderdale, FL M.D.	1.1	102	Ocean City, NJ	(7.1)	162	Goldsboro, NC	(12.0)
43	Mobile, AL	0.9	103	Lima, OH	(7.2)	163	Bakersfield, CA	(12.1)
44	Mansfield, OH	0.5	104	Crestview-Fort Walton Beach, FL	(7.3)	163	Lafayette, LA	(12.1)
45	Sherman-Denison, TX	0.0	104	Muskegon-Norton Shores, MI	(7.3)	165	Colorado Springs, CO	(12.3)
46	Syracuse, NY	(0.2)	106	Pine Bluff, AR	(7.6)	165	South Bend-Mishawaka, IN-MI	(12.3)
47	Williamsport, PA	(0.5)	107	Allentown, PA-NJ	(7.7)	167	Denver-Aurora, CO	(12.4)
48	Flint, MI	(0.6)	107	Ames, IA	(7.7)	168	Des Moines-West Des Moines, IA	(12.5)
48	Oklahoma City, OK	(0.6)	109	Yuba City, CA	(7.8)	168	Eugene-Springfield, OR	(12.5)
48	Springfield, MO	(0.6)	110	Lafayette, IN	(7.9)	168	Miami (greater), FL	(12.5)
51	Evansville, IN-KY	(0.8)	111	Farmington, NM	(8.0)	168	San Antonio, TX	(12.5)
52	Dayton, OH	(0.9)	111	Sebastian-Vero Beach, FL	(8.0)	172	Prescott, AZ	(12.6)
53	Wausau, WI	(1.3)	113	Morristown, TN	(8.1)	172	Winchester, VA-WV	(12.6)
54	Lawton, OK	(1.4)	113	Raleigh-Cary, NC	(8.1)	174	Ann Arbor, MI	(12.7)
55	Akron, OH	(1.5)	115	Augusta, GA-SC	(8.2)	174	Pittsburgh, PA	(12.7)
56	Albany-Schenectady-Troy, NY	(1.8)	116	Fayetteville, NC	(8.5)	174	Provo-Orem, UT	(12.7)
56	Anderson, SC	(1.8)	117	Fort Wayne, IN	(8.6)	177	Port St. Lucie, FL	(12.8)
58	Kokomo, IN	(1.9)	117	Olympia, WA	(8.6)	178	Asheville, NC	(12.9)
59	Cleveland-Elyria-Mentor, OH	(2.1)	119	Greenville, SC	(8.7)	179	McAllen-Edinburg-Mission, TX	(13.0)
60	Hanford-Corcoran, CA	(2.3)	120	Houma, LA	(8.8)	180	Florence, SC	(13.1)

Note: All listings are for Metropolitan Statistical Areas (M.S.A.s) except for those ending with "M.D." Listings with "M.D." are Metropolitan Divisions which are smaller parts of eleven large M.S.A.s. See explanatory note at beginning of metropolitan area section.

Rank Order - Metro Area (continued)

RANK	METROPOLITAN AREA	% CHANGE	RANK	METROPOLITAN AREA	% CHANGE	RANK	METROPOLITAN AREA	% CHANGE
180	Omaha-Council Bluffs, NE-IA	(13.1)	243	Palm Coast, FL	(20.4)	NA	Cape Girardeau, MO-IL**	NA
182	Baltimore-Towson, MD	(13.4)	245	Elmira, NY	(20.5)	NA	Champaign-Urbana, IL**	NA
182	Bangor, ME	(13.4)	246	Logan, UT-ID	(21.3)	NA	Chicago (greater), IL-IN-WI**	NA
184	Ocala, FL	(13.6)	247	Oxnard-Thousand Oaks, CA	(21.5)	NA	Chicago-Joilet-Naperville, IL M.D.**	NA
185	Seattle-Bellevue-Everett, WA M.D.	(13.8)	247	Phoenix-Mesa-Scottsdale, AZ	(21.5)	NA	Columbus, GA-AL**	NA
186	Iowa City, IA	(13.9)	247	Yakima, WA	(21.5)	NA	Cumberland, MD-WV**	NA
187	Riverside-San Bernardino, CA	(14.0)	250	Amarillo, TX	(21.6)	NA	Dalton, GA**	NA
188	Pascagoula, MS	(14.2)	251	Punta Gorda, FL	(21.7)	NA	Danville, IL**	NA
189	Ogden-Clearfield, UT	(14.5)	252	Dallas-Plano-Irving, TX M.D.	(22.2)	NA	Davenport, IA-IL**	NA
189	San Francisco-S. Mateo, CA M.D.	(14.5)	252	Longview, WA	(22.2)	NA	Decatur, AL**	NA
191	Seattle (greater), WA	(14.7)	252	Yuma, AZ	(22.2)	NA	Decatur, IL**	NA
192	Salt Lake City, UT	(14.8)	255	Odessa, TX	(22.3)	NA	Detroit (greater), MI**	NA
193	Corvallis, OR	(14.9)	256	Killeen-Temple-Fort Hood, TX	(22.6)	NA	Detroit-Livonia-Dearborn, MI M.D.**	NA
194	Hot Springs, AR	(15.0)	257	Joplin, MO	(22.7)	NA	Dothan, AL**	NA
194	Stockton, CA	(15.0)	258	Valdosta, GA	(22.8)	NA	Duluth, MN-WI**	NA
196	Fond du Lac, WI	(15.1)	258	Waco, TX	(22.8)	NA	Durham-Chapel Hill, NC**	NA
197	Wichita, KS	(15.2)	258	West Palm Beach, FL M.D.	(22.8)	NA	Elizabethtown, KY**	NA
198	Fort Worth-Arlington, TX M.D.	(15.3)	261	Harrisonburg, VA	(23.0)	NA	Fairbanks, AK**	NA
198	Richmond, VA	(15.3)	262	Idaho Falls, ID	(23.2)	NA	Fargo, ND-MN**	NA
200	Anchorage, AK	(15.4)	262	Vallejo-Fairfield, CA	(23.2)	NA	Florence-Muscle Shoals, AL**	NA
200	Hartford, CT	(15.4)	264	Green Bay, WI	(23.5)	NA	Fort Smith, AR-OK**	NA
200	Los Angeles (greater), CA	(15.4)	264	Wenatchee, WA	(23.5)	NA	Gadsden, AL**	NA
200	Miami-Dade County, FL M.D.	(15.4)	266	Salisbury, MD	(23.9)	NA	Gainesville, FL**	NA
204	Monroe, LA	(15.6)	267	Spartanburg, SC	(24.2)	NA	Gary, IN M.D.**	NA
205	State College, PA	(16.1)	268	Chico, CA	(24.4)	NA	Grand Forks, ND-MN**	NA
206	Brownsville-Harlingen, TX	(16.3)	269	Modesto, CA	(24.7)	NA	Great Falls, MT**	NA
206	Sacramento, CA	(16.3)	269	Napa, CA	(24.7)	NA	Gulfport-Biloxi, MS**	NA
208	Austin-Round Rock, TX	(16.4)	269	Salem, OR	(24.7)	NA	Hagerstown-Martinsburg, MD-WV**	NA
209	Santa Rosa-Petaluma, CA	(16.5)	272	Bethesda-Frederick, MD M.D.	(24.8)	NA	Holland-Grand Haven, MI**	NA
210	Washington, DC-VA-MD-WV M.D.	(16.6)	273	San Angelo, TX	(24.9)	NA	Houston, TX**	NA
211	Hinesville, GA	(16.8)	274	Oshkosh-Neenah, WI	(25.0)	NA	Huntsville, AL**	NA
211	Jacksonville, NC	(16.8)	275	Dubuque, IA	(25.4)	NA	Jacksonville, FL**	NA
211	Los Angeles County, CA M.D.	(16.8)	275	Tampa-St Petersburg, FL	(25.4)	NA	Kankakee-Bradley, IL**	NA
211	Rocky Mount, NC	(16.8)	277	Casper, WY	(25.6)	NA	Kansas City, MO-KS**	NA
211	San Jose, CA	(16.8)	278	Charlottesville, VA	(25.9)	NA	La Crosse, WI-MN**	NA
216	Lakeland, FL	(17.0)	279	Corpus Christi, TX	(26.2)	NA	Lake Co.-Kenosha Co., IL-WI M.D.**	NA
217	Tacoma, WA M.D.	(17.2)	280	Bellingham, WA	(26.7)	NA	Lexington-Fayette, KY**	NA
218	Flagstaff, AZ	(17.3)	280	New Orleans, LA	(26.7)	NA	Manchester-Nashua, NH**	NA
219	Chattanooga, TN-GA	(17.6)	282	Grand Rapids-Wyoming, MI	(26.8)	NA	Manhattan, KS**	NA
220	Washington (greater) DC-VA-MD-WV	(18.0)	283	Laredo, TX	(28.7)	NA	Mankato-North Mankato, MN**	NA
221	Abilene, TX	(18.1)	284	Cape Coral-Fort Myers, FL	(28.9)	NA	Minneapolis-St. Paul, MN-WI**	NA
221	Clarksville, TN-KY	(18.1)	285	Saginaw, MI	(29.3)	NA	Missoula, MT**	NA
223	Orlando, FL	(18.2)	286	Lake Havasu City-Kingman, AZ	(29.4)	NA	Montgomery, AL**	NA
223	San Francisco (greater), CA	(18.2)	287	Wichita Falls, TX	(29.6)	NA	New Haven-Milford, CT**	NA
225	Bowling Green, KY	(18.3)	288	Waterloo-Cedar Falls, IA	(30.0)	NA	North Port-Bradenton-Sarasota, FL**	NA
226	Boise City-Nampa, ID	(18.5)	289	Sheboygan, WI	(30.1)	NA	Norwich-New London, CT**	NA
227	Springfield, OH	(18.9)	290	Salinas, CA	(30.7)	NA	Owensboro, KY**	NA
228	Bay City, MI	(19.0)	291	Longview, TX	(31.0)	NA	Peoria, IL**	NA
228	Milwaukee, WI	(19.0)	292	San Diego, CA	(31.1)	NA	Pueblo, CO**	NA
230	College Station-Bryan, TX	(19.2)	293	Appleton, WI	(31.6)	NA	Rochester, MN**	NA
231	Cheyenne, WY	(19.4)	294	Las Vegas-Paradise, NV	(32.7)	NA	Rockford, IL**	NA
232	Dallas (greater), TX	(19.8)	295	Reno-Sparks, NV	(33.2)	NA	Santa Fe, NM**	NA
232	El Paso, TX	(19.8)	296	Charlotte-Gastonia, NC-SC	(35.5)	NA	Savannah, GA**	NA
234	Cedar Rapids, IA	(19.9)	297	Sumter, SC	(36.4)	NA	Springfield, IL**	NA
235	Lawrence, KS	(20.0)	NA	Albuquerque, NM**	NA	NA	St. Cloud, MN**	NA
235	Lincoln, NE	(20.0)	NA	Anniston-Oxford, AL**	NA	NA	Terre Haute, IN**	NA
237	Greeley, CO	(20.2)	NA	Atlanta, GA**	NA	NA	Toledo, OH**	NA
237	Jackson, TN	(20.2)	NA	Auburn, AL**	NA	NA	Tucson, AZ**	NA
237	Midland, TX	(20.2)	NA	Billings, MT**	NA	NA	Tuscaloosa, AL**	NA
237	Myrtle Beach, SC	(20.2)	NA	Birmingham-Hoover, AL**	NA	NA	Warren-Farmington Hills, MI M.D.**	NA
241	Memphis, TN-MS-AR	(20.3)	NA	Bloomington-Normal, IL**	NA	NA	Wilmington, NC**	NA
241	Oakland-Fremont, CA M.D.	(20.3)	NA	Boulder, CO**	NA	NA	Winston-Salem, NC**	NA
243	Mount Vernon-Anacortes, WA	(20.4)	NA	Canton, OH**	NA			

Source: CQ Press using reported data from the F.B.I. "Crime in the United States 2011"
*Includes murder, rape, robbery, aggravated assault, burglary, larceny-theft, and motor vehicle theft.
**Not available.

Alpha Order - Metro Area

5. Violent Crimes in 2011
National Total = 1,203,564 Violent Crimes*

RANK	METROPOLITAN AREA	CRIMES
264	Abilene, TX	502
111	Akron, OH	2,281
101	Albany-Schenectady-Troy, NY	2,472
202	Albany, GA	841
53	Albuquerque, NM	5,938
178	Alexandria, LA	1,053
128	Allentown, PA-NJ	1,765
308	Altoona, PA	326
156	Amarillo, TX	1,318
324	Ames, IA	250
103	Anchorage, AK	2,454
176	Anderson, SC	1,103
177	Ann Arbor, MI	1,066
236	Anniston-Oxford, AL	607
310	Appleton, WI	321
188	Asheville, NC	938
218	Athens-Clarke County, GA	734
12	Atlanta, GA	21,403
150	Atlantic City, NJ	1,396
316	Auburn, AL	296
118	Augusta, GA-SC	2,035
63	Austin-Round Rock, TX	5,032
67	Bakersfield, CA	4,447
16	Baltimore-Towson, MD	17,681
355	Bangor, ME	123
184	Barnstable Town, MA	985
66	Baton Rouge, LA	4,752
199	Battle Creek, MI	853
317	Bay City, MI	295
115	Beaumont-Port Arthur, TX	2,167
284	Bellingham, WA	439
260	Bend, OR	528
110	Bethesda-Frederick, MD M.D.	2,282
287	Billings, MT	418
255	Binghamton, NY	548
52	Birmingham-Hoover, AL	5,942
326	Bismarck, ND	245
326	Blacksburg, VA	245
257	Bloomington-Normal, IL	546
297	Bloomington, IN	378
157	Boise City-Nampa, ID	1,303
17	Boston (greater), MA-NH	17,153
32	Boston-Quincy, MA M.D.	9,937
223	Boulder, CO	697
335	Bowling Green, KY	207
207	Bremerton-Silverdale, WA	810
95	Bridgeport-Stamford, CT	2,645
166	Brownsville-Harlingen, TX	1,217
244	Brunswick, GA	575
64	Buffalo-Niagara Falls, NY	5,010
234	Burlington, NC	644
72	Cambridge-Newton, MA M.D.	3,813
68	Camden, NJ M.D.	4,412
167	Canton, OH	1,211
114	Cape Coral-Fort Myers, FL	2,213
280	Cape Girardeau, MO-IL	448
352	Carson City, NV	148
342	Casper, WY	188
270	Cedar Rapids, IA	478
155	Champaign-Urbana, IL	1,321

RANK	METROPOLITAN AREA	CRIMES
159	Charleston, WV	1,286
42	Charlotte-Gastonia, NC-SC	7,621
304	Charlottesville, VA	337
93	Chattanooga, TN-GA	2,673
332	Cheyenne, WY	226
NA	Chicago (greater), IL-IN-WI**	NA
NA	Chicago-Joilet-Naperville, IL M.D.**	NA
243	Chico, CA	576
51	Cincinnati-Middletown, OH-KY-IN	6,287
168	Clarksville, TN-KY	1,204
39	Cleveland-Elyria-Mentor, OH	8,411
219	Cleveland, TN	733
203	College Station-Bryan, TX	838
104	Colorado Springs, CO	2,449
220	Columbia, MO	729
165	Columbus, GA-AL	1,220
354	Columbus, IN	126
48	Columbus, OH	6,664
107	Corpus Christi, TX	2,346
357	Corvallis, OR	97
211	Crestview-Fort Walton Beach, FL	782
303	Cumberland, MD-WV	338
10	Dallas (greater), TX	23,316
22	Dallas-Plano-Irving, TX M.D.	14,562
309	Dalton, GA	322
269	Danville, IL	482
334	Danville, VA	214
141	Davenport, IA-IL	1,586
105	Dayton, OH	2,443
302	Decatur, AL	342
245	Decatur, IL	567
98	Deltona-Daytona Beach, FL	2,511
34	Denver-Aurora, CO	9,181
140	Des Moines-West Des Moines, IA	1,590
8	Detroit (greater), MI	24,633
13	Detroit-Livonia-Dearborn, MI M.D.	19,145
239	Dothan, AL	590
181	Dover, DE	1,020
353	Dubuque, IA	146
NA	Duluth, MN-WI**	NA
112	Durham-Chapel Hill, NC	2,253
328	Eau Claire, WI	244
75	Edison, NJ M.D.	3,554
270	El Centro, CA	478
83	El Paso, TX	3,325
356	Elizabethtown, KY	117
345	Elmira, NY	177
224	Erie, PA	692
182	Eugene-Springfield, OR	1,001
192	Evansville, IN-KY	912
340	Fairbanks, AK	192
NA	Fargo, ND-MN**	NA
206	Farmington, NM	822
127	Fayetteville, NC	1,795
246	Flagstaff, AZ	565
74	Flint, MI	3,579
304	Florence-Muscle Shoals, AL	337
153	Florence, SC	1,369
344	Fond du Lac, WI	184
232	Fort Collins-Loveland, CO	653

RANK	METROPOLITAN AREA	CRIMES
37	Fort Lauderdale, FL M.D.	8,749
161	Fort Smith, AR-OK	1,257
189	Fort Wayne, IN	935
36	Fort Worth-Arlington, TX M.D.	8,754
62	Fresno, CA	5,172
262	Gadsden, AL	513
139	Gainesville, FL	1,603
319	Gainesville, GA	284
113	Gary, IN M.D.	2,242
335	Glens Falls, NY	207
252	Goldsboro, NC	551
NA	Grand Forks, ND-MN**	NA
278	Grand Junction, CO	450
94	Grand Rapids-Wyoming, MI	2,672
338	Great Falls, MT	204
216	Greeley, CO	754
281	Green Bay, WI	446
79	Greenville, SC	3,478
247	Gulfport-Biloxi, MS	563
221	Hagerstown-Martinsburg, MD-WV	717
258	Hanford-Corcoran, CA	542
132	Harrisburg-Carlisle, PA	1,691
351	Harrisonburg, VA	150
89	Hartford, CT	2,999
205	Hickory, NC	823
321	Hinesville, GA	269
290	Holland-Grand Haven, MI	401
266	Hot Springs, AR	496
230	Houma, LA	661
6	Houston, TX	33,444
117	Huntsville, AL	2,106
323	Idaho Falls, ID	255
31	Indianapolis, IN	10,348
300	Iowa City, IA	368
44	Jacksonville, FL	7,141
285	Jacksonville, NC	426
116	Jackson, MS	2,149
197	Jackson, TN	866
294	Janesville, WI	393
273	Jefferson City, MO	473
233	Johnson City, TN	650
296	Johnstown, PA	379
275	Jonesboro, AR	467
249	Joplin, MO	552
282	Kankakee-Bradley, IL	440
33	Kansas City, MO-KS	9,750
231	Kennewick-Pasco-Richland, WA	656
151	Killeen-Temple-Fort Hood, TX	1,382
172	Kingsport, TN-VA	1,136
307	Kingston, NY	335
86	Knoxville, TN	3,240
322	Kokomo, IN	264
NA	La Crosse, WI-MN**	NA
253	Lafayette, IN	550
143	Lafayette, LA	1,561
152	Lake Co.-Kenosha Co., IL-WI M.D.	1,381
289	Lake Havasu City-Kingman, AZ	409
96	Lakeland, FL	2,543
187	Lancaster, PA	946
129	Lansing-East Lansing, MI	1,718

Note: All listings are for Metropolitan Statistical Areas (M.S.A.s) except for those ending with "M.D." Listings with "M.D." are Metropolitan Divisions which are smaller parts of eleven large M.S.A.s. See explanatory note at beginning of metropolitan area section.

18   Metro Areas

Alpha Order - Metro Area (continued)

RANK	METROPOLITAN AREA	CRIMES
163	Laredo, TX	1,236
212	Las Cruces, NM	778
26	Las Vegas-Paradise, NV	12,732
295	Lawrence, KS	390
196	Lawton, OK	875
330	Lebanon, PA	240
348	Lewiston-Auburn, ME	166
125	Lexington-Fayette, KY	1,808
263	Lima, OH	504
183	Lincoln, NE	989
60	Little Rock, AR	5,260
358	Logan, UT-ID	61
201	Longview, TX	843
313	Longview, WA	315
4	Los Angeles County, CA M.D.	46,116
3	Los Angeles (greater), CA	52,624
59	Louisville, KY-IN	5,413
119	Lubbock, TX	1,965
282	Lynchburg, VA	440
192	Macon, GA	912
209	Madera, CA	799
162	Madison, WI	1,245
180	Manchester-Nashua, NH	1,021
299	Manhattan, KS	369
NA	Mankato-North Mankato, MN**	NA
331	Mansfield, OH	227
108	McAllen-Edinburg-Mission, TX	2,337
238	Medford, OR	596
24	Memphis, TN-MS-AR	13,007
148	Merced, CA	1,409
5	Miami (greater), FL	33,654
15	Miami-Dade County, FL M.D.	18,320
342	Michigan City-La Porte, IN	188
291	Midland, TX	399
46	Milwaukee, WI	7,003
NA	Minneapolis-St. Paul, MN-WI**	NA
320	Missoula, MT	276
97	Mobile, AL	2,524
99	Modesto, CA	2,484
171	Monroe, LA	1,139
298	Monroe, MI	377
175	Montgomery, AL	1,121
272	Morristown, TN	474
329	Mount Vernon-Anacortes, WA	242
237	Muncie, IN	602
217	Muskegon-Norton Shores, MI	746
124	Myrtle Beach, SC	1,822
277	Napa, CA	452
179	Naples-Marco Island, FL	1,028
30	Nashville-Davidson, TN	10,440
69	Nassau-Suffolk, NY M.D.	4,370
88	New Haven-Milford, CT	3,008
55	New Orleans, LA	5,782
1	New York (greater), NY-NJ-PA	77,029
2	New York-W. Plains NY-NJ M.D.	60,749
40	Newark-Union, NJ-PA M.D.	8,356
77	North Port-Bradenton-Sarasota, FL	3,518
242	Norwich-New London, CT	583
21	Oakland-Fremont, CA M.D.	14,712
134	Ocala, FL	1,668
315	Ocean City, NJ	309
186	Odessa, TX	951
204	Ogden-Clearfield, UT	827
47	Oklahoma City, OK	6,689
240	Olympia, WA	587
82	Omaha-Council Bluffs, NE-IA	3,349
25	Orlando, FL	12,887
310	Oshkosh-Neenah, WI	321
349	Owensboro, KY	164
130	Oxnard-Thousand Oaks, CA	1,705
85	Palm Bay-Melbourne, FL	3,262
314	Palm Coast, FL	311
190	Panama City-Lynn Haven, FL	915
255	Pascagoula, MS	548
92	Peabody, MA M.D.	2,776
106	Pensacola, FL	2,397
147	Peoria, IL	1,467
7	Philadelphia (greater) PA-NJ-MD-DE	31,880
9	Philadelphia, PA M.D.	23,595
19	Phoenix-Mesa-Scottsdale, AZ	16,152
213	Pine Bluff, AR	777
45	Pittsburgh, PA	7,084
258	Pittsfield, MA	542
340	Pocatello, ID	192
146	Port St. Lucie, FL	1,481
54	Portland-Vancouver, OR-WA	5,849
228	Portland, ME	672
137	Poughkeepsie, NY	1,623
215	Prescott, AZ	766
292	Provo-Orem, UT	398
198	Pueblo, CO	861
293	Punta Gorda, FL	396
276	Racine, WI	455
91	Raleigh-Cary, NC	2,785
261	Rapid City, SD	519
160	Reading, PA	1,272
158	Redding, CA	1,302
133	Reno-Sparks, NV	1,680
90	Richmond, VA	2,990
20	Riverside-San Bernardino, CA	15,172
200	Roanoke, VA	850
NA	Rochester, MN**	NA
87	Rochester, NY	3,064
100	Rockford, IL	2,476
235	Rockingham County, NH M.D.	627
214	Rocky Mount, NC	770
267	Rome, GA	486
35	Sacramento, CA	9,136
142	Saginaw, MI	1,572
194	Salem, OR	885
120	Salinas, CA	1,951
229	Salisbury, MD	664
78	Salt Lake City, UT	3,481
318	San Angelo, TX	287
38	San Antonio, TX	8,709
29	San Diego, CA	11,009
11	San Francisco (greater), CA	22,294
43	San Francisco-S. Mateo, CA M.D.	7,582
65	San Jose, CA	4,760
226	San Luis Obispo, CA	680
333	Sandusky, OH	224
50	Santa Ana-Anaheim, CA M.D.	6,508
135	Santa Barbara-Santa Maria, CA	1,657
170	Santa Cruz-Watsonville, CA	1,169
249	Santa Fe, NM	552
131	Santa Rosa-Petaluma, CA	1,702
169	Savannah, GA	1,202
144	Scranton--Wilkes-Barre, PA	1,523
28	Seattle (greater), WA	11,536
41	Seattle-Bellevue-Everett, WA M.D.	8,160
278	Sebastian-Vero Beach, FL	450
350	Sheboygan, WI	158
306	Sherman-Denison, TX	336
286	Sioux City, IA-NE-SD	419
265	Sioux Falls, SD	497
174	South Bend-Mishawaka, IN-MI	1,123
149	Spartanburg, SC	1,401
136	Spokane, WA	1,644
145	Springfield, IL	1,500
80	Springfield, MA	3,477
123	Springfield, MO	1,867
288	Springfield, OH	411
347	State College, PA	171
56	Stockton, CA	5,694
NA	St. Cloud, MN**	NA
301	St. Joseph, MO-KS	352
23	St. Louis, MO-IL	13,992
253	Sumter, SC	550
122	Syracuse, NY	1,907
81	Tacoma, WA M.D.	3,376
102	Tallahassee, FL	2,462
27	Tampa-St Petersburg, FL	12,277
312	Terre Haute, IN	317
191	Texarkana, TX-Texarkana, AR	913
84	Toledo, OH	3,289
194	Topeka, KS	885
138	Trenton-Ewing, NJ	1,604
70	Tucson, AZ	4,309
61	Tulsa, OK	5,250
185	Tuscaloosa, AL	979
210	Tyler, TX	791
222	Utica-Rome, NY	699
268	Valdosta, GA	485
126	Vallejo-Fairfield, CA	1,802
241	Victoria, TX	584
57	Virginia Beach-Norfolk, VA-NC	5,488
121	Visalia-Porterville, CA	1,942
173	Waco, TX	1,126
274	Warner Robins, GA	470
57	Warren-Farmington Hills, MI M.D.	5,488
14	Washington (greater) DC-VA-MD-WV	18,908
18	Washington, DC-VA-MD-WV M.D.	16,626
248	Waterloo-Cedar Falls, IA	559
339	Wausau, WI	200
345	Wenatchee, WA	177
49	West Palm Beach, FL M.D.	6,585
249	Wichita Falls, TX	552
73	Wichita, KS	3,619
335	Williamsport, PA	207
71	Wilmington, DE-MD-NJ M.D.	3,873
163	Wilmington, NC	1,236
325	Winchester, VA-WV	246
109	Winston-Salem, NC	2,307
76	Worcester, MA	3,528
208	Yakima, WA	807
154	York-Hanover, PA	1,324
225	Yuba City, CA	684
227	Yuma, AZ	676

Source: Reported data from the F.B.I. "Crime in the United States 2011"
*Violent crimes are offenses of murder, forcible rape, robbery, and aggravated assault.
**Not available.

Rank Order - Metro Area

5. Violent Crimes in 2011 (continued)
National Total = 1,203,564 Violent Crimes*

RANK	METROPOLITAN AREA	CRIMES	RANK	METROPOLITAN AREA	CRIMES	RANK	METROPOLITAN AREA	CRIMES
1	New York (greater), NY-NJ-PA	77,029	61	Tulsa, OK	5,250	121	Visalia-Porterville, CA	1,942
2	New York-W. Plains NY-NJ M.D.	60,749	62	Fresno, CA	5,172	122	Syracuse, NY	1,907
3	Los Angeles (greater), CA	52,624	63	Austin-Round Rock, TX	5,032	123	Springfield, MO	1,867
4	Los Angeles County, CA M.D.	46,116	64	Buffalo-Niagara Falls, NY	5,010	124	Myrtle Beach, SC	1,822
5	Miami (greater), FL	33,654	65	San Jose, CA	4,760	125	Lexington-Fayette, KY	1,808
6	Houston, TX	33,444	66	Baton Rouge, LA	4,752	126	Vallejo-Fairfield, CA	1,802
7	Philadelphia (greater) PA-NJ-MD-DE	31,880	67	Bakersfield, CA	4,447	127	Fayetteville, NC	1,795
8	Detroit (greater), MI	24,633	68	Camden, NJ M.D.	4,412	128	Allentown, PA-NJ	1,765
9	Philadelphia, PA M.D.	23,595	69	Nassau-Suffolk, NY M.D.	4,370	129	Lansing-East Lansing, MI	1,718
10	Dallas (greater), TX	23,316	70	Tucson, AZ	4,309	130	Oxnard-Thousand Oaks, CA	1,705
11	San Francisco (greater), CA	22,294	71	Wilmington, DE-MD-NJ M.D.	3,873	131	Santa Rosa-Petaluma, CA	1,702
12	Atlanta, GA	21,403	72	Cambridge-Newton, MA M.D.	3,813	132	Harrisburg-Carlisle, PA	1,691
13	Detroit-Livonia-Dearborn, MI M.D.	19,145	73	Wichita, KS	3,619	133	Reno-Sparks, NV	1,680
14	Washington (greater) DC-VA-MD-WV	18,908	74	Flint, MI	3,579	134	Ocala, FL	1,668
15	Miami-Dade County, FL M.D.	18,320	75	Edison, NJ M.D.	3,554	135	Santa Barbara-Santa Maria, CA	1,657
16	Baltimore-Towson, MD	17,681	76	Worcester, MA	3,528	136	Spokane, WA	1,644
17	Boston (greater), MA-NH	17,153	77	North Port-Bradenton-Sarasota, FL	3,518	137	Poughkeepsie, NY	1,623
18	Washington, DC-VA-MD-WV M.D.	16,626	78	Salt Lake City, UT	3,481	138	Trenton-Ewing, NJ	1,604
19	Phoenix-Mesa-Scottsdale, AZ	16,152	79	Greenville, SC	3,478	139	Gainesville, FL	1,603
20	Riverside-San Bernardino, CA	15,172	80	Springfield, MA	3,477	140	Des Moines-West Des Moines, IA	1,590
21	Oakland-Fremont, CA M.D.	14,712	81	Tacoma, WA M.D.	3,376	141	Davenport, IA-IL	1,586
22	Dallas-Plano-Irving, TX M.D.	14,562	82	Omaha-Council Bluffs, NE-IA	3,349	142	Saginaw, MI	1,572
23	St. Louis, MO-IL	13,992	83	El Paso, TX	3,325	143	Lafayette, LA	1,561
24	Memphis, TN-MS-AR	13,007	84	Toledo, OH	3,289	144	Scranton--Wilkes-Barre, PA	1,523
25	Orlando, FL	12,887	85	Palm Bay-Melbourne, FL	3,262	145	Springfield, IL	1,500
26	Las Vegas-Paradise, NV	12,732	86	Knoxville, TN	3,240	146	Port St. Lucie, FL	1,481
27	Tampa-St Petersburg, FL	12,277	87	Rochester, NY	3,064	147	Peoria, IL	1,467
28	Seattle (greater), WA	11,536	88	New Haven-Milford, CT	3,008	148	Merced, CA	1,409
29	San Diego, CA	11,009	89	Hartford, CT	2,999	149	Spartanburg, SC	1,401
30	Nashville-Davidson, TN	10,440	90	Richmond, VA	2,990	150	Atlantic City, NJ	1,396
31	Indianapolis, IN	10,348	91	Raleigh-Cary, NC	2,785	151	Killeen-Temple-Fort Hood, TX	1,382
32	Boston-Quincy, MA M.D.	9,937	92	Peabody, MA M.D.	2,776	152	Lake Co.-Kenosha Co., IL-WI M.D.	1,381
33	Kansas City, MO-KS	9,750	93	Chattanooga, TN-GA	2,673	153	Florence, SC	1,369
34	Denver-Aurora, CO	9,181	94	Grand Rapids-Wyoming, MI	2,672	154	York-Hanover, PA	1,324
35	Sacramento, CA	9,136	95	Bridgeport-Stamford, CT	2,645	155	Champaign-Urbana, IL	1,321
36	Fort Worth-Arlington, TX M.D.	8,754	96	Lakeland, FL	2,543	156	Amarillo, TX	1,318
37	Fort Lauderdale, FL M.D.	8,749	97	Mobile, AL	2,524	157	Boise City-Nampa, ID	1,303
38	San Antonio, TX	8,709	98	Deltona-Daytona Beach, FL	2,511	158	Redding, CA	1,302
39	Cleveland-Elyria-Mentor, OH	8,411	99	Modesto, CA	2,484	159	Charleston, WV	1,286
40	Newark-Union, NJ-PA M.D.	8,356	100	Rockford, IL	2,476	160	Reading, PA	1,272
41	Seattle-Bellevue-Everett, WA M.D.	8,160	101	Albany-Schenectady-Troy, NY	2,472	161	Fort Smith, AR-OK	1,257
42	Charlotte-Gastonia, NC-SC	7,621	102	Tallahassee, FL	2,462	162	Madison, WI	1,245
43	San Francisco-S. Mateo, CA M.D.	7,582	103	Anchorage, AK	2,454	163	Laredo, TX	1,236
44	Jacksonville, FL	7,141	104	Colorado Springs, CO	2,449	163	Wilmington, NC	1,236
45	Pittsburgh, PA	7,084	105	Dayton, OH	2,443	165	Columbus, GA-AL	1,220
46	Milwaukee, WI	7,003	106	Pensacola, FL	2,397	166	Brownsville-Harlingen, TX	1,217
47	Oklahoma City, OK	6,689	107	Corpus Christi, TX	2,346	167	Canton, OH	1,211
48	Columbus, OH	6,664	108	McAllen-Edinburg-Mission, TX	2,337	168	Clarksville, TN-KY	1,204
49	West Palm Beach, FL M.D.	6,585	109	Winston-Salem, NC	2,307	169	Savannah, GA	1,202
50	Santa Ana-Anaheim, CA M.D.	6,508	110	Bethesda-Frederick, MD M.D.	2,282	170	Santa Cruz-Watsonville, CA	1,169
51	Cincinnati-Middletown, OH-KY-IN	6,287	111	Akron, OH	2,281	171	Monroe, LA	1,139
52	Birmingham-Hoover, AL	5,942	112	Durham-Chapel Hill, NC	2,253	172	Kingsport, TN-VA	1,136
53	Albuquerque, NM	5,938	113	Gary, IN M.D.	2,242	173	Waco, TX	1,126
54	Portland-Vancouver, OR-WA	5,849	114	Cape Coral-Fort Myers, FL	2,213	174	South Bend-Mishawaka, IN-MI	1,123
55	New Orleans, LA	5,782	115	Beaumont-Port Arthur, TX	2,167	175	Montgomery, AL	1,121
56	Stockton, CA	5,694	116	Jackson, MS	2,149	176	Anderson, SC	1,103
57	Virginia Beach-Norfolk, VA-NC	5,488	117	Huntsville, AL	2,106	177	Ann Arbor, MI	1,066
57	Warren-Farmington Hills, MI M.D.	5,488	118	Augusta, GA-SC	2,035	178	Alexandria, LA	1,053
59	Louisville, KY-IN	5,413	119	Lubbock, TX	1,965	179	Naples-Marco Island, FL	1,028
60	Little Rock, AR	5,260	120	Salinas, CA	1,951	180	Manchester-Nashua, NH	1,021

Note: All listings are for Metropolitan Statistical Areas (M.S.A.s) except for those ending with "M.D." Listings with "M.D." are Metropolitan Divisions which are smaller parts of eleven large M.S.A.s. See explanatory note at beginning of metropolitan area section.

Rank Order - Metro Area (continued)

RANK	METROPOLITAN AREA	CRIMES
181	Dover, DE	1,020
182	Eugene-Springfield, OR	1,001
183	Lincoln, NE	989
184	Barnstable Town, MA	985
185	Tuscaloosa, AL	979
186	Odessa, TX	951
187	Lancaster, PA	946
188	Asheville, NC	938
189	Fort Wayne, IN	935
190	Panama City-Lynn Haven, FL	915
191	Texarkana, TX-Texarkana, AR	913
192	Evansville, IN-KY	912
192	Macon, GA	912
194	Salem, OR	885
194	Topeka, KS	885
196	Lawton, OK	875
197	Jackson, TN	866
198	Pueblo, CO	861
199	Battle Creek, MI	853
200	Roanoke, VA	850
201	Longview, TX	843
202	Albany, GA	841
203	College Station-Bryan, TX	838
204	Ogden-Clearfield, UT	827
205	Hickory, NC	823
206	Farmington, NM	822
207	Bremerton-Silverdale, WA	810
208	Yakima, WA	807
209	Madera, CA	799
210	Tyler, TX	791
211	Crestview-Fort Walton Beach, FL	782
212	Las Cruces, NM	778
213	Pine Bluff, AR	777
214	Rocky Mount, NC	770
215	Prescott, AZ	766
216	Greeley, CO	754
217	Muskegon-Norton Shores, MI	746
218	Athens-Clarke County, GA	734
219	Cleveland, TN	733
220	Columbia, MO	729
221	Hagerstown-Martinsburg, MD-WV	717
222	Utica-Rome, NY	699
223	Boulder, CO	697
224	Erie, PA	692
225	Yuba City, CA	684
226	San Luis Obispo, CA	680
227	Yuma, AZ	676
228	Portland, ME	672
229	Salisbury, MD	664
230	Houma, LA	661
231	Kennewick-Pasco-Richland, WA	656
232	Fort Collins-Loveland, CO	653
233	Johnson City, TN	650
234	Burlington, NC	644
235	Rockingham County, NH M.D.	627
236	Anniston-Oxford, AL	607
237	Muncie, IN	602
238	Medford, OR	596
239	Dothan, AL	590
240	Olympia, WA	587
241	Victoria, TX	584
242	Norwich-New London, CT	583
243	Chico, CA	576
244	Brunswick, GA	575
245	Decatur, IL	567
246	Flagstaff, AZ	565
247	Gulfport-Biloxi, MS	563
248	Waterloo-Cedar Falls, IA	559
249	Joplin, MO	552
249	Santa Fe, NM	552
249	Wichita Falls, TX	552
252	Goldsboro, NC	551
253	Lafayette, IN	550
253	Sumter, SC	550
255	Binghamton, NY	548
255	Pascagoula, MS	548
257	Bloomington-Normal, IL	546
258	Hanford-Corcoran, CA	542
258	Pittsfield, MA	542
260	Bend, OR	528
261	Rapid City, SD	519
262	Gadsden, AL	513
263	Lima, OH	504
264	Abilene, TX	502
265	Sioux Falls, SD	497
266	Hot Springs, AR	496
267	Rome, GA	486
268	Valdosta, GA	485
269	Danville, IL	482
270	Cedar Rapids, IA	478
270	El Centro, CA	478
272	Morristown, TN	474
273	Jefferson City, MO	473
274	Warner Robins, GA	470
275	Jonesboro, AR	467
276	Racine, WI	455
277	Napa, CA	452
278	Grand Junction, CO	450
278	Sebastian-Vero Beach, FL	450
280	Cape Girardeau, MO-IL	448
281	Green Bay, WI	446
282	Kankakee-Bradley, IL	440
282	Lynchburg, VA	440
284	Bellingham, WA	439
285	Jacksonville, NC	426
286	Sioux City, IA-NE-SD	419
287	Billings, MT	418
288	Springfield, OH	411
289	Lake Havasu City-Kingman, AZ	409
290	Holland-Grand Haven, MI	401
291	Midland, TX	399
292	Provo-Orem, UT	398
293	Punta Gorda, FL	396
294	Janesville, WI	393
295	Lawrence, KS	390
296	Johnstown, PA	379
297	Bloomington, IN	378
298	Monroe, MI	377
299	Manhattan, KS	369
300	Iowa City, IA	368
301	St. Joseph, MO-KS	352
302	Decatur, AL	342
303	Cumberland, MD-WV	338
304	Charlottesville, VA	337
304	Florence-Muscle Shoals, AL	337
306	Sherman-Denison, TX	336
307	Kingston, NY	335
308	Altoona, PA	326
309	Dalton, GA	322
310	Appleton, WI	321
310	Oshkosh-Neenah, WI	321
312	Terre Haute, IN	317
313	Longview, WA	315
314	Palm Coast, FL	311
315	Ocean City, NJ	309
316	Auburn, AL	296
317	Bay City, MI	295
318	San Angelo, TX	287
319	Gainesville, GA	284
320	Missoula, MT	276
321	Hinesville, GA	269
322	Kokomo, IN	264
323	Idaho Falls, ID	255
324	Ames, IA	250
325	Winchester, VA-WV	246
326	Bismarck, ND	245
326	Blacksburg, VA	245
328	Eau Claire, WI	244
329	Mount Vernon-Anacortes, WA	242
330	Lebanon, PA	240
331	Mansfield, OH	227
332	Cheyenne, WY	226
333	Sandusky, OH	224
334	Danville, VA	214
335	Bowling Green, KY	207
335	Glens Falls, NY	207
335	Williamsport, PA	207
338	Great Falls, MT	204
339	Wausau, WI	200
340	Fairbanks, AK	192
340	Pocatello, ID	192
342	Casper, WY	188
342	Michigan City-La Porte, IN	188
344	Fond du Lac, WI	184
345	Elmira, NY	177
345	Wenatchee, WA	177
347	State College, PA	171
348	Lewiston-Auburn, ME	166
349	Owensboro, KY	164
350	Sheboygan, WI	158
351	Harrisonburg, VA	150
352	Carson City, NV	148
353	Dubuque, IA	146
354	Columbus, IN	126
355	Bangor, ME	123
356	Elizabethtown, KY	117
357	Corvallis, OR	97
358	Logan, UT-ID	61
NA	Chicago (greater), IL-IN-WI**	NA
NA	Chicago-Joilet-Naperville, IL M.D.**	NA
NA	Duluth, MN-WI**	NA
NA	Fargo, ND-MN**	NA
NA	Grand Forks, ND-MN**	NA
NA	La Crosse, WI-MN**	NA
NA	Mankato-North Mankato, MN**	NA
NA	Minneapolis-St. Paul, MN-WI**	NA
NA	Rochester, MN**	NA
NA	St. Cloud, MN**	NA

Source: Reported data from the F.B.I. "Crime in the United States 2011"
*Violent crimes are offenses of murder, forcible rape, robbery, and aggravated assault.
**Not available.

Alpha Order - Metro Area

6. Violent Crime Rate in 2011
National Rate = 386.3 Violent Crimes per 100,000 Population*

RANK	METROPOLITAN AREA	RATE	RANK	METROPOLITAN AREA	RATE	RANK	METROPOLITAN AREA	RATE
230	Abilene, TX	297.5	122	Charleston, WV	422.1	88	Fort Lauderdale, FL M.D.	493.8
208	Akron, OH	324.1	119	Charlotte-Gastonia, NC-SC	428.1	129	Fort Smith, AR-OK	417.4
247	Albany-Schenectady-Troy, NY	282.6	330	Charlottesville, VA	165.2	293	Fort Wayne, IN	223.5
59	Albany, GA	527.7	79	Chattanooga, TN-GA	501.0	142	Fort Worth-Arlington, TX M.D.	401.4
19	Albuquerque, NM	662.0	278	Cheyenne, WY	244.4	49	Fresno, CA	549.4
16	Alexandria, LA	677.9	NA	Chicago (greater), IL-IN-WI**	NA	91	Gadsden, AL	488.9
304	Allentown, PA-NJ	214.2	NA	Chicago-Joilet-Naperville, IL M.D.**	NA	32	Gainesville, FL	598.4
266	Altoona, PA	255.7	264	Chico, CA	258.8	336	Gainesville, GA	156.0
68	Amarillo, TX	516.6	233	Cincinnati-Middletown, OH-KY-IN	294.5	215	Gary, IN M.D.	315.0
249	Ames, IA	277.7	113	Clarksville, TN-KY	435.9	333	Glens Falls, NY	159.8
5	Anchorage, AK	789.2	140	Cleveland-Elyria-Mentor, OH	404.6	107	Goldsboro, NC	443.7
40	Anderson, SC	582.7	27	Cleveland, TN	627.4	NA	Grand Forks, ND-MN**	NA
219	Ann Arbor, MI	309.4	172	College Station-Bryan, TX	358.9	226	Grand Junction, CO	301.4
71	Anniston-Oxford, AL	509.5	163	Colorado Springs, CO	372.8	185	Grand Rapids-Wyoming, MI	345.4
349	Appleton, WI	141.6	125	Columbia, MO	420.4	274	Great Falls, MT	248.6
299	Asheville, NC	218.0	134	Columbus, GA-AL	409.0	237	Greeley, CO	293.1
159	Athens-Clarke County, GA	376.3	331	Columbus, IN	163.2	347	Green Bay, WI	145.0
143	Atlanta, GA	400.9	170	Columbus, OH	362.6	53	Greenville, SC	539.7
74	Atlantic City, NJ	506.8	54	Corpus Christi, TX	536.6	291	Gulfport-Biloxi, MS	225.4
307	Auburn, AL	210.0	353	Corvallis, OR	112.2	260	Hagerstown-Martinsburg, MD-WV	264.9
171	Augusta, GA-SC	360.9	120	Crestview-Fort Walton Beach, FL	426.7	182	Hanford-Corcoran, CA	350.2
244	Austin-Round Rock, TX	287.1	204	Cumberland, MD-WV	324.9	221	Harrisburg-Carlisle, PA	306.8
64	Bakersfield, CA	523.5	173	Dallas (greater), TX	358.4	352	Harrisonburg, VA	118.4
25	Baltimore-Towson, MD	646.2	194	Dallas-Plano-Irving, TX M.D.	336.7	235	Hartford, CT	293.4
356	Bangor, ME	79.9	293	Dalton, GA	223.5	295	Hickory, NC	222.4
104	Barnstable Town, MA	453.5	36	Danville, IL	588.7	191	Hinesville, GA	340.8
37	Baton Rouge, LA	586.8	313	Danville, VA	198.5	340	Holland-Grand Haven, MI	152.1
28	Battle Creek, MI	627.0	131	Davenport, IA-IL	416.1	69	Hot Springs, AR	512.7
252	Bay City, MI	273.9	240	Dayton, OH	290.1	216	Houma, LA	314.6
50	Beaumont-Port Arthur, TX	545.9	298	Decatur, AL	221.3	48	Houston, TX	550.8
303	Bellingham, WA	214.9	70	Decatur, IL	510.3	78	Huntsville, AL	501.9
200	Bend, OR	331.2	80	Deltona-Daytona Beach, FL	500.9	316	Idaho Falls, ID	193.3
319	Bethesda-Frederick, MD M.D.	187.6	177	Denver-Aurora, CO	354.8	39	Indianapolis, IN	586.2
262	Billings, MT	262.1	249	Des Moines-West Des Moines, IA	277.7	283	Iowa City, IA	239.9
301	Binghamton, NY	216.7	42	Detroit (greater), MI	573.8	63	Jacksonville, FL	523.6
62	Birmingham-Hoover, AL	524.2	1	Detroit-Livonia-Dearborn, MI M.D.	1,052.4	284	Jacksonville, NC	236.6
297	Bismarck, ND	221.5	141	Dothan, AL	403.2	146	Jackson, MS	397.2
344	Blacksburg, VA	148.6	30	Dover, DE	622.1	9	Jackson, TN	743.6
210	Bloomington-Normal, IL	321.0	337	Dubuque, IA	155.1	280	Janesville, WI	244.1
315	Bloomington, IN	195.1	NA	Duluth, MN-WI**	NA	216	Jefferson City, MO	314.6
309	Boise City-Nampa, ID	209.0	108	Durham-Chapel Hill, NC	441.1	207	Johnson City, TN	324.2
162	Boston (greater), MA-NH	374.7	342	Eau Claire, WI	150.8	261	Johnstown, PA	262.9
66	Boston-Quincy, MA M.D.	523.2	341	Edison, NJ M.D.	151.4	155	Jonesboro, AR	383.0
286	Boulder, CO	232.6	256	El Centro, CA	270.7	218	Joplin, MO	313.4
331	Bowling Green, KY	163.2	135	El Paso, TX	406.7	150	Kankakee-Bradley, IL	386.7
212	Bremerton-Silverdale, WA	317.6	355	Elizabethtown, KY	97.0	97	Kansas City, MO-KS	476.8
234	Bridgeport-Stamford, CT	293.6	314	Elmira, NY	198.4	267	Kennewick-Pasco-Richland, WA	254.9
235	Brownsville-Harlingen, TX	293.4	277	Erie, PA	245.9	197	Killeen-Temple-Fort Hood, TX	334.0
76	Brunswick, GA	505.1	248	Eugene-Springfield, OR	281.6	169	Kingsport, TN-VA	363.4
110	Buffalo-Niagara Falls, NY	439.2	269	Evansville, IN-KY	252.9	322	Kingston, NY	182.7
124	Burlington, NC	420.8	46	Fairbanks, AK	560.7	103	Knoxville, TN	460.0
270	Cambridge-Newton, MA M.D.	252.1	NA	Fargo, ND-MN**	NA	258	Kokomo, IN	266.2
179	Camden, NJ M.D.	351.6	29	Farmington, NM	625.1	NA	La Crosse, WI-MN**	NA
228	Canton, OH	299.2	93	Fayetteville, NC	483.8	255	Lafayette, IN	271.2
178	Cape Coral-Fort Myers, FL	352.8	132	Flagstaff, AZ	414.5	45	Lafayette, LA	565.1
102	Cape Girardeau, MO-IL	463.7	3	Flint, MI	841.2	334	Lake Co.-Kenosha Co., IL-WI M.D.	158.2
259	Carson City, NV	265.5	290	Florence-Muscle Shoals, AL	227.9	312	Lake Havasu City-Kingman, AZ	201.5
276	Casper, WY	247.2	22	Florence, SC	658.3	130	Lakeland, FL	416.7
320	Cedar Rapids, IA	184.3	325	Fond du Lac, WI	180.3	324	Lancaster, PA	181.5
44	Champaign-Urbana, IL	568.0	304	Fort Collins-Loveland, CO	214.2	166	Lansing-East Lansing, MI	370.5

Note: All listings are for Metropolitan Statistical Areas (M.S.A.s) except for those ending with "M.D." Listings with "M.D." are Metropolitan Divisions which are smaller parts of eleven large M.S.A.s. See explanatory note at beginning of metropolitan area section.

Alpha Order - Metro Area (continued)

RANK	METROPOLITAN AREA	RATE
94	Laredo, TX	483.6
168	Las Cruces, NM	367.7
24	Las Vegas-Paradise, NV	647.0
183	Lawrence, KS	349.7
14	Lawton, OK	697.6
326	Lebanon, PA	179.1
338	Lewiston-Auburn, ME	154.1
156	Lexington-Fayette, KY	380.3
98	Lima, OH	473.6
205	Lincoln, NE	324.4
8	Little Rock, AR	746.0
358	Logan, UT-ID	47.7
153	Longview, TX	385.1
225	Longview, WA	302.8
101	Los Angeles County, CA M.D.	464.2
138	Los Angeles (greater), CA	405.4
127	Louisville, KY-IN	419.0
17	Lubbock, TX	675.5
328	Lynchburg, VA	172.1
149	Macon, GA	387.5
64	Madera, CA	523.5
299	Madison, WI	218.0
268	Manchester-Nashua, NH	254.5
243	Manhattan, KS	288.5
NA	Mankato-North Mankato, MN**	NA
323	Mansfield, OH	182.2
232	McAllen-Edinburg-Mission, TX	295.4
239	Medford, OR	290.2
2	Memphis, TN-MS-AR	980.4
51	Merced, CA	544.4
33	Miami (greater), FL	596.7
11	Miami-Dade County, FL M.D.	724.0
329	Michigan City-La Porte, IN	167.8
246	Midland, TX	285.5
105	Milwaukee, WI	448.1
NA	Minneapolis-St. Paul, MN-WI**	NA
272	Missoula, MT	250.3
31	Mobile, AL	608.2
95	Modesto, CA	477.2
26	Monroe, LA	639.7
275	Monroe, MI	248.2
229	Montgomery, AL	297.9
187	Morristown, TN	343.9
311	Mount Vernon-Anacortes, WA	203.8
72	Muncie, IN	509.0
116	Muskegon-Norton Shores, MI	433.6
18	Myrtle Beach, SC	668.8
202	Napa, CA	327.3
214	Naples-Marco Island, FL	315.4
23	Nashville-Davidson, TN	650.8
339	Nassau-Suffolk, NY M.D.	153.6
165	New Haven-Milford, CT	371.2
90	New Orleans, LA	490.6
136	New York (greater), NY-NJ-PA	406.0
67	New York-W. Plains NY-NJ M.D.	522.5
148	Newark-Union, NJ-PA M.D.	387.8
87	North Port-Bradenton-Sarasota, FL	494.2
145	Norwich-New London, CT	397.8
43	Oakland-Fremont, CA M.D.	568.2
84	Ocala, FL	496.7
213	Ocean City, NJ	316.6
15	Odessa, TX	679.2
346	Ogden-Clearfield, UT	148.3
58	Oklahoma City, OK	528.2
289	Olympia, WA	229.1
154	Omaha-Council Bluffs, NE-IA	383.8
34	Orlando, FL	595.7
317	Oshkosh-Neenah, WI	191.4
348	Owensboro, KY	141.9
310	Oxnard-Thousand Oaks, CA	204.7
35	Palm Bay-Melbourne, FL	592.2
211	Palm Coast, FL	320.6
55	Panama City-Lynn Haven, FL	534.6
195	Pascagoula, MS	336.5
164	Peabody, MA M.D.	371.3
60	Pensacola, FL	526.7
152	Peoria, IL	385.7
56	Philadelphia (greater) PA-NJ-MD-DE	532.3
38	Philadelphia, PA M.D.	586.7
157	Phoenix-Mesa-Scottsdale, AZ	379.8
7	Pine Bluff, AR	769.2
227	Pittsburgh, PA	299.7
133	Pittsfield, MA	410.5
308	Pocatello, ID	209.5
186	Port St. Lucie, FL	344.5
263	Portland-Vancouver, OR-WA	259.7
351	Portland, ME	130.7
282	Poughkeepsie, NY	241.0
174	Prescott, AZ	357.9
357	Provo-Orem, UT	74.1
57	Pueblo, CO	532.0
279	Punta Gorda, FL	244.2
288	Racine, WI	231.8
281	Raleigh-Cary, NC	243.3
137	Rapid City, SD	405.7
220	Reading, PA	308.2
10	Redding, CA	726.1
147	Reno-Sparks, NV	391.6
285	Richmond, VA	234.8
176	Riverside-San Bernardino, CA	354.9
254	Roanoke, VA	272.1
NA	Rochester, MN**	NA
242	Rochester, NY	289.3
13	Rockford, IL	706.5
343	Rockingham County, NH M.D.	149.7
81	Rocky Mount, NC	499.0
83	Rome, GA	498.0
126	Sacramento, CA	420.2
6	Saginaw, MI	785.9
292	Salem, OR	224.1
100	Salinas, CA	464.6
61	Salisbury, MD	525.4
222	Salt Lake City, UT	303.8
271	San Angelo, TX	251.4
144	San Antonio, TX	398.1
180	San Diego, CA	351.5
73	San Francisco (greater), CA	508.3
123	San Francisco-S. Mateo, CA M.D.	421.9
265	San Jose, CA	256.1
273	San Luis Obispo, CA	249.3
238	Sandusky, OH	290.4
306	Santa Ana-Anaheim, CA M.D.	213.7
151	Santa Barbara-Santa Maria, CA	386.4
109	Santa Cruz-Watsonville, CA	440.4
158	Santa Fe, NM	378.6
184	Santa Rosa-Petaluma, CA	347.7
190	Savannah, GA	341.3
257	Scranton--Wilkes-Barre, PA	269.4
201	Seattle (greater), WA	330.2
222	Seattle-Bellevue-Everett, WA M.D.	303.8
209	Sebastian-Vero Beach, FL	321.6
350	Sheboygan, WI	136.2
253	Sherman-Denison, TX	272.2
241	Sioux City, IA-NE-SD	289.9
302	Sioux Falls, SD	215.1
181	South Bend-Mishawaka, IN-MI	350.3
92	Spartanburg, SC	487.1
188	Spokane, WA	343.5
12	Springfield, IL	711.6
82	Springfield, MA	498.7
121	Springfield, MO	426.0
231	Springfield, OH	296.9
354	State College, PA	110.7
4	Stockton, CA	821.2
NA	St. Cloud, MN**	NA
251	St. Joseph, MO-KS	275.4
86	St. Louis, MO-IL	495.4
75	Sumter, SC	505.9
245	Syracuse, NY	286.5
128	Tacoma, WA M.D.	418.0
20	Tallahassee, FL	661.1
114	Tampa-St Petersburg, FL	435.2
321	Terre Haute, IN	182.9
21	Texarkana, TX-Texarkana, AR	660.1
77	Toledo, OH	504.5
160	Topeka, KS	376.0
112	Trenton-Ewing, NJ	436.2
117	Tucson, AZ	433.4
47	Tulsa, OK	554.1
106	Tuscaloosa, AL	444.0
167	Tyler, TX	369.4
287	Utica-Rome, NY	232.4
189	Valdosta, GA	342.9
118	Vallejo-Fairfield, CA	430.9
85	Victoria, TX	495.7
205	Virginia Beach-Norfolk, VA-NC	324.4
115	Visalia-Porterville, CA	434.1
99	Waco, TX	469.5
198	Warner Robins, GA	331.6
296	Warren-Farmington Hills, MI M.D.	221.8
196	Washington (greater) DC-VA-MD-WV	334.6
161	Washington, DC-VA-MD-WV M.D.	374.9
199	Waterloo-Cedar Falls, IA	331.4
345	Wausau, WI	148.5
335	Wenatchee, WA	157.2
89	West Palm Beach, FL M.D.	492.1
175	Wichita Falls, TX	357.3
41	Wichita, KS	577.2
327	Williamsport, PA	177.7
52	Wilmington, DE-MD-NJ M.D.	543.7
193	Wilmington, NC	336.9
318	Winchester, VA-WV	189.6
96	Winston-Salem, NC	476.9
111	Worcester, MA	439.1
203	Yakima, WA	326.7
224	York-Hanover, PA	303.4
139	Yuba City, CA	405.1
192	Yuma, AZ	340.5

Source: Reported data from the F.B.I. "Crime in the United States 2011"

*Violent crimes are offenses of murder, forcible rape, robbery, and aggravated assault.

**Not available.

Rank Order - Metro Area

6. Violent Crime Rate in 2011 (continued)
National Rate = 386.3 Violent Crimes per 100,000 Population*

RANK	METROPOLITAN AREA	RATE
1	Detroit-Livonia-Dearborn, MI M.D.	1,052.4
2	Memphis, TN-MS-AR	980.4
3	Flint, MI	841.2
4	Stockton, CA	821.2
5	Anchorage, AK	789.2
6	Saginaw, MI	785.9
7	Pine Bluff, AR	769.2
8	Little Rock, AR	746.0
9	Jackson, TN	743.6
10	Redding, CA	726.1
11	Miami-Dade County, FL M.D.	724.0
12	Springfield, IL	711.6
13	Rockford, IL	706.5
14	Lawton, OK	697.6
15	Odessa, TX	679.2
16	Alexandria, LA	677.9
17	Lubbock, TX	675.5
18	Myrtle Beach, SC	668.8
19	Albuquerque, NM	662.0
20	Tallahassee, FL	661.1
21	Texarkana, TX-Texarkana, AR	660.1
22	Florence, SC	658.3
23	Nashville-Davidson, TN	650.8
24	Las Vegas-Paradise, NV	647.0
25	Baltimore-Towson, MD	646.2
26	Monroe, LA	639.7
27	Cleveland, TN	627.4
28	Battle Creek, MI	627.0
29	Farmington, NM	625.1
30	Dover, DE	622.1
31	Mobile, AL	608.2
32	Gainesville, FL	598.4
33	Miami (greater), FL	596.7
34	Orlando, FL	595.7
35	Palm Bay-Melbourne, FL	592.2
36	Danville, IL	588.7
37	Baton Rouge, LA	586.8
38	Philadelphia, PA M.D.	586.7
39	Indianapolis, IN	586.2
40	Anderson, SC	582.7
41	Wichita, KS	577.2
42	Detroit (greater), MI	573.8
43	Oakland-Fremont, CA M.D.	568.2
44	Champaign-Urbana, IL	568.0
45	Lafayette, LA	565.1
46	Fairbanks, AK	560.7
47	Tulsa, OK	554.1
48	Houston, TX	550.8
49	Fresno, CA	549.4
50	Beaumont-Port Arthur, TX	545.9
51	Merced, CA	544.4
52	Wilmington, DE-MD-NJ M.D.	543.7
53	Greenville, SC	539.7
54	Corpus Christi, TX	536.6
55	Panama City-Lynn Haven, FL	534.6
56	Philadelphia (greater) PA-NJ-MD-DE	532.3
57	Pueblo, CO	532.0
58	Oklahoma City, OK	528.2
59	Albany, GA	527.7
60	Pensacola, FL	526.7
61	Salisbury, MD	525.4
62	Birmingham-Hoover, AL	524.2
63	Jacksonville, FL	523.6
64	Bakersfield, CA	523.5
64	Madera, CA	523.5
66	Boston-Quincy, MA M.D.	523.2
67	New York-W. Plains NY-NJ M.D.	522.5
68	Amarillo, TX	516.6
69	Hot Springs, AR	512.7
70	Decatur, IL	510.3
71	Anniston-Oxford, AL	509.5
72	Muncie, IN	509.0
73	San Francisco (greater), CA	508.3
74	Atlantic City, NJ	506.8
75	Sumter, SC	505.9
76	Brunswick, GA	505.1
77	Toledo, OH	504.5
78	Huntsville, AL	501.9
79	Chattanooga, TN-GA	501.0
80	Deltona-Daytona Beach, FL	500.9
81	Rocky Mount, NC	499.0
82	Springfield, MA	498.7
83	Rome, GA	498.0
84	Ocala, FL	496.7
85	Victoria, TX	495.7
86	St. Louis, MO-IL	495.4
87	North Port-Bradenton-Sarasota, FL	494.2
88	Fort Lauderdale, FL M.D.	493.8
89	West Palm Beach, FL M.D.	492.1
90	New Orleans, LA	490.6
91	Gadsden, AL	488.9
92	Spartanburg, SC	487.1
93	Fayetteville, NC	483.8
94	Laredo, TX	483.6
95	Modesto, CA	477.2
96	Winston-Salem, NC	476.9
97	Kansas City, MO-KS	476.8
98	Lima, OH	473.6
99	Waco, TX	469.5
100	Salinas, CA	464.6
101	Los Angeles County, CA M.D.	464.2
102	Cape Girardeau, MO-IL	463.7
103	Knoxville, TN	460.0
104	Barnstable Town, MA	453.5
105	Milwaukee, WI	448.1
106	Tuscaloosa, AL	444.0
107	Goldsboro, NC	443.7
108	Durham-Chapel Hill, NC	441.1
109	Santa Cruz-Watsonville, CA	440.4
110	Buffalo-Niagara Falls, NY	439.2
111	Worcester, MA	439.1
112	Trenton-Ewing, NJ	436.2
113	Clarksville, TN-KY	435.9
114	Tampa-St Petersburg, FL	435.2
115	Visalia-Porterville, CA	434.1
116	Muskegon-Norton Shores, MI	433.6
117	Tucson, AZ	433.4
118	Vallejo-Fairfield, CA	430.9
119	Charlotte-Gastonia, NC-SC	428.1
120	Crestview-Fort Walton Beach, FL	426.7
121	Springfield, MO	426.0
122	Charleston, WV	422.1
123	San Francisco-S. Mateo, CA M.D.	421.9
124	Burlington, NC	420.8
125	Columbia, MO	420.4
126	Sacramento, CA	420.2
127	Louisville, KY-IN	419.0
128	Tacoma, WA M.D.	418.0
129	Fort Smith, AR-OK	417.4
130	Lakeland, FL	416.7
131	Davenport, IA-IL	416.1
132	Flagstaff, AZ	414.5
133	Pittsfield, MA	410.5
134	Columbus, GA-AL	409.0
135	El Paso, TX	406.7
136	New York (greater), NY-NJ-PA	406.0
137	Rapid City, SD	405.7
138	Los Angeles (greater), CA	405.4
139	Yuba City, CA	405.1
140	Cleveland-Elyria-Mentor, OH	404.6
141	Dothan, AL	403.2
142	Fort Worth-Arlington, TX M.D.	401.4
143	Atlanta, GA	400.9
144	San Antonio, TX	398.1
145	Norwich-New London, CT	397.8
146	Jackson, MS	397.2
147	Reno-Sparks, NV	391.6
148	Newark-Union, NJ-PA M.D.	387.8
149	Macon, GA	387.5
150	Kankakee-Bradley, IL	386.7
151	Santa Barbara-Santa Maria, CA	386.4
152	Peoria, IL	385.7
153	Longview, TX	385.1
154	Omaha-Council Bluffs, NE-IA	383.8
155	Jonesboro, AR	383.0
156	Lexington-Fayette, KY	380.3
157	Phoenix-Mesa-Scottsdale, AZ	379.8
158	Santa Fe, NM	378.6
159	Athens-Clarke County, GA	376.3
160	Topeka, KS	376.0
161	Washington, DC-VA-MD-WV M.D.	374.9
162	Boston (greater), MA-NH	374.7
163	Colorado Springs, CO	372.8
164	Peabody, MA M.D.	371.3
165	New Haven-Milford, CT	371.2
166	Lansing-East Lansing, MI	370.5
167	Tyler, TX	369.4
168	Las Cruces, NM	367.7
169	Kingsport, TN-VA	363.4
170	Columbus, OH	362.6
171	Augusta, GA-SC	360.9
172	College Station-Bryan, TX	358.9
173	Dallas (greater), TX	358.4
174	Prescott, AZ	357.9
175	Wichita Falls, TX	357.3
176	Riverside-San Bernardino, CA	354.9
177	Denver-Aurora, CO	354.8
178	Cape Coral-Fort Myers, FL	352.8
179	Camden, NJ M.D.	351.6
180	San Diego, CA	351.5

Note: All listings are for Metropolitan Statistical Areas (M.S.A.s) except for those ending with "M.D." Listings with "M.D." are Metropolitan Divisions which are smaller parts of eleven large M.S.A.s. See explanatory note at beginning of metropolitan area section.

Rank Order - Metro Area (continued)

RANK	METROPOLITAN AREA	RATE
181	South Bend-Mishawaka, IN-MI	350.3
182	Hanford-Corcoran, CA	350.2
183	Lawrence, KS	349.7
184	Santa Rosa-Petaluma, CA	347.7
185	Grand Rapids-Wyoming, MI	345.4
186	Port St. Lucie, FL	344.5
187	Morristown, TN	343.9
188	Spokane, WA	343.5
189	Valdosta, GA	342.9
190	Savannah, GA	341.3
191	Hinesville, GA	340.8
192	Yuma, AZ	340.5
193	Wilmington, NC	336.9
194	Dallas-Plano-Irving, TX M.D.	336.7
195	Pascagoula, MS	336.5
196	Washington (greater) DC-VA-MD-WV	334.6
197	Killeen-Temple-Fort Hood, TX	334.0
198	Warner Robins, GA	331.6
199	Waterloo-Cedar Falls, IA	331.4
200	Bend, OR	331.2
201	Seattle (greater), WA	330.2
202	Napa, CA	327.3
203	Yakima, WA	326.7
204	Cumberland, MD-WV	324.9
205	Lincoln, NE	324.4
205	Virginia Beach-Norfolk, VA-NC	324.4
207	Johnson City, TN	324.2
208	Akron, OH	324.1
209	Sebastian-Vero Beach, FL	321.6
210	Bloomington-Normal, IL	321.0
211	Palm Coast, FL	320.6
212	Bremerton-Silverdale, WA	317.6
213	Ocean City, NJ	316.6
214	Naples-Marco Island, FL	315.4
215	Gary, IN M.D.	315.0
216	Houma, LA	314.6
216	Jefferson City, MO	314.6
218	Joplin, MO	313.4
219	Ann Arbor, MI	309.4
220	Reading, PA	308.2
221	Harrisburg-Carlisle, PA	306.8
222	Salt Lake City, UT	303.8
222	Seattle-Bellevue-Everett, WA M.D.	303.8
224	York-Hanover, PA	303.4
225	Longview, WA	302.8
226	Grand Junction, CO	301.4
227	Pittsburgh, PA	299.7
228	Canton, OH	299.2
229	Montgomery, AL	297.9
230	Abilene, TX	297.5
231	Springfield, OH	296.9
232	McAllen-Edinburg-Mission, TX	295.4
233	Cincinnati-Middletown, OH-KY-IN	294.5
234	Bridgeport-Stamford, CT	293.6
235	Brownsville-Harlingen, TX	293.4
235	Hartford, CT	293.4
237	Greeley, CO	293.1
238	Sandusky, OH	290.4
239	Medford, OR	290.2
240	Dayton, OH	290.1
241	Sioux City, IA-NE-SD	289.9
242	Rochester, NY	289.3
243	Manhattan, KS	288.5
244	Austin-Round Rock, TX	287.1
245	Syracuse, NY	286.5
246	Midland, TX	285.5
247	Albany-Schenectady-Troy, NY	282.6
248	Eugene-Springfield, OR	281.6
249	Ames, IA	277.7
249	Des Moines-West Des Moines, IA	277.7
251	St. Joseph, MO-KS	275.4
252	Bay City, MI	273.9
253	Sherman-Denison, TX	272.2
254	Roanoke, VA	272.1
255	Lafayette, IN	271.2
256	El Centro, CA	270.7
257	Scranton--Wilkes-Barre, PA	269.4
258	Kokomo, IN	266.2
259	Carson City, NV	265.5
260	Hagerstown-Martinsburg, MD-WV	264.9
261	Johnstown, PA	262.9
262	Billings, MT	262.1
263	Portland-Vancouver, OR-WA	259.7
264	Chico, CA	258.8
265	San Jose, CA	256.1
266	Altoona, PA	255.7
267	Kennewick-Pasco-Richland, WA	254.9
268	Manchester-Nashua, NH	254.5
269	Evansville, IN-KY	252.9
270	Cambridge-Newton, MA M.D.	252.1
271	San Angelo, TX	251.4
272	Missoula, MT	250.3
273	San Luis Obispo, CA	249.3
274	Great Falls, MT	248.6
275	Monroe, MI	248.2
276	Casper, WY	247.2
277	Erie, PA	245.9
278	Cheyenne, WY	244.4
279	Punta Gorda, FL	244.2
280	Janesville, WI	244.1
281	Raleigh-Cary, NC	243.3
282	Poughkeepsie, NY	241.0
283	Iowa City, IA	239.9
284	Jacksonville, NC	236.6
285	Richmond, VA	234.8
286	Boulder, CO	232.6
287	Utica-Rome, NY	232.4
288	Racine, WI	231.8
289	Olympia, WA	229.1
290	Florence-Muscle Shoals, AL	227.9
291	Gulfport-Biloxi, MS	225.4
292	Salem, OR	224.1
293	Dalton, GA	223.5
293	Fort Wayne, IN	223.5
295	Hickory, NC	222.4
296	Warren-Farmington Hills, MI M.D.	221.8
297	Bismarck, ND	221.5
298	Decatur, AL	221.3
299	Asheville, NC	218.0
299	Madison, WI	218.0
301	Binghamton, NY	216.7
302	Sioux Falls, SD	215.1
303	Bellingham, WA	214.9
304	Allentown, PA-NJ	214.2
304	Fort Collins-Loveland, CO	214.2
306	Santa Ana-Anaheim, CA M.D.	213.7
307	Auburn, AL	210.0
308	Pocatello, ID	209.5
309	Boise City-Nampa, ID	209.0
310	Oxnard-Thousand Oaks, CA	204.7
311	Mount Vernon-Anacortes, WA	203.8
312	Lake Havasu City-Kingman, AZ	201.5
313	Danville, VA	198.5
314	Elmira, NY	198.4
315	Bloomington, IN	195.1
316	Idaho Falls, ID	193.3
317	Oshkosh-Neenah, WI	191.4
318	Winchester, VA-WV	189.6
319	Bethesda-Frederick, MD M.D.	187.6
320	Cedar Rapids, IA	184.3
321	Terre Haute, IN	182.9
322	Kingston, NY	182.7
323	Mansfield, OH	182.2
324	Lancaster, PA	181.5
325	Fond du Lac, WI	180.3
326	Lebanon, PA	179.1
327	Williamsport, PA	177.7
328	Lynchburg, VA	172.1
329	Michigan City-La Porte, IN	167.8
330	Charlottesville, VA	165.2
331	Bowling Green, KY	163.2
331	Columbus, IN	163.2
333	Glens Falls, NY	159.8
334	Lake Co.-Kenosha Co., IL-WI M.D.	158.2
335	Wenatchee, WA	157.2
336	Gainesville, GA	156.0
337	Dubuque, IA	155.1
338	Lewiston-Auburn, ME	154.1
339	Nassau-Suffolk, NY M.D.	153.6
340	Holland-Grand Haven, MI	152.1
341	Edison, NJ M.D.	151.4
342	Eau Claire, WI	150.8
343	Rockingham County, NH M.D.	149.7
344	Blacksburg, VA	148.6
345	Wausau, WI	148.5
346	Ogden-Clearfield, UT	148.3
347	Green Bay, WI	145.0
348	Owensboro, KY	141.9
349	Appleton, WI	141.6
350	Sheboygan, WI	136.2
351	Portland, ME	130.7
352	Harrisonburg, VA	118.4
353	Corvallis, OR	112.2
354	State College, PA	110.7
355	Elizabethtown, KY	97.0
356	Bangor, ME	79.9
357	Provo-Orem, UT	74.1
358	Logan, UT-ID	47.7
NA	Chicago (greater), IL-IN-WI**	NA
NA	Chicago-Joilet-Naperville, IL M.D.**	NA
NA	Duluth, MN-WI**	NA
NA	Fargo, ND-MN**	NA
NA	Grand Forks, ND-MN**	NA
NA	La Crosse, WI-MN**	NA
NA	Mankato-North Mankato, MN**	NA
NA	Minneapolis-St. Paul, MN-WI**	NA
NA	Rochester, MN**	NA
NA	St. Cloud, MN**	NA

Source: Reported data from the F.B.I. "Crime in the United States 2011"
*Violent crimes are offenses of murder, forcible rape, robbery, and aggravated assault.
**Not available.

Alpha Order - Metro Area

7. Percent Change in Violent Crime Rate: 2010 to 2011
National Percent Change = 4.5% Decrease*

RANK	METROPOLITAN AREA	% CHANGE	RANK	METROPOLITAN AREA	% CHANGE	RANK	METROPOLITAN AREA	% CHANGE
315	Abilene, TX	(29.7)	NA	Charleston, WV**	NA	78	Fort Lauderdale, FL M.D.	2.2
42	Akron, OH	6.4	NA	Charlotte-Gastonia, NC-SC**	NA	97	Fort Smith, AR-OK	(0.4)
231	Albany-Schenectady-Troy, NY	(9.0)	299	Charlottesville, VA	(18.9)	46	Fort Wayne, IN	5.9
190	Albany, GA	(6.8)	160	Chattanooga, TN-GA	(4.1)	102	Fort Worth-Arlington, TX M.D.	(0.7)
112	Albuquerque, NM	(1.3)	11	Cheyenne, WY	22.7	76	Fresno, CA	2.3
43	Alexandria, LA	6.3	NA	Chicago (greater), IL-IN-WI**	NA	NA	Gadsden, AL**	NA
179	Allentown, PA-NJ	(6.1)	NA	Chicago-Joilet-Naperville, IL M.D.**	NA	158	Gainesville, FL	(4.0)
52	Altoona, PA	5.0	309	Chico, CA	(24.5)	248	Gainesville, GA	(10.6)
90	Amarillo, TX	0.7	180	Cincinnati-Middletown, OH-KY-IN	(6.2)	NA	Gary, IN M.D.**	NA
200	Ames, IA	(7.3)	40	Clarksville, TN-KY	7.0	35	Glens Falls, NY	9.2
133	Anchorage, AK	(2.9)	132	Cleveland-Elyria-Mentor, OH	(2.7)	284	Goldsboro, NC	(14.8)
101	Anderson, SC	(0.6)	26	Cleveland, TN	13.4	NA	Grand Forks, ND-MN**	NA
219	Ann Arbor, MI	(8.6)	94	College Station-Bryan, TX	0.4	26	Grand Junction, CO	13.4
NA	Anniston-Oxford, AL**	NA	300	Colorado Springs, CO	(19.4)	256	Grand Rapids-Wyoming, MI	(11.4)
233	Appleton, WI	(9.1)	70	Columbia, MO	3.0	NA	Great Falls, MT**	NA
167	Asheville, NC	(5.1)	NA	Columbus, GA-AL**	NA	31	Greeley, CO	10.7
94	Athens-Clarke County, GA	0.4	21	Columbus, IN	14.9	209	Green Bay, WI	(7.8)
139	Atlanta, GA	(3.1)	120	Columbus, OH	(1.7)	57	Greenville, SC	4.1
163	Atlantic City, NJ	(4.3)	256	Corpus Christi, TX	(11.4)	83	Gulfport-Biloxi, MS	1.6
NA	Auburn, AL**	NA	154	Corvallis, OR	(3.9)	38	Hagerstown-Martinsburg, MD-WV	7.8
270	Augusta, GA-SC	(12.6)	20	Crestview-Fort Walton Beach, FL	15.3	108	Hanford-Corcoran, CA	(1.0)
266	Austin-Round Rock, TX	(12.4)	NA	Cumberland, MD-WV**	NA	88	Harrisburg-Carlisle, PA	0.9
259	Bakersfield, CA	(11.7)	153	Dallas (greater), TX	(3.8)	81	Harrisonburg, VA	1.7
174	Baltimore-Towson, MD	(5.7)	174	Dallas-Plano-Irving, TX M.D.	(5.7)	112	Hartford, CT	(1.3)
17	Bangor, ME	16.8	250	Dalton, GA	(10.8)	60	Hickory, NC	3.6
56	Barnstable Town, MA	4.3	133	Danville, IL	(2.9)	243	Hinesville, GA	(10.1)
NA	Baton Rouge, LA**	NA	160	Danville, VA	(4.1)	289	Holland-Grand Haven, MI	(15.4)
243	Battle Creek, MI	(10.1)	NA	Davenport, IA-IL**	NA	223	Hot Springs, AR	(8.8)
296	Bay City, MI	(18.3)	209	Dayton, OH	(7.8)	295	Houma, LA	(18.2)
32	Beaumont-Port Arthur, TX	9.6	NA	Decatur, AL**	NA	NA	Houston, TX**	NA
301	Bellingham, WA	(19.5)	108	Decatur, IL	(1.0)	NA	Huntsville, AL**	NA
36	Bend, OR	8.6	212	Deltona-Daytona Beach, FL	(7.9)	278	Idaho Falls, ID	(14.2)
239	Bethesda-Frederick, MD M.D.	(9.7)	49	Denver-Aurora, CO	5.3	NA	Indianapolis, IN**	NA
NA	Billings, MT**	NA	154	Des Moines-West Des Moines, IA	(3.9)	65	Iowa City, IA	3.4
121	Binghamton, NY	(2.1)	NA	Detroit (greater), MI**	NA	178	Jacksonville, FL	(6.0)
NA	Birmingham-Hoover, AL**	NA	171	Detroit-Livonia-Dearborn, MI M.D.	(5.3)	NA	Jacksonville, NC**	NA
139	Bismarck, ND	(3.1)	NA	Dothan, AL**	NA	154	Jackson, MS	(3.9)
276	Blacksburg, VA	(14.0)	30	Dover, DE	11.4	25	Jackson, TN	13.5
273	Bloomington-Normal, IL	(13.5)	319	Dubuque, IA	(63.3)	112	Janesville, WI	(1.3)
307	Bloomington, IN	(23.6)	NA	Duluth, MN-WI**	NA	39	Jefferson City, MO	7.4
146	Boise City-Nampa, ID	(3.4)	68	Durham-Chapel Hill, NC	3.3	192	Johnson City, TN	(6.9)
208	Boston (greater), MA-NH	(7.7)	102	Eau Claire, WI	(0.7)	8	Johnstown, PA	25.7
201	Boston-Quincy, MA M.D.	(7.4)	133	Edison, NJ M.D.	(2.9)	129	Jonesboro, AR	(2.6)
16	Boulder, CO	17.6	312	El Centro, CA	(25.8)	291	Joplin, MO	(16.7)
41	Bowling Green, KY	6.7	242	El Paso, TX	(10.0)	NA	Kankakee-Bradley, IL**	NA
310	Bremerton-Silverdale, WA	(24.9)	318	Elizabethtown, KY	(51.3)	NA	Kansas City, MO-KS**	NA
58	Bridgeport-Stamford, CT	3.9	286	Elmira, NY	(14.9)	37	Kennewick-Pasco-Richland, WA	8.0
264	Brownsville-Harlingen, TX	(12.3)	233	Erie, PA	(9.1)	303	Killeen-Temple-Fort Hood, TX	(19.8)
254	Brunswick, GA	(11.1)	NA	Eugene-Springfield, OR**	NA	76	Kingsport, TN-VA	2.3
235	Buffalo-Niagara Falls, NY	(9.2)	NA	Evansville, IN-KY**	NA	301	Kingston, NY	(19.5)
63	Burlington, NC	3.5	313	Fairbanks, AK	(28.4)	112	Knoxville, TN	(1.3)
286	Cambridge-Newton, MA M.D.	(14.9)	NA	Fargo, ND-MN**	NA	7	Kokomo, IN	28.4
47	Camden, NJ M.D.	5.7	141	Farmington, NM	(3.2)	NA	La Crosse, WI-MN**	NA
14	Canton, OH	21.2	87	Fayetteville, NC	1.0	4	Lafayette, IN	38.7
219	Cape Coral-Fort Myers, FL	(8.6)	71	Flagstaff, AZ	2.9	227	Lafayette, LA	(8.9)
279	Cape Girardeau, MO-IL	(14.4)	81	Flint, MI	1.7	NA	Lake Co.-Kenosha Co., IL-WI M.D.**	NA
239	Carson City, NV	(9.7)	NA	Florence-Muscle Shoals, AL**	NA	NA	Lake Havasu City-Kingman, AZ**	NA
6	Casper, WY	31.7	164	Florence, SC	(4.5)	72	Lakeland, FL	2.7
164	Cedar Rapids, IA	(4.5)	65	Fond du Lac, WI	3.4	127	Lancaster, PA	(2.4)
NA	Champaign-Urbana, IL**	NA	245	Fort Collins-Loveland, CO	(10.2)	253	Lansing-East Lansing, MI	(11.0)

Note: All listings are for Metropolitan Statistical Areas (M.S.A.s) except for those ending with "M.D." Listings with "M.D." are Metropolitan Divisions which are smaller parts of eleven large M.S.A.s. See explanatory note at beginning of metropolitan area section.

Alpha Order - Metro Area (continued)

RANK	METROPOLITAN AREA	% CHANGE	RANK	METROPOLITAN AREA	% CHANGE	RANK	METROPOLITAN AREA	% CHANGE
188	Laredo, TX	(6.6)	NA	Oklahoma City, OK**	NA	97	Savannah, GA	(0.4)
52	Las Cruces, NM	5.0	201	Olympia, WA	(7.4)	28	Scranton--Wilkes-Barre, PA	12.8
288	Las Vegas-Paradise, NV	(15.2)	102	Omaha-Council Bluffs, NE-IA	(0.7)	185	Seattle (greater), WA	(6.5)
237	Lawrence, KS	(9.6)	133	Orlando, FL	(2.9)	160	Seattle-Bellevue-Everett, WA M.D.	(4.1)
237	Lawton, OK	(9.6)	NA	Oshkosh-Neenah, WI**	NA	112	Sebastian-Vero Beach, FL	(1.3)
171	Lebanon, PA	(5.3)	12	Owensboro, KY	22.4	NA	Sheboygan, WI**	NA
145	Lewiston-Auburn, ME	(3.3)	173	Oxnard-Thousand Oaks, CA	(5.5)	133	Sherman-Denison, TX	(2.9)
NA	Lexington-Fayette, KY**	NA	92	Palm Bay-Melbourne, FL	0.5	13	Sioux City, IA-NE-SD	21.4
19	Lima, OH	15.8	5	Palm Coast, FL	36.1	199	Sioux Falls, SD	(7.2)
308	Lincoln, NE	(24.0)	72	Panama City-Lynn Haven, FL	2.7	92	South Bend-Mishawaka, IN-MI	0.5
112	Little Rock, AR	(1.3)	10	Pascagoula, MS	24.0	111	Spartanburg, SC	(1.2)
311	Logan, UT-ID	(25.1)	83	Peabody, MA M.D.	1.6	102	Spokane, WA	(0.7)
298	Longview, TX	(18.6)	206	Pensacola, FL	(7.6)	292	Springfield, IL	(16.8)
141	Longview, WA	(3.2)	167	Peoria, IL	(5.1)	275	Springfield, MA	(13.9)
223	Los Angeles County, CA M.D.	(8.8)	149	Philadelphia (greater) PA-NJ-MD-DE	(3.5)	167	Springfield, MO	(5.1)
215	Los Angeles (greater), CA	(8.4)	141	Philadelphia, PA M.D.	(3.2)	293	Springfield, OH	(17.6)
45	Louisville, KY-IN	6.0	75	Phoenix-Mesa-Scottsdale, AZ	2.4	59	State College, PA	3.7
290	Lubbock, TX	(16.4)	138	Pine Bluff, AR	(3.0)	79	Stockton, CA	2.0
317	Lynchburg, VA	(40.1)	180	Pittsburgh, PA	(6.2)	NA	St. Cloud, MN**	NA
304	Macon, GA	(20.0)	236	Pittsfield, MA	(9.5)	206	St. Joseph, MO-KS	(7.6)
15	Madera, CA	21.1	150	Pocatello, ID	(3.6)	97	St. Louis, MO-IL	(0.4)
219	Madison, WI	(8.6)	195	Port St. Lucie, FL	(7.1)	314	Sumter, SC	(28.6)
18	Manchester-Nashua, NH	16.5	NA	Portland-Vancouver, OR-WA**	NA	121	Syracuse, NY	(2.1)
264	Manhattan, KS	(12.3)	121	Portland, ME	(2.1)	258	Tacoma, WA M.D.	(11.5)
NA	Mankato-North Mankato, MN**	NA	222	Poughkeepsie, NY	(8.7)	283	Tallahassee, FL	(14.7)
74	Mansfield, OH	2.5	34	Prescott, AZ	9.4	272	Tampa-St Petersburg, FL	(13.0)
214	McAllen-Edinburg-Mission, TX	(8.0)	231	Provo-Orem, UT	(9.0)	NA	Terre Haute, IN**	NA
32	Medford, OR	9.6	NA	Pueblo, CO**	NA	249	Texarkana, TX-Texarkana, AR	(10.7)
129	Memphis, TN-MS-AR	(2.6)	85	Punta Gorda, FL	1.5	54	Toledo, OH	4.4
185	Merced, CA	(6.5)	215	Racine, WI	(8.4)	158	Topeka, KS	(4.0)
121	Miami (greater), FL	(2.1)	96	Raleigh-Cary, NC	0.3	128	Trenton-Ewing, NJ	(2.5)
112	Miami-Dade County, FL M.D.	(1.3)	119	Rapid City, SD	(1.5)	80	Tucson, AZ	1.8
305	Michigan City-La Porte, IN	(21.0)	185	Reading, PA	(6.5)	201	Tulsa, OK	(7.4)
284	Midland, TX	(14.8)	227	Redding, CA	(8.9)	NA	Tuscaloosa, AL**	NA
146	Milwaukee, WI	(3.4)	205	Reno-Sparks, NV	(7.5)	255	Tyler, TX	(11.3)
NA	Minneapolis-St. Paul, MN-WI**	NA	271	Richmond, VA	(12.8)	250	Utica-Rome, NY	(10.8)
NA	Missoula, MT**	NA	151	Riverside-San Bernardino, CA	(3.7)	166	Valdosta, GA	(4.6)
24	Mobile, AL	13.9	245	Roanoke, VA	(10.2)	227	Vallejo-Fairfield, CA	(8.9)
209	Modesto, CA	(7.8)	NA	Rochester, MN**	NA	269	Victoria, TX	(12.5)
2	Monroe, LA	49.0	223	Rochester, NY	(8.8)	151	Virginia Beach-Norfolk, VA-NC	(3.7)
250	Monroe, MI	(10.8)	195	Rockford, IL	(7.1)	223	Visalia-Porterville, CA	(8.8)
NA	Montgomery, AL**	NA	63	Rockingham County, NH M.D.	3.5	273	Waco, TX	(13.5)
247	Morristown, TN	(10.5)	297	Rocky Mount, NC	(18.5)	183	Warner Robins, GA	(6.3)
125	Mount Vernon-Anacortes, WA	(2.3)	65	Rome, GA	3.4	NA	Warren-Farmington Hills, MI M.D.**	NA
1	Muncie, IN	102.3	262	Sacramento, CA	(12.1)	261	Washington (greater) DC-VA-MD-WV	(11.9)
212	Muskegon-Norton Shores, MI	(7.9)	239	Saginaw, MI	(9.7)	266	Washington, DC-VA-MD-WV M.D.	(12.4)
60	Myrtle Beach, SC	3.6	192	Salem, OR	(6.9)	263	Waterloo-Cedar Falls, IA	(12.2)
316	Napa, CA	(31.8)	183	Salinas, CA	(6.3)	22	Wausau, WI	14.8
91	Naples-Marco Island, FL	0.6	306	Salisbury, MD	(21.5)	176	Wenatchee, WA	(5.9)
86	Nashville-Davidson, TN	1.2	281	Salt Lake City, UT	(14.5)	227	West Palm Beach, FL M.D.	(8.9)
180	Nassau-Suffolk, NY M.D.	(6.2)	218	San Angelo, TX	(8.5)	108	Wichita Falls, TX	(1.0)
260	New Haven-Milford, CT	(11.8)	294	San Antonio, TX	(17.7)	102	Wichita, KS	(0.7)
51	New Orleans, LA	5.2	195	San Diego, CA	(7.1)	48	Williamsport, PA	5.6
60	New York (greater), NY-NJ-PA	3.6	154	San Francisco (greater), CA	(3.9)	279	Wilmington, DE-MD-NJ M.D.	(14.4)
49	New York-W. Plains NY-NJ M.D.	5.3	195	San Francisco-S. Mateo, CA M.D.	(7.1)	201	Wilmington, NC	(7.4)
97	Newark-Union, NJ-PA M.D.	(0.4)	141	San Jose, CA	(3.2)	23	Winchester, VA-WV	14.1
146	North Port-Bradenton-Sarasota, FL	(3.4)	188	San Luis Obispo, CA	(6.6)	54	Winston-Salem, NC	4.4
89	Norwich-New London, CT	0.8	129	Sandusky, OH	(2.6)	190	Worcester, MA	(6.8)
125	Oakland-Fremont, CA M.D.	(2.3)	176	Santa Ana-Anaheim, CA M.D.	(5.9)	167	Yakima, WA	(5.1)
194	Ocala, FL	(7.0)	281	Santa Barbara-Santa Maria, CA	(14.5)	3	York-Hanover, PA	45.5
9	Ocean City, NJ	24.7	277	Santa Cruz-Watsonville, CA	(14.1)	29	Yuba City, CA	11.9
69	Odessa, TX	3.2	44	Santa Fe, NM	6.1	215	Yuma, AZ	(8.4)
107	Ogden-Clearfield, UT	(0.9)	266	Santa Rosa-Petaluma, CA	(12.4)			

Source: CQ Press using reported data from the F.B.I. "Crime in the United States 2011"
*Violent crimes are offenses of murder, forcible rape, robbery, and aggravated assault.
**Not available.

Rank Order - Metro Area

7. Percent Change in Violent Crime Rate: 2010 to 2011 (continued)
National Percent Change = 4.5% Decrease*

RANK	METROPOLITAN AREA	% CHANGE	RANK	METROPOLITAN AREA	% CHANGE	RANK	METROPOLITAN AREA	% CHANGE
1	Muncie, IN	102.3	60	Myrtle Beach, SC	3.6	121	Binghamton, NY	(2.1)
2	Monroe, LA	49.0	60	New York (greater), NY-NJ-PA	3.6	121	Miami (greater), FL	(2.1)
3	York-Hanover, PA	45.5	63	Burlington, NC	3.5	121	Portland, ME	(2.1)
4	Lafayette, IN	38.7	63	Rockingham County, NH M.D.	3.5	121	Syracuse, NY	(2.1)
5	Palm Coast, FL	36.1	65	Fond du Lac, WI	3.4	125	Mount Vernon-Anacortes, WA	(2.3)
6	Casper, WY	31.7	65	Iowa City, IA	3.4	125	Oakland-Fremont, CA M.D.	(2.3)
7	Kokomo, IN	28.4	65	Rome, GA	3.4	127	Lancaster, PA	(2.4)
8	Johnstown, PA	25.7	68	Durham-Chapel Hill, NC	3.3	128	Trenton-Ewing, NJ	(2.5)
9	Ocean City, NJ	24.7	69	Odessa, TX	3.2	129	Jonesboro, AR	(2.6)
10	Pascagoula, MS	24.0	70	Columbia, MO	3.0	129	Memphis, TN-MS-AR	(2.6)
11	Cheyenne, WY	22.7	71	Flagstaff, AZ	2.9	129	Sandusky, OH	(2.6)
12	Owensboro, KY	22.4	72	Lakeland, FL	2.7	132	Cleveland-Elyria-Mentor, OH	(2.7)
13	Sioux City, IA-NE-SD	21.4	72	Panama City-Lynn Haven, FL	2.7	133	Anchorage, AK	(2.9)
14	Canton, OH	21.2	74	Mansfield, OH	2.5	133	Danville, IL	(2.9)
15	Madera, CA	21.1	75	Phoenix-Mesa-Scottsdale, AZ	2.4	133	Edison, NJ M.D.	(2.9)
16	Boulder, CO	17.6	76	Fresno, CA	2.3	133	Orlando, FL	(2.9)
17	Bangor, ME	16.8	76	Kingsport, TN-VA	2.3	133	Sherman-Denison, TX	(2.9)
18	Manchester-Nashua, NH	16.5	78	Fort Lauderdale, FL M.D.	2.2	138	Pine Bluff, AR	(3.0)
19	Lima, OH	15.8	79	Stockton, CA	2.0	139	Atlanta, GA	(3.1)
20	Crestview-Fort Walton Beach, FL	15.3	80	Tucson, AZ	1.8	139	Bismarck, ND	(3.1)
21	Columbus, IN	14.9	81	Flint, MI	1.7	141	Farmington, NM	(3.2)
22	Wausau, WI	14.8	81	Harrisonburg, VA	1.7	141	Longview, WA	(3.2)
23	Winchester, VA-WV	14.1	83	Gulfport-Biloxi, MS	1.6	141	Philadelphia, PA M.D.	(3.2)
24	Mobile, AL	13.9	83	Peabody, MA M.D.	1.6	141	San Jose, CA	(3.2)
25	Jackson, TN	13.5	85	Punta Gorda, FL	1.5	145	Lewiston-Auburn, ME	(3.3)
26	Cleveland, TN	13.4	86	Nashville-Davidson, TN	1.2	146	Boise City-Nampa, ID	(3.4)
26	Grand Junction, CO	13.4	87	Fayetteville, NC	1.0	146	Milwaukee, WI	(3.4)
28	Scranton--Wilkes-Barre, PA	12.8	88	Harrisburg-Carlisle, PA	0.9	146	North Port-Bradenton-Sarasota, FL	(3.4)
29	Yuba City, CA	11.9	89	Norwich-New London, CT	0.8	149	Philadelphia (greater) PA-NJ-MD-DE	(3.5)
30	Dover, DE	11.4	90	Amarillo, TX	0.7	150	Pocatello, ID	(3.6)
31	Greeley, CO	10.7	91	Naples-Marco Island, FL	0.6	151	Riverside-San Bernardino, CA	(3.7)
32	Beaumont-Port Arthur, TX	9.6	92	Palm Bay-Melbourne, FL	0.5	151	Virginia Beach-Norfolk, VA-NC	(3.7)
32	Medford, OR	9.6	92	South Bend-Mishawaka, IN-MI	0.5	153	Dallas (greater), TX	(3.8)
34	Prescott, AZ	9.4	94	Athens-Clarke County, GA	0.4	154	Corvallis, OR	(3.9)
35	Glens Falls, NY	9.2	94	College Station-Bryan, TX	0.4	154	Des Moines-West Des Moines, IA	(3.9)
36	Bend, OR	8.6	96	Raleigh-Cary, NC	0.3	154	Jackson, MS	(3.9)
37	Kennewick-Pasco-Richland, WA	8.0	97	Fort Smith, AR-OK	(0.4)	154	San Francisco (greater), CA	(3.9)
38	Hagerstown-Martinsburg, MD-WV	7.8	97	Newark-Union, NJ-PA M.D.	(0.4)	158	Gainesville, FL	(4.0)
39	Jefferson City, MO	7.4	97	Savannah, GA	(0.4)	158	Topeka, KS	(4.0)
40	Clarksville, TN-KY	7.0	97	St. Louis, MO-IL	(0.4)	160	Chattanooga, TN-GA	(4.1)
41	Bowling Green, KY	6.7	101	Anderson, SC	(0.6)	160	Danville, VA	(4.1)
42	Akron, OH	6.4	102	Eau Claire, WI	(0.7)	160	Seattle-Bellevue-Everett, WA M.D.	(4.1)
43	Alexandria, LA	6.3	102	Fort Worth-Arlington, TX M.D.	(0.7)	163	Atlantic City, NJ	(4.3)
44	Santa Fe, NM	6.1	102	Omaha-Council Bluffs, NE-IA	(0.7)	164	Cedar Rapids, IA	(4.5)
45	Louisville, KY-IN	6.0	102	Spokane, WA	(0.7)	164	Florence, SC	(4.5)
46	Fort Wayne, IN	5.9	102	Wichita, KS	(0.7)	166	Valdosta, GA	(4.6)
47	Camden, NJ M.D.	5.7	107	Ogden-Clearfield, UT	(0.9)	167	Asheville, NC	(5.1)
48	Williamsport, PA	5.6	108	Decatur, IL	(1.0)	167	Peoria, IL	(5.1)
49	Denver-Aurora, CO	5.3	108	Hanford-Corcoran, CA	(1.0)	167	Springfield, MO	(5.1)
49	New York-W. Plains NY-NJ M.D.	5.3	108	Wichita Falls, TX	(1.0)	167	Yakima, WA	(5.1)
51	New Orleans, LA	5.2	111	Spartanburg, SC	(1.2)	171	Detroit-Livonia-Dearborn, MI M.D.	(5.3)
52	Altoona, PA	5.0	112	Albuquerque, NM	(1.3)	171	Lebanon, PA	(5.3)
52	Las Cruces, NM	5.0	112	Hartford, CT	(1.3)	173	Oxnard-Thousand Oaks, CA	(5.5)
54	Toledo, OH	4.4	112	Janesville, WI	(1.3)	174	Baltimore-Towson, MD	(5.7)
54	Winston-Salem, NC	4.4	112	Knoxville, TN	(1.3)	174	Dallas-Plano-Irving, TX M.D.	(5.7)
56	Barnstable Town, MA	4.3	112	Little Rock, AR	(1.3)	176	Santa Ana-Anaheim, CA M.D.	(5.9)
57	Greenville, SC	4.1	112	Miami-Dade County, FL M.D.	(1.3)	176	Wenatchee, WA	(5.9)
58	Bridgeport-Stamford, CT	3.9	112	Sebastian-Vero Beach, FL	(1.3)	178	Jacksonville, FL	(6.0)
59	State College, PA	3.7	119	Rapid City, SD	(1.5)	179	Allentown, PA-NJ	(6.1)
60	Hickory, NC	3.6	120	Columbus, OH	(1.7)	180	Cincinnati-Middletown, OH-KY-IN	(6.2)

Note: All listings are for Metropolitan Statistical Areas (M.S.A.s) except for those ending with "M.D." Listings with "M.D." are Metropolitan Divisions which are smaller parts of eleven large M.S.A.s. See explanatory note at beginning of metropolitan area section.

Rank Order - Metro Area (continued)

RANK	METROPOLITAN AREA	% CHANGE
180	Nassau-Suffolk, NY M.D.	(6.2)
180	Pittsburgh, PA	(6.2)
183	Salinas, CA	(6.3)
183	Warner Robins, GA	(6.3)
185	Merced, CA	(6.5)
185	Reading, PA	(6.5)
185	Seattle (greater), WA	(6.5)
188	Laredo, TX	(6.6)
188	San Luis Obispo, CA	(6.6)
190	Albany, GA	(6.8)
190	Worcester, MA	(6.8)
192	Johnson City, TN	(6.9)
192	Salem, OR	(6.9)
194	Ocala, FL	(7.0)
195	Port St. Lucie, FL	(7.1)
195	Rockford, IL	(7.1)
195	San Diego, CA	(7.1)
195	San Francisco-S. Mateo, CA M.D.	(7.1)
199	Sioux Falls, SD	(7.2)
200	Ames, IA	(7.3)
201	Boston-Quincy, MA M.D.	(7.4)
201	Olympia, WA	(7.4)
201	Tulsa, OK	(7.4)
201	Wilmington, NC	(7.4)
205	Reno-Sparks, NV	(7.5)
206	Pensacola, FL	(7.6)
206	St. Joseph, MO-KS	(7.6)
208	Boston (greater), MA-NH	(7.7)
209	Dayton, OH	(7.8)
209	Green Bay, WI	(7.8)
209	Modesto, CA	(7.8)
212	Deltona-Daytona Beach, FL	(7.9)
212	Muskegon-Norton Shores, MI	(7.9)
214	McAllen-Edinburg-Mission, TX	(8.0)
215	Los Angeles (greater), CA	(8.4)
215	Racine, WI	(8.4)
215	Yuma, AZ	(8.4)
218	San Angelo, TX	(8.5)
219	Ann Arbor, MI	(8.6)
219	Cape Coral-Fort Myers, FL	(8.6)
219	Madison, WI	(8.6)
222	Poughkeepsie, NY	(8.7)
223	Hot Springs, AR	(8.8)
223	Los Angeles County, CA M.D.	(8.8)
223	Rochester, NY	(8.8)
223	Visalia-Porterville, CA	(8.8)
227	Lafayette, LA	(8.9)
227	Redding, CA	(8.9)
227	Vallejo-Fairfield, CA	(8.9)
227	West Palm Beach, FL M.D.	(8.9)
231	Albany-Schenectady-Troy, NY	(9.0)
231	Provo-Orem, UT	(9.0)
233	Appleton, WI	(9.1)
233	Erie, PA	(9.1)
235	Buffalo-Niagara Falls, NY	(9.2)
236	Pittsfield, MA	(9.5)
237	Lawrence, KS	(9.6)
237	Lawton, OK	(9.6)
239	Bethesda-Frederick, MD M.D.	(9.7)
239	Carson City, NV	(9.7)
239	Saginaw, MI	(9.7)
242	El Paso, TX	(10.0)
243	Battle Creek, MI	(10.1)
243	Hinesville, GA	(10.1)
245	Fort Collins-Loveland, CO	(10.2)
245	Roanoke, VA	(10.2)
247	Morristown, TN	(10.5)
248	Gainesville, GA	(10.6)
249	Texarkana, TX-Texarkana, AR	(10.7)
250	Dalton, GA	(10.8)
250	Monroe, MI	(10.8)
250	Utica-Rome, NY	(10.8)
253	Lansing-East Lansing, MI	(11.0)
254	Brunswick, GA	(11.1)
255	Tyler, TX	(11.3)
256	Corpus Christi, TX	(11.4)
256	Grand Rapids-Wyoming, MI	(11.4)
258	Tacoma, WA M.D.	(11.5)
259	Bakersfield, CA	(11.7)
260	New Haven-Milford, CT	(11.8)
261	Washington (greater) DC-VA-MD-WV	(11.9)
262	Sacramento, CA	(12.1)
263	Waterloo-Cedar Falls, IA	(12.2)
264	Brownsville-Harlingen, TX	(12.3)
264	Manhattan, KS	(12.3)
266	Austin-Round Rock, TX	(12.4)
266	Santa Rosa-Petaluma, CA	(12.4)
266	Washington, DC-VA-MD-WV M.D.	(12.4)
269	Victoria, TX	(12.5)
270	Augusta, GA-SC	(12.6)
271	Richmond, VA	(12.8)
272	Tampa-St Petersburg, FL	(13.0)
273	Bloomington-Normal, IL	(13.5)
273	Waco, TX	(13.5)
275	Springfield, MA	(13.9)
276	Blacksburg, VA	(14.0)
277	Santa Cruz-Watsonville, CA	(14.1)
278	Idaho Falls, ID	(14.2)
279	Cape Girardeau, MO-IL	(14.4)
279	Wilmington, DE-MD-NJ M.D.	(14.4)
281	Salt Lake City, UT	(14.5)
281	Santa Barbara-Santa Maria, CA	(14.5)
283	Tallahassee, FL	(14.7)
284	Goldsboro, NC	(14.8)
284	Midland, TX	(14.8)
286	Cambridge-Newton, MA M.D.	(14.9)
286	Elmira, NY	(14.9)
288	Las Vegas-Paradise, NV	(15.2)
289	Holland-Grand Haven, MI	(15.4)
290	Lubbock, TX	(16.4)
291	Joplin, MO	(16.7)
292	Springfield, IL	(16.8)
293	Springfield, OH	(17.6)
294	San Antonio, TX	(17.7)
295	Houma, LA	(18.2)
296	Bay City, MI	(18.3)
297	Rocky Mount, NC	(18.5)
298	Longview, TX	(18.6)
299	Charlottesville, VA	(18.9)
300	Colorado Springs, CO	(19.4)
301	Bellingham, WA	(19.5)
301	Kingston, NY	(19.5)
303	Killeen-Temple-Fort Hood, TX	(19.8)
304	Macon, GA	(20.0)
305	Michigan City-La Porte, IN	(21.0)
306	Salisbury, MD	(21.5)
307	Bloomington, IN	(23.6)
308	Lincoln, NE	(24.0)
309	Chico, CA	(24.5)
310	Bremerton-Silverdale, WA	(24.9)
311	Logan, UT-ID	(25.1)
312	El Centro, CA	(25.8)
313	Fairbanks, AK	(28.4)
314	Sumter, SC	(28.6)
315	Abilene, TX	(29.7)
316	Napa, CA	(31.8)
317	Lynchburg, VA	(40.1)
318	Elizabethtown, KY	(51.3)
319	Dubuque, IA	(63.3)
NA	Anniston-Oxford, AL**	NA
NA	Auburn, AL**	NA
NA	Baton Rouge, LA**	NA
NA	Billings, MT**	NA
NA	Birmingham-Hoover, AL**	NA
NA	Champaign-Urbana, IL**	NA
NA	Charleston, WV**	NA
NA	Charlotte-Gastonia, NC-SC**	NA
NA	Chicago (greater), IL-IN-WI**	NA
NA	Chicago-Joilet-Naperville, IL M.D.**	NA
NA	Columbus, GA-AL**	NA
NA	Cumberland, MD-WV**	NA
NA	Davenport, IA-IL**	NA
NA	Decatur, AL**	NA
NA	Detroit (greater), MI**	NA
NA	Dothan, AL**	NA
NA	Duluth, MN-WI**	NA
NA	Eugene-Springfield, OR**	NA
NA	Evansville, IN-KY**	NA
NA	Fargo, ND-MN**	NA
NA	Florence-Muscle Shoals, AL**	NA
NA	Gadsden, AL**	NA
NA	Gary, IN M.D.**	NA
NA	Grand Forks, ND-MN**	NA
NA	Great Falls, MT**	NA
NA	Houston, TX**	NA
NA	Huntsville, AL**	NA
NA	Indianapolis, IN**	NA
NA	Jacksonville, NC**	NA
NA	Kankakee-Bradley, IL**	NA
NA	Kansas City, MO-KS**	NA
NA	La Crosse, WI-MN**	NA
NA	Lake Co.-Kenosha Co., IL-WI M.D.**	NA
NA	Lake Havasu City-Kingman, AZ**	NA
NA	Lexington-Fayette, KY**	NA
NA	Mankato-North Mankato, MN**	NA
NA	Minneapolis-St. Paul, MN-WI**	NA
NA	Missoula, MT**	NA
NA	Montgomery, AL**	NA
NA	Oklahoma City, OK**	NA
NA	Oshkosh-Neenah, WI**	NA
NA	Portland-Vancouver, OR-WA**	NA
NA	Pueblo, CO**	NA
NA	Rochester, MN**	NA
NA	Sheboygan, WI**	NA
NA	St. Cloud, MN**	NA
NA	Terre Haute, IN**	NA
NA	Tuscaloosa, AL**	NA
NA	Warren-Farmington Hills, MI M.D.**	NA

Source: CQ Press using reported data from the F.B.I. "Crime in the United States 2011"
*Violent crimes are offenses of murder, forcible rape, robbery, and aggravated assault.
**Not available.

Alpha Order - Metro Area

8. Percent Change in Violent Crime Rate: 2007 to 2011
National Percent Change = 18.1% Decrease*

RANK	METROPOLITAN AREA	% CHANGE
290	Abilene, TX	(37.3)
44	Akron, OH	3.5
162	Albany-Schenectady-Troy, NY	(16.6)
26	Albany, GA	11.8
NA	Albuquerque, NM**	NA
251	Alexandria, LA	(27.4)
170	Allentown, PA-NJ	(17.3)
132	Altoona, PA	(13.5)
280	Amarillo, TX	(34.6)
137	Ames, IA	(13.8)
83	Anchorage, AK	(5.0)
118	Anderson, SC	(10.7)
97	Ann Arbor, MI	(7.8)
NA	Anniston-Oxford, AL**	NA
9	Appleton, WI	34.3
221	Asheville, NC	(22.8)
45	Athens-Clarke County, GA	3.4
NA	Atlanta, GA**	NA
141	Atlantic City, NJ	(14.0)
NA	Auburn, AL**	NA
142	Augusta, GA-SC	(14.1)
162	Austin-Round Rock, TX	(16.6)
110	Bakersfield, CA	(9.6)
176	Baltimore-Towson, MD	(18.3)
14	Bangor, ME	29.9
20	Barnstable Town, MA	19.0
187	Baton Rouge, LA	(19.4)
251	Battle Creek, MI	(27.4)
48	Bay City, MI	2.4
88	Beaumont-Port Arthur, TX	(6.4)
98	Bellingham, WA	(8.0)
4	Bend, OR	49.9
254	Bethesda-Frederick, MD M.D.	(27.9)
NA	Billings, MT**	NA
28	Binghamton, NY	11.0
NA	Birmingham-Hoover, AL**	NA
12	Bismarck, ND	32.2
263	Blacksburg, VA	(28.9)
NA	Bloomington-Normal, IL**	NA
182	Bloomington, IN	(18.9)
209	Boise City-Nampa, ID	(22.0)
70	Boston (greater), MA-NH	(3.2)
106	Boston-Quincy, MA M.D.	(8.9)
NA	Boulder, CO**	NA
302	Bowling Green, KY	(50.8)
246	Bremerton-Silverdale, WA	(26.8)
78	Bridgeport-Stamford, CT	(4.3)
255	Brownsville-Harlingen, TX	(28.2)
297	Brunswick, GA	(38.6)
85	Buffalo-Niagara Falls, NY	(5.9)
91	Burlington, NC	(7.0)
36	Cambridge-Newton, MA M.D.	6.5
55	Camden, NJ M.D.	0.6
NA	Canton, OH**	NA
291	Cape Coral-Fort Myers, FL	(37.8)
NA	Cape Girardeau, MO-IL**	NA
255	Carson City, NV	(28.2)
52	Casper, WY	1.7
236	Cedar Rapids, IA	(25.6)
NA	Champaign-Urbana, IL**	NA

RANK	METROPOLITAN AREA	% CHANGE
54	Charleston, WV	0.7
300	Charlotte-Gastonia, NC-SC	(40.6)
291	Charlottesville, VA	(37.8)
230	Chattanooga, TN-GA	(24.5)
10	Cheyenne, WY	33.3
NA	Chicago (greater), IL-IN-WI**	NA
NA	Chicago-Joilet-Naperville, IL M.D.**	NA
301	Chico, CA	(42.8)
184	Cincinnati-Middletown, OH-KY-IN	(19.1)
227	Clarksville, TN-KY	(23.6)
94	Cleveland-Elyria-Mentor, OH	(7.3)
157	Cleveland, TN	(16.1)
273	College Station-Bryan, TX	(31.8)
219	Colorado Springs, CO	(22.7)
184	Columbia, MO	(19.1)
NA	Columbus, GA-AL**	NA
1	Columbus, IN	60.6
178	Columbus, OH	(18.6)
197	Corpus Christi, TX	(21.0)
184	Corvallis, OR	(19.1)
40	Crestview-Fort Walton Beach, FL	5.7
NA	Cumberland, MD-WV**	NA
263	Dallas (greater), TX	(28.9)
281	Dallas-Plano-Irving, TX M.D.	(34.7)
283	Dalton, GA	(35.7)
NA	Danville, IL**	NA
202	Danville, VA	(21.4)
NA	Davenport, IA-IL**	NA
67	Dayton, OH	(2.8)
NA	Decatur, AL**	NA
NA	Decatur, IL**	NA
146	Deltona-Daytona Beach, FL	(14.6)
69	Denver-Aurora, CO	(3.0)
253	Des Moines-West Des Moines, IA	(27.6)
NA	Detroit (greater), MI**	NA
137	Detroit-Livonia-Dearborn, MI M.D.	(13.8)
NA	Dothan, AL**	NA
59	Dover, DE	(0.3)
304	Dubuque, IA	(69.3)
NA	Duluth, MN-WI**	NA
NA	Durham-Chapel Hill, NC**	NA
3	Eau Claire, WI	50.3
107	Edison, NJ M.D.	(9.1)
190	El Centro, CA	(19.6)
53	El Paso, TX	1.6
NA	Elizabethtown, KY**	NA
258	Elmira, NY	(28.4)
144	Erie, PA	(14.4)
103	Eugene-Springfield, OR	(8.5)
74	Evansville, IN-KY	(3.7)
NA	Fairbanks, AK**	NA
NA	Fargo, ND-MN**	NA
33	Farmington, NM	7.8
205	Fayetteville, NC	(21.7)
99	Flagstaff, AZ	(8.2)
58	Flint, MI	(0.1)
NA	Florence-Muscle Shoals, AL**	NA
294	Florence, SC	(38.2)
148	Fond du Lac, WI	(14.7)
86	Fort Collins-Loveland, CO	(6.0)

RANK	METROPOLITAN AREA	% CHANGE
178	Fort Lauderdale, FL M.D.	(18.6)
NA	Fort Smith, AR-OK**	NA
43	Fort Wayne, IN	4.0
161	Fort Worth-Arlington, TX M.D.	(16.5)
29	Fresno, CA	10.9
NA	Gadsden, AL**	NA
288	Gainesville, FL	(36.5)
277	Gainesville, GA	(33.1)
NA	Gary, IN M.D.**	NA
123	Glens Falls, NY	(11.7)
80	Goldsboro, NC	(4.7)
NA	Grand Forks, ND-MN**	NA
125	Grand Junction, CO	(12.3)
180	Grand Rapids-Wyoming, MI	(18.8)
NA	Great Falls, MT**	NA
84	Greeley, CO	(5.1)
296	Green Bay, WI	(38.4)
213	Greenville, SC	(22.1)
NA	Gulfport-Biloxi, MS**	NA
NA	Hagerstown-Martinsburg, MD-WV**	NA
21	Hanford-Corcoran, CA	17.1
77	Harrisburg-Carlisle, PA	(4.1)
255	Harrisonburg, VA	(28.2)
55	Hartford, CT	0.6
203	Hickory, NC	(21.5)
193	Hinesville, GA	(20.1)
NA	Holland-Grand Haven, MI**	NA
99	Hot Springs, AR	(8.2)
284	Houma, LA	(35.8)
NA	Houston, TX**	NA
NA	Huntsville, AL**	NA
275	Idaho Falls, ID	(32.3)
114	Indianapolis, IN	(10.1)
112	Iowa City, IA	(10.0)
NA	Jacksonville, FL**	NA
298	Jacksonville, NC	(38.7)
64	Jackson, MS	(1.9)
120	Jackson, TN	(11.2)
39	Janesville, WI	6.0
67	Jefferson City, MO	(2.8)
217	Johnson City, TN	(22.5)
18	Johnstown, PA	21.3
102	Jonesboro, AR	(8.3)
215	Joplin, MO	(22.4)
NA	Kankakee-Bradley, IL**	NA
NA	Kansas City, MO-KS**	NA
47	Kennewick-Pasco-Richland, WA	2.7
154	Killeen-Temple-Fort Hood, TX	(15.6)
70	Kingsport, TN-VA	(3.2)
245	Kingston, NY	(26.7)
128	Knoxville, TN	(12.9)
70	Kokomo, IN	(3.2)
NA	La Crosse, WI-MN**	NA
27	Lafayette, IN	11.5
263	Lafayette, LA	(28.9)
NA	Lake Co.-Kenosha Co., IL-WI M.D.**	NA
261	Lake Havasu City-Kingman, AZ	(28.6)
209	Lakeland, FL	(22.0)
117	Lancaster, PA	(10.5)
170	Lansing-East Lansing, MI	(17.3)

Note: All listings are for Metropolitan Statistical Areas (M.S.A.s) except for those ending with "M.D." Listings with "M.D." are Metropolitan Divisions which are smaller parts of eleven large M.S.A.s. See explanatory note at beginning of metropolitan area section.

Alpha Order - Metro Area (continued)

RANK	METROPOLITAN AREA	% CHANGE	RANK	METROPOLITAN AREA	% CHANGE	RANK	METROPOLITAN AREA	% CHANGE
145	Laredo, TX	(14.5)	51	Oklahoma City, OK	2.2	295	Savannah, GA	(38.3)
173	Las Cruces, NM	(17.4)	32	Olympia, WA	8.9	87	Scranton--Wilkes-Barre, PA	(6.2)
249	Las Vegas-Paradise, NV	(27.1)	90	Omaha-Council Bluffs, NE-IA	(6.7)	143	Seattle (greater), WA	(14.3)
152	Lawrence, KS	(15.2)	266	Orlando, FL	(29.5)	119	Seattle-Bellevue-Everett, WA M.D.	(10.8)
270	Lawton, OK	(30.4)	166	Oshkosh-Neenah, WI	(17.1)	105	Sebastian-Vero Beach, FL	(8.8)
258	Lebanon, PA	(28.4)	NA	Owensboro, KY**	NA	31	Sheboygan, WI	9.1
35	Lewiston-Auburn, ME	6.6	221	Oxnard-Thousand Oaks, CA	(22.8)	34	Sherman-Denison, TX	7.0
NA	Lexington-Fayette, KY**	NA	154	Palm Bay-Melbourne, FL	(15.6)	79	Sioux City, IA-NE-SD	(4.4)
22	Lima, OH	16.9	63	Palm Coast, FL	(1.5)	38	Sioux Falls, SD	6.2
272	Lincoln, NE	(31.7)	120	Panama City-Lynn Haven, FL	(11.2)	116	South Bend-Mishawaka, IN-MI	(10.4)
115	Little Rock, AR	(10.3)	11	Pascagoula, MS	33.2	276	Spartanburg, SC	(33.0)
285	Logan, UT-ID	(35.9)	57	Peabody, MA M.D.	0.1	207	Spokane, WA	(21.8)
286	Longview, TX	(36.4)	192	Pensacola, FL	(20.0)	NA	Springfield, IL**	NA
46	Longview, WA	3.2	NA	Peoria, IL**	NA	134	Springfield, MA	(13.6)
250	Los Angeles County, CA M.D.	(27.3)	152	Philadelphia (greater) PA-NJ-MD-DE	(15.2)	92	Springfield, MO	(7.2)
246	Los Angeles (greater), CA	(26.8)	170	Philadelphia, PA M.D.	(17.3)	165	Springfield, OH	(17.0)
70	Louisville, KY-IN	(3.2)	218	Phoenix-Mesa-Scottsdale, AZ	(22.6)	30	State College, PA	10.1
151	Lubbock, TX	(15.1)	200	Pine Bluff, AR	(21.2)	92	Stockton, CA	(7.2)
242	Lynchburg, VA	(26.4)	169	Pittsburgh, PA	(17.2)	NA	St. Cloud, MN**	NA
140	Macon, GA	(13.9)	49	Pittsfield, MA	2.3	76	St. Joseph, MO-KS	(4.0)
42	Madera, CA	4.4	66	Pocatello, ID	(2.3)	96	St. Louis, MO-IL	(7.7)
99	Madison, WI	(8.2)	286	Port St. Lucie, FL	(36.4)	303	Sumter, SC	(65.3)
NA	Manchester-Nashua, NH**	NA	166	Portland-Vancouver, OR-WA	(17.1)	107	Syracuse, NY	(9.1)
NA	Manhattan, KS**	NA	75	Portland, ME	(3.9)	197	Tacoma, WA M.D.	(21.0)
NA	Mankato-North Mankato, MN**	NA	157	Poughkeepsie, NY	(16.1)	224	Tallahassee, FL	(23.0)
112	Mansfield, OH	(10.0)	81	Prescott, AZ	(4.8)	293	Tampa-St Petersburg, FL	(38.1)
131	McAllen-Edinburg-Mission, TX	(13.4)	126	Provo-Orem, UT	(12.7)	NA	Terre Haute, IN**	NA
23	Medford, OR	15.8	NA	Pueblo, CO**	NA	219	Texarkana, TX-Texarkana, AR	(22.7)
189	Memphis, TN-MS-AR	(19.5)	299	Punta Gorda, FL	(40.2)	160	Toledo, OH	(16.4)
94	Merced, CA	(7.3)	221	Racine, WI	(22.8)	111	Topeka, KS	(9.8)
236	Miami (greater), FL	(25.6)	235	Raleigh-Cary, NC	(25.3)	60	Trenton-Ewing, NJ	(0.5)
246	Miami-Dade County, FL M.D.	(26.8)	19	Rapid City, SD	20.5	166	Tucson, AZ	(17.1)
137	Michigan City-La Porte, IN	(13.8)	61	Reading, PA	(0.9)	146	Tulsa, OK	(14.6)
174	Midland, TX	(18.1)	2	Redding, CA	54.4	NA	Tuscaloosa, AL**	NA
242	Milwaukee, WI	(26.4)	229	Reno-Sparks, NV	(24.3)	268	Tyler, TX	(29.6)
NA	Minneapolis-St. Paul, MN-WI**	NA	282	Richmond, VA	(35.6)	205	Utica-Rome, NY	(21.7)
NA	Missoula, MT**	NA	234	Riverside-San Bernardino, CA	(25.1)	236	Valdosta, GA	(25.6)
8	Mobile, AL	35.6	278	Roanoke, VA	(33.3)	262	Vallejo-Fairfield, CA	(28.7)
224	Modesto, CA	(23.0)	NA	Rochester, MN**	NA	16	Victoria, TX	26.6
6	Monroe, LA	44.7	122	Rochester, NY	(11.3)	241	Virginia Beach-Norfolk, VA-NC	(26.3)
13	Monroe, MI	31.7	NA	Rockford, IL**	NA	157	Visalia-Porterville, CA	(16.1)
NA	Montgomery, AL**	NA	15	Rockingham County, NH M.D.	27.3	271	Waco, TX	(30.8)
215	Morristown, TN	(22.4)	164	Rocky Mount, NC	(16.7)	156	Warner Robins, GA	(16.0)
41	Mount Vernon-Anacortes, WA	5.1	25	Rome, GA	13.5	NA	Warren-Farmington Hills, MI M.D.**	NA
7	Muncie, IN	39.5	204	Sacramento, CA	(21.6)	232	Washington (greater) DC-VA-MD-WV	(24.6)
136	Muskegon-Norton Shores, MI	(13.7)	244	Saginaw, MI	(26.6)	228	Washington, DC-VA-MD-WV M.D.	(24.2)
266	Myrtle Beach, SC	(29.5)	232	Salem, OR	(24.6)	209	Waterloo-Cedar Falls, IA	(22.0)
81	Napa, CA	(4.8)	132	Salinas, CA	(13.5)	214	Wausau, WI	(22.3)
236	Naples-Marco Island, FL	(25.6)	279	Salisbury, MD	(33.5)	180	Wenatchee, WA	(18.8)
195	Nashville-Davidson, TN	(20.3)	176	Salt Lake City, UT	(18.3)	274	West Palm Beach, FL M.D.	(32.2)
134	Nassau-Suffolk, NY M.D.	(13.6)	269	San Angelo, TX	(29.7)	187	Wichita Falls, TX	(19.4)
NA	New Haven-Milford, CT**	NA	129	San Antonio, TX	(13.1)	150	Wichita, KS	(14.9)
288	New Orleans, LA	(36.5)	230	San Diego, CA	(24.5)	17	Williamsport, PA	25.3
65	New York (greater), NY-NJ-PA	(2.0)	197	San Francisco (greater), CA	(21.0)	182	Wilmington, DE-MD-NJ M.D.	(18.9)
61	New York-W. Plains NY-NJ M.D.	(0.9)	226	San Francisco-S. Mateo, CA M.D.	(23.4)	196	Wilmington, NC	(20.5)
49	Newark-Union, NJ-PA M.D.	2.3	207	San Jose, CA	(21.8)	104	Winchester, VA-WV	(8.6)
NA	North Port-Bradenton-Sarasota, FL**	NA	260	San Luis Obispo, CA	(28.5)	NA	Winston-Salem, NC**	NA
NA	Norwich-New London, CT**	NA	109	Sandusky, OH	(9.4)	23	Worcester, MA	15.8
190	Oakland-Fremont, CA M.D.	(19.6)	209	Santa Ana-Anaheim, CA M.D.	(22.0)	148	Yakima, WA	(14.7)
240	Ocala, FL	(26.0)	89	Santa Barbara-Santa Maria, CA	(6.6)	36	York-Hanover, PA	6.5
126	Ocean City, NJ	(12.7)	124	Santa Cruz-Watsonville, CA	(12.2)	129	Yuba City, CA	(13.1)
5	Odessa, TX	45.1	NA	Santa Fe, NM**	NA	200	Yuma, AZ	(21.2)
193	Ogden-Clearfield, UT	(20.1)	175	Santa Rosa-Petaluma, CA	(18.2)			

Source: CQ Press using reported data from the F.B.I. "Crime in the United States 2011"
*Violent crimes are offenses of murder, forcible rape, robbery, and aggravated assault.
**Not available.

Rank Order - Metro Area

8. Percent Change in Violent Crime Rate: 2007 to 2011 (continued)
National Percent Change = 18.1% Decrease*

RANK	METROPOLITAN AREA	% CHANGE	RANK	METROPOLITAN AREA	% CHANGE	RANK	METROPOLITAN AREA	% CHANGE
1	Columbus, IN	60.6	61	New York-W. Plains NY-NJ M.D.	(0.9)	120	Panama City-Lynn Haven, FL	(11.2)
2	Redding, CA	54.4	61	Reading, PA	(0.9)	122	Rochester, NY	(11.3)
3	Eau Claire, WI	50.3	63	Palm Coast, FL	(1.5)	123	Glens Falls, NY	(11.7)
4	Bend, OR	49.9	64	Jackson, MS	(1.9)	124	Santa Cruz-Watsonville, CA	(12.2)
5	Odessa, TX	45.1	65	New York (greater), NY-NJ-PA	(2.0)	125	Grand Junction, CO	(12.3)
6	Monroe, LA	44.7	66	Pocatello, ID	(2.3)	126	Ocean City, NJ	(12.7)
7	Muncie, IN	39.5	67	Dayton, OH	(2.8)	126	Provo-Orem, UT	(12.7)
8	Mobile, AL	35.6	67	Jefferson City, MO	(2.8)	128	Knoxville, TN	(12.9)
9	Appleton, WI	34.3	69	Denver-Aurora, CO	(3.0)	129	San Antonio, TX	(13.1)
10	Cheyenne, WY	33.3	70	Boston (greater), MA-NH	(3.2)	129	Yuba City, CA	(13.1)
11	Pascagoula, MS	33.2	70	Kingsport, TN-VA	(3.2)	131	McAllen-Edinburg-Mission, TX	(13.4)
12	Bismarck, ND	32.2	70	Kokomo, IN	(3.2)	132	Altoona, PA	(13.5)
13	Monroe, MI	31.7	70	Louisville, KY-IN	(3.2)	132	Salinas, CA	(13.5)
14	Bangor, ME	29.9	74	Evansville, IN-KY	(3.7)	134	Nassau-Suffolk, NY M.D.	(13.6)
15	Rockingham County, NH M.D.	27.3	75	Portland, ME	(3.9)	134	Springfield, MA	(13.6)
16	Victoria, TX	26.6	76	St. Joseph, MO-KS	(4.0)	136	Muskegon-Norton Shores, MI	(13.7)
17	Williamsport, PA	25.3	77	Harrisburg-Carlisle, PA	(4.1)	137	Ames, IA	(13.8)
18	Johnstown, PA	21.3	78	Bridgeport-Stamford, CT	(4.3)	137	Detroit-Livonia-Dearborn, MI M.D.	(13.8)
19	Rapid City, SD	20.5	79	Sioux City, IA-NE-SD	(4.4)	137	Michigan City-La Porte, IN	(13.8)
20	Barnstable Town, MA	19.0	80	Goldsboro, NC	(4.7)	140	Macon, GA	(13.9)
21	Hanford-Corcoran, CA	17.1	81	Napa, CA	(4.8)	141	Atlantic City, NJ	(14.0)
22	Lima, OH	16.9	81	Prescott, AZ	(4.8)	142	Augusta, GA-SC	(14.1)
23	Medford, OR	15.8	83	Anchorage, AK	(5.0)	143	Seattle (greater), WA	(14.3)
23	Worcester, MA	15.8	84	Greeley, CO	(5.1)	144	Erie, PA	(14.4)
25	Rome, GA	13.5	85	Buffalo-Niagara Falls, NY	(5.9)	145	Laredo, TX	(14.5)
26	Albany, GA	11.8	86	Fort Collins-Loveland, CO	(6.0)	146	Deltona-Daytona Beach, FL	(14.6)
27	Lafayette, IN	11.5	87	Scranton--Wilkes-Barre, PA	(6.2)	146	Tulsa, OK	(14.6)
28	Binghamton, NY	11.0	88	Beaumont-Port Arthur, TX	(6.4)	148	Fond du Lac, WI	(14.7)
29	Fresno, CA	10.9	89	Santa Barbara-Santa Maria, CA	(6.6)	148	Yakima, WA	(14.7)
30	State College, PA	10.1	90	Omaha-Council Bluffs, NE-IA	(6.7)	150	Wichita, KS	(14.9)
31	Sheboygan, WI	9.1	91	Burlington, NC	(7.0)	151	Lubbock, TX	(15.1)
32	Olympia, WA	8.9	92	Springfield, MO	(7.2)	152	Lawrence, KS	(15.2)
33	Farmington, NM	7.8	92	Stockton, CA	(7.2)	152	Philadelphia (greater) PA-NJ-MD-DE	(15.2)
34	Sherman-Denison, TX	7.0	94	Cleveland-Elyria-Mentor, OH	(7.3)	154	Killeen-Temple-Fort Hood, TX	(15.6)
35	Lewiston-Auburn, ME	6.6	94	Merced, CA	(7.3)	154	Palm Bay-Melbourne, FL	(15.6)
36	Cambridge-Newton, MA M.D.	6.5	96	St. Louis, MO-IL	(7.7)	156	Warner Robins, GA	(16.0)
36	York-Hanover, PA	6.5	97	Ann Arbor, MI	(7.8)	157	Cleveland, TN	(16.1)
38	Sioux Falls, SD	6.2	98	Bellingham, WA	(8.0)	157	Poughkeepsie, NY	(16.1)
39	Janesville, WI	6.0	99	Flagstaff, AZ	(8.2)	157	Visalia-Porterville, CA	(16.1)
40	Crestview-Fort Walton Beach, FL	5.7	99	Hot Springs, AR	(8.2)	160	Toledo, OH	(16.4)
41	Mount Vernon-Anacortes, WA	5.1	99	Madison, WI	(8.2)	161	Fort Worth-Arlington, TX M.D.	(16.5)
42	Madera, CA	4.4	102	Jonesboro, AR	(8.3)	162	Albany-Schenectady-Troy, NY	(16.6)
43	Fort Wayne, IN	4.0	103	Eugene-Springfield, OR	(8.5)	162	Austin-Round Rock, TX	(16.6)
44	Akron, OH	3.5	104	Winchester, VA-WV	(8.6)	164	Rocky Mount, NC	(16.7)
45	Athens-Clarke County, GA	3.4	105	Sebastian-Vero Beach, FL	(8.8)	165	Springfield, OH	(17.0)
46	Longview, WA	3.2	106	Boston-Quincy, MA M.D.	(8.9)	166	Oshkosh-Neenah, WI	(17.1)
47	Kennewick-Pasco-Richland, WA	2.7	107	Edison, NJ M.D.	(9.1)	166	Portland-Vancouver, OR-WA	(17.1)
48	Bay City, MI	2.4	107	Syracuse, NY	(9.1)	166	Tucson, AZ	(17.1)
49	Newark-Union, NJ-PA M.D.	2.3	109	Sandusky, OH	(9.4)	169	Pittsburgh, PA	(17.2)
49	Pittsfield, MA	2.3	110	Bakersfield, CA	(9.6)	170	Allentown, PA-NJ	(17.3)
51	Oklahoma City, OK	2.2	111	Topeka, KS	(9.8)	170	Lansing-East Lansing, MI	(17.3)
52	Casper, WY	1.7	112	Iowa City, IA	(10.0)	170	Philadelphia, PA M.D.	(17.3)
53	El Paso, TX	1.6	112	Mansfield, OH	(10.0)	173	Las Cruces, NM	(17.4)
54	Charleston, WV	0.7	114	Indianapolis, IN	(10.1)	174	Midland, TX	(18.1)
55	Camden, NJ M.D.	0.6	115	Little Rock, AR	(10.3)	175	Santa Rosa-Petaluma, CA	(18.2)
55	Hartford, CT	0.6	116	South Bend-Mishawaka, IN-MI	(10.4)	176	Baltimore-Towson, MD	(18.3)
57	Peabody, MA M.D.	0.1	117	Lancaster, PA	(10.5)	176	Salt Lake City, UT	(18.3)
58	Flint, MI	(0.1)	118	Anderson, SC	(10.7)	178	Columbus, OH	(18.6)
59	Dover, DE	(0.3)	119	Seattle-Bellevue-Everett, WA M.D.	(10.8)	178	Fort Lauderdale, FL M.D.	(18.6)
60	Trenton-Ewing, NJ	(0.5)	120	Jackson, TN	(11.2)	180	Grand Rapids-Wyoming, MI	(18.8)

Note: All listings are for Metropolitan Statistical Areas (M.S.A.s) except for those ending with "M.D." Listings with "M.D." are Metropolitan Divisions which are smaller parts of eleven large M.S.A.s. See explanatory note at beginning of metropolitan area section.

Rank Order - Metro Area (continued)

RANK	METROPOLITAN AREA	% CHANGE	RANK	METROPOLITAN AREA	% CHANGE	RANK	METROPOLITAN AREA	% CHANGE
180	Wenatchee, WA	(18.8)	244	Saginaw, MI	(26.6)	NA	Atlanta, GA**	NA
182	Bloomington, IN	(18.9)	245	Kingston, NY	(26.7)	NA	Auburn, AL**	NA
182	Wilmington, DE-MD-NJ M.D.	(18.9)	246	Bremerton-Silverdale, WA	(26.8)	NA	Billings, MT**	NA
184	Cincinnati-Middletown, OH-KY-IN	(19.1)	246	Los Angeles (greater), CA	(26.8)	NA	Birmingham-Hoover, AL**	NA
184	Columbia, MO	(19.1)	246	Miami-Dade County, FL M.D.	(26.8)	NA	Bloomington-Normal, IL**	NA
184	Corvallis, OR	(19.1)	249	Las Vegas-Paradise, NV	(27.1)	NA	Boulder, CO**	NA
187	Baton Rouge, LA	(19.4)	250	Los Angeles County, CA M.D.	(27.3)	NA	Canton, OH**	NA
187	Wichita Falls, TX	(19.4)	251	Alexandria, LA	(27.4)	NA	Cape Girardeau, MO-IL**	NA
189	Memphis, TN-MS-AR	(19.5)	251	Battle Creek, MI	(27.4)	NA	Champaign-Urbana, IL**	NA
190	El Centro, CA	(19.6)	253	Des Moines-West Des Moines, IA	(27.6)	NA	Chicago (greater), IL-IN-WI**	NA
190	Oakland-Fremont, CA M.D.	(19.6)	254	Bethesda-Frederick, MD M.D.	(27.9)	NA	Chicago-Joilet-Naperville, IL M.D.**	NA
192	Pensacola, FL	(20.0)	255	Brownsville-Harlingen, TX	(28.2)	NA	Columbus, GA-AL**	NA
193	Hinesville, GA	(20.1)	255	Carson City, NV	(28.2)	NA	Cumberland, MD-WV**	NA
193	Ogden-Clearfield, UT	(20.1)	255	Harrisonburg, VA	(28.2)	NA	Danville, IL**	NA
195	Nashville-Davidson, TN	(20.3)	258	Elmira, NY	(28.4)	NA	Davenport, IA-IL**	NA
196	Wilmington, NC	(20.5)	258	Lebanon, PA	(28.4)	NA	Decatur, AL**	NA
197	Corpus Christi, TX	(21.0)	260	San Luis Obispo, CA	(28.5)	NA	Decatur, IL**	NA
197	San Francisco (greater), CA	(21.0)	261	Lake Havasu City-Kingman, AZ	(28.6)	NA	Detroit (greater), MI**	NA
197	Tacoma, WA M.D.	(21.0)	262	Vallejo-Fairfield, CA	(28.7)	NA	Dothan, AL**	NA
200	Pine Bluff, AR	(21.2)	263	Blacksburg, VA	(28.9)	NA	Duluth, MN-WI**	NA
200	Yuma, AZ	(21.2)	263	Dallas (greater), TX	(28.9)	NA	Durham-Chapel Hill, NC**	NA
202	Danville, VA	(21.4)	263	Lafayette, LA	(28.9)	NA	Elizabethtown, KY**	NA
203	Hickory, NC	(21.5)	266	Myrtle Beach, SC	(29.5)	NA	Fairbanks, AK**	NA
204	Sacramento, CA	(21.6)	266	Orlando, FL	(29.5)	NA	Fargo, ND-MN**	NA
205	Fayetteville, NC	(21.7)	268	Tyler, TX	(29.6)	NA	Florence-Muscle Shoals, AL**	NA
205	Utica-Rome, NY	(21.7)	269	San Angelo, TX	(29.7)	NA	Fort Smith, AR-OK**	NA
207	San Jose, CA	(21.8)	270	Lawton, OK	(30.4)	NA	Gadsden, AL**	NA
207	Spokane, WA	(21.8)	271	Waco, TX	(30.8)	NA	Gary, IN M.D.**	NA
209	Boise City-Nampa, ID	(22.0)	272	Lincoln, NE	(31.7)	NA	Grand Forks, ND-MN**	NA
209	Lakeland, FL	(22.0)	273	College Station-Bryan, TX	(31.8)	NA	Great Falls, MT**	NA
209	Santa Ana-Anaheim, CA M.D.	(22.0)	274	West Palm Beach, FL M.D.	(32.2)	NA	Gulfport-Biloxi, MS**	NA
209	Waterloo-Cedar Falls, IA	(22.0)	275	Idaho Falls, ID	(32.3)	NA	Hagerstown-Martinsburg, MD-WV**	NA
213	Greenville, SC	(22.1)	276	Spartanburg, SC	(33.0)	NA	Holland-Grand Haven, MI**	NA
214	Wausau, WI	(22.3)	277	Gainesville, GA	(33.1)	NA	Houston, TX**	NA
215	Joplin, MO	(22.4)	278	Roanoke, VA	(33.3)	NA	Huntsville, AL**	NA
215	Morristown, TN	(22.4)	279	Salisbury, MD	(33.5)	NA	Jacksonville, FL**	NA
217	Johnson City, TN	(22.5)	280	Amarillo, TX	(34.6)	NA	Kankakee-Bradley, IL**	NA
218	Phoenix-Mesa-Scottsdale, AZ	(22.6)	281	Dallas-Plano-Irving, TX M.D.	(34.7)	NA	Kansas City, MO-KS**	NA
219	Colorado Springs, CO	(22.7)	282	Richmond, VA	(35.6)	NA	La Crosse, WI-MN**	NA
219	Texarkana, TX-Texarkana, AR	(22.7)	283	Dalton, GA	(35.7)	NA	Lake Co.-Kenosha Co., IL-WI M.D.**	NA
221	Asheville, NC	(22.8)	284	Houma, LA	(35.8)	NA	Lexington-Fayette, KY**	NA
221	Oxnard-Thousand Oaks, CA	(22.8)	285	Logan, UT-ID	(35.9)	NA	Manchester-Nashua, NH**	NA
221	Racine, WI	(22.8)	286	Longview, TX	(36.4)	NA	Manhattan, KS**	NA
224	Modesto, CA	(23.0)	286	Port St. Lucie, FL	(36.4)	NA	Mankato-North Mankato, MN**	NA
224	Tallahassee, FL	(23.0)	288	Gainesville, FL	(36.5)	NA	Minneapolis-St. Paul, MN-WI**	NA
226	San Francisco-S. Mateo, CA M.D.	(23.4)	288	New Orleans, LA	(36.5)	NA	Missoula, MT**	NA
227	Clarksville, TN-KY	(23.6)	290	Abilene, TX	(37.3)	NA	Montgomery, AL**	NA
228	Washington, DC-VA-MD-WV M.D.	(24.2)	291	Cape Coral-Fort Myers, FL	(37.8)	NA	New Haven-Milford, CT**	NA
229	Reno-Sparks, NV	(24.3)	291	Charlottesville, VA	(37.8)	NA	North Port-Bradenton-Sarasota, FL**	NA
230	Chattanooga, TN-GA	(24.5)	293	Tampa-St Petersburg, FL	(38.1)	NA	Norwich-New London, CT**	NA
230	San Diego, CA	(24.5)	294	Florence, SC	(38.2)	NA	Owensboro, KY**	NA
232	Salem, OR	(24.6)	295	Savannah, GA	(38.3)	NA	Peoria, IL**	NA
232	Washington (greater) DC-VA-MD-WV	(24.6)	296	Green Bay, WI	(38.4)	NA	Pueblo, CO**	NA
234	Riverside-San Bernardino, CA	(25.1)	297	Brunswick, GA	(38.6)	NA	Rochester, MN**	NA
235	Raleigh-Cary, NC	(25.3)	298	Jacksonville, NC	(38.7)	NA	Rockford, IL**	NA
236	Cedar Rapids, IA	(25.6)	299	Punta Gorda, FL	(40.2)	NA	Santa Fe, NM**	NA
236	Miami (greater), FL	(25.6)	300	Charlotte-Gastonia, NC-SC	(40.6)	NA	Springfield, IL**	NA
236	Naples-Marco Island, FL	(25.6)	301	Chico, CA	(42.8)	NA	St. Cloud, MN**	NA
236	Valdosta, GA	(25.6)	302	Bowling Green, KY	(50.8)	NA	Terre Haute, IN**	NA
240	Ocala, FL	(26.0)	303	Sumter, SC	(65.3)	NA	Tuscaloosa, AL**	NA
241	Virginia Beach-Norfolk, VA-NC	(26.3)	304	Dubuque, IA	(69.3)	NA	Warren-Farmington Hills, MI M.D.**	NA
242	Lynchburg, VA	(26.4)	NA	Albuquerque, NM**	NA	NA	Winston-Salem, NC**	NA
242	Milwaukee, WI	(26.4)	NA	Anniston-Oxford, AL**	NA			

Source: CQ Press using reported data from the F.B.I. "Crime in the United States 2011"
*Violent crimes are offenses of murder, forcible rape, robbery, and aggravated assault.
**Not available.

Alpha Order - Metro Area

9. Murders in 2011
National Total = 14,612 Murders*

RANK	METROPOLITAN AREA	MURDERS
246	Abilene, TX	5
97	Akron, OH	33
166	Albany-Schenectady-Troy, NY	13
145	Albany, GA	16
81	Albuquerque, NM	45
246	Alexandria, LA	5
118	Allentown, PA-NJ	23
321	Altoona, PA	2
170	Amarillo, TX	12
359	Ames, IA	0
166	Anchorage, AK	13
151	Anderson, SC	15
204	Ann Arbor, MI	8
159	Anniston-Oxford, AL	14
321	Appleton, WI	2
170	Asheville, NC	12
230	Athens-Clarke County, GA	6
13	Atlanta, GA	319
119	Atlantic City, NJ	22
290	Auburn, AL	3
73	Augusta, GA-SC	50
73	Austin-Round Rock, TX	50
79	Bakersfield, CA	46
17	Baltimore-Towson, MD	256
219	Bangor, ME	7
290	Barnstable Town, MA	3
39	Baton Rouge, LA	96
204	Battle Creek, MI	8
290	Bay City, MI	3
108	Beaumont-Port Arthur, TX	26
290	Bellingham, WA	3
321	Bend, OR	2
133	Bethesda-Frederick, MD M.D.	18
290	Billings, MT	3
290	Binghamton, NY	3
36	Birmingham-Hoover, AL	101
290	Bismarck, ND	3
290	Blacksburg, VA	3
321	Bloomington-Normal, IL	2
230	Bloomington, IN	6
204	Boise City-Nampa, ID	8
30	Boston (greater), MA-NH	129
41	Boston-Quincy, MA M.D.	94
268	Boulder, CO	4
290	Bowling Green, KY	3
290	Bremerton-Silverdale, WA	3
99	Bridgeport-Stamford, CT	32
204	Brownsville-Harlingen, TX	8
219	Brunswick, GA	7
81	Buffalo-Niagara Falls, NY	45
290	Burlington, NC	3
159	Cambridge-Newton, MA M.D.	14
61	Camden, NJ M.D.	65
151	Canton, OH	15
88	Cape Coral-Fort Myers, FL	38
341	Cape Girardeau, MO-IL	1
268	Carson City, NV	4
321	Casper, WY	2
321	Cedar Rapids, IA	2
230	Champaign-Urbana, IL	6

RANK	METROPOLITAN AREA	MURDERS
130	Charleston, WV	19
48	Charlotte-Gastonia, NC-SC	86
230	Charlottesville, VA	6
93	Chattanooga, TN-GA	34
321	Cheyenne, WY	2
3	Chicago (greater), IL-IN-WI	609
6	Chicago-Joilet-Naperville, IL M.D.	540
204	Chico, CA	8
37	Cincinnati-Middletown, OH-KY-IN	99
179	Clarksville, TN-KY	11
37	Cleveland-Elyria-Mentor, OH	99
219	Cleveland, TN	7
246	College Station-Bryan, TX	5
101	Colorado Springs, CO	31
268	Columbia, MO	4
114	Columbus, GA-AL	24
341	Columbus, IN	1
35	Columbus, OH	104
133	Corpus Christi, TX	18
290	Corvallis, OR	3
268	Crestview-Fort Walton Beach, FL	4
230	Cumberland, MD-WV	6
14	Dallas (greater), TX	294
23	Dallas-Plano-Irving, TX M.D.	200
321	Dalton, GA	2
290	Danville, IL	3
179	Danville, VA	11
204	Davenport, IA-IL	8
71	Dayton, OH	51
290	Decatur, AL	3
186	Decatur, IL	10
119	Deltona-Daytona Beach, FL	22
55	Denver-Aurora, CO	71
195	Des Moines-West Des Moines, IA	9
8	Detroit (greater), MI	416
10	Detroit-Livonia-Dearborn, MI M.D.	370
246	Dothan, AL	5
219	Dover, DE	7
341	Dubuque, IA	1
290	Duluth, MN-WI	3
89	Durham-Chapel Hill, NC	37
359	Eau Claire, WI	0
106	Edison, NJ M.D.	29
290	El Centro, CA	3
133	El Paso, TX	18
321	Elizabethtown, KY	2
341	Elmira, NY	1
204	Erie, PA	8
290	Eugene-Springfield, OR	3
219	Evansville, IN-KY	7
321	Fairbanks, AK	2
341	Fargo, ND-MN	1
246	Farmington, NM	5
97	Fayetteville, NC	33
246	Flagstaff, AZ	5
62	Flint, MI	64
290	Florence-Muscle Shoals, AL	3
159	Florence, SC	14
321	Fond du Lac, WI	2
268	Fort Collins-Loveland, CO	4

RANK	METROPOLITAN AREA	MURDERS
66	Fort Lauderdale, FL M.D.	59
195	Fort Smith, AR-OK	9
108	Fort Wayne, IN	26
41	Fort Worth-Arlington, TX M.D.	94
70	Fresno, CA	52
246	Gadsden, AL	5
166	Gainesville, FL	13
246	Gainesville, GA	5
64	Gary, IN M.D.	63
170	Glens Falls, NY	12
186	Goldsboro, NC	10
359	Grand Forks, ND-MN	0
290	Grand Junction, CO	3
125	Grand Rapids-Wyoming, MI	20
321	Great Falls, MT	2
230	Greeley, CO	6
321	Green Bay, WI	2
84	Greenville, SC	42
124	Gulfport-Biloxi, MS	21
195	Hagerstown-Martinsburg, MD-WV	9
204	Hanford-Corcoran, CA	8
125	Harrisburg-Carlisle, PA	20
321	Harrisonburg, VA	2
90	Hartford, CT	36
119	Hickory, NC	22
268	Hinesville, GA	4
321	Holland-Grand Haven, MI	2
268	Hot Springs, AR	4
230	Houma, LA	6
12	Houston, TX	330
130	Huntsville, AL	19
230	Idaho Falls, ID	6
34	Indianapolis, IN	107
290	Iowa City, IA	3
46	Jacksonville, FL	87
268	Jacksonville, NC	4
60	Jackson, MS	66
195	Jackson, TN	9
268	Janesville, WI	4
219	Jefferson City, MO	7
230	Johnson City, TN	6
268	Johnstown, PA	4
268	Jonesboro, AR	4
290	Joplin, MO	3
268	Kankakee-Bradley, IL	4
27	Kansas City, MO-KS	161
246	Kennewick-Pasco-Richland, WA	5
133	Killeen-Temple-Fort Hood, TX	18
195	Kingsport, TN-VA	9
321	Kingston, NY	2
93	Knoxville, TN	34
246	Kokomo, IN	5
359	La Crosse, WI-MN	0
290	Lafayette, IN	3
170	Lafayette, LA	12
230	Lake Co.-Kenosha Co., IL-WI M.D.	6
170	Lake Havasu City-Kingman, AZ	12
111	Lakeland, FL	25
219	Lancaster, PA	7
133	Lansing-East Lansing, MI	18

Note: All listings are for Metropolitan Statistical Areas (M.S.A.s) except for those ending with "M.D." Listings with "M.D." are Metropolitan Divisions which are smaller parts of eleven large M.S.A.s. See explanatory note at beginning of metropolitan area section.

Alpha Order - Metro Area (continued)

RANK	METROPOLITAN AREA	MURDERS
179	Laredo, TX	11
219	Las Cruces, NM	7
43	Las Vegas-Paradise, NV	93
359	Lawrence, KS	0
204	Lawton, OK	8
341	Lebanon, PA	1
268	Lewiston-Auburn, ME	4
142	Lexington-Fayette, KY	17
321	Lima, OH	2
268	Lincoln, NE	4
57	Little Rock, AR	69
359	Logan, UT-ID	0
179	Longview, TX	11
268	Longview, WA	4
5	Los Angeles County, CA M.D.	568
2	Los Angeles (greater), CA	641
68	Louisville, KY-IN	57
179	Lubbock, TX	11
230	Lynchburg, VA	6
133	Macon, GA	18
246	Madera, CA	5
186	Madison, WI	10
204	Manchester-Nashua, NH	8
246	Manhattan, KS	5
341	Mankato-North Mankato, MN	1
290	Mansfield, OH	3
91	McAllen-Edinburg-Mission, TX	35
186	Medford, OR	10
28	Memphis, TN-MS-AR	141
159	Merced, CA	14
11	Miami (greater), FL	344
20	Miami-Dade County, FL M.D.	218
268	Michigan City-La Porte, IN	4
230	Midland, TX	6
44	Milwaukee, WI	92
66	Minneapolis-St. Paul, MN-WI	59
341	Missoula, MT	1
76	Mobile, AL	47
93	Modesto, CA	34
195	Monroe, LA	9
290	Monroe, MI	3
87	Montgomery, AL	39
290	Morristown, TN	3
290	Mount Vernon-Anacortes, WA	3
321	Muncie, IN	2
219	Muskegon-Norton Shores, MI	7
114	Myrtle Beach, SC	24
290	Napa, CA	3
186	Naples-Marco Island, FL	10
50	Nashville-Davidson, TN	78
69	Nassau-Suffolk, NY M.D.	55
73	New Haven-Milford, CT	50
15	New Orleans, LA	279
1	New York (greater), NY-NJ-PA	852
4	New York-W. Plains NY-NJ M.D.	596
26	Newark-Union, NJ-PA M.D.	172
99	North Port-Bradenton-Sarasota, FL	32
246	Norwich-New London, CT	5
24	Oakland-Fremont, CA M.D.	196
159	Ocala, FL	14
341	Ocean City, NJ	1
179	Odessa, TX	11
204	Ogden-Clearfield, UT	8

RANK	METROPOLITAN AREA	MURDERS
50	Oklahoma City, OK	78
268	Olympia, WA	4
71	Omaha-Council Bluffs, NE-IA	51
31	Orlando, FL	122
341	Oshkosh-Neenah, WI	1
341	Owensboro, KY	1
151	Oxnard-Thousand Oaks, CA	15
151	Palm Bay-Melbourne, FL	15
341	Palm Coast, FL	1
170	Panama City-Lynn Haven, FL	12
246	Pascagoula, MS	5
125	Peabody, MA M.D.	20
133	Pensacola, FL	18
119	Peoria, IL	22
7	Philadelphia (greater) PA-NJ-MD-DE	486
9	Philadelphia, PA M.D.	386
22	Phoenix-Mesa-Scottsdale, AZ	209
151	Pine Bluff, AR	15
45	Pittsburgh, PA	90
268	Pittsfield, MA	4
290	Pocatello, ID	3
119	Port St. Lucie, FL	22
76	Portland-Vancouver, OR-WA	47
246	Portland, ME	5
145	Poughkeepsie, NY	16
142	Prescott, AZ	17
246	Provo-Orem, UT	5
166	Pueblo, CO	13
321	Punta Gorda, FL	2
219	Racine, WI	7
103	Raleigh-Cary, NC	30
268	Rapid City, SD	4
130	Reading, PA	19
230	Redding, CA	6
114	Reno-Sparks, NV	24
55	Richmond, VA	71
25	Riverside-San Bernardino, CA	185
186	Roanoke, VA	10
341	Rochester, MN	1
83	Rochester, NY	43
107	Rockford, IL	27
341	Rockingham County, NH M.D.	1
133	Rocky Mount, NC	18
246	Rome, GA	5
40	Sacramento, CA	95
159	Saginaw, MI	14
170	Salem, OR	12
93	Salinas, CA	34
230	Salisbury, MD	6
114	Salt Lake City, UT	24
359	San Angelo, TX	0
32	San Antonio, TX	111
49	San Diego, CA	82
16	San Francisco (greater), CA	264
58	San Francisco-S. Mateo, CA M.D.	68
65	San Jose, CA	61
246	San Luis Obispo, CA	5
341	Sandusky, OH	1
53	Santa Ana-Anaheim, CA M.D.	73
186	Santa Barbara-Santa Maria, CA	10
186	Santa Cruz-Watsonville, CA	10
268	Santa Fe, NM	4
179	Santa Rosa-Petaluma, CA	11

RANK	METROPOLITAN AREA	MURDERS
103	Savannah, GA	30
151	Scranton--Wilkes-Barre, PA	15
53	Seattle (greater), WA	73
76	Seattle-Bellevue-Everett, WA M.D.	47
246	Sebastian-Vero Beach, FL	5
341	Sheboygan, WI	1
246	Sherman-Denison, TX	5
321	Sioux City, IA-NE-SD	2
246	Sioux Falls, SD	5
145	South Bend-Mishawaka, IN-MI	16
170	Spartanburg, SC	12
219	Spokane, WA	7
195	Springfield, IL	9
111	Springfield, MA	25
195	Springfield, MO	9
290	Springfield, OH	3
359	State College, PA	0
46	Stockton, CA	87
359	St. Cloud, MN	0
268	St. Joseph, MO-KS	4
21	St. Louis, MO-IL	215
142	Sumter, SC	17
151	Syracuse, NY	15
108	Tacoma, WA M.D.	26
133	Tallahassee, FL	18
29	Tampa-St Petersburg, FL	134
230	Terre Haute, IN	6
186	Texarkana, TX-Texarkana, AR	10
85	Toledo, OH	40
151	Topeka, KS	15
111	Trenton-Ewing, NJ	25
52	Tucson, AZ	75
62	Tulsa, OK	64
195	Tuscaloosa, AL	9
204	Tyler, TX	8
204	Utica-Rome, NY	8
204	Valdosta, GA	8
103	Vallejo-Fairfield, CA	30
290	Victoria, TX	3
32	Virginia Beach-Norfolk, VA-NC	111
85	Visalia-Porterville, CA	40
170	Waco, TX	12
246	Warner Robins, GA	5
79	Warren-Farmington Hills, MI M.D.	46
18	Washington (greater) DC-VA-MD-WV	251
19	Washington, DC-VA-MD-WV M.D.	233
268	Waterloo-Cedar Falls, IA	4
359	Wausau, WI	0
230	Wenatchee, WA	6
59	West Palm Beach, FL M.D.	67
341	Wichita Falls, TX	1
101	Wichita, KS	31
341	Williamsport, PA	1
91	Wilmington, DE-MD-NJ M.D.	35
145	Wilmington, NC	16
290	Winchester, VA-WV	3
125	Winston-Salem, NC	20
145	Worcester, MA	16
145	Yakima, WA	16
125	York-Hanover, PA	20
204	Yuba City, CA	8
159	Yuma, AZ	14

Source: Reported data from the F.B.I. "Crime in the United States 2011"
*Includes nonnegligent manslaughter.

Rank Order - Metro Area

9. Murders in 2011 (continued)
National Total = 14,612 Murders*

RANK	METROPOLITAN AREA	MURDERS
1	New York (greater), NY-NJ-PA	852
2	Los Angeles (greater), CA	641
3	Chicago (greater), IL-IN-WI	609
4	New York-W. Plains NY-NJ M.D.	596
5	Los Angeles County, CA M.D.	568
6	Chicago-Joilet-Naperville, IL M.D.	540
7	Philadelphia (greater) PA-NJ-MD-DE	486
8	Detroit (greater), MI	416
9	Philadelphia, PA M.D.	386
10	Detroit-Livonia-Dearborn, MI M.D.	370
11	Miami (greater), FL	344
12	Houston, TX	330
13	Atlanta, GA	319
14	Dallas (greater), TX	294
15	New Orleans, LA	279
16	San Francisco (greater), CA	264
17	Baltimore-Towson, MD	256
18	Washington (greater) DC-VA-MD-WV	251
19	Washington, DC-VA-MD-WV M.D.	233
20	Miami-Dade County, FL M.D.	218
21	St. Louis, MO-IL	215
22	Phoenix-Mesa-Scottsdale, AZ	209
23	Dallas-Plano-Irving, TX M.D.	200
24	Oakland-Fremont, CA M.D.	196
25	Riverside-San Bernardino, CA	185
26	Newark-Union, NJ-PA M.D.	172
27	Kansas City, MO-KS	161
28	Memphis, TN-MS-AR	141
29	Tampa-St Petersburg, FL	134
30	Boston (greater), MA-NH	129
31	Orlando, FL	122
32	San Antonio, TX	111
32	Virginia Beach-Norfolk, VA-NC	111
34	Indianapolis, IN	107
35	Columbus, OH	104
36	Birmingham-Hoover, AL	101
37	Cincinnati-Middletown, OH-KY-IN	99
37	Cleveland-Elyria-Mentor, OH	99
39	Baton Rouge, LA	96
40	Sacramento, CA	95
41	Boston-Quincy, MA M.D.	94
41	Fort Worth-Arlington, TX M.D.	94
43	Las Vegas-Paradise, NV	93
44	Milwaukee, WI	92
45	Pittsburgh, PA	90
46	Jacksonville, FL	87
46	Stockton, CA	87
48	Charlotte-Gastonia, NC-SC	86
49	San Diego, CA	82
50	Nashville-Davidson, TN	78
50	Oklahoma City, OK	78
52	Tucson, AZ	75
53	Santa Ana-Anaheim, CA M.D.	73
53	Seattle (greater), WA	73
55	Denver-Aurora, CO	71
55	Richmond, VA	71
57	Little Rock, AR	69
58	San Francisco-S. Mateo, CA M.D.	68
59	West Palm Beach, FL M.D.	67
60	Jackson, MS	66
61	Camden, NJ M.D.	65
62	Flint, MI	64
62	Tulsa, OK	64
64	Gary, IN M.D.	63
65	San Jose, CA	61
66	Fort Lauderdale, FL M.D.	59
66	Minneapolis-St. Paul, MN-WI	59
68	Louisville, KY-IN	57
69	Nassau-Suffolk, NY M.D.	55
70	Fresno, CA	52
71	Dayton, OH	51
71	Omaha-Council Bluffs, NE-IA	51
73	Augusta, GA-SC	50
73	Austin-Round Rock, TX	50
73	New Haven-Milford, CT	50
76	Mobile, AL	47
76	Portland-Vancouver, OR-WA	47
76	Seattle-Bellevue-Everett, WA M.D.	47
79	Bakersfield, CA	46
79	Warren-Farmington Hills, MI M.D.	46
81	Albuquerque, NM	45
81	Buffalo-Niagara Falls, NY	45
83	Rochester, NY	43
84	Greenville, SC	42
85	Toledo, OH	40
85	Visalia-Porterville, CA	40
87	Montgomery, AL	39
88	Cape Coral-Fort Myers, FL	38
89	Durham-Chapel Hill, NC	37
90	Hartford, CT	36
91	McAllen-Edinburg-Mission, TX	35
91	Wilmington, DE-MD-NJ M.D.	35
93	Chattanooga, TN-GA	34
93	Knoxville, TN	34
93	Modesto, CA	34
93	Salinas, CA	34
97	Akron, OH	33
97	Fayetteville, NC	33
99	Bridgeport-Stamford, CT	32
99	North Port-Bradenton-Sarasota, FL	32
101	Colorado Springs, CO	31
101	Wichita, KS	31
103	Raleigh-Cary, NC	30
103	Savannah, GA	30
103	Vallejo-Fairfield, CA	30
106	Edison, NJ M.D.	29
107	Rockford, IL	27
108	Beaumont-Port Arthur, TX	26
108	Fort Wayne, IN	26
108	Tacoma, WA M.D.	26
111	Lakeland, FL	25
111	Springfield, MA	25
111	Trenton-Ewing, NJ	25
114	Columbus, GA-AL	24
114	Myrtle Beach, SC	24
114	Reno-Sparks, NV	24
114	Salt Lake City, UT	24
118	Allentown, PA-NJ	23
119	Atlantic City, NJ	22
119	Deltona-Daytona Beach, FL	22
119	Hickory, NC	22
119	Peoria, IL	22
119	Port St. Lucie, FL	22
124	Gulfport-Biloxi, MS	21
125	Grand Rapids-Wyoming, MI	20
125	Harrisburg-Carlisle, PA	20
125	Peabody, MA M.D.	20
125	Winston-Salem, NC	20
125	York-Hanover, PA	20
130	Charleston, WV	19
130	Huntsville, AL	19
130	Reading, PA	19
133	Bethesda-Frederick, MD M.D.	18
133	Corpus Christi, TX	18
133	El Paso, TX	18
133	Killeen-Temple-Fort Hood, TX	18
133	Lansing-East Lansing, MI	18
133	Macon, GA	18
133	Pensacola, FL	18
133	Rocky Mount, NC	18
133	Tallahassee, FL	18
142	Lexington-Fayette, KY	17
142	Prescott, AZ	17
142	Sumter, SC	17
145	Albany, GA	16
145	Poughkeepsie, NY	16
145	South Bend-Mishawaka, IN-MI	16
145	Wilmington, NC	16
145	Worcester, MA	16
145	Yakima, WA	16
151	Anderson, SC	15
151	Canton, OH	15
151	Oxnard-Thousand Oaks, CA	15
151	Palm Bay-Melbourne, FL	15
151	Pine Bluff, AR	15
151	Scranton--Wilkes-Barre, PA	15
151	Syracuse, NY	15
151	Topeka, KS	15
159	Anniston-Oxford, AL	14
159	Cambridge-Newton, MA M.D.	14
159	Florence, SC	14
159	Merced, CA	14
159	Ocala, FL	14
159	Saginaw, MI	14
159	Yuma, AZ	14
166	Albany-Schenectady-Troy, NY	13
166	Anchorage, AK	13
166	Gainesville, FL	13
166	Pueblo, CO	13
170	Amarillo, TX	12
170	Asheville, NC	12
170	Glens Falls, NY	12
170	Lafayette, LA	12
170	Lake Havasu City-Kingman, AZ	12
170	Panama City-Lynn Haven, FL	12
170	Salem, OR	12
170	Spartanburg, SC	12
170	Waco, TX	12
179	Clarksville, TN-KY	11
179	Danville, VA	11

Note: All listings are for Metropolitan Statistical Areas (M.S.A.s) except for those ending with "M.D." Listings with "M.D." are Metropolitan Divisions which are smaller parts of eleven large M.S.A.s. See explanatory note at beginning of metropolitan area section.

Rank Order - Metro Area (continued)

RANK	METROPOLITAN AREA	MURDERS
179	Laredo, TX	11
179	Longview, TX	11
179	Lubbock, TX	11
179	Odessa, TX	11
179	Santa Rosa-Petaluma, CA	11
186	Decatur, IL	10
186	Goldsboro, NC	10
186	Madison, WI	10
186	Medford, OR	10
186	Naples-Marco Island, FL	10
186	Roanoke, VA	10
186	Santa Barbara-Santa Maria, CA	10
186	Santa Cruz-Watsonville, CA	10
186	Texarkana, TX-Texarkana, AR	10
195	Des Moines-West Des Moines, IA	9
195	Fort Smith, AR-OK	9
195	Hagerstown-Martinsburg, MD-WV	9
195	Jackson, TN	9
195	Kingsport, TN-VA	9
195	Monroe, LA	9
195	Springfield, IL	9
195	Springfield, MO	9
195	Tuscaloosa, AL	9
204	Ann Arbor, MI	8
204	Battle Creek, MI	8
204	Boise City-Nampa, ID	8
204	Brownsville-Harlingen, TX	8
204	Chico, CA	8
204	Davenport, IA-IL	8
204	Erie, PA	8
204	Hanford-Corcoran, CA	8
204	Lawton, OK	8
204	Manchester-Nashua, NH	8
204	Ogden-Clearfield, UT	8
204	Tyler, TX	8
204	Utica-Rome, NY	8
204	Valdosta, GA	8
204	Yuba City, CA	8
219	Bangor, ME	7
219	Brunswick, GA	7
219	Cleveland, TN	7
219	Dover, DE	7
219	Evansville, IN-KY	7
219	Jefferson City, MO	7
219	Lancaster, PA	7
219	Las Cruces, NM	7
219	Muskegon-Norton Shores, MI	7
219	Racine, WI	7
219	Spokane, WA	7
230	Athens-Clarke County, GA	6
230	Bloomington, IN	6
230	Champaign-Urbana, IL	6
230	Charlottesville, VA	6
230	Cumberland, MD-WV	6
230	Greeley, CO	6
230	Houma, LA	6
230	Idaho Falls, ID	6
230	Johnson City, TN	6
230	Lake Co.-Kenosha Co., IL-WI M.D.	6
230	Lynchburg, VA	6
230	Midland, TX	6
230	Redding, CA	6
230	Salisbury, MD	6
230	Terre Haute, IN	6
230	Wenatchee, WA	6
246	Abilene, TX	5
246	Alexandria, LA	5
246	College Station-Bryan, TX	5
246	Dothan, AL	5
246	Farmington, NM	5
246	Flagstaff, AZ	5
246	Gadsden, AL	5
246	Gainesville, GA	5
246	Kennewick-Pasco-Richland, WA	5
246	Kokomo, IN	5
246	Madera, CA	5
246	Manhattan, KS	5
246	Norwich-New London, CT	5
246	Pascagoula, MS	5
246	Portland, ME	5
246	Provo-Orem, UT	5
246	Rome, GA	5
246	San Luis Obispo, CA	5
246	Sebastian-Vero Beach, FL	5
246	Sherman-Denison, TX	5
246	Sioux Falls, SD	5
246	Warner Robins, GA	5
268	Boulder, CO	4
268	Carson City, NV	4
268	Columbia, MO	4
268	Crestview-Fort Walton Beach, FL	4
268	Fort Collins-Loveland, CO	4
268	Hinesville, GA	4
268	Hot Springs, AR	4
268	Jacksonville, NC	4
268	Janesville, WI	4
268	Johnstown, PA	4
268	Jonesboro, AR	4
268	Kankakee-Bradley, IL	4
268	Lewiston-Auburn, ME	4
268	Lincoln, NE	4
268	Longview, WA	4
268	Michigan City-La Porte, IN	4
268	Olympia, WA	4
268	Pittsfield, MA	4
268	Rapid City, SD	4
268	Santa Fe, NM	4
268	St. Joseph, MO-KS	4
268	Waterloo-Cedar Falls, IA	4
290	Auburn, AL	3
290	Barnstable Town, MA	3
290	Bay City, MI	3
290	Bellingham, WA	3
290	Billings, MT	3
290	Binghamton, NY	3
290	Bismarck, ND	3
290	Blacksburg, VA	3
290	Bowling Green, KY	3
290	Bremerton-Silverdale, WA	3
290	Burlington, NC	3
290	Corvallis, OR	3
290	Danville, IL	3
290	Decatur, AL	3
290	Duluth, MN-WI	3
290	El Centro, CA	3
290	Eugene-Springfield, OR	3
290	Florence-Muscle Shoals, AL	3
290	Grand Junction, CO	3
290	Iowa City, IA	3
290	Joplin, MO	3
290	Lafayette, IN	3
290	Mansfield, OH	3
290	Monroe, MI	3
290	Morristown, TN	3
290	Mount Vernon-Anacortes, WA	3
290	Napa, CA	3
290	Pocatello, ID	3
290	Springfield, OH	3
290	Victoria, TX	3
290	Winchester, VA-WV	3
321	Altoona, PA	2
321	Appleton, WI	2
321	Bend, OR	2
321	Bloomington-Normal, IL	2
321	Casper, WY	2
321	Cedar Rapids, IA	2
321	Cheyenne, WY	2
321	Dalton, GA	2
321	Elizabethtown, KY	2
321	Fairbanks, AK	2
321	Fond du Lac, WI	2
321	Great Falls, MT	2
321	Green Bay, WI	2
321	Harrisonburg, VA	2
321	Holland-Grand Haven, MI	2
321	Kingston, NY	2
321	Lima, OH	2
321	Muncie, IN	2
321	Punta Gorda, FL	2
321	Sioux City, IA-NE-SD	2
341	Cape Girardeau, MO-IL	1
341	Columbus, IN	1
341	Dubuque, IA	1
341	Elmira, NY	1
341	Fargo, ND-MN	1
341	Lebanon, PA	1
341	Mankato-North Mankato, MN	1
341	Missoula, MT	1
341	Ocean City, NJ	1
341	Oshkosh-Neenah, WI	1
341	Owensboro, KY	1
341	Palm Coast, FL	1
341	Rochester, MN	1
341	Rockingham County, NH M.D.	1
341	Sandusky, OH	1
341	Sheboygan, WI	1
341	Wichita Falls, TX	1
341	Williamsport, PA	1
359	Ames, IA	0
359	Eau Claire, WI	0
359	Grand Forks, ND-MN	0
359	La Crosse, WI-MN	0
359	Lawrence, KS	0
359	Logan, UT-ID	0
359	San Angelo, TX	0
359	State College, PA	0
359	St. Cloud, MN	0
359	Wausau, WI	0

Source: Reported data from the F.B.I. "Crime in the United States 2011"
*Includes nonnegligent manslaughter.

Alpha Order - Metro Area

10. Murder Rate in 2011
National Rate = 4.7 Murders per 100,000 Population*

RANK	METROPOLITAN AREA	RATE	RANK	METROPOLITAN AREA	RATE	RANK	METROPOLITAN AREA	RATE
220	Abilene, TX	3.0	69	Charleston, WV	6.2	203	Fort Lauderdale, FL M.D.	3.3
129	Akron, OH	4.7	124	Charlotte-Gastonia, NC-SC	4.8	220	Fort Smith, AR-OK	3.0
310	Albany-Schenectady-Troy, NY	1.5	225	Charlottesville, VA	2.9	69	Fort Wayne, IN	6.2
15	Albany, GA	10.0	64	Chattanooga, TN-GA	6.4	153	Fort Worth-Arlington, TX M.D.	4.3
110	Albuquerque, NM	5.0	264	Cheyenne, WY	2.2	96	Fresno, CA	5.5
211	Alexandria, LA	3.2	64	Chicago (greater), IL-IN-WI	6.4	124	Gadsden, AL	4.8
229	Allentown, PA-NJ	2.8	55	Chicago-Joilet-Naperville, IL M.D.	6.8	116	Gainesville, FL	4.9
306	Altoona, PA	1.6	188	Chico, CA	3.6	235	Gainesville, GA	2.7
129	Amarillo, TX	4.7	137	Cincinnati-Middletown, OH-KY-IN	4.6	22	Gary, IN M.D.	8.9
359	Ames, IA	0.0	172	Clarksville, TN-KY	4.0	20	Glens Falls, NY	9.3
161	Anchorage, AK	4.2	124	Cleveland-Elyria-Mentor, OH	4.8	31	Goldsboro, NC	8.1
38	Anderson, SC	7.9	79	Cleveland, TN	6.0	359	Grand Forks, ND-MN	0.0
257	Ann Arbor, MI	2.3	273	College Station-Bryan, TX	2.1	280	Grand Junction, CO	2.0
9	Anniston-Oxford, AL	11.8	129	Colorado Springs, CO	4.7	243	Grand Rapids-Wyoming, MI	2.6
341	Appleton, WI	0.9	257	Columbia, MO	2.3	251	Great Falls, MT	2.4
229	Asheville, NC	2.8	34	Columbus, GA-AL	8.0	257	Greeley, CO	2.3
214	Athens-Clarke County, GA	3.1	319	Columbus, IN	1.3	351	Green Bay, WI	0.7
79	Atlanta, GA	6.0	90	Columbus, OH	5.7	61	Greenville, SC	6.5
34	Atlantic City, NJ	8.0	164	Corpus Christi, TX	4.1	30	Gulfport-Biloxi, MS	8.4
273	Auburn, AL	2.1	196	Corvallis, OR	3.5	203	Hagerstown-Martinsburg, MD-WV	3.3
22	Augusta, GA-SC	8.9	264	Crestview-Fort Walton Beach, FL	2.2	102	Hanford-Corcoran, CA	5.2
225	Austin-Round Rock, TX	2.9	86	Cumberland, MD-WV	5.8	188	Harrisburg-Carlisle, PA	3.6
97	Bakersfield, CA	5.4	141	Dallas (greater), TX	4.5	306	Harrisonburg, VA	1.6
19	Baltimore-Towson, MD	9.4	137	Dallas-Plano-Irving, TX M.D.	4.6	196	Hartford, CT	3.5
141	Bangor, ME	4.5	315	Dalton, GA	1.4	82	Hickory, NC	5.9
315	Barnstable Town, MA	1.4	183	Danville, IL	3.7	104	Hinesville, GA	5.1
8	Baton Rouge, LA	11.9	14	Danville, VA	10.2	348	Holland-Grand Haven, MI	0.8
82	Battle Creek, MI	5.9	273	Davenport, IA-IL	2.1	164	Hot Springs, AR	4.1
229	Bay City, MI	2.8	73	Dayton, OH	6.1	225	Houma, LA	2.9
59	Beaumont-Port Arthur, TX	6.6	288	Decatur, AL	1.9	97	Houston, TX	5.4
310	Bellingham, WA	1.5	21	Decatur, IL	9.0	141	Huntsville, AL	4.5
319	Bend, OR	1.3	147	Deltona-Daytona Beach, FL	4.4	141	Idaho Falls, ID	4.5
310	Bethesda-Frederick, MD M.D.	1.5	235	Denver-Aurora, CO	2.7	73	Indianapolis, IN	6.1
288	Billings, MT	1.9	306	Des Moines-West Des Moines, IA	1.6	280	Iowa City, IA	2.0
327	Binghamton, NY	1.2	17	Detroit (greater), MI	9.7	64	Jacksonville, FL	6.4
22	Birmingham-Hoover, AL	8.9	2	Detroit-Livonia-Dearborn, MI M.D.	20.3	264	Jacksonville, NC	2.2
235	Bismarck, ND	2.7	201	Dothan, AL	3.4	7	Jackson, MS	12.2
296	Blacksburg, VA	1.8	153	Dover, DE	4.3	42	Jackson, TN	7.7
327	Bloomington-Normal, IL	1.2	332	Dubuque, IA	1.1	248	Janesville, WI	2.5
214	Bloomington, IN	3.1	332	Duluth, MN-WI	1.1	129	Jefferson City, MO	4.7
319	Boise City-Nampa, ID	1.3	48	Durham-Chapel Hill, NC	7.2	220	Johnson City, TN	3.0
229	Boston (greater), MA-NH	2.8	359	Eau Claire, WI	0.0	229	Johnstown, PA	2.8
116	Boston-Quincy, MA M.D.	4.9	327	Edison, NJ M.D.	1.2	203	Jonesboro, AR	3.3
319	Boulder, CO	1.3	301	El Centro, CA	1.7	301	Joplin, MO	1.7
251	Bowling Green, KY	2.4	264	El Paso, TX	2.2	196	Kankakee-Bradley, IL	3.5
327	Bremerton-Silverdale, WA	1.2	301	Elizabethtown, KY	1.7	38	Kansas City, MO-KS	7.9
188	Bridgeport-Stamford, CT	3.6	332	Elmira, NY	1.1	288	Kennewick-Pasco-Richland, WA	1.9
288	Brownsville-Harlingen, TX	1.9	229	Erie, PA	2.8	153	Killeen-Temple-Fort Hood, TX	4.3
73	Brunswick, GA	6.1	348	Eugene-Springfield, OR	0.8	225	Kingsport, TN-VA	2.9
174	Buffalo-Niagara Falls, NY	3.9	288	Evansville, IN-KY	1.9	332	Kingston, NY	1.1
280	Burlington, NC	2.0	86	Fairbanks, AK	5.8	124	Knoxville, TN	4.8
341	Cambridge-Newton, MA M.D.	0.9	356	Fargo, ND-MN	0.5	110	Kokomo, IN	5.0
102	Camden, NJ M.D.	5.2	177	Farmington, NM	3.8	359	La Crosse, WI-MN	0.0
183	Canton, OH	3.7	22	Fayetteville, NC	8.9	310	Lafayette, IN	1.5
73	Cape Coral-Fort Myers, FL	6.1	183	Flagstaff, AZ	3.7	153	Lafayette, LA	4.3
336	Cape Girardeau, MO-IL	1.0	4	Flint, MI	15.0	351	Lake Co.-Kenosha Co., IL-WI M.D.	0.7
48	Carson City, NV	7.2	280	Florence-Muscle Shoals, AL	2.0	82	Lake Havasu City-Kingman, AZ	5.9
243	Casper, WY	2.6	58	Florence, SC	6.7	164	Lakeland, FL	4.1
348	Cedar Rapids, IA	0.8	280	Fond du Lac, WI	2.0	319	Lancaster, PA	1.3
243	Champaign-Urbana, IL	2.6	319	Fort Collins-Loveland, CO	1.3	174	Lansing-East Lansing, MI	3.9

Note: All listings are for Metropolitan Statistical Areas (M.S.A.s) except for those ending with "M.D." Listings with "M.D." are Metropolitan Divisions which are smaller parts of eleven large M.S.A.s. See explanatory note at beginning of metropolitan area section.

Alpha Order - Metro Area (continued)

RANK	METROPOLITAN AREA	RATE	RANK	METROPOLITAN AREA	RATE	RANK	METROPOLITAN AREA	RATE
153	Laredo, TX	4.3	69	Oklahoma City, OK	6.2	29	Savannah, GA	8.5
203	Las Cruces, NM	3.3	306	Olympia, WA	1.6	235	Scranton--Wilkes-Barre, PA	2.7
129	Las Vegas-Paradise, NV	4.7	86	Omaha-Council Bluffs, NE-IA	5.8	273	Seattle (greater), WA	2.1
359	Lawrence, KS	0.0	93	Orlando, FL	5.6	301	Seattle-Bellevue-Everett, WA M.D.	1.7
64	Lawton, OK	6.4	354	Oshkosh-Neenah, WI	0.6	188	Sebastian-Vero Beach, FL	3.6
351	Lebanon, PA	0.7	341	Owensboro, KY	0.9	341	Sheboygan, WI	0.9
183	Lewiston-Auburn, ME	3.7	296	Oxnard-Thousand Oaks, CA	1.8	164	Sherman-Denison, TX	4.1
188	Lexington-Fayette, KY	3.6	235	Palm Bay-Melbourne, FL	2.7	315	Sioux City, IA-NE-SD	1.4
288	Lima, OH	1.9	336	Palm Coast, FL	1.0	264	Sioux Falls, SD	2.2
319	Lincoln, NE	1.3	53	Panama City-Lynn Haven, FL	7.0	110	South Bend-Mishawaka, IN-MI	5.0
16	Little Rock, AR	9.8	214	Pascagoula, MS	3.1	161	Spartanburg, SC	4.2
359	Logan, UT-ID	0.0	235	Peabody, MA M.D.	2.7	310	Spokane, WA	1.5
110	Longview, TX	5.0	172	Pensacola, FL	4.0	153	Springfield, IL	4.3
177	Longview, WA	3.8	86	Peoria, IL	5.8	188	Springfield, MA	3.6
90	Los Angeles County, CA M.D.	5.7	31	Philadelphia (greater) PA-NJ-MD-DE	8.1	273	Springfield, MO	2.1
116	Los Angeles (greater), CA	4.9	18	Philadelphia, PA M.D.	9.6	264	Springfield, OH	2.2
147	Louisville, KY-IN	4.4	116	Phoenix-Mesa-Scottsdale, AZ	4.9	359	State College, PA	0.0
177	Lubbock, TX	3.8	5	Pine Bluff, AR	14.8	6	Stockton, CA	12.5
257	Lynchburg, VA	2.3	177	Pittsburgh, PA	3.8	359	St. Cloud, MN	0.0
44	Macon, GA	7.6	220	Pittsfield, MA	3.0	214	St. Joseph, MO-KS	3.1
203	Madera, CA	3.3	203	Pocatello, ID	3.3	44	St. Louis, MO-IL	7.6
296	Madison, WI	1.8	104	Port St. Lucie, FL	5.1	3	Sumter, SC	15.6
280	Manchester-Nashua, NH	2.0	273	Portland-Vancouver, OR-WA	2.1	257	Syracuse, NY	2.3
174	Manhattan, KS	3.9	336	Portland, ME	1.0	211	Tacoma, WA M.D.	3.2
336	Mankato-North Mankato, MN	1.0	251	Poughkeepsie, NY	2.4	124	Tallahassee, FL	4.8
251	Mansfield, OH	2.4	38	Prescott, AZ	7.9	129	Tampa-St Petersburg, FL	4.7
147	McAllen-Edinburg-Mission, TX	4.4	341	Provo-Orem, UT	0.9	196	Terre Haute, IN	3.5
116	Medford, OR	4.9	34	Pueblo, CO	8.0	48	Texarkana, TX-Texarkana, AR	7.2
12	Memphis, TN-MS-AR	10.6	327	Punta Gorda, FL	1.2	73	Toledo, OH	6.1
97	Merced, CA	5.4	188	Racine, WI	3.6	64	Topeka, KS	6.4
73	Miami (greater), FL	6.1	243	Raleigh-Cary, NC	2.6	55	Trenton-Ewing, NJ	6.8
28	Miami-Dade County, FL M.D.	8.6	214	Rapid City, SD	3.1	47	Tucson, AZ	7.5
188	Michigan City-La Porte, IN	3.6	137	Reading, PA	4.6	55	Tulsa, OK	6.8
153	Midland, TX	4.3	203	Redding, CA	3.3	164	Tuscaloosa, AL	4.1
82	Milwaukee, WI	5.9	93	Reno-Sparks, NV	5.6	183	Tyler, TX	3.7
296	Minneapolis-St. Paul, MN-WI	1.8	93	Richmond, VA	5.6	235	Utica-Rome, NY	2.7
341	Missoula, MT	0.9	153	Riverside-San Bernardino, CA	4.3	90	Valdosta, GA	5.7
11	Mobile, AL	11.3	211	Roanoke, VA	3.2	48	Vallejo-Fairfield, CA	7.2
61	Modesto, CA	6.5	356	Rochester, MN	0.5	248	Victoria, TX	2.5
104	Monroe, LA	5.1	164	Rochester, NY	4.1	59	Virginia Beach-Norfolk, VA-NC	6.6
280	Monroe, MI	2.0	42	Rockford, IL	7.7	22	Visalia-Porterville, CA	8.9
13	Montgomery, AL	10.4	358	Rockingham County, NH M.D.	0.2	110	Waco, TX	5.0
264	Morristown, TN	2.2	10	Rocky Mount, NC	11.7	196	Warner Robins, GA	3.5
248	Mount Vernon-Anacortes, WA	2.5	104	Rome, GA	5.1	288	Warren-Farmington Hills, MI M.D.	1.9
301	Muncie, IN	1.7	147	Sacramento, CA	4.4	147	Washington (greater) DC-VA-MD-WV	4.4
164	Muskegon-Norton Shores, MI	4.1	53	Saginaw, MI	7.0	100	Washington, DC-VA-MD-WV M.D.	5.3
27	Myrtle Beach, SC	8.8	220	Salem, OR	3.0	251	Waterloo-Cedar Falls, IA	2.4
264	Napa, CA	2.2	31	Salinas, CA	8.1	359	Wausau, WI	0.0
214	Naples-Marco Island, FL	3.1	129	Salisbury, MD	4.7	100	Wenatchee, WA	5.3
116	Nashville-Davidson, TN	4.9	273	Salt Lake City, UT	2.1	110	West Palm Beach, FL M.D.	5.0
288	Nassau-Suffolk, NY M.D.	1.9	359	San Angelo, TX	0.0	354	Wichita Falls, TX	0.6
69	New Haven-Milford, CT	6.2	104	San Antonio, TX	5.1	116	Wichita, KS	4.9
1	New Orleans, LA	23.7	243	San Diego, CA	2.6	341	Williamsport, PA	0.9
141	New York (greater), NY-NJ-PA	4.5	79	San Francisco (greater), CA	6.0	116	Wilmington, DE-MD-NJ M.D.	4.9
104	New York-W. Plains NY-NJ M.D.	5.1	177	San Francisco-S. Mateo, CA M.D.	3.8	147	Wilmington, NC	4.4
34	Newark-Union, NJ-PA M.D.	8.0	203	San Jose, CA	3.3	257	Winchester, VA-WV	2.3
141	North Port-Bradenton-Sarasota, FL	4.5	296	San Luis Obispo, CA	1.8	164	Winston-Salem, NC	4.1
201	Norwich-New London, CT	3.4	319	Sandusky, OH	1.3	280	Worcester, MA	2.0
44	Oakland-Fremont, CA M.D.	7.6	251	Santa Ana-Anaheim, CA M.D.	2.4	61	Yakima, WA	6.5
161	Ocala, FL	4.2	257	Santa Barbara-Santa Maria, CA	2.3	137	York-Hanover, PA	4.6
336	Ocean City, NJ	1.0	177	Santa Cruz-Watsonville, CA	3.8	129	Yuba City, CA	4.7
38	Odessa, TX	7.9	235	Santa Fe, NM	2.7	52	Yuma, AZ	7.1
315	Ogden-Clearfield, UT	1.4	264	Santa Rosa-Petaluma, CA	2.2			

Source: Reported data from the F.B.I. "Crime in the United States 2011"
*Includes nonnegligent manslaughter.

Rank Order - Metro Area

10. Murder Rate in 2011 (continued)
National Rate = 4.7 Murders per 100,000 Population*

RANK	METROPOLITAN AREA	RATE
1	New Orleans, LA	23.7
2	Detroit-Livonia-Dearborn, MI M.D.	20.3
3	Sumter, SC	15.6
4	Flint, MI	15.0
5	Pine Bluff, AR	14.8
6	Stockton, CA	12.5
7	Jackson, MS	12.2
8	Baton Rouge, LA	11.9
9	Anniston-Oxford, AL	11.8
10	Rocky Mount, NC	11.7
11	Mobile, AL	11.3
12	Memphis, TN-MS-AR	10.6
13	Montgomery, AL	10.4
14	Danville, VA	10.2
15	Albany, GA	10.0
16	Little Rock, AR	9.8
17	Detroit (greater), MI	9.7
18	Philadelphia, PA M.D.	9.6
19	Baltimore-Towson, MD	9.4
20	Glens Falls, NY	9.3
21	Decatur, IL	9.0
22	Augusta, GA-SC	8.9
22	Birmingham-Hoover, AL	8.9
22	Fayetteville, NC	8.9
22	Gary, IN M.D.	8.9
22	Visalia-Porterville, CA	8.9
27	Myrtle Beach, SC	8.8
28	Miami-Dade County, FL M.D.	8.6
29	Savannah, GA	8.5
30	Gulfport-Biloxi, MS	8.4
31	Goldsboro, NC	8.1
31	Philadelphia (greater) PA-NJ-MD-DE	8.1
31	Salinas, CA	8.1
34	Atlantic City, NJ	8.0
34	Columbus, GA-AL	8.0
34	Newark-Union, NJ-PA M.D.	8.0
34	Pueblo, CO	8.0
38	Anderson, SC	7.9
38	Kansas City, MO-KS	7.9
38	Odessa, TX	7.9
38	Prescott, AZ	7.9
42	Jackson, TN	7.7
42	Rockford, IL	7.7
44	Macon, GA	7.6
44	Oakland-Fremont, CA M.D.	7.6
44	St. Louis, MO-IL	7.6
47	Tucson, AZ	7.5
48	Carson City, NV	7.2
48	Durham-Chapel Hill, NC	7.2
48	Texarkana, TX-Texarkana, AR	7.2
48	Vallejo-Fairfield, CA	7.2
52	Yuma, AZ	7.1
53	Panama City-Lynn Haven, FL	7.0
53	Saginaw, MI	7.0
55	Chicago-Joilet-Naperville, IL M.D.	6.8
55	Trenton-Ewing, NJ	6.8
55	Tulsa, OK	6.8
58	Florence, SC	6.7
59	Beaumont-Port Arthur, TX	6.6
59	Virginia Beach-Norfolk, VA-NC	6.6
61	Greenville, SC	6.5
61	Modesto, CA	6.5
61	Yakima, WA	6.5
64	Chattanooga, TN-GA	6.4
64	Chicago (greater), IL-IN-WI	6.4
64	Jacksonville, FL	6.4
64	Lawton, OK	6.4
64	Topeka, KS	6.4
69	Charleston, WV	6.2
69	Fort Wayne, IN	6.2
69	New Haven-Milford, CT	6.2
69	Oklahoma City, OK	6.2
73	Brunswick, GA	6.1
73	Cape Coral-Fort Myers, FL	6.1
73	Dayton, OH	6.1
73	Indianapolis, IN	6.1
73	Miami (greater), FL	6.1
73	Toledo, OH	6.1
79	Atlanta, GA	6.0
79	Cleveland, TN	6.0
79	San Francisco (greater), CA	6.0
82	Battle Creek, MI	5.9
82	Hickory, NC	5.9
82	Lake Havasu City-Kingman, AZ	5.9
82	Milwaukee, WI	5.9
86	Cumberland, MD-WV	5.8
86	Fairbanks, AK	5.8
86	Omaha-Council Bluffs, NE-IA	5.8
86	Peoria, IL	5.8
90	Columbus, OH	5.7
90	Los Angeles County, CA M.D.	5.7
90	Valdosta, GA	5.7
93	Orlando, FL	5.6
93	Reno-Sparks, NV	5.6
93	Richmond, VA	5.6
96	Fresno, CA	5.5
97	Bakersfield, CA	5.4
97	Houston, TX	5.4
97	Merced, CA	5.4
100	Washington, DC-VA-MD-WV M.D.	5.3
100	Wenatchee, WA	5.3
102	Camden, NJ M.D.	5.2
102	Hanford-Corcoran, CA	5.2
104	Hinesville, GA	5.1
104	Monroe, LA	5.1
104	New York-W. Plains NY-NJ M.D.	5.1
104	Port St. Lucie, FL	5.1
104	Rome, GA	5.1
104	San Antonio, TX	5.1
110	Albuquerque, NM	5.0
110	Kokomo, IN	5.0
110	Longview, TX	5.0
110	South Bend-Mishawaka, IN-MI	5.0
110	Waco, TX	5.0
110	West Palm Beach, FL M.D.	5.0
116	Boston-Quincy, MA M.D.	4.9
116	Gainesville, FL	4.9
116	Los Angeles (greater), CA	4.9
116	Medford, OR	4.9
116	Nashville-Davidson, TN	4.9
116	Phoenix-Mesa-Scottsdale, AZ	4.9
116	Wichita, KS	4.9
116	Wilmington, DE-MD-NJ M.D.	4.9
124	Charlotte-Gastonia, NC-SC	4.8
124	Cleveland-Elyria-Mentor, OH	4.8
124	Gadsden, AL	4.8
124	Knoxville, TN	4.8
124	Tallahassee, FL	4.8
129	Akron, OH	4.7
129	Amarillo, TX	4.7
129	Colorado Springs, CO	4.7
129	Jefferson City, MO	4.7
129	Las Vegas-Paradise, NV	4.7
129	Salisbury, MD	4.7
129	Tampa-St Petersburg, FL	4.7
129	Yuba City, CA	4.7
137	Cincinnati-Middletown, OH-KY-IN	4.6
137	Dallas-Plano-Irving, TX M.D.	4.6
137	Reading, PA	4.6
137	York-Hanover, PA	4.6
141	Bangor, ME	4.5
141	Dallas (greater), TX	4.5
141	Huntsville, AL	4.5
141	Idaho Falls, ID	4.5
141	New York (greater), NY-NJ-PA	4.5
141	North Port-Bradenton-Sarasota, FL	4.5
147	Deltona-Daytona Beach, FL	4.4
147	Louisville, KY-IN	4.4
147	McAllen-Edinburg-Mission, TX	4.4
147	Sacramento, CA	4.4
147	Washington (greater) DC-VA-MD-WV	4.4
147	Wilmington, NC	4.4
153	Dover, DE	4.3
153	Fort Worth-Arlington, TX M.D.	4.3
153	Killeen-Temple-Fort Hood, TX	4.3
153	Lafayette, LA	4.3
153	Laredo, TX	4.3
153	Midland, TX	4.3
153	Riverside-San Bernardino, CA	4.3
153	Springfield, IL	4.3
161	Anchorage, AK	4.2
161	Ocala, FL	4.2
161	Spartanburg, SC	4.2
164	Corpus Christi, TX	4.1
164	Hot Springs, AR	4.1
164	Lakeland, FL	4.1
164	Muskegon-Norton Shores, MI	4.1
164	Rochester, NY	4.1
164	Sherman-Denison, TX	4.1
164	Tuscaloosa, AL	4.1
164	Winston-Salem, NC	4.1
172	Clarksville, TN-KY	4.0
172	Pensacola, FL	4.0
174	Buffalo-Niagara Falls, NY	3.9
174	Lansing-East Lansing, MI	3.9
174	Manhattan, KS	3.9
177	Farmington, NM	3.8
177	Longview, WA	3.8
177	Lubbock, TX	3.8
177	Pittsburgh, PA	3.8

Note: All listings are for Metropolitan Statistical Areas (M.S.A.s) except for those ending with "M.D." Listings with "M.D." are Metropolitan Divisions which are smaller parts of eleven large M.S.A.s. See explanatory note at beginning of metropolitan area section.

Rank Order - Metro Area (continued)

RANK	METROPOLITAN AREA	RATE	RANK	METROPOLITAN AREA	RATE	RANK	METROPOLITAN AREA	RATE
177	San Francisco-S. Mateo, CA M.D.	3.8	243	Champaign-Urbana, IL	2.6	306	Des Moines-West Des Moines, IA	1.6
177	Santa Cruz-Watsonville, CA	3.8	243	Grand Rapids-Wyoming, MI	2.6	306	Harrisonburg, VA	1.6
183	Canton, OH	3.7	243	Raleigh-Cary, NC	2.6	306	Olympia, WA	1.6
183	Danville, IL	3.7	243	San Diego, CA	2.6	310	Albany-Schenectady-Troy, NY	1.5
183	Flagstaff, AZ	3.7	248	Janesville, WI	2.5	310	Bellingham, WA	1.5
183	Lewiston-Auburn, ME	3.7	248	Mount Vernon-Anacortes, WA	2.5	310	Bethesda-Frederick, MD M.D.	1.5
183	Tyler, TX	3.7	248	Victoria, TX	2.5	310	Lafayette, IN	1.5
188	Bridgeport-Stamford, CT	3.6	251	Bowling Green, KY	2.4	310	Spokane, WA	1.5
188	Chico, CA	3.6	251	Great Falls, MT	2.4	315	Barnstable Town, MA	1.4
188	Harrisburg-Carlisle, PA	3.6	251	Mansfield, OH	2.4	315	Dalton, GA	1.4
188	Lexington-Fayette, KY	3.6	251	Poughkeepsie, NY	2.4	315	Ogden-Clearfield, UT	1.4
188	Michigan City-La Porte, IN	3.6	251	Santa Ana-Anaheim, CA M.D.	2.4	315	Sioux City, IA-NE-SD	1.4
188	Racine, WI	3.6	251	Waterloo-Cedar Falls, IA	2.4	319	Bend, OR	1.3
188	Sebastian-Vero Beach, FL	3.6	257	Ann Arbor, MI	2.3	319	Boise City-Nampa, ID	1.3
188	Springfield, MA	3.6	257	Columbia, MO	2.3	319	Boulder, CO	1.3
196	Corvallis, OR	3.5	257	Greeley, CO	2.3	319	Columbus, IN	1.3
196	Hartford, CT	3.5	257	Lynchburg, VA	2.3	319	Fort Collins-Loveland, CO	1.3
196	Kankakee-Bradley, IL	3.5	257	Santa Barbara-Santa Maria, CA	2.3	319	Lancaster, PA	1.3
196	Terre Haute, IN	3.5	257	Syracuse, NY	2.3	319	Lincoln, NE	1.3
196	Warner Robins, GA	3.5	257	Winchester, VA-WV	2.3	319	Sandusky, OH	1.3
201	Dothan, AL	3.4	264	Cheyenne, WY	2.2	327	Binghamton, NY	1.2
201	Norwich-New London, CT	3.4	264	Crestview-Fort Walton Beach, FL	2.2	327	Bloomington-Normal, IL	1.2
203	Fort Lauderdale, FL M.D.	3.3	264	El Paso, TX	2.2	327	Bremerton-Silverdale, WA	1.2
203	Hagerstown-Martinsburg, MD-WV	3.3	264	Jacksonville, NC	2.2	327	Edison, NJ M.D.	1.2
203	Jonesboro, AR	3.3	264	Morristown, TN	2.2	327	Punta Gorda, FL	1.2
203	Las Cruces, NM	3.3	264	Napa, CA	2.2	332	Dubuque, IA	1.1
203	Madera, CA	3.3	264	Santa Rosa-Petaluma, CA	2.2	332	Duluth, MN-WI	1.1
203	Pocatello, ID	3.3	264	Sioux Falls, SD	2.2	332	Elmira, NY	1.1
203	Redding, CA	3.3	264	Springfield, OH	2.2	332	Kingston, NY	1.1
203	San Jose, CA	3.3	273	Auburn, AL	2.1	336	Cape Girardeau, MO-IL	1.0
211	Alexandria, LA	3.2	273	College Station-Bryan, TX	2.1	336	Mankato-North Mankato, MN	1.0
211	Roanoke, VA	3.2	273	Davenport, IA-IL	2.1	336	Ocean City, NJ	1.0
211	Tacoma, WA M.D.	3.2	273	Portland-Vancouver, OR-WA	2.1	336	Palm Coast, FL	1.0
214	Athens-Clarke County, GA	3.1	273	Salt Lake City, UT	2.1	336	Portland, ME	1.0
214	Bloomington, IN	3.1	273	Seattle (greater), WA	2.1	341	Appleton, WI	0.9
214	Naples-Marco Island, FL	3.1	273	Springfield, MO	2.1	341	Cambridge-Newton, MA M.D.	0.9
214	Pascagoula, MS	3.1	280	Burlington, NC	2.0	341	Missoula, MT	0.9
214	Rapid City, SD	3.1	280	Florence-Muscle Shoals, AL	2.0	341	Owensboro, KY	0.9
214	St. Joseph, MO-KS	3.1	280	Fond du Lac, WI	2.0	341	Provo-Orem, UT	0.9
220	Abilene, TX	3.0	280	Grand Junction, CO	2.0	341	Sheboygan, WI	0.9
220	Fort Smith, AR-OK	3.0	280	Iowa City, IA	2.0	341	Williamsport, PA	0.9
220	Johnson City, TN	3.0	280	Manchester-Nashua, NH	2.0	348	Cedar Rapids, IA	0.8
220	Pittsfield, MA	3.0	280	Monroe, MI	2.0	348	Eugene-Springfield, OR	0.8
220	Salem, OR	3.0	280	Worcester, MA	2.0	348	Holland-Grand Haven, MI	0.8
225	Austin-Round Rock, TX	2.9	288	Billings, MT	1.9	351	Green Bay, WI	0.7
225	Charlottesville, VA	2.9	288	Brownsville-Harlingen, TX	1.9	351	Lake Co.-Kenosha Co., IL-WI M.D.	0.7
225	Houma, LA	2.9	288	Decatur, AL	1.9	351	Lebanon, PA	0.7
225	Kingsport, TN-VA	2.9	288	Evansville, IN-KY	1.9	354	Oshkosh-Neenah, WI	0.6
229	Allentown, PA-NJ	2.8	288	Kennewick-Pasco-Richland, WA	1.9	354	Wichita Falls, TX	0.6
229	Asheville, NC	2.8	288	Lima, OH	1.9	356	Fargo, ND-MN	0.5
229	Bay City, MI	2.8	288	Nassau-Suffolk, NY M.D.	1.9	356	Rochester, MN	0.5
229	Boston (greater), MA-NH	2.8	288	Warren-Farmington Hills, MI M.D.	1.9	358	Rockingham County, NH M.D.	0.2
229	Erie, PA	2.8	296	Blacksburg, VA	1.8	359	Ames, IA	0.0
229	Johnstown, PA	2.8	296	Madison, WI	1.8	359	Eau Claire, WI	0.0
235	Bismarck, ND	2.7	296	Minneapolis-St. Paul, MN-WI	1.8	359	Grand Forks, ND-MN	0.0
235	Denver-Aurora, CO	2.7	296	Oxnard-Thousand Oaks, CA	1.8	359	La Crosse, WI-MN	0.0
235	Gainesville, GA	2.7	296	San Luis Obispo, CA	1.8	359	Lawrence, KS	0.0
235	Palm Bay-Melbourne, FL	2.7	301	El Centro, CA	1.7	359	Logan, UT-ID	0.0
235	Peabody, MA M.D.	2.7	301	Elizabethtown, KY	1.7	359	San Angelo, TX	0.0
235	Santa Fe, NM	2.7	301	Joplin, MO	1.7	359	State College, PA	0.0
235	Scranton--Wilkes-Barre, PA	2.7	301	Muncie, IN	1.7	359	St. Cloud, MN	0.0
235	Utica-Rome, NY	2.7	301	Seattle-Bellevue-Everett, WA M.D.	1.7	359	Wausau, WI	0.0
243	Casper, WY	2.6	306	Altoona, PA	1.6			

Source: Reported data from the F.B.I. "Crime in the United States 2011"
*Includes nonnegligent manslaughter.

Alpha Order - Metro Area

11. Percent Change in Murder Rate: 2010 to 2011
National Percent Change = 1.5% Decrease*

RANK	METROPOLITAN AREA	% CHANGE
163	Abilene, TX	(3.2)
83	Akron, OH	27.0
132	Albany-Schenectady-Troy, NY	0.0
106	Albany, GA	14.9
201	Albuquerque, NM	(13.8)
274	Alexandria, LA	(44.8)
223	Allentown, PA-NJ	(20.0)
21	Altoona, PA	100.0
210	Amarillo, TX	(17.5)
305	Ames, IA	(100.0)
132	Anchorage, AK	0.0
59	Anderson, SC	49.1
45	Ann Arbor, MI	64.3
NA	Anniston-Oxford, AL**	NA
NA	Appleton, WI***	NA
62	Asheville, NC	47.4
240	Athens-Clarke County, GA	(26.2)
152	Atlanta, GA	(1.6)
132	Atlantic City, NJ	0.0
NA	Auburn, AL**	NA
200	Augusta, GA-SC	(12.7)
203	Austin-Round Rock, TX	(14.7)
263	Bakersfield, CA	(40.0)
188	Baltimore-Towson, MD	(8.7)
19	Bangor, ME	125.0
10	Barnstable Town, MA	180.0
NA	Baton Rouge, LA**	NA
77	Battle Creek, MI	31.1
5	Bay City, MI	211.1
97	Beaumont-Port Arthur, TX	17.9
263	Bellingham, WA	(40.0)
300	Bend, OR	(69.8)
227	Bethesda-Frederick, MD M.D.	(21.1)
NA	Billings, MT**	NA
290	Binghamton, NY	(52.0)
NA	Birmingham-Hoover, AL**	NA
55	Bismarck, ND	50.0
268	Blacksburg, VA	(41.9)
21	Bloomington-Normal, IL	100.0
61	Bloomington, IN	47.6
216	Boise City-Nampa, ID	(18.8)
223	Boston (greater), MA-NH	(20.0)
206	Boston-Quincy, MA M.D.	(15.5)
271	Boulder, CO	(43.5)
NA	Bowling Green, KY***	NA
6	Bremerton-Silverdale, WA	200.0
176	Bridgeport-Stamford, CT	(5.3)
246	Brownsville-Harlingen, TX	(29.6)
128	Brunswick, GA	3.4
258	Buffalo-Niagara Falls, NY	(36.1)
298	Burlington, NC	(66.1)
250	Cambridge-Newton, MA M.D.	(30.8)
85	Camden, NJ M.D.	26.8
60	Canton, OH	48.0
73	Cape Coral-Fort Myers, FL	35.6
191	Cape Girardeau, MO-IL	(9.1)
NA	Carson City, NV***	NA
255	Casper, WY	(33.3)
132	Cedar Rapids, IA	0.0
NA	Champaign-Urbana, IL**	NA

RANK	METROPOLITAN AREA	% CHANGE
NA	Charleston, WV**	NA
NA	Charlotte-Gastonia, NC-SC**	NA
165	Charlottesville, VA	(3.3)
71	Chattanooga, TN-GA	39.1
NA	Cheyenne, WY***	NA
NA	Chicago (greater), IL-IN-WI**	NA
NA	Chicago-Joilet-Naperville, IL M.D.**	NA
109	Chico, CA	12.5
114	Cincinnati-Middletown, OH-KY-IN	9.5
253	Clarksville, TN-KY	(32.2)
154	Cleveland-Elyria-Mentor, OH	(2.0)
NA	Cleveland, TN***	NA
270	College Station-Bryan, TX	(43.2)
83	Colorado Springs, CO	27.0
168	Columbia, MO	(4.2)
NA	Columbus, GA-AL**	NA
NA	Columbus, IN***	NA
153	Columbus, OH	(1.7)
211	Corpus Christi, TX	(18.0)
NA	Corvallis, OR***	NA
79	Crestview-Fort Walton Beach, FL	29.4
NA	Cumberland, MD-WV**	NA
169	Dallas (greater), TX	(4.3)
155	Dallas-Plano-Irving, TX M.D.	(2.1)
295	Dalton, GA	(63.2)
9	Danville, IL	184.6
193	Danville, VA	(9.7)
NA	Davenport, IA-IL**	NA
88	Dayton, OH	24.5
NA	Decatur, AL**	NA
16	Decatur, IL	136.8
79	Deltona-Daytona Beach, FL	29.4
120	Denver-Aurora, CO	8.0
132	Des Moines-West Des Moines, IA	0.0
NA	Detroit (greater), MI**	NA
112	Detroit-Livonia-Dearborn, MI M.D.	11.5
NA	Dothan, AL**	NA
102	Dover, DE	16.2
NA	Dubuque, IA***	NA
228	Duluth, MN-WI	(21.4)
131	Durham-Chapel Hill, NC	1.4
305	Eau Claire, WI	(100.0)
245	Edison, NJ M.D.	(29.4)
177	El Centro, CA	(5.6)
14	El Paso, TX	144.4
NA	Elizabethtown, KY***	NA
301	Elmira, NY	(76.1)
262	Erie, PA	(39.1)
NA	Eugene-Springfield, OR**	NA
209	Evansville, IN-KY	(17.4)
NA	Fairbanks, AK***	NA
285	Fargo, ND-MN	(50.0)
93	Farmington, NM	18.8
69	Fayetteville, NC	41.3
234	Flagstaff, AZ	(22.9)
118	Flint, MI	8.7
NA	Florence-Muscle Shoals, AL**	NA
257	Florence, SC	(35.6)
21	Fond du Lac, WI	100.0
NA	Fort Collins-Loveland, CO***	NA

RANK	METROPOLITAN AREA	% CHANGE
179	Fort Lauderdale, FL M.D.	(5.7)
259	Fort Smith, AR-OK	(36.2)
129	Fort Wayne, IN	3.3
196	Fort Worth-Arlington, TX M.D.	(10.4)
218	Fresno, CA	(19.1)
NA	Gadsden, AL**	NA
132	Gainesville, FL	0.0
82	Gainesville, GA	28.6
NA	Gary, IN M.D.**	NA
NA	Glens Falls, NY***	NA
105	Goldsboro, NC	15.7
305	Grand Forks, ND-MN	(100.0)
132	Grand Junction, CO	0.0
95	Grand Rapids-Wyoming, MI	18.2
NA	Great Falls, MT**	NA
32	Greeley, CO	91.7
248	Green Bay, WI	(30.0)
69	Greenville, SC	41.3
42	Gulfport-Biloxi, MS	68.0
2	Hagerstown-Martinsburg, MD-WV	371.4
12	Hanford-Corcoran, CA	160.0
130	Harrisburg-Carlisle, PA	2.9
21	Harrisonburg, VA	100.0
231	Hartford, CT	(22.2)
41	Hickory, NC	68.6
276	Hinesville, GA	(47.4)
NA	Holland-Grand Haven, MI***	NA
292	Hot Springs, AR	(54.4)
288	Houma, LA	(50.8)
NA	Houston, TX**	NA
NA	Huntsville, AL**	NA
30	Idaho Falls, ID	95.7
NA	Indianapolis, IN**	NA
49	Iowa City, IA	53.8
198	Jacksonville, FL	(11.1)
NA	Jacksonville, NC**	NA
99	Jackson, MS	17.3
37	Jackson, TN	75.0
132	Janesville, WI	0.0
38	Jefferson City, MO	74.1
92	Johnson City, TN	20.0
132	Johnstown, PA	0.0
221	Jonesboro, AR	(19.5)
132	Joplin, MO	0.0
NA	Kankakee-Bradley, IL**	NA
NA	Kansas City, MO-KS**	NA
174	Kennewick-Pasco-Richland, WA	(5.0)
156	Killeen-Temple-Fort Hood, TX	(2.3)
261	Kingsport, TN-VA	(37.0)
132	Kingston, NY	0.0
167	Knoxville, TN	(4.0)
43	Kokomo, IN	66.7
305	La Crosse, WI-MN	(100.0)
55	Lafayette, IN	50.0
269	Lafayette, LA	(42.7)
NA	Lake Co.-Kenosha Co., IL-WI M.D.**	NA
NA	Lake Havasu City-Kingman, AZ**	NA
222	Lakeland, FL	(19.6)
243	Lancaster, PA	(27.8)
66	Lansing-East Lansing, MI	44.4

Note: All listings are for Metropolitan Statistical Areas (M.S.A.s) except for those ending with "M.D." Listings with "M.D." are Metropolitan Divisions which are smaller parts of eleven large M.S.A.s. See explanatory note at beginning of metropolitan area section.

Alpha Order - Metro Area (continued)

RANK	METROPOLITAN AREA	% CHANGE
172	Laredo, TX	(4.4)
228	Las Cruces, NM	(21.4)
247	Las Vegas-Paradise, NV	(29.9)
132	Lawrence, KS	0.0
65	Lawton, OK	45.5
302	Lebanon, PA	(81.6)
75	Lewiston-Auburn, ME	32.1
NA	Lexington-Fayette, KY**	NA
289	Lima, OH	(51.3)
33	Lincoln, NE	85.7
47	Little Rock, AR	55.6
132	Logan, UT-ID	0.0
281	Longview, TX	(47.9)
21	Longview, WA	100.0
192	Los Angeles County, CA M.D.	(9.5)
184	Los Angeles (greater), CA	(7.5)
195	Louisville, KY-IN	(10.2)
124	Lubbock, TX	5.6
297	Lynchburg, VA	(64.1)
260	Macon, GA	(36.7)
285	Madera, CA	(50.0)
21	Madison, WI	100.0
8	Manchester-Nashua, NH	185.7
216	Manhattan, KS	(18.8)
299	Mankato-North Mankato, MN	(68.8)
238	Mansfield, OH	(25.0)
169	McAllen-Edinburg-Mission, TX	(4.3)
4	Medford, OR	226.7
90	Memphis, TN-MS-AR	23.3
282	Merced, CA	(48.6)
185	Miami (greater), FL	(7.6)
166	Miami-Dade County, FL M.D.	(3.4)
223	Michigan City-La Porte, IN	(20.0)
31	Midland, TX	95.5
187	Milwaukee, WI	(7.8)
238	Minneapolis-St. Paul, MN-WI	(25.0)
NA	Missoula, MT**	NA
51	Mobile, AL	52.7
103	Modesto, CA	16.1
273	Monroe, LA	(44.0)
49	Monroe, MI	53.8
NA	Montgomery, AL**	NA
283	Morristown, TN	(48.8)
NA	Mount Vernon-Anacortes, WA***	NA
NA	Muncie, IN***	NA
36	Muskegon-Norton Shores, MI	78.3
58	Myrtle Beach, SC	49.2
63	Napa, CA	46.7
190	Naples-Marco Island, FL	(8.8)
226	Nashville-Davidson, TN	(21.0)
252	Nassau-Suffolk, NY M.D.	(32.1)
89	New Haven-Milford, CT	24.0
108	New Orleans, LA	13.9
169	New York (greater), NY-NJ-PA	(4.3)
177	New York-W. Plains NY-NJ M.D.	(5.6)
104	Newark-Union, NJ-PA M.D.	15.9
87	North Port-Bradenton-Sarasota, FL	25.0
161	Norwich-New London, CT	(2.9)
151	Oakland-Fremont, CA M.D.	(1.3)
47	Ocala, FL	55.6
291	Ocean City, NJ	(52.4)
53	Odessa, TX	51.9
182	Ogden-Clearfield, UT	(6.7)

RANK	METROPOLITAN AREA	% CHANGE
117	Oklahoma City, OK	8.8
132	Olympia, WA	0.0
81	Omaha-Council Bluffs, NE-IA	28.9
101	Orlando, FL	16.7
NA	Oshkosh-Neenah, WI**	NA
285	Owensboro, KY	(50.0)
212	Oxnard-Thousand Oaks, CA	(18.2)
241	Palm Bay-Melbourne, FL	(27.0)
NA	Palm Coast, FL***	NA
160	Panama City-Lynn Haven, FL	(2.8)
215	Pascagoula, MS	(18.4)
183	Peabody, MA M.D.	(6.9)
276	Pensacola, FL	(47.4)
233	Peoria, IL	(22.7)
127	Philadelphia (greater) PA-NJ-MD-DE	3.8
125	Philadelphia, PA M.D.	5.5
197	Phoenix-Mesa-Scottsdale, AZ	(10.9)
44	Pine Bluff, AR	64.4
218	Pittsburgh, PA	(19.1)
3	Pittsfield, MA	275.0
6	Pocatello, ID	200.0
123	Port St. Lucie, FL	6.2
NA	Portland-Vancouver, OR-WA**	NA
276	Portland, ME	(47.4)
279	Poughkeepsie, NY	(47.8)
15	Prescott, AZ	139.4
212	Provo-Orem, UT	(18.2)
NA	Pueblo, CO**	NA
21	Punta Gorda, FL	100.0
194	Racine, WI	(10.0)
235	Raleigh-Cary, NC	(23.5)
162	Rapid City, SD	(3.1)
67	Reading, PA	43.8
20	Redding, CA	106.3
74	Reno-Sparks, NV	33.3
231	Richmond, VA	(22.2)
172	Riverside-San Bernardino, CA	(4.4)
284	Roanoke, VA	(49.2)
132	Rochester, MN	0.0
207	Rochester, NY	(16.3)
94	Rockford, IL	18.5
303	Rockingham County, NH M.D.	(85.7)
107	Rocky Mount, NC	14.7
46	Rome, GA	59.4
126	Sacramento, CA	4.8
21	Saginaw, MI	100.0
18	Salem, OR	130.8
237	Salinas, CA	(24.3)
279	Salisbury, MD	(47.8)
242	Salt Lake City, UT	(27.6)
305	San Angelo, TX	(100.0)
119	San Antonio, TX	8.5
95	San Diego, CA	18.2
163	San Francisco (greater), CA	(3.2)
174	San Francisco-S. Mateo, CA M.D.	(5.0)
17	San Jose, CA	135.7
212	San Luis Obispo, CA	(18.2)
NA	Sandusky, OH***	NA
116	Santa Ana-Anaheim, CA M.D.	9.1
204	Santa Barbara-Santa Maria, CA	(14.8)
251	Santa Cruz-Watsonville, CA	(30.9)
294	Santa Fe, NM	(59.1)
39	Santa Rosa-Petaluma, CA	69.2

RANK	METROPOLITAN AREA	% CHANGE
78	Savannah, GA	30.8
91	Scranton--Wilkes-Barre, PA	22.7
188	Seattle (greater), WA	(8.7)
205	Seattle-Bellevue-Everett, WA M.D.	(15.0)
NA	Sebastian-Vero Beach, FL***	NA
NA	Sheboygan, WI**	NA
293	Sherman-Denison, TX	(54.9)
NA	Sioux City, IA-NE-SD***	NA
35	Sioux Falls, SD	83.3
21	South Bend-Mishawaka, IN-MI	100.0
220	Spartanburg, SC	(19.2)
263	Spokane, WA	(40.0)
156	Springfield, IL	(2.3)
159	Springfield, MA	(2.7)
248	Springfield, MO	(30.0)
236	Springfield, OH	(24.1)
132	State College, PA	0.0
72	Stockton, CA	35.9
305	St. Cloud, MN	(100.0)
272	St. Joseph, MO-KS	(43.6)
158	St. Louis, MO-IL	(2.6)
11	Sumter, SC	173.7
254	Syracuse, NY	(32.4)
180	Tacoma, WA M.D.	(5.9)
186	Tallahassee, FL	(7.7)
115	Tampa-St Petersburg, FL	9.3
NA	Terre Haute, IN**	NA
13	Texarkana, TX-Texarkana, AR	148.3
52	Toledo, OH	52.5
121	Topeka, KS	6.7
86	Trenton-Ewing, NJ	25.9
181	Tucson, AZ	(6.3)
122	Tulsa, OK	6.3
NA	Tuscaloosa, AL**	NA
266	Tyler, TX	(41.3)
109	Utica-Rome, NY	12.5
55	Valdosta, GA	50.0
198	Vallejo-Fairfield, CA	(11.1)
296	Victoria, TX	(63.8)
132	Virginia Beach-Norfolk, VA-NC	0.0
113	Visalia-Porterville, CA	11.2
76	Waco, TX	31.6
267	Warner Robins, GA	(41.7)
NA	Warren-Farmington Hills, MI M.D.**	NA
208	Washington (greater) DC-VA-MD-WV	(17.0)
202	Washington, DC-VA-MD-WV M.D.	(14.5)
132	Waterloo-Cedar Falls, IA	0.0
132	Wausau, WI	0.0
1	Wenatchee, WA	488.9
230	West Palm Beach, FL M.D.	(21.9)
304	Wichita Falls, TX	(87.5)
40	Wichita, KS	69.0
275	Williamsport, PA	(47.1)
244	Wilmington, DE-MD-NJ M.D.	(27.9)
63	Wilmington, NC	46.7
67	Winchester, VA-WV	43.8
100	Winston-Salem, NC	17.1
98	Worcester, MA	17.6
256	Yakima, WA	(35.0)
34	York-Hanover, PA	84.0
111	Yuba City, CA	11.9
54	Yuma, AZ	51.1

Source: CQ Press using reported data from the F.B.I. "Crime in the United States 2011"
*Includes nonnegligent manslaughter. **Not available. ***These metro areas had murder rates of 0 in 2010 but had at least one murder in 2011. Calculating percent increase from zero results in an infinite number. This is shown as "NA."

Rank Order - Metro Area

11. Percent Change in Murder Rate: 2010 to 2011 (continued)
National Percent Change = 1.5% Decrease*

RANK	METROPOLITAN AREA	% CHANGE	RANK	METROPOLITAN AREA	% CHANGE	RANK	METROPOLITAN AREA	% CHANGE
1	Wenatchee, WA	488.9	61	Bloomington, IN	47.6	121	Topeka, KS	6.7
2	Hagerstown-Martinsburg, MD-WV	371.4	62	Asheville, NC	47.4	122	Tulsa, OK	6.3
3	Pittsfield, MA	275.0	63	Napa, CA	46.7	123	Port St. Lucie, FL	6.2
4	Medford, OR	226.7	63	Wilmington, NC	46.7	124	Lubbock, TX	5.6
5	Bay City, MI	211.1	65	Lawton, OK	45.5	125	Philadelphia, PA M.D.	5.5
6	Bremerton-Silverdale, WA	200.0	66	Lansing-East Lansing, MI	44.4	126	Sacramento, CA	4.8
6	Pocatello, ID	200.0	67	Reading, PA	43.8	127	Philadelphia (greater) PA-NJ-MD-DE	3.8
8	Manchester-Nashua, NH	185.7	67	Winchester, VA-WV	43.8	128	Brunswick, GA	3.4
9	Danville, IL	184.6	69	Fayetteville, NC	41.3	129	Fort Wayne, IN	3.3
10	Barnstable Town, MA	180.0	69	Greenville, SC	41.3	130	Harrisburg-Carlisle, PA	2.9
11	Sumter, SC	173.7	71	Chattanooga, TN-GA	39.1	131	Durham-Chapel Hill, NC	1.4
12	Hanford-Corcoran, CA	160.0	72	Stockton, CA	35.9	132	Albany-Schenectady-Troy, NY	0.0
13	Texarkana, TX-Texarkana, AR	148.3	73	Cape Coral-Fort Myers, FL	35.6	132	Anchorage, AK	0.0
14	El Paso, TX	144.4	74	Reno-Sparks, NV	33.3	132	Atlantic City, NJ	0.0
15	Prescott, AZ	139.4	75	Lewiston-Auburn, ME	32.1	132	Cedar Rapids, IA	0.0
16	Decatur, IL	136.8	76	Waco, TX	31.6	132	Des Moines-West Des Moines, IA	0.0
17	San Jose, CA	135.7	77	Battle Creek, MI	31.1	132	Gainesville, FL	0.0
18	Salem, OR	130.8	78	Savannah, GA	30.8	132	Grand Junction, CO	0.0
19	Bangor, ME	125.0	79	Crestview-Fort Walton Beach, FL	29.4	132	Janesville, WI	0.0
20	Redding, CA	106.3	79	Deltona-Daytona Beach, FL	29.4	132	Johnstown, PA	0.0
21	Altoona, PA	100.0	81	Omaha-Council Bluffs, NE-IA	28.9	132	Joplin, MO	0.0
21	Bloomington-Normal, IL	100.0	82	Gainesville, GA	28.6	132	Kingston, NY	0.0
21	Fond du Lac, WI	100.0	83	Akron, OH	27.0	132	Lawrence, KS	0.0
21	Harrisonburg, VA	100.0	83	Colorado Springs, CO	27.0	132	Logan, UT-ID	0.0
21	Longview, WA	100.0	85	Camden, NJ M.D.	26.8	132	Olympia, WA	0.0
21	Madison, WI	100.0	86	Trenton-Ewing, NJ	25.9	132	Rochester, MN	0.0
21	Punta Gorda, FL	100.0	87	North Port-Bradenton-Sarasota, FL	25.0	132	State College, PA	0.0
21	Saginaw, MI	100.0	88	Dayton, OH	24.5	132	Virginia Beach-Norfolk, VA-NC	0.0
21	South Bend-Mishawaka, IN-MI	100.0	89	New Haven-Milford, CT	24.0	132	Waterloo-Cedar Falls, IA	0.0
30	Idaho Falls, ID	95.7	90	Memphis, TN-MS-AR	23.3	132	Wausau, WI	0.0
31	Midland, TX	95.5	91	Scranton--Wilkes-Barre, PA	22.7	151	Oakland-Fremont, CA M.D.	(1.3)
32	Greeley, CO	91.7	92	Johnson City, TN	20.0	152	Atlanta, GA	(1.6)
33	Lincoln, NE	85.7	93	Farmington, NM	18.8	153	Columbus, OH	(1.7)
34	York-Hanover, PA	84.0	94	Rockford, IL	18.5	154	Cleveland-Elyria-Mentor, OH	(2.0)
35	Sioux Falls, SD	83.3	95	Grand Rapids-Wyoming, MI	18.2	155	Dallas-Plano-Irving, TX M.D.	(2.1)
36	Muskegon-Norton Shores, MI	78.3	95	San Diego, CA	18.2	156	Killeen-Temple-Fort Hood, TX	(2.3)
37	Jackson, TN	75.0	97	Beaumont-Port Arthur, TX	17.9	156	Springfield, IL	(2.3)
38	Jefferson City, MO	74.1	98	Worcester, MA	17.6	158	St. Louis, MO-IL	(2.6)
39	Santa Rosa-Petaluma, CA	69.2	99	Jackson, MS	17.3	159	Springfield, MA	(2.7)
40	Wichita, KS	69.0	100	Winston-Salem, NC	17.1	160	Panama City-Lynn Haven, FL	(2.8)
41	Hickory, NC	68.6	101	Orlando, FL	16.7	161	Norwich-New London, CT	(2.9)
42	Gulfport-Biloxi, MS	68.0	102	Dover, DE	16.2	162	Rapid City, SD	(3.1)
43	Kokomo, IN	66.7	103	Modesto, CA	16.1	163	Abilene, TX	(3.2)
44	Pine Bluff, AR	64.4	104	Newark-Union, NJ-PA M.D.	15.9	163	San Francisco (greater), CA	(3.2)
45	Ann Arbor, MI	64.3	105	Goldsboro, NC	15.7	165	Charlottesville, VA	(3.3)
46	Rome, GA	59.4	106	Albany, GA	14.9	166	Miami-Dade County, FL M.D.	(3.4)
47	Little Rock, AR	55.6	107	Rocky Mount, NC	14.7	167	Knoxville, TN	(4.0)
47	Ocala, FL	55.6	108	New Orleans, LA	13.9	168	Columbia, MO	(4.2)
49	Iowa City, IA	53.8	109	Chico, CA	12.5	169	Dallas (greater), TX	(4.3)
49	Monroe, MI	53.8	109	Utica-Rome, NY	12.5	169	McAllen-Edinburg-Mission, TX	(4.3)
51	Mobile, AL	52.7	111	Yuba City, CA	11.9	169	New York (greater), NY-NJ-PA	(4.3)
52	Toledo, OH	52.5	112	Detroit-Livonia-Dearborn, MI M.D.	11.5	172	Laredo, TX	(4.4)
53	Odessa, TX	51.9	113	Visalia-Porterville, CA	11.2	172	Riverside-San Bernardino, CA	(4.4)
54	Yuma, AZ	51.1	114	Cincinnati-Middletown, OH-KY-IN	9.5	174	Kennewick-Pasco-Richland, WA	(5.0)
55	Bismarck, ND	50.0	115	Tampa-St Petersburg, FL	9.3	174	San Francisco-S. Mateo, CA M.D.	(5.0)
55	Lafayette, IN	50.0	116	Santa Ana-Anaheim, CA M.D.	9.1	176	Bridgeport-Stamford, CT	(5.3)
55	Valdosta, GA	50.0	117	Oklahoma City, OK	8.8	177	El Centro, CA	(5.6)
58	Myrtle Beach, SC	49.2	118	Flint, MI	8.7	177	New York-W. Plains NY-NJ M.D.	(5.6)
59	Anderson, SC	49.1	119	San Antonio, TX	8.5	179	Fort Lauderdale, FL M.D.	(5.7)
60	Canton, OH	48.0	120	Denver-Aurora, CO	8.0	180	Tacoma, WA M.D.	(5.9)

Note: All listings are for Metropolitan Statistical Areas (M.S.A.s) except for those ending with "M.D." Listings with "M.D." are Metropolitan Divisions which are smaller parts of eleven large M.S.A.s. See explanatory note at beginning of metropolitan area section.

Rank Order - Metro Area (continued)

RANK	METROPOLITAN AREA	% CHANGE
181	Tucson, AZ	(6.3)
182	Ogden-Clearfield, UT	(6.7)
183	Peabody, MA M.D.	(6.9)
184	Los Angeles (greater), CA	(7.5)
185	Miami (greater), FL	(7.6)
186	Tallahassee, FL	(7.7)
187	Milwaukee, WI	(7.8)
188	Baltimore-Towson, MD	(8.7)
188	Seattle (greater), WA	(8.7)
190	Naples-Marco Island, FL	(8.8)
191	Cape Girardeau, MO-IL	(9.1)
192	Los Angeles County, CA M.D.	(9.5)
193	Danville, VA	(9.7)
194	Racine, WI	(10.0)
195	Louisville, KY-IN	(10.2)
196	Fort Worth-Arlington, TX M.D.	(10.4)
197	Phoenix-Mesa-Scottsdale, AZ	(10.9)
198	Jacksonville, FL	(11.1)
198	Vallejo-Fairfield, CA	(11.1)
200	Augusta, GA-SC	(12.7)
201	Albuquerque, NM	(13.8)
202	Washington, DC-VA-MD-WV M.D.	(14.5)
203	Austin-Round Rock, TX	(14.7)
204	Santa Barbara-Santa Maria, CA	(14.8)
205	Seattle-Bellevue-Everett, WA M.D.	(15.0)
206	Boston-Quincy, MA M.D.	(15.5)
207	Rochester, NY	(16.3)
208	Washington (greater) DC-VA-MD-WV	(17.0)
209	Evansville, IN-KY	(17.4)
210	Amarillo, TX	(17.5)
211	Corpus Christi, TX	(18.0)
212	Oxnard-Thousand Oaks, CA	(18.2)
212	Provo-Orem, UT	(18.2)
212	San Luis Obispo, CA	(18.2)
215	Pascagoula, MS	(18.4)
216	Boise City-Nampa, ID	(18.8)
216	Manhattan, KS	(18.8)
218	Fresno, CA	(19.1)
218	Pittsburgh, PA	(19.1)
220	Spartanburg, SC	(19.2)
221	Jonesboro, AR	(19.5)
222	Lakeland, FL	(19.6)
223	Allentown, PA-NJ	(20.0)
223	Boston (greater), MA-NH	(20.0)
223	Michigan City-La Porte, IN	(20.0)
226	Nashville-Davidson, TN	(21.0)
227	Bethesda-Frederick, MD M.D.	(21.1)
228	Duluth, MN-WI	(21.4)
228	Las Cruces, NM	(21.4)
230	West Palm Beach, FL M.D.	(21.9)
231	Hartford, CT	(22.2)
231	Richmond, VA	(22.2)
233	Peoria, IL	(22.7)
234	Flagstaff, AZ	(22.9)
235	Raleigh-Cary, NC	(23.5)
236	Springfield, OH	(24.1)
237	Salinas, CA	(24.3)
238	Mansfield, OH	(25.0)
238	Minneapolis-St. Paul, MN-WI	(25.0)
240	Athens-Clarke County, GA	(26.2)
241	Palm Bay-Melbourne, FL	(27.0)
242	Salt Lake City, UT	(27.6)
243	Lancaster, PA	(27.8)
244	Wilmington, DE-MD-NJ M.D.	(27.9)
245	Edison, NJ M.D.	(29.4)
246	Brownsville-Harlingen, TX	(29.6)
247	Las Vegas-Paradise, NV	(29.9)
248	Green Bay, WI	(30.0)
248	Springfield, MO	(30.0)
250	Cambridge-Newton, MA M.D.	(30.8)
251	Santa Cruz-Watsonville, CA	(30.9)
252	Nassau-Suffolk, NY M.D.	(32.1)
253	Clarksville, TN-KY	(32.2)
254	Syracuse, NY	(32.4)
255	Casper, WY	(33.3)
256	Yakima, WA	(35.0)
257	Florence, SC	(35.6)
258	Buffalo-Niagara Falls, NY	(36.1)
259	Fort Smith, AR-OK	(36.2)
260	Macon, GA	(36.7)
261	Kingsport, TN-VA	(37.0)
262	Erie, PA	(39.1)
263	Bakersfield, CA	(40.0)
263	Bellingham, WA	(40.0)
263	Spokane, WA	(40.0)
266	Tyler, TX	(41.3)
267	Warner Robins, GA	(41.7)
268	Blacksburg, VA	(41.9)
269	Lafayette, LA	(42.7)
270	College Station-Bryan, TX	(43.2)
271	Boulder, CO	(43.5)
272	St. Joseph, MO-KS	(43.6)
273	Monroe, LA	(44.0)
274	Alexandria, LA	(44.8)
275	Williamsport, PA	(47.1)
276	Hinesville, GA	(47.4)
276	Pensacola, FL	(47.4)
276	Portland, ME	(47.4)
279	Poughkeepsie, NY	(47.8)
279	Salisbury, MD	(47.8)
281	Longview, TX	(47.9)
282	Merced, CA	(48.6)
283	Morristown, TN	(48.8)
284	Roanoke, VA	(49.2)
285	Fargo, ND-MN	(50.0)
285	Madera, CA	(50.0)
285	Owensboro, KY	(50.0)
288	Houma, LA	(50.8)
289	Lima, OH	(51.3)
290	Binghamton, NY	(52.0)
291	Ocean City, NJ	(52.4)
292	Hot Springs, AR	(54.4)
293	Sherman-Denison, TX	(54.9)
294	Santa Fe, NM	(59.1)
295	Dalton, GA	(63.2)
296	Victoria, TX	(63.8)
297	Lynchburg, VA	(64.1)
298	Burlington, NC	(66.1)
299	Mankato-North Mankato, MN	(68.8)
300	Bend, OR	(69.8)
301	Elmira, NY	(76.1)
302	Lebanon, PA	(81.6)
303	Rockingham County, NH M.D.	(85.7)
304	Wichita Falls, TX	(87.5)
305	Ames, IA	(100.0)
305	Eau Claire, WI	(100.0)
305	Grand Forks, ND-MN	(100.0)
305	La Crosse, WI-MN	(100.0)
305	San Angelo, TX	(100.0)
305	St. Cloud, MN	(100.0)
NA	Anniston-Oxford, AL**	NA
NA	Appleton, WI***	NA
NA	Auburn, AL**	NA
NA	Baton Rouge, LA**	NA
NA	Billings, MT**	NA
NA	Birmingham-Hoover, AL**	NA
NA	Bowling Green, KY***	NA
NA	Carson City, NV***	NA
NA	Champaign-Urbana, IL**	NA
NA	Charleston, WV**	NA
NA	Charlotte-Gastonia, NC-SC**	NA
NA	Cheyenne, WY***	NA
NA	Chicago (greater), IL-IN-WI**	NA
NA	Chicago-Joilet-Naperville, IL M.D.**	NA
NA	Cleveland, TN***	NA
NA	Columbus, GA-AL**	NA
NA	Columbus, IN***	NA
NA	Corvallis, OR***	NA
NA	Cumberland, MD-WV**	NA
NA	Davenport, IA-IL**	NA
NA	Decatur, AL**	NA
NA	Detroit (greater), MI**	NA
NA	Dothan, AL**	NA
NA	Dubuque, IA***	NA
NA	Elizabethtown, KY***	NA
NA	Eugene-Springfield, OR**	NA
NA	Fairbanks, AK***	NA
NA	Florence-Muscle Shoals, AL**	NA
NA	Fort Collins-Loveland, CO***	NA
NA	Gadsden, AL**	NA
NA	Gary, IN M.D.**	NA
NA	Glens Falls, NY***	NA
NA	Great Falls, MT**	NA
NA	Holland-Grand Haven, MI***	NA
NA	Houston, TX**	NA
NA	Huntsville, AL**	NA
NA	Indianapolis, IN**	NA
NA	Jacksonville, NC**	NA
NA	Kankakee-Bradley, IL**	NA
NA	Kansas City, MO-KS**	NA
NA	Lake Co.-Kenosha Co., IL-WI M.D.**	NA
NA	Lake Havasu City-Kingman, AZ**	NA
NA	Lexington-Fayette, KY**	NA
NA	Missoula, MT**	NA
NA	Montgomery, AL**	NA
NA	Mount Vernon-Anacortes, WA***	NA
NA	Muncie, IN***	NA
NA	Oshkosh-Neenah, WI**	NA
NA	Palm Coast, FL***	NA
NA	Portland-Vancouver, OR-WA**	NA
NA	Pueblo, CO**	NA
NA	Sandusky, OH***	NA
NA	Sebastian-Vero Beach, FL***	NA
NA	Sheboygan, WI**	NA
NA	Sioux City, IA-NE-SD***	NA
NA	Terre Haute, IN**	NA
NA	Tuscaloosa, AL**	NA
NA	Warren-Farmington Hills, MI M.D.**	NA

Source: CQ Press using reported data from the F.B.I. "Crime in the United States 2011"
*Includes nonnegligent manslaughter. **Not available. ***These metro areas had murder rates of 0 in 2010 but had at least one murder in 2011. Calculating percent increase from zero results in an infinite number. This is shown as "NA."

Alpha Order - Metro Area

12. Percent Change in Murder Rate: 2007 to 2011
National Percent Change = 17.4% Decrease*

RANK	METROPOLITAN AREA	% CHANGE	RANK	METROPOLITAN AREA	% CHANGE	RANK	METROPOLITAN AREA	% CHANGE
278	Abilene, TX	(52.4)	20	Charleston, WV	138.5	261	Fort Lauderdale, FL M.D.	(43.1)
61	Akron, OH	30.6	227	Charlotte-Gastonia, NC-SC	(32.4)	89	Fort Smith, AR-OK	11.1
103	Albany-Schenectady-Troy, NY	0.0	87	Charlottesville, VA	11.5	123	Fort Wayne, IN	(1.6)
92	Albany, GA	9.9	38	Chattanooga, TN-GA	77.8	135	Fort Worth-Arlington, TX M.D.	(4.4)
248	Albuquerque, NM	(39.0)	34	Cheyenne, WY	83.3	225	Fresno, CA	(32.1)
277	Alexandria, LA	(52.2)	NA	Chicago (greater), IL-IN-WI**	NA	NA	Gadsden, AL**	NA
249	Allentown, PA-NJ	(39.1)	NA	Chicago-Joilet-Naperville, IL M.D.**	NA	39	Gainesville, FL	69.0
230	Altoona, PA	(33.3)	159	Chico, CA	(14.3)	73	Gainesville, GA	22.7
250	Amarillo, TX	(39.7)	126	Cincinnati-Middletown, OH-KY-IN	(2.1)	NA	Gary, IN M.D.**	NA
303	Ames, IA	(100.0)	217	Clarksville, TN-KY	(29.8)	20	Glens Falls, NY	138.5
255	Anchorage, AK	(41.7)	181	Cleveland-Elyria-Mentor, OH	(21.3)	272	Goldsboro, NC	(50.9)
14	Anderson, SC	182.1	24	Cleveland, TN	122.2	303	Grand Forks, ND-MN	(100.0)
57	Ann Arbor, MI	35.3	255	College Station-Bryan, TX	(41.7)	59	Grand Junction, CO	33.3
NA	Anniston-Oxford, AL**	NA	133	Colorado Springs, CO	(4.1)	199	Grand Rapids-Wyoming, MI	(25.7)
35	Appleton, WI	80.0	212	Columbia, MO	(28.1)	NA	Great Falls, MT**	NA
267	Asheville, NC	(46.2)	NA	Columbus, GA-AL**	NA	170	Greeley, CO	(17.9)
274	Athens-Clarke County, GA	(51.6)	276	Columbus, IN	(51.9)	267	Green Bay, WI	(46.2)
220	Atlanta, GA	(31.0)	94	Columbus, OH	5.6	103	Greenville, SC	0.0
47	Atlantic City, NJ	45.5	196	Corpus Christi, TX	(25.5)	NA	Gulfport-Biloxi, MS**	NA
NA	Auburn, AL**	NA	51	Corvallis, OR	40.0	NA	Hagerstown-Martinsburg, MD-WV**	NA
67	Augusta, GA-SC	27.1	103	Crestview-Fort Walton Beach, FL	0.0	90	Hanford-Corcoran, CA	10.6
98	Austin-Round Rock, TX	3.6	NA	Cumberland, MD-WV**	NA	148	Harrisburg-Carlisle, PA	(10.0)
159	Bakersfield, CA	(14.3)	187	Dallas (greater), TX	(23.7)	NA	Harrisonburg, VA***	NA
218	Baltimore-Towson, MD	(29.9)	215	Dallas-Plano-Irving, TX M.D.	(29.2)	189	Hartford, CT	(23.9)
26	Bangor, ME	114.3	243	Dalton, GA	(36.4)	83	Hickory, NC	13.5
42	Barnstable Town, MA	55.6	NA	Danville, IL**	NA	189	Hinesville, GA	(23.9)
234	Baton Rouge, LA	(33.5)	78	Danville, VA	20.0	NA	Holland-Grand Haven, MI**	NA
203	Battle Creek, MI	(26.3)	NA	Davenport, IA-IL**	NA	288	Hot Springs, AR	(60.6)
191	Bay City, MI	(24.3)	63	Dayton, OH	29.8	271	Houma, LA	(50.8)
159	Beaumont-Port Arthur, TX	(14.3)	NA	Decatur, AL***	NA	NA	Houston, TX**	NA
55	Bellingham, WA	36.4	NA	Decatur, IL**	NA	NA	Huntsville, AL**	NA
NA	Bend, OR***	NA	91	Deltona-Daytona Beach, FL	10.0	2	Idaho Falls, ID	462.5
237	Bethesda-Frederick, MD M.D.	(34.8)	178	Denver-Aurora, CO	(20.6)	180	Indianapolis, IN	(20.8)
NA	Billings, MT**	NA	71	Des Moines-West Des Moines, IA	23.1	NA	Iowa City, IA***	NA
193	Binghamton, NY	(25.0)	NA	Detroit (greater), MI**	NA	253	Jacksonville, FL	(40.7)
NA	Birmingham-Hoover, AL**	NA	141	Detroit-Livonia-Dearborn, MI M.D.	(7.7)	297	Jacksonville, NC	(69.4)
16	Bismarck, ND	170.0	NA	Dothan, AL**	NA	123	Jackson, MS	(1.6)
302	Blacksburg, VA	(91.5)	62	Dover, DE	30.3	206	Jackson, TN	(26.7)
NA	Bloomington-Normal, IL**	NA	103	Dubuque, IA	0.0	175	Janesville, WI	(19.4)
50	Bloomington, IN	40.9	206	Duluth, MN-WI	(26.7)	23	Jefferson City, MO	123.8
291	Boise City-Nampa, ID	(63.9)	NA	Durham-Chapel Hill, NC**	NA	48	Johnson City, TN	42.9
103	Boston (greater), MA-NH	0.0	303	Eau Claire, WI	(100.0)	27	Johnstown, PA	100.0
131	Boston-Quincy, MA M.D.	(3.9)	193	Edison, NJ M.D.	(25.0)	193	Jonesboro, AR	(25.0)
NA	Boulder, CO**	NA	224	El Centro, CA	(32.0)	290	Joplin, MO	(63.8)
17	Bowling Green, KY	166.7	171	El Paso, TX	(18.5)	NA	Kankakee-Bradley, IL**	NA
10	Bremerton-Silverdale, WA	200.0	244	Elizabethtown, KY	(37.0)	NA	Kansas City, MO-KS**	NA
53	Bridgeport-Stamford, CT	38.5	293	Elmira, NY	(67.6)	85	Kennewick-Pasco-Richland, WA	11.8
279	Brownsville-Harlingen, TX	(52.5)	42	Erie, PA	55.6	177	Killeen-Temple-Fort Hood, TX	(20.4)
296	Brunswick, GA	(69.0)	17	Eugene-Springfield, OR	166.7	87	Kingsport, TN-VA	11.5
205	Buffalo-Niagara Falls, NY	(26.4)	85	Evansville, IN-KY	11.8	221	Kingston, NY	(31.3)
294	Burlington, NC	(67.7)	NA	Fairbanks, AK**	NA	159	Knoxville, TN	(14.3)
103	Cambridge-Newton, MA M.D.	0.0	295	Fargo, ND-MN	(68.8)	3	Kokomo, IN	400.0
93	Camden, NJ M.D.	6.1	298	Farmington, NM	(69.6)	303	La Crosse, WI-MN	(100.0)
NA	Canton, OH**	NA	100	Fayetteville, NC	2.3	55	Lafayette, IN	36.4
188	Cape Coral-Fort Myers, FL	(23.8)	44	Flagstaff, AZ	54.2	284	Lafayette, LA	(54.3)
NA	Cape Girardeau, MO-IL**	NA	37	Flint, MI	78.6	NA	Lake Co.-Kenosha Co., IL-WI M.D.**	NA
4	Carson City, NV	300.0	NA	Florence-Muscle Shoals, AL**	NA	203	Lake Havasu City-Kingman, AZ	(26.3)
280	Casper, WY	(53.6)	286	Florence, SC	(55.0)	196	Lakeland, FL	(25.5)
230	Cedar Rapids, IA	(33.3)	NA	Fond du Lac, WI***	NA	265	Lancaster, PA	(45.8)
NA	Champaign-Urbana, IL**	NA	140	Fort Collins-Loveland, CO	(7.1)	166	Lansing-East Lansing, MI	(15.2)

Note: All listings are for Metropolitan Statistical Areas (M.S.A.s) except for those ending with "M.D." Listings with "M.D." are Metropolitan Divisions which are smaller parts of eleven large M.S.A.s. See explanatory note at beginning of metropolitan area section.

Alpha Order - Metro Area (continued)

RANK	METROPOLITAN AREA	% CHANGE
183	Laredo, TX	(21.8)
240	Las Cruces, NM	(35.3)
264	Las Vegas-Paradise, NV	(45.3)
303	Lawrence, KS	(100.0)
219	Lawton, OK	(30.4)
154	Lebanon, PA	(12.5)
103	Lewiston-Auburn, ME	0.0
NA	Lexington-Fayette, KY**	NA
103	Lima, OH	0.0
280	Lincoln, NE	(53.6)
200	Little Rock, AR	(25.8)
103	Logan, UT-ID	0.0
82	Longview, TX	13.6
68	Longview, WA	26.7
235	Los Angeles County, CA M.D.	(34.5)
229	Los Angeles (greater), CA	(32.9)
246	Louisville, KY-IN	(38.0)
230	Lubbock, TX	(33.3)
143	Lynchburg, VA	(8.0)
254	Macon, GA	(41.5)
129	Madera, CA	(2.9)
148	Madison, WI	(10.0)
NA	Manchester-Nashua, NH**	NA
NA	Manhattan, KS**	NA
NA	Mankato-North Mankato, MN**	NA
287	Mansfield, OH	(56.4)
158	McAllen-Edinburg-Mission, TX	(13.7)
9	Medford, OR	226.7
151	Memphis, TN-MS-AR	(10.9)
178	Merced, CA	(20.6)
183	Miami (greater), FL	(21.8)
146	Miami-Dade County, FL M.D.	(9.5)
259	Michigan City-La Porte, IN	(42.9)
58	Midland, TX	34.4
174	Milwaukee, WI	(19.2)
241	Minneapolis-St. Paul, MN-WI	(35.7)
NA	Missoula, MT**	NA
202	Mobile, AL	(26.1)
69	Modesto, CA	25.0
25	Monroe, LA	121.7
8	Monroe, MI	233.3
NA	Montgomery, AL**	NA
252	Morristown, TN	(40.5)
46	Mount Vernon-Anacortes, WA	47.1
32	Muncie, IN	88.9
1	Muskegon-Norton Shores, MI	583.3
36	Myrtle Beach, SC	79.6
273	Napa, CA	(51.1)
246	Naples-Marco Island, FL	(38.0)
211	Nashville-Davidson, TN	(27.9)
103	Nassau-Suffolk, NY M.D.	0.0
NA	New Haven-Milford, CT**	NA
167	New Orleans, LA	(16.0)
103	New York (greater), NY-NJ-PA	0.0
96	New York-W. Plains NY-NJ M.D.	4.1
130	Newark-Union, NJ-PA M.D.	(3.6)
NA	North Port-Bradenton-Sarasota, FL**	NA
NA	Norwich-New London, CT**	NA
192	Oakland-Fremont, CA M.D.	(24.8)
127	Ocala, FL	(2.3)
103	Ocean City, NJ	0.0
66	Odessa, TX	27.4
51	Ogden-Clearfield, UT	40.0
137	Oklahoma City, OK	(4.6)
242	Olympia, WA	(36.0)
101	Omaha-Council Bluffs, NE-IA	1.8
185	Orlando, FL	(22.2)
270	Oshkosh-Neenah, WI	(50.0)
NA	Owensboro, KY**	NA
159	Oxnard-Thousand Oaks, CA	(14.3)
283	Palm Bay-Melbourne, FL	(54.2)
299	Palm Coast, FL	(77.8)
48	Panama City-Lynn Haven, FL	42.9
289	Pascagoula, MS	(63.5)
73	Peabody, MA M.D.	22.7
201	Pensacola, FL	(25.9)
NA	Peoria, IL**	NA
164	Philadelphia (greater) PA-NJ-MD-DE	(14.7)
173	Philadelphia, PA M.D.	(18.6)
251	Phoenix-Mesa-Scottsdale, AZ	(40.2)
165	Pine Bluff, AR	(14.9)
153	Pittsburgh, PA	(11.6)
6	Pittsfield, MA	275.0
NA	Pocatello, ID***	NA
54	Port St. Lucie, FL	37.8
136	Portland-Vancouver, OR-WA	(4.5)
168	Portland, ME	(16.7)
216	Poughkeepsie, NY	(29.4)
14	Prescott, AZ	182.1
22	Provo-Orem, UT	125.0
NA	Pueblo, CO**	NA
300	Punta Gorda, FL	(81.5)
99	Racine, WI	2.9
209	Raleigh-Cary, NC	(27.8)
138	Rapid City, SD	(6.1)
60	Reading, PA	31.4
266	Redding, CA	(45.9)
97	Reno-Sparks, NV	3.7
238	Richmond, VA	(34.9)
228	Riverside-San Bernardino, CA	(32.8)
79	Roanoke, VA	18.5
285	Rochester, MN	(54.5)
196	Rochester, NY	(25.5)
NA	Rockford, IL**	NA
103	Rockingham County, NH M.D.	0.0
169	Rocky Mount, NC	(17.6)
76	Rome, GA	21.4
145	Sacramento, CA	(8.3)
236	Saginaw, MI	(34.6)
10	Salem, OR	200.0
80	Salinas, CA	14.1
84	Salisbury, MD	11.9
269	Salt Lake City, UT	(48.8)
303	San Angelo, TX	(100.0)
213	San Antonio, TX	(28.2)
209	San Diego, CA	(27.8)
222	San Francisco (greater), CA	(31.8)
263	San Francisco-S. Mateo, CA M.D.	(44.1)
81	San Jose, CA	13.8
148	San Luis Obispo, CA	(10.0)
103	Sandusky, OH	0.0
141	Santa Ana-Anaheim, CA M.D.	(7.7)
143	Santa Barbara-Santa Maria, CA	(8.0)
40	Santa Cruz-Watsonville, CA	58.3
NA	Santa Fe, NM**	NA
64	Santa Rosa-Petaluma, CA	29.4
121	Savannah, GA	(1.2)
139	Scranton--Wilkes-Barre, PA	(6.9)
226	Seattle (greater), WA	(32.3)
262	Seattle-Bellevue-Everett, WA M.D.	(43.3)
19	Sebastian-Vero Beach, FL	140.0
103	Sheboygan, WI	0.0
70	Sherman-Denison, TX	24.2
103	Sioux City, IA-NE-SD	0.0
41	Sioux Falls, SD	57.1
75	South Bend-Mishawaka, IN-MI	22.0
282	Spartanburg, SC	(53.8)
274	Spokane, WA	(51.6)
NA	Springfield, IL**	NA
176	Springfield, MA	(20.0)
154	Springfield, MO	(12.5)
245	Springfield, OH	(37.1)
303	State College, PA	(100.0)
30	Stockton, CA	89.4
303	St. Cloud, MN	(100.0)
29	St. Joseph, MO-KS	93.8
122	St. Louis, MO-IL	(1.3)
33	Sumter, SC	83.5
258	Syracuse, NY	(42.5)
103	Tacoma, WA M.D.	0.0
27	Tallahassee, FL	100.0
152	Tampa-St Petersburg, FL	(11.3)
NA	Terre Haute, IN**	NA
239	Texarkana, TX-Texarkana, AR	(35.1)
12	Toledo, OH	190.5
71	Topeka, KS	23.1
134	Trenton-Ewing, NJ	(4.2)
128	Tucson, AZ	(2.6)
156	Tulsa, OK	(12.8)
NA	Tuscaloosa, AL**	NA
147	Tyler, TX	(9.8)
208	Utica-Rome, NY	(27.0)
7	Valdosta, GA	256.3
132	Vallejo-Fairfield, CA	(4.0)
214	Victoria, TX	(28.6)
171	Virginia Beach-Norfolk, VA-NC	(18.5)
120	Visalia-Porterville, CA	(1.1)
65	Waco, TX	28.2
45	Warner Robins, GA	52.2
NA	Warren-Farmington Hills, MI M.D.**	NA
259	Washington (greater) DC-VA-MD-WV	(42.9)
257	Washington, DC-VA-MD-WV M.D.	(42.4)
186	Waterloo-Cedar Falls, IA	(22.6)
303	Wausau, WI	(100.0)
31	Wenatchee, WA	89.3
230	West Palm Beach, FL M.D.	(33.3)
301	Wichita Falls, TX	(85.4)
223	Wichita, KS	(31.9)
292	Williamsport, PA	(65.4)
125	Wilmington, DE-MD-NJ M.D.	(2.0)
182	Wilmington, NC	(21.4)
13	Winchester, VA-WV	187.5
NA	Winston-Salem, NC**	NA
157	Worcester, MA	(13.0)
102	Yakima, WA	1.6
77	York-Hanover, PA	21.1
5	Yuba City, CA	291.7
95	Yuma, AZ	4.4

Source: CQ Press using reported data from the F.B.I. "Crime in the United States 2011"
*Includes nonnegligent manslaughter. **Not available. ***These metro areas had murder rates of 0 in 2007 but had at least one murder in 2011. Calculating percent increase from zero results in an infinite number. This is shown as "NA."

12. Percent Change in Murder Rate: 2007 to 2011 (continued)
National Percent Change = 17.4% Decrease*

Rank Order - Metro Area

RANK	METROPOLITAN AREA	% CHANGE	RANK	METROPOLITAN AREA	% CHANGE	RANK	METROPOLITAN AREA	% CHANGE
1	Muskegon-Norton Shores, MI	583.3	61	Akron, OH	30.6	121	Savannah, GA	(1.2)
2	Idaho Falls, ID	462.5	62	Dover, DE	30.3	122	St. Louis, MO-IL	(1.3)
3	Kokomo, IN	400.0	63	Dayton, OH	29.8	123	Fort Wayne, IN	(1.6)
4	Carson City, NV	300.0	64	Santa Rosa-Petaluma, CA	29.4	123	Jackson, MS	(1.6)
5	Yuba City, CA	291.7	65	Waco, TX	28.2	125	Wilmington, DE-MD-NJ M.D.	(2.0)
6	Pittsfield, MA	275.0	66	Odessa, TX	27.4	126	Cincinnati-Middletown, OH-KY-IN	(2.1)
7	Valdosta, GA	256.3	67	Augusta, GA-SC	27.1	127	Ocala, FL	(2.3)
8	Monroe, MI	233.3	68	Longview, WA	26.7	128	Tucson, AZ	(2.6)
9	Medford, OR	226.7	69	Modesto, CA	25.0	129	Madera, CA	(2.9)
10	Bremerton-Silverdale, WA	200.0	70	Sherman-Denison, TX	24.2	130	Newark-Union, NJ-PA M.D.	(3.6)
10	Salem, OR	200.0	71	Des Moines-West Des Moines, IA	23.1	131	Boston-Quincy, MA M.D.	(3.9)
12	Toledo, OH	190.5	71	Topeka, KS	23.1	132	Vallejo-Fairfield, CA	(4.0)
13	Winchester, VA-WV	187.5	73	Gainesville, GA	22.7	133	Colorado Springs, CO	(4.1)
14	Anderson, SC	182.1	73	Peabody, MA M.D.	22.7	134	Trenton-Ewing, NJ	(4.2)
14	Prescott, AZ	182.1	75	South Bend-Mishawaka, IN-MI	22.0	135	Fort Worth-Arlington, TX M.D.	(4.4)
16	Bismarck, ND	170.0	76	Rome, GA	21.4	136	Portland-Vancouver, OR-WA	(4.5)
17	Bowling Green, KY	166.7	77	York-Hanover, PA	21.1	137	Oklahoma City, OK	(4.6)
17	Eugene-Springfield, OR	166.7	78	Danville, VA	20.0	138	Rapid City, SD	(6.1)
19	Sebastian-Vero Beach, FL	140.0	79	Roanoke, VA	18.5	139	Scranton--Wilkes-Barre, PA	(6.9)
20	Charleston, WV	138.5	80	Salinas, CA	14.1	140	Fort Collins-Loveland, CO	(7.1)
20	Glens Falls, NY	138.5	81	San Jose, CA	13.8	141	Detroit-Livonia-Dearborn, MI M.D.	(7.7)
22	Provo-Orem, UT	125.0	82	Longview, TX	13.6	141	Santa Ana-Anaheim, CA M.D.	(7.7)
23	Jefferson City, MO	123.8	83	Hickory, NC	13.5	143	Lynchburg, VA	(8.0)
24	Cleveland, TN	122.2	84	Salisbury, MD	11.9	143	Santa Barbara-Santa Maria, CA	(8.0)
25	Monroe, LA	121.7	85	Evansville, IN-KY	11.8	145	Sacramento, CA	(8.3)
26	Bangor, ME	114.3	85	Kennewick-Pasco-Richland, WA	11.8	146	Miami-Dade County, FL M.D.	(9.5)
27	Johnstown, PA	100.0	87	Charlottesville, VA	11.5	147	Tyler, TX	(9.8)
27	Tallahassee, FL	100.0	87	Kingsport, TN-VA	11.5	148	Harrisburg-Carlisle, PA	(10.0)
29	St. Joseph, MO-KS	93.8	89	Fort Smith, AR-OK	11.1	148	Madison, WI	(10.0)
30	Stockton, CA	89.4	90	Hanford-Corcoran, CA	10.6	148	San Luis Obispo, CA	(10.0)
31	Wenatchee, WA	89.3	91	Deltona-Daytona Beach, FL	10.0	151	Memphis, TN-MS-AR	(10.9)
32	Muncie, IN	88.9	92	Albany, GA	9.9	152	Tampa-St Petersburg, FL	(11.3)
33	Sumter, SC	83.5	93	Camden, NJ M.D.	6.1	153	Pittsburgh, PA	(11.6)
34	Cheyenne, WY	83.3	94	Columbus, OH	5.6	154	Lebanon, PA	(12.5)
35	Appleton, WI	80.0	95	Yuma, AZ	4.4	154	Springfield, MO	(12.5)
36	Myrtle Beach, SC	79.6	96	New York-W. Plains NY-NJ M.D.	4.1	156	Tulsa, OK	(12.8)
37	Flint, MI	78.6	97	Reno-Sparks, NV	3.7	157	Worcester, MA	(13.0)
38	Chattanooga, TN-GA	77.8	98	Austin-Round Rock, TX	3.6	158	McAllen-Edinburg-Mission, TX	(13.7)
39	Gainesville, FL	69.0	99	Racine, WI	2.9	159	Bakersfield, CA	(14.3)
40	Santa Cruz-Watsonville, CA	58.3	100	Fayetteville, NC	2.3	159	Beaumont-Port Arthur, TX	(14.3)
41	Sioux Falls, SD	57.1	101	Omaha-Council Bluffs, NE-IA	1.8	159	Chico, CA	(14.3)
42	Barnstable Town, MA	55.6	102	Yakima, WA	1.6	159	Knoxville, TN	(14.3)
42	Erie, PA	55.6	103	Albany-Schenectady-Troy, NY	0.0	159	Oxnard-Thousand Oaks, CA	(14.3)
44	Flagstaff, AZ	54.2	103	Boston (greater), MA-NH	0.0	164	Philadelphia (greater) PA-NJ-MD-DE	(14.7)
45	Warner Robins, GA	52.2	103	Cambridge-Newton, MA M.D.	0.0	165	Pine Bluff, AR	(14.9)
46	Mount Vernon-Anacortes, WA	47.1	103	Crestview-Fort Walton Beach, FL	0.0	166	Lansing-East Lansing, MI	(15.2)
47	Atlantic City, NJ	45.5	103	Dubuque, IA	0.0	167	New Orleans, LA	(16.0)
48	Johnson City, TN	42.9	103	Greenville, SC	0.0	168	Portland, ME	(16.7)
48	Panama City-Lynn Haven, FL	42.9	103	Lewiston-Auburn, ME	0.0	169	Rocky Mount, NC	(17.6)
50	Bloomington, IN	40.9	103	Lima, OH	0.0	170	Greeley, CO	(17.9)
51	Corvallis, OR	40.0	103	Logan, UT-ID	0.0	171	El Paso, TX	(18.5)
51	Ogden-Clearfield, UT	40.0	103	Nassau-Suffolk, NY M.D.	0.0	171	Virginia Beach-Norfolk, VA-NC	(18.5)
53	Bridgeport-Stamford, CT	38.5	103	New York (greater), NY-NJ-PA	0.0	173	Philadelphia, PA M.D.	(18.6)
54	Port St. Lucie, FL	37.8	103	Ocean City, NJ	0.0	174	Milwaukee, WI	(19.2)
55	Bellingham, WA	36.4	103	Rockingham County, NH M.D.	0.0	175	Janesville, WI	(19.4)
55	Lafayette, IN	36.4	103	Sandusky, OH	0.0	176	Springfield, MA	(20.0)
57	Ann Arbor, MI	35.3	103	Sheboygan, WI	0.0	177	Killeen-Temple-Fort Hood, TX	(20.4)
58	Midland, TX	34.4	103	Sioux City, IA-NE-SD	0.0	178	Denver-Aurora, CO	(20.6)
59	Grand Junction, CO	33.3	103	Tacoma, WA M.D.	0.0	178	Merced, CA	(20.6)
60	Reading, PA	31.4	120	Visalia-Porterville, CA	(1.1)	180	Indianapolis, IN	(20.8)

Note: All listings are for Metropolitan Statistical Areas (M.S.A.s) except for those ending with "M.D." Listings with "M.D." are Metropolitan Divisions which are smaller parts of eleven large M.S.A.s. See explanatory note at beginning of metropolitan area section.

Rank Order - Metro Area (continued)

RANK	METROPOLITAN AREA	% CHANGE
181	Cleveland-Elyria-Mentor, OH	(21.3)
182	Wilmington, NC	(21.4)
183	Laredo, TX	(21.8)
183	Miami (greater), FL	(21.8)
185	Orlando, FL	(22.2)
186	Waterloo-Cedar Falls, IA	(22.6)
187	Dallas (greater), TX	(23.7)
188	Cape Coral-Fort Myers, FL	(23.8)
189	Hartford, CT	(23.9)
189	Hinesville, GA	(23.9)
191	Bay City, MI	(24.3)
192	Oakland-Fremont, CA M.D.	(24.8)
193	Binghamton, NY	(25.0)
193	Edison, NJ M.D.	(25.0)
193	Jonesboro, AR	(25.0)
196	Corpus Christi, TX	(25.5)
196	Lakeland, FL	(25.5)
196	Rochester, NY	(25.5)
199	Grand Rapids-Wyoming, MI	(25.7)
200	Little Rock, AR	(25.8)
201	Pensacola, FL	(25.9)
202	Mobile, AL	(26.1)
203	Battle Creek, MI	(26.3)
203	Lake Havasu City-Kingman, AZ	(26.3)
205	Buffalo-Niagara Falls, NY	(26.4)
206	Duluth, MN-WI	(26.7)
206	Jackson, TN	(26.7)
208	Utica-Rome, NY	(27.0)
209	Raleigh-Cary, NC	(27.8)
209	San Diego, CA	(27.8)
211	Nashville-Davidson, TN	(27.9)
212	Columbia, MO	(28.1)
213	San Antonio, TX	(28.2)
214	Victoria, TX	(28.6)
215	Dallas-Plano-Irving, TX M.D.	(29.2)
216	Poughkeepsie, NY	(29.4)
217	Clarksville, TN-KY	(29.8)
218	Baltimore-Towson, MD	(29.9)
219	Lawton, OK	(30.4)
220	Atlanta, GA	(31.0)
221	Kingston, NY	(31.3)
222	San Francisco (greater), CA	(31.8)
223	Wichita, KS	(31.9)
224	El Centro, CA	(32.0)
225	Fresno, CA	(32.1)
226	Seattle (greater), WA	(32.3)
227	Charlotte-Gastonia, NC-SC	(32.4)
228	Riverside-San Bernardino, CA	(32.8)
229	Los Angeles (greater), CA	(32.9)
230	Altoona, PA	(33.3)
230	Cedar Rapids, IA	(33.3)
230	Lubbock, TX	(33.3)
230	West Palm Beach, FL M.D.	(33.3)
234	Baton Rouge, LA	(33.5)
235	Los Angeles County, CA M.D.	(34.5)
236	Saginaw, MI	(34.6)
237	Bethesda-Frederick, MD M.D.	(34.8)
238	Richmond, VA	(34.9)
239	Texarkana, TX-Texarkana, AR	(35.1)
240	Las Cruces, NM	(35.3)
241	Minneapolis-St. Paul, MN-WI	(35.7)
242	Olympia, WA	(36.0)
243	Dalton, GA	(36.4)
244	Elizabethtown, KY	(37.0)
245	Springfield, OH	(37.1)
246	Louisville, KY-IN	(38.0)
246	Naples-Marco Island, FL	(38.0)
248	Albuquerque, NM	(39.0)
249	Allentown, PA-NJ	(39.1)
250	Amarillo, TX	(39.7)
251	Phoenix-Mesa-Scottsdale, AZ	(40.2)
252	Morristown, TN	(40.5)
253	Jacksonville, FL	(40.7)
254	Macon, GA	(41.5)
255	Anchorage, AK	(41.7)
255	College Station-Bryan, TX	(41.7)
257	Washington, DC-VA-MD-WV M.D.	(42.4)
258	Syracuse, NY	(42.5)
259	Michigan City-La Porte, IN	(42.9)
259	Washington (greater) DC-VA-MD-WV	(42.9)
261	Fort Lauderdale, FL M.D.	(43.1)
262	Seattle-Bellevue-Everett, WA M.D.	(43.3)
263	San Francisco-S. Mateo, CA M.D.	(44.1)
264	Las Vegas-Paradise, NV	(45.3)
265	Lancaster, PA	(45.8)
266	Redding, CA	(45.9)
267	Asheville, NC	(46.2)
267	Green Bay, WI	(46.2)
269	Salt Lake City, UT	(48.8)
270	Oshkosh-Neenah, WI	(50.0)
271	Houma, LA	(50.8)
272	Goldsboro, NC	(50.9)
273	Napa, CA	(51.1)
274	Athens-Clarke County, GA	(51.6)
274	Spokane, WA	(51.6)
276	Columbus, IN	(51.9)
277	Alexandria, LA	(52.2)
278	Abilene, TX	(52.4)
279	Brownsville-Harlingen, TX	(52.5)
280	Casper, WY	(53.6)
280	Lincoln, NE	(53.6)
282	Spartanburg, SC	(53.8)
283	Palm Bay-Melbourne, FL	(54.2)
284	Lafayette, LA	(54.3)
285	Rochester, MN	(54.5)
286	Florence, SC	(55.0)
287	Mansfield, OH	(56.4)
288	Hot Springs, AR	(60.6)
289	Pascagoula, MS	(63.5)
290	Joplin, MO	(63.8)
291	Boise City-Nampa, ID	(63.9)
292	Williamsport, PA	(65.4)
293	Elmira, NY	(67.6)
294	Burlington, NC	(67.7)
295	Fargo, ND-MN	(68.8)
296	Brunswick, GA	(69.0)
297	Jacksonville, NC	(69.4)
298	Farmington, NM	(69.6)
299	Palm Coast, FL	(77.8)
300	Punta Gorda, FL	(81.5)
301	Wichita Falls, TX	(85.4)
302	Blacksburg, VA	(91.5)
303	Ames, IA	(100.0)
303	Eau Claire, WI	(100.0)
303	Grand Forks, ND-MN	(100.0)
303	La Crosse, WI-MN	(100.0)
303	Lawrence, KS	(100.0)
303	San Angelo, TX	(100.0)
303	State College, PA	(100.0)
303	St. Cloud, MN	(100.0)
303	Wausau, WI	(100.0)
NA	Anniston-Oxford, AL**	NA
NA	Auburn, AL**	NA
NA	Bend, OR***	NA
NA	Billings, MT**	NA
NA	Birmingham-Hoover, AL**	NA
NA	Bloomington-Normal, IL**	NA
NA	Boulder, CO**	NA
NA	Canton, OH**	NA
NA	Cape Girardeau, MO-IL**	NA
NA	Champaign-Urbana, IL**	NA
NA	Chicago (greater), IL-IN-WI**	NA
NA	Chicago-Joilet-Naperville, IL M.D.**	NA
NA	Columbus, GA-AL**	NA
NA	Cumberland, MD-WV**	NA
NA	Danville, IL**	NA
NA	Davenport, IA-IL**	NA
NA	Decatur, AL***	NA
NA	Decatur, IL**	NA
NA	Detroit (greater), MI**	NA
NA	Dothan, AL**	NA
NA	Durham-Chapel Hill, NC**	NA
NA	Fairbanks, AK**	NA
NA	Florence-Muscle Shoals, AL**	NA
NA	Fond du Lac, WI***	NA
NA	Gadsden, AL**	NA
NA	Gary, IN M.D.**	NA
NA	Great Falls, MT**	NA
NA	Gulfport-Biloxi, MS**	NA
NA	Hagerstown-Martinsburg, MD-WV**	NA
NA	Harrisonburg, VA***	NA
NA	Holland-Grand Haven, MI**	NA
NA	Houston, TX**	NA
NA	Huntsville, AL**	NA
NA	Iowa City, IA***	NA
NA	Kankakee-Bradley, IL**	NA
NA	Kansas City, MO-KS**	NA
NA	Lake Co.-Kenosha Co., IL-WI M.D.**	NA
NA	Lexington-Fayette, KY**	NA
NA	Manchester-Nashua, NH**	NA
NA	Manhattan, KS**	NA
NA	Mankato-North Mankato, MN**	NA
NA	Missoula, MT**	NA
NA	Montgomery, AL**	NA
NA	New Haven-Milford, CT**	NA
NA	North Port-Bradenton-Sarasota, FL**	NA
NA	Norwich-New London, CT**	NA
NA	Owensboro, KY**	NA
NA	Peoria, IL**	NA
NA	Pocatello, ID***	NA
NA	Pueblo, CO**	NA
NA	Rockford, IL**	NA
NA	Santa Fe, NM**	NA
NA	Springfield, IL**	NA
NA	Terre Haute, IN**	NA
NA	Tuscaloosa, AL**	NA
NA	Warren-Farmington Hills, MI M.D.**	NA
NA	Winston-Salem, NC**	NA

Source: CQ Press using reported data from the F.B.I. "Crime in the United States 2011"
*Includes nonnegligent manslaughter. **Not available. ***These metro areas had murder rates of 0 in 2007 but had at least one murder in 2011. Calculating percent increase from zero results in an infinite number. This is shown as "NA."

Alpha Order - Metro Area

13. Rapes in 2011
National Total = 83,425 Rapes*

RANK	METROPOLITAN AREA	RAPES
300	Abilene, TX	36
72	Akron, OH	261
109	Albany-Schenectady-Troy, NY	157
252	Albany, GA	51
58	Albuquerque, NM	355
248	Alexandria, LA	53
114	Allentown, PA-NJ	154
242	Altoona, PA	56
154	Amarillo, TX	112
317	Ames, IA	30
69	Anchorage, AK	289
224	Anderson, SC	64
106	Ann Arbor, MI	169
277	Anniston-Oxford, AL	43
270	Appleton, WI	45
206	Asheville, NC	73
274	Athens-Clarke County, GA	44
13	Atlanta, GA	1,099
235	Atlantic City, NJ	60
312	Auburn, AL	32
86	Augusta, GA-SC	205
52	Austin-Round Rock, TX	399
94	Bakersfield, CA	184
30	Baltimore-Towson, MD	681
339	Bangor, ME	21
168	Barnstable Town, MA	99
117	Baton Rouge, LA	149
193	Battle Creek, MI	83
204	Bay City, MI	74
128	Beaumont-Port Arthur, TX	137
175	Bellingham, WA	94
245	Bend, OR	55
118	Bethesda-Frederick, MD M.D.	146
280	Billings, MT	42
239	Binghamton, NY	59
50	Birmingham-Hoover, AL	417
282	Bismarck, ND	41
245	Blacksburg, VA	55
175	Bloomington-Normal, IL	94
277	Bloomington, IN	43
109	Boise City-Nampa, ID	157
15	Boston (greater), MA-NH	1,026
43	Boston-Quincy, MA M.D.	532
196	Boulder, CO	81
292	Bowling Green, KY	38
143	Bremerton-Silverdale, WA	122
79	Bridgeport-Stamford, CT	228
181	Brownsville-Harlingen, TX	92
317	Brunswick, GA	30
74	Buffalo-Niagara Falls, NY	258
323	Burlington, NC	28
71	Cambridge-Newton, MA M.D.	262
76	Camden, NJ M.D.	245
136	Canton, OH	127
159	Cape Coral-Fort Myers, FL	107
302	Cape Girardeau, MO-IL	35
358	Carson City, NV	0
349	Casper, WY	16
226	Cedar Rapids, IA	63
133	Champaign-Urbana, IL	129

RANK	METROPOLITAN AREA	RAPES
191	Charleston, WV	84
48	Charlotte-Gastonia, NC-SC	438
245	Charlottesville, VA	55
180	Chattanooga, TN-GA	93
288	Cheyenne, WY	39
NA	Chicago (greater), IL-IN-WI**	NA
NA	Chicago-Joilet-Naperville, IL M.D.**	NA
202	Chico, CA	75
35	Cincinnati-Middletown, OH-KY-IN	659
157	Clarksville, TN-KY	109
32	Cleveland-Elyria-Mentor, OH	677
309	Cleveland, TN	33
208	College Station-Bryan, TX	72
54	Colorado Springs, CO	395
270	Columbia, MO	45
211	Columbus, GA-AL	69
352	Columbus, IN	13
19	Columbus, OH	822
72	Corpus Christi, TX	261
346	Corvallis, OR	18
235	Crestview-Fort Walton Beach, FL	60
302	Cumberland, MD-WV	35
4	Dallas (greater), TX	1,753
16	Dallas-Plano-Irving, TX M.D.	1,018
317	Dalton, GA	30
197	Danville, IL	78
292	Danville, VA	38
100	Davenport, IA-IL	175
68	Dayton, OH	291
297	Decatur, AL	37
309	Decatur, IL	33
147	Deltona-Daytona Beach, FL	117
10	Denver-Aurora, CO	1,290
99	Des Moines-West Des Moines, IA	177
8	Detroit (greater), MI	1,387
20	Detroit-Livonia-Dearborn, MI M.D.	773
274	Dothan, AL	44
189	Dover, DE	85
339	Dubuque, IA	21
NA	Duluth, MN-WI**	NA
147	Durham-Chapel Hill, NC	117
285	Eau Claire, WI	40
93	Edison, NJ M.D.	185
314	El Centro, CA	31
77	El Paso, TX	241
297	Elizabethtown, KY	37
352	Elmira, NY	13
133	Erie, PA	129
146	Eugene-Springfield, OR	118
175	Evansville, IN-KY	94
347	Fairbanks, AK	17
NA	Fargo, ND-MN**	NA
162	Farmington, NM	104
197	Fayetteville, NC	78
211	Flagstaff, AZ	69
78	Flint, MI	234
336	Florence-Muscle Shoals, AL	22
235	Florence, SC	60
274	Fond du Lac, WI	44
172	Fort Collins-Loveland, CO	96

RANK	METROPOLITAN AREA	RAPES
45	Fort Lauderdale, FL M.D.	473
124	Fort Smith, AR-OK	139
144	Fort Wayne, IN	120
26	Fort Worth-Arlington, TX M.D.	735
115	Fresno, CA	152
280	Gadsden, AL	42
142	Gainesville, FL	124
309	Gainesville, GA	33
95	Gary, IN M.D.	182
305	Glens Falls, NY	34
357	Goldsboro, NC	6
NA	Grand Forks, ND-MN**	NA
181	Grand Junction, CO	92
61	Grand Rapids-Wyoming, MI	331
349	Great Falls, MT	16
216	Greeley, CO	67
204	Green Bay, WI	74
83	Greenville, SC	217
197	Gulfport-Biloxi, MS	78
305	Hagerstown-Martinsburg, MD-WV	34
317	Hanford-Corcoran, CA	30
96	Harrisburg-Carlisle, PA	181
305	Harrisonburg, VA	34
87	Hartford, CT	201
257	Hickory, NC	50
349	Hinesville, GA	16
136	Holland-Grand Haven, MI	127
252	Hot Springs, AR	51
250	Houma, LA	52
5	Houston, TX	1,628
154	Huntsville, AL	112
292	Idaho Falls, ID	38
41	Indianapolis, IN	569
258	Iowa City, IA	49
47	Jacksonville, FL	439
220	Jacksonville, NC	66
100	Jackson, MS	175
230	Jackson, TN	61
288	Janesville, WI	39
336	Jefferson City, MO	22
343	Johnson City, TN	19
252	Johnstown, PA	51
239	Jonesboro, AR	59
220	Joplin, MO	66
239	Kankakee-Bradley, IL	59
27	Kansas City, MO-KS	730
184	Kennewick-Pasco-Richland, WA	90
126	Killeen-Temple-Fort Hood, TX	138
163	Kingsport, TN-VA	103
277	Kingston, NY	43
90	Knoxville, TN	190
335	Kokomo, IN	23
NA	La Crosse, WI-MN**	NA
228	Lafayette, IN	62
242	Lafayette, LA	56
92	Lake Co.-Kenosha Co., IL-WI M.D.	188
270	Lake Havasu City-Kingman, AZ	45
120	Lakeland, FL	143
150	Lancaster, PA	115
83	Lansing-East Lansing, MI	217

Note: All listings are for Metropolitan Statistical Areas (M.S.A.s) except for those ending with "M.D." Listings with "M.D." are Metropolitan Divisions which are smaller parts of eleven large M.S.A.s. See explanatory note at beginning of metropolitan area section.

Alpha Order - Metro Area (continued)

RANK	METROPOLITAN AREA	RAPES
191	Laredo, TX	84
230	Las Cruces, NM	61
21	Las Vegas-Paradise, NV	769
288	Lawrence, KS	39
226	Lawton, OK	63
329	Lebanon, PA	26
297	Lewiston-Auburn, ME	37
112	Lexington-Fayette, KY	155
216	Lima, OH	67
103	Lincoln, NE	174
62	Little Rock, AR	327
352	Logan, UT-ID	13
200	Longview, TX	76
189	Longview, WA	85
2	Los Angeles County, CA M.D.	1,904
1	Los Angeles (greater), CA	2,314
59	Louisville, KY-IN	349
175	Lubbock, TX	94
252	Lynchburg, VA	51
252	Macon, GA	51
325	Madera, CA	27
120	Madison, WI	143
136	Manchester-Nashua, NH	127
258	Manhattan, KS	49
NA	Mankato-North Mankato, MN**	NA
262	Mansfield, OH	48
80	McAllen-Edinburg-Mission, TX	225
209	Medford, OR	71
39	Memphis, TN-MS-AR	578
230	Merced, CA	61
7	Miami (greater), FL	1,451
36	Miami-Dade County, FL M.D.	638
329	Michigan City-La Porte, IN	26
336	Midland, TX	22
66	Milwaukee, WI	295
NA	Minneapolis-St. Paul, MN-WI**	NA
292	Missoula, MT	38
186	Mobile, AL	87
147	Modesto, CA	117
288	Monroe, LA	39
214	Monroe, MI	68
200	Montgomery, AL	76
325	Morristown, TN	27
265	Mount Vernon-Anacortes, WA	47
230	Muncie, IN	61
165	Muskegon-Norton Shores, MI	101
98	Myrtle Beach, SC	178
305	Napa, CA	34
270	Naples-Marco Island, FL	45
38	Nashville-Davidson, TN	596
152	Nassau-Suffolk, NY M.D.	114
150	New Haven-Milford, CT	115
65	New Orleans, LA	310
3	New York (greater), NY-NJ-PA	1,896
9	New York-W. Plains NY-NJ M.D.	1,351
75	Newark-Union, NJ-PA M.D.	246
89	North Port-Bradenton-Sarasota, FL	194
235	Norwich-New London, CT	60
40	Oakland-Fremont, CA M.D.	574
107	Ocala, FL	162
352	Ocean City, NJ	13
292	Odessa, TX	38
116	Ogden-Clearfield, UT	150
44	Oklahoma City, OK	511
210	Olympia, WA	70
57	Omaha-Council Bluffs, NE-IA	366
31	Orlando, FL	679
333	Oshkosh-Neenah, WI	24
242	Owensboro, KY	56
165	Oxnard-Thousand Oaks, CA	101
103	Palm Bay-Melbourne, FL	174
343	Palm Coast, FL	19
228	Panama City-Lynn Haven, FL	62
211	Pascagoula, MS	69
144	Peabody, MA M.D.	120
88	Pensacola, FL	198
136	Peoria, IL	127
5	Philadelphia (greater) PA-NJ-MD-DE	1,628
11	Philadelphia, PA M.D.	1,203
12	Phoenix-Mesa-Scottsdale, AZ	1,156
258	Pine Bluff, AR	49
49	Pittsburgh, PA	425
216	Pittsfield, MA	67
342	Pocatello, ID	20
174	Port St. Lucie, FL	95
25	Portland-Vancouver, OR-WA	743
129	Portland, ME	135
172	Poughkeepsie, NY	96
302	Prescott, AZ	35
164	Provo-Orem, UT	102
282	Pueblo, CO	41
314	Punta Gorda, FL	31
325	Racine, WI	27
81	Raleigh-Cary, NC	223
136	Rapid City, SD	127
230	Reading, PA	61
170	Redding, CA	98
185	Reno-Sparks, NV	88
91	Richmond, VA	189
23	Riverside-San Bernardino, CA	757
206	Roanoke, VA	73
NA	Rochester, MN**	NA
82	Rochester, NY	220
105	Rockford, IL	171
154	Rockingham County, NH M.D.	112
339	Rocky Mount, NC	21
323	Rome, GA	28
42	Sacramento, CA	542
188	Saginaw, MI	86
186	Salem, OR	87
175	Salinas, CA	94
325	Salisbury, MD	27
46	Salt Lake City, UT	457
262	San Angelo, TX	48
33	San Antonio, TX	676
34	San Diego, CA	660
18	San Francisco (greater), CA	891
63	San Francisco-S. Mateo, CA M.D.	317
55	San Jose, CA	368
183	San Luis Obispo, CA	91
356	Sandusky, OH	12
51	Santa Ana-Anaheim, CA M.D.	410
131	Santa Barbara-Santa Maria, CA	130
202	Santa Cruz-Watsonville, CA	75
317	Santa Fe, NM	30
126	Santa Rosa-Petaluma, CA	138
214	Savannah, GA	68
160	Scranton--Wilkes-Barre, PA	106
14	Seattle (greater), WA	1,044
24	Seattle-Bellevue-Everett, WA M.D.	749
312	Sebastian-Vero Beach, FL	32
347	Sheboygan, WI	17
343	Sherman-Denison, TX	19
267	Sioux City, IA-NE-SD	46
136	Sioux Falls, SD	127
157	South Bend-Mishawaka, IN-MI	109
193	Spartanburg, SC	83
135	Spokane, WA	128
122	Springfield, IL	140
85	Springfield, MA	216
130	Springfield, MO	133
300	Springfield, OH	36
265	State College, PA	47
122	Stockton, CA	140
NA	St. Cloud, MN**	NA
322	St. Joseph, MO-KS	29
28	St. Louis, MO-IL	713
332	Sumter, SC	25
112	Syracuse, NY	155
66	Tacoma, WA M.D.	295
109	Tallahassee, FL	157
29	Tampa-St Petersburg, FL	687
282	Terre Haute, IN	41
216	Texarkana, TX-Texarkana, AR	67
100	Toledo, OH	175
220	Topeka, KS	66
248	Trenton-Ewing, NJ	53
70	Tucson, AZ	284
52	Tulsa, OK	399
224	Tuscaloosa, AL	64
167	Tyler, TX	100
267	Utica-Rome, NY	46
285	Valdosta, GA	40
153	Vallejo-Fairfield, CA	113
223	Victoria, TX	65
56	Virginia Beach-Norfolk, VA-NC	367
168	Visalia-Porterville, CA	99
131	Waco, TX	130
314	Warner Robins, GA	31
37	Warren-Farmington Hills, MI M.D.	614
17	Washington (greater) DC-VA-MD-WV	909
22	Washington, DC-VA-MD-WV M.D.	763
195	Waterloo-Cedar Falls, IA	82
258	Wausau, WI	49
329	Wenatchee, WA	26
60	West Palm Beach, FL M.D.	340
267	Wichita Falls, TX	46
64	Wichita, KS	312
333	Williamsport, PA	24
97	Wilmington, DE-MD-NJ M.D.	180
171	Wilmington, NC	97
285	Winchester, VA-WV	40
119	Winston-Salem, NC	144
108	Worcester, MA	160
160	Yakima, WA	106
124	York-Hanover, PA	139
250	Yuba City, CA	52
262	Yuma, AZ	48

Source: Reported data from the F.B.I. "Crime in the United States 2011"

*Forcible rape is the carnal knowledge of a female forcibly and against her will. Assaults or attempts to commit rape by force or threat of force are included. However, statutory rape without force and other sex offenses are excluded. **Not available

Rank Order - Metro Area

13. Rapes in 2011 (continued)
National Total = 83,425 Rapes*

RANK	METROPOLITAN AREA	RAPES	RANK	METROPOLITAN AREA	RAPES	RANK	METROPOLITAN AREA	RAPES
1	Los Angeles (greater), CA	2,314	61	Grand Rapids-Wyoming, MI	331	120	Madison, WI	143
2	Los Angeles County, CA M.D.	1,904	62	Little Rock, AR	327	122	Springfield, IL	140
3	New York (greater), NY-NJ-PA	1,896	63	San Francisco-S. Mateo, CA M.D.	317	122	Stockton, CA	140
4	Dallas (greater), TX	1,753	64	Wichita, KS	312	124	Fort Smith, AR-OK	139
5	Houston, TX	1,628	65	New Orleans, LA	310	124	York-Hanover, PA	139
5	Philadelphia (greater) PA-NJ-MD-DE	1,628	66	Milwaukee, WI	295	126	Killeen-Temple-Fort Hood, TX	138
7	Miami (greater), FL	1,451	66	Tacoma, WA M.D.	295	126	Santa Rosa-Petaluma, CA	138
8	Detroit (greater), MI	1,387	68	Dayton, OH	291	128	Beaumont-Port Arthur, TX	137
9	New York-W. Plains NY-NJ M.D.	1,351	69	Anchorage, AK	289	129	Portland, ME	135
10	Denver-Aurora, CO	1,290	70	Tucson, AZ	284	130	Springfield, MO	133
11	Philadelphia, PA M.D.	1,203	71	Cambridge-Newton, MA M.D.	262	131	Santa Barbara-Santa Maria, CA	130
12	Phoenix-Mesa-Scottsdale, AZ	1,156	72	Akron, OH	261	131	Waco, TX	130
13	Atlanta, GA	1,099	72	Corpus Christi, TX	261	133	Champaign-Urbana, IL	129
14	Seattle (greater), WA	1,044	74	Buffalo-Niagara Falls, NY	258	133	Erie, PA	129
15	Boston (greater), MA-NH	1,026	75	Newark-Union, NJ-PA M.D.	246	135	Spokane, WA	128
16	Dallas-Plano-Irving, TX M.D.	1,018	76	Camden, NJ M.D.	245	136	Canton, OH	127
17	Washington (greater) DC-VA-MD-WV	909	77	El Paso, TX	241	136	Holland-Grand Haven, MI	127
18	San Francisco (greater), CA	891	78	Flint, MI	234	136	Manchester-Nashua, NH	127
19	Columbus, OH	822	79	Bridgeport-Stamford, CT	228	136	Peoria, IL	127
20	Detroit-Livonia-Dearborn, MI M.D.	773	80	McAllen-Edinburg-Mission, TX	225	136	Rapid City, SD	127
21	Las Vegas-Paradise, NV	769	81	Raleigh-Cary, NC	223	136	Sioux Falls, SD	127
22	Washington, DC-VA-MD-WV M.D.	763	82	Rochester, NY	220	142	Gainesville, FL	124
23	Riverside-San Bernardino, CA	757	83	Greenville, SC	217	143	Bremerton-Silverdale, WA	122
24	Seattle-Bellevue-Everett, WA M.D.	749	83	Lansing-East Lansing, MI	217	144	Fort Wayne, IN	120
25	Portland-Vancouver, OR-WA	743	85	Springfield, MA	216	144	Peabody, MA M.D.	120
26	Fort Worth-Arlington, TX M.D.	735	86	Augusta, GA-SC	205	146	Eugene-Springfield, OR	118
27	Kansas City, MO-KS	730	87	Hartford, CT	201	147	Deltona-Daytona Beach, FL	117
28	St. Louis, MO-IL	713	88	Pensacola, FL	198	147	Durham-Chapel Hill, NC	117
29	Tampa-St Petersburg, FL	687	89	North Port-Bradenton-Sarasota, FL	194	147	Modesto, CA	117
30	Baltimore-Towson, MD	681	90	Knoxville, TN	190	150	Lancaster, PA	115
31	Orlando, FL	679	91	Richmond, VA	189	150	New Haven-Milford, CT	115
32	Cleveland-Elyria-Mentor, OH	677	92	Lake Co.-Kenosha Co., IL-WI M.D.	188	152	Nassau-Suffolk, NY M.D.	114
33	San Antonio, TX	676	93	Edison, NJ M.D.	185	153	Vallejo-Fairfield, CA	113
34	San Diego, CA	660	94	Bakersfield, CA	184	154	Amarillo, TX	112
35	Cincinnati-Middletown, OH-KY-IN	659	95	Gary, IN M.D.	182	154	Huntsville, AL	112
36	Miami-Dade County, FL M.D.	638	96	Harrisburg-Carlisle, PA	181	154	Rockingham County, NH M.D.	112
37	Warren-Farmington Hills, MI M.D.	614	97	Wilmington, DE-MD-NJ M.D.	180	157	Clarksville, TN-KY	109
38	Nashville-Davidson, TN	596	98	Myrtle Beach, SC	178	157	South Bend-Mishawaka, IN-MI	109
39	Memphis, TN-MS-AR	578	99	Des Moines-West Des Moines, IA	177	159	Cape Coral-Fort Myers, FL	107
40	Oakland-Fremont, CA M.D.	574	100	Davenport, IA-IL	175	160	Scranton--Wilkes-Barre, PA	106
41	Indianapolis, IN	569	100	Jackson, MS	175	160	Yakima, WA	106
42	Sacramento, CA	542	100	Toledo, OH	175	162	Farmington, NM	104
43	Boston-Quincy, MA M.D.	532	103	Lincoln, NE	174	163	Kingsport, TN-VA	103
44	Oklahoma City, OK	511	103	Palm Bay-Melbourne, FL	174	164	Provo-Orem, UT	102
45	Fort Lauderdale, FL M.D.	473	105	Rockford, IL	171	165	Muskegon-Norton Shores, MI	101
46	Salt Lake City, UT	457	106	Ann Arbor, MI	169	165	Oxnard-Thousand Oaks, CA	101
47	Jacksonville, FL	439	107	Ocala, FL	162	167	Tyler, TX	100
48	Charlotte-Gastonia, NC-SC	438	108	Worcester, MA	160	168	Barnstable Town, MA	99
49	Pittsburgh, PA	425	109	Albany-Schenectady-Troy, NY	157	168	Visalia-Porterville, CA	99
50	Birmingham-Hoover, AL	417	109	Boise City-Nampa, ID	157	170	Redding, CA	98
51	Santa Ana-Anaheim, CA M.D.	410	109	Tallahassee, FL	157	171	Wilmington, NC	97
52	Austin-Round Rock, TX	399	112	Lexington-Fayette, KY	155	172	Fort Collins-Loveland, CO	96
52	Tulsa, OK	399	112	Syracuse, NY	155	172	Poughkeepsie, NY	96
54	Colorado Springs, CO	395	114	Allentown, PA-NJ	154	174	Port St. Lucie, FL	95
55	San Jose, CA	368	115	Fresno, CA	152	175	Bellingham, WA	94
56	Virginia Beach-Norfolk, VA-NC	367	116	Ogden-Clearfield, UT	150	175	Bloomington-Normal, IL	94
57	Omaha-Council Bluffs, NE-IA	366	117	Baton Rouge, LA	149	175	Evansville, IN-KY	94
58	Albuquerque, NM	355	118	Bethesda-Frederick, MD M.D.	146	175	Lubbock, TX	94
59	Louisville, KY-IN	349	119	Winston-Salem, NC	144	175	Salinas, CA	94
60	West Palm Beach, FL M.D.	340	120	Lakeland, FL	143	180	Chattanooga, TN-GA	93

Note: All listings are for Metropolitan Statistical Areas (M.S.A.s) except for those ending with "M.D." Listings with "M.D." are Metropolitan Divisions which are smaller parts of eleven large M.S.A.s. See explanatory note at beginning of metropolitan area section.

Rank Order - Metro Area (continued)

RANK	METROPOLITAN AREA	RAPES
181	Brownsville-Harlingen, TX	92
181	Grand Junction, CO	92
183	San Luis Obispo, CA	91
184	Kennewick-Pasco-Richland, WA	90
185	Reno-Sparks, NV	88
186	Mobile, AL	87
186	Salem, OR	87
188	Saginaw, MI	86
189	Dover, DE	85
189	Longview, WA	85
191	Charleston, WV	84
191	Laredo, TX	84
193	Battle Creek, MI	83
193	Spartanburg, SC	83
195	Waterloo-Cedar Falls, IA	82
196	Boulder, CO	81
197	Danville, IL	78
197	Fayetteville, NC	78
197	Gulfport-Biloxi, MS	78
200	Longview, TX	76
200	Montgomery, AL	76
202	Chico, CA	75
202	Santa Cruz-Watsonville, CA	75
204	Bay City, MI	74
204	Green Bay, WI	74
206	Asheville, NC	73
206	Roanoke, VA	73
208	College Station-Bryan, TX	72
209	Medford, OR	71
210	Olympia, WA	70
211	Columbus, GA-AL	69
211	Flagstaff, AZ	69
211	Pascagoula, MS	69
214	Monroe, MI	68
214	Savannah, GA	68
216	Greeley, CO	67
216	Lima, OH	67
216	Pittsfield, MA	67
216	Texarkana, TX-Texarkana, AR	67
220	Jacksonville, NC	66
220	Joplin, MO	66
220	Topeka, KS	66
223	Victoria, TX	65
224	Anderson, SC	64
224	Tuscaloosa, AL	64
226	Cedar Rapids, IA	63
226	Lawton, OK	63
228	Lafayette, IN	62
228	Panama City-Lynn Haven, FL	62
230	Jackson, TN	61
230	Las Cruces, NM	61
230	Merced, CA	61
230	Muncie, IN	61
230	Reading, PA	61
235	Atlantic City, NJ	60
235	Crestview-Fort Walton Beach, FL	60
235	Florence, SC	60
235	Norwich-New London, CT	60
239	Binghamton, NY	59
239	Jonesboro, AR	59
239	Kankakee-Bradley, IL	59
242	Altoona, PA	56
242	Lafayette, LA	56
242	Owensboro, KY	56
245	Bend, OR	55
245	Blacksburg, VA	55
245	Charlottesville, VA	55
248	Alexandria, LA	53
248	Trenton-Ewing, NJ	53
250	Houma, LA	52
250	Yuba City, CA	52
252	Albany, GA	51
252	Hot Springs, AR	51
252	Johnstown, PA	51
252	Lynchburg, VA	51
252	Macon, GA	51
257	Hickory, NC	50
258	Iowa City, IA	49
258	Manhattan, KS	49
258	Pine Bluff, AR	49
258	Wausau, WI	49
262	Mansfield, OH	48
262	San Angelo, TX	48
262	Yuma, AZ	48
265	Mount Vernon-Anacortes, WA	47
265	State College, PA	47
267	Sioux City, IA-NE-SD	46
267	Utica-Rome, NY	46
267	Wichita Falls, TX	46
270	Appleton, WI	45
270	Columbia, MO	45
270	Lake Havasu City-Kingman, AZ	45
270	Naples-Marco Island, FL	45
274	Athens-Clarke County, GA	44
274	Dothan, AL	44
274	Fond du Lac, WI	44
277	Anniston-Oxford, AL	43
277	Bloomington, IN	43
277	Kingston, NY	43
280	Billings, MT	42
280	Gadsden, AL	42
282	Bismarck, ND	41
282	Pueblo, CO	41
282	Terre Haute, IN	41
285	Eau Claire, WI	40
285	Valdosta, GA	40
285	Winchester, VA-WV	40
288	Cheyenne, WY	39
288	Janesville, WI	39
288	Lawrence, KS	39
288	Monroe, LA	39
292	Bowling Green, KY	38
292	Danville, VA	38
292	Idaho Falls, ID	38
292	Missoula, MT	38
292	Odessa, TX	38
297	Decatur, AL	37
297	Elizabethtown, KY	37
297	Lewiston-Auburn, ME	37
300	Abilene, TX	36
300	Springfield, OH	36
302	Cape Girardeau, MO-IL	35
302	Cumberland, MD-WV	35
302	Prescott, AZ	35
305	Glens Falls, NY	34
305	Hagerstown-Martinsburg, MD-WV	34
305	Harrisonburg, VA	34
305	Napa, CA	34
309	Cleveland, TN	33
309	Decatur, IL	33
309	Gainesville, GA	33
312	Auburn, AL	32
312	Sebastian-Vero Beach, FL	32
314	El Centro, CA	31
314	Punta Gorda, FL	31
314	Warner Robins, GA	31
317	Ames, IA	30
317	Brunswick, GA	30
317	Dalton, GA	30
317	Hanford-Corcoran, CA	30
317	Santa Fe, NM	30
322	St. Joseph, MO-KS	29
323	Burlington, NC	28
323	Rome, GA	28
325	Madera, CA	27
325	Morristown, TN	27
325	Racine, WI	27
325	Salisbury, MD	27
329	Lebanon, PA	26
329	Michigan City-La Porte, IN	26
329	Wenatchee, WA	26
332	Sumter, SC	25
333	Oshkosh-Neenah, WI	24
333	Williamsport, PA	24
335	Kokomo, IN	23
336	Florence-Muscle Shoals, AL	22
336	Jefferson City, MO	22
336	Midland, TX	22
339	Bangor, ME	21
339	Dubuque, IA	21
339	Rocky Mount, NC	21
342	Pocatello, ID	20
343	Johnson City, TN	19
343	Palm Coast, FL	19
343	Sherman-Denison, TX	19
346	Corvallis, OR	18
347	Fairbanks, AK	17
347	Sheboygan, WI	17
349	Casper, WY	16
349	Great Falls, MT	16
349	Hinesville, GA	16
352	Columbus, IN	13
352	Elmira, NY	13
352	Logan, UT-ID	13
352	Ocean City, NJ	13
356	Sandusky, OH	12
357	Goldsboro, NC	6
358	Carson City, NV	0
NA	Chicago (greater), IL-IN-WI**	NA
NA	Chicago-Joilet-Naperville, IL M.D.**	NA
NA	Duluth, MN-WI**	NA
NA	Fargo, ND-MN**	NA
NA	Grand Forks, ND-MN**	NA
NA	La Crosse, WI-MN**	NA
NA	Mankato-North Mankato, MN**	NA
NA	Minneapolis-St. Paul, MN-WI**	NA
NA	Rochester, MN**	NA
NA	St. Cloud, MN**	NA

Source: Reported data from the F.B.I. "Crime in the United States 2011"
*Forcible rape is the carnal knowledge of a female forcibly and against her will. Assaults or attempts to commit rape by force or threat of force are included. However, statutory rape without force and other sex offenses are excluded. **Not available

Alpha Order - Metro Area

14. Rape Rate in 2011
National Rate = 26.8 Rapes per 100,000 Population*

RANK	METROPOLITAN AREA	RATE	RANK	METROPOLITAN AREA	RATE	RANK	METROPOLITAN AREA	RATE
270	Abilene, TX	21.3	175	Charleston, WV	27.6	191	Fort Lauderdale, FL M.D.	26.7
82	Akron, OH	37.1	220	Charlotte-Gastonia, NC-SC	24.6	48	Fort Smith, AR-OK	46.2
309	Albany-Schenectady-Troy, NY	18.0	181	Charlottesville, VA	27.0	164	Fort Wayne, IN	28.7
129	Albany, GA	32.0	316	Chattanooga, TN-GA	17.4	107	Fort Worth-Arlington, TX M.D.	33.7
74	Albuquerque, NM	39.6	65	Cheyenne, WY	42.2	323	Fresno, CA	16.1
104	Alexandria, LA	34.1	NA	Chicago (greater), IL-IN-WI**	NA	72	Gadsden, AL	40.0
304	Allentown, PA-NJ	18.7	NA	Chicago-Joilet-Naperville, IL M.D.**	NA	47	Gainesville, FL	46.3
55	Altoona, PA	43.9	107	Chico, CA	33.7	308	Gainesville, GA	18.1
55	Amarillo, TX	43.9	140	Cincinnati-Middletown, OH-KY-IN	30.9	206	Gary, IN M.D.	25.6
114	Ames, IA	33.3	76	Clarksville, TN-KY	39.5	197	Glens Falls, NY	26.3
3	Anchorage, AK	92.9	122	Cleveland-Elyria-Mentor, OH	32.6	356	Goldsboro, NC	4.8
106	Anderson, SC	33.8	170	Cleveland, TN	28.2	NA	Grand Forks, ND-MN**	NA
34	Ann Arbor, MI	49.1	143	College Station-Bryan, TX	30.8	10	Grand Junction, CO	61.6
91	Anniston-Oxford, AL	36.1	12	Colorado Springs, CO	60.1	62	Grand Rapids-Wyoming, MI	42.8
287	Appleton, WI	19.9	204	Columbia, MO	25.9	294	Great Falls, MT	19.5
320	Asheville, NC	17.0	239	Columbus, GA-AL	23.1	202	Greeley, CO	26.0
247	Athens-Clarke County, GA	22.6	321	Columbus, IN	16.8	226	Green Bay, WI	24.1
278	Atlanta, GA	20.6	54	Columbus, OH	44.7	107	Greenville, SC	33.7
263	Atlantic City, NJ	21.8	13	Corpus Christi, TX	59.7	138	Gulfport-Biloxi, MS	31.2
245	Auburn, AL	22.7	275	Corvallis, OR	20.8	347	Hagerstown-Martinsburg, MD-WV	12.6
87	Augusta, GA-SC	36.4	121	Crestview-Fort Walton Beach, FL	32.7	297	Hanford-Corcoran, CA	19.4
244	Austin-Round Rock, TX	22.8	110	Cumberland, MD-WV	33.6	120	Harrisburg-Carlisle, PA	32.8
265	Bakersfield, CA	21.7	186	Dallas (greater), TX	26.9	188	Harrisonburg, VA	26.8
215	Baltimore-Towson, MD	24.9	230	Dallas-Plano-Irving, TX M.D.	23.5	291	Hartford, CT	19.7
342	Bangor, ME	13.6	275	Dalton, GA	20.8	344	Hickory, NC	13.5
52	Barnstable Town, MA	45.6	2	Danville, IL	95.3	282	Hinesville, GA	20.3
306	Baton Rouge, LA	18.4	94	Danville, VA	35.2	41	Holland-Grand Haven, MI	48.2
11	Battle Creek, MI	61.0	50	Davenport, IA-IL	45.9	23	Hot Springs, AR	52.7
6	Bay City, MI	68.7	98	Dayton, OH	34.6	217	Houma, LA	24.8
100	Beaumont-Port Arthur, TX	34.5	227	Decatur, AL	23.9	188	Houston, TX	26.8
49	Bellingham, WA	46.0	157	Decatur, IL	29.7	191	Huntsville, AL	26.7
100	Bend, OR	34.5	234	Deltona-Daytona Beach, FL	23.3	162	Idaho Falls, ID	28.8
349	Bethesda-Frederick, MD M.D.	12.0	31	Denver-Aurora, CO	49.8	127	Indianapolis, IN	32.2
197	Billings, MT	26.3	140	Des Moines-West Des Moines, IA	30.9	130	Iowa City, IA	31.9
234	Binghamton, NY	23.3	124	Detroit (greater), MI	32.3	127	Jacksonville, FL	32.2
84	Birmingham-Hoover, AL	36.8	63	Detroit-Livonia-Dearborn, MI M.D.	42.5	85	Jacksonville, NC	36.7
82	Bismarck, ND	37.1	151	Dothan, AL	30.1	124	Jackson, MS	32.3
111	Blacksburg, VA	33.4	25	Dover, DE	51.8	24	Jackson, TN	52.4
17	Bloomington-Normal, IL	55.3	252	Dubuque, IA	22.3	224	Janesville, WI	24.2
253	Bloomington, IN	22.2	NA	Duluth, MN-WI**	NA	334	Jefferson City, MO	14.6
211	Boise City-Nampa, ID	25.2	242	Durham-Chapel Hill, NC	22.9	354	Johnson City, TN	9.5
250	Boston (greater), MA-NH	22.4	219	Eau Claire, WI	24.7	93	Johnstown, PA	35.4
172	Boston-Quincy, MA M.D.	28.0	355	Edison, NJ M.D.	7.9	39	Jonesboro, AR	48.4
181	Boulder, CO	27.0	314	El Centro, CA	17.6	80	Joplin, MO	37.5
152	Bowling Green, KY	30.0	158	El Paso, TX	29.5	25	Kankakee-Bradley, IL	51.8
43	Bremerton-Silverdale, WA	47.8	146	Elizabethtown, KY	30.7	92	Kansas City, MO-KS	35.7
208	Bridgeport-Stamford, CT	25.3	334	Elmira, NY	14.6	95	Kennewick-Pasco-Richland, WA	35.0
253	Brownsville-Harlingen, TX	22.2	51	Erie, PA	45.8	114	Killeen-Temple-Fort Hood, TX	33.3
195	Brunswick, GA	26.4	116	Eugene-Springfield, OR	33.2	118	Kingsport, TN-VA	32.9
247	Buffalo-Niagara Falls, NY	22.6	201	Evansville, IN-KY	26.1	230	Kingston, NY	23.5
307	Burlington, NC	18.3	33	Fairbanks, AK	49.6	181	Knoxville, TN	27.0
317	Cambridge-Newton, MA M.D.	17.3	NA	Fargo, ND-MN**	NA	237	Kokomo, IN	23.2
294	Camden, NJ M.D.	19.5	5	Farmington, NM	79.1	NA	La Crosse, WI-MN**	NA
136	Canton, OH	31.4	272	Fayetteville, NC	21.0	147	Lafayette, IN	30.6
319	Cape Coral-Fort Myers, FL	17.1	29	Flagstaff, AZ	50.6	282	Lafayette, LA	20.3
89	Cape Girardeau, MO-IL	36.2	19	Flint, MI	55.0	268	Lake Co.-Kenosha Co., IL-WI M.D.	21.5
358	Carson City, NV	0.0	330	Florence-Muscle Shoals, AL	14.9	253	Lake Havasu City-Kingman, AZ	22.2
272	Casper, WY	21.0	160	Florence, SC	28.9	232	Lakeland, FL	23.4
223	Cedar Rapids, IA	24.3	59	Fond du Lac, WI	43.1	257	Lancaster, PA	22.1
16	Champaign-Urbana, IL	55.5	135	Fort Collins-Loveland, CO	31.5	44	Lansing-East Lansing, MI	46.8

Note: All listings are for Metropolitan Statistical Areas (M.S.A.s) except for those ending with "M.D." Listings with "M.D." are Metropolitan Divisions which are smaller parts of eleven large M.S.A.s. See explanatory note at beginning of metropolitan area section.

Alpha Order - Metro Area (continued)

RANK	METROPOLITAN AREA	RATE
118	Laredo, TX	32.9
162	Las Cruces, NM	28.8
77	Las Vegas-Paradise, NV	39.1
95	Lawrence, KS	35.0
30	Lawton, OK	50.2
297	Lebanon, PA	19.4
103	Lewiston-Auburn, ME	34.4
122	Lexington-Fayette, KY	32.6
9	Lima, OH	63.0
15	Lincoln, NE	57.1
46	Little Rock, AR	46.4
352	Logan, UT-ID	10.2
97	Longview, TX	34.7
4	Longview, WA	81.7
300	Los Angeles County, CA M.D.	19.2
311	Los Angeles (greater), CA	17.8
181	Louisville, KY-IN	27.0
124	Lubbock, TX	32.3
287	Lynchburg, VA	19.9
265	Macon, GA	21.7
312	Madera, CA	17.7
214	Madison, WI	25.0
133	Manchester-Nashua, NH	31.7
79	Manhattan, KS	38.3
NA	Mankato-North Mankato, MN**	NA
78	Mansfield, OH	38.5
167	McAllen-Edinburg-Mission, TX	28.4
98	Medford, OR	34.6
57	Memphis, TN-MS-AR	43.6
229	Merced, CA	23.6
205	Miami (greater), FL	25.7
211	Miami-Dade County, FL M.D.	25.2
237	Michigan City-La Porte, IN	23.2
326	Midland, TX	15.7
303	Milwaukee, WI	18.9
NA	Minneapolis-St. Paul, MN-WI**	NA
100	Missoula, MT	34.5
272	Mobile, AL	21.0
249	Modesto, CA	22.5
261	Monroe, LA	21.9
53	Monroe, MI	44.8
285	Montgomery, AL	20.2
292	Morristown, TN	19.6
74	Mount Vernon-Anacortes, WA	39.6
27	Muncie, IN	51.6
14	Muskegon-Norton Shores, MI	58.7
8	Myrtle Beach, SC	65.3
220	Napa, CA	24.6
340	Naples-Marco Island, FL	13.8
81	Nashville-Davidson, TN	37.2
357	Nassau-Suffolk, NY M.D.	4.0
339	New Haven-Milford, CT	14.2
197	New Orleans, LA	26.3
353	New York (greater), NY-NJ-PA	10.0
350	New York-W. Plains NY-NJ M.D.	11.6
351	Newark-Union, NJ-PA M.D.	11.4
176	North Port-Bradenton-Sarasota, FL	27.3
70	Norwich-New London, CT	40.9
253	Oakland-Fremont, CA M.D.	22.2
41	Ocala, FL	48.2
346	Ocean City, NJ	13.3
180	Odessa, TX	27.1
186	Ogden-Clearfield, UT	26.9
71	Oklahoma City, OK	40.4
176	Olympia, WA	27.3
69	Omaha-Council Bluffs, NE-IA	41.9
136	Orlando, FL	31.4
337	Oshkosh-Neenah, WI	14.3
37	Owensboro, KY	48.5
348	Oxnard-Thousand Oaks, CA	12.1
134	Palm Bay-Melbourne, FL	31.6
292	Palm Coast, FL	19.6
89	Panama City-Lynn Haven, FL	36.2
64	Pascagoula, MS	42.4
325	Peabody, MA M.D.	16.0
58	Pensacola, FL	43.5
111	Peoria, IL	33.4
178	Philadelphia (greater) PA-NJ-MD-DE	27.2
153	Philadelphia, PA M.D.	29.9
178	Phoenix-Mesa-Scottsdale, AZ	27.2
37	Pine Bluff, AR	48.5
309	Pittsburgh, PA	18.0
28	Pittsfield, MA	50.8
263	Pocatello, ID	21.8
257	Port St. Lucie, FL	22.1
117	Portland-Vancouver, OR-WA	33.0
197	Portland, ME	26.3
337	Poughkeepsie, NY	14.3
322	Prescott, AZ	16.4
302	Provo-Orem, UT	19.0
208	Pueblo, CO	25.3
301	Punta Gorda, FL	19.1
340	Racine, WI	13.8
294	Raleigh-Cary, NC	19.5
1	Rapid City, SD	99.3
331	Reading, PA	14.8
21	Redding, CA	54.7
281	Reno-Sparks, NV	20.5
331	Richmond, VA	14.8
312	Riverside-San Bernardino, CA	17.7
232	Roanoke, VA	23.4
NA	Rochester, MN**	NA
275	Rochester, NY	20.8
35	Rockford, IL	48.8
191	Rockingham County, NH M.D.	26.7
342	Rocky Mount, NC	13.6
164	Rome, GA	28.7
215	Sacramento, CA	24.9
60	Saginaw, MI	43.0
260	Salem, OR	22.0
250	Salinas, CA	22.4
269	Salisbury, MD	21.4
73	Salt Lake City, UT	39.9
68	San Angelo, TX	42.0
140	San Antonio, TX	30.9
271	San Diego, CA	21.1
282	San Francisco (greater), CA	20.3
314	San Francisco-S. Mateo, CA M.D.	17.6
290	San Jose, CA	19.8
111	San Luis Obispo, CA	33.4
327	Sandusky, OH	15.6
344	Santa Ana-Anaheim, CA M.D.	13.5
149	Santa Barbara-Santa Maria, CA	30.3
168	Santa Cruz-Watsonville, CA	28.3
278	Santa Fe, NM	20.6
170	Santa Rosa-Petaluma, CA	28.2
299	Savannah, GA	19.3
304	Scranton--Wilkes-Barre, PA	18.7
153	Seattle (greater), WA	29.9
174	Seattle-Bellevue-Everett, WA M.D.	27.9
242	Sebastian-Vero Beach, FL	22.9
333	Sheboygan, WI	14.7
328	Sherman-Denison, TX	15.4
132	Sioux City, IA-NE-SD	31.8
19	Sioux Falls, SD	55.0
105	South Bend-Mishawaka, IN-MI	34.0
160	Spartanburg, SC	28.9
191	Spokane, WA	26.7
7	Springfield, IL	66.4
139	Springfield, MA	31.0
149	Springfield, MO	30.3
202	Springfield, OH	26.0
148	State College, PA	30.4
285	Stockton, CA	20.2
NA	St. Cloud, MN**	NA
245	St. Joseph, MO-KS	22.7
211	St. Louis, MO-IL	25.2
241	Sumter, SC	23.0
234	Syracuse, NY	23.3
86	Tacoma, WA M.D.	36.5
65	Tallahassee, FL	42.2
222	Tampa-St Petersburg, FL	24.4
228	Terre Haute, IN	23.7
39	Texarkana, TX-Texarkana, AR	48.4
188	Toledo, OH	26.8
172	Topeka, KS	28.0
336	Trenton-Ewing, NJ	14.4
166	Tucson, AZ	28.6
67	Tulsa, OK	42.1
159	Tuscaloosa, AL	29.0
45	Tyler, TX	46.7
329	Utica-Rome, NY	15.3
168	Valdosta, GA	28.3
181	Vallejo-Fairfield, CA	27.0
18	Victoria, TX	55.2
265	Virginia Beach-Norfolk, VA-NC	21.7
257	Visalia-Porterville, CA	22.1
22	Waco, TX	54.2
261	Warner Robins, GA	21.9
217	Warren-Farmington Hills, MI M.D.	24.8
323	Washington (greater) DC-VA-MD-WV	16.1
318	Washington, DC-VA-MD-WV M.D.	17.2
36	Waterloo-Cedar Falls, IA	48.6
87	Wausau, WI	36.4
239	Wenatchee, WA	23.1
207	West Palm Beach, FL M.D.	25.4
155	Wichita Falls, TX	29.8
31	Wichita, KS	49.8
278	Williamsport, PA	20.6
208	Wilmington, DE-MD-NJ M.D.	25.3
195	Wilmington, NC	26.4
143	Winchester, VA-WV	30.8
155	Winston-Salem, NC	29.8
287	Worcester, MA	19.9
61	Yakima, WA	42.9
130	York-Hanover, PA	31.9
143	Yuba City, CA	30.8
224	Yuma, AZ	24.2

Source: Reported data from the F.B.I. "Crime in the United States 2011"
*Forcible rape is the carnal knowledge of a female forcibly and against her will. Assaults or attempts to commit rape by force or threat of force are included. However, statutory rape without force and other sex offenses are excluded. **Not available

14. Rape Rate in 2011 (continued)
National Rate = 26.8 Rapes per 100,000 Population*

Rank Order - Metro Area

RANK	METROPOLITAN AREA	RATE
1	Rapid City, SD	99.3
2	Danville, IL	95.3
3	Anchorage, AK	92.9
4	Longview, WA	81.7
5	Farmington, NM	79.1
6	Bay City, MI	68.7
7	Springfield, IL	66.4
8	Myrtle Beach, SC	65.3
9	Lima, OH	63.0
10	Grand Junction, CO	61.6
11	Battle Creek, MI	61.0
12	Colorado Springs, CO	60.1
13	Corpus Christi, TX	59.7
14	Muskegon-Norton Shores, MI	58.7
15	Lincoln, NE	57.1
16	Champaign-Urbana, IL	55.5
17	Bloomington-Normal, IL	55.3
18	Victoria, TX	55.2
19	Flint, MI	55.0
19	Sioux Falls, SD	55.0
21	Redding, CA	54.7
22	Waco, TX	54.2
23	Hot Springs, AR	52.7
24	Jackson, TN	52.4
25	Dover, DE	51.8
25	Kankakee-Bradley, IL	51.8
27	Muncie, IN	51.6
28	Pittsfield, MA	50.8
29	Flagstaff, AZ	50.6
30	Lawton, OK	50.2
31	Denver-Aurora, CO	49.8
31	Wichita, KS	49.8
33	Fairbanks, AK	49.6
34	Ann Arbor, MI	49.1
35	Rockford, IL	48.8
36	Waterloo-Cedar Falls, IA	48.6
37	Owensboro, KY	48.5
37	Pine Bluff, AR	48.5
39	Jonesboro, AR	48.4
39	Texarkana, TX-Texarkana, AR	48.4
41	Holland-Grand Haven, MI	48.2
41	Ocala, FL	48.2
43	Bremerton-Silverdale, WA	47.8
44	Lansing-East Lansing, MI	46.8
45	Tyler, TX	46.7
46	Little Rock, AR	46.4
47	Gainesville, FL	46.3
48	Fort Smith, AR-OK	46.2
49	Bellingham, WA	46.0
50	Davenport, IA-IL	45.9
51	Erie, PA	45.8
52	Barnstable Town, MA	45.6
53	Monroe, MI	44.8
54	Columbus, OH	44.7
55	Altoona, PA	43.9
55	Amarillo, TX	43.9
57	Memphis, TN-MS-AR	43.6
58	Pensacola, FL	43.5
59	Fond du Lac, WI	43.1
60	Saginaw, MI	43.0
61	Yakima, WA	42.9
62	Grand Rapids-Wyoming, MI	42.8
63	Detroit-Livonia-Dearborn, MI M.D.	42.5
64	Pascagoula, MS	42.4
65	Cheyenne, WY	42.2
65	Tallahassee, FL	42.2
67	Tulsa, OK	42.1
68	San Angelo, TX	42.0
69	Omaha-Council Bluffs, NE-IA	41.9
70	Norwich-New London, CT	40.9
71	Oklahoma City, OK	40.4
72	Gadsden, AL	40.0
73	Salt Lake City, UT	39.9
74	Albuquerque, NM	39.6
74	Mount Vernon-Anacortes, WA	39.6
76	Clarksville, TN-KY	39.5
77	Las Vegas-Paradise, NV	39.1
78	Mansfield, OH	38.5
79	Manhattan, KS	38.3
80	Joplin, MO	37.5
81	Nashville-Davidson, TN	37.2
82	Akron, OH	37.1
82	Bismarck, ND	37.1
84	Birmingham-Hoover, AL	36.8
85	Jacksonville, NC	36.7
86	Tacoma, WA M.D.	36.5
87	Augusta, GA-SC	36.4
87	Wausau, WI	36.4
89	Cape Girardeau, MO-IL	36.2
89	Panama City-Lynn Haven, FL	36.2
91	Anniston-Oxford, AL	36.1
92	Kansas City, MO-KS	35.7
93	Johnstown, PA	35.4
94	Danville, VA	35.2
95	Kennewick-Pasco-Richland, WA	35.0
95	Lawrence, KS	35.0
97	Longview, TX	34.7
98	Dayton, OH	34.6
98	Medford, OR	34.6
100	Beaumont-Port Arthur, TX	34.5
100	Bend, OR	34.5
100	Missoula, MT	34.5
103	Lewiston-Auburn, ME	34.4
104	Alexandria, LA	34.1
105	South Bend-Mishawaka, IN-MI	34.0
106	Anderson, SC	33.8
107	Chico, CA	33.7
107	Fort Worth-Arlington, TX M.D.	33.7
107	Greenville, SC	33.7
110	Cumberland, MD-WV	33.6
111	Blacksburg, VA	33.4
111	Peoria, IL	33.4
111	San Luis Obispo, CA	33.4
114	Ames, IA	33.3
114	Killeen-Temple-Fort Hood, TX	33.3
116	Eugene-Springfield, OR	33.2
117	Portland-Vancouver, OR-WA	33.0
118	Kingsport, TN-VA	32.9
118	Laredo, TX	32.9
120	Harrisburg-Carlisle, PA	32.8
121	Crestview-Fort Walton Beach, FL	32.7
122	Cleveland-Elyria-Mentor, OH	32.6
122	Lexington-Fayette, KY	32.6
124	Detroit (greater), MI	32.3
124	Jackson, MS	32.3
124	Lubbock, TX	32.3
127	Indianapolis, IN	32.2
127	Jacksonville, FL	32.2
129	Albany, GA	32.0
130	Iowa City, IA	31.9
130	York-Hanover, PA	31.9
132	Sioux City, IA-NE-SD	31.8
133	Manchester-Nashua, NH	31.7
134	Palm Bay-Melbourne, FL	31.6
135	Fort Collins-Loveland, CO	31.5
136	Canton, OH	31.4
136	Orlando, FL	31.4
138	Gulfport-Biloxi, MS	31.2
139	Springfield, MA	31.0
140	Cincinnati-Middletown, OH-KY-IN	30.9
140	Des Moines-West Des Moines, IA	30.9
140	San Antonio, TX	30.9
143	College Station-Bryan, TX	30.8
143	Winchester, VA-WV	30.8
143	Yuba City, CA	30.8
146	Elizabethtown, KY	30.7
147	Lafayette, IN	30.6
148	State College, PA	30.4
149	Santa Barbara-Santa Maria, CA	30.3
149	Springfield, MO	30.3
151	Dothan, AL	30.1
152	Bowling Green, KY	30.0
153	Philadelphia, PA M.D.	29.9
153	Seattle (greater), WA	29.9
155	Wichita Falls, TX	29.8
155	Winston-Salem, NC	29.8
157	Decatur, IL	29.7
158	El Paso, TX	29.5
159	Tuscaloosa, AL	29.0
160	Florence, SC	28.9
160	Spartanburg, SC	28.9
162	Idaho Falls, ID	28.8
162	Las Cruces, NM	28.8
164	Fort Wayne, IN	28.7
164	Rome, GA	28.7
166	Tucson, AZ	28.6
167	McAllen-Edinburg-Mission, TX	28.4
168	Santa Cruz-Watsonville, CA	28.3
168	Valdosta, GA	28.3
170	Cleveland, TN	28.2
170	Santa Rosa-Petaluma, CA	28.2
172	Boston-Quincy, MA M.D.	28.0
172	Topeka, KS	28.0
174	Seattle-Bellevue-Everett, WA M.D.	27.9
175	Charleston, WV	27.6
176	North Port-Bradenton-Sarasota, FL	27.3
176	Olympia, WA	27.3
178	Philadelphia (greater) PA-NJ-MD-DE	27.2
178	Phoenix-Mesa-Scottsdale, AZ	27.2
180	Odessa, TX	27.1

Note: All listings are for Metropolitan Statistical Areas (M.S.A.s) except for those ending with "M.D." Listings with "M.D." are Metropolitan Divisions which are smaller parts of eleven large M.S.A.s. See explanatory note at beginning of metropolitan area section.

Rank Order - Metro Area (continued)

RANK	METROPOLITAN AREA	RATE
181	Boulder, CO	27.0
181	Charlottesville, VA	27.0
181	Knoxville, TN	27.0
181	Louisville, KY-IN	27.0
181	Vallejo-Fairfield, CA	27.0
186	Dallas (greater), TX	26.9
186	Ogden-Clearfield, UT	26.9
188	Harrisonburg, VA	26.8
188	Houston, TX	26.8
188	Toledo, OH	26.8
191	Fort Lauderdale, FL M.D.	26.7
191	Huntsville, AL	26.7
191	Rockingham County, NH M.D.	26.7
191	Spokane, WA	26.7
195	Brunswick, GA	26.4
195	Wilmington, NC	26.4
197	Billings, MT	26.3
197	Glens Falls, NY	26.3
197	New Orleans, LA	26.3
197	Portland, ME	26.3
201	Evansville, IN-KY	26.1
202	Greeley, CO	26.0
202	Springfield, OH	26.0
204	Columbia, MO	25.9
205	Miami (greater), FL	25.7
206	Gary, IN M.D.	25.6
207	West Palm Beach, FL M.D.	25.4
208	Bridgeport-Stamford, CT	25.3
208	Pueblo, CO	25.3
208	Wilmington, DE-MD-NJ M.D.	25.3
211	Boise City-Nampa, ID	25.2
211	Miami-Dade County, FL M.D.	25.2
211	St. Louis, MO-IL	25.2
214	Madison, WI	25.0
215	Baltimore-Towson, MD	24.9
215	Sacramento, CA	24.9
217	Houma, LA	24.8
217	Warren-Farmington Hills, MI M.D.	24.8
219	Eau Claire, WI	24.7
220	Charlotte-Gastonia, NC-SC	24.6
220	Napa, CA	24.6
222	Tampa-St Petersburg, FL	24.4
223	Cedar Rapids, IA	24.3
224	Janesville, WI	24.2
224	Yuma, AZ	24.2
226	Green Bay, WI	24.1
227	Decatur, AL	23.9
228	Terre Haute, IN	23.7
229	Merced, CA	23.6
230	Dallas-Plano-Irving, TX M.D.	23.5
230	Kingston, NY	23.5
232	Lakeland, FL	23.4
232	Roanoke, VA	23.4
234	Binghamton, NY	23.3
234	Deltona-Daytona Beach, FL	23.3
234	Syracuse, NY	23.3
237	Kokomo, IN	23.2
237	Michigan City-La Porte, IN	23.2
239	Columbus, GA-AL	23.1
239	Wenatchee, WA	23.1
241	Sumter, SC	23.0
242	Durham-Chapel Hill, NC	22.9
242	Sebastian-Vero Beach, FL	22.9
244	Austin-Round Rock, TX	22.8
245	Auburn, AL	22.7
245	St. Joseph, MO-KS	22.7
247	Athens-Clarke County, GA	22.6
247	Buffalo-Niagara Falls, NY	22.6
249	Modesto, CA	22.5
250	Boston (greater), MA-NH	22.4
250	Salinas, CA	22.4
252	Dubuque, IA	22.3
253	Bloomington, IN	22.2
253	Brownsville-Harlingen, TX	22.2
253	Lake Havasu City-Kingman, AZ	22.2
253	Oakland-Fremont, CA M.D.	22.2
257	Lancaster, PA	22.1
257	Port St. Lucie, FL	22.1
257	Visalia-Porterville, CA	22.1
260	Salem, OR	22.0
261	Monroe, LA	21.9
261	Warner Robins, GA	21.9
263	Atlantic City, NJ	21.8
263	Pocatello, ID	21.8
265	Bakersfield, CA	21.7
265	Macon, GA	21.7
265	Virginia Beach-Norfolk, VA-NC	21.7
268	Lake Co.-Kenosha Co., IL-WI M.D.	21.5
269	Salisbury, MD	21.4
270	Abilene, TX	21.3
271	San Diego, CA	21.1
272	Casper, WY	21.0
272	Fayetteville, NC	21.0
272	Mobile, AL	21.0
275	Corvallis, OR	20.8
275	Dalton, GA	20.8
275	Rochester, NY	20.8
278	Atlanta, GA	20.6
278	Santa Fe, NM	20.6
278	Williamsport, PA	20.6
281	Reno-Sparks, NV	20.5
282	Hinesville, GA	20.3
282	Lafayette, LA	20.3
282	San Francisco (greater), CA	20.3
285	Montgomery, AL	20.2
285	Stockton, CA	20.2
287	Appleton, WI	19.9
287	Lynchburg, VA	19.9
287	Worcester, MA	19.9
290	San Jose, CA	19.8
291	Hartford, CT	19.7
292	Morristown, TN	19.6
292	Palm Coast, FL	19.6
294	Camden, NJ M.D.	19.5
294	Great Falls, MT	19.5
294	Raleigh-Cary, NC	19.5
297	Hanford-Corcoran, CA	19.4
297	Lebanon, PA	19.4
299	Savannah, GA	19.3
300	Los Angeles County, CA M.D.	19.2
301	Punta Gorda, FL	19.1
302	Provo-Orem, UT	19.0
303	Milwaukee, WI	18.9
304	Allentown, PA-NJ	18.7
304	Scranton--Wilkes-Barre, PA	18.7
306	Baton Rouge, LA	18.4
307	Burlington, NC	18.3
308	Gainesville, GA	18.1
309	Albany-Schenectady-Troy, NY	18.0
309	Pittsburgh, PA	18.0
311	Los Angeles (greater), CA	17.8
312	Madera, CA	17.7
312	Riverside-San Bernardino, CA	17.7
314	El Centro, CA	17.6
314	San Francisco-S. Mateo, CA M.D.	17.6
316	Chattanooga, TN-GA	17.4
317	Cambridge-Newton, MA M.D.	17.3
318	Washington, DC-VA-MD-WV M.D.	17.2
319	Cape Coral-Fort Myers, FL	17.1
320	Asheville, NC	17.0
321	Columbus, IN	16.8
322	Prescott, AZ	16.4
323	Fresno, CA	16.1
323	Washington (greater) DC-VA-MD-WV	16.1
325	Peabody, MA M.D.	16.0
326	Midland, TX	15.7
327	Sandusky, OH	15.6
328	Sherman-Denison, TX	15.4
329	Utica-Rome, NY	15.3
330	Florence-Muscle Shoals, AL	14.9
331	Reading, PA	14.8
331	Richmond, VA	14.8
333	Sheboygan, WI	14.7
334	Elmira, NY	14.6
334	Jefferson City, MO	14.6
336	Trenton-Ewing, NJ	14.4
337	Oshkosh-Neenah, WI	14.3
337	Poughkeepsie, NY	14.3
339	New Haven-Milford, CT	14.2
340	Naples-Marco Island, FL	13.8
340	Racine, WI	13.8
342	Bangor, ME	13.6
342	Rocky Mount, NC	13.6
344	Hickory, NC	13.5
344	Santa Ana-Anaheim, CA M.D.	13.5
346	Ocean City, NJ	13.3
347	Hagerstown-Martinsburg, MD-WV	12.6
348	Oxnard-Thousand Oaks, CA	12.1
349	Bethesda-Frederick, MD M.D.	12.0
350	New York-W. Plains NY-NJ M.D.	11.6
351	Newark-Union, NJ-PA M.D.	11.4
352	Logan, UT-ID	10.2
353	New York (greater), NY-NJ-PA	10.0
354	Johnson City, TN	9.5
355	Edison, NJ M.D.	7.9
356	Goldsboro, NC	4.8
357	Nassau-Suffolk, NY M.D.	4.0
358	Carson City, NV	0.0
NA	Chicago (greater), IL-IN-WI**	NA
NA	Chicago-Joilet-Naperville, IL M.D.**	NA
NA	Duluth, MN-WI**	NA
NA	Fargo, ND-MN**	NA
NA	Grand Forks, ND-MN**	NA
NA	La Crosse, WI-MN**	NA
NA	Mankato-North Mankato, MN**	NA
NA	Minneapolis-St. Paul, MN-WI**	NA
NA	Rochester, MN**	NA
NA	St. Cloud, MN**	NA

Source: Reported data from the F.B.I. "Crime in the United States 2011"
*Forcible rape is the carnal knowledge of a female forcibly and against her will. Assaults or attempts to commit rape by force or threat of force are included. However, statutory rape without force and other sex offenses are excluded. **Not available

Alpha Order - Metro Area

15. Percent Change in Rape Rate: 2010 to 2011
National Percent Change = 3.2% Decrease*

RANK	METROPOLITAN AREA	% CHANGE	RANK	METROPOLITAN AREA	% CHANGE	RANK	METROPOLITAN AREA	% CHANGE
317	Abilene, TX	(56.4)	NA	Charleston, WV**	NA	73	Fort Lauderdale, FL M.D.	8.1
213	Akron, OH	(9.3)	NA	Charlotte-Gastonia, NC-SC**	NA	62	Fort Smith, AR-OK	11.3
249	Albany-Schenectady-Troy, NY	(14.3)	236	Charlottesville, VA	(12.9)	124	Fort Wayne, IN	0.0
22	Albany, GA	28.5	309	Chattanooga, TN-GA	(33.6)	91	Fort Worth-Arlington, TX M.D.	5.3
230	Albuquerque, NM	(11.6)	173	Cheyenne, WY	(5.4)	264	Fresno, CA	(17.4)
10	Alexandria, LA	47.6	NA	Chicago (greater), IL-IN-WI**	NA	NA	Gadsden, AL**	NA
200	Allentown, PA-NJ	(7.9)	NA	Chicago-Joilet-Naperville, IL M.D.**	NA	194	Gainesville, FL	(7.6)
46	Altoona, PA	15.5	268	Chico, CA	(18.6)	184	Gainesville, GA	(6.2)
79	Amarillo, TX	7.6	162	Cincinnati-Middletown, OH-KY-IN	(4.6)	NA	Gary, IN M.D.**	NA
275	Ames, IA	(20.1)	97	Clarksville, TN-KY	4.2	136	Glens Falls, NY	(1.1)
73	Anchorage, AK	8.1	113	Cleveland-Elyria-Mentor, OH	1.6	283	Goldsboro, NC	(21.3)
190	Anderson, SC	(7.1)	21	Cleveland, TN	28.8	NA	Grand Forks, ND-MN**	NA
54	Ann Arbor, MI	13.7	301	College Station-Bryan, TX	(29.0)	27	Grand Junction, CO	24.2
NA	Anniston-Oxford, AL**	NA	192	Colorado Springs, CO	(7.3)	205	Grand Rapids-Wyoming, MI	(8.4)
188	Appleton, WI	(7.0)	196	Columbia, MO	(7.8)	NA	Great Falls, MT**	NA
285	Asheville, NC	(22.0)	NA	Columbus, GA-AL**	NA	169	Greeley, CO	(5.1)
48	Athens-Clarke County, GA	15.3	315	Columbus, IN	(52.3)	282	Green Bay, WI	(21.2)
140	Atlanta, GA	(1.4)	101	Columbus, OH	3.5	104	Greenville, SC	2.7
48	Atlantic City, NJ	15.3	60	Corpus Christi, TX	11.8	228	Gulfport-Biloxi, MS	(11.4)
NA	Auburn, AL**	NA	122	Corvallis, OR	0.5	300	Hagerstown-Martinsburg, MD-WV	(28.0)
149	Augusta, GA-SC	(2.7)	65	Crestview-Fort Walton Beach, FL	10.5	118	Hanford-Corcoran, CA	1.0
195	Austin-Round Rock, TX	(7.7)	NA	Cumberland, MD-WV**	NA	159	Harrisburg-Carlisle, PA	(4.4)
71	Bakersfield, CA	9.0	162	Dallas (greater), TX	(4.6)	44	Harrisonburg, VA	16.5
90	Baltimore-Towson, MD	5.5	225	Dallas-Plano-Irving, TX M.D.	(10.6)	62	Hartford, CT	11.3
77	Bangor, ME	7.9	253	Dalton, GA	(14.8)	286	Hickory, NC	(22.4)
24	Barnstable Town, MA	26.3	33	Danville, IL	19.3	201	Hinesville, GA	(8.1)
NA	Baton Rouge, LA**	NA	16	Danville, VA	38.0	261	Holland-Grand Haven, MI	(16.9)
271	Battle Creek, MI	(19.0)	NA	Davenport, IA-IL**	NA	132	Hot Springs, AR	(0.9)
234	Bay City, MI	(12.0)	70	Dayton, OH	9.1	67	Houma, LA	10.2
207	Beaumont-Port Arthur, TX	(8.5)	NA	Decatur, AL**	NA	NA	Houston, TX**	NA
103	Bellingham, WA	2.9	91	Decatur, IL	5.3	NA	Huntsville, AL**	NA
34	Bend, OR	19.0	273	Deltona-Daytona Beach, FL	(19.7)	108	Idaho Falls, ID	2.5
176	Bethesda-Frederick, MD M.D.	(5.5)	112	Denver-Aurora, CO	1.8	NA	Indianapolis, IN**	NA
NA	Billings, MT**	NA	215	Des Moines-West Des Moines, IA	(9.4)	274	Iowa City, IA	(19.8)
53	Binghamton, NY	14.8	NA	Detroit (greater), MI**	NA	97	Jacksonville, FL	4.2
NA	Birmingham-Hoover, AL**	NA	114	Detroit-Livonia-Dearborn, MI M.D.	1.4	NA	Jacksonville, NC**	NA
61	Bismarck, ND	11.7	NA	Dothan, AL**	NA	119	Jackson, MS	0.9
39	Blacksburg, VA	16.8	37	Dover, DE	18.0	15	Jackson, TN	39.0
29	Bloomington-Normal, IL	22.1	208	Dubuque, IA	(8.6)	297	Janesville, WI	(26.4)
291	Bloomington, IN	(24.5)	NA	Duluth, MN-WI**	NA	223	Jefferson City, MO	(10.4)
294	Boise City-Nampa, ID	(25.2)	152	Durham-Chapel Hill, NC	(3.4)	319	Johnson City, TN	(58.1)
132	Boston (greater), MA-NH	(0.9)	216	Eau Claire, WI	(9.5)	2	Johnstown, PA	112.0
99	Boston-Quincy, MA M.D.	4.1	138	Edison, NJ M.D.	(1.2)	50	Jonesboro, AR	15.2
12	Boulder, CO	42.9	51	El Centro, CA	15.0	253	Joplin, MO	(14.8)
288	Bowling Green, KY	(23.7)	123	El Paso, TX	0.3	NA	Kankakee-Bradley, IL**	NA
305	Bremerton-Silverdale, WA	(30.2)	11	Elizabethtown, KY	45.5	NA	Kansas City, MO-KS**	NA
8	Bridgeport-Stamford, CT	58.1	45	Elmira, NY	15.9	46	Kennewick-Pasco-Richland, WA	15.5
230	Brownsville-Harlingen, TX	(11.6)	150	Erie, PA	(3.0)	277	Killeen-Temple-Fort Hood, TX	(20.7)
102	Brunswick, GA	3.1	NA	Eugene-Springfield, OR**	NA	177	Kingsport, TN-VA	(5.7)
235	Buffalo-Niagara Falls, NY	(12.7)	131	Evansville, IN-KY	(0.8)	17	Kingston, NY	36.6
31	Burlington, NC	21.2	320	Fairbanks, AK	(74.3)	179	Knoxville, TN	(5.9)
116	Cambridge-Newton, MA M.D.	1.2	NA	Fargo, ND-MN**	NA	266	Kokomo, IN	(18.0)
64	Camden, NJ M.D.	10.8	88	Farmington, NM	5.7	NA	La Crosse, WI-MN**	NA
110	Canton, OH	2.3	132	Fayetteville, NC	(0.9)	38	Lafayette, IN	17.2
290	Cape Coral-Fort Myers, FL	(24.3)	96	Flagstaff, AZ	4.3	57	Lafayette, LA	12.8
39	Cape Girardeau, MO-IL	16.8	109	Flint, MI	2.4	NA	Lake Co.-Kenosha Co., IL-WI M.D.**	NA
321	Carson City, NV	(100.0)	NA	Florence-Muscle Shoals, AL**	NA	NA	Lake Havasu City-Kingman, AZ**	NA
7	Casper, WY	62.8	162	Florence, SC	(4.6)	78	Lakeland, FL	7.8
68	Cedar Rapids, IA	9.5	13	Fond du Lac, WI	39.5	170	Lancaster, PA	(5.2)
NA	Champaign-Urbana, IL**	NA	258	Fort Collins-Loveland, CO	(16.7)	148	Lansing-East Lansing, MI	(2.5)

Note: All listings are for Metropolitan Statistical Areas (M.S.A.s) except for those ending with "M.D." Listings with "M.D." are Metropolitan Divisions which are smaller parts of eleven large M.S.A.s. See explanatory note at beginning of metropolitan area section.

Alpha Order - Metro Area (continued)

RANK	METROPOLITAN AREA	% CHANGE	RANK	METROPOLITAN AREA	% CHANGE	RANK	METROPOLITAN AREA	% CHANGE
138	Laredo, TX	(1.2)	196	Oklahoma City, OK	(7.8)	179	Savannah, GA	(5.9)
157	Las Cruces, NM	(4.3)	271	Olympia, WA	(19.0)	247	Scranton--Wilkes-Barre, PA	(14.2)
142	Las Vegas-Paradise, NV	(1.8)	76	Omaha-Council Bluffs, NE-IA	8.0	226	Seattle (greater), WA	(10.7)
218	Lawrence, KS	(9.6)	167	Orlando, FL	(4.8)	222	Seattle-Bellevue-Everett, WA M.D.	(10.3)
232	Lawton, OK	(11.8)	NA	Oshkosh-Neenah, WI**	NA	39	Sebastian-Vero Beach, FL	16.8
82	Lebanon, PA	6.6	25	Owensboro, KY	25.6	NA	Sheboygan, WI**	NA
196	Lewiston-Auburn, ME	(7.8)	187	Oxnard-Thousand Oaks, CA	(6.9)	6	Sioux City, IA-NE-SD	71.9
NA	Lexington-Fayette, KY**	NA	129	Palm Bay-Melbourne, FL	(0.3)	23	Sioux Falls, SD	27.0
43	Lima, OH	16.7	35	Palm Coast, FL	18.8	124	South Bend-Mishawaka, IN-MI	0.0
39	Lincoln, NE	16.8	140	Panama City-Lynn Haven, FL	(1.4)	124	Spartanburg, SC	0.0
143	Little Rock, AR	(2.1)	298	Pascagoula, MS	(27.1)	245	Spokane, WA	(14.1)
318	Logan, UT-ID	(56.8)	292	Peabody, MA M.D.	(24.9)	173	Springfield, IL	(5.4)
289	Longview, TX	(24.2)	281	Pensacola, FL	(21.1)	299	Springfield, MA	(27.9)
252	Longview, WA	(14.5)	220	Peoria, IL	(9.7)	227	Springfield, MO	(10.9)
208	Los Angeles County, CA M.D.	(8.6)	162	Philadelphia (greater) PA-NJ-MD-DE	(4.6)	220	Springfield, OH	(9.7)
210	Los Angeles (greater), CA	(8.7)	193	Philadelphia, PA M.D.	(7.4)	3	State College, PA	87.7
124	Louisville, KY-IN	0.0	93	Phoenix-Mesa-Scottsdale, AZ	5.0	255	Stockton, CA	(15.1)
307	Lubbock, TX	(32.3)	237	Pine Bluff, AR	(13.2)	NA	St. Cloud, MN**	NA
216	Lynchburg, VA	(9.5)	83	Pittsburgh, PA	6.5	110	St. Joseph, MO-KS	2.3
247	Macon, GA	(14.2)	18	Pittsfield, MA	34.7	151	St. Louis, MO-IL	(3.1)
313	Madera, CA	(45.4)	310	Pocatello, ID	(40.1)	302	Sumter, SC	(29.2)
100	Madison, WI	3.7	279	Port St. Lucie, FL	(20.8)	106	Syracuse, NY	2.6
160	Manchester-Nashua, NH	(4.5)	NA	Portland-Vancouver, OR-WA**	NA	232	Tacoma, WA M.D.	(11.8)
124	Manhattan, KS	0.0	205	Portland, ME	(8.4)	256	Tallahassee, FL	(16.1)
NA	Mankato-North Mankato, MN**	NA	120	Poughkeepsie, NY	0.7	203	Tampa-St Petersburg, FL	(8.3)
115	Mansfield, OH	1.3	303	Prescott, AZ	(29.9)	NA	Terre Haute, IN**	NA
143	McAllen-Edinburg-Mission, TX	(2.1)	244	Provo-Orem, UT	(14.0)	56	Texarkana, TX-Texarkana, AR	13.3
188	Medford, OR	(7.0)	NA	Pueblo, CO**	NA	172	Toledo, OH	(5.3)
173	Memphis, TN-MS-AR	(5.4)	19	Punta Gorda, FL	31.7	136	Topeka, KS	(1.1)
267	Merced, CA	(18.3)	237	Racine, WI	(13.2)	1	Trenton-Ewing, NJ	121.5
72	Miami (greater), FL	8.9	32	Raleigh-Cary, NC	21.1	28	Tucson, AZ	22.2
36	Miami-Dade County, FL M.D.	18.3	86	Rapid City, SD	6.3	130	Tulsa, OK	(0.5)
304	Michigan City-La Porte, IN	(30.1)	160	Reading, PA	(4.5)	NA	Tuscaloosa, AL**	NA
316	Midland, TX	(53.4)	258	Redding, CA	(16.7)	249	Tyler, TX	(14.3)
89	Milwaukee, WI	5.6	269	Reno-Sparks, NV	(18.7)	296	Utica-Rome, NY	(26.1)
NA	Minneapolis-St. Paul, MN-WI**	NA	185	Richmond, VA	(6.3)	65	Valdosta, GA	10.5
NA	Missoula, MT**	NA	237	Riverside-San Bernardino, CA	(13.2)	287	Vallejo-Fairfield, CA	(23.1)
263	Mobile, AL	(17.3)	106	Roanoke, VA	2.6	117	Victoria, TX	1.1
242	Modesto, CA	(13.8)	NA	Rochester, MN**	NA	84	Virginia Beach-Norfolk, VA-NC	6.4
186	Monroe, LA	(6.4)	179	Rochester, NY	(5.9)	154	Visalia-Porterville, CA	(3.5)
279	Monroe, MI	(20.8)	203	Rockford, IL	(8.3)	81	Waco, TX	6.9
NA	Montgomery, AL**	NA	73	Rockingham County, NH M.D.	8.1	146	Warner Robins, GA	(2.2)
265	Morristown, TN	(17.6)	311	Rocky Mount, NC	(42.9)	NA	Warren-Farmington Hills, MI M.D.**	NA
157	Mount Vernon-Anacortes, WA	(4.3)	29	Rome, GA	22.1	218	Washington (greater) DC-VA-MD-WV	(9.6)
4	Muncie, IN	85.6	162	Sacramento, CA	(4.6)	223	Washington, DC-VA-MD-WV M.D.	(10.4)
256	Muskegon-Norton Shores, MI	(16.1)	312	Saginaw, MI	(43.4)	20	Waterloo-Cedar Falls, IA	30.6
9	Myrtle Beach, SC	52.9	240	Salem, OR	(13.4)	5	Wausau, WI	78.4
51	Napa, CA	15.0	59	Salinas, CA	12.0	314	Wenatchee, WA	(46.8)
261	Naples-Marco Island, FL	(16.9)	295	Salisbury, MD	(25.4)	168	West Palm Beach, FL M.D.	(4.9)
213	Nashville-Davidson, TN	(9.3)	241	Salt Lake City, UT	(13.6)	191	Wichita Falls, TX	(7.2)
284	Nassau-Suffolk, NY M.D.	(21.6)	276	San Angelo, TX	(20.2)	183	Wichita, KS	(6.0)
196	New Haven-Milford, CT	(7.8)	170	San Antonio, TX	(5.2)	242	Williamsport, PA	(13.8)
104	New Orleans, LA	2.7	156	San Diego, CA	(4.1)	152	Wilmington, DE-MD-NJ M.D.	(3.4)
135	New York (greater), NY-NJ-PA	(1.0)	249	San Francisco (greater), CA	(14.3)	177	Wilmington, NC	(5.7)
95	New York-W. Plains NY-NJ M.D.	4.5	121	San Francisco-S. Mateo, CA M.D.	0.6	308	Winchester, VA-WV	(32.6)
260	Newark-Union, NJ-PA M.D.	(16.8)	211	San Jose, CA	(8.8)	147	Winston-Salem, NC	(2.3)
80	North Port-Bradenton-Sarasota, FL	7.5	68	San Luis Obispo, CA	9.5	270	Worcester, MA	(18.8)
55	Norwich-New London, CT	13.6	202	Sandusky, OH	(8.2)	143	Yakima, WA	(2.1)
277	Oakland-Fremont, CA M.D.	(20.7)	211	Santa Ana-Anaheim, CA M.D.	(8.8)	14	York-Hanover, PA	39.3
58	Ocala, FL	12.4	179	Santa Barbara-Santa Maria, CA	(5.9)	155	Yuba City, CA	(4.0)
292	Ocean City, NJ	(24.9)	84	Santa Cruz-Watsonville, CA	6.4	26	Yuma, AZ	24.7
93	Odessa, TX	5.0	306	Santa Fe, NM	(32.2)			
245	Ogden-Clearfield, UT	(14.1)	87	Santa Rosa-Petaluma, CA	6.0			

Source: CQ Press using reported data from the F.B.I. "Crime in the United States 2011"
*Forcible rape is the carnal knowledge of a female forcibly and against her will. Assaults or attempts to commit rape by force or threat of force are included. However, statutory rape without force and other sex offenses are excluded. **Not available

15. Percent Change in Rape Rate: 2010 to 2011 (continued)
National Percent Change = 3.2% Decrease*

Rank Order - Metro Area

RANK	METROPOLITAN AREA	% CHANGE	RANK	METROPOLITAN AREA	% CHANGE	RANK	METROPOLITAN AREA	% CHANGE
1	Trenton-Ewing, NJ	121.5	61	Bismarck, ND	11.7	121	San Francisco-S. Mateo, CA M.D.	0.6
2	Johnstown, PA	112.0	62	Fort Smith, AR-OK	11.3	122	Corvallis, OR	0.5
3	State College, PA	87.7	62	Hartford, CT	11.3	123	El Paso, TX	0.3
4	Muncie, IN	85.6	64	Camden, NJ M.D.	10.8	124	Fort Wayne, IN	0.0
5	Wausau, WI	78.4	65	Crestview-Fort Walton Beach, FL	10.5	124	Louisville, KY-IN	0.0
6	Sioux City, IA-NE-SD	71.9	65	Valdosta, GA	10.5	124	Manhattan, KS	0.0
7	Casper, WY	62.8	67	Houma, LA	10.2	124	South Bend-Mishawaka, IN-MI	0.0
8	Bridgeport-Stamford, CT	58.1	68	Cedar Rapids, IA	9.5	124	Spartanburg, SC	0.0
9	Myrtle Beach, SC	52.9	68	San Luis Obispo, CA	9.5	129	Palm Bay-Melbourne, FL	(0.3)
10	Alexandria, LA	47.6	70	Dayton, OH	9.1	130	Tulsa, OK	(0.5)
11	Elizabethtown, KY	45.5	71	Bakersfield, CA	9.0	131	Evansville, IN-KY	(0.8)
12	Boulder, CO	42.9	72	Miami (greater), FL	8.9	132	Boston (greater), MA-NH	(0.9)
13	Fond du Lac, WI	39.5	73	Anchorage, AK	8.1	132	Fayetteville, NC	(0.9)
14	York-Hanover, PA	39.3	73	Fort Lauderdale, FL M.D.	8.1	132	Hot Springs, AR	(0.9)
15	Jackson, TN	39.0	73	Rockingham County, NH M.D.	8.1	135	New York (greater), NY-NJ-PA	(1.0)
16	Danville, VA	38.0	76	Omaha-Council Bluffs, NE-IA	8.0	136	Glens Falls, NY	(1.1)
17	Kingston, NY	36.6	77	Bangor, ME	7.9	136	Topeka, KS	(1.1)
18	Pittsfield, MA	34.7	78	Lakeland, FL	7.8	138	Edison, NJ M.D.	(1.2)
19	Punta Gorda, FL	31.7	79	Amarillo, TX	7.6	138	Laredo, TX	(1.2)
20	Waterloo-Cedar Falls, IA	30.6	80	North Port-Bradenton-Sarasota, FL	7.5	140	Atlanta, GA	(1.4)
21	Cleveland, TN	28.8	81	Waco, TX	6.9	140	Panama City-Lynn Haven, FL	(1.4)
22	Albany, GA	28.5	82	Lebanon, PA	6.6	142	Las Vegas-Paradise, NV	(1.8)
23	Sioux Falls, SD	27.0	83	Pittsburgh, PA	6.5	143	Little Rock, AR	(2.1)
24	Barnstable Town, MA	26.3	84	Santa Cruz-Watsonville, CA	6.4	143	McAllen-Edinburg-Mission, TX	(2.1)
25	Owensboro, KY	25.6	84	Virginia Beach-Norfolk, VA-NC	6.4	143	Yakima, WA	(2.1)
26	Yuma, AZ	24.7	86	Rapid City, SD	6.3	146	Warner Robins, GA	(2.2)
27	Grand Junction, CO	24.2	87	Santa Rosa-Petaluma, CA	6.0	147	Winston-Salem, NC	(2.3)
28	Tucson, AZ	22.2	88	Farmington, NM	5.7	148	Lansing-East Lansing, MI	(2.5)
29	Bloomington-Normal, IL	22.1	89	Milwaukee, WI	5.6	149	Augusta, GA-SC	(2.7)
29	Rome, GA	22.1	90	Baltimore-Towson, MD	5.5	150	Erie, PA	(3.0)
31	Burlington, NC	21.2	91	Decatur, IL	5.3	151	St. Louis, MO-IL	(3.1)
32	Raleigh-Cary, NC	21.1	91	Fort Worth-Arlington, TX M.D.	5.3	152	Durham-Chapel Hill, NC	(3.4)
33	Danville, IL	19.3	93	Odessa, TX	5.0	152	Wilmington, DE-MD-NJ M.D.	(3.4)
34	Bend, OR	19.0	93	Phoenix-Mesa-Scottsdale, AZ	5.0	154	Visalia-Porterville, CA	(3.5)
35	Palm Coast, FL	18.8	95	New York-W. Plains NY-NJ M.D.	4.5	155	Yuba City, CA	(4.0)
36	Miami-Dade County, FL M.D.	18.3	96	Flagstaff, AZ	4.3	156	San Diego, CA	(4.1)
37	Dover, DE	18.0	97	Clarksville, TN-KY	4.2	157	Las Cruces, NM	(4.3)
38	Lafayette, IN	17.2	97	Jacksonville, FL	4.2	157	Mount Vernon-Anacortes, WA	(4.3)
39	Blacksburg, VA	16.8	99	Boston-Quincy, MA M.D.	4.1	159	Harrisburg-Carlisle, PA	(4.4)
39	Cape Girardeau, MO-IL	16.8	100	Madison, WI	3.7	160	Manchester-Nashua, NH	(4.5)
39	Lincoln, NE	16.8	101	Columbus, OH	3.5	160	Reading, PA	(4.5)
39	Sebastian-Vero Beach, FL	16.8	102	Brunswick, GA	3.1	162	Cincinnati-Middletown, OH-KY-IN	(4.6)
43	Lima, OH	16.7	103	Bellingham, WA	2.9	162	Dallas (greater), TX	(4.6)
44	Harrisonburg, VA	16.5	104	Greenville, SC	2.7	162	Florence, SC	(4.6)
45	Elmira, NY	15.9	104	New Orleans, LA	2.7	162	Philadelphia (greater) PA-NJ-MD-DE	(4.6)
46	Altoona, PA	15.5	106	Roanoke, VA	2.6	162	Sacramento, CA	(4.6)
46	Kennewick-Pasco-Richland, WA	15.5	106	Syracuse, NY	2.6	167	Orlando, FL	(4.8)
48	Athens-Clarke County, GA	15.3	108	Idaho Falls, ID	2.5	168	West Palm Beach, FL M.D.	(4.9)
48	Atlantic City, NJ	15.3	109	Flint, MI	2.4	169	Greeley, CO	(5.1)
50	Jonesboro, AR	15.2	110	Canton, OH	2.3	170	Lancaster, PA	(5.2)
51	El Centro, CA	15.0	110	St. Joseph, MO-KS	2.3	170	San Antonio, TX	(5.2)
51	Napa, CA	15.0	112	Denver-Aurora, CO	1.8	172	Toledo, OH	(5.3)
53	Binghamton, NY	14.8	113	Cleveland-Elyria-Mentor, OH	1.6	173	Cheyenne, WY	(5.4)
54	Ann Arbor, MI	13.7	114	Detroit-Livonia-Dearborn, MI M.D.	1.4	173	Memphis, TN-MS-AR	(5.4)
55	Norwich-New London, CT	13.6	115	Mansfield, OH	1.3	173	Springfield, IL	(5.4)
56	Texarkana, TX-Texarkana, AR	13.3	116	Cambridge-Newton, MA M.D.	1.2	176	Bethesda-Frederick, MD M.D.	(5.5)
57	Lafayette, LA	12.8	117	Victoria, TX	1.1	177	Kingsport, TN-VA	(5.7)
58	Ocala, FL	12.4	118	Hanford-Corcoran, CA	1.0	177	Wilmington, NC	(5.7)
59	Salinas, CA	12.0	119	Jackson, MS	0.9	179	Knoxville, TN	(5.9)
60	Corpus Christi, TX	11.8	120	Poughkeepsie, NY	0.7	179	Rochester, NY	(5.9)

Note: All listings are for Metropolitan Statistical Areas (M.S.A.s) except for those ending with "M.D." Listings with "M.D." are Metropolitan Divisions which are smaller parts of eleven large M.S.A.s. See explanatory note at beginning of metropolitan area section.

Rank Order - Metro Area (continued)

RANK	METROPOLITAN AREA	% CHANGE	RANK	METROPOLITAN AREA	% CHANGE	RANK	METROPOLITAN AREA	% CHANGE
179	Santa Barbara-Santa Maria, CA	(5.9)	244	Provo-Orem, UT	(14.0)	307	Lubbock, TX	(32.3)
179	Savannah, GA	(5.9)	245	Ogden-Clearfield, UT	(14.1)	308	Winchester, VA-WV	(32.6)
183	Wichita, KS	(6.0)	245	Spokane, WA	(14.1)	309	Chattanooga, TN-GA	(33.6)
184	Gainesville, GA	(6.2)	247	Macon, GA	(14.2)	310	Pocatello, ID	(40.1)
185	Richmond, VA	(6.3)	247	Scranton--Wilkes-Barre, PA	(14.2)	311	Rocky Mount, NC	(42.9)
186	Monroe, LA	(6.4)	249	Albany-Schenectady-Troy, NY	(14.3)	312	Saginaw, MI	(43.4)
187	Oxnard-Thousand Oaks, CA	(6.9)	249	San Francisco (greater), CA	(14.3)	313	Madera, CA	(45.4)
188	Appleton, WI	(7.0)	249	Tyler, TX	(14.3)	314	Wenatchee, WA	(46.8)
188	Medford, OR	(7.0)	252	Longview, WA	(14.5)	315	Columbus, IN	(52.3)
190	Anderson, SC	(7.1)	253	Dalton, GA	(14.8)	316	Midland, TX	(53.4)
191	Wichita Falls, TX	(7.2)	253	Joplin, MO	(14.8)	317	Abilene, TX	(56.4)
192	Colorado Springs, CO	(7.3)	255	Stockton, CA	(15.1)	318	Logan, UT-ID	(56.8)
193	Philadelphia, PA M.D.	(7.4)	256	Muskegon-Norton Shores, MI	(16.1)	319	Johnson City, TN	(58.1)
194	Gainesville, FL	(7.6)	256	Tallahassee, FL	(16.1)	320	Fairbanks, AK	(74.3)
195	Austin-Round Rock, TX	(7.7)	258	Fort Collins-Loveland, CO	(16.7)	321	Carson City, NV	(100.0)
196	Columbia, MO	(7.8)	258	Redding, CA	(16.7)	NA	Anniston-Oxford, AL**	NA
196	Lewiston-Auburn, ME	(7.8)	260	Newark-Union, NJ-PA M.D.	(16.8)	NA	Auburn, AL**	NA
196	New Haven-Milford, CT	(7.8)	261	Holland-Grand Haven, MI	(16.9)	NA	Baton Rouge, LA**	NA
196	Oklahoma City, OK	(7.8)	261	Naples-Marco Island, FL	(16.9)	NA	Billings, MT**	NA
200	Allentown, PA-NJ	(7.9)	263	Mobile, AL	(17.3)	NA	Birmingham-Hoover, AL**	NA
201	Hinesville, GA	(8.1)	264	Fresno, CA	(17.4)	NA	Champaign-Urbana, IL**	NA
202	Sandusky, OH	(8.2)	265	Morristown, TN	(17.6)	NA	Charleston, WV**	NA
203	Rockford, IL	(8.3)	266	Kokomo, IN	(18.0)	NA	Charlotte-Gastonia, NC-SC**	NA
203	Tampa-St Petersburg, FL	(8.3)	267	Merced, CA	(18.3)	NA	Chicago (greater), IL-IN-WI**	NA
205	Grand Rapids-Wyoming, MI	(8.4)	268	Chico, CA	(18.6)	NA	Chicago-Joilet-Naperville, IL M.D.**	NA
205	Portland, ME	(8.4)	269	Reno-Sparks, NV	(18.7)	NA	Columbus, GA-AL**	NA
207	Beaumont-Port Arthur, TX	(8.5)	270	Worcester, MA	(18.8)	NA	Cumberland, MD-WV**	NA
208	Dubuque, IA	(8.6)	271	Battle Creek, MI	(19.0)	NA	Davenport, IA-IL**	NA
208	Los Angeles County, CA M.D.	(8.6)	271	Olympia, WA	(19.0)	NA	Decatur, AL**	NA
210	Los Angeles (greater), CA	(8.7)	273	Deltona-Daytona Beach, FL	(19.7)	NA	Detroit (greater), MI**	NA
211	San Jose, CA	(8.8)	274	Iowa City, IA	(19.8)	NA	Dothan, AL**	NA
211	Santa Ana-Anaheim, CA M.D.	(8.8)	275	Ames, IA	(20.1)	NA	Duluth, MN-WI**	NA
213	Akron, OH	(9.3)	276	San Angelo, TX	(20.2)	NA	Eugene-Springfield, OR**	NA
213	Nashville-Davidson, TN	(9.3)	277	Killeen-Temple-Fort Hood, TX	(20.7)	NA	Fargo, ND-MN**	NA
215	Des Moines-West Des Moines, IA	(9.4)	277	Oakland-Fremont, CA M.D.	(20.7)	NA	Florence-Muscle Shoals, AL**	NA
216	Eau Claire, WI	(9.5)	279	Monroe, MI	(20.8)	NA	Gadsden, AL**	NA
216	Lynchburg, VA	(9.5)	279	Port St. Lucie, FL	(20.8)	NA	Gary, IN M.D.**	NA
218	Lawrence, KS	(9.6)	281	Pensacola, FL	(21.1)	NA	Grand Forks, ND-MN**	NA
218	Washington (greater) DC-VA-MD-WV	(9.6)	282	Green Bay, WI	(21.2)	NA	Great Falls, MT**	NA
220	Peoria, IL	(9.7)	283	Goldsboro, NC	(21.3)	NA	Houston, TX**	NA
220	Springfield, OH	(9.7)	284	Nassau-Suffolk, NY M.D.	(21.6)	NA	Huntsville, AL**	NA
222	Seattle-Bellevue-Everett, WA M.D.	(10.3)	285	Asheville, NC	(22.0)	NA	Indianapolis, IN**	NA
223	Jefferson City, MO	(10.4)	286	Hickory, NC	(22.4)	NA	Jacksonville, NC**	NA
223	Washington, DC-VA-MD-WV M.D.	(10.4)	287	Vallejo-Fairfield, CA	(23.1)	NA	Kankakee-Bradley, IL**	NA
225	Dallas-Plano-Irving, TX M.D.	(10.6)	288	Bowling Green, KY	(23.7)	NA	Kansas City, MO-KS**	NA
226	Seattle (greater), WA	(10.7)	289	Longview, TX	(24.2)	NA	La Crosse, WI-MN**	NA
227	Springfield, MO	(10.9)	290	Cape Coral-Fort Myers, FL	(24.3)	NA	Lake Co.-Kenosha Co., IL-WI M.D.**	NA
228	Gulfport-Biloxi, MS	(11.4)	291	Bloomington, IN	(24.5)	NA	Lake Havasu City-Kingman, AZ**	NA
229	Sherman-Denison, TX	(11.5)	292	Ocean City, NJ	(24.9)	NA	Lexington-Fayette, KY**	NA
230	Albuquerque, NM	(11.6)	292	Peabody, MA M.D.	(24.9)	NA	Mankato-North Mankato, MN**	NA
230	Brownsville-Harlingen, TX	(11.6)	294	Boise City-Nampa, ID	(25.2)	NA	Minneapolis-St. Paul, MN-WI**	NA
232	Lawton, OK	(11.8)	295	Salisbury, MD	(25.4)	NA	Missoula, MT**	NA
232	Tacoma, WA M.D.	(11.8)	296	Utica-Rome, NY	(26.1)	NA	Montgomery, AL**	NA
234	Bay City, MI	(12.0)	297	Janesville, WI	(26.4)	NA	Oshkosh-Neenah, WI**	NA
235	Buffalo-Niagara Falls, NY	(12.7)	298	Pascagoula, MS	(27.1)	NA	Portland-Vancouver, OR-WA**	NA
236	Charlottesville, VA	(12.9)	299	Springfield, MA	(27.9)	NA	Pueblo, CO**	NA
237	Pine Bluff, AR	(13.2)	300	Hagerstown-Martinsburg, MD-WV	(28.0)	NA	Rochester, MN**	NA
237	Racine, WI	(13.2)	301	College Station-Bryan, TX	(29.0)	NA	Sheboygan, WI**	NA
237	Riverside-San Bernardino, CA	(13.2)	302	Sumter, SC	(29.2)	NA	St. Cloud, MN**	NA
240	Salem, OR	(13.4)	303	Prescott, AZ	(29.9)	NA	Terre Haute, IN**	NA
241	Salt Lake City, UT	(13.6)	304	Michigan City-La Porte, IN	(30.1)	NA	Tuscaloosa, AL**	NA
242	Modesto, CA	(13.8)	305	Bremerton-Silverdale, WA	(30.2)	NA	Warren-Farmington Hills, MI M.D.**	NA
242	Williamsport, PA	(13.8)	306	Santa Fe, NM	(32.2)			

Source: CQ Press using reported data from the F.B.I. "Crime in the United States 2011"
*Forcible rape is the carnal knowledge of a female forcibly and against her will. Assaults or attempts to commit rape by force or threat of force are included. However, statutory rape without force and other sex offenses are excluded. **Not available

Alpha Order - Metro Area

16. Percent Change in Rape Rate: 2007 to 2011
National Percent Change = 12.4% Decrease*

RANK	METROPOLITAN AREA	% CHANGE	RANK	METROPOLITAN AREA	% CHANGE	RANK	METROPOLITAN AREA	% CHANGE
306	Abilene, TX	(67.4)	54	Charleston, WV	11.7	81	Fort Lauderdale, FL M.D.	1.5
187	Akron, OH	(16.1)	226	Charlotte-Gastonia, NC-SC	(22.2)	NA	Fort Smith, AR-OK**	NA
175	Albany-Schenectady-Troy, NY	(14.7)	168	Charlottesville, VA	(13.5)	47	Fort Wayne, IN	14.3
17	Albany, GA	35.6	303	Chattanooga, TN-GA	(50.8)	146	Fort Worth-Arlington, TX M.D.	(11.8)
241	Albuquerque, NM	(24.9)	66	Cheyenne, WY	7.7	220	Fresno, CA	(21.1)
36	Alexandria, LA	16.4	NA	Chicago (greater), IL-IN-WI**	NA	NA	Gadsden, AL**	NA
21	Allentown, PA-NJ	31.7	NA	Chicago-Joilet-Naperville, IL M.D.**	NA	240	Gainesville, FL	(24.8)
9	Altoona, PA	67.6	292	Chico, CA	(42.7)	157	Gainesville, GA	(12.6)
233	Amarillo, TX	(23.7)	255	Cincinnati-Middletown, OH-KY-IN	(28.6)	NA	Gary, IN M.D.**	NA
76	Ames, IA	2.5	87	Clarksville, TN-KY	(0.5)	197	Glens Falls, NY	(16.8)
67	Anchorage, AK	7.0	123	Cleveland-Elyria-Mentor, OH	(7.9)	300	Goldsboro, NC	(50.0)
114	Anderson, SC	(5.6)	159	Cleveland, TN	(12.7)	NA	Grand Forks, ND-MN**	NA
58	Ann Arbor, MI	10.8	271	College Station-Bryan, TX	(32.5)	10	Grand Junction, CO	63.4
NA	Anniston-Oxford, AL**	NA	84	Colorado Springs, CO	0.7	118	Grand Rapids-Wyoming, MI	(7.2)
154	Appleton, WI	(12.3)	59	Columbia, MO	10.2	NA	Great Falls, MT**	NA
214	Asheville, NC	(18.7)	NA	Columbus, GA-AL**	NA	219	Greeley, CO	(20.5)
179	Athens-Clarke County, GA	(15.0)	98	Columbus, IN	(3.4)	235	Green Bay, WI	(24.2)
78	Atlanta, GA	2.0	208	Columbus, OH	(17.7)	188	Greenville, SC	(16.2)
133	Atlantic City, NJ	(9.2)	192	Corpus Christi, TX	(16.4)	NA	Gulfport-Biloxi, MS**	NA
NA	Auburn, AL**	NA	166	Corvallis, OR	(13.3)	NA	Hagerstown-Martinsburg, MD-WV**	NA
172	Augusta, GA-SC	(14.2)	99	Crestview-Fort Walton Beach, FL	(3.5)	93	Hanford-Corcoran, CA	(1.5)
269	Austin-Round Rock, TX	(32.1)	NA	Cumberland, MD-WV**	NA	65	Harrisburg-Carlisle, PA	8.6
108	Bakersfield, CA	(4.8)	177	Dallas (greater), TX	(14.9)	12	Harrisonburg, VA	53.1
23	Baltimore-Towson, MD	29.0	201	Dallas-Plano-Irving, TX M.D.	(17.0)	63	Hartford, CT	8.8
13	Bangor, ME	41.7	62	Dalton, GA	8.9	291	Hickory, NC	(42.6)
8	Barnstable Town, MA	71.4	NA	Danville, IL**	NA	288	Hinesville, GA	(42.0)
241	Baton Rouge, LA	(24.9)	3	Danville, VA	134.7	NA	Holland-Grand Haven, MI**	NA
277	Battle Creek, MI	(37.0)	NA	Davenport, IA-IL**	NA	5	Hot Springs, AR	111.6
26	Bay City, MI	25.4	162	Dayton, OH	(12.8)	232	Houma, LA	(23.5)
264	Beaumont-Port Arthur, TX	(30.9)	NA	Decatur, AL**	NA	NA	Houston, TX**	NA
91	Bellingham, WA	(1.3)	NA	Decatur, IL**	NA	NA	Huntsville, AL**	NA
90	Bend, OR	(1.1)	260	Deltona-Daytona Beach, FL	(29.8)	274	Idaho Falls, ID	(34.8)
203	Bethesda-Frederick, MD M.D.	(17.2)	37	Denver-Aurora, CO	16.1	142	Indianapolis, IN	(11.0)
NA	Billings, MT**	NA	273	Des Moines-West Des Moines, IA	(34.7)	16	Iowa City, IA	39.9
145	Binghamton, NY	(11.7)	NA	Detroit (greater), MI**	NA	44	Jacksonville, FL	14.6
NA	Birmingham-Hoover, AL**	NA	24	Detroit-Livonia-Dearborn, MI M.D.	26.9	170	Jacksonville, NC	(14.1)
166	Bismarck, ND	(13.3)	NA	Dothan, AL**	NA	241	Jackson, MS	(24.9)
52	Blacksburg, VA	12.1	117	Dover, DE	(6.8)	29	Jackson, TN	24.2
NA	Bloomington-Normal, IL**	NA	204	Dubuque, IA	(17.4)	204	Janesville, WI	(17.4)
120	Bloomington, IN	(7.5)	NA	Duluth, MN-WI**	NA	299	Jefferson City, MO	(48.2)
296	Boise City-Nampa, ID	(46.8)	NA	Durham-Chapel Hill, NC**	NA	297	Johnson City, TN	(47.2)
75	Boston (greater), MA-NH	3.2	11	Eau Claire, WI	54.4	1	Johnstown, PA	372.0
68	Boston-Quincy, MA M.D.	5.7	125	Edison, NJ M.D.	(8.1)	32	Jonesboro, AR	20.1
NA	Boulder, CO**	NA	80	El Centro, CA	1.7	95	Joplin, MO	(1.8)
276	Bowling Green, KY	(35.1)	234	El Paso, TX	(24.0)	NA	Kankakee-Bradley, IL**	NA
289	Bremerton-Silverdale, WA	(42.2)	137	Elizabethtown, KY	(9.7)	NA	Kansas City, MO-KS**	NA
18	Bridgeport-Stamford, CT	34.6	170	Elmira, NY	(14.1)	163	Kennewick-Pasco-Richland, WA	(12.9)
154	Brownsville-Harlingen, TX	(12.3)	61	Erie, PA	9.3	238	Killeen-Temple-Fort Hood, TX	(24.5)
89	Brunswick, GA	(0.8)	31	Eugene-Springfield, OR	20.3	190	Kingsport, TN-VA	(16.3)
228	Buffalo-Niagara Falls, NY	(22.9)	111	Evansville, IN-KY	(5.4)	71	Kingston, NY	4.9
224	Burlington, NC	(21.5)	NA	Fairbanks, AK**	NA	128	Knoxville, TN	(8.8)
59	Cambridge-Newton, MA M.D.	10.2	NA	Fargo, ND-MN**	NA	97	Kokomo, IN	(2.5)
70	Camden, NJ M.D.	5.4	106	Farmington, NM	(4.2)	NA	La Crosse, WI-MN**	NA
NA	Canton, OH**	NA	220	Fayetteville, NC	(21.1)	94	Lafayette, IN	(1.6)
293	Cape Coral-Fort Myers, FL	(43.2)	198	Flagstaff, AZ	(16.9)	304	Lafayette, LA	(53.7)
NA	Cape Girardeau, MO-IL**	NA	64	Flint, MI	8.7	NA	Lake Co.-Kenosha Co., IL-WI M.D.**	NA
308	Carson City, NV	(100.0)	NA	Florence-Muscle Shoals, AL**	NA	22	Lake Havasu City-Kingman, AZ	29.8
239	Casper, WY	(24.7)	279	Florence, SC	(38.0)	262	Lakeland, FL	(30.4)
41	Cedar Rapids, IA	15.2	25	Fond du Lac, WI	26.4	72	Lancaster, PA	3.8
NA	Champaign-Urbana, IL**	NA	198	Fort Collins-Loveland, CO	(16.9)	184	Lansing-East Lansing, MI	(15.8)

Note: All listings are for Metropolitan Statistical Areas (M.S.A.s) except for those ending with "M.D." Listings with "M.D." are Metropolitan Divisions which are smaller parts of eleven large M.S.A.s. See explanatory note at beginning of metropolitan area section.

Alpha Order - Metro Area (continued)

RANK	METROPOLITAN AREA	% CHANGE
110	Laredo, TX	(4.9)
286	Las Cruces, NM	(41.8)
181	Las Vegas-Paradise, NV	(15.6)
270	Lawrence, KS	(32.3)
268	Lawton, OK	(31.6)
275	Lebanon, PA	(34.9)
113	Lewiston-Auburn, ME	(5.5)
NA	Lexington-Fayette, KY**	NA
74	Lima, OH	3.4
14	Lincoln, NE	40.6
104	Little Rock, AR	(3.9)
305	Logan, UT-ID	(55.3)
300	Longview, TX	(50.0)
85	Longview, WA	0.5
194	Los Angeles County, CA M.D.	(16.5)
207	Los Angeles (greater), CA	(17.6)
46	Louisville, KY-IN	14.4
248	Lubbock, TX	(26.1)
228	Lynchburg, VA	(22.9)
230	Macon, GA	(23.0)
177	Madera, CA	(14.9)
52	Madison, WI	12.1
NA	Manchester-Nashua, NH**	NA
NA	Manhattan, KS**	NA
NA	Mankato-North Mankato, MN**	NA
249	Mansfield, OH	(26.2)
39	McAllen-Edinburg-Mission, TX	15.4
42	Medford, OR	15.0
119	Memphis, TN-MS-AR	(7.4)
245	Merced, CA	(25.6)
150	Miami (greater), FL	(12.0)
195	Miami-Dade County, FL M.D.	(16.6)
91	Michigan City-La Porte, IN	(1.3)
307	Midland, TX	(71.0)
209	Milwaukee, WI	(17.8)
NA	Minneapolis-St. Paul, MN-WI**	NA
NA	Missoula, MT**	NA
43	Mobile, AL	14.8
186	Modesto, CA	(16.0)
156	Monroe, LA	(12.4)
7	Monroe, MI	99.1
NA	Montgomery, AL**	NA
285	Morristown, TN	(41.0)
57	Mount Vernon-Anacortes, WA	10.9
116	Muncie, IN	(6.4)
130	Muskegon-Norton Shores, MI	(9.0)
39	Myrtle Beach, SC	15.4
49	Napa, CA	13.4
252	Naples-Marco Island, FL	(27.4)
85	Nashville-Davidson, TN	0.5
295	Nassau-Suffolk, NY M.D.	(45.2)
NA	New Haven-Milford, CT**	NA
150	New Orleans, LA	(12.0)
83	New York (greater), NY-NJ-PA	1.0
48	New York-W. Plains NY-NJ M.D.	13.7
165	Newark-Union, NJ-PA M.D.	(13.0)
NA	North Port-Bradenton-Sarasota, FL**	NA
NA	Norwich-New London, CT**	NA
235	Oakland-Fremont, CA M.D.	(24.2)
77	Ocala, FL	2.1
302	Ocean City, NJ	(50.2)
6	Odessa, TX	105.3
121	Ogden-Clearfield, UT	(7.6)
111	Oklahoma City, OK	(5.4)
106	Olympia, WA	(4.2)
55	Omaha-Council Bluffs, NE-IA	11.4
225	Orlando, FL	(21.9)
143	Oshkosh-Neenah, WI	(11.2)
NA	Owensboro, KY**	NA
264	Oxnard-Thousand Oaks, CA	(30.9)
125	Palm Bay-Melbourne, FL	(8.1)
104	Palm Coast, FL	(3.9)
294	Panama City-Lynn Haven, FL	(43.9)
28	Pascagoula, MS	25.1
231	Peabody, MA M.D.	(23.4)
115	Pensacola, FL	(6.0)
NA	Peoria, IL**	NA
130	Philadelphia (greater) PA-NJ-MD-DE	(9.0)
146	Philadelphia, PA M.D.	(11.8)
99	Phoenix-Mesa-Scottsdale, AZ	(3.5)
130	Pine Bluff, AR	(9.0)
146	Pittsburgh, PA	(11.8)
51	Pittsfield, MA	12.4
204	Pocatello, ID	(17.4)
282	Port St. Lucie, FL	(39.5)
184	Portland-Vancouver, OR-WA	(15.8)
163	Portland, ME	(12.9)
216	Poughkeepsie, NY	(19.2)
138	Prescott, AZ	(9.9)
87	Provo-Orem, UT	(0.5)
NA	Pueblo, CO**	NA
69	Punta Gorda, FL	5.5
133	Racine, WI	(9.2)
99	Raleigh-Cary, NC	(3.5)
56	Rapid City, SD	11.3
211	Reading, PA	(18.2)
198	Redding, CA	(16.9)
278	Reno-Sparks, NV	(37.9)
266	Richmond, VA	(31.2)
256	Riverside-San Bernardino, CA	(29.2)
247	Roanoke, VA	(25.7)
NA	Rochester, MN**	NA
153	Rochester, NY	(12.2)
NA	Rockford, IL**	NA
44	Rockingham County, NH M.D.	14.6
284	Rocky Mount, NC	(40.6)
35	Rome, GA	19.6
157	Sacramento, CA	(12.6)
223	Saginaw, MI	(21.2)
272	Salem, OR	(34.3)
245	Salinas, CA	(25.6)
298	Salisbury, MD	(47.4)
196	Salt Lake City, UT	(16.7)
135	San Angelo, TX	(9.5)
251	San Antonio, TX	(27.0)
152	San Diego, CA	(12.1)
217	San Francisco (greater), CA	(19.4)
128	San Francisco-S. Mateo, CA M.D.	(8.8)
123	San Jose, CA	(7.9)
212	San Luis Obispo, CA	(18.5)
19	Sandusky, OH	34.5
218	Santa Ana-Anaheim, CA M.D.	(19.6)
227	Santa Barbara-Santa Maria, CA	(22.3)
159	Santa Cruz-Watsonville, CA	(12.7)
NA	Santa Fe, NM**	NA
173	Santa Rosa-Petaluma, CA	(14.5)
280	Savannah, GA	(38.1)
146	Scranton--Wilkes-Barre, PA	(11.8)
210	Seattle (greater), WA	(17.9)
215	Seattle-Bellevue-Everett, WA M.D.	(18.9)
192	Sebastian-Vero Beach, FL	(16.4)
282	Sheboygan, WI	(39.5)
122	Sherman-Denison, TX	(7.8)
108	Sioux City, IA-NE-SD	(4.8)
38	Sioux Falls, SD	16.0
190	South Bend-Mishawaka, IN-MI	(16.3)
201	Spartanburg, SC	(17.0)
82	Spokane, WA	1.1
NA	Springfield, IL**	NA
220	Springfield, MA	(21.1)
27	Springfield, MO	25.2
257	Springfield, OH	(29.5)
4	State College, PA	114.1
188	Stockton, CA	(16.2)
NA	St. Cloud, MN**	NA
32	St. Joseph, MO-KS	20.1
30	St. Louis, MO-IL	21.7
290	Sumter, SC	(42.4)
73	Syracuse, NY	3.6
175	Tacoma, WA M.D.	(14.7)
263	Tallahassee, FL	(30.8)
257	Tampa-St Petersburg, FL	(29.5)
NA	Terre Haute, IN**	NA
96	Texarkana, TX-Texarkana, AR	(2.4)
159	Toledo, OH	(12.7)
141	Topeka, KS	(10.8)
34	Trenton-Ewing, NJ	20.0
254	Tucson, AZ	(28.1)
180	Tulsa, OK	(15.1)
NA	Tuscaloosa, AL**	NA
169	Tyler, TX	(13.8)
103	Utica-Rome, NY	(3.8)
267	Valdosta, GA	(31.3)
127	Vallejo-Fairfield, CA	(8.5)
15	Victoria, TX	40.5
261	Virginia Beach-Norfolk, VA-NC	(30.0)
250	Visalia-Porterville, CA	(26.8)
235	Waco, TX	(24.2)
79	Warner Robins, GA	1.9
NA	Warren-Farmington Hills, MI M.D.**	NA
182	Washington (greater) DC-VA-MD-WV	(15.7)
182	Washington, DC-VA-MD-WV M.D.	(15.7)
135	Waterloo-Cedar Falls, IA	(9.5)
2	Wausau, WI	165.7
281	Wenatchee, WA	(39.2)
213	West Palm Beach, FL M.D.	(18.6)
50	Wichita Falls, TX	13.3
174	Wichita, KS	(14.6)
102	Williamsport, PA	(3.7)
139	Wilmington, DE-MD-NJ M.D.	(10.6)
287	Wilmington, NC	(41.9)
259	Winchester, VA-WV	(29.7)
NA	Winston-Salem, NC**	NA
253	Worcester, MA	(27.6)
244	Yakima, WA	(25.4)
20	York-Hanover, PA	32.9
144	Yuba City, CA	(11.5)
140	Yuma, AZ	(10.7)

Source: CQ Press using reported data from the F.B.I. "Crime in the United States 2011"
*Forcible rape is the carnal knowledge of a female forcibly and against her will. Assaults or attempts to commit rape by force or threat of force are included. However, statutory rape without force and other sex offenses are excluded. **Not available

Rank Order - Metro Area

16. Percent Change in Rape Rate: 2007 to 2011 (continued)
National Percent Change = 12.4% Decrease*

RANK	METROPOLITAN AREA	% CHANGE
1	Johnstown, PA	372.0
2	Wausau, WI	165.7
3	Danville, VA	134.7
4	State College, PA	114.1
5	Hot Springs, AR	111.6
6	Odessa, TX	105.3
7	Monroe, MI	99.1
8	Barnstable Town, MA	71.4
9	Altoona, PA	67.6
10	Grand Junction, CO	63.4
11	Eau Claire, WI	54.4
12	Harrisonburg, VA	53.1
13	Bangor, ME	41.7
14	Lincoln, NE	40.6
15	Victoria, TX	40.5
16	Iowa City, IA	39.9
17	Albany, GA	35.6
18	Bridgeport-Stamford, CT	34.6
19	Sandusky, OH	34.5
20	York-Hanover, PA	32.9
21	Allentown, PA-NJ	31.7
22	Lake Havasu City-Kingman, AZ	29.8
23	Baltimore-Towson, MD	29.0
24	Detroit-Livonia-Dearborn, MI M.D.	26.9
25	Fond du Lac, WI	26.4
26	Bay City, MI	25.4
27	Springfield, MO	25.2
28	Pascagoula, MS	25.1
29	Jackson, TN	24.2
30	St. Louis, MO-IL	21.7
31	Eugene-Springfield, OR	20.3
32	Jonesboro, AR	20.1
32	St. Joseph, MO-KS	20.1
34	Trenton-Ewing, NJ	20.0
35	Rome, GA	19.6
36	Alexandria, LA	16.4
37	Denver-Aurora, CO	16.1
38	Sioux Falls, SD	16.0
39	McAllen-Edinburg-Mission, TX	15.4
39	Myrtle Beach, SC	15.4
41	Cedar Rapids, IA	15.2
42	Medford, OR	15.0
43	Mobile, AL	14.8
44	Jacksonville, FL	14.6
44	Rockingham County, NH M.D.	14.6
46	Louisville, KY-IN	14.4
47	Fort Wayne, IN	14.3
48	New York-W. Plains NY-NJ M.D.	13.7
49	Napa, CA	13.4
50	Wichita Falls, TX	13.3
51	Pittsfield, MA	12.4
52	Blacksburg, VA	12.1
52	Madison, WI	12.1
54	Charleston, WV	11.7
55	Omaha-Council Bluffs, NE-IA	11.4
56	Rapid City, SD	11.3
57	Mount Vernon-Anacortes, WA	10.9
58	Ann Arbor, MI	10.8
59	Cambridge-Newton, MA M.D.	10.2
59	Columbia, MO	10.2
61	Erie, PA	9.3
62	Dalton, GA	8.9
63	Hartford, CT	8.8
64	Flint, MI	8.7
65	Harrisburg-Carlisle, PA	8.6
66	Cheyenne, WY	7.7
67	Anchorage, AK	7.0
68	Boston-Quincy, MA M.D.	5.7
69	Punta Gorda, FL	5.5
70	Camden, NJ M.D.	5.4
71	Kingston, NY	4.9
72	Lancaster, PA	3.8
73	Syracuse, NY	3.6
74	Lima, OH	3.4
75	Boston (greater), MA-NH	3.2
76	Ames, IA	2.5
77	Ocala, FL	2.1
78	Atlanta, GA	2.0
79	Warner Robins, GA	1.9
80	El Centro, CA	1.7
81	Fort Lauderdale, FL M.D.	1.5
82	Spokane, WA	1.1
83	New York (greater), NY-NJ-PA	1.0
84	Colorado Springs, CO	0.7
85	Longview, WA	0.5
85	Nashville-Davidson, TN	0.5
87	Clarksville, TN-KY	(0.5)
87	Provo-Orem, UT	(0.5)
89	Brunswick, GA	(0.8)
90	Bend, OR	(1.1)
91	Bellingham, WA	(1.3)
91	Michigan City-La Porte, IN	(1.3)
93	Hanford-Corcoran, CA	(1.5)
94	Lafayette, IN	(1.6)
95	Joplin, MO	(1.8)
96	Texarkana, TX-Texarkana, AR	(2.4)
97	Kokomo, IN	(2.5)
98	Columbus, IN	(3.4)
99	Crestview-Fort Walton Beach, FL	(3.5)
99	Phoenix-Mesa-Scottsdale, AZ	(3.5)
99	Raleigh-Cary, NC	(3.5)
102	Williamsport, PA	(3.7)
103	Utica-Rome, NY	(3.8)
104	Little Rock, AR	(3.9)
104	Palm Coast, FL	(3.9)
106	Farmington, NM	(4.2)
106	Olympia, WA	(4.2)
108	Bakersfield, CA	(4.8)
108	Sioux City, IA-NE-SD	(4.8)
110	Laredo, TX	(4.9)
111	Evansville, IN-KY	(5.4)
111	Oklahoma City, OK	(5.4)
113	Lewiston-Auburn, ME	(5.5)
114	Anderson, SC	(5.6)
115	Pensacola, FL	(6.0)
116	Muncie, IN	(6.4)
117	Dover, DE	(6.8)
118	Grand Rapids-Wyoming, MI	(7.2)
119	Memphis, TN-MS-AR	(7.4)
120	Bloomington, IN	(7.5)
121	Ogden-Clearfield, UT	(7.6)
122	Sherman-Denison, TX	(7.8)
123	Cleveland-Elyria-Mentor, OH	(7.9)
123	San Jose, CA	(7.9)
125	Edison, NJ M.D.	(8.1)
125	Palm Bay-Melbourne, FL	(8.1)
127	Vallejo-Fairfield, CA	(8.5)
128	Knoxville, TN	(8.8)
128	San Francisco-S. Mateo, CA M.D.	(8.8)
130	Muskegon-Norton Shores, MI	(9.0)
130	Philadelphia (greater) PA-NJ-MD-DE	(9.0)
130	Pine Bluff, AR	(9.0)
133	Atlantic City, NJ	(9.2)
133	Racine, WI	(9.2)
135	San Angelo, TX	(9.5)
135	Waterloo-Cedar Falls, IA	(9.5)
137	Elizabethtown, KY	(9.7)
138	Prescott, AZ	(9.9)
139	Wilmington, DE-MD-NJ M.D.	(10.6)
140	Yuma, AZ	(10.7)
141	Topeka, KS	(10.8)
142	Indianapolis, IN	(11.0)
143	Oshkosh-Neenah, WI	(11.2)
144	Yuba City, CA	(11.5)
145	Binghamton, NY	(11.7)
146	Fort Worth-Arlington, TX M.D.	(11.8)
146	Philadelphia, PA M.D.	(11.8)
146	Pittsburgh, PA	(11.8)
146	Scranton--Wilkes-Barre, PA	(11.8)
150	Miami (greater), FL	(12.0)
150	New Orleans, LA	(12.0)
152	San Diego, CA	(12.1)
153	Rochester, NY	(12.2)
154	Appleton, WI	(12.3)
154	Brownsville-Harlingen, TX	(12.3)
156	Monroe, LA	(12.4)
157	Gainesville, GA	(12.6)
157	Sacramento, CA	(12.6)
159	Cleveland, TN	(12.7)
159	Santa Cruz-Watsonville, CA	(12.7)
159	Toledo, OH	(12.7)
162	Dayton, OH	(12.8)
163	Kennewick-Pasco-Richland, WA	(12.9)
163	Portland, ME	(12.9)
165	Newark-Union, NJ-PA M.D.	(13.0)
166	Bismarck, ND	(13.3)
166	Corvallis, OR	(13.3)
168	Charlottesville, VA	(13.5)
169	Tyler, TX	(13.8)
170	Elmira, NY	(14.1)
170	Jacksonville, NC	(14.1)
172	Augusta, GA-SC	(14.2)
173	Santa Rosa-Petaluma, CA	(14.5)
174	Wichita, KS	(14.6)
175	Albany-Schenectady-Troy, NY	(14.7)
175	Tacoma, WA M.D.	(14.7)
177	Dallas (greater), TX	(14.9)
177	Madera, CA	(14.9)
179	Athens-Clarke County, GA	(15.0)
180	Tulsa, OK	(15.1)

Note: All listings are for Metropolitan Statistical Areas (M.S.A.s) except for those ending with "M.D." Listings with "M.D." are Metropolitan Divisions which are smaller parts of eleven large M.S.A.s. See explanatory note at beginning of metropolitan area section.

Rank Order - Metro Area (continued)

RANK	METROPOLITAN AREA	% CHANGE
181	Las Vegas-Paradise, NV	(15.6)
182	Washington (greater) DC-VA-MD-WV	(15.7)
182	Washington, DC-VA-MD-WV M.D.	(15.7)
184	Lansing-East Lansing, MI	(15.8)
184	Portland-Vancouver, OR-WA	(15.8)
186	Modesto, CA	(16.0)
187	Akron, OH	(16.1)
188	Greenville, SC	(16.2)
188	Stockton, CA	(16.2)
190	Kingsport, TN-VA	(16.3)
190	South Bend-Mishawaka, IN-MI	(16.3)
192	Corpus Christi, TX	(16.4)
192	Sebastian-Vero Beach, FL	(16.4)
194	Los Angeles County, CA M.D.	(16.5)
195	Miami-Dade County, FL M.D.	(16.6)
196	Salt Lake City, UT	(16.7)
197	Glens Falls, NY	(16.8)
198	Flagstaff, AZ	(16.9)
198	Fort Collins-Loveland, CO	(16.9)
198	Redding, CA	(16.9)
201	Dallas-Plano-Irving, TX M.D.	(17.0)
201	Spartanburg, SC	(17.0)
203	Bethesda-Frederick, MD M.D.	(17.2)
204	Dubuque, IA	(17.4)
204	Janesville, WI	(17.4)
204	Pocatello, ID	(17.4)
207	Los Angeles (greater), CA	(17.6)
208	Columbus, OH	(17.7)
209	Milwaukee, WI	(17.8)
210	Seattle (greater), WA	(17.9)
211	Reading, PA	(18.2)
212	San Luis Obispo, CA	(18.5)
213	West Palm Beach, FL M.D.	(18.6)
214	Asheville, NC	(18.7)
215	Seattle-Bellevue-Everett, WA M.D.	(18.9)
216	Poughkeepsie, NY	(19.2)
217	San Francisco (greater), CA	(19.4)
218	Santa Ana-Anaheim, CA M.D.	(19.6)
219	Greeley, CO	(20.5)
220	Fayetteville, NC	(21.1)
220	Fresno, CA	(21.1)
220	Springfield, MA	(21.1)
223	Saginaw, MI	(21.2)
224	Burlington, NC	(21.5)
225	Orlando, FL	(21.9)
226	Charlotte-Gastonia, NC-SC	(22.2)
227	Santa Barbara-Santa Maria, CA	(22.3)
228	Buffalo-Niagara Falls, NY	(22.9)
228	Lynchburg, VA	(22.9)
230	Macon, GA	(23.0)
231	Peabody, MA M.D.	(23.4)
232	Houma, LA	(23.5)
233	Amarillo, TX	(23.7)
234	El Paso, TX	(24.0)
235	Green Bay, WI	(24.2)
235	Oakland-Fremont, CA M.D.	(24.2)
235	Waco, TX	(24.2)
238	Killeen-Temple-Fort Hood, TX	(24.5)
239	Casper, WY	(24.7)
240	Gainesville, FL	(24.8)
241	Albuquerque, NM	(24.9)
241	Baton Rouge, LA	(24.9)
241	Jackson, MS	(24.9)
244	Yakima, WA	(25.4)
245	Merced, CA	(25.6)
245	Salinas, CA	(25.6)
247	Roanoke, VA	(25.7)
248	Lubbock, TX	(26.1)
249	Mansfield, OH	(26.2)
250	Visalia-Porterville, CA	(26.8)
251	San Antonio, TX	(27.0)
252	Naples-Marco Island, FL	(27.4)
253	Worcester, MA	(27.6)
254	Tucson, AZ	(28.1)
255	Cincinnati-Middletown, OH-KY-IN	(28.6)
256	Riverside-San Bernardino, CA	(29.2)
257	Springfield, OH	(29.5)
257	Tampa-St Petersburg, FL	(29.5)
259	Winchester, VA-WV	(29.7)
260	Deltona-Daytona Beach, FL	(29.8)
261	Virginia Beach-Norfolk, VA-NC	(30.0)
262	Lakeland, FL	(30.4)
263	Tallahassee, FL	(30.8)
264	Beaumont-Port Arthur, TX	(30.9)
264	Oxnard-Thousand Oaks, CA	(30.9)
266	Richmond, VA	(31.2)
267	Valdosta, GA	(31.3)
268	Lawton, OK	(31.6)
269	Austin-Round Rock, TX	(32.1)
270	Lawrence, KS	(32.3)
271	College Station-Bryan, TX	(32.5)
272	Salem, OR	(34.3)
273	Des Moines-West Des Moines, IA	(34.7)
274	Idaho Falls, ID	(34.8)
275	Lebanon, PA	(34.9)
276	Bowling Green, KY	(35.1)
277	Battle Creek, MI	(37.0)
278	Reno-Sparks, NV	(37.9)
279	Florence, SC	(38.0)
280	Savannah, GA	(38.1)
281	Wenatchee, WA	(39.2)
282	Port St. Lucie, FL	(39.5)
282	Sheboygan, WI	(39.5)
284	Rocky Mount, NC	(40.6)
285	Morristown, TN	(41.0)
286	Las Cruces, NM	(41.8)
287	Wilmington, NC	(41.9)
288	Hinesville, GA	(42.0)
289	Bremerton-Silverdale, WA	(42.2)
290	Sumter, SC	(42.4)
291	Hickory, NC	(42.6)
292	Chico, CA	(42.7)
293	Cape Coral-Fort Myers, FL	(43.2)
294	Panama City-Lynn Haven, FL	(43.9)
295	Nassau-Suffolk, NY M.D.	(45.2)
296	Boise City-Nampa, ID	(46.8)
297	Johnson City, TN	(47.2)
298	Salisbury, MD	(47.4)
299	Jefferson City, MO	(48.2)
300	Goldsboro, NC	(50.0)
300	Longview, TX	(50.0)
302	Ocean City, NJ	(50.2)
303	Chattanooga, TN-GA	(50.8)
304	Lafayette, LA	(53.7)
305	Logan, UT-ID	(55.3)
306	Abilene, TX	(67.4)
307	Midland, TX	(71.0)
308	Carson City, NV	(100.0)
NA	Anniston-Oxford, AL**	NA
NA	Auburn, AL**	NA
NA	Billings, MT**	NA
NA	Birmingham-Hoover, AL**	NA
NA	Bloomington-Normal, IL**	NA
NA	Boulder, CO**	NA
NA	Canton, OH**	NA
NA	Cape Girardeau, MO-IL**	NA
NA	Champaign-Urbana, IL**	NA
NA	Chicago (greater), IL-IN-WI**	NA
NA	Chicago-Joilet-Naperville, IL M.D.**	NA
NA	Columbus, GA-AL**	NA
NA	Cumberland, MD-WV**	NA
NA	Danville, IL**	NA
NA	Davenport, IA-IL**	NA
NA	Decatur, AL**	NA
NA	Decatur, IL**	NA
NA	Detroit (greater), MI**	NA
NA	Dothan, AL**	NA
NA	Duluth, MN-WI**	NA
NA	Durham-Chapel Hill, NC**	NA
NA	Fairbanks, AK**	NA
NA	Fargo, ND-MN**	NA
NA	Florence-Muscle Shoals, AL**	NA
NA	Fort Smith, AR-OK**	NA
NA	Gadsden, AL**	NA
NA	Gary, IN M.D.**	NA
NA	Grand Forks, ND-MN**	NA
NA	Great Falls, MT**	NA
NA	Gulfport-Biloxi, MS**	NA
NA	Hagerstown-Martinsburg, MD-WV**	NA
NA	Holland-Grand Haven, MI**	NA
NA	Houston, TX**	NA
NA	Huntsville, AL**	NA
NA	Kankakee-Bradley, IL**	NA
NA	Kansas City, MO-KS**	NA
NA	La Crosse, WI-MN**	NA
NA	Lake Co.-Kenosha Co., IL-WI M.D.**	NA
NA	Lexington-Fayette, KY**	NA
NA	Manchester-Nashua, NH**	NA
NA	Manhattan, KS**	NA
NA	Mankato-North Mankato, MN**	NA
NA	Minneapolis-St. Paul, MN-WI**	NA
NA	Missoula, MT**	NA
NA	Montgomery, AL**	NA
NA	New Haven-Milford, CT**	NA
NA	North Port-Bradenton-Sarasota, FL**	NA
NA	Norwich-New London, CT**	NA
NA	Owensboro, KY**	NA
NA	Peoria, IL**	NA
NA	Pueblo, CO**	NA
NA	Rochester, MN**	NA
NA	Rockford, IL**	NA
NA	Santa Fe, NM**	NA
NA	Springfield, IL**	NA
NA	St. Cloud, MN**	NA
NA	Terre Haute, IN**	NA
NA	Tuscaloosa, AL**	NA
NA	Warren-Farmington Hills, MI M.D.**	NA
NA	Winston-Salem, NC**	NA

Source: CQ Press using reported data from the F.B.I. "Crime in the United States 2011"
*Forcible rape is the carnal knowledge of a female forcibly and against her will. Assaults or attempts to commit rape by force or threat of force are included. However, statutory rape without force and other sex offenses are excluded. **Not available

Alpha Order - Metro Area

17. Robberies in 2011
National Total = 354,396 Robberies*

RANK	METROPOLITAN AREA	ROBBERY
232	Abilene, TX	122
88	Akron, OH	900
98	Albany-Schenectady-Troy, NY	763
185	Albany, GA	202
76	Albuquerque, NM	1,168
196	Alexandria, LA	182
111	Allentown, PA-NJ	609
323	Altoona, PA	48
171	Amarillo, TX	241
363	Ames, IA	13
135	Anchorage, AK	471
219	Anderson, SC	138
183	Ann Arbor, MI	214
240	Anniston-Oxford, AL	113
338	Appleton, WI	33
162	Asheville, NC	271
212	Athens-Clarke County, GA	147
13	Atlanta, GA	8,147
112	Atlantic City, NJ	603
256	Auburn, AL	94
99	Augusta, GA-SC	743
69	Austin-Round Rock, TX	1,317
82	Bakersfield, CA	1,029
19	Baltimore-Towson, MD	5,968
324	Bangor, ME	47
246	Barnstable Town, MA	106
70	Baton Rouge, LA	1,290
217	Battle Creek, MI	139
328	Bay City, MI	45
106	Beaumont-Port Arthur, TX	627
283	Bellingham, WA	74
328	Bend, OR	45
83	Bethesda-Frederick, MD M.D.	1,005
332	Billings, MT	41
228	Binghamton, NY	125
60	Birmingham-Hoover, AL	1,704
360	Bismarck, ND	16
355	Blacksburg, VA	24
264	Bloomington-Normal, IL	87
291	Bloomington, IN	69
257	Boise City-Nampa, ID	91
24	Boston (greater), MA-NH	4,583
36	Boston-Quincy, MA M.D.	3,059
264	Boulder, CO	87
295	Bowling Green, KY	67
236	Bremerton-Silverdale, WA	117
79	Bridgeport-Stamford, CT	1,094
174	Brownsville-Harlingen, TX	233
207	Brunswick, GA	151
54	Buffalo-Niagara Falls, NY	1,946
221	Burlington, NC	135
95	Cambridge-Newton, MA M.D.	810
62	Camden, NJ M.D.	1,686
118	Canton, OH	579
113	Cape Coral-Fort Myers, FL	602
244	Cape Girardeau, MO-IL	107
360	Carson City, NV	16
357	Casper, WY	23
264	Cedar Rapids, IA	87
178	Champaign-Urbana, IL	219

RANK	METROPOLITAN AREA	ROBBERY
185	Charleston, WV	202
50	Charlotte-Gastonia, NC-SC	2,211
269	Charlottesville, VA	86
129	Chattanooga, TN-GA	502
345	Cheyenne, WY	30
5	Chicago (greater), IL-IN-WI	18,100
6	Chicago-Joilet-Naperville, IL M.D.	16,870
206	Chico, CA	158
41	Cincinnati-Middletown, OH-KY-IN	2,891
187	Clarksville, TN-KY	199
26	Cleveland-Elyria-Mentor, OH	4,194
316	Cleveland, TN	56
232	College Station-Bryan, TX	122
133	Colorado Springs, CO	478
196	Columbia, MO	182
138	Columbus, GA-AL	465
355	Columbus, IN	24
29	Columbus, OH	3,768
144	Corpus Christi, TX	398
360	Corvallis, OR	16
240	Crestview-Fort Walton Beach, FL	113
288	Cumberland, MD-WV	70
14	Dallas (greater), TX	8,090
21	Dallas-Plano-Irving, TX M.D.	5,865
333	Dalton, GA	40
271	Danville, IL	84
283	Danville, VA	74
184	Davenport, IA-IL	210
80	Dayton, OH	1,072
293	Decatur, AL	68
223	Decatur, IL	133
126	Deltona-Daytona Beach, FL	510
46	Denver-Aurora, CO	2,270
166	Des Moines-West Des Moines, IA	254
16	Detroit (greater), MI	7,029
20	Detroit-Livonia-Dearborn, MI M.D.	5,921
230	Dothan, AL	124
190	Dover, DE	193
338	Dubuque, IA	33
226	Duluth, MN-WI	127
91	Durham-Chapel Hill, NC	824
343	Eau Claire, WI	31
68	Edison, NJ M.D.	1,351
257	El Centro, CA	91
129	El Paso, TX	502
327	Elizabethtown, KY	46
348	Elmira, NY	28
191	Erie, PA	191
166	Eugene-Springfield, OR	254
193	Evansville, IN-KY	189
336	Fairbanks, AK	36
300	Fargo, ND-MN	64
318	Farmington, NM	53
103	Fayetteville, NC	676
314	Flagstaff, AZ	57
85	Flint, MI	926
297	Florence-Muscle Shoals, AL	65
178	Florence, SC	219
363	Fond du Lac, WI	13
303	Fort Collins-Loveland, CO	62

RANK	METROPOLITAN AREA	ROBBERY
34	Fort Lauderdale, FL M.D.	3,474
227	Fort Smith, AR-OK	126
150	Fort Wayne, IN	341
49	Fort Worth-Arlington, TX M.D.	2,225
66	Fresno, CA	1,379
270	Gadsden, AL	85
160	Gainesville, FL	283
274	Gainesville, GA	82
92	Gary, IN M.D.	822
359	Glens Falls, NY	18
225	Goldsboro, NC	128
365	Grand Forks, ND-MN	12
321	Grand Junction, CO	52
104	Grand Rapids-Wyoming, MI	668
338	Great Falls, MT	33
250	Greeley, CO	101
316	Green Bay, WI	56
123	Greenville, SC	533
189	Gulfport-Biloxi, MS	194
212	Hagerstown-Martinsburg, MD-WV	147
251	Hanford-Corcoran, CA	97
116	Harrisburg-Carlisle, PA	581
358	Harrisonburg, VA	21
77	Hartford, CT	1,134
193	Hickory, NC	189
307	Hinesville, GA	60
351	Holland-Grand Haven, MI	26
295	Hot Springs, AR	67
212	Houma, LA	147
8	Houston, TX	11,530
131	Huntsville, AL	498
365	Idaho Falls, ID	12
32	Indianapolis, IN	3,599
350	Iowa City, IA	27
56	Jacksonville, FL	1,870
303	Jacksonville, NC	62
84	Jackson, MS	940
203	Jackson, TN	170
252	Janesville, WI	96
288	Jefferson City, MO	70
264	Johnson City, TN	87
263	Johnstown, PA	88
254	Jonesboro, AR	95
283	Joplin, MO	74
216	Kankakee-Bradley, IL	141
44	Kansas City, MO-KS	2,462
264	Kennewick-Pasco-Richland, WA	87
157	Killeen-Temple-Fort Hood, TX	301
222	Kingsport, TN-VA	134
297	Kingston, NY	65
94	Knoxville, TN	818
278	Kokomo, IN	80
347	La Crosse, WI-MN	29
300	Lafayette, IN	64
155	Lafayette, LA	317
142	Lake Co.-Kenosha Co., IL-WI M.D.	408
314	Lake Havasu City-Kingman, AZ	57
125	Lakeland, FL	528
150	Lancaster, PA	341
149	Lansing-East Lansing, MI	343

Note: All listings are for Metropolitan Statistical Areas (M.S.A.s) except for those ending with "M.D." Listings with "M.D." are Metropolitan Divisions which are smaller parts of eleven large M.S.A.s. See explanatory note at beginning of metropolitan area section.

Alpha Order - Metro Area (continued)

RANK	METROPOLITAN AREA	ROBBERY
177	Laredo, TX	222
259	Las Cruces, NM	90
31	Las Vegas-Paradise, NV	3,764
333	Lawrence, KS	40
198	Lawton, OK	180
280	Lebanon, PA	77
307	Lewiston-Auburn, ME	60
108	Lexington-Fayette, KY	623
236	Lima, OH	117
200	Lincoln, NE	177
72	Little Rock, AR	1,268
368	Logan, UT-ID	5
220	Longview, TX	136
307	Longview, WA	60
4	Los Angeles County, CA M.D.	19,902
3	Los Angeles (greater), CA	22,147
53	Louisville, KY-IN	1,977
154	Lubbock, TX	322
262	Lynchburg, VA	89
156	Macon, GA	305
217	Madera, CA	139
148	Madison, WI	344
164	Manchester-Nashua, NH	262
324	Manhattan, KS	47
351	Mankato-North Mankato, MN	26
242	Mansfield, OH	112
136	McAllen-Edinburg-Mission, TX	468
286	Medford, OR	73
33	Memphis, TN-MS-AR	3,480
161	Merced, CA	274
9	Miami (greater), FL	11,512
18	Miami-Dade County, FL M.D.	6,157
303	Michigan City-La Porte, IN	62
303	Midland, TX	62
35	Milwaukee, WI	3,311
38	Minneapolis-St. Paul, MN-WI	2,998
351	Missoula, MT	26
89	Mobile, AL	894
100	Modesto, CA	702
209	Monroe, LA	150
287	Monroe, MI	71
140	Montgomery, AL	432
279	Morristown, TN	79
300	Mount Vernon-Anacortes, WA	64
236	Muncie, IN	117
204	Muskegon-Norton Shores, MI	165
141	Myrtle Beach, SC	410
291	Napa, CA	69
181	Naples-Marco Island, FL	215
45	Nashville-Davidson, TN	2,316
57	Nassau-Suffolk, NY M.D.	1,851
73	New Haven-Milford, CT	1,246
58	New Orleans, LA	1,781
1	New York (greater), NY-NJ-PA	31,628
2	New York-W. Plains NY-NJ M.D.	23,931
25	Newark-Union, NJ-PA M.D.	4,495
90	North Port-Bradenton-Sarasota, FL	831
244	Norwich-New London, CT	107
17	Oakland-Fremont, CA M.D.	6,604
191	Ocala, FL	191
271	Ocean City, NJ	84
254	Odessa, TX	95
207	Ogden-Clearfield, UT	151
64	Oklahoma City, OK	1,501
259	Olympia, WA	90
97	Omaha-Council Bluffs, NE-IA	789
39	Orlando, FL	2,968
351	Oshkosh-Neenah, WI	26
331	Owensboro, KY	42
110	Oxnard-Thousand Oaks, CA	616
120	Palm Bay-Melbourne, FL	561
335	Palm Coast, FL	37
201	Panama City-Lynn Haven, FL	173
234	Pascagoula, MS	120
109	Peabody, MA M.D.	618
116	Pensacola, FL	581
146	Peoria, IL	371
7	Philadelphia (greater) PA-NJ-MD-DE	13,057
11	Philadelphia, PA M.D.	10,007
22	Phoenix-Mesa-Scottsdale, AZ	5,354
205	Pine Bluff, AR	163
51	Pittsburgh, PA	2,150
311	Pittsfield, MA	58
367	Pocatello, ID	7
144	Port St. Lucie, FL	398
61	Portland-Vancouver, OR-WA	1,697
195	Portland, ME	186
122	Poughkeepsie, NY	542
342	Prescott, AZ	32
311	Provo-Orem, UT	58
199	Pueblo, CO	179
318	Punta Gorda, FL	53
175	Racine, WI	225
85	Raleigh-Cary, NC	926
311	Rapid City, SD	58
139	Reading, PA	451
224	Redding, CA	132
133	Reno-Sparks, NV	478
75	Richmond, VA	1,208
23	Riverside-San Bernardino, CA	4,931
181	Roanoke, VA	215
293	Rochester, MN	68
81	Rochester, NY	1,036
105	Rockford, IL	630
252	Rockingham County, NH M.D.	96
187	Rocky Mount, NC	199
280	Rome, GA	77
43	Sacramento, CA	2,848
176	Saginaw, MI	224
202	Salem, OR	171
119	Salinas, CA	572
228	Salisbury, MD	125
93	Salt Lake City, UT	819
328	San Angelo, TX	45
52	San Antonio, TX	2,050
37	San Diego, CA	3,050
10	San Francisco (greater), CA	10,369
30	San Francisco-S. Mateo, CA M.D.	3,765
63	San Jose, CA	1,614
277	San Luis Obispo, CA	81
318	Sandusky, OH	53
47	Santa Ana-Anaheim, CA M.D.	2,245
158	Santa Barbara-Santa Maria, CA	298
169	Santa Cruz-Watsonville, CA	252
247	Santa Fe, NM	103
173	Santa Rosa-Petaluma, CA	234
121	Savannah, GA	548
143	Scranton--Wilkes-Barre, PA	400
27	Seattle (greater), WA	3,808
42	Seattle-Bellevue-Everett, WA M.D.	2,888
274	Sebastian-Vero Beach, FL	82
345	Sheboygan, WI	30
307	Sherman-Denison, TX	60
336	Sioux City, IA-NE-SD	36
280	Sioux Falls, SD	77
127	South Bend-Mishawaka, IN-MI	509
166	Spartanburg, SC	254
115	Spokane, WA	582
159	Springfield, IL	296
96	Springfield, MA	793
152	Springfield, MO	330
180	Springfield, OH	216
343	State College, PA	31
59	Stockton, CA	1,723
321	St. Cloud, MN	52
273	St. Joseph, MO-KS	83
28	St. Louis, MO-IL	3,784
239	Sumter, SC	116
132	Syracuse, NY	495
87	Tacoma, WA M.D.	920
107	Tallahassee, FL	624
40	Tampa-St Petersburg, FL	2,960
243	Terre Haute, IN	110
234	Texarkana, TX-Texarkana, AR	120
71	Toledo, OH	1,285
170	Topeka, KS	242
102	Trenton-Ewing, NJ	691
65	Tucson, AZ	1,406
74	Tulsa, OK	1,236
165	Tuscaloosa, AL	261
248	Tyler, TX	102
215	Utica-Rome, NY	146
230	Valdosta, GA	124
101	Vallejo-Fairfield, CA	694
274	Victoria, TX	82
48	Virginia Beach-Norfolk, VA-NC	2,227
153	Visalia-Porterville, CA	325
162	Waco, TX	271
211	Warner Robins, GA	149
78	Warren-Farmington Hills, MI M.D.	1,108
12	Washington (greater) DC-VA-MD-WV	9,005
15	Washington, DC-VA-MD-WV M.D.	8,000
297	Waterloo-Cedar Falls, IA	65
348	Wausau, WI	28
338	Wenatchee, WA	33
55	West Palm Beach, FL M.D.	1,881
209	Wichita Falls, TX	150
124	Wichita, KS	529
288	Williamsport, PA	70
67	Wilmington, DE-MD-NJ M.D.	1,364
147	Wilmington, NC	360
324	Winchester, VA-WV	47
127	Winston-Salem, NC	509
114	Worcester, MA	593
172	Yakima, WA	236
137	York-Hanover, PA	466
248	Yuba City, CA	102
259	Yuma, AZ	90

Source: Reported data from the F.B.I. "Crime in the United States 2011"
*Robbery is the taking of anything of value by force or threat of force. Attempts are included.

Rank Order - Metro Area

17. Robberies in 2011 (continued)
National Total = 354,396 Robberies*

RANK	METROPOLITAN AREA	ROBBERY
1	New York (greater), NY-NJ-PA	31,628
2	New York-W. Plains NY-NJ M.D.	23,931
3	Los Angeles (greater), CA	22,147
4	Los Angeles County, CA M.D.	19,902
5	Chicago (greater), IL-IN-WI	18,100
6	Chicago-Joilet-Naperville, IL M.D.	16,870
7	Philadelphia (greater) PA-NJ-MD-DE	13,057
8	Houston, TX	11,530
9	Miami (greater), FL	11,512
10	San Francisco (greater), CA	10,369
11	Philadelphia, PA M.D.	10,007
12	Washington (greater) DC-VA-MD-WV	9,005
13	Atlanta, GA	8,147
14	Dallas (greater), TX	8,090
15	Washington, DC-VA-MD-WV M.D.	8,000
16	Detroit (greater), MI	7,029
17	Oakland-Fremont, CA M.D.	6,604
18	Miami-Dade County, FL M.D.	6,157
19	Baltimore-Towson, MD	5,968
20	Detroit-Livonia-Dearborn, MI M.D.	5,921
21	Dallas-Plano-Irving, TX M.D.	5,865
22	Phoenix-Mesa-Scottsdale, AZ	5,354
23	Riverside-San Bernardino, CA	4,931
24	Boston (greater), MA-NH	4,583
25	Newark-Union, NJ-PA M.D.	4,495
26	Cleveland-Elyria-Mentor, OH	4,194
27	Seattle (greater), WA	3,808
28	St. Louis, MO-IL	3,784
29	Columbus, OH	3,768
30	San Francisco-S. Mateo, CA M.D.	3,765
31	Las Vegas-Paradise, NV	3,764
32	Indianapolis, IN	3,599
33	Memphis, TN-MS-AR	3,480
34	Fort Lauderdale, FL M.D.	3,474
35	Milwaukee, WI	3,311
36	Boston-Quincy, MA M.D.	3,059
37	San Diego, CA	3,050
38	Minneapolis-St. Paul, MN-WI	2,998
39	Orlando, FL	2,968
40	Tampa-St Petersburg, FL	2,960
41	Cincinnati-Middletown, OH-KY-IN	2,891
42	Seattle-Bellevue-Everett, WA M.D.	2,888
43	Sacramento, CA	2,848
44	Kansas City, MO-KS	2,462
45	Nashville-Davidson, TN	2,316
46	Denver-Aurora, CO	2,270
47	Santa Ana-Anaheim, CA M.D.	2,245
48	Virginia Beach-Norfolk, VA-NC	2,227
49	Fort Worth-Arlington, TX M.D.	2,225
50	Charlotte-Gastonia, NC-SC	2,211
51	Pittsburgh, PA	2,150
52	San Antonio, TX	2,050
53	Louisville, KY-IN	1,977
54	Buffalo-Niagara Falls, NY	1,946
55	West Palm Beach, FL M.D.	1,881
56	Jacksonville, FL	1,870
57	Nassau-Suffolk, NY M.D.	1,851
58	New Orleans, LA	1,781
59	Stockton, CA	1,723
60	Birmingham-Hoover, AL	1,704
61	Portland-Vancouver, OR-WA	1,697
62	Camden, NJ M.D.	1,686
63	San Jose, CA	1,614
64	Oklahoma City, OK	1,501
65	Tucson, AZ	1,406
66	Fresno, CA	1,379
67	Wilmington, DE-MD-NJ M.D.	1,364
68	Edison, NJ M.D.	1,351
69	Austin-Round Rock, TX	1,317
70	Baton Rouge, LA	1,290
71	Toledo, OH	1,285
72	Little Rock, AR	1,268
73	New Haven-Milford, CT	1,246
74	Tulsa, OK	1,236
75	Richmond, VA	1,208
76	Albuquerque, NM	1,168
77	Hartford, CT	1,134
78	Warren-Farmington Hills, MI M.D.	1,108
79	Bridgeport-Stamford, CT	1,094
80	Dayton, OH	1,072
81	Rochester, NY	1,036
82	Bakersfield, CA	1,029
83	Bethesda-Frederick, MD M.D.	1,005
84	Jackson, MS	940
85	Flint, MI	926
85	Raleigh-Cary, NC	926
87	Tacoma, WA M.D.	920
88	Akron, OH	900
89	Mobile, AL	894
90	North Port-Bradenton-Sarasota, FL	831
91	Durham-Chapel Hill, NC	824
92	Gary, IN M.D.	822
93	Salt Lake City, UT	819
94	Knoxville, TN	818
95	Cambridge-Newton, MA M.D.	810
96	Springfield, MA	793
97	Omaha-Council Bluffs, NE-IA	789
98	Albany-Schenectady-Troy, NY	763
99	Augusta, GA-SC	743
100	Modesto, CA	702
101	Vallejo-Fairfield, CA	694
102	Trenton-Ewing, NJ	691
103	Fayetteville, NC	676
104	Grand Rapids-Wyoming, MI	668
105	Rockford, IL	630
106	Beaumont-Port Arthur, TX	627
107	Tallahassee, FL	624
108	Lexington-Fayette, KY	623
109	Peabody, MA M.D.	618
110	Oxnard-Thousand Oaks, CA	616
111	Allentown, PA-NJ	609
112	Atlantic City, NJ	603
113	Cape Coral-Fort Myers, FL	602
114	Worcester, MA	593
115	Spokane, WA	582
116	Harrisburg-Carlisle, PA	581
116	Pensacola, FL	581
118	Canton, OH	579
119	Salinas, CA	572
120	Palm Bay-Melbourne, FL	561
121	Savannah, GA	548
122	Poughkeepsie, NY	542
123	Greenville, SC	533
124	Wichita, KS	529
125	Lakeland, FL	528
126	Deltona-Daytona Beach, FL	510
127	South Bend-Mishawaka, IN-MI	509
127	Winston-Salem, NC	509
129	Chattanooga, TN-GA	502
129	El Paso, TX	502
131	Huntsville, AL	498
132	Syracuse, NY	495
133	Colorado Springs, CO	478
133	Reno-Sparks, NV	478
135	Anchorage, AK	471
136	McAllen-Edinburg-Mission, TX	468
137	York-Hanover, PA	466
138	Columbus, GA-AL	465
139	Reading, PA	451
140	Montgomery, AL	432
141	Myrtle Beach, SC	410
142	Lake Co.-Kenosha Co., IL-WI M.D.	408
143	Scranton--Wilkes-Barre, PA	400
144	Corpus Christi, TX	398
144	Port St. Lucie, FL	398
146	Peoria, IL	371
147	Wilmington, NC	360
148	Madison, WI	344
149	Lansing-East Lansing, MI	343
150	Fort Wayne, IN	341
150	Lancaster, PA	341
152	Springfield, MO	330
153	Visalia-Porterville, CA	325
154	Lubbock, TX	322
155	Lafayette, LA	317
156	Macon, GA	305
157	Killeen-Temple-Fort Hood, TX	301
158	Santa Barbara-Santa Maria, CA	298
159	Springfield, IL	296
160	Gainesville, FL	283
161	Merced, CA	274
162	Asheville, NC	271
162	Waco, TX	271
164	Manchester-Nashua, NH	262
165	Tuscaloosa, AL	261
166	Des Moines-West Des Moines, IA	254
166	Eugene-Springfield, OR	254
166	Spartanburg, SC	254
169	Santa Cruz-Watsonville, CA	252
170	Topeka, KS	242
171	Amarillo, TX	241
172	Yakima, WA	236
173	Santa Rosa-Petaluma, CA	234
174	Brownsville-Harlingen, TX	233
175	Racine, WI	225
176	Saginaw, MI	224
177	Laredo, TX	222
178	Champaign-Urbana, IL	219
178	Florence, SC	219
180	Springfield, OH	216

Note: All listings are for Metropolitan Statistical Areas (M.S.A.s) except for those ending with "M.D." Listings with "M.D." are Metropolitan Divisions which are smaller parts of eleven large M.S.A.s. See explanatory note at beginning of metropolitan area section.

Rank Order - Metro Area (continued)

RANK	METROPOLITAN AREA	ROBBERY	RANK	METROPOLITAN AREA	ROBBERY	RANK	METROPOLITAN AREA	ROBBERY
181	Naples-Marco Island, FL	215	244	Cape Girardeau, MO-IL	107	307	Hinesville, GA	60
181	Roanoke, VA	215	244	Norwich-New London, CT	107	307	Lewiston-Auburn, ME	60
183	Ann Arbor, MI	214	246	Barnstable Town, MA	106	307	Longview, WA	60
184	Davenport, IA-IL	210	247	Santa Fe, NM	103	307	Sherman-Denison, TX	60
185	Albany, GA	202	248	Tyler, TX	102	311	Pittsfield, MA	58
185	Charleston, WV	202	248	Yuba City, CA	102	311	Provo-Orem, UT	58
187	Clarksville, TN-KY	199	250	Greeley, CO	101	311	Rapid City, SD	58
187	Rocky Mount, NC	199	251	Hanford-Corcoran, CA	97	314	Flagstaff, AZ	57
189	Gulfport-Biloxi, MS	194	252	Janesville, WI	96	314	Lake Havasu City-Kingman, AZ	57
190	Dover, DE	193	252	Rockingham County, NH M.D.	96	316	Cleveland, TN	56
191	Erie, PA	191	254	Jonesboro, AR	95	316	Green Bay, WI	56
191	Ocala, FL	191	254	Odessa, TX	95	318	Farmington, NM	53
193	Evansville, IN-KY	189	256	Auburn, AL	94	318	Punta Gorda, FL	53
193	Hickory, NC	189	257	Boise City-Nampa, ID	91	318	Sandusky, OH	53
195	Portland, ME	186	257	El Centro, CA	91	321	Grand Junction, CO	52
196	Alexandria, LA	182	259	Las Cruces, NM	90	321	St. Cloud, MN	52
196	Columbia, MO	182	259	Olympia, WA	90	323	Altoona, PA	48
198	Lawton, OK	180	259	Yuma, AZ	90	324	Bangor, ME	47
199	Pueblo, CO	179	262	Lynchburg, VA	89	324	Manhattan, KS	47
200	Lincoln, NE	177	263	Johnstown, PA	88	324	Winchester, VA-WV	47
201	Panama City-Lynn Haven, FL	173	264	Bloomington-Normal, IL	87	327	Elizabethtown, KY	46
202	Salem, OR	171	264	Boulder, CO	87	328	Bay City, MI	45
203	Jackson, TN	170	264	Cedar Rapids, IA	87	328	Bend, OR	45
204	Muskegon-Norton Shores, MI	165	264	Johnson City, TN	87	328	San Angelo, TX	45
205	Pine Bluff, AR	163	264	Kennewick-Pasco-Richland, WA	87	331	Owensboro, KY	42
206	Chico, CA	158	269	Charlottesville, VA	86	332	Billings, MT	41
207	Brunswick, GA	151	270	Gadsden, AL	85	333	Dalton, GA	40
207	Ogden-Clearfield, UT	151	271	Danville, IL	84	333	Lawrence, KS	40
209	Monroe, LA	150	271	Ocean City, NJ	84	335	Palm Coast, FL	37
209	Wichita Falls, TX	150	273	St. Joseph, MO-KS	83	336	Fairbanks, AK	36
211	Warner Robins, GA	149	274	Gainesville, GA	82	336	Sioux City, IA-NE-SD	36
212	Athens-Clarke County, GA	147	274	Sebastian-Vero Beach, FL	82	338	Appleton, WI	33
212	Hagerstown-Martinsburg, MD-WV	147	274	Victoria, TX	82	338	Dubuque, IA	33
212	Houma, LA	147	277	San Luis Obispo, CA	81	338	Great Falls, MT	33
215	Utica-Rome, NY	146	278	Kokomo, IN	80	338	Wenatchee, WA	33
216	Kankakee-Bradley, IL	141	279	Morristown, TN	79	342	Prescott, AZ	32
217	Battle Creek, MI	139	280	Lebanon, PA	77	343	Eau Claire, WI	31
217	Madera, CA	139	280	Rome, GA	77	343	State College, PA	31
219	Anderson, SC	138	280	Sioux Falls, SD	77	345	Cheyenne, WY	30
220	Longview, TX	136	283	Bellingham, WA	74	345	Sheboygan, WI	30
221	Burlington, NC	135	283	Danville, VA	74	347	La Crosse, WI-MN	29
222	Kingsport, TN-VA	134	283	Joplin, MO	74	348	Elmira, NY	28
223	Decatur, IL	133	286	Medford, OR	73	348	Wausau, WI	28
224	Redding, CA	132	287	Monroe, MI	71	350	Iowa City, IA	27
225	Goldsboro, NC	128	288	Cumberland, MD-WV	70	351	Holland-Grand Haven, MI	26
226	Duluth, MN-WI	127	288	Jefferson City, MO	70	351	Mankato-North Mankato, MN	26
227	Fort Smith, AR-OK	126	288	Williamsport, PA	70	351	Missoula, MT	26
228	Binghamton, NY	125	291	Bloomington, IN	69	351	Oshkosh-Neenah, WI	26
228	Salisbury, MD	125	291	Napa, CA	69	355	Blacksburg, VA	24
230	Dothan, AL	124	293	Decatur, AL	68	355	Columbus, IN	24
230	Valdosta, GA	124	293	Rochester, MN	68	357	Casper, WY	23
232	Abilene, TX	122	295	Bowling Green, KY	67	358	Harrisonburg, VA	21
232	College Station-Bryan, TX	122	295	Hot Springs, AR	67	359	Glens Falls, NY	18
234	Pascagoula, MS	120	297	Florence-Muscle Shoals, AL	65	360	Bismarck, ND	16
234	Texarkana, TX-Texarkana, AR	120	297	Kingston, NY	65	360	Carson City, NV	16
236	Bremerton-Silverdale, WA	117	297	Waterloo-Cedar Falls, IA	65	360	Corvallis, OR	16
236	Lima, OH	117	300	Fargo, ND-MN	64	363	Ames, IA	13
236	Muncie, IN	117	300	Lafayette, IN	64	363	Fond du Lac, WI	13
239	Sumter, SC	116	300	Mount Vernon-Anacortes, WA	64	365	Grand Forks, ND-MN	12
240	Anniston-Oxford, AL	113	303	Fort Collins-Loveland, CO	62	365	Idaho Falls, ID	12
240	Crestview-Fort Walton Beach, FL	113	303	Jacksonville, NC	62	367	Pocatello, ID	7
242	Mansfield, OH	112	303	Michigan City-La Porte, IN	62	368	Logan, UT-ID	5
243	Terre Haute, IN	110	303	Midland, TX	62			

Source: Reported data from the F.B.I. "Crime in the United States 2011"
*Robbery is the taking of anything of value by force or threat of force. Attempts are included.

Alpha Order - Metro Area

18. Robbery Rate in 2011
National Rate = 113.7 Robberies per 100,000 Population*

RANK	METROPOLITAN AREA	RATE	RANK	METROPOLITAN AREA	RATE	RANK	METROPOLITAN AREA	RATE
208	Abilene, TX	72.3	226	Charleston, WV	66.3	24	Fort Lauderdale, FL M.D.	196.1
83	Akron, OH	127.9	89	Charlotte-Gastonia, NC-SC	124.2	293	Fort Smith, AR-OK	41.8
169	Albany-Schenectady-Troy, NY	87.2	291	Charlottesville, VA	42.2	182	Fort Wayne, IN	81.5
86	Albany, GA	126.7	156	Chattanooga, TN-GA	94.1	136	Fort Worth-Arlington, TX M.D.	102.0
80	Albuquerque, NM	130.2	323	Cheyenne, WY	32.4	58	Fresno, CA	146.5
100	Alexandria, LA	117.2	27	Chicago (greater), IL-IN-WI	190.7	183	Gadsden, AL	81.0
197	Allentown, PA-NJ	73.9	13	Chicago-Joilet-Naperville, IL M.D.	213.4	124	Gainesville, FL	105.6
303	Altoona, PA	37.6	212	Chico, CA	71.0	280	Gainesville, GA	45.0
154	Amarillo, TX	94.5	70	Cincinnati-Middletown, OH-KY-IN	135.4	103	Gary, IN M.D.	115.5
360	Ames, IA	14.4	209	Clarksville, TN-KY	72.0	361	Glens Falls, NY	13.9
54	Anchorage, AK	151.5	21	Cleveland-Elyria-Mentor, OH	201.8	132	Goldsboro, NC	103.1
204	Anderson, SC	72.9	270	Cleveland, TN	47.9	363	Grand Forks, ND-MN	12.0
235	Ann Arbor, MI	62.1	261	College Station-Bryan, TX	52.3	316	Grand Junction, CO	34.8
153	Anniston-Oxford, AL	94.8	205	Colorado Springs, CO	72.8	174	Grand Rapids-Wyoming, MI	86.4
356	Appleton, WI	14.6	130	Columbia, MO	105.0	297	Great Falls, MT	40.2
233	Asheville, NC	63.0	49	Columbus, GA-AL	155.9	299	Greeley, CO	39.3
191	Athens-Clarke County, GA	75.4	326	Columbus, IN	31.1	351	Green Bay, WI	18.2
53	Atlanta, GA	152.6	18	Columbus, OH	205.0	179	Greenville, SC	82.7
8	Atlantic City, NJ	218.9	160	Corpus Christi, TX	91.0	189	Gulfport-Biloxi, MS	77.7
225	Auburn, AL	66.7	350	Corvallis, OR	18.5	256	Hagerstown-Martinsburg, MD-WV	54.3
75	Augusta, GA-SC	131.8	237	Crestview-Fort Walton Beach, FL	61.7	234	Hanford-Corcoran, CA	62.7
194	Austin-Round Rock, TX	75.2	224	Cumberland, MD-WV	67.3	125	Harrisburg-Carlisle, PA	105.4
93	Bakersfield, CA	121.1	88	Dallas (greater), TX	124.3	353	Harrisonburg, VA	16.6
9	Baltimore-Towson, MD	218.1	69	Dallas-Plano-Irving, TX M.D.	135.6	113	Hartford, CT	110.9
327	Bangor, ME	30.5	336	Dalton, GA	27.8	264	Hickory, NC	51.1
267	Barnstable Town, MA	48.8	134	Danville, IL	102.6	190	Hinesville, GA	76.0
44	Baton Rouge, LA	159.3	221	Danville, VA	68.6	365	Holland-Grand Haven, MI	9.9
135	Battle Creek, MI	102.2	255	Davenport, IA-IL	55.1	218	Hot Springs, AR	69.3
293	Bay City, MI	41.8	85	Dayton, OH	127.3	215	Houma, LA	70.0
47	Beaumont-Port Arthur, TX	158.0	284	Decatur, AL	44.0	28	Houston, TX	189.9
307	Bellingham, WA	36.2	95	Decatur, IL	119.7	96	Huntsville, AL	118.7
334	Bend, OR	28.2	138	Deltona-Daytona Beach, FL	101.7	366	Idaho Falls, ID	9.1
181	Bethesda-Frederick, MD M.D.	82.6	167	Denver-Aurora, CO	87.7	20	Indianapolis, IN	203.9
341	Billings, MT	25.7	282	Des Moines-West Des Moines, IA	44.4	352	Iowa City, IA	17.6
266	Binghamton, NY	49.4	40	Detroit (greater), MI	163.7	67	Jacksonville, FL	137.1
57	Birmingham-Hoover, AL	150.3	1	Detroit-Livonia-Dearborn, MI M.D.	325.5	318	Jacksonville, NC	34.4
359	Bismarck, ND	14.5	176	Dothan, AL	84.7	34	Jackson, MS	173.7
356	Blacksburg, VA	14.6	99	Dover, DE	117.7	59	Jackson, TN	146.0
263	Bloomington-Normal, IL	51.2	314	Dubuque, IA	35.1	243	Janesville, WI	59.6
311	Bloomington, IN	35.6	279	Duluth, MN-WI	45.1	275	Jefferson City, MO	46.6
356	Boise City-Nampa, ID	14.6	42	Durham-Chapel Hill, NC	161.3	287	Johnson City, TN	43.4
140	Boston (greater), MA-NH	100.1	349	Eau Claire, WI	19.2	239	Johnstown, PA	61.1
43	Boston-Quincy, MA M.D.	161.1	248	Edison, NJ M.D.	57.5	188	Jonesboro, AR	77.9
332	Boulder, CO	29.0	262	El Centro, CA	51.5	292	Joplin, MO	42.0
259	Bowling Green, KY	52.8	238	El Paso, TX	61.4	90	Kankakee-Bradley, IL	123.9
276	Bremerton-Silverdale, WA	45.9	301	Elizabethtown, KY	38.2	94	Kansas City, MO-KS	120.4
92	Bridgeport-Stamford, CT	121.4	325	Elmira, NY	31.4	319	Kennewick-Pasco-Richland, WA	33.8
252	Brownsville-Harlingen, TX	56.2	222	Erie, PA	67.9	206	Killeen-Temple-Fort Hood, TX	72.7
74	Brunswick, GA	132.6	210	Eugene-Springfield, OR	71.5	289	Kingsport, TN-VA	42.9
35	Buffalo-Niagara Falls, NY	170.6	260	Evansville, IN-KY	52.4	312	Kingston, NY	35.5
166	Burlington, NC	88.2	128	Fairbanks, AK	105.1	102	Knoxville, TN	116.1
258	Cambridge-Newton, MA M.D.	53.6	328	Fargo, ND-MN	30.2	185	Kokomo, IN	80.7
72	Camden, NJ M.D.	134.4	296	Farmington, NM	40.3	345	La Crosse, WI-MN	21.6
62	Canton, OH	143.1	30	Fayetteville, NC	182.2	324	Lafayette, IN	31.6
148	Cape Coral-Fort Myers, FL	96.0	293	Flagstaff, AZ	41.8	105	Lafayette, LA	114.8
114	Cape Girardeau, MO-IL	110.7	11	Flint, MI	217.6	273	Lake Co.-Kenosha Co., IL-WI M.D.	46.8
333	Carson City, NV	28.7	284	Florence-Muscle Shoals, AL	44.0	335	Lake Havasu City-Kingman, AZ	28.1
328	Casper, WY	30.2	126	Florence, SC	105.3	173	Lakeland, FL	86.5
320	Cedar Rapids, IA	33.6	362	Fond du Lac, WI	12.7	228	Lancaster, PA	65.4
155	Champaign-Urbana, IL	94.2	347	Fort Collins-Loveland, CO	20.3	196	Lansing-East Lansing, MI	74.0

Note: All listings are for Metropolitan Statistical Areas (M.S.A.s) except for those ending with "M.D." Listings with "M.D." are Metropolitan Divisions which are smaller parts of eleven large M.S.A.s. See explanatory note at beginning of metropolitan area section.

Alpha Order - Metro Area (continued)

RANK	METROPOLITAN AREA	RATE	RANK	METROPOLITAN AREA	RATE	RANK	METROPOLITAN AREA	RATE
170	Laredo, TX	86.9	97	Oklahoma City, OK	118.5	50	Savannah, GA	155.6
290	Las Cruces, NM	42.5	314	Olympia, WA	35.1	213	Scranton--Wilkes-Barre, PA	70.7
26	Las Vegas-Paradise, NV	191.3	163	Omaha-Council Bluffs, NE-IA	90.4	119	Seattle (greater), WA	109.0
310	Lawrence, KS	35.9	66	Orlando, FL	137.2	120	Seattle-Bellevue-Everett, WA M.D.	107.5
61	Lawton, OK	143.5	354	Oshkosh-Neenah, WI	15.5	245	Sebastian-Vero Beach, FL	58.6
248	Lebanon, PA	57.5	305	Owensboro, KY	36.3	340	Sheboygan, WI	25.9
253	Lewiston-Auburn, ME	55.7	197	Oxnard-Thousand Oaks, CA	73.9	268	Sherman-Denison, TX	48.6
77	Lexington-Fayette, KY	131.1	137	Palm Bay-Melbourne, FL	101.9	342	Sioux City, IA-NE-SD	24.9
117	Lima, OH	110.0	302	Palm Coast, FL	38.1	321	Sioux Falls, SD	33.3
246	Lincoln, NE	58.1	139	Panama City-Lynn Haven, FL	101.1	46	South Bend-Mishawaka, IN-MI	158.8
32	Little Rock, AR	179.8	200	Pascagoula, MS	73.7	165	Spartanburg, SC	88.3
368	Logan, UT-ID	3.9	179	Peabody, MA M.D.	82.7	91	Spokane, WA	121.6
235	Longview, TX	62.1	84	Pensacola, FL	127.7	65	Springfield, IL	140.4
247	Longview, WA	57.7	145	Peoria, IL	97.5	109	Springfield, MA	113.7
22	Los Angeles County, CA M.D.	200.3	10	Philadelphia (greater) PA-NJ-MD-DE	218.0	193	Springfield, MO	75.3
35	Los Angeles (greater), CA	170.6	4	Philadelphia, PA M.D.	248.8	48	Springfield, OH	156.0
52	Louisville, KY-IN	153.0	87	Phoenix-Mesa-Scottsdale, AZ	125.9	348	State College, PA	20.1
114	Lubbock, TX	110.7	41	Pine Bluff, AR	161.4	5	Stockton, CA	248.5
316	Lynchburg, VA	34.8	160	Pittsburgh, PA	91.0	337	St. Cloud, MN	27.3
81	Macon, GA	129.6	286	Pittsfield, MA	43.9	231	St. Joseph, MO-KS	64.9
159	Madera, CA	91.1	367	Pocatello, ID	7.6	73	St. Louis, MO-IL	134.0
241	Madison, WI	60.2	158	Port St. Lucie, FL	92.6	122	Sumter, SC	106.7
229	Manchester-Nashua, NH	65.3	191	Portland-Vancouver, OR-WA	75.4	195	Syracuse, NY	74.4
304	Manhattan, KS	36.8	307	Portland, ME	36.2	108	Tacoma, WA M.D.	113.9
339	Mankato-North Mankato, MN	26.7	186	Poughkeepsie, NY	80.5	37	Tallahassee, FL	167.6
164	Mansfield, OH	89.9	355	Prescott, AZ	15.0	131	Tampa-St Petersburg, FL	104.9
244	McAllen-Edinburg-Mission, TX	59.2	364	Provo-Orem, UT	10.8	232	Terre Haute, IN	63.5
312	Medford, OR	35.5	116	Pueblo, CO	110.6	171	Texarkana, TX-Texarkana, AR	86.8
2	Memphis, TN-MS-AR	262.3	322	Punta Gorda, FL	32.7	23	Toledo, OH	197.1
123	Merced, CA	105.9	107	Racine, WI	114.6	133	Topeka, KS	102.8
19	Miami (greater), FL	204.1	184	Raleigh-Cary, NC	80.9	29	Trenton-Ewing, NJ	187.9
6	Miami-Dade County, FL M.D.	243.3	277	Rapid City, SD	45.3	63	Tucson, AZ	141.4
254	Michigan City-La Porte, IN	55.3	118	Reading, PA	109.3	79	Tulsa, OK	130.4
282	Midland, TX	44.4	202	Redding, CA	73.6	98	Tuscaloosa, AL	118.4
14	Milwaukee, WI	211.9	112	Reno-Sparks, NV	111.4	272	Tyler, TX	47.6
162	Minneapolis-St. Paul, MN-WI	90.7	151	Richmond, VA	94.9	269	Utica-Rome, NY	48.5
343	Missoula, MT	23.6	104	Riverside-San Bernardino, CA	115.4	167	Valdosta, GA	87.7
12	Mobile, AL	215.4	219	Roanoke, VA	68.8	39	Vallejo-Fairfield, CA	165.9
71	Modesto, CA	134.9	305	Rochester, MN	36.3	216	Victoria, TX	69.6
178	Monroe, LA	84.2	144	Rochester, NY	97.8	76	Virginia Beach-Norfolk, VA-NC	131.6
274	Monroe, MI	46.7	32	Rockford, IL	179.8	207	Visalia-Porterville, CA	72.6
105	Montgomery, AL	114.8	344	Rockingham County, NH M.D.	22.9	110	Waco, TX	113.0
250	Morristown, TN	57.3	82	Rocky Mount, NC	128.9	128	Warner Robins, GA	105.1
257	Mount Vernon-Anacortes, WA	53.9	187	Rome, GA	78.9	281	Warren-Farmington Hills, MI M.D.	44.8
141	Muncie, IN	98.9	78	Sacramento, CA	131.0	44	Washington (greater) DC-VA-MD-WV	159.3
149	Muskegon-Norton Shores, MI	95.9	111	Saginaw, MI	112.0	31	Washington, DC-VA-MD-WV M.D.	180.4
56	Myrtle Beach, SC	150.5	288	Salem, OR	43.3	300	Waterloo-Cedar Falls, IA	38.5
265	Napa, CA	50.0	68	Salinas, CA	136.2	346	Wausau, WI	20.8
227	Naples-Marco Island, FL	66.0	141	Salisbury, MD	98.9	331	Wenatchee, WA	29.3
60	Nashville-Davidson, TN	144.4	210	Salt Lake City, UT	71.5	64	West Palm Beach, FL M.D.	140.6
230	Nassau-Suffolk, NY M.D.	65.0	298	San Angelo, TX	39.4	147	Wichita Falls, TX	97.1
51	New Haven-Milford, CT	153.8	157	San Antonio, TX	93.7	177	Wichita, KS	84.4
55	New Orleans, LA	151.1	146	San Diego, CA	97.4	242	Williamsport, PA	60.1
38	New York (greater), NY-NJ-PA	166.7	7	San Francisco (greater), CA	236.4	25	Wilmington, DE-MD-NJ M.D.	191.5
17	New York-W. Plains NY-NJ M.D.	205.8	15	San Francisco-S. Mateo, CA M.D.	209.5	143	Wilmington, NC	98.1
16	Newark-Union, NJ-PA M.D.	208.6	171	San Jose, CA	86.8	307	Winchester, VA-WV	36.2
101	North Port-Bradenton-Sarasota, FL	116.7	330	San Luis Obispo, CA	29.7	127	Winston-Salem, NC	105.2
203	Norwich-New London, CT	73.0	220	Sandusky, OH	68.7	199	Worcester, MA	73.8
3	Oakland-Fremont, CA M.D.	255.0	200	Santa Ana-Anaheim, CA M.D.	73.7	150	Yakima, WA	95.5
251	Ocala, FL	56.9	217	Santa Barbara-Santa Maria, CA	69.5	121	York-Hanover, PA	106.8
175	Ocean City, NJ	86.1	151	Santa Cruz-Watsonville, CA	94.9	240	Yuba City, CA	60.4
223	Odessa, TX	67.8	213	Santa Fe, NM	70.7	277	Yuma, AZ	45.3
338	Ogden-Clearfield, UT	27.1	271	Santa Rosa-Petaluma, CA	47.8			

Source: Reported data from the F.B.I. "Crime in the United States 2011"
*Robbery is the taking of anything of value by force or threat of force. Attempts are included.

18. Robbery Rate in 2011 (continued)
National Rate = 113.7 Robberies per 100,000 Population*

Rank Order - Metro Area

RANK	METROPOLITAN AREA	RATE	RANK	METROPOLITAN AREA	RATE	RANK	METROPOLITAN AREA	RATE
1	Detroit-Livonia-Dearborn, MI M.D.	325.5	61	Lawton, OK	143.5	121	York-Hanover, PA	106.8
2	Memphis, TN-MS-AR	262.3	62	Canton, OH	143.1	122	Sumter, SC	106.7
3	Oakland-Fremont, CA M.D.	255.0	63	Tucson, AZ	141.4	123	Merced, CA	105.9
4	Philadelphia, PA M.D.	248.8	64	West Palm Beach, FL M.D.	140.6	124	Gainesville, FL	105.6
5	Stockton, CA	248.5	65	Springfield, IL	140.4	125	Harrisburg-Carlisle, PA	105.4
6	Miami-Dade County, FL M.D.	243.3	66	Orlando, FL	137.2	126	Florence, SC	105.3
7	San Francisco (greater), CA	236.4	67	Jacksonville, FL	137.1	127	Winston-Salem, NC	105.2
8	Atlantic City, NJ	218.9	68	Salinas, CA	136.2	128	Fairbanks, AK	105.1
9	Baltimore-Towson, MD	218.1	69	Dallas-Plano-Irving, TX M.D.	135.6	128	Warner Robins, GA	105.1
10	Philadelphia (greater) PA-NJ-MD-DE	218.0	70	Cincinnati-Middletown, OH-KY-IN	135.4	130	Columbia, MO	105.0
11	Flint, MI	217.6	71	Modesto, CA	134.9	131	Tampa-St Petersburg, FL	104.9
12	Mobile, AL	215.4	72	Camden, NJ M.D.	134.4	132	Goldsboro, NC	103.1
13	Chicago-Joilet-Naperville, IL M.D.	213.4	73	St. Louis, MO-IL	134.0	133	Topeka, KS	102.8
14	Milwaukee, WI	211.9	74	Brunswick, GA	132.6	134	Danville, IL	102.6
15	San Francisco-S. Mateo, CA M.D.	209.5	75	Augusta, GA-SC	131.8	135	Battle Creek, MI	102.2
16	Newark-Union, NJ-PA M.D.	208.6	76	Virginia Beach-Norfolk, VA-NC	131.6	136	Fort Worth-Arlington, TX M.D.	102.0
17	New York-W. Plains NY-NJ M.D.	205.8	77	Lexington-Fayette, KY	131.1	137	Palm Bay-Melbourne, FL	101.9
18	Columbus, OH	205.0	78	Sacramento, CA	131.0	138	Deltona-Daytona Beach, FL	101.7
19	Miami (greater), FL	204.1	79	Tulsa, OK	130.4	139	Panama City-Lynn Haven, FL	101.1
20	Indianapolis, IN	203.9	80	Albuquerque, NM	130.2	140	Boston (greater), MA-NH	100.1
21	Cleveland-Elyria-Mentor, OH	201.8	81	Macon, GA	129.6	141	Muncie, IN	98.9
22	Los Angeles County, CA M.D.	200.3	82	Rocky Mount, NC	128.9	141	Salisbury, MD	98.9
23	Toledo, OH	197.1	83	Akron, OH	127.9	143	Wilmington, NC	98.1
24	Fort Lauderdale, FL M.D.	196.1	84	Pensacola, FL	127.7	144	Rochester, NY	97.8
25	Wilmington, DE-MD-NJ M.D.	191.5	85	Dayton, OH	127.3	145	Peoria, IL	97.5
26	Las Vegas-Paradise, NV	191.3	86	Albany, GA	126.7	146	San Diego, CA	97.4
27	Chicago (greater), IL-IN-WI	190.7	87	Phoenix-Mesa-Scottsdale, AZ	125.9	147	Wichita Falls, TX	97.1
28	Houston, TX	189.9	88	Dallas (greater), TX	124.3	148	Cape Coral-Fort Myers, FL	96.0
29	Trenton-Ewing, NJ	187.9	89	Charlotte-Gastonia, NC-SC	124.2	149	Muskegon-Norton Shores, MI	95.9
30	Fayetteville, NC	182.2	90	Kankakee-Bradley, IL	123.9	150	Yakima, WA	95.5
31	Washington, DC-VA-MD-WV M.D.	180.4	91	Spokane, WA	121.6	151	Richmond, VA	94.9
32	Little Rock, AR	179.8	92	Bridgeport-Stamford, CT	121.4	151	Santa Cruz-Watsonville, CA	94.9
32	Rockford, IL	179.8	93	Bakersfield, CA	121.1	153	Anniston-Oxford, AL	94.8
34	Jackson, MS	173.7	94	Kansas City, MO-KS	120.4	154	Amarillo, TX	94.5
35	Buffalo-Niagara Falls, NY	170.6	95	Decatur, IL	119.7	155	Champaign-Urbana, IL	94.2
35	Los Angeles (greater), CA	170.6	96	Huntsville, AL	118.7	156	Chattanooga, TN-GA	94.1
37	Tallahassee, FL	167.6	97	Oklahoma City, OK	118.5	157	San Antonio, TX	93.7
38	New York (greater), NY-NJ-PA	166.7	98	Tuscaloosa, AL	118.4	158	Port St. Lucie, FL	92.6
39	Vallejo-Fairfield, CA	165.9	99	Dover, DE	117.7	159	Madera, CA	91.1
40	Detroit (greater), MI	163.7	100	Alexandria, LA	117.2	160	Corpus Christi, TX	91.0
41	Pine Bluff, AR	161.4	101	North Port-Bradenton-Sarasota, FL	116.7	160	Pittsburgh, PA	91.0
42	Durham-Chapel Hill, NC	161.3	102	Knoxville, TN	116.1	162	Minneapolis-St. Paul, MN-WI	90.7
43	Boston-Quincy, MA M.D.	161.1	103	Gary, IN M.D.	115.5	163	Omaha-Council Bluffs, NE-IA	90.4
44	Baton Rouge, LA	159.3	104	Riverside-San Bernardino, CA	115.4	164	Mansfield, OH	89.9
44	Washington (greater) DC-VA-MD-WV	159.3	105	Lafayette, LA	114.8	165	Spartanburg, SC	88.3
46	South Bend-Mishawaka, IN-MI	158.8	105	Montgomery, AL	114.8	166	Burlington, NC	88.2
47	Beaumont-Port Arthur, TX	158.0	107	Racine, WI	114.6	167	Denver-Aurora, CO	87.7
48	Springfield, OH	156.0	108	Tacoma, WA M.D.	113.9	167	Valdosta, GA	87.7
49	Columbus, GA-AL	155.9	109	Springfield, MA	113.7	169	Albany-Schenectady-Troy, NY	87.2
50	Savannah, GA	155.6	110	Waco, TX	113.0	170	Laredo, TX	86.9
51	New Haven-Milford, CT	153.8	111	Saginaw, MI	112.0	171	San Jose, CA	86.8
52	Louisville, KY-IN	153.0	112	Reno-Sparks, NV	111.4	171	Texarkana, TX-Texarkana, AR	86.8
53	Atlanta, GA	152.6	113	Hartford, CT	110.9	173	Lakeland, FL	86.5
54	Anchorage, AK	151.5	114	Cape Girardeau, MO-IL	110.7	174	Grand Rapids-Wyoming, MI	86.4
55	New Orleans, LA	151.1	114	Lubbock, TX	110.7	175	Ocean City, NJ	86.1
56	Myrtle Beach, SC	150.5	116	Pueblo, CO	110.6	176	Dothan, AL	84.7
57	Birmingham-Hoover, AL	150.3	117	Lima, OH	110.0	177	Wichita, KS	84.4
58	Fresno, CA	146.5	118	Reading, PA	109.3	178	Monroe, LA	84.2
59	Jackson, TN	146.0	119	Seattle (greater), WA	109.0	179	Greenville, SC	82.7
60	Nashville-Davidson, TN	144.4	120	Seattle-Bellevue-Everett, WA M.D.	107.5	179	Peabody, MA M.D.	82.7

Note: All listings are for Metropolitan Statistical Areas (M.S.A.s) except for those ending with "M.D." Listings with "M.D." are Metropolitan Divisions which are smaller parts of eleven large M.S.A.s. See explanatory note at beginning of metropolitan area section.

Rank Order - Metro Area (continued)

RANK	METROPOLITAN AREA	RATE
181	Bethesda-Frederick, MD M.D.	82.6
182	Fort Wayne, IN	81.5
183	Gadsden, AL	81.0
184	Raleigh-Cary, NC	80.9
185	Kokomo, IN	80.7
186	Poughkeepsie, NY	80.5
187	Rome, GA	78.9
188	Jonesboro, AR	77.9
189	Gulfport-Biloxi, MS	77.7
190	Hinesville, GA	76.0
191	Athens-Clarke County, GA	75.4
191	Portland-Vancouver, OR-WA	75.4
193	Springfield, MO	75.3
194	Austin-Round Rock, TX	75.2
195	Syracuse, NY	74.4
196	Lansing-East Lansing, MI	74.0
197	Allentown, PA-NJ	73.9
197	Oxnard-Thousand Oaks, CA	73.9
199	Worcester, MA	73.8
200	Pascagoula, MS	73.7
200	Santa Ana-Anaheim, CA M.D.	73.7
202	Redding, CA	73.6
203	Norwich-New London, CT	73.0
204	Anderson, SC	72.9
205	Colorado Springs, CO	72.8
206	Killeen-Temple-Fort Hood, TX	72.7
207	Visalia-Porterville, CA	72.6
208	Abilene, TX	72.3
209	Clarksville, TN-KY	72.0
210	Eugene-Springfield, OR	71.5
210	Salt Lake City, UT	71.5
212	Chico, CA	71.0
213	Santa Fe, NM	70.7
213	Scranton--Wilkes-Barre, PA	70.7
215	Houma, LA	70.0
216	Victoria, TX	69.6
217	Santa Barbara-Santa Maria, CA	69.5
218	Hot Springs, AR	69.3
219	Roanoke, VA	68.8
220	Sandusky, OH	68.7
221	Danville, VA	68.6
222	Erie, PA	67.9
223	Odessa, TX	67.8
224	Cumberland, MD-WV	67.3
225	Auburn, AL	66.7
226	Charleston, WV	66.3
227	Naples-Marco Island, FL	66.0
228	Lancaster, PA	65.4
229	Manchester-Nashua, NH	65.3
230	Nassau-Suffolk, NY M.D.	65.0
231	St. Joseph, MO-KS	64.9
232	Terre Haute, IN	63.5
233	Asheville, NC	63.0
234	Hanford-Corcoran, CA	62.7
235	Ann Arbor, MI	62.1
235	Longview, TX	62.1
237	Crestview-Fort Walton Beach, FL	61.7
238	El Paso, TX	61.4
239	Johnstown, PA	61.1
240	Yuba City, CA	60.4
241	Madison, WI	60.2
242	Williamsport, PA	60.1
243	Janesville, WI	59.6
244	McAllen-Edinburg-Mission, TX	59.2
245	Sebastian-Vero Beach, FL	58.6
246	Lincoln, NE	58.1
247	Longview, WA	57.7
248	Edison, NJ M.D.	57.5
248	Lebanon, PA	57.5
250	Morristown, TN	57.3
251	Ocala, FL	56.9
252	Brownsville-Harlingen, TX	56.2
253	Lewiston-Auburn, ME	55.7
254	Michigan City-La Porte, IN	55.3
255	Davenport, IA-IL	55.1
256	Hagerstown-Martinsburg, MD-WV	54.3
257	Mount Vernon-Anacortes, WA	53.9
258	Cambridge-Newton, MA M.D.	53.6
259	Bowling Green, KY	52.8
260	Evansville, IN-KY	52.4
261	College Station-Bryan, TX	52.3
262	El Centro, CA	51.5
263	Bloomington-Normal, IL	51.2
264	Hickory, NC	51.1
265	Napa, CA	50.0
266	Binghamton, NY	49.4
267	Barnstable Town, MA	48.8
268	Sherman-Denison, TX	48.6
269	Utica-Rome, NY	48.5
270	Cleveland, TN	47.9
271	Santa Rosa-Petaluma, CA	47.8
272	Tyler, TX	47.6
273	Lake Co.-Kenosha Co., IL-WI M.D.	46.8
274	Monroe, MI	46.7
275	Jefferson City, MO	46.6
276	Bremerton-Silverdale, WA	45.9
277	Rapid City, SD	45.3
277	Yuma, AZ	45.3
279	Duluth, MN-WI	45.1
280	Gainesville, GA	45.0
281	Warren-Farmington Hills, MI M.D.	44.8
282	Des Moines-West Des Moines, IA	44.4
282	Midland, TX	44.4
284	Decatur, AL	44.0
284	Florence-Muscle Shoals, AL	44.0
286	Pittsfield, MA	43.9
287	Johnson City, TN	43.4
288	Salem, OR	43.3
289	Kingsport, TN-VA	42.9
290	Las Cruces, NM	42.5
291	Charlottesville, VA	42.2
292	Joplin, MO	42.0
293	Bay City, MI	41.8
293	Flagstaff, AZ	41.8
293	Fort Smith, AR-OK	41.8
296	Farmington, NM	40.3
297	Great Falls, MT	40.2
298	San Angelo, TX	39.4
299	Greeley, CO	39.3
300	Waterloo-Cedar Falls, IA	38.5
301	Elizabethtown, KY	38.2
302	Palm Coast, FL	38.1
303	Altoona, PA	37.6
304	Manhattan, KS	36.8
305	Owensboro, KY	36.3
305	Rochester, MN	36.3
307	Bellingham, WA	36.2
307	Portland, ME	36.2
307	Winchester, VA-WV	36.2
310	Lawrence, KS	35.9
311	Bloomington, IN	35.6
312	Kingston, NY	35.5
312	Medford, OR	35.5
314	Dubuque, IA	35.1
314	Olympia, WA	35.1
316	Grand Junction, CO	34.8
316	Lynchburg, VA	34.8
318	Jacksonville, NC	34.4
319	Kennewick-Pasco-Richland, WA	33.8
320	Cedar Rapids, IA	33.6
321	Sioux Falls, SD	33.3
322	Punta Gorda, FL	32.7
323	Cheyenne, WY	32.4
324	Lafayette, IN	31.6
325	Elmira, NY	31.4
326	Columbus, IN	31.1
327	Bangor, ME	30.5
328	Casper, WY	30.2
328	Fargo, ND-MN	30.2
330	San Luis Obispo, CA	29.7
331	Wenatchee, WA	29.3
332	Boulder, CO	29.0
333	Carson City, NV	28.7
334	Bend, OR	28.2
335	Lake Havasu City-Kingman, AZ	28.1
336	Dalton, GA	27.8
337	St. Cloud, MN	27.3
338	Ogden-Clearfield, UT	27.1
339	Mankato-North Mankato, MN	26.7
340	Sheboygan, WI	25.9
341	Billings, MT	25.7
342	Sioux City, IA-NE-SD	24.9
343	Missoula, MT	23.6
344	Rockingham County, NH M.D.	22.9
345	La Crosse, WI-MN	21.6
346	Wausau, WI	20.8
347	Fort Collins-Loveland, CO	20.3
348	State College, PA	20.1
349	Eau Claire, WI	19.2
350	Corvallis, OR	18.5
351	Green Bay, WI	18.2
352	Iowa City, IA	17.6
353	Harrisonburg, VA	16.6
354	Oshkosh-Neenah, WI	15.5
355	Prescott, AZ	15.0
356	Appleton, WI	14.6
356	Blacksburg, VA	14.6
356	Boise City-Nampa, ID	14.6
359	Bismarck, ND	14.5
360	Ames, IA	14.4
361	Glens Falls, NY	13.9
362	Fond du Lac, WI	12.7
363	Grand Forks, ND-MN	12.0
364	Provo-Orem, UT	10.8
365	Holland-Grand Haven, MI	9.9
366	Idaho Falls, ID	9.1
367	Pocatello, ID	7.6
368	Logan, UT-ID	3.9

Source: Reported data from the F.B.I. "Crime in the United States 2011"
*Robbery is the taking of anything of value by force or threat of force. Attempts are included.

Alpha Order - Metro Area

19. Percent Change in Robbery Rate: 2010 to 2011
National Percent Change = 4.7% Decrease*

RANK	METROPOLITAN AREA	% CHANGE	RANK	METROPOLITAN AREA	% CHANGE	RANK	METROPOLITAN AREA	% CHANGE
139	Abilene, TX	(0.6)	NA	Charleston, WV**	NA	53	Fort Lauderdale, FL M.D.	11.2
30	Akron, OH	21.7	NA	Charlotte-Gastonia, NC-SC**	NA	279	Fort Smith, AR-OK	(18.0)
239	Albany-Schenectady-Troy, NY	(11.5)	83	Charlottesville, VA	5.5	134	Fort Wayne, IN	0.2
263	Albany, GA	(15.8)	295	Chattanooga, TN-GA	(21.3)	195	Fort Worth-Arlington, TX M.D.	(6.3)
92	Albuquerque, NM	4.7	22	Cheyenne, WY	29.6	141	Fresno, CA	(0.7)
237	Alexandria, LA	(11.4)	NA	Chicago (greater), IL-IN-WI**	NA	NA	Gadsden, AL**	NA
294	Allentown, PA-NJ	(21.0)	NA	Chicago-Joilet-Naperville, IL M.D.**	NA	209	Gainesville, FL	(7.9)
306	Altoona, PA	(24.5)	133	Chico, CA	0.4	169	Gainesville, GA	(3.4)
176	Amarillo, TX	(4.4)	254	Cincinnati-Middletown, OH-KY-IN	(14.3)	NA	Gary, IN M.D.**	NA
39	Ames, IA	16.1	84	Clarksville, TN-KY	5.3	25	Glens Falls, NY	26.4
110	Anchorage, AK	2.0	152	Cleveland-Elyria-Mentor, OH	(1.8)	298	Goldsboro, NC	(23.2)
172	Anderson, SC	(4.0)	15	Cleveland, TN	36.5	19	Grand Forks, ND-MN	33.3
234	Ann Arbor, MI	(11.0)	290	College Station-Bryan, TX	(20.4)	47	Grand Junction, CO	13.7
NA	Anniston-Oxford, AL**	NA	288	Colorado Springs, CO	(20.0)	192	Grand Rapids-Wyoming, MI	(5.8)
81	Appleton, WI	5.8	24	Columbia, MO	27.3	NA	Great Falls, MT**	NA
86	Asheville, NC	5.2	NA	Columbus, GA-AL**	NA	21	Greeley, CO	30.6
75	Athens-Clarke County, GA	7.0	67	Columbus, IN	8.4	309	Green Bay, WI	(25.4)
112	Atlanta, GA	1.9	172	Columbus, OH	(4.0)	219	Greenville, SC	(9.5)
230	Atlantic City, NJ	(10.8)	273	Corpus Christi, TX	(17.1)	256	Gulfport-Biloxi, MS	(14.6)
NA	Auburn, AL**	NA	183	Corvallis, OR	(5.1)	211	Hagerstown-Martinsburg, MD-WV	(8.1)
263	Augusta, GA-SC	(15.8)	165	Crestview-Fort Walton Beach, FL	(3.1)	53	Hanford-Corcoran, CA	11.2
226	Austin-Round Rock, TX	(10.5)	NA	Cumberland, MD-WV**	NA	240	Harrisburg-Carlisle, PA	(11.8)
283	Bakersfield, CA	(18.4)	183	Dallas (greater), TX	(5.1)	18	Harrisonburg, VA	35.0
113	Baltimore-Towson, MD	1.7	176	Dallas-Plano-Irving, TX M.D.	(4.4)	100	Hartford, CT	3.8
50	Bangor, ME	12.1	258	Dalton, GA	(15.0)	146	Hickory, NC	(1.5)
260	Barnstable Town, MA	(15.3)	280	Danville, IL	(18.2)	302	Hinesville, GA	(23.7)
NA	Baton Rouge, LA**	NA	77	Danville, VA	6.7	230	Holland-Grand Haven, MI	(10.8)
200	Battle Creek, MI	(6.8)	NA	Davenport, IA-IL**	NA	308	Hot Springs, AR	(25.0)
275	Bay City, MI	(17.7)	232	Dayton, OH	(10.9)	246	Houma, LA	(12.6)
135	Beaumont-Port Arthur, TX	0.1	NA	Decatur, AL**	NA	NA	Houston, TX**	NA
316	Bellingham, WA	(28.5)	204	Decatur, IL	(7.0)	NA	Huntsville, AL**	NA
216	Bend, OR	(8.7)	103	Deltona-Daytona Beach, FL	3.6	296	Idaho Falls, ID	(22.2)
255	Bethesda-Frederick, MD M.D.	(14.5)	62	Denver-Aurora, CO	9.8	NA	Indianapolis, IN**	NA
NA	Billings, MT**	NA	188	Des Moines-West Des Moines, IA	(5.7)	324	Iowa City, IA	(33.1)
165	Binghamton, NY	(3.1)	NA	Detroit (greater), MI**	NA	206	Jacksonville, FL	(7.4)
NA	Birmingham-Hoover, AL**	NA	196	Detroit-Livonia-Dearborn, MI M.D.	(6.5)	NA	Jacksonville, NC**	NA
257	Bismarck, ND	(14.7)	NA	Dothan, AL**	NA	291	Jackson, MS	(20.5)
328	Blacksburg, VA	(42.7)	99	Dover, DE	3.9	79	Jackson, TN	6.0
322	Bloomington-Normal, IL	(31.3)	211	Dubuque, IA	(8.1)	242	Janesville, WI	(12.0)
314	Bloomington, IN	(26.7)	129	Duluth, MN-WI	0.7	44	Jefferson City, MO	14.2
287	Boise City-Nampa, ID	(19.8)	79	Durham-Chapel Hill, NC	6.0	87	Johnson City, TN	5.1
160	Boston (greater), MA-NH	(2.3)	57	Eau Claire, WI	10.3	13	Johnstown, PA	37.3
144	Boston-Quincy, MA M.D.	(1.2)	170	Edison, NJ M.D.	(3.8)	3	Jonesboro, AR	55.2
27	Boulder, CO	23.4	272	El Centro, CA	(16.9)	245	Joplin, MO	(12.5)
72	Bowling Green, KY	7.5	244	El Paso, TX	(12.4)	NA	Kankakee-Bradley, IL**	NA
178	Bremerton-Silverdale, WA	(4.6)	43	Elizabethtown, KY	14.4	NA	Kansas City, MO-KS**	NA
62	Bridgeport-Stamford, CT	9.8	319	Elmira, NY	(29.9)	228	Kennewick-Pasco-Richland, WA	(10.6)
317	Brownsville-Harlingen, TX	(28.6)	243	Erie, PA	(12.3)	310	Killeen-Temple-Fort Hood, TX	(26.1)
237	Brunswick, GA	(11.4)	NA	Eugene-Springfield, OR**	NA	45	Kingsport, TN-VA	14.1
158	Buffalo-Niagara Falls, NY	(2.1)	70	Evansville, IN-KY	7.8	120	Kingston, NY	1.4
9	Burlington, NC	40.0	34	Fairbanks, AK	18.4	211	Knoxville, TN	(8.1)
249	Cambridge-Newton, MA M.D.	(13.0)	14	Fargo, ND-MN	36.7	37	Kokomo, IN	17.3
73	Camden, NJ M.D.	7.4	6	Farmington, NM	46.0	304	La Crosse, WI-MN	(23.9)
20	Canton, OH	32.7	69	Fayetteville, NC	7.9	154	Lafayette, IN	(1.9)
175	Cape Coral-Fort Myers, FL	(4.2)	232	Flagstaff, AZ	(10.9)	202	Lafayette, LA	(6.9)
5	Cape Girardeau, MO-IL	54.4	152	Flint, MI	(1.8)	NA	Lake Co.-Kenosha Co., IL-WI M.D.**	NA
293	Carson City, NV	(20.9)	NA	Florence-Muscle Shoals, AL**	NA	NA	Lake Havasu City-Kingman, AZ**	NA
164	Casper, WY	(2.9)	320	Florence, SC	(30.6)	165	Lakeland, FL	(3.1)
323	Cedar Rapids, IA	(32.7)	148	Fond du Lac, WI	(1.6)	130	Lancaster, PA	0.6
NA	Champaign-Urbana, IL**	NA	315	Fort Collins-Loveland, CO	(27.0)	207	Lansing-East Lansing, MI	(7.7)

Note: All listings are for Metropolitan Statistical Areas (M.S.A.s) except for those ending with "M.D." Listings with "M.D." are Metropolitan Divisions which are smaller parts of eleven large M.S.A.s. See explanatory note at beginning of metropolitan area section.

Alpha Order - Metro Area (continued)

RANK	METROPOLITAN AREA	% CHANGE
121	Laredo, TX	1.3
33	Las Cruces, NM	19.0
291	Las Vegas-Paradise, NV	(20.5)
321	Lawrence, KS	(31.1)
7	Lawton, OK	43.9
2	Lebanon, PA	72.7
199	Lewiston-Auburn, ME	(6.7)
NA	Lexington-Fayette, KY**	NA
127	Lima, OH	0.9
168	Lincoln, NE	(3.3)
123	Little Rock, AR	1.1
136	Logan, UT-ID	0.0
302	Longview, TX	(23.7)
28	Longview, WA	23.3
221	Los Angeles County, CA M.D.	(9.7)
224	Los Angeles (greater), CA	(10.0)
139	Louisville, KY-IN	(0.6)
217	Lubbock, TX	(9.0)
241	Lynchburg, VA	(11.9)
269	Macon, GA	(16.7)
76	Madera, CA	6.8
277	Madison, WI	(17.9)
40	Manchester-Nashua, NH	16.0
91	Manhattan, KS	4.8
10	Mankato-North Mankato, MN	39.8
38	Mansfield, OH	17.1
276	McAllen-Edinburg-Mission, TX	(17.8)
48	Medford, OR	13.4
188	Memphis, TN-MS-AR	(5.7)
158	Merced, CA	(2.1)
108	Miami (greater), FL	2.8
106	Miami-Dade County, FL M.D.	3.0
325	Michigan City-La Porte, IN	(33.7)
260	Midland, TX	(15.3)
113	Milwaukee, WI	1.7
151	Minneapolis-St. Paul, MN-WI	(1.7)
NA	Missoula, MT**	NA
29	Mobile, AL	22.1
218	Modesto, CA	(9.2)
26	Monroe, LA	24.9
285	Monroe, MI	(19.3)
NA	Montgomery, AL**	NA
267	Morristown, TN	(16.4)
31	Mount Vernon-Anacortes, WA	20.6
95	Muncie, IN	4.5
210	Muskegon-Norton Shores, MI	(8.0)
154	Myrtle Beach, SC	(1.9)
178	Napa, CA	(4.6)
84	Naples-Marco Island, FL	5.3
98	Nashville-Davidson, TN	4.0
172	Nassau-Suffolk, NY M.D.	(4.0)
138	New Haven-Milford, CT	(0.5)
50	New Orleans, LA	12.1
118	New York (greater), NY-NJ-PA	1.5
123	New York-W. Plains NY-NJ M.D.	1.1
71	Newark-Union, NJ-PA M.D.	7.6
188	North Port-Bradenton-Sarasota, FL	(5.7)
265	Norwich-New London, CT	(15.9)
128	Oakland-Fremont, CA M.D.	0.8
289	Ocala, FL	(20.3)
17	Ocean City, NJ	35.6
267	Odessa, TX	(16.4)
304	Ogden-Clearfield, UT	(23.9)

RANK	METROPOLITAN AREA	% CHANGE
58	Oklahoma City, OK	10.1
96	Olympia, WA	4.2
200	Omaha-Council Bluffs, NE-IA	(6.8)
180	Orlando, FL	(4.8)
NA	Oshkosh-Neenah, WI**	NA
8	Owensboro, KY	42.4
182	Oxnard-Thousand Oaks, CA	(5.0)
97	Palm Bay-Melbourne, FL	4.1
106	Palm Coast, FL	3.0
78	Panama City-Lynn Haven, FL	6.4
102	Pascagoula, MS	3.7
41	Peabody, MA M.D.	15.2
161	Pensacola, FL	(2.4)
156	Peoria, IL	(2.0)
156	Philadelphia (greater) PA-NJ-MD-DE	(2.0)
142	Philadelphia, PA M.D.	(1.0)
118	Phoenix-Mesa-Scottsdale, AZ	1.5
197	Pine Bluff, AR	(6.6)
188	Pittsburgh, PA	(5.7)
4	Pittsfield, MA	55.1
329	Pocatello, ID	(50.6)
52	Port St. Lucie, FL	11.3
NA	Portland-Vancouver, OR-WA**	NA
281	Portland, ME	(18.3)
186	Poughkeepsie, NY	(5.6)
16	Prescott, AZ	36.4
300	Provo-Orem, UT	(23.4)
NA	Pueblo, CO**	NA
58	Punta Gorda, FL	10.1
92	Racine, WI	4.7
73	Raleigh-Cary, NC	7.4
214	Rapid City, SD	(8.5)
117	Reading, PA	1.6
162	Redding, CA	(2.5)
183	Reno-Sparks, NV	(5.1)
259	Richmond, VA	(15.1)
137	Riverside-San Bernardino, CA	(0.3)
122	Roanoke, VA	1.2
90	Rochester, MN	4.9
145	Rochester, NY	(1.4)
49	Rockford, IL	12.5
252	Rockingham County, NH M.D.	(13.9)
307	Rocky Mount, NC	(24.8)
310	Rome, GA	(26.1)
281	Sacramento, CA	(18.3)
250	Saginaw, MI	(13.3)
170	Salem, OR	(3.8)
162	Salinas, CA	(2.5)
327	Salisbury, MD	(39.7)
271	Salt Lake City, UT	(16.8)
286	San Angelo, TX	(19.6)
313	San Antonio, TX	(26.3)
228	San Diego, CA	(10.6)
146	San Francisco (greater), CA	(1.5)
186	San Francisco-S. Mateo, CA M.D.	(5.6)
67	San Jose, CA	8.4
253	San Luis Obispo, CA	(14.2)
1	Sandusky, OH	94.6
248	Santa Ana-Anaheim, CA M.D.	(12.9)
219	Santa Barbara-Santa Maria, CA	(9.5)
221	Santa Cruz-Watsonville, CA	(9.7)
46	Santa Fe, NM	14.0
284	Santa Rosa-Petaluma, CA	(19.0)

RANK	METROPOLITAN AREA	% CHANGE
132	Savannah, GA	0.5
42	Scranton--Wilkes-Barre, PA	14.6
215	Seattle (greater), WA	(8.6)
194	Seattle-Bellevue-Everett, WA M.D.	(6.2)
226	Sebastian-Vero Beach, FL	(10.5)
NA	Sheboygan, WI**	NA
125	Sherman-Denison, TX	1.0
100	Sioux City, IA-NE-SD	3.8
11	Sioux Falls, SD	39.3
35	South Bend-Mishawaka, IN-MI	18.3
130	Spartanburg, SC	0.6
64	Spokane, WA	9.3
297	Springfield, IL	(22.6)
225	Springfield, MA	(10.2)
204	Springfield, MO	(7.0)
148	Springfield, OH	(1.6)
246	State College, PA	(12.6)
208	Stockton, CA	(7.8)
66	St. Cloud, MN	8.8
64	St. Joseph, MO-KS	9.3
82	St. Louis, MO-IL	5.6
326	Sumter, SC	(37.0)
202	Syracuse, NY	(6.9)
262	Tacoma, WA M.D.	(15.5)
105	Tallahassee, FL	3.2
269	Tampa-St Petersburg, FL	(16.7)
NA	Terre Haute, IN**	NA
310	Texarkana, TX-Texarkana, AR	(26.1)
61	Toledo, OH	9.9
104	Topeka, KS	3.3
113	Trenton-Ewing, NJ	1.7
87	Tucson, AZ	5.1
274	Tulsa, OK	(17.5)
NA	Tuscaloosa, AL**	NA
301	Tyler, TX	(23.6)
299	Utica-Rome, NY	(23.3)
53	Valdosta, GA	11.2
266	Vallejo-Fairfield, CA	(16.0)
197	Victoria, TX	(6.6)
143	Virginia Beach-Norfolk, VA-NC	(1.1)
318	Visalia-Porterville, CA	(28.7)
60	Waco, TX	10.0
36	Warner Robins, GA	18.2
NA	Warren-Farmington Hills, MI M.D.**	NA
236	Washington (greater) DC-VA-MD-WV	(11.3)
235	Washington, DC-VA-MD-WV M.D.	(11.1)
250	Waterloo-Cedar Falls, IA	(13.3)
12	Wausau, WI	37.7
22	Wenatchee, WA	29.6
223	West Palm Beach, FL M.D.	(9.8)
113	Wichita Falls, TX	1.7
109	Wichita, KS	2.7
87	Williamsport, PA	5.1
277	Wilmington, DE-MD-NJ M.D.	(17.9)
180	Wilmington, NC	(4.8)
94	Winchester, VA-WV	4.6
110	Winston-Salem, NC	2.0
125	Worcester, MA	1.0
148	Yakima, WA	(1.6)
32	York-Hanover, PA	20.0
193	Yuba City, CA	(5.9)
56	Yuma, AZ	10.8

Source: CQ Press using reported data from the F.B.I. "Crime in the United States 2011"
*Robbery is the taking of anything of value by force or threat of force. Attempts are included.
**Not available.

Rank Order - Metro Area
19. Percent Change in Robbery Rate: 2010 to 2011 (continued)
National Percent Change = 4.7% Decrease*

RANK	METROPOLITAN AREA	% CHANGE	RANK	METROPOLITAN AREA	% CHANGE	RANK	METROPOLITAN AREA	% CHANGE
1	Sandusky, OH	94.6	61	Toledo, OH	9.9	121	Laredo, TX	1.3
2	Lebanon, PA	72.7	62	Bridgeport-Stamford, CT	9.8	122	Roanoke, VA	1.2
3	Jonesboro, AR	55.2	62	Denver-Aurora, CO	9.8	123	Little Rock, AR	1.1
4	Pittsfield, MA	55.1	64	Spokane, WA	9.3	123	New York-W. Plains NY-NJ M.D.	1.1
5	Cape Girardeau, MO-IL	54.4	64	St. Joseph, MO-KS	9.3	125	Sherman-Denison, TX	1.0
6	Farmington, NM	46.0	66	St. Cloud, MN	8.8	125	Worcester, MA	1.0
7	Lawton, OK	43.9	67	Columbus, IN	8.4	127	Lima, OH	0.9
8	Owensboro, KY	42.4	67	San Jose, CA	8.4	128	Oakland-Fremont, CA M.D.	0.8
9	Burlington, NC	40.0	69	Fayetteville, NC	7.9	129	Duluth, MN-WI	0.7
10	Mankato-North Mankato, MN	39.8	70	Evansville, IN-KY	7.8	130	Lancaster, PA	0.6
11	Sioux Falls, SD	39.3	71	Newark-Union, NJ-PA M.D.	7.6	130	Spartanburg, SC	0.6
12	Wausau, WI	37.7	72	Bowling Green, KY	7.5	132	Savannah, GA	0.5
13	Johnstown, PA	37.3	73	Camden, NJ M.D.	7.4	133	Chico, CA	0.4
14	Fargo, ND-MN	36.7	73	Raleigh-Cary, NC	7.4	134	Fort Wayne, IN	0.2
15	Cleveland, TN	36.5	75	Athens-Clarke County, GA	7.0	135	Beaumont-Port Arthur, TX	0.1
16	Prescott, AZ	36.4	76	Madera, CA	6.8	136	Logan, UT-ID	0.0
17	Ocean City, NJ	35.6	77	Danville, VA	6.7	137	Riverside-San Bernardino, CA	(0.3)
18	Harrisonburg, VA	35.0	78	Panama City-Lynn Haven, FL	6.4	138	New Haven-Milford, CT	(0.5)
19	Grand Forks, ND-MN	33.3	79	Durham-Chapel Hill, NC	6.0	139	Abilene, TX	(0.6)
20	Canton, OH	32.7	79	Jackson, TN	6.0	139	Louisville, KY-IN	(0.6)
21	Greeley, CO	30.6	81	Appleton, WI	5.8	141	Fresno, CA	(0.7)
22	Cheyenne, WY	29.6	82	St. Louis, MO-IL	5.6	142	Philadelphia, PA M.D.	(1.0)
22	Wenatchee, WA	29.6	83	Charlottesville, VA	5.5	143	Virginia Beach-Norfolk, VA-NC	(1.1)
24	Columbia, MO	27.3	84	Clarksville, TN-KY	5.3	144	Boston-Quincy, MA M.D.	(1.2)
25	Glens Falls, NY	26.4	84	Naples-Marco Island, FL	5.3	145	Rochester, NY	(1.4)
26	Monroe, LA	24.9	86	Asheville, NC	5.2	146	Hickory, NC	(1.5)
27	Boulder, CO	23.4	87	Johnson City, TN	5.1	146	San Francisco (greater), CA	(1.5)
28	Longview, WA	23.3	87	Tucson, AZ	5.1	148	Fond du Lac, WI	(1.6)
29	Mobile, AL	22.1	87	Williamsport, PA	5.1	148	Springfield, OH	(1.6)
30	Akron, OH	21.7	90	Rochester, MN	4.9	148	Yakima, WA	(1.6)
31	Mount Vernon-Anacortes, WA	20.6	91	Manhattan, KS	4.8	151	Minneapolis-St. Paul, MN-WI	(1.7)
32	York-Hanover, PA	20.0	92	Albuquerque, NM	4.7	152	Cleveland-Elyria-Mentor, OH	(1.8)
33	Las Cruces, NM	19.0	92	Racine, WI	4.7	152	Flint, MI	(1.8)
34	Fairbanks, AK	18.4	94	Winchester, VA-WV	4.6	154	Lafayette, IN	(1.9)
35	South Bend-Mishawaka, IN-MI	18.3	95	Muncie, IN	4.5	154	Myrtle Beach, SC	(1.9)
36	Warner Robins, GA	18.2	96	Olympia, WA	4.2	156	Peoria, IL	(2.0)
37	Kokomo, IN	17.3	97	Palm Bay-Melbourne, FL	4.1	156	Philadelphia (greater) PA-NJ-MD-DE	(2.0)
38	Mansfield, OH	17.1	98	Nashville-Davidson, TN	4.0	158	Buffalo-Niagara Falls, NY	(2.1)
39	Ames, IA	16.1	99	Dover, DE	3.9	158	Merced, CA	(2.1)
40	Manchester-Nashua, NH	16.0	100	Hartford, CT	3.8	160	Boston (greater), MA-NH	(2.3)
41	Peabody, MA M.D.	15.2	100	Sioux City, IA-NE-SD	3.8	161	Pensacola, FL	(2.4)
42	Scranton--Wilkes-Barre, PA	14.6	102	Pascagoula, MS	3.7	162	Redding, CA	(2.5)
43	Elizabethtown, KY	14.4	103	Deltona-Daytona Beach, FL	3.6	162	Salinas, CA	(2.5)
44	Jefferson City, MO	14.2	104	Topeka, KS	3.3	164	Casper, WY	(2.9)
45	Kingsport, TN-VA	14.1	105	Tallahassee, FL	3.2	165	Binghamton, NY	(3.1)
46	Santa Fe, NM	14.0	106	Miami-Dade County, FL M.D.	3.0	165	Crestview-Fort Walton Beach, FL	(3.1)
47	Grand Junction, CO	13.7	106	Palm Coast, FL	3.0	165	Lakeland, FL	(3.1)
48	Medford, OR	13.4	108	Miami (greater), FL	2.8	168	Lincoln, NE	(3.3)
49	Rockford, IL	12.5	109	Wichita, KS	2.7	169	Gainesville, GA	(3.4)
50	Bangor, ME	12.1	110	Anchorage, AK	2.0	170	Edison, NJ M.D.	(3.8)
50	New Orleans, LA	12.1	110	Winston-Salem, NC	2.0	170	Salem, OR	(3.8)
52	Port St. Lucie, FL	11.3	112	Atlanta, GA	1.9	172	Anderson, SC	(4.0)
53	Fort Lauderdale, FL M.D.	11.2	113	Baltimore-Towson, MD	1.7	172	Columbus, OH	(4.0)
53	Hanford-Corcoran, CA	11.2	113	Milwaukee, WI	1.7	172	Nassau-Suffolk, NY M.D.	(4.0)
53	Valdosta, GA	11.2	113	Trenton-Ewing, NJ	1.7	175	Cape Coral-Fort Myers, FL	(4.2)
56	Yuma, AZ	10.8	113	Wichita Falls, TX	1.7	176	Amarillo, TX	(4.4)
57	Eau Claire, WI	10.3	117	Reading, PA	1.6	176	Dallas-Plano-Irving, TX M.D.	(4.4)
58	Oklahoma City, OK	10.1	118	New York (greater), NY-NJ-PA	1.5	178	Bremerton-Silverdale, WA	(4.6)
58	Punta Gorda, FL	10.1	118	Phoenix-Mesa-Scottsdale, AZ	1.5	178	Napa, CA	(4.6)
60	Waco, TX	10.0	120	Kingston, NY	1.4	180	Orlando, FL	(4.8)

Note: All listings are for Metropolitan Statistical Areas (M.S.A.s) except for those ending with "M.D." Listings with "M.D." are Metropolitan Divisions which are smaller parts of eleven large M.S.A.s. See explanatory note at beginning of metropolitan area section.

Rank Order - Metro Area (continued)

RANK	METROPOLITAN AREA	% CHANGE	RANK	METROPOLITAN AREA	% CHANGE	RANK	METROPOLITAN AREA	% CHANGE
180	Wilmington, NC	(4.8)	244	El Paso, TX	(12.4)	307	Rocky Mount, NC	(24.8)
182	Oxnard-Thousand Oaks, CA	(5.0)	245	Joplin, MO	(12.5)	308	Hot Springs, AR	(25.0)
183	Corvallis, OR	(5.1)	246	Houma, LA	(12.6)	309	Green Bay, WI	(25.4)
183	Dallas (greater), TX	(5.1)	246	State College, PA	(12.6)	310	Killeen-Temple-Fort Hood, TX	(26.1)
183	Reno-Sparks, NV	(5.1)	248	Santa Ana-Anaheim, CA M.D.	(12.9)	310	Rome, GA	(26.1)
186	Poughkeepsie, NY	(5.6)	249	Cambridge-Newton, MA M.D.	(13.0)	310	Texarkana, TX-Texarkana, AR	(26.1)
186	San Francisco-S. Mateo, CA M.D.	(5.6)	250	Saginaw, MI	(13.3)	313	San Antonio, TX	(26.3)
188	Des Moines-West Des Moines, IA	(5.7)	250	Waterloo-Cedar Falls, IA	(13.3)	314	Bloomington, IN	(26.7)
188	Memphis, TN-MS-AR	(5.7)	252	Rockingham County, NH M.D.	(13.9)	315	Fort Collins-Loveland, CO	(27.0)
188	North Port-Bradenton-Sarasota, FL	(5.7)	253	San Luis Obispo, CA	(14.2)	316	Bellingham, WA	(28.5)
188	Pittsburgh, PA	(5.7)	254	Cincinnati-Middletown, OH-KY-IN	(14.3)	317	Brownsville-Harlingen, TX	(28.6)
192	Grand Rapids-Wyoming, MI	(5.8)	255	Bethesda-Frederick, MD M.D.	(14.5)	318	Visalia-Porterville, CA	(28.7)
193	Yuba City, CA	(5.9)	256	Gulfport-Biloxi, MS	(14.6)	319	Elmira, NY	(29.9)
194	Seattle-Bellevue-Everett, WA M.D.	(6.2)	257	Bismarck, ND	(14.7)	320	Florence, SC	(30.6)
195	Fort Worth-Arlington, TX M.D.	(6.3)	258	Dalton, GA	(15.0)	321	Lawrence, KS	(31.1)
196	Detroit-Livonia-Dearborn, MI M.D.	(6.5)	259	Richmond, VA	(15.1)	322	Bloomington-Normal, IL	(31.3)
197	Pine Bluff, AR	(6.6)	260	Barnstable Town, MA	(15.3)	323	Cedar Rapids, IA	(32.7)
197	Victoria, TX	(6.6)	260	Midland, TX	(15.3)	324	Iowa City, IA	(33.1)
199	Lewiston-Auburn, ME	(6.7)	262	Tacoma, WA M.D.	(15.5)	325	Michigan City-La Porte, IN	(33.7)
200	Battle Creek, MI	(6.8)	263	Albany, GA	(15.8)	326	Sumter, SC	(37.0)
200	Omaha-Council Bluffs, NE-IA	(6.8)	263	Augusta, GA-SC	(15.8)	327	Salisbury, MD	(39.7)
202	Lafayette, LA	(6.9)	265	Norwich-New London, CT	(15.9)	328	Blacksburg, VA	(42.7)
202	Syracuse, NY	(6.9)	266	Vallejo-Fairfield, CA	(16.0)	329	Pocatello, ID	(50.6)
204	Decatur, IL	(7.0)	267	Morristown, TN	(16.4)	NA	Anniston-Oxford, AL**	NA
204	Springfield, MO	(7.0)	267	Odessa, TX	(16.4)	NA	Auburn, AL**	NA
206	Jacksonville, FL	(7.4)	269	Macon, GA	(16.7)	NA	Baton Rouge, LA**	NA
207	Lansing-East Lansing, MI	(7.7)	269	Tampa-St Petersburg, FL	(16.7)	NA	Billings, MT**	NA
208	Stockton, CA	(7.8)	271	Salt Lake City, UT	(16.8)	NA	Birmingham-Hoover, AL**	NA
209	Gainesville, FL	(7.9)	272	El Centro, CA	(16.9)	NA	Champaign-Urbana, IL**	NA
210	Muskegon-Norton Shores, MI	(8.0)	273	Corpus Christi, TX	(17.1)	NA	Charleston, WV**	NA
211	Dubuque, IA	(8.1)	274	Tulsa, OK	(17.5)	NA	Charlotte-Gastonia, NC-SC**	NA
211	Hagerstown-Martinsburg, MD-WV	(8.1)	275	Bay City, MI	(17.7)	NA	Chicago (greater), IL-IN-WI**	NA
211	Knoxville, TN	(8.1)	276	McAllen-Edinburg-Mission, TX	(17.8)	NA	Chicago-Joilet-Naperville, IL M.D.**	NA
214	Rapid City, SD	(8.5)	277	Madison, WI	(17.9)	NA	Columbus, GA-AL**	NA
215	Seattle (greater), WA	(8.6)	277	Wilmington, DE-MD-NJ M.D.	(17.9)	NA	Cumberland, MD-WV**	NA
216	Bend, OR	(8.7)	279	Fort Smith, AR-OK	(18.0)	NA	Davenport, IA-IL**	NA
217	Lubbock, TX	(9.0)	280	Danville, IL	(18.2)	NA	Decatur, AL**	NA
218	Modesto, CA	(9.2)	281	Portland, ME	(18.3)	NA	Detroit (greater), MI**	NA
219	Greenville, SC	(9.5)	281	Sacramento, CA	(18.3)	NA	Dothan, AL**	NA
219	Santa Barbara-Santa Maria, CA	(9.5)	283	Bakersfield, CA	(18.4)	NA	Eugene-Springfield, OR**	NA
221	Los Angeles County, CA M.D.	(9.7)	284	Santa Rosa-Petaluma, CA	(19.0)	NA	Florence-Muscle Shoals, AL**	NA
221	Santa Cruz-Watsonville, CA	(9.7)	285	Monroe, MI	(19.3)	NA	Gadsden, AL**	NA
223	West Palm Beach, FL M.D.	(9.8)	286	San Angelo, TX	(19.6)	NA	Gary, IN M.D.**	NA
224	Los Angeles (greater), CA	(10.0)	287	Boise City-Nampa, ID	(19.8)	NA	Great Falls, MT**	NA
225	Springfield, MA	(10.2)	288	Colorado Springs, CO	(20.0)	NA	Houston, TX**	NA
226	Austin-Round Rock, TX	(10.5)	289	Ocala, FL	(20.3)	NA	Huntsville, AL**	NA
226	Sebastian-Vero Beach, FL	(10.5)	290	College Station-Bryan, TX	(20.4)	NA	Indianapolis, IN**	NA
228	Kennewick-Pasco-Richland, WA	(10.6)	291	Jackson, MS	(20.5)	NA	Jacksonville, NC**	NA
228	San Diego, CA	(10.6)	291	Las Vegas-Paradise, NV	(20.5)	NA	Kankakee-Bradley, IL**	NA
230	Atlantic City, NJ	(10.8)	293	Carson City, NV	(20.9)	NA	Kansas City, MO-KS**	NA
230	Holland-Grand Haven, MI	(10.8)	294	Allentown, PA-NJ	(21.0)	NA	Lake Co.-Kenosha Co., IL-WI M.D.**	NA
232	Dayton, OH	(10.9)	295	Chattanooga, TN-GA	(21.3)	NA	Lake Havasu City-Kingman, AZ**	NA
232	Flagstaff, AZ	(10.9)	296	Idaho Falls, ID	(22.2)	NA	Lexington-Fayette, KY**	NA
234	Ann Arbor, MI	(11.0)	297	Springfield, IL	(22.6)	NA	Missoula, MT**	NA
235	Washington, DC-VA-MD-WV M.D.	(11.1)	298	Goldsboro, NC	(23.2)	NA	Montgomery, AL**	NA
236	Washington (greater) DC-VA-MD-WV	(11.3)	299	Utica-Rome, NY	(23.3)	NA	Oshkosh-Neenah, WI**	NA
237	Alexandria, LA	(11.4)	300	Provo-Orem, UT	(23.4)	NA	Portland-Vancouver, OR-WA**	NA
237	Brunswick, GA	(11.4)	301	Tyler, TX	(23.6)	NA	Pueblo, CO**	NA
239	Albany-Schenectady-Troy, NY	(11.5)	302	Hinesville, GA	(23.7)	NA	Sheboygan, WI**	NA
240	Harrisburg-Carlisle, PA	(11.8)	302	Longview, TX	(23.7)	NA	Terre Haute, IN**	NA
241	Lynchburg, VA	(11.9)	304	La Crosse, WI-MN	(23.9)	NA	Tuscaloosa, AL**	NA
242	Janesville, WI	(12.0)	304	Ogden-Clearfield, UT	(23.9)	NA	Warren-Farmington Hills, MI M.D.**	NA
243	Erie, PA	(12.3)	306	Altoona, PA	(24.5)			

Source: CQ Press using reported data from the F.B.I. "Crime in the United States 2011"
*Robbery is the taking of anything of value by force or threat of force. Attempts are included.
**Not available.

Alpha Order - Metro Area

20. Percent Change in Robbery Rate: 2007 to 2011
National Percent Change = 23.3% Decrease*

RANK	METROPOLITAN AREA	% CHANGE	RANK	METROPOLITAN AREA	% CHANGE	RANK	METROPOLITAN AREA	% CHANGE
259	Abilene, TX	(34.1)	113	Charleston, WV	(12.5)	117	Fort Lauderdale, FL M.D.	(13.1)
79	Akron, OH	(6.3)	312	Charlotte-Gastonia, NC-SC	(51.7)	242	Fort Smith, AR-OK	(31.1)
148	Albany-Schenectady-Troy, NY	(17.5)	303	Charlottesville, VA	(45.9)	201	Fort Wayne, IN	(24.5)
92	Albany, GA	(8.7)	212	Chattanooga, TN-GA	(27.1)	223	Fort Worth-Arlington, TX M.D.	(28.2)
267	Albuquerque, NM	(36.0)	2	Cheyenne, WY	87.3	89	Fresno, CA	(8.0)
111	Alexandria, LA	(12.4)	NA	Chicago (greater), IL-IN-WI**	NA	NA	Gadsden, AL**	NA
248	Allentown, PA-NJ	(32.1)	NA	Chicago-Joliet-Naperville, IL M.D.**	NA	276	Gainesville, FL	(37.6)
312	Altoona, PA	(51.7)	115	Chico, CA	(12.9)	186	Gainesville, GA	(22.8)
306	Amarillo, TX	(47.2)	123	Cincinnati-Middletown, OH-KY-IN	(13.8)	NA	Gary, IN M.D.**	NA
248	Ames, IA	(32.1)	213	Clarksville, TN-KY	(27.3)	8	Glens Falls, NY	51.1
49	Anchorage, AK	0.5	143	Cleveland-Elyria-Mentor, OH	(17.3)	105	Goldsboro, NC	(12.1)
78	Anderson, SC	(6.2)	128	Cleveland, TN	(15.2)	41	Grand Forks, ND-MN	5.3
154	Ann Arbor, MI	(18.4)	273	College Station-Bryan, TX	(37.3)	76	Grand Junction, CO	(5.9)
NA	Anniston-Oxford, AL**	NA	178	Colorado Springs, CO	(22.0)	200	Grand Rapids-Wyoming, MI	(24.1)
100	Appleton, WI	(10.4)	46	Columbia, MO	2.6	NA	Great Falls, MT**	NA
189	Asheville, NC	(23.0)	NA	Columbus, GA-AL**	NA	9	Greeley, CO	50.0
209	Athens-Clarke County, GA	(26.1)	25	Columbus, IN	10.7	282	Green Bay, WI	(39.5)
262	Atlanta, GA	(34.6)	167	Columbus, OH	(19.9)	293	Greenville, SC	(42.1)
117	Atlantic City, NJ	(13.1)	261	Corpus Christi, TX	(34.4)	NA	Gulfport-Biloxi, MS**	NA
NA	Auburn, AL**	NA	91	Corvallis, OR	(8.4)	NA	Hagerstown-Martinsburg, MD-WV**	NA
180	Augusta, GA-SC	(22.1)	187	Crestview-Fort Walton Beach, FL	(22.9)	49	Hanford-Corcoran, CA	0.5
237	Austin-Round Rock, TX	(30.1)	NA	Cumberland, MD-WV**	NA	142	Harrisburg-Carlisle, PA	(16.9)
129	Bakersfield, CA	(15.3)	279	Dallas (greater), TX	(38.5)	314	Harrisonburg, VA	(52.7)
158	Baltimore-Towson, MD	(19.0)	292	Dallas-Plano-Irving, TX M.D.	(41.4)	135	Hartford, CT	(15.9)
13	Bangor, ME	31.5	163	Dalton, GA	(19.4)	208	Hickory, NC	(26.0)
5	Barnstable Town, MA	54.9	NA	Danville, IL**	NA	52	Hinesville, GA	(0.8)
119	Baton Rouge, LA	(13.3)	285	Danville, VA	(40.1)	NA	Holland-Grand Haven, MI**	NA
145	Battle Creek, MI	(17.4)	NA	Davenport, IA-IL**	NA	302	Hot Springs, AR	(45.8)
214	Bay City, MI	(27.4)	51	Dayton, OH	(0.3)	36	Houma, LA	6.2
81	Beaumont-Port Arthur, TX	(6.5)	NA	Decatur, AL**	NA	NA	Houston, TX**	NA
132	Bellingham, WA	(15.6)	NA	Decatur, IL**	NA	NA	Huntsville, AL**	NA
226	Bend, OR	(28.4)	241	Deltona-Daytona Beach, FL	(30.7)	266	Idaho Falls, ID	(35.9)
218	Bethesda-Frederick, MD M.D.	(27.7)	83	Denver-Aurora, CO	(6.9)	177	Indianapolis, IN	(21.4)
NA	Billings, MT**	NA	307	Des Moines-West Des Moines, IA	(48.1)	305	Iowa City, IA	(46.2)
24	Binghamton, NY	11.5	NA	Detroit (greater), MI**	NA	311	Jacksonville, FL	(49.4)
NA	Birmingham-Hoover, AL**	NA	150	Detroit-Livonia-Dearborn, MI M.D.	(17.8)	316	Jacksonville, NC	(54.8)
33	Bismarck, ND	6.6	NA	Dothan, AL**	NA	95	Jackson, MS	(9.3)
304	Blacksburg, VA	(46.1)	15	Dover, DE	26.0	291	Jackson, TN	(41.3)
NA	Bloomington-Normal, IL**	NA	16	Dubuque, IA	20.6	194	Janesville, WI	(23.4)
275	Bloomington, IN	(37.5)	160	Duluth, MN-WI	(19.2)	7	Jefferson City, MO	54.3
254	Boise City-Nampa, ID	(33.6)	NA	Durham-Chapel Hill, NC**	NA	28	Johnson City, TN	9.6
82	Boston (greater), MA-NH	(6.6)	1	Eau Claire, WI	100.0	37	Johnstown, PA	6.1
90	Boston-Quincy, MA M.D.	(8.3)	101	Edison, NJ M.D.	(10.7)	114	Jonesboro, AR	(12.8)
NA	Boulder, CO**	NA	108	El Centro, CA	(12.3)	264	Joplin, MO	(35.1)
268	Bowling Green, KY	(36.2)	130	El Paso, TX	(15.4)	NA	Kankakee-Bradley, IL**	NA
38	Bremerton-Silverdale, WA	5.8	69	Elizabethtown, KY	(5.2)	NA	Kansas City, MO-KS**	NA
64	Bridgeport-Stamford, CT	(4.5)	270	Elmira, NY	(37.2)	184	Kennewick-Pasco-Richland, WA	(22.7)
236	Brownsville-Harlingen, TX	(29.9)	282	Erie, PA	(39.5)	205	Killeen-Temple-Fort Hood, TX	(25.4)
160	Brunswick, GA	(19.2)	70	Eugene-Springfield, OR	(5.3)	39	Kingsport, TN-VA	5.7
64	Buffalo-Niagara Falls, NY	(4.5)	206	Evansville, IN-KY	(25.5)	55	Kingston, NY	(1.7)
125	Burlington, NC	(14.3)	NA	Fairbanks, AK**	NA	108	Knoxville, TN	(12.3)
137	Cambridge-Newton, MA M.D.	(16.3)	5	Fargo, ND-MN	54.9	17	Kokomo, IN	19.6
59	Camden, NJ M.D.	(2.6)	45	Farmington, NM	3.3	106	La Crosse, WI-MN	(12.2)
NA	Canton, OH**	NA	74	Fayetteville, NC	(5.6)	220	Lafayette, IN	(28.0)
298	Cape Coral-Fort Myers, FL	(43.0)	238	Flagstaff, AZ	(30.4)	232	Lafayette, LA	(29.5)
NA	Cape Girardeau, MO-IL**	NA	33	Flint, MI	6.6	NA	Lake Co.-Kenosha Co., IL-WI M.D.**	NA
198	Carson City, NV	(23.9)	NA	Florence-Muscle Shoals, AL**	NA	222	Lake Havasu City-Kingman, AZ	(28.1)
76	Casper, WY	(5.9)	265	Florence, SC	(35.3)	251	Lakeland, FL	(33.3)
296	Cedar Rapids, IA	(42.7)	282	Fond du Lac, WI	(39.5)	145	Lancaster, PA	(17.4)
NA	Champaign-Urbana, IL**	NA	62	Fort Collins-Loveland, CO	(2.9)	132	Lansing-East Lansing, MI	(15.6)

Note: All listings are for Metropolitan Statistical Areas (M.S.A.s) except for those ending with "M.D." Listings with "M.D." are Metropolitan Divisions which are smaller parts of eleven large M.S.A.s. See explanatory note at beginning of metropolitan area section.

Alpha Order - Metro Area (continued)

RANK	METROPOLITAN AREA	% CHANGE
281	Laredo, TX	(39.4)
256	Las Cruces, NM	(33.9)
299	Las Vegas-Paradise, NV	(43.3)
278	Lawrence, KS	(37.9)
137	Lawton, OK	(16.3)
57	Lebanon, PA	(2.2)
14	Lewiston-Auburn, ME	29.8
NA	Lexington-Fayette, KY**	NA
122	Lima, OH	(13.7)
68	Lincoln, NE	(5.1)
175	Little Rock, AR	(21.2)
104	Logan, UT-ID	(11.4)
308	Longview, TX	(48.3)
94	Longview, WA	(9.0)
223	Los Angeles County, CA M.D.	(28.2)
223	Los Angeles (greater), CA	(28.2)
152	Louisville, KY-IN	(18.1)
29	Lubbock, TX	9.1
246	Lynchburg, VA	(31.9)
176	Macon, GA	(21.3)
21	Madera, CA	14.9
206	Madison, WI	(25.5)
NA	Manchester-Nashua, NH**	NA
NA	Manhattan, KS**	NA
NA	Mankato-North Mankato, MN**	NA
11	Mansfield, OH	40.2
152	McAllen-Edinburg-Mission, TX	(18.1)
22	Medford, OR	14.1
273	Memphis, TN-MS-AR	(37.3)
30	Merced, CA	9.0
238	Miami (greater), FL	(30.4)
259	Miami-Dade County, FL M.D.	(34.1)
285	Michigan City-La Porte, IN	(40.1)
247	Midland, TX	(32.0)
160	Milwaukee, WI	(19.2)
253	Minneapolis-St. Paul, MN-WI	(33.4)
NA	Missoula, MT**	NA
96	Mobile, AL	(9.5)
130	Modesto, CA	(15.4)
87	Monroe, LA	(7.7)
19	Monroe, MI	15.3
NA	Montgomery, AL**	NA
167	Morristown, TN	(19.9)
72	Mount Vernon-Anacortes, WA	(5.4)
3	Muncie, IN	68.8
47	Muskegon-Norton Shores, MI	1.8
182	Myrtle Beach, SC	(22.5)
154	Napa, CA	(18.4)
111	Naples-Marco Island, FL	(12.4)
214	Nashville-Davidson, TN	(27.4)
96	Nassau-Suffolk, NY M.D.	(9.5)
NA	New Haven-Milford, CT**	NA
233	New Orleans, LA	(29.7)
86	New York (greater), NY-NJ-PA	(7.3)
98	New York-W. Plains NY-NJ M.D.	(9.9)
23	Newark-Union, NJ-PA M.D.	13.7
NA	North Port-Bradenton-Sarasota, FL**	NA
NA	Norwich-New London, CT**	NA
195	Oakland-Fremont, CA M.D.	(23.5)
251	Ocala, FL	(33.3)
169	Ocean City, NJ	(20.2)
137	Odessa, TX	(16.3)
256	Ogden-Clearfield, UT	(33.9)

RANK	METROPOLITAN AREA	% CHANGE
136	Oklahoma City, OK	(16.0)
67	Olympia, WA	(4.9)
170	Omaha-Council Bluffs, NE-IA	(20.6)
308	Orlando, FL	(48.3)
270	Oshkosh-Neenah, WI	(37.2)
NA	Owensboro, KY**	NA
220	Oxnard-Thousand Oaks, CA	(28.0)
189	Palm Bay-Melbourne, FL	(23.0)
276	Palm Coast, FL	(37.6)
60	Panama City-Lynn Haven, FL	(2.8)
250	Pascagoula, MS	(32.4)
19	Peabody, MA M.D.	15.3
165	Pensacola, FL	(19.5)
NA	Peoria, IL**	NA
148	Philadelphia (greater) PA-NJ-MD-DE	(17.5)
170	Philadelphia, PA M.D.	(20.6)
233	Phoenix-Mesa-Scottsdale, AZ	(29.7)
288	Pine Bluff, AR	(40.7)
184	Pittsburgh, PA	(22.7)
35	Pittsfield, MA	6.3
301	Pocatello, ID	(44.9)
192	Port St. Lucie, FL	(23.3)
204	Portland-Vancouver, OR-WA	(25.0)
85	Portland, ME	(7.2)
72	Poughkeepsie, NY	(5.4)
195	Prescott, AZ	(23.5)
287	Provo-Orem, UT	(40.3)
NA	Pueblo, CO**	NA
240	Punta Gorda, FL	(30.6)
243	Racine, WI	(31.7)
227	Raleigh-Cary, NC	(28.6)
10	Rapid City, SD	40.7
74	Reading, PA	(5.6)
39	Redding, CA	5.7
243	Reno-Sparks, NV	(31.7)
300	Richmond, VA	(43.7)
210	Riverside-San Bernardino, CA	(26.5)
258	Roanoke, VA	(34.0)
170	Rochester, MN	(20.6)
165	Rochester, NY	(19.5)
NA	Rockford, IL**	NA
18	Rockingham County, NH M.D.	18.0
294	Rocky Mount, NC	(42.3)
48	Rome, GA	0.9
235	Sacramento, CA	(29.8)
269	Saginaw, MI	(36.8)
203	Salem, OR	(24.8)
115	Salinas, CA	(12.9)
315	Salisbury, MD	(53.5)
211	Salt Lake City, UT	(26.7)
127	San Angelo, TX	(15.1)
243	San Antonio, TX	(31.7)
263	San Diego, CA	(34.8)
199	San Francisco (greater), CA	(24.0)
202	San Francisco-S. Mateo, CA M.D.	(24.6)
79	San Jose, CA	(6.3)
143	San Luis Obispo, CA	(17.3)
42	Sandusky, OH	4.7
217	Santa Ana-Anaheim, CA M.D.	(27.6)
102	Santa Barbara-Santa Maria, CA	(11.2)
126	Santa Cruz-Watsonville, CA	(14.8)
NA	Santa Fe, NM**	NA
151	Santa Rosa-Petaluma, CA	(17.9)

RANK	METROPOLITAN AREA	% CHANGE
289	Savannah, GA	(41.1)
66	Scranton--Wilkes-Barre, PA	(4.7)
145	Seattle (greater), WA	(17.4)
140	Seattle-Bellevue-Everett, WA M.D.	(16.7)
197	Sebastian-Vero Beach, FL	(23.7)
106	Sheboygan, WI	(12.2)
12	Sherman-Denison, TX	32.1
52	Sioux City, IA-NE-SD	(0.8)
4	Sioux Falls, SD	59.3
88	South Bend-Mishawaka, IN-MI	(7.9)
310	Spartanburg, SC	(48.7)
26	Spokane, WA	10.5
NA	Springfield, IL**	NA
140	Springfield, MA	(16.7)
70	Springfield, MO	(5.3)
124	Springfield, OH	(14.0)
158	State College, PA	(19.0)
154	Stockton, CA	(18.4)
60	St. Cloud, MN	(2.8)
32	St. Joseph, MO-KS	6.9
120	St. Louis, MO-IL	(13.6)
189	Sumter, SC	(23.0)
120	Syracuse, NY	(13.6)
163	Tacoma, WA M.D.	(19.4)
187	Tallahassee, FL	(22.9)
295	Tampa-St Petersburg, FL	(42.6)
NA	Terre Haute, IN**	NA
270	Texarkana, TX-Texarkana, AR	(37.2)
58	Toledo, OH	(2.4)
219	Topeka, KS	(27.8)
99	Trenton-Ewing, NJ	(10.1)
174	Tucson, AZ	(20.7)
44	Tulsa, OK	4.1
NA	Tuscaloosa, AL**	NA
290	Tyler, TX	(41.2)
170	Utica-Rome, NY	(20.6)
227	Valdosta, GA	(28.6)
108	Vallejo-Fairfield, CA	(12.3)
62	Victoria, TX	(2.9)
229	Virginia Beach-Norfolk, VA-NC	(28.7)
255	Visalia-Porterville, CA	(33.7)
157	Waco, TX	(18.8)
55	Warner Robins, GA	(1.7)
NA	Warren-Farmington Hills, MI M.D.**	NA
183	Washington (greater) DC-VA-MD-WV	(22.6)
178	Washington, DC-VA-MD-WV M.D.	(22.0)
216	Waterloo-Cedar Falls, IA	(27.5)
180	Wausau, WI	(22.1)
84	Wenatchee, WA	(7.0)
296	West Palm Beach, FL M.D.	(42.7)
280	Wichita Falls, TX	(39.2)
132	Wichita, KS	(15.6)
27	Williamsport, PA	9.9
102	Wilmington, DE-MD-NJ M.D.	(11.2)
231	Wilmington, NC	(28.8)
93	Winchester, VA-WV	(8.8)
NA	Winston-Salem, NC**	NA
31	Worcester, MA	7.6
42	Yakima, WA	4.7
54	York-Hanover, PA	(1.6)
192	Yuba City, CA	(23.3)
229	Yuma, AZ	(28.7)

Source: CQ Press using reported data from the F.B.I. "Crime in the United States 2011"
*Robbery is the taking of anything of value by force or threat of force. Attempts are included.
**Not available.

Rank Order - Metro Area

20. Percent Change in Robbery Rate: 2007 to 2011 (continued)
National Percent Change = 23.3% Decrease*

RANK	METROPOLITAN AREA	% CHANGE	RANK	METROPOLITAN AREA	% CHANGE	RANK	METROPOLITAN AREA	% CHANGE
1	Eau Claire, WI	100.0	60	St. Cloud, MN	(2.8)	120	Syracuse, NY	(13.6)
2	Cheyenne, WY	87.3	62	Fort Collins-Loveland, CO	(2.9)	122	Lima, OH	(13.7)
3	Muncie, IN	68.8	62	Victoria, TX	(2.9)	123	Cincinnati-Middletown, OH-KY-IN	(13.8)
4	Sioux Falls, SD	59.3	64	Bridgeport-Stamford, CT	(4.5)	124	Springfield, OH	(14.0)
5	Barnstable Town, MA	54.9	64	Buffalo-Niagara Falls, NY	(4.5)	125	Burlington, NC	(14.3)
5	Fargo, ND-MN	54.9	66	Scranton--Wilkes-Barre, PA	(4.7)	126	Santa Cruz-Watsonville, CA	(14.8)
7	Jefferson City, MO	54.3	67	Olympia, WA	(4.9)	127	San Angelo, TX	(15.1)
8	Glens Falls, NY	51.1	68	Lincoln, NE	(5.1)	128	Cleveland, TN	(15.2)
9	Greeley, CO	50.0	69	Elizabethtown, KY	(5.2)	129	Bakersfield, CA	(15.3)
10	Rapid City, SD	40.7	70	Eugene-Springfield, OR	(5.3)	130	El Paso, TX	(15.4)
11	Mansfield, OH	40.2	70	Springfield, MO	(5.3)	130	Modesto, CA	(15.4)
12	Sherman-Denison, TX	32.1	72	Mount Vernon-Anacortes, WA	(5.4)	132	Bellingham, WA	(15.6)
13	Bangor, ME	31.5	72	Poughkeepsie, NY	(5.4)	132	Lansing-East Lansing, MI	(15.6)
14	Lewiston-Auburn, ME	29.8	74	Fayetteville, NC	(5.6)	132	Wichita, KS	(15.6)
15	Dover, DE	26.0	74	Reading, PA	(5.6)	135	Hartford, CT	(15.9)
16	Dubuque, IA	20.6	76	Casper, WY	(5.9)	136	Oklahoma City, OK	(16.0)
17	Kokomo, IN	19.6	76	Grand Junction, CO	(5.9)	137	Cambridge-Newton, MA M.D.	(16.3)
18	Rockingham County, NH M.D.	18.0	78	Anderson, SC	(6.2)	137	Lawton, OK	(16.3)
19	Monroe, MI	15.3	79	Akron, OH	(6.3)	137	Odessa, TX	(16.3)
19	Peabody, MA M.D.	15.3	79	San Jose, CA	(6.3)	140	Seattle-Bellevue-Everett, WA M.D.	(16.7)
21	Madera, CA	14.9	81	Beaumont-Port Arthur, TX	(6.5)	140	Springfield, MA	(16.7)
22	Medford, OR	14.1	82	Boston (greater), MA-NH	(6.6)	142	Harrisburg-Carlisle, PA	(16.9)
23	Newark-Union, NJ-PA M.D.	13.7	83	Denver-Aurora, CO	(6.9)	143	Cleveland-Elyria-Mentor, OH	(17.3)
24	Binghamton, NY	11.5	84	Wenatchee, WA	(7.0)	143	San Luis Obispo, CA	(17.3)
25	Columbus, IN	10.7	85	Portland, ME	(7.2)	145	Battle Creek, MI	(17.4)
26	Spokane, WA	10.5	86	New York (greater), NY-NJ-PA	(7.3)	145	Lancaster, PA	(17.4)
27	Williamsport, PA	9.9	87	Monroe, LA	(7.7)	145	Seattle (greater), WA	(17.4)
28	Johnson City, TN	9.6	88	South Bend-Mishawaka, IN-MI	(7.9)	148	Albany-Schenectady-Troy, NY	(17.5)
29	Lubbock, TX	9.1	89	Fresno, CA	(8.0)	148	Philadelphia (greater) PA-NJ-MD-DE	(17.5)
30	Merced, CA	9.0	90	Boston-Quincy, MA M.D.	(8.3)	150	Detroit-Livonia-Dearborn, MI M.D.	(17.8)
31	Worcester, MA	7.6	91	Corvallis, OR	(8.4)	151	Santa Rosa-Petaluma, CA	(17.9)
32	St. Joseph, MO-KS	6.9	92	Albany, GA	(8.7)	152	Louisville, KY-IN	(18.1)
33	Bismarck, ND	6.6	93	Winchester, VA-WV	(8.8)	152	McAllen-Edinburg-Mission, TX	(18.1)
33	Flint, MI	6.6	94	Longview, WA	(9.0)	154	Ann Arbor, MI	(18.4)
35	Pittsfield, MA	6.3	95	Jackson, MS	(9.3)	154	Napa, CA	(18.4)
36	Houma, LA	6.2	96	Mobile, AL	(9.5)	154	Stockton, CA	(18.4)
37	Johnstown, PA	6.1	96	Nassau-Suffolk, NY M.D.	(9.5)	157	Waco, TX	(18.8)
38	Bremerton-Silverdale, WA	5.8	98	New York-W. Plains NY-NJ M.D.	(9.9)	158	Baltimore-Towson, MD	(19.0)
39	Kingsport, TN-VA	5.7	99	Trenton-Ewing, NJ	(10.1)	158	State College, PA	(19.0)
39	Redding, CA	5.7	100	Appleton, WI	(10.4)	160	Brunswick, GA	(19.2)
41	Grand Forks, ND-MN	5.3	101	Edison, NJ M.D.	(10.7)	160	Duluth, MN-WI	(19.2)
42	Sandusky, OH	4.7	102	Santa Barbara-Santa Maria, CA	(11.2)	160	Milwaukee, WI	(19.2)
42	Yakima, WA	4.7	102	Wilmington, DE-MD-NJ M.D.	(11.2)	163	Dalton, GA	(19.4)
44	Tulsa, OK	4.1	104	Logan, UT-ID	(11.4)	163	Tacoma, WA M.D.	(19.4)
45	Farmington, NM	3.3	105	Goldsboro, NC	(12.1)	165	Pensacola, FL	(19.5)
46	Columbia, MO	2.6	106	La Crosse, WI-MN	(12.2)	165	Rochester, NY	(19.5)
47	Muskegon-Norton Shores, MI	1.8	106	Sheboygan, WI	(12.2)	167	Columbus, OH	(19.9)
48	Rome, GA	0.9	108	El Centro, CA	(12.3)	167	Morristown, TN	(19.9)
49	Anchorage, AK	0.5	108	Knoxville, TN	(12.3)	169	Ocean City, NJ	(20.2)
49	Hanford-Corcoran, CA	0.5	108	Vallejo-Fairfield, CA	(12.3)	170	Omaha-Council Bluffs, NE-IA	(20.6)
51	Dayton, OH	(0.3)	111	Alexandria, LA	(12.4)	170	Philadelphia, PA M.D.	(20.6)
52	Hinesville, GA	(0.8)	111	Naples-Marco Island, FL	(12.4)	170	Rochester, MN	(20.6)
52	Sioux City, IA-NE-SD	(0.8)	113	Charleston, WV	(12.5)	170	Utica-Rome, NY	(20.6)
54	York-Hanover, PA	(1.6)	114	Jonesboro, AR	(12.8)	174	Tucson, AZ	(20.7)
55	Kingston, NY	(1.7)	115	Chico, CA	(12.9)	175	Little Rock, AR	(21.2)
55	Warner Robins, GA	(1.7)	115	Salinas, CA	(12.9)	176	Macon, GA	(21.3)
57	Lebanon, PA	(2.2)	117	Atlantic City, NJ	(13.1)	177	Indianapolis, IN	(21.4)
58	Toledo, OH	(2.4)	117	Fort Lauderdale, FL M.D.	(13.1)	178	Colorado Springs, CO	(22.0)
59	Camden, NJ M.D.	(2.6)	119	Baton Rouge, LA	(13.3)	178	Washington, DC-VA-MD-WV M.D.	(22.0)
60	Panama City-Lynn Haven, FL	(2.8)	120	St. Louis, MO-IL	(13.6)	180	Augusta, GA-SC	(22.1)

Note: All listings are for Metropolitan Statistical Areas (M.S.A.s) except for those ending with "M.D." Listings with "M.D." are Metropolitan Divisions which are smaller parts of eleven large M.S.A.s. See explanatory note at beginning of metropolitan area section.

Rank Order - Metro Area (continued)

RANK	METROPOLITAN AREA	% CHANGE	RANK	METROPOLITAN AREA	% CHANGE	RANK	METROPOLITAN AREA	% CHANGE
180	Wausau, WI	(22.1)	243	Reno-Sparks, NV	(31.7)	307	Des Moines-West Des Moines, IA	(48.1)
182	Myrtle Beach, SC	(22.5)	243	San Antonio, TX	(31.7)	308	Longview, TX	(48.3)
183	Washington (greater) DC-VA-MD-WV	(22.6)	246	Lynchburg, VA	(31.9)	308	Orlando, FL	(48.3)
184	Kennewick-Pasco-Richland, WA	(22.7)	247	Midland, TX	(32.0)	310	Spartanburg, SC	(48.7)
184	Pittsburgh, PA	(22.7)	248	Allentown, PA-NJ	(32.1)	311	Jacksonville, FL	(49.4)
186	Gainesville, GA	(22.8)	248	Ames, IA	(32.1)	312	Altoona, PA	(51.7)
187	Crestview-Fort Walton Beach, FL	(22.9)	250	Pascagoula, MS	(32.4)	312	Charlotte-Gastonia, NC-SC	(51.7)
187	Tallahassee, FL	(22.9)	251	Lakeland, FL	(33.3)	314	Harrisonburg, VA	(52.7)
189	Asheville, NC	(23.0)	251	Ocala, FL	(33.3)	315	Salisbury, MD	(53.5)
189	Palm Bay-Melbourne, FL	(23.0)	253	Minneapolis-St. Paul, MN-WI	(33.4)	316	Jacksonville, NC	(54.8)
189	Sumter, SC	(23.0)	254	Boise City-Nampa, ID	(33.6)	NA	Anniston-Oxford, AL**	NA
192	Port St. Lucie, FL	(23.3)	255	Visalia-Porterville, CA	(33.7)	NA	Auburn, AL**	NA
192	Yuba City, CA	(23.3)	256	Las Cruces, NM	(33.9)	NA	Billings, MT**	NA
194	Janesville, WI	(23.4)	256	Ogden-Clearfield, UT	(33.9)	NA	Birmingham-Hoover, AL**	NA
195	Oakland-Fremont, CA M.D.	(23.5)	258	Roanoke, VA	(34.0)	NA	Bloomington-Normal, IL**	NA
195	Prescott, AZ	(23.5)	259	Abilene, TX	(34.1)	NA	Boulder, CO**	NA
197	Sebastian-Vero Beach, FL	(23.7)	259	Miami-Dade County, FL M.D.	(34.1)	NA	Canton, OH**	NA
198	Carson City, NV	(23.9)	261	Corpus Christi, TX	(34.4)	NA	Cape Girardeau, MO-IL**	NA
199	San Francisco (greater), CA	(24.0)	262	Atlanta, GA	(34.6)	NA	Champaign-Urbana, IL**	NA
200	Grand Rapids-Wyoming, MI	(24.1)	263	San Diego, CA	(34.8)	NA	Chicago (greater), IL-IN-WI**	NA
201	Fort Wayne, IN	(24.5)	264	Joplin, MO	(35.1)	NA	Chicago-Joilet-Naperville, IL M.D.**	NA
202	San Francisco-S. Mateo, CA M.D.	(24.6)	265	Florence, SC	(35.3)	NA	Columbus, GA-AL**	NA
203	Salem, OR	(24.8)	266	Idaho Falls, ID	(35.9)	NA	Cumberland, MD-WV**	NA
204	Portland-Vancouver, OR-WA	(25.0)	267	Albuquerque, NM	(36.0)	NA	Danville, IL**	NA
205	Killeen-Temple-Fort Hood, TX	(25.4)	268	Bowling Green, KY	(36.2)	NA	Davenport, IA-IL**	NA
206	Evansville, IN-KY	(25.5)	269	Saginaw, MI	(36.8)	NA	Decatur, AL**	NA
206	Madison, WI	(25.5)	270	Elmira, NY	(37.2)	NA	Decatur, IL**	NA
208	Hickory, NC	(26.0)	270	Oshkosh-Neenah, WI	(37.2)	NA	Detroit (greater), MI**	NA
209	Athens-Clarke County, GA	(26.1)	270	Texarkana, TX-Texarkana, AR	(37.2)	NA	Dothan, AL**	NA
210	Riverside-San Bernardino, CA	(26.5)	273	College Station-Bryan, TX	(37.3)	NA	Durham-Chapel Hill, NC**	NA
211	Salt Lake City, UT	(26.7)	273	Memphis, TN-MS-AR	(37.3)	NA	Fairbanks, AK**	NA
212	Chattanooga, TN-GA	(27.1)	275	Bloomington, IN	(37.5)	NA	Florence-Muscle Shoals, AL**	NA
213	Clarksville, TN-KY	(27.3)	276	Gainesville, FL	(37.6)	NA	Gadsden, AL**	NA
214	Bay City, MI	(27.4)	276	Palm Coast, FL	(37.6)	NA	Gary, IN M.D.**	NA
214	Nashville-Davidson, TN	(27.4)	278	Lawrence, KS	(37.9)	NA	Great Falls, MT**	NA
216	Waterloo-Cedar Falls, IA	(27.5)	279	Dallas (greater), TX	(38.5)	NA	Gulfport-Biloxi, MS**	NA
217	Santa Ana-Anaheim, CA M.D.	(27.6)	280	Wichita Falls, TX	(39.2)	NA	Hagerstown-Martinsburg, MD-WV**	NA
218	Bethesda-Frederick, MD M.D.	(27.7)	281	Laredo, TX	(39.4)	NA	Holland-Grand Haven, MI**	NA
219	Topeka, KS	(27.8)	282	Erie, PA	(39.5)	NA	Houston, TX**	NA
220	Lafayette, IN	(28.0)	282	Fond du Lac, WI	(39.5)	NA	Huntsville, AL**	NA
220	Oxnard-Thousand Oaks, CA	(28.0)	282	Green Bay, WI	(39.5)	NA	Kankakee-Bradley, IL**	NA
222	Lake Havasu City-Kingman, AZ	(28.1)	285	Danville, VA	(40.1)	NA	Kansas City, MO-KS**	NA
223	Fort Worth-Arlington, TX M.D.	(28.2)	285	Michigan City-La Porte, IN	(40.1)	NA	Lake Co.-Kenosha Co., IL-WI M.D.**	NA
223	Los Angeles County, CA M.D.	(28.2)	287	Provo-Orem, UT	(40.3)	NA	Lexington-Fayette, KY**	NA
223	Los Angeles (greater), CA	(28.2)	288	Pine Bluff, AR	(40.7)	NA	Manchester-Nashua, NH**	NA
226	Bend, OR	(28.4)	289	Savannah, GA	(41.1)	NA	Manhattan, KS**	NA
227	Raleigh-Cary, NC	(28.6)	290	Tyler, TX	(41.2)	NA	Mankato-North Mankato, MN**	NA
227	Valdosta, GA	(28.6)	291	Jackson, TN	(41.3)	NA	Missoula, MT**	NA
229	Virginia Beach-Norfolk, VA-NC	(28.7)	292	Dallas-Plano-Irving, TX M.D.	(41.4)	NA	Montgomery, AL**	NA
229	Yuma, AZ	(28.7)	293	Greenville, SC	(42.1)	NA	New Haven-Milford, CT**	NA
231	Wilmington, NC	(28.8)	294	Rocky Mount, NC	(42.3)	NA	North Port-Bradenton-Sarasota, FL**	NA
232	Lafayette, LA	(29.5)	295	Tampa-St Petersburg, Fl	(42.6)	NA	Norwich-New London, CT**	NA
233	New Orleans, LA	(29.7)	296	Cedar Rapids, IA	(42.7)	NA	Owensboro, KY**	NA
233	Phoenix-Mesa-Scottsdale, AZ	(29.7)	296	West Palm Beach, FL M.D.	(42.7)	NA	Peoria, IL**	NA
235	Sacramento, CA	(29.8)	298	Cape Coral-Fort Myers, FL	(43.0)	NA	Pueblo, CO**	NA
236	Brownsville-Harlingen, TX	(29.9)	299	Las Vegas-Paradise, NV	(43.3)	NA	Rockford, IL**	NA
237	Austin-Round Rock, TX	(30.1)	300	Richmond, VA	(43.7)	NA	Santa Fe, NM**	NA
238	Flagstaff, AZ	(30.4)	301	Pocatello, ID	(44.9)	NA	Springfield, IL**	NA
238	Miami (greater), FL	(30.4)	302	Hot Springs, AR	(45.8)	NA	Terre Haute, IN**	NA
240	Punta Gorda, FL	(30.6)	303	Charlottesville, VA	(45.9)	NA	Tuscaloosa, AL**	NA
241	Deltona-Daytona Beach, FL	(30.7)	304	Blacksburg, VA	(46.1)	NA	Warren-Farmington Hills, MI M.D.**	NA
242	Fort Smith, AR-OK	(31.1)	305	Iowa City, IA	(46.2)	NA	Winston-Salem, NC**	NA
243	Racine, WI	(31.7)	306	Amarillo, TX	(47.2)			

Source: CQ Press using reported data from the F.B.I. "Crime in the United States 2011"
*Robbery is the taking of anything of value by force or threat of force. Attempts are included.
**Not available.

Alpha Order - Metro Area

21. Aggravated Assaults in 2011
National Total = 751,373 Aggravated Assaults*

RANK	METROPOLITAN AREA	ASSAULTS
270	Abilene, TX	339
134	Akron, OH	1,087
108	Albany-Schenectady-Troy, NY	1,539
206	Albany, GA	572
47	Albuquerque, NM	4,370
168	Alexandria, LA	813
148	Allentown, PA-NJ	979
314	Altoona, PA	220
155	Amarillo, TX	953
317	Ames, IA	207
95	Anchorage, AK	1,681
163	Anderson, SC	886
182	Ann Arbor, MI	675
237	Anniston-Oxford, AL	437
305	Appleton, WI	241
202	Asheville, NC	582
215	Athens-Clarke County, GA	537
14	Atlanta, GA	11,838
179	Atlantic City, NJ	711
327	Auburn, AL	167
141	Augusta, GA-SC	1,037
62	Austin-Round Rock, TX	3,266
64	Bakersfield, CA	3,188
17	Baltimore-Towson, MD	10,776
366	Bangor, ME	48
171	Barnstable Town, MA	777
63	Baton Rouge, LA	3,217
196	Battle Creek, MI	623
325	Bay City, MI	173
116	Beaumont-Port Arthur, TX	1,377
296	Bellingham, WA	268
240	Bend, OR	426
132	Bethesda-Frederick, MD M.D.	1,113
273	Billings, MT	332
264	Binghamton, NY	361
51	Birmingham-Hoover, AL	3,720
324	Bismarck, ND	185
331	Blacksburg, VA	163
263	Bloomington-Normal, IL	363
298	Bloomington, IN	260
140	Boise City-Nampa, ID	1,047
15	Boston (greater), MA-NH	11,415
34	Boston-Quincy, MA M.D.	6,252
218	Boulder, CO	525
354	Bowling Green, KY	99
207	Bremerton-Silverdale, WA	568
119	Bridgeport-Stamford, CT	1,291
165	Brownsville-Harlingen, TX	884
255	Brunswick, GA	387
67	Buffalo-Niagara Falls, NY	2,761
230	Burlington, NC	478
70	Cambridge-Newton, MA M.D.	2,727
79	Camden, NJ M.D.	2,416
227	Canton, OH	490
114	Cape Coral-Fort Myers, FL	1,466
286	Cape Girardeau, MO-IL	305
347	Carson City, NV	128
341	Casper, WY	147
277	Cedar Rapids, IA	326
152	Champaign-Urbana, IL	967

RANK	METROPOLITAN AREA	ASSAULTS
147	Charleston, WV	981
40	Charlotte-Gastonia, NC-SC	4,886
322	Charlottesville, VA	190
87	Chattanooga, TN-GA	2,044
339	Cheyenne, WY	155
7	Chicago (greater), IL-IN-WI	19,478
8	Chicago-Joilet-Naperville, IL M.D.	17,524
271	Chico, CA	335
73	Cincinnati-Middletown, OH-KY-IN	2,638
164	Clarksville, TN-KY	885
57	Cleveland-Elyria-Mentor, OH	3,441
188	Cleveland, TN	637
187	College Station-Bryan, TX	639
107	Colorado Springs, CO	1,545
225	Columbia, MO	498
184	Columbus, GA-AL	662
360	Columbus, IN	88
90	Columbus, OH	1,970
96	Corpus Christi, TX	1,669
365	Corvallis, OR	60
201	Crestview-Fort Walton Beach, FL	605
312	Cumberland, MD-WV	227
11	Dallas (greater), TX	13,179
28	Dallas-Plano-Irving, TX M.D.	7,479
302	Dalton, GA	250
279	Danville, IL	317
358	Danville, VA	91
126	Davenport, IA-IL	1,193
142	Dayton, OH	1,029
310	Decatur, AL	234
254	Decatur, IL	391
91	Deltona-Daytona Beach, FL	1,862
39	Denver-Aurora, CO	5,550
130	Des Moines-West Des Moines, IA	1,150
10	Detroit (greater), MI	15,801
12	Detroit-Livonia-Dearborn, MI M.D.	12,081
245	Dothan, AL	417
176	Dover, DE	735
358	Dubuque, IA	91
276	Duluth, MN-WI	327
120	Durham-Chapel Hill, NC	1,275
325	Eau Claire, WI	173
89	Edison, NJ M.D.	1,989
267	El Centro, CA	353
74	El Paso, TX	2,564
368	Elizabethtown, KY	32
346	Elmira, NY	135
262	Erie, PA	364
192	Eugene-Springfield, OR	626
197	Evansville, IN-KY	622
344	Fairbanks, AK	137
260	Fargo, ND-MN	372
185	Farmington, NM	660
144	Fayetteville, NC	1,008
238	Flagstaff, AZ	434
80	Flint, MI	2,355
303	Florence-Muscle Shoals, AL	247
135	Florence, SC	1,076
349	Fond du Lac, WI	125
226	Fort Collins-Loveland, CO	491

RANK	METROPOLITAN AREA	ASSAULTS
42	Fort Lauderdale, FL M.D.	4,743
146	Fort Smith, AR-OK	983
235	Fort Wayne, IN	448
37	Fort Worth-Arlington, TX M.D.	5,700
54	Fresno, CA	3,589
256	Gadsden, AL	381
127	Gainesville, FL	1,183
330	Gainesville, GA	164
129	Gary, IN M.D.	1,175
342	Glens Falls, NY	143
251	Goldsboro, NC	407
343	Grand Forks, ND-MN	140
287	Grand Junction, CO	303
98	Grand Rapids-Wyoming, MI	1,653
340	Great Falls, MT	153
204	Greeley, CO	580
280	Green Bay, WI	314
72	Greenville, SC	2,686
294	Gulfport-Biloxi, MS	270
217	Hagerstown-Martinsburg, MD-WV	527
251	Hanford-Corcoran, CA	407
161	Harrisburg-Carlisle, PA	909
356	Harrisonburg, VA	93
102	Hartford, CT	1,628
208	Hickory, NC	562
323	Hinesville, GA	189
304	Holland-Grand Haven, MI	246
258	Hot Springs, AR	374
233	Houma, LA	456
6	Houston, TX	19,956
113	Huntsville, AL	1,477
319	Idaho Falls, ID	199
35	Indianapolis, IN	6,073
291	Iowa City, IA	289
41	Jacksonville, FL	4,745
289	Jacksonville, NC	294
151	Jackson, MS	968
192	Jackson, TN	626
299	Janesville, WI	254
258	Jefferson City, MO	374
213	Johnson City, TN	538
306	Johnstown, PA	236
284	Jonesboro, AR	309
249	Joplin, MO	409
306	Kankakee-Bradley, IL	236
33	Kansas City, MO-KS	6,397
231	Kennewick-Pasco-Richland, WA	474
159	Killeen-Temple-Fort Hood, TX	925
162	Kingsport, TN-VA	890
313	Kingston, NY	225
83	Knoxville, TN	2,198
336	Kokomo, IN	156
327	La Crosse, WI-MN	167
243	Lafayette, IN	421
128	Lafayette, LA	1,176
170	Lake Co.-Kenosha Co., IL-WI M.D.	779
288	Lake Havasu City-Kingman, AZ	295
92	Lakeland, FL	1,847
229	Lancaster, PA	483
131	Lansing-East Lansing, MI	1,140

Note: All listings are for Metropolitan Statistical Areas (M.S.A.s) except for those ending with "M.D." Listings with "M.D." are Metropolitan Divisions which are smaller parts of eleven large M.S.A.s. See explanatory note at beginning of metropolitan area section.

Alpha Order - Metro Area (continued)

RANK	METROPOLITAN AREA	ASSAULTS
160	Laredo, TX	919
198	Las Cruces, NM	620
26	Las Vegas-Paradise, NV	8,106
282	Lawrence, KS	311
194	Lawton, OK	624
345	Lebanon, PA	136
362	Lewiston-Auburn, ME	65
143	Lexington-Fayette, KY	1,013
278	Lima, OH	318
189	Lincoln, NE	634
53	Little Rock, AR	3,596
367	Logan, UT-ID	43
198	Longview, TX	620
329	Longview, WA	166
4	Los Angeles County, CA M.D.	23,742
3	Los Angeles (greater), CA	27,522
65	Louisville, KY-IN	3,030
109	Lubbock, TX	1,538
289	Lynchburg, VA	294
213	Macon, GA	538
190	Madera, CA	628
174	Madison, WI	748
194	Manchester-Nashua, NH	624
296	Manhattan, KS	268
361	Mankato-North Mankato, MN	72
364	Mansfield, OH	64
103	McAllen-Edinburg-Mission, TX	1,609
236	Medford, OR	442
23	Memphis, TN-MS-AR	8,808
137	Merced, CA	1,060
5	Miami (greater), FL	20,347
16	Miami-Dade County, FL M.D.	11,307
355	Michigan City-La Porte, IN	96
284	Midland, TX	309
61	Milwaukee, WI	3,305
43	Minneapolis-St. Paul, MN-WI	4,636
315	Missoula, MT	211
111	Mobile, AL	1,496
101	Modesto, CA	1,631
157	Monroe, LA	941
309	Monroe, MI	235
205	Montgomery, AL	574
261	Morristown, TN	365
347	Mount Vernon-Anacortes, WA	128
242	Muncie, IN	422
232	Muskegon-Norton Shores, MI	473
125	Myrtle Beach, SC	1,210
268	Napa, CA	346
173	Naples-Marco Island, FL	758
29	Nashville-Davidson, TN	7,450
81	Nassau-Suffolk, NY M.D.	2,350
106	New Haven-Milford, CT	1,597
59	New Orleans, LA	3,412
1	New York (greater), NY-NJ-PA	42,653
2	New York-W. Plains NY-NJ M.D.	34,871
56	Newark-Union, NJ-PA M.D.	3,443
77	North Port-Bradenton-Sarasota, FL	2,461
248	Norwich-New London, CT	411
30	Oakland-Fremont, CA M.D.	7,338
118	Ocala, FL	1,301
315	Ocean City, NJ	211
169	Odessa, TX	807
221	Ogden-Clearfield, UT	518

RANK	METROPOLITAN AREA	ASSAULTS
44	Oklahoma City, OK	4,599
241	Olympia, WA	423
85	Omaha-Council Bluffs, NE-IA	2,143
22	Orlando, FL	9,118
294	Oshkosh-Neenah, WI	270
362	Owensboro, KY	65
149	Oxnard-Thousand Oaks, CA	973
76	Palm Bay-Melbourne, FL	2,512
299	Palm Coast, FL	254
183	Panama City-Lynn Haven, FL	668
266	Pascagoula, MS	354
88	Peabody, MA M.D.	2,018
105	Pensacola, FL	1,600
156	Peoria, IL	947
9	Philadelphia (greater) PA-NJ-MD-DE	16,709
13	Philadelphia, PA M.D.	11,999
19	Phoenix-Mesa-Scottsdale, AZ	9,433
212	Pine Bluff, AR	550
46	Pittsburgh, PA	4,419
247	Pittsfield, MA	413
332	Pocatello, ID	162
153	Port St. Lucie, FL	966
60	Portland-Vancouver, OR-WA	3,362
268	Portland, ME	346
150	Poughkeepsie, NY	969
181	Prescott, AZ	682
311	Provo-Orem, UT	233
190	Pueblo, CO	628
283	Punta Gorda, FL	310
320	Racine, WI	196
104	Raleigh-Cary, NC	1,606
275	Rapid City, SD	330
175	Reading, PA	741
136	Redding, CA	1,066
133	Reno-Sparks, NV	1,090
110	Richmond, VA	1,522
20	Riverside-San Bernardino, CA	9,299
211	Roanoke, VA	552
334	Rochester, MN	159
94	Rochester, NY	1,765
99	Rockford, IL	1,648
244	Rockingham County, NH M.D.	418
216	Rocky Mount, NC	532
257	Rome, GA	376
38	Sacramento, CA	5,651
122	Saginaw, MI	1,248
200	Salem, OR	615
121	Salinas, CA	1,251
222	Salisbury, MD	506
84	Salt Lake City, UT	2,181
321	San Angelo, TX	194
36	San Antonio, TX	5,872
31	San Diego, CA	7,217
18	San Francisco (greater), CA	10,770
58	San Francisco-S. Mateo, CA M.D.	3,432
71	San Jose, CA	2,717
223	San Luis Obispo, CA	503
335	Sandusky, OH	158
49	Santa Ana-Anaheim, CA M.D.	3,780
124	Santa Barbara-Santa Maria, CA	1,219
167	Santa Cruz-Watsonville, CA	832
246	Santa Fe, NM	415
117	Santa Rosa-Petaluma, CA	1,319

RANK	METROPOLITAN AREA	ASSAULTS
210	Savannah, GA	556
145	Scranton--Wilkes-Barre, PA	1,002
32	Seattle (greater), WA	6,611
45	Seattle-Bellevue-Everett, WA M.D.	4,476
274	Sebastian-Vero Beach, FL	331
353	Sheboygan, WI	110
301	Sherman-Denison, TX	252
271	Sioux City, IA-NE-SD	335
292	Sioux Falls, SD	288
228	South Bend-Mishawaka, IN-MI	489
139	Spartanburg, SC	1,052
158	Spokane, WA	927
138	Springfield, IL	1,055
78	Springfield, MA	2,443
115	Springfield, MO	1,395
336	Springfield, OH	156
356	State College, PA	93
50	Stockton, CA	3,744
318	St. Cloud, MN	204
306	St. Joseph, MO-KS	236
21	St. Louis, MO-IL	9,280
253	Sumter, SC	392
123	Syracuse, NY	1,242
86	Tacoma, WA M.D.	2,135
97	Tallahassee, FL	1,663
25	Tampa-St Petersburg, FL	8,496
333	Terre Haute, IN	160
177	Texarkana, TX-Texarkana, AR	716
93	Toledo, OH	1,789
208	Topeka, KS	562
166	Trenton-Ewing, NJ	835
75	Tucson, AZ	2,544
55	Tulsa, OK	3,551
186	Tuscaloosa, AL	645
203	Tyler, TX	581
224	Utica-Rome, NY	499
281	Valdosta, GA	313
154	Vallejo-Fairfield, CA	965
238	Victoria, TX	434
66	Virginia Beach-Norfolk, VA-NC	2,783
112	Visalia-Porterville, CA	1,478
178	Waco, TX	713
293	Warner Robins, GA	285
51	Warren-Farmington Hills, MI M.D.	3,720
24	Washington (greater) DC-VA-MD-WV	8,743
27	Washington, DC-VA-MD-WV M.D.	7,630
250	Waterloo-Cedar Falls, IA	408
350	Wausau, WI	123
351	Wenatchee, WA	112
48	West Palm Beach, FL M.D.	4,297
265	Wichita Falls, TX	355
69	Wichita, KS	2,747
351	Williamsport, PA	112
82	Wilmington, DE-MD-NJ M.D.	2,294
172	Wilmington, NC	763
336	Winchester, VA-WV	156
100	Winston-Salem, NC	1,634
68	Worcester, MA	2,759
234	Yakima, WA	449
180	York-Hanover, PA	699
220	Yuba City, CA	522
219	Yuma, AZ	524

Source: Reported data from the F.B.I. "Crime in the United States 2011"
*Aggravated assault is an attack for the purpose of inflicting severe bodily injury.

Rank Order - Metro Area

21. Aggravated Assaults in 2011 (continued)
National Total = 751,373 Aggravated Assaults*

RANK	METROPOLITAN AREA	ASSAULTS	RANK	METROPOLITAN AREA	ASSAULTS	RANK	METROPOLITAN AREA	ASSAULTS
1	New York (greater), NY-NJ-PA	42,653	61	Milwaukee, WI	3,305	121	Salinas, CA	1,251
2	New York-W. Plains NY-NJ M.D.	34,871	62	Austin-Round Rock, TX	3,266	122	Saginaw, MI	1,248
3	Los Angeles (greater), CA	27,522	63	Baton Rouge, LA	3,217	123	Syracuse, NY	1,242
4	Los Angeles County, CA M.D.	23,742	64	Bakersfield, CA	3,188	124	Santa Barbara-Santa Maria, CA	1,219
5	Miami (greater), FL	20,347	65	Louisville, KY-IN	3,030	125	Myrtle Beach, SC	1,210
6	Houston, TX	19,956	66	Virginia Beach-Norfolk, VA-NC	2,783	126	Davenport, IA-IL	1,193
7	Chicago (greater), IL-IN-WI	19,478	67	Buffalo-Niagara Falls, NY	2,761	127	Gainesville, FL	1,183
8	Chicago-Joilet-Naperville, IL M.D.	17,524	68	Worcester, MA	2,759	128	Lafayette, LA	1,176
9	Philadelphia (greater) PA-NJ-MD-DE	16,709	69	Wichita, KS	2,747	129	Gary, IN M.D.	1,175
10	Detroit (greater), MI	15,801	70	Cambridge-Newton, MA M.D.	2,727	130	Des Moines-West Des Moines, IA	1,150
11	Dallas (greater), TX	13,179	71	San Jose, CA	2,717	131	Lansing-East Lansing, MI	1,140
12	Detroit-Livonia-Dearborn, MI M.D.	12,081	72	Greenville, SC	2,686	132	Bethesda-Frederick, MD M.D.	1,113
13	Philadelphia, PA M.D.	11,999	73	Cincinnati-Middletown, OH-KY-IN	2,638	133	Reno-Sparks, NV	1,090
14	Atlanta, GA	11,838	74	El Paso, TX	2,564	134	Akron, OH	1,087
15	Boston (greater), MA-NH	11,415	75	Tucson, AZ	2,544	135	Florence, SC	1,076
16	Miami-Dade County, FL M.D.	11,307	76	Palm Bay-Melbourne, FL	2,512	136	Redding, CA	1,066
17	Baltimore-Towson, MD	10,776	77	North Port-Bradenton-Sarasota, FL	2,461	137	Merced, CA	1,060
18	San Francisco (greater), CA	10,770	78	Springfield, MA	2,443	138	Springfield, IL	1,055
19	Phoenix-Mesa-Scottsdale, AZ	9,433	79	Camden, NJ M.D.	2,416	139	Spartanburg, SC	1,052
20	Riverside-San Bernardino, CA	9,299	80	Flint, MI	2,355	140	Boise City-Nampa, ID	1,047
21	St. Louis, MO-IL	9,280	81	Nassau-Suffolk, NY M.D.	2,350	141	Augusta, GA-SC	1,037
22	Orlando, FL	9,118	82	Wilmington, DE-MD-NJ M.D.	2,294	142	Dayton, OH	1,029
23	Memphis, TN-MS-AR	8,808	83	Knoxville, TN	2,198	143	Lexington-Fayette, KY	1,013
24	Washington (greater) DC-VA-MD-WV	8,743	84	Salt Lake City, UT	2,181	144	Fayetteville, NC	1,008
25	Tampa-St Petersburg, FL	8,496	85	Omaha-Council Bluffs, NE-IA	2,143	145	Scranton--Wilkes-Barre, PA	1,002
26	Las Vegas-Paradise, NV	8,106	86	Tacoma, WA M.D.	2,135	146	Fort Smith, AR-OK	983
27	Washington, DC-VA-MD-WV M.D.	7,630	87	Chattanooga, TN-GA	2,044	147	Charleston, WV	981
28	Dallas-Plano-Irving, TX M.D.	7,479	88	Peabody, MA M.D.	2,018	148	Allentown, PA-NJ	979
29	Nashville-Davidson, TN	7,450	89	Edison, NJ M.D.	1,989	149	Oxnard-Thousand Oaks, CA	973
30	Oakland-Fremont, CA M.D.	7,338	90	Columbus, OH	1,970	150	Poughkeepsie, NY	969
31	San Diego, CA	7,217	91	Deltona-Daytona Beach, FL	1,862	151	Jackson, MS	968
32	Seattle (greater), WA	6,611	92	Lakeland, FL	1,847	152	Champaign-Urbana, IL	967
33	Kansas City, MO-KS	6,397	93	Toledo, OH	1,789	153	Port St. Lucie, FL	966
34	Boston-Quincy, MA M.D.	6,252	94	Rochester, NY	1,765	154	Vallejo-Fairfield, CA	965
35	Indianapolis, IN	6,073	95	Anchorage, AK	1,681	155	Amarillo, TX	953
36	San Antonio, TX	5,872	96	Corpus Christi, TX	1,669	156	Peoria, IL	947
37	Fort Worth-Arlington, TX M.D.	5,700	97	Tallahassee, FL	1,663	157	Monroe, LA	941
38	Sacramento, CA	5,651	98	Grand Rapids-Wyoming, MI	1,653	158	Spokane, WA	927
39	Denver-Aurora, CO	5,550	99	Rockford, IL	1,648	159	Killeen-Temple-Fort Hood, TX	925
40	Charlotte-Gastonia, NC-SC	4,886	100	Winston-Salem, NC	1,634	160	Laredo, TX	919
41	Jacksonville, FL	4,745	101	Modesto, CA	1,631	161	Harrisburg-Carlisle, PA	909
42	Fort Lauderdale, FL M.D.	4,743	102	Hartford, CT	1,628	162	Kingsport, TN-VA	890
43	Minneapolis-St. Paul, MN-WI	4,636	103	McAllen-Edinburg-Mission, TX	1,609	163	Anderson, SC	886
44	Oklahoma City, OK	4,599	104	Raleigh-Cary, NC	1,606	164	Clarksville, TN-KY	885
45	Seattle-Bellevue-Everett, WA M.D.	4,476	105	Pensacola, FL	1,600	165	Brownsville-Harlingen, TX	884
46	Pittsburgh, PA	4,419	106	New Haven-Milford, CT	1,597	166	Trenton-Ewing, NJ	835
47	Albuquerque, NM	4,370	107	Colorado Springs, CO	1,545	167	Santa Cruz-Watsonville, CA	832
48	West Palm Beach, FL M.D.	4,297	108	Albany-Schenectady-Troy, NY	1,539	168	Alexandria, LA	813
49	Santa Ana-Anaheim, CA M.D.	3,780	109	Lubbock, TX	1,538	169	Odessa, TX	807
50	Stockton, CA	3,744	110	Richmond, VA	1,522	170	Lake Co.-Kenosha Co., IL-WI M.D.	779
51	Birmingham-Hoover, AL	3,720	111	Mobile, AL	1,496	171	Barnstable Town, MA	777
51	Warren-Farmington Hills, MI M.D.	3,720	112	Visalia-Porterville, CA	1,478	172	Wilmington, NC	763
53	Little Rock, AR	3,596	113	Huntsville, AL	1,477	173	Naples-Marco Island, FL	758
54	Fresno, CA	3,589	114	Cape Coral-Fort Myers, FL	1,466	174	Madison, WI	748
55	Tulsa, OK	3,551	115	Springfield, MO	1,395	175	Reading, PA	741
56	Newark-Union, NJ-PA M.D.	3,443	116	Beaumont-Port Arthur, TX	1,377	176	Dover, DE	735
57	Cleveland-Elyria-Mentor, OH	3,441	117	Santa Rosa-Petaluma, CA	1,319	177	Texarkana, TX-Texarkana, AR	716
58	San Francisco-S. Mateo, CA M.D.	3,432	118	Ocala, FL	1,301	178	Waco, TX	713
59	New Orleans, LA	3,412	119	Bridgeport-Stamford, CT	1,291	179	Atlantic City, NJ	711
60	Portland-Vancouver, OR-WA	3,362	120	Durham-Chapel Hill, NC	1,275	180	York-Hanover, PA	699

Note: All listings are for Metropolitan Statistical Areas (M.S.A.s) except for those ending with "M.D." Listings with "M.D." are Metropolitan Divisions which are smaller parts of eleven large M.S.A.s. See explanatory note at beginning of metropolitan area section.

Rank Order - Metro Area (continued)

RANK	METROPOLITAN AREA	ASSAULTS
181	Prescott, AZ	682
182	Ann Arbor, MI	675
183	Panama City-Lynn Haven, FL	668
184	Columbus, GA-AL	662
185	Farmington, NM	660
186	Tuscaloosa, AL	645
187	College Station-Bryan, TX	639
188	Cleveland, TN	637
189	Lincoln, NE	634
190	Madera, CA	628
190	Pueblo, CO	628
192	Eugene-Springfield, OR	626
192	Jackson, TN	626
194	Lawton, OK	624
194	Manchester-Nashua, NH	624
196	Battle Creek, MI	623
197	Evansville, IN-KY	622
198	Las Cruces, NM	620
198	Longview, TX	620
200	Salem, OR	615
201	Crestview-Fort Walton Beach, FL	605
202	Asheville, NC	582
203	Tyler, TX	581
204	Greeley, CO	580
205	Montgomery, AL	574
206	Albany, GA	572
207	Bremerton-Silverdale, WA	568
208	Hickory, NC	562
208	Topeka, KS	562
210	Savannah, GA	556
211	Roanoke, VA	552
212	Pine Bluff, AR	550
213	Johnson City, TN	538
213	Macon, GA	538
215	Athens-Clarke County, GA	537
216	Rocky Mount, NC	532
217	Hagerstown-Martinsburg, MD-WV	527
218	Boulder, CO	525
219	Yuma, AZ	524
220	Yuba City, CA	522
221	Ogden-Clearfield, UT	518
222	Salisbury, MD	506
223	San Luis Obispo, CA	503
224	Utica-Rome, NY	499
225	Columbia, MO	498
226	Fort Collins-Loveland, CO	491
227	Canton, OH	490
228	South Bend-Mishawaka, IN-MI	489
229	Lancaster, PA	483
230	Burlington, NC	478
231	Kennewick-Pasco-Richland, WA	474
232	Muskegon-Norton Shores, MI	473
233	Houma, LA	456
234	Yakima, WA	449
235	Fort Wayne, IN	448
236	Medford, OR	442
237	Anniston-Oxford, AL	437
238	Flagstaff, AZ	434
238	Victoria, TX	434
240	Bend, OR	426
241	Olympia, WA	423
242	Muncie, IN	422
243	Lafayette, IN	421
244	Rockingham County, NH M.D.	418
245	Dothan, AL	417
246	Santa Fe, NM	415
247	Pittsfield, MA	413
248	Norwich-New London, CT	411
249	Joplin, MO	409
250	Waterloo-Cedar Falls, IA	408
251	Goldsboro, NC	407
251	Hanford-Corcoran, CA	407
253	Sumter, SC	392
254	Decatur, IL	391
255	Brunswick, GA	387
256	Gadsden, AL	381
257	Rome, GA	376
258	Hot Springs, AR	374
258	Jefferson City, MO	374
260	Fargo, ND-MN	372
261	Morristown, TN	365
262	Erie, PA	364
263	Bloomington-Normal, IL	363
264	Binghamton, NY	361
265	Wichita Falls, TX	355
266	Pascagoula, MS	354
267	El Centro, CA	353
268	Napa, CA	346
268	Portland, ME	346
270	Abilene, TX	339
271	Chico, CA	335
271	Sioux City, IA-NE-SD	335
273	Billings, MT	332
274	Sebastian-Vero Beach, FL	331
275	Rapid City, SD	330
276	Duluth, MN-WI	327
277	Cedar Rapids, IA	326
278	Lima, OH	318
279	Danville, IL	317
280	Green Bay, WI	314
281	Valdosta, GA	313
282	Lawrence, KS	311
283	Punta Gorda, FL	310
284	Jonesboro, AR	309
284	Midland, TX	309
286	Cape Girardeau, MO-IL	305
287	Grand Junction, CO	303
288	Lake Havasu City-Kingman, AZ	295
289	Jacksonville, NC	294
289	Lynchburg, VA	294
291	Iowa City, IA	289
292	Sioux Falls, SD	288
293	Warner Robins, GA	285
294	Gulfport-Biloxi, MS	270
294	Oshkosh-Neenah, WI	270
296	Bellingham, WA	268
296	Manhattan, KS	268
298	Bloomington, IN	260
299	Janesville, WI	254
299	Palm Coast, FL	254
301	Sherman-Denison, TX	252
302	Dalton, GA	250
303	Florence-Muscle Shoals, AL	247
304	Holland-Grand Haven, MI	246
305	Appleton, WI	241
306	Johnstown, PA	236
306	Kankakee-Bradley, IL	236
306	St. Joseph, MO-KS	236
309	Monroe, MI	235
310	Decatur, AL	234
311	Provo-Orem, UT	233
312	Cumberland, MD-WV	227
313	Kingston, NY	225
314	Altoona, PA	220
315	Missoula, MT	211
315	Ocean City, NJ	211
317	Ames, IA	207
318	St. Cloud, MN	204
319	Idaho Falls, ID	199
320	Racine, WI	196
321	San Angelo, TX	194
322	Charlottesville, VA	190
323	Hinesville, GA	189
324	Bismarck, ND	185
325	Bay City, MI	173
325	Eau Claire, WI	173
327	Auburn, AL	167
327	La Crosse, WI-MN	167
329	Longview, WA	166
330	Gainesville, GA	164
331	Blacksburg, VA	163
332	Pocatello, ID	162
333	Terre Haute, IN	160
334	Rochester, MN	159
335	Sandusky, OH	158
336	Kokomo, IN	156
336	Springfield, OH	156
336	Winchester, VA-WV	156
339	Cheyenne, WY	155
340	Great Falls, MT	153
341	Casper, WY	147
342	Glens Falls, NY	143
343	Grand Forks, ND-MN	140
344	Fairbanks, AK	137
345	Lebanon, PA	136
346	Elmira, NY	135
347	Carson City, NV	128
347	Mount Vernon-Anacortes, WA	128
349	Fond du Lac, WI	125
350	Wausau, WI	123
351	Wenatchee, WA	112
351	Williamsport, PA	112
353	Sheboygan, WI	110
354	Bowling Green, KY	99
355	Michigan City-La Porte, IN	96
356	Harrisonburg, VA	93
356	State College, PA	93
358	Danville, VA	91
358	Dubuque, IA	91
360	Columbus, IN	88
361	Mankato-North Mankato, MN	72
362	Lewiston-Auburn, ME	65
362	Owensboro, KY	65
364	Mansfield, OH	64
365	Corvallis, OR	60
366	Bangor, ME	48
367	Logan, UT-ID	43
368	Elizabethtown, KY	32

Source: Reported data from the F.B.I. "Crime in the United States 2011"
*Aggravated assault is an attack for the purpose of inflicting severe bodily injury.

Alpha Order - Metro Area

22. Aggravated Assault Rate in 2011
National Rate = 241.1 Aggravated Assaults per 100,000 Population*

RANK	METROPOLITAN AREA	RATE	RANK	METROPOLITAN AREA	RATE	RANK	METROPOLITAN AREA	RATE
216	Abilene, TX	200.9	90	Charleston, WV	322.0	138	Fort Lauderdale, FL M.D.	267.7
284	Akron, OH	154.5	129	Charlotte-Gastonia, NC-SC	274.5	89	Fort Smith, AR-OK	326.4
247	Albany-Schenectady-Troy, NY	176.0	343	Charlottesville, VA	93.2	329	Fort Wayne, IN	107.1
67	Albany, GA	358.9	50	Chattanooga, TN-GA	383.1	145	Fort Worth-Arlington, TX M.D.	261.4
21	Albuquerque, NM	487.2	257	Cheyenne, WY	167.6	52	Fresno, CA	381.2
14	Alexandria, LA	523.4	209	Chicago (greater), IL-IN-WI	205.2	62	Gadsden, AL	363.1
318	Allentown, PA-NJ	118.8	187	Chicago-Joilet-Naperville, IL M.D.	221.6	31	Gainesville, FL	441.6
252	Altoona, PA	172.6	291	Chico, CA	150.5	349	Gainesville, GA	90.1
55	Amarillo, TX	373.5	311	Cincinnati-Middletown, OH-KY-IN	123.6	264	Gary, IN M.D.	165.1
174	Ames, IA	230.0	93	Clarksville, TN-KY	320.4	325	Glens Falls, NY	110.4
9	Anchorage, AK	540.6	263	Cleveland-Elyria-Mentor, OH	165.5	88	Goldsboro, NC	327.8
23	Anderson, SC	468.0	7	Cleveland, TN	545.2	301	Grand Forks, ND-MN	140.2
220	Ann Arbor, MI	195.9	131	College Station-Bryan, TX	273.7	213	Grand Junction, CO	203.0
59	Anniston-Oxford, AL	366.8	166	Colorado Springs, CO	235.2	197	Grand Rapids-Wyoming, MI	213.7
332	Appleton, WI	106.3	117	Columbia, MO	287.2	233	Great Falls, MT	186.5
302	Asheville, NC	135.3	184	Columbus, GA-AL	221.9	179	Greeley, CO	225.5
127	Athens-Clarke County, GA	275.3	323	Columbus, IN	114.0	333	Green Bay, WI	102.1
185	Atlanta, GA	221.8	328	Columbus, OH	107.2	35	Greenville, SC	416.8
147	Atlantic City, NJ	258.1	51	Corpus Christi, TX	381.8	326	Gulfport-Biloxi, MS	108.1
319	Auburn, AL	118.5	359	Corvallis, OR	69.4	221	Hagerstown-Martinsburg, MD-WV	194.7
238	Augusta, GA-SC	183.9	83	Crestview-Fort Walton Beach, FL	330.1	143	Hanford-Corcoran, CA	263.0
234	Austin-Round Rock, TX	186.4	190	Cumberland, MD-WV	218.2	266	Harrisburg-Carlisle, PA	164.9
53	Bakersfield, CA	375.3	214	Dallas (greater), TX	202.6	358	Harrisonburg, VA	73.4
43	Baltimore-Towson, MD	393.8	251	Dallas-Plano-Irving, TX M.D.	172.9	276	Hartford, CT	159.3
367	Bangor, ME	31.2	250	Dalton, GA	173.5	287	Hickory, NC	151.8
68	Barnstable Town, MA	357.7	47	Danville, IL	387.2	162	Hinesville, GA	239.4
42	Baton Rouge, LA	397.2	354	Danville, VA	84.4	342	Holland-Grand Haven, MI	93.3
25	Battle Creek, MI	457.9	101	Davenport, IA-IL	313.0	48	Hot Springs, AR	386.6
272	Bay City, MI	160.6	314	Dayton, OH	122.2	193	Houma, LA	217.1
75	Beaumont-Port Arthur, TX	346.9	288	Decatur, AL	151.4	85	Houston, TX	328.7
304	Bellingham, WA	131.2	71	Decatur, IL	351.9	70	Huntsville, AL	352.0
139	Bend, OR	267.2	56	Deltona-Daytona Beach, FL	371.4	290	Idaho Falls, ID	150.9
347	Bethesda-Frederick, MD M.D.	91.5	196	Denver-Aurora, CO	214.5	78	Indianapolis, IN	344.0
204	Billings, MT	208.2	217	Des Moines-West Des Moines, IA	200.8	230	Iowa City, IA	188.4
298	Binghamton, NY	142.8	58	Detroit (greater), MI	368.1	74	Jacksonville, FL	347.9
87	Birmingham-Hoover, AL	328.2	1	Detroit-Livonia-Dearborn, MI M.D.	664.1	269	Jacksonville, NC	163.3
258	Bismarck, ND	167.2	118	Dothan, AL	285.0	242	Jackson, MS	178.9
338	Blacksburg, VA	98.8	27	Dover, DE	448.2	11	Jackson, TN	537.5
198	Bloomington-Normal, IL	213.4	339	Dubuque, IA	96.7	278	Janesville, WI	157.7
303	Bloomington, IN	134.2	321	Duluth, MN-WI	116.0	156	Jefferson City, MO	248.8
256	Boise City-Nampa, ID	168.0	153	Durham-Chapel Hill, NC	249.6	137	Johnson City, TN	268.3
154	Boston (greater), MA-NH	249.3	331	Eau Claire, WI	106.9	268	Johnstown, PA	163.7
84	Boston-Quincy, MA M.D.	329.2	353	Edison, NJ M.D.	84.7	151	Jonesboro, AR	253.4
249	Boulder, CO	175.2	218	El Centro, CA	199.9	170	Joplin, MO	232.2
356	Bowling Green, KY	78.1	98	El Paso, TX	313.6	208	Kankakee-Bradley, IL	207.4
183	Bremerton-Silverdale, WA	222.7	368	Elizabethtown, KY	26.5	102	Kansas City, MO-KS	312.8
297	Bridgeport-Stamford, CT	143.3	289	Elmira, NY	151.3	237	Kennewick-Pasco-Richland, WA	184.2
199	Brownsville-Harlingen, TX	213.1	306	Erie, PA	129.3	182	Killeen-Temple-Fort Hood, TX	223.5
80	Brunswick, GA	339.9	246	Eugene-Springfield, OR	176.1	119	Kingsport, TN-VA	284.7
160	Buffalo-Niagara Falls, NY	242.1	253	Evansville, IN-KY	172.5	312	Kingston, NY	122.7
104	Burlington, NC	312.3	41	Fairbanks, AK	400.1	105	Knoxville, TN	312.1
240	Cambridge-Newton, MA M.D.	180.3	248	Fargo, ND-MN	175.7	279	Kokomo, IN	157.3
224	Camden, NJ M.D.	192.5	18	Farmington, NM	501.9	309	La Crosse, WI-MN	124.3
315	Canton, OH	121.1	132	Fayetteville, NC	271.7	207	Lafayette, IN	207.6
168	Cape Coral-Fort Myers, FL	233.7	95	Flagstaff, AZ	318.4	33	Lafayette, LA	425.7
97	Cape Girardeau, MO-IL	315.7	6	Flint, MI	553.5	350	Lake Co.-Kenosha Co., IL-WI M.D.	89.3
176	Carson City, NV	229.6	259	Florence-Muscle Shoals, AL	167.1	295	Lake Havasu City-Kingman, AZ	145.3
223	Casper, WY	193.3	16	Florence, SC	517.4	107	Lakeland, FL	302.6
307	Cedar Rapids, IA	125.7	313	Fond du Lac, WI	122.5	345	Lancaster, PA	92.7
36	Champaign-Urbana, IL	415.8	270	Fort Collins-Loveland, CO	161.1	157	Lansing-East Lansing, MI	245.9

Note: All listings are for Metropolitan Statistical Areas (M.S.A.s) except for those ending with "M.D." Listings with "M.D." are Metropolitan Divisions which are smaller parts of eleven large M.S.A.s. See explanatory note at beginning of metropolitan area section.

Alpha Order - Metro Area (continued)

RANK	METROPOLITAN AREA	RATE
66	Laredo, TX	359.6
114	Las Cruces, NM	293.0
37	Las Vegas-Paradise, NV	411.9
126	Lawrence, KS	278.8
20	Lawton, OK	497.5
334	Lebanon, PA	101.5
361	Lewiston-Auburn, ME	60.4
199	Lexington-Fayette, KY	213.1
110	Lima, OH	298.8
205	Lincoln, NE	208.0
17	Little Rock, AR	510.0
366	Logan, UT-ID	33.7
123	Longview, TX	283.3
275	Longview, WA	159.6
163	Los Angeles County, CA M.D.	239.0
201	Los Angeles (greater), CA	212.0
167	Louisville, KY-IN	234.5
12	Lubbock, TX	528.7
322	Lynchburg, VA	115.0
177	Macon, GA	228.6
38	Madera, CA	411.4
305	Madison, WI	131.0
281	Manchester-Nashua, NH	155.5
203	Manhattan, KS	209.6
357	Mankato-North Mankato, MN	73.9
364	Mansfield, OH	51.4
212	McAllen-Edinburg-Mission, TX	203.4
195	Medford, OR	215.2
2	Memphis, TN-MS-AR	663.9
39	Merced, CA	409.6
63	Miami (greater), FL	360.7
28	Miami-Dade County, FL M.D.	446.8
351	Michigan City-La Porte, IN	85.7
189	Midland, TX	221.1
202	Milwaukee, WI	211.5
299	Minneapolis-St. Paul, MN-WI	140.3
225	Missoula, MT	191.4
65	Mobile, AL	360.5
99	Modesto, CA	313.4
13	Monroe, LA	528.5
282	Monroe, MI	154.7
286	Montgomery, AL	152.5
140	Morristown, TN	264.8
327	Mount Vernon-Anacortes, WA	107.8
69	Muncie, IN	356.8
128	Muskegon-Norton Shores, MI	274.9
30	Myrtle Beach, SC	444.2
152	Napa, CA	250.6
169	Naples-Marco Island, FL	232.6
24	Nashville-Davidson, TN	464.4
355	Nassau-Suffolk, NY M.D.	82.6
219	New Haven-Milford, CT	197.1
116	New Orleans, LA	289.5
180	New York (greater), NY-NJ-PA	224.8
109	New York-W. Plains NY-NJ M.D.	299.9
274	Newark-Union, NJ-PA M.D.	159.8
76	North Port-Bradenton-Sarasota, FL	345.7
124	Norwich-New London, CT	280.4
122	Oakland-Fremont, CA M.D.	283.4
46	Ocala, FL	387.4
194	Ocean City, NJ	216.2
5	Odessa, TX	576.4
344	Ogden-Clearfield, UT	92.9
61	Oklahoma City, OK	363.2
264	Olympia, WA	165.1
158	Omaha-Council Bluffs, NE-IA	245.6
34	Orlando, FL	421.4
271	Oshkosh-Neenah, WI	161.0
363	Owensboro, KY	56.3
320	Oxnard-Thousand Oaks, CA	116.8
26	Palm Bay-Melbourne, FL	456.1
144	Palm Coast, FL	261.9
44	Panama City-Lynn Haven, FL	390.3
192	Pascagoula, MS	217.4
134	Peabody, MA M.D.	269.9
72	Pensacola, FL	351.6
155	Peoria, IL	249.0
125	Philadelphia (greater) PA-NJ-MD-DE	279.0
111	Philadelphia, PA M.D.	298.4
185	Phoenix-Mesa-Scottsdale, AZ	221.8
8	Pine Bluff, AR	544.5
231	Pittsburgh, PA	186.9
102	Pittsfield, MA	312.8
244	Pocatello, ID	176.7
181	Port St. Lucie, FL	224.7
293	Portland-Vancouver, OR-WA	149.3
360	Portland, ME	67.3
296	Poughkeepsie, NY	143.9
94	Prescott, AZ	318.7
365	Provo-Orem, UT	43.4
45	Pueblo, CO	388.1
226	Punta Gorda, FL	191.2
335	Racine, WI	99.9
299	Raleigh-Cary, NC	140.3
148	Rapid City, SD	258.0
241	Reading, PA	179.5
4	Redding, CA	594.5
150	Reno-Sparks, NV	254.1
317	Richmond, VA	119.5
191	Riverside-San Bernardino, CA	217.5
244	Roanoke, VA	176.7
352	Rochester, MN	84.8
260	Rochester, NY	166.7
22	Rockford, IL	470.2
336	Rockingham County, NH M.D.	99.8
77	Rocky Mount, NC	344.7
49	Rome, GA	385.3
146	Sacramento, CA	259.9
3	Saginaw, MI	623.9
280	Salem, OR	155.7
112	Salinas, CA	297.9
40	Salisbury, MD	400.3
228	Salt Lake City, UT	190.3
255	San Angelo, TX	169.9
136	San Antonio, TX	268.4
173	San Diego, CA	230.4
159	San Francisco (greater), CA	245.5
227	San Francisco-S. Mateo, CA M.D.	191.0
294	San Jose, CA	146.2
236	San Luis Obispo, CA	184.4
210	Sandusky, OH	204.8
310	Santa Ana-Anaheim, CA M.D.	124.1
121	Santa Barbara-Santa Maria, CA	284.2
99	Santa Cruz-Watsonville, CA	313.4
119	Santa Fe, NM	284.7
135	Santa Rosa-Petaluma, CA	269.4
277	Savannah, GA	157.9
243	Scranton--Wilkes-Barre, PA	177.2
229	Seattle (greater), WA	189.2
261	Seattle-Bellevue-Everett, WA M.D.	166.6
165	Sebastian-Vero Beach, FL	236.6
341	Sheboygan, WI	94.8
211	Sherman-Denison, TX	204.2
171	Sioux City, IA-NE-SD	231.8
308	Sioux Falls, SD	124.7
285	South Bend-Mishawaka, IN-MI	152.6
60	Spartanburg, SC	365.8
222	Spokane, WA	193.7
19	Springfield, IL	500.5
73	Springfield, MA	350.4
96	Springfield, MO	318.3
324	Springfield, OH	112.7
362	State College, PA	60.2
10	Stockton, CA	540.0
329	St. Cloud, MN	107.1
235	St. Joseph, MO-KS	184.6
86	St. Louis, MO-IL	328.6
64	Sumter, SC	360.6
232	Syracuse, NY	186.6
141	Tacoma, WA M.D.	264.3
29	Tallahassee, FL	446.5
108	Tampa-St Petersburg, FL	301.2
346	Terre Haute, IN	92.3
15	Texarkana, TX-Texarkana, AR	517.7
130	Toledo, OH	274.4
164	Topeka, KS	238.8
178	Trenton-Ewing, NJ	227.1
149	Tucson, AZ	255.9
54	Tulsa, OK	374.8
115	Tuscaloosa, AL	292.5
133	Tyler, TX	271.3
262	Utica-Rome, NY	165.9
188	Valdosta, GA	221.3
172	Vallejo-Fairfield, CA	230.7
57	Victoria, TX	368.4
267	Virginia Beach-Norfolk, VA-NC	164.5
82	Visalia-Porterville, CA	330.4
113	Waco, TX	297.3
215	Warner Robins, GA	201.1
292	Warren-Farmington Hills, MI M.D.	150.4
282	Washington (greater) DC-VA-MD-WV	154.7
254	Washington, DC-VA-MD-WV M.D.	172.0
161	Waterloo-Cedar Falls, IA	241.9
348	Wausau, WI	91.3
337	Wenatchee, WA	99.4
92	West Palm Beach, FL M.D.	321.1
175	Wichita Falls, TX	229.8
32	Wichita, KS	438.1
340	Williamsport, PA	96.2
90	Wilmington, DE-MD-NJ M.D.	322.0
205	Wilmington, NC	208.0
316	Winchester, VA-WV	120.2
81	Winston-Salem, NC	337.8
79	Worcester, MA	343.4
239	Yakima, WA	181.7
273	York-Hanover, PA	160.2
106	Yuba City, CA	309.1
142	Yuma, AZ	264.0

Source: Reported data from the F.B.I. "Crime in the United States 2011"
*Aggravated assault is an attack for the purpose of inflicting severe bodily injury.

Rank Order - Metro Area

22. Aggravated Assault Rate in 2011 (continued)
National Rate = 241.1 Aggravated Assaults per 100,000 Population*

RANK	METROPOLITAN AREA	RATE	RANK	METROPOLITAN AREA	RATE	RANK	METROPOLITAN AREA	RATE
1	Detroit-Livonia-Dearborn, MI M.D.	664.1	61	Oklahoma City, OK	363.2	121	Santa Barbara-Santa Maria, CA	284.2
2	Memphis, TN-MS-AR	663.9	62	Gadsden, AL	363.1	122	Oakland-Fremont, CA M.D.	283.4
3	Saginaw, MI	623.9	63	Miami (greater), FL	360.7	123	Longview, TX	283.3
4	Redding, CA	594.5	64	Sumter, SC	360.6	124	Norwich-New London, CT	280.4
5	Odessa, TX	576.4	65	Mobile, AL	360.5	125	Philadelphia (greater) PA-NJ-MD-DE	279.0
6	Flint, MI	553.5	66	Laredo, TX	359.6	126	Lawrence, KS	278.8
7	Cleveland, TN	545.2	67	Albany, GA	358.9	127	Athens-Clarke County, GA	275.3
8	Pine Bluff, AR	544.5	68	Barnstable Town, MA	357.7	128	Muskegon-Norton Shores, MI	274.9
9	Anchorage, AK	540.6	69	Muncie, IN	356.8	129	Charlotte-Gastonia, NC-SC	274.5
10	Stockton, CA	540.0	70	Huntsville, AL	352.0	130	Toledo, OH	274.4
11	Jackson, TN	537.5	71	Decatur, IL	351.9	131	College Station-Bryan, TX	273.7
12	Lubbock, TX	528.7	72	Pensacola, FL	351.6	132	Fayetteville, NC	271.7
13	Monroe, LA	528.5	73	Springfield, MA	350.4	133	Tyler, TX	271.3
14	Alexandria, LA	523.4	74	Jacksonville, FL	347.9	134	Peabody, MA M.D.	269.9
15	Texarkana, TX-Texarkana, AR	517.7	75	Beaumont-Port Arthur, TX	346.9	135	Santa Rosa-Petaluma, CA	269.4
16	Florence, SC	517.4	76	North Port-Bradenton-Sarasota, FL	345.7	136	San Antonio, TX	268.4
17	Little Rock, AR	510.0	77	Rocky Mount, NC	344.7	137	Johnson City, TN	268.3
18	Farmington, NM	501.9	78	Indianapolis, IN	344.0	138	Fort Lauderdale, FL M.D.	267.7
19	Springfield, IL	500.5	79	Worcester, MA	343.4	139	Bend, OR	267.2
20	Lawton, OK	497.5	80	Brunswick, GA	339.9	140	Morristown, TN	264.8
21	Albuquerque, NM	487.2	81	Winston-Salem, NC	337.8	141	Tacoma, WA M.D.	264.3
22	Rockford, IL	470.2	82	Visalia-Porterville, CA	330.4	142	Yuma, AZ	264.0
23	Anderson, SC	468.0	83	Crestview-Fort Walton Beach, FL	330.1	143	Hanford-Corcoran, CA	263.0
24	Nashville-Davidson, TN	464.4	84	Boston-Quincy, MA M.D.	329.2	144	Palm Coast, FL	261.9
25	Battle Creek, MI	457.9	85	Houston, TX	328.7	145	Fort Worth-Arlington, TX M.D.	261.4
26	Palm Bay-Melbourne, FL	456.1	86	St. Louis, MO-IL	328.6	146	Sacramento, CA	259.9
27	Dover, DE	448.2	87	Birmingham-Hoover, AL	328.2	147	Atlantic City, NJ	258.1
28	Miami-Dade County, FL M.D.	446.8	88	Goldsboro, NC	327.8	148	Rapid City, SD	258.0
29	Tallahassee, FL	446.5	89	Fort Smith, AR-OK	326.4	149	Tucson, AZ	255.9
30	Myrtle Beach, SC	444.2	90	Charleston, WV	322.0	150	Reno-Sparks, NV	254.1
31	Gainesville, FL	441.6	90	Wilmington, DE-MD-NJ M.D.	322.0	151	Jonesboro, AR	253.4
32	Wichita, KS	438.1	92	West Palm Beach, FL M.D.	321.1	152	Napa, CA	250.6
33	Lafayette, LA	425.7	93	Clarksville, TN-KY	320.4	153	Durham-Chapel Hill, NC	249.6
34	Orlando, FL	421.4	94	Prescott, AZ	318.7	154	Boston (greater), MA-NH	249.3
35	Greenville, SC	416.8	95	Flagstaff, AZ	318.4	155	Peoria, IL	249.0
36	Champaign-Urbana, IL	415.8	96	Springfield, MO	318.3	156	Jefferson City, MO	248.8
37	Las Vegas-Paradise, NV	411.9	97	Cape Girardeau, MO-IL	315.7	157	Lansing-East Lansing, MI	245.9
38	Madera, CA	411.4	98	El Paso, TX	313.6	158	Omaha-Council Bluffs, NE-IA	245.6
39	Merced, CA	409.6	99	Modesto, CA	313.4	159	San Francisco (greater), CA	245.5
40	Salisbury, MD	400.3	99	Santa Cruz-Watsonville, CA	313.4	160	Buffalo-Niagara Falls, NY	242.1
41	Fairbanks, AK	400.1	101	Davenport, IA-IL	313.0	161	Waterloo-Cedar Falls, IA	241.9
42	Baton Rouge, LA	397.2	102	Kansas City, MO-KS	312.8	162	Hinesville, GA	239.4
43	Baltimore-Towson, MD	393.8	102	Pittsfield, MA	312.8	163	Los Angeles County, CA M.D.	239.0
44	Panama City-Lynn Haven, FL	390.3	104	Burlington, NC	312.3	164	Topeka, KS	238.8
45	Pueblo, CO	388.1	105	Knoxville, TN	312.1	165	Sebastian-Vero Beach, FL	236.6
46	Ocala, FL	387.4	106	Yuba City, CA	309.1	166	Colorado Springs, CO	235.2
47	Danville, IL	387.2	107	Lakeland, FL	302.6	167	Louisville, KY-IN	234.5
48	Hot Springs, AR	386.6	108	Tampa-St Petersburg, FL	301.2	168	Cape Coral-Fort Myers, FL	233.7
49	Rome, GA	385.3	109	New York-W. Plains NY-NJ M.D.	299.9	169	Naples-Marco Island, FL	232.6
50	Chattanooga, TN-GA	383.1	110	Lima, OH	298.8	170	Joplin, MO	232.2
51	Corpus Christi, TX	381.8	111	Philadelphia, PA M.D.	298.4	171	Sioux City, IA-NE-SD	231.8
52	Fresno, CA	381.2	112	Salinas, CA	297.9	172	Vallejo-Fairfield, CA	230.7
53	Bakersfield, CA	375.3	113	Waco, TX	297.3	173	San Diego, CA	230.4
54	Tulsa, OK	374.8	114	Las Cruces, NM	293.0	174	Ames, IA	230.0
55	Amarillo, TX	373.5	115	Tuscaloosa, AL	292.5	175	Wichita Falls, TX	229.8
56	Deltona-Daytona Beach, FL	371.4	116	New Orleans, LA	289.5	176	Carson City, NV	229.6
57	Victoria, TX	368.4	117	Columbia, MO	287.2	177	Macon, GA	228.6
58	Detroit (greater), MI	368.1	118	Dothan, AL	285.0	178	Trenton-Ewing, NJ	227.1
59	Anniston-Oxford, AL	366.8	119	Kingsport, TN-VA	284.7	179	Greeley, CO	225.5
60	Spartanburg, SC	365.8	119	Santa Fe, NM	284.7	180	New York (greater), NY-NJ-PA	224.8

Note: All listings are for Metropolitan Statistical Areas (M.S.A.s) except for those ending with "M.D." Listings with "M.D." are Metropolitan Divisions which are smaller parts of eleven large M.S.A.s. See explanatory note at beginning of metropolitan area section.

Rank Order - Metro Area (continued)

RANK	METROPOLITAN AREA	RATE
181	Port St. Lucie, FL	224.7
182	Killeen-Temple-Fort Hood, TX	223.5
183	Bremerton-Silverdale, WA	222.7
184	Columbus, GA-AL	221.9
185	Atlanta, GA	221.8
185	Phoenix-Mesa-Scottsdale, AZ	221.8
187	Chicago-Joilet-Naperville, IL M.D.	221.6
188	Valdosta, GA	221.3
189	Midland, TX	221.1
190	Cumberland, MD-WV	218.2
191	Riverside-San Bernardino, CA	217.5
192	Pascagoula, MS	217.4
193	Houma, LA	217.1
194	Ocean City, NJ	216.2
195	Medford, OR	215.2
196	Denver-Aurora, CO	214.5
197	Grand Rapids-Wyoming, MI	213.7
198	Bloomington-Normal, IL	213.4
199	Brownsville-Harlingen, TX	213.1
199	Lexington-Fayette, KY	213.1
201	Los Angeles (greater), CA	212.0
202	Milwaukee, WI	211.5
203	Manhattan, KS	209.6
204	Billings, MT	208.2
205	Lincoln, NE	208.0
205	Wilmington, NC	208.0
207	Lafayette, IN	207.6
208	Kankakee-Bradley, IL	207.4
209	Chicago (greater), IL-IN-WI	205.2
210	Sandusky, OH	204.8
211	Sherman-Denison, TX	204.2
212	McAllen-Edinburg-Mission, TX	203.4
213	Grand Junction, CO	203.0
214	Dallas (greater), TX	202.6
215	Warner Robins, GA	201.1
216	Abilene, TX	200.9
217	Des Moines-West Des Moines, IA	200.8
218	El Centro, CA	199.9
219	New Haven-Milford, CT	197.1
220	Ann Arbor, MI	195.9
221	Hagerstown-Martinsburg, MD-WV	194.7
222	Spokane, WA	193.7
223	Casper, WY	193.3
224	Camden, NJ M.D.	192.5
225	Missoula, MT	191.4
226	Punta Gorda, FL	191.2
227	San Francisco-S. Mateo, CA M.D.	191.0
228	Salt Lake City, UT	190.3
229	Seattle (greater), WA	189.2
230	Iowa City, IA	188.4
231	Pittsburgh, PA	186.9
232	Syracuse, NY	186.6
233	Great Falls, MT	186.5
234	Austin-Round Rock, TX	186.4
235	St. Joseph, MO-KS	184.6
236	San Luis Obispo, CA	184.4
237	Kennewick-Pasco-Richland, WA	184.2
238	Augusta, GA-SC	183.9
239	Yakima, WA	181.7
240	Cambridge-Newton, MA M.D.	180.3
241	Reading, PA	179.5
242	Jackson, MS	178.9
243	Scranton--Wilkes-Barre, PA	177.2
244	Pocatello, ID	176.7
244	Roanoke, VA	176.7
246	Eugene-Springfield, OR	176.1
247	Albany-Schenectady-Troy, NY	176.0
248	Fargo, ND-MN	175.7
249	Boulder, CO	175.2
250	Dalton, GA	173.5
251	Dallas-Plano-Irving, TX M.D.	172.9
252	Altoona, PA	172.6
253	Evansville, IN-KY	172.5
254	Washington, DC-VA-MD-WV M.D.	172.0
255	San Angelo, TX	169.9
256	Boise City-Nampa, ID	168.0
257	Cheyenne, WY	167.6
258	Bismarck, ND	167.2
259	Florence-Muscle Shoals, AL	167.1
260	Rochester, NY	166.7
261	Seattle-Bellevue-Everett, WA M.D.	166.6
262	Utica-Rome, NY	165.9
263	Cleveland-Elyria-Mentor, OH	165.5
264	Gary, IN M.D.	165.1
264	Olympia, WA	165.1
266	Harrisburg-Carlisle, PA	164.9
267	Virginia Beach-Norfolk, VA-NC	164.5
268	Johnstown, PA	163.7
269	Jacksonville, NC	163.3
270	Fort Collins-Loveland, CO	161.1
271	Oshkosh-Neenah, WI	161.0
272	Bay City, MI	160.6
273	York-Hanover, PA	160.2
274	Newark-Union, NJ-PA M.D.	159.8
275	Longview, WA	159.6
276	Hartford, CT	159.3
277	Savannah, GA	157.9
278	Janesville, WI	157.7
279	Kokomo, IN	157.3
280	Salem, OR	155.7
281	Manchester-Nashua, NH	155.5
282	Monroe, MI	154.7
282	Washington (greater) DC-VA-MD-WV	154.7
284	Akron, OH	154.5
285	South Bend-Mishawaka, IN-MI	152.6
286	Montgomery, AL	152.5
287	Hickory, NC	151.8
288	Decatur, AL	151.4
289	Elmira, NY	151.3
290	Idaho Falls, ID	150.9
291	Chico, CA	150.5
292	Warren-Farmington Hills, MI M.D.	150.4
293	Portland-Vancouver, OR-WA	149.3
294	San Jose, CA	146.2
295	Lake Havasu City-Kingman, AZ	145.3
296	Poughkeepsie, NY	143.9
297	Bridgeport-Stamford, CT	143.3
298	Binghamton, NY	142.8
299	Minneapolis-St. Paul, MN-WI	140.3
299	Raleigh-Cary, NC	140.3
301	Grand Forks, ND-MN	140.2
302	Asheville, NC	135.3
303	Bloomington, IN	134.2
304	Bellingham, WA	131.2
305	Madison, WI	131.0
306	Erie, PA	129.3
307	Cedar Rapids, IA	125.7
308	Sioux Falls, SD	124.7
309	La Crosse, WI-MN	124.3
310	Santa Ana-Anaheim, CA M.D.	124.1
311	Cincinnati-Middletown, OH-KY-IN	123.6
312	Kingston, NY	122.7
313	Fond du Lac, WI	122.5
314	Dayton, OH	122.2
315	Canton, OH	121.1
316	Winchester, VA-WV	120.2
317	Richmond, VA	119.5
318	Allentown, PA-NJ	118.8
319	Auburn, AL	118.5
320	Oxnard-Thousand Oaks, CA	116.8
321	Duluth, MN-WI	116.0
322	Lynchburg, VA	115.0
323	Columbus, IN	114.0
324	Springfield, OH	112.7
325	Glens Falls, NY	110.4
326	Gulfport-Biloxi, MS	108.1
327	Mount Vernon-Anacortes, WA	107.8
328	Columbus, OH	107.2
329	Fort Wayne, IN	107.1
329	St. Cloud, MN	107.1
331	Eau Claire, WI	106.9
332	Appleton, WI	106.3
333	Green Bay, WI	102.1
334	Lebanon, PA	101.5
335	Racine, WI	99.9
336	Rockingham County, NH M.D.	99.8
337	Wenatchee, WA	99.4
338	Blacksburg, VA	98.8
339	Dubuque, IA	96.7
340	Williamsport, PA	96.2
341	Sheboygan, WI	94.8
342	Holland-Grand Haven, MI	93.3
343	Charlottesville, VA	93.2
344	Ogden-Clearfield, UT	92.9
345	Lancaster, PA	92.7
346	Terre Haute, IN	92.3
347	Bethesda-Frederick, MD M.D.	91.5
348	Wausau, WI	91.3
349	Gainesville, GA	90.1
350	Lake Co.-Kenosha Co., IL-WI M.D.	89.3
351	Michigan City-La Porte, IN	85.7
352	Rochester, MN	84.8
353	Edison, NJ M.D.	84.7
354	Danville, VA	84.4
355	Nassau-Suffolk, NY M.D.	82.6
356	Bowling Green, KY	78.1
357	Mankato-North Mankato, MN	73.9
358	Harrisonburg, VA	73.4
359	Corvallis, OR	69.4
360	Portland, ME	67.3
361	Lewiston-Auburn, ME	60.4
362	State College, PA	60.2
363	Owensboro, KY	56.3
364	Mansfield, OH	51.4
365	Provo-Orem, UT	43.4
366	Logan, UT-ID	33.7
367	Bangor, ME	31.2
368	Elizabethtown, KY	26.5

Source: Reported data from the F.B.I. "Crime in the United States 2011"
*Aggravated assault is an attack for the purpose of inflicting severe bodily injury.

Alpha Order - Metro Area

23. Percent Change in Aggravated Assault Rate: 2010 to 2011
National Percent Change = 4.6% Decrease*

RANK	METROPOLITAN AREA	% CHANGE	RANK	METROPOLITAN AREA	% CHANGE	RANK	METROPOLITAN AREA	% CHANGE
320	Abilene, TX	(32.7)	NA	Charleston, WV**	NA	148	Fort Lauderdale, FL M.D.	(3.9)
107	Akron, OH	(0.3)	NA	Charlotte-Gastonia, NC-SC**	NA	93	Fort Smith, AR-OK	1.4
195	Albany-Schenectady-Troy, NY	(7.1)	317	Charlottesville, VA	(28.1)	38	Fort Wayne, IN	12.5
180	Albany, GA	(6.1)	83	Chattanooga, TN-GA	2.9	96	Fort Worth-Arlington, TX M.D.	1.0
121	Albuquerque, NM	(1.7)	12	Cheyenne, WY	29.4	71	Fresno, CA	5.0
53	Alexandria, LA	9.8	NA	Chicago (greater), IL-IN-WI**	NA	NA	Gadsden, AL**	NA
62	Allentown, PA-NJ	7.1	NA	Chicago-Joilet-Naperville, IL M.D.**	NA	131	Gainesville, FL	(2.7)
42	Altoona, PA	11.4	322	Chico, CA	(33.9)	280	Gainesville, GA	(15.4)
90	Amarillo, TX	1.5	80	Cincinnati-Middletown, OH-KY-IN	3.3	NA	Gary, IN M.D.**	NA
177	Ames, IA	(5.9)	57	Clarksville, TN-KY	8.5	90	Glens Falls, NY	1.5
177	Anchorage, AK	(5.9)	152	Cleveland-Elyria-Mentor, OH	(4.5)	251	Goldsboro, NC	(12.1)
105	Anderson, SC	(0.1)	52	Cleveland, TN	9.9	22	Grand Forks, ND-MN	17.5
255	Ann Arbor, MI	(12.5)	41	College Station-Bryan, TX	11.9	47	Grand Junction, CO	10.6
NA	Anniston-Oxford, AL**	NA	307	Colorado Springs, CO	(22.4)	272	Grand Rapids-Wyoming, MI	(14.2)
245	Appleton, WI	(11.8)	131	Columbia, MO	(2.7)	NA	Great Falls, MT**	NA
201	Asheville, NC	(7.4)	NA	Columbus, GA-AL**	NA	54	Greeley, CO	9.4
124	Athens-Clarke County, GA	(1.9)	7	Columbus, IN	46.0	97	Green Bay, WI	0.9
186	Atlanta, GA	(6.5)	98	Columbus, OH	0.8	63	Greenville, SC	7.0
101	Atlantic City, NJ	0.2	259	Corpus Christi, TX	(12.8)	18	Gulfport-Biloxi, MS	19.3
NA	Auburn, AL**	NA	222	Corvallis, OR	(9.4)	26	Hagerstown-Martinsburg, MD-WV	15.7
249	Augusta, GA-SC	(11.9)	17	Crestview-Fort Walton Beach, FL	19.9	154	Hanford-Corcoran, CA	(4.7)
264	Austin-Round Rock, TX	(13.6)	NA	Cumberland, MD-WV**	NA	39	Harrisburg-Carlisle, PA	12.4
228	Bakersfield, CA	(9.7)	135	Dallas (greater), TX	(2.9)	215	Harrisonburg, VA	(8.6)
232	Baltimore-Towson, MD	(9.9)	180	Dallas-Plano-Irving, TX M.D.	(6.1)	168	Hartford, CT	(5.4)
23	Bangor, ME	17.3	212	Dalton, GA	(8.5)	63	Hickory, NC	7.0
70	Barnstable Town, MA	5.1	137	Danville, IL	(3.1)	142	Hinesville, GA	(3.4)
NA	Baton Rouge, LA**	NA	303	Danville, VA	(20.3)	282	Holland-Grand Haven, MI	(15.7)
232	Battle Creek, MI	(9.9)	NA	Davenport, IA-IL**	NA	161	Hot Springs, AR	(5.2)
306	Bay City, MI	(21.7)	222	Dayton, OH	(9.4)	304	Houma, LA	(21.4)
25	Beaumont-Port Arthur, TX	16.8	NA	Decatur, AL**	NA	NA	Houston, TX**	NA
307	Bellingham, WA	(22.4)	111	Decatur, IL	(0.9)	NA	Huntsville, AL**	NA
43	Bend, OR	11.0	235	Deltona-Daytona Beach, FL	(10.1)	293	Idaho Falls, ID	(17.6)
165	Bethesda-Frederick, MD M.D.	(5.3)	76	Denver-Aurora, CO	4.2	NA	Indianapolis, IN**	NA
NA	Billings, MT**	NA	130	Des Moines-West Des Moines, IA	(2.6)	32	Iowa City, IA	14.3
140	Binghamton, NY	(3.3)	NA	Detroit (greater), MI**	NA	183	Jacksonville, FL	(6.2)
NA	Birmingham-Hoover, AL**	NA	171	Detroit-Livonia-Dearborn, MI M.D.	(5.5)	NA	Jacksonville, NC**	NA
165	Bismarck, ND	(5.3)	NA	Dothan, AL**	NA	23	Jackson, MS	17.3
275	Blacksburg, VA	(14.5)	34	Dover, DE	12.8	33	Jackson, TN	13.0
278	Bloomington-Normal, IL	(14.8)	326	Dubuque, IA	(73.2)	54	Janesville, WI	9.4
310	Bloomington, IN	(23.4)	195	Duluth, MN-WI	(7.1)	65	Jefferson City, MO	6.7
81	Boise City-Nampa, ID	3.2	85	Durham-Chapel Hill, NC	2.3	154	Johnson City, TN	(4.7)
237	Boston (greater), MA-NH	(10.2)	78	Eau Claire, WI	3.9	35	Johnstown, PA	12.7
241	Boston-Quincy, MA M.D.	(10.9)	126	Edison, NJ M.D.	(2.1)	277	Jonesboro, AR	(14.7)
30	Boulder, CO	14.4	319	El Centro, CA	(30.0)	296	Joplin, MO	(17.8)
16	Bowling Green, KY	20.9	240	El Paso, TX	(10.8)	NA	Kankakee-Bradley, IL**	NA
313	Bremerton-Silverdale, WA	(27.2)	327	Elizabethtown, KY	(81.7)	NA	Kansas City, MO-KS**	NA
174	Bridgeport-Stamford, CT	(5.8)	244	Elmira, NY	(11.6)	43	Kennewick-Pasco-Richland, WA	11.0
188	Brownsville-Harlingen, TX	(6.6)	212	Erie, PA	(8.5)	293	Killeen-Temple-Fort Hood, TX	(17.6)
252	Brunswick, GA	(12.2)	NA	Eugene-Springfield, OR**	NA	85	Kingsport, TN-VA	2.3
259	Buffalo-Niagara Falls, NY	(12.8)	NA	Evansville, IN-KY**	NA	318	Kingston, NY	(29.3)
138	Burlington, NC	(3.2)	302	Fairbanks, AK	(20.2)	88	Knoxville, TN	2.0
288	Cambridge-Newton, MA M.D.	(16.6)	18	Fargo, ND-MN	19.3	6	Kokomo, IN	46.7
79	Camden, NJ M.D.	3.6	195	Farmington, NM	(7.1)	51	La Crosse, WI-MN	10.0
30	Canton, OH	14.4	146	Fayetteville, NC	(3.8)	5	Lafayette, IN	52.4
228	Cape Coral-Fort Myers, FL	(9.7)	69	Flagstaff, AZ	5.2	228	Lafayette, LA	(9.7)
315	Cape Girardeau, MO-IL	(27.9)	83	Flint, MI	2.9	NA	Lake Co.-Kenosha Co., IL-WI M.D.**	NA
237	Carson City, NV	(10.2)	NA	Florence-Muscle Shoals, AL**	NA	NA	Lake Havasu City-Kingman, AZ**	NA
10	Casper, WY	38.3	77	Florence, SC	4.1	74	Lakeland, FL	4.5
72	Cedar Rapids, IA	4.8	168	Fond du Lac, WI	(5.4)	140	Lancaster, PA	(3.3)
NA	Champaign-Urbana, IL**	NA	191	Fort Collins-Loveland, CO	(6.9)	267	Lansing-East Lansing, MI	(13.8)

Note: All listings are for Metropolitan Statistical Areas (M.S.A.s) except for those ending with "M.D." Listings with "M.D." are Metropolitan Divisions which are smaller parts of eleven large M.S.A.s. See explanatory note at beginning of metropolitan area section.

Alpha Order - Metro Area (continued)

RANK	METROPOLITAN AREA	% CHANGE	RANK	METROPOLITAN AREA	% CHANGE	RANK	METROPOLITAN AREA	% CHANGE
218	Laredo, TX	(8.7)	NA	Oklahoma City, OK**	NA	121	Savannah, GA	(1.7)
73	Las Cruces, NM	4.6	203	Olympia, WA	(7.5)	27	Scranton--Wilkes-Barre, PA	15.6
263	Las Vegas-Paradise, NV	(13.5)	107	Omaha-Council Bluffs, NE-IA	(0.3)	151	Seattle (greater), WA	(4.4)
174	Lawrence, KS	(5.8)	128	Orlando, FL	(2.4)	116	Seattle-Bellevue-Everett, WA M.D.	(1.4)
297	Lawton, OK	(18.5)	NA	Oshkosh-Neenah, WI**	NA	121	Sebastian-Vero Beach, FL	(1.7)
312	Lebanon, PA	(24.2)	36	Owensboro, KY	12.6	NA	Sheboygan, WI**	NA
94	Lewiston-Auburn, ME	1.2	168	Oxnard-Thousand Oaks, CA	(5.4)	110	Sherman-Denison, TX	(0.7)
NA	Lexington-Fayette, KY**	NA	104	Palm Bay-Melbourne, FL	0.0	21	Sioux City, IA-NE-SD	18.1
14	Lima, OH	23.4	8	Palm Coast, FL	43.8	311	Sioux Falls, SD	(23.6)
323	Lincoln, NE	(34.4)	85	Panama City-Lynn Haven, FL	2.3	272	South Bend-Mishawaka, IN-MI	(14.2)
131	Little Rock, AR	(2.7)	4	Pascagoula, MS	57.2	116	Spartanburg, SC	(1.4)
191	Logan, UT-ID	(6.9)	101	Peabody, MA M.D.	0.2	143	Spokane, WA	(3.7)
283	Longview, TX	(15.8)	188	Pensacola, FL	(6.6)	285	Springfield, IL	(16.5)
165	Longview, WA	(5.3)	161	Peoria, IL	(5.2)	264	Springfield, MA	(13.6)
209	Los Angeles County, CA M.D.	(8.0)	156	Philadelphia (greater) PA-NJ-MD-DE	(4.8)	146	Springfield, MO	(3.8)
195	Los Angeles (greater), CA	(7.1)	156	Philadelphia, PA M.D.	(4.8)	321	Springfield, OH	(33.7)
40	Louisville, KY-IN	12.0	82	Phoenix-Mesa-Scottsdale, AZ	3.0	241	State College, PA	(10.9)
291	Lubbock, TX	(16.8)	124	Pine Bluff, AR	(1.9)	61	Stockton, CA	7.4
325	Lynchburg, VA	(47.6)	200	Pittsburgh, PA	(7.2)	57	St. Cloud, MN	8.5
305	Macon, GA	(21.6)	298	Pittsfield, MA	(19.2)	254	St. Joseph, MO-KS	(12.4)
11	Madera, CA	33.6	60	Pocatello, ID	7.5	128	St. Louis, MO-IL	(2.4)
188	Madison, WI	(6.6)	245	Port St. Lucie, FL	(11.8)	316	Sumter, SC	(28.0)
15	Manchester-Nashua, NH	21.3	NA	Portland-Vancouver, OR-WA**	NA	105	Syracuse, NY	(0.1)
285	Manhattan, KS	(16.5)	28	Portland, ME	14.8	228	Tacoma, WA M.D.	(9.7)
314	Mankato-North Mankato, MN	(27.6)	232	Poughkeepsie, NY	(9.9)	300	Tallahassee, FL	(19.8)
269	Mansfield, OH	(14.0)	50	Prescott, AZ	10.1	253	Tampa-St Petersburg, FL	(12.3)
172	McAllen-Edinburg-Mission, TX	(5.6)	120	Provo-Orem, UT	(1.6)	NA	Terre Haute, IN**	NA
48	Medford, OR	10.5	NA	Pueblo, CO**	NA	235	Texarkana, TX-Texarkana, AR	(10.1)
116	Memphis, TN-MS-AR	(1.4)	127	Punta Gorda, FL	(2.3)	95	Toledo, OH	1.1
174	Merced, CA	(5.8)	299	Racine, WI	(19.3)	201	Topeka, KS	(7.4)
161	Miami (greater), FL	(5.2)	160	Raleigh-Cary, NC	(5.1)	221	Trenton-Ewing, NJ	(9.3)
149	Miami-Dade County, FL M.D.	(4.3)	136	Rapid City, SD	(3.0)	116	Tucson, AZ	(1.4)
183	Michigan City-La Porte, IN	(6.2)	245	Reading, PA	(11.8)	149	Tulsa, OK	(4.3)
239	Midland, TX	(10.4)	220	Redding, CA	(9.1)	NA	Tuscaloosa, AL**	NA
215	Milwaukee, WI	(8.6)	210	Reno-Sparks, NV	(8.1)	204	Tyler, TX	(7.6)
211	Minneapolis-St. Paul, MN-WI	(8.2)	243	Richmond, VA	(11.2)	156	Utica-Rome, NY	(4.8)
NA	Missoula, MT**	NA	153	Riverside-San Bernardino, CA	(4.6)	245	Valdosta, GA	(11.8)
43	Mobile, AL	11.0	271	Roanoke, VA	(14.1)	109	Vallejo-Fairfield, CA	(0.6)
193	Modesto, CA	(7.0)	292	Rochester, MN	(17.4)	274	Victoria, TX	(14.4)
3	Monroe, LA	60.4	257	Rochester, NY	(12.7)	193	Virginia Beach-Norfolk, VA-NC	(7.0)
156	Monroe, MI	(4.8)	262	Rockford, IL	(13.1)	143	Visalia-Porterville, CA	(3.7)
NA	Montgomery, AL**	NA	57	Rockingham County, NH M.D.	8.5	309	Waco, TX	(22.9)
207	Morristown, TN	(7.9)	280	Rocky Mount, NC	(15.4)	279	Warner Robins, GA	(15.0)
249	Mount Vernon-Anacortes, WA	(11.9)	46	Rome, GA	10.7	NA	Warren-Farmington Hills, MI M.D.**	NA
1	Muncie, IN	175.9	227	Sacramento, CA	(9.6)	257	Washington (greater) DC-VA-MD-WV	(12.7)
186	Muskegon-Norton Shores, MI	(6.5)	173	Saginaw, MI	(5.7)	268	Washington, DC-VA-MD-WV M.D.	(13.9)
101	Myrtle Beach, SC	0.2	207	Salem, OR	(7.9)	293	Waterloo-Cedar Falls, IA	(17.6)
324	Napa, CA	(38.1)	212	Salinas, CA	(8.5)	131	Wausau, WI	(2.7)
99	Naples-Marco Island, FL	0.7	275	Salisbury, MD	(14.5)	111	Wenatchee, WA	(0.9)
89	Nashville-Davidson, TN	1.6	266	Salt Lake City, UT	(13.7)	215	West Palm Beach, FL M.D.	(8.6)
183	Nassau-Suffolk, NY M.D.	(6.2)	111	San Angelo, TX	(0.9)	100	Wichita Falls, TX	0.5
300	New Haven-Milford, CT	(19.8)	284	San Antonio, TX	(16.0)	115	Wichita, KS	(1.2)
90	New Orleans, LA	1.5	180	San Diego, CA	(6.1)	36	Williamsport, PA	12.6
66	New York (greater), NY-NJ-PA	5.6	161	San Francisco (greater), CA	(5.2)	256	Wilmington, DE-MD-NJ M.D.	(12.6)
56	New York-W. Plains NY-NJ M.D.	8.7	226	San Francisco-S. Mateo, CA M.D.	(9.5)	222	Wilmington, NC	(9.4)
218	Newark-Union, NJ-PA M.D.	(8.7)	222	San Jose, CA	(9.4)	9	Winchester, VA-WV	42.8
143	North Port-Bradenton-Sarasota, FL	(3.7)	204	San Luis Obispo, CA	(7.6)	66	Winston-Salem, NC	5.6
74	Norwich-New London, CT	4.5	288	Sandusky, OH	(16.6)	204	Worcester, MA	(7.6)
138	Oakland-Fremont, CA M.D.	(3.2)	114	Santa Ana-Anaheim, CA M.D.	(1.1)	179	Yakima, WA	(6.0)
195	Ocala, FL	(7.1)	285	Santa Barbara-Santa Maria, CA	(16.5)	2	York-Hanover, PA	70.4
13	Ocean City, NJ	26.7	288	Santa Cruz-Watsonville, CA	(16.6)	20	Yuba City, CA	18.2
68	Odessa, TX	5.5	49	Santa Fe, NM	10.3	269	Yuma, AZ	(14.0)
29	Ogden-Clearfield, UT	14.5	261	Santa Rosa-Petaluma, CA	(13.0)			

Source: CQ Press using reported data from the F.B.I. "Crime in the United States 2011"
*Aggravated assault is an attack for the purpose of inflicting severe bodily injury.
**Not available.

Rank Order - Metro Area
23. Percent Change in Aggravated Assault Rate: 2010 to 2011 (continued)
National Percent Change = 4.6% Decrease*

RANK	METROPOLITAN AREA	% CHANGE
1	Muncie, IN	175.9
2	York-Hanover, PA	70.4
3	Monroe, LA	60.4
4	Pascagoula, MS	57.2
5	Lafayette, IN	52.4
6	Kokomo, IN	46.7
7	Columbus, IN	46.0
8	Palm Coast, FL	43.8
9	Winchester, VA-WV	42.8
10	Casper, WY	38.3
11	Madera, CA	33.6
12	Cheyenne, WY	29.4
13	Ocean City, NJ	26.7
14	Lima, OH	23.4
15	Manchester-Nashua, NH	21.3
16	Bowling Green, KY	20.9
17	Crestview-Fort Walton Beach, FL	19.9
18	Fargo, ND-MN	19.3
18	Gulfport-Biloxi, MS	19.3
20	Yuba City, CA	18.2
21	Sioux City, IA-NE-SD	18.1
22	Grand Forks, ND-MN	17.5
23	Bangor, ME	17.3
23	Jackson, MS	17.3
25	Beaumont-Port Arthur, TX	16.8
26	Hagerstown-Martinsburg, MD-WV	15.7
27	Scranton--Wilkes-Barre, PA	15.6
28	Portland, ME	14.8
29	Ogden-Clearfield, UT	14.5
30	Boulder, CO	14.4
30	Canton, OH	14.4
32	Iowa City, IA	14.3
33	Jackson, TN	13.0
34	Dover, DE	12.8
35	Johnstown, PA	12.7
36	Owensboro, KY	12.6
36	Williamsport, PA	12.6
38	Fort Wayne, IN	12.5
39	Harrisburg-Carlisle, PA	12.4
40	Louisville, KY-IN	12.0
41	College Station-Bryan, TX	11.9
42	Altoona, PA	11.4
43	Bend, OR	11.0
43	Kennewick-Pasco-Richland, WA	11.0
43	Mobile, AL	11.0
46	Rome, GA	10.7
47	Grand Junction, CO	10.6
48	Medford, OR	10.5
49	Santa Fe, NM	10.3
50	Prescott, AZ	10.1
51	La Crosse, WI-MN	10.0
52	Cleveland, TN	9.9
53	Alexandria, LA	9.8
54	Greeley, CO	9.4
54	Janesville, WI	9.4
56	New York-W. Plains NY-NJ M.D.	8.7
57	Clarksville, TN-KY	8.5
57	Rockingham County, NH M.D.	8.5
57	St. Cloud, MN	8.5
60	Pocatello, ID	7.5

RANK	METROPOLITAN AREA	% CHANGE
61	Stockton, CA	7.4
62	Allentown, PA-NJ	7.1
63	Greenville, SC	7.0
63	Hickory, NC	7.0
65	Jefferson City, MO	6.7
66	New York (greater), NY-NJ-PA	5.6
66	Winston-Salem, NC	5.6
68	Odessa, TX	5.5
69	Flagstaff, AZ	5.2
70	Barnstable Town, MA	5.1
71	Fresno, CA	5.0
72	Cedar Rapids, IA	4.8
73	Las Cruces, NM	4.6
74	Lakeland, FL	4.5
74	Norwich-New London, CT	4.5
76	Denver-Aurora, CO	4.2
77	Florence, SC	4.1
78	Eau Claire, WI	3.9
79	Camden, NJ M.D.	3.6
80	Cincinnati-Middletown, OH-KY-IN	3.3
81	Boise City-Nampa, ID	3.2
82	Phoenix-Mesa-Scottsdale, AZ	3.0
83	Chattanooga, TN-GA	2.9
83	Flint, MI	2.9
85	Durham-Chapel Hill, NC	2.3
85	Kingsport, TN-VA	2.3
85	Panama City-Lynn Haven, FL	2.3
88	Knoxville, TN	2.0
89	Nashville-Davidson, TN	1.6
90	Amarillo, TX	1.5
90	Glens Falls, NY	1.5
90	New Orleans, LA	1.5
93	Fort Smith, AR-OK	1.4
94	Lewiston-Auburn, ME	1.2
95	Toledo, OH	1.1
96	Fort Worth-Arlington, TX M.D.	1.0
97	Green Bay, WI	0.9
98	Columbus, OH	0.8
99	Naples-Marco Island, FL	0.7
100	Wichita Falls, TX	0.5
101	Atlantic City, NJ	0.2
101	Myrtle Beach, SC	0.2
101	Peabody, MA M.D.	0.2
104	Palm Bay-Melbourne, FL	0.0
105	Anderson, SC	(0.1)
105	Syracuse, NY	(0.1)
107	Akron, OH	(0.3)
107	Omaha-Council Bluffs, NE-IA	(0.3)
109	Vallejo-Fairfield, CA	(0.6)
110	Sherman-Denison, TX	(0.7)
111	Decatur, IL	(0.9)
111	San Angelo, TX	(0.9)
111	Wenatchee, WA	(0.9)
114	Santa Ana-Anaheim, CA M.D.	(1.1)
115	Wichita, KS	(1.2)
116	Memphis, TN-MS-AR	(1.4)
116	Seattle-Bellevue-Everett, WA M.D.	(1.4)
116	Spartanburg, SC	(1.4)
116	Tucson, AZ	(1.4)
120	Provo-Orem, UT	(1.6)

RANK	METROPOLITAN AREA	% CHANGE
121	Albuquerque, NM	(1.7)
121	Savannah, GA	(1.7)
121	Sebastian-Vero Beach, FL	(1.7)
124	Athens-Clarke County, GA	(1.9)
124	Pine Bluff, AR	(1.9)
126	Edison, NJ M.D.	(2.1)
127	Punta Gorda, FL	(2.3)
128	Orlando, FL	(2.4)
128	St. Louis, MO-IL	(2.4)
130	Des Moines-West Des Moines, IA	(2.6)
131	Columbia, MO	(2.7)
131	Gainesville, FL	(2.7)
131	Little Rock, AR	(2.7)
131	Wausau, WI	(2.7)
135	Dallas (greater), TX	(2.9)
136	Rapid City, SD	(3.0)
137	Danville, IL	(3.1)
138	Burlington, NC	(3.2)
138	Oakland-Fremont, CA M.D.	(3.2)
140	Binghamton, NY	(3.3)
140	Lancaster, PA	(3.3)
142	Hinesville, GA	(3.4)
143	North Port-Bradenton-Sarasota, FL	(3.7)
143	Spokane, WA	(3.7)
143	Visalia-Porterville, CA	(3.7)
146	Fayetteville, NC	(3.8)
146	Springfield, MO	(3.8)
148	Fort Lauderdale, FL M.D.	(3.9)
149	Miami-Dade County, FL M.D.	(4.3)
149	Tulsa, OK	(4.3)
151	Seattle (greater), WA	(4.4)
152	Cleveland-Elyria-Mentor, OH	(4.5)
153	Riverside-San Bernardino, CA	(4.6)
154	Hanford-Corcoran, CA	(4.7)
154	Johnson City, TN	(4.7)
156	Monroe, MI	(4.8)
156	Philadelphia (greater) PA-NJ-MD-DE	(4.8)
156	Philadelphia, PA M.D.	(4.8)
156	Utica-Rome, NY	(4.8)
160	Raleigh-Cary, NC	(5.1)
161	Hot Springs, AR	(5.2)
161	Miami (greater), FL	(5.2)
161	Peoria, IL	(5.2)
161	San Francisco (greater), CA	(5.2)
165	Bethesda-Frederick, MD M.D.	(5.3)
165	Bismarck, ND	(5.3)
165	Longview, WA	(5.3)
168	Fond du Lac, WI	(5.4)
168	Hartford, CT	(5.4)
168	Oxnard-Thousand Oaks, CA	(5.4)
171	Detroit-Livonia-Dearborn, MI M.D.	(5.5)
172	McAllen-Edinburg-Mission, TX	(5.6)
173	Saginaw, MI	(5.7)
174	Bridgeport-Stamford, CT	(5.8)
174	Lawrence, KS	(5.8)
174	Merced, CA	(5.8)
177	Ames, IA	(5.9)
177	Anchorage, AK	(5.9)
179	Yakima, WA	(6.0)
180	Albany, GA	(6.1)

Note: All listings are for Metropolitan Statistical Areas (M.S.A.s) except for those ending with "M.D." Listings with "M.D." are Metropolitan Divisions which are smaller parts of eleven large M.S.A.s. See explanatory note at beginning of metropolitan area section.

Rank Order - Metro Area (continued)

RANK	METROPOLITAN AREA	% CHANGE
180	Dallas-Plano-Irving, TX M.D.	(6.1)
180	San Diego, CA	(6.1)
183	Jacksonville, FL	(6.2)
183	Michigan City-La Porte, IN	(6.2)
183	Nassau-Suffolk, NY M.D.	(6.2)
186	Atlanta, GA	(6.5)
186	Muskegon-Norton Shores, MI	(6.5)
188	Brownsville-Harlingen, TX	(6.6)
188	Madison, WI	(6.6)
188	Pensacola, FL	(6.6)
191	Fort Collins-Loveland, CO	(6.9)
191	Logan, UT-ID	(6.9)
193	Modesto, CA	(7.0)
193	Virginia Beach-Norfolk, VA-NC	(7.0)
195	Albany-Schenectady-Troy, NY	(7.1)
195	Duluth, MN-WI	(7.1)
195	Farmington, NM	(7.1)
195	Los Angeles (greater), CA	(7.1)
195	Ocala, FL	(7.1)
200	Pittsburgh, PA	(7.2)
201	Asheville, NC	(7.4)
201	Topeka, KS	(7.4)
203	Olympia, WA	(7.5)
204	San Luis Obispo, CA	(7.6)
204	Tyler, TX	(7.6)
204	Worcester, MA	(7.6)
207	Morristown, TN	(7.9)
207	Salem, OR	(7.9)
209	Los Angeles County, CA M.D.	(8.0)
210	Reno-Sparks, NV	(8.1)
211	Minneapolis-St. Paul, MN-WI	(8.2)
212	Dalton, GA	(8.5)
212	Erie, PA	(8.5)
212	Salinas, CA	(8.5)
215	Harrisonburg, VA	(8.6)
215	Milwaukee, WI	(8.6)
215	West Palm Beach, FL M.D.	(8.6)
218	Laredo, TX	(8.7)
218	Newark-Union, NJ-PA M.D.	(8.7)
220	Redding, CA	(9.1)
221	Trenton-Ewing, NJ	(9.3)
222	Corvallis, OR	(9.4)
222	Dayton, OH	(9.4)
222	San Jose, CA	(9.4)
222	Wilmington, NC	(9.4)
226	San Francisco-S. Mateo, CA M.D.	(9.5)
227	Sacramento, CA	(9.6)
228	Bakersfield, CA	(9.7)
228	Cape Coral-Fort Myers, FL	(9.7)
228	Lafayette, LA	(9.7)
228	Tacoma, WA M.D.	(9.7)
232	Baltimore-Towson, MD	(9.9)
232	Battle Creek, MI	(9.9)
232	Poughkeepsie, NY	(9.9)
235	Deltona-Daytona Beach, FL	(10.1)
235	Texarkana, TX-Texarkana, AR	(10.1)
237	Boston (greater), MA-NH	(10.2)
237	Carson City, NV	(10.2)
239	Midland, TX	(10.4)
240	El Paso, TX	(10.8)
241	Boston-Quincy, MA M.D.	(10.9)
241	State College, PA	(10.9)
243	Richmond, VA	(11.2)
244	Elmira, NY	(11.6)
245	Appleton, WI	(11.8)
245	Port St. Lucie, FL	(11.8)
245	Reading, PA	(11.8)
245	Valdosta, GA	(11.8)
249	Augusta, GA-SC	(11.9)
249	Mount Vernon-Anacortes, WA	(11.9)
251	Goldsboro, NC	(12.1)
252	Brunswick, GA	(12.2)
253	Tampa-St Petersburg, FL	(12.3)
254	St. Joseph, MO-KS	(12.4)
255	Ann Arbor, MI	(12.5)
256	Wilmington, DE-MD-NJ M.D.	(12.6)
257	Rochester, NY	(12.7)
257	Washington (greater) DC-VA-MD-WV	(12.7)
259	Buffalo-Niagara Falls, NY	(12.8)
259	Corpus Christi, TX	(12.8)
261	Santa Rosa-Petaluma, CA	(13.0)
262	Rockford, IL	(13.1)
263	Las Vegas-Paradise, NV	(13.5)
264	Austin-Round Rock, TX	(13.6)
264	Springfield, MA	(13.6)
266	Salt Lake City, UT	(13.7)
267	Lansing-East Lansing, MI	(13.8)
268	Washington, DC-VA-MD-WV M.D.	(13.9)
269	Mansfield, OH	(14.0)
269	Yuma, AZ	(14.0)
271	Roanoke, VA	(14.1)
272	Grand Rapids-Wyoming, MI	(14.2)
272	South Bend-Mishawaka, IN-MI	(14.2)
274	Victoria, TX	(14.4)
275	Blacksburg, VA	(14.5)
275	Salisbury, MD	(14.5)
277	Jonesboro, AR	(14.7)
278	Bloomington-Normal, IL	(14.8)
279	Warner Robins, GA	(15.0)
280	Gainesville, GA	(15.4)
280	Rocky Mount, NC	(15.4)
282	Holland-Grand Haven, MI	(15.7)
283	Longview, TX	(15.8)
284	San Antonio, TX	(16.0)
285	Manhattan, KS	(16.5)
285	Santa Barbara-Santa Maria, CA	(16.5)
285	Springfield, IL	(16.5)
288	Cambridge-Newton, MA M.D.	(16.6)
288	Sandusky, OH	(16.6)
288	Santa Cruz-Watsonville, CA	(16.6)
291	Lubbock, TX	(16.8)
292	Rochester, MN	(17.4)
293	Idaho Falls, ID	(17.6)
293	Killeen-Temple-Fort Hood, TX	(17.6)
293	Waterloo-Cedar Falls, IA	(17.6)
296	Joplin, MO	(17.8)
297	Lawton, OK	(18.5)
298	Pittsfield, MA	(19.2)
299	Racine, WI	(19.3)
300	New Haven-Milford, CT	(19.8)
300	Tallahassee, FL	(19.8)
302	Fairbanks, AK	(20.2)
303	Danville, VA	(20.3)
304	Houma, LA	(21.4)
305	Macon, GA	(21.6)
306	Bay City, MI	(21.7)
307	Bellingham, WA	(22.4)
307	Colorado Springs, CO	(22.4)
309	Waco, TX	(22.9)
310	Bloomington, IN	(23.4)
311	Sioux Falls, SD	(23.6)
312	Lebanon, PA	(24.2)
313	Bremerton-Silverdale, WA	(27.2)
314	Mankato-North Mankato, MN	(27.6)
315	Cape Girardeau, MO-IL	(27.9)
316	Sumter, SC	(28.0)
317	Charlottesville, VA	(28.1)
318	Kingston, NY	(29.3)
319	El Centro, CA	(30.0)
320	Abilene, TX	(32.7)
321	Springfield, OH	(33.7)
322	Chico, CA	(33.9)
323	Lincoln, NE	(34.4)
324	Napa, CA	(38.1)
325	Lynchburg, VA	(47.6)
326	Dubuque, IA	(73.2)
327	Elizabethtown, KY	(81.7)
NA	Anniston-Oxford, AL**	NA
NA	Auburn, AL**	NA
NA	Baton Rouge, LA**	NA
NA	Billings, MT**	NA
NA	Birmingham-Hoover, AL**	NA
NA	Champaign-Urbana, IL**	NA
NA	Charleston, WV**	NA
NA	Charlotte-Gastonia, NC-SC**	NA
NA	Chicago (greater), IL-IN-WI**	NA
NA	Chicago-Joilet-Naperville, IL M.D.**	NA
NA	Columbus, GA-AL**	NA
NA	Cumberland, MD-WV**	NA
NA	Davenport, IA-IL**	NA
NA	Decatur, AL**	NA
NA	Detroit (greater), MI**	NA
NA	Dothan, AL**	NA
NA	Eugene-Springfield, OR**	NA
NA	Evansville, IN-KY**	NA
NA	Florence-Muscle Shoals, AL**	NA
NA	Gadsden, AL**	NA
NA	Gary, IN M.D.**	NA
NA	Great Falls, MT**	NA
NA	Houston, TX**	NA
NA	Huntsville, AL**	NA
NA	Indianapolis, IN**	NA
NA	Jacksonville, NC**	NA
NA	Kankakee-Bradley, IL**	NA
NA	Kansas City, MO-KS**	NA
NA	Lake Co.-Kenosha Co., IL-WI M.D.**	NA
NA	Lake Havasu City-Kingman, AZ**	NA
NA	Lexington-Fayette, KY**	NA
NA	Missoula, MT**	NA
NA	Montgomery, AL**	NA
NA	Oklahoma City, OK**	NA
NA	Oshkosh-Neenah, WI**	NA
NA	Portland-Vancouver, OR-WA**	NA
NA	Pueblo, CO**	NA
NA	Sheboygan, WI**	NA
NA	Terre Haute, IN**	NA
NA	Tuscaloosa, AL**	NA
NA	Warren-Farmington Hills, MI M.D.**	NA

Source: CQ Press using reported data from the F.B.I. "Crime in the United States 2011"

*Aggravated assault is an attack for the purpose of inflicting severe bodily injury.

**Not available.

Alpha Order - Metro Area

24. Percent Change in Aggravated Assault Rate: 2007 to 2011
National Percent Change = 16.1% Decrease*

RANK	METROPOLITAN AREA	% CHANGE	RANK	METROPOLITAN AREA	% CHANGE	RANK	METROPOLITAN AREA	% CHANGE
272	Abilene, TX	(31.4)	65	Charleston, WV	1.9	223	Fort Lauderdale, FL M.D.	(23.3)
28	Akron, OH	19.9	285	Charlotte-Gastonia, NC-SC	(35.5)	NA	Fort Smith, AR-OK**	NA
173	Albany-Schenectady-Troy, NY	(16.3)	298	Charlottesville, VA	(39.5)	14	Fort Wayne, IN	41.9
29	Albany, GA	19.4	217	Chattanooga, TN-GA	(22.7)	143	Fort Worth-Arlington, TX M.D.	(11.6)
NA	Albuquerque, NM**	NA	18	Cheyenne, WY	33.3	23	Fresno, CA	23.9
273	Alexandria, LA	(31.5)	NA	Chicago (greater), IL-IN-WI**	NA	NA	Gadsden, AL**	NA
131	Allentown, PA-NJ	(9.5)	NA	Chicago-Joilet-Naperville, IL M.D.**	NA	294	Gainesville, FL	(37.7)
126	Altoona, PA	(8.8)	308	Chico, CA	(51.1)	301	Gainesville, GA	(40.7)
273	Amarillo, TX	(31.5)	213	Cincinnati-Middletown, OH-KY-IN	(22.4)	NA	Gary, IN M.D.**	NA
153	Ames, IA	(13.5)	236	Clarksville, TN-KY	(24.7)	192	Glens Falls, NY	(19.0)
115	Anchorage, AK	(7.8)	45	Cleveland-Elyria-Mentor, OH	9.6	67	Goldsboro, NC	1.7
149	Anderson, SC	(12.7)	175	Cleveland, TN	(16.9)	42	Grand Forks, ND-MN	12.2
120	Ann Arbor, MI	(8.2)	268	College Station-Bryan, TX	(30.5)	231	Grand Junction, CO	(24.1)
NA	Anniston-Oxford, AL**	NA	254	Colorado Springs, CO	(27.5)	188	Grand Rapids-Wyoming, MI	(18.5)
7	Appleton, WI	61.6	244	Columbia, MO	(26.4)	NA	Great Falls, MT**	NA
214	Asheville, NC	(22.5)	NA	Columbus, GA-AL**	NA	124	Greeley, CO	(8.7)
27	Athens-Clarke County, GA	20.3	2	Columbus, IN	113.1	300	Green Bay, WI	(40.6)
NA	Atlanta, GA**	NA	177	Columbus, OH	(17.2)	176	Greenville, SC	(17.1)
172	Atlantic City, NJ	(16.2)	180	Corpus Christi, TX	(17.6)	NA	Gulfport-Biloxi, MS**	NA
NA	Auburn, AL**	NA	233	Corvallis, OR	(24.6)	NA	Hagerstown-Martinsburg, MD-WV**	NA
124	Augusta, GA-SC	(8.7)	37	Crestview-Fort Walton Beach, FL	14.8	23	Hanford-Corcoran, CA	23.9
110	Austin-Round Rock, TX	(6.8)	NA	Cumberland, MD-WV**	NA	58	Harrisburg-Carlisle, PA	4.0
118	Bakersfield, CA	(7.9)	224	Dallas (greater), TX	(23.4)	281	Harrisonburg, VA	(34.6)
196	Baltimore-Towson, MD	(19.5)	269	Dallas-Plano-Irving, TX M.D.	(30.6)	32	Hartford, CT	16.3
31	Bangor, ME	16.9	299	Dalton, GA	(40.5)	186	Hickory, NC	(18.2)
44	Barnstable Town, MA	11.0	NA	Danville, IL**	NA	212	Hinesville, GA	(22.2)
206	Baton Rouge, LA	(20.9)	244	Danville, VA	(26.4)	NA	Holland-Grand Haven, MI**	NA
257	Battle Creek, MI	(27.9)	NA	Davenport, IA-IL**	NA	82	Hot Springs, AR	(2.3)
55	Bay City, MI	6.1	89	Dayton, OH	(3.3)	305	Houma, LA	(43.7)
86	Beaumont-Port Arthur, TX	(2.7)	NA	Decatur, AL**	NA	NA	Houston, TX**	NA
123	Bellingham, WA	(8.3)	NA	Decatur, IL**	NA	NA	Huntsville, AL**	NA
4	Bend, OR	82.1	115	Deltona-Daytona Beach, FL	(7.8)	277	Idaho Falls, ID	(33.3)
265	Bethesda-Frederick, MD M.D.	(29.2)	99	Denver-Aurora, CO	(4.8)	75	Indianapolis, IN	(1.4)
NA	Billings, MT**	NA	196	Des Moines-West Des Moines, IA	(19.5)	140	Iowa City, IA	(10.8)
33	Binghamton, NY	16.0	NA	Detroit (greater), MI**	NA	NA	Jacksonville, FL**	NA
NA	Birmingham-Hoover, AL**	NA	154	Detroit-Livonia-Dearborn, MI M.D.	(13.6)	292	Jacksonville, NC	(37.2)
10	Bismarck, ND	52.0	NA	Dothan, AL**	NA	39	Jackson, MS	13.4
232	Blacksburg, VA	(24.5)	101	Dover, DE	(5.0)	70	Jackson, TN	0.3
NA	Bloomington-Normal, IL**	NA	311	Dubuque, IA	(78.4)	20	Janesville, WI	31.2
166	Bloomington, IN	(14.8)	264	Duluth, MN-WI	(28.9)	104	Jefferson City, MO	(5.4)
155	Boise City-Nampa, ID	(13.8)	NA	Durham-Chapel Hill, NC**	NA	239	Johnson City, TN	(25.2)
84	Boston (greater), MA-NH	(2.4)	12	Eau Claire, WI	44.3	49	Johnstown, PA	9.0
134	Boston-Quincy, MA M.D.	(10.3)	115	Edison, NJ M.D.	(7.8)	139	Jonesboro, AR	(10.7)
NA	Boulder, CO**	NA	215	El Centro, CA	(22.6)	211	Joplin, MO	(21.7)
309	Bowling Green, KY	(61.4)	45	El Paso, TX	9.6	NA	Kankakee-Bradley, IL**	NA
254	Bremerton-Silverdale, WA	(27.5)	NA	Elizabethtown, KY**	NA	NA	Kansas City, MO-KS**	NA
130	Bridgeport-Stamford, CT	(9.4)	250	Elmira, NY	(26.8)	39	Kennewick-Pasco-Richland, WA	13.4
262	Brownsville-Harlingen, TX	(28.8)	75	Erie, PA	(1.4)	134	Killeen-Temple-Fort Hood, TX	(10.3)
307	Brunswick, GA	(44.4)	155	Eugene-Springfield, OR	(13.8)	87	Kingsport, TN-VA	(2.8)
95	Buffalo-Niagara Falls, NY	(4.4)	56	Evansville, IN-KY	5.8	282	Kingston, NY	(35.1)
82	Burlington, NC	(2.3)	NA	Fairbanks, AK**	NA	152	Knoxville, TN	(13.4)
36	Cambridge-Newton, MA M.D.	15.5	11	Fargo, ND-MN	45.4	159	Kokomo, IN	(13.9)
63	Camden, NJ M.D.	2.3	41	Farmington, NM	12.6	92	La Crosse, WI-MN	(3.9)
NA	Canton, OH**	NA	267	Fayetteville, NC	(30.3)	21	Lafayette, IN	24.2
283	Cape Coral-Fort Myers, FL	(35.2)	88	Flagstaff, AZ	(3.0)	244	Lafayette, LA	(26.4)
NA	Cape Girardeau, MO-IL**	NA	95	Flint, MI	(4.4)	NA	Lake Co.-Kenosha Co., IL-WI M.D.**	NA
261	Carson City, NV	(28.5)	NA	Florence-Muscle Shoals, AL**	NA	278	Lake Havasu City-Kingman, AZ	(33.4)
49	Casper, WY	9.0	295	Florence, SC	(38.4)	179	Lakeland, FL	(17.3)
233	Cedar Rapids, IA	(24.6)	210	Fond du Lac, WI	(21.6)	113	Lancaster, PA	(7.2)
NA	Champaign-Urbana, IL**	NA	92	Fort Collins-Loveland, CO	(3.9)	183	Lansing-East Lansing, MI	(18.0)

Note: All listings are for Metropolitan Statistical Areas (M.S.A.s) except for those ending with "M.D." Listings with "M.D." are Metropolitan Divisions which are smaller parts of eleven large M.S.A.s. See explanatory note at beginning of metropolitan area section.

Alpha Order - Metro Area (continued)

RANK	METROPOLITAN AREA	% CHANGE
106	Laredo, TX	(6.0)
133	Las Cruces, NM	(10.2)
174	Las Vegas-Paradise, NV	(16.8)
114	Lawrence, KS	(7.4)
279	Lawton, OK	(33.5)
291	Lebanon, PA	(36.9)
78	Lewiston-Auburn, ME	(1.9)
NA	Lexington-Fayette, KY**	NA
15	Lima, OH	39.0
306	Lincoln, NE	(43.8)
105	Little Rock, AR	(5.8)
262	Logan, UT-ID	(28.8)
271	Longview, TX	(31.2)
47	Longview, WA	9.5
252	Los Angeles County, CA M.D.	(27.1)
243	Los Angeles (greater), CA	(26.2)
51	Louisville, KY-IN	8.9
183	Lubbock, TX	(18.0)
240	Lynchburg, VA	(25.4)
109	Macon, GA	(6.5)
60	Madera, CA	3.4
72	Madison, WI	(0.9)
NA	Manchester-Nashua, NH**	NA
NA	Manhattan, KS**	NA
NA	Mankato-North Mankato, MN**	NA
289	Mansfield, OH	(36.3)
168	McAllen-Edinburg-Mission, TX	(14.9)
38	Medford, OR	14.6
134	Memphis, TN-MS-AR	(10.3)
129	Merced, CA	(9.3)
225	Miami (greater), FL	(23.5)
220	Miami-Dade County, FL M.D.	(22.9)
30	Michigan City-La Porte, IN	18.4
79	Midland, TX	(2.2)
276	Milwaukee, WI	(33.2)
248	Minneapolis-St. Paul, MN-WI	(26.7)
NA	Missoula, MT**	NA
3	Mobile, AL	103.8
248	Modesto, CA	(26.7)
6	Monroe, LA	63.3
22	Monroe, MI	24.1
NA	Montgomery, AL**	NA
204	Morristown, TN	(20.8)
52	Mount Vernon-Anacortes, WA	8.3
13	Muncie, IN	42.6
200	Muskegon-Norton Shores, MI	(19.9)
288	Myrtle Beach, SC	(35.9)
79	Napa, CA	(2.2)
259	Naples-Marco Island, FL	(28.3)
194	Nashville-Davidson, TN	(19.1)
162	Nassau-Suffolk, NY M.D.	(14.5)
NA	New Haven-Milford, CT**	NA
303	New Orleans, LA	(42.1)
64	New York (greater), NY-NJ-PA	2.2
57	New York-W. Plains NY-NJ M.D.	5.6
120	Newark-Union, NJ-PA M.D.	(8.2)
NA	North Port-Bradenton-Sarasota, FL**	NA
NA	Norwich-New London, CT**	NA
170	Oakland-Fremont, CA M.D.	(15.2)
254	Ocala, FL	(27.5)
99	Ocean City, NJ	(4.8)
8	Odessa, TX	56.8
190	Ogden-Clearfield, UT	(18.8)

RANK	METROPOLITAN AREA	% CHANGE
43	Oklahoma City, OK	11.1
34	Olympia, WA	15.9
91	Omaha-Council Bluffs, NE-IA	(3.5)
204	Orlando, FL	(20.8)
165	Oshkosh-Neenah, WI	(14.7)
NA	Owensboro, KY**	NA
186	Oxnard-Thousand Oaks, CA	(18.2)
155	Palm Bay-Melbourne, FL	(13.8)
48	Palm Coast, FL	9.3
127	Panama City-Lynn Haven, FL	(9.0)
1	Pascagoula, MS	114.8
79	Peabody, MA M.D.	(2.2)
209	Pensacola, FL	(21.5)
NA	Peoria, IL**	NA
159	Philadelphia (greater) PA-NJ-MD-DE	(13.9)
166	Philadelphia, PA M.D.	(14.8)
195	Phoenix-Mesa-Scottsdale, AZ	(19.4)
161	Pine Bluff, AR	(14.0)
168	Pittsburgh, PA	(14.9)
71	Pittsfield, MA	(0.4)
68	Pocatello, ID	1.4
302	Port St. Lucie, FL	(41.0)
150	Portland-Vancouver, OR-WA	(12.8)
62	Portland, ME	2.4
203	Poughkeepsie, NY	(20.5)
101	Prescott, AZ	(5.0)
120	Provo-Orem, UT	(8.2)
NA	Pueblo, CO**	NA
304	Punta Gorda, FL	(43.3)
148	Racine, WI	(12.2)
241	Raleigh-Cary, NC	(25.6)
26	Rapid City, SD	21.6
59	Reading, PA	3.5
5	Redding, CA	80.8
196	Reno-Sparks, NV	(19.5)
258	Richmond, VA	(28.0)
227	Riverside-San Bernardino, CA	(23.7)
280	Roanoke, VA	(34.4)
191	Rochester, MN	(18.9)
101	Rochester, NY	(5.0)
NA	Rockford, IL**	NA
17	Rockingham County, NH M.D.	33.8
66	Rocky Mount, NC	1.8
34	Rome, GA	15.9
181	Sacramento, CA	(17.8)
233	Saginaw, MI	(24.6)
230	Salem, OR	(24.0)
151	Salinas, CA	(13.2)
237	Salisbury, MD	(24.9)
162	Salt Lake City, UT	(14.5)
286	San Angelo, TX	(35.6)
74	San Antonio, TX	(1.2)
201	San Diego, CA	(20.2)
182	San Francisco (greater), CA	(17.9)
215	San Francisco-S. Mateo, CA M.D.	(22.6)
269	San Jose, CA	(30.6)
275	San Luis Obispo, CA	(31.7)
171	Sandusky, OH	(15.4)
189	Santa Ana-Anaheim, CA M.D.	(18.7)
89	Santa Barbara-Santa Maria, CA	(3.3)
145	Santa Cruz-Watsonville, CA	(11.9)
NA	Santa Fe, NM**	NA
192	Santa Rosa-Petaluma, CA	(19.0)

RANK	METROPOLITAN AREA	% CHANGE
290	Savannah, GA	(36.7)
107	Scranton--Wilkes-Barre, PA	(6.1)
141	Seattle (greater), WA	(11.5)
95	Seattle-Bellevue-Everett, WA M.D.	(4.4)
94	Sebastian-Vero Beach, FL	(4.2)
16	Sheboygan, WI	35.0
60	Sherman-Denison, TX	3.4
98	Sioux City, IA-NE-SD	(4.7)
108	Sioux Falls, SD	(6.2)
146	South Bend-Mishawaka, IN-MI	(12.1)
260	Spartanburg, SC	(28.4)
284	Spokane, WA	(35.4)
NA	Springfield, IL**	NA
144	Springfield, MA	(11.7)
132	Springfield, MO	(9.8)
177	Springfield, OH	(17.2)
73	State College, PA	(1.1)
77	Stockton, CA	(1.7)
111	St. Cloud, MN	(7.0)
134	St. Joseph, MO-KS	(10.3)
111	St. Louis, MO-IL	(7.0)
310	Sumter, SC	(71.6)
118	Syracuse, NY	(7.9)
217	Tacoma, WA M.D.	(22.7)
219	Tallahassee, FL	(22.8)
293	Tampa-St Petersburg, FL	(37.3)
NA	Terre Haute, IN**	NA
207	Texarkana, TX-Texarkana, AR	(21.0)
241	Toledo, OH	(25.6)
69	Topeka, KS	0.4
53	Trenton-Ewing, NJ	7.9
155	Tucson, AZ	(13.8)
199	Tulsa, OK	(19.6)
NA	Tuscaloosa, AL**	NA
266	Tyler, TX	(29.6)
221	Utica-Rome, NY	(23.2)
238	Valdosta, GA	(25.1)
297	Vallejo-Fairfield, CA	(39.0)
19	Victoria, TX	32.9
229	Virginia Beach-Norfolk, VA-NC	(23.9)
138	Visalia-Porterville, CA	(10.4)
287	Waco, TX	(35.8)
228	Warner Robins, GA	(23.8)
NA	Warren-Farmington Hills, MI M.D.**	NA
250	Washington (greater) DC-VA-MD-WV	(26.8)
247	Washington, DC-VA-MD-WV M.D.	(26.5)
221	Waterloo-Cedar Falls, IA	(23.2)
296	Wausau, WI	(38.6)
185	Wenatchee, WA	(18.1)
253	West Palm Beach, FL M.D.	(27.4)
128	Wichita Falls, TX	(9.2)
162	Wichita, KS	(14.5)
9	Williamsport, PA	52.2
226	Wilmington, DE-MD-NJ M.D.	(23.6)
141	Wilmington, NC	(11.5)
84	Winchester, VA-WV	(2.4)
NA	Winston-Salem, NC**	NA
25	Worcester, MA	22.3
202	Yakima, WA	(20.3)
53	York-Hanover, PA	7.9
146	Yuba City, CA	(12.1)
208	Yuma, AZ	(21.1)

Source: CQ Press using reported data from the F.B.I. "Crime in the United States 2011"
*Aggravated assault is an attack for the purpose of inflicting severe bodily injury.
**Not available.

Rank Order - Metro Area

24. Percent Change in Aggravated Assault Rate: 2007 to 2011 (continued)
National Percent Change = 16.1% Decrease*

RANK	METROPOLITAN AREA	% CHANGE	RANK	METROPOLITAN AREA	% CHANGE	RANK	METROPOLITAN AREA	% CHANGE
1	Pascagoula, MS	114.8	60	Sherman-Denison, TX	3.4	120	Newark-Union, NJ-PA M.D.	(8.2)
2	Columbus, IN	113.1	62	Portland, ME	2.4	120	Provo-Orem, UT	(8.2)
3	Mobile, AL	103.8	63	Camden, NJ M.D.	2.3	123	Bellingham, WA	(8.3)
4	Bend, OR	82.1	64	New York (greater), NY-NJ-PA	2.2	124	Augusta, GA-SC	(8.7)
5	Redding, CA	80.8	65	Charleston, WV	1.9	124	Greeley, CO	(8.7)
6	Monroe, LA	63.3	66	Rocky Mount, NC	1.8	126	Altoona, PA	(8.8)
7	Appleton, WI	61.6	67	Goldsboro, NC	1.7	127	Panama City-Lynn Haven, FL	(9.0)
8	Odessa, TX	56.8	68	Pocatello, ID	1.4	128	Wichita Falls, TX	(9.2)
9	Williamsport, PA	52.2	69	Topeka, KS	0.4	129	Merced, CA	(9.3)
10	Bismarck, ND	52.0	70	Jackson, TN	0.3	130	Bridgeport-Stamford, CT	(9.4)
11	Fargo, ND-MN	45.4	71	Pittsfield, MA	(0.4)	131	Allentown, PA-NJ	(9.5)
12	Eau Claire, WI	44.3	72	Madison, WI	(0.9)	132	Springfield, MO	(9.8)
13	Muncie, IN	42.6	73	State College, PA	(1.1)	133	Las Cruces, NM	(10.2)
14	Fort Wayne, IN	41.9	74	San Antonio, TX	(1.2)	134	Boston-Quincy, MA M.D.	(10.3)
15	Lima, OH	39.0	75	Erie, PA	(1.4)	134	Killeen-Temple-Fort Hood, TX	(10.3)
16	Sheboygan, WI	35.0	75	Indianapolis, IN	(1.4)	134	Memphis, TN-MS-AR	(10.3)
17	Rockingham County, NH M.D.	33.8	77	Stockton, CA	(1.7)	134	St. Joseph, MO-KS	(10.3)
18	Cheyenne, WY	33.3	78	Lewiston-Auburn, ME	(1.9)	138	Visalia-Porterville, CA	(10.4)
19	Victoria, TX	32.9	79	Midland, TX	(2.2)	139	Jonesboro, AR	(10.7)
20	Janesville, WI	31.2	79	Napa, CA	(2.2)	140	Iowa City, IA	(10.8)
21	Lafayette, IN	24.2	79	Peabody, MA M.D.	(2.2)	141	Seattle (greater), WA	(11.5)
22	Monroe, MI	24.1	82	Burlington, NC	(2.3)	141	Wilmington, NC	(11.5)
23	Fresno, CA	23.9	82	Hot Springs, AR	(2.3)	143	Fort Worth-Arlington, TX M.D.	(11.6)
23	Hanford-Corcoran, CA	23.9	84	Boston (greater), MA-NH	(2.4)	144	Springfield, MA	(11.7)
25	Worcester, MA	22.3	84	Winchester, VA-WV	(2.4)	145	Santa Cruz-Watsonville, CA	(11.9)
26	Rapid City, SD	21.6	86	Beaumont-Port Arthur, TX	(2.7)	146	South Bend-Mishawaka, IN-MI	(12.1)
27	Athens-Clarke County, GA	20.3	87	Kingsport, TN-VA	(2.8)	146	Yuba City, CA	(12.1)
28	Akron, OH	19.9	88	Flagstaff, AZ	(3.0)	148	Racine, WI	(12.2)
29	Albany, GA	19.4	89	Dayton, OH	(3.3)	149	Anderson, SC	(12.7)
30	Michigan City-La Porte, IN	18.4	89	Santa Barbara-Santa Maria, CA	(3.3)	150	Portland-Vancouver, OR-WA	(12.8)
31	Bangor, ME	16.9	91	Omaha-Council Bluffs, NE-IA	(3.5)	151	Salinas, CA	(13.2)
32	Hartford, CT	16.3	92	Fort Collins-Loveland, CO	(3.9)	152	Knoxville, TN	(13.4)
33	Binghamton, NY	16.0	92	La Crosse, WI-MN	(3.9)	153	Ames, IA	(13.5)
34	Olympia, WA	15.9	94	Sebastian-Vero Beach, FL	(4.2)	154	Detroit-Livonia-Dearborn, MI M.D.	(13.6)
34	Rome, GA	15.9	95	Buffalo-Niagara Falls, NY	(4.4)	155	Boise City-Nampa, ID	(13.8)
36	Cambridge-Newton, MA M.D.	15.5	95	Flint, MI	(4.4)	155	Eugene-Springfield, OR	(13.8)
37	Crestview-Fort Walton Beach, FL	14.8	95	Seattle-Bellevue-Everett, WA M.D.	(4.4)	155	Palm Bay-Melbourne, FL	(13.8)
38	Medford, OR	14.6	98	Sioux City, IA-NE-SD	(4.7)	155	Tucson, AZ	(13.8)
39	Jackson, MS	13.4	99	Denver-Aurora, CO	(4.8)	159	Kokomo, IN	(13.9)
39	Kennewick-Pasco-Richland, WA	13.4	99	Ocean City, NJ	(4.8)	159	Philadelphia (greater) PA-NJ-MD-DE	(13.9)
41	Farmington, NM	12.6	101	Dover, DE	(5.0)	161	Pine Bluff, AR	(14.0)
42	Grand Forks, ND-MN	12.2	101	Prescott, AZ	(5.0)	162	Nassau-Suffolk, NY M.D.	(14.5)
43	Oklahoma City, OK	11.1	101	Rochester, NY	(5.0)	162	Salt Lake City, UT	(14.5)
44	Barnstable Town, MA	11.0	104	Jefferson City, MO	(5.4)	162	Wichita, KS	(14.5)
45	Cleveland-Elyria-Mentor, OH	9.6	105	Little Rock, AR	(5.8)	165	Oshkosh-Neenah, WI	(14.7)
45	El Paso, TX	9.6	106	Laredo, TX	(6.0)	166	Bloomington, IN	(14.8)
47	Longview, WA	9.5	107	Scranton--Wilkes-Barre, PA	(6.1)	166	Philadelphia, PA M.D.	(14.8)
48	Palm Coast, FL	9.3	108	Sioux Falls, SD	(6.2)	168	McAllen-Edinburg-Mission, TX	(14.9)
49	Casper, WY	9.0	109	Macon, GA	(6.5)	168	Pittsburgh, PA	(14.9)
49	Johnstown, PA	9.0	110	Austin-Round Rock, TX	(6.8)	170	Oakland-Fremont, CA M.D.	(15.2)
51	Louisville, KY-IN	8.9	111	St. Cloud, MN	(7.0)	171	Sandusky, OH	(15.4)
52	Mount Vernon-Anacortes, WA	8.3	111	St. Louis, MO-IL	(7.0)	172	Atlantic City, NJ	(16.2)
53	Trenton-Ewing, NJ	7.9	113	Lancaster, PA	(7.2)	173	Albany-Schenectady-Troy, NY	(16.3)
53	York-Hanover, PA	7.9	114	Lawrence, KS	(7.4)	174	Las Vegas-Paradise, NV	(16.8)
55	Bay City, MI	6.1	115	Anchorage, AK	(7.8)	175	Cleveland, TN	(16.9)
56	Evansville, IN-KY	5.8	115	Deltona-Daytona Beach, FL	(7.8)	176	Greenville, SC	(17.1)
57	New York-W. Plains NY-NJ M.D.	5.6	115	Edison, NJ M.D.	(7.8)	177	Columbus, OH	(17.2)
58	Harrisburg-Carlisle, PA	4.0	118	Bakersfield, CA	(7.9)	177	Springfield, OH	(17.2)
59	Reading, PA	3.5	118	Syracuse, NY	(7.9)	179	Lakeland, FL	(17.3)
60	Madera, CA	3.4	120	Ann Arbor, MI	(8.2)	180	Corpus Christi, TX	(17.6)

Note: All listings are for Metropolitan Statistical Areas (M.S.A.s) except for those ending with "M.D." Listings with "M.D." are Metropolitan Divisions which are smaller parts of eleven large M.S.A.s. See explanatory note at beginning of metropolitan area section.

Rank Order - Metro Area (continued)

RANK	METROPOLITAN AREA	% CHANGE	RANK	METROPOLITAN AREA	% CHANGE	RANK	METROPOLITAN AREA	% CHANGE
181	Sacramento, CA	(17.8)	244	Columbia, MO	(26.4)	307	Brunswick, GA	(44.4)
182	San Francisco (greater), CA	(17.9)	244	Danville, VA	(26.4)	308	Chico, CA	(51.1)
183	Lansing-East Lansing, MI	(18.0)	244	Lafayette, LA	(26.4)	309	Bowling Green, KY	(61.4)
183	Lubbock, TX	(18.0)	247	Washington, DC-VA-MD-WV M.D.	(26.5)	310	Sumter, SC	(71.6)
185	Wenatchee, WA	(18.1)	248	Minneapolis-St. Paul, MN-WI	(26.7)	311	Dubuque, IA	(78.4)
186	Hickory, NC	(18.2)	248	Modesto, CA	(26.7)	NA	Albuquerque, NM**	NA
186	Oxnard-Thousand Oaks, CA	(18.2)	250	Elmira, NY	(26.8)	NA	Anniston-Oxford, AL**	NA
188	Grand Rapids-Wyoming, MI	(18.5)	250	Washington (greater) DC-VA-MD-WV	(26.8)	NA	Atlanta, GA**	NA
189	Santa Ana-Anaheim, CA M.D.	(18.7)	252	Los Angeles County, CA M.D.	(27.1)	NA	Auburn, AL**	NA
190	Ogden-Clearfield, UT	(18.8)	253	West Palm Beach, FL M.D.	(27.4)	NA	Billings, MT**	NA
191	Rochester, MN	(18.9)	254	Bremerton-Silverdale, WA	(27.5)	NA	Birmingham-Hoover, AL**	NA
192	Glens Falls, NY	(19.0)	254	Colorado Springs, CO	(27.5)	NA	Bloomington-Normal, IL**	NA
192	Santa Rosa-Petaluma, CA	(19.0)	254	Ocala, FL	(27.5)	NA	Boulder, CO**	NA
194	Nashville-Davidson, TN	(19.1)	257	Battle Creek, MI	(27.9)	NA	Canton, OH**	NA
195	Phoenix-Mesa-Scottsdale, AZ	(19.4)	258	Richmond, VA	(28.0)	NA	Cape Girardeau, MO-IL**	NA
196	Baltimore-Towson, MD	(19.5)	259	Naples-Marco Island, FL	(28.3)	NA	Champaign-Urbana, IL**	NA
196	Des Moines-West Des Moines, IA	(19.5)	260	Spartanburg, SC	(28.4)	NA	Chicago (greater), IL-IN-WI**	NA
196	Reno-Sparks, NV	(19.5)	261	Carson City, NV	(28.5)	NA	Chicago-Joilet-Naperville, IL M.D.**	NA
199	Tulsa, OK	(19.6)	262	Brownsville-Harlingen, TX	(28.8)	NA	Columbus, GA-AL**	NA
200	Muskegon-Norton Shores, MI	(19.9)	262	Logan, UT-ID	(28.8)	NA	Cumberland, MD-WV**	NA
201	San Diego, CA	(20.2)	264	Duluth, MN-WI	(28.9)	NA	Danville, IL**	NA
202	Yakima, WA	(20.3)	265	Bethesda-Frederick, MD M.D.	(29.2)	NA	Davenport, IA-IL**	NA
203	Poughkeepsie, NY	(20.5)	266	Tyler, TX	(29.6)	NA	Decatur, AL**	NA
204	Morristown, TN	(20.8)	267	Fayetteville, NC	(30.3)	NA	Decatur, IL**	NA
204	Orlando, FL	(20.8)	268	College Station-Bryan, TX	(30.5)	NA	Detroit (greater), MI**	NA
206	Baton Rouge, LA	(20.9)	269	Dallas-Plano-Irving, TX M.D.	(30.6)	NA	Dothan, AL**	NA
207	Texarkana, TX-Texarkana, AR	(21.0)	269	San Jose, CA	(30.6)	NA	Durham-Chapel Hill, NC**	NA
208	Yuma, AZ	(21.1)	271	Longview, TX	(31.2)	NA	Elizabethtown, KY**	NA
209	Pensacola, FL	(21.5)	272	Abilene, TX	(31.4)	NA	Fairbanks, AK**	NA
210	Fond du Lac, WI	(21.6)	273	Alexandria, LA	(31.5)	NA	Florence-Muscle Shoals, AL**	NA
211	Joplin, MO	(21.7)	273	Amarillo, TX	(31.5)	NA	Fort Smith, AR-OK**	NA
212	Hinesville, GA	(22.2)	275	San Luis Obispo, CA	(31.7)	NA	Gadsden, AL**	NA
213	Cincinnati-Middletown, OH-KY-IN	(22.4)	276	Milwaukee, WI	(33.2)	NA	Gary, IN M.D.**	NA
214	Asheville, NC	(22.5)	277	Idaho Falls, ID	(33.3)	NA	Great Falls, MT**	NA
215	El Centro, CA	(22.6)	278	Lake Havasu City-Kingman, AZ	(33.4)	NA	Gulfport-Biloxi, MS**	NA
215	San Francisco-S. Mateo, CA M.D.	(22.6)	279	Lawton, OK	(33.5)	NA	Hagerstown-Martinsburg, MD-WV**	NA
217	Chattanooga, TN-GA	(22.7)	280	Roanoke, VA	(34.4)	NA	Holland-Grand Haven, MI**	NA
217	Tacoma, WA M.D.	(22.7)	281	Harrisonburg, VA	(34.6)	NA	Houston, TX**	NA
219	Tallahassee, FL	(22.8)	282	Kingston, NY	(35.1)	NA	Huntsville, AL**	NA
220	Miami-Dade County, FL M.D.	(22.9)	283	Cape Coral-Fort Myers, FL	(35.2)	NA	Jacksonville, FL**	NA
221	Utica-Rome, NY	(23.2)	284	Spokane, WA	(35.4)	NA	Kankakee-Bradley, IL**	NA
221	Waterloo-Cedar Falls, IA	(23.2)	285	Charlotte-Gastonia, NC-SC	(35.5)	NA	Kansas City, MO-KS**	NA
223	Fort Lauderdale, FL M.D.	(23.3)	286	San Angelo, TX	(35.6)	NA	Lake Co.-Kenosha Co., IL-WI M.D.**	NA
224	Dallas (greater), TX	(23.4)	287	Waco, TX	(35.8)	NA	Lexington-Fayette, KY**	NA
225	Miami (greater), FL	(23.5)	288	Myrtle Beach, SC	(35.9)	NA	Manchester-Nashua, NH**	NA
226	Wilmington, DE-MD-NJ M.D.	(23.6)	289	Mansfield, OH	(36.3)	NA	Manhattan, KS**	NA
227	Riverside-San Bernardino, CA	(23.7)	290	Savannah, GA	(36.7)	NA	Mankato-North Mankato, MN**	NA
228	Warner Robins, GA	(23.8)	291	Lebanon, PA	(36.9)	NA	Missoula, MT**	NA
229	Virginia Beach-Norfolk, VA-NC	(23.9)	292	Jacksonville, NC	(37.2)	NA	Montgomery, AL**	NA
230	Salem, OR	(24.0)	293	Tampa-St Petersburg, FL	(37.3)	NA	New Haven-Milford, CT**	NA
231	Grand Junction, CO	(24.1)	294	Gainesville, FL	(37.7)	NA	North Port-Bradenton-Sarasota, FL**	NA
232	Blacksburg, VA	(24.5)	295	Florence, SC	(38.4)	NA	Norwich-New London, CT**	NA
233	Cedar Rapids, IA	(24.6)	296	Wausau, WI	(38.6)	NA	Owensboro, KY**	NA
233	Corvallis, OR	(24.6)	297	Vallejo-Fairfield, CA	(39.0)	NA	Peoria, IL**	NA
233	Saginaw, MI	(24.6)	298	Charlottesville, VA	(39.5)	NA	Pueblo, CO**	NA
236	Clarksville, TN-KY	(24.7)	299	Dalton, GA	(40.5)	NA	Rockford, IL**	NA
237	Salisbury, MD	(24.9)	300	Green Bay, WI	(40.6)	NA	Santa Fe, NM**	NA
238	Valdosta, GA	(25.1)	301	Gainesville, GA	(40.7)	NA	Springfield, IL**	NA
239	Johnson City, TN	(25.2)	302	Port St. Lucie, FL	(41.0)	NA	Terre Haute, IN**	NA
240	Lynchburg, VA	(25.4)	303	New Orleans, LA	(42.1)	NA	Tuscaloosa, AL**	NA
241	Raleigh-Cary, NC	(25.6)	304	Punta Gorda, FL	(43.3)	NA	Warren-Farmington Hills, MI M.D.**	NA
241	Toledo, OH	(25.6)	305	Houma, LA	(43.7)	NA	Winston-Salem, NC**	NA
243	Los Angeles (greater), CA	(26.2)	306	Lincoln, NE	(43.8)			

Source: CQ Press using reported data from the F.B.I. "Crime in the United States 2011"

*Aggravated assault is an attack for the purpose of inflicting severe bodily injury.

**Not available.

Alpha Order - Metro Area

25. Property Crimes in 2011
National Total = 9,063,173 Property Crimes*

RANK	METROPOLITAN AREA	CRIMES
257	Abilene, TX	5,112
92	Akron, OH	23,158
95	Albany-Schenectady-Troy, NY	21,818
208	Albany, GA	6,958
68	Albuquerque, NM	36,335
212	Alexandria, LA	6,795
109	Allentown, PA-NJ	18,765
346	Altoona, PA	2,529
165	Amarillo, TX	10,315
352	Ames, IA	2,351
166	Anchorage, AK	10,268
173	Anderson, SC	9,699
193	Ann Arbor, MI	7,935
258	Anniston-Oxford, AL	5,089
299	Appleton, WI	3,839
156	Asheville, NC	10,898
202	Athens-Clarke County, GA	7,269
10	Atlanta, GA	189,614
176	Atlantic City, NJ	9,392
273	Auburn, AL	4,587
90	Augusta, GA-SC	24,543
46	Austin-Round Rock, TX	60,429
76	Bakersfield, CA	30,071
28	Baltimore-Towson, MD	83,249
283	Bangor, ME	4,316
225	Barnstable Town, MA	6,051
72	Baton Rouge, LA	32,994
253	Battle Creek, MI	5,227
357	Bay City, MI	2,113
125	Beaumont-Port Arthur, TX	15,375
220	Bellingham, WA	6,395
262	Bend, OR	4,914
94	Bethesda-Frederick, MD M.D.	22,508
238	Billings, MT	5,521
215	Binghamton, NY	6,648
57	Birmingham-Hoover, AL	46,401
340	Bismarck, ND	2,700
286	Blacksburg, VA	4,137
305	Bloomington-Normal, IL	3,697
244	Bloomington, IN	5,378
141	Boise City-Nampa, ID	12,681
24	Boston (greater), MA-NH	96,552
63	Boston-Quincy, MA M.D.	44,643
217	Boulder, CO	6,465
316	Bowling Green, KY	3,380
198	Bremerton-Silverdale, WA	7,477
118	Bridgeport-Stamford, CT	17,390
119	Brownsville-Harlingen, TX	17,055
251	Brunswick, GA	5,269
69	Buffalo-Niagara Falls, NY	33,597
227	Burlington, NC	6,003
82	Cambridge-Newton, MA M.D.	27,064
70	Camden, NJ M.D.	33,497
144	Canton, OH	12,522
117	Cape Coral-Fort Myers, FL	17,498
307	Cape Girardeau, MO-IL	3,563
366	Carson City, NV	1,275
348	Casper, WY	2,438
221	Cedar Rapids, IA	6,332
233	Champaign-Urbana, IL	5,812

RANK	METROPOLITAN AREA	CRIMES
184	Charleston, WV	8,970
44	Charlotte-Gastonia, NC-SC	61,156
287	Charlottesville, VA	4,082
102	Chattanooga, TN-GA	19,799
344	Cheyenne, WY	2,559
3	Chicago (greater), IL-IN-WI	264,951
7	Chicago-Joilet-Naperville, IL M.D.	222,513
246	Chico, CA	5,375
34	Cincinnati-Middletown, OH-KY-IN	74,691
194	Clarksville, TN-KY	7,851
42	Cleveland-Elyria-Mentor, OH	61,589
308	Cleveland, TN	3,555
199	College Station-Bryan, TX	7,463
107	Colorado Springs, CO	19,159
237	Columbia, MO	5,570
124	Columbus, GA-AL	15,752
322	Columbus, IN	3,213
32	Columbus, OH	76,800
110	Corpus Christi, TX	18,593
355	Corvallis, OR	2,229
252	Crestview-Fort Walton Beach, FL	5,251
328	Cumberland, MD-WV	3,023
6	Dallas (greater), TX	227,610
13	Dallas-Plano-Irving, TX M.D.	146,720
284	Dalton, GA	4,286
319	Danville, IL	3,309
336	Danville, VA	2,800
152	Davenport, IA-IL	11,228
80	Dayton, OH	28,957
295	Decatur, AL	3,952
317	Decatur, IL	3,374
111	Deltona-Daytona Beach, FL	18,295
36	Denver-Aurora, CO	70,741
114	Des Moines-West Des Moines, IA	17,711
17	Detroit (greater), MI	123,574
33	Detroit-Livonia-Dearborn, MI M.D.	74,812
281	Dothan, AL	4,399
228	Dover, DE	5,992
360	Dubuque, IA	1,911
177	Duluth, MN-WI	9,228
105	Durham-Chapel Hill, NC	19,386
314	Eau Claire, WI	3,410
61	Edison, NJ M.D.	45,227
231	El Centro, CA	5,899
104	El Paso, TX	19,492
361	Elizabethtown, KY	1,875
358	Elmira, NY	2,101
197	Erie, PA	7,580
142	Eugene-Springfield, OR	12,639
170	Evansville, IN-KY	9,933
364	Fairbanks, AK	1,396
282	Fargo, ND-MN	4,390
338	Farmington, NM	2,758
97	Fayetteville, NC	20,252
274	Flagstaff, AZ	4,585
120	Flint, MI	16,535
306	Florence-Muscle Shoals, AL	3,681
164	Florence, SC	10,357
363	Fond du Lac, WI	1,625
196	Fort Collins-Loveland, CO	7,666

RANK	METROPOLITAN AREA	CRIMES
35	Fort Lauderdale, FL M.D.	70,949
187	Fort Smith, AR-OK	8,423
151	Fort Wayne, IN	11,612
30	Fort Worth-Arlington, TX M.D.	80,890
64	Fresno, CA	40,767
271	Gadsden, AL	4,624
178	Gainesville, FL	9,204
277	Gainesville, GA	4,505
86	Gary, IN M.D.	24,767
356	Glens Falls, NY	2,135
255	Goldsboro, NC	5,186
354	Grand Forks, ND-MN	2,280
288	Grand Junction, CO	4,062
113	Grand Rapids-Wyoming, MI	17,875
330	Great Falls, MT	2,947
243	Greeley, CO	5,401
240	Green Bay, WI	5,464
91	Greenville, SC	23,542
169	Gulfport-Biloxi, MS	10,007
229	Hagerstown-Martinsburg, MD-WV	5,978
310	Hanford-Corcoran, CA	3,436
145	Harrisburg-Carlisle, PA	12,111
362	Harrisonburg, VA	1,663
85	Hartford, CT	24,976
139	Hickory, NC	12,944
345	Hinesville, GA	2,552
264	Holland-Grand Haven, MI	4,842
248	Hot Springs, AR	5,309
207	Houma, LA	6,968
8	Houston, TX	217,186
130	Huntsville, AL	14,721
339	Idaho Falls, ID	2,718
39	Indianapolis, IN	66,511
335	Iowa City, IA	2,810
53	Jacksonville, FL	50,233
242	Jacksonville, NC	5,420
103	Jackson, MS	19,594
267	Jackson, TN	4,723
263	Janesville, WI	4,877
303	Jefferson City, MO	3,720
224	Johnson City, TN	6,065
329	Johnstown, PA	2,971
266	Jonesboro, AR	4,795
216	Joplin, MO	6,483
320	Kankakee-Bradley, IL	3,291
38	Kansas City, MO-KS	69,682
211	Kennewick-Pasco-Richland, WA	6,798
150	Killeen-Temple-Fort Hood, TX	11,663
167	Kingsport, TN-VA	10,219
311	Kingston, NY	3,435
83	Knoxville, TN	26,908
313	Kokomo, IN	3,417
326	La Crosse, WI-MN	3,113
248	Lafayette, IN	5,309
159	Lafayette, LA	10,781
115	Lake Co.-Kenosha Co., IL-WI M.D.	17,671
218	Lake Havasu City-Kingman, AZ	6,463
99	Lakeland, FL	20,106
161	Lancaster, PA	10,586
153	Lansing-East Lansing, MI	11,083

Note: All listings are for Metropolitan Statistical Areas (M.S.A.s) except for those ending with "M.D." Listings with "M.D." are Metropolitan Divisions which are smaller parts of eleven large M.S.A.s. See explanatory note at beginning of metropolitan area section.

Alpha Order - Metro Area (continued)

RANK	METROPOLITAN AREA	CRIMES
158	Laredo, TX	10,851
210	Las Cruces, NM	6,800
49	Las Vegas-Paradise, NV	53,676
278	Lawrence, KS	4,488
232	Lawton, OK	5,890
349	Lebanon, PA	2,421
325	Lewiston-Auburn, ME	3,181
108	Lexington-Fayette, KY	19,120
291	Lima, OH	3,981
155	Lincoln, NE	10,926
67	Little Rock, AR	36,551
365	Logan, UT-ID	1,356
201	Longview, TX	7,366
311	Longview, WA	3,435
5	Los Angeles County, CA M.D.	228,136
2	Los Angeles (greater), CA	289,794
54	Louisville, KY-IN	48,790
134	Lubbock, TX	13,652
256	Lynchburg, VA	5,178
138	Macon, GA	12,988
301	Madera, CA	3,805
129	Madison, WI	14,773
175	Manchester-Nashua, NH	9,416
343	Manhattan, KS	2,561
334	Mankato-North Mankato, MN	2,825
241	Mansfield, OH	5,462
75	McAllen-Edinburg-Mission, TX	31,295
209	Medford, OR	6,891
45	Memphis, TN-MS-AR	60,532
179	Merced, CA	9,132
4	Miami (greater), FL	236,524
19	Miami-Dade County, FL M.D.	119,789
289	Michigan City-La Porte, IN	4,044
300	Midland, TX	3,816
52	Milwaukee, WI	51,249
25	Minneapolis-St. Paul, MN-WI	94,005
333	Missoula, MT	2,861
101	Mobile, AL	19,948
106	Modesto, CA	19,187
190	Monroe, LA	8,059
298	Monroe, MI	3,852
125	Montgomery, AL	15,375
269	Morristown, TN	4,704
250	Mount Vernon-Anacortes, WA	5,293
318	Muncie, IN	3,352
205	Muskegon-Norton Shores, MI	7,092
128	Myrtle Beach, SC	15,229
337	Napa, CA	2,799
223	Naples-Marco Island, FL	6,077
50	Nashville-Davidson, TN	53,243
58	Nassau-Suffolk, NY M.D.	45,975
88	New Haven-Milford, CT	24,656
65	New Orleans, LA	39,982
1	New York (greater), NY-NJ-PA	330,926
9	New York-W. Plains NY-NJ M.D.	195,039
62	Newark-Union, NJ-PA M.D.	44,685
84	North Port-Bradenton-Sarasota, FL	25,997
321	Norwich-New London, CT	3,260
29	Oakland-Fremont, CA M.D.	82,633
188	Ocala, FL	8,381
276	Ocean City, NJ	4,544
285	Odessa, TX	4,238
131	Ogden-Clearfield, UT	14,294
48	Oklahoma City, OK	54,100
204	Olympia, WA	7,123
78	Omaha-Council Bluffs, NE-IA	29,276
31	Orlando, FL	79,243
323	Oshkosh-Neenah, WI	3,195
327	Owensboro, KY	3,050
132	Oxnard-Thousand Oaks, CA	14,169
112	Palm Bay-Melbourne, FL	18,155
359	Palm Coast, FL	2,064
200	Panama City-Lynn Haven, FL	7,424
247	Pascagoula, MS	5,358
123	Peabody, MA M.D.	15,786
121	Pensacola, FL	16,320
160	Peoria, IL	10,660
11	Philadelphia (greater) PA-NJ-MD-DE	164,536
21	Philadelphia, PA M.D.	108,364
12	Phoenix-Mesa-Scottsdale, AZ	155,482
259	Pine Bluff, AR	5,059
60	Pittsburgh, PA	45,480
324	Pittsfield, MA	3,183
341	Pocatello, ID	2,611
147	Port St. Lucie, FL	12,063
37	Portland-Vancouver, OR-WA	70,657
136	Portland, ME	13,262
137	Poughkeepsie, NY	13,115
270	Prescott, AZ	4,627
149	Provo-Orem, UT	11,834
203	Pueblo, CO	7,136
290	Punta Gorda, FL	4,037
236	Racine, WI	5,652
77	Raleigh-Cary, NC	29,712
304	Rapid City, SD	3,713
183	Reading, PA	8,987
261	Redding, CA	4,954
162	Reno-Sparks, NV	10,452
73	Richmond, VA	31,776
18	Riverside-San Bernardino, CA	120,476
192	Roanoke, VA	7,975
315	Rochester, MN	3,382
81	Rochester, NY	27,384
157	Rockford, IL	10,868
181	Rockingham County, NH M.D.	9,059
226	Rocky Mount, NC	6,022
302	Rome, GA	3,724
43	Sacramento, CA	61,437
260	Saginaw, MI	4,982
154	Salem, OR	11,001
172	Salinas, CA	9,893
292	Salisbury, MD	3,966
56	Salt Lake City, UT	47,286
294	San Angelo, TX	3,958
22	San Antonio, TX	102,108
40	San Diego, CA	65,102
14	San Francisco (greater), CA	135,104
51	San Francisco-S. Mateo, CA M.D.	52,471
66	San Jose, CA	39,884
222	San Luis Obispo, CA	6,196
353	Sandusky, OH	2,329
41	Santa Ana-Anaheim, CA M.D.	61,658
180	Santa Barbara-Santa Maria, CA	9,083
185	Santa Cruz-Watsonville, CA	8,744
244	Santa Fe, NM	5,378
189	Santa Rosa-Petaluma, CA	8,307
140	Savannah, GA	12,773
142	Scranton--Wilkes-Barre, PA	12,639
16	Seattle (greater), WA	132,146
23	Seattle-Bellevue-Everett, WA M.D.	100,812
293	Sebastian-Vero Beach, FL	3,959
351	Sheboygan, WI	2,393
296	Sherman-Denison, TX	3,905
280	Sioux City, IA-NE-SD	4,410
239	Sioux Falls, SD	5,513
148	South Bend-Mishawaka, IN-MI	11,866
168	Spartanburg, SC	10,201
89	Spokane, WA	24,591
182	Springfield, IL	9,045
98	Springfield, MA	20,210
99	Springfield, MO	20,106
234	Springfield, OH	5,755
347	State College, PA	2,470
79	Stockton, CA	29,142
272	St. Cloud, MN	4,611
265	St. Joseph, MO-KS	4,826
26	St. Louis, MO-IL	88,365
297	Sumter, SC	3,866
122	Syracuse, NY	15,860
74	Tacoma, WA M.D.	31,334
133	Tallahassee, FL	13,737
27	Tampa-St Petersburg, FL	87,498
214	Terre Haute, IN	6,697
219	Texarkana, TX-Texarkana, AR	6,428
NA	Toledo, OH**	NA
171	Topeka, KS	9,911
191	Trenton-Ewing, NJ	8,010
NA	Tucson, AZ**	NA
71	Tulsa, OK	33,176
195	Tuscaloosa, AL	7,791
206	Tyler, TX	6,995
213	Utica-Rome, NY	6,710
279	Valdosta, GA	4,415
146	Vallejo-Fairfield, CA	12,087
275	Victoria, TX	4,548
47	Virginia Beach-Norfolk, VA-NC	56,010
127	Visalia-Porterville, CA	15,334
174	Waco, TX	9,548
230	Warner Robins, GA	5,947
55	Warren-Farmington Hills, MI M.D.	48,762
15	Washington (greater) DC-VA-MD-WV	134,852
20	Washington, DC-VA-MD-WV M.D.	112,344
309	Waterloo-Cedar Falls, IA	3,447
350	Wausau, WI	2,415
331	Wenatchee, WA	2,932
59	West Palm Beach, FL M.D.	45,786
235	Wichita Falls, TX	5,681
87	Wichita, KS	24,709
342	Williamsport, PA	2,565
93	Wilmington, DE-MD-NJ M.D.	22,675
135	Wilmington, NC	13,480
331	Winchester, VA-WV	2,932
96	Winston-Salem, NC	21,438
116	Worcester, MA	17,516
163	Yakima, WA	10,418
186	York-Hanover, PA	8,717
268	Yuba City, CA	4,716
254	Yuma, AZ	5,222

Source: Reported data from the F.B.I. "Crime in the United States 2011"
*Property crimes are offenses of burglary, larceny-theft, and motor vehicle theft. Attempts are included.
**Not available.

Rank Order - Metro Area

25. Property Crimes in 2011 (continued)
National Total = 9,063,173 Property Crimes*

RANK	METROPOLITAN AREA	CRIMES	RANK	METROPOLITAN AREA	CRIMES	RANK	METROPOLITAN AREA	CRIMES
1	New York (greater), NY-NJ-PA	330,926	61	Edison, NJ M.D.	45,227	121	Pensacola, FL	16,320
2	Los Angeles (greater), CA	289,794	62	Newark-Union, NJ-PA M.D.	44,685	122	Syracuse, NY	15,860
3	Chicago (greater), IL-IN-WI	264,951	63	Boston-Quincy, MA M.D.	44,643	123	Peabody, MA M.D.	15,786
4	Miami (greater), FL	236,524	64	Fresno, CA	40,767	124	Columbus, GA-AL	15,752
5	Los Angeles County, CA M.D.	228,136	65	New Orleans, LA	39,982	125	Beaumont-Port Arthur, TX	15,375
6	Dallas (greater), TX	227,610	66	San Jose, CA	39,884	125	Montgomery, AL	15,375
7	Chicago-Joilet-Naperville, IL M.D.	222,513	67	Little Rock, AR	36,551	127	Visalia-Porterville, CA	15,334
8	Houston, TX	217,186	68	Albuquerque, NM	36,335	128	Myrtle Beach, SC	15,229
9	New York-W. Plains NY-NJ M.D.	195,039	69	Buffalo-Niagara Falls, NY	33,597	129	Madison, WI	14,773
10	Atlanta, GA	189,614	70	Camden, NJ M.D.	33,497	130	Huntsville, AL	14,721
11	Philadelphia (greater) PA-NJ-MD-DE	164,536	71	Tulsa, OK	33,176	131	Ogden-Clearfield, UT	14,294
12	Phoenix-Mesa-Scottsdale, AZ	155,482	72	Baton Rouge, LA	32,994	132	Oxnard-Thousand Oaks, CA	14,169
13	Dallas-Plano-Irving, TX M.D.	146,720	73	Richmond, VA	31,776	133	Tallahassee, FL	13,737
14	San Francisco (greater), CA	135,104	74	Tacoma, WA M.D.	31,334	134	Lubbock, TX	13,652
15	Washington (greater) DC-VA-MD-WV	134,852	75	McAllen-Edinburg-Mission, TX	31,295	135	Wilmington, NC	13,480
16	Seattle (greater), WA	132,146	76	Bakersfield, CA	30,071	136	Portland, ME	13,262
17	Detroit (greater), MI	123,574	77	Raleigh-Cary, NC	29,712	137	Poughkeepsie, NY	13,115
18	Riverside-San Bernardino, CA	120,476	78	Omaha-Council Bluffs, NE-IA	29,276	138	Macon, GA	12,988
19	Miami-Dade County, FL M.D.	119,789	79	Stockton, CA	29,142	139	Hickory, NC	12,944
20	Washington, DC-VA-MD-WV M.D.	112,344	80	Dayton, OH	28,957	140	Savannah, GA	12,773
21	Philadelphia, PA M.D.	108,364	81	Rochester, NY	27,384	141	Boise City-Nampa, ID	12,681
22	San Antonio, TX	102,108	82	Cambridge-Newton, MA M.D.	27,064	142	Eugene-Springfield, OR	12,639
23	Seattle-Bellevue-Everett, WA M.D.	100,812	83	Knoxville, TN	26,908	142	Scranton--Wilkes-Barre, PA	12,639
24	Boston (greater), MA-NH	96,552	84	North Port-Bradenton-Sarasota, FL	25,997	144	Canton, OH	12,522
25	Minneapolis-St. Paul, MN-WI	94,005	85	Hartford, CT	24,976	145	Harrisburg-Carlisle, PA	12,111
26	St. Louis, MO-IL	88,365	86	Gary, IN M.D.	24,767	146	Vallejo-Fairfield, CA	12,087
27	Tampa-St Petersburg, FL	87,498	87	Wichita, KS	24,709	147	Port St. Lucie, FL	12,063
28	Baltimore-Towson, MD	83,249	88	New Haven-Milford, CT	24,656	148	South Bend-Mishawaka, IN-MI	11,866
29	Oakland-Fremont, CA M.D.	82,633	89	Spokane, WA	24,591	149	Provo-Orem, UT	11,834
30	Fort Worth-Arlington, TX M.D.	80,890	90	Augusta, GA-SC	24,543	150	Killeen-Temple-Fort Hood, TX	11,663
31	Orlando, FL	79,243	91	Greenville, SC	23,542	151	Fort Wayne, IN	11,612
32	Columbus, OH	76,800	92	Akron, OH	23,158	152	Davenport, IA-IL	11,228
33	Detroit-Livonia-Dearborn, MI M.D.	74,812	93	Wilmington, DE-MD-NJ M.D.	22,675	153	Lansing-East Lansing, MI	11,083
34	Cincinnati-Middletown, OH-KY-IN	74,691	94	Bethesda-Frederick, MD M.D.	22,508	154	Salem, OR	11,001
35	Fort Lauderdale, FL M.D.	70,949	95	Albany-Schenectady-Troy, NY	21,818	155	Lincoln, NE	10,926
36	Denver-Aurora, CO	70,741	96	Winston-Salem, NC	21,438	156	Asheville, NC	10,898
37	Portland-Vancouver, OR-WA	70,657	97	Fayetteville, NC	20,252	157	Rockford, IL	10,868
38	Kansas City, MO-KS	69,682	98	Springfield, MA	20,210	158	Laredo, TX	10,851
39	Indianapolis, IN	66,511	99	Lakeland, FL	20,106	159	Lafayette, LA	10,781
40	San Diego, CA	65,102	99	Springfield, MO	20,106	160	Peoria, IL	10,660
41	Santa Ana-Anaheim, CA M.D.	61,658	101	Mobile, AL	19,948	161	Lancaster, PA	10,586
42	Cleveland-Elyria-Mentor, OH	61,589	102	Chattanooga, TN-GA	19,799	162	Reno-Sparks, NV	10,452
43	Sacramento, CA	61,437	103	Jackson, MS	19,594	163	Yakima, WA	10,418
44	Charlotte-Gastonia, NC-SC	61,156	104	El Paso, TX	19,492	164	Florence, SC	10,357
45	Memphis, TN-MS-AR	60,532	105	Durham-Chapel Hill, NC	19,386	165	Amarillo, TX	10,315
46	Austin-Round Rock, TX	60,429	106	Modesto, CA	19,187	166	Anchorage, AK	10,268
47	Virginia Beach-Norfolk, VA-NC	56,010	107	Colorado Springs, CO	19,159	167	Kingsport, TN-VA	10,219
48	Oklahoma City, OK	54,100	108	Lexington-Fayette, KY	19,120	168	Spartanburg, SC	10,201
49	Las Vegas-Paradise, NV	53,676	109	Allentown, PA-NJ	18,765	169	Gulfport-Biloxi, MS	10,007
50	Nashville-Davidson, TN	53,243	110	Corpus Christi, TX	18,593	170	Evansville, IN-KY	9,933
51	San Francisco-S. Mateo, CA M.D.	52,471	111	Deltona-Daytona Beach, FL	18,295	171	Topeka, KS	9,911
52	Milwaukee, WI	51,249	112	Palm Bay-Melbourne, FL	18,155	172	Salinas, CA	9,893
53	Jacksonville, FL	50,233	113	Grand Rapids-Wyoming, MI	17,875	173	Anderson, SC	9,699
54	Louisville, KY-IN	48,790	114	Des Moines-West Des Moines, IA	17,711	174	Waco, TX	9,548
55	Warren-Farmington Hills, MI M.D.	48,762	115	Lake Co.-Kenosha Co., IL-WI M.D.	17,671	175	Manchester-Nashua, NH	9,416
56	Salt Lake City, UT	47,286	116	Worcester, MA	17,516	176	Atlantic City, NJ	9,392
57	Birmingham-Hoover, AL	46,401	117	Cape Coral-Fort Myers, FL	17,498	177	Duluth, MN-WI	9,228
58	Nassau-Suffolk, NY M.D.	45,975	118	Bridgeport-Stamford, CT	17,390	178	Gainesville, FL	9,204
59	West Palm Beach, FL M.D.	45,786	119	Brownsville-Harlingen, TX	17,055	179	Merced, CA	9,132
60	Pittsburgh, PA	45,480	120	Flint, MI	16,535	180	Santa Barbara-Santa Maria, CA	9,083

Note: All listings are for Metropolitan Statistical Areas (M.S.A.s) except for those ending with "M.D." Listings with "M.D." are Metropolitan Divisions which are smaller parts of eleven large M.S.A.s. See explanatory note at beginning of metropolitan area section.

Rank Order - Metro Area (continued)

RANK	METROPOLITAN AREA	CRIMES	RANK	METROPOLITAN AREA	CRIMES	RANK	METROPOLITAN AREA	CRIMES
181	Rockingham County, NH M.D.	9,059	244	Bloomington, IN	5,378	307	Cape Girardeau, MO-IL	3,563
182	Springfield, IL	9,045	244	Santa Fe, NM	5,378	308	Cleveland, TN	3,555
183	Reading, PA	8,987	246	Chico, CA	5,375	309	Waterloo-Cedar Falls, IA	3,447
184	Charleston, WV	8,970	247	Pascagoula, MS	5,358	310	Hanford-Corcoran, CA	3,436
185	Santa Cruz-Watsonville, CA	8,744	248	Hot Springs, AR	5,309	311	Kingston, NY	3,435
186	York-Hanover, PA	8,717	248	Lafayette, IN	5,309	311	Longview, WA	3,435
187	Fort Smith, AR-OK	8,423	250	Mount Vernon-Anacortes, WA	5,293	313	Kokomo, IN	3,417
188	Ocala, FL	8,381	251	Brunswick, GA	5,269	314	Eau Claire, WI	3,410
189	Santa Rosa-Petaluma, CA	8,307	252	Crestview-Fort Walton Beach, FL	5,251	315	Rochester, MN	3,382
190	Monroe, LA	8,059	253	Battle Creek, MI	5,227	316	Bowling Green, KY	3,380
191	Trenton-Ewing, NJ	8,010	254	Yuma, AZ	5,222	317	Decatur, IL	3,374
192	Roanoke, VA	7,975	255	Goldsboro, NC	5,186	318	Muncie, IN	3,352
193	Ann Arbor, MI	7,935	256	Lynchburg, VA	5,178	319	Danville, IL	3,309
194	Clarksville, TN-KY	7,851	257	Abilene, TX	5,112	320	Kankakee-Bradley, IL	3,291
195	Tuscaloosa, AL	7,791	258	Anniston-Oxford, AL	5,089	321	Norwich-New London, CT	3,260
196	Fort Collins-Loveland, CO	7,666	259	Pine Bluff, AR	5,059	322	Columbus, IN	3,213
197	Erie, PA	7,580	260	Saginaw, MI	4,982	323	Oshkosh-Neenah, WI	3,195
198	Bremerton-Silverdale, WA	7,477	261	Redding, CA	4,954	324	Pittsfield, MA	3,183
199	College Station-Bryan, TX	7,463	262	Bend, OR	4,914	325	Lewiston-Auburn, ME	3,181
200	Panama City-Lynn Haven, FL	7,424	263	Janesville, WI	4,877	326	La Crosse, WI-MN	3,113
201	Longview, TX	7,366	264	Holland-Grand Haven, MI	4,842	327	Owensboro, KY	3,050
202	Athens-Clarke County, GA	7,269	265	St. Joseph, MO-KS	4,826	328	Cumberland, MD-WV	3,023
203	Pueblo, CO	7,136	266	Jonesboro, AR	4,795	329	Johnstown, PA	2,971
204	Olympia, WA	7,123	267	Jackson, TN	4,723	330	Great Falls, MT	2,947
205	Muskegon-Norton Shores, MI	7,092	268	Yuba City, CA	4,716	331	Wenatchee, WA	2,932
206	Tyler, TX	6,995	269	Morristown, TN	4,704	331	Winchester, VA-WV	2,932
207	Houma, LA	6,968	270	Prescott, AZ	4,627	333	Missoula, MT	2,861
208	Albany, GA	6,958	271	Gadsden, AL	4,624	334	Mankato-North Mankato, MN	2,825
209	Medford, OR	6,891	272	St. Cloud, MN	4,611	335	Iowa City, IA	2,810
210	Las Cruces, NM	6,800	273	Auburn, AL	4,587	336	Danville, VA	2,800
211	Kennewick-Pasco-Richland, WA	6,798	274	Flagstaff, AZ	4,585	337	Napa, CA	2,799
212	Alexandria, LA	6,795	275	Victoria, TX	4,548	338	Farmington, NM	2,758
213	Utica-Rome, NY	6,710	276	Ocean City, NJ	4,544	339	Idaho Falls, ID	2,718
214	Terre Haute, IN	6,697	277	Gainesville, GA	4,505	340	Bismarck, ND	2,700
215	Binghamton, NY	6,648	278	Lawrence, KS	4,488	341	Pocatello, ID	2,611
216	Joplin, MO	6,483	279	Valdosta, GA	4,415	342	Williamsport, PA	2,565
217	Boulder, CO	6,465	280	Sioux City, IA-NE-SD	4,410	343	Manhattan, KS	2,561
218	Lake Havasu City-Kingman, AZ	6,463	281	Dothan, AL	4,399	344	Cheyenne, WY	2,559
219	Texarkana, TX-Texarkana, AR	6,428	282	Fargo, ND-MN	4,390	345	Hinesville, GA	2,552
220	Bellingham, WA	6,395	283	Bangor, ME	4,316	346	Altoona, PA	2,529
221	Cedar Rapids, IA	6,332	284	Dalton, GA	4,286	347	State College, PA	2,470
222	San Luis Obispo, CA	6,196	285	Odessa, TX	4,238	348	Casper, WY	2,438
223	Naples-Marco Island, FL	6,077	286	Blacksburg, VA	4,137	349	Lebanon, PA	2,421
224	Johnson City, TN	6,065	287	Charlottesville, VA	4,082	350	Wausau, WI	2,415
225	Barnstable Town, MA	6,051	288	Grand Junction, CO	4,062	351	Sheboygan, WI	2,393
226	Rocky Mount, NC	6,022	289	Michigan City-La Porte, IN	4,044	352	Ames, IA	2,351
227	Burlington, NC	6,003	290	Punta Gorda, FL	4,037	353	Sandusky, OH	2,329
228	Dover, DE	5,992	291	Lima, OH	3,981	354	Grand Forks, ND-MN	2,280
229	Hagerstown-Martinsburg, MD-WV	5,978	292	Salisbury, MD	3,966	355	Corvallis, OR	2,229
230	Warner Robins, GA	5,947	293	Sebastian-Vero Beach, FL	3,959	356	Glens Falls, NY	2,135
231	El Centro, CA	5,899	294	San Angelo, TX	3,958	357	Bay City, MI	2,113
232	Lawton, OK	5,890	295	Decatur, AL	3,952	358	Elmira, NY	2,101
233	Champaign-Urbana, IL	5,812	296	Sherman-Denison, TX	3,905	359	Palm Coast, FL	2,064
234	Springfield, OH	5,755	297	Sumter, SC	3,866	360	Dubuque, IA	1,911
235	Wichita Falls, TX	5,681	298	Monroe, MI	3,852	361	Elizabethtown, KY	1,875
236	Racine, WI	5,652	299	Appleton, WI	3,839	362	Harrisonburg, VA	1,663
237	Columbia, MO	5,570	300	Midland, TX	3,816	363	Fond du Lac, WI	1,625
238	Billings, MT	5,521	301	Madera, CA	3,805	364	Fairbanks, AK	1,396
239	Sioux Falls, SD	5,513	302	Rome, GA	3,724	365	Logan, UT-ID	1,356
240	Green Bay, WI	5,464	303	Jefferson City, MO	3,720	366	Carson City, NV	1,275
241	Mansfield, OH	5,462	304	Rapid City, SD	3,713	NA	Toledo, OH**	NA
242	Jacksonville, NC	5,420	305	Bloomington-Normal, IL	3,697	NA	Tucson, AZ**	NA
243	Greeley, CO	5,401	306	Florence-Muscle Shoals, AL	3,681			

Source: Reported data from the F.B.I. "Crime in the United States 2011"
*Property crimes are offenses of burglary, larceny-theft, and motor vehicle theft. Attempts are included.
**Not available.

Alpha Order - Metro Area

26. Property Crime Rate in 2011
National Rate = 2,908.7 Property Crimes per 100,000 Population*

RANK	METROPOLITAN AREA	RATE	RANK	METROPOLITAN AREA	RATE	RANK	METROPOLITAN AREA	RATE
181	Abilene, TX	3,029.7	193	Charleston, WV	2,944.1	61	Fort Lauderdale, FL M.D.	4,004.1
149	Akron, OH	3,290.8	128	Charlotte-Gastonia, NC-SC	3,435.5	218	Fort Smith, AR-OK	2,797.0
264	Albany-Schenectady-Troy, NY	2,494.5	335	Charlottesville, VA	2,001.3	226	Fort Wayne, IN	2,775.4
28	Albany, GA	4,365.7	85	Chattanooga, TN-GA	3,711.0	86	Fort Worth-Arlington, TX M.D.	3,708.9
55	Albuquerque, NM	4,050.7	227	Cheyenne, WY	2,767.3	31	Fresno, CA	4,330.5
27	Alexandria, LA	4,374.6	220	Chicago (greater), IL-IN-WI	2,791.5	25	Gadsden, AL	4,406.6
293	Allentown, PA-NJ	2,277.8	214	Chicago-Joilet-Naperville, IL M.D.	2,814.2	127	Gainesville, FL	3,435.9
337	Altoona, PA	1,983.6	276	Chico, CA	2,414.8	269	Gainesville, GA	2,474.6
56	Amarillo, TX	4,042.9	118	Cincinnati-Middletown, OH-KY-IN	3,498.9	121	Gary, IN M.D.	3,480.0
244	Ames, IA	2,611.9	208	Clarksville, TN-KY	2,842.2	360	Glens Falls, NY	1,648.6
145	Anchorage, AK	3,302.0	189	Cleveland-Elyria-Mentor, OH	2,962.8	43	Goldsboro, NC	4,176.3
8	Anderson, SC	5,123.5	177	Cleveland, TN	3,042.8	292	Grand Forks, ND-MN	2,283.8
289	Ann Arbor, MI	2,303.1	160	College Station-Bryan, TX	3,196.5	234	Grand Junction, CO	2,721.1
34	Anniston-Oxford, AL	4,271.3	196	Colorado Springs, CO	2,916.7	288	Grand Rapids-Wyoming, MI	2,310.7
358	Appleton, WI	1,693.8	158	Columbia, MO	3,212.0	105	Great Falls, MT	3,591.8
258	Asheville, NC	2,533.0	5	Columbus, GA-AL	5,280.5	318	Greeley, CO	2,099.7
84	Athens-Clarke County, GA	3,726.2	44	Columbus, IN	4,162.7	354	Green Bay, WI	1,776.5
111	Atlanta, GA	3,552.0	42	Columbus, OH	4,178.7	99	Greenville, SC	3,653.3
132	Atlantic City, NJ	3,409.5	35	Corpus Christi, TX	4,252.8	60	Gulfport-Biloxi, MS	4,006.6
155	Auburn, AL	3,255.0	252	Corvallis, OR	2,577.2	301	Hagerstown-Martinsburg, MD-WV	2,208.4
29	Augusta, GA-SC	4,352.2	205	Crestview-Fort Walton Beach, FL	2,864.9	300	Hanford-Corcoran, CA	2,219.9
124	Austin-Round Rock, TX	3,448.3	197	Cumberland, MD-WV	2,905.4	304	Harrisburg-Carlisle, PA	2,197.1
113	Bakersfield, CA	3,539.8	119	Dallas (greater), TX	3,498.5	365	Harrisonburg, VA	1,312.3
179	Baltimore-Towson, MD	3,042.5	135	Dallas-Plano-Irving, TX M.D.	3,392.5	271	Hartford, CT	2,443.4
216	Bangor, ME	2,804.4	188	Dalton, GA	2,974.3	120	Hickory, NC	3,497.1
222	Barnstable Town, MA	2,785.9	57	Danville, IL	4,041.7	156	Hinesville, GA	3,232.8
53	Baton Rouge, LA	4,074.2	246	Danville, VA	2,596.6	348	Holland-Grand Haven, MI	1,836.9
74	Battle Creek, MI	3,842.2	192	Davenport, IA-IL	2,945.4	3	Hot Springs, AR	5,487.3
339	Bay City, MI	1,962.1	126	Dayton, OH	3,438.6	142	Houma, LA	3,316.8
71	Beaumont-Port Arthur, TX	3,873.5	254	Decatur, AL	2,556.8	108	Houston, TX	3,576.9
167	Bellingham, WA	3,130.3	180	Decatur, IL	3,036.9	116	Huntsville, AL	3,508.3
174	Bend, OR	3,082.6	101	Deltona-Daytona Beach, FL	3,649.3	325	Idaho Falls, ID	2,060.9
347	Bethesda-Frederick, MD M.D.	1,850.1	231	Denver-Aurora, CO	2,733.7	81	Indianapolis, IN	3,767.9
123	Billings, MT	3,462.4	173	Des Moines-West Des Moines, IA	3,093.0	349	Iowa City, IA	1,832.0
242	Binghamton, NY	2,629.2	204	Detroit (greater), MI	2,878.5	92	Jacksonville, FL	3,682.9
50	Birmingham-Hoover, AL	4,093.7	48	Detroit-Livonia-Dearborn, MI M.D.	4,112.3	186	Jacksonville, NC	3,010.7
273	Bismarck, ND	2,440.9	187	Dothan, AL	3,006.0	103	Jackson, MS	3,621.1
260	Blacksburg, VA	2,508.7	98	Dover, DE	3,654.3	54	Jackson, TN	4,055.2
308	Bloomington-Normal, IL	2,173.7	329	Dubuque, IA	2,029.9	182	Janesville, WI	3,028.6
225	Bloomington, IN	2,776.5	152	Duluth, MN-WI	3,274.9	270	Jefferson City, MO	2,474.2
327	Boise City-Nampa, ID	2,034.2	77	Durham-Chapel Hill, NC	3,795.6	184	Johnson City, TN	3,024.8
316	Boston (greater), MA-NH	2,109.0	317	Eau Claire, WI	2,106.9	324	Johnstown, PA	2,061.2
285	Boston-Quincy, MA M.D.	2,350.5	342	Edison, NJ M.D.	1,926.2	65	Jonesboro, AR	3,932.2
311	Boulder, CO	2,157.2	140	El Centro, CA	3,340.7	93	Joplin, MO	3,680.3
238	Bowling Green, KY	2,665.1	281	El Paso, TX	2,384.4	201	Kankakee-Bradley, IL	2,892.1
194	Bremerton-Silverdale, WA	2,931.3	364	Elizabethtown, KY	1,555.2	133	Kansas City, MO-KS	3,407.4
341	Bridgeport-Stamford, CT	1,930.0	284	Elmira, NY	2,354.6	239	Kennewick-Pasco-Richland, WA	2,641.9
49	Brownsville-Harlingen, TX	4,111.9	236	Erie, PA	2,693.1	213	Killeen-Temple-Fort Hood, TX	2,818.3
18	Brunswick, GA	4,628.1	110	Eugene-Springfield, OR	3,555.7	153	Kingsport, TN-VA	3,268.8
191	Buffalo-Niagara Falls, NY	2,945.5	229	Evansville, IN-KY	2,754.5	345	Kingston, NY	1,873.8
66	Burlington, NC	3,922.3	52	Fairbanks, AK	4,076.7	75	Knoxville, TN	3,820.4
353	Cambridge-Newton, MA M.D.	1,789.7	322	Fargo, ND-MN	2,073.1	125	Kokomo, IN	3,444.8
237	Camden, NJ M.D.	2,669.4	319	Farmington, NM	2,097.4	287	La Crosse, WI-MN	2,317.7
172	Canton, OH	3,094.0	4	Fayetteville, NC	5,458.3	243	Lafayette, IN	2,617.6
221	Cape Coral-Fort Myers, FL	2,789.9	137	Flagstaff, AZ	3,363.3	67	Lafayette, LA	3,902.7
90	Cape Girardeau, MO-IL	3,687.6	69	Flint, MI	3,886.3	332	Lake Co.-Kenosha Co., IL-WI M.D.	2,024.8
291	Carson City, NV	2,287.4	267	Florence-Muscle Shoals, AL	2,489.8	162	Lake Havasu City-Kingman, AZ	3,183.4
159	Casper, WY	3,205.5	10	Florence, SC	4,980.3	147	Lakeland, FL	3,294.4
272	Cedar Rapids, IA	2,442.0	363	Fond du Lac, WI	1,592.0	328	Lancaster, PA	2,031.5
261	Champaign-Urbana, IL	2,498.8	259	Fort Collins-Loveland, CO	2,514.7	278	Lansing-East Lansing, MI	2,390.2

Note: All listings are for Metropolitan Statistical Areas (M.S.A.s) except for those ending with "M.D." Listings with "M.D." are Metropolitan Divisions which are smaller parts of eleven large M.S.A.s. See explanatory note at beginning of metropolitan area section.

Alpha Order - Metro Area (continued)

RANK	METROPOLITAN AREA	RATE
36	Laredo, TX	4,245.8
157	Las Cruces, NM	3,214.0
233	Las Vegas-Paradise, NV	2,727.8
58	Lawrence, KS	4,024.0
13	Lawton, OK	4,696.0
350	Lebanon, PA	1,806.8
190	Lewiston-Auburn, ME	2,953.9
59	Lexington-Fayette, KY	4,022.2
83	Lima, OH	3,741.2
107	Lincoln, NE	3,584.0
6	Little Rock, AR	5,184.2
366	Logan, UT-ID	1,061.4
136	Longview, TX	3,365.3
144	Longview, WA	3,302.3
290	Los Angeles County, CA M.D.	2,296.5
297	Los Angeles (greater), CA	2,232.7
79	Louisville, KY-IN	3,776.4
14	Lubbock, TX	4,693.3
331	Lynchburg, VA	2,025.4
2	Macon, GA	5,518.6
265	Madera, CA	2,492.8
249	Madison, WI	2,586.9
286	Manchester-Nashua, NH	2,346.7
334	Manhattan, KS	2,002.5
200	Mankato-North Mankato, MN	2,897.8
26	Mansfield, OH	4,384.8
63	McAllen-Edinburg-Mission, TX	3,956.0
138	Medford, OR	3,355.4
20	Memphis, TN-MS-AR	4,562.8
115	Merced, CA	3,528.6
41	Miami (greater), FL	4,193.3
12	Miami-Dade County, FL M.D.	4,733.9
104	Michigan City-La Porte, IN	3,609.6
232	Midland, TX	2,730.6
151	Milwaukee, WI	3,279.5
207	Minneapolis-St. Paul, MN-WI	2,844.6
248	Missoula, MT	2,594.6
11	Mobile, AL	4,807.0
91	Modesto, CA	3,686.3
21	Monroe, LA	4,526.1
256	Monroe, MI	2,535.8
51	Montgomery, AL	4,085.4
131	Morristown, TN	3,412.7
22	Mount Vernon-Anacortes, WA	4,457.8
209	Muncie, IN	2,834.1
47	Muskegon-Norton Shores, MI	4,121.9
1	Myrtle Beach, SC	5,590.1
330	Napa, CA	2,027.0
346	Naples-Marco Island, FL	1,864.7
141	Nashville-Davidson, TN	3,318.8
361	Nassau-Suffolk, NY M.D.	1,615.6
178	New Haven-Milford, CT	3,042.6
134	New Orleans, LA	3,392.8
355	New York (greater), NY-NJ-PA	1,744.1
359	New York-W. Plains NY-NJ M.D.	1,677.6
321	Newark-Union, NJ-PA M.D.	2,073.7
100	North Port-Bradenton-Sarasota, FL	3,652.0
299	Norwich-New London, CT	2,224.3
161	Oakland-Fremont, CA M.D.	3,191.2
262	Ocala, FL	2,495.7
16	Ocean City, NJ	4,656.3
183	Odessa, TX	3,026.8
253	Ogden-Clearfield, UT	2,562.8

RANK	METROPOLITAN AREA	RATE
33	Oklahoma City, OK	4,271.9
224	Olympia, WA	2,780.0
139	Omaha-Council Bluffs, NE-IA	3,355.0
96	Orlando, FL	3,662.7
344	Oshkosh-Neenah, WI	1,904.9
240	Owensboro, KY	2,639.7
356	Oxnard-Thousand Oaks, CA	1,701.0
146	Palm Bay-Melbourne, FL	3,296.2
313	Palm Coast, FL	2,127.8
30	Panama City-Lynn Haven, FL	4,337.6
150	Pascagoula, MS	3,290.0
315	Peabody, MA M.D.	2,111.3
106	Pensacola, FL	3,585.9
217	Peoria, IL	2,802.9
230	Philadelphia (greater) PA-NJ-MD-DE	2,747.3
235	Philadelphia, PA M.D.	2,694.4
97	Phoenix-Mesa-Scottsdale, AZ	3,656.5
9	Pine Bluff, AR	5,008.1
343	Pittsburgh, PA	1,924.0
277	Pittsfield, MA	2,411.0
206	Pocatello, ID	2,848.6
215	Port St. Lucie, FL	2,806.1
166	Portland-Vancouver, OR-WA	3,137.6
251	Portland, ME	2,580.0
340	Poughkeepsie, NY	1,947.8
310	Prescott, AZ	2,161.9
302	Provo-Orem, UT	2,203.8
24	Pueblo, CO	4,409.5
268	Punta Gorda, FL	2,489.5
203	Racine, WI	2,879.9
247	Raleigh-Cary, NC	2,595.3
198	Rapid City, SD	2,902.6
307	Reading, PA	2,177.3
228	Redding, CA	2,762.9
274	Reno-Sparks, NV	2,436.3
263	Richmond, VA	2,495.6
212	Riverside-San Bernardino, CA	2,818.5
255	Roanoke, VA	2,552.9
351	Rochester, MN	1,804.3
250	Rochester, NY	2,585.7
171	Rockford, IL	3,100.9
309	Rockingham County, NH M.D.	2,162.5
68	Rocky Mount, NC	3,902.2
76	Rome, GA	3,816.2
211	Sacramento, CA	2,825.5
266	Saginaw, MI	2,490.8
223	Salem, OR	2,785.8
283	Salinas, CA	2,355.8
165	Salisbury, MD	3,137.9
46	Salt Lake City, UT	4,126.6
122	San Angelo, TX	3,466.6
15	San Antonio, TX	4,667.6
320	San Diego, CA	2,078.8
175	San Francisco (greater), CA	3,080.1
195	San Francisco-S. Mateo, CA M.D.	2,920.0
312	San Jose, CA	2,146.0
294	San Luis Obispo, CA	2,271.2
185	Sandusky, OH	3,019.4
333	Santa Ana-Anaheim, CA M.D.	2,024.5
314	Santa Barbara-Santa Maria, CA	2,117.9
148	Santa Cruz-Watsonville, CA	3,293.8
88	Santa Fe, NM	3,689.0
357	Santa Rosa-Petaluma, CA	1,696.8

RANK	METROPOLITAN AREA	RATE
102	Savannah, GA	3,626.8
296	Scranton--Wilkes-Barre, PA	2,235.3
78	Seattle (greater), WA	3,782.3
82	Seattle-Bellevue-Everett, WA M.D.	3,753.1
210	Sebastian-Vero Beach, FL	2,829.7
323	Sheboygan, WI	2,062.8
164	Sherman-Denison, TX	3,164.0
176	Sioux City, IA-NE-SD	3,051.3
279	Sioux Falls, SD	2,386.2
87	South Bend-Mishawaka, IN-MI	3,701.8
112	Spartanburg, SC	3,546.7
7	Spokane, WA	5,138.0
32	Springfield, IL	4,290.8
199	Springfield, MA	2,898.9
19	Springfield, MO	4,587.3
45	Springfield, OH	4,157.2
362	State College, PA	1,598.9
39	Stockton, CA	4,203.0
275	St. Cloud, MN	2,419.8
80	St. Joseph, MO-KS	3,775.8
168	St. Louis, MO-IL	3,128.9
109	Sumter, SC	3,556.3
282	Syracuse, NY	2,383.0
70	Tacoma, WA M.D.	3,879.4
89	Tallahassee, FL	3,688.6
170	Tampa-St Petersburg, FL	3,101.5
72	Terre Haute, IN	3,864.3
17	Texarkana, TX-Texarkana, AR	4,647.7
NA	Toledo, OH**	NA
38	Topeka, KS	4,211.1
306	Trenton-Ewing, NJ	2,178.2
NA	Tucson, AZ**	NA
117	Tulsa, OK	3,501.4
114	Tuscaloosa, AL	3,533.0
154	Tyler, TX	3,266.8
298	Utica-Rome, NY	2,231.1
169	Valdosta, GA	3,121.8
202	Vallejo-Fairfield, CA	2,890.2
73	Victoria, TX	3,860.4
143	Virginia Beach-Norfolk, VA-NC	3,310.9
129	Visalia-Porterville, CA	3,427.5
62	Waco, TX	3,980.8
40	Warner Robins, GA	4,195.7
338	Warren-Farmington Hills, MI M.D.	1,971.1
280	Washington (greater) DC-VA-MD-WV	2,386.0
257	Washington, DC-VA-MD-WV M.D.	2,533.1
326	Waterloo-Cedar Falls, IA	2,043.3
352	Wausau, WI	1,793.6
245	Wenatchee, WA	2,603.4
130	West Palm Beach, FL M.D.	3,421.7
94	Wichita Falls, TX	3,677.3
64	Wichita, KS	3,940.7
303	Williamsport, PA	2,202.1
163	Wilmington, DE-MD-NJ M.D.	3,183.1
95	Wilmington, NC	3,673.9
295	Winchester, VA-WV	2,259.7
23	Winston-Salem, NC	4,431.4
305	Worcester, MA	2,180.2
37	Yakima, WA	4,217.0
336	York-Hanover, PA	1,997.7
219	Yuba City, CA	2,792.9
241	Yuma, AZ	2,630.4

Source: Reported data from the F.B.I. "Crime in the United States 2011"
*Property crimes are offenses of burglary, larceny-theft, and motor vehicle theft. Attempts are included.
**Not available.

Rank Order - Metro Area

26. Property Crime Rate in 2011 (continued)
National Rate = 2,908.7 Property Crimes per 100,000 Population*

RANK	METROPOLITAN AREA	RATE	RANK	METROPOLITAN AREA	RATE	RANK	METROPOLITAN AREA	RATE
1	Myrtle Beach, SC	5,590.1	61	Fort Lauderdale, FL M.D.	4,004.1	121	Gary, IN M.D.	3,480.0
2	Macon, GA	5,518.6	62	Waco, TX	3,980.8	122	San Angelo, TX	3,466.6
3	Hot Springs, AR	5,487.3	63	McAllen-Edinburg-Mission, TX	3,956.0	123	Billings, MT	3,462.4
4	Fayetteville, NC	5,458.3	64	Wichita, KS	3,940.7	124	Austin-Round Rock, TX	3,448.3
5	Columbus, GA-AL	5,280.5	65	Jonesboro, AR	3,932.2	125	Kokomo, IN	3,444.8
6	Little Rock, AR	5,184.2	66	Burlington, NC	3,922.3	126	Dayton, OH	3,438.6
7	Spokane, WA	5,138.0	67	Lafayette, LA	3,902.7	127	Gainesville, FL	3,435.9
8	Anderson, SC	5,123.5	68	Rocky Mount, NC	3,902.2	128	Charlotte-Gastonia, NC-SC	3,435.5
9	Pine Bluff, AR	5,008.1	69	Flint, MI	3,886.3	129	Visalia-Porterville, CA	3,427.5
10	Florence, SC	4,980.3	70	Tacoma, WA M.D.	3,879.4	130	West Palm Beach, FL M.D.	3,421.7
11	Mobile, AL	4,807.0	71	Beaumont-Port Arthur, TX	3,873.5	131	Morristown, TN	3,412.7
12	Miami-Dade County, FL M.D.	4,733.9	72	Terre Haute, IN	3,864.3	132	Atlantic City, NJ	3,409.5
13	Lawton, OK	4,696.0	73	Victoria, TX	3,860.4	133	Kansas City, MO-KS	3,407.4
14	Lubbock, TX	4,693.3	74	Battle Creek, MI	3,842.2	134	New Orleans, LA	3,392.8
15	San Antonio, TX	4,667.6	75	Knoxville, TN	3,820.4	135	Dallas-Plano-Irving, TX M.D.	3,392.5
16	Ocean City, NJ	4,656.3	76	Rome, GA	3,816.2	136	Longview, TX	3,365.3
17	Texarkana, TX-Texarkana, AR	4,647.7	77	Durham-Chapel Hill, NC	3,795.6	137	Flagstaff, AZ	3,363.3
18	Brunswick, GA	4,628.1	78	Seattle (greater), WA	3,782.3	138	Medford, OR	3,355.4
19	Springfield, MO	4,587.3	79	Louisville, KY-IN	3,776.4	139	Omaha-Council Bluffs, NE-IA	3,355.0
20	Memphis, TN-MS-AR	4,562.8	80	St. Joseph, MO-KS	3,775.8	140	El Centro, CA	3,340.7
21	Monroe, LA	4,526.1	81	Indianapolis, IN	3,767.9	141	Nashville-Davidson, TN	3,318.8
22	Mount Vernon-Anacortes, WA	4,457.8	82	Seattle-Bellevue-Everett, WA M.D.	3,753.1	142	Houma, LA	3,316.8
23	Winston-Salem, NC	4,431.4	83	Lima, OH	3,741.2	143	Virginia Beach-Norfolk, VA-NC	3,310.9
24	Pueblo, CO	4,409.5	84	Athens-Clarke County, GA	3,726.2	144	Longview, WA	3,302.3
25	Gadsden, AL	4,406.6	85	Chattanooga, TN-GA	3,711.0	145	Anchorage, AK	3,302.0
26	Mansfield, OH	4,384.8	86	Fort Worth-Arlington, TX M.D.	3,708.9	146	Palm Bay-Melbourne, FL	3,296.2
27	Alexandria, LA	4,374.6	87	South Bend-Mishawaka, IN-MI	3,701.8	147	Lakeland, FL	3,294.4
28	Albany, GA	4,365.7	88	Santa Fe, NM	3,689.0	148	Santa Cruz-Watsonville, CA	3,293.8
29	Augusta, GA-SC	4,352.2	89	Tallahassee, FL	3,688.6	149	Akron, OH	3,290.8
30	Panama City-Lynn Haven, FL	4,337.6	90	Cape Girardeau, MO-IL	3,687.6	150	Pascagoula, MS	3,290.0
31	Fresno, CA	4,330.5	91	Modesto, CA	3,686.3	151	Milwaukee, WI	3,279.5
32	Springfield, IL	4,290.8	92	Jacksonville, FL	3,682.9	152	Duluth, MN-WI	3,274.9
33	Oklahoma City, OK	4,271.9	93	Joplin, MO	3,680.3	153	Kingsport, TN-VA	3,268.8
34	Anniston-Oxford, AL	4,271.3	94	Wichita Falls, TX	3,677.3	154	Tyler, TX	3,266.8
35	Corpus Christi, TX	4,252.8	95	Wilmington, NC	3,673.9	155	Auburn, AL	3,255.0
36	Laredo, TX	4,245.8	96	Orlando, FL	3,662.7	156	Hinesville, GA	3,232.8
37	Yakima, WA	4,217.0	97	Phoenix-Mesa-Scottsdale, AZ	3,656.5	157	Las Cruces, NM	3,214.0
38	Topeka, KS	4,211.1	98	Dover, DE	3,654.3	158	Columbia, MO	3,212.0
39	Stockton, CA	4,203.0	99	Greenville, SC	3,653.3	159	Casper, WY	3,205.5
40	Warner Robins, GA	4,195.7	100	North Port-Bradenton-Sarasota, FL	3,652.0	160	College Station-Bryan, TX	3,196.5
41	Miami (greater), FL	4,193.3	101	Deltona-Daytona Beach, FL	3,649.3	161	Oakland-Fremont, CA M.D.	3,191.2
42	Columbus, OH	4,178.7	102	Savannah, GA	3,626.8	162	Lake Havasu City-Kingman, AZ	3,183.4
43	Goldsboro, NC	4,176.3	103	Jackson, MS	3,621.1	163	Wilmington, DE-MD-NJ M.D.	3,183.1
44	Columbus, IN	4,162.7	104	Michigan City-La Porte, IN	3,609.6	164	Sherman-Denison, TX	3,164.0
45	Springfield, OH	4,157.2	105	Great Falls, MT	3,591.8	165	Salisbury, MD	3,137.9
46	Salt Lake City, UT	4,126.6	106	Pensacola, FL	3,585.9	166	Portland-Vancouver, OR-WA	3,137.6
47	Muskegon-Norton Shores, MI	4,121.9	107	Lincoln, NE	3,584.0	167	Bellingham, WA	3,130.3
48	Detroit-Livonia-Dearborn, MI M.D.	4,112.3	108	Houston, TX	3,576.9	168	St. Louis, MO-IL	3,128.9
49	Brownsville-Harlingen, TX	4,111.9	109	Sumter, SC	3,556.3	169	Valdosta, GA	3,121.8
50	Birmingham-Hoover, AL	4,093.7	110	Eugene-Springfield, OR	3,555.7	170	Tampa-St Petersburg, FL	3,101.5
51	Montgomery, AL	4,085.4	111	Atlanta, GA	3,552.0	171	Rockford, IL	3,100.9
52	Fairbanks, AK	4,076.7	112	Spartanburg, SC	3,546.7	172	Canton, OH	3,094.0
53	Baton Rouge, LA	4,074.2	113	Bakersfield, CA	3,539.8	173	Des Moines-West Des Moines, IA	3,093.0
54	Jackson, TN	4,055.2	114	Tuscaloosa, AL	3,533.0	174	Bend, OR	3,082.6
55	Albuquerque, NM	4,050.7	115	Merced, CA	3,528.6	175	San Francisco (greater), CA	3,080.1
56	Amarillo, TX	4,042.9	116	Huntsville, AL	3,508.3	176	Sioux City, IA-NE-SD	3,051.3
57	Danville, IL	4,041.7	117	Tulsa, OK	3,501.4	177	Cleveland, TN	3,042.8
58	Lawrence, KS	4,024.0	118	Cincinnati-Middletown, OH-KY-IN	3,498.9	178	New Haven-Milford, CT	3,042.6
59	Lexington-Fayette, KY	4,022.2	119	Dallas (greater), TX	3,498.5	179	Baltimore-Towson, MD	3,042.5
60	Gulfport-Biloxi, MS	4,006.6	120	Hickory, NC	3,497.1	180	Decatur, IL	3,036.9

Note: All listings are for Metropolitan Statistical Areas (M.S.A.s) except for those ending with "M.D." Listings with "M.D." are Metropolitan Divisions which are smaller parts of eleven large M.S.A.s. See explanatory note at beginning of metropolitan area section.

Rank Order - Metro Area (continued)

RANK	METROPOLITAN AREA	RATE	RANK	METROPOLITAN AREA	RATE	RANK	METROPOLITAN AREA	RATE
181	Abilene, TX	3,029.7	244	Ames, IA	2,611.9	307	Reading, PA	2,177.3
182	Janesville, WI	3,028.6	245	Wenatchee, WA	2,603.4	308	Bloomington-Normal, IL	2,173.7
183	Odessa, TX	3,026.8	246	Danville, VA	2,596.6	309	Rockingham County, NH M.D.	2,162.5
184	Johnson City, TN	3,024.8	247	Raleigh-Cary, NC	2,595.3	310	Prescott, AZ	2,161.9
185	Sandusky, OH	3,019.4	248	Missoula, MT	2,594.6	311	Boulder, CO	2,157.2
186	Jacksonville, NC	3,010.7	249	Madison, WI	2,586.9	312	San Jose, CA	2,146.0
187	Dothan, AL	3,006.0	250	Rochester, NY	2,585.7	313	Palm Coast, FL	2,127.8
188	Dalton, GA	2,974.3	251	Portland, ME	2,580.0	314	Santa Barbara-Santa Maria, CA	2,117.9
189	Cleveland-Elyria-Mentor, OH	2,962.8	252	Corvallis, OR	2,577.2	315	Peabody, MA M.D.	2,111.3
190	Lewiston-Auburn, ME	2,953.9	253	Ogden-Clearfield, UT	2,562.8	316	Boston (greater), MA-NH	2,109.0
191	Buffalo-Niagara Falls, NY	2,945.5	254	Decatur, AL	2,556.8	317	Eau Claire, WI	2,106.9
192	Davenport, IA-IL	2,945.4	255	Roanoke, VA	2,552.9	318	Greeley, CO	2,099.7
193	Charleston, WV	2,944.1	256	Monroe, MI	2,535.8	319	Farmington, NM	2,097.4
194	Bremerton-Silverdale, WA	2,931.3	257	Washington, DC-VA-MD-WV M.D.	2,533.1	320	San Diego, CA	2,078.8
195	San Francisco-S. Mateo, CA M.D.	2,920.0	258	Asheville, NC	2,533.0	321	Newark-Union, NJ-PA M.D.	2,073.7
196	Colorado Springs, CO	2,916.7	259	Fort Collins-Loveland, CO	2,514.7	322	Fargo, ND-MN	2,073.1
197	Cumberland, MD-WV	2,905.4	260	Blacksburg, VA	2,508.7	323	Sheboygan, WI	2,062.8
198	Rapid City, SD	2,902.6	261	Champaign-Urbana, IL	2,498.8	324	Johnstown, PA	2,061.2
199	Springfield, MA	2,898.9	262	Ocala, FL	2,495.7	325	Idaho Falls, ID	2,060.9
200	Mankato-North Mankato, MN	2,897.8	263	Richmond, VA	2,495.6	326	Waterloo-Cedar Falls, IA	2,043.3
201	Kankakee-Bradley, IL	2,892.1	264	Albany-Schenectady-Troy, NY	2,494.5	327	Boise City-Nampa, ID	2,034.2
202	Vallejo-Fairfield, CA	2,890.2	265	Madera, CA	2,492.8	328	Lancaster, PA	2,031.5
203	Racine, WI	2,879.9	266	Saginaw, MI	2,490.8	329	Dubuque, IA	2,029.9
204	Detroit (greater), MI	2,878.5	267	Florence-Muscle Shoals, AL	2,489.8	330	Napa, CA	2,027.0
205	Crestview-Fort Walton Beach, FL	2,864.9	268	Punta Gorda, FL	2,489.5	331	Lynchburg, VA	2,025.4
206	Pocatello, ID	2,848.6	269	Gainesville, GA	2,474.6	332	Lake Co.-Kenosha Co., IL-WI M.D.	2,024.8
207	Minneapolis-St. Paul, MN-WI	2,844.6	270	Jefferson City, MO	2,474.2	333	Santa Ana-Anaheim, CA M.D.	2,024.5
208	Clarksville, TN-KY	2,842.2	271	Hartford, CT	2,443.4	334	Manhattan, KS	2,002.5
209	Muncie, IN	2,834.1	272	Cedar Rapids, IA	2,442.0	335	Charlottesville, VA	2,001.3
210	Sebastian-Vero Beach, FL	2,829.7	273	Bismarck, ND	2,440.9	336	York-Hanover, PA	1,997.7
211	Sacramento, CA	2,825.5	274	Reno-Sparks, NV	2,436.3	337	Altoona, PA	1,983.6
212	Riverside-San Bernardino, CA	2,818.5	275	St. Cloud, MN	2,419.8	338	Warren-Farmington Hills, MI M.D.	1,971.1
213	Killeen-Temple-Fort Hood, TX	2,818.3	276	Chico, CA	2,414.8	339	Bay City, MI	1,962.1
214	Chicago-Joilet-Naperville, IL M.D.	2,814.2	277	Pittsfield, MA	2,411.0	340	Poughkeepsie, NY	1,947.8
215	Port St. Lucie, FL	2,806.1	278	Lansing-East Lansing, MI	2,390.2	341	Bridgeport-Stamford, CT	1,930.0
216	Bangor, ME	2,804.4	279	Sioux Falls, SD	2,386.2	342	Edison, NJ M.D.	1,926.2
217	Peoria, IL	2,802.9	280	Washington (greater) DC-VA-MD-WV	2,386.0	343	Pittsburgh, PA	1,924.0
218	Fort Smith, AR-OK	2,797.0	281	El Paso, TX	2,384.4	344	Oshkosh-Neenah, WI	1,904.9
219	Yuba City, CA	2,792.9	282	Syracuse, NY	2,383.0	345	Kingston, NY	1,873.8
220	Chicago (greater), IL-IN-WI	2,791.5	283	Salinas, CA	2,355.8	346	Naples-Marco Island, FL	1,864.7
221	Cape Coral-Fort Myers, FL	2,789.9	284	Elmira, NY	2,354.6	347	Bethesda-Frederick, MD M.D.	1,850.1
222	Barnstable Town, MA	2,785.9	285	Boston-Quincy, MA M.D.	2,350.5	348	Holland-Grand Haven, MI	1,836.9
223	Salem, OR	2,785.8	286	Manchester-Nashua, NH	2,346.7	349	Iowa City, IA	1,832.0
224	Olympia, WA	2,780.0	287	La Crosse, WI-MN	2,317.7	350	Lebanon, PA	1,806.8
225	Bloomington, IN	2,776.5	288	Grand Rapids-Wyoming, MI	2,310.7	351	Rochester, MN	1,804.3
226	Fort Wayne, IN	2,775.4	289	Ann Arbor, MI	2,303.1	352	Wausau, WI	1,793.6
227	Cheyenne, WY	2,767.3	290	Los Angeles County, CA M.D.	2,296.5	353	Cambridge-Newton, MA M.D.	1,789.7
228	Redding, CA	2,762.9	291	Carson City, NV	2,287.4	354	Green Bay, WI	1,776.5
229	Evansville, IN-KY	2,754.5	292	Grand Forks, ND-MN	2,283.8	355	New York (greater), NY-NJ-PA	1,744.1
230	Philadelphia (greater) PA-NJ-MD-DE	2,747.3	293	Allentown, PA-NJ	2,277.8	356	Oxnard-Thousand Oaks, CA	1,701.0
231	Denver-Aurora, CO	2,733.7	294	San Luis Obispo, CA	2,271.2	357	Santa Rosa-Petaluma, CA	1,696.8
232	Midland, TX	2,730.6	295	Winchester, VA-WV	2,259.7	358	Appleton, WI	1,693.8
233	Las Vegas-Paradise, NV	2,727.8	296	Scranton--Wilkes-Barre, PA	2,235.3	359	New York-W. Plains NY-NJ M.D.	1,677.6
234	Grand Junction, CO	2,721.1	297	Los Angeles (greater), CA	2,232.7	360	Glens Falls, NY	1,648.6
235	Philadelphia, PA M.D.	2,694.4	298	Utica-Rome, NY	2,231.1	361	Nassau-Suffolk, NY M.D.	1,615.6
236	Erie, PA	2,693.1	299	Norwich-New London, CT	2,224.3	362	State College, PA	1,598.9
237	Camden, NJ M.D.	2,669.4	300	Hanford-Corcoran, CA	2,219.9	363	Fond du Lac, WI	1,592.0
238	Bowling Green, KY	2,665.1	301	Hagerstown-Martinsburg, MD-WV	2,208.4	364	Elizabethtown, KY	1,555.2
239	Kennewick-Pasco-Richland, WA	2,641.9	302	Provo-Orem, UT	2,203.8	365	Harrisonburg, VA	1,312.3
240	Owensboro, KY	2,639.7	303	Williamsport, PA	2,202.1	366	Logan, UT-ID	1,061.4
241	Yuma, AZ	2,630.4	304	Harrisburg-Carlisle, PA	2,197.1	NA	Toledo, OH**	NA
242	Binghamton, NY	2,629.2	305	Worcester, MA	2,180.2	NA	Tucson, AZ**	NA
243	Lafayette, IN	2,617.6	306	Trenton-Ewing, NJ	2,178.2			

Source: Reported data from the F.B.I. "Crime in the United States 2011"

*Property crimes are offenses of burglary, larceny-theft, and motor vehicle theft. Attempts are included.

**Not available.

Alpha Order - Metro Area

27. Percent Change in Property Crime Rate: 2010 to 2011
National Percent Change = 1.3% Decrease*

RANK	METROPOLITAN AREA	% CHANGE	RANK	METROPOLITAN AREA	% CHANGE	RANK	METROPOLITAN AREA	% CHANGE
320	Abilene, TX	(16.2)	NA	Charleston, WV**	NA	76	Fort Lauderdale, FL M.D.	4.3
92	Akron, OH	3.3	NA	Charlotte-Gastonia, NC-SC**	NA	262	Fort Smith, AR-OK	(7.2)
265	Albany-Schenectady-Troy, NY	(7.4)	301	Charlottesville, VA	(12.0)	95	Fort Wayne, IN	3.2
199	Albany, GA	(3.3)	177	Chattanooga, TN-GA	(2.1)	230	Fort Worth-Arlington, TX M.D.	(5.0)
80	Albuquerque, NM	4.0	283	Cheyenne, WY	(8.9)	109	Fresno, CA	1.9
225	Alexandria, LA	(4.8)	NA	Chicago (greater), IL-IN-WI**	NA	NA	Gadsden, AL**	NA
152	Allentown, PA-NJ	(0.9)	NA	Chicago-Joilet-Naperville, IL M.D.**	NA	209	Gainesville, FL	(3.9)
23	Altoona, PA	9.5	291	Chico, CA	(9.7)	104	Gainesville, GA	2.4
319	Amarillo, TX	(16.0)	69	Cincinnati-Middletown, OH-KY-IN	4.7	NA	Gary, IN M.D.**	NA
92	Ames, IA	3.3	58	Clarksville, TN-KY	5.8	49	Glens Falls, NY	6.5
242	Anchorage, AK	(5.8)	73	Cleveland-Elyria-Mentor, OH	4.5	265	Goldsboro, NC	(7.4)
27	Anderson, SC	8.8	24	Cleveland, TN	9.2	80	Grand Forks, ND-MN	4.0
318	Ann Arbor, MI	(15.1)	304	College Station-Bryan, TX	(12.4)	63	Grand Junction, CO	5.5
NA	Anniston-Oxford, AL**	NA	292	Colorado Springs, CO	(9.8)	272	Grand Rapids-Wyoming, MI	(8.0)
324	Appleton, WI	(20.7)	39	Columbia, MO	7.6	NA	Great Falls, MT**	NA
95	Asheville, NC	3.2	NA	Columbus, GA-AL**	NA	223	Greeley, CO	(4.7)
197	Athens-Clarke County, GA	(3.1)	8	Columbus, IN	14.4	199	Green Bay, WI	(3.3)
103	Atlanta, GA	2.6	169	Columbus, OH	(1.9)	52	Greenville, SC	6.3
212	Atlantic City, NJ	(4.0)	280	Corpus Christi, TX	(8.6)	259	Gulfport-Biloxi, MS	(7.0)
NA	Auburn, AL**	NA	4	Corvallis, OR	17.5	42	Hagerstown-Martinsburg, MD-WV	7.4
289	Augusta, GA-SC	(9.6)	180	Crestview-Fort Walton Beach, FL	(2.2)	10	Hanford-Corcoran, CA	13.2
285	Austin-Round Rock, TX	(9.1)	NA	Cumberland, MD-WV**	NA	89	Harrisburg-Carlisle, PA	3.6
223	Bakersfield, CA	(4.7)	196	Dallas (greater), TX	(3.0)	259	Harrisonburg, VA	(7.0)
165	Baltimore-Towson, MD	(1.6)	173	Dallas-Plano-Irving, TX M.D.	(2.0)	203	Hartford, CT	(3.5)
288	Bangor, ME	(9.5)	189	Dalton, GA	(2.6)	21	Hickory, NC	10.0
250	Barnstable Town, MA	(6.3)	100	Danville, IL	2.8	262	Hinesville, GA	(7.2)
NA	Baton Rouge, LA**	NA	264	Danville, VA	(7.3)	84	Holland-Grand Haven, MI	3.8
86	Battle Creek, MI	3.7	NA	Davenport, IA-IL**	NA	152	Hot Springs, AR	(0.9)
323	Bay City, MI	(20.6)	106	Dayton, OH	2.3	217	Houma, LA	(4.2)
134	Beaumont-Port Arthur, TX	0.2	NA	Decatur, AL**	NA	NA	Houston, TX**	NA
177	Bellingham, WA	(2.1)	297	Decatur, IL	(11.5)	NA	Huntsville, AL**	NA
86	Bend, OR	3.7	145	Deltona-Daytona Beach, FL	(0.6)	99	Idaho Falls, ID	3.1
274	Bethesda-Frederick, MD M.D.	(8.1)	164	Denver-Aurora, CO	(1.4)	NA	Indianapolis, IN**	NA
NA	Billings, MT**	NA	30	Des Moines-West Des Moines, IA	8.6	42	Iowa City, IA	7.4
67	Binghamton, NY	4.9	NA	Detroit (greater), MI**	NA	185	Jacksonville, FL	(2.4)
NA	Birmingham-Hoover, AL**	NA	155	Detroit-Livonia-Dearborn, MI M.D.	(1.0)	NA	Jacksonville, NC**	NA
1	Bismarck, ND	37.5	NA	Dothan, AL**	NA	212	Jackson, MS	(4.0)
155	Blacksburg, VA	(1.0)	46	Dover, DE	7.2	310	Jackson, TN	(13.4)
293	Bloomington-Normal, IL	(9.9)	237	Dubuque, IA	(5.4)	100	Janesville, WI	2.8
268	Bloomington, IN	(7.6)	NA	Duluth, MN-WI**	NA	159	Jefferson City, MO	(1.1)
165	Boise City-Nampa, ID	(1.6)	137	Durham-Chapel Hill, NC	0.1	119	Johnson City, TN	1.4
206	Boston (greater), MA-NH	(3.7)	95	Eau Claire, WI	3.2	18	Johnstown, PA	10.6
185	Boston-Quincy, MA M.D.	(2.4)	75	Edison, NJ M.D.	4.4	11	Jonesboro, AR	12.8
241	Boulder, CO	(5.5)	173	El Centro, CA	(2.0)	148	Joplin, MO	(0.8)
230	Bowling Green, KY	(5.0)	309	El Paso, TX	(13.2)	NA	Kankakee-Bradley, IL**	NA
48	Bremerton-Silverdale, WA	6.7	252	Elizabethtown, KY	(6.4)	NA	Kansas City, MO-KS**	NA
33	Bridgeport-Stamford, CT	8.3	24	Elmira, NY	9.2	19	Kennewick-Pasco-Richland, WA	10.1
294	Brownsville-Harlingen, TX	(10.6)	32	Erie, PA	8.4	310	Killeen-Temple-Fort Hood, TX	(13.4)
306	Brunswick, GA	(12.7)	NA	Eugene-Springfield, OR**	NA	115	Kingsport, TN-VA	1.7
230	Buffalo-Niagara Falls, NY	(5.0)	133	Evansville, IN-KY	0.3	180	Kingston, NY	(2.2)
104	Burlington, NC	2.4	132	Fairbanks, AK	0.6	122	Knoxville, TN	1.2
280	Cambridge-Newton, MA M.D.	(8.6)	258	Fargo, ND-MN	(6.8)	16	Kokomo, IN	10.8
54	Camden, NJ M.D.	6.1	219	Farmington, NM	(4.4)	125	La Crosse, WI-MN	1.1
3	Canton, OH	21.1	73	Fayetteville, NC	4.5	76	Lafayette, IN	4.3
84	Cape Coral-Fort Myers, FL	3.8	217	Flagstaff, AZ	(4.2)	250	Lafayette, LA	(6.3)
148	Cape Girardeau, MO-IL	(0.8)	65	Flint, MI	5.4	NA	Lake Co.-Kenosha Co., IL-WI M.D.**	NA
15	Carson City, NV	11.3	NA	Florence-Muscle Shoals, AL**	NA	NA	Lake Havasu City-Kingman, AZ**	NA
308	Casper, WY	(13.0)	92	Florence, SC	3.3	257	Lakeland, FL	(6.7)
208	Cedar Rapids, IA	(3.8)	282	Fond du Lac, WI	(8.7)	38	Lancaster, PA	7.8
NA	Champaign-Urbana, IL**	NA	188	Fort Collins-Loveland, CO	(2.5)	248	Lansing-East Lansing, MI	(6.2)

Note: All listings are for Metropolitan Statistical Areas (M.S.A.s) except for those ending with "M.D." Listings with "M.D." are Metropolitan Divisions which are smaller parts of eleven large M.S.A.s. See explanatory note at beginning of metropolitan area section.

Alpha Order - Metro Area (continued)

RANK	METROPOLITAN AREA	% CHANGE	RANK	METROPOLITAN AREA	% CHANGE	RANK	METROPOLITAN AREA	% CHANGE
305	Laredo, TX	(12.6)	116	Oklahoma City, OK	1.5	173	Savannah, GA	(2.0)
49	Las Cruces, NM	6.5	307	Olympia, WA	(12.9)	140	Scranton--Wilkes-Barre, PA	(0.1)
255	Las Vegas-Paradise, NV	(6.6)	29	Omaha-Council Bluffs, NE-IA	8.7	198	Seattle (greater), WA	(3.2)
69	Lawrence, KS	4.7	109	Orlando, FL	1.9	199	Seattle-Bellevue-Everett, WA M.D.	(3.3)
237	Lawton, OK	(5.4)	NA	Oshkosh-Neenah, WI**	NA	275	Sebastian-Vero Beach, FL	(8.4)
24	Lebanon, PA	9.2	19	Owensboro, KY	10.1	NA	Sheboygan, WI**	NA
2	Lewiston-Auburn, ME	22.9	315	Oxnard-Thousand Oaks, CA	(14.3)	56	Sherman-Denison, TX	6.0
NA	Lexington-Fayette, KY**	NA	79	Palm Bay-Melbourne, FL	4.2	7	Sioux City, IA-NE-SD	16.2
173	Lima, OH	(2.0)	272	Palm Coast, FL	(8.0)	129	Sioux Falls, SD	0.9
148	Lincoln, NE	(0.8)	220	Panama City-Lynn Haven, FL	(4.5)	226	South Bend-Mishawaka, IN-MI	(4.9)
66	Little Rock, AR	5.1	180	Pascagoula, MS	(2.2)	129	Spartanburg, SC	0.9
237	Logan, UT-ID	(5.4)	212	Peabody, MA M.D.	(4.0)	107	Spokane, WA	2.0
296	Longview, TX	(11.0)	27	Pensacola, FL	8.8	255	Springfield, IL	(6.6)
235	Longview, WA	(5.3)	47	Peoria, IL	7.0	233	Springfield, MA	(5.2)
194	Los Angeles County, CA M.D.	(2.8)	95	Philadelphia (greater) PA-NJ-MD-DE	3.2	209	Springfield, MO	(3.9)
169	Los Angeles (greater), CA	(1.9)	80	Philadelphia, PA M.D.	4.0	113	Springfield, OH	1.8
45	Louisville, KY-IN	7.3	91	Phoenix-Mesa-Scottsdale, AZ	3.4	205	State College, PA	(3.6)
226	Lubbock, TX	(4.9)	30	Pine Bluff, AR	8.6	109	Stockton, CA	1.9
128	Lynchburg, VA	1.0	189	Pittsburgh, PA	(2.6)	22	St. Cloud, MN	9.6
90	Macon, GA	3.5	206	Pittsfield, MA	(3.7)	36	St. Joseph, MO-KS	8.0
9	Madera, CA	13.7	100	Pocatello, ID	2.8	155	St. Louis, MO-IL	(1.0)
162	Madison, WI	(1.3)	40	Port St. Lucie, FL	7.5	325	Sumter, SC	(24.9)
54	Manchester-Nashua, NH	6.1	NA	Portland-Vancouver, OR-WA**	NA	237	Syracuse, NY	(5.4)
202	Manhattan, KS	(3.4)	76	Portland, ME	4.3	189	Tacoma, WA M.D.	(2.6)
6	Mankato-North Mankato, MN	16.6	246	Poughkeepsie, NY	(6.1)	113	Tallahassee, FL	1.8
61	Mansfield, OH	5.7	143	Prescott, AZ	(0.4)	275	Tampa-St Petersburg, FL	(8.4)
322	McAllen-Edinburg-Mission, TX	(17.5)	67	Provo-Orem, UT	4.9	NA	Terre Haute, IN**	NA
5	Medford, OR	17.0	NA	Pueblo, CO**	NA	13	Texarkana, TX-Texarkana, AR	11.9
162	Memphis, TN-MS-AR	(1.3)	246	Punta Gorda, FL	(6.1)	NA	Toledo, OH**	NA
49	Merced, CA	6.5	40	Racine, WI	7.5	146	Topeka, KS	(0.7)
129	Miami (greater), FL	0.9	52	Raleigh-Cary, NC	6.3	69	Trenton-Ewing, NJ	4.7
122	Miami-Dade County, FL M.D.	1.2	109	Rapid City, SD	1.9	NA	Tucson, AZ**	NA
235	Michigan City-La Porte, IN	(5.3)	139	Reading, PA	0.0	116	Tulsa, OK	1.5
312	Midland, TX	(13.6)	62	Redding, CA	5.6	NA	Tuscaloosa, AL**	NA
185	Milwaukee, WI	(2.4)	302	Reno-Sparks, NV	(12.2)	298	Tyler, TX	(11.8)
168	Minneapolis-St. Paul, MN-WI	(1.7)	169	Richmond, VA	(1.9)	253	Utica-Rome, NY	(6.5)
NA	Missoula, MT**	NA	72	Riverside-San Bernardino, CA	4.6	313	Valdosta, GA	(13.7)
83	Mobile, AL	3.9	215	Roanoke, VA	(4.1)	242	Vallejo-Fairfield, CA	(5.8)
275	Modesto, CA	(8.4)	143	Rochester, MN	(0.4)	134	Victoria, TX	0.2
270	Monroe, LA	(7.7)	278	Rochester, NY	(8.5)	226	Virginia Beach-Norfolk, VA-NC	(4.9)
140	Monroe, MI	(0.1)	278	Rockford, IL	(8.5)	233	Visalia-Porterville, CA	(5.2)
NA	Montgomery, AL**	NA	37	Rockingham County, NH M.D.	7.9	194	Waco, TX	(2.8)
270	Morristown, TN	(7.7)	42	Rocky Mount, NC	7.4	14	Warner Robins, GA	11.6
289	Mount Vernon-Anacortes, WA	(9.6)	63	Rome, GA	5.5	NA	Warren-Farmington Hills, MI M.D.**	NA
34	Muncie, IN	8.2	284	Sacramento, CA	(9.0)	253	Washington (greater) DC-VA-MD-WV	(6.5)
155	Muskegon-Norton Shores, MI	(1.0)	300	Saginaw, MI	(11.9)	248	Washington, DC-VA-MD-WV M.D.	(6.2)
146	Myrtle Beach, SC	(0.7)	120	Salem, OR	1.3	298	Waterloo-Cedar Falls, IA	(11.8)
192	Napa, CA	(2.7)	259	Salinas, CA	(7.0)	137	Wausau, WI	0.1
58	Naples-Marco Island, FL	5.8	313	Salisbury, MD	(13.7)	203	Wenatchee, WA	(3.5)
177	Nashville-Davidson, TN	(2.1)	265	Salt Lake City, UT	(7.4)	215	West Palm Beach, FL M.D.	(4.1)
209	Nassau-Suffolk, NY M.D.	(3.9)	320	San Angelo, TX	(16.2)	302	Wichita Falls, TX	(12.2)
184	New Haven-Milford, CT	(2.3)	295	San Antonio, TX	(10.8)	86	Wichita, KS	3.7
NA	New Orleans, LA**	NA	242	San Diego, CA	(5.8)	17	Williamsport, PA	10.7
116	New York (greater), NY-NJ-PA	1.5	152	San Francisco (greater), CA	(0.9)	220	Wilmington, DE-MD-NJ M.D.	(4.5)
125	New York-W. Plains NY-NJ M.D.	1.1	192	San Francisco-S. Mateo, CA M.D.	(2.7)	169	Wilmington, NC	(1.9)
57	Newark-Union, NJ-PA M.D.	5.9	226	San Jose, CA	(4.9)	180	Winchester, VA-WV	(2.2)
159	North Port-Bradenton-Sarasota, FL	(1.1)	161	San Luis Obispo, CA	(1.2)	58	Winston-Salem, NC	5.8
268	Norwich-New London, CT	(7.6)	34	Sandusky, OH	8.2	120	Worcester, MA	1.3
134	Oakland-Fremont, CA M.D.	0.2	122	Santa Ana-Anaheim, CA M.D.	1.2	285	Yakima, WA	(9.1)
125	Ocala, FL	1.1	148	Santa Barbara-Santa Maria, CA	(0.8)	220	York-Hanover, PA	(4.5)
165	Ocean City, NJ	(1.6)	107	Santa Cruz-Watsonville, CA	2.0	12	Yuba City, CA	12.6
317	Odessa, TX	(14.8)	245	Santa Fe, NM	(6.0)	142	Yuma, AZ	(0.2)
316	Ogden-Clearfield, UT	(14.7)	285	Santa Rosa-Petaluma, CA	(9.1)			

Source: CQ Press using reported data from the F.B.I. "Crime in the United States 2011"
*Property crimes are offenses of burglary, larceny-theft, and motor vehicle theft. Attempts are included.
**Not available.

Rank Order - Metro Area

27. Percent Change in Property Crime Rate: 2010 to 2011 (continued)
National Percent Change = 1.3% Decrease*

RANK	METROPOLITAN AREA	% CHANGE	RANK	METROPOLITAN AREA	% CHANGE	RANK	METROPOLITAN AREA	% CHANGE
1	Bismarck, ND	37.5	61	Mansfield, OH	5.7	120	Worcester, MA	1.3
2	Lewiston-Auburn, ME	22.9	62	Redding, CA	5.6	122	Knoxville, TN	1.2
3	Canton, OH	21.1	63	Grand Junction, CO	5.5	122	Miami-Dade County, FL M.D.	1.2
4	Corvallis, OR	17.5	63	Rome, GA	5.5	122	Santa Ana-Anaheim, CA M.D.	1.2
5	Medford, OR	17.0	65	Flint, MI	5.4	125	La Crosse, WI-MN	1.1
6	Mankato-North Mankato, MN	16.6	66	Little Rock, AR	5.1	125	New York-W. Plains NY-NJ M.D.	1.1
7	Sioux City, IA-NE-SD	16.2	67	Binghamton, NY	4.9	125	Ocala, FL	1.1
8	Columbus, IN	14.4	67	Provo-Orem, UT	4.9	128	Lynchburg, VA	1.0
9	Madera, CA	13.7	69	Cincinnati-Middletown, OH-KY-IN	4.7	129	Miami (greater), FL	0.9
10	Hanford-Corcoran, CA	13.2	69	Lawrence, KS	4.7	129	Sioux Falls, SD	0.9
11	Jonesboro, AR	12.8	69	Trenton-Ewing, NJ	4.7	129	Spartanburg, SC	0.9
12	Yuba City, CA	12.6	72	Riverside-San Bernardino, CA	4.6	132	Fairbanks, AK	0.6
13	Texarkana, TX-Texarkana, AR	11.9	73	Cleveland-Elyria-Mentor, OH	4.5	133	Evansville, IN-KY	0.3
14	Warner Robins, GA	11.6	73	Fayetteville, NC	4.5	134	Beaumont-Port Arthur, TX	0.2
15	Carson City, NV	11.3	75	Edison, NJ M.D.	4.4	134	Oakland-Fremont, CA M.D.	0.2
16	Kokomo, IN	10.8	76	Fort Lauderdale, FL M.D.	4.3	134	Victoria, TX	0.2
17	Williamsport, PA	10.7	76	Lafayette, IN	4.3	137	Durham-Chapel Hill, NC	0.1
18	Johnstown, PA	10.6	76	Portland, ME	4.3	137	Wausau, WI	0.1
19	Kennewick-Pasco-Richland, WA	10.1	79	Palm Bay-Melbourne, FL	4.2	139	Reading, PA	0.0
19	Owensboro, KY	10.1	80	Albuquerque, NM	4.0	140	Monroe, MI	(0.1)
21	Hickory, NC	10.0	80	Grand Forks, ND-MN	4.0	140	Scranton--Wilkes-Barre, PA	(0.1)
22	St. Cloud, MN	9.6	80	Philadelphia, PA M.D.	4.0	142	Yuma, AZ	(0.2)
23	Altoona, PA	9.5	83	Mobile, AL	3.9	143	Prescott, AZ	(0.4)
24	Cleveland, TN	9.2	84	Cape Coral-Fort Myers, FL	3.8	143	Rochester, MN	(0.4)
24	Elmira, NY	9.2	84	Holland-Grand Haven, MI	3.8	145	Deltona-Daytona Beach, FL	(0.6)
24	Lebanon, PA	9.2	86	Battle Creek, MI	3.7	146	Myrtle Beach, SC	(0.7)
27	Anderson, SC	8.8	86	Bend, OR	3.7	146	Topeka, KS	(0.7)
27	Pensacola, FL	8.8	86	Wichita, KS	3.7	148	Cape Girardeau, MO-IL	(0.8)
29	Omaha-Council Bluffs, NE-IA	8.7	89	Harrisburg-Carlisle, PA	3.6	148	Joplin, MO	(0.8)
30	Des Moines-West Des Moines, IA	8.6	90	Macon, GA	3.5	148	Lincoln, NE	(0.8)
30	Pine Bluff, AR	8.6	91	Phoenix-Mesa-Scottsdale, AZ	3.4	148	Santa Barbara-Santa Maria, CA	(0.8)
32	Erie, PA	8.4	92	Akron, OH	3.3	152	Allentown, PA-NJ	(0.9)
33	Bridgeport-Stamford, CT	8.3	92	Ames, IA	3.3	152	Hot Springs, AR	(0.9)
34	Muncie, IN	8.2	92	Florence, SC	3.3	152	San Francisco (greater), CA	(0.9)
34	Sandusky, OH	8.2	95	Asheville, NC	3.2	155	Blacksburg, VA	(1.0)
36	St. Joseph, MO-KS	8.0	95	Eau Claire, WI	3.2	155	Detroit-Livonia-Dearborn, MI M.D.	(1.0)
37	Rockingham County, NH M.D.	7.9	95	Fort Wayne, IN	3.2	155	Muskegon-Norton Shores, MI	(1.0)
38	Lancaster, PA	7.8	95	Philadelphia (greater) PA-NJ-MD-DE	3.2	155	St. Louis, MO-IL	(1.0)
39	Columbia, MO	7.6	99	Idaho Falls, ID	3.1	159	Jefferson City, MO	(1.1)
40	Port St. Lucie, FL	7.5	100	Danville, IL	2.8	159	North Port-Bradenton-Sarasota, FL	(1.1)
40	Racine, WI	7.5	100	Janesville, WI	2.8	161	San Luis Obispo, CA	(1.2)
42	Hagerstown-Martinsburg, MD-WV	7.4	100	Pocatello, ID	2.8	162	Madison, WI	(1.3)
42	Iowa City, IA	7.4	103	Atlanta, GA	2.6	162	Memphis, TN-MS-AR	(1.3)
42	Rocky Mount, NC	7.4	104	Burlington, NC	2.4	164	Denver-Aurora, CO	(1.4)
45	Louisville, KY-IN	7.3	104	Gainesville, GA	2.4	165	Baltimore-Towson, MD	(1.6)
46	Dover, DE	7.2	106	Dayton, OH	2.3	165	Boise City-Nampa, ID	(1.6)
47	Peoria, IL	7.0	107	Santa Cruz-Watsonville, CA	2.0	165	Ocean City, NJ	(1.6)
48	Bremerton-Silverdale, WA	6.7	107	Spokane, WA	2.0	168	Minneapolis-St. Paul, MN-WI	(1.7)
49	Glens Falls, NY	6.5	109	Fresno, CA	1.9	169	Columbus, OH	(1.9)
49	Las Cruces, NM	6.5	109	Orlando, FL	1.9	169	Los Angeles (greater), CA	(1.9)
49	Merced, CA	6.5	109	Rapid City, SD	1.9	169	Richmond, VA	(1.9)
52	Greenville, SC	6.3	109	Stockton, CA	1.9	169	Wilmington, NC	(1.9)
52	Raleigh-Cary, NC	6.3	113	Springfield, OH	1.8	173	Dallas-Plano-Irving, TX M.D.	(2.0)
54	Camden, NJ M.D.	6.1	113	Tallahassee, FL	1.8	173	El Centro, CA	(2.0)
54	Manchester-Nashua, NH	6.1	115	Kingsport, TN-VA	1.7	173	Lima, OH	(2.0)
56	Sherman-Denison, TX	6.0	116	New York (greater), NY-NJ-PA	1.5	173	Savannah, GA	(2.0)
57	Newark-Union, NJ-PA M.D.	5.9	116	Oklahoma City, OK	1.5	177	Bellingham, WA	(2.1)
58	Clarksville, TN-KY	5.8	116	Tulsa, OK	1.5	177	Chattanooga, TN-GA	(2.1)
58	Naples-Marco Island, FL	5.8	119	Johnson City, TN	1.4	177	Nashville-Davidson, TN	(2.1)
58	Winston-Salem, NC	5.8	120	Salem, OR	1.3	180	Crestview-Fort Walton Beach, FL	(2.2)

Note: All listings are for Metropolitan Statistical Areas (M.S.A.s) except for those ending with "M.D." Listings with "M.D." are Metropolitan Divisions which are smaller parts of eleven large M.S.A.s. See explanatory note at beginning of metropolitan area section.

Rank Order - Metro Area (continued)

RANK	METROPOLITAN AREA	% CHANGE
180	Kingston, NY	(2.2)
180	Pascagoula, MS	(2.2)
180	Winchester, VA-WV	(2.2)
184	New Haven-Milford, CT	(2.3)
185	Boston-Quincy, MA M.D.	(2.4)
185	Jacksonville, FL	(2.4)
185	Milwaukee, WI	(2.4)
188	Fort Collins-Loveland, CO	(2.5)
189	Dalton, GA	(2.6)
189	Pittsburgh, PA	(2.6)
189	Tacoma, WA M.D.	(2.6)
192	Napa, CA	(2.7)
192	San Francisco-S. Mateo, CA M.D.	(2.7)
194	Los Angeles County, CA M.D.	(2.8)
194	Waco, TX	(2.8)
196	Dallas (greater), TX	(3.0)
197	Athens-Clarke County, GA	(3.1)
198	Seattle (greater), WA	(3.2)
199	Albany, GA	(3.3)
199	Green Bay, WI	(3.3)
199	Seattle-Bellevue-Everett, WA M.D.	(3.3)
202	Manhattan, KS	(3.4)
203	Hartford, CT	(3.5)
203	Wenatchee, WA	(3.5)
205	State College, PA	(3.6)
206	Boston (greater), MA-NH	(3.7)
206	Pittsfield, MA	(3.7)
208	Cedar Rapids, IA	(3.8)
209	Gainesville, FL	(3.9)
209	Nassau-Suffolk, NY M.D.	(3.9)
209	Springfield, MO	(3.9)
212	Atlantic City, NJ	(4.0)
212	Jackson, MS	(4.0)
212	Peabody, MA M.D.	(4.0)
215	Roanoke, VA	(4.1)
215	West Palm Beach, FL M.D.	(4.1)
217	Flagstaff, AZ	(4.2)
217	Houma, LA	(4.2)
219	Farmington, NM	(4.4)
220	Panama City-Lynn Haven, FL	(4.5)
220	Wilmington, DE-MD-NJ M.D.	(4.5)
220	York-Hanover, PA	(4.5)
223	Bakersfield, CA	(4.7)
223	Greeley, CO	(4.7)
225	Alexandria, LA	(4.8)
226	Lubbock, TX	(4.9)
226	San Jose, CA	(4.9)
226	South Bend-Mishawaka, IN-MI	(4.9)
226	Virginia Beach-Norfolk, VA-NC	(4.9)
230	Bowling Green, KY	(5.0)
230	Buffalo-Niagara Falls, NY	(5.0)
230	Fort Worth-Arlington, TX M.D.	(5.0)
233	Springfield, MA	(5.2)
233	Visalia-Porterville, CA	(5.2)
235	Longview, WA	(5.3)
235	Michigan City-La Porte, IN	(5.3)
237	Dubuque, IA	(5.4)
237	Lawton, OK	(5.4)
237	Logan, UT-ID	(5.4)
237	Syracuse, NY	(5.4)
241	Boulder, CO	(5.5)
242	Anchorage, AK	(5.8)
242	San Diego, CA	(5.8)
242	Vallejo-Fairfield, CA	(5.8)
245	Santa Fe, NM	(6.0)
246	Poughkeepsie, NY	(6.1)
246	Punta Gorda, FL	(6.1)
248	Lansing-East Lansing, MI	(6.2)
248	Washington, DC-VA-MD-WV M.D.	(6.2)
250	Barnstable Town, MA	(6.3)
250	Lafayette, LA	(6.3)
252	Elizabethtown, KY	(6.4)
253	Utica-Rome, NY	(6.5)
253	Washington (greater) DC-VA-MD-WV	(6.5)
255	Las Vegas-Paradise, NV	(6.6)
255	Springfield, IL	(6.6)
257	Lakeland, FL	(6.7)
258	Fargo, ND-MN	(6.8)
259	Gulfport-Biloxi, MS	(7.0)
259	Harrisonburg, VA	(7.0)
259	Salinas, CA	(7.0)
262	Fort Smith, AR-OK	(7.2)
262	Hinesville, GA	(7.2)
264	Danville, VA	(7.3)
265	Albany-Schenectady-Troy, NY	(7.4)
265	Goldsboro, NC	(7.4)
265	Salt Lake City, UT	(7.4)
268	Bloomington, IN	(7.6)
268	Norwich-New London, CT	(7.6)
270	Monroe, LA	(7.7)
270	Morristown, TN	(7.7)
272	Grand Rapids-Wyoming, MI	(8.0)
272	Palm Coast, FL	(8.0)
274	Bethesda-Frederick, MD M.D.	(8.1)
275	Modesto, CA	(8.4)
275	Sebastian-Vero Beach, FL	(8.4)
275	Tampa-St Petersburg, FL	(8.4)
278	Rochester, NY	(8.5)
278	Rockford, IL	(8.5)
280	Cambridge-Newton, MA M.D.	(8.6)
280	Corpus Christi, TX	(8.6)
282	Fond du Lac, WI	(8.7)
283	Cheyenne, WY	(8.9)
284	Sacramento, CA	(9.0)
285	Austin-Round Rock, TX	(9.1)
285	Santa Rosa-Petaluma, CA	(9.1)
285	Yakima, WA	(9.1)
288	Bangor, ME	(9.5)
289	Augusta, GA-SC	(9.6)
289	Mount Vernon-Anacortes, WA	(9.6)
291	Chico, CA	(9.7)
292	Colorado Springs, CO	(9.8)
293	Bloomington-Normal, IL	(9.9)
294	Brownsville-Harlingen, TX	(10.6)
295	San Antonio, TX	(10.8)
296	Longview, TX	(11.0)
297	Decatur, IL	(11.5)
298	Tyler, TX	(11.8)
298	Waterloo-Cedar Falls, IA	(11.8)
300	Saginaw, MI	(11.9)
301	Charlottesville, VA	(12.0)
302	Reno-Sparks, NV	(12.2)
302	Wichita Falls, TX	(12.2)
304	College Station-Bryan, TX	(12.4)
305	Laredo, TX	(12.6)
306	Brunswick, GA	(12.7)
307	Olympia, WA	(12.9)
308	Casper, WY	(13.0)
309	El Paso, TX	(13.2)
310	Jackson, TN	(13.4)
310	Killeen-Temple-Fort Hood, TX	(13.4)
312	Midland, TX	(13.6)
313	Salisbury, MD	(13.7)
313	Valdosta, GA	(13.7)
315	Oxnard-Thousand Oaks, CA	(14.3)
316	Ogden-Clearfield, UT	(14.7)
317	Odessa, TX	(14.8)
318	Ann Arbor, MI	(15.1)
319	Amarillo, TX	(16.0)
320	Abilene, TX	(16.2)
320	San Angelo, TX	(16.2)
322	McAllen-Edinburg-Mission, TX	(17.5)
323	Bay City, MI	(20.6)
324	Appleton, WI	(20.7)
325	Sumter, SC	(24.9)
NA	Anniston-Oxford, AL**	NA
NA	Auburn, AL**	NA
NA	Baton Rouge, LA**	NA
NA	Billings, MT**	NA
NA	Birmingham-Hoover, AL**	NA
NA	Champaign-Urbana, IL**	NA
NA	Charleston, WV**	NA
NA	Charlotte-Gastonia, NC-SC**	NA
NA	Chicago (greater), IL-IN-WI**	NA
NA	Chicago-Joilet-Naperville, IL M.D.**	NA
NA	Columbus, GA-AL**	NA
NA	Cumberland, MD-WV**	NA
NA	Davenport, IA-IL**	NA
NA	Decatur, AL**	NA
NA	Detroit (greater), MI**	NA
NA	Dothan, AL**	NA
NA	Duluth, MN-WI**	NA
NA	Eugene-Springfield, OR**	NA
NA	Florence-Muscle Shoals, AL**	NA
NA	Gadsden, AL**	NA
NA	Gary, IN M.D.**	NA
NA	Great Falls, MT**	NA
NA	Houston, TX**	NA
NA	Huntsville, AL**	NA
NA	Indianapolis, IN**	NA
NA	Jacksonville, NC**	NA
NA	Kankakee-Bradley, IL**	NA
NA	Kansas City, MO-KS**	NA
NA	Lake Co.-Kenosha Co., IL-WI M.D.**	NA
NA	Lake Havasu City-Kingman, AZ**	NA
NA	Lexington-Fayette, KY**	NA
NA	Missoula, MT**	NA
NA	Montgomery, AL**	NA
NA	New Orleans, LA**	NA
NA	Oshkosh-Neenah, WI**	NA
NA	Portland-Vancouver, OR-WA**	NA
NA	Pueblo, CO**	NA
NA	Sheboygan, WI**	NA
NA	Terre Haute, IN**	NA
NA	Toledo, OH**	NA
NA	Tucson, AZ**	NA
NA	Tuscaloosa, AL**	NA
NA	Warren-Farmington Hills, MI M.D.**	NA

Source: CQ Press using reported data from the F.B.I. "Crime in the United States 2011"
*Property crimes are offenses of burglary, larceny-theft, and motor vehicle theft. Attempts are included.
**Not available.

Alpha Order - Metro Area

28. Percent Change in Property Crime Rate: 2007 to 2011
National Percent Change = 11.2% Decrease*

RANK	METROPOLITAN AREA	% CHANGE	RANK	METROPOLITAN AREA	% CHANGE	RANK	METROPOLITAN AREA	% CHANGE
215	Abilene, TX	(15.5)	168	Charleston, WV	(11.7)	34	Fort Lauderdale, FL M.D.	4.3
64	Akron, OH	(2.0)	309	Charlotte-Gastonia, NC-SC	(34.8)	205	Fort Smith, AR-OK	(14.6)
48	Albany-Schenectady-Troy, NY	0.2	284	Charlottesville, VA	(24.7)	139	Fort Wayne, IN	(9.4)
83	Albany, GA	(5.0)	225	Chattanooga, TN-GA	(16.6)	209	Fort Worth-Arlington, TX M.D.	(15.1)
165	Albuquerque, NM	(11.2)	268	Cheyenne, WY	(22.1)	23	Fresno, CA	8.2
66	Alexandria, LA	(2.1)	NA	Chicago (greater), IL-IN-WI**	NA	NA	Gadsden, AL**	NA
102	Allentown, PA-NJ	(6.7)	NA	Chicago-Joilet-Naperville, IL M.D.**	NA	NA	Gainesville, FL**	NA
163	Altoona, PA	(11.1)	262	Chico, CA	(21.8)	147	Gainesville, GA	(9.8)
246	Amarillo, TX	(19.6)	38	Cincinnati-Middletown, OH-KY-IN	3.6	NA	Gary, IN M.D.**	NA
108	Ames, IA	(7.0)	230	Clarksville, TN-KY	(17.1)	154	Glens Falls, NY	(10.5)
232	Anchorage, AK	(17.5)	61	Cleveland-Elyria-Mentor, OH	(1.4)	182	Goldsboro, NC	(12.7)
53	Anderson, SC	(0.7)	153	Cleveland, TN	(10.3)	198	Grand Forks, ND-MN	(14.2)
190	Ann Arbor, MI	(13.3)	232	College Station-Bryan, TX	(17.5)	132	Grand Junction, CO	(9.0)
NA	Anniston-Oxford, AL**	NA	157	Colorado Springs, CO	(10.7)	294	Grand Rapids-Wyoming, MI	(27.9)
307	Appleton, WI	(34.3)	26	Columbia, MO	6.2	NA	Great Falls, MT**	NA
172	Asheville, NC	(11.9)	NA	Columbus, GA-AL**	NA	264	Greeley, CO	(21.9)
159	Athens-Clarke County, GA	(10.8)	23	Columbus, IN	8.2	265	Green Bay, WI	(22.0)
124	Atlanta, GA	(8.1)	137	Columbus, OH	(9.3)	96	Greenville, SC	(6.3)
80	Atlantic City, NJ	(4.9)	289	Corpus Christi, TX	(26.8)	NA	Gulfport-Biloxi, MS**	NA
NA	Auburn, AL**	NA	206	Corvallis, OR	(14.8)	NA	Hagerstown-Martinsburg, MD-WV**	NA
120	Augusta, GA-SC	(7.7)	132	Crestview-Fort Walton Beach, FL	(9.0)	78	Hanford-Corcoran, CA	(4.8)
222	Austin-Round Rock, TX	(16.4)	NA	Cumberland, MD-WV**	NA	22	Harrisburg-Carlisle, PA	8.6
180	Bakersfield, CA	(12.5)	239	Dallas (greater), TX	(18.8)	272	Harrisonburg, VA	(22.5)
176	Baltimore-Towson, MD	(12.3)	254	Dallas-Plano-Irving, TX M.D.	(20.7)	228	Hartford, CT	(17.0)
198	Bangor, ME	(14.2)	NA	Dalton, GA**	NA	57	Hickory, NC	(1.0)
37	Barnstable Town, MA	3.7	NA	Danville, IL**	NA	222	Hinesville, GA	(16.4)
115	Baton Rouge, LA	(7.3)	135	Danville, VA	(9.1)	NA	Holland-Grand Haven, MI**	NA
105	Battle Creek, MI	(6.8)	NA	Davenport, IA-IL**	NA	216	Hot Springs, AR	(15.6)
256	Bay City, MI	(21.3)	53	Dayton, OH	(0.7)	83	Houma, LA	(5.0)
83	Beaumont-Port Arthur, TX	(5.0)	NA	Decatur, AL**	NA	NA	Houston, TX**	NA
293	Bellingham, WA	(27.7)	NA	Decatur, IL**	NA	NA	Huntsville, AL**	NA
149	Bend, OR	(10.0)	51	Deltona-Daytona Beach, FL	(0.6)	269	Idaho Falls, ID	(22.2)
282	Bethesda-Frederick, MD M.D.	(24.5)	191	Denver-Aurora, CO	(13.4)	141	Indianapolis, IN	(9.6)
NA	Billings, MT**	NA	160	Des Moines-West Des Moines, IA	(10.9)	202	Iowa City, IA	(14.4)
21	Binghamton, NY	10.7	NA	Detroit (greater), MI**	NA	262	Jacksonville, FL	(21.8)
NA	Birmingham-Hoover, AL**	NA	NA	Detroit-Livonia-Dearborn, MI M.D.**	NA	202	Jacksonville, NC	(14.4)
12	Bismarck, ND	14.1	NA	Dothan, AL**	NA	98	Jackson, MS	(6.4)
154	Blacksburg, VA	(10.5)	9	Dover, DE	17.4	260	Jackson, TN	(21.7)
NA	Bloomington-Normal, IL**	NA	220	Dubuque, IA	(16.3)	160	Janesville, WI	(10.9)
57	Bloomington, IN	(1.0)	117	Duluth, MN-WI	(7.4)	98	Jefferson City, MO	(6.4)
237	Boise City-Nampa, ID	(18.1)	NA	Durham-Chapel Hill, NC**	NA	71	Johnson City, TN	(2.5)
119	Boston (greater), MA-NH	(7.5)	120	Eau Claire, WI	(7.7)	55	Johnstown, PA	(0.8)
176	Boston-Quincy, MA M.D.	(12.3)	39	Edison, NJ M.D.	2.8	165	Jonesboro, AR	(11.2)
NA	Boulder, CO**	NA	160	El Centro, CA	(10.9)	276	Joplin, MO	(22.8)
208	Bowling Green, KY	(14.9)	274	El Paso, TX	(22.6)	NA	Kankakee-Bradley, IL**	NA
15	Bremerton-Silverdale, WA	13.2	115	Elizabethtown, KY	(7.3)	NA	Kansas City, MO-KS**	NA
74	Bridgeport-Stamford, CT	(3.5)	247	Elmira, NY	(19.7)	120	Kennewick-Pasco-Richland, WA	(7.7)
212	Brownsville-Harlingen, TX	(15.3)	3	Erie, PA	25.3	279	Killeen-Temple-Fort Hood, TX	(23.3)
43	Brunswick, GA	1.5	185	Eugene-Springfield, OR	(12.8)	169	Kingsport, TN-VA	(11.8)
73	Buffalo-Niagara Falls, NY	(3.1)	50	Evansville, IN-KY	(0.5)	12	Kingston, NY	14.1
33	Burlington, NC	4.6	NA	Fairbanks, AK**	NA	69	Knoxville, TN	(2.3)
169	Cambridge-Newton, MA M.D.	(11.8)	191	Fargo, ND-MN	(13.4)	63	Kokomo, IN	(1.8)
32	Camden, NJ M.D.	4.8	169	Farmington, NM	(11.8)	117	La Crosse, WI-MN	(7.4)
NA	Canton, OH**	NA	110	Fayetteville, NC	(7.1)	141	Lafayette, IN	(9.6)
292	Cape Coral-Fort Myers, FL	(27.6)	238	Flagstaff, AZ	(18.2)	132	Lafayette, LA	(9.0)
NA	Cape Girardeau, MO-IL**	NA	55	Flint, MI	(0.8)	NA	Lake Co.-Kenosha Co., IL-WI M.D.**	NA
11	Carson City, NV	15.5	NA	Florence-Muscle Shoals, AL**	NA	296	Lake Havasu City-Kingman, AZ	(29.5)
291	Casper, WY	(27.2)	126	Florence, SC	(8.2)	220	Lakeland, FL	(16.3)
245	Cedar Rapids, IA	(19.4)	209	Fond du Lac, WI	(15.1)	89	Lancaster, PA	(5.2)
NA	Champaign-Urbana, IL**	NA	149	Fort Collins-Loveland, CO	(10.0)	124	Lansing-East Lansing, MI	(8.1)

Note: All listings are for Metropolitan Statistical Areas (M.S.A.s) except for those ending with "M.D." Listings with "M.D." are Metropolitan Divisions which are smaller parts of eleven large M.S.A.s. See explanatory note at beginning of metropolitan area section.

Alpha Order - Metro Area (continued)

RANK	METROPOLITAN AREA	% CHANGE	RANK	METROPOLITAN AREA	% CHANGE	RANK	METROPOLITAN AREA	% CHANGE
298	Laredo, TX	(30.1)	57	Oklahoma City, OK	(1.0)	NA	Savannah, GA**	NA
25	Las Cruces, NM	7.4	147	Olympia, WA	(9.8)	75	Scranton--Wilkes-Barre, PA	(4.0)
306	Las Vegas-Paradise, NV	(34.0)	194	Omaha-Council Bluffs, NE-IA	(13.8)	206	Seattle (greater), WA	(14.8)
249	Lawrence, KS	(20.4)	217	Orlando, FL	(16.0)	196	Seattle-Bellevue-Everett, WA M.D.	(14.1)
31	Lawton, OK	5.1	288	Oshkosh-Neenah, WI	(25.7)	123	Sebastian-Vero Beach, FL	(7.9)
26	Lebanon, PA	6.2	NA	Owensboro, KY**	NA	303	Sheboygan, WI	(31.7)
6	Lewiston-Auburn, ME	20.7	256	Oxnard-Thousand Oaks, CA	(21.3)	51	Sherman-Denison, TX	(0.6)
NA	Lexington-Fayette, KY**	NA	78	Palm Bay-Melbourne, FL	(4.8)	2	Sioux City, IA-NE-SD	28.8
141	Lima, OH	(9.6)	274	Palm Coast, FL	(22.6)	5	Sioux Falls, SD	20.9
239	Lincoln, NE	(18.8)	35	Panama City-Lynn Haven, FL	4.2	179	South Bend-Mishawaka, IN-MI	(12.4)
96	Little Rock, AR	(6.3)	231	Pascagoula, MS	(17.2)	276	Spartanburg, SC	(22.8)
252	Logan, UT-ID	(20.5)	42	Peabody, MA M.D.	2.1	1	Spokane, WA	34.9
300	Longview, TX	(30.3)	29	Pensacola, FL	6.0	NA	Springfield, IL**	NA
281	Longview, WA	(23.9)	NA	Peoria, IL**	NA	67	Springfield, MA	(2.2)
201	Los Angeles County, CA M.D.	(14.3)	80	Philadelphia (greater) PA-NJ-MD-DE	(4.9)	49	Springfield, MO	0.1
186	Los Angeles (greater), CA	(12.9)	112	Philadelphia, PA M.D.	(7.2)	243	Springfield, OH	(19.1)
41	Louisville, KY-IN	2.5	259	Phoenix-Mesa-Scottsdale, AZ	(21.4)	232	State College, PA	(17.5)
90	Lubbock, TX	(5.3)	87	Pine Bluff, AR	(5.1)	222	Stockton, CA	(16.4)
47	Lynchburg, VA	0.4	174	Pittsburgh, PA	(12.0)	93	St. Cloud, MN	(5.8)
26	Macon, GA	6.2	18	Pittsfield, MA	11.3	87	St. Joseph, MO-KS	(5.1)
10	Madera, CA	16.5	72	Pocatello, ID	(2.8)	156	St. Louis, MO-IL	(10.6)
175	Madison, WI	(12.1)	130	Port St. Lucie, FL	(8.6)	294	Sumter, SC	(27.9)
NA	Manchester-Nashua, NH**	NA	163	Portland-Vancouver, OR-WA	(11.1)	44	Syracuse, NY	1.0
NA	Manhattan, KS**	NA	35	Portland, ME	4.2	226	Tacoma, WA M.D.	(16.8)
NA	Mankato-North Mankato, MN**	NA	60	Poughkeepsie, NY	(1.2)	112	Tallahassee, FL	(7.2)
44	Mansfield, OH	1.0	194	Prescott, AZ	(13.8)	278	Tampa-St Petersburg, FL	(23.2)
188	McAllen-Edinburg-Mission, TX	(13.0)	182	Provo-Orem, UT	(12.7)	NA	Terre Haute, IN**	NA
19	Medford, OR	11.1	NA	Pueblo, CO**	NA	14	Texarkana, TX-Texarkana, AR	13.6
252	Memphis, TN-MS-AR	(20.5)	244	Punta Gorda, FL	(19.2)	NA	Toledo, OH**	NA
92	Merced, CA	(5.6)	141	Racine, WI	(9.6)	131	Topeka, KS	(8.8)
152	Miami (greater), FL	(10.2)	95	Raleigh-Cary, NC	(6.1)	39	Trenton-Ewing, NJ	2.8
191	Miami-Dade County, FL M.D.	(13.4)	20	Rapid City, SD	10.9	NA	Tucson, AZ**	NA
151	Michigan City-La Porte, IN	(10.1)	102	Reading, PA	(6.7)	126	Tulsa, OK	(8.2)
249	Midland, TX	(20.4)	8	Redding, CA	18.7	NA	Tuscaloosa, AL**	NA
236	Milwaukee, WI	(17.9)	308	Reno-Sparks, NV	(34.5)	137	Tyler, TX	(9.3)
242	Minneapolis-St. Paul, MN-WI	(19.0)	182	Richmond, VA	(12.7)	135	Utica-Rome, NY	(9.1)
NA	Missoula, MT**	NA	176	Riverside-San Bernardino, CA	(12.3)	272	Valdosta, GA	(22.5)
69	Mobile, AL	(2.3)	128	Roanoke, VA	(8.3)	270	Vallejo-Fairfield, CA	(22.3)
286	Modesto, CA	(24.9)	167	Rochester, MN	(11.4)	30	Victoria, TX	5.8
248	Monroe, LA	(20.3)	83	Rochester, NY	(5.0)	75	Virginia Beach-Norfolk, VA-NC	(4.0)
7	Monroe, MI	20.6	NA	Rockford, IL**	NA	146	Visalia-Porterville, CA	(9.7)
NA	Montgomery, AL**	NA	4	Rockingham County, NH M.D.	22.5	260	Waco, TX	(21.7)
98	Morristown, TN	(6.4)	227	Rocky Mount, NC	(16.9)	16	Warner Robins, GA	11.8
255	Mount Vernon-Anacortes, WA	(21.2)	77	Rome, GA	(4.2)	NA	Warren-Farmington Hills, MI M.D.**	NA
139	Muncie, IN	(9.4)	214	Sacramento, CA	(15.4)	228	Washington (greater) DC-VA-MD-WV	(17.0)
101	Muskegon-Norton Shores, MI	(6.6)	298	Saginaw, MI	(30.1)	212	Washington, DC-VA-MD-WV M.D.	(15.3)
241	Myrtle Beach, SC	(18.9)	284	Salem, OR	(24.7)	302	Waterloo-Cedar Falls, IA	(31.2)
290	Napa, CA	(27.1)	305	Salinas, CA	(33.4)	44	Wausau, WI	1.0
62	Naples-Marco Island, FL	(1.6)	265	Salisbury, MD	(22.0)	280	Wenatchee, WA	(23.7)
141	Nashville-Davidson, TN	(9.6)	204	Salt Lake City, UT	(14.5)	256	West Palm Beach, FL M.D.	(21.3)
64	Nassau-Suffolk, NY M.D.	(2.0)	282	San Angelo, TX	(24.5)	301	Wichita Falls, TX	(30.4)
NA	New Haven-Milford, CT**	NA	180	San Antonio, TX	(12.5)	211	Wichita, KS	(15.2)
287	New Orleans, LA	(25.0)	304	San Diego, CA	(32.1)	67	Williamsport, PA	(2.2)
80	New York (greater), NY-NJ-PA	(4.9)	235	San Francisco (greater), CA	(17.7)	106	Wilmington, DE-MD-NJ M.D.	(6.9)
106	New York-W. Plains NY-NJ M.D.	(6.9)	188	San Francisco-S. Mateo, CA M.D.	(13.0)	NA	Wilmington, NC**	NA
94	Newark-Union, NJ-PA M.D.	(6.0)	218	San Jose, CA	(16.1)	186	Winchester, VA-WV	(12.9)
NA	North Port-Bradenton-Sarasota, FL**	NA	110	San Luis Obispo, CA	(7.1)	NA	Winston-Salem, NC**	NA
NA	Norwich-New London, CT**	NA	172	Sandusky, OH	(11.9)	17	Worcester, MA	11.5
249	Oakland-Fremont, CA M.D.	(20.4)	112	Santa Ana-Anaheim, CA M.D.	(7.2)	265	Yakima, WA	(22.0)
157	Ocala, FL	(10.7)	91	Santa Barbara-Santa Maria, CA	(5.4)	196	York-Hanover, PA	(14.1)
102	Ocean City, NJ	(6.7)	128	Santa Cruz-Watsonville, CA	(8.3)	108	Yuba City, CA	(7.0)
297	Odessa, TX	(29.6)	NA	Santa Fe, NM**	NA	271	Yuma, AZ	(22.4)
198	Ogden-Clearfield, UT	(14.2)	218	Santa Rosa-Petaluma, CA	(16.1)			

Source: CQ Press using reported data from the F.B.I. "Crime in the United States 2011"

*Property crimes are offenses of burglary, larceny-theft, and motor vehicle theft. Attempts are included.

**Not available.

Rank Order - Metro Area

28. Percent Change in Property Crime Rate: 2007 to 2011 (continued)
National Percent Change = 11.2% Decrease*

RANK	METROPOLITAN AREA	% CHANGE	RANK	METROPOLITAN AREA	% CHANGE	RANK	METROPOLITAN AREA	% CHANGE
1	Spokane, WA	34.9	61	Cleveland-Elyria-Mentor, OH	(1.4)	120	Eau Claire, WI	(7.7)
2	Sioux City, IA-NE-SD	28.8	62	Naples-Marco Island, FL	(1.6)	120	Kennewick-Pasco-Richland, WA	(7.7)
3	Erie, PA	25.3	63	Kokomo, IN	(1.8)	123	Sebastian-Vero Beach, FL	(7.9)
4	Rockingham County, NH M.D.	22.5	64	Akron, OH	(2.0)	124	Atlanta, GA	(8.1)
5	Sioux Falls, SD	20.9	64	Nassau-Suffolk, NY M.D.	(2.0)	124	Lansing-East Lansing, MI	(8.1)
6	Lewiston-Auburn, ME	20.7	66	Alexandria, LA	(2.1)	126	Florence, SC	(8.2)
7	Monroe, MI	20.6	67	Springfield, MA	(2.2)	126	Tulsa, OK	(8.2)
8	Redding, CA	18.7	67	Williamsport, PA	(2.2)	128	Roanoke, VA	(8.3)
9	Dover, DE	17.4	69	Knoxville, TN	(2.3)	128	Santa Cruz-Watsonville, CA	(8.3)
10	Madera, CA	16.5	69	Mobile, AL	(2.3)	130	Port St. Lucie, FL	(8.6)
11	Carson City, NV	15.5	71	Johnson City, TN	(2.5)	131	Topeka, KS	(8.8)
12	Bismarck, ND	14.1	72	Pocatello, ID	(2.8)	132	Crestview-Fort Walton Beach, FL	(9.0)
12	Kingston, NY	14.1	73	Buffalo-Niagara Falls, NY	(3.1)	132	Grand Junction, CO	(9.0)
14	Texarkana, TX-Texarkana, AR	13.6	74	Bridgeport-Stamford, CT	(3.5)	132	Lafayette, LA	(9.0)
15	Bremerton-Silverdale, WA	13.2	75	Scranton--Wilkes-Barre, PA	(4.0)	135	Danville, VA	(9.1)
16	Warner Robins, GA	11.8	75	Virginia Beach-Norfolk, VA-NC	(4.0)	135	Utica-Rome, NY	(9.1)
17	Worcester, MA	11.5	77	Rome, GA	(4.2)	137	Columbus, OH	(9.3)
18	Pittsfield, MA	11.3	78	Hanford-Corcoran, CA	(4.8)	137	Tyler, TX	(9.3)
19	Medford, OR	11.1	78	Palm Bay-Melbourne, FL	(4.8)	139	Fort Wayne, IN	(9.4)
20	Rapid City, SD	10.9	80	Atlantic City, NJ	(4.9)	139	Muncie, IN	(9.4)
21	Binghamton, NY	10.7	80	New York (greater), NY-NJ-PA	(4.9)	141	Indianapolis, IN	(9.6)
22	Harrisburg-Carlisle, PA	8.6	80	Philadelphia (greater) PA-NJ-MD-DE	(4.9)	141	Lafayette, IN	(9.6)
23	Columbus, IN	8.2	83	Albany, GA	(5.0)	141	Lima, OH	(9.6)
23	Fresno, CA	8.2	83	Beaumont-Port Arthur, TX	(5.0)	141	Nashville-Davidson, TN	(9.6)
25	Las Cruces, NM	7.4	83	Houma, LA	(5.0)	141	Racine, WI	(9.6)
26	Columbia, MO	6.2	83	Rochester, NY	(5.0)	146	Visalia-Porterville, CA	(9.7)
26	Lebanon, PA	6.2	87	Pine Bluff, AR	(5.1)	147	Gainesville, GA	(9.8)
26	Macon, GA	6.2	87	St. Joseph, MO-KS	(5.1)	147	Olympia, WA	(9.8)
29	Pensacola, FL	6.0	89	Lancaster, PA	(5.2)	149	Bend, OR	(10.0)
30	Victoria, TX	5.8	90	Lubbock, TX	(5.3)	149	Fort Collins-Loveland, CO	(10.0)
31	Lawton, OK	5.1	91	Santa Barbara-Santa Maria, CA	(5.4)	151	Michigan City-La Porte, IN	(10.1)
32	Camden, NJ M.D.	4.8	92	Merced, CA	(5.6)	152	Miami (greater), FL	(10.2)
33	Burlington, NC	4.6	93	St. Cloud, MN	(5.8)	153	Cleveland, TN	(10.3)
34	Fort Lauderdale, FL M.D.	4.3	94	Newark-Union, NJ-PA M.D.	(6.0)	154	Blacksburg, VA	(10.5)
35	Panama City-Lynn Haven, FL	4.2	95	Raleigh-Cary, NC	(6.1)	154	Glens Falls, NY	(10.5)
35	Portland, ME	4.2	96	Greenville, SC	(6.3)	156	St. Louis, MO-IL	(10.6)
37	Barnstable Town, MA	3.7	96	Little Rock, AR	(6.3)	157	Colorado Springs, CO	(10.7)
38	Cincinnati-Middletown, OH-KY-IN	3.6	98	Jackson, MS	(6.4)	157	Ocala, FL	(10.7)
39	Edison, NJ M.D.	2.8	98	Jefferson City, MO	(6.4)	159	Athens-Clarke County, GA	(10.8)
39	Trenton-Ewing, NJ	2.8	98	Morristown, TN	(6.4)	160	Des Moines-West Des Moines, IA	(10.9)
41	Louisville, KY-IN	2.5	101	Muskegon-Norton Shores, MI	(6.6)	160	El Centro, CA	(10.9)
42	Peabody, MA M.D.	2.1	102	Allentown, PA-NJ	(6.7)	160	Janesville, WI	(10.9)
43	Brunswick, GA	1.5	102	Ocean City, NJ	(6.7)	163	Altoona, PA	(11.1)
44	Mansfield, OH	1.0	102	Reading, PA	(6.7)	163	Portland-Vancouver, OR-WA	(11.1)
44	Syracuse, NY	1.0	105	Battle Creek, MI	(6.8)	165	Albuquerque, NM	(11.2)
44	Wausau, WI	1.0	106	New York-W. Plains NY-NJ M.D.	(6.9)	165	Jonesboro, AR	(11.2)
47	Lynchburg, VA	0.4	106	Wilmington, DE-MD-NJ M.D.	(6.9)	167	Rochester, MN	(11.4)
48	Albany-Schenectady-Troy, NY	0.2	108	Ames, IA	(7.0)	168	Charleston, WV	(11.7)
49	Springfield, MO	0.1	108	Yuba City, CA	(7.0)	169	Cambridge-Newton, MA M.D.	(11.8)
50	Evansville, IN-KY	(0.5)	110	Fayetteville, NC	(7.1)	169	Farmington, NM	(11.8)
51	Deltona-Daytona Beach, FL	(0.6)	110	San Luis Obispo, CA	(7.1)	169	Kingsport, TN-VA	(11.8)
51	Sherman-Denison, TX	(0.6)	112	Philadelphia, PA M.D.	(7.2)	172	Asheville, NC	(11.9)
53	Anderson, SC	(0.7)	112	Santa Ana-Anaheim, CA M.D.	(7.2)	172	Sandusky, OH	(11.9)
53	Dayton, OH	(0.7)	112	Tallahassee, FL	(7.2)	174	Pittsburgh, PA	(12.0)
55	Flint, MI	(0.8)	115	Baton Rouge, LA	(7.3)	175	Madison, WI	(12.1)
55	Johnstown, PA	(0.8)	115	Elizabethtown, KY	(7.3)	176	Baltimore-Towson, MD	(12.3)
57	Bloomington, IN	(1.0)	117	Duluth, MN-WI	(7.4)	176	Boston-Quincy, MA M.D.	(12.3)
57	Hickory, NC	(1.0)	117	La Crosse, WI-MN	(7.4)	176	Riverside-San Bernardino, CA	(12.3)
57	Oklahoma City, OK	(1.0)	119	Boston (greater), MA-NH	(7.5)	179	South Bend-Mishawaka, IN-MI	(12.4)
60	Poughkeepsie, NY	(1.2)	120	Augusta, GA-SC	(7.7)	180	Bakersfield, CA	(12.5)

Note: All listings are for Metropolitan Statistical Areas (M.S.A.s) except for those ending with "M.D." Listings with "M.D." are Metropolitan Divisions which are smaller parts of eleven large M.S.A.s. See explanatory note at beginning of metropolitan area section.

Rank Order - Metro Area (continued)

RANK	METROPOLITAN AREA	% CHANGE	RANK	METROPOLITAN AREA	% CHANGE	RANK	METROPOLITAN AREA	% CHANGE
180	San Antonio, TX	(12.5)	244	Punta Gorda, FL	(19.2)	307	Appleton, WI	(34.3)
182	Goldsboro, NC	(12.7)	245	Cedar Rapids, IA	(19.4)	308	Reno-Sparks, NV	(34.5)
182	Provo-Orem, UT	(12.7)	246	Amarillo, TX	(19.6)	309	Charlotte-Gastonia, NC-SC	(34.8)
182	Richmond, VA	(12.7)	247	Elmira, NY	(19.7)	NA	Anniston-Oxford, AL**	NA
185	Eugene-Springfield, OR	(12.8)	248	Monroe, LA	(20.3)	NA	Auburn, AL**	NA
186	Los Angeles (greater), CA	(12.9)	249	Lawrence, KS	(20.4)	NA	Billings, MT**	NA
186	Winchester, VA-WV	(12.9)	249	Midland, TX	(20.4)	NA	Birmingham-Hoover, AL**	NA
188	McAllen-Edinburg-Mission, TX	(13.0)	249	Oakland-Fremont, CA M.D.	(20.4)	NA	Bloomington-Normal, IL**	NA
188	San Francisco-S. Mateo, CA M.D.	(13.0)	252	Logan, UT-ID	(20.5)	NA	Boulder, CO**	NA
190	Ann Arbor, MI	(13.3)	252	Memphis, TN-MS-AR	(20.5)	NA	Canton, OH**	NA
191	Denver-Aurora, CO	(13.4)	254	Dallas-Plano-Irving, TX M.D.	(20.7)	NA	Cape Girardeau, MO-IL**	NA
191	Fargo, ND-MN	(13.4)	255	Mount Vernon-Anacortes, WA	(21.2)	NA	Champaign-Urbana, IL**	NA
191	Miami-Dade County, FL M.D.	(13.4)	256	Bay City, MI	(21.3)	NA	Chicago (greater), IL-IN-WI**	NA
194	Omaha-Council Bluffs, NE-IA	(13.8)	256	Oxnard-Thousand Oaks, CA	(21.3)	NA	Chicago-Joilet-Naperville, IL M.D.**	NA
194	Prescott, AZ	(13.8)	256	West Palm Beach, FL M.D.	(21.3)	NA	Columbus, GA-AL**	NA
196	Seattle-Bellevue-Everett, WA M.D.	(14.1)	259	Phoenix-Mesa-Scottsdale, AZ	(21.4)	NA	Cumberland, MD-WV**	NA
196	York-Hanover, PA	(14.1)	260	Jackson, TN	(21.7)	NA	Dalton, GA**	NA
198	Bangor, ME	(14.2)	260	Waco, TX	(21.7)	NA	Danville, IL**	NA
198	Grand Forks, ND-MN	(14.2)	262	Chico, CA	(21.8)	NA	Davenport, IA-IL**	NA
198	Ogden-Clearfield, UT	(14.2)	262	Jacksonville, FL	(21.8)	NA	Decatur, AL**	NA
201	Los Angeles County, CA M.D.	(14.3)	264	Greeley, CO	(21.9)	NA	Decatur, IL**	NA
202	Iowa City, IA	(14.4)	265	Green Bay, WI	(22.0)	NA	Detroit (greater), MI**	NA
202	Jacksonville, NC	(14.4)	265	Salisbury, MD	(22.0)	NA	Detroit-Livonia-Dearborn, MI M.D.**	NA
204	Salt Lake City, UT	(14.5)	265	Yakima, WA	(22.0)	NA	Dothan, AL**	NA
205	Fort Smith, AR-OK	(14.6)	268	Cheyenne, WY	(22.1)	NA	Durham-Chapel Hill, NC**	NA
206	Corvallis, OR	(14.8)	269	Idaho Falls, ID	(22.2)	NA	Fairbanks, AK**	NA
206	Seattle (greater), WA	(14.8)	270	Vallejo-Fairfield, CA	(22.3)	NA	Florence-Muscle Shoals, AL**	NA
208	Bowling Green, KY	(14.9)	271	Yuma, AZ	(22.4)	NA	Gadsden, AL**	NA
209	Fond du Lac, WI	(15.1)	272	Harrisonburg, VA	(22.5)	NA	Gainesville, FL**	NA
209	Fort Worth-Arlington, TX M.D.	(15.1)	272	Valdosta, GA	(22.5)	NA	Gary, IN M.D.**	NA
211	Wichita, KS	(15.2)	274	El Paso, TX	(22.6)	NA	Great Falls, MT**	NA
212	Brownsville-Harlingen, TX	(15.3)	274	Palm Coast, FL	(22.6)	NA	Gulfport-Biloxi, MS**	NA
212	Washington, DC-VA-MD-WV M.D.	(15.3)	276	Joplin, MO	(22.8)	NA	Hagerstown-Martinsburg, MD-WV**	NA
214	Sacramento, CA	(15.4)	276	Spartanburg, SC	(22.8)	NA	Holland-Grand Haven, MI**	NA
215	Abilene, TX	(15.5)	278	Tampa-St Petersburg, FL	(23.2)	NA	Houston, TX**	NA
216	Hot Springs, AR	(15.6)	279	Killeen-Temple-Fort Hood, TX	(23.3)	NA	Huntsville, AL**	NA
217	Orlando, FL	(16.0)	280	Wenatchee, WA	(23.7)	NA	Kankakee-Bradley, IL**	NA
218	San Jose, CA	(16.1)	281	Longview, WA	(23.9)	NA	Kansas City, MO-KS**	NA
218	Santa Rosa-Petaluma, CA	(16.1)	282	Bethesda-Frederick, MD M.D.	(24.5)	NA	Lake Co.-Kenosha Co., IL-WI M.D.**	NA
220	Dubuque, IA	(16.3)	282	San Angelo, TX	(24.5)	NA	Lexington-Fayette, KY**	NA
220	Lakeland, FL	(16.3)	284	Charlottesville, VA	(24.7)	NA	Manchester-Nashua, NH**	NA
222	Austin-Round Rock, TX	(16.4)	284	Salem, OR	(24.7)	NA	Manhattan, KS**	NA
222	Hinesville, GA	(16.4)	286	Modesto, CA	(24.9)	NA	Mankato-North Mankato, MN**	NA
222	Stockton, CA	(16.4)	287	New Orleans, LA	(25.0)	NA	Missoula, MT**	NA
225	Chattanooga, TN-GA	(16.6)	288	Oshkosh-Neenah, WI	(25.7)	NA	Montgomery, AL**	NA
226	Tacoma, WA M.D.	(16.8)	289	Corpus Christi, TX	(26.8)	NA	New Haven-Milford, CT**	NA
227	Rocky Mount, NC	(16.9)	290	Napa, CA	(27.1)	NA	North Port-Bradenton-Sarasota, FL**	NA
228	Hartford, CT	(17.0)	291	Casper, WY	(27.2)	NA	Norwich-New London, CT**	NA
228	Washington (greater) DC-VA-MD-WV	(17.0)	292	Cape Coral-Fort Myers, FL	(27.6)	NA	Owensboro, KY**	NA
230	Clarksville, TN-KY	(17.1)	293	Bellingham, WA	(27.7)	NA	Peoria, IL**	NA
231	Pascagoula, MS	(17.2)	294	Grand Rapids-Wyoming, MI	(27.9)	NA	Pueblo, CO**	NA
232	Anchorage, AK	(17.5)	294	Sumter, SC	(27.9)	NA	Rockford, IL**	NA
232	College Station-Bryan, TX	(17.5)	296	Lake Havasu City-Kingman, AZ	(29.5)	NA	Santa Fe, NM**	NA
232	State College, PA	(17.5)	297	Odessa, TX	(29.6)	NA	Savannah, GA**	NA
235	San Francisco (greater), CA	(17.7)	298	Laredo, TX	(30.1)	NA	Springfield, IL**	NA
236	Milwaukee, WI	(17.9)	298	Saginaw, MI	(30.1)	NA	Terre Haute, IN**	NA
237	Boise City-Nampa, ID	(18.1)	300	Longview, TX	(30.3)	NA	Toledo, OH**	NA
238	Flagstaff, AZ	(18.2)	301	Wichita Falls, TX	(30.4)	NA	Tucson, AZ**	NA
239	Dallas (greater), TX	(18.8)	302	Waterloo-Cedar Falls, IA	(31.2)	NA	Tuscaloosa, AL**	NA
239	Lincoln, NE	(18.8)	303	Sheboygan, WI	(31.7)	NA	Warren-Farmington Hills, MI M.D.**	NA
241	Myrtle Beach, SC	(18.9)	304	San Diego, CA	(32.1)	NA	Wilmington, NC**	NA
242	Minneapolis-St. Paul, MN-WI	(19.0)	305	Salinas, CA	(33.4)	NA	Winston-Salem, NC**	NA
243	Springfield, OH	(19.1)	306	Las Vegas-Paradise, NV	(34.0)			

Source: CQ Press using reported data from the F.B.I. "Crime in the United States 2011"
*Property crimes are offenses of burglary, larceny-theft, and motor vehicle theft. Attempts are included.
**Not available.

Alpha Order - Metro Area

29. Burglaries in 2011
National Total = 2,188,005 Burglaries*

RANK	METROPOLITAN AREA	BURGLARY	RANK	METROPOLITAN AREA	BURGLARY	RANK	METROPOLITAN AREA	BURGLARY
250	Abilene, TX	1,338	185	Charleston, WV	2,118	33	Fort Lauderdale, FL M.D.	18,814
82	Akron, OH	6,771	40	Charlotte-Gastonia, NC-SC	15,339	173	Fort Smith, AR-OK	2,322
113	Albany-Schenectady-Troy, NY	4,480	345	Charlottesville, VA	503	170	Fort Wayne, IN	2,369
194	Albany, GA	1,966	106	Chattanooga, TN-GA	4,910	24	Fort Worth-Arlington, TX M.D.	21,185
69	Albuquerque, NM	8,561	358	Cheyenne, WY	394	61	Fresno, CA	9,938
209	Alexandria, LA	1,752	4	Chicago (greater), IL-IN-WI	56,203	253	Gadsden, AL	1,266
142	Allentown, PA-NJ	3,192	9	Chicago-Joilet-Naperville, IL M.D.	46,751	184	Gainesville, FL	2,119
343	Altoona, PA	527	226	Chico, CA	1,564	269	Gainesville, GA	1,124
176	Amarillo, TX	2,296	32	Cincinnati-Middletown, OH-KY-IN	18,934	92	Gary, IN M.D.	6,196
347	Ames, IA	497	167	Clarksville, TN-KY	2,405	355	Glens Falls, NY	404
260	Anchorage, AK	1,161	31	Cleveland-Elyria-Mentor, OH	19,368	218	Goldsboro, NC	1,651
151	Anderson, SC	2,720	305	Cleveland, TN	799	349	Grand Forks, ND-MN	463
196	Ann Arbor, MI	1,957	214	College Station-Bryan, TX	1,676	316	Grand Junction, CO	722
211	Anniston-Oxford, AL	1,727	119	Colorado Springs, CO	4,144	107	Grand Rapids-Wyoming, MI	4,887
338	Appleton, WI	558	283	Columbia, MO	1,045	361	Great Falls, MT	344
140	Asheville, NC	3,273	116	Columbus, GA-AL	4,285	268	Greeley, CO	1,126
200	Athens-Clarke County, GA	1,892	353	Columbus, IN	419	285	Green Bay, WI	1,031
7	Atlanta, GA	51,978	23	Columbus, OH	21,407	95	Greenville, SC	5,832
182	Atlantic City, NJ	2,144	130	Corpus Christi, TX	3,623	149	Gulfport-Biloxi, MS	2,768
281	Auburn, AL	1,054	357	Corvallis, OR	397	224	Hagerstown-Martinsburg, MD-WV	1,603
85	Augusta, GA-SC	6,650	287	Crestview-Fort Walton Beach, FL	997	299	Hanford-Corcoran, CA	859
53	Austin-Round Rock, TX	10,820	311	Cumberland, MD-WV	771	162	Harrisburg-Carlisle, PA	2,474
63	Bakersfield, CA	9,460	2	Dallas (greater), TX	60,036	365	Harrisonburg, VA	266
36	Baltimore-Towson, MD	17,846	10	Dallas-Plano-Irving, TX M.D.	38,851	105	Hartford, CT	5,000
292	Bangor, ME	921	289	Dalton, GA	974	118	Hickory, NC	4,173
177	Barnstable Town, MA	2,295	262	Danville, IL	1,153	303	Hinesville, GA	829
68	Baton Rouge, LA	8,771	319	Danville, VA	714	290	Holland-Grand Haven, MI	967
212	Battle Creek, MI	1,714	172	Davenport, IA-IL	2,351	208	Hot Springs, AR	1,758
340	Bay City, MI	538	72	Dayton, OH	8,023	212	Houma, LA	1,714
111	Beaumont-Port Arthur, TX	4,555	240	Decatur, AL	1,464	5	Houston, TX	54,694
243	Bellingham, WA	1,448	252	Decatur, IL	1,312	114	Huntsville, AL	4,347
307	Bend, OR	791	108	Deltona-Daytona Beach, FL	4,692	336	Idaho Falls, ID	571
124	Bethesda-Frederick, MD M.D.	3,903	46	Denver-Aurora, CO	13,399	35	Indianapolis, IN	18,232
300	Billings, MT	851	126	Des Moines-West Des Moines, IA	3,848	337	Iowa City, IA	568
257	Binghamton, NY	1,215	13	Detroit (greater), MI	33,968	49	Jacksonville, FL	11,429
43	Birmingham-Hoover, AL	14,658	19	Detroit-Livonia-Dearborn, MI M.D.	23,057	231	Jacksonville, NC	1,524
352	Bismarck, ND	436	278	Dothan, AL	1,078	87	Jackson, MS	6,492
318	Blacksburg, VA	716	261	Dover, DE	1,158	242	Jackson, TN	1,455
293	Bloomington-Normal, IL	901	346	Dubuque, IA	499	275	Janesville, WI	1,086
273	Bloomington, IN	1,096	205	Duluth, MN-WI	1,842	308	Jefferson City, MO	778
165	Boise City-Nampa, ID	2,414	86	Durham-Chapel Hill, NC	6,576	235	Johnson City, TN	1,515
28	Boston (greater), MA-NH	20,033	310	Eau Claire, WI	774	312	Johnstown, PA	767
65	Boston-Quincy, MA M.D.	9,258	66	Edison, NJ M.D.	9,173	210	Jonesboro, AR	1,750
267	Boulder, CO	1,134	191	El Centro, CA	1,987	249	Joplin, MO	1,352
325	Bowling Green, KY	654	160	El Paso, TX	2,505	313	Kankakee-Bradley, IL	754
187	Bremerton-Silverdale, WA	2,029	362	Elizabethtown, KY	342	41	Kansas City, MO-KS	15,241
131	Bridgeport-Stamford, CT	3,602	354	Elmira, NY	407	244	Kennewick-Pasco-Richland, WA	1,423
143	Brownsville-Harlingen, TX	3,189	189	Erie, PA	1,997	125	Killeen-Temple-Fort Hood, TX	3,897
245	Brunswick, GA	1,422	161	Eugene-Springfield, OR	2,493	175	Kingsport, TN-VA	2,301
71	Buffalo-Niagara Falls, NY	8,075	183	Evansville, IN-KY	2,127	314	Kingston, NY	749
216	Burlington, NC	1,656	368	Fairbanks, AK	143	89	Knoxville, TN	6,321
97	Cambridge-Newton, MA M.D.	5,666	322	Fargo, ND-MN	697	304	Kokomo, IN	826
74	Camden, NJ M.D.	7,892	339	Farmington, NM	543	331	La Crosse, WI-MN	608
127	Canton, OH	3,782	79	Fayetteville, NC	7,286	263	Lafayette, IN	1,146
101	Cape Coral-Fort Myers, FL	5,326	342	Flagstaff, AZ	528	179	Lafayette, LA	2,195
317	Cape Girardeau, MO-IL	717	84	Flint, MI	6,684	141	Lake Co.-Kenosha Co., IL-WI M.D.	3,256
364	Carson City, NV	316	291	Florence-Muscle Shoals, AL	954	217	Lake Havasu City-Kingman, AZ	1,653
355	Casper, WY	404	153	Florence, SC	2,658	94	Lakeland, FL	6,057
234	Cedar Rapids, IA	1,517	366	Fond du Lac, WI	238	202	Lancaster, PA	1,881
230	Champaign-Urbana, IL	1,525	277	Fort Collins-Loveland, CO	1,081	139	Lansing-East Lansing, MI	3,278

Note: All listings are for Metropolitan Statistical Areas (M.S.A.s) except for those ending with "M.D." Listings with "M.D." are Metropolitan Divisions which are smaller parts of eleven large M.S.A.s. See explanatory note at beginning of metropolitan area section.

Alpha Order - Metro Area (continued)

RANK	METROPOLITAN AREA	BURGLARY	RANK	METROPOLITAN AREA	BURGLARY	RANK	METROPOLITAN AREA	BURGLARY
199	Laredo, TX	1,907	44	Oklahoma City, OK	14,513	144	Savannah, GA	3,053
204	Las Cruces, NM	1,863	198	Olympia, WA	1,916	158	Scranton--Wilkes-Barre, PA	2,569
39	Las Vegas-Paradise, NV	15,978	98	Omaha-Council Bluffs, NE-IA	5,618	15	Seattle (greater), WA	29,558
327	Lawrence, KS	642	20	Orlando, FL	22,072	22	Seattle-Bellevue-Everett, WA M.D.	21,770
186	Lawton, OK	2,086	330	Oshkosh-Neenah, WI	627	272	Sebastian-Vero Beach, FL	1,107
351	Lebanon, PA	446	319	Owensboro, KY	714	360	Sheboygan, WI	364
302	Lewiston-Auburn, ME	839	154	Oxnard-Thousand Oaks, CA	2,654	286	Sherman-Denison, TX	1,003
115	Lexington-Fayette, KY	4,317	110	Palm Bay-Melbourne, FL	4,616	295	Sioux City, IA-NE-SD	889
259	Lima, OH	1,180	344	Palm Coast, FL	505	274	Sioux Falls, SD	1,095
233	Lincoln, NE	1,523	221	Panama City-Lynn Haven, FL	1,628	129	South Bend-Mishawaka, IN-MI	3,657
56	Little Rock, AR	10,365	221	Pascagoula, MS	1,628	150	Spartanburg, SC	2,750
367	Logan, UT-ID	218	133	Peabody, MA M.D.	3,561	102	Spokane, WA	5,254
207	Longview, TX	1,801	121	Pensacola, FL	3,963	171	Springfield, IL	2,357
323	Longview, WA	683	145	Peoria, IL	2,974	96	Springfield, MA	5,731
8	Los Angeles County, CA M.D.	49,328	14	Philadelphia (greater) PA-NJ-MD-DE	33,415	132	Springfield, MO	3,601
1	Los Angeles (greater), CA	60,048	30	Philadelphia, PA M.D.	19,982	203	Springfield, OH	1,868
48	Louisville, KY-IN	12,607	11	Phoenix-Mesa-Scottsdale, AZ	37,510	350	State College, PA	460
123	Lubbock, TX	3,923	188	Pine Bluff, AR	2,008	73	Stockton, CA	7,931
276	Lynchburg, VA	1,085	60	Pittsburgh, PA	10,106	315	St. Cloud, MN	745
135	Macon, GA	3,434	281	Pittsfield, MA	1,054	266	St. Joseph, MO-KS	1,140
221	Madera, CA	1,628	363	Pocatello, ID	335	25	St. Louis, MO-IL	21,019
163	Madison, WI	2,470	137	Port St. Lucie, FL	3,360	256	Sumter, SC	1,219
200	Manchester-Nashua, NH	1,892	51	Portland-Vancouver, OR-WA	11,047	134	Syracuse, NY	3,543
329	Manhattan, KS	628	146	Portland, ME	2,919	76	Tacoma, WA M.D.	7,788
332	Mankato-North Mankato, MN	604	168	Poughkeepsie, NY	2,384	109	Tallahassee, FL	4,644
236	Mansfield, OH	1,492	271	Prescott, AZ	1,115	21	Tampa-St Petersburg, FL	21,996
90	McAllen-Edinburg-Mission, TX	6,316	219	Provo-Orem, UT	1,635	220	Terre Haute, IN	1,632
298	Medford, OR	860	197	Pueblo, CO	1,923	206	Texarkana, TX-Texarkana, AR	1,828
34	Memphis, TN-MS-AR	18,756	264	Punta Gorda, FL	1,144	58	Toledo, OH	10,299
157	Merced, CA	2,604	228	Racine, WI	1,558	164	Topeka, KS	2,425
6	Miami (greater), FL	54,367	77	Raleigh-Cary, NC	7,574	177	Trenton-Ewing, NJ	2,295
18	Miami-Dade County, FL M.D.	24,227	319	Rapid City, SD	714	70	Tucson, AZ	8,408
306	Michigan City-La Porte, IN	796	174	Reading, PA	2,303	57	Tulsa, OK	10,324
301	Midland, TX	848	246	Redding, CA	1,416	180	Tuscaloosa, AL	2,194
64	Milwaukee, WI	9,400	152	Reno-Sparks, NV	2,718	224	Tyler, TX	1,603
37	Minneapolis-St. Paul, MN-WI	17,198	88	Richmond, VA	6,433	227	Utica-Rome, NY	1,561
359	Missoula, MT	389	12	Riverside-San Bernardino, CA	34,714	251	Valdosta, GA	1,330
93	Mobile, AL	6,149	231	Roanoke, VA	1,524	122	Vallejo-Fairfield, CA	3,960
100	Modesto, CA	5,346	324	Rochester, MN	663	254	Victoria, TX	1,234
156	Monroe, LA	2,611	91	Rochester, NY	6,232	59	Virginia Beach-Norfolk, VA-NC	10,284
269	Monroe, MI	1,124	148	Rockford, IL	2,793	120	Visalia-Porterville, CA	3,986
117	Montgomery, AL	4,249	229	Rockingham County, NH M.D.	1,548	165	Waco, TX	2,414
284	Morristown, TN	1,035	192	Rocky Mount, NC	1,980	265	Warner Robins, GA	1,143
255	Mount Vernon-Anacortes, WA	1,228	297	Rome, GA	869	52	Warren-Farmington Hills, MI M.D.	10,911
309	Muncie, IN	775	42	Sacramento, CA	14,730	27	Washington (greater) DC-VA-MD-WV	20,115
239	Muskegon-Norton Shores, MI	1,470	190	Saginaw, MI	1,993	38	Washington, DC-VA-MD-WV M.D.	16,212
136	Myrtle Beach, SC	3,404	193	Salem, OR	1,967	288	Waterloo-Cedar Falls, IA	994
328	Napa, CA	631	155	Salinas, CA	2,650	348	Wausau, WI	494
237	Naples-Marco Island, FL	1,485	280	Salisbury, MD	1,056	334	Wenatchee, WA	582
45	Nashville-Davidson, TN	13,474	81	Salt Lake City, UT	6,881	50	West Palm Beach, FL M.D.	11,326
75	Nassau-Suffolk, NY M.D.	7,889	296	San Angelo, TX	886	238	Wichita Falls, TX	1,476
112	New Haven-Milford, CT	4,526	26	San Antonio, TX	20,168	103	Wichita, KS	5,204
62	New Orleans, LA	9,562	47	San Diego, CA	13,326	341	Williamsport, PA	531
3	New York (greater), NY-NJ-PA	56,514	17	San Francisco (greater), CA	28,864	99	Wilmington, DE-MD-NJ M.D.	5,541
16	New York-W. Plains NY-NJ M.D.	29,019	67	San Francisco-S. Mateo, CA M.D.	8,844	128	Wilmington, NC	3,748
55	Newark-Union, NJ-PA M.D.	10,433	77	San Jose, CA	7,574	335	Winchester, VA-WV	573
82	North Port-Bradenton-Sarasota, FL	6,771	247	San Luis Obispo, CA	1,411	80	Winston-Salem, NC	7,071
326	Norwich-New London, CT	647	333	Sandusky, OH	596	104	Worcester, MA	5,085
29	Oakland-Fremont, CA M.D.	20,020	54	Santa Ana-Anaheim, CA M.D.	10,720	138	Yakima, WA	3,351
159	Ocala, FL	2,540	181	Santa Barbara-Santa Maria, CA	2,167	248	York-Hanover, PA	1,385
279	Ocean City, NJ	1,075	195	Santa Cruz-Watsonville, CA	1,958	258	Yuba City, CA	1,187
294	Odessa, TX	900	147	Santa Fe, NM	2,867	240	Yuma, AZ	1,464
169	Ogden-Clearfield, UT	2,378	215	Santa Rosa-Petaluma, CA	1,664			

Source: Reported data from the F.B.I. "Crime in the United States 2011"

*Burglary is the unlawful entry of a structure to commit a felony or theft. Attempts are included.

Rank Order - Metro Area

29. Burglaries in 2011 (continued)
National Total = 2,188,005 Burglaries*

RANK	METROPOLITAN AREA	BURGLARY	RANK	METROPOLITAN AREA	BURGLARY	RANK	METROPOLITAN AREA	BURGLARY
1	Los Angeles (greater), CA	60,048	61	Fresno, CA	9,938	121	Pensacola, FL	3,963
2	Dallas (greater), TX	60,036	62	New Orleans, LA	9,562	122	Vallejo-Fairfield, CA	3,960
3	New York (greater), NY-NJ-PA	56,514	63	Bakersfield, CA	9,460	123	Lubbock, TX	3,923
4	Chicago (greater), IL-IN-WI	56,203	64	Milwaukee, WI	9,400	124	Bethesda-Frederick, MD M.D.	3,903
5	Houston, TX	54,694	65	Boston-Quincy, MA M.D.	9,258	125	Killeen-Temple-Fort Hood, TX	3,897
6	Miami (greater), FL	54,367	66	Edison, NJ M.D.	9,173	126	Des Moines-West Des Moines, IA	3,848
7	Atlanta, GA	51,978	67	San Francisco-S. Mateo, CA M.D.	8,844	127	Canton, OH	3,782
8	Los Angeles County, CA M.D.	49,328	68	Baton Rouge, LA	8,771	128	Wilmington, NC	3,748
9	Chicago-Joilet-Naperville, IL M.D.	46,751	69	Albuquerque, NM	8,561	129	South Bend-Mishawaka, IN-MI	3,657
10	Dallas-Plano-Irving, TX M.D.	38,851	70	Tucson, AZ	8,408	130	Corpus Christi, TX	3,623
11	Phoenix-Mesa-Scottsdale, AZ	37,510	71	Buffalo-Niagara Falls, NY	8,075	131	Bridgeport-Stamford, CT	3,602
12	Riverside-San Bernardino, CA	34,714	72	Dayton, OH	8,023	132	Springfield, MO	3,601
13	Detroit (greater), MI	33,968	73	Stockton, CA	7,931	133	Peabody, MA M.D.	3,561
14	Philadelphia (greater) PA-NJ-MD-DE	33,415	74	Camden, NJ M.D.	7,892	134	Syracuse, NY	3,543
15	Seattle (greater), WA	29,558	75	Nassau-Suffolk, NY M.D.	7,889	135	Macon, GA	3,434
16	New York-W. Plains NY-NJ M.D.	29,019	76	Tacoma, WA M.D.	7,788	136	Myrtle Beach, SC	3,404
17	San Francisco (greater), CA	28,864	77	Raleigh-Cary, NC	7,574	137	Port St. Lucie, FL	3,360
18	Miami-Dade County, FL M.D.	24,227	77	San Jose, CA	7,574	138	Yakima, WA	3,351
19	Detroit-Livonia-Dearborn, MI M.D.	23,057	79	Fayetteville, NC	7,286	139	Lansing-East Lansing, MI	3,278
20	Orlando, FL	22,072	80	Winston-Salem, NC	7,071	140	Asheville, NC	3,273
21	Tampa-St Petersburg, FL	21,996	81	Salt Lake City, UT	6,881	141	Lake Co.-Kenosha Co., IL-WI M.D.	3,256
22	Seattle-Bellevue-Everett, WA M.D.	21,770	82	Akron, OH	6,771	142	Allentown, PA-NJ	3,192
23	Columbus, OH	21,407	82	North Port-Bradenton-Sarasota, FL	6,771	143	Brownsville-Harlingen, TX	3,189
24	Fort Worth-Arlington, TX M.D.	21,185	84	Flint, MI	6,684	144	Savannah, GA	3,053
25	St. Louis, MO-IL	21,019	85	Augusta, GA-SC	6,650	145	Peoria, IL	2,974
26	San Antonio, TX	20,168	86	Durham-Chapel Hill, NC	6,576	146	Portland, ME	2,919
27	Washington (greater) DC-VA-MD-WV	20,115	87	Jackson, MS	6,492	147	Santa Fe, NM	2,867
28	Boston (greater), MA-NH	20,033	88	Richmond, VA	6,433	148	Rockford, IL	2,793
29	Oakland-Fremont, CA M.D.	20,020	89	Knoxville, TN	6,321	149	Gulfport-Biloxi, MS	2,768
30	Philadelphia, PA M.D.	19,982	90	McAllen-Edinburg-Mission, TX	6,316	150	Spartanburg, SC	2,750
31	Cleveland-Elyria-Mentor, OH	19,368	91	Rochester, NY	6,232	151	Anderson, SC	2,720
32	Cincinnati-Middletown, OH-KY-IN	18,934	92	Gary, IN M.D.	6,196	152	Reno-Sparks, NV	2,718
33	Fort Lauderdale, FL M.D.	18,814	93	Mobile, AL	6,149	153	Florence, SC	2,658
34	Memphis, TN-MS-AR	18,756	94	Lakeland, FL	6,057	154	Oxnard-Thousand Oaks, CA	2,654
35	Indianapolis, IN	18,232	95	Greenville, SC	5,832	155	Salinas, CA	2,650
36	Baltimore-Towson, MD	17,846	96	Springfield, MA	5,731	156	Monroe, LA	2,611
37	Minneapolis-St. Paul, MN-WI	17,198	97	Cambridge-Newton, MA M.D.	5,666	157	Merced, CA	2,604
38	Washington, DC-VA-MD-WV M.D.	16,212	98	Omaha-Council Bluffs, NE-IA	5,618	158	Scranton--Wilkes-Barre, PA	2,569
39	Las Vegas-Paradise, NV	15,978	99	Wilmington, DE-MD-NJ M.D.	5,541	159	Ocala, FL	2,540
40	Charlotte-Gastonia, NC-SC	15,339	100	Modesto, CA	5,346	160	El Paso, TX	2,505
41	Kansas City, MO-KS	15,241	101	Cape Coral-Fort Myers, FL	5,326	161	Eugene-Springfield, OR	2,493
42	Sacramento, CA	14,730	102	Spokane, WA	5,254	162	Harrisburg-Carlisle, PA	2,474
43	Birmingham-Hoover, AL	14,658	103	Wichita, KS	5,204	163	Madison, WI	2,470
44	Oklahoma City, OK	14,513	104	Worcester, MA	5,085	164	Topeka, KS	2,425
45	Nashville-Davidson, TN	13,474	105	Hartford, CT	5,000	165	Boise City-Nampa, ID	2,414
46	Denver-Aurora, CO	13,399	106	Chattanooga, TN-GA	4,910	165	Waco, TX	2,414
47	San Diego, CA	13,326	107	Grand Rapids-Wyoming, MI	4,887	167	Clarksville, TN-KY	2,405
48	Louisville, KY-IN	12,607	108	Deltona-Daytona Beach, FL	4,692	168	Poughkeepsie, NY	2,384
49	Jacksonville, FL	11,429	109	Tallahassee, FL	4,644	169	Ogden-Clearfield, UT	2,378
50	West Palm Beach, FL M.D.	11,326	110	Palm Bay-Melbourne, FL	4,616	170	Fort Wayne, IN	2,369
51	Portland-Vancouver, OR-WA	11,047	111	Beaumont-Port Arthur, TX	4,555	171	Springfield, IL	2,357
52	Warren-Farmington Hills, MI M.D.	10,911	112	New Haven-Milford, CT	4,526	172	Davenport, IA-IL	2,351
53	Austin-Round Rock, TX	10,820	113	Albany-Schenectady-Troy, NY	4,480	173	Fort Smith, AR-OK	2,322
54	Santa Ana-Anaheim, CA M.D.	10,720	114	Huntsville, AL	4,347	174	Reading, PA	2,303
55	Newark-Union, NJ-PA M.D.	10,433	115	Lexington-Fayette, KY	4,317	175	Kingsport, TN-VA	2,301
56	Little Rock, AR	10,365	116	Columbus, GA-AL	4,285	176	Amarillo, TX	2,296
57	Tulsa, OK	10,324	117	Montgomery, AL	4,249	177	Barnstable Town, MA	2,295
58	Toledo, OH	10,299	118	Hickory, NC	4,173	177	Trenton-Ewing, NJ	2,295
59	Virginia Beach-Norfolk, VA-NC	10,284	119	Colorado Springs, CO	4,144	179	Lafayette, LA	2,195
60	Pittsburgh, PA	10,106	120	Visalia-Porterville, CA	3,986	180	Tuscaloosa, AL	2,194

Note: All listings are for Metropolitan Statistical Areas (M.S.A.s) except for those ending with "M.D." Listings with "M.D." are Metropolitan Divisions which are smaller parts of eleven large M.S.A.s. See explanatory note at beginning of metropolitan area section.

Rank Order - Metro Area (continued)

RANK	METROPOLITAN AREA	BURGLARY	RANK	METROPOLITAN AREA	BURGLARY	RANK	METROPOLITAN AREA	BURGLARY
181	Santa Barbara-Santa Maria, CA	2,167	244	Kennewick-Pasco-Richland, WA	1,423	307	Bend, OR	791
182	Atlantic City, NJ	2,144	245	Brunswick, GA	1,422	308	Jefferson City, MO	778
183	Evansville, IN-KY	2,127	246	Redding, CA	1,416	309	Muncie, IN	775
184	Gainesville, FL	2,119	247	San Luis Obispo, CA	1,411	310	Eau Claire, WI	774
185	Charleston, WV	2,118	248	York-Hanover, PA	1,385	311	Cumberland, MD-WV	771
186	Lawton, OK	2,086	249	Joplin, MO	1,352	312	Johnstown, PA	767
187	Bremerton-Silverdale, WA	2,029	250	Abilene, TX	1,338	313	Kankakee-Bradley, IL	754
188	Pine Bluff, AR	2,008	251	Valdosta, GA	1,330	314	Kingston, NY	749
189	Erie, PA	1,997	252	Decatur, IL	1,312	315	St. Cloud, MN	745
190	Saginaw, MI	1,993	253	Gadsden, AL	1,266	316	Grand Junction, CO	722
191	El Centro, CA	1,987	254	Victoria, TX	1,234	317	Cape Girardeau, MO-IL	717
192	Rocky Mount, NC	1,980	255	Mount Vernon-Anacortes, WA	1,228	318	Blacksburg, VA	716
193	Salem, OR	1,967	256	Sumter, SC	1,219	319	Danville, VA	714
194	Albany, GA	1,966	257	Binghamton, NY	1,215	319	Owensboro, KY	714
195	Santa Cruz-Watsonville, CA	1,958	258	Yuba City, CA	1,187	319	Rapid City, SD	714
196	Ann Arbor, MI	1,957	259	Lima, OH	1,180	322	Fargo, ND-MN	697
197	Pueblo, CO	1,923	260	Anchorage, AK	1,161	323	Longview, WA	683
198	Olympia, WA	1,916	261	Dover, DE	1,158	324	Rochester, MN	663
199	Laredo, TX	1,907	262	Danville, IL	1,153	325	Bowling Green, KY	654
200	Athens-Clarke County, GA	1,892	263	Lafayette, IN	1,146	326	Norwich-New London, CT	647
200	Manchester-Nashua, NH	1,892	264	Punta Gorda, FL	1,144	327	Lawrence, KS	642
202	Lancaster, PA	1,881	265	Warner Robins, GA	1,143	328	Napa, CA	631
203	Springfield, OH	1,868	266	St. Joseph, MO-KS	1,140	329	Manhattan, KS	628
204	Las Cruces, NM	1,863	267	Boulder, CO	1,134	330	Oshkosh-Neenah, WI	627
205	Duluth, MN-WI	1,842	268	Greeley, CO	1,126	331	La Crosse, WI-MN	608
206	Texarkana, TX-Texarkana, AR	1,828	269	Gainesville, GA	1,124	332	Mankato-North Mankato, MN	604
207	Longview, TX	1,801	269	Monroe, MI	1,124	333	Sandusky, OH	596
208	Hot Springs, AR	1,758	271	Prescott, AZ	1,115	334	Wenatchee, WA	582
209	Alexandria, LA	1,752	272	Sebastian-Vero Beach, FL	1,107	335	Winchester, VA-WV	573
210	Jonesboro, AR	1,750	273	Bloomington, IN	1,096	336	Idaho Falls, ID	571
211	Anniston-Oxford, AL	1,727	274	Sioux Falls, SD	1,095	337	Iowa City, IA	568
212	Battle Creek, MI	1,714	275	Janesville, WI	1,086	338	Appleton, WI	558
212	Houma, LA	1,714	276	Lynchburg, VA	1,085	339	Farmington, NM	543
214	College Station-Bryan, TX	1,676	277	Fort Collins-Loveland, CO	1,081	340	Bay City, MI	538
215	Santa Rosa-Petaluma, CA	1,664	278	Dothan, AL	1,078	341	Williamsport, PA	531
216	Burlington, NC	1,656	279	Ocean City, NJ	1,075	342	Flagstaff, AZ	528
217	Lake Havasu City-Kingman, AZ	1,653	280	Salisbury, MD	1,056	343	Altoona, PA	527
218	Goldsboro, NC	1,651	281	Auburn, AL	1,054	344	Palm Coast, FL	505
219	Provo-Orem, UT	1,635	281	Pittsfield, MA	1,054	345	Charlottesville, VA	503
220	Terre Haute, IN	1,632	283	Columbia, MO	1,045	346	Dubuque, IA	499
221	Madera, CA	1,628	284	Morristown, TN	1,035	347	Ames, IA	497
221	Panama City-Lynn Haven, FL	1,628	285	Green Bay, WI	1,031	348	Wausau, WI	494
221	Pascagoula, MS	1,628	286	Sherman-Denison, TX	1,003	349	Grand Forks, ND-MN	463
224	Hagerstown-Martinsburg, MD-WV	1,603	287	Crestview-Fort Walton Beach, FL	997	350	State College, PA	460
224	Tyler, TX	1,603	288	Waterloo-Cedar Falls, IA	994	351	Lebanon, PA	446
226	Chico, CA	1,564	289	Dalton, GA	974	352	Bismarck, ND	436
227	Utica-Rome, NY	1,561	290	Holland-Grand Haven, MI	967	353	Columbus, IN	419
228	Racine, WI	1,558	291	Florence-Muscle Shoals, AL	954	354	Elmira, NY	407
229	Rockingham County, NH M.D.	1,548	292	Bangor, ME	921	355	Casper, WY	404
230	Champaign-Urbana, IL	1,525	293	Bloomington-Normal, IL	901	355	Glens Falls, NY	404
231	Jacksonville, NC	1,524	294	Odessa, TX	900	357	Corvallis, OR	397
231	Roanoke, VA	1,524	295	Sioux City, IA-NE-SD	889	358	Cheyenne, WY	394
233	Lincoln, NE	1,523	296	San Angelo, TX	886	359	Missoula, MT	389
234	Cedar Rapids, IA	1,517	297	Rome, GA	869	360	Sheboygan, WI	364
235	Johnson City, TN	1,515	298	Medford, OR	860	361	Great Falls, MT	344
236	Mansfield, OH	1,492	299	Hanford-Corcoran, CA	859	362	Elizabethtown, KY	342
237	Naples-Marco Island, FL	1,485	300	Billings, MT	851	363	Pocatello, ID	335
238	Wichita Falls, TX	1,476	301	Midland, TX	848	364	Carson City, NV	316
239	Muskegon-Norton Shores, MI	1,470	302	Lewiston-Auburn, ME	839	365	Harrisonburg, VA	266
240	Decatur, AL	1,464	303	Hinesville, GA	829	366	Fond du Lac, WI	238
240	Yuma, AZ	1,464	304	Kokomo, IN	826	367	Logan, UT-ID	218
242	Jackson, TN	1,455	305	Cleveland, TN	799	368	Fairbanks, AK	143
243	Bellingham, WA	1,448	306	Michigan City-La Porte, IN	796			

Source: Reported data from the F.B.I. "Crime in the United States 2011"
*Burglary is the unlawful entry of a structure to commit a felony or theft. Attempts are included.

Alpha Order - Metro Area

30. Burglary Rate in 2011
National Rate = 702.2 Burglaries per 100,000 Population*

RANK	METROPOLITAN AREA	RATE	RANK	METROPOLITAN AREA	RATE	RANK	METROPOLITAN AREA	RATE
151	Abilene, TX	793.0	196	Charleston, WV	695.2	61	Fort Lauderdale, FL M.D.	1,061.8
85	Akron, OH	962.2	120	Charlotte-Gastonia, NC-SC	861.7	165	Fort Smith, AR-OK	771.1
271	Albany-Schenectady-Troy, NY	512.2	364	Charlottesville, VA	246.6	244	Fort Wayne, IN	566.2
34	Albany, GA	1,233.5	103	Chattanooga, TN-GA	920.3	81	Fort Worth-Arlington, TX M.D.	971.4
89	Albuquerque, NM	954.4	313	Cheyenne, WY	426.1	63	Fresno, CA	1,055.7
47	Alexandria, LA	1,127.9	233	Chicago (greater), IL-IN-WI	592.2	35	Gadsden, AL	1,206.5
327	Allentown, PA-NJ	387.5	235	Chicago-Joilet-Naperville, IL M.D.	591.3	154	Gainesville, FL	791.0
319	Altoona, PA	413.4	194	Chico, CA	702.6	223	Gainesville, GA	617.4
107	Amarillo, TX	899.9	113	Cincinnati-Middletown, OH-KY-IN	887.0	117	Gary, IN M.D.	870.6
253	Ames, IA	552.2	117	Clarksville, TN-KY	870.6	356	Glens Falls, NY	312.0
333	Anchorage, AK	373.4	100	Cleveland-Elyria-Mentor, OH	931.7	22	Goldsboro, NC	1,329.5
14	Anderson, SC	1,436.8	197	Cleveland, TN	683.9	293	Grand Forks, ND-MN	463.8
241	Ann Arbor, MI	568.0	185	College Station-Bryan, TX	717.9	287	Grand Junction, CO	483.7
13	Anniston-Oxford, AL	1,449.5	218	Colorado Springs, CO	630.9	216	Grand Rapids-Wyoming, MI	631.7
365	Appleton, WI	246.2	229	Columbia, MO	602.6	316	Great Falls, MT	419.3
168	Asheville, NC	760.7	15	Columbus, GA-AL	1,436.4	306	Greeley, CO	437.7
82	Athens-Clarke County, GA	969.9	255	Columbus, IN	542.8	349	Green Bay, WI	335.2
80	Atlanta, GA	973.7	41	Columbus, OH	1,164.8	105	Greenville, SC	905.0
160	Atlantic City, NJ	778.3	133	Corpus Christi, TX	828.7	54	Gulfport-Biloxi, MS	1,108.3
173	Auburn, AL	747.9	295	Corvallis, OR	459.0	233	Hagerstown-Martinsburg, MD-WV	592.2
40	Augusta, GA-SC	1,179.2	254	Crestview-Fort Walton Beach, FL	544.0	251	Hanford-Corcoran, CA	555.0
223	Austin-Round Rock, TX	617.4	179	Cumberland, MD-WV	741.0	302	Harrisburg-Carlisle, PA	448.8
52	Bakersfield, CA	1,113.6	101	Dallas (greater), TX	922.8	367	Harrisonburg, VA	209.9
210	Baltimore-Towson, MD	652.2	108	Dallas-Plano-Irving, TX M.D.	898.3	283	Hartford, CT	489.2
232	Bangor, ME	598.4	199	Dalton, GA	675.9	48	Hickory, NC	1,127.4
62	Barnstable Town, MA	1,056.6	18	Danville, IL	1,408.3	64	Hinesville, GA	1,050.1
58	Baton Rouge, LA	1,083.1	203	Danville, VA	662.1	338	Holland-Grand Haven, MI	366.8
29	Battle Creek, MI	1,259.9	225	Davenport, IA-IL	616.7	4	Hot Springs, AR	1,817.1
274	Bay City, MI	499.6	90	Dayton, OH	952.7	137	Houma, LA	815.9
42	Beaumont-Port Arthur, TX	1,147.6	93	Decatur, AL	947.1	106	Houston, TX	900.8
188	Bellingham, WA	708.8	39	Decatur, IL	1,180.9	66	Huntsville, AL	1,036.0
279	Bend, OR	496.2	98	Deltona-Daytona Beach, FL	935.9	309	Idaho Falls, ID	432.9
352	Bethesda-Frederick, MD M.D.	320.8	266	Denver-Aurora, CO	517.8	68	Indianapolis, IN	1,032.9
256	Billings, MT	533.7	201	Des Moines-West Des Moines, IA	672.0	335	Iowa City, IA	370.3
288	Binghamton, NY	480.5	152	Detroit (greater), MI	791.2	129	Jacksonville, FL	837.9
24	Birmingham-Hoover, AL	1,293.2	28	Detroit-Livonia-Dearborn, MI M.D.	1,267.4	123	Jacksonville, NC	846.5
324	Bismarck, ND	394.2	183	Dothan, AL	736.6	36	Jackson, MS	1,199.8
308	Blacksburg, VA	434.2	191	Dover, DE	706.2	31	Jackson, TN	1,249.3
261	Bloomington-Normal, IL	529.7	260	Dubuque, IA	530.0	200	Janesville, WI	674.4
245	Bloomington, IN	565.8	209	Duluth, MN-WI	653.7	267	Jefferson City, MO	517.5
329	Boise City-Nampa, ID	387.2	25	Durham-Chapel Hill, NC	1,287.5	170	Johnson City, TN	755.6
307	Boston (greater), MA-NH	437.6	289	Eau Claire, WI	478.2	258	Johnstown, PA	532.1
285	Boston-Quincy, MA M.D.	487.4	326	Edison, NJ M.D.	390.7	16	Jonesboro, AR	1,435.1
330	Boulder, CO	378.4	49	El Centro, CA	1,125.3	167	Joplin, MO	767.5
270	Bowling Green, KY	515.7	357	El Paso, TX	306.4	202	Kankakee-Bradley, IL	662.6
148	Bremerton-Silverdale, WA	795.5	361	Elizabethtown, KY	283.7	176	Kansas City, MO-KS	745.3
323	Bridgeport-Stamford, CT	399.8	297	Elmira, NY	456.1	252	Kennewick-Pasco-Richland, WA	553.0
166	Brownsville-Harlingen, TX	768.9	187	Erie, PA	709.5	95	Killeen-Temple-Fort Hood, TX	941.7
32	Brunswick, GA	1,249.0	195	Eugene-Springfield, OR	701.3	184	Kingsport, TN-VA	736.0
189	Buffalo-Niagara Falls, NY	708.0	236	Evansville, IN-KY	589.8	321	Kingston, NY	408.6
59	Burlington, NC	1,082.0	318	Fairbanks, AK	417.6	109	Knoxville, TN	897.5
331	Cambridge-Newton, MA M.D.	374.7	351	Fargo, ND-MN	329.1	131	Kokomo, IN	832.7
219	Camden, NJ M.D.	628.9	320	Farmington, NM	412.9	301	La Crosse, WI-MN	452.7
99	Canton, OH	934.5	3	Fayetteville, NC	1,963.7	246	Lafayette, IN	565.0
122	Cape Coral-Fort Myers, FL	849.2	328	Flagstaff, AZ	387.3	149	Lafayette, LA	794.6
178	Cape Girardeau, MO-IL	742.1	7	Flint, MI	1,571.0	334	Lake Co.-Kenosha Co., IL-WI M.D.	373.1
243	Carson City, NV	566.9	211	Florence-Muscle Shoals, AL	645.3	138	Lake Havasu City-Kingman, AZ	814.2
259	Casper, WY	531.2	27	Florence, SC	1,278.1	78	Lakeland, FL	992.5
239	Cedar Rapids, IA	585.1	366	Fond du Lac, WI	233.2	341	Lancaster, PA	361.0
207	Champaign-Urbana, IL	655.7	343	Fort Collins-Loveland, CO	354.6	190	Lansing-East Lansing, MI	706.9

Note: All listings are for Metropolitan Statistical Areas (M.S.A.s) except for those ending with "M.D." Listings with "M.D." are Metropolitan Divisions which are smaller parts of eleven large M.S.A.s. See explanatory note at beginning of metropolitan area section.

Alpha Order - Metro Area (continued)

RANK	METROPOLITAN AREA	RATE
175	Laredo, TX	746.2
115	Las Cruces, NM	880.5
141	Las Vegas-Paradise, NV	812.0
240	Lawrence, KS	575.6
5	Lawton, OK	1,663.1
350	Lebanon, PA	332.9
159	Lewiston-Auburn, ME	779.1
104	Lexington-Fayette, KY	908.2
53	Lima, OH	1,108.9
274	Lincoln, NE	499.6
9	Little Rock, AR	1,470.1
368	Logan, UT-ID	170.6
134	Longview, TX	822.8
206	Longview, WA	656.6
278	Los Angeles County, CA M.D.	496.6
294	Los Angeles (greater), CA	462.6
79	Louisville, KY-IN	975.8
21	Lubbock, TX	1,348.6
315	Lynchburg, VA	424.4
12	Macon, GA	1,459.1
60	Madera, CA	1,066.6
310	Madison, WI	432.5
292	Manchester-Nashua, NH	471.5
281	Manhattan, KS	491.1
221	Mankato-North Mankato, MN	619.6
37	Mansfield, OH	1,197.8
145	McAllen-Edinburg-Mission, TX	798.4
317	Medford, OR	418.8
17	Memphis, TN-MS-AR	1,413.8
74	Merced, CA	1,006.2
84	Miami (greater), FL	963.9
86	Miami-Dade County, FL M.D.	957.4
186	Michigan City-La Porte, IN	710.5
228	Midland, TX	606.8
230	Milwaukee, WI	601.5
264	Minneapolis-St. Paul, MN-WI	520.4
346	Missoula, MT	352.8
8	Mobile, AL	1,481.8
70	Modesto, CA	1,027.1
10	Monroe, LA	1,466.4
180	Monroe, MI	739.9
46	Montgomery, AL	1,129.0
171	Morristown, TN	750.9
67	Mount Vernon-Anacortes, WA	1,034.2
208	Muncie, IN	655.3
121	Muskegon-Norton Shores, MI	854.4
30	Myrtle Beach, SC	1,249.5
296	Napa, CA	457.0
299	Naples-Marco Island, FL	455.7
127	Nashville-Davidson, TN	839.9
362	Nassau-Suffolk, NY M.D.	277.2
247	New Haven-Milford, CT	558.5
142	New Orleans, LA	811.4
359	New York (greater), NY-NJ-PA	297.8
363	New York-W. Plains NY-NJ M.D.	249.6
286	Newark-Union, NJ-PA M.D.	484.2
91	North Port-Bradenton-Sarasota, FL	951.2
304	Norwich-New London, CT	441.5
163	Oakland-Fremont, CA M.D.	773.2
169	Ocala, FL	756.4
55	Ocean City, NJ	1,101.6
213	Odessa, TX	642.8
312	Ogden-Clearfield, UT	426.4
43	Oklahoma City, OK	1,146.0
174	Olympia, WA	747.8
212	Omaha-Council Bluffs, NE-IA	643.8
72	Orlando, FL	1,020.2
332	Oshkosh-Neenah, WI	373.8
222	Owensboro, KY	617.9
353	Oxnard-Thousand Oaks, CA	318.6
128	Palm Bay-Melbourne, FL	838.1
263	Palm Coast, FL	520.6
91	Panama City-Lynn Haven, FL	951.2
75	Pascagoula, MS	999.6
290	Peabody, MA M.D.	476.3
116	Pensacola, FL	870.8
156	Peoria, IL	782.0
250	Philadelphia (greater) PA-NJ-MD-DE	557.9
277	Philadelphia, PA M.D.	496.8
114	Phoenix-Mesa-Scottsdale, AZ	882.1
1	Pine Bluff, AR	1,987.8
311	Pittsburgh, PA	427.5
145	Pittsfield, MA	798.4
339	Pocatello, ID	365.5
157	Port St. Lucie, FL	781.6
282	Portland-Vancouver, OR-WA	490.6
242	Portland, ME	567.9
344	Poughkeepsie, NY	354.1
262	Prescott, AZ	521.0
358	Provo-Orem, UT	304.5
38	Pueblo, CO	1,188.3
192	Punta Gorda, FL	705.5
150	Racine, WI	793.8
204	Raleigh-Cary, NC	661.6
248	Rapid City, SD	558.2
249	Reading, PA	558.0
155	Redding, CA	789.7
214	Reno-Sparks, NV	633.6
273	Richmond, VA	505.2
140	Riverside-San Bernardino, CA	812.1
284	Roanoke, VA	487.8
345	Rochester, MN	353.7
238	Rochester, NY	588.4
147	Rockford, IL	796.9
336	Rockingham County, NH M.D.	369.5
26	Rocky Mount, NC	1,283.0
112	Rome, GA	890.5
198	Sacramento, CA	677.4
76	Saginaw, MI	996.4
276	Salem, OR	498.1
217	Salinas, CA	631.0
130	Salisbury, MD	835.5
231	Salt Lake City, UT	600.5
162	San Angelo, TX	776.0
102	San Antonio, TX	921.9
314	San Diego, CA	425.5
205	San Francisco (greater), CA	658.0
280	San Francisco-S. Mateo, CA M.D.	492.2
322	San Jose, CA	407.5
268	San Luis Obispo, CA	517.2
164	Sandusky, OH	772.7
347	Santa Ana-Anaheim, CA M.D.	352.0
272	Santa Barbara-Santa Maria, CA	505.3
181	Santa Cruz-Watsonville, CA	737.6
2	Santa Fe, NM	1,966.6
348	Santa Rosa-Petaluma, CA	339.9
119	Savannah, GA	866.9
300	Scranton--Wilkes-Barre, PA	454.3
125	Seattle (greater), WA	846.0
143	Seattle-Bellevue-Everett, WA M.D.	810.5
152	Sebastian-Vero Beach, FL	791.2
355	Sheboygan, WI	313.8
139	Sherman-Denison, TX	812.7
226	Sioux City, IA-NE-SD	615.1
291	Sioux Falls, SD	474.0
45	South Bend-Mishawaka, IN-MI	1,140.9
87	Spartanburg, SC	956.1
56	Spokane, WA	1,097.8
51	Springfield, IL	1,118.1
135	Springfield, MA	822.0
136	Springfield, MO	821.6
20	Springfield, OH	1,349.4
359	State College, PA	297.8
44	Stockton, CA	1,143.8
325	St. Cloud, MN	391.0
110	St. Joseph, MO-KS	891.9
177	St. Louis, MO-IL	744.3
50	Sumter, SC	1,121.4
257	Syracuse, NY	532.3
83	Tacoma, WA M.D.	964.2
33	Tallahassee, FL	1,247.0
158	Tampa-St Petersburg, FL	779.7
95	Terre Haute, IN	941.7
23	Texarkana, TX-Texarkana, AR	1,321.7
6	Toledo, OH	1,579.8
69	Topeka, KS	1,030.4
220	Trenton-Ewing, NJ	624.1
126	Tucson, AZ	845.8
57	Tulsa, OK	1,089.6
77	Tuscaloosa, AL	994.9
172	Tyler, TX	748.6
265	Utica-Rome, NY	519.0
97	Valdosta, GA	940.4
94	Vallejo-Fairfield, CA	946.9
65	Victoria, TX	1,047.4
227	Virginia Beach-Norfolk, VA-NC	607.9
111	Visalia-Porterville, CA	891.0
73	Waco, TX	1,006.5
144	Warner Robins, GA	806.4
305	Warren-Farmington Hills, MI M.D.	441.1
342	Washington (greater) DC-VA-MD-WV	355.9
339	Washington, DC-VA-MD-WV M.D.	365.5
237	Waterloo-Cedar Falls, IA	589.2
337	Wausau, WI	366.9
269	Wenatchee, WA	516.8
124	West Palm Beach, FL M.D.	846.4
88	Wichita Falls, TX	955.4
132	Wichita, KS	830.0
298	Williamsport, PA	455.9
161	Wilmington, DE-MD-NJ M.D.	777.8
71	Wilmington, NC	1,021.5
303	Winchester, VA-WV	441.6
11	Winston-Salem, NC	1,461.6
215	Worcester, MA	632.9
19	Yakima, WA	1,356.4
354	York-Hanover, PA	317.4
193	Yuba City, CA	703.0
182	Yuma, AZ	737.4

Source: Reported data from the F.B.I. "Crime in the United States 2011"
*Burglary is the unlawful entry of a structure to commit a felony or theft. Attempts are included.

Rank Order - Metro Area

30. Burglary Rate in 2011 (continued)
National Rate = 702.2 Burglaries per 100,000 Population*

RANK	METROPOLITAN AREA	RATE
1	Pine Bluff, AR	1,987.8
2	Santa Fe, NM	1,966.6
3	Fayetteville, NC	1,963.7
4	Hot Springs, AR	1,817.1
5	Lawton, OK	1,663.1
6	Toledo, OH	1,579.8
7	Flint, MI	1,571.0
8	Mobile, AL	1,481.8
9	Little Rock, AR	1,470.1
10	Monroe, LA	1,466.4
11	Winston-Salem, NC	1,461.6
12	Macon, GA	1,459.1
13	Anniston-Oxford, AL	1,449.5
14	Anderson, SC	1,436.8
15	Columbus, GA-AL	1,436.4
16	Jonesboro, AR	1,435.1
17	Memphis, TN-MS-AR	1,413.8
18	Danville, IL	1,408.3
19	Yakima, WA	1,356.4
20	Springfield, OH	1,349.4
21	Lubbock, TX	1,348.6
22	Goldsboro, NC	1,329.5
23	Texarkana, TX-Texarkana, AR	1,321.7
24	Birmingham-Hoover, AL	1,293.2
25	Durham-Chapel Hill, NC	1,287.5
26	Rocky Mount, NC	1,283.0
27	Florence, SC	1,278.1
28	Detroit-Livonia-Dearborn, MI M.D.	1,267.4
29	Battle Creek, MI	1,259.9
30	Myrtle Beach, SC	1,249.5
31	Jackson, TN	1,249.3
32	Brunswick, GA	1,249.0
33	Tallahassee, FL	1,247.0
34	Albany, GA	1,233.5
35	Gadsden, AL	1,206.5
36	Jackson, MS	1,199.8
37	Mansfield, OH	1,197.8
38	Pueblo, CO	1,188.3
39	Decatur, IL	1,180.9
40	Augusta, GA-SC	1,179.2
41	Columbus, OH	1,164.8
42	Beaumont-Port Arthur, TX	1,147.6
43	Oklahoma City, OK	1,146.0
44	Stockton, CA	1,143.8
45	South Bend-Mishawaka, IN-MI	1,140.9
46	Montgomery, AL	1,129.0
47	Alexandria, LA	1,127.9
48	Hickory, NC	1,127.4
49	El Centro, CA	1,125.3
50	Sumter, SC	1,121.4
51	Springfield, IL	1,118.1
52	Bakersfield, CA	1,113.6
53	Lima, OH	1,108.9
54	Gulfport-Biloxi, MS	1,108.3
55	Ocean City, NJ	1,101.6
56	Spokane, WA	1,097.8
57	Tulsa, OK	1,089.6
58	Baton Rouge, LA	1,083.1
59	Burlington, NC	1,082.0
60	Madera, CA	1,066.5
61	Fort Lauderdale, FL M.D.	1,061.8
62	Barnstable Town, MA	1,056.6
63	Fresno, CA	1,055.7
64	Hinesville, GA	1,050.1
65	Victoria, TX	1,047.4
66	Huntsville, AL	1,036.0
67	Mount Vernon-Anacortes, WA	1,034.2
68	Indianapolis, IN	1,032.9
69	Topeka, KS	1,030.4
70	Modesto, CA	1,027.1
71	Wilmington, NC	1,021.5
72	Orlando, FL	1,020.2
73	Waco, TX	1,006.5
74	Merced, CA	1,006.2
75	Pascagoula, MS	999.6
76	Saginaw, MI	996.4
77	Tuscaloosa, AL	994.9
78	Lakeland, FL	992.5
79	Louisville, KY-IN	975.8
80	Atlanta, GA	973.7
81	Fort Worth-Arlington, TX M.D.	971.4
82	Athens-Clarke County, GA	969.9
83	Tacoma, WA M.D.	964.2
84	Miami (greater), FL	963.9
85	Akron, OH	962.2
86	Miami-Dade County, FL M.D.	957.4
87	Spartanburg, SC	956.1
88	Wichita Falls, TX	955.4
89	Albuquerque, NM	954.4
90	Dayton, OH	952.7
91	North Port-Bradenton-Sarasota, FL	951.2
91	Panama City-Lynn Haven, FL	951.2
93	Decatur, AL	947.1
94	Vallejo-Fairfield, CA	946.9
95	Killeen-Temple-Fort Hood, TX	941.7
95	Terre Haute, IN	941.7
97	Valdosta, GA	940.4
98	Deltona-Daytona Beach, FL	935.9
99	Canton, OH	934.5
100	Cleveland-Elyria-Mentor, OH	931.7
101	Dallas (greater), TX	922.8
102	San Antonio, TX	921.9
103	Chattanooga, TN-GA	920.3
104	Lexington-Fayette, KY	908.2
105	Greenville, SC	905.0
106	Houston, TX	900.8
107	Amarillo, TX	899.9
108	Dallas-Plano-Irving, TX M.D.	898.3
109	Knoxville, TN	897.5
110	St. Joseph, MO-KS	891.9
111	Visalia-Porterville, CA	891.0
112	Rome, GA	890.5
113	Cincinnati-Middletown, OH-KY-IN	887.0
114	Phoenix-Mesa-Scottsdale, AZ	882.1
115	Las Cruces, NM	880.5
116	Pensacola, FL	870.8
117	Clarksville, TN-KY	870.6
117	Gary, IN M.D.	870.6
119	Savannah, GA	866.9
120	Charlotte-Gastonia, NC-SC	861.7
121	Muskegon-Norton Shores, MI	854.4
122	Cape Coral-Fort Myers, FL	849.2
123	Jacksonville, NC	846.5
124	West Palm Beach, FL M.D.	846.4
125	Seattle (greater), WA	846.0
126	Tucson, AZ	845.8
127	Nashville-Davidson, TN	839.9
128	Palm Bay-Melbourne, FL	838.1
129	Jacksonville, FL	837.9
130	Salisbury, MD	835.5
131	Kokomo, IN	832.7
132	Wichita, KS	830.0
133	Corpus Christi, TX	828.7
134	Longview, TX	822.8
135	Springfield, MA	822.0
136	Springfield, MO	821.6
137	Houma, LA	815.9
138	Lake Havasu City-Kingman, AZ	814.2
139	Sherman-Denison, TX	812.7
140	Riverside-San Bernardino, CA	812.1
141	Las Vegas-Paradise, NV	812.0
142	New Orleans, LA	811.4
143	Seattle-Bellevue-Everett, WA M.D.	810.5
144	Warner Robins, GA	806.4
145	McAllen-Edinburg-Mission, TX	798.4
145	Pittsfield, MA	798.4
147	Rockford, IL	796.9
148	Bremerton-Silverdale, WA	795.5
149	Lafayette, LA	794.6
150	Racine, WI	793.8
151	Abilene, TX	793.0
152	Detroit (greater), MI	791.2
152	Sebastian-Vero Beach, FL	791.2
154	Gainesville, FL	791.0
155	Redding, CA	789.7
156	Peoria, IL	782.0
157	Port St. Lucie, FL	781.6
158	Tampa-St Petersburg, FL	779.7
159	Lewiston-Auburn, ME	779.1
160	Atlantic City, NJ	778.3
161	Wilmington, DE-MD-NJ M.D.	777.8
162	San Angelo, TX	776.0
163	Oakland-Fremont, CA M.D.	773.2
164	Sandusky, OH	772.7
165	Fort Smith, AR-OK	771.1
166	Brownsville-Harlingen, TX	768.9
167	Joplin, MO	767.5
168	Asheville, NC	760.7
169	Ocala, FL	756.4
170	Johnson City, TN	755.6
171	Morristown, TN	750.9
172	Tyler, TX	748.6
173	Auburn, AL	747.9
174	Olympia, WA	747.8
175	Laredo, TX	746.2
176	Kansas City, MO-KS	745.3
177	St. Louis, MO-IL	744.3
178	Cape Girardeau, MO-IL	742.1
179	Cumberland, MD-WV	741.0
180	Monroe, MI	739.9

Note: All listings are for Metropolitan Statistical Areas (M.S.A.s) except for those ending with "M.D." Listings with "M.D." are Metropolitan Divisions which are smaller parts of eleven large M.S.A.s. See explanatory note at beginning of metropolitan area section.

Rank Order - Metro Area (continued)

RANK	METROPOLITAN AREA	RATE	RANK	METROPOLITAN AREA	RATE	RANK	METROPOLITAN AREA	RATE
181	Santa Cruz-Watsonville, CA	737.6	244	Fort Wayne, IN	566.2	307	Boston (greater), MA-NH	437.6
182	Yuma, AZ	737.4	245	Bloomington, IN	565.8	308	Blacksburg, VA	434.2
183	Dothan, AL	736.6	246	Lafayette, IN	565.0	309	Idaho Falls, ID	432.9
184	Kingsport, TN-VA	736.0	247	New Haven-Milford, CT	558.5	310	Madison, WI	432.5
185	College Station-Bryan, TX	717.9	248	Rapid City, SD	558.2	311	Pittsburgh, PA	427.5
186	Michigan City-La Porte, IN	710.5	249	Reading, PA	558.0	312	Ogden-Clearfield, UT	426.4
187	Erie, PA	709.5	250	Philadelphia (greater) PA-NJ-MD-DE	557.9	313	Cheyenne, WY	426.1
188	Bellingham, WA	708.8	251	Hanford-Corcoran, CA	555.0	314	San Diego, CA	425.5
189	Buffalo-Niagara Falls, NY	708.0	252	Kennewick-Pasco-Richland, WA	553.0	315	Lynchburg, VA	424.4
190	Lansing-East Lansing, MI	706.9	253	Ames, IA	552.2	316	Great Falls, MT	419.3
191	Dover, DE	706.2	254	Crestview-Fort Walton Beach, FL	544.0	317	Medford, OR	418.8
192	Punta Gorda, FL	705.5	255	Columbus, IN	542.8	318	Fairbanks, AK	417.6
193	Yuba City, CA	703.0	256	Billings, MT	533.7	319	Altoona, PA	413.4
194	Chico, CA	702.6	257	Syracuse, NY	532.3	320	Farmington, NM	412.9
195	Eugene-Springfield, OR	701.3	258	Johnstown, PA	532.1	321	Kingston, NY	408.6
196	Charleston, WV	695.2	259	Casper, WY	531.2	322	San Jose, CA	407.5
197	Cleveland, TN	683.9	260	Dubuque, IA	530.0	323	Bridgeport-Stamford, CT	399.8
198	Sacramento, CA	677.4	261	Bloomington-Normal, IL	529.7	324	Bismarck, ND	394.2
199	Dalton, GA	675.9	262	Prescott, AZ	521.0	325	St. Cloud, MN	391.0
200	Janesville, WI	674.4	263	Palm Coast, FL	520.6	326	Edison, NJ M.D.	390.7
201	Des Moines-West Des Moines, IA	672.0	264	Minneapolis-St. Paul, MN-WI	520.4	327	Allentown, PA-NJ	387.5
202	Kankakee-Bradley, IL	662.6	265	Utica-Rome, NY	519.0	328	Flagstaff, AZ	387.3
203	Danville, VA	662.1	266	Denver-Aurora, CO	517.8	329	Boise City-Nampa, ID	387.2
204	Raleigh-Cary, NC	661.6	267	Jefferson City, MO	517.5	330	Boulder, CO	378.4
205	San Francisco (greater), CA	658.0	268	San Luis Obispo, CA	517.2	331	Cambridge-Newton, MA M.D.	374.7
206	Longview, WA	656.6	269	Wenatchee, WA	516.8	332	Oshkosh-Neenah, WI	373.8
207	Champaign-Urbana, IL	655.7	270	Bowling Green, KY	515.7	333	Anchorage, AK	373.4
208	Muncie, IN	655.3	271	Albany-Schenectady-Troy, NY	512.2	334	Lake Co.-Kenosha Co., IL-WI M.D.	373.1
209	Duluth, MN-WI	653.7	272	Santa Barbara-Santa Maria, CA	505.3	335	Iowa City, IA	370.3
210	Baltimore-Towson, MD	652.2	273	Richmond, VA	505.2	336	Rockingham County, NH M.D.	369.5
211	Florence-Muscle Shoals, AL	645.3	274	Bay City, MI	499.6	337	Wausau, WI	366.9
212	Omaha-Council Bluffs, NE-IA	643.8	274	Lincoln, NE	499.6	338	Holland-Grand Haven, MI	366.8
213	Odessa, TX	642.8	276	Salem, OR	498.1	339	Pocatello, ID	365.5
214	Reno-Sparks, NV	633.6	277	Philadelphia, PA M.D.	496.8	339	Washington, DC-VA-MD-WV M.D.	365.5
215	Worcester, MA	632.9	278	Los Angeles County, CA M.D.	496.6	341	Lancaster, PA	361.0
216	Grand Rapids-Wyoming, MI	631.7	279	Bend, OR	496.2	342	Washington (greater) DC-VA-MD-WV	355.9
217	Salinas, CA	631.0	280	San Francisco-S. Mateo, CA M.D.	492.2	343	Fort Collins-Loveland, CO	354.6
218	Colorado Springs, CO	630.9	281	Manhattan, KS	491.1	344	Poughkeepsie, NY	354.1
219	Camden, NJ M.D.	628.9	282	Portland-Vancouver, OR-WA	490.6	345	Rochester, MN	353.7
220	Trenton-Ewing, NJ	624.1	283	Hartford, CT	489.2	346	Missoula, MT	352.8
221	Mankato-North Mankato, MN	619.6	284	Roanoke, VA	487.8	347	Santa Ana-Anaheim, CA M.D.	352.0
222	Owensboro, KY	617.9	285	Boston-Quincy, MA M.D.	487.4	348	Santa Rosa-Petaluma, CA	339.9
223	Austin-Round Rock, TX	617.4	286	Newark-Union, NJ-PA M.D.	484.2	349	Green Bay, WI	335.2
223	Gainesville, GA	617.4	287	Grand Junction, CO	483.7	350	Lebanon, PA	332.9
225	Davenport, IA-IL	616.7	288	Binghamton, NY	480.5	351	Fargo, ND-MN	329.1
226	Sioux City, IA-NE-SD	615.1	289	Eau Claire, WI	478.2	352	Bethesda-Frederick, MD M.D.	320.8
227	Virginia Beach-Norfolk, VA-NC	607.9	290	Peabody, MA M.D.	476.3	353	Oxnard-Thousand Oaks, CA	318.6
228	Midland, TX	606.8	291	Sioux Falls, SD	474.0	354	York-Hanover, PA	317.4
229	Columbia, MO	602.6	292	Manchester-Nashua, NH	471.5	355	Sheboygan, WI	313.8
230	Milwaukee, WI	601.5	293	Grand Forks, ND-MN	463.8	356	Glens Falls, NY	312.0
231	Salt Lake City, UT	600.5	294	Los Angeles (greater), CA	462.6	357	El Paso, TX	306.4
232	Bangor, ME	598.4	295	Corvallis, OR	459.0	358	Provo-Orem, UT	304.5
233	Chicago (greater), IL-IN-WI	592.2	296	Napa, CA	457.0	359	New York (greater), NY-NJ-PA	297.8
233	Hagerstown-Martinsburg, MD-WV	592.2	297	Elmira, NY	456.1	359	State College, PA	297.8
235	Chicago-Joilet-Naperville, IL M.D.	591.3	298	Williamsport, PA	455.9	361	Elizabethtown, KY	283.7
236	Evansville, IN-KY	589.8	299	Naples-Marco Island, FL	455.7	362	Nassau-Suffolk, NY M.D.	277.2
237	Waterloo-Cedar Falls, IA	589.2	300	Scranton--Wilkes-Barre, PA	454.3	363	New York-W. Plains NY-NJ M.D.	249.6
238	Rochester, NY	588.4	301	La Crosse, WI-MN	452.7	364	Charlottesville, VA	246.6
239	Cedar Rapids, IA	585.1	302	Harrisburg-Carlisle, PA	448.8	365	Appleton, WI	246.2
240	Lawrence, KS	575.6	303	Winchester, VA-WV	441.6	366	Fond du Lac, WI	233.2
241	Ann Arbor, MI	568.0	304	Norwich-New London, CT	441.5	367	Harrisonburg, VA	209.9
242	Portland, ME	567.9	305	Warren-Farmington Hills, MI M.D.	441.1	368	Logan, UT-ID	170.6
243	Carson City, NV	566.9	306	Greeley, CO	437.7			

Source: Reported data from the F.B.I. "Crime in the United States 2011"
*Burglary is the unlawful entry of a structure to commit a felony or theft. Attempts are included.

Alpha Order - Metro Area

31. Percent Change in Burglary Rate: 2010 to 2011
National Percent Change = 0.2% Increase*

RANK	METROPOLITAN AREA	% CHANGE	RANK	METROPOLITAN AREA	% CHANGE	RANK	METROPOLITAN AREA	% CHANGE
320	Abilene, TX	(21.4)	NA	Charleston, WV**	NA	66	Fort Lauderdale, FL M.D.	8.8
141	Akron, OH	1.5	NA	Charlotte-Gastonia, NC-SC**	NA	180	Fort Smith, AR-OK	(1.6)
154	Albany-Schenectady-Troy, NY	0.0	325	Charlottesville, VA	(26.0)	263	Fort Wayne, IN	(9.8)
282	Albany, GA	(13.0)	188	Chattanooga, TN-GA	(2.0)	149	Fort Worth-Arlington, TX M.D.	0.6
119	Albuquerque, NM	3.7	26	Cheyenne, WY	16.1	77	Fresno, CA	7.7
234	Alexandria, LA	(6.3)	NA	Chicago (greater), IL-IN-WI**	NA	NA	Gadsden, AL**	NA
268	Allentown, PA-NJ	(10.3)	NA	Chicago-Joilet-Naperville, IL M.D.**	NA	279	Gainesville, FL	(12.5)
200	Altoona, PA	(2.8)	297	Chico, CA	(15.6)	103	Gainesville, GA	4.8
319	Amarillo, TX	(20.9)	61	Cincinnati-Middletown, OH-KY-IN	9.3	NA	Gary, IN M.D.**	NA
28	Ames, IA	15.4	127	Clarksville, TN-KY	2.7	210	Glens Falls, NY	(3.7)
268	Anchorage, AK	(10.3)	114	Cleveland-Elyria-Mentor, OH	4.0	317	Goldsboro, NC	(20.7)
50	Anderson, SC	10.7	177	Cleveland, TN	(1.4)	51	Grand Forks, ND-MN	10.6
289	Ann Arbor, MI	(13.9)	271	College Station-Bryan, TX	(10.7)	83	Grand Junction, CO	7.2
NA	Anniston-Oxford, AL**	NA	250	Colorado Springs, CO	(8.4)	301	Grand Rapids-Wyoming, MI	(16.3)
328	Appleton, WI	(35.0)	7	Columbia, MO	32.5	NA	Great Falls, MT**	NA
141	Asheville, NC	1.5	NA	Columbus, GA-AL**	NA	157	Greeley, CO	(0.2)
222	Athens-Clarke County, GA	(4.7)	178	Columbus, IN	(1.5)	266	Green Bay, WI	(10.2)
137	Atlanta, GA	1.7	158	Columbus, OH	(0.3)	86	Greenville, SC	6.8
102	Atlantic City, NJ	5.0	251	Corpus Christi, TX	(8.7)	246	Gulfport-Biloxi, MS	(8.1)
NA	Auburn, AL**	NA	16	Corvallis, OR	21.0	10	Hagerstown-Martinsburg, MD-WV	25.0
282	Augusta, GA-SC	(13.0)	303	Crestview-Fort Walton Beach, FL	(16.6)	97	Hanford-Corcoran, CA	5.7
310	Austin-Round Rock, TX	(18.1)	NA	Cumberland, MD-WV**	NA	38	Harrisburg-Carlisle, PA	12.4
203	Bakersfield, CA	(3.0)	161	Dallas (greater), TX	(0.4)	295	Harrisonburg, VA	(15.5)
150	Baltimore-Towson, MD	0.4	170	Dallas-Plano-Irving, TX M.D.	(1.0)	95	Hartford, CT	5.9
107	Bangor, ME	4.4	251	Dalton, GA	(8.7)	36	Hickory, NC	12.9
228	Barnstable Town, MA	(5.4)	178	Danville, IL	(1.5)	152	Hinesville, GA	0.3
NA	Baton Rouge, LA**	NA	278	Danville, VA	(12.4)	193	Holland-Grand Haven, MI	(2.6)
53	Battle Creek, MI	10.0	NA	Davenport, IA-IL**	NA	244	Hot Springs, AR	(7.4)
310	Bay City, MI	(18.1)	137	Dayton, OH	1.7	17	Houma, LA	19.8
166	Beaumont-Port Arthur, TX	(0.8)	NA	Decatur, AL**	NA	NA	Houston, TX**	NA
133	Bellingham, WA	2.1	324	Decatur, IL	(25.4)	NA	Huntsville, AL**	NA
158	Bend, OR	(0.3)	193	Deltona-Daytona Beach, FL	(2.6)	220	Idaho Falls, ID	(4.6)
193	Bethesda-Frederick, MD M.D.	(2.6)	188	Denver-Aurora, CO	(2.0)	NA	Indianapolis, IN**	NA
NA	Billings, MT**	NA	70	Des Moines-West Des Moines, IA	8.7	34	Iowa City, IA	13.7
94	Binghamton, NY	6.0	NA	Detroit (greater), MI**	NA	253	Jacksonville, FL	(8.8)
NA	Birmingham-Hoover, AL**	NA	154	Detroit-Livonia-Dearborn, MI M.D.	0.0	NA	Jacksonville, NC**	NA
1	Bismarck, ND	79.6	NA	Dothan, AL**	NA	193	Jackson, MS	(2.6)
282	Blacksburg, VA	(13.0)	143	Dover, DE	1.3	226	Jackson, TN	(5.1)
270	Bloomington-Normal, IL	(10.5)	265	Dubuque, IA	(9.9)	46	Janesville, WI	11.1
322	Bloomington, IN	(23.8)	73	Duluth, MN-WI	8.2	181	Jefferson City, MO	(1.7)
207	Boise City-Nampa, ID	(3.3)	107	Durham-Chapel Hill, NC	4.4	172	Johnson City, TN	(1.2)
220	Boston (greater), MA-NH	(4.6)	106	Eau Claire, WI	4.5	8	Johnstown, PA	28.9
181	Boston-Quincy, MA M.D.	(1.7)	41	Edison, NJ M.D.	12.1	112	Jonesboro, AR	4.1
192	Boulder, CO	(2.4)	145	El Centro, CA	1.0	44	Joplin, MO	11.4
316	Bowling Green, KY	(20.6)	291	El Paso, TX	(14.2)	NA	Kankakee-Bradley, IL**	NA
39	Bremerton-Silverdale, WA	12.3	309	Elizabethtown, KY	(18.0)	NA	Kansas City, MO-KS**	NA
76	Bridgeport-Stamford, CT	7.8	162	Elmira, NY	(0.5)	20	Kennewick-Pasco-Richland, WA	19.4
287	Brownsville-Harlingen, TX	(13.5)	46	Erie, PA	11.1	230	Killeen-Temple-Fort Hood, TX	(5.6)
312	Brunswick, GA	(18.3)	NA	Eugene-Springfield, OR**	NA	239	Kingsport, TN-VA	(7.0)
222	Buffalo-Niagara Falls, NY	(4.7)	35	Evansville, IN-KY	13.2	123	Kingston, NY	3.2
117	Burlington, NC	3.8	227	Fairbanks, AK	(5.3)	257	Knoxville, TN	(9.1)
260	Cambridge-Newton, MA M.D.	(9.5)	246	Fargo, ND-MN	(8.1)	49	Kokomo, IN	10.8
31	Camden, NJ M.D.	14.4	313	Farmington, NM	(18.4)	109	La Crosse, WI-MN	4.3
13	Canton, OH	23.3	40	Fayetteville, NC	12.2	42	Lafayette, IN	11.9
121	Cape Coral-Fort Myers, FL	3.5	234	Flagstaff, AZ	(6.3)	300	Lafayette, LA	(16.0)
191	Cape Girardeau, MO-IL	(2.2)	114	Flint, MI	4.0	NA	Lake Co.-Kenosha Co., IL-WI M.D.**	NA
45	Carson City, NV	11.2	NA	Florence-Muscle Shoals, AL**	NA	NA	Lake Havasu City-Kingman, AZ**	NA
314	Casper, WY	(19.9)	145	Florence, SC	1.0	136	Lakeland, FL	1.8
134	Cedar Rapids, IA	2.0	329	Fond du Lac, WI	(36.2)	82	Lancaster, PA	7.3
NA	Champaign-Urbana, IL**	NA	237	Fort Collins-Loveland, CO	(6.7)	57	Lansing-East Lansing, MI	9.7

Note: All listings are for Metropolitan Statistical Areas (M.S.A.s) except for those ending with "M.D." Listings with "M.D." are Metropolitan Divisions which are smaller parts of eleven large M.S.A.s. See explanatory note at beginning of metropolitan area section.

Alpha Order - Metro Area (continued)

RANK	METROPOLITAN AREA	% CHANGE
232	Laredo, TX	(6.2)
96	Las Cruces, NM	5.8
263	Las Vegas-Paradise, NV	(9.8)
116	Lawrence, KS	3.9
147	Lawton, OK	0.9
224	Lebanon, PA	(4.9)
2	Lewiston-Auburn, ME	72.3
NA	Lexington-Fayette, KY**	NA
188	Lima, OH	(2.0)
218	Lincoln, NE	(4.4)
111	Little Rock, AR	4.2
154	Logan, UT-ID	0.0
218	Longview, TX	(4.4)
294	Longview, WA	(15.2)
158	Los Angeles County, CA M.D.	(0.3)
164	Los Angeles (greater), CA	(0.6)
72	Louisville, KY-IN	8.6
57	Lubbock, TX	9.7
19	Lynchburg, VA	19.7
193	Macon, GA	(2.6)
5	Madera, CA	34.7
241	Madison, WI	(7.1)
137	Manchester-Nashua, NH	1.7
63	Manhattan, KS	9.1
3	Mankato-North Mankato, MN	48.2
172	Mansfield, OH	(1.2)
320	McAllen-Edinburg-Mission, TX	(21.4)
128	Medford, OR	2.5
170	Memphis, TN-MS-AR	(1.0)
87	Merced, CA	6.6
117	Miami (greater), FL	3.8
105	Miami-Dade County, FL M.D.	4.6
308	Michigan City-La Porte, IN	(17.5)
326	Midland, TX	(26.1)
80	Milwaukee, WI	7.4
119	Minneapolis-St. Paul, MN-WI	3.7
NA	Missoula, MT**	NA
24	Mobile, AL	17.1
184	Modesto, CA	(1.8)
246	Monroe, LA	(8.1)
29	Monroe, MI	15.2
NA	Montgomery, AL**	NA
279	Morristown, TN	(12.5)
61	Mount Vernon-Anacortes, WA	9.3
21	Muncie, IN	18.2
288	Muskegon-Norton Shores, MI	(13.8)
231	Myrtle Beach, SC	(6.1)
207	Napa, CA	(3.3)
11	Naples-Marco Island, FL	23.7
166	Nashville-Davidson, TN	(0.8)
97	Nassau-Suffolk, NY M.D.	5.7
92	New Haven-Milford, CT	6.1
77	New Orleans, LA	7.7
87	New York (greater), NY-NJ-PA	6.6
123	New York-W. Plains NY-NJ M.D.	3.2
37	Newark-Union, NJ-PA M.D.	12.7
229	North Port-Bradenton-Sarasota, FL	(5.5)
301	Norwich-New London, CT	(16.3)
147	Oakland-Fremont, CA M.D.	0.9
83	Ocala, FL	7.2
214	Ocean City, NJ	(4.0)
327	Odessa, TX	(26.6)
305	Ogden-Clearfield, UT	(16.9)
212	Oklahoma City, OK	(3.8)
241	Olympia, WA	(7.1)
52	Omaha-Council Bluffs, NE-IA	10.4
140	Orlando, FL	1.6
NA	Oshkosh-Neenah, WI**	NA
4	Owensboro, KY	34.8
297	Oxnard-Thousand Oaks, CA	(15.6)
90	Palm Bay-Melbourne, FL	6.3
253	Palm Coast, FL	(8.8)
213	Panama City-Lynn Haven, FL	(3.9)
307	Pascagoula, MS	(17.3)
246	Peabody, MA M.D.	(8.1)
100	Pensacola, FL	5.3
22	Peoria, IL	17.4
66	Philadelphia (greater) PA-NJ-MD-DE	8.8
53	Philadelphia, PA M.D.	10.0
48	Phoenix-Mesa-Scottsdale, AZ	10.9
33	Pine Bluff, AR	14.0
166	Pittsburgh, PA	(0.8)
79	Pittsfield, MA	7.5
286	Pocatello, ID	(13.3)
57	Port St. Lucie, FL	9.7
NA	Portland-Vancouver, OR-WA**	NA
63	Portland, ME	9.1
132	Poughkeepsie, NY	2.2
129	Prescott, AZ	2.4
199	Provo-Orem, UT	(2.7)
NA	Pueblo, CO**	NA
205	Punta Gorda, FL	(3.1)
9	Racine, WI	27.9
100	Raleigh-Cary, NC	5.3
126	Rapid City, SD	3.1
90	Reading, PA	6.3
216	Redding, CA	(4.3)
209	Reno-Sparks, NV	(3.6)
135	Richmond, VA	1.9
66	Riverside-San Bernardino, CA	8.8
175	Roanoke, VA	(1.3)
25	Rochester, MN	16.4
232	Rochester, NY	(6.2)
305	Rockford, IL	(16.9)
74	Rockingham County, NH M.D.	8.0
74	Rocky Mount, NC	8.0
164	Rome, GA	(0.6)
275	Sacramento, CA	(11.9)
256	Saginaw, MI	(9.0)
43	Salem, OR	11.8
281	Salinas, CA	(12.8)
318	Salisbury, MD	(20.8)
315	Salt Lake City, UT	(20.2)
323	San Angelo, TX	(24.0)
289	San Antonio, TX	(13.9)
239	San Diego, CA	(7.0)
150	San Francisco (greater), CA	0.4
172	San Francisco-S. Mateo, CA M.D.	(1.2)
206	San Jose, CA	(3.2)
258	San Luis Obispo, CA	(9.3)
15	Sandusky, OH	22.1
186	Santa Ana-Anaheim, CA M.D.	(1.9)
109	Santa Barbara-Santa Maria, CA	4.3
70	Santa Cruz-Watsonville, CA	8.7
261	Santa Fe, NM	(9.7)
295	Santa Rosa-Petaluma, CA	(15.5)
285	Savannah, GA	(13.2)
184	Scranton--Wilkes-Barre, PA	(1.8)
131	Seattle (greater), WA	2.3
104	Seattle-Bellevue-Everett, WA M.D.	4.7
253	Sebastian-Vero Beach, FL	(8.8)
NA	Sheboygan, WI**	NA
30	Sherman-Denison, TX	14.8
17	Sioux City, IA-NE-SD	19.8
273	Sioux Falls, SD	(11.2)
181	South Bend-Mishawaka, IN-MI	(1.7)
66	Spartanburg, SC	8.8
123	Spokane, WA	3.2
304	Springfield, IL	(16.8)
243	Springfield, MA	(7.2)
186	Springfield, MO	(1.9)
92	Springfield, OH	6.1
14	State College, PA	22.5
129	Stockton, CA	2.4
6	St. Cloud, MN	33.9
169	St. Joseph, MO-KS	(0.9)
85	St. Louis, MO-IL	7.1
292	Sumter, SC	(14.4)
299	Syracuse, NY	(15.8)
210	Tacoma, WA M.D.	(3.7)
99	Tallahassee, FL	5.6
245	Tampa-St Petersburg, FL	(8.0)
NA	Terre Haute, IN**	NA
32	Texarkana, TX-Texarkana, AR	14.2
23	Toledo, OH	17.3
57	Topeka, KS	9.7
12	Trenton-Ewing, NJ	23.4
80	Tucson, AZ	7.4
122	Tulsa, OK	3.3
NA	Tuscaloosa, AL**	NA
276	Tyler, TX	(12.0)
143	Utica-Rome, NY	1.3
293	Valdosta, GA	(15.1)
162	Vallejo-Fairfield, CA	(0.5)
63	Victoria, TX	9.1
152	Virginia Beach-Norfolk, VA-NC	0.3
175	Visalia-Porterville, CA	(1.3)
238	Waco, TX	(6.8)
236	Warner Robins, GA	(6.5)
NA	Warren-Farmington Hills, MI M.D.**	NA
261	Washington (greater) DC-VA-MD-WV	(9.7)
274	Washington, DC-VA-MD-WV M.D.	(11.3)
272	Waterloo-Cedar Falls, IA	(11.0)
215	Wausau, WI	(4.1)
53	Wenatchee, WA	10.0
225	West Palm Beach, FL M.D.	(5.0)
276	Wichita Falls, TX	(12.0)
216	Wichita, KS	(4.3)
27	Williamsport, PA	15.6
193	Wilmington, DE-MD-NJ M.D.	(2.6)
259	Wilmington, NC	(9.4)
266	Winchester, VA-WV	(10.2)
56	Winston-Salem, NC	9.9
89	Worcester, MA	6.5
203	Yakima, WA	(3.0)
202	York-Hanover, PA	(2.9)
112	Yuba City, CA	4.1
200	Yuma, AZ	(2.8)

Source: CQ Press using reported data from the F.B.I. "Crime in the United States 2011"
*Burglary is the unlawful entry of a structure to commit a felony or theft. Attempts are included.
**Not available.

Rank Order - Metro Area
31. Percent Change in Burglary Rate: 2010 to 2011 (continued)
National Percent Change = 0.2% Increase*

RANK	METROPOLITAN AREA	% CHANGE	RANK	METROPOLITAN AREA	% CHANGE	RANK	METROPOLITAN AREA	% CHANGE
1	Bismarck, ND	79.6	61	Cincinnati-Middletown, OH-KY-IN	9.3	121	Cape Coral-Fort Myers, FL	3.5
2	Lewiston-Auburn, ME	72.3	61	Mount Vernon-Anacortes, WA	9.3	122	Tulsa, OK	3.3
3	Mankato-North Mankato, MN	48.2	63	Manhattan, KS	9.1	123	Kingston, NY	3.2
4	Owensboro, KY	34.8	63	Portland, ME	9.1	123	New York-W. Plains NY-NJ M.D.	3.2
5	Madera, CA	34.7	63	Victoria, TX	9.1	123	Spokane, WA	3.2
6	St. Cloud, MN	33.9	66	Fort Lauderdale, FL M.D.	8.8	126	Rapid City, SD	3.1
7	Columbia, MO	32.5	66	Philadelphia (greater) PA-NJ-MD-DE	8.8	127	Clarksville, TN-KY	2.7
8	Johnstown, PA	28.9	66	Riverside-San Bernardino, CA	8.8	128	Medford, OR	2.5
9	Racine, WI	27.9	66	Spartanburg, SC	8.8	129	Prescott, AZ	2.4
10	Hagerstown-Martinsburg, MD-WV	25.0	70	Des Moines-West Des Moines, IA	8.7	129	Stockton, CA	2.4
11	Naples-Marco Island, FL	23.7	70	Santa Cruz-Watsonville, CA	8.7	131	Seattle (greater), WA	2.3
12	Trenton-Ewing, NJ	23.4	72	Louisville, KY-IN	8.6	132	Poughkeepsie, NY	2.2
13	Canton, OH	23.3	73	Duluth, MN-WI	8.2	133	Bellingham, WA	2.1
14	State College, PA	22.5	74	Rockingham County, NH M.D.	8.0	134	Cedar Rapids, IA	2.0
15	Sandusky, OH	22.1	74	Rocky Mount, NC	8.0	135	Richmond, VA	1.9
16	Corvallis, OR	21.0	76	Bridgeport-Stamford, CT	7.8	136	Lakeland, FL	1.8
17	Houma, LA	19.8	77	Fresno, CA	7.7	137	Atlanta, GA	1.7
17	Sioux City, IA-NE-SD	19.8	77	New Orleans, LA	7.7	137	Dayton, OH	1.7
19	Lynchburg, VA	19.7	79	Pittsfield, MA	7.5	137	Manchester-Nashua, NH	1.7
20	Kennewick-Pasco-Richland, WA	19.4	80	Milwaukee, WI	7.4	140	Orlando, FL	1.6
21	Muncie, IN	18.2	80	Tucson, AZ	7.4	141	Akron, OH	1.5
22	Peoria, IL	17.4	82	Lancaster, PA	7.3	141	Asheville, NC	1.5
23	Toledo, OH	17.3	83	Grand Junction, CO	7.2	143	Dover, DE	1.3
24	Mobile, AL	17.1	83	Ocala, FL	7.2	143	Utica-Rome, NY	1.3
25	Rochester, MN	16.4	85	St. Louis, MO-IL	7.1	145	El Centro, CA	1.0
26	Cheyenne, WY	16.1	86	Greenville, SC	6.8	145	Florence, SC	1.0
27	Williamsport, PA	15.6	87	Merced, CA	6.6	147	Lawton, OK	0.9
28	Ames, IA	15.4	87	New York (greater), NY-NJ-PA	6.6	147	Oakland-Fremont, CA M.D.	0.9
29	Monroe, MI	15.2	89	Worcester, MA	6.5	149	Fort Worth-Arlington, TX M.D.	0.6
30	Sherman-Denison, TX	14.8	90	Palm Bay-Melbourne, FL	6.3	150	Baltimore-Towson, MD	0.4
31	Camden, NJ M.D.	14.4	90	Reading, PA	6.3	150	San Francisco (greater), CA	0.4
32	Texarkana, TX-Texarkana, AR	14.2	92	New Haven-Milford, CT	6.1	152	Hinesville, GA	0.3
33	Pine Bluff, AR	14.0	92	Springfield, OH	6.1	152	Virginia Beach-Norfolk, VA-NC	0.3
34	Iowa City, IA	13.7	94	Binghamton, NY	6.0	154	Albany-Schenectady-Troy, NY	0.0
35	Evansville, IN-KY	13.2	95	Hartford, CT	5.9	154	Detroit-Livonia-Dearborn, MI M.D.	0.0
36	Hickory, NC	12.9	96	Las Cruces, NM	5.8	154	Logan, UT-ID	0.0
37	Newark-Union, NJ-PA M.D.	12.7	97	Hanford-Corcoran, CA	5.7	157	Greeley, CO	(0.2)
38	Harrisburg-Carlisle, PA	12.4	97	Nassau-Suffolk, NY M.D.	5.7	158	Bend, OR	(0.3)
39	Bremerton-Silverdale, WA	12.3	99	Tallahassee, FL	5.6	158	Columbus, OH	(0.3)
40	Fayetteville, NC	12.2	100	Pensacola, FL	5.3	158	Los Angeles County, CA M.D.	(0.3)
41	Edison, NJ M.D.	12.1	100	Raleigh-Cary, NC	5.3	161	Dallas (greater), TX	(0.4)
42	Lafayette, IN	11.9	102	Atlantic City, NJ	5.0	162	Elmira, NY	(0.5)
43	Salem, OR	11.8	103	Gainesville, GA	4.8	162	Vallejo-Fairfield, CA	(0.5)
44	Joplin, MO	11.4	104	Seattle-Bellevue-Everett, WA M.D.	4.7	164	Los Angeles (greater), CA	(0.6)
45	Carson City, NV	11.2	105	Miami-Dade County, FL M.D.	4.6	164	Rome, GA	(0.6)
46	Erie, PA	11.1	106	Eau Claire, WI	4.5	166	Beaumont-Port Arthur, TX	(0.8)
46	Janesville, WI	11.1	107	Bangor, ME	4.4	166	Nashville-Davidson, TN	(0.8)
48	Phoenix-Mesa-Scottsdale, AZ	10.9	107	Durham-Chapel Hill, NC	4.4	166	Pittsburgh, PA	(0.8)
49	Kokomo, IN	10.8	109	La Crosse, WI-MN	4.3	169	St. Joseph, MO-KS	(0.9)
50	Anderson, SC	10.7	109	Santa Barbara-Santa Maria, CA	4.3	170	Dallas-Plano-Irving, TX M.D.	(1.0)
51	Grand Forks, ND-MN	10.6	111	Little Rock, AR	4.2	170	Memphis, TN-MS-AR	(1.0)
52	Omaha-Council Bluffs, NE-IA	10.4	112	Jonesboro, AR	4.1	172	Johnson City, TN	(1.2)
53	Battle Creek, MI	10.0	112	Yuba City, CA	4.1	172	Mansfield, OH	(1.2)
53	Philadelphia, PA M.D.	10.0	114	Cleveland-Elyria-Mentor, OH	4.0	172	San Francisco-S. Mateo, CA M.D.	(1.2)
53	Wenatchee, WA	10.0	114	Flint, MI	4.0	175	Roanoke, VA	(1.3)
56	Winston-Salem, NC	9.9	116	Lawrence, KS	3.9	175	Visalia-Porterville, CA	(1.3)
57	Lansing-East Lansing, MI	9.7	117	Burlington, NC	3.8	177	Cleveland, TN	(1.4)
57	Lubbock, TX	9.7	117	Miami (greater), FL	3.8	178	Columbus, IN	(1.5)
57	Port St. Lucie, FL	9.7	119	Albuquerque, NM	3.7	178	Danville, IL	(1.5)
57	Topeka, KS	9.7	119	Minneapolis-St. Paul, MN-WI	3.7	180	Fort Smith, AR-OK	(1.6)

Note: All listings are for Metropolitan Statistical Areas (M.S.A.s) except for those ending with "M.D." Listings with "M.D." are Metropolitan Divisions which are smaller parts of eleven large M.S.A.s. See explanatory note at beginning of metropolitan area section.

Rank Order - Metro Area (continued)

RANK	METROPOLITAN AREA	% CHANGE
181	Boston-Quincy, MA M.D.	(1.7)
181	Jefferson City, MO	(1.7)
181	South Bend-Mishawaka, IN-MI	(1.7)
184	Modesto, CA	(1.8)
184	Scranton--Wilkes-Barre, PA	(1.8)
186	Santa Ana-Anaheim, CA M.D.	(1.9)
186	Springfield, MO	(1.9)
188	Chattanooga, TN-GA	(2.0)
188	Denver-Aurora, CO	(2.0)
188	Lima, OH	(2.0)
191	Cape Girardeau, MO-IL	(2.2)
192	Boulder, CO	(2.4)
193	Bethesda-Frederick, MD M.D.	(2.6)
193	Deltona-Daytona Beach, FL	(2.6)
193	Holland-Grand Haven, MI	(2.6)
193	Jackson, MS	(2.6)
193	Macon, GA	(2.6)
193	Wilmington, DE-MD-NJ M.D.	(2.6)
199	Provo-Orem, UT	(2.7)
200	Altoona, PA	(2.8)
200	Yuma, AZ	(2.8)
202	York-Hanover, PA	(2.9)
203	Bakersfield, CA	(3.0)
203	Yakima, WA	(3.0)
205	Punta Gorda, FL	(3.1)
206	San Jose, CA	(3.2)
207	Boise City-Nampa, ID	(3.3)
207	Napa, CA	(3.3)
209	Reno-Sparks, NV	(3.6)
210	Glens Falls, NY	(3.7)
210	Tacoma, WA M.D.	(3.7)
212	Oklahoma City, OK	(3.8)
213	Panama City-Lynn Haven, FL	(3.9)
214	Ocean City, NJ	(4.0)
215	Wausau, WI	(4.1)
216	Redding, CA	(4.3)
216	Wichita, KS	(4.3)
218	Lincoln, NE	(4.4)
218	Longview, TX	(4.4)
220	Boston (greater), MA-NH	(4.6)
220	Idaho Falls, ID	(4.6)
222	Athens-Clarke County, GA	(4.7)
222	Buffalo-Niagara Falls, NY	(4.7)
224	Lebanon, PA	(4.9)
225	West Palm Beach, FL M.D.	(5.0)
226	Jackson, TN	(5.1)
227	Fairbanks, AK	(5.3)
228	Barnstable Town, MA	(5.4)
229	North Port-Bradenton-Sarasota, FL	(5.5)
230	Killeen-Temple-Fort Hood, TX	(5.6)
231	Myrtle Beach, SC	(6.1)
232	Laredo, TX	(6.2)
232	Rochester, NY	(6.2)
234	Alexandria, LA	(6.3)
234	Flagstaff, AZ	(6.3)
236	Warner Robins, GA	(6.5)
237	Fort Collins-Loveland, CO	(6.7)
238	Waco, TX	(6.8)
239	Kingsport, TN-VA	(7.0)
239	San Diego, CA	(7.0)
241	Madison, WI	(7.1)
241	Olympia, WA	(7.1)
243	Springfield, MA	(7.2)
244	Hot Springs, AR	(7.4)
245	Tampa-St Petersburg, FL	(8.0)
246	Fargo, ND-MN	(8.1)
246	Gulfport-Biloxi, MS	(8.1)
246	Monroe, LA	(8.1)
246	Peabody, MA M.D.	(8.1)
250	Colorado Springs, CO	(8.4)
251	Corpus Christi, TX	(8.7)
251	Dalton, GA	(8.7)
253	Jacksonville, FL	(8.8)
253	Palm Coast, FL	(8.8)
253	Sebastian-Vero Beach, FL	(8.8)
256	Saginaw, MI	(9.0)
257	Knoxville, TN	(9.1)
258	San Luis Obispo, CA	(9.3)
259	Wilmington, NC	(9.4)
260	Cambridge-Newton, MA M.D.	(9.5)
261	Santa Fe, NM	(9.7)
261	Washington (greater) DC-VA-MD-WV	(9.7)
263	Fort Wayne, IN	(9.8)
263	Las Vegas-Paradise, NV	(9.8)
265	Dubuque, IA	(9.9)
266	Green Bay, WI	(10.2)
266	Winchester, VA-WV	(10.2)
268	Allentown, PA-NJ	(10.3)
268	Anchorage, AK	(10.3)
270	Bloomington-Normal, IL	(10.5)
271	College Station-Bryan, TX	(10.7)
272	Waterloo-Cedar Falls, IA	(11.0)
273	Sioux Falls, SD	(11.2)
274	Washington, DC-VA-MD-WV M.D.	(11.3)
275	Sacramento, CA	(11.9)
276	Tyler, TX	(12.0)
276	Wichita Falls, TX	(12.0)
278	Danville, VA	(12.4)
279	Gainesville, FL	(12.5)
279	Morristown, TN	(12.5)
281	Salinas, CA	(12.8)
282	Albany, GA	(13.0)
282	Augusta, GA-SC	(13.0)
282	Blacksburg, VA	(13.0)
285	Savannah, GA	(13.2)
286	Pocatello, ID	(13.3)
287	Brownsville-Harlingen, TX	(13.5)
288	Muskegon-Norton Shores, MI	(13.8)
289	Ann Arbor, MI	(13.9)
289	San Antonio, TX	(13.9)
291	El Paso, TX	(14.2)
292	Sumter, SC	(14.4)
293	Valdosta, GA	(15.1)
294	Longview, WA	(15.2)
295	Harrisonburg, VA	(15.5)
295	Santa Rosa-Petaluma, CA	(15.5)
297	Chico, CA	(15.6)
297	Oxnard-Thousand Oaks, CA	(15.6)
299	Syracuse, NY	(15.8)
300	Lafayette, LA	(16.0)
301	Grand Rapids-Wyoming, MI	(16.3)
301	Norwich-New London, CT	(16.3)
303	Crestview-Fort Walton Beach, FL	(16.6)
304	Springfield, IL	(16.8)
305	Ogden-Clearfield, UT	(16.9)
305	Rockford, IL	(16.9)
307	Pascagoula, MS	(17.3)
308	Michigan City-La Porte, IN	(17.5)
309	Elizabethtown, KY	(18.0)
310	Austin-Round Rock, TX	(18.1)
310	Bay City, MI	(18.1)
312	Brunswick, GA	(18.3)
313	Farmington, NM	(18.4)
314	Casper, WY	(19.9)
315	Salt Lake City, UT	(20.2)
316	Bowling Green, KY	(20.6)
317	Goldsboro, NC	(20.7)
318	Salisbury, MD	(20.8)
319	Amarillo, TX	(20.9)
320	Abilene, TX	(21.4)
320	McAllen-Edinburg-Mission, TX	(21.4)
322	Bloomington, IN	(23.8)
323	San Angelo, TX	(24.0)
324	Decatur, IL	(25.4)
325	Charlottesville, VA	(26.0)
326	Midland, TX	(26.1)
327	Odessa, TX	(26.6)
328	Appleton, WI	(35.0)
329	Fond du Lac, WI	(36.2)
NA	Anniston-Oxford, AL**	NA
NA	Auburn, AL**	NA
NA	Baton Rouge, LA**	NA
NA	Billings, MT**	NA
NA	Birmingham-Hoover, AL**	NA
NA	Champaign-Urbana, IL**	NA
NA	Charleston, WV**	NA
NA	Charlotte-Gastonia, NC-SC**	NA
NA	Chicago (greater), IL-IN-WI**	NA
NA	Chicago-Joilet-Naperville, IL M.D.**	NA
NA	Columbus, GA-AL**	NA
NA	Cumberland, MD-WV**	NA
NA	Davenport, IA-IL**	NA
NA	Decatur, AL**	NA
NA	Detroit (greater), MI**	NA
NA	Dothan, AL**	NA
NA	Eugene-Springfield, OR**	NA
NA	Florence-Muscle Shoals, AL**	NA
NA	Gadsden, AL**	NA
NA	Gary, IN M.D.**	NA
NA	Great Falls, MT**	NA
NA	Houston, TX**	NA
NA	Huntsville, AL**	NA
NA	Indianapolis, IN**	NA
NA	Jacksonville, NC**	NA
NA	Kankakee-Bradley, IL**	NA
NA	Kansas City, MO-KS**	NA
NA	Lake Co.-Kenosha Co., IL-WI M.D.**	NA
NA	Lake Havasu City-Kingman, AZ**	NA
NA	Lexington-Fayette, KY**	NA
NA	Missoula, MT**	NA
NA	Montgomery, AL**	NA
NA	Oshkosh-Neenah, WI**	NA
NA	Portland-Vancouver, OR-WA**	NA
NA	Pueblo, CO**	NA
NA	Sheboygan, WI**	NA
NA	Terre Haute, IN**	NA
NA	Tuscaloosa, AL**	NA
NA	Warren-Farmington Hills, MI M.D.**	NA

Source: CQ Press using reported data from the F.B.I. "Crime in the United States 2011"
*Burglary is the unlawful entry of a structure to commit a felony or theft. Attempts are included.
**Not available.

Alpha Order - Metro Area

32. Percent Change in Burglary Rate: 2007 to 2011
National Percent Change = 3.3% Decrease*

RANK	METROPOLITAN AREA	% CHANGE	RANK	METROPOLITAN AREA	% CHANGE	RANK	METROPOLITAN AREA	% CHANGE
268	Abilene, TX	(22.1)	159	Charleston, WV	(3.4)	9	Fort Lauderdale, FL M.D.	34.4
40	Akron, OH	16.5	310	Charlotte-Gastonia, NC-SC	(34.9)	171	Fort Smith, AR-OK	(4.9)
98	Albany-Schenectady-Troy, NY	3.8	313	Charlottesville, VA	(39.5)	214	Fort Wayne, IN	(10.9)
157	Albany, GA	(3.1)	136	Chattanooga, TN-GA	(1.3)	139	Fort Worth-Arlington, TX M.D.	(1.4)
167	Albuquerque, NM	(4.7)	161	Cheyenne, WY	(3.6)	12	Fresno, CA	32.5
150	Alexandria, LA	(2.6)	NA	Chicago (greater), IL-IN-WI**	NA	NA	Gadsden, AL**	NA
181	Allentown, PA-NJ	(7.0)	NA	Chicago-Joilet-Naperville, IL M.D.**	NA	311	Gainesville, FL	(36.0)
280	Altoona, PA	(24.6)	248	Chico, CA	(17.5)	78	Gainesville, GA	7.7
262	Amarillo, TX	(21.1)	41	Cincinnati-Middletown, OH-KY-IN	16.3	NA	Gary, IN M.D.**	NA
301	Ames, IA	(29.9)	236	Clarksville, TN-KY	(14.8)	78	Glens Falls, NY	7.7
291	Anchorage, AK	(26.7)	52	Cleveland-Elyria-Mentor, OH	14.4	196	Goldsboro, NC	(9.1)
115	Anderson, SC	1.4	168	Cleveland, TN	(4.8)	95	Grand Forks, ND-MN	4.2
187	Ann Arbor, MI	(7.6)	282	College Station-Bryan, TX	(25.0)	184	Grand Junction, CO	(7.5)
NA	Anniston-Oxford, AL**	NA	144	Colorado Springs, CO	(2.1)	243	Grand Rapids-Wyoming, MI	(16.9)
299	Appleton, WI	(29.3)	78	Columbia, MO	7.7	NA	Great Falls, MT**	NA
198	Asheville, NC	(9.2)	NA	Columbus, GA-AL**	NA	275	Greeley, CO	(23.8)
110	Athens-Clarke County, GA	2.1	64	Columbus, IN	11.8	261	Green Bay, WI	(21.0)
141	Atlanta, GA	(1.6)	126	Columbus, OH	(0.4)	189	Greenville, SC	(7.8)
95	Atlantic City, NJ	4.2	294	Corpus Christi, TX	(27.2)	NA	Gulfport-Biloxi, MS**	NA
NA	Auburn, AL**	NA	221	Corvallis, OR	(12.1)	NA	Hagerstown-Martinsburg, MD-WV**	NA
35	Augusta, GA-SC	17.3	245	Crestview-Fort Walton Beach, FL	(17.1)	20	Hanford-Corcoran, CA	24.1
265	Austin-Round Rock, TX	(21.7)	NA	Cumberland, MD-WV**	NA	25	Harrisburg-Carlisle, PA	21.1
81	Bakersfield, CA	7.6	205	Dallas (greater), TX	(9.9)	315	Harrisonburg, VA	(41.9)
193	Baltimore-Towson, MD	(8.8)	228	Dallas-Plano-Irving, TX M.D.	(13.9)	174	Hartford, CT	(5.6)
56	Bangor, ME	12.9	123	Dalton, GA	(0.1)	74	Hickory, NC	9.3
56	Barnstable Town, MA	12.9	NA	Danville, IL**	NA	66	Hinesville, GA	11.3
121	Baton Rouge, LA	0.3	202	Danville, VA	(9.8)	NA	Holland-Grand Haven, MI**	NA
32	Battle Creek, MI	18.8	NA	Davenport, IA-IL**	NA	142	Hot Springs, AR	(1.9)
200	Bay City, MI	(9.5)	33	Dayton, OH	18.6	1	Houma, LA	60.0
102	Beaumont-Port Arthur, TX	3.1	NA	Decatur, AL**	NA	NA	Houston, TX**	NA
212	Bellingham, WA	(10.7)	NA	Decatur, IL**	NA	NA	Huntsville, AL**	NA
308	Bend, OR	(33.3)	139	Deltona-Daytona Beach, FL	(1.4)	274	Idaho Falls, ID	(23.7)
234	Bethesda-Frederick, MD M.D.	(14.5)	255	Denver-Aurora, CO	(19.2)	91	Indianapolis, IN	4.9
NA	Billings, MT**	NA	72	Des Moines-West Des Moines, IA	9.8	205	Iowa City, IA	(9.9)
5	Binghamton, NY	38.7	NA	Detroit (greater), MI**	NA	291	Jacksonville, FL	(26.7)
NA	Birmingham-Hoover, AL**	NA	116	Detroit-Livonia-Dearborn, MI M.D.	1.3	259	Jacksonville, NC	(20.6)
73	Bismarck, ND	9.7	NA	Dothan, AL**	NA	102	Jackson, MS	3.1
265	Blacksburg, VA	(21.7)	46	Dover, DE	15.6	166	Jackson, TN	(4.6)
NA	Bloomington-Normal, IL**	NA	305	Dubuque, IA	(31.1)	60	Janesville, WI	12.4
239	Bloomington, IN	(16.1)	132	Duluth, MN-WI	(0.9)	104	Jefferson City, MO	3.0
282	Boise City-Nampa, ID	(25.0)	NA	Durham-Chapel Hill, NC**	NA	89	Johnson City, TN	5.4
179	Boston (greater), MA-NH	(6.9)	62	Eau Claire, WI	12.2	10	Johnstown, PA	34.3
162	Boston-Quincy, MA M.D.	(4.1)	43	Edison, NJ M.D.	16.2	253	Jonesboro, AR	(18.9)
NA	Boulder, CO**	NA	179	El Centro, CA	(6.9)	240	Joplin, MO	(16.5)
284	Bowling Green, KY	(25.1)	252	El Paso, TX	(18.7)	NA	Kankakee-Bradley, IL**	NA
21	Bremerton-Silverdale, WA	22.7	275	Elizabethtown, KY	(23.8)	NA	Kansas City, MO-KS**	NA
34	Bridgeport-Stamford, CT	17.8	191	Elmira, NY	(8.1)	159	Kennewick-Pasco-Richland, WA	(3.4)
272	Brownsville-Harlingen, TX	(23.3)	15	Erie, PA	30.7	264	Killeen-Temple-Fort Hood, TX	(21.6)
41	Brunswick, GA	16.3	271	Eugene-Springfield, OR	(22.9)	177	Kingsport, TN-VA	(6.2)
110	Buffalo-Niagara Falls, NY	2.1	59	Evansville, IN-KY	12.5	27	Kingston, NY	20.0
82	Burlington, NC	7.5	NA	Fairbanks, AK**	NA	130	Knoxville, TN	(0.7)
225	Cambridge-Newton, MA M.D.	(13.0)	297	Fargo, ND-MN	(28.0)	29	Kokomo, IN	19.3
21	Camden, NJ M.D.	22.7	316	Farmington, NM	(46.8)	36	La Crosse, WI-MN	16.9
NA	Canton, OH**	NA	58	Fayetteville, NC	12.7	219	Lafayette, IN	(11.7)
272	Cape Coral-Fort Myers, FL	(23.3)	309	Flagstaff, AZ	(34.7)	228	Lafayette, LA	(13.9)
NA	Cape Girardeau, MO-IL**	NA	23	Flint, MI	22.3	NA	Lake Co.-Kenosha Co., IL-WI M.D.**	NA
69	Carson City, NV	10.4	NA	Florence-Muscle Shoals, AL**	NA	295	Lake Havasu City-Kingman, AZ	(27.6)
314	Casper, WY	(41.1)	168	Florence, SC	(4.8)	212	Lakeland, FL	(10.7)
136	Cedar Rapids, IA	(1.3)	77	Fond du Lac, WI	7.8	202	Lancaster, PA	(9.8)
NA	Champaign-Urbana, IL**	NA	248	Fort Collins-Loveland, CO	(17.5)	70	Lansing-East Lansing, MI	10.2

Note: All listings are for Metropolitan Statistical Areas (M.S.A.s) except for those ending with "M.D." Listings with "M.D." are Metropolitan Divisions which are smaller parts of eleven large M.S.A.s. See explanatory note at beginning of metropolitan area section.

Alpha Order - Metro Area (continued)

RANK	METROPOLITAN AREA	% CHANGE	RANK	METROPOLITAN AREA	% CHANGE	RANK	METROPOLITAN AREA	% CHANGE
222	Laredo, TX	(12.2)	84	Oklahoma City, OK	6.8	154	Savannah, GA	(2.8)
18	Las Cruces, NM	26.7	37	Olympia, WA	16.7	112	Scranton--Wilkes-Barre, PA	1.9
281	Las Vegas-Paradise, NV	(24.7)	135	Omaha-Council Bluffs, NE-IA	(1.1)	143	Seattle (greater), WA	(2.0)
164	Lawrence, KS	(4.4)	223	Orlando, FL	(12.5)	154	Seattle-Bellevue-Everett, WA M.D.	(2.8)
63	Lawton, OK	12.0	278	Oshkosh-Neenah, WI	(24.3)	129	Sebastian-Vero Beach, FL	(0.5)
14	Lebanon, PA	31.0	NA	Owensboro, KY**	NA	312	Sheboygan, WI	(37.6)
7	Lewiston-Auburn, ME	38.0	287	Oxnard-Thousand Oaks, CA	(25.8)	126	Sherman-Denison, TX	(0.4)
NA	Lexington-Fayette, KY**	NA	175	Palm Bay-Melbourne, FL	(5.9)	19	Sioux City, IA-NE-SD	25.9
85	Lima, OH	6.6	278	Palm Coast, FL	(24.3)	16	Sioux Falls, SD	30.3
303	Lincoln, NE	(30.7)	126	Panama City-Lynn Haven, FL	(0.4)	37	South Bend-Mishawaka, IN-MI	16.7
107	Little Rock, AR	2.4	237	Pascagoula, MS	(14.9)	254	Spartanburg, SC	(19.1)
306	Logan, UT-ID	(32.1)	217	Peabody, MA M.D.	(11.5)	3	Spokane, WA	48.0
290	Longview, TX	(26.6)	86	Pensacola, FL	6.5	NA	Springfield, IL**	NA
302	Longview, WA	(30.5)	NA	Peoria, IL**	NA	87	Springfield, MA	6.1
208	Los Angeles County, CA M.D.	(10.4)	88	Philadelphia (greater) PA-NJ-MD-DE	5.6	92	Springfield, MO	4.7
217	Los Angeles (greater), CA	(11.5)	119	Philadelphia, PA M.D.	0.6	90	Springfield, OH	5.1
75	Louisville, KY-IN	8.7	199	Phoenix-Mesa-Scottsdale, AZ	(9.3)	122	State College, PA	0.2
146	Lubbock, TX	(2.2)	109	Pine Bluff, AR	2.3	94	Stockton, CA	4.6
31	Lynchburg, VA	19.1	178	Pittsburgh, PA	(6.3)	39	St. Cloud, MN	16.6
47	Macon, GA	15.3	68	Pittsfield, MA	10.6	98	St. Joseph, MO-KS	3.8
4	Madera, CA	47.2	176	Pocatello, ID	(6.0)	65	St. Louis, MO-IL	11.4
299	Madison, WI	(29.3)	146	Port St. Lucie, FL	(2.2)	298	Sumter, SC	(28.1)
NA	Manchester-Nashua, NH**	NA	207	Portland-Vancouver, OR-WA	(10.3)	163	Syracuse, NY	(4.3)
NA	Manhattan, KS**	NA	67	Portland, ME	11.2	118	Tacoma, WA M.D.	0.7
NA	Mankato-North Mankato, MN**	NA	76	Poughkeepsie, NY	7.9	168	Tallahassee, FL	(4.8)
131	Mansfield, OH	(0.8)	209	Prescott, AZ	(10.5)	259	Tampa-St Petersburg, FL	(20.6)
232	McAllen-Edinburg-Mission, TX	(14.4)	251	Provo-Orem, UT	(18.3)	NA	Terre Haute, IN**	NA
232	Medford, OR	(14.4)	NA	Pueblo, CO**	NA	6	Texarkana, TX-Texarkana, AR	38.3
191	Memphis, TN-MS-AR	(8.1)	171	Punta Gorda, FL	(4.9)	8	Toledo, OH	37.7
105	Merced, CA	2.9	30	Racine, WI	19.2	49	Topeka, KS	15.2
158	Miami (greater), FL	(3.2)	173	Raleigh-Cary, NC	(5.4)	11	Trenton-Ewing, NJ	33.8
228	Miami-Dade County, FL M.D.	(13.9)	61	Rapid City, SD	12.3	101	Tucson, AZ	3.5
98	Michigan City-La Porte, IN	3.8	53	Reading, PA	14.0	107	Tulsa, OK	2.4
289	Midland, TX	(26.4)	17	Redding, CA	28.8	NA	Tuscaloosa, AL**	NA
150	Milwaukee, WI	(2.6)	265	Reno-Sparks, NV	(21.7)	183	Tyler, TX	(7.2)
257	Minneapolis-St. Paul, MN-WI	(20.0)	193	Richmond, VA	(8.8)	220	Utica-Rome, NY	(12.0)
NA	Missoula, MT**	NA	132	Riverside-San Bernardino, CA	(0.9)	148	Valdosta, GA	(2.5)
51	Mobile, AL	14.9	190	Roanoke, VA	(7.9)	24	Vallejo-Fairfield, CA	21.9
214	Modesto, CA	(10.9)	196	Rochester, MN	(9.1)	26	Victoria, TX	21.0
120	Monroe, LA	0.5	47	Rochester, NY	15.3	114	Virginia Beach-Norfolk, VA-NC	1.5
2	Monroe, MI	55.5	NA	Rockford, IL**	NA	92	Visalia-Porterville, CA	4.7
NA	Montgomery, AL**	NA	45	Rockingham County, NH M.D.	15.7	247	Waco, TX	(17.2)
202	Morristown, TN	(9.8)	216	Rocky Mount, NC	(11.2)	240	Warner Robins, GA	(16.5)
117	Mount Vernon-Anacortes, WA	1.2	83	Rome, GA	7.1	NA	Warren-Farmington Hills, MI M.D.**	NA
132	Muncie, IN	(0.9)	224	Sacramento, CA	(12.6)	209	Washington (greater) DC-VA-MD-WV	(10.5)
44	Muskegon-Norton Shores, MI	15.9	304	Saginaw, MI	(30.9)	201	Washington, DC-VA-MD-WV M.D.	(9.6)
231	Myrtle Beach, SC	(14.3)	184	Salem, OR	(7.5)	287	Waterloo-Cedar Falls, IA	(25.8)
277	Napa, CA	(24.2)	235	Salinas, CA	(14.7)	148	Wausau, WI	(2.5)
136	Naples-Marco Island, FL	(1.3)	269	Salisbury, MD	(22.6)	184	Wenatchee, WA	(7.5)
71	Nashville-Davidson, TN	9.9	270	Salt Lake City, UT	(22.8)	258	West Palm Beach, FL M.D.	(20.5)
28	Nassau-Suffolk, NY M.D.	19.5	256	San Angelo, TX	(19.3)	285	Wichita Falls, TX	(25.2)
NA	New Haven-Milford, CT**	NA	244	San Antonio, TX	(17.0)	227	Wichita, KS	(13.5)
307	New Orleans, LA	(32.9)	286	San Diego, CA	(25.3)	211	Williamsport, PA	(10.6)
112	New York (greater), NY-NJ-PA	1.9	164	San Francisco (greater), CA	(4.4)	97	Wilmington, DE-MD-NJ M.D.	4.0
195	New York-W. Plains NY-NJ M.D.	(9.0)	182	San Francisco-S. Mateo, CA M.D.	(7.1)	262	Wilmington, NC	(21.1)
50	Newark-Union, NJ-PA M.D.	15.0	225	San Jose, CA	(13.0)	187	Winchester, VA-WV	(7.6)
NA	North Port-Bradenton-Sarasota, FL**	NA	124	San Luis Obispo, CA	(0.3)	NA	Winston-Salem, NC**	NA
NA	Norwich-New London, CT**	NA	153	Sandusky, OH	(2.7)	13	Worcester, MA	31.3
154	Oakland-Fremont, CA M.D.	(2.8)	238	Santa Ana-Anaheim, CA M.D.	(15.9)	106	Yakima, WA	2.8
144	Ocala, FL	(2.1)	124	Santa Barbara-Santa Maria, CA	(0.3)	250	York-Hanover, PA	(18.2)
55	Ocean City, NJ	13.4	54	Santa Cruz-Watsonville, CA	13.7	242	Yuba City, CA	(16.6)
296	Odessa, TX	(27.7)	NA	Santa Fe, NM**	NA	150	Yuma, AZ	(2.6)
245	Ogden-Clearfield, UT	(17.1)	291	Santa Rosa-Petaluma, CA	(26.7)			

Source: CQ Press using reported data from the F.B.I. "Crime in the United States 2011"
*Burglary is the unlawful entry of a structure to commit a felony or theft. Attempts are included.
**Not available.

32. Percent Change in Burglary Rate: 2007 to 2011 (continued)
National Percent Change = 3.3% Decrease*

Rank Order - Metro Area

RANK	METROPOLITAN AREA	% CHANGE	RANK	METROPOLITAN AREA	% CHANGE	RANK	METROPOLITAN AREA	% CHANGE
1	Houma, LA	60.0	61	Rapid City, SD	12.3	121	Baton Rouge, LA	0.3
2	Monroe, MI	55.5	62	Eau Claire, WI	12.2	122	State College, PA	0.2
3	Spokane, WA	48.0	63	Lawton, OK	12.0	123	Dalton, GA	(0.1)
4	Madera, CA	47.2	64	Columbus, IN	11.8	124	San Luis Obispo, CA	(0.3)
5	Binghamton, NY	38.7	65	St. Louis, MO-IL	11.4	124	Santa Barbara-Santa Maria, CA	(0.3)
6	Texarkana, TX-Texarkana, AR	38.3	66	Hinesville, GA	11.3	126	Columbus, OH	(0.4)
7	Lewiston-Auburn, ME	38.0	67	Portland, ME	11.2	126	Panama City-Lynn Haven, FL	(0.4)
8	Toledo, OH	37.7	68	Pittsfield, MA	10.6	126	Sherman-Denison, TX	(0.4)
9	Fort Lauderdale, FL M.D.	34.4	69	Carson City, NV	10.4	129	Sebastian-Vero Beach, FL	(0.5)
10	Johnstown, PA	34.3	70	Lansing-East Lansing, MI	10.2	130	Knoxville, TN	(0.7)
11	Trenton-Ewing, NJ	33.8	71	Nashville-Davidson, TN	9.9	131	Mansfield, OH	(0.8)
12	Fresno, CA	32.5	72	Des Moines-West Des Moines, IA	9.8	132	Duluth, MN-WI	(0.9)
13	Worcester, MA	31.3	73	Bismarck, ND	9.7	132	Muncie, IN	(0.9)
14	Lebanon, PA	31.0	74	Hickory, NC	9.3	132	Riverside-San Bernardino, CA	(0.9)
15	Erie, PA	30.7	75	Louisville, KY-IN	8.7	135	Omaha-Council Bluffs, NE-IA	(1.1)
16	Sioux Falls, SD	30.3	76	Poughkeepsie, NY	7.9	136	Cedar Rapids, IA	(1.3)
17	Redding, CA	28.8	77	Fond du Lac, WI	7.8	136	Chattanooga, TN-GA	(1.3)
18	Las Cruces, NM	26.7	78	Columbia, MO	7.7	136	Naples-Marco Island, FL	(1.3)
19	Sioux City, IA-NE-SD	25.9	78	Gainesville, GA	7.7	139	Deltona-Daytona Beach, FL	(1.4)
20	Hanford-Corcoran, CA	24.1	78	Glens Falls, NY	7.7	139	Fort Worth-Arlington, TX M.D.	(1.4)
21	Bremerton-Silverdale, WA	22.7	81	Bakersfield, CA	7.6	141	Atlanta, GA	(1.6)
21	Camden, NJ M.D.	22.7	82	Burlington, NC	7.5	142	Hot Springs, AR	(1.9)
23	Flint, MI	22.3	83	Rome, GA	7.1	143	Seattle (greater), WA	(2.0)
24	Vallejo-Fairfield, CA	21.9	84	Oklahoma City, OK	6.8	144	Colorado Springs, CO	(2.1)
25	Harrisburg-Carlisle, PA	21.1	85	Lima, OH	6.6	144	Ocala, FL	(2.1)
26	Victoria, TX	21.0	86	Pensacola, FL	6.5	146	Lubbock, TX	(2.2)
27	Kingston, NY	20.0	87	Springfield, MA	6.1	146	Port St. Lucie, FL	(2.2)
28	Nassau-Suffolk, NY M.D.	19.5	88	Philadelphia (greater) PA-NJ-MD-DE	5.6	148	Valdosta, GA	(2.5)
29	Kokomo, IN	19.3	89	Johnson City, TN	5.4	148	Wausau, WI	(2.5)
30	Racine, WI	19.2	90	Springfield, OH	5.1	150	Alexandria, LA	(2.6)
31	Lynchburg, VA	19.1	91	Indianapolis, IN	4.9	150	Milwaukee, WI	(2.6)
32	Battle Creek, MI	18.8	92	Springfield, MO	4.7	150	Yuma, AZ	(2.6)
33	Dayton, OH	18.6	92	Visalia-Porterville, CA	4.7	153	Sandusky, OH	(2.7)
34	Bridgeport-Stamford, CT	17.8	94	Stockton, CA	4.6	154	Oakland-Fremont, CA M.D.	(2.8)
35	Augusta, GA-SC	17.3	95	Atlantic City, NJ	4.2	154	Savannah, GA	(2.8)
36	La Crosse, WI-MN	16.9	95	Grand Forks, ND-MN	4.2	154	Seattle-Bellevue-Everett, WA M.D.	(2.8)
37	Olympia, WA	16.7	97	Wilmington, DE-MD-NJ M.D.	4.0	157	Albany, GA	(3.1)
37	South Bend-Mishawaka, IN-MI	16.7	98	Albany-Schenectady-Troy, NY	3.8	158	Miami (greater), FL	(3.2)
39	St. Cloud, MN	16.6	98	Michigan City-La Porte, IN	3.8	159	Charleston, WV	(3.4)
40	Akron, OH	16.5	98	St. Joseph, MO-KS	3.8	159	Kennewick-Pasco-Richland, WA	(3.4)
41	Brunswick, GA	16.3	101	Tucson, AZ	3.5	161	Cheyenne, WY	(3.6)
41	Cincinnati-Middletown, OH-KY-IN	16.3	102	Beaumont-Port Arthur, TX	3.1	162	Boston-Quincy, MA M.D.	(4.1)
43	Edison, NJ M.D.	16.2	102	Jackson, MS	3.1	163	Syracuse, NY	(4.3)
44	Muskegon-Norton Shores, MI	15.9	104	Jefferson City, MO	3.0	164	Lawrence, KS	(4.4)
45	Rockingham County, NH M.D.	15.7	105	Merced, CA	2.9	164	San Francisco (greater), CA	(4.4)
46	Dover, DE	15.6	106	Yakima, WA	2.8	166	Jackson, TN	(4.6)
47	Macon, GA	15.3	107	Little Rock, AR	2.4	167	Albuquerque, NM	(4.7)
47	Rochester, NY	15.3	107	Tulsa, OK	2.4	168	Cleveland, TN	(4.8)
49	Topeka, KS	15.2	109	Pine Bluff, AR	2.3	168	Florence, SC	(4.8)
50	Newark-Union, NJ-PA M.D.	15.0	110	Athens-Clarke County, GA	2.1	168	Tallahassee, FL	(4.8)
51	Mobile, AL	14.9	110	Buffalo-Niagara Falls, NY	2.1	171	Fort Smith, AR-OK	(4.9)
52	Cleveland-Elyria-Mentor, OH	14.4	112	New York (greater), NY-NJ-PA	1.9	171	Punta Gorda, FL	(4.9)
53	Reading, PA	14.0	112	Scranton--Wilkes-Barre, PA	1.9	173	Raleigh-Cary, NC	(5.4)
54	Santa Cruz-Watsonville, CA	13.7	114	Virginia Beach-Norfolk, VA-NC	1.5	174	Hartford, CT	(5.6)
55	Ocean City, NJ	13.4	115	Anderson, SC	1.4	175	Palm Bay-Melbourne, FL	(5.9)
56	Bangor, ME	12.9	116	Detroit-Livonia-Dearborn, MI M.D.	1.3	176	Pocatello, ID	(6.0)
56	Barnstable Town, MA	12.9	117	Mount Vernon-Anacortes, WA	1.2	177	Kingsport, TN-VA	(6.2)
58	Fayetteville, NC	12.7	118	Tacoma, WA M.D.	0.7	178	Pittsburgh, PA	(6.3)
59	Evansville, IN-KY	12.5	119	Philadelphia, PA M.D.	0.6	179	Boston (greater), MA-NH	(6.9)
60	Janesville, WI	12.4	120	Monroe, LA	0.5	179	El Centro, CA	(6.9)

Note: All listings are for Metropolitan Statistical Areas (M.S.A.s) except for those ending with "M.D." Listings with "M.D." are Metropolitan Divisions which are smaller parts of eleven large M.S.A.s. See explanatory note at beginning of metropolitan area section.

Rank Order - Metro Area (continued)

RANK	METROPOLITAN AREA	% CHANGE	RANK	METROPOLITAN AREA	% CHANGE	RANK	METROPOLITAN AREA	% CHANGE
181	Allentown, PA-NJ	(7.0)	244	San Antonio, TX	(17.0)	307	New Orleans, LA	(32.9)
182	San Francisco-S. Mateo, CA M.D.	(7.1)	245	Crestview-Fort Walton Beach, FL	(17.1)	308	Bend, OR	(33.3)
183	Tyler, TX	(7.2)	245	Ogden-Clearfield, UT	(17.1)	309	Flagstaff, AZ	(34.7)
184	Grand Junction, CO	(7.5)	247	Waco, TX	(17.2)	310	Charlotte-Gastonia, NC-SC	(34.9)
184	Salem, OR	(7.5)	248	Chico, CA	(17.5)	311	Gainesville, FL	(36.0)
184	Wenatchee, WA	(7.5)	248	Fort Collins-Loveland, CO	(17.5)	312	Sheboygan, WI	(37.6)
187	Ann Arbor, MI	(7.6)	250	York-Hanover, PA	(18.2)	313	Charlottesville, VA	(39.5)
187	Winchester, VA-WV	(7.6)	251	Provo-Orem, UT	(18.3)	314	Casper, WY	(41.1)
189	Greenville, SC	(7.8)	252	El Paso, TX	(18.7)	315	Harrisonburg, VA	(41.9)
190	Roanoke, VA	(7.9)	253	Jonesboro, AR	(18.9)	316	Farmington, NM	(46.8)
191	Elmira, NY	(8.1)	254	Spartanburg, SC	(19.1)	NA	Anniston-Oxford, AL**	NA
191	Memphis, TN-MS-AR	(8.1)	255	Denver-Aurora, CO	(19.2)	NA	Auburn, AL**	NA
193	Baltimore-Towson, MD	(8.8)	256	San Angelo, TX	(19.3)	NA	Billings, MT**	NA
193	Richmond, VA	(8.8)	257	Minneapolis-St. Paul, MN-WI	(20.0)	NA	Birmingham-Hoover, AL**	NA
195	New York-W. Plains NY-NJ M.D.	(9.0)	258	West Palm Beach, FL M.D.	(20.5)	NA	Bloomington-Normal, IL**	NA
196	Goldsboro, NC	(9.1)	259	Jacksonville, NC	(20.6)	NA	Boulder, CO**	NA
196	Rochester, MN	(9.1)	259	Tampa-St Petersburg, FL	(20.6)	NA	Canton, OH**	NA
198	Asheville, NC	(9.2)	261	Green Bay, WI	(21.0)	NA	Cape Girardeau, MO-IL**	NA
199	Phoenix-Mesa-Scottsdale, AZ	(9.3)	262	Amarillo, TX	(21.1)	NA	Champaign-Urbana, IL**	NA
200	Bay City, MI	(9.5)	262	Wilmington, NC	(21.1)	NA	Chicago (greater), IL-IN-WI**	NA
201	Washington, DC-VA-MD-WV M.D.	(9.6)	264	Killeen-Temple-Fort Hood, TX	(21.6)	NA	Chicago-Joilet-Naperville, IL M.D.**	NA
202	Danville, VA	(9.8)	265	Austin-Round Rock, TX	(21.7)	NA	Columbus, GA-AL**	NA
202	Lancaster, PA	(9.8)	265	Blacksburg, VA	(21.7)	NA	Cumberland, MD-WV**	NA
202	Morristown, TN	(9.8)	265	Reno-Sparks, NV	(21.7)	NA	Danville, IL**	NA
205	Dallas (greater), TX	(9.9)	268	Abilene, TX	(22.1)	NA	Davenport, IA-IL**	NA
205	Iowa City, IA	(9.9)	269	Salisbury, MD	(22.6)	NA	Decatur, AL**	NA
207	Portland-Vancouver, OR-WA	(10.3)	270	Salt Lake City, UT	(22.8)	NA	Decatur, IL**	NA
208	Los Angeles County, CA M.D.	(10.4)	271	Eugene-Springfield, OR	(22.9)	NA	Detroit (greater), MI**	NA
209	Prescott, AZ	(10.5)	272	Brownsville-Harlingen, TX	(23.3)	NA	Dothan, AL**	NA
209	Washington (greater) DC-VA-MD-WV	(10.5)	272	Cape Coral-Fort Myers, FL	(23.3)	NA	Durham-Chapel Hill, NC**	NA
211	Williamsport, PA	(10.6)	274	Idaho Falls, ID	(23.7)	NA	Fairbanks, AK**	NA
212	Bellingham, WA	(10.7)	275	Elizabethtown, KY	(23.8)	NA	Florence-Muscle Shoals, AL**	NA
212	Lakeland, FL	(10.7)	275	Greeley, CO	(23.8)	NA	Gadsden, AL**	NA
214	Fort Wayne, IN	(10.9)	277	Napa, CA	(24.2)	NA	Gary, IN M.D.**	NA
214	Modesto, CA	(10.9)	278	Oshkosh-Neenah, WI	(24.3)	NA	Great Falls, MT**	NA
216	Rocky Mount, NC	(11.2)	278	Palm Coast, FL	(24.3)	NA	Gulfport-Biloxi, MS**	NA
217	Los Angeles (greater), CA	(11.5)	280	Altoona, PA	(24.6)	NA	Hagerstown-Martinsburg, MD-WV**	NA
217	Peabody, MA M.D.	(11.5)	281	Las Vegas-Paradise, NV	(24.7)	NA	Holland-Grand Haven, MI**	NA
219	Lafayette, IN	(11.7)	282	Boise City-Nampa, ID	(25.0)	NA	Houston, TX**	NA
220	Utica-Rome, NY	(12.0)	282	College Station-Bryan, TX	(25.0)	NA	Huntsville, AL**	NA
221	Corvallis, OR	(12.1)	284	Bowling Green, KY	(25.1)	NA	Kankakee-Bradley, IL**	NA
222	Laredo, TX	(12.2)	285	Wichita Falls, TX	(25.2)	NA	Kansas City, MO-KS**	NA
223	Orlando, FL	(12.5)	286	San Diego, CA	(25.3)	NA	Lake Co.-Kenosha Co., IL-WI M.D.**	NA
224	Sacramento, CA	(12.6)	287	Oxnard-Thousand Oaks, CA	(25.8)	NA	Lexington-Fayette, KY**	NA
225	Cambridge-Newton, MA M.D.	(13.0)	287	Waterloo-Cedar Falls, IA	(25.8)	NA	Manchester-Nashua, NH**	NA
225	San Jose, CA	(13.0)	289	Midland, TX	(26.4)	NA	Manhattan, KS**	NA
227	Wichita, KS	(13.5)	290	Longview, TX	(26.6)	NA	Mankato-North Mankato, MN**	NA
228	Dallas-Plano-Irving, TX M.D.	(13.9)	291	Anchorage, AK	(26.7)	NA	Missoula, MT**	NA
228	Lafayette, LA	(13.9)	291	Jacksonville, FL	(26.7)	NA	Montgomery, AL**	NA
228	Miami-Dade County, FL M.D.	(13.9)	291	Santa Rosa-Petaluma, CA	(26.7)	NA	New Haven-Milford, CT**	NA
231	Myrtle Beach, SC	(14.3)	294	Corpus Christi, TX	(27.2)	NA	North Port-Bradenton-Sarasota, FL**	NA
232	McAllen-Edinburg-Mission, TX	(14.4)	295	Lake Havasu City-Kingman, AZ	(27.6)	NA	Norwich-New London, CT**	NA
232	Medford, OR	(14.4)	296	Odessa, TX	(27.7)	NA	Owensboro, KY**	NA
234	Bethesda-Frederick, MD M.D.	(14.5)	297	Fargo, ND-MN	(28.0)	NA	Peoria, IL**	NA
235	Salinas, CA	(14.7)	298	Sumter, SC	(28.1)	NA	Pueblo, CO**	NA
236	Clarksville, TN-KY	(14.8)	299	Appleton, WI	(29.3)	NA	Rockford, IL**	NA
237	Pascagoula, MS	(14.9)	299	Madison, WI	(29.3)	NA	Santa Fe, NM**	NA
238	Santa Ana-Anaheim, CA M.D.	(15.9)	301	Ames, IA	(29.9)	NA	Springfield, IL**	NA
239	Bloomington, IN	(16.1)	302	Longview, WA	(30.5)	NA	Terre Haute, IN**	NA
240	Joplin, MO	(16.5)	303	Lincoln, NE	(30.7)	NA	Tuscaloosa, AL**	NA
240	Warner Robins, GA	(16.5)	304	Saginaw, MI	(30.9)	NA	Warren-Farmington Hills, MI M.D.**	NA
242	Yuba City, CA	(16.6)	305	Dubuque, IA	(31.1)	NA	Winston-Salem, NC**	NA
243	Grand Rapids-Wyoming, MI	(16.9)	306	Logan, UT-ID	(32.1)			

Source: CQ Press using reported data from the F.B.I. "Crime in the United States 2011"
*Burglary is the unlawful entry of a structure to commit a felony or theft. Attempts are included.
**Not available.

Alpha Order - Metro Area

33. Larceny-Thefts in 2011
National Total = 6,159,795 Larceny-Thefts*

RANK	METROPOLITAN AREA	THEFTS
254	Abilene, TX	3,569
97	Akron, OH	15,125
89	Albany-Schenectady-Troy, NY	16,592
214	Albany, GA	4,660
66	Albuquerque, NM	24,236
217	Alexandria, LA	4,622
98	Allentown, PA-NJ	14,607
345	Altoona, PA	1,922
161	Amarillo, TX	7,346
350	Ames, IA	1,775
147	Anchorage, AK	8,456
182	Anderson, SC	6,078
193	Ann Arbor, MI	5,538
273	Anniston-Oxford, AL	3,169
272	Appleton, WI	3,174
171	Asheville, NC	6,860
204	Athens-Clarke County, GA	5,018
11	Atlanta, GA	117,515
169	Atlantic City, NJ	6,916
259	Auburn, AL	3,400
93	Augusta, GA-SC	15,767
37	Austin-Round Rock, TX	46,845
94	Bakersfield, CA	15,725
28	Baltimore-Towson, MD	57,896
269	Bangor, ME	3,255
255	Barnstable Town, MA	3,565
73	Baton Rouge, LA	23,099
264	Battle Creek, MI	3,355
358	Bay City, MI	1,504
130	Beaumont-Port Arthur, TX	10,000
212	Bellingham, WA	4,721
237	Bend, OR	3,950
87	Bethesda-Frederick, MD M.D.	17,153
227	Billings, MT	4,264
198	Binghamton, NY	5,257
62	Birmingham-Hoover, AL	28,634
333	Bismarck, ND	2,098
267	Blacksburg, VA	3,279
298	Bloomington-Normal, IL	2,699
235	Bloomington, IN	3,964
132	Boise City-Nampa, ID	9,801
23	Boston (greater), MA-NH	69,260
59	Boston-Quincy, MA M.D.	31,919
205	Boulder, CO	5,000
303	Bowling Green, KY	2,571
210	Bremerton-Silverdale, WA	4,870
113	Bridgeport-Stamford, CT	11,989
104	Brownsville-Harlingen, TX	13,416
248	Brunswick, GA	3,678
69	Buffalo-Niagara Falls, NY	23,609
230	Burlington, NC	4,122
76	Cambridge-Newton, MA M.D.	19,920
70	Camden, NJ M.D.	23,547
154	Canton, OH	8,203
120	Cape Coral-Fort Myers, FL	11,375
297	Cape Girardeau, MO-IL	2,737
366	Carson City, NV	890
343	Casper, WY	1,936
220	Cedar Rapids, IA	4,536
232	Champaign-Urbana, IL	4,103
181	Charleston, WV	6,281
41	Charlotte-Gastonia, NC-SC	42,346
263	Charlottesville, VA	3,362
103	Chattanooga, TN-GA	13,471
334	Cheyenne, WY	2,068
3	Chicago (greater), IL-IN-WI	181,610
5	Chicago-Joilet-Naperville, IL M.D.	151,642
271	Chico, CA	3,196
31	Cincinnati-Middletown, OH-KY-IN	52,640
202	Clarksville, TN-KY	5,036
51	Cleveland-Elyria-Mentor, OH	36,321
306	Cleveland, TN	2,554
190	College Station-Bryan, TX	5,576
102	Colorado Springs, CO	13,623
225	Columbia, MO	4,324
128	Columbus, GA-AL	10,158
308	Columbus, IN	2,524
33	Columbus, OH	51,050
99	Corpus Christi, TX	14,374
351	Corvallis, OR	1,756
234	Crestview-Fort Walton Beach, FL	4,037
327	Cumberland, MD-WV	2,194
7	Dallas (greater), TX	148,365
14	Dallas-Plano-Irving, TX M.D.	93,801
280	Dalton, GA	3,047
336	Danville, IL	2,054
339	Danville, VA	1,970
149	Davenport, IA-IL	8,365
79	Dayton, OH	19,431
324	Decatur, AL	2,217
344	Decatur, IL	1,933
110	Deltona-Daytona Beach, FL	12,577
34	Denver-Aurora, CO	49,825
109	Des Moines-West Des Moines, IA	12,748
22	Detroit (greater), MI	70,238
48	Detroit-Livonia-Dearborn, MI M.D.	36,700
279	Dothan, AL	3,079
216	Dover, DE	4,641
361	Dubuque, IA	1,353
167	Duluth, MN-WI	7,007
115	Durham-Chapel Hill, NC	11,889
307	Eau Claire, WI	2,546
54	Edison, NJ M.D.	34,239
274	El Centro, CA	3,158
95	El Paso, TX	15,277
360	Elizabethtown, KY	1,455
355	Elmira, NY	1,653
197	Erie, PA	5,378
137	Eugene-Springfield, OR	9,217
159	Evansville, IN-KY	7,379
364	Fairbanks, AK	1,170
256	Fargo, ND-MN	3,483
335	Farmington, NM	2,058
114	Fayetteville, NC	11,923
238	Flagstaff, AZ	3,941
146	Flint, MI	8,478
305	Florence-Muscle Shoals, AL	2,564
166	Florence, SC	7,120
363	Fond du Lac, WI	1,323
179	Fort Collins-Loveland, CO	6,315
35	Fort Lauderdale, FL M.D.	47,633
189	Fort Smith, AR-OK	5,712
143	Fort Wayne, IN	8,736
29	Fort Worth-Arlington, TX M.D.	54,564
68	Fresno, CA	23,759
283	Gadsden, AL	2,996
176	Gainesville, FL	6,642
278	Gainesville, GA	3,087
90	Gary, IN M.D.	16,095
354	Glens Falls, NY	1,672
270	Goldsboro, NC	3,249
352	Grand Forks, ND-MN	1,689
276	Grand Junction, CO	3,118
112	Grand Rapids-Wyoming, MI	12,141
311	Great Falls, MT	2,488
236	Greeley, CO	3,955
228	Green Bay, WI	4,237
91	Greenville, SC	15,954
174	Gulfport-Biloxi, MS	6,721
233	Hagerstown-Martinsburg, MD-WV	4,073
328	Hanford-Corcoran, CA	2,188
138	Harrisburg-Carlisle, PA	9,105
362	Harrisonburg, VA	1,325
84	Hartford, CT	17,926
153	Hickory, NC	8,223
357	Hinesville, GA	1,589
246	Holland-Grand Haven, MI	3,764
268	Hot Springs, AR	3,263
208	Houma, LA	4,944
8	Houston, TX	141,881
136	Huntsville, AL	9,323
337	Idaho Falls, ID	2,008
42	Indianapolis, IN	42,016
330	Iowa City, IA	2,145
50	Jacksonville, FL	36,366
252	Jacksonville, NC	3,621
122	Jackson, MS	11,228
285	Jackson, TN	2,966
249	Janesville, WI	3,656
289	Jefferson City, MO	2,807
226	Johnson City, TN	4,296
332	Johnstown, PA	2,117
287	Jonesboro, AR	2,902
215	Joplin, MO	4,649
315	Kankakee-Bradley, IL	2,435
36	Kansas City, MO-KS	46,852
209	Kennewick-Pasco-Richland, WA	4,872
160	Killeen-Temple-Fort Hood, TX	7,362
157	Kingsport, TN-VA	7,473
302	Kingston, NY	2,588
81	Knoxville, TN	18,935
313	Kokomo, IN	2,467
316	La Crosse, WI-MN	2,398
241	Lafayette, IN	3,880
155	Lafayette, LA	8,180
101	Lake Co.-Kenosha Co., IL-WI M.D.	13,873
222	Lake Havasu City-Kingman, AZ	4,469
106	Lakeland, FL	13,213
150	Lancaster, PA	8,349
162	Lansing-East Lansing, MI	7,304

Note: All listings are for Metropolitan Statistical Areas (M.S.A.s) except for those ending with "M.D." Listings with "M.D." are Metropolitan Divisions which are smaller parts of eleven large M.S.A.s. See explanatory note at beginning of metropolitan area section.

Alpha Order - Metro Area (continued)

RANK	METROPOLITAN AREA	THEFTS
148	Laredo, TX	8,436
221	Las Cruces, NM	4,514
61	Las Vegas-Paradise, NV	29,435
251	Lawrence, KS	3,632
253	Lawton, OK	3,575
347	Lebanon, PA	1,901
321	Lewiston-Auburn, ME	2,279
100	Lexington-Fayette, KY	13,948
301	Lima, OH	2,624
139	Lincoln, NE	9,019
67	Little Rock, AR	23,864
365	Logan, UT-ID	1,093
206	Longview, TX	4,998
314	Longview, WA	2,451
9	Los Angeles County, CA M.D.	138,325
2	Los Angeles (greater), CA	183,422
58	Louisville, KY-IN	32,953
141	Lubbock, TX	8,959
242	Lynchburg, VA	3,867
144	Macon, GA	8,632
356	Madera, CA	1,603
116	Madison, WI	11,755
164	Manchester-Nashua, NH	7,202
348	Manhattan, KS	1,863
331	Mankato-North Mankato, MN	2,126
243	Mansfield, OH	3,808
71	McAllen-Edinburg-Mission, TX	23,319
188	Medford, OR	5,783
46	Memphis, TN-MS-AR	37,358
194	Merced, CA	5,496
4	Miami (greater), FL	163,975
16	Miami-Dade County, FL M.D.	84,714
281	Michigan City-La Porte, IN	3,014
291	Midland, TX	2,797
49	Milwaukee, WI	36,584
21	Minneapolis-St. Paul, MN-WI	70,653
319	Missoula, MT	2,346
111	Mobile, AL	12,518
124	Modesto, CA	10,620
199	Monroe, LA	5,224
309	Monroe, MI	2,513
129	Montgomery, AL	10,032
257	Morristown, TN	3,419
244	Mount Vernon-Anacortes, WA	3,801
318	Muncie, IN	2,354
196	Muskegon-Norton Shores, MI	5,394
123	Myrtle Beach, SC	10,687
346	Napa, CA	1,919
223	Naples-Marco Island, FL	4,377
47	Nashville-Davidson, TN	36,858
53	Nassau-Suffolk, NY M.D.	35,720
85	New Haven-Milford, CT	17,775
63	New Orleans, LA	26,334
1	New York (greater), NY-NJ-PA	247,703
6	New York-W. Plains NY-NJ M.D.	151,598
64	Newark-Union, NJ-PA M.D.	26,146
82	North Port-Bradenton-Sarasota, FL	18,320
312	Norwich-New London, CT	2,471
38	Oakland-Fremont, CA M.D.	45,716
192	Ocala, FL	5,549
260	Ocean City, NJ	3,395
277	Odessa, TX	3,096
121	Ogden-Clearfield, UT	11,249

RANK	METROPOLITAN AREA	THEFTS
55	Oklahoma City, OK	34,142
211	Olympia, WA	4,861
75	Omaha-Council Bluffs, NE-IA	19,995
32	Orlando, FL	51,775
310	Oshkosh-Neenah, WI	2,508
325	Owensboro, KY	2,212
125	Oxnard-Thousand Oaks, CA	10,501
108	Palm Bay-Melbourne, FL	12,791
359	Palm Coast, FL	1,484
195	Panama City-Lynn Haven, FL	5,472
261	Pascagoula, MS	3,393
127	Peabody, MA M.D.	10,223
118	Pensacola, FL	11,529
163	Peoria, IL	7,237
10	Philadelphia (greater) PA-NJ-MD-DE	118,163
19	Philadelphia, PA M.D.	78,819
12	Phoenix-Mesa-Scottsdale, AZ	104,351
300	Pine Bluff, AR	2,648
57	Pittsburgh, PA	33,523
338	Pittsfield, MA	1,998
329	Pocatello, ID	2,187
152	Port St. Lucie, FL	8,247
30	Portland-Vancouver, OR-WA	52,921
131	Portland, ME	9,891
126	Poughkeepsie, NY	10,321
266	Prescott, AZ	3,305
133	Provo-Orem, UT	9,754
213	Pueblo, CO	4,683
293	Punta Gorda, FL	2,780
240	Racine, WI	3,890
74	Raleigh-Cary, NC	20,449
290	Rapid City, SD	2,806
184	Reading, PA	6,037
283	Redding, CA	2,996
172	Reno-Sparks, NV	6,842
72	Richmond, VA	23,295
24	Riverside-San Bernardino, CA	68,600
185	Roanoke, VA	6,035
303	Rochester, MN	2,571
77	Rochester, NY	19,901
158	Rockford, IL	7,439
165	Rockingham County, NH M.D.	7,198
245	Rocky Mount, NC	3,792
299	Rome, GA	2,683
44	Sacramento, CA	37,938
294	Saginaw, MI	2,753
151	Salem, OR	8,270
191	Salinas, CA	5,573
292	Salisbury, MD	2,786
52	Salt Lake City, UT	35,817
286	San Angelo, TX	2,923
20	San Antonio, TX	74,936
43	San Diego, CA	40,420
17	San Francisco (greater), CA	83,296
45	San Francisco-S. Mateo, CA M.D.	37,580
65	San Jose, CA	25,429
224	San Luis Obispo, CA	4,360
353	Sandusky, OH	1,685
39	Santa Ana-Anaheim, CA M.D.	45,097
178	Santa Barbara-Santa Maria, CA	6,367
186	Santa Cruz-Watsonville, CA	5,964
322	Santa Fe, NM	2,252
183	Santa Rosa-Petaluma, CA	6,041

RANK	METROPOLITAN AREA	THEFTS
142	Savannah, GA	8,838
135	Scranton--Wilkes-Barre, PA	9,410
15	Seattle (greater), WA	86,948
25	Seattle-Bellevue-Everett, WA M.D.	67,561
296	Sebastian-Vero Beach, FL	2,742
341	Sheboygan, WI	1,947
295	Sherman-Denison, TX	2,750
265	Sioux City, IA-NE-SD	3,311
231	Sioux Falls, SD	4,107
156	South Bend-Mishawaka, IN-MI	7,611
175	Spartanburg, SC	6,651
88	Spokane, WA	16,771
177	Springfield, IL	6,396
107	Springfield, MA	12,993
96	Springfield, MO	15,223
250	Springfield, OH	3,649
340	State College, PA	1,952
83	Stockton, CA	18,193
247	St. Cloud, MN	3,681
262	St. Joseph, MO-KS	3,379
27	St. Louis, MO-IL	60,465
317	Sumter, SC	2,387
117	Syracuse, NY	11,673
80	Tacoma, WA M.D.	19,387
145	Tallahassee, FL	8,548
26	Tampa-St Petersburg, FL	60,961
218	Terre Haute, IN	4,607
229	Texarkana, TX-Texarkana, AR	4,191
NA	Toledo, OH**	NA
173	Topeka, KS	6,775
203	Trenton-Ewing, NJ	5,035
NA	Tucson, AZ**	NA
78	Tulsa, OK	19,575
200	Tuscaloosa, AL	5,162
201	Tyler, TX	5,055
207	Utica-Rome, NY	4,965
288	Valdosta, GA	2,889
180	Vallejo-Fairfield, CA	6,298
275	Victoria, TX	3,151
40	Virginia Beach-Norfolk, VA-NC	42,961
134	Visalia-Porterville, CA	9,433
170	Waco, TX	6,875
219	Warner Robins, GA	4,543
56	Warren-Farmington Hills, MI M.D.	33,538
13	Washington (greater) DC-VA-MD-WV	100,012
18	Washington, DC-VA-MD-WV M.D.	82,859
320	Waterloo-Cedar Falls, IA	2,307
349	Wausau, WI	1,844
326	Wenatchee, WA	2,199
60	West Palm Beach, FL M.D.	31,628
239	Wichita Falls, TX	3,936
86	Wichita, KS	17,318
342	Williamsport, PA	1,943
92	Wilmington, DE-MD-NJ M.D.	15,797
140	Wilmington, NC	9,008
323	Winchester, VA-WV	2,219
105	Winston-Salem, NC	13,401
119	Worcester, MA	11,392
187	Yakima, WA	5,802
168	York-Hanover, PA	6,941
282	Yuba City, CA	3,010
258	Yuma, AZ	3,403

Source: Reported data from the F.B.I. "Crime in the United States 2011"
*Larceny-theft is the unlawful taking of property. Attempts are included.
**Not available.

Rank Order - Metro Area

33. Larceny-Thefts in 2011 (continued)
National Total = 6,159,795 Larceny-Thefts*

RANK	METROPOLITAN AREA	THEFTS	RANK	METROPOLITAN AREA	THEFTS	RANK	METROPOLITAN AREA	THEFTS
1	New York (greater), NY-NJ-PA	247,703	61	Las Vegas-Paradise, NV	29,435	121	Ogden-Clearfield, UT	11,249
2	Los Angeles (greater), CA	183,422	62	Birmingham-Hoover, AL	28,634	122	Jackson, MS	11,228
3	Chicago (greater), IL-IN-WI	181,610	63	New Orleans, LA	26,334	123	Myrtle Beach, SC	10,687
4	Miami (greater), FL	163,975	64	Newark-Union, NJ-PA M.D.	26,146	124	Modesto, CA	10,620
5	Chicago-Joilet-Naperville, IL M.D.	151,642	65	San Jose, CA	25,429	125	Oxnard-Thousand Oaks, CA	10,501
6	New York-W. Plains NY-NJ M.D.	151,598	66	Albuquerque, NM	24,236	126	Poughkeepsie, NY	10,321
7	Dallas (greater), TX	148,365	67	Little Rock, AR	23,864	127	Peabody, MA M.D.	10,223
8	Houston, TX	141,881	68	Fresno, CA	23,759	128	Columbus, GA-AL	10,158
9	Los Angeles County, CA M.D.	138,325	69	Buffalo-Niagara Falls, NY	23,609	129	Montgomery, AL	10,032
10	Philadelphia (greater) PA-NJ-MD-DE	118,163	70	Camden, NJ M.D.	23,547	130	Beaumont-Port Arthur, TX	10,000
11	Atlanta, GA	117,515	71	McAllen-Edinburg-Mission, TX	23,319	131	Portland, ME	9,891
12	Phoenix-Mesa-Scottsdale, AZ	104,351	72	Richmond, VA	23,295	132	Boise City-Nampa, ID	9,801
13	Washington (greater) DC-VA-MD-WV	100,012	73	Baton Rouge, LA	23,099	133	Provo-Orem, UT	9,754
14	Dallas-Plano-Irving, TX M.D.	93,801	74	Raleigh-Cary, NC	20,449	134	Visalia-Porterville, CA	9,433
15	Seattle (greater), WA	86,948	75	Omaha-Council Bluffs, NE-IA	19,995	135	Scranton--Wilkes-Barre, PA	9,410
16	Miami-Dade County, FL M.D.	84,714	76	Cambridge-Newton, MA M.D.	19,920	136	Huntsville, AL	9,323
17	San Francisco (greater), CA	83,296	77	Rochester, NY	19,901	137	Eugene-Springfield, OR	9,217
18	Washington, DC-VA-MD-WV M.D.	82,859	78	Tulsa, OK	19,575	138	Harrisburg-Carlisle, PA	9,105
19	Philadelphia, PA M.D.	78,819	79	Dayton, OH	19,431	139	Lincoln, NE	9,019
20	San Antonio, TX	74,936	80	Tacoma, WA M.D.	19,387	140	Wilmington, NC	9,008
21	Minneapolis-St. Paul, MN-WI	70,653	81	Knoxville, TN	18,935	141	Lubbock, TX	8,959
22	Detroit (greater), MI	70,238	82	North Port-Bradenton-Sarasota, FL	18,320	142	Savannah, GA	8,838
23	Boston (greater), MA-NH	69,260	83	Stockton, CA	18,193	143	Fort Wayne, IN	8,736
24	Riverside-San Bernardino, CA	68,600	84	Hartford, CT	17,926	144	Macon, GA	8,632
25	Seattle-Bellevue-Everett, WA M.D.	67,561	85	New Haven-Milford, CT	17,775	145	Tallahassee, FL	8,548
26	Tampa-St Petersburg, FL	60,961	86	Wichita, KS	17,318	146	Flint, MI	8,478
27	St. Louis, MO-IL	60,465	87	Bethesda-Frederick, MD M.D.	17,153	147	Anchorage, AK	8,456
28	Baltimore-Towson, MD	57,896	88	Spokane, WA	16,771	148	Laredo, TX	8,436
29	Fort Worth-Arlington, TX M.D.	54,564	89	Albany-Schenectady-Troy, NY	16,592	149	Davenport, IA-IL	8,365
30	Portland-Vancouver, OR-WA	52,921	90	Gary, IN M.D.	16,095	150	Lancaster, PA	8,349
31	Cincinnati-Middletown, OH-KY-IN	52,640	91	Greenville, SC	15,954	151	Salem, OR	8,270
32	Orlando, FL	51,775	92	Wilmington, DE-MD-NJ M.D.	15,797	152	Port St. Lucie, FL	8,247
33	Columbus, OH	51,050	93	Augusta, GA-SC	15,767	153	Hickory, NC	8,223
34	Denver-Aurora, CO	49,825	94	Bakersfield, CA	15,725	154	Canton, OH	8,203
35	Fort Lauderdale, FL M.D.	47,633	95	El Paso, TX	15,277	155	Lafayette, LA	8,180
36	Kansas City, MO-KS	46,852	96	Springfield, MO	15,223	156	South Bend-Mishawaka, IN-MI	7,611
37	Austin-Round Rock, TX	46,845	97	Akron, OH	15,125	157	Kingsport, TN-VA	7,473
38	Oakland-Fremont, CA M.D.	45,716	98	Allentown, PA-NJ	14,607	158	Rockford, IL	7,439
39	Santa Ana-Anaheim, CA M.D.	45,097	99	Corpus Christi, TX	14,374	159	Evansville, IN-KY	7,379
40	Virginia Beach-Norfolk, VA-NC	42,961	100	Lexington-Fayette, KY	13,948	160	Killeen-Temple-Fort Hood, TX	7,362
41	Charlotte-Gastonia, NC-SC	42,346	101	Lake Co.-Kenosha Co., IL-WI M.D.	13,873	161	Amarillo, TX	7,346
42	Indianapolis, IN	42,016	102	Colorado Springs, CO	13,623	162	Lansing-East Lansing, MI	7,304
43	San Diego, CA	40,420	103	Chattanooga, TN-GA	13,471	163	Peoria, IL	7,237
44	Sacramento, CA	37,938	104	Brownsville-Harlingen, TX	13,416	164	Manchester-Nashua, NH	7,202
45	San Francisco-S. Mateo, CA M.D.	37,580	105	Winston-Salem, NC	13,401	165	Rockingham County, NH M.D.	7,198
46	Memphis, TN-MS-AR	37,358	106	Lakeland, FL	13,213	166	Florence, SC	7,120
47	Nashville-Davidson, TN	36,858	107	Springfield, MA	12,993	167	Duluth, MN-WI	7,007
48	Detroit-Livonia-Dearborn, MI M.D.	36,700	108	Palm Bay-Melbourne, FL	12,791	168	York-Hanover, PA	6,941
49	Milwaukee, WI	36,584	109	Des Moines-West Des Moines, IA	12,748	169	Atlantic City, NJ	6,916
50	Jacksonville, FL	36,366	110	Deltona-Daytona Beach, FL	12,577	170	Waco, TX	6,875
51	Cleveland-Elyria-Mentor, OH	36,321	111	Mobile, AL	12,518	171	Asheville, NC	6,860
52	Salt Lake City, UT	35,817	112	Grand Rapids-Wyoming, MI	12,141	172	Reno-Sparks, NV	6,842
53	Nassau-Suffolk, NY M.D.	35,720	113	Bridgeport-Stamford, CT	11,989	173	Topeka, KS	6,775
54	Edison, NJ M.D.	34,239	114	Fayetteville, NC	11,923	174	Gulfport-Biloxi, MS	6,721
55	Oklahoma City, OK	34,142	115	Durham-Chapel Hill, NC	11,889	175	Spartanburg, SC	6,651
56	Warren-Farmington Hills, MI M.D.	33,538	116	Madison, WI	11,755	176	Gainesville, FL	6,642
57	Pittsburgh, PA	33,523	117	Syracuse, NY	11,673	177	Springfield, IL	6,396
58	Louisville, KY-IN	32,953	118	Pensacola, FL	11,529	178	Santa Barbara-Santa Maria, CA	6,367
59	Boston-Quincy, MA M.D.	31,919	119	Worcester, MA	11,392	179	Fort Collins-Loveland, CO	6,315
60	West Palm Beach, FL M.D.	31,628	120	Cape Coral-Fort Myers, FL	11,375	180	Vallejo-Fairfield, CA	6,298

Note: All listings are for Metropolitan Statistical Areas (M.S.A.s) except for those ending with "M.D." Listings with "M.D." are Metropolitan Divisions which are smaller parts of eleven large M.S.A.s. See explanatory note at beginning of metropolitan area section.

Rank Order - Metro Area (continued)

RANK	METROPOLITAN AREA	THEFTS	RANK	METROPOLITAN AREA	THEFTS	RANK	METROPOLITAN AREA	THEFTS
181	Charleston, WV	6,281	244	Mount Vernon-Anacortes, WA	3,801	307	Eau Claire, WI	2,546
182	Anderson, SC	6,078	245	Rocky Mount, NC	3,792	308	Columbus, IN	2,524
183	Santa Rosa-Petaluma, CA	6,041	246	Holland-Grand Haven, MI	3,764	309	Monroe, MI	2,513
184	Reading, PA	6,037	247	St. Cloud, MN	3,681	310	Oshkosh-Neenah, WI	2,508
185	Roanoke, VA	6,035	248	Brunswick, GA	3,678	311	Great Falls, MT	2,488
186	Santa Cruz-Watsonville, CA	5,964	249	Janesville, WI	3,656	312	Norwich-New London, CT	2,471
187	Yakima, WA	5,802	250	Springfield, OH	3,649	313	Kokomo, IN	2,467
188	Medford, OR	5,783	251	Lawrence, KS	3,632	314	Longview, WA	2,451
189	Fort Smith, AR-OK	5,712	252	Jacksonville, NC	3,621	315	Kankakee-Bradley, IL	2,435
190	College Station-Bryan, TX	5,576	253	Lawton, OK	3,575	316	La Crosse, WI-MN	2,398
191	Salinas, CA	5,573	254	Abilene, TX	3,569	317	Sumter, SC	2,387
192	Ocala, FL	5,549	255	Barnstable Town, MA	3,565	318	Muncie, IN	2,354
193	Ann Arbor, MI	5,538	256	Fargo, ND-MN	3,483	319	Missoula, MT	2,346
194	Merced, CA	5,496	257	Morristown, TN	3,419	320	Waterloo-Cedar Falls, IA	2,307
195	Panama City-Lynn Haven, FL	5,472	258	Yuma, AZ	3,403	321	Lewiston-Auburn, ME	2,279
196	Muskegon-Norton Shores, MI	5,394	259	Auburn, AL	3,400	322	Santa Fe, NM	2,252
197	Erie, PA	5,378	260	Ocean City, NJ	3,395	323	Winchester, VA-WV	2,219
198	Binghamton, NY	5,257	261	Pascagoula, MS	3,393	324	Decatur, AL	2,217
199	Monroe, LA	5,224	262	St. Joseph, MO-KS	3,379	325	Owensboro, KY	2,212
200	Tuscaloosa, AL	5,162	263	Charlottesville, VA	3,362	326	Wenatchee, WA	2,199
201	Tyler, TX	5,055	264	Battle Creek, MI	3,355	327	Cumberland, MD-WV	2,194
202	Clarksville, TN-KY	5,036	265	Sioux City, IA-NE-SD	3,311	328	Hanford-Corcoran, CA	2,188
203	Trenton-Ewing, NJ	5,035	266	Prescott, AZ	3,305	329	Pocatello, ID	2,187
204	Athens-Clarke County, GA	5,018	267	Blacksburg, VA	3,279	330	Iowa City, IA	2,145
205	Boulder, CO	5,000	268	Hot Springs, AR	3,263	331	Mankato-North Mankato, MN	2,126
206	Longview, TX	4,998	269	Bangor, ME	3,255	332	Johnstown, PA	2,117
207	Utica-Rome, NY	4,965	270	Goldsboro, NC	3,249	333	Bismarck, ND	2,098
208	Houma, LA	4,944	271	Chico, CA	3,196	334	Cheyenne, WY	2,068
209	Kennewick-Pasco-Richland, WA	4,872	272	Appleton, WI	3,174	335	Farmington, NM	2,058
210	Bremerton-Silverdale, WA	4,870	273	Anniston-Oxford, AL	3,169	336	Danville, IL	2,054
211	Olympia, WA	4,861	274	El Centro, CA	3,158	337	Idaho Falls, ID	2,008
212	Bellingham, WA	4,721	275	Victoria, TX	3,151	338	Pittsfield, MA	1,998
213	Pueblo, CO	4,683	276	Grand Junction, CO	3,118	339	Danville, VA	1,970
214	Albany, GA	4,660	277	Odessa, TX	3,096	340	State College, PA	1,952
215	Joplin, MO	4,649	278	Gainesville, GA	3,087	341	Sheboygan, WI	1,947
216	Dover, DE	4,641	279	Dothan, AL	3,079	342	Williamsport, PA	1,943
217	Alexandria, LA	4,622	280	Dalton, GA	3,047	343	Casper, WY	1,936
218	Terre Haute, IN	4,607	281	Michigan City-La Porte, IN	3,014	344	Decatur, IL	1,933
219	Warner Robins, GA	4,543	282	Yuba City, CA	3,010	345	Altoona, PA	1,922
220	Cedar Rapids, IA	4,536	283	Gadsden, AL	2,996	346	Napa, CA	1,919
221	Las Cruces, NM	4,514	283	Redding, CA	2,996	347	Lebanon, PA	1,901
222	Lake Havasu City-Kingman, AZ	4,469	285	Jackson, TN	2,966	348	Manhattan, KS	1,863
223	Naples-Marco Island, FL	4,377	286	San Angelo, TX	2,923	349	Wausau, WI	1,844
224	San Luis Obispo, CA	4,360	287	Jonesboro, AR	2,902	350	Ames, IA	1,775
225	Columbia, MO	4,324	288	Valdosta, GA	2,889	351	Corvallis, OR	1,756
226	Johnson City, TN	4,296	289	Jefferson City, MO	2,807	352	Grand Forks, ND-MN	1,689
227	Billings, MT	4,264	290	Rapid City, SD	2,806	353	Sandusky, OH	1,685
228	Green Bay, WI	4,237	291	Midland, TX	2,797	354	Glens Falls, NY	1,672
229	Texarkana, TX-Texarkana, AR	4,191	292	Salisbury, MD	2,786	355	Elmira, NY	1,653
230	Burlington, NC	4,122	293	Punta Gorda, FL	2,780	356	Madera, CA	1,603
231	Sioux Falls, SD	4,107	294	Saginaw, MI	2,753	357	Hinesville, GA	1,589
232	Champaign-Urbana, IL	4,103	295	Sherman-Denison, TX	2,750	358	Bay City, MI	1,504
233	Hagerstown-Martinsburg, MD-WV	4,073	296	Sebastian-Vero Beach, FL	2,742	359	Palm Coast, FL	1,484
234	Crestview-Fort Walton Beach, FL	4,037	297	Cape Girardeau, MO-IL	2,737	360	Elizabethtown, KY	1,455
235	Bloomington, IN	3,964	298	Bloomington-Normal, IL	2,699	361	Dubuque, IA	1,353
236	Greeley, CO	3,955	299	Rome, GA	2,683	362	Harrisonburg, VA	1,325
237	Bend, OR	3,950	300	Pine Bluff, AR	2,648	363	Fond du Lac, WI	1,323
238	Flagstaff, AZ	3,941	301	Lima, OH	2,624	364	Fairbanks, AK	1,170
239	Wichita Falls, TX	3,936	302	Kingston, NY	2,588	365	Logan, UT-ID	1,093
240	Racine, WI	3,890	303	Bowling Green, KY	2,571	366	Carson City, NV	890
241	Lafayette, IN	3,880	303	Rochester, MN	2,571	NA	Toledo, OH**	NA
242	Lynchburg, VA	3,867	305	Florence-Muscle Shoals, AL	2,564	NA	Tucson, AZ**	NA
243	Mansfield, OH	3,808	306	Cleveland, TN	2,554			

Source: Reported data from the F.B.I. "Crime in the United States 2011"
*Larceny-theft is the unlawful taking of property. Attempts are included.
**Not available.

Alpha Order - Metro Area

34. Larceny-Theft Rate in 2011
National Rate = 1,976.9 Larceny-Thefts per 100,000 Population*

RANK	METROPOLITAN AREA	RATE	RANK	METROPOLITAN AREA	RATE	RANK	METROPOLITAN AREA	RATE
179	Abilene, TX	2,115.2	196	Charleston, WV	2,061.5	64	Fort Lauderdale, FL M.D.	2,688.3
168	Akron, OH	2,149.3	120	Charlotte-Gastonia, NC-SC	2,378.9	234	Fort Smith, AR-OK	1,896.8
233	Albany-Schenectady-Troy, NY	1,897.0	285	Charlottesville, VA	1,648.3	188	Fort Wayne, IN	2,088.0
38	Albany, GA	2,923.8	89	Chattanooga, TN-GA	2,524.9	97	Fort Worth-Arlington, TX M.D.	2,501.8
58	Albuquerque, NM	2,701.9	146	Cheyenne, WY	2,236.3	90	Fresno, CA	2,523.8
32	Alexandria, LA	2,975.6	226	Chicago (greater), IL-IN-WI	1,913.4	45	Gadsden, AL	2,855.2
257	Allentown, PA-NJ	1,773.1	224	Chicago-Joilet-Naperville, IL M.D.	1,917.8	103	Gainesville, FL	2,479.5
313	Altoona, PA	1,507.5	325	Chico, CA	1,435.8	272	Gainesville, GA	1,695.7
42	Amarillo, TX	2,879.2	108	Cincinnati-Middletown, OH-KY-IN	2,465.9	144	Gary, IN M.D.	2,261.5
215	Ames, IA	1,972.0	247	Clarksville, TN-KY	1,823.1	356	Glens Falls, NY	1,291.1
57	Anchorage, AK	2,719.3	264	Cleveland-Elyria-Mentor, OH	1,747.2	77	Goldsboro, NC	2,616.4
20	Anderson, SC	3,210.7	162	Cleveland, TN	2,186.0	273	Grand Forks, ND-MN	1,691.8
289	Ann Arbor, MI	1,607.4	116	College Station-Bryan, TX	2,388.3	187	Grand Junction, CO	2,088.7
70	Anniston-Oxford, AL	2,659.8	192	Colorado Springs, CO	2,074.0	302	Grand Rapids-Wyoming, MI	1,569.5
335	Appleton, WI	1,400.4	98	Columbia, MO	2,493.5	29	Great Falls, MT	3,032.3
295	Asheville, NC	1,594.4	9	Columbus, GA-AL	3,405.2	306	Greeley, CO	1,537.5
80	Athens-Clarke County, GA	2,572.3	15	Columbus, IN	3,270.0	340	Green Bay, WI	1,377.5
156	Atlanta, GA	2,201.4	53	Columbus, OH	2,777.7	105	Greenville, SC	2,475.8
93	Atlantic City, NJ	2,510.7	14	Corpus Christi, TX	3,287.8	61	Gulfport-Biloxi, MS	2,691.0
112	Auburn, AL	2,412.7	202	Corvallis, OR	2,030.3	315	Hagerstown-Martinsburg, MD-WV	1,504.7
52	Augusta, GA-SC	2,795.9	155	Crestview-Fort Walton Beach, FL	2,202.6	331	Hanford-Corcoran, CA	1,413.6
67	Austin-Round Rock, TX	2,673.2	182	Cumberland, MD-WV	2,108.7	283	Harrisburg-Carlisle, PA	1,651.8
244	Bakersfield, CA	1,851.1	142	Dallas (greater), TX	2,280.5	365	Harrisonburg, VA	1,045.6
178	Baltimore-Towson, MD	2,115.9	165	Dallas-Plano-Irving, TX M.D.	2,168.9	262	Hartford, CT	1,753.7
180	Bangor, ME	2,115.0	181	Dalton, GA	2,114.5	151	Hickory, NC	2,221.6
287	Barnstable Town, MA	1,641.3	95	Danville, IL	2,508.8	207	Hinesville, GA	2,012.9
46	Baton Rouge, LA	2,852.4	246	Danville, VA	1,826.9	327	Holland-Grand Haven, MI	1,427.9
106	Battle Creek, MI	2,466.1	159	Davenport, IA-IL	2,194.4	11	Hot Springs, AR	3,372.6
337	Bay City, MI	1,396.6	135	Dayton, OH	2,307.4	125	Houma, LA	2,353.4
91	Beaumont-Port Arthur, TX	2,519.4	326	Decatur, AL	1,434.3	130	Houston, TX	2,336.7
134	Bellingham, WA	2,310.9	266	Decatur, IL	1,739.9	150	Huntsville, AL	2,221.9
104	Bend, OR	2,477.9	96	Deltona-Daytona Beach, FL	2,508.7	309	Idaho Falls, ID	1,522.5
334	Bethesda-Frederick, MD M.D.	1,409.9	221	Denver-Aurora, CO	1,925.4	118	Indianapolis, IN	2,380.2
66	Billings, MT	2,674.1	149	Des Moines-West Des Moines, IA	2,226.3	336	Iowa City, IA	1,398.4
190	Binghamton, NY	2,079.0	288	Detroit (greater), MI	1,636.1	68	Jacksonville, FL	2,666.3
88	Birmingham-Hoover, AL	2,526.2	205	Detroit-Livonia-Dearborn, MI M.D.	2,017.4	208	Jacksonville, NC	2,011.4
235	Bismarck, ND	1,896.7	184	Dothan, AL	2,104.0	191	Jackson, MS	2,075.0
212	Blacksburg, VA	1,988.4	49	Dover, DE	2,830.3	84	Jackson, TN	2,546.6
298	Bloomington-Normal, IL	1,586.9	324	Dubuque, IA	1,437.2	143	Janesville, WI	2,270.4
198	Bloomington, IN	2,046.5	101	Duluth, MN-WI	2,486.7	241	Jefferson City, MO	1,867.0
301	Boise City-Nampa, ID	1,572.2	131	Durham-Chapel Hill, NC	2,327.7	169	Johnson City, TN	2,142.6
311	Boston (greater), MA-NH	1,512.8	300	Eau Claire, WI	1,573.0	320	Johnstown, PA	1,468.7
275	Boston-Quincy, MA M.D.	1,680.6	322	Edison, NJ M.D.	1,458.2	119	Jonesboro, AR	2,379.8
278	Boulder, CO	1,668.3	251	El Centro, CA	1,788.4	73	Joplin, MO	2,639.1
203	Bowling Green, KY	2,027.2	239	El Paso, TX	1,868.8	171	Kankakee-Bradley, IL	2,139.9
229	Bremerton-Silverdale, WA	1,909.3	363	Elizabethtown, KY	1,206.8	139	Kansas City, MO-KS	2,291.0
350	Bridgeport-Stamford, CT	1,330.6	243	Elmira, NY	1,852.5	236	Kennewick-Pasco-Richland, WA	1,893.4
17	Brownsville-Harlingen, TX	3,234.6	228	Erie, PA	1,910.7	255	Killeen-Temple-Fort Hood, TX	1,779.0
18	Brunswick, GA	3,230.6	78	Eugene-Springfield, OR	2,593.0	115	Kingsport, TN-VA	2,390.5
194	Buffalo-Niagara Falls, NY	2,069.9	199	Evansville, IN-KY	2,046.2	333	Kingston, NY	1,411.8
60	Burlington, NC	2,693.3	8	Fairbanks, AK	3,416.8	63	Knoxville, TN	2,688.4
352	Cambridge-Newton, MA M.D.	1,317.2	286	Fargo, ND-MN	1,644.8	100	Kokomo, IN	2,487.1
238	Camden, NJ M.D.	1,876.5	303	Farmington, NM	1,565.0	253	La Crosse, WI-MN	1,785.4
204	Canton, OH	2,026.8	19	Fayetteville, NC	3,213.5	227	Lafayette, IN	1,913.0
249	Cape Coral-Fort Myers, FL	1,813.7	41	Flagstaff, AZ	2,890.9	33	Lafayette, LA	2,961.2
48	Cape Girardeau, MO-IL	2,832.7	210	Flint, MI	1,992.6	297	Lake Co.-Kenosha Co., IL-WI M.D.	1,589.6
293	Carson City, NV	1,596.7	267	Florence-Muscle Shoals, AL	1,734.2	157	Lake Havasu City-Kingman, AZ	2,201.3
85	Casper, WY	2,545.5	7	Florence, SC	3,423.7	166	Lakeland, FL	2,165.0
263	Cedar Rapids, IA	1,749.4	355	Fond du Lac, WI	1,296.1	291	Lancaster, PA	1,602.2
260	Champaign-Urbana, IL	1,764.1	193	Fort Collins-Loveland, CO	2,071.5	299	Lansing-East Lansing, MI	1,575.2

Note: All listings are for Metropolitan Statistical Areas (M.S.A.s) except for those ending with "M.D." Listings with "M.D." are Metropolitan Divisions which are smaller parts of eleven large M.S.A.s. See explanatory note at beginning of metropolitan area section.

Alpha Order - Metro Area (continued)

RANK	METROPOLITAN AREA	RATE
13	Laredo, TX	3,300.8
173	Las Cruces, NM	2,133.5
316	Las Vegas-Paradise, NV	1,495.9
16	Lawrence, KS	3,256.5
47	Lawton, OK	2,850.3
328	Lebanon, PA	1,418.7
177	Lewiston-Auburn, ME	2,116.3
36	Lexington-Fayette, KY	2,934.2
107	Lima, OH	2,466.0
34	Lincoln, NE	2,958.5
10	Little Rock, AR	3,384.7
366	Logan, UT-ID	855.5
141	Longview, TX	2,283.5
124	Longview, WA	2,356.3
338	Los Angeles County, CA M.D.	1,392.4
332	Los Angeles (greater), CA	1,413.2
82	Louisville, KY-IN	2,550.6
26	Lubbock, TX	3,079.9
312	Lynchburg, VA	1,512.6
2	Macon, GA	3,667.7
364	Madera, CA	1,050.2
197	Madison, WI	2,058.4
250	Manchester-Nashua, NH	1,794.9
323	Manhattan, KS	1,456.7
164	Mankato-North Mankato, MN	2,180.8
27	Mansfield, OH	3,057.0
35	McAllen-Edinburg-Mission, TX	2,947.8
51	Medford, OR	2,815.9
50	Memphis, TN-MS-AR	2,816.0
175	Merced, CA	2,123.6
39	Miami (greater), FL	2,907.1
12	Miami-Dade County, FL M.D.	3,347.8
62	Michigan City-La Porte, IN	2,690.2
209	Midland, TX	2,001.4
128	Milwaukee, WI	2,341.1
172	Minneapolis-St. Paul, MN-WI	2,137.9
174	Missoula, MT	2,127.5
31	Mobile, AL	3,016.5
201	Modesto, CA	2,040.3
37	Monroe, LA	2,933.9
281	Monroe, MI	1,654.3
69	Montgomery, AL	2,665.7
102	Morristown, TN	2,480.4
22	Mount Vernon-Anacortes, WA	3,201.2
211	Muncie, IN	1,990.3
24	Muskegon-Norton Shores, MI	3,135.0
1	Myrtle Beach, SC	3,922.9
339	Napa, CA	1,389.7
349	Naples-Marco Island, FL	1,343.0
136	Nashville-Davidson, TN	2,297.5
360	Nassau-Suffolk, NY M.D.	1,255.3
161	New Haven-Milford, CT	2,193.4
147	New Orleans, LA	2,234.6
353	New York (greater), NY-NJ-PA	1,305.5
354	New York-W. Plains NY-NJ M.D.	1,304.0
362	Newark-Union, NJ-PA M.D.	1,213.3
79	North Port-Bradenton-Sarasota, FL	2,573.6
274	Norwich-New London, CT	1,686.0
259	Oakland-Fremont, CA M.D.	1,765.5
282	Ocala, FL	1,652.4
4	Ocean City, NJ	3,478.9
153	Odessa, TX	2,211.2
206	Ogden-Clearfield, UT	2,016.9
59	Oklahoma City, OK	2,696.0
232	Olympia, WA	1,897.2
138	Omaha-Council Bluffs, NE-IA	2,291.4
114	Orlando, FL	2,393.1
317	Oshkosh-Neenah, WI	1,495.3
225	Owensboro, KY	1,914.4
359	Oxnard-Thousand Oaks, CA	1,260.6
132	Palm Bay-Melbourne, FL	2,322.3
308	Palm Coast, FL	1,529.9
23	Panama City-Lynn Haven, FL	3,197.1
189	Pascagoula, MS	2,083.4
347	Peabody, MA M.D.	1,367.3
87	Pensacola, FL	2,533.2
230	Peoria, IL	1,902.8
214	Philadelphia (greater) PA-NJ-MD-DE	1,973.0
216	Philadelphia, PA M.D.	1,959.8
111	Phoenix-Mesa-Scottsdale, AZ	2,454.0
76	Pine Bluff, AR	2,621.3
329	Pittsburgh, PA	1,418.2
310	Pittsfield, MA	1,513.4
117	Pocatello, ID	2,386.0
223	Port St. Lucie, FL	1,918.4
126	Portland-Vancouver, OR-WA	2,350.1
222	Portland, ME	1,924.2
307	Poughkeepsie, NY	1,532.9
305	Prescott, AZ	1,544.2
248	Provo-Orem, UT	1,816.5
40	Pueblo, CO	2,893.7
269	Punta Gorda, FL	1,714.4
213	Racine, WI	1,982.1
252	Raleigh-Cary, NC	1,786.2
160	Rapid City, SD	2,193.6
321	Reading, PA	1,462.6
277	Redding, CA	1,670.9
294	Reno-Sparks, NV	1,594.9
245	Richmond, VA	1,829.5
290	Riverside-San Bernardino, CA	1,604.9
219	Roanoke, VA	1,931.8
342	Rochester, MN	1,371.6
237	Rochester, NY	1,879.1
176	Rockford, IL	2,122.5
268	Rockingham County, NH M.D.	1,718.3
109	Rocky Mount, NC	2,457.2
56	Rome, GA	2,749.4
265	Sacramento, CA	1,744.8
341	Saginaw, MI	1,376.4
185	Salem, OR	2,094.2
351	Salinas, CA	1,327.1
154	Salisbury, MD	2,204.3
25	Salt Lake City, UT	3,125.7
81	San Angelo, TX	2,560.1
6	San Antonio, TX	3,425.5
357	San Diego, CA	1,290.7
231	San Francisco (greater), CA	1,899.0
186	San Francisco-S. Mateo, CA M.D.	2,091.3
345	San Jose, CA	1,368.2
292	San Luis Obispo, CA	1,598.2
163	Sandusky, OH	2,184.5
319	Santa Ana-Anaheim, CA M.D.	1,480.7
318	Santa Barbara-Santa Maria, CA	1,484.6
145	Santa Cruz-Watsonville, CA	2,246.6
304	Santa Fe, NM	1,544.8
361	Santa Rosa-Petaluma, CA	1,234.0
94	Savannah, GA	2,509.5
280	Scranton--Wilkes-Barre, PA	1,664.2
99	Seattle (greater), WA	2,488.7
92	Seattle-Bellevue-Everett, WA M.D.	2,515.2
216	Sebastian-Vero Beach, FL	1,959.8
276	Sheboygan, WI	1,678.3
148	Sherman-Denison, TX	2,228.1
140	Sioux City, IA-NE-SD	2,290.9
256	Sioux Falls, SD	1,777.6
121	South Bend-Mishawaka, IN-MI	2,374.4
133	Spartanburg, SC	2,312.4
3	Spokane, WA	3,504.1
28	Springfield, IL	3,034.1
242	Springfield, MA	1,863.7
5	Springfield, MO	3,473.2
74	Springfield, OH	2,635.9
358	State College, PA	1,263.6
75	Stockton, CA	2,623.9
220	St. Cloud, MN	1,931.7
72	St. Joseph, MO-KS	2,643.7
170	St. Louis, MO-IL	2,141.0
158	Sumter, SC	2,195.8
261	Syracuse, NY	1,753.9
113	Tacoma, WA M.D.	2,400.3
137	Tallahassee, FL	2,295.3
167	Tampa-St Petersburg, FL	2,160.8
71	Terre Haute, IN	2,658.3
30	Texarkana, TX-Texarkana, AR	3,030.3
NA	Toledo, OH**	NA
43	Topeka, KS	2,878.6
344	Trenton-Ewing, NJ	1,369.2
NA	Tucson, AZ**	NA
195	Tulsa, OK	2,065.9
129	Tuscaloosa, AL	2,340.9
123	Tyler, TX	2,360.7
284	Utica-Rome, NY	1,650.9
200	Valdosta, GA	2,042.8
314	Vallejo-Fairfield, CA	1,506.0
65	Victoria, TX	2,674.6
86	Virginia Beach-Norfolk, VA-NC	2,539.6
183	Visalia-Porterville, CA	2,108.5
44	Waco, TX	2,866.4
21	Warner Robins, GA	3,205.1
348	Warren-Farmington Hills, MI M.D.	1,355.7
258	Washington (greater) DC-VA-MD-WV	1,769.6
240	Washington, DC-VA-MD-WV M.D.	1,868.3
346	Waterloo-Cedar Falls, IA	1,367.5
343	Wausau, WI	1,369.5
218	Wenatchee, WA	1,952.5
122	West Palm Beach, FL M.D.	2,363.6
83	Wichita Falls, TX	2,547.7
55	Wichita, KS	2,762.0
279	Williamsport, PA	1,668.1
152	Wilmington, DE-MD-NJ M.D.	2,217.5
110	Wilmington, NC	2,455.1
271	Winchester, VA-WV	1,710.2
54	Winston-Salem, NC	2,770.1
330	Worcester, MA	1,417.9
127	Yakima, WA	2,348.5
296	York-Hanover, PA	1,590.7
254	Yuba City, CA	1,782.6
270	Yuma, AZ	1,714.2

Source: Reported data from the F.B.I. "Crime in the United States 2011"
*Larceny-theft is the unlawful taking of property. Attempts are included.
**Not available.

Rank Order - Metro Area

34. Larceny-Theft Rate in 2011 (continued)
National Rate = 1,976.9 Larceny-Thefts per 100,000 Population*

RANK	METROPOLITAN AREA	RATE	RANK	METROPOLITAN AREA	RATE	RANK	METROPOLITAN AREA	RATE
1	Myrtle Beach, SC	3,922.9	61	Gulfport-Biloxi, MS	2,691.0	121	South Bend-Mishawaka, IN-MI	2,374.4
2	Macon, GA	3,667.7	62	Michigan City-La Porte, IN	2,690.2	122	West Palm Beach, FL M.D.	2,363.6
3	Spokane, WA	3,504.1	63	Knoxville, TN	2,688.4	123	Tyler, TX	2,360.7
4	Ocean City, NJ	3,478.9	64	Fort Lauderdale, FL M.D.	2,688.3	124	Longview, WA	2,356.3
5	Springfield, MO	3,473.2	65	Victoria, TX	2,674.6	125	Houma, LA	2,353.4
6	San Antonio, TX	3,425.5	66	Billings, MT	2,674.1	126	Portland-Vancouver, OR-WA	2,350.1
7	Florence, SC	3,423.7	67	Austin-Round Rock, TX	2,673.2	127	Yakima, WA	2,348.5
8	Fairbanks, AK	3,416.8	68	Jacksonville, FL	2,666.3	128	Milwaukee, WI	2,341.1
9	Columbus, GA-AL	3,405.2	69	Montgomery, AL	2,665.7	129	Tuscaloosa, AL	2,340.9
10	Little Rock, AR	3,384.7	70	Anniston-Oxford, AL	2,659.8	130	Houston, TX	2,336.7
11	Hot Springs, AR	3,372.6	71	Terre Haute, IN	2,658.3	131	Durham-Chapel Hill, NC	2,327.7
12	Miami-Dade County, FL M.D.	3,347.8	72	St. Joseph, MO-KS	2,643.7	132	Palm Bay-Melbourne, FL	2,322.3
13	Laredo, TX	3,300.8	73	Joplin, MO	2,639.1	133	Spartanburg, SC	2,312.4
14	Corpus Christi, TX	3,287.8	74	Springfield, OH	2,635.9	134	Bellingham, WA	2,310.9
15	Columbus, IN	3,270.0	75	Stockton, CA	2,623.9	135	Dayton, OH	2,307.4
16	Lawrence, KS	3,256.5	76	Pine Bluff, AR	2,621.3	136	Nashville-Davidson, TN	2,297.5
17	Brownsville-Harlingen, TX	3,234.6	77	Goldsboro, NC	2,616.4	137	Tallahassee, FL	2,295.3
18	Brunswick, GA	3,230.6	78	Eugene-Springfield, OR	2,593.0	138	Omaha-Council Bluffs, NE-IA	2,291.4
19	Fayetteville, NC	3,213.5	79	North Port-Bradenton-Sarasota, FL	2,573.6	139	Kansas City, MO-KS	2,291.0
20	Anderson, SC	3,210.7	80	Athens-Clarke County, GA	2,572.3	140	Sioux City, IA-NE-SD	2,290.9
21	Warner Robins, GA	3,205.1	81	San Angelo, TX	2,560.1	141	Longview, TX	2,283.5
22	Mount Vernon-Anacortes, WA	3,201.2	82	Louisville, KY-IN	2,550.6	142	Dallas (greater), TX	2,280.5
23	Panama City-Lynn Haven, FL	3,197.1	83	Wichita Falls, TX	2,547.7	143	Janesville, WI	2,270.4
24	Muskegon-Norton Shores, MI	3,135.0	84	Jackson, TN	2,546.6	144	Gary, IN M.D.	2,261.5
25	Salt Lake City, UT	3,125.7	85	Casper, WY	2,545.5	145	Santa Cruz-Watsonville, CA	2,246.6
26	Lubbock, TX	3,079.9	86	Virginia Beach-Norfolk, VA-NC	2,539.6	146	Cheyenne, WY	2,236.3
27	Mansfield, OH	3,057.0	87	Pensacola, FL	2,533.2	147	New Orleans, LA	2,234.6
28	Springfield, IL	3,034.1	88	Birmingham-Hoover, AL	2,526.2	148	Sherman-Denison, TX	2,228.1
29	Great Falls, MT	3,032.3	89	Chattanooga, TN-GA	2,524.9	149	Des Moines-West Des Moines, IA	2,226.3
30	Texarkana, TX-Texarkana, AR	3,030.3	90	Fresno, CA	2,523.8	150	Huntsville, AL	2,221.9
31	Mobile, AL	3,016.5	91	Beaumont-Port Arthur, TX	2,519.4	151	Hickory, NC	2,221.6
32	Alexandria, LA	2,975.6	92	Seattle-Bellevue-Everett, WA M.D.	2,515.2	152	Wilmington, DE-MD-NJ M.D.	2,217.5
33	Lafayette, LA	2,961.2	93	Atlantic City, NJ	2,510.7	153	Odessa, TX	2,211.2
34	Lincoln, NE	2,958.5	94	Savannah, GA	2,509.5	154	Salisbury, MD	2,204.3
35	McAllen-Edinburg-Mission, TX	2,947.8	95	Danville, IL	2,508.8	155	Crestview-Fort Walton Beach, FL	2,202.6
36	Lexington-Fayette, KY	2,934.2	96	Deltona-Daytona Beach, FL	2,508.7	156	Atlanta, GA	2,201.4
37	Monroe, LA	2,933.9	97	Fort Worth-Arlington, TX M.D.	2,501.8	157	Lake Havasu City-Kingman, AZ	2,201.3
38	Albany, GA	2,923.8	98	Columbia, MO	2,493.5	158	Sumter, SC	2,195.8
39	Miami (greater), FL	2,907.1	99	Seattle (greater), WA	2,488.7	159	Davenport, IA-IL	2,194.4
40	Pueblo, CO	2,893.7	100	Kokomo, IN	2,487.1	160	Rapid City, SD	2,193.6
41	Flagstaff, AZ	2,890.9	101	Duluth, MN-WI	2,486.7	161	New Haven-Milford, CT	2,193.4
42	Amarillo, TX	2,879.2	102	Morristown, TN	2,480.4	162	Cleveland, TN	2,186.0
43	Topeka, KS	2,878.6	103	Gainesville, FL	2,479.5	163	Sandusky, OH	2,184.5
44	Waco, TX	2,866.4	104	Bend, OR	2,477.9	164	Mankato-North Mankato, MN	2,180.8
45	Gadsden, AL	2,855.2	105	Greenville, SC	2,475.8	165	Dallas-Plano-Irving, TX M.D.	2,168.9
46	Baton Rouge, LA	2,852.4	106	Battle Creek, MI	2,466.1	166	Lakeland, FL	2,165.0
47	Lawton, OK	2,850.3	107	Lima, OH	2,466.0	167	Tampa-St Petersburg, FL	2,160.8
48	Cape Girardeau, MO-IL	2,832.7	108	Cincinnati-Middletown, OH-KY-IN	2,465.9	168	Akron, OH	2,149.3
49	Dover, DE	2,830.3	109	Rocky Mount, NC	2,457.2	169	Johnson City, TN	2,142.6
50	Memphis, TN-MS-AR	2,816.0	110	Wilmington, NC	2,455.1	170	St. Louis, MO-IL	2,141.0
51	Medford, OR	2,815.9	111	Phoenix-Mesa-Scottsdale, AZ	2,454.0	171	Kankakee-Bradley, IL	2,139.9
52	Augusta, GA-SC	2,795.9	112	Auburn, AL	2,412.7	172	Minneapolis-St. Paul, MN-WI	2,137.9
53	Columbus, OH	2,777.7	113	Tacoma, WA M.D.	2,400.3	173	Las Cruces, NM	2,133.5
54	Winston-Salem, NC	2,770.1	114	Orlando, FL	2,393.1	174	Missoula, MT	2,127.5
55	Wichita, KS	2,762.0	115	Kingsport, TN-VA	2,390.5	175	Merced, CA	2,123.6
56	Rome, GA	2,749.4	116	College Station-Bryan, TX	2,388.3	176	Rockford, IL	2,122.5
57	Anchorage, AK	2,719.3	117	Pocatello, ID	2,386.0	177	Lewiston-Auburn, ME	2,116.3
58	Albuquerque, NM	2,701.9	118	Indianapolis, IN	2,380.2	178	Baltimore-Towson, MD	2,115.9
59	Oklahoma City, OK	2,696.0	119	Jonesboro, AR	2,379.8	179	Abilene, TX	2,115.2
60	Burlington, NC	2,693.3	120	Charlotte-Gastonia, NC-SC	2,378.9	180	Bangor, ME	2,115.0

Note: All listings are for Metropolitan Statistical Areas (M.S.A.s) except for those ending with "M.D." Listings with "M.D." are Metropolitan Divisions which are smaller parts of eleven large M.S.A.s. See explanatory note at beginning of metropolitan area section.

Rank Order - Metro Area (continued)

RANK	METROPOLITAN AREA	RATE
181	Dalton, GA	2,114.5
182	Cumberland, MD-WV	2,108.7
183	Visalia-Porterville, CA	2,108.5
184	Dothan, AL	2,104.0
185	Salem, OR	2,094.2
186	San Francisco-S. Mateo, CA M.D.	2,091.3
187	Grand Junction, CO	2,088.7
188	Fort Wayne, IN	2,088.0
189	Pascagoula, MS	2,083.4
190	Binghamton, NY	2,079.0
191	Jackson, MS	2,075.0
192	Colorado Springs, CO	2,074.0
193	Fort Collins-Loveland, CO	2,071.5
194	Buffalo-Niagara Falls, NY	2,069.9
195	Tulsa, OK	2,065.9
196	Charleston, WV	2,061.5
197	Madison, WI	2,058.4
198	Bloomington, IN	2,046.5
199	Evansville, IN-KY	2,046.2
200	Valdosta, GA	2,042.8
201	Modesto, CA	2,040.3
202	Corvallis, OR	2,030.3
203	Bowling Green, KY	2,027.2
204	Canton, OH	2,026.8
205	Detroit-Livonia-Dearborn, MI M.D.	2,017.4
206	Ogden-Clearfield, UT	2,016.9
207	Hinesville, GA	2,012.9
208	Jacksonville, NC	2,011.4
209	Midland, TX	2,001.4
210	Flint, MI	1,992.6
211	Muncie, IN	1,990.3
212	Blacksburg, VA	1,988.4
213	Racine, WI	1,982.1
214	Philadelphia (greater) PA-NJ-MD-DE	1,973.0
215	Ames, IA	1,972.0
216	Philadelphia, PA M.D.	1,959.8
216	Sebastian-Vero Beach, FL	1,959.8
218	Wenatchee, WA	1,952.5
219	Roanoke, VA	1,931.8
220	St. Cloud, MN	1,931.7
221	Denver-Aurora, CO	1,925.4
222	Portland, ME	1,924.2
223	Port St. Lucie, FL	1,918.4
224	Chicago-Joilet-Naperville, IL M.D.	1,917.8
225	Owensboro, KY	1,914.4
226	Chicago (greater), IL-IN-WI	1,913.4
227	Lafayette, IN	1,913.0
228	Erie, PA	1,910.7
229	Bremerton-Silverdale, WA	1,909.3
230	Peoria, IL	1,902.8
231	San Francisco (greater), CA	1,899.0
232	Olympia, WA	1,897.2
233	Albany-Schenectady-Troy, NY	1,897.0
234	Fort Smith, AR-OK	1,896.8
235	Bismarck, ND	1,896.7
236	Kennewick-Pasco-Richland, WA	1,893.4
237	Rochester, NY	1,879.1
238	Camden, NJ M.D.	1,876.5
239	El Paso, TX	1,868.8
240	Washington, DC-VA-MD-WV M.D.	1,868.3
241	Jefferson City, MO	1,867.0
242	Springfield, MA	1,863.7
243	Elmira, NY	1,852.5
244	Bakersfield, CA	1,851.1
245	Richmond, VA	1,829.5
246	Danville, VA	1,826.9
247	Clarksville, TN-KY	1,823.1
248	Provo-Orem, UT	1,816.5
249	Cape Coral-Fort Myers, FL	1,813.7
250	Manchester-Nashua, NH	1,794.9
251	El Centro, CA	1,788.4
252	Raleigh-Cary, NC	1,786.2
253	La Crosse, WI-MN	1,785.4
254	Yuba City, CA	1,782.6
255	Killeen-Temple-Fort Hood, TX	1,779.0
256	Sioux Falls, SD	1,777.6
257	Allentown, PA-NJ	1,773.1
258	Washington (greater) DC-VA-MD-WV	1,769.6
259	Oakland-Fremont, CA M.D.	1,765.5
260	Champaign-Urbana, IL	1,764.1
261	Syracuse, NY	1,753.9
262	Hartford, CT	1,753.7
263	Cedar Rapids, IA	1,749.4
264	Cleveland-Elyria-Mentor, OH	1,747.2
265	Sacramento, CA	1,744.8
266	Decatur, IL	1,739.9
267	Florence-Muscle Shoals, AL	1,734.2
268	Rockingham County, NH M.D.	1,718.3
269	Punta Gorda, FL	1,714.4
270	Yuma, AZ	1,714.2
271	Winchester, VA-WV	1,710.2
272	Gainesville, GA	1,695.7
273	Grand Forks, ND-MN	1,691.8
274	Norwich-New London, CT	1,686.0
275	Boston-Quincy, MA M.D.	1,680.6
276	Sheboygan, WI	1,678.3
277	Redding, CA	1,670.9
278	Boulder, CO	1,668.3
279	Williamsport, PA	1,668.1
280	Scranton--Wilkes-Barre, PA	1,664.2
281	Monroe, MI	1,654.3
282	Ocala, FL	1,652.4
283	Harrisburg-Carlisle, PA	1,651.8
284	Utica-Rome, NY	1,650.9
285	Charlottesville, VA	1,648.3
286	Fargo, ND-MN	1,644.8
287	Barnstable Town, MA	1,641.3
288	Detroit (greater), MI	1,636.1
289	Ann Arbor, MI	1,607.4
290	Riverside-San Bernardino, CA	1,604.9
291	Lancaster, PA	1,602.2
292	San Luis Obispo, CA	1,598.2
293	Carson City, NV	1,596.7
294	Reno-Sparks, NV	1,594.9
295	Asheville, NC	1,594.4
296	York-Hanover, PA	1,590.7
297	Lake Co.-Kenosha Co., IL-WI M.D.	1,589.6
298	Bloomington-Normal, IL	1,586.9
299	Lansing-East Lansing, MI	1,575.2
300	Eau Claire, WI	1,573.0
301	Boise City-Nampa, ID	1,572.2
302	Grand Rapids-Wyoming, MI	1,569.5
303	Farmington, NM	1,565.0
304	Santa Fe, NM	1,544.8
305	Prescott, AZ	1,544.2
306	Greeley, CO	1,537.5
307	Poughkeepsie, NY	1,532.9
308	Palm Coast, FL	1,529.9
309	Idaho Falls, ID	1,522.5
310	Pittsfield, MA	1,513.4
311	Boston (greater), MA-NH	1,512.8
312	Lynchburg, VA	1,512.6
313	Altoona, PA	1,507.5
314	Vallejo-Fairfield, CA	1,506.0
315	Hagerstown-Martinsburg, MD-WV	1,504.7
316	Las Vegas-Paradise, NV	1,495.9
317	Oshkosh-Neenah, WI	1,495.3
318	Santa Barbara-Santa Maria, CA	1,484.6
319	Santa Ana-Anaheim, CA M.D.	1,480.7
320	Johnstown, PA	1,468.7
321	Reading, PA	1,462.6
322	Edison, NJ M.D.	1,458.2
323	Manhattan, KS	1,456.7
324	Dubuque, IA	1,437.2
325	Chico, CA	1,435.8
326	Decatur, AL	1,434.3
327	Holland-Grand Haven, MI	1,427.9
328	Lebanon, PA	1,418.7
329	Pittsburgh, PA	1,418.2
330	Worcester, MA	1,417.9
331	Hanford-Corcoran, CA	1,413.6
332	Los Angeles (greater), CA	1,413.2
333	Kingston, NY	1,411.8
334	Bethesda-Frederick, MD M.D.	1,409.9
335	Appleton, WI	1,400.4
336	Iowa City, IA	1,398.4
337	Bay City, MI	1,396.6
338	Los Angeles County, CA M.D.	1,392.4
339	Napa, CA	1,389.7
340	Green Bay, WI	1,377.5
341	Saginaw, MI	1,376.4
342	Rochester, MN	1,371.6
343	Wausau, WI	1,369.5
344	Trenton-Ewing, NJ	1,369.2
345	San Jose, CA	1,368.2
346	Waterloo-Cedar Falls, IA	1,367.5
347	Peabody, MA M.D.	1,367.3
348	Warren-Farmington Hills, MI M.D.	1,355.7
349	Naples-Marco Island, FL	1,343.0
350	Bridgeport-Stamford, CT	1,330.6
351	Salinas, CA	1,327.1
352	Cambridge-Newton, MA M.D.	1,317.2
353	New York (greater), NY-NJ-PA	1,305.5
354	New York-W. Plains NY-NJ M.D.	1,304.0
355	Fond du Lac, WI	1,296.1
356	Glens Falls, NY	1,291.1
357	San Diego, CA	1,290.7
358	State College, PA	1,263.6
359	Oxnard-Thousand Oaks, CA	1,260.6
360	Nassau-Suffolk, NY M.D.	1,255.3
361	Santa Rosa-Petaluma, CA	1,234.0
362	Newark-Union, NJ-PA M.D.	1,213.3
363	Elizabethtown, KY	1,206.8
364	Madera, CA	1,050.2
365	Harrisonburg, VA	1,045.6
366	Logan, UT-ID	855.5
NA	Toledo, OH**	NA
NA	Tucson, AZ**	NA

Source: Reported data from the F.B.I. "Crime in the United States 2011"

*Larceny-theft is the unlawful taking of property. Attempts are included.

**Not available.

Alpha Order - Metro Area

35. Percent Change in Larceny-Theft Rate: 2010 to 2011
National Percent Change = 1.4% Decrease*

RANK	METROPOLITAN AREA	% CHANGE	RANK	METROPOLITAN AREA	% CHANGE	RANK	METROPOLITAN AREA	% CHANGE
312	Abilene, TX	(14.0)	NA	Charleston, WV**	NA	87	Fort Lauderdale, FL M.D.	3.4
83	Akron, OH	3.6	NA	Charlotte-Gastonia, NC-SC**	NA	287	Fort Smith, AR-OK	(9.5)
275	Albany-Schenectady-Troy, NY	(8.6)	291	Charlottesville, VA	(10.1)	48	Fort Wayne, IN	6.2
69	Albany, GA	4.3	182	Chattanooga, TN-GA	(2.1)	260	Fort Worth-Arlington, TX M.D.	(7.0)
67	Albuquerque, NM	4.5	302	Cheyenne, WY	(11.9)	139	Fresno, CA	0.4
252	Alexandria, LA	(6.3)	NA	Chicago (greater), IL-IN-WI**	NA	NA	Gadsden, AL**	NA
127	Allentown, PA-NJ	0.9	NA	Chicago-Joilet-Naperville, IL M.D.**	NA	150	Gainesville, FL	0.1
12	Altoona, PA	14.4	283	Chico, CA	(9.3)	114	Gainesville, GA	1.9
321	Amarillo, TX	(15.1)	74	Cincinnati-Middletown, OH-KY-IN	3.9	NA	Gary, IN M.D.**	NA
142	Ames, IA	0.3	41	Clarksville, TN-KY	7.0	30	Glens Falls, NY	8.6
204	Anchorage, AK	(3.3)	91	Cleveland-Elyria-Mentor, OH	3.2	142	Goldsboro, NC	0.3
54	Anderson, SC	5.6	15	Cleveland, TN	12.2	122	Grand Forks, ND-MN	1.3
319	Ann Arbor, MI	(14.5)	305	College Station-Bryan, TX	(12.1)	67	Grand Junction, CO	4.5
NA	Anniston-Oxford, AL**	NA	285	Colorado Springs, CO	(9.4)	210	Grand Rapids-Wyoming, MI	(3.7)
325	Appleton, WI	(18.0)	94	Columbia, MO	2.9	NA	Great Falls, MT**	NA
74	Asheville, NC	3.9	NA	Columbus, GA-AL**	NA	245	Greeley, CO	(5.7)
159	Athens-Clarke County, GA	(0.6)	10	Columbus, IN	15.1	177	Green Bay, WI	(1.6)
92	Atlanta, GA	3.1	173	Columbus, OH	(1.4)	57	Greenville, SC	5.3
254	Atlantic City, NJ	(6.5)	279	Corpus Christi, TX	(8.8)	254	Gulfport-Biloxi, MS	(6.5)
NA	Auburn, AL**	NA	8	Corvallis, OR	16.5	80	Hagerstown-Martinsburg, MD-WV	3.7
273	Augusta, GA-SC	(8.0)	94	Crestview-Fort Walton Beach, FL	2.9	2	Hanford-Corcoran, CA	23.1
259	Austin-Round Rock, TX	(6.8)	NA	Cumberland, MD-WV**	NA	132	Harrisburg-Carlisle, PA	0.7
221	Bakersfield, CA	(4.2)	210	Dallas (greater), TX	(3.7)	243	Harrisonburg, VA	(5.5)
164	Baltimore-Towson, MD	(0.9)	180	Dallas-Plano-Irving, TX M.D.	(2.0)	250	Hartford, CT	(5.9)
309	Bangor, ME	(12.9)	156	Dalton, GA	(0.3)	19	Hickory, NC	9.6
260	Barnstable Town, MA	(7.0)	59	Danville, IL	5.0	296	Hinesville, GA	(10.7)
NA	Baton Rouge, LA**	NA	229	Danville, VA	(4.7)	59	Holland-Grand Haven, MI	5.0
107	Battle Creek, MI	2.3	NA	Davenport, IA-IL**	NA	74	Hot Springs, AR	3.9
326	Bay City, MI	(21.4)	94	Dayton, OH	2.9	287	Houma, LA	(9.5)
124	Beaumont-Port Arthur, TX	1.2	NA	Decatur, AL**	NA	NA	Houston, TX**	NA
192	Bellingham, WA	(2.6)	122	Decatur, IL	1.3	NA	Huntsville, AL**	NA
59	Bend, OR	5.0	104	Deltona-Daytona Beach, FL	2.4	69	Idaho Falls, ID	4.3
275	Bethesda-Frederick, MD M.D.	(8.6)	171	Denver-Aurora, CO	(1.3)	NA	Indianapolis, IN**	NA
NA	Billings, MT**	NA	29	Des Moines-West Des Moines, IA	8.7	38	Iowa City, IA	7.4
89	Binghamton, NY	3.3	NA	Detroit (greater), MI**	NA	152	Jacksonville, FL	(0.1)
NA	Birmingham-Hoover, AL**	NA	150	Detroit-Livonia-Dearborn, MI M.D.	0.1	NA	Jacksonville, NC**	NA
1	Bismarck, ND	30.5	NA	Dothan, AL**	NA	218	Jackson, MS	(4.0)
116	Blacksburg, VA	1.8	17	Dover, DE	11.4	323	Jackson, TN	(16.5)
285	Bloomington-Normal, IL	(9.4)	196	Dubuque, IA	(2.9)	125	Janesville, WI	1.1
215	Bloomington, IN	(3.8)	246	Duluth, MN-WI	(5.8)	152	Jefferson City, MO	(0.1)
166	Boise City-Nampa, ID	(1.0)	170	Durham-Chapel Hill, NC	(1.2)	118	Johnson City, TN	1.7
207	Boston (greater), MA-NH	(3.5)	79	Eau Claire, WI	3.8	51	Johnstown, PA	5.7
182	Boston-Quincy, MA M.D.	(2.1)	98	Edison, NJ M.D.	2.7	7	Jonesboro, AR	17.7
266	Boulder, CO	(7.4)	196	El Centro, CA	(2.9)	221	Joplin, MO	(4.2)
142	Bowling Green, KY	0.3	310	El Paso, TX	(13.2)	NA	Kankakee-Bradley, IL**	NA
121	Bremerton-Silverdale, WA	1.5	210	Elizabethtown, KY	(3.7)	NA	Kansas City, MO-KS**	NA
31	Bridgeport-Stamford, CT	8.5	14	Elmira, NY	12.7	46	Kennewick-Pasco-Richland, WA	6.3
280	Brownsville-Harlingen, TX	(8.9)	33	Erie, PA	8.2	324	Killeen-Temple-Fort Hood, TX	(16.9)
293	Brunswick, GA	(10.2)	NA	Eugene-Springfield, OR**	NA	64	Kingsport, TN-VA	4.7
226	Buffalo-Niagara Falls, NY	(4.5)	204	Evansville, IN-KY	(3.3)	204	Kingston, NY	(3.3)
107	Burlington, NC	2.3	102	Fairbanks, AK	2.6	57	Knoxville, TN	5.3
270	Cambridge-Newton, MA M.D.	(7.8)	251	Fargo, ND-MN	(6.1)	31	Kokomo, IN	8.5
110	Camden, NJ M.D.	2.2	131	Farmington, NM	0.8	132	La Crosse, WI-MN	0.7
4	Canton, OH	21.0	126	Fayetteville, NC	1.0	98	Lafayette, IN	2.7
51	Cape Coral-Fort Myers, FL	5.7	220	Flagstaff, AZ	(4.1)	198	Lafayette, LA	(3.0)
155	Cape Girardeau, MO-IL	(0.2)	51	Flint, MI	5.7	NA	Lake Co.-Kenosha Co., IL-WI M.D.**	NA
11	Carson City, NV	14.6	NA	Florence-Muscle Shoals, AL**	NA	NA	Lake Havasu City-Kingman, AZ**	NA
296	Casper, WY	(10.7)	74	Florence, SC	3.9	283	Lakeland, FL	(9.3)
229	Cedar Rapids, IA	(4.7)	178	Fond du Lac, WI	(1.7)	35	Lancaster, PA	7.9
NA	Champaign-Urbana, IL**	NA	160	Fort Collins-Loveland, CO	(0.7)	308	Lansing-East Lansing, MI	(12.3)

Note: All listings are for Metropolitan Statistical Areas (M.S.A.s) except for those ending with "M.D." Listings with "M.D." are Metropolitan Divisions which are smaller parts of eleven large M.S.A.s. See explanatory note at beginning of metropolitan area section.

Alpha Order - Metro Area (continued)

RANK	METROPOLITAN AREA	% CHANGE
293	Laredo, TX	(10.2)
54	Las Cruces, NM	5.6
239	Las Vegas-Paradise, NV	(5.3)
80	Lawrence, KS	3.7
270	Lawton, OK	(7.8)
13	Lebanon, PA	13.6
16	Lewiston-Auburn, ME	11.6
NA	Lexington-Fayette, KY**	NA
194	Lima, OH	(2.7)
156	Lincoln, NE	(0.3)
54	Little Rock, AR	5.6
257	Logan, UT-ID	(6.7)
307	Longview, TX	(12.2)
215	Longview, WA	(3.8)
186	Los Angeles County, CA M.D.	(2.2)
169	Los Angeles (greater), CA	(1.1)
44	Louisville, KY-IN	6.5
302	Lubbock, TX	(11.9)
199	Lynchburg, VA	(3.1)
23	Macon, GA	9.4
74	Madera, CA	3.9
147	Madison, WI	0.2
33	Manchester-Nashua, NH	8.2
272	Manhattan, KS	(7.9)
19	Mankato-North Mankato, MN	9.6
35	Mansfield, OH	7.9
318	McAllen-Edinburg-Mission, TX	(14.4)
3	Medford, OR	21.8
142	Memphis, TN-MS-AR	0.3
42	Merced, CA	6.8
139	Miami (greater), FL	0.4
135	Miami-Dade County, FL M.D.	0.5
179	Michigan City-La Porte, IN	(1.9)
282	Midland, TX	(9.2)
243	Milwaukee, WI	(5.5)
187	Minneapolis-St. Paul, MN-WI	(2.3)
NA	Missoula, MT**	NA
158	Mobile, AL	(0.4)
295	Modesto, CA	(10.6)
265	Monroe, LA	(7.3)
199	Monroe, MI	(3.1)
NA	Montgomery, AL**	NA
263	Morristown, TN	(7.1)
322	Mount Vernon-Anacortes, WA	(16.0)
38	Muncie, IN	7.4
83	Muskegon-Norton Shores, MI	3.6
87	Myrtle Beach, SC	3.4
221	Napa, CA	(4.2)
132	Naples-Marco Island, FL	0.7
189	Nashville-Davidson, TN	(2.4)
236	Nassau-Suffolk, NY M.D.	(5.2)
227	New Haven-Milford, CT	(4.6)
27	New Orleans, LA	8.8
139	New York (greater), NY-NJ-PA	0.4
127	New York-W. Plains NY-NJ M.D.	0.9
94	Newark-Union, NJ-PA M.D.	2.9
127	North Port-Bradenton-Sarasota, FL	0.9
235	Norwich-New London, CT	(5.0)
175	Oakland-Fremont, CA M.D.	(1.5)
166	Ocala, FL	(1.0)
162	Ocean City, NJ	(0.8)
300	Odessa, TX	(11.3)
312	Ogden-Clearfield, UT	(14.0)
113	Oklahoma City, OK	2.0
319	Olympia, WA	(14.5)
43	Omaha-Council Bluffs, NE-IA	6.6
114	Orlando, FL	1.9
NA	Oshkosh-Neenah, WI**	NA
71	Owensboro, KY	4.2
315	Oxnard-Thousand Oaks, CA	(14.2)
89	Palm Bay-Melbourne, FL	3.3
254	Palm Coast, FL	(6.5)
224	Panama City-Lynn Haven, FL	(4.4)
44	Pascagoula, MS	6.5
246	Peabody, MA M.D.	(5.8)
25	Pensacola, FL	9.2
65	Peoria, IL	4.6
119	Philadelphia (greater) PA-NJ-MD-DE	1.6
104	Philadelphia, PA M.D.	2.4
110	Phoenix-Mesa-Scottsdale, AZ	2.2
62	Pine Bluff, AR	4.9
194	Pittsburgh, PA	(2.7)
281	Pittsfield, MA	(9.0)
46	Pocatello, ID	6.3
48	Port St. Lucie, FL	6.2
NA	Portland-Vancouver, OR-WA**	NA
98	Portland, ME	2.7
274	Poughkeepsie, NY	(8.1)
166	Prescott, AZ	(1.0)
50	Provo-Orem, UT	5.9
NA	Pueblo, CO**	NA
267	Punta Gorda, FL	(7.5)
104	Racine, WI	2.4
22	Raleigh-Cary, NC	9.5
135	Rapid City, SD	0.5
107	Reading, PA	2.3
40	Redding, CA	7.2
317	Reno-Sparks, NV	(14.3)
190	Richmond, VA	(2.5)
85	Riverside-San Bernardino, CA	3.5
241	Roanoke, VA	(5.4)
210	Rochester, MN	(3.7)
289	Rochester, NY	(9.9)
246	Rockford, IL	(5.8)
37	Rockingham County, NH M.D.	7.7
26	Rocky Mount, NC	9.0
23	Rome, GA	9.4
269	Sacramento, CA	(7.6)
315	Saginaw, MI	(14.2)
164	Salem, OR	(0.9)
290	Salinas, CA	(10.0)
291	Salisbury, MD	(10.1)
246	Salt Lake City, UT	(5.8)
311	San Angelo, TX	(13.6)
298	San Antonio, TX	(10.9)
210	San Diego, CA	(3.7)
180	San Francisco (greater), CA	(2.0)
190	San Francisco-S. Mateo, CA M.D.	(2.5)
236	San Jose, CA	(5.2)
162	San Luis Obispo, CA	(0.8)
116	Sandusky, OH	1.8
98	Santa Ana-Anaheim, CA M.D.	2.7
171	Santa Barbara-Santa Maria, CA	(1.3)
182	Santa Cruz-Watsonville, CA	(2.1)
187	Santa Fe, NM	(2.3)
260	Santa Rosa-Petaluma, CA	(7.0)
110	Savannah, GA	2.2
160	Scranton--Wilkes-Barre, PA	(0.7)
229	Seattle (greater), WA	(4.7)
239	Seattle-Bellevue-Everett, WA M.D.	(5.3)
263	Sebastian-Vero Beach, FL	(7.1)
NA	Sheboygan, WI**	NA
92	Sherman-Denison, TX	3.1
9	Sioux City, IA-NE-SD	15.4
85	Sioux Falls, SD	3.5
257	South Bend-Mishawaka, IN-MI	(6.7)
199	Spartanburg, SC	(3.1)
80	Spokane, WA	3.7
182	Springfield, IL	(2.1)
199	Springfield, MA	(3.1)
227	Springfield, MO	(4.6)
119	Springfield, OH	1.6
277	State College, PA	(8.7)
73	Stockton, CA	4.0
63	St. Cloud, MN	4.8
19	St. Joseph, MO-KS	9.6
173	St. Louis, MO-IL	(1.4)
327	Sumter, SC	(30.2)
175	Syracuse, NY	(1.5)
192	Tacoma, WA M.D.	(2.6)
147	Tallahassee, FL	0.2
267	Tampa-St Petersburg, FL	(7.5)
NA	Terre Haute, IN**	NA
18	Texarkana, TX-Texarkana, AR	10.4
NA	Toledo, OH**	NA
234	Topeka, KS	(4.9)
209	Trenton-Ewing, NJ	(3.6)
NA	Tucson, AZ**	NA
142	Tulsa, OK	0.3
NA	Tuscaloosa, AL**	NA
299	Tyler, TX	(11.2)
277	Utica-Rome, NY	(8.7)
301	Valdosta, GA	(11.8)
241	Vallejo-Fairfield, CA	(5.4)
199	Victoria, TX	(3.1)
236	Virginia Beach-Norfolk, VA-NC	(5.2)
229	Visalia-Porterville, CA	(4.7)
147	Waco, TX	0.2
5	Warner Robins, GA	18.3
NA	Warren-Farmington Hills, MI M.D.**	NA
229	Washington (greater) DC-VA-MD-WV	(4.7)
218	Washington, DC-VA-MD-WV M.D.	(4.0)
305	Waterloo-Cedar Falls, IA	(12.1)
135	Wausau, WI	0.5
253	Wenatchee, WA	(6.4)
217	West Palm Beach, FL M.D.	(3.9)
304	Wichita Falls, TX	(12.0)
65	Wichita, KS	4.6
27	Williamsport, PA	8.8
207	Wilmington, DE-MD-NJ M.D.	(3.5)
102	Wilmington, NC	2.6
152	Winchester, VA-WV	(0.1)
72	Winston-Salem, NC	4.1
135	Worcester, MA	0.5
314	Yakima, WA	(14.1)
224	York-Hanover, PA	(4.4)
6	Yuba City, CA	18.0
127	Yuma, AZ	0.9

Source: CQ Press using reported data from the F.B.I. "Crime in the United States 2011"
*Larceny-theft is the unlawful taking of property. Attempts are included.
**Not available.

Rank Order - Metro Area

35. Percent Change in Larceny-Theft Rate: 2010 to 2011 (continued)
National Percent Change = 1.4% Decrease*

RANK	METROPOLITAN AREA	% CHANGE	RANK	METROPOLITAN AREA	% CHANGE	RANK	METROPOLITAN AREA	% CHANGE
1	Bismarck, ND	30.5	59	Holland-Grand Haven, MI	5.0	121	Bremerton-Silverdale, WA	1.5
2	Hanford-Corcoran, CA	23.1	62	Pine Bluff, AR	4.9	122	Decatur, IL	1.3
3	Medford, OR	21.8	63	St. Cloud, MN	4.8	122	Grand Forks, ND-MN	1.3
4	Canton, OH	21.0	64	Kingsport, TN-VA	4.7	124	Beaumont-Port Arthur, TX	1.2
5	Warner Robins, GA	18.3	65	Peoria, IL	4.6	125	Janesville, WI	1.1
6	Yuba City, CA	18.0	65	Wichita, KS	4.6	126	Fayetteville, NC	1.0
7	Jonesboro, AR	17.7	67	Albuquerque, NM	4.5	127	Allentown, PA-NJ	0.9
8	Corvallis, OR	16.5	67	Grand Junction, CO	4.5	127	New York-W. Plains NY-NJ M.D.	0.9
9	Sioux City, IA-NE-SD	15.4	69	Albany, GA	4.3	127	North Port-Bradenton-Sarasota, FL	0.9
10	Columbus, IN	15.1	69	Idaho Falls, ID	4.3	127	Yuma, AZ	0.9
11	Carson City, NV	14.6	71	Owensboro, KY	4.2	131	Farmington, NM	0.8
12	Altoona, PA	14.4	72	Winston-Salem, NC	4.1	132	Harrisburg-Carlisle, PA	0.7
13	Lebanon, PA	13.6	73	Stockton, CA	4.0	132	La Crosse, WI-MN	0.7
14	Elmira, NY	12.7	74	Asheville, NC	3.9	132	Naples-Marco Island, FL	0.7
15	Cleveland, TN	12.2	74	Cincinnati-Middletown, OH-KY-IN	3.9	135	Miami-Dade County, FL M.D.	0.5
16	Lewiston-Auburn, ME	11.6	74	Florence, SC	3.9	135	Rapid City, SD	0.5
17	Dover, DE	11.4	74	Hot Springs, AR	3.9	135	Wausau, WI	0.5
18	Texarkana, TX-Texarkana, AR	10.4	74	Madera, CA	3.9	135	Worcester, MA	0.5
19	Hickory, NC	9.6	79	Eau Claire, WI	3.8	139	Fresno, CA	0.4
19	Mankato-North Mankato, MN	9.6	80	Hagerstown-Martinsburg, MD-WV	3.7	139	Miami (greater), FL	0.4
19	St. Joseph, MO-KS	9.6	80	Lawrence, KS	3.7	139	New York (greater), NY-NJ-PA	0.4
22	Raleigh-Cary, NC	9.5	80	Spokane, WA	3.7	142	Ames, IA	0.3
23	Macon, GA	9.4	83	Akron, OH	3.6	142	Bowling Green, KY	0.3
23	Rome, GA	9.4	83	Muskegon-Norton Shores, MI	3.6	142	Goldsboro, NC	0.3
25	Pensacola, FL	9.2	85	Riverside-San Bernardino, CA	3.5	142	Memphis, TN-MS-AR	0.3
26	Rocky Mount, NC	9.0	85	Sioux Falls, SD	3.5	142	Tulsa, OK	0.3
27	New Orleans, LA	8.8	87	Fort Lauderdale, FL M.D.	3.4	147	Madison, WI	0.2
27	Williamsport, PA	8.8	87	Myrtle Beach, SC	3.4	147	Tallahassee, FL	0.2
29	Des Moines-West Des Moines, IA	8.7	89	Binghamton, NY	3.3	147	Waco, TX	0.2
30	Glens Falls, NY	8.6	89	Palm Bay-Melbourne, FL	3.3	150	Detroit-Livonia-Dearborn, MI M.D.	0.1
31	Bridgeport-Stamford, CT	8.5	91	Cleveland-Elyria-Mentor, OH	3.2	150	Gainesville, FL	0.1
31	Kokomo, IN	8.5	92	Atlanta, GA	3.1	152	Jacksonville, FL	(0.1)
33	Erie, PA	8.2	92	Sherman-Denison, TX	3.1	152	Jefferson City, MO	(0.1)
33	Manchester-Nashua, NH	8.2	94	Columbia, MO	2.9	152	Winchester, VA-WV	(0.1)
35	Lancaster, PA	7.9	94	Crestview-Fort Walton Beach, FL	2.9	155	Cape Girardeau, MO-IL	(0.2)
35	Mansfield, OH	7.9	94	Dayton, OH	2.9	156	Dalton, GA	(0.3)
37	Rockingham County, NH M.D.	7.7	94	Newark-Union, NJ-PA M.D.	2.9	156	Lincoln, NE	(0.3)
38	Iowa City, IA	7.4	98	Edison, NJ M.D.	2.7	158	Mobile, AL	(0.4)
38	Muncie, IN	7.4	98	Lafayette, IN	2.7	159	Athens-Clarke County, GA	(0.6)
40	Redding, CA	7.2	98	Portland, ME	2.7	160	Fort Collins-Loveland, CO	(0.7)
41	Clarksville, TN-KY	7.0	98	Santa Ana-Anaheim, CA M.D.	2.7	160	Scranton--Wilkes-Barre, PA	(0.7)
42	Merced, CA	6.8	102	Fairbanks, AK	2.6	162	Ocean City, NJ	(0.8)
43	Omaha-Council Bluffs, NE-IA	6.6	102	Wilmington, NC	2.6	162	San Luis Obispo, CA	(0.8)
44	Louisville, KY-IN	6.5	104	Deltona-Daytona Beach, FL	2.4	164	Baltimore-Towson, MD	(0.9)
44	Pascagoula, MS	6.5	104	Philadelphia, PA M.D.	2.4	164	Salem, OR	(0.9)
46	Kennewick-Pasco-Richland, WA	6.3	104	Racine, WI	2.4	166	Boise City-Nampa, ID	(1.0)
46	Pocatello, ID	6.3	107	Battle Creek, MI	2.3	166	Ocala, FL	(1.0)
48	Fort Wayne, IN	6.2	107	Burlington, NC	2.3	166	Prescott, AZ	(1.0)
48	Port St. Lucie, FL	6.2	107	Reading, PA	2.3	169	Los Angeles (greater), CA	(1.1)
50	Provo-Orem, UT	5.9	110	Camden, NJ M.D.	2.2	170	Durham-Chapel Hill, NC	(1.2)
51	Cape Coral-Fort Myers, FL	5.7	110	Phoenix-Mesa-Scottsdale, AZ	2.2	171	Denver-Aurora, CO	(1.3)
51	Flint, MI	5.7	110	Savannah, GA	2.2	171	Santa Barbara-Santa Maria, CA	(1.3)
51	Johnstown, PA	5.7	113	Oklahoma City, OK	2.0	173	Columbus, OH	(1.4)
54	Anderson, SC	5.6	114	Gainesville, GA	1.9	173	St. Louis, MO-IL	(1.4)
54	Las Cruces, NM	5.6	114	Orlando, FL	1.9	175	Oakland-Fremont, CA M.D.	(1.5)
54	Little Rock, AR	5.6	116	Blacksburg, VA	1.8	175	Syracuse, NY	(1.5)
57	Greenville, SC	5.3	116	Sandusky, OH	1.8	177	Green Bay, WI	(1.6)
57	Knoxville, TN	5.3	118	Johnson City, TN	1.7	178	Fond du Lac, WI	(1.7)
59	Bend, OR	5.0	119	Philadelphia (greater) PA-NJ-MD-DE	1.6	179	Michigan City-La Porte, IN	(1.9)
59	Danville, IL	5.0	119	Springfield, OH	1.6	180	Dallas-Plano-Irving, TX M.D.	(2.0)

Note: All listings are for Metropolitan Statistical Areas (M.S.A.s) except for those ending with "M.D." Listings with "M.D." are Metropolitan Divisions which are smaller parts of eleven large M.S.A.s. See explanatory note at beginning of metropolitan area section.

Rank Order - Metro Area (continued)

RANK	METROPOLITAN AREA	% CHANGE	RANK	METROPOLITAN AREA	% CHANGE	RANK	METROPOLITAN AREA	% CHANGE
180	San Francisco (greater), CA	(2.0)	243	Milwaukee, WI	(5.5)	307	Longview, TX	(12.2)
182	Boston-Quincy, MA M.D.	(2.1)	245	Greeley, CO	(5.7)	308	Lansing-East Lansing, MI	(12.3)
182	Chattanooga, TN-GA	(2.1)	246	Duluth, MN-WI	(5.8)	309	Bangor, ME	(12.9)
182	Santa Cruz-Watsonville, CA	(2.1)	246	Peabody, MA M.D.	(5.8)	310	El Paso, TX	(13.2)
182	Springfield, IL	(2.1)	246	Rockford, IL	(5.8)	311	San Angelo, TX	(13.6)
186	Los Angeles County, CA M.D.	(2.2)	246	Salt Lake City, UT	(5.8)	312	Abilene, TX	(14.0)
187	Minneapolis-St. Paul, MN-WI	(2.3)	250	Hartford, CT	(5.9)	312	Ogden-Clearfield, UT	(14.0)
187	Santa Fe, NM	(2.3)	251	Fargo, ND-MN	(6.1)	314	Yakima, WA	(14.1)
189	Nashville-Davidson, TN	(2.4)	252	Alexandria, LA	(6.3)	315	Oxnard-Thousand Oaks, CA	(14.2)
190	Richmond, VA	(2.5)	253	Wenatchee, WA	(6.4)	315	Saginaw, MI	(14.2)
190	San Francisco-S. Mateo, CA M.D.	(2.5)	254	Atlantic City, NJ	(6.5)	317	Reno-Sparks, NV	(14.3)
192	Bellingham, WA	(2.6)	254	Gulfport-Biloxi, MS	(6.5)	318	McAllen-Edinburg-Mission, TX	(14.4)
192	Tacoma, WA M.D.	(2.6)	254	Palm Coast, FL	(6.5)	319	Ann Arbor, MI	(14.5)
194	Lima, OH	(2.7)	257	Logan, UT-ID	(6.7)	319	Olympia, WA	(14.5)
194	Pittsburgh, PA	(2.7)	257	South Bend-Mishawaka, IN-MI	(6.7)	321	Amarillo, TX	(15.1)
196	Dubuque, IA	(2.9)	259	Austin-Round Rock, TX	(6.8)	322	Mount Vernon-Anacortes, WA	(16.0)
196	El Centro, CA	(2.9)	260	Barnstable Town, MA	(7.0)	323	Jackson, TN	(16.5)
198	Lafayette, LA	(3.0)	260	Fort Worth-Arlington, TX M.D.	(7.0)	324	Killeen-Temple-Fort Hood, TX	(16.9)
199	Lynchburg, VA	(3.1)	260	Santa Rosa-Petaluma, CA	(7.0)	325	Appleton, WI	(18.0)
199	Monroe, MI	(3.1)	263	Morristown, TN	(7.1)	326	Bay City, MI	(21.4)
199	Spartanburg, SC	(3.1)	263	Sebastian-Vero Beach, FL	(7.1)	327	Sumter, SC	(30.2)
199	Springfield, MA	(3.1)	265	Monroe, LA	(7.3)	NA	Anniston-Oxford, AL**	NA
199	Victoria, TX	(3.1)	266	Boulder, CO	(7.4)	NA	Auburn, AL**	NA
204	Anchorage, AK	(3.3)	267	Punta Gorda, FL	(7.5)	NA	Baton Rouge, LA**	NA
204	Evansville, IN-KY	(3.3)	267	Tampa-St Petersburg, FL	(7.5)	NA	Billings, MT**	NA
204	Kingston, NY	(3.3)	269	Sacramento, CA	(7.6)	NA	Birmingham-Hoover, AL**	NA
207	Boston (greater), MA-NH	(3.5)	270	Cambridge-Newton, MA M.D.	(7.8)	NA	Champaign-Urbana, IL**	NA
207	Wilmington, DE-MD-NJ M.D.	(3.5)	270	Lawton, OK	(7.8)	NA	Charleston, WV**	NA
209	Trenton-Ewing, NJ	(3.6)	272	Manhattan, KS	(7.9)	NA	Charlotte-Gastonia, NC-SC**	NA
210	Dallas (greater), TX	(3.7)	273	Augusta, GA-SC	(8.0)	NA	Chicago (greater), IL-IN-WI**	NA
210	Elizabethtown, KY	(3.7)	274	Poughkeepsie, NY	(8.1)	NA	Chicago-Joilet-Naperville, IL M.D.**	NA
210	Grand Rapids-Wyoming, MI	(3.7)	275	Albany-Schenectady-Troy, NY	(8.6)	NA	Columbus, GA-AL**	NA
210	Rochester, MN	(3.7)	275	Bethesda-Frederick, MD M.D.	(8.6)	NA	Cumberland, MD-WV**	NA
210	San Diego, CA	(3.7)	277	State College, PA	(8.7)	NA	Davenport, IA-IL**	NA
215	Bloomington, IN	(3.8)	277	Utica-Rome, NY	(8.7)	NA	Decatur, AL**	NA
215	Longview, WA	(3.8)	279	Corpus Christi, TX	(8.8)	NA	Detroit (greater), MI**	NA
217	West Palm Beach, FL M.D.	(3.9)	280	Brownsville-Harlingen, TX	(8.9)	NA	Dothan, AL**	NA
218	Jackson, MS	(4.0)	281	Pittsfield, MA	(9.0)	NA	Eugene-Springfield, OR**	NA
218	Washington, DC-VA-MD-WV M.D.	(4.0)	282	Midland, TX	(9.2)	NA	Florence-Muscle Shoals, AL**	NA
220	Flagstaff, AZ	(4.1)	283	Chico, CA	(9.3)	NA	Gadsden, AL**	NA
221	Bakersfield, CA	(4.2)	283	Lakeland, FL	(9.3)	NA	Gary, IN M.D.**	NA
221	Joplin, MO	(4.2)	285	Bloomington-Normal, IL	(9.4)	NA	Great Falls, MT**	NA
221	Napa, CA	(4.2)	285	Colorado Springs, CO	(9.4)	NA	Houston, TX**	NA
224	Panama City-Lynn Haven, FL	(4.4)	287	Fort Smith, AR-OK	(9.5)	NA	Huntsville, AL**	NA
224	York-Hanover, PA	(4.4)	287	Houma, LA	(9.5)	NA	Indianapolis, IN**	NA
226	Buffalo-Niagara Falls, NY	(4.5)	289	Rochester, NY	(9.9)	NA	Jacksonville, NC**	NA
227	New Haven-Milford, CT	(4.6)	290	Salinas, CA	(10.0)	NA	Kankakee-Bradley, IL**	NA
227	Springfield, MO	(4.6)	291	Charlottesville, VA	(10.1)	NA	Kansas City, MO-KS**	NA
229	Cedar Rapids, IA	(4.7)	291	Salisbury, MD	(10.1)	NA	Lake Co.-Kenosha Co., IL-WI M.D.**	NA
229	Danville, VA	(4.7)	293	Brunswick, GA	(10.2)	NA	Lake Havasu City-Kingman, AZ**	NA
229	Seattle (greater), WA	(4.7)	293	Laredo, TX	(10.2)	NA	Lexington-Fayette, KY**	NA
229	Visalia-Porterville, CA	(4.7)	295	Modesto, CA	(10.6)	NA	Missoula, MT**	NA
229	Washington (greater) DC-VA-MD-WV	(4.7)	296	Casper, WY	(10.7)	NA	Montgomery, AL**	NA
234	Topeka, KS	(4.9)	296	Hinesville, GA	(10.7)	NA	Oshkosh-Neenah, WI**	NA
235	Norwich-New London, CT	(5.0)	298	San Antonio, TX	(10.9)	NA	Portland-Vancouver, OR-WA**	NA
236	Nassau-Suffolk, NY M.D.	(5.2)	299	Tyler, TX	(11.2)	NA	Pueblo, CO**	NA
236	San Jose, CA	(5.2)	300	Odessa, TX	(11.3)	NA	Sheboygan, WI**	NA
236	Virginia Beach-Norfolk, VA-NC	(5.2)	301	Valdosta, GA	(11.8)	NA	Terre Haute, IN**	NA
239	Las Vegas-Paradise, NV	(5.3)	302	Cheyenne, WY	(11.9)	NA	Toledo, OH**	NA
239	Seattle-Bellevue-Everett, WA M.D.	(5.3)	302	Lubbock, TX	(11.9)	NA	Tucson, AZ**	NA
241	Roanoke, VA	(5.4)	304	Wichita Falls, TX	(12.0)	NA	Tuscaloosa, AL**	NA
241	Vallejo-Fairfield, CA	(5.4)	305	College Station-Bryan, TX	(12.1)	NA	Warren-Farmington Hills, MI M.D.**	NA
243	Harrisonburg, VA	(5.5)	305	Waterloo-Cedar Falls, IA	(12.1)			

Source: CQ Press using reported data from the F.B.I. "Crime in the United States 2011"
*Larceny-theft is the unlawful taking of property. Attempts are included.
**Not available.

Alpha Order - Metro Area

36. Percent Change in Larceny-Theft Rate: 2007 to 2011
National Percent Change = 9.5% Decrease*

RANK	METROPOLITAN AREA	% CHANGE	RANK	METROPOLITAN AREA	% CHANGE	RANK	METROPOLITAN AREA	% CHANGE
169	Abilene, TX	(10.0)	188	Charleston, WV	(11.1)	53	Fort Lauderdale, FL M.D.	1.0
98	Akron, OH	(5.1)	305	Charlotte-Gastonia, NC-SC	(30.4)	231	Fort Smith, AR-OK	(15.8)
47	Albany-Schenectady-Troy, NY	1.7	269	Charlottesville, VA	(21.5)	114	Fort Wayne, IN	(6.2)
80	Albany, GA	(2.7)	259	Chattanooga, TN-GA	(20.4)	247	Fort Worth-Arlington, TX M.D.	(18.2)
84	Albuquerque, NM	(3.3)	287	Cheyenne, WY	(24.9)	48	Fresno, CA	1.5
72	Alexandria, LA	(1.5)	NA	Chicago (greater), IL-IN-WI**	NA	NA	Gadsden, AL**	NA
103	Allentown, PA-NJ	(5.5)	NA	Chicago-Joilet-Naperville, IL M.D.**	NA	NA	Gainesville, FL**	NA
94	Altoona, PA	(4.3)	269	Chico, CA	(21.5)	148	Gainesville, GA	(8.7)
217	Amarillo, TX	(14.2)	37	Cincinnati-Middletown, OH-KY-IN	3.5	NA	Gary, IN M.D.**	NA
34	Ames, IA	4.4	232	Clarksville, TN-KY	(16.0)	212	Glens Falls, NY	(13.9)
181	Anchorage, AK	(10.8)	57	Cleveland-Elyria-Mentor, OH	0.4	205	Goldsboro, NC	(13.2)
66	Anderson, SC	(1.1)	179	Cleveland, TN	(10.7)	237	Grand Forks, ND-MN	(16.6)
197	Ann Arbor, MI	(12.3)	209	College Station-Bryan, TX	(13.6)	116	Grand Junction, CO	(6.4)
NA	Anniston-Oxford, AL**	NA	179	Colorado Springs, CO	(10.7)	306	Grand Rapids-Wyoming, MI	(31.0)
311	Appleton, WI	(34.4)	20	Columbia, MO	8.9	NA	Great Falls, MT**	NA
191	Asheville, NC	(11.4)	NA	Columbus, GA-AL**	NA	250	Greeley, CO	(18.7)
196	Athens-Clarke County, GA	(12.2)	37	Columbus, IN	3.5	258	Green Bay, WI	(20.3)
100	Atlanta, GA	(5.3)	136	Columbus, OH	(7.4)	80	Greenville, SC	(2.7)
102	Atlantic City, NJ	(5.4)	291	Corpus Christi, TX	(25.8)	NA	Gulfport-Biloxi, MS**	NA
NA	Auburn, AL**	NA	214	Corvallis, OR	(14.1)	NA	Hagerstown-Martinsburg, MD-WV**	NA
194	Augusta, GA-SC	(12.0)	88	Crestview-Fort Walton Beach, FL	(3.8)	111	Hanford-Corcoran, CA	(5.8)
206	Austin-Round Rock, TX	(13.5)	NA	Cumberland, MD-WV**	NA	27	Harrisburg-Carlisle, PA	5.9
264	Bakersfield, CA	(20.8)	253	Dallas (greater), TX	(19.2)	210	Harrisonburg, VA	(13.8)
141	Baltimore-Towson, MD	(7.9)	254	Dallas-Plano-Irving, TX M.D.	(19.8)	227	Hartford, CT	(15.1)
256	Bangor, ME	(20.1)	127	Dalton, GA	(7.0)	62	Hickory, NC	(0.6)
51	Barnstable Town, MA	1.2	NA	Danville, IL**	NA	298	Hinesville, GA	(27.8)
97	Baton Rouge, LA	(4.6)	125	Danville, VA	(6.9)	NA	Holland-Grand Haven, MI**	NA
203	Battle Creek, MI	(13.1)	NA	Davenport, IA-IL**	NA	263	Hot Springs, AR	(20.6)
268	Bay City, MI	(21.3)	66	Dayton, OH	(1.1)	229	Houma, LA	(15.5)
91	Beaumont-Port Arthur, TX	(4.0)	NA	Decatur, AL**	NA	NA	Houston, TX**	NA
303	Bellingham, WA	(30.0)	NA	Decatur, IL**	NA	NA	Huntsville, AL**	NA
49	Bend, OR	1.4	25	Deltona-Daytona Beach, FL	6.0	255	Idaho Falls, ID	(19.9)
275	Bethesda-Frederick, MD M.D.	(22.8)	111	Denver-Aurora, CO	(5.8)	165	Indianapolis, IN	(9.9)
NA	Billings, MT**	NA	212	Des Moines-West Des Moines, IA	(13.9)	220	Iowa City, IA	(14.5)
28	Binghamton, NY	5.5	NA	Detroit (greater), MI**	NA	219	Jacksonville, FL	(14.3)
NA	Birmingham-Hoover, AL**	NA	160	Detroit-Livonia-Dearborn, MI M.D.	(9.4)	162	Jacksonville, NC	(9.6)
11	Bismarck, ND	16.4	NA	Dothan, AL**	NA	165	Jackson, MS	(9.9)
127	Blacksburg, VA	(7.0)	7	Dover, DE	22.4	271	Jackson, TN	(21.7)
NA	Bloomington-Normal, IL**	NA	123	Dubuque, IA	(6.7)	220	Janesville, WI	(14.5)
33	Bloomington, IN	4.9	133	Duluth, MN-WI	(7.2)	127	Jefferson City, MO	(7.0)
193	Boise City-Nampa, ID	(11.7)	NA	Durham-Chapel Hill, NC**	NA	80	Johnson City, TN	(2.7)
98	Boston (greater), MA-NH	(5.1)	165	Eau Claire, WI	(9.9)	108	Johnstown, PA	(5.7)
177	Boston-Quincy, MA M.D.	(10.6)	45	Edison, NJ M.D.	2.3	103	Jonesboro, AR	(5.5)
NA	Boulder, CO**	NA	75	El Centro, CA	(1.9)	283	Joplin, MO	(23.9)
194	Bowling Green, KY	(12.0)	242	El Paso, TX	(17.5)	NA	Kankakee-Bradley, IL**	NA
24	Bremerton-Silverdale, WA	7.0	68	Elizabethtown, KY	(1.3)	NA	Kansas City, MO-KS**	NA
108	Bridgeport-Stamford, CT	(5.7)	266	Elmira, NY	(21.1)	125	Kennewick-Pasco-Richland, WA	(6.9)
172	Brownsville-Harlingen, TX	(10.3)	4	Erie, PA	27.0	276	Killeen-Temple-Fort Hood, TX	(23.0)
50	Brunswick, GA	1.3	70	Eugene-Springfield, OR	(1.4)	185	Kingsport, TN-VA	(10.9)
60	Buffalo-Niagara Falls, NY	0.0	76	Evansville, IN-KY	(2.3)	14	Kingston, NY	14.7
25	Burlington, NC	6.0	NA	Fairbanks, AK**	NA	46	Knoxville, TN	1.8
147	Cambridge-Newton, MA M.D.	(8.6)	120	Fargo, ND-MN	(6.6)	118	Kokomo, IN	(6.5)
29	Camden, NJ M.D.	5.2	16	Farmington, NM	13.0	185	La Crosse, WI-MN	(10.9)
NA	Canton, OH**	NA	222	Fayetteville, NC	(14.6)	150	Lafayette, IN	(8.8)
281	Cape Coral-Fort Myers, FL	(23.8)	214	Flagstaff, AZ	(14.1)	76	Lafayette, LA	(2.3)
NA	Cape Girardeau, MO-IL**	NA	162	Flint, MI	(9.6)	NA	Lake Co.-Kenosha Co., IL-WI M.D.**	NA
6	Carson City, NV	23.0	NA	Florence-Muscle Shoals, AL**	NA	292	Lake Havasu City-Kingman, AZ	(26.6)
265	Casper, WY	(21.0)	120	Florence, SC	(6.6)	222	Lakeland, FL	(14.6)
276	Cedar Rapids, IA	(23.0)	246	Fond du Lac, WI	(18.0)	61	Lancaster, PA	(0.4)
NA	Champaign-Urbana, IL**	NA	100	Fort Collins-Loveland, CO	(5.3)	200	Lansing-East Lansing, MI	(12.5)

Note: All listings are for Metropolitan Statistical Areas (M.S.A.s) except for those ending with "M.D." Listings with "M.D." are Metropolitan Divisions which are smaller parts of eleven large M.S.A.s. See explanatory note at beginning of metropolitan area section.

Alpha Order - Metro Area (continued)

RANK	METROPOLITAN AREA	% CHANGE
296	Laredo, TX	(27.5)
42	Las Cruces, NM	2.8
278	Las Vegas-Paradise, NV	(23.4)
278	Lawrence, KS	(23.4)
30	Lawton, OK	5.0
35	Lebanon, PA	4.2
10	Lewiston-Auburn, ME	18.9
NA	Lexington-Fayette, KY**	NA
214	Lima, OH	(14.1)
233	Lincoln, NE	(16.2)
139	Little Rock, AR	(7.8)
242	Logan, UT-ID	(17.5)
304	Longview, TX	(30.3)
274	Longview, WA	(22.2)
148	Los Angeles County, CA M.D.	(8.7)
118	Los Angeles (greater), CA	(6.5)
30	Louisville, KY-IN	5.0
127	Lubbock, TX	(7.0)
63	Lynchburg, VA	(0.7)
21	Macon, GA	7.9
79	Madera, CA	(2.4)
105	Madison, WI	(5.6)
NA	Manchester-Nashua, NH**	NA
NA	Manhattan, KS**	NA
NA	Mankato-North Mankato, MN**	NA
53	Mansfield, OH	1.0
145	McAllen-Edinburg-Mission, TX	(8.4)
9	Medford, OR	20.5
272	Memphis, TN-MS-AR	(21.9)
108	Merced, CA	(5.7)
134	Miami (greater), FL	(7.3)
143	Miami-Dade County, FL M.D.	(8.0)
190	Michigan City-La Porte, IN	(11.2)
240	Midland, TX	(17.4)
234	Milwaukee, WI	(16.3)
234	Minneapolis-St. Paul, MN-WI	(16.3)
NA	Missoula, MT**	NA
105	Mobile, AL	(5.6)
299	Modesto, CA	(28.2)
292	Monroe, LA	(26.6)
15	Monroe, MI	13.7
NA	Montgomery, AL**	NA
89	Morristown, TN	(3.9)
284	Mount Vernon-Anacortes, WA	(24.3)
206	Muncie, IN	(13.5)
146	Muskegon-Norton Shores, MI	(8.5)
251	Myrtle Beach, SC	(18.8)
294	Napa, CA	(27.1)
44	Naples-Marco Island, FL	2.4
197	Nashville-Davidson, TN	(12.3)
74	Nassau-Suffolk, NY M.D.	(1.8)
NA	New Haven-Milford, CT**	NA
236	New Orleans, LA	(16.4)
86	New York (greater), NY-NJ-PA	(3.5)
94	New York-W. Plains NY-NJ M.D.	(4.3)
144	Newark-Union, NJ-PA M.D.	(8.2)
NA	North Port-Bradenton-Sarasota, FL**	NA
NA	Norwich-New London, CT**	NA
238	Oakland-Fremont, CA M.D.	(16.9)
170	Ocala, FL	(10.2)
173	Ocean City, NJ	(10.4)
301	Odessa, TX	(28.7)
188	Ogden-Clearfield, UT	(11.1)
70	Oklahoma City, OK	(1.4)
185	Olympia, WA	(10.9)
226	Omaha-Council Bluffs, NE-IA	(15.0)
192	Orlando, FL	(11.5)
288	Oshkosh-Neenah, WI	(25.0)
NA	Owensboro, KY**	NA
242	Oxnard-Thousand Oaks, CA	(17.5)
58	Palm Bay-Melbourne, FL	0.1
248	Palm Coast, FL	(18.3)
21	Panama City-Lynn Haven, FL	7.9
181	Pascagoula, MS	(10.8)
40	Peabody, MA M.D.	3.4
19	Pensacola, FL	9.1
NA	Peoria, IL**	NA
76	Philadelphia (greater) PA-NJ-MD-DE	(2.3)
87	Philadelphia, PA M.D.	(3.7)
203	Phoenix-Mesa-Scottsdale, AZ	(13.1)
131	Pine Bluff, AR	(7.1)
153	Pittsburgh, PA	(9.1)
12	Pittsfield, MA	15.2
65	Pocatello, ID	(1.0)
141	Port St. Lucie, FL	(7.9)
123	Portland-Vancouver, OR-WA	(6.7)
36	Portland, ME	4.1
68	Poughkeepsie, NY	(1.3)
201	Prescott, AZ	(12.6)
160	Provo-Orem, UT	(9.4)
NA	Pueblo, CO**	NA
266	Punta Gorda, FL	(21.1)
224	Racine, WI	(14.7)
89	Raleigh-Cary, NC	(3.9)
18	Rapid City, SD	10.6
91	Reading, PA	(4.0)
13	Redding, CA	15.0
312	Reno-Sparks, NV	(36.2)
173	Richmond, VA	(10.4)
181	Riverside-San Bernardino, CA	(10.8)
134	Roanoke, VA	(7.3)
164	Rochester, MN	(9.7)
105	Rochester, NY	(5.6)
NA	Rockford, IL**	NA
3	Rockingham County, NH M.D.	27.6
242	Rocky Mount, NC	(17.5)
96	Rome, GA	(4.4)
137	Sacramento, CA	(7.5)
290	Saginaw, MI	(25.7)
281	Salem, OR	(23.8)
309	Salinas, CA	(32.7)
256	Salisbury, MD	(20.1)
165	Salt Lake City, UT	(9.9)
285	San Angelo, TX	(24.6)
173	San Antonio, TX	(10.4)
273	San Diego, CA	(22.1)
206	San Francisco (greater), CA	(13.5)
152	San Francisco-S. Mateo, CA M.D.	(9.0)
210	San Jose, CA	(13.8)
157	San Luis Obispo, CA	(9.3)
202	Sandusky, OH	(12.8)
52	Santa Ana-Anaheim, CA M.D.	1.1
73	Santa Barbara-Santa Maria, CA	(1.6)
228	Santa Cruz-Watsonville, CA	(15.3)
NA	Santa Fe, NM**	NA
155	Santa Rosa-Petaluma, CA	(9.2)
NA	Savannah, GA**	NA
93	Scranton--Wilkes-Barre, PA	(4.2)
176	Seattle (greater), WA	(10.5)
155	Seattle-Bellevue-Everett, WA M.D.	(9.2)
116	Sebastian-Vero Beach, FL	(6.4)
307	Sheboygan, WI	(31.2)
55	Sherman-Denison, TX	0.8
2	Sioux City, IA-NE-SD	30.4
8	Sioux Falls, SD	20.6
262	South Bend-Mishawaka, IN-MI	(20.5)
278	Spartanburg, SC	(23.4)
1	Spokane, WA	42.5
NA	Springfield, IL**	NA
58	Springfield, MA	0.1
64	Springfield, MO	(0.8)
286	Springfield, OH	(24.8)
259	State College, PA	(20.4)
240	Stockton, CA	(17.4)
153	St. Cloud, MN	(9.1)
131	St. Joseph, MO-KS	(7.1)
197	St. Louis, MO-IL	(12.3)
289	Sumter, SC	(25.5)
30	Syracuse, NY	5.0
224	Tacoma, WA M.D.	(14.7)
85	Tallahassee, FL	(3.4)
248	Tampa-St Petersburg, FL	(18.3)
NA	Terre Haute, IN**	NA
23	Texarkana, TX-Texarkana, AR	7.1
NA	Toledo, OH**	NA
217	Topeka, KS	(14.2)
113	Trenton-Ewing, NJ	(5.9)
NA	Tucson, AZ**	NA
137	Tulsa, OK	(7.5)
NA	Tuscaloosa, AL**	NA
157	Tyler, TX	(9.3)
120	Utica-Rome, NY	(6.6)
296	Valdosta, GA	(27.5)
310	Vallejo-Fairfield, CA	(33.6)
43	Victoria, TX	2.5
80	Virginia Beach-Norfolk, VA-NC	(2.7)
150	Visalia-Porterville, CA	(8.8)
259	Waco, TX	(20.4)
5	Warner Robins, GA	24.5
NA	Warren-Farmington Hills, MI M.D.**	NA
181	Washington (greater) DC-VA-MD-WV	(10.8)
139	Washington, DC-VA-MD-WV M.D.	(7.8)
308	Waterloo-Cedar Falls, IA	(32.5)
37	Wausau, WI	3.5
295	Wenatchee, WA	(27.3)
239	West Palm Beach, FL M.D.	(17.1)
302	Wichita Falls, TX	(29.7)
229	Wichita, KS	(15.5)
41	Williamsport, PA	3.0
115	Wilmington, DE-MD-NJ M.D.	(6.3)
157	Wilmington, NC	(9.3)
177	Winchester, VA-WV	(10.6)
NA	Winston-Salem, NC**	NA
17	Worcester, MA	11.5
300	Yakima, WA	(28.4)
170	York-Hanover, PA	(10.2)
55	Yuba City, CA	0.8
251	Yuma, AZ	(18.8)

Source: CQ Press using reported data from the F.B.I. "Crime in the United States 2011"
*Larceny-theft is the unlawful taking of property. Attempts are included.
**Not available.

Rank Order - Metro Area
36. Percent Change in Larceny-Theft Rate: 2007 to 2011 (continued)
National Percent Change = 9.5% Decrease*

RANK	METROPOLITAN AREA	% CHANGE	RANK	METROPOLITAN AREA	% CHANGE	RANK	METROPOLITAN AREA	% CHANGE
1	Spokane, WA	42.5	61	Lancaster, PA	(0.4)	120	Florence, SC	(6.6)
2	Sioux City, IA-NE-SD	30.4	62	Hickory, NC	(0.6)	120	Utica-Rome, NY	(6.6)
3	Rockingham County, NH M.D.	27.6	63	Lynchburg, VA	(0.7)	123	Dubuque, IA	(6.7)
4	Erie, PA	27.0	64	Springfield, MO	(0.8)	123	Portland-Vancouver, OR-WA	(6.7)
5	Warner Robins, GA	24.5	65	Pocatello, ID	(1.0)	125	Danville, VA	(6.9)
6	Carson City, NV	23.0	66	Anderson, SC	(1.1)	125	Kennewick-Pasco-Richland, WA	(6.9)
7	Dover, DE	22.4	66	Dayton, OH	(1.1)	127	Blacksburg, VA	(7.0)
8	Sioux Falls, SD	20.6	68	Elizabethtown, KY	(1.3)	127	Dalton, GA	(7.0)
9	Medford, OR	20.5	68	Poughkeepsie, NY	(1.3)	127	Jefferson City, MO	(7.0)
10	Lewiston-Auburn, ME	18.9	70	Eugene-Springfield, OR	(1.4)	127	Lubbock, TX	(7.0)
11	Bismarck, ND	16.4	70	Oklahoma City, OK	(1.4)	131	Pine Bluff, AR	(7.1)
12	Pittsfield, MA	15.2	72	Alexandria, LA	(1.5)	131	St. Joseph, MO-KS	(7.1)
13	Redding, CA	15.0	73	Santa Barbara-Santa Maria, CA	(1.6)	133	Duluth, MN-WI	(7.2)
14	Kingston, NY	14.7	74	Nassau-Suffolk, NY M.D.	(1.8)	134	Miami (greater), FL	(7.3)
15	Monroe, MI	13.7	75	El Centro, CA	(1.9)	134	Roanoke, VA	(7.3)
16	Farmington, NM	13.0	76	Evansville, IN-KY	(2.3)	136	Columbus, OH	(7.4)
17	Worcester, MA	11.5	76	Lafayette, LA	(2.3)	137	Sacramento, CA	(7.5)
18	Rapid City, SD	10.6	76	Philadelphia (greater) PA-NJ-MD-DE	(2.3)	137	Tulsa, OK	(7.5)
19	Pensacola, FL	9.1	79	Madera, CA	(2.4)	139	Little Rock, AR	(7.8)
20	Columbia, MO	8.9	80	Albany, GA	(2.7)	139	Washington, DC-VA-MD-WV M.D.	(7.8)
21	Macon, GA	7.9	80	Greenville, SC	(2.7)	141	Baltimore-Towson, MD	(7.9)
21	Panama City-Lynn Haven, FL	7.9	80	Johnson City, TN	(2.7)	141	Port St. Lucie, FL	(7.9)
23	Texarkana, TX-Texarkana, AR	7.1	80	Virginia Beach-Norfolk, VA-NC	(2.7)	143	Miami-Dade County, FL M.D.	(8.0)
24	Bremerton-Silverdale, WA	7.0	84	Albuquerque, NM	(3.3)	144	Newark-Union, NJ-PA M.D.	(8.2)
25	Burlington, NC	6.0	85	Tallahassee, FL	(3.4)	145	McAllen-Edinburg-Mission, TX	(8.4)
25	Deltona-Daytona Beach, FL	6.0	86	New York (greater), NY-NJ-PA	(3.5)	146	Muskegon-Norton Shores, MI	(8.5)
27	Harrisburg-Carlisle, PA	5.9	87	Philadelphia, PA M.D.	(3.7)	147	Cambridge-Newton, MA M.D.	(8.6)
28	Binghamton, NY	5.5	88	Crestview-Fort Walton Beach, FL	(3.8)	148	Gainesville, GA	(8.7)
29	Camden, NJ M.D.	5.2	89	Morristown, TN	(3.9)	148	Los Angeles County, CA M.D.	(8.7)
30	Lawton, OK	5.0	89	Raleigh-Cary, NC	(3.9)	150	Lafayette, IN	(8.8)
30	Louisville, KY-IN	5.0	91	Beaumont-Port Arthur, TX	(4.0)	150	Visalia-Porterville, CA	(8.8)
30	Syracuse, NY	5.0	91	Reading, PA	(4.0)	152	San Francisco-S. Mateo, CA M.D.	(9.0)
33	Bloomington, IN	4.9	93	Scranton--Wilkes-Barre, PA	(4.2)	153	Pittsburgh, PA	(9.1)
34	Ames, IA	4.4	94	Altoona, PA	(4.3)	153	St. Cloud, MN	(9.1)
35	Lebanon, PA	4.2	94	New York-W. Plains NY-NJ M.D.	(4.3)	155	Santa Rosa-Petaluma, CA	(9.2)
36	Portland, ME	4.1	96	Rome, GA	(4.4)	155	Seattle-Bellevue-Everett, WA M.D.	(9.2)
37	Cincinnati-Middletown, OH-KY-IN	3.5	97	Baton Rouge, LA	(4.6)	157	San Luis Obispo, CA	(9.3)
37	Columbus, IN	3.5	98	Akron, OH	(5.1)	157	Tyler, TX	(9.3)
37	Wausau, WI	3.5	98	Boston (greater), MA-NH	(5.1)	157	Wilmington, NC	(9.3)
40	Peabody, MA M.D.	3.4	100	Atlanta, GA	(5.3)	160	Detroit-Livonia-Dearborn, MI M.D.	(9.4)
41	Williamsport, PA	3.0	100	Fort Collins-Loveland, CO	(5.3)	160	Provo-Orem, UT	(9.4)
42	Las Cruces, NM	2.8	102	Atlantic City, NJ	(5.4)	162	Flint, MI	(9.6)
43	Victoria, TX	2.5	103	Allentown, PA-NJ	(5.5)	162	Jacksonville, NC	(9.6)
44	Naples-Marco Island, FL	2.4	103	Jonesboro, AR	(5.5)	164	Rochester, MN	(9.7)
45	Edison, NJ M.D.	2.3	105	Madison, WI	(5.6)	165	Eau Claire, WI	(9.9)
46	Knoxville, TN	1.8	105	Mobile, AL	(5.6)	165	Indianapolis, IN	(9.9)
47	Albany-Schenectady-Troy, NY	1.7	105	Rochester, NY	(5.6)	165	Jackson, MS	(9.9)
48	Fresno, CA	1.5	108	Bridgeport-Stamford, CT	(5.7)	165	Salt Lake City, UT	(9.9)
49	Bend, OR	1.4	108	Johnstown, PA	(5.7)	169	Abilene, TX	(10.0)
50	Brunswick, GA	1.3	108	Merced, CA	(5.7)	170	Ocala, FL	(10.2)
51	Barnstable Town, MA	1.2	111	Denver-Aurora, CO	(5.8)	170	York-Hanover, PA	(10.2)
52	Santa Ana-Anaheim, CA M.D.	1.1	111	Hanford-Corcoran, CA	(5.8)	172	Brownsville-Harlingen, TX	(10.3)
53	Fort Lauderdale, FL M.D.	1.0	113	Trenton-Ewing, NJ	(5.9)	173	Ocean City, NJ	(10.4)
53	Mansfield, OH	1.0	114	Fort Wayne, IN	(6.2)	173	Richmond, VA	(10.4)
55	Sherman-Denison, TX	0.8	115	Wilmington, DE-MD-NJ M.D.	(6.3)	173	San Antonio, TX	(10.4)
55	Yuba City, CA	0.8	116	Grand Junction, CO	(6.4)	176	Seattle (greater), WA	(10.5)
57	Cleveland-Elyria-Mentor, OH	0.4	116	Sebastian-Vero Beach, FL	(6.4)	177	Boston-Quincy, MA M.D.	(10.6)
58	Palm Bay-Melbourne, FL	0.1	118	Kokomo, IN	(6.5)	177	Winchester, VA-WV	(10.6)
58	Springfield, MA	0.1	118	Los Angeles (greater), CA	(6.5)	179	Cleveland, TN	(10.7)
60	Buffalo-Niagara Falls, NY	0.0	120	Fargo, ND-MN	(6.6)	179	Colorado Springs, CO	(10.7)

Note: All listings are for Metropolitan Statistical Areas (M.S.A.s) except for those ending with "M.D." Listings with "M.D." are Metropolitan Divisions which are smaller parts of eleven large M.S.A.s. See explanatory note at beginning of metropolitan area section.

Rank Order - Metro Area (continued)

RANK	METROPOLITAN AREA	% CHANGE
181	Anchorage, AK	(10.8)
181	Pascagoula, MS	(10.8)
181	Riverside-San Bernardino, CA	(10.8)
181	Washington (greater) DC-VA-MD-WV	(10.8)
185	Kingsport, TN-VA	(10.9)
185	La Crosse, WI-MN	(10.9)
185	Olympia, WA	(10.9)
188	Charleston, WV	(11.1)
188	Ogden-Clearfield, UT	(11.1)
190	Michigan City-La Porte, IN	(11.2)
191	Asheville, NC	(11.4)
192	Orlando, FL	(11.5)
193	Boise City-Nampa, ID	(11.7)
194	Augusta, GA-SC	(12.0)
194	Bowling Green, KY	(12.0)
196	Athens-Clarke County, GA	(12.2)
197	Ann Arbor, MI	(12.3)
197	Nashville-Davidson, TN	(12.3)
197	St. Louis, MO-IL	(12.3)
200	Lansing-East Lansing, MI	(12.5)
201	Prescott, AZ	(12.6)
202	Sandusky, OH	(12.8)
203	Battle Creek, MI	(13.1)
203	Phoenix-Mesa-Scottsdale, AZ	(13.1)
205	Goldsboro, NC	(13.2)
206	Austin-Round Rock, TX	(13.5)
206	Muncie, IN	(13.5)
206	San Francisco (greater), CA	(13.5)
209	College Station-Bryan, TX	(13.6)
210	Harrisonburg, VA	(13.8)
210	San Jose, CA	(13.8)
212	Des Moines-West Des Moines, IA	(13.9)
212	Glens Falls, NY	(13.9)
214	Corvallis, OR	(14.1)
214	Flagstaff, AZ	(14.1)
214	Lima, OH	(14.1)
217	Amarillo, TX	(14.2)
217	Topeka, KS	(14.2)
219	Jacksonville, FL	(14.3)
220	Iowa City, IA	(14.5)
220	Janesville, WI	(14.5)
222	Fayetteville, NC	(14.6)
222	Lakeland, FL	(14.6)
224	Racine, WI	(14.7)
224	Tacoma, WA M.D.	(14.7)
226	Omaha-Council Bluffs, NE-IA	(15.0)
227	Hartford, CT	(15.1)
228	Santa Cruz-Watsonville, CA	(15.3)
229	Houma, LA	(15.5)
229	Wichita, KS	(15.5)
231	Fort Smith, AR-OK	(15.8)
232	Clarksville, TN-KY	(16.0)
233	Lincoln, NE	(16.2)
234	Milwaukee, WI	(16.3)
234	Minneapolis-St. Paul, MN-WI	(16.3)
236	New Orleans, LA	(16.4)
237	Grand Forks, ND-MN	(16.6)
238	Oakland-Fremont, CA M.D.	(16.9)
239	West Palm Beach, FL M.D.	(17.1)
240	Midland, TX	(17.4)
240	Stockton, CA	(17.4)
242	El Paso, TX	(17.5)
242	Logan, UT-ID	(17.5)
242	Oxnard-Thousand Oaks, CA	(17.5)
242	Rocky Mount, NC	(17.5)
246	Fond du Lac, WI	(18.0)
247	Fort Worth-Arlington, TX M.D.	(18.2)
248	Palm Coast, FL	(18.3)
248	Tampa-St Petersburg, FL	(18.3)
250	Greeley, CO	(18.7)
251	Myrtle Beach, SC	(18.8)
251	Yuma, AZ	(18.8)
253	Dallas (greater), TX	(19.2)
254	Dallas-Plano-Irving, TX M.D.	(19.8)
255	Idaho Falls, ID	(19.9)
256	Bangor, ME	(20.1)
256	Salisbury, MD	(20.1)
258	Green Bay, WI	(20.3)
259	Chattanooga, TN-GA	(20.4)
259	State College, PA	(20.4)
259	Waco, TX	(20.4)
262	South Bend-Mishawaka, IN-MI	(20.5)
263	Hot Springs, AR	(20.6)
264	Bakersfield, CA	(20.8)
265	Casper, WY	(21.0)
266	Elmira, NY	(21.1)
266	Punta Gorda, FL	(21.1)
268	Bay City, MI	(21.3)
269	Charlottesville, VA	(21.5)
269	Chico, CA	(21.5)
271	Jackson, TN	(21.7)
272	Memphis, TN-MS-AR	(21.9)
273	San Diego, CA	(22.1)
274	Longview, WA	(22.2)
275	Bethesda-Frederick, MD M.D.	(22.8)
276	Cedar Rapids, IA	(23.0)
276	Killeen-Temple-Fort Hood, TX	(23.0)
278	Las Vegas-Paradise, NV	(23.4)
278	Lawrence, KS	(23.4)
278	Spartanburg, SC	(23.4)
281	Cape Coral-Fort Myers, FL	(23.8)
281	Salem, OR	(23.8)
283	Joplin, MO	(23.9)
284	Mount Vernon-Anacortes, WA	(24.3)
285	San Angelo, TX	(24.6)
286	Springfield, OH	(24.8)
287	Cheyenne, WY	(24.9)
288	Oshkosh-Neenah, WI	(25.0)
289	Sumter, SC	(25.5)
290	Saginaw, MI	(25.7)
291	Corpus Christi, TX	(25.8)
292	Lake Havasu City-Kingman, AZ	(26.6)
292	Monroe, LA	(26.6)
294	Napa, CA	(27.1)
295	Wenatchee, WA	(27.3)
296	Laredo, TX	(27.5)
296	Valdosta, GA	(27.5)
298	Hinesville, GA	(27.8)
299	Modesto, CA	(28.2)
300	Yakima, WA	(28.4)
301	Odessa, TX	(28.7)
302	Wichita Falls, TX	(29.7)
303	Bellingham, WA	(30.0)
304	Longview, TX	(30.3)
305	Charlotte-Gastonia, NC-SC	(30.4)
306	Grand Rapids-Wyoming, MI	(31.0)
307	Sheboygan, WI	(31.2)
308	Waterloo-Cedar Falls, IA	(32.5)
309	Salinas, CA	(32.7)
310	Vallejo-Fairfield, CA	(33.6)
311	Appleton, WI	(34.4)
312	Reno-Sparks, NV	(36.2)
NA	Anniston-Oxford, AL**	NA
NA	Auburn, AL**	NA
NA	Billings, MT**	NA
NA	Birmingham-Hoover, AL**	NA
NA	Bloomington-Normal, IL**	NA
NA	Boulder, CO**	NA
NA	Canton, OH**	NA
NA	Cape Girardeau, MO-IL**	NA
NA	Champaign-Urbana, IL**	NA
NA	Chicago (greater), IL-IN-WI**	NA
NA	Chicago-Joilet-Naperville, IL M.D.**	NA
NA	Columbus, GA-AL**	NA
NA	Cumberland, MD-WV**	NA
NA	Danville, IL**	NA
NA	Davenport, IA-IL**	NA
NA	Decatur, AL**	NA
NA	Decatur, IL**	NA
NA	Detroit (greater), MI**	NA
NA	Dothan, AL**	NA
NA	Durham-Chapel Hill, NC**	NA
NA	Fairbanks, AK**	NA
NA	Florence-Muscle Shoals, AL**	NA
NA	Gadsden, AL**	NA
NA	Gainesville, FL**	NA
NA	Gary, IN M.D.**	NA
NA	Great Falls, MT**	NA
NA	Gulfport-Biloxi, MS**	NA
NA	Hagerstown-Martinsburg, MD-WV**	NA
NA	Holland-Grand Haven, MI**	NA
NA	Houston, TX**	NA
NA	Huntsville, AL**	NA
NA	Kankakee-Bradley, IL**	NA
NA	Kansas City, MO-KS**	NA
NA	Lake Co.-Kenosha Co., IL-WI M.D.**	NA
NA	Lexington-Fayette, KY**	NA
NA	Manchester-Nashua, NH**	NA
NA	Manhattan, KS**	NA
NA	Mankato-North Mankato, MN**	NA
NA	Missoula, MT**	NA
NA	Montgomery, AL**	NA
NA	New Haven-Milford, CT**	NA
NA	North Port-Bradenton-Sarasota, FL**	NA
NA	Norwich-New London, CT**	NA
NA	Owensboro, KY**	NA
NA	Peoria, IL**	NA
NA	Pueblo, CO**	NA
NA	Rockford, IL**	NA
NA	Santa Fe, NM**	NA
NA	Savannah, GA**	NA
NA	Springfield, IL**	NA
NA	Terre Haute, IN**	NA
NA	Toledo, OH**	NA
NA	Tucson, AZ**	NA
NA	Tuscaloosa, AL**	NA
NA	Warren-Farmington Hills, MI M.D.**	NA
NA	Winston-Salem, NC**	NA

Source: CQ Press using reported data from the F.B.I. "Crime in the United States 2011"
*Larceny-theft is the unlawful taking of property. Attempts are included.
**Not available.

Alpha Order - Metro Area

37. Motor Vehicle Thefts in 2011
National Total = 715,373 Motor Vehicle Thefts*

RANK	METROPOLITAN AREA	THEFTS	RANK	METROPOLITAN AREA	THEFTS	RANK	METROPOLITAN AREA	THEFTS
275	Abilene, TX	205	161	Charleston, WV	571	50	Fort Lauderdale, FL M.D.	4,502
109	Akron, OH	1,262	59	Charlotte-Gastonia, NC-SC	3,471	204	Fort Smith, AR-OK	389
143	Albany-Schenectady-Troy, NY	746	266	Charlottesville, VA	217	176	Fort Wayne, IN	507
216	Albany, GA	332	101	Chattanooga, TN-GA	1,418	46	Fort Worth-Arlington, TX M.D.	5,141
58	Albuquerque, NM	3,538	337	Cheyenne, WY	97	33	Fresno, CA	7,070
194	Alexandria, LA	421	3	Chicago (greater), IL-IN-WI	27,138	208	Gadsden, AL	362
121	Allentown, PA-NJ	966	5	Chicago-Joilet-Naperville, IL M.D.	24,120	188	Gainesville, FL	443
347	Altoona, PA	80	154	Chico, CA	615	230	Gainesville, GA	294
147	Amarillo, TX	673	64	Cincinnati-Middletown, OH-KY-IN	3,117	72	Gary, IN M.D.	2,476
348	Ames, IA	79	196	Clarksville, TN-KY	410	362	Glens Falls, NY	59
150	Anchorage, AK	651	41	Cleveland-Elyria-Mentor, OH	5,900	234	Goldsboro, NC	286
127	Anderson, SC	901	278	Cleveland, TN	202	319	Grand Forks, ND-MN	128
189	Ann Arbor, MI	440	271	College Station-Bryan, TX	211	265	Grand Junction, CO	222
282	Anniston-Oxford, AL	193	102	Colorado Springs, CO	1,392	131	Grand Rapids-Wyoming, MI	847
331	Appleton, WI	107	279	Columbia, MO	201	326	Great Falls, MT	115
139	Asheville, NC	765	105	Columbus, GA-AL	1,309	221	Greeley, CO	320
209	Athens-Clarke County, GA	359	239	Columbus, IN	270	280	Green Bay, WI	196
8	Atlanta, GA	20,121	52	Columbus, OH	4,343	91	Greenville, SC	1,756
216	Atlantic City, NJ	332	157	Corpus Christi, TX	596	173	Gulfport-Biloxi, MS	518
316	Auburn, AL	133	351	Corvallis, OR	76	227	Hagerstown-Martinsburg, MD-WV	302
78	Augusta, GA-SC	2,126	266	Crestview-Fort Walton Beach, FL	217	204	Hanford-Corcoran, CA	389
70	Austin-Round Rock, TX	2,764	364	Cumberland, MD-WV	58	170	Harrisburg-Carlisle, PA	532
47	Bakersfield, CA	4,886	10	Dallas (greater), TX	19,209	355	Harrisonburg, VA	72
31	Baltimore-Towson, MD	7,507	18	Dallas-Plano-Irving, TX M.D.	14,068	80	Hartford, CT	2,050
310	Bangor, ME	140	242	Dalton, GA	265	164	Hickory, NC	548
285	Barnstable Town, MA	191	333	Danville, IL	102	315	Hinesville, GA	134
112	Baton Rouge, LA	1,124	324	Danville, VA	116	328	Holland-Grand Haven, MI	111
299	Battle Creek, MI	158	174	Davenport, IA-IL	512	233	Hot Springs, AR	288
356	Bay City, MI	71	97	Dayton, OH	1,503	225	Houma, LA	310
135	Beaumont-Port Arthur, TX	820	238	Decatur, AL	271	7	Houston, TX	20,611
260	Bellingham, WA	226	318	Decatur, IL	129	115	Huntsville, AL	1,051
291	Bend, OR	173	119	Deltona-Daytona Beach, FL	1,026	312	Idaho Falls, ID	139
100	Bethesda-Frederick, MD M.D.	1,452	30	Denver-Aurora, CO	7,517	38	Indianapolis, IN	6,263
199	Billings, MT	406	113	Des Moines-West Des Moines, IA	1,115	337	Iowa City, IA	97
290	Binghamton, NY	176	9	Detroit (greater), MI	19,368	73	Jacksonville, FL	2,438
65	Birmingham-Hoover, AL	3,109	15	Detroit-Livonia-Dearborn, MI M.D.	15,055	237	Jacksonville, NC	275
295	Bismarck, ND	166	253	Dothan, AL	242	85	Jackson, MS	1,874
308	Blacksburg, VA	142	282	Dover, DE	193	227	Jackson, TN	302
337	Bloomington-Normal, IL	97	362	Dubuque, IA	59	313	Janesville, WI	135
222	Bloomington, IN	318	207	Duluth, MN-WI	379	313	Jefferson City, MO	135
180	Boise City-Nampa, ID	466	125	Durham-Chapel Hill, NC	921	248	Johnson City, TN	254
32	Boston (greater), MA-NH	7,259	342	Eau Claire, WI	90	344	Johnstown, PA	87
60	Boston-Quincy, MA M.D.	3,466	88	Edison, NJ M.D.	1,815	307	Jonesboro, AR	143
218	Boulder, CO	331	141	El Centro, CA	754	179	Joplin, MO	482
301	Bowling Green, KY	155	92	El Paso, TX	1,710	333	Kankakee-Bradley, IL	102
159	Bremerton-Silverdale, WA	578	349	Elizabethtown, KY	78	29	Kansas City, MO-KS	7,589
90	Bridgeport-Stamford, CT	1,799	368	Elmira, NY	41	177	Kennewick-Pasco-Richland, WA	503
184	Brownsville-Harlingen, TX	450	275	Erie, PA	205	201	Killeen-Temple-Fort Hood, TX	404
294	Brunswick, GA	169	123	Eugene-Springfield, OR	929	186	Kingsport, TN-VA	445
84	Buffalo-Niagara Falls, NY	1,913	191	Evansville, IN-KY	427	335	Kingston, NY	98
262	Burlington, NC	225	345	Fairbanks, AK	83	96	Knoxville, TN	1,652
99	Cambridge-Newton, MA M.D.	1,478	272	Fargo, ND-MN	210	321	Kokomo, IN	124
79	Camden, NJ M.D.	2,058	300	Farmington, NM	157	331	La Crosse, WI-MN	107
169	Canton, OH	537	116	Fayetteville, NC	1,043	235	Lafayette, IN	283
137	Cape Coral-Fort Myers, FL	797	324	Flagstaff, AZ	116	199	Lafayette, LA	406
330	Cape Girardeau, MO-IL	109	103	Flint, MI	1,373	167	Lake Co.-Kenosha Co., IL-WI M.D.	542
358	Carson City, NV	69	296	Florence-Muscle Shoals, AL	163	213	Lake Havasu City-Kingman, AZ	341
335	Casper, WY	98	158	Florence, SC	579	132	Lakeland, FL	836
236	Cedar Rapids, IA	279	359	Fond du Lac, WI	64	210	Lancaster, PA	356
287	Champaign-Urbana, IL	184	239	Fort Collins-Loveland, CO	270	178	Lansing-East Lansing, MI	501

Note: All listings are for Metropolitan Statistical Areas (M.S.A.s) except for those ending with "M.D." Listings with "M.D." are Metropolitan Divisions which are smaller parts of eleven large M.S.A.s. See explanatory note at beginning of metropolitan area section.

Alpha Order - Metro Area (continued)

RANK	METROPOLITAN AREA	THEFTS
175	Laredo, TX	508
193	Las Cruces, NM	423
27	Las Vegas-Paradise, NV	8,263
270	Lawrence, KS	214
258	Lawton, OK	229
353	Lebanon, PA	74
360	Lewiston-Auburn, ME	63
130	Lexington-Fayette, KY	855
289	Lima, OH	177
206	Lincoln, NE	384
76	Little Rock, AR	2,322
367	Logan, UT-ID	45
162	Longview, TX	567
229	Longview, WA	301
2	Los Angeles County, CA M.D.	40,483
1	Los Angeles (greater), CA	46,324
62	Louisville, KY-IN	3,230
138	Lubbock, TX	770
260	Lynchburg, VA	226
124	Macon, GA	922
160	Madera, CA	574
164	Madison, WI	548
220	Manchester-Nashua, NH	322
357	Manhattan, KS	70
340	Mankato-North Mankato, MN	95
298	Mansfield, OH	162
95	McAllen-Edinburg-Mission, TX	1,660
252	Medford, OR	248
51	Memphis, TN-MS-AR	4,418
118	Merced, CA	1,032
11	Miami (greater), FL	18,182
24	Miami-Dade County, FL M.D.	10,848
257	Michigan City-La Porte, IN	234
293	Midland, TX	171
45	Milwaukee, WI	5,265
39	Minneapolis-St. Paul, MN-WI	6,154
320	Missoula, MT	126
107	Mobile, AL	1,281
63	Modesto, CA	3,221
263	Monroe, LA	224
268	Monroe, MI	215
114	Montgomery, AL	1,094
249	Morristown, TN	250
243	Mount Vernon-Anacortes, WA	264
264	Muncie, IN	223
259	Muskegon-Norton Shores, MI	228
111	Myrtle Beach, SC	1,138
251	Napa, CA	249
268	Naples-Marco Island, FL	215
67	Nashville-Davidson, TN	2,911
74	Nassau-Suffolk, NY M.D.	2,366
75	New Haven-Milford, CT	2,355
55	New Orleans, LA	4,086
4	New York (greater), NY-NJ-PA	26,709
17	New York-W. Plains NY-NJ M.D.	14,422
28	Newark-Union, NJ-PA M.D.	8,106
126	North Port-Bradenton-Sarasota, FL	906
308	Norwich-New London, CT	142
13	Oakland-Fremont, CA M.D.	16,897
231	Ocala, FL	292
353	Ocean City, NJ	74
253	Odessa, TX	242
148	Ogden-Clearfield, UT	667

RANK	METROPOLITAN AREA	THEFTS
43	Oklahoma City, OK	5,445
212	Olympia, WA	346
57	Omaha-Council Bluffs, NE-IA	3,663
44	Orlando, FL	5,396
361	Oshkosh-Neenah, WI	60
321	Owensboro, KY	124
120	Oxnard-Thousand Oaks, CA	1,014
142	Palm Bay-Melbourne, FL	748
352	Palm Coast, FL	75
219	Panama City-Lynn Haven, FL	324
214	Pascagoula, MS	337
82	Peabody, MA M.D.	2,002
133	Pensacola, FL	828
185	Peoria, IL	449
21	Philadelphia (greater) PA-NJ-MD-DE	12,958
25	Philadelphia, PA M.D.	9,563
19	Phoenix-Mesa-Scottsdale, AZ	13,621
202	Pine Bluff, AR	403
86	Pittsburgh, PA	1,851
317	Pittsfield, MA	131
343	Pocatello, ID	89
182	Port St. Lucie, FL	456
37	Portland-Vancouver, OR-WA	6,689
183	Portland, ME	452
196	Poughkeepsie, NY	410
274	Prescott, AZ	207
186	Provo-Orem, UT	445
171	Pueblo, CO	530
327	Punta Gorda, FL	113
277	Racine, WI	204
93	Raleigh-Cary, NC	1,689
282	Rapid City, SD	193
151	Reading, PA	647
167	Redding, CA	542
128	Reno-Sparks, NV	892
81	Richmond, VA	2,048
12	Riverside-San Bernardino, CA	17,162
195	Roanoke, VA	416
305	Rochester, MN	148
110	Rochester, NY	1,251
153	Rockford, IL	636
223	Rockingham County, NH M.D.	313
249	Rocky Mount, NC	250
292	Rome, GA	172
26	Sacramento, CA	8,769
256	Saginaw, MI	236
140	Salem, OR	764
94	Salinas, CA	1,670
321	Salisbury, MD	124
48	Salt Lake City, UT	4,588
304	San Angelo, TX	149
34	San Antonio, TX	7,004
23	San Diego, CA	11,356
6	San Francisco (greater), CA	22,944
40	San Francisco-S. Mateo, CA M.D.	6,047
35	San Jose, CA	6,881
192	San Luis Obispo, CA	425
366	Sandusky, OH	48
42	Santa Ana-Anaheim, CA M.D.	5,841
163	Santa Barbara-Santa Maria, CA	549
134	Santa Cruz-Watsonville, CA	822
246	Santa Fe, NM	259
155	Santa Rosa-Petaluma, CA	602

RANK	METROPOLITAN AREA	THEFTS
129	Savannah, GA	882
149	Scranton--Wilkes-Barre, PA	660
14	Seattle (greater), WA	15,640
22	Seattle-Bellevue-Everett, WA M.D.	11,481
329	Sebastian-Vero Beach, FL	110
346	Sheboygan, WI	82
302	Sherman-Denison, TX	152
272	Sioux City, IA-NE-SD	210
224	Sioux Falls, SD	311
156	South Bend-Mishawaka, IN-MI	598
136	Spartanburg, SC	800
71	Spokane, WA	2,566
231	Springfield, IL	292
98	Springfield, MA	1,486
106	Springfield, MO	1,282
255	Springfield, OH	238
364	State College, PA	58
66	Stockton, CA	3,018
286	St. Cloud, MN	185
226	St. Joseph, MO-KS	307
35	St. Louis, MO-IL	6,881
245	Sumter, SC	260
152	Syracuse, NY	644
54	Tacoma, WA M.D.	4,159
166	Tallahassee, FL	545
49	Tampa-St Petersburg, FL	4,541
181	Terre Haute, IN	458
198	Texarkana, TX-Texarkana, AR	409
89	Toledo, OH	1,808
145	Topeka, KS	711
146	Trenton-Ewing, NJ	680
56	Tucson, AZ	3,827
61	Tulsa, OK	3,277
190	Tuscaloosa, AL	435
214	Tyler, TX	337
287	Utica-Rome, NY	184
280	Valdosta, GA	196
87	Vallejo-Fairfield, CA	1,829
296	Victoria, TX	163
69	Virginia Beach-Norfolk, VA-NC	2,765
83	Visalia-Porterville, CA	1,915
246	Waco, TX	259
244	Warner Robins, GA	261
53	Warren-Farmington Hills, MI M.D.	4,313
16	Washington (greater) DC-VA-MD-WV	14,725
20	Washington, DC-VA-MD-WV M.D.	13,273
306	Waterloo-Cedar Falls, IA	146
350	Wausau, WI	77
303	Wenatchee, WA	151
68	West Palm Beach, FL M.D.	2,832
241	Wichita Falls, TX	269
77	Wichita, KS	2,187
341	Williamsport, PA	91
104	Wilmington, DE-MD-NJ M.D.	1,337
144	Wilmington, NC	724
310	Winchester, VA-WV	140
121	Winston-Salem, NC	966
117	Worcester, MA	1,039
108	Yakima, WA	1,265
203	York-Hanover, PA	391
172	Yuba City, CA	519
211	Yuma, AZ	355

Source: Reported data from the F.B.I. "Crime in the United States 2011"
*Motor vehicle theft includes the theft or attempted theft of a self-propelled vehicle. Excludes motorboats, construction equipment, airplanes, and farming equipment.

37. Motor Vehicle Thefts in 2011 (continued)
National Total = 715,373 Motor Vehicle Thefts*

RANK	METROPOLITAN AREA	THEFTS
1	Los Angeles (greater), CA	46,324
2	Los Angeles County, CA M.D.	40,483
3	Chicago (greater), IL-IN-WI	27,138
4	New York (greater), NY-NJ-PA	26,709
5	Chicago-Joilet-Naperville, IL M.D.	24,120
6	San Francisco (greater), CA	22,944
7	Houston, TX	20,611
8	Atlanta, GA	20,121
9	Detroit (greater), MI	19,368
10	Dallas (greater), TX	19,209
11	Miami (greater), FL	18,182
12	Riverside-San Bernardino, CA	17,162
13	Oakland-Fremont, CA M.D.	16,897
14	Seattle (greater), WA	15,640
15	Detroit-Livonia-Dearborn, MI M.D.	15,055
16	Washington (greater) DC-VA-MD-WV	14,725
17	New York-W. Plains NY-NJ M.D.	14,422
18	Dallas-Plano-Irving, TX M.D.	14,068
19	Phoenix-Mesa-Scottsdale, AZ	13,621
20	Washington, DC-VA-MD-WV M.D.	13,273
21	Philadelphia (greater) PA-NJ-MD-DE	12,958
22	Seattle-Bellevue-Everett, WA M.D.	11,481
23	San Diego, CA	11,356
24	Miami-Dade County, FL M.D.	10,848
25	Philadelphia, PA M.D.	9,563
26	Sacramento, CA	8,769
27	Las Vegas-Paradise, NV	8,263
28	Newark-Union, NJ-PA M.D.	8,106
29	Kansas City, MO-KS	7,589
30	Denver-Aurora, CO	7,517
31	Baltimore-Towson, MD	7,507
32	Boston (greater), MA-NH	7,259
33	Fresno, CA	7,070
34	San Antonio, TX	7,004
35	San Jose, CA	6,881
35	St. Louis, MO-IL	6,881
37	Portland-Vancouver, OR-WA	6,689
38	Indianapolis, IN	6,263
39	Minneapolis-St. Paul, MN-WI	6,154
40	San Francisco-S. Mateo, CA M.D.	6,047
41	Cleveland-Elyria-Mentor, OH	5,900
42	Santa Ana-Anaheim, CA M.D.	5,841
43	Oklahoma City, OK	5,445
44	Orlando, FL	5,396
45	Milwaukee, WI	5,265
46	Fort Worth-Arlington, TX M.D.	5,141
47	Bakersfield, CA	4,886
48	Salt Lake City, UT	4,588
49	Tampa-St Petersburg, FL	4,541
50	Fort Lauderdale, FL M.D.	4,502
51	Memphis, TN-MS-AR	4,418
52	Columbus, OH	4,343
53	Warren-Farmington Hills, MI M.D.	4,313
54	Tacoma, WA M.D.	4,159
55	New Orleans, LA	4,086
56	Tucson, AZ	3,827
57	Omaha-Council Bluffs, NE-IA	3,663
58	Albuquerque, NM	3,538
59	Charlotte-Gastonia, NC-SC	3,471
60	Boston-Quincy, MA M.D.	3,466
61	Tulsa, OK	3,277
62	Louisville, KY-IN	3,230
63	Modesto, CA	3,221
64	Cincinnati-Middletown, OH-KY-IN	3,117
65	Birmingham-Hoover, AL	3,109
66	Stockton, CA	3,018
67	Nashville-Davidson, TN	2,911
68	West Palm Beach, FL M.D.	2,832
69	Virginia Beach-Norfolk, VA-NC	2,765
70	Austin-Round Rock, TX	2,764
71	Spokane, WA	2,566
72	Gary, IN M.D.	2,476
73	Jacksonville, FL	2,438
74	Nassau-Suffolk, NY M.D.	2,366
75	New Haven-Milford, CT	2,355
76	Little Rock, AR	2,322
77	Wichita, KS	2,187
78	Augusta, GA-SC	2,126
79	Camden, NJ M.D.	2,058
80	Hartford, CT	2,050
81	Richmond, VA	2,048
82	Peabody, MA M.D.	2,002
83	Visalia-Porterville, CA	1,915
84	Buffalo-Niagara Falls, NY	1,913
85	Jackson, MS	1,874
86	Pittsburgh, PA	1,851
87	Vallejo-Fairfield, CA	1,829
88	Edison, NJ M.D.	1,815
89	Toledo, OH	1,808
90	Bridgeport-Stamford, CT	1,799
91	Greenville, SC	1,756
92	El Paso, TX	1,710
93	Raleigh-Cary, NC	1,689
94	Salinas, CA	1,670
95	McAllen-Edinburg-Mission, TX	1,660
96	Knoxville, TN	1,652
97	Dayton, OH	1,503
98	Springfield, MA	1,486
99	Cambridge-Newton, MA M.D.	1,478
100	Bethesda-Frederick, MD M.D.	1,452
101	Chattanooga, TN-GA	1,418
102	Colorado Springs, CO	1,392
103	Flint, MI	1,373
104	Wilmington, DE-MD-NJ M.D.	1,337
105	Columbus, GA-AL	1,309
106	Springfield, MO	1,282
107	Mobile, AL	1,281
108	Yakima, WA	1,265
109	Akron, OH	1,262
110	Rochester, NY	1,251
111	Myrtle Beach, SC	1,138
112	Baton Rouge, LA	1,124
113	Des Moines-West Des Moines, IA	1,115
114	Montgomery, AL	1,094
115	Huntsville, AL	1,051
116	Fayetteville, NC	1,043
117	Worcester, MA	1,039
118	Merced, CA	1,032
119	Deltona-Daytona Beach, FL	1,026
120	Oxnard-Thousand Oaks, CA	1,014
121	Allentown, PA-NJ	966
121	Winston-Salem, NC	966
123	Eugene-Springfield, OR	929
124	Macon, GA	922
125	Durham-Chapel Hill, NC	921
126	North Port-Bradenton-Sarasota, FL	906
127	Anderson, SC	901
128	Reno-Sparks, NV	892
129	Savannah, GA	882
130	Lexington-Fayette, KY	855
131	Grand Rapids-Wyoming, MI	847
132	Lakeland, FL	836
133	Pensacola, FL	828
134	Santa Cruz-Watsonville, CA	822
135	Beaumont-Port Arthur, TX	820
136	Spartanburg, SC	800
137	Cape Coral-Fort Myers, FL	797
138	Lubbock, TX	770
139	Asheville, NC	765
140	Salem, OR	764
141	El Centro, CA	754
142	Palm Bay-Melbourne, FL	748
143	Albany-Schenectady-Troy, NY	746
144	Wilmington, NC	724
145	Topeka, KS	711
146	Trenton-Ewing, NJ	680
147	Amarillo, TX	673
148	Ogden-Clearfield, UT	667
149	Scranton--Wilkes-Barre, PA	660
150	Anchorage, AK	651
151	Reading, PA	647
152	Syracuse, NY	644
153	Rockford, IL	636
154	Chico, CA	615
155	Santa Rosa-Petaluma, CA	602
156	South Bend-Mishawaka, IN-MI	598
157	Corpus Christi, TX	596
158	Florence, SC	579
159	Bremerton-Silverdale, WA	578
160	Madera, CA	574
161	Charleston, WV	571
162	Longview, TX	567
163	Santa Barbara-Santa Maria, CA	549
164	Hickory, NC	548
164	Madison, WI	548
166	Tallahassee, FL	545
167	Lake Co.-Kenosha Co., IL-WI M.D.	542
167	Redding, CA	542
169	Canton, OH	537
170	Harrisburg-Carlisle, PA	532
171	Pueblo, CO	530
172	Yuba City, CA	519
173	Gulfport-Biloxi, MS	518
174	Davenport, IA-IL	512
175	Laredo, TX	508
176	Fort Wayne, IN	507
177	Kennewick-Pasco-Richland, WA	503
178	Lansing-East Lansing, MI	501
179	Joplin, MO	482
180	Boise City-Nampa, ID	466

Note: All listings are for Metropolitan Statistical Areas (M.S.A.s) except for those ending with "M.D." Listings with "M.D." are Metropolitan Divisions which are smaller parts of eleven large M.S.A.s. See explanatory note at beginning of metropolitan area section.

Rank Order - Metro Area (continued)

RANK	METROPOLITAN AREA	THEFTS
181	Terre Haute, IN	458
182	Port St. Lucie, FL	456
183	Portland, ME	452
184	Brownsville-Harlingen, TX	450
185	Peoria, IL	449
186	Kingsport, TN-VA	445
186	Provo-Orem, UT	445
188	Gainesville, FL	443
189	Ann Arbor, MI	440
190	Tuscaloosa, AL	435
191	Evansville, IN-KY	427
192	San Luis Obispo, CA	425
193	Las Cruces, NM	423
194	Alexandria, LA	421
195	Roanoke, VA	416
196	Clarksville, TN-KY	410
196	Poughkeepsie, NY	410
198	Texarkana, TX-Texarkana, AR	409
199	Billings, MT	406
199	Lafayette, LA	406
201	Killeen-Temple-Fort Hood, TX	404
202	Pine Bluff, AR	403
203	York-Hanover, PA	391
204	Fort Smith, AR-OK	389
204	Hanford-Corcoran, CA	389
206	Lincoln, NE	384
207	Duluth, MN-WI	379
208	Gadsden, AL	362
209	Athens-Clarke County, GA	359
210	Lancaster, PA	356
211	Yuma, AZ	355
212	Olympia, WA	346
213	Lake Havasu City-Kingman, AZ	341
214	Pascagoula, MS	337
214	Tyler, TX	337
216	Albany, GA	332
216	Atlantic City, NJ	332
218	Boulder, CO	331
219	Panama City-Lynn Haven, FL	324
220	Manchester-Nashua, NH	322
221	Greeley, CO	320
222	Bloomington, IN	318
223	Rockingham County, NH M.D.	313
224	Sioux Falls, SD	311
225	Houma, LA	310
226	St. Joseph, MO-KS	307
227	Hagerstown-Martinsburg, MD-WV	302
227	Jackson, TN	302
229	Longview, WA	301
230	Gainesville, GA	294
231	Ocala, FL	292
231	Springfield, IL	292
233	Hot Springs, AR	288
234	Goldsboro, NC	286
235	Lafayette, IN	283
236	Cedar Rapids, IA	279
237	Jacksonville, NC	275
238	Decatur, AL	271
239	Columbus, IN	270
239	Fort Collins-Loveland, CO	270
241	Wichita Falls, TX	269
242	Dalton, GA	265
243	Mount Vernon-Anacortes, WA	264
244	Warner Robins, GA	261
245	Sumter, SC	260
246	Santa Fe, NM	259
246	Waco, TX	259
248	Johnson City, TN	254
249	Morristown, TN	250
249	Rocky Mount, NC	250
251	Napa, CA	249
252	Medford, OR	248
253	Dothan, AL	242
253	Odessa, TX	242
255	Springfield, OH	238
256	Saginaw, MI	236
257	Michigan City-La Porte, IN	234
258	Lawton, OK	229
259	Muskegon-Norton Shores, MI	228
260	Bellingham, WA	226
260	Lynchburg, VA	226
262	Burlington, NC	225
263	Monroe, LA	224
264	Muncie, IN	223
265	Grand Junction, CO	222
266	Charlottesville, VA	217
266	Crestview-Fort Walton Beach, FL	217
268	Monroe, MI	215
268	Naples-Marco Island, FL	215
270	Lawrence, KS	214
271	College Station-Bryan, TX	211
272	Fargo, ND-MN	210
272	Sioux City, IA-NE-SD	210
274	Prescott, AZ	207
275	Abilene, TX	205
275	Erie, PA	205
277	Racine, WI	204
278	Cleveland, TN	202
279	Columbia, MO	201
280	Green Bay, WI	196
280	Valdosta, GA	196
282	Anniston-Oxford, AL	193
282	Dover, DE	193
282	Rapid City, SD	193
285	Barnstable Town, MA	191
286	St. Cloud, MN	185
287	Champaign-Urbana, IL	184
287	Utica-Rome, NY	184
289	Lima, OH	177
290	Binghamton, NY	176
291	Bend, OR	173
292	Rome, GA	172
293	Midland, TX	171
294	Brunswick, GA	169
295	Bismarck, ND	166
296	Florence-Muscle Shoals, AL	163
296	Victoria, TX	163
298	Mansfield, OH	162
299	Battle Creek, MI	158
300	Farmington, NM	157
301	Bowling Green, KY	155
302	Sherman-Denison, TX	152
303	Wenatchee, WA	151
304	San Angelo, TX	149
305	Rochester, MN	148
306	Waterloo-Cedar Falls, IA	146
307	Jonesboro, AR	143
308	Blacksburg, VA	142
308	Norwich-New London, CT	142
310	Bangor, ME	140
310	Winchester, VA-WV	140
312	Idaho Falls, ID	139
313	Janesville, WI	135
313	Jefferson City, MO	135
315	Hinesville, GA	134
316	Auburn, AL	133
317	Pittsfield, MA	131
318	Decatur, IL	129
319	Grand Forks, ND-MN	128
320	Missoula, MT	126
321	Kokomo, IN	124
321	Owensboro, KY	124
321	Salisbury, MD	124
324	Danville, VA	116
324	Flagstaff, AZ	116
326	Great Falls, MT	115
327	Punta Gorda, FL	113
328	Holland-Grand Haven, MI	111
329	Sebastian-Vero Beach, FL	110
330	Cape Girardeau, MO-IL	109
331	Appleton, WI	107
331	La Crosse, WI-MN	107
333	Danville, IL	102
333	Kankakee-Bradley, IL	102
335	Casper, WY	98
335	Kingston, NY	98
337	Bloomington-Normal, IL	97
337	Cheyenne, WY	97
337	Iowa City, IA	97
340	Mankato-North Mankato, MN	95
341	Williamsport, PA	91
342	Eau Claire, WI	90
343	Pocatello, ID	89
344	Johnstown, PA	87
345	Fairbanks, AK	83
346	Sheboygan, WI	82
347	Altoona, PA	80
348	Ames, IA	79
349	Elizabethtown, KY	78
350	Wausau, WI	77
351	Corvallis, OR	76
352	Palm Coast, FL	75
353	Lebanon, PA	74
353	Ocean City, NJ	74
355	Harrisonburg, VA	72
356	Bay City, MI	71
357	Manhattan, KS	70
358	Carson City, NV	69
359	Fond du Lac, WI	64
360	Lewiston-Auburn, ME	63
361	Oshkosh-Neenah, WI	60
362	Dubuque, IA	59
362	Glens Falls, NY	59
364	Cumberland, MD-WV	58
364	State College, PA	58
366	Sandusky, OH	48
367	Logan, UT-ID	45
368	Elmira, NY	41

Source: Reported data from the F.B.I. "Crime in the United States 2011"
*Motor vehicle theft includes the theft or attempted theft of a self-propelled vehicle. Excludes motorboats, construction equipment, airplanes, and farming equipment.

Alpha Order - Metro Area

38. Motor Vehicle Theft Rate in 2011
National Rate = 229.6 Motor Vehicle Thefts per 100,000 Population*

RANK	METROPOLITAN AREA	RATE	RANK	METROPOLITAN AREA	RATE	RANK	METROPOLITAN AREA	RATE
251	Abilene, TX	121.5	146	Charleston, WV	187.4	99	Fort Lauderdale, FL M.D.	254.1
162	Akron, OH	179.3	138	Charlotte-Gastonia, NC-SC	195.0	231	Fort Smith, AR-OK	129.2
318	Albany-Schenectady-Troy, NY	85.3	285	Charlottesville, VA	106.4	252	Fort Wayne, IN	121.2
124	Albany, GA	208.3	90	Chattanooga, TN-GA	265.8	111	Fort Worth-Arlington, TX M.D.	235.7
31	Albuquerque, NM	394.4	288	Cheyenne, WY	104.9	2	Fresno, CA	751.0
88	Alexandria, LA	271.0	77	Chicago (greater), IL-IN-WI	285.9	49	Gadsden, AL	345.0
264	Allentown, PA-NJ	117.3	64	Chicago-Joilet-Naperville, IL M.D.	305.1	179	Gainesville, FL	165.4
345	Altoona, PA	62.7	83	Chico, CA	276.3	186	Gainesville, GA	161.5
93	Amarillo, TX	263.8	206	Cincinnati-Middletown, OH-KY-IN	146.0	45	Gary, IN M.D.	347.9
314	Ames, IA	87.8	198	Clarksville, TN-KY	148.4	364	Glens Falls, NY	45.6
121	Anchorage, AK	209.3	78	Cleveland-Elyria-Mentor, OH	283.8	113	Goldsboro, NC	230.3
10	Anderson, SC	476.0	172	Cleveland, TN	172.9	233	Grand Forks, ND-MN	128.2
235	Ann Arbor, MI	127.7	305	College Station-Bryan, TX	90.4	197	Grand Junction, CO	148.7
184	Anniston-Oxford, AL	162.0	118	Colorado Springs, CO	211.9	276	Grand Rapids-Wyoming, MI	109.5
362	Appleton, WI	47.2	269	Columbia, MO	115.9	211	Great Falls, MT	140.2
166	Asheville, NC	177.8	13	Columbus, GA-AL	438.8	243	Greeley, CO	124.4
151	Athens-Clarke County, GA	184.0	43	Columbus, IN	349.8	343	Green Bay, WI	63.7
35	Atlanta, GA	376.9	110	Columbus, OH	236.3	87	Greenville, SC	272.5
254	Atlantic City, NJ	120.5	218	Corpus Christi, TX	136.3	126	Gulfport-Biloxi, MS	207.4
303	Auburn, AL	94.4	311	Corvallis, OR	87.9	272	Hagerstown-Martinsburg, MD-WV	111.6
34	Augusta, GA-SC	377.0	258	Crestview-Fort Walton Beach, FL	118.4	100	Hanford-Corcoran, CA	251.3
190	Austin-Round Rock, TX	157.7	357	Cumberland, MD-WV	55.7	301	Harrisburg-Carlisle, PA	96.5
5	Bakersfield, CA	575.2	71	Dallas (greater), TX	295.3	356	Harrisonburg, VA	56.8
84	Baltimore-Towson, MD	274.4	56	Dallas-Plano-Irving, TX M.D.	325.3	130	Hartford, CT	200.6
304	Bangor, ME	91.0	152	Dalton, GA	183.9	200	Hickory, NC	148.1
311	Barnstable Town, MA	87.9	242	Danville, IL	124.6	175	Hinesville, GA	169.7
213	Baton Rouge, LA	138.8	282	Danville, VA	107.6	365	Holland-Grand Haven, MI	42.1
267	Battle Creek, MI	116.1	223	Davenport, IA-IL	134.3	68	Hot Springs, AR	297.7
341	Bay City, MI	65.9	165	Dayton, OH	178.5	201	Houma, LA	147.6
128	Beaumont-Port Arthur, TX	206.6	169	Decatur, AL	175.3	50	Houston, TX	339.4
273	Bellingham, WA	110.6	267	Decatur, IL	116.1	101	Huntsville, AL	250.5
277	Bend, OR	108.5	129	Deltona-Daytona Beach, FL	204.7	287	Idaho Falls, ID	105.4
256	Bethesda-Frederick, MD M.D.	119.4	75	Denver-Aurora, CO	290.5	42	Indianapolis, IN	354.8
98	Billings, MT	254.6	139	Des Moines-West Des Moines, IA	194.7	344	Iowa City, IA	63.2
338	Binghamton, NY	69.6	11	Detroit (greater), MI	451.2	164	Jacksonville, FL	178.7
85	Birmingham-Hoover, AL	274.3	1	Detroit-Livonia-Dearborn, MI M.D.	827.6	194	Jacksonville, NC	152.8
196	Bismarck, ND	150.1	179	Dothan, AL	165.4	47	Jackson, MS	346.3
317	Blacksburg, VA	86.1	263	Dover, DE	117.7	96	Jackson, TN	259.3
355	Bloomington-Normal, IL	57.0	345	Dubuque, IA	62.7	320	Janesville, WI	83.8
181	Bloomington, IN	164.2	222	Duluth, MN-WI	134.5	306	Jefferson City, MO	89.8
333	Boise City-Nampa, ID	74.8	159	Durham-Chapel Hill, NC	180.3	238	Johnson City, TN	126.7
189	Boston (greater), MA-NH	158.6	358	Eau Claire, WI	55.6	352	Johnstown, PA	60.4
154	Boston-Quincy, MA M.D.	182.5	330	Edison, NJ M.D.	77.3	264	Jonesboro, AR	117.3
274	Boulder, CO	110.4	20	El Centro, CA	427.0	86	Joplin, MO	273.6
249	Bowling Green, KY	122.2	122	El Paso, TX	209.2	307	Kankakee-Bradley, IL	89.6
114	Bremerton-Silverdale, WA	226.6	342	Elizabethtown, KY	64.7	38	Kansas City, MO-KS	371.1
132	Bridgeport-Stamford, CT	199.7	363	Elmira, NY	45.9	137	Kennewick-Pasco-Richland, WA	195.5
277	Brownsville-Harlingen, TX	108.5	335	Erie, PA	72.8	294	Killeen-Temple-Fort Hood, TX	97.6
198	Brunswick, GA	148.4	94	Eugene-Springfield, OR	261.4	208	Kingsport, TN-VA	142.3
177	Buffalo-Niagara Falls, NY	167.7	258	Evansville, IN-KY	118.4	361	Kingston, NY	53.5
203	Burlington, NC	147.0	106	Fairbanks, AK	242.4	112	Knoxville, TN	234.6
293	Cambridge-Newton, MA M.D.	97.7	290	Fargo, ND-MN	99.2	241	Kokomo, IN	125.0
182	Camden, NJ M.D.	164.0	256	Farmington, NM	119.4	324	La Crosse, WI-MN	79.7
226	Canton, OH	132.7	79	Fayetteville, NC	281.1	212	Lafayette, IN	139.5
237	Cape Coral-Fort Myers, FL	127.1	319	Flagstaff, AZ	85.1	203	Lafayette, LA	147.0
271	Cape Girardeau, MO-IL	112.8	57	Flint, MI	322.7	349	Lake Co.-Kenosha Co., IL-WI M.D.	62.1
245	Carson City, NV	123.8	275	Florence-Muscle Shoals, AL	110.3	176	Lake Havasu City-Kingman, AZ	168.0
232	Casper, WY	128.9	80	Florence, SC	278.4	217	Lakeland, FL	137.0
282	Cedar Rapids, IA	107.6	345	Fond du Lac, WI	62.7	339	Lancaster, PA	68.3
325	Champaign-Urbana, IL	79.1	309	Fort Collins-Loveland, CO	88.6	279	Lansing-East Lansing, MI	108.0

Note: All listings are for Metropolitan Statistical Areas (M.S.A.s) except for those ending with "M.D." Listings with "M.D." are Metropolitan Divisions which are smaller parts of eleven large M.S.A.s. See explanatory note at beginning of metropolitan area section.

Alpha Order - Metro Area (continued)

RANK	METROPOLITAN AREA	RATE	RANK	METROPOLITAN AREA	RATE	RANK	METROPOLITAN AREA	RATE
134	Laredo, TX	198.8	16	Oklahoma City, OK	430.0	102	Savannah, GA	250.4
131	Las Cruces, NM	199.9	220	Olympia, WA	135.0	266	Scranton--Wilkes-Barre, PA	116.7
21	Las Vegas-Paradise, NV	419.9	22	Omaha-Council Bluffs, NE-IA	419.8	12	Seattle (greater), WA	447.7
141	Lawrence, KS	191.9	104	Orlando, FL	249.4	19	Seattle-Bellevue-Everett, WA M.D.	427.4
153	Lawton, OK	182.6	367	Oshkosh-Neenah, WI	35.8	327	Sebastian-Vero Beach, FL	78.6
359	Lebanon, PA	55.2	284	Owensboro, KY	107.3	336	Sheboygan, WI	70.7
353	Lewiston-Auburn, ME	58.5	250	Oxnard-Thousand Oaks, CA	121.7	246	Sherman-Denison, TX	123.2
161	Lexington-Fayette, KY	179.9	219	Palm Bay-Melbourne, FL	135.8	207	Sioux City, IA-NE-SD	145.3
178	Lima, OH	166.3	330	Palm Coast, FL	77.3	221	Sioux Falls, SD	134.6
239	Lincoln, NE	126.0	143	Panama City-Lynn Haven, FL	189.3	147	South Bend-Mishawaka, IN-MI	186.6
54	Little Rock, AR	329.3	127	Pascagoula, MS	206.9	81	Spartanburg, SC	278.1
368	Logan, UT-ID	35.2	89	Peabody, MA M.D.	267.8	6	Spokane, WA	536.1
97	Longview, TX	259.0	155	Pensacola, FL	181.9	215	Springfield, IL	138.5
76	Longview, WA	289.4	260	Peoria, IL	118.1	117	Springfield, MA	213.1
24	Los Angeles County, CA M.D.	407.5	116	Philadelphia (greater) PA-NJ-MD-DE	216.4	72	Springfield, MO	292.5
41	Los Angeles (greater), CA	356.9	109	Philadelphia, PA M.D.	237.8	174	Springfield, OH	171.9
103	Louisville, KY-IN	250.0	59	Phoenix-Mesa-Scottsdale, AZ	320.3	366	State College, PA	37.5
91	Lubbock, TX	264.7	28	Pine Bluff, AR	398.9	15	Stockton, CA	435.3
310	Lynchburg, VA	88.4	328	Pittsburgh, PA	78.3	296	St. Cloud, MN	97.1
32	Macon, GA	391.8	290	Pittsfield, MA	99.2	107	St. Joseph, MO-KS	240.2
37	Madera, CA	376.1	296	Pocatello, ID	97.1	105	St. Louis, MO-IL	243.6
302	Madison, WI	96.0	286	Port St. Lucie, FL	106.1	108	Sumter, SC	239.2
323	Manchester-Nashua, NH	80.3	69	Portland-Vancouver, OR-WA	297.0	299	Syracuse, NY	96.8
360	Manhattan, KS	54.7	311	Portland, ME	87.9	8	Tacoma, WA M.D.	514.9
295	Mankato-North Mankato, MN	97.4	351	Poughkeepsie, NY	60.9	205	Tallahassee, FL	146.3
229	Mansfield, OH	130.1	300	Prescott, AZ	96.7	187	Tampa-St Petersburg, FL	161.0
120	McAllen-Edinburg-Mission, TX	209.8	322	Provo-Orem, UT	82.9	92	Terre Haute, IN	264.3
253	Medford, OR	120.8	55	Pueblo, CO	327.5	70	Texarkana, TX-Texarkana, AR	295.7
53	Memphis, TN-MS-AR	333.0	337	Punta Gorda, FL	69.7	82	Toledo, OH	277.3
29	Merced, CA	398.8	289	Racine, WI	103.9	66	Topeka, KS	302.1
58	Miami (greater), FL	322.3	202	Raleigh-Cary, NC	147.5	149	Trenton-Ewing, NJ	184.9
17	Miami-Dade County, FL M.D.	428.7	195	Rapid City, SD	150.9	33	Tucson, AZ	385.0
123	Michigan City-La Porte, IN	208.9	192	Reading, PA	156.8	48	Tulsa, OK	345.9
248	Midland, TX	122.4	65	Redding, CA	302.3	135	Tuscaloosa, AL	197.3
51	Milwaukee, WI	336.9	125	Reno-Sparks, NV	207.9	191	Tyler, TX	157.4
148	Minneapolis-St. Paul, MN-WI	186.2	188	Richmond, VA	160.8	350	Utica-Rome, NY	61.2
270	Missoula, MT	114.3	26	Riverside-San Bernardino, CA	401.5	214	Valdosta, GA	138.6
62	Mobile, AL	308.7	225	Roanoke, VA	133.2	14	Vallejo-Fairfield, CA	437.3
4	Modesto, CA	618.8	326	Rochester, MN	79.0	216	Victoria, TX	138.4
240	Monroe, LA	125.8	260	Rochester, NY	118.1	183	Virginia Beach-Norfolk, VA-NC	163.4
209	Monroe, MI	141.5	156	Rockford, IL	181.5	18	Visalia-Porterville, CA	428.1
73	Montgomery, AL	290.7	334	Rockingham County, NH M.D.	74.7	279	Waco, TX	108.0
158	Morristown, TN	181.4	184	Rocky Mount, NC	162.0	150	Warner Robins, GA	184.1
115	Mount Vernon-Anacortes, WA	222.3	168	Rome, GA	176.3	170	Warren-Farmington Hills, MI M.D.	174.3
144	Muncie, IN	188.5	25	Sacramento, CA	403.3	95	Washington (greater) DC-VA-MD-WV	260.5
227	Muskegon-Norton Shores, MI	132.5	262	Saginaw, MI	118.0	67	Washington, DC-VA-MD-WV M.D.	299.3
23	Myrtle Beach, SC	417.7	140	Salem, OR	193.5	316	Waterloo-Cedar Falls, IA	86.5
159	Napa, CA	180.3	30	Salinas, CA	397.7	354	Wausau, WI	57.2
340	Naples-Marco Island, FL	66.0	292	Salisbury, MD	98.1	224	Wenatchee, WA	134.1
156	Nashville-Davidson, TN	181.5	27	Salt Lake City, UT	400.4	119	West Palm Beach, FL M.D.	211.6
321	Nassau-Suffolk, NY M.D.	83.1	228	San Angelo, TX	130.5	171	Wichita Falls, TX	174.1
74	New Haven-Milford, CT	290.6	60	San Antonio, TX	320.2	44	Wichita, KS	348.8
46	New Orleans, LA	346.7	40	San Diego, CA	362.6	329	Williamsport, PA	78.1
210	New York (greater), NY-NJ-PA	140.8	7	San Francisco (greater), CA	523.1	145	Wilmington, DE-MD-NJ M.D.	187.7
244	New York-W. Plains NY-NJ M.D.	124.1	52	San Francisco-S. Mateo, CA M.D.	336.5	135	Wilmington, NC	197.3
36	Newark-Union, NJ-PA M.D.	376.2	39	San Jose, CA	370.2	281	Winchester, VA-WV	107.9
236	North Port-Bradenton-Sarasota, FL	127.3	193	San Luis Obispo, CA	155.8	132	Winston-Salem, NC	199.7
298	Norwich-New London, CT	96.9	348	Sandusky, OH	62.2	230	Worcester, MA	129.3
3	Oakland-Fremont, CA M.D.	652.5	142	Santa Ana-Anaheim, CA M.D.	191.8	9	Yakima, WA	512.0
315	Ocala, FL	87.0	234	Santa Barbara-Santa Maria, CA	128.0	307	York-Hanover, PA	89.6
332	Ocean City, NJ	75.8	61	Santa Cruz-Watsonville, CA	309.6	63	Yuba City, CA	307.4
173	Odessa, TX	172.8	167	Santa Fe, NM	177.7	163	Yuma, AZ	178.8
255	Ogden-Clearfield, UT	119.6	247	Santa Rosa-Petaluma, CA	123.0			

Source: Reported data from the F.B.I. "Crime in the United States 2011"
*Motor vehicle theft includes the theft or attempted theft of a self-propelled vehicle. Excludes motorboats, construction equipment, airplanes, and farming equipment.

Rank Order - Metro Area

38. Motor Vehicle Theft Rate in 2011 (continued)
National Rate = 229.6 Motor Vehicle Thefts per 100,000 Population*

RANK	METROPOLITAN AREA	RATE	RANK	METROPOLITAN AREA	RATE	RANK	METROPOLITAN AREA	RATE
1	Detroit-Livonia-Dearborn, MI M.D.	827.6	61	Santa Cruz-Watsonville, CA	309.6	121	Anchorage, AK	209.3
2	Fresno, CA	751.0	62	Mobile, AL	308.7	122	El Paso, TX	209.2
3	Oakland-Fremont, CA M.D.	652.5	63	Yuba City, CA	307.4	123	Michigan City-La Porte, IN	208.9
4	Modesto, CA	618.8	64	Chicago-Joilet-Naperville, IL M.D.	305.1	124	Albany, GA	208.3
5	Bakersfield, CA	575.2	65	Redding, CA	302.3	125	Reno-Sparks, NV	207.9
6	Spokane, WA	536.1	66	Topeka, KS	302.1	126	Gulfport-Biloxi, MS	207.4
7	San Francisco (greater), CA	523.1	67	Washington, DC-VA-MD-WV M.D.	299.3	127	Pascagoula, MS	206.9
8	Tacoma, WA M.D.	514.9	68	Hot Springs, AR	297.7	128	Beaumont-Port Arthur, TX	206.6
9	Yakima, WA	512.0	69	Portland-Vancouver, OR-WA	297.0	129	Deltona-Daytona Beach, FL	204.7
10	Anderson, SC	476.0	70	Texarkana, TX-Texarkana, AR	295.7	130	Hartford, CT	200.6
11	Detroit (greater), MI	451.2	71	Dallas (greater), TX	295.3	131	Las Cruces, NM	199.9
12	Seattle (greater), WA	447.7	72	Springfield, MO	292.5	132	Bridgeport-Stamford, CT	199.7
13	Columbus, GA-AL	438.8	73	Montgomery, AL	290.7	132	Winston-Salem, NC	199.7
14	Vallejo-Fairfield, CA	437.3	74	New Haven-Milford, CT	290.6	134	Laredo, TX	198.8
15	Stockton, CA	435.3	75	Denver-Aurora, CO	290.5	135	Tuscaloosa, AL	197.3
16	Oklahoma City, OK	430.0	76	Longview, WA	289.4	135	Wilmington, NC	197.3
17	Miami-Dade County, FL M.D.	428.7	77	Chicago (greater), IL-IN-WI	285.9	137	Kennewick-Pasco-Richland, WA	195.5
18	Visalia-Porterville, CA	428.1	78	Cleveland-Elyria-Mentor, OH	283.8	138	Charlotte-Gastonia, NC-SC	195.0
19	Seattle-Bellevue-Everett, WA M.D.	427.4	79	Fayetteville, NC	281.1	139	Des Moines-West Des Moines, IA	194.7
20	El Centro, CA	427.0	80	Florence, SC	278.4	140	Salem, OR	193.5
21	Las Vegas-Paradise, NV	419.9	81	Spartanburg, SC	278.1	141	Lawrence, KS	191.9
22	Omaha-Council Bluffs, NE-IA	419.8	82	Toledo, OH	277.3	142	Santa Ana-Anaheim, CA M.D.	191.8
23	Myrtle Beach, SC	417.7	83	Chico, CA	276.3	143	Panama City-Lynn Haven, FL	189.3
24	Los Angeles County, CA M.D.	407.5	84	Baltimore-Towson, MD	274.4	144	Muncie, IN	188.5
25	Sacramento, CA	403.3	85	Birmingham-Hoover, AL	274.3	145	Wilmington, DE-MD-NJ M.D.	187.7
26	Riverside-San Bernardino, CA	401.5	86	Joplin, MO	273.6	146	Charleston, WV	187.4
27	Salt Lake City, UT	400.4	87	Greenville, SC	272.5	147	South Bend-Mishawaka, IN-MI	186.6
28	Pine Bluff, AR	398.9	88	Alexandria, LA	271.0	148	Minneapolis-St. Paul, MN-WI	186.2
29	Merced, CA	398.8	89	Peabody, MA M.D.	267.8	149	Trenton-Ewing, NJ	184.9
30	Salinas, CA	397.7	90	Chattanooga, TN-GA	265.8	150	Warner Robins, GA	184.1
31	Albuquerque, NM	394.4	91	Lubbock, TX	264.7	151	Athens-Clarke County, GA	184.0
32	Macon, GA	391.8	92	Terre Haute, IN	264.3	152	Dalton, GA	183.9
33	Tucson, AZ	385.0	93	Amarillo, TX	263.8	153	Lawton, OK	182.6
34	Augusta, GA-SC	377.0	94	Eugene-Springfield, OR	261.4	154	Boston-Quincy, MA M.D.	182.5
35	Atlanta, GA	376.9	95	Washington (greater) DC-VA-MD-WV	260.5	155	Pensacola, FL	181.9
36	Newark-Union, NJ-PA M.D.	376.2	96	Jackson, TN	259.3	156	Nashville-Davidson, TN	181.5
37	Madera, CA	376.1	97	Longview, TX	259.0	156	Rockford, IL	181.5
38	Kansas City, MO-KS	371.1	98	Billings, MT	254.6	158	Morristown, TN	181.4
39	San Jose, CA	370.2	99	Fort Lauderdale, FL M.D.	254.1	159	Durham-Chapel Hill, NC	180.3
40	San Diego, CA	362.6	100	Hanford-Corcoran, CA	251.3	159	Napa, CA	180.3
41	Los Angeles (greater), CA	356.9	101	Huntsville, AL	250.5	161	Lexington-Fayette, KY	179.9
42	Indianapolis, IN	354.8	102	Savannah, GA	250.4	162	Akron, OH	179.3
43	Columbus, IN	349.8	103	Louisville, KY-IN	250.0	163	Yuma, AZ	178.8
44	Wichita, KS	348.8	104	Orlando, FL	249.4	164	Jacksonville, FL	178.7
45	Gary, IN M.D.	347.9	105	St. Louis, MO-IL	243.6	165	Dayton, OH	178.5
46	New Orleans, LA	346.7	106	Fairbanks, AK	242.4	166	Asheville, NC	177.8
47	Jackson, MS	346.3	107	St. Joseph, MO-KS	240.2	167	Santa Fe, NM	177.7
48	Tulsa, OK	345.9	108	Sumter, SC	239.2	168	Rome, GA	176.3
49	Gadsden, AL	345.0	109	Philadelphia, PA M.D.	237.8	169	Decatur, AL	175.3
50	Houston, TX	339.4	110	Columbus, OH	236.3	170	Warren-Farmington Hills, MI M.D.	174.3
51	Milwaukee, WI	336.9	111	Fort Worth-Arlington, TX M.D.	235.7	171	Wichita Falls, TX	174.1
52	San Francisco-S. Mateo, CA M.D.	336.5	112	Knoxville, TN	234.6	172	Cleveland, TN	172.9
53	Memphis, TN-MS-AR	333.0	113	Goldsboro, NC	230.3	173	Odessa, TX	172.8
54	Little Rock, AR	329.3	114	Bremerton-Silverdale, WA	226.6	174	Springfield, OH	171.9
55	Pueblo, CO	327.5	115	Mount Vernon-Anacortes, WA	222.3	175	Hinesville, GA	169.7
56	Dallas-Plano-Irving, TX M.D.	325.3	116	Philadelphia (greater) PA-NJ-MD-DE	216.4	176	Lake Havasu City-Kingman, AZ	168.0
57	Flint, MI	322.7	117	Springfield, MA	213.1	177	Buffalo-Niagara Falls, NY	167.7
58	Miami (greater), FL	322.3	118	Colorado Springs, CO	211.9	178	Lima, OH	166.3
59	Phoenix-Mesa-Scottsdale, AZ	320.3	119	West Palm Beach, FL M.D.	211.6	179	Dothan, AL	165.4
60	San Antonio, TX	320.2	120	McAllen-Edinburg-Mission, TX	209.8	179	Gainesville, FL	165.4

Note: All listings are for Metropolitan Statistical Areas (M.S.A.s) except for those ending with "M.D." Listings with "M.D." are Metropolitan Divisions which are smaller parts of eleven large M.S.A.s. See explanatory note at beginning of metropolitan area section.

Rank Order - Metro Area (continued)

RANK	METROPOLITAN AREA	RATE	RANK	METROPOLITAN AREA	RATE	RANK	METROPOLITAN AREA	RATE
181	Bloomington, IN	164.2	244	New York-W. Plains NY-NJ M.D.	124.1	307	Kankakee-Bradley, IL	89.6
182	Camden, NJ M.D.	164.0	245	Carson City, NV	123.8	307	York-Hanover, PA	89.6
183	Virginia Beach-Norfolk, VA-NC	163.4	246	Sherman-Denison, TX	123.2	309	Fort Collins-Loveland, CO	88.6
184	Anniston-Oxford, AL	162.0	247	Santa Rosa-Petaluma, CA	123.0	310	Lynchburg, VA	88.4
184	Rocky Mount, NC	162.0	248	Midland, TX	122.4	311	Barnstable Town, MA	87.9
186	Gainesville, GA	161.5	249	Bowling Green, KY	122.2	311	Corvallis, OR	87.9
187	Tampa-St Petersburg, FL	161.0	250	Oxnard-Thousand Oaks, CA	121.7	311	Portland, ME	87.9
188	Richmond, VA	160.8	251	Abilene, TX	121.5	314	Ames, IA	87.8
189	Boston (greater), MA-NH	158.6	252	Fort Wayne, IN	121.2	315	Ocala, FL	87.0
190	Austin-Round Rock, TX	157.7	253	Medford, OR	120.8	316	Waterloo-Cedar Falls, IA	86.5
191	Tyler, TX	157.4	254	Atlantic City, NJ	120.5	317	Blacksburg, VA	86.1
192	Reading, PA	156.8	255	Ogden-Clearfield, UT	119.6	318	Albany-Schenectady-Troy, NY	85.3
193	San Luis Obispo, CA	155.8	256	Bethesda-Frederick, MD M.D.	119.4	319	Flagstaff, AZ	85.1
194	Jacksonville, NC	152.8	256	Farmington, NM	119.4	320	Janesville, WI	83.8
195	Rapid City, SD	150.9	258	Crestview-Fort Walton Beach, FL	118.4	321	Nassau-Suffolk, NY M.D.	83.1
196	Bismarck, ND	150.1	258	Evansville, IN-KY	118.4	322	Provo-Orem, UT	82.9
197	Grand Junction, CO	148.7	260	Peoria, IL	118.1	323	Manchester-Nashua, NH	80.3
198	Brunswick, GA	148.4	260	Rochester, NY	118.1	324	La Crosse, WI-MN	79.7
198	Clarksville, TN-KY	148.4	262	Saginaw, MI	118.0	325	Champaign-Urbana, IL	79.1
200	Hickory, NC	148.1	263	Dover, DE	117.7	326	Rochester, MN	79.0
201	Houma, LA	147.6	264	Allentown, PA-NJ	117.3	327	Sebastian-Vero Beach, FL	78.6
202	Raleigh-Cary, NC	147.5	264	Jonesboro, AR	117.3	328	Pittsburgh, PA	78.3
203	Burlington, NC	147.0	266	Scranton--Wilkes-Barre, PA	116.7	329	Williamsport, PA	78.1
203	Lafayette, LA	147.0	267	Battle Creek, MI	116.1	330	Edison, NJ M.D.	77.3
205	Tallahassee, FL	146.3	267	Decatur, IL	116.1	330	Palm Coast, FL	77.3
206	Cincinnati-Middletown, OH-KY-IN	146.0	269	Columbia, MO	115.9	332	Ocean City, NJ	75.8
207	Sioux City, IA-NE-SD	145.3	270	Missoula, MT	114.3	333	Boise City-Nampa, ID	74.8
208	Kingsport, TN-VA	142.3	271	Cape Girardeau, MO-IL	112.8	334	Rockingham County, NH M.D.	74.7
209	Monroe, MI	141.5	272	Hagerstown-Martinsburg, MD-WV	111.6	335	Erie, PA	72.8
210	New York (greater), NY-NJ-PA	140.8	273	Bellingham, WA	110.6	336	Sheboygan, WI	70.7
211	Great Falls, MT	140.2	274	Boulder, CO	110.4	337	Punta Gorda, FL	69.7
212	Lafayette, IN	139.5	275	Florence-Muscle Shoals, AL	110.3	338	Binghamton, NY	69.6
213	Baton Rouge, LA	138.8	276	Grand Rapids-Wyoming, MI	109.5	339	Lancaster, PA	68.3
214	Valdosta, GA	138.6	277	Bend, OR	108.5	340	Naples-Marco Island, FL	66.0
215	Springfield, IL	138.5	277	Brownsville-Harlingen, TX	108.5	341	Bay City, MI	65.9
216	Victoria, TX	138.4	279	Lansing-East Lansing, MI	108.0	342	Elizabethtown, KY	64.7
217	Lakeland, FL	137.0	279	Waco, TX	108.0	343	Green Bay, WI	63.7
218	Corpus Christi, TX	136.3	281	Winchester, VA-WV	107.9	344	Iowa City, IA	63.2
219	Palm Bay-Melbourne, FL	135.8	282	Cedar Rapids, IA	107.6	345	Altoona, PA	62.7
220	Olympia, WA	135.0	282	Danville, VA	107.6	345	Dubuque, IA	62.7
221	Sioux Falls, SD	134.6	284	Owensboro, KY	107.3	345	Fond du Lac, WI	62.7
222	Duluth, MN-WI	134.5	285	Charlottesville, VA	106.4	348	Sandusky, OH	62.2
223	Davenport, IA-IL	134.3	286	Port St. Lucie, FL	106.1	349	Lake Co.-Kenosha Co., IL-WI M.D.	62.1
224	Wenatchee, WA	134.1	287	Idaho Falls, ID	105.4	350	Utica-Rome, NY	61.2
225	Roanoke, VA	133.2	288	Cheyenne, WY	104.9	351	Poughkeepsie, NY	60.9
226	Canton, OH	132.7	289	Racine, WI	103.9	352	Johnstown, PA	60.4
227	Muskegon-Norton Shores, MI	132.5	290	Fargo, ND-MN	99.2	353	Lewiston-Auburn, ME	58.5
228	San Angelo, TX	130.5	290	Pittsfield, MA	99.2	354	Wausau, WI	57.2
229	Mansfield, OH	130.1	292	Salisbury, MD	98.1	355	Bloomington-Normal, IL	57.0
230	Worcester, MA	129.3	293	Cambridge-Newton, MA M.D.	97.7	356	Harrisonburg, VA	56.8
231	Fort Smith, AR-OK	129.2	294	Killeen-Temple-Fort Hood, TX	97.6	357	Cumberland, MD-WV	55.7
232	Casper, WY	128.9	295	Mankato-North Mankato, MN	97.4	358	Eau Claire, WI	55.6
233	Grand Forks, ND-MN	128.2	296	Pocatello, ID	97.1	359	Lebanon, PA	55.2
234	Santa Barbara-Santa Maria, CA	128.0	296	St. Cloud, MN	97.1	360	Manhattan, KS	54.7
235	Ann Arbor, MI	127.7	298	Norwich-New London, CT	96.9	361	Kingston, NY	53.5
236	North Port-Bradenton-Sarasota, FL	127.3	299	Syracuse, NY	96.8	362	Appleton, WI	47.2
237	Cape Coral-Fort Myers, FL	127.1	300	Prescott, AZ	96.7	363	Elmira, NY	45.9
238	Johnson City, TN	126.7	301	Harrisburg-Carlisle, PA	96.5	364	Glens Falls, NY	45.6
239	Lincoln, NE	126.0	302	Madison, WI	96.0	365	Holland-Grand Haven, MI	42.1
240	Monroe, LA	125.8	303	Auburn, AL	94.4	366	State College, PA	37.5
241	Kokomo, IN	125.0	304	Bangor, ME	91.0	367	Oshkosh-Neenah, WI	35.8
242	Danville, IL	124.6	305	College Station-Bryan, TX	90.4	368	Logan, UT-ID	35.2
243	Greeley, CO	124.4	306	Jefferson City, MO	89.8			

Source: Reported data from the F.B.I. "Crime in the United States 2011"
*Motor vehicle theft includes the theft or attempted theft of a self-propelled vehicle. Excludes motorboats, construction equipment, airplanes, and farming equipment.

Alpha Order - Metro Area

39. Percent Change in Motor Vehicle Theft Rate: 2010 to 2011
National Percent Change = 4.0% Decrease*

RANK	METROPOLITAN AREA	% CHANGE	RANK	METROPOLITAN AREA	% CHANGE	RANK	METROPOLITAN AREA	% CHANGE
289	Abilene, TX	(18.2)	NA	Charleston, WV**	NA	164	Fort Lauderdale, FL M.D.	(4.1)
64	Akron, OH	9.8	NA	Charlotte-Gastonia, NC-SC**	NA	161	Fort Smith, AR-OK	(3.9)
297	Albany-Schenectady-Troy, NY	(19.1)	149	Charlottesville, VA	(2.5)	18	Fort Wayne, IN	27.3
318	Albany, GA	(28.5)	149	Chattanooga, TN-GA	(2.5)	184	Fort Worth-Arlington, TX M.D.	(5.7)
124	Albuquerque, NM	1.3	295	Cheyenne, WY	(19.0)	141	Fresno, CA	(0.9)
21	Alexandria, LA	27.1	NA	Chicago (greater), IL-IN-WI**	NA	NA	Gadsden, AL**	NA
72	Allentown, PA-NJ	8.9	NA	Chicago-Joilet-Naperville, IL M.D.**	NA	261	Gainesville, FL	(14.7)
206	Altoona, PA	(7.8)	80	Chico, CA	6.6	137	Gainesville, GA	(0.4)
202	Amarillo, TX	(7.4)	194	Cincinnati-Middletown, OH-KY-IN	(6.8)	NA	Gary, IN M.D.**	NA
88	Ames, IA	5.4	69	Clarksville, TN-KY	9.0	14	Glens Falls, NY	29.5
313	Anchorage, AK	(24.4)	51	Cleveland-Elyria-Mentor, OH	15.3	117	Goldsboro, NC	1.7
15	Anderson, SC	29.2	39	Cleveland, TN	18.7	36	Grand Forks, ND-MN	19.5
316	Ann Arbor, MI	(26.8)	321	College Station-Bryan, TX	(30.5)	50	Grand Junction, CO	15.7
NA	Anniston-Oxford, AL**	NA	281	Colorado Springs, CO	(17.3)	263	Grand Rapids-Wyoming, MI	(15.0)
178	Appleton, WI	(5.6)	77	Columbia, MO	7.1	NA	Great Falls, MT**	NA
91	Asheville, NC	4.4	NA	Columbus, GA-AL**	NA	188	Greeley, CO	(6.2)
310	Athens-Clarke County, GA	(22.5)	7	Columbus, IN	40.7	123	Green Bay, WI	1.4
116	Atlanta, GA	1.9	254	Columbus, OH	(13.9)	53	Greenville, SC	14.4
147	Atlantic City, NJ	(2.1)	156	Corpus Christi, TX	(3.1)	214	Gulfport-Biloxi, MS	(8.6)
NA	Auburn, AL**	NA	30	Corvallis, OR	22.6	269	Hagerstown-Martinsburg, MD-WV	(15.5)
229	Augusta, GA-SC	(10.8)	251	Crestview-Fort Walton Beach, FL	(13.1)	246	Hanford-Corcoran, CA	(12.7)
204	Austin-Round Rock, TX	(7.7)	NA	Cumberland, MD-WV**	NA	42	Harrisburg-Carlisle, PA	18.4
216	Bakersfield, CA	(9.2)	174	Dallas (greater), TX	(5.3)	115	Harrisonburg, VA	2.0
224	Baltimore-Towson, MD	(10.2)	169	Dallas-Plano-Irving, TX M.D.	(4.9)	155	Hartford, CT	(3.0)
169	Bangor, ME	(4.9)	165	Dalton, GA	(4.2)	159	Hickory, NC	(3.7)
161	Barnstable Town, MA	(3.9)	56	Danville, IL	13.0	189	Hinesville, GA	(6.3)
NA	Baton Rouge, LA**	NA	278	Danville, VA	(16.9)	28	Holland-Grand Haven, MI	23.8
306	Battle Creek, MI	(20.9)	NA	Davenport, IA-IL**	NA	220	Hot Springs, AR	(9.6)
311	Bay City, MI	(23.1)	143	Dayton, OH	(1.3)	283	Houma, LA	(17.4)
186	Beaumont-Port Arthur, TX	(6.1)	NA	Decatur, AL**	NA	NA	Houston, TX**	NA
268	Bellingham, WA	(15.4)	241	Decatur, IL	(11.7)	NA	Huntsville, AL**	NA
191	Bend, OR	(6.5)	309	Deltona-Daytona Beach, FL	(22.0)	26	Idaho Falls, ID	24.1
271	Bethesda-Frederick, MD M.D.	(15.6)	135	Denver-Aurora, CO	(0.3)	NA	Indianapolis, IN**	NA
NA	Billings, MT**	NA	79	Des Moines-West Des Moines, IA	6.9	298	Iowa City, IA	(19.2)
3	Binghamton, NY	71.4	NA	Detroit (greater), MI**	NA	157	Jacksonville, FL	(3.3)
NA	Birmingham-Hoover, AL**	NA	168	Detroit-Livonia-Dearborn, MI M.D.	(4.8)	NA	Jacksonville, NC**	NA
4	Bismarck, ND	47.0	NA	Dothan, AL**	NA	206	Jackson, MS	(7.8)
100	Blacksburg, VA	3.5	324	Dover, DE	(32.1)	279	Jackson, TN	(17.2)
291	Bloomington-Normal, IL	(18.3)	286	Dubuque, IA	(17.8)	218	Janesville, WI	(9.4)
32	Bloomington, IN	21.5	NA	Duluth, MN-WI**	NA	256	Jefferson City, MO	(14.1)
178	Boise City-Nampa, ID	(5.6)	233	Durham-Chapel Hill, NC	(11.1)	49	Johnson City, TN	15.9
149	Boston (greater), MA-NH	(2.5)	303	Eau Claire, WI	(19.9)	142	Johnstown, PA	(1.1)
191	Boston-Quincy, MA M.D.	(6.5)	127	Edison, NJ M.D.	0.9	6	Jonesboro, AR	41.2
43	Boulder, CO	17.9	178	El Centro, CA	(5.6)	113	Joplin, MO	2.2
219	Bowling Green, KY	(9.5)	244	El Paso, TX	(12.1)	NA	Kankakee-Bradley, IL**	NA
5	Bremerton-Silverdale, WA	44.1	110	Elizabethtown, KY	2.4	NA	Kansas City, MO-KS**	NA
75	Bridgeport-Stamford, CT	7.7	263	Elmira, NY	(15.0)	19	Kennewick-Pasco-Richland, WA	27.2
325	Brownsville-Harlingen, TX	(33.3)	216	Erie, PA	(9.2)	257	Killeen-Temple-Fort Hood, TX	(14.2)
273	Brunswick, GA	(15.8)	NA	Eugene-Springfield, OR**	NA	109	Kingsport, TN-VA	2.5
228	Buffalo-Niagara Falls, NY	(10.7)	67	Evansville, IN-KY	9.4	232	Kingston, NY	(11.0)
173	Burlington, NC	(5.0)	255	Fairbanks, AK	(14.0)	129	Knoxville, TN	0.7
265	Cambridge-Newton, MA M.D.	(15.1)	257	Fargo, ND-MN	(14.2)	2	Kokomo, IN	90.3
22	Camden, NJ M.D.	25.4	229	Farmington, NM	(10.8)	210	La Crosse, WI-MN	(8.2)
67	Canton, OH	9.4	154	Fayetteville, NC	(2.8)	146	Lafayette, IN	(1.6)
274	Cape Coral-Fort Myers, FL	(15.9)	104	Flagstaff, AZ	3.0	250	Lafayette, LA	(12.9)
194	Cape Girardeau, MO-IL	(6.8)	61	Flint, MI	10.5	NA	Lake Co.-Kenosha Co., IL-WI M.D.**	NA
293	Carson City, NV	(18.8)	NA	Florence-Muscle Shoals, AL**	NA	NA	Lake Havasu City-Kingman, AZ**	NA
315	Casper, WY	(26.3)	82	Florence, SC	6.5	292	Lakeland, FL	(18.4)
285	Cedar Rapids, IA	(17.5)	80	Fond du Lac, WI	6.6	65	Lancaster, PA	9.6
NA	Champaign-Urbana, IL**	NA	308	Fort Collins-Loveland, CO	(21.9)	117	Lansing-East Lansing, MI	1.7

Note: All listings are for Metropolitan Statistical Areas (M.S.A.s) except for those ending with "M.D." Listings with "M.D." are Metropolitan Divisions which are smaller parts of eleven large M.S.A.s. See explanatory note at beginning of metropolitan area section.

Alpha Order - Metro Area (continued)

RANK	METROPOLITAN AREA	% CHANGE	RANK	METROPOLITAN AREA	% CHANGE	RANK	METROPOLITAN AREA	% CHANGE
327	Laredo, TX	(48.3)	52	Oklahoma City, OK	14.9	114	Savannah, GA	2.1
35	Las Cruces, NM	19.8	301	Olympia, WA	(19.6)	48	Scranton--Wilkes-Barre, PA	16.6
169	Las Vegas-Paradise, NV	(4.9)	40	Omaha-Council Bluffs, NE-IA	18.5	167	Seattle (greater), WA	(4.4)
13	Lawrence, KS	29.7	106	Orlando, FL	2.8	178	Seattle-Bellevue-Everett, WA M.D.	(5.6)
289	Lawton, OK	(18.2)	NA	Oshkosh-Neenah, WI**	NA	323	Sebastian-Vero Beach, FL	(31.2)
144	Lebanon, PA	(1.4)	84	Owensboro, KY	6.2	NA	Sheboygan, WI**	NA
83	Lewiston-Auburn, ME	6.4	247	Oxnard-Thousand Oaks, CA	(12.8)	85	Sherman-Denison, TX	6.1
NA	Lexington-Fayette, KY**	NA	86	Palm Bay-Melbourne, FL	5.9	55	Sioux City, IA-NE-SD	13.9
59	Lima, OH	11.2	317	Palm Coast, FL	(27.8)	43	Sioux Falls, SD	17.9
97	Lincoln, NE	3.7	208	Panama City-Lynn Haven, FL	(7.9)	134	South Bend-Mishawaka, IN-MI	(0.2)
97	Little Rock, AR	3.7	94	Pascagoula, MS	4.3	60	Spartanburg, SC	10.8
117	Logan, UT-ID	1.7	47	Peabody, MA M.D.	16.7	222	Spokane, WA	(10.1)
299	Longview, TX	(19.4)	31	Pensacola, FL	22.2	215	Springfield, IL	(9.1)
73	Longview, WA	8.8	235	Peoria, IL	(11.2)	261	Springfield, MA	(14.7)
202	Los Angeles County, CA M.D.	(7.4)	91	Philadelphia (greater) PA-NJ-MD-DE	4.4	135	Springfield, MO	(0.3)
196	Los Angeles (greater), CA	(6.9)	89	Philadelphia, PA M.D.	5.0	307	Springfield, OH	(21.5)
63	Louisville, KY-IN	10.1	169	Phoenix-Mesa-Scottsdale, AZ	(4.9)	43	State College, PA	17.9
25	Lubbock, TX	24.3	74	Pine Bluff, AR	8.5	224	Stockton, CA	(10.2)
138	Lynchburg, VA	(0.8)	227	Pittsburgh, PA	(10.4)	8	St. Cloud, MN	32.8
295	Macon, GA	(19.0)	107	Pittsfield, MA	2.7	11	St. Joseph, MO-KS	30.6
158	Madera, CA	(3.6)	211	Pocatello, ID	(8.3)	276	St. Louis, MO-IL	(16.6)
189	Madison, WI	(6.3)	46	Port St. Lucie, FL	17.4	266	Sumter, SC	(15.2)
211	Manchester-Nashua, NH	(8.3)	NA	Portland-Vancouver, OR-WA**	NA	204	Syracuse, NY	(7.7)
9	Manhattan, KS	32.1	58	Portland, ME	12.1	138	Tacoma, WA M.D.	(0.8)
19	Mankato-North Mankato, MN	27.2	107	Poughkeepsie, NY	2.7	161	Tallahassee, FL	(3.9)
17	Mansfield, OH	27.8	178	Prescott, AZ	(5.6)	305	Tampa-St Petersburg, FL	(20.4)
326	McAllen-Edinburg-Mission, TX	(37.6)	54	Provo-Orem, UT	14.2	NA	Terre Haute, IN**	NA
286	Medford, OR	(17.8)	NA	Pueblo, CO**	NA	37	Texarkana, TX-Texarkana, AR	19.3
260	Memphis, TN-MS-AR	(14.4)	144	Punta Gorda, FL	(1.4)	24	Toledo, OH	24.5
96	Merced, CA	4.1	272	Racine, WI	(15.7)	69	Topeka, KS	9.0
148	Miami (greater), FL	(2.2)	302	Raleigh-Cary, NC	(19.7)	38	Trenton-Ewing, NJ	19.0
138	Miami-Dade County, FL M.D.	(0.8)	29	Rapid City, SD	22.7	281	Tucson, AZ	(17.3)
132	Michigan City-La Porte, IN	0.4	320	Reading, PA	(29.5)	104	Tulsa, OK	3.0
222	Midland, TX	(10.1)	12	Redding, CA	30.0	NA	Tuscaloosa, AL**	NA
91	Milwaukee, WI	4.4	299	Reno-Sparks, NV	(19.4)	294	Tyler, TX	(18.9)
213	Minneapolis-St. Paul, MN-WI	(8.5)	177	Richmond, VA	(5.5)	200	Utica-Rome, NY	(7.3)
NA	Missoula, MT**	NA	126	Riverside-San Bernardino, CA	1.0	319	Valdosta, GA	(28.8)
199	Mobile, AL	(7.2)	87	Roanoke, VA	5.8	277	Vallejo-Fairfield, CA	(16.8)
233	Modesto, CA	(11.1)	186	Rochester, MN	(6.1)	103	Victoria, TX	3.1
235	Monroe, LA	(11.2)	99	Rochester, NY	3.6	279	Virginia Beach-Norfolk, VA-NC	(17.2)
314	Monroe, MI	(25.8)	100	Rockford, IL	3.5	257	Visalia-Porterville, CA	(14.2)
NA	Montgomery, AL**	NA	62	Rockingham County, NH M.D.	10.3	322	Waco, TX	(30.6)
77	Morristown, TN	7.1	269	Rocky Mount, NC	(15.5)	149	Warner Robins, GA	(2.5)
23	Mount Vernon-Anacortes, WA	25.0	267	Rome, GA	(15.3)	NA	Warren-Farmington Hills, MI M.D.**	NA
238	Muncie, IN	(11.3)	224	Sacramento, CA	(10.2)	247	Washington (greater) DC-VA-MD-WV	(12.8)
220	Muskegon-Norton Shores, MI	(9.6)	209	Saginaw, MI	(8.0)	247	Washington, DC-VA-MD-WV M.D.	(12.8)
283	Myrtle Beach, SC	(17.4)	117	Salem, OR	1.7	240	Waterloo-Cedar Falls, IA	(11.6)
57	Napa, CA	12.7	40	Salinas, CA	18.5	26	Wausau, WI	24.1
65	Naples-Marco Island, FL	9.6	312	Salisbury, MD	(24.2)	175	Wenatchee, WA	(5.4)
165	Nashville-Davidson, TN	(4.2)	102	Salt Lake City, UT	3.3	153	West Palm Beach, FL M.D.	(2.6)
253	Nassau-Suffolk, NY M.D.	(13.5)	252	San Angelo, TX	(13.3)	275	Wichita Falls, TX	(16.1)
131	New Haven-Milford, CT	0.6	122	San Antonio, TX	1.5	34	Wichita, KS	19.9
NA	New Orleans, LA**	NA	235	San Diego, CA	(11.2)	16	Williamsport, PA	28.9
125	New York (greater), NY-NJ-PA	1.2	117	San Francisco (greater), CA	1.7	304	Wilmington, DE-MD-NJ M.D.	(20.0)
133	New York-W. Plains NY-NJ M.D.	0.3	178	San Francisco-S. Mateo, CA M.D.	(5.6)	243	Wilmington, NC	(11.9)
76	Newark-Union, NJ-PA M.D.	7.6	184	San Jose, CA	(5.7)	111	Winchester, VA-WV	2.3
196	North Port-Bradenton-Sarasota, FL	(6.9)	10	San Luis Obispo, CA	31.7	111	Winston-Salem, NC	2.3
200	Norwich-New London, CT	(7.3)	1	Sandusky, OH	374.8	238	Worcester, MA	(11.3)
94	Oakland-Fremont, CA M.D.	4.3	160	Santa Ana-Anaheim, CA M.D.	(3.8)	128	Yakima, WA	0.8
196	Ocala, FL	(6.9)	245	Santa Barbara-Santa Maria, CA	(12.6)	242	York-Hanover, PA	(11.8)
175	Ocean City, NJ	(5.4)	33	Santa Cruz-Watsonville, CA	20.8	90	Yuba City, CA	4.5
193	Odessa, TX	(6.6)	69	Santa Fe, NM	9.0	129	Yuma, AZ	0.7
286	Ogden-Clearfield, UT	(17.8)	231	Santa Rosa-Petaluma, CA	(10.9)			

Source: CQ Press using reported data from the F.B.I. "Crime in the United States 2011"
*Motor vehicle theft includes the theft or attempted theft of a self-propelled vehicle. Excludes motorboats, construction equipment, airplanes, and farming equipment. **Not available.

Rank Order - Metro Area

39. Percent Change in Motor Vehicle Theft Rate: 2010 to 2011 (continued)
National Percent Change = 4.0% Decrease*

RANK	METROPOLITAN AREA	% CHANGE	RANK	METROPOLITAN AREA	% CHANGE	RANK	METROPOLITAN AREA	% CHANGE
1	Sandusky, OH	374.8	61	Flint, MI	10.5	117	San Francisco (greater), CA	1.7
2	Kokomo, IN	90.3	62	Rockingham County, NH M.D.	10.3	122	San Antonio, TX	1.5
3	Binghamton, NY	71.4	63	Louisville, KY-IN	10.1	123	Green Bay, WI	1.4
4	Bismarck, ND	47.0	64	Akron, OH	9.8	124	Albuquerque, NM	1.3
5	Bremerton-Silverdale, WA	44.1	65	Lancaster, PA	9.6	125	New York (greater), NY-NJ-PA	1.2
6	Jonesboro, AR	41.2	65	Naples-Marco Island, FL	9.6	126	Riverside-San Bernardino, CA	1.0
7	Columbus, IN	40.7	67	Canton, OH	9.4	127	Edison, NJ M.D.	0.9
8	St. Cloud, MN	32.8	67	Evansville, IN-KY	9.4	128	Yakima, WA	0.8
9	Manhattan, KS	32.1	69	Clarksville, TN-KY	9.0	129	Knoxville, TN	0.7
10	San Luis Obispo, CA	31.7	69	Santa Fe, NM	9.0	129	Yuma, AZ	0.7
11	St. Joseph, MO-KS	30.6	69	Topeka, KS	9.0	131	New Haven-Milford, CT	0.6
12	Redding, CA	30.0	72	Allentown, PA-NJ	8.9	132	Michigan City-La Porte, IN	0.4
13	Lawrence, KS	29.7	73	Longview, WA	8.8	133	New York-W. Plains NY-NJ M.D.	0.3
14	Glens Falls, NY	29.5	74	Pine Bluff, AR	8.5	134	South Bend-Mishawaka, IN-MI	(0.2)
15	Anderson, SC	29.2	75	Bridgeport-Stamford, CT	7.7	135	Denver-Aurora, CO	(0.3)
16	Williamsport, PA	28.9	76	Newark-Union, NJ-PA M.D.	7.6	135	Springfield, MO	(0.3)
17	Mansfield, OH	27.8	77	Columbia, MO	7.1	137	Gainesville, GA	(0.4)
18	Fort Wayne, IN	27.3	77	Morristown, TN	7.1	138	Lynchburg, VA	(0.8)
19	Kennewick-Pasco-Richland, WA	27.2	79	Des Moines-West Des Moines, IA	6.9	138	Miami-Dade County, FL M.D.	(0.8)
19	Mankato-North Mankato, MN	27.2	80	Chico, CA	6.6	138	Tacoma, WA M.D.	(0.8)
21	Alexandria, LA	27.1	80	Fond du Lac, WI	6.6	141	Fresno, CA	(0.9)
22	Camden, NJ M.D.	25.4	82	Florence, SC	6.5	142	Johnstown, PA	(1.1)
23	Mount Vernon-Anacortes, WA	25.0	83	Lewiston-Auburn, ME	6.4	143	Dayton, OH	(1.3)
24	Toledo, OH	24.5	84	Owensboro, KY	6.2	144	Lebanon, PA	(1.4)
25	Lubbock, TX	24.3	85	Sherman-Denison, TX	6.1	144	Punta Gorda, FL	(1.4)
26	Idaho Falls, ID	24.1	86	Palm Bay-Melbourne, FL	5.9	146	Lafayette, IN	(1.6)
26	Wausau, WI	24.1	87	Roanoke, VA	5.8	147	Atlantic City, NJ	(2.1)
28	Holland-Grand Haven, MI	23.8	88	Ames, IA	5.4	148	Miami (greater), FL	(2.2)
29	Rapid City, SD	22.7	89	Philadelphia, PA M.D.	5.0	149	Boston (greater), MA-NH	(2.5)
30	Corvallis, OR	22.6	90	Yuba City, CA	4.5	149	Charlottesville, VA	(2.5)
31	Pensacola, FL	22.2	91	Asheville, NC	4.4	149	Chattanooga, TN-GA	(2.5)
32	Bloomington, IN	21.5	91	Milwaukee, WI	4.4	149	Warner Robins, GA	(2.5)
33	Santa Cruz-Watsonville, CA	20.8	91	Philadelphia (greater) PA-NJ-MD-DE	4.4	153	West Palm Beach, FL M.D.	(2.6)
34	Wichita, KS	19.9	94	Oakland-Fremont, CA M.D.	4.3	154	Fayetteville, NC	(2.8)
35	Las Cruces, NM	19.8	94	Pascagoula, MS	4.3	155	Hartford, CT	(3.0)
36	Grand Forks, ND-MN	19.5	96	Merced, CA	4.1	156	Corpus Christi, TX	(3.1)
37	Texarkana, TX-Texarkana, AR	19.3	97	Lincoln, NE	3.7	157	Jacksonville, FL	(3.3)
38	Trenton-Ewing, NJ	19.0	97	Little Rock, AR	3.7	158	Madera, CA	(3.6)
39	Cleveland, TN	18.7	99	Rochester, NY	3.6	159	Hickory, NC	(3.7)
40	Omaha-Council Bluffs, NE-IA	18.5	100	Blacksburg, VA	3.5	160	Santa Ana-Anaheim, CA M.D.	(3.8)
40	Salinas, CA	18.5	100	Rockford, IL	3.5	161	Barnstable Town, MA	(3.9)
42	Harrisburg-Carlisle, PA	18.4	102	Salt Lake City, UT	3.3	161	Fort Smith, AR-OK	(3.9)
43	Boulder, CO	17.9	103	Victoria, TX	3.1	161	Tallahassee, FL	(3.9)
43	Sioux Falls, SD	17.9	104	Flagstaff, AZ	3.0	164	Fort Lauderdale, FL M.D.	(4.1)
43	State College, PA	17.9	104	Tulsa, OK	3.0	165	Dalton, GA	(4.2)
46	Port St. Lucie, FL	17.4	106	Orlando, FL	2.8	165	Nashville-Davidson, TN	(4.2)
47	Peabody, MA M.D.	16.7	107	Pittsfield, MA	2.7	167	Seattle (greater), WA	(4.4)
48	Scranton--Wilkes-Barre, PA	16.6	107	Poughkeepsie, NY	2.7	168	Detroit-Livonia-Dearborn, MI M.D.	(4.8)
49	Johnson City, TN	15.9	109	Kingsport, TN-VA	2.5	169	Bangor, ME	(4.9)
50	Grand Junction, CO	15.7	110	Elizabethtown, KY	2.4	169	Dallas-Plano-Irving, TX M.D.	(4.9)
51	Cleveland-Elyria-Mentor, OH	15.3	111	Winchester, VA-WV	2.3	169	Las Vegas-Paradise, NV	(4.9)
52	Oklahoma City, OK	14.9	111	Winston-Salem, NC	2.3	169	Phoenix-Mesa-Scottsdale, AZ	(4.9)
53	Greenville, SC	14.4	113	Joplin, MO	2.2	173	Burlington, NC	(5.0)
54	Provo-Orem, UT	14.2	114	Savannah, GA	2.1	174	Dallas (greater), TX	(5.3)
55	Sioux City, IA-NE-SD	13.9	115	Harrisonburg, VA	2.0	175	Ocean City, NJ	(5.4)
56	Danville, IL	13.0	116	Atlanta, GA	1.9	175	Wenatchee, WA	(5.4)
57	Napa, CA	12.7	117	Goldsboro, NC	1.7	177	Richmond, VA	(5.5)
58	Portland, ME	12.1	117	Lansing-East Lansing, MI	1.7	178	Appleton, WI	(5.6)
59	Lima, OH	11.2	117	Logan, UT-ID	1.7	178	Boise City-Nampa, ID	(5.6)
60	Spartanburg, SC	10.8	117	Salem, OR	1.7	178	El Centro, CA	(5.6)

Note: All listings are for Metropolitan Statistical Areas (M.S.A.s) except for those ending with "M.D." Listings with "M.D." are Metropolitan Divisions which are smaller parts of eleven large M.S.A.s. See explanatory note at beginning of metropolitan area section.

Rank Order - Metro Area (continued)

RANK	METROPOLITAN AREA	% CHANGE
178	Prescott, AZ	(5.6)
178	San Francisco-S. Mateo, CA M.D.	(5.6)
178	Seattle-Bellevue-Everett, WA M.D.	(5.6)
184	Fort Worth-Arlington, TX M.D.	(5.7)
184	San Jose, CA	(5.7)
186	Beaumont-Port Arthur, TX	(6.1)
186	Rochester, MN	(6.1)
188	Greeley, CO	(6.2)
189	Hinesville, GA	(6.3)
189	Madison, WI	(6.3)
191	Bend, OR	(6.5)
191	Boston-Quincy, MA M.D.	(6.5)
193	Odessa, TX	(6.6)
194	Cape Girardeau, MO-IL	(6.8)
194	Cincinnati-Middletown, OH-KY-IN	(6.8)
196	Los Angeles (greater), CA	(6.9)
196	North Port-Bradenton-Sarasota, FL	(6.9)
196	Ocala, FL	(6.9)
199	Mobile, AL	(7.2)
200	Norwich-New London, CT	(7.3)
200	Utica-Rome, NY	(7.3)
202	Amarillo, TX	(7.4)
202	Los Angeles County, CA M.D.	(7.4)
204	Austin-Round Rock, TX	(7.7)
204	Syracuse, NY	(7.7)
206	Altoona, PA	(7.8)
206	Jackson, MS	(7.8)
208	Panama City-Lynn Haven, FL	(7.9)
209	Saginaw, MI	(8.0)
210	La Crosse, WI-MN	(8.2)
211	Manchester-Nashua, NH	(8.3)
211	Pocatello, ID	(8.3)
213	Minneapolis-St. Paul, MN-WI	(8.5)
214	Gulfport-Biloxi, MS	(8.6)
215	Springfield, IL	(9.1)
216	Bakersfield, CA	(9.2)
216	Erie, PA	(9.2)
218	Janesville, WI	(9.4)
219	Bowling Green, KY	(9.5)
220	Hot Springs, AR	(9.6)
220	Muskegon-Norton Shores, MI	(9.6)
222	Midland, TX	(10.1)
222	Spokane, WA	(10.1)
224	Baltimore-Towson, MD	(10.2)
224	Sacramento, CA	(10.2)
224	Stockton, CA	(10.2)
227	Pittsburgh, PA	(10.4)
228	Buffalo-Niagara Falls, NY	(10.7)
229	Augusta, GA-SC	(10.8)
229	Farmington, NM	(10.8)
231	Santa Rosa-Petaluma, CA	(10.9)
232	Kingston, NY	(11.0)
233	Durham-Chapel Hill, NC	(11.1)
233	Modesto, CA	(11.1)
235	Monroe, LA	(11.2)
235	Peoria, IL	(11.2)
235	San Diego, CA	(11.2)
238	Muncie, IN	(11.3)
238	Worcester, MA	(11.3)
240	Waterloo-Cedar Falls, IA	(11.6)
241	Decatur, IL	(11.7)
242	York-Hanover, PA	(11.8)
243	Wilmington, NC	(11.9)
244	El Paso, TX	(12.1)
245	Santa Barbara-Santa Maria, CA	(12.6)
246	Hanford-Corcoran, CA	(12.7)
247	Oxnard-Thousand Oaks, CA	(12.8)
247	Washington (greater) DC-VA-MD-WV	(12.8)
247	Washington, DC-VA-MD-WV M.D.	(12.8)
250	Lafayette, LA	(12.9)
251	Crestview-Fort Walton Beach, FL	(13.1)
252	San Angelo, TX	(13.3)
253	Nassau-Suffolk, NY M.D.	(13.5)
254	Columbus, OH	(13.9)
255	Fairbanks, AK	(14.0)
256	Jefferson City, MO	(14.1)
257	Fargo, ND-MN	(14.2)
257	Killeen-Temple-Fort Hood, TX	(14.2)
257	Visalia-Porterville, CA	(14.2)
260	Memphis, TN-MS-AR	(14.4)
261	Gainesville, FL	(14.7)
261	Springfield, MA	(14.7)
263	Elmira, NY	(15.0)
263	Grand Rapids-Wyoming, MI	(15.0)
265	Cambridge-Newton, MA M.D.	(15.1)
266	Sumter, SC	(15.2)
267	Rome, GA	(15.3)
268	Bellingham, WA	(15.4)
269	Hagerstown-Martinsburg, MD-WV	(15.5)
269	Rocky Mount, NC	(15.5)
271	Bethesda-Frederick, MD M.D.	(15.6)
272	Racine, WI	(15.7)
273	Brunswick, GA	(15.8)
274	Cape Coral-Fort Myers, FL	(15.9)
275	Wichita Falls, TX	(16.1)
276	St. Louis, MO-IL	(16.6)
277	Vallejo-Fairfield, CA	(16.8)
278	Danville, VA	(16.9)
279	Jackson, TN	(17.2)
279	Virginia Beach-Norfolk, VA-NC	(17.2)
281	Colorado Springs, CO	(17.3)
281	Tucson, AZ	(17.3)
283	Houma, LA	(17.4)
283	Myrtle Beach, SC	(17.4)
285	Cedar Rapids, IA	(17.5)
286	Dubuque, IA	(17.8)
286	Medford, OR	(17.8)
286	Ogden-Clearfield, UT	(17.8)
289	Abilene, TX	(18.2)
289	Lawton, OK	(18.2)
291	Bloomington-Normal, IL	(18.3)
292	Lakeland, FL	(18.4)
293	Carson City, NV	(18.8)
294	Tyler, TX	(18.9)
295	Cheyenne, WY	(19.0)
295	Macon, GA	(19.0)
297	Albany-Schenectady-Troy, NY	(19.1)
298	Iowa City, IA	(19.2)
299	Longview, TX	(19.4)
299	Reno-Sparks, NV	(19.4)
301	Olympia, WA	(19.6)
302	Raleigh-Cary, NC	(19.7)
303	Eau Claire, WI	(19.9)
304	Wilmington, DE-MD-NJ M.D.	(20.0)
305	Tampa-St Petersburg, FL	(20.4)
306	Battle Creek, MI	(20.9)
307	Springfield, OH	(21.5)
308	Fort Collins-Loveland, CO	(21.9)
309	Deltona-Daytona Beach, FL	(22.0)
310	Athens-Clarke County, GA	(22.5)
311	Bay City, MI	(23.1)
312	Salisbury, MD	(24.2)
313	Anchorage, AK	(24.4)
314	Monroe, MI	(25.8)
315	Casper, WY	(26.3)
316	Ann Arbor, MI	(26.8)
317	Palm Coast, FL	(27.8)
318	Albany, GA	(28.5)
319	Valdosta, GA	(28.8)
320	Reading, PA	(29.5)
321	College Station-Bryan, TX	(30.5)
322	Waco, TX	(30.6)
323	Sebastian-Vero Beach, FL	(31.2)
324	Dover, DE	(32.1)
325	Brownsville-Harlingen, TX	(33.3)
326	McAllen-Edinburg-Mission, TX	(37.6)
327	Laredo, TX	(48.3)
NA	Anniston-Oxford, AL**	NA
NA	Auburn, AL**	NA
NA	Baton Rouge, LA**	NA
NA	Billings, MT**	NA
NA	Birmingham-Hoover, AL**	NA
NA	Champaign-Urbana, IL**	NA
NA	Charleston, WV**	NA
NA	Charlotte-Gastonia, NC-SC**	NA
NA	Chicago (greater), IL-IN-WI**	NA
NA	Chicago-Joilet-Naperville, IL M.D.**	NA
NA	Columbus, GA-AL**	NA
NA	Cumberland, MD-WV**	NA
NA	Davenport, IA-IL**	NA
NA	Decatur, AL**	NA
NA	Detroit (greater), MI**	NA
NA	Dothan, AL**	NA
NA	Duluth, MN-WI**	NA
NA	Eugene-Springfield, OR**	NA
NA	Florence-Muscle Shoals, AL**	NA
NA	Gadsden, AL**	NA
NA	Gary, IN M.D.**	NA
NA	Great Falls, MT**	NA
NA	Houston, TX**	NA
NA	Huntsville, AL**	NA
NA	Indianapolis, IN**	NA
NA	Jacksonville, NC**	NA
NA	Kankakee-Bradley, IL**	NA
NA	Kansas City, MO-KS**	NA
NA	Lake Co.-Kenosha Co., IL-WI M.D.**	NA
NA	Lake Havasu City-Kingman, AZ**	NA
NA	Lexington-Fayette, KY**	NA
NA	Missoula, MT**	NA
NA	Montgomery, AL**	NA
NA	New Orleans, LA**	NA
NA	Oshkosh-Neenah, WI**	NA
NA	Portland-Vancouver, OR-WA**	NA
NA	Pueblo, CO**	NA
NA	Sheboygan, WI**	NA
NA	Terre Haute, IN**	NA
NA	Tuscaloosa, AL**	NA
NA	Warren-Farmington Hills, MI M.D.**	NA

Source: CQ Press using reported data from the F.B.I. "Crime in the United States 2011"
*Motor vehicle theft includes the theft or attempted theft of a self-propelled vehicle. Excludes motorboats, construction equipment, airplanes, and farming equipment. **Not available.

Alpha Order - Metro Area

40. Percent Change in Motor Vehicle Theft Rate: 2007 to 2011
National Percent Change = 37.1% Decrease*

RANK	METROPOLITAN AREA	% CHANGE	RANK	METROPOLITAN AREA	% CHANGE	RANK	METROPOLITAN AREA	% CHANGE
229	Abilene, TX	(44.1)	169	Charleston, WV	(36.8)	144	Fort Lauderdale, FL M.D.	(34.8)
128	Akron, OH	(32.5)	310	Charlotte-Gastonia, NC-SC	(63.2)	185	Fort Smith, AR-OK	(38.8)
144	Albany-Schenectady-Troy, NY	(34.8)	108	Charlottesville, VA	(29.5)	201	Fort Wayne, IN	(40.4)
135	Albany, GA	(33.5)	69	Chattanooga, TN-GA	(22.8)	96	Fort Worth-Arlington, TX M.D.	(27.9)
256	Albuquerque, NM	(48.4)	65	Cheyenne, WY	(22.3)	14	Fresno, CA	4.7
24	Alexandria, LA	(6.2)	NA	Chicago (greater), IL-IN-WI**	NA	NA	Gadsden, AL**	NA
61	Allentown, PA-NJ	(21.6)	NA	Chicago-Joilet-Naperville, IL M.D.**	NA	262	Gainesville, FL	(49.1)
210	Altoona, PA	(41.6)	119	Chico, CA	(31.8)	256	Gainesville, GA	(48.4)
271	Amarillo, TX	(50.7)	166	Cincinnati-Middletown, OH-KY-IN	(36.7)	NA	Gary, IN M.D.**	NA
138	Ames, IA	(33.7)	173	Clarksville, TN-KY	(37.4)	34	Glens Falls, NY	(13.0)
283	Anchorage, AK	(52.9)	166	Cleveland-Elyria-Mentor, OH	(36.7)	78	Goldsboro, NC	(24.9)
21	Anderson, SC	(3.8)	70	Cleveland, TN	(22.9)	113	Grand Forks, ND-MN	(31.0)
188	Ann Arbor, MI	(39.3)	196	College Station-Bryan, TX	(40.0)	172	Grand Junction, CO	(37.1)
NA	Anniston-Oxford, AL**	NA	106	Colorado Springs, CO	(29.4)	154	Grand Rapids-Wyoming, MI	(35.8)
258	Appleton, WI	(48.5)	135	Columbia, MO	(33.5)	NA	Great Falls, MT**	NA
78	Asheville, NC	(24.9)	NA	Columbus, GA-AL**	NA	234	Greeley, CO	(44.4)
182	Athens-Clarke County, GA	(38.6)	1	Columbus, IN	73.3	258	Green Bay, WI	(48.5)
115	Atlanta, GA	(31.5)	242	Columbus, OH	(45.9)	93	Greenville, SC	(27.0)
143	Atlantic City, NJ	(34.7)	235	Corpus Christi, TX	(44.6)	NA	Gulfport-Biloxi, MS**	NA
NA	Auburn, AL**	NA	156	Corvallis, OR	(36.0)	NA	Hagerstown-Martinsburg, MD-WV**	NA
104	Augusta, GA-SC	(29.0)	208	Crestview-Fort Walton Beach, FL	(41.3)	142	Hanford-Corcoran, CA	(34.4)
161	Austin-Round Rock, TX	(36.3)	NA	Cumberland, MD-WV**	NA	13	Harrisburg-Carlisle, PA	5.1
37	Bakersfield, CA	(14.4)	156	Dallas (greater), TX	(36.0)	282	Harrisonburg, VA	(52.4)
194	Baltimore-Towson, MD	(39.9)	180	Dallas-Plano-Irving, TX M.D.	(38.4)	229	Hartford, CT	(44.1)
18	Bangor, ME	(1.4)	NA	Dalton, GA**	NA	231	Hickory, NC	(44.2)
125	Barnstable Town, MA	(32.4)	NA	Danville, IL**	NA	4	Hinesville, GA	23.7
298	Baton Rouge, LA	(57.4)	134	Danville, VA	(33.4)	NA	Holland-Grand Haven, MI**	NA
255	Battle Creek, MI	(47.9)	NA	Davenport, IA-IL**	NA	83	Hot Springs, AR	(25.2)
304	Bay City, MI	(60.4)	237	Dayton, OH	(45.1)	81	Houma, LA	(25.1)
190	Beaumont-Port Arthur, TX	(39.4)	NA	Decatur, AL**	NA	NA	Houston, TX**	NA
279	Bellingham, WA	(52.1)	NA	Decatur, IL**	NA	NA	Huntsville, AL**	NA
289	Bend, OR	(54.8)	214	Deltona-Daytona Beach, FL	(42.4)	209	Idaho Falls, ID	(41.5)
277	Bethesda-Frederick, MD M.D.	(52.0)	183	Denver-Aurora, CO	(38.7)	140	Indianapolis, IN	(34.1)
NA	Billings, MT**	NA	100	Des Moines-West Des Moines, IA	(28.3)	129	Iowa City, IA	(32.6)
6	Binghamton, NY	19.8	NA	Detroit (greater), MI**	NA	306	Jacksonville, FL	(60.9)
NA	Birmingham-Hoover, AL**	NA	NA	Detroit-Livonia-Dearborn, MI M.D.**	NA	124	Jacksonville, NC	(32.3)
16	Bismarck, ND	(0.5)	NA	Dothan, AL**	NA	36	Jackson, MS	(14.0)
66	Blacksburg, VA	(22.5)	176	Dover, DE	(37.9)	299	Jackson, TN	(57.8)
NA	Bloomington-Normal, IL**	NA	240	Dubuque, IA	(45.7)	212	Janesville, WI	(42.0)
27	Bloomington, IN	(8.7)	117	Duluth, MN-WI	(31.6)	133	Jefferson City, MO	(33.3)
304	Boise City-Nampa, ID	(60.4)	NA	Durham-Chapel Hill, NC**	NA	110	Johnson City, TN	(30.2)
90	Boston (greater), MA-NH	(26.5)	268	Eau Claire, WI	(50.3)	272	Johnstown, PA	(51.1)
175	Boston-Quincy, MA M.D.	(37.6)	115	Edison, NJ M.D.	(31.5)	44	Jonesboro, AR	(18.3)
NA	Boulder, CO**	NA	203	El Centro, CA	(40.5)	95	Joplin, MO	(27.5)
33	Bowling Green, KY	(12.8)	280	El Paso, TX	(52.3)	NA	Kankakee-Bradley, IL**	NA
2	Bremerton-Silverdale, WA	45.0	59	Elizabethtown, KY	(21.5)	NA	Kansas City, MO-KS**	NA
49	Bridgeport-Stamford, CT	(20.1)	260	Elmira, NY	(48.8)	71	Kennewick-Pasco-Richland, WA	(23.3)
293	Brownsville-Harlingen, TX	(56.4)	101	Erie, PA	(28.5)	205	Killeen-Temple-Fort Hood, TX	(40.6)
266	Brunswick, GA	(49.9)	272	Eugene-Springfield, OR	(51.1)	201	Kingsport, TN-VA	(40.4)
191	Buffalo-Niagara Falls, NY	(39.5)	53	Evansville, IN-KY	(21.0)	73	Kingston, NY	(24.1)
96	Burlington, NC	(27.9)	NA	Fairbanks, AK**	NA	152	Knoxville, TN	(35.5)
179	Cambridge-Newton, MA M.D.	(38.1)	222	Fargo, ND-MN	(43.5)	39	Kokomo, IN	(16.1)
144	Camden, NJ M.D.	(34.8)	237	Farmington, NM	(45.1)	98	La Crosse, WI-MN	(28.1)
NA	Canton, OH**	NA	78	Fayetteville, NC	(24.9)	30	Lafayette, IN	(11.4)
311	Cape Coral-Fort Myers, FL	(65.1)	239	Flagstaff, AZ	(45.4)	292	Lafayette, LA	(56.2)
NA	Cape Girardeau, MO-IL**	NA	75	Flint, MI	(24.5)	NA	Lake Co.-Kenosha Co., IL-WI M.D.**	NA
92	Carson City, NV	(26.6)	NA	Florence-Muscle Shoals, AL**	NA	296	Lake Havasu City-Kingman, AZ	(57.0)
286	Casper, WY	(53.6)	135	Florence, SC	(33.5)	280	Lakeland, FL	(52.3)
148	Cedar Rapids, IA	(35.0)	48	Fond du Lac, WI	(19.7)	261	Lancaster, PA	(49.0)
NA	Champaign-Urbana, IL**	NA	267	Fort Collins-Loveland, CO	(50.1)	121	Lansing-East Lansing, MI	(32.1)

Note: All listings are for Metropolitan Statistical Areas (M.S.A.s) except for those ending with "M.D." Listings with "M.D." are Metropolitan Divisions which are smaller parts of eleven large M.S.A.s. See explanatory note at beginning of metropolitan area section.

Alpha Order - Metro Area (continued)

RANK	METROPOLITAN AREA	% CHANGE
313	Laredo, TX	(70.2)
28	Las Cruces, NM	(10.3)
308	Las Vegas-Paradise, NV	(61.7)
22	Lawrence, KS	(5.1)
119	Lawton, OK	(31.8)
151	Lebanon, PA	(35.4)
220	Lewiston-Auburn, ME	(43.0)
NA	Lexington-Fayette, KY**	NA
88	Lima, OH	(26.3)
57	Lincoln, NE	(21.3)
68	Little Rock, AR	(22.7)
84	Logan, UT-ID	(25.6)
193	Longview, TX	(39.8)
51	Longview, WA	(20.9)
123	Los Angeles County, CA M.D.	(32.2)
131	Los Angeles (greater), CA	(32.8)
109	Louisville, KY-IN	(29.8)
17	Lubbock, TX	(1.1)
160	Lynchburg, VA	(36.1)
90	Macon, GA	(26.5)
10	Madera, CA	10.6
165	Madison, WI	(36.6)
NA	Manchester-Nashua, NH**	NA
NA	Manhattan, KS**	NA
NA	Mankato-North Mankato, MN**	NA
5	Mansfield, OH	21.8
249	McAllen-Edinburg-Mission, TX	(47.1)
174	Medford, OR	(37.5)
232	Memphis, TN-MS-AR	(44.3)
58	Merced, CA	(21.4)
203	Miami (greater), FL	(40.5)
198	Miami-Dade County, FL M.D.	(40.1)
111	Michigan City-La Porte, IN	(30.7)
138	Midland, TX	(33.7)
211	Milwaukee, WI	(41.9)
196	Minneapolis-St. Paul, MN-WI	(40.0)
NA	Missoula, MT**	NA
103	Mobile, AL	(28.9)
125	Modesto, CA	(32.4)
218	Monroe, LA	(42.6)
42	Monroe, MI	(17.6)
NA	Montgomery, AL**	NA
54	Morristown, TN	(21.1)
242	Mount Vernon-Anacortes, WA	(45.9)
9	Muncie, IN	14.0
254	Muskegon-Norton Shores, MI	(47.5)
114	Myrtle Beach, SC	(31.3)
140	Napa, CA	(34.1)
242	Naples-Marco Island, FL	(45.9)
171	Nashville-Davidson, TN	(37.0)
192	Nassau-Suffolk, NY M.D.	(39.7)
NA	New Haven-Milford, CT**	NA
240	New Orleans, LA	(45.7)
81	New York (greater), NY-NJ-PA	(25.1)
74	New York-W. Plains NY-NJ M.D.	(24.4)
45	Newark-Union, NJ-PA M.D.	(18.6)
NA	North Port-Bradenton-Sarasota, FL**	NA
NA	Norwich-New London, CT**	NA
194	Oakland-Fremont, CA M.D.	(39.9)
277	Ocala, FL	(52.0)
221	Ocean City, NJ	(43.3)
232	Odessa, TX	(44.3)
207	Ogden-Clearfield, UT	(40.9)

RANK	METROPOLITAN AREA	% CHANGE
38	Oklahoma City, OK	(15.2)
295	Olympia, WA	(56.9)
67	Omaha-Council Bluffs, NE-IA	(22.6)
262	Orlando, FL	(49.1)
284	Oshkosh-Neenah, WI	(53.3)
NA	Owensboro, KY**	NA
200	Oxnard-Thousand Oaks, CA	(40.3)
246	Palm Bay-Melbourne, FL	(46.3)
302	Palm Coast, FL	(59.1)
63	Panama City-Lynn Haven, FL	(22.2)
290	Pascagoula, MS	(55.6)
3	Peabody, MA M.D.	29.7
87	Pensacola, FL	(25.9)
NA	Peoria, IL**	NA
163	Philadelphia (greater) PA-NJ-MD-DE	(36.5)
166	Philadelphia, PA M.D.	(36.7)
309	Phoenix-Mesa-Scottsdale, AZ	(62.6)
63	Pine Bluff, AR	(22.2)
287	Pittsburgh, PA	(54.0)
72	Pittsfield, MA	(23.8)
86	Pocatello, ID	(25.7)
228	Port St. Lucie, FL	(44.0)
156	Portland-Vancouver, OR-WA	(36.0)
77	Portland, ME	(24.8)
118	Poughkeepsie, NY	(31.7)
187	Prescott, AZ	(39.0)
222	Provo-Orem, UT	(43.5)
NA	Pueblo, CO**	NA
300	Punta Gorda, FL	(58.1)
252	Racine, WI	(47.4)
99	Raleigh-Cary, NC	(28.2)
11	Rapid City, SD	10.1
275	Reading, PA	(51.3)
8	Redding, CA	15.9
264	Reno-Sparks, NV	(49.2)
185	Richmond, VA	(38.8)
129	Riverside-San Bernardino, CA	(32.6)
62	Roanoke, VA	(22.1)
176	Rochester, MN	(37.9)
248	Rochester, NY	(46.7)
NA	Rockford, IL**	NA
75	Rockingham County, NH M.D.	(24.5)
198	Rocky Mount, NC	(40.1)
155	Rome, GA	(35.9)
206	Sacramento, CA	(40.7)
291	Saginaw, MI	(56.0)
284	Salem, OR	(53.3)
276	Salinas, CA	(51.8)
252	Salisbury, MD	(47.4)
112	Salt Lake City, UT	(30.9)
235	San Angelo, TX	(44.6)
46	San Antonio, TX	(19.6)
293	San Diego, CA	(56.4)
188	San Francisco (greater), CA	(39.3)
163	San Francisco-S. Mateo, CA M.D.	(36.5)
88	San Jose, CA	(26.3)
23	San Luis Obispo, CA	(5.6)
274	Sandusky, OH	(51.2)
156	Santa Ana-Anaheim, CA M.D.	(36.0)
219	Santa Barbara-Santa Maria, CA	(42.7)
12	Santa Cruz-Watsonville, CA	6.6
NA	Santa Fe, NM**	NA
183	Santa Rosa-Petaluma, CA	(38.7)

RANK	METROPOLITAN AREA	% CHANGE
216	Savannah, GA	(42.5)
46	Scranton--Wilkes-Barre, PA	(19.6)
222	Seattle (greater), WA	(43.5)
227	Seattle-Bellevue-Everett, WA M.D.	(43.9)
297	Sebastian-Vero Beach, FL	(57.3)
26	Sheboygan, WI	(7.3)
56	Sherman-Denison, TX	(21.2)
7	Sioux City, IA-NE-SD	17.2
15	Sioux Falls, SD	(0.1)
102	South Bend-Mishawaka, IN-MI	(28.8)
105	Spartanburg, SC	(29.1)
32	Spokane, WA	(11.9)
NA	Springfield, IL**	NA
144	Springfield, MA	(34.8)
19	Springfield, MO	(1.9)
268	Springfield, OH	(50.3)
106	State College, PA	(29.4)
216	Stockton, CA	(42.5)
29	St. Cloud, MN	(11.2)
31	St. Joseph, MO-KS	(11.8)
176	St. Louis, MO-IL	(37.9)
225	Sumter, SC	(43.7)
94	Syracuse, NY	(27.2)
213	Tacoma, WA M.D.	(42.2)
265	Tallahassee, FL	(49.3)
307	Tampa-St Petersburg, FL	(61.0)
NA	Terre Haute, IN**	NA
20	Texarkana, TX-Texarkana, AR	(3.6)
54	Toledo, OH	(21.1)
43	Topeka, KS	(18.0)
25	Trenton-Ewing, NJ	(6.4)
301	Tucson, AZ	(58.4)
132	Tulsa, OK	(33.0)
NA	Tuscaloosa, AL**	NA
40	Tyler, TX	(17.3)
169	Utica-Rome, NY	(36.8)
226	Valdosta, GA	(43.8)
149	Vallejo-Fairfield, CA	(35.2)
50	Victoria, TX	(20.8)
121	Virginia Beach-Norfolk, VA-NC	(32.1)
125	Visalia-Porterville, CA	(32.4)
303	Waco, TX	(59.7)
35	Warner Robins, GA	(13.6)
NA	Warren-Farmington Hills, MI M.D.**	NA
251	Washington (greater) DC-VA-MD-WV	(47.2)
247	Washington, DC-VA-MD-WV M.D.	(46.6)
214	Waterloo-Cedar Falls, IA	(42.4)
84	Wausau, WI	(25.6)
51	Wenatchee, WA	(20.9)
270	West Palm Beach, FL M.D.	(50.6)
288	Wichita Falls, TX	(54.6)
41	Wichita, KS	(17.5)
149	Williamsport, PA	(35.2)
181	Wilmington, DE-MD-NJ M.D.	(38.5)
NA	Wilmington, NC**	NA
249	Winchester, VA-WV	(47.1)
NA	Winston-Salem, NC**	NA
153	Worcester, MA	(35.6)
161	Yakima, WA	(36.3)
245	York-Hanover, PA	(46.0)
59	Yuba City, CA	(21.5)
312	Yuma, AZ	(65.5)

Source: CQ Press using reported data from the F.B.I. "Crime in the United States 2011"
*Motor vehicle theft includes the theft or attempted theft of a self-propelled vehicle. Excludes motorboats, construction equipment, airplanes, and farming equipment. **Not available.

Rank Order - Metro Area

40. Percent Change in Motor Vehicle Theft Rate: 2007 to 2011 (continued)
National Percent Change = 37.1% Decrease*

RANK	METROPOLITAN AREA	% CHANGE	RANK	METROPOLITAN AREA	% CHANGE	RANK	METROPOLITAN AREA	% CHANGE
1	Columbus, IN	73.3	61	Allentown, PA-NJ	(21.6)	121	Lansing-East Lansing, MI	(32.1)
2	Bremerton-Silverdale, WA	45.0	62	Roanoke, VA	(22.1)	121	Virginia Beach-Norfolk, VA-NC	(32.1)
3	Peabody, MA M.D.	29.7	63	Panama City-Lynn Haven, FL	(22.2)	123	Los Angeles County, CA M.D.	(32.2)
4	Hinesville, GA	23.7	63	Pine Bluff, AR	(22.2)	124	Jacksonville, NC	(32.3)
5	Mansfield, OH	21.8	65	Cheyenne, WY	(22.3)	125	Barnstable Town, MA	(32.4)
6	Binghamton, NY	19.8	66	Blacksburg, VA	(22.5)	125	Modesto, CA	(32.4)
7	Sioux City, IA-NE-SD	17.2	67	Omaha-Council Bluffs, NE-IA	(22.6)	125	Visalia-Porterville, CA	(32.4)
8	Redding, CA	15.9	68	Little Rock, AR	(22.7)	128	Akron, OH	(32.5)
9	Muncie, IN	14.0	69	Chattanooga, TN-GA	(22.8)	129	Iowa City, IA	(32.6)
10	Madera, CA	10.6	70	Cleveland, TN	(22.9)	129	Riverside-San Bernardino, CA	(32.6)
11	Rapid City, SD	10.1	71	Kennewick-Pasco-Richland, WA	(23.3)	131	Los Angeles (greater), CA	(32.8)
12	Santa Cruz-Watsonville, CA	6.6	72	Pittsfield, MA	(23.8)	132	Tulsa, OK	(33.0)
13	Harrisburg-Carlisle, PA	5.1	73	Kingston, NY	(24.1)	133	Jefferson City, MO	(33.3)
14	Fresno, CA	4.7	74	New York-W. Plains NY-NJ M.D.	(24.4)	134	Danville, VA	(33.4)
15	Sioux Falls, SD	(0.1)	75	Flint, MI	(24.5)	135	Albany, GA	(33.5)
16	Bismarck, ND	(0.5)	75	Rockingham County, NH M.D.	(24.5)	135	Columbia, MO	(33.5)
17	Lubbock, TX	(1.1)	77	Portland, ME	(24.8)	135	Florence, SC	(33.5)
18	Bangor, ME	(1.4)	78	Asheville, NC	(24.9)	138	Ames, IA	(33.7)
19	Springfield, MO	(1.9)	78	Fayetteville, NC	(24.9)	138	Midland, TX	(33.7)
20	Texarkana, TX-Texarkana, AR	(3.6)	78	Goldsboro, NC	(24.9)	140	Indianapolis, IN	(34.1)
21	Anderson, SC	(3.8)	81	Houma, LA	(25.1)	140	Napa, CA	(34.1)
22	Lawrence, KS	(5.1)	81	New York (greater), NY-NJ-PA	(25.1)	142	Hanford-Corcoran, CA	(34.4)
23	San Luis Obispo, CA	(5.6)	83	Hot Springs, AR	(25.2)	143	Atlantic City, NJ	(34.7)
24	Alexandria, LA	(6.2)	84	Logan, UT-ID	(25.6)	144	Albany-Schenectady-Troy, NY	(34.8)
25	Trenton-Ewing, NJ	(6.4)	84	Wausau, WI	(25.6)	144	Camden, NJ M.D.	(34.8)
26	Sheboygan, WI	(7.3)	86	Pocatello, ID	(25.7)	144	Fort Lauderdale, FL M.D.	(34.8)
27	Bloomington, IN	(8.7)	87	Pensacola, FL	(25.9)	144	Springfield, MA	(34.8)
28	Las Cruces, NM	(10.3)	88	Lima, OH	(26.3)	148	Cedar Rapids, IA	(35.0)
29	St. Cloud, MN	(11.2)	88	San Jose, CA	(26.3)	149	Vallejo-Fairfield, CA	(35.2)
30	Lafayette, IN	(11.4)	90	Boston (greater), MA-NH	(26.5)	149	Williamsport, PA	(35.2)
31	St. Joseph, MO-KS	(11.8)	90	Macon, GA	(26.5)	151	Lebanon, PA	(35.4)
32	Spokane, WA	(11.9)	92	Carson City, NV	(26.6)	152	Knoxville, TN	(35.5)
33	Bowling Green, KY	(12.8)	93	Greenville, SC	(27.0)	153	Worcester, MA	(35.6)
34	Glens Falls, NY	(13.0)	94	Syracuse, NY	(27.2)	154	Grand Rapids-Wyoming, MI	(35.8)
35	Warner Robins, GA	(13.6)	95	Joplin, MO	(27.5)	155	Rome, GA	(35.9)
36	Jackson, MS	(14.0)	96	Burlington, NC	(27.9)	156	Corvallis, OR	(36.0)
37	Bakersfield, CA	(14.4)	96	Fort Worth-Arlington, TX M.D.	(27.9)	156	Dallas (greater), TX	(36.0)
38	Oklahoma City, OK	(15.2)	98	La Crosse, WI-MN	(28.1)	156	Portland-Vancouver, OR-WA	(36.0)
39	Kokomo, IN	(16.1)	99	Raleigh-Cary, NC	(28.2)	156	Santa Ana-Anaheim, CA M.D.	(36.0)
40	Tyler, TX	(17.3)	100	Des Moines-West Des Moines, IA	(28.3)	160	Lynchburg, VA	(36.1)
41	Wichita, KS	(17.5)	101	Erie, PA	(28.5)	161	Austin-Round Rock, TX	(36.3)
42	Monroe, MI	(17.6)	102	South Bend-Mishawaka, IN-MI	(28.8)	161	Yakima, WA	(36.3)
43	Topeka, KS	(18.0)	103	Mobile, AL	(28.9)	163	Philadelphia (greater) PA-NJ-MD-DE	(36.5)
44	Jonesboro, AR	(18.3)	104	Augusta, GA-SC	(29.0)	163	San Francisco-S. Mateo, CA M.D.	(36.5)
45	Newark-Union, NJ-PA M.D.	(18.6)	105	Spartanburg, SC	(29.1)	165	Madison, WI	(36.6)
46	San Antonio, TX	(19.6)	106	Colorado Springs, CO	(29.4)	166	Cincinnati-Middletown, OH-KY-IN	(36.7)
46	Scranton--Wilkes-Barre, PA	(19.6)	106	State College, PA	(29.4)	166	Cleveland-Elyria-Mentor, OH	(36.7)
48	Fond du Lac, WI	(19.7)	108	Charlottesville, VA	(29.5)	166	Philadelphia, PA M.D.	(36.7)
49	Bridgeport-Stamford, CT	(20.1)	109	Louisville, KY-IN	(29.8)	169	Charleston, WV	(36.8)
50	Victoria, TX	(20.8)	110	Johnson City, TN	(30.2)	169	Utica-Rome, NY	(36.8)
51	Longview, WA	(20.9)	111	Michigan City-La Porte, IN	(30.7)	171	Nashville-Davidson, TN	(37.0)
51	Wenatchee, WA	(20.9)	112	Salt Lake City, UT	(30.9)	172	Grand Junction, CO	(37.1)
53	Evansville, IN-KY	(21.0)	113	Grand Forks, ND-MN	(31.0)	173	Clarksville, TN-KY	(37.4)
54	Morristown, TN	(21.1)	114	Myrtle Beach, SC	(31.3)	174	Medford, OR	(37.5)
54	Toledo, OH	(21.1)	115	Atlanta, GA	(31.5)	175	Boston-Quincy, MA M.D.	(37.6)
56	Sherman-Denison, TX	(21.2)	115	Edison, NJ M.D.	(31.5)	176	Dover, DE	(37.9)
57	Lincoln, NE	(21.3)	117	Duluth, MN-WI	(31.6)	176	Rochester, MN	(37.9)
58	Merced, CA	(21.4)	118	Poughkeepsie, NY	(31.7)	176	St. Louis, MO-IL	(37.9)
59	Elizabethtown, KY	(21.5)	119	Chico, CA	(31.8)	179	Cambridge-Newton, MA M.D.	(38.1)
59	Yuba City, CA	(21.5)	119	Lawton, OK	(31.8)	180	Dallas-Plano-Irving, TX M.D.	(38.4)

Note: All listings are for Metropolitan Statistical Areas (M.S.A.s) except for those ending with "M.D." Listings with "M.D." are Metropolitan Divisions which are smaller parts of eleven large M.S.A.s. See explanatory note at beginning of metropolitan area section.

Rank Order - Metro Area (continued)

RANK	METROPOLITAN AREA	% CHANGE
181	Wilmington, DE-MD-NJ M.D.	(38.5)
182	Athens-Clarke County, GA	(38.6)
183	Denver-Aurora, CO	(38.7)
183	Santa Rosa-Petaluma, CA	(38.7)
185	Fort Smith, AR-OK	(38.8)
185	Richmond, VA	(38.8)
187	Prescott, AZ	(39.0)
188	Ann Arbor, MI	(39.3)
188	San Francisco (greater), CA	(39.3)
190	Beaumont-Port Arthur, TX	(39.4)
191	Buffalo-Niagara Falls, NY	(39.5)
192	Nassau-Suffolk, NY M.D.	(39.7)
193	Longview, TX	(39.8)
194	Baltimore-Towson, MD	(39.9)
194	Oakland-Fremont, CA M.D.	(39.9)
196	College Station-Bryan, TX	(40.0)
196	Minneapolis-St. Paul, MN-WI	(40.0)
198	Miami-Dade County, FL M.D.	(40.1)
198	Rocky Mount, NC	(40.1)
200	Oxnard-Thousand Oaks, CA	(40.3)
201	Fort Wayne, IN	(40.4)
201	Kingsport, TN-VA	(40.4)
203	El Centro, CA	(40.5)
203	Miami (greater), FL	(40.5)
205	Killeen-Temple-Fort Hood, TX	(40.6)
206	Sacramento, CA	(40.7)
207	Ogden-Clearfield, UT	(40.9)
208	Crestview-Fort Walton Beach, FL	(41.3)
209	Idaho Falls, ID	(41.5)
210	Altoona, PA	(41.6)
211	Milwaukee, WI	(41.9)
212	Janesville, WI	(42.0)
213	Tacoma, WA M.D.	(42.2)
214	Deltona-Daytona Beach, FL	(42.4)
214	Waterloo-Cedar Falls, IA	(42.4)
216	Savannah, GA	(42.5)
216	Stockton, CA	(42.5)
218	Monroe, LA	(42.6)
219	Santa Barbara-Santa Maria, CA	(42.7)
220	Lewiston-Auburn, ME	(43.0)
221	Ocean City, NJ	(43.3)
222	Fargo, ND-MN	(43.5)
222	Provo-Orem, UT	(43.5)
222	Seattle (greater), WA	(43.5)
225	Sumter, SC	(43.7)
226	Valdosta, GA	(43.8)
227	Seattle-Bellevue-Everett, WA M.D.	(43.9)
228	Port St. Lucie, FL	(44.0)
229	Abilene, TX	(44.1)
229	Hartford, CT	(44.1)
231	Hickory, NC	(44.2)
232	Memphis, TN-MS-AR	(44.3)
232	Odessa, TX	(44.3)
234	Greeley, CO	(44.4)
235	Corpus Christi, TX	(44.6)
235	San Angelo, TX	(44.6)
237	Dayton, OH	(45.1)
237	Farmington, NM	(45.1)
239	Flagstaff, AZ	(45.4)
240	Dubuque, IA	(45.7)
240	New Orleans, LA	(45.7)
242	Columbus, OH	(45.9)
242	Mount Vernon-Anacortes, WA	(45.9)
242	Naples-Marco Island, FL	(45.9)
245	York-Hanover, PA	(46.0)
246	Palm Bay-Melbourne, FL	(46.3)
247	Washington, DC-VA-MD-WV M.D.	(46.6)
248	Rochester, NY	(46.7)
249	McAllen-Edinburg-Mission, TX	(47.1)
249	Winchester, VA-WV	(47.1)
251	Washington (greater) DC-VA-MD-WV	(47.2)
252	Racine, WI	(47.4)
252	Salisbury, MD	(47.4)
254	Muskegon-Norton Shores, MI	(47.5)
255	Battle Creek, MI	(47.9)
256	Albuquerque, NM	(48.4)
256	Gainesville, GA	(48.4)
258	Appleton, WI	(48.5)
258	Green Bay, WI	(48.5)
260	Elmira, NY	(48.8)
261	Lancaster, PA	(49.0)
262	Gainesville, FL	(49.1)
262	Orlando, FL	(49.1)
264	Reno-Sparks, NV	(49.2)
265	Tallahassee, FL	(49.3)
266	Brunswick, GA	(49.9)
267	Fort Collins-Loveland, CO	(50.1)
268	Eau Claire, WI	(50.3)
268	Springfield, OH	(50.3)
270	West Palm Beach, FL M.D.	(50.6)
271	Amarillo, TX	(50.7)
272	Eugene-Springfield, OR	(51.1)
272	Johnstown, PA	(51.1)
274	Sandusky, OH	(51.2)
275	Reading, PA	(51.3)
276	Salinas, CA	(51.8)
277	Bethesda-Frederick, MD M.D.	(52.0)
277	Ocala, FL	(52.0)
279	Bellingham, WA	(52.1)
280	El Paso, TX	(52.3)
280	Lakeland, FL	(52.3)
282	Harrisonburg, VA	(52.4)
283	Anchorage, AK	(52.9)
284	Oshkosh-Neenah, WI	(53.3)
284	Salem, OR	(53.3)
286	Casper, WY	(53.6)
287	Pittsburgh, PA	(54.0)
288	Wichita Falls, TX	(54.6)
289	Bend, OR	(54.8)
290	Pascagoula, MS	(55.6)
291	Saginaw, MI	(56.0)
292	Lafayette, LA	(56.2)
293	Brownsville-Harlingen, TX	(56.4)
293	San Diego, CA	(56.4)
295	Olympia, WA	(56.9)
296	Lake Havasu City-Kingman, AZ	(57.0)
297	Sebastian-Vero Beach, FL	(57.3)
298	Baton Rouge, LA	(57.4)
299	Jackson, TN	(57.8)
300	Punta Gorda, FL	(58.1)
301	Tucson, AZ	(58.4)
302	Palm Coast, FL	(59.1)
303	Waco, TX	(59.7)
304	Bay City, MI	(60.4)
304	Boise City-Nampa, ID	(60.4)
306	Jacksonville, FL	(60.9)
307	Tampa-St Petersburg, FL	(61.0)
308	Las Vegas-Paradise, NV	(61.7)
309	Phoenix-Mesa-Scottsdale, AZ	(62.6)
310	Charlotte-Gastonia, NC-SC	(63.2)
311	Cape Coral-Fort Myers, FL	(65.1)
312	Yuma, AZ	(65.5)
313	Laredo, TX	(70.2)
NA	Anniston-Oxford, AL**	NA
NA	Auburn, AL**	NA
NA	Billings, MT**	NA
NA	Birmingham-Hoover, AL**	NA
NA	Bloomington-Normal, IL**	NA
NA	Boulder, CO**	NA
NA	Canton, OH**	NA
NA	Cape Girardeau, MO-IL**	NA
NA	Champaign-Urbana, IL**	NA
NA	Chicago (greater), IL-IN-WI**	NA
NA	Chicago-Joilet-Naperville, IL M.D.**	NA
NA	Columbus, GA-AL**	NA
NA	Cumberland, MD-WV**	NA
NA	Dalton, GA**	NA
NA	Danville, IL**	NA
NA	Davenport, IA-IL**	NA
NA	Decatur, AL**	NA
NA	Decatur, IL**	NA
NA	Detroit (greater), MI**	NA
NA	Detroit-Livonia-Dearborn, MI M.D.**	NA
NA	Dothan, AL**	NA
NA	Durham-Chapel Hill, NC**	NA
NA	Fairbanks, AK**	NA
NA	Florence-Muscle Shoals, AL**	NA
NA	Gadsden, AL**	NA
NA	Gary, IN M.D.**	NA
NA	Great Falls, MT**	NA
NA	Gulfport-Biloxi, MS**	NA
NA	Hagerstown-Martinsburg, MD-WV**	NA
NA	Holland-Grand Haven, MI**	NA
NA	Houston, TX**	NA
NA	Huntsville, AL**	NA
NA	Kankakee-Bradley, IL**	NA
NA	Kansas City, MO-KS**	NA
NA	Lake Co.-Kenosha Co., IL-WI M.D.**	NA
NA	Lexington-Fayette, KY**	NA
NA	Manchester-Nashua, NH**	NA
NA	Manhattan, KS**	NA
NA	Mankato-North Mankato, MN**	NA
NA	Missoula, MT**	NA
NA	Montgomery, AL**	NA
NA	New Haven-Milford, CT**	NA
NA	North Port-Bradenton-Sarasota, FL**	NA
NA	Norwich-New London, CT**	NA
NA	Owensboro, KY**	NA
NA	Peoria, IL**	NA
NA	Pueblo, CO**	NA
NA	Rockford, IL**	NA
NA	Santa Fe, NM**	NA
NA	Springfield, IL**	NA
NA	Terre Haute, IN**	NA
NA	Tuscaloosa, AL**	NA
NA	Warren-Farmington Hills, MI M.D.**	NA
NA	Wilmington, NC**	NA
NA	Winston-Salem, NC**	NA

Source: CQ Press using reported data from the F.B.I. "Crime in the United States 2011"
*Motor vehicle theft includes the theft or attempted theft of a self-propelled vehicle. Excludes motorboats, construction equipment, airplanes, and farming equipment. **Not available.

Rank Order - Metro Area (continued)

RANK	METROPOLITAN AREA	% CHANGE
181	Wilmington, DE-MD-NJ M.D.	(38.5)
182	Athens-Clarke County, GA	(38.6)
183	Denver-Aurora, CO	(38.7)
183	Santa Rosa-Petaluma, CA	(38.7)
185	Fort Smith, AR-OK	(38.8)
185	Richmond, VA	(38.8)
187	Prescott, AZ	(39.0)
188	Ann Arbor, MI	(39.3)
188	San Francisco (greater), CA	(39.3)
190	Beaumont-Port Arthur, TX	(39.4)
191	Buffalo-Niagara Falls, NY	(39.5)
192	Nassau-Suffolk, NY M.D.	(39.7)
193	Longview, TX	(39.8)
194	Baltimore-Towson, MD	(39.9)
194	Oakland-Fremont, CA M.D.	(39.9)
196	College Station-Bryan, TX	(40.0)
196	Minneapolis-St. Paul, MN-WI	(40.0)
198	Miami-Dade County, FL M.D.	(40.1)
198	Rocky Mount, NC	(40.1)
200	Oxnard-Thousand Oaks, CA	(40.3)
201	Fort Wayne, IN	(40.4)
201	Kingsport, TN-VA	(40.4)
203	El Centro, CA	(40.5)
203	Miami (greater), FL	(40.5)
205	Killeen-Temple-Fort Hood, TX	(40.6)
206	Sacramento, CA	(40.7)
207	Ogden-Clearfield, UT	(40.9)
208	Crestview-Fort Walton Beach, FL	(41.3)
209	Idaho Falls, ID	(41.5)
210	Altoona, PA	(41.6)
211	Milwaukee, WI	(41.9)
212	Janesville, WI	(42.0)
213	Tacoma, WA M.D.	(42.2)
214	Deltona-Daytona Beach, FL	(42.4)
214	Waterloo-Cedar Falls, IA	(42.4)
216	Savannah, GA	(42.5)
216	Stockton, CA	(42.5)
218	Monroe, LA	(42.6)
219	Santa Barbara-Santa Maria, CA	(42.7)
220	Lewiston-Auburn, ME	(43.0)
221	Ocean City, NJ	(43.3)
222	Fargo, ND-MN	(43.5)
222	Provo-Orem, UT	(43.5)
222	Seattle (greater), WA	(43.5)
225	Sumter, SC	(43.7)
226	Valdosta, GA	(43.8)
227	Seattle-Bellevue-Everett, WA M.D.	(43.9)
228	Port St. Lucie, FL	(44.0)
229	Abilene, TX	(44.1)
229	Hartford, CT	(44.1)
231	Hickory, NC	(44.2)
232	Memphis, TN-MS-AR	(44.3)
232	Odessa, TX	(44.3)
234	Greeley, CO	(44.4)
235	Corpus Christi, TX	(44.6)
235	San Angelo, TX	(44.6)
237	Dayton, OH	(45.1)
237	Farmington, NM	(45.1)
239	Flagstaff, AZ	(45.4)
240	Dubuque, IA	(45.7)
240	New Orleans, LA	(45.7)
242	Columbus, OH	(45.9)
242	Mount Vernon-Anacortes, WA	(45.9)
242	Naples-Marco Island, FL	(45.9)
245	York-Hanover, PA	(46.0)
246	Palm Bay-Melbourne, FL	(46.3)
247	Washington, DC-VA-MD-WV M.D.	(46.6)
248	Rochester, NY	(46.7)
249	McAllen-Edinburg-Mission, TX	(47.1)
249	Winchester, VA-WV	(47.1)
251	Washington (greater) DC-VA-MD-WV	(47.2)
252	Racine, WI	(47.4)
252	Salisbury, MD	(47.4)
254	Muskegon-Norton Shores, MI	(47.5)
255	Battle Creek, MI	(47.9)
256	Albuquerque, NM	(48.4)
256	Gainesville, GA	(48.4)
258	Appleton, WI	(48.5)
258	Green Bay, WI	(48.5)
260	Elmira, NY	(48.8)
261	Lancaster, PA	(49.0)
262	Gainesville, FL	(49.1)
262	Orlando, FL	(49.1)
264	Reno-Sparks, NV	(49.2)
265	Tallahassee, FL	(49.3)
266	Brunswick, GA	(49.9)
267	Fort Collins-Loveland, CO	(50.1)
268	Eau Claire, WI	(50.3)
268	Springfield, OH	(50.3)
270	West Palm Beach, FL M.D.	(50.6)
271	Amarillo, TX	(50.7)
272	Eugene-Springfield, OR	(51.1)
272	Johnstown, PA	(51.1)
274	Sandusky, OH	(51.2)
275	Reading, PA	(51.3)
276	Salinas, CA	(51.8)
277	Bethesda-Frederick, MD M.D.	(52.0)
277	Ocala, FL	(52.0)
279	Bellingham, WA	(52.1)
280	El Paso, TX	(52.3)
280	Lakeland, FL	(52.3)
282	Harrisonburg, VA	(52.4)
283	Anchorage, AK	(52.9)
284	Oshkosh-Neenah, WI	(53.3)
284	Salem, OR	(53.3)
286	Casper, WY	(53.6)
287	Pittsburgh, PA	(54.0)
288	Wichita Falls, TX	(54.6)
289	Bend, OR	(54.8)
290	Pascagoula, MS	(55.6)
291	Saginaw, MI	(56.0)
292	Lafayette, LA	(56.2)
293	Brownsville-Harlingen, TX	(56.4)
293	San Diego, CA	(56.4)
295	Olympia, WA	(56.9)
296	Lake Havasu City-Kingman, AZ	(57.0)
297	Sebastian-Vero Beach, FL	(57.3)
298	Baton Rouge, LA	(57.4)
299	Jackson, TN	(57.8)
300	Punta Gorda, FL	(58.1)
301	Tucson, AZ	(58.4)
302	Palm Coast, FL	(59.1)
303	Waco, TX	(59.7)
304	Bay City, MI	(60.4)
304	Boise City-Nampa, ID	(60.4)
306	Jacksonville, FL	(60.9)
307	Tampa-St Petersburg, FL	(61.0)
308	Las Vegas-Paradise, NV	(61.7)
309	Phoenix-Mesa-Scottsdale, AZ	(62.6)
310	Charlotte-Gastonia, NC-SC	(63.2)
311	Cape Coral-Fort Myers, FL	(65.1)
312	Yuma, AZ	(65.5)
313	Laredo, TX	(70.2)
NA	Anniston-Oxford, AL**	NA
NA	Auburn, AL**	NA
NA	Billings, MT**	NA
NA	Birmingham-Hoover, AL**	NA
NA	Bloomington-Normal, IL**	NA
NA	Boulder, CO**	NA
NA	Canton, OH**	NA
NA	Cape Girardeau, MO-IL**	NA
NA	Champaign-Urbana, IL**	NA
NA	Chicago (greater), IL-IN-WI**	NA
NA	Chicago-Joilet-Naperville, IL M.D.**	NA
NA	Columbus, GA-AL**	NA
NA	Cumberland, MD-WV**	NA
NA	Dalton, GA**	NA
NA	Danville, IL**	NA
NA	Davenport, IA-IL**	NA
NA	Decatur, AL**	NA
NA	Decatur, IL**	NA
NA	Detroit (greater), MI**	NA
NA	Detroit-Livonia-Dearborn, MI M.D.**	NA
NA	Dothan, AL**	NA
NA	Durham-Chapel Hill, NC**	NA
NA	Fairbanks, AK**	NA
NA	Florence-Muscle Shoals, AL**	NA
NA	Gadsden, AL**	NA
NA	Gary, IN M.D.**	NA
NA	Great Falls, MT**	NA
NA	Gulfport-Biloxi, MS**	NA
NA	Hagerstown-Martinsburg, MD-WV**	NA
NA	Holland-Grand Haven, MI**	NA
NA	Houston, TX**	NA
NA	Huntsville, AL**	NA
NA	Kankakee-Bradley, IL**	NA
NA	Kansas City, MO-KS**	NA
NA	Lake Co.-Kenosha Co., IL-WI M.D.**	NA
NA	Lexington-Fayette, KY**	NA
NA	Manchester-Nashua, NH**	NA
NA	Manhattan, KS**	NA
NA	Mankato-North Mankato, MN**	NA
NA	Missoula, MT**	NA
NA	Montgomery, AL**	NA
NA	New Haven-Milford, CT**	NA
NA	North Port-Bradenton-Sarasota, FL**	NA
NA	Norwich-New London, CT**	NA
NA	Owensboro, KY**	NA
NA	Peoria, IL**	NA
NA	Pueblo, CO**	NA
NA	Rockford, IL**	NA
NA	Santa Fe, NM**	NA
NA	Springfield, IL**	NA
NA	Terre Haute, IN**	NA
NA	Tuscaloosa, AL**	NA
NA	Warren-Farmington Hills, MI M.D.**	NA
NA	Wilmington, NC**	NA
NA	Winston-Salem, NC**	NA

Source: CQ Press using reported data from the F.B.I. "Crime in the United States 2011"
*Motor vehicle theft includes the theft or attempted theft of a self-propelled vehicle. Excludes motorboats, construction equipment, airplanes, and farming equipment. **Not available.

II. City Crime Statistics
(for cities larger than 75,000 population)

Crimes in 2011 164	Property Crimes in 2011. 260
Crime Rate in 2011 168	Property Crime Rate in 2011 264
Percent Change in Crime Rate: 2010 to 2011. 172	Percent Change in Property Crime Rate: 2010 to 2011 . . . 268
Percent Change in Crime Rate: 2007 to 2011. 176	Percent Change in Property Crime Rate: 2007 to 2011 . . . 272
Violent Crimes in 2011. 180	Burglaries in 2011. 276
Violent Crime Rate in 2011 184	Burglary Rate in 2011. 280
Percent Change in Violent Crime Rate: 2010 to 2011 188	Percent Change in Burglary Rate: 2010 to 2011. 284
Percent Change in Violent Crime Rate: 2007 to 2011 192	Percent Change in Burglary Rate: 2007 to 2011. 288
Murders in 2011 196	Larceny-Thefts in 2011. 292
Murder Rate in 2011 200	Larceny-Theft Rate in 2011 296
Percent Change in Murder Rate: 2010 to 2011. 204	Percent Change in Larceny-Theft Rate: 2010 to 2011 300
Percent Change in Murder Rate: 2007 to 2011. 208	Percent Change in Larceny-Theft Rate: 2007 to 2011 304
Rapes in 2011 212	Motor Vehicle Thefts in 2011 308
Rape Rate in 2011 216	Motor Vehicle Theft Rate in 2011. 312
Percent Change in Rape Rate: 2010 to 2011. 220	Percent Change in Motor Vehicle Theft Rate:
Percent Change in Rape Rate: 2007 to 2011. 224	2010 to 2011. 316
Robberies in 2011 228	Percent Change in Motor Vehicle Theft Rate:
Robbery Rate in 2011 232	2007 to 2011. 320
Percent Change in Robbery Rate: 2010 to 2011. 236	Police Officers in 2011 324
Percent Change in Robbery Rate: 2007 to 2011. 240	Rate of Police Officers in 2011. 328
Aggravated Assaults in 2011. 244	Percent Change in Rate of Police Officers: 2010 to 2011. . 332
Aggravated Assault Rate in 2011 248	Percent Change in Rate of Police Officers:
Percent Change in Aggravated Assault Rate:	2007 to 2011. 336
2010 to 2011. 252	
Percent Change in Aggravated Assault Rate:	
2007 to 2011. 256	

Please note the following for Tables 41 through 84 and 88 through 90:

- All listings are for cities of 75,000 or more in population that reported data to the F.B.I. for 2011.

Alpha Order - City

41. Crimes in 2011
National Total = 10,266,737 Crimes*

RANK	CITY	CRIMES
205	Abilene, TX	4,812
79	Akron, OH	12,643
180	Albany, GA	5,359
175	Albany, NY	5,550
28	Albuquerque, NM	32,183
285	Alexandria, VA	3,433
386	Alhambra, CA	2,043
189	Allentown, PA	5,222
412	Allen, TX	1,598
94	Amarillo, TX	10,611
378	Amherst, NY	2,128
101	Anaheim, CA	9,774
83	Anchorage, AK	11,843
323	Ann Arbor, MI	2,810
210	Antioch, CA	4,691
424	Arlington Heights, IL	1,131
48	Arlington, TX	19,082
338	Arvada, CO	2,708
217	Asheville, NC	4,393
185	Athens-Clarke, GA	5,290
21	Atlanta, GA	36,241
88	Aurora, CO	11,323
215	Aurora, IL	4,457
13	Austin, TX	45,721
236	Avondale, AZ	4,165
55	Bakersfield, CA	16,706
399	Baldwin Park, CA	1,843
17	Baltimore, MD	38,709
63	Baton Rouge, LA	15,134
123	Beaumont, TX	7,725
393	Beaverton, OR	1,945
270	Bellevue, WA	3,679
380	Bellflower, CA	2,118
251	Bellingham, WA	3,937
347	Bend, OR	2,620
176	Berkeley, CA	5,546
384	Bethlehem, PA	2,081
194	Billings, MT	5,006
44	Birmingham, AL	21,004
383	Bloomington, IL	2,101
294	Bloomington, IN	3,316
NA	Bloomington, MN**	NA
319	Boca Raton, FL	2,854
162	Boise, ID	5,838
38	Boston, MA	24,697
329	Boulder, CO	2,766
417	Brick Twnshp, NJ	1,413
136	Bridgeport, CT	7,054
218	Brockton, MA	4,389
353	Broken Arrow, OK	2,431
NA	Brooklyn Park, MN**	NA
110	Brownsville, TX	8,687
293	Bryan, TX	3,331
382	Buena Park, CA	2,109
51	Buffalo, NY	17,555
333	Burbank, CA	2,746
275	Cambridge, MA	3,638
141	Camden, NJ	6,614
414	Canton Twnshp, MI	1,527
231	Cape Coral, FL	4,225
375	Carlsbad, CA	2,180
428	Carmel, IN	848
282	Carrollton, TX	3,528
316	Carson, CA	2,936
373	Cary, NC	2,201
187	Cedar Rapids, IA	5,237
416	Centennial, CO	1,515
312	Champaign, IL	3,013
118	Chandler, AZ	8,097
237	Charleston, SC	4,152
19	Charlotte, NC	36,795
82	Chattanooga, TN	12,095

RANK	CITY	CRIMES
317	Cheektowaga, NY	2,928
119	Chesapeake, VA	8,055
NA	Chicago, IL**	NA
358	Chico, CA	2,360
425	Chino Hills, CA	1,046
363	Chino, CA	2,319
166	Chula Vista, CA	5,677
362	Cicero, IL	2,325
39	Cincinnati, OH	23,529
272	Citrus Heights, CA	3,667
409	Clarkstown, NY	1,617
192	Clarksville, TN	5,100
200	Clearwater, FL	4,930
31	Cleveland, OH	30,749
396	Clifton, NJ	1,853
347	Clinton Twnshp, MI	2,620
238	Clovis, CA	4,144
297	College Station, TX	3,281
368	Colonie, NY	2,251
50	Colorado Springs, CO	17,731
202	Columbia, MO	4,845
74	Columbus, GA	13,383
10	Columbus, OH	54,228
252	Compton, CA	3,932
229	Concord, CA	4,233
302	Concord, NC	3,204
299	Coral Springs, FL	3,271
280	Corona, CA	3,554
53	Corpus Christi, TX	16,884
265	Costa Mesa, CA	3,765
377	Cranston, RI	2,147
7	Dallas, TX	70,189
385	Daly City, CA	2,064
404	Danbury, CT	1,752
174	Davenport, IA	5,560
250	Davie, FL	3,984
103	Dayton, OH	9,678
242	Dearborn, MI	4,116
294	Decatur, IL	3,316
328	Deerfield Beach, FL	2,781
276	Denton, TX	3,626
35	Denver, CO	26,203
84	Des Moines, IA	11,796
8	Detroit, MI	59,063
228	Downey, CA	4,266
NA	Duluth, MN**	NA
76	Durham, NC	12,977
199	Edinburg, TX	4,934
392	Edison Twnshp, NJ	1,974
405	Edmond, OK	1,704
313	El Cajon, CA	2,997
339	El Monte, CA	2,707
47	El Paso, TX	19,170
359	Elgin, IL	2,355
146	Elizabeth, NJ	6,414
262	Elk Grove, CA	3,793
235	Erie, PA	4,169
269	Escondido, CA	3,705
115	Eugene, OR	8,338
161	Evansville, IN	5,947
120	Everett, WA	7,953
289	Fairfield, CA	3,399
227	Fall River, MA	4,276
308	Fargo, ND	3,055
418	Farmington Hills, MI	1,367
67	Fayetteville, NC	14,022
429	Fishers, IN	711
106	Flint, MI	9,010
197	Fontana, CA	4,955
209	Fort Collins, CO	4,692
85	Fort Lauderdale, FL	11,757
184	Fort Smith, AR	5,304

RANK	CITY	CRIMES
100	Fort Wayne, IN	9,821
15	Fort Worth, TX	39,686
224	Fremont, CA	4,336
32	Fresno, CA	28,336
349	Frisco, TX	2,582
258	Fullerton, CA	3,856
151	Gainesville, FL	6,268
260	Garden Grove, CA	3,836
105	Garland, TX	9,213
159	Gary, IN	5,977
249	Gilbert, AZ	4,032
57	Glendale, AZ	15,852
268	Glendale, CA	3,710
127	Grand Prairie, TX	7,547
126	Grand Rapids, MI	7,569
341	Greece, NY	2,679
279	Greeley, CO	3,555
326	Green Bay, WI	2,793
208	Gresham, OR	4,727
389	Hamilton Twnshp, NJ	2,002
221	Hammond, IN	4,366
168	Hampton, VA	5,623
133	Hartford, CT	7,141
331	Hawthorne, CA	2,747
222	Hayward, CA	4,361
261	Hemet, CA	3,833
182	Henderson, NV	5,348
350	Hesperia, CA	2,562
114	Hialeah, FL	8,353
167	High Point, NC	5,657
372	Hillsboro, OR	2,211
112	Hollywood, FL	8,449
367	Hoover, AL	2,253
2	Houston, TX	129,228
195	Huntington Beach, CA	4,995
89	Huntsville, AL	11,267
131	Independence, MO	7,190
9	Indianapolis, IN	56,137
310	Indio, CA	3,040
290	Inglewood, CA	3,390
288	Irvine, CA	3,400
129	Irving, TX	7,308
14	Jacksonville, FL	41,295
66	Jackson, MS	14,431
125	Jersey City, NJ	7,607
430	Johns Creek, GA	609
220	Joliet, IL	4,378
108	Kansas City, KS	8,830
30	Kansas City, MO	31,081
319	Kennewick, WA	2,854
296	Kenosha, WI	3,310
173	Kent, WA	5,566
158	Killeen, TX	6,025
65	Knoxville, TN	14,570
128	Lafayette, LA	7,354
426	Lake Forest, CA	1,036
165	Lakeland, FL	5,695
422	Lakewood Twnshp, NJ	1,165
381	Lakewood, CA	2,113
140	Lakewood, CO	6,809
245	Lancaster, CA	4,067
178	Lansing, MI	5,456
86	Laredo, TX	11,539
287	Largo, FL	3,421
196	Las Cruces, NM	4,970
12	Las Vegas, NV	52,239
240	Lawrence, KS	4,128
300	Lawrence, MA	3,245
149	Lawton, OK	6,360
390	League City, TX	1,979
370	Lee's Summit, MO	2,223
298	Lewisville, TX	3,278

II. City Crime Statistics
(for cities larger than 75,000 population)

Crimes in 2011 164	Property Crimes in 2011. 260
Crime Rate in 2011 168	Property Crime Rate in 2011 264
Percent Change in Crime Rate: 2010 to 2011. 172	Percent Change in Property Crime Rate: 2010 to 2011 . . . 268
Percent Change in Crime Rate: 2007 to 2011. 176	Percent Change in Property Crime Rate: 2007 to 2011 . . . 272
Violent Crimes in 2011. 180	Burglaries in 2011. 276
Violent Crime Rate in 2011 184	Burglary Rate in 2011. 280
Percent Change in Violent Crime Rate: 2010 to 2011 188	Percent Change in Burglary Rate: 2010 to 2011. 284
Percent Change in Violent Crime Rate: 2007 to 2011 192	Percent Change in Burglary Rate: 2007 to 2011. 288
Murders in 2011 196	Larceny-Thefts in 2011. 292
Murder Rate in 2011 200	Larceny-Theft Rate in 2011 296
Percent Change in Murder Rate: 2010 to 2011. 204	Percent Change in Larceny-Theft Rate: 2010 to 2011 300
Percent Change in Murder Rate: 2007 to 2011. 208	Percent Change in Larceny-Theft Rate: 2007 to 2011 304
Rapes in 2011 212	Motor Vehicle Thefts in 2011 308
Rape Rate in 2011 216	Motor Vehicle Theft Rate in 2011. 312
Percent Change in Rape Rate: 2010 to 2011. 220	Percent Change in Motor Vehicle Theft Rate:
Percent Change in Rape Rate: 2007 to 2011. 224	2010 to 2011. 316
Robberies in 2011 228	Percent Change in Motor Vehicle Theft Rate:
Robbery Rate in 2011 232	2007 to 2011. 320
Percent Change in Robbery Rate: 2010 to 2011. 236	Police Officers in 2011 324
Percent Change in Robbery Rate: 2007 to 2011. 240	Rate of Police Officers in 2011. 328
Aggravated Assaults in 2011. 244	Percent Change in Rate of Police Officers: 2010 to 2011. . 332
Aggravated Assault Rate in 2011 248	Percent Change in Rate of Police Officers:
Percent Change in Aggravated Assault Rate:	2007 to 2011. 336
2010 to 2011. 252	
Percent Change in Aggravated Assault Rate:	
2007 to 2011. 256	

Please note the following for Tables 41 through 84 and 88 through 90:

- All listings are for cities of 75,000 or more in population that reported data to the F.B.I. for 2011.

Alpha Order - City

41. Crimes in 2011
National Total = 10,266,737 Crimes*

RANK	CITY	CRIMES
205	Abilene, TX	4,812
79	Akron, OH	12,643
180	Albany, GA	5,359
175	Albany, NY	5,550
28	Albuquerque, NM	32,183
285	Alexandria, VA	3,433
386	Alhambra, CA	2,043
189	Allentown, PA	5,222
412	Allen, TX	1,598
94	Amarillo, TX	10,611
378	Amherst, NY	2,128
101	Anaheim, CA	9,774
83	Anchorage, AK	11,843
323	Ann Arbor, MI	2,810
210	Antioch, CA	4,691
424	Arlington Heights, IL	1,131
48	Arlington, TX	19,082
338	Arvada, CO	2,708
217	Asheville, NC	4,393
185	Athens-Clarke, GA	5,290
21	Atlanta, GA	36,241
88	Aurora, CO	11,323
215	Aurora, IL	4,457
13	Austin, TX	45,721
236	Avondale, AZ	4,165
55	Bakersfield, CA	16,706
399	Baldwin Park, CA	1,843
17	Baltimore, MD	38,709
63	Baton Rouge, LA	15,134
123	Beaumont, TX	7,725
393	Beaverton, OR	1,945
270	Bellevue, WA	3,679
380	Bellflower, CA	2,118
251	Bellingham, WA	3,937
347	Bend, OR	2,620
176	Berkeley, CA	5,546
384	Bethlehem, PA	2,081
194	Billings, MT	5,006
44	Birmingham, AL	21,004
383	Bloomington, IL	2,101
294	Bloomington, IN	3,316
NA	Bloomington, MN**	NA
319	Boca Raton, FL	2,854
162	Boise, ID	5,838
38	Boston, MA	24,697
329	Boulder, CO	2,766
417	Brick Twnshp, NJ	1,413
136	Bridgeport, CT	7,054
218	Brockton, MA	4,389
353	Broken Arrow, OK	2,431
NA	Brooklyn Park, MN**	NA
110	Brownsville, TX	8,687
293	Bryan, TX	3,331
382	Buena Park, CA	2,109
51	Buffalo, NY	17,555
333	Burbank, CA	2,746
275	Cambridge, MA	3,638
141	Camden, NJ	6,614
414	Canton Twnshp, MI	1,527
231	Cape Coral, FL	4,225
375	Carlsbad, CA	2,180
428	Carmel, IN	848
282	Carrollton, TX	3,528
316	Carson, CA	2,936
373	Cary, NC	2,201
187	Cedar Rapids, IA	5,237
416	Centennial, CO	1,515
312	Champaign, IL	3,013
118	Chandler, AZ	8,097
237	Charleston, SC	4,152
19	Charlotte, NC	36,795
82	Chattanooga, TN	12,095

RANK	CITY	CRIMES
317	Cheektowaga, NY	2,928
119	Chesapeake, VA	8,055
NA	Chicago, IL**	NA
358	Chico, CA	2,360
425	Chino Hills, CA	1,046
363	Chino, CA	2,319
166	Chula Vista, CA	5,677
362	Cicero, IL	2,325
39	Cincinnati, OH	23,529
272	Citrus Heights, CA	3,667
409	Clarkstown, NY	1,617
192	Clarksville, TN	5,100
200	Clearwater, FL	4,930
31	Cleveland, OH	30,749
396	Clifton, NJ	1,853
347	Clinton Twnshp, MI	2,620
238	Clovis, CA	4,144
297	College Station, TX	3,281
368	Colonie, NY	2,251
50	Colorado Springs, CO	17,731
202	Columbia, MO	4,845
74	Columbus, GA	13,383
10	Columbus, OH	54,228
252	Compton, CA	3,932
229	Concord, CA	4,233
302	Concord, NC	3,204
299	Coral Springs, FL	3,271
280	Corona, CA	3,554
53	Corpus Christi, TX	16,884
265	Costa Mesa, CA	3,765
377	Cranston, RI	2,147
7	Dallas, TX	70,189
385	Daly City, CA	2,064
404	Danbury, CT	1,752
174	Davenport, IA	5,560
250	Davie, FL	3,984
103	Dayton, OH	9,678
242	Dearborn, MI	4,116
294	Decatur, IL	3,316
328	Deerfield Beach, FL	2,781
276	Denton, TX	3,626
35	Denver, CO	26,203
84	Des Moines, IA	11,796
8	Detroit, MI	59,063
228	Downey, CA	4,266
NA	Duluth, MN**	NA
76	Durham, NC	12,977
199	Edinburg, TX	4,934
392	Edison Twnshp, NJ	1,974
405	Edmond, OK	1,704
313	El Cajon, CA	2,997
339	El Monte, CA	2,707
47	El Paso, TX	19,170
359	Elgin, IL	2,355
146	Elizabeth, NJ	6,414
262	Elk Grove, CA	3,793
235	Erie, PA	4,169
269	Escondido, CA	3,705
115	Eugene, OR	8,338
161	Evansville, IN	5,947
120	Everett, WA	7,953
289	Fairfield, CA	3,399
227	Fall River, MA	4,276
308	Fargo, ND	3,055
418	Farmington Hills, MI	1,367
67	Fayetteville, NC	14,022
429	Fishers, IN	711
106	Flint, MI	9,010
197	Fontana, CA	4,955
209	Fort Collins, CO	4,692
85	Fort Lauderdale, FL	11,757
184	Fort Smith, AR	5,304

RANK	CITY	CRIMES
100	Fort Wayne, IN	9,821
15	Fort Worth, TX	39,686
224	Fremont, CA	4,336
32	Fresno, CA	28,336
349	Frisco, TX	2,582
258	Fullerton, CA	3,856
151	Gainesville, FL	6,268
260	Garden Grove, CA	3,836
105	Garland, TX	9,213
159	Gary, IN	5,977
249	Gilbert, AZ	4,032
57	Glendale, AZ	15,852
268	Glendale, CA	3,710
127	Grand Prairie, TX	7,547
126	Grand Rapids, MI	7,569
341	Greece, NY	2,679
279	Greeley, CO	3,555
326	Green Bay, WI	2,793
208	Gresham, OR	4,727
389	Hamilton Twnshp, NJ	2,002
221	Hammond, IN	4,366
168	Hampton, VA	5,623
133	Hartford, CT	7,141
331	Hawthorne, CA	2,747
222	Hayward, CA	4,361
261	Hemet, CA	3,833
182	Henderson, NV	5,348
350	Hesperia, CA	2,562
114	Hialeah, FL	8,353
167	High Point, NC	5,657
372	Hillsboro, OR	2,211
112	Hollywood, FL	8,449
367	Hoover, AL	2,253
2	Houston, TX	129,228
195	Huntington Beach, CA	4,995
89	Huntsville, AL	11,267
131	Independence, MO	7,190
9	Indianapolis, IN	56,137
310	Indio, CA	3,040
290	Inglewood, CA	3,390
288	Irvine, CA	3,400
129	Irving, TX	7,308
14	Jacksonville, FL	41,295
66	Jackson, MS	14,431
125	Jersey City, NJ	7,607
430	Johns Creek, GA	609
220	Joliet, IL	4,378
108	Kansas City, KS	8,830
30	Kansas City, MO	31,081
319	Kennewick, WA	2,854
296	Kenosha, WI	3,310
173	Kent, WA	5,566
158	Killeen, TX	6,025
65	Knoxville, TN	14,570
128	Lafayette, LA	7,354
426	Lake Forest, CA	1,036
165	Lakeland, FL	5,695
422	Lakewood Twnshp, NJ	1,165
381	Lakewood, CA	2,113
140	Lakewood, CO	6,809
245	Lancaster, CA	4,067
178	Lansing, MI	5,456
86	Laredo, TX	11,539
287	Largo, FL	3,421
196	Las Cruces, NM	4,970
12	Las Vegas, NV	52,239
240	Lawrence, KS	4,128
300	Lawrence, MA	3,245
149	Lawton, OK	6,360
390	League City, TX	1,979
370	Lee's Summit, MO	2,223
298	Lewisville, TX	3,278

Alpha Order - City (continued)

RANK	CITY	CRIMES
71	Lexington, KY	13,789
90	Lincoln, NE	11,155
49	Little Rock, AR	18,409
386	Livermore, CA	2,043
366	Livonia, MI	2,276
59	Long Beach, CA	15,673
374	Longmont, CO	2,196
232	Longview, TX	4,214
3	Los Angeles, CA	106,375
23	Louisville, KY	36,035
254	Lowell, MA	3,896
69	Lubbock, TX	13,878
331	Lynchburg, VA	2,747
286	Lynn, MA	3,424
113	Macon, GA	8,373
109	Madison, WI	8,751
205	Manchester, NH	4,812
157	McAllen, TX	6,121
307	McKinney, TX	3,067
226	Medford, OR	4,282
207	Melbourne, FL	4,760
11	Memphis, TN	52,691
406	Menifee, CA	1,664
273	Merced, CA	3,662
423	Meridian, ID	1,157
52	Mesa, AZ	16,955
137	Mesquite, TX	6,939
95	Miami Beach, FL	10,472
147	Miami Gardens, FL	6,396
33	Miami, FL	27,770
277	Midland, TX	3,621
22	Milwaukee, WI	36,066
40	Minneapolis, MN	22,912
266	Miramar, FL	3,722
420	Mission Viejo, CA	1,295
321	Mission, TX	2,851
62	Mobile, AL	15,269
98	Modesto, CA	10,307
87	Montgomery, AL	11,451
143	Moreno Valley, CA	6,494
177	Murfreesboro, TN	5,505
411	Murrieta, CA	1,600
340	Nampa, ID	2,702
400	Napa, CA	1,839
371	Naperville, IL	2,222
360	Nashua, NH	2,342
20	Nashville, TN	36,495
216	New Bedford, MA	4,422
116	New Haven, CT	8,227
54	New Orleans, LA	16,761
413	New Rochelle, NY	1,557
1	New York, NY	191,666
75	Newark, NJ	13,259
361	Newport Beach, CA	2,339
138	Newport News, VA	6,886
421	Newton, MA	1,261
72	Norfolk, VA	13,682
271	Norman, OK	3,671
153	North Charleston, SC	6,232
344	Norwalk, CA	2,645
369	Norwalk, CT	2,240
34	Oakland, CA	27,556
214	Oceanside, CA	4,469
255	Odessa, TX	3,882
419	O'Fallon, MO	1,296
204	Ogden, UT	4,821
16	Oklahoma City, OK	39,221
354	Olathe, KS	2,430
43	Omaha, NE	21,073
181	Ontario, CA	5,351
324	Orange, CA	2,809
357	Orem, UT	2,367
45	Orlando, FL	19,736

RANK	CITY	CRIMES
225	Overland Park, KS	4,304
241	Oxnard, CA	4,118
291	Palm Bay, FL	3,340
248	Palmdale, CA	4,058
243	Pasadena, CA	4,107
163	Pasadena, TX	5,832
154	Paterson, NJ	6,222
398	Pearland, TX	1,851
186	Pembroke Pines, FL	5,254
193	Peoria, AZ	5,075
152	Peoria, IL	6,252
5	Philadelphia, PA	77,885
6	Phoenix, AZ	72,568
81	Pittsburgh, PA	12,539
130	Plano, TX	7,193
234	Plantation, FL	4,205
179	Pomona, CA	5,371
145	Pompano Beach, FL	6,441
230	Port St. Lucie, FL	4,232
27	Portland, OR	33,059
164	Portsmouth, VA	5,787
311	Provo, UT	3,037
150	Pueblo, CO	6,325
376	Quincy, MA	2,170
253	Racine, WI	3,929
64	Raleigh, NC	14,966
427	Ramapo, NY	993
233	Rancho Cucamon., CA	4,208
247	Reading, PA	4,059
244	Redding, CA	4,097
406	Redwood City, CA	1,664
124	Reno, NV	7,658
213	Renton, WA	4,515
284	Rialto, CA	3,458
314	Richardson, TX	2,981
172	Richmond, CA	5,581
99	Richmond, VA	10,075
402	Rio Rancho, NM	1,799
93	Riverside, CA	10,941
188	Roanoke, VA	5,224
NA	Rochester, MN**	NA
77	Rochester, NY	12,963
104	Rockford, IL	9,228
263	Roseville, CA	3,789
402	Roswell, GA	1,799
351	Round Rock, TX	2,561
42	Sacramento, CA	21,917
144	Salem, OR	6,479
169	Salinas, CA	5,607
68	Salt Lake City, UT	14,011
256	San Angelo, TX	3,874
4	San Antonio, TX	87,906
97	San Bernardino, CA	10,322
26	San Diego, CA	34,813
18	San Francisco, CA	38,260
37	San Jose, CA	25,178
278	San Leandro, CA	3,572
408	San Marcos, CA	1,657
391	San Mateo, CA	1,978
346	Sandy Springs, GA	2,628
334	Sandy, UT	2,738
121	Santa Ana, CA	7,888
306	Santa Barbara, CA	3,075
305	Santa Clara, CA	3,110
322	Santa Clarita, CA	2,830
304	Santa Maria, CA	3,145
291	Santa Monica, CA	3,340
219	Santa Rosa, CA	4,388
96	Savannah, GA	10,468
134	Scottsdale, AZ	7,124
327	Scranton, PA	2,782
24	Seattle, WA	35,456
91	Shreveport, LA	11,128
401	Simi Valley, CA	1,813

RANK	CITY	CRIMES
259	Sioux City, IA	3,846
191	Sioux Falls, SD	5,147
388	Somerville, MA	2,024
139	South Bend, IN	6,840
283	South Gate, CA	3,473
335	Sparks, NV	2,732
190	Spokane Valley, WA	5,176
56	Spokane, WA	16,343
111	Springfield, IL	8,454
107	Springfield, MA	8,946
58	Springfield, MO	15,724
356	Stamford, CT	2,376
318	Sterling Heights, MI	2,874
46	Stockton, CA	19,618
223	St. Joseph, MO	4,337
29	St. Louis, MO	31,619
70	St. Paul, MN	13,817
61	St. Petersburg, FL	15,335
345	Suffolk, VA	2,640
415	Sugar Land, TX	1,525
379	Sunnyvale, CA	2,120
257	Sunrise, FL	3,859
336	Surprise, AZ	2,729
142	Syracuse, NY	6,577
73	Tacoma, WA	13,569
92	Tallahassee, FL	11,024
80	Tampa, FL	12,621
352	Temecula, CA	2,501
102	Tempe, AZ	9,720
239	Thornton, CO	4,133
394	Thousand Oaks, CA	1,925
NA	Toledo, OH**	NA
301	Toms River Twnshp, NJ	3,236
116	Topeka, KS	8,227
315	Torrance, CA	2,952
364	Tracy, CA	2,316
264	Trenton, NJ	3,778
397	Troy, MI	1,852
NA	Tucson, AZ**	NA
36	Tulsa, OK	25,883
203	Tuscaloosa, AL	4,834
410	Tustin, CA	1,610
198	Tyler, TX	4,944
343	Upper Darby Twnshp, PA	2,656
395	Vacaville, CA	1,872
156	Vallejo, CA	6,147
135	Vancouver, WA	7,080
274	Ventura, CA	3,646
211	Victorville, CA	4,617
78	Virginia Beach, VA	12,909
169	Visalia, CA	5,607
355	Vista, CA	2,412
132	Waco, TX	7,188
212	Warren, MI	4,572
365	Warwick, RI	2,278
25	Washington, DC	35,297
200	Waterbury, CT	4,930
281	West Covina, CA	3,529
303	West Jordan, UT	3,149
155	West Palm Beach, FL	6,152
160	West Valley, UT	5,956
337	Westland, MI	2,728
330	Westminster, CA	2,752
309	Westminster, CO	3,048
325	Whittier, CA	2,802
183	Wichita Falls, TX	5,335
41	Wichita, KS	22,406
148	Wilmington, NC	6,370
60	Winston-Salem, NC	15,439
342	Woodbridge Twnshp, NJ	2,665
122	Worcester, MA	7,877
171	Yakima, WA	5,601
246	Yonkers, NY	4,060
267	Yuma, AZ	3,717

Source: CQ Press using reported data from the F.B.I. "Crime in the United States 2011"
*Includes murder, rape, robbery, aggravated assault, burglary, larceny-theft, and motor vehicle theft.
**Not available.

41. Crimes in 2011 (continued)
National Total = 10,266,737 Crimes*

RANK	CITY	CRIMES	RANK	CITY	CRIMES	RANK	CITY	CRIMES
1	New York, NY	191,666	73	Tacoma, WA	13,569	145	Pompano Beach, FL	6,441
2	Houston, TX	129,228	74	Columbus, GA	13,383	146	Elizabeth, NJ	6,414
3	Los Angeles, CA	106,375	75	Newark, NJ	13,259	147	Miami Gardens, FL	6,396
4	San Antonio, TX	87,906	76	Durham, NC	12,977	148	Wilmington, NC	6,370
5	Philadelphia, PA	77,885	77	Rochester, NY	12,963	149	Lawton, OK	6,360
6	Phoenix, AZ	72,568	78	Virginia Beach, VA	12,909	150	Pueblo, CO	6,325
7	Dallas, TX	70,189	79	Akron, OH	12,643	151	Gainesville, FL	6,268
8	Detroit, MI	59,063	80	Tampa, FL	12,621	152	Peoria, IL	6,252
9	Indianapolis, IN	56,137	81	Pittsburgh, PA	12,539	153	North Charleston, SC	6,232
10	Columbus, OH	54,228	82	Chattanooga, TN	12,095	154	Paterson, NJ	6,222
11	Memphis, TN	52,691	83	Anchorage, AK	11,843	155	West Palm Beach, FL	6,152
12	Las Vegas, NV	52,239	84	Des Moines, IA	11,796	156	Vallejo, CA	6,147
13	Austin, TX	45,721	85	Fort Lauderdale, FL	11,757	157	McAllen, TX	6,121
14	Jacksonville, FL	41,295	86	Laredo, TX	11,539	158	Killeen, TX	6,025
15	Fort Worth, TX	39,686	87	Montgomery, AL	11,451	159	Gary, IN	5,977
16	Oklahoma City, OK	39,221	88	Aurora, CO	11,323	160	West Valley, UT	5,956
17	Baltimore, MD	38,709	89	Huntsville, AL	11,267	161	Evansville, IN	5,947
18	San Francisco, CA	38,260	90	Lincoln, NE	11,155	162	Boise, ID	5,838
19	Charlotte, NC	36,795	91	Shreveport, LA	11,128	163	Pasadena, TX	5,832
20	Nashville, TN	36,495	92	Tallahassee, FL	11,024	164	Portsmouth, VA	5,787
21	Atlanta, GA	36,241	93	Riverside, CA	10,941	165	Lakeland, FL	5,695
22	Milwaukee, WI	36,066	94	Amarillo, TX	10,611	166	Chula Vista, CA	5,677
23	Louisville, KY	36,035	95	Miami Beach, FL	10,472	167	High Point, NC	5,657
24	Seattle, WA	35,456	96	Savannah, GA	10,468	168	Hampton, VA	5,623
25	Washington, DC	35,297	97	San Bernardino, CA	10,322	169	Salinas, CA	5,607
26	San Diego, CA	34,813	98	Modesto, CA	10,307	169	Visalia, CA	5,607
27	Portland, OR	33,059	99	Richmond, VA	10,075	171	Yakima, WA	5,601
28	Albuquerque, NM	32,183	100	Fort Wayne, IN	9,821	172	Richmond, CA	5,581
29	St. Louis, MO	31,619	101	Anaheim, CA	9,774	173	Kent, WA	5,566
30	Kansas City, MO	31,081	102	Tempe, AZ	9,720	174	Davenport, IA	5,560
31	Cleveland, OH	30,749	103	Dayton, OH	9,678	175	Albany, NY	5,550
32	Fresno, CA	28,336	104	Rockford, IL	9,228	176	Berkeley, CA	5,546
33	Miami, FL	27,770	105	Garland, TX	9,213	177	Murfreesboro, TN	5,505
34	Oakland, CA	27,556	106	Flint, MI	9,010	178	Lansing, MI	5,456
35	Denver, CO	26,203	107	Springfield, MA	8,946	179	Pomona, CA	5,371
36	Tulsa, OK	25,883	108	Kansas City, KS	8,830	180	Albany, GA	5,359
37	San Jose, CA	25,178	109	Madison, WI	8,751	181	Ontario, CA	5,351
38	Boston, MA	24,697	110	Brownsville, TX	8,687	182	Henderson, NV	5,348
39	Cincinnati, OH	23,529	111	Springfield, IL	8,454	183	Wichita Falls, TX	5,335
40	Minneapolis, MN	22,912	112	Hollywood, FL	8,449	184	Fort Smith, AR	5,304
41	Wichita, KS	22,406	113	Macon, GA	8,373	185	Athens-Clarke, GA	5,290
42	Sacramento, CA	21,917	114	Hialeah, FL	8,353	186	Pembroke Pines, FL	5,254
43	Omaha, NE	21,073	115	Eugene, OR	8,338	187	Cedar Rapids, IA	5,237
44	Birmingham, AL	21,004	116	New Haven, CT	8,227	188	Roanoke, VA	5,224
45	Orlando, FL	19,736	116	Topeka, KS	8,227	189	Allentown, PA	5,222
46	Stockton, CA	19,618	118	Chandler, AZ	8,097	190	Spokane Valley, WA	5,176
47	El Paso, TX	19,170	119	Chesapeake, VA	8,055	191	Sioux Falls, SD	5,147
48	Arlington, TX	19,082	120	Everett, WA	7,953	192	Clarksville, TN	5,100
49	Little Rock, AR	18,409	121	Santa Ana, CA	7,888	193	Peoria, AZ	5,075
50	Colorado Springs, CO	17,731	122	Worcester, MA	7,877	194	Billings, MT	5,006
51	Buffalo, NY	17,555	123	Beaumont, TX	7,725	195	Huntington Beach, CA	4,995
52	Mesa, AZ	16,955	124	Reno, NV	7,658	196	Las Cruces, NM	4,970
53	Corpus Christi, TX	16,884	125	Jersey City, NJ	7,607	197	Fontana, CA	4,955
54	New Orleans, LA	16,761	126	Grand Rapids, MI	7,569	198	Tyler, TX	4,944
55	Bakersfield, CA	16,706	127	Grand Prairie, TX	7,547	199	Edinburg, TX	4,934
56	Spokane, WA	16,343	128	Lafayette, LA	7,354	200	Clearwater, FL	4,930
57	Glendale, AZ	15,852	129	Irving, TX	7,308	200	Waterbury, CT	4,930
58	Springfield, MO	15,724	130	Plano, TX	7,193	202	Columbia, MO	4,845
59	Long Beach, CA	15,673	131	Independence, MO	7,190	203	Tuscaloosa, AL	4,834
60	Winston-Salem, NC	15,439	132	Waco, TX	7,188	204	Ogden, UT	4,821
61	St. Petersburg, FL	15,335	133	Hartford, CT	7,141	205	Abilene, TX	4,812
62	Mobile, AL	15,269	134	Scottsdale, AZ	7,124	205	Manchester, NH	4,812
63	Baton Rouge, LA	15,134	135	Vancouver, WA	7,080	207	Melbourne, FL	4,760
64	Raleigh, NC	14,966	136	Bridgeport, CT	7,054	208	Gresham, OR	4,727
65	Knoxville, TN	14,570	137	Mesquite, TX	6,939	209	Fort Collins, CO	4,692
66	Jackson, MS	14,431	138	Newport News, VA	6,886	210	Antioch, CA	4,691
67	Fayetteville, NC	14,022	139	South Bend, IN	6,840	211	Victorville, CA	4,617
68	Salt Lake City, UT	14,011	140	Lakewood, CO	6,809	212	Warren, MI	4,572
69	Lubbock, TX	13,878	141	Camden, NJ	6,614	213	Renton, WA	4,515
70	St. Paul, MN	13,817	142	Syracuse, NY	6,577	214	Oceanside, CA	4,469
71	Lexington, KY	13,789	143	Moreno Valley, CA	6,494	215	Aurora, IL	4,457
72	Norfolk, VA	13,682	144	Salem, OR	6,479	216	New Bedford, MA	4,422

Rank Order - City (continued)

RANK	CITY	CRIMES
217	Asheville, NC	4,393
218	Brockton, MA	4,389
219	Santa Rosa, CA	4,388
220	Joliet, IL	4,378
221	Hammond, IN	4,366
222	Hayward, CA	4,361
223	St. Joseph, MO	4,337
224	Fremont, CA	4,336
225	Overland Park, KS	4,304
226	Medford, OR	4,282
227	Fall River, MA	4,276
228	Downey, CA	4,266
229	Concord, CA	4,233
230	Port St. Lucie, FL	4,232
231	Cape Coral, FL	4,225
232	Longview, TX	4,214
233	Rancho Cucamon., CA	4,208
234	Plantation, FL	4,205
235	Erie, PA	4,169
236	Avondale, AZ	4,165
237	Charleston, SC	4,152
238	Clovis, CA	4,144
239	Thornton, CO	4,133
240	Lawrence, KS	4,128
241	Oxnard, CA	4,118
242	Dearborn, MI	4,116
243	Pasadena, CA	4,107
244	Redding, CA	4,097
245	Lancaster, CA	4,067
246	Yonkers, NY	4,060
247	Reading, PA	4,059
248	Palmdale, CA	4,058
249	Gilbert, AZ	4,032
250	Davie, FL	3,984
251	Bellingham, WA	3,937
252	Compton, CA	3,932
253	Racine, WI	3,929
254	Lowell, MA	3,896
255	Odessa, TX	3,882
256	San Angelo, TX	3,874
257	Sunrise, FL	3,859
258	Fullerton, CA	3,856
259	Sioux City, IA	3,846
260	Garden Grove, CA	3,836
261	Hemet, CA	3,833
262	Elk Grove, CA	3,793
263	Roseville, CA	3,789
264	Trenton, NJ	3,778
265	Costa Mesa, CA	3,765
266	Miramar, FL	3,722
267	Yuma, AZ	3,717
268	Glendale, CA	3,710
269	Escondido, CA	3,705
270	Bellevue, WA	3,679
271	Norman, OK	3,671
272	Citrus Heights, CA	3,667
273	Merced, CA	3,662
274	Ventura, CA	3,646
275	Cambridge, MA	3,638
276	Denton, TX	3,626
277	Midland, TX	3,621
278	San Leandro, CA	3,572
279	Greeley, CO	3,555
280	Corona, CA	3,554
281	West Covina, CA	3,529
282	Carrollton, TX	3,528
283	South Gate, CA	3,473
284	Rialto, CA	3,458
285	Alexandria, VA	3,433
286	Lynn, MA	3,424
287	Largo, FL	3,421
288	Irvine, CA	3,400
289	Fairfield, CA	3,399
290	Inglewood, CA	3,390
291	Palm Bay, FL	3,340
291	Santa Monica, CA	3,340
293	Bryan, TX	3,331
294	Bloomington, IN	3,316
294	Decatur, IL	3,316
296	Kenosha, WI	3,310
297	College Station, TX	3,281
298	Lewisville, TX	3,278
299	Coral Springs, FL	3,271
300	Lawrence, MA	3,245
301	Toms River Twnshp, NJ	3,236
302	Concord, NC	3,204
303	West Jordan, UT	3,149
304	Santa Maria, CA	3,145
305	Santa Clara, CA	3,110
306	Santa Barbara, CA	3,075
307	McKinney, TX	3,067
308	Fargo, ND	3,055
309	Westminster, CO	3,048
310	Indio, CA	3,040
311	Provo, UT	3,037
312	Champaign, IL	3,013
313	El Cajon, CA	2,997
314	Richardson, TX	2,981
315	Torrance, CA	2,952
316	Carson, CA	2,936
317	Cheektowaga, NY	2,928
318	Sterling Heights, MI	2,874
319	Boca Raton, FL	2,854
319	Kennewick, WA	2,854
321	Mission, TX	2,851
322	Santa Clarita, CA	2,830
323	Ann Arbor, MI	2,810
324	Orange, CA	2,809
325	Whittier, CA	2,802
326	Green Bay, WI	2,793
327	Scranton, PA	2,782
328	Deerfield Beach, FL	2,781
329	Boulder, CO	2,766
330	Westminster, CA	2,752
331	Hawthorne, CA	2,747
331	Lynchburg, VA	2,747
333	Burbank, CA	2,746
334	Sandy, UT	2,738
335	Sparks, NV	2,732
336	Surprise, AZ	2,729
337	Westland, MI	2,728
338	Arvada, CO	2,708
339	El Monte, CA	2,707
340	Nampa, ID	2,702
341	Greece, NY	2,679
342	Woodbridge Twnshp, NJ	2,665
343	Upper Darby Twnshp, PA	2,656
344	Norwalk, CA	2,645
345	Suffolk, VA	2,640
346	Sandy Springs, GA	2,628
347	Bend, OR	2,620
347	Clinton Twnshp, MI	2,620
349	Frisco, TX	2,582
350	Hesperia, CA	2,562
351	Round Rock, TX	2,561
352	Temecula, CA	2,501
353	Broken Arrow, OK	2,431
354	Olathe, KS	2,430
355	Vista, CA	2,412
356	Stamford, CT	2,376
357	Orem, UT	2,367
358	Chico, CA	2,360
359	Elgin, IL	2,355
360	Nashua, NH	2,342
361	Newport Beach, CA	2,339
362	Cicero, IL	2,325
363	Chino, CA	2,319
364	Tracy, CA	2,316
365	Warwick, RI	2,278
366	Livonia, MI	2,276
367	Hoover, AL	2,253
368	Colonie, NY	2,251
369	Norwalk, CT	2,240
370	Lee's Summit, MO	2,223
371	Naperville, IL	2,222
372	Hillsboro, OR	2,211
373	Cary, NC	2,201
374	Longmont, CO	2,196
375	Carlsbad, CA	2,180
376	Quincy, MA	2,170
377	Cranston, RI	2,147
378	Amherst, NY	2,128
379	Sunnyvale, CA	2,120
380	Bellflower, CA	2,118
381	Lakewood, CA	2,113
382	Buena Park, CA	2,109
383	Bloomington, IL	2,101
384	Bethlehem, PA	2,081
385	Daly City, CA	2,064
386	Alhambra, CA	2,043
386	Livermore, CA	2,043
388	Somerville, MA	2,024
389	Hamilton Twnshp, NJ	2,002
390	League City, TX	1,979
391	San Mateo, CA	1,978
392	Edison Twnshp, NJ	1,974
393	Beaverton, OR	1,945
394	Thousand Oaks, CA	1,925
395	Vacaville, CA	1,872
396	Clifton, NJ	1,853
397	Troy, MI	1,852
398	Pearland, TX	1,851
399	Baldwin Park, CA	1,843
400	Napa, CA	1,839
401	Simi Valley, CA	1,813
402	Rio Rancho, NM	1,799
402	Roswell, GA	1,799
404	Danbury, CT	1,752
405	Edmond, OK	1,704
406	Menifee, CA	1,664
406	Redwood City, CA	1,664
408	San Marcos, CA	1,657
409	Clarkstown, NY	1,617
410	Tustin, CA	1,610
411	Murrieta, CA	1,600
412	Allen, TX	1,598
413	New Rochelle, NY	1,557
414	Canton Twnshp, MI	1,527
415	Sugar Land, TX	1,525
416	Centennial, CO	1,515
417	Brick Twnshp, NJ	1,413
418	Farmington Hills, MI	1,367
419	O'Fallon, MO	1,296
420	Mission Viejo, CA	1,295
421	Newton, MA	1,261
422	Lakewood Twnshp, NJ	1,165
423	Meridian, ID	1,157
424	Arlington Heights, IL	1,131
425	Chino Hills, CA	1,046
426	Lake Forest, CA	1,036
427	Ramapo, NY	993
428	Carmel, IN	848
429	Fishers, IN	711
430	Johns Creek, GA	609
NA	Bloomington, MN**	NA
NA	Brooklyn Park, MN**	NA
NA	Chicago, IL**	NA
NA	Duluth, MN**	NA
NA	Rochester, MN**	NA
NA	Toledo, OH**	NA
NA	Tucson, AZ**	NA

Source: CQ Press using reported data from the F.B.I. "Crime in the United States 2011"
*Includes murder, rape, robbery, aggravated assault, burglary, larceny-theft, and motor vehicle theft.
**Not available.

Alpha Order - City

42. Crime Rate in 2011
National Rate = 3,295.0 Crimes per 100,000 Population*

RANK	CITY	RATE
200	Abilene, TX	4,025.9
47	Akron, OH	6,345.1
31	Albany, GA	6,830.8
91	Albany, NY	5,646.2
77	Albuquerque, NM	5,830.7
355	Alexandria, VA	2,423.8
353	Alhambra, CA	2,430.2
173	Allentown, PA	4,410.2
406	Allen, TX	1,857.7
100	Amarillo, TX	5,449.7
407	Amherst, NY	1,809.4
296	Anaheim, CA	2,872.9
202	Anchorage, AK	3,988.1
349	Ann Arbor, MI	2,468.2
161	Antioch, CA	4,529.1
418	Arlington Heights, IL	1,501.5
116	Arlington, TX	5,114.1
344	Arvada, CO	2,500.8
113	Asheville, NC	5,201.9
162	Athens-Clarke, GA	4,517.0
9	Atlanta, GA	8,516.6
242	Aurora, CO	3,423.5
371	Aurora, IL	2,245.4
88	Austin, TX	5,665.4
104	Avondale, AZ	5,386.9
146	Bakersfield, CA	4,751.9
356	Baldwin Park, CA	2,416.2
53	Baltimore, MD	6,175.2
40	Baton Rouge, LA	6,534.8
45	Beaumont, TX	6,395.7
378	Beaverton, OR	2,143.0
289	Bellevue, WA	2,960.2
312	Bellflower, CA	2,732.3
140	Bellingham, WA	4,792.2
248	Bend, OR	3,382.6
133	Berkeley, CA	4,869.1
305	Bethlehem, PA	2,766.5
145	Billings, MT	4,763.3
3	Birmingham, AL	9,849.1
311	Bloomington, IL	2,734.2
193	Bloomington, IN	4,103.1
NA	Bloomington, MN**	NA
254	Boca Raton, FL	3,336.4
301	Boise, ID	2,807.5
204	Boston, MA	3,974.7
302	Boulder, CO	2,791.7
405	Brick Twnshp, NJ	1,875.9
131	Bridgeport, CT	4,881.8
151	Brockton, MA	4,650.3
352	Broken Arrow, OK	2,433.2
NA	Brooklyn Park, MN**	NA
134	Brownsville, TX	4,861.1
182	Bryan, TX	4,281.3
335	Buena Park, CA	2,588.5
37	Buffalo, NY	6,688.0
330	Burbank, CA	2,626.4
238	Cambridge, MA	3,438.5
8	Camden, NJ	8,522.8
409	Canton Twnshp, MI	1,694.7
318	Cape Coral, FL	2,701.3
386	Carlsbad, CA	2,045.7
428	Carmel, IN	1,065.4
293	Carrollton, TX	2,901.2
273	Carson, CA	3,164.1
411	Cary, NC	1,607.2
192	Cedar Rapids, IA	4,124.0
420	Centennial, CO	1,483.5
220	Champaign, IL	3,706.1
249	Chandler, AZ	3,381.3
244	Charleston, SC	3,417.8
150	Charlotte, NC	4,660.7
22	Chattanooga, TN	7,148.9
221	Cheektowaga, NY	3,697.2
232	Chesapeake, VA	3,582.2
NA	Chicago, IL**	NA
316	Chico, CA	2,706.4
423	Chino Hills, CA	1,382.2
291	Chino, CA	2,939.2
366	Chula Vista, CA	2,300.4
307	Cicero, IL	2,763.1
15	Cincinnati, OH	7,918.0
175	Citrus Heights, CA	4,351.0
387	Clarkstown, NY	2,041.1
212	Clarksville, TN	3,802.3
163	Clearwater, FL	4,516.6
16	Cleveland, OH	7,743.3
374	Clifton, NJ	2,195.1
315	Clinton Twnshp, MI	2,708.8
181	Clovis, CA	4,283.0
241	College Station, TX	3,423.7
295	Colonie, NY	2,887.7
189	Colorado Springs, CO	4,185.0
170	Columbia, MO	4,449.3
25	Columbus, GA	6,956.4
28	Columbus, OH	6,885.1
198	Compton, CA	4,029.1
240	Concord, CA	3,427.5
201	Concord, NC	4,001.5
322	Coral Springs, FL	2,664.9
365	Corona, CA	2,305.3
102	Corpus Christi, TX	5,417.8
247	Costa Mesa, CA	3,384.2
319	Cranston, RI	2,674.1
82	Dallas, TX	5,739.0
390	Daly City, CA	2,017.4
376	Danbury, CT	2,161.8
97	Davenport, IA	5,548.5
184	Davie, FL	4,272.6
30	Dayton, OH	6,833.2
188	Dearborn, MI	4,196.6
177	Decatur, IL	4,343.1
226	Deerfield Beach, FL	3,657.3
275	Denton, TX	3,132.1
180	Denver, CO	4,291.3
80	Des Moines, IA	5,768.3
11	Detroit, MI	8,281.0
214	Downey, CA	3,772.4
NA	Duluth, MN**	NA
94	Durham, NC	5,612.3
50	Edinburg, TX	6,267.6
398	Edison Twnshp, NJ	1,968.1
382	Edmond, OK	2,071.1
286	El Cajon, CA	2,977.7
360	El Monte, CA	2,357.8
294	El Paso, TX	2,892.4
375	Elgin, IL	2,170.2
115	Elizabeth, NJ	5,115.4
351	Elk Grove, CA	2,450.0
194	Erie, PA	4,082.8
338	Escondido, CA	2,544.6
110	Eugene, OR	5,282.3
120	Evansville, IN	5,038.6
18	Everett, WA	7,600.7
272	Fairfield, CA	3,189.8
142	Fall River, MA	4,783.1
297	Fargo, ND	2,846.4
408	Farmington Hills, MI	1,715.6
26	Fayetteville, NC	6,903.3
429	Fishers, IN	921.2
7	Flint, MI	8,802.5
345	Fontana, CA	2,497.8
268	Fort Collins, CO	3,202.9
23	Fort Lauderdale, FL	7,007.5
57	Fort Smith, AR	6,106.3
208	Fort Wayne, IN	3,851.6
111	Fort Worth, TX	5,243.9
395	Fremont, CA	2,001.8
89	Fresno, CA	5,661.8
377	Frisco, TX	2,161.6
299	Fullerton, CA	2,819.7
125	Gainesville, FL	4,972.7
372	Garden Grove, CA	2,218.7
203	Garland, TX	3,977.1
19	Gary, IN	7,406.1
403	Gilbert, AZ	1,907.2
27	Glendale, AZ	6,894.2
402	Glendale, CA	1,912.6
187	Grand Prairie, TX	4,214.2
199	Grand Rapids, MI	4,028.2
303	Greece, NY	2,775.4
217	Greeley, CO	3,761.6
320	Green Bay, WI	2,672.5
172	Gresham, OR	4,429.4
370	Hamilton Twnshp, NJ	2,255.5
105	Hammond, IN	5,374.0
197	Hampton, VA	4,043.1
84	Hartford, CT	5,712.5
267	Hawthorne, CA	3,221.0
284	Hayward, CA	2,989.4
138	Hemet, CA	4,816.4
384	Henderson, NV	2,057.7
300	Hesperia, CA	2,808.2
224	Hialeah, FL	3,667.9
106	High Point, NC	5,352.2
358	Hillsboro, OR	2,388.1
72	Hollywood, FL	5,921.4
310	Hoover, AL	2,747.2
63	Houston, TX	6,028.5
334	Huntington Beach, CA	2,598.5
51	Huntsville, AL	6,225.8
55	Independence, MO	6,131.9
32	Indianapolis, IN	6,738.9
205	Indio, CA	3,951.6
280	Inglewood, CA	3,055.1
413	Irvine, CA	1,582.3
257	Irving, TX	3,309.2
128	Jacksonville, FL	4,948.9
10	Jackson, MS	8,285.6
279	Jersey City, NJ	3,062.1
430	Johns Creek, GA	783.4
287	Joliet, IL	2,960.6
64	Kansas City, KS	6,018.6
33	Kansas City, MO	6,735.4
213	Kennewick, WA	3,801.4
255	Kenosha, WI	3,321.6
70	Kent, WA	5,930.0
158	Killeen, TX	4,612.9
13	Knoxville, TN	8,072.6
61	Lafayette, LA	6,041.4
425	Lake Forest, CA	1,325.3
81	Lakeland, FL	5,767.1
426	Lakewood Twnshp, NJ	1,250.6
333	Lakewood, CO	2,609.0
148	Lakewood, CO	4,680.7
337	Lancaster, CA	2,566.4
143	Lansing, MI	4,777.1
141	Laredo, TX	4,786.8
176	Largo, FL	4,346.6
121	Las Cruces, NM	5,035.0
233	Las Vegas, NV	3,581.8
149	Lawrence, KS	4,680.3
186	Lawrence, MA	4,222.9
42	Lawton, OK	6,496.2
364	League City, TX	2,319.6
354	Lee's Summit, MO	2,424.3
251	Lewisville, TX	3,369.1

168 Cities

Alpha Order - City (continued)

RANK	CITY	RATE
153	Lexington, KY	4,629.6
183	Lincoln, NE	4,279.1
5	Little Rock, AR	9,441.1
346	Livermore, CA	2,493.9
361	Livonia, MI	2,349.6
252	Long Beach, CA	3,351.1
343	Longmont, CO	2,501.9
114	Longview, TX	5,129.8
304	Los Angeles, CA	2,772.2
103	Louisville, KY	5,417.6
229	Lowell, MA	3,635.4
73	Lubbock, TX	5,920.5
231	Lynchburg, VA	3,592.2
215	Lynn, MA	3,767.6
6	Macon, GA	9,046.6
218	Madison, WI	3,736.2
174	Manchester, NH	4,386.2
157	McAllen, TX	4,615.8
367	McKinney, TX	2,290.9
90	Medford, OR	5,656.2
54	Melbourne, FL	6,173.4
14	Memphis, TN	8,072.5
380	Menifee, CA	2,121.6
160	Merced, CA	4,584.0
416	Meridian, ID	1,523.9
210	Mesa, AZ	3,807.9
135	Mesquite, TX	4,860.4
1	Miami Beach, FL	11,769.6
75	Miami Gardens, FL	5,888.0
29	Miami, FL	6,858.5
271	Midland, TX	3,190.7
62	Milwaukee, WI	6,036.9
69	Minneapolis, MN	5,943.0
282	Miramar, FL	3,008.8
424	Mission Viejo, CA	1,371.8
230	Mission, TX	3,623.6
59	Mobile, AL	6,062.3
119	Modesto, CA	5,064.1
98	Montgomery, AL	5,538.5
256	Moreno Valley, CA	3,319.4
122	Murfreesboro, TN	5,016.6
415	Murrieta, CA	1,528.4
260	Nampa, ID	3,276.8
359	Napa, CA	2,363.2
414	Naperville, IL	1,561.7
317	Nashua, NH	2,704.2
68	Nashville, TN	5,955.6
155	New Bedford, MA	4,623.2
48	New Haven, CT	6,327.5
137	New Orleans, LA	4,830.6
391	New Rochelle, NY	2,011.4
363	New York, NY	2,334.0
144	Newark, NJ	4,768.3
313	Newport Beach, CA	2,713.9
216	Newport News, VA	3,765.4
421	Newton, MA	1,472.0
96	Norfolk, VA	5,568.5
261	Norman, OK	3,274.4
49	North Charleston, SC	6,320.1
347	Norwalk, CA	2,476.8
332	Norwalk, CT	2,611.9
24	Oakland, CA	6,970.6
325	Oceanside, CA	2,643.6
211	Odessa, TX	3,804.3
410	O'Fallon, MO	1,627.8
86	Ogden, UT	5,710.5
36	Oklahoma City, OK	6,690.6
401	Olathe, KS	1,918.4
117	Omaha, NE	5,107.3
266	Ontario, CA	3,226.4
388	Orange, CA	2,035.2
329	Orem, UT	2,629.0
12	Orlando, FL	8,170.6

RANK	CITY	RATE
350	Overland Park, KS	2,466.9
385	Oxnard, CA	2,056.7
270	Palm Bay, FL	3,193.2
331	Palmdale, CA	2,625.8
288	Pasadena, CA	2,960.3
209	Pasadena, TX	3,832.3
185	Paterson, NJ	4,241.7
397	Pearland, TX	1,986.6
253	Pembroke Pines, FL	3,349.5
262	Peoria, AZ	3,248.1
101	Peoria, IL	5,419.9
118	Philadelphia, PA	5,087.6
127	Phoenix, AZ	4,949.7
196	Pittsburgh, PA	4,063.1
314	Plano, TX	2,711.2
130	Plantation, FL	4,883.1
234	Pomona, CA	3,561.4
46	Pompano Beach, FL	6,364.2
340	Port St. Lucie, FL	2,536.5
95	Portland, OR	5,603.3
67	Portsmouth, VA	5,986.0
324	Provo, UT	2,648.7
76	Pueblo, CO	5,832.1
362	Quincy, MA	2,337.5
126	Racine, WI	4,960.6
225	Raleigh, NC	3,659.0
427	Ramapo, NY	1,176.1
341	Rancho Cucamon., CA	2,516.6
159	Reading, PA	4,593.6
167	Redding, CA	4,506.3
379	Redwood City, CA	2,141.1
250	Reno, NV	3,371.8
129	Renton, WA	4,888.8
237	Rialto, CA	3,446.4
290	Richardson, TX	2,942.4
108	Richmond, CA	5,319.3
132	Richmond, VA	4,875.3
389	Rio Rancho, NM	2,032.8
235	Riverside, CA	3,558.7
107	Roanoke, VA	5,320.2
NA	Rochester, MN**	NA
56	Rochester, NY	6,128.8
65	Rockford, IL	6,018.4
274	Roseville, CA	3,152.7
393	Roswell, GA	2,009.9
342	Round Rock, TX	2,511.1
152	Sacramento, CA	4,643.7
191	Salem, OR	4,145.7
222	Salinas, CA	3,683.7
20	Salt Lake City, UT	7,372.7
195	San Angelo, TX	4,071.0
43	San Antonio, TX	6,485.9
136	San Bernardino, CA	4,859.9
326	San Diego, CA	2,643.5
147	San Francisco, CA	4,696.2
328	San Jose, CA	2,630.8
190	San Leandro, CA	4,156.0
399	San Marcos, CA	1,954.8
392	San Mateo, CA	2,011.2
306	Sandy Springs, GA	2,763.7
278	Sandy, UT	3,071.3
357	Santa Ana, CA	2,402.4
239	Santa Barbara, CA	3,437.7
327	Santa Clara, CA	2,639.2
412	Santa Clarita, CA	1,586.4
276	Santa Maria, CA	3,122.4
223	Santa Monica, CA	3,678.8
336	Santa Rosa, CA	2,584.4
155	Savannah, GA	4,623.2
265	Scottsdale, AZ	3,231.4
227	Scranton, PA	3,644.6
83	Seattle, WA	5,735.3
99	Shreveport, LA	5,532.6
422	Simi Valley, CA	1,442.3

RANK	CITY	RATE
154	Sioux City, IA	4,627.2
258	Sioux Falls, SD	3,304.4
323	Somerville, MA	2,655.6
35	South Bend, IN	6,726.7
228	South Gate, CA	3,636.4
283	Sparks, NV	3,001.4
87	Spokane Valley, WA	5,677.7
17	Spokane, WA	7,701.9
21	Springfield, IL	7,250.4
79	Springfield, MA	5,809.4
4	Springfield, MO	9,822.7
400	Stamford, CT	1,933.8
373	Sterling Heights, MI	2,217.6
38	Stockton, CA	6,647.1
93	St. Joseph, MO	5,628.2
2	St. Louis, MO	9,866.9
139	St. Paul, MN	4,803.2
52	St. Petersburg, FL	6,180.9
277	Suffolk, VA	3,084.3
404	Sugar Land, TX	1,895.0
419	Sunnyvale, CA	1,495.8
166	Sunrise, FL	4,508.7
368	Surprise, AZ	2,289.8
165	Syracuse, NY	4,510.3
34	Tacoma, WA	6,733.7
66	Tallahassee, FL	5,996.3
219	Tampa, FL	3,709.0
348	Temecula, CA	2,469.5
71	Tempe, AZ	5,926.5
243	Thornton, CO	3,420.2
417	Thousand Oaks, CA	1,501.9
NA	Toledo, OH**	NA
236	Toms River Twnshp, NJ	3,535.0
44	Topeka, KS	6,413.2
394	Torrance, CA	2,006.1
308	Tracy, CA	2,760.5
171	Trenton, NJ	4,434.5
369	Troy, MI	2,288.7
NA	Tucson, AZ**	NA
41	Tulsa, OK	6,534.4
109	Tuscaloosa, AL	5,317.8
381	Tustin, CA	2,106.6
124	Tyler, TX	4,997.0
269	Upper Darby Twnshp, PA	3,197.7
395	Vacaville, CA	2,001.8
112	Vallejo, CA	5,240.2
179	Vancouver, WA	4,308.4
246	Ventura, CA	3,385.8
207	Victorville, CA	3,937.2
292	Virginia Beach, VA	2,912.5
169	Visalia, CA	4,453.4
339	Vista, CA	2,540.6
92	Waco, TX	5,640.7
245	Warren, MI	3,413.1
309	Warwick, RI	2,758.8
85	Washington, DC	5,711.5
168	Waterbury, CT	4,458.7
259	West Covina, CA	3,287.5
285	West Jordan, UT	2,978.8
58	West Palm Beach, FL	6,074.2
164	West Valley, UT	4,512.8
263	Westland, MI	3,246.4
281	Westminster, CA	3,032.3
298	Westminster, CO	2,823.2
264	Whittier, CA	3,245.5
123	Wichita Falls, TX	4,997.5
78	Wichita, KS	5,822.8
74	Wilmington, NC	5,907.7
39	Winston-Salem, NC	6,639.6
321	Woodbridge Twnshp, NJ	2,667.3
178	Worcester, MA	4,324.6
60	Yakima, WA	6,055.4
383	Yonkers, NY	2,062.4
206	Yuma, AZ	3,938.3

Source: CQ Press using reported data from the F.B.I. "Crime in the United States 2011"
*Includes murder, rape, robbery, aggravated assault, burglary, larceny-theft, and motor vehicle theft.
**Not available.

Rank Order - City

42. Crime Rate in 2011 (continued)
National Rate = 3,295.0 Crimes per 100,000 Population*

RANK	CITY	RATE	RANK	CITY	RATE	RANK	CITY	RATE
1	Miami Beach, FL	11,769.6	73	Lubbock, TX	5,920.5	145	Billings, MT	4,763.3
2	St. Louis, MO	9,866.9	74	Wilmington, NC	5,907.7	146	Bakersfield, CA	4,751.9
3	Birmingham, AL	9,849.1	75	Miami Gardens, FL	5,888.0	147	San Francisco, CA	4,696.2
4	Springfield, MO	9,822.7	76	Pueblo, CO	5,832.1	148	Lakewood, CO	4,680.7
5	Little Rock, AR	9,441.1	77	Albuquerque, NM	5,830.7	149	Lawrence, KS	4,680.3
6	Macon, GA	9,046.6	78	Wichita, KS	5,822.8	150	Charlotte, NC	4,660.7
7	Flint, MI	8,802.5	79	Springfield, MA	5,809.4	151	Brockton, MA	4,650.3
8	Camden, NJ	8,522.8	80	Des Moines, IA	5,768.3	152	Sacramento, CA	4,643.7
9	Atlanta, GA	8,516.6	81	Lakeland, FL	5,767.1	153	Lexington, KY	4,629.6
10	Jackson, MS	8,285.6	82	Dallas, TX	5,739.0	154	Sioux City, IA	4,627.2
11	Detroit, MI	8,281.0	83	Seattle, WA	5,735.3	155	New Bedford, MA	4,623.2
12	Orlando, FL	8,170.6	84	Hartford, CT	5,712.5	155	Savannah, GA	4,623.2
13	Knoxville, TN	8,072.6	85	Washington, DC	5,711.5	157	McAllen, TX	4,615.8
14	Memphis, TN	8,072.5	86	Ogden, UT	5,710.5	158	Killeen, TX	4,612.9
15	Cincinnati, OH	7,918.0	87	Spokane Valley, WA	5,677.7	159	Reading, PA	4,593.6
16	Cleveland, OH	7,743.3	88	Austin, TX	5,665.4	160	Merced, CA	4,584.0
17	Spokane, WA	7,701.9	89	Fresno, CA	5,661.8	161	Antioch, CA	4,529.1
18	Everett, WA	7,600.7	90	Medford, OR	5,656.2	162	Athens-Clarke, GA	4,517.0
19	Gary, IN	7,406.1	91	Albany, NY	5,646.2	163	Clearwater, FL	4,516.6
20	Salt Lake City, UT	7,372.7	92	Waco, TX	5,640.7	164	West Valley, UT	4,512.8
21	Springfield, IL	7,250.4	93	St. Joseph, MO	5,628.2	165	Syracuse, NY	4,510.3
22	Chattanooga, TN	7,148.9	94	Durham, NC	5,612.3	166	Sunrise, FL	4,508.7
23	Fort Lauderdale, FL	7,007.5	95	Portland, OR	5,603.3	167	Redding, CA	4,506.3
24	Oakland, CA	6,970.6	96	Norfolk, VA	5,568.5	168	Waterbury, CT	4,458.7
25	Columbus, GA	6,956.4	97	Davenport, IA	5,548.5	169	Visalia, CA	4,453.4
26	Fayetteville, NC	6,903.8	98	Montgomery, AL	5,538.5	170	Columbia, MO	4,449.3
27	Glendale, AZ	6,894.2	99	Shreveport, LA	5,532.6	171	Trenton, NJ	4,434.5
28	Columbus, OH	6,885.1	100	Amarillo, TX	5,449.7	172	Gresham, OR	4,429.4
29	Miami, FL	6,858.5	101	Peoria, IL	5,419.9	173	Allentown, PA	4,410.2
30	Dayton, OH	6,833.2	102	Corpus Christi, TX	5,417.8	174	Manchester, NH	4,386.2
31	Albany, GA	6,830.8	103	Louisville, KY	5,417.6	175	Citrus Heights, CA	4,351.0
32	Indianapolis, IN	6,738.9	104	Avondale, AZ	5,386.9	176	Largo, FL	4,346.6
33	Kansas City, MO	6,735.4	105	Hammond, IN	5,374.0	177	Decatur, IL	4,343.1
34	Tacoma, WA	6,733.7	106	High Point, NC	5,352.2	178	Worcester, MA	4,324.6
35	South Bend, IN	6,726.7	107	Roanoke, VA	5,320.2	179	Vancouver, WA	4,308.4
36	Oklahoma City, OK	6,690.6	108	Richmond, CA	5,319.3	180	Denver, CO	4,291.3
37	Buffalo, NY	6,688.0	109	Tuscaloosa, AL	5,317.8	181	Clovis, CA	4,283.0
38	Stockton, CA	6,647.1	110	Eugene, OR	5,282.3	182	Bryan, TX	4,281.3
39	Winston-Salem, NC	6,639.6	111	Fort Worth, TX	5,243.9	183	Lincoln, NE	4,279.1
40	Baton Rouge, LA	6,534.8	112	Vallejo, CA	5,240.2	184	Davie, FL	4,272.6
41	Tulsa, OK	6,534.4	113	Asheville, NC	5,201.9	185	Paterson, NJ	4,241.5
42	Lawton, OK	6,496.2	114	Longview, TX	5,129.8	186	Lawrence, MA	4,222.9
43	San Antonio, TX	6,485.9	115	Elizabeth, NJ	5,115.4	187	Grand Prairie, TX	4,214.2
44	Topeka, KS	6,413.2	116	Arlington, TX	5,114.1	188	Dearborn, MI	4,196.6
45	Beaumont, TX	6,395.7	117	Omaha, NE	5,107.3	189	Colorado Springs, CO	4,185.0
46	Pompano Beach, FL	6,364.2	118	Philadelphia, PA	5,087.6	190	San Leandro, CA	4,156.0
47	Akron, OH	6,345.1	119	Modesto, CA	5,064.1	191	Salem, OR	4,145.7
48	New Haven, CT	6,327.5	120	Evansville, IN	5,038.6	192	Cedar Rapids, IA	4,124.0
49	North Charleston, SC	6,320.1	121	Las Cruces, NM	5,035.0	193	Bloomington, IN	4,103.1
50	Edinburg, TX	6,267.6	122	Murfreesboro, TN	5,016.6	194	Erie, PA	4,082.8
51	Huntsville, AL	6,225.8	123	Wichita Falls, TX	4,997.5	195	San Angelo, TX	4,071.0
52	St. Petersburg, FL	6,180.9	124	Tyler, TX	4,997.0	196	Pittsburgh, PA	4,063.1
53	Baltimore, MD	6,175.2	125	Gainesville, FL	4,972.7	197	Hampton, VA	4,043.1
54	Melbourne, FL	6,173.4	126	Racine, WI	4,960.6	198	Compton, CA	4,029.1
55	Independence, MO	6,131.9	127	Phoenix, AZ	4,949.7	199	Grand Rapids, MI	4,028.2
56	Rochester, NY	6,128.8	128	Jacksonville, FL	4,948.9	200	Abilene, TX	4,025.9
57	Fort Smith, AR	6,106.3	129	Renton, WA	4,888.8	201	Concord, NC	4,001.5
58	West Palm Beach, FL	6,074.2	130	Plantation, FL	4,883.1	202	Anchorage, AK	3,988.1
59	Mobile, AL	6,062.3	131	Bridgeport, CT	4,881.8	203	Garland, TX	3,977.1
60	Yakima, WA	6,055.4	132	Richmond, VA	4,875.3	204	Boston, MA	3,974.7
61	Lafayette, LA	6,041.4	133	Berkeley, CA	4,869.1	205	Indio, CA	3,951.6
62	Milwaukee, WI	6,036.9	134	Brownsville, TX	4,861.1	206	Yuma, AZ	3,938.3
63	Houston, TX	6,028.5	135	Mesquite, TX	4,860.4	207	Victorville, CA	3,937.2
64	Kansas City, KS	6,018.6	136	San Bernardino, CA	4,859.9	208	Fort Wayne, IN	3,851.6
65	Rockford, IL	6,018.4	137	New Orleans, LA	4,830.6	209	Pasadena, TX	3,832.3
66	Tallahassee, FL	5,996.3	138	Hemet, CA	4,816.4	210	Mesa, AZ	3,807.9
67	Portsmouth, VA	5,986.0	139	St. Paul, MN	4,803.2	211	Odessa, TX	3,804.3
68	Nashville, TN	5,955.6	140	Bellingham, WA	4,792.2	212	Clarksville, TN	3,802.3
69	Minneapolis, MN	5,943.0	141	Laredo, TX	4,786.8	213	Kennewick, WA	3,801.5
70	Kent, WA	5,930.0	142	Fall River, MA	4,783.1	214	Downey, CA	3,772.4
71	Tempe, AZ	5,926.5	143	Lansing, MI	4,777.1	215	Lynn, MA	3,767.6
72	Hollywood, FL	5,921.4	144	Newark, NJ	4,768.3	216	Newport News, VA	3,765.4

Rank Order - City (continued)

RANK	CITY	RATE	RANK	CITY	RATE	RANK	CITY	RATE
217	Greeley, CO	3,761.6	290	Richardson, TX	2,942.4	364	League City, TX	2,319.6
218	Madison, WI	3,736.2	291	Chino, CA	2,939.2	365	Corona, CA	2,305.3
219	Tampa, FL	3,709.0	292	Virginia Beach, VA	2,912.5	366	Chula Vista, CA	2,300.4
220	Champaign, IL	3,706.1	293	Carrollton, TX	2,901.2	367	McKinney, TX	2,290.9
221	Cheektowaga, NY	3,697.2	294	El Paso, TX	2,892.4	368	Surprise, AZ	2,289.8
222	Salinas, CA	3,683.7	295	Colonie, NY	2,887.7	369	Troy, MI	2,288.7
223	Santa Monica, CA	3,678.8	296	Anaheim, CA	2,872.9	370	Hamilton Twnshp, NJ	2,255.5
224	Hialeah, FL	3,667.9	297	Fargo, ND	2,846.4	371	Aurora, IL	2,245.4
225	Raleigh, NC	3,659.0	298	Westminster, CO	2,823.2	372	Garden Grove, CA	2,218.7
226	Deerfield Beach, FL	3,657.3	299	Fullerton, CA	2,819.7	373	Sterling Heights, MI	2,217.6
227	Scranton, PA	3,644.6	300	Hesperia, CA	2,808.2	374	Clifton, NJ	2,195.1
228	South Gate, CA	3,636.4	301	Boise, ID	2,807.5	375	Elgin, IL	2,170.2
229	Lowell, MA	3,635.4	302	Boulder, CO	2,791.7	376	Danbury, CT	2,161.8
230	Mission, TX	3,623.6	303	Greece, NY	2,775.4	377	Frisco, TX	2,161.6
231	Lynchburg, VA	3,592.2	304	Los Angeles, CA	2,772.2	378	Beaverton, OR	2,143.0
232	Chesapeake, VA	3,582.2	305	Bethlehem, PA	2,766.5	379	Redwood City, CA	2,141.1
233	Las Vegas, NV	3,581.8	306	Sandy Springs, GA	2,763.7	380	Menifee, CA	2,121.6
234	Pomona, CA	3,561.4	307	Cicero, IL	2,763.1	381	Tustin, CA	2,106.6
235	Riverside, CA	3,558.7	308	Tracy, CA	2,760.5	382	Edmond, OK	2,071.1
236	Toms River Twnshp, NJ	3,535.0	309	Warwick, RI	2,758.8	383	Yonkers, NY	2,062.4
237	Rialto, CA	3,446.4	310	Hoover, AL	2,747.2	384	Henderson, NV	2,057.7
238	Cambridge, MA	3,438.5	311	Bloomington, IL	2,734.2	385	Oxnard, CA	2,056.7
239	Santa Barbara, CA	3,437.7	312	Bellflower, CA	2,732.3	386	Carlsbad, CA	2,045.7
240	Concord, CA	3,427.5	313	Newport Beach, CA	2,713.9	387	Clarkstown, NY	2,041.1
241	College Station, TX	3,423.7	314	Plano, TX	2,711.2	388	Orange, CA	2,035.2
242	Aurora, CO	3,423.5	315	Clinton Twnshp, MI	2,708.8	389	Rio Rancho, NM	2,032.8
243	Thornton, CO	3,420.2	316	Chico, CA	2,706.4	390	Daly City, CA	2,017.4
244	Charleston, SC	3,417.8	317	Nashua, NH	2,704.2	391	New Rochelle, NY	2,011.4
245	Warren, MI	3,413.1	318	Cape Coral, FL	2,701.3	392	San Mateo, CA	2,011.2
246	Ventura, CA	3,385.8	319	Cranston, RI	2,674.1	393	Roswell, GA	2,009.9
247	Costa Mesa, CA	3,384.2	320	Green Bay, WI	2,672.5	394	Torrance, CA	2,006.1
248	Bend, OR	3,382.6	321	Woodbridge Twnshp, NJ	2,667.3	395	Fremont, CA	2,001.8
249	Chandler, AZ	3,381.3	322	Coral Springs, FL	2,664.9	395	Vacaville, CA	2,001.8
250	Reno, NV	3,371.8	323	Somerville, MA	2,655.6	397	Pearland, TX	1,986.6
251	Lewisville, TX	3,369.1	324	Provo, UT	2,648.7	398	Edison Twnshp, NJ	1,968.1
252	Long Beach, CA	3,351.1	325	Oceanside, CA	2,643.6	399	San Marcos, CA	1,954.8
253	Pembroke Pines, FL	3,349.5	326	San Diego, CA	2,643.5	400	Stamford, CT	1,933.8
254	Boca Raton, FL	3,336.4	327	Santa Clara, CA	2,639.2	401	Olathe, KS	1,918.4
255	Kenosha, WI	3,321.6	328	San Jose, CA	2,630.8	402	Glendale, CA	1,912.6
256	Moreno Valley, CA	3,319.4	329	Orem, UT	2,629.0	403	Gilbert, AZ	1,907.2
257	Irving, TX	3,309.2	330	Burbank, CA	2,626.4	404	Sugar Land, TX	1,895.0
258	Sioux Falls, SD	3,304.4	331	Palmdale, CA	2,625.8	405	Brick Twnshp, NJ	1,875.9
259	West Covina, CA	3,287.5	332	Norwalk, CT	2,611.9	406	Allen, TX	1,857.7
260	Nampa, ID	3,276.8	333	Lakewood, CA	2,609.0	407	Amherst, NY	1,809.4
261	Norman, OK	3,274.4	334	Huntington Beach, CA	2,598.5	408	Farmington Hills, MI	1,715.6
262	Peoria, AZ	3,248.1	335	Buena Park, CA	2,588.5	409	Canton Twnshp, MI	1,694.7
263	Westland, MI	3,246.4	336	Santa Rosa, CA	2,584.4	410	O'Fallon, MO	1,627.8
264	Whittier, CA	3,245.5	337	Lancaster, CA	2,566.4	411	Cary, NC	1,607.1
265	Scottsdale, AZ	3,231.4	338	Escondido, CA	2,544.6	412	Santa Clarita, CA	1,586.4
266	Ontario, CA	3,226.4	339	Vista, CA	2,540.6	413	Irvine, CA	1,582.3
267	Hawthorne, CA	3,221.0	340	Port St. Lucie, FL	2,536.5	414	Naperville, IL	1,561.7
268	Fort Collins, CO	3,202.9	341	Rancho Cucamon., CA	2,516.6	415	Murrieta, CA	1,528.4
269	Upper Darby Twnshp, PA	3,197.7	342	Round Rock, TX	2,511.1	416	Meridian, ID	1,523.9
270	Palm Bay, FL	3,193.2	343	Longmont, CO	2,501.9	417	Thousand Oaks, CA	1,501.9
271	Midland, TX	3,190.7	344	Arvada, CO	2,500.8	418	Arlington Heights, IL	1,501.5
272	Fairfield, CA	3,189.8	345	Fontana, CA	2,497.8	419	Sunnyvale, CA	1,495.8
273	Carson, CA	3,164.1	346	Livermore, CA	2,493.9	420	Centennial, CO	1,483.5
274	Roseville, CA	3,152.7	347	Norwalk, CA	2,476.8	421	Newton, MA	1,472.0
275	Denton, TX	3,132.1	348	Temecula, CA	2,469.5	422	Simi Valley, CA	1,442.3
276	Santa Maria, CA	3,122.4	349	Ann Arbor, MI	2,468.2	423	Chino Hills, CA	1,382.2
277	Suffolk, VA	3,084.3	350	Overland Park, KS	2,466.9	424	Mission Viejo, CA	1,371.8
278	Sandy, UT	3,071.3	351	Elk Grove, CA	2,450.0	425	Lake Forest, CA	1,325.3
279	Jersey City, NJ	3,062.1	352	Broken Arrow, OK	2,433.2	426	Lakewood Twnshp, NJ	1,250.6
280	Inglewood, CA	3,055.1	353	Alhambra, CA	2,430.2	427	Ramapo, NY	1,176.1
281	Westminster, CA	3,032.3	354	Lee's Summit, MO	2,424.3	428	Carmel, IN	1,065.4
282	Miramar, FL	3,008.8	355	Alexandria, VA	2,423.8	429	Fishers, IN	921.2
283	Sparks, NV	3,001.4	356	Baldwin Park, CA	2,416.4	430	Johns Creek, GA	783.4
284	Hayward, CA	2,989.4	357	Santa Ana, CA	2,402.4	NA	Bloomington, MN**	NA
285	West Jordan, UT	2,978.8	358	Hillsboro, OR	2,388.1	NA	Brooklyn Park, MN**	NA
286	El Cajon, CA	2,977.7	359	Napa, CA	2,363.2	NA	Chicago, IL**	NA
287	Joliet, IL	2,960.6	360	El Monte, CA	2,357.8	NA	Duluth, MN**	NA
288	Pasadena, CA	2,960.3	361	Livonia, MI	2,349.6	NA	Rochester, MN**	NA
289	Bellevue, WA	2,960.2	362	Quincy, MA	2,337.5	NA	Toledo, OH**	NA
			363	New York, NY	2,334.0	NA	Tucson, AZ**	NA

Source: CQ Press using reported data from the F.B.I. "Crime in the United States 2011"
*Includes murder, rape, robbery, aggravated assault, burglary, larceny-theft, and motor vehicle theft.
**Not available.

Alpha Order - City

43. Percent Change in Crime Rate: 2010 to 2011
National Percent Change = 1.7% Decrease*

RANK	CITY	% CHANGE	RANK	CITY	% CHANGE	RANK	CITY	% CHANGE
369	Abilene, TX	(14.0)	194	Cheektowaga, NY	(2.4)	102	Fort Wayne, IN	3.1
88	Akron, OH	4.3	212	Chesapeake, VA	(3.3)	161	Fort Worth, TX	(0.6)
365	Albany, GA	(13.4)	NA	Chicago, IL**	NA	384	Fremont, CA	(16.1)
277	Albany, NY	(6.9)	329	Chico, CA	(10.6)	154	Fresno, CA	(0.2)
92	Albuquerque, NM	3.7	197	Chino Hills, CA	(2.6)	345	Frisco, TX	(11.5)
76	Alexandria, VA	5.3	42	Chino, CA	8.8	350	Fullerton, CA	(12.1)
302	Alhambra, CA	(8.6)	306	Chula Vista, CA	(8.9)	292	Gainesville, FL	(7.9)
392	Allentown, PA	(17.8)	NA	Cicero, IL**	NA	329	Garden Grove, CA	(10.6)
171	Allen, TX	(1.1)	39	Cincinnati, OH	9.1	208	Garland, TX	(3.2)
379	Amarillo, TX	(15.3)	377	Citrus Heights, CA	(14.8)	NA	Gary, IN**	NA
320	Amherst, NY	(9.6)	331	Clarkstown, NY	(10.7)	230	Gilbert, AZ	(4.2)
131	Anaheim, CA	0.9	183	Clarksville, TN	(1.9)	9	Glendale, AZ	16.7
299	Anchorage, AK	(8.4)	268	Clearwater, FL	(6.7)	251	Glendale, CA	(5.7)
375	Ann Arbor, MI	(14.4)	16	Cleveland, OH	13.9	361	Grand Prairie, TX	(13.0)
8	Antioch, CA	16.8	NA	Clifton, NJ**	NA	393	Grand Rapids, MI	(18.0)
319	Arlington Heights, IL	(9.5)	224	Clinton Twnshp, MI	(4.0)	226	Greece, NY	(4.1)
291	Arlington, TX	(7.8)	33	Clovis, CA	10.0	105	Greeley, CO	2.8
256	Arvada, CO	(5.9)	76	College Station, TX	5.3	304	Green Bay, WI	(8.7)
193	Asheville, NC	(2.3)	218	Colonie, NY	(3.8)	143	Gresham, OR	0.4
220	Athens-Clarke, GA	(3.9)	341	Colorado Springs, CO	(11.2)	122	Hamilton Twnshp, NJ	1.4
2	Atlanta, GA	25.0	70	Columbia, MO	5.9	325	Hammond, IN	(9.9)
216	Aurora, CO	(3.7)	337	Columbus, GA	(11.1)	117	Hampton, VA	2.0
337	Aurora, IL	(11.1)	233	Columbus, OH	(4.3)	135	Hartford, CT	0.8
308	Austin, TX	(9.1)	293	Compton, CA	(8.0)	245	Hawthorne, CA	(5.3)
18	Avondale, AZ	13.2	218	Concord, CA	(3.8)	183	Hayward, CA	(1.9)
299	Bakersfield, CA	(8.4)	298	Concord, NC	(8.1)	50	Hemet, CA	8.1
281	Baldwin Park, CA	(7.1)	55	Coral Springs, FL	7.7	244	Henderson, NV	(5.2)
80	Baltimore, MD	5.1	247	Corona, CA	(5.4)	19	Hesperia, CA	13.1
NA	Baton Rouge, LA**	NA	315	Corpus Christi, TX	(9.3)	312	Hialeah, FL	(9.2)
114	Beaumont, TX	2.3	42	Costa Mesa, CA	8.8	108	High Point, NC	2.7
148	Beaverton, OR	0.1	68	Cranston, RI	6.3	NA	Hillsboro, OR**	NA
208	Bellevue, WA	(3.2)	114	Dallas, TX	2.3	58	Hollywood, FL	7.6
312	Bellflower, CA	(9.2)	148	Daly City, CA	0.1	NA	Hoover, AL**	NA
173	Bellingham, WA	(1.2)	55	Danbury, CT	7.7	154	Houston, TX	(0.2)
123	Bend, OR	1.3	NA	Davenport, IA**	NA	180	Huntington Beach, CA	(1.8)
404	Berkeley, CA	(22.8)	176	Davie, FL	(1.3)	NA	Huntsville, AL**	NA
345	Bethlehem, PA	(11.5)	148	Dayton, OH	0.1	214	Independence, MO	(3.6)
NA	Billings, MT**	NA	379	Dearborn, MI	(15.3)	NA	Indianapolis, IN**	NA
NA	Birmingham, AL**	NA	317	Decatur, IL	(9.4)	22	Indio, CA	11.3
365	Bloomington, IL	(13.4)	263	Deerfield Beach, FL	(6.4)	197	Inglewood, CA	(2.6)
369	Bloomington, IN	(14.0)	22	Denton, TX	11.3	6	Irvine, CA	17.8
NA	Bloomington, MN**	NA	45	Denver, CO	8.7	389	Irving, TX	(17.5)
52	Boca Raton, FL	7.8	60	Des Moines, IA	7.5	242	Jacksonville, FL	(5.1)
286	Boise, ID	(7.5)	12	Detroit, MI	15.0	214	Jackson, MS	(3.6)
208	Boston, MA	(3.2)	283	Downey, CA	(7.2)	234	Jersey City, NJ	(4.4)
248	Boulder, CO	(5.5)	NA	Duluth, MN**	NA	408	Johns Creek, GA	(32.4)
126	Brick Twnshp, NJ	1.1	124	Durham, NC	1.2	251	Joliet, IL	(5.7)
24	Bridgeport, CT	11.2	197	Edinburg, TX	(2.6)	124	Kansas City, KS	1.2
47	Brockton, MA	8.6	63	Edison Twnshp, NJ	6.8	NA	Kansas City, MO**	NA
40	Broken Arrow, OK	8.9	191	Edmond, OK	(2.2)	248	Kennewick, WA	(5.5)
NA	Brooklyn Park, MN**	NA	333	El Cajon, CA	(10.9)	120	Kenosha, WI	1.5
344	Brownsville, TX	(11.4)	326	El Monte, CA	(10.1)	113	Kent, WA	2.4
398	Bryan, TX	(20.5)	333	El Paso, TX	(10.9)	387	Killeen, TX	(17.2)
293	Buena Park, CA	(8.0)	293	Elgin, IL	(8.0)	67	Knoxville, TN	6.4
NA	Buffalo, NY**	NA	75	Elizabeth, NJ	5.6	350	Lafayette, LA	(12.1)
268	Burbank, CA	(6.7)	267	Elk Grove, CA	(6.6)	234	Lake Forest, CA	(4.4)
141	Cambridge, MA	0.5	65	Erie, PA	6.7	183	Lakeland, FL	(1.9)
1	Camden, NJ	26.2	403	Escondido, CA	(22.7)	399	Lakewood Twnshp, NJ	(21.4)
345	Canton Twnshp, MI	(11.5)	42	Eugene, OR	8.8	263	Lakewood, CA	(6.4)
65	Cape Coral, FL	6.7	202	Evansville, IN	(2.7)	163	Lakewood, CO	(0.8)
117	Carlsbad, CA	2.0	293	Everett, WA	(8.0)	345	Lancaster, CA	(11.5)
395	Carmel, IN	(18.7)	376	Fairfield, CA	(14.7)	173	Lansing, MI	(1.2)
105	Carrollton, TX	2.8	188	Fall River, MA	(2.1)	355	Laredo, TX	(12.4)
94	Carson, CA	3.5	285	Fargo, ND	(7.4)	391	Largo, FL	(17.6)
171	Cary, NC	(1.1)	337	Farmington Hills, MI	(11.1)	100	Las Cruces, NM	3.2
151	Cedar Rapids, IA	0.0	79	Fayetteville, NC	5.2	312	Las Vegas, NV	(9.2)
308	Centennial, CO	(9.1)	268	Fishers, IN	(6.7)	96	Lawrence, KS	3.4
NA	Champaign, IL**	NA	24	Flint, MI	11.2	195	Lawrence, MA	(2.5)
158	Chandler, AZ	(0.4)	48	Fontana, CA	8.3	180	Lawton, OK	(1.8)
306	Charleston, SC	(8.9)	336	Fort Collins, CO	(11.0)	386	League City, TX	(17.0)
258	Charlotte, NC	(6.1)	10	Fort Lauderdale, FL	15.8	236	Lee's Summit, MO	(4.5)
163	Chattanooga, TN	(0.8)	226	Fort Smith, AR	(4.1)	204	Lewisville, TX	(3.0)

Alpha Order - City (continued)

RANK	CITY	% CHANGE	RANK	CITY	% CHANGE	RANK	CITY	% CHANGE
NA	Lexington, KY**	NA	178	Overland Park, KS	(1.5)	15	Sioux City, IA	14.0
208	Lincoln, NE	(3.2)	388	Oxnard, CA	(17.4)	160	Sioux Falls, SD	(0.5)
108	Little Rock, AR	2.7	27	Palm Bay, FL	10.7	283	Somerville, MA	(7.2)
197	Livermore, CA	(2.6)	286	Palmdale, CA	(7.5)	83	South Bend, IN	5.0
260	Livonia, MI	(6.2)	289	Pasadena, CA	(7.6)	36	South Gate, CA	9.3
51	Long Beach, CA	7.9	317	Pasadena, TX	(9.4)	349	Sparks, NV	(12.0)
327	Longmont, CO	(10.4)	117	Paterson, NJ	2.0	17	Spokane Valley, WA	13.5
389	Longview, TX	(17.5)	191	Pearland, TX	(2.2)	224	Spokane, WA	(4.0)
230	Los Angeles, CA	(4.2)	277	Pembroke Pines, FL	(6.9)	250	Springfield, IL	(5.6)
92	Louisville, KY	3.7	84	Peoria, AZ	4.6	279	Springfield, MA	(7.0)
400	Lowell, MA	(21.5)	105	Peoria, IL	2.8	268	Springfield, MO	(6.7)
261	Lubbock, TX	(6.3)	91	Philadelphia, PA	3.9	111	Stamford, CT	2.5
286	Lynchburg, VA	(7.5)	31	Phoenix, AZ	10.2	NA	Sterling Heights, MI**	NA
154	Lynn, MA	(0.2)	323	Pittsburgh, PA	(9.8)	220	Stockton, CA	(3.9)
128	Macon, GA	1.0	85	Plano, TX	4.5	36	St. Joseph, MO	9.3
163	Madison, WI	(0.8)	110	Plantation, FL	2.6	85	St. Louis, MO	4.5
29	Manchester, NH	10.3	128	Pomona, CA	1.0	197	St. Paul, MN	(2.6)
396	McAllen, TX	(19.3)	38	Pompano Beach, FL	9.2	308	St. Petersburg, FL	(9.1)
239	McKinney, TX	(4.7)	12	Port St. Lucie, FL	15.0	14	Suffolk, VA	14.5
5	Medford, OR	18.2	139	Portland, OR	0.6	401	Sugar Land, TX	(21.8)
29	Melbourne, FL	10.3	186	Portsmouth, VA	(2.0)	385	Sunnyvale, CA	(16.3)
94	Memphis, TN	3.5	68	Provo, UT	6.3	254	Sunrise, FL	(5.8)
407	Menifee, CA	(30.5)	NA	Pueblo, CO**	NA	120	Surprise, AZ	1.5
73	Merced, CA	5.8	220	Quincy, MA	(3.9)	353	Syracuse, NY	(12.2)
372	Meridian, ID	(14.3)	61	Racine, WI	7.3	266	Tacoma, WA	(6.5)
96	Mesa, AZ	3.4	89	Raleigh, NC	4.2	135	Tallahassee, FL	0.8
279	Mesquite, TX	(7.0)	45	Ramapo, NY	8.7	245	Tampa, FL	(5.3)
52	Miami Beach, FL	7.8	33	Rancho Cucamon., CA	10.0	87	Temecula, CA	4.4
145	Miami Gardens, FL	0.2	382	Reading, PA	(15.6)	26	Tempe, AZ	10.8
10	Miami, FL	15.8	58	Redding, CA	7.6	NA	Thornton, CO**	NA
356	Midland, TX	(12.6)	354	Redwood City, CA	(12.3)	372	Thousand Oaks, CA	(14.3)
220	Milwaukee, WI	(3.9)	363	Reno, NV	(13.2)	NA	Toledo, OH**	NA
111	Minneapolis, MN	2.5	406	Renton, WA	(29.9)	6	Toms River Twnshp, NJ	17.8
394	Miramar, FL	(18.6)	21	Rialto, CA	11.7	186	Topeka, KS	(2.0)
52	Mission Viejo, CA	7.8	226	Richardson, TX	(4.1)	328	Torrance, CA	(10.5)
402	Mission, TX	(22.3)	242	Richmond, CA	(5.1)	138	Tracy, CA	0.7
NA	Mobile, AL**	NA	158	Richmond, VA	(0.4)	154	Trenton, NJ	(0.2)
230	Modesto, CA	(4.2)	40	Rio Rancho, NM	8.9	116	Troy, MI	2.2
NA	Montgomery, AL**	NA	256	Riverside, CA	(5.9)	NA	Tucson, AZ**	NA
32	Moreno Valley, CA	10.1	275	Roanoke, VA	(6.8)	145	Tulsa, OK	0.2
80	Murfreesboro, TN	5.1	NA	Rochester, MN**	NA	NA	Tuscaloosa, AL**	NA
70	Murrieta, CA	5.9	337	Rochester, NY	(11.1)	315	Tustin, CA	(9.3)
62	Nampa, ID	7.2	268	Rockford, IL	(6.7)	357	Tyler, TX	(12.8)
169	Napa, CA	(1.0)	304	Roseville, CA	(8.7)	145	Upper Darby Twnshp, PA	0.2
NA	Naperville, IL**	NA	368	Roswell, GA	(13.8)	367	Vacaville, CA	(13.7)
180	Nashua, NH	(1.8)	333	Round Rock, TX	(10.9)	126	Vallejo, CA	1.1
188	Nashville, TN	(2.1)	323	Sacramento, CA	(9.8)	152	Vancouver, WA	(0.1)
359	New Bedford, MA	(12.9)	173	Salem, OR	(1.2)	240	Ventura, CA	(4.8)
372	New Haven, CT	(14.3)	301	Salinas, CA	(8.5)	73	Victorville, CA	5.8
20	New Orleans, LA	13.0	364	Salt Lake City, UT	(13.3)	322	Virginia Beach, VA	(9.7)
96	New Rochelle, NY	3.4	381	San Angelo, TX	(15.5)	254	Visalia, CA	(5.8)
96	New York, NY	3.4	268	San Antonio, TX	(6.7)	261	Vista, CA	(6.3)
28	Newark, NJ	10.5	302	San Bernardino, CA	(8.6)	178	Waco, TX	(1.5)
206	Newport Beach, CA	(3.1)	236	San Diego, CA	(4.5)	131	Warren, MI	0.9
188	Newport News, VA	(2.1)	131	San Francisco, CA	0.9	70	Warwick, RI	5.9
241	Newton, MA	(5.0)	131	San Jose, CA	0.9	162	Washington, DC	(0.7)
331	Norfolk, VA	(10.7)	263	San Leandro, CA	(6.4)	213	Waterbury, CT	(3.5)
169	Norman, OK	(1.0)	361	San Marcos, CA	(13.0)	80	West Covina, CA	5.1
290	North Charleston, SC	(7.7)	378	San Marcos, CA	(15.1)	281	West Jordan, UT	(7.1)
143	Norwalk, CA	0.4	397	Sandy Springs, GA	(19.8)	76	West Palm Beach, FL	5.3
152	Norwalk, CT	(0.1)	195	Sandy, UT	(2.5)	357	West Valley, UT	(12.8)
3	Oakland, CA	21.1	128	Santa Ana, CA	1.0	320	Westland, MI	(9.6)
135	Oceanside, CA	0.8	103	Santa Barbara, CA	3.0	203	Westminster, CA	(2.9)
308	Odessa, TX	(9.1)	275	Santa Clara, CA	(6.8)	350	Westminster, CO	(12.1)
168	O'Fallon, MO	(0.9)	341	Santa Clarita, CA	(11.2)	238	Whittier, CA	(4.6)
268	Ogden, UT	(6.7)	343	Santa Maria, CA	(11.3)	359	Wichita Falls, TX	(12.9)
163	Oklahoma City, OK	(0.8)	293	Santa Monica, CA	(8.0)	100	Wichita, KS	3.2
226	Olathe, KS	(4.1)	383	Santa Rosa, CA	(15.9)	251	Wilmington, NC	(5.7)
3	Omaha, NE	21.1	204	Savannah, GA	(3.0)	90	Winston-Salem, NC	4.0
141	Ontario, CA	0.5	55	Scottsdale, AZ	7.7	63	Woodbridge Twnshp, NJ	6.8
103	Orange, CA	3.0	176	Scranton, PA	(1.3)	163	Worcester, MA	(0.8)
258	Orem, UT	(6.1)	206	Seattle, WA	(3.1)	371	Yakima, WA	(14.1)
49	Orlando, FL	8.2	139	Shreveport, LA	0.6	35	Yonkers, NY	9.7
			405	Simi Valley, CA	(24.9)	216	Yuma, AZ	(3.7)

Source: CQ Press using reported data from the F.B.I. "Crime in the United States 2011"
*Includes murder, rape, robbery, aggravated assault, burglary, larceny-theft, and motor vehicle theft.
**Not available.

43. Percent Change in Crime Rate: 2010 to 2011 (continued)
National Percent Change = 1.7% Decrease*

RANK	CITY	% CHANGE
1	Camden, NJ	26.2
2	Atlanta, GA	25.0
3	Oakland, CA	21.1
3	Omaha, NE	21.1
5	Medford, OR	18.2
6	Irvine, CA	17.8
6	Toms River Twnshp, NJ	17.8
8	Antioch, CA	16.8
9	Glendale, AZ	16.7
10	Fort Lauderdale, FL	15.8
10	Miami, FL	15.8
12	Detroit, MI	15.0
12	Port St. Lucie, FL	15.0
14	Suffolk, VA	14.5
15	Sioux City, IA	14.0
16	Cleveland, OH	13.9
17	Spokane Valley, WA	13.5
18	Avondale, AZ	13.2
19	Hesperia, CA	13.1
20	New Orleans, LA	13.0
21	Rialto, CA	11.7
22	Denton, TX	11.3
22	Indio, CA	11.3
24	Bridgeport, CT	11.2
24	Flint, MI	11.2
26	Tempe, AZ	10.8
27	Palm Bay, FL	10.7
28	Newark, NJ	10.5
29	Manchester, NH	10.3
29	Melbourne, FL	10.3
31	Phoenix, AZ	10.2
32	Moreno Valley, CA	10.1
33	Clovis, CA	10.0
33	Rancho Cucamon., CA	10.0
35	Yonkers, NY	9.7
36	South Gate, CA	9.3
36	St. Joseph, MO	9.3
38	Pompano Beach, FL	9.2
39	Cincinnati, OH	9.1
40	Broken Arrow, OK	8.9
40	Rio Rancho, NM	8.9
42	Chino, CA	8.8
42	Costa Mesa, CA	8.8
42	Eugene, OR	8.8
45	Denver, CO	8.7
45	Ramapo, NY	8.7
47	Brockton, MA	8.6
48	Fontana, CA	8.3
49	Orlando, FL	8.2
50	Hemet, CA	8.1
51	Long Beach, CA	7.9
52	Boca Raton, FL	7.8
52	Miami Beach, FL	7.8
52	Mission Viejo, CA	7.8
55	Coral Springs, FL	7.7
55	Danbury, CT	7.7
55	Scottsdale, AZ	7.7
58	Hollywood, FL	7.6
58	Redding, CA	7.6
60	Des Moines, IA	7.5
61	Racine, WI	7.3
62	Nampa, ID	7.2
63	Edison Twnshp, NJ	6.8
63	Woodbridge Twnshp, NJ	6.8
65	Cape Coral, FL	6.7
65	Erie, PA	6.7
67	Knoxville, TN	6.4
68	Cranston, RI	6.3
68	Provo, UT	6.3
70	Columbia, MO	5.9
70	Murrieta, CA	5.9
70	Warwick, RI	5.9

RANK	CITY	% CHANGE
73	Merced, CA	5.8
73	Victorville, CA	5.8
75	Elizabeth, NJ	5.6
76	Alexandria, VA	5.3
76	College Station, TX	5.3
76	West Palm Beach, FL	5.3
79	Fayetteville, NC	5.2
80	Baltimore, MD	5.1
80	Murfreesboro, TN	5.1
80	West Covina, CA	5.1
83	South Bend, IN	5.0
84	Peoria, AZ	4.6
85	Plano, TX	4.5
85	St. Louis, MO	4.5
87	Temecula, CA	4.4
88	Akron, OH	4.3
89	Raleigh, NC	4.2
90	Winston-Salem, NC	4.0
91	Philadelphia, PA	3.9
92	Albuquerque, NM	3.7
92	Louisville, KY	3.7
94	Carson, CA	3.5
94	Memphis, TN	3.5
96	Lawrence, KS	3.4
96	Mesa, AZ	3.4
96	New Rochelle, NY	3.4
96	New York, NY	3.4
100	Las Cruces, NM	3.2
100	Wichita, KS	3.2
102	Fort Wayne, IN	3.1
103	Orange, CA	3.0
103	Santa Barbara, CA	3.0
105	Carrollton, TX	2.8
105	Greeley, CO	2.8
105	Peoria, IL	2.8
108	High Point, NC	2.7
108	Little Rock, AR	2.7
110	Plantation, FL	2.6
111	Minneapolis, MN	2.5
111	Stamford, CT	2.5
113	Kent, WA	2.4
114	Beaumont, TX	2.3
114	Dallas, TX	2.3
116	Troy, MI	2.2
117	Carlsbad, CA	2.0
117	Hampton, VA	2.0
117	Paterson, NJ	2.0
120	Kenosha, WI	1.5
120	Surprise, AZ	1.5
122	Hamilton Twnshp, NJ	1.4
123	Bend, OR	1.3
124	Durham, NC	1.2
124	Kansas City, KS	1.2
126	Brick Twnshp, NJ	1.1
126	Vallejo, CA	1.1
128	Macon, GA	1.0
128	Pomona, CA	1.0
128	Santa Ana, CA	1.0
131	Anaheim, CA	0.9
131	San Francisco, CA	0.9
131	San Jose, CA	0.9
131	Warren, MI	0.9
135	Hartford, CT	0.8
135	Oceanside, CA	0.8
135	Tallahassee, FL	0.8
138	Tracy, CA	0.7
139	Portland, OR	0.6
139	Shreveport, LA	0.6
141	Cambridge, MA	0.5
141	Ontario, CA	0.5
143	Gresham, OR	0.4
143	Norwalk, CA	0.4

RANK	CITY	% CHANGE
145	Miami Gardens, FL	0.2
145	Tulsa, OK	0.2
145	Upper Darby Twnshp, PA	0.2
148	Beaverton, OR	0.1
148	Daly City, CA	0.1
148	Dayton, OH	0.1
151	Cedar Rapids, IA	0.0
152	Norwalk, CT	(0.1)
152	Vancouver, WA	(0.1)
154	Fresno, CA	(0.2)
154	Houston, TX	(0.2)
154	Lynn, MA	(0.2)
154	Trenton, NJ	(0.2)
158	Chandler, AZ	(0.4)
158	Richmond, VA	(0.4)
160	Sioux Falls, SD	(0.5)
161	Fort Worth, TX	(0.6)
162	Washington, DC	(0.7)
163	Chattanooga, TN	(0.8)
163	Lakewood, CO	(0.8)
163	Madison, WI	(0.8)
163	Oklahoma City, OK	(0.8)
163	Worcester, MA	(0.8)
168	O'Fallon, MO	(0.9)
169	Napa, CA	(1.0)
169	Norman, OK	(1.0)
171	Allen, TX	(1.1)
171	Cary, NC	(1.1)
173	Bellingham, WA	(1.2)
173	Lansing, MI	(1.2)
173	Salem, OR	(1.2)
176	Davie, FL	(1.3)
176	Scranton, PA	(1.3)
178	Overland Park, KS	(1.5)
178	Waco, TX	(1.5)
180	Huntington Beach, CA	(1.8)
180	Lawton, OK	(1.8)
180	Nashua, NH	(1.8)
183	Clarksville, TN	(1.9)
183	Hayward, CA	(1.9)
183	Lakeland, FL	(1.9)
186	Portsmouth, VA	(2.0)
186	Topeka, KS	(2.0)
188	Fall River, MA	(2.1)
188	Nashville, TN	(2.1)
188	Newport News, VA	(2.1)
191	Edmond, OK	(2.2)
191	Pearland, TX	(2.2)
193	Asheville, NC	(2.3)
194	Cheektowaga, NY	(2.4)
195	Lawrence, MA	(2.5)
195	Sandy, UT	(2.5)
197	Chino Hills, CA	(2.6)
197	Edinburg, TX	(2.6)
197	Inglewood, CA	(2.6)
197	Livermore, CA	(2.6)
197	St. Paul, MN	(2.6)
202	Evansville, IN	(2.7)
203	Westminster, CA	(2.9)
204	Lewisville, TX	(3.0)
204	Savannah, GA	(3.0)
206	Newport Beach, CA	(3.1)
206	Seattle, WA	(3.1)
208	Bellevue, WA	(3.2)
208	Boston, MA	(3.2)
208	Garland, TX	(3.2)
208	Lincoln, NE	(3.2)
212	Chesapeake, VA	(3.3)
213	Waterbury, CT	(3.5)
214	Independence, MO	(3.6)
214	Jackson, MS	(3.6)
216	Aurora, CO	(3.7)

Rank Order - City (continued)

RANK	CITY	% CHANGE
216	Yuma, AZ	(3.7)
218	Colonie, NY	(3.8)
218	Concord, CA	(3.8)
220	Athens-Clarke, GA	(3.9)
220	Milwaukee, WI	(3.9)
220	Quincy, MA	(3.9)
220	Stockton, CA	(3.9)
224	Clinton Twnshp, MI	(4.0)
224	Spokane, WA	(4.0)
226	Fort Smith, AR	(4.1)
226	Greece, NY	(4.1)
226	Olathe, KS	(4.1)
226	Richardson, TX	(4.1)
230	Gilbert, AZ	(4.2)
230	Los Angeles, CA	(4.2)
230	Modesto, CA	(4.2)
233	Columbus, OH	(4.3)
234	Jersey City, NJ	(4.4)
234	Lake Forest, CA	(4.4)
236	Lee's Summit, MO	(4.5)
236	San Diego, CA	(4.5)
238	Whittier, CA	(4.6)
239	McKinney, TX	(4.7)
240	Ventura, CA	(4.8)
241	Newton, MA	(5.0)
242	Jacksonville, FL	(5.1)
242	Richmond, CA	(5.1)
244	Henderson, NV	(5.2)
245	Hawthorne, CA	(5.3)
245	Tampa, FL	(5.3)
247	Corona, CA	(5.4)
248	Boulder, CO	(5.5)
248	Kennewick, WA	(5.5)
250	Springfield, IL	(5.6)
251	Glendale, CA	(5.7)
251	Joliet, IL	(5.7)
251	Wilmington, NC	(5.7)
254	Sunrise, FL	(5.8)
254	Visalia, CA	(5.8)
256	Arvada, CO	(5.9)
256	Riverside, CA	(5.9)
258	Charlotte, NC	(6.1)
258	Orem, UT	(6.1)
260	Livonia, MI	(6.2)
261	Lubbock, TX	(6.3)
261	Vista, CA	(6.3)
263	Deerfield Beach, FL	(6.4)
263	Lakewood, CA	(6.4)
263	San Leandro, CA	(6.4)
266	Tacoma, WA	(6.5)
267	Elk Grove, CA	(6.6)
268	Burbank, CA	(6.7)
268	Clearwater, FL	(6.7)
268	Fishers, IN	(6.7)
268	Ogden, UT	(6.7)
268	Rockford, IL	(6.7)
268	San Antonio, TX	(6.7)
268	Springfield, MO	(6.7)
275	Roanoke, VA	(6.8)
275	Santa Clara, CA	(6.8)
277	Albany, NY	(6.9)
277	Pembroke Pines, FL	(6.9)
279	Mesquite, TX	(7.0)
279	Springfield, MA	(7.0)
281	Baldwin Park, CA	(7.1)
281	West Jordan, UT	(7.1)
283	Downey, CA	(7.2)
283	Somerville, MA	(7.2)
285	Fargo, ND	(7.4)
286	Boise, ID	(7.5)
286	Lynchburg, VA	(7.5)
286	Palmdale, CA	(7.5)
289	Pasadena, CA	(7.6)

RANK	CITY	% CHANGE
290	North Charleston, SC	(7.7)
291	Arlington, TX	(7.8)
292	Gainesville, FL	(7.9)
293	Buena Park, CA	(8.0)
293	Compton, CA	(8.0)
293	Elgin, IL	(8.0)
293	Everett, WA	(8.0)
293	Santa Monica, CA	(8.0)
298	Concord, NC	(8.1)
299	Anchorage, AK	(8.4)
299	Bakersfield, CA	(8.4)
301	Salinas, CA	(8.5)
302	Alhambra, CA	(8.6)
302	San Bernardino, CA	(8.6)
304	Green Bay, WI	(8.7)
304	Roseville, CA	(8.7)
306	Charleston, SC	(8.9)
306	Chula Vista, CA	(8.9)
308	Austin, TX	(9.1)
308	Centennial, CO	(9.1)
308	Odessa, TX	(9.1)
308	St. Petersburg, FL	(9.1)
312	Bellflower, CA	(9.2)
312	Hialeah, FL	(9.2)
312	Las Vegas, NV	(9.2)
315	Corpus Christi, TX	(9.3)
315	Tustin, CA	(9.3)
317	Decatur, IL	(9.4)
317	Pasadena, TX	(9.4)
319	Arlington Heights, IL	(9.5)
320	Amherst, NY	(9.6)
320	Westland, MI	(9.6)
322	Virginia Beach, VA	(9.7)
323	Pittsburgh, PA	(9.8)
323	Sacramento, CA	(9.8)
325	Hammond, IN	(9.9)
326	El Monte, CA	(10.1)
327	Longmont, CO	(10.4)
328	Torrance, CA	(10.5)
329	Chico, CA	(10.6)
329	Garden Grove, CA	(10.6)
331	Clarkstown, NY	(10.7)
331	Norfolk, VA	(10.7)
333	El Cajon, CA	(10.9)
333	El Paso, TX	(10.9)
333	Round Rock, TX	(10.9)
336	Fort Collins, CO	(11.0)
337	Aurora, IL	(11.1)
337	Columbus, GA	(11.1)
337	Farmington Hills, MI	(11.1)
337	Rochester, NY	(11.1)
341	Colorado Springs, CO	(11.2)
341	Santa Clarita, CA	(11.2)
343	Santa Maria, CA	(11.3)
344	Brownsville, TX	(11.4)
345	Bethlehem, PA	(11.5)
345	Canton Twnshp, MI	(11.5)
345	Frisco, TX	(11.5)
345	Lancaster, CA	(11.5)
349	Sparks, NV	(12.0)
350	Fullerton, CA	(12.1)
350	Lafayette, LA	(12.1)
350	Westminster, CO	(12.1)
353	Syracuse, NY	(12.2)
354	Redwood City, CA	(12.3)
355	Laredo, TX	(12.4)
356	Midland, TX	(12.6)
357	Tyler, TX	(12.8)
357	West Valley, UT	(12.8)
359	New Bedford, MA	(12.9)
359	Wichita Falls, TX	(12.9)
361	Grand Prairie, TX	(13.0)
361	San Marcos, CA	(13.0)
363	Reno, NV	(13.2)

RANK	CITY	% CHANGE
364	Salt Lake City, UT	(13.3)
365	Albany, GA	(13.4)
365	Bloomington, IL	(13.4)
367	Vacaville, CA	(13.7)
368	Roswell, GA	(13.8)
369	Abilene, TX	(14.0)
369	Bloomington, IN	(14.0)
371	Yakima, WA	(14.1)
372	Meridian, ID	(14.3)
372	New Haven, CT	(14.3)
372	Thousand Oaks, CA	(14.3)
375	Ann Arbor, MI	(14.4)
376	Fairfield, CA	(14.7)
377	Citrus Heights, CA	(14.8)
378	San Mateo, CA	(15.1)
379	Amarillo, TX	(15.3)
379	Dearborn, MI	(15.3)
381	San Angelo, TX	(15.5)
382	Reading, PA	(15.6)
383	Santa Rosa, CA	(15.9)
384	Fremont, CA	(16.1)
385	Sunnyvale, CA	(16.3)
386	League City, TX	(17.0)
387	Killeen, TX	(17.2)
388	Oxnard, CA	(17.4)
389	Irving, TX	(17.5)
389	Longview, TX	(17.5)
391	Largo, FL	(17.6)
392	Allentown, PA	(17.8)
393	Grand Rapids, MI	(18.0)
394	Miramar, FL	(18.6)
395	Carmel, IN	(18.7)
396	McAllen, TX	(19.3)
397	Sandy Springs, GA	(19.8)
398	Bryan, TX	(20.5)
399	Lakewood Twnshp, NJ	(21.4)
400	Lowell, MA	(21.5)
401	Sugar Land, TX	(21.8)
402	Mission, TX	(22.3)
403	Escondido, CA	(22.7)
404	Berkeley, CA	(22.8)
405	Simi Valley, CA	(24.9)
406	Renton, WA	(29.9)
407	Menifee, CA	(30.5)
408	Johns Creek, GA	(32.4)
NA	Baton Rouge, LA**	NA
NA	Billings, MT**	NA
NA	Birmingham, AL**	NA
NA	Bloomington, MN**	NA
NA	Brooklyn Park, MN**	NA
NA	Buffalo, NY**	NA
NA	Champaign, IL**	NA
NA	Chicago, IL**	NA
NA	Cicero, IL**	NA
NA	Clifton, NJ**	NA
NA	Davenport, IA**	NA
NA	Duluth, MN**	NA
NA	Gary, IN**	NA
NA	Hillsboro, OR**	NA
NA	Hoover, AL**	NA
NA	Huntsville, AL**	NA
NA	Indianapolis, IN**	NA
NA	Kansas City, MO**	NA
NA	Lexington, KY**	NA
NA	Mobile, AL**	NA
NA	Montgomery, AL**	NA
NA	Naperville, IL**	NA
NA	Pueblo, CO**	NA
NA	Rochester, MN**	NA
NA	Sterling Heights, MI**	NA
NA	Thornton, CO**	NA
NA	Toledo, OH**	NA
NA	Tucson, AZ**	NA
NA	Tuscaloosa, AL**	NA

Source: CQ Press using reported data from the F.B.I. "Crime in the United States 2011"
*Includes murder, rape, robbery, aggravated assault, burglary, larceny-theft, and motor vehicle theft.
**Not available.

Alpha Order - City

44. Percent Change in Crime Rate: 2007 to 2011
National Percent Change = 12.1% Decrease*

RANK	CITY	% CHANGE	RANK	CITY	% CHANGE	RANK	CITY	% CHANGE
236	Abilene, TX	(17.2)	13	Cheektowaga, NY	15.7	167	Fort Wayne, IN	(11.8)
24	Akron, OH	9.8	76	Chesapeake, VA	(2.5)	206	Fort Worth, TX	(14.5)
226	Albany, GA	(16.4)	NA	Chicago, IL**	NA	360	Fremont, CA	(30.3)
73	Albany, NY	(1.4)	353	Chico, CA	(29.2)	23	Fresno, CA	11.3
186	Albuquerque, NM	(13.0)	152	Chino Hills, CA	(10.8)	354	Frisco, TX	(29.4)
128	Alexandria, VA	(8.5)	190	Chino, CA	(13.2)	245	Fullerton, CA	(17.9)
158	Alhambra, CA	(11.4)	384	Chula Vista, CA	(38.6)	300	Gainesville, FL	(22.1)
320	Allentown, PA	(23.6)	NA	Cicero, IL**	NA	315	Garden Grove, CA	(23.0)
275	Allen, TX	(19.7)	25	Cincinnati, OH	9.1	85	Garland, TX	(3.6)
310	Amarillo, TX	(22.7)	NA	Citrus Heights, CA**	NA	4	Gary, IN	34.7
41	Amherst, NY	3.8	101	Clarkstown, NY	(5.8)	323	Gilbert, AZ	(24.0)
101	Anaheim, CA	(5.8)	324	Clarksville, TN	(24.1)	8	Glendale, AZ	23.7
222	Anchorage, AK	(16.1)	179	Clearwater, FL	(12.5)	96	Glendale, CA	(5.3)
137	Ann Arbor, MI	(9.3)	51	Cleveland, OH	1.8	224	Grand Prairie, TX	(16.2)
12	Antioch, CA	16.0	252	Clifton, NJ	(18.4)	380	Grand Rapids, MI	(35.5)
NA	Arlington Heights, IL**	NA	56	Clinton Twnshp, MI	0.7	21	Greece, NY	13.9
274	Arlington, TX	(19.6)	5	Clovis, CA	33.3	206	Greeley, CO	(14.5)
110	Arvada, CO	(6.3)	110	College Station, TX	(6.3)	310	Green Bay, WI	(22.7)
284	Asheville, NC	(20.2)	131	Colonie, NY	(8.8)	141	Gresham, OR	(9.5)
193	Athens-Clarke, GA	(13.6)	215	Colorado Springs, CO	(15.5)	32	Hamilton Twnshp, NJ	6.0
91	Atlanta, GA	(4.4)	26	Columbia, MO	8.0	117	Hammond, IN	(6.9)
298	Aurora, CO	(21.9)	186	Columbus, GA	(13.0)	29	Hampton, VA	7.3
NA	Aurora, IL**	NA	176	Columbus, OH	(12.3)	239	Hartford, CT	(17.4)
241	Austin, TX	(17.7)	182	Compton, CA	(12.7)	64	Hawthorne, CA	0.0
NA	Avondale, AZ**	NA	321	Concord, CA	(23.7)	325	Hayward, CA	(24.2)
220	Bakersfield, CA	(15.9)	313	Concord, NC	(22.9)	87	Hemet, CA	(3.8)
188	Baldwin Park, CA	(13.1)	37	Coral Springs, FL	4.4	329	Henderson, NV	(24.9)
89	Baltimore, MD	(3.9)	262	Corona, CA	(18.9)	39	Hesperia, CA	4.1
127	Baton Rouge, LA	(8.2)	338	Corpus Christi, TX	(26.5)	339	Hialeah, FL	(26.8)
138	Beaumont, TX	(9.4)	45	Costa Mesa, CA	3.4	267	High Point, NC	(19.2)
317	Beaverton, OR	(23.4)	60	Cranston, RI	0.3	352	Hillsboro, OR	(28.9)
252	Bellevue, WA	(18.4)	339	Dallas, TX	(26.8)	14	Hollywood, FL	15.2
368	Bellflower, CA	(32.8)	217	Daly City, CA	(15.6)	NA	Hoover, AL**	NA
356	Bellingham, WA	(29.8)	31	Danbury, CT	6.1	163	Houston, TX	(11.6)
261	Bend, OR	(18.8)	NA	Davenport, IA**	NA	19	Huntington Beach, CA	14.9
382	Berkeley, CA	(36.4)	113	Davie, FL	(6.5)	NA	Huntsville, AL**	NA
289	Bethlehem, PA	(21.1)	168	Dayton, OH	(11.9)	322	Independence, MO	(23.9)
NA	Billings, MT**	NA	276	Dearborn, MI	(19.8)	149	Indianapolis, IN	(10.6)
NA	Birmingham, AL**	NA	NA	Decatur, IL**	NA	51	Indio, CA	1.8
NA	Bloomington, IL**	NA	122	Deerfield Beach, FL	(7.6)	179	Inglewood, CA	(12.5)
154	Bloomington, IN	(10.9)	124	Denton, TX	(7.8)	104	Irvine, CA	(6.0)
NA	Bloomington, MN**	NA	95	Denver, CO	(5.2)	370	Irving, TX	(33.3)
291	Boca Raton, FL	(21.2)	226	Des Moines, IA	(16.4)	336	Jacksonville, FL	(26.3)
248	Boise, ID	(18.1)	130	Detroit, MI	(8.6)	39	Jackson, MS	4.1
330	Boston, MA	(25.1)	110	Downey, CA	(6.3)	281	Jersey City, NJ	(20.1)
83	Boulder, CO	(3.3)	NA	Duluth, MN**	NA	NA	Johns Creek, GA**	NA
57	Brick Twnshp, NJ	0.6	NA	Durham, NC**	NA	NA	Joliet, IL**	NA
243	Bridgeport, CT	(17.8)	26	Edinburg, TX	8.0	287	Kansas City, KS	(20.6)
NA	Brockton, MA**	NA	288	Edison Twnshp, NJ	(20.9)	NA	Kansas City, MO**	NA
54	Broken Arrow, OK	1.3	230	Edmond, OK	(16.7)	122	Kennewick, WA	(7.6)
NA	Brooklyn Park, MN**	NA	385	El Cajon, CA	(38.9)	200	Kenosha, WI	(14.1)
234	Brownsville, TX	(16.9)	224	El Monte, CA	(16.2)	124	Kent, WA	(7.8)
358	Bryan, TX	(30.2)	281	El Paso, TX	(20.1)	335	Killeen, TX	(26.0)
185	Buena Park, CA	(12.9)	NA	Elgin, IL**	NA	69	Knoxville, TN	(0.8)
NA	Buffalo, NY**	NA	41	Elizabeth, NJ	3.8	246	Lafayette, LA	(18.0)
138	Burbank, CA	(9.4)	267	Elk Grove, CA	(19.2)	163	Lake Forest, CA	(11.6)
196	Cambridge, MA	(13.8)	16	Erie, PA	15.1	174	Lakeland, FL	(12.1)
34	Camden, NJ	5.9	363	Escondido, CA	(31.9)	390	Lakewood Twnshp, NJ	(46.8)
151	Canton Twnshp, MI	(10.7)	97	Eugene, OR	(5.4)	351	Lakewood, CA	(28.8)
346	Cape Coral, FL	(27.7)	68	Evansville, IN	(0.6)	66	Lakewood, CO	(0.5)
355	Carlsbad, CA	(29.7)	267	Everett, WA	(19.2)	388	Lancaster, CA	(41.9)
381	Carmel, IN	(36.3)	364	Fairfield, CA	(32.1)	55	Lansing, MI	1.1
191	Carrollton, TX	(13.3)	NA	Fall River, MA**	NA	361	Laredo, TX	(30.5)
136	Carson, CA	(9.2)	201	Fargo, ND	(14.2)	116	Largo, FL	(6.7)
256	Cary, NC	(18.6)	243	Farmington Hills, MI	(17.8)	105	Las Cruces, NM	(6.1)
292	Cedar Rapids, IA	(21.4)	236	Fayetteville, NC	(17.2)	373	Las Vegas, NV	(33.8)
258	Centennial, CO	(18.7)	350	Fishers, IN	(28.7)	307	Lawrence, KS	(22.5)
NA	Champaign, IL**	NA	48	Flint, MI	2.3	3	Lawrence, MA	36.4
81	Chandler, AZ	(3.1)	182	Fontana, CA	(12.7)	72	Lawton, OK	(1.2)
344	Charleston, SC	(27.5)	202	Fort Collins, CO	(14.3)	158	League City, TX	(11.4)
387	Charlotte, NC	(41.6)	11	Fort Lauderdale, FL	17.3	296	Lee's Summit, MO	(21.7)
318	Chattanooga, TN	(23.5)	251	Fort Smith, AR	(18.2)	22	Lewisville, TX	11.4

Alpha Order - City (continued)

RANK	CITY	% CHANGE
NA	Lexington, KY**	NA
286	Lincoln, NE	(20.4)
131	Little Rock, AR	(8.8)
149	Livermore, CA	(10.6)
170	Livonia, MI	(12.0)
82	Long Beach, CA	(3.2)
NA	Longmont, CO**	NA
365	Longview, TX	(32.2)
235	Los Angeles, CA	(17.0)
62	Louisville, KY	0.1
154	Lowell, MA	(10.9)
121	Lubbock, TX	(7.1)
146	Lynchburg, VA	(10.1)
131	Lynn, MA	(8.8)
84	Macon, GA	(3.4)
119	Madison, WI	(7.0)
NA	Manchester, NH**	NA
348	McAllen, TX	(27.8)
105	McKinney, TX	(6.1)
14	Medford, OR	15.2
53	Melbourne, FL	1.4
271	Memphis, TN	(19.4)
NA	Menifee, CA**	NA
265	Merced, CA	(19.1)
313	Meridian, ID	(22.9)
298	Mesa, AZ	(21.9)
35	Mesquite, TX	5.1
18	Miami Beach, FL	15.0
385	Miami Gardens, FL	(38.9)
46	Miami, FL	3.1
248	Midland, TX	(18.1)
332	Milwaukee, WI	(25.2)
294	Minneapolis, MN	(21.5)
303	Miramar, FL	(22.2)
113	Mission Viejo, CA	(6.5)
145	Mission, TX	(10.0)
NA	Mobile, AL**	NA
300	Modesto, CA	(22.1)
NA	Montgomery, AL**	NA
209	Moreno Valley, CA	(14.6)
71	Murfreesboro, TN	(1.0)
346	Murrieta, CA	(27.7)
92	Nampa, ID	(4.8)
367	Napa, CA	(32.6)
NA	Naperville, IL**	NA
NA	Nashua, NH**	NA
221	Nashville, TN	(16.0)
57	New Bedford, MA	0.6
NA	New Haven, CT**	NA
389	New Orleans, LA	(44.0)
162	New Rochelle, NY	(11.5)
90	New York, NY	(4.0)
48	Newark, NJ	2.3
135	Newport Beach, CA	(9.1)
305	Newport News, VA	(22.4)
170	Newton, MA	(12.0)
99	Norfolk, VA	(5.6)
148	Norman, OK	(10.4)
369	North Charleston, SC	(32.9)
271	Norwalk, CA	(19.4)
66	Norwalk, CT	(0.5)
163	Oakland, CA	(11.6)
278	Oceanside, CA	(20.0)
327	Odessa, TX	(24.5)
373	O'Fallon, MO	(33.8)
240	Ogden, UT	(17.6)
69	Oklahoma City, OK	(0.8)
NA	Olathe, KS**	NA
93	Omaha, NE	(5.1)
215	Ontario, CA	(15.5)
229	Orange, CA	(16.6)
231	Orem, UT	(16.8)
297	Orlando, FL	(21.8)
131	Overland Park, KS	(8.8)
330	Oxnard, CA	(25.1)
105	Palm Bay, FL	(6.1)
358	Palmdale, CA	(30.2)
209	Pasadena, CA	(14.6)
74	Pasadena, TX	(1.5)
29	Paterson, NJ	7.3
337	Pearland, TX	(26.4)
157	Pembroke Pines, FL	(11.3)
304	Peoria, AZ	(22.3)
NA	Peoria, IL**	NA
170	Philadelphia, PA	(12.0)
326	Phoenix, AZ	(24.4)
342	Pittsburgh, PA	(27.1)
256	Plano, TX	(18.6)
93	Plantation, FL	(5.1)
202	Pomona, CA	(14.3)
64	Pompano Beach, FL	0.0
77	Port St. Lucie, FL	(2.7)
206	Portland, OR	(14.5)
44	Portsmouth, VA	3.6
168	Provo, UT	(11.9)
NA	Pueblo, CO**	NA
60	Quincy, MA	0.3
176	Racine, WI	(12.3)
142	Raleigh, NC	(9.6)
7	Ramapo, NY	30.5
41	Rancho Cucamon., CA	3.8
252	Reading, PA	(18.4)
6	Redding, CA	32.8
305	Redwood City, CA	(22.4)
375	Reno, NV	(33.9)
365	Renton, WA	(32.2)
20	Rialto, CA	14.3
181	Richardson, TX	(12.6)
264	Richmond, CA	(19.0)
192	Richmond, VA	(13.4)
318	Rio Rancho, NM	(23.5)
252	Riverside, CA	(18.4)
248	Roanoke, VA	(18.1)
NA	Rochester, MN**	NA
119	Rochester, NY	(7.0)
246	Rockford, IL	(18.0)
265	Roseville, CA	(19.1)
342	Roswell, GA	(27.1)
75	Round Rock, TX	(2.3)
345	Sacramento, CA	(27.6)
281	Salem, OR	(20.1)
371	Salinas, CA	(33.4)
292	Salt Lake City, UT	(21.4)
334	San Angelo, TX	(25.6)
115	San Antonio, TX	(6.6)
285	San Bernardino, CA	(20.3)
376	San Diego, CA	(34.0)
219	San Francisco, CA	(15.7)
163	San Jose, CA	(11.6)
349	San Leandro, CA	(28.6)
278	San Marcos, CA	(20.0)
310	San Mateo, CA	(22.7)
378	Sandy Springs, GA	(34.9)
231	Sandy, UT	(16.8)
222	Santa Ana, CA	(16.1)
28	Santa Barbara, CA	7.5
289	Santa Clara, CA	(21.1)
378	Santa Clarita, CA	(34.9)
231	Santa Maria, CA	(16.8)
170	Santa Monica, CA	(12.0)
156	Santa Rosa, CA	(11.1)
197	Savannah, GA	(13.9)
158	Scottsdale, AZ	(11.4)
32	Scranton, PA	6.0
152	Seattle, WA	(10.8)
316	Shreveport, LA	(23.1)
362	Simi Valley, CA	(31.0)
10	Sioux City, IA	19.4
16	Sioux Falls, SD	15.1
307	Somerville, MA	(22.5)
128	South Bend, IN	(8.5)
47	South Gate, CA	2.6
377	Sparks, NV	(34.1)
2	Spokane Valley, WA	51.7
9	Spokane, WA	20.3
NA	Springfield, IL**	NA
176	Springfield, MA	(12.3)
87	Springfield, MO	(3.8)
38	Stamford, CT	4.2
NA	Sterling Heights, MI**	NA
195	Stockton, CA	(13.7)
62	St. Joseph, MO	0.1
238	St. Louis, MO	(17.3)
79	St. Paul, MN	(2.9)
271	St. Petersburg, FL	(19.4)
138	Suffolk, VA	(9.4)
117	Sugar Land, TX	(6.9)
357	Sunnyvale, CA	(30.0)
80	Sunrise, FL	(3.0)
204	Surprise, AZ	(14.4)
211	Syracuse, NY	(14.7)
300	Tacoma, WA	(22.1)
105	Tallahassee, FL	(6.1)
383	Tampa, FL	(38.5)
267	Temecula, CA	(19.2)
241	Tempe, AZ	(17.7)
NA	Thornton, CO**	NA
144	Thousand Oaks, CA	(9.9)
NA	Toledo, OH**	NA
1	Toms River Twnshp, NJ	54.5
126	Topeka, KS	(8.0)
258	Torrance, CA	(18.7)
188	Tracy, CA	(13.1)
78	Trenton, NJ	(2.8)
97	Troy, MI	(5.4)
NA	Tucson, AZ**	NA
184	Tulsa, OK	(12.8)
NA	Tuscaloosa, AL**	NA
197	Tustin, CA	(13.9)
109	Tyler, TX	(6.2)
101	Upper Darby Twnshp, PA	(5.8)
262	Vacaville, CA	(18.9)
204	Vallejo, CA	(14.4)
85	Vancouver, WA	(3.6)
217	Ventura, CA	(15.6)
174	Victorville, CA	(12.1)
146	Virginia Beach, VA	(10.1)
158	Visalia, CA	(11.4)
211	Vista, CA	(14.7)
328	Waco, TX	(24.6)
NA	Warren, MI**	NA
NA	Warwick, RI**	NA
100	Washington, DC	(5.7)
294	Waterbury, CT	(21.5)
228	West Covina, CA	(16.5)
278	West Jordan, UT	(20.0)
339	West Palm Beach, FL	(26.8)
333	West Valley, UT	(25.3)
197	Westland, MI	(13.9)
143	Westminster, CA	(9.7)
258	Westminster, CO	(18.7)
50	Whittier, CA	2.2
371	Wichita Falls, TX	(33.4)
193	Wichita, KS	(13.6)
211	Wilmington, NC	(14.7)
NA	Winston-Salem, NC**	NA
214	Woodbridge Twnshp, NJ	(15.4)
57	Worcester, MA	0.6
276	Yakima, WA	(19.8)
36	Yonkers, NY	5.0
307	Yuma, AZ	(22.5)

Source: CQ Press using reported data from the F.B.I. "Crime in the United States 2011"
*Includes murder, rape, robbery, aggravated assault, burglary, larceny-theft, and motor vehicle theft.
**Not available.

Rank Order - City

44. Percent Change in Crime Rate: 2007 to 2011 (continued)
National Percent Change = 12.1% Decrease*

RANK	CITY	% CHANGE	RANK	CITY	% CHANGE	RANK	CITY	% CHANGE
1	Toms River Twnshp, NJ	54.5	73	Albany, NY	(1.4)	145	Mission, TX	(10.0)
2	Spokane Valley, WA	51.7	74	Pasadena, TX	(1.5)	146	Lynchburg, VA	(10.1)
3	Lawrence, MA	36.4	75	Round Rock, TX	(2.3)	146	Virginia Beach, VA	(10.1)
4	Gary, IN	34.7	76	Chesapeake, VA	(2.5)	148	Norman, OK	(10.4)
5	Clovis, CA	33.3	77	Port St. Lucie, FL	(2.7)	149	Indianapolis, IN	(10.6)
6	Redding, CA	32.8	78	Trenton, NJ	(2.8)	149	Livermore, CA	(10.6)
7	Ramapo, NY	30.5	79	St. Paul, MN	(2.9)	151	Canton Twnshp, MI	(10.7)
8	Glendale, AZ	23.7	80	Sunrise, FL	(3.0)	152	Chino Hills, CA	(10.8)
9	Spokane, WA	20.3	81	Chandler, AZ	(3.1)	152	Seattle, WA	(10.8)
10	Sioux City, IA	19.4	82	Long Beach, CA	(3.2)	154	Bloomington, IN	(10.9)
11	Fort Lauderdale, FL	17.3	83	Boulder, CO	(3.3)	154	Lowell, MA	(10.9)
12	Antioch, CA	16.0	84	Macon, GA	(3.4)	156	Santa Rosa, CA	(11.1)
13	Cheektowaga, NY	15.7	85	Garland, TX	(3.6)	157	Pembroke Pines, FL	(11.3)
14	Hollywood, FL	15.2	85	Vancouver, WA	(3.6)	158	Alhambra, CA	(11.4)
14	Medford, OR	15.2	87	Hemet, CA	(3.8)	158	League City, TX	(11.4)
16	Erie, PA	15.1	87	Springfield, MO	(3.8)	158	Scottsdale, AZ	(11.4)
16	Sioux Falls, SD	15.1	89	Baltimore, MD	(3.9)	158	Visalia, CA	(11.4)
18	Miami Beach, FL	15.0	90	New York, NY	(4.0)	162	New Rochelle, NY	(11.5)
19	Huntington Beach, CA	14.9	91	Atlanta, GA	(4.4)	163	Houston, TX	(11.6)
20	Rialto, CA	14.3	92	Nampa, ID	(4.8)	163	Lake Forest, CA	(11.6)
21	Greece, NY	13.9	93	Omaha, NE	(5.1)	163	Oakland, CA	(11.6)
22	Lewisville, TX	11.4	93	Plantation, FL	(5.1)	163	San Jose, CA	(11.6)
23	Fresno, CA	11.3	95	Denver, CO	(5.2)	167	Fort Wayne, IN	(11.8)
24	Akron, OH	9.8	96	Glendale, CA	(5.3)	168	Dayton, OH	(11.9)
25	Cincinnati, OH	9.1	97	Eugene, OR	(5.4)	168	Provo, UT	(11.9)
26	Columbia, MO	8.0	97	Troy, MI	(5.4)	170	Livonia, MI	(12.0)
26	Edinburg, TX	8.0	99	Norfolk, VA	(5.6)	170	Newton, MA	(12.0)
28	Santa Barbara, CA	7.5	100	Washington, DC	(5.7)	170	Philadelphia, PA	(12.0)
29	Hampton, VA	7.3	101	Anaheim, CA	(5.8)	170	Santa Monica, CA	(12.0)
29	Paterson, NJ	7.3	101	Clarkstown, NY	(5.8)	174	Lakeland, FL	(12.1)
31	Danbury, CT	6.1	101	Upper Darby Twnshp, PA	(5.8)	174	Victorville, CA	(12.1)
32	Hamilton Twnshp, NJ	6.0	104	Irvine, CA	(6.0)	176	Columbus, OH	(12.3)
32	Scranton, PA	6.0	105	Las Cruces, NM	(6.1)	176	Racine, WI	(12.3)
34	Camden, NJ	5.9	105	McKinney, TX	(6.1)	176	Springfield, MA	(12.3)
35	Mesquite, TX	5.1	105	Palm Bay, FL	(6.1)	179	Clearwater, FL	(12.5)
36	Yonkers, NY	5.0	105	Tallahassee, FL	(6.1)	179	Inglewood, CA	(12.5)
37	Coral Springs, FL	4.4	109	Tyler, TX	(6.2)	181	Richardson, TX	(12.6)
38	Stamford, CT	4.2	110	Arvada, CO	(6.3)	182	Compton, CA	(12.7)
39	Hesperia, CA	4.1	110	College Station, TX	(6.3)	182	Fontana, CA	(12.7)
39	Jackson, MS	4.1	110	Downey, CA	(6.3)	184	Tulsa, OK	(12.8)
41	Amherst, NY	3.8	113	Davie, FL	(6.5)	185	Buena Park, CA	(12.9)
41	Elizabeth, NJ	3.8	113	Mission Viejo, CA	(6.5)	186	Albuquerque, NM	(13.0)
41	Rancho Cucamon., CA	3.8	115	San Antonio, TX	(6.6)	186	Columbus, GA	(13.0)
44	Portsmouth, VA	3.6	116	Largo, FL	(6.7)	188	Baldwin Park, CA	(13.1)
45	Costa Mesa, CA	3.4	117	Hammond, IN	(6.9)	188	Tracy, CA	(13.1)
46	Miami, FL	3.1	117	Sugar Land, TX	(6.9)	190	Chino, CA	(13.2)
47	South Gate, CA	2.6	119	Madison, WI	(7.0)	191	Carrollton, TX	(13.3)
48	Flint, MI	2.3	119	Rochester, NY	(7.0)	192	Richmond, VA	(13.4)
48	Newark, NJ	2.3	121	Lubbock, TX	(7.1)	193	Athens-Clarke, GA	(13.6)
50	Whittier, CA	2.2	122	Deerfield Beach, FL	(7.6)	193	Wichita, KS	(13.6)
51	Cleveland, OH	1.8	122	Kennewick, WA	(7.6)	195	Stockton, CA	(13.7)
51	Indio, CA	1.8	124	Denton, TX	(7.8)	196	Cambridge, MA	(13.8)
53	Melbourne, FL	1.4	124	Kent, WA	(7.8)	197	Savannah, GA	(13.9)
54	Broken Arrow, OK	1.3	126	Topeka, KS	(8.0)	197	Tustin, CA	(13.9)
55	Lansing, MI	1.1	127	Baton Rouge, LA	(8.2)	197	Westland, MI	(13.9)
56	Clinton Twnshp, MI	0.7	128	Alexandria, VA	(8.5)	200	Kenosha, WI	(14.1)
57	Brick Twnshp, NJ	0.6	128	South Bend, IN	(8.5)	201	Fargo, ND	(14.2)
57	New Bedford, MA	0.6	130	Detroit, MI	(8.6)	202	Fort Collins, CO	(14.3)
57	Worcester, MA	0.6	131	Colonie, NY	(8.8)	202	Pomona, CA	(14.3)
60	Cranston, RI	0.3	131	Little Rock, AR	(8.8)	204	Surprise, AZ	(14.4)
60	Quincy, MA	0.3	131	Lynn, MA	(8.8)	204	Vallejo, CA	(14.4)
62	Louisville, KY	0.1	131	Overland Park, KS	(8.8)	206	Fort Worth, TX	(14.5)
62	St. Joseph, MO	0.1	135	Newport Beach, CA	(9.1)	206	Greeley, CO	(14.5)
64	Hawthorne, CA	0.0	136	Carson, CA	(9.2)	206	Portland, OR	(14.5)
64	Pompano Beach, FL	0.0	137	Ann Arbor, MI	(9.3)	209	Moreno Valley, CA	(14.6)
66	Lakewood, CO	(0.5)	138	Beaumont, TX	(9.4)	209	Pasadena, CA	(14.6)
66	Norwalk, CT	(0.5)	138	Burbank, CA	(9.4)	211	Syracuse, NY	(14.7)
68	Evansville, IN	(0.6)	138	Suffolk, VA	(9.4)	211	Vista, CA	(14.7)
69	Knoxville, TN	(0.8)	141	Gresham, OR	(9.5)	211	Wilmington, NC	(14.7)
69	Oklahoma City, OK	(0.8)	142	Raleigh, NC	(9.6)	214	Woodbridge Twnshp, NJ	(15.4)
71	Murfreesboro, TN	(1.0)	143	Westminster, CA	(9.7)	215	Colorado Springs, CO	(15.5)
72	Lawton, OK	(1.2)	144	Thousand Oaks, CA	(9.9)	215	Ontario, CA	(15.5)

Rank Order - City (continued)

RANK	CITY	% CHANGE	RANK	CITY	% CHANGE	RANK	CITY	% CHANGE
217	Daly City, CA	(15.6)	289	Santa Clara, CA	(21.1)	364	Fairfield, CA	(32.1)
217	Ventura, CA	(15.6)	291	Boca Raton, FL	(21.2)	365	Longview, TX	(32.2)
219	San Francisco, CA	(15.7)	292	Cedar Rapids, IA	(21.4)	365	Renton, WA	(32.2)
220	Bakersfield, CA	(15.9)	292	Salt Lake City, UT	(21.4)	367	Napa, CA	(32.6)
221	Nashville, TN	(16.0)	294	Minneapolis, MN	(21.5)	368	Bellflower, CA	(32.8)
222	Anchorage, AK	(16.1)	294	Waterbury, CT	(21.5)	369	North Charleston, SC	(32.9)
222	Santa Ana, CA	(16.1)	296	Lee's Summit, MO	(21.7)	370	Irving, TX	(33.3)
224	El Monte, CA	(16.2)	297	Orlando, FL	(21.8)	371	Salinas, CA	(33.4)
224	Grand Prairie, TX	(16.2)	298	Aurora, CO	(21.9)	371	Wichita Falls, TX	(33.4)
226	Albany, GA	(16.4)	298	Mesa, AZ	(21.9)	373	Las Vegas, NV	(33.8)
226	Des Moines, IA	(16.4)	300	Gainesville, FL	(22.1)	373	O'Fallon, MO	(33.8)
228	West Covina, CA	(16.5)	300	Modesto, CA	(22.1)	375	Reno, NV	(33.9)
229	Orange, CA	(16.6)	300	Tacoma, WA	(22.1)	376	San Diego, CA	(34.0)
230	Edmond, OK	(16.7)	303	Miramar, FL	(22.2)	377	Sparks, NV	(34.1)
231	Orem, UT	(16.8)	304	Peoria, AZ	(22.3)	378	Sandy Springs, GA	(34.9)
231	Sandy, UT	(16.8)	305	Newport News, VA	(22.4)	378	Santa Clarita, CA	(34.9)
231	Santa Maria, CA	(16.8)	305	Redwood City, CA	(22.4)	380	Grand Rapids, MI	(35.5)
234	Brownsville, TX	(16.9)	307	Lawrence, KS	(22.5)	381	Carmel, IN	(36.3)
235	Los Angeles, CA	(17.0)	307	Somerville, MA	(22.5)	382	Berkeley, CA	(36.4)
236	Abilene, TX	(17.2)	307	Yuma, AZ	(22.5)	383	Tampa, FL	(38.5)
236	Fayetteville, NC	(17.2)	310	Amarillo, TX	(22.7)	384	Chula Vista, CA	(38.6)
238	St. Louis, MO	(17.3)	310	Green Bay, WI	(22.7)	385	El Cajon, CA	(38.9)
239	Hartford, CT	(17.4)	310	San Mateo, CA	(22.7)	385	Miami Gardens, FL	(38.9)
240	Ogden, UT	(17.6)	313	Concord, NC	(22.9)	387	Charlotte, NC	(41.6)
241	Austin, TX	(17.7)	313	Meridian, ID	(22.9)	388	Lancaster, CA	(41.9)
241	Tempe, AZ	(17.7)	315	Garden Grove, CA	(23.0)	389	New Orleans, LA	(44.0)
243	Bridgeport, CT	(17.8)	316	Shreveport, LA	(23.1)	390	Lakewood Twnshp, NJ	(46.8)
243	Farmington Hills, MI	(17.8)	317	Beaverton, OR	(23.4)	NA	Arlington Heights, IL**	NA
245	Fullerton, CA	(17.9)	318	Chattanooga, TN	(23.5)	NA	Aurora, IL**	NA
246	Lafayette, LA	(18.0)	318	Rio Rancho, NM	(23.5)	NA	Avondale, AZ**	NA
246	Rockford, IL	(18.0)	320	Allentown, PA	(23.6)	NA	Billings, MT**	NA
248	Boise, ID	(18.1)	321	Concord, CA	(23.7)	NA	Birmingham, AL**	NA
248	Midland, TX	(18.1)	322	Independence, MO	(23.9)	NA	Bloomington, IL**	NA
248	Roanoke, VA	(18.1)	323	Gilbert, AZ	(24.0)	NA	Bloomington, MN**	NA
251	Fort Smith, AR	(18.2)	324	Clarksville, TN	(24.1)	NA	Brockton, MA**	NA
252	Bellevue, WA	(18.4)	325	Hayward, CA	(24.2)	NA	Brooklyn Park, MN**	NA
252	Clifton, NJ	(18.4)	326	Phoenix, AZ	(24.4)	NA	Buffalo, NY**	NA
252	Reading, PA	(18.4)	327	Odessa, TX	(24.5)	NA	Champaign, IL**	NA
252	Riverside, CA	(18.4)	328	Waco, TX	(24.6)	NA	Chicago, IL**	NA
256	Cary, NC	(18.6)	329	Henderson, NV	(24.9)	NA	Cicero, IL**	NA
256	Plano, TX	(18.6)	330	Boston, MA	(25.1)	NA	Citrus Heights, CA**	NA
258	Centennial, CO	(18.7)	330	Oxnard, CA	(25.1)	NA	Davenport, IA**	NA
258	Torrance, CA	(18.7)	332	Milwaukee, WI	(25.2)	NA	Decatur, IL**	NA
258	Westminster, CO	(18.7)	333	West Valley, UT	(25.3)	NA	Duluth, MN**	NA
261	Bend, OR	(18.8)	334	San Angelo, TX	(25.6)	NA	Durham, NC**	NA
262	Corona, CA	(18.9)	335	Killeen, TX	(26.0)	NA	Elgin, IL**	NA
262	Vacaville, CA	(18.9)	336	Jacksonville, FL	(26.3)	NA	Fall River, MA**	NA
264	Richmond, CA	(19.0)	337	Pearland, TX	(26.4)	NA	Hoover, AL**	NA
265	Merced, CA	(19.1)	338	Corpus Christi, TX	(26.5)	NA	Huntsville, AL**	NA
265	Roseville, CA	(19.1)	339	Dallas, TX	(26.8)	NA	Johns Creek, GA**	NA
267	Elk Grove, CA	(19.2)	339	Hialeah, FL	(26.8)	NA	Joliet, IL**	NA
267	Everett, WA	(19.2)	339	West Palm Beach, FL	(26.8)	NA	Kansas City, MO**	NA
267	High Point, NC	(19.2)	342	Pittsburgh, PA	(27.1)	NA	Lexington, KY**	NA
267	Temecula, CA	(19.2)	342	Roswell, GA	(27.1)	NA	Longmont, CO**	NA
271	Memphis, TN	(19.4)	344	Charleston, SC	(27.5)	NA	Manchester, NH**	NA
271	Norwalk, CA	(19.4)	345	Sacramento, CA	(27.6)	NA	Menifee, CA**	NA
271	St. Petersburg, FL	(19.4)	346	Cape Coral, FL	(27.7)	NA	Mobile, AL**	NA
274	Arlington, TX	(19.6)	346	Murrieta, CA	(27.7)	NA	Montgomery, AL**	NA
275	Allen, TX	(19.7)	348	McAllen, TX	(27.8)	NA	Naperville, IL**	NA
276	Dearborn, MI	(19.8)	349	San Leandro, CA	(28.6)	NA	Nashua, NH**	NA
276	Yakima, WA	(19.8)	350	Fishers, IN	(28.7)	NA	New Haven, CT**	NA
278	Oceanside, CA	(20.0)	351	Lakewood, CA	(28.8)	NA	Olathe, KS**	NA
278	San Marcos, CA	(20.0)	352	Hillsboro, OR	(28.9)	NA	Peoria, IL**	NA
278	West Jordan, UT	(20.0)	353	Chico, CA	(29.2)	NA	Pueblo, CO**	NA
281	El Paso, TX	(20.1)	354	Frisco, TX	(29.4)	NA	Rochester, MN**	NA
281	Jersey City, NJ	(20.1)	355	Carlsbad, CA	(29.7)	NA	Springfield, IL**	NA
281	Salem, OR	(20.1)	356	Bellingham, WA	(29.8)	NA	Sterling Heights, MI**	NA
284	Asheville, NC	(20.2)	357	Sunnyvale, CA	(30.0)	NA	Thornton, CO**	NA
285	San Bernardino, CA	(20.3)	358	Bryan, TX	(30.2)	NA	Toledo, OH**	NA
286	Lincoln, NE	(20.4)	358	Palmdale, CA	(30.2)	NA	Tucson, AZ**	NA
287	Kansas City, KS	(20.6)	360	Fremont, CA	(30.3)	NA	Tuscaloosa, AL**	NA
288	Edison Twnshp, NJ	(20.9)	361	Laredo, TX	(30.5)	NA	Warren, MI**	NA
289	Bethlehem, PA	(21.1)	362	Simi Valley, CA	(31.0)	NA	Warwick, RI**	NA
			363	Escondido, CA	(31.9)	NA	Winston-Salem, NC**	NA

Source: CQ Press using reported data from the F.B.I. "Crime in the United States 2011"
*Includes murder, rape, robbery, aggravated assault, burglary, larceny-theft, and motor vehicle theft.
**Not available.

Alpha Order - City

45. Violent Crimes in 2011
National Total = 1,203,564 Violent Crimes*

RANK	CITY	CRIMES	RANK	CITY	CRIMES	RANK	CITY	CRIMES
242	Abilene, TX	428	366	Cheektowaga, NY	175	152	Fort Wayne, IN	785
74	Akron, OH	1,779	133	Chesapeake, VA	892	29	Fort Worth, TX	4,569
181	Albany, GA	640	NA	Chicago, IL**	NA	262	Fremont, CA	384
127	Albany, NY	939	325	Chico, CA	245	47	Fresno, CA	2,915
30	Albuquerque, NM	4,207	423	Chino Hills, CA	68	391	Frisco, TX	122
317	Alexandria, VA	252	321	Chino, CA	247	293	Fullerton, CA	306
376	Alhambra, CA	152	174	Chula Vista, CA	670	131	Gainesville, FL	912
180	Allentown, PA	647	279	Cicero, IL	344	231	Garden Grove, CA	449
419	Allen, TX	72	44	Cincinnati, OH	3,067	206	Garland, TX	530
107	Amarillo, TX	1,223	282	Citrus Heights, CA	334	182	Gary, IN	639
390	Amherst, NY	124	406	Clarkstown, NY	100	362	Gilbert, AZ	178
105	Anaheim, CA	1,281	136	Clarksville, TN	883	114	Glendale, AZ	1,114
58	Anchorage, AK	2,388	149	Clearwater, FL	801	316	Glendale, CA	258
314	Ann Arbor, MI	261	20	Cleveland, OH	5,426	193	Grand Prairie, TX	591
143	Antioch, CA	818	342	Clifton, NJ	215	96	Grand Rapids, MI	1,395
428	Arlington Heights, IL	48	294	Clinton Twnshp, MI	303	385	Greece, NY	135
67	Arlington, TX	1,874	346	Clovis, CA	211	235	Greeley, CO	437
372	Arvada, CO	162	300	College Station, TX	288	264	Green Bay, WI	373
232	Asheville, NC	444	426	Colonie, NY	54	250	Gresham, OR	416
249	Athens-Clarke, GA	417	69	Colorado Springs, CO	1,865	357	Hamilton Twnshp, NJ	185
16	Atlanta, GA	6,097	196	Columbia, MO	582	205	Hammond, IN	547
91	Aurora, CO	1,448	128	Columbus, GA	933	277	Hampton, VA	350
183	Aurora, IL	636	23	Columbus, OH	5,185	80	Hartford, CT	1,639
37	Austin, TX	3,471	120	Compton, CA	1,067	185	Hawthorne, CA	623
322	Avondale, AZ	246	239	Concord, CA	430	198	Hayward, CA	579
68	Bakersfield, CA	1,866	413	Concord, NC	93	271	Hemet, CA	361
328	Baldwin Park, CA	242	331	Coral Springs, FL	236	200	Henderson, NV	571
9	Baltimore, MD	8,885	352	Corona, CA	200	289	Hesperia, CA	313
56	Baton Rouge, LA	2,468	64	Corpus Christi, TX	1,987	137	Hialeah, FL	860
118	Beaumont, TX	1,069	334	Costa Mesa, CA	231	192	High Point, NC	600
370	Beaverton, OR	166	403	Cranston, RI	104	379	Hillsboro, OR	146
382	Bellevue, WA	140	10	Dallas, TX	8,330	176	Hollywood, FL	660
302	Bellflower, CA	286	359	Daly City, CA	184	424	Hoover, AL	59
353	Bellingham, WA	199	371	Danbury, CT	164	2	Houston, TX	20,892
350	Bend, OR	204	179	Davenport, IA	652	252	Huntington Beach, CA	406
223	Berkeley, CA	482	276	Davie, FL	357	87	Huntsville, AL	1,518
341	Bethlehem, PA	219	98	Dayton, OH	1,355	217	Independence, MO	499
289	Billings, MT	313	273	Dearborn, MI	359	8	Indianapolis, IN	9,170
43	Birmingham, AL	3,163	224	Decatur, IL	481	239	Indio, CA	430
271	Bloomington, IL	361	270	Deerfield Beach, FL	366	147	Inglewood, CA	808
327	Bloomington, IN	244	291	Denton, TX	311	393	Irvine, CA	120
NA	Bloomington, MN**	NA	35	Denver, CO	3,708	211	Irving, TX	514
362	Boca Raton, FL	178	118	Des Moines, IA	1,069	24	Jacksonville, FL	5,182
213	Boise, ID	510	5	Detroit, MI	15,245	81	Jackson, MS	1,620
22	Boston, MA	5,252	258	Downey, CA	390	65	Jersey City, NJ	1,906
310	Boulder, CO	275	NA	Duluth, MN**	NA	430	Johns Creek, GA	35
406	Brick Twnshp, NJ	100	77	Durham, NC	1,707	210	Joliet, IL	517
92	Bridgeport, CT	1,447	304	Edinburg, TX	282	126	Kansas City, KS	947
111	Brockton, MA	1,160	381	Edison Twnshp, NJ	142	19	Kansas City, MO	5,536
380	Broken Arrow, OK	144	425	Edmond, OK	58	337	Kennewick, WA	226
NA	Brooklyn Park, MN**	NA	207	El Cajon, CA	529	308	Kenosha, WI	279
216	Brownsville, TX	500	247	El Monte, CA	421	199	Kent, WA	577
243	Bryan, TX	425	50	El Paso, TX	2,858	144	Killeen, TX	815
335	Buena Park, CA	230	301	Elgin, IL	287	78	Knoxville, TN	1,691
40	Buffalo, NY	3,250	99	Elizabeth, NJ	1,315	140	Lafayette, LA	843
355	Burbank, CA	191	208	Elk Grove, CA	523	415	Lake Forest, CA	89
227	Cambridge, MA	479	238	Erie, PA	431	204	Lakeland, FL	548
61	Camden, NJ	2,152	218	Escondido, CA	495	414	Lakewood Twnshp, NJ	92
386	Canton Twnshp, MI	132	228	Eugene, OR	460	343	Lakewood, CA	214
332	Cape Coral, FL	235	220	Evansville, IN	491	189	Lakewood, CO	615
347	Carlsbad, CA	210	230	Everett, WA	450	138	Lancaster, CA	851
431	Carmel, IN	17	243	Fairfield, CA	425	110	Lansing, MI	1,169
349	Carrollton, TX	206	117	Fall River, MA	1,089	112	Laredo, TX	1,120
232	Carson, CA	444	262	Fargo, ND	384	264	Largo, FL	373
399	Cary, NC	108	404	Farmington Hills, MI	101	245	Las Cruces, NM	424
275	Cedar Rapids, IA	358	121	Fayetteville, NC	1,050	6	Las Vegas, NV	10,813
372	Centennial, CO	162	432	Fishers, IN	11	281	Lawrence, KS	335
162	Champaign, IL	732	57	Flint, MI	2,392	157	Lawrence, MA	764
173	Chandler, AZ	681	164	Fontana, CA	720	142	Lawton, OK	829
254	Charleston, SC	398	248	Fort Collins, CO	420	412	League City, TX	94
28	Charlotte, NC	4,787	84	Fort Lauderdale, FL	1,565	401	Lee's Summit, MO	107
90	Chattanooga, TN	1,460	190	Fort Smith, AR	601	360	Lewisville, TX	183

Alpha Order - City (continued)

RANK	CITY	CRIMES
97	Lexington, KY	1,358
125	Lincoln, NE	966
48	Little Rock, AR	2,905
312	Livermore, CA	267
369	Livonia, MI	168
51	Long Beach, CA	2,857
330	Longmont, CO	238
251	Longview, TX	412
3	Los Angeles, CA	20,045
32	Louisville, KY	4,086
150	Lowell, MA	795
72	Lubbock, TX	1,800
309	Lynchburg, VA	278
148	Lynn, MA	804
201	Macon, GA	566
144	Madison, WI	815
188	Manchester, NH	618
322	McAllen, TX	246
329	McKinney, TX	241
260	Medford, OR	387
159	Melbourne, FL	750
7	Memphis, TN	10,336
427	Menifee, CA	53
214	Merced, CA	503
399	Meridian, ID	108
71	Mesa, AZ	1,838
255	Mesquite, TX	397
135	Miami Beach, FL	887
123	Miami Gardens, FL	999
27	Miami, FL	4,849
282	Midland, TX	334
17	Milwaukee, WI	5,969
34	Minneapolis, MN	3,722
211	Miramar, FL	514
418	Mission Viejo, CA	79
406	Mission, TX	100
82	Mobile, AL	1,619
95	Modesto, CA	1,413
167	Montgomery, AL	707
162	Moreno Valley, CA	732
177	Murfreesboro, TN	654
402	Murrieta, CA	105
336	Nampa, ID	227
340	Napa, CA	224
397	Naperville, IL	112
345	Nashua, NH	212
12	Nashville, TN	7,239
116	New Bedford, MA	1,093
75	New Haven, CT	1,748
52	New Orleans, LA	2,748
343	New Rochelle, NY	214
1	New York, NY	51,209
41	Newark, NJ	3,243
394	Newport Beach, CA	116
139	Newport News, VA	845
417	Newton, MA	80
94	Norfolk, VA	1,424
355	Norman, OK	191
178	North Charleston, SC	653
266	Norwalk, CA	371
285	Norwalk, CT	326
15	Oakland, CA	6,652
186	Oceanside, CA	620
160	Odessa, TX	748
422	O'Fallon, MO	71
257	Ogden, UT	392
25	Oklahoma City, OK	5,108
337	Olathe, KS	226
59	Omaha, NE	2,309
219	Ontario, CA	493
374	Orange, CA	157
429	Orem, UT	45
53	Orlando, FL	2,591

RANK	CITY	CRIMES
299	Overland Park, KS	289
187	Oxnard, CA	619
190	Palm Bay, FL	601
152	Palmdale, CA	785
236	Pasadena, CA	435
201	Pasadena, TX	566
89	Paterson, NJ	1,490
389	Pearland, TX	125
292	Pembroke Pines, FL	310
295	Peoria, AZ	301
146	Peoria, IL	814
4	Philadelphia, PA	18,268
11	Phoenix, AZ	8,089
55	Pittsburgh, PA	2,476
241	Plano, TX	429
297	Plantation, FL	292
129	Pomona, CA	927
130	Pompano Beach, FL	917
266	Port St. Lucie, FL	371
45	Portland, OR	3,037
203	Portsmouth, VA	550
378	Provo, UT	149
141	Pueblo, CO	831
256	Quincy, MA	394
287	Racine, WI	324
76	Raleigh, NC	1,724
398	Ramapo, NY	110
296	Rancho Cucamon., CA	293
158	Reading, PA	758
168	Redding, CA	701
364	Redwood City, CA	177
115	Reno, NV	1,108
297	Renton, WA	292
226	Rialto, CA	480
368	Richardson, TX	173
122	Richmond, CA	1,035
93	Richmond, VA	1,428
361	Rio Rancho, NM	180
101	Riverside, CA	1,310
194	Roanoke, VA	589
NA	Rochester, MN**	NA
63	Rochester, NY	2,029
62	Rockford, IL	2,106
319	Roseville, CA	248
419	Roswell, GA	72
396	Round Rock, TX	115
39	Sacramento, CA	3,354
209	Salem, OR	519
113	Salinas, CA	1,115
108	Salt Lake City, UT	1,213
318	San Angelo, TX	250
13	San Antonio, TX	7,038
70	San Bernardino, CA	1,861
26	San Diego, CA	5,104
21	San Francisco, CA	5,374
42	San Jose, CA	3,206
269	San Leandro, CA	367
333	San Marcos, CA	233
322	San Mateo, CA	246
375	Sandy Springs, GA	153
392	Sandy, UT	121
100	Santa Ana, CA	1,313
288	Santa Barbara, CA	319
364	Santa Clara, CA	177
313	Santa Clarita, CA	262
166	Santa Maria, CA	716
268	Santa Monica, CA	369
172	Santa Rosa, CA	682
134	Savannah, GA	889
253	Scottsdale, AZ	400
337	Scranton, PA	226
36	Seattle, WA	3,664
86	Shreveport, LA	1,544
394	Simi Valley, CA	116

RANK	CITY	CRIMES
280	Sioux City, IA	339
234	Sioux Falls, SD	440
304	Somerville, MA	282
161	South Bend, IN	744
197	South Gate, CA	580
303	Sparks, NV	285
366	Spokane Valley, WA	175
103	Spokane, WA	1,304
106	Springfield, IL	1,278
83	Springfield, MA	1,581
102	Springfield, MO	1,306
259	Stamford, CT	389
351	Sterling Heights, MI	203
31	Stockton, CA	4,155
306	St. Joseph, MO	281
18	St. Louis, MO	5,950
66	St. Paul, MN	1,885
54	St. Petersburg, FL	2,532
315	Suffolk, VA	259
410	Sugar Land, TX	96
377	Sunnyvale, CA	150
311	Sunrise, FL	269
387	Surprise, AZ	131
104	Syracuse, NY	1,302
88	Tacoma, WA	1,507
79	Tallahassee, FL	1,661
60	Tampa, FL	2,228
411	Temecula, CA	95
151	Tempe, AZ	787
170	Thornton, CO	695
384	Thousand Oaks, CA	137
49	Toledo, OH	2,868
404	Toms River Twnshp, NJ	101
169	Topeka, KS	698
357	Torrance, CA	185
383	Tracy, CA	138
109	Trenton, NJ	1,208
419	Troy, MI	72
38	Tucson, AZ	3,440
33	Tulsa, OK	3,960
237	Tuscaloosa, AL	432
409	Tustin, CA	97
214	Tyler, TX	503
246	Upper Darby Twnshp, PA	423
354	Vacaville, CA	195
132	Vallejo, CA	903
184	Vancouver, WA	633
285	Ventura, CA	326
171	Victorville, CA	686
154	Virginia Beach, VA	776
222	Visalia, CA	486
260	Vista, CA	387
156	Waco, TX	766
165	Warren, MI	719
416	Warwick, RI	84
14	Washington, DC	6,985
273	Waterbury, CT	359
307	West Covina, CA	280
347	West Jordan, UT	210
155	West Palm Beach, FL	769
195	West Valley, UT	588
278	Westland, MI	348
319	Westminster, CA	248
325	Westminster, CO	245
282	Whittier, CA	334
229	Wichita Falls, TX	459
46	Wichita, KS	2,950
175	Wilmington, NC	662
84	Winston-Salem, NC	1,565
388	Woodbridge Twnshp, NJ	127
72	Worcester, MA	1,800
224	Yakima, WA	481
124	Yonkers, NY	992
221	Yuma, AZ	490

Source: Reported data from the F.B.I. "Crime in the United States 2011"
*Violent crimes are offenses of murder, forcible rape, robbery, and aggravated assault.
**Not available.

Rank Order - City

45. Violent Crimes in 2011 (continued)
National Total = 1,203,564 Violent Crimes*

RANK	CITY	CRIMES
1	New York, NY	51,209
2	Houston, TX	20,892
3	Los Angeles, CA	20,045
4	Philadelphia, PA	18,268
5	Detroit, MI	15,245
6	Las Vegas, NV	10,813
7	Memphis, TN	10,336
8	Indianapolis, IN	9,170
9	Baltimore, MD	8,885
10	Dallas, TX	8,330
11	Phoenix, AZ	8,089
12	Nashville, TN	7,239
13	San Antonio, TX	7,038
14	Washington, DC	6,985
15	Oakland, CA	6,652
16	Atlanta, GA	6,097
17	Milwaukee, WI	5,969
18	St. Louis, MO	5,950
19	Kansas City, MO	5,536
20	Cleveland, OH	5,426
21	San Francisco, CA	5,374
22	Boston, MA	5,252
23	Columbus, OH	5,185
24	Jacksonville, FL	5,182
25	Oklahoma City, OK	5,108
26	San Diego, CA	5,104
27	Miami, FL	4,849
28	Charlotte, NC	4,787
29	Fort Worth, TX	4,569
30	Albuquerque, NM	4,207
31	Stockton, CA	4,155
32	Louisville, KY	4,086
33	Tulsa, OK	3,960
34	Minneapolis, MN	3,722
35	Denver, CO	3,708
36	Seattle, WA	3,664
37	Austin, TX	3,471
38	Tucson, AZ	3,440
39	Sacramento, CA	3,354
40	Buffalo, NY	3,250
41	Newark, NJ	3,243
42	San Jose, CA	3,206
43	Birmingham, AL	3,163
44	Cincinnati, OH	3,067
45	Portland, OR	3,037
46	Wichita, KS	2,950
47	Fresno, CA	2,915
48	Little Rock, AR	2,905
49	Toledo, OH	2,868
50	El Paso, TX	2,858
51	Long Beach, CA	2,857
52	New Orleans, LA	2,748
53	Orlando, FL	2,591
54	St. Petersburg, FL	2,532
55	Pittsburgh, PA	2,476
56	Baton Rouge, LA	2,468
57	Flint, MI	2,392
58	Anchorage, AK	2,388
59	Omaha, NE	2,309
60	Tampa, FL	2,228
61	Camden, NJ	2,152
62	Rockford, IL	2,106
63	Rochester, NY	2,029
64	Corpus Christi, TX	1,987
65	Jersey City, NJ	1,906
66	St. Paul, MN	1,885
67	Arlington, TX	1,874
68	Bakersfield, CA	1,866
69	Colorado Springs, CO	1,865
70	San Bernardino, CA	1,861
71	Mesa, AZ	1,838
72	Lubbock, TX	1,800

RANK	CITY	CRIMES
72	Worcester, MA	1,800
74	Akron, OH	1,779
75	New Haven, CT	1,748
76	Raleigh, NC	1,724
77	Durham, NC	1,707
78	Knoxville, TN	1,691
79	Tallahassee, FL	1,661
80	Hartford, CT	1,639
81	Jackson, MS	1,620
82	Mobile, AL	1,619
83	Springfield, MA	1,581
84	Fort Lauderdale, FL	1,565
84	Winston-Salem, NC	1,565
86	Shreveport, LA	1,544
87	Huntsville, AL	1,518
88	Tacoma, WA	1,507
89	Paterson, NJ	1,490
90	Chattanooga, TN	1,460
91	Aurora, CO	1,448
92	Bridgeport, CT	1,447
93	Richmond, VA	1,428
94	Norfolk, VA	1,424
95	Modesto, CA	1,413
96	Grand Rapids, MI	1,395
97	Lexington, KY	1,358
98	Dayton, OH	1,355
99	Elizabeth, NJ	1,315
100	Santa Ana, CA	1,313
101	Riverside, CA	1,310
102	Springfield, MO	1,306
103	Spokane, WA	1,304
104	Syracuse, NY	1,302
105	Anaheim, CA	1,281
106	Springfield, IL	1,278
107	Amarillo, TX	1,223
108	Salt Lake City, UT	1,213
109	Trenton, NJ	1,208
110	Lansing, MI	1,169
111	Brockton, MA	1,160
112	Laredo, TX	1,120
113	Salinas, CA	1,115
114	Glendale, AZ	1,114
115	Reno, NV	1,108
116	New Bedford, MA	1,093
117	Fall River, MA	1,089
118	Beaumont, TX	1,069
118	Des Moines, IA	1,069
120	Compton, CA	1,067
121	Fayetteville, NC	1,050
122	Richmond, CA	1,035
123	Miami Gardens, FL	999
124	Yonkers, NY	992
125	Lincoln, NE	966
126	Kansas City, KS	947
127	Albany, NY	939
128	Columbus, GA	933
129	Pomona, CA	927
130	Pompano Beach, FL	917
131	Gainesville, FL	912
132	Vallejo, CA	903
133	Chesapeake, VA	892
134	Savannah, GA	889
135	Miami Beach, FL	887
136	Clarksville, TN	883
137	Hialeah, FL	860
138	Lancaster, CA	851
139	Newport News, VA	845
140	Lafayette, LA	843
141	Pueblo, CO	831
142	Lawton, OK	829
143	Antioch, CA	818
144	Killeen, TX	815

RANK	CITY	CRIMES
144	Madison, WI	815
146	Peoria, IL	814
147	Inglewood, CA	808
148	Lynn, MA	804
149	Clearwater, FL	801
150	Lowell, MA	795
151	Tempe, AZ	787
152	Fort Wayne, IN	785
152	Palmdale, CA	785
154	Virginia Beach, VA	776
155	West Palm Beach, FL	769
156	Waco, TX	766
157	Lawrence, MA	764
158	Reading, PA	758
159	Melbourne, FL	750
160	Odessa, TX	748
161	South Bend, IN	744
162	Champaign, IL	732
162	Moreno Valley, CA	732
164	Fontana, CA	720
165	Warren, MI	719
166	Santa Maria, CA	716
167	Montgomery, AL	707
168	Redding, CA	701
169	Topeka, KS	698
170	Thornton, CO	695
171	Victorville, CA	686
172	Santa Rosa, CA	682
173	Chandler, AZ	681
174	Chula Vista, CA	670
175	Wilmington, NC	662
176	Hollywood, FL	660
177	Murfreesboro, TN	654
178	North Charleston, SC	653
179	Davenport, IA	652
180	Allentown, PA	647
181	Albany, GA	640
182	Gary, IN	639
183	Aurora, IL	636
184	Vancouver, WA	633
185	Hawthorne, CA	623
186	Oceanside, CA	620
187	Oxnard, CA	619
188	Manchester, NH	618
189	Lakewood, CO	615
190	Fort Smith, AR	601
190	Palm Bay, FL	601
192	High Point, NC	600
193	Grand Prairie, TX	591
194	Roanoke, VA	589
195	West Valley, UT	588
196	Columbia, MO	582
197	South Gate, CA	580
198	Hayward, CA	579
199	Kent, WA	577
200	Henderson, NV	571
201	Macon, GA	566
201	Pasadena, TX	566
203	Portsmouth, VA	550
204	Lakeland, FL	548
205	Hammond, IN	547
206	Garland, TX	530
207	El Cajon, CA	529
208	Elk Grove, CA	523
209	Salem, OR	519
210	Joliet, IL	517
211	Irving, TX	514
211	Miramar, FL	514
213	Boise, ID	510
214	Merced, CA	503
214	Tyler, TX	503
216	Brownsville, TX	500

Rank Order - City (continued)

RANK	CITY	CRIMES
217	Independence, MO	499
218	Escondido, CA	495
219	Ontario, CA	493
220	Evansville, IN	491
221	Yuma, AZ	490
222	Visalia, CA	486
223	Berkeley, CA	482
224	Decatur, IL	481
224	Yakima, WA	481
226	Rialto, CA	480
227	Cambridge, MA	479
228	Eugene, OR	460
229	Wichita Falls, TX	459
230	Everett, WA	450
231	Garden Grove, CA	449
232	Asheville, NC	444
232	Carson, CA	444
234	Sioux Falls, SD	440
235	Greeley, CO	437
236	Pasadena, CA	435
237	Tuscaloosa, AL	432
238	Erie, PA	431
239	Concord, CA	430
239	Indio, CA	430
241	Plano, TX	429
242	Abilene, TX	428
243	Bryan, TX	425
243	Fairfield, CA	425
245	Las Cruces, NM	424
246	Upper Darby Twnshp, PA	423
247	El Monte, CA	421
248	Fort Collins, CO	420
249	Athens-Clarke, GA	417
250	Gresham, OR	416
251	Longview, TX	412
252	Huntington Beach, CA	406
253	Scottsdale, AZ	400
254	Charleston, SC	398
255	Mesquite, TX	397
256	Quincy, MA	394
257	Ogden, UT	392
258	Downey, CA	390
259	Stamford, CT	389
260	Medford, OR	387
260	Vista, CA	387
262	Fargo, ND	384
262	Fremont, CA	384
264	Green Bay, WI	373
264	Largo, FL	373
266	Norwalk, CA	371
266	Port St. Lucie, FL	371
268	Santa Monica, CA	369
269	San Leandro, CA	367
270	Deerfield Beach, FL	366
271	Bloomington, IL	361
271	Hemet, CA	361
273	Dearborn, MI	359
273	Waterbury, CT	359
275	Cedar Rapids, IA	358
276	Davie, FL	357
277	Hampton, VA	350
278	Westland, MI	348
279	Cicero, IL	344
280	Sioux City, IA	339
281	Lawrence, KS	335
282	Citrus Heights, CA	334
282	Midland, TX	334
282	Whittier, CA	334
285	Norwalk, CT	326
285	Ventura, CA	326
287	Racine, WI	324
288	Santa Barbara, CA	319
289	Billings, MT	313
289	Hesperia, CA	313
291	Denton, TX	311
292	Pembroke Pines, FL	310
293	Fullerton, CA	306
294	Clinton Twnshp, MI	303
295	Peoria, AZ	301
296	Rancho Cucamon., CA	293
297	Plantation, FL	292
297	Renton, WA	292
299	Overland Park, KS	289
300	College Station, TX	288
301	Elgin, IL	287
302	Bellflower, CA	286
303	Sparks, NV	285
304	Edinburg, TX	282
304	Somerville, MA	282
306	St. Joseph, MO	281
307	West Covina, CA	280
308	Kenosha, WI	279
309	Lynchburg, VA	278
310	Boulder, CO	275
311	Sunrise, FL	269
312	Livermore, CA	267
313	Santa Clarita, CA	262
314	Ann Arbor, MI	261
315	Suffolk, VA	259
316	Glendale, CA	258
317	Alexandria, VA	252
318	San Angelo, TX	250
319	Roseville, CA	248
319	Westminster, CA	248
321	Chino, CA	247
322	Avondale, AZ	246
322	McAllen, TX	246
322	San Mateo, CA	246
325	Chico, CA	245
325	Westminster, CO	245
327	Bloomington, IN	244
328	Baldwin Park, CA	242
329	McKinney, TX	241
330	Longmont, CO	238
331	Coral Springs, FL	236
332	Cape Coral, FL	235
333	San Marcos, CA	233
334	Costa Mesa, CA	231
335	Buena Park, CA	230
336	Nampa, ID	227
337	Kennewick, WA	226
337	Olathe, KS	226
337	Scranton, PA	226
340	Napa, CA	224
341	Bethlehem, PA	219
342	Clifton, NJ	215
343	Lakewood, CA	214
343	New Rochelle, NY	214
345	Nashua, NH	212
346	Clovis, CA	211
347	Carlsbad, CA	210
347	West Jordan, UT	210
349	Carrollton, TX	206
350	Bend, OR	204
351	Sterling Heights, MI	203
352	Corona, CA	200
353	Bellingham, WA	199
354	Vacaville, CA	195
355	Burbank, CA	191
355	Norman, OK	191
357	Hamilton Twnshp, NJ	185
357	Torrance, CA	185
359	Daly City, CA	184
360	Lewisville, TX	183
361	Rio Rancho, NM	180
362	Boca Raton, FL	178
362	Gilbert, AZ	178
364	Redwood City, CA	177
364	Santa Clara, CA	177
366	Cheektowaga, NY	175
366	Spokane Valley, WA	175
368	Richardson, TX	173
369	Livonia, MI	168
370	Beaverton, OR	166
371	Danbury, CT	164
372	Arvada, CO	162
372	Centennial, CO	162
374	Orange, CA	157
375	Sandy Springs, GA	153
376	Alhambra, CA	152
377	Sunnyvale, CA	150
378	Provo, UT	149
379	Hillsboro, OR	146
380	Broken Arrow, OK	144
381	Edison Twnshp, NJ	142
382	Bellevue, WA	140
383	Tracy, CA	138
384	Thousand Oaks, CA	137
385	Greece, NY	135
386	Canton Twnshp, MI	132
387	Surprise, AZ	131
388	Woodbridge Twnshp, NJ	127
389	Pearland, TX	125
390	Amherst, NY	124
391	Frisco, TX	122
392	Sandy, UT	121
393	Irvine, CA	120
394	Newport Beach, CA	116
394	Simi Valley, CA	116
396	Round Rock, TX	115
397	Naperville, IL	112
398	Ramapo, NY	110
399	Cary, NC	108
399	Meridian, ID	108
401	Lee's Summit, MO	107
402	Murrieta, CA	105
403	Cranston, RI	104
404	Farmington Hills, MI	101
404	Toms River Twnshp, NJ	101
406	Brick Twnshp, NJ	100
406	Clarkstown, NY	100
406	Mission, TX	100
409	Tustin, CA	97
410	Sugar Land, TX	96
411	Temecula, CA	95
412	League City, TX	94
413	Concord, NC	93
414	Lakewood Twnshp, NJ	92
415	Lake Forest, CA	89
416	Warwick, RI	84
417	Newton, MA	80
418	Mission Viejo, CA	79
419	Allen, TX	72
419	Roswell, GA	72
419	Troy, MI	72
422	O'Fallon, MO	71
423	Chino Hills, CA	68
424	Hoover, AL	59
425	Edmond, OK	58
426	Colonie, NY	54
427	Menifee, CA	53
428	Arlington Heights, IL	48
429	Orem, UT	45
430	Johns Creek, GA	35
431	Carmel, IN	17
432	Fishers, IN	11
NA	Bloomington, MN**	NA
NA	Brooklyn Park, MN**	NA
NA	Chicago, IL**	NA
NA	Duluth, MN**	NA
NA	Rochester, MN**	NA

Source: Reported data from the F.B.I. "Crime in the United States 2011"
*Violent crimes are offenses of murder, forcible rape, robbery, and aggravated assault.
**Not available.

Alpha Order - City

46. Violent Crime Rate in 2011
National Rate = 386.3 Violent Crimes per 100,000 Population*

RANK	CITY	RATE
248	Abilene, TX	358.1
60	Akron, OH	892.8
71	Albany, GA	815.8
51	Albany, NY	955.3
84	Albuquerque, NM	762.2
355	Alexandria, VA	177.9
351	Alhambra, CA	180.8
153	Allentown, PA	546.4
418	Allen, TX	83.7
122	Amarillo, TX	628.1
406	Amherst, NY	105.4
235	Anaheim, CA	376.5
72	Anchorage, AK	804.2
323	Ann Arbor, MI	229.3
76	Antioch, CA	789.8
427	Arlington Heights, IL	63.7
174	Arlington, TX	502.2
372	Arvada, CO	149.6
160	Asheville, NC	525.8
252	Athens-Clarke, GA	356.1
9	Atlanta, GA	1,432.8
196	Aurora, CO	437.8
269	Aurora, IL	320.4
198	Austin, TX	430.1
270	Avondale, AZ	318.2
159	Bakersfield, CA	530.8
271	Baldwin Park, CA	317.3
11	Baltimore, MD	1,417.4
31	Baton Rouge, LA	1,065.7
61	Beaumont, TX	885.0
348	Beaverton, OR	182.9
400	Bellevue, WA	112.6
240	Bellflower, CA	369.0
321	Bellingham, WA	242.2
312	Bend, OR	263.4
206	Berkeley, CA	423.2
291	Bethlehem, PA	291.1
286	Billings, MT	297.8
8	Birmingham, AL	1,483.2
185	Bloomington, IL	469.8
283	Bloomington, IN	301.9
NA	Bloomington, MN**	NA
335	Boca Raton, FL	208.1
319	Boise, ID	245.3
68	Boston, MA	845.2
302	Boulder, CO	277.6
383	Brick Twnshp, NJ	132.8
38	Bridgeport, CT	1,001.4
18	Brockton, MA	1,229.1
375	Broken Arrow, OK	144.1
NA	Brooklyn Park, MN**	NA
300	Brownsville, TX	279.8
154	Bryan, TX	546.2
296	Buena Park, CA	282.3
17	Buffalo, NY	1,238.2
349	Burbank, CA	182.7
193	Cambridge, MA	452.7
1	Camden, NJ	2,773.1
374	Canton Twnshp, MI	146.5
370	Cape Coral, FL	150.2
342	Carlsbad, CA	197.1
431	Carmel, IN	21.4
362	Carrollton, TX	169.4
181	Carson, CA	478.5
421	Cary, NC	78.9
297	Cedar Rapids, IA	281.9
367	Centennial, CO	158.6
58	Champaign, IL	900.4
294	Chandler, AZ	284.4
266	Charleston, SC	327.6
135	Charlotte, NC	606.4
65	Chattanooga, TN	863.0
329	Cheektowaga, NY	221.0
223	Chesapeake, VA	396.7
NA	Chicago, IL**	NA
298	Chico, CA	281.0
414	Chino Hills, CA	89.9
277	Chino, CA	313.1
307	Chula Vista, CA	271.5
215	Cicero, IL	408.8
33	Cincinnati, OH	1,032.1
224	Citrus Heights, CA	396.3
392	Clarkstown, NY	126.2
110	Clarksville, TN	658.3
91	Clearwater, FL	733.8
14	Cleveland, OH	1,366.4
316	Clifton, NJ	254.7
276	Clinton Twnshp, MI	313.3
331	Clovis, CA	218.1
285	College Station, TX	300.5
425	Colonie, NY	69.3
195	Colorado Springs, CO	440.2
158	Columbia, MO	534.5
177	Columbus, GA	485.0
110	Columbus, OH	658.3
29	Compton, CA	1,093.4
254	Concord, CA	348.2
396	Concord, NC	116.1
344	Coral Springs, FL	192.3
386	Corona, CA	129.7
119	Corpus Christi, TX	637.6
336	Costa Mesa, CA	207.6
387	Cranston, RI	129.5
105	Dallas, TX	681.1
353	Daly City, CA	179.8
339	Danbury, CT	202.4
115	Davenport, IA	650.7
231	Davie, FL	382.9
50	Dayton, OH	956.7
243	Dearborn, MI	366.0
120	Decatur, IL	630.0
179	Deerfield Beach, FL	481.3
309	Denton, TX	268.6
133	Denver, CO	607.3
162	Des Moines, IA	522.7
3	Detroit, MI	2,137.4
257	Downey, CA	344.9
NA	Duluth, MN**	NA
90	Durham, NC	738.2
247	Edinburg, TX	358.2
377	Edison Twnshp, NJ	141.6
424	Edmond, OK	70.5
161	El Cajon, CA	525.6
242	El Monte, CA	366.7
197	El Paso, TX	431.2
310	Elgin, IL	264.5
32	Elizabeth, NJ	1,048.8
262	Elk Grove, CA	337.8
208	Erie, PA	422.1
260	Escondido, CA	340.0
290	Eugene, OR	291.4
210	Evansville, IN	416.0
198	Everett, WA	430.1
221	Fairfield, CA	398.8
19	Fall River, MA	1,218.1
249	Fargo, ND	357.8
391	Farmington Hills, MI	126.8
167	Fayetteville, NC	517.0
432	Fishers, IN	14.3
2	Flint, MI	2,336.9
246	Fontana, CA	363.0
293	Fort Collins, CO	286.7
53	Fort Lauderdale, FL	932.8
103	Fort Smith, AR	691.9
280	Fort Wayne, IN	307.9
136	Fort Worth, TX	603.7
356	Fremont, CA	177.3
142	Fresno, CA	582.4
407	Frisco, TX	102.1
327	Fullerton, CA	223.8
97	Gainesville, FL	723.5
315	Garden Grove, CA	259.7
324	Garland, TX	228.8
75	Gary, IN	791.8
417	Gilbert, AZ	84.2
178	Glendale, AZ	484.5
382	Glendale, CA	133.0
265	Grand Prairie, TX	330.0
87	Grand Rapids, MI	742.4
378	Greece, NY	139.9
189	Greeley, CO	462.4
250	Green Bay, WI	356.9
226	Gresham, OR	389.8
334	Hamilton Twnshp, NJ	208.4
106	Hammond, IN	673.3
317	Hampton, VA	251.7
16	Hartford, CT	1,311.1
95	Hawthorne, CA	730.5
222	Hayward, CA	396.9
192	Hemet, CA	453.6
330	Henderson, NV	219.7
258	Hesperia, CA	343.1
234	Hialeah, FL	377.6
147	High Point, NC	567.7
368	Hillsboro, OR	157.7
188	Hollywood, FL	462.6
423	Hoover, AL	71.9
46	Houston, TX	974.6
332	Huntington Beach, CA	211.2
69	Huntsville, AL	838.8
204	Independence, MO	425.6
27	Indianapolis, IN	1,100.8
150	Indio, CA	558.9
96	Inglewood, CA	728.2
428	Irvine, CA	55.8
322	Irving, TX	232.7
125	Jacksonville, FL	621.0
54	Jackson, MS	930.1
81	Jersey City, NJ	767.2
430	Johns Creek, GA	45.0
253	Joliet, IL	349.6
116	Kansas City, KS	645.5
20	Kansas City, MO	1,199.7
284	Kennewick, WA	301.0
299	Kenosha, WI	280.0
126	Kent, WA	614.7
123	Killeen, TX	624.0
52	Knoxville, TN	936.9
102	Lafayette, LA	692.5
397	Lake Forest, CA	113.9
151	Lakeland, FL	554.9
410	Lakewood Twnshp, NJ	98.8
311	Lakewood, CA	264.2
207	Lakewood, CO	422.8
156	Lancaster, CA	537.0
35	Lansing, MI	1,023.5
186	Laredo, TX	464.6
184	Largo, FL	473.9
201	Las Cruces, NM	429.5
89	Las Vegas, NV	741.4
233	Lawrence, KS	379.8
43	Lawrence, MA	994.2
67	Lawton, OK	846.7
402	League City, TX	110.2
395	Lee's Summit, MO	116.7
346	Lewisville, TX	188.1

184 Cities

Alpha Order - City (continued)

RANK	CITY	RATE
191	Lexington, KY	455.9
238	Lincoln, NE	370.6
7	Little Rock, AR	1,489.8
267	Livermore, CA	325.9
359	Livonia, MI	173.4
132	Long Beach, CA	610.9
308	Longmont, CO	271.2
175	Longview, TX	501.5
163	Los Angeles, CA	522.4
129	Louisville, KY	614.3
88	Lowell, MA	741.8
79	Lubbock, TX	767.9
245	Lynchburg, VA	363.5
62	Lynn, MA	884.7
131	Macon, GA	611.5
255	Madison, WI	348.0
148	Manchester, NH	563.3
347	McAllen, TX	185.5
352	McKinney, TX	180.0
169	Medford, OR	511.2
47	Melbourne, FL	972.7
6	Memphis, TN	1,583.5
426	Menifee, CA	67.6
121	Merced, CA	629.6
376	Meridian, ID	142.3
213	Mesa, AZ	412.8
301	Mesquite, TX	278.1
42	Miami Beach, FL	996.9
55	Miami Gardens, FL	919.7
21	Miami, FL	1,197.6
289	Midland, TX	294.3
40	Milwaukee, WI	999.1
48	Minneapolis, MN	965.4
211	Miramar, FL	415.5
418	Mission Viejo, CA	83.7
388	Mission, TX	127.1
117	Mobile, AL	642.8
101	Modesto, CA	694.2
259	Montgomery, AL	342.0
236	Moreno Valley, CA	374.2
139	Murfreesboro, TN	596.0
409	Murrieta, CA	100.3
304	Nampa, ID	275.3
292	Napa, CA	287.8
422	Naperville, IL	78.7
320	Nashua, NH	244.8
23	Nashville, TN	1,181.3
25	New Bedford, MA	1,142.7
15	New Haven, CT	1,344.4
74	New Orleans, LA	792.0
303	New Rochelle, NY	276.5
124	New York, NY	623.6
24	Newark, NJ	1,166.3
380	Newport Beach, CA	134.6
190	Newport News, VA	462.1
412	Newton, MA	93.4
143	Norfolk, VA	579.6
361	Norman, OK	170.4
108	North Charleston, SC	662.2
256	Norwalk, CA	347.4
232	Norwalk, CT	380.1
5	Oakland, CA	1,682.7
241	Oceanside, CA	366.8
92	Odessa, TX	733.0
415	O'Fallon, MO	89.2
187	Ogden, UT	464.3
64	Oklahoma City, OK	871.4
354	Olathe, KS	178.4
149	Omaha, NE	559.6
287	Ontario, CA	297.3
398	Orange, CA	113.8
429	Orem, UT	50.0
30	Orlando, FL	1,072.7
363	Overland Park, KS	165.6
279	Oxnard, CA	309.2
145	Palm Bay, FL	574.6
172	Palmdale, CA	507.9
275	Pasadena, CA	313.5
237	Pasadena, TX	371.9
37	Paterson, NJ	1,015.8
381	Pearland, TX	134.2
341	Pembroke Pines, FL	197.6
343	Peoria, AZ	192.6
100	Peoria, IL	705.7
22	Philadelphia, PA	1,193.3
152	Phoenix, AZ	551.7
73	Pittsburgh, PA	802.3
365	Plano, TX	161.7
261	Plantation, FL	339.1
126	Pomona, CA	614.7
56	Pompano Beach, FL	906.1
328	Port St. Lucie, FL	222.4
168	Portland, OR	514.8
146	Portsmouth, VA	568.9
385	Provo, UT	130.0
83	Pueblo, CO	766.2
205	Quincy, MA	424.4
214	Racine, WI	409.1
209	Raleigh, NC	421.5
384	Ramapo, NY	130.3
357	Rancho Cucamon., CA	175.2
66	Reading, PA	857.8
77	Redding, CA	771.0
325	Redwood City, CA	227.7
176	Reno, NV	487.8
273	Renton, WA	316.2
182	Rialto, CA	478.4
360	Richardson, TX	170.8
45	Richmond, CA	986.5
104	Richmond, VA	691.0
338	Rio Rancho, NM	203.4
203	Riverside, CA	426.1
138	Roanoke, VA	599.9
NA	Rochester, MN**	NA
49	Rochester, NY	959.3
13	Rockford, IL	1,373.5
337	Roseville, CA	206.4
420	Roswell, GA	80.4
399	Round Rock, TX	112.8
99	Sacramento, CA	710.6
264	Salem, OR	332.1
93	Salinas, CA	732.5
118	Salt Lake City, UT	638.3
313	San Angelo, TX	262.7
165	San Antonio, TX	519.3
63	San Bernardino, CA	876.2
227	San Diego, CA	387.6
109	San Francisco, CA	659.6
263	San Jose, CA	335.0
202	San Leandro, CA	427.0
305	San Marcos, CA	274.9
318	San Mateo, CA	250.1
366	Sandy Springs, GA	160.9
379	Sandy, UT	135.7
220	Santa Ana, CA	399.9
251	Santa Barbara, CA	356.6
370	Santa Clara, CA	150.2
373	Santa Clarita, CA	146.9
98	Santa Maria, CA	710.9
218	Santa Monica, CA	406.4
219	Santa Rosa, CA	401.7
225	Savannah, GA	392.6
350	Scottsdale, AZ	181.4
288	Scranton, PA	296.1
140	Seattle, WA	592.7
80	Shreveport, LA	767.6
413	Simi Valley, CA	92.3
216	Sioux City, IA	407.9
295	Sioux Falls, SD	282.5
239	Somerville, MA	370.0
94	South Bend, IN	731.7
133	South Gate, CA	607.3
277	Sparks, NV	313.1
345	Spokane Valley, WA	192.0
128	Spokane, WA	614.5
28	Springfield, IL	1,096.1
34	Springfield, MA	1,026.7
70	Springfield, MO	815.9
272	Stamford, CT	316.6
369	Sterling Heights, MI	156.6
12	Stockton, CA	1,407.8
244	St. Joseph, MO	364.7
4	St. Louis, MO	1,856.7
112	St. Paul, MN	655.3
36	St. Petersburg, FL	1,020.5
282	Suffolk, VA	302.6
394	Sugar Land, TX	119.3
405	Sunnyvale, CA	105.8
274	Sunrise, FL	314.3
403	Surprise, AZ	109.9
59	Syracuse, NY	892.9
86	Tacoma, WA	747.9
57	Tallahassee, FL	903.5
113	Tampa, FL	654.7
411	Temecula, CA	93.8
180	Tempe, AZ	479.9
144	Thornton, CO	575.1
404	Thousand Oaks, CA	106.9
41	Toledo, OH	997.8
401	Toms River Twnshp, NJ	110.3
155	Topeka, KS	544.1
393	Torrance, CA	125.7
364	Tracy, CA	164.5
10	Trenton, NJ	1,417.9
416	Troy, MI	89.0
114	Tucson, AZ	652.2
39	Tulsa, OK	999.7
183	Tuscaloosa, AL	475.2
390	Tustin, CA	126.9
171	Tyler, TX	508.4
170	Upper Darby Twnshp, PA	509.3
333	Vacaville, CA	208.5
78	Vallejo, CA	769.8
230	Vancouver, WA	385.2
281	Ventura, CA	302.7
141	Victorville, CA	585.0
358	Virginia Beach, VA	175.1
229	Visalia, CA	386.0
217	Vista, CA	407.6
137	Waco, TX	601.1
157	Warren, MI	536.7
408	Warwick, RI	101.7
26	Washington, DC	1,130.3
268	Waterbury, CT	324.7
314	West Covina, CA	260.8
340	West Jordan, UT	198.7
85	West Palm Beach, FL	759.3
194	West Valley, UT	445.5
212	Westland, MI	414.1
306	Westminster, CA	273.3
326	Westminster, CO	226.9
228	Whittier, CA	386.9
200	Wichita Falls, TX	430.0
82	Wichita, KS	766.6
130	Wilmington, NC	614.0
107	Winston-Salem, NC	673.0
388	Woodbridge Twnshp, NJ	127.1
44	Worcester, MA	988.2
164	Yakima, WA	520.0
173	Yonkers, NY	503.9
166	Yuma, AZ	519.2

Source: CQ Press using reported data from the F.B.I. "Crime in the United States 2011"
*Violent crimes are offenses of murder, forcible rape, robbery, and aggravated assault.
**Not available.

Rank Order - City

46. Violent Crime Rate in 2011 (continued)
National Rate = 386.3 Violent Crimes per 100,000 Population*

RANK	CITY	RATE	RANK	CITY	RATE	RANK	CITY	RATE
1	Camden, NJ	2,773.1	73	Pittsburgh, PA	802.3	145	Palm Bay, FL	574.6
2	Flint, MI	2,336.9	74	New Orleans, LA	792.0	146	Portsmouth, VA	568.9
3	Detroit, MI	2,137.4	75	Gary, IN	791.8	147	High Point, NC	567.7
4	St. Louis, MO	1,856.7	76	Antioch, CA	789.8	148	Manchester, NH	563.3
5	Oakland, CA	1,682.7	77	Redding, CA	771.0	149	Omaha, NE	559.6
6	Memphis, TN	1,583.5	78	Vallejo, CA	769.8	150	Indio, CA	558.9
7	Little Rock, AR	1,489.8	79	Lubbock, TX	767.9	151	Lakeland, FL	554.9
8	Birmingham, AL	1,483.2	80	Shreveport, LA	767.6	152	Phoenix, AZ	551.7
9	Atlanta, GA	1,432.8	81	Jersey City, NJ	767.2	153	Allentown, PA	546.4
10	Trenton, NJ	1,417.9	82	Wichita, KS	766.6	154	Bryan, TX	546.2
11	Baltimore, MD	1,417.4	83	Pueblo, CO	766.2	155	Topeka, KS	544.1
12	Stockton, CA	1,407.8	84	Albuquerque, NM	762.2	156	Lancaster, CA	537.0
13	Rockford, IL	1,373.5	85	West Palm Beach, FL	759.3	157	Warren, MI	536.7
14	Cleveland, OH	1,366.4	86	Tacoma, WA	747.9	158	Columbia, MO	534.5
15	New Haven, CT	1,344.4	87	Grand Rapids, MI	742.4	159	Bakersfield, CA	530.8
16	Hartford, CT	1,311.1	88	Lowell, MA	741.8	160	Asheville, NC	525.8
17	Buffalo, NY	1,238.2	89	Las Vegas, NV	741.4	161	El Cajon, CA	525.6
18	Brockton, MA	1,229.1	90	Durham, NC	738.2	162	Des Moines, IA	522.7
19	Fall River, MA	1,218.1	91	Clearwater, FL	733.8	163	Los Angeles, CA	522.4
20	Kansas City, MO	1,199.7	92	Odessa, TX	733.0	164	Yakima, WA	520.0
21	Miami, FL	1,197.6	93	Salinas, CA	732.5	165	San Antonio, TX	519.3
22	Philadelphia, PA	1,193.3	94	South Bend, IN	731.7	166	Yuma, AZ	519.2
23	Nashville, TN	1,181.3	95	Hawthorne, CA	730.5	167	Fayetteville, NC	517.0
24	Newark, NJ	1,166.3	96	Inglewood, CA	728.2	168	Portland, OR	514.8
25	New Bedford, MA	1,142.7	97	Gainesville, FL	723.5	169	Medford, OR	511.2
26	Washington, DC	1,130.3	98	Santa Maria, CA	710.9	170	Upper Darby Twnshp, PA	509.3
27	Indianapolis, IN	1,100.8	99	Sacramento, CA	710.6	171	Tyler, TX	508.4
28	Springfield, IL	1,096.1	100	Peoria, IL	705.7	172	Palmdale, CA	507.9
29	Compton, CA	1,093.4	101	Modesto, CA	694.2	173	Yonkers, NY	503.9
30	Orlando, FL	1,072.7	102	Lafayette, LA	692.5	174	Arlington, TX	502.2
31	Baton Rouge, LA	1,065.7	103	Fort Smith, AR	691.9	175	Longview, TX	501.5
32	Elizabeth, NJ	1,048.8	104	Richmond, VA	691.0	176	Reno, NV	487.8
33	Cincinnati, OH	1,032.1	105	Dallas, TX	681.1	177	Columbus, GA	485.0
34	Springfield, MA	1,026.7	106	Hammond, IN	673.3	178	Glendale, AZ	484.5
35	Lansing, MI	1,023.5	107	Winston-Salem, NC	673.0	179	Deerfield Beach, FL	481.3
36	St. Petersburg, FL	1,020.5	108	North Charleston, SC	662.2	180	Tempe, AZ	479.9
37	Paterson, NJ	1,015.8	109	San Francisco, CA	659.6	181	Carson, CA	478.5
38	Bridgeport, CT	1,001.4	110	Clarksville, TN	658.3	182	Rialto, CA	478.4
39	Tulsa, OK	999.7	110	Columbus, OH	658.3	183	Tuscaloosa, AL	475.2
40	Milwaukee, WI	999.1	112	St. Paul, MN	655.3	184	Largo, FL	473.9
41	Toledo, OH	997.8	113	Tampa, FL	654.7	185	Bloomington, IL	469.8
42	Miami Beach, FL	996.9	114	Tucson, AZ	652.2	186	Laredo, TX	464.6
43	Lawrence, MA	994.2	115	Davenport, IA	650.7	187	Ogden, UT	464.3
44	Worcester, MA	988.2	116	Kansas City, KS	645.5	188	Hollywood, FL	462.6
45	Richmond, CA	986.5	117	Mobile, AL	642.8	189	Greeley, CO	462.4
46	Houston, TX	974.6	118	Salt Lake City, UT	638.3	190	Newport News, VA	462.1
47	Melbourne, FL	972.7	119	Corpus Christi, TX	637.6	191	Lexington, KY	455.9
48	Minneapolis, MN	965.4	120	Decatur, IL	630.0	192	Hemet, CA	453.6
49	Rochester, NY	959.3	121	Merced, CA	629.6	193	Cambridge, MA	452.7
50	Dayton, OH	956.7	122	Amarillo, TX	628.1	194	West Valley, UT	445.5
51	Albany, NY	955.3	123	Killeen, TX	624.0	195	Colorado Springs, CO	440.2
52	Knoxville, TN	936.9	124	New York, NY	623.6	196	Aurora, CO	437.8
53	Fort Lauderdale, FL	932.8	125	Jacksonville, FL	621.0	197	El Paso, TX	431.2
54	Jackson, MS	930.1	126	Kent, WA	614.7	198	Austin, TX	430.1
55	Miami Gardens, FL	919.7	126	Pomona, CA	614.7	198	Everett, WA	430.1
56	Pompano Beach, FL	906.1	128	Spokane, WA	614.5	200	Wichita Falls, TX	430.0
57	Tallahassee, FL	903.5	129	Louisville, KY	614.3	201	Las Cruces, NM	429.5
58	Champaign, IL	900.4	130	Wilmington, NC	614.0	202	San Leandro, CA	427.0
59	Syracuse, NY	892.9	131	Macon, GA	611.5	203	Riverside, CA	426.1
60	Akron, OH	892.8	132	Long Beach, CA	610.9	204	Independence, MO	425.6
61	Beaumont, TX	885.0	133	Denver, CO	607.3	205	Quincy, MA	424.4
62	Lynn, MA	884.7	133	South Gate, CA	607.3	206	Berkeley, CA	423.2
63	San Bernardino, CA	876.2	135	Charlotte, NC	606.4	207	Lakewood, CO	422.8
64	Oklahoma City, OK	871.4	136	Fort Worth, TX	603.7	208	Erie, PA	422.1
65	Chattanooga, TN	863.0	137	Waco, TX	601.1	209	Raleigh, NC	421.5
66	Reading, PA	857.8	138	Roanoke, VA	599.9	210	Evansville, IN	416.0
67	Lawton, OK	846.7	139	Murfreesboro, TN	596.0	211	Miramar, FL	415.5
68	Boston, MA	845.2	140	Seattle, WA	592.7	212	Westland, MI	414.1
69	Huntsville, AL	838.8	141	Victorville, CA	585.0	213	Mesa, AZ	412.8
70	Springfield, MO	815.9	142	Fresno, CA	582.4	214	Racine, WI	409.1
71	Albany, GA	815.8	143	Norfolk, VA	579.6	215	Cicero, IL	408.8
72	Anchorage, AK	804.2	144	Thornton, CO	575.1	216	Sioux City, IA	407.9

Rank Order - City (continued)

RANK	CITY	RATE	RANK	CITY	RATE	RANK	CITY	RATE
217	Vista, CA	407.6	290	Eugene, OR	291.4	364	Tracy, CA	164.5
218	Santa Monica, CA	406.4	291	Bethlehem, PA	291.1	365	Plano, TX	161.7
219	Santa Rosa, CA	401.7	292	Napa, CA	287.8	366	Sandy Springs, GA	160.9
220	Santa Ana, CA	399.9	293	Fort Collins, CO	286.7	367	Centennial, CO	158.6
221	Fairfield, CA	398.8	294	Chandler, AZ	284.4	368	Hillsboro, OR	157.7
222	Hayward, CA	396.9	295	Sioux Falls, SD	282.5	369	Sterling Heights, MI	156.6
223	Chesapeake, VA	396.7	296	Buena Park, CA	282.3	370	Cape Coral, FL	150.2
224	Citrus Heights, CA	396.3	297	Cedar Rapids, IA	281.9	370	Santa Clara, CA	150.2
225	Savannah, GA	392.6	298	Chico, CA	281.0	372	Arvada, CO	149.6
226	Gresham, OR	389.8	299	Kenosha, WI	280.0	373	Santa Clarita, CA	146.9
227	San Diego, CA	387.6	300	Brownsville, TX	279.8	374	Canton Twnshp, MI	146.5
228	Whittier, CA	386.9	301	Mesquite, TX	278.1	375	Broken Arrow, OK	144.1
229	Visalia, CA	386.0	302	Boulder, CO	277.6	376	Meridian, ID	142.3
230	Vancouver, WA	385.2	303	New Rochelle, NY	276.5	377	Edison Twnshp, NJ	141.6
231	Davie, FL	382.9	304	Nampa, ID	275.3	378	Greece, NY	139.9
232	Norwalk, CT	380.1	305	San Marcos, CA	274.9	379	Sandy, UT	135.7
233	Lawrence, KS	379.8	306	Westminster, CA	273.3	380	Newport Beach, CA	134.6
234	Hialeah, FL	377.6	307	Chula Vista, CA	271.5	381	Pearland, TX	134.2
235	Anaheim, CA	376.5	308	Longmont, CO	271.2	382	Glendale, CA	133.0
236	Moreno Valley, CA	374.2	309	Denton, TX	268.6	383	Brick Twnshp, NJ	132.8
237	Pasadena, TX	371.9	310	Elgin, IL	264.5	384	Ramapo, NY	130.3
238	Lincoln, NE	370.6	311	Lakewood, CA	264.2	385	Provo, UT	130.0
239	Somerville, MA	370.0	312	Bend, OR	263.4	386	Corona, CA	129.7
240	Bellflower, CA	369.0	313	San Angelo, TX	262.7	387	Cranston, RI	129.5
241	Oceanside, CA	366.8	314	West Covina, CA	260.8	388	Mission, TX	127.1
242	El Monte, CA	366.7	315	Garden Grove, CA	259.7	388	Woodbridge Twnshp, NJ	127.1
243	Dearborn, MI	366.0	316	Clifton, NJ	254.7	390	Tustin, CA	126.9
244	St. Joseph, MO	364.7	317	Hampton, VA	251.7	391	Farmington Hills, MI	126.8
245	Lynchburg, VA	363.5	318	San Mateo, CA	250.1	392	Clarkstown, NY	126.2
246	Fontana, CA	363.0	319	Boise, ID	245.3	393	Torrance, CA	125.7
247	Edinburg, TX	358.2	320	Nashua, NH	244.8	394	Sugar Land, TX	119.3
248	Abilene, TX	358.1	321	Bellingham, WA	242.2	395	Lee's Summit, MO	116.7
249	Fargo, ND	357.8	322	Irving, TX	232.7	396	Concord, NC	116.1
250	Green Bay, WI	356.9	323	Ann Arbor, MI	229.3	397	Lake Forest, CA	113.9
251	Santa Barbara, CA	356.6	324	Garland, TX	228.8	398	Orange, CA	113.8
252	Athens-Clarke, GA	356.1	325	Redwood City, CA	227.7	399	Round Rock, TX	112.8
253	Joliet, IL	349.6	326	Westminster, CO	226.9	400	Bellevue, WA	112.6
254	Concord, CA	348.2	327	Fullerton, CA	223.8	401	Toms River Twnshp, NJ	110.3
255	Madison, WI	348.0	328	Port St. Lucie, FL	222.4	402	League City, TX	110.2
256	Norwalk, CA	347.4	329	Cheektowaga, NY	221.0	403	Surprise, AZ	109.9
257	Downey, CA	344.9	330	Henderson, NV	219.7	404	Thousand Oaks, CA	106.9
258	Hesperia, CA	343.1	331	Clovis, CA	218.1	405	Sunnyvale, CA	105.8
259	Montgomery, AL	342.0	332	Huntington Beach, CA	211.2	406	Amherst, NY	105.4
260	Escondido, CA	340.0	333	Vacaville, CA	208.5	407	Frisco, TX	102.1
261	Plantation, FL	339.1	334	Hamilton Twnshp, NJ	208.4	408	Warwick, RI	101.7
262	Elk Grove, CA	337.8	335	Boca Raton, FL	208.1	409	Murrieta, CA	100.3
263	San Jose, CA	335.0	336	Costa Mesa, CA	207.6	410	Lakewood Twnshp, NJ	98.8
264	Salem, OR	332.1	337	Roseville, CA	206.4	411	Temecula, CA	93.8
265	Grand Prairie, TX	330.0	338	Rio Rancho, NM	203.4	412	Newton, MA	93.4
266	Charleston, SC	327.6	339	Danbury, CT	202.4	413	Simi Valley, CA	92.3
267	Livermore, CA	325.9	340	West Jordan, UT	198.7	414	Chino Hills, CA	89.9
268	Waterbury, CT	324.7	341	Pembroke Pines, FL	197.6	415	O'Fallon, MO	89.2
269	Aurora, IL	320.4	342	Carlsbad, CA	197.1	416	Troy, MI	89.0
270	Avondale, AZ	318.2	343	Peoria, AZ	192.6	417	Gilbert, AZ	84.2
271	Baldwin Park, CA	317.3	344	Coral Springs, FL	192.3	418	Allen, TX	83.7
272	Stamford, CT	316.6	345	Spokane Valley, WA	192.0	418	Mission Viejo, CA	83.7
273	Renton, WA	316.2	346	Lewisville, TX	188.1	420	Roswell, GA	80.4
274	Sunrise, FL	314.3	347	McAllen, TX	185.5	421	Cary, NC	78.9
275	Pasadena, CA	313.5	348	Beaverton, OR	182.9	422	Naperville, IL	78.7
276	Clinton Twnshp, MI	313.3	349	Burbank, CA	182.7	423	Hoover, AL	71.9
277	Chino, CA	313.1	350	Scottsdale, AZ	181.4	424	Edmond, OK	70.5
277	Sparks, NV	313.1	351	Alhambra, CA	180.8	425	Colonie, NY	69.3
279	Oxnard, CA	309.2	352	McKinney, TX	180.0	426	Menifee, CA	67.6
280	Fort Wayne, IN	307.9	353	Daly City, CA	179.8	427	Arlington Heights, IL	63.7
281	Ventura, CA	302.7	354	Olathe, KS	178.4	428	Irvine, CA	55.8
282	Suffolk, VA	302.6	355	Alexandria, VA	177.9	429	Orem, UT	50.0
283	Bloomington, IN	301.9	356	Fremont, CA	177.3	430	Johns Creek, GA	45.0
284	Kennewick, WA	301.0	357	Rancho Cucamon., CA	175.2	431	Carmel, IN	21.4
285	College Station, TX	300.5	358	Virginia Beach, VA	175.1	432	Fishers, IN	14.3
286	Billings, MT	297.8	359	Livonia, MI	173.4	NA	Bloomington, MN**	NA
287	Ontario, CA	297.3	360	Richardson, TX	170.8	NA	Brooklyn Park, MN**	NA
288	Scranton, PA	296.1	361	Norman, OK	170.4	NA	Chicago, IL**	NA
289	Midland, TX	294.3	362	Carrollton, TX	169.4	NA	Duluth, MN**	NA
			363	Overland Park, KS	165.6	NA	Rochester, MN**	NA

Source: CQ Press using reported data from the F.B.I. "Crime in the United States 2011"
*Violent crimes are offenses of murder, forcible rape, robbery, and aggravated assault.
**Not available.

Alpha Order - City

47. Percent Change in Violent Crime Rate: 2010 to 2011
National Percent Change = 4.5% Decrease*

RANK	CITY	% CHANGE	RANK	CITY	% CHANGE	RANK	CITY	% CHANGE
386	Abilene, TX	(27.6)	50	Cheektowaga, NY	9.3	75	Fort Wayne, IN	6.1
46	Akron, OH	10.3	96	Chesapeake, VA	3.4	82	Fort Worth, TX	5.0
350	Albany, GA	(17.5)	NA	Chicago, IL**	NA	382	Fremont, CA	(25.3)
272	Albany, NY	(9.7)	158	Chico, CA	(1.8)	236	Fresno, CA	(6.9)
173	Albuquerque, NM	(3.1)	340	Chino Hills, CA	(16.3)	277	Frisco, TX	(10.0)
151	Alexandria, VA	(1.5)	138	Chino, CA	(0.2)	393	Fullerton, CA	(29.9)
346	Alhambra, CA	(16.9)	216	Chula Vista, CA	(6.2)	233	Gainesville, FL	(6.7)
357	Allentown, PA	(19.0)	NA	Cicero, IL**	NA	363	Garden Grove, CA	(19.9)
27	Allen, TX	15.1	198	Cincinnati, OH	(4.9)	98	Garland, TX	3.2
122	Amarillo, TX	1.0	316	Citrus Heights, CA	(13.1)	NA	Gary, IN**	NA
175	Amherst, NY	(3.3)	59	Clarkstown, NY	7.5	299	Gilbert, AZ	(11.6)
48	Anaheim, CA	9.8	94	Clarksville, TN	3.9	12	Glendale, AZ	23.5
184	Anchorage, AK	(4.0)	135	Clearwater, FL	0.0	202	Glendale, CA	(5.5)
273	Ann Arbor, MI	(9.8)	80	Cleveland, OH	5.4	249	Grand Prairie, TX	(8.1)
229	Antioch, CA	(6.6)	NA	Clifton, NJ**	NA	320	Grand Rapids, MI	(13.5)
37	Arlington Heights, IL	12.0	328	Clinton Twnshp, MI	(15.0)	52	Greece, NY	8.4
132	Arlington, TX	0.1	9	Clovis, CA	26.7	122	Greeley, CO	1.0
21	Arvada, CO	18.8	14	College Station, TX	20.8	165	Green Bay, WI	(2.3)
216	Asheville, NC	(6.2)	144	Colonie, NY	(1.1)	328	Gresham, OR	(15.0)
53	Athens-Clarke, GA	8.3	282	Colorado Springs, CO	(10.5)	126	Hamilton Twnshp, NJ	0.8
3	Atlanta, GA	33.7	90	Columbia, MO	4.3	372	Hammond, IN	(22.6)
159	Aurora, CO	(1.9)	288	Columbus, GA	(10.9)	244	Hampton, VA	(7.9)
301	Aurora, IL	(11.9)	233	Columbus, OH	(6.7)	117	Hartford, CT	1.4
271	Austin, TX	(9.6)	372	Compton, CA	(22.6)	216	Hawthorne, CA	(6.2)
4	Avondale, AZ	32.0	376	Concord, CA	(22.8)	303	Hayward, CA	(12.0)
337	Bakersfield, CA	(15.9)	406	Concord, NC	(42.8)	278	Hemet, CA	(10.1)
175	Baldwin Park, CA	(3.3)	223	Coral Springs, FL	(6.3)	67	Henderson, NV	6.9
168	Baltimore, MD	(2.6)	137	Corona, CA	(0.1)	73	Hesperia, CA	6.3
NA	Baton Rouge, LA**	NA	293	Corpus Christi, TX	(11.3)	319	Hialeah, FL	(13.4)
58	Beaumont, TX	7.6	190	Costa Mesa, CA	(4.5)	156	High Point, NC	(1.7)
388	Beaverton, OR	(28.1)	273	Cranston, RI	(9.8)	NA	Hillsboro, OR**	NA
90	Bellevue, WA	4.3	170	Dallas, TX	(2.8)	42	Hollywood, FL	10.8
401	Bellflower, CA	(35.3)	385	Daly City, CA	(26.7)	NA	Hoover, AL**	NA
395	Bellingham, WA	(30.3)	1	Danbury, CT	41.7	147	Houston, TX	(1.2)
331	Bend, OR	(15.2)	NA	Davenport, IA**	NA	259	Huntington Beach, CA	(9.0)
354	Berkeley, CA	(18.5)	175	Davie, FL	(3.3)	NA	Huntsville, AL**	NA
251	Bethlehem, PA	(8.4)	178	Dayton, OH	(3.4)	70	Independence, MO	6.5
NA	Billings, MT**	NA	356	Dearborn, MI	(18.9)	NA	Indianapolis, IN**	NA
NA	Birmingham, AL**	NA	126	Decatur, IL	0.8	43	Indio, CA	10.6
269	Bloomington, IL	(9.3)	334	Deerfield Beach, FL	(15.6)	174	Inglewood, CA	(3.2)
389	Bloomington, IN	(28.7)	85	Denton, TX	4.8	124	Irvine, CA	0.9
NA	Bloomington, MN**	NA	37	Denver, CO	12.0	266	Irving, TX	(9.2)
105	Boca Raton, FL	2.5	147	Des Moines, IA	(1.2)	229	Jacksonville, FL	(6.6)
223	Boise, ID	(6.3)	33	Detroit, MI	13.2	205	Jackson, MS	(5.7)
227	Boston, MA	(6.5)	225	Downey, CA	(6.4)	106	Jersey City, NJ	2.4
5	Boulder, CO	31.2	NA	Duluth, MN**	NA	407	Johns Creek, GA	(46.1)
114	Brick Twnshp, NJ	1.6	67	Durham, NC	6.9	171	Joliet, IL	(3.0)
153	Bridgeport, CT	(1.6)	25	Edinburg, TX	15.9	34	Kansas City, KS	12.8
86	Brockton, MA	4.6	124	Edison Twnshp, NJ	0.9	NA	Kansas City, MO**	NA
153	Broken Arrow, OK	(1.6)	366	Edmond, OK	(20.6)	323	Kennewick, WA	(13.7)
NA	Brooklyn Park, MN**	NA	7	El Cajon, CA	28.1	103	Kenosha, WI	2.6
282	Brownsville, TX	(10.5)	383	El Monte, CA	(25.5)	81	Kent, WA	5.2
130	Bryan, TX	0.4	209	El Paso, TX	(5.9)	377	Killeen, TX	(23.0)
225	Buena Park, CA	(6.4)	361	Elgin, IL	(19.7)	142	Knoxville, TN	(0.9)
NA	Buffalo, NY**	NA	196	Elizabeth, NJ	(4.7)	328	Lafayette, LA	(15.0)
326	Burbank, CA	(14.6)	264	Elk Grove, CA	(9.1)	216	Lake Forest, CA	(6.2)
100	Cambridge, MA	3.1	282	Erie, PA	(10.5)	29	Lakeland, FL	14.3
20	Camden, NJ	19.1	363	Escondido, CA	(19.9)	403	Lakewood Twnshp, NJ	(36.2)
307	Canton Twnshp, MI	(12.5)	61	Eugene, OR	7.4	396	Lakewood, CA	(30.5)
310	Cape Coral, FL	(12.7)	156	Evansville, IN	(1.7)	190	Lakewood, CO	(4.5)
115	Carlsbad, CA	1.5	365	Everett, WA	(20.1)	293	Lancaster, CA	(11.3)
410	Carmel, IN	(63.5)	348	Fairfield, CA	(17.2)	238	Lansing, MI	(7.0)
15	Carrollton, TX	20.5	128	Fall River, MA	0.6	216	Laredo, TX	(6.2)
297	Carson, CA	(11.4)	23	Fargo, ND	18.1	398	Largo, FL	(31.6)
238	Cary, NC	(7.0)	344	Farmington Hills, MI	(16.6)	108	Las Cruces, NM	2.2
181	Cedar Rapids, IA	(3.6)	162	Fayetteville, NC	(2.2)	347	Las Vegas, NV	(17.0)
150	Centennial, CO	(1.4)	405	Fishers, IN	(39.9)	321	Lawrence, KS	(13.6)
NA	Champaign, IL**	NA	76	Flint, MI	5.8	48	Lawrence, MA	9.8
141	Chandler, AZ	(0.5)	244	Fontana, CA	(7.9)	216	Lawton, OK	(6.2)
280	Charleston, SC	(10.2)	266	Fort Collins, CO	(9.2)	19	League City, TX	19.4
144	Charlotte, NC	(1.1)	7	Fort Lauderdale, FL	28.1	78	Lee's Summit, MO	5.5
188	Chattanooga, TN	(4.4)	286	Fort Smith, AR	(10.7)	327	Lewisville, TX	(14.7)

Alpha Order - City (continued)

RANK	CITY	% CHANGE
NA	Lexington, KY**	NA
379	Lincoln, NE	(23.5)
162	Little Rock, AR	(2.2)
350	Livermore, CA	(17.5)
138	Livonia, MI	(0.2)
95	Long Beach, CA	3.8
313	Longmont, CO	(12.9)
399	Longview, TX	(32.4)
229	Los Angeles, CA	(6.6)
83	Louisville, KY	4.9
402	Lowell, MA	(35.8)
307	Lubbock, TX	(12.5)
332	Lynchburg, VA	(15.4)
135	Lynn, MA	0.0
377	Macon, GA	(23.0)
289	Madison, WI	(11.1)
39	Manchester, NH	11.9
342	McAllen, TX	(16.5)
36	McKinney, TX	12.1
11	Medford, OR	25.3
43	Melbourne, FL	10.6
102	Memphis, TN	2.7
409	Menifee, CA	(51.5)
289	Merced, CA	(11.1)
186	Meridian, ID	(4.2)
88	Mesa, AZ	4.4
375	Mesquite, TX	(22.7)
115	Miami Beach, FL	1.5
190	Miami Gardens, FL	(4.5)
54	Miami, FL	8.1
366	Midland, TX	(20.6)
187	Milwaukee, WI	(4.3)
251	Minneapolis, MN	(8.4)
311	Miramar, FL	(12.8)
31	Mission Viejo, CA	13.3
147	Mission, TX	(1.2)
NA	Mobile, AL**	NA
119	Modesto, CA	1.2
NA	Montgomery, AL**	NA
111	Moreno Valley, CA	2.0
57	Murfreesboro, TN	7.9
77	Murrieta, CA	5.7
335	Nampa, ID	(15.7)
293	Napa, CA	(11.3)
NA	Naperville, IL**	NA
13	Nashua, NH	22.5
92	Nashville, TN	4.1
300	New Bedford, MA	(11.7)
335	New Haven, CT	(15.7)
51	New Orleans, LA	8.8
213	New Rochelle, NY	(6.1)
63	New York, NY	7.2
31	Newark, NJ	13.3
207	Newport Beach, CA	(5.8)
200	Newport News, VA	(5.3)
259	Newton, MA	(9.0)
213	Norfolk, VA	(6.1)
2	Norman, OK	37.8
372	North Charleston, SC	(22.6)
369	Norwalk, CA	(20.9)
209	Norwalk, CT	(5.9)
47	Oakland, CA	10.0
159	Oceanside, CA	(1.9)
103	Odessa, TX	2.6
117	O'Fallon, MO	1.4
26	Ogden, UT	15.6
211	Oklahoma City, OK	(6.0)
92	Olathe, KS	4.1
28	Omaha, NE	14.9
354	Ontario, CA	(18.5)
88	Orange, CA	4.4
397	Orem, UT	(31.2)
132	Orlando, FL	0.1

RANK	CITY	% CHANGE
107	Overland Park, KS	2.3
332	Oxnard, CA	(15.4)
30	Palm Bay, FL	14.0
281	Palmdale, CA	(10.4)
352	Pasadena, CA	(18.2)
293	Pasadena, TX	(11.3)
199	Paterson, NJ	(5.1)
183	Pearland, TX	(3.9)
78	Pembroke Pines, FL	5.5
55	Peoria, AZ	8.0
244	Peoria, IL	(7.9)
131	Philadelphia, PA	0.3
70	Phoenix, AZ	6.5
286	Pittsburgh, PA	(10.7)
285	Plano, TX	(10.6)
143	Plantation, FL	(1.0)
65	Pomona, CA	7.0
216	Pompano Beach, FL	(6.2)
211	Port St. Lucie, FL	(6.0)
197	Portland, OR	(4.8)
238	Portsmouth, VA	(7.0)
371	Provo, UT	(21.1)
NA	Pueblo, CO**	NA
242	Quincy, MA	(7.4)
318	Racine, WI	(13.3)
113	Raleigh, NC	1.7
10	Ramapo, NY	26.3
255	Rancho Cucamon., CA	(8.9)
259	Reading, PA	(9.0)
289	Redding, CA	(11.1)
169	Redwood City, CA	(2.7)
241	Reno, NV	(7.2)
390	Renton, WA	(28.9)
190	Rialto, CA	(4.5)
244	Richardson, TX	(7.9)
317	Richmond, CA	(13.2)
202	Richmond, VA	(5.5)
40	Rio Rancho, NM	11.4
292	Riverside, CA	(11.2)
338	Roanoke, VA	(16.0)
NA	Rochester, MN**	NA
306	Rochester, NY	(12.3)
204	Rockford, IL	(5.6)
384	Roseville, CA	(26.0)
408	Roswell, GA	(47.6)
55	Round Rock, TX	8.0
353	Sacramento, CA	(18.3)
64	Salem, OR	7.1
264	Salinas, CA	(9.1)
301	Salt Lake City, UT	(11.9)
304	San Angelo, TX	(12.2)
324	San Antonio, TX	(14.3)
59	San Bernardino, CA	7.5
270	San Diego, CA	(9.4)
213	San Francisco, CA	(6.1)
121	San Jose, CA	1.1
179	San Leandro, CA	(3.5)
171	San Marcos, CA	(3.0)
366	San Mateo, CA	(20.6)
392	Sandy Springs, GA	(29.4)
360	Sandy, UT	(19.3)
276	Santa Ana, CA	(9.9)
278	Santa Barbara, CA	(10.1)
235	Santa Clara, CA	(6.8)
400	Santa Clarita, CA	(33.2)
357	Santa Maria, CA	(19.0)
259	Santa Monica, CA	(9.0)
348	Santa Rosa, CA	(17.2)
159	Savannah, GA	(1.9)
22	Scottsdale, AZ	18.5
259	Scranton, PA	(9.0)
86	Seattle, WA	4.6
132	Shreveport, LA	0.1
313	Simi Valley, CA	(12.9)

RANK	CITY	% CHANGE
18	Sioux City, IA	19.5
207	Sioux Falls, SD	(5.8)
24	Somerville, MA	17.5
108	South Bend, IN	2.2
165	South Gate, CA	(2.3)
362	Sparks, NV	(19.8)
110	Spokane Valley, WA	2.1
153	Spokane, WA	(1.6)
297	Springfield, IL	(11.4)
380	Springfield, MA	(24.2)
179	Springfield, MO	(3.5)
41	Stamford, CT	10.9
NA	Sterling Heights, MI**	NA
112	Stockton, CA	1.9
266	St. Joseph, MO	(9.2)
73	St. Louis, MO	6.3
311	St. Paul, MN	(12.8)
273	St. Petersburg, FL	(9.8)
151	Suffolk, VA	(1.5)
393	Sugar Land, TX	(29.9)
339	Sunnyvale, CA	(16.1)
340	Sunrise, FL	(16.3)
188	Surprise, AZ	(4.4)
205	Syracuse, NY	(5.7)
304	Tacoma, WA	(12.2)
307	Tallahassee, FL	(12.5)
83	Tampa, FL	4.9
6	Temecula, CA	29.9
69	Tempe, AZ	6.6
NA	Thornton, CO**	NA
195	Thousand Oaks, CA	(4.6)
45	Toledo, OH	10.4
62	Toms River Twnshp, NJ	7.3
162	Topeka, KS	(2.2)
404	Torrance, CA	(39.1)
140	Tracy, CA	(0.4)
144	Trenton, NJ	(1.1)
17	Troy, MI	20.4
98	Tucson, AZ	3.2
254	Tulsa, OK	(8.6)
NA	Tuscaloosa, AL**	NA
387	Tustin, CA	(27.7)
370	Tyler, TX	(21.0)
250	Upper Darby Twnshp, PA	(8.3)
391	Vacaville, CA	(29.3)
65	Vallejo, CA	7.0
184	Vancouver, WA	(4.0)
15	Ventura, CA	20.5
128	Victorville, CA	0.6
236	Virginia Beach, VA	(6.9)
342	Visalia, CA	(16.5)
229	Vista, CA	(6.6)
255	Waco, TX	(8.9)
243	Warren, MI	(7.8)
119	Warwick, RI	1.2
255	Washington, DC	(8.9)
182	Waterbury, CT	(3.8)
321	West Covina, CA	(13.6)
357	West Jordan, UT	(19.0)
167	West Palm Beach, FL	(2.5)
251	West Valley, UT	(8.4)
325	Westland, MI	(14.5)
201	Westminster, CA	(5.4)
70	Westminster, CO	6.5
244	Whittier, CA	(7.9)
227	Wichita Falls, TX	(6.5)
190	Wichita, KS	(4.5)
313	Wilmington, NC	(12.9)
97	Winston-Salem, NC	3.3
381	Woodbridge Twnshp, NJ	(25.0)
100	Worcester, MA	3.1
255	Yakima, WA	(8.9)
35	Yonkers, NY	12.2
344	Yuma, AZ	(16.6)

Source: CQ Press using reported data from the F.B.I. "Crime in the United States 2011"
*Violent crimes are offenses of murder, forcible rape, robbery, and aggravated assault.
**Not available.

Rank Order - City

47. Percent Change in Violent Crime Rate: 2010 to 2011 (continued)
National Percent Change = 4.5% Decrease*

RANK	CITY	% CHANGE	RANK	CITY	% CHANGE	RANK	CITY	% CHANGE
1	Danbury, CT	41.7	73	Hesperia, CA	6.3	144	Colonie, NY	(1.1)
2	Norman, OK	37.8	73	St. Louis, MO	6.3	144	Trenton, NJ	(1.1)
3	Atlanta, GA	33.7	75	Fort Wayne, IN	6.1	147	Des Moines, IA	(1.2)
4	Avondale, AZ	32.0	76	Flint, MI	5.8	147	Houston, TX	(1.2)
5	Boulder, CO	31.2	77	Murrieta, CA	5.7	147	Mission, TX	(1.2)
6	Temecula, CA	29.9	78	Lee's Summit, MO	5.5	150	Centennial, CO	(1.4)
7	El Cajon, CA	28.1	78	Pembroke Pines, FL	5.5	151	Alexandria, VA	(1.5)
7	Fort Lauderdale, FL	28.1	80	Cleveland, OH	5.4	151	Suffolk, VA	(1.5)
9	Clovis, CA	26.7	81	Kent, WA	5.2	153	Bridgeport, CT	(1.6)
10	Ramapo, NY	26.3	82	Fort Worth, TX	5.0	153	Broken Arrow, OK	(1.6)
11	Medford, OR	25.3	83	Louisville, KY	4.9	153	Spokane, WA	(1.6)
12	Glendale, AZ	23.5	83	Tampa, FL	4.9	156	Evansville, IN	(1.7)
13	Nashua, NH	22.5	85	Denton, TX	4.8	156	High Point, NC	(1.7)
14	College Station, TX	20.8	86	Brockton, MA	4.6	158	Chico, CA	(1.8)
15	Carrollton, TX	20.5	86	Seattle, WA	4.6	159	Aurora, CO	(1.9)
15	Ventura, CA	20.5	88	Mesa, AZ	4.4	159	Oceanside, CA	(1.9)
17	Troy, MI	20.4	88	Orange, CA	4.4	159	Savannah, GA	(1.9)
18	Sioux City, IA	19.5	90	Bellevue, WA	4.3	162	Fayetteville, NC	(2.2)
19	League City, TX	19.4	90	Columbia, MO	4.3	162	Little Rock, AR	(2.2)
20	Camden, NJ	19.1	92	Nashville, TN	4.1	162	Topeka, KS	(2.2)
21	Arvada, CO	18.8	92	Olathe, KS	4.1	165	Green Bay, WI	(2.3)
22	Scottsdale, AZ	18.5	94	Clarksville, TN	3.9	165	South Gate, CA	(2.3)
23	Fargo, ND	18.1	95	Long Beach, CA	3.8	167	West Palm Beach, FL	(2.5)
24	Somerville, MA	17.5	96	Chesapeake, VA	3.4	168	Baltimore, MD	(2.6)
25	Edinburg, TX	15.9	97	Winston-Salem, NC	3.3	169	Redwood City, CA	(2.7)
26	Ogden, UT	15.6	98	Garland, TX	3.2	170	Dallas, TX	(2.8)
27	Allen, TX	15.1	98	Tucson, AZ	3.2	171	Joliet, IL	(3.0)
28	Omaha, NE	14.9	100	Cambridge, MA	3.1	171	San Marcos, CA	(3.0)
29	Lakeland, FL	14.3	100	Worcester, MA	3.1	173	Albuquerque, NM	(3.1)
30	Palm Bay, FL	14.0	102	Memphis, TN	2.7	174	Inglewood, CA	(3.2)
31	Mission Viejo, CA	13.3	103	Kenosha, WI	2.6	175	Amherst, NY	(3.3)
31	Newark, NJ	13.3	103	Odessa, TX	2.6	175	Baldwin Park, CA	(3.3)
33	Detroit, MI	13.2	105	Boca Raton, FL	2.5	175	Davie, FL	(3.3)
34	Kansas City, KS	12.8	106	Jersey City, NJ	2.4	178	Dayton, OH	(3.4)
35	Yonkers, NY	12.2	107	Overland Park, KS	2.3	179	San Leandro, CA	(3.5)
36	McKinney, TX	12.1	108	Las Cruces, NM	2.2	179	Springfield, MO	(3.5)
37	Arlington Heights, IL	12.0	108	South Bend, IN	2.2	181	Cedar Rapids, IA	(3.6)
37	Denver, CO	12.0	110	Spokane Valley, WA	2.1	182	Waterbury, CT	(3.8)
39	Manchester, NH	11.9	111	Moreno Valley, CA	2.0	183	Pearland, TX	(3.9)
40	Rio Rancho, NM	11.4	112	Stockton, CA	1.9	184	Anchorage, AK	(4.0)
41	Stamford, CT	10.9	113	Raleigh, NC	1.7	184	Vancouver, WA	(4.0)
42	Hollywood, FL	10.8	114	Brick Twnshp, NJ	1.6	186	Meridian, ID	(4.2)
43	Indio, CA	10.6	115	Carlsbad, CA	1.5	187	Milwaukee, WI	(4.3)
43	Melbourne, FL	10.6	115	Miami Beach, FL	1.5	188	Chattanooga, TN	(4.4)
45	Toledo, OH	10.4	117	Hartford, CT	1.4	188	Surprise, AZ	(4.4)
46	Akron, OH	10.3	117	O'Fallon, MO	1.4	190	Costa Mesa, CA	(4.5)
47	Oakland, CA	10.0	119	Modesto, CA	1.2	190	Lakewood, CO	(4.5)
48	Anaheim, CA	9.8	119	Warwick, RI	1.2	190	Miami Gardens, FL	(4.5)
48	Lawrence, MA	9.8	121	San Jose, CA	1.1	190	Rialto, CA	(4.5)
50	Cheektowaga, NY	9.3	122	Amarillo, TX	1.0	190	Wichita, KS	(4.5)
51	New Orleans, LA	8.8	122	Greeley, CO	1.0	195	Thousand Oaks, CA	(4.6)
52	Greece, NY	8.4	124	Edison Twnshp, NJ	0.9	196	Elizabeth, NJ	(4.7)
53	Athens-Clarke, GA	8.3	124	Irvine, CA	0.9	197	Portland, OR	(4.8)
54	Miami, FL	8.1	126	Decatur, IL	0.8	198	Cincinnati, OH	(4.9)
55	Peoria, AZ	8.0	126	Hamilton Twnshp, NJ	0.8	199	Paterson, NJ	(5.1)
55	Round Rock, TX	8.0	128	Fall River, MA	0.6	200	Newport News, VA	(5.3)
57	Murfreesboro, TN	7.9	128	Victorville, CA	0.6	201	Westminster, CA	(5.4)
58	Beaumont, TX	7.6	130	Bryan, TX	0.4	202	Glendale, CA	(5.5)
59	Clarkstown, NY	7.5	131	Philadelphia, PA	0.3	202	Richmond, VA	(5.5)
59	San Bernardino, CA	7.5	132	Arlington, TX	0.1	204	Rockford, IL	(5.6)
61	Eugene, OR	7.4	132	Orlando, FL	0.1	205	Jackson, MS	(5.7)
62	Toms River Twnshp, NJ	7.3	132	Shreveport, LA	0.1	205	Syracuse, NY	(5.7)
63	New York, NY	7.2	135	Clearwater, FL	0.0	207	Newport Beach, CA	(5.8)
64	Salem, OR	7.1	135	Lynn, MA	0.0	207	Sioux Falls, SD	(5.8)
65	Pomona, CA	7.0	137	Corona, CA	(0.1)	209	El Paso, TX	(5.9)
65	Vallejo, CA	7.0	138	Chino, CA	(0.2)	209	Norwalk, CT	(5.9)
67	Durham, NC	6.9	138	Livonia, MI	(0.2)	211	Oklahoma City, OK	(6.0)
67	Henderson, NV	6.9	140	Tracy, CA	(0.4)	211	Port St. Lucie, FL	(6.0)
69	Tempe, AZ	6.6	141	Chandler, AZ	(0.5)	213	New Rochelle, NY	(6.1)
70	Independence, MO	6.5	142	Knoxville, TN	(0.9)	213	Norfolk, VA	(6.1)
70	Phoenix, AZ	6.5	143	Plantation, FL	(1.0)	213	San Francisco, CA	(6.1)
70	Westminster, CO	6.5	144	Charlotte, NC	(1.1)	216	Asheville, NC	(6.2)

Rank Order - City (continued)

RANK	CITY	% CHANGE	RANK	CITY	% CHANGE	RANK	CITY	% CHANGE
216	Chula Vista, CA	(6.2)	289	Merced, CA	(11.1)	363	Garden Grove, CA	(19.9)
216	Hawthorne, CA	(6.2)	289	Redding, CA	(11.1)	365	Everett, WA	(20.1)
216	Lake Forest, CA	(6.2)	292	Riverside, CA	(11.2)	366	Edmond, OK	(20.6)
216	Laredo, TX	(6.2)	293	Corpus Christi, TX	(11.3)	366	Midland, TX	(20.6)
216	Lawton, OK	(6.2)	293	Lancaster, CA	(11.3)	366	San Mateo, CA	(20.6)
216	Pompano Beach, FL	(6.2)	293	Napa, CA	(11.3)	369	Norwalk, CA	(20.9)
223	Boise, ID	(6.3)	293	Pasadena, TX	(11.3)	370	Tyler, TX	(21.0)
223	Coral Springs, FL	(6.3)	297	Carson, CA	(11.4)	371	Provo, UT	(21.1)
225	Buena Park, CA	(6.4)	297	Springfield, IL	(11.4)	372	Compton, CA	(22.6)
225	Downey, CA	(6.4)	299	Gilbert, AZ	(11.6)	372	Hammond, IN	(22.6)
227	Boston, MA	(6.5)	300	New Bedford, MA	(11.7)	372	North Charleston, SC	(22.6)
227	Wichita Falls, TX	(6.5)	301	Aurora, IL	(11.9)	375	Mesquite, TX	(22.7)
229	Antioch, CA	(6.6)	301	Salt Lake City, UT	(11.9)	376	Concord, CA	(22.8)
229	Jacksonville, FL	(6.6)	303	Hayward, CA	(12.0)	377	Killeen, TX	(23.0)
229	Los Angeles, CA	(6.6)	304	San Angelo, TX	(12.2)	377	Macon, GA	(23.0)
229	Vista, CA	(6.6)	304	Tacoma, WA	(12.2)	379	Lincoln, NE	(23.5)
233	Columbus, OH	(6.7)	306	Rochester, NY	(12.3)	380	Springfield, MA	(24.2)
233	Gainesville, FL	(6.7)	307	Canton Twnshp, MI	(12.5)	381	Woodbridge Twnshp, NJ	(25.0)
235	Santa Clara, CA	(6.8)	307	Lubbock, TX	(12.5)	382	Fremont, CA	(25.3)
236	Fresno, CA	(6.9)	307	Tallahassee, FL	(12.5)	383	El Monte, CA	(25.5)
236	Virginia Beach, VA	(6.9)	310	Cape Coral, FL	(12.7)	384	Roseville, CA	(26.0)
238	Cary, NC	(7.0)	311	Miramar, FL	(12.8)	385	Daly City, CA	(26.7)
238	Lansing, MI	(7.0)	311	St. Paul, MN	(12.8)	386	Abilene, TX	(27.6)
238	Portsmouth, VA	(7.0)	313	Longmont, CO	(12.9)	387	Tustin, CA	(27.7)
241	Reno, NV	(7.2)	313	Simi Valley, CA	(12.9)	388	Beaverton, OR	(28.1)
242	Quincy, MA	(7.4)	313	Wilmington, NC	(12.9)	389	Bloomington, IN	(28.7)
243	Warren, MI	(7.8)	316	Citrus Heights, CA	(13.1)	390	Renton, WA	(28.9)
244	Fontana, CA	(7.9)	317	Richmond, CA	(13.2)	391	Vacaville, CA	(29.3)
244	Hampton, VA	(7.9)	318	Racine, WI	(13.3)	392	Sandy Springs, GA	(29.4)
244	Peoria, IL	(7.9)	319	Hialeah, FL	(13.4)	393	Fullerton, CA	(29.9)
244	Richardson, TX	(7.9)	320	Grand Rapids, MI	(13.5)	393	Sugar Land, TX	(29.9)
244	Whittier, CA	(7.9)	321	Lawrence, KS	(13.6)	395	Bellingham, WA	(30.3)
249	Grand Prairie, TX	(8.1)	321	West Covina, CA	(13.6)	396	Lakewood, CA	(30.5)
250	Upper Darby Twnshp, PA	(8.3)	323	Kennewick, WA	(13.7)	397	Orem, UT	(31.2)
251	Bethlehem, PA	(8.4)	324	San Antonio, TX	(14.3)	398	Largo, FL	(31.6)
251	Minneapolis, MN	(8.4)	325	Westland, MI	(14.5)	399	Longview, TX	(32.4)
251	West Valley, UT	(8.4)	326	Burbank, CA	(14.6)	400	Santa Clarita, CA	(33.2)
254	Tulsa, OK	(8.6)	327	Lewisville, TX	(14.7)	401	Bellflower, CA	(35.3)
255	Rancho Cucamon., CA	(8.9)	328	Clinton Twnshp, MI	(15.0)	402	Lowell, MA	(35.8)
255	Waco, TX	(8.9)	328	Gresham, OR	(15.0)	403	Lakewood Twnshp, NJ	(36.2)
255	Washington, DC	(8.9)	328	Lafayette, LA	(15.0)	404	Torrance, CA	(39.1)
255	Yakima, WA	(8.9)	331	Bend, OR	(15.2)	405	Fishers, IN	(39.9)
259	Huntington Beach, CA	(9.0)	332	Lynchburg, VA	(15.4)	406	Concord, NC	(42.8)
259	Newton, MA	(9.0)	332	Oxnard, CA	(15.4)	407	Johns Creek, GA	(46.1)
259	Reading, PA	(9.0)	334	Deerfield Beach, FL	(15.6)	408	Roswell, GA	(47.6)
259	Santa Monica, CA	(9.0)	335	Nampa, ID	(15.7)	409	Menifee, CA	(51.5)
259	Scranton, PA	(9.0)	335	New Haven, CT	(15.7)	410	Carmel, IN	(63.5)
264	Elk Grove, CA	(9.1)	337	Bakersfield, CA	(15.9)	NA	Baton Rouge, LA**	NA
264	Salinas, CA	(9.1)	338	Roanoke, VA	(16.0)	NA	Billings, MT**	NA
266	Fort Collins, CO	(9.2)	339	Sunnyvale, CA	(16.1)	NA	Birmingham, AL**	NA
266	Irving, TX	(9.2)	340	Chino Hills, CA	(16.3)	NA	Bloomington, MN**	NA
266	St. Joseph, MO	(9.2)	340	Sunrise, FL	(16.3)	NA	Brooklyn Park, MN**	NA
269	Bloomington, IL	(9.3)	342	McAllen, TX	(16.5)	NA	Buffalo, NY**	NA
270	San Diego, CA	(9.4)	342	Visalia, CA	(16.5)	NA	Champaign, IL**	NA
271	Austin, TX	(9.6)	344	Farmington Hills, MI	(16.6)	NA	Chicago, IL**	NA
272	Albany, NY	(9.7)	344	Yuma, AZ	(16.6)	NA	Cicero, IL**	NA
273	Ann Arbor, MI	(9.8)	346	Alhambra, CA	(16.9)	NA	Clifton, NJ**	NA
273	Cranston, RI	(9.8)	347	Las Vegas, NV	(17.0)	NA	Davenport, IA**	NA
273	St. Petersburg, FL	(9.8)	348	Fairfield, CA	(17.2)	NA	Duluth, MN**	NA
276	Santa Ana, CA	(9.9)	348	Santa Rosa, CA	(17.2)	NA	Gary, IN**	NA
277	Frisco, TX	(10.0)	350	Albany, GA	(17.5)	NA	Hillsboro, OR**	NA
278	Hemet, CA	(10.1)	350	Livermore, CA	(17.5)	NA	Hoover, AL**	NA
278	Santa Barbara, CA	(10.1)	352	Pasadena, CA	(18.2)	NA	Huntsville, AL**	NA
280	Charleston, SC	(10.2)	353	Sacramento, CA	(18.3)	NA	Indianapolis, IN**	NA
281	Palmdale, CA	(10.4)	354	Berkeley, CA	(18.5)	NA	Kansas City, MO**	NA
282	Brownsville, TX	(10.5)	354	Ontario, CA	(18.5)	NA	Lexington, KY**	NA
282	Colorado Springs, CO	(10.5)	356	Dearborn, MI	(18.9)	NA	Mobile, AL**	NA
282	Erie, PA	(10.5)	357	Allentown, PA	(19.0)	NA	Montgomery, AL**	NA
285	Plano, TX	(10.6)	357	Santa Maria, CA	(19.0)	NA	Naperville, IL**	NA
286	Fort Smith, AR	(10.7)	357	West Jordan, UT	(19.0)	NA	Pueblo, CO**	NA
286	Pittsburgh, PA	(10.7)	360	Sandy, UT	(19.3)	NA	Rochester, MN**	NA
288	Columbus, GA	(10.9)	361	Elgin, IL	(19.7)	NA	Sterling Heights, MI**	NA
289	Madison, WI	(11.1)	362	Sparks, NV	(19.8)	NA	Thornton, CO**	NA
			363	Escondido, CA	(19.9)	NA	Tuscaloosa, AL**	NA

Source: CQ Press using reported data from the F.B.I. "Crime in the United States 2011"
*Violent crimes are offenses of murder, forcible rape, robbery, and aggravated assault.
**Not available.

Alpha Order - City

48. Percent Change in Violent Crime Rate: 2007 to 2011
National Percent Change = 18.1% Decrease*

RANK	CITY	% CHANGE	RANK	CITY	% CHANGE	RANK	CITY	% CHANGE
344	Abilene, TX	(37.9)	216	Cheektowaga, NY	(22.6)	51	Fort Wayne, IN	0.4
17	Akron, OH	18.9	119	Chesapeake, VA	(9.6)	117	Fort Worth, TX	(9.5)
72	Albany, GA	(3.8)	NA	Chicago, IL**	NA	367	Fremont, CA	(41.1)
208	Albany, NY	(20.5)	378	Chico, CA	(45.8)	119	Fresno, CA	(9.6)
222	Albuquerque, NM	(23.0)	100	Chino Hills, CA	(7.1)	42	Frisco, TX	2.8
318	Alexandria, VA	(33.7)	34	Chino, CA	8.9	331	Fullerton, CA	(35.9)
374	Alhambra, CA	(44.4)	327	Chula Vista, CA	(35.5)	283	Gainesville, FL	(30.2)
304	Allentown, PA	(32.5)	NA	Cicero, IL**	NA	311	Garden Grove, CA	(33.0)
28	Allen, TX	13.4	76	Cincinnati, OH	(4.4)	322	Garland, TX	(34.6)
331	Amarillo, TX	(35.9)	NA	Citrus Heights, CA**	NA	25	Gary, IN	14.9
154	Amherst, NY	(14.1)	20	Clarkstown, NY	17.2	251	Gilbert, AZ	(26.3)
134	Anaheim, CA	(11.3)	234	Clarksville, TN	(24.0)	197	Glendale, AZ	(19.5)
79	Anchorage, AK	(5.0)	115	Clearwater, FL	(9.1)	277	Glendale, CA	(29.1)
142	Ann Arbor, MI	(13.0)	95	Cleveland, OH	(6.7)	155	Grand Prairie, TX	(14.3)
89	Antioch, CA	(6.4)	113	Clifton, NJ	(8.7)	230	Grand Rapids, MI	(23.8)
NA	Arlington Heights, IL**	NA	60	Clinton Twnshp, MI	(1.4)	38	Greece, NY	6.8
266	Arlington, TX	(27.8)	5	Clovis, CA	51.9	53	Greeley, CO	(0.8)
262	Arvada, CO	(27.5)	124	College Station, TX	(10.2)	371	Green Bay, WI	(42.1)
237	Asheville, NC	(24.1)	342	Colonie, NY	(37.5)	187	Gresham, OR	(18.7)
102	Athens-Clarke, GA	(7.2)	177	Colorado Springs, CO	(17.0)	71	Hamilton Twnshp, NJ	(3.7)
137	Atlanta, GA	(11.8)	180	Columbia, MO	(17.2)	190	Hammond, IN	(18.9)
203	Aurora, CO	(20.2)	286	Columbus, GA	(30.4)	285	Hampton, VA	(30.3)
NA	Aurora, IL**	NA	217	Columbus, OH	(22.7)	22	Hartford, CT	15.7
207	Austin, TX	(20.4)	325	Compton, CA	(35.3)	185	Hawthorne, CA	(18.3)
NA	Avondale, AZ**	NA	147	Concord, CA	(13.5)	338	Hayward, CA	(36.7)
149	Bakersfield, CA	(13.7)	393	Concord, NC	(71.3)	300	Hemet, CA	(32.0)
133	Baldwin Park, CA	(10.9)	166	Coral Springs, FL	(16.1)	93	Henderson, NV	(6.6)
145	Baltimore, MD	(13.1)	369	Corona, CA	(41.4)	105	Hesperia, CA	(7.6)
98	Baton Rouge, LA	(6.9)	219	Corpus Christi, TX	(22.8)	333	Hialeah, FL	(36.0)
122	Beaumont, TX	(9.8)	136	Costa Mesa, CA	(11.6)	302	High Point, NC	(32.2)
238	Beaverton, OR	(24.2)	85	Cranston, RI	(5.8)	257	Hillsboro, OR	(26.9)
66	Bellevue, WA	(2.9)	337	Dallas, TX	(36.3)	183	Hollywood, FL	(17.9)
377	Bellflower, CA	(45.7)	350	Daly City, CA	(38.3)	NA	Hoover, AL**	NA
58	Bellingham, WA	(1.2)	30	Danbury, CT	10.8	150	Houston, TX	(13.9)
13	Bend, OR	27.7	NA	Davenport, IA**	NA	31	Huntington Beach, CA	9.5
309	Berkeley, CA	(32.9)	55	Davie, FL	(0.9)	NA	Huntsville, AL**	NA
212	Bethlehem, PA	(21.4)	97	Dayton, OH	(6.8)	376	Independence, MO	(44.6)
NA	Billings, MT**	NA	267	Dearborn, MI	(27.9)	131	Indianapolis, IN	(10.8)
NA	Birmingham, AL**	NA	NA	Decatur, IL**	NA	12	Indio, CA	30.8
NA	Bloomington, IL**	NA	254	Deerfield Beach, FL	(26.4)	192	Inglewood, CA	(19.0)
239	Bloomington, IN	(24.3)	169	Denton, TX	(16.4)	211	Irvine, CA	(21.2)
NA	Bloomington, MN**	NA	64	Denver, CO	(2.0)	340	Irving, TX	(37.2)
227	Boca Raton, FL	(23.4)	314	Des Moines, IA	(33.4)	355	Jacksonville, FL	(39.2)
241	Boise, ID	(24.6)	93	Detroit, MI	(6.6)	36	Jackson, MS	8.0
256	Boston, MA	(26.8)	255	Downey, CA	(26.7)	229	Jersey City, NJ	(23.7)
23	Boulder, CO	15.4	NA	Duluth, MN**	NA	NA	Johns Creek, GA**	NA
39	Brick Twnshp, NJ	6.7	NA	Durham, NC**	NA	NA	Joliet, IL**	NA
152	Bridgeport, CT	(14.0)	102	Edinburg, TX	(7.2)	197	Kansas City, KS	(19.5)
NA	Brockton, MA**	NA	343	Edison Twnshp, NJ	(37.6)	NA	Kansas City, MO**	NA
293	Broken Arrow, OK	(31.1)	362	Edmond, OK	(40.3)	197	Kennewick, WA	(19.5)
NA	Brooklyn Park, MN**	NA	66	El Cajon, CA	(2.9)	232	Kenosha, WI	(23.9)
373	Brownsville, TX	(43.7)	316	El Monte, CA	(33.6)	62	Kent, WA	(1.7)
348	Bryan, TX	(38.2)	41	El Paso, TX	3.2	203	Killeen, TX	(20.2)
275	Buena Park, CA	(28.9)	NA	Elgin, IL**	NA	171	Knoxville, TN	(16.5)
NA	Buffalo, NY**	NA	6	Elizabeth, NJ	40.3	353	Lafayette, LA	(38.8)
281	Burbank, CA	(30.1)	105	Elk Grove, CA	(7.6)	90	Lake Forest, CA	(6.5)
35	Cambridge, MA	8.8	210	Erie, PA	(20.9)	164	Lakeland, FL	(15.8)
14	Camden, NJ	24.8	292	Escondido, CA	(31.0)	389	Lakewood Twnshp, NJ	(62.4)
19	Canton Twnshp, MI	17.4	50	Eugene, OR	0.9	385	Lakewood, CA	(53.7)
362	Cape Coral, FL	(40.3)	112	Evansville, IN	(8.4)	78	Lakewood, CO	(4.8)
367	Carlsbad, CA	(41.1)	241	Everett, WA	(24.6)	366	Lancaster, CA	(40.9)
386	Carmel, IN	(54.2)	312	Fairfield, CA	(33.1)	90	Lansing, MI	(6.5)
138	Carrollton, TX	(11.9)	NA	Fall River, MA**	NA	201	Laredo, TX	(19.8)
320	Carson, CA	(34.0)	10	Fargo, ND	33.6	346	Largo, FL	(38.0)
306	Cary, NC	(32.7)	276	Farmington Hills, MI	(29.0)	147	Las Cruces, NM	(13.5)
279	Cedar Rapids, IA	(29.7)	321	Fayetteville, NC	(34.5)	259	Las Vegas, NV	(27.1)
150	Centennial, CO	(13.9)	392	Fishers, IN	(66.3)	169	Lawrence, KS	(16.4)
NA	Champaign, IL**	NA	57	Flint, MI	(1.1)	8	Lawrence, MA	38.4
146	Chandler, AZ	(13.3)	271	Fontana, CA	(28.5)	296	Lawton, OK	(31.6)
388	Charleston, SC	(60.6)	124	Fort Collins, CO	(10.2)	142	League City, TX	(13.0)
351	Charlotte, NC	(38.5)	24	Fort Lauderdale, FL	15.1	127	Lee's Summit, MO	(10.5)
314	Chattanooga, TN	(33.4)	251	Fort Smith, AR	(26.3)	58	Lewisville, TX	(1.2)

Alpha Order - City (continued)

RANK	CITY	% CHANGE
NA	Lexington, KY**	NA
300	Lincoln, NE	(32.0)
110	Little Rock, AR	(7.9)
3	Livermore, CA	54.7
33	Livonia, MI	9.1
160	Long Beach, CA	(15.5)
NA	Longmont, CO**	NA
381	Longview, TX	(47.7)
260	Los Angeles, CA	(27.3)
117	Louisville, KY	(9.5)
141	Lowell, MA	(12.7)
165	Lubbock, TX	(15.9)
248	Lynchburg, VA	(25.6)
172	Lynn, MA	(16.6)
214	Macon, GA	(22.1)
86	Madison, WI	(6.0)
NA	Manchester, NH**	NA
327	McAllen, TX	(35.5)
172	McKinney, TX	(16.6)
7	Medford, OR	38.8
74	Melbourne, FL	(4.0)
189	Memphis, TN	(18.8)
NA	Menifee, CA**	NA
196	Merced, CA	(19.4)
215	Meridian, ID	(22.5)
162	Mesa, AZ	(15.6)
335	Mesquite, TX	(36.2)
194	Miami Beach, FL	(19.3)
384	Miami Gardens, FL	(52.3)
200	Miami, FL	(19.7)
135	Midland, TX	(11.5)
273	Milwaukee, WI	(28.8)
330	Minneapolis, MN	(35.8)
209	Miramar, FL	(20.8)
66	Mission Viejo, CA	(2.9)
127	Mission, TX	(10.5)
NA	Mobile, AL**	NA
69	Modesto, CA	(3.1)
NA	Montgomery, AL**	NA
288	Moreno Valley, CA	(30.5)
177	Murfreesboro, TN	(17.0)
172	Murrieta, CA	(16.6)
157	Nampa, ID	(14.9)
244	Napa, CA	(24.8)
NA	Naperville, IL**	NA
NA	Nashua, NH**	NA
213	Nashville, TN	(21.7)
70	New Bedford, MA	(3.4)
NA	New Haven, CT**	NA
382	New Orleans, LA	(49.4)
100	New Rochelle, NY	(7.1)
47	New York, NY	1.6
9	Newark, NJ	36.8
339	Newport Beach, CA	(37.1)
313	Newport News, VA	(33.2)
56	Newton, MA	(1.0)
294	Norfolk, VA	(31.3)
52	Norman, OK	(0.2)
390	North Charleston, SC	(62.5)
359	Norwalk, CA	(39.7)
90	Norwalk, CT	(6.5)
140	Oakland, CA	(12.3)
309	Oceanside, CA	(32.9)
11	Odessa, TX	32.8
18	O'Fallon, MO	17.7
265	Ogden, UT	(27.6)
43	Oklahoma City, OK	2.4
NA	Olathe, KS**	NA
88	Omaha, NE	(6.3)
354	Ontario, CA	(38.9)
370	Orange, CA	(41.9)
295	Orem, UT	(31.5)
372	Orlando, FL	(43.6)

RANK	CITY	% CHANGE
123	Overland Park, KS	(9.9)
297	Oxnard, CA	(31.8)
87	Palm Bay, FL	(6.2)
289	Palmdale, CA	(30.8)
352	Pasadena, CA	(38.7)
157	Pasadena, TX	(14.9)
45	Paterson, NJ	1.7
203	Pearland, TX	(20.2)
223	Pembroke Pines, FL	(23.1)
202	Peoria, AZ	(20.1)
NA	Peoria, IL**	NA
193	Philadelphia, PA	(19.1)
230	Phoenix, AZ	(23.8)
262	Pittsburgh, PA	(27.5)
344	Plano, TX	(37.9)
75	Plantation, FL	(4.3)
219	Pomona, CA	(22.8)
261	Pompano Beach, FL	(27.4)
186	Port St. Lucie, FL	(18.6)
246	Portland, OR	(25.1)
270	Portsmouth, VA	(28.3)
131	Provo, UT	(10.8)
NA	Pueblo, CO**	NA
4	Quincy, MA	53.3
333	Racine, WI	(36.0)
250	Raleigh, NC	(26.2)
1	Ramapo, NY	55.5
180	Rancho Cucamon., CA	(17.2)
104	Reading, PA	(7.4)
2	Redding, CA	54.8
383	Redwood City, CA	(50.2)
290	Reno, NV	(30.9)
232	Renton, WA	(23.9)
329	Rialto, CA	(35.7)
364	Richardson, TX	(40.5)
179	Richmond, CA	(17.1)
267	Richmond, VA	(27.9)
361	Rio Rancho, NM	(40.1)
305	Riverside, CA	(32.6)
357	Roanoke, VA	(39.5)
NA	Rochester, MN**	NA
162	Rochester, NY	(15.6)
48	Rockford, IL	1.4
364	Roseville, CA	(40.5)
391	Roswell, GA	(62.6)
61	Round Rock, TX	(1.6)
335	Sacramento, CA	(36.2)
139	Salem, OR	(12.0)
107	Salinas, CA	(7.8)
234	Salt Lake City, UT	(24.0)
323	San Angelo, TX	(34.8)
95	San Antonio, TX	(6.7)
184	San Bernardino, CA	(18.2)
219	San Diego, CA	(22.8)
240	San Francisco, CA	(24.5)
175	San Jose, CA	(16.7)
356	San Leandro, CA	(39.3)
226	San Marcos, CA	(23.3)
247	San Mateo, CA	(25.3)
359	Sandy Springs, GA	(39.7)
297	Sandy, UT	(31.8)
281	Santa Ana, CA	(30.1)
297	Santa Barbara, CA	(31.8)
273	Santa Clara, CA	(28.8)
306	Santa Clarita, CA	(32.7)
49	Santa Maria, CA	1.0
358	Santa Monica, CA	(39.6)
194	Santa Rosa, CA	(19.3)
347	Savannah, GA	(38.1)
65	Scottsdale, AZ	(2.6)
84	Scranton, PA	(5.5)
82	Seattle, WA	(5.4)
283	Shreveport, LA	(30.2)
341	Simi Valley, CA	(37.4)

RANK	CITY	% CHANGE
116	Sioux City, IA	(9.3)
37	Sioux Falls, SD	7.5
80	Somerville, MA	(5.1)
80	South Bend, IN	(5.1)
40	South Gate, CA	3.9
217	Sparks, NV	(22.7)
374	Spokane Valley, WA	(44.4)
107	Spokane, WA	(7.8)
NA	Springfield, IL**	NA
245	Springfield, MA	(25.0)
21	Springfield, MO	16.8
29	Stamford, CT	12.6
NA	Sterling Heights, MI**	NA
53	Stockton, CA	(0.8)
16	St. Joseph, MO	22.3
160	St. Louis, MO	(15.5)
228	St. Paul, MN	(23.5)
319	St. Petersburg, FL	(33.9)
234	Suffolk, VA	(24.0)
62	Sugar Land, TX	(1.7)
127	Sunnyvale, CA	(10.5)
308	Sunrise, FL	(32.8)
278	Surprise, AZ	(29.4)
142	Syracuse, NY	(13.0)
271	Tacoma, WA	(28.5)
206	Tallahassee, FL	(20.3)
348	Tampa, FL	(38.2)
387	Temecula, CA	(57.6)
124	Tempe, AZ	(10.2)
NA	Thornton, CO**	NA
111	Thousand Oaks, CA	(8.3)
187	Toledo, OH	(18.7)
159	Toms River Twnshp, NJ	(15.3)
107	Topeka, KS	(7.8)
380	Torrance, CA	(47.6)
44	Tracy, CA	1.8
45	Trenton, NJ	1.7
121	Troy, MI	(9.7)
176	Tucson, AZ	(16.8)
168	Tulsa, OK	(16.2)
NA	Tuscaloosa, AL**	NA
324	Tustin, CA	(35.2)
257	Tyler, TX	(26.9)
15	Upper Darby Twnshp, PA	23.4
249	Vacaville, CA	(26.1)
182	Vallejo, CA	(17.5)
73	Vancouver, WA	(3.9)
152	Ventura, CA	(14.0)
99	Victorville, CA	(7.0)
280	Virginia Beach, VA	(29.9)
303	Visalia, CA	(32.4)
286	Vista, CA	(30.4)
325	Waco, TX	(35.3)
155	Warren, MI	(14.3)
NA	Warwick, RI**	NA
166	Washington, DC	(16.1)
130	Waterbury, CT	(10.7)
269	West Covina, CA	(28.1)
82	West Jordan, UT	(5.4)
316	West Palm Beach, FL	(33.6)
114	West Valley, UT	(8.9)
241	Westland, MI	(24.6)
290	Westminster, CA	(30.9)
32	Westminster, CO	9.2
76	Whittier, CA	(4.4)
251	Wichita Falls, TX	(26.3)
190	Wichita, KS	(18.9)
262	Wilmington, NC	(27.5)
NA	Winston-Salem, NC**	NA
379	Woodbridge Twnshp, NJ	(46.3)
27	Worcester, MA	13.5
223	Yakima, WA	(23.1)
26	Yonkers, NY	13.7
225	Yuma, AZ	(23.2)

Source: CQ Press using reported data from the F.B.I. "Crime in the United States 2011"
*Violent crimes are offenses of murder, forcible rape, robbery, and aggravated assault.
**Not available.

Rank Order - City

48. Percent Change in Violent Crime Rate: 2007 to 2011 (continued)
National Percent Change = 18.1% Decrease*

RANK	CITY	% CHANGE	RANK	CITY	% CHANGE	RANK	CITY	% CHANGE
1	Ramapo, NY	55.5	73	Vancouver, WA	(3.9)	145	Baltimore, MD	(13.1)
2	Redding, CA	54.8	74	Melbourne, FL	(4.0)	146	Chandler, AZ	(13.3)
3	Livermore, CA	54.7	75	Plantation, FL	(4.3)	147	Concord, CA	(13.5)
4	Quincy, MA	53.3	76	Cincinnati, OH	(4.4)	147	Las Cruces, NM	(13.5)
5	Clovis, CA	51.9	76	Whittier, CA	(4.4)	149	Bakersfield, CA	(13.7)
6	Elizabeth, NJ	40.3	78	Lakewood, CO	(4.8)	150	Centennial, CO	(13.9)
7	Medford, OR	38.8	79	Anchorage, AK	(5.0)	150	Houston, TX	(13.9)
8	Lawrence, MA	38.4	80	Somerville, MA	(5.1)	152	Bridgeport, CT	(14.0)
9	Newark, NJ	36.8	80	South Bend, IN	(5.1)	152	Ventura, CA	(14.0)
10	Fargo, ND	33.6	82	Seattle, WA	(5.4)	154	Amherst, NY	(14.1)
11	Odessa, TX	32.8	82	West Jordan, UT	(5.4)	155	Grand Prairie, TX	(14.3)
12	Indio, CA	30.8	84	Scranton, PA	(5.5)	155	Warren, MI	(14.3)
13	Bend, OR	27.7	85	Cranston, RI	(5.8)	157	Nampa, ID	(14.9)
14	Camden, NJ	24.8	86	Madison, WI	(6.0)	157	Pasadena, TX	(14.9)
15	Upper Darby Twnshp, PA	23.4	87	Palm Bay, FL	(6.2)	159	Toms River Twnshp, NJ	(15.3)
16	St. Joseph, MO	22.3	88	Omaha, NE	(6.3)	160	Long Beach, CA	(15.5)
17	Akron, OH	18.9	89	Antioch, CA	(6.4)	160	St. Louis, MO	(15.5)
18	O'Fallon, MO	17.7	90	Lake Forest, CA	(6.5)	162	Mesa, AZ	(15.6)
19	Canton Twnshp, MI	17.4	90	Lansing, MI	(6.5)	162	Rochester, NY	(15.6)
20	Clarkstown, NY	17.2	90	Norwalk, CT	(6.5)	164	Lakeland, FL	(15.8)
21	Springfield, MO	16.8	93	Detroit, MI	(6.6)	165	Lubbock, TX	(15.9)
22	Hartford, CT	15.7	93	Henderson, NV	(6.6)	166	Coral Springs, FL	(16.1)
23	Boulder, CO	15.4	95	Cleveland, OH	(6.7)	166	Washington, DC	(16.1)
24	Fort Lauderdale, FL	15.1	95	San Antonio, TX	(6.7)	168	Tulsa, OK	(16.2)
25	Gary, IN	14.9	97	Dayton, OH	(6.8)	169	Denton, TX	(16.4)
26	Yonkers, NY	13.7	98	Baton Rouge, LA	(6.9)	169	Lawrence, KS	(16.4)
27	Worcester, MA	13.5	99	Victorville, CA	(7.0)	171	Knoxville, TN	(16.5)
28	Allen, TX	13.4	100	Chino Hills, CA	(7.1)	172	Lynn, MA	(16.6)
29	Stamford, CT	12.6	100	New Rochelle, NY	(7.1)	172	McKinney, TX	(16.6)
30	Danbury, CT	10.8	102	Athens-Clarke, GA	(7.2)	172	Murrieta, CA	(16.6)
31	Huntington Beach, CA	9.5	102	Edinburg, TX	(7.2)	175	San Jose, CA	(16.7)
32	Westminster, CO	9.2	104	Reading, PA	(7.4)	176	Tucson, AZ	(16.8)
33	Livonia, MI	9.1	105	Elk Grove, CA	(7.6)	177	Colorado Springs, CO	(17.0)
34	Chino, CA	8.9	105	Hesperia, CA	(7.6)	177	Murfreesboro, TN	(17.0)
35	Cambridge, MA	8.8	107	Salinas, CA	(7.8)	179	Richmond, CA	(17.1)
36	Jackson, MS	8.0	107	Spokane, WA	(7.8)	180	Columbia, MO	(17.2)
37	Sioux Falls, SD	7.5	107	Topeka, KS	(7.8)	180	Rancho Cucamon., CA	(17.2)
38	Greece, NY	6.8	110	Little Rock, AR	(7.9)	182	Vallejo, CA	(17.5)
39	Brick Twnshp, NJ	6.7	111	Thousand Oaks, CA	(8.3)	183	Hollywood, FL	(17.9)
40	South Gate, CA	3.9	112	Evansville, IN	(8.4)	184	San Bernardino, CA	(18.2)
41	El Paso, TX	3.2	113	Clifton, NJ	(8.7)	185	Hawthorne, CA	(18.3)
42	Frisco, TX	2.8	114	West Valley, UT	(8.9)	186	Port St. Lucie, FL	(18.6)
43	Oklahoma City, OK	2.4	115	Clearwater, FL	(9.1)	187	Gresham, OR	(18.7)
44	Tracy, CA	1.8	116	Sioux City, IA	(9.3)	187	Toledo, OH	(18.7)
45	Paterson, NJ	1.7	117	Fort Worth, TX	(9.5)	189	Memphis, TN	(18.8)
45	Trenton, NJ	1.7	117	Louisville, KY	(9.5)	190	Hammond, IN	(18.9)
47	New York, NY	1.6	119	Chesapeake, VA	(9.6)	190	Wichita, KS	(18.9)
48	Rockford, IL	1.4	119	Fresno, CA	(9.6)	192	Inglewood, CA	(19.0)
49	Santa Maria, CA	1.0	121	Troy, MI	(9.7)	193	Philadelphia, PA	(19.1)
50	Eugene, OR	0.9	122	Beaumont, TX	(9.8)	194	Miami Beach, FL	(19.3)
51	Fort Wayne, IN	0.4	123	Overland Park, KS	(9.9)	194	Santa Rosa, CA	(19.3)
52	Norman, OK	(0.2)	124	College Station, TX	(10.2)	196	Merced, CA	(19.4)
53	Greeley, CO	(0.8)	124	Fort Collins, CO	(10.2)	197	Glendale, AZ	(19.5)
53	Stockton, CA	(0.8)	124	Tempe, AZ	(10.2)	197	Kansas City, KS	(19.5)
55	Davie, FL	(0.9)	127	Lee's Summit, MO	(10.5)	197	Kennewick, WA	(19.5)
56	Newton, MA	(1.0)	127	Mission, TX	(10.5)	200	Miami, FL	(19.7)
57	Flint, MI	(1.1)	127	Sunnyvale, CA	(10.5)	201	Laredo, TX	(19.8)
58	Bellingham, WA	(1.2)	130	Waterbury, CT	(10.7)	202	Peoria, AZ	(20.1)
58	Lewisville, TX	(1.2)	131	Indianapolis, IN	(10.8)	203	Aurora, CO	(20.2)
60	Clinton Twnshp, MI	(1.4)	131	Provo, UT	(10.8)	203	Killeen, TX	(20.2)
61	Round Rock, TX	(1.6)	133	Baldwin Park, CA	(10.9)	203	Pearland, TX	(20.2)
62	Kent, WA	(1.7)	134	Anaheim, CA	(11.3)	206	Tallahassee, FL	(20.3)
62	Sugar Land, TX	(1.7)	135	Midland, TX	(11.5)	207	Austin, TX	(20.4)
64	Denver, CO	(2.0)	136	Costa Mesa, CA	(11.6)	208	Albany, NY	(20.5)
65	Scottsdale, AZ	(2.6)	137	Atlanta, GA	(11.8)	209	Miramar, FL	(20.8)
66	Bellevue, WA	(2.9)	138	Carrollton, TX	(11.9)	210	Erie, PA	(20.9)
66	El Cajon, CA	(2.9)	139	Salem, OR	(12.0)	211	Irvine, CA	(21.2)
66	Mission Viejo, CA	(2.9)	140	Oakland, CA	(12.3)	212	Bethlehem, PA	(21.4)
69	Modesto, CA	(3.1)	141	Lowell, MA	(12.7)	213	Nashville, TN	(21.7)
70	New Bedford, MA	(3.4)	142	Ann Arbor, MI	(13.0)	214	Macon, GA	(22.1)
71	Hamilton Twnshp, NJ	(3.7)	142	League City, TX	(13.0)	215	Meridian, ID	(22.5)
72	Albany, GA	(3.8)	142	Syracuse, NY	(13.0)	216	Cheektowaga, NY	(22.6)

Rank Order - City (continued)

RANK	CITY	% CHANGE	RANK	CITY	% CHANGE	RANK	CITY	% CHANGE
217	Columbus, OH	(22.7)	290	Reno, NV	(30.9)	364	Richardson, TX	(40.5)
217	Sparks, NV	(22.7)	290	Westminster, CA	(30.9)	364	Roseville, CA	(40.5)
219	Corpus Christi, TX	(22.8)	292	Escondido, CA	(31.0)	366	Lancaster, CA	(40.9)
219	Pomona, CA	(22.8)	293	Broken Arrow, OK	(31.1)	367	Carlsbad, CA	(41.1)
219	San Diego, CA	(22.8)	294	Norfolk, VA	(31.3)	367	Fremont, CA	(41.1)
222	Albuquerque, NM	(23.0)	295	Orem, UT	(31.5)	369	Corona, CA	(41.4)
223	Pembroke Pines, FL	(23.1)	296	Lawton, OK	(31.6)	370	Orange, CA	(41.9)
223	Yakima, WA	(23.1)	297	Oxnard, CA	(31.8)	371	Green Bay, WI	(42.1)
225	Yuma, AZ	(23.2)	297	Sandy, UT	(31.8)	372	Orlando, FL	(43.6)
226	San Marcos, CA	(23.3)	297	Santa Barbara, CA	(31.8)	373	Brownsville, TX	(43.7)
227	Boca Raton, FL	(23.4)	300	Hemet, CA	(32.0)	374	Alhambra, CA	(44.4)
228	St. Paul, MN	(23.5)	300	Lincoln, NE	(32.0)	374	Spokane Valley, WA	(44.4)
229	Jersey City, NJ	(23.7)	302	High Point, NC	(32.2)	376	Independence, MO	(44.6)
230	Grand Rapids, MI	(23.8)	303	Visalia, CA	(32.4)	377	Bellflower, CA	(45.7)
230	Phoenix, AZ	(23.8)	304	Allentown, PA	(32.5)	378	Chico, CA	(45.8)
232	Kenosha, WI	(23.9)	305	Riverside, CA	(32.6)	379	Woodbridge Twnshp, NJ	(46.3)
232	Renton, WA	(23.9)	306	Cary, NC	(32.7)	380	Torrance, CA	(47.6)
234	Clarksville, TN	(24.0)	306	Santa Clarita, CA	(32.7)	381	Longview, TX	(47.7)
234	Salt Lake City, UT	(24.0)	308	Sunrise, FL	(32.8)	382	New Orleans, LA	(49.4)
234	Suffolk, VA	(24.0)	309	Berkeley, CA	(32.9)	383	Redwood City, CA	(50.2)
237	Asheville, NC	(24.1)	309	Oceanside, CA	(32.9)	384	Miami Gardens, FL	(52.3)
238	Beaverton, OR	(24.2)	311	Garden Grove, CA	(33.0)	385	Lakewood, CA	(53.7)
239	Bloomington, IN	(24.3)	312	Fairfield, CA	(33.1)	386	Carmel, IN	(54.2)
240	San Francisco, CA	(24.5)	313	Newport News, VA	(33.2)	387	Temecula, CA	(57.6)
241	Boise, ID	(24.6)	314	Chattanooga, TN	(33.4)	388	Charleston, SC	(60.6)
241	Everett, WA	(24.6)	314	Des Moines, IA	(33.4)	389	Lakewood Twnshp, NJ	(62.4)
241	Westland, MI	(24.6)	316	El Monte, CA	(33.6)	390	North Charleston, SC	(62.5)
244	Napa, CA	(24.8)	316	West Palm Beach, FL	(33.6)	391	Roswell, GA	(62.6)
245	Springfield, MA	(25.0)	318	Alexandria, VA	(33.7)	392	Fishers, IN	(66.3)
246	Portland, OR	(25.1)	319	St. Petersburg, FL	(33.9)	393	Concord, NC	(71.3)
247	San Mateo, CA	(25.3)	320	Carson, CA	(34.0)	NA	Arlington Heights, IL**	NA
248	Lynchburg, VA	(25.6)	321	Fayetteville, NC	(34.5)	NA	Aurora, IL**	NA
249	Vacaville, CA	(26.1)	322	Garland, TX	(34.6)	NA	Avondale, AZ**	NA
250	Raleigh, NC	(26.2)	323	San Angelo, TX	(34.8)	NA	Billings, MT**	NA
251	Fort Smith, AR	(26.3)	324	Tustin, CA	(35.2)	NA	Birmingham, AL**	NA
251	Gilbert, AZ	(26.3)	325	Compton, CA	(35.3)	NA	Bloomington, IL**	NA
251	Wichita Falls, TX	(26.3)	325	Waco, TX	(35.3)	NA	Bloomington, MN**	NA
254	Deerfield Beach, FL	(26.4)	327	Chula Vista, CA	(35.5)	NA	Brockton, MA**	NA
255	Downey, CA	(26.7)	327	McAllen, TX	(35.5)	NA	Brooklyn Park, MN**	NA
256	Boston, MA	(26.8)	329	Rialto, CA	(35.7)	NA	Buffalo, NY**	NA
257	Hillsboro, OR	(26.9)	330	Minneapolis, MN	(35.8)	NA	Champaign, IL**	NA
257	Tyler, TX	(26.9)	331	Amarillo, TX	(35.9)	NA	Chicago, IL**	NA
259	Las Vegas, NV	(27.1)	331	Fullerton, CA	(35.9)	NA	Cicero, IL**	NA
260	Los Angeles, CA	(27.3)	333	Hialeah, FL	(36.0)	NA	Citrus Heights, CA**	NA
261	Pompano Beach, FL	(27.4)	333	Racine, WI	(36.0)	NA	Davenport, IA**	NA
262	Arvada, CO	(27.5)	335	Mesquite, TX	(36.2)	NA	Decatur, IL**	NA
262	Pittsburgh, PA	(27.5)	335	Sacramento, CA	(36.2)	NA	Duluth, MN**	NA
262	Wilmington, NC	(27.5)	337	Dallas, TX	(36.3)	NA	Durham, NC**	NA
265	Ogden, UT	(27.6)	338	Hayward, CA	(36.7)	NA	Elgin, IL**	NA
266	Arlington, TX	(27.8)	339	Newport Beach, CA	(37.1)	NA	Fall River, MA**	NA
267	Dearborn, MI	(27.9)	340	Irving, TX	(37.2)	NA	Hoover, AL**	NA
267	Richmond, VA	(27.9)	341	Simi Valley, CA	(37.4)	NA	Huntsville, AL**	NA
269	West Covina, CA	(28.1)	342	Colonie, NY	(37.5)	NA	Johns Creek, GA**	NA
270	Portsmouth, VA	(28.3)	343	Edison Twnshp, NJ	(37.6)	NA	Joliet, IL**	NA
271	Fontana, CA	(28.5)	344	Abilene, TX	(37.9)	NA	Kansas City, MO**	NA
271	Tacoma, WA	(28.5)	344	Plano, TX	(37.9)	NA	Lexington, KY**	NA
273	Milwaukee, WI	(28.8)	346	Largo, FL	(38.0)	NA	Longmont, CO**	NA
273	Santa Clara, CA	(28.8)	347	Savannah, GA	(38.1)	NA	Manchester, NH**	NA
275	Buena Park, CA	(28.9)	348	Bryan, TX	(38.2)	NA	Menifee, CA**	NA
276	Farmington Hills, MI	(29.0)	348	Tampa, FL	(38.2)	NA	Mobile, AL**	NA
277	Glendale, CA	(29.1)	350	Daly City, CA	(38.3)	NA	Montgomery, AL**	NA
278	Surprise, AZ	(29.4)	351	Charlotte, NC	(38.5)	NA	Naperville, IL**	NA
279	Cedar Rapids, IA	(29.7)	352	Pasadena, CA	(38.7)	NA	Nashua, NH**	NA
280	Virginia Beach, VA	(29.9)	353	Lafayette, LA	(38.8)	NA	New Haven, CT**	NA
281	Burbank, CA	(30.1)	354	Ontario, CA	(38.9)	NA	Olathe, KS**	NA
281	Santa Ana, CA	(30.1)	355	Jacksonville, FL	(39.2)	NA	Peoria, IL**	NA
283	Gainesville, FL	(30.2)	356	San Leandro, CA	(39.3)	NA	Pueblo, CO**	NA
283	Shreveport, LA	(30.2)	357	Roanoke, VA	(39.5)	NA	Rochester, MN**	NA
285	Hampton, VA	(30.3)	358	Santa Monica, CA	(39.6)	NA	Springfield, IL**	NA
286	Columbus, GA	(30.4)	359	Norwalk, CA	(39.7)	NA	Sterling Heights, MI**	NA
286	Vista, CA	(30.4)	359	Sandy Springs, GA	(39.7)	NA	Thornton, CO**	NA
288	Moreno Valley, CA	(30.5)	361	Rio Rancho, NM	(40.1)	NA	Tuscaloosa, AL**	NA
289	Palmdale, CA	(30.8)	362	Cape Coral, FL	(40.3)	NA	Warwick, RI**	NA
			362	Edmond, OK	(40.3)	NA	Winston-Salem, NC**	NA

Source: CQ Press using reported data from the F.B.I. "Crime in the United States 2011"
*Violent crimes are offenses of murder, forcible rape, robbery, and aggravated assault.
**Not available.

Alpha Order - City

49. Murders in 2011
National Total = 14,612 Murders*

RANK	CITY	MURDERS
194	Abilene, TX	5
66	Akron, OH	27
112	Albany, GA	13
221	Albany, NY	4
50	Albuquerque, NM	35
332	Alexandria, VA	1
332	Alhambra, CA	1
133	Allentown, PA	10
390	Allen, TX	0
133	Amarillo, TX	10
390	Amherst, NY	0
100	Anaheim, CA	15
120	Anchorage, AK	12
390	Ann Arbor, MI	0
194	Antioch, CA	5
282	Arlington Heights, IL	2
80	Arlington, TX	22
332	Arvada, CO	1
194	Asheville, NC	5
174	Athens-Clarke, GA	6
19	Atlanta, GA	88
141	Aurora, CO	9
282	Aurora, IL	2
64	Austin, TX	28
174	Avondale, AZ	6
88	Bakersfield, CA	18
332	Baldwin Park, CA	1
8	Baltimore, MD	196
26	Baton Rouge, LA	64
112	Beaumont, TX	13
390	Beaverton, OR	0
332	Bellevue, WA	1
221	Bellflower, CA	4
332	Bellingham, WA	1
332	Bend, OR	1
332	Berkeley, CA	1
247	Bethlehem, PA	3
282	Billings, MT	2
32	Birmingham, AL	54
332	Bloomington, IL	1
221	Bloomington, IN	4
390	Bloomington, MN	0
390	Boca Raton, FL	0
332	Boise, ID	1
27	Boston, MA	63
282	Boulder, CO	2
390	Brick Twnshp, NJ	0
84	Bridgeport, CT	20
141	Brockton, MA	9
390	Broken Arrow, OK	0
194	Brooklyn Park, MN	5
332	Brownsville, TX	1
282	Bryan, TX	2
247	Buena Park, CA	3
47	Buffalo, NY	36
332	Burbank, CA	1
194	Cambridge, MA	5
41	Camden, NJ	47
390	Canton Twnshp, MI	0
247	Cape Coral, FL	3
221	Carlsbad, CA	4
332	Carmel, IN	1
247	Carrollton, TX	3
194	Carson, CA	5
332	Cary, NC	1
282	Cedar Rapids, IA	2
390	Centennial, CO	0
332	Champaign, IL	1
282	Chandler, AZ	2
126	Charleston, SC	11
31	Charlotte, NC	56
76	Chattanooga, TN	24

RANK	CITY	MURDERS
282	Cheektowaga, NY	2
120	Chesapeake, VA	12
2	Chicago, IL	431
194	Chico, CA	5
390	Chino Hills, CA	0
282	Chino, CA	2
174	Chula Vista, CA	6
332	Cicero, IL	1
28	Cincinnati, OH	61
332	Citrus Heights, CA	1
390	Clarkstown, NY	0
149	Clarksville, TN	8
133	Clearwater, FL	10
23	Cleveland, OH	74
282	Clifton, NJ	2
332	Clinton Twnshp, MI	1
221	Clovis, CA	4
332	College Station, TX	1
282	Colonie, NY	2
70	Colorado Springs, CO	26
282	Columbia, MO	2
100	Columbus, GA	15
20	Columbus, OH	87
92	Compton, CA	17
164	Concord, CA	7
282	Concord, NC	2
332	Coral Springs, FL	1
282	Corona, CA	2
120	Corpus Christi, TX	12
221	Costa Mesa, CA	4
332	Cranston, RI	1
9	Dallas, TX	133
332	Daly City, CA	1
332	Danbury, CT	1
194	Davenport, IA	5
332	Davie, FL	1
54	Dayton, OH	33
247	Dearborn, MI	3
133	Decatur, IL	10
332	Deerfield Beach, FL	1
282	Denton, TX	2
52	Denver, CO	34
149	Des Moines, IA	8
3	Detroit, MI	344
282	Downey, CA	2
390	Duluth, MN	0
66	Durham, NC	27
332	Edinburg, TX	1
282	Edison Twnshp, NJ	2
332	Edmond, OK	1
282	El Cajon, CA	2
332	El Monte, CA	1
98	El Paso, TX	16
194	Elgin, IL	5
92	Elizabeth, NJ	17
247	Elk Grove, CA	3
174	Erie, PA	6
247	Escondido, CA	3
390	Eugene, OR	0
247	Evansville, IN	3
194	Everett, WA	5
194	Fairfield, CA	5
282	Fall River, MA	2
332	Fargo, ND	1
282	Farmington Hills, MI	2
73	Fayetteville, NC	25
390	Fishers, IN	0
33	Flint, MI	52
194	Fontana, CA	5
247	Fort Collins, CO	3
120	Fort Lauderdale, FL	12
194	Fort Smith, AR	5

RANK	CITY	MURDERS
76	Fort Wayne, IN	24
39	Fort Worth, TX	48
282	Fremont, CA	2
50	Fresno, CA	35
247	Frisco, TX	3
282	Fullerton, CA	2
174	Gainesville, FL	6
282	Garden Grove, CA	2
194	Garland, TX	5
58	Gary, IN	30
282	Gilbert, AZ	2
80	Glendale, AZ	22
390	Glendale, CA	0
141	Grand Prairie, TX	9
133	Grand Rapids, MI	10
390	Greece, NY	0
332	Greeley, CO	1
282	Green Bay, WI	2
332	Gresham, OR	1
390	Hamilton Twnshp, NJ	0
141	Hammond, IN	9
141	Hampton, VA	9
66	Hartford, CT	27
194	Hawthorne, CA	5
164	Hayward, CA	7
194	Hemet, CA	5
282	Henderson, NV	2
282	Hesperia, CA	2
221	Hialeah, FL	4
247	High Point, NC	3
332	Hillsboro, OR	1
221	Hollywood, FL	4
390	Hoover, AL	0
7	Houston, TX	198
221	Huntington Beach, CA	4
112	Huntsville, AL	13
282	Independence, MO	2
16	Indianapolis, IN	96
247	Indio, CA	3
112	Inglewood, CA	13
282	Irvine, CA	2
149	Irving, TX	8
24	Jacksonville, FL	71
33	Jackson, MS	52
88	Jersey City, NJ	18
390	Johns Creek, GA	0
149	Joliet, IL	8
66	Kansas City, KS	27
13	Kansas City, MO	108
282	Kennewick, WA	2
390	Kenosha, WI	0
332	Kent, WA	1
100	Killeen, TX	15
92	Knoxville, TN	17
174	Lafayette, LA	6
282	Lake Forest, CA	2
174	Lakeland, FL	6
282	Lakewood Twnshp, NJ	2
282	Lakewood, CA	2
149	Lakewood, CO	8
221	Lancaster, CA	4
149	Lansing, MI	8
126	Laredo, TX	11
332	Largo, FL	1
247	Las Cruces, NM	3
22	Las Vegas, NV	82
390	Lawrence, KS	0
133	Lawrence, MA	10
149	Lawton, OK	8
247	League City, TX	3
390	Lee's Summit, MO	0
247	Lewisville, TX	3

Alpha Order - City (continued)

RANK	CITY	MURDERS
107	Lexington, KY	14
221	Lincoln, NE	4
46	Little Rock, AR	37
247	Livermore, CA	3
332	Livonia, MI	1
73	Long Beach, CA	25
332	Longmont, CO	1
221	Longview, TX	4
5	Los Angeles, CA	297
39	Louisville, KY	48
247	Lowell, MA	3
149	Lubbock, TX	8
247	Lynchburg, VA	3
247	Lynn, MA	3
112	Macon, GA	13
149	Madison, WI	8
282	Manchester, NH	2
221	McAllen, TX	4
332	McKinney, TX	1
174	Medford, OR	6
247	Melbourne, FL	3
10	Memphis, TN	117
282	Menifee, CA	2
149	Merced, CA	8
282	Meridian, ID	2
88	Mesa, AZ	18
282	Mesquite, TX	2
221	Miami Beach, FL	4
76	Miami Gardens, FL	24
25	Miami, FL	68
221	Midland, TX	4
21	Milwaukee, WI	85
55	Minneapolis, MN	32
221	Miramar, FL	4
390	Mission Viejo, CA	0
282	Mission, TX	2
58	Mobile, AL	30
107	Modesto, CA	14
56	Montgomery, AL	31
164	Moreno Valley, CA	7
247	Murfreesboro, TN	3
282	Murrieta, CA	2
390	Nampa, ID	0
332	Napa, CA	1
282	Naperville, IL	2
247	Nashua, NH	3
36	Nashville, TN	50
221	New Bedford, MA	4
52	New Haven, CT	34
6	New Orleans, LA	200
282	New Rochelle, NY	2
1	New York, NY	515
17	Newark, NJ	94
390	Newport Beach, CA	0
100	Newport News, VA	15
390	Newton, MA	0
62	Norfolk, VA	29
282	Norman, OK	2
194	North Charleston, SC	5
194	Norwalk, CA	5
247	Norwalk, CT	3
15	Oakland, CA	104
164	Oceanside, CA	7
174	Odessa, TX	6
390	O'Fallon, MO	0
282	Ogden, UT	2
29	Oklahoma City, OK	58
174	Olathe, KS	6
43	Omaha, NE	43
174	Ontario, CA	6
247	Orange, CA	3
390	Orem, UT	0
62	Orlando, FL	29

RANK	CITY	MURDERS
282	Overland Park, KS	2
149	Oxnard, CA	8
282	Palm Bay, FL	2
141	Palmdale, CA	9
164	Pasadena, CA	7
194	Pasadena, TX	5
92	Paterson, NJ	17
282	Pearland, TX	2
221	Pembroke Pines, FL	4
282	Peoria, AZ	2
98	Peoria, IL	16
4	Philadelphia, PA	324
11	Phoenix, AZ	116
42	Pittsburgh, PA	44
194	Plano, TX	5
332	Plantation, FL	1
126	Pomona, CA	11
194	Pompano Beach, FL	5
174	Port St. Lucie, FL	6
84	Portland, OR	20
120	Portsmouth, VA	12
221	Provo, UT	4
120	Pueblo, CO	12
332	Quincy, MA	1
194	Racine, WI	5
92	Raleigh, NC	17
390	Ramapo, NY	0
174	Rancho Cucamon., CA	6
112	Reading, PA	13
247	Redding, CA	3
390	Redwood City, CA	0
107	Reno, NV	14
332	Renton, WA	1
174	Rialto, CA	6
390	Richardson, TX	0
70	Richmond, CA	26
47	Richmond, VA	36
390	Rio Rancho, NM	0
112	Riverside, CA	13
149	Roanoke, VA	8
332	Rochester, MN	1
56	Rochester, NY	31
82	Rockford, IL	21
332	Roseville, CA	1
390	Roswell, GA	0
282	Round Rock, TX	2
47	Sacramento, CA	36
247	Salem, OR	3
100	Salinas, CA	15
174	Salt Lake City, UT	6
390	San Angelo, TX	0
18	San Antonio, TX	89
58	San Bernardino, CA	30
45	San Diego, CA	38
36	San Francisco, CA	50
44	San Jose, CA	39
164	San Leandro, CA	7
390	San Marcos, CA	0
332	San Mateo, CA	1
332	Sandy Springs, GA	1
332	Sandy, UT	1
112	Santa Ana, CA	13
390	Santa Barbara, CA	0
282	Santa Clara, CA	2
194	Santa Clarita, CA	5
164	Santa Maria, CA	7
332	Santa Monica, CA	1
194	Santa Rosa, CA	5
70	Savannah, GA	26
221	Scottsdale, AZ	4
247	Scranton, PA	3
84	Seattle, WA	20
92	Shreveport, LA	17
390	Simi Valley, CA	0

RANK	CITY	MURDERS
332	Sioux City, IA	1
194	Sioux Falls, SD	5
390	Somerville, MA	0
141	South Bend, IN	9
174	South Gate, CA	6
164	Sparks, NV	7
390	Spokane Valley, WA	0
221	Spokane, WA	4
149	Springfield, IL	8
84	Springfield, MA	20
194	Springfield, MO	5
174	Stamford, CT	6
332	Sterling Heights, MI	1
29	Stockton, CA	58
221	St. Joseph, MO	4
12	St. Louis, MO	113
149	St. Paul, MN	8
82	St. Petersburg, FL	21
247	Suffolk, VA	3
332	Sugar Land, TX	1
247	Sunnyvale, CA	3
247	Sunrise, FL	3
390	Surprise, AZ	0
126	Syracuse, NY	11
126	Tacoma, WA	11
133	Tallahassee, FL	10
64	Tampa, FL	28
390	Temecula, CA	0
194	Tempe, AZ	5
390	Thornton, CO	0
332	Thousand Oaks, CA	1
58	Toledo, OH	30
332	Toms River Twnshp, NJ	1
100	Topeka, KS	15
282	Torrance, CA	2
390	Tracy, CA	0
79	Trenton, NJ	23
390	Troy, MI	0
35	Tucson, AZ	51
38	Tulsa, OK	49
247	Tuscaloosa, AL	3
332	Tustin, CA	1
247	Tyler, TX	3
247	Upper Darby Twnshp, PA	3
247	Vacaville, CA	3
88	Vallejo, CA	18
141	Vancouver, WA	9
332	Ventura, CA	1
174	Victorville, CA	6
100	Virginia Beach, VA	15
149	Visalia, CA	8
390	Vista, CA	0
126	Waco, TX	11
174	Warren, MI	6
390	Warwick, RI	0
13	Washington, DC	108
164	Waterbury, CT	7
332	West Covina, CA	1
390	West Jordan, UT	0
107	West Palm Beach, FL	14
221	West Valley, UT	4
332	Westland, MI	1
247	Westminster, CA	3
221	Westminster, CO	4
221	Whittier, CA	4
332	Wichita Falls, TX	1
73	Wichita, KS	25
133	Wilmington, NC	10
107	Winston-Salem, NC	14
332	Woodbridge Twnshp, NJ	1
126	Worcester, MA	11
174	Yakima, WA	6
164	Yonkers, NY	7
221	Yuma, AZ	4

Source: Reported data from the F.B.I. "Crime in the United States 2011"
*Includes nonnegligent manslaughter.

Rank Order - City

49. Murders in 2011 (continued)
National Total = 14,612 Murders*

RANK	CITY	MURDERS
1	New York, NY	515
2	Chicago, IL	431
3	Detroit, MI	344
4	Philadelphia, PA	324
5	Los Angeles, CA	297
6	New Orleans, LA	200
7	Houston, TX	198
8	Baltimore, MD	196
9	Dallas, TX	133
10	Memphis, TN	117
11	Phoenix, AZ	116
12	St. Louis, MO	113
13	Kansas City, MO	108
13	Washington, DC	108
15	Oakland, CA	104
16	Indianapolis, IN	96
17	Newark, NJ	94
18	San Antonio, TX	89
19	Atlanta, GA	88
20	Columbus, OH	87
21	Milwaukee, WI	85
22	Las Vegas, NV	82
23	Cleveland, OH	74
24	Jacksonville, FL	71
25	Miami, FL	68
26	Baton Rouge, LA	64
27	Boston, MA	63
28	Cincinnati, OH	61
29	Oklahoma City, OK	58
29	Stockton, CA	58
31	Charlotte, NC	56
32	Birmingham, AL	54
33	Flint, MI	52
33	Jackson, MS	52
35	Tucson, AZ	51
36	Nashville, TN	50
36	San Francisco, CA	50
38	Tulsa, OK	49
39	Fort Worth, TX	48
39	Louisville, KY	48
41	Camden, NJ	47
42	Pittsburgh, PA	44
43	Omaha, NE	43
44	San Jose, CA	39
45	San Diego, CA	38
46	Little Rock, AR	37
47	Buffalo, NY	36
47	Richmond, VA	36
47	Sacramento, CA	36
50	Albuquerque, NM	35
50	Fresno, CA	35
52	Denver, CO	34
52	New Haven, CT	34
54	Dayton, OH	33
55	Minneapolis, MN	32
56	Montgomery, AL	31
56	Rochester, NY	31
58	Gary, IN	30
58	Mobile, AL	30
58	San Bernardino, CA	30
58	Toledo, OH	30
62	Norfolk, VA	29
62	Orlando, FL	29
64	Austin, TX	28
64	Tampa, FL	28
66	Akron, OH	27
66	Durham, NC	27
66	Hartford, CT	27
66	Kansas City, KS	27
70	Colorado Springs, CO	26
70	Richmond, CA	26
70	Savannah, GA	26
73	Fayetteville, NC	25
73	Long Beach, CA	25
73	Wichita, KS	25
76	Chattanooga, TN	24
76	Fort Wayne, IN	24
76	Miami Gardens, FL	24
79	Trenton, NJ	23
80	Arlington, TX	22
80	Glendale, AZ	22
82	Rockford, IL	21
82	St. Petersburg, FL	21
84	Bridgeport, CT	20
84	Portland, OR	20
84	Seattle, WA	20
84	Springfield, MA	20
88	Bakersfield, CA	18
88	Jersey City, NJ	18
88	Mesa, AZ	18
88	Vallejo, CA	18
92	Compton, CA	17
92	Elizabeth, NJ	17
92	Knoxville, TN	17
92	Paterson, NJ	17
92	Raleigh, NC	17
92	Shreveport, LA	17
98	El Paso, TX	16
98	Peoria, IL	16
100	Anaheim, CA	15
100	Columbus, GA	15
100	Killeen, TX	15
100	Newport News, VA	15
100	Salinas, CA	15
100	Topeka, KS	15
100	Virginia Beach, VA	15
107	Lexington, KY	14
107	Modesto, CA	14
107	Reno, NV	14
107	West Palm Beach, FL	14
107	Winston-Salem, NC	14
112	Albany, GA	13
112	Beaumont, TX	13
112	Huntsville, AL	13
112	Inglewood, CA	13
112	Macon, GA	13
112	Reading, PA	13
112	Riverside, CA	13
112	Santa Ana, CA	13
120	Anchorage, AK	12
120	Chesapeake, VA	12
120	Corpus Christi, TX	12
120	Fort Lauderdale, FL	12
120	Portsmouth, VA	12
120	Pueblo, CO	12
126	Charleston, SC	11
126	Laredo, TX	11
126	Pomona, CA	11
126	Syracuse, NY	11
126	Tacoma, WA	11
126	Waco, TX	11
126	Worcester, MA	11
133	Allentown, PA	10
133	Amarillo, TX	10
133	Clearwater, FL	10
133	Decatur, IL	10
133	Grand Rapids, MI	10
133	Lawrence, MA	10
133	Tallahassee, FL	10
133	Wilmington, NC	10
141	Aurora, CO	9
141	Brockton, MA	9
141	Grand Prairie, TX	9
141	Hammond, IN	9
141	Hampton, VA	9
141	Palmdale, CA	9
141	South Bend, IN	9
141	Vancouver, WA	9
149	Clarksville, TN	8
149	Des Moines, IA	8
149	Irving, TX	8
149	Joliet, IL	8
149	Lakewood, CO	8
149	Lansing, MI	8
149	Lawton, OK	8
149	Lubbock, TX	8
149	Madison, WI	8
149	Merced, CA	8
149	Oxnard, CA	8
149	Roanoke, VA	8
149	Springfield, IL	8
149	St. Paul, MN	8
149	Visalia, CA	8
164	Concord, CA	7
164	Hayward, CA	7
164	Moreno Valley, CA	7
164	Oceanside, CA	7
164	Pasadena, CA	7
164	San Leandro, CA	7
164	Santa Maria, CA	7
164	Sparks, NV	7
164	Waterbury, CT	7
164	Yonkers, NY	7
174	Athens-Clarke, GA	6
174	Avondale, AZ	6
174	Chula Vista, CA	6
174	Erie, PA	6
174	Gainesville, FL	6
174	Lafayette, LA	6
174	Lakeland, FL	6
174	Medford, OR	6
174	Odessa, TX	6
174	Olathe, KS	6
174	Ontario, CA	6
174	Port St. Lucie, FL	6
174	Rancho Cucamon., CA	6
174	Rialto, CA	6
174	Salt Lake City, UT	6
174	South Gate, CA	6
174	Stamford, CT	6
174	Victorville, CA	6
174	Warren, MI	6
174	Yakima, WA	6
194	Abilene, TX	5
194	Antioch, CA	5
194	Asheville, NC	5
194	Brooklyn Park, MN	5
194	Cambridge, MA	5
194	Carson, CA	5
194	Chico, CA	5
194	Davenport, IA	5
194	Elgin, IL	5
194	Everett, WA	5
194	Fairfield, CA	5
194	Fontana, CA	5
194	Fort Smith, AR	5
194	Garland, TX	5
194	Hawthorne, CA	5
194	Hemet, CA	5
194	North Charleston, SC	5
194	Norwalk, CA	5
194	Pasadena, TX	5
194	Plano, TX	5
194	Pompano Beach, FL	5
194	Racine, WI	5
194	Santa Clarita, CA	5

Rank Order - City (continued)

RANK	CITY	MURDERS
194	Santa Rosa, CA	5
194	Sioux Falls, SD	5
194	Springfield, MO	5
194	Tempe, AZ	5
221	Albany, NY	4
221	Bellflower, CA	4
221	Bloomington, IN	4
221	Carlsbad, CA	4
221	Clovis, CA	4
221	Costa Mesa, CA	4
221	Hialeah, FL	4
221	Hollywood, FL	4
221	Huntington Beach, CA	4
221	Lancaster, CA	4
221	Lincoln, NE	4
221	Longview, TX	4
221	McAllen, TX	4
221	Miami Beach, FL	4
221	Midland, TX	4
221	Miramar, FL	4
221	New Bedford, MA	4
221	Pembroke Pines, FL	4
221	Provo, UT	4
221	Scottsdale, AZ	4
221	Spokane, WA	4
221	St. Joseph, MO	4
221	West Valley, UT	4
221	Westminster, CO	4
221	Whittier, CA	4
221	Yuma, AZ	4
247	Bethlehem, PA	3
247	Buena Park, CA	3
247	Cape Coral, FL	3
247	Carrollton, TX	3
247	Dearborn, MI	3
247	Elk Grove, CA	3
247	Escondido, CA	3
247	Evansville, IN	3
247	Fort Collins, CO	3
247	Frisco, TX	3
247	High Point, NC	3
247	Indio, CA	3
247	Las Cruces, NM	3
247	League City, TX	3
247	Lewisville, TX	3
247	Livermore, CA	3
247	Lowell, MA	3
247	Lynchburg, VA	3
247	Lynn, MA	3
247	Melbourne, FL	3
247	Murfreesboro, TN	3
247	Nashua, NH	3
247	Norwalk, CT	3
247	Orange, CA	3
247	Redding, CA	3
247	Salem, OR	3
247	Scranton, PA	3
247	Suffolk, VA	3
247	Sunnyvale, CA	3
247	Sunrise, FL	3
247	Tuscaloosa, AL	3
247	Tyler, TX	3
247	Upper Darby Twnshp, PA	3
247	Vacaville, CA	3
247	Westminster, CA	3
282	Arlington Heights, IL	2
282	Aurora, IL	2
282	Billings, MT	2
282	Boulder, CO	2
282	Bryan, TX	2
282	Cedar Rapids, IA	2
282	Chandler, AZ	2
282	Cheektowaga, NY	2
282	Chino, CA	2
282	Clifton, NJ	2
282	Colonie, NY	2
282	Columbia, MO	2
282	Concord, NC	2
282	Corona, CA	2
282	Denton, TX	2
282	Downey, CA	2
282	Edison Twnshp, NJ	2
282	El Cajon, CA	2
282	Fall River, MA	2
282	Farmington Hills, MI	2
282	Fremont, CA	2
282	Fullerton, CA	2
282	Garden Grove, CA	2
282	Gilbert, AZ	2
282	Green Bay, WI	2
282	Henderson, NV	2
282	Hesperia, CA	2
282	Independence, MO	2
282	Irvine, CA	2
282	Kennewick, WA	2
282	Lake Forest, CA	2
282	Lakewood Twnshp, NJ	2
282	Lakewood, CA	2
282	Manchester, NH	2
282	Menifee, CA	2
282	Meridian, ID	2
282	Mesquite, TX	2
282	Mission, TX	2
282	Murrieta, CA	2
282	Naperville, IL	2
282	New Rochelle, NY	2
282	Norman, OK	2
282	Ogden, UT	2
282	Overland Park, KS	2
282	Palm Bay, FL	2
282	Pearland, TX	2
282	Peoria, AZ	2
282	Round Rock, TX	2
282	Santa Clara, CA	2
282	Torrance, CA	2
332	Alexandria, VA	1
332	Alhambra, CA	1
332	Arvada, CO	1
332	Baldwin Park, CA	1
332	Bellevue, WA	1
332	Bellingham, WA	1
332	Bend, OR	1
332	Berkeley, CA	1
332	Bloomington, IL	1
332	Boise, ID	1
332	Brownsville, TX	1
332	Burbank, CA	1
332	Carmel, IN	1
332	Cary, NC	1
332	Champaign, IL	1
332	Cicero, IL	1
332	Citrus Heights, CA	1
332	Clinton Twnshp, MI	1
332	College Station, TX	1
332	Coral Springs, FL	1
332	Cranston, RI	1
332	Daly City, CA	1
332	Danbury, CT	1
332	Davie, FL	1
332	Deerfield Beach, FL	1
332	Edinburg, TX	1
332	Edmond, OK	1
332	El Monte, CA	1
332	Fargo, ND	1
332	Greeley, CO	1
332	Gresham, OR	1
332	Hillsboro, OR	1
332	Kent, WA	1
332	Largo, FL	1
332	Livonia, MI	1
332	Longmont, CO	1
332	McKinney, TX	1
332	Napa, CA	1
332	Plantation, FL	1
332	Quincy, MA	1
332	Renton, WA	1
332	Rochester, MN	1
332	Roseville, CA	1
332	San Mateo, CA	1
332	Sandy Springs, GA	1
332	Sandy, UT	1
332	Santa Monica, CA	1
332	Sioux City, IA	1
332	Sterling Heights, MI	1
332	Sugar Land, TX	1
332	Thousand Oaks, CA	1
332	Toms River Twnshp, NJ	1
332	Tustin, CA	1
332	Ventura, CA	1
332	West Covina, CA	1
332	Westland, MI	1
332	Wichita Falls, TX	1
332	Woodbridge Twnshp, NJ	1
390	Allen, TX	0
390	Amherst, NY	0
390	Ann Arbor, MI	0
390	Beaverton, OR	0
390	Bloomington, MN	0
390	Boca Raton, FL	0
390	Brick Twnshp, NJ	0
390	Broken Arrow, OK	0
390	Canton Twnshp, MI	0
390	Centennial, CO	0
390	Chino Hills, CA	0
390	Clarkstown, NY	0
390	Duluth, MN	0
390	Eugene, OR	0
390	Fishers, IN	0
390	Glendale, CA	0
390	Greece, NY	0
390	Hamilton Twnshp, NJ	0
390	Hoover, AL	0
390	Johns Creek, GA	0
390	Kenosha, WI	0
390	Lawrence, KS	0
390	Lee's Summit, MO	0
390	Mission Viejo, CA	0
390	Nampa, ID	0
390	Newport Beach, CA	0
390	Newton, MA	0
390	O'Fallon, MO	0
390	Orem, UT	0
390	Ramapo, NY	0
390	Redwood City, CA	0
390	Richardson, TX	0
390	Rio Rancho, NM	0
390	Roswell, GA	0
390	San Angelo, TX	0
390	San Marcos, CA	0
390	Santa Barbara, CA	0
390	Simi Valley, CA	0
390	Somerville, MA	0
390	Spokane Valley, WA	0
390	Surprise, AZ	0
390	Temecula, CA	0
390	Thornton, CO	0
390	Tracy, CA	0
390	Troy, MI	0
390	Vista, CA	0
390	Warwick, RI	0
390	West Jordan, UT	0

Source: Reported data from the F.B.I. "Crime in the United States 2011"
*Includes nonnegligent manslaughter.

Alpha Order - City

50. Murder Rate in 2011
National Rate = 4.7 Murders per 100,000 Population*

RANK	CITY	RATE
189	Abilene, TX	4.2
48	Akron, OH	13.6
32	Albany, GA	16.6
194	Albany, NY	4.1
124	Albuquerque, NM	6.3
385	Alexandria, VA	0.7
333	Alhambra, CA	1.2
91	Allentown, PA	8.4
390	Allen, TX	0.0
161	Amarillo, TX	5.1
390	Amherst, NY	0.0
188	Anaheim, CA	4.4
198	Anchorage, AK	4.0
390	Ann Arbor, MI	0.0
174	Antioch, CA	4.8
258	Arlington Heights, IL	2.7
139	Arlington, TX	5.9
366	Arvada, CO	0.9
139	Asheville, NC	5.9
161	Athens-Clarke, GA	5.1
21	Atlanta, GA	20.7
258	Aurora, CO	2.7
358	Aurora, IL	1.0
221	Austin, TX	3.5
101	Avondale, AZ	7.8
161	Bakersfield, CA	5.1
322	Baldwin Park, CA	1.3
8	Baltimore, MD	31.3
10	Baton Rouge, LA	27.6
70	Beaumont, TX	10.8
390	Beaverton, OR	0.0
378	Bellevue, WA	0.8
159	Bellflower, CA	5.2
333	Bellingham, WA	1.2
322	Bend, OR	1.3
366	Berkeley, CA	0.9
198	Bethlehem, PA	4.0
298	Billings, MT	1.9
14	Birmingham, AL	25.3
322	Bloomington, IL	1.3
169	Bloomington, IN	4.9
390	Bloomington, MN	0.0
390	Boca Raton, FL	0.0
389	Boise, ID	0.5
73	Boston, MA	10.1
293	Boulder, CO	2.0
390	Brick Twnshp, NJ	0.0
44	Bridgeport, CT	13.8
79	Brockton, MA	9.5
390	Broken Arrow, OK	0.0
119	Brooklyn Park, MN	6.5
388	Brownsville, TX	0.6
262	Bryan, TX	2.6
210	Buena Park, CA	3.7
46	Buffalo, NY	13.7
358	Burbank, CA	1.0
178	Cambridge, MA	4.7
1	Camden, NJ	60.6
390	Canton Twnshp, MI	0.0
298	Cape Coral, FL	1.9
209	Carlsbad, CA	3.8
322	Carmel, IN	1.3
269	Carrollton, TX	2.5
153	Carson, CA	5.4
385	Cary, NC	0.7
316	Cedar Rapids, IA	1.6
390	Centennial, CO	0.0
333	Champaign, IL	1.2
378	Chandler, AZ	0.8
85	Charleston, SC	9.1
112	Charlotte, NC	7.1
39	Chattanooga, TN	14.2

RANK	CITY	RATE
269	Cheektowaga, NY	2.5
156	Chesapeake, VA	5.3
33	Chicago, IL	15.9
146	Chico, CA	5.7
390	Chino Hills, CA	0.0
269	Chino, CA	2.5
280	Chula Vista, CA	2.4
333	Cicero, IL	1.2
22	Cincinnati, OH	20.5
333	Citrus Heights, CA	1.2
390	Clarkstown, NY	0.0
135	Clarksville, TN	6.0
83	Clearwater, FL	9.2
25	Cleveland, OH	18.6
280	Clifton, NJ	2.4
358	Clinton Twnshp, MI	1.0
194	Clovis, CA	4.1
358	College Station, TX	1.0
262	Colonie, NY	2.6
132	Colorado Springs, CO	6.1
307	Columbia, MO	1.8
101	Columbus, GA	7.8
68	Columbus, OH	11.0
29	Compton, CA	17.4
146	Concord, CA	5.7
269	Concord, NC	2.5
378	Coral Springs, FL	0.8
322	Corona, CA	1.3
203	Corpus Christi, TX	3.9
213	Costa Mesa, CA	3.6
333	Cranston, RI	1.2
69	Dallas, TX	10.9
358	Daly City, CA	1.0
333	Danbury, CT	1.2
166	Davenport, IA	5.0
346	Davie, FL	1.1
17	Dayton, OH	23.3
243	Dearborn, MI	3.1
50	Decatur, IL	13.1
322	Deerfield Beach, FL	1.3
313	Denton, TX	1.7
148	Denver, CO	5.6
203	Des Moines, IA	3.9
4	Detroit, MI	48.2
307	Downey, CA	1.8
390	Duluth, MN	0.0
59	Durham, NC	11.7
322	Edinburg, TX	1.3
293	Edison Twnshp, NJ	2.0
333	Edmond, OK	1.2
293	El Cajon, CA	2.0
366	El Monte, CA	0.9
280	El Paso, TX	2.4
183	Elgin, IL	4.6
48	Elizabeth, NJ	13.6
298	Elk Grove, CA	1.9
139	Erie, PA	5.9
288	Escondido, CA	2.1
390	Eugene, OR	0.0
269	Evansville, IN	2.5
174	Everett, WA	4.8
178	Fairfield, CA	4.7
284	Fall River, MA	2.2
366	Fargo, ND	0.9
269	Farmington Hills, MI	2.5
55	Fayetteville, NC	12.3
390	Fishers, IN	0.0
3	Flint, MI	50.8
269	Fontana, CA	2.5
293	Fort Collins, CO	2.0
108	Fort Lauderdale, FL	7.2
144	Fort Smith, AR	5.8

RANK	CITY	RATE
80	Fort Wayne, IN	9.4
124	Fort Worth, TX	6.3
366	Fremont, CA	0.9
113	Fresno, CA	7.0
269	Frisco, TX	2.5
317	Fullerton, CA	1.5
174	Gainesville, FL	4.8
333	Garden Grove, CA	1.2
284	Garland, TX	2.2
5	Gary, IN	37.2
366	Gilbert, AZ	0.9
78	Glendale, AZ	9.6
390	Glendale, CA	0.0
166	Grand Prairie, TX	5.0
156	Grand Rapids, MI	5.3
390	Greece, NY	0.0
346	Greeley, CO	1.1
298	Green Bay, WI	1.9
366	Gresham, OR	0.9
390	Hamilton Twnshp, NJ	0.0
66	Hammond, IN	11.1
119	Hampton, VA	6.5
19	Hartford, CT	21.6
139	Hawthorne, CA	5.9
174	Hayward, CA	4.8
124	Hemet, CA	6.3
378	Henderson, NV	0.8
284	Hesperia, CA	2.2
307	Hialeah, FL	1.8
253	High Point, NC	2.8
346	Hillsboro, OR	1.1
253	Hollywood, FL	2.8
390	Hoover, AL	0.0
83	Houston, TX	9.2
288	Huntington Beach, CA	2.1
108	Huntsville, AL	7.2
313	Independence, MO	1.7
63	Indianapolis, IN	11.5
203	Indio, CA	3.9
59	Inglewood, CA	11.7
366	Irvine, CA	0.9
213	Irving, TX	3.6
88	Jacksonville, FL	8.5
9	Jackson, MS	29.9
108	Jersey City, NJ	7.2
390	Johns Creek, GA	0.0
153	Joliet, IL	5.4
26	Kansas City, KS	18.4
16	Kansas City, MO	23.4
258	Kennewick, WA	2.7
390	Kenosha, WI	0.0
346	Kent, WA	1.1
63	Killeen, TX	11.5
80	Knoxville, TN	9.4
169	Lafayette, LA	4.9
262	Lake Forest, CA	2.6
132	Lakeland, FL	6.1
288	Lakewood Twnshp, NJ	2.1
269	Lakewood, CA	2.5
150	Lakewood, CO	5.5
269	Lancaster, CA	2.5
113	Lansing, MI	7.0
183	Laredo, TX	4.6
322	Largo, FL	1.3
246	Las Cruces, NM	3.0
148	Las Vegas, NV	5.6
390	Lawrence, KS	0.0
51	Lawrence, MA	13.0
93	Lawton, OK	8.2
221	League City, TX	3.5
390	Lee's Summit, MO	0.0
243	Lewisville, TX	3.1

Alpha Order - City (continued)

RANK	CITY	RATE
178	Lexington, KY	4.7
317	Lincoln, NE	1.5
24	Little Rock, AR	19.0
210	Livermore, CA	3.7
358	Livonia, MI	1.0
156	Long Beach, CA	5.3
346	Longmont, CO	1.1
169	Longview, TX	4.9
103	Los Angeles, CA	7.7
108	Louisville, KY	7.2
253	Lowell, MA	2.8
229	Lubbock, TX	3.4
203	Lynchburg, VA	3.9
233	Lynn, MA	3.3
42	Macon, GA	14.0
229	Madison, WI	3.4
307	Manchester, NH	1.8
246	McAllen, TX	3.0
385	McKinney, TX	0.7
99	Medford, OR	7.9
203	Melbourne, FL	3.9
27	Memphis, TN	17.9
262	Menifee, CA	2.6
74	Merced, CA	10.0
262	Meridian, ID	2.6
198	Mesa, AZ	4.0
319	Mesquite, TX	1.4
186	Miami Beach, FL	4.5
18	Miami Gardens, FL	22.1
31	Miami, FL	16.8
221	Midland, TX	3.5
39	Milwaukee, WI	14.2
92	Minneapolis, MN	8.3
238	Miramar, FL	3.2
390	Mission Viejo, CA	0.0
269	Mission, TX	2.5
57	Mobile, AL	11.9
115	Modesto, CA	6.9
35	Montgomery, AL	15.0
213	Moreno Valley, CA	3.6
258	Murfreesboro, TN	2.7
298	Murrieta, CA	1.9
390	Nampa, ID	0.0
322	Napa, CA	1.3
319	Naperville, IL	1.4
221	Nashua, NH	3.5
93	Nashville, TN	8.2
189	New Bedford, MA	4.2
13	New Haven, CT	26.2
2	New Orleans, LA	57.6
262	New Rochelle, NY	2.6
124	New York, NY	6.3
7	Newark, NJ	33.8
390	Newport Beach, CA	0.0
93	Newport News, VA	8.2
390	Newton, MA	0.0
58	Norfolk, VA	11.8
307	Norman, OK	1.8
161	North Charleston, SC	5.1
178	Norwalk, CA	4.7
221	Norwalk, CT	3.5
12	Oakland, CA	26.3
194	Oceanside, CA	4.1
139	Odessa, TX	5.9
390	O'Fallon, MO	0.0
280	Ogden, UT	2.4
75	Oklahoma City, OK	9.9
178	Olathe, KS	4.7
71	Omaha, NE	10.4
213	Ontario, CA	3.6
284	Orange, CA	2.2
390	Orem, UT	0.0
56	Orlando, FL	12.0

RANK	CITY	RATE
346	Overland Park, KS	1.1
198	Oxnard, CA	4.0
298	Palm Bay, FL	1.9
144	Palmdale, CA	5.8
166	Pasadena, CA	5.0
233	Pasadena, TX	3.3
62	Paterson, NJ	11.6
288	Pearland, TX	2.1
262	Pembroke Pines, FL	2.6
322	Peoria, AZ	1.3
43	Peoria, IL	13.9
20	Philadelphia, PA	21.2
99	Phoenix, AZ	7.9
38	Pittsburgh, PA	14.3
298	Plano, TX	1.9
333	Plantation, FL	1.2
107	Pomona, CA	7.3
169	Pompano Beach, FL	4.9
213	Port St. Lucie, FL	3.6
229	Portland, OR	3.4
53	Portsmouth, VA	12.4
221	Provo, UT	3.5
66	Pueblo, CO	11.1
346	Quincy, MA	1.1
124	Racine, WI	6.3
189	Raleigh, NC	4.2
390	Ramapo, NY	0.0
213	Rancho Cucamon., CA	3.6
36	Reading, PA	14.7
233	Redding, CA	3.3
390	Redwood City, CA	0.0
131	Reno, NV	6.2
346	Renton, WA	1.1
135	Rialto, CA	6.0
390	Richardson, TX	0.0
15	Richmond, CA	24.8
29	Richmond, VA	17.4
390	Rio Rancho, NM	0.0
189	Riverside, CA	4.2
97	Roanoke, VA	8.1
366	Rochester, MN	0.9
36	Rochester, NY	14.7
46	Rockford, IL	13.7
378	Roseville, CA	0.8
390	Roswell, GA	0.0
293	Round Rock, TX	2.0
105	Sacramento, CA	7.6
298	Salem, OR	1.9
75	Salinas, CA	9.9
238	Salt Lake City, UT	3.2
390	San Angelo, TX	0.0
118	San Antonio, TX	6.6
41	San Bernardino, CA	14.1
251	San Diego, CA	2.9
132	San Francisco, CA	6.1
194	San Jose, CA	4.1
97	San Leandro, CA	8.1
390	San Marcos, CA	0.0
358	San Mateo, CA	1.0
346	Sandy Springs, GA	1.1
346	Sandy, UT	1.1
198	Santa Ana, CA	4.0
390	Santa Barbara, CA	0.0
313	Santa Clara, CA	1.7
253	Santa Clarita, CA	2.8
115	Santa Maria, CA	6.9
346	Santa Monica, CA	1.1
251	Santa Rosa, CA	2.9
63	Savannah, GA	11.5
307	Scottsdale, AZ	1.8
203	Scranton, PA	3.9
238	Seattle, WA	3.2
88	Shreveport, LA	8.5
390	Simi Valley, CA	0.0

RANK	CITY	RATE
333	Sioux City, IA	1.2
238	Sioux Falls, SD	3.2
390	Somerville, MA	0.0
86	South Bend, IN	8.9
124	South Gate, CA	6.3
103	Sparks, NV	7.7
390	Spokane Valley, WA	0.0
298	Spokane, WA	1.9
115	Springfield, IL	6.9
51	Springfield, MA	13.0
243	Springfield, MO	3.1
169	Stamford, CT	4.9
378	Sterling Heights, MI	0.8
23	Stockton, CA	19.7
159	St. Joseph, MO	5.2
6	St. Louis, MO	35.3
253	St. Paul, MN	2.8
88	St. Petersburg, FL	8.5
221	Suffolk, VA	3.5
333	Sugar Land, TX	1.2
288	Sunnyvale, CA	2.1
221	Sunrise, FL	3.5
390	Surprise, AZ	0.0
106	Syracuse, NY	7.5
150	Tacoma, WA	5.5
153	Tallahassee, FL	5.4
93	Tampa, FL	8.2
390	Temecula, CA	0.0
246	Tempe, AZ	3.0
390	Thornton, CO	0.0
378	Thousand Oaks, CA	0.8
71	Toledo, OH	10.4
346	Toms River Twnshp, NJ	1.1
59	Topeka, KS	11.7
319	Torrance, CA	1.4
390	Tracy, CA	0.0
11	Trenton, NJ	27.0
390	Troy, MI	0.0
77	Tucson, AZ	9.7
53	Tulsa, OK	12.4
233	Tuscaloosa, AL	3.3
322	Tustin, CA	1.3
246	Tyler, TX	3.0
213	Upper Darby Twnshp, PA	3.6
238	Vacaville, CA	3.2
34	Vallejo, CA	15.3
150	Vancouver, WA	5.5
366	Ventura, CA	0.9
161	Victorville, CA	5.1
229	Virginia Beach, VA	3.4
123	Visalia, CA	6.4
390	Vista, CA	0.0
87	Waco, TX	8.6
186	Warren, MI	4.5
390	Warwick, RI	0.0
28	Washington, DC	17.5
124	Waterbury, CT	6.3
366	West Covina, CA	0.9
390	West Jordan, UT	0.0
44	West Palm Beach, FL	13.8
246	West Valley, UT	3.0
333	Westland, MI	1.2
233	Westminster, CA	3.3
210	Westminster, CO	3.7
183	Whittier, CA	4.6
366	Wichita Falls, TX	0.9
119	Wichita, KS	6.5
82	Wilmington, NC	9.3
135	Winston-Salem, NC	6.0
358	Woodbridge Twnshp, NJ	1.0
135	Worcester, MA	6.0
119	Yakima, WA	6.5
213	Yonkers, NY	3.6
189	Yuma, AZ	4.2

Source: CQ Press using reported data from the F.B.I. "Crime in the United States 2011"
*Includes nonnegligent manslaughter.

50. Murder Rate in 2011 (continued)
National Rate = 4.7 Murders per 100,000 Population*

RANK	CITY	RATE
1	Camden, NJ	60.6
2	New Orleans, LA	57.6
3	Flint, MI	50.8
4	Detroit, MI	48.2
5	Gary, IN	37.2
6	St. Louis, MO	35.3
7	Newark, NJ	33.8
8	Baltimore, MD	31.3
9	Jackson, MS	29.9
10	Baton Rouge, LA	27.6
11	Trenton, NJ	27.0
12	Oakland, CA	26.3
13	New Haven, CT	26.2
14	Birmingham, AL	25.3
15	Richmond, CA	24.8
16	Kansas City, MO	23.4
17	Dayton, OH	23.3
18	Miami Gardens, FL	22.1
19	Hartford, CT	21.6
20	Philadelphia, PA	21.2
21	Atlanta, GA	20.7
22	Cincinnati, OH	20.5
23	Stockton, CA	19.7
24	Little Rock, AR	19.0
25	Cleveland, OH	18.6
26	Kansas City, KS	18.4
27	Memphis, TN	17.9
28	Washington, DC	17.5
29	Compton, CA	17.4
29	Richmond, VA	17.4
31	Miami, FL	16.8
32	Albany, GA	16.6
33	Chicago, IL	15.9
34	Vallejo, CA	15.3
35	Montgomery, AL	15.0
36	Reading, PA	14.7
36	Rochester, NY	14.7
38	Pittsburgh, PA	14.3
39	Chattanooga, TN	14.2
39	Milwaukee, WI	14.2
41	San Bernardino, CA	14.1
42	Macon, GA	14.0
43	Peoria, IL	13.9
44	Bridgeport, CT	13.8
44	West Palm Beach, FL	13.8
46	Buffalo, NY	13.7
46	Rockford, IL	13.7
48	Akron, OH	13.6
48	Elizabeth, NJ	13.6
50	Decatur, IL	13.1
51	Lawrence, MA	13.0
51	Springfield, MA	13.0
53	Portsmouth, VA	12.4
53	Tulsa, OK	12.4
55	Fayetteville, NC	12.3
56	Orlando, FL	12.0
57	Mobile, AL	11.9
58	Norfolk, VA	11.8
59	Durham, NC	11.7
59	Inglewood, CA	11.7
59	Topeka, KS	11.7
62	Paterson, NJ	11.6
63	Indianapolis, IN	11.5
63	Killeen, TX	11.5
63	Savannah, GA	11.5
66	Hammond, IN	11.1
66	Pueblo, CO	11.1
68	Columbus, OH	11.0
69	Dallas, TX	10.9
70	Beaumont, TX	10.8
71	Omaha, NE	10.4
71	Toledo, OH	10.4
73	Boston, MA	10.1
74	Merced, CA	10.0
75	Oklahoma City, OK	9.9
75	Salinas, CA	9.9
77	Tucson, AZ	9.7
78	Glendale, AZ	9.6
79	Brockton, MA	9.5
80	Fort Wayne, IN	9.4
80	Knoxville, TN	9.4
82	Wilmington, NC	9.3
83	Clearwater, FL	9.2
83	Houston, TX	9.2
85	Charleston, SC	9.1
86	South Bend, IN	8.9
87	Waco, TX	8.6
88	Jacksonville, FL	8.5
88	Shreveport, LA	8.5
88	St. Petersburg, FL	8.5
91	Allentown, PA	8.4
92	Minneapolis, MN	8.3
93	Lawton, OK	8.2
93	Nashville, TN	8.2
93	Newport News, VA	8.2
93	Tampa, FL	8.2
97	Roanoke, VA	8.1
97	San Leandro, CA	8.1
99	Medford, OR	7.9
99	Phoenix, AZ	7.9
101	Avondale, AZ	7.8
101	Columbus, GA	7.8
103	Los Angeles, CA	7.7
103	Sparks, NV	7.7
105	Sacramento, CA	7.6
106	Syracuse, NY	7.5
107	Pomona, CA	7.3
108	Fort Lauderdale, FL	7.2
108	Huntsville, AL	7.2
108	Jersey City, NJ	7.2
108	Louisville, KY	7.2
112	Charlotte, NC	7.1
113	Fresno, CA	7.0
113	Lansing, MI	7.0
115	Modesto, CA	6.9
115	Santa Maria, CA	6.9
115	Springfield, IL	6.9
118	San Antonio, TX	6.6
119	Brooklyn Park, MN	6.5
119	Hampton, VA	6.5
119	Wichita, KS	6.5
119	Yakima, WA	6.5
123	Visalia, CA	6.4
124	Albuquerque, NM	6.3
124	Fort Worth, TX	6.3
124	Hemet, CA	6.3
124	New York, NY	6.3
124	Racine, WI	6.3
124	South Gate, CA	6.3
124	Waterbury, CT	6.3
131	Reno, NV	6.2
132	Colorado Springs, CO	6.1
132	Lakeland, FL	6.1
132	San Francisco, CA	6.1
135	Clarksville, TN	6.0
135	Rialto, CA	6.0
135	Winston-Salem, NC	6.0
135	Worcester, MA	6.0
139	Arlington, TX	5.9
139	Asheville, NC	5.9
139	Erie, PA	5.9
139	Hawthorne, CA	5.9
139	Odessa, TX	5.9
144	Fort Smith, AR	5.8
144	Palmdale, CA	5.8
146	Chico, CA	5.7
146	Concord, CA	5.7
148	Denver, CO	5.6
148	Las Vegas, NV	5.6
150	Lakewood, CO	5.5
150	Tacoma, WA	5.5
150	Vancouver, WA	5.5
153	Carson, CA	5.4
153	Joliet, IL	5.4
153	Tallahassee, FL	5.4
156	Chesapeake, VA	5.3
156	Grand Rapids, MI	5.3
156	Long Beach, CA	5.3
159	Bellflower, CA	5.2
159	St. Joseph, MO	5.2
161	Amarillo, TX	5.1
161	Athens-Clarke, GA	5.1
161	Bakersfield, CA	5.1
161	North Charleston, SC	5.1
161	Victorville, CA	5.1
166	Davenport, IA	5.0
166	Grand Prairie, TX	5.0
166	Pasadena, CA	5.0
169	Bloomington, IN	4.9
169	Lafayette, LA	4.9
169	Longview, TX	4.9
169	Pompano Beach, FL	4.9
169	Stamford, CT	4.9
174	Antioch, CA	4.8
174	Everett, WA	4.8
174	Gainesville, FL	4.8
174	Hayward, CA	4.8
178	Cambridge, MA	4.7
178	Fairfield, CA	4.7
178	Lexington, KY	4.7
178	Norwalk, CA	4.7
178	Olathe, KS	4.7
183	Elgin, IL	4.6
183	Laredo, TX	4.6
183	Whittier, CA	4.6
186	Miami Beach, FL	4.5
186	Warren, MI	4.5
188	Anaheim, CA	4.4
189	Abilene, TX	4.2
189	New Bedford, MA	4.2
189	Raleigh, NC	4.2
189	Riverside, CA	4.2
189	Yuma, AZ	4.2
194	Albany, NY	4.1
194	Clovis, CA	4.1
194	Oceanside, CA	4.1
194	San Jose, CA	4.1
198	Anchorage, AK	4.0
198	Bethlehem, PA	4.0
198	Mesa, AZ	4.0
198	Oxnard, CA	4.0
198	Santa Ana, CA	4.0
203	Corpus Christi, TX	3.9
203	Des Moines, IA	3.9
203	Indio, CA	3.9
203	Lynchburg, VA	3.9
203	Melbourne, FL	3.9
203	Scranton, PA	3.9
209	Carlsbad, CA	3.8
210	Buena Park, CA	3.7
210	Livermore, CA	3.7
210	Westminster, CO	3.7
213	Costa Mesa, CA	3.6
213	Irving, TX	3.6
213	Moreno Valley, CA	3.6
213	Ontario, CA	3.6

Rank Order - City (continued)

RANK	CITY	RATE	RANK	CITY	RATE	RANK	CITY	RATE
213	Port St. Lucie, FL	3.6	288	Lakewood Twnshp, NJ	2.1	358	San Mateo, CA	1.0
213	Rancho Cucamon., CA	3.6	288	Pearland, TX	2.1	358	Woodbridge Twnshp, NJ	1.0
213	Upper Darby Twnshp, PA	3.6	288	Sunnyvale, CA	2.1	366	Arvada, CO	0.9
213	Yonkers, NY	3.6	293	Boulder, CO	2.0	366	Berkeley, CA	0.9
221	Austin, TX	3.5	293	Edison Twnshp, NJ	2.0	366	El Monte, CA	0.9
221	League City, TX	3.5	293	El Cajon, CA	2.0	366	Fargo, ND	0.9
221	Midland, TX	3.5	293	Fort Collins, CO	2.0	366	Fremont, CA	0.9
221	Nashua, NH	3.5	293	Round Rock, TX	2.0	366	Gilbert, AZ	0.9
221	Norwalk, CT	3.5	298	Billings, MT	1.9	366	Gresham, OR	0.9
221	Provo, UT	3.5	298	Cape Coral, FL	1.9	366	Irvine, CA	0.9
221	Suffolk, VA	3.5	298	Elk Grove, CA	1.9	366	Rochester, MN	0.9
221	Sunrise, FL	3.5	298	Green Bay, WI	1.9	366	Ventura, CA	0.9
229	Lubbock, TX	3.4	298	Murrieta, CA	1.9	366	West Covina, CA	0.9
229	Madison, WI	3.4	298	Palm Bay, FL	1.9	366	Wichita Falls, TX	0.9
229	Portland, OR	3.4	298	Plano, TX	1.9	378	Bellevue, WA	0.8
229	Virginia Beach, VA	3.4	298	Salem, OR	1.9	378	Chandler, AZ	0.8
233	Lynn, MA	3.3	298	Spokane, WA	1.9	378	Coral Springs, FL	0.8
233	Pasadena, TX	3.3	307	Columbia, MO	1.8	378	Henderson, NV	0.8
233	Redding, CA	3.3	307	Downey, CA	1.8	378	Roseville, CA	0.8
233	Tuscaloosa, AL	3.3	307	Hialeah, FL	1.8	378	Sterling Heights, MI	0.8
233	Westminster, CA	3.3	307	Manchester, NH	1.8	378	Thousand Oaks, CA	0.8
238	Miramar, FL	3.2	307	Norman, OK	1.8	385	Alexandria, VA	0.7
238	Salt Lake City, UT	3.2	307	Scottsdale, AZ	1.8	385	Cary, NC	0.7
238	Seattle, WA	3.2	313	Denton, TX	1.7	385	McKinney, TX	0.7
238	Sioux Falls, SD	3.2	313	Independence, MO	1.7	388	Brownsville, TX	0.6
238	Vacaville, CA	3.2	313	Santa Clara, CA	1.7	389	Boise, ID	0.5
243	Dearborn, MI	3.1	316	Cedar Rapids, IA	1.6	390	Allen, TX	0.0
243	Lewisville, TX	3.1	317	Fullerton, CA	1.5	390	Amherst, NY	0.0
243	Springfield, MO	3.1	317	Lincoln, NE	1.5	390	Ann Arbor, MI	0.0
246	Las Cruces, NM	3.0	319	Mesquite, TX	1.4	390	Beaverton, OR	0.0
246	McAllen, TX	3.0	319	Naperville, IL	1.4	390	Bloomington, MN	0.0
246	Tempe, AZ	3.0	319	Torrance, CA	1.4	390	Boca Raton, FL	0.0
246	Tyler, TX	3.0	322	Baldwin Park, CA	1.3	390	Brick Twnshp, NJ	0.0
246	West Valley, UT	3.0	322	Bend, OR	1.3	390	Broken Arrow, OK	0.0
251	San Diego, CA	2.9	322	Bloomington, IL	1.3	390	Canton Twnshp, MI	0.0
251	Santa Rosa, CA	2.9	322	Carmel, IN	1.3	390	Centennial, CO	0.0
253	High Point, NC	2.8	322	Corona, CA	1.3	390	Chino Hills, CA	0.0
253	Hollywood, FL	2.8	322	Deerfield Beach, FL	1.3	390	Clarkstown, NY	0.0
253	Lowell, MA	2.8	322	Edinburg, TX	1.3	390	Duluth, MN	0.0
253	Santa Clarita, CA	2.8	322	Largo, FL	1.3	390	Eugene, OR	0.0
253	St. Paul, MN	2.8	322	Napa, CA	1.3	390	Fishers, IN	0.0
258	Arlington Heights, IL	2.7	322	Peoria, AZ	1.3	390	Glendale, CA	0.0
258	Aurora, CO	2.7	322	Tustin, CA	1.3	390	Greece, NY	0.0
258	Kennewick, WA	2.7	333	Alhambra, CA	1.2	390	Hamilton Twnshp, NJ	0.0
258	Murfreesboro, TN	2.7	333	Bellingham, WA	1.2	390	Hoover, AL	0.0
262	Bryan, TX	2.6	333	Champaign, IL	1.2	390	Johns Creek, GA	0.0
262	Colonie, NY	2.6	333	Cicero, IL	1.2	390	Kenosha, WI	0.0
262	Lake Forest, CA	2.6	333	Citrus Heights, CA	1.2	390	Lawrence, KS	0.0
262	Menifee, CA	2.6	333	Cranston, RI	1.2	390	Lee's Summit, MO	0.0
262	Meridian, ID	2.6	333	Danbury, CT	1.2	390	Mission Viejo, CA	0.0
262	New Rochelle, NY	2.6	333	Edmond, OK	1.2	390	Nampa, ID	0.0
262	Pembroke Pines, FL	2.6	333	Garden Grove, CA	1.2	390	Newport Beach, CA	0.0
269	Carrollton, TX	2.5	333	Plantation, FL	1.2	390	Newton, MA	0.0
269	Cheektowaga, NY	2.5	333	Sioux City, IA	1.2	390	O'Fallon, MO	0.0
269	Chino, CA	2.5	333	Sugar Land, TX	1.2	390	Orem, UT	0.0
269	Concord, NC	2.5	333	Westland, MI	1.2	390	Ramapo, NY	0.0
269	Evansville, IN	2.5	346	Davie, FL	1.1	390	Redwood City, CA	0.0
269	Farmington Hills, MI	2.5	346	Greeley, CO	1.1	390	Richardson, TX	0.0
269	Fontana, CA	2.5	346	Hillsboro, OR	1.1	390	Rio Rancho, NM	0.0
269	Frisco, TX	2.5	346	Kent, WA	1.1	390	Roswell, GA	0.0
269	Lakewood, CA	2.5	346	Longmont, CO	1.1	390	San Angelo, TX	0.0
269	Lancaster, CA	2.5	346	Overland Park, KS	1.1	390	San Marcos, CA	0.0
269	Mission, TX	2.5	346	Quincy, MA	1.1	390	Santa Barbara, CA	0.0
280	Chula Vista, CA	2.4	346	Renton, WA	1.1	390	Simi Valley, CA	0.0
280	Clifton, NJ	2.4	346	Sandy Springs, GA	1.1	390	Somerville, MA	0.0
280	El Paso, TX	2.4	346	Sandy, UT	1.1	390	Spokane Valley, WA	0.0
280	Ogden, UT	2.4	346	Santa Monica, CA	1.1	390	Surprise, AZ	0.0
284	Fall River, MA	2.2	346	Toms River Twnshp, NJ	1.1	390	Temecula, CA	0.0
284	Garland, TX	2.2	358	Aurora, IL	1.0	390	Thornton, CO	0.0
284	Hesperia, CA	2.2	358	Burbank, CA	1.0	390	Tracy, CA	0.0
284	Orange, CA	2.2	358	Clinton Twnshp, MI	1.0	390	Troy, MI	0.0
288	Escondido, CA	2.1	358	College Station, TX	1.0	390	Vista, CA	0.0
288	Huntington Beach, CA	2.1	358	Daly City, CA	1.0	390	Warwick, RI	0.0
			358	Livonia, MI	1.0	390	West Jordan, UT	0.0

Source: CQ Press using reported data from the F.B.I. "Crime in the United States 2011"
*Includes nonnegligent manslaughter.

Alpha Order - City

51. Percent Change in Murder Rate: 2010 to 2011
National Percent Change = 1.5% Decrease*

RANK	CITY	% CHANGE	RANK	CITY	% CHANGE	RANK	CITY	% CHANGE
97	Abilene, TX	23.5	41	Cheektowaga, NY	92.3	130	Fort Wayne, IN	5.6
93	Akron, OH	27.1	83	Chesapeake, VA	32.5	257	Fort Worth, TX	(25.0)
121	Albany, GA	9.9	135	Chicago, IL	4.6	290	Fremont, CA	(40.0)
47	Albany, NY	86.4	2	Chico, CA	375.0	256	Fresno, CA	(24.7)
241	Albuquerque, NM	(18.2)	362	Chino Hills, CA	(100.0)	NA	Frisco, TX***	NA
298	Alexandria, VA	(46.2)	NA	Chino, CA***	NA	282	Fullerton, CA	(34.8)
340	Alhambra, CA	(65.7)	17	Chula Vista, CA	166.7	72	Gainesville, FL	41.2
145	Allentown, PA	1.2	NA	Cicero, IL**	NA	278	Garden Grove, CA	(33.3)
146	Allen, TX	0.0	146	Cincinnati, OH	0.0	274	Garland, TX	(31.3)
202	Amarillo, TX	(3.8)	353	Citrus Heights, CA	(74.5)	NA	Gary, IN**	NA
362	Amherst, NY	(100.0)	146	Clarkstown, NY	0.0	331	Gilbert, AZ	(60.9)
26	Anaheim, CA	109.5	237	Clarksville, TN	(15.5)	35	Glendale, AZ	95.9
223	Anchorage, AK	(11.1)	36	Clearwater, FL	95.7	146	Glendale, CA	0.0
146	Ann Arbor, MI	0.0	195	Cleveland, OH	(2.1)	27	Grand Prairie, TX	108.3
335	Antioch, CA	(62.2)	NA	Clifton, NJ**	NA	117	Grand Rapids, MI	12.8
NA	Arlington Heights, IL***	NA	356	Clinton Twnshp, MI	(84.1)	362	Greece, NY	(100.0)
74	Arlington, TX	40.5	37	Clovis, CA	95.2	146	Greeley, CO	0.0
146	Arvada, CO	0.0	349	College Station, TX	(70.6)	206	Green Bay, WI	(5.0)
21	Asheville, NC	126.9	NA	Colonie, NY***	NA	358	Gresham, OR	(86.8)
114	Athens-Clarke, GA	15.9	100	Colorado Springs, CO	22.0	362	Hamilton Twnshp, NJ	(100.0)
104	Atlanta, GA	19.7	287	Columbia, MO	(37.9)	236	Hammond, IN	(15.3)
334	Aurora, CO	(62.0)	200	Columbus, GA	(3.7)	277	Hampton, VA	(33.0)
325	Aurora, IL	(56.5)	218	Columbus, OH	(9.8)	138	Hartford, CT	4.3
265	Austin, TX	(27.1)	280	Compton, CA	(34.6)	297	Hawthorne, CA	(44.9)
NA	Avondale, AZ***	NA	51	Concord, CA	72.7	299	Hayward, CA	(46.7)
301	Bakersfield, CA	(48.5)	295	Concord, NC	(43.2)	293	Hemet, CA	(42.2)
303	Baldwin Park, CA	(50.0)	146	Coral Springs, FL	0.0	351	Henderson, NV	(73.3)
220	Baltimore, MD	(10.1)	146	Corona, CA	0.0	204	Hesperia, CA	(4.3)
NA	Baton Rouge, LA**	NA	272	Corpus Christi, TX	(30.4)	343	Hialeah, FL	(67.3)
108	Beaumont, TX	18.7	6	Costa Mesa, CA	300.0	66	High Point, NC	47.4
146	Beaverton, OR	0.0	146	Cranston, RI	0.0	NA	Hillsboro, OR**	NA
NA	Bellevue, WA***	NA	199	Dallas, TX	(3.5)	294	Hollywood, FL	(42.9)
7	Bellflower, CA	271.4	303	Daly City, CA	(50.0)	NA	Hoover, AL**	NA
316	Bellingham, WA	(52.0)	316	Danbury, CT	(52.0)	253	Houston, TX	(22.0)
354	Bend, OR	(79.4)	NA	Davenport, IA**	NA	25	Huntington Beach, CA	110.0
355	Berkeley, CA	(81.6)	339	Davie, FL	(65.6)	NA	Huntsville, AL**	NA
NA	Bethlehem, PA***	NA	136	Dayton, OH	4.5	352	Independence, MO	(74.2)
NA	Billings, MT**	NA	234	Dearborn, MI	(13.9)	NA	Indianapolis, IN**	NA
NA	Birmingham, AL**	NA	19	Decatur, IL	147.2	338	Indio, CA	(65.2)
146	Bloomington, IL	0.0	146	Deerfield Beach, FL	0.0	279	Inglewood, CA	(34.3)
8	Bloomington, IN	250.0	269	Denton, TX	(29.2)	NA	Irvine, CA***	NA
146	Bloomington, MN	0.0	58	Denver, CO	55.6	96	Irving, TX	24.1
362	Boca Raton, FL	(100.0)	86	Des Moines, IA	30.0	227	Jacksonville, FL	(12.4)
342	Boise, ID	(66.7)	76	Detroit, MI	39.7	92	Jackson, MS	27.2
221	Boston, MA	(10.6)	344	Downey, CA	(67.9)	270	Jersey City, NJ	(29.4)
303	Boulder, CO	(50.0)	362	Duluth, MN	(100.0)	146	Johns Creek, GA	0.0
362	Brick Twnshp, NJ	(100.0)	107	Durham, NC	19.4	259	Joliet, IL	(26.0)
229	Bridgeport, CT	(12.7)	315	Edinburg, TX	(51.9)	129	Kansas City, KS	5.7
195	Brockton, MA	(2.1)	146	Edison Twnshp, NJ	0.0	NA	Kansas City, MO**	NA
362	Broken Arrow, OK	(100.0)	146	Edmond, OK	0.0	NA	Kennewick, WA***	NA
NA	Brooklyn Park, MN**	NA	NA	El Cajon, CA***	NA	362	Kenosha, WI	(100.0)
357	Brownsville, TX	(84.6)	336	El Monte, CA	(64.0)	319	Kent, WA	(52.2)
311	Bryan, TX	(50.9)	12	El Paso, TX	200.0	88	Killeen, TX	27.8
NA	Buena Park, CA***	NA	95	Elgin, IL	24.3	113	Knoxville, TN	16.0
NA	Buffalo, NY**	NA	84	Elizabeth, NJ	32.0	321	Lafayette, LA	(52.9)
NA	Burbank, CA***	NA	79	Elk Grove, CA	35.7	NA	Lake Forest, CA***	NA
NA	Cambridge, MA***	NA	302	Erie, PA	(48.7)	316	Lakeland, FL	(52.0)
87	Camden, NJ	29.5	146	Escondido, CA	0.0	333	Lakewood Twnshp, NJ	(61.8)
146	Canton Twnshp, MI	0.0	146	Eugene, OR	0.0	NA	Lakewood, CA**	NA
146	Cape Coral, FL	0.0	292	Evansville, IN	(41.9)	1	Lakewood, CO	685.7
NA	Carlsbad, CA***	NA	203	Everett, WA	(4.0)	300	Lancaster, CA	(46.8)
NA	Carmel, IN***	NA	289	Fairfield, CA	(39.0)	251	Lansing, MI	(21.3)
245	Carrollton, TX	(19.4)	330	Fall River, MA	(60.7)	110	Laredo, TX	17.9
239	Carson, CA	(16.9)	NA	Fargo, ND***	NA	346	Largo, FL	(68.3)
146	Cary, NC	0.0	41	Farmington Hills, MI	92.3	198	Las Cruces, NM	(3.2)
30	Cedar Rapids, IA	100.0	62	Fayetteville, NC	50.0	260	Las Vegas, NV	(26.3)
146	Centennial, CO	0.0	146	Fishers, IN	0.0	146	Lawrence, KS	0.0
NA	Champaign, IL**	NA	134	Flint, MI	4.7	217	Lawrence, MA	(9.7)
345	Chandler, AZ	(68.0)	245	Fontana, CA	(19.4)	18	Lawton, OK	148.5
126	Charleston, SC	7.1	NA	Fort Collins, CO**	NA	16	League City, TX	169.2
210	Charlotte, NC	(6.6)	45	Fort Lauderdale, FL	89.5	362	Lee's Summit, MO	(100.0)
78	Chattanooga, TN	36.5	240	Fort Smith, AR	(17.1)	119	Lewisville, TX	10.7

Alpha Order - City (continued)

RANK	CITY	% CHANGE	RANK	CITY	% CHANGE	RANK	CITY	% CHANGE
NA	Lexington, KY**	NA	NA	Overland Park, KS***	NA	NA	Sioux City, IA***	NA
46	Lincoln, NE	87.5	205	Oxnard, CA	(4.8)	52	Sioux Falls, SD	68.4
68	Little Rock, AR	46.2	314	Palm Bay, FL	(51.3)	146	Somerville, MA	0.0
NA	Livermore, CA***	NA	125	Palmdale, CA	7.4	61	South Bend, IN	53.4
325	Livonia, MI	(56.5)	20	Pasadena, CA	138.1	233	South Gate, CA	(13.7)
255	Long Beach, CA	(23.2)	274	Pasadena, TX	(31.3)	224	Sparks, NV	(11.5)
146	Longmont, CO	0.0	208	Paterson, NJ	(5.7)	362	Spokane Valley, WA	(100.0)
332	Longview, TX	(61.7)	284	Pearland, TX	(36.4)	286	Spokane, WA	(36.7)
144	Los Angeles, CA	1.3	200	Pembroke Pines, FL	(3.7)	116	Springfield, IL	15.0
226	Louisville, KY	(12.2)	341	Peoria, AZ	(65.8)	94	Springfield, MA	25.0
14	Lowell, MA	180.0	266	Peoria, IL	(27.6)	324	Springfield, MO	(55.7)
254	Lubbock, TX	(22.7)	124	Philadelphia, PA	8.2	11	Stamford, CT	206.3
261	Lynchburg, VA	(26.4)	139	Phoenix, AZ	3.9	NA	Sterling Heights, MI**	NA
208	Lynn, MA	(5.7)	243	Pittsburgh, PA	(18.8)	111	Stockton, CA	17.3
296	Macon, GA	(43.3)	79	Plano, TX	35.7	250	St. Joseph, MO	(21.2)
4	Madison, WI	325.0	303	Plantation, FL	(50.0)	230	St. Louis, MO	(12.8)
30	Manchester, NH	100.0	273	Pomona, CA	(30.5)	311	St. Paul, MN	(50.9)
244	McAllen, TX	(18.9)	267	Pompano Beach, FL	(27.9)	53	St. Petersburg, FL	60.4
146	McKinney, TX	0.0	30	Port St. Lucie, FL	100.0	146	Suffolk, VA	0.0
40	Medford, OR	92.7	230	Portland, OR	(12.8)	NA	Sugar Land, TX***	NA
327	Melbourne, FL	(56.7)	225	Portsmouth, VA	(12.1)	NA	Sunnyvale, CA***	NA
81	Memphis, TN	35.6	28	Provo, UT	105.9	55	Sunrise, FL	59.1
NA	Menifee, CA***	NA	NA	Pueblo, CO**	NA	146	Surprise, AZ	0.0
118	Merced, CA	11.1	361	Quincy, MA	(91.0)	276	Syracuse, NY	(31.8)
285	Meridian, ID	(36.6)	283	Racine, WI	(35.1)	252	Tacoma, WA	(21.4)
101	Mesa, AZ	21.2	90	Raleigh, NC	27.3	264	Tallahassee, FL	(27.0)
350	Mesquite, TX	(73.1)	362	Ramapo, NY	(100.0)	133	Tampa, FL	5.1
309	Miami Beach, FL	(50.5)	9	Rancho Cucamon., CA	227.3	362	Temecula, CA	(100.0)
120	Miami Gardens, FL	10.5	105	Reading, PA	19.5	322	Tempe, AZ	(53.1)
122	Miami, FL	9.1	62	Redding, CA	50.0	NA	Thornton, CO**	NA
39	Midland, TX	94.4	362	Redwood City, CA	(100.0)	146	Thousand Oaks, CA	0.0
213	Milwaukee, WI	(8.4)	59	Reno, NV	55.0	69	Toledo, OH	42.5
232	Minneapolis, MN	(13.5)	NA	Renton, WA***	NA	337	Toms River Twnshp, NJ	(64.5)
329	Miramar, FL	(59.5)	237	Rialto, CA	(15.5)	136	Topeka, KS	4.5
146	Mission Viejo, CA	0.0	146	Richardson, TX	0.0	303	Torrance, CA	(50.0)
222	Mission, TX	(10.7)	99	Richmond, CA	22.2	362	Tracy, CA	(100.0)
NA	Mobile, AL**	NA	228	Richmond, VA	(12.6)	62	Trenton, NJ	50.0
73	Modesto, CA	40.8	146	Rio Rancho, NM	0.0	362	Troy, MI	(100.0)
NA	Montgomery, AL**	NA	75	Riverside, CA	40.0	146	Tucson, AZ	0.0
320	Moreno Valley, CA	(52.6)	235	Roanoke, VA	(14.7)	215	Tulsa, OK	(9.5)
291	Murfreesboro, TN	(41.3)	219	Rochester, MN	(10.0)	NA	Tuscaloosa, AL**	NA
43	Murrieta, CA	90.0	263	Rochester, NY	(26.9)	211	Tustin, CA	(7.1)
362	Nampa, ID	(100.0)	143	Rockford, IL	2.2	303	Tyler, TX	(50.0)
146	Napa, CA	0.0	146	Roseville, CA	0.0	270	Upper Darby Twnshp, PA	(29.4)
NA	Naperville, IL**	NA	146	Roswell, GA	0.0	197	Vacaville, CA	(3.0)
13	Nashua, NH	191.7	NA	Round Rock, TX***	NA	142	Vallejo, CA	2.7
212	Nashville, TN	(7.9)	123	Sacramento, CA	8.6	NA	Vancouver, WA***	NA
90	New Bedford, MA	27.3	10	Salem, OR	216.7	347	Ventura, CA	(69.0)
71	New Haven, CT	42.4	257	Salinas, CA	(25.0)	146	Victorville, CA	0.0
111	New Orleans, LA	17.3	268	Salt Lake City, UT	(28.9)	127	Virginia Beach, VA	6.3
48	New Rochelle, NY	85.7	362	San Angelo, TX	(100.0)	82	Visalia, CA	33.3
194	New York, NY	(1.6)	115	San Antonio, TX	15.8	362	Vista, CA	(100.0)
131	Newark, NJ	5.3	216	San Bernardino, CA	(9.6)	23	Waco, TX	120.5
146	Newport Beach, CA	0.0	85	San Diego, CA	31.8	109	Warren, MI	18.4
247	Newport News, VA	(19.6)	140	San Francisco, CA	3.4	146	Warwick, RI	0.0
146	Newton, MA	0.0	37	San Jose, CA	95.2	249	Washington, DC	(20.1)
242	Norfolk, VA	(18.6)	56	San Leandro, CA	58.8	77	Waterbury, CT	37.0
146	Norman, OK	0.0	362	San Marcos, CA	(100.0)	NA	West Covina, CA***	NA
328	North Charleston, SC	(57.9)	214	San Mateo, CA	(9.1)	362	West Jordan, UT	(100.0)
103	Norwalk, CA	20.5	359	Sandy Springs, GA	(86.9)	262	West Palm Beach, FL	(26.6)
310	Norwalk, CT	(50.7)	146	Sandy, UT	0.0	288	West Valley, UT	(38.8)
105	Oakland, CA	19.5	313	Santa Ana, CA	(51.2)	348	Westland, MI	(70.0)
50	Oceanside, CA	78.3	362	Santa Barbara, CA	(100.0)	62	Westminster, CA	50.0
34	Odessa, TX	96.7	207	Santa Clara, CA	(5.6)	5	Westminster, CO	311.1
146	O'Fallon, MO	0.0	3	Santa Clarita, CA	366.7	49	Whittier, CA	84.0
30	Ogden, UT	100.0	29	Santa Maria, CA	102.9	360	Wichita Falls, TX	(87.1)
131	Oklahoma City, OK	5.3	146	Santa Monica, CA	0.0	60	Wichita, KS	54.8
67	Olathe, KS	46.9	22	Santa Rosa, CA	123.1	44	Wilmington, NC	89.8
69	Omaha, NE	42.5	102	Savannah, GA	21.1	89	Winston-Salem, NC	27.7
24	Ontario, CA	111.8	128	Scottsdale, AZ	5.9	146	Woodbridge Twnshp, NJ	0.0
146	Orange, CA	0.0	15	Scranton, PA	178.6	57	Worcester, MA	57.9
362	Orem, UT	(100.0)	141	Seattle, WA	3.2	323	Yakima, WA	(53.6)
54	Orlando, FL	60.0	280	Shreveport, LA	(34.6)	248	Yonkers, NY	(20.0)
			362	Simi Valley, CA	(100.0)	97	Yuma, AZ	23.5

Source: CQ Press using reported data from the F.B.I. "Crime in the United States 2011"
*Includes nonnegligent manslaughter. **Not available. ***These cities had murder rates of 0 in 2010 but had at least one murder in 2011. Calculating percent increase from zero results in an infinite number. These are shown as "NA."

Rank Order - City

51. Percent Change in Murder Rate: 2010 to 2011 (continued)
National Percent Change = 1.5% Decrease*

RANK	CITY	% CHANGE	RANK	CITY	% CHANGE	RANK	CITY	% CHANGE
1	Lakewood, CO	685.7	73	Modesto, CA	40.8	145	Allentown, PA	1.2
2	Chico, CA	375.0	74	Arlington, TX	40.5	146	Allen, TX	0.0
3	Santa Clarita, CA	366.7	75	Riverside, CA	40.0	146	Ann Arbor, MI	0.0
4	Madison, WI	325.0	76	Detroit, MI	39.7	146	Arvada, CO	0.0
5	Westminster, CO	311.1	77	Waterbury, CT	37.0	146	Beaverton, OR	0.0
6	Costa Mesa, CA	300.0	78	Chattanooga, TN	36.5	146	Bloomington, IL	0.0
7	Bellflower, CA	271.4	79	Elk Grove, CA	35.7	146	Bloomington, MN	0.0
8	Bloomington, IN	250.0	79	Plano, TX	35.7	146	Canton Twnshp, MI	0.0
9	Rancho Cucamon., CA	227.3	81	Memphis, TN	35.6	146	Cape Coral, FL	0.0
10	Salem, OR	216.7	82	Visalia, CA	33.3	146	Cary, NC	0.0
11	Stamford, CT	206.3	83	Chesapeake, VA	32.5	146	Centennial, CO	0.0
12	El Paso, TX	200.0	84	Elizabeth, NJ	32.0	146	Cincinnati, OH	0.0
13	Nashua, NH	191.7	85	San Diego, CA	31.8	146	Clarkstown, NY	0.0
14	Lowell, MA	180.0	86	Des Moines, IA	30.0	146	Coral Springs, FL	0.0
15	Scranton, PA	178.6	87	Camden, NJ	29.5	146	Corona, CA	0.0
16	League City, TX	169.2	88	Killeen, TX	27.8	146	Cranston, RI	0.0
17	Chula Vista, CA	166.7	89	Winston-Salem, NC	27.7	146	Deerfield Beach, FL	0.0
18	Lawton, OK	148.5	90	New Bedford, MA	27.3	146	Edison Twnshp, NJ	0.0
19	Decatur, IL	147.2	90	Raleigh, NC	27.3	146	Edmond, OK	0.0
20	Pasadena, CA	138.1	92	Jackson, MS	27.2	146	Escondido, CA	0.0
21	Asheville, NC	126.9	93	Akron, OH	27.1	146	Eugene, OR	0.0
22	Santa Rosa, CA	123.1	94	Springfield, MA	25.0	146	Fishers, IN	0.0
23	Waco, TX	120.5	95	Elgin, IL	24.3	146	Glendale, CA	0.0
24	Ontario, CA	111.8	96	Irving, TX	24.1	146	Greeley, CO	0.0
25	Huntington Beach, CA	110.0	97	Abilene, TX	23.5	146	Johns Creek, GA	0.0
26	Anaheim, CA	109.5	97	Yuma, AZ	23.5	146	Lawrence, KS	0.0
27	Grand Prairie, TX	108.3	99	Richmond, CA	22.2	146	Longmont, CO	0.0
28	Provo, UT	105.9	100	Colorado Springs, CO	22.0	146	McKinney, TX	0.0
29	Santa Maria, CA	102.9	101	Mesa, AZ	21.2	146	Mission Viejo, CA	0.0
30	Cedar Rapids, IA	100.0	102	Savannah, GA	21.1	146	Napa, CA	0.0
30	Manchester, NH	100.0	103	Norwalk, CA	20.5	146	Newport Beach, CA	0.0
30	Ogden, UT	100.0	104	Atlanta, GA	19.7	146	Newton, MA	0.0
30	Port St. Lucie, FL	100.0	105	Oakland, CA	19.5	146	Norman, OK	0.0
34	Odessa, TX	96.7	105	Reading, PA	19.5	146	O'Fallon, MO	0.0
35	Glendale, AZ	95.9	107	Durham, NC	19.4	146	Orange, CA	0.0
36	Clearwater, FL	95.7	108	Beaumont, TX	18.7	146	Richardson, TX	0.0
37	Clovis, CA	95.2	109	Warren, MI	18.4	146	Rio Rancho, NM	0.0
37	San Jose, CA	95.2	110	Laredo, TX	17.9	146	Roseville, CA	0.0
39	Midland, TX	94.4	111	New Orleans, LA	17.3	146	Roswell, GA	0.0
40	Medford, OR	92.7	111	Stockton, CA	17.3	146	Sandy, UT	0.0
41	Cheektowaga, NY	92.3	113	Knoxville, TN	16.0	146	Santa Monica, CA	0.0
41	Farmington Hills, MI	92.3	114	Athens-Clarke, GA	15.9	146	Somerville, MA	0.0
43	Murrieta, CA	90.0	115	San Antonio, TX	15.8	146	Suffolk, VA	0.0
44	Wilmington, NC	89.8	116	Springfield, IL	15.0	146	Surprise, AZ	0.0
45	Fort Lauderdale, FL	89.5	117	Grand Rapids, MI	12.8	146	Thousand Oaks, CA	0.0
46	Lincoln, NE	87.5	118	Merced, CA	11.1	146	Tucson, AZ	0.0
47	Albany, NY	86.4	119	Lewisville, TX	10.7	146	Victorville, CA	0.0
48	New Rochelle, NY	85.7	120	Miami Gardens, FL	10.5	146	Warwick, RI	0.0
49	Whittier, CA	84.0	121	Albany, GA	9.9	146	Woodbridge Twnshp, NJ	0.0
50	Oceanside, CA	78.3	122	Miami, FL	9.1	194	New York, NY	(1.6)
51	Concord, CA	72.7	123	Sacramento, CA	8.6	195	Brockton, MA	(2.1)
52	Sioux Falls, SD	68.4	124	Philadelphia, PA	8.2	195	Cleveland, OH	(2.1)
53	St. Petersburg, FL	60.4	125	Palmdale, CA	7.4	197	Vacaville, CA	(3.0)
54	Orlando, FL	60.0	126	Charleston, SC	7.1	198	Las Cruces, NM	(3.2)
55	Sunrise, FL	59.1	127	Virginia Beach, VA	6.3	199	Dallas, TX	(3.5)
56	San Leandro, CA	58.8	128	Scottsdale, AZ	5.9	200	Columbus, GA	(3.7)
57	Worcester, MA	57.9	129	Kansas City, KS	5.7	200	Pembroke Pines, FL	(3.7)
58	Denver, CO	55.6	130	Fort Wayne, IN	5.6	202	Amarillo, TX	(3.8)
59	Reno, NV	55.0	131	Newark, NJ	5.3	203	Everett, WA	(4.0)
60	Wichita, KS	54.8	131	Oklahoma City, OK	5.3	204	Hesperia, CA	(4.3)
61	South Bend, IN	53.4	133	Tampa, FL	5.1	205	Oxnard, CA	(4.8)
62	Fayetteville, NC	50.0	134	Flint, MI	4.7	206	Green Bay, WI	(5.0)
62	Redding, CA	50.0	135	Chicago, IL	4.6	207	Santa Clara, CA	(5.6)
62	Trenton, NJ	50.0	136	Dayton, OH	4.5	208	Lynn, MA	(5.7)
62	Westminster, CA	50.0	136	Topeka, KS	4.5	208	Paterson, NJ	(5.7)
66	High Point, NC	47.4	138	Hartford, CT	4.3	210	Charlotte, NC	(6.6)
67	Olathe, KS	46.9	139	Phoenix, AZ	3.9	211	Tustin, CA	(7.1)
68	Little Rock, AR	46.2	140	San Francisco, CA	3.4	212	Nashville, TN	(7.9)
69	Omaha, NE	42.5	141	Seattle, WA	3.2	213	Milwaukee, WI	(8.4)
69	Toledo, OH	42.5	142	Vallejo, CA	2.7	214	San Mateo, CA	(9.1)
71	New Haven, CT	42.4	143	Rockford, IL	2.2	215	Tulsa, OK	(9.5)
72	Gainesville, FL	41.2	144	Los Angeles, CA	1.3	216	San Bernardino, CA	(9.6)

Rank Order - City (continued)

RANK	CITY	% CHANGE	RANK	CITY	% CHANGE	RANK	CITY	% CHANGE
217	Lawrence, MA	(9.7)	290	Fremont, CA	(40.0)	362	Brick Twnshp, NJ	(100.0)
218	Columbus, OH	(9.8)	291	Murfreesboro, TN	(41.3)	362	Broken Arrow, OK	(100.0)
219	Rochester, MN	(10.0)	292	Evansville, IN	(41.9)	362	Chino Hills, CA	(100.0)
220	Baltimore, MD	(10.1)	293	Hemet, CA	(42.2)	362	Duluth, MN	(100.0)
221	Boston, MA	(10.6)	294	Hollywood, FL	(42.9)	362	Greece, NY	(100.0)
222	Mission, TX	(10.7)	295	Concord, NC	(43.2)	362	Hamilton Twnshp, NJ	(100.0)
223	Anchorage, AK	(11.1)	296	Macon, GA	(43.3)	362	Kenosha, WI	(100.0)
224	Sparks, NV	(11.5)	297	Hawthorne, CA	(44.9)	362	Lee's Summit, MO	(100.0)
225	Portsmouth, VA	(12.1)	298	Alexandria, VA	(46.2)	362	Nampa, ID	(100.0)
226	Louisville, KY	(12.2)	299	Hayward, CA	(46.7)	362	Orem, UT	(100.0)
227	Jacksonville, FL	(12.4)	300	Lancaster, CA	(46.8)	362	Ramapo, NY	(100.0)
228	Richmond, VA	(12.6)	301	Bakersfield, CA	(48.5)	362	Redwood City, CA	(100.0)
229	Bridgeport, CT	(12.7)	302	Erie, PA	(48.7)	362	San Angelo, TX	(100.0)
230	Portland, OR	(12.8)	303	Baldwin Park, CA	(50.0)	362	San Marcos, CA	(100.0)
230	St. Louis, MO	(12.8)	303	Boulder, CO	(50.0)	362	Santa Barbara, CA	(100.0)
232	Minneapolis, MN	(13.5)	303	Daly City, CA	(50.0)	362	Simi Valley, CA	(100.0)
233	South Gate, CA	(13.7)	303	Plantation, FL	(50.0)	362	Spokane Valley, WA	(100.0)
234	Dearborn, MI	(13.9)	303	Torrance, CA	(50.0)	362	Temecula, CA	(100.0)
235	Roanoke, VA	(14.7)	303	Tyler, TX	(50.0)	362	Tracy, CA	(100.0)
236	Hammond, IN	(15.3)	309	Miami Beach, FL	(50.5)	362	Troy, MI	(100.0)
237	Clarksville, TN	(15.5)	310	Norwalk, CT	(50.7)	362	Vista, CA	(100.0)
237	Rialto, CA	(15.5)	311	Bryan, TX	(50.9)	362	West Jordan, UT	(100.0)
239	Carson, CA	(16.9)	311	St. Paul, MN	(50.9)	NA	Arlington Heights, IL***	NA
240	Fort Smith, AR	(17.1)	313	Santa Ana, CA	(51.2)	NA	Avondale, AZ***	NA
241	Albuquerque, NM	(18.2)	314	Palm Bay, FL	(51.3)	NA	Baton Rouge, LA**	NA
242	Norfolk, VA	(18.6)	315	Edinburg, TX	(51.9)	NA	Bellevue, WA***	NA
243	Pittsburgh, PA	(18.8)	316	Bellingham, WA	(52.0)	NA	Bethlehem, PA***	NA
244	McAllen, TX	(18.9)	316	Danbury, CT	(52.0)	NA	Billings, MT**	NA
245	Carrollton, TX	(19.4)	316	Lakeland, FL	(52.0)	NA	Birmingham, AL**	NA
245	Fontana, CA	(19.4)	319	Kent, WA	(52.2)	NA	Brooklyn Park, MN**	NA
247	Newport News, VA	(19.6)	320	Moreno Valley, CA	(52.6)	NA	Buena Park, CA***	NA
248	Yonkers, NY	(20.0)	321	Lafayette, LA	(52.9)	NA	Buffalo, NY**	NA
249	Washington, DC	(20.1)	322	Tempe, AZ	(53.1)	NA	Burbank, CA***	NA
250	St. Joseph, MO	(21.2)	323	Yakima, WA	(53.6)	NA	Cambridge, MA***	NA
251	Lansing, MI	(21.3)	324	Springfield, MO	(55.7)	NA	Carlsbad, CA***	NA
252	Tacoma, WA	(21.4)	325	Aurora, IL	(56.5)	NA	Carmel, IN***	NA
253	Houston, TX	(22.0)	325	Livonia, MI	(56.5)	NA	Champaign, IL**	NA
254	Lubbock, TX	(22.7)	327	Melbourne, FL	(56.7)	NA	Chino, CA***	NA
255	Long Beach, CA	(23.2)	328	North Charleston, SC	(57.9)	NA	Cicero, IL**	NA
256	Fresno, CA	(24.7)	329	Miramar, FL	(59.5)	NA	Clifton, NJ**	NA
257	Fort Worth, TX	(25.0)	330	Fall River, MA	(60.7)	NA	Colonie, NY**	NA
257	Salinas, CA	(25.0)	331	Gilbert, AZ	(60.9)	NA	Davenport, IA**	NA
259	Joliet, IL	(26.0)	332	Longview, TX	(61.7)	NA	El Cajon, CA***	NA
260	Las Vegas, NV	(26.3)	333	Lakewood Twnshp, NJ	(61.8)	NA	Fargo, ND***	NA
261	Lynchburg, VA	(26.4)	334	Aurora, CO	(62.0)	NA	Fort Collins, CO**	NA
262	West Palm Beach, FL	(26.6)	335	Antioch, CA	(62.2)	NA	Frisco, TX***	NA
263	Rochester, NY	(26.9)	336	El Monte, CA	(64.0)	NA	Gary, IN**	NA
264	Tallahassee, FL	(27.0)	337	Toms River Twnshp, NJ	(64.5)	NA	Hillsboro, OR**	NA
265	Austin, TX	(27.1)	338	Indio, CA	(65.2)	NA	Hoover, AL**	NA
266	Peoria, IL	(27.6)	339	Davie, FL	(65.6)	NA	Huntsville, AL**	NA
267	Pompano Beach, FL	(27.9)	340	Alhambra, CA	(65.7)	NA	Indianapolis, IN**	NA
268	Salt Lake City, UT	(28.9)	341	Peoria, AZ	(65.8)	NA	Irvine, CA***	NA
269	Denton, TX	(29.2)	342	Boise, ID	(66.7)	NA	Kansas City, MO**	NA
270	Jersey City, NJ	(29.4)	343	Hialeah, FL	(67.3)	NA	Kennewick, WA***	NA
270	Upper Darby Twnshp, PA	(29.4)	344	Downey, CA	(67.9)	NA	Lake Forest, CA***	NA
272	Corpus Christi, TX	(30.4)	345	Chandler, AZ	(68.0)	NA	Lakewood, CA**	NA
273	Pomona, CA	(30.5)	346	Largo, FL	(68.3)	NA	Lexington, KY**	NA
274	Garland, TX	(31.3)	347	Ventura, CA	(69.0)	NA	Livermore, CA***	NA
274	Pasadena, TX	(31.3)	348	Westland, MI	(70.0)	NA	Menifee, CA***	NA
276	Syracuse, NY	(31.8)	349	College Station, TX	(70.6)	NA	Mobile, AL**	NA
277	Hampton, VA	(33.0)	350	Mesquite, TX	(73.1)	NA	Montgomery, AL**	NA
278	Garden Grove, CA	(33.3)	351	Henderson, NV	(73.3)	NA	Naperville, IL**	NA
279	Inglewood, CA	(34.3)	352	Independence, MO	(74.2)	NA	Overland Park, KS***	NA
280	Compton, CA	(34.6)	353	Citrus Heights, CA	(74.5)	NA	Pueblo, CO**	NA
280	Shreveport, LA	(34.6)	354	Bend, OR	(79.4)	NA	Renton, WA***	NA
282	Fullerton, CA	(34.8)	355	Berkeley, CA	(81.6)	NA	Round Rock, TX***	NA
283	Racine, WI	(35.1)	356	Clinton Twnshp, MI	(84.1)	NA	Sioux City, IA***	NA
284	Pearland, TX	(36.4)	357	Brownsville, TX	(84.6)	NA	Sterling Heights, MI**	NA
285	Meridian, ID	(36.6)	358	Gresham, OR	(86.8)	NA	Sugar Land, TX***	NA
286	Spokane, WA	(36.7)	359	Sandy Springs, GA	(86.9)	NA	Sunnyvale, CA***	NA
287	Columbia, MO	(37.9)	360	Wichita Falls, TX	(87.1)	NA	Thornton, CO**	NA
288	West Valley, UT	(38.8)	361	Quincy, MA	(91.0)	NA	Tuscaloosa, AL**	NA
289	Fairfield, CA	(39.0)	362	Amherst, NY	(100.0)	NA	Vancouver, WA***	NA
			362	Boca Raton, FL	(100.0)	NA	West Covina, CA***	NA

Source: CQ Press using reported data from the F.B.I. "Crime in the United States 2011"
*Includes nonnegligent manslaughter. **Not available. ***These cities had murder rates of 0 in 2010 but had at least one murder in 2011. Calculating percent increase from zero results in an infinite number. These are shown as "NA."

Alpha Order - City

52. Percent Change in Murder Rate: 2007 to 2011
National Percent Change = 17.4% Decrease*

RANK	CITY	% CHANGE	RANK	CITY	% CHANGE	RANK	CITY	% CHANGE
271	Abilene, TX	(46.8)	NA	Cheektowaga, NY***	NA	130	Fort Wayne, IN	(3.1)
65	Akron, OH	29.5	124	Chesapeake, VA	(1.9)	202	Fort Worth, TX	(26.7)
87	Albany, GA	3.8	94	Chicago, IL	1.3	319	Fremont, CA	(64.0)
67	Albany, NY	28.1	56	Chico, CA	42.5	232	Fresno, CA	(36.4)
214	Albuquerque, NM	(31.5)	354	Chino Hills, CA	(100.0)	19	Frisco, TX	127.3
351	Alexandria, VA	(86.3)	NA	Chino, CA***	NA	312	Fullerton, CA	(59.5)
78	Alhambra, CA	9.1	228	Chula Vista, CA	(35.1)	86	Gainesville, FL	4.3
301	Allentown, PA	(54.8)	NA	Cicero, IL**	NA	334	Garden Grove, CA	(75.0)
95	Allen, TX	0.0	80	Cincinnati, OH	7.9	213	Garland, TX	(31.3)
281	Amarillo, TX	(49.5)	NA	Citrus Heights, CA**	NA	280	Gary, IN	(49.2)
354	Amherst, NY	(100.0)	95	Clarkstown, NY	0.0	40	Gilbert, AZ	80.0
164	Anaheim, CA	(13.7)	197	Clarksville, TN	(24.1)	47	Glendale, AZ	60.0
275	Anchorage, AK	(48.1)	120	Clearwater, FL	(1.1)	354	Glendale, CA	(100.0)
95	Ann Arbor, MI	0.0	148	Cleveland, OH	(9.3)	63	Grand Prairie, TX	31.6
289	Antioch, CA	(51.0)	NA	Clifton, NJ***	NA	279	Grand Rapids, MI	(49.0)
NA	Arlington Heights, IL**	NA	324	Clinton Twnshp, MI	(67.7)	95	Greece, NY	0.0
45	Arlington, TX	68.6	NA	Clovis, CA***	NA	334	Greeley, CO	(75.0)
348	Arvada, CO	(84.2)	196	College Station, TX	(23.1)	134	Green Bay, WI	(5.0)
309	Asheville, NC	(56.9)	25	Colonie, NY	100.0	151	Gresham, OR	(10.0)
177	Athens-Clarke, GA	(17.7)	169	Colorado Springs, CO	(15.3)	95	Hamilton Twnshp, NJ	0.0
182	Atlanta, GA	(20.1)	256	Columbia, MO	(41.9)	257	Hammond, IN	(42.5)
255	Aurora, CO	(41.3)	242	Columbus, GA	(38.6)	48	Hampton, VA	54.8
350	Aurora, IL	(85.5)	90	Columbus, OH	2.8	161	Hartford, CT	(13.3)
171	Austin, TX	(16.7)	301	Compton, CA	(54.8)	282	Hawthorne, CA	(49.6)
NA	Avondale, AZ**	NA	17	Concord, CA	128.0	170	Hayward, CA	(15.8)
79	Bakersfield, CA	8.5	338	Concord, NC	(77.5)	50	Hemet, CA	50.0
352	Baldwin Park, CA	(87.1)	320	Coral Springs, FL	(65.2)	339	Henderson, NV	(77.8)
209	Baltimore, MD	(30.8)	314	Corona, CA	(60.6)	316	Hesperia, CA	(62.1)
156	Baton Rouge, LA	(11.3)	223	Corpus Christi, TX	(33.9)	263	Hialeah, FL	(43.8)
184	Beaumont, TX	(21.2)	NA	Costa Mesa, CA***	NA	342	High Point, NC	(78.6)
95	Beaverton, OR	0.0	NA	Cranston, RI***	NA	NA	Hillsboro, OR***	NA
NA	Bellevue, WA***	NA	217	Dallas, TX	(32.3)	327	Hollywood, FL	(68.5)
192	Bellflower, CA	(22.4)	NA	Daly City, CA***	NA	NA	Hoover, AL**	NA
297	Bellingham, WA	(53.8)	293	Danbury, CT	(52.0)	261	Houston, TX	(43.2)
NA	Bend, OR***	NA	NA	Davenport, IA**	NA	NA	Huntington Beach, CA***	NA
346	Berkeley, CA	(81.6)	95	Davie, FL	0.0	NA	Huntsville, AL**	NA
290	Bethlehem, PA	(51.2)	66	Dayton, OH	29.4	332	Independence, MO	(73.4)
NA	Billings, MT**	NA	7	Dearborn, MI	181.8	181	Indianapolis, IN	(19.6)
NA	Birmingham, AL**	NA	NA	Decatur, IL**	NA	46	Indio, CA	62.5
NA	Bloomington, IL**	NA	334	Deerfield Beach, FL	(75.0)	207	Inglewood, CA	(29.1)
3	Bloomington, IN	226.7	135	Denton, TX	(5.6)	303	Irvine, CA	(55.0)
95	Bloomington, MN	0.0	215	Denver, CO	(31.7)	187	Irving, TX	(21.7)
354	Boca Raton, FL	(100.0)	34	Des Moines, IA	85.7	266	Jacksonville, FL	(44.8)
353	Boise, ID	(90.0)	83	Detroit, MI	5.2	74	Jackson, MS	14.1
144	Boston, MA	(8.2)	219	Downey, CA	(33.3)	161	Jersey City, NJ	(13.3)
38	Boulder, CO	81.8	354	Duluth, MN	(100.0)	NA	Johns Creek, GA**	NA
95	Brick Twnshp, NJ	0.0	NA	Durham, NC**	NA	157	Joliet, IL	(11.5)
60	Bridgeport, CT	35.3	139	Edinburg, TX	(7.1)	62	Kansas City, KS	32.4
178	Brockton, MA	(18.8)	NA	Edison Twnshp, NJ***	NA	NA	Kansas City, MO**	NA
354	Broken Arrow, OK	(100.0)	297	Edmond, OK	(53.8)	44	Kennewick, WA	68.8
49	Brooklyn Park, MN	51.2	300	El Cajon, CA	(54.5)	354	Kenosha, WI	(100.0)
342	Brownsville, TX	(78.6)	345	El Monte, CA	(81.3)	337	Kent, WA	(77.1)
307	Bryan, TX	(55.9)	166	El Paso, TX	(14.3)	95	Killeen, TX	0.0
127	Buena Park, CA	(2.6)	11	Elgin, IL	142.1	231	Knoxville, TN	(36.1)
NA	Buffalo, NY**	NA	82	Elizabeth, NJ	7.1	317	Lafayette, LA	(62.6)
321	Burbank, CA	(65.5)	59	Elk Grove, CA	35.7	25	Lake Forest, CA	100.0
NA	Cambridge, MA***	NA	23	Erie, PA	103.4	141	Lakeland, FL	(7.6)
75	Camden, NJ	13.9	208	Escondido, CA	(30.0)	290	Lakewood Twnshp, NJ	(51.2)
354	Canton Twnshp, MI	(100.0)	354	Eugene, OR	(100.0)	283	Lakewood, CA	(50.0)
243	Cape Coral, FL	(38.7)	53	Evansville, IN	47.1	1	Lakewood, CO	685.7
39	Carlsbad, CA	81.0	218	Everett, WA	(32.4)	330	Lancaster, CA	(69.9)
178	Carmel, IN	(18.8)	205	Fairfield, CA	(28.8)	288	Lansing, MI	(50.4)
246	Carrollton, TX	(39.0)	NA	Fall River, MA**	NA	91	Laredo, TX	2.2
325	Carson, CA	(68.2)	331	Fargo, ND	(72.7)	344	Largo, FL	(80.9)
189	Cary, NC	(22.2)	NA	Farmington Hills, MI***	NA	307	Las Cruces, NM	(55.9)
219	Cedar Rapids, IA	(33.3)	126	Fayetteville, NC	(2.4)	237	Las Vegas, NV	(37.1)
95	Centennial, CO	0.0	95	Fishers, IN	0.0	95	Lawrence, KS	0.0
NA	Champaign, IL**	NA	31	Flint, MI	96.1	16	Lawrence, MA	128.1
339	Chandler, AZ	(77.8)	265	Fontana, CA	(44.4)	184	Lawton, OK	(21.2)
222	Charleston, SC	(33.6)	10	Fort Collins, CO	150.0	NA	League City, TX***	NA
215	Charlotte, NC	(31.7)	268	Fort Lauderdale, FL	(45.9)	95	Lee's Summit, MO	0.0
25	Chattanooga, TN	100.0	131	Fort Smith, AR	(3.3)	5	Lewisville, TX	210.0

Alpha Order - City (continued)

RANK	CITY	% CHANGE
NA	Lexington, KY**	NA
249	Lincoln, NE	(40.0)
212	Little Rock, AR	(31.2)
6	Livermore, CA	208.3
95	Livonia, MI	0.0
250	Long Beach, CA	(40.4)
NA	Longmont, CO**	NA
199	Longview, TX	(24.6)
198	Los Angeles, CA	(24.5)
234	Louisville, KY	(36.8)
132	Lowell, MA	(3.4)
292	Lubbock, TX	(51.4)
9	Lynchburg, VA	160.0
318	Lynn, MA	(63.7)
251	Macon, GA	(40.7)
129	Madison, WI	(2.9)
NA	Manchester, NH**	NA
227	McAllen, TX	(34.8)
159	McKinney, TX	(12.5)
NA	Medford, OR***	NA
50	Melbourne, FL	50.0
137	Memphis, TN	(6.3)
NA	Menifee, CA**	NA
77	Merced, CA	11.1
NA	Meridian, ID***	NA
171	Mesa, AZ	(16.7)
328	Mesquite, TX	(68.9)
125	Miami Beach, FL	(2.2)
147	Miami Gardens, FL	(9.1)
158	Miami, FL	(11.6)
153	Midland, TX	(10.3)
192	Milwaukee, WI	(22.4)
225	Minneapolis, MN	(34.6)
274	Miramar, FL	(47.5)
95	Mission Viejo, CA	0.0
171	Mission, TX	(16.7)
NA	Mobile, AL**	NA
64	Modesto, CA	30.2
NA	Montgomery, AL**	NA
273	Moreno Valley, CA	(47.1)
230	Murfreesboro, TN	(35.7)
243	Murrieta, CA	(38.7)
354	Nampa, ID	(100.0)
323	Napa, CA	(67.5)
95	Naperville, IL	0.0
NA	Nashua, NH**	NA
232	Nashville, TN	(36.4)
33	New Bedford, MA	90.9
NA	New Haven, CT**	NA
247	New Orleans, LA	(39.2)
34	New Rochelle, NY	85.7
84	New York, NY	5.0
146	Newark, NJ	(8.9)
354	Newport Beach, CA	(100.0)
275	Newport News, VA	(48.1)
95	Newton, MA	0.0
264	Norfolk, VA	(44.1)
297	Norman, OK	(53.8)
347	North Charleston, SC	(82.7)
176	Norwalk, CA	(17.5)
128	Norwalk, CT	(2.8)
160	Oakland, CA	(13.2)
18	Oceanside, CA	127.8
137	Odessa, TX	(6.3)
95	O'Fallon, MO	0.0
234	Ogden, UT	(36.8)
140	Oklahoma City, OK	(7.5)
NA	Olathe, KS**	NA
81	Omaha, NE	7.2
310	Ontario, CA	(57.6)
4	Orange, CA	214.3
354	Orem, UT	(100.0)
211	Orlando, FL	(31.0)

RANK	CITY	% CHANGE
145	Overland Park, KS	(8.3)
171	Oxnard, CA	(16.7)
315	Palm Bay, FL	(62.0)
200	Palmdale, CA	(24.7)
224	Pasadena, CA	(34.2)
14	Pasadena, TX	135.7
69	Paterson, NJ	22.1
189	Pearland, TX	(22.2)
NA	Pembroke Pines, FL***	NA
326	Peoria, AZ	(68.3)
122	Peoria, IL	(1.4)
191	Philadelphia, PA	(22.3)
258	Phoenix, AZ	(42.8)
168	Pittsburgh, PA	(14.4)
12	Plano, TX	137.5
333	Plantation, FL	(73.9)
311	Pomona, CA	(58.0)
278	Pompano Beach, FL	(48.4)
8	Port St. Lucie, FL	176.9
175	Portland, OR	(17.1)
201	Portsmouth, VA	(26.2)
NA	Provo, UT***	NA
NA	Pueblo, CO**	NA
283	Quincy, MA	(50.0)
204	Racine, WI	(28.4)
219	Raleigh, NC	(33.3)
95	Ramapo, NY	0.0
22	Rancho Cucamon., CA	111.8
29	Reading, PA	98.6
NA	Redding, CA***	NA
354	Redwood City, CA	(100.0)
186	Reno, NV	(21.5)
229	Renton, WA	(35.3)
313	Rialto, CA	(59.7)
354	Richardson, TX	(100.0)
269	Richmond, CA	(46.0)
225	Richmond, VA	(34.6)
354	Rio Rancho, NM	(100.0)
84	Riverside, CA	5.0
37	Roanoke, VA	84.1
303	Rochester, MN	(55.0)
248	Rochester, NY	(39.3)
92	Rockford, IL	1.5
155	Roseville, CA	(11.1)
354	Roswell, GA	(100.0)
25	Round Rock, TX	100.0
183	Sacramento, CA	(20.8)
95	Salem, OR	0.0
89	Salinas, CA	3.1
322	Salt Lake City, UT	(66.3)
354	San Angelo, TX	(100.0)
206	San Antonio, TX	(29.0)
237	San Bernardino, CA	(37.1)
241	San Diego, CA	(38.3)
305	San Francisco, CA	(55.1)
72	San Jose, CA	17.1
NA	San Leandro, CA***	NA
354	San Marcos, CA	(100.0)
NA	San Mateo, CA***	NA
349	Sandy Springs, GA	(84.3)
95	Sandy, UT	0.0
254	Santa Ana, CA	(41.2)
354	Santa Barbara, CA	(100.0)
236	Santa Clara, CA	(37.0)
2	Santa Clarita, CA	366.7
30	Santa Maria, CA	97.1
294	Santa Monica, CA	(52.2)
76	Santa Rosa, CA	11.5
142	Savannah, GA	(8.0)
166	Scottsdale, AZ	(14.3)
58	Scranton, PA	39.3
188	Seattle, WA	(22.0)
296	Shreveport, LA	(52.8)
354	Simi Valley, CA	(100.0)

RANK	CITY	% CHANGE
283	Sioux City, IA	(50.0)
15	Sioux Falls, SD	128.6
354	Somerville, MA	(100.0)
61	South Bend, IN	32.8
209	South Gate, CA	(30.8)
21	Sparks, NV	120.0
95	Spokane Valley, WA	0.0
328	Spokane, WA	(68.9)
92	Springfield, IL	1.5
123	Springfield, MA	(1.5)
136	Springfield, MO	(6.1)
32	Stamford, CT	96.0
NA	Sterling Heights, MI**	NA
24	Stockton, CA	101.0
34	St. Joseph, MO	85.7
154	St. Louis, MO	(10.9)
270	St. Paul, MN	(46.2)
180	St. Petersburg, FL	(19.0)
54	Suffolk, VA	45.8
NA	Sugar Land, TX***	NA
57	Sunnyvale, CA	40.0
272	Sunrise, FL	(47.0)
354	Surprise, AZ	(100.0)
267	Syracuse, NY	(44.9)
194	Tacoma, WA	(22.5)
43	Tallahassee, FL	74.2
121	Tampa, FL	(1.2)
354	Temecula, CA	(100.0)
277	Tempe, AZ	(48.3)
NA	Thornton, CO**	NA
283	Thousand Oaks, CA	(50.0)
13	Toledo, OH	136.4
NA	Toms River Twnshp, NJ***	NA
71	Topeka, KS	19.4
95	Torrance, CA	0.0
354	Tracy, CA	(100.0)
149	Trenton, NJ	(9.7)
354	Troy, MI	(100.0)
88	Tucson, AZ	3.2
165	Tulsa, OK	(13.9)
NA	Tuscaloosa, AL**	NA
306	Tustin, CA	(55.2)
55	Tyler, TX	42.9
259	Upper Darby Twnshp, PA	(42.9)
251	Vacaville, CA	(40.7)
70	Vallejo, CA	19.5
68	Vancouver, WA	27.9
151	Ventura, CA	(10.0)
251	Victorville, CA	(40.7)
143	Virginia Beach, VA	(8.1)
239	Visalia, CA	(37.9)
354	Vista, CA	(100.0)
42	Waco, TX	75.5
163	Warren, MI	(13.5)
NA	Warwick, RI**	NA
261	Washington, DC	(43.2)
20	Waterbury, CT	125.0
295	West Covina, CA	(52.6)
354	West Jordan, UT	(100.0)
73	West Palm Beach, FL	16.9
245	West Valley, UT	(38.8)
283	Westland, MI	(50.0)
50	Westminster, CA	50.0
NA	Westminster, CO***	NA
133	Whittier, CA	(4.2)
341	Wichita Falls, TX	(78.0)
260	Wichita, KS	(43.0)
149	Wilmington, NC	(9.7)
NA	Winston-Salem, NC**	NA
95	Woodbridge Twnshp, NJ	0.0
41	Worcester, MA	76.5
195	Yakima, WA	(22.6)
203	Yonkers, NY	(28.0)
240	Yuma, AZ	(38.2)

Source: CQ Press using reported data from the F.B.I. "Crime in the United States 2011"
*Includes nonnegligent manslaughter. **Not available. ***These cities had murder rates of 0 in 2007 but had at least one murder in 2011. Calculating percent increase from zero results in an infinite number. These are shown as "NA."

52. Percent Change in Murder Rate: 2007 to 2011 (continued)
National Percent Change = 17.4% Decrease*

RANK	CITY	% CHANGE	RANK	CITY	% CHANGE	RANK	CITY	% CHANGE
1	Lakewood, CO	685.7	73	West Palm Beach, FL	16.9	145	Overland Park, KS	(8.3)
2	Santa Clarita, CA	366.7	74	Jackson, MS	14.1	146	Newark, NJ	(8.9)
3	Bloomington, IN	226.7	75	Camden, NJ	13.9	147	Miami Gardens, FL	(9.1)
4	Orange, CA	214.3	76	Santa Rosa, CA	11.5	148	Cleveland, OH	(9.3)
5	Lewisville, TX	210.0	77	Merced, CA	11.1	149	Trenton, NJ	(9.7)
6	Livermore, CA	208.3	78	Alhambra, CA	9.1	149	Wilmington, NC	(9.7)
7	Dearborn, MI	181.8	79	Bakersfield, CA	8.5	151	Gresham, OR	(10.0)
8	Port St. Lucie, FL	176.9	80	Cincinnati, OH	7.9	151	Ventura, CA	(10.0)
9	Lynchburg, VA	160.0	81	Omaha, NE	7.2	153	Midland, TX	(10.3)
10	Fort Collins, CO	150.0	82	Elizabeth, NJ	7.1	154	St. Louis, MO	(10.9)
11	Elgin, IL	142.1	83	Detroit, MI	5.2	155	Roseville, CA	(11.1)
12	Plano, TX	137.5	84	New York, NY	5.0	156	Baton Rouge, LA	(11.3)
13	Toledo, OH	136.4	84	Riverside, CA	5.0	157	Joliet, IL	(11.5)
14	Pasadena, TX	135.7	86	Gainesville, FL	4.3	158	Miami, FL	(11.6)
15	Sioux Falls, SD	128.6	87	Albany, GA	3.8	159	McKinney, TX	(12.5)
16	Lawrence, MA	128.1	88	Tucson, AZ	3.2	160	Oakland, CA	(13.2)
17	Concord, CA	128.0	89	Salinas, CA	3.1	161	Hartford, CT	(13.3)
18	Oceanside, CA	127.8	90	Columbus, OH	2.8	161	Jersey City, NJ	(13.3)
19	Frisco, TX	127.3	91	Laredo, TX	2.2	163	Warren, MI	(13.5)
20	Waterbury, CT	125.0	92	Rockford, IL	1.5	164	Anaheim, CA	(13.7)
21	Sparks, NV	120.0	92	Springfield, IL	1.5	165	Tulsa, OK	(13.9)
22	Rancho Cucamon., CA	111.8	94	Chicago, IL	1.3	166	El Paso, TX	(14.3)
23	Erie, PA	103.4	95	Allen, TX	0.0	166	Scottsdale, AZ	(14.3)
24	Stockton, CA	101.0	95	Ann Arbor, MI	0.0	168	Pittsburgh, PA	(14.4)
25	Chattanooga, TN	100.0	95	Beaverton, OR	0.0	169	Colorado Springs, CO	(15.3)
25	Colonie, NY	100.0	95	Bloomington, MN	0.0	170	Hayward, CA	(15.8)
25	Lake Forest, CA	100.0	95	Brick Twnshp, NJ	0.0	171	Austin, TX	(16.7)
25	Round Rock, TX	100.0	95	Centennial, CO	0.0	171	Mesa, AZ	(16.7)
29	Reading, PA	98.6	95	Clarkstown, NY	0.0	171	Mission, TX	(16.7)
30	Santa Maria, CA	97.1	95	Davie, FL	0.0	171	Oxnard, CA	(16.7)
31	Flint, MI	96.1	95	Fishers, IN	0.0	175	Portland, OR	(17.1)
32	Stamford, CT	96.0	95	Greece, NY	0.0	176	Norwalk, CA	(17.5)
33	New Bedford, MA	90.9	95	Hamilton Twnshp, NJ	0.0	177	Athens-Clarke, GA	(17.7)
34	Des Moines, IA	85.7	95	Killeen, TX	0.0	178	Brockton, MA	(18.8)
34	New Rochelle, NY	85.7	95	Lawrence, KS	0.0	178	Carmel, IN	(18.8)
34	St. Joseph, MO	85.7	95	Lee's Summit, MO	0.0	180	St. Petersburg, FL	(19.0)
37	Roanoke, VA	84.1	95	Livonia, MI	0.0	181	Indianapolis, IN	(19.6)
38	Boulder, CO	81.8	95	Mission Viejo, CA	0.0	182	Atlanta, GA	(20.1)
39	Carlsbad, CA	81.0	95	Naperville, IL	0.0	183	Sacramento, CA	(20.8)
40	Gilbert, AZ	80.0	95	Newton, MA	0.0	184	Beaumont, TX	(21.2)
41	Worcester, MA	76.5	95	O'Fallon, MO	0.0	184	Lawton, OK	(21.2)
42	Waco, TX	75.5	95	Ramapo, NY	0.0	186	Reno, NV	(21.5)
43	Tallahassee, FL	74.2	95	Salem, OR	0.0	187	Irving, TX	(21.7)
44	Kennewick, WA	68.8	95	Sandy, UT	0.0	188	Seattle, WA	(22.0)
45	Arlington, TX	68.6	95	Spokane Valley, WA	0.0	189	Cary, NC	(22.2)
46	Indio, CA	62.5	95	Torrance, CA	0.0	189	Pearland, TX	(22.2)
47	Glendale, AZ	60.0	95	Woodbridge Twnshp, NJ	0.0	191	Philadelphia, PA	(22.3)
48	Hampton, VA	54.8	120	Clearwater, FL	(1.1)	192	Bellflower, CA	(22.4)
49	Brooklyn Park, MN	51.2	121	Tampa, FL	(1.2)	192	Milwaukee, WI	(22.4)
50	Hemet, CA	50.0	122	Peoria, IL	(1.4)	194	Tacoma, WA	(22.5)
50	Melbourne, FL	50.0	123	Springfield, MA	(1.5)	195	Yakima, WA	(22.6)
50	Westminster, CA	50.0	124	Chesapeake, VA	(1.9)	196	College Station, TX	(23.1)
53	Evansville, IN	47.1	125	Miami Beach, FL	(2.2)	197	Clarksville, TN	(24.1)
54	Suffolk, VA	45.8	126	Fayetteville, NC	(2.4)	198	Los Angeles, CA	(24.5)
55	Tyler, TX	42.9	127	Buena Park, CA	(2.6)	199	Longview, TX	(24.6)
56	Chico, CA	42.5	128	Norwalk, CT	(2.8)	200	Palmdale, CA	(24.7)
57	Sunnyvale, CA	40.0	129	Madison, WI	(2.9)	201	Portsmouth, VA	(26.2)
58	Scranton, PA	39.3	130	Fort Wayne, IN	(3.1)	202	Fort Worth, TX	(26.7)
59	Elk Grove, CA	35.7	131	Fort Smith, AR	(3.3)	203	Yonkers, NY	(28.0)
60	Bridgeport, CT	35.3	132	Lowell, MA	(3.4)	204	Racine, WI	(28.4)
61	South Bend, IN	32.8	133	Whittier, CA	(4.2)	205	Fairfield, CA	(28.8)
62	Kansas City, KS	32.4	134	Green Bay, WI	(5.0)	206	San Antonio, TX	(29.0)
63	Grand Prairie, TX	31.6	135	Denton, TX	(5.6)	207	Inglewood, CA	(29.1)
64	Modesto, CA	30.2	136	Springfield, MO	(6.1)	208	Escondido, CA	(30.0)
65	Akron, OH	29.5	137	Memphis, TN	(6.3)	209	Baltimore, MD	(30.8)
66	Dayton, OH	29.4	137	Odessa, TX	(6.3)	209	South Gate, CA	(30.8)
67	Albany, NY	28.1	139	Edinburg, TX	(7.1)	211	Orlando, FL	(31.0)
68	Vancouver, WA	27.9	140	Oklahoma City, OK	(7.5)	212	Little Rock, AR	(31.2)
69	Paterson, NJ	22.1	141	Lakeland, FL	(7.6)	213	Garland, TX	(31.3)
70	Vallejo, CA	19.5	142	Savannah, GA	(8.0)	214	Albuquerque, NM	(31.5)
71	Topeka, KS	19.4	143	Virginia Beach, VA	(8.1)	215	Charlotte, NC	(31.7)
72	San Jose, CA	17.1	144	Boston, MA	(8.2)	215	Denver, CO	(31.7)

Rank Order - City (continued)

RANK	CITY	% CHANGE	RANK	CITY	% CHANGE	RANK	CITY	% CHANGE
217	Dallas, TX	(32.3)	290	Bethlehem, PA	(51.2)	354	Newport Beach, CA	(100.0)
218	Everett, WA	(32.4)	290	Lakewood Twnshp, NJ	(51.2)	354	Orem, UT	(100.0)
219	Cedar Rapids, IA	(33.3)	292	Lubbock, TX	(51.4)	354	Redwood City, CA	(100.0)
219	Downey, CA	(33.3)	293	Danbury, CT	(52.0)	354	Richardson, TX	(100.0)
219	Raleigh, NC	(33.3)	294	Santa Monica, CA	(52.2)	354	Rio Rancho, NM	(100.0)
222	Charleston, SC	(33.6)	295	West Covina, CA	(52.6)	354	Roswell, GA	(100.0)
223	Corpus Christi, TX	(33.9)	296	Shreveport, LA	(52.8)	354	San Angelo, TX	(100.0)
224	Pasadena, CA	(34.2)	297	Bellingham, WA	(53.8)	354	San Marcos, CA	(100.0)
225	Minneapolis, MN	(34.6)	297	Edmond, OK	(53.8)	354	Santa Barbara, CA	(100.0)
225	Richmond, VA	(34.6)	297	Norman, OK	(53.8)	354	Simi Valley, CA	(100.0)
227	McAllen, TX	(34.8)	300	El Cajon, CA	(54.5)	354	Somerville, MA	(100.0)
228	Chula Vista, CA	(35.1)	301	Allentown, PA	(54.8)	354	Surprise, AZ	(100.0)
229	Renton, WA	(35.3)	301	Compton, CA	(54.8)	354	Temecula, CA	(100.0)
230	Murfreesboro, TN	(35.7)	303	Irvine, CA	(55.0)	354	Tracy, CA	(100.0)
231	Knoxville, TN	(36.1)	303	Rochester, MN	(55.0)	354	Troy, MI	(100.0)
232	Fresno, CA	(36.4)	305	San Francisco, CA	(55.1)	354	Vista, CA	(100.0)
232	Nashville, TN	(36.4)	306	Tustin, CA	(55.2)	354	West Jordan, UT	(100.0)
234	Louisville, KY	(36.8)	307	Bryan, TX	(55.9)	NA	Arlington Heights, IL**	NA
234	Ogden, UT	(36.8)	307	Las Cruces, NM	(55.9)	NA	Avondale, AZ**	NA
236	Santa Clara, CA	(37.0)	309	Asheville, NC	(56.9)	NA	Bellevue, WA***	NA
237	Las Vegas, NV	(37.1)	310	Ontario, CA	(57.6)	NA	Bend, OR***	NA
237	San Bernardino, CA	(37.1)	311	Pomona, CA	(58.0)	NA	Billings, MT**	NA
239	Visalia, CA	(37.9)	312	Fullerton, CA	(59.5)	NA	Birmingham, AL**	NA
240	Yuma, AZ	(38.2)	313	Rialto, CA	(59.7)	NA	Bloomington, IL**	NA
241	San Diego, CA	(38.3)	314	Corona, CA	(60.6)	NA	Buffalo, NY**	NA
242	Columbus, GA	(38.6)	315	Palm Bay, FL	(62.0)	NA	Cambridge, MA***	NA
243	Cape Coral, FL	(38.7)	316	Hesperia, CA	(62.1)	NA	Champaign, IL**	NA
243	Murrieta, CA	(38.7)	317	Lafayette, LA	(62.6)	NA	Cheektowaga, NY***	NA
245	West Valley, UT	(38.8)	318	Lynn, MA	(63.7)	NA	Chino, CA***	NA
246	Carrollton, TX	(39.0)	319	Fremont, CA	(64.0)	NA	Cicero, IL**	NA
247	New Orleans, LA	(39.2)	320	Coral Springs, FL	(65.2)	NA	Citrus Heights, CA**	NA
248	Rochester, NY	(39.3)	321	Burbank, CA	(65.5)	NA	Clifton, NJ***	NA
249	Lincoln, NE	(40.0)	322	Salt Lake City, UT	(66.3)	NA	Clovis, CA***	NA
250	Long Beach, CA	(40.4)	323	Napa, CA	(67.5)	NA	Costa Mesa, CA***	NA
251	Macon, GA	(40.7)	324	Clinton Twnshp, MI	(67.7)	NA	Cranston, RI***	NA
251	Vacaville, CA	(40.7)	325	Carson, CA	(68.2)	NA	Daly City, CA***	NA
251	Victorville, CA	(40.7)	326	Peoria, AZ	(68.3)	NA	Davenport, IA**	NA
254	Santa Ana, CA	(41.2)	327	Hollywood, FL	(68.5)	NA	Decatur, IL**	NA
255	Aurora, CO	(41.3)	328	Mesquite, TX	(68.9)	NA	Durham, NC**	NA
256	Columbia, MO	(41.9)	328	Spokane, WA	(68.9)	NA	Edison Twnshp, NJ***	NA
257	Hammond, IN	(42.5)	330	Lancaster, CA	(69.9)	NA	Fall River, MA**	NA
258	Phoenix, AZ	(42.8)	331	Fargo, ND	(72.7)	NA	Farmington Hills, MI***	NA
259	Upper Darby Twnshp, PA	(42.9)	332	Independence, MO	(73.4)	NA	Hillsboro, OR***	NA
260	Wichita, KS	(43.0)	333	Plantation, FL	(73.9)	NA	Hoover, AL**	NA
261	Houston, TX	(43.2)	334	Deerfield Beach, FL	(75.0)	NA	Huntington Beach, CA***	NA
261	Washington, DC	(43.2)	334	Garden Grove, CA	(75.0)	NA	Huntsville, AL**	NA
263	Hialeah, FL	(43.8)	334	Greeley, CO	(75.0)	NA	Johns Creek, GA**	NA
264	Norfolk, VA	(44.1)	337	Kent, WA	(77.1)	NA	Kansas City, MO**	NA
265	Fontana, CA	(44.4)	338	Concord, NC	(77.5)	NA	Kansas City, TX***	NA
266	Jacksonville, FL	(44.8)	339	Chandler, AZ	(77.8)	NA	Lexington, KY**	NA
267	Syracuse, NY	(44.9)	339	Henderson, NV	(77.8)	NA	Longmont, CO**	NA
268	Fort Lauderdale, FL	(45.9)	341	Wichita Falls, TX	(78.0)	NA	Manchester, NH**	NA
269	Richmond, CA	(46.0)	342	Brownsville, TX	(78.6)	NA	Medford, OR**	NA
270	St. Paul, MN	(46.2)	342	High Point, NC	(78.6)	NA	Menifee, CA**	NA
271	Abilene, TX	(46.8)	344	Largo, FL	(80.9)	NA	Meridian, ID***	NA
272	Sunrise, FL	(47.0)	345	El Monte, CA	(81.3)	NA	Mobile, AL**	NA
273	Moreno Valley, CA	(47.1)	346	Berkeley, CA	(81.6)	NA	Montgomery, AL**	NA
274	Miramar, FL	(47.5)	347	North Charleston, SC	(82.7)	NA	Nashua, NH**	NA
275	Anchorage, AK	(48.1)	348	Arvada, CO	(84.2)	NA	New Haven, CT**	NA
275	Newport News, VA	(48.1)	349	Sandy Springs, GA	(84.3)	NA	Olathe, KS**	NA
277	Tempe, AZ	(48.3)	350	Aurora, IL	(85.5)	NA	Pembroke Pines, FL***	NA
278	Pompano Beach, FL	(48.4)	351	Alexandria, VA	(86.3)	NA	Provo, UT***	NA
279	Grand Rapids, MI	(49.0)	352	Baldwin Park, CA	(87.1)	NA	Pueblo, CO**	NA
280	Gary, IN	(49.2)	353	Boise, ID	(90.0)	NA	Redding, CA***	NA
281	Amarillo, TX	(49.5)	354	Amherst, NY	(100.0)	NA	San Leandro, CA***	NA
282	Hawthorne, CA	(49.6)	354	Boca Raton, FL	(100.0)	NA	San Mateo, CA***	NA
283	Lakewood, CA	(50.0)	354	Broken Arrow, OK	(100.0)	NA	Sterling Heights, MI**	NA
283	Quincy, MA	(50.0)	354	Canton Twnshp, MI	(100.0)	NA	Sugar Land, TX***	NA
283	Sioux City, IA	(50.0)	354	Chino Hills, CA	(100.0)	NA	Thornton, CO**	NA
283	Thousand Oaks, CA	(50.0)	354	Duluth, MN	(100.0)	NA	Toms River Twnshp, NJ***	NA
283	Westland, MI	(50.0)	354	Eugene, OR	(100.0)	NA	Tuscaloosa, AL**	NA
288	Lansing, MI	(50.4)	354	Glendale, CA	(100.0)	NA	Warwick, RI**	NA
289	Antioch, CA	(51.0)	354	Kenosha, WI	(100.0)	NA	Westminster, CO***	NA
			354	Nampa, ID	(100.0)	NA	Winston-Salem, NC**	NA

Source: CQ Press using reported data from the F.B.I. "Crime in the United States 2011"
*Includes nonnegligent manslaughter. **Not available. ***These cities had murder rates of 0 in 2007 but had at least one murder in 2011. Calculating percent increase from zero results in an infinite number. These are shown as "NA."

Alpha Order - City

53. Rapes in 2011
National Total = 83,425 Rapes*

RANK	CITY	RAPES
226	Abilene, TX	33
47	Akron, OH	165
197	Albany, GA	37
226	Albany, NY	33
27	Albuquerque, NM	264
356	Alexandria, VA	14
400	Alhambra, CA	7
120	Allentown, PA	61
370	Allen, TX	12
71	Amarillo, TX	104
400	Amherst, NY	7
69	Anaheim, CA	105
22	Anchorage, AK	283
205	Ann Arbor, MI	36
305	Antioch, CA	21
415	Arlington Heights, IL	5
51	Arlington, TX	136
272	Arvada, CO	25
296	Asheville, NC	22
250	Athens-Clarke, GA	30
50	Atlanta, GA	148
41	Aurora, CO	183
128	Aurora, IL	58
35	Austin, TX	211
408	Avondale, AZ	6
187	Bakersfield, CA	39
387	Baldwin Park, CA	9
19	Baltimore, MD	341
151	Baton Rouge, LA	51
112	Beaumont, TX	65
305	Beaverton, OR	21
290	Bellevue, WA	23
356	Bellflower, CA	14
213	Bellingham, WA	35
272	Bend, OR	25
323	Berkeley, CA	19
341	Bethlehem, PA	17
205	Billings, MT	36
43	Birmingham, AL	182
103	Bloomington, IL	69
333	Bloomington, IN	18
NA	Bloomington, MN**	NA
290	Boca Raton, FL	23
110	Boise, ID	66
24	Boston, MA	271
213	Boulder, CO	35
400	Brick Twnshp, NJ	7
63	Bridgeport, CT	116
120	Brockton, MA	61
296	Broken Arrow, OK	22
NA	Brooklyn Park, MN**	NA
197	Brownsville, TX	37
296	Bryan, TX	22
395	Buena Park, CA	8
59	Buffalo, NY	121
341	Burbank, CA	17
282	Cambridge, MA	24
110	Camden, NJ	66
305	Canton Twnshp, MI	21
356	Cape Coral, FL	14
374	Carlsbad, CA	11
395	Carmel, IN	8
418	Carrollton, TX	4
366	Carson, CA	13
366	Cary, NC	13
178	Cedar Rapids, IA	41
262	Centennial, CO	27
136	Champaign, IL	56
117	Chandler, AZ	62
250	Charleston, SC	30
33	Charlotte, NC	218
205	Chattanooga, TN	36
380	Cheektowaga, NY	10
165	Chesapeake, VA	46
NA	Chicago, IL**	NA
197	Chico, CA	37
418	Chino Hills, CA	4
387	Chino, CA	9
219	Chula Vista, CA	34
282	Cicero, IL	24
41	Cincinnati, OH	183
350	Citrus Heights, CA	15
415	Clarkstown, NY	5
120	Clarksville, TN	61
180	Clearwater, FL	40
16	Cleveland, OH	354
380	Clifton, NJ	10
290	Clinton Twnshp, MI	23
268	Clovis, CA	26
244	College Station, TX	31
431	Colonie, NY	0
20	Colorado Springs, CO	319
197	Columbia, MO	37
180	Columbus, GA	40
6	Columbus, OH	565
169	Compton, CA	45
323	Concord, CA	19
395	Concord, NC	8
418	Coral Springs, FL	4
380	Corona, CA	10
38	Corpus Christi, TX	194
250	Costa Mesa, CA	30
333	Cranston, RI	18
10	Dallas, TX	428
356	Daly City, CA	14
219	Danbury, CT	34
145	Davenport, IA	53
341	Davie, FL	17
76	Dayton, OH	98
296	Dearborn, MI	22
356	Decatur, IL	14
290	Deerfield Beach, FL	23
145	Denton, TX	53
13	Denver, CO	396
72	Des Moines, IA	103
11	Detroit, MI	427
290	Downey, CA	23
NA	Duluth, MN**	NA
113	Durham, NC	64
258	Edinburg, TX	28
387	Edison Twnshp, NJ	9
400	Edmond, OK	7
258	El Cajon, CA	28
226	El Monte, CA	33
34	El Paso, TX	217
93	Elgin, IL	78
192	Elizabeth, NJ	38
333	Elk Grove, CA	18
95	Erie, PA	77
258	Escondido, CA	28
93	Eugene, OR	78
136	Evansville, IN	56
157	Everett, WA	49
305	Fairfield, CA	21
149	Fall River, MA	52
176	Fargo, ND	42
374	Farmington Hills, MI	11
136	Fayetteville, NC	56
431	Fishers, IN	0
88	Flint, MI	85
187	Fontana, CA	39
136	Fort Collins, CO	56
83	Fort Lauderdale, FL	91
114	Fort Smith, AR	63
80	Fort Wayne, IN	94
17	Fort Worth, TX	350
213	Fremont, CA	35
151	Fresno, CA	51
408	Frisco, TX	6
272	Fullerton, CA	25
90	Gainesville, FL	82
323	Garden Grove, CA	19
140	Garland, TX	55
163	Gary, IN	47
305	Gilbert, AZ	21
173	Glendale, AZ	44
356	Glendale, CA	14
103	Grand Prairie, TX	69
91	Grand Rapids, MI	81
408	Greece, NY	6
192	Greeley, CO	38
143	Green Bay, WI	54
244	Gresham, OR	31
380	Hamilton Twnshp, NJ	10
169	Hammond, IN	45
323	Hampton, VA	19
272	Hawthorne, CA	25
173	Hayward, CA	44
350	Hemet, CA	15
128	Henderson, NV	58
272	Hesperia, CA	25
244	Hialeah, FL	31
272	High Point, NC	25
290	Hillsboro, OR	23
163	Hollywood, FL	47
400	Hoover, AL	7
4	Houston, TX	771
219	Huntington Beach, CA	34
151	Huntsville, AL	51
169	Independence, MO	45
9	Indianapolis, IN	435
282	Indio, CA	24
226	Inglewood, CA	33
374	Irvine, CA	11
272	Irving, TX	25
17	Jacksonville, FL	350
56	Jackson, MS	126
157	Jersey City, NJ	49
422	Johns Creek, GA	3
250	Joliet, IL	30
78	Kansas City, KS	95
26	Kansas City, MO	265
262	Kennewick, WA	27
154	Kenosha, WI	50
123	Kent, WA	60
103	Killeen, TX	69
80	Knoxville, TN	94
350	Lafayette, LA	15
430	Lake Forest, CA	1
205	Lakeland, FL	36
408	Lakewood Twnshp, NJ	6
387	Lakewood, CA	9
87	Lakewood, CO	88
176	Lancaster, CA	42
84	Lansing, MI	90
98	Laredo, TX	76
237	Largo, FL	32
341	Las Cruces, NM	17
5	Las Vegas, NV	651
226	Lawrence, KS	33
370	Lawrence, MA	12
134	Lawton, OK	57
305	League City, TX	21
333	Lee's Summit, MO	18
296	Lewisville, TX	22

212 Cities

Alpha Order - City (continued)

RANK	CITY	RAPES	RANK	CITY	RAPES	RANK	CITY	RAPES
69	Lexington, KY	105	123	Overland Park, KS	60	205	Sioux City, IA	36
46	Lincoln, NE	166	268	Oxnard, CA	26	67	Sioux Falls, SD	108
49	Little Rock, AR	161	296	Palm Bay, FL	22	341	Somerville, MA	17
356	Livermore, CA	14	192	Palmdale, CA	38	123	South Bend, IN	60
323	Livonia, MI	19	268	Pasadena, CA	26	380	South Gate, CA	10
64	Long Beach, CA	112	117	Pasadena, TX	62	165	Sparks, NV	46
333	Longmont, CO	18	187	Paterson, NJ	39	296	Spokane Valley, WA	22
314	Longview, TX	20	350	Pearland, TX	15	89	Spokane, WA	84
3	Los Angeles, CA	828	258	Pembroke Pines, FL	28	72	Springfield, IL	103
30	Louisville, KY	227	213	Peoria, AZ	35	244	Springfield, MA	31
205	Lowell, MA	36	226	Peoria, IL	33	66	Springfield, MO	110
101	Lubbock, TX	70	2	Philadelphia, PA	833	237	Stamford, CT	32
296	Lynchburg, VA	22	7	Phoenix, AZ	559	374	Sterling Heights, MI	11
257	Lynn, MA	29	107	Pittsburgh, PA	67	84	Stockton, CA	90
226	Macon, GA	33	180	Plano, TX	40	305	St. Joseph, MO	21
99	Madison, WI	74	350	Plantation, FL	15	40	St. Louis, MO	188
103	Manchester, NH	69	143	Pomona, CA	54	45	St. Paul, MN	169
262	McAllen, TX	27	178	Pompano Beach, FL	41	84	St. Petersburg, FL	90
226	McKinney, TX	33	250	Port St. Lucie, FL	30	323	Suffolk, VA	19
192	Medford, OR	38	28	Portland, OR	258	415	Sugar Land, TX	5
272	Melbourne, FL	25	165	Portsmouth, VA	46	305	Sunnyvale, CA	21
12	Memphis, TN	398	262	Provo, UT	27	387	Sunrise, FL	9
427	Menifee, CA	2	180	Pueblo, CO	40	370	Surprise, AZ	12
314	Merced, CA	20	244	Quincy, MA	31	114	Syracuse, NY	63
323	Meridian, ID	19	356	Racine, WI	14	57	Tacoma, WA	125
53	Mesa, AZ	131	55	Raleigh, NC	127	68	Tallahassee, FL	107
395	Mesquite, TX	8	422	Ramapo, NY	3	128	Tampa, FL	58
180	Miami Beach, FL	40	366	Rancho Cucamon., CA	13	400	Temecula, CA	7
323	Miami Gardens, FL	19	296	Reading, PA	22	169	Tempe, AZ	45
77	Miami, FL	96	114	Redding, CA	63	154	Thornton, CO	50
305	Midland, TX	21	268	Redwood City, CA	26	380	Thousand Oaks, CA	10
38	Milwaukee, WI	194	262	Reno, NV	27	58	Toledo, OH	124
14	Minneapolis, MN	386	226	Renton, WA	33	422	Toms River Twnshp, NJ	3
180	Miramar, FL	40	333	Rialto, CA	18	145	Topeka, KS	53
422	Mission Viejo, CA	3	387	Richardson, TX	9	341	Torrance, CA	17
408	Mission, TX	6	187	Richmond, CA	39	370	Tracy, CA	12
159	Mobile, AL	48	173	Richmond, VA	44	272	Trenton, NJ	25
107	Modesto, CA	67	356	Rio Rancho, NM	14	341	Troy, MI	17
192	Montgomery, AL	38	134	Riverside, CA	57	36	Tucson, AZ	204
237	Moreno Valley, CA	32	226	Roanoke, VA	33	25	Tulsa, OK	266
250	Murfreesboro, TN	30	NA	Rochester, MN**	NA	187	Tuscaloosa, AL	39
366	Murrieta, CA	13	78	Rochester, NY	95	400	Tustin, CA	7
197	Nampa, ID	37	64	Rockford, IL	112	165	Tyler, TX	46
282	Napa, CA	24	282	Roseville, CA	24	314	Upper Darby Twnshp, PA	20
418	Naperville, IL	4	374	Roswell, GA	11	314	Vacaville, CA	20
282	Nashua, NH	24	272	Round Rock, TX	25	145	Vallejo, CA	53
15	Nashville, TN	373	52	Sacramento, CA	134	74	Vancouver, WA	102
127	New Bedford, MA	59	237	Salem, OR	32	314	Ventura, CA	20
140	New Haven, CT	55	219	Salinas, CA	34	197	Victorville, CA	37
48	New Orleans, LA	163	61	Salt Lake City, UT	119	123	Virginia Beach, VA	60
427	New Rochelle, NY	2	237	San Angelo, TX	32	180	Visalia, CA	40
1	New York, NY	1,092	8	San Antonio, TX	492	237	Vista, CA	32
128	Newark, NJ	58	95	San Bernardino, CA	77	101	Waco, TX	70
349	Newport Beach, CA	16	21	San Diego, CA	293	100	Warren, MI	73
149	Newport News, VA	52	53	San Francisco, CA	131	282	Warwick, RI	24
427	Newton, MA	2	31	San Jose, CA	226	44	Washington, DC	172
91	Norfolk, VA	81	323	San Leandro, CA	19	387	Waterbury, CT	9
107	Norman, OK	67	323	San Marcos, CA	19	314	West Covina, CA	20
213	North Charleston, SC	35	314	San Mateo, CA	20	244	West Jordan, UT	31
380	Norwalk, CA	10	408	Sandy Springs, GA	6	159	West Palm Beach, FL	48
350	Norwalk, CT	15	341	Sandy, UT	17	95	West Valley, UT	77
37	Oakland, CA	202	117	Santa Ana, CA	62	154	Westland, MI	50
128	Oceanside, CA	58	197	Santa Barbara, CA	37	374	Westminster, CA	11
197	Odessa, TX	37	356	Santa Clara, CA	14	219	Westminster, CO	34
422	O'Fallon, MO	3	333	Santa Clarita, CA	18	400	Whittier, CA	7
314	Ogden, UT	20	333	Santa Maria, CA	18	250	Wichita Falls, TX	30
23	Oklahoma City, OK	277	282	Santa Monica, CA	24	29	Wichita, KS	238
159	Olathe, KS	48	128	Santa Rosa, CA	58	237	Wilmington, NC	32
32	Omaha, NE	220	205	Savannah, GA	36	82	Winston-Salem, NC	93
262	Ontario, CA	27	219	Scottsdale, AZ	34	395	Woodbridge Twnshp, NJ	8
408	Orange, CA	6	219	Scranton, PA	34	205	Worcester, MA	36
314	Orem, UT	20	75	Seattle, WA	100	159	Yakima, WA	48
61	Orlando, FL	119	59	Shreveport, LA	121	213	Yonkers, NY	35
			387	Simi Valley, CA	9	226	Yuma, AZ	33

Source: Reported data from the F.B.I. "Crime in the United States 2011"

*Forcible rape is the carnal knowledge of a female forcibly and against her will. Assaults or attempts to commit rape by force or threat of force are included. However, statutory rape without force and other sex offenses are excluded. **Not available

Rank Order - City

53. Rapes in 2011 (continued)
National Total = 83,425 Rapes*

RANK	CITY	RAPES	RANK	CITY	RAPES	RANK	CITY	RAPES
1	New York, NY	1,092	72	Springfield, IL	103	145	Davenport, IA	53
2	Philadelphia, PA	833	74	Vancouver, WA	102	145	Denton, TX	53
3	Los Angeles, CA	828	75	Seattle, WA	100	145	Topeka, KS	53
4	Houston, TX	771	76	Dayton, OH	98	145	Vallejo, CA	53
5	Las Vegas, NV	651	77	Miami, FL	96	149	Fall River, MA	52
6	Columbus, OH	565	78	Kansas City, KS	95	149	Newport News, VA	52
7	Phoenix, AZ	559	78	Rochester, NY	95	151	Baton Rouge, LA	51
8	San Antonio, TX	492	80	Fort Wayne, IN	94	151	Fresno, CA	51
9	Indianapolis, IN	435	80	Knoxville, TN	94	151	Huntsville, AL	51
10	Dallas, TX	428	82	Winston-Salem, NC	93	154	Kenosha, WI	50
11	Detroit, MI	427	83	Fort Lauderdale, FL	91	154	Thornton, CO	50
12	Memphis, TN	398	84	Lansing, MI	90	154	Westland, MI	50
13	Denver, CO	396	84	Stockton, CA	90	157	Everett, WA	49
14	Minneapolis, MN	386	84	St. Petersburg, FL	90	157	Jersey City, NJ	49
15	Nashville, TN	373	87	Lakewood, CO	88	159	Mobile, AL	48
16	Cleveland, OH	354	88	Flint, MI	85	159	Olathe, KS	48
17	Fort Worth, TX	350	89	Spokane, WA	84	159	West Palm Beach, FL	48
17	Jacksonville, FL	350	90	Gainesville, FL	82	159	Yakima, WA	48
19	Baltimore, MD	341	91	Grand Rapids, MI	81	163	Gary, IN	47
20	Colorado Springs, CO	319	91	Norfolk, VA	81	163	Hollywood, FL	47
21	San Diego, CA	293	93	Elgin, IL	78	165	Chesapeake, VA	46
22	Anchorage, AK	283	93	Eugene, OR	78	165	Portsmouth, VA	46
23	Oklahoma City, OK	277	95	Erie, PA	77	165	Sparks, NV	46
24	Boston, MA	271	95	San Bernardino, CA	77	165	Tyler, TX	46
25	Tulsa, OK	266	95	West Valley, UT	77	169	Compton, CA	45
26	Kansas City, MO	265	98	Laredo, TX	76	169	Hammond, IN	45
27	Albuquerque, NM	264	99	Madison, WI	74	169	Independence, MO	45
28	Portland, OR	258	100	Warren, MI	73	169	Tempe, AZ	45
29	Wichita, KS	238	101	Lubbock, TX	70	173	Glendale, AZ	44
30	Louisville, KY	227	101	Waco, TX	70	173	Hayward, CA	44
31	San Jose, CA	226	103	Bloomington, IL	69	173	Richmond, VA	44
32	Omaha, NE	220	103	Grand Prairie, TX	69	176	Fargo, ND	42
33	Charlotte, NC	218	103	Killeen, TX	69	176	Lancaster, CA	42
34	El Paso, TX	217	103	Manchester, NH	69	178	Cedar Rapids, IA	41
35	Austin, TX	211	107	Modesto, CA	67	178	Pompano Beach, FL	41
36	Tucson, AZ	204	107	Norman, OK	67	180	Clearwater, FL	40
37	Oakland, CA	202	107	Pittsburgh, PA	67	180	Columbus, GA	40
38	Corpus Christi, TX	194	110	Boise, ID	66	180	Miami Beach, FL	40
38	Milwaukee, WI	194	110	Camden, NJ	66	180	Miramar, FL	40
40	St. Louis, MO	188	112	Beaumont, TX	65	180	Plano, TX	40
41	Aurora, CO	183	113	Durham, NC	64	180	Pueblo, CO	40
41	Cincinnati, OH	183	114	Fort Smith, AR	63	180	Visalia, CA	40
43	Birmingham, AL	182	114	Redding, CA	63	187	Bakersfield, CA	39
44	Washington, DC	172	114	Syracuse, NY	63	187	Fontana, CA	39
45	St. Paul, MN	169	117	Chandler, AZ	62	187	Paterson, NJ	39
46	Lincoln, NE	166	117	Pasadena, TX	62	187	Richmond, CA	39
47	Akron, OH	165	117	Santa Ana, CA	62	187	Tuscaloosa, AL	39
48	New Orleans, LA	163	120	Allentown, PA	61	192	Elizabeth, NJ	38
49	Little Rock, AR	161	120	Brockton, MA	61	192	Greeley, CO	38
50	Atlanta, GA	148	120	Clarksville, TN	61	192	Medford, OR	38
51	Arlington, TX	136	123	Kent, WA	60	192	Montgomery, AL	38
52	Sacramento, CA	134	123	Overland Park, KS	60	192	Palmdale, CA	38
53	Mesa, AZ	131	123	South Bend, IN	60	197	Albany, GA	37
53	San Francisco, CA	131	123	Virginia Beach, VA	60	197	Brownsville, TX	37
55	Raleigh, NC	127	127	New Bedford, MA	59	197	Chico, CA	37
56	Jackson, MS	126	128	Aurora, IL	58	197	Columbia, MO	37
57	Tacoma, WA	125	128	Henderson, NV	58	197	Nampa, ID	37
58	Toledo, OH	124	128	Newark, NJ	58	197	Odessa, TX	37
59	Buffalo, NY	121	128	Oceanside, CA	58	197	Santa Barbara, CA	37
59	Shreveport, LA	121	128	Santa Rosa, CA	58	197	Victorville, CA	37
61	Orlando, FL	119	128	Tampa, FL	58	205	Ann Arbor, MI	36
61	Salt Lake City, UT	119	134	Lawton, OK	57	205	Billings, MT	36
63	Bridgeport, CT	116	134	Riverside, CA	57	205	Chattanooga, TN	36
64	Long Beach, CA	112	136	Champaign, IL	56	205	Lakeland, FL	36
64	Rockford, IL	112	136	Evansville, IN	56	205	Lowell, MA	36
66	Springfield, MO	110	136	Fayetteville, NC	56	205	Savannah, GA	36
67	Sioux Falls, SD	108	136	Fort Collins, CO	56	205	Sioux City, IA	36
68	Tallahassee, FL	107	140	Garland, TX	55	205	Worcester, MA	36
69	Anaheim, CA	105	140	Hartford, CT	55	213	Bellingham, WA	35
69	Lexington, KY	105	140	New Haven, CT	55	213	Boulder, CO	35
71	Amarillo, TX	104	143	Green Bay, WI	54	213	Fremont, CA	35
72	Des Moines, IA	103	143	Pomona, CA	54	213	North Charleston, SC	35

Rank Order - City (continued)

RANK	CITY	RAPES
213	Peoria, AZ	35
213	Yonkers, NY	35
219	Chula Vista, CA	34
219	Danbury, CT	34
219	Huntington Beach, CA	34
219	Salinas, CA	34
219	Scottsdale, AZ	34
219	Scranton, PA	34
219	Westminster, CO	34
226	Abilene, TX	33
226	Albany, NY	33
226	El Monte, CA	33
226	Inglewood, CA	33
226	Lawrence, KS	33
226	Macon, GA	33
226	McKinney, TX	33
226	Peoria, IL	33
226	Renton, WA	33
226	Roanoke, VA	33
226	Yuma, AZ	33
237	Largo, FL	32
237	Moreno Valley, CA	32
237	Salem, OR	32
237	San Angelo, TX	32
237	Stamford, CT	32
237	Vista, CA	32
237	Wilmington, NC	32
244	College Station, TX	31
244	Gresham, OR	31
244	Hialeah, FL	31
244	Quincy, MA	31
244	Springfield, MA	31
244	West Jordan, UT	31
250	Athens-Clarke, GA	30
250	Charleston, SC	30
250	Costa Mesa, CA	30
250	Joliet, IL	30
250	Murfreesboro, TN	30
250	Port St. Lucie, FL	30
250	Wichita Falls, TX	30
257	Lynn, MA	29
258	Edinburg, TX	28
258	El Cajon, CA	28
258	Escondido, CA	28
258	Pembroke Pines, FL	28
262	Centennial, CO	27
262	Kennewick, WA	27
262	McAllen, TX	27
262	Ontario, CA	27
262	Provo, UT	27
262	Reno, NV	27
268	Clovis, CA	26
268	Oxnard, CA	26
268	Pasadena, CA	26
268	Redwood City, CA	26
272	Arvada, CO	25
272	Bend, OR	25
272	Fullerton, CA	25
272	Hawthorne, CA	25
272	Hesperia, CA	25
272	High Point, NC	25
272	Irving, TX	25
272	Melbourne, FL	25
272	Round Rock, TX	25
272	Trenton, NJ	25
282	Cambridge, MA	24
282	Cicero, IL	24
282	Indio, CA	24
282	Napa, CA	24
282	Nashua, NH	24
282	Roseville, CA	24
282	Santa Monica, CA	24
282	Warwick, RI	24
290	Bellevue, WA	23
290	Boca Raton, FL	23
290	Clinton Twnshp, MI	23
290	Deerfield Beach, FL	23
290	Downey, CA	23
290	Hillsboro, OR	23
296	Asheville, NC	22
296	Broken Arrow, OK	22
296	Bryan, TX	22
296	Dearborn, MI	22
296	Lewisville, TX	22
296	Lynchburg, VA	22
296	Palm Bay, FL	22
296	Reading, PA	22
296	Spokane Valley, WA	22
305	Antioch, CA	21
305	Beaverton, OR	21
305	Canton Twnshp, MI	21
305	Fairfield, CA	21
305	Gilbert, AZ	21
305	League City, TX	21
305	Midland, TX	21
305	St. Joseph, MO	21
305	Sunnyvale, CA	21
314	Longview, TX	20
314	Merced, CA	20
314	Ogden, UT	20
314	Orem, UT	20
314	San Mateo, CA	20
314	Upper Darby Twnshp, PA	20
314	Vacaville, CA	20
314	Ventura, CA	20
314	West Covina, CA	20
323	Berkeley, CA	19
323	Concord, CA	19
323	Garden Grove, CA	19
323	Hampton, VA	19
323	Livonia, MI	19
323	Meridian, ID	19
323	Miami Gardens, FL	19
323	San Leandro, CA	19
323	San Marcos, CA	19
323	Suffolk, VA	19
333	Bloomington, IN	18
333	Cranston, RI	18
333	Elk Grove, CA	18
333	Lee's Summit, MO	18
333	Longmont, CO	18
333	Rialto, CA	18
333	Santa Clarita, CA	18
333	Santa Maria, CA	18
341	Bethlehem, PA	17
341	Burbank, CA	17
341	Davie, FL	17
341	Las Cruces, NM	17
341	Sandy, UT	17
341	Somerville, MA	17
341	Torrance, CA	17
341	Troy, MI	17
349	Newport Beach, CA	16
350	Citrus Heights, CA	15
350	Hemet, CA	15
350	Lafayette, LA	15
350	Norwalk, CT	15
350	Pearland, TX	15
350	Plantation, FL	15
356	Alexandria, VA	14
356	Bellflower, CA	14
356	Cape Coral, FL	14
356	Daly City, CA	14
356	Decatur, IL	14
356	Glendale, CA	14
356	Livermore, CA	14
356	Racine, WI	14
356	Rio Rancho, NM	14
356	Santa Clara, CA	14
366	Carson, CA	13
366	Cary, NC	13
366	Murrieta, CA	13
366	Rancho Cucamon., CA	13
370	Allen, TX	12
370	Lawrence, MA	12
370	Surprise, AZ	12
370	Tracy, CA	12
374	Carlsbad, CA	11
374	Farmington Hills, MI	11
374	Irvine, CA	11
374	Roswell, GA	11
374	Sterling Heights, MI	11
374	Westminster, CA	11
380	Cheektowaga, NY	10
380	Clifton, NJ	10
380	Corona, CA	10
380	Hamilton Twnshp, NJ	10
380	Norwalk, CA	10
380	South Gate, CA	10
380	Thousand Oaks, CA	10
387	Baldwin Park, CA	9
387	Chino, CA	9
387	Edison Twnshp, NJ	9
387	Lakewood, CA	9
387	Richardson, TX	9
387	Simi Valley, CA	9
387	Sunrise, FL	9
387	Waterbury, CT	9
395	Buena Park, CA	8
395	Carmel, IN	8
395	Concord, NC	8
395	Mesquite, TX	8
395	Woodbridge Twnshp, NJ	8
400	Alhambra, CA	7
400	Amherst, NY	7
400	Brick Twnshp, NJ	7
400	Edmond, OK	7
400	Hoover, AL	7
400	Temecula, CA	7
400	Tustin, CA	7
400	Whittier, CA	7
408	Avondale, AZ	6
408	Frisco, TX	6
408	Greece, NY	6
408	Lakewood Twnshp, NJ	6
408	Mission, TX	6
408	Orange, CA	6
408	Sandy Springs, GA	6
415	Arlington Heights, IL	5
415	Clarkstown, NY	5
415	Sugar Land, TX	5
418	Carrollton, TX	4
418	Chino Hills, CA	4
418	Coral Springs, FL	4
418	Naperville, IL	4
422	Johns Creek, GA	3
422	Mission Viejo, CA	3
422	O'Fallon, MO	3
422	Ramapo, NY	3
422	Toms River Twnshp, NJ	3
427	Menifee, CA	2
427	New Rochelle, NY	2
427	Newton, MA	2
430	Lake Forest, CA	1
431	Colonie, NY	0
431	Fishers, IN	0
NA	Bloomington, MN**	NA
NA	Brooklyn Park, MN**	NA
NA	Chicago, IL**	NA
NA	Duluth, MN**	NA
NA	Rochester, MN**	NA

Source: Reported data from the F.B.I. "Crime in the United States 2011"
*Forcible rape is the carnal knowledge of a female forcibly and against her will. Assaults or attempts to commit rape by force or threat of force are included. However, statutory rape without force and other sex offenses are excluded. **Not available

Alpha Order - City

54. Rape Rate in 2011
National Rate = 26.8 Rapes per 100,000 Population*

RANK	CITY	RATE	RANK	CITY	RATE	RANK	CITY	RATE
214	Abilene, TX	27.6	357	Cheektowaga, NY	12.6	131	Fort Wayne, IN	36.9
9	Akron, OH	82.8	283	Chesapeake, VA	20.5	89	Fort Worth, TX	46.2
85	Albany, GA	47.2	NA	Chicago, IL**	NA	335	Fremont, CA	16.2
159	Albany, NY	33.6	109	Chico, CA	42.4	377	Fresno, CA	10.2
80	Albuquerque, NM	47.8	415	Chino Hills, CA	5.3	417	Frisco, TX	5.0
382	Alexandria, VA	9.9	368	Chino, CA	11.4	313	Fullerton, CA	18.3
395	Alhambra, CA	8.3	349	Chula Vista, CA	13.8	26	Gainesville, FL	65.1
72	Allentown, PA	51.5	204	Cicero, IL	28.5	373	Garden Grove, CA	11.0
347	Allen, TX	14.0	39	Cincinnati, OH	61.6	247	Garland, TX	23.7
64	Amarillo, TX	53.4	321	Citrus Heights, CA	17.8	51	Gary, IN	58.2
413	Amherst, NY	6.0	409	Clarkstown, NY	6.3	382	Gilbert, AZ	9.9
185	Anaheim, CA	30.9	93	Clarksville, TN	45.5	300	Glendale, AZ	19.1
2	Anchorage, AK	95.3	133	Clearwater, FL	36.6	403	Glendale, CA	7.2
178	Ann Arbor, MI	31.6	4	Cleveland, OH	89.1	124	Grand Prairie, TX	38.5
287	Antioch, CA	20.3	364	Clifton, NJ	11.8	105	Grand Rapids, MI	43.1
406	Arlington Heights, IL	6.6	246	Clinton Twnshp, MI	23.8	411	Greece, NY	6.2
135	Arlington, TX	36.4	222	Clovis, CA	26.9	119	Greeley, CO	40.2
254	Arvada, CO	23.1	171	College Station, TX	32.3	71	Green Bay, WI	51.7
228	Asheville, NC	26.1	431	Colonie, NY	0.0	200	Gresham, OR	29.0
232	Athens-Clarke, GA	25.6	14	Colorado Springs, CO	75.3	369	Hamilton Twnshp, NJ	11.3
151	Atlanta, GA	34.8	157	Columbia, MO	34.0	56	Hammond, IN	55.4
57	Aurora, CO	55.3	281	Columbus, GA	20.8	351	Hampton, VA	13.7
198	Aurora, IL	29.2	19	Columbus, OH	71.7	100	Hartford, CT	44.0
228	Austin, TX	26.1	90	Compton, CA	46.1	195	Hawthorne, CA	29.3
399	Avondale, AZ	7.8	342	Concord, CA	15.4	189	Hayward, CA	30.2
371	Bakersfield, CA	11.1	381	Concord, NC	10.0	304	Hemet, CA	18.8
364	Baldwin Park, CA	11.8	422	Coral Springs, FL	3.3	263	Henderson, NV	22.3
60	Baltimore, MD	54.4	407	Corona, CA	6.5	217	Hesperia, CA	27.4
271	Baton Rouge, LA	22.0	34	Corpus Christi, TX	62.3	353	Hialeah, FL	13.6
63	Beaumont, TX	53.8	221	Costa Mesa, CA	27.0	247	High Point, NC	23.7
254	Beaverton, OR	23.1	259	Cranston, RI	22.4	236	Hillsboro, OR	24.8
309	Bellevue, WA	18.5	149	Dallas, TX	35.0	166	Hollywood, FL	32.9
316	Bellflower, CA	18.1	351	Daly City, CA	13.7	392	Hoover, AL	8.5
108	Bellingham, WA	42.6	111	Danbury, CT	42.0	140	Houston, TX	36.0
171	Bend, OR	32.3	66	Davenport, IA	52.9	323	Huntington Beach, CA	17.7
331	Berkeley, CA	16.7	315	Davie, FL	18.2	208	Huntsville, AL	28.2
257	Bethlehem, PA	22.6	22	Dayton, OH	69.2	125	Independence, MO	38.4
153	Billings, MT	34.3	259	Dearborn, MI	22.4	68	Indianapolis, IN	52.2
6	Birmingham, AL	85.3	313	Decatur, IL	18.3	183	Indio, CA	31.2
3	Bloomington, IL	89.8	189	Deerfield Beach, FL	30.2	192	Inglewood, CA	29.7
263	Bloomington, IN	22.3	92	Denton, TX	45.8	416	Irvine, CA	5.1
NA	Bloomington, MN**	NA	27	Denver, CO	64.9	369	Irving, TX	11.3
222	Boca Raton, FL	26.9	75	Des Moines, IA	50.4	112	Jacksonville, FL	41.9
177	Boise, ID	31.7	44	Detroit, MI	59.9	17	Jackson, MS	72.3
102	Boston, MA	43.6	287	Downey, CA	20.3	294	Jersey City, NJ	19.7
147	Boulder, CO	35.3	NA	Duluth, MN**	NA	419	Johns Creek, GA	3.9
387	Brick Twnshp, NJ	9.3	212	Durham, NC	27.7	287	Joliet, IL	20.3
11	Bridgeport, CT	80.3	145	Edinburg, TX	35.6	28	Kansas City, KS	64.8
29	Brockton, MA	64.6	389	Edison Twnshp, NJ	9.0	55	Kansas City, MO	57.4
271	Broken Arrow, OK	22.0	392	Edmond, OK	8.5	140	Kennewick, WA	36.0
NA	Brooklyn Park, MN**	NA	210	El Cajon, CA	27.8	76	Kenosha, WI	50.2
282	Brownsville, TX	20.7	202	El Monte, CA	28.7	30	Kent, WA	63.9
207	Bryan, TX	28.3	168	El Paso, TX	32.7	67	Killeen, TX	52.8
384	Buena Park, CA	9.8	18	Elgin, IL	71.9	69	Knoxville, TN	52.1
90	Buffalo, NY	46.1	188	Elizabeth, NJ	30.3	359	Lafayette, LA	12.3
333	Burbank, CA	16.3	366	Elk Grove, CA	11.6	430	Lake Forest, CA	1.3
256	Cambridge, MA	22.7	13	Erie, PA	75.4	134	Lakeland, FL	36.5
7	Camden, NJ	85.0	299	Escondido, CA	19.2	408	Lakewood Twnshp, NJ	6.4
253	Canton Twnshp, MI	23.3	78	Eugene, OR	49.4	371	Lakewood, CA	11.1
389	Cape Coral, FL	9.0	82	Evansville, IN	47.4	42	Lakewood, CO	60.5
376	Carlsbad, CA	10.3	87	Everett, WA	46.8	225	Lancaster, CA	26.5
378	Carmel, IN	10.1	294	Fairfield, CA	19.7	12	Lansing, MI	78.8
422	Carrollton, TX	3.3	51	Fall River, MA	58.2	181	Laredo, TX	31.5
347	Carson, CA	14.0	122	Fargo, ND	39.1	116	Largo, FL	40.7
385	Cary, NC	9.5	349	Farmington Hills, MI	13.8	328	Las Cruces, NM	17.2
171	Cedar Rapids, IA	32.3	214	Fayetteville, NC	27.6	98	Las Vegas, NV	44.6
226	Centennial, CO	26.4	431	Fishers, IN	0.0	129	Lawrence, KS	37.4
23	Champaign, IL	68.9	8	Flint, MI	83.0	341	Lawrence, MA	15.6
231	Chandler, AZ	25.9	294	Fontana, CA	19.7	51	Lawton, OK	58.2
237	Charleston, SC	24.7	126	Fort Collins, CO	38.2	238	League City, TX	24.6
214	Charlotte, NC	27.6	62	Fort Lauderdale, FL	54.2	297	Lee's Summit, MO	19.6
276	Chattanooga, TN	21.3	16	Fort Smith, AR	72.5	257	Lewisville, TX	22.6

Alpha Order - City (continued)

RANK	CITY	RATE
147	Lexington, KY	35.3
31	Lincoln, NE	63.7
10	Little Rock, AR	82.6
329	Livermore, CA	17.1
297	Livonia, MI	19.6
245	Long Beach, CA	23.9
283	Longmont, CO	20.5
242	Longview, TX	24.3
274	Los Angeles, CA	21.6
156	Louisville, KY	34.1
159	Lowell, MA	33.6
191	Lubbock, TX	29.9
201	Lynchburg, VA	28.8
175	Lynn, MA	31.9
143	Macon, GA	35.7
178	Madison, WI	31.6
32	Manchester, NH	62.9
286	McAllen, TX	20.4
238	McKinney, TX	24.6
76	Medford, OR	50.2
170	Melbourne, FL	32.4
40	Memphis, TN	61.0
427	Menifee, CA	2.6
233	Merced, CA	25.0
233	Meridian, ID	25.0
194	Mesa, AZ	29.4
414	Mesquite, TX	5.6
95	Miami Beach, FL	45.0
325	Miami Gardens, FL	17.5
247	Miami, FL	23.7
309	Midland, TX	18.5
169	Milwaukee, WI	32.5
1	Minneapolis, MN	100.1
171	Miramar, FL	32.3
425	Mission Viejo, CA	3.2
402	Mission, TX	7.6
300	Mobile, AL	19.1
166	Modesto, CA	32.9
312	Montgomery, AL	18.4
332	Moreno Valley, CA	16.4
219	Murfreesboro, TN	27.3
358	Murrieta, CA	12.4
96	Nampa, ID	44.9
186	Napa, CA	30.8
426	Naperville, IL	2.8
212	Nashua, NH	27.7
41	Nashville, TN	60.9
38	New Bedford, MA	61.7
110	New Haven, CT	42.3
86	New Orleans, LA	47.0
427	New Rochelle, NY	2.6
355	New York, NY	13.3
280	Newark, NJ	20.9
306	Newport Beach, CA	18.6
205	Newport News, VA	28.4
429	Newton, MA	2.3
165	Norfolk, VA	33.0
45	Norman, OK	59.8
146	North Charleston, SC	35.5
386	Norwalk, CA	9.4
325	Norwalk, CT	17.5
73	Oakland, CA	51.1
153	Oceanside, CA	34.3
136	Odessa, TX	36.3
420	O'Fallon, MO	3.8
247	Ogden, UT	23.7
84	Oklahoma City, OK	47.3
128	Olathe, KS	37.9
65	Omaha, NE	53.3
333	Ontario, CA	16.3
418	Orange, CA	4.3
267	Orem, UT	22.2
79	Orlando, FL	49.3

RANK	CITY	RATE
152	Overland Park, KS	34.4
356	Oxnard, CA	13.0
278	Palm Bay, FL	21.0
238	Palmdale, CA	24.6
305	Pasadena, CA	18.7
116	Pasadena, TX	40.7
224	Paterson, NJ	26.6
337	Pearland, TX	16.1
318	Pembroke Pines, FL	17.9
259	Peoria, AZ	22.4
203	Peoria, IL	28.6
60	Philadelphia, PA	54.4
127	Phoenix, AZ	38.1
273	Pittsburgh, PA	21.7
344	Plano, TX	15.1
327	Plantation, FL	17.4
142	Pomona, CA	35.8
118	Pompano Beach, FL	40.5
317	Port St. Lucie, FL	18.0
101	Portland, OR	43.7
81	Portsmouth, VA	47.6
252	Provo, UT	23.5
131	Pueblo, CO	36.9
164	Quincy, MA	33.4
323	Racine, WI	17.7
184	Raleigh, NC	31.1
421	Ramapo, NY	3.6
399	Rancho Cucamon., CA	7.8
235	Reading, PA	24.9
20	Redding, CA	69.3
163	Redwood City, CA	33.5
362	Reno, NV	11.9
143	Renton, WA	35.7
318	Rialto, CA	17.9
391	Richardson, TX	8.9
130	Richmond, CA	37.2
276	Richmond, VA	21.3
340	Rio Rancho, NM	15.8
309	Riverside, CA	18.5
159	Roanoke, VA	33.6
NA	Rochester, MN**	NA
96	Rochester, NY	44.9
15	Rockford, IL	73.0
292	Roseville, CA	20.0
359	Roswell, GA	12.3
241	Round Rock, TX	24.5
205	Sacramento, CA	28.4
283	Salem, OR	20.5
263	Salinas, CA	22.3
33	Salt Lake City, UT	62.6
159	San Angelo, TX	33.6
136	San Antonio, TX	36.3
136	San Bernardino, CA	36.3
267	San Diego, CA	22.2
337	San Francisco, CA	16.1
251	San Jose, CA	23.6
270	San Leandro, CA	22.1
259	San Marcos, CA	22.4
287	San Mateo, CA	20.3
409	Sandy Springs, GA	6.3
300	Sandy, UT	19.1
303	Santa Ana, CA	18.9
113	Santa Barbara, CA	41.4
362	Santa Clara, CA	11.9
378	Santa Clarita, CA	10.1
318	Santa Maria, CA	17.9
226	Santa Monica, CA	26.4
155	Santa Rosa, CA	34.2
339	Savannah, GA	15.9
342	Scottsdale, AZ	15.4
99	Scranton, PA	44.5
335	Seattle, WA	16.2
43	Shreveport, LA	60.2
403	Simi Valley, CA	7.2

RANK	CITY	RATE
103	Sioux City, IA	43.3
20	Sioux Falls, SD	69.3
263	Somerville, MA	22.3
47	South Bend, IN	59.0
374	South Gate, CA	10.5
74	Sparks, NV	50.5
243	Spokane Valley, WA	24.1
121	Spokane, WA	39.6
5	Springfield, IL	88.3
291	Springfield, MA	20.1
24	Springfield, MO	68.7
230	Stamford, CT	26.0
392	Sterling Heights, MI	8.5
187	Stockton, CA	30.5
219	St. Joseph, MO	27.3
48	St. Louis, MO	58.7
48	St. Paul, MN	58.7
136	St. Petersburg, FL	36.3
267	Suffolk, VA	22.2
411	Sugar Land, TX	6.2
345	Sunnyvale, CA	14.8
374	Sunrise, FL	10.5
378	Surprise, AZ	10.1
104	Syracuse, NY	43.2
36	Tacoma, WA	62.0
51	Tallahassee, FL	58.2
330	Tampa, FL	17.0
405	Temecula, CA	6.9
217	Tempe, AZ	27.4
113	Thornton, CO	41.4
399	Thousand Oaks, CA	7.8
105	Toledo, OH	43.1
422	Toms River Twnshp, NJ	3.3
115	Topeka, KS	41.3
366	Torrance, CA	11.6
346	Tracy, CA	14.3
195	Trenton, NJ	29.3
278	Troy, MI	21.0
123	Tucson, AZ	38.7
25	Tulsa, OK	67.2
107	Tuscaloosa, AL	42.9
388	Tustin, CA	9.2
88	Tyler, TX	46.5
243	Upper Darby Twnshp, PA	24.1
275	Vacaville, CA	21.4
94	Vallejo, CA	45.2
35	Vancouver, WA	62.1
306	Ventura, CA	18.6
178	Victorville, CA	31.6
354	Virginia Beach, VA	13.5
176	Visalia, CA	31.8
158	Vista, CA	33.7
58	Waco, TX	54.9
59	Warren, MI	54.5
199	Warwick, RI	29.1
210	Washington, DC	27.8
396	Waterbury, CT	8.1
306	West Covina, CA	18.6
195	West Jordan, UT	29.3
82	West Palm Beach, FL	47.4
50	West Valley, UT	58.3
46	Westland, MI	59.5
361	Westminster, CA	12.1
181	Westminster, CO	31.5
396	Whittier, CA	8.1
209	Wichita Falls, TX	28.1
37	Wichita, KS	61.9
192	Wilmington, NC	29.7
120	Winston-Salem, NC	40.0
398	Woodbridge Twnshp, NJ	8.0
293	Worcester, MA	19.8
70	Yakima, WA	51.9
321	Yonkers, NY	17.8
149	Yuma, AZ	35.0

Source: CQ Press using reported data from the F.B.I. "Crime in the United States 2011"
*Forcible rape is the carnal knowledge of a female forcibly and against her will. Assaults or attempts to commit rape by force or threat of force are included. However, statutory rape without force and other sex offenses are excluded. **Not available

54. Rape Rate in 2011 (continued)
National Rate = 26.8 Rapes per 100,000 Population*

RANK	CITY	RATE	RANK	CITY	RATE	RANK	CITY	RATE
1	Minneapolis, MN	100.1	73	Oakland, CA	51.1	145	Edinburg, TX	35.6
2	Anchorage, AK	95.3	74	Sparks, NV	50.5	146	North Charleston, SC	35.5
3	Bloomington, IL	89.8	75	Des Moines, IA	50.4	147	Boulder, CO	35.3
4	Cleveland, OH	89.1	76	Kenosha, WI	50.2	147	Lexington, KY	35.3
5	Springfield, IL	88.3	76	Medford, OR	50.2	149	Dallas, TX	35.0
6	Birmingham, AL	85.3	78	Eugene, OR	49.4	149	Yuma, AZ	35.0
7	Camden, NJ	85.0	79	Orlando, FL	49.3	151	Atlanta, GA	34.8
8	Flint, MI	83.0	80	Albuquerque, NM	47.8	152	Overland Park, KS	34.4
9	Akron, OH	82.8	81	Portsmouth, VA	47.6	153	Billings, MT	34.3
10	Little Rock, AR	82.6	82	Evansville, IN	47.4	153	Oceanside, CA	34.3
11	Bridgeport, CT	80.3	82	West Palm Beach, FL	47.4	155	Santa Rosa, CA	34.2
12	Lansing, MI	78.8	84	Oklahoma City, OK	47.3	156	Louisville, KY	34.1
13	Erie, PA	75.4	85	Albany, GA	47.2	157	Columbia, MO	34.0
14	Colorado Springs, CO	75.3	86	New Orleans, LA	47.0	158	Vista, CA	33.7
15	Rockford, IL	73.0	87	Everett, WA	46.8	159	Albany, NY	33.6
16	Fort Smith, AR	72.5	88	Tyler, TX	46.5	159	Lowell, MA	33.6
17	Jackson, MS	72.3	89	Fort Worth, TX	46.2	159	Roanoke, VA	33.6
18	Elgin, IL	71.9	90	Buffalo, NY	46.1	159	San Angelo, TX	33.6
19	Columbus, OH	71.7	90	Compton, CA	46.1	163	Redwood City, CA	33.5
20	Redding, CA	69.3	92	Denton, TX	45.8	164	Quincy, MA	33.4
20	Sioux Falls, SD	69.3	93	Clarksville, TN	45.5	165	Norfolk, VA	33.0
22	Dayton, OH	69.2	94	Vallejo, CA	45.2	166	Hollywood, FL	32.9
23	Champaign, IL	68.9	95	Miami Beach, FL	45.0	166	Modesto, CA	32.9
24	Springfield, MO	68.7	96	Nampa, ID	44.9	168	El Paso, TX	32.7
25	Tulsa, OK	67.2	96	Rochester, NY	44.9	169	Milwaukee, WI	32.5
26	Gainesville, FL	65.1	98	Las Vegas, NV	44.6	170	Melbourne, FL	32.4
27	Denver, CO	64.9	99	Scranton, PA	44.5	171	Bend, OR	32.3
28	Kansas City, KS	64.8	100	Hartford, CT	44.0	171	Cedar Rapids, IA	32.3
29	Brockton, MA	64.6	101	Portland, OR	43.7	171	College Station, TX	32.3
30	Kent, WA	63.9	102	Boston, MA	43.6	171	Miramar, FL	32.3
31	Lincoln, NE	63.7	103	Sioux City, IA	43.3	175	Lynn, MA	31.9
32	Manchester, NH	62.9	104	Syracuse, NY	43.2	176	Visalia, CA	31.8
33	Salt Lake City, UT	62.6	105	Grand Rapids, MI	43.1	177	Boise, ID	31.7
34	Corpus Christi, TX	62.3	105	Toledo, OH	43.1	178	Ann Arbor, MI	31.6
35	Vancouver, WA	62.1	107	Tuscaloosa, AL	42.9	178	Madison, WI	31.6
36	Tacoma, WA	62.0	108	Bellingham, WA	42.6	178	Victorville, CA	31.6
37	Wichita, KS	61.9	109	Chico, CA	42.4	181	Laredo, TX	31.5
38	New Bedford, MA	61.7	110	New Haven, CT	42.3	181	Westminster, CO	31.5
39	Cincinnati, OH	61.6	111	Danbury, CT	42.0	183	Indio, CA	31.2
40	Memphis, TN	61.0	112	Jacksonville, FL	41.9	184	Raleigh, NC	31.1
41	Nashville, TN	60.9	113	Santa Barbara, CA	41.4	185	Anaheim, CA	30.9
42	Lakewood, CO	60.5	113	Thornton, CO	41.4	186	Napa, CA	30.8
43	Shreveport, LA	60.2	115	Topeka, KS	41.3	187	Stockton, CA	30.5
44	Detroit, MI	59.9	116	Largo, FL	40.7	188	Elizabeth, NJ	30.3
45	Norman, OK	59.8	116	Pasadena, TX	40.7	189	Deerfield Beach, FL	30.2
46	Westland, MI	59.5	118	Pompano Beach, FL	40.5	189	Hayward, CA	30.2
47	South Bend, IN	59.0	119	Greeley, CO	40.2	191	Lubbock, TX	29.9
48	St. Louis, MO	58.7	120	Winston-Salem, NC	40.0	192	Inglewood, CA	29.7
48	St. Paul, MN	58.7	121	Spokane, WA	39.6	192	Wilmington, NC	29.7
50	West Valley, UT	58.3	122	Fargo, ND	39.1	194	Mesa, AZ	29.4
51	Fall River, MA	58.2	123	Tucson, AZ	38.7	195	Hawthorne, CA	29.3
51	Gary, IN	58.2	124	Grand Prairie, TX	38.5	195	Trenton, NJ	29.3
51	Lawton, OK	58.2	125	Independence, MO	38.4	195	West Jordan, UT	29.3
51	Tallahassee, FL	58.2	126	Fort Collins, CO	38.2	198	Aurora, IL	29.2
55	Kansas City, MO	57.4	127	Phoenix, AZ	38.1	199	Warwick, RI	29.1
56	Hammond, IN	55.4	128	Olathe, KS	37.9	200	Gresham, OR	29.0
57	Aurora, CO	55.3	129	Lawrence, KS	37.4	201	Lynchburg, VA	28.8
58	Waco, TX	54.9	130	Richmond, CA	37.2	202	El Monte, CA	28.7
59	Warren, MI	54.5	131	Fort Wayne, IN	36.9	203	Peoria, IL	28.6
60	Baltimore, MD	54.4	131	Pueblo, CO	36.9	204	Cicero, IL	28.5
60	Philadelphia, PA	54.4	133	Clearwater, FL	36.6	205	Newport News, VA	28.4
62	Fort Lauderdale, FL	54.2	134	Lakeland, FL	36.5	205	Sacramento, CA	28.4
63	Beaumont, TX	53.8	135	Arlington, TX	36.4	207	Bryan, TX	28.3
64	Amarillo, TX	53.4	136	Odessa, TX	36.3	208	Huntsville, AL	28.2
65	Omaha, NE	53.3	136	San Antonio, TX	36.3	209	Wichita Falls, TX	28.1
66	Davenport, IA	52.9	136	San Bernardino, CA	36.3	210	El Cajon, CA	27.8
67	Killeen, TX	52.8	136	St. Petersburg, FL	36.3	210	Washington, DC	27.8
68	Indianapolis, IN	52.2	140	Houston, TX	36.0	212	Durham, NC	27.7
69	Knoxville, TN	52.1	140	Kennewick, WA	36.0	212	Nashua, NH	27.7
70	Yakima, WA	51.9	142	Pomona, CA	35.8	214	Abilene, TX	27.6
71	Green Bay, WI	51.7	143	Macon, GA	35.7	214	Charlotte, NC	27.6
72	Allentown, PA	51.5	143	Renton, WA	35.7	214	Fayetteville, NC	27.6

Rank Order - City (continued)

RANK	CITY	RATE
217	Hesperia, CA	27.4
217	Tempe, AZ	27.4
219	Murfreesboro, TN	27.3
219	St. Joseph, MO	27.3
221	Costa Mesa, CA	27.0
222	Boca Raton, FL	26.9
222	Clovis, CA	26.9
224	Paterson, NJ	26.6
225	Lancaster, CA	26.5
226	Centennial, CO	26.4
226	Santa Monica, CA	26.4
228	Asheville, NC	26.1
228	Austin, TX	26.1
230	Stamford, CT	26.0
231	Chandler, AZ	25.9
232	Athens-Clarke, GA	25.6
233	Merced, CA	25.0
233	Meridian, ID	25.0
235	Reading, PA	24.9
236	Hillsboro, OR	24.8
237	Charleston, SC	24.7
238	League City, TX	24.6
238	McKinney, TX	24.6
238	Palmdale, CA	24.6
241	Round Rock, TX	24.5
242	Longview, TX	24.3
243	Spokane Valley, WA	24.1
243	Upper Darby Twnshp, PA	24.1
245	Long Beach, CA	23.9
246	Clinton Twnshp, MI	23.8
247	Garland, TX	23.7
247	High Point, NC	23.7
247	Miami, FL	23.7
247	Ogden, UT	23.7
251	San Jose, CA	23.6
252	Provo, UT	23.5
253	Canton Twnshp, MI	23.3
254	Arvada, CO	23.1
254	Beaverton, OR	23.1
256	Cambridge, MA	22.7
257	Bethlehem, PA	22.6
257	Lewisville, TX	22.6
259	Cranston, RI	22.4
259	Dearborn, MI	22.4
259	Peoria, AZ	22.4
259	San Marcos, CA	22.4
263	Bloomington, IN	22.3
263	Henderson, NV	22.3
263	Salinas, CA	22.3
263	Somerville, MA	22.3
267	Orem, UT	22.2
267	San Diego, CA	22.2
267	Suffolk, VA	22.2
270	San Leandro, CA	22.1
271	Baton Rouge, LA	22.0
271	Broken Arrow, OK	22.0
273	Pittsburgh, PA	21.7
274	Los Angeles, CA	21.6
275	Vacaville, CA	21.4
276	Chattanooga, TN	21.3
276	Richmond, VA	21.3
278	Palm Bay, FL	21.0
278	Troy, MI	21.0
280	Newark, NJ	20.9
281	Columbus, GA	20.8
282	Brownsville, TX	20.7
283	Chesapeake, VA	20.5
283	Longmont, CO	20.5
283	Salem, OR	20.5
286	McAllen, TX	20.4
287	Antioch, CA	20.3
287	Downey, CA	20.3
287	Joliet, IL	20.3

RANK	CITY	RATE
287	San Mateo, CA	20.3
291	Springfield, MA	20.1
292	Roseville, CA	20.0
293	Worcester, MA	19.8
294	Fairfield, CA	19.7
294	Fontana, CA	19.7
294	Jersey City, NJ	19.7
297	Lee's Summit, MO	19.6
297	Livonia, MI	19.6
299	Escondido, CA	19.2
300	Glendale, AZ	19.1
300	Mobile, AL	19.1
300	Sandy, UT	19.1
303	Santa Ana, CA	18.9
304	Hemet, CA	18.8
305	Pasadena, CA	18.7
306	Newport Beach, CA	18.6
306	Ventura, CA	18.6
306	West Covina, CA	18.6
309	Bellevue, WA	18.5
309	Midland, TX	18.5
309	Riverside, CA	18.5
312	Montgomery, AL	18.4
313	Decatur, IL	18.3
313	Fullerton, CA	18.3
315	Davie, FL	18.2
316	Bellflower, CA	18.1
317	Port St. Lucie, FL	18.0
318	Pembroke Pines, FL	17.9
318	Rialto, CA	17.9
318	Santa Maria, CA	17.9
321	Citrus Heights, CA	17.8
321	Yonkers, NY	17.8
323	Huntington Beach, CA	17.7
323	Racine, WI	17.7
325	Miami Gardens, FL	17.5
325	Norwalk, CT	17.5
327	Plantation, FL	17.4
328	Las Cruces, NM	17.2
329	Livermore, CA	17.1
330	Tampa, FL	17.0
331	Berkeley, CA	16.7
332	Moreno Valley, CA	16.4
333	Burbank, CA	16.3
333	Ontario, CA	16.3
335	Fremont, CA	16.2
335	Seattle, WA	16.2
337	Pearland, TX	16.1
337	San Francisco, CA	16.1
339	Savannah, GA	15.9
340	Rio Rancho, NM	15.8
341	Lawrence, MA	15.6
342	Concord, CA	15.4
342	Scottsdale, AZ	15.4
344	Plano, TX	15.1
345	Sunnyvale, CA	14.8
346	Tracy, CA	14.3
347	Allen, TX	14.0
347	Carson, CA	14.0
349	Chula Vista, CA	13.8
349	Farmington Hills, MI	13.8
351	Daly City, CA	13.7
351	Hampton, VA	13.7
353	Hialeah, FL	13.6
354	Virginia Beach, VA	13.5
355	New York, NY	13.3
356	Oxnard, CA	13.0
357	Cheektowaga, NY	12.6
358	Murrieta, CA	12.4
359	Lafayette, LA	12.3
359	Roswell, GA	12.3
361	Westminster, CA	12.1
362	Reno, NV	11.9
362	Santa Clara, CA	11.9

RANK	CITY	RATE
364	Baldwin Park, CA	11.8
364	Clifton, NJ	11.8
366	Elk Grove, CA	11.6
366	Torrance, CA	11.6
368	Chino, CA	11.4
369	Hamilton Twnshp, NJ	11.3
369	Irving, TX	11.3
371	Bakersfield, CA	11.1
371	Lakewood, CA	11.1
373	Garden Grove, CA	11.0
374	South Gate, CA	10.5
374	Sunrise, FL	10.5
376	Carlsbad, CA	10.3
377	Fresno, CA	10.2
378	Carmel, IN	10.1
378	Santa Clarita, CA	10.1
378	Surprise, AZ	10.1
381	Concord, NC	10.0
382	Alexandria, VA	9.9
382	Gilbert, AZ	9.9
384	Buena Park, CA	9.8
385	Cary, NC	9.5
386	Norwalk, CA	9.4
387	Brick Twnshp, NJ	9.3
388	Tustin, CA	9.2
389	Cape Coral, FL	9.0
389	Edison Twnshp, NJ	9.0
391	Richardson, TX	8.9
392	Edmond, OK	8.5
392	Hoover, AL	8.5
392	Sterling Heights, MI	8.5
395	Alhambra, CA	8.3
396	Waterbury, CT	8.1
396	Whittier, CA	8.1
398	Woodbridge Twnshp, NJ	8.0
399	Avondale, AZ	7.8
399	Rancho Cucamon., CA	7.8
399	Thousand Oaks, CA	7.8
402	Mission, TX	7.6
403	Glendale, CA	7.2
403	Simi Valley, CA	7.2
405	Temecula, CA	6.9
406	Arlington Heights, IL	6.6
407	Corona, CA	6.5
408	Lakewood Twnshp, NJ	6.4
409	Clarkstown, NY	6.3
409	Sandy Springs, GA	6.3
411	Greece, NY	6.2
411	Sugar Land, TX	6.2
413	Amherst, NY	6.0
414	Mesquite, TX	5.6
415	Chino Hills, CA	5.3
416	Irvine, CA	5.1
417	Frisco, TX	5.0
418	Orange, CA	4.3
419	Johns Creek, GA	3.9
420	O'Fallon, MO	3.8
421	Ramapo, NY	3.6
422	Carrollton, TX	3.3
422	Coral Springs, FL	3.3
422	Toms River Twnshp, NJ	3.3
425	Mission Viejo, CA	3.2
426	Naperville, IL	2.8
427	Menifee, CA	2.6
427	New Rochelle, NY	2.6
429	Newton, MA	2.3
430	Lake Forest, CA	1.3
431	Colonie, NY	0.0
431	Fishers, IN	0.0
NA	Bloomington, MN**	NA
NA	Brooklyn Park, MN**	NA
NA	Chicago, IL**	NA
NA	Duluth, MN**	NA
NA	Rochester, MN**	NA

Source: CQ Press using reported data from the F.B.I. "Crime in the United States 2011"
*Forcible rape is the carnal knowledge of a female forcibly and against her will. Assaults or attempts to commit rape by force or threat of force are included. However, statutory rape without force and other sex offenses are excluded. **Not available

Alpha Order - City

55. Percent Change in Rape Rate: 2010 to 2011
National Percent Change = 3.2% Decrease*

RANK	CITY	% CHANGE	RANK	CITY	% CHANGE	RANK	CITY	% CHANGE
394	Abilene, TX	(52.6)	385	Cheektowaga, NY	(43.2)	183	Fort Wayne, IN	(1.3)
134	Akron, OH	7.1	22	Chesapeake, VA	78.3	121	Fort Worth, TX	8.5
77	Albany, GA	23.2	NA	Chicago, IL**	NA	281	Fremont, CA	(16.9)
323	Albany, NY	(25.8)	310	Chico, CA	(22.8)	339	Fresno, CA	(29.2)
311	Albuquerque, NM	(22.9)	302	Chino Hills, CA	(20.9)	400	Frisco, TX	(56.1)
333	Alexandria, VA	(27.7)	326	Chino, CA	(26.0)	213	Fullerton, CA	(6.2)
252	Alhambra, CA	(11.7)	382	Chula Vista, CA	(41.5)	250	Gainesville, FL	(11.5)
275	Allentown, PA	(16.7)	NA	Cicero, IL**	NA	275	Garden Grove, CA	(16.7)
152	Allen, TX	4.5	255	Cincinnati, OH	(12.1)	55	Garland, TX	34.7
106	Amarillo, TX	11.7	376	Citrus Heights, CA	(39.9)	NA	Gary, IN**	NA
286	Amherst, NY	(17.8)	76	Clarkstown, NY	23.5	289	Gilbert, AZ	(18.2)
84	Anaheim, CA	18.8	151	Clarksville, TN	4.6	166	Glendale, AZ	2.1
148	Anchorage, AK	4.8	110	Clearwater, FL	10.6	274	Glendale, CA	(16.3)
287	Ann Arbor, MI	(17.9)	107	Cleveland, OH	11.4	196	Grand Prairie, TX	(2.8)
358	Antioch, CA	(35.1)	NA	Clifton, NJ**	NA	227	Grand Rapids, MI	(8.3)
206	Arlington Heights, IL	(4.3)	264	Clinton Twnshp, MI	(12.8)	393	Greece, NY	(52.3)
89	Arlington, TX	17.4	275	Clovis, CA	(16.7)	230	Greeley, CO	(9.0)
284	Arvada, CO	(17.5)	309	College Station, TX	(22.7)	200	Green Bay, WI	(3.0)
358	Asheville, NC	(35.1)	409	Colonie, NY	(100.0)	340	Gresham, OR	(29.3)
180	Athens-Clarke, GA	(0.4)	212	Colorado Springs, CO	(6.1)	3	Hamilton Twnshp, NJ	242.4
9	Atlanta, GA	109.6	207	Columbia, MO	(5.0)	34	Hammond, IN	56.5
192	Aurora, CO	(2.3)	171	Columbus, GA	1.0	346	Hampton, VA	(31.8)
298	Aurora, IL	(20.4)	189	Columbus, OH	(2.0)	83	Hartford, CT	20.2
304	Austin, TX	(21.6)	26	Compton, CA	73.3	321	Hawthorne, CA	(25.6)
403	Avondale, AZ	(64.2)	348	Concord, CA	(32.8)	230	Hayward, CA	(9.0)
120	Bakersfield, CA	8.8	369	Concord, NC	(37.9)	292	Hemet, CA	(19.3)
101	Baldwin Park, CA	13.5	388	Coral Springs, FL	(47.6)	28	Henderson, NV	68.9
59	Baltimore, MD	31.4	353	Corona, CA	(33.7)	240	Hesperia, CA	(9.9)
NA	Baton Rouge, LA**	NA	213	Corpus Christi, TX	(6.2)	322	Hialeah, FL	(25.7)
236	Beaumont, TX	(9.4)	259	Costa Mesa, CA	(12.3)	247	High Point, NC	(10.9)
341	Beaverton, OR	(30.0)	143	Cranston, RI	5.7	NA	Hillsboro, OR**	NA
6	Bellevue, WA	137.2	234	Dallas, TX	(9.3)	88	Hollywood, FL	17.5
387	Bellflower, CA	(45.2)	36	Daly City, CA	55.7	NA	Hoover, AL**	NA
216	Bellingham, WA	(6.6)	31	Danbury, CT	62.8	96	Houston, TX	15.4
19	Bend, OR	83.5	NA	Davenport, IA**	NA	129	Huntington Beach, CA	7.3
320	Berkeley, CA	(25.4)	295	Davie, FL	(19.8)	NA	Huntsville, AL**	NA
222	Bethlehem, PA	(7.4)	97	Dayton, OH	14.6	123	Independence, MO	8.2
NA	Billings, MT**	NA	370	Dearborn, MI	(38.3)	NA	Indianapolis, IN**	NA
NA	Birmingham, AL**	NA	345	Decatur, IL	(31.5)	263	Indio, CA	(12.6)
37	Bloomington, IL	55.1	210	Deerfield Beach, FL	(5.3)	155	Inglewood, CA	4.2
389	Bloomington, IN	(48.0)	267	Denton, TX	(13.1)	399	Irvine, CA	(54.1)
NA	Bloomington, MN**	NA	129	Denver, CO	7.3	358	Irving, TX	(35.1)
21	Boca Raton, FL	79.3	195	Des Moines, IA	(2.7)	119	Jacksonville, FL	9.1
328	Boise, ID	(26.6)	56	Detroit, MI	33.1	74	Jackson, MS	24.7
112	Boston, MA	9.8	68	Downey, CA	27.7	117	Jersey City, NJ	9.4
140	Boulder, CO	6.3	NA	Duluth, MN**	NA	396	Johns Creek, GA	(53.0)
143	Brick Twnshp, NJ	5.7	125	Durham, NC	7.8	187	Joliet, IL	(1.5)
13	Bridgeport, CT	95.4	92	Edinburg, TX	16.3	41	Kansas City, KS	50.3
190	Brockton, MA	(2.1)	20	Edison Twnshp, NJ	80.0	NA	Kansas City, MO**	NA
342	Broken Arrow, OK	(30.8)	303	Edmond, OK	(21.3)	185	Kennewick, WA	(1.4)
NA	Brooklyn Park, MN**	NA	24	El Cajon, CA	74.8	81	Kenosha, WI	21.3
82	Brownsville, TX	20.3	62	El Monte, CA	29.3	289	Kent, WA	(18.2)
367	Bryan, TX	(37.3)	99	El Paso, TX	13.9	337	Killeen, TX	(28.9)
376	Buena Park, CA	(39.9)	240	Elgin, IL	(9.9)	301	Knoxville, TN	(20.7)
NA	Buffalo, NY**	NA	228	Elizabeth, NJ	(8.7)	337	Lafayette, LA	(28.9)
61	Burbank, CA	29.4	85	Elk Grove, CA	18.4	408	Lake Forest, CA	(87.7)
105	Cambridge, MA	11.8	173	Erie, PA	0.7	27	Lakeland, FL	73.0
224	Camden, NJ	(7.9)	329	Escondido, CA	(27.0)	220	Lakewood Twnshp, NJ	(7.2)
375	Canton Twnshp, MI	(39.8)	211	Eugene, OR	(5.4)	383	Lakewood, CA	(42.5)
366	Cape Coral, FL	(37.1)	260	Evansville, IN	(12.4)	248	Lakewood, CO	(11.0)
390	Carlsbad, CA	(48.2)	372	Everett, WA	(38.8)	356	Lancaster, CA	(34.4)
238	Carmel, IN	(9.8)	99	Fairfield, CA	13.9	229	Lansing, MI	(8.8)
139	Carrollton, TX	6.5	175	Fall River, MA	0.5	219	Laredo, TX	(6.8)
126	Carson, CA	7.7	249	Fargo, ND	(11.3)	315	Largo, FL	(23.8)
205	Cary, NC	(4.0)	350	Farmington Hills, MI	(33.0)	40	Las Cruces, NM	52.2
72	Cedar Rapids, IA	26.7	173	Fayetteville, NC	0.7	200	Las Vegas, NV	(3.0)
45	Centennial, CO	45.1	409	Fishers, IN	(100.0)	257	Lawrence, KS	(12.2)
NA	Champaign, IL**	NA	185	Flint, MI	(1.4)	234	Lawrence, MA	(9.3)
160	Chandler, AZ	2.8	162	Fontana, CA	2.6	246	Lawton, OK	(10.7)
32	Charleston, SC	61.4	283	Fort Collins, CO	(17.1)	166	League City, TX	2.1
225	Charlotte, NC	(8.0)	52	Fort Lauderdale, FL	38.3	171	Lee's Summit, MO	1.0
395	Chattanooga, TN	(52.9)	272	Fort Smith, AR	(15.7)	168	Lewisville, TX	1.8

Alpha Order - City (continued)

RANK	CITY	% CHANGE
NA	Lexington, KY**	NA
95	Lincoln, NE	15.6
137	Little Rock, AR	7.0
264	Livermore, CA	(12.8)
78	Livonia, MI	22.5
285	Long Beach, CA	(17.6)
2	Longmont, CO	266.1
397	Longview, TX	(53.6)
242	Los Angeles, CA	(10.0)
207	Louisville, KY	(5.0)
347	Lowell, MA	(32.1)
318	Lubbock, TX	(25.1)
279	Lynchburg, VA	(16.8)
348	Lynn, MA	(32.8)
215	Macon, GA	(6.3)
268	Madison, WI	(13.4)
116	Manchester, NH	9.6
11	McAllen, TX	96.2
112	McKinney, TX	9.8
295	Medford, OR	(19.8)
242	Melbourne, FL	(10.0)
193	Memphis, TN	(2.6)
401	Menifee, CA	(60.0)
380	Merced, CA	(41.3)
138	Meridian, ID	6.8
129	Mesa, AZ	7.3
217	Mesquite, TX	(6.7)
169	Miami Beach, FL	1.6
311	Miami Gardens, FL	(22.9)
7	Miami, FL	127.9
398	Midland, TX	(53.9)
178	Milwaukee, WI	0.0
254	Minneapolis, MN	(11.9)
126	Miramar, FL	7.7
374	Mission Viejo, CA	(39.6)
308	Mission, TX	(22.4)
NA	Mobile, AL**	NA
123	Modesto, CA	8.2
NA	Montgomery, AL**	NA
188	Moreno Valley, CA	(1.8)
293	Murfreesboro, TN	(19.5)
63	Murrieta, CA	29.2
324	Nampa, ID	(25.9)
109	Napa, CA	10.8
NA	Naperville, IL**	NA
371	Nashua, NH	(38.6)
165	Nashville, TN	2.4
297	New Bedford, MA	(19.9)
317	New Haven, CT	(24.6)
92	New Orleans, LA	16.3
402	New Rochelle, NY	(61.8)
129	New York, NY	7.3
324	Newark, NJ	(25.9)
1	Newport Beach, CA	279.6
351	Newport News, VA	(33.2)
405	Newton, MA	(68.1)
270	Norfolk, VA	(14.1)
46	Norman, OK	42.0
342	North Charleston, SC	(30.8)
344	Norwalk, CA	(31.4)
75	Norwalk, CT	24.1
354	Oakland, CA	(34.1)
70	Oceanside, CA	27.0
163	Odessa, TX	2.5
33	O'Fallon, MO	58.3
294	Ogden, UT	(19.7)
299	Oklahoma City, OK	(20.5)
91	Olathe, KS	16.6
69	Omaha, NE	27.5
381	Ontario, CA	(41.4)
12	Orange, CA	95.5
117	Orem, UT	9.4
147	Orlando, FL	4.9

RANK	CITY	% CHANGE
38	Overland Park, KS	53.6
66	Oxnard, CA	28.7
98	Palm Bay, FL	14.1
253	Palmdale, CA	(11.8)
64	Pasadena, CA	29.0
264	Pasadena, TX	(12.8)
251	Paterson, NJ	(11.6)
225	Pearland, TX	(8.0)
8	Pembroke Pines, FL	121.0
217	Peoria, AZ	(6.7)
145	Peoria, IL	5.5
245	Philadelphia, PA	(10.2)
102	Phoenix, AZ	12.7
160	Pittsburgh, PA	2.8
299	Plano, TX	(20.5)
145	Plantation, FL	5.5
43	Pomona, CA	47.9
279	Pompano Beach, FL	(16.8)
357	Port St. Lucie, FL	(34.8)
134	Portland, OR	7.1
4	Portsmouth, VA	178.4
376	Provo, UT	(39.9)
NA	Pueblo, CO**	NA
53	Quincy, MA	36.9
313	Racine, WI	(23.7)
58	Raleigh, NC	31.8
51	Ramapo, NY	38.5
183	Rancho Cucamon., CA	(1.3)
204	Reading, PA	(3.5)
156	Redding, CA	3.9
35	Redwood City, CA	55.8
383	Reno, NV	(42.5)
379	Renton, WA	(40.8)
386	Rialto, CA	(44.4)
336	Richardson, TX	(28.8)
262	Richmond, CA	(12.5)
112	Richmond, VA	9.8
10	Rio Rancho, NM	97.5
334	Riverside, CA	(28.3)
87	Roanoke, VA	17.9
NA	Rochester, MN**	NA
223	Rochester, NY	(7.6)
158	Rockford, IL	3.7
47	Roseville, CA	40.8
355	Roswell, GA	(34.2)
150	Round Rock, TX	4.7
291	Sacramento, CA	(18.6)
352	Salem, OR	(33.4)
48	Salinas, CA	40.3
315	Salt Lake City, UT	(23.8)
363	San Angelo, TX	(35.4)
122	San Antonio, TX	8.4
115	San Bernardino, CA	9.7
193	San Diego, CA	(2.6)
182	San Francisco, CA	(0.6)
237	San Jose, CA	(9.6)
25	San Leandro, CA	74.0
90	San Marcos, CA	17.3
304	San Mateo, CA	(21.6)
406	Sandy Springs, GA	(71.0)
230	Sandy, UT	(9.0)
329	Santa Ana, CA	(27.0)
70	Santa Barbara, CA	27.0
15	Santa Clara, CA	91.9
287	Santa Clarita, CA	(17.9)
391	Santa Maria, CA	(50.8)
14	Santa Monica, CA	92.7
203	Santa Rosa, CA	(3.4)
104	Savannah, GA	12.0
126	Scottsdale, AZ	7.7
50	Scranton, PA	39.1
152	Seattle, WA	4.5
181	Shreveport, LA	(0.5)
368	Simi Valley, CA	(37.4)

RANK	CITY	% CHANGE
30	Sioux City, IA	64.6
94	Sioux Falls, SD	16.1
48	Somerville, MA	40.3
86	South Bend, IN	18.2
307	South Gate, CA	(22.2)
57	Sparks, NV	31.9
392	Spokane Valley, WA	(51.9)
175	Spokane, WA	0.5
179	Springfield, IL	(0.3)
407	Springfield, MA	(76.0)
244	Springfield, MO	(10.1)
29	Stamford, CT	67.7
NA	Sterling Heights, MI**	NA
275	Stockton, CA	(16.7)
157	St. Joseph, MO	3.8
108	St. Louis, MO	11.0
238	St. Paul, MN	(9.8)
273	St. Petersburg, FL	(15.8)
141	Suffolk, VA	6.2
327	Sugar Land, TX	(26.2)
313	Sunnyvale, CA	(23.7)
332	Sunrise, FL	(27.1)
335	Surprise, AZ	(28.4)
268	Syracuse, NY	(13.4)
257	Tacoma, WA	(12.2)
306	Tallahassee, FL	(21.9)
73	Tampa, FL	25.9
5	Temecula, CA	137.9
111	Tempe, AZ	10.0
NA	Thornton, CO**	NA
373	Thousand Oaks, CA	(39.5)
198	Toledo, OH	(2.9)
362	Toms River Twnshp, NJ	(35.3)
170	Topeka, KS	1.5
270	Torrance, CA	(14.1)
60	Tracy, CA	30.0
17	Trenton, NJ	87.8
18	Troy, MI	85.8
64	Tucson, AZ	29.0
148	Tulsa, OK	4.8
NA	Tuscaloosa, AL**	NA
319	Tustin, CA	(25.2)
142	Tyler, TX	5.9
103	Upper Darby Twnshp, PA	12.1
329	Vacaville, CA	(27.0)
260	Vallejo, CA	(12.4)
221	Vancouver, WA	(7.3)
80	Ventura, CA	21.6
196	Victorville, CA	(2.8)
134	Virginia Beach, VA	7.1
39	Visalia, CA	52.9
42	Vista, CA	49.1
53	Waco, TX	36.9
154	Warren, MI	4.4
23	Warwick, RI	75.3
233	Washington, DC	(9.2)
44	Waterbury, CT	47.3
159	West Covina, CA	3.3
282	West Jordan, UT	(17.0)
190	West Palm Beach, FL	(2.1)
163	West Valley, UT	2.5
133	Westland, MI	7.2
365	Westminster, CA	(36.3)
177	Westminster, CO	0.3
404	Whittier, CA	(66.9)
364	Wichita Falls, TX	(35.7)
209	Wichita, KS	(5.2)
361	Wilmington, NC	(35.2)
198	Winston-Salem, NC	(2.9)
255	Woodbridge Twnshp, NJ	(12.1)
16	Worcester, MA	90.4
202	Yakima, WA	(3.2)
79	Yonkers, NY	21.9
66	Yuma, AZ	28.7

Source: CQ Press using reported data from the F.B.I. "Crime in the United States 2011"
*Forcible rape is the carnal knowledge of a female forcibly and against her will. Assaults or attempts to commit rape by force or threat of force are included. However, statutory rape without force and other sex offenses are excluded. **Not available

55. Percent Change in Rape Rate: 2010 to 2011 (continued)
National Percent Change = 3.2% Decrease*

RANK	CITY	% CHANGE	RANK	CITY	% CHANGE	RANK	CITY	% CHANGE
1	Newport Beach, CA	279.6	73	Tampa, FL	25.9	145	Peoria, IL	5.5
2	Longmont, CO	266.1	74	Jackson, MS	24.7	145	Plantation, FL	5.5
3	Hamilton Twnshp, NJ	242.4	75	Norwalk, CT	24.1	147	Orlando, FL	4.9
4	Portsmouth, VA	178.4	76	Clarkstown, NY	23.5	148	Anchorage, AK	4.8
5	Temecula, CA	137.9	77	Albany, GA	23.2	148	Tulsa, OK	4.8
6	Bellevue, WA	137.2	78	Livonia, MI	22.5	150	Round Rock, TX	4.7
7	Miami, FL	127.9	79	Yonkers, NY	21.9	151	Clarksville, TN	4.6
8	Pembroke Pines, FL	121.0	80	Ventura, CA	21.6	152	Allen, TX	4.5
9	Atlanta, GA	109.6	81	Kenosha, WI	21.3	152	Seattle, WA	4.5
10	Rio Rancho, NM	97.5	82	Brownsville, TX	20.3	154	Warren, MI	4.4
11	McAllen, TX	96.2	83	Hartford, CT	20.2	155	Inglewood, CA	4.2
12	Orange, CA	95.5	84	Anaheim, CA	18.8	156	Redding, CA	3.9
13	Bridgeport, CT	95.4	85	Elk Grove, CA	18.4	157	St. Joseph, MO	3.8
14	Santa Monica, CA	92.7	86	South Bend, IN	18.2	158	Rockford, IL	3.7
15	Santa Clara, CA	91.9	87	Roanoke, VA	17.9	159	West Covina, CA	3.3
16	Worcester, MA	90.4	88	Hollywood, FL	17.5	160	Chandler, AZ	2.8
17	Trenton, NJ	87.8	89	Arlington, TX	17.4	160	Pittsburgh, PA	2.8
18	Troy, MI	85.8	90	San Marcos, CA	17.3	162	Fontana, CA	2.6
19	Bend, OR	83.5	91	Olathe, KS	16.6	163	Odessa, TX	2.5
20	Edison Twnshp, NJ	80.0	92	Edinburg, TX	16.3	163	West Valley, UT	2.5
21	Boca Raton, FL	79.3	92	New Orleans, LA	16.3	165	Nashville, TN	2.4
22	Chesapeake, VA	78.3	94	Sioux Falls, SD	16.1	166	Glendale, AZ	2.1
23	Warwick, RI	75.3	95	Lincoln, NE	15.6	166	League City, TX	2.1
24	El Cajon, CA	74.8	96	Houston, TX	15.4	168	Lewisville, TX	1.8
25	San Leandro, CA	74.0	97	Dayton, OH	14.6	169	Miami Beach, FL	1.6
26	Compton, CA	73.3	98	Palm Bay, FL	14.1	170	Topeka, KS	1.5
27	Lakeland, FL	73.0	99	El Paso, TX	13.9	171	Columbus, GA	1.0
28	Henderson, NV	68.9	99	Fairfield, CA	13.9	171	Lee's Summit, MO	1.0
29	Stamford, CT	67.7	101	Baldwin Park, CA	13.5	173	Erie, PA	0.7
30	Sioux City, IA	64.6	102	Phoenix, AZ	12.7	173	Fayetteville, NC	0.7
31	Danbury, CT	62.8	103	Upper Darby Twnshp, PA	12.1	175	Fall River, MA	0.5
32	Charleston, SC	61.4	104	Savannah, GA	12.0	175	Spokane, WA	0.5
33	O'Fallon, MO	58.3	105	Cambridge, MA	11.8	177	Westminster, CO	0.3
34	Hammond, IN	56.5	106	Amarillo, TX	11.7	178	Milwaukee, WI	0.0
35	Redwood City, CA	55.8	107	Cleveland, OH	11.4	179	Springfield, IL	(0.3)
36	Daly City, CA	55.7	108	St. Louis, MO	11.0	180	Athens-Clarke, GA	(0.4)
37	Bloomington, IL	55.1	109	Napa, CA	10.8	181	Shreveport, LA	(0.5)
38	Overland Park, KS	53.6	110	Clearwater, FL	10.6	182	San Francisco, CA	(0.6)
39	Visalia, CA	52.9	111	Tempe, AZ	10.0	183	Fort Wayne, IN	(1.3)
40	Las Cruces, NM	52.2	112	Boston, MA	9.8	183	Rancho Cucamon., CA	(1.3)
41	Kansas City, KS	50.3	112	McKinney, TX	9.8	185	Flint, MI	(1.4)
42	Vista, CA	49.1	112	Richmond, VA	9.8	185	Kennewick, WA	(1.4)
43	Pomona, CA	47.9	115	San Bernardino, CA	9.7	187	Joliet, IL	(1.5)
44	Waterbury, CT	47.3	116	Manchester, NH	9.6	188	Moreno Valley, CA	(1.8)
45	Centennial, CO	45.1	117	Jersey City, NJ	9.4	189	Columbus, OH	(2.0)
46	Norman, OK	42.0	117	Orem, UT	9.4	190	Brockton, MA	(2.1)
47	Roseville, CA	40.8	119	Jacksonville, FL	9.1	190	West Palm Beach, FL	(2.1)
48	Salinas, CA	40.3	120	Bakersfield, CA	8.8	192	Aurora, CO	(2.3)
48	Somerville, MA	40.3	121	Fort Worth, TX	8.5	193	Memphis, TN	(2.6)
50	Scranton, PA	39.1	122	San Antonio, TX	8.4	193	San Diego, CA	(2.6)
51	Ramapo, NY	38.5	123	Independence, MO	8.2	195	Des Moines, IA	(2.7)
52	Fort Lauderdale, FL	38.3	123	Modesto, CA	8.2	196	Grand Prairie, TX	(2.8)
53	Quincy, MA	36.9	125	Durham, NC	7.8	196	Victorville, CA	(2.8)
53	Waco, TX	36.9	126	Carson, CA	7.7	198	Toledo, OH	(2.9)
55	Garland, TX	34.7	126	Miramar, FL	7.7	198	Winston-Salem, NC	(2.9)
56	Detroit, MI	33.1	126	Scottsdale, AZ	7.7	200	Green Bay, WI	(3.0)
57	Sparks, NV	31.9	129	Denver, CO	7.3	200	Las Vegas, NV	(3.0)
58	Raleigh, NC	31.8	129	Huntington Beach, CA	7.3	202	Yakima, WA	(3.2)
59	Baltimore, MD	31.4	129	Mesa, AZ	7.3	203	Santa Rosa, CA	(3.4)
60	Tracy, CA	30.0	129	New York, NY	7.3	204	Reading, PA	(3.5)
61	Burbank, CA	29.4	133	Westland, MI	7.2	205	Cary, NC	(4.0)
62	El Monte, CA	29.3	134	Akron, OH	7.1	206	Arlington Heights, IL	(4.3)
63	Murrieta, CA	29.2	134	Portland, OR	7.1	207	Columbia, MO	(5.0)
64	Pasadena, CA	29.0	134	Virginia Beach, VA	7.1	207	Louisville, KY	(5.0)
64	Tucson, AZ	29.0	137	Little Rock, AR	7.0	209	Wichita, KS	(5.2)
66	Oxnard, CA	28.7	138	Meridian, ID	6.8	210	Deerfield Beach, FL	(5.3)
66	Yuma, AZ	28.7	139	Carrollton, TX	6.5	211	Eugene, OR	(5.4)
68	Downey, CA	27.7	140	Boulder, CO	6.3	212	Colorado Springs, CO	(6.1)
69	Omaha, NE	27.5	141	Suffolk, VA	6.2	213	Corpus Christi, TX	(6.2)
70	Oceanside, CA	27.0	142	Tyler, TX	5.9	213	Fullerton, CA	(6.2)
70	Santa Barbara, CA	27.0	143	Brick Twnshp, NJ	5.7	215	Macon, GA	(6.3)
72	Cedar Rapids, IA	26.7	143	Cranston, RI	5.7	216	Bellingham, WA	(6.6)

Rank Order - City (continued)

RANK	CITY	% CHANGE	RANK	CITY	% CHANGE	RANK	CITY	% CHANGE
217	Mesquite, TX	(6.7)	289	Kent, WA	(18.2)	364	Wichita Falls, TX	(35.7)
217	Peoria, AZ	(6.7)	291	Sacramento, CA	(18.6)	365	Westminster, CA	(36.3)
219	Laredo, TX	(6.8)	292	Hemet, CA	(19.3)	366	Cape Coral, FL	(37.1)
220	Lakewood Twnshp, NJ	(7.2)	293	Murfreesboro, TN	(19.5)	367	Bryan, TX	(37.3)
221	Vancouver, WA	(7.3)	294	Ogden, UT	(19.7)	368	Simi Valley, CA	(37.4)
222	Bethlehem, PA	(7.4)	295	Davie, FL	(19.8)	369	Concord, NC	(37.9)
223	Rochester, NY	(7.6)	295	Medford, OR	(19.8)	370	Dearborn, MI	(38.3)
224	Camden, NJ	(7.9)	297	New Bedford, MA	(19.9)	371	Nashua, NH	(38.6)
225	Charlotte, NC	(8.0)	298	Aurora, IL	(20.4)	372	Everett, WA	(38.8)
225	Pearland, TX	(8.0)	299	Oklahoma City, OK	(20.5)	373	Thousand Oaks, CA	(39.5)
227	Grand Rapids, MI	(8.3)	299	Plano, TX	(20.5)	374	Mission Viejo, CA	(39.6)
228	Elizabeth, NJ	(8.7)	301	Knoxville, TN	(20.7)	375	Canton Twnshp, MI	(39.8)
229	Lansing, MI	(8.8)	302	Chino Hills, CA	(20.9)	376	Buena Park, CA	(39.9)
230	Greeley, CO	(9.0)	303	Edmond, OK	(21.3)	376	Citrus Heights, CA	(39.9)
230	Hayward, CA	(9.0)	304	Austin, TX	(21.6)	376	Provo, UT	(39.9)
230	Sandy, UT	(9.0)	304	San Mateo, CA	(21.6)	379	Renton, WA	(40.8)
233	Washington, DC	(9.2)	306	Tallahassee, FL	(21.9)	380	Merced, CA	(41.3)
234	Dallas, TX	(9.3)	307	South Gate, CA	(22.2)	381	Ontario, CA	(41.4)
234	Lawrence, MA	(9.3)	308	Mission, TX	(22.4)	382	Chula Vista, CA	(41.5)
236	Beaumont, TX	(9.4)	309	College Station, TX	(22.7)	383	Lakewood, CA	(42.5)
237	San Jose, CA	(9.6)	310	Chico, CA	(22.8)	383	Reno, NV	(42.5)
238	Carmel, IN	(9.8)	311	Albuquerque, NM	(22.9)	385	Cheektowaga, NY	(43.2)
238	St. Paul, MN	(9.8)	311	Miami Gardens, FL	(22.9)	386	Rialto, CA	(44.4)
240	Elgin, IL	(9.9)	313	Racine, WI	(23.7)	387	Bellflower, CA	(45.2)
240	Hesperia, CA	(9.9)	313	Sunnyvale, CA	(23.7)	388	Coral Springs, FL	(47.6)
242	Los Angeles, CA	(10.0)	315	Largo, FL	(23.8)	389	Bloomington, IN	(48.0)
242	Melbourne, FL	(10.0)	315	Salt Lake City, UT	(23.8)	390	Carlsbad, CA	(48.2)
244	Springfield, MO	(10.1)	317	New Haven, CT	(24.6)	391	Santa Maria, CA	(50.8)
245	Philadelphia, PA	(10.2)	318	Lubbock, TX	(25.1)	392	Spokane Valley, WA	(51.9)
246	Lawton, OK	(10.7)	319	Tustin, CA	(25.2)	393	Greece, NY	(52.3)
247	High Point, NC	(10.9)	320	Berkeley, CA	(25.4)	394	Abilene, TX	(52.6)
248	Lakewood, CO	(11.0)	321	Hawthorne, CA	(25.6)	395	Chattanooga, TN	(52.9)
249	Fargo, ND	(11.3)	322	Hialeah, FL	(25.7)	396	Johns Creek, GA	(53.0)
250	Gainesville, FL	(11.5)	323	Albany, NY	(25.8)	397	Longview, TX	(53.6)
251	Paterson, NJ	(11.6)	324	Nampa, ID	(25.9)	398	Midland, TX	(53.9)
252	Alhambra, CA	(11.7)	324	Newark, NJ	(25.9)	399	Irvine, CA	(54.1)
253	Palmdale, CA	(11.8)	326	Chino, CA	(26.0)	400	Frisco, TX	(56.1)
254	Minneapolis, MN	(11.9)	327	Sugar Land, TX	(26.2)	401	Menifee, CA	(60.0)
255	Cincinnati, OH	(12.1)	328	Boise, ID	(26.6)	402	New Rochelle, NY	(61.8)
255	Woodbridge Twnshp, NJ	(12.1)	329	Escondido, CA	(27.0)	403	Avondale, AZ	(64.2)
257	Lawrence, KS	(12.2)	329	Santa Ana, CA	(27.0)	404	Whittier, CA	(66.9)
257	Tacoma, WA	(12.2)	329	Vacaville, CA	(27.0)	405	Newton, MA	(68.1)
259	Costa Mesa, CA	(12.3)	332	Sunrise, FL	(27.1)	406	Sandy Springs, GA	(71.0)
260	Evansville, IN	(12.4)	333	Alexandria, VA	(27.7)	407	Springfield, MA	(76.0)
260	Vallejo, CA	(12.4)	334	Riverside, CA	(28.3)	408	Lake Forest, CA	(87.7)
262	Richmond, CA	(12.5)	335	Surprise, AZ	(28.4)	409	Colonie, NY	(100.0)
263	Indio, CA	(12.6)	336	Richardson, TX	(28.8)	409	Fishers, IN	(100.0)
264	Clinton Twnshp, MI	(12.8)	337	Killeen, TX	(28.9)	NA	Baton Rouge, LA**	NA
264	Livermore, CA	(12.8)	337	Lafayette, LA	(28.9)	NA	Billings, MT**	NA
264	Pasadena, TX	(12.8)	339	Fresno, CA	(29.2)	NA	Birmingham, AL**	NA
267	Denton, TX	(13.1)	340	Gresham, OR	(29.3)	NA	Bloomington, MN**	NA
268	Madison, WI	(13.4)	341	Beaverton, OR	(30.0)	NA	Brooklyn Park, MN**	NA
268	Syracuse, NY	(13.4)	342	Broken Arrow, OK	(30.8)	NA	Buffalo, NY**	NA
270	Norfolk, VA	(14.1)	342	North Charleston, SC	(30.8)	NA	Champaign, IL**	NA
270	Torrance, CA	(14.1)	344	Norwalk, CA	(31.4)	NA	Chicago, IL**	NA
272	Fort Smith, AR	(15.7)	345	Decatur, IL	(31.5)	NA	Cicero, IL**	NA
273	St. Petersburg, FL	(15.8)	346	Hampton, VA	(31.8)	NA	Clifton, NJ**	NA
274	Glendale, CA	(16.3)	347	Lowell, MA	(32.1)	NA	Davenport, IA**	NA
275	Allentown, PA	(16.7)	348	Concord, CA	(32.8)	NA	Duluth, MN**	NA
275	Clovis, CA	(16.7)	348	Lynn, MA	(32.8)	NA	Gary, IN**	NA
275	Garden Grove, CA	(16.7)	350	Farmington Hills, MI	(33.0)	NA	Hillsboro, OR**	NA
275	Stockton, CA	(16.7)	351	Newport News, VA	(33.2)	NA	Hoover, AL**	NA
279	Lynchburg, VA	(16.8)	352	Salem, OR	(33.4)	NA	Huntsville, AL**	NA
279	Pompano Beach, FL	(16.8)	353	Corona, CA	(33.7)	NA	Indianapolis, IN**	NA
281	Fremont, CA	(16.9)	354	Oakland, CA	(34.1)	NA	Kansas City, MO**	NA
282	West Jordan, UT	(17.0)	355	Roswell, GA	(34.2)	NA	Lexington, KY**	NA
283	Fort Collins, CO	(17.1)	356	Lancaster, CA	(34.4)	NA	Mobile, AL**	NA
284	Arvada, CO	(17.5)	357	Port St. Lucie, FL	(34.8)	NA	Montgomery, AL**	NA
285	Long Beach, CA	(17.6)	358	Antioch, CA	(35.1)	NA	Naperville, IL**	NA
286	Amherst, NY	(17.8)	358	Asheville, NC	(35.1)	NA	Pueblo, CO**	NA
287	Ann Arbor, MI	(17.9)	358	Irving, TX	(35.1)	NA	Rochester, MN**	NA
287	Santa Clarita, CA	(17.9)	361	Wilmington, NC	(35.2)	NA	Sterling Heights, MI**	NA
289	Gilbert, AZ	(18.2)	362	Toms River Twnshp, NJ	(35.3)	NA	Thornton, CO**	NA
			363	San Angelo, TX	(35.4)	NA	Tuscaloosa, AL**	NA

Source: CQ Press using reported data from the F.B.I. "Crime in the United States 2011"
*Forcible rape is the carnal knowledge of a female forcibly and against her will. Assaults or attempts to commit rape by force or threat of force are included. However, statutory rape without force and other sex offenses are excluded. **Not available

Alpha Order - City

56. Percent Change in Rape Rate: 2007 to 2011
National Percent Change = 12.4% Decrease*

RANK	CITY	% CHANGE	RANK	CITY	% CHANGE	RANK	CITY	% CHANGE
376	Abilene, TX	(64.4)	352	Cheektowaga, NY	(50.2)	100	Fort Wayne, IN	7.9
122	Akron, OH	(0.7)	328	Chesapeake, VA	(41.4)	153	Fort Worth, TX	(7.4)
93	Albany, GA	10.8	NA	Chicago, IL**	NA	149	Fremont, CA	(6.9)
281	Albany, NY	(29.9)	343	Chico, CA	(46.6)	356	Fresno, CA	(51.4)
220	Albuquerque, NM	(20.1)	51	Chino Hills, CA	35.9	306	Frisco, TX	(35.1)
252	Alexandria, VA	(24.4)	58	Chino, CA	31.0	325	Fullerton, CA	(40.2)
158	Alhambra, CA	(8.8)	344	Chula Vista, CA	(47.1)	250	Gainesville, FL	(24.2)
6	Allentown, PA	176.9	NA	Cicero, IL**	NA	347	Garden Grove, CA	(47.6)
95	Allen, TX	10.2	303	Cincinnati, OH	(34.6)	121	Garland, TX	(0.4)
226	Amarillo, TX	(21.2)	NA	Citrus Heights, CA**	NA	123	Gary, IN	(0.9)
198	Amherst, NY	(16.7)	316	Clarkstown, NY	(37.6)	166	Gilbert, AZ	(10.8)
99	Anaheim, CA	8.0	216	Clarksville, TN	(19.8)	205	Glendale, AZ	(17.7)
107	Anchorage, AK	5.4	83	Clearwater, FL	15.8	77	Glendale, CA	20.0
78	Ann Arbor, MI	19.2	111	Cleveland, OH	4.8	207	Grand Prairie, TX	(17.9)
242	Antioch, CA	(23.4)	15	Clifton, NJ	87.3	76	Grand Rapids, MI	20.1
NA	Arlington Heights, IL**	NA	141	Clinton Twnshp, MI	(4.0)	268	Greece, NY	(27.9)
179	Arlington, TX	(13.1)	97	Clovis, CA	8.5	265	Greeley, CO	(27.0)
195	Arvada, CO	(16.3)	311	College Station, TX	(36.3)	236	Green Bay, WI	(22.8)
278	Asheville, NC	(29.5)	392	Colonie, NY	(100.0)	367	Gresham, OR	(61.5)
244	Athens-Clarke, GA	(23.6)	126	Colorado Springs, CO	(1.2)	40	Hamilton Twnshp, NJ	44.9
82	Atlanta, GA	16.8	98	Columbia, MO	8.3	22	Hammond, IN	72.1
168	Aurora, CO	(11.0)	287	Columbus, GA	(31.1)	368	Hampton, VA	(61.9)
NA	Aurora, IL**	NA	221	Columbus, OH	(20.2)	145	Hartford, CT	(5.6)
331	Austin, TX	(43.0)	109	Compton, CA	5.3	150	Hawthorne, CA	(7.0)
NA	Avondale, AZ**	NA	39	Concord, CA	45.3	170	Hayward, CA	(11.4)
183	Bakersfield, CA	(14.0)	383	Concord, NC	(69.9)	371	Hemet, CA	(62.5)
320	Baldwin Park, CA	(37.9)	317	Coral Springs, FL	(37.7)	190	Henderson, NV	(15.2)
9	Baltimore, MD	132.5	375	Corona, CA	(64.3)	174	Hesperia, CA	(11.9)
283	Baton Rouge, LA	(30.2)	258	Corpus Christi, TX	(25.0)	285	Hialeah, FL	(30.3)
199	Beaumont, TX	(17.1)	247	Costa Mesa, CA	(23.9)	324	High Point, NC	(39.7)
106	Beaverton, OR	5.5	10	Cranston, RI	126.3	330	Hillsboro, OR	(42.5)
250	Bellevue, WA	(24.2)	188	Dallas, TX	(15.0)	233	Hollywood, FL	(22.2)
341	Bellflower, CA	(46.0)	155	Daly City, CA	(8.1)	NA	Hoover, AL**	NA
89	Bellingham, WA	12.1	26	Danbury, CT	68.0	88	Houston, TX	12.5
72	Bend, OR	21.4	NA	Davenport, IA**	NA	79	Huntington Beach, CA	18.8
278	Berkeley, CA	(29.5)	270	Davie, FL	(28.1)	NA	Huntsville, AL**	NA
288	Bethlehem, PA	(31.3)	152	Dayton, OH	(7.2)	150	Independence, MO	(7.0)
NA	Billings, MT**	NA	246	Dearborn, MI	(23.8)	201	Indianapolis, IN	(17.5)
NA	Birmingham, AL**	NA	NA	Decatur, IL**	NA	221	Indio, CA	(20.2)
NA	Bloomington, IL**	NA	169	Deerfield Beach, FL	(11.2)	18	Inglewood, CA	80.0
310	Bloomington, IN	(35.9)	288	Denton, TX	(31.3)	340	Irvine, CA	(45.7)
NA	Bloomington, MN**	NA	62	Denver, CO	25.8	261	Irving, TX	(26.1)
38	Boca Raton, FL	46.2	345	Des Moines, IA	(47.4)	54	Jacksonville, FL	34.3
350	Boise, ID	(48.3)	34	Detroit, MI	51.3	163	Jackson, MS	(10.0)
128	Boston, MA	(1.8)	58	Downey, CA	31.0	118	Jersey City, NJ	1.0
179	Boulder, CO	(13.1)	NA	Duluth, MN**	NA	NA	Johns Creek, GA**	NA
8	Brick Twnshp, NJ	138.5	NA	Durham, NC**	NA	NA	Joliet, IL**	NA
44	Bridgeport, CT	43.6	65	Edinburg, TX	24.0	115	Kansas City, KS	2.0
41	Brockton, MA	44.8	NA	Edison Twnshp, NJ***	NA	NA	Kansas City, MO**	NA
207	Broken Arrow, OK	(17.9)	382	Edmond, OK	(68.5)	325	Kennewick, WA	(40.2)
NA	Brooklyn Park, MN**	NA	74	El Cajon, CA	20.9	103	Kenosha, WI	5.9
20	Brownsville, TX	74.0	46	El Monte, CA	42.8	195	Kent, WA	(16.3)
335	Bryan, TX	(43.8)	230	El Paso, TX	(22.0)	298	Killeen, TX	(32.9)
304	Buena Park, CA	(34.7)	NA	Elgin, IL**	NA	176	Knoxville, TN	(12.4)
NA	Buffalo, NY**	NA	32	Elizabeth, NJ	52.3	390	Lafayette, LA	(79.3)
69	Burbank, CA	22.6	286	Elk Grove, CA	(30.5)	391	Lake Forest, CA	(83.5)
14	Cambridge, MA	90.8	114	Erie, PA	2.3	187	Lakeland, FL	(14.9)
120	Camden, NJ	0.2	157	Escondido, CA	(8.6)	3	Lakewood Twnshp, NJ	357.1
130	Canton Twnshp, MI	(2.1)	56	Eugene, OR	32.4	347	Lakewood, CA	(47.6)
374	Cape Coral, FL	(64.0)	136	Evansville, IN	(2.7)	116	Lakewood, CO	1.7
257	Carlsbad, CA	(24.8)	248	Everett, WA	(24.1)	307	Lancaster, CA	(35.2)
11	Carmel, IN	110.4	329	Fairfield, CA	(41.9)	136	Lansing, MI	(2.7)
49	Carrollton, TX	37.5	NA	Fall River, MA**	NA	182	Laredo, TX	(13.9)
57	Carson, CA	32.1	332	Fargo, ND	(43.3)	184	Largo, FL	(14.1)
124	Cary, NC	(1.0)	193	Farmington Hills, MI	(15.9)	370	Las Cruces, NM	(62.2)
81	Cedar Rapids, IA	18.3	202	Fayetteville, NC	(17.6)	200	Las Vegas, NV	(17.3)
248	Centennial, CO	(24.1)	392	Fishers, IN	(100.0)	280	Lawrence, KS	(29.8)
NA	Champaign, IL**	NA	172	Flint, MI	(11.6)	263	Lawrence, MA	(26.8)
61	Chandler, AZ	27.6	213	Fontana, CA	(19.3)	295	Lawton, OK	(32.6)
357	Charleston, SC	(51.8)	275	Fort Collins, CO	(28.6)	147	League City, TX	(6.1)
273	Charlotte, NC	(28.3)	17	Fort Lauderdale, FL	81.9	29	Lee's Summit, MO	63.3
381	Chattanooga, TN	(67.6)	230	Fort Smith, AR	(22.0)	112	Lewisville, TX	4.6

Alpha Order - City (continued)

RANK	CITY	% CHANGE	RANK	CITY	% CHANGE	RANK	CITY	% CHANGE
NA	Lexington, KY**	NA	28	Overland Park, KS	66.2	164	Sioux City, IA	(10.2)
50	Lincoln, NE	37.0	262	Oxnard, CA	(26.6)	104	Sioux Falls, SD	5.8
65	Little Rock, AR	24.0	253	Palm Bay, FL	(24.5)	135	Somerville, MA	(2.6)
213	Livermore, CA	(19.3)	113	Palmdale, CA	2.9	155	South Bend, IN	(8.1)
282	Livonia, MI	(30.0)	202	Pasadena, CA	(17.6)	322	South Gate, CA	(39.0)
207	Long Beach, CA	(17.9)	223	Pasadena, TX	(21.1)	70	Sparks, NV	22.0
NA	Longmont, CO**	NA	36	Paterson, NJ	51.1	53	Spokane Valley, WA	34.6
378	Longview, TX	(66.0)	361	Pearland, TX	(54.6)	166	Spokane, WA	(10.8)
197	Los Angeles, CA	(16.6)	24	Pembroke Pines, FL	70.5	NA	Springfield, IL**	NA
96	Louisville, KY	9.6	215	Peoria, AZ	(19.4)	380	Springfield, MA	(66.6)
228	Lowell, MA	(21.5)	NA	Peoria, IL**	NA	43	Springfield, MO	43.7
314	Lubbock, TX	(36.7)	211	Philadelphia, PA	(18.3)	146	Stamford, CT	(5.8)
188	Lynchburg, VA	(15.0)	84	Phoenix, AZ	15.5	NA	Sterling Heights, MI**	NA
317	Lynn, MA	(37.7)	346	Pittsburgh, PA	(47.5)	181	Stockton, CA	(13.6)
235	Macon, GA	(22.6)	238	Plano, TX	(23.0)	31	St. Joseph, MO	52.5
64	Madison, WI	24.9	16	Plantation, FL	87.1	216	St. Louis, MO	(19.8)
NA	Manchester, NH**	NA	21	Pomona, CA	73.8	154	St. Paul, MN	(7.8)
133	McAllen, TX	(2.4)	293	Pompano Beach, FL	(32.5)	177	St. Petersburg, FL	(12.5)
327	McKinney, TX	(40.7)	360	Port St. Lucie, FL	(53.8)	260	Suffolk, VA	(25.8)
75	Medford, OR	20.4	194	Portland, OR	(16.0)	383	Sugar Land, TX	(69.9)
27	Melbourne, FL	67.9	55	Portsmouth, VA	34.1	60	Sunnyvale, CA	28.7
160	Memphis, TN	(9.6)	139	Provo, UT	(3.3)	140	Sunrise, FL	(3.7)
NA	Menifee, CA**	NA	NA	Pueblo, CO**	NA	300	Surprise, AZ	(33.6)
283	Merced, CA	(30.2)	13	Quincy, MA	90.9	161	Syracuse, NY	(9.8)
321	Meridian, ID	(38.1)	349	Racine, WI	(48.1)	178	Tacoma, WA	(12.8)
244	Mesa, AZ	(23.6)	85	Raleigh, NC	15.2	290	Tallahassee, FL	(31.5)
148	Mesquite, TX	(6.7)	6	Ramapo, NY	176.9	273	Tampa, FL	(28.3)
296	Miami Beach, FL	(32.7)	266	Rancho Cucamon., CA	(27.1)	342	Temecula, CA	(46.1)
385	Miami Gardens, FL	(71.7)	355	Reading, PA	(50.7)	259	Tempe, AZ	(25.5)
24	Miami, FL	70.5	255	Redding, CA	(24.7)	NA	Thornton, CO**	NA
379	Midland, TX	(66.5)	92	Redwood City, CA	11.7	351	Thousand Oaks, CA	(48.7)
223	Milwaukee, WI	(21.1)	386	Reno, NV	(73.2)	191	Toledo, OH	(15.3)
206	Minneapolis, MN	(17.8)	210	Renton, WA	(18.1)	389	Toms River Twnshp, NJ	(77.7)
48	Miramar, FL	41.7	270	Rialto, CA	(28.1)	102	Topeka, KS	7.0
5	Mission Viejo, CA	190.9	364	Richardson, TX	(59.2)	223	Torrance, CA	(21.1)
315	Mission, TX	(37.2)	68	Richmond, CA	22.8	1	Tracy, CA	495.8
NA	Mobile, AL**	NA	236	Richmond, VA	(22.8)	30	Trenton, NJ	62.8
107	Modesto, CA	5.4	301	Rio Rancho, NM	(34.4)	23	Troy, MI	70.7
NA	Montgomery, AL**	NA	323	Riverside, CA	(39.1)	263	Tucson, AZ	(26.8)
359	Moreno Valley, CA	(52.7)	337	Roanoke, VA	(44.5)	185	Tulsa, OK	(14.3)
159	Murfreesboro, TN	(9.3)	NA	Rochester, MN**	NA	NA	Tuscaloosa, AL**	NA
35	Murrieta, CA	51.2	240	Rochester, NY	(23.2)	369	Tustin, CA	(62.1)
301	Nampa, ID	(34.4)	119	Rockford, IL	0.6	254	Tyler, TX	(24.6)
42	Napa, CA	44.6	270	Roseville, CA	(28.1)	105	Upper Darby Twnshp, PA	5.7
NA	Naperville, IL**	NA	309	Roswell, GA	(35.6)	241	Vacaville, CA	(23.3)
NA	Nashua, NH**	NA	86	Round Rock, TX	14.0	12	Vallejo, CA	102.7
80	Nashville, TN	18.5	293	Sacramento, CA	(32.5)	191	Vancouver, WA	(15.3)
47	New Bedford, MA	42.5	339	Salem, OR	(45.3)	268	Ventura, CA	(27.9)
NA	New Haven, CT**	NA	312	Salinas, CA	(36.5)	94	Victorville, CA	10.5
161	New Orleans, LA	(9.8)	129	Salt Lake City, UT	(2.0)	299	Virginia Beach, VA	(33.2)
313	New Rochelle, NY	(36.6)	308	San Angelo, TX	(35.5)	131	Visalia, CA	(2.2)
63	New York, NY	25.5	255	San Antonio, TX	(24.7)	73	Vista, CA	21.2
132	Newark, NJ	(2.3)	127	San Bernardino, CA	(1.6)	276	Waco, TX	(29.2)
4	Newport Beach, CA	272.0	144	San Diego, CA	(5.5)	175	Warren, MI	(12.0)
338	Newport News, VA	(44.6)	143	San Francisco, CA	(5.3)	NA	Warwick, RI**	NA
387	Newton, MA	(76.3)	116	San Jose, CA	1.7	186	Washington, DC	(14.7)
234	Norfolk, VA	(22.5)	45	San Leandro, CA	43.5	357	Waterbury, CT	(51.8)
19	Norman, OK	77.4	37	San Marcos, CA	49.3	142	West Covina, CA	(4.1)
377	North Charleston, SC	(65.9)	133	San Mateo, CA	(2.4)	243	West Jordan, UT	(23.5)
277	Norwalk, CA	(29.3)	388	Sandy Springs, GA	(77.5)	91	West Palm Beach, FL	11.8
87	Norwalk, CT	13.6	296	Sandy, UT	(32.7)	239	West Valley, UT	(23.1)
292	Oakland, CA	(32.2)	124	Santa Ana, CA	(1.0)	52	Westland, MI	35.5
89	Oceanside, CA	12.1	219	Santa Barbara, CA	(19.9)	354	Westminster, CA	(50.6)
2	Odessa, TX	397.3	364	Santa Clara, CA	(59.2)	33	Westminster, CO	52.2
373	O'Fallon, MO	(63.8)	229	Santa Clarita, CA	(21.7)	333	Whittier, CA	(43.4)
335	Ogden, UT	(43.8)	366	Santa Maria, CA	(60.7)	165	Wichita Falls, TX	(10.5)
227	Oklahoma City, OK	(21.3)	232	Santa Monica, CA	(22.1)	202	Wichita, KS	(17.6)
NA	Olathe, KS**	NA	212	Santa Rosa, CA	(18.4)	353	Wilmington, NC	(50.3)
71	Omaha, NE	21.7	363	Savannah, GA	(57.6)	NA	Winston-Salem, NC**	NA
319	Ontario, CA	(37.8)	171	Scottsdale, AZ	(11.5)	334	Woodbridge Twnshp, NJ	(43.7)
266	Orange, CA	(27.1)	65	Scranton, PA	24.0	372	Worcester, MA	(62.6)
172	Orem, UT	(11.6)	110	Seattle, WA	5.2	305	Yakima, WA	(34.8)
291	Orlando, FL	(31.7)	101	Shreveport, LA	7.3	216	Yonkers, NY	(19.8)
			362	Simi Valley, CA	(55.8)	138	Yuma, AZ	(2.8)

Source: CQ Press using reported data from the F.B.I. "Crime in the United States 2011"
*Forcible rape is the carnal knowledge of a female forcibly and against her will. **Not available. ***Edison Twnshp, NJ had a rape rate of 0 i 2007 but had 9 rapes in 2011. Calculating percent increase from zero results in an infinite number. This is shown as "NA."

Rank Order - City
56. Percent Change in Rape Rate: 2007 to 2011 (continued)
National Percent Change = 12.4% Decrease*

RANK	CITY	% CHANGE	RANK	CITY	% CHANGE	RANK	CITY	% CHANGE
1	Tracy, CA	495.8	73	Vista, CA	21.2	145	Hartford, CT	(5.6)
2	Odessa, TX	397.3	74	El Cajon, CA	20.9	146	Stamford, CT	(5.8)
3	Lakewood Twnshp, NJ	357.1	75	Medford, OR	20.4	147	League City, TX	(6.1)
4	Newport Beach, CA	272.0	76	Grand Rapids, MI	20.1	148	Mesquite, TX	(6.7)
5	Mission Viejo, CA	190.9	77	Glendale, CA	20.0	149	Fremont, CA	(6.9)
6	Allentown, PA	176.9	78	Ann Arbor, MI	19.2	150	Hawthorne, CA	(7.0)
6	Ramapo, NY	176.9	79	Huntington Beach, CA	18.8	150	Independence, MO	(7.0)
8	Brick Twnshp, NJ	138.5	80	Nashville, TN	18.5	152	Dayton, OH	(7.2)
9	Baltimore, MD	132.5	81	Cedar Rapids, IA	18.3	153	Fort Worth, TX	(7.4)
10	Cranston, RI	126.3	82	Atlanta, GA	16.8	154	St. Paul, MN	(7.8)
11	Carmel, IN	110.4	83	Clearwater, FL	15.8	155	Daly City, CA	(8.1)
12	Vallejo, CA	102.7	84	Phoenix, AZ	15.5	155	South Bend, IN	(8.1)
13	Quincy, MA	90.9	85	Raleigh, NC	15.2	157	Escondido, CA	(8.6)
14	Cambridge, MA	90.8	86	Round Rock, TX	14.0	158	Alhambra, CA	(8.8)
15	Clifton, NJ	87.3	87	Norwalk, CT	13.6	159	Murfreesboro, TN	(9.3)
16	Plantation, FL	87.1	88	Houston, TX	12.5	160	Memphis, TN	(9.6)
17	Fort Lauderdale, FL	81.9	89	Bellingham, WA	12.1	161	New Orleans, LA	(9.8)
18	Inglewood, CA	80.0	89	Oceanside, CA	12.1	161	Syracuse, NY	(9.8)
19	Norman, OK	77.4	91	West Palm Beach, FL	11.8	163	Jackson, MS	(10.0)
20	Brownsville, TX	74.0	92	Redwood City, CA	11.7	164	Sioux City, IA	(10.2)
21	Pomona, CA	73.8	93	Albany, GA	10.8	165	Wichita Falls, TX	(10.5)
22	Hammond, IN	72.1	94	Victorville, CA	10.5	166	Gilbert, AZ	(10.8)
23	Troy, MI	70.7	95	Allen, TX	10.2	166	Spokane, WA	(10.8)
24	Miami, FL	70.5	96	Louisville, KY	9.6	168	Aurora, CO	(11.0)
24	Pembroke Pines, FL	70.5	97	Clovis, CA	8.5	169	Deerfield Beach, FL	(11.2)
26	Danbury, CT	68.0	98	Columbia, MO	8.3	170	Hayward, CA	(11.4)
27	Melbourne, FL	67.9	99	Anaheim, CA	8.0	171	Scottsdale, AZ	(11.5)
28	Overland Park, KS	66.2	100	Fort Wayne, IN	7.9	172	Flint, MI	(11.6)
29	Lee's Summit, MO	63.3	101	Shreveport, LA	7.3	172	Orem, UT	(11.6)
30	Trenton, NJ	62.8	102	Topeka, KS	7.0	174	Hesperia, CA	(11.9)
31	St. Joseph, MO	52.5	103	Kenosha, WI	5.9	175	Warren, MI	(12.0)
32	Elizabeth, NJ	52.3	104	Sioux Falls, SD	5.8	176	Knoxville, TN	(12.4)
33	Westminster, CO	52.2	105	Upper Darby Twnshp, PA	5.7	177	St. Petersburg, FL	(12.5)
34	Detroit, MI	51.3	106	Beaverton, OR	5.5	178	Tacoma, WA	(12.8)
35	Murrieta, CA	51.2	107	Anchorage, AK	5.4	179	Arlington, TX	(13.1)
36	Paterson, NJ	51.1	107	Modesto, CA	5.4	179	Boulder, CO	(13.1)
37	San Marcos, CA	49.3	109	Compton, CA	5.3	181	Stockton, CA	(13.6)
38	Boca Raton, FL	46.2	110	Seattle, WA	5.2	182	Laredo, TX	(13.9)
39	Concord, CA	45.3	111	Cleveland, OH	4.8	183	Bakersfield, CA	(14.0)
40	Hamilton Twnshp, NJ	44.9	112	Lewisville, TX	4.6	184	Largo, FL	(14.1)
41	Brockton, MA	44.8	113	Palmdale, CA	2.9	185	Tulsa, OK	(14.3)
42	Napa, CA	44.6	114	Erie, PA	2.3	186	Washington, DC	(14.7)
43	Springfield, MO	43.7	115	Kansas City, KS	2.0	187	Lakeland, FL	(14.9)
44	Bridgeport, CT	43.6	116	Lakewood, CO	1.7	188	Dallas, TX	(15.0)
45	San Leandro, CA	43.5	116	San Jose, CA	1.7	188	Lynchburg, VA	(15.0)
46	El Monte, CA	42.8	118	Jersey City, NJ	1.0	190	Henderson, NV	(15.2)
47	New Bedford, MA	42.5	119	Rockford, IL	0.6	191	Toledo, OH	(15.3)
48	Miramar, FL	41.7	120	Camden, NJ	0.2	191	Vancouver, WA	(15.3)
49	Carrollton, TX	37.5	121	Garland, TX	(0.4)	193	Farmington Hills, MI	(15.9)
50	Lincoln, NE	37.0	122	Akron, OH	(0.7)	194	Portland, OR	(16.0)
51	Chino Hills, CA	35.9	123	Gary, IN	(0.9)	195	Arvada, CO	(16.3)
52	Westland, MI	35.5	124	Cary, NC	(1.0)	195	Kent, WA	(16.3)
53	Spokane Valley, WA	34.6	124	Santa Ana, CA	(1.0)	197	Los Angeles, CA	(16.6)
54	Jacksonville, FL	34.3	126	Colorado Springs, CO	(1.2)	198	Amherst, NY	(16.7)
55	Portsmouth, VA	34.1	127	San Bernardino, CA	(1.6)	199	Beaumont, TX	(17.1)
56	Eugene, OR	32.4	128	Boston, MA	(1.8)	200	Las Vegas, NV	(17.3)
57	Carson, CA	32.1	129	Salt Lake City, UT	(2.0)	201	Indianapolis, IN	(17.5)
58	Chino, CA	31.0	130	Canton Twnshp, MI	(2.1)	202	Fayetteville, NC	(17.6)
58	Downey, CA	31.0	131	Visalia, CA	(2.2)	202	Pasadena, CA	(17.6)
60	Sunnyvale, CA	28.7	132	Newark, NJ	(2.3)	202	Wichita, KS	(17.6)
61	Chandler, AZ	27.6	133	McAllen, TX	(2.4)	205	Glendale, AZ	(17.7)
62	Denver, CO	25.8	133	San Mateo, CA	(2.4)	206	Minneapolis, MN	(17.8)
63	New York, NY	25.5	135	Somerville, MA	(2.6)	207	Broken Arrow, OK	(17.9)
64	Madison, WI	24.9	136	Evansville, IN	(2.7)	207	Grand Prairie, TX	(17.9)
65	Edinburg, TX	24.0	136	Lansing, MI	(2.7)	207	Long Beach, CA	(17.9)
65	Little Rock, AR	24.0	138	Yuma, AZ	(2.8)	210	Renton, WA	(18.1)
65	Scranton, PA	24.0	139	Provo, UT	(3.3)	211	Philadelphia, PA	(18.3)
68	Richmond, CA	22.8	140	Sunrise, FL	(3.7)	212	Santa Rosa, CA	(18.4)
69	Burbank, CA	22.6	141	Clinton Twnshp, MI	(4.0)	213	Fontana, CA	(19.3)
70	Sparks, NV	22.0	142	West Covina, CA	(4.1)	213	Livermore, CA	(19.3)
71	Omaha, NE	21.7	143	San Francisco, CA	(5.3)	215	Peoria, AZ	(19.4)
72	Bend, OR	21.4	144	San Diego, CA	(5.5)	216	Clarksville, TN	(19.8)

Rank Order - City (continued)

RANK	CITY	% CHANGE	RANK	CITY	% CHANGE	RANK	CITY	% CHANGE
216	St. Louis, MO	(19.8)	290	Tallahassee, FL	(31.5)	364	Richardson, TX	(59.2)
216	Yonkers, NY	(19.8)	291	Orlando, FL	(31.7)	364	Santa Clara, CA	(59.2)
219	Santa Barbara, CA	(19.9)	292	Oakland, CA	(32.2)	366	Santa Maria, CA	(60.7)
220	Albuquerque, NM	(20.1)	293	Pompano Beach, FL	(32.5)	367	Gresham, OR	(61.5)
221	Columbus, OH	(20.2)	293	Sacramento, CA	(32.5)	368	Hampton, VA	(61.9)
221	Indio, CA	(20.2)	295	Lawton, OK	(32.6)	369	Tustin, CA	(62.1)
223	Milwaukee, WI	(21.1)	296	Miami Beach, FL	(32.7)	370	Las Cruces, NM	(62.2)
223	Pasadena, TX	(21.1)	296	Sandy, UT	(32.7)	371	Hemet, CA	(62.5)
223	Torrance, CA	(21.1)	298	Killeen, TX	(32.9)	372	Worcester, MA	(62.6)
226	Amarillo, TX	(21.2)	299	Virginia Beach, VA	(33.2)	373	O'Fallon, MO	(63.8)
227	Oklahoma City, OK	(21.3)	300	Surprise, AZ	(33.6)	374	Cape Coral, FL	(64.0)
228	Lowell, MA	(21.5)	301	Nampa, ID	(34.4)	375	Corona, CA	(64.3)
229	Santa Clarita, CA	(21.7)	301	Rio Rancho, NM	(34.4)	376	Abilene, TX	(64.4)
230	El Paso, TX	(22.0)	303	Cincinnati, OH	(34.6)	377	North Charleston, SC	(65.9)
230	Fort Smith, AR	(22.0)	304	Buena Park, CA	(34.7)	378	Longview, TX	(66.0)
232	Santa Monica, CA	(22.1)	305	Yakima, WA	(34.8)	379	Midland, TX	(66.5)
233	Hollywood, FL	(22.2)	306	Frisco, TX	(35.1)	380	Springfield, MA	(66.6)
234	Norfolk, VA	(22.5)	307	Lancaster, CA	(35.2)	381	Chattanooga, TN	(67.6)
235	Macon, GA	(22.6)	308	San Angelo, TX	(35.5)	382	Edmond, OK	(68.5)
236	Green Bay, WI	(22.8)	309	Roswell, GA	(35.6)	383	Concord, NC	(69.9)
236	Richmond, VA	(22.8)	310	Bloomington, IN	(35.9)	383	Sugar Land, TX	(69.9)
238	Plano, TX	(23.0)	311	College Station, TX	(36.3)	385	Miami Gardens, FL	(71.7)
239	West Valley, UT	(23.1)	312	Salinas, CA	(36.5)	386	Reno, NV	(73.2)
240	Rochester, NY	(23.2)	313	New Rochelle, NY	(36.6)	387	Newton, MA	(76.3)
241	Vacaville, CA	(23.3)	314	Lubbock, TX	(36.7)	388	Sandy Springs, GA	(77.5)
242	Antioch, CA	(23.4)	315	Mission, TX	(37.2)	389	Toms River Twnshp, NJ	(77.7)
243	West Jordan, UT	(23.5)	316	Clarkstown, NY	(37.6)	390	Lafayette, LA	(79.3)
244	Athens-Clarke, GA	(23.6)	317	Coral Springs, FL	(37.7)	391	Lake Forest, CA	(83.5)
244	Mesa, AZ	(23.6)	317	Lynn, MA	(37.7)	392	Colonie, NY	(100.0)
246	Dearborn, MI	(23.8)	319	Ontario, CA	(37.8)	392	Fishers, IN	(100.0)
247	Costa Mesa, CA	(23.9)	320	Baldwin Park, CA	(37.9)	NA	Arlington Heights, IL**	NA
248	Centennial, CO	(24.1)	321	Meridian, ID	(38.1)	NA	Aurora, IL**	NA
248	Everett, WA	(24.1)	322	South Gate, CA	(39.0)	NA	Avondale, AZ**	NA
250	Bellevue, WA	(24.2)	323	Riverside, CA	(39.1)	NA	Billings, MT**	NA
250	Gainesville, FL	(24.2)	324	High Point, NC	(39.7)	NA	Birmingham, AL**	NA
252	Alexandria, VA	(24.4)	325	Fullerton, CA	(40.2)	NA	Bloomington, IL**	NA
253	Palm Bay, FL	(24.5)	325	Kennewick, WA	(40.2)	NA	Bloomington, MN**	NA
254	Tyler, TX	(24.6)	327	McKinney, TX	(40.7)	NA	Brooklyn Park, MN**	NA
255	Redding, CA	(24.7)	328	Chesapeake, VA	(41.4)	NA	Buffalo, NY**	NA
255	San Antonio, TX	(24.7)	329	Fairfield, CA	(41.9)	NA	Champaign, IL**	NA
257	Carlsbad, CA	(24.8)	330	Hillsboro, OR	(42.5)	NA	Chicago, IL**	NA
258	Corpus Christi, TX	(25.0)	331	Austin, TX	(43.0)	NA	Cicero, IL**	NA
259	Tempe, AZ	(25.5)	332	Fargo, ND	(43.3)	NA	Citrus Heights, CA**	NA
260	Suffolk, VA	(25.8)	333	Whittier, CA	(43.4)	NA	Davenport, IA**	NA
261	Irving, TX	(26.1)	334	Woodbridge Twnshp, NJ	(43.7)	NA	Decatur, IL**	NA
262	Oxnard, CA	(26.6)	335	Bryan, TX	(43.8)	NA	Duluth, MN**	NA
263	Lawrence, MA	(26.8)	335	Ogden, UT	(43.8)	NA	Durham, NC**	NA
263	Tucson, AZ	(26.8)	337	Roanoke, VA	(44.5)	NA	Edison Twnshp, NJ***	NA
265	Greeley, CO	(27.0)	338	Newport News, VA	(44.6)	NA	Elgin, IL**	NA
266	Orange, CA	(27.1)	339	Salem, OR	(45.3)	NA	Fall River, MA**	NA
266	Rancho Cucamon., CA	(27.1)	340	Irvine, CA	(45.7)	NA	Hoover, AL**	NA
268	Greece, NY	(27.9)	341	Bellflower, CA	(46.0)	NA	Huntsville, AL**	NA
268	Ventura, CA	(27.9)	342	Temecula, CA	(46.1)	NA	Johns Creek, GA**	NA
270	Davie, FL	(28.1)	343	Chico, CA	(46.6)	NA	Joliet, IL**	NA
270	Rialto, CA	(28.1)	344	Chula Vista, CA	(47.1)	NA	Kansas City, MO**	NA
270	Roseville, CA	(28.1)	345	Des Moines, IA	(47.4)	NA	Lexington, KY**	NA
273	Charlotte, NC	(28.3)	346	Pittsburgh, PA	(47.5)	NA	Longmont, CO**	NA
273	Tampa, FL	(28.3)	347	Garden Grove, CA	(47.6)	NA	Manchester, NH**	NA
275	Fort Collins, CO	(28.6)	347	Lakewood, CA	(47.6)	NA	Menifee, CA**	NA
276	Waco, TX	(29.2)	349	Racine, WI	(48.1)	NA	Mobile, AL**	NA
277	Norwalk, CA	(29.3)	350	Boise, ID	(48.3)	NA	Montgomery, AL**	NA
278	Asheville, NC	(29.5)	351	Thousand Oaks, CA	(48.7)	NA	Naperville, IL**	NA
278	Berkeley, CA	(29.5)	352	Cheektowaga, NY	(50.2)	NA	Nashua, NH**	NA
280	Lawrence, KS	(29.8)	353	Wilmington, NC	(50.3)	NA	New Haven, CT**	NA
281	Albany, NY	(29.9)	354	Westminster, CA	(50.6)	NA	Olathe, KS**	NA
282	Livonia, MI	(30.0)	355	Reading, PA	(50.7)	NA	Peoria, IL**	NA
283	Baton Rouge, LA	(30.2)	356	Fresno, CA	(51.4)	NA	Pueblo, CO**	NA
283	Merced, CA	(30.2)	357	Charleston, SC	(51.8)	NA	Rochester, MN**	NA
285	Hialeah, FL	(30.3)	357	Waterbury, CT	(51.8)	NA	Springfield, IL**	NA
286	Elk Grove, CA	(30.5)	359	Moreno Valley, CA	(52.7)	NA	Sterling Heights, MI**	NA
287	Columbus, GA	(31.1)	360	Port St. Lucie, FL	(53.8)	NA	Thornton, CO**	NA
288	Bethlehem, PA	(31.3)	361	Pearland, TX	(54.6)	NA	Tuscaloosa, AL**	NA
288	Denton, TX	(31.3)	362	Simi Valley, CA	(55.8)	NA	Warwick, RI**	NA
			363	Savannah, GA	(57.6)	NA	Winston-Salem, NC**	NA

Source: CQ Press using reported data from the F.B.I. "Crime in the United States 2011"
*Forcible rape is the carnal knowledge of a female forcibly and against her will. **Not available. ***Edison Twnshp, NJ had a rape rate of 0 i 2007 but had 9 rapes in 2011. Calculating percent increase from zero results in an infinite number. This is shown as "NA."

Alpha Order - City

57. Robberies in 2011
National Total = 354,396 Robberies*

RANK	CITY	ROBBERY
249	Abilene, TX	120
64	Akron, OH	718
200	Albany, GA	176
132	Albany, NY	320
50	Albuquerque, NM	998
238	Alexandria, VA	129
346	Alhambra, CA	57
128	Allentown, PA	339
426	Allen, TX	17
162	Amarillo, TX	235
370	Amherst, NY	41
99	Anaheim, CA	446
93	Anchorage, AK	465
336	Ann Arbor, MI	59
139	Antioch, CA	290
426	Arlington Heights, IL	17
82	Arlington, TX	540
392	Arvada, CO	34
191	Asheville, NC	181
235	Athens-Clarke, GA	132
19	Atlanta, GA	2,343
86	Aurora, CO	504
213	Aurora, IL	158
44	Austin, TX	1,106
268	Avondale, AZ	103
81	Bakersfield, CA	548
291	Baldwin Park, CA	90
10	Baltimore, MD	3,457
53	Baton Rouge, LA	893
121	Beaumont, TX	356
385	Beaverton, OR	36
339	Bellevue, WA	58
253	Bellflower, CA	116
349	Bellingham, WA	55
410	Bend, OR	27
126	Berkeley, CA	340
280	Bethlehem, PA	97
385	Billings, MT	36
49	Birmingham, AL	1,011
339	Bloomington, IL	58
339	Bloomington, IN	58
370	Bloomington, MN	41
330	Boca Raton, FL	63
336	Boise, ID	59
23	Boston, MA	1,904
387	Boulder, CO	35
421	Brick Twnshp, NJ	20
73	Bridgeport, CT	610
167	Brockton, MA	232
370	Broken Arrow, OK	41
268	Brooklyn Park, MN	103
259	Brownsville, TX	109
308	Bryan, TX	78
309	Buena Park, CA	76
32	Buffalo, NY	1,459
322	Burbank, CA	68
221	Cambridge, MA	152
55	Camden, NJ	857
397	Canton Twnshp, MI	32
339	Cape Coral, FL	58
387	Carlsbad, CA	35
437	Carmel, IN	2
287	Carrollton, TX	93
262	Carson, CA	106
370	Cary, NC	41
297	Cedar Rapids, IA	86
417	Centennial, CO	23
263	Champaign, IL	105
206	Chandler, AZ	171
211	Charleston, SC	162
29	Charlotte, NC	1,612
113	Chattanooga, TN	385

RANK	CITY	ROBBERY
304	Cheektowaga, NY	80
154	Chesapeake, VA	246
2	Chicago, IL	13,975
288	Chico, CA	92
428	Chino Hills, CA	16
339	Chino, CA	58
166	Chula Vista, CA	233
211	Cicero, IL	162
26	Cincinnati, OH	1,773
242	Citrus Heights, CA	127
401	Clarkstown, NY	31
241	Clarksville, TN	128
190	Clearwater, FL	182
15	Cleveland, OH	3,156
271	Clifton, NJ	101
320	Clinton Twnshp, MI	71
349	Clovis, CA	55
397	College Station, TX	32
397	Colonie, NY	32
98	Colorado Springs, CO	449
210	Columbia, MO	166
105	Columbus, GA	413
14	Columbus, OH	3,244
115	Compton, CA	380
209	Concord, CA	167
381	Concord, NC	37
291	Coral Springs, FL	90
263	Corona, CA	105
118	Corpus Christi, TX	370
298	Costa Mesa, CA	83
404	Cranston, RI	30
7	Dallas, TX	4,066
336	Daly City, CA	59
309	Danbury, CT	76
255	Davenport, IA	113
263	Davie, FL	105
70	Dayton, OH	638
266	Dearborn, MI	104
245	Decatur, IL	124
233	Deerfield Beach, FL	134
349	Denton, TX	55
42	Denver, CO	1,143
170	Des Moines, IA	216
6	Detroit, MI	4,962
174	Downey, CA	204
299	Duluth, MN	82
65	Durham, NC	699
352	Edinburg, TX	54
328	Edison Twnshp, NJ	65
421	Edmond, OK	20
183	El Cajon, CA	187
179	El Monte, CA	196
94	El Paso, TX	464
299	Elgin, IL	82
61	Elizabeth, NJ	723
278	Elk Grove, CA	98
223	Erie, PA	150
196	Escondido, CA	177
196	Eugene, OR	177
219	Evansville, IN	154
227	Everett, WA	143
225	Fairfield, CA	148
143	Fall River, MA	274
364	Fargo, ND	47
409	Farmington Hills, MI	28
89	Fayetteville, NC	495
435	Fishers, IN	8
74	Flint, MI	607
159	Fontana, CA	241
366	Fort Collins, CO	46
57	Fort Lauderdale, FL	771
273	Fort Smith, AR	100

RANK	CITY	ROBBERY
134	Fort Wayne, IN	310
37	Fort Worth, TX	1,267
215	Fremont, CA	156
48	Fresno, CA	1,020
417	Frisco, TX	23
266	Fullerton, CA	104
186	Gainesville, FL	184
206	Garden Grove, CA	171
153	Garland, TX	247
131	Gary, IN	328
347	Gilbert, AZ	56
103	Glendale, AZ	431
260	Glendale, CA	108
176	Grand Prairie, TX	201
94	Grand Rapids, MI	464
361	Greece, NY	48
314	Greeley, CO	75
361	Green Bay, WI	48
204	Gresham, OR	172
303	Hamilton Twnshp, NJ	81
186	Hammond, IN	184
218	Hampton, VA	155
76	Hartford, CT	602
136	Hawthorne, CA	302
120	Hayward, CA	360
245	Hemet, CA	124
178	Henderson, NV	197
283	Hesperia, CA	95
152	Hialeah, FL	253
177	High Point, NC	200
387	Hillsboro, OR	35
147	Hollywood, FL	269
387	Hoover, AL	35
5	Houston, TX	8,054
260	Huntington Beach, CA	108
110	Huntsville, AL	405
256	Independence, MO	110
11	Indianapolis, IN	3,372
256	Indio, CA	110
124	Inglewood, CA	343
375	Irvine, CA	40
222	Irving, TX	151
31	Jacksonville, FL	1,578
56	Jackson, MS	808
51	Jersey City, NJ	961
431	Johns Creek, GA	13
296	Joliet, IL	87
138	Kansas City, KS	291
27	Kansas City, MO	1,665
387	Kennewick, WA	35
277	Kenosha, WI	99
172	Kent, WA	210
204	Killeen, TX	172
80	Knoxville, TN	559
167	Lafayette, LA	232
420	Lake Forest, CA	22
229	Lakeland, FL	140
401	Lakewood Twnshp, NJ	31
278	Lakewood, CA	98
236	Lakewood, CO	131
145	Lancaster, CA	273
142	Lansing, MI	275
171	Laredo, TX	215
271	Largo, FL	101
322	Las Cruces, NM	68
9	Las Vegas, NV	3,493
381	Lawrence, KS	37
158	Lawrence, MA	244
201	Lawton, OK	175
381	League City, TX	37
404	Lee's Summit, MO	30
354	Lewisville, TX	53

Alpha Order - City (continued)

RANK	CITY	ROBBERY	RANK	CITY	ROBBERY	RANK	CITY	ROBBERY
88	Lexington, KY	496	380	Overland Park, KS	38	392	Sioux City, IA	34
196	Lincoln, NE	177	143	Oxnard, CA	274	314	Sioux Falls, SD	75
54	Little Rock, AR	858	280	Palm Bay, FL	97	291	Somerville, MA	90
377	Livermore, CA	39	154	Palmdale, CA	246	109	South Bend, IN	406
375	Livonia, MI	40	195	Pasadena, CA	178	147	South Gate, CA	269
36	Long Beach, CA	1,320	231	Pasadena, TX	135	314	Sparks, NV	75
396	Longmont, CO	33	60	Paterson, NJ	751	339	Spokane Valley, WA	58
256	Longview, TX	110	407	Pearland, TX	29	92	Spokane, WA	484
3	Los Angeles, CA	10,077	250	Pembroke Pines, FL	119	150	Springfield, IL	258
28	Louisville, KY	1,643	347	Peoria, AZ	56	83	Springfield, MA	532
208	Lowell, MA	168	140	Peoria, IL	288	141	Springfield, MO	286
133	Lubbock, TX	313	4	Philadelphia, PA	8,246	182	Stamford, CT	190
318	Lynchburg, VA	72	13	Phoenix, AZ	3,324	401	Sterling Heights, MI	31
191	Lynn, MA	181	43	Pittsburgh, PA	1,126	35	Stockton, CA	1,323
154	Macon, GA	246	228	Plano, TX	142	299	St. Joseph, MO	82
146	Madison, WI	272	238	Plantation, FL	129	20	St. Louis, MO	2,127
191	Manchester, NH	181	128	Pomona, CA	339	75	St. Paul, MN	604
318	McAllen, TX	72	124	Pompano Beach, FL	343	62	St. Petersburg, FL	720
367	McKinney, TX	44	332	Port St. Lucie, FL	61	309	Suffolk, VA	76
334	Medford, OR	60	52	Portland, OR	917	407	Sugar Land, TX	29
213	Melbourne, FL	158	162	Portsmouth, VA	235	322	Sunnyvale, CA	68
17	Memphis, TN	3,083	412	Provo, UT	26	273	Sunrise, FL	100
417	Menifee, CA	23	203	Pueblo, CO	173	356	Surprise, AZ	51
224	Merced, CA	149	289	Quincy, MA	91	111	Syracuse, NY	388
436	Meridian, ID	3	184	Racine, WI	186	99	Tacoma, WA	446
87	Mesa, AZ	497	68	Raleigh, NC	680	85	Tallahassee, FL	511
196	Mesquite, TX	177	415	Ramapo, NY	24	78	Tampa, FL	587
118	Miami Beach, FL	370	268	Rancho Cucamon., CA	103	352	Temecula, CA	54
105	Miami Gardens, FL	413	116	Reading, PA	377	161	Tempe, AZ	237
21	Miami, FL	2,002	273	Redding, CA	100	359	Thornton, CO	50
339	Midland, TX	58	330	Redwood City, CA	63	392	Thousand Oaks, CA	34
18	Milwaukee, WI	2,963	114	Reno, NV	383	41	Toledo, OH	1,152
30	Minneapolis, MN	1,589	254	Renton, WA	115	332	Toms River Twnshp, NJ	61
181	Miramar, FL	192	174	Rialto, CA	204	162	Topeka, KS	235
404	Mission Viejo, CA	30	309	Richardson, TX	76	289	Torrance, CA	91
381	Mission, TX	37	135	Richmond, CA	303	322	Tracy, CA	68
71	Mobile, AL	637	69	Richmond, VA	676	84	Trenton, NJ	519
104	Modesto, CA	425	429	Rio Rancho, NM	15	430	Troy, MI	14
123	Montgomery, AL	354	97	Riverside, CA	458	39	Tucson, AZ	1,163
130	Moreno Valley, CA	330	201	Roanoke, VA	175	46	Tulsa, OK	1,090
236	Murfreesboro, TN	131	328	Rochester, MN	65	180	Tuscaloosa, AL	194
392	Murrieta, CA	34	59	Rochester, NY	755	377	Tustin, CA	39
433	Nampa, ID	9	79	Rockford, IL	566	306	Tyler, TX	79
364	Napa, CA	47	368	Roseville, CA	43	160	Upper Darby Twnshp, PA	240
415	Naperville, IL	24	397	Roswell, GA	32	356	Vacaville, CA	51
359	Nashua, NH	50	377	Round Rock, TX	39	102	Vallejo, CA	435
24	Nashville, TN	1,889	40	Sacramento, CA	1,162	185	Vancouver, WA	185
137	New Bedford, MA	294	250	Salem, OR	119	231	Ventura, CA	135
58	New Haven, CT	766	117	Salinas, CA	374	149	Victorville, CA	261
47	New Orleans, LA	1,059	126	Salt Lake City, UT	340	107	Virginia Beach, VA	412
252	New Rochelle, NY	118	369	San Angelo, TX	42	283	Visalia, CA	95
1	New York, NY	19,773	25	San Antonio, TX	1,785	248	Vista, CA	121
22	Newark, NJ	1,977	62	San Bernardino, CA	720	157	Waco, TX	245
410	Newport Beach, CA	27	33	San Diego, CA	1,456	215	Warren, MI	156
111	Newport News, VA	388	16	San Francisco, CA	3,088	425	Warwick, RI	18
424	Newton, MA	19	45	San Jose, CA	1,101	8	Washington, DC	3,756
72	Norfolk, VA	625	169	San Leandro, CA	217	189	Waterbury, CT	183
356	Norman, OK	51	334	San Marcos, CA	60	245	West Covina, CA	124
186	North Charleston, SC	184	321	San Mateo, CA	69	414	West Jordan, UT	25
230	Norwalk, CA	138	286	Sandy Springs, GA	94	162	West Palm Beach, FL	235
291	Norwalk, CT	90	412	Sandy, UT	26	243	West Valley, UT	126
12	Oakland, CA	3,365	77	Santa Ana, CA	591	295	Westland, MI	88
191	Oceanside, CA	181	304	Santa Barbara, CA	80	306	Westminster, CA	79
317	Odessa, TX	73	326	Santa Clara, CA	67	361	Westminster, CO	48
433	O'Fallon, MO	9	309	Santa Clarita, CA	76	273	Whittier, CA	100
282	Ogden, UT	96	220	Santa Maria, CA	153	226	Wichita Falls, TX	147
38	Oklahoma City, OK	1,232	238	Santa Monica, CA	129	90	Wichita, KS	490
421	Olathe, KS	20	233	Santa Rosa, CA	134	151	Wilmington, NC	254
67	Omaha, NE	696	91	Savannah, GA	488	101	Winston-Salem, NC	444
173	Ontario, CA	209	244	Scottsdale, AZ	125	355	Woodbridge Twnshp, NJ	52
299	Orange, CA	82	283	Scranton, PA	95	108	Worcester, MA	411
432	Orem, UT	10	34	Seattle, WA	1,418	215	Yakima, WA	156
66	Orlando, FL	697	122	Shreveport, LA	355	96	Yonkers, NY	463
			370	Simi Valley, CA	41	327	Yuma, AZ	66

Source: Reported data from the F.B.I. "Crime in the United States 2011"
*Robbery is the taking of anything of value by force or threat of force. Attempts are included.

57. Robberies in 2011 (continued)
National Total = 354,396 Robberies*

RANK	CITY	ROBBERY	RANK	CITY	ROBBERY	RANK	CITY	ROBBERY
1	New York, NY	19,773	73	Bridgeport, CT	610	145	Lancaster, CA	273
2	Chicago, IL	13,975	74	Flint, MI	607	146	Madison, WI	272
3	Los Angeles, CA	10,077	75	St. Paul, MN	604	147	Hollywood, FL	269
4	Philadelphia, PA	8,246	76	Hartford, CT	602	147	South Gate, CA	269
5	Houston, TX	8,054	77	Santa Ana, CA	591	149	Victorville, CA	261
6	Detroit, MI	4,962	78	Tampa, FL	587	150	Springfield, IL	258
7	Dallas, TX	4,066	79	Rockford, IL	566	151	Wilmington, NC	254
8	Washington, DC	3,756	80	Knoxville, TN	559	152	Hialeah, FL	253
9	Las Vegas, NV	3,493	81	Bakersfield, CA	548	153	Garland, TX	247
10	Baltimore, MD	3,457	82	Arlington, TX	540	154	Chesapeake, VA	246
11	Indianapolis, IN	3,372	83	Springfield, MA	532	154	Macon, GA	246
12	Oakland, CA	3,365	84	Trenton, NJ	519	154	Palmdale, CA	246
13	Phoenix, AZ	3,324	85	Tallahassee, FL	511	157	Waco, TX	245
14	Columbus, OH	3,244	86	Aurora, CO	504	158	Lawrence, MA	244
15	Cleveland, OH	3,156	87	Mesa, AZ	497	159	Fontana, CA	241
16	San Francisco, CA	3,088	88	Lexington, KY	496	160	Upper Darby Twnshp, PA	240
17	Memphis, TN	3,083	89	Fayetteville, NC	495	161	Tempe, AZ	237
18	Milwaukee, WI	2,963	90	Wichita, KS	490	162	Amarillo, TX	235
19	Atlanta, GA	2,343	91	Savannah, GA	488	162	Portsmouth, VA	235
20	St. Louis, MO	2,127	92	Spokane, WA	484	162	Topeka, KS	235
21	Miami, FL	2,002	93	Anchorage, AK	465	162	West Palm Beach, FL	235
22	Newark, NJ	1,977	94	El Paso, TX	464	166	Chula Vista, CA	233
23	Boston, MA	1,904	94	Grand Rapids, MI	464	167	Brockton, MA	232
24	Nashville, TN	1,889	96	Yonkers, NY	463	167	Lafayette, LA	232
25	San Antonio, TX	1,785	97	Riverside, CA	458	169	San Leandro, CA	217
26	Cincinnati, OH	1,773	98	Colorado Springs, CO	449	170	Des Moines, IA	216
27	Kansas City, MO	1,665	99	Anaheim, CA	446	171	Laredo, TX	215
28	Louisville, KY	1,643	99	Tacoma, WA	446	172	Kent, WA	210
29	Charlotte, NC	1,612	101	Winston-Salem, NC	444	173	Ontario, CA	209
30	Minneapolis, MN	1,589	102	Vallejo, CA	435	174	Downey, CA	204
31	Jacksonville, FL	1,578	103	Glendale, AZ	431	174	Rialto, CA	204
32	Buffalo, NY	1,459	104	Modesto, CA	425	176	Grand Prairie, TX	201
33	San Diego, CA	1,456	105	Columbus, GA	413	177	High Point, NC	200
34	Seattle, WA	1,418	105	Miami Gardens, FL	413	178	Henderson, NV	197
35	Stockton, CA	1,323	107	Virginia Beach, VA	412	179	El Monte, CA	196
36	Long Beach, CA	1,320	108	Worcester, MA	411	180	Tuscaloosa, AL	194
37	Fort Worth, TX	1,267	109	South Bend, IN	406	181	Miramar, FL	192
38	Oklahoma City, OK	1,232	110	Huntsville, AL	405	182	Stamford, CT	190
39	Tucson, AZ	1,163	111	Newport News, VA	388	183	El Cajon, CA	187
40	Sacramento, CA	1,162	111	Syracuse, NY	388	184	Racine, WI	186
41	Toledo, OH	1,152	113	Chattanooga, TN	385	185	Vancouver, WA	185
42	Denver, CO	1,143	114	Reno, NV	383	186	Gainesville, FL	184
43	Pittsburgh, PA	1,126	115	Compton, CA	380	186	Hammond, IN	184
44	Austin, TX	1,106	116	Reading, PA	377	186	North Charleston, SC	184
45	San Jose, CA	1,101	117	Salinas, CA	374	189	Waterbury, CT	183
46	Tulsa, OK	1,090	118	Corpus Christi, TX	370	190	Clearwater, FL	182
47	New Orleans, LA	1,059	118	Miami Beach, FL	370	191	Asheville, NC	181
48	Fresno, CA	1,020	120	Hayward, CA	360	191	Lynn, MA	181
49	Birmingham, AL	1,011	121	Beaumont, TX	356	191	Manchester, NH	181
50	Albuquerque, NM	998	122	Shreveport, LA	355	191	Oceanside, CA	181
51	Jersey City, NJ	961	123	Montgomery, AL	354	195	Pasadena, CA	178
52	Portland, OR	917	124	Inglewood, CA	343	196	Escondido, CA	177
53	Baton Rouge, LA	893	124	Pompano Beach, FL	343	196	Eugene, OR	177
54	Little Rock, AR	858	126	Berkeley, CA	340	196	Lincoln, NE	177
55	Camden, NJ	857	126	Salt Lake City, UT	340	196	Mesquite, TX	177
56	Jackson, MS	808	128	Allentown, PA	339	200	Albany, GA	176
57	Fort Lauderdale, FL	771	128	Pomona, CA	339	201	Lawton, OK	175
58	New Haven, CT	766	130	Moreno Valley, CA	330	201	Roanoke, VA	175
59	Rochester, NY	755	131	Gary, IN	328	203	Pueblo, CO	173
60	Paterson, NJ	751	132	Albany, NY	320	204	Gresham, OR	172
61	Elizabeth, NJ	723	133	Lubbock, TX	313	204	Killeen, TX	172
62	San Bernardino, CA	720	134	Fort Wayne, IN	310	206	Chandler, AZ	171
62	St. Petersburg, FL	720	135	Richmond, CA	303	206	Garden Grove, CA	171
64	Akron, OH	718	136	Hawthorne, CA	302	208	Lowell, MA	168
65	Durham, NC	699	137	New Bedford, MA	294	209	Concord, CA	167
66	Orlando, FL	697	138	Kansas City, KS	291	210	Columbia, MO	166
67	Omaha, NE	696	139	Antioch, CA	290	211	Charleston, SC	162
68	Raleigh, NC	680	140	Peoria, IL	288	211	Cicero, IL	162
69	Richmond, VA	676	141	Springfield, MO	286	213	Aurora, IL	158
70	Dayton, OH	638	142	Lansing, MI	275	213	Melbourne, FL	158
71	Mobile, AL	637	143	Fall River, MA	274	215	Fremont, CA	156
72	Norfolk, VA	625	143	Oxnard, CA	274	215	Warren, MI	156

Rank Order - City (continued)

RANK	CITY	ROBBERY
215	Yakima, WA	156
218	Hampton, VA	155
219	Evansville, IN	154
220	Santa Maria, CA	153
221	Cambridge, MA	152
222	Irving, TX	151
223	Erie, PA	150
224	Merced, CA	149
225	Fairfield, CA	148
226	Wichita Falls, TX	147
227	Everett, WA	143
228	Plano, TX	142
229	Lakeland, FL	140
230	Norwalk, CA	138
231	Pasadena, TX	135
231	Ventura, CA	135
233	Deerfield Beach, FL	134
233	Santa Rosa, CA	134
235	Athens-Clarke, GA	132
236	Lakewood, CO	131
236	Murfreesboro, TN	131
238	Alexandria, VA	129
238	Plantation, FL	129
238	Santa Monica, CA	129
241	Clarksville, TN	128
242	Citrus Heights, CA	127
243	West Valley, UT	126
244	Scottsdale, AZ	125
245	Decatur, IL	124
245	Hemet, CA	124
245	West Covina, CA	124
248	Vista, CA	121
249	Abilene, TX	120
250	Pembroke Pines, FL	119
250	Salem, OR	119
252	New Rochelle, NY	118
253	Bellflower, CA	116
254	Renton, WA	115
255	Davenport, IA	113
256	Independence, MO	110
256	Indio, CA	110
256	Longview, TX	110
259	Brownsville, TX	109
260	Glendale, CA	108
260	Huntington Beach, CA	108
262	Carson, CA	106
263	Champaign, IL	105
263	Corona, CA	105
263	Davie, FL	105
266	Dearborn, MI	104
266	Fullerton, CA	104
268	Avondale, AZ	103
268	Brooklyn Park, MN	103
268	Rancho Cucamon., CA	103
271	Clifton, NJ	101
271	Largo, FL	101
273	Fort Smith, AR	100
273	Redding, CA	100
273	Sunrise, FL	100
273	Whittier, CA	100
277	Kenosha, WI	99
278	Elk Grove, CA	98
278	Lakewood, CA	98
280	Bethlehem, PA	97
280	Palm Bay, FL	97
282	Ogden, UT	96
283	Hesperia, CA	95
283	Scranton, PA	95
283	Visalia, CA	95
286	Sandy Springs, GA	94
287	Carrollton, TX	93
288	Chico, CA	92
289	Quincy, MA	91
289	Torrance, CA	91
291	Baldwin Park, CA	90
291	Coral Springs, FL	90
291	Norwalk, CT	90
291	Somerville, MA	90
295	Westland, MI	88
296	Joliet, IL	87
297	Cedar Rapids, IA	86
298	Costa Mesa, CA	83
299	Duluth, MN	82
299	Elgin, IL	82
299	Orange, CA	82
299	St. Joseph, MO	82
303	Hamilton Twnshp, NJ	81
304	Cheektowaga, NY	80
304	Santa Barbara, CA	80
306	Tyler, TX	79
306	Westminster, CA	79
308	Bryan, TX	78
309	Buena Park, CA	76
309	Danbury, CT	76
309	Richardson, TX	76
309	Santa Clarita, CA	76
309	Suffolk, VA	76
314	Greeley, CO	75
314	Sioux Falls, SD	75
314	Sparks, NV	75
317	Odessa, TX	73
318	Lynchburg, VA	72
318	McAllen, TX	72
320	Clinton Twnshp, MI	71
321	San Mateo, CA	69
322	Burbank, CA	68
322	Las Cruces, NM	68
322	Sunnyvale, CA	68
322	Tracy, CA	68
326	Santa Clara, CA	67
327	Yuma, AZ	66
328	Edison Twnshp, NJ	65
328	Rochester, MN	65
330	Boca Raton, FL	63
330	Redwood City, CA	63
332	Port St. Lucie, FL	61
332	Toms River Twnshp, NJ	61
334	Medford, OR	60
334	San Marcos, CA	60
336	Ann Arbor, MI	59
336	Boise, ID	59
336	Daly City, CA	59
339	Bellevue, WA	58
339	Bloomington, IL	58
339	Bloomington, IN	58
339	Cape Coral, FL	58
339	Chino, CA	58
339	Midland, TX	58
339	Spokane Valley, WA	58
346	Alhambra, CA	57
347	Gilbert, AZ	56
347	Peoria, AZ	56
349	Bellingham, WA	55
349	Clovis, CA	55
349	Denton, TX	55
352	Edinburg, TX	54
352	Temecula, CA	54
354	Lewisville, TX	53
355	Woodbridge Twnshp, NJ	52
356	Norman, OK	51
356	Surprise, AZ	51
356	Vacaville, CA	51
359	Nashua, NH	50
359	Thornton, CO	50
361	Greece, NY	48
361	Green Bay, WI	48
361	Westminster, CO	48
364	Fargo, ND	47
364	Napa, CA	47
366	Fort Collins, CO	46
367	McKinney, TX	44
368	Roseville, CA	43
369	San Angelo, TX	42
370	Amherst, NY	41
370	Bloomington, MN	41
370	Broken Arrow, OK	41
370	Cary, NC	41
370	Simi Valley, CA	41
375	Irvine, CA	40
375	Livonia, MI	40
377	Livermore, CA	39
377	Round Rock, TX	39
377	Tustin, CA	39
380	Overland Park, KS	38
381	Concord, NC	37
381	Lawrence, KS	37
381	League City, TX	37
381	Mission, TX	37
385	Beaverton, OR	36
385	Billings, MT	36
387	Boulder, CO	35
387	Carlsbad, CA	35
387	Hillsboro, OR	35
387	Hoover, AL	35
387	Kennewick, WA	35
392	Arvada, CO	34
392	Murrieta, CA	34
392	Sioux City, IA	34
392	Thousand Oaks, CA	34
396	Longmont, CO	33
397	Canton Twnshp, MI	32
397	College Station, TX	32
397	Colonie, NY	32
397	Roswell, GA	32
401	Clarkstown, NY	31
401	Lakewood Twnshp, NJ	31
401	Sterling Heights, MI	31
404	Cranston, RI	30
404	Lee's Summit, MO	30
404	Mission Viejo, CA	30
407	Pearland, TX	29
407	Sugar Land, TX	29
409	Farmington Hills, MI	28
410	Bend, OR	27
410	Newport Beach, CA	27
412	Provo, UT	26
412	Sandy, UT	26
414	West Jordan, UT	25
415	Naperville, IL	24
415	Ramapo, NY	24
417	Centennial, CO	23
417	Frisco, TX	23
417	Menifee, CA	23
420	Lake Forest, CA	22
421	Brick Twnshp, NJ	20
421	Edmond, OK	20
421	Olathe, KS	20
424	Newton, MA	19
425	Warwick, RI	18
426	Allen, TX	17
426	Arlington Heights, IL	17
428	Chino Hills, CA	16
429	Rio Rancho, NM	15
430	Troy, MI	14
431	Johns Creek, GA	13
432	Orem, UT	10
433	Nampa, ID	9
433	O'Fallon, MO	9
435	Fishers, IN	8
436	Meridian, ID	3
437	Carmel, IN	2

Source: Reported data from the F.B.I. "Crime in the United States 2011"
*Robbery is the taking of anything of value by force or threat of force. Attempts are included.

Alpha Order - City

58. Robbery Rate in 2011
National Rate = 113.7 Robberies per 100,000 Population*

RANK	CITY	RATE	RANK	CITY	RATE	RANK	CITY	RATE
260	Abilene, TX	100.4	259	Cheektowaga, NY	101.0	218	Fort Wayne, IN	121.6
48	Akron, OH	360.3	248	Chesapeake, VA	109.4	158	Fort Worth, TX	167.4
107	Albany, GA	224.3	17	Chicago, IL	516.9	306	Fremont, CA	72.0
56	Albany, NY	325.5	255	Chico, CA	105.5	124	Fresno, CA	203.8
141	Albuquerque, NM	180.8	423	Chino Hills, CA	21.1	425	Frisco, TX	19.3
277	Alexandria, VA	91.1	303	Chino, CA	73.5	293	Fullerton, CA	76.1
319	Alhambra, CA	67.8	268	Chula Vista, CA	94.4	184	Gainesville, FL	146.0
72	Allentown, PA	286.3	128	Cicero, IL	192.5	263	Garden Grove, CA	98.9
424	Allen, TX	19.8	9	Cincinnati, OH	596.6	250	Garland, TX	106.6
222	Amarillo, TX	120.7	179	Citrus Heights, CA	150.7	34	Gary, IN	406.4
390	Amherst, NY	34.9	376	Clarkstown, NY	39.1	412	Gilbert, AZ	26.5
204	Anaheim, CA	131.1	267	Clarksville, TN	95.4	135	Glendale, AZ	187.4
169	Anchorage, AK	156.6	159	Clearwater, FL	166.7	340	Glendale, CA	55.7
347	Ann Arbor, MI	51.8	3	Cleveland, OH	794.8	241	Grand Prairie, TX	112.2
75	Antioch, CA	280.0	223	Clifton, NJ	119.6	86	Grand Rapids, MI	246.9
418	Arlington Heights, IL	22.6	304	Clinton Twnshp, MI	73.4	350	Greece, NY	49.7
185	Arlington, TX	144.7	337	Clovis, CA	56.8	289	Greeley, CO	79.4
401	Arvada, CO	31.4	393	College Station, TX	33.4	360	Green Bay, WI	45.9
116	Asheville, NC	214.3	372	Colonie, NY	41.1	165	Gresham, OR	161.2
238	Athens-Clarke, GA	112.7	252	Colorado Springs, CO	106.0	276	Hamilton Twnshp, NJ	91.3
15	Atlanta, GA	550.6	175	Columbia, MO	152.4	104	Hammond, IN	226.5
175	Aurora, CO	152.4	115	Columbus, GA	214.7	244	Hampton, VA	111.4
288	Aurora, IL	79.6	33	Columbus, OH	411.9	21	Hartford, CT	481.6
193	Austin, TX	137.0	38	Compton, CA	389.4	50	Hawthorne, CA	354.1
201	Avondale, AZ	133.2	196	Concord, CA	135.2	87	Hayward, CA	246.8
170	Bakersfield, CA	155.9	359	Concord, NC	46.2	171	Hemet, CA	155.8
227	Baldwin Park, CA	118.0	305	Coral Springs, FL	73.3	296	Henderson, NV	75.8
14	Baltimore, MD	551.5	317	Corona, CA	68.1	258	Hesperia, CA	104.1
40	Baton Rouge, LA	385.6	225	Corpus Christi, TX	118.7	245	Hialeah, FL	111.1
67	Beaumont, TX	294.7	301	Costa Mesa, CA	74.6	132	High Point, NC	189.2
375	Beaverton, OR	39.7	380	Cranston, RI	37.4	378	Hillsboro, OR	37.8
357	Bellevue, WA	46.7	54	Dallas, TX	332.5	134	Hollywood, FL	188.5
181	Bellflower, CA	149.6	334	Daly City, CA	57.7	367	Hoover, AL	42.7
321	Bellingham, WA	66.9	271	Danbury, CT	93.8	43	Houston, TX	375.7
390	Bend, OR	34.9	237	Davenport, IA	112.8	339	Huntington Beach, CA	56.2
66	Berkeley, CA	298.5	239	Davie, FL	112.6	108	Huntsville, AL	223.8
208	Bethlehem, PA	129.0	26	Dayton, OH	450.5	271	Independence, MO	93.8
392	Billings, MT	34.3	252	Dearborn, MI	106.0	35	Indianapolis, IN	404.8
22	Birmingham, AL	474.1	164	Decatur, IL	162.4	188	Indio, CA	143.0
298	Bloomington, IL	75.5	149	Deerfield Beach, FL	176.2	59	Inglewood, CA	309.1
307	Bloomington, IN	71.8	355	Denton, TX	47.5	426	Irvine, CA	18.6
351	Bloomington, MN	49.1	136	Denver, CO	187.2	316	Irving, TX	68.4
302	Boca Raton, FL	73.6	254	Des Moines, IA	105.6	133	Jacksonville, FL	189.1
408	Boise, ID	28.4	5	Detroit, MI	695.7	24	Jackson, MS	463.9
63	Boston, MA	306.4	142	Downey, CA	180.4	39	Jersey City, NJ	386.8
388	Boulder, CO	35.3	269	Duluth, MN	94.3	430	Johns Creek, GA	16.7
411	Brick Twnshp, NJ	26.6	65	Durham, NC	302.3	333	Joliet, IL	58.8
30	Bridgeport, CT	422.2	315	Edinburg, TX	68.6	127	Kansas City, KS	198.3
89	Brockton, MA	245.8	324	Edison Twnshp, NJ	64.8	47	Kansas City, MO	360.8
373	Broken Arrow, OK	41.0	414	Edmond, OK	24.3	358	Kennewick, WA	46.6
197	Brooklyn Park, MN	134.9	139	El Cajon, CA	185.8	262	Kenosha, WI	99.3
329	Brownsville, TX	61.0	153	El Monte, CA	170.7	109	Kent, WA	223.7
261	Bryan, TX	100.3	312	El Paso, TX	70.0	202	Killeen, TX	131.7
273	Buena Park, CA	93.3	297	Elgin, IL	75.6	58	Knoxville, TN	309.7
13	Buffalo, NY	555.8	12	Elizabeth, NJ	576.6	131	Lafayette, LA	190.6
323	Burbank, CA	65.0	326	Elk Grove, CA	63.3	410	Lake Forest, CA	28.1
187	Cambridge, MA	143.7	183	Erie, PA	146.9	190	Lakeland, FL	141.8
1	Camden, NJ	1,104.3	218	Escondido, CA	121.6	394	Lakewood Twnshp, NJ	33.3
387	Canton Twnshp, MI	35.5	242	Eugene, OR	112.1	221	Lakewood, CA	121.0
381	Cape Coral, FL	37.1	205	Evansville, IN	130.5	278	Lakewood, CO	90.1
396	Carlsbad, CA	32.8	195	Everett, WA	136.7	151	Lancaster, CA	172.3
437	Carmel, IN	2.5	191	Fairfield, CA	138.9	93	Lansing, MI	240.8
292	Carrollton, TX	76.5	62	Fall River, MA	306.5	280	Laredo, TX	89.2
235	Carson, CA	114.2	364	Fargo, ND	43.8	209	Largo, FL	128.3
405	Cary, NC	29.9	389	Farmington Hills, MI	35.1	314	Las Cruces, NM	68.9
320	Cedar Rapids, IA	67.7	91	Fayetteville, NC	243.7	95	Las Vegas, NV	239.5
419	Centennial, CO	22.5	435	Fishers, IN	10.4	369	Lawrence, KS	42.0
206	Champaign, IL	129.2	10	Flint, MI	593.0	57	Lawrence, MA	317.5
309	Chandler, AZ	71.4	220	Fontana, CA	121.5	145	Lawton, OK	178.7
200	Charleston, SC	133.4	401	Fort Collins, CO	31.4	365	League City, TX	43.4
123	Charlotte, NC	204.2	25	Fort Lauderdale, FL	459.5	397	Lee's Summit, MO	32.7
102	Chattanooga, TN	227.6	233	Fort Smith, AR	115.1	341	Lewisville, TX	54.5

Alpha Order - City (continued)

RANK	CITY	RATE
160	Lexington, KY	166.5
318	Lincoln, NE	67.9
28	Little Rock, AR	440.0
354	Livermore, CA	47.6
371	Livonia, MI	41.3
73	Long Beach, CA	282.2
379	Longmont, CO	37.6
198	Longview, TX	133.9
80	Los Angeles, CA	262.6
85	Louisville, KY	247.0
168	Lowell, MA	156.8
199	Lubbock, TX	133.5
270	Lynchburg, VA	94.2
126	Lynn, MA	199.2
79	Macon, GA	265.8
230	Madison, WI	116.1
163	Manchester, NH	165.0
343	McAllen, TX	54.3
395	McKinney, TX	32.9
290	Medford, OR	79.3
122	Melbourne, FL	204.9
23	Memphis, TN	472.3
406	Menifee, CA	29.3
138	Merced, CA	186.5
436	Meridian, ID	4.0
243	Mesa, AZ	111.6
217	Mesquite, TX	124.0
31	Miami Beach, FL	415.8
41	Miami Gardens, FL	380.2
20	Miami, FL	494.4
348	Midland, TX	51.1
19	Milwaukee, WI	496.0
32	Minneapolis, MN	412.2
173	Miramar, FL	155.2
400	Mission Viejo, CA	31.8
356	Mission, TX	47.0
82	Mobile, AL	252.9
121	Modesto, CA	208.8
152	Montgomery, AL	171.2
154	Moreno Valley, CA	168.7
224	Murfreesboro, TN	119.4
399	Murrieta, CA	32.5
434	Nampa, ID	10.9
330	Napa, CA	60.4
428	Naperville, IL	16.9
334	Nashua, NH	57.7
60	Nashville, TN	308.3
61	New Bedford, MA	307.4
11	New Haven, CT	589.1
64	New Orleans, LA	305.2
175	New Rochelle, NY	152.4
93	New York, NY	240.8
4	Newark, NJ	711.0
403	Newport Beach, CA	31.3
118	Newport News, VA	212.2
420	Newton, MA	22.2
81	Norfolk, VA	254.4
361	Norman, OK	45.5
137	North Charleston, SC	186.6
206	Norwalk, CA	129.2
256	Norwalk, CT	104.9
2	Oakland, CA	851.2
249	Oceanside, CA	107.1
308	Odessa, TX	71.5
432	O'Fallon, MO	11.3
236	Ogden, UT	113.7
119	Oklahoma City, OK	210.2
431	Olathe, KS	15.8
154	Omaha, NE	168.7
213	Ontario, CA	126.0
332	Orange, CA	59.4
433	Orem, UT	11.1
71	Orlando, FL	288.6

RANK	CITY	RATE
421	Overland Park, KS	21.8
194	Oxnard, CA	136.8
275	Palm Bay, FL	92.7
167	Palmdale, CA	159.2
209	Pasadena, CA	128.3
282	Pasadena, TX	88.7
18	Paterson, NJ	512.0
404	Pearland, TX	31.1
295	Pembroke Pines, FL	75.9
384	Peoria, AZ	35.8
84	Peoria, IL	249.7
16	Philadelphia, PA	538.6
103	Phoenix, AZ	226.7
46	Pittsburgh, PA	364.9
344	Plano, TX	53.5
180	Plantation, FL	149.8
106	Pomona, CA	224.8
53	Pompano Beach, FL	338.9
382	Port St. Lucie, FL	36.6
172	Portland, OR	155.4
92	Portsmouth, VA	243.1
417	Provo, UT	22.7
166	Pueblo, CO	159.5
265	Quincy, MA	98.0
98	Racine, WI	234.8
161	Raleigh, NC	166.3
408	Ramapo, NY	28.4
328	Rancho Cucamon., CA	61.6
29	Reading, PA	426.6
247	Redding, CA	110.0
285	Redwood City, CA	81.1
157	Reno, NV	168.6
215	Renton, WA	124.5
125	Rialto, CA	203.3
300	Richardson, TX	75.0
70	Richmond, CA	288.8
55	Richmond, VA	327.1
428	Rio Rancho, NM	16.9
182	Riverside, CA	149.0
147	Roanoke, VA	178.2
330	Rochester, MN	60.4
49	Rochester, NY	357.0
45	Rockford, IL	369.1
384	Roseville, CA	35.8
384	Roswell, GA	35.8
377	Round Rock, TX	38.2
88	Sacramento, CA	246.2
293	Salem, OR	76.1
90	Salinas, CA	245.7
144	Salt Lake City, UT	178.9
363	San Angelo, TX	44.1
202	San Antonio, TX	131.7
52	San Bernardino, CA	339.0
246	San Diego, CA	110.6
42	San Francisco, CA	379.0
234	San Jose, CA	115.0
83	San Leandro, CA	252.5
310	San Marcos, CA	70.8
311	San Mateo, CA	70.2
263	Sandy Springs, GA	98.9
407	Sandy, UT	29.2
143	Santa Ana, CA	180.0
279	Santa Barbara, CA	89.4
336	Santa Clara, CA	56.9
368	Santa Clarita, CA	42.6
178	Santa Maria, CA	151.9
189	Santa Monica, CA	142.1
291	Santa Rosa, CA	78.9
114	Savannah, GA	215.5
338	Scottsdale, AZ	56.7
215	Scranton, PA	124.5
100	Seattle, WA	229.4
148	Shreveport, LA	176.5
398	Simi Valley, CA	32.6

RANK	CITY	RATE
374	Sioux City, IA	40.9
352	Sioux Falls, SD	48.2
226	Somerville, MA	118.1
37	South Bend, IN	399.3
74	South Gate, CA	281.7
284	Sparks, NV	82.4
325	Spokane Valley, WA	63.6
101	Spokane, WA	228.1
111	Springfield, IL	221.3
51	Springfield, MA	345.5
145	Springfield, MO	178.7
174	Stamford, CT	154.6
415	Sterling Heights, MI	23.9
27	Stockton, CA	448.3
251	St. Joseph, MO	106.4
6	St. Louis, MO	663.7
120	St. Paul, MN	210.0
68	St. Petersburg, FL	290.2
281	Suffolk, VA	88.8
383	Sugar Land, TX	36.0
353	Sunnyvale, CA	48.0
228	Sunrise, FL	116.8
366	Surprise, AZ	42.8
78	Syracuse, NY	266.1
111	Tacoma, WA	221.3
76	Tallahassee, FL	277.9
150	Tampa, FL	172.5
345	Temecula, CA	53.3
186	Tempe, AZ	144.5
370	Thornton, CO	41.4
412	Thousand Oaks, CA	26.5
36	Toledo, OH	400.8
322	Toms River Twnshp, NJ	66.6
140	Topeka, KS	183.2
327	Torrance, CA	61.8
285	Tracy, CA	81.1
7	Trenton, NJ	609.2
427	Troy, MI	17.3
113	Tucson, AZ	220.5
77	Tulsa, OK	275.2
117	Tuscaloosa, AL	213.4
349	Tustin, CA	51.0
287	Tyler, TX	79.8
69	Upper Darby Twnshp, PA	289.0
341	Vacaville, CA	54.5
44	Vallejo, CA	370.8
239	Vancouver, WA	112.6
214	Ventura, CA	125.4
110	Victorville, CA	222.6
274	Virginia Beach, VA	93.0
298	Visalia, CA	75.5
211	Vista, CA	127.5
129	Waco, TX	192.3
229	Warren, MI	116.5
421	Warwick, RI	21.8
8	Washington, DC	607.8
162	Waterbury, CT	165.5
232	West Covina, CA	115.5
416	West Jordan, UT	23.6
99	West Palm Beach, FL	232.0
266	West Valley, UT	95.5
257	Westland, MI	104.7
283	Westminster, CA	87.0
362	Westminster, CO	44.5
231	Whittier, CA	115.8
192	Wichita Falls, TX	137.7
212	Wichita, KS	127.3
96	Wilmington, NC	235.6
130	Winston-Salem, NC	190.9
346	Woodbridge Twnshp, NJ	52.0
105	Worcester, MA	225.6
154	Yakima, WA	168.7
97	Yonkers, NY	235.2
313	Yuma, AZ	69.9

Source: CQ Press using reported data from the F.B.I. "Crime in the United States 2011"
*Robbery is the taking of anything of value by force or threat of force. Attempts are included.

58. Robbery Rate in 2011 (continued)
National Rate = 113.7 Robberies per 100,000 Population*

Rank Order - City

RANK	CITY	RATE
1	Camden, NJ	1,104.3
2	Oakland, CA	851.2
3	Cleveland, OH	794.8
4	Newark, NJ	711.0
5	Detroit, MI	695.7
6	St. Louis, MO	663.7
7	Trenton, NJ	609.2
8	Washington, DC	607.8
9	Cincinnati, OH	596.6
10	Flint, MI	593.0
11	New Haven, CT	589.1
12	Elizabeth, NJ	576.6
13	Buffalo, NY	555.8
14	Baltimore, MD	551.5
15	Atlanta, GA	550.6
16	Philadelphia, PA	538.6
17	Chicago, IL	516.9
18	Paterson, NJ	512.0
19	Milwaukee, WI	496.0
20	Miami, FL	494.4
21	Hartford, CT	481.6
22	Birmingham, AL	474.1
23	Memphis, TN	472.3
24	Jackson, MS	463.9
25	Fort Lauderdale, FL	459.5
26	Dayton, OH	450.5
27	Stockton, CA	448.3
28	Little Rock, AR	440.0
29	Reading, PA	426.6
30	Bridgeport, CT	422.2
31	Miami Beach, FL	415.8
32	Minneapolis, MN	412.2
33	Columbus, OH	411.9
34	Gary, IN	406.4
35	Indianapolis, IN	404.8
36	Toledo, OH	400.8
37	South Bend, IN	399.3
38	Compton, CA	389.4
39	Jersey City, NJ	386.8
40	Baton Rouge, LA	385.6
41	Miami Gardens, FL	380.2
42	San Francisco, CA	379.0
43	Houston, TX	375.7
44	Vallejo, CA	370.8
45	Rockford, IL	369.1
46	Pittsburgh, PA	364.9
47	Kansas City, MO	360.8
48	Akron, OH	360.3
49	Rochester, NY	357.0
50	Hawthorne, CA	354.1
51	Springfield, MA	345.5
52	San Bernardino, CA	339.0
53	Pompano Beach, FL	338.9
54	Dallas, TX	332.5
55	Richmond, VA	327.1
56	Albany, NY	325.5
57	Lawrence, MA	317.5
58	Knoxville, TN	309.7
59	Inglewood, CA	309.1
60	Nashville, TN	308.3
61	New Bedford, MA	307.4
62	Fall River, MA	306.5
63	Boston, MA	306.4
64	New Orleans, LA	305.2
65	Durham, NC	302.3
66	Berkeley, CA	298.5
67	Beaumont, TX	294.7
68	St. Petersburg, FL	290.2
69	Upper Darby Twnshp, PA	289.0
70	Richmond, CA	288.8
71	Orlando, FL	288.6
72	Allentown, PA	286.3
73	Long Beach, CA	282.2
74	South Gate, CA	281.7
75	Antioch, CA	280.0
76	Tallahassee, FL	277.9
77	Tulsa, OK	275.2
78	Syracuse, NY	266.1
79	Macon, GA	265.8
80	Los Angeles, CA	262.6
81	Norfolk, VA	254.4
82	Mobile, AL	252.9
83	San Leandro, CA	252.5
84	Peoria, IL	249.7
85	Louisville, KY	247.0
86	Grand Rapids, MI	246.9
87	Hayward, CA	246.8
88	Sacramento, CA	246.2
89	Brockton, MA	245.8
90	Salinas, CA	245.7
91	Fayetteville, NC	243.7
92	Portsmouth, VA	243.1
93	Lansing, MI	240.8
93	New York, NY	240.8
95	Las Vegas, NV	239.5
96	Wilmington, NC	235.6
97	Yonkers, NY	235.2
98	Racine, WI	234.8
99	West Palm Beach, FL	232.0
100	Seattle, WA	229.4
101	Spokane, WA	228.1
102	Chattanooga, TN	227.6
103	Phoenix, AZ	226.7
104	Hammond, IN	226.5
105	Worcester, MA	225.6
106	Pomona, CA	224.8
107	Albany, GA	224.3
108	Huntsville, AL	223.8
109	Kent, WA	223.7
110	Victorville, CA	222.6
111	Springfield, IL	221.3
111	Tacoma, WA	221.3
113	Tucson, AZ	220.5
114	Savannah, GA	215.5
115	Columbus, GA	214.7
116	Asheville, NC	214.3
117	Tuscaloosa, AL	213.4
118	Newport News, VA	212.2
119	Oklahoma City, OK	210.2
120	St. Paul, MN	210.0
121	Modesto, CA	208.8
122	Melbourne, FL	204.9
123	Charlotte, NC	204.2
124	Fresno, CA	203.8
125	Rialto, CA	203.3
126	Lynn, MA	199.2
127	Kansas City, KS	198.3
128	Cicero, IL	192.5
129	Waco, TX	192.3
130	Winston-Salem, NC	190.9
131	Lafayette, LA	190.6
132	High Point, NC	189.2
133	Jacksonville, FL	189.1
134	Hollywood, FL	188.5
135	Glendale, AZ	187.4
136	Denver, CO	187.2
137	North Charleston, SC	186.6
138	Merced, CA	186.5
139	El Cajon, CA	185.8
140	Topeka, KS	183.2
141	Albuquerque, NM	180.8
142	Downey, CA	180.4
143	Santa Ana, CA	180.0
144	Salt Lake City, UT	178.9
145	Lawton, OK	178.7
145	Springfield, MO	178.7
147	Roanoke, VA	178.2
148	Shreveport, LA	176.5
149	Deerfield Beach, FL	176.2
150	Tampa, FL	172.5
151	Lancaster, CA	172.3
152	Montgomery, AL	171.2
153	El Monte, CA	170.7
154	Moreno Valley, CA	168.7
154	Omaha, NE	168.7
154	Yakima, WA	168.7
157	Reno, NV	168.6
158	Fort Worth, TX	167.4
159	Clearwater, FL	166.7
160	Lexington, KY	166.5
161	Raleigh, NC	166.3
162	Waterbury, CT	165.5
163	Manchester, NH	165.0
164	Decatur, IL	162.4
165	Gresham, OR	161.2
166	Pueblo, CO	159.5
167	Palmdale, CA	159.2
168	Lowell, MA	156.8
169	Anchorage, AK	156.6
170	Bakersfield, CA	155.9
171	Hemet, CA	155.8
172	Portland, OR	155.4
173	Miramar, FL	155.2
174	Stamford, CT	154.6
175	Aurora, CO	152.4
175	Columbia, MO	152.4
175	New Rochelle, NY	152.4
178	Santa Maria, CA	151.9
179	Citrus Heights, CA	150.7
180	Plantation, FL	149.8
181	Bellflower, CA	149.6
182	Riverside, CA	149.0
183	Erie, PA	146.9
184	Gainesville, FL	146.0
185	Arlington, TX	144.7
186	Tempe, AZ	144.5
187	Cambridge, MA	143.7
188	Indio, CA	143.0
189	Santa Monica, CA	142.1
190	Lakeland, FL	141.8
191	Fairfield, CA	138.9
192	Wichita Falls, TX	137.7
193	Austin, TX	137.0
194	Oxnard, CA	136.8
195	Everett, WA	136.7
196	Concord, CA	135.2
197	Brooklyn Park, MN	134.9
198	Longview, TX	133.9
199	Lubbock, TX	133.5
200	Charleston, SC	133.4
201	Avondale, AZ	133.2
202	Killeen, TX	131.7
202	San Antonio, TX	131.7
204	Anaheim, CA	131.1
205	Evansville, IN	130.5
206	Champaign, IL	129.2
206	Norwalk, CA	129.2
208	Bethlehem, PA	129.0
209	Largo, FL	128.3
209	Pasadena, CA	128.3
211	Vista, CA	127.5
212	Wichita, KS	127.3
213	Ontario, CA	126.0
214	Ventura, CA	125.4
215	Renton, WA	124.5
215	Scranton, PA	124.5

Rank Order - City (continued)

RANK	CITY	RATE
217	Mesquite, TX	124.0
218	Escondido, CA	121.6
218	Fort Wayne, IN	121.6
220	Fontana, CA	121.5
221	Lakewood, CA	121.0
222	Amarillo, TX	120.7
223	Clifton, NJ	119.6
224	Murfreesboro, TN	119.4
225	Corpus Christi, TX	118.7
226	Somerville, MA	118.1
227	Baldwin Park, CA	118.0
228	Sunrise, FL	116.8
229	Warren, MI	116.5
230	Madison, WI	116.1
231	Whittier, CA	115.8
232	West Covina, CA	115.5
233	Fort Smith, AR	115.1
234	San Jose, CA	115.0
235	Carson, CA	114.2
236	Ogden, UT	113.7
237	Davenport, IA	112.8
238	Athens-Clarke, GA	112.7
239	Davie, FL	112.6
239	Vancouver, WA	112.6
241	Grand Prairie, TX	112.2
242	Eugene, OR	112.1
243	Mesa, AZ	111.6
244	Hampton, VA	111.4
245	Hialeah, FL	111.1
246	San Diego, CA	110.6
247	Redding, CA	110.0
248	Chesapeake, VA	109.4
249	Oceanside, CA	107.1
250	Garland, TX	106.6
251	St. Joseph, MO	106.4
252	Colorado Springs, CO	106.0
252	Dearborn, MI	106.0
254	Des Moines, IA	105.6
255	Chico, CA	105.5
256	Norwalk, CT	104.9
257	Westland, MI	104.7
258	Hesperia, CA	104.1
259	Cheektowaga, NY	101.0
260	Abilene, TX	100.4
261	Bryan, TX	100.3
262	Kenosha, WI	99.3
263	Garden Grove, CA	98.9
263	Sandy Springs, GA	98.9
265	Quincy, MA	98.0
266	West Valley, UT	95.5
267	Clarksville, TN	95.4
268	Chula Vista, CA	94.4
269	Duluth, MN	94.3
270	Lynchburg, VA	94.2
271	Danbury, CT	93.8
271	Independence, MO	93.8
273	Buena Park, CA	93.3
274	Virginia Beach, VA	93.0
275	Palm Bay, FL	92.7
276	Hamilton Twnshp, NJ	91.3
277	Alexandria, VA	91.1
278	Lakewood, CO	90.1
279	Santa Barbara, CA	89.4
280	Laredo, TX	89.2
281	Suffolk, VA	88.8
282	Pasadena, TX	88.7
283	Westminster, CA	87.0
284	Sparks, NV	82.4
285	Redwood City, CA	81.1
285	Tracy, CA	81.1
287	Tyler, TX	79.8
288	Aurora, IL	79.6
289	Greeley, CO	79.4
290	Medford, OR	79.3
291	Santa Rosa, CA	78.9
292	Carrollton, TX	76.5
293	Fullerton, CA	76.1
293	Salem, OR	76.1
295	Pembroke Pines, FL	75.9
296	Henderson, NV	75.8
297	Elgin, IL	75.6
298	Bloomington, IL	75.5
298	Visalia, CA	75.5
300	Richardson, TX	75.0
301	Costa Mesa, CA	74.6
302	Boca Raton, FL	73.6
303	Chino, CA	73.5
304	Clinton Twnshp, MI	73.4
305	Coral Springs, FL	73.3
306	Fremont, CA	72.0
307	Bloomington, IN	71.8
308	Odessa, TX	71.5
309	Chandler, AZ	71.4
310	San Marcos, CA	70.8
311	San Mateo, CA	70.2
312	El Paso, TX	70.0
313	Yuma, AZ	69.9
314	Las Cruces, NM	68.9
315	Edinburg, TX	68.6
316	Irving, TX	68.4
317	Corona, CA	68.1
318	Lincoln, NE	67.9
319	Alhambra, CA	67.8
320	Cedar Rapids, IA	67.7
321	Bellingham, WA	66.9
322	Toms River Twnshp, NJ	66.6
323	Burbank, CA	65.0
324	Edison Twnshp, NJ	64.8
325	Spokane Valley, WA	63.6
326	Elk Grove, CA	63.3
327	Torrance, CA	61.8
328	Rancho Cucamon., CA	61.6
329	Brownsville, TX	61.0
330	Napa, CA	60.4
330	Rochester, MN	60.4
332	Orange, CA	59.4
333	Joliet, IL	58.8
334	Daly City, CA	57.7
334	Nashua, NH	57.7
336	Santa Clara, CA	56.9
337	Clovis, CA	56.8
338	Scottsdale, AZ	56.7
339	Huntington Beach, CA	56.2
340	Glendale, CA	55.7
341	Lewisville, TX	54.5
341	Vacaville, CA	54.5
343	McAllen, TX	54.3
344	Plano, TX	53.5
345	Temecula, CA	53.3
346	Woodbridge Twnshp, NJ	52.0
347	Ann Arbor, MI	51.8
348	Midland, TX	51.1
349	Tustin, CA	51.0
350	Greece, NY	49.7
351	Bloomington, MN	49.1
352	Sioux Falls, SD	48.2
353	Sunnyvale, CA	48.0
354	Livermore, CA	47.6
355	Denton, TX	47.5
356	Mission, TX	47.0
357	Bellevue, WA	46.7
358	Kennewick, WA	46.6
359	Concord, NC	46.2
360	Green Bay, WI	45.9
361	Norman, OK	45.5
362	Westminster, CO	44.5
363	San Angelo, TX	44.1
364	Fargo, ND	43.8
365	League City, TX	43.4
366	Surprise, AZ	42.8
367	Hoover, AL	42.7
368	Santa Clarita, CA	42.6
369	Lawrence, KS	42.0
370	Thornton, CO	41.4
371	Livonia, MI	41.3
372	Colonie, NY	41.1
373	Broken Arrow, OK	41.0
374	Sioux City, IA	40.9
375	Beaverton, OR	39.7
376	Clarkstown, NY	39.1
377	Round Rock, TX	38.2
378	Hillsboro, OR	37.8
379	Longmont, CO	37.6
380	Cranston, RI	37.4
381	Cape Coral, FL	37.1
382	Port St. Lucie, FL	36.6
383	Sugar Land, TX	36.0
384	Peoria, AZ	35.8
384	Roseville, CA	35.8
384	Roswell, GA	35.8
387	Canton Twnshp, MI	35.5
388	Boulder, CO	35.3
389	Farmington Hills, MI	35.1
390	Amherst, NY	34.9
390	Bend, OR	34.9
392	Billings, MT	34.3
393	College Station, TX	33.4
394	Lakewood Twnshp, NJ	33.3
395	McKinney, TX	32.9
396	Carlsbad, CA	32.8
397	Lee's Summit, MO	32.7
398	Simi Valley, CA	32.6
399	Murrieta, CA	32.5
400	Mission Viejo, CA	31.8
401	Arvada, CO	31.4
401	Fort Collins, CO	31.4
403	Newport Beach, CA	31.3
404	Pearland, TX	31.1
405	Cary, NC	29.9
406	Menifee, CA	29.3
407	Sandy, UT	29.2
408	Boise, ID	28.4
408	Ramapo, NY	28.4
410	Lake Forest, CA	28.1
411	Brick Twnshp, NJ	26.6
412	Gilbert, AZ	26.5
412	Thousand Oaks, CA	26.5
414	Edmond, OK	24.3
415	Sterling Heights, MI	23.9
416	West Jordan, UT	23.6
417	Provo, UT	22.7
418	Arlington Heights, IL	22.6
419	Centennial, CO	22.5
420	Newton, MA	22.2
421	Overland Park, KS	21.8
421	Warwick, RI	21.8
423	Chino Hills, CA	21.1
424	Allen, TX	19.8
425	Frisco, TX	19.3
426	Irvine, CA	18.6
427	Troy, MI	17.3
428	Naperville, IL	16.9
428	Rio Rancho, NM	16.9
430	Johns Creek, GA	16.7
431	Olathe, KS	15.8
432	O'Fallon, MO	11.3
433	Orem, UT	11.1
434	Nampa, ID	10.9
435	Fishers, IN	10.4
436	Meridian, ID	4.0
437	Carmel, IN	2.5

Source: CQ Press using reported data from the F.B.I. "Crime in the United States 2011"
*Robbery is the taking of anything of value by force or threat of force. Attempts are included.

Alpha Order - City

59. Percent Change in Robbery Rate: 2010 to 2011
National Percent Change = 4.7% Decrease*

RANK	CITY	% CHANGE
115	Abilene, TX	4.8
38	Akron, OH	23.1
337	Albany, GA	(19.3)
213	Albany, NY	(4.5)
114	Albuquerque, NM	4.9
78	Alexandria, VA	11.4
380	Alhambra, CA	(29.7)
388	Allentown, PA	(32.5)
179	Allen, TX	(1.5)
202	Amarillo, TX	(3.4)
63	Amherst, NY	15.6
263	Anaheim, CA	(9.8)
159	Anchorage, AK	0.1
360	Ann Arbor, MI	(23.8)
248	Antioch, CA	(8.6)
24	Arlington Heights, IL	35.3
119	Arlington, TX	4.4
51	Arvada, CO	20.3
159	Asheville, NC	0.1
63	Athens-Clarke, GA	15.6
21	Atlanta, GA	36.6
190	Aurora, CO	(2.4)
39	Aurora, IL	22.8
279	Austin, TX	(11.4)
15	Avondale, AZ	41.0
336	Bakersfield, CA	(18.9)
271	Baldwin Park, CA	(10.7)
110	Baltimore, MD	5.8
NA	Baton Rouge, LA**	NA
127	Beaumont, TX	3.4
322	Beaverton, OR	(17.1)
148	Bellevue, WA	1.1
399	Bellflower, CA	(38.1)
367	Bellingham, WA	(25.7)
267	Bend, OR	(10.5)
313	Berkeley, CA	(16.0)
297	Bethlehem, PA	(13.7)
NA	Billings, MT**	NA
NA	Birmingham, AL**	NA
364	Bloomington, IL	(25.2)
373	Bloomington, IN	(27.9)
283	Bloomington, MN	(11.7)
27	Boca Raton, FL	30.3
150	Boise, ID	0.7
137	Boston, MA	2.5
49	Boulder, CO	20.9
334	Brick Twnshp, NJ	(18.7)
117	Bridgeport, CT	4.5
227	Brockton, MA	(6.5)
14	Broken Arrow, OK	42.9
NA	Brooklyn Park, MN**	NA
390	Brownsville, TX	(33.4)
313	Bryan, TX	(16.0)
253	Buena Park, CA	(9.1)
NA	Buffalo, NY**	NA
386	Burbank, CA	(31.5)
252	Cambridge, MA	(8.9)
41	Camden, NJ	22.7
23	Canton Twnshp, MI	35.5
232	Cape Coral, FL	(7.0)
340	Carlsbad, CA	(19.6)
2	Carmel, IN	78.6
6	Carrollton, TX	59.0
335	Carson, CA	(18.8)
48	Cary, NC	21.1
376	Cedar Rapids, IA	(28.7)
303	Centennial, CO	(14.4)
NA	Champaign, IL**	NA
279	Chandler, AZ	(11.4)
122	Charleston, SC	3.8
256	Charlotte, NC	(9.2)
356	Chattanooga, TN	(23.3)

RANK	CITY	% CHANGE
10	Cheektowaga, NY	49.0
267	Chesapeake, VA	(10.5)
131	Chicago, IL	3.1
136	Chico, CA	2.6
185	Chino Hills, CA	(1.9)
332	Chino, CA	(18.6)
305	Chula Vista, CA	(14.9)
NA	Cicero, IL**	NA
225	Cincinnati, OH	(6.3)
329	Citrus Heights, CA	(17.9)
290	Clarkstown, NY	(12.5)
163	Clarksville, TN	(0.2)
374	Clearwater, FL	(28.1)
104	Cleveland, OH	6.5
NA	Clifton, NJ**	NA
96	Clinton Twnshp, MI	7.5
172	Clovis, CA	(1.0)
389	College Station, TX	(32.9)
142	Colonie, NY	2.2
341	Colorado Springs, CO	(19.8)
51	Columbia, MO	20.3
318	Columbus, GA	(16.9)
218	Columbus, OH	(5.2)
356	Compton, CA	(23.3)
174	Concord, CA	(1.2)
406	Concord, NC	(44.5)
54	Coral Springs, FL	19.4
61	Corona, CA	16.0
287	Corpus Christi, TX	(12.3)
279	Costa Mesa, CA	(11.4)
35	Cranston, RI	24.7
199	Dallas, TX	(3.2)
405	Daly City, CA	(44.0)
4	Danbury, CT	65.7
NA	Davenport, IA**	NA
71	Davie, FL	13.4
287	Dayton, OH	(12.3)
387	Dearborn, MI	(31.6)
270	Decatur, IL	(10.6)
307	Deerfield Beach, FL	(15.1)
232	Denton, TX	(7.0)
39	Denver, CO	22.8
213	Des Moines, IA	(4.5)
75	Detroit, MI	13.0
196	Downey, CA	(3.0)
283	Duluth, MN	(11.7)
98	Durham, NC	7.2
58	Edinburg, TX	17.1
32	Edison Twnshp, NJ	25.1
103	Edmond, OK	6.6
123	El Cajon, CA	3.7
346	El Monte, CA	(21.5)
250	El Paso, TX	(8.7)
328	Elgin, IL	(17.7)
205	Elizabeth, NJ	(4.0)
316	Elk Grove, CA	(16.6)
282	Erie, PA	(11.6)
337	Escondido, CA	(19.3)
141	Eugene, OR	2.3
105	Evansville, IN	6.4
363	Everett, WA	(24.9)
348	Fairfield, CA	(21.7)
86	Fall River, MA	9.2
34	Fargo, ND	24.8
1	Farmington Hills, MI	110.2
84	Fayetteville, NC	10.1
393	Fishers, IN	(34.2)
201	Flint, MI	(3.3)
192	Fontana, CA	(2.5)
293	Fort Collins, CO	(13.0)
22	Fort Lauderdale, FL	36.4
342	Fort Smith, AR	(20.1)

RANK	CITY	% CHANGE
169	Fort Wayne, IN	(0.5)
223	Fort Worth, TX	(6.1)
348	Fremont, CA	(21.7)
199	Fresno, CA	(3.2)
213	Frisco, TX	(4.5)
383	Fullerton, CA	(30.1)
302	Gainesville, FL	(14.3)
271	Garden Grove, CA	(10.7)
73	Garland, TX	13.2
NA	Gary, IN**	NA
226	Gilbert, AZ	(6.4)
54	Glendale, AZ	19.4
240	Glendale, CA	(7.8)
196	Grand Prairie, TX	(3.0)
256	Grand Rapids, MI	(9.2)
3	Greece, NY	76.2
25	Greeley, CO	31.7
384	Green Bay, WI	(30.6)
223	Gresham, OR	(6.1)
324	Hamilton Twnshp, NJ	(17.4)
324	Hammond, IN	(17.4)
241	Hampton, VA	(8.0)
108	Hartford, CT	6.1
111	Hawthorne, CA	5.7
251	Hayward, CA	(8.8)
283	Hemet, CA	(11.7)
109	Henderson, NV	6.0
18	Hesperia, CA	38.1
220	Hialeah, FL	(5.4)
261	High Point, NC	(9.5)
NA	Hillsboro, OR**	NA
70	Hollywood, FL	13.6
NA	Hoover, AL**	NA
259	Houston, TX	(9.3)
163	Huntington Beach, CA	(0.2)
NA	Huntsville, AL**	NA
238	Independence, MO	(7.6)
NA	Indianapolis, IN**	NA
71	Indio, CA	13.4
253	Inglewood, CA	(9.1)
148	Irvine, CA	1.1
321	Irving, TX	(17.0)
244	Jacksonville, FL	(8.2)
366	Jackson, MS	(25.6)
157	Jersey City, NJ	0.2
353	Johns Creek, GA	(23.0)
380	Joliet, IL	(29.7)
177	Kansas City, KS	(1.3)
NA	Kansas City, MO**	NA
330	Kennewick, WA	(18.1)
81	Kenosha, WI	10.5
43	Kent, WA	22.2
398	Killeen, TX	(37.7)
241	Knoxville, TN	(8.0)
246	Lafayette, LA	(8.4)
390	Lake Forest, CA	(33.4)
209	Lakeland, FL	(4.2)
411	Lakewood Twnshp, NJ	(52.4)
369	Lakewood, CA	(26.4)
244	Lakewood, CO	(8.2)
155	Lancaster, CA	0.4
129	Lansing, MI	3.2
179	Laredo, TX	(1.5)
375	Largo, FL	(28.5)
94	Las Cruces, NM	7.8
310	Las Vegas, NV	(15.3)
395	Lawrence, KS	(35.3)
20	Lawrence, MA	37.4
13	Lawton, OK	45.5
8	League City, TX	54.4
81	Lee's Summit, MO	10.5
370	Lewisville, TX	(26.5)

236 Cities

Alpha Order - City (continued)

RANK	CITY	% CHANGE
NA	Lexington, KY**	NA
198	Lincoln, NE	(3.1)
174	Little Rock, AR	(1.2)
370	Livermore, CA	(26.5)
157	Livonia, MI	0.2
90	Long Beach, CA	8.5
234	Longmont, CO	(7.2)
348	Longview, TX	(21.7)
239	Los Angeles, CA	(7.7)
184	Louisville, KY	(1.8)
305	Lowell, MA	(14.9)
234	Lubbock, TX	(7.2)
221	Lynchburg, VA	(5.6)
323	Lynn, MA	(17.3)
316	Macon, GA	(16.6)
307	Madison, WI	(15.1)
62	Manchester, NH	15.8
396	McAllen, TX	(36.4)
69	McKinney, TX	13.8
12	Medford, OR	45.8
80	Melbourne, FL	10.8
183	Memphis, TN	(1.7)
400	Menifee, CA	(38.8)
137	Merced, CA	2.5
414	Meridian, ID	(73.5)
174	Mesa, AZ	(1.2)
151	Mesquite, TX	0.6
121	Miami Beach, FL	3.9
56	Miami Gardens, FL	19.3
57	Miami, FL	17.3
297	Midland, TX	(13.7)
137	Milwaukee, WI	2.5
167	Minneapolis, MN	(0.4)
126	Miramar, FL	3.5
7	Mission Viejo, CA	58.2
253	Mission, TX	(9.1)
NA	Mobile, AL**	NA
166	Modesto, CA	(0.3)
NA	Montgomery, AL**	NA
273	Moreno Valley, CA	(10.8)
297	Murfreesboro, TN	(13.7)
133	Murrieta, CA	2.8
407	Nampa, ID	(46.0)
124	Napa, CA	3.6
NA	Naperville, IL**	NA
106	Nashua, NH	6.3
116	Nashville, TN	4.6
147	New Bedford, MA	1.3
227	New Haven, CT	(6.5)
68	New Orleans, LA	14.1
50	New Rochelle, NY	20.7
140	New York, NY	2.4
36	Newark, NJ	24.3
401	Newport Beach, CA	(39.0)
73	Newport News, VA	13.2
37	Newton, MA	24.0
162	Norfolk, VA	(0.1)
16	Norman, OK	40.9
397	North Charleston, SC	(36.7)
318	Norwalk, CA	(16.9)
385	Norwalk, CT	(30.9)
53	Oakland, CA	19.6
113	Oceanside, CA	5.2
361	Odessa, TX	(24.3)
134	O'Fallon, MO	2.7
312	Ogden, UT	(15.8)
93	Oklahoma City, OK	8.1
378	Olathe, KS	(28.8)
92	Omaha, NE	8.4
243	Ontario, CA	(8.1)
11	Orange, CA	45.9
401	Orem, UT	(39.0)
129	Orlando, FL	3.2

RANK	CITY	% CHANGE
90	Overland Park, KS	8.5
345	Oxnard, CA	(21.4)
5	Palm Bay, FL	59.6
267	Palmdale, CA	(10.5)
185	Pasadena, CA	(1.9)
295	Pasadena, TX	(13.3)
193	Paterson, NJ	(2.6)
182	Pearland, TX	(1.6)
45	Pembroke Pines, FL	21.6
300	Peoria, AZ	(14.1)
227	Peoria, IL	(6.5)
155	Philadelphia, PA	0.4
95	Phoenix, AZ	7.7
207	Pittsburgh, PA	(4.1)
188	Plano, TX	(2.0)
134	Plantation, FL	2.7
107	Pomona, CA	6.2
210	Pompano Beach, FL	(4.3)
44	Port St. Lucie, FL	22.0
292	Portland, OR	(12.7)
248	Portsmouth, VA	(8.6)
171	Provo, UT	(0.9)
NA	Pueblo, CO**	NA
344	Quincy, MA	(21.0)
207	Racine, WI	(4.1)
89	Raleigh, NC	8.6
19	Ramapo, NY	37.9
185	Rancho Cucamon., CA	(1.9)
262	Reading, PA	(9.6)
210	Redding, CA	(4.3)
291	Redwood City, CA	(12.6)
194	Reno, NV	(2.7)
382	Renton, WA	(30.0)
117	Rialto, CA	4.5
295	Richardson, TX	(13.3)
368	Richmond, CA	(26.2)
246	Richmond, VA	(8.4)
327	Rio Rancho, NM	(17.6)
266	Riverside, CA	(10.4)
205	Roanoke, VA	(4.0)
85	Rochester, MN	9.4
273	Rochester, NY	(10.8)
59	Rockford, IL	16.5
410	Roseville, CA	(50.7)
412	Roswell, GA	(53.0)
47	Round Rock, TX	21.3
351	Sacramento, CA	(22.0)
152	Salem, OR	0.5
195	Salinas, CA	(2.9)
278	Salt Lake City, UT	(11.3)
332	San Angelo, TX	(18.6)
352	San Antonio, TX	(22.3)
100	San Bernardino, CA	6.9
276	San Diego, CA	(11.2)
190	San Francisco, CA	(2.4)
67	San Jose, CA	14.3
218	San Leandro, CA	(5.2)
311	San Marcos, CA	(15.4)
343	San Mateo, CA	(20.6)
376	Sandy Springs, GA	(28.7)
331	Sandy, UT	(18.2)
304	Santa Ana, CA	(14.8)
315	Santa Barbara, CA	(16.4)
124	Santa Clara, CA	3.6
403	Santa Clarita, CA	(41.0)
286	Santa Maria, CA	(12.2)
365	Santa Monica, CA	(25.3)
362	Santa Rosa, CA	(24.8)
161	Savannah, GA	0.0
26	Scottsdale, AZ	30.6
294	Scranton, PA	(13.1)
167	Seattle, WA	(0.4)
170	Shreveport, LA	(0.6)
98	Simi Valley, CA	7.2

RANK	CITY	% CHANGE
101	Sioux City, IA	6.8
16	Sioux Falls, SD	40.9
30	Somerville, MA	25.8
41	South Bend, IN	22.7
318	South Gate, CA	(16.9)
372	Sparks, NV	(26.9)
188	Spokane Valley, WA	(2.0)
97	Spokane, WA	7.3
354	Springfield, IL	(23.1)
256	Springfield, MA	(9.2)
260	Springfield, MO	(9.4)
32	Stamford, CT	25.1
NA	Sterling Heights, MI**	NA
236	Stockton, CA	(7.3)
65	St. Joseph, MO	15.4
79	St. Louis, MO	10.9
276	St. Paul, MN	(11.2)
222	St. Petersburg, FL	(6.0)
210	Suffolk, VA	(4.3)
409	Sugar Land, TX	(50.0)
87	Sunnyvale, CA	9.1
309	Sunrise, FL	(15.2)
76	Surprise, AZ	12.9
203	Syracuse, NY	(3.8)
324	Tacoma, WA	(17.4)
178	Tallahassee, FL	(1.4)
287	Tampa, FL	(12.3)
28	Temecula, CA	30.0
231	Tempe, AZ	(6.7)
NA	Thornton, CO**	NA
393	Thousand Oaks, CA	(34.2)
66	Toledo, OH	15.3
29	Toms River Twnshp, NJ	25.9
127	Topeka, KS	3.4
404	Torrance, CA	(42.9)
60	Tracy, CA	16.2
144	Trenton, NJ	1.8
9	Troy, MI	53.1
101	Tucson, AZ	6.8
347	Tulsa, OK	(21.6)
NA	Tuscaloosa, AL**	NA
392	Tustin, CA	(33.5)
337	Tyler, TX	(19.3)
217	Upper Darby Twnshp, PA	(4.8)
379	Vacaville, CA	(29.2)
237	Vallejo, CA	(7.5)
88	Vancouver, WA	8.9
46	Ventura, CA	21.5
144	Victorville, CA	1.8
204	Virginia Beach, VA	(3.9)
408	Visalia, CA	(46.4)
112	Vista, CA	5.6
31	Waco, TX	25.3
264	Warren, MI	(9.9)
355	Warwick, RI	(23.2)
230	Washington, DC	(6.6)
143	Waterbury, CT	2.0
146	West Covina, CA	1.4
413	West Jordan, UT	(54.2)
275	West Palm Beach, FL	(11.0)
265	West Valley, UT	(10.2)
213	Westland, MI	(4.5)
359	Westminster, CA	(23.6)
152	Westminster, CO	0.5
179	Whittier, CA	(1.5)
120	Wichita Falls, TX	4.2
163	Wichita, KS	(0.2)
301	Wilmington, NC	(14.2)
172	Winston-Salem, NC	(1.0)
358	Woodbridge Twnshp, NJ	(23.5)
77	Worcester, MA	11.5
152	Yakima, WA	0.5
132	Yonkers, NY	3.0
83	Yuma, AZ	10.3

Source: CQ Press using reported data from the F.B.I. "Crime in the United States 2011"
*Robbery is the taking of anything of value by force or threat of force. Attempts are included.
**Not available.

Rank Order - City

59. Percent Change in Robbery Rate: 2010 to 2011 (continued)
National Percent Change = 4.7% Decrease*

RANK	CITY	% CHANGE	RANK	CITY	% CHANGE	RANK	CITY	% CHANGE
1	Farmington Hills, MI	110.2	73	Garland, TX	13.2	144	Victorville, CA	1.8
2	Carmel, IN	78.6	73	Newport News, VA	13.2	146	West Covina, CA	1.4
3	Greece, NY	76.2	75	Detroit, MI	13.0	147	New Bedford, MA	1.3
4	Danbury, CT	65.7	76	Surprise, AZ	12.9	148	Bellevue, WA	1.1
5	Palm Bay, FL	59.6	77	Worcester, MA	11.5	148	Irvine, CA	1.1
6	Carrollton, TX	59.0	78	Alexandria, VA	11.4	150	Boise, ID	0.7
7	Mission Viejo, CA	58.2	79	St. Louis, MO	10.9	151	Mesquite, TX	0.6
8	League City, TX	54.4	80	Melbourne, FL	10.8	152	Salem, OR	0.5
9	Troy, MI	53.1	81	Kenosha, WI	10.5	152	Westminster, CO	0.5
10	Cheektowaga, NY	49.0	81	Lee's Summit, MO	10.5	152	Yakima, WA	0.5
11	Orange, CA	45.9	83	Yuma, AZ	10.3	155	Lancaster, CA	0.4
12	Medford, OR	45.8	84	Fayetteville, NC	10.1	155	Philadelphia, PA	0.4
13	Lawton, OK	45.5	85	Rochester, MN	9.4	157	Jersey City, NJ	0.2
14	Broken Arrow, OK	42.9	86	Fall River, MA	9.2	157	Livonia, MI	0.2
15	Avondale, AZ	41.0	87	Sunnyvale, CA	9.1	159	Anchorage, AK	0.1
16	Norman, OK	40.9	88	Vancouver, WA	8.9	159	Asheville, NC	0.1
16	Sioux Falls, SD	40.9	89	Raleigh, NC	8.6	161	Savannah, GA	0.0
18	Hesperia, CA	38.1	90	Long Beach, CA	8.5	162	Norfolk, VA	(0.1)
19	Ramapo, NY	37.9	90	Overland Park, KS	8.5	163	Clarksville, TN	(0.2)
20	Lawrence, MA	37.4	92	Omaha, NE	8.4	163	Huntington Beach, CA	(0.2)
21	Atlanta, GA	36.6	93	Oklahoma City, OK	8.1	163	Wichita, KS	(0.2)
22	Fort Lauderdale, FL	36.4	94	Las Cruces, NM	7.8	166	Modesto, CA	(0.3)
23	Canton Twnshp, MI	35.5	95	Phoenix, AZ	7.7	167	Minneapolis, MN	(0.4)
24	Arlington Heights, IL	35.3	96	Clinton Twnshp, MI	7.5	167	Seattle, WA	(0.4)
25	Greeley, CO	31.7	97	Spokane, WA	7.3	169	Fort Wayne, IN	(0.5)
26	Scottsdale, AZ	30.6	98	Durham, NC	7.2	170	Shreveport, LA	(0.6)
27	Boca Raton, FL	30.3	98	Simi Valley, CA	7.2	171	Provo, UT	(0.9)
28	Temecula, CA	30.0	100	San Bernardino, CA	6.9	172	Clovis, CA	(1.0)
29	Toms River Twnshp, NJ	25.9	101	Sioux City, IA	6.8	172	Winston-Salem, NC	(1.0)
30	Somerville, MA	25.8	101	Tucson, AZ	6.8	174	Concord, CA	(1.2)
31	Waco, TX	25.3	103	Edmond, OK	6.6	174	Little Rock, AR	(1.2)
32	Edison Twnshp, NJ	25.1	104	Cleveland, OH	6.5	174	Mesa, AZ	(1.2)
32	Stamford, CT	25.1	105	Evansville, IN	6.4	177	Kansas City, KS	(1.3)
34	Fargo, ND	24.8	106	Nashua, NH	6.3	178	Tallahassee, FL	(1.4)
35	Cranston, RI	24.7	107	Pomona, CA	6.2	179	Allen, TX	(1.5)
36	Newark, NJ	24.3	108	Hartford, CT	6.1	179	Laredo, TX	(1.5)
37	Newton, MA	24.0	109	Henderson, NV	6.0	179	Whittier, CA	(1.5)
38	Akron, OH	23.1	110	Baltimore, MD	5.8	182	Pearland, TX	(1.6)
39	Aurora, IL	22.8	111	Hawthorne, CA	5.7	183	Memphis, TN	(1.7)
39	Denver, CO	22.8	112	Vista, CA	5.6	184	Louisville, KY	(1.8)
41	Camden, NJ	22.7	113	Oceanside, CA	5.2	185	Chino Hills, CA	(1.9)
41	South Bend, IN	22.7	114	Albuquerque, NM	4.9	185	Pasadena, CA	(1.9)
43	Kent, WA	22.2	115	Abilene, TX	4.8	185	Rancho Cucamon., CA	(1.9)
44	Port St. Lucie, FL	22.0	116	Nashville, TN	4.6	188	Plano, TX	(2.0)
45	Pembroke Pines, FL	21.6	117	Bridgeport, CT	4.5	188	Spokane Valley, WA	(2.0)
46	Ventura, CA	21.5	117	Rialto, CA	4.5	190	Aurora, CO	(2.4)
47	Round Rock, TX	21.3	119	Arlington, TX	4.4	190	San Francisco, CA	(2.4)
48	Cary, NC	21.1	120	Wichita Falls, TX	4.2	192	Fontana, CA	(2.5)
49	Boulder, CO	20.9	121	Miami Beach, FL	3.9	193	Paterson, NJ	(2.6)
50	New Rochelle, NY	20.7	122	Charleston, SC	3.8	194	Reno, NV	(2.7)
51	Arvada, CO	20.3	123	El Cajon, CA	3.7	195	Salinas, CA	(2.9)
51	Columbia, MO	20.3	124	Napa, CA	3.6	196	Downey, CA	(3.0)
53	Oakland, CA	19.6	124	Santa Clara, CA	3.6	196	Grand Prairie, TX	(3.0)
54	Coral Springs, FL	19.4	126	Miramar, FL	3.5	198	Lincoln, NE	(3.1)
54	Glendale, AZ	19.4	127	Beaumont, TX	3.4	199	Dallas, TX	(3.2)
56	Miami Gardens, FL	19.3	127	Topeka, KS	3.4	199	Fresno, CA	(3.2)
57	Miami, FL	17.3	129	Lansing, MI	3.2	201	Flint, MI	(3.3)
58	Edinburg, TX	17.1	129	Orlando, FL	3.2	202	Amarillo, TX	(3.4)
59	Rockford, IL	16.5	131	Chicago, IL	3.1	203	Syracuse, NY	(3.8)
60	Tracy, CA	16.2	132	Yonkers, NY	3.0	204	Virginia Beach, VA	(3.9)
61	Corona, CA	16.0	133	Murrieta, CA	2.8	205	Elizabeth, NJ	(4.0)
62	Manchester, NH	15.8	134	O'Fallon, MO	2.7	205	Roanoke, VA	(4.0)
63	Amherst, NY	15.6	134	Plantation, FL	2.7	207	Pittsburgh, PA	(4.1)
63	Athens-Clarke, GA	15.6	136	Chico, CA	2.6	207	Racine, WI	(4.1)
65	St. Joseph, MO	15.4	137	Boston, MA	2.5	209	Lakeland, FL	(4.2)
66	Toledo, OH	15.3	137	Merced, CA	2.5	210	Pompano Beach, FL	(4.3)
67	San Jose, CA	14.3	137	Milwaukee, WI	2.5	210	Redding, CA	(4.3)
68	New Orleans, LA	14.1	140	New York, NY	2.4	210	Suffolk, VA	(4.3)
69	McKinney, TX	13.8	141	Eugene, OR	2.3	213	Albany, NY	(4.5)
70	Hollywood, FL	13.6	142	Colonie, NY	2.2	213	Des Moines, IA	(4.5)
71	Davie, FL	13.4	143	Waterbury, CT	2.0	213	Frisco, TX	(4.5)
71	Indio, CA	13.4	144	Trenton, NJ	1.8	213	Westland, MI	(4.5)

238   Cities

Rank Order - City (continued)

RANK	CITY	% CHANGE
217	Upper Darby Twnshp, PA	(4.8)
218	Columbus, OH	(5.2)
218	San Leandro, CA	(5.2)
220	Hialeah, FL	(5.4)
221	Lynchburg, VA	(5.6)
222	St. Petersburg, FL	(6.0)
223	Fort Worth, TX	(6.1)
223	Gresham, OR	(6.1)
225	Cincinnati, OH	(6.3)
226	Gilbert, AZ	(6.4)
227	Brockton, MA	(6.5)
227	New Haven, CT	(6.5)
227	Peoria, IL	(6.5)
230	Washington, DC	(6.6)
231	Tempe, AZ	(6.7)
232	Cape Coral, FL	(7.0)
232	Denton, TX	(7.0)
234	Longmont, CO	(7.2)
234	Lubbock, TX	(7.2)
236	Stockton, CA	(7.3)
237	Vallejo, CA	(7.5)
238	Independence, MO	(7.6)
239	Los Angeles, CA	(7.7)
240	Glendale, CA	(7.8)
241	Hampton, VA	(8.0)
241	Knoxville, TN	(8.0)
243	Ontario, CA	(8.1)
244	Jacksonville, FL	(8.2)
244	Lakewood, CO	(8.2)
246	Lafayette, LA	(8.4)
246	Richmond, VA	(8.4)
248	Antioch, CA	(8.6)
248	Portsmouth, VA	(8.6)
250	El Paso, TX	(8.7)
251	Hayward, CA	(8.8)
252	Cambridge, MA	(8.9)
253	Buena Park, CA	(9.1)
253	Inglewood, CA	(9.1)
253	Mission, TX	(9.1)
256	Charlotte, NC	(9.2)
256	Grand Rapids, MI	(9.2)
256	Springfield, MA	(9.2)
259	Houston, TX	(9.3)
260	Springfield, MO	(9.4)
261	High Point, NC	(9.5)
262	Reading, PA	(9.6)
263	Anaheim, CA	(9.8)
264	Warren, MI	(9.9)
265	West Valley, UT	(10.2)
266	Riverside, CA	(10.4)
267	Bend, OR	(10.5)
267	Chesapeake, VA	(10.5)
267	Palmdale, CA	(10.5)
270	Decatur, IL	(10.6)
271	Baldwin Park, CA	(10.7)
271	Garden Grove, CA	(10.7)
273	Moreno Valley, CA	(10.8)
273	Rochester, NY	(10.8)
275	West Palm Beach, FL	(11.0)
276	San Diego, CA	(11.2)
276	St. Paul, MN	(11.2)
278	Salt Lake City, UT	(11.3)
279	Austin, TX	(11.4)
279	Chandler, AZ	(11.4)
279	Costa Mesa, CA	(11.4)
282	Erie, PA	(11.6)
283	Bloomington, MN	(11.7)
283	Duluth, MN	(11.7)
283	Hemet, CA	(11.7)
286	Santa Maria, CA	(12.2)
287	Corpus Christi, TX	(12.3)
287	Dayton, OH	(12.3)
287	Tampa, FL	(12.3)
290	Clarkstown, NY	(12.5)
291	Redwood City, CA	(12.6)
292	Portland, OR	(12.7)
293	Fort Collins, CO	(13.0)
294	Scranton, PA	(13.1)
295	Pasadena, TX	(13.3)
295	Richardson, TX	(13.3)
297	Bethlehem, PA	(13.7)
297	Midland, TX	(13.7)
297	Murfreesboro, TN	(13.7)
300	Peoria, AZ	(14.1)
301	Wilmington, NC	(14.2)
302	Gainesville, FL	(14.3)
303	Centennial, CO	(14.4)
304	Santa Ana, CA	(14.8)
305	Chula Vista, CA	(14.9)
305	Lowell, MA	(14.9)
307	Deerfield Beach, FL	(15.1)
307	Madison, WI	(15.1)
309	Sunrise, FL	(15.2)
310	Las Vegas, NV	(15.3)
311	San Marcos, CA	(15.4)
312	Ogden, UT	(15.8)
313	Berkeley, CA	(16.0)
313	Bryan, TX	(16.0)
315	Santa Barbara, CA	(16.4)
316	Elk Grove, CA	(16.6)
316	Macon, GA	(16.6)
318	Columbus, GA	(16.9)
318	Norwalk, CA	(16.9)
318	South Gate, CA	(16.9)
321	Irving, TX	(17.0)
322	Beaverton, OR	(17.1)
323	Lynn, MA	(17.3)
324	Hamilton Twnshp, NJ	(17.4)
324	Hammond, IN	(17.4)
324	Tacoma, WA	(17.4)
327	Rio Rancho, NM	(17.6)
328	Elgin, IL	(17.7)
329	Citrus Heights, CA	(17.9)
330	Kennewick, WA	(18.1)
331	Sandy, UT	(18.2)
332	Chino, CA	(18.6)
332	San Angelo, TX	(18.6)
334	Brick Twnshp, NJ	(18.7)
335	Carson, CA	(18.8)
336	Bakersfield, CA	(18.9)
337	Albany, GA	(19.3)
337	Escondido, CA	(19.3)
337	Tyler, TX	(19.3)
340	Carlsbad, CA	(19.6)
341	Colorado Springs, CO	(19.8)
342	Fort Smith, AR	(20.1)
343	San Mateo, CA	(20.6)
344	Quincy, MA	(21.0)
345	Oxnard, CA	(21.4)
346	El Monte, CA	(21.5)
347	Tulsa, OK	(21.6)
348	Fairfield, CA	(21.7)
348	Fremont, CA	(21.7)
348	Longview, TX	(21.7)
351	Sacramento, CA	(22.0)
352	San Antonio, TX	(22.3)
353	Johns Creek, GA	(23.0)
354	Springfield, IL	(23.1)
355	Warwick, RI	(23.2)
356	Chattanooga, TN	(23.3)
356	Compton, CA	(23.3)
358	Woodbridge Twnshp, NJ	(23.5)
359	Westminster, CA	(23.6)
360	Ann Arbor, MI	(23.8)
361	Odessa, TX	(24.3)
362	Santa Rosa, CA	(24.8)
363	Everett, WA	(24.9)
364	Bloomington, IL	(25.2)
365	Santa Monica, CA	(25.3)
366	Jackson, MS	(25.6)
367	Bellingham, WA	(25.7)
368	Richmond, CA	(26.2)
369	Lakewood, CA	(26.4)
370	Lewisville, TX	(26.5)
370	Livermore, CA	(26.5)
372	Sparks, NV	(26.9)
373	Bloomington, IN	(27.9)
374	Clearwater, FL	(28.1)
375	Largo, FL	(28.5)
376	Cedar Rapids, IA	(28.7)
376	Sandy Springs, GA	(28.7)
378	Olathe, KS	(28.8)
379	Vacaville, CA	(29.2)
380	Alhambra, CA	(29.7)
380	Joliet, IL	(29.7)
382	Renton, WA	(30.0)
383	Fullerton, CA	(30.1)
384	Green Bay, WI	(30.6)
385	Norwalk, CT	(30.9)
386	Burbank, CA	(31.5)
387	Dearborn, MI	(31.6)
388	Allentown, PA	(32.5)
389	College Station, TX	(32.9)
390	Brownsville, TX	(33.4)
390	Lake Forest, CA	(33.4)
392	Tustin, CA	(33.5)
393	Fishers, IN	(34.2)
393	Thousand Oaks, CA	(34.2)
395	Lawrence, KS	(35.3)
396	McAllen, TX	(36.4)
397	North Charleston, SC	(36.7)
398	Killeen, TX	(37.7)
399	Bellflower, CA	(38.1)
400	Menifee, CA	(38.8)
401	Newport Beach, CA	(39.0)
401	Orem, UT	(39.0)
403	Santa Clarita, CA	(41.0)
404	Torrance, CA	(42.9)
405	Daly City, CA	(44.0)
406	Concord, NC	(44.5)
407	Nampa, ID	(46.0)
408	Visalia, CA	(46.4)
409	Sugar Land, TX	(50.0)
410	Roseville, CA	(50.7)
411	Lakewood Twnshp, NJ	(52.4)
412	Roswell, GA	(53.0)
413	West Jordan, UT	(54.2)
414	Meridian, ID	(73.5)
NA	Baton Rouge, LA**	NA
NA	Billings, MT**	NA
NA	Birmingham, AL**	NA
NA	Brooklyn Park, MN**	NA
NA	Buffalo, NY**	NA
NA	Champaign, IL**	NA
NA	Cicero, IL**	NA
NA	Clifton, NJ**	NA
NA	Davenport, IA**	NA
NA	Gary, IN**	NA
NA	Hillsboro, OR**	NA
NA	Hoover, AL**	NA
NA	Huntsville, AL**	NA
NA	Indianapolis, IN**	NA
NA	Kansas City, MO**	NA
NA	Lexington, KY**	NA
NA	Mobile, AL**	NA
NA	Montgomery, AL**	NA
NA	Naperville, IL**	NA
NA	Pueblo, CO**	NA
NA	Sterling Heights, MI**	NA
NA	Thornton, CO**	NA
NA	Tuscaloosa, AL**	NA

Source: CQ Press using reported data from the F.B.I. "Crime in the United States 2011"
*Robbery is the taking of anything of value by force or threat of force. Attempts are included.
**Not available.

Alpha Order - City

60. Percent Change in Robbery Rate: 2007 to 2011
National Percent Change = 23.3% Decrease*

RANK	CITY	% CHANGE	RANK	CITY	% CHANGE	RANK	CITY	% CHANGE
266	Abilene, TX	(31.1)	75	Cheektowaga, NY	(4.8)	216	Fort Wayne, IN	(25.8)
51	Akron, OH	3.0	209	Chesapeake, VA	(25.1)	261	Fort Worth, TX	(30.7)
157	Albany, GA	(17.8)	77	Chicago, IL	(5.3)	323	Fremont, CA	(37.5)
163	Albany, NY	(18.7)	224	Chico, CA	(26.7)	127	Fresno, CA	(12.8)
303	Albuquerque, NM	(35.5)	303	Chino Hills, CA	(35.5)	150	Frisco, TX	(16.8)
193	Alexandria, VA	(22.5)	361	Chino, CA	(44.1)	367	Fullerton, CA	(45.3)
400	Alhambra, CA	(69.0)	378	Chula Vista, CA	(47.9)	286	Gainesville, FL	(33.3)
363	Allentown, PA	(44.3)	NA	Cicero, IL**	NA	322	Garden Grove, CA	(37.2)
31	Allen, TX	11.2	57	Cincinnati, OH	1.1	235	Garland, TX	(28.0)
376	Amarillo, TX	(47.6)	NA	Citrus Heights, CA**	NA	22	Gary, IN	21.7
152	Amherst, NY	(17.1)	46	Clarkstown, NY	6.3	66	Gilbert, AZ	(2.2)
202	Anaheim, CA	(24.4)	267	Clarksville, TN	(31.3)	133	Glendale, AZ	(13.4)
64	Anchorage, AK	(1.8)	211	Clearwater, FL	(25.3)	281	Glendale, CA	(32.9)
115	Ann Arbor, MI	(11.3)	129	Cleveland, OH	(13.1)	187	Grand Prairie, TX	(21.3)
259	Antioch, CA	(30.5)	125	Clifton, NJ	(12.3)	243	Grand Rapids, MI	(29.0)
NA	Arlington Heights, IL**	NA	83	Clinton Twnshp, MI	(6.4)	29	Greece, NY	15.6
229	Arlington, TX	(27.4)	35	Clovis, CA	9.7	10	Greeley, CO	50.1
237	Arvada, CO	(28.1)	363	College Station, TX	(44.3)	382	Green Bay, WI	(48.4)
272	Asheville, NC	(31.8)	8	Colonie, NY	51.7	89	Gresham, OR	(7.0)
107	Athens-Clarke, GA	(10.0)	206	Colorado Springs, CO	(24.9)	176	Hamilton Twnshp, NJ	(20.1)
197	Atlanta, GA	(23.5)	49	Columbia, MO	3.3	318	Hammond, IN	(36.9)
172	Aurora, CO	(19.6)	293	Columbus, GA	(34.4)	311	Hampton, VA	(35.9)
166	Aurora, IL	(19.1)	185	Columbus, OH	(21.2)	86	Hartford, CT	(6.6)
277	Austin, TX	(32.6)	173	Compton, CA	(19.8)	173	Hawthorne, CA	(19.8)
NA	Avondale, AZ**	NA	329	Concord, CA	(38.8)	303	Hayward, CA	(35.5)
181	Bakersfield, CA	(21.0)	402	Concord, NC	(70.8)	206	Hemet, CA	(24.9)
115	Baldwin Park, CA	(11.3)	40	Coral Springs, FL	8.1	144	Henderson, NV	(16.1)
117	Baltimore, MD	(11.6)	361	Corona, CA	(44.1)	105	Hesperia, CA	(9.7)
130	Baton Rouge, LA	(13.2)	270	Corpus Christi, TX	(31.6)	387	Hialeah, FL	(52.3)
47	Beaumont, TX	4.3	44	Costa Mesa, CA	6.4	358	High Point, NC	(43.9)
328	Beaverton, OR	(38.6)	237	Cranston, RI	(28.1)	386	Hillsboro, OR	(51.8)
101	Bellevue, WA	(9.0)	347	Dallas, TX	(42.9)	312	Hollywood, FL	(36.1)
391	Bellflower, CA	(54.3)	399	Daly City, CA	(68.8)	NA	Hoover, AL**	NA
123	Bellingham, WA	(12.0)	61	Danbury, CT	(0.1)	243	Houston, TX	(29.0)
293	Bend, OR	(34.4)	NA	Davenport, IA**	NA	42	Huntington Beach, CA	7.5
250	Berkeley, CA	(29.8)	197	Davie, FL	(23.5)	NA	Huntsville, AL**	NA
81	Bethlehem, PA	(6.0)	85	Dayton, OH	(6.5)	290	Independence, MO	(33.7)
NA	Billings, MT**	NA	288	Dearborn, MI	(33.4)	178	Indianapolis, IN	(20.2)
NA	Birmingham, AL**	NA	NA	Decatur, IL**	NA	91	Indio, CA	(7.8)
NA	Bloomington, IL**	NA	83	Deerfield Beach, FL	(6.4)	267	Inglewood, CA	(31.3)
267	Bloomington, IN	(31.3)	303	Denton, TX	(35.5)	140	Irvine, CA	(14.7)
195	Bloomington, MN	(22.8)	54	Denver, CO	2.7	358	Irving, TX	(43.9)
196	Boca Raton, FL	(22.9)	375	Des Moines, IA	(47.4)	384	Jacksonville, FL	(51.6)
151	Boise, ID	(17.0)	98	Detroit, MI	(8.9)	78	Jackson, MS	(5.5)
166	Boston, MA	(19.1)	270	Downey, CA	(31.6)	214	Jersey City, NJ	(25.4)
24	Boulder, CO	18.9	242	Duluth, MN	(28.7)	NA	Johns Creek, GA**	NA
3	Brick Twnshp, NJ	72.7	NA	Durham, NC**	NA	371	Joliet, IL	(45.8)
137	Bridgeport, CT	(13.9)	93	Edinburg, TX	(8.0)	345	Kansas City, KS	(41.9)
28	Brockton, MA	16.3	211	Edison Twnshp, NJ	(25.3)	NA	Kansas City, MO**	NA
15	Broken Arrow, OK	35.8	333	Edmond, OK	(38.9)	76	Kennewick, WA	(5.1)
173	Brooklyn Park, MN	(19.8)	91	El Cajon, CA	(7.8)	285	Kenosha, WI	(33.1)
377	Brownsville, TX	(47.8)	106	El Monte, CA	(9.8)	41	Kent, WA	7.9
249	Bryan, TX	(29.5)	96	El Paso, TX	(8.6)	275	Killeen, TX	(32.1)
350	Buena Park, CA	(43.1)	117	Elgin, IL	(11.6)	149	Knoxville, TN	(16.6)
NA	Buffalo, NY**	NA	25	Elizabeth, NJ	18.3	272	Lafayette, LA	(31.8)
255	Burbank, CA	(30.4)	352	Elk Grove, CA	(43.2)	281	Lake Forest, CA	(32.9)
64	Cambridge, MA	(1.8)	353	Erie, PA	(43.3)	309	Lakeland, FL	(35.8)
30	Camden, NJ	11.7	346	Escondido, CA	(42.0)	405	Lakewood Twnshp, NJ	(76.0)
5	Canton Twnshp, MI	64.4	96	Eugene, OR	(8.6)	396	Lakewood, CA	(60.9)
329	Cape Coral, FL	(38.8)	146	Evansville, IN	(16.2)	154	Lakewood, CO	(17.3)
397	Carlsbad, CA	(64.6)	302	Everett, WA	(35.3)	347	Lancaster, CA	(42.9)
404	Carmel, IN	(74.2)	286	Fairfield, CA	(33.3)	56	Lansing, MI	1.7
163	Carrollton, TX	(18.7)	NA	Fall River, MA**	NA	337	Laredo, TX	(39.3)
383	Carson, CA	(51.0)	9	Fargo, ND	51.6	217	Largo, FL	(26.1)
343	Cary, NC	(41.1)	50	Farmington Hills, MI	3.2	317	Las Cruces, NM	(36.8)
324	Cedar Rapids, IA	(38.3)	162	Fayetteville, NC	(18.5)	329	Las Vegas, NV	(38.8)
333	Centennial, CO	(38.9)	347	Fishers, IN	(42.9)	341	Lawrence, KS	(40.0)
NA	Champaign, IL**	NA	48	Flint, MI	3.5	2	Lawrence, MA	74.7
228	Chandler, AZ	(27.2)	221	Fontana, CA	(26.5)	142	Lawton, OK	(15.6)
371	Charleston, SC	(45.8)	19	Fort Collins, CO	24.6	20	League City, TX	24.4
389	Charlotte, NC	(53.1)	26	Fort Lauderdale, FL	17.4	296	Lee's Summit, MO	(35.0)
279	Chattanooga, TN	(32.7)	276	Fort Smith, AR	(32.5)	229	Lewisville, TX	(27.4)

Alpha Order - City (continued)

RANK	CITY	% CHANGE	RANK	CITY	% CHANGE	RANK	CITY	% CHANGE
NA	Lexington, KY**	NA	255	Overland Park, KS	(30.4)	53	Sioux City, IA	2.8
73	Lincoln, NE	(4.5)	355	Oxnard, CA	(43.7)	7	Sioux Falls, SD	59.1
179	Little Rock, AR	(20.5)	110	Palm Bay, FL	(10.3)	220	Somerville, MA	(26.4)
356	Livermore, CA	(43.8)	321	Palmdale, CA	(37.1)	88	South Bend, IN	(6.9)
17	Livonia, MI	28.3	325	Pasadena, CA	(38.4)	133	South Gate, CA	(13.4)
114	Long Beach, CA	(11.2)	135	Pasadena, TX	(13.5)	373	Sparks, NV	(46.6)
NA	Longmont, CO**	NA	38	Paterson, NJ	9.1	74	Spokane Valley, WA	(4.6)
369	Longview, TX	(45.4)	200	Pearland, TX	(24.1)	37	Spokane, WA	9.2
204	Los Angeles, CA	(24.6)	184	Pembroke Pines, FL	(21.1)	185	Springfield, IL	(21.2)
168	Louisville, KY	(19.3)	380	Peoria, AZ	(48.3)	201	Springfield, MA	(24.3)
284	Lowell, MA	(33.0)	232	Peoria, IL	(27.6)	94	Springfield, MO	(8.5)
32	Lubbock, TX	10.3	204	Philadelphia, PA	(24.6)	12	Stamford, CT	43.3
181	Lynchburg, VA	(21.0)	248	Phoenix, AZ	(29.3)	NA	Sterling Heights, MI**	NA
98	Lynn, MA	(8.9)	241	Pittsburgh, PA	(28.6)	155	Stockton, CA	(17.5)
158	Macon, GA	(18.0)	136	Plano, TX	(13.7)	27	St. Joseph, MO	16.8
227	Madison, WI	(27.1)	130	Plantation, FL	(13.2)	147	St. Louis, MO	(16.3)
NA	Manchester, NH**	NA	237	Pomona, CA	(28.1)	223	St. Paul, MN	(26.6)
325	McAllen, TX	(38.4)	187	Pompano Beach, FL	(21.3)	247	St. Petersburg, FL	(29.2)
121	McKinney, TX	(11.8)	44	Port St. Lucie, FL	6.4	117	Suffolk, VA	(11.6)
16	Medford, OR	29.8	298	Portland, OR	(35.1)	199	Sugar Land, TX	(23.9)
94	Melbourne, FL	(8.5)	203	Portsmouth, VA	(24.5)	58	Sunnyvale, CA	0.8
298	Memphis, TN	(35.1)	211	Provo, UT	(25.3)	370	Sunrise, FL	(45.5)
NA	Menifee, CA**	NA	NA	Pueblo, CO**	NA	20	Surprise, AZ	24.4
72	Merced, CA	(4.1)	18	Quincy, MA	27.9	148	Syracuse, NY	(16.5)
398	Meridian, ID	(67.7)	290	Racine, WI	(33.7)	279	Tacoma, WA	(32.7)
160	Mesa, AZ	(18.2)	225	Raleigh, NC	(26.9)	190	Tallahassee, FL	(21.7)
155	Mesquite, TX	(17.5)	4	Ramapo, NY	67.1	385	Tampa, FL	(51.7)
170	Miami Beach, FL	(19.5)	90	Rancho Cucamon., CA	(7.2)	325	Temecula, CA	(38.4)
367	Miami Gardens, FL	(45.3)	108	Reading, PA	(10.1)	208	Tempe, AZ	(25.0)
176	Miami, FL	(20.1)	60	Redding, CA	0.5	NA	Thornton, CO**	NA
261	Midland, TX	(30.7)	261	Redwood City, CA	(30.7)	127	Thousand Oaks, CA	(12.8)
170	Milwaukee, WI	(19.5)	253	Reno, NV	(30.0)	69	Toledo, OH	(3.0)
337	Minneapolis, MN	(39.3)	234	Renton, WA	(27.9)	14	Toms River Twnshp, NJ	36.8
126	Miramar, FL	(12.4)	245	Rialto, CA	(29.1)	231	Topeka, KS	(27.5)
39	Mission Viejo, CA	8.2	363	Richardson, TX	(44.3)	393	Torrance, CA	(58.5)
67	Mission, TX	(2.7)	340	Richmond, CA	(39.8)	70	Tracy, CA	(3.9)
NA	Mobile, AL**	NA	303	Richmond, VA	(35.5)	139	Trenton, NJ	(14.5)
70	Modesto, CA	(3.9)	251	Rio Rancho, NM	(29.9)	253	Troy, MI	(30.0)
NA	Montgomery, AL**	NA	296	Riverside, CA	(35.0)	169	Tucson, AZ	(19.4)
255	Moreno Valley, CA	(30.4)	336	Roanoke, VA	(39.1)	55	Tulsa, OK	2.6
144	Murfreesboro, TN	(16.1)	192	Rochester, MN	(21.9)	NA	Tuscaloosa, AL**	NA
261	Murrieta, CA	(30.7)	240	Rochester, NY	(28.5)	363	Tustin, CA	(44.3)
380	Nampa, ID	(48.3)	103	Rockford, IL	(9.2)	335	Tyler, TX	(39.0)
190	Napa, CA	(21.7)	395	Roseville, CA	(60.1)	32	Upper Darby Twnshp, PA	10.3
11	Naperville, IL	44.4	401	Roswell, GA	(70.3)	329	Vacaville, CA	(38.8)
NA	Nashua, NH**	NA	6	Round Rock, TX	62.6	23	Vallejo, CA	19.9
265	Nashville, TN	(30.9)	354	Sacramento, CA	(43.6)	36	Vancouver, WA	9.3
62	New Bedford, MA	(0.7)	112	Salem, OR	(10.9)	130	Ventura, CA	(13.2)
NA	New Haven, CT**	NA	79	Salinas, CA	(5.6)	117	Victorville, CA	(11.6)
344	New Orleans, LA	(41.7)	315	Salt Lake City, UT	(36.5)	225	Virginia Beach, VA	(26.9)
80	New Rochelle, NY	(5.8)	165	San Angelo, TX	(18.9)	350	Visalia, CA	(43.1)
102	New York, NY	(9.1)	245	San Antonio, TX	(29.1)	277	Vista, CA	(32.6)
1	Newark, NJ	80.9	181	San Bernardino, CA	(21.0)	138	Waco, TX	(14.3)
388	Newport Beach, CA	(52.5)	288	San Diego, CA	(33.4)	233	Warren, MI	(27.7)
221	Newport News, VA	(26.5)	218	San Francisco, CA	(26.3)	NA	Warwick, RI**	NA
13	Newton, MA	41.4	59	San Jose, CA	0.6	110	Washington, DC	(10.3)
314	Norfolk, VA	(36.3)	313	San Leandro, CA	(36.2)	124	Waterbury, CT	(12.2)
103	Norman, OK	(9.2)	358	San Marcos, CA	(43.9)	251	West Covina, CA	(29.9)
403	North Charleston, SC	(73.6)	309	San Mateo, CA	(35.8)	390	West Jordan, UT	(53.5)
303	Norwalk, CA	(35.5)	356	Sandy Springs, GA	(43.8)	394	West Palm Beach, FL	(59.0)
218	Norwalk, CT	(26.3)	143	Sandy, UT	(15.9)	210	West Valley, UT	(25.2)
67	Oakland, CA	(2.7)	189	Santa Ana, CA	(21.4)	194	Westland, MI	(22.6)
260	Oceanside, CA	(30.6)	180	Santa Barbara, CA	(20.7)	319	Westminster, CA	(37.0)
215	Odessa, TX	(25.5)	140	Santa Clara, CA	(14.7)	63	Westminster, CO	(1.3)
235	O'Fallon, MO	(28.0)	300	Santa Clarita, CA	(35.2)	281	Whittier, CA	(32.9)
295	Ogden, UT	(34.7)	82	Santa Maria, CA	(6.2)	342	Wichita Falls, TX	(40.4)
161	Oklahoma City, OK	(18.4)	374	Santa Monica, CA	(46.7)	159	Wichita, KS	(18.1)
NA	Olathe, KS**	NA	108	Santa Rosa, CA	(10.1)	292	Wilmington, NC	(33.8)
112	Omaha, NE	(10.9)	339	Savannah, GA	(39.6)	NA	Winston-Salem, NC**	NA
319	Ontario, CA	(37.0)	87	Scottsdale, AZ	(6.7)	379	Woodbridge Twnshp, NJ	(48.1)
255	Orange, CA	(30.4)	98	Scranton, PA	(8.9)	43	Worcester, MA	6.9
274	Orem, UT	(31.9)	121	Seattle, WA	(11.8)	52	Yakima, WA	2.9
392	Orlando, FL	(57.8)	300	Shreveport, LA	(35.2)	34	Yonkers, NY	9.9
			316	Simi Valley, CA	(36.6)	153	Yuma, AZ	(17.2)

Source: CQ Press using reported data from the F.B.I. "Crime in the United States 2011"
*Robbery is the taking of anything of value by force or threat of force. Attempts are included.
**Not available.

Rank Order - City

60. Percent Change in Robbery Rate: 2007 to 2011 (continued)
National Percent Change = 23.3% Decrease*

RANK	CITY	% CHANGE	RANK	CITY	% CHANGE	RANK	CITY	% CHANGE
1	Newark, NJ	80.9	73	Lincoln, NE	(4.5)	144	Murfreesboro, TN	(16.1)
2	Lawrence, MA	74.7	74	Spokane Valley, WA	(4.6)	146	Evansville, IN	(16.2)
3	Brick Twnshp, NJ	72.7	75	Cheektowaga, NY	(4.8)	147	St. Louis, MO	(16.3)
4	Ramapo, NY	67.1	76	Kennewick, WA	(5.1)	148	Syracuse, NY	(16.5)
5	Canton Twnshp, MI	64.4	77	Chicago, IL	(5.3)	149	Knoxville, TN	(16.6)
6	Round Rock, TX	62.6	78	Jackson, MS	(5.5)	150	Frisco, TX	(16.8)
7	Sioux Falls, SD	59.1	79	Salinas, CA	(5.6)	151	Boise, ID	(17.0)
8	Colonie, NY	51.7	80	New Rochelle, NY	(5.8)	152	Amherst, NY	(17.1)
9	Fargo, ND	51.6	81	Bethlehem, PA	(6.0)	153	Yuma, AZ	(17.2)
10	Greeley, CO	50.1	82	Santa Maria, CA	(6.2)	154	Lakewood, CO	(17.3)
11	Naperville, IL	44.4	83	Clinton Twnshp, MI	(6.4)	155	Mesquite, TX	(17.5)
12	Stamford, CT	43.3	83	Deerfield Beach, FL	(6.4)	155	Stockton, CA	(17.5)
13	Newton, MA	41.4	85	Dayton, OH	(6.5)	157	Albany, GA	(17.8)
14	Toms River Twnshp, NJ	36.8	86	Hartford, CT	(6.6)	158	Macon, GA	(18.0)
15	Broken Arrow, OK	35.8	87	Scottsdale, AZ	(6.7)	159	Wichita, KS	(18.1)
16	Medford, OR	29.8	88	South Bend, IN	(6.9)	160	Mesa, AZ	(18.2)
17	Livonia, MI	28.3	89	Gresham, OR	(7.0)	161	Oklahoma City, OK	(18.4)
18	Quincy, MA	27.9	90	Rancho Cucamon., CA	(7.2)	162	Fayetteville, NC	(18.5)
19	Fort Collins, CO	24.6	91	El Cajon, CA	(7.8)	163	Albany, NY	(18.7)
20	League City, TX	24.4	91	Indio, CA	(7.8)	163	Carrollton, TX	(18.7)
20	Surprise, AZ	24.4	93	Edinburg, TX	(8.0)	165	San Angelo, TX	(18.9)
22	Gary, IN	21.7	94	Melbourne, FL	(8.5)	166	Aurora, IL	(19.1)
23	Vallejo, CA	19.9	94	Springfield, MO	(8.5)	166	Boston, MA	(19.1)
24	Boulder, CO	18.9	96	El Paso, TX	(8.6)	168	Louisville, KY	(19.3)
25	Elizabeth, NJ	18.3	96	Eugene, OR	(8.6)	169	Tucson, AZ	(19.4)
26	Fort Lauderdale, FL	17.4	98	Detroit, MI	(8.9)	170	Miami Beach, FL	(19.5)
27	St. Joseph, MO	16.8	98	Lynn, MA	(8.9)	170	Milwaukee, WI	(19.5)
28	Brockton, MA	16.3	98	Scranton, PA	(8.9)	172	Aurora, CO	(19.6)
29	Greece, NY	15.6	101	Bellevue, WA	(9.0)	173	Brooklyn Park, MN	(19.8)
30	Camden, NJ	11.7	102	New York, NY	(9.1)	173	Compton, CA	(19.8)
31	Allen, TX	11.2	103	Norman, OK	(9.2)	173	Hawthorne, CA	(19.8)
32	Lubbock, TX	10.3	103	Rockford, IL	(9.2)	176	Hamilton Twnshp, NJ	(20.1)
32	Upper Darby Twnshp, PA	10.3	105	Hesperia, CA	(9.7)	176	Miami, FL	(20.1)
34	Yonkers, NY	9.9	106	El Monte, CA	(9.8)	178	Indianapolis, IN	(20.2)
35	Clovis, CA	9.7	107	Athens-Clarke, GA	(10.0)	179	Little Rock, AR	(20.5)
36	Vancouver, WA	9.3	108	Reading, PA	(10.1)	180	Santa Barbara, CA	(20.7)
37	Spokane, WA	9.2	108	Santa Rosa, CA	(10.1)	181	Bakersfield, CA	(21.0)
38	Paterson, NJ	9.1	110	Palm Bay, FL	(10.3)	181	Lynchburg, VA	(21.0)
39	Mission Viejo, CA	8.2	110	Washington, DC	(10.3)	181	San Bernardino, CA	(21.0)
40	Coral Springs, FL	8.1	112	Omaha, NE	(10.9)	184	Pembroke Pines, FL	(21.1)
41	Kent, WA	7.9	112	Salem, OR	(10.9)	185	Columbus, OH	(21.2)
42	Huntington Beach, CA	7.5	114	Long Beach, CA	(11.2)	185	Springfield, IL	(21.2)
43	Worcester, MA	6.9	115	Ann Arbor, MI	(11.3)	187	Grand Prairie, TX	(21.3)
44	Costa Mesa, CA	6.4	115	Baldwin Park, CA	(11.3)	187	Pompano Beach, FL	(21.3)
44	Port St. Lucie, FL	6.4	117	Baltimore, MD	(11.6)	189	Santa Ana, CA	(21.4)
46	Clarkstown, NY	6.3	117	Elgin, IL	(11.6)	190	Napa, CA	(21.7)
47	Beaumont, TX	4.3	117	Suffolk, VA	(11.6)	190	Tallahassee, FL	(21.7)
48	Flint, MI	3.5	117	Victorville, CA	(11.6)	192	Rochester, MN	(21.9)
49	Columbia, MO	3.3	121	McKinney, TX	(11.8)	193	Alexandria, VA	(22.5)
50	Farmington Hills, MI	3.2	121	Seattle, WA	(11.8)	194	Westland, MI	(22.6)
51	Akron, OH	3.0	123	Bellingham, WA	(12.0)	195	Bloomington, MN	(22.8)
52	Yakima, WA	2.9	124	Waterbury, CT	(12.2)	196	Boca Raton, FL	(22.9)
53	Sioux City, IA	2.8	125	Clifton, NJ	(12.3)	197	Atlanta, GA	(23.5)
54	Denver, CO	2.7	126	Miramar, FL	(12.4)	197	Davie, FL	(23.5)
55	Tulsa, OK	2.6	127	Fresno, CA	(12.8)	199	Sugar Land, TX	(23.9)
56	Lansing, MI	1.7	127	Thousand Oaks, CA	(12.8)	200	Pearland, TX	(24.1)
57	Cincinnati, OH	1.1	129	Cleveland, OH	(13.1)	201	Springfield, MA	(24.3)
58	Sunnyvale, CA	0.8	130	Baton Rouge, LA	(13.2)	202	Anaheim, CA	(24.4)
59	San Jose, CA	0.6	130	Plantation, FL	(13.2)	203	Portsmouth, VA	(24.5)
60	Redding, CA	0.5	130	Ventura, CA	(13.2)	204	Los Angeles, CA	(24.6)
61	Danbury, CT	(0.1)	133	Glendale, AZ	(13.4)	204	Philadelphia, PA	(24.6)
62	New Bedford, MA	(0.7)	133	South Gate, CA	(13.4)	206	Colorado Springs, CO	(24.9)
63	Westminster, CO	(1.3)	135	Pasadena, TX	(13.5)	206	Hemet, CA	(24.9)
64	Anchorage, AK	(1.8)	136	Plano, TX	(13.7)	208	Tempe, AZ	(25.0)
64	Cambridge, MA	(1.8)	137	Bridgeport, CT	(13.9)	209	Chesapeake, VA	(25.1)
66	Gilbert, AZ	(2.2)	138	Waco, TX	(14.3)	210	West Valley, UT	(25.2)
67	Mission, TX	(2.7)	139	Trenton, NJ	(14.5)	211	Clearwater, FL	(25.3)
67	Oakland, CA	(2.7)	140	Irvine, CA	(14.7)	211	Edison Twnshp, NJ	(25.3)
69	Toledo, OH	(3.0)	140	Santa Clara, CA	(14.7)	211	Provo, UT	(25.3)
70	Modesto, CA	(3.9)	142	Lawton, OK	(15.6)	214	Jersey City, NJ	(25.4)
70	Tracy, CA	(3.9)	143	Sandy, UT	(15.9)	215	Odessa, TX	(25.5)
72	Merced, CA	(4.1)	144	Henderson, NV	(16.1)	216	Fort Wayne, IN	(25.8)

Rank Order - City (continued)

RANK	CITY	% CHANGE	RANK	CITY	% CHANGE	RANK	CITY	% CHANGE
217	Largo, FL	(26.1)	290	Independence, MO	(33.7)	363	College Station, TX	(44.3)
218	Norwalk, CT	(26.3)	290	Racine, WI	(33.7)	363	Richardson, TX	(44.3)
218	San Francisco, CA	(26.3)	292	Wilmington, NC	(33.8)	363	Tustin, CA	(44.3)
220	Somerville, MA	(26.4)	293	Bend, OR	(34.4)	367	Fullerton, CA	(45.3)
221	Fontana, CA	(26.5)	293	Columbus, GA	(34.4)	367	Miami Gardens, FL	(45.3)
221	Newport News, VA	(26.5)	295	Ogden, UT	(34.7)	369	Longview, TX	(45.4)
223	St. Paul, MN	(26.6)	296	Lee's Summit, MO	(35.0)	370	Sunrise, FL	(45.5)
224	Chico, CA	(26.7)	296	Riverside, CA	(35.0)	371	Charleston, SC	(45.8)
225	Raleigh, NC	(26.9)	298	Memphis, TN	(35.1)	371	Joliet, IL	(45.8)
225	Virginia Beach, VA	(26.9)	298	Portland, OR	(35.1)	373	Sparks, NV	(46.6)
227	Madison, WI	(27.1)	300	Santa Clarita, CA	(35.2)	374	Santa Monica, CA	(46.7)
228	Chandler, AZ	(27.2)	300	Shreveport, LA	(35.2)	375	Des Moines, IA	(47.4)
229	Arlington, TX	(27.4)	302	Everett, WA	(35.3)	376	Amarillo, TX	(47.6)
229	Lewisville, TX	(27.4)	303	Albuquerque, NM	(35.5)	377	Brownsville, TX	(47.8)
231	Topeka, KS	(27.5)	303	Chino Hills, CA	(35.5)	378	Chula Vista, CA	(47.9)
232	Peoria, IL	(27.6)	303	Denton, TX	(35.5)	379	Woodbridge Twnshp, NJ	(48.1)
233	Warren, MI	(27.7)	303	Hayward, CA	(35.5)	380	Nampa, ID	(48.3)
234	Renton, WA	(27.9)	303	Norwalk, CA	(35.5)	380	Peoria, AZ	(48.3)
235	Garland, TX	(28.0)	303	Richmond, VA	(35.5)	382	Green Bay, WI	(48.4)
235	O'Fallon, MO	(28.0)	309	Lakeland, FL	(35.8)	383	Carson, CA	(51.0)
237	Arvada, CO	(28.1)	309	San Mateo, CA	(35.8)	384	Jacksonville, FL	(51.6)
237	Cranston, RI	(28.1)	311	Hampton, VA	(35.9)	385	Tampa, FL	(51.7)
237	Pomona, CA	(28.1)	312	Hollywood, FL	(36.1)	386	Hillsboro, OR	(51.8)
240	Rochester, NY	(28.5)	313	San Leandro, CA	(36.2)	387	Hialeah, FL	(52.3)
241	Pittsburgh, PA	(28.6)	314	Norfolk, VA	(36.3)	388	Newport Beach, CA	(52.5)
242	Duluth, MN	(28.7)	315	Salt Lake City, UT	(36.5)	389	Charlotte, NC	(53.1)
243	Grand Rapids, MI	(29.0)	316	Simi Valley, CA	(36.6)	390	West Jordan, UT	(53.5)
243	Houston, TX	(29.0)	317	Las Cruces, NM	(36.8)	391	Bellflower, CA	(54.3)
245	Rialto, CA	(29.1)	318	Hammond, IN	(36.9)	392	Orlando, FL	(57.8)
245	San Antonio, TX	(29.1)	319	Ontario, CA	(37.0)	393	Torrance, CA	(58.5)
247	St. Petersburg, FL	(29.2)	319	Westminster, CA	(37.0)	394	West Palm Beach, FL	(59.0)
248	Phoenix, AZ	(29.3)	321	Palmdale, CA	(37.1)	395	Roseville, CA	(60.1)
249	Bryan, TX	(29.5)	322	Garden Grove, CA	(37.2)	396	Lakewood, CA	(60.9)
250	Berkeley, CA	(29.8)	323	Fremont, CA	(37.5)	397	Carlsbad, CA	(64.6)
251	Rio Rancho, NM	(29.9)	324	Cedar Rapids, IA	(38.3)	398	Meridian, ID	(67.7)
251	West Covina, CA	(29.9)	325	McAllen, TX	(38.4)	399	Daly City, CA	(68.8)
253	Reno, NV	(30.0)	325	Pasadena, CA	(38.4)	400	Alhambra, CA	(69.0)
253	Troy, MI	(30.0)	325	Temecula, CA	(38.4)	401	Roswell, GA	(70.3)
255	Burbank, CA	(30.4)	328	Beaverton, OR	(38.6)	402	Concord, NC	(70.8)
255	Moreno Valley, CA	(30.4)	329	Cape Coral, FL	(38.8)	403	North Charleston, SC	(73.6)
255	Orange, CA	(30.4)	329	Concord, CA	(38.8)	404	Carmel, IN	(74.2)
255	Overland Park, KS	(30.4)	329	Las Vegas, NV	(38.8)	405	Lakewood Twnshp, NJ	(76.0)
259	Antioch, CA	(30.5)	329	Vacaville, CA	(38.8)	NA	Arlington Heights, IL**	NA
260	Oceanside, CA	(30.6)	333	Centennial, CO	(38.9)	NA	Avondale, AZ**	NA
261	Fort Worth, TX	(30.7)	333	Edmond, OK	(38.9)	NA	Billings, MT**	NA
261	Midland, TX	(30.7)	335	Tyler, TX	(39.0)	NA	Birmingham, AL**	NA
261	Murrieta, CA	(30.7)	336	Roanoke, VA	(39.1)	NA	Bloomington, IL**	NA
261	Redwood City, CA	(30.7)	337	Laredo, TX	(39.3)	NA	Buffalo, NY**	NA
265	Nashville, TN	(30.9)	337	Minneapolis, MN	(39.3)	NA	Champaign, IL**	NA
266	Abilene, TX	(31.1)	339	Savannah, GA	(39.6)	NA	Cicero, IL**	NA
267	Bloomington, IN	(31.3)	340	Richmond, CA	(39.8)	NA	Citrus Heights, CA**	NA
267	Clarksville, TN	(31.3)	341	Lawrence, KS	(40.0)	NA	Davenport, IA**	NA
267	Inglewood, CA	(31.3)	342	Wichita Falls, TX	(40.4)	NA	Decatur, IL**	NA
270	Corpus Christi, TX	(31.6)	343	Cary, NC	(41.1)	NA	Durham, NC**	NA
270	Downey, CA	(31.6)	344	New Orleans, LA	(41.7)	NA	Fall River, MA**	NA
272	Asheville, NC	(31.8)	345	Kansas City, KS	(41.9)	NA	Hoover, AL**	NA
272	Lafayette, LA	(31.8)	346	Escondido, CA	(42.0)	NA	Huntsville, AL**	NA
274	Orem, UT	(31.9)	347	Dallas, TX	(42.9)	NA	Johns Creek, GA**	NA
275	Killeen, TX	(32.1)	347	Fishers, IN	(42.9)	NA	Kansas City, MO**	NA
276	Fort Smith, AR	(32.5)	347	Lancaster, CA	(42.9)	NA	Lexington, KY**	NA
277	Austin, TX	(32.6)	350	Buena Park, CA	(43.1)	NA	Longmont, CO**	NA
277	Vista, CA	(32.6)	350	Visalia, CA	(43.1)	NA	Manchester, NH**	NA
279	Chattanooga, TN	(32.7)	352	Elk Grove, CA	(43.2)	NA	Menifee, CA**	NA
279	Tacoma, WA	(32.7)	353	Erie, PA	(43.3)	NA	Mobile, AL**	NA
281	Glendale, CA	(32.9)	354	Sacramento, CA	(43.6)	NA	Montgomery, AL**	NA
281	Lake Forest, CA	(32.9)	355	Oxnard, CA	(43.7)	NA	Nashua, NH**	NA
281	Whittier, CA	(32.9)	356	Livermore, CA	(43.8)	NA	New Haven, CT**	NA
284	Lowell, MA	(33.0)	356	Sandy Springs, GA	(43.8)	NA	Olathe, KS**	NA
285	Kenosha, WI	(33.1)	358	High Point, NC	(43.9)	NA	Pueblo, CO**	NA
286	Fairfield, CA	(33.3)	358	Irving, TX	(43.9)	NA	Sterling Heights, MI**	NA
286	Gainesville, FL	(33.3)	358	San Marcos, CA	(43.9)	NA	Thornton, CO**	NA
288	Dearborn, MI	(33.4)	361	Chino, CA	(44.1)	NA	Tuscaloosa, AL**	NA
288	San Diego, CA	(33.4)	361	Corona, CA	(44.1)	NA	Warwick, RI**	NA
			363	Allentown, PA	(44.3)	NA	Winston-Salem, NC**	NA

Source: CQ Press using reported data from the F.B.I. "Crime in the United States 2011"
*Robbery is the taking of anything of value by force or threat of force. Attempts are included.
**Not available.

Alpha Order - City

61. Aggravated Assaults in 2011
National Total = 751,373 Aggravated Assaults*

RANK	CITY	ASSAULTS
233	Abilene, TX	270
92	Akron, OH	869
170	Albany, GA	414
133	Albany, NY	582
24	Albuquerque, NM	2,910
352	Alexandria, VA	108
376	Alhambra, CA	87
251	Allentown, PA	237
422	Allen, TX	43
91	Amarillo, TX	874
388	Amherst, NY	76
106	Anaheim, CA	715
51	Anchorage, AK	1,628
302	Ann Arbor, MI	166
147	Antioch, CA	502
431	Arlington Heights, IL	24
67	Arlington, TX	1,176
359	Arvada, CO	102
254	Asheville, NC	236
247	Athens-Clarke, GA	249
17	Atlanta, GA	3,518
100	Aurora, CO	752
169	Aurora, IL	418
35	Austin, TX	2,126
339	Avondale, AZ	131
63	Bakersfield, CA	1,261
334	Baldwin Park, CA	142
11	Baltimore, MD	4,891
54	Baton Rouge, LA	1,460
119	Beaumont, TX	635
351	Beaverton, OR	109
407	Bellevue, WA	58
325	Bellflower, CA	152
352	Bellingham, WA	108
328	Bend, OR	151
343	Berkeley, CA	122
359	Bethlehem, PA	102
249	Billings, MT	239
40	Birmingham, AL	1,916
258	Bloomington, IL	233
303	Bloomington, IN	164
393	Bloomington, MN	70
369	Boca Raton, FL	92
179	Boise, ID	384
21	Boston, MA	3,014
277	Boulder, CO	203
390	Brick Twnshp, NJ	73
107	Bridgeport, CT	701
93	Brockton, MA	858
383	Broken Arrow, OK	81
359	Brooklyn Park, MN	102
194	Brownsville, TX	353
205	Bryan, TX	323
331	Buena Park, CA	143
50	Buffalo, NY	1,634
356	Burbank, CA	105
66	Camden, NJ	1,182
215	Cambridge, MA	298
385	Canton Twnshp, MI	79
311	Cape Coral, FL	160
311	Carlsbad, CA	160
436	Carmel, IN	6
355	Carrollton, TX	106
207	Carson, CA	320
413	Cary, NC	53
260	Cedar Rapids, IA	229
348	Centennial, CO	112
135	Champaign, IL	570
163	Chandler, AZ	446
283	Charleston, SC	195
26	Charlotte, NC	2,901
78	Chattanooga, TN	1,015

RANK	CITY	ASSAULTS
379	Cheektowaga, NY	83
130	Chesapeake, VA	588
2	Chicago, IL	12,408
349	Chico, CA	111
419	Chino Hills, CA	48
293	Chino, CA	178
172	Chula Vista, CA	397
318	Cicero, IL	157
73	Cincinnati, OH	1,050
284	Citrus Heights, CA	191
400	Clarkstown, NY	64
111	Clarksville, TN	686
136	Clearwater, FL	569
42	Cleveland, OH	1,842
359	Clifton, NJ	102
273	Clinton Twnshp, MI	208
341	Clovis, CA	126
261	College Station, TX	224
432	Colonie, NY	20
71	Colorado Springs, CO	1,071
182	Columbia, MO	377
161	Columbus, GA	465
62	Columbus, OH	1,289
122	Compton, CA	625
251	Concord, CA	237
420	Concord, NC	46
335	Coral Springs, FL	141
379	Corona, CA	83
55	Corpus Christi, TX	1,411
347	Costa Mesa, CA	114
411	Cranston, RI	55
14	Dallas, TX	3,703
350	Daly City, CA	110
413	Danbury, CT	53
155	Davenport, IA	481
255	Davie, FL	234
132	Dayton, OH	586
259	Dearborn, MI	230
202	Decatur, IL	333
273	Deerfield Beach, FL	208
279	Denton, TX	201
34	Denver, CO	2,135
103	Des Moines, IA	742
4	Detroit, MI	9,512
308	Downey, CA	161
303	Duluth, MN	164
83	Durham, NC	917
280	Edinburg, TX	199
396	Edison Twnshp, NJ	66
428	Edmond, OK	30
210	El Cajon, CA	312
284	El Monte, CA	191
33	El Paso, TX	2,161
343	Elgin, IL	122
141	Elizabeth, NJ	537
171	Elk Grove, CA	404
281	Erie, PA	198
221	Escondido, CA	287
276	Eugene, OR	205
225	Evansville, IN	278
241	Everett, WA	253
244	Fairfield, CA	251
99	Fall River, MA	761
217	Fargo, ND	294
403	Farmington Hills, MI	60
158	Fayetteville, NC	474
437	Fishers, IN	3
49	Flint, MI	1,648
165	Fontana, CA	435
208	Fort Collins, CO	315
109	Fort Lauderdale, FL	691
166	Fort Smith, AR	433

RANK	CITY	ASSAULTS
193	Fort Wayne, IN	357
25	Fort Worth, TX	2,904
284	Fremont, CA	191
45	Fresno, CA	1,809
373	Frisco, TX	90
295	Fullerton, CA	175
118	Gainesville, FL	640
239	Garden Grove, CA	257
263	Garland, TX	223
255	Gary, IN	234
364	Gilbert, AZ	99
124	Glendale, AZ	617
336	Glendale, CA	136
210	Grand Prairie, TX	312
94	Grand Rapids, MI	840
383	Greece, NY	81
205	Greeley, CO	323
234	Green Bay, WI	269
269	Gresham, OR	212
366	Hamilton Twnshp, NJ	94
213	Hammond, IN	309
301	Hampton, VA	167
81	Hartford, CT	955
219	Hawthorne, CA	291
300	Hayward, CA	168
267	Hemet, CA	217
209	Henderson, NV	314
284	Hesperia, CA	191
134	Hialeah, FL	572
186	High Point, NC	372
376	Hillsboro, OR	87
198	Hollywood, FL	340
434	Hoover, AL	17
3	Houston, TX	11,869
238	Huntington Beach, CA	260
74	Huntsville, AL	1,049
197	Independence, MO	342
9	Indianapolis, IN	5,267
218	Indio, CA	293
168	Inglewood, CA	419
395	Irvine, CA	67
203	Irving, TX	330
20	Jacksonville, FL	3,183
120	Jackson, MS	634
90	Jersey City, NJ	878
433	Johns Creek, GA	19
175	Joliet, IL	392
143	Kansas City, KS	534
18	Kansas City, MO	3,498
307	Kennewick, WA	162
340	Kenosha, WI	130
214	Kent, WA	306
138	Killeen, TX	559
77	Knoxville, TN	1,021
128	Lafayette, LA	590
400	Lake Forest, CA	64
187	Lakeland, FL	366
413	Lakewood Twnshp, NJ	53
356	Lakewood, CA	105
177	Lakewood, CO	388
144	Lancaster, CA	532
97	Lansing, MI	796
96	Laredo, TX	818
249	Largo, FL	239
201	Las Cruces, NM	336
8	Las Vegas, NV	6,587
237	Lawrence, KS	265
149	Lawrence, MA	498
129	Lawton, OK	589
427	League City, TX	33
404	Lee's Summit, MO	59
356	Lewisville, TX	105

Alpha Order - City (continued)

RANK	CITY	ASSAULTS
102	Lexington, KY	743
123	Lincoln, NE	619
41	Little Rock, AR	1,849
270	Livermore, CA	211
352	Livonia, MI	108
58	Long Beach, CA	1,400
289	Longmont, CO	186
225	Longview, TX	278
6	Los Angeles, CA	8,843
32	Louisville, KY	2,168
130	Lowell, MA	588
56	Lubbock, TX	1,409
290	Lynchburg, VA	181
127	Lynn, MA	591
228	Macon, GA	274
162	Madison, WI	461
187	Manchester, NH	366
331	McAllen, TX	143
305	McKinney, TX	163
223	Medford, OR	283
137	Melbourne, FL	564
7	Memphis, TN	6,738
430	Menifee, CA	26
204	Merced, CA	326
378	Meridian, ID	84
65	Mesa, AZ	1,192
271	Mesquite, TX	210
159	Miami Beach, FL	473
139	Miami Gardens, FL	543
29	Miami, FL	2,683
244	Midland, TX	251
27	Milwaukee, WI	2,727
47	Minneapolis, MN	1,715
225	Miramar, FL	278
420	Mission Viejo, CA	46
411	Mission, TX	55
87	Mobile, AL	904
85	Modesto, CA	907
222	Montgomery, AL	284
192	Moreno Valley, CA	363
151	Murfreesboro, TN	490
410	Murrieta, CA	56
290	Nampa, ID	181
325	Napa, CA	152
382	Naperville, IL	82
337	Nashua, NH	135
10	Nashville, TN	4,927
104	New Bedford, MA	736
89	New Haven, CT	893
61	New Orleans, LA	1,326
369	New Rochelle, NY	92
1	New York, NY	29,829
69	Newark, NJ	1,114
390	Newport Beach, CA	73
176	Newport News, VA	390
404	Newton, MA	59
110	Norfolk, VA	689
392	Norman, OK	71
167	North Charleston, SC	429
265	Norwalk, CA	218
265	Norwalk, CT	218
22	Oakland, CA	2,981
184	Oceanside, CA	374
121	Odessa, TX	632
404	O'Fallon, MO	59
228	Ogden, UT	274
15	Oklahoma City, OK	3,541
325	Olathe, KS	152
59	Omaha, NE	1,350
244	Ontario, CA	251
396	Orange, CA	66
435	Orem, UT	15
46	Orlando, FL	1,746

RANK	CITY	ASSAULTS
288	Overland Park, KS	189
212	Oxnard, CA	311
156	Palm Bay, FL	480
150	Palmdale, CA	492
261	Pasadena, CA	224
191	Pasadena, TX	364
113	Paterson, NJ	683
385	Pearland, TX	79
316	Pembroke Pines, FL	159
273	Peoria, AZ	208
157	Peoria, IL	477
5	Philadelphia, PA	8,865
13	Phoenix, AZ	4,090
64	Pittsburgh, PA	1,239
248	Plano, TX	242
330	Plantation, FL	147
146	Pomona, CA	523
145	Pompano Beach, FL	528
228	Port St. Lucie, FL	274
42	Portland, OR	1,842
239	Portsmouth, VA	257
369	Provo, UT	92
125	Pueblo, CO	606
231	Quincy, MA	271
346	Racine, WI	119
88	Raleigh, NC	900
379	Ramapo, NY	83
298	Rancho Cucamon., CA	171
195	Reading, PA	346
142	Redding, CA	535
374	Redwood City, CA	88
112	Reno, NV	684
331	Renton, WA	143
242	Rialto, CA	252
374	Richardson, TX	88
115	Richmond, CA	667
114	Richmond, VA	672
328	Rio Rancho, NM	151
98	Riverside, CA	782
185	Roanoke, VA	373
359	Rochester, MN	102
68	Rochester, NY	1,148
57	Rockford, IL	1,407
292	Roseville, CA	180
429	Roswell, GA	29
418	Round Rock, TX	49
38	Sacramento, CA	2,022
190	Salem, OR	365
108	Salinas, CA	692
101	Salt Lake City, UT	748
294	San Angelo, TX	176
12	San Antonio, TX	4,672
75	San Bernardino, CA	1,034
19	San Diego, CA	3,317
37	San Francisco, CA	2,105
44	San Jose, CA	1,840
342	San Leandro, CA	124
323	San Marcos, CA	154
321	San Mateo, CA	156
416	Sandy Springs, GA	52
387	Sandy, UT	77
116	Santa Ana, CA	647
278	Santa Barbara, CA	202
366	Santa Clara, CA	94
305	Santa Clarita, CA	163
140	Santa Maria, CA	538
268	Santa Monica, CA	215
153	Santa Rosa, CA	485
199	Savannah, GA	339
251	Scottsdale, AZ	237
366	Scranton, PA	94
35	Seattle, WA	2,126
72	Shreveport, LA	1,051
396	Simi Valley, CA	66

RANK	CITY	ASSAULTS
236	Sioux City, IA	268
242	Sioux Falls, SD	252
295	Somerville, MA	175
234	South Bend, IN	269
216	South Gate, CA	295
318	Sparks, NV	157
365	Spokane Valley, WA	95
105	Spokane, WA	732
84	Springfield, IL	909
80	Springfield, MA	998
86	Springfield, MO	905
308	Stamford, CT	161
311	Sterling Heights, MI	160
28	Stockton, CA	2,684
297	St. Joseph, MO	174
16	St. Louis, MO	3,522
70	St. Paul, MN	1,104
48	St. Petersburg, FL	1,701
308	Suffolk, VA	161
402	Sugar Land, TX	61
407	Sunnyvale, CA	58
318	Sunrise, FL	157
394	Surprise, AZ	68
94	Syracuse, NY	840
82	Tacoma, WA	925
76	Tallahassee, FL	1,033
53	Tampa, FL	1,555
426	Temecula, CA	34
148	Tempe, AZ	500
126	Thornton, CO	595
369	Thousand Oaks, CA	92
52	Toledo, OH	1,562
425	Toms River Twnshp, NJ	36
174	Topeka, KS	395
389	Torrance, CA	75
407	Tracy, CA	58
117	Trenton, NJ	641
424	Troy, MI	41
38	Tucson, AZ	2,022
30	Tulsa, OK	2,555
282	Tuscaloosa, AL	196
417	Tustin, CA	50
183	Tyler, TX	375
311	Upper Darby Twnshp, PA	160
345	Vacaville, CA	121
172	Vallejo, CA	397
200	Vancouver, WA	337
299	Ventura, CA	170
180	Victorville, CA	382
220	Virginia Beach, VA	289
196	Visalia, CA	343
255	Vista, CA	234
164	Waco, TX	440
154	Warren, MI	484
423	Warwick, RI	42
23	Washington, DC	2,949
311	Waterbury, CT	160
337	West Covina, CA	135
323	West Jordan, UT	154
160	West Palm Beach, FL	472
181	West Valley, UT	381
272	Westland, MI	209
322	Westminster, CA	155
316	Westminster, CO	159
263	Whittier, CA	223
224	Wichita Falls, TX	281
31	Wichita, KS	2,197
187	Wilmington, NC	366
79	Winston-Salem, NC	1,014
396	Woodbridge Twnshp, NJ	66
60	Worcester, MA	1,342
231	Yakima, WA	271
152	Yonkers, NY	487
178	Yuma, AZ	387

Source: Reported data from the F.B.I. "Crime in the United States 2011"
*Aggravated assault is an attack for the purpose of inflicting severe bodily injury.

Rank Order - City

61. Aggravated Assaults in 2011 (continued)
National Total = 751,373 Aggravated Assaults*

RANK	CITY	ASSAULTS	RANK	CITY	ASSAULTS	RANK	CITY	ASSAULTS
1	New York, NY	29,829	73	Cincinnati, OH	1,050	145	Pompano Beach, FL	528
2	Chicago, IL	12,408	74	Huntsville, AL	1,049	146	Pomona, CA	523
3	Houston, TX	11,869	75	San Bernardino, CA	1,034	147	Antioch, CA	502
4	Detroit, MI	9,512	76	Tallahassee, FL	1,033	148	Tempe, AZ	500
5	Philadelphia, PA	8,865	77	Knoxville, TN	1,021	149	Lawrence, MA	498
6	Los Angeles, CA	8,843	78	Chattanooga, TN	1,015	150	Palmdale, CA	492
7	Memphis, TN	6,738	79	Winston-Salem, NC	1,014	151	Murfreesboro, TN	490
8	Las Vegas, NV	6,587	80	Springfield, MA	998	152	Yonkers, NY	487
9	Indianapolis, IN	5,267	81	Hartford, CT	955	153	Santa Rosa, CA	485
10	Nashville, TN	4,927	82	Tacoma, WA	925	154	Warren, MI	484
11	Baltimore, MD	4,891	83	Durham, NC	917	155	Davenport, IA	481
12	San Antonio, TX	4,672	84	Springfield, IL	909	156	Palm Bay, FL	480
13	Phoenix, AZ	4,090	85	Modesto, CA	907	157	Peoria, IL	477
14	Dallas, TX	3,703	86	Springfield, MO	905	158	Fayetteville, NC	474
15	Oklahoma City, OK	3,541	87	Mobile, AL	904	159	Miami Beach, FL	473
16	St. Louis, MO	3,522	88	Raleigh, NC	900	160	West Palm Beach, FL	472
17	Atlanta, GA	3,518	89	New Haven, CT	893	161	Columbus, GA	465
18	Kansas City, MO	3,498	90	Jersey City, NJ	878	162	Madison, WI	461
19	San Diego, CA	3,317	91	Amarillo, TX	874	163	Chandler, AZ	446
20	Jacksonville, FL	3,183	92	Akron, OH	869	164	Waco, TX	440
21	Boston, MA	3,014	93	Brockton, MA	858	165	Fontana, CA	435
22	Oakland, CA	2,981	94	Grand Rapids, MI	840	166	Fort Smith, AR	433
23	Washington, DC	2,949	94	Syracuse, NY	840	167	North Charleston, SC	429
24	Albuquerque, NM	2,910	96	Laredo, TX	818	168	Inglewood, CA	419
25	Fort Worth, TX	2,904	97	Lansing, MI	796	169	Aurora, IL	418
26	Charlotte, NC	2,901	98	Riverside, CA	782	170	Albany, GA	414
27	Milwaukee, WI	2,727	99	Fall River, MA	761	171	Elk Grove, CA	404
28	Stockton, CA	2,684	100	Aurora, CO	752	172	Chula Vista, CA	397
29	Miami, FL	2,683	101	Salt Lake City, UT	748	172	Vallejo, CA	397
30	Tulsa, OK	2,555	102	Lexington, KY	743	174	Topeka, KS	395
31	Wichita, KS	2,197	103	Des Moines, IA	742	175	Joliet, IL	392
32	Louisville, KY	2,168	104	New Bedford, MA	736	176	Newport News, VA	390
33	El Paso, TX	2,161	105	Spokane, WA	732	177	Lakewood, CO	388
34	Denver, CO	2,135	106	Anaheim, CA	715	178	Yuma, AZ	387
35	Austin, TX	2,126	107	Bridgeport, CT	701	179	Boise, ID	384
35	Seattle, WA	2,126	108	Salinas, CA	692	180	Victorville, CA	382
37	San Francisco, CA	2,105	109	Fort Lauderdale, FL	691	181	West Valley, UT	381
38	Sacramento, CA	2,022	110	Norfolk, VA	689	182	Columbia, MO	377
38	Tucson, AZ	2,022	111	Clarksville, TN	686	183	Tyler, TX	375
40	Birmingham, AL	1,916	112	Reno, NV	684	184	Oceanside, CA	374
41	Little Rock, AR	1,849	113	Paterson, NJ	683	185	Roanoke, VA	373
42	Cleveland, OH	1,842	114	Richmond, VA	672	186	High Point, NC	372
42	Portland, OR	1,842	115	Richmond, CA	667	187	Lakeland, FL	366
44	San Jose, CA	1,840	116	Santa Ana, CA	647	187	Manchester, NH	366
45	Fresno, CA	1,809	117	Trenton, NJ	641	187	Wilmington, NC	366
46	Orlando, FL	1,746	118	Gainesville, FL	640	190	Salem, OR	365
47	Minneapolis, MN	1,715	119	Beaumont, TX	635	191	Pasadena, TX	364
48	St. Petersburg, FL	1,701	120	Jackson, MS	634	192	Moreno Valley, CA	363
49	Flint, MI	1,648	121	Odessa, TX	632	193	Fort Wayne, IN	357
50	Buffalo, NY	1,634	122	Compton, CA	625	194	Brownsville, TX	353
51	Anchorage, AK	1,628	123	Lincoln, NE	619	195	Reading, PA	346
52	Toledo, OH	1,562	124	Glendale, AZ	617	196	Visalia, CA	343
53	Tampa, FL	1,555	125	Pueblo, CO	606	197	Independence, MO	342
54	Baton Rouge, LA	1,460	126	Thornton, CO	595	198	Hollywood, FL	340
55	Corpus Christi, TX	1,411	127	Lynn, MA	591	199	Savannah, GA	339
56	Lubbock, TX	1,409	128	Lafayette, LA	590	200	Vancouver, WA	337
57	Rockford, IL	1,407	129	Lawton, OK	589	201	Las Cruces, NM	336
58	Long Beach, CA	1,400	130	Chesapeake, VA	588	202	Decatur, IL	333
59	Omaha, NE	1,350	130	Lowell, MA	588	203	Irving, TX	330
60	Worcester, MA	1,342	132	Dayton, OH	586	204	Merced, CA	326
61	New Orleans, LA	1,326	133	Albany, NY	582	205	Bryan, TX	323
62	Columbus, OH	1,289	134	Hialeah, FL	572	205	Greeley, CO	323
63	Bakersfield, CA	1,261	135	Champaign, IL	570	207	Carson, CA	320
64	Pittsburgh, PA	1,239	136	Clearwater, FL	569	208	Fort Collins, CO	315
65	Mesa, AZ	1,192	137	Melbourne, FL	564	209	Henderson, NV	314
66	Camden, NJ	1,182	138	Killeen, TX	559	210	El Cajon, CA	312
67	Arlington, TX	1,176	139	Miami Gardens, FL	543	210	Grand Prairie, TX	312
68	Rochester, NY	1,148	140	Santa Maria, CA	538	212	Oxnard, CA	311
69	Newark, NJ	1,114	141	Elizabeth, NJ	537	213	Hammond, IN	309
70	St. Paul, MN	1,104	142	Redding, CA	535	214	Kent, WA	306
71	Colorado Springs, CO	1,071	143	Kansas City, KS	534	215	Cambridge, MA	298
72	Shreveport, LA	1,051	144	Lancaster, CA	532	216	South Gate, CA	295

Rank Order - City (continued)

RANK	CITY	ASSAULTS
217	Fargo, ND	294
218	Indio, CA	293
219	Hawthorne, CA	291
220	Virginia Beach, VA	289
221	Escondido, CA	287
222	Montgomery, AL	284
223	Medford, OR	283
224	Wichita Falls, TX	281
225	Evansville, IN	278
225	Longview, TX	278
225	Miramar, FL	278
228	Macon, GA	274
228	Ogden, UT	274
228	Port St. Lucie, FL	274
231	Quincy, MA	271
231	Yakima, WA	271
233	Abilene, TX	270
234	Green Bay, WI	269
234	South Bend, IN	269
236	Sioux City, IA	268
237	Lawrence, KS	265
238	Huntington Beach, CA	260
239	Garden Grove, CA	257
239	Portsmouth, VA	257
241	Everett, WA	253
242	Rialto, CA	252
242	Sioux Falls, SD	252
244	Fairfield, CA	251
244	Midland, TX	251
244	Ontario, CA	251
247	Athens-Clarke, GA	249
248	Plano, TX	242
249	Billings, MT	239
249	Largo, FL	239
251	Allentown, PA	237
251	Concord, CA	237
251	Scottsdale, AZ	237
254	Asheville, NC	236
255	Davie, FL	234
255	Gary, IN	234
255	Vista, CA	234
258	Bloomington, IL	233
259	Dearborn, MI	230
260	Cedar Rapids, IA	229
261	College Station, TX	224
261	Pasadena, CA	224
263	Garland, TX	223
263	Whittier, CA	223
265	Norwalk, CA	218
265	Norwalk, CT	218
267	Hemet, CA	217
268	Santa Monica, CA	215
269	Gresham, OR	212
270	Livermore, CA	211
271	Mesquite, TX	210
272	Westland, MI	209
273	Clinton Twnshp, MI	208
273	Deerfield Beach, FL	208
273	Peoria, AZ	208
276	Eugene, OR	205
277	Boulder, CO	203
278	Santa Barbara, CA	202
279	Denton, TX	201
280	Edinburg, TX	199
281	Erie, PA	198
282	Tuscaloosa, AL	196
283	Charleston, SC	195
284	Citrus Heights, CA	191
284	El Monte, CA	191
284	Fremont, CA	191
284	Hesperia, CA	191
288	Overland Park, KS	189
289	Longmont, CO	186
290	Lynchburg, VA	181
290	Nampa, ID	181
292	Roseville, CA	180
293	Chino, CA	178
294	San Angelo, TX	176
295	Fullerton, CA	175
295	Somerville, MA	175
297	St. Joseph, MO	174
298	Rancho Cucamon., CA	171
299	Ventura, CA	170
300	Hayward, CA	168
301	Hampton, VA	167
302	Ann Arbor, MI	166
303	Bloomington, IN	164
303	Duluth, MN	164
305	McKinney, TX	163
305	Santa Clarita, CA	163
307	Kennewick, WA	162
308	Downey, CA	161
308	Stamford, CT	161
308	Suffolk, VA	161
311	Cape Coral, FL	160
311	Carlsbad, CA	160
311	Sterling Heights, MI	160
311	Upper Darby Twnshp, PA	160
311	Waterbury, CT	160
316	Pembroke Pines, FL	159
316	Westminster, CO	159
318	Cicero, IL	157
318	Sparks, NV	157
318	Sunrise, FL	157
321	San Mateo, CA	156
322	Westminster, CA	155
323	San Marcos, CA	154
323	West Jordan, UT	154
325	Bellflower, CA	152
325	Napa, CA	152
325	Olathe, KS	152
328	Bend, OR	151
328	Rio Rancho, NM	151
330	Plantation, FL	147
331	Buena Park, CA	143
331	McAllen, TX	143
331	Renton, WA	143
334	Baldwin Park, CA	142
335	Coral Springs, FL	141
336	Glendale, CA	136
337	Nashua, NH	135
337	West Covina, CA	135
339	Avondale, AZ	131
340	Kenosha, WI	130
341	Clovis, CA	126
342	San Leandro, CA	124
343	Berkeley, CA	122
343	Elgin, IL	122
345	Vacaville, CA	121
346	Racine, WI	119
347	Costa Mesa, CA	114
348	Centennial, CO	112
349	Chico, CA	111
350	Daly City, CA	110
351	Beaverton, OR	109
352	Alexandria, VA	108
352	Bellingham, WA	108
352	Livonia, MI	108
355	Carrollton, TX	106
356	Burbank, CA	105
356	Lakewood, CA	105
356	Lewisville, TX	105
359	Arvada, CO	102
359	Bethlehem, PA	102
359	Brooklyn Park, MN	102
359	Clifton, NJ	102
359	Rochester, MN	102
364	Gilbert, AZ	99
365	Spokane Valley, WA	95
366	Hamilton Twnshp, NJ	94
366	Santa Clara, CA	94
366	Scranton, PA	94
369	Boca Raton, FL	92
369	New Rochelle, NY	92
369	Provo, UT	92
369	Thousand Oaks, CA	92
373	Frisco, TX	90
374	Redwood City, CA	88
374	Richardson, TX	88
376	Alhambra, CA	87
376	Hillsboro, OR	87
378	Meridian, ID	84
379	Cheektowaga, NY	83
379	Corona, CA	83
379	Ramapo, NY	83
382	Naperville, IL	82
383	Broken Arrow, OK	81
383	Greece, NY	81
385	Canton Twnshp, MI	79
385	Pearland, TX	79
387	Sandy, UT	77
388	Amherst, NY	76
389	Torrance, CA	75
390	Brick Twnshp, NJ	73
390	Newport Beach, CA	73
392	Norman, OK	71
393	Bloomington, MN	70
394	Surprise, AZ	68
395	Irvine, CA	67
396	Edison Twnshp, NJ	66
396	Orange, CA	66
396	Simi Valley, CA	66
396	Woodbridge Twnshp, NJ	66
400	Clarkstown, NY	64
400	Lake Forest, CA	64
402	Sugar Land, TX	61
403	Farmington Hills, MI	60
404	Lee's Summit, MO	59
404	Newton, MA	59
404	O'Fallon, MO	59
407	Bellevue, WA	58
407	Sunnyvale, CA	58
407	Tracy, CA	58
410	Murrieta, CA	56
411	Cranston, RI	55
411	Mission, TX	55
413	Cary, NC	53
413	Danbury, CT	53
413	Lakewood Twnshp, NJ	53
416	Sandy Springs, GA	52
417	Tustin, CA	50
418	Round Rock, TX	49
419	Chino Hills, CA	48
420	Concord, NC	46
420	Mission Viejo, CA	46
422	Allen, TX	43
423	Warwick, RI	42
424	Troy, MI	41
425	Toms River Twnshp, NJ	36
426	Temecula, CA	34
427	League City, TX	33
428	Edmond, OK	30
429	Roswell, GA	29
430	Menifee, CA	26
431	Arlington Heights, IL	24
432	Colonie, NY	20
433	Johns Creek, GA	19
434	Hoover, AL	17
435	Orem, UT	15
436	Carmel, IN	6
437	Fishers, IN	3

Source: Reported data from the F.B.I. "Crime in the United States 2011"

*Aggravated assault is an attack for the purpose of inflicting severe bodily injury.

Alpha Order - City

62. Aggravated Assault Rate in 2011
National Rate = 241.1 Aggravated Assaults per 100,000 Population*

RANK	CITY	RATE	RANK	CITY	RATE	RANK	CITY	RATE
233	Abilene, TX	225.9	355	Cheektowaga, NY	104.8	315	Fort Wayne, IN	140.0
94	Akron, OH	436.1	197	Chesapeake, VA	261.5	113	Fort Worth, TX	383.7
60	Albany, GA	527.7	82	Chicago, IL	458.9	371	Fremont, CA	88.2
43	Albany, NY	592.1	329	Chico, CA	127.3	129	Fresno, CA	361.5
61	Albuquerque, NM	527.2	403	Chino Hills, CA	63.4	387	Frisco, TX	75.3
385	Alexandria, VA	76.3	236	Chino, CA	225.6	328	Fullerton, CA	128.0
357	Alhambra, CA	103.5	294	Chula Vista, CA	160.9	67	Gainesville, FL	507.7
257	Allentown, PA	200.2	272	Cicero, IL	186.6	307	Garden Grove, CA	148.6
416	Allen, TX	50.0	134	Cincinnati, OH	353.3	365	Garland, TX	96.3
89	Amarillo, TX	448.9	232	Citrus Heights, CA	226.6	178	Gary, IN	289.9
401	Amherst, NY	64.6	382	Clarkstown, NY	80.8	420	Gilbert, AZ	46.8
251	Anaheim, CA	210.2	66	Clarksville, TN	511.5	189	Glendale, AZ	268.3
55	Anchorage, AK	548.2	65	Clearwater, FL	521.3	391	Glendale, CA	70.1
310	Ann Arbor, MI	145.8	80	Cleveland, OH	463.9	282	Grand Prairie, TX	174.2
74	Antioch, CA	484.7	334	Clifton, NJ	120.8	90	Grand Rapids, MI	447.1
430	Arlington Heights, IL	31.9	245	Clinton Twnshp, MI	215.0	378	Greece, NY	83.9
162	Arlington, TX	315.2	324	Clovis, CA	130.2	144	Greeley, CO	341.8
367	Arvada, CO	94.2	225	College Station, TX	233.7	202	Green Bay, WI	257.4
183	Asheville, NC	279.5	432	Colonie, NY	25.7	258	Gresham, OR	198.7
248	Athens-Clarke, GA	212.6	205	Colorado Springs, CO	252.8	354	Hamilton Twnshp, NJ	105.9
12	Atlanta, GA	826.7	138	Columbia, MO	346.2	118	Hammond, IN	380.3
230	Aurora, CO	227.4	216	Columbus, GA	241.7	336	Hampton, VA	120.1
250	Aurora, IL	210.6	291	Columbus, OH	163.7	17	Hartford, CT	764.0
195	Austin, TX	263.4	33	Compton, CA	640.4	145	Hawthorne, CA	341.2
288	Avondale, AZ	169.4	269	Concord, CA	191.9	340	Hayward, CA	115.2
132	Bakersfield, CA	358.7	406	Concord, NC	57.5	187	Hemet, CA	272.7
273	Baldwin Park, CA	186.2	341	Coral Springs, FL	114.9	334	Henderson, NV	120.8
14	Baltimore, MD	780.3	410	Corona, CA	53.8	252	Hesperia, CA	209.4
36	Baton Rouge, LA	630.4	87	Corpus Christi, TX	452.8	208	Hialeah, FL	251.2
62	Beaumont, TX	525.7	358	Costa Mesa, CA	102.5	135	High Point, NC	352.0
336	Beaverton, OR	120.1	395	Cranston, RI	68.5	368	Hillsboro, OR	94.0
421	Bellevue, WA	46.7	170	Dallas, TX	302.8	218	Hollywood, FL	238.3
263	Bellflower, CA	196.1	350	Daly City, CA	107.5	434	Hoover, AL	20.7
321	Bellingham, WA	131.5	398	Danbury, CT	65.4	53	Houston, TX	553.7
265	Bend, OR	195.0	76	Davenport, IA	480.0	318	Huntington Beach, CA	135.3
353	Berkeley, CA	107.1	210	Davie, FL	250.9	45	Huntsville, AL	579.6
317	Bethlehem, PA	135.6	102	Dayton, OH	413.8	177	Independence, MO	291.7
230	Billings, MT	227.4	224	Dearborn, MI	234.5	35	Indianapolis, IN	632.3
10	Birmingham, AL	898.4	94	Decatur, IL	436.1	117	Indio, CA	380.9
169	Bloomington, IL	303.2	186	Deerfield Beach, FL	273.5	121	Inglewood, CA	377.6
256	Bloomington, IN	202.9	283	Denton, TX	173.6	431	Irvine, CA	31.2
379	Bloomington, MN	83.8	136	Denver, CO	349.6	306	Irving, TX	149.4
350	Boca Raton, FL	107.5	128	Des Moines, IA	362.8	116	Jacksonville, FL	381.5
277	Boise, ID	184.7	3	Detroit, MI	1,333.6	125	Jackson, MS	364.0
72	Boston, MA	485.1	314	Downey, CA	142.4	133	Jersey City, NJ	353.4
254	Boulder, CO	204.9	270	Duluth, MN	188.7	433	Johns Creek, GA	24.4
364	Brick Twnshp, NJ	96.9	109	Durham, NC	396.6	193	Joliet, IL	265.1
72	Bridgeport, CT	485.1	205	Edinburg, TX	252.8	125	Kansas City, KS	364.0
9	Brockton, MA	909.1	397	Edison Twnshp, NJ	65.8	18	Kansas City, MO	758.0
381	Broken Arrow, OK	81.1	426	Edmond, OK	36.5	243	Kennewick, WA	215.8
319	Brooklyn Park, MN	133.6	164	El Cajon, CA	310.0	323	Kenosha, WI	130.5
259	Brownsville, TX	197.5	289	El Monte, CA	166.4	155	Kent, WA	326.0
101	Bryan, TX	415.1	154	El Paso, TX	326.1	100	Killeen, TX	428.0
281	Buena Park, CA	175.5	343	Elgin, IL	112.4	49	Knoxville, TN	565.7
37	Buffalo, NY	622.5	99	Elizabeth, NJ	428.3	74	Lafayette, LA	484.7
362	Burbank, CA	100.4	198	Elk Grove, CA	261.0	380	Lake Forest, CA	81.9
181	Cambridge, MA	281.7	266	Erie, PA	193.9	123	Lakeland, FL	370.6
2	Camden, NJ	1,523.1	260	Escondido, CA	197.1	408	Lakewood Twnshp, NJ	56.9
372	Canton Twnshp, MI	87.7	325	Eugene, OR	129.9	326	Lakewood, CA	129.6
359	Cape Coral, FL	102.3	223	Evansville, IN	235.5	191	Lakewood, CO	266.7
303	Carlsbad, CA	150.1	215	Everett, WA	241.8	151	Lancaster, CA	335.7
436	Carmel, IN	7.5	222	Fairfield, CA	235.6	25	Lansing, MI	697.0
373	Carrollton, TX	87.2	11	Fall River, MA	851.2	148	Laredo, TX	339.3
141	Carson, CA	344.9	185	Fargo, ND	273.9	168	Largo, FL	303.7
424	Cary, NC	38.7	387	Farmington Hills, MI	75.3	146	Las Cruces, NM	340.4
280	Cedar Rapids, IA	180.3	227	Fayetteville, NC	233.4	88	Las Vegas, NV	451.6
346	Centennial, CO	109.7	437	Fishers, IN	3.9	172	Lawrence, KS	300.5
24	Champaign, IL	701.1	1	Flint, MI	1,610.1	30	Lawrence, MA	648.1
273	Chandler, AZ	186.2	242	Fontana, CA	219.3	40	Lawton, OK	601.6
295	Charleston, SC	160.5	245	Fort Collins, CO	215.0	424	League City, TX	38.7
124	Charlotte, NC	367.5	104	Fort Lauderdale, FL	411.9	402	Lee's Summit, MO	64.3
42	Chattanooga, TN	599.9	69	Fort Smith, AR	498.5	348	Lewisville, TX	107.9

Alpha Order - City (continued)

RANK	CITY	RATE
211	Lexington, KY	249.5
219	Lincoln, NE	237.5
6	Little Rock, AR	948.3
201	Livermore, CA	257.6
344	Livonia, MI	111.5
173	Long Beach, CA	299.3
249	Longmont, CO	211.9
149	Longview, TX	338.4
228	Los Angeles, CA	230.5
156	Louisville, KY	325.9
54	Lowell, MA	548.7
41	Lubbock, TX	601.1
221	Lynchburg, VA	236.7
29	Lynn, MA	650.3
174	Macon, GA	296.0
262	Madison, WI	196.8
152	Manchester, NH	333.6
349	McAllen, TX	107.8
333	McKinney, TX	121.8
122	Medford, OR	373.8
22	Melbourne, FL	731.5
5	Memphis, TN	1,032.3
428	Menifee, CA	33.2
106	Merced, CA	408.1
345	Meridian, ID	110.6
190	Mesa, AZ	267.7
309	Mesquite, TX	147.1
59	Miami Beach, FL	531.6
68	Miami Gardens, FL	499.9
28	Miami, FL	662.6
238	Midland, TX	221.2
85	Milwaukee, WI	456.5
93	Minneapolis, MN	444.8
237	Miramar, FL	224.7
417	Mission Viejo, CA	48.7
392	Mission, TX	69.9
131	Mobile, AL	358.9
92	Modesto, CA	445.6
316	Montgomery, AL	137.4
275	Moreno Valley, CA	185.5
91	Murfreesboro, TN	446.5
411	Murrieta, CA	53.5
241	Nampa, ID	219.5
264	Napa, CA	195.3
405	Naperville, IL	57.6
298	Nashua, NH	155.9
13	Nashville, TN	804.0
16	New Bedford, MA	769.5
26	New Haven, CT	686.8
115	New Orleans, LA	382.2
339	New Rochelle, NY	118.9
127	New York, NY	363.2
108	Newark, NJ	400.6
377	Newport Beach, CA	84.7
247	Newport News, VA	213.3
394	Newton, MA	68.9
182	Norfolk, VA	280.4
404	Norman, OK	63.3
97	North Charleston, SC	435.1
255	Norwalk, CA	204.1
204	Norwalk, CT	254.2
19	Oakland, CA	754.1
238	Oceanside, CA	221.2
38	Odessa, TX	619.3
389	O'Fallon, MO	74.1
159	Ogden, UT	324.6
39	Oklahoma City, OK	604.1
338	Olathe, KS	120.0
153	Omaha, NE	327.2
301	Ontario, CA	151.3
419	Orange, CA	47.8
435	Orem, UT	16.7
23	Orlando, FL	722.8

RANK	CITY	RATE
347	Overland Park, KS	108.3
299	Oxnard, CA	155.3
82	Palm Bay, FL	458.9
161	Palmdale, CA	318.4
293	Pasadena, CA	161.5
217	Pasadena, TX	239.2
79	Paterson, NJ	465.6
376	Pearland, TX	84.8
361	Pembroke Pines, FL	101.4
320	Peoria, AZ	133.1
103	Peoria, IL	413.5
46	Philadelphia, PA	579.1
184	Phoenix, AZ	279.0
107	Pittsburgh, PA	401.5
370	Plano, TX	91.2
286	Plantation, FL	170.7
137	Pomona, CA	346.8
64	Pompano Beach, FL	521.7
290	Port St. Lucie, FL	164.2
163	Portland, OR	312.2
192	Portsmouth, VA	265.8
383	Provo, UT	80.2
52	Pueblo, CO	558.8
176	Quincy, MA	291.9
302	Racine, WI	150.2
240	Raleigh, NC	220.0
363	Ramapo, NY	98.3
359	Rancho Cucamon., CA	102.3
111	Reading, PA	391.6
44	Redding, CA	588.4
342	Redwood City, CA	113.2
171	Reno, NV	301.2
300	Renton, WA	154.8
208	Rialto, CA	251.2
374	Richardson, TX	86.9
34	Richmond, CA	635.7
158	Richmond, VA	325.2
287	Rio Rancho, NM	170.6
203	Riverside, CA	254.4
119	Roanoke, VA	379.9
366	Rochester, MN	94.8
57	Rochester, NY	542.8
7	Rockford, IL	917.6
304	Roseville, CA	149.8
429	Roswell, GA	32.4
418	Round Rock, TX	48.0
98	Sacramento, CA	428.4
226	Salem, OR	233.6
86	Salinas, CA	454.6
110	Salt Lake City, UT	393.6
276	San Angelo, TX	184.9
142	San Antonio, TX	344.7
71	San Bernardino, CA	486.8
207	San Diego, CA	251.9
199	San Francisco, CA	258.4
268	San Jose, CA	192.3
313	San Leandro, CA	144.3
279	San Marcos, CA	181.7
296	San Mateo, CA	158.6
409	Sandy Springs, GA	54.7
375	Sandy, UT	86.4
260	Santa Ana, CA	197.1
234	Santa Barbara, CA	225.8
384	Santa Clara, CA	79.8
369	Santa Clarita, CA	91.4
58	Santa Maria, CA	534.1
220	Santa Monica, CA	236.8
180	Santa Rosa, CA	285.7
305	Savannah, GA	149.7
350	Scottsdale, AZ	107.5
332	Scranton, PA	123.1
143	Seattle, WA	343.9
63	Shreveport, LA	522.5
412	Simi Valley, CA	52.5

RANK	CITY	RATE
160	Sioux City, IA	322.4
292	Sioux Falls, SD	161.8
229	Somerville, MA	229.6
194	South Bend, IN	264.5
165	South Gate, CA	308.9
284	Sparks, NV	172.5
356	Spokane Valley, WA	104.2
140	Spokane, WA	345.0
15	Springfield, IL	779.6
30	Springfield, MA	648.1
50	Springfield, MO	565.3
322	Stamford, CT	131.0
331	Sterling Heights, MI	123.5
8	Stockton, CA	909.4
234	St. Joseph, MO	225.8
4	St. Louis, MO	1,099.1
112	St. Paul, MN	383.8
27	St. Petersburg, FL	685.6
271	Suffolk, VA	188.1
386	Sugar Land, TX	75.8
422	Sunnyvale, CA	40.9
278	Sunrise, FL	183.4
407	Surprise, AZ	57.1
47	Syracuse, NY	576.0
81	Tacoma, WA	459.0
51	Tallahassee, FL	561.9
84	Tampa, FL	457.0
427	Temecula, CA	33.6
167	Tempe, AZ	304.9
70	Thornton, CO	492.4
390	Thousand Oaks, CA	71.8
56	Toledo, OH	543.5
423	Toms River Twnshp, NJ	39.3
166	Topeka, KS	307.9
413	Torrance, CA	51.0
393	Tracy, CA	69.1
20	Trenton, NJ	752.4
415	Troy, MI	50.7
114	Tucson, AZ	383.3
32	Tulsa, OK	645.0
244	Tuscaloosa, AL	215.6
398	Tustin, CA	65.4
120	Tyler, TX	379.0
267	Upper Darby Twnshp, PA	192.6
327	Vacaville, CA	129.4
149	Vallejo, CA	338.4
253	Vancouver, WA	205.1
297	Ventura, CA	157.9
157	Victorville, CA	325.8
400	Virginia Beach, VA	65.2
188	Visalia, CA	272.4
214	Vista, CA	246.5
139	Waco, TX	345.3
130	Warren, MI	361.3
414	Warwick, RI	50.9
77	Washington, DC	477.2
312	Waterbury, CT	144.7
330	West Covina, CA	125.8
311	West Jordan, UT	145.7
78	West Palm Beach, FL	466.0
179	West Valley, UT	288.7
212	Westland, MI	248.7
285	Westminster, CA	170.8
308	Westminster, CO	147.3
200	Whittier, CA	258.3
196	Wichita Falls, TX	263.2
48	Wichita, KS	571.0
147	Wilmington, NC	339.4
94	Winston-Salem, NC	436.1
396	Woodbridge Twnshp, NJ	66.1
21	Worcester, MA	736.8
175	Yakima, WA	293.0
213	Yonkers, NY	247.4
105	Yuma, AZ	410.0

Source: CQ Press using reported data from the F.B.I. "Crime in the United States 2011"
*Aggravated assault is an attack for the purpose of inflicting severe bodily injury.

Rank Order - City

62. Aggravated Assault Rate in 2011 (continued)
National Rate = 241.1 Aggravated Assaults per 100,000 Population*

RANK	CITY	RATE	RANK	CITY	RATE	RANK	CITY	RATE
1	Flint, MI	1,610.1	72	Bridgeport, CT	485.1	145	Hawthorne, CA	341.2
2	Camden, NJ	1,523.1	74	Antioch, CA	484.7	146	Las Cruces, NM	340.4
3	Detroit, MI	1,333.6	74	Lafayette, LA	484.7	147	Wilmington, NC	339.4
4	St. Louis, MO	1,099.1	76	Davenport, IA	480.0	148	Laredo, TX	339.3
5	Memphis, TN	1,032.3	77	Washington, DC	477.2	149	Longview, TX	338.4
6	Little Rock, AR	948.3	78	West Palm Beach, FL	466.0	149	Vallejo, CA	338.4
7	Rockford, IL	917.6	79	Paterson, NJ	465.6	151	Lancaster, CA	335.7
8	Stockton, CA	909.4	80	Cleveland, OH	463.9	152	Manchester, NH	333.6
9	Brockton, MA	909.1	81	Tacoma, WA	459.0	153	Omaha, NE	327.2
10	Birmingham, AL	898.4	82	Chicago, IL	458.9	154	El Paso, TX	326.1
11	Fall River, MA	851.2	82	Palm Bay, FL	458.9	155	Kent, WA	326.0
12	Atlanta, GA	826.7	84	Tampa, FL	457.0	156	Louisville, KY	325.9
13	Nashville, TN	804.0	85	Milwaukee, WI	456.5	157	Victorville, CA	325.8
14	Baltimore, MD	780.3	86	Salinas, CA	454.6	158	Richmond, VA	325.2
15	Springfield, IL	779.6	87	Corpus Christi, TX	452.8	159	Ogden, UT	324.6
16	New Bedford, MA	769.5	88	Las Vegas, NV	451.6	160	Sioux City, IA	322.4
17	Hartford, CT	764.0	89	Amarillo, TX	448.9	161	Palmdale, CA	318.4
18	Kansas City, MO	758.0	90	Grand Rapids, MI	447.1	162	Arlington, TX	315.2
19	Oakland, CA	754.1	91	Murfreesboro, TN	446.5	163	Portland, OR	312.2
20	Trenton, NJ	752.4	92	Modesto, CA	445.6	164	El Cajon, CA	310.0
21	Worcester, MA	736.8	93	Minneapolis, MN	444.8	165	South Gate, CA	308.9
22	Melbourne, FL	731.5	94	Akron, OH	436.1	166	Topeka, KS	307.9
23	Orlando, FL	722.8	94	Decatur, IL	436.1	167	Tempe, AZ	304.9
24	Champaign, IL	701.1	94	Winston-Salem, NC	436.1	168	Largo, FL	303.7
25	Lansing, MI	697.0	97	North Charleston, SC	435.1	169	Bloomington, IL	303.2
26	New Haven, CT	686.8	98	Sacramento, CA	428.4	170	Dallas, TX	302.8
27	St. Petersburg, FL	685.6	99	Elizabeth, NJ	428.3	171	Reno, NV	301.2
28	Miami, FL	662.6	100	Killeen, TX	428.0	172	Lawrence, KS	300.5
29	Lynn, MA	650.3	101	Bryan, TX	415.1	173	Long Beach, CA	299.3
30	Lawrence, MA	648.1	102	Dayton, OH	413.8	174	Macon, GA	296.0
30	Springfield, MA	648.1	103	Peoria, IL	413.5	175	Yakima, WA	293.0
32	Tulsa, OK	645.0	104	Fort Lauderdale, FL	411.9	176	Quincy, MA	291.9
33	Compton, CA	640.4	105	Yuma, AZ	410.0	177	Independence, MO	291.7
34	Richmond, CA	635.7	106	Merced, CA	408.1	178	Gary, IN	289.9
35	Indianapolis, IN	632.3	107	Pittsburgh, PA	401.5	179	West Valley, UT	288.7
36	Baton Rouge, LA	630.4	108	Newark, NJ	400.6	180	Santa Rosa, CA	285.7
37	Buffalo, NY	622.5	109	Durham, NC	396.6	181	Cambridge, MA	281.7
38	Odessa, TX	619.3	110	Salt Lake City, UT	393.6	182	Norfolk, VA	280.4
39	Oklahoma City, OK	604.1	111	Reading, PA	391.6	183	Asheville, NC	279.5
40	Lawton, OK	601.6	112	St. Paul, MN	383.8	184	Phoenix, AZ	279.0
41	Lubbock, TX	601.1	113	Fort Worth, TX	383.7	185	Fargo, ND	273.9
42	Chattanooga, TN	599.9	114	Tucson, AZ	383.3	186	Deerfield Beach, FL	273.5
43	Albany, NY	592.1	115	New Orleans, LA	382.2	187	Hemet, CA	272.7
44	Redding, CA	588.4	116	Jacksonville, FL	381.5	188	Visalia, CA	272.4
45	Huntsville, AL	579.6	117	Indio, CA	380.9	189	Glendale, AZ	268.3
46	Philadelphia, PA	579.1	118	Hammond, IN	380.3	190	Mesa, AZ	267.7
47	Syracuse, NY	576.0	119	Roanoke, VA	379.9	191	Lakewood, CO	266.7
48	Wichita, KS	571.0	120	Tyler, TX	379.0	192	Portsmouth, VA	265.8
49	Knoxville, TN	565.7	121	Inglewood, CA	377.6	193	Joliet, IL	265.1
50	Springfield, MO	565.3	122	Medford, OR	373.8	194	South Bend, IN	264.5
51	Tallahassee, FL	561.9	123	Lakeland, FL	370.6	195	Austin, TX	263.4
52	Pueblo, CO	558.8	124	Charlotte, NC	367.5	196	Wichita Falls, TX	263.2
53	Houston, TX	553.7	125	Jackson, MS	364.0	197	Chesapeake, VA	261.5
54	Lowell, MA	548.7	125	Kansas City, KS	364.0	198	Elk Grove, CA	261.0
55	Anchorage, AK	548.2	127	New York, NY	363.2	199	San Francisco, CA	258.4
56	Toledo, OH	543.5	128	Des Moines, IA	362.8	200	Whittier, CA	258.3
57	Rochester, NY	542.8	129	Fresno, CA	361.5	201	Livermore, CA	257.6
58	Santa Maria, CA	534.1	130	Warren, MI	361.3	202	Green Bay, WI	257.4
59	Miami Beach, FL	531.6	131	Mobile, AL	358.9	203	Riverside, CA	254.4
60	Albany, GA	527.7	132	Bakersfield, CA	358.7	204	Norwalk, CT	254.2
61	Albuquerque, NM	527.2	133	Jersey City, NJ	353.4	205	Colorado Springs, CO	252.8
62	Beaumont, TX	525.7	134	Cincinnati, OH	353.3	205	Edinburg, TX	252.8
63	Shreveport, LA	522.5	135	High Point, NC	352.0	207	San Diego, CA	251.9
64	Pompano Beach, FL	521.7	136	Denver, CO	349.6	208	Hialeah, FL	251.2
65	Clearwater, FL	521.3	137	Pomona, CA	346.8	208	Rialto, CA	251.2
66	Clarksville, TN	511.5	138	Columbia, MO	346.2	210	Davie, FL	250.9
67	Gainesville, FL	507.7	139	Waco, TX	345.3	211	Lexington, KY	249.5
68	Miami Gardens, FL	499.9	140	Spokane, WA	345.0	212	Westland, MI	248.7
69	Fort Smith, AR	498.5	141	Carson, CA	344.9	213	Yonkers, NY	247.4
70	Thornton, CO	492.4	142	San Antonio, TX	344.7	214	Vista, CA	246.5
71	San Bernardino, CA	486.8	143	Seattle, WA	343.9	215	Everett, WA	241.8
72	Boston, MA	485.1	144	Greeley, CO	341.8	216	Columbus, GA	241.7

Rank Order - City (continued)

RANK	CITY	RATE
217	Pasadena, TX	239.2
218	Hollywood, FL	238.3
219	Lincoln, NE	237.5
220	Santa Monica, CA	236.8
221	Lynchburg, VA	236.7
222	Fairfield, CA	235.6
223	Evansville, IN	235.5
224	Dearborn, MI	234.5
225	College Station, TX	233.7
226	Salem, OR	233.6
227	Fayetteville, NC	233.4
228	Los Angeles, CA	230.5
229	Somerville, MA	229.6
230	Aurora, CO	227.4
230	Billings, MT	227.4
232	Citrus Heights, CA	226.6
233	Abilene, TX	225.9
234	Santa Barbara, CA	225.8
234	St. Joseph, MO	225.8
236	Chino, CA	225.6
237	Miramar, FL	224.7
238	Midland, TX	221.2
238	Oceanside, CA	221.2
240	Raleigh, NC	220.0
241	Nampa, ID	219.5
242	Fontana, CA	219.3
243	Kennewick, WA	215.8
244	Tuscaloosa, AL	215.6
245	Clinton Twnshp, MI	215.0
245	Fort Collins, CO	215.0
247	Newport News, VA	213.3
248	Athens-Clarke, GA	212.6
249	Longmont, CO	211.9
250	Aurora, IL	210.6
251	Anaheim, CA	210.2
252	Hesperia, CA	209.4
253	Vancouver, WA	205.1
254	Boulder, CO	204.9
255	Norwalk, CA	204.1
256	Bloomington, IN	202.9
257	Allentown, PA	200.2
258	Gresham, OR	198.7
259	Brownsville, TX	197.5
260	Escondido, CA	197.1
260	Santa Ana, CA	197.1
262	Madison, WI	196.8
263	Bellflower, CA	196.1
264	Napa, CA	195.3
265	Bend, OR	195.0
266	Erie, PA	193.9
267	Upper Darby Twnshp, PA	192.6
268	San Jose, CA	192.3
269	Concord, CA	191.9
270	Duluth, MN	188.7
271	Suffolk, VA	188.1
272	Cicero, IL	186.6
273	Baldwin Park, CA	186.2
273	Chandler, AZ	186.2
275	Moreno Valley, CA	185.5
276	San Angelo, TX	184.9
277	Boise, ID	184.7
278	Sunrise, FL	183.4
279	San Marcos, CA	181.7
280	Cedar Rapids, IA	180.3
281	Buena Park, CA	175.5
282	Grand Prairie, TX	174.2
283	Denton, TX	173.6
284	Sparks, NV	172.5
285	Westminster, CA	170.8
286	Plantation, FL	170.7
287	Rio Rancho, NM	170.6
288	Avondale, AZ	169.4
289	El Monte, CA	166.4
290	Port St. Lucie, FL	164.2
291	Columbus, OH	163.7
292	Sioux Falls, SD	161.8
293	Pasadena, CA	161.5
294	Chula Vista, CA	160.9
295	Charleston, SC	160.5
296	San Mateo, CA	158.6
297	Ventura, CA	157.9
298	Nashua, NH	155.9
299	Oxnard, CA	155.3
300	Renton, WA	154.8
301	Ontario, CA	151.3
302	Racine, WI	150.2
303	Carlsbad, CA	150.1
304	Roseville, CA	149.8
305	Savannah, GA	149.7
306	Irving, TX	149.4
307	Garden Grove, CA	148.6
308	Westminster, CO	147.3
309	Mesquite, TX	147.1
310	Ann Arbor, MI	145.8
311	West Jordan, UT	145.7
312	Waterbury, CT	144.7
313	San Leandro, CA	144.3
314	Downey, CA	142.4
315	Fort Wayne, IN	140.0
316	Montgomery, AL	137.4
317	Bethlehem, PA	135.6
318	Huntington Beach, CA	135.3
319	Brooklyn Park, MN	133.6
320	Peoria, AZ	133.1
321	Bellingham, WA	131.5
322	Stamford, CT	131.0
323	Kenosha, WI	130.5
324	Clovis, CA	130.2
325	Eugene, OR	129.9
326	Lakewood, CA	129.6
327	Vacaville, CA	129.4
328	Fullerton, CA	128.0
329	Chico, CA	127.3
330	West Covina, CA	125.8
331	Sterling Heights, MI	123.5
332	Scranton, PA	123.1
333	McKinney, TX	121.8
334	Clifton, NJ	120.8
334	Henderson, NV	120.8
336	Beaverton, OR	120.1
336	Hampton, VA	120.1
338	Olathe, KS	120.0
339	New Rochelle, NY	118.9
340	Hayward, CA	115.2
341	Coral Springs, FL	114.9
342	Redwood City, CA	113.2
343	Elgin, IL	112.4
344	Livonia, MI	111.5
345	Meridian, ID	110.6
346	Centennial, CO	109.7
347	Overland Park, KS	108.3
348	Lewisville, TX	107.9
349	McAllen, TX	107.8
350	Boca Raton, FL	107.5
350	Daly City, CA	107.5
350	Scottsdale, AZ	107.5
353	Berkeley, CA	107.1
354	Hamilton Twnshp, NJ	105.9
355	Cheektowaga, NY	104.8
356	Spokane Valley, WA	104.2
357	Alhambra, CA	103.5
358	Costa Mesa, CA	102.5
359	Cape Coral, FL	102.3
359	Rancho Cucamon., CA	102.3
361	Pembroke Pines, FL	101.4
362	Burbank, CA	100.4
363	Ramapo, NY	98.3
364	Brick Twnshp, NJ	96.9
365	Garland, TX	96.3
366	Rochester, MN	94.8
367	Arvada, CO	94.2
368	Hillsboro, OR	94.0
369	Santa Clarita, CA	91.4
370	Plano, TX	91.2
371	Fremont, CA	88.2
372	Canton Twnshp, MI	87.7
373	Carrollton, TX	87.2
374	Richardson, TX	86.9
375	Sandy, UT	86.4
376	Pearland, TX	84.8
377	Newport Beach, CA	84.7
378	Greece, NY	83.9
379	Bloomington, MN	83.8
380	Lake Forest, CA	81.9
381	Broken Arrow, OK	81.1
382	Clarkstown, NY	80.8
383	Provo, UT	80.2
384	Santa Clara, CA	79.8
385	Alexandria, VA	76.3
386	Sugar Land, TX	75.8
387	Farmington Hills, MI	75.3
387	Frisco, TX	75.3
389	O'Fallon, MO	74.1
390	Thousand Oaks, CA	71.8
391	Glendale, CA	70.1
392	Mission, TX	69.9
393	Tracy, CA	69.1
394	Newton, MA	68.9
395	Cranston, RI	68.5
396	Woodbridge Twnshp, NJ	66.1
397	Edison Twnshp, NJ	65.8
398	Danbury, CT	65.4
398	Tustin, CA	65.4
400	Virginia Beach, VA	65.2
401	Amherst, NY	64.6
402	Lee's Summit, MO	64.3
403	Chino Hills, CA	63.4
404	Norman, OK	63.3
405	Naperville, IL	57.6
406	Concord, NC	57.5
407	Surprise, AZ	57.1
408	Lakewood Twnshp, NJ	56.9
409	Sandy Springs, GA	54.7
410	Corona, CA	53.8
411	Murrieta, CA	53.5
412	Simi Valley, CA	52.5
413	Torrance, CA	51.0
414	Warwick, RI	50.9
415	Troy, MI	50.7
416	Allen, TX	50.0
417	Mission Viejo, CA	48.7
418	Round Rock, TX	48.0
419	Orange, CA	47.8
420	Gilbert, AZ	46.8
421	Bellevue, WA	46.7
422	Sunnyvale, CA	40.9
423	Toms River Twnshp, NJ	39.3
424	Cary, NC	38.7
424	League City, TX	38.7
426	Edmond, OK	36.5
427	Temecula, CA	33.6
428	Menifee, CA	33.2
429	Roswell, GA	32.4
430	Arlington Heights, IL	31.9
431	Irvine, CA	31.2
432	Colonie, NY	25.7
433	Johns Creek, GA	24.4
434	Hoover, AL	20.7
435	Orem, UT	16.7
436	Carmel, IN	7.5
437	Fishers, IN	3.9

Source: CQ Press using reported data from the F.B.I. "Crime in the United States 2011"

*Aggravated assault is an attack for the purpose of inflicting severe bodily injury.

Alpha Order - City

63. Percent Change in Aggravated Assault Rate: 2010 to 2011
National Percent Change = 4.6% Decrease*

RANK	CITY	% CHANGE	RANK	CITY	% CHANGE	RANK	CITY	% CHANGE
395	Abilene, TX	(32.9)	190	Cheektowaga, NY	(5.5)	44	Fort Wayne, IN	14.9
118	Akron, OH	1.7	85	Chesapeake, VA	6.3	58	Fort Worth, TX	10.9
348	Albany, GA	(19.7)	190	Chicago, IL	(5.5)	387	Fremont, CA	(29.2)
275	Albany, NY	(11.6)	138	Chico, CA	0.0	223	Fresno, CA	(7.7)
174	Albuquerque, NM	(3.2)	340	Chino Hills, CA	(18.5)	224	Frisco, TX	(7.9)
236	Alexandria, VA	(8.9)	73	Chino, CA	8.5	392	Fullerton, CA	(32.1)
185	Alhambra, CA	(4.4)	105	Chula Vista, CA	4.4	179	Gainesville, FL	(3.8)
62	Allentown, PA	10.8	NA	Cicero, IL**	NA	375	Garden Grove, CA	(25.1)
16	Allen, TX	27.9	151	Cincinnati, OH	(1.4)	252	Garland, TX	(9.8)
125	Amarillo, TX	1.1	186	Citrus Heights, CA	(4.7)	NA	Gary, IN**	NA
212	Amherst, NY	(7.2)	29	Clarkstown, NY	19.5	261	Gilbert, AZ	(10.9)
20	Anaheim, CA	23.9	99	Clarksville, TN	4.9	18	Glendale, AZ	26.6
206	Anchorage, AK	(6.4)	52	Clearwater, FL	12.4	159	Glendale, CA	(2.1)
150	Ann Arbor, MI	(1.3)	113	Cleveland, OH	2.8	293	Grand Prairie, TX	(13.5)
160	Antioch, CA	(2.2)	NA	Clifton, NJ**	NA	322	Grand Rapids, MI	(16.4)
184	Arlington Heights, IL	(4.2)	345	Clinton Twnshp, MI	(19.4)	117	Greece, NY	1.8
179	Arlington, TX	(3.8)	1	Clovis, CA	62.1	170	Greeley, CO	(3.0)
12	Arvada, CO	32.9	4	College Station, TX	52.0	94	Green Bay, WI	5.6
224	Asheville, NC	(7.9)	147	Colonie, NY	(0.8)	324	Gresham, OR	(16.8)
90	Athens-Clarke, GA	5.7	224	Colorado Springs, CO	(7.9)	37	Hamilton Twnshp, NJ	16.6
13	Atlanta, GA	30.3	139	Columbia, MO	(0.3)	389	Hammond, IN	(30.5)
132	Aurora, CO	0.5	200	Columbus, GA	(6.1)	156	Hampton, VA	(2.0)
343	Aurora, IL	(19.0)	276	Columbus, OH	(11.7)	163	Hartford, CT	(2.3)
210	Austin, TX	(7.0)	372	Compton, CA	(24.8)	292	Hawthorne, CA	(13.3)
9	Avondale, AZ	35.8	398	Concord, CA	(33.4)	324	Hayward, CA	(16.8)
304	Bakersfield, CA	(14.3)	409	Concord, NC	(42.1)	214	Hemet, CA	(7.3)
116	Baldwin Park, CA	1.9	319	Coral Springs, FL	(16.1)	114	Henderson, NV	2.6
240	Baltimore, MD	(9.1)	257	Corona, CA	(10.3)	166	Hesperia, CA	(2.6)
NA	Baton Rouge, LA**	NA	272	Corpus Christi, TX	(11.5)	309	Hialeah, FL	(14.8)
55	Beaumont, TX	12.1	125	Costa Mesa, CA	1.1	109	High Point, NC	3.5
390	Beaverton, OR	(30.7)	372	Cranston, RI	(24.8)	NA	Hillsboro, OR**	NA
293	Bellevue, WA	(13.5)	152	Dallas, TX	(1.6)	69	Hollywood, FL	9.1
397	Bellflower, CA	(33.3)	337	Daly City, CA	(18.3)	NA	Hoover, AL**	NA
406	Bellingham, WA	(37.2)	48	Danbury, CT	13.0	104	Houston, TX	4.7
355	Bend, OR	(21.2)	NA	Davenport, IA**	NA	305	Huntington Beach, CA	(14.4)
357	Berkeley, CA	(21.4)	218	Davie, FL	(7.4)	NA	Huntsville, AL**	NA
196	Bethlehem, PA	(5.8)	99	Dayton, OH	4.9	47	Independence, MO	14.0
NA	Billings, MT**	NA	232	Dearborn, MI	(8.6)	NA	Indianapolis, IN**	NA
NA	Birmingham, AL**	NA	88	Decatur, IL	6.0	46	Indio, CA	14.6
311	Bloomington, IL	(15.3)	330	Deerfield Beach, FL	(17.1)	110	Inglewood, CA	3.3
384	Bloomington, IN	(27.4)	41	Denton, TX	15.7	27	Irvine, CA	20.9
3	Bloomington, MN	54.0	82	Denver, CO	7.4	168	Irving, TX	(2.8)
334	Boca Raton, FL	(17.5)	139	Des Moines, IA	(0.3)	212	Jacksonville, FL	(7.2)
160	Boise, ID	(2.2)	56	Detroit, MI	11.9	15	Jackson, MS	29.4
280	Boston, MA	(12.3)	270	Downey, CA	(11.4)	94	Jersey City, NJ	5.6
7	Boulder, CO	41.2	177	Duluth, MN	(3.6)	412	Johns Creek, GA	(54.3)
66	Brick Twnshp, NJ	10.1	85	Durham, NC	6.3	83	Joliet, IL	6.6
285	Bridgeport, CT	(12.8)	39	Edinburg, TX	16.4	36	Kansas City, KS	17.2
71	Brockton, MA	8.7	346	Edison Twnshp, NJ	(19.5)	NA	Kansas City, MO**	NA
176	Broken Arrow, OK	(3.5)	394	Edmond, OK	(32.4)	313	Kennewick, WA	(15.5)
NA	Brooklyn Park, MN**	NA	6	El Cajon, CA	44.1	206	Kenosha, WI	(6.4)
149	Brownsville, TX	(1.2)	400	El Monte, CA	(33.5)	118	Kent, WA	1.7
58	Bryan, TX	10.9	218	El Paso, TX	(7.4)	328	Killeen, TX	(17.0)
181	Buena Park, CA	(3.9)	383	Elgin, IL	(27.1)	90	Knoxville, TN	5.7
NA	Buffalo, NY**	NA	200	Elizabeth, NJ	(6.1)	321	Lafayette, LA	(16.3)
193	Burbank, CA	(5.7)	230	Elk Grove, CA	(8.3)	30	Lake Forest, CA	19.4
78	Cambridge, MA	7.8	272	Erie, PA	(11.5)	25	Lakeland, FL	22.1
33	Camden, NJ	18.2	347	Escondido, CA	(19.6)	358	Lakewood Twnshp, NJ	(21.6)
305	Canton Twnshp, MI	(14.4)	32	Eugene, OR	18.5	403	Lakewood, CA	(34.0)
276	Cape Coral, FL	(11.7)	167	Evansville, IN	(2.7)	175	Lakewood, CO	(3.3)
51	Carlsbad, CA	12.5	278	Everett, WA	(12.0)	297	Lancaster, CA	(13.7)
414	Carmel, IN	(83.7)	316	Fairfield, CA	(15.6)	252	Lansing, MI	(9.8)
129	Carrollton, TX	0.9	153	Fall River, MA	(1.8)	221	Laredo, TX	(7.5)
243	Carson, CA	(9.2)	23	Fargo, ND	22.4	398	Largo, FL	(33.4)
361	Cary, NC	(21.8)	400	Farmington Hills, MI	(33.5)	142	Las Cruces, NM	(0.5)
96	Cedar Rapids, IA	5.3	302	Fayetteville, NC	(14.1)	342	Las Vegas, NV	(18.9)
193	Centennial, CO	(5.7)	381	Fishers, IN	(26.4)	247	Lawrence, KS	(9.5)
NA	Champaign, IL**	NA	66	Flint, MI	10.1	130	Lawrence, MA	0.8
97	Chandler, AZ	5.0	268	Fontana, CA	(11.3)	313	Lawton, OK	(15.5)
371	Charleston, SC	(24.5)	228	Fort Collins, CO	(8.0)	139	League City, TX	(0.3)
99	Charlotte, NC	4.9	33	Fort Lauderdale, FL	18.2	74	Lee's Summit, MO	8.4
70	Chattanooga, TN	9.0	214	Fort Smith, AR	(7.3)	263	Lewisville, TX	(11.0)

Alpha Order - City (continued)

RANK	CITY	% CHANGE
NA	Lexington, KY**	NA
402	Lincoln, NE	(33.8)
183	Little Rock, AR	(4.0)
330	Livermore, CA	(17.1)
165	Livonia, MI	(2.5)
115	Long Beach, CA	2.3
350	Longmont, CO	(19.8)
396	Longview, TX	(33.1)
189	Los Angeles, CA	(5.2)
53	Louisville, KY	12.3
408	Lowell, MA	(40.4)
286	Lubbock, TX	(12.9)
338	Lynchburg, VA	(18.4)
68	Lynn, MA	9.7
386	Macon, GA	(28.3)
247	Madison, WI	(9.5)
64	Manchester, NH	10.3
279	McAllen, TX	(12.1)
53	McKinney, TX	12.3
14	Medford, OR	30.2
49	Melbourne, FL	12.6
102	Memphis, TN	4.8
413	Menifee, CA	(60.9)
302	Merced, CA	(14.1)
105	Meridian, ID	4.4
85	Mesa, AZ	6.3
404	Mesquite, TX	(34.7)
131	Miami Beach, FL	0.6
328	Miami Gardens, FL	(17.0)
134	Miami, FL	0.3
336	Midland, TX	(18.0)
261	Milwaukee, WI	(10.9)
299	Minneapolis, MN	(13.9)
362	Miramar, FL	(22.1)
135	Mission Viejo, CA	0.2
71	Mission, TX	8.7
NA	Mobile, AL**	NA
125	Modesto, CA	1.1
NA	Montgomery, AL**	NA
28	Moreno Valley, CA	20.8
31	Murfreesboro, TN	18.9
120	Murrieta, CA	1.5
255	Nampa, ID	(9.9)
335	Napa, CA	(17.6)
NA	Naperville, IL**	NA
2	Nashua, NH	56.8
107	Nashville, TN	4.2
313	New Bedford, MA	(15.5)
366	New Haven, CT	(22.9)
112	New Orleans, LA	3.1
379	New Rochelle, NY	(25.8)
58	New York, NY	10.9
128	Newark, NJ	1.0
163	Newport Beach, CA	(2.3)
301	Newport News, VA	(14.0)
267	Newton, MA	(11.2)
247	Norfolk, VA	(9.5)
11	Norman, OK	33.3
283	North Charleston, SC	(12.6)
368	Norwalk, CA	(23.3)
65	Norwalk, CT	10.2
97	Oakland, CA	5.0
236	Oceanside, CA	(8.9)
84	Odessa, TX	6.4
142	O'Fallon, MO	(0.5)
8	Ogden, UT	37.7
238	Oklahoma City, OK	(9.0)
89	Olathe, KS	5.8
40	Omaha, NE	15.9
370	Ontario, CA	(23.5)
376	Orange, CA	(25.3)
411	Orem, UT	(49.5)
156	Orlando, FL	(2.0)
240	Overland Park, KS	(9.1)
282	Oxnard, CA	(12.4)
75	Palm Bay, FL	8.3
258	Palmdale, CA	(10.4)
391	Pasadena, CA	(31.6)
255	Pasadena, TX	(9.9)
214	Paterson, NJ	(7.3)
169	Pearland, TX	(2.9)
265	Pembroke Pines, FL	(11.1)
23	Peoria, AZ	22.4
233	Peoria, IL	(8.7)
123	Philadelphia, PA	1.2
102	Phoenix, AZ	4.8
320	Pittsburgh, PA	(16.2)
297	Plano, TX	(13.7)
181	Plantation, FL	(3.9)
90	Pomona, CA	5.7
200	Pompano Beach, FL	(6.1)
214	Port St. Lucie, FL	(7.3)
153	Portland, OR	(1.8)
312	Portsmouth, VA	(15.4)
352	Provo, UT	(20.7)
NA	Pueblo, CO**	NA
156	Quincy, MA	(2.0)
363	Racine, WI	(22.5)
203	Raleigh, NC	(6.2)
19	Ramapo, NY	24.9
310	Rancho Cucamon., CA	(15.2)
247	Reading, PA	(9.5)
299	Redding, CA	(13.9)
160	Redwood City, CA	(2.2)
229	Reno, NV	(8.1)
374	Renton, WA	(25.0)
199	Rialto, CA	(6.0)
132	Richardson, TX	0.5
209	Richmond, CA	(6.9)
170	Richmond, VA	(3.0)
63	Rio Rancho, NM	10.7
259	Riverside, CA	(10.6)
363	Roanoke, VA	(22.5)
343	Rochester, MN	(19.0)
288	Rochester, NY	(13.1)
286	Rockford, IL	(12.9)
359	Roseville, CA	(21.7)
410	Roswell, GA	(44.6)
170	Round Rock, TX	(3.0)
323	Sacramento, CA	(16.5)
43	Salem, OR	15.2
288	Salinas, CA	(13.1)
252	Salt Lake City, UT	(9.8)
177	San Angelo, TX	(3.6)
291	San Antonio, TX	(13.2)
75	San Bernardino, CA	8.3
245	San Diego, CA	(9.4)
270	San Francisco, CA	(11.4)
188	San Jose, CA	(5.1)
233	San Leandro, CA	(8.7)
121	San Marcos, CA	1.3
351	San Mateo, CA	(20.5)
218	Sandy Springs, GA	(7.4)
359	Sandy, UT	(21.7)
144	Santa Ana, CA	(0.7)
263	Santa Barbara, CA	(11.0)
341	Santa Clara, CA	(18.8)
393	Santa Clarita, CA	(32.2)
348	Santa Maria, CA	(19.7)
155	Santa Monica, CA	(1.9)
324	Santa Rosa, CA	(16.8)
210	Savannah, GA	(7.0)
45	Scottsdale, AZ	14.7
333	Scranton, PA	(17.3)
77	Seattle, WA	8.2
121	Shreveport, LA	1.3
327	Simi Valley, CA	(16.9)
38	Sioux City, IA	16.5
352	Sioux Falls, SD	(20.7)
56	Somerville, MA	11.9
354	South Bend, IN	(21.0)
35	South Gate, CA	17.9
376	Sparks, NV	(25.3)
5	Spokane Valley, WA	49.9
208	Spokane, WA	(6.7)
235	Springfield, IL	(8.8)
381	Springfield, MA	(26.4)
136	Springfield, MO	0.1
247	Stamford, CT	(9.5)
NA	Sterling Heights, MI**	NA
78	Stockton, CA	7.8
338	St. Joseph, MO	(18.4)
107	St. Louis, MO	4.2
293	St. Paul, MN	(13.5)
272	St. Petersburg, FL	(11.5)
148	Suffolk, VA	(1.1)
317	Sugar Land, TX	(15.8)
405	Sunnyvale, CA	(34.8)
330	Sunrise, FL	(17.1)
240	Surprise, AZ	(9.1)
190	Syracuse, NY	(5.5)
244	Tacoma, WA	(9.3)
318	Tallahassee, FL	(16.0)
49	Tampa, FL	12.6
17	Temecula, CA	27.8
42	Tempe, AZ	15.4
NA	Thornton, CO**	NA
21	Thousand Oaks, CA	23.8
81	Toledo, OH	7.6
196	Toms River Twnshp, NJ	(5.8)
198	Topeka, KS	(5.9)
407	Torrance, CA	(37.7)
288	Tracy, CA	(13.1)
203	Trenton, NJ	(6.2)
123	Troy, MI	1.2
144	Tucson, AZ	(0.7)
170	Tulsa, OK	(3.0)
NA	Tuscaloosa, AL**	NA
367	Tustin, CA	(23.1)
368	Tyler, TX	(23.3)
308	Upper Darby Twnshp, PA	(14.5)
388	Vacaville, CA	(30.2)
10	Vallejo, CA	34.2
265	Vancouver, WA	(11.1)
26	Ventura, CA	21.6
136	Victorville, CA	0.1
296	Virginia Beach, VA	(13.6)
224	Visalia, CA	(7.9)
305	Vista, CA	(14.4)
376	Waco, TX	(25.3)
238	Warren, MI	(9.0)
231	Warwick, RI	(8.5)
268	Washington, DC	(11.3)
280	Waterbury, CT	(12.3)
380	West Covina, CA	(25.9)
221	West Jordan, UT	(7.5)
110	West Palm Beach, FL	3.3
245	West Valley, UT	(9.4)
355	Westland, MI	(21.2)
58	Westminster, CA	10.9
78	Westminster, CO	7.8
205	Whittier, CA	(6.3)
187	Wichita Falls, TX	(5.0)
193	Wichita, KS	(5.7)
260	Wilmington, NC	(10.7)
90	Winston-Salem, NC	5.7
385	Woodbridge Twnshp, NJ	(27.6)
144	Worcester, MA	(0.7)
284	Yakima, WA	(12.7)
22	Yonkers, NY	22.7
363	Yuma, AZ	(22.5)

Source: CQ Press using reported data from the F.B.I. "Crime in the United States 2011"
*Aggravated assault is an attack for the purpose of inflicting severe bodily injury.
**Not available.

63. Percent Change in Aggravated Assault Rate: 2010 to 2011 (continued)
National Percent Change = 4.6% Decrease*

RANK	CITY	% CHANGE
1	Clovis, CA	62.1
2	Nashua, NH	56.8
3	Bloomington, MN	54.0
4	College Station, TX	52.0
5	Spokane Valley, WA	49.9
6	El Cajon, CA	44.1
7	Boulder, CO	41.2
8	Ogden, UT	37.7
9	Avondale, AZ	35.8
10	Vallejo, CA	34.2
11	Norman, OK	33.3
12	Arvada, CO	32.9
13	Atlanta, GA	30.3
14	Medford, OR	30.2
15	Jackson, MS	29.4
16	Allen, TX	27.9
17	Temecula, CA	27.8
18	Glendale, AZ	26.6
19	Ramapo, NY	24.9
20	Anaheim, CA	23.9
21	Thousand Oaks, CA	23.8
22	Yonkers, NY	22.7
23	Fargo, ND	22.4
23	Peoria, AZ	22.4
25	Lakeland, FL	22.1
26	Ventura, CA	21.6
27	Irvine, CA	20.9
28	Moreno Valley, CA	20.8
29	Clarkstown, NY	19.5
30	Lake Forest, CA	19.4
31	Murfreesboro, TN	18.9
32	Eugene, OR	18.5
33	Camden, NJ	18.2
33	Fort Lauderdale, FL	18.2
35	South Gate, CA	17.9
36	Kansas City, KS	17.2
37	Hamilton Twnshp, NJ	16.6
38	Sioux City, IA	16.5
39	Edinburg, TX	16.4
40	Omaha, NE	15.9
41	Denton, TX	15.7
42	Tempe, AZ	15.4
43	Salem, OR	15.2
44	Fort Wayne, IN	14.9
45	Scottsdale, AZ	14.7
46	Indio, CA	14.6
47	Independence, MO	14.0
48	Danbury, CT	13.0
49	Melbourne, FL	12.6
49	Tampa, FL	12.6
51	Carlsbad, CA	12.5
52	Clearwater, FL	12.4
53	Louisville, KY	12.3
53	McKinney, TX	12.3
55	Beaumont, TX	12.1
56	Detroit, MI	11.9
56	Somerville, MA	11.9
58	Bryan, TX	10.9
58	Fort Worth, TX	10.9
58	New York, NY	10.9
58	Westminster, CA	10.9
62	Allentown, PA	10.8
63	Rio Rancho, NM	10.7
64	Manchester, NH	10.3
65	Norwalk, CT	10.2
66	Brick Twnshp, NJ	10.1
66	Flint, MI	10.1
68	Lynn, MA	9.7
69	Hollywood, FL	9.1
70	Chattanooga, TN	9.0
71	Brockton, MA	8.7
71	Mission, TX	8.7
73	Chino, CA	8.5
74	Lee's Summit, MO	8.4
75	Palm Bay, FL	8.3
75	San Bernardino, CA	8.3
77	Seattle, WA	8.2
78	Cambridge, MA	7.8
78	Stockton, CA	7.8
78	Westminster, CO	7.8
81	Toledo, OH	7.6
82	Denver, CO	7.4
83	Joliet, IL	6.6
84	Odessa, TX	6.4
85	Chesapeake, VA	6.3
85	Durham, NC	6.3
85	Mesa, AZ	6.3
88	Decatur, IL	6.0
89	Olathe, KS	5.8
90	Athens-Clarke, GA	5.7
90	Knoxville, TN	5.7
90	Pomona, CA	5.7
90	Winston-Salem, NC	5.7
94	Green Bay, WI	5.6
94	Jersey City, NJ	5.6
96	Cedar Rapids, IA	5.3
97	Chandler, AZ	5.0
97	Oakland, CA	5.0
99	Charlotte, NC	4.9
99	Clarksville, TN	4.9
99	Dayton, OH	4.9
102	Memphis, TN	4.8
102	Phoenix, AZ	4.8
104	Houston, TX	4.7
105	Chula Vista, CA	4.4
105	Meridian, ID	4.4
107	Nashville, TN	4.2
107	St. Louis, MO	4.2
109	High Point, NC	3.5
110	Inglewood, CA	3.3
110	West Palm Beach, FL	3.3
112	New Orleans, LA	3.1
113	Cleveland, OH	2.8
114	Henderson, NV	2.6
115	Long Beach, CA	2.3
116	Baldwin Park, CA	1.9
117	Greece, NY	1.8
118	Akron, OH	1.7
118	Kent, WA	1.7
120	Murrieta, CA	1.5
121	San Marcos, CA	1.3
121	Shreveport, LA	1.3
123	Philadelphia, PA	1.2
123	Troy, MI	1.2
125	Amarillo, TX	1.1
125	Costa Mesa, CA	1.1
125	Modesto, CA	1.1
128	Newark, NJ	1.0
129	Carrollton, TX	0.9
130	Lawrence, MA	0.8
131	Miami Beach, FL	0.6
132	Aurora, CO	0.5
132	Richardson, TX	0.5
134	Miami, FL	0.3
135	Mission Viejo, CA	0.2
136	Springfield, MO	0.1
136	Victorville, CA	0.1
138	Chico, CA	0.0
139	Columbia, MO	(0.3)
139	Des Moines, IA	(0.3)
139	League City, TX	(0.3)
142	Las Cruces, NM	(0.5)
142	O'Fallon, MO	(0.5)
144	Santa Ana, CA	(0.7)
144	Tucson, AZ	(0.7)
144	Worcester, MA	(0.7)
147	Colonie, NY	(0.8)
148	Suffolk, VA	(1.1)
149	Brownsville, TX	(1.2)
150	Ann Arbor, MI	(1.3)
151	Cincinnati, OH	(1.4)
152	Dallas, TX	(1.6)
153	Fall River, MA	(1.8)
153	Portland, OR	(1.8)
155	Santa Monica, CA	(1.9)
156	Hampton, VA	(2.0)
156	Orlando, FL	(2.0)
156	Quincy, MA	(2.0)
159	Glendale, CA	(2.1)
160	Antioch, CA	(2.2)
160	Boise, ID	(2.2)
160	Redwood City, CA	(2.2)
163	Hartford, CT	(2.3)
163	Newport Beach, CA	(2.3)
165	Livonia, MI	(2.5)
166	Hesperia, CA	(2.6)
167	Evansville, IN	(2.7)
168	Irving, TX	(2.8)
169	Pearland, TX	(2.9)
170	Greeley, CO	(3.0)
170	Richmond, VA	(3.0)
170	Round Rock, TX	(3.0)
170	Tulsa, OK	(3.0)
174	Albuquerque, NM	(3.2)
175	Lakewood, CO	(3.3)
176	Broken Arrow, OK	(3.5)
177	Duluth, MN	(3.6)
177	San Angelo, TX	(3.6)
179	Arlington, TX	(3.8)
179	Gainesville, FL	(3.8)
181	Buena Park, CA	(3.9)
181	Plantation, FL	(3.9)
183	Little Rock, AR	(4.0)
184	Arlington Heights, IL	(4.2)
185	Alhambra, CA	(4.4)
186	Citrus Heights, CA	(4.7)
187	Wichita Falls, TX	(5.0)
188	San Jose, CA	(5.1)
189	Los Angeles, CA	(5.2)
190	Cheektowaga, NY	(5.5)
190	Chicago, IL	(5.5)
190	Syracuse, NY	(5.5)
193	Burbank, CA	(5.7)
193	Centennial, CO	(5.7)
193	Wichita, KS	(5.7)
196	Bethlehem, PA	(5.8)
196	Toms River Twnshp, NJ	(5.8)
198	Topeka, KS	(5.9)
199	Rialto, CA	(6.0)
200	Columbus, GA	(6.1)
200	Elizabeth, NJ	(6.1)
200	Pompano Beach, FL	(6.1)
203	Raleigh, NC	(6.2)
203	Trenton, NJ	(6.2)
205	Whittier, CA	(6.3)
206	Anchorage, AK	(6.4)
206	Kenosha, WI	(6.4)
208	Spokane, WA	(6.7)
209	Richmond, CA	(6.9)
210	Austin, TX	(7.0)
210	Savannah, GA	(7.0)
212	Amherst, NY	(7.2)
212	Jacksonville, FL	(7.2)
214	Fort Smith, AR	(7.3)
214	Hemet, CA	(7.3)
214	Paterson, NJ	(7.3)

Rank Order - City (continued)

RANK	CITY	% CHANGE	RANK	CITY	% CHANGE	RANK	CITY	% CHANGE
214	Port St. Lucie, FL	(7.3)	288	Tracy, CA	(13.1)	363	Roanoke, VA	(22.5)
218	Davie, FL	(7.4)	291	San Antonio, TX	(13.2)	363	Yuma, AZ	(22.5)
218	El Paso, TX	(7.4)	292	Hawthorne, CA	(13.3)	366	New Haven, CT	(22.9)
218	Sandy Springs, GA	(7.4)	293	Bellevue, WA	(13.5)	367	Tustin, CA	(23.1)
221	Laredo, TX	(7.5)	293	Grand Prairie, TX	(13.5)	368	Norwalk, CA	(23.3)
221	West Jordan, UT	(7.5)	293	St. Paul, MN	(13.5)	368	Tyler, TX	(23.3)
223	Fresno, CA	(7.7)	296	Virginia Beach, VA	(13.6)	370	Ontario, CA	(23.5)
224	Asheville, NC	(7.9)	297	Lancaster, CA	(13.7)	371	Charleston, SC	(24.5)
224	Colorado Springs, CO	(7.9)	297	Plano, TX	(13.7)	372	Compton, CA	(24.8)
224	Frisco, TX	(7.9)	299	Minneapolis, MN	(13.9)	372	Cranston, RI	(24.8)
224	Visalia, CA	(7.9)	299	Redding, CA	(13.9)	374	Renton, WA	(25.0)
228	Fort Collins, CO	(8.0)	301	Newport News, VA	(14.0)	375	Garden Grove, CA	(25.1)
229	Reno, NV	(8.1)	302	Fayetteville, NC	(14.1)	376	Orange, CA	(25.3)
230	Elk Grove, CA	(8.3)	302	Merced, CA	(14.1)	376	Sparks, NV	(25.3)
231	Warwick, RI	(8.5)	304	Bakersfield, CA	(14.3)	376	Waco, TX	(25.3)
232	Dearborn, MI	(8.6)	305	Canton Twnshp, MI	(14.4)	379	New Rochelle, NY	(25.8)
233	Peoria, IL	(8.7)	305	Huntington Beach, CA	(14.4)	380	West Covina, CA	(25.9)
233	San Leandro, CA	(8.7)	305	Vista, CA	(14.4)	381	Fishers, IN	(26.4)
235	Springfield, IL	(8.8)	308	Upper Darby Twnshp, PA	(14.5)	381	Springfield, MA	(26.4)
236	Alexandria, VA	(8.9)	309	Hialeah, FL	(14.8)	383	Elgin, IL	(27.1)
236	Oceanside, CA	(8.9)	310	Rancho Cucamon., CA	(15.2)	384	Bloomington, IN	(27.4)
238	Oklahoma City, OK	(9.0)	311	Bloomington, IL	(15.3)	385	Woodbridge Twnshp, NJ	(27.6)
238	Warren, MI	(9.0)	312	Portsmouth, VA	(15.4)	386	Macon, GA	(28.3)
240	Baltimore, MD	(9.1)	313	Kennewick, WA	(15.5)	387	Fremont, CA	(29.2)
240	Overland Park, KS	(9.1)	313	Lawton, OK	(15.5)	388	Vacaville, CA	(30.2)
240	Surprise, AZ	(9.1)	313	New Bedford, MA	(15.5)	389	Hammond, IN	(30.5)
243	Carson, CA	(9.2)	316	Fairfield, CA	(15.6)	390	Beaverton, OR	(30.7)
244	Tacoma, WA	(9.3)	317	Sugar Land, TX	(15.8)	391	Pasadena, CA	(31.6)
245	San Diego, CA	(9.4)	318	Tallahassee, FL	(16.0)	392	Fullerton, CA	(32.1)
245	West Valley, UT	(9.4)	319	Coral Springs, FL	(16.1)	393	Santa Clarita, CA	(32.2)
247	Lawrence, KS	(9.5)	320	Pittsburgh, PA	(16.2)	394	Edmond, OK	(32.4)
247	Madison, WI	(9.5)	321	Lafayette, LA	(16.3)	395	Abilene, TX	(32.9)
247	Norfolk, VA	(9.5)	322	Grand Rapids, MI	(16.4)	396	Longview, TX	(33.1)
247	Reading, PA	(9.5)	323	Sacramento, CA	(16.5)	397	Bellflower, CA	(33.3)
247	Stamford, CT	(9.5)	324	Gresham, OR	(16.8)	398	Concord, CA	(33.4)
252	Garland, TX	(9.8)	324	Hayward, CA	(16.8)	398	Largo, FL	(33.4)
252	Lansing, MI	(9.8)	324	Santa Rosa, CA	(16.8)	400	El Monte, CA	(33.5)
252	Salt Lake City, UT	(9.8)	327	Simi Valley, CA	(16.9)	400	Farmington Hills, MI	(33.5)
255	Nampa, ID	(9.9)	328	Killeen, TX	(17.0)	402	Lincoln, NE	(33.8)
255	Pasadena, TX	(9.9)	328	Miami Gardens, FL	(17.0)	403	Lakewood, CA	(34.0)
257	Corona, CA	(10.3)	330	Deerfield Beach, FL	(17.1)	404	Mesquite, TX	(34.7)
258	Palmdale, CA	(10.4)	330	Livermore, CA	(17.1)	405	Sunnyvale, CA	(34.8)
259	Riverside, CA	(10.6)	330	Sunrise, FL	(17.1)	406	Bellingham, WA	(37.2)
260	Wilmington, NC	(10.7)	333	Scranton, PA	(17.3)	407	Torrance, CA	(37.7)
261	Gilbert, AZ	(10.9)	334	Boca Raton, FL	(17.5)	408	Lowell, MA	(40.4)
261	Milwaukee, WI	(10.9)	335	Napa, CA	(17.6)	409	Concord, NC	(42.1)
263	Lewisville, TX	(11.0)	336	Midland, TX	(18.0)	410	Roswell, GA	(44.6)
263	Santa Barbara, CA	(11.0)	337	Daly City, CA	(18.3)	411	Orem, UT	(49.5)
265	Pembroke Pines, FL	(11.1)	338	Lynchburg, VA	(18.4)	412	Johns Creek, GA	(54.3)
265	Vancouver, WA	(11.1)	338	St. Joseph, MO	(18.4)	413	Menifee, CA	(60.9)
267	Newton, MA	(11.2)	340	Chino Hills, CA	(18.5)	414	Carmel, IN	(83.7)
268	Fontana, CA	(11.3)	341	Santa Clara, CA	(18.8)	NA	Baton Rouge, LA**	NA
268	Washington, DC	(11.3)	342	Las Vegas, NV	(18.9)	NA	Billings, MT**	NA
270	Downey, CA	(11.4)	343	Aurora, IL	(19.0)	NA	Birmingham, AL**	NA
270	San Francisco, CA	(11.4)	343	Rochester, MN	(19.0)	NA	Brooklyn Park, MN**	NA
272	Corpus Christi, TX	(11.5)	345	Clinton Twnshp, MI	(19.4)	NA	Buffalo, NY**	NA
272	Erie, PA	(11.5)	346	Edison Twnshp, NJ	(19.5)	NA	Champaign, IL**	NA
272	St. Petersburg, FL	(11.5)	347	Escondido, CA	(19.6)	NA	Cicero, IL**	NA
275	Albany, NY	(11.6)	348	Albany, GA	(19.7)	NA	Clifton, NJ**	NA
276	Cape Coral, FL	(11.7)	348	Santa Maria, CA	(19.7)	NA	Davenport, IA**	NA
276	Columbus, OH	(11.7)	350	Longmont, CO	(19.8)	NA	Gary, IN**	NA
278	Everett, WA	(12.0)	351	San Mateo, CA	(20.5)	NA	Hillsboro, OR**	NA
279	McAllen, TX	(12.1)	352	Provo, UT	(20.7)	NA	Hoover, AL**	NA
280	Boston, MA	(12.3)	352	Sioux Falls, SD	(20.7)	NA	Huntsville, AL**	NA
280	Waterbury, CT	(12.3)	354	South Bend, IN	(21.0)	NA	Indianapolis, IN**	NA
282	Oxnard, CA	(12.4)	355	Bend, OR	(21.2)	NA	Kansas City, MO**	NA
283	North Charleston, SC	(12.6)	355	Westland, MI	(21.2)	NA	Lexington, KY**	NA
284	Yakima, WA	(12.7)	357	Berkeley, CA	(21.4)	NA	Mobile, AL**	NA
285	Bridgeport, CT	(12.8)	358	Lakewood Twnshp, NJ	(21.6)	NA	Montgomery, AL**	NA
286	Lubbock, TX	(12.9)	359	Roseville, CA	(21.7)	NA	Naperville, IL**	NA
286	Rockford, IL	(12.9)	359	Sandy, UT	(21.7)	NA	Pueblo, CO**	NA
288	Rochester, NY	(13.1)	361	Cary, NC	(21.8)	NA	Sterling Heights, MI**	NA
288	Salinas, CA	(13.1)	362	Miramar, FL	(22.1)	NA	Thornton, CO**	NA
			363	Racine, WI	(22.5)	NA	Tuscaloosa, AL**	NA

Source: CQ Press using reported data from the F.B.I. "Crime in the United States 2011"
*Aggravated assault is an attack for the purpose of inflicting severe bodily injury.
**Not available.

Alpha Order - City

64. Percent Change in Aggravated Assault Rate: 2007 to 2011
National Percent Change = 16.1% Decrease*

RANK	CITY	% CHANGE	RANK	CITY	% CHANGE	RANK	CITY	% CHANGE
326	Abilene, TX	(34.6)	308	Cheektowaga, NY	(32.0)	15	Fort Wayne, IN	41.4
13	Akron, OH	42.0	73	Chesapeake, VA	3.6	70	Fort Worth, TX	4.6
78	Albany, GA	2.2	263	Chicago, IL	(25.6)	382	Fremont, CA	(46.8)
223	Albany, NY	(21.0)	394	Chico, CA	(56.2)	121	Fresno, CA	(4.5)
200	Albuquerque, NM	(17.7)	62	Chino Hills, CA	7.8	46	Frisco, TX	11.9
364	Alexandria, VA	(42.5)	10	Chino, CA	52.9	271	Fullerton, CA	(27.1)
60	Alhambra, CA	8.2	246	Chula Vista, CA	(23.5)	293	Gainesville, FL	(30.1)
236	Allentown, PA	(22.4)	NA	Cicero, IL**	NA	275	Garden Grove, CA	(27.3)
39	Allen, TX	15.7	131	Cincinnati, OH	(6.1)	375	Garland, TX	(44.8)
318	Amarillo, TX	(33.1)	NA	Citrus Heights, CA**	NA	23	Gary, IN	29.7
156	Amherst, NY	(9.9)	21	Clarkstown, NY	32.9	347	Gilbert, AZ	(38.0)
110	Anaheim, CA	(3.4)	240	Clarksville, TN	(22.8)	254	Glendale, AZ	(24.8)
132	Anchorage, AK	(6.9)	118	Clearwater, FL	(4.0)	276	Glendale, CA	(28.1)
207	Ann Arbor, MI	(18.4)	71	Cleveland, OH	4.2	148	Grand Prairie, TX	(9.2)
32	Antioch, CA	20.0	166	Clifton, NJ	(11.4)	241	Grand Rapids, MI	(22.9)
NA	Arlington Heights, IL**	NA	80	Clinton Twnshp, MI	1.7	67	Greece, NY	5.5
293	Arlington, TX	(30.1)	3	Clovis, CA	94.3	110	Greeley, CO	(3.4)
271	Arvada, CO	(27.1)	69	College Station, TX	4.9	371	Green Bay, WI	(43.8)
177	Asheville, NC	(14.7)	399	Colonie, NY	(66.2)	172	Gresham, OR	(13.4)
106	Athens-Clarke, GA	(2.8)	197	Colorado Springs, CO	(17.4)	43	Hamilton Twnshp, NJ	12.3
104	Atlanta, GA	(2.6)	257	Columbia, MO	(25.3)	152	Hammond, IN	(9.4)
233	Aurora, CO	(22.2)	265	Columbus, GA	(26.0)	208	Hampton, VA	(18.5)
344	Aurora, IL	(37.5)	278	Columbus, OH	(28.3)	17	Hartford, CT	40.0
143	Austin, TX	(8.2)	368	Compton, CA	(43.0)	189	Hawthorne, CA	(16.5)
NA	Avondale, AZ**	NA	42	Concord, CA	13.8	370	Hayward, CA	(43.6)
160	Bakersfield, CA	(10.4)	403	Concord, NC	(71.6)	315	Hemet, CA	(32.7)
117	Baldwin Park, CA	(3.9)	257	Coral Springs, FL	(25.3)	68	Henderson, NV	5.0
192	Baltimore, MD	(16.9)	303	Corona, CA	(31.2)	120	Hesperia, CA	(4.4)
93	Baton Rouge, LA	(1.2)	218	Corpus Christi, TX	(19.7)	255	Hialeah, FL	(24.9)
180	Beaumont, TX	(15.2)	222	Costa Mesa, CA	(20.7)	227	High Point, NC	(21.5)
234	Beaverton, OR	(22.3)	152	Cranston, RI	(9.4)	86	Hillsboro, OR	0.0
37	Bellevue, WA	15.9	288	Dallas, TX	(29.4)	55	Hollywood, FL	9.6
341	Bellflower, CA	(37.3)	35	Daly City, CA	17.6	NA	Hoover, AL**	NA
77	Bellingham, WA	2.3	64	Danbury, CT	6.7	89	Houston, TX	(0.2)
9	Bend, OR	54.3	NA	Davenport, IA**	NA	63	Huntington Beach, CA	7.7
352	Berkeley, CA	(39.4)	34	Davie, FL	18.0	NA	Huntsville, AL**	NA
288	Bethlehem, PA	(29.4)	145	Dayton, OH	(8.6)	386	Independence, MO	(49.7)
NA	Billings, MT**	NA	267	Dearborn, MI	(26.3)	104	Indianapolis, IN	(2.6)
NA	Birmingham, AL**	NA	NA	Decatur, IL**	NA	5	Indio, CA	65.1
NA	Bloomington, IL**	NA	331	Deerfield Beach, FL	(35.8)	152	Inglewood, CA	(9.4)
226	Bloomington, IN	(21.4)	108	Denton, TX	(3.0)	193	Irvine, CA	(17.0)
50	Bloomington, MN	10.3	138	Denver, CO	(7.4)	327	Irving, TX	(34.7)
287	Boca Raton, FL	(29.3)	261	Des Moines, IA	(25.4)	327	Jacksonville, FL	(34.7)
201	Boise, ID	(17.9)	138	Detroit, MI	(7.4)	20	Jackson, MS	38.0
315	Boston, MA	(32.7)	252	Downey, CA	(24.6)	244	Jersey City, NJ	(23.1)
30	Boulder, CO	21.2	334	Duluth, MN	(36.1)	NA	Johns Creek, GA**	NA
142	Brick Twnshp, NJ	(8.0)	NA	Durham, NC**	NA	96	Joliet, IL	(1.6)
220	Bridgeport, CT	(20.2)	157	Edinburg, TX	(10.1)	127	Kansas City, KS	(4.9)
NA	Brockton, MA**	NA	391	Edison Twnshp, NJ	(53.1)	NA	Kansas City, MO**	NA
380	Broken Arrow, OK	(46.3)	256	Edmond, OK	(25.2)	201	Kennewick, WA	(17.9)
373	Brooklyn Park, MN	(44.6)	90	El Cajon, CA	(0.7)	245	Kenosha, WI	(23.3)
379	Brownsville, TX	(45.9)	388	El Monte, CA	(50.8)	109	Kent, WA	(3.3)
352	Bryan, TX	(39.4)	52	El Paso, TX	9.9	175	Killeen, TX	(14.1)
204	Buena Park, CA	(18.0)	47	Elgin, IL	11.3	187	Knoxville, TN	(16.4)
NA	Buffalo, NY**	NA	4	Elizabeth, NJ	88.1	345	Lafayette, LA	(37.9)
321	Burbank, CA	(33.8)	49	Elk Grove, CA	10.5	38	Lake Forest, CA	15.8
58	Cambridge, MA	9.2	97	Erie, PA	(1.8)	123	Lakeland, FL	(4.7)
19	Camden, NJ	39.0	249	Escondido, CA	(23.8)	389	Lakewood Twnshp, NJ	(51.9)
44	Canton Twnshp, MI	12.0	84	Eugene, OR	1.3	375	Lakewood, CA	(44.8)
340	Cape Coral, FL	(37.1)	129	Evansville, IN	(5.0)	107	Lakewood, CO	(2.9)
320	Carlsbad, CA	(33.6)	190	Everett, WA	(16.7)	355	Lancaster, CA	(39.9)
404	Carmel, IN	(75.5)	309	Fairfield, CA	(32.1)	145	Lansing, MI	(8.6)
126	Carrollton, TX	(4.8)	NA	Fall River, MA**	NA	170	Laredo, TX	(13.2)
264	Carson, CA	(25.7)	6	Fargo, ND	64.3	369	Largo, FL	(43.4)
298	Cary, NC	(30.9)	363	Farmington Hills, MI	(41.3)	83	Las Cruces, NM	1.5
300	Cedar Rapids, IA	(31.0)	384	Fayetteville, NC	(47.5)	219	Las Vegas, NV	(19.8)
103	Centennial, CO	(2.5)	402	Fishers, IN	(71.3)	148	Lawrence, KS	(9.2)
NA	Champaign, IL**	NA	112	Flint, MI	(3.6)	24	Lawrence, MA	27.2
155	Chandler, AZ	(9.7)	291	Fontana, CA	(30.0)	329	Lawton, OK	(35.2)
400	Charleston, SC	(69.1)	158	Fort Collins, CO	(10.3)	360	League City, TX	(40.9)
270	Charlotte, NC	(26.9)	54	Fort Lauderdale, FL	9.7	130	Lee's Summit, MO	(5.7)
310	Chattanooga, TN	(32.2)	262	Fort Smith, AR	(25.5)	36	Lewisville, TX	16.5

Alpha Order - City (continued)

RANK	CITY	% CHANGE	RANK	CITY	% CHANGE	RANK	CITY	% CHANGE
NA	Lexington, KY**	NA	195	Overland Park, KS	(17.1)	158	Sioux City, IA	(10.3)
372	Lincoln, NE	(44.1)	196	Oxnard, CA	(17.3)	99	Sioux Falls, SD	(2.2)
101	Little Rock, AR	(2.3)	115	Palm Bay, FL	(3.8)	44	Somerville, MA	12.0
1	Livermore, CA	149.1	283	Palmdale, CA	(29.1)	102	South Bend, IN	(2.4)
41	Livonia, MI	14.1	359	Pasadena, CA	(40.8)	22	South Gate, CA	32.6
208	Long Beach, CA	(18.5)	179	Pasadena, TX	(15.1)	186	Sparks, NV	(16.3)
NA	Longmont, CO**	NA	137	Paterson, NJ	(7.3)	397	Spokane Valley, WA	(60.1)
382	Longview, TX	(46.8)	121	Pearland, TX	(4.5)	181	Spokane, WA	(15.3)
300	Los Angeles, CA	(31.0)	313	Pembroke Pines, FL	(32.5)	351	Springfield, IL	(39.2)
95	Louisville, KY	(1.4)	127	Peoria, AZ	(4.9)	239	Springfield, MA	(22.7)
115	Lowell, MA	(3.8)	94	Peoria, IL	(1.3)	25	Springfield, MO	25.1
208	Lubbock, TX	(18.5)	170	Philadelphia, PA	(13.2)	144	Stamford, CT	(8.5)
284	Lynchburg, VA	(29.2)	229	Phoenix, AZ	(21.7)	NA	Sterling Heights, MI**	NA
191	Lynn, MA	(16.8)	257	Pittsburgh, PA	(25.3)	56	Stockton, CA	9.5
250	Macon, GA	(24.4)	385	Plano, TX	(48.7)	31	St. Joseph, MO	21.1
60	Madison, WI	8.2	80	Plantation, FL	1.7	178	St. Louis, MO	(15.0)
NA	Manchester, NH**	NA	232	Pomona, CA	(22.1)	246	St. Paul, MN	(23.5)
347	McAllen, TX	(38.0)	295	Pompano Beach, FL	(30.2)	336	St. Petersburg, FL	(36.6)
161	McKinney, TX	(10.6)	197	Port St. Lucie, FL	(17.4)	284	Suffolk, VA	(29.2)
16	Medford, OR	40.8	221	Portland, OR	(20.4)	14	Sugar Land, TX	41.9
123	Melbourne, FL	(4.7)	339	Portsmouth, VA	(36.7)	281	Sunnyvale, CA	(28.9)
148	Memphis, TN	(9.2)	167	Provo, UT	(12.0)	234	Sunrise, FL	(22.3)
NA	Menifee, CA**	NA	NA	Pueblo, CO**	NA	367	Surprise, AZ	(42.9)
253	Merced, CA	(24.7)	7	Quincy, MA	61.6	163	Syracuse, NY	(10.8)
181	Meridian, ID	(15.3)	347	Racine, WI	(38.0)	277	Tacoma, WA	(28.2)
173	Mesa, AZ	(13.5)	284	Raleigh, NC	(29.2)	211	Tallahassee, FL	(18.6)
381	Mesquite, TX	(46.5)	11	Ramapo, NY	50.1	307	Tampa, FL	(31.9)
204	Miami Beach, FL	(18.0)	243	Rancho Cucamon., CA	(23.0)	401	Temecula, CA	(71.1)
395	Miami Gardens, FL	(56.5)	90	Reading, PA	(0.7)	79	Tempe, AZ	1.8
224	Miami, FL	(21.1)	2	Redding, CA	98.3	NA	Thornton, CO**	NA
48	Midland, TX	10.7	398	Redwood City, CA	(63.4)	75	Thousand Oaks, CA	3.3
341	Milwaukee, WI	(37.3)	271	Reno, NV	(27.1)	279	Toledo, OH	(28.4)
330	Minneapolis, MN	(35.5)	229	Renton, WA	(21.7)	361	Toms River Twnshp, NJ	(41.1)
288	Miramar, FL	(29.4)	354	Rialto, CA	(39.8)	65	Topeka, KS	6.6
168	Mission Viejo, CA	(12.6)	313	Richardson, TX	(32.5)	306	Torrance, CA	(31.8)
165	Mission, TX	(11.0)	85	Richmond, CA	0.2	123	Tracy, CA	(4.7)
NA	Mobile, AL**	NA	201	Richmond, VA	(17.9)	33	Trenton, NJ	18.6
112	Modesto, CA	(3.6)	361	Rio Rancho, NM	(41.1)	185	Troy, MI	(16.1)
NA	Montgomery, AL**	NA	300	Riverside, CA	(31.0)	176	Tucson, AZ	(14.5)
271	Moreno Valley, CA	(27.1)	357	Roanoke, VA	(40.1)	238	Tulsa, OK	(22.5)
199	Murfreesboro, TN	(17.5)	319	Rochester, MN	(33.4)	NA	Tuscaloosa, AL**	NA
174	Murrieta, CA	(14.0)	99	Rochester, NY	(2.2)	181	Tustin, CA	(15.3)
112	Nampa, ID	(3.6)	66	Rockford, IL	6.5	250	Tyler, TX	(24.4)
296	Napa, CA	(30.3)	325	Roseville, CA	(34.5)	8	Upper Darby Twnshp, PA	58.5
52	Naperville, IL	9.9	393	Roswell, GA	(55.7)	214	Vacaville, CA	(19.1)
NA	Nashua, NH**	NA	291	Round Rock, TX	(30.0)	364	Vallejo, CA	(42.5)
216	Nashville, TN	(19.5)	305	Sacramento, CA	(31.5)	132	Vancouver, WA	(6.9)
134	New Bedford, MA	(7.1)	140	Salem, OR	(7.5)	169	Ventura, CA	(12.7)
NA	New Haven, CT**	NA	134	Salinas, CA	(7.1)	119	Victorville, CA	(4.3)
396	New Orleans, LA	(57.3)	212	Salt Lake City, UT	(18.8)	322	Virginia Beach, VA	(33.9)
147	New Rochelle, NY	(8.8)	343	San Angelo, TX	(37.4)	303	Visalia, CA	(31.2)
57	New York, NY	9.4	51	San Antonio, TX	10.1	311	Vista, CA	(32.3)
88	Newark, NJ	(0.1)	187	San Bernardino, CA	(16.4)	373	Waco, TX	(44.6)
358	Newport Beach, CA	(40.3)	206	San Diego, CA	(18.2)	151	Warren, MI	(9.3)
336	Newport News, VA	(36.6)	228	San Francisco, CA	(21.6)	NA	Warwick, RI**	NA
86	Newton, MA	0.0	268	San Jose, CA	(26.4)	225	Washington, DC	(21.3)
269	Norfolk, VA	(26.5)	387	San Leandro, CA	(50.5)	134	Waterbury, CT	(7.1)
248	Norman, OK	(23.6)	184	San Marcos, CA	(15.4)	280	West Covina, CA	(28.8)
390	North Charleston, SC	(53.0)	236	San Mateo, CA	(22.4)	28	West Jordan, UT	21.4
366	Norwalk, CA	(42.8)	98	Sandy Springs, GA	(2.1)	162	West Palm Beach, FL	(10.7)
73	Norwalk, CT	3.6	332	Sandy, UT	(35.9)	76	West Valley, UT	2.8
216	Oakland, CA	(19.5)	345	Santa Ana, CA	(37.9)	312	Westland, MI	(32.4)
350	Oceanside, CA	(38.5)	336	Santa Barbara, CA	(36.6)	265	Westminster, CA	(26.0)
17	Odessa, TX	40.0	282	Santa Clara, CA	(29.0)	72	Westminster, CO	3.8
12	O'Fallon, MO	49.4	324	Santa Clarita, CA	(34.3)	29	Whittier, CA	21.3
241	Ogden, UT	(22.9)	59	Santa Maria, CA	8.3	193	Wichita Falls, TX	(17.0)
39	Oklahoma City, OK	15.7	334	Santa Monica, CA	(36.1)	212	Wichita, KS	(18.8)
NA	Olathe, KS**	NA	231	Santa Rosa, CA	(21.8)	215	Wilmington, NC	(19.4)
141	Omaha, NE	(7.6)	323	Savannah, GA	(34.0)	NA	Winston-Salem, NC**	NA
355	Ontario, CA	(39.9)	82	Scottsdale, AZ	1.6	378	Woodbridge Twnshp, NJ	(45.6)
392	Orange, CA	(53.9)	163	Scranton, PA	(10.8)	27	Worcester, MA	22.1
377	Orem, UT	(45.2)	92	Seattle, WA	(0.9)	298	Yakima, WA	(30.9)
333	Orlando, FL	(36.0)	297	Shreveport, LA	(30.7)	26	Yonkers, NY	22.5
			317	Simi Valley, CA	(33.0)	257	Yuma, AZ	(25.3)

Source: CQ Press using reported data from the F.B.I. "Crime in the United States 2011"
*Aggravated assault is an attack for the purpose of inflicting severe bodily injury.
**Not available.

Rank Order - City
64. Percent Change in Aggravated Assault Rate: 2007 to 2011 (continued)
National Percent Change = 16.1% Decrease*

RANK	CITY	% CHANGE	RANK	CITY	% CHANGE	RANK	CITY	% CHANGE
1	Livermore, CA	149.1	73	Chesapeake, VA	3.6	145	Dayton, OH	(8.6)
2	Redding, CA	98.3	73	Norwalk, CT	3.6	145	Lansing, MI	(8.6)
3	Clovis, CA	94.3	75	Thousand Oaks, CA	3.3	147	New Rochelle, NY	(8.8)
4	Elizabeth, NJ	88.1	76	West Valley, UT	2.8	148	Grand Prairie, TX	(9.2)
5	Indio, CA	65.1	77	Bellingham, WA	2.3	148	Lawrence, KS	(9.2)
6	Fargo, ND	64.3	78	Albany, GA	2.2	148	Memphis, TN	(9.2)
7	Quincy, MA	61.6	79	Tempe, AZ	1.8	151	Warren, MI	(9.3)
8	Upper Darby Twnshp, PA	58.5	80	Clinton Twnshp, MI	1.7	152	Cranston, RI	(9.4)
9	Bend, OR	54.3	80	Plantation, FL	1.7	152	Hammond, IN	(9.4)
10	Chino, CA	52.9	82	Scottsdale, AZ	1.6	152	Inglewood, CA	(9.4)
11	Ramapo, NY	50.1	83	Las Cruces, NM	1.5	155	Chandler, AZ	(9.7)
12	O'Fallon, MO	49.4	84	Eugene, OR	1.3	156	Amherst, NY	(9.9)
13	Akron, OH	42.0	85	Richmond, CA	0.2	157	Edinburg, TX	(10.1)
14	Sugar Land, TX	41.9	86	Hillsboro, OR	0.0	158	Fort Collins, CO	(10.3)
15	Fort Wayne, IN	41.4	86	Newton, MA	0.0	158	Sioux City, IA	(10.3)
16	Medford, OR	40.8	88	Newark, NJ	(0.1)	160	Bakersfield, CA	(10.4)
17	Hartford, CT	40.0	89	Houston, TX	(0.2)	161	McKinney, TX	(10.6)
17	Odessa, TX	40.0	90	El Cajon, CA	(0.7)	162	West Palm Beach, FL	(10.7)
19	Camden, NJ	39.0	90	Reading, PA	(0.7)	163	Scranton, PA	(10.8)
20	Jackson, MS	38.0	92	Seattle, WA	(0.9)	163	Syracuse, NY	(10.8)
21	Clarkstown, NY	32.9	93	Baton Rouge, LA	(1.2)	165	Mission, TX	(11.0)
22	South Gate, CA	32.6	94	Peoria, IL	(1.3)	166	Clifton, NJ	(11.4)
23	Gary, IN	29.7	95	Louisville, KY	(1.4)	167	Provo, UT	(12.0)
24	Lawrence, MA	27.2	96	Joliet, IL	(1.6)	168	Mission Viejo, CA	(12.6)
25	Springfield, MO	25.1	97	Erie, PA	(1.8)	169	Ventura, CA	(12.7)
26	Yonkers, NY	22.5	98	Sandy Springs, GA	(2.1)	170	Laredo, TX	(13.2)
27	Worcester, MA	22.1	99	Rochester, NY	(2.2)	170	Philadelphia, PA	(13.2)
28	West Jordan, UT	21.4	99	Sioux Falls, SD	(2.2)	172	Gresham, OR	(13.4)
29	Whittier, CA	21.3	101	Little Rock, AR	(2.3)	173	Mesa, AZ	(13.5)
30	Boulder, CO	21.2	102	South Bend, IN	(2.4)	174	Murrieta, CA	(14.0)
31	St. Joseph, MO	21.1	103	Centennial, CO	(2.5)	175	Killeen, TX	(14.1)
32	Antioch, CA	20.0	104	Atlanta, GA	(2.6)	176	Tucson, AZ	(14.5)
33	Trenton, NJ	18.6	104	Indianapolis, IN	(2.6)	177	Asheville, NC	(14.7)
34	Davie, FL	18.0	106	Athens-Clarke, GA	(2.8)	178	St. Louis, MO	(15.0)
35	Daly City, CA	17.6	107	Lakewood, CO	(2.9)	179	Pasadena, TX	(15.1)
36	Lewisville, TX	16.5	108	Denton, TX	(3.0)	180	Beaumont, TX	(15.2)
37	Bellevue, WA	15.9	109	Kent, WA	(3.3)	181	Meridian, ID	(15.3)
38	Lake Forest, CA	15.8	110	Anaheim, CA	(3.4)	181	Spokane, WA	(15.3)
39	Allen, TX	15.7	110	Greeley, CO	(3.4)	181	Tustin, CA	(15.3)
39	Oklahoma City, OK	15.7	112	Flint, MI	(3.6)	184	San Marcos, CA	(15.4)
41	Livonia, MI	14.1	112	Modesto, CA	(3.6)	185	Troy, MI	(16.1)
42	Concord, CA	13.8	112	Nampa, ID	(3.6)	186	Sparks, NV	(16.3)
43	Hamilton Twnshp, NJ	12.3	115	Lowell, MA	(3.8)	187	Knoxville, TN	(16.4)
44	Canton Twnshp, MI	12.0	115	Palm Bay, FL	(3.8)	187	San Bernardino, CA	(16.4)
44	Somerville, MA	12.0	117	Baldwin Park, CA	(3.9)	189	Hawthorne, CA	(16.5)
46	Frisco, TX	11.9	118	Clearwater, FL	(4.0)	190	Everett, WA	(16.7)
47	Elgin, IL	11.3	119	Victorville, CA	(4.3)	191	Lynn, MA	(16.8)
48	Midland, TX	10.7	120	Hesperia, CA	(4.4)	192	Baltimore, MD	(16.9)
49	Elk Grove, CA	10.5	121	Fresno, CA	(4.5)	193	Irvine, CA	(17.0)
50	Bloomington, MN	10.3	121	Pearland, TX	(4.5)	193	Wichita Falls, TX	(17.0)
51	San Antonio, TX	10.1	123	Lakeland, FL	(4.7)	195	Overland Park, KS	(17.1)
52	El Paso, TX	9.9	123	Melbourne, FL	(4.7)	196	Oxnard, CA	(17.3)
52	Naperville, IL	9.9	123	Tracy, CA	(4.7)	197	Colorado Springs, CO	(17.4)
54	Fort Lauderdale, FL	9.7	126	Carrollton, TX	(4.8)	197	Port St. Lucie, FL	(17.4)
55	Hollywood, FL	9.6	127	Kansas City, KS	(4.9)	199	Murfreesboro, TN	(17.5)
56	Stockton, CA	9.5	127	Peoria, AZ	(4.9)	200	Albuquerque, NM	(17.7)
57	New York, NY	9.4	129	Evansville, IN	(5.0)	201	Boise, ID	(17.9)
58	Cambridge, MA	9.2	130	Lee's Summit, MO	(5.7)	201	Kennewick, WA	(17.9)
59	Santa Maria, CA	8.3	131	Cincinnati, OH	(6.1)	201	Richmond, VA	(17.9)
60	Alhambra, CA	8.2	132	Anchorage, AK	(6.9)	204	Buena Park, CA	(18.0)
60	Madison, WI	8.2	132	Vancouver, WA	(6.9)	204	Miami Beach, FL	(18.0)
62	Chino Hills, CA	7.8	134	New Bedford, MA	(7.1)	206	San Diego, CA	(18.2)
63	Huntington Beach, CA	7.7	134	Salinas, CA	(7.1)	207	Ann Arbor, MI	(18.4)
64	Danbury, CT	6.7	134	Waterbury, CT	(7.1)	208	Hampton, VA	(18.5)
65	Topeka, KS	6.6	137	Paterson, NJ	(7.3)	208	Long Beach, CA	(18.5)
66	Rockford, IL	6.5	138	Denver, CO	(7.4)	208	Lubbock, TX	(18.5)
67	Greece, NY	5.5	138	Detroit, MI	(7.4)	211	Tallahassee, FL	(18.6)
68	Henderson, NV	5.0	140	Salem, OR	(7.5)	212	Salt Lake City, UT	(18.8)
69	College Station, TX	4.9	141	Omaha, NE	(7.6)	212	Wichita, KS	(18.8)
70	Fort Worth, TX	4.6	142	Brick Twnshp, NJ	(8.0)	214	Vacaville, CA	(19.1)
71	Cleveland, OH	4.2	143	Austin, TX	(8.2)	215	Wilmington, NC	(19.4)
72	Westminster, CO	3.8	144	Stamford, CT	(8.5)	216	Nashville, TN	(19.5)

Rank Order - City (continued)

RANK	CITY	% CHANGE	RANK	CITY	% CHANGE	RANK	CITY	% CHANGE
216	Oakland, CA	(19.5)	288	Miramar, FL	(29.4)	364	Alexandria, VA	(42.5)
218	Corpus Christi, TX	(19.7)	291	Fontana, CA	(30.0)	364	Vallejo, CA	(42.5)
219	Las Vegas, NV	(19.8)	291	Round Rock, TX	(30.0)	366	Norwalk, CA	(42.8)
220	Bridgeport, CT	(20.2)	293	Arlington, TX	(30.1)	367	Surprise, AZ	(42.9)
221	Portland, OR	(20.4)	293	Gainesville, FL	(30.1)	368	Compton, CA	(43.0)
222	Costa Mesa, CA	(20.7)	295	Pompano Beach, FL	(30.2)	369	Largo, FL	(43.4)
223	Albany, NY	(21.0)	296	Napa, CA	(30.3)	370	Hayward, CA	(43.6)
224	Miami, FL	(21.1)	297	Shreveport, LA	(30.7)	371	Green Bay, WI	(43.8)
225	Washington, DC	(21.3)	298	Cary, NC	(30.9)	372	Lincoln, NE	(44.1)
226	Bloomington, IN	(21.4)	298	Yakima, WA	(30.9)	373	Brooklyn Park, MN	(44.6)
227	High Point, NC	(21.5)	300	Cedar Rapids, IA	(31.0)	373	Waco, TX	(44.6)
228	San Francisco, CA	(21.6)	300	Los Angeles, CA	(31.0)	375	Garland, TX	(44.8)
229	Phoenix, AZ	(21.7)	300	Riverside, CA	(31.0)	375	Lakewood, CA	(44.8)
229	Renton, WA	(21.7)	303	Corona, CA	(31.2)	377	Orem, UT	(45.2)
231	Santa Rosa, CA	(21.8)	303	Visalia, CA	(31.2)	378	Woodbridge Twnshp, NJ	(45.6)
232	Pomona, CA	(22.1)	305	Sacramento, CA	(31.5)	379	Brownsville, TX	(45.9)
233	Aurora, CO	(22.2)	306	Torrance, CA	(31.8)	380	Broken Arrow, OK	(46.3)
234	Beaverton, OR	(22.3)	307	Tampa, FL	(31.9)	381	Mesquite, TX	(46.5)
234	Sunrise, FL	(22.3)	308	Cheektowaga, NY	(32.0)	382	Fremont, CA	(46.8)
236	Allentown, PA	(22.4)	309	Fairfield, CA	(32.1)	382	Longview, TX	(46.8)
236	San Mateo, CA	(22.4)	310	Chattanooga, TN	(32.2)	384	Fayetteville, NC	(47.5)
238	Tulsa, OK	(22.5)	311	Vista, CA	(32.3)	385	Plano, TX	(48.7)
239	Springfield, MA	(22.7)	312	Westland, MI	(32.4)	386	Independence, MO	(49.7)
240	Clarksville, TN	(22.8)	313	Pembroke Pines, FL	(32.5)	387	San Leandro, CA	(50.5)
241	Grand Rapids, MI	(22.9)	313	Richardson, TX	(32.5)	388	El Monte, CA	(50.8)
241	Ogden, UT	(22.9)	315	Boston, MA	(32.7)	389	Lakewood Twnshp, NJ	(51.9)
243	Rancho Cucamon., CA	(23.0)	315	Hemet, CA	(32.7)	390	North Charleston, SC	(53.0)
244	Jersey City, NJ	(23.1)	317	Simi Valley, CA	(33.0)	391	Edison Twnshp, NJ	(53.1)
245	Kenosha, WI	(23.3)	318	Amarillo, TX	(33.1)	392	Orange, CA	(53.9)
246	Chula Vista, CA	(23.5)	319	Rochester, MN	(33.4)	393	Roswell, GA	(55.7)
246	St. Paul, MN	(23.5)	320	Carlsbad, CA	(33.6)	394	Chico, CA	(56.2)
248	Norman, OK	(23.6)	321	Burbank, CA	(33.8)	395	Miami Gardens, FL	(56.5)
249	Escondido, CA	(23.8)	322	Virginia Beach, VA	(33.9)	396	New Orleans, LA	(57.3)
250	Macon, GA	(24.4)	323	Savannah, GA	(34.0)	397	Spokane Valley, WA	(60.1)
250	Tyler, TX	(24.4)	324	Santa Clarita, CA	(34.3)	398	Redwood City, CA	(63.4)
252	Downey, CA	(24.6)	325	Roseville, CA	(34.5)	399	Colonie, NY	(66.2)
253	Merced, CA	(24.7)	326	Abilene, TX	(34.6)	400	Charleston, SC	(69.1)
254	Glendale, AZ	(24.8)	327	Irving, TX	(34.7)	401	Temecula, CA	(71.1)
255	Hialeah, FL	(24.9)	327	Jacksonville, FL	(34.7)	402	Fishers, IN	(71.3)
256	Edmond, OK	(25.2)	329	Lawton, OK	(35.2)	403	Concord, NC	(71.6)
257	Columbia, MO	(25.3)	330	Minneapolis, MN	(35.5)	404	Carmel, IN	(75.5)
257	Coral Springs, FL	(25.3)	331	Deerfield Beach, FL	(35.8)	NA	Arlington Heights, IL**	NA
257	Pittsburgh, PA	(25.3)	332	Sandy, UT	(35.9)	NA	Avondale, AZ**	NA
257	Yuma, AZ	(25.3)	333	Orlando, FL	(36.0)	NA	Billings, MT**	NA
261	Des Moines, IA	(25.4)	334	Duluth, MN	(36.1)	NA	Birmingham, AL**	NA
262	Fort Smith, AR	(25.5)	334	Santa Monica, CA	(36.1)	NA	Bloomington, IL**	NA
263	Chicago, IL	(25.6)	336	Newport News, VA	(36.6)	NA	Brockton, MA**	NA
264	Carson, CA	(25.7)	336	Santa Barbara, CA	(36.6)	NA	Buffalo, NY**	NA
265	Columbus, GA	(26.0)	336	St. Petersburg, FL	(36.6)	NA	Champaign, IL**	NA
265	Westminster, CA	(26.0)	339	Portsmouth, VA	(36.7)	NA	Cicero, IL**	NA
267	Dearborn, MI	(26.3)	340	Cape Coral, FL	(37.1)	NA	Citrus Heights, CA**	NA
268	San Jose, CA	(26.4)	341	Bellflower, CA	(37.3)	NA	Davenport, IA**	NA
269	Norfolk, VA	(26.5)	341	Milwaukee, WI	(37.3)	NA	Decatur, IL**	NA
270	Charlotte, NC	(26.9)	343	San Angelo, TX	(37.4)	NA	Durham, NC**	NA
271	Arvada, CO	(27.1)	344	Aurora, IL	(37.5)	NA	Fall River, MA**	NA
271	Fullerton, CA	(27.1)	345	Lafayette, LA	(37.9)	NA	Hoover, AL**	NA
271	Moreno Valley, CA	(27.1)	345	Santa Ana, CA	(37.9)	NA	Huntsville, AL**	NA
271	Reno, NV	(27.1)	347	Gilbert, AZ	(38.0)	NA	Johns Creek, GA**	NA
275	Garden Grove, CA	(27.3)	347	McAllen, TX	(38.0)	NA	Kansas City, MO**	NA
276	Glendale, CA	(28.1)	347	Racine, WI	(38.0)	NA	Lexington, KY**	NA
277	Tacoma, WA	(28.2)	350	Oceanside, CA	(38.5)	NA	Longmont, CO**	NA
278	Columbus, OH	(28.3)	351	Springfield, IL	(39.2)	NA	Manchester, NH**	NA
279	Toledo, OH	(28.4)	352	Berkeley, CA	(39.4)	NA	Menifee, CA**	NA
280	West Covina, CA	(28.8)	352	Bryan, TX	(39.4)	NA	Mobile, AL**	NA
281	Sunnyvale, CA	(28.9)	354	Rialto, CA	(39.8)	NA	Montgomery, AL**	NA
282	Santa Clara, CA	(29.0)	355	Lancaster, CA	(39.9)	NA	Nashua, NH**	NA
283	Palmdale, CA	(29.1)	355	Ontario, CA	(39.9)	NA	New Haven, CT**	NA
284	Lynchburg, VA	(29.2)	357	Roanoke, VA	(40.1)	NA	Olathe, KS**	NA
284	Raleigh, NC	(29.2)	358	Newport Beach, CA	(40.3)	NA	Pueblo, CO**	NA
284	Suffolk, VA	(29.2)	359	Pasadena, CA	(40.8)	NA	Sterling Heights, MI**	NA
287	Boca Raton, FL	(29.3)	360	League City, TX	(40.9)	NA	Thornton, CO**	NA
288	Bethlehem, PA	(29.4)	361	Rio Rancho, NM	(41.1)	NA	Tuscaloosa, AL**	NA
288	Dallas, TX	(29.4)	361	Toms River Twnshp, NJ	(41.1)	NA	Warwick, RI**	NA
			363	Farmington Hills, MI	(41.3)	NA	Winston-Salem, NC**	NA

Source: CQ Press using reported data from the F.B.I. "Crime in the United States 2011"
*Aggravated assault is an attack for the purpose of inflicting severe bodily injury.
**Not available.

Alpha Order - City

65. Property Crimes in 2011
National Total = 9,063,173 Property Crimes*

RANK	CITY	CRIMES	RANK	CITY	CRIMES	RANK	CITY	CRIMES
201	Abilene, TX	4,384	310	Cheektowaga, NY	2,753	98	Fort Wayne, IN	9,036
79	Akron, OH	10,864	118	Chesapeake, VA	7,163	16	Fort Worth, TX	35,117
183	Albany, GA	4,719	2	Chicago, IL	118,239	216	Fremont, CA	3,952
189	Albany, NY	4,611	368	Chico, CA	2,115	32	Fresno, CA	25,421
29	Albuquerque, NM	27,976	430	Chino Hills, CA	978	340	Frisco, TX	2,460
278	Alexandria, VA	3,181	372	Chino, CA	2,072	247	Fullerton, CA	3,550
385	Alhambra, CA	1,891	170	Chula Vista, CA	5,007	155	Gainesville, FL	5,356
191	Allentown, PA	4,575	379	Cicero, IL	1,981	258	Garden Grove, CA	3,387
412	Allen, TX	1,526	39	Cincinnati, OH	20,462	101	Garland, TX	8,683
96	Amarillo, TX	9,388	260	Citrus Heights, CA	3,333	156	Gary, IN	5,338
377	Amherst, NY	2,004	413	Clarkstown, NY	1,517	228	Gilbert, AZ	3,854
103	Anaheim, CA	8,493	209	Clarksville, TN	4,217	56	Glendale, AZ	14,738
95	Anchorage, AK	9,455	211	Clearwater, FL	4,129	255	Glendale, CA	3,452
327	Ann Arbor, MI	2,549	33	Cleveland, OH	25,323	120	Grand Prairie, TX	6,956
225	Antioch, CA	3,873	406	Clifton, NJ	1,638	135	Grand Rapids, MI	6,174
427	Arlington Heights, IL	1,083	352	Clinton Twnshp, MI	2,317	329	Greece, NY	2,544
46	Arlington, TX	17,208	218	Clovis, CA	3,933	284	Greeley, CO	3,118
328	Arvada, CO	2,546	293	College Station, TX	2,993	344	Green Bay, WI	2,420
217	Asheville, NC	3,949	361	Colonie, NY	2,197	203	Gresham, OR	4,311
177	Athens-Clarke, GA	4,873	49	Colorado Springs, CO	15,866	392	Hamilton Twnshp, NJ	1,817
22	Atlanta, GA	30,144	206	Columbia, MO	4,263	232	Hammond, IN	3,819
89	Aurora, CO	9,875	70	Columbus, GA	12,450	159	Hampton, VA	5,273
231	Aurora, IL	3,821	9	Columbus, OH	49,043	148	Hartford, CT	5,502
13	Austin, TX	42,250	302	Compton, CA	2,865	366	Hawthorne, CA	2,124
220	Avondale, AZ	3,919	233	Concord, CA	3,803	236	Hayward, CA	3,782
55	Bakersfield, CA	14,840	285	Concord, NC	3,111	254	Hemet, CA	3,472
410	Baldwin Park, CA	1,601	291	Coral Springs, FL	3,035	180	Henderson, NV	4,777
25	Baltimore, MD	29,824	259	Corona, CA	3,354	357	Hesperia, CA	2,249
69	Baton Rouge, LA	12,666	54	Corpus Christi, TX	14,897	114	Hialeah, FL	7,493
125	Beaumont, TX	6,656	250	Costa Mesa, CA	3,534	169	High Point, NC	5,057
395	Beaverton, OR	1,779	375	Cranston, RI	2,043	374	Hillsboro, OR	2,065
249	Bellevue, WA	3,539	7	Dallas, TX	61,859	111	Hollywood, FL	7,789
390	Bellflower, CA	1,832	387	Daly City, CA	1,880	362	Hoover, AL	2,194
239	Bellingham, WA	3,738	411	Danbury, CT	1,588	3	Houston, TX	108,336
345	Bend, OR	2,416	174	Davenport, IA	4,908	190	Huntington Beach, CA	4,589
168	Berkeley, CA	5,064	243	Davie, FL	3,627	90	Huntsville, AL	9,749
389	Bethlehem, PA	1,862	105	Dayton, OH	8,323	124	Independence, MO	6,691
186	Billings, MT	4,693	237	Dearborn, MI	3,757	10	Indianapolis, IN	46,967
45	Birmingham, AL	17,841	304	Decatur, IL	2,835	320	Indio, CA	2,610
399	Bloomington, IL	1,740	346	Deerfield Beach, FL	2,415	322	Inglewood, CA	2,582
288	Bloomington, IN	3,072	264	Denton, TX	3,315	267	Irvine, CA	3,280
281	Bloomington, MN	3,151	35	Denver, CO	22,495	121	Irving, TX	6,794
313	Boca Raton, FL	2,676	81	Des Moines, IA	10,727	15	Jacksonville, FL	36,113
157	Boise, ID	5,328	11	Detroit, MI	43,818	66	Jackson, MS	12,811
41	Boston, MA	19,445	224	Downey, CA	3,876	143	Jersey City, NJ	5,701
333	Boulder, CO	2,491	202	Duluth, MN	4,346	435	Johns Creek, GA	574
422	Brick Twnshp, NJ	1,313	77	Durham, NC	11,270	226	Joliet, IL	3,861
144	Bridgeport, CT	5,607	187	Edinburg, TX	4,652	108	Kansas City, KS	7,883
271	Brockton, MA	3,229	390	Edison Twnshp, NJ	1,832	31	Kansas City, MO	25,545
353	Broken Arrow, OK	2,287	405	Edmond, OK	1,646	317	Kennewick, WA	2,628
303	Brooklyn Park, MN	2,844	338	El Cajon, CA	2,468	292	Kenosha, WI	3,031
106	Brownsville, TX	8,187	354	El Monte, CA	2,286	172	Kent, WA	4,989
299	Bryan, TX	2,906	48	El Paso, TX	16,312	163	Killeen, TX	5,210
388	Buena Park, CA	1,879	373	Elgin, IL	2,068	64	Knoxville, TN	12,879
58	Buffalo, NY	14,305	167	Elizabeth, NJ	5,099	130	Lafayette, LA	6,511
326	Burbank, CA	2,555	269	Elk Grove, CA	3,270	431	Lake Forest, CA	947
279	Cambridge, MA	3,159	239	Erie, PA	3,738	164	Lakeland, FL	5,147
196	Camden, NJ	4,462	274	Escondido, CA	3,210	428	Lakewood Twnshp, NJ	1,073
419	Canton Twnshp, MI	1,395	109	Eugene, OR	7,878	384	Lakewood, CA	1,899
215	Cape Coral, FL	3,990	150	Evansville, IN	5,456	134	Lakewood, CO	6,194
380	Carlsbad, CA	1,970	113	Everett, WA	7,503	273	Lancaster, CA	3,216
433	Carmel, IN	831	295	Fairfield, CA	2,974	204	Lansing, MI	4,287
262	Carrollton, TX	3,322	277	Fall River, MA	3,187	83	Laredo, TX	10,419
332	Carson, CA	2,492	314	Fargo, ND	2,671	290	Largo, FL	3,048
371	Cary, NC	2,093	423	Farmington Hills, MI	1,266	193	Las Cruces, NM	4,546
175	Cedar Rapids, IA	4,879	63	Fayetteville, NC	12,972	14	Las Vegas, NV	41,426
420	Centennial, CO	1,353	434	Fishers, IN	700	235	Lawrence, KS	3,793
355	Champaign, IL	2,281	126	Flint, MI	6,618	334	Lawrence, MA	2,481
115	Chandler, AZ	7,416	207	Fontana, CA	4,235	146	Lawton, OK	5,531
238	Charleston, SC	3,754	205	Fort Collins, CO	4,272	386	League City, TX	1,885
19	Charlotte, NC	32,008	85	Fort Lauderdale, FL	10,192	367	Lee's Summit, MO	2,116
82	Chattanooga, TN	10,635	185	Fort Smith, AR	4,703	287	Lewisville, TX	3,095

Alpha Order - City (continued)

RANK	CITY	CRIMES	RANK	CITY	CRIMES	RANK	CITY	CRIMES
71	Lexington, KY	12,431	213	Overland Park, KS	4,015	251	Sioux City, IA	3,507
86	Lincoln, NE	10,189	252	Oxnard, CA	3,499	184	Sioux Falls, SD	4,707
50	Little Rock, AR	15,504	312	Palm Bay, FL	2,739	398	Somerville, MA	1,742
396	Livermore, CA	1,776	268	Palmdale, CA	3,273	136	South Bend, IN	6,096
370	Livonia, MI	2,108	242	Pasadena, CA	3,672	300	South Gate, CA	2,893
65	Long Beach, CA	12,816	160	Pasadena, TX	5,266	341	Sparks, NV	2,447
382	Longmont, CO	1,958	182	Paterson, NJ	4,732	171	Spokane Valley, WA	5,001
234	Longview, TX	3,802	402	Pearland, TX	1,726	53	Spokane, WA	15,039
4	Los Angeles, CA	86,330	173	Pembroke Pines, FL	4,944	117	Springfield, IL	7,176
20	Louisville, KY	31,949	181	Peoria, AZ	4,774	116	Springfield, MA	7,365
286	Lowell, MA	3,101	151	Peoria, IL	5,438	57	Springfield, MO	14,418
74	Lubbock, TX	12,078	8	Philadelphia, PA	59,617	378	Stamford, CT	1,987
337	Lynchburg, VA	2,469	6	Phoenix, AZ	64,479	314	Sterling Heights, MI	2,671
318	Lynn, MA	2,620	87	Pittsburgh, PA	10,063	51	Stockton, CA	15,463
110	Macon, GA	7,807	122	Plano, TX	6,764	212	St. Joseph, MO	4,056
107	Madison, WI	7,936	222	Plantation, FL	3,913	30	St. Louis, MO	25,669
210	Manchester, NH	4,194	197	Pomona, CA	4,444	76	St. Paul, MN	11,932
140	McAllen, TX	5,875	147	Pompano Beach, FL	5,524	67	St. Petersburg, FL	12,803
305	McKinney, TX	2,826	226	Port St. Lucie, FL	3,861	348	Suffolk, VA	2,381
223	Medford, OR	3,895	24	Portland, OR	30,022	417	Sugar Land, TX	1,429
214	Melbourne, FL	4,010	162	Portsmouth, VA	5,237	380	Sunnyvale, CA	1,970
12	Memphis, TN	42,355	301	Provo, UT	2,888	246	Sunrise, FL	3,590
409	Menifee, CA	1,611	149	Pueblo, CO	5,494	321	Surprise, AZ	2,598
279	Merced, CA	3,159	396	Quincy, MA	1,776	158	Syracuse, NY	5,275
429	Meridian, ID	1,049	245	Racine, WI	3,605	75	Tacoma, WA	12,062
52	Mesa, AZ	15,117	62	Raleigh, NC	13,242	97	Tallahassee, FL	9,363
129	Mesquite, TX	6,542	432	Ramapo, NY	883	84	Tampa, FL	10,393
92	Miami Beach, FL	9,585	221	Rancho Cucamon., CA	3,915	347	Temecula, CA	2,406
152	Miami Gardens, FL	5,397	265	Reading, PA	3,301	99	Tempe, AZ	8,933
34	Miami, FL	22,921	257	Redding, CA	3,396	256	Thornton, CO	3,438
266	Midland, TX	3,287	416	Redwood City, CA	1,487	393	Thousand Oaks, CA	1,788
23	Milwaukee, WI	30,097	128	Reno, NV	6,550	NA	Toledo, OH**	NA
42	Minneapolis, MN	19,190	208	Renton, WA	4,223	282	Toms River Twnshp, NJ	3,135
275	Miramar, FL	3,208	294	Rialto, CA	2,978	112	Topeka, KS	7,529
425	Mission Viejo, CA	1,216	306	Richardson, TX	2,808	308	Torrance, CA	2,767
311	Mission, TX	2,751	193	Richmond, CA	4,546	364	Tracy, CA	2,178
61	Mobile, AL	13,650	102	Richmond, VA	8,647	323	Trenton, NJ	2,570
100	Modesto, CA	8,894	407	Rio Rancho, NM	1,619	394	Troy, MI	1,780
80	Montgomery, AL	10,744	91	Riverside, CA	9,631	NA	Tucson, AZ**	NA
141	Moreno Valley, CA	5,762	188	Roanoke, VA	4,635	37	Tulsa, OK	21,923
179	Murfreesboro, TN	4,851	350	Rochester, MN	2,323	200	Tuscaloosa, AL	4,402
415	Murrieta, CA	1,495	78	Rochester, NY	10,934	414	Tustin, CA	1,513
335	Nampa, ID	2,475	119	Rockford, IL	7,122	198	Tyler, TX	4,441
408	Napa, CA	1,615	248	Roseville, CA	3,541	358	Upper Darby Twnshp, PA	2,233
369	Naperville, IL	2,110	401	Roswell, GA	1,727	404	Vacaville, CA	1,677
365	Nashua, NH	2,130	342	Round Rock, TX	2,446	161	Vallejo, CA	5,244
27	Nashville, TN	29,256	44	Sacramento, CA	18,563	132	Vancouver, WA	6,447
261	New Bedford, MA	3,329	139	Salem, OR	5,960	263	Ventura, CA	3,320
131	New Haven, CT	6,479	195	Salinas, CA	4,492	219	Victorville, CA	3,931
59	New Orleans, LA	14,013	68	Salt Lake City, UT	12,798	73	Virginia Beach, VA	12,133
421	New Rochelle, NY	1,343	244	San Angelo, TX	3,624	165	Visalia, CA	5,121
1	New York, NY	140,457	5	San Antonio, TX	80,868	376	Vista, CA	2,025
88	Newark, NJ	10,016	104	San Bernardino, CA	8,461	133	Waco, TX	6,422
359	Newport Beach, CA	2,223	26	San Diego, CA	29,709	229	Warren, MI	3,853
138	Newport News, VA	6,041	18	San Francisco, CA	32,886	362	Warwick, RI	2,194
426	Newton, MA	1,181	36	San Jose, CA	21,972	28	Washington, DC	28,312
72	Norfolk, VA	12,258	276	San Leandro, CA	3,205	192	Waterbury, CT	4,571
253	Norman, OK	3,480	418	San Marcos, CA	1,424	270	West Covina, CA	3,249
145	North Charleston, SC	5,579	400	San Mateo, CA	1,732	297	West Jordan, UT	2,939
356	Norwalk, CA	2,274	335	Sandy Springs, GA	2,475	153	West Palm Beach, FL	5,383
383	Norwalk, CT	1,914	319	Sandy, UT	2,617	154	West Valley, UT	5,368
38	Oakland, CA	20,904	127	Santa Ana, CA	6,575	349	Westland, MI	2,380
230	Oceanside, CA	3,849	309	Santa Barbara, CA	2,756	331	Westminster, CA	2,504
283	Odessa, TX	3,134	298	Santa Clara, CA	2,933	307	Westminster, CO	2,803
424	O'Fallon, MO	1,225	324	Santa Clarita, CA	2,568	338	Whittier, CA	2,468
199	Ogden, UT	4,429	343	Santa Maria, CA	2,429	176	Wichita Falls, TX	4,876
17	Oklahoma City, OK	34,113	296	Santa Monica, CA	2,971	40	Wichita, KS	19,456
360	Olathe, KS	2,204	241	Santa Rosa, CA	3,706	142	Wilmington, NC	5,708
43	Omaha, NE	18,764	94	Savannah, GA	9,579	60	Winston-Salem, NC	13,874
178	Ontario, CA	4,858	123	Scottsdale, AZ	6,724	330	Woodbridge Twnshp, NJ	2,538
316	Orange, CA	2,652	325	Scranton, PA	2,556	137	Worcester, MA	6,077
351	Orem, UT	2,322	21	Seattle, WA	31,792	166	Yakima, WA	5,120
47	Orlando, FL	17,145	93	Shreveport, LA	9,584	289	Yonkers, NY	3,068
			403	Simi Valley, CA	1,697	272	Yuma, AZ	3,227

Source: Reported data from the F.B.I. "Crime in the United States 2011"
*Property crimes are offenses of burglary, larceny-theft, and motor vehicle theft. Attempts are included.
**Not available.

Rank Order - City

65. Property Crimes in 2011 (continued)
National Total = 9,063,173 Property Crimes*

RANK	CITY	CRIMES	RANK	CITY	CRIMES	RANK	CITY	CRIMES
1	New York, NY	140,457	73	Virginia Beach, VA	12,133	145	North Charleston, SC	5,579
2	Chicago, IL	118,239	74	Lubbock, TX	12,078	146	Lawton, OK	5,531
3	Houston, TX	108,336	75	Tacoma, WA	12,062	147	Pompano Beach, FL	5,524
4	Los Angeles, CA	86,330	76	St. Paul, MN	11,932	148	Hartford, CT	5,502
5	San Antonio, TX	80,868	77	Durham, NC	11,270	149	Pueblo, CO	5,494
6	Phoenix, AZ	64,479	78	Rochester, NY	10,934	150	Evansville, IN	5,456
7	Dallas, TX	61,859	79	Akron, OH	10,864	151	Peoria, IL	5,438
8	Philadelphia, PA	59,617	80	Montgomery, AL	10,744	152	Miami Gardens, FL	5,397
9	Columbus, OH	49,043	81	Des Moines, IA	10,727	153	West Palm Beach, FL	5,383
10	Indianapolis, IN	46,967	82	Chattanooga, TN	10,635	154	West Valley, UT	5,368
11	Detroit, MI	43,818	83	Laredo, TX	10,419	155	Gainesville, FL	5,356
12	Memphis, TN	42,355	84	Tampa, FL	10,393	156	Gary, IN	5,338
13	Austin, TX	42,250	85	Fort Lauderdale, FL	10,192	157	Boise, ID	5,328
14	Las Vegas, NV	41,426	86	Lincoln, NE	10,189	158	Syracuse, NY	5,275
15	Jacksonville, FL	36,113	87	Pittsburgh, PA	10,063	159	Hampton, VA	5,273
16	Fort Worth, TX	35,117	88	Newark, NJ	10,016	160	Pasadena, TX	5,266
17	Oklahoma City, OK	34,113	89	Aurora, CO	9,875	161	Vallejo, CA	5,244
18	San Francisco, CA	32,886	90	Huntsville, AL	9,749	162	Portsmouth, VA	5,237
19	Charlotte, NC	32,008	91	Riverside, CA	9,631	163	Killeen, TX	5,210
20	Louisville, KY	31,949	92	Miami Beach, FL	9,585	164	Lakeland, FL	5,147
21	Seattle, WA	31,792	93	Shreveport, LA	9,584	165	Visalia, CA	5,121
22	Atlanta, GA	30,144	94	Savannah, GA	9,579	166	Yakima, WA	5,120
23	Milwaukee, WI	30,097	95	Anchorage, AK	9,455	167	Elizabeth, NJ	5,099
24	Portland, OR	30,022	96	Amarillo, TX	9,388	168	Berkeley, CA	5,064
25	Baltimore, MD	29,824	97	Tallahassee, FL	9,363	169	High Point, NC	5,057
26	San Diego, CA	29,709	98	Fort Wayne, IN	9,036	170	Chula Vista, CA	5,007
27	Nashville, TN	29,256	99	Tempe, AZ	8,933	171	Spokane Valley, WA	5,001
28	Washington, DC	28,312	100	Modesto, CA	8,894	172	Kent, WA	4,989
29	Albuquerque, NM	27,976	101	Garland, TX	8,683	173	Pembroke Pines, FL	4,944
30	St. Louis, MO	25,669	102	Richmond, VA	8,647	174	Davenport, IA	4,908
31	Kansas City, MO	25,545	103	Anaheim, CA	8,493	175	Cedar Rapids, IA	4,879
32	Fresno, CA	25,421	104	San Bernardino, CA	8,461	176	Wichita Falls, TX	4,876
33	Cleveland, OH	25,323	105	Dayton, OH	8,323	177	Athens-Clarke, GA	4,873
34	Miami, FL	22,921	106	Brownsville, TX	8,187	178	Ontario, CA	4,858
35	Denver, CO	22,495	107	Madison, WI	7,936	179	Murfreesboro, TN	4,851
36	San Jose, CA	21,972	108	Kansas City, KS	7,883	180	Henderson, NV	4,777
37	Tulsa, OK	21,923	109	Eugene, OR	7,878	181	Peoria, AZ	4,774
38	Oakland, CA	20,904	110	Macon, GA	7,807	182	Paterson, NJ	4,732
39	Cincinnati, OH	20,462	111	Hollywood, FL	7,789	183	Albany, GA	4,719
40	Wichita, KS	19,456	112	Topeka, KS	7,529	184	Sioux Falls, SD	4,707
41	Boston, MA	19,445	113	Everett, WA	7,503	185	Fort Smith, AR	4,703
42	Minneapolis, MN	19,190	114	Hialeah, FL	7,493	186	Billings, MT	4,693
43	Omaha, NE	18,764	115	Chandler, AZ	7,416	187	Edinburg, TX	4,652
44	Sacramento, CA	18,563	116	Springfield, MA	7,365	188	Roanoke, VA	4,635
45	Birmingham, AL	17,841	117	Springfield, IL	7,176	189	Albany, NY	4,611
46	Arlington, TX	17,208	118	Chesapeake, VA	7,163	190	Huntington Beach, CA	4,589
47	Orlando, FL	17,145	119	Rockford, IL	7,122	191	Allentown, PA	4,575
48	El Paso, TX	16,312	120	Grand Prairie, TX	6,956	192	Waterbury, CT	4,571
49	Colorado Springs, CO	15,866	121	Irving, TX	6,794	193	Las Cruces, NM	4,546
50	Little Rock, AR	15,504	122	Plano, TX	6,764	193	Richmond, CA	4,546
51	Stockton, CA	15,463	123	Scottsdale, AZ	6,724	195	Salinas, CA	4,492
52	Mesa, AZ	15,117	124	Independence, MO	6,691	196	Camden, NJ	4,462
53	Spokane, WA	15,039	125	Beaumont, TX	6,656	197	Pomona, CA	4,444
54	Corpus Christi, TX	14,897	126	Flint, MI	6,618	198	Tyler, TX	4,441
55	Bakersfield, CA	14,840	127	Santa Ana, CA	6,575	199	Ogden, UT	4,429
56	Glendale, AZ	14,738	128	Reno, NV	6,550	200	Tuscaloosa, AL	4,402
57	Springfield, MO	14,418	129	Mesquite, TX	6,542	201	Abilene, TX	4,384
58	Buffalo, NY	14,305	130	Lafayette, LA	6,511	202	Duluth, MN	4,346
59	New Orleans, LA	14,013	131	New Haven, CT	6,479	203	Gresham, OR	4,311
60	Winston-Salem, NC	13,874	132	Vancouver, WA	6,447	204	Lansing, MI	4,287
61	Mobile, AL	13,650	133	Waco, TX	6,422	205	Fort Collins, CO	4,272
62	Raleigh, NC	13,242	134	Lakewood, CO	6,194	206	Columbia, MO	4,263
63	Fayetteville, NC	12,972	135	Grand Rapids, MI	6,174	207	Fontana, CA	4,235
64	Knoxville, TN	12,879	136	South Bend, IN	6,096	208	Renton, WA	4,223
65	Long Beach, CA	12,816	137	Worcester, MA	6,077	209	Clarksville, TN	4,217
66	Jackson, MS	12,811	138	Newport News, VA	6,041	210	Manchester, NH	4,194
67	St. Petersburg, FL	12,803	139	Salem, OR	5,960	211	Clearwater, FL	4,129
68	Salt Lake City, UT	12,798	140	McAllen, TX	5,875	212	St. Joseph, MO	4,056
69	Baton Rouge, LA	12,666	141	Moreno Valley, CA	5,762	213	Overland Park, KS	4,015
70	Columbus, GA	12,450	142	Wilmington, NC	5,708	214	Melbourne, FL	4,010
71	Lexington, KY	12,431	143	Jersey City, NJ	5,701	215	Cape Coral, FL	3,990
72	Norfolk, VA	12,258	144	Bridgeport, CT	5,607	216	Fremont, CA	3,952

Rank Order - City (continued)

RANK	CITY	CRIMES	RANK	CITY	CRIMES	RANK	CITY	CRIMES
217	Asheville, NC	3,949	290	Largo, FL	3,048	364	Tracy, CA	2,178
218	Clovis, CA	3,933	291	Coral Springs, FL	3,035	365	Nashua, NH	2,130
219	Victorville, CA	3,931	292	Kenosha, WI	3,031	366	Hawthorne, CA	2,124
220	Avondale, AZ	3,919	293	College Station, TX	2,993	367	Lee's Summit, MO	2,116
221	Rancho Cucamon., CA	3,915	294	Rialto, CA	2,978	368	Chico, CA	2,115
222	Plantation, FL	3,913	295	Fairfield, CA	2,974	369	Naperville, IL	2,110
223	Medford, OR	3,895	296	Santa Monica, CA	2,971	370	Livonia, MI	2,108
224	Downey, CA	3,876	297	West Jordan, UT	2,939	371	Cary, NC	2,093
225	Antioch, CA	3,873	298	Santa Clara, CA	2,933	372	Chino, CA	2,072
226	Joliet, IL	3,861	299	Bryan, TX	2,906	373	Elgin, IL	2,068
226	Port St. Lucie, FL	3,861	300	South Gate, CA	2,893	374	Hillsboro, OR	2,065
228	Gilbert, AZ	3,854	301	Provo, UT	2,888	375	Cranston, RI	2,043
229	Warren, MI	3,853	302	Compton, CA	2,865	376	Vista, CA	2,025
230	Oceanside, CA	3,849	303	Brooklyn Park, MN	2,844	377	Amherst, NY	2,004
231	Aurora, IL	3,821	304	Decatur, IL	2,835	378	Stamford, CT	1,987
232	Hammond, IN	3,819	305	McKinney, TX	2,826	379	Cicero, IL	1,981
233	Concord, CA	3,803	306	Richardson, TX	2,808	380	Carlsbad, CA	1,970
234	Longview, TX	3,802	307	Westminster, CO	2,803	380	Sunnyvale, CA	1,970
235	Lawrence, KS	3,793	308	Torrance, CA	2,767	382	Longmont, CO	1,958
236	Hayward, CA	3,782	309	Santa Barbara, CA	2,756	383	Norwalk, CT	1,914
237	Dearborn, MI	3,757	310	Cheektowaga, NY	2,753	384	Lakewood, CA	1,899
238	Charleston, SC	3,754	311	Mission, TX	2,751	385	Alhambra, CA	1,891
239	Bellingham, WA	3,738	312	Palm Bay, FL	2,739	386	League City, TX	1,885
239	Erie, PA	3,738	313	Boca Raton, FL	2,676	387	Daly City, CA	1,880
241	Santa Rosa, CA	3,706	314	Fargo, ND	2,671	388	Buena Park, CA	1,879
242	Pasadena, CA	3,672	314	Sterling Heights, MI	2,671	389	Bethlehem, PA	1,862
243	Davie, FL	3,627	316	Orange, CA	2,652	390	Bellflower, CA	1,832
244	San Angelo, TX	3,624	317	Kennewick, WA	2,628	390	Edison Twnshp, NJ	1,832
245	Racine, WI	3,605	318	Lynn, MA	2,620	392	Hamilton Twnshp, NJ	1,817
246	Sunrise, FL	3,590	319	Sandy, UT	2,617	393	Thousand Oaks, CA	1,788
247	Fullerton, CA	3,550	320	Indio, CA	2,610	394	Troy, MI	1,780
248	Roseville, CA	3,541	321	Surprise, AZ	2,598	395	Beaverton, OR	1,779
249	Bellevue, WA	3,539	322	Inglewood, CA	2,582	396	Livermore, CA	1,776
250	Costa Mesa, CA	3,534	323	Trenton, NJ	2,570	396	Quincy, MA	1,776
251	Sioux City, IA	3,507	324	Santa Clarita, CA	2,568	398	Somerville, MA	1,742
252	Oxnard, CA	3,499	325	Scranton, PA	2,556	399	Bloomington, IL	1,740
253	Norman, OK	3,480	326	Burbank, CA	2,555	400	San Mateo, CA	1,732
254	Hemet, CA	3,472	327	Ann Arbor, MI	2,549	401	Roswell, GA	1,727
255	Glendale, CA	3,452	328	Arvada, CO	2,546	402	Pearland, TX	1,726
256	Thornton, CO	3,438	329	Greece, NY	2,544	403	Simi Valley, CA	1,697
257	Redding, CA	3,396	330	Woodbridge Twnshp, NJ	2,538	404	Vacaville, CA	1,677
258	Garden Grove, CA	3,387	331	Westminster, CA	2,504	405	Edmond, OK	1,646
259	Corona, CA	3,354	332	Carson, CA	2,492	406	Clifton, NJ	1,638
260	Citrus Heights, CA	3,333	333	Boulder, CO	2,491	407	Rio Rancho, NM	1,619
261	New Bedford, MA	3,329	334	Lawrence, MA	2,481	408	Napa, CA	1,615
262	Carrollton, TX	3,322	335	Nampa, ID	2,475	409	Menifee, CA	1,611
263	Ventura, CA	3,320	335	Sandy Springs, GA	2,475	410	Baldwin Park, CA	1,601
264	Denton, TX	3,315	337	Lynchburg, VA	2,469	411	Danbury, CT	1,588
265	Reading, PA	3,301	338	El Cajon, CA	2,468	412	Allen, TX	1,526
266	Midland, TX	3,287	338	Whittier, CA	2,468	413	Clarkstown, NY	1,517
267	Irvine, CA	3,280	340	Frisco, TX	2,460	414	Tustin, CA	1,513
268	Palmdale, CA	3,273	341	Sparks, NV	2,447	415	Murrieta, CA	1,495
269	Elk Grove, CA	3,270	342	Round Rock, TX	2,446	416	Redwood City, CA	1,487
270	West Covina, CA	3,249	343	Santa Maria, CA	2,429	417	Sugar Land, TX	1,429
271	Brockton, MA	3,229	344	Green Bay, WI	2,420	418	San Marcos, CA	1,424
272	Yuma, AZ	3,227	345	Bend, OR	2,416	419	Canton Twnshp, MI	1,395
273	Lancaster, CA	3,216	346	Deerfield Beach, FL	2,415	420	Centennial, CO	1,353
274	Escondido, CA	3,210	347	Temecula, CA	2,406	421	New Rochelle, NY	1,343
275	Miramar, FL	3,208	348	Suffolk, VA	2,381	422	Brick Twnshp, NJ	1,313
276	San Leandro, CA	3,205	349	Westland, MI	2,380	423	Farmington Hills, MI	1,266
277	Fall River, MA	3,187	350	Rochester, MN	2,323	424	O'Fallon, MO	1,225
278	Alexandria, VA	3,181	351	Orem, UT	2,322	425	Mission Viejo, CA	1,216
279	Cambridge, MA	3,159	352	Clinton Twnshp, MI	2,317	426	Newton, MA	1,181
279	Merced, CA	3,159	353	Broken Arrow, OK	2,287	427	Arlington Heights, IL	1,083
281	Bloomington, MN	3,151	354	El Monte, CA	2,286	428	Lakewood Twnshp, NJ	1,073
282	Toms River Twnshp, NJ	3,135	355	Champaign, IL	2,281	429	Meridian, ID	1,049
283	Odessa, TX	3,134	356	Norwalk, CA	2,274	430	Chino Hills, CA	978
284	Greeley, CO	3,118	357	Hesperia, CA	2,249	431	Lake Forest, CA	947
285	Concord, NC	3,111	358	Upper Darby Twnshp, PA	2,233	432	Ramapo, NY	883
286	Lowell, MA	3,101	359	Newport Beach, CA	2,223	433	Carmel, IN	831
287	Lewisville, TX	3,095	360	Olathe, KS	2,204	434	Fishers, IN	700
288	Bloomington, IN	3,072	361	Colonie, NY	2,197	435	Johns Creek, GA	574
289	Yonkers, NY	3,068	362	Hoover, AL	2,194	NA	Toledo, OH**	NA
			362	Warwick, RI	2,194	NA	Tucson, AZ**	NA

Source: Reported data from the F.B.I. "Crime in the United States 2011"
*Property crimes are offenses of burglary, larceny-theft, and motor vehicle theft. Attempts are included.
**Not available.

Alpha Order - City

66. Property Crime Rate in 2011
National Rate = 2,908.7 Property Crimes per 100,000 Population*

RANK	CITY	RATE	RANK	CITY	RATE	RANK	CITY	RATE
193	Abilene, TX	3,667.8	202	Cheektowaga, NY	3,476.3	198	Fort Wayne, IN	3,543.7
50	Akron, OH	5,452.3	224	Chesapeake, VA	3,185.5	110	Fort Worth, TX	4,640.2
27	Albany, GA	6,015.0	132	Chicago, IL	4,373.2	397	Fremont, CA	1,824.5
107	Albany, NY	4,690.9	321	Chico, CA	2,425.5	78	Fresno, CA	5,079.3
80	Albuquerque, NM	5,068.5	428	Chino Hills, CA	1,292.3	370	Frisco, TX	2,059.4
347	Alexandria, VA	2,245.9	292	Chino, CA	2,626.1	297	Fullerton, CA	2,596.0
346	Alhambra, CA	2,249.4	374	Chula Vista, CA	2,028.9	140	Gainesville, FL	4,249.1
172	Allentown, PA	3,863.8	328	Cicero, IL	2,354.3	381	Garden Grove, CA	1,959.0
402	Allen, TX	1,774.0	13	Cincinnati, OH	6,885.9	183	Garland, TX	3,748.3
96	Amarillo, TX	4,821.6	160	Citrus Heights, CA	3,954.7	15	Gary, IN	6,614.3
409	Amherst, NY	1,703.9	386	Clarkstown, NY	1,914.9	398	Gilbert, AZ	1,823.0
310	Anaheim, CA	2,496.3	230	Clarksville, TN	3,144.0	19	Glendale, AZ	6,409.7
225	Anchorage, AK	3,184.0	180	Clearwater, FL	3,782.8	400	Glendale, CA	1,779.6
348	Ann Arbor, MI	2,239.0	21	Cleveland, OH	6,376.9	169	Grand Prairie, TX	3,884.1
185	Antioch, CA	3,739.3	382	Clifton, NJ	1,940.4	217	Grand Rapids, MI	3,285.8
420	Arlington Heights, IL	1,437.7	324	Clinton Twnshp, MI	2,395.5	291	Greece, NY	2,635.5
113	Arlington, TX	4,611.8	153	Clovis, CA	4,064.9	215	Greeley, CO	3,299.2
329	Arvada, CO	2,351.2	234	College Station, TX	3,123.2	333	Green Bay, WI	2,315.6
108	Asheville, NC	4,676.1	275	Colonie, NY	2,818.5	155	Gresham, OR	4,039.6
147	Athens-Clarke, GA	4,160.9	184	Colorado Springs, CO	3,744.8	372	Hamilton Twnshp, NJ	2,047.1
12	Atlanta, GA	7,083.8	164	Columbia, MO	3,914.8	106	Hammond, IN	4,700.7
253	Aurora, CO	2,985.7	17	Columbus, GA	6,471.4	179	Hampton, VA	3,791.4
384	Aurora, IL	1,925.0	23	Columbus, OH	6,226.8	130	Hartford, CT	4,401.4
67	Austin, TX	5,235.3	260	Compton, CA	2,935.8	311	Hawthorne, CA	2,490.5
79	Avondale, AZ	5,068.7	241	Concord, CA	3,079.3	300	Hayward, CA	2,592.5
142	Bakersfield, CA	4,221.1	168	Concord, NC	3,885.4	134	Hemet, CA	4,362.8
367	Baldwin Park, CA	2,099.0	315	Coral Springs, FL	2,472.6	393	Henderson, NV	1,838.0
103	Baltimore, MD	4,757.8	358	Corona, CA	2,175.6	316	Hesperia, CA	2,465.1
47	Baton Rouge, LA	5,469.1	100	Corpus Christi, TX	4,780.2	216	Hialeah, FL	3,290.3
45	Beaumont, TX	5,510.6	227	Costa Mesa, CA	3,176.5	98	High Point, NC	4,784.5
379	Beaverton, OR	1,960.1	306	Cranston, RI	2,544.5	351	Hillsboro, OR	2,230.4
271	Bellevue, WA	2,847.5	82	Dallas, TX	5,057.9	48	Hollywood, FL	5,458.8
327	Bellflower, CA	2,363.4	394	Daly City, CA	1,837.5	288	Hoover, AL	2,675.2
121	Bellingham, WA	4,550.0	380	Danbury, CT	1,959.5	84	Houston, TX	5,053.9
235	Bend, OR	3,119.2	93	Davenport, IA	4,897.9	325	Huntington Beach, CA	2,387.3
127	Berkeley, CA	4,445.9	167	Davie, FL	3,889.7	56	Huntsville, AL	5,387.0
314	Bethlehem, PA	2,475.4	33	Dayton, OH	5,876.5	37	Independence, MO	5,706.4
126	Billings, MT	4,465.5	174	Dearborn, MI	3,830.6	41	Indianapolis, IN	5,638.1
4	Birmingham, AL	8,365.9	191	Decatur, IL	3,713.1	209	Indio, CA	3,392.7
343	Bloomington, IL	2,264.4	228	Deerfield Beach, FL	3,176.0	332	Inglewood, CA	2,326.9
178	Bloomington, IN	3,801.2	269	Denton, TX	2,863.5	417	Irvine, CA	1,526.5
181	Bloomington, MN	3,772.2	192	Denver, CO	3,684.0	242	Irving, TX	3,076.4
233	Boca Raton, FL	3,128.3	65	Des Moines, IA	5,245.5	136	Jacksonville, FL	4,327.9
303	Boise, ID	2,562.2	25	Detroit, MI	6,143.5	7	Jackson, MS	7,355.5
232	Boston, MA	3,129.4	204	Downey, CA	3,427.5	339	Jersey City, NJ	2,294.9
309	Boulder, CO	2,514.1	87	Duluth, MN	4,999.4	435	Johns Creek, GA	738.4
405	Brick Twnshp, NJ	1,743.2	94	Durham, NC	4,874.0	294	Joliet, IL	2,611.0
170	Bridgeport, CT	3,880.4	32	Edinburg, TX	5,909.4	57	Kansas City, KS	5,373.1
206	Brockton, MA	3,421.3	396	Edison Twnshp, NJ	1,826.5	42	Kansas City, MO	5,535.7
340	Broken Arrow, OK	2,289.1	376	Edmond, OK	2,000.6	199	Kennewick, WA	3,500.4
190	Brooklyn Park, MN	3,724.2	319	El Cajon, CA	2,452.1	247	Kenosha, WI	3,041.6
116	Brownsville, TX	4,581.3	377	El Monte, CA	1,991.1	59	Kent, WA	5,315.3
188	Bryan, TX	3,735.0	317	El Paso, TX	2,461.1	158	Killeen, TX	3,988.9
336	Buena Park, CA	2,306.2	389	Elgin, IL	1,905.7	9	Knoxville, TN	7,135.7
51	Buffalo, NY	5,449.9	152	Elizabeth, NJ	4,066.6	58	Lafayette, LA	5,348.9
320	Burbank, CA	2,443.7	365	Elk Grove, CA	2,112.2	430	Lake Forest, CA	1,211.4
253	Cambridge, MA	2,985.7	194	Erie, PA	3,660.7	68	Lakeland, FL	5,212.2
36	Camden, NJ	5,749.1	353	Escondido, CA	2,204.6	431	Lakewood Twnshp, NJ	1,151.9
414	Canton Twnshp, MI	1,548.2	88	Eugene, OR	4,990.9	330	Lakewood, CA	2,344.8
304	Cape Coral, FL	2,551.0	112	Evansville, IN	4,622.6	139	Lakewood, CO	4,257.9
392	Carlsbad, CA	1,848.6	8	Everett, WA	7,170.6	373	Lancaster, CA	2,029.4
433	Carmel, IN	1,044.0	277	Fairfield, CA	2,790.9	182	Lansing, MI	3,753.6
284	Carrollton, TX	2,731.8	197	Fall River, MA	3,564.9	137	Laredo, TX	4,322.2
287	Carson, CA	2,685.6	313	Fargo, ND	2,488.6	171	Largo, FL	3,872.6
416	Cary, NC	1,528.3	412	Farmington Hills, MI	1,588.9	114	Las Cruces, NM	4,605.4
173	Cedar Rapids, IA	3,842.1	20	Fayetteville, NC	6,386.8	273	Las Vegas, NV	2,840.4
427	Centennial, CO	1,324.8	434	Fishers, IN	906.9	138	Lawrence, KS	4,300.5
276	Champaign, IL	2,805.7	18	Flint, MI	6,465.6	221	Lawrence, MA	3,228.7
237	Chandler, AZ	3,096.9	361	Fontana, CA	2,134.9	40	Lawton, OK	5,649.4
238	Charleston, SC	3,090.2	263	Fort Collins, CO	2,916.2	352	League City, TX	2,209.4
154	Charlotte, NC	4,054.3	26	Fort Lauderdale, FL	6,074.7	335	Lee's Summit, MO	2,307.6
22	Chattanooga, TN	6,285.9	55	Fort Smith, AR	5,414.4	226	Lewisville, TX	3,181.0

Alpha Order - City (continued)

RANK	CITY	RATE
146	Lexington, KY	4,173.6
165	Lincoln, NE	3,908.5
6	Little Rock, AR	7,951.3
359	Livermore, CA	2,168.0
357	Livonia, MI	2,176.1
282	Long Beach, CA	2,740.3
350	Longmont, CO	2,230.8
111	Longview, TX	4,628.2
345	Los Angeles, CA	2,249.8
97	Louisville, KY	4,803.3
265	Lowell, MA	2,893.6
73	Lubbock, TX	5,152.6
221	Lynchburg, VA	3,228.7
267	Lynn, MA	2,882.9
3	Macon, GA	8,435.1
210	Madison, WI	3,388.2
175	Manchester, NH	3,822.9
128	McAllen, TX	4,430.3
366	McKinney, TX	2,110.9
74	Medford, OR	5,145.0
69	Melbourne, FL	5,200.7
16	Memphis, TN	6,489.0
371	Menifee, CA	2,054.1
161	Merced, CA	3,954.4
424	Meridian, ID	1,381.7
208	Mesa, AZ	3,395.1
115	Mesquite, TX	4,582.3
1	Miami Beach, FL	10,772.7
92	Miami Gardens, FL	4,968.3
38	Miami, FL	5,660.9
264	Midland, TX	2,896.4
86	Milwaukee, WI	5,037.8
91	Minneapolis, MN	4,977.6
299	Miramar, FL	2,593.3
429	Mission Viejo, CA	1,288.1
200	Mission, TX	3,496.5
53	Mobile, AL	5,419.5
133	Modesto, CA	4,369.9
70	Montgomery, AL	5,196.5
259	Moreno Valley, CA	2,945.2
129	Murfreesboro, TN	4,420.6
421	Murrieta, CA	1,428.1
252	Nampa, ID	3,001.5
368	Napa, CA	2,075.3
418	Naperville, IL	1,483.0
318	Nashua, NH	2,459.4
101	Nashville, TN	4,774.2
201	New Bedford, MA	3,480.4
90	New Haven, CT	4,983.1
156	New Orleans, LA	4,038.6
407	New Rochelle, NY	1,735.0
408	New York, NY	1,710.4
196	Newark, NJ	3,602.0
301	Newport Beach, CA	2,579.3
214	Newport News, VA	3,303.3
425	Newton, MA	1,378.6
89	Norfolk, VA	4,988.9
236	Norman, OK	3,104.0
39	North Charleston, SC	5,657.9
363	Norwalk, CA	2,129.4
349	Norwalk, CT	2,231.8
62	Oakland, CA	5,287.9
342	Oceanside, CA	2,276.8
243	Odessa, TX	3,071.3
415	O'Fallon, MO	1,538.6
64	Ogden, UT	5,246.2
35	Oklahoma City, OK	5,819.3
406	Olathe, KS	1,739.9
122	Omaha, NE	4,547.7
262	Ontario, CA	2,929.1
385	Orange, CA	1,921.5
302	Orem, UT	2,579.1
10	Orlando, FL	7,098.0
337	Overland Park, KS	2,301.2
404	Oxnard, CA	1,747.5
293	Palm Bay, FL	2,618.6
364	Palmdale, CA	2,117.8
290	Pasadena, CA	2,646.8
203	Pasadena, TX	3,460.4
223	Paterson, NJ	3,226.0
391	Pearland, TX	1,852.5
229	Pembroke Pines, FL	3,151.9
244	Peoria, AZ	3,055.4
105	Peoria, IL	4,714.2
166	Philadelphia, PA	3,894.3
131	Phoenix, AZ	4,398.0
219	Pittsburgh, PA	3,260.8
305	Plano, TX	2,549.5
123	Plantation, FL	4,544.0
257	Pomona, CA	2,946.8
49	Pompano Beach, FL	5,458.2
334	Port St. Lucie, FL	2,314.1
77	Portland, OR	5,088.6
54	Portsmouth, VA	5,417.1
308	Provo, UT	2,518.8
81	Pueblo, CO	5,065.8
388	Quincy, MA	1,913.1
120	Racine, WI	4,551.5
220	Raleigh, NC	3,237.5
432	Ramapo, NY	1,045.8
331	Rancho Cucamon., CA	2,341.3
186	Reading, PA	3,735.7
187	Redding, CA	3,735.3
387	Redwood City, CA	1,913.3
266	Reno, NV	2,883.9
118	Renton, WA	4,572.6
255	Rialto, CA	2,968.0
280	Richardson, TX	2,771.7
135	Richmond, CA	4,332.8
145	Richmond, VA	4,184.3
395	Rio Rancho, NM	1,829.4
231	Riverside, CA	3,132.6
104	Roanoke, VA	4,720.4
360	Rochester, MN	2,159.1
71	Rochester, NY	5,169.5
109	Rockford, IL	4,644.9
258	Roseville, CA	2,946.3
383	Roswell, GA	1,929.4
323	Round Rock, TX	2,398.3
162	Sacramento, CA	3,933.1
176	Salem, OR	3,813.6
256	Salinas, CA	2,951.2
14	Salt Lake City, UT	6,734.4
177	San Angelo, TX	3,808.3
30	San Antonio, TX	5,966.6
159	San Bernardino, CA	3,983.7
344	San Diego, CA	2,255.9
157	San Francisco, CA	4,036.6
338	San Jose, CA	2,295.8
189	San Leandro, CA	3,729.0
410	San Marcos, CA	1,679.9
403	San Mateo, CA	1,761.1
295	Sandy Springs, GA	2,602.8
261	Sandy, UT	2,935.5
375	Santa Ana, CA	2,002.5
240	Santa Barbara, CA	3,081.1
312	Santa Clara, CA	2,489.0
419	Santa Clarita, CA	1,439.5
322	Santa Maria, CA	2,411.6
218	Santa Monica, CA	3,272.4
355	Santa Rosa, CA	2,182.7
141	Savannah, GA	4,230.6
246	Scottsdale, AZ	3,050.0
212	Scranton, PA	3,348.5
75	Seattle, WA	5,142.6
102	Shreveport, LA	4,765.0
426	Simi Valley, CA	1,350.1
143	Sioux City, IA	4,219.4
250	Sioux Falls, SD	3,022.0
341	Somerville, MA	2,285.6
28	South Bend, IN	5,995.0
248	South Gate, CA	3,029.1
286	Sparks, NV	2,688.3
46	Spokane Valley, WA	5,485.8
11	Spokane, WA	7,087.4
24	Springfield, IL	6,154.4
99	Springfield, MA	4,782.7
2	Springfield, MO	9,006.9
411	Stamford, CT	1,617.2
369	Sterling Heights, MI	2,060.9
66	Stockton, CA	5,239.3
63	St. Joseph, MO	5,263.5
5	St. Louis, MO	8,010.2
148	St. Paul, MN	4,147.9
72	St. Petersburg, FL	5,160.3
278	Suffolk, VA	2,781.7
401	Sugar Land, TX	1,775.7
423	Sunnyvale, CA	1,390.0
144	Sunrise, FL	4,194.4
356	Surprise, AZ	2,179.9
195	Syracuse, NY	3,617.4
29	Tacoma, WA	5,985.8
76	Tallahassee, FL	5,092.8
245	Tampa, FL	3,054.2
326	Temecula, CA	2,375.7
52	Tempe, AZ	5,446.7
272	Thornton, CO	2,845.1
422	Thousand Oaks, CA	1,395.0
NA	Toledo, OH**	NA
205	Toms River Twnshp, NJ	3,424.6
34	Topeka, KS	5,869.1
390	Torrance, CA	1,880.4
297	Tracy, CA	2,596.0
251	Trenton, NJ	3,016.6
354	Troy, MI	2,199.7
NA	Tucson, AZ**	NA
44	Tulsa, OK	5,534.7
95	Tuscaloosa, AL	4,842.5
378	Tustin, CA	1,979.6
124	Tyler, TX	4,488.6
285	Upper Darby Twnshp, PA	2,688.5
399	Vacaville, CA	1,793.3
125	Vallejo, CA	4,470.4
163	Vancouver, WA	3,923.2
239	Ventura, CA	3,083.1
211	Victorville, CA	3,352.2
283	Virginia Beach, VA	2,737.4
150	Visalia, CA	4,067.4
362	Vista, CA	2,133.0
85	Waco, TX	5,039.6
268	Warren, MI	2,876.4
289	Warwick, RI	2,657.1
116	Washington, DC	4,581.3
149	Waterbury, CT	4,134.0
249	West Covina, CA	3,026.7
279	West Jordan, UT	2,780.2
60	West Palm Beach, FL	5,314.9
151	West Valley, UT	4,067.3
274	Westland, MI	2,832.3
281	Westminster, CA	2,759.0
296	Westminster, CO	2,596.3
270	Whittier, CA	2,858.7
119	Wichita Falls, TX	4,567.6
83	Wichita, KS	5,056.2
61	Wilmington, NC	5,293.7
30	Winston-Salem, NC	5,966.6
307	Woodbridge Twnshp, NJ	2,540.2
213	Worcester, MA	3,336.4
43	Yakima, WA	5,535.4
413	Yonkers, NY	1,558.5
207	Yuma, AZ	3,419.1

Source: CQ Press using reported data from the F.B.I. "Crime in the United States 2011"
*Property crimes are offenses of burglary, larceny-theft, and motor vehicle theft. Attempts are included.
**Not available.

66. Property Crime Rate in 2011 (continued)
National Rate = 2,908.7 Property Crimes per 100,000 Population*

RANK	CITY	RATE	RANK	CITY	RATE	RANK	CITY	RATE
1	Miami Beach, FL	10,772.7	73	Lubbock, TX	5,152.6	145	Richmond, VA	4,184.3
2	Springfield, MO	9,006.9	74	Medford, OR	5,145.0	146	Lexington, KY	4,173.6
3	Macon, GA	8,435.1	75	Seattle, WA	5,142.6	147	Athens-Clarke, GA	4,160.9
4	Birmingham, AL	8,365.9	76	Tallahassee, FL	5,092.8	148	St. Paul, MN	4,147.9
5	St. Louis, MO	8,010.2	77	Portland, OR	5,088.6	149	Waterbury, CT	4,134.0
6	Little Rock, AR	7,951.3	78	Fresno, CA	5,079.3	150	Visalia, CA	4,067.4
7	Jackson, MS	7,355.5	79	Avondale, AZ	5,068.7	151	West Valley, UT	4,067.3
8	Everett, WA	7,170.6	80	Albuquerque, NM	5,068.5	152	Elizabeth, NJ	4,066.6
9	Knoxville, TN	7,135.7	81	Pueblo, CO	5,065.8	153	Clovis, CA	4,064.9
10	Orlando, FL	7,098.0	82	Dallas, TX	5,057.9	154	Charlotte, NC	4,054.3
11	Spokane, WA	7,087.4	83	Wichita, KS	5,056.2	155	Gresham, OR	4,039.6
12	Atlanta, GA	7,083.8	84	Houston, TX	5,053.9	156	New Orleans, LA	4,038.6
13	Cincinnati, OH	6,885.9	85	Waco, TX	5,039.6	157	San Francisco, CA	4,036.6
14	Salt Lake City, UT	6,734.4	86	Milwaukee, WI	5,037.8	158	Killeen, TX	3,988.9
15	Gary, IN	6,614.3	87	Duluth, MN	4,999.4	159	San Bernardino, CA	3,983.7
16	Memphis, TN	6,489.0	88	Eugene, OR	4,990.9	160	Citrus Heights, CA	3,954.7
17	Columbus, GA	6,471.4	89	Norfolk, VA	4,988.9	161	Merced, CA	3,954.4
18	Flint, MI	6,465.6	90	New Haven, CT	4,983.1	162	Sacramento, CA	3,933.1
19	Glendale, AZ	6,409.7	91	Minneapolis, MN	4,977.6	163	Vancouver, WA	3,923.2
20	Fayetteville, NC	6,386.8	92	Miami Gardens, FL	4,968.3	164	Columbia, MO	3,914.8
21	Cleveland, OH	6,376.9	93	Davenport, IA	4,897.9	165	Lincoln, NE	3,908.5
22	Chattanooga, TN	6,285.9	94	Durham, NC	4,874.0	166	Philadelphia, PA	3,894.3
23	Columbus, OH	6,226.8	95	Tuscaloosa, AL	4,842.5	167	Davie, FL	3,889.7
24	Springfield, IL	6,154.4	96	Amarillo, TX	4,821.6	168	Concord, NC	3,885.4
25	Detroit, MI	6,143.5	97	Louisville, KY	4,803.3	169	Grand Prairie, TX	3,884.1
26	Fort Lauderdale, FL	6,074.7	98	High Point, NC	4,784.5	170	Bridgeport, CT	3,880.4
27	Albany, GA	6,015.0	99	Springfield, MA	4,782.7	171	Largo, FL	3,872.6
28	South Bend, IN	5,995.0	100	Corpus Christi, TX	4,780.2	172	Allentown, PA	3,863.8
29	Tacoma, WA	5,985.8	101	Nashville, TN	4,774.2	173	Cedar Rapids, IA	3,842.1
30	San Antonio, TX	5,966.6	102	Shreveport, LA	4,765.0	174	Dearborn, MI	3,830.6
30	Winston-Salem, NC	5,966.6	103	Baltimore, MD	4,757.8	175	Manchester, NH	3,822.9
32	Edinburg, TX	5,909.4	104	Roanoke, VA	4,720.4	176	Salem, OR	3,813.6
33	Dayton, OH	5,876.5	105	Peoria, IL	4,714.2	177	San Angelo, TX	3,808.3
34	Topeka, KS	5,869.1	106	Hammond, IN	4,700.7	178	Bloomington, IN	3,801.2
35	Oklahoma City, OK	5,819.3	107	Albany, NY	4,690.9	179	Hampton, VA	3,791.4
36	Camden, NJ	5,749.7	108	Asheville, NC	4,676.1	180	Clearwater, FL	3,782.8
37	Independence, MO	5,706.4	109	Rockford, IL	4,644.9	181	Bloomington, MN	3,772.2
38	Miami, FL	5,660.9	110	Fort Worth, TX	4,640.2	182	Lansing, MI	3,753.6
39	North Charleston, SC	5,657.9	111	Longview, TX	4,628.2	183	Garland, TX	3,748.3
40	Lawton, OK	5,649.4	112	Evansville, IN	4,622.6	184	Colorado Springs, CO	3,744.8
41	Indianapolis, IN	5,638.1	113	Arlington, TX	4,611.8	185	Antioch, CA	3,739.3
42	Kansas City, MO	5,535.7	114	Las Cruces, NM	4,605.4	186	Reading, PA	3,735.7
43	Yakima, WA	5,535.4	115	Mesquite, TX	4,582.3	187	Redding, CA	3,735.3
44	Tulsa, OK	5,534.7	116	Brownsville, TX	4,581.3	188	Bryan, TX	3,735.0
45	Beaumont, TX	5,510.6	116	Washington, DC	4,581.3	189	San Leandro, CA	3,729.0
46	Spokane Valley, WA	5,485.8	118	Renton, WA	4,572.6	190	Brooklyn Park, MN	3,724.2
47	Baton Rouge, LA	5,469.1	119	Wichita Falls, TX	4,567.6	191	Decatur, IL	3,713.1
48	Hollywood, FL	5,458.8	120	Racine, WI	4,551.5	192	Denver, CO	3,684.0
49	Pompano Beach, FL	5,458.2	121	Bellingham, WA	4,550.0	193	Abilene, TX	3,667.8
50	Akron, OH	5,452.3	122	Omaha, NE	4,547.7	194	Erie, PA	3,660.7
51	Buffalo, NY	5,449.9	123	Plantation, FL	4,544.0	195	Syracuse, NY	3,617.4
52	Tempe, AZ	5,446.7	124	Tyler, TX	4,488.6	196	Newark, NJ	3,602.0
53	Mobile, AL	5,419.5	125	Vallejo, CA	4,470.4	197	Fall River, MA	3,564.9
54	Portsmouth, VA	5,417.1	126	Billings, MT	4,465.5	198	Fort Wayne, IN	3,543.7
55	Fort Smith, AR	5,414.4	127	Berkeley, CA	4,445.9	199	Kennewick, WA	3,500.4
56	Huntsville, AL	5,387.0	128	McAllen, TX	4,430.3	200	Mission, TX	3,496.5
57	Kansas City, KS	5,373.1	129	Murfreesboro, TN	4,420.6	201	New Bedford, MA	3,480.4
58	Lafayette, LA	5,348.9	130	Hartford, CT	4,401.4	202	Cheektowaga, NY	3,476.3
59	Kent, WA	5,315.3	131	Phoenix, AZ	4,398.0	203	Pasadena, TX	3,460.4
60	West Palm Beach, FL	5,314.9	132	Chicago, IL	4,373.2	204	Downey, CA	3,427.5
61	Wilmington, NC	5,293.7	133	Modesto, CA	4,369.9	205	Toms River Twnshp, NJ	3,424.6
62	Oakland, CA	5,287.9	134	Hemet, CA	4,362.8	206	Brockton, MA	3,421.3
63	St. Joseph, MO	5,263.5	135	Richmond, CA	4,332.8	207	Yuma, AZ	3,419.1
64	Ogden, UT	5,246.2	136	Jacksonville, FL	4,327.9	208	Mesa, AZ	3,395.1
65	Des Moines, IA	5,245.5	137	Laredo, TX	4,322.2	209	Indio, CA	3,392.7
66	Stockton, CA	5,239.3	138	Lawrence, KS	4,300.5	210	Madison, WI	3,388.2
67	Austin, TX	5,235.3	139	Lakewood, CO	4,257.9	211	Victorville, CA	3,352.2
68	Lakeland, FL	5,212.2	140	Gainesville, FL	4,249.1	212	Scranton, PA	3,348.5
69	Melbourne, FL	5,200.7	141	Savannah, GA	4,230.6	213	Worcester, MA	3,336.4
70	Montgomery, AL	5,196.5	142	Bakersfield, CA	4,221.1	214	Newport News, VA	3,303.3
71	Rochester, NY	5,169.5	143	Sioux City, IA	4,219.4	215	Greeley, CO	3,299.2
72	St. Petersburg, FL	5,160.3	144	Sunrise, FL	4,194.4	216	Hialeah, FL	3,290.3

Rank Order - City (continued)

RANK	CITY	RATE	RANK	CITY	RATE	RANK	CITY	RATE
217	Grand Rapids, MI	3,285.8	290	Pasadena, CA	2,646.8	364	Palmdale, CA	2,117.8
218	Santa Monica, CA	3,272.4	291	Greece, NY	2,635.5	365	Elk Grove, CA	2,112.2
219	Pittsburgh, PA	3,260.8	292	Chino, CA	2,626.1	366	McKinney, TX	2,110.9
220	Raleigh, NC	3,237.5	293	Palm Bay, FL	2,618.6	367	Baldwin Park, CA	2,099.0
221	Lawrence, MA	3,228.7	294	Joliet, IL	2,611.0	368	Napa, CA	2,075.3
221	Lynchburg, VA	3,228.7	295	Sandy Springs, GA	2,602.8	369	Sterling Heights, MI	2,060.9
223	Paterson, NJ	3,226.0	296	Westminster, CO	2,596.3	370	Frisco, TX	2,059.4
224	Chesapeake, VA	3,185.5	297	Fullerton, CA	2,596.0	371	Menifee, CA	2,054.1
225	Anchorage, AK	3,184.0	297	Tracy, CA	2,596.0	372	Hamilton Twnshp, NJ	2,047.1
226	Lewisville, TX	3,181.0	299	Miramar, FL	2,593.3	373	Lancaster, CA	2,029.4
227	Costa Mesa, CA	3,176.5	300	Hayward, CA	2,592.5	374	Chula Vista, CA	2,028.9
228	Deerfield Beach, FL	3,176.0	301	Newport Beach, CA	2,579.3	375	Santa Ana, CA	2,002.5
229	Pembroke Pines, FL	3,151.9	302	Orem, UT	2,579.1	376	Edmond, OK	2,000.6
230	Clarksville, TN	3,144.0	303	Boise, ID	2,562.2	377	El Monte, CA	1,991.1
231	Riverside, CA	3,132.6	304	Cape Coral, FL	2,551.0	378	Tustin, CA	1,979.6
232	Boston, MA	3,129.4	305	Plano, TX	2,549.5	379	Beaverton, OR	1,960.1
233	Boca Raton, FL	3,128.3	306	Cranston, RI	2,544.5	380	Danbury, CT	1,959.5
234	College Station, TX	3,123.2	307	Woodbridge Twnshp, NJ	2,540.2	381	Garden Grove, CA	1,959.0
235	Bend, OR	3,119.2	308	Provo, UT	2,518.8	382	Clifton, NJ	1,940.4
236	Norman, OK	3,104.0	309	Boulder, CO	2,514.1	383	Roswell, GA	1,929.4
237	Chandler, AZ	3,096.9	310	Anaheim, CA	2,496.3	384	Aurora, IL	1,925.0
238	Charleston, SC	3,090.2	311	Hawthorne, CA	2,490.5	385	Orange, CA	1,921.5
239	Ventura, CA	3,083.1	312	Santa Clara, CA	2,489.0	386	Clarkstown, NY	1,914.9
240	Santa Barbara, CA	3,081.1	313	Fargo, ND	2,488.6	387	Redwood City, CA	1,913.3
241	Concord, CA	3,079.3	314	Bethlehem, PA	2,475.4	388	Quincy, MA	1,913.1
242	Irving, TX	3,076.4	315	Coral Springs, FL	2,472.6	389	Elgin, IL	1,905.7
243	Odessa, TX	3,071.3	316	Hesperia, CA	2,465.1	390	Torrance, CA	1,880.4
244	Peoria, AZ	3,055.4	317	El Paso, TX	2,461.1	391	Pearland, TX	1,852.5
245	Tampa, FL	3,054.2	318	Nashua, NH	2,459.4	392	Carlsbad, CA	1,848.6
246	Scottsdale, AZ	3,050.0	319	El Cajon, CA	2,452.1	393	Henderson, NV	1,838.0
247	Kenosha, WI	3,041.6	320	Burbank, CA	2,443.7	394	Daly City, CA	1,837.5
248	South Gate, CA	3,029.1	321	Chico, CA	2,425.5	395	Rio Rancho, NM	1,829.4
249	West Covina, CA	3,026.7	322	Santa Maria, CA	2,411.6	396	Edison Twnshp, NJ	1,826.5
250	Sioux Falls, SD	3,022.0	323	Round Rock, TX	2,398.3	397	Fremont, CA	1,824.5
251	Trenton, NJ	3,016.6	324	Clinton Twnshp, MI	2,395.5	398	Gilbert, AZ	1,823.0
252	Nampa, ID	3,001.5	325	Huntington Beach, CA	2,387.3	399	Vacaville, CA	1,793.3
253	Aurora, CO	2,985.7	326	Temecula, CA	2,375.7	400	Glendale, CA	1,779.6
253	Cambridge, MA	2,985.7	327	Bellflower, CA	2,363.4	401	Sugar Land, TX	1,775.7
255	Rialto, CA	2,968.0	328	Cicero, IL	2,354.3	402	Allen, TX	1,774.0
256	Salinas, CA	2,951.2	329	Arvada, CO	2,351.2	403	San Mateo, CA	1,761.1
257	Pomona, CA	2,946.8	330	Lakewood, CA	2,344.8	404	Oxnard, CA	1,747.5
258	Roseville, CA	2,946.3	331	Rancho Cucamon., CA	2,341.3	405	Brick Twnshp, NJ	1,743.2
259	Moreno Valley, CA	2,945.2	332	Inglewood, CA	2,326.9	406	Olathe, KS	1,739.9
260	Compton, CA	2,935.8	333	Green Bay, WI	2,315.6	407	New Rochelle, NY	1,735.0
261	Sandy, UT	2,935.5	334	Port St. Lucie, FL	2,314.1	408	New York, NY	1,710.4
262	Ontario, CA	2,929.1	335	Lee's Summit, MO	2,307.6	409	Amherst, NY	1,703.9
263	Fort Collins, CO	2,916.2	336	Buena Park, CA	2,306.2	410	San Marcos, CA	1,679.9
264	Midland, TX	2,896.4	337	Overland Park, KS	2,301.2	411	Stamford, CT	1,617.2
265	Lowell, MA	2,893.6	338	San Jose, CA	2,295.8	412	Farmington Hills, MI	1,588.9
266	Reno, NV	2,883.9	339	Jersey City, NJ	2,294.9	413	Yonkers, NY	1,558.5
267	Lynn, MA	2,882.9	340	Broken Arrow, OK	2,289.1	414	Canton Twnshp, MI	1,548.2
268	Warren, MI	2,876.3	341	Somerville, MA	2,285.6	415	O'Fallon, MO	1,538.6
269	Denton, TX	2,863.5	342	Oceanside, CA	2,276.8	416	Cary, NC	1,528.3
270	Whittier, CA	2,858.7	343	Bloomington, IL	2,264.4	417	Irvine, CA	1,526.5
271	Bellevue, WA	2,847.5	344	San Diego, CA	2,255.9	418	Naperville, IL	1,483.0
272	Thornton, CO	2,845.1	345	Los Angeles, CA	2,249.8	419	Santa Clarita, CA	1,439.5
273	Las Vegas, NV	2,840.4	346	Alhambra, CA	2,249.4	420	Arlington Heights, IL	1,437.7
274	Westland, MI	2,832.3	347	Alexandria, VA	2,245.9	421	Murrieta, CA	1,428.1
275	Colonie, NY	2,818.5	348	Ann Arbor, MI	2,239.0	422	Thousand Oaks, CA	1,395.0
276	Champaign, IL	2,805.7	349	Norwalk, CT	2,231.8	423	Sunnyvale, CA	1,390.0
277	Fairfield, CA	2,790.9	350	Longmont, CO	2,230.8	424	Meridian, ID	1,381.7
278	Suffolk, VA	2,781.7	351	Hillsboro, OR	2,230.4	425	Newton, MA	1,378.6
279	West Jordan, UT	2,780.2	352	League City, TX	2,209.4	426	Simi Valley, CA	1,350.1
280	Richardson, TX	2,771.7	353	Escondido, CA	2,204.6	427	Centennial, CO	1,324.8
281	Westminster, CA	2,759.0	354	Troy, MI	2,199.7	428	Chino Hills, CA	1,292.3
282	Long Beach, CA	2,740.3	355	Santa Rosa, CA	2,182.7	429	Mission Viejo, CA	1,288.1
283	Virginia Beach, VA	2,737.4	356	Surprise, AZ	2,179.9	430	Lake Forest, CA	1,211.4
284	Carrollton, TX	2,731.8	357	Livonia, MI	2,176.1	431	Lakewood Twnshp, NJ	1,151.9
285	Upper Darby Twnshp, PA	2,688.5	358	Corona, CA	2,175.6	432	Ramapo, NY	1,045.8
286	Sparks, NV	2,688.3	359	Livermore, CA	2,168.0	433	Carmel, IN	1,044.0
287	Carson, CA	2,685.6	360	Rochester, MN	2,159.1	434	Fishers, IN	906.9
288	Hoover, AL	2,675.2	361	Fontana, CA	2,134.9	435	Johns Creek, GA	738.4
289	Warwick, RI	2,657.1	362	Vista, CA	2,133.0	NA	Toledo, OH**	NA
			363	Norwalk, CA	2,129.4	NA	Tucson, AZ**	NA

Source: CQ Press using reported data from the F.B.I. "Crime in the United States 2011"
*Property crimes are offenses of burglary, larceny-theft, and motor vehicle theft. Attempts are included.
**Not available.

Alpha Order - City

67. Percent Change in Property Crime Rate: 2010 to 2011
National Percent Change = 1.3% Decrease*

RANK	CITY	% CHANGE	RANK	CITY	% CHANGE	RANK	CITY	% CHANGE
358	Abilene, TX	(12.4)	208	Cheektowaga, NY	(3.0)	120	Fort Wayne, IN	2.8
108	Akron, OH	3.4	232	Chesapeake, VA	(4.1)	183	Fort Worth, TX	(1.3)
360	Albany, GA	(12.8)	112	Chicago, IL	3.2	381	Fremont, CA	(15.1)
273	Albany, NY	(6.3)	346	Chico, CA	(11.5)	146	Fresno, CA	0.7
89	Albuquerque, NM	4.8	186	Chino Hills, CA	(1.5)	346	Frisco, TX	(11.5)
78	Alexandria, VA	5.9	40	Chino, CA	10.0	329	Fullerton, CA	(10.2)
301	Alhambra, CA	(7.9)	320	Chula Vista, CA	(9.3)	305	Gainesville, FL	(8.1)
394	Allentown, PA	(17.6)	NA	Cicero, IL**	NA	320	Garden Grove, CA	(9.3)
189	Allen, TX	(1.7)	30	Cincinnati, OH	11.6	221	Garland, TX	(3.6)
392	Amarillo, TX	(17.0)	379	Citrus Heights, CA	(15.0)	NA	Gary, IN**	NA
326	Amherst, NY	(10.0)	352	Clarkstown, NY	(11.7)	226	Gilbert, AZ	(3.8)
168	Anaheim, CA	(0.3)	208	Clarksville, TN	(3.0)	12	Glendale, AZ	16.3
322	Anchorage, AK	(9.5)	301	Clearwater, FL	(7.9)	258	Glendale, CA	(5.7)
377	Ann Arbor, MI	(14.8)	13	Cleveland, OH	15.9	365	Grand Prairie, TX	(13.4)
4	Antioch, CA	23.3	NA	Clifton, NJ**	NA	398	Grand Rapids, MI	(18.9)
329	Arlington Heights, IL	(10.2)	200	Clinton Twnshp, MI	(2.3)	239	Greece, NY	(4.7)
311	Arlington, TX	(8.5)	48	Clovis, CA	9.2	114	Greeley, CO	3.1
290	Arvada, CO	(7.2)	99	College Station, TX	4.0	323	Green Bay, WI	(9.6)
192	Asheville, NC	(1.8)	226	Colonie, NY	(3.8)	123	Gresham, OR	2.1
243	Athens-Clarke, GA	(4.8)	341	Colorado Springs, CO	(11.3)	134	Hamilton Twnshp, NJ	1.5
3	Atlanta, GA	23.4	76	Columbia, MO	6.1	298	Hammond, IN	(7.7)
230	Aurora, CO	(3.9)	338	Columbus, GA	(11.1)	121	Hampton, VA	2.7
336	Aurora, IL	(11.0)	232	Columbus, OH	(4.1)	149	Hartford, CT	0.6
316	Austin, TX	(9.0)	177	Compton, CA	(1.0)	251	Hawthorne, CA	(5.1)
24	Avondale, AZ	12.2	177	Concord, CA	(1.0)	166	Hayward, CA	(0.2)
294	Bakersfield, CA	(7.4)	274	Concord, NC	(6.4)	36	Hemet, CA	10.5
295	Baldwin Park, CA	(7.6)	52	Coral Springs, FL	9.0	275	Henderson, NV	(6.5)
64	Baltimore, MD	7.7	258	Corona, CA	(5.7)	17	Hesperia, CA	14.2
NA	Baton Rouge, LA**	NA	316	Corpus Christi, TX	(9.0)	312	Hialeah, FL	(8.7)
134	Beaumont, TX	1.5	43	Costa Mesa, CA	9.8	112	High Point, NC	3.2
100	Beaverton, OR	3.9	69	Cranston, RI	7.2	NA	Hillsboro, OR**	NA
218	Bellevue, WA	(3.5)	114	Dallas, TX	3.1	67	Hollywood, FL	7.3
211	Bellflower, CA	(3.1)	101	Daly City, CA	3.8	NA	Hoover, AL**	NA
139	Bellingham, WA	1.1	84	Danbury, CT	5.1	161	Houston, TX	0.0
116	Bend, OR	3.0	NA	Davenport, IA**	NA	180	Huntington Beach, CA	(1.1)
407	Berkeley, CA	(23.2)	180	Davie, FL	(1.1)	NA	Huntsville, AL**	NA
357	Bethlehem, PA	(11.9)	146	Dayton, OH	0.7	236	Independence, MO	(4.3)
NA	Billings, MT**	NA	378	Dearborn, MI	(14.9)	NA	Indianapolis, IN**	NA
NA	Birmingham, AL**	NA	334	Decatur, IL	(10.9)	31	Indio, CA	11.4
371	Bloomington, IL	(14.2)	243	Deerfield Beach, FL	(4.8)	202	Inglewood, CA	(2.4)
359	Bloomington, IN	(12.6)	26	Denton, TX	11.9	6	Irvine, CA	18.5
189	Bloomington, MN	(1.7)	61	Denver, CO	8.2	396	Irving, TX	(18.0)
61	Boca Raton, FL	8.2	58	Des Moines, IA	8.5	246	Jacksonville, FL	(4.9)
295	Boise, ID	(7.6)	14	Detroit, MI	15.6	216	Jackson, MS	(3.3)
200	Boston, MA	(2.3)	293	Downey, CA	(7.3)	275	Jersey City, NJ	(6.5)
309	Boulder, CO	(8.3)	NA	Duluth, MN**	NA	411	Johns Creek, GA	(31.3)
139	Brick Twnshp, NJ	1.1	154	Durham, NC	0.3	266	Joliet, IL	(6.1)
15	Bridgeport, CT	15.0	218	Edinburg, TX	(3.5)	164	Kansas City, KS	(0.1)
38	Brockton, MA	10.1	67	Edison Twnshp, NJ	7.3	NA	Kansas City, MO**	NA
44	Broken Arrow, OK	9.7	185	Edmond, OK	(1.4)	239	Kennewick, WA	(4.7)
NA	Brooklyn Park, MN**	NA	389	El Cajon, CA	(16.4)	136	Kenosha, WI	1.4
346	Brownsville, TX	(11.5)	278	El Monte, CA	(6.6)	123	Kent, WA	2.1
404	Bryan, TX	(22.8)	352	El Paso, TX	(11.7)	387	Killeen, TX	(16.2)
307	Buena Park, CA	(8.2)	266	Elgin, IL	(6.1)	65	Knoxville, TN	7.5
NA	Buffalo, NY**	NA	56	Elizabeth, NJ	8.7	352	Lafayette, LA	(11.7)
266	Burbank, CA	(6.1)	271	Elk Grove, CA	(6.2)	236	Lake Forest, CA	(4.3)
159	Cambridge, MA	0.1	48	Erie, PA	9.2	216	Lakeland, FL	(3.3)
1	Camden, NJ	29.9	406	Escondido, CA	(23.1)	402	Lakewood Twnshp, NJ	(19.8)
342	Canton Twnshp, MI	(11.4)	54	Eugene, OR	8.8	204	Lakewood, CA	(2.6)
63	Cape Coral, FL	8.1	206	Evansville, IN	(2.8)	170	Lakewood, CO	(0.4)
127	Carlsbad, CA	2.0	288	Everett, WA	(7.1)	350	Lancaster, CA	(11.6)
390	Carmel, IN	(16.6)	373	Fairfield, CA	(14.3)	152	Lansing, MI	0.5
130	Carrollton, TX	1.8	208	Fall River, MA	(3.0)	361	Laredo, TX	(13.0)
74	Carson, CA	6.7	329	Fargo, ND	(10.2)	383	Largo, FL	(15.5)
175	Cary, NC	(0.8)	333	Farmington Hills, MI	(10.7)	109	Las Cruces, NM	3.3
154	Cedar Rapids, IA	0.3	78	Fayetteville, NC	5.9	286	Las Vegas, NV	(6.9)
326	Centennial, CO	(10.0)	263	Fishers, IN	(5.9)	83	Lawrence, KS	5.2
NA	Champaign, IL**	NA	22	Flint, MI	13.2	261	Lawrence, MA	(5.8)
170	Chandler, AZ	(0.4)	28	Fontana, CA	11.7	177	Lawton, OK	(1.0)
312	Charleston, SC	(8.7)	338	Fort Collins, CO	(11.1)	397	League City, TX	(18.3)
284	Charlotte, NC	(6.8)	18	Fort Lauderdale, FL	14.1	246	Lee's Summit, MO	(4.9)
166	Chattanooga, TN	(0.2)	215	Fort Smith, AR	(3.2)	198	Lewisville, TX	(2.2)

Alpha Order - City (continued)

RANK	CITY	% CHANGE
NA	Lexington, KY**	NA
174	Lincoln, NE	(0.7)
102	Little Rock, AR	3.7
157	Livermore, CA	0.2
280	Livonia, MI	(6.7)
54	Long Beach, CA	8.8
326	Longmont, CO	(10.0)
383	Longview, TX	(15.5)
221	Los Angeles, CA	(3.6)
104	Louisville, KY	3.6
391	Lowell, MA	(16.8)
253	Lubbock, TX	(5.2)
275	Lynchburg, VA	(6.5)
168	Lynn, MA	(0.3)
109	Macon, GA	3.3
153	Madison, WI	0.4
38	Manchester, NH	10.1
400	McAllen, TX	(19.4)
263	McKinney, TX	(5.9)
8	Medford, OR	17.5
37	Melbourne, FL	10.3
102	Memphis, TN	3.7
409	Menifee, CA	(29.5)
50	Merced, CA	9.1
382	Meridian, ID	(15.2)
109	Mesa, AZ	3.3
261	Mesquite, TX	(5.8)
59	Miami Beach, FL	8.4
139	Miami Gardens, FL	1.1
8	Miami, FL	17.5
350	Midland, TX	(11.6)
226	Milwaukee, WI	(3.8)
88	Minneapolis, MN	4.9
401	Miramar, FL	(19.5)
66	Mission Viejo, CA	7.4
405	Mission, TX	(22.9)
NA	Mobile, AL**	NA
250	Modesto, CA	(5.0)
NA	Montgomery, AL**	NA
32	Moreno Valley, CA	11.3
91	Murfreesboro, TN	4.7
78	Murrieta, CA	5.9
42	Nampa, ID	9.9
149	Napa, CA	0.6
NA	Naperville, IL**	NA
224	Nashua, NH	(3.7)
221	Nashville, TN	(3.6)
363	New Bedford, MA	(13.3)
370	New Haven, CT	(13.9)
20	New Orleans, LA	13.8
84	New Rochelle, NY	5.1
123	New York, NY	2.1
44	Newark, NJ	9.7
207	Newport Beach, CA	(2.9)
189	Newport News, VA	(1.7)
239	Newton, MA	(4.7)
340	Norfolk, VA	(11.2)
203	Norman, OK	(2.5)
257	North Charleston, SC	(5.6)
84	Norwalk, CA	5.1
143	Norwalk, CT	0.9
2	Oakland, CA	25.1
137	Oceanside, CA	1.3
342	Odessa, TX	(11.4)
180	O'Fallon, MO	(1.1)
307	Ogden, UT	(8.2)
161	Oklahoma City, OK	0.0
246	Olathe, KS	(4.9)
5	Omaha, NE	21.9
117	Ontario, CA	2.9
117	Orange, CA	2.9
255	Orem, UT	(5.5)
47	Orlando, FL	9.5
192	Overland Park, KS	(1.8)
395	Oxnard, CA	(17.8)
40	Palm Bay, FL	10.0
280	Palmdale, CA	(6.7)
266	Pasadena, CA	(6.1)
319	Pasadena, TX	(9.2)
95	Paterson, NJ	4.4
197	Pearland, TX	(2.1)
295	Pembroke Pines, FL	(7.6)
95	Peoria, AZ	4.4
92	Peoria, IL	4.6
87	Philadelphia, PA	5.0
35	Phoenix, AZ	10.7
323	Pittsburgh, PA	(9.6)
81	Plano, TX	5.6
117	Plantation, FL	2.9
164	Pomona, CA	(0.1)
24	Pompano Beach, FL	12.2
8	Port St. Lucie, FL	17.5
138	Portland, OR	1.2
186	Portsmouth, VA	(1.5)
60	Provo, UT	8.3
NA	Pueblo, CO**	NA
211	Quincy, MA	(3.1)
44	Racine, WI	9.7
92	Raleigh, NC	4.6
72	Ramapo, NY	6.9
28	Rancho Cucamon., CA	11.7
392	Reading, PA	(17.0)
23	Redding, CA	12.4
363	Redwood City, CA	(13.3)
371	Reno, NV	(14.2)
410	Renton, WA	(30.0)
16	Rialto, CA	14.8
226	Richardson, TX	(3.8)
211	Richmond, CA	(3.1)
149	Richmond, VA	0.6
57	Rio Rancho, NM	8.6
251	Riverside, CA	(5.1)
255	Roanoke, VA	(5.5)
278	Rochester, MN	(6.6)
334	Rochester, NY	(10.9)
288	Rockford, IL	(7.1)
290	Roseville, CA	(7.2)
342	Roswell, GA	(11.4)
352	Round Rock, TX	(11.7)
304	Sacramento, CA	(8.0)
194	Salem, OR	(1.9)
310	Salinas, CA	(8.4)
365	Salt Lake City, UT	(13.4)
385	San Angelo, TX	(15.7)
265	San Antonio, TX	(6.0)
346	San Bernardino, CA	(11.5)
224	San Diego, CA	(3.7)
123	San Francisco, CA	2.1
143	San Jose, CA	0.9
280	San Leandro, CA	(6.7)
375	San Marcos, CA	(14.4)
373	San Mateo, CA	(14.3)
399	Sandy Springs, GA	(19.1)
188	Sandy, UT	(1.6)
107	Santa Ana, CA	3.5
89	Santa Barbara, CA	4.8
284	Santa Clara, CA	(6.8)
305	Santa Clarita, CA	(8.1)
312	Santa Maria, CA	(8.7)
301	Santa Monica, CA	(7.9)
385	Santa Rosa, CA	(15.7)
211	Savannah, GA	(3.1)
70	Scottsdale, AZ	7.1
172	Scranton, PA	(0.6)
230	Seattle, WA	(3.9)
146	Shreveport, LA	0.7
408	Simi Valley, CA	(25.6)
21	Sioux City, IA	13.5
161	Sioux Falls, SD	0.0
332	Somerville, MA	(10.3)
82	South Bend, IN	5.3
26	South Gate, CA	11.9
336	Sparks, NV	(11.0)
19	Spokane Valley, WA	13.9
235	Spokane, WA	(4.2)
238	Springfield, IL	(4.5)
198	Springfield, MA	(2.2)
287	Springfield, MO	(7.0)
142	Stamford, CT	1.0
NA	Sterling Heights, MI**	NA
254	Stockton, CA	(5.4)
34	St. Joseph, MO	10.9
97	St. Louis, MO	4.1
175	St. Paul, MN	(0.8)
316	St. Petersburg, FL	(9.0)
11	Suffolk, VA	16.5
403	Sugar Land, TX	(21.2)
388	Sunnyvale, CA	(16.3)
246	Sunrise, FL	(4.9)
130	Surprise, AZ	1.8
369	Syracuse, NY	(13.6)
258	Tacoma, WA	(5.7)
104	Tallahassee, FL	3.6
290	Tampa, FL	(7.2)
104	Temecula, CA	3.6
33	Tempe, AZ	11.2
NA	Thornton, CO**	NA
379	Thousand Oaks, CA	(15.0)
NA	Toledo, OH**	NA
7	Toms River Twnshp, NJ	18.1
195	Topeka, KS	(2.0)
298	Torrance, CA	(7.7)
145	Tracy, CA	0.8
157	Trenton, NJ	0.2
132	Troy, MI	1.6
NA	Tucson, AZ**	NA
127	Tulsa, OK	2.0
NA	Tuscaloosa, AL**	NA
300	Tustin, CA	(7.8)
352	Tyler, TX	(11.7)
127	Upper Darby Twnshp, PA	2.0
342	Vacaville, CA	(11.4)
159	Vallejo, CA	0.1
154	Vancouver, WA	0.3
280	Ventura, CA	(6.7)
73	Victorville, CA	6.8
325	Virginia Beach, VA	(9.8)
239	Visalia, CA	(4.7)
271	Vista, CA	(6.2)
172	Waco, TX	(0.6)
121	Warren, MI	2.7
77	Warwick, RI	6.0
132	Washington, DC	1.6
218	Waterbury, CT	(3.5)
70	West Covina, CA	7.1
266	West Jordan, UT	(6.1)
75	West Palm Beach, FL	6.5
362	West Valley, UT	(13.2)
315	Westland, MI	(8.9)
204	Westminster, CA	(2.6)
365	Westminster, CO	(13.4)
232	Whittier, CA	(4.1)
365	Wichita Falls, TX	(13.4)
94	Wichita, KS	4.5
243	Wilmington, NC	(4.8)
97	Winston-Salem, NC	4.1
50	Woodbridge Twnshp, NJ	9.1
195	Worcester, MA	(2.0)
376	Yakima, WA	(14.5)
53	Yonkers, NY	8.9
183	Yuma, AZ	(1.3)

Source: CQ Press using reported data from the F.B.I. "Crime in the United States 2011"
*Property crimes are offenses of burglary, larceny-theft, and motor vehicle theft. Attempts are included.
**Not available.

Rank Order - City
67. Percent Change in Property Crime Rate: 2010 to 2011 (continued)
National Percent Change = 1.3% Decrease*

RANK	CITY	% CHANGE	RANK	CITY	% CHANGE	RANK	CITY	% CHANGE
1	Camden, NJ	29.9	73	Victorville, CA	6.8	145	Tracy, CA	0.8
2	Oakland, CA	25.1	74	Carson, CA	6.7	146	Dayton, OH	0.7
3	Atlanta, GA	23.4	75	West Palm Beach, FL	6.5	146	Fresno, CA	0.7
4	Antioch, CA	23.3	76	Columbia, MO	6.1	146	Shreveport, LA	0.7
5	Omaha, NE	21.9	77	Warwick, RI	6.0	149	Hartford, CT	0.6
6	Irvine, CA	18.5	78	Alexandria, VA	5.9	149	Napa, CA	0.6
7	Toms River Twnshp, NJ	18.1	78	Fayetteville, NC	5.9	149	Richmond, VA	0.6
8	Medford, OR	17.5	78	Murrieta, CA	5.9	152	Lansing, MI	0.5
8	Miami, FL	17.5	81	Plano, TX	5.6	153	Madison, WI	0.4
8	Port St. Lucie, FL	17.5	82	South Bend, IN	5.3	154	Cedar Rapids, IA	0.3
11	Suffolk, VA	16.5	83	Lawrence, KS	5.2	154	Durham, NC	0.3
12	Glendale, AZ	16.3	84	Danbury, CT	5.1	154	Vancouver, WA	0.3
13	Cleveland, OH	15.9	84	New Rochelle, NY	5.1	157	Livermore, CA	0.2
14	Detroit, MI	15.6	84	Norwalk, CA	5.1	157	Trenton, NJ	0.2
15	Bridgeport, CT	15.0	87	Philadelphia, PA	5.0	159	Cambridge, MA	0.1
16	Rialto, CA	14.8	88	Minneapolis, MN	4.9	159	Vallejo, CA	0.1
17	Hesperia, CA	14.2	89	Albuquerque, NM	4.8	161	Houston, TX	0.0
18	Fort Lauderdale, FL	14.1	89	Santa Barbara, CA	4.8	161	Oklahoma City, OK	0.0
19	Spokane Valley, WA	13.9	91	Murfreesboro, TN	4.7	161	Sioux Falls, SD	0.0
20	New Orleans, LA	13.8	92	Peoria, IL	4.6	164	Kansas City, KS	(0.1)
21	Sioux City, IA	13.5	92	Raleigh, NC	4.6	164	Pomona, CA	(0.1)
22	Flint, MI	13.2	94	Wichita, KS	4.5	166	Chattanooga, TN	(0.2)
23	Redding, CA	12.4	95	Paterson, NJ	4.4	166	Hayward, CA	(0.2)
24	Avondale, AZ	12.2	95	Peoria, AZ	4.4	168	Anaheim, CA	(0.3)
24	Pompano Beach, FL	12.2	97	St. Louis, MO	4.1	168	Lynn, MA	(0.3)
26	Denton, TX	11.9	97	Winston-Salem, NC	4.1	170	Chandler, AZ	(0.4)
26	South Gate, CA	11.9	99	College Station, TX	4.0	170	Lakewood, CO	(0.4)
28	Fontana, CA	11.7	100	Beaverton, OR	3.9	172	Scranton, PA	(0.6)
28	Rancho Cucamon., CA	11.7	101	Daly City, CA	3.8	172	Waco, TX	(0.6)
30	Cincinnati, OH	11.6	102	Little Rock, AR	3.7	174	Lincoln, NE	(0.7)
31	Indio, CA	11.4	102	Memphis, TN	3.7	175	Cary, NC	(0.8)
32	Moreno Valley, CA	11.3	104	Louisville, KY	3.6	175	St. Paul, MN	(0.8)
33	Tempe, AZ	11.2	104	Tallahassee, FL	3.6	177	Compton, CA	(1.0)
34	St. Joseph, MO	10.9	104	Temecula, CA	3.6	177	Concord, CA	(1.0)
35	Phoenix, AZ	10.7	107	Santa Ana, CA	3.5	177	Lawton, OK	(1.0)
36	Hemet, CA	10.5	108	Akron, OH	3.4	180	Davie, FL	(1.1)
37	Melbourne, FL	10.3	109	Las Cruces, NM	3.3	180	Huntington Beach, CA	(1.1)
38	Brockton, MA	10.1	109	Macon, GA	3.3	180	O'Fallon, MO	(1.1)
38	Manchester, NH	10.1	109	Mesa, AZ	3.3	183	Fort Worth, TX	(1.3)
40	Chino, CA	10.0	112	Chicago, IL	3.2	183	Yuma, AZ	(1.3)
40	Palm Bay, FL	10.0	112	High Point, NC	3.2	185	Edmond, OK	(1.4)
42	Nampa, ID	9.9	114	Dallas, TX	3.1	186	Chino Hills, CA	(1.5)
43	Costa Mesa, CA	9.8	114	Greeley, CO	3.1	186	Portsmouth, VA	(1.5)
44	Broken Arrow, OK	9.7	116	Bend, OR	3.0	188	Sandy, UT	(1.6)
44	Newark, NJ	9.7	117	Ontario, CA	2.9	189	Allen, TX	(1.7)
44	Racine, WI	9.7	117	Orange, CA	2.9	189	Bloomington, MN	(1.7)
47	Orlando, FL	9.5	117	Plantation, FL	2.9	189	Newport News, VA	(1.7)
48	Clovis, CA	9.2	120	Fort Wayne, IN	2.8	192	Asheville, NC	(1.8)
48	Erie, PA	9.2	121	Hampton, VA	2.7	192	Overland Park, KS	(1.8)
50	Merced, CA	9.1	121	Warren, MI	2.7	194	Salem, OR	(1.9)
50	Woodbridge Twnshp, NJ	9.1	123	Gresham, OR	2.1	195	Topeka, KS	(2.0)
52	Coral Springs, FL	9.0	123	Kent, WA	2.1	195	Worcester, MA	(2.0)
53	Yonkers, NY	8.9	123	New York, NY	2.1	197	Pearland, TX	(2.1)
54	Eugene, OR	8.8	123	San Francisco, CA	2.1	198	Lewisville, TX	(2.2)
54	Long Beach, CA	8.8	127	Carlsbad, CA	2.0	198	Springfield, MA	(2.2)
56	Elizabeth, NJ	8.7	127	Tulsa, OK	2.0	200	Boston, MA	(2.3)
57	Rio Rancho, NM	8.6	127	Upper Darby Twnshp, PA	2.0	200	Clinton Twnshp, MI	(2.3)
58	Des Moines, IA	8.5	130	Carrollton, TX	1.8	202	Inglewood, CA	(2.4)
59	Miami Beach, FL	8.4	130	Surprise, AZ	1.8	203	Norman, OK	(2.5)
60	Provo, UT	8.3	132	Troy, MI	1.6	204	Lakewood, CA	(2.6)
61	Boca Raton, FL	8.2	132	Washington, DC	1.6	204	Westminster, CA	(2.6)
61	Denver, CO	8.2	134	Beaumont, TX	1.5	206	Evansville, IN	(2.8)
63	Cape Coral, FL	8.1	134	Hamilton Twnshp, NJ	1.5	207	Newport Beach, CA	(2.9)
64	Baltimore, MD	7.7	136	Kenosha, WI	1.4	208	Cheektowaga, NY	(3.0)
65	Knoxville, TN	7.5	137	Oceanside, CA	1.3	208	Clarksville, TN	(3.0)
66	Mission Viejo, CA	7.4	138	Portland, OR	1.2	208	Fall River, MA	(3.0)
67	Edison Twnshp, NJ	7.3	139	Bellingham, WA	1.1	211	Bellflower, CA	(3.1)
67	Hollywood, FL	7.3	139	Brick Twnshp, NJ	1.1	211	Quincy, MA	(3.1)
69	Cranston, RI	7.2	139	Miami Gardens, FL	1.1	211	Richmond, CA	(3.1)
70	Scottsdale, AZ	7.1	142	Stamford, CT	1.0	211	Savannah, GA	(3.1)
70	West Covina, CA	7.1	143	Norwalk, CT	0.9	215	Fort Smith, AR	(3.2)
72	Ramapo, NY	6.9	143	San Jose, CA	0.9	216	Jackson, MS	(3.3)

Rank Order - City (continued)

RANK	CITY	% CHANGE	RANK	CITY	% CHANGE	RANK	CITY	% CHANGE
216	Lakeland, FL	(3.3)	290	Arvada, CO	(7.2)	363	Redwood City, CA	(13.3)
218	Bellevue, WA	(3.5)	290	Roseville, CA	(7.2)	365	Grand Prairie, TX	(13.4)
218	Edinburg, TX	(3.5)	290	Tampa, FL	(7.2)	365	Salt Lake City, UT	(13.4)
218	Waterbury, CT	(3.5)	293	Downey, CA	(7.3)	365	Westminster, CO	(13.4)
221	Garland, TX	(3.6)	294	Bakersfield, CA	(7.4)	365	Wichita Falls, TX	(13.4)
221	Los Angeles, CA	(3.6)	295	Baldwin Park, CA	(7.6)	369	Syracuse, NY	(13.6)
221	Nashville, TN	(3.6)	295	Boise, ID	(7.6)	370	New Haven, CT	(13.9)
224	Nashua, NH	(3.7)	295	Pembroke Pines, FL	(7.6)	371	Bloomington, IL	(14.2)
224	San Diego, CA	(3.7)	298	Hammond, IN	(7.7)	371	Reno, NV	(14.2)
226	Colonie, NY	(3.8)	298	Torrance, CA	(7.7)	373	Fairfield, CA	(14.3)
226	Gilbert, AZ	(3.8)	300	Tustin, CA	(7.8)	373	San Mateo, CA	(14.3)
226	Milwaukee, WI	(3.8)	301	Alhambra, CA	(7.9)	375	San Marcos, CA	(14.4)
226	Richardson, TX	(3.8)	301	Clearwater, FL	(7.9)	376	Yakima, WA	(14.5)
230	Aurora, CO	(3.9)	301	Santa Monica, CA	(7.9)	377	Ann Arbor, MI	(14.8)
230	Seattle, WA	(3.9)	304	Sacramento, CA	(8.0)	378	Dearborn, MI	(14.9)
232	Chesapeake, VA	(4.1)	305	Gainesville, FL	(8.1)	379	Citrus Heights, CA	(15.0)
232	Columbus, OH	(4.1)	305	Santa Clarita, CA	(8.1)	379	Thousand Oaks, CA	(15.0)
232	Whittier, CA	(4.1)	307	Buena Park, CA	(8.2)	381	Fremont, CA	(15.1)
235	Spokane, WA	(4.2)	307	Ogden, UT	(8.2)	382	Meridian, ID	(15.2)
236	Independence, MO	(4.3)	309	Boulder, CO	(8.3)	383	Largo, FL	(15.5)
236	Lake Forest, CA	(4.3)	310	Salinas, CA	(8.4)	383	Longview, TX	(15.5)
238	Springfield, IL	(4.5)	311	Arlington, TX	(8.5)	385	San Angelo, TX	(15.7)
239	Greece, NY	(4.7)	312	Charleston, SC	(8.7)	385	Santa Rosa, CA	(15.7)
239	Kennewick, WA	(4.7)	312	Hialeah, FL	(8.7)	387	Killeen, TX	(16.2)
239	Newton, MA	(4.7)	312	Santa Maria, CA	(8.7)	388	Sunnyvale, CA	(16.3)
239	Visalia, CA	(4.7)	315	Westland, MI	(8.9)	389	El Cajon, CA	(16.4)
243	Athens-Clarke, GA	(4.8)	316	Austin, TX	(9.0)	390	Carmel, IN	(16.6)
243	Deerfield Beach, FL	(4.8)	316	Corpus Christi, TX	(9.0)	391	Lowell, MA	(16.8)
243	Wilmington, NC	(4.8)	316	St. Petersburg, FL	(9.0)	392	Amarillo, TX	(17.0)
246	Jacksonville, FL	(4.9)	319	Pasadena, TX	(9.2)	392	Reading, PA	(17.0)
246	Lee's Summit, MO	(4.9)	320	Chula Vista, CA	(9.3)	394	Allentown, PA	(17.6)
246	Olathe, KS	(4.9)	320	Garden Grove, CA	(9.3)	395	Oxnard, CA	(17.8)
246	Sunrise, FL	(4.9)	322	Anchorage, AK	(9.5)	396	Irving, TX	(18.0)
250	Modesto, CA	(5.0)	323	Green Bay, WI	(9.6)	397	League City, TX	(18.3)
251	Hawthorne, CA	(5.1)	323	Pittsburgh, PA	(9.6)	398	Grand Rapids, MI	(18.9)
251	Riverside, CA	(5.1)	325	Virginia Beach, VA	(9.8)	399	Sandy Springs, GA	(19.1)
253	Lubbock, TX	(5.2)	326	Amherst, NY	(10.0)	400	McAllen, TX	(19.4)
254	Stockton, CA	(5.4)	326	Centennial, CO	(10.0)	401	Miramar, FL	(19.5)
255	Orem, UT	(5.5)	326	Longmont, CO	(10.0)	402	Lakewood Twnshp, NJ	(19.8)
255	Roanoke, VA	(5.5)	329	Arlington Heights, IL	(10.2)	403	Sugar Land, TX	(21.2)
257	North Charleston, SC	(5.6)	329	Fargo, ND	(10.2)	404	Bryan, TX	(22.8)
258	Corona, CA	(5.7)	329	Fullerton, CA	(10.2)	405	Mission, TX	(22.9)
258	Glendale, CA	(5.7)	332	Somerville, MA	(10.3)	406	Escondido, CA	(23.1)
258	Tacoma, WA	(5.7)	333	Farmington Hills, MI	(10.7)	407	Berkeley, CA	(23.2)
261	Lawrence, MA	(5.8)	334	Decatur, IL	(10.9)	408	Simi Valley, CA	(25.6)
261	Mesquite, TX	(5.8)	334	Rochester, NY	(10.9)	409	Menifee, CA	(29.5)
263	Fishers, IN	(5.9)	336	Aurora, IL	(11.0)	410	Renton, WA	(30.0)
263	McKinney, TX	(5.9)	336	Sparks, NV	(11.0)	411	Johns Creek, GA	(31.3)
265	San Antonio, TX	(6.0)	338	Columbus, GA	(11.1)	NA	Baton Rouge, LA**	NA
266	Burbank, CA	(6.1)	338	Fort Collins, CO	(11.1)	NA	Billings, MT**	NA
266	Elgin, IL	(6.1)	340	Norfolk, VA	(11.2)	NA	Birmingham, AL**	NA
266	Joliet, IL	(6.1)	341	Colorado Springs, CO	(11.3)	NA	Brooklyn Park, MN**	NA
266	Pasadena, CA	(6.1)	342	Canton Twnshp, MI	(11.4)	NA	Buffalo, NY**	NA
266	West Jordan, UT	(6.1)	342	Odessa, TX	(11.4)	NA	Champaign, IL**	NA
271	Elk Grove, CA	(6.2)	342	Roswell, GA	(11.4)	NA	Cicero, IL**	NA
271	Vista, CA	(6.2)	342	Vacaville, CA	(11.4)	NA	Clifton, NJ**	NA
273	Albany, NY	(6.3)	346	Brownsville, TX	(11.5)	NA	Davenport, IA**	NA
274	Concord, NC	(6.4)	346	Chico, CA	(11.5)	NA	Duluth, MN**	NA
275	Henderson, NV	(6.5)	346	Frisco, TX	(11.5)	NA	Gary, IN**	NA
275	Jersey City, NJ	(6.5)	346	San Bernardino, CA	(11.5)	NA	Hillsboro, OR**	NA
275	Lynchburg, VA	(6.5)	350	Lancaster, CA	(11.6)	NA	Hoover, AL**	NA
278	El Monte, CA	(6.6)	350	Midland, TX	(11.6)	NA	Huntsville, AL**	NA
278	Rochester, MN	(6.6)	352	Clarkstown, NY	(11.7)	NA	Indianapolis, IN**	NA
280	Livonia, MI	(6.7)	352	El Paso, TX	(11.7)	NA	Kansas City, MO**	NA
280	Palmdale, CA	(6.7)	352	Lafayette, LA	(11.7)	NA	Lexington, KY**	NA
280	San Leandro, CA	(6.7)	352	Round Rock, TX	(11.7)	NA	Mobile, AL**	NA
280	Ventura, CA	(6.7)	352	Tyler, TX	(11.7)	NA	Montgomery, AL**	NA
284	Charlotte, NC	(6.8)	357	Bethlehem, PA	(11.9)	NA	Naperville, IL**	NA
284	Santa Clara, CA	(6.8)	358	Abilene, TX	(12.4)	NA	Pueblo, CO**	NA
286	Las Vegas, NV	(6.9)	359	Bloomington, IN	(12.6)	NA	Sterling Heights, MI**	NA
287	Springfield, MO	(7.0)	360	Albany, GA	(12.8)	NA	Thornton, CO**	NA
288	Everett, WA	(7.1)	361	Laredo, TX	(13.0)	NA	Toledo, OH**	NA
288	Rockford, IL	(7.1)	362	West Valley, UT	(13.2)	NA	Tucson, AZ**	NA
			363	New Bedford, MA	(13.3)	NA	Tuscaloosa, AL**	NA

Source: CQ Press using reported data from the F.B.I. "Crime in the United States 2011"
*Property crimes are offenses of burglary, larceny-theft, and motor vehicle theft. Attempts are included.
**Not available.

Alpha Order - City

68. Percent Change in Property Crime Rate: 2007 to 2011
National Percent Change = 11.2% Decrease*

RANK	CITY	% CHANGE
223	Abilene, TX	(14.4)
33	Akron, OH	8.4
266	Albany, GA	(17.9)
47	Albany, NY	3.7
181	Albuquerque, NM	(11.2)
117	Alexandria, VA	(5.6)
130	Alhambra, CA	(6.9)
318	Allentown, PA	(22.2)
298	Allen, TX	(20.7)
293	Amarillo, TX	(20.6)
43	Amherst, NY	5.2
105	Anaheim, CA	(4.9)
271	Anchorage, AK	(18.5)
152	Ann Arbor, MI	(8.9)
12	Antioch, CA	22.1
NA	Arlington Heights, IL**	NA
273	Arlington, TX	(18.6)
103	Arvada, CO	(4.5)
290	Asheville, NC	(19.8)
218	Athens-Clarke, GA	(14.1)
91	Atlanta, GA	(2.8)
317	Aurora, CO	(22.1)
347	Aurora, IL	(25.4)
261	Austin, TX	(17.4)
NA	Avondale, AZ**	NA
245	Bakersfield, CA	(16.2)
211	Baldwin Park, CA	(13.4)
74	Baltimore, MD	(0.8)
146	Baton Rouge, LA	(8.4)
157	Beaumont, TX	(9.3)
332	Beaverton, OR	(23.3)
280	Bellevue, WA	(19.0)
371	Bellflower, CA	(30.2)
374	Bellingham, WA	(30.9)
310	Bend, OR	(21.2)
393	Berkeley, CA	(36.7)
307	Bethlehem, PA	(21.1)
NA	Billings, MT**	NA
NA	Birmingham, AL**	NA
NA	Bloomington, IL**	NA
162	Bloomington, IN	(9.6)
119	Bloomington, MN	(5.7)
306	Boca Raton, FL	(21.0)
261	Boise, ID	(17.4)
343	Boston, MA	(24.6)
108	Boulder, CO	(5.0)
68	Brick Twnshp, NJ	0.2
275	Bridgeport, CT	(18.8)
95	Brockton, MA	(3.0)
45	Broken Arrow, OK	4.4
235	Brooklyn Park, MN	(15.6)
223	Brownsville, TX	(14.4)
366	Bryan, TX	(28.8)
169	Buena Park, CA	(10.5)
NA	Buffalo, NY**	NA
140	Burbank, CA	(7.4)
248	Cambridge, MA	(16.5)
79	Camden, NJ	(1.3)
200	Canton Twnshp, MI	(12.7)
355	Cape Coral, FL	(26.8)
364	Carlsbad, CA	(28.2)
392	Carmel, IN	(35.8)
211	Carrollton, TX	(13.4)
90	Carson, CA	(2.7)
264	Cary, NC	(17.7)
298	Cedar Rapids, IA	(20.7)
284	Centennial, CO	(19.3)
NA	Champaign, IL**	NA
84	Chandler, AZ	(2.1)
291	Charleston, SC	(20.4)
398	Charlotte, NC	(42.0)
315	Chattanooga, TN	(21.9)
15	Cheektowaga, NY	19.4
81	Chesapeake, VA	(1.5)
85	Chicago, IL	(2.2)
353	Chico, CA	(26.6)
178	Chino Hills, CA	(11.0)
229	Chino, CA	(15.2)
397	Chula Vista, CA	(39.0)
NA	Cicero, IL**	NA
26	Cincinnati, OH	11.5
NA	Citrus Heights, CA**	NA
136	Clarkstown, NY	(7.0)
337	Clarksville, TN	(24.2)
208	Clearwater, FL	(13.1)
46	Cleveland, OH	3.8
287	Clifton, NJ	(19.5)
62	Clinton Twnshp, MI	1.0
5	Clovis, CA	32.4
122	College Station, TX	(5.9)
142	Colonie, NY	(7.7)
233	Colorado Springs, CO	(15.4)
24	Columbia, MO	12.6
182	Columbus, GA	(11.3)
178	Columbus, OH	(11.0)
65	Compton, CA	0.5
344	Concord, CA	(24.7)
275	Concord, NC	(18.8)
38	Coral Springs, FL	6.4
255	Corona, CA	(17.0)
359	Corpus Christi, TX	(26.9)
44	Costa Mesa, CA	4.6
63	Cranston, RI	0.6
347	Dallas, TX	(25.4)
198	Daly City, CA	(12.4)
42	Danbury, CT	5.6
NA	Davenport, IA**	NA
136	Davie, FL	(7.0)
200	Dayton, OH	(12.7)
278	Dearborn, MI	(18.9)
NA	Decatur, IL**	NA
102	Deerfield Beach, FL	(3.9)
130	Denton, TX	(6.9)
119	Denver, CO	(5.7)
219	Des Moines, IA	(14.2)
157	Detroit, MI	(9.3)
99	Downey, CA	(3.5)
85	Duluth, MN	(2.2)
NA	Durham, NC**	NA
30	Edinburg, TX	9.1
283	Edison Twnshp, NJ	(19.2)
235	Edmond, OK	(15.6)
401	El Cajon, CA	(43.3)
188	El Monte, CA	(12.0)
330	El Paso, TX	(23.1)
323	Elgin, IL	(22.4)
91	Elizabeth, NJ	(2.8)
302	Elk Grove, CA	(20.8)
13	Erie, PA	21.5
378	Escondido, CA	(32.0)
119	Eugene, OR	(5.7)
70	Evansville, IN	0.1
278	Everett, WA	(18.9)
378	Fairfield, CA	(32.0)
NA	Fall River, MA**	NA
270	Fargo, ND	(18.4)
252	Farmington Hills, MI	(16.8)
233	Fayetteville, NC	(15.4)
362	Fishers, IN	(27.4)
49	Flint, MI	3.5
156	Fontana, CA	(9.2)
227	Fort Collins, CO	(14.7)
17	Fort Lauderdale, FL	17.6
259	Fort Smith, AR	(17.1)
200	Fort Wayne, IN	(12.7)
229	Fort Worth, TX	(15.2)
367	Fremont, CA	(29.0)
21	Fresno, CA	14.4
372	Frisco, TX	(30.5)
239	Fullerton, CA	(15.8)
293	Gainesville, FL	(20.6)
312	Garden Grove, CA	(21.5)
74	Garland, TX	(0.8)
3	Gary, IN	37.5
334	Gilbert, AZ	(23.9)
8	Glendale, AZ	28.9
94	Glendale, CA	(2.9)
247	Grand Prairie, TX	(16.3)
394	Grand Rapids, MI	(37.7)
22	Greece, NY	14.3
244	Greeley, CO	(16.1)
271	Green Bay, WI	(18.5)
148	Gresham, OR	(8.5)
35	Hamilton Twnshp, NJ	7.1
105	Hammond, IN	(4.9)
27	Hampton, VA	11.3
334	Hartford, CT	(23.9)
36	Hawthorne, CA	7.0
315	Hayward, CA	(21.9)
65	Hemet, CA	0.5
353	Henderson, NV	(26.6)
39	Hesperia, CA	6.0
349	Hialeah, FL	(25.6)
260	High Point, NC	(17.3)
368	Hillsboro, OR	(29.1)
16	Hollywood, FL	19.3
NA	Hoover, AL**	NA
180	Houston, TX	(11.1)
19	Huntington Beach, CA	15.4
NA	Huntsville, AL**	NA
313	Independence, MO	(21.7)
173	Indianapolis, IN	(10.6)
83	Indio, CA	(1.8)
167	Inglewood, CA	(10.2)
115	Irvine, CA	(5.4)
381	Irving, TX	(33.0)
336	Jacksonville, FL	(24.0)
48	Jackson, MS	3.6
275	Jersey City, NJ	(18.8)
NA	Johns Creek, GA**	NA
95	Joliet, IL	(3.0)
298	Kansas City, KS	(20.7)
NA	Kansas City, MO**	NA
126	Kennewick, WA	(6.4)
208	Kenosha, WI	(13.1)
148	Kent, WA	(8.5)
355	Killeen, TX	(26.8)
58	Knoxville, TN	1.7
219	Lafayette, LA	(14.2)
190	Lake Forest, CA	(12.1)
186	Lakeland, FL	(11.7)
402	Lakewood Twnshp, NJ	(44.9)
337	Lakewood, CA	(24.2)
72	Lakewood, CO	0.0
399	Lancaster, CA	(42.1)
50	Lansing, MI	3.4
376	Laredo, TX	(31.4)
73	Largo, FL	(0.6)
112	Las Cruces, NM	(5.3)
388	Las Vegas, NV	(35.3)
328	Lawrence, KS	(23.0)
4	Lawrence, MA	35.7
41	Lawton, OK	5.8
182	League City, TX	(11.3)
318	Lee's Summit, MO	(22.2)
25	Lewisville, TX	12.2

272 Cities

Alpha Order - City (continued)

RANK	CITY	% CHANGE
NA	Lexington, KY**	NA
281	Lincoln, NE	(19.1)
152	Little Rock, AR	(8.9)
241	Livermore, CA	(15.9)
211	Livonia, MI	(13.4)
70	Long Beach, CA	0.1
NA	Longmont, CO**	NA
369	Longview, TX	(29.9)
219	Los Angeles, CA	(14.2)
60	Louisville, KY	1.5
169	Lowell, MA	(10.5)
117	Lubbock, TX	(5.6)
144	Lynchburg, VA	(7.9)
124	Lynn, MA	(6.1)
82	Macon, GA	(1.7)
138	Madison, WI	(7.1)
NA	Manchester, NH**	NA
363	McAllen, TX	(27.5)
109	McKinney, TX	(5.1)
23	Medford, OR	13.2
53	Melbourne, FL	2.5
287	Memphis, TN	(19.5)
NA	Menifee, CA**	NA
281	Merced, CA	(19.1)
328	Meridian, ID	(23.0)
327	Mesa, AZ	(22.6)
29	Mesquite, TX	9.5
14	Miami Beach, FL	19.7
390	Miami Gardens, FL	(35.5)
28	Miami, FL	9.6
274	Midland, TX	(18.7)
340	Milwaukee, WI	(24.4)
268	Minneapolis, MN	(18.0)
323	Miramar, FL	(22.4)
128	Mission Viejo, CA	(6.7)
164	Mission, TX	(9.9)
NA	Mobile, AL**	NA
340	Modesto, CA	(24.4)
NA	Montgomery, AL**	NA
190	Moreno Valley, CA	(12.1)
58	Murfreesboro, TN	1.7
365	Murrieta, CA	(28.4)
101	Nampa, ID	(3.8)
382	Napa, CA	(33.6)
143	Naperville, IL	(7.8)
NA	Nashua, NH**	NA
223	Nashville, TN	(14.4)
57	New Bedford, MA	2.0
NA	New Haven, CT**	NA
400	New Orleans, LA	(42.8)
195	New Rochelle, NY	(12.2)
122	New York, NY	(5.9)
115	Newark, NJ	(5.4)
130	Newport Beach, CA	(6.9)
293	Newport News, VA	(20.6)
200	Newton, MA	(12.7)
79	Norfolk, VA	(1.3)
177	Norman, OK	(10.9)
352	North Charleston, SC	(26.1)
228	Norwalk, CA	(14.8)
63	Norwalk, CT	0.6
184	Oakland, CA	(11.4)
261	Oceanside, CA	(17.4)
377	Odessa, TX	(31.6)
389	O'Fallon, MO	(35.4)
250	Ogden, UT	(16.6)
77	Oklahoma City, OK	(1.2)
NA	Olathe, KS**	NA
105	Omaha, NE	(4.9)
190	Ontario, CA	(12.1)
223	Orange, CA	(14.4)
248	Orem, UT	(16.5)
255	Orlando, FL	(17.0)

RANK	CITY	% CHANGE
150	Overland Park, KS	(8.7)
333	Oxnard, CA	(23.8)
124	Palm Bay, FL	(6.1)
370	Palmdale, CA	(30.0)
169	Pasadena, CA	(10.5)
68	Pasadena, TX	0.2
30	Paterson, NJ	9.1
355	Pearland, TX	(26.8)
168	Pembroke Pines, FL	(10.4)
326	Peoria, AZ	(22.5)
56	Peoria, IL	2.3
161	Philadelphia, PA	(9.5)
342	Phoenix, AZ	(24.5)
359	Pittsburgh, PA	(26.9)
254	Plano, TX	(16.9)
110	Plantation, FL	(5.2)
197	Pomona, CA	(12.3)
37	Pompano Beach, FL	6.7
74	Port St. Lucie, FL	(0.8)
210	Portland, OR	(13.3)
32	Portsmouth, VA	8.7
188	Provo, UT	(12.0)
NA	Pueblo, CO**	NA
130	Quincy, MA	(6.9)
157	Racine, WI	(9.3)
130	Raleigh, NC	(6.9)
9	Ramapo, NY	28.0
40	Rancho Cucamon., CA	5.9
293	Reading, PA	(20.6)
7	Redding, CA	29.0
252	Redwood City, CA	(16.8)
384	Reno, NV	(34.4)
380	Renton, WA	(32.7)
6	Rialto, CA	30.7
165	Richardson, TX	(10.0)
285	Richmond, CA	(19.4)
169	Richmond, VA	(10.5)
307	Rio Rancho, NM	(21.1)
241	Riverside, CA	(15.9)
219	Roanoke, VA	(14.2)
255	Rochester, MN	(17.0)
112	Rochester, NY	(5.3)
323	Rockford, IL	(22.4)
255	Roseville, CA	(17.0)
337	Roswell, GA	(24.2)
87	Round Rock, TX	(2.3)
350	Sacramento, CA	(25.8)
302	Salem, OR	(20.8)
394	Salinas, CA	(37.7)
307	Salt Lake City, UT	(21.1)
346	San Angelo, TX	(24.8)
127	San Antonio, TX	(6.6)
298	San Bernardino, CA	(20.7)
391	San Diego, CA	(35.6)
217	San Francisco, CA	(14.0)
175	San Jose, CA	(10.8)
361	San Leandro, CA	(27.1)
285	San Marcos, CA	(19.4)
320	San Mateo, CA	(22.3)
385	Sandy Springs, GA	(34.6)
241	Sandy, UT	(15.9)
199	Santa Ana, CA	(12.6)
20	Santa Barbara, CA	15.2
293	Santa Clara, CA	(20.6)
386	Santa Clarita, CA	(35.1)
305	Santa Maria, CA	(20.9)
128	Santa Monica, CA	(6.7)
160	Santa Rosa, CA	(9.4)
173	Savannah, GA	(10.6)
187	Scottsdale, AZ	(11.8)
34	Scranton, PA	7.2
184	Seattle, WA	(11.4)
314	Shreveport, LA	(21.8)
372	Simi Valley, CA	(30.5)

RANK	CITY	% CHANGE
11	Sioux City, IA	23.1
18	Sioux Falls, SD	15.9
344	Somerville, MA	(24.7)
152	South Bend, IN	(8.9)
55	South Gate, CA	2.4
387	Sparks, NV	(35.2)
1	Spokane Valley, WA	61.5
10	Spokane, WA	23.5
88	Springfield, IL	(2.4)
155	Springfield, MA	(9.0)
112	Springfield, MO	(5.3)
52	Stamford, CT	2.7
NA	Sterling Heights, MI**	NA
250	Stockton, CA	(16.6)
77	St. Joseph, MO	(1.2)
264	St. Louis, MO	(17.7)
61	St. Paul, MN	1.4
238	St. Petersburg, FL	(15.7)
141	Suffolk, VA	(7.5)
139	Sugar Land, TX	(7.3)
375	Sunnyvale, CA	(31.1)
67	Sunrise, FL	0.3
214	Surprise, AZ	(13.5)
229	Syracuse, NY	(15.2)
310	Tacoma, WA	(21.2)
95	Tallahassee, FL	(3.0)
396	Tampa, FL	(38.6)
245	Temecula, CA	(16.2)
269	Tempe, AZ	(18.3)
NA	Thornton, CO**	NA
166	Thousand Oaks, CA	(10.1)
NA	Toledo, OH**	NA
2	Toms River Twnshp, NJ	58.7
145	Topeka, KS	(8.0)
235	Torrance, CA	(15.6)
215	Tracy, CA	(13.9)
104	Trenton, NJ	(4.7)
110	Troy, MI	(5.2)
NA	Tucson, AZ**	NA
195	Tulsa, OK	(12.2)
NA	Tuscaloosa, AL**	NA
190	Tustin, CA	(12.1)
98	Tyler, TX	(3.1)
163	Upper Darby Twnshp, PA	(9.8)
266	Vacaville, CA	(17.9)
215	Vallejo, CA	(13.9)
100	Vancouver, WA	(3.6)
239	Ventura, CA	(15.8)
207	Victorville, CA	(13.0)
146	Virginia Beach, VA	(8.4)
150	Visalia, CA	(8.7)
175	Vista, CA	(10.8)
330	Waco, TX	(23.1)
NA	Warren, MI**	NA
NA	Warwick, RI**	NA
91	Washington, DC	(2.8)
320	Waterbury, CT	(22.3)
232	West Covina, CA	(15.3)
302	West Jordan, UT	(20.8)
350	West Palm Beach, FL	(25.8)
355	West Valley, UT	(26.8)
190	Westland, MI	(12.1)
130	Westminster, CA	(6.9)
292	Westminster, CO	(20.5)
51	Whittier, CA	3.2
383	Wichita Falls, TX	(34.0)
200	Wichita, KS	(12.7)
205	Wilmington, NC	(12.9)
NA	Winston-Salem, NC**	NA
205	Woodbridge Twnshp, NJ	(12.9)
89	Worcester, MA	(2.6)
287	Yakima, WA	(19.5)
53	Yonkers, NY	2.5
320	Yuma, AZ	(22.3)

Source: CQ Press using reported data from the F.B.I. "Crime in the United States 2011"
*Property crimes are offenses of burglary, larceny-theft, and motor vehicle theft. Attempts are included.
**Not available.

Rank Order - City

68. Percent Change in Property Crime Rate: 2007 to 2011 (continued)
National Percent Change = 11.2% Decrease*

RANK	CITY	% CHANGE	RANK	CITY	% CHANGE	RANK	CITY	% CHANGE
1	Spokane Valley, WA	61.5	73	Largo, FL	(0.6)	145	Topeka, KS	(8.0)
2	Toms River Twnshp, NJ	58.7	74	Baltimore, MD	(0.8)	146	Baton Rouge, LA	(8.4)
3	Gary, IN	37.5	74	Garland, TX	(0.8)	146	Virginia Beach, VA	(8.4)
4	Lawrence, MA	35.7	74	Port St. Lucie, FL	(0.8)	148	Gresham, OR	(8.5)
5	Clovis, CA	32.4	77	Oklahoma City, OK	(1.2)	148	Kent, WA	(8.5)
6	Rialto, CA	30.7	77	St. Joseph, MO	(1.2)	150	Overland Park, KS	(8.7)
7	Redding, CA	29.0	79	Camden, NJ	(1.3)	150	Visalia, CA	(8.7)
8	Glendale, AZ	28.9	79	Norfolk, VA	(1.3)	152	Ann Arbor, MI	(8.9)
9	Ramapo, NY	28.0	81	Chesapeake, VA	(1.5)	152	Little Rock, AR	(8.9)
10	Spokane, WA	23.5	82	Macon, GA	(1.7)	152	South Bend, IN	(8.9)
11	Sioux City, IA	23.1	83	Indio, CA	(1.8)	155	Springfield, MA	(9.0)
12	Antioch, CA	22.1	84	Chandler, AZ	(2.1)	156	Fontana, CA	(9.2)
13	Erie, PA	21.5	85	Chicago, IL	(2.2)	157	Beaumont, TX	(9.3)
14	Miami Beach, FL	19.7	85	Duluth, MN	(2.2)	157	Detroit, MI	(9.3)
15	Cheektowaga, NY	19.4	87	Round Rock, TX	(2.3)	157	Racine, WI	(9.3)
16	Hollywood, FL	19.3	88	Springfield, IL	(2.4)	160	Santa Rosa, CA	(9.4)
17	Fort Lauderdale, FL	17.6	89	Worcester, MA	(2.6)	161	Philadelphia, PA	(9.5)
18	Sioux Falls, SD	15.9	90	Carson, CA	(2.7)	162	Bloomington, IN	(9.6)
19	Huntington Beach, CA	15.4	91	Atlanta, GA	(2.8)	163	Upper Darby Twnshp, PA	(9.8)
20	Santa Barbara, CA	15.2	91	Elizabeth, NJ	(2.8)	164	Mission, TX	(9.9)
21	Fresno, CA	14.4	91	Washington, DC	(2.8)	165	Richardson, TX	(10.0)
22	Greece, NY	14.3	94	Glendale, CA	(2.9)	166	Thousand Oaks, CA	(10.1)
23	Medford, OR	13.2	95	Brockton, MA	(3.0)	167	Inglewood, CA	(10.2)
24	Columbia, MO	12.6	95	Joliet, IL	(3.0)	168	Pembroke Pines, FL	(10.4)
25	Lewisville, TX	12.2	95	Tallahassee, FL	(3.0)	169	Buena Park, CA	(10.5)
26	Cincinnati, OH	11.5	98	Tyler, TX	(3.1)	169	Lowell, MA	(10.5)
27	Hampton, VA	11.3	99	Downey, CA	(3.5)	169	Pasadena, CA	(10.5)
28	Miami, FL	9.6	100	Vancouver, WA	(3.6)	169	Richmond, VA	(10.5)
29	Mesquite, TX	9.5	101	Nampa, ID	(3.8)	173	Indianapolis, IN	(10.6)
30	Edinburg, TX	9.1	102	Deerfield Beach, FL	(3.9)	173	Savannah, GA	(10.6)
30	Paterson, NJ	9.1	103	Arvada, CO	(4.5)	175	San Jose, CA	(10.8)
32	Portsmouth, VA	8.7	104	Trenton, NJ	(4.7)	175	Vista, CA	(10.8)
33	Akron, OH	8.4	105	Anaheim, CA	(4.9)	177	Norman, OK	(10.9)
34	Scranton, PA	7.2	105	Hammond, IN	(4.9)	178	Chino Hills, CA	(11.0)
35	Hamilton Twnshp, NJ	7.1	105	Omaha, NE	(4.9)	178	Columbus, OH	(11.0)
36	Hawthorne, CA	7.0	108	Boulder, CO	(5.0)	180	Houston, TX	(11.1)
37	Pompano Beach, FL	6.7	109	McKinney, TX	(5.1)	181	Albuquerque, NM	(11.2)
38	Coral Springs, FL	6.4	110	Plantation, FL	(5.2)	182	Columbus, GA	(11.3)
39	Hesperia, CA	6.0	110	Troy, MI	(5.2)	182	League City, TX	(11.3)
40	Rancho Cucamon., CA	5.9	112	Las Cruces, NM	(5.3)	184	Oakland, CA	(11.4)
41	Lawton, OK	5.8	112	Rochester, NY	(5.3)	184	Seattle, WA	(11.4)
42	Danbury, CT	5.6	112	Springfield, MO	(5.3)	186	Lakeland, FL	(11.7)
43	Amherst, NY	5.2	115	Irvine, CA	(5.4)	187	Scottsdale, AZ	(11.8)
44	Costa Mesa, CA	4.6	115	Newark, NJ	(5.4)	188	El Monte, CA	(12.0)
45	Broken Arrow, OK	4.4	117	Alexandria, VA	(5.6)	188	Provo, UT	(12.0)
46	Cleveland, OH	3.8	117	Lubbock, TX	(5.6)	190	Lake Forest, CA	(12.1)
47	Albany, NY	3.7	119	Bloomington, MN	(5.7)	190	Moreno Valley, CA	(12.1)
48	Jackson, MS	3.6	119	Denver, CO	(5.7)	190	Ontario, CA	(12.1)
49	Flint, MI	3.5	119	Eugene, OR	(5.7)	190	Tustin, CA	(12.1)
50	Lansing, MI	3.4	122	College Station, TX	(5.9)	190	Westland, MI	(12.1)
51	Whittier, CA	3.2	122	New York, NY	(5.9)	195	New Rochelle, NY	(12.2)
52	Stamford, CT	2.7	124	Lynn, MA	(6.1)	195	Tulsa, OK	(12.2)
53	Melbourne, FL	2.5	124	Palm Bay, FL	(6.1)	197	Pomona, CA	(12.3)
53	Yonkers, NY	2.5	126	Kennewick, WA	(6.4)	198	Daly City, CA	(12.4)
55	South Gate, CA	2.4	127	San Antonio, TX	(6.6)	199	Santa Ana, CA	(12.6)
56	Peoria, IL	2.3	128	Mission Viejo, CA	(6.7)	200	Canton Twnshp, MI	(12.7)
57	New Bedford, MA	2.0	128	Santa Monica, CA	(6.7)	200	Dayton, OH	(12.7)
58	Knoxville, TN	1.7	130	Alhambra, CA	(6.9)	200	Fort Wayne, IN	(12.7)
58	Murfreesboro, TN	1.7	130	Denton, TX	(6.9)	200	Newton, MA	(12.7)
60	Louisville, KY	1.5	130	Newport Beach, CA	(6.9)	200	Wichita, KS	(12.7)
61	St. Paul, MN	1.4	130	Quincy, MA	(6.9)	205	Wilmington, NC	(12.9)
62	Clinton Twnshp, MI	1.0	130	Raleigh, NC	(6.9)	205	Woodbridge Twnshp, NJ	(12.9)
63	Cranston, RI	0.6	130	Westminster, CA	(6.9)	207	Victorville, CA	(13.0)
63	Norwalk, CT	0.6	136	Clarkstown, NY	(7.0)	208	Clearwater, FL	(13.1)
65	Compton, CA	0.5	136	Davie, FL	(7.0)	208	Kenosha, WI	(13.1)
65	Hemet, CA	0.5	138	Madison, WI	(7.1)	210	Portland, OR	(13.3)
67	Sunrise, FL	0.3	139	Sugar Land, TX	(7.3)	211	Baldwin Park, CA	(13.4)
68	Brick Twnshp, NJ	0.2	140	Burbank, CA	(7.4)	211	Carrollton, TX	(13.4)
68	Pasadena, TX	0.2	141	Suffolk, VA	(7.5)	211	Livonia, MI	(13.4)
70	Evansville, IN	0.1	142	Colonie, NY	(7.7)	214	Surprise, AZ	(13.5)
70	Long Beach, CA	0.1	143	Naperville, IL	(7.8)	215	Tracy, CA	(13.9)
72	Lakewood, CO	0.0	144	Lynchburg, VA	(7.9)	215	Vallejo, CA	(13.9)

Rank Order - City (continued)

RANK	CITY	% CHANGE	RANK	CITY	% CHANGE	RANK	CITY	% CHANGE
217	San Francisco, CA	(14.0)	290	Asheville, NC	(19.8)	364	Carlsbad, CA	(28.2)
218	Athens-Clarke, GA	(14.1)	291	Charleston, SC	(20.4)	365	Murrieta, CA	(28.4)
219	Des Moines, IA	(14.2)	292	Westminster, CO	(20.5)	366	Bryan, TX	(28.8)
219	Lafayette, LA	(14.2)	293	Amarillo, TX	(20.6)	367	Fremont, CA	(29.0)
219	Los Angeles, CA	(14.2)	293	Gainesville, FL	(20.6)	368	Hillsboro, OR	(29.1)
219	Roanoke, VA	(14.2)	293	Newport News, VA	(20.6)	369	Longview, TX	(29.9)
223	Abilene, TX	(14.4)	293	Reading, PA	(20.6)	370	Palmdale, CA	(30.0)
223	Brownsville, TX	(14.4)	293	Santa Clara, CA	(20.6)	371	Bellflower, CA	(30.2)
223	Nashville, TN	(14.4)	298	Allen, TX	(20.7)	372	Frisco, TX	(30.5)
223	Orange, CA	(14.4)	298	Cedar Rapids, IA	(20.7)	372	Simi Valley, CA	(30.5)
227	Fort Collins, CO	(14.7)	298	Kansas City, KS	(20.7)	374	Bellingham, WA	(30.9)
228	Norwalk, CA	(14.8)	298	San Bernardino, CA	(20.7)	375	Sunnyvale, CA	(31.1)
229	Chino, CA	(15.2)	302	Elk Grove, CA	(20.8)	376	Laredo, TX	(31.4)
229	Fort Worth, TX	(15.2)	302	Salem, OR	(20.8)	377	Odessa, TX	(31.6)
229	Syracuse, NY	(15.2)	302	West Jordan, UT	(20.8)	378	Escondido, CA	(32.0)
232	West Covina, CA	(15.3)	305	Santa Maria, CA	(20.9)	378	Fairfield, CA	(32.0)
233	Colorado Springs, CO	(15.4)	306	Boca Raton, FL	(21.0)	380	Renton, WA	(32.7)
233	Fayetteville, NC	(15.4)	307	Bethlehem, PA	(21.1)	381	Irving, TX	(33.0)
235	Brooklyn Park, MN	(15.6)	307	Rio Rancho, NM	(21.1)	382	Napa, CA	(33.6)
235	Edmond, OK	(15.6)	307	Salt Lake City, UT	(21.1)	383	Wichita Falls, TX	(34.0)
235	Torrance, CA	(15.6)	310	Bend, OR	(21.2)	384	Reno, NV	(34.4)
238	St. Petersburg, FL	(15.7)	310	Tacoma, WA	(21.2)	385	Sandy Springs, GA	(34.6)
239	Fullerton, CA	(15.8)	312	Garden Grove, CA	(21.5)	386	Santa Clarita, CA	(35.1)
239	Ventura, CA	(15.8)	313	Independence, MO	(21.7)	387	Sparks, NV	(35.2)
241	Livermore, CA	(15.9)	314	Shreveport, LA	(21.8)	388	Las Vegas, NV	(35.3)
241	Riverside, CA	(15.9)	315	Chattanooga, TN	(21.9)	389	O'Fallon, MO	(35.4)
241	Sandy, UT	(15.9)	315	Hayward, CA	(21.9)	390	Miami Gardens, FL	(35.5)
244	Greeley, CO	(16.1)	317	Aurora, CO	(22.1)	391	San Diego, CA	(35.6)
245	Bakersfield, CA	(16.2)	318	Allentown, PA	(22.2)	392	Carmel, IN	(35.8)
245	Temecula, CA	(16.2)	318	Lee's Summit, MO	(22.2)	393	Berkeley, CA	(36.7)
247	Grand Prairie, TX	(16.3)	320	San Mateo, CA	(22.3)	394	Grand Rapids, MI	(37.7)
248	Cambridge, MA	(16.5)	320	Waterbury, CT	(22.3)	394	Salinas, CA	(37.7)
248	Orem, UT	(16.5)	320	Yuma, AZ	(22.3)	396	Tampa, FL	(38.6)
250	Ogden, UT	(16.6)	323	Elgin, IL	(22.4)	397	Chula Vista, CA	(39.0)
250	Stockton, CA	(16.6)	323	Miramar, FL	(22.4)	398	Charlotte, NC	(42.0)
252	Farmington Hills, MI	(16.8)	323	Rockford, IL	(22.4)	399	Lancaster, CA	(42.1)
252	Redwood City, CA	(16.8)	326	Peoria, AZ	(22.5)	400	New Orleans, LA	(42.8)
254	Plano, TX	(16.9)	327	Mesa, AZ	(22.6)	401	El Cajon, CA	(43.3)
255	Corona, CA	(17.0)	328	Lawrence, KS	(23.0)	402	Lakewood Twnshp, NJ	(44.9)
255	Orlando, FL	(17.0)	328	Meridian, ID	(23.0)	NA	Arlington Heights, IL**	NA
255	Rochester, MN	(17.0)	330	El Paso, TX	(23.1)	NA	Avondale, AZ**	NA
255	Roseville, CA	(17.0)	330	Waco, TX	(23.1)	NA	Billings, MT**	NA
259	Fort Smith, AR	(17.1)	332	Beaverton, OR	(23.3)	NA	Birmingham, AL**	NA
260	High Point, NC	(17.3)	333	Oxnard, CA	(23.8)	NA	Bloomington, IL**	NA
261	Austin, TX	(17.4)	334	Gilbert, AZ	(23.9)	NA	Buffalo, NY**	NA
261	Boise, ID	(17.4)	334	Hartford, CT	(23.9)	NA	Champaign, IL**	NA
261	Oceanside, CA	(17.4)	336	Jacksonville, FL	(24.0)	NA	Cicero, IL**	NA
264	Cary, NC	(17.7)	337	Clarksville, TN	(24.2)	NA	Citrus Heights, CA**	NA
264	St. Louis, MO	(17.7)	337	Lakewood, CA	(24.2)	NA	Davenport, IA**	NA
266	Albany, GA	(17.9)	337	Roswell, GA	(24.2)	NA	Decatur, IL**	NA
266	Vacaville, CA	(17.9)	340	Milwaukee, WI	(24.4)	NA	Durham, NC**	NA
268	Minneapolis, MN	(18.0)	340	Modesto, CA	(24.4)	NA	Fall River, MA**	NA
269	Tempe, AZ	(18.3)	342	Phoenix, AZ	(24.5)	NA	Hoover, AL**	NA
270	Fargo, ND	(18.4)	343	Boston, MA	(24.6)	NA	Huntsville, AL**	NA
271	Anchorage, AK	(18.5)	344	Concord, CA	(24.7)	NA	Johns Creek, GA**	NA
271	Green Bay, WI	(18.5)	344	Somerville, MA	(24.7)	NA	Kansas City, MO**	NA
273	Arlington, TX	(18.6)	346	San Angelo, TX	(24.8)	NA	Lexington, KY**	NA
274	Midland, TX	(18.7)	347	Aurora, IL	(25.4)	NA	Longmont, CO**	NA
275	Bridgeport, CT	(18.8)	347	Dallas, TX	(25.4)	NA	Manchester, NH**	NA
275	Concord, NC	(18.8)	349	Hialeah, FL	(25.6)	NA	Menifee, CA**	NA
275	Jersey City, NJ	(18.8)	350	Sacramento, CA	(25.8)	NA	Mobile, AL**	NA
278	Dearborn, MI	(18.9)	350	West Palm Beach, FL	(25.8)	NA	Montgomery, AL**	NA
278	Everett, WA	(18.9)	352	North Charleston, SC	(26.1)	NA	Nashua, NH**	NA
280	Bellevue, WA	(19.0)	353	Chico, CA	(26.6)	NA	New Haven, CT**	NA
281	Lincoln, NE	(19.1)	353	Henderson, NV	(26.6)	NA	Olathe, KS**	NA
281	Merced, CA	(19.1)	355	Cape Coral, FL	(26.8)	NA	Pueblo, CO**	NA
283	Edison Twnshp, NJ	(19.2)	355	Killeen, TX	(26.8)	NA	Sterling Heights, MI**	NA
284	Centennial, CO	(19.3)	355	Pearland, TX	(26.8)	NA	Thornton, CO**	NA
285	Richmond, CA	(19.4)	355	West Valley, UT	(26.8)	NA	Toledo, OH**	NA
285	San Marcos, CA	(19.4)	359	Corpus Christi, TX	(26.9)	NA	Tucson, AZ**	NA
287	Clifton, NJ	(19.5)	359	Pittsburgh, PA	(26.9)	NA	Tuscaloosa, AL**	NA
287	Memphis, TN	(19.5)	361	San Leandro, CA	(27.1)	NA	Warren, MI**	NA
287	Yakima, WA	(19.5)	362	Fishers, IN	(27.4)	NA	Warwick, RI**	NA
			363	McAllen, TX	(27.5)	NA	Winston-Salem, NC**	NA

Source: CQ Press using reported data from the F.B.I. "Crime in the United States 2011"
*Property crimes are offenses of burglary, larceny-theft, and motor vehicle theft. Attempts are included.
**Not available.

Alpha Order - City

69. Burglaries in 2011
National Total = 2,188,005 Burglaries*

RANK	CITY	BURGLARY	RANK	CITY	BURGLARY	RANK	CITY	BURGLARY
181	Abilene, TX	1,119	379	Cheektowaga, NY	362	112	Fort Wayne, IN	1,888
48	Akron, OH	4,268	162	Chesapeake, VA	1,237	15	Fort Worth, TX	10,058
155	Albany, GA	1,332	2	Chicago, IL	26,420	165	Fremont, CA	1,206
225	Albany, NY	895	333	Chico, CA	487	34	Fresno, CA	5,713
31	Albuquerque, NM	5,985	411	Chino Hills, CA	264	334	Frisco, TX	483
405	Alexandria, VA	303	318	Chino, CA	530	278	Fullerton, CA	643
397	Alhambra, CA	312	241	Chula Vista, CA	807	193	Gainesville, FL	1,063
184	Allentown, PA	1,101	270	Cicero, IL	668	258	Garden Grove, CA	717
417	Allen, TX	248	29	Cincinnati, OH	6,674	95	Garland, TX	2,244
108	Amarillo, TX	2,016	289	Citrus Heights, CA	607	84	Gary, IN	2,618
423	Amherst, NY	221	435	Clarkstown, NY	111	233	Gilbert, AZ	823
141	Anaheim, CA	1,410	153	Clarksville, TN	1,333	90	Glendale, AZ	2,442
188	Anchorage, AK	1,080	256	Clearwater, FL	719	282	Glendale, CA	623
316	Ann Arbor, MI	534	14	Cleveland, OH	10,706	117	Grand Prairie, TX	1,808
152	Antioch, CA	1,335	398	Clifton, NJ	311	110	Grand Rapids, MI	1,952
427	Arlington Heights, IL	170	312	Clinton Twnshp, MI	545	382	Greece, NY	355
45	Arlington, TX	4,388	219	Clovis, CA	914	294	Greeley, CO	593
403	Arvada, CO	304	276	College Station, TX	651	341	Green Bay, WI	467
251	Asheville, NC	753	421	Colonie, NY	224	254	Gresham, OR	751
146	Athens-Clarke, GA	1,359	66	Colorado Springs, CO	3,323	325	Hamilton Twnshp, NJ	513
23	Atlanta, GA	7,499	245	Columbia, MO	798	197	Hammond, IN	1,032
98	Aurora, CO	2,144	65	Columbus, GA	3,342	236	Hampton, VA	820
209	Aurora, IL	947	9	Columbus, OH	15,169	157	Hartford, CT	1,271
25	Austin, TX	7,042	244	Compton, CA	800	293	Hawthorne, CA	598
260	Avondale, AZ	712	223	Concord, CA	898	202	Hayward, CA	988
46	Bakersfield, CA	4,321	346	Concord, NC	452	169	Hemet, CA	1,173
395	Baldwin Park, CA	315	280	Coral Springs, FL	633	156	Henderson, NV	1,280
17	Baltimore, MD	8,615	263	Corona, CA	705	270	Hesperia, CA	668
50	Baton Rouge, LA	4,220	83	Corpus Christi, TX	2,668	191	Hialeah, FL	1,069
106	Beaumont, TX	2,035	321	Costa Mesa, CA	524	158	High Point, NC	1,266
420	Beaverton, OR	227	344	Cranston, RI	461	415	Hillsboro, OR	252
289	Bellevue, WA	607	3	Dallas, TX	18,727	103	Hollywood, FL	2,054
336	Bellflower, CA	481	393	Daly City, CA	322	357	Hoover, AL	422
277	Bellingham, WA	646	386	Danbury, CT	343	1	Houston, TX	27,459
378	Bend, OR	365	174	Davenport, IA	1,140	251	Huntington Beach, CA	753
205	Berkeley, CA	976	261	Davie, FL	709	82	Huntsville, AL	2,677
372	Bethlehem, PA	371	71	Dayton, OH	3,121	168	Independence, MO	1,178
269	Billings, MT	669	287	Dearborn, MI	612	10	Indianapolis, IN	15,122
33	Birmingham, AL	5,806	174	Decatur, IL	1,140	247	Indio, CA	788
345	Bloomington, IL	460	302	Deerfield Beach, FL	569	303	Inglewood, CA	568
292	Bloomington, IN	601	306	Denton, TX	565	325	Irvine, CA	513
416	Bloomington, MN	251	39	Denver, CO	4,868	130	Irving, TX	1,603
332	Boca Raton, FL	495	88	Des Moines, IA	2,493	19	Jacksonville, FL	8,518
239	Boise, ID	809	7	Detroit, MI	15,994	40	Jackson, MS	4,722
61	Boston, MA	3,482	248	Downey, CA	769	142	Jersey City, NJ	1,402
341	Boulder, CO	467	250	Duluth, MN	756	433	Johns Creek, GA	131
389	Brick Twnshp, NJ	331	57	Durham, NC	3,874	210	Joliet, IL	939
133	Bridgeport, CT	1,540	249	Edinburg, TX	758	116	Kansas City, KS	1,827
196	Brockton, MA	1,037	386	Edison Twnshp, NJ	343	27	Kansas City, MO	6,848
354	Broken Arrow, OK	426	398	Edmond, OK	311	363	Kennewick, WA	404
330	Brooklyn Park, MN	506	291	El Cajon, CA	603	305	Kenosha, WI	566
200	Brownsville, TX	1,009	313	El Monte, CA	544	164	Kent, WA	1,223
265	Bryan, TX	681	115	El Paso, TX	1,859	107	Killeen, TX	2,034
400	Buena Park, CA	310	309	Elgin, IL	555	85	Knoxville, TN	2,544
43	Buffalo, NY	4,473	173	Elizabeth, NJ	1,162	166	Lafayette, LA	1,194
366	Burbank, CA	395	272	Elk Grove, CA	664	431	Lake Forest, CA	140
315	Cambridge, MA	539	163	Erie, PA	1,233	153	Lakeland, FL	1,333
138	Camden, NJ	1,436	308	Escondido, CA	557	412	Lakewood Twnshp, NJ	261
422	Canton Twnshp, MI	222	136	Eugene, OR	1,440	388	Lakewood, CA	341
198	Cape Coral, FL	1,023	189	Evansville, IN	1,074	212	Lakewood, CO	935
339	Carlsbad, CA	468	172	Everett, WA	1,163	203	Lancaster, CA	986
436	Carmel, IN	69	301	Fairfield, CA	572	127	Lansing, MI	1,650
224	Carrollton, TX	896	230	Fall River, MA	863	118	Laredo, TX	1,790
299	Carson, CA	573	356	Fargo, ND	423	284	Largo, FL	617
374	Cary, NC	370	410	Farmington Hills, MI	267	180	Las Cruces, NM	1,120
185	Cedar Rapids, IA	1,099	51	Fayetteville, NC	4,204	12	Las Vegas, NV	12,662
391	Centennial, CO	325	437	Fishers, IN	57	331	Lawrence, KS	502
297	Champaign, IL	586	60	Flint, MI	3,628	264	Lawrence, MA	682
150	Chandler, AZ	1,344	195	Fontana, CA	1,041	109	Lawton, OK	1,960
319	Charleston, SC	527	307	Fort Collins, CO	560	371	League City, TX	374
18	Charlotte, NC	8,536	72	Fort Lauderdale, FL	3,102	391	Lee's Summit, MO	325
86	Chattanooga, TN	2,503	182	Fort Smith, AR	1,110	299	Lewisville, TX	573

Alpha Order - City (continued)

RANK	CITY	BURGLARY
78	Lexington, KY	2,724
143	Lincoln, NE	1,401
42	Little Rock, AR	4,655
376	Livermore, CA	366
401	Livonia, MI	308
68	Long Beach, CA	3,275
407	Longmont, CO	298
237	Longview, TX	819
6	Los Angeles, CA	17,264
21	Louisville, KY	8,127
219	Lowell, MA	914
63	Lubbock, TX	3,410
323	Lynchburg, VA	515
257	Lynn, MA	718
97	Macon, GA	2,154
136	Madison, WI	1,440
222	Manchester, NH	902
328	McAllen, TX	511
281	McKinney, TX	626
374	Medford, OR	370
229	Melbourne, FL	873
11	Memphis, TN	13,254
348	Menifee, CA	450
242	Merced, CA	802
430	Meridian, ID	156
77	Mesa, AZ	2,769
123	Mesquite, TX	1,704
171	Miami Beach, FL	1,171
134	Miami Gardens, FL	1,485
36	Miami, FL	5,141
259	Midland, TX	715
30	Milwaukee, WI	6,669
37	Minneapolis, MN	5,104
204	Miramar, FL	981
426	Mission Viejo, CA	193
343	Mission, TX	464
55	Mobile, AL	4,058
99	Modesto, CA	2,121
75	Montgomery, AL	2,885
100	Moreno Valley, CA	2,095
144	Murfreesboro, TN	1,383
383	Murrieta, CA	348
324	Nampa, ID	514
385	Napa, CA	344
406	Naperville, IL	300
380	Nashua, NH	360
22	Nashville, TN	7,541
206	New Bedford, MA	969
140	New Haven, CT	1,413
58	New Orleans, LA	3,857
428	New Rochelle, NY	166
5	New York, NY	18,159
91	Newark, NJ	2,396
350	Newport Beach, CA	441
186	Newport News, VA	1,094
425	Newton, MA	212
94	Norfolk, VA	2,256
267	Norman, OK	677
201	North Charleston, SC	999
337	Norwalk, CA	476
408	Norwalk, CT	297
35	Oakland, CA	5,170
246	Oceanside, CA	792
284	Odessa, TX	617
432	O'Fallon, MO	135
231	Ogden, UT	858
16	Oklahoma City, OK	9,855
414	Olathe, KS	259
67	Omaha, NE	3,321
210	Ontario, CA	939
349	Orange, CA	445
428	Orem, UT	166
52	Orlando, FL	4,165
339	Overland Park, KS	468
298	Oxnard, CA	577
240	Palm Bay, FL	808
207	Palmdale, CA	959
199	Pasadena, CA	1,011
179	Pasadena, TX	1,124
118	Paterson, NJ	1,790
389	Pearland, TX	331
194	Pembroke Pines, FL	1,059
187	Peoria, AZ	1,088
121	Peoria, IL	1,721
13	Philadelphia, PA	12,057
4	Phoenix, AZ	18,666
81	Pittsburgh, PA	2,686
167	Plano, TX	1,193
255	Plantation, FL	748
227	Pomona, CA	890
151	Pompano Beach, FL	1,343
178	Port St. Lucie, FL	1,128
47	Portland, OR	4,303
149	Portsmouth, VA	1,348
370	Provo, UT	386
131	Pueblo, CO	1,590
310	Quincy, MA	551
161	Racine, WI	1,239
74	Raleigh, NC	2,985
434	Ramapo, NY	119
169	Rancho Cucamon., CA	1,173
145	Reading, PA	1,380
233	Redding, CA	823
352	Redwood City, CA	436
129	Reno, NV	1,618
217	Renton, WA	917
213	Rialto, CA	934
266	Richardson, TX	680
126	Richmond, CA	1,651
113	Richmond, VA	1,886
403	Rio Rancho, NM	304
101	Riverside, CA	2,080
215	Roanoke, VA	928
355	Rochester, MN	425
64	Rochester, NY	3,384
111	Rockford, IL	1,890
316	Roseville, CA	534
363	Roswell, GA	404
367	Round Rock, TX	394
53	Sacramento, CA	4,141
226	Salem, OR	891
174	Salinas, CA	1,140
125	Salt Lake City, UT	1,658
243	San Angelo, TX	801
8	San Antonio, TX	15,334
92	San Bernardino, CA	2,359
32	San Diego, CA	5,840
44	San Francisco, CA	4,408
49	San Jose, CA	4,223
268	San Leandro, CA	671
381	San Marcos, CA	358
402	San Mateo, CA	306
296	Sandy Springs, GA	587
351	Sandy, UT	438
192	Santa Ana, CA	1,067
314	Santa Barbara, CA	541
360	Santa Clara, CA	409
304	Santa Clarita, CA	567
275	Santa Maria, CA	655
334	Santa Monica, CA	483
279	Santa Rosa, CA	637
96	Savannah, GA	2,241
139	Scottsdale, AZ	1,424
283	Scranton, PA	620
28	Seattle, WA	6,807
76	Shreveport, LA	2,775
396	Simi Valley, CA	314
261	Sioux City, IA	709
228	Sioux Falls, SD	880
359	Somerville, MA	415
93	South Bend, IN	2,335
358	South Gate, CA	418
274	Sparks, NV	656
217	Spokane Valley, WA	917
73	Spokane, WA	3,030
114	Springfield, IL	1,883
87	Springfield, MA	2,499
104	Springfield, MO	2,053
409	Stamford, CT	282
347	Sterling Heights, MI	451
54	Stockton, CA	4,133
221	St. Joseph, MO	907
26	St. Louis, MO	7,015
70	St. Paul, MN	3,197
62	St. Petersburg, FL	3,412
322	Suffolk, VA	518
424	Sugar Land, TX	220
368	Sunnyvale, CA	393
216	Sunrise, FL	919
284	Surprise, AZ	617
122	Syracuse, NY	1,705
80	Tacoma, WA	2,709
69	Tallahassee, FL	3,252
79	Tampa, FL	2,718
311	Temecula, CA	547
132	Tempe, AZ	1,579
325	Thornton, CO	513
394	Thousand Oaks, CA	319
20	Toledo, OH	8,366
295	Toms River Twnshp, NJ	589
120	Topeka, KS	1,727
329	Torrance, CA	509
369	Tracy, CA	390
177	Trenton, NJ	1,138
419	Troy, MI	236
38	Tucson, AZ	4,979
24	Tulsa, OK	7,353
159	Tuscaloosa, AL	1,249
418	Tustin, CA	243
232	Tyler, TX	834
384	Upper Darby Twnshp, PA	347
412	Vacaville, CA	261
89	Vallejo, CA	2,468
208	Vancouver, WA	950
273	Ventura, CA	657
146	Victorville, CA	1,359
105	Virginia Beach, VA	2,038
182	Visalia, CA	1,110
338	Vista, CA	469
124	Waco, TX	1,670
190	Warren, MI	1,070
376	Warwick, RI	366
59	Washington, DC	3,849
238	Waterbury, CT	818
320	West Covina, CA	526
362	West Jordan, UT	405
148	West Palm Beach, FL	1,354
214	West Valley, UT	929
288	Westland, MI	610
360	Westminster, CA	409
365	Westminster, CO	397
353	Whittier, CA	435
160	Wichita Falls, TX	1,241
56	Wichita, KS	4,005
135	Wilmington, NC	1,454
41	Winston-Salem, NC	4,680
372	Woodbridge Twnshp, NJ	371
102	Worcester, MA	2,066
128	Yakima, WA	1,619
251	Yonkers, NY	753
235	Yuma, AZ	822

Source: Reported data from the F.B.I. "Crime in the United States 2011"
*Burglary is the unlawful entry of a structure to commit a felony or theft. Attempts are included.

Rank Order - City

69. Burglaries in 2011 (continued)
National Total = 2,188,005 Burglaries*

RANK	CITY	BURGLARY	RANK	CITY	BURGLARY	RANK	CITY	BURGLARY
1	Houston, TX	27,459	73	Spokane, WA	3,030	145	Reading, PA	1,380
2	Chicago, IL	26,420	74	Raleigh, NC	2,985	146	Athens-Clarke, GA	1,359
3	Dallas, TX	18,727	75	Montgomery, AL	2,885	146	Victorville, CA	1,359
4	Phoenix, AZ	18,666	76	Shreveport, LA	2,775	148	West Palm Beach, FL	1,354
5	New York, NY	18,159	77	Mesa, AZ	2,769	149	Portsmouth, VA	1,348
6	Los Angeles, CA	17,264	78	Lexington, KY	2,724	150	Chandler, AZ	1,344
7	Detroit, MI	15,994	79	Tampa, FL	2,718	151	Pompano Beach, FL	1,343
8	San Antonio, TX	15,334	80	Tacoma, WA	2,709	152	Antioch, CA	1,335
9	Columbus, OH	15,169	81	Pittsburgh, PA	2,686	153	Clarksville, TN	1,333
10	Indianapolis, IN	15,122	82	Huntsville, AL	2,677	153	Lakeland, FL	1,333
11	Memphis, TN	13,254	83	Corpus Christi, TX	2,668	155	Albany, GA	1,332
12	Las Vegas, NV	12,662	84	Gary, IN	2,618	156	Henderson, NV	1,280
13	Philadelphia, PA	12,057	85	Knoxville, TN	2,544	157	Hartford, CT	1,271
14	Cleveland, OH	10,706	86	Chattanooga, TN	2,503	158	High Point, NC	1,266
15	Fort Worth, TX	10,058	87	Springfield, MA	2,499	159	Tuscaloosa, AL	1,249
16	Oklahoma City, OK	9,855	88	Des Moines, IA	2,493	160	Wichita Falls, TX	1,241
17	Baltimore, MD	8,615	89	Vallejo, CA	2,468	161	Racine, WI	1,239
18	Charlotte, NC	8,536	90	Glendale, AZ	2,442	162	Chesapeake, VA	1,237
19	Jacksonville, FL	8,518	91	Newark, NJ	2,396	163	Erie, PA	1,233
20	Toledo, OH	8,366	92	San Bernardino, CA	2,359	164	Kent, WA	1,223
21	Louisville, KY	8,127	93	South Bend, IN	2,335	165	Fremont, CA	1,206
22	Nashville, TN	7,541	94	Norfolk, VA	2,256	166	Lafayette, LA	1,194
23	Atlanta, GA	7,499	95	Garland, TX	2,244	167	Plano, TX	1,193
24	Tulsa, OK	7,353	96	Savannah, GA	2,241	168	Independence, MO	1,178
25	Austin, TX	7,042	97	Macon, GA	2,154	169	Hemet, CA	1,173
26	St. Louis, MO	7,015	98	Aurora, CO	2,144	169	Rancho Cucamon., CA	1,173
27	Kansas City, MO	6,848	99	Modesto, CA	2,121	171	Miami Beach, FL	1,171
28	Seattle, WA	6,807	100	Moreno Valley, CA	2,095	172	Everett, WA	1,163
29	Cincinnati, OH	6,674	101	Riverside, CA	2,080	173	Elizabeth, NJ	1,162
30	Milwaukee, WI	6,669	102	Worcester, MA	2,066	174	Davenport, IA	1,140
31	Albuquerque, NM	5,985	103	Hollywood, FL	2,054	174	Decatur, IL	1,140
32	San Diego, CA	5,840	104	Springfield, MO	2,053	174	Salinas, CA	1,140
33	Birmingham, AL	5,806	105	Virginia Beach, VA	2,038	177	Trenton, NJ	1,138
34	Fresno, CA	5,713	106	Beaumont, TX	2,035	178	Port St. Lucie, FL	1,128
35	Oakland, CA	5,170	107	Killeen, TX	2,034	179	Pasadena, TX	1,124
36	Miami, FL	5,141	108	Amarillo, TX	2,016	180	Las Cruces, NM	1,120
37	Minneapolis, MN	5,104	109	Lawton, OK	1,960	181	Abilene, TX	1,119
38	Tucson, AZ	4,979	110	Grand Rapids, MI	1,952	182	Fort Smith, AR	1,110
39	Denver, CO	4,868	111	Rockford, IL	1,890	182	Visalia, CA	1,110
40	Jackson, MS	4,722	112	Fort Wayne, IN	1,888	184	Allentown, PA	1,101
41	Winston-Salem, NC	4,680	113	Richmond, VA	1,886	185	Cedar Rapids, IA	1,099
42	Little Rock, AR	4,655	114	Springfield, IL	1,883	186	Newport News, VA	1,094
43	Buffalo, NY	4,473	115	El Paso, TX	1,859	187	Peoria, AZ	1,088
44	San Francisco, CA	4,408	116	Kansas City, KS	1,827	188	Anchorage, AK	1,080
45	Arlington, TX	4,388	117	Grand Prairie, TX	1,808	189	Evansville, IN	1,074
46	Bakersfield, CA	4,321	118	Laredo, TX	1,790	190	Warren, MI	1,070
47	Portland, OR	4,303	118	Paterson, NJ	1,790	191	Hialeah, FL	1,069
48	Akron, OH	4,268	120	Topeka, KS	1,727	192	Santa Ana, CA	1,067
49	San Jose, CA	4,223	121	Peoria, IL	1,721	193	Gainesville, FL	1,063
50	Baton Rouge, LA	4,220	122	Syracuse, NY	1,705	194	Pembroke Pines, FL	1,059
51	Fayetteville, NC	4,204	123	Mesquite, TX	1,704	195	Fontana, CA	1,041
52	Orlando, FL	4,165	124	Waco, TX	1,670	196	Brockton, MA	1,037
53	Sacramento, CA	4,141	125	Salt Lake City, UT	1,658	197	Hammond, IN	1,032
54	Stockton, CA	4,133	126	Richmond, CA	1,651	198	Cape Coral, FL	1,023
55	Mobile, AL	4,058	127	Lansing, MI	1,650	199	Pasadena, CA	1,011
56	Wichita, KS	4,005	128	Yakima, WA	1,619	200	Brownsville, TX	1,009
57	Durham, NC	3,874	129	Reno, NV	1,618	201	North Charleston, SC	999
58	New Orleans, LA	3,857	130	Irving, TX	1,603	202	Hayward, CA	988
59	Washington, DC	3,849	131	Pueblo, CO	1,590	203	Lancaster, CA	986
60	Flint, MI	3,628	132	Tempe, AZ	1,579	204	Miramar, FL	981
61	Boston, MA	3,482	133	Bridgeport, CT	1,540	205	Berkeley, CA	976
62	St. Petersburg, FL	3,412	134	Miami Gardens, FL	1,485	206	New Bedford, MA	969
63	Lubbock, TX	3,410	135	Wilmington, NC	1,454	207	Palmdale, CA	959
64	Rochester, NY	3,384	136	Eugene, OR	1,440	208	Vancouver, WA	950
65	Columbus, GA	3,342	136	Madison, WI	1,440	209	Aurora, IL	947
66	Colorado Springs, CO	3,323	138	Camden, NJ	1,436	210	Joliet, IL	939
67	Omaha, NE	3,321	139	Scottsdale, AZ	1,424	210	Ontario, CA	939
68	Long Beach, CA	3,275	140	New Haven, CT	1,413	212	Lakewood, CO	935
69	Tallahassee, FL	3,252	141	Anaheim, CA	1,410	213	Rialto, CA	934
70	St. Paul, MN	3,197	142	Jersey City, NJ	1,402	214	West Valley, UT	929
71	Dayton, OH	3,121	143	Lincoln, NE	1,401	215	Roanoke, VA	928
72	Fort Lauderdale, FL	3,102	144	Murfreesboro, TN	1,383	216	Sunrise, FL	919

Rank Order - City (continued)

RANK	CITY	BURGLARY	RANK	CITY	BURGLARY	RANK	CITY	BURGLARY
217	Renton, WA	917	289	Citrus Heights, CA	607	363	Roswell, GA	404
217	Spokane Valley, WA	917	291	El Cajon, CA	603	365	Westminster, CO	397
219	Clovis, CA	914	292	Bloomington, IN	601	366	Burbank, CA	395
219	Lowell, MA	914	293	Hawthorne, CA	598	367	Round Rock, TX	394
221	St. Joseph, MO	907	294	Greeley, CO	593	368	Sunnyvale, CA	393
222	Manchester, NH	902	295	Toms River Twnshp, NJ	589	369	Tracy, CA	390
223	Concord, CA	898	296	Sandy Springs, GA	587	370	Provo, UT	386
224	Carrollton, TX	896	297	Champaign, IL	586	371	League City, TX	374
225	Albany, NY	895	298	Oxnard, CA	577	372	Bethlehem, PA	371
226	Salem, OR	891	299	Carson, CA	573	372	Woodbridge Twnshp, NJ	371
227	Pomona, CA	890	299	Lewisville, TX	573	374	Cary, NC	370
228	Sioux Falls, SD	880	301	Fairfield, CA	572	374	Medford, OR	370
229	Melbourne, FL	873	302	Deerfield Beach, FL	569	376	Livermore, CA	366
230	Fall River, MA	863	303	Inglewood, CA	568	376	Warwick, RI	366
231	Ogden, UT	858	304	Santa Clarita, CA	567	378	Bend, OR	365
232	Tyler, TX	834	305	Kenosha, WI	566	379	Cheektowaga, NY	362
233	Gilbert, AZ	823	306	Denton, TX	565	380	Nashua, NH	360
233	Redding, CA	823	307	Fort Collins, CO	560	381	San Marcos, CA	358
235	Yuma, AZ	822	308	Escondido, CA	557	382	Greece, NY	355
236	Hampton, VA	820	309	Elgin, IL	555	383	Murrieta, CA	348
237	Longview, TX	819	310	Quincy, MA	551	384	Upper Darby Twnshp, PA	347
238	Waterbury, CT	818	311	Temecula, CA	547	385	Napa, CA	344
239	Boise, ID	809	312	Clinton Twnshp, MI	545	386	Danbury, CT	343
240	Palm Bay, FL	808	313	El Monte, CA	544	386	Edison Twnshp, NJ	343
241	Chula Vista, CA	807	314	Santa Barbara, CA	541	388	Lakewood, CA	341
242	Merced, CA	802	315	Cambridge, MA	539	389	Brick Twnshp, NJ	331
243	San Angelo, TX	801	316	Ann Arbor, MI	534	389	Pearland, TX	331
244	Compton, CA	800	316	Roseville, CA	534	391	Centennial, CO	325
245	Columbia, MO	798	318	Chino, CA	530	391	Lee's Summit, MO	325
246	Oceanside, CA	792	319	Charleston, SC	527	393	Daly City, CA	322
247	Indio, CA	788	320	West Covina, CA	526	394	Thousand Oaks, CA	319
248	Downey, CA	769	321	Costa Mesa, CA	524	395	Baldwin Park, CA	315
249	Edinburg, TX	758	322	Suffolk, VA	518	396	Simi Valley, CA	314
250	Duluth, MN	756	323	Lynchburg, VA	515	397	Alhambra, CA	312
251	Asheville, NC	753	324	Nampa, ID	514	398	Clifton, NJ	311
251	Huntington Beach, CA	753	325	Hamilton Twnshp, NJ	513	398	Edmond, OK	311
251	Yonkers, NY	753	325	Irvine, CA	513	400	Buena Park, CA	310
254	Gresham, OR	751	325	Thornton, CO	513	401	Livonia, MI	308
255	Plantation, FL	748	328	McAllen, TX	511	402	San Mateo, CA	306
256	Clearwater, FL	719	329	Torrance, CA	509	403	Arvada, CO	304
257	Lynn, MA	718	330	Brooklyn Park, MN	506	403	Rio Rancho, NM	304
258	Garden Grove, CA	717	331	Lawrence, KS	502	405	Alexandria, VA	303
259	Midland, TX	715	332	Boca Raton, FL	495	406	Naperville, IL	300
260	Avondale, AZ	712	333	Chico, CA	487	407	Longmont, CO	298
261	Davie, FL	709	334	Frisco, TX	483	408	Norwalk, CT	297
261	Sioux City, IA	709	334	Santa Monica, CA	483	409	Stamford, CT	282
263	Corona, CA	705	336	Bellflower, CA	481	410	Farmington Hills, MI	267
264	Lawrence, MA	682	337	Norwalk, CA	476	411	Chino Hills, CA	264
265	Bryan, TX	681	338	Vista, CA	469	412	Lakewood Twnshp, NJ	261
266	Richardson, TX	680	339	Carlsbad, CA	468	412	Vacaville, CA	261
267	Norman, OK	677	339	Overland Park, KS	468	414	Olathe, KS	259
268	San Leandro, CA	671	341	Boulder, CO	467	415	Hillsboro, OR	252
269	Billings, MT	669	341	Green Bay, WI	467	416	Bloomington, MN	251
270	Cicero, IL	668	343	Mission, TX	464	417	Allen, TX	248
270	Hesperia, CA	668	344	Cranston, RI	461	418	Tustin, CA	243
272	Elk Grove, CA	664	345	Bloomington, IL	460	419	Troy, MI	236
273	Ventura, CA	657	346	Concord, NC	452	420	Beaverton, OR	227
274	Sparks, NV	656	347	Sterling Heights, MI	451	421	Colonie, NY	224
275	Santa Maria, CA	655	348	Menifee, CA	450	422	Canton Twnshp, MI	222
276	College Station, TX	651	349	Orange, CA	445	423	Amherst, NY	221
277	Bellingham, WA	646	350	Newport Beach, CA	441	424	Sugar Land, TX	220
278	Fullerton, CA	643	351	Sandy, UT	438	425	Newton, MA	212
279	Santa Rosa, CA	637	352	Redwood City, CA	436	426	Mission Viejo, CA	193
280	Coral Springs, FL	633	353	Whittier, CA	435	427	Arlington Heights, IL	170
281	McKinney, TX	626	354	Broken Arrow, OK	426	428	New Rochelle, NY	166
282	Glendale, CA	623	355	Rochester, MN	425	428	Orem, UT	166
283	Scranton, PA	620	356	Fargo, ND	423	430	Meridian, ID	156
284	Largo, FL	617	357	Hoover, AL	422	431	Lake Forest, CA	140
284	Odessa, TX	617	358	South Gate, CA	418	432	O'Fallon, MO	135
284	Surprise, AZ	617	359	Somerville, MA	415	433	Johns Creek, GA	131
287	Dearborn, MI	612	360	Santa Clara, CA	409	434	Ramapo, NY	119
288	Westland, MI	610	360	Westminster, CA	409	435	Clarkstown, NY	111
289	Bellevue, WA	607	362	West Jordan, UT	405	436	Carmel, IN	69
			363	Kennewick, WA	404	437	Fishers, IN	57

Source: Reported data from the F.B.I. "Crime in the United States 2011"
*Burglary is the unlawful entry of a structure to commit a felony or theft. Attempts are included.

Alpha Order - City

70. Burglary Rate in 2011
National Rate = 702.2 Burglaries per 100,000 Population*

RANK	CITY	RATE	RANK	CITY	RATE	RANK	CITY	RATE
149	Abilene, TX	936.2	326	Cheektowaga, NY	457.1	203	Fort Wayne, IN	740.4
14	Akron, OH	2,142.0	288	Chesapeake, VA	550.1	71	Fort Worth, TX	1,329.0
32	Albany, GA	1,697.8	141	Chicago, IL	977.2	287	Fremont, CA	556.8
158	Albany, NY	910.5	286	Chico, CA	558.5	102	Fresno, CA	1,141.5
116	Albuquerque, NM	1,084.3	379	Chino Hills, CA	348.8	355	Frisco, TX	404.3
424	Alexandria, VA	213.9	232	Chino, CA	671.7	318	Fullerton, CA	470.2
372	Alhambra, CA	371.1	390	Chula Vista, CA	327.0	179	Gainesville, FL	843.3
151	Allentown, PA	929.8	189	Cicero, IL	793.9	352	Garden Grove, CA	414.7
402	Allen, TX	288.3	10	Cincinnati, OH	2,245.9	142	Garland, TX	968.7
125	Amarillo, TX	1,035.4	217	Citrus Heights, CA	720.2	2	Gary, IN	3,244.0
429	Amherst, NY	187.9	435	Clarkstown, NY	140.1	359	Gilbert, AZ	389.3
353	Anaheim, CA	414.4	137	Clarksville, TN	993.8	121	Glendale, AZ	1,062.1
376	Anchorage, AK	363.7	235	Clearwater, FL	658.7	393	Glendale, CA	321.2
320	Ann Arbor, MI	469.0	6	Cleveland, OH	2,696.0	132	Grand Prairie, TX	1,009.6
78	Antioch, CA	1,288.9	373	Clifton, NJ	368.4	124	Grand Rapids, MI	1,038.9
421	Arlington Heights, IL	225.7	282	Clinton Twnshp, MI	563.5	374	Greece, NY	367.8
97	Arlington, TX	1,176.0	147	Clovis, CA	944.7	245	Greeley, CO	627.5
405	Arvada, CO	280.7	226	College Station, TX	679.3	331	Green Bay, WI	446.8
161	Asheville, NC	891.7	404	Colonie, NY	287.4	220	Gresham, OR	703.7
100	Athens-Clarke, GA	1,160.4	194	Colorado Springs, CO	784.3	271	Hamilton Twnshp, NJ	578.0
27	Atlanta, GA	1,762.3	207	Columbia, MO	732.8	83	Hammond, IN	1,270.3
238	Aurora, CO	648.2	29	Columbus, GA	1,737.1	267	Hampton, VA	589.6
313	Aurora, IL	477.1	20	Columbus, OH	1,926.0	128	Hartford, CT	1,016.8
166	Austin, TX	872.6	183	Compton, CA	819.8	222	Hawthorne, CA	701.2
153	Avondale, AZ	920.9	212	Concord, CA	727.1	227	Hayward, CA	677.3
89	Bakersfield, CA	1,229.1	280	Concord, NC	564.5	50	Hemet, CA	1,474.0
354	Baldwin Park, CA	413.0	298	Coral Springs, FL	515.7	307	Henderson, NV	492.5
62	Baltimore, MD	1,374.3	325	Corona, CA	457.3	208	Hesperia, CA	732.2
24	Baton Rouge, LA	1,822.2	176	Corpus Christi, TX	856.1	319	Hialeah, FL	469.4
33	Beaumont, TX	1,684.8	317	Costa Mesa, CA	471.0	94	High Point, NC	1,197.8
414	Beaverton, OR	250.1	272	Cranston, RI	574.2	411	Hillsboro, OR	272.2
311	Bellevue, WA	488.4	44	Dallas, TX	1,531.2	54	Hollywood, FL	1,439.5
251	Bellflower, CA	620.5	398	Daly City, CA	314.7	299	Hoover, AL	514.6
193	Bellingham, WA	786.3	347	Danbury, CT	423.2	80	Houston, TX	1,281.0
316	Bend, OR	471.2	103	Davenport, IA	1,137.6	358	Huntington Beach, CA	391.7
175	Berkeley, CA	856.9	198	Davie, FL	760.4	49	Huntsville, AL	1,479.2
306	Bethlehem, PA	493.2	12	Dayton, OH	2,203.6	134	Independence, MO	1,004.6
242	Billings, MT	636.6	246	Dearborn, MI	624.0	25	Indianapolis, IN	1,815.3
4	Birmingham, AL	2,722.5	45	Decatur, IL	1,493.1	126	Indio, CA	1,024.3
262	Bloomington, IL	598.6	200	Deerfield Beach, FL	748.3	300	Inglewood, CA	511.9
201	Bloomington, IN	743.7	312	Denton, TX	488.0	419	Irvine, CA	238.7
400	Bloomington, MN	300.5	188	Denver, CO	797.2	213	Irving, TX	725.9
269	Boca Raton, FL	578.7	92	Des Moines, IA	1,219.1	127	Jacksonville, FL	1,020.8
360	Boise, ID	389.0	11	Detroit, MI	2,242.4	5	Jackson, MS	2,711.1
285	Boston, MA	560.4	225	Downey, CA	680.0	281	Jersey City, NJ	564.4
315	Boulder, CO	471.3	170	Duluth, MN	869.7	433	Johns Creek, GA	168.5
339	Brick Twnshp, NJ	439.4	35	Durham, NC	1,675.4	243	Joliet, IL	635.0
120	Bridgeport, CT	1,065.8	144	Edinburg, TX	962.9	86	Kansas City, KS	1,245.3
114	Brockton, MA	1,098.7	385	Edison Twnshp, NJ	342.0	47	Kansas City, MO	1,484.0
345	Broken Arrow, OK	426.4	368	Edmond, OK	378.0	292	Kennewick, WA	538.1
234	Brooklyn Park, MN	662.6	261	El Cajon, CA	599.1	276	Kenosha, WI	568.0
279	Brownsville, TX	564.6	314	El Monte, CA	473.8	77	Kent, WA	1,303.0
165	Bryan, TX	875.3	406	El Paso, TX	280.5	43	Killeen, TX	1,557.3
367	Buena Park, CA	380.5	302	Elgin, IL	511.5	56	Knoxville, TN	1,409.5
31	Buffalo, NY	1,704.1	152	Elizabeth, NJ	926.7	140	Lafayette, LA	980.9
369	Burbank, CA	377.8	344	Elk Grove, CA	428.9	431	Lake Forest, CA	179.1
303	Cambridge, MA	509.4	93	Erie, PA	1,207.5	65	Lakeland, FL	1,349.9
22	Camden, NJ	1,850.3	364	Escondido, CA	382.5	407	Lakewood Twnshp, NJ	280.2
418	Canton Twnshp, MI	246.4	157	Eugene, OR	912.3	349	Lakewood, CA	421.0
236	Cape Coral, FL	654.1	159	Evansville, IN	909.9	241	Lakewood, CO	642.7
340	Carlsbad, CA	439.2	110	Everett, WA	1,111.5	249	Lancaster, CA	622.2
436	Carmel, IN	86.7	294	Fairfield, CA	536.8	53	Lansing, MI	1,444.7
206	Carrollton, TX	736.8	143	Fall River, MA	965.3	202	Laredo, TX	742.6
253	Carson, CA	617.5	357	Fargo, ND	394.1	195	Largo, FL	783.9
412	Cary, NC	270.2	388	Farmington Hills, MI	335.1	104	Las Cruces, NM	1,134.6
173	Cedar Rapids, IA	865.4	16	Fayetteville, NC	2,069.8	172	Las Vegas, NV	868.2
394	Centennial, CO	318.2	437	Fishers, IN	73.8	275	Lawrence, KS	569.2
215	Champaign, IL	720.8	1	Flint, MI	3,544.5	162	Lawrence, MA	887.5
283	Chandler, AZ	561.2	296	Fontana, CA	524.8	19	Lawton, OK	2,002.0
343	Charleston, SC	433.8	366	Fort Collins, CO	382.3	341	League City, TX	438.4
117	Charlotte, NC	1,081.2	23	Fort Lauderdale, FL	1,848.9	378	Lee's Summit, MO	354.4
48	Chattanooga, TN	1,479.4	81	Fort Smith, AR	1,277.9	268	Lewisville, TX	588.9

Alpha Order - City (continued)

RANK	CITY	RATE	RANK	CITY	RATE	RANK	CITY	RATE
155	Lexington, KY	914.6	413	Overland Park, KS	268.2	177	Sioux City, IA	853.0
293	Lincoln, NE	537.4	403	Oxnard, CA	288.2	278	Sioux Falls, SD	565.0
7	Little Rock, AR	2,387.3	197	Palm Bay, FL	772.5	289	Somerville, MA	544.5
331	Livermore, CA	446.8	251	Palmdale, CA	620.5	9	South Bend, IN	2,296.3
395	Livonia, MI	318.0	211	Pasadena, CA	728.7	342	South Gate, CA	437.7
223	Long Beach, CA	700.2	205	Pasadena, TX	738.6	216	Sparks, NV	720.7
386	Longmont, CO	339.5	91	Paterson, NJ	1,220.3	133	Spokane Valley, WA	1,005.9
136	Longview, TX	997.0	377	Pearland, TX	355.3	55	Spokane, WA	1,427.9
329	Los Angeles, CA	449.9	230	Pembroke Pines, FL	675.1	37	Springfield, IL	1,614.9
90	Louisville, KY	1,221.8	224	Peoria, AZ	696.3	36	Springfield, MA	1,622.8
178	Lowell, MA	852.9	46	Peoria, IL	1,491.9	79	Springfield, MO	1,282.5
52	Lubbock, TX	1,454.8	192	Philadelphia, PA	787.6	420	Stamford, CT	229.5
231	Lynchburg, VA	673.5	82	Phoenix, AZ	1,273.2	380	Sterling Heights, MI	348.0
191	Lynn, MA	790.1	169	Pittsburgh, PA	870.4	57	Stockton, CA	1,400.4
8	Macon, GA	2,327.3	330	Plano, TX	449.7	96	St. Joseph, MO	1,177.0
255	Madison, WI	614.8	171	Plantation, FL	868.6	13	St. Louis, MO	2,189.1
182	Manchester, NH	822.2	265	Pomona, CA	590.1	111	St. Paul, MN	1,111.4
362	McAllen, TX	385.3	72	Pompano Beach, FL	1,327.0	61	St. Petersburg, FL	1,375.2
322	McKinney, TX	467.6	229	Port St. Lucie, FL	676.1	257	Suffolk, VA	605.2
310	Medford, OR	488.7	210	Portland, OR	729.4	410	Sugar Land, TX	273.4
106	Melbourne, FL	1,132.2	59	Portsmouth, VA	1,394.3	409	Sunnyvale, CA	277.3
17	Memphis, TN	2,030.6	387	Provo, UT	336.7	118	Sunrise, FL	1,073.7
273	Menifee, CA	573.8	51	Pueblo, CO	1,466.1	297	Surprise, AZ	517.7
135	Merced, CA	1,003.9	264	Quincy, MA	593.5	98	Syracuse, NY	1,169.2
426	Meridian, ID	205.5	41	Racine, WI	1,564.3	68	Tacoma, WA	1,344.4
250	Mesa, AZ	621.9	209	Raleigh, NC	729.8	26	Tallahassee, FL	1,768.9
95	Mesquite, TX	1,193.6	434	Ramapo, NY	140.9	187	Tampa, FL	798.7
74	Miami Beach, FL	1,316.1	221	Rancho Cucamon., CA	701.5	291	Temecula, CA	540.1
64	Miami Gardens, FL	1,367.1	42	Reading, PA	1,561.7	145	Tempe, AZ	962.8
84	Miami, FL	1,269.7	160	Redding, CA	905.2	346	Thornton, CO	424.5
244	Midland, TX	630.0	284	Redwood City, CA	561.0	416	Thousand Oaks, CA	248.9
108	Milwaukee, WI	1,116.3	218	Reno, NV	712.4	3	Toledo, OH	2,910.7
73	Minneapolis, MN	1,323.9	138	Renton, WA	992.9	240	Toms River Twnshp, NJ	643.4
190	Miramar, FL	793.0	150	Rialto, CA	930.9	67	Topeka, KS	1,346.2
428	Mission Viejo, CA	204.4	233	Richardson, TX	671.2	383	Torrance, CA	345.9
266	Mission, TX	589.7	40	Richmond, CA	1,573.6	323	Tracy, CA	464.9
38	Mobile, AL	1,611.2	156	Richmond, VA	912.6	70	Trenton, NJ	1,335.7
122	Modesto, CA	1,042.1	384	Rio Rancho, NM	343.5	401	Troy, MI	291.6
58	Montgomery, AL	1,395.4	228	Riverside, CA	676.5	148	Tucson, AZ	943.9
119	Moreno Valley, CA	1,070.9	146	Roanoke, VA	945.1	21	Tulsa, OK	1,856.3
85	Murfreesboro, TN	1,260.3	356	Rochester, MN	395.0	63	Tuscaloosa, AL	1,374.0
389	Murrieta, CA	332.4	39	Rochester, NY	1,599.9	396	Tustin, CA	317.9
247	Nampa, ID	623.3	87	Rockford, IL	1,232.6	180	Tyler, TX	842.9
337	Napa, CA	442.1	334	Roseville, CA	444.3	350	Upper Darby Twnshp, PA	417.8
425	Naperville, IL	210.9	327	Roswell, GA	451.4	408	Vacaville, CA	279.1
351	Nashua, NH	415.7	361	Round Rock, TX	386.3	15	Vallejo, CA	2,103.9
88	Nashville, TN	1,230.6	164	Sacramento, CA	877.4	270	Vancouver, WA	578.1
130	New Bedford, MA	1,013.1	274	Salem, OR	570.1	256	Ventura, CA	610.1
115	New Haven, CT	1,086.8	199	Salinas, CA	749.0	101	Victorville, CA	1,158.9
109	New Orleans, LA	1,111.6	167	Salt Lake City, UT	872.5	324	Virginia Beach, VA	459.8
423	New Rochelle, NY	214.4	181	San Angelo, TX	841.7	163	Visalia, CA	881.6
422	New York, NY	221.1	107	San Antonio, TX	1,131.4	305	Vista, CA	494.0
174	Newark, NJ	861.7	112	San Bernardino, CA	1,110.7	75	Waco, TX	1,310.5
301	Newport Beach, CA	511.7	335	San Diego, CA	443.5	186	Warren, MI	798.8
263	Newport News, VA	598.2	290	San Francisco, CA	541.1	336	Warwick, RI	443.2
417	Newton, MA	247.5	338	San Jose, CA	441.2	248	Washington, DC	622.8
154	Norfolk, VA	918.2	196	San Leandro, CA	780.7	204	Waterbury, CT	739.8
260	Norman, OK	603.9	348	San Marcos, CA	422.3	309	West Covina, CA	490.0
130	North Charleston, SC	1,013.1	399	San Mateo, CA	311.1	363	West Jordan, UT	383.1
333	Norwalk, CA	445.7	254	Sandy Springs, GA	617.3	69	West Palm Beach, FL	1,336.9
382	Norwalk, CT	346.3	308	Sandy, UT	491.3	219	West Valley, UT	703.9
76	Oakland, CA	1,307.8	391	Santa Ana, CA	325.0	213	Westland, MI	725.9
321	Oceanside, CA	468.5	258	Santa Barbara, CA	604.8	328	Westminster, CA	450.7
259	Odessa, TX	604.6	381	Santa Clara, CA	347.1	375	Westminster, CO	367.7
432	O'Fallon, MO	169.6	397	Santa Clarita, CA	317.8	304	Whittier, CA	503.9
129	Ogden, UT	1,016.3	237	Santa Maria, CA	650.3	99	Wichita Falls, TX	1,162.5
34	Oklahoma City, OK	1,681.5	295	Santa Monica, CA	532.0	123	Wichita, KS	1,040.8
427	Olathe, KS	204.5	370	Santa Rosa, CA	375.2	66	Wilmington, NC	1,348.5
185	Omaha, NE	804.9	139	Savannah, GA	989.7	18	Winston-Salem, NC	2,012.7
277	Ontario, CA	566.2	239	Scottsdale, AZ	645.9	371	Woodbridge Twnshp, NJ	371.3
392	Orange, CA	322.4	184	Scranton, PA	812.2	105	Worcester, MA	1,134.3
430	Orem, UT	184.4	113	Seattle, WA	1,101.1	28	Yakima, WA	1,750.3
30	Orlando, FL	1,724.3	60	Shreveport, LA	1,379.7	364	Yonkers, NY	382.5
			415	Simi Valley, CA	249.8	168	Yuma, AZ	870.9

Source: CQ Press using reported data from the F.B.I. "Crime in the United States 2011"
*Burglary is the unlawful entry of a structure to commit a felony or theft. Attempts are included.

Rank Order - City

70. Burglary Rate in 2011 (continued)
National Rate = 702.2 Burglaries per 100,000 Population*

RANK	CITY	RATE	RANK	CITY	RATE	RANK	CITY	RATE
1	Flint, MI	3,544.5	73	Minneapolis, MN	1,323.9	145	Tempe, AZ	962.8
2	Gary, IN	3,244.0	74	Miami Beach, FL	1,316.1	146	Roanoke, VA	945.1
3	Toledo, OH	2,910.7	75	Waco, TX	1,310.5	147	Clovis, CA	944.7
4	Birmingham, AL	2,722.5	76	Oakland, CA	1,307.8	148	Tucson, AZ	943.9
5	Jackson, MS	2,711.1	77	Kent, WA	1,303.0	149	Abilene, TX	936.2
6	Cleveland, OH	2,696.0	78	Antioch, CA	1,288.9	150	Rialto, CA	930.9
7	Little Rock, AR	2,387.3	79	Springfield, MO	1,282.5	151	Allentown, PA	929.8
8	Macon, GA	2,327.3	80	Houston, TX	1,281.0	152	Elizabeth, NJ	926.7
9	South Bend, IN	2,296.3	81	Fort Smith, AR	1,277.9	153	Avondale, AZ	920.9
10	Cincinnati, OH	2,245.9	82	Phoenix, AZ	1,273.2	154	Norfolk, VA	918.2
11	Detroit, MI	2,242.4	83	Hammond, IN	1,270.3	155	Lexington, KY	914.6
12	Dayton, OH	2,203.6	84	Miami, FL	1,269.7	156	Richmond, VA	912.6
13	St. Louis, MO	2,189.1	85	Murfreesboro, TN	1,260.3	157	Eugene, OR	912.3
14	Akron, OH	2,142.0	86	Kansas City, KS	1,245.3	158	Albany, NY	910.5
15	Vallejo, CA	2,103.9	87	Rockford, IL	1,232.6	159	Evansville, IN	909.9
16	Fayetteville, NC	2,069.8	88	Nashville, TN	1,230.6	160	Redding, CA	905.2
17	Memphis, TN	2,030.6	89	Bakersfield, CA	1,229.1	161	Asheville, NC	891.7
18	Winston-Salem, NC	2,012.7	90	Louisville, KY	1,221.8	162	Lawrence, MA	887.5
19	Lawton, OK	2,002.0	91	Paterson, NJ	1,220.3	163	Visalia, CA	881.6
20	Columbus, OH	1,926.0	92	Des Moines, IA	1,219.1	164	Sacramento, CA	877.4
21	Tulsa, OK	1,856.3	93	Erie, PA	1,207.5	165	Bryan, TX	875.3
22	Camden, NJ	1,850.4	94	High Point, NC	1,197.8	166	Austin, TX	872.6
23	Fort Lauderdale, FL	1,848.9	95	Mesquite, TX	1,193.6	167	Salt Lake City, UT	872.5
24	Baton Rouge, LA	1,822.2	96	St. Joseph, MO	1,177.0	168	Yuma, AZ	870.9
25	Indianapolis, IN	1,815.3	97	Arlington, TX	1,176.0	169	Pittsburgh, PA	870.4
26	Tallahassee, FL	1,768.9	98	Syracuse, NY	1,169.2	170	Duluth, MN	869.7
27	Atlanta, GA	1,762.3	99	Wichita Falls, TX	1,162.5	171	Plantation, FL	868.6
28	Yakima, WA	1,750.3	100	Athens-Clarke, GA	1,160.4	172	Las Vegas, NV	868.2
29	Columbus, GA	1,737.1	101	Victorville, CA	1,158.9	173	Cedar Rapids, IA	865.4
30	Orlando, FL	1,724.3	102	Fresno, CA	1,141.5	174	Newark, NJ	861.7
31	Buffalo, NY	1,704.1	103	Davenport, IA	1,137.6	175	Berkeley, CA	856.9
32	Albany, GA	1,697.8	104	Las Cruces, NM	1,134.6	176	Corpus Christi, TX	856.1
33	Beaumont, TX	1,684.8	105	Worcester, MA	1,134.3	177	Sioux City, IA	853.0
34	Oklahoma City, OK	1,681.1	106	Melbourne, FL	1,132.2	178	Lowell, MA	852.9
35	Durham, NC	1,675.4	107	San Antonio, TX	1,131.4	179	Gainesville, FL	843.3
36	Springfield, MA	1,622.8	108	Milwaukee, WI	1,116.3	180	Tyler, TX	842.9
37	Springfield, IL	1,614.9	109	New Orleans, LA	1,111.6	181	San Angelo, TX	841.7
38	Mobile, AL	1,611.2	110	Everett, WA	1,111.5	182	Manchester, NH	822.2
39	Rochester, NY	1,599.9	111	St. Paul, MN	1,111.4	183	Compton, CA	819.8
40	Richmond, CA	1,573.6	112	San Bernardino, CA	1,110.7	184	Scranton, PA	812.2
41	Racine, WI	1,564.3	113	Seattle, WA	1,101.1	185	Omaha, NE	804.9
42	Reading, PA	1,561.7	114	Brockton, MA	1,098.7	186	Warren, MI	798.8
43	Killeen, TX	1,557.3	115	New Haven, CT	1,086.8	187	Tampa, FL	798.7
44	Dallas, TX	1,531.2	116	Albuquerque, NM	1,084.3	188	Denver, CO	797.2
45	Decatur, IL	1,493.1	117	Charlotte, NC	1,081.2	189	Cicero, IL	793.9
46	Peoria, IL	1,491.9	118	Sunrise, FL	1,073.7	190	Miramar, FL	793.0
47	Kansas City, MO	1,484.0	119	Moreno Valley, CA	1,070.9	191	Lynn, MA	790.1
48	Chattanooga, TN	1,479.4	120	Bridgeport, CT	1,065.8	192	Philadelphia, PA	787.6
49	Huntsville, AL	1,479.2	121	Glendale, AZ	1,062.1	193	Bellingham, WA	786.3
50	Hemet, CA	1,474.0	122	Modesto, CA	1,042.1	194	Colorado Springs, CO	784.3
51	Pueblo, CO	1,466.1	123	Wichita, KS	1,040.8	195	Largo, FL	783.9
52	Lubbock, TX	1,454.8	124	Grand Rapids, MI	1,038.9	196	San Leandro, CA	780.7
53	Lansing, MI	1,444.7	125	Amarillo, TX	1,035.4	197	Palm Bay, FL	772.5
54	Hollywood, FL	1,439.5	126	Indio, CA	1,024.3	198	Davie, FL	760.4
55	Spokane, WA	1,427.9	127	Jacksonville, FL	1,020.8	199	Salinas, CA	749.0
56	Knoxville, TN	1,409.5	128	Hartford, CT	1,016.8	200	Deerfield Beach, FL	748.3
57	Stockton, CA	1,400.4	129	Ogden, UT	1,016.3	201	Bloomington, IN	743.7
58	Montgomery, AL	1,395.4	130	New Bedford, MA	1,013.1	202	Laredo, TX	742.6
59	Portsmouth, VA	1,394.3	130	North Charleston, SC	1,013.1	203	Fort Wayne, IN	740.4
60	Shreveport, LA	1,379.7	132	Grand Prairie, TX	1,009.6	204	Waterbury, CT	739.8
61	St. Petersburg, FL	1,375.2	133	Spokane Valley, WA	1,005.9	205	Pasadena, TX	738.6
62	Baltimore, MD	1,374.3	134	Independence, MO	1,004.6	206	Carrollton, TX	736.8
63	Tuscaloosa, AL	1,374.0	135	Merced, CA	1,003.9	207	Columbia, MO	732.8
64	Miami Gardens, FL	1,367.1	136	Longview, TX	997.0	208	Hesperia, CA	732.2
65	Lakeland, FL	1,349.9	137	Clarksville, TN	993.8	209	Raleigh, NC	729.8
66	Wilmington, NC	1,348.5	138	Renton, WA	992.9	210	Portland, OR	729.3
67	Topeka, KS	1,346.2	139	Savannah, GA	989.7	211	Pasadena, CA	728.7
68	Tacoma, WA	1,344.4	140	Lafayette, LA	980.9	212	Concord, CA	727.1
69	West Palm Beach, FL	1,336.9	141	Chicago, IL	977.2	213	Irving, TX	725.9
70	Trenton, NJ	1,335.7	142	Garland, TX	968.7	213	Westland, MI	725.9
71	Fort Worth, TX	1,329.0	143	Fall River, MA	965.3	215	Champaign, IL	720.8
72	Pompano Beach, FL	1,327.0	144	Edinburg, TX	962.9	216	Sparks, NV	720.7

Rank Order - City (continued)

RANK	CITY	RATE
217	Citrus Heights, CA	720.2
218	Reno, NV	712.4
219	West Valley, UT	703.9
220	Gresham, OR	703.7
221	Rancho Cucamon., CA	701.5
222	Hawthorne, CA	701.2
223	Long Beach, CA	700.2
224	Peoria, AZ	696.3
225	Downey, CA	680.0
226	College Station, TX	679.3
227	Hayward, CA	677.3
228	Riverside, CA	676.5
229	Port St. Lucie, FL	676.1
230	Pembroke Pines, FL	675.1
231	Lynchburg, VA	673.5
232	Chino, CA	671.7
233	Richardson, TX	671.2
234	Brooklyn Park, MN	662.6
235	Clearwater, FL	658.7
236	Cape Coral, FL	654.1
237	Santa Maria, CA	650.3
238	Aurora, CO	648.2
239	Scottsdale, AZ	645.9
240	Toms River Twnshp, NJ	643.4
241	Lakewood, CO	642.7
242	Billings, MT	636.6
243	Joliet, IL	635.0
244	Midland, TX	630.0
245	Greeley, CO	627.5
246	Dearborn, MI	624.0
247	Nampa, ID	623.3
248	Washington, DC	622.8
249	Lancaster, CA	622.2
250	Mesa, AZ	621.9
251	Bellflower, CA	620.5
251	Palmdale, CA	620.5
253	Carson, CA	617.5
254	Sandy Springs, GA	617.3
255	Madison, WI	614.8
256	Ventura, CA	610.1
257	Suffolk, VA	605.2
258	Santa Barbara, CA	604.8
259	Odessa, TX	604.6
260	Norman, OK	603.9
261	El Cajon, CA	599.1
262	Bloomington, IL	598.6
263	Newport News, VA	598.2
264	Quincy, MA	593.5
265	Pomona, CA	590.1
266	Mission, TX	589.7
267	Hampton, VA	589.6
268	Lewisville, TX	588.9
269	Boca Raton, FL	578.7
270	Vancouver, WA	578.1
271	Hamilton Twnshp, NJ	578.0
272	Cranston, RI	574.2
273	Menifee, CA	573.8
274	Salem, OR	570.1
275	Lawrence, KS	569.2
276	Kenosha, WI	568.0
277	Ontario, CA	566.2
278	Sioux Falls, SD	565.0
279	Brownsville, TX	564.6
280	Concord, NC	564.5
281	Jersey City, NJ	564.4
282	Clinton Twnshp, MI	563.5
283	Chandler, AZ	561.2
284	Redwood City, CA	561.0
285	Boston, MA	560.4
286	Chico, CA	558.5
287	Fremont, CA	556.8
288	Chesapeake, VA	550.1
289	Somerville, MA	544.5
290	San Francisco, CA	541.1
291	Temecula, CA	540.1
292	Kennewick, WA	538.1
293	Lincoln, NE	537.4
294	Fairfield, CA	536.8
295	Santa Monica, CA	532.0
296	Fontana, CA	524.8
297	Surprise, AZ	517.7
298	Coral Springs, FL	515.7
299	Hoover, AL	514.6
300	Inglewood, CA	511.9
301	Newport Beach, CA	511.7
302	Elgin, IL	511.5
303	Cambridge, MA	509.4
304	Whittier, CA	503.9
305	Vista, CA	494.0
306	Bethlehem, PA	493.2
307	Henderson, NV	492.5
308	Sandy, UT	491.3
309	West Covina, CA	490.0
310	Medford, OR	488.7
311	Bellevue, WA	488.4
312	Denton, TX	488.0
313	Aurora, IL	477.1
314	El Monte, CA	473.8
315	Boulder, CO	471.3
316	Bend, OR	471.2
317	Costa Mesa, CA	471.0
318	Fullerton, CA	470.2
319	Hialeah, FL	469.4
320	Ann Arbor, MI	469.0
321	Oceanside, CA	468.5
322	McKinney, TX	467.6
323	Tracy, CA	464.9
324	Virginia Beach, VA	459.8
325	Corona, CA	457.3
326	Cheektowaga, NY	457.1
327	Roswell, GA	451.4
328	Westminster, CA	450.7
329	Los Angeles, CA	449.9
330	Plano, TX	449.7
331	Green Bay, WI	446.8
331	Livermore, CA	446.8
333	Norwalk, CA	445.7
334	Roseville, CA	444.3
335	San Diego, CA	443.5
336	Warwick, RI	443.2
337	Napa, CA	442.1
338	San Jose, CA	441.2
339	Brick Twnshp, NJ	439.4
340	Carlsbad, CA	439.2
341	League City, TX	438.4
342	South Gate, CA	437.7
343	Charleston, SC	433.8
344	Elk Grove, CA	428.9
345	Broken Arrow, OK	426.4
346	Thornton, CO	424.5
347	Danbury, CT	423.2
348	San Marcos, CA	422.3
349	Lakewood, CA	421.0
350	Upper Darby Twnshp, PA	417.8
351	Nashua, NH	415.7
352	Garden Grove, CA	414.7
353	Anaheim, CA	414.4
354	Baldwin Park, CA	413.0
355	Frisco, TX	404.3
356	Rochester, MN	395.0
357	Fargo, ND	394.1
358	Huntington Beach, CA	391.7
359	Gilbert, AZ	389.3
360	Boise, ID	389.0
361	Round Rock, TX	386.3
362	McAllen, TX	385.3
363	West Jordan, UT	383.1
364	Escondido, CA	382.5
364	Yonkers, NY	382.5
366	Fort Collins, CO	382.3
367	Buena Park, CA	380.5
368	Edmond, OK	378.0
369	Burbank, CA	377.8
370	Santa Rosa, CA	375.2
371	Woodbridge Twnshp, NJ	371.3
372	Alhambra, CA	371.1
373	Clifton, NJ	368.4
374	Greece, NY	367.8
375	Westminster, CO	367.7
376	Anchorage, AK	363.7
377	Pearland, TX	355.3
378	Lee's Summit, MO	354.4
379	Chino Hills, CA	348.8
380	Sterling Heights, MI	348.0
381	Santa Clara, CA	347.1
382	Norwalk, CT	346.3
383	Torrance, CA	345.9
384	Rio Rancho, NM	343.5
385	Edison Twnshp, NJ	342.0
386	Longmont, CO	339.5
387	Provo, UT	336.7
388	Farmington Hills, MI	335.1
389	Murrieta, CA	332.4
390	Chula Vista, CA	327.0
391	Santa Ana, CA	325.0
392	Orange, CA	322.4
393	Glendale, CA	321.2
394	Centennial, CO	318.2
395	Livonia, MI	318.0
396	Tustin, CA	317.9
397	Santa Clarita, CA	317.8
398	Daly City, CA	314.7
399	San Mateo, CA	311.1
400	Bloomington, MN	300.5
401	Troy, MI	291.6
402	Allen, TX	288.3
403	Oxnard, CA	288.2
404	Colonie, NY	287.4
405	Arvada, CO	280.7
406	El Paso, TX	280.5
407	Lakewood Twnshp, NJ	280.2
408	Vacaville, CA	279.1
409	Sunnyvale, CA	277.3
410	Sugar Land, TX	273.4
411	Hillsboro, OR	272.2
412	Cary, NC	270.2
413	Overland Park, KS	268.2
414	Beaverton, OR	250.1
415	Simi Valley, CA	249.8
416	Thousand Oaks, CA	248.9
417	Newton, MA	247.5
418	Canton Twnshp, MI	246.4
419	Irvine, CA	238.7
420	Stamford, CT	229.5
421	Arlington Heights, IL	225.7
422	New York, NY	221.1
423	New Rochelle, NY	214.4
424	Alexandria, VA	213.9
425	Naperville, IL	210.9
426	Meridian, ID	205.5
427	Olathe, KS	204.5
428	Mission Viejo, CA	204.4
429	Amherst, NY	187.9
430	Orem, UT	184.4
431	Lake Forest, CA	179.1
432	O'Fallon, MO	169.6
433	Johns Creek, GA	168.5
434	Ramapo, NY	140.9
435	Clarkstown, NY	140.1
436	Carmel, IN	86.7
437	Fishers, IN	73.8

Source: CQ Press using reported data from the F.B.I. "Crime in the United States 2011"
*Burglary is the unlawful entry of a structure to commit a felony or theft. Attempts are included.

Alpha Order - City

71. Percent Change in Burglary Rate: 2010 to 2011
National Percent Change = 0.2% Increase*

RANK	CITY	% CHANGE	RANK	CITY	% CHANGE	RANK	CITY	% CHANGE
360	Abilene, TX	(18.3)	365	Cheektowaga, NY	(18.7)	328	Fort Wayne, IN	(11.1)
161	Akron, OH	3.8	144	Chesapeake, VA	5.2	130	Fort Worth, TX	6.1
385	Albany, GA	(23.9)	136	Chicago, IL	5.7	217	Fremont, CA	(2.0)
301	Albany, NY	(8.8)	411	Chico, CA	(32.6)	144	Fresno, CA	5.2
105	Albuquerque, NM	8.2	96	Chino Hills, CA	8.8	119	Frisco, TX	7.1
164	Alexandria, VA	3.1	40	Chino, CA	18.0	291	Fullerton, CA	(7.9)
299	Alhambra, CA	(8.6)	209	Chula Vista, CA	(1.4)	365	Gainesville, FL	(18.7)
387	Allentown, PA	(24.0)	NA	Cicero, IL**	NA	348	Garden Grove, CA	(14.9)
372	Allen, TX	(19.2)	60	Cincinnati, OH	15.0	195	Garland, TX	(0.4)
385	Amarillo, TX	(23.9)	373	Citrus Heights, CA	(19.5)	NA	Gary, IN**	NA
269	Amherst, NY	(5.9)	407	Clarkstown, NY	(29.6)	134	Gilbert, AZ	5.9
336	Anaheim, CA	(12.0)	296	Clarksville, TN	(8.4)	58	Glendale, AZ	15.1
343	Anchorage, AK	(13.7)	321	Clearwater, FL	(10.4)	211	Glendale, CA	(1.5)
191	Ann Arbor, MI	0.0	47	Cleveland, OH	16.6	346	Grand Prairie, TX	(14.4)
33	Antioch, CA	21.1	NA	Clifton, NJ**	NA	401	Grand Rapids, MI	(28.2)
129	Arlington Heights, IL	6.3	194	Clinton Twnshp, MI	(0.3)	333	Greece, NY	(11.6)
263	Arlington, TX	(5.3)	36	Clovis, CA	20.0	102	Greeley, CO	8.5
383	Arvada, CO	(22.0)	18	College Station, TX	26.5	375	Green Bay, WI	(20.3)
285	Asheville, NC	(7.5)	230	Colonie, NY	(2.8)	119	Gresham, OR	7.1
214	Athens-Clarke, GA	(1.8)	312	Colorado Springs, CO	(9.6)	29	Hamilton Twnshp, NJ	21.8
42	Atlanta, GA	17.9	4	Columbia, MO	37.3	309	Hammond, IN	(9.5)
296	Aurora, CO	(8.4)	282	Columbus, GA	(7.2)	77	Hampton, VA	12.3
184	Aurora, IL	1.4	224	Columbus, OH	(2.3)	22	Hartford, CT	25.4
378	Austin, TX	(20.6)	307	Compton, CA	(9.1)	317	Hawthorne, CA	(10.0)
259	Avondale, AZ	(5.2)	248	Concord, CA	(3.7)	323	Hayward, CA	(10.8)
239	Bakersfield, CA	(3.2)	95	Concord, NC	9.2	25	Hemet, CA	23.2
155	Baldwin Park, CA	4.1	16	Coral Springs, FL	26.8	180	Henderson, NV	1.7
52	Baltimore, MD	16.1	111	Corona, CA	7.9	158	Hesperia, CA	3.9
NA	Baton Rouge, LA**	NA	274	Corpus Christi, TX	(6.3)	279	Hialeah, FL	(6.8)
66	Beaumont, TX	14.4	73	Costa Mesa, CA	13.5	249	High Point, NC	(4.0)
39	Beaverton, OR	18.7	35	Cranston, RI	20.4	NA	Hillsboro, OR**	NA
256	Bellevue, WA	(5.0)	179	Dallas, TX	2.1	78	Hollywood, FL	12.1
91	Bellflower, CA	9.4	243	Daly City, CA	(3.4)	NA	Hoover, AL**	NA
104	Bellingham, WA	8.3	8	Danbury, CT	33.2	149	Houston, TX	4.6
237	Bend, OR	(3.1)	NA	Davenport, IA**	NA	206	Huntington Beach, CA	(1.2)
370	Berkeley, CA	(19.1)	335	Davie, FL	(11.8)	NA	Huntsville, AL**	NA
363	Bethlehem, PA	(18.4)	200	Dayton, OH	(0.7)	224	Independence, MO	(2.3)
NA	Billings, MT**	NA	138	Dearborn, MI	5.6	NA	Indianapolis, IN**	NA
NA	Birmingham, AL**	NA	394	Decatur, IL	(26.2)	149	Indio, CA	4.6
315	Bloomington, IL	(9.8)	239	Deerfield Beach, FL	(3.2)	298	Inglewood, CA	(8.5)
412	Bloomington, IN	(34.0)	84	Denton, TX	10.1	107	Irvine, CA	8.0
85	Bloomington, MN	10.0	114	Denver, CO	7.5	293	Irving, TX	(8.2)
93	Boca Raton, FL	9.3	86	Des Moines, IA	9.8	337	Jacksonville, FL	(12.4)
315	Boise, ID	(9.8)	40	Detroit, MI	18.0	217	Jackson, MS	(2.0)
188	Boston, MA	0.6	80	Downey, CA	10.9	309	Jersey City, NJ	(9.5)
220	Boulder, CO	(2.1)	33	Duluth, MN	21.1	413	Johns Creek, GA	(36.5)
147	Brick Twnshp, NJ	5.0	117	Durham, NC	7.3	191	Joliet, IL	0.0
177	Bridgeport, CT	2.2	402	Edinburg, TX	(28.5)	279	Kansas City, KS	(6.8)
6	Brockton, MA	35.3	168	Edison Twnshp, NJ	2.8	NA	Kansas City, MO**	NA
42	Broken Arrow, OK	17.9	351	Edmond, OK	(15.3)	256	Kennewick, WA	(5.0)
NA	Brooklyn Park, MN**	NA	174	El Cajon, CA	2.4	277	Kenosha, WI	(6.6)
379	Brownsville, TX	(21.0)	255	El Monte, CA	(4.9)	86	Kent, WA	9.8
392	Bryan, TX	(25.9)	319	El Paso, TX	(10.3)	284	Killeen, TX	(7.4)
345	Buena Park, CA	(14.3)	10	Elgin, IL	29.7	249	Knoxville, TN	(4.0)
NA	Buffalo, NY**	NA	15	Elizabeth, NJ	26.9	379	Lafayette, LA	(21.0)
360	Burbank, CA	(18.3)	276	Elk Grove, CA	(6.5)	353	Lake Forest, CA	(15.7)
67	Cambridge, MA	14.3	72	Erie, PA	13.6	54	Lakeland, FL	15.6
2	Camden, NJ	44.2	399	Escondido, CA	(27.6)	356	Lakewood Twnshp, NJ	(17.2)
357	Canton Twnshp, MI	(17.5)	106	Eugene, OR	8.1	124	Lakewood, CA	6.8
237	Cape Coral, FL	(3.1)	226	Evansville, IN	(2.4)	264	Lakewood, CO	(5.4)
82	Carlsbad, CA	10.6	79	Everett, WA	11.1	322	Lancaster, CA	(10.5)
414	Carmel, IN	(45.5)	393	Fairfield, CA	(26.1)	60	Lansing, MI	15.0
114	Carrollton, TX	7.5	290	Fall River, MA	(7.8)	269	Laredo, TX	(5.9)
11	Carson, CA	29.4	190	Fargo, ND	0.2	98	Largo, FL	8.6
403	Cary, NC	(28.6)	325	Farmington Hills, MI	(10.9)	202	Las Cruces, NM	(0.8)
93	Cedar Rapids, IA	9.3	89	Fayetteville, NC	9.7	327	Las Vegas, NV	(11.0)
62	Centennial, CO	14.9	410	Fishers, IN	(31.9)	174	Lawrence, KS	2.4
NA	Champaign, IL**	NA	130	Flint, MI	6.1	277	Lawrence, MA	(6.6)
206	Chandler, AZ	(1.2)	21	Fontana, CA	25.7	148	Lawton, OK	4.9
350	Charleston, SC	(15.2)	357	Fort Collins, CO	(17.5)	246	League City, TX	(3.6)
285	Charlotte, NC	(7.5)	32	Fort Lauderdale, FL	21.2	113	Lee's Summit, MO	7.6
259	Chattanooga, TN	(5.2)	173	Fort Smith, AR	2.5	245	Lewisville, TX	(3.5)

Alpha Order - City (continued)

RANK	CITY	% CHANGE
NA	Lexington, KY**	NA
254	Lincoln, NE	(4.7)
98	Little Rock, AR	8.6
204	Livermore, CA	(1.0)
334	Livonia, MI	(11.7)
83	Long Beach, CA	10.5
293	Longmont, CO	(8.2)
304	Longview, TX	(8.9)
200	Los Angeles, CA	(0.7)
166	Louisville, KY	2.9
212	Lowell, MA	(1.6)
114	Lubbock, TX	7.5
46	Lynchburg, VA	16.9
64	Lynn, MA	14.7
233	Macon, GA	(2.9)
328	Madison, WI	(11.1)
217	Manchester, NH	(2.0)
398	McAllen, TX	(27.0)
188	McKinney, TX	0.6
259	Medford, OR	(5.2)
67	Melbourne, FL	14.3
152	Memphis, TN	4.5
408	Menifee, CA	(30.3)
26	Merced, CA	22.9
388	Meridian, ID	(24.2)
158	Mesa, AZ	3.9
89	Mesquite, TX	9.7
230	Miami Beach, FL	(2.8)
69	Miami Gardens, FL	14.0
30	Miami, FL	21.5
384	Midland, TX	(22.5)
91	Milwaukee, WI	9.4
126	Minneapolis, MN	6.7
406	Miramar, FL	(28.8)
56	Mission Viejo, CA	15.2
338	Mission, TX	(12.5)
NA	Mobile, AL**	NA
220	Modesto, CA	(2.1)
NA	Montgomery, AL**	NA
65	Moreno Valley, CA	14.6
146	Murfreesboro, TN	5.1
370	Murrieta, CA	(19.1)
47	Nampa, ID	16.6
180	Napa, CA	1.7
NA	Naperville, IL**	NA
312	Nashua, NH	(9.6)
216	Nashville, TN	(1.9)
396	New Bedford, MA	(26.6)
235	New Haven, CT	(3.0)
118	New Orleans, LA	7.2
75	New Rochelle, NY	12.8
168	New York, NY	2.8
23	Newark, NJ	25.3
209	Newport Beach, CA	(1.4)
275	Newport News, VA	(6.4)
28	Newton, MA	22.0
195	Norfolk, VA	(0.4)
355	Norman, OK	(16.9)
153	North Charleston, SC	4.3
156	Norwalk, CA	4.0
304	Norwalk, CT	(8.9)
107	Oakland, CA	8.0
127	Oceanside, CA	6.5
391	Odessa, TX	(25.5)
166	O'Fallon, MO	2.9
252	Ogden, UT	(4.5)
233	Oklahoma City, OK	(2.9)
130	Olathe, KS	6.1
27	Omaha, NE	22.8
58	Ontario, CA	15.1
86	Orange, CA	9.8
400	Orem, UT	(28.1)
163	Orlando, FL	3.2

RANK	CITY	% CHANGE
226	Overland Park, KS	(2.4)
409	Oxnard, CA	(30.6)
111	Palm Bay, FL	7.9
256	Palmdale, CA	(5.0)
17	Pasadena, CA	26.6
241	Pasadena, TX	(3.3)
37	Paterson, NJ	19.8
195	Pearland, TX	(0.4)
314	Pembroke Pines, FL	(9.7)
14	Peoria, AZ	27.0
45	Peoria, IL	17.1
70	Philadelphia, PA	13.7
20	Phoenix, AZ	25.8
289	Pittsburgh, PA	(7.7)
186	Plano, TX	1.1
259	Plantation, FL	(5.2)
158	Pomona, CA	3.9
24	Pompano Beach, FL	23.8
31	Port St. Lucie, FL	21.3
193	Portland, OR	(0.1)
143	Portsmouth, VA	5.3
119	Provo, UT	7.1
NA	Pueblo, CO**	NA
130	Quincy, MA	6.1
9	Racine, WI	32.2
184	Raleigh, NC	1.4
49	Ramapo, NY	16.2
3	Rancho Cucamon., CA	41.0
323	Reading, PA	(10.8)
228	Redding, CA	(2.5)
309	Redwood City, CA	(9.5)
241	Reno, NV	(3.3)
394	Renton, WA	(26.2)
13	Rialto, CA	28.1
62	Richardson, TX	14.9
122	Richmond, CA	7.0
141	Richmond, VA	5.4
338	Rio Rancho, NM	(12.5)
208	Riverside, CA	(1.3)
182	Roanoke, VA	1.5
156	Rochester, MN	4.0
264	Rochester, NY	(5.4)
367	Rockford, IL	(18.9)
214	Roseville, CA	(1.8)
318	Roswell, GA	(10.1)
285	Round Rock, TX	(7.5)
357	Sacramento, CA	(17.5)
176	Salem, OR	2.3
377	Salinas, CA	(20.4)
404	Salt Lake City, UT	(28.7)
390	San Angelo, TX	(25.0)
306	San Antonio, TX	(9.0)
252	San Bernardino, CA	(4.5)
301	San Diego, CA	(8.8)
230	San Francisco, CA	(2.8)
98	San Jose, CA	8.6
243	San Leandro, CA	(3.4)
187	San Marcos, CA	1.0
38	San Mateo, CA	19.2
203	Santa Ana, CA	(0.9)
124	Santa Barbara, CA	6.8
364	Santa Clara, CA	(18.5)
266	Santa Clarita, CA	(5.6)
75	Santa Maria, CA	12.8
74	Santa Monica, CA	13.1
381	Santa Rosa, CA	(21.6)
360	Savannah, GA	(18.3)
49	Scottsdale, AZ	16.2
342	Scranton, PA	(13.5)
134	Seattle, WA	5.9
141	Shreveport, LA	5.4
381	Simi Valley, CA	(21.6)

RANK	CITY	% CHANGE
56	Sioux City, IA	15.2
293	Sioux Falls, SD	(8.2)
351	Somerville, MA	(15.3)
107	South Bend, IN	8.0
341	South Gate, CA	(13.0)
267	Sparks, NV	(5.7)
140	Spokane Valley, WA	5.5
182	Spokane, WA	1.5
338	Springfield, IL	(12.5)
269	Springfield, MA	(5.9)
291	Springfield, MO	(7.9)
367	Stamford, CT	(18.9)
NA	Sterling Heights, MI**	NA
301	Stockton, CA	(8.8)
171	St. Joseph, MO	2.7
53	St. Louis, MO	16.0
103	St. Paul, MN	8.4
273	St. Petersburg, FL	(6.0)
7	Suffolk, VA	34.2
235	Sugar Land, TX	(3.0)
300	Sunnyvale, CA	(8.7)
49	Sunrise, FL	16.2
98	Surprise, AZ	8.6
397	Syracuse, NY	(26.7)
282	Tacoma, WA	(7.2)
136	Tallahassee, FL	5.7
331	Tampa, FL	(11.3)
162	Temecula, CA	3.4
44	Tempe, AZ	17.6
NA	Thornton, CO**	NA
344	Thousand Oaks, CA	(13.8)
19	Toledo, OH	26.1
54	Toms River Twnshp, NJ	15.6
138	Topeka, KS	5.6
269	Torrance, CA	(5.9)
70	Tracy, CA	13.7
12	Trenton, NJ	29.0
375	Troy, MI	(20.3)
199	Tucson, AZ	(0.5)
177	Tulsa, OK	2.2
NA	Tuscaloosa, AL**	NA
220	Tustin, CA	(2.1)
367	Tyler, TX	(18.9)
154	Upper Darby Twnshp, PA	4.2
374	Vacaville, CA	(20.1)
123	Vallejo, CA	6.9
165	Vancouver, WA	3.0
220	Ventura, CA	(2.1)
127	Victorville, CA	6.5
279	Virginia Beach, VA	(6.8)
325	Visalia, CA	(10.9)
204	Vista, CA	(1.0)
319	Waco, TX	(10.3)
80	Warren, MI	10.9
212	Warwick, RI	(1.6)
331	Washington, DC	(11.3)
168	Waterbury, CT	2.8
229	West Covina, CA	(2.7)
346	West Jordan, UT	(14.4)
97	West Palm Beach, FL	8.7
354	West Valley, UT	(15.8)
308	Westland, MI	(9.4)
246	Westminster, CA	(3.6)
389	Westminster, CO	(24.7)
195	Whittier, CA	(0.4)
328	Wichita Falls, TX	(11.1)
285	Wichita, KS	(7.5)
251	Wilmington, NC	(4.3)
149	Winston-Salem, NC	4.6
5	Woodbridge Twnshp, NJ	37.1
107	Worcester, MA	8.0
172	Yakima, WA	2.6
1	Yonkers, NY	46.3
267	Yuma, AZ	(5.7)

Source: CQ Press using reported data from the F.B.I. "Crime in the United States 2011"
*Burglary is the unlawful entry of a structure to commit a felony or theft. Attempts are included.
**Not available.

71. Percent Change in Burglary Rate: 2010 to 2011 (continued)
National Percent Change = 0.2% Increase*

Rank Order - City

RANK	CITY	% CHANGE	RANK	CITY	% CHANGE	RANK	CITY	% CHANGE
1	Yonkers, NY	46.3	73	Costa Mesa, CA	13.5	144	Fresno, CA	5.2
2	Camden, NJ	44.2	74	Santa Monica, CA	13.1	146	Murfreesboro, TN	5.1
3	Rancho Cucamon., CA	41.0	75	New Rochelle, NY	12.8	147	Brick Twnshp, NJ	5.0
4	Columbia, MO	37.3	75	Santa Maria, CA	12.8	148	Lawton, OK	4.9
5	Woodbridge Twnshp, NJ	37.1	77	Hampton, VA	12.3	149	Houston, TX	4.6
6	Brockton, MA	35.3	78	Hollywood, FL	12.1	149	Indio, CA	4.6
7	Suffolk, VA	34.2	79	Everett, WA	11.1	149	Winston-Salem, NC	4.6
8	Danbury, CT	33.2	80	Downey, CA	10.9	152	Memphis, TN	4.5
9	Racine, WI	32.2	80	Warren, MI	10.9	153	North Charleston, SC	4.3
10	Elgin, IL	29.7	82	Carlsbad, CA	10.6	154	Upper Darby Twnshp, PA	4.2
11	Carson, CA	29.4	83	Long Beach, CA	10.5	155	Baldwin Park, CA	4.1
12	Trenton, NJ	29.0	84	Denton, TX	10.1	156	Norwalk, CA	4.0
13	Rialto, CA	28.1	85	Bloomington, MN	10.0	156	Rochester, MN	4.0
14	Peoria, AZ	27.0	86	Des Moines, IA	9.8	158	Hesperia, CA	3.9
15	Elizabeth, NJ	26.9	86	Kent, WA	9.8	158	Mesa, AZ	3.9
16	Coral Springs, FL	26.8	86	Orange, CA	9.8	158	Pomona, CA	3.9
17	Pasadena, CA	26.6	89	Fayetteville, NC	9.7	161	Akron, OH	3.8
18	College Station, TX	26.5	89	Mesquite, TX	9.7	162	Temecula, CA	3.4
19	Toledo, OH	26.1	91	Bellflower, CA	9.4	163	Orlando, FL	3.2
20	Phoenix, AZ	25.8	91	Milwaukee, WI	9.4	164	Alexandria, VA	3.1
21	Fontana, CA	25.7	93	Boca Raton, FL	9.3	165	Vancouver, WA	3.0
22	Hartford, CT	25.4	93	Cedar Rapids, IA	9.3	166	Louisville, KY	2.9
23	Newark, NJ	25.3	95	Concord, NC	9.2	166	O'Fallon, MO	2.9
24	Pompano Beach, FL	23.8	96	Chino Hills, CA	8.8	168	Edison Twnshp, NJ	2.8
25	Hemet, CA	23.2	97	West Palm Beach, FL	8.7	168	New York, NY	2.8
26	Merced, CA	22.9	98	Largo, FL	8.6	168	Waterbury, CT	2.8
27	Omaha, NE	22.8	98	Little Rock, AR	8.6	171	St. Joseph, MO	2.7
28	Newton, MA	22.0	98	San Jose, CA	8.6	172	Yakima, WA	2.6
29	Hamilton Twnshp, NJ	21.8	98	Surprise, AZ	8.6	173	Fort Smith, AR	2.5
30	Miami, FL	21.5	102	Greeley, CO	8.5	174	El Cajon, CA	2.4
31	Port St. Lucie, FL	21.3	103	St. Paul, MN	8.4	174	Lawrence, KS	2.4
32	Fort Lauderdale, FL	21.2	104	Bellingham, WA	8.3	176	Salem, OR	2.3
33	Antioch, CA	21.1	105	Albuquerque, NM	8.2	177	Bridgeport, CT	2.2
33	Duluth, MN	21.1	106	Eugene, OR	8.1	177	Tulsa, OK	2.2
35	Cranston, RI	20.4	107	Irvine, CA	8.0	179	Dallas, TX	2.1
36	Clovis, CA	20.0	107	Oakland, CA	8.0	180	Henderson, NV	1.7
37	Paterson, NJ	19.8	107	South Bend, IN	8.0	180	Napa, CA	1.7
38	San Mateo, CA	19.2	107	Worcester, MA	8.0	182	Roanoke, VA	1.5
39	Beaverton, OR	18.7	111	Corona, CA	7.9	182	Spokane, WA	1.5
40	Chino, CA	18.0	111	Palm Bay, FL	7.9	184	Aurora, IL	1.4
40	Detroit, MI	18.0	113	Lee's Summit, MO	7.6	184	Raleigh, NC	1.4
42	Atlanta, GA	17.9	114	Carrollton, TX	7.5	186	Plano, TX	1.1
42	Broken Arrow, OK	17.9	114	Denver, CO	7.5	187	San Marcos, CA	1.0
44	Tempe, AZ	17.6	114	Lubbock, TX	7.5	188	Boston, MA	0.6
45	Peoria, IL	17.1	117	Durham, NC	7.3	188	McKinney, TX	0.6
46	Lynchburg, VA	16.9	118	New Orleans, LA	7.2	190	Fargo, ND	0.2
47	Cleveland, OH	16.6	119	Frisco, TX	7.1	191	Ann Arbor, MI	0.0
47	Nampa, ID	16.6	119	Gresham, OR	7.1	191	Joliet, IL	0.0
49	Ramapo, NY	16.2	119	Provo, UT	7.1	193	Portland, OR	(0.1)
49	Scottsdale, AZ	16.2	122	Richmond, CA	7.0	194	Clinton Twnshp, MI	(0.3)
49	Sunrise, FL	16.2	123	Vallejo, CA	6.9	195	Garland, TX	(0.4)
52	Baltimore, MD	16.1	124	Lakewood, CA	6.8	195	Norfolk, VA	(0.4)
53	St. Louis, MO	16.0	124	Santa Barbara, CA	6.8	195	Pearland, TX	(0.4)
54	Lakeland, FL	15.6	126	Minneapolis, MN	6.7	195	Whittier, CA	(0.4)
54	Toms River Twnshp, NJ	15.6	127	Oceanside, CA	6.5	199	Tucson, AZ	(0.5)
56	Mission Viejo, CA	15.2	127	Victorville, CA	6.5	200	Dayton, OH	(0.7)
56	Sioux City, IA	15.2	129	Arlington Heights, IL	6.3	200	Los Angeles, CA	(0.7)
58	Glendale, AZ	15.1	130	Flint, MI	6.1	202	Las Cruces, NM	(0.8)
58	Ontario, CA	15.1	130	Fort Worth, TX	6.1	203	Santa Ana, CA	(0.9)
60	Cincinnati, OH	15.0	130	Olathe, KS	6.1	204	Livermore, CA	(1.0)
60	Lansing, MI	15.0	130	Quincy, MA	6.1	204	Vista, CA	(1.0)
62	Centennial, CO	14.9	134	Gilbert, AZ	5.9	206	Chandler, AZ	(1.2)
62	Richardson, TX	14.9	134	Seattle, WA	5.9	206	Huntington Beach, CA	(1.2)
64	Lynn, MA	14.7	136	Chicago, IL	5.7	208	Riverside, CA	(1.3)
65	Moreno Valley, CA	14.6	136	Tallahassee, FL	5.7	209	Chula Vista, CA	(1.4)
66	Beaumont, TX	14.4	138	Dearborn, MI	5.6	209	Newport Beach, CA	(1.4)
67	Cambridge, MA	14.3	138	Topeka, KS	5.6	211	Glendale, CA	(1.5)
67	Melbourne, FL	14.3	140	Spokane Valley, WA	5.5	212	Lowell, MA	(1.6)
69	Miami Gardens, FL	14.0	141	Richmond, VA	5.4	212	Warwick, RI	(1.6)
70	Philadelphia, PA	13.7	141	Shreveport, LA	5.4	214	Athens-Clarke, GA	(1.8)
70	Tracy, CA	13.7	143	Portsmouth, VA	5.3	214	Roseville, CA	(1.8)
72	Erie, PA	13.6	144	Chesapeake, VA	5.2	216	Nashville, TN	(1.9)

Rank Order - City (continued)

RANK	CITY	% CHANGE	RANK	CITY	% CHANGE	RANK	CITY	% CHANGE
217	Fremont, CA	(2.0)	290	Fall River, MA	(7.8)	364	Santa Clara, CA	(18.5)
217	Jackson, MS	(2.0)	291	Fullerton, CA	(7.9)	365	Cheektowaga, NY	(18.7)
217	Manchester, NH	(2.0)	291	Springfield, MO	(7.9)	365	Gainesville, FL	(18.7)
220	Boulder, CO	(2.1)	293	Irving, TX	(8.2)	367	Rockford, IL	(18.9)
220	Modesto, CA	(2.1)	293	Longmont, CO	(8.2)	367	Stamford, CT	(18.9)
220	Tustin, CA	(2.1)	293	Sioux Falls, SD	(8.2)	367	Tyler, TX	(18.9)
220	Ventura, CA	(2.1)	296	Aurora, CO	(8.4)	370	Berkeley, CA	(19.1)
224	Columbus, OH	(2.3)	296	Clarksville, TN	(8.4)	370	Murrieta, CA	(19.1)
224	Independence, MO	(2.3)	298	Inglewood, CA	(8.5)	372	Allen, TX	(19.2)
226	Evansville, IN	(2.4)	299	Alhambra, CA	(8.6)	373	Citrus Heights, CA	(19.5)
226	Overland Park, KS	(2.4)	300	Sunnyvale, CA	(8.7)	374	Vacaville, CA	(20.1)
228	Redding, CA	(2.5)	301	Albany, NY	(8.8)	375	Green Bay, WI	(20.3)
229	West Covina, CA	(2.7)	301	San Diego, CA	(8.8)	375	Troy, MI	(20.3)
230	Colonie, NY	(2.8)	301	Stockton, CA	(8.8)	377	Salinas, CA	(20.4)
230	Miami Beach, FL	(2.8)	304	Longview, TX	(8.9)	378	Austin, TX	(20.6)
230	San Francisco, CA	(2.8)	304	Norwalk, CT	(8.9)	379	Brownsville, TX	(21.0)
233	Macon, GA	(2.9)	306	San Antonio, TX	(9.0)	379	Lafayette, LA	(21.0)
233	Oklahoma City, OK	(2.9)	307	Compton, CA	(9.1)	381	Santa Rosa, CA	(21.6)
235	New Haven, CT	(3.0)	308	Westland, MI	(9.4)	381	Simi Valley, CA	(21.6)
235	Sugar Land, TX	(3.0)	309	Hammond, IN	(9.5)	383	Arvada, CO	(22.0)
237	Bend, OR	(3.1)	309	Jersey City, NJ	(9.5)	384	Midland, TX	(22.5)
237	Cape Coral, FL	(3.1)	309	Redwood City, CA	(9.5)	385	Albany, GA	(23.9)
239	Bakersfield, CA	(3.2)	312	Colorado Springs, CO	(9.6)	385	Amarillo, TX	(23.9)
239	Deerfield Beach, FL	(3.2)	312	Nashua, NH	(9.6)	387	Allentown, PA	(24.0)
241	Pasadena, TX	(3.3)	314	Pembroke Pines, FL	(9.7)	388	Meridian, ID	(24.2)
241	Reno, NV	(3.3)	315	Bloomington, IL	(9.8)	389	Westminster, CO	(24.7)
243	Daly City, CA	(3.4)	315	Boise, ID	(9.8)	390	San Angelo, TX	(25.0)
243	San Leandro, CA	(3.4)	317	Hawthorne, CA	(10.0)	391	Odessa, TX	(25.5)
245	Lewisville, TX	(3.5)	318	Roswell, GA	(10.1)	392	Bryan, TX	(25.9)
246	League City, TX	(3.6)	319	El Paso, TX	(10.3)	393	Fairfield, CA	(26.1)
246	Westminster, CA	(3.6)	319	Waco, TX	(10.3)	394	Decatur, IL	(26.2)
248	Concord, CA	(3.7)	321	Clearwater, FL	(10.4)	394	Renton, WA	(26.2)
249	High Point, NC	(4.0)	322	Lancaster, CA	(10.5)	396	New Bedford, MA	(26.6)
249	Knoxville, TN	(4.0)	323	Hayward, CA	(10.8)	397	Syracuse, NY	(26.7)
251	Wilmington, NC	(4.3)	323	Reading, PA	(10.8)	398	McAllen, TX	(27.0)
252	Ogden, UT	(4.5)	325	Farmington Hills, MI	(10.9)	399	Escondido, CA	(27.6)
252	San Bernardino, CA	(4.5)	325	Visalia, CA	(10.9)	400	Orem, UT	(28.1)
254	Lincoln, NE	(4.7)	327	Las Vegas, NV	(11.0)	401	Grand Rapids, MI	(28.2)
255	El Monte, CA	(4.9)	328	Fort Wayne, IN	(11.1)	402	Edinburg, TX	(28.5)
256	Bellevue, WA	(5.0)	328	Madison, WI	(11.1)	403	Cary, NC	(28.6)
256	Kennewick, WA	(5.0)	328	Wichita Falls, TX	(11.1)	404	Salt Lake City, UT	(28.7)
256	Palmdale, CA	(5.0)	331	Tampa, FL	(11.3)	404	Sandy Springs, GA	(28.7)
259	Avondale, AZ	(5.2)	331	Washington, DC	(11.3)	406	Miramar, FL	(28.8)
259	Chattanooga, TN	(5.2)	333	Greece, NY	(11.6)	407	Clarkstown, NY	(29.6)
259	Medford, OR	(5.2)	334	Livonia, MI	(11.7)	408	Menifee, CA	(30.3)
259	Plantation, FL	(5.2)	335	Davie, FL	(11.8)	409	Oxnard, CA	(30.6)
263	Arlington, TX	(5.3)	336	Anaheim, CA	(12.0)	410	Fishers, IN	(31.9)
264	Lakewood, CO	(5.4)	337	Jacksonville, FL	(12.4)	411	Chico, CA	(32.6)
264	Rochester, NY	(5.4)	338	Mission, TX	(12.5)	412	Bloomington, IN	(34.0)
266	Santa Clarita, CA	(5.6)	338	Rio Rancho, NM	(12.5)	413	Johns Creek, GA	(36.5)
267	Sparks, NV	(5.7)	338	Springfield, IL	(12.5)	414	Carmel, IN	(45.5)
267	Yuma, AZ	(5.7)	341	South Gate, CA	(13.0)	NA	Baton Rouge, LA**	NA
269	Amherst, NY	(5.9)	342	Scranton, PA	(13.5)	NA	Billings, MT**	NA
269	Laredo, TX	(5.9)	343	Anchorage, AK	(13.7)	NA	Birmingham, AL**	NA
269	Springfield, MA	(5.9)	344	Thousand Oaks, CA	(13.8)	NA	Brooklyn Park, MN**	NA
269	Torrance, CA	(5.9)	345	Buena Park, CA	(14.3)	NA	Buffalo, NY**	NA
273	St. Petersburg, FL	(6.0)	346	Grand Prairie, TX	(14.4)	NA	Champaign, IL**	NA
274	Corpus Christi, TX	(6.3)	346	West Jordan, UT	(14.4)	NA	Cicero, IL**	NA
275	Newport News, VA	(6.4)	348	Garden Grove, CA	(14.9)	NA	Clifton, NJ**	NA
276	Elk Grove, CA	(6.5)	349	Sandy, UT	(15.1)	NA	Davenport, IA**	NA
277	Kenosha, WI	(6.6)	350	Charleston, SC	(15.2)	NA	Gary, IN**	NA
277	Lawrence, MA	(6.6)	351	Edmond, OK	(15.3)	NA	Hillsboro, OR**	NA
279	Hialeah, FL	(6.8)	351	Somerville, MA	(15.3)	NA	Hoover, AL**	NA
279	Kansas City, KS	(6.8)	353	Lake Forest, CA	(15.7)	NA	Huntsville, AL**	NA
279	Virginia Beach, VA	(6.8)	354	West Valley, UT	(15.8)	NA	Indianapolis, IN**	NA
282	Columbus, GA	(7.2)	355	Norman, OK	(16.9)	NA	Kansas City, MO**	NA
282	Tacoma, WA	(7.2)	356	Lakewood Twnshp, NJ	(17.2)	NA	Lexington, KY**	NA
284	Killeen, TX	(7.4)	357	Canton Twnshp, MI	(17.5)	NA	Mobile, AL**	NA
285	Asheville, NC	(7.5)	357	Fort Collins, CO	(17.5)	NA	Montgomery, AL**	NA
285	Charlotte, NC	(7.5)	357	Sacramento, CA	(17.5)	NA	Naperville, IL**	NA
285	Round Rock, TX	(7.5)	360	Abilene, TX	(18.3)	NA	Pueblo, CO**	NA
285	Wichita, KS	(7.5)	360	Burbank, CA	(18.3)	NA	Sterling Heights, MI**	NA
289	Pittsburgh, PA	(7.7)	360	Savannah, GA	(18.3)	NA	Thornton, CO**	NA
			363	Bethlehem, PA	(18.4)	NA	Tuscaloosa, AL**	NA

Source: CQ Press using reported data from the F.B.I. "Crime in the United States 2011"
*Burglary is the unlawful entry of a structure to commit a felony or theft. Attempts are included.
**Not available.

Alpha Order - City

72. Percent Change in Burglary Rate: 2007 to 2011
National Percent Change = 3.3% Decrease*

RANK	CITY	% CHANGE	RANK	CITY	% CHANGE	RANK	CITY	% CHANGE
277	Abilene, TX	(18.9)	63	Cheektowaga, NY	20.2	242	Fort Wayne, IN	(13.6)
24	Akron, OH	34.7	169	Chesapeake, VA	(1.9)	159	Fort Worth, TX	(1.0)
259	Albany, GA	(16.0)	84	Chicago, IL	11.5	241	Fremont, CA	(13.2)
229	Albany, NY	(11.4)	398	Chico, CA	(43.1)	19	Fresno, CA	38.3
159	Albuquerque, NM	(1.0)	183	Chino Hills, CA	(4.4)	355	Frisco, TX	(30.0)
279	Alexandria, VA	(19.0)	214	Chino, CA	(8.7)	350	Fullerton, CA	(28.7)
314	Alhambra, CA	(23.6)	380	Chula Vista, CA	(34.6)	395	Gainesville, FL	(40.0)
333	Allentown, PA	(25.2)	NA	Cicero, IL**	NA	289	Garden Grove, CA	(20.3)
390	Allen, TX	(37.9)	62	Cincinnati, OH	20.4	121	Garland, TX	4.3
330	Amarillo, TX	(25.0)	NA	Citrus Heights, CA**	NA	3	Gary, IN	80.3
115	Amherst, NY	4.9	297	Clarkstown, NY	(21.0)	282	Gilbert, AZ	(19.2)
320	Anaheim, CA	(24.0)	332	Clarksville, TN	(25.1)	177	Glendale, AZ	(3.8)
351	Anchorage, AK	(28.9)	269	Clearwater, FL	(17.9)	114	Glendale, CA	5.2
204	Ann Arbor, MI	(7.3)	29	Cleveland, OH	31.0	146	Grand Prairie, TX	1.1
42	Antioch, CA	28.0	329	Clifton, NJ	(24.9)	320	Grand Rapids, MI	(24.0)
NA	Arlington Heights, IL**	NA	139	Clinton Twnshp, MI	2.3	54	Greece, NY	22.8
166	Arlington, TX	(1.6)	10	Clovis, CA	51.3	279	Greeley, CO	(19.0)
358	Arvada, CO	(30.2)	112	College Station, TX	5.9	295	Green Bay, WI	(20.9)
382	Asheville, NC	(35.9)	266	Colonie, NY	(17.5)	92	Gresham, OR	10.1
147	Athens-Clarke, GA	0.7	208	Colorado Springs, CO	(7.7)	11	Hamilton Twnshp, NJ	50.6
162	Atlanta, GA	(1.1)	68	Columbia, MO	17.9	158	Hammond, IN	(0.8)
246	Aurora, CO	(14.1)	47	Columbus, GA	23.8	84	Hampton, VA	11.5
218	Aurora, IL	(9.5)	164	Columbus, OH	(1.4)	102	Hartford, CT	8.4
303	Austin, TX	(22.1)	48	Compton, CA	23.7	26	Hawthorne, CA	33.1
NA	Avondale, AZ**	NA	98	Concord, CA	8.9	163	Hayward, CA	(1.3)
89	Bakersfield, CA	10.8	327	Concord, NC	(24.5)	35	Hemet, CA	29.9
263	Baldwin Park, CA	(16.8)	17	Coral Springs, FL	41.7	361	Henderson, NV	(30.8)
70	Baltimore, MD	16.2	116	Corona, CA	4.8	53	Hesperia, CA	22.9
103	Baton Rouge, LA	8.2	345	Corpus Christi, TX	(28.0)	399	Hialeah, FL	(44.0)
105	Beaumont, TX	7.9	145	Costa Mesa, CA	1.6	385	High Point, NC	(36.4)
368	Beaverton, OR	(32.3)	21	Cranston, RI	35.9	402	Hillsboro, OR	(46.0)
154	Bellevue, WA	(0.3)	255	Dallas, TX	(15.6)	15	Hollywood, FL	47.7
247	Bellflower, CA	(14.2)	99	Daly City, CA	8.8	NA	Hoover, AL**	NA
243	Bellingham, WA	(13.8)	52	Danbury, CT	23.0	181	Houston, TX	(4.3)
396	Bend, OR	(40.4)	NA	Davenport, IA**	NA	179	Huntington Beach, CA	(3.9)
339	Berkeley, CA	(25.9)	73	Davie, FL	14.5	NA	Huntsville, AL**	NA
271	Bethlehem, PA	(18.1)	119	Dayton, OH	4.7	260	Independence, MO	(16.1)
NA	Billings, MT**	NA	165	Dearborn, MI	(1.5)	104	Indianapolis, IN	8.1
NA	Birmingham, AL**	NA	NA	Decatur, IL**	NA	181	Indio, CA	(4.3)
NA	Bloomington, IL**	NA	150	Deerfield Beach, FL	0.2	359	Inglewood, CA	(30.7)
312	Bloomington, IN	(23.0)	308	Denton, TX	(22.6)	326	Irvine, CA	(24.3)
368	Bloomington, MN	(32.3)	286	Denver, CO	(19.7)	266	Irving, TX	(17.5)
336	Boca Raton, FL	(25.5)	80	Des Moines, IA	12.3	341	Jacksonville, FL	(26.8)
317	Boise, ID	(23.9)	100	Detroit, MI	8.7	60	Jackson, MS	22.1
237	Boston, MA	(12.9)	86	Downey, CA	11.4	219	Jersey City, NJ	(9.7)
111	Boulder, CO	6.2	131	Duluth, MN	3.3	NA	Johns Creek, GA**	NA
20	Brick Twnshp, NJ	37.4	NA	Durham, NC**	NA	110	Joliet, IL	6.5
59	Bridgeport, CT	22.2	168	Edinburg, TX	(1.7)	299	Kansas City, KS	(21.3)
12	Brockton, MA	48.9	307	Edison Twnshp, NJ	(22.4)	NA	Kansas City, MO**	NA
223	Broken Arrow, OK	(10.5)	317	Edmond, OK	(23.9)	156	Kennewick, WA	(0.4)
314	Brooklyn Park, MN	(23.6)	195	El Cajon, CA	(6.3)	348	Kenosha, WI	(28.4)
359	Brownsville, TX	(30.7)	192	El Monte, CA	(5.9)	144	Kent, WA	1.7
397	Bryan, TX	(40.9)	284	El Paso, TX	(19.6)	355	Killeen, TX	(30.0)
344	Buena Park, CA	(27.5)	128	Elgin, IL	3.7	133	Knoxville, TN	3.1
NA	Buffalo, NY**	NA	13	Elizabeth, NJ	48.1	293	Lafayette, LA	(20.5)
276	Burbank, CA	(18.6)	389	Elk Grove, CA	(37.7)	380	Lake Forest, CA	(34.6)
305	Cambridge, MA	(22.2)	14	Erie, PA	47.9	78	Lakeland, FL	12.4
37	Camden, NJ	29.5	387	Escondido, CA	(36.8)	405	Lakewood Twnshp, NJ	(58.0)
300	Canton Twnshp, MI	(21.6)	270	Eugene, OR	(18.0)	268	Lakewood, CA	(17.7)
354	Cape Coral, FL	(29.5)	189	Evansville, IN	(5.6)	193	Lakewood, CO	(6.1)
295	Carlsbad, CA	(20.9)	301	Everett, WA	(21.8)	401	Lancaster, CA	(44.3)
404	Carmel, IN	(56.3)	272	Fairfield, CA	(18.2)	28	Lansing, MI	31.1
142	Carrollton, TX	1.8	NA	Fall River, MA**	NA	232	Laredo, TX	(12.5)
22	Carson, CA	35.8	374	Fargo, ND	(33.1)	141	Largo, FL	2.0
364	Cary, NC	(31.1)	378	Farmington Hills, MI	(33.9)	71	Las Cruces, NM	16.0
154	Cedar Rapids, IA	(0.3)	173	Fayetteville, NC	(3.1)	317	Las Vegas, NV	(23.9)
234	Centennial, CO	(12.6)	375	Fishers, IN	(33.2)	197	Lawrence, KS	(6.8)
NA	Champaign, IL**	NA	44	Flint, MI	26.9	18	Lawrence, MA	38.7
74	Chandler, AZ	14.4	159	Fontana, CA	(1.0)	83	Lawton, OK	11.8
385	Charleston, SC	(36.4)	345	Fort Collins, CO	(28.0)	261	League City, TX	(16.3)
393	Charlotte, NC	(38.8)	8	Fort Lauderdale, FL	53.4	323	Lee's Summit, MO	(24.1)
177	Chattanooga, TN	(3.8)	135	Fort Smith, AR	2.9	129	Lewisville, TX	3.5

Alpha Order - City (continued)

RANK	CITY	% CHANGE
NA	Lexington, KY**	NA
366	Lincoln, NE	(31.3)
81	Little Rock, AR	12.1
198	Livermore, CA	(6.9)
343	Livonia, MI	(27.3)
75	Long Beach, CA	14.2
NA	Longmont, CO**	NA
365	Longview, TX	(31.2)
228	Los Angeles, CA	(11.3)
149	Louisville, KY	0.5
209	Lowell, MA	(7.9)
157	Lubbock, TX	(0.7)
166	Lynchburg, VA	(1.6)
388	Lynn, MA	(37.2)
94	Macon, GA	9.6
372	Madison, WI	(32.7)
NA	Manchester, NH**	NA
394	McAllen, TX	(39.5)
122	McKinney, TX	4.0
250	Medford, OR	(14.6)
185	Melbourne, FL	(5.0)
199	Memphis, TN	(7.0)
NA	Menifee, CA**	NA
193	Merced, CA	(6.1)
357	Meridian, ID	(30.1)
174	Mesa, AZ	(3.3)
7	Mesquite, TX	67.4
258	Miami Beach, FL	(15.7)
281	Miami Gardens, FL	(19.1)
105	Miami, FL	7.9
305	Midland, TX	(22.2)
133	Milwaukee, WI	3.1
289	Minneapolis, MN	(20.3)
237	Miramar, FL	(12.9)
187	Mission Viejo, CA	(5.2)
113	Mission, TX	5.5
NA	Mobile, AL**	NA
171	Modesto, CA	(2.2)
NA	Montgomery, AL**	NA
116	Moreno Valley, CA	4.8
31	Murfreesboro, TN	30.6
370	Murrieta, CA	(32.5)
273	Nampa, ID	(18.3)
347	Napa, CA	(28.1)
57	Naperville, IL	22.3
NA	Nashua, NH**	NA
76	Nashville, TN	13.6
122	New Bedford, MA	4.0
NA	New Haven, CT**	NA
403	New Orleans, LA	(51.3)
371	New Rochelle, NY	(32.6)
240	New York, NY	(13.1)
45	Newark, NJ	26.1
383	Newport Beach, CA	(36.2)
373	Newport News, VA	(32.9)
87	Newton, MA	11.3
50	Norfolk, VA	23.5
298	Norman, OK	(21.2)
330	North Charleston, SC	(25.0)
211	Norwalk, CA	(8.1)
135	Norwalk, CT	2.9
95	Oakland, CA	9.4
200	Oceanside, CA	(7.1)
376	Odessa, TX	(33.4)
273	O'Fallon, MO	(18.3)
245	Ogden, UT	(13.9)
78	Oklahoma City, OK	12.4
NA	Olathe, KS**	NA
124	Omaha, NE	3.9
138	Ontario, CA	2.5
183	Orange, CA	(4.4)
362	Orem, UT	(30.9)
200	Orlando, FL	(7.1)

RANK	CITY	% CHANGE
252	Overland Park, KS	(14.7)
391	Oxnard, CA	(38.0)
231	Palm Bay, FL	(11.7)
335	Palmdale, CA	(25.4)
38	Pasadena, CA	28.6
126	Pasadena, TX	3.8
48	Paterson, NJ	23.7
392	Pearland, TX	(38.1)
46	Pembroke Pines, FL	23.9
311	Peoria, AZ	(22.9)
23	Peoria, IL	35.2
169	Philadelphia, PA	(1.9)
140	Phoenix, AZ	2.2
293	Pittsburgh, PA	(20.5)
255	Plano, TX	(15.6)
151	Plantation, FL	0.0
190	Pomona, CA	(5.8)
57	Pompano Beach, FL	22.3
126	Port St. Lucie, FL	3.8
277	Portland, OR	(18.9)
40	Portsmouth, VA	28.3
289	Provo, UT	(20.3)
NA	Pueblo, CO**	NA
209	Quincy, MA	(7.9)
27	Racine, WI	31.2
216	Raleigh, NC	(9.1)
93	Ramapo, NY	9.8
5	Rancho Cucamon., CA	69.8
109	Reading, PA	7.1
31	Redding, CA	30.6
1	Redwood City, CA	109.1
263	Reno, NV	(16.8)
232	Renton, WA	(12.5)
38	Rialto, CA	28.6
250	Richardson, TX	(14.6)
43	Richmond, CA	27.5
190	Richmond, VA	(5.8)
399	Rio Rancho, NM	(44.0)
216	Riverside, CA	(9.1)
254	Roanoke, VA	(15.4)
255	Rochester, MN	(15.6)
41	Rochester, NY	28.1
348	Rockford, IL	(28.4)
314	Roseville, CA	(23.6)
284	Roswell, GA	(19.6)
77	Round Rock, TX	13.4
336	Sacramento, CA	(25.5)
176	Salem, OR	(3.7)
219	Salinas, CA	(9.7)
320	Salt Lake City, UT	(24.0)
289	San Angelo, TX	(20.3)
226	San Antonio, TX	(11.0)
116	San Bernardino, CA	4.8
342	San Diego, CA	(27.2)
301	San Francisco, CA	(21.8)
204	San Jose, CA	(7.3)
313	San Leandro, CA	(23.2)
273	San Marcos, CA	(18.3)
66	San Mateo, CA	18.0
379	Sandy Springs, GA	(34.0)
234	Sandy, UT	(12.6)
97	Santa Ana, CA	9.2
225	Santa Barbara, CA	(10.6)
366	Santa Clara, CA	(31.3)
352	Santa Clarita, CA	(29.1)
100	Santa Maria, CA	8.7
362	Santa Monica, CA	(30.9)
287	Santa Rosa, CA	(19.9)
226	Savannah, GA	(11.0)
153	Scottsdale, AZ	(0.2)
68	Scranton, PA	17.9
107	Seattle, WA	7.6
175	Shreveport, LA	(3.6)
352	Simi Valley, CA	(29.1)

RANK	CITY	% CHANGE
56	Sioux City, IA	22.4
36	Sioux Falls, SD	29.8
207	Somerville, MA	(7.4)
51	South Bend, IN	23.3
188	South Gate, CA	(5.3)
328	Sparks, NV	(24.7)
4	Spokane Valley, WA	75.5
33	Spokane, WA	30.2
55	Springfield, IL	22.6
61	Springfield, MA	21.0
221	Springfield, MO	(9.8)
265	Stamford, CT	(17.4)
NA	Sterling Heights, MI**	NA
137	Stockton, CA	2.7
91	St. Joseph, MO	10.7
120	St. Louis, MO	4.6
82	St. Paul, MN	12.0
212	St. Petersburg, FL	(8.2)
89	Suffolk, VA	10.8
108	Sugar Land, TX	7.3
172	Sunnyvale, CA	(2.8)
25	Sunrise, FL	34.0
180	Surprise, AZ	(4.1)
213	Syracuse, NY	(8.4)
147	Tacoma, WA	0.7
96	Tallahassee, FL	9.3
383	Tampa, FL	(36.2)
324	Temecula, CA	(24.2)
230	Tempe, AZ	(11.6)
NA	Thornton, CO**	NA
340	Thousand Oaks, CA	(26.5)
16	Toledo, OH	45.7
2	Toms River Twnshp, NJ	85.9
72	Topeka, KS	15.2
124	Torrance, CA	3.9
88	Tracy, CA	11.1
29	Trenton, NJ	31.0
239	Troy, MI	(13.0)
132	Tucson, AZ	3.2
129	Tulsa, OK	3.5
NA	Tuscaloosa, AL**	NA
310	Tustin, CA	(22.8)
151	Tyler, TX	0.0
65	Upper Darby Twnshp, PA	18.3
222	Vacaville, CA	(10.0)
6	Vallejo, CA	68.8
204	Vancouver, WA	(7.3)
249	Ventura, CA	(14.5)
186	Victorville, CA	(5.1)
200	Virginia Beach, VA	(7.1)
203	Visalia, CA	(7.2)
334	Vista, CA	(25.3)
282	Waco, TX	(19.2)
34	Warren, MI	30.0
NA	Warwick, RI**	NA
196	Washington, DC	(6.5)
215	Waterbury, CT	(9.0)
303	West Covina, CA	(22.1)
377	West Jordan, UT	(33.7)
253	West Palm Beach, FL	(15.0)
309	West Valley, UT	(22.7)
223	Westland, MI	(10.5)
324	Westminster, CA	(24.2)
243	Westminster, CO	(13.8)
142	Whittier, CA	1.8
336	Wichita Falls, TX	(25.5)
248	Wichita, KS	(14.4)
288	Wilmington, NC	(20.2)
NA	Winston-Salem, NC**	NA
262	Woodbridge Twnshp, NJ	(16.5)
9	Worcester, MA	52.5
64	Yakima, WA	20.1
66	Yonkers, NY	18.0
236	Yuma, AZ	(12.8)

Source: CQ Press using reported data from the F.B.I. "Crime in the United States 2011"
*Burglary is the unlawful entry of a structure to commit a felony or theft. Attempts are included.
**Not available.

Rank Order - City

72. Percent Change in Burglary Rate: 2007 to 2011 (continued)
National Percent Change = 3.3% Decrease*

RANK	CITY	% CHANGE	RANK	CITY	% CHANGE	RANK	CITY	% CHANGE
1	Redwood City, CA	109.1	73	Davie, FL	14.5	145	Costa Mesa, CA	1.6
2	Toms River Twnshp, NJ	85.9	74	Chandler, AZ	14.4	146	Grand Prairie, TX	1.1
3	Gary, IN	80.3	75	Long Beach, CA	14.2	147	Athens-Clarke, GA	0.7
4	Spokane Valley, WA	75.5	76	Nashville, TN	13.6	147	Tacoma, WA	0.7
5	Rancho Cucamon., CA	69.8	77	Round Rock, TX	13.4	149	Louisville, KY	0.5
6	Vallejo, CA	68.8	78	Lakeland, FL	12.4	150	Deerfield Beach, FL	0.2
7	Mesquite, TX	67.4	78	Oklahoma City, OK	12.4	151	Plantation, FL	0.0
8	Fort Lauderdale, FL	53.4	80	Des Moines, IA	12.3	151	Tyler, TX	0.0
9	Worcester, MA	52.5	81	Little Rock, AR	12.1	153	Scottsdale, AZ	(0.2)
10	Clovis, CA	51.3	82	St. Paul, MN	12.0	154	Bellevue, WA	(0.3)
11	Hamilton Twnshp, NJ	50.6	83	Lawton, OK	11.8	154	Cedar Rapids, IA	(0.3)
12	Brockton, MA	48.9	84	Chicago, IL	11.5	156	Kennewick, WA	(0.4)
13	Elizabeth, NJ	48.1	84	Hampton, VA	11.5	157	Lubbock, TX	(0.7)
14	Erie, PA	47.9	86	Downey, CA	11.4	158	Hammond, IN	(0.8)
15	Hollywood, FL	47.7	87	Newton, MA	11.3	159	Albuquerque, NM	(1.0)
16	Toledo, OH	45.7	88	Tracy, CA	11.1	159	Fontana, CA	(1.0)
17	Coral Springs, FL	41.7	89	Bakersfield, CA	10.8	159	Fort Worth, TX	(1.0)
18	Lawrence, MA	38.7	89	Suffolk, VA	10.8	162	Atlanta, GA	(1.1)
19	Fresno, CA	38.3	91	St. Joseph, MO	10.7	163	Hayward, CA	(1.3)
20	Brick Twnshp, NJ	37.4	92	Gresham, OR	10.1	164	Columbus, OH	(1.4)
21	Cranston, RI	35.9	93	Ramapo, NY	9.8	165	Dearborn, MI	(1.5)
22	Carson, CA	35.8	94	Macon, GA	9.6	166	Arlington, TX	(1.6)
23	Peoria, IL	35.2	95	Oakland, CA	9.4	166	Lynchburg, VA	(1.6)
24	Akron, OH	34.7	96	Tallahassee, FL	9.3	168	Edinburg, TX	(1.7)
25	Sunrise, FL	34.0	97	Santa Ana, CA	9.2	169	Chesapeake, VA	(1.9)
26	Hawthorne, CA	33.1	98	Concord, CA	8.9	169	Philadelphia, PA	(1.9)
27	Racine, WI	31.2	99	Daly City, CA	8.8	171	Modesto, CA	(2.2)
28	Lansing, MI	31.1	100	Detroit, MI	8.7	172	Sunnyvale, CA	(2.8)
29	Cleveland, OH	31.0	100	Santa Maria, CA	8.7	173	Fayetteville, NC	(3.1)
29	Trenton, NJ	31.0	102	Hartford, CT	8.4	174	Mesa, AZ	(3.3)
31	Murfreesboro, TN	30.6	103	Baton Rouge, LA	8.2	175	Shreveport, LA	(3.6)
31	Redding, CA	30.6	104	Indianapolis, IN	8.1	176	Salem, OR	(3.7)
33	Spokane, WA	30.2	105	Beaumont, TX	7.9	177	Chattanooga, TN	(3.8)
34	Warren, MI	30.0	105	Miami, FL	7.9	177	Glendale, AZ	(3.8)
35	Hemet, CA	29.9	107	Seattle, WA	7.6	179	Huntington Beach, CA	(3.9)
36	Sioux Falls, SD	29.8	108	Sugar Land, TX	7.3	180	Surprise, AZ	(4.1)
37	Camden, NJ	29.5	109	Reading, PA	7.1	181	Houston, TX	(4.3)
38	Pasadena, CA	28.6	110	Joliet, IL	6.5	181	Indio, CA	(4.3)
38	Rialto, CA	28.6	111	Boulder, CO	6.2	183	Chino Hills, CA	(4.4)
40	Portsmouth, VA	28.3	112	College Station, TX	5.9	183	Orange, CA	(4.4)
41	Rochester, NY	28.1	113	Mission, TX	5.5	185	Melbourne, FL	(5.0)
42	Antioch, CA	28.0	114	Glendale, CA	5.2	186	Victorville, CA	(5.1)
43	Richmond, CA	27.5	115	Amherst, NY	4.9	187	Mission Viejo, CA	(5.2)
44	Flint, MI	26.9	116	Corona, CA	4.8	188	South Gate, CA	(5.3)
45	Newark, NJ	26.1	116	Moreno Valley, CA	4.8	189	Evansville, IN	(5.6)
46	Pembroke Pines, FL	23.9	116	San Bernardino, CA	4.8	190	Pomona, CA	(5.8)
47	Columbus, GA	23.8	119	Dayton, OH	4.7	190	Richmond, VA	(5.8)
48	Compton, CA	23.7	120	St. Louis, MO	4.6	192	El Monte, CA	(5.9)
48	Paterson, NJ	23.7	121	Garland, TX	4.3	193	Lakewood, CO	(6.1)
50	Norfolk, VA	23.5	122	McKinney, TX	4.0	193	Merced, CA	(6.1)
51	South Bend, IN	23.3	122	New Bedford, MA	4.0	195	El Cajon, CA	(6.3)
52	Danbury, CT	23.0	124	Omaha, NE	3.9	196	Washington, DC	(6.5)
53	Hesperia, CA	22.9	124	Torrance, CA	3.9	197	Lawrence, KS	(6.8)
54	Greece, NY	22.8	126	Pasadena, TX	3.8	198	Livermore, CA	(6.9)
55	Springfield, IL	22.6	126	Port St. Lucie, FL	3.8	199	Memphis, TN	(7.0)
56	Sioux City, IA	22.4	128	Elgin, IL	3.7	200	Oceanside, CA	(7.1)
57	Naperville, IL	22.3	129	Lewisville, TX	3.5	200	Orlando, FL	(7.1)
57	Pompano Beach, FL	22.3	129	Tulsa, OK	3.5	200	Virginia Beach, VA	(7.1)
59	Bridgeport, CT	22.2	131	Duluth, MN	3.3	203	Visalia, CA	(7.2)
60	Jackson, MS	22.1	132	Tucson, AZ	3.2	204	Ann Arbor, MI	(7.3)
61	Springfield, MA	21.0	133	Knoxville, TN	3.1	204	San Jose, CA	(7.3)
62	Cincinnati, OH	20.4	133	Milwaukee, WI	3.1	204	Vancouver, WA	(7.3)
63	Cheektowaga, NY	20.2	135	Fort Smith, AR	2.9	207	Somerville, MA	(7.4)
64	Yakima, WA	20.1	135	Norwalk, CT	2.9	208	Colorado Springs, CO	(7.7)
65	Upper Darby Twnshp, PA	18.3	137	Stockton, CA	2.7	209	Lowell, MA	(7.9)
66	San Mateo, CA	18.0	138	Ontario, CA	2.5	209	Quincy, MA	(7.9)
66	Yonkers, NY	18.0	139	Clinton Twnshp, MI	2.3	211	Norwalk, CA	(8.1)
68	Columbia, MO	17.9	140	Phoenix, AZ	2.2	212	St. Petersburg, FL	(8.2)
68	Scranton, PA	17.9	141	Largo, FL	2.0	213	Syracuse, NY	(8.4)
70	Baltimore, MD	16.2	142	Carrollton, TX	1.8	214	Chino, CA	(8.7)
71	Las Cruces, NM	16.0	142	Whittier, CA	1.8	215	Waterbury, CT	(9.0)
72	Topeka, KS	15.2	144	Kent, WA	1.7	216	Raleigh, NC	(9.1)

Rank Order - City (continued)

RANK	CITY	% CHANGE
216	Riverside, CA	(9.1)
218	Aurora, IL	(9.5)
219	Jersey City, NJ	(9.7)
219	Salinas, CA	(9.7)
221	Springfield, MO	(9.8)
222	Vacaville, CA	(10.0)
223	Broken Arrow, OK	(10.5)
223	Westland, MI	(10.5)
225	Santa Barbara, CA	(10.6)
226	San Antonio, TX	(11.0)
226	Savannah, GA	(11.0)
228	Los Angeles, CA	(11.3)
229	Albany, NY	(11.4)
230	Tempe, AZ	(11.6)
231	Palm Bay, FL	(11.7)
232	Laredo, TX	(12.5)
232	Renton, WA	(12.5)
234	Centennial, CO	(12.6)
234	Sandy, UT	(12.6)
236	Yuma, AZ	(12.8)
237	Boston, MA	(12.9)
237	Miramar, FL	(12.9)
239	Troy, MI	(13.0)
240	New York, NY	(13.1)
241	Fremont, CA	(13.2)
242	Fort Wayne, IN	(13.6)
243	Bellingham, WA	(13.8)
243	Westminster, CO	(13.8)
245	Ogden, UT	(13.9)
246	Aurora, CO	(14.1)
247	Bellflower, CA	(14.2)
248	Wichita, KS	(14.4)
249	Ventura, CA	(14.5)
250	Medford, OR	(14.6)
250	Richardson, TX	(14.6)
252	Overland Park, KS	(14.7)
253	West Palm Beach, FL	(15.0)
254	Roanoke, VA	(15.4)
255	Dallas, TX	(15.6)
255	Plano, TX	(15.6)
255	Rochester, MN	(15.6)
258	Miami Beach, FL	(15.7)
259	Albany, GA	(16.0)
260	Independence, MO	(16.1)
261	League City, TX	(16.3)
262	Woodbridge Twnshp, NJ	(16.5)
263	Baldwin Park, CA	(16.8)
263	Reno, NV	(16.8)
265	Stamford, CT	(17.4)
266	Colonie, NY	(17.5)
266	Irving, TX	(17.5)
268	Lakewood, CA	(17.7)
269	Clearwater, FL	(17.9)
270	Eugene, OR	(18.0)
271	Bethlehem, PA	(18.1)
272	Fairfield, CA	(18.2)
273	Nampa, ID	(18.3)
273	O'Fallon, MO	(18.3)
273	San Marcos, CA	(18.3)
276	Burbank, CA	(18.6)
277	Abilene, TX	(18.9)
277	Portland, OR	(18.9)
279	Alexandria, VA	(19.0)
279	Greeley, CO	(19.0)
281	Miami Gardens, FL	(19.1)
282	Gilbert, AZ	(19.2)
282	Waco, TX	(19.2)
284	El Paso, TX	(19.6)
284	Roswell, GA	(19.6)
286	Denver, CO	(19.7)
287	Santa Rosa, CA	(19.9)
288	Wilmington, NC	(20.2)
289	Garden Grove, CA	(20.3)

RANK	CITY	% CHANGE
289	Minneapolis, MN	(20.3)
289	Provo, UT	(20.3)
289	San Angelo, TX	(20.3)
293	Lafayette, LA	(20.5)
293	Pittsburgh, PA	(20.5)
295	Carlsbad, CA	(20.9)
295	Green Bay, WI	(20.9)
297	Clarkstown, NY	(21.0)
298	Norman, OK	(21.2)
299	Kansas City, KS	(21.3)
300	Canton Twnshp, MI	(21.6)
301	Everett, WA	(21.8)
301	San Francisco, CA	(21.8)
303	Austin, TX	(22.1)
303	West Covina, CA	(22.1)
305	Cambridge, MA	(22.2)
305	Midland, TX	(22.2)
307	Edison Twnshp, NJ	(22.4)
308	Denton, TX	(22.6)
309	West Valley, UT	(22.7)
310	Tustin, CA	(22.8)
311	Peoria, AZ	(22.9)
312	Bloomington, IN	(23.0)
313	San Leandro, CA	(23.2)
314	Alhambra, CA	(23.6)
314	Brooklyn Park, MN	(23.6)
314	Roseville, CA	(23.6)
317	Boise, ID	(23.9)
317	Edmond, OK	(23.9)
317	Las Vegas, NV	(23.9)
320	Anaheim, CA	(24.0)
320	Grand Rapids, MI	(24.0)
320	Salt Lake City, UT	(24.0)
323	Lee's Summit, MO	(24.1)
324	Temecula, CA	(24.2)
324	Westminster, CA	(24.2)
326	Irvine, CA	(24.3)
327	Concord, NC	(24.5)
328	Sparks, NV	(24.7)
329	Clifton, NJ	(24.9)
330	Amarillo, TX	(25.0)
330	North Charleston, SC	(25.0)
332	Clarksville, TN	(25.1)
333	Allentown, PA	(25.2)
334	Vista, CA	(25.3)
335	Palmdale, CA	(25.4)
336	Boca Raton, FL	(25.5)
336	Sacramento, CA	(25.5)
336	Wichita Falls, TX	(25.5)
339	Berkeley, CA	(25.9)
340	Thousand Oaks, CA	(26.5)
341	Jacksonville, FL	(26.8)
342	San Diego, CA	(27.2)
343	Livonia, MI	(27.3)
344	Buena Park, CA	(27.5)
345	Corpus Christi, TX	(28.0)
345	Fort Collins, CO	(28.0)
347	Napa, CA	(28.1)
348	Kenosha, WI	(28.4)
348	Rockford, IL	(28.4)
350	Fullerton, CA	(28.7)
351	Anchorage, AK	(28.9)
352	Santa Clarita, CA	(29.1)
352	Simi Valley, CA	(29.1)
354	Cape Coral, FL	(29.5)
355	Frisco, TX	(30.0)
355	Killeen, TX	(30.0)
357	Meridian, ID	(30.1)
358	Arvada, CO	(30.2)
359	Brownsville, TX	(30.7)
359	Inglewood, CA	(30.7)
361	Henderson, NV	(30.8)
362	Orem, UT	(30.9)
362	Santa Monica, CA	(30.9)

RANK	CITY	% CHANGE
364	Cary, NC	(31.1)
365	Longview, TX	(31.2)
366	Lincoln, NE	(31.3)
366	Santa Clara, CA	(31.3)
368	Beaverton, OR	(32.3)
368	Bloomington, MN	(32.3)
370	Murrieta, CA	(32.5)
371	New Rochelle, NY	(32.6)
372	Madison, WI	(32.7)
373	Newport News, VA	(32.9)
374	Fargo, ND	(33.1)
375	Fishers, IN	(33.2)
376	Odessa, TX	(33.4)
377	West Jordan, UT	(33.7)
378	Farmington Hills, MI	(33.9)
379	Sandy Springs, GA	(34.0)
380	Chula Vista, CA	(34.6)
380	Lake Forest, CA	(34.6)
382	Asheville, NC	(35.9)
383	Newport Beach, CA	(36.2)
383	Tampa, FL	(36.2)
385	Charleston, SC	(36.4)
385	High Point, NC	(36.4)
387	Escondido, CA	(36.8)
388	Lynn, MA	(37.2)
389	Elk Grove, CA	(37.7)
390	Allen, TX	(37.9)
391	Oxnard, CA	(38.0)
392	Pearland, TX	(38.1)
393	Charlotte, NC	(38.8)
394	McAllen, TX	(39.5)
395	Gainesville, FL	(40.0)
396	Bend, OR	(40.4)
397	Bryan, TX	(40.9)
398	Chico, CA	(43.1)
399	Hialeah, FL	(44.0)
399	Rio Rancho, NM	(44.0)
401	Lancaster, CA	(44.3)
402	Hillsboro, OR	(46.0)
403	New Orleans, LA	(51.3)
404	Carmel, IN	(56.3)
405	Lakewood Twnshp, NJ	(58.0)
NA	Arlington Heights, IL**	NA
NA	Avondale, AZ**	NA
NA	Billings, MT**	NA
NA	Birmingham, AL**	NA
NA	Bloomington, IL**	NA
NA	Buffalo, NY**	NA
NA	Champaign, IL**	NA
NA	Cicero, IL**	NA
NA	Citrus Heights, CA**	NA
NA	Davenport, IA**	NA
NA	Decatur, IL**	NA
NA	Durham, NC**	NA
NA	Fall River, MA**	NA
NA	Hoover, AL**	NA
NA	Huntsville, AL**	NA
NA	Johns Creek, GA**	NA
NA	Kansas City, MO**	NA
NA	Lexington, KY**	NA
NA	Longmont, CO**	NA
NA	Manchester, NH**	NA
NA	Menifee, CA**	NA
NA	Mobile, AL**	NA
NA	Montgomery, AL**	NA
NA	Nashua, NH**	NA
NA	New Haven, CT**	NA
NA	Olathe, KS**	NA
NA	Pueblo, CO**	NA
NA	Sterling Heights, MI**	NA
NA	Thornton, CO**	NA
NA	Tuscaloosa, AL**	NA
NA	Warwick, RI**	NA
NA	Winston-Salem, NC**	NA

Source: CQ Press using reported data from the F.B.I. "Crime in the United States 2011"
*Burglary is the unlawful entry of a structure to commit a felony or theft. Attempts are included.
**Not available.

Alpha Order - City

73. Larceny-Thefts in 2011
National Total = 6,159,795 Larceny-Thefts*

RANK	CITY	THEFTS
191	Abilene, TX	3,093
103	Akron, OH	5,790
187	Albany, GA	3,174
160	Albany, NY	3,514
24	Albuquerque, NM	19,168
238	Alexandria, VA	2,506
376	Alhambra, CA	1,362
194	Allentown, PA	3,041
396	Allen, TX	1,207
91	Amarillo, TX	6,756
334	Amherst, NY	1,736
99	Anaheim, CA	5,964
75	Anchorage, AK	7,750
312	Ann Arbor, MI	1,918
354	Antioch, CA	1,571
425	Arlington Heights, IL	892
44	Arlington, TX	11,757
292	Arvada, CO	2,053
206	Asheville, NC	2,875
182	Athens-Clarke, GA	3,273
27	Atlanta, GA	17,274
86	Aurora, CO	6,861
218	Aurora, IL	2,740
9	Austin, TX	33,069
199	Avondale, AZ	2,975
69	Bakersfield, CA	8,123
426	Baldwin Park, CA	883
28	Baltimore, MD	17,010
73	Baton Rouge, LA	7,946
130	Beaumont, TX	4,336
370	Beaverton, OR	1,410
213	Bellevue, WA	2,775
422	Bellflower, CA	907
201	Bellingham, WA	2,961
302	Bend, OR	1,978
163	Berkeley, CA	3,460
372	Bethlehem, PA	1,405
147	Billings, MT	3,689
52	Birmingham, AL	10,522
392	Bloomington, IL	1,231
258	Bloomington, IN	2,300
210	Bloomington, MN	2,813
288	Boca Raton, FL	2,067
129	Boise, ID	4,347
34	Boston, MA	14,064
315	Boulder, CO	1,899
417	Brick Twnshp, NJ	960
195	Bridgeport, CT	3,025
326	Brockton, MA	1,805
336	Broken Arrow, OK	1,728
273	Brooklyn Park, MN	2,203
83	Brownsville, TX	7,015
279	Bryan, TX	2,130
393	Buena Park, CA	1,230
64	Buffalo, NY	8,711
310	Burbank, CA	1,926
242	Cambridge, MA	2,465
269	Camden, NJ	2,226
410	Canton Twnshp, MI	1,094
208	Cape Coral, FL	2,855
374	Carlsbad, CA	1,375
432	Carmel, IN	729
278	Carrollton, TX	2,152
377	Carson, CA	1,360
346	Cary, NC	1,658
155	Cedar Rapids, IA	3,566
418	Centennial, CO	957
349	Champaign, IL	1,599
105	Chandler, AZ	5,741
202	Charleston, SC	2,957
20	Charlotte, NC	21,371
78	Chattanooga, TN	7,338

RANK	CITY	THEFTS
261	Cheektowaga, NY	2,294
106	Chesapeake, VA	5,601
2	Chicago, IL	72,373
380	Chico, CA	1,337
434	Chino Hills, CA	624
379	Chino, CA	1,341
179	Chula Vista, CA	3,316
413	Cicero, IL	1,042
40	Cincinnati, OH	12,512
248	Citrus Heights, CA	2,386
375	Clarkstown, NY	1,370
223	Clarksville, TN	2,666
185	Clearwater, FL	3,252
51	Cleveland, OH	10,524
408	Clifton, NJ	1,131
353	Clinton Twnshp, MI	1,576
231	Clovis, CA	2,608
262	College Station, TX	2,289
307	Colonie, NY	1,955
48	Colorado Springs, CO	11,375
178	Columbia, MO	3,323
71	Columbus, GA	8,059
10	Columbus, OH	30,259
397	Compton, CA	1,202
264	Concord, CA	2,268
236	Concord, NC	2,528
266	Coral Springs, FL	2,238
260	Corona, CA	2,298
43	Corpus Christi, TX	11,762
217	Costa Mesa, CA	2,743
369	Cranston, RI	1,423
8	Dallas, TX	35,148
381	Daly City, CA	1,308
399	Danbury, CT	1,183
159	Davenport, IA	3,529
228	Davie, FL	2,640
127	Dayton, OH	4,569
219	Dearborn, MI	2,705
352	Decatur, IL	1,581
347	Deerfield Beach, FL	1,651
230	Denton, TX	2,632
35	Denver, CO	14,040
77	Des Moines, IA	7,400
29	Detroit, MI	16,456
291	Downey, CA	2,054
168	Duluth, MN	3,424
89	Durham, NC	6,768
149	Edinburg, TX	3,666
388	Edison Twnshp, NJ	1,279
387	Edmond, OK	1,280
366	El Cajon, CA	1,443
405	El Monte, CA	1,136
37	El Paso, TX	12,997
368	Elgin, IL	1,425
227	Elizabeth, NJ	2,641
263	Elk Grove, CA	2,282
245	Erie, PA	2,404
277	Escondido, CA	2,156
100	Eugene, OR	5,862
136	Evansville, IN	4,151
108	Everett, WA	5,415
290	Fairfield, CA	2,055
296	Fall River, MA	2,027
281	Fargo, ND	2,120
424	Farmington Hills, MI	895
70	Fayetteville, NC	8,088
433	Fishers, IN	626
271	Flint, MI	2,220
244	Fontana, CA	2,411
157	Fort Collins, CO	3,553
94	Fort Lauderdale, FL	6,489
172	Fort Smith, AR	3,389

RANK	CITY	THEFTS
89	Fort Wayne, IN	6,768
15	Fort Worth, TX	22,617
256	Fremont, CA	2,303
33	Fresno, CA	14,928
317	Frisco, TX	1,878
235	Fullerton, CA	2,548
140	Gainesville, FL	4,003
265	Garden Grove, CA	2,242
102	Garland, TX	5,794
310	Gary, IN	1,926
205	Gilbert, AZ	2,896
50	Glendale, AZ	10,838
238	Glendale, CA	2,506
131	Grand Prairie, TX	4,330
142	Grand Rapids, MI	3,897
285	Greece, NY	2,081
251	Greeley, CO	2,377
321	Green Bay, WI	1,852
203	Gresham, OR	2,943
398	Hamilton Twnshp, NJ	1,198
256	Hammond, IN	2,303
135	Hampton, VA	4,180
174	Hartford, CT	3,372
405	Hawthorne, CA	1,136
341	Hayward, CA	1,693
313	Hemet, CA	1,911
192	Henderson, NV	3,069
400	Hesperia, CA	1,181
107	Hialeah, FL	5,473
158	High Point, NC	3,550
343	Hillsboro, OR	1,683
113	Hollywood, FL	5,163
345	Hoover, AL	1,663
3	Houston, TX	68,596
154	Huntington Beach, CA	3,584
96	Huntsville, AL	6,306
119	Independence, MO	4,785
11	Indianapolis, IN	26,588
364	Indio, CA	1,453
363	Inglewood, CA	1,459
225	Irvine, CA	2,649
126	Irving, TX	4,590
12	Jacksonville, FL	25,733
92	Jackson, MS	6,632
165	Jersey City, NJ	3,439
435	Johns Creek, GA	432
215	Joliet, IL	2,751
118	Kansas City, KS	4,792
30	Kansas City, MO	15,305
289	Kennewick, WA	2,056
253	Kenosha, WI	2,329
198	Kent, WA	2,977
197	Killeen, TX	2,989
58	Knoxville, TN	9,515
117	Lafayette, LA	5,040
430	Lake Forest, CA	763
152	Lakeland, FL	3,612
428	Lakewood Twnshp, NJ	786
382	Lakewood, CA	1,295
120	Lakewood, CO	4,771
322	Lancaster, CA	1,843
247	Lansing, MI	2,397
68	Laredo, TX	8,143
254	Largo, FL	2,327
188	Las Cruces, NM	3,164
17	Las Vegas, NV	21,977
190	Lawrence, KS	3,098
429	Lawrence, MA	773
175	Lawton, OK	3,365
364	League City, TX	1,453
344	Lee's Summit, MO	1,676
270	Lewisville, TX	2,223

Alpha Order - City (continued)

RANK	CITY	THEFTS
62	Lexington, KY	9,036
67	Lincoln, NE	8,424
54	Little Rock, AR	9,756
386	Livermore, CA	1,283
350	Livonia, MI	1,589
79	Long Beach, CA	7,329
355	Longmont, CO	1,559
219	Longview, TX	2,705
5	Los Angeles, CA	53,469
19	Louisville, KY	21,560
308	Lowell, MA	1,941
72	Lubbock, TX	7,975
320	Lynchburg, VA	1,855
355	Lynn, MA	1,559
114	Macon, GA	5,104
98	Madison, WI	6,152
189	Manchester, NH	3,136
111	McAllen, TX	5,184
284	McKinney, TX	2,085
173	Medford, OR	3,375
196	Melbourne, FL	3,021
13	Memphis, TN	25,667
423	Menifee, CA	901
294	Merced, CA	2,044
427	Meridian, ID	863
46	Mesa, AZ	11,407
134	Mesquite, TX	4,197
74	Miami Beach, FL	7,838
183	Miami Gardens, FL	3,270
32	Miami, FL	15,080
243	Midland, TX	2,435
25	Milwaukee, WI	18,890
41	Minneapolis, MN	12,311
304	Miramar, FL	1,969
416	Mission Viejo, CA	983
282	Mission, TX	2,094
63	Mobile, AL	8,891
109	Modesto, CA	5,410
81	Montgomery, AL	7,043
214	Moreno Valley, CA	2,767
180	Murfreesboro, TN	3,283
414	Murrieta, CA	1,031
319	Nampa, ID	1,864
407	Napa, CA	1,132
330	Naperville, IL	1,768
341	Nashua, NH	1,693
23	Nashville, TN	19,987
297	New Bedford, MA	2,018
137	New Haven, CT	4,124
76	New Orleans, LA	7,616
409	New Rochelle, NY	1,100
1	New York, NY	112,864
141	Newark, NJ	3,921
339	Newport Beach, CA	1,702
125	Newport News, VA	4,592
419	Newton, MA	942
61	Norfolk, VA	9,217
224	Norman, OK	2,656
138	North Charleston, SC	4,092
404	Norwalk, CA	1,156
366	Norwalk, CT	1,443
59	Oakland, CA	9,429
221	Oceanside, CA	2,704
252	Odessa, TX	2,336
412	O'Fallon, MO	1,061
181	Ogden, UT	3,279
21	Oklahoma City, OK	20,199
329	Olathe, KS	1,774
38	Omaha, NE	12,793
193	Ontario, CA	3,057
299	Orange, CA	2,001
287	Orem, UT	2,069
45	Orlando, FL	11,669
186	Overland Park, KS	3,237
234	Oxnard, CA	2,563
327	Palm Bay, FL	1,786
314	Palmdale, CA	1,906
249	Pasadena, CA	2,382
145	Pasadena, TX	3,728
316	Paterson, NJ	1,888
384	Pearland, TX	1,289
153	Pembroke Pines, FL	3,591
176	Peoria, AZ	3,360
163	Peoria, IL	3,460
6	Philadelphia, PA	40,113
7	Phoenix, AZ	38,258
84	Pittsburgh, PA	6,897
112	Plano, TX	5,182
204	Plantation, FL	2,929
233	Pomona, CA	2,578
143	Pompano Beach, FL	3,852
232	Port St. Lucie, FL	2,590
16	Portland, OR	22,494
150	Portsmouth, VA	3,623
246	Provo, UT	2,400
167	Pueblo, CO	3,434
411	Quincy, MA	1,087
268	Racine, WI	2,227
60	Raleigh, NC	9,343
431	Ramapo, NY	740
250	Rancho Cucamon., CA	2,381
360	Reading, PA	1,501
267	Redding, CA	2,237
420	Redwood City, CA	918
132	Reno, NV	4,311
216	Renton, WA	2,748
358	Rialto, CA	1,524
309	Richardson, TX	1,934
357	Richmond, CA	1,533
101	Richmond, VA	5,833
395	Rio Rancho, NM	1,208
97	Riverside, CA	6,278
168	Roanoke, VA	3,424
325	Rochester, MN	1,809
87	Rochester, NY	6,849
121	Rockford, IL	4,746
212	Roseville, CA	2,786
391	Roswell, GA	1,262
299	Round Rock, TX	2,001
49	Sacramento, CA	11,087
122	Salem, OR	4,641
276	Salinas, CA	2,189
55	Salt Lake City, UT	9,654
222	San Angelo, TX	2,685
4	San Antonio, TX	59,641
128	San Bernardino, CA	4,446
26	San Diego, CA	17,610
14	San Francisco, CA	24,304
39	San Jose, CA	12,628
305	San Leandro, CA	1,957
421	San Marcos, CA	908
385	San Mateo, CA	1,288
336	Sandy Springs, GA	1,728
301	Sandy, UT	1,986
133	Santa Ana, CA	4,222
280	Santa Barbara, CA	2,124
274	Santa Clara, CA	2,202
331	Santa Clarita, CA	1,766
359	Santa Maria, CA	1,510
258	Santa Monica, CA	2,300
211	Santa Rosa, CA	2,794
93	Savannah, GA	6,608
116	Scottsdale, AZ	5,054
324	Scranton, PA	1,810
18	Seattle, WA	21,585
95	Shreveport, LA	6,371
389	Simi Valley, CA	1,278
229	Sioux City, IA	2,635
156	Sioux Falls, SD	3,554
401	Somerville, MA	1,178
166	South Bend, IN	3,437
383	South Gate, CA	1,294
348	Sparks, NV	1,600
151	Spokane Valley, WA	3,613
53	Spokane, WA	10,231
115	Springfield, IL	5,076
139	Springfield, MA	4,072
47	Springfield, MO	11,391
361	Stamford, CT	1,498
293	Sterling Heights, MI	2,047
56	Stockton, CA	9,651
207	St. Joseph, MO	2,870
31	St. Louis, MO	15,285
85	St. Paul, MN	6,890
65	St. Petersburg, FL	8,544
332	Suffolk, VA	1,757
402	Sugar Land, TX	1,176
378	Sunnyvale, CA	1,351
237	Sunrise, FL	2,511
318	Surprise, AZ	1,873
184	Syracuse, NY	3,261
80	Tacoma, WA	7,228
104	Tallahassee, FL	5,748
82	Tampa, FL	7,042
340	Temecula, CA	1,700
88	Tempe, AZ	6,804
226	Thornton, CO	2,644
371	Thousand Oaks, CA	1,409
NA	Toledo, OH**	NA
240	Toms River Twnshp, NJ	2,499
110	Topeka, KS	5,213
305	Torrance, CA	1,957
351	Tracy, CA	1,585
415	Trenton, NJ	993
373	Troy, MI	1,402
NA	Tucson, AZ**	NA
42	Tulsa, OK	12,136
200	Tuscaloosa, AL	2,963
403	Tustin, CA	1,167
170	Tyler, TX	3,423
333	Upper Darby Twnshp, PA	1,744
390	Vacaville, CA	1,265
338	Vallejo, CA	1,716
123	Vancouver, WA	4,629
241	Ventura, CA	2,468
283	Victorville, CA	2,086
57	Virginia Beach, VA	9,645
162	Visalia, CA	3,466
394	Vista, CA	1,213
124	Waco, TX	4,593
303	Warren, MI	1,975
335	Warwick, RI	1,734
22	Washington, DC	20,124
177	Waterbury, CT	3,326
272	West Covina, CA	2,212
255	West Jordan, UT	2,314
148	West Palm Beach, FL	3,685
146	West Valley, UT	3,711
362	Westland, MI	1,470
323	Westminster, CA	1,815
286	Westminster, CO	2,077
328	Whittier, CA	1,779
171	Wichita Falls, TX	3,398
36	Wichita, KS	13,550
144	Wilmington, NC	3,843
66	Winston-Salem, NC	8,522
295	Woodbridge Twnshp, NJ	2,030
161	Worcester, MA	3,481
209	Yakima, WA	2,841
298	Yonkers, NY	2,017
275	Yuma, AZ	2,196

Source: Reported data from the F.B.I. "Crime in the United States 2011"
*Larceny-theft is the unlawful taking of property. Attempts are included.
**Not available.

73. Larceny-Thefts in 2011 (continued)
National Total = 6,159,795 Larceny-Thefts*

RANK	CITY	THEFTS
1	New York, NY	112,864
2	Chicago, IL	72,373
3	Houston, TX	68,596
4	San Antonio, TX	59,641
5	Los Angeles, CA	53,469
6	Philadelphia, PA	40,113
7	Phoenix, AZ	38,258
8	Dallas, TX	35,148
9	Austin, TX	33,069
10	Columbus, OH	30,259
11	Indianapolis, IN	26,588
12	Jacksonville, FL	25,733
13	Memphis, TN	25,667
14	San Francisco, CA	24,304
15	Fort Worth, TX	22,617
16	Portland, OR	22,494
17	Las Vegas, NV	21,977
18	Seattle, WA	21,585
19	Louisville, KY	21,560
20	Charlotte, NC	21,371
21	Oklahoma City, OK	20,199
22	Washington, DC	20,124
23	Nashville, TN	19,987
24	Albuquerque, NM	19,168
25	Milwaukee, WI	18,890
26	San Diego, CA	17,610
27	Atlanta, GA	17,274
28	Baltimore, MD	17,010
29	Detroit, MI	16,456
30	Kansas City, MO	15,305
31	St. Louis, MO	15,285
32	Miami, FL	15,080
33	Fresno, CA	14,928
34	Boston, MA	14,064
35	Denver, CO	14,040
36	Wichita, KS	13,550
37	El Paso, TX	12,997
38	Omaha, NE	12,793
39	San Jose, CA	12,628
40	Cincinnati, OH	12,512
41	Minneapolis, MN	12,311
42	Tulsa, OK	12,136
43	Corpus Christi, TX	11,762
44	Arlington, TX	11,757
45	Orlando, FL	11,669
46	Mesa, AZ	11,407
47	Springfield, MO	11,391
48	Colorado Springs, CO	11,375
49	Sacramento, CA	11,087
50	Glendale, AZ	10,838
51	Cleveland, OH	10,524
52	Birmingham, AL	10,522
53	Spokane, WA	10,231
54	Little Rock, AR	9,756
55	Salt Lake City, UT	9,654
56	Stockton, CA	9,651
57	Virginia Beach, VA	9,645
58	Knoxville, TN	9,515
59	Oakland, CA	9,429
60	Raleigh, NC	9,343
61	Norfolk, VA	9,217
62	Lexington, KY	9,036
63	Mobile, AL	8,891
64	Buffalo, NY	8,711
65	St. Petersburg, FL	8,544
66	Winston-Salem, NC	8,522
67	Lincoln, NE	8,424
68	Laredo, TX	8,143
69	Bakersfield, CA	8,123
70	Fayetteville, NC	8,088
71	Columbus, GA	8,059
72	Lubbock, TX	7,975
73	Baton Rouge, LA	7,946
74	Miami Beach, FL	7,838
75	Anchorage, AK	7,750
76	New Orleans, LA	7,616
77	Des Moines, IA	7,400
78	Chattanooga, TN	7,338
79	Long Beach, CA	7,329
80	Tacoma, WA	7,228
81	Montgomery, AL	7,043
82	Tampa, FL	7,042
83	Brownsville, TX	7,015
84	Pittsburgh, PA	6,897
85	St. Paul, MN	6,890
86	Aurora, CO	6,861
87	Rochester, NY	6,849
88	Tempe, AZ	6,804
89	Durham, NC	6,768
89	Fort Wayne, IN	6,768
91	Amarillo, TX	6,756
92	Jackson, MS	6,632
93	Savannah, GA	6,608
94	Fort Lauderdale, FL	6,489
95	Shreveport, LA	6,371
96	Huntsville, AL	6,306
97	Riverside, CA	6,278
98	Madison, WI	6,152
99	Anaheim, CA	5,964
100	Eugene, OR	5,862
101	Richmond, VA	5,833
102	Garland, TX	5,794
103	Akron, OH	5,790
104	Tallahassee, FL	5,748
105	Chandler, AZ	5,741
106	Chesapeake, VA	5,601
107	Hialeah, FL	5,473
108	Everett, WA	5,415
109	Modesto, CA	5,410
110	Topeka, KS	5,213
111	McAllen, TX	5,184
112	Plano, TX	5,182
113	Hollywood, FL	5,163
114	Macon, GA	5,104
115	Springfield, IL	5,076
116	Scottsdale, AZ	5,054
117	Lafayette, LA	5,040
118	Kansas City, KS	4,792
119	Independence, MO	4,785
120	Lakewood, CO	4,771
121	Rockford, IL	4,746
122	Salem, OR	4,641
123	Vancouver, WA	4,629
124	Waco, TX	4,593
125	Newport News, VA	4,592
126	Irving, TX	4,590
127	Dayton, OH	4,569
128	San Bernardino, CA	4,446
129	Boise, ID	4,347
130	Beaumont, TX	4,336
131	Grand Prairie, TX	4,330
132	Reno, NV	4,311
133	Santa Ana, CA	4,222
134	Mesquite, TX	4,197
135	Hampton, VA	4,180
136	Evansville, IN	4,151
137	New Haven, CT	4,124
138	North Charleston, SC	4,092
139	Springfield, MA	4,072
140	Gainesville, FL	4,003
141	Newark, NJ	3,921
142	Grand Rapids, MI	3,897
143	Pompano Beach, FL	3,852
144	Wilmington, NC	3,843
145	Pasadena, TX	3,728
146	West Valley, UT	3,711
147	Billings, MT	3,689
148	West Palm Beach, FL	3,685
149	Edinburg, TX	3,666
150	Portsmouth, VA	3,623
151	Spokane Valley, WA	3,613
152	Lakeland, FL	3,612
153	Pembroke Pines, FL	3,591
154	Huntington Beach, CA	3,584
155	Cedar Rapids, IA	3,566
156	Sioux Falls, SD	3,554
157	Fort Collins, CO	3,553
158	High Point, NC	3,550
159	Davenport, IA	3,529
160	Albany, NY	3,514
161	Worcester, MA	3,481
162	Visalia, CA	3,466
163	Berkeley, CA	3,460
163	Peoria, IL	3,460
165	Jersey City, NJ	3,439
166	South Bend, IN	3,437
167	Pueblo, CO	3,434
168	Duluth, MN	3,424
168	Roanoke, VA	3,424
170	Tyler, TX	3,423
171	Wichita Falls, TX	3,398
172	Fort Smith, AR	3,389
173	Medford, OR	3,375
174	Hartford, CT	3,372
175	Lawton, OK	3,365
176	Peoria, AZ	3,360
177	Waterbury, CT	3,326
178	Columbia, MO	3,323
179	Chula Vista, CA	3,316
180	Murfreesboro, TN	3,283
181	Ogden, UT	3,279
182	Athens-Clarke, GA	3,273
183	Miami Gardens, FL	3,270
184	Syracuse, NY	3,261
185	Clearwater, FL	3,252
186	Overland Park, KS	3,237
187	Albany, GA	3,174
188	Las Cruces, NM	3,164
189	Manchester, NH	3,136
190	Lawrence, KS	3,098
191	Abilene, TX	3,093
192	Henderson, NV	3,069
193	Ontario, CA	3,057
194	Allentown, PA	3,041
195	Bridgeport, CT	3,025
196	Melbourne, FL	3,021
197	Killeen, TX	2,989
198	Kent, WA	2,977
199	Avondale, AZ	2,975
200	Tuscaloosa, AL	2,963
201	Bellingham, WA	2,961
202	Charleston, SC	2,957
203	Gresham, OR	2,943
204	Plantation, FL	2,929
205	Gilbert, AZ	2,896
206	Asheville, NC	2,875
207	St. Joseph, MO	2,870
208	Cape Coral, FL	2,855
209	Yakima, WA	2,841
210	Bloomington, MN	2,813
211	Santa Rosa, CA	2,794
212	Roseville, CA	2,786
213	Bellevue, WA	2,775
214	Moreno Valley, CA	2,767
215	Joliet, IL	2,751
216	Renton, WA	2,748

Rank Order - City (continued)

RANK	CITY	THEFTS	RANK	CITY	THEFTS	RANK	CITY	THEFTS
217	Costa Mesa, CA	2,743	290	Fairfield, CA	2,055	364	Indio, CA	1,453
218	Aurora, IL	2,740	291	Downey, CA	2,054	364	League City, TX	1,453
219	Dearborn, MI	2,705	292	Arvada, CO	2,053	366	El Cajon, CA	1,443
219	Longview, TX	2,705	293	Sterling Heights, MI	2,047	366	Norwalk, CT	1,443
221	Oceanside, CA	2,704	294	Merced, CA	2,044	368	Elgin, IL	1,425
222	San Angelo, TX	2,685	295	Woodbridge Twnshp, NJ	2,030	369	Cranston, RI	1,423
223	Clarksville, TN	2,666	296	Fall River, MA	2,027	370	Beaverton, OR	1,410
224	Norman, OK	2,656	297	New Bedford, MA	2,018	371	Thousand Oaks, CA	1,409
225	Irvine, CA	2,649	298	Yonkers, NY	2,017	372	Bethlehem, PA	1,405
226	Thornton, CO	2,644	299	Orange, CA	2,001	373	Troy, MI	1,402
227	Elizabeth, NJ	2,641	299	Round Rock, TX	2,001	374	Carlsbad, CA	1,375
228	Davie, FL	2,640	301	Sandy, UT	1,986	375	Clarkstown, NY	1,370
229	Sioux City, IA	2,635	302	Bend, OR	1,978	376	Alhambra, CA	1,362
230	Denton, TX	2,632	303	Warren, MI	1,975	377	Carson, CA	1,360
231	Clovis, CA	2,608	304	Miramar, FL	1,969	378	Sunnyvale, CA	1,351
232	Port St. Lucie, FL	2,590	305	San Leandro, CA	1,957	379	Chino, CA	1,341
233	Pomona, CA	2,578	305	Torrance, CA	1,957	380	Chico, CA	1,337
234	Oxnard, CA	2,563	307	Colonie, NY	1,955	381	Daly City, CA	1,308
235	Fullerton, CA	2,548	308	Lowell, MA	1,941	382	Lakewood, CA	1,295
236	Concord, NC	2,528	309	Richardson, TX	1,934	383	South Gate, CA	1,294
237	Sunrise, FL	2,511	310	Burbank, CA	1,926	384	Pearland, TX	1,289
238	Alexandria, VA	2,506	310	Gary, IN	1,926	385	San Mateo, CA	1,288
238	Glendale, CA	2,506	312	Ann Arbor, MI	1,918	386	Livermore, CA	1,283
240	Toms River Twnshp, NJ	2,499	313	Hemet, CA	1,911	387	Edmond, OK	1,280
241	Ventura, CA	2,468	314	Palmdale, CA	1,906	388	Edison Twnshp, NJ	1,279
242	Cambridge, MA	2,465	315	Boulder, CO	1,899	389	Simi Valley, CA	1,278
243	Midland, TX	2,435	316	Paterson, NJ	1,888	390	Vacaville, CA	1,265
244	Fontana, CA	2,411	317	Frisco, TX	1,878	391	Roswell, GA	1,262
245	Erie, PA	2,404	318	Surprise, AZ	1,873	392	Bloomington, IL	1,231
246	Provo, UT	2,400	319	Nampa, ID	1,864	393	Buena Park, CA	1,230
247	Lansing, MI	2,397	320	Lynchburg, VA	1,855	394	Vista, CA	1,213
248	Citrus Heights, CA	2,386	321	Green Bay, WI	1,852	395	Rio Rancho, NM	1,208
249	Pasadena, CA	2,382	322	Lancaster, CA	1,843	396	Allen, TX	1,207
250	Rancho Cucamon., CA	2,381	323	Westminster, CA	1,815	397	Compton, CA	1,202
251	Greeley, CO	2,377	324	Scranton, PA	1,810	398	Hamilton Twnshp, NJ	1,198
252	Odessa, TX	2,336	325	Rochester, MN	1,809	399	Danbury, CT	1,183
253	Kenosha, WI	2,329	326	Brockton, MA	1,805	400	Hesperia, CA	1,181
254	Largo, FL	2,327	327	Palm Bay, FL	1,786	401	Somerville, MA	1,178
255	West Jordan, UT	2,314	328	Whittier, CA	1,779	402	Sugar Land, TX	1,176
256	Fremont, CA	2,303	329	Olathe, KS	1,774	403	Tustin, CA	1,167
256	Hammond, IN	2,303	330	Naperville, IL	1,768	404	Norwalk, CA	1,156
258	Bloomington, IN	2,300	331	Santa Clarita, CA	1,766	405	El Monte, CA	1,136
258	Santa Monica, CA	2,300	332	Suffolk, VA	1,757	405	Hawthorne, CA	1,136
260	Corona, CA	2,298	333	Upper Darby Twnshp, PA	1,744	407	Napa, CA	1,132
261	Cheektowaga, NY	2,294	334	Amherst, NY	1,736	408	Clifton, NJ	1,131
262	College Station, TX	2,289	335	Warwick, RI	1,734	409	New Rochelle, NY	1,100
263	Elk Grove, CA	2,282	336	Broken Arrow, OK	1,728	410	Canton Twnshp, MI	1,094
264	Concord, CA	2,268	336	Sandy Springs, GA	1,728	411	Quincy, MA	1,087
265	Garden Grove, CA	2,242	338	Vallejo, CA	1,716	412	O'Fallon, MO	1,061
266	Coral Springs, FL	2,238	339	Newport Beach, CA	1,702	413	Cicero, IL	1,042
267	Redding, CA	2,237	340	Temecula, CA	1,700	414	Murrieta, CA	1,031
268	Racine, WI	2,227	341	Hayward, CA	1,693	415	Trenton, NJ	993
269	Camden, NJ	2,226	341	Nashua, NH	1,693	416	Mission Viejo, CA	983
270	Lewisville, TX	2,223	343	Hillsboro, OR	1,683	417	Brick Twnshp, NJ	960
271	Flint, MI	2,220	344	Lee's Summit, MO	1,676	418	Centennial, CO	957
272	West Covina, CA	2,212	345	Hoover, AL	1,663	419	Newton, MA	942
273	Brooklyn Park, MN	2,203	346	Cary, NC	1,658	420	Redwood City, CA	918
274	Santa Clara, CA	2,202	347	Deerfield Beach, FL	1,651	421	San Marcos, CA	908
275	Yuma, AZ	2,196	348	Sparks, NV	1,600	422	Bellflower, CA	907
276	Salinas, CA	2,189	349	Champaign, IL	1,599	423	Menifee, CA	901
277	Escondido, CA	2,156	350	Livonia, MI	1,589	424	Farmington Hills, MI	895
278	Carrollton, TX	2,152	351	Tracy, CA	1,585	425	Arlington Heights, IL	892
279	Bryan, TX	2,130	352	Decatur, IL	1,581	426	Baldwin Park, CA	883
280	Santa Barbara, CA	2,124	353	Clinton Twnshp, MI	1,576	427	Meridian, ID	863
281	Fargo, ND	2,120	354	Antioch, CA	1,571	428	Lakewood Twnshp, NJ	786
282	Mission, TX	2,094	355	Longmont, CO	1,559	429	Lawrence, MA	773
283	Victorville, CA	2,086	355	Lynn, MA	1,559	430	Lake Forest, CA	763
284	McKinney, TX	2,085	357	Richmond, CA	1,533	431	Ramapo, NY	740
285	Greece, NY	2,081	358	Rialto, CA	1,524	432	Carmel, IN	729
286	Westminster, CO	2,077	359	Santa Maria, CA	1,510	433	Fishers, IN	626
287	Orem, UT	2,069	360	Reading, PA	1,501	434	Chino Hills, CA	624
288	Boca Raton, FL	2,067	361	Stamford, CT	1,498	435	Johns Creek, GA	432
289	Kennewick, WA	2,056	362	Westland, MI	1,470	NA	Toledo, OH**	NA
			363	Inglewood, CA	1,459	NA	Tucson, AZ**	NA

Source: Reported data from the F.B.I. "Crime in the United States 2011"
*Larceny-theft is the unlawful taking of property. Attempts are included.
**Not available.

Alpha Order - City

74. Larceny-Theft Rate in 2011
National Rate = 1,976.9 Larceny-Thefts per 100,000 Population*

RANK	CITY	RATE
174	Abilene, TX	2,587.7
136	Akron, OH	2,905.8
27	Albany, GA	4,045.7
58	Albany, NY	3,574.9
69	Albuquerque, NM	3,472.7
299	Alexandria, VA	1,769.3
320	Alhambra, CA	1,620.2
175	Allentown, PA	2,568.2
361	Allen, TX	1,403.2
70	Amarillo, TX	3,469.8
344	Amherst, NY	1,476.1
301	Anaheim, CA	1,753.0
172	Anchorage, AK	2,609.8
313	Ann Arbor, MI	1,684.7
338	Antioch, CA	1,516.8
403	Arlington Heights, IL	1,184.2
110	Arlington, TX	3,150.9
275	Arvada, CO	1,895.9
77	Asheville, NC	3,404.4
152	Athens-Clarke, GA	2,794.7
26	Atlanta, GA	4,059.4
249	Aurora, CO	2,074.4
366	Aurora, IL	1,380.4
23	Austin, TX	4,097.7
38	Avondale, AZ	3,847.8
209	Bakersfield, CA	2,310.5
411	Baldwin Park, CA	1,157.6
159	Baltimore, MD	2,713.6
75	Baton Rouge, LA	3,431.0
56	Beaumont, TX	3,589.8
332	Beaverton, OR	1,553.6
228	Bellevue, WA	2,232.8
407	Bellflower, CA	1,170.1
55	Bellingham, WA	3,604.2
178	Bend, OR	2,553.7
118	Berkeley, CA	3,037.7
279	Bethlehem, PA	1,867.8
65	Billings, MT	3,510.2
8	Birmingham, AL	4,933.9
321	Bloomington, IL	1,602.0
142	Bloomington, IN	2,846.0
82	Bloomington, MN	3,367.5
192	Boca Raton, FL	2,416.4
247	Boise, ID	2,090.5
224	Boston, MA	2,263.4
270	Boulder, CO	1,916.6
393	Brick Twnshp, NJ	1,274.5
244	Bridgeport, CT	2,093.5
271	Brockton, MA	1,912.5
304	Broken Arrow, OK	1,729.6
138	Brooklyn Park, MN	2,884.8
32	Brownsville, TX	3,925.4
157	Bryan, TX	2,737.6
339	Buena Park, CA	1,509.6
84	Buffalo, NY	3,318.7
285	Burbank, CA	1,842.1
206	Cambridge, MA	2,329.8
140	Camden, NJ	2,868.4
401	Canton Twnshp, MI	1,214.1
288	Cape Coral, FL	1,825.4
386	Carlsbad, CA	1,290.3
430	Carmel, IN	915.9
298	Carrollton, TX	1,769.7
347	Carson, CA	1,465.6
402	Cary, NC	1,210.7
151	Cedar Rapids, IA	2,808.1
429	Centennial, CO	937.1
263	Champaign, IL	1,966.8
195	Chandler, AZ	2,397.4
188	Charleston, SC	2,434.1
160	Charlotte, NC	2,707.0
17	Chattanooga, TN	4,337.2

RANK	CITY	RATE
137	Cheektowaga, NY	2,896.7
184	Chesapeake, VA	2,490.8
164	Chicago, IL	2,676.8
335	Chico, CA	1,533.3
433	Chino Hills, CA	824.5
311	Chino, CA	1,699.6
373	Chula Vista, CA	1,343.7
395	Cicero, IL	1,238.4
18	Cincinnati, OH	4,210.5
145	Citrus Heights, CA	2,831.0
305	Clarkstown, NY	1,729.3
260	Clarksville, TN	1,987.7
128	Clearwater, FL	2,979.3
168	Cleveland, OH	2,650.2
374	Clifton, NJ	1,339.8
319	Clinton Twnshp, MI	1,629.4
162	Clovis, CA	2,695.5
197	College Station, TX	2,388.6
182	Colonie, NY	2,508.0
163	Colorado Springs, CO	2,684.8
117	Columbia, MO	3,051.6
19	Columbus, GA	4,189.0
39	Columbus, OH	3,841.9
398	Compton, CA	1,231.7
286	Concord, CA	1,836.4
109	Concord, NC	3,157.3
289	Coral Springs, FL	1,823.3
342	Corona, CA	1,490.6
43	Corpus Christi, TX	3,774.3
185	Costa Mesa, CA	2,465.6
296	Cranston, RI	1,772.3
139	Dallas, TX	2,873.9
390	Daly City, CA	1,278.4
351	Danbury, CT	1,459.7
61	Davenport, IA	3,521.7
144	Davie, FL	2,831.2
96	Dayton, OH	3,226.0
153	Dearborn, MI	2,758.0
251	Decatur, IL	2,070.7
234	Deerfield Beach, FL	2,171.2
222	Denton, TX	2,273.5
211	Denver, CO	2,299.3
52	Des Moines, IA	3,618.6
210	Detroit, MI	2,307.2
292	Downey, CA	1,816.3
30	Duluth, MN	3,938.8
134	Durham, NC	2,927.0
13	Edinburg, TX	4,656.9
392	Edison Twnshp, NJ	1,275.2
331	Edmond, OK	1,555.7
355	El Cajon, CA	1,433.7
425	El Monte, CA	989.5
265	El Paso, TX	1,961.0
381	Elgin, IL	1,313.2
240	Elizabeth, NJ	2,106.3
346	Elk Grove, CA	1,474.0
203	Erie, PA	2,354.3
343	Escondido, CA	1,480.7
48	Eugene, OR	3,713.7
63	Evansville, IN	3,516.9
5	Everett, WA	5,175.1
268	Fairfield, CA	1,928.5
223	Fall River, MA	2,267.4
261	Fargo, ND	1,975.2
414	Farmington Hills, MI	1,123.2
28	Fayetteville, NC	3,982.1
434	Fishers, IN	811.0
235	Flint, MI	2,168.9
400	Fontana, CA	1,215.4
190	Fort Collins, CO	2,425.4
37	Fort Lauderdale, FL	3,867.6
35	Fort Smith, AR	3,901.6

RANK	CITY	RATE
167	Fort Wayne, IN	2,654.3
125	Fort Worth, TX	2,988.5
419	Fremont, CA	1,063.2
127	Fresno, CA	2,982.7
326	Frisco, TX	1,572.2
281	Fullerton, CA	1,863.3
102	Gainesville, FL	3,175.7
383	Garden Grove, CA	1,296.8
183	Garland, TX	2,501.2
198	Gary, IN	2,386.5
368	Gilbert, AZ	1,369.9
12	Glendale, AZ	4,713.6
385	Glendale, CA	1,291.9
191	Grand Prairie, TX	2,417.8
250	Grand Rapids, MI	2,074.0
236	Greece, NY	2,155.9
180	Greeley, CO	2,515.2
297	Green Bay, WI	1,772.1
154	Gresham, OR	2,757.7
372	Hamilton Twnshp, NJ	1,349.7
143	Hammond, IN	2,834.7
122	Hampton, VA	3,005.5
161	Hartford, CT	2,697.5
377	Hawthorne, CA	1,332.0
410	Hayward, CA	1,160.5
194	Hemet, CA	2,401.3
405	Henderson, NV	1,180.8
384	Hesperia, CA	1,294.5
193	Hialeah, FL	2,403.3
83	High Point, NC	3,358.7
290	Hillsboro, OR	1,817.8
53	Hollywood, FL	3,618.4
258	Hoover, AL	2,027.8
98	Houston, TX	3,200.0
280	Huntington Beach, CA	1,864.5
68	Huntsville, AL	3,484.5
24	Independence, MO	4,080.8
100	Indianapolis, IN	3,191.7
277	Indio, CA	1,888.7
380	Inglewood, CA	1,314.9
397	Irvine, CA	1,232.8
248	Irving, TX	2,078.4
114	Jacksonville, FL	3,083.9
41	Jackson, MS	3,807.8
364	Jersey City, NJ	1,384.3
435	Johns Creek, GA	555.7
282	Joliet, IL	1,860.3
89	Kansas City, KS	3,266.3
85	Kansas City, MO	3,316.7
156	Kennewick, WA	2,738.5
205	Kenosha, WI	2,337.2
104	Kent, WA	3,171.7
217	Killeen, TX	2,288.4
4	Knoxville, TN	5,271.8
22	Lafayette, LA	4,140.4
427	Lake Forest, CA	976.1
50	Lakeland, FL	3,657.7
432	Lakewood Twnshp, NJ	843.8
323	Lakewood, CA	1,599.0
87	Lakewood, CO	3,279.7
409	Lancaster, CA	1,163.0
243	Lansing, MI	2,098.7
81	Laredo, TX	3,378.0
131	Largo, FL	2,956.6
97	Las Cruces, NM	3,205.3
340	Las Vegas, NV	1,506.8
64	Lawrence, KS	3,512.5
423	Lawrence, MA	1,005.9
74	Lawton, OK	3,437.0
310	League City, TX	1,703.0
287	Lee's Summit, MO	1,827.8
218	Lewisville, TX	2,284.8

296 Cities

Alpha Order - City (continued)

RANK	CITY	RATE
119	Lexington, KY	3,033.8
95	Lincoln, NE	3,231.5
7	Little Rock, AR	5,003.4
329	Livermore, CA	1,566.2
318	Livonia, MI	1,640.4
328	Long Beach, CA	1,567.1
295	Longmont, CO	1,776.2
86	Longview, TX	3,292.8
363	Los Angeles, CA	1,393.4
93	Louisville, KY	3,241.4
293	Lowell, MA	1,811.2
78	Lubbock, TX	3,402.2
189	Lynchburg, VA	2,425.8
307	Lynn, MA	1,715.4
3	Macon, GA	5,514.6
170	Madison, WI	2,626.5
141	Manchester, NH	2,858.5
34	McAllen, TX	3,909.2
330	McKinney, TX	1,557.4
14	Medford, OR	4,458.2
33	Melbourne, FL	3,918.0
31	Memphis, TN	3,932.3
412	Menifee, CA	1,148.8
177	Merced, CA	2,558.6
413	Meridian, ID	1,136.7
176	Mesa, AZ	2,561.9
132	Mesquite, TX	2,939.8
1	Miami Beach, FL	8,809.2
120	Miami Gardens, FL	3,010.3
46	Miami, FL	3,724.4
238	Midland, TX	2,145.6
108	Milwaukee, WI	3,161.9
99	Minneapolis, MN	3,193.1
324	Miramar, FL	1,591.7
420	Mission Viejo, CA	1,041.3
165	Mission, TX	2,661.4
60	Mobile, AL	3,530.0
166	Modesto, CA	2,658.1
76	Montgomery, AL	3,406.5
358	Moreno Valley, CA	1,414.3
124	Murfreesboro, TN	2,991.7
426	Murrieta, CA	984.9
225	Nampa, ID	2,260.5
352	Napa, CA	1,454.7
394	Naperville, IL	1,242.6
266	Nashua, NH	1,954.8
90	Nashville, TN	3,261.6
239	New Bedford, MA	2,109.8
103	New Haven, CT	3,171.8
230	New Orleans, LA	2,195.0
357	New Rochelle, NY	1,421.0
367	New York, NY	1,374.4
359	Newark, NJ	1,410.1
262	Newport Beach, CA	1,974.8
181	Newport News, VA	2,511.0
415	Newton, MA	1,099.6
44	Norfolk, VA	3,751.3
202	Norman, OK	2,369.1
20	North Charleston, SC	4,149.8
417	Norwalk, CA	1,082.5
314	Norwalk, CT	1,682.6
199	Oakland, CA	2,385.2
322	Oceanside, CA	1,599.5
216	Odessa, TX	2,289.2
376	O'Fallon, MO	1,332.6
36	Ogden, UT	3,884.0
72	Oklahoma City, OK	3,445.7
362	Olathe, KS	1,400.5
112	Omaha, NE	3,100.5
284	Ontario, CA	1,843.2
353	Orange, CA	1,449.8
212	Orem, UT	2,298.0
9	Orlando, FL	4,830.9
283	Overland Park, KS	1,855.3
389	Oxnard, CA	1,280.1
309	Palm Bay, FL	1,707.5
396	Palmdale, CA	1,233.3
306	Pasadena, CA	1,717.0
187	Pasadena, TX	2,449.7
387	Paterson, NJ	1,287.1
365	Pearland, TX	1,383.5
215	Pembroke Pines, FL	2,289.3
237	Peoria, AZ	2,150.5
123	Peoria, IL	2,999.5
171	Philadelphia, PA	2,620.3
173	Phoenix, AZ	2,609.5
227	Pittsburgh, PA	2,234.9
267	Plano, TX	1,953.2
79	Plantation, FL	3,401.3
308	Pomona, CA	1,709.4
42	Pompano Beach, FL	3,806.1
333	Port St. Lucie, FL	1,552.3
40	Portland, OR	3,812.6
45	Portsmouth, VA	3,747.6
246	Provo, UT	2,093.2
107	Pueblo, CO	3,166.4
406	Quincy, MA	1,170.9
150	Racine, WI	2,811.7
219	Raleigh, NC	2,284.3
431	Ramapo, NY	876.2
356	Rancho Cucamon., CA	1,423.9
312	Reading, PA	1,698.7
186	Redding, CA	2,460.5
404	Redwood City, CA	1,181.2
274	Reno, NV	1,898.1
129	Renton, WA	2,975.5
337	Rialto, CA	1,518.9
273	Richardson, TX	1,909.0
350	Richmond, CA	1,461.1
146	Richmond, VA	2,822.6
369	Rio Rancho, NM	1,365.0
256	Riverside, CA	2,042.0
67	Roanoke, VA	3,487.1
315	Rochester, MN	1,681.3
94	Rochester, NY	3,238.1
113	Rockford, IL	3,095.3
208	Roseville, CA	2,318.1
360	Roswell, GA	1,409.9
264	Round Rock, TX	1,962.0
204	Sacramento, CA	2,349.1
130	Salem, OR	2,969.6
354	Salinas, CA	1,438.1
6	Salt Lake City, UT	5,080.0
147	San Angelo, TX	2,821.5
15	San Antonio, TX	4,400.4
245	San Bernardino, CA	2,093.3
375	San Diego, CA	1,337.2
126	San Francisco, CA	2,983.2
379	San Jose, CA	1,319.5
221	San Leandro, CA	2,276.9
418	San Marcos, CA	1,071.2
382	San Mateo, CA	1,309.6
291	Sandy Springs, GA	1,817.2
229	Sandy, UT	2,227.7
388	Santa Ana, CA	1,285.9
200	Santa Barbara, CA	2,374.5
278	Santa Clara, CA	1,868.7
424	Santa Clarita, CA	989.9
341	Santa Maria, CA	1,499.2
179	Santa Monica, CA	2,533.3
317	Santa Rosa, CA	1,645.6
135	Savannah, GA	2,918.4
213	Scottsdale, AZ	2,292.5
201	Scranton, PA	2,371.2
66	Seattle, WA	3,491.5
106	Shreveport, LA	3,167.5
422	Simi Valley, CA	1,016.7
105	Sioux City, IA	3,170.2
220	Sioux Falls, SD	2,281.7
334	Somerville, MA	1,545.6
80	South Bend, IN	3,380.0
370	South Gate, CA	1,354.9
300	Sparks, NV	1,757.8
29	Spokane Valley, WA	3,963.2
10	Spokane, WA	4,821.5
16	Springfield, IL	4,353.3
169	Springfield, MA	2,644.3
2	Springfield, MO	7,115.9
399	Stamford, CT	1,219.2
325	Sterling Heights, MI	1,579.5
88	Stockton, CA	3,270.0
46	St. Joseph, MO	3,724.4
11	St. Louis, MO	4,769.8
196	St. Paul, MN	2,395.1
73	St. Petersburg, FL	3,443.7
255	Suffolk, VA	2,052.7
349	Sugar Land, TX	1,461.3
428	Sunnyvale, CA	953.2
133	Sunrise, FL	2,933.8
327	Surprise, AZ	1,571.6
226	Syracuse, NY	2,236.3
57	Tacoma, WA	3,586.9
111	Tallahassee, FL	3,126.5
252	Tampa, FL	2,069.4
316	Temecula, CA	1,678.6
21	Tempe, AZ	4,148.6
232	Thornton, CO	2,188.0
416	Thousand Oaks, CA	1,099.3
NA	Toledo, OH**	NA
158	Toms River Twnshp, NJ	2,729.9
25	Topeka, KS	4,063.7
378	Torrance, CA	1,330.0
276	Tracy, CA	1,889.2
408	Trenton, NJ	1,165.5
303	Troy, MI	1,732.6
NA	Tucson, AZ**	NA
116	Tulsa, OK	3,063.9
91	Tuscaloosa, AL	3,259.5
336	Tustin, CA	1,526.9
71	Tyler, TX	3,459.7
242	Upper Darby Twnshp, PA	2,099.7
371	Vacaville, CA	1,352.7
348	Vallejo, CA	1,462.9
148	Vancouver, WA	2,816.9
214	Ventura, CA	2,291.9
294	Victorville, CA	1,778.9
233	Virginia Beach, VA	2,176.1
155	Visalia, CA	2,752.9
391	Vista, CA	1,277.7
54	Waco, TX	3,604.3
345	Warren, MI	1,474.4
241	Warwick, RI	2,100.0
92	Washington, DC	3,256.3
121	Waterbury, CT	3,008.0
253	West Covina, CA	2,060.6
231	West Jordan, UT	2,188.9
51	West Palm Beach, FL	3,638.4
149	West Valley, UT	2,811.8
302	Westland, MI	1,749.4
259	Westminster, CA	1,999.9
269	Westminster, CO	1,923.8
253	Whittier, CA	2,060.6
101	Wichita Falls, TX	3,183.0
62	Wichita, KS	3,521.3
59	Wilmington, NC	3,564.1
49	Winston-Salem, NC	3,664.9
257	Woodbridge Twnshp, NJ	2,031.7
272	Worcester, MA	1,911.1
115	Yakima, WA	3,071.5
421	Yonkers, NY	1,024.6
207	Yuma, AZ	2,326.7

Source: CQ Press using reported data from the F.B.I. "Crime in the United States 2011"
*Larceny-theft is the unlawful taking of property. Attempts are included.
**Not available.

Rank Order - City

74. Larceny-Theft Rate in 2011 (continued)
National Rate = 1,976.9 Larceny-Thefts per 100,000 Population*

RANK	CITY	RATE
1	Miami Beach, FL	8,809.2
2	Springfield, MO	7,115.9
3	Macon, GA	5,514.6
4	Knoxville, TN	5,271.8
5	Everett, WA	5,175.1
6	Salt Lake City, UT	5,080.0
7	Little Rock, AR	5,003.4
8	Birmingham, AL	4,933.9
9	Orlando, FL	4,830.9
10	Spokane, WA	4,821.5
11	St. Louis, MO	4,769.8
12	Glendale, AZ	4,713.6
13	Edinburg, TX	4,656.9
14	Medford, OR	4,458.2
15	San Antonio, TX	4,400.4
16	Springfield, IL	4,353.3
17	Chattanooga, TN	4,337.2
18	Cincinnati, OH	4,210.5
19	Columbus, GA	4,189.0
20	North Charleston, SC	4,149.8
21	Tempe, AZ	4,148.6
22	Lafayette, LA	4,140.4
23	Austin, TX	4,097.7
24	Independence, MO	4,080.8
25	Topeka, KS	4,063.7
26	Atlanta, GA	4,059.4
27	Albany, GA	4,045.7
28	Fayetteville, NC	3,982.1
29	Spokane Valley, WA	3,963.2
30	Duluth, MN	3,938.8
31	Memphis, TN	3,932.3
32	Brownsville, TX	3,925.4
33	Melbourne, FL	3,918.0
34	McAllen, TX	3,909.2
35	Fort Smith, AR	3,901.6
36	Ogden, UT	3,884.0
37	Fort Lauderdale, FL	3,867.6
38	Avondale, AZ	3,847.8
39	Columbus, OH	3,841.9
40	Portland, OR	3,812.6
41	Jackson, MS	3,807.8
42	Pompano Beach, FL	3,806.1
43	Corpus Christi, TX	3,774.3
44	Norfolk, VA	3,751.3
45	Portsmouth, VA	3,747.6
46	Miami, FL	3,724.4
46	St. Joseph, MO	3,724.4
48	Eugene, OR	3,713.7
49	Winston-Salem, NC	3,664.9
50	Lakeland, FL	3,657.7
51	West Palm Beach, FL	3,638.4
52	Des Moines, IA	3,618.6
53	Hollywood, FL	3,618.4
54	Waco, TX	3,604.3
55	Bellingham, WA	3,604.2
56	Beaumont, TX	3,589.8
57	Tacoma, WA	3,586.9
58	Albany, NY	3,574.9
59	Wilmington, NC	3,564.1
60	Mobile, AL	3,530.6
61	Davenport, IA	3,521.7
62	Wichita, KS	3,521.3
63	Evansville, IN	3,516.9
64	Lawrence, KS	3,512.5
65	Billings, MT	3,510.2
66	Seattle, WA	3,491.5
67	Roanoke, VA	3,487.1
68	Huntsville, AL	3,484.5
69	Albuquerque, NM	3,472.7
70	Amarillo, TX	3,469.8
71	Tyler, TX	3,459.7
72	Oklahoma City, OK	3,445.7
73	St. Petersburg, FL	3,443.7
74	Lawton, OK	3,437.0
75	Baton Rouge, LA	3,431.0
76	Montgomery, AL	3,406.5
77	Asheville, NC	3,404.4
78	Lubbock, TX	3,402.2
79	Plantation, FL	3,401.3
80	South Bend, IN	3,380.0
81	Laredo, TX	3,378.0
82	Bloomington, MN	3,367.5
83	High Point, NC	3,358.7
84	Buffalo, NY	3,318.7
85	Kansas City, MO	3,316.7
86	Longview, TX	3,292.8
87	Lakewood, CO	3,279.7
88	Stockton, CA	3,270.0
89	Kansas City, KS	3,266.3
90	Nashville, TN	3,261.6
91	Tuscaloosa, AL	3,259.5
92	Washington, DC	3,256.3
93	Louisville, KY	3,241.4
94	Rochester, NY	3,238.1
95	Lincoln, NE	3,231.5
96	Dayton, OH	3,226.0
97	Las Cruces, NM	3,205.3
98	Houston, TX	3,200.0
99	Minneapolis, MN	3,193.3
100	Indianapolis, IN	3,191.7
101	Wichita Falls, TX	3,183.0
102	Gainesville, FL	3,175.7
103	New Haven, CT	3,171.8
104	Kent, WA	3,171.7
105	Sioux City, IA	3,170.2
106	Shreveport, LA	3,167.5
107	Pueblo, CO	3,166.4
108	Milwaukee, WI	3,161.9
109	Concord, NC	3,157.3
110	Arlington, TX	3,150.9
111	Tallahassee, FL	3,126.5
112	Omaha, NE	3,100.5
113	Rockford, IL	3,095.3
114	Jacksonville, FL	3,083.9
115	Yakima, WA	3,071.5
116	Tulsa, OK	3,063.9
117	Columbia, MO	3,051.6
118	Berkeley, CA	3,037.7
119	Lexington, KY	3,033.8
120	Miami Gardens, FL	3,010.3
121	Waterbury, CT	3,008.0
122	Hampton, VA	3,005.5
123	Peoria, IL	2,999.5
124	Murfreesboro, TN	2,991.7
125	Fort Worth, TX	2,988.5
126	San Francisco, CA	2,983.2
127	Fresno, CA	2,982.7
128	Clearwater, FL	2,979.3
129	Renton, WA	2,975.5
130	Salem, OR	2,969.6
131	Largo, FL	2,956.6
132	Mesquite, TX	2,939.8
133	Sunrise, FL	2,933.8
134	Durham, NC	2,927.0
135	Savannah, GA	2,918.4
136	Akron, OH	2,905.8
137	Cheektowaga, NY	2,896.7
138	Brooklyn Park, MN	2,884.8
139	Dallas, TX	2,873.9
140	Camden, NJ	2,868.4
141	Manchester, NH	2,858.5
142	Bloomington, IN	2,846.0
143	Hammond, IN	2,834.7
144	Davie, FL	2,831.2
145	Citrus Heights, CA	2,831.0
146	Richmond, VA	2,822.6
147	San Angelo, TX	2,821.5
148	Vancouver, WA	2,816.9
149	West Valley, UT	2,811.8
150	Racine, WI	2,811.7
151	Cedar Rapids, IA	2,808.1
152	Athens-Clarke, GA	2,794.7
153	Dearborn, MI	2,758.0
154	Gresham, OR	2,757.7
155	Visalia, CA	2,752.9
156	Kennewick, WA	2,738.5
157	Bryan, TX	2,737.6
158	Toms River Twnshp, NJ	2,729.9
159	Baltimore, MD	2,713.6
160	Charlotte, NC	2,707.0
161	Hartford, CT	2,697.5
162	Clovis, CA	2,695.5
163	Colorado Springs, CO	2,684.8
164	Chicago, IL	2,676.8
165	Mission, TX	2,661.4
166	Modesto, CA	2,658.1
167	Fort Wayne, IN	2,654.3
168	Cleveland, OH	2,650.2
169	Springfield, MA	2,644.3
170	Madison, WI	2,626.5
171	Philadelphia, PA	2,620.3
172	Anchorage, AK	2,609.8
173	Phoenix, AZ	2,609.5
174	Abilene, TX	2,587.7
175	Allentown, PA	2,568.2
176	Mesa, AZ	2,561.9
177	Merced, CA	2,558.6
178	Bend, OR	2,553.7
179	Santa Monica, CA	2,533.3
180	Greeley, CO	2,515.2
181	Newport News, VA	2,511.0
182	Colonie, NY	2,508.0
183	Garland, TX	2,501.2
184	Chesapeake, VA	2,490.8
185	Costa Mesa, CA	2,465.6
186	Redding, CA	2,460.5
187	Pasadena, TX	2,449.7
188	Charleston, SC	2,434.1
189	Lynchburg, VA	2,425.8
190	Fort Collins, CO	2,425.4
191	Grand Prairie, TX	2,417.8
192	Boca Raton, FL	2,416.4
193	Hialeah, FL	2,403.3
194	Hemet, CA	2,401.3
195	Chandler, AZ	2,397.4
196	St. Paul, MN	2,395.1
197	College Station, TX	2,388.6
198	Gary, IN	2,386.5
199	Oakland, CA	2,385.2
200	Santa Barbara, CA	2,374.5
201	Scranton, PA	2,371.2
202	Norman, OK	2,369.1
203	Erie, PA	2,354.3
204	Sacramento, CA	2,349.1
205	Kenosha, WI	2,337.2
206	Cambridge, MA	2,329.8
207	Yuma, AZ	2,326.7
208	Roseville, CA	2,318.1
209	Bakersfield, CA	2,310.5
210	Detroit, MI	2,307.2
211	Denver, CO	2,299.3
212	Orem, UT	2,298.0
213	Scottsdale, AZ	2,292.5
214	Ventura, CA	2,291.9
215	Pembroke Pines, FL	2,289.3
216	Odessa, TX	2,289.2

Rank Order - City (continued)

RANK	CITY	RATE	RANK	CITY	RATE	RANK	CITY	RATE
217	Killeen, TX	2,288.4	290	Hillsboro, OR	1,817.8	364	Jersey City, NJ	1,384.3
218	Lewisville, TX	2,284.8	291	Sandy Springs, GA	1,817.2	365	Pearland, TX	1,383.5
219	Raleigh, NC	2,284.3	292	Downey, CA	1,816.3	366	Aurora, IL	1,380.4
220	Sioux Falls, SD	2,281.7	293	Lowell, MA	1,811.2	367	New York, NY	1,374.4
221	San Leandro, CA	2,276.9	294	Victorville, CA	1,778.9	368	Gilbert, AZ	1,369.9
222	Denton, TX	2,273.5	295	Longmont, CO	1,776.2	369	Rio Rancho, NM	1,365.0
223	Fall River, MA	2,267.4	296	Cranston, RI	1,772.3	370	South Gate, CA	1,354.9
224	Boston, MA	2,263.4	297	Green Bay, WI	1,772.1	371	Vacaville, CA	1,352.7
225	Nampa, ID	2,260.5	298	Carrollton, TX	1,769.7	372	Hamilton Twnshp, NJ	1,349.7
226	Syracuse, NY	2,236.3	299	Alexandria, VA	1,769.3	373	Chula Vista, CA	1,343.7
227	Pittsburgh, PA	2,234.9	300	Sparks, NV	1,757.8	374	Clifton, NJ	1,339.8
228	Bellevue, WA	2,232.8	301	Anaheim, CA	1,753.0	375	San Diego, CA	1,337.2
229	Sandy, UT	2,227.7	302	Westland, MI	1,749.4	376	O'Fallon, MO	1,332.6
230	New Orleans, LA	2,195.0	303	Troy, MI	1,732.6	377	Hawthorne, CA	1,332.0
231	West Jordan, UT	2,188.9	304	Broken Arrow, OK	1,729.6	378	Torrance, CA	1,330.0
232	Thornton, CO	2,188.0	305	Clarkstown, NY	1,729.3	379	San Jose, CA	1,319.5
233	Virginia Beach, VA	2,176.1	306	Pasadena, CA	1,717.0	380	Inglewood, CA	1,314.9
234	Deerfield Beach, FL	2,171.2	307	Lynn, MA	1,715.4	381	Elgin, IL	1,313.2
235	Flint, MI	2,168.9	308	Pomona, CA	1,709.4	382	San Mateo, CA	1,309.6
236	Greece, NY	2,155.9	309	Palm Bay, FL	1,707.5	383	Garden Grove, CA	1,296.8
237	Peoria, AZ	2,150.5	310	League City, TX	1,703.0	384	Hesperia, CA	1,294.5
238	Midland, TX	2,145.6	311	Chino, CA	1,699.6	385	Glendale, CA	1,291.9
239	New Bedford, MA	2,109.8	312	Reading, PA	1,698.7	386	Carlsbad, CA	1,290.3
240	Elizabeth, NJ	2,106.3	313	Ann Arbor, MI	1,684.7	387	Paterson, NJ	1,287.1
241	Warwick, RI	2,100.0	314	Norwalk, CT	1,682.6	388	Santa Ana, CA	1,285.9
242	Upper Darby Twnshp, PA	2,099.7	315	Rochester, MN	1,681.3	389	Oxnard, CA	1,280.1
243	Lansing, MI	2,098.7	316	Temecula, CA	1,678.6	390	Daly City, CA	1,278.4
244	Bridgeport, CT	2,093.5	317	Santa Rosa, CA	1,645.6	391	Vista, CA	1,277.7
245	San Bernardino, CA	2,093.3	318	Livonia, MI	1,640.4	392	Edison Twnshp, NJ	1,275.2
246	Provo, UT	2,093.2	319	Clinton Twnshp, MI	1,629.4	393	Brick Twnshp, NJ	1,274.5
247	Boise, ID	2,090.5	320	Alhambra, CA	1,620.2	394	Naperville, IL	1,242.6
248	Irving, TX	2,078.4	321	Bloomington, IL	1,602.0	395	Cicero, IL	1,238.4
249	Aurora, CO	2,074.4	322	Oceanside, CA	1,599.5	396	Palmdale, CA	1,233.3
250	Grand Rapids, MI	2,074.0	323	Lakewood, CA	1,599.0	397	Irvine, CA	1,232.8
251	Decatur, IL	2,070.7	324	Miramar, FL	1,591.7	398	Compton, CA	1,231.7
252	Tampa, FL	2,069.4	325	Sterling Heights, MI	1,579.5	399	Stamford, CT	1,219.2
253	West Covina, CA	2,060.6	326	Frisco, TX	1,572.2	400	Fontana, CA	1,215.4
253	Whittier, CA	2,060.6	327	Surprise, AZ	1,571.6	401	Canton Twnshp, MI	1,214.1
255	Suffolk, VA	2,052.7	328	Long Beach, CA	1,567.1	402	Cary, NC	1,210.7
256	Riverside, CA	2,042.0	329	Livermore, CA	1,566.2	403	Arlington Heights, IL	1,184.2
257	Woodbridge Twnshp, NJ	2,031.7	330	McKinney, TX	1,557.4	404	Redwood City, CA	1,181.2
258	Hoover, AL	2,027.8	331	Edmond, OK	1,555.7	405	Henderson, NV	1,180.8
259	Westminster, CA	1,999.9	332	Beaverton, OR	1,553.6	406	Quincy, MA	1,170.9
260	Clarksville, TN	1,987.7	333	Port St. Lucie, FL	1,552.3	407	Bellflower, CA	1,170.1
261	Fargo, ND	1,975.2	334	Somerville, MA	1,545.6	408	Trenton, NJ	1,165.5
262	Newport Beach, CA	1,974.8	335	Chico, CA	1,533.3	409	Lancaster, CA	1,163.0
263	Champaign, IL	1,966.8	336	Tustin, CA	1,526.9	410	Hayward, CA	1,160.5
264	Round Rock, TX	1,962.0	337	Rialto, CA	1,518.9	411	Baldwin Park, CA	1,157.6
265	El Paso, TX	1,961.0	338	Antioch, CA	1,516.8	412	Menifee, CA	1,148.8
266	Nashua, NH	1,954.8	339	Buena Park, CA	1,509.6	413	Meridian, ID	1,136.7
267	Plano, TX	1,953.2	340	Las Vegas, NV	1,506.8	414	Farmington Hills, MI	1,123.2
268	Fairfield, CA	1,928.5	341	Santa Maria, CA	1,499.2	415	Newton, MA	1,099.6
269	Westminster, CO	1,923.8	342	Corona, CA	1,490.6	416	Thousand Oaks, CA	1,099.3
270	Boulder, CO	1,916.6	343	Escondido, CA	1,480.7	417	Norwalk, CA	1,082.5
271	Brockton, MA	1,912.5	344	Amherst, NY	1,476.1	418	San Marcos, CA	1,071.2
272	Worcester, MA	1,911.1	345	Warren, MI	1,474.4	419	Fremont, CA	1,063.2
273	Richardson, TX	1,909.0	346	Elk Grove, CA	1,474.0	420	Mission Viejo, CA	1,041.3
274	Reno, NV	1,898.1	347	Carson, CA	1,465.6	421	Yonkers, NY	1,024.6
275	Arvada, CO	1,895.9	348	Vallejo, CA	1,462.9	422	Simi Valley, CA	1,016.7
276	Tracy, CA	1,889.2	349	Sugar Land, TX	1,461.3	423	Lawrence, MA	1,005.9
277	Indio, CA	1,888.7	350	Richmond, CA	1,461.1	424	Santa Clarita, CA	989.9
278	Santa Clara, CA	1,868.7	351	Danbury, CT	1,459.7	425	El Monte, CA	989.5
279	Bethlehem, PA	1,867.8	352	Napa, CA	1,454.7	426	Murrieta, CA	984.9
280	Huntington Beach, CA	1,864.5	353	Orange, CA	1,449.8	427	Lake Forest, CA	976.1
281	Fullerton, CA	1,863.3	354	Salinas, CA	1,438.1	428	Sunnyvale, CA	953.2
282	Joliet, IL	1,860.3	355	El Cajon, CA	1,433.7	429	Centennial, CO	937.1
283	Overland Park, KS	1,855.3	356	Rancho Cucamon., CA	1,423.9	430	Carmel, IN	915.9
284	Ontario, CA	1,843.2	357	New Rochelle, NY	1,421.0	431	Ramapo, NY	876.5
285	Burbank, CA	1,842.1	358	Moreno Valley, CA	1,414.3	432	Lakewood Twnshp, NJ	843.8
286	Concord, CA	1,836.4	359	Newark, NJ	1,410.1	433	Chino Hills, CA	824.5
287	Lee's Summit, MO	1,827.8	360	Roswell, GA	1,409.9	434	Fishers, IN	811.0
288	Cape Coral, FL	1,825.4	361	Allen, TX	1,403.2	435	Johns Creek, GA	555.7
289	Coral Springs, FL	1,823.3	362	Olathe, KS	1,400.5	NA	Toledo, OH**	NA
			363	Los Angeles, CA	1,393.4	NA	Tucson, AZ**	NA

Source: CQ Press using reported data from the F.B.I. "Crime in the United States 2011"
*Larceny-theft is the unlawful taking of property. Attempts are included.
**Not available.

Alpha Order - City

75. Percent Change in Larceny-Theft Rate: 2010 to 2011
National Percent Change = 1.4% Decrease*

RANK	CITY	% CHANGE	RANK	CITY	% CHANGE	RANK	CITY	% CHANGE
333	Abilene, TX	(10.3)	167	Cheektowaga, NY	0.0	73	Fort Wayne, IN	6.0
126	Akron, OH	2.1	249	Chesapeake, VA	(5.1)	230	Fort Worth, TX	(4.2)
243	Albany, GA	(4.9)	136	Chicago, IL	1.5	400	Fremont, CA	(20.8)
245	Albany, NY	(5.0)	289	Chico, CA	(7.3)	188	Fresno, CA	(1.3)
94	Albuquerque, NM	4.4	270	Chino Hills, CA	(6.5)	373	Frisco, TX	(14.7)
120	Alexandria, VA	2.4	49	Chino, CA	8.9	351	Fullerton, CA	(12.2)
254	Alhambra, CA	(5.7)	251	Chula Vista, CA	(5.4)	225	Gainesville, FL	(3.8)
384	Allentown, PA	(16.7)	NA	Cicero, IL**	NA	281	Garden Grove, CA	(7.0)
129	Allen, TX	1.9	29	Cincinnati, OH	12.8	222	Garland, TX	(3.7)
379	Amarillo, TX	(15.6)	335	Citrus Heights, CA	(10.6)	NA	Gary, IN**	NA
335	Amherst, NY	(10.6)	334	Clarkstown, NY	(10.4)	260	Gilbert, AZ	(6.0)
145	Anaheim, CA	1.1	179	Clarksville, TN	(0.4)	17	Glendale, AZ	16.4
289	Anchorage, AK	(7.3)	264	Clearwater, FL	(6.3)	292	Glendale, CA	(7.4)
390	Ann Arbor, MI	(17.6)	32	Cleveland, OH	12.0	351	Grand Prairie, TX	(12.2)
1	Antioch, CA	47.7	NA	Clifton, NJ**	NA	366	Grand Rapids, MI	(13.8)
359	Arlington Heights, IL	(12.7)	206	Clinton Twnshp, MI	(2.5)	253	Greece, NY	(5.6)
323	Arlington, TX	(9.4)	66	Clovis, CA	6.5	124	Greeley, CO	2.2
230	Arvada, CO	(4.2)	146	College Station, TX	1.0	264	Green Bay, WI	(6.3)
181	Asheville, NC	(0.5)	208	Colonie, NY	(2.8)	98	Gresham, OR	4.2
237	Athens-Clarke, GA	(4.4)	344	Colorado Springs, CO	(11.4)	263	Hamilton Twnshp, NJ	(6.1)
5	Atlanta, GA	22.8	148	Columbia, MO	0.9	274	Hammond, IN	(6.8)
204	Aurora, CO	(2.4)	367	Columbus, GA	(13.9)	114	Hampton, VA	2.7
370	Aurora, IL	(14.4)	218	Columbus, OH	(3.5)	278	Hartford, CT	(6.9)
264	Austin, TX	(6.3)	251	Compton, CA	(5.4)	162	Hawthorne, CA	0.4
4	Avondale, AZ	24.2	81	Concord, CA	5.4	133	Hayward, CA	1.7
323	Bakersfield, CA	(9.4)	278	Concord, NC	(6.9)	94	Hemet, CA	4.4
245	Baldwin Park, CA	(5.0)	77	Coral Springs, FL	5.7	308	Henderson, NV	(8.4)
66	Baltimore, MD	6.5	274	Corona, CA	(6.8)	31	Hesperia, CA	12.2
NA	Baton Rouge, LA**	NA	332	Corpus Christi, TX	(9.8)	301	Hialeah, FL	(8.0)
208	Beaumont, TX	(2.8)	40	Costa Mesa, CA	10.9	77	High Point, NC	5.7
136	Beaverton, OR	1.5	71	Cranston, RI	6.1	NA	Hillsboro, OR**	NA
196	Bellevue, WA	(1.8)	101	Dallas, TX	3.9	61	Hollywood, FL	7.7
260	Bellflower, CA	(6.0)	26	Daly City, CA	13.1	NA	Hoover, AL**	NA
171	Bellingham, WA	(0.2)	150	Danbury, CT	0.8	199	Houston, TX	(2.1)
100	Bend, OR	4.1	NA	Davenport, IA**	NA	176	Huntington Beach, CA	(0.3)
407	Berkeley, CA	(26.4)	139	Davie, FL	1.4	NA	Huntsville, AL**	NA
328	Bethlehem, PA	(9.6)	136	Dayton, OH	1.5	254	Independence, MO	(5.7)
NA	Billings, MT**	NA	388	Dearborn, MI	(17.4)	NA	Indianapolis, IN**	NA
NA	Birmingham, AL**	NA	91	Decatur, IL	4.7	2	Indio, CA	26.7
380	Bloomington, IL	(15.8)	274	Deerfield Beach, FL	(6.8)	46	Inglewood, CA	9.8
272	Bloomington, IN	(6.6)	23	Denton, TX	14.1	9	Irvine, CA	21.9
207	Bloomington, MN	(2.6)	60	Denver, CO	7.8	403	Irving, TX	(21.9)
57	Boca Raton, FL	8.0	61	Des Moines, IA	7.7	198	Jacksonville, FL	(1.9)
296	Boise, ID	(7.6)	22	Detroit, MI	14.7	221	Jackson, MS	(3.6)
208	Boston, MA	(2.8)	392	Downey, CA	(18.1)	297	Jersey City, NJ	(7.7)
345	Boulder, CO	(11.7)	156	Duluth, MN	0.5	411	Johns Creek, GA	(29.3)
139	Brick Twnshp, NJ	1.4	199	Durham, NC	(2.1)	305	Joliet, IL	(8.3)
8	Bridgeport, CT	22.3	70	Edinburg, TX	6.2	165	Kansas City, KS	0.3
79	Brockton, MA	5.5	86	Edison Twnshp, NJ	4.9	NA	Kansas City, MO**	NA
56	Broken Arrow, OK	8.2	130	Edmond, OK	1.8	264	Kennewick, WA	(6.3)
NA	Brooklyn Park, MN**	NA	397	El Cajon, CA	(19.4)	108	Kenosha, WI	3.3
318	Brownsville, TX	(9.2)	146	El Monte, CA	1.0	126	Kent, WA	2.1
401	Bryan, TX	(21.6)	347	El Paso, TX	(11.9)	399	Killeen, TX	(20.7)
245	Buena Park, CA	(5.0)	370	Elgin, IL	(14.4)	37	Knoxville, TN	11.3
NA	Buffalo, NY**	NA	167	Elizabeth, NJ	0.0	321	Lafayette, LA	(9.3)
192	Burbank, CA	(1.6)	245	Elk Grove, CA	(5.0)	156	Lake Forest, CA	0.5
194	Cambridge, MA	(1.7)	47	Erie, PA	9.1	299	Lakeland, FL	(7.9)
20	Camden, NJ	15.4	377	Escondido, CA	(15.3)	389	Lakewood Twnshp, NJ	(17.5)
303	Canton Twnshp, MI	(8.2)	41	Eugene, OR	10.8	176	Lakewood, CA	(0.3)
28	Cape Coral, FL	12.9	218	Evansville, IN	(3.5)	130	Lakewood, CO	1.8
188	Carlsbad, CA	(1.3)	285	Everett, WA	(7.1)	340	Lancaster, CA	(10.9)
354	Carmel, IN	(12.3)	292	Fairfield, CA	(7.4)	292	Lansing, MI	(7.4)
114	Carrollton, TX	2.7	139	Fall River, MA	1.4	339	Laredo, TX	(10.8)
240	Carson, CA	(4.7)	337	Fargo, ND	(10.7)	395	Largo, FL	(19.1)
55	Cary, NC	8.4	315	Farmington Hills, MI	(9.1)	112	Las Cruces, NM	2.8
194	Cedar Rapids, IA	(1.7)	88	Fayetteville, NC	4.8	229	Las Vegas, NV	(4.0)
386	Centennial, CO	(17.3)	191	Fishers, IN	(1.4)	97	Lawrence, KS	4.3
NA	Champaign, IL**	NA	6	Flint, MI	22.4	409	Lawrence, MA	(26.7)
156	Chandler, AZ	0.5	45	Fontana, CA	9.9	218	Lawton, OK	(3.5)
318	Charleston, SC	(9.2)	318	Fort Collins, CO	(9.2)	398	League City, TX	(20.6)
243	Charlotte, NC	(4.9)	34	Fort Lauderdale, FL	11.9	273	Lee's Summit, MO	(6.7)
130	Chattanooga, TN	1.8	241	Fort Smith, AR	(4.8)	171	Lewisville, TX	(0.2)

Alpha Order - City (continued)

RANK	CITY	% CHANGE
NA	Lexington, KY**	NA
171	Lincoln, NE	(0.2)
121	Little Rock, AR	2.3
117	Livermore, CA	2.5
239	Livonia, MI	(4.6)
38	Long Beach, CA	11.0
312	Longmont, CO	(9.0)
381	Longview, TX	(16.1)
215	Los Angeles, CA	(3.1)
108	Louisville, KY	3.3
393	Lowell, MA	(18.3)
347	Lubbock, TX	(11.9)
346	Lynchburg, VA	(11.8)
285	Lynn, MA	(7.1)
50	Macon, GA	8.8
101	Madison, WI	3.9
21	Manchester, NH	15.0
383	McAllen, TX	(16.2)
287	McKinney, TX	(7.2)
6	Medford, OR	22.4
44	Melbourne, FL	10.2
79	Memphis, TN	5.5
410	Menifee, CA	(29.2)
117	Merced, CA	2.5
362	Meridian, ID	(13.2)
101	Mesa, AZ	3.9
323	Mesquite, TX	(9.4)
36	Miami Beach, FL	11.4
254	Miami Gardens, FL	(5.7)
18	Miami, FL	15.8
299	Midland, TX	(7.9)
330	Milwaukee, WI	(9.7)
71	Minneapolis, MN	6.1
368	Miramar, FL	(14.0)
63	Mission Viejo, CA	7.5
404	Mission, TX	(22.4)
NA	Mobile, AL**	NA
264	Modesto, CA	(6.3)
NA	Montgomery, AL**	NA
63	Moreno Valley, CA	7.5
101	Murfreesboro, TN	3.9
10	Murrieta, CA	20.6
43	Nampa, ID	10.6
179	Napa, CA	(0.4)
NA	Naperville, IL**	NA
212	Nashua, NH	(3.0)
222	Nashville, TN	(3.7)
230	New Bedford, MA	(4.2)
391	New Haven, CT	(17.8)
11	New Orleans, LA	19.6
117	New Rochelle, NY	2.5
111	New York, NY	2.9
57	Newark, NJ	8.0
167	Newport Beach, CA	0.0
156	Newport News, VA	0.5
321	Newton, MA	(9.3)
360	Norfolk, VA	(12.9)
156	Norman, OK	0.5
297	North Charleston, SC	(7.7)
68	Norwalk, CA	6.4
106	Norwalk, CT	3.6
3	Oakland, CA	26.6
182	Oceanside, CA	(0.6)
289	Odessa, TX	(7.3)
184	O'Fallon, MO	(0.9)
315	Ogden, UT	(9.1)
176	Oklahoma City, OK	(0.3)
302	Olathe, KS	(8.1)
12	Omaha, NE	19.1
156	Ontario, CA	0.5
116	Orange, CA	2.6
204	Orem, UT	(2.4)
32	Orlando, FL	12.0

RANK	CITY	% CHANGE
202	Overland Park, KS	(2.2)
354	Oxnard, CA	(12.3)
50	Palm Bay, FL	8.8
230	Palmdale, CA	(4.2)
363	Pasadena, CA	(13.4)
351	Pasadena, TX	(12.2)
395	Paterson, NJ	(19.1)
230	Pearland, TX	(4.2)
274	Pembroke Pines, FL	(6.8)
152	Peoria, AZ	0.6
167	Peoria, IL	0.0
121	Philadelphia, PA	2.3
73	Phoenix, AZ	6.0
312	Pittsburgh, PA	(9.0)
65	Plano, TX	6.7
76	Plantation, FL	5.8
54	Pomona, CA	8.5
41	Pompano Beach, FL	10.8
24	Port St. Lucie, FL	13.8
121	Portland, OR	2.3
228	Portsmouth, VA	(3.9)
50	Provo, UT	8.8
NA	Pueblo, CO**	NA
303	Quincy, MA	(8.2)
143	Racine, WI	1.2
83	Raleigh, NC	5.3
88	Ramapo, NY	4.8
162	Rancho Cucamon., CA	0.4
357	Reading, PA	(12.6)
19	Redding, CA	15.6
341	Redwood City, CA	(11.1)
386	Reno, NV	(17.3)
412	Renton, WA	(29.9)
30	Rialto, CA	12.6
323	Richardson, TX	(9.4)
162	Richmond, CA	0.4
196	Richmond, VA	(1.8)
15	Rio Rancho, NM	16.9
230	Riverside, CA	(4.2)
308	Roanoke, VA	(8.4)
305	Rochester, MN	(8.3)
363	Rochester, NY	(13.4)
216	Rockford, IL	(3.2)
308	Roseville, CA	(8.4)
330	Roswell, GA	(9.7)
341	Round Rock, TX	(11.1)
183	Sacramento, CA	(0.7)
208	Salem, OR	(2.8)
374	Salinas, CA	(14.9)
343	Salt Lake City, UT	(11.2)
357	San Angelo, TX	(12.6)
264	San Antonio, TX	(6.3)
378	San Bernardino, CA	(15.4)
203	San Diego, CA	(2.3)
124	San Francisco, CA	2.2
152	San Jose, CA	0.6
270	San Leandro, CA	(6.5)
375	San Marcos, CA	(15.0)
385	San Mateo, CA	(17.1)
369	Sandy Springs, GA	(14.2)
187	Sandy, UT	(1.2)
94	Santa Ana, CA	4.4
83	Santa Barbara, CA	5.3
238	Santa Clara, CA	(4.5)
311	Santa Clarita, CA	(8.9)
349	Santa Maria, CA	(12.0)
356	Santa Monica, CA	(12.4)
370	Santa Rosa, CA	(14.4)
126	Savannah, GA	2.1
81	Scottsdale, AZ	5.4
93	Scranton, PA	4.6
281	Seattle, WA	(7.0)
166	Shreveport, LA	0.2
408	Simi Valley, CA	(26.6)

RANK	CITY	% CHANGE
25	Sioux City, IA	13.5
150	Sioux Falls, SD	0.8
305	Somerville, MA	(8.3)
110	South Bend, IN	3.2
152	South Gate, CA	0.6
350	Sparks, NV	(12.1)
15	Spokane Valley, WA	16.9
222	Spokane, WA	(3.7)
185	Springfield, IL	(1.0)
135	Springfield, MA	1.6
281	Springfield, MO	(7.0)
86	Stamford, CT	4.9
NA	Sterling Heights, MI**	NA
186	Stockton, CA	(1.1)
38	St. Joseph, MO	11.0
106	St. Louis, MO	3.6
188	St. Paul, MN	(1.3)
278	St. Petersburg, FL	(6.9)
27	Suffolk, VA	13.0
402	Sugar Land, TX	(21.7)
394	Sunnyvale, CA	(18.8)
337	Sunrise, FL	(10.7)
148	Surprise, AZ	0.9
225	Syracuse, NY	(3.8)
295	Tacoma, WA	(7.5)
112	Tallahassee, FL	2.8
225	Tampa, FL	(3.8)
88	Temecula, CA	4.8
34	Tempe, AZ	11.9
NA	Thornton, CO**	NA
376	Thousand Oaks, CA	(15.1)
NA	Toledo, OH**	NA
13	Toms River Twnshp, NJ	18.0
258	Topeka, KS	(5.8)
281	Torrance, CA	(7.0)
143	Tracy, CA	1.2
405	Trenton, NJ	(24.5)
98	Troy, MI	4.2
NA	Tucson, AZ**	NA
133	Tulsa, OK	1.7
NA	Tuscaloosa, AL**	NA
260	Tustin, CA	(6.0)
327	Tyler, TX	(9.5)
139	Upper Darby Twnshp, PA	1.4
312	Vacaville, CA	(9.0)
171	Vallejo, CA	(0.2)
152	Vancouver, WA	0.6
328	Ventura, CA	(9.6)
73	Victorville, CA	6.0
315	Virginia Beach, VA	(9.1)
192	Visalia, CA	(1.6)
259	Vista, CA	(5.9)
91	Waco, TX	4.7
230	Warren, MI	(4.2)
47	Warwick, RI	9.1
53	Washington, DC	8.6
250	Waterbury, CT	(5.2)
14	West Covina, CA	17.1
241	West Jordan, UT	(4.8)
59	West Palm Beach, FL	7.9
381	West Valley, UT	(16.1)
287	Westland, MI	(7.2)
212	Westminster, CA	(3.0)
360	Westminster, CO	(12.9)
212	Whittier, CA	(3.0)
365	Wichita Falls, TX	(13.6)
68	Wichita, KS	6.4
216	Wilmington, NC	(3.2)
105	Winston-Salem, NC	3.8
85	Woodbridge Twnshp, NJ	5.2
254	Worcester, MA	(5.7)
406	Yakima, WA	(24.7)
199	Yonkers, NY	(2.1)
171	Yuma, AZ	(0.2)

Source: CQ Press using reported data from the F.B.I. "Crime in the United States 2011"
*Larceny-theft is the unlawful taking of property. Attempts are included.
**Not available.

Rank Order - City

75. Percent Change in Larceny-Theft Rate: 2010 to 2011 (continued)
National Percent Change = 1.4% Decrease*

RANK	CITY	% CHANGE	RANK	CITY	% CHANGE	RANK	CITY	% CHANGE
1	Antioch, CA	47.7	73	Fort Wayne, IN	6.0	145	Anaheim, CA	1.1
2	Indio, CA	26.7	73	Phoenix, AZ	6.0	146	College Station, TX	1.0
3	Oakland, CA	26.6	73	Victorville, CA	6.0	146	El Monte, CA	1.0
4	Avondale, AZ	24.2	76	Plantation, FL	5.8	148	Columbia, MO	0.9
5	Atlanta, GA	22.8	77	Coral Springs, FL	5.7	148	Surprise, AZ	0.9
6	Flint, MI	22.4	77	High Point, NC	5.7	150	Danbury, CT	0.8
6	Medford, OR	22.4	79	Brockton, MA	5.5	150	Sioux Falls, SD	0.8
8	Bridgeport, CT	22.3	79	Memphis, TN	5.5	152	Peoria, AZ	0.6
9	Irvine, CA	21.9	81	Concord, CA	5.4	152	San Jose, CA	0.6
10	Murrieta, CA	20.6	81	Scottsdale, AZ	5.4	152	South Gate, CA	0.6
11	New Orleans, LA	19.6	83	Raleigh, NC	5.3	152	Vancouver, WA	0.6
12	Omaha, NE	19.1	83	Santa Barbara, CA	5.3	156	Chandler, AZ	0.5
13	Toms River Twnshp, NJ	18.0	85	Woodbridge Twnshp, NJ	5.2	156	Duluth, MN	0.5
14	West Covina, CA	17.1	86	Edison Twnshp, NJ	4.9	156	Lake Forest, CA	0.5
15	Rio Rancho, NM	16.9	86	Stamford, CT	4.9	156	Newport News, VA	0.5
15	Spokane Valley, WA	16.9	88	Fayetteville, NC	4.8	156	Norman, OK	0.5
17	Glendale, AZ	16.4	88	Ramapo, NY	4.8	156	Ontario, CA	0.5
18	Miami, FL	15.8	88	Temecula, CA	4.8	162	Hawthorne, CA	0.4
19	Redding, CA	15.6	91	Decatur, IL	4.7	162	Rancho Cucamon., CA	0.4
20	Camden, NJ	15.4	91	Waco, TX	4.7	162	Richmond, CA	0.4
21	Manchester, NH	15.0	93	Scranton, PA	4.6	165	Kansas City, KS	0.3
22	Detroit, MI	14.7	94	Albuquerque, NM	4.4	166	Shreveport, LA	0.2
23	Denton, TX	14.1	94	Hemet, CA	4.4	167	Cheektowaga, NY	0.0
24	Port St. Lucie, FL	13.8	94	Santa Ana, CA	4.4	167	Elizabeth, NJ	0.0
25	Sioux City, IA	13.5	97	Lawrence, KS	4.3	167	Newport Beach, CA	0.0
26	Daly City, CA	13.1	98	Gresham, OR	4.2	167	Peoria, IL	0.0
27	Suffolk, VA	13.0	98	Troy, MI	4.2	171	Bellingham, WA	(0.2)
28	Cape Coral, FL	12.9	100	Bend, OR	4.1	171	Lewisville, TX	(0.2)
29	Cincinnati, OH	12.8	101	Dallas, TX	3.9	171	Lincoln, NE	(0.2)
30	Rialto, CA	12.6	101	Madison, WI	3.9	171	Vallejo, CA	(0.2)
31	Hesperia, CA	12.2	101	Mesa, AZ	3.9	171	Yuma, AZ	(0.2)
32	Cleveland, OH	12.0	101	Murfreesboro, TN	3.9	176	Huntington Beach, CA	(0.3)
32	Orlando, FL	12.0	105	Winston-Salem, NC	3.8	176	Lakewood, CA	(0.3)
34	Fort Lauderdale, FL	11.9	106	Norwalk, CT	3.6	176	Oklahoma City, OK	(0.3)
34	Tempe, AZ	11.9	106	St. Louis, MO	3.6	179	Clarksville, TN	(0.4)
36	Miami Beach, FL	11.4	108	Kenosha, WI	3.3	179	Napa, CA	(0.4)
37	Knoxville, TN	11.3	108	Louisville, KY	3.3	181	Asheville, NC	(0.5)
38	Long Beach, CA	11.0	110	South Bend, IN	3.2	182	Oceanside, CA	(0.6)
38	St. Joseph, MO	11.0	111	New York, NY	2.9	183	Sacramento, CA	(0.7)
40	Costa Mesa, CA	10.9	112	Las Cruces, NM	2.8	184	O'Fallon, MO	(0.9)
41	Eugene, OR	10.8	112	Tallahassee, FL	2.8	185	Springfield, IL	(1.0)
41	Pompano Beach, FL	10.8	114	Carrollton, TX	2.7	186	Stockton, CA	(1.1)
43	Nampa, ID	10.6	114	Hampton, VA	2.7	187	Sandy, UT	(1.2)
44	Melbourne, FL	10.2	116	Orange, CA	2.6	188	Carlsbad, CA	(1.3)
45	Fontana, CA	9.9	117	Livermore, CA	2.5	188	Fresno, CA	(1.3)
46	Inglewood, CA	9.8	117	Merced, CA	2.5	188	St. Paul, MN	(1.3)
47	Erie, PA	9.1	117	New Rochelle, NY	2.5	191	Fishers, IN	(1.4)
47	Warwick, RI	9.1	120	Alexandria, VA	2.4	192	Burbank, CA	(1.6)
49	Chino, CA	8.9	121	Little Rock, AR	2.3	192	Visalia, CA	(1.6)
50	Macon, GA	8.8	121	Philadelphia, PA	2.3	194	Cambridge, MA	(1.7)
50	Palm Bay, FL	8.8	121	Portland, OR	2.3	194	Cedar Rapids, IA	(1.7)
50	Provo, UT	8.8	124	Greeley, CO	2.2	196	Bellevue, WA	(1.8)
53	Washington, DC	8.6	124	San Francisco, CA	2.2	196	Richmond, VA	(1.8)
54	Pomona, CA	8.5	126	Akron, OH	2.1	198	Jacksonville, FL	(1.9)
55	Cary, NC	8.4	126	Kent, WA	2.1	199	Durham, NC	(2.1)
56	Broken Arrow, OK	8.2	126	Savannah, GA	2.1	199	Houston, TX	(2.1)
57	Boca Raton, FL	8.0	129	Allen, TX	1.9	199	Yonkers, NY	(2.1)
57	Newark, NJ	8.0	130	Chattanooga, TN	1.8	202	Overland Park, KS	(2.2)
59	West Palm Beach, FL	7.9	130	Edmond, OK	1.8	203	San Diego, CA	(2.3)
60	Denver, CO	7.8	130	Lakewood, CO	1.8	204	Aurora, CO	(2.4)
61	Des Moines, IA	7.7	133	Hayward, CA	1.7	204	Orem, UT	(2.4)
61	Hollywood, FL	7.7	133	Tulsa, OK	1.7	206	Clinton Twnshp, MI	(2.5)
63	Mission Viejo, CA	7.5	135	Springfield, MA	1.6	207	Bloomington, MN	(2.6)
63	Moreno Valley, CA	7.5	136	Beaverton, OR	1.5	208	Beaumont, TX	(2.8)
65	Plano, TX	6.7	136	Chicago, IL	1.5	208	Boston, MA	(2.8)
66	Baltimore, MD	6.5	136	Dayton, OH	1.5	208	Colonie, NY	(2.8)
66	Clovis, CA	6.5	139	Brick Twnshp, NJ	1.4	208	Salem, OR	(2.8)
68	Norwalk, CA	6.4	139	Davie, FL	1.4	212	Nashua, NH	(3.0)
68	Wichita, KS	6.4	139	Fall River, MA	1.4	212	Westminster, CA	(3.0)
70	Edinburg, TX	6.2	139	Upper Darby Twnshp, PA	1.4	212	Whittier, CA	(3.0)
71	Cranston, RI	6.1	143	Racine, WI	1.2	215	Los Angeles, CA	(3.1)
71	Minneapolis, MN	6.1	143	Tracy, CA	1.2	216	Rockford, IL	(3.2)

Rank Order - City (continued)

RANK	CITY	% CHANGE	RANK	CITY	% CHANGE	RANK	CITY	% CHANGE
216	Wilmington, NC	(3.2)	289	Chico, CA	(7.3)	363	Rochester, NY	(13.4)
218	Columbus, OH	(3.5)	289	Odessa, TX	(7.3)	365	Wichita Falls, TX	(13.6)
218	Evansville, IN	(3.5)	292	Fairfield, CA	(7.4)	366	Grand Rapids, MI	(13.8)
218	Lawton, OK	(3.5)	292	Glendale, CA	(7.4)	367	Columbus, GA	(13.9)
221	Jackson, MS	(3.6)	292	Lansing, MI	(7.4)	368	Miramar, FL	(14.0)
222	Garland, TX	(3.7)	295	Tacoma, WA	(7.5)	369	Sandy Springs, GA	(14.2)
222	Nashville, TN	(3.7)	296	Boise, ID	(7.6)	370	Aurora, IL	(14.4)
222	Spokane, WA	(3.7)	297	Jersey City, NJ	(7.7)	370	Elgin, IL	(14.4)
225	Gainesville, FL	(3.8)	297	North Charleston, SC	(7.7)	370	Santa Rosa, CA	(14.4)
225	Syracuse, NY	(3.8)	299	Lakeland, FL	(7.9)	373	Frisco, TX	(14.7)
225	Tampa, FL	(3.8)	299	Midland, TX	(7.9)	374	Salinas, CA	(14.9)
228	Portsmouth, VA	(3.9)	301	Hialeah, FL	(8.0)	375	San Marcos, CA	(15.0)
229	Las Vegas, NV	(4.0)	302	Olathe, KS	(8.1)	376	Thousand Oaks, CA	(15.1)
230	Arvada, CO	(4.2)	303	Canton Twnshp, MI	(8.2)	377	Escondido, CA	(15.3)
230	Fort Worth, TX	(4.2)	303	Quincy, MA	(8.2)	378	San Bernardino, CA	(15.4)
230	New Bedford, MA	(4.2)	305	Joliet, IL	(8.3)	379	Amarillo, TX	(15.6)
230	Palmdale, CA	(4.2)	305	Rochester, MN	(8.3)	380	Bloomington, IL	(15.8)
230	Pearland, TX	(4.2)	305	Somerville, MA	(8.3)	381	Longview, TX	(16.1)
230	Riverside, CA	(4.2)	308	Henderson, NV	(8.4)	381	West Valley, UT	(16.1)
230	Warren, MI	(4.2)	308	Roanoke, VA	(8.4)	383	McAllen, TX	(16.2)
237	Athens-Clarke, GA	(4.4)	308	Roseville, CA	(8.4)	384	Allentown, PA	(16.7)
238	Santa Clara, CA	(4.5)	311	Santa Clarita, CA	(8.9)	385	San Mateo, CA	(17.1)
239	Livonia, MI	(4.6)	312	Longmont, CO	(9.0)	386	Centennial, CO	(17.3)
240	Carson, CA	(4.7)	312	Pittsburgh, PA	(9.0)	386	Reno, NV	(17.3)
241	Fort Smith, AR	(4.8)	312	Vacaville, CA	(9.0)	388	Dearborn, MI	(17.4)
241	West Jordan, UT	(4.8)	315	Farmington Hills, MI	(9.1)	389	Lakewood Twnshp, NJ	(17.5)
243	Albany, GA	(4.9)	315	Ogden, UT	(9.1)	390	Ann Arbor, MI	(17.6)
243	Charlotte, NC	(4.9)	315	Virginia Beach, VA	(9.1)	391	New Haven, CT	(17.8)
245	Albany, NY	(5.0)	318	Brownsville, TX	(9.2)	392	Downey, CA	(18.1)
245	Baldwin Park, CA	(5.0)	318	Charleston, SC	(9.2)	393	Lowell, MA	(18.3)
245	Buena Park, CA	(5.0)	318	Fort Collins, CO	(9.2)	394	Sunnyvale, CA	(18.8)
245	Elk Grove, CA	(5.0)	321	Lafayette, LA	(9.3)	395	Largo, FL	(19.1)
249	Chesapeake, VA	(5.1)	321	Newton, MA	(9.3)	395	Paterson, NJ	(19.1)
250	Waterbury, CT	(5.2)	323	Arlington, TX	(9.4)	397	El Cajon, CA	(19.4)
251	Chula Vista, CA	(5.4)	323	Bakersfield, CA	(9.4)	398	League City, TX	(20.6)
251	Compton, CA	(5.4)	323	Mesquite, TX	(9.4)	399	Killeen, TX	(20.7)
253	Greece, NY	(5.6)	323	Richardson, TX	(9.4)	400	Fremont, CA	(20.8)
254	Alhambra, CA	(5.7)	327	Tyler, TX	(9.5)	401	Bryan, TX	(21.6)
254	Independence, MO	(5.7)	328	Bethlehem, PA	(9.6)	402	Sugar Land, TX	(21.7)
254	Miami Gardens, FL	(5.7)	328	Ventura, CA	(9.6)	403	Irving, TX	(21.9)
254	Worcester, MA	(5.7)	330	Milwaukee, WI	(9.7)	404	Mission, TX	(22.4)
258	Topeka, KS	(5.8)	330	Roswell, GA	(9.7)	405	Trenton, NJ	(24.5)
259	Vista, CA	(5.9)	332	Corpus Christi, TX	(9.8)	406	Yakima, WA	(24.7)
260	Bellflower, CA	(6.0)	333	Abilene, TX	(10.3)	407	Berkeley, CA	(26.4)
260	Gilbert, AZ	(6.0)	334	Clarkstown, NY	(10.4)	408	Simi Valley, CA	(26.6)
260	Tustin, CA	(6.0)	335	Amherst, NY	(10.6)	409	Lawrence, MA	(26.7)
263	Hamilton Twnshp, NJ	(6.1)	335	Citrus Heights, CA	(10.6)	410	Menifee, CA	(29.2)
264	Austin, TX	(6.3)	337	Fargo, ND	(10.7)	411	Johns Creek, GA	(29.3)
264	Clearwater, FL	(6.3)	337	Sunrise, FL	(10.7)	412	Renton, WA	(29.9)
264	Green Bay, WI	(6.3)	339	Laredo, TX	(10.8)	NA	Baton Rouge, LA**	NA
264	Kennewick, WA	(6.3)	340	Lancaster, CA	(10.9)	NA	Billings, MT**	NA
264	Modesto, CA	(6.3)	341	Redwood City, CA	(11.1)	NA	Birmingham, AL**	NA
264	San Antonio, TX	(6.3)	341	Round Rock, TX	(11.1)	NA	Brooklyn Park, MN**	NA
270	Chino Hills, CA	(6.5)	343	Salt Lake City, UT	(11.2)	NA	Buffalo, NY**	NA
270	San Leandro, CA	(6.5)	344	Colorado Springs, CO	(11.4)	NA	Champaign, IL**	NA
272	Bloomington, IN	(6.6)	345	Boulder, CO	(11.7)	NA	Cicero, IL**	NA
273	Lee's Summit, MO	(6.7)	346	Lynchburg, VA	(11.8)	NA	Clifton, NJ**	NA
274	Corona, CA	(6.8)	347	El Paso, TX	(11.9)	NA	Davenport, IA**	NA
274	Deerfield Beach, FL	(6.8)	347	Lubbock, TX	(11.9)	NA	Gary, IN**	NA
274	Hammond, IN	(6.8)	349	Santa Maria, CA	(12.0)	NA	Hillsboro, OR**	NA
274	Pembroke Pines, FL	(6.8)	350	Sparks, NV	(12.1)	NA	Hoover, AL**	NA
278	Concord, NC	(6.9)	351	Fullerton, CA	(12.2)	NA	Huntsville, AL**	NA
278	Hartford, CT	(6.9)	351	Grand Prairie, TX	(12.2)	NA	Indianapolis, IN**	NA
278	St. Petersburg, FL	(6.9)	351	Pasadena, TX	(12.2)	NA	Kansas City, MO**	NA
281	Garden Grove, CA	(7.0)	354	Carmel, IN	(12.3)	NA	Lexington, KY**	NA
281	Seattle, WA	(7.0)	354	Oxnard, CA	(12.3)	NA	Mobile, AL**	NA
281	Springfield, MO	(7.0)	356	Santa Monica, CA	(12.4)	NA	Montgomery, AL**	NA
281	Torrance, CA	(7.0)	357	Reading, PA	(12.6)	NA	Naperville, IL**	NA
285	Everett, WA	(7.1)	357	San Angelo, TX	(12.6)	NA	Pueblo, CO**	NA
285	Lynn, MA	(7.1)	359	Arlington Heights, IL	(12.7)	NA	Sterling Heights, MI**	NA
287	McKinney, TX	(7.2)	360	Norfolk, VA	(12.9)	NA	Thornton, CO**	NA
287	Westland, MI	(7.2)	360	Westminster, CO	(12.9)	NA	Toledo, OH**	NA
289	Anchorage, AK	(7.3)	362	Meridian, ID	(13.2)	NA	Tucson, AZ**	NA
			363	Pasadena, CA	(13.4)	NA	Tuscaloosa, AL**	NA

Source: CQ Press using reported data from the F.B.I. "Crime in the United States 2011"
*Larceny-theft is the unlawful taking of property. Attempts are included.
**Not available.

Alpha Order - City

76. Percent Change in Larceny-Theft Rate: 2007 to 2011
National Percent Change = 9.5% Decrease*

RANK	CITY	% CHANGE	RANK	CITY	% CHANGE	RANK	CITY	% CHANGE
201	Abilene, TX	(10.0)	19	Cheektowaga, NY	22.4	199	Fort Wayne, IN	(9.8)
81	Akron, OH	1.5	81	Chesapeake, VA	1.5	312	Fort Worth, TX	(19.8)
270	Albany, GA	(15.9)	192	Chicago, IL	(8.8)	375	Fremont, CA	(31.1)
37	Albany, NY	12.0	328	Chico, CA	(21.4)	51	Fresno, CA	7.9
124	Albuquerque, NM	(4.4)	206	Chino Hills, CA	(10.7)	379	Frisco, TX	(32.1)
129	Alexandria, VA	(4.6)	225	Chino, CA	(12.5)	190	Fullerton, CA	(8.7)
48	Alhambra, CA	9.3	338	Chula Vista, CA	(22.5)	203	Gainesville, FL	(10.4)
318	Allentown, PA	(20.3)	NA	Cicero, IL**	NA	294	Garden Grove, CA	(18.2)
292	Allen, TX	(17.9)	32	Cincinnati, OH	13.5	94	Garland, TX	(1.0)
243	Amarillo, TX	(14.0)	NA	Citrus Heights, CA**	NA	33	Gary, IN	12.3
59	Amherst, NY	5.8	113	Clarkstown, NY	(3.6)	312	Gilbert, AZ	(19.8)
71	Anaheim, CA	3.2	332	Clarksville, TN	(21.7)	2	Glendale, AZ	75.7
214	Anchorage, AK	(11.7)	173	Clearwater, FL	(7.7)	78	Glendale, CA	2.0
161	Ann Arbor, MI	(6.9)	64	Cleveland, OH	4.2	276	Grand Prairie, TX	(16.5)
6	Antioch, CA	35.0	311	Clifton, NJ	(19.5)	402	Grand Rapids, MI	(42.4)
NA	Arlington Heights, IL**	NA	50	Clinton Twnshp, MI	8.6	36	Greece, NY	12.2
333	Arlington, TX	(21.8)	12	Clovis, CA	27.1	226	Greeley, CO	(12.6)
70	Arvada, CO	3.4	157	College Station, TX	(6.7)	261	Green Bay, WI	(15.4)
216	Asheville, NC	(11.9)	136	Colonie, NY	(4.9)	84	Gresham, OR	1.3
287	Athens-Clarke, GA	(17.4)	263	Colorado Springs, CO	(15.5)	87	Hamilton Twnshp, NJ	0.6
91	Atlanta, GA	(0.8)	24	Columbia, MO	16.3	133	Hammond, IN	(4.8)
289	Aurora, CO	(17.7)	263	Columbus, GA	(15.5)	23	Hampton, VA	18.7
365	Aurora, IL	(27.4)	186	Columbus, OH	(8.5)	348	Hartford, CT	(24.3)
254	Austin, TX	(14.8)	30	Compton, CA	14.3	22	Hawthorne, CA	19.7
NA	Avondale, AZ**	NA	349	Concord, CA	(24.4)	308	Hayward, CA	(19.3)
356	Bakersfield, CA	(25.3)	245	Concord, NC	(14.1)	153	Hemet, CA	(6.6)
33	Baldwin Park, CA	12.3	74	Coral Springs, FL	2.8	173	Henderson, NV	(7.7)
85	Baltimore, MD	1.2	242	Corona, CA	(13.9)	77	Hesperia, CA	2.2
197	Baton Rouge, LA	(9.0)	359	Corpus Christi, TX	(25.4)	248	Hialeah, FL	(14.2)
220	Beaumont, TX	(12.2)	38	Costa Mesa, CA	11.6	111	High Point, NC	(3.5)
314	Beaverton, OR	(19.9)	109	Cranston, RI	(3.4)	324	Hillsboro, OR	(21.0)
267	Bellevue, WA	(15.7)	356	Dallas, TX	(25.3)	16	Hollywood, FL	23.3
381	Bellflower, CA	(32.7)	192	Daly City, CA	(8.8)	NA	Hoover, AL**	NA
381	Bellingham, WA	(32.7)	49	Danbury, CT	9.1	167	Houston, TX	(7.2)
220	Bend, OR	(12.2)	NA	Davenport, IA**	NA	11	Huntington Beach, CA	28.7
398	Berkeley, CA	(37.8)	168	Davie, FL	(7.5)	NA	Huntsville, AL**	NA
323	Bethlehem, PA	(20.9)	205	Dayton, OH	(10.5)	314	Independence, MO	(19.9)
NA	Billings, MT**	NA	245	Dearborn, MI	(14.1)	228	Indianapolis, IN	(12.9)
NA	Birmingham, AL**	NA	NA	Decatur, IL**	NA	33	Indio, CA	12.3
NA	Bloomington, IL**	NA	105	Deerfield Beach, FL	(2.7)	14	Inglewood, CA	25.0
133	Bloomington, IN	(4.8)	92	Denton, TX	(0.9)	69	Irvine, CA	3.5
86	Bloomington, MN	1.0	31	Denver, CO	13.7	391	Irving, TX	(35.2)
303	Boca Raton, FL	(19.1)	303	Des Moines, IA	(19.1)	278	Jacksonville, FL	(16.6)
228	Boise, ID	(12.9)	140	Detroit, MI	(5.0)	122	Jackson, MS	(4.3)
342	Boston, MA	(22.8)	184	Downey, CA	(8.4)	296	Jersey City, NJ	(18.4)
189	Boulder, CO	(8.6)	97	Duluth, MN	(1.6)	NA	Johns Creek, GA**	NA
150	Brick Twnshp, NJ	(6.1)	NA	Durham, NC**	NA	148	Joliet, IL	(6.0)
377	Bridgeport, CT	(31.8)	21	Edinburg, TX	20.0	241	Kansas City, KS	(13.8)
280	Brockton, MA	(16.7)	314	Edison Twnshp, NJ	(19.9)	NA	Kansas City, MO**	NA
43	Broken Arrow, OK	10.8	219	Edmond, OK	(12.0)	166	Kennewick, WA	(7.1)
152	Brooklyn Park, MN	(6.4)	399	El Cajon, CA	(38.5)	122	Kenosha, WI	(4.3)
180	Brownsville, TX	(8.2)	215	El Monte, CA	(11.8)	129	Kent, WA	(4.6)
346	Bryan, TX	(23.2)	282	El Paso, TX	(16.9)	344	Killeen, TX	(23.0)
55	Buena Park, CA	7.5	352	Elgin, IL	(24.9)	54	Knoxville, TN	7.6
NA	Buffalo, NY**	NA	257	Elizabeth, NJ	(15.1)	180	Lafayette, LA	(8.2)
61	Burbank, CA	5.0	161	Elk Grove, CA	(6.9)	104	Lake Forest, CA	(2.6)
236	Cambridge, MA	(13.3)	27	Erie, PA	16.2	270	Lakeland, FL	(15.9)
99	Camden, NJ	(2.0)	299	Escondido, CA	(18.6)	385	Lakewood Twnshp, NJ	(34.0)
180	Canton Twnshp, MI	(8.2)	56	Eugene, OR	7.0	328	Lakewood, CA	(21.4)
343	Cape Coral, FL	(22.9)	67	Evansville, IN	3.6	41	Lakewood, CO	10.9
364	Carlsbad, CA	(27.2)	151	Everett, WA	(6.2)	393	Lancaster, CA	(35.5)
380	Carmel, IN	(32.4)	376	Fairfield, CA	(31.5)	144	Lansing, MI	(5.2)
284	Carrollton, TX	(17.2)	NA	Fall River, MA**	NA	370	Laredo, TX	(29.1)
233	Carson, CA	(13.2)	216	Fargo, ND	(11.9)	67	Largo, FL	3.6
227	Cary, NC	(12.7)	147	Farmington Hills, MI	(5.9)	206	Las Cruces, NM	(10.7)
347	Cedar Rapids, IA	(24.2)	303	Fayetteville, NC	(19.1)	360	Las Vegas, NV	(25.6)
293	Centennial, CO	(18.1)	350	Fishers, IN	(24.7)	363	Lawrence, KS	(26.2)
NA	Champaign, IL**	NA	257	Flint, MI	(15.1)	233	Lawrence, MA	(13.2)
76	Chandler, AZ	2.4	66	Fontana, CA	3.8	58	Lawton, OK	6.1
228	Charleston, SC	(12.9)	195	Fort Collins, CO	(8.9)	179	League City, TX	(8.1)
400	Charlotte, NC	(38.6)	47	Fort Lauderdale, FL	10.5	291	Lee's Summit, MO	(17.8)
362	Chattanooga, TN	(25.9)	319	Fort Smith, AR	(20.4)	28	Lewisville, TX	15.9

Alpha Order - City (continued)

RANK	CITY	% CHANGE	RANK	CITY	% CHANGE	RANK	CITY	% CHANGE
NA	Lexington, KY**	NA	140	Overland Park, KS	(5.0)	15	Sioux City, IA	24.6
278	Lincoln, NE	(16.6)	281	Oxnard, CA	(16.8)	29	Sioux Falls, SD	14.8
261	Little Rock, AR	(15.4)	88	Palm Bay, FL	(0.4)	355	Somerville, MA	(25.2)
284	Livermore, CA	(17.2)	369	Palmdale, CA	(28.3)	320	South Bend, IN	(20.5)
190	Livonia, MI	(8.7)	276	Pasadena, CA	(16.5)	17	South Gate, CA	22.7
72	Long Beach, CA	3.0	83	Pasadena, TX	1.4	394	Sparks, NV	(36.9)
NA	Longmont, CO**	NA	136	Paterson, NJ	(4.9)	3	Spokane Valley, WA	70.0
365	Longview, TX	(27.4)	334	Pearland, TX	(22.2)	8	Spokane, WA	33.0
168	Los Angeles, CA	(7.5)	259	Pembroke Pines, FL	(15.2)	161	Springfield, IL	(6.9)
53	Louisville, KY	7.8	251	Peoria, AZ	(14.4)	255	Springfield, MA	(14.9)
96	Lowell, MA	(1.4)	121	Peoria, IL	(4.2)	132	Springfield, MO	(4.7)
183	Lubbock, TX	(8.3)	117	Philadelphia, PA	(4.0)	44	Stamford, CT	10.7
148	Lynchburg, VA	(6.0)	303	Phoenix, AZ	(19.1)	NA	Sterling Heights, MI**	NA
13	Lynn, MA	25.3	335	Pittsburgh, PA	(22.3)	288	Stockton, CA	(17.5)
89	Macon, GA	(0.5)	289	Plano, TX	(17.7)	119	St. Joseph, MO	(4.1)
63	Madison, WI	4.6	144	Plantation, FL	(5.2)	295	St. Louis, MO	(18.3)
NA	Manchester, NH**	NA	243	Pomona, CA	(14.0)	75	St. Paul, MN	2.5
341	McAllen, TX	(22.6)	41	Pompano Beach, FL	10.9	157	St. Petersburg, FL	(6.7)
146	McKinney, TX	(5.6)	95	Port St. Lucie, FL	(1.2)	210	Suffolk, VA	(11.1)
20	Medford, OR	20.5	153	Portland, OR	(6.6)	140	Sugar Land, TX	(5.0)
40	Melbourne, FL	11.0	65	Portsmouth, VA	4.1	388	Sunnyvale, CA	(34.5)
321	Memphis, TN	(20.6)	127	Provo, UT	(4.5)	136	Sunrise, FL	(4.9)
NA	Menifee, CA**	NA	NA	Pueblo, CO**	NA	198	Surprise, AZ	(9.5)
324	Merced, CA	(21.0)	157	Quincy, MA	(6.7)	237	Syracuse, NY	(13.5)
297	Meridian, ID	(18.5)	309	Racine, WI	(19.4)	328	Tacoma, WA	(21.4)
284	Mesa, AZ	(17.2)	124	Raleigh, NC	(4.4)	116	Tallahassee, FL	(3.9)
90	Mesquite, TX	(0.6)	7	Ramapo, NY	33.1	384	Tampa, FL	(32.8)
5	Miami Beach, FL	36.3	119	Rancho Cucamon., CA	(4.1)	161	Temecula, CA	(6.9)
401	Miami Gardens, FL	(39.4)	338	Reading, PA	(22.5)	206	Tempe, AZ	(10.7)
18	Miami, FL	22.5	10	Redding, CA	29.9	NA	Thornton, CO**	NA
270	Midland, TX	(15.9)	377	Redwood City, CA	(31.8)	101	Thousand Oaks, CA	(2.2)
356	Milwaukee, WI	(25.3)	397	Reno, NV	(37.6)	NA	Toledo, OH**	NA
202	Minneapolis, MN	(10.2)	387	Renton, WA	(34.3)	4	Toms River Twnshp, NJ	57.5
317	Miramar, FL	(20.2)	1	Rialto, CA	117.0	222	Topeka, KS	(12.3)
98	Mission Viejo, CA	(1.7)	168	Richardson, TX	(7.5)	263	Torrance, CA	(15.5)
168	Mission, TX	(7.5)	338	Richmond, CA	(22.5)	253	Tracy, CA	(14.7)
NA	Mobile, AL**	NA	161	Richmond, VA	(6.9)	374	Trenton, NJ	(30.8)
371	Modesto, CA	(29.5)	102	Rio Rancho, NM	(2.4)	103	Troy, MI	(2.5)
NA	Montgomery, AL**	NA	240	Riverside, CA	(13.7)	NA	Tucson, AZ**	NA
282	Moreno Valley, CA	(16.9)	228	Roanoke, VA	(12.9)	238	Tulsa, OK	(13.6)
136	Murfreesboro, TN	(4.9)	250	Rochester, MN	(14.3)	NA	Tuscaloosa, AL**	NA
307	Murrieta, CA	(19.2)	140	Rochester, NY	(5.0)	109	Tustin, CA	(3.4)
45	Nampa, ID	10.6	309	Rockford, IL	(19.4)	133	Tyler, TX	(4.8)
390	Napa, CA	(34.7)	209	Roseville, CA	(11.0)	213	Upper Darby Twnshp, PA	(11.6)
203	Naperville, IL	(10.4)	335	Roswell, GA	(22.3)	251	Vacaville, CA	(14.4)
NA	Nashua, NH**	NA	117	Round Rock, TX	(4.0)	403	Vallejo, CA	(45.8)
301	Nashville, TN	(19.0)	274	Sacramento, CA	(16.2)	92	Vancouver, WA	(0.9)
62	New Bedford, MA	4.8	297	Salem, OR	(18.5)	222	Ventura, CA	(12.3)
NA	New Haven, CT**	NA	396	Salinas, CA	(37.3)	210	Victorville, CA	(11.1)
386	New Orleans, LA	(34.2)	301	Salt Lake City, UT	(19.0)	175	Virginia Beach, VA	(7.8)
184	New Rochelle, NY	(8.4)	351	San Angelo, TX	(24.8)	115	Visalia, CA	(3.7)
99	New York, NY	(2.0)	127	San Antonio, TX	(4.5)	45	Vista, CA	10.6
200	Newark, NJ	(9.9)	331	San Bernardino, CA	(21.5)	326	Waco, TX	(21.3)
39	Newport Beach, CA	11.1	367	San Diego, CA	(27.5)	274	Warren, MI	(16.2)
232	Newport News, VA	(13.1)	157	San Francisco, CA	(6.7)	NA	Warwick, RI**	NA
267	Newton, MA	(15.7)	153	San Jose, CA	(6.6)	24	Washington, DC	16.3
106	Norfolk, VA	(2.8)	186	San Leandro, CA	(8.5)	354	Waterbury, CT	(25.0)
113	Norman, OK	(3.6)	186	San Marcos, CA	(8.5)	168	West Covina, CA	(7.5)
326	North Charleston, SC	(21.3)	360	San Mateo, CA	(25.6)	269	West Jordan, UT	(15.8)
255	Norwalk, CA	(14.9)	381	Sandy Springs, GA	(32.7)	337	West Palm Beach, FL	(22.4)
72	Norwalk, CT	3.0	273	Sandy, UT	(16.0)	352	West Valley, UT	(24.9)
60	Oakland, CA	5.6	153	Santa Ana, CA	(6.6)	233	Westland, MI	(13.2)
248	Oceanside, CA	(14.2)	9	Santa Barbara, CA	31.6	80	Westminster, CA	1.6
372	Odessa, TX	(30.2)	263	Santa Clara, CA	(15.5)	300	Westminster, CO	(18.8)
395	O'Fallon, MO	(37.0)	391	Santa Clarita, CA	(35.2)	24	Whittier, CA	16.3
224	Ogden, UT	(12.4)	322	Santa Maria, CA	(20.7)	388	Wichita Falls, TX	(34.5)
106	Oklahoma City, OK	(2.8)	57	Santa Monica, CA	6.9	212	Wichita, KS	(11.5)
NA	Olathe, KS**	NA	108	Santa Rosa, CA	(3.2)	124	Wilmington, NC	(4.4)
111	Omaha, NE	(3.5)	129	Savannah, GA	(4.6)	NA	Winston-Salem, NC**	NA
195	Ontario, CA	(8.9)	177	Scottsdale, AZ	(8.0)	177	Woodbridge Twnshp, NJ	(8.0)
192	Orange, CA	(8.8)	51	Scranton, PA	7.9	216	Worcester, MA	(11.9)
245	Orem, UT	(14.1)	176	Seattle, WA	(7.9)	372	Yakima, WA	(30.2)
259	Orlando, FL	(15.2)	344	Shreveport, LA	(23.0)	79	Yonkers, NY	1.8
			368	Simi Valley, CA	(27.9)	238	Yuma, AZ	(13.6)

Source: CQ Press using reported data from the F.B.I. "Crime in the United States 2011"
*Larceny-theft is the unlawful taking of property. Attempts are included.
**Not available.

Rank Order - City

76. Percent Change in Larceny-Theft Rate: 2007 to 2011 (continued)
National Percent Change = 9.5% Decrease*

RANK	CITY	% CHANGE	RANK	CITY	% CHANGE	RANK	CITY	% CHANGE
1	Rialto, CA	117.0	72	Norwalk, CT	3.0	144	Plantation, FL	(5.2)
2	Glendale, AZ	75.7	74	Coral Springs, FL	2.8	146	McKinney, TX	(5.6)
3	Spokane Valley, WA	70.0	75	St. Paul, MN	2.5	147	Farmington Hills, MI	(5.9)
4	Toms River Twnshp, NJ	57.5	76	Chandler, AZ	2.4	148	Joliet, IL	(6.0)
5	Miami Beach, FL	36.3	77	Hesperia, CA	2.2	148	Lynchburg, VA	(6.0)
6	Antioch, CA	35.0	78	Glendale, CA	2.0	150	Brick Twnshp, NJ	(6.1)
7	Ramapo, NY	33.1	79	Yonkers, NY	1.8	151	Everett, WA	(6.2)
8	Spokane, WA	33.0	80	Westminster, CA	1.6	152	Brooklyn Park, MN	(6.4)
9	Santa Barbara, CA	31.6	81	Akron, OH	1.5	153	Hemet, CA	(6.6)
10	Redding, CA	29.9	81	Chesapeake, VA	1.5	153	Portland, OR	(6.6)
11	Huntington Beach, CA	28.7	83	Pasadena, TX	1.4	153	San Jose, CA	(6.6)
12	Clovis, CA	27.1	84	Gresham, OR	1.3	153	Santa Ana, CA	(6.6)
13	Lynn, MA	25.3	85	Baltimore, MD	1.2	157	College Station, TX	(6.7)
14	Inglewood, CA	25.0	86	Bloomington, MN	1.0	157	Quincy, MA	(6.7)
15	Sioux City, IA	24.6	87	Hamilton Twnshp, NJ	0.6	157	San Francisco, CA	(6.7)
16	Hollywood, FL	23.3	88	Palm Bay, FL	(0.4)	157	St. Petersburg, FL	(6.7)
17	South Gate, CA	22.7	89	Macon, GA	(0.5)	161	Ann Arbor, MI	(6.9)
18	Miami, FL	22.5	90	Mesquite, TX	(0.6)	161	Elk Grove, CA	(6.9)
19	Cheektowaga, NY	22.4	91	Atlanta, GA	(0.8)	161	Richmond, VA	(6.9)
20	Medford, OR	20.5	92	Denton, TX	(0.9)	161	Springfield, IL	(6.9)
21	Edinburg, TX	20.0	92	Vancouver, WA	(0.9)	161	Temecula, CA	(6.9)
22	Hawthorne, CA	19.7	94	Garland, TX	(1.0)	166	Kennewick, WA	(7.1)
23	Hampton, VA	18.7	95	Port St. Lucie, FL	(1.2)	167	Houston, TX	(7.2)
24	Columbia, MO	16.3	96	Lowell, MA	(1.4)	168	Davie, FL	(7.5)
24	Washington, DC	16.3	97	Duluth, MN	(1.6)	168	Los Angeles, CA	(7.5)
24	Whittier, CA	16.3	98	Mission Viejo, CA	(1.7)	168	Mission, TX	(7.5)
27	Erie, PA	16.2	99	Camden, NJ	(2.0)	168	Richardson, TX	(7.5)
28	Lewisville, TX	15.9	99	New York, NY	(2.0)	168	West Covina, CA	(7.5)
29	Sioux Falls, SD	14.8	101	Thousand Oaks, CA	(2.2)	173	Clearwater, FL	(7.7)
30	Compton, CA	14.3	102	Rio Rancho, NM	(2.4)	173	Henderson, NV	(7.7)
31	Denver, CO	13.7	103	Troy, MI	(2.5)	175	Virginia Beach, VA	(7.8)
32	Cincinnati, OH	13.5	104	Lake Forest, CA	(2.6)	176	Seattle, WA	(7.9)
33	Baldwin Park, CA	12.3	105	Deerfield Beach, FL	(2.7)	177	Scottsdale, AZ	(8.0)
33	Gary, IN	12.3	106	Norfolk, VA	(2.8)	177	Woodbridge Twnshp, NJ	(8.0)
33	Indio, CA	12.3	106	Oklahoma City, OK	(2.8)	179	League City, TX	(8.1)
36	Greece, NY	12.2	108	Santa Rosa, CA	(3.2)	180	Brownsville, TX	(8.2)
37	Albany, NY	12.0	109	Cranston, RI	(3.4)	180	Canton Twnshp, MI	(8.2)
38	Costa Mesa, CA	11.6	109	Tustin, CA	(3.4)	180	Lafayette, LA	(8.2)
39	Newport Beach, CA	11.1	111	High Point, NC	(3.5)	183	Lubbock, TX	(8.3)
40	Melbourne, FL	11.0	111	Omaha, NE	(3.5)	184	Downey, CA	(8.4)
41	Lakewood, CO	10.9	113	Clarkstown, NY	(3.6)	184	New Rochelle, NY	(8.4)
41	Pompano Beach, FL	10.9	113	Norman, OK	(3.6)	186	Columbus, OH	(8.5)
43	Broken Arrow, OK	10.8	115	Visalia, CA	(3.7)	186	San Leandro, CA	(8.5)
44	Stamford, CT	10.7	116	Tallahassee, FL	(3.9)	186	San Marcos, CA	(8.5)
45	Nampa, ID	10.6	117	Philadelphia, PA	(4.0)	189	Boulder, CO	(8.6)
45	Vista, CA	10.6	117	Round Rock, TX	(4.0)	190	Fullerton, CA	(8.7)
47	Fort Lauderdale, FL	10.5	119	Rancho Cucamon., CA	(4.1)	190	Livonia, MI	(8.7)
48	Alhambra, CA	9.3	119	St. Joseph, MO	(4.1)	192	Chicago, IL	(8.8)
49	Danbury, CT	9.1	121	Peoria, IL	(4.2)	192	Daly City, CA	(8.8)
50	Clinton Twnshp, MI	8.6	122	Jackson, MS	(4.3)	192	Orange, CA	(8.8)
51	Fresno, CA	7.9	122	Kenosha, WI	(4.3)	195	Fort Collins, CO	(8.9)
51	Scranton, PA	7.9	124	Albuquerque, NM	(4.4)	195	Ontario, CA	(8.9)
53	Louisville, KY	7.8	124	Raleigh, NC	(4.4)	197	Baton Rouge, LA	(9.0)
54	Knoxville, TN	7.6	124	Wilmington, NC	(4.4)	198	Surprise, AZ	(9.5)
55	Buena Park, CA	7.5	127	Provo, UT	(4.5)	199	Fort Wayne, IN	(9.8)
56	Eugene, OR	7.0	127	San Antonio, TX	(4.5)	200	Newark, NJ	(9.9)
57	Santa Monica, CA	6.9	129	Alexandria, VA	(4.6)	201	Abilene, TX	(10.0)
58	Lawton, OK	6.1	129	Kent, WA	(4.6)	202	Minneapolis, MN	(10.2)
59	Amherst, NY	5.8	129	Savannah, GA	(4.6)	203	Gainesville, FL	(10.4)
60	Oakland, CA	5.6	132	Springfield, MO	(4.7)	203	Naperville, IL	(10.4)
61	Burbank, CA	5.0	133	Bloomington, IN	(4.8)	205	Dayton, OH	(10.5)
62	New Bedford, MA	4.8	133	Hammond, IN	(4.8)	206	Chino Hills, CA	(10.7)
63	Madison, WI	4.6	133	Tyler, TX	(4.8)	206	Las Cruces, NM	(10.7)
64	Cleveland, OH	4.2	136	Colonie, NY	(4.9)	206	Tempe, AZ	(10.7)
65	Portsmouth, VA	4.1	136	Murfreesboro, TN	(4.9)	209	Roseville, CA	(11.0)
66	Fontana, CA	3.8	136	Paterson, NJ	(4.9)	210	Suffolk, VA	(11.1)
67	Evansville, IN	3.6	136	Sunrise, FL	(4.9)	210	Victorville, CA	(11.1)
67	Largo, FL	3.6	140	Detroit, MI	(5.0)	212	Wichita, KS	(11.5)
69	Irvine, CA	3.5	140	Overland Park, KS	(5.0)	213	Upper Darby Twnshp, PA	(11.6)
70	Arvada, CO	3.4	140	Rochester, NY	(5.0)	214	Anchorage, AK	(11.7)
71	Anaheim, CA	3.2	140	Sugar Land, TX	(5.0)	215	El Monte, CA	(11.8)
72	Long Beach, CA	3.0	144	Lansing, MI	(5.2)	216	Asheville, NC	(11.9)

Rank Order - City (continued)

RANK	CITY	% CHANGE
216	Fargo, ND	(11.9)
216	Worcester, MA	(11.9)
219	Edmond, OK	(12.0)
220	Beaumont, TX	(12.2)
220	Bend, OR	(12.2)
222	Topeka, KS	(12.3)
222	Ventura, CA	(12.3)
224	Ogden, UT	(12.4)
225	Chino, CA	(12.5)
226	Greeley, CO	(12.6)
227	Cary, NC	(12.7)
228	Boise, ID	(12.9)
228	Charleston, SC	(12.9)
228	Indianapolis, IN	(12.9)
228	Roanoke, VA	(12.9)
232	Newport News, VA	(13.1)
233	Carson, CA	(13.2)
233	Lawrence, MA	(13.2)
233	Westland, MI	(13.2)
236	Cambridge, MA	(13.3)
237	Syracuse, NY	(13.5)
238	Tulsa, OK	(13.6)
238	Yuma, AZ	(13.6)
240	Riverside, CA	(13.7)
241	Kansas City, KS	(13.8)
242	Corona, CA	(13.9)
243	Amarillo, TX	(14.0)
243	Pomona, CA	(14.0)
245	Concord, NC	(14.1)
245	Dearborn, MI	(14.1)
245	Orem, UT	(14.1)
248	Hialeah, FL	(14.2)
248	Oceanside, CA	(14.2)
250	Rochester, MN	(14.3)
251	Peoria, AZ	(14.4)
251	Vacaville, CA	(14.4)
253	Tracy, CA	(14.7)
254	Austin, TX	(14.8)
255	Norwalk, CA	(14.9)
255	Springfield, MA	(14.9)
257	Elizabeth, NJ	(15.1)
257	Flint, MI	(15.1)
259	Orlando, FL	(15.2)
259	Pembroke Pines, FL	(15.2)
261	Green Bay, WI	(15.4)
261	Little Rock, AR	(15.4)
263	Colorado Springs, CO	(15.5)
263	Columbus, GA	(15.5)
263	Santa Clara, CA	(15.5)
263	Torrance, CA	(15.5)
267	Bellevue, WA	(15.7)
267	Newton, MA	(15.7)
269	West Jordan, UT	(15.8)
270	Albany, GA	(15.9)
270	Lakeland, FL	(15.9)
270	Midland, TX	(15.9)
273	Sandy, UT	(16.0)
274	Sacramento, CA	(16.2)
274	Warren, MI	(16.2)
276	Grand Prairie, TX	(16.5)
276	Pasadena, CA	(16.5)
278	Jacksonville, FL	(16.6)
278	Lincoln, NE	(16.6)
280	Brockton, MA	(16.7)
281	Oxnard, CA	(16.8)
282	El Paso, TX	(16.9)
282	Moreno Valley, CA	(16.9)
284	Carrollton, TX	(17.2)
284	Livermore, CA	(17.2)
284	Mesa, AZ	(17.2)
287	Athens-Clarke, GA	(17.4)
288	Stockton, CA	(17.5)
289	Aurora, CO	(17.7)
289	Plano, TX	(17.7)
291	Lee's Summit, MO	(17.8)
292	Allen, TX	(17.9)
293	Centennial, CO	(18.1)
294	Garden Grove, CA	(18.2)
295	St. Louis, MO	(18.3)
296	Jersey City, NJ	(18.4)
297	Meridian, ID	(18.5)
297	Salem, OR	(18.5)
299	Escondido, CA	(18.6)
300	Westminster, CO	(18.8)
301	Nashville, TN	(19.0)
301	Salt Lake City, UT	(19.0)
303	Boca Raton, FL	(19.1)
303	Des Moines, IA	(19.1)
303	Fayetteville, NC	(19.1)
303	Phoenix, AZ	(19.1)
307	Murrieta, CA	(19.2)
308	Hayward, CA	(19.3)
309	Racine, WI	(19.4)
309	Rockford, IL	(19.4)
311	Clifton, NJ	(19.5)
312	Fort Worth, TX	(19.8)
312	Gilbert, AZ	(19.8)
314	Beaverton, OR	(19.9)
314	Edison Twnshp, NJ	(19.9)
314	Independence, MO	(19.9)
317	Miramar, FL	(20.2)
318	Allentown, PA	(20.3)
319	Fort Smith, AR	(20.4)
320	South Bend, IN	(20.5)
321	Memphis, TN	(20.6)
322	Santa Maria, CA	(20.7)
323	Bethlehem, PA	(20.9)
324	Hillsboro, OR	(21.0)
324	Merced, CA	(21.0)
326	North Charleston, SC	(21.3)
326	Waco, TX	(21.3)
328	Chico, CA	(21.4)
328	Lakewood, CA	(21.4)
328	Tacoma, WA	(21.4)
331	San Bernardino, CA	(21.5)
332	Clarksville, TN	(21.7)
333	Arlington, TX	(21.8)
334	Pearland, TX	(22.2)
335	Pittsburgh, PA	(22.3)
335	Roswell, GA	(22.3)
337	West Palm Beach, FL	(22.4)
338	Chula Vista, CA	(22.5)
338	Reading, PA	(22.5)
338	Richmond, CA	(22.5)
341	McAllen, TX	(22.6)
342	Boston, MA	(22.8)
343	Cape Coral, FL	(22.9)
344	Killeen, TX	(23.0)
344	Shreveport, LA	(23.0)
346	Bryan, TX	(23.2)
347	Cedar Rapids, IA	(24.2)
348	Hartford, CT	(24.3)
349	Concord, CA	(24.4)
350	Fishers, IN	(24.7)
351	San Angelo, TX	(24.8)
352	Elgin, IL	(24.9)
352	West Valley, UT	(24.9)
354	Waterbury, CT	(25.0)
355	Somerville, MA	(25.2)
356	Bakersfield, CA	(25.3)
356	Dallas, TX	(25.3)
356	Milwaukee, WI	(25.3)
359	Corpus Christi, TX	(25.4)
360	Las Vegas, NV	(25.6)
360	San Mateo, CA	(25.6)
362	Chattanooga, TN	(25.9)
363	Lawrence, KS	(26.2)
364	Carlsbad, CA	(27.2)
365	Aurora, IL	(27.4)
365	Longview, TX	(27.4)
367	San Diego, CA	(27.5)
368	Simi Valley, CA	(27.9)
369	Palmdale, CA	(28.3)
370	Laredo, TX	(29.1)
371	Modesto, CA	(29.5)
372	Odessa, TX	(30.2)
372	Yakima, WA	(30.2)
374	Trenton, NJ	(30.8)
375	Fremont, CA	(31.1)
376	Fairfield, CA	(31.5)
377	Bridgeport, CT	(31.8)
377	Redwood City, CA	(31.8)
379	Frisco, TX	(32.1)
380	Carmel, IN	(32.4)
381	Bellflower, CA	(32.7)
381	Bellingham, WA	(32.7)
381	Sandy Springs, GA	(32.7)
384	Tampa, FL	(32.8)
385	Lakewood Twnshp, NJ	(34.0)
386	New Orleans, LA	(34.2)
387	Renton, WA	(34.3)
388	Sunnyvale, CA	(34.5)
388	Wichita Falls, TX	(34.5)
390	Napa, CA	(34.7)
391	Irving, TX	(35.2)
391	Santa Clarita, CA	(35.2)
393	Lancaster, CA	(35.5)
394	Sparks, NV	(36.9)
395	O'Fallon, MO	(37.0)
396	Salinas, CA	(37.3)
397	Reno, NV	(37.6)
398	Berkeley, CA	(37.8)
399	El Cajon, CA	(38.5)
400	Charlotte, NC	(38.6)
401	Miami Gardens, FL	(39.4)
402	Grand Rapids, MI	(42.4)
403	Vallejo, CA	(45.8)
NA	Arlington Heights, IL**	NA
NA	Avondale, AZ**	NA
NA	Billings, MT**	NA
NA	Birmingham, AL**	NA
NA	Bloomington, IL**	NA
NA	Buffalo, NY**	NA
NA	Champaign, IL**	NA
NA	Cicero, IL**	NA
NA	Citrus Heights, CA**	NA
NA	Davenport, IA**	NA
NA	Decatur, IL**	NA
NA	Durham, NC**	NA
NA	Fall River, MA**	NA
NA	Hoover, AL**	NA
NA	Huntsville, AL**	NA
NA	Johns Creek, GA**	NA
NA	Kansas City, MO**	NA
NA	Lexington, KY**	NA
NA	Longmont, CO**	NA
NA	Manchester, NH**	NA
NA	Menifee, CA**	NA
NA	Mobile, AL**	NA
NA	Montgomery, AL**	NA
NA	Nashua, NH**	NA
NA	New Haven, CT**	NA
NA	Olathe, KS**	NA
NA	Pueblo, CO**	NA
NA	Sterling Heights, MI**	NA
NA	Thornton, CO**	NA
NA	Toledo, OH**	NA
NA	Tucson, AZ**	NA
NA	Tuscaloosa, AL**	NA
NA	Warwick, RI**	NA
NA	Winston-Salem, NC**	NA

Source: CQ Press using reported data from the F.B.I. "Crime in the United States 2011"
*Larceny-theft is the unlawful taking of property. Attempts are included.
**Not available.

Alpha Order - City

77. Motor Vehicle Thefts in 2011
National Total = 715,373 Motor Vehicle Thefts*

RANK	CITY	THEFTS	RANK	CITY	THEFTS	RANK	CITY	THEFTS
312	Abilene, TX	172	391	Cheektowaga, NY	97	191	Fort Wayne, IN	380
105	Akron, OH	806	216	Chesapeake, VA	325	37	Fort Worth, TX	2,442
281	Albany, GA	213	1	Chicago, IL	19,446	169	Fremont, CA	443
290	Albany, NY	202	233	Chico, CA	291	16	Fresno, CA	4,780
32	Albuquerque, NM	2,823	398	Chino Hills, CA	90	389	Frisco, TX	99
192	Alexandria, VA	372	292	Chino, CA	201	197	Fullerton, CA	359
278	Alhambra, CA	217	92	Chula Vista, CA	884	234	Gainesville, FL	290
173	Allentown, PA	433	248	Cicero, IL	271	174	Garden Grove, CA	428
409	Allen, TX	71	65	Cincinnati, OH	1,276	125	Garland, TX	645
137	Amarillo, TX	616	208	Citrus Heights, CA	340	107	Gary, IN	794
420	Amherst, NY	47	425	Clarkstown, NY	36	352	Gilbert, AZ	135
72	Anaheim, CA	1,119	277	Clarksville, TN	218	57	Glendale, AZ	1,458
134	Anchorage, AK	625	328	Clearwater, FL	158	220	Glendale, CA	323
391	Ann Arbor, MI	97	21	Cleveland, OH	4,093	102	Grand Prairie, TX	818
84	Antioch, CA	967	293	Clifton, NJ	196	216	Grand Rapids, MI	325
434	Arlington Heights, IL	21	293	Clinton Twnshp, MI	196	375	Greece, NY	108
75	Arlington, TX	1,063	181	Clovis, CA	411	336	Greeley, CO	148
303	Arvada, CO	189	417	College Station, TX	53	386	Green Bay, WI	101
222	Asheville, NC	321	435	Colonie, NY	18	136	Gresham, OR	617
263	Athens-Clarke, GA	241	69	Colorado Springs, CO	1,168	378	Hamilton Twnshp, NJ	106
13	Atlanta, GA	5,371	340	Columbia, MO	142	162	Hammond, IN	484
93	Aurora, CO	870	79	Columbus, GA	1,049	246	Hampton, VA	273
354	Aurora, IL	134	24	Columbus, OH	3,615	98	Hartford, CT	859
42	Austin, TX	2,139	95	Compton, CA	863	186	Hawthorne, CA	390
271	Avondale, AZ	232	129	Concord, CA	637	73	Hayward, CA	1,101
39	Bakersfield, CA	2,396	357	Concord, NC	131	188	Hemet, CA	388
184	Baldwin Park, CA	403	319	Coral Springs, FL	164	174	Henderson, NV	428
19	Baltimore, MD	4,199	201	Corona, CA	351	185	Hesperia, CA	400
155	Baton Rouge, LA	500	166	Corpus Christi, TX	467	85	Hialeah, FL	951
235	Beaumont, TX	285	250	Costa Mesa, CA	267	263	High Point, NC	241
340	Beaverton, OR	142	324	Cranston, RI	159	359	Hillsboro, OR	130
330	Bellevue, WA	157	6	Dallas, TX	7,984	145	Hollywood, FL	572
168	Bellflower, CA	444	260	Daly City, CA	250	374	Hoover, AL	109
357	Bellingham, WA	131	412	Danbury, CT	62	3	Houston, TX	12,281
408	Bend, OR	73	266	Davenport, IA	239	259	Huntington Beach, CA	252
132	Berkeley, CA	628	241	Davie, FL	278	114	Huntsville, AL	766
403	Bethlehem, PA	86	130	Dayton, OH	633	116	Independence, MO	728
211	Billings, MT	335	170	Dearborn, MI	440	14	Indianapolis, IN	5,257
54	Birmingham, AL	1,513	371	Decatur, IL	114	193	Indio, CA	369
419	Bloomington, IL	49	295	Deerfield Beach, FL	195	148	Inglewood, CA	555
314	Bloomington, IN	171	365	Denton, TX	118	365	Irvine, CA	118
401	Bloomington, MN	87	25	Denver, CO	3,587	139	Irving, TX	601
371	Boca Raton, FL	114	100	Des Moines, IA	834	47	Jacksonville, FL	1,862
312	Boise, ID	172	4	Detroit, MI	11,368	58	Jackson, MS	1,457
46	Boston, MA	1,899	78	Downey, CA	1,053	97	Jersey City, NJ	860
364	Boulder, CO	125	318	Duluth, MN	166	437	Johns Creek, GA	11
433	Brick Twnshp, NJ	22	132	Durham, NC	628	314	Joliet, IL	171
80	Bridgeport, CT	1,042	273	Edinburg, TX	228	67	Kansas City, KS	1,264
189	Brockton, MA	387	283	Edison Twnshp, NJ	210	28	Kansas City, MO	3,392
355	Broken Arrow, OK	133	416	Edmond, OK	55	317	Kennewick, WA	168
352	Brooklyn Park, MN	135	178	El Cajon, CA	422	351	Kenosha, WI	136
320	Brownsville, TX	163	138	El Monte, CA	606	110	Kent, WA	789
395	Bryan, TX	95	59	El Paso, TX	1,456	305	Killeen, TX	187
209	Buena Park, CA	339	400	Elgin, IL	88	101	Knoxville, TN	820
71	Buffalo, NY	1,121	63	Elizabeth, NJ	1,296	243	Lafayette, LA	277
270	Burbank, CA	234	218	Elk Grove, CA	324	422	Lake Forest, CA	44
332	Cambridge, MA	155	386	Erie, PA	101	290	Lakeland, FL	202
106	Camden, NJ	800	156	Escondido, CA	497	431	Lakewood Twnshp, NJ	26
405	Canton Twnshp, MI	79	143	Eugene, OR	576	253	Lakewood, CA	263
373	Cape Coral, FL	112	272	Evansville, IN	231	157	Lakewood, CO	488
361	Carlsbad, CA	127	89	Everett, WA	925	189	Lancaster, CA	387
426	Carmel, IN	33	202	Fairfield, CA	347	265	Lansing, MI	240
245	Carrollton, TX	274	230	Fall River, MA	297	159	Laredo, TX	486
146	Carson, CA	559	360	Fargo, ND	128	382	Largo, FL	104
411	Cary, NC	65	382	Farmington Hills, MI	104	254	Las Cruces, NM	262
280	Cedar Rapids, IA	214	121	Fayetteville, NC	680	9	Las Vegas, NV	6,787
409	Centennial, CO	71	436	Fishers, IN	17	298	Lawrence, KS	193
394	Champaign, IL	96	113	Flint, MI	770	81	Lawrence, MA	1,026
212	Chandler, AZ	331	112	Fontana, CA	783	286	Lawton, OK	206
249	Charleston, SC	270	324	Fort Collins, CO	159	415	League City, TX	58
44	Charlotte, NC	2,101	139	Fort Lauderdale, FL	601	369	Lee's Summit, MO	115
107	Chattanooga, TN	794	288	Fort Smith, AR	204	228	Lewisville, TX	299

308 Cities

Alpha Order - City (continued)

RANK	CITY	THEFTS
123	Lexington, KY	671
194	Lincoln, NE	364
74	Little Rock, AR	1,093
361	Livermore, CA	127
282	Livonia, MI	211
41	Long Beach, CA	2,212
386	Longmont, CO	101
241	Longview, TX	278
2	Los Angeles, CA	15,597
40	Louisville, KY	2,262
261	Lowell, MA	246
120	Lubbock, TX	693
389	Lynchburg, VA	99
205	Lynn, MA	343
150	Macon, GA	549
203	Madison, WI	344
331	Manchester, NH	156
309	McAllen, TX	180
369	McKinney, TX	115
334	Medford, OR	150
367	Melbourne, FL	116
26	Memphis, TN	3,434
255	Menifee, CA	260
223	Merced, CA	313
428	Meridian, ID	30
87	Mesa, AZ	941
128	Mesquite, TX	641
143	Miami Beach, FL	576
126	Miami Gardens, FL	642
34	Miami, FL	2,700
349	Midland, TX	137
17	Milwaukee, WI	4,538
50	Minneapolis, MN	1,775
256	Miramar, FL	258
424	Mission Viejo, CA	40
298	Mission, TX	193
118	Mobile, AL	701
60	Modesto, CA	1,363
103	Montgomery, AL	816
91	Moreno Valley, CA	900
306	Murfreesboro, TN	185
367	Murrieta, CA	116
391	Nampa, ID	97
344	Napa, CA	139
423	Naperville, IL	42
406	Nashua, NH	77
51	Nashville, TN	1,728
207	New Bedford, MA	342
86	New Haven, CT	942
36	New Orleans, LA	2,540
406	New Rochelle, NY	77
5	New York, NY	9,434
23	Newark, NJ	3,699
404	Newport Beach, CA	80
199	Newport News, VA	355
430	Newton, MA	27
111	Norfolk, VA	785
337	Norman, OK	147
157	North Charleston, SC	488
126	Norwalk, CA	642
310	Norwalk, CT	174
10	Oakland, CA	6,305
200	Oceanside, CA	353
308	Odessa, TX	181
429	O'Fallon, MO	29
232	Ogden, UT	292
22	Oklahoma City, OK	4,059
314	Olathe, KS	171
35	Omaha, NE	2,650
96	Ontario, CA	862
286	Orange, CA	206
401	Orem, UT	87
62	Orlando, FL	1,311
224	Overland Park, KS	310
197	Oxnard, CA	359
338	Palm Bay, FL	145
183	Palmdale, CA	408
239	Pasadena, CA	279
180	Pasadena, TX	414
77	Paterson, NJ	1,054
378	Pearland, TX	106
231	Pembroke Pines, FL	294
215	Peoria, AZ	326
257	Peoria, IL	257
8	Philadelphia, PA	7,447
7	Phoenix, AZ	7,555
163	Pittsburgh, PA	480
187	Plano, TX	389
268	Plantation, FL	236
82	Pomona, CA	976
213	Pompano Beach, FL	329
339	Port St. Lucie, FL	143
31	Portland, OR	3,225
251	Portsmouth, VA	266
385	Provo, UT	102
165	Pueblo, CO	470
346	Quincy, MA	138
344	Racine, WI	139
90	Raleigh, NC	914
432	Ramapo, NY	24
196	Rancho Cucamon., CA	361
179	Reading, PA	420
210	Redding, CA	336
355	Redwood City, CA	133
135	Reno, NV	621
147	Renton, WA	558
153	Rialto, CA	520
297	Richardson, TX	194
61	Richmond, CA	1,362
88	Richmond, VA	928
377	Rio Rancho, NM	107
66	Riverside, CA	1,273
236	Roanoke, VA	283
399	Rochester, MN	89
118	Rochester, NY	701
159	Rockford, IL	486
275	Roseville, CA	221
413	Roswell, GA	61
418	Round Rock, TX	51
30	Sacramento, CA	3,335
174	Salem, OR	428
70	Salinas, CA	1,163
55	Salt Lake City, UT	1,486
346	San Angelo, TX	138
12	San Antonio, TX	5,893
53	San Bernardino, CA	1,656
11	San Diego, CA	6,259
20	San Francisco, CA	4,174
15	San Jose, CA	5,121
142	San Leandro, CA	577
328	San Marcos, CA	158
346	San Mateo, CA	138
322	Sandy Springs, GA	160
298	Sandy, UT	193
64	Santa Ana, CA	1,286
397	Santa Barbara, CA	91
221	Santa Clara, CA	322
269	Santa Clarita, CA	235
252	Santa Maria, CA	264
304	Santa Monica, CA	188
244	Santa Rosa, CA	275
115	Savannah, GA	730
261	Scottsdale, AZ	246
363	Scranton, PA	126
27	Seattle, WA	3,400
172	Shreveport, LA	438
381	Simi Valley, CA	105
320	Sioux City, IA	163
246	Sioux Falls, SD	273
335	Somerville, MA	149
218	South Bend, IN	324
68	South Gate, CA	1,181
301	Sparks, NV	191
164	Spokane Valley, WA	471
49	Spokane, WA	1,778
278	Springfield, IL	217
107	Springfield, MA	794
83	Springfield, MO	974
285	Stamford, CT	207
311	Sterling Heights, MI	173
52	Stockton, CA	1,679
239	St. Joseph, MO	279
29	St. Louis, MO	3,369
48	St. Paul, MN	1,845
99	St. Petersburg, FL	847
378	Suffolk, VA	106
426	Sugar Land, TX	33
274	Sunnyvale, CA	226
322	Sunrise, FL	160
375	Surprise, AZ	108
225	Syracuse, NY	309
43	Tacoma, WA	2,125
195	Tallahassee, FL	363
130	Tampa, FL	633
324	Temecula, CA	159
149	Tempe, AZ	550
237	Thornton, CO	281
414	Thousand Oaks, CA	60
56	Toledo, OH	1,465
420	Toms River Twnshp, NJ	47
141	Topeka, KS	589
226	Torrance, CA	301
289	Tracy, CA	203
171	Trenton, NJ	439
340	Troy, MI	142
33	Tucson, AZ	2,746
38	Tulsa, OK	2,434
302	Tuscaloosa, AL	190
384	Tustin, CA	103
307	Tyler, TX	184
340	Upper Darby Twnshp, PA	142
333	Vacaville, CA	151
76	Vallejo, CA	1,060
94	Vancouver, WA	868
295	Ventura, CA	195
159	Victorville, CA	486
167	Virginia Beach, VA	450
151	Visalia, CA	545
205	Vista, CA	343
324	Waco, TX	159
104	Warren, MI	808
396	Warwick, RI	94
18	Washington, DC	4,339
177	Waterbury, CT	427
154	West Covina, CA	511
276	West Jordan, UT	220
203	West Palm Beach, FL	344
116	West Valley, UT	728
227	Westland, MI	300
238	Westminster, CA	280
213	Westminster, CO	329
258	Whittier, CA	254
267	Wichita Falls, TX	237
45	Wichita, KS	1,901
181	Wilmington, NC	411
122	Winston-Salem, NC	672
349	Woodbridge Twnshp, NJ	137
152	Worcester, MA	530
124	Yakima, WA	660
229	Yonkers, NY	298
284	Yuma, AZ	209

Source: Reported data from the F.B.I. "Crime in the United States 2011"
*Motor vehicle theft includes the theft or attempted theft of a self-propelled vehicle. Excludes motorboats, construction equipment, airplanes, and farming equipment. **Not available.

77. Motor Vehicle Thefts in 2011 (continued)
National Total = 715,373 Motor Vehicle Thefts*

RANK	CITY	THEFTS
1	Chicago, IL	19,446
2	Los Angeles, CA	15,597
3	Houston, TX	12,281
4	Detroit, MI	11,368
5	New York, NY	9,434
6	Dallas, TX	7,984
7	Phoenix, AZ	7,555
8	Philadelphia, PA	7,447
9	Las Vegas, NV	6,787
10	Oakland, CA	6,305
11	San Diego, CA	6,259
12	San Antonio, TX	5,893
13	Atlanta, GA	5,371
14	Indianapolis, IN	5,257
15	San Jose, CA	5,121
16	Fresno, CA	4,780
17	Milwaukee, WI	4,538
18	Washington, DC	4,339
19	Baltimore, MD	4,199
20	San Francisco, CA	4,174
21	Cleveland, OH	4,093
22	Oklahoma City, OK	4,059
23	Newark, NJ	3,699
24	Columbus, OH	3,615
25	Denver, CO	3,587
26	Memphis, TN	3,434
27	Seattle, WA	3,400
28	Kansas City, MO	3,392
29	St. Louis, MO	3,369
30	Sacramento, CA	3,335
31	Portland, OR	3,225
32	Albuquerque, NM	2,823
33	Tucson, AZ	2,746
34	Miami, FL	2,700
35	Omaha, NE	2,650
36	New Orleans, LA	2,540
37	Fort Worth, TX	2,442
38	Tulsa, OK	2,434
39	Bakersfield, CA	2,396
40	Louisville, KY	2,262
41	Long Beach, CA	2,212
42	Austin, TX	2,139
43	Tacoma, WA	2,125
44	Charlotte, NC	2,101
45	Wichita, KS	1,901
46	Boston, MA	1,899
47	Jacksonville, FL	1,862
48	St. Paul, MN	1,845
49	Spokane, WA	1,778
50	Minneapolis, MN	1,775
51	Nashville, TN	1,728
52	Stockton, CA	1,679
53	San Bernardino, CA	1,656
54	Birmingham, AL	1,513
55	Salt Lake City, UT	1,486
56	Toledo, OH	1,465
57	Glendale, AZ	1,458
58	Jackson, MS	1,457
59	El Paso, TX	1,456
60	Modesto, CA	1,363
61	Richmond, CA	1,362
62	Orlando, FL	1,311
63	Elizabeth, NJ	1,296
64	Santa Ana, CA	1,286
65	Cincinnati, OH	1,276
66	Riverside, CA	1,273
67	Kansas City, KS	1,264
68	South Gate, CA	1,181
69	Colorado Springs, CO	1,168
70	Salinas, CA	1,163
71	Buffalo, NY	1,121
72	Anaheim, CA	1,119
73	Hayward, CA	1,101
74	Little Rock, AR	1,093
75	Arlington, TX	1,063
76	Vallejo, CA	1,060
77	Paterson, NJ	1,054
78	Downey, CA	1,053
79	Columbus, GA	1,049
80	Bridgeport, CT	1,042
81	Lawrence, MA	1,026
82	Pomona, CA	976
83	Springfield, MO	974
84	Antioch, CA	967
85	Hialeah, FL	951
86	New Haven, CT	942
87	Mesa, AZ	941
88	Richmond, VA	928
89	Everett, WA	925
90	Raleigh, NC	914
91	Moreno Valley, CA	900
92	Chula Vista, CA	884
93	Aurora, CO	870
94	Vancouver, WA	868
95	Compton, CA	863
96	Ontario, CA	862
97	Jersey City, NJ	860
98	Hartford, CT	859
99	St. Petersburg, FL	847
100	Des Moines, IA	834
101	Knoxville, TN	820
102	Grand Prairie, TX	818
103	Montgomery, AL	816
104	Warren, MI	808
105	Akron, OH	806
106	Camden, NJ	800
107	Chattanooga, TN	794
107	Gary, IN	794
107	Springfield, MA	794
110	Kent, WA	789
111	Norfolk, VA	785
112	Fontana, CA	783
113	Flint, MI	770
114	Huntsville, AL	766
115	Savannah, GA	730
116	Independence, MO	728
116	West Valley, UT	728
118	Mobile, AL	701
118	Rochester, NY	701
120	Lubbock, TX	693
121	Fayetteville, NC	680
122	Winston-Salem, NC	672
123	Lexington, KY	671
124	Yakima, WA	660
125	Garland, TX	645
126	Miami Gardens, FL	642
126	Norwalk, CA	642
128	Mesquite, TX	641
129	Concord, CA	637
130	Dayton, OH	633
130	Tampa, FL	633
132	Berkeley, CA	628
132	Durham, NC	628
134	Anchorage, AK	625
135	Reno, NV	621
136	Gresham, OR	617
137	Amarillo, TX	616
138	El Monte, CA	606
139	Fort Lauderdale, FL	601
139	Irving, TX	601
141	Topeka, KS	589
142	San Leandro, CA	577
143	Eugene, OR	576
143	Miami Beach, FL	576
145	Hollywood, FL	572
146	Carson, CA	559
147	Renton, WA	558
148	Inglewood, CA	555
149	Tempe, AZ	550
150	Macon, GA	549
151	Visalia, CA	545
152	Worcester, MA	530
153	Rialto, CA	520
154	West Covina, CA	511
155	Baton Rouge, LA	500
156	Escondido, CA	497
157	Lakewood, CO	488
157	North Charleston, SC	488
159	Laredo, TX	486
159	Rockford, IL	486
159	Victorville, CA	486
162	Hammond, IN	484
163	Pittsburgh, PA	480
164	Spokane Valley, WA	471
165	Pueblo, CO	470
166	Corpus Christi, TX	467
167	Virginia Beach, VA	450
168	Bellflower, CA	444
169	Fremont, CA	443
170	Dearborn, MI	440
171	Trenton, NJ	439
172	Shreveport, LA	438
173	Allentown, PA	433
174	Garden Grove, CA	428
174	Henderson, NV	428
174	Salem, OR	428
177	Waterbury, CT	427
178	El Cajon, CA	422
179	Reading, PA	420
180	Pasadena, TX	414
181	Clovis, CA	411
181	Wilmington, NC	411
183	Palmdale, CA	408
184	Baldwin Park, CA	403
185	Hesperia, CA	400
186	Hawthorne, CA	390
187	Plano, TX	389
188	Hemet, CA	388
189	Brockton, MA	387
189	Lancaster, CA	387
191	Fort Wayne, IN	380
192	Alexandria, VA	372
193	Indio, CA	369
194	Lincoln, NE	364
195	Tallahassee, FL	363
196	Rancho Cucamon., CA	361
197	Fullerton, CA	359
197	Oxnard, CA	359
199	Newport News, VA	355
200	Oceanside, CA	353
201	Corona, CA	351
202	Fairfield, CA	347
203	Madison, WI	344
203	West Palm Beach, FL	344
205	Lynn, MA	343
205	Vista, CA	343
207	New Bedford, MA	342
208	Citrus Heights, CA	340
209	Buena Park, CA	339
210	Redding, CA	336
211	Billings, MT	335
212	Chandler, AZ	331
213	Pompano Beach, FL	329
213	Westminster, CO	329
215	Peoria, AZ	326
216	Chesapeake, VA	325

Rank Order - City (continued)

RANK	CITY	THEFTS
216	Grand Rapids, MI	325
218	Elk Grove, CA	324
218	South Bend, IN	324
220	Glendale, CA	323
221	Santa Clara, CA	322
222	Asheville, NC	321
223	Merced, CA	313
224	Overland Park, KS	310
225	Syracuse, NY	309
226	Torrance, CA	301
227	Westland, MI	300
228	Lewisville, TX	299
229	Yonkers, NY	298
230	Fall River, MA	297
231	Pembroke Pines, FL	294
232	Ogden, UT	292
233	Chico, CA	291
234	Gainesville, FL	290
235	Beaumont, TX	285
236	Roanoke, VA	283
237	Thornton, CO	281
238	Westminster, CA	280
239	Pasadena, CA	279
239	St. Joseph, MO	279
241	Davie, FL	278
241	Longview, TX	278
243	Lafayette, LA	277
244	Santa Rosa, CA	275
245	Carrollton, TX	274
246	Hampton, VA	273
246	Sioux Falls, SD	273
248	Cicero, IL	271
249	Charleston, SC	270
250	Costa Mesa, CA	267
251	Portsmouth, VA	266
252	Santa Maria, CA	264
253	Lakewood, CA	263
254	Las Cruces, NM	262
255	Menifee, CA	260
256	Miramar, FL	258
257	Peoria, IL	257
258	Whittier, CA	254
259	Huntington Beach, CA	252
260	Daly City, CA	250
261	Lowell, MA	246
261	Scottsdale, AZ	246
263	Athens-Clarke, GA	241
263	High Point, NC	241
265	Lansing, MI	240
266	Davenport, IA	239
267	Wichita Falls, TX	237
268	Plantation, FL	236
269	Santa Clarita, CA	235
270	Burbank, CA	234
271	Avondale, AZ	232
272	Evansville, IN	231
273	Edinburg, TX	228
274	Sunnyvale, CA	226
275	Roseville, CA	221
276	West Jordan, UT	220
277	Clarksville, TN	218
278	Alhambra, CA	217
278	Springfield, IL	217
280	Cedar Rapids, IA	214
281	Albany, GA	213
282	Livonia, MI	211
283	Edison Twnshp, NJ	210
284	Yuma, AZ	209
285	Stamford, CT	207
286	Lawton, OK	206
286	Orange, CA	206
288	Fort Smith, AR	204
289	Tracy, CA	203
290	Albany, NY	202
290	Lakeland, FL	202
292	Chino, CA	201
293	Clifton, NJ	196
293	Clinton Twnshp, MI	196
295	Deerfield Beach, FL	195
295	Ventura, CA	195
297	Richardson, TX	194
298	Lawrence, KS	193
298	Mission, TX	193
298	Sandy, UT	193
301	Sparks, NV	191
302	Tuscaloosa, AL	190
303	Arvada, CO	189
304	Santa Monica, CA	188
305	Killeen, TX	187
306	Murfreesboro, TN	185
307	Tyler, TX	184
308	Odessa, TX	181
309	McAllen, TX	180
310	Norwalk, CT	174
311	Sterling Heights, MI	173
312	Abilene, TX	172
312	Boise, ID	172
314	Bloomington, IN	171
314	Joliet, IL	171
314	Olathe, KS	171
317	Kennewick, WA	168
318	Duluth, MN	166
319	Coral Springs, FL	164
320	Brownsville, TX	163
320	Sioux City, IA	163
322	Sandy Springs, GA	160
322	Sunrise, FL	160
324	Cranston, RI	159
324	Fort Collins, CO	159
324	Temecula, CA	159
324	Waco, TX	159
328	Clearwater, FL	158
328	San Marcos, CA	158
330	Bellevue, WA	157
331	Manchester, NH	156
332	Cambridge, MA	155
333	Vacaville, CA	151
334	Medford, OR	150
335	Somerville, MA	149
336	Greeley, CO	148
337	Norman, OK	147
338	Palm Bay, FL	145
339	Port St. Lucie, FL	143
340	Beaverton, OR	142
340	Columbia, MO	142
340	Troy, MI	142
340	Upper Darby Twnshp, PA	142
344	Napa, CA	139
344	Racine, WI	139
346	Quincy, MA	138
346	San Angelo, TX	138
346	San Mateo, CA	138
349	Midland, TX	137
349	Woodbridge Twnshp, NJ	137
351	Kenosha, WI	136
352	Brooklyn Park, MN	135
352	Gilbert, AZ	135
354	Aurora, IL	134
355	Broken Arrow, OK	133
355	Redwood City, CA	133
357	Bellingham, WA	131
357	Concord, NC	131
359	Hillsboro, OR	130
360	Fargo, ND	128
361	Carlsbad, CA	127
361	Livermore, CA	127
363	Scranton, PA	126
364	Boulder, CO	125
365	Denton, TX	118
365	Irvine, CA	118
367	Melbourne, FL	116
367	Murrieta, CA	116
369	Lee's Summit, MO	115
369	McKinney, TX	115
371	Boca Raton, FL	114
371	Decatur, IL	114
373	Cape Coral, FL	112
374	Hoover, AL	109
375	Greece, NY	108
375	Surprise, AZ	108
377	Rio Rancho, NM	107
378	Hamilton Twnshp, NJ	106
378	Pearland, TX	106
378	Suffolk, VA	106
381	Simi Valley, CA	105
382	Farmington Hills, MI	104
382	Largo, FL	104
384	Tustin, CA	103
385	Provo, UT	102
386	Erie, PA	101
386	Green Bay, WI	101
386	Longmont, CO	101
389	Frisco, TX	99
389	Lynchburg, VA	99
391	Ann Arbor, MI	97
391	Cheektowaga, NY	97
391	Nampa, ID	97
394	Champaign, IL	96
395	Bryan, TX	95
396	Warwick, RI	94
397	Santa Barbara, CA	91
398	Chino Hills, CA	90
399	Rochester, MN	89
400	Elgin, IL	88
401	Bloomington, MN	87
401	Orem, UT	87
403	Bethlehem, PA	86
404	Newport Beach, CA	80
405	Canton Twnshp, MI	79
406	Nashua, NH	77
406	New Rochelle, NY	77
408	Bend, OR	73
409	Allen, TX	71
409	Centennial, CO	71
411	Cary, NC	65
412	Danbury, CT	62
413	Roswell, GA	61
414	Thousand Oaks, CA	60
415	League City, TX	58
416	Edmond, OK	55
417	College Station, TX	53
418	Round Rock, TX	51
419	Bloomington, IL	49
420	Amherst, NY	47
420	Toms River Twnshp, NJ	47
422	Lake Forest, CA	44
423	Naperville, IL	42
424	Mission Viejo, CA	40
425	Clarkstown, NY	36
426	Carmel, IN	33
426	Sugar Land, TX	33
428	Meridian, ID	30
429	O'Fallon, MO	29
430	Newton, MA	27
431	Lakewood Twnshp, NJ	26
432	Ramapo, NY	24
433	Brick Twnshp, NJ	22
434	Arlington Heights, IL	21
435	Colonie, NY	18
436	Fishers, IN	17
437	Johns Creek, GA	11

Source: Reported data from the F.B.I. "Crime in the United States 2011"
*Motor vehicle theft includes the theft or attempted theft of a self-propelled vehicle. Excludes motorboats, construction equipment, airplanes, and farming equipment. **Not available.

Alpha Order - City

78. Motor Vehicle Theft Rate in 2011
National Rate = 229.6 Motor Vehicle Thefts per 100,000 Population*

RANK	CITY	RATE
332	Abilene, TX	143.9
131	Akron, OH	404.5
202	Albany, GA	271.5
263	Albany, NY	205.5
90	Albuquerque, NM	511.4
208	Alexandria, VA	262.6
211	Alhambra, CA	258.1
143	Allentown, PA	365.7
404	Allen, TX	82.5
176	Amarillo, TX	316.4
426	Amherst, NY	40.0
165	Anaheim, CA	328.9
250	Anchorage, AK	210.5
399	Ann Arbor, MI	85.2
15	Antioch, CA	933.6
433	Arlington Heights, IL	27.9
189	Arlington, TX	284.9
297	Arvada, CO	174.5
140	Asheville, NC	380.1
262	Athens-Clarke, GA	205.8
6	Atlanta, GA	1,262.2
207	Aurora, CO	263.0
411	Aurora, IL	67.5
205	Austin, TX	265.0
181	Avondale, AZ	300.1
42	Bakersfield, CA	681.5
77	Baldwin Park, CA	528.3
44	Baltimore, MD	669.9
245	Baton Rouge, LA	215.9
221	Beaumont, TX	236.0
316	Beaverton, OR	156.5
357	Bellevue, WA	126.3
67	Bellflower, CA	572.8
312	Bellingham, WA	159.5
390	Bend, OR	94.2
71	Berkeley, CA	551.3
375	Bethlehem, PA	114.3
173	Billings, MT	318.8
37	Birmingham, AL	709.5
414	Bloomington, IL	63.8
248	Bloomington, IN	211.6
382	Bloomington, MN	104.2
347	Boca Raton, FL	133.3
402	Boise, ID	82.7
179	Boston, MA	305.6
358	Boulder, CO	126.2
431	Brick Twnshp, NJ	29.2
33	Bridgeport, CT	721.1
128	Brockton, MA	410.0
348	Broken Arrow, OK	133.1
293	Brooklyn Park, MN	176.8
392	Brownsville, TX	91.2
363	Bryan, TX	122.1
125	Buena Park, CA	416.1
120	Buffalo, NY	427.1
232	Burbank, CA	223.8
328	Cambridge, MA	146.5
11	Camden, NJ	1,030.9
396	Canton Twnshp, MI	87.7
407	Cape Coral, FL	71.6
368	Carlsbad, CA	119.2
424	Carmel, IN	41.5
230	Carrollton, TX	225.3
59	Carson, CA	602.4
420	Cary, NC	47.5
302	Cedar Rapids, IA	168.5
408	Centennial, CO	69.5
370	Champaign, IL	118.1
339	Chandler, AZ	138.2
237	Charleston, SC	222.3
203	Charlotte, NC	266.1
102	Chattanooga, TN	469.3

RANK	CITY	RATE
362	Cheektowaga, NY	122.5
331	Chesapeake, VA	144.5
34	Chicago, IL	719.2
161	Chico, CA	333.7
369	Chino Hills, CA	118.9
213	Chino, CA	254.8
147	Chula Vista, CA	358.2
171	Cicero, IL	322.1
119	Cincinnati, OH	429.4
132	Citrus Heights, CA	403.4
422	Clarkstown, NY	45.4
309	Clarksville, TN	162.5
330	Clearwater, FL	144.8
12	Cleveland, OH	1,030.7
224	Clifton, NJ	232.2
268	Clinton Twnshp, MI	202.6
121	Clovis, CA	424.8
416	College Station, TX	55.3
435	Colonie, NY	23.1
193	Colorado Springs, CO	275.7
355	Columbia, MO	130.4
74	Columbus, GA	545.3
107	Columbus, OH	459.0
18	Compton, CA	884.3
85	Concord, CA	515.8
308	Concord, NC	163.6
345	Coral Springs, FL	133.6
228	Corona, CA	227.7
321	Corpus Christi, TX	149.9
219	Costa Mesa, CA	240.0
272	Cranston, RI	198.0
47	Dallas, TX	652.8
216	Daly City, CA	244.4
406	Danbury, CT	76.5
220	Davenport, IA	238.5
182	Davie, FL	298.1
114	Dayton, OH	446.9
113	Dearborn, MI	448.6
322	Decatur, IL	149.3
212	Deerfield Beach, FL	256.4
383	Denton, TX	101.9
64	Denver, CO	587.4
129	Des Moines, IA	407.8
2	Detroit, MI	1,593.9
16	Downey, CA	931.1
280	Duluth, MN	191.0
201	Durham, NC	271.6
186	Edinburg, TX	289.6
254	Edison Twnshp, NJ	209.4
412	Edmond, OK	66.8
123	El Cajon, CA	419.3
79	El Monte, CA	527.8
240	El Paso, TX	219.7
405	Elgin, IL	81.1
10	Elizabeth, NJ	1,033.6
255	Elk Grove, CA	209.3
387	Erie, PA	98.9
154	Escondido, CA	341.3
144	Eugene, OR	364.9
276	Evansville, IN	195.7
19	Everett, WA	884.0
166	Fairfield, CA	325.6
162	Fall River, MA	332.2
367	Fargo, ND	119.3
354	Farmington Hills, MI	130.5
160	Fayetteville, NC	334.8
436	Fishers, IN	22.0
29	Flint, MI	752.3
134	Fontana, CA	394.7
381	Fort Collins, CO	108.5
147	Fort Lauderdale, FL	358.2
222	Fort Smith, AR	234.9

RANK	CITY	RATE
324	Fort Wayne, IN	149.0
169	Fort Worth, TX	322.7
266	Fremont, CA	204.5
14	Fresno, CA	955.1
401	Frisco, TX	82.9
209	Fullerton, CA	262.5
225	Gainesville, FL	230.1
214	Garden Grove, CA	247.6
191	Garland, TX	278.4
13	Gary, IN	983.8
413	Gilbert, AZ	63.9
52	Glendale, AZ	634.1
305	Glendale, CA	166.5
109	Grand Prairie, TX	456.8
298	Grand Rapids, MI	173.0
378	Greece, NY	111.9
315	Greeley, CO	156.6
388	Green Bay, WI	96.6
65	Gresham, OR	578.2
366	Hamilton Twnshp, NJ	119.4
61	Hammond, IN	595.7
274	Hampton, VA	196.3
41	Hartford, CT	687.2
108	Hawthorne, CA	457.3
28	Hayward, CA	754.7
95	Hemet, CA	487.5
307	Henderson, NV	164.7
115	Hesperia, CA	438.4
124	Hialeah, FL	417.6
227	High Point, NC	228.0
335	Hillsboro, OR	140.4
133	Hollywood, FL	400.9
349	Hoover, AL	132.9
66	Houston, TX	572.9
352	Huntington Beach, CA	131.1
122	Huntsville, AL	423.3
54	Independence, MO	620.9
53	Indianapolis, IN	631.1
97	Indio, CA	479.7
92	Inglewood, CA	500.2
417	Irvine, CA	54.9
199	Irving, TX	272.1
235	Jacksonville, FL	223.1
23	Jackson, MS	836.5
151	Jersey City, NJ	346.2
437	Johns Creek, GA	14.2
372	Joliet, IL	115.6
20	Kansas City, KS	861.6
30	Kansas City, MO	735.1
232	Kennewick, WA	223.8
341	Kenosha, WI	136.5
21	Kent, WA	840.6
333	Killeen, TX	143.2
110	Knoxville, TN	454.3
229	Lafayette, LA	227.6
415	Lake Forest, CA	56.3
264	Lakeland, FL	204.6
433	Lakewood Twnshp, NJ	27.9
168	Lakewood, CA	324.7
158	Lakewood, CO	335.5
217	Lancaster, CA	244.2
252	Lansing, MI	210.1
269	Laredo, TX	201.6
350	Largo, FL	132.1
204	Las Cruces, NM	265.4
103	Las Vegas, NV	465.3
241	Lawrence, KS	218.8
3	Lawrence, MA	1,335.2
251	Lawton, OK	210.4
410	League City, TX	68.0
359	Lee's Summit, MO	125.4
178	Lewisville, TX	307.3

Alpha Order - City (continued)

RANK	CITY	RATE	RANK	CITY	RATE	RANK	CITY	RATE
230	Lexington, KY	225.3	291	Overland Park, KS	177.7	275	Sioux City, IA	196.1
337	Lincoln, NE	139.6	289	Oxnard, CA	179.3	296	Sioux Falls, SD	175.3
69	Little Rock, AR	560.5	338	Palm Bay, FL	138.6	277	Somerville, MA	195.5
318	Livermore, CA	155.0	206	Palmdale, CA	264.0	174	South Bend, IN	318.6
242	Livonia, MI	217.8	270	Pasadena, CA	201.1	7	South Gate, CA	1,236.6
101	Long Beach, CA	473.0	200	Pasadena, TX	272.0	253	Sparks, NV	209.8
373	Longmont, CO	115.1	35	Paterson, NJ	718.5	84	Spokane Valley, WA	516.7
157	Longview, TX	338.4	376	Pearland, TX	113.8	22	Spokane, WA	837.9
130	Los Angeles, CA	406.5	281	Pembroke Pines, FL	187.4	284	Springfield, IL	186.1
155	Louisville, KY	340.1	258	Peoria, AZ	208.6	86	Springfield, MA	515.6
226	Lowell, MA	229.5	236	Peoria, IL	222.8	56	Springfield, MO	608.5
183	Lubbock, TX	295.6	96	Philadelphia, PA	486.5	302	Stamford, CT	168.5
356	Lynchburg, VA	129.5	87	Phoenix, AZ	515.3	346	Sterling Heights, MI	133.5
141	Lynn, MA	377.4	317	Pittsburgh, PA	155.5	68	Stockton, CA	568.9
62	Macon, GA	593.2	327	Plano, TX	146.6	145	St. Joseph, MO	362.1
326	Madison, WI	146.9	195	Plantation, FL	274.1	9	St. Louis, MO	1,051.3
334	Manchester, NH	142.2	49	Pomona, CA	647.2	51	St. Paul, MN	641.4
342	McAllen, TX	135.7	167	Pompano Beach, FL	325.1	153	St. Petersburg, FL	341.4
397	McKinney, TX	85.9	398	Port St. Lucie, FL	85.7	361	Suffolk, VA	123.8
271	Medford, OR	198.1	73	Portland, OR	546.6	425	Sugar Land, TX	41.0
320	Melbourne, FL	150.4	194	Portsmouth, VA	275.1	312	Sunnyvale, CA	159.5
80	Memphis, TN	526.1	394	Provo, UT	89.0	282	Sunrise, FL	186.9
163	Menifee, CA	331.5	117	Pueblo, CO	433.4	393	Surprise, AZ	90.6
136	Merced, CA	391.8	325	Quincy, MA	148.7	247	Syracuse, NY	211.9
427	Meridian, ID	39.5	294	Racine, WI	175.5	8	Tacoma, WA	1,054.5
249	Mesa, AZ	211.3	234	Raleigh, NC	223.5	273	Tallahassee, FL	197.4
112	Mesquite, TX	449.0	432	Ramapo, NY	28.4	285	Tampa, FL	186.0
48	Miami Beach, FL	647.4	245	Rancho Cucamon., CA	215.9	314	Temecula, CA	157.0
63	Miami Gardens, FL	591.0	99	Reading, PA	475.3	159	Tempe, AZ	335.3
46	Miami, FL	666.8	142	Redding, CA	369.6	223	Thornton, CO	232.5
365	Midland, TX	120.7	299	Redwood City, CA	171.1	421	Thousand Oaks, CA	46.8
27	Milwaukee, WI	759.6	197	Reno, NV	273.4	91	Toledo, OH	509.7
104	Minneapolis, MN	460.4	57	Renton, WA	604.2	418	Toms River Twnshp, NJ	51.3
258	Miramar, FL	208.6	83	Rialto, CA	518.3	106	Topeka, KS	459.1
423	Mission Viejo, CA	42.4	279	Richardson, TX	191.5	264	Torrance, CA	204.6
215	Mission, TX	245.3	5	Richmond, CA	1,298.1	218	Tracy, CA	242.0
192	Mobile, AL	278.3	111	Richmond, VA	449.1	87	Trenton, NJ	515.3
45	Modesto, CA	669.7	364	Rio Rancho, NM	120.9	294	Troy, MI	175.5
134	Montgomery, AL	394.7	127	Riverside, CA	414.1	81	Tucson, AZ	520.6
105	Moreno Valley, CA	460.0	188	Roanoke, VA	288.2	55	Tulsa, OK	614.5
301	Murfreesboro, TN	168.6	402	Rochester, MN	82.7	256	Tuscaloosa, AL	209.0
380	Murrieta, CA	110.8	164	Rochester, NY	331.4	344	Tustin, CA	134.8
371	Nampa, ID	117.6	175	Rockford, IL	317.0	285	Tyler, TX	186.0
290	Napa, CA	178.6	287	Roseville, CA	183.9	300	Upper Darby Twnshp, PA	171.0
430	Naperville, IL	29.5	409	Roswell, GA	68.1	311	Vacaville, CA	161.5
395	Nashua, NH	88.9	419	Round Rock, TX	50.0	17	Vallejo, CA	903.6
190	Nashville, TN	282.0	38	Sacramento, CA	706.6	78	Vancouver, WA	528.2
149	New Bedford, MA	357.6	196	Salem, OR	273.9	288	Ventura, CA	181.1
32	New Haven, CT	724.5	26	Salinas, CA	764.1	126	Victorville, CA	414.4
31	New Orleans, LA	732.0	24	Salt Lake City, UT	781.9	385	Virginia Beach, VA	101.5
386	New Rochelle, NY	99.5	329	San Angelo, TX	145.0	118	Visalia, CA	432.9
374	New York, NY	114.9	116	San Antonio, TX	434.8	146	Vista, CA	361.3
4	Newark, NJ	1,330.3	25	San Bernardino, CA	779.7	360	Waco, TX	124.8
391	Newport Beach, CA	92.8	99	San Diego, CA	475.3	58	Warren, MI	603.2
278	Newport News, VA	194.1	89	San Francisco, CA	512.3	376	Warwick, RI	113.8
429	Newton, MA	31.5	76	San Jose, CA	535.1	39	Washington, DC	702.1
172	Norfolk, VA	319.5	43	San Leandro, CA	671.3	138	Waterbury, CT	386.2
352	Norman, OK	131.1	283	San Marcos, CA	186.4	98	West Covina, CA	476.0
93	North Charleston, SC	494.9	336	San Mateo, CA	140.3	260	West Jordan, UT	208.1
60	Norwalk, CA	601.2	304	Sandy Springs, GA	168.3	156	West Palm Beach, FL	339.6
267	Norwalk, CT	202.9	244	Sandy, UT	216.5	70	West Valley, UT	551.6
1	Oakland, CA	1,594.9	137	Santa Ana, CA	391.7	150	Westland, MI	357.0
257	Oceanside, CA	208.8	384	Santa Barbara, CA	101.7	177	Westminster, CA	308.5
292	Odessa, TX	177.4	198	Santa Clara, CA	273.3	180	Westminster, CO	304.7
428	O'Fallon, MO	36.4	351	Santa Clarita, CA	131.7	184	Whittier, CA	294.2
152	Ogden, UT	345.9	210	Santa Maria, CA	262.1	238	Wichita Falls, TX	222.0
40	Oklahoma City, OK	692.4	261	Santa Monica, CA	207.1	94	Wichita, KS	494.0
343	Olathe, KS	135.0	310	Santa Rosa, CA	162.0	139	Wilmington, NC	381.2
50	Omaha, NE	642.3	170	Savannah, GA	322.4	187	Winston-Salem, NC	289.0
82	Ontario, CA	519.7	379	Scottsdale, AZ	111.6	340	Woodbridge Twnshp, NJ	137.1
322	Orange, CA	149.3	306	Scranton, PA	165.1	185	Worcester, MA	291.0
388	Orem, UT	96.6	72	Seattle, WA	550.0	36	Yakima, WA	713.5
75	Orlando, FL	542.7	242	Shreveport, LA	217.8	319	Yonkers, NY	151.4
			400	Simi Valley, CA	83.5	239	Yuma, AZ	221.4

Source: CQ Press using reported data from the F.B.I. "Crime in the United States 2011"
*Motor vehicle theft includes the theft or attempted theft of a self-propelled vehicle. Excludes motorboats, construction equipment, airplanes, and farming equipment. **Not available.

Rank Order - City

78. Motor Vehicle Theft Rate in 2011 (continued)
National Rate = 229.6 Motor Vehicle Thefts per 100,000 Population*

RANK	CITY	RATE	RANK	CITY	RATE	RANK	CITY	RATE
1	Oakland, CA	1,594.9	73	Portland, OR	546.6	145	St. Joseph, MO	362.1
2	Detroit, MI	1,593.9	74	Columbus, GA	545.3	146	Vista, CA	361.3
3	Lawrence, MA	1,335.2	75	Orlando, FL	542.7	147	Chula Vista, CA	358.2
4	Newark, NJ	1,330.3	76	San Jose, CA	535.1	147	Fort Lauderdale, FL	358.2
5	Richmond, CA	1,298.1	77	Baldwin Park, CA	528.3	149	New Bedford, MA	357.6
6	Atlanta, GA	1,262.2	78	Vancouver, WA	528.2	150	Westland, MI	357.0
7	South Gate, CA	1,236.6	79	El Monte, CA	527.8	151	Jersey City, NJ	346.2
8	Tacoma, WA	1,054.5	80	Memphis, TN	526.1	152	Ogden, UT	345.9
9	St. Louis, MO	1,051.3	81	Tucson, AZ	520.6	153	St. Petersburg, FL	341.4
10	Elizabeth, NJ	1,033.6	82	Ontario, CA	519.7	154	Escondido, CA	341.3
11	Camden, NJ	1,030.9	83	Rialto, CA	518.3	155	Louisville, KY	340.1
12	Cleveland, OH	1,030.7	84	Spokane Valley, WA	516.7	156	West Palm Beach, FL	339.6
13	Gary, IN	983.8	85	Concord, CA	515.8	157	Longview, TX	338.4
14	Fresno, CA	955.1	86	Springfield, MA	515.6	158	Lakewood, CO	335.5
15	Antioch, CA	933.6	87	Phoenix, AZ	515.3	159	Tempe, AZ	335.3
16	Downey, CA	931.1	87	Trenton, NJ	515.3	160	Fayetteville, NC	334.8
17	Vallejo, CA	903.6	89	San Francisco, CA	512.3	161	Chico, CA	333.7
18	Compton, CA	884.3	90	Albuquerque, NM	511.4	162	Fall River, MA	332.2
19	Everett, WA	884.0	91	Toledo, OH	509.7	163	Menifee, CA	331.5
20	Kansas City, KS	861.6	92	Inglewood, CA	500.2	164	Rochester, NY	331.4
21	Kent, WA	840.6	93	North Charleston, SC	494.9	165	Anaheim, CA	328.9
22	Spokane, WA	837.9	94	Wichita, KS	494.0	166	Fairfield, CA	325.6
23	Jackson, MS	836.5	95	Hemet, CA	487.5	167	Pompano Beach, FL	325.1
24	Salt Lake City, UT	781.9	96	Philadelphia, PA	486.5	168	Lakewood, CA	324.7
25	San Bernardino, CA	779.7	97	Indio, CA	479.7	169	Fort Worth, TX	322.7
26	Salinas, CA	764.1	98	West Covina, CA	476.0	170	Savannah, GA	322.4
27	Milwaukee, WI	759.6	99	Reading, PA	475.3	171	Cicero, IL	322.1
28	Hayward, CA	754.7	99	San Diego, CA	475.3	172	Norfolk, VA	319.5
29	Flint, MI	752.3	101	Long Beach, CA	473.0	173	Billings, MT	318.8
30	Kansas City, MO	735.1	102	Chattanooga, TN	469.3	174	South Bend, IN	318.6
31	New Orleans, LA	732.0	103	Las Vegas, NV	465.3	175	Rockford, IL	317.0
32	New Haven, CT	724.5	104	Minneapolis, MN	460.4	176	Amarillo, TX	316.4
33	Bridgeport, CT	721.1	105	Moreno Valley, CA	460.0	177	Westminster, CA	308.5
34	Chicago, IL	719.2	106	Topeka, KS	459.1	178	Lewisville, TX	307.3
35	Paterson, NJ	718.5	107	Columbus, OH	459.0	179	Boston, MA	305.6
36	Yakima, WA	713.5	108	Hawthorne, CA	457.3	180	Westminster, CO	304.7
37	Birmingham, AL	709.5	109	Grand Prairie, TX	456.8	181	Avondale, AZ	300.1
38	Sacramento, CA	706.6	110	Knoxville, TN	454.3	182	Davie, FL	298.1
39	Washington, DC	702.1	111	Richmond, VA	449.1	183	Lubbock, TX	295.6
40	Oklahoma City, OK	692.4	112	Mesquite, TX	449.0	184	Whittier, CA	294.2
41	Hartford, CT	687.2	113	Dearborn, MI	448.6	185	Worcester, MA	291.0
42	Bakersfield, CA	681.5	114	Dayton, OH	446.9	186	Edinburg, TX	289.6
43	San Leandro, CA	671.3	115	Hesperia, CA	438.4	187	Winston-Salem, NC	289.0
44	Baltimore, MD	669.9	116	San Antonio, TX	434.8	188	Roanoke, VA	288.2
45	Modesto, CA	669.7	117	Pueblo, CO	433.4	189	Arlington, TX	284.9
46	Miami, FL	666.8	118	Visalia, CA	432.9	190	Nashville, TN	282.0
47	Dallas, TX	652.8	119	Cincinnati, OH	429.4	191	Garland, TX	278.4
48	Miami Beach, FL	647.4	120	Buffalo, NY	427.1	192	Mobile, AL	278.3
49	Pomona, CA	647.2	121	Clovis, CA	424.8	193	Colorado Springs, CO	275.7
50	Omaha, NE	642.3	122	Huntsville, AL	423.3	194	Portsmouth, VA	275.1
51	St. Paul, MN	641.4	123	El Cajon, CA	419.3	195	Plantation, FL	274.1
52	Glendale, AZ	634.1	124	Hialeah, FL	417.6	196	Salem, OR	273.9
53	Indianapolis, IN	631.1	125	Buena Park, CA	416.1	197	Reno, NV	273.4
54	Independence, MO	620.9	126	Victorville, CA	414.4	198	Santa Clara, CA	273.3
55	Tulsa, OK	614.5	127	Riverside, CA	414.1	199	Irving, TX	272.1
56	Springfield, MO	608.5	128	Brockton, MA	410.0	200	Pasadena, TX	272.0
57	Renton, WA	604.2	129	Des Moines, IA	407.8	201	Durham, NC	271.6
58	Warren, MI	603.2	130	Los Angeles, CA	406.5	202	Albany, GA	271.5
59	Carson, CA	602.4	131	Akron, OH	404.5	203	Charlotte, NC	266.1
60	Norwalk, CA	601.2	132	Citrus Heights, CA	403.4	204	Las Cruces, NM	265.4
61	Hammond, IN	595.7	133	Hollywood, FL	400.9	205	Austin, TX	265.0
62	Macon, GA	593.2	134	Fontana, CA	394.7	206	Palmdale, CA	264.0
63	Miami Gardens, FL	591.0	134	Montgomery, AL	394.7	207	Aurora, CO	263.0
64	Denver, CO	587.4	136	Merced, CA	391.8	208	Alexandria, VA	262.6
65	Gresham, OR	578.2	137	Santa Ana, CA	391.7	209	Fullerton, CA	262.5
66	Houston, TX	572.9	138	Waterbury, CT	386.2	210	Santa Maria, CA	262.1
67	Bellflower, CA	572.8	139	Wilmington, NC	381.2	211	Alhambra, CA	258.1
68	Stockton, CA	568.9	140	Asheville, NC	380.1	212	Deerfield Beach, FL	256.4
69	Little Rock, AR	560.5	141	Lynn, MA	377.4	213	Chino, CA	254.8
70	West Valley, UT	551.6	142	Redding, CA	369.6	214	Garden Grove, CA	247.6
71	Berkeley, CA	551.3	143	Allentown, PA	365.7	215	Mission, TX	245.3
72	Seattle, WA	550.0	144	Eugene, OR	364.9	216	Daly City, CA	244.4

Rank Order - City (continued)

RANK	CITY	RATE
217	Lancaster, CA	244.2
218	Tracy, CA	242.0
219	Costa Mesa, CA	240.0
220	Davenport, IA	238.5
221	Beaumont, TX	236.0
222	Fort Smith, AR	234.9
223	Thornton, CO	232.5
224	Clifton, NJ	232.2
225	Gainesville, FL	230.1
226	Lowell, MA	229.5
227	High Point, NC	228.0
228	Corona, CA	227.7
229	Lafayette, LA	227.6
230	Carrollton, TX	225.3
230	Lexington, KY	225.3
232	Burbank, CA	223.8
232	Kennewick, WA	223.8
234	Raleigh, NC	223.5
235	Jacksonville, FL	223.1
236	Peoria, IL	222.8
237	Charleston, SC	222.3
238	Wichita Falls, TX	222.0
239	Yuma, AZ	221.4
240	El Paso, TX	219.7
241	Lawrence, KS	218.8
242	Livonia, MI	217.8
242	Shreveport, LA	217.8
244	Sandy, UT	216.5
245	Baton Rouge, LA	215.9
245	Rancho Cucamon., CA	215.9
247	Syracuse, NY	211.9
248	Bloomington, IN	211.6
249	Mesa, AZ	211.3
250	Anchorage, AK	210.5
251	Lawton, OK	210.4
252	Lansing, MI	210.1
253	Sparks, NV	209.8
254	Edison Twnshp, NJ	209.4
255	Elk Grove, CA	209.3
256	Tuscaloosa, AL	209.0
257	Oceanside, CA	208.8
258	Miramar, FL	208.6
258	Peoria, AZ	208.6
260	West Jordan, UT	208.1
261	Santa Monica, CA	207.1
262	Athens-Clarke, GA	205.8
263	Albany, NY	205.5
264	Lakeland, FL	204.6
264	Torrance, CA	204.6
266	Fremont, CA	204.5
267	Norwalk, CT	202.9
268	Clinton Twnshp, MI	202.6
269	Laredo, TX	201.6
270	Pasadena, CA	201.1
271	Medford, OR	198.1
272	Cranston, RI	198.0
273	Tallahassee, FL	197.4
274	Hampton, VA	196.3
275	Sioux City, IA	196.1
276	Evansville, IN	195.7
277	Somerville, MA	195.5
278	Newport News, VA	194.1
279	Richardson, TX	191.5
280	Duluth, MN	191.0
281	Pembroke Pines, FL	187.4
282	Sunrise, FL	186.9
283	San Marcos, CA	186.4
284	Springfield, IL	186.1
285	Tampa, FL	186.0
285	Tyler, TX	186.0
287	Roseville, CA	183.9
288	Ventura, CA	181.1
289	Oxnard, CA	179.3
290	Napa, CA	178.6
291	Overland Park, KS	177.7
292	Odessa, TX	177.4
293	Brooklyn Park, MN	176.8
294	Racine, WI	175.5
294	Troy, MI	175.5
296	Sioux Falls, SD	175.3
297	Arvada, CO	174.5
298	Grand Rapids, MI	173.0
299	Redwood City, CA	171.1
300	Upper Darby Twnshp, PA	171.0
301	Murfreesboro, TN	168.6
302	Cedar Rapids, IA	168.5
302	Stamford, CT	168.5
304	Sandy Springs, GA	168.3
305	Glendale, CA	166.5
306	Scranton, PA	165.1
307	Henderson, NV	164.7
308	Concord, NC	163.6
309	Clarksville, TN	162.5
310	Santa Rosa, CA	162.0
311	Vacaville, CA	161.5
312	Bellingham, WA	159.5
312	Sunnyvale, CA	159.5
314	Temecula, CA	157.0
315	Greeley, CO	156.6
316	Beaverton, OR	156.5
317	Pittsburgh, PA	155.5
318	Livermore, CA	155.0
319	Yonkers, NY	151.4
320	Melbourne, FL	150.4
321	Corpus Christi, TX	149.9
322	Decatur, IL	149.3
322	Orange, CA	149.3
324	Fort Wayne, IN	149.0
325	Quincy, MA	148.7
326	Madison, WI	146.9
327	Plano, TX	146.6
328	Cambridge, MA	146.5
329	San Angelo, TX	145.0
330	Clearwater, FL	144.8
331	Chesapeake, VA	144.5
332	Abilene, TX	143.9
333	Killeen, TX	143.2
334	Manchester, NH	142.2
335	Hillsboro, OR	140.4
336	San Mateo, CA	140.3
337	Lincoln, NE	139.6
338	Palm Bay, FL	138.6
339	Chandler, AZ	138.2
340	Woodbridge Twnshp, NJ	137.1
341	Kenosha, WI	136.5
342	McAllen, TX	135.7
343	Olathe, KS	135.0
344	Tustin, CA	134.8
345	Coral Springs, FL	133.6
346	Sterling Heights, MI	133.5
347	Boca Raton, FL	133.3
348	Broken Arrow, OK	133.1
349	Hoover, AL	132.9
350	Largo, FL	132.1
351	Santa Clarita, CA	131.7
352	Huntington Beach, CA	131.1
352	Norman, OK	131.1
354	Farmington Hills, MI	130.5
355	Columbia, MO	130.4
356	Lynchburg, VA	129.5
357	Bellevue, WA	126.3
358	Boulder, CO	126.2
359	Lee's Summit, MO	125.4
360	Waco, TX	124.8
361	Suffolk, VA	123.8
362	Cheektowaga, NY	122.5
363	Bryan, TX	122.1
364	Rio Rancho, NM	120.9
365	Midland, TX	120.7
366	Hamilton Twnshp, NJ	119.4
367	Fargo, ND	119.3
368	Carlsbad, CA	119.2
369	Chino Hills, CA	118.9
370	Champaign, IL	118.1
371	Nampa, ID	117.6
372	Joliet, IL	115.6
373	Longmont, CO	115.1
374	New York, NY	114.9
375	Bethlehem, PA	114.3
376	Pearland, TX	113.8
376	Warwick, RI	113.8
378	Greece, NY	111.9
379	Scottsdale, AZ	111.6
380	Murrieta, CA	110.8
381	Fort Collins, CO	108.5
382	Bloomington, MN	104.2
383	Denton, TX	101.9
384	Santa Barbara, CA	101.7
385	Virginia Beach, VA	101.5
386	New Rochelle, NY	99.5
387	Erie, PA	98.9
388	Green Bay, WI	96.6
388	Orem, UT	96.6
390	Bend, OR	94.2
391	Newport Beach, CA	92.8
392	Brownsville, TX	91.2
393	Surprise, AZ	90.6
394	Provo, UT	89.0
395	Nashua, NH	88.9
396	Canton Twnshp, MI	87.7
397	McKinney, TX	85.9
398	Port St. Lucie, FL	85.7
399	Ann Arbor, MI	85.2
400	Simi Valley, CA	83.5
401	Frisco, TX	82.9
402	Boise, ID	82.7
402	Rochester, MN	82.7
404	Allen, TX	82.5
405	Elgin, IL	81.1
406	Danbury, CT	76.5
407	Cape Coral, FL	71.6
408	Centennial, CO	69.5
409	Roswell, GA	68.1
410	League City, TX	68.0
411	Aurora, IL	67.5
412	Edmond, OK	66.8
413	Gilbert, AZ	63.9
414	Bloomington, IL	63.8
415	Lake Forest, CA	56.3
416	College Station, TX	55.3
417	Irvine, CA	54.9
418	Toms River Twnshp, NJ	51.3
419	Round Rock, TX	50.0
420	Cary, NC	47.5
421	Thousand Oaks, CA	46.8
422	Clarkstown, NY	45.4
423	Mission Viejo, CA	42.4
424	Carmel, IN	41.5
425	Sugar Land, TX	41.0
426	Amherst, NY	40.0
427	Meridian, ID	39.5
428	O'Fallon, MO	36.4
429	Newton, MA	31.5
430	Naperville, IL	29.5
431	Brick Twnshp, NJ	29.2
432	Ramapo, NY	28.4
433	Arlington Heights, IL	27.9
433	Lakewood Twnshp, NJ	27.9
435	Colonie, NY	23.1
436	Fishers, IN	22.0
437	Johns Creek, GA	14.2

Source: CQ Press using reported data from the F.B.I. "Crime in the United States 2011"
*Motor vehicle theft includes the theft or attempted theft of a self-propelled vehicle. Excludes motorboats, construction equipment, airplanes, and farming equipment. **Not available.

Alpha Order - City

79. Percent Change in Motor Vehicle Theft Rate: 2010 to 2011
National Percent Change = 4.0% Decrease*

RANK	CITY	% CHANGE	RANK	CITY	% CHANGE	RANK	CITY	% CHANGE
211	Abilene, TX	(7.5)	166	Cheektowaga, NY	(2.2)	21	Fort Wayne, IN	33.4
66	Akron, OH	11.1	313	Chesapeake, VA	(16.8)	166	Fort Worth, TX	(2.2)
393	Albany, GA	(33.9)	99	Chicago, IL	6.8	285	Fremont, CA	(14.3)
313	Albany, NY	(16.8)	26	Chico, CA	29.3	136	Fresno, CA	1.7
147	Albuquerque, NM	0.6	85	Chino Hills, CA	8.1	360	Frisco, TX	(23.4)
13	Alexandria, VA	40.3	156	Chino, CA	(0.7)	133	Fullerton, CA	2.2
329	Alhambra, CA	(18.8)	366	Chula Vista, CA	(26.0)	331	Gainesville, FL	(19.0)
192	Allentown, PA	(4.9)	NA	Cicero, IL**	NA	249	Garden Grove, CA	(10.9)
51	Allen, TX	15.4	258	Cincinnati, OH	(11.6)	265	Garland, TX	(12.1)
205	Amarillo, TX	(6.9)	385	Citrus Heights, CA	(31.8)	NA	Gary, IN**	NA
208	Amherst, NY	(7.2)	64	Clarkstown, NY	11.3	248	Gilbert, AZ	(10.8)
70	Anaheim, CA	10.2	146	Clarksville, TN	0.8	47	Glendale, AZ	17.1
364	Anchorage, AK	(24.8)	361	Clearwater, FL	(23.9)	151	Glendale, CA	(0.1)
370	Ann Arbor, MI	(26.2)	32	Cleveland, OH	25.4	315	Grand Prairie, TX	(17.1)
156	Antioch, CA	(0.7)	NA	Clifton, NJ**	NA	273	Grand Rapids, MI	(12.8)
270	Arlington Heights, IL	(12.5)	197	Clinton Twnshp, MI	(5.9)	3	Greece, NY	72.2
266	Arlington, TX	(12.2)	107	Clovis, CA	5.5	163	Greeley, CO	(1.8)
231	Arvada, CO	(9.6)	408	College Station, TX	(45.1)	250	Green Bay, WI	(11.0)
145	Asheville, NC	1.0	411	Colonie, NY	(58.6)	253	Gresham, OR	(11.1)
351	Athens-Clarke, GA	(22.1)	292	Colorado Springs, CO	(14.8)	58	Hamilton Twnshp, NJ	13.7
20	Atlanta, GA	34.3	151	Columbia, MO	(0.1)	218	Hammond, IN	(8.1)
184	Aurora, CO	(4.2)	151	Columbus, GA	(0.1)	325	Hampton, VA	(17.8)
292	Aurora, IL	(14.8)	288	Columbus, OH	(14.5)	127	Hartford, CT	3.1
199	Austin, TX	(6.2)	49	Compton, CA	16.3	263	Hawthorne, CA	(11.9)
389	Avondale, AZ	(33.2)	304	Concord, CA	(15.9)	82	Hayward, CA	8.3
210	Bakersfield, CA	(7.4)	388	Concord, NC	(32.9)	87	Hemet, CA	8.0
337	Baldwin Park, CA	(19.5)	173	Coral Springs, FL	(3.0)	290	Henderson, NV	(14.7)
171	Baltimore, MD	(2.8)	336	Corona, CA	(19.4)	8	Hesperia, CA	45.4
NA	Baton Rouge, LA**	NA	178	Corpus Christi, TX	(3.8)	290	Hialeah, FL	(14.7)
245	Beaumont, TX	(10.6)	198	Costa Mesa, CA	(6.0)	79	High Point, NC	9.1
83	Beaverton, OR	8.2	261	Cranston, RI	(11.8)	NA	Hillsboro, OR**	NA
351	Bellevue, WA	(22.1)	136	Dallas, TX	1.7	233	Hollywood, FL	(9.8)
223	Bellflower, CA	(8.8)	351	Daly City, CA	(22.1)	NA	Hoover, AL**	NA
169	Bellingham, WA	(2.7)	355	Danbury, CT	(22.3)	134	Houston, TX	2.0
119	Bend, OR	4.1	NA	Davenport, IA**	NA	250	Huntington Beach, CA	(11.0)
216	Berkeley, CA	(7.9)	95	Davie, FL	7.1	NA	Huntsville, AL**	NA
323	Bethlehem, PA	(17.5)	142	Dayton, OH	1.5	132	Independence, MO	2.3
NA	Billings, MT**	NA	348	Dearborn, MI	(21.3)	NA	Indianapolis, IN**	NA
NA	Birmingham, AL**	NA	255	Decatur, IL	(11.3)	310	Indio, CA	(16.5)
243	Bloomington, IL	(10.5)	77	Deerfield Beach, FL	9.5	344	Inglewood, CA	(20.2)
37	Bloomington, IN	22.4	320	Denton, TX	(17.4)	162	Irvine, CA	(1.4)
175	Bloomington, MN	(3.2)	69	Denver, CO	10.5	238	Irving, TX	(10.0)
97	Boca Raton, FL	7.0	62	Des Moines, IA	11.8	206	Jacksonville, FL	(7.0)
95	Boise, ID	7.1	57	Detroit, MI	13.8	200	Jackson, MS	(6.3)
176	Boston, MA	(3.4)	93	Downey, CA	7.3	113	Jersey City, NJ	4.8
11	Boulder, CO	40.7	NA	Duluth, MN**	NA	399	Johns Creek, GA	(39.3)
400	Brick Twnshp, NJ	(40.4)	258	Durham, NC	(11.6)	155	Joliet, IL	(0.4)
48	Bridgeport, CT	16.7	366	Edinburg, TX	(26.0)	73	Kansas City, KS	9.8
294	Brockton, MA	(14.9)	17	Edison Twnshp, NJ	35.6	NA	Kansas City, MO**	NA
114	Broken Arrow, OK	4.7	34	Edmond, OK	23.7	39	Kennewick, WA	21.7
NA	Brooklyn Park, MN**	NA	370	El Cajon, CA	(26.2)	103	Kenosha, WI	6.4
389	Brownsville, TX	(33.2)	333	El Monte, CA	(19.3)	214	Kent, WA	(7.7)
372	Bryan, TX	(26.4)	258	El Paso, TX	(11.6)	374	Killeen, TX	(26.6)
274	Buena Park, CA	(12.9)	332	Elgin, IL	(19.1)	119	Knoxville, TN	4.1
NA	Buffalo, NY**	NA	54	Elizabeth, NJ	14.2	229	Lafayette, LA	(9.4)
308	Burbank, CA	(16.2)	278	Elk Grove, CA	(13.2)	383	Lake Forest, CA	(31.2)
261	Cambridge, MA	(11.8)	366	Erie, PA	(26.0)	339	Lakeland, FL	(19.7)
4	Camden, NJ	57.1	404	Escondido, CA	(42.2)	413	Lakewood Twnshp, NJ	(63.0)
382	Canton Twnshp, MI	(29.8)	202	Eugene, OR	(6.6)	347	Lakewood, CA	(21.0)
108	Cape Coral, FL	5.4	81	Evansville, IN	8.6	239	Lakewood, CO	(10.1)
67	Carlsbad, CA	10.9	358	Everett, WA	(23.1)	318	Lancaster, CA	(17.3)
295	Carmel, IN	(15.1)	378	Fairfield, CA	(27.7)	160	Lansing, MI	(1.3)
320	Carrollton, TX	(17.4)	295	Fall River, MA	(15.1)	409	Laredo, TX	(48.5)
41	Carson, CA	20.0	380	Fargo, ND	(28.8)	398	Largo, FL	(36.6)
110	Cary, NC	5.1	350	Farmington Hills, MI	(22.0)	17	Las Cruces, NM	35.6
222	Cedar Rapids, IA	(8.6)	176	Fayetteville, NC	(3.4)	217	Las Vegas, NV	(8.0)
53	Centennial, CO	14.5	391	Fishers, IN	(33.3)	24	Lawrence, KS	31.7
NA	Champaign, IL**	NA	30	Flint, MI	25.9	40	Lawrence, MA	21.0
257	Chandler, AZ	(11.4)	135	Fontana, CA	1.8	254	Lawton, OK	(11.2)
55	Charleston, SC	14.1	365	Fort Collins, CO	(25.5)	394	League City, TX	(34.0)
346	Charlotte, NC	(20.4)	111	Fort Lauderdale, FL	4.9	233	Lee's Summit, MO	(9.8)
164	Chattanooga, TN	(1.9)	189	Fort Smith, AR	(4.6)	275	Lewisville, TX	(13.1)

Alpha Order - City (continued)

RANK	CITY	% CHANGE
NA	Lexington, KY**	NA
118	Lincoln, NE	4.2
173	Little Rock, AR	(3.0)
307	Livermore, CA	(16.1)
280	Livonia, MI	(13.8)
151	Long Beach, CA	(0.1)
375	Longmont, CO	(26.9)
372	Longview, TX	(26.4)
221	Los Angeles, CA	(8.4)
73	Louisville, KY	9.8
403	Lowell, MA	(41.7)
23	Lubbock, TX	33.1
124	Lynchburg, VA	3.5
101	Lynn, MA	6.5
299	Macon, GA	(15.4)
181	Madison, WI	(4.1)
179	Manchester, NH	(3.9)
410	McAllen, TX	(54.8)
282	McKinney, TX	(13.9)
239	Medford, OR	(10.1)
255	Melbourne, FL	(11.3)
233	Memphis, TN	(9.8)
381	Menifee, CA	(29.5)
29	Merced, CA	26.0
344	Meridian, ID	(20.2)
194	Mesa, AZ	(5.0)
303	Mesquite, TX	(15.8)
181	Miami Beach, FL	(4.1)
59	Miami Gardens, FL	13.4
42	Miami, FL	19.9
243	Midland, TX	(10.5)
103	Milwaukee, WI	6.4
204	Minneapolis, MN	(6.7)
327	Miramar, FL	(18.5)
339	Mission Viejo, CA	(19.7)
405	Mission, TX	(42.8)
NA	Mobile, AL**	NA
184	Modesto, CA	(4.2)
NA	Montgomery, AL**	NA
50	Moreno Valley, CA	15.8
46	Murfreesboro, TN	18.0
220	Murrieta, CA	(8.3)
356	Nampa, ID	(22.7)
105	Napa, CA	6.1
NA	Naperville, IL**	NA
52	Nashua, NH	14.9
223	Nashville, TN	(8.8)
320	New Bedford, MA	(17.4)
246	New Haven, CT	(10.7)
83	New Orleans, LA	8.2
22	New Rochelle, NY	33.2
208	New York, NY	(7.2)
128	Newark, NJ	3.0
406	Newport Beach, CA	(43.3)
272	Newport News, VA	(12.7)
139	Newton, MA	1.6
330	Norfolk, VA	(18.9)
25	Norman, OK	30.6
200	North Charleston, SC	(6.3)
124	Norwalk, CA	3.5
165	Norwalk, CT	(2.1)
11	Oakland, CA	40.7
109	Oceanside, CA	5.2
196	Odessa, TX	(5.6)
337	O'Fallon, MO	(19.5)
226	Ogden, UT	(8.9)
71	Oklahoma City, OK	9.9
42	Olathe, KS	19.9
16	Omaha, NE	35.8
149	Ontario, CA	0.0
206	Orange, CA	(7.0)
315	Orem, UT	(17.1)
78	Orlando, FL	9.3

RANK	CITY	% CHANGE
119	Overland Park, KS	4.1
379	Oxnard, CA	(28.3)
6	Palm Bay, FL	46.2
342	Palmdale, CA	(20.1)
358	Pasadena, CA	(23.1)
101	Pasadena, TX	6.5
5	Paterson, NJ	50.0
31	Pearland, TX	25.7
230	Pembroke Pines, FL	(9.5)
280	Peoria, AZ	(13.8)
187	Peoria, IL	(4.4)
93	Philadelphia, PA	7.3
128	Phoenix, AZ	3.0
366	Pittsburgh, PA	(26.0)
106	Plano, TX	5.7
188	Plantation, FL	(4.5)
339	Pomona, CA	(19.7)
227	Pompano Beach, FL	(9.0)
2	Port St. Lucie, FL	77.1
192	Portland, OR	(4.9)
144	Portsmouth, VA	1.1
136	Provo, UT	1.7
NA	Pueblo, CO**	NA
91	Quincy, MA	7.4
214	Racine, WI	(7.7)
89	Raleigh, NC	7.8
15	Ramapo, NY	37.9
44	Rancho Cucamon., CA	19.6
401	Reading, PA	(41.0)
14	Redding, CA	39.6
392	Redwood City, CA	(33.7)
312	Reno, NV	(16.6)
397	Renton, WA	(35.9)
139	Rialto, CA	1.6
148	Richardson, TX	0.1
304	Richmond, CA	(15.9)
99	Richmond, VA	6.8
171	Rio Rancho, NM	(2.8)
287	Riverside, CA	(14.4)
61	Roanoke, VA	12.0
318	Rochester, MN	(17.3)
241	Rochester, NY	(10.2)
60	Rockford, IL	13.1
190	Roseville, CA	(4.7)
402	Roswell, GA	(41.2)
407	Round Rock, TX	(44.4)
309	Sacramento, CA	(16.4)
149	Salem, OR	0.0
27	Salinas, CA	29.2
202	Salt Lake City, UT	(6.6)
299	San Angelo, TX	(15.4)
97	San Antonio, TX	7.0
232	San Bernardino, CA	(9.7)
168	San Diego, CA	(2.3)
91	San Francisco, CA	7.4
181	San Jose, CA	(4.1)
250	San Leandro, CA	(11.0)
395	San Marcos, CA	(34.5)
396	San Mateo, CA	(34.6)
376	Sandy Springs, GA	(27.3)
9	Sandy, UT	45.1
116	Santa Ana, CA	4.5
285	Santa Barbara, CA	(14.3)
194	Santa Clara, CA	(5.0)
213	Santa Clarita, CA	(7.6)
377	Santa Maria, CA	(27.4)
76	Santa Monica, CA	9.6
283	Santa Rosa, CA	(14.0)
80	Savannah, GA	8.9
180	Scottsdale, AZ	(4.0)
131	Scranton, PA	2.4
158	Seattle, WA	(1.2)
317	Shreveport, LA	(17.2)
362	Simi Valley, CA	(24.2)

RANK	CITY	% CHANGE
90	Sioux City, IA	7.7
36	Sioux Falls, SD	23.5
242	Somerville, MA	(10.4)
71	South Bend, IN	9.9
10	South Gate, CA	44.3
324	Sparks, NV	(17.7)
73	Spokane Valley, WA	9.8
297	Spokane, WA	(15.2)
227	Springfield, IL	(9.0)
223	Springfield, MA	(8.8)
191	Springfield, MO	(4.8)
88	Stamford, CT	7.9
NA	Sterling Heights, MI**	NA
328	Stockton, CA	(18.6)
6	St. Joseph, MO	46.2
269	St. Louis, MO	(12.4)
266	St. Paul, MN	(12.2)
387	St. Petersburg, FL	(32.7)
115	Suffolk, VA	4.6
412	Sugar Land, TX	(61.2)
275	Sunnyvale, CA	(13.1)
218	Sunrise, FL	(8.1)
302	Surprise, AZ	(15.6)
348	Syracuse, NY	(21.3)
126	Tacoma, WA	3.4
160	Tallahassee, FL	(1.3)
357	Tampa, FL	(22.8)
211	Temecula, CA	(7.5)
237	Tempe, AZ	(9.9)
NA	Thornton, CO**	NA
333	Thousand Oaks, CA	(19.3)
19	Toledo, OH	34.4
1	Toms River Twnshp, NJ	80.0
55	Topeka, KS	14.1
284	Torrance, CA	(14.2)
333	Tracy, CA	(19.3)
45	Trenton, NJ	18.9
28	Troy, MI	28.5
342	Tucson, AZ	(20.1)
130	Tulsa, OK	2.8
NA	Tuscaloosa, AL**	NA
384	Tustin, CA	(31.7)
310	Tyler, TX	(16.5)
122	Upper Darby Twnshp, PA	4.0
288	Vacaville, CA	(14.5)
268	Vallejo, CA	(12.3)
186	Vancouver, WA	(4.3)
33	Ventura, CA	24.7
65	Victorville, CA	11.2
386	Virginia Beach, VA	(31.9)
233	Visalia, CA	(9.8)
279	Vista, CA	(13.4)
363	Waco, TX	(24.5)
63	Warren, MI	11.6
270	Warwick, RI	(12.5)
275	Washington, DC	(13.1)
158	Waterbury, CT	(1.2)
301	West Covina, CA	(15.5)
169	West Jordan, UT	(2.7)
264	West Palm Beach, FL	(12.0)
68	West Valley, UT	10.8
298	Westland, MI	(15.3)
139	Westminster, CA	1.6
143	Westminster, CO	1.3
306	Whittier, CA	(16.0)
351	Wichita Falls, TX	(22.1)
38	Wichita, KS	21.9
326	Wilmington, NC	(18.1)
111	Winston-Salem, NC	4.9
85	Woodbridge Twnshp, NJ	8.1
246	Worcester, MA	(10.7)
123	Yakima, WA	3.8
34	Yonkers, NY	23.7
116	Yuma, AZ	4.5

Source: CQ Press using reported data from the F.B.I. "Crime in the United States 2011"
*Motor vehicle theft includes the theft or attempted theft of a self-propelled vehicle. Excludes motorboats, construction equipment, airplanes, and farming equipment. **Not available.

Rank Order - City
79. Percent Change in Motor Vehicle Theft Rate: 2010 to 2011 (continued)
National Percent Change = 4.0% Decrease*

RANK	CITY	% CHANGE	RANK	CITY	% CHANGE	RANK	CITY	% CHANGE
1	Toms River Twnshp, NJ	80.0	73	Kansas City, KS	9.8	145	Asheville, NC	1.0
2	Port St. Lucie, FL	77.1	73	Louisville, KY	9.8	146	Clarksville, TN	0.8
3	Greece, NY	72.2	73	Spokane Valley, WA	9.8	147	Albuquerque, NM	0.6
4	Camden, NJ	57.1	76	Santa Monica, CA	9.6	148	Richardson, TX	0.1
5	Paterson, NJ	50.0	77	Deerfield Beach, FL	9.5	149	Ontario, CA	0.0
6	Palm Bay, FL	46.2	78	Orlando, FL	9.3	149	Salem, OR	0.0
6	St. Joseph, MO	46.2	79	High Point, NC	9.1	151	Columbia, MO	(0.1)
8	Hesperia, CA	45.4	80	Savannah, GA	8.9	151	Columbus, GA	(0.1)
9	Sandy, UT	45.1	81	Evansville, IN	8.6	151	Glendale, CA	(0.1)
10	South Gate, CA	44.3	82	Hayward, CA	8.3	151	Long Beach, CA	(0.1)
11	Boulder, CO	40.7	83	Beaverton, OR	8.2	155	Joliet, IL	(0.4)
11	Oakland, CA	40.7	83	New Orleans, LA	8.2	156	Antioch, CA	(0.7)
13	Alexandria, VA	40.3	85	Chino Hills, CA	8.1	156	Chino, CA	(0.7)
14	Redding, CA	39.6	85	Woodbridge Twnshp, NJ	8.1	158	Seattle, WA	(1.2)
15	Ramapo, NY	37.9	87	Hemet, CA	8.0	158	Waterbury, CT	(1.2)
16	Omaha, NE	35.8	88	Stamford, CT	7.9	160	Lansing, MI	(1.3)
17	Edison Twnshp, NJ	35.6	89	Raleigh, NC	7.8	160	Tallahassee, FL	(1.3)
17	Las Cruces, NM	35.6	90	Sioux City, IA	7.7	162	Irvine, CA	(1.4)
19	Toledo, OH	34.4	91	Quincy, MA	7.4	163	Greeley, CO	(1.8)
20	Atlanta, GA	34.3	91	San Francisco, CA	7.4	164	Chattanooga, TN	(1.9)
21	Fort Wayne, IN	33.4	93	Downey, CA	7.3	165	Norwalk, CT	(2.1)
22	New Rochelle, NY	33.2	93	Philadelphia, PA	7.3	166	Cheektowaga, NY	(2.2)
23	Lubbock, TX	33.1	95	Boise, ID	7.1	166	Fort Worth, TX	(2.2)
24	Lawrence, KS	31.7	95	Davie, FL	7.1	168	San Diego, CA	(2.3)
25	Norman, OK	30.6	97	Boca Raton, FL	7.0	169	Bellingham, WA	(2.7)
26	Chico, CA	29.3	97	San Antonio, TX	7.0	169	West Jordan, UT	(2.7)
27	Salinas, CA	29.2	99	Chicago, IL	6.8	171	Baltimore, MD	(2.8)
28	Troy, MI	28.5	99	Richmond, VA	6.8	171	Rio Rancho, NM	(2.8)
29	Merced, CA	26.0	101	Lynn, MA	6.5	173	Coral Springs, FL	(3.0)
30	Flint, MI	25.9	101	Pasadena, TX	6.5	173	Little Rock, AR	(3.0)
31	Pearland, TX	25.7	103	Kenosha, WI	6.4	175	Bloomington, MN	(3.2)
32	Cleveland, OH	25.4	103	Milwaukee, WI	6.4	176	Boston, MA	(3.4)
33	Ventura, CA	24.7	105	Napa, CA	6.1	176	Fayetteville, NC	(3.4)
34	Edmond, OK	23.7	106	Plano, TX	5.7	178	Corpus Christi, TX	(3.8)
34	Yonkers, NY	23.7	107	Clovis, CA	5.5	179	Manchester, NH	(3.9)
36	Sioux Falls, SD	23.5	108	Cape Coral, FL	5.4	180	Scottsdale, AZ	(4.0)
37	Bloomington, IN	22.4	109	Oceanside, CA	5.2	181	Madison, WI	(4.1)
38	Wichita, KS	21.9	110	Cary, NC	5.1	181	Miami Beach, FL	(4.1)
39	Kennewick, WA	21.7	111	Fort Lauderdale, FL	4.9	181	San Jose, CA	(4.1)
40	Lawrence, MA	21.0	111	Winston-Salem, NC	4.9	184	Aurora, CO	(4.2)
41	Carson, CA	20.0	113	Jersey City, NJ	4.8	184	Modesto, CA	(4.2)
42	Miami, FL	19.9	114	Broken Arrow, OK	4.7	186	Vancouver, WA	(4.3)
42	Olathe, KS	19.9	115	Suffolk, VA	4.6	187	Peoria, IL	(4.4)
44	Rancho Cucamon., CA	19.6	116	Santa Ana, CA	4.5	188	Plantation, FL	(4.5)
45	Trenton, NJ	18.9	116	Yuma, AZ	4.5	189	Fort Smith, AR	(4.6)
46	Murfreesboro, TN	18.0	118	Lincoln, NE	4.2	190	Roseville, CA	(4.7)
47	Glendale, AZ	17.1	119	Bend, OR	4.1	191	Springfield, MO	(4.8)
48	Bridgeport, CT	16.7	119	Knoxville, TN	4.1	192	Allentown, PA	(4.9)
49	Compton, CA	16.3	119	Overland Park, KS	4.1	192	Portland, OR	(4.9)
50	Moreno Valley, CA	15.8	122	Upper Darby Twnshp, PA	4.0	194	Mesa, AZ	(5.0)
51	Allen, TX	15.4	123	Yakima, WA	3.8	194	Santa Clara, CA	(5.0)
52	Nashua, NH	14.9	124	Lynchburg, VA	3.5	196	Odessa, TX	(5.6)
53	Centennial, CO	14.5	124	Norwalk, CA	3.5	197	Clinton Twnshp, MI	(5.9)
54	Elizabeth, NJ	14.2	126	Tacoma, WA	3.4	198	Costa Mesa, CA	(6.0)
55	Charleston, SC	14.1	127	Hartford, CT	3.1	199	Austin, TX	(6.2)
55	Topeka, KS	14.1	128	Newark, NJ	3.0	200	Jackson, MS	(6.3)
57	Detroit, MI	13.8	128	Phoenix, AZ	3.0	200	North Charleston, SC	(6.3)
58	Hamilton Twnshp, NJ	13.7	130	Tulsa, OK	2.8	202	Eugene, OR	(6.6)
59	Miami Gardens, FL	13.4	131	Scranton, PA	2.4	202	Salt Lake City, UT	(6.6)
60	Rockford, IL	13.1	132	Independence, MO	2.3	204	Minneapolis, MN	(6.7)
61	Roanoke, VA	12.0	133	Fullerton, CA	2.2	205	Amarillo, TX	(6.9)
62	Des Moines, IA	11.8	134	Houston, TX	2.0	206	Jacksonville, FL	(7.0)
63	Warren, MI	11.6	135	Fontana, CA	1.8	206	Orange, CA	(7.0)
64	Clarkstown, NY	11.3	136	Dallas, TX	1.7	208	Amherst, NY	(7.2)
65	Victorville, CA	11.2	136	Fresno, CA	1.7	208	New York, NY	(7.2)
66	Akron, OH	11.1	136	Provo, UT	1.7	210	Bakersfield, CA	(7.4)
67	Carlsbad, CA	10.9	139	Newton, MA	1.6	211	Abilene, TX	(7.5)
68	West Valley, UT	10.8	139	Rialto, CA	1.6	211	Temecula, CA	(7.5)
69	Denver, CO	10.5	139	Westminster, CA	1.6	213	Santa Clarita, CA	(7.6)
70	Anaheim, CA	10.2	142	Dayton, OH	1.5	214	Kent, WA	(7.7)
71	Oklahoma City, OK	9.9	143	Westminster, CO	1.3	214	Racine, WI	(7.7)
71	South Bend, IN	9.9	144	Portsmouth, VA	1.1	216	Berkeley, CA	(7.9)

Rank Order - City (continued)

RANK	CITY	% CHANGE	RANK	CITY	% CHANGE	RANK	CITY	% CHANGE
217	Las Vegas, NV	(8.0)	290	Henderson, NV	(14.7)	364	Anchorage, AK	(24.8)
218	Hammond, IN	(8.1)	290	Hialeah, FL	(14.7)	365	Fort Collins, CO	(25.5)
218	Sunrise, FL	(8.1)	292	Aurora, IL	(14.8)	366	Chula Vista, CA	(26.0)
220	Murrieta, CA	(8.3)	292	Colorado Springs, CO	(14.8)	366	Edinburg, TX	(26.0)
221	Los Angeles, CA	(8.4)	294	Brockton, MA	(14.9)	366	Erie, PA	(26.0)
222	Cedar Rapids, IA	(8.6)	295	Carmel, IN	(15.1)	366	Pittsburgh, PA	(26.0)
223	Bellflower, CA	(8.8)	295	Fall River, MA	(15.1)	370	Ann Arbor, MI	(26.2)
223	Nashville, TN	(8.8)	297	Spokane, WA	(15.2)	370	El Cajon, CA	(26.2)
223	Springfield, MA	(8.8)	298	Westland, MI	(15.3)	372	Bryan, TX	(26.4)
226	Ogden, UT	(8.9)	299	Macon, GA	(15.4)	372	Longview, TX	(26.4)
227	Pompano Beach, FL	(9.0)	299	San Angelo, TX	(15.4)	374	Killeen, TX	(26.6)
227	Springfield, IL	(9.0)	301	West Covina, CA	(15.5)	375	Longmont, CO	(26.9)
229	Lafayette, LA	(9.4)	302	Surprise, AZ	(15.6)	376	Sandy Springs, GA	(27.3)
230	Pembroke Pines, FL	(9.5)	303	Mesquite, TX	(15.8)	377	Santa Maria, CA	(27.4)
231	Arvada, CO	(9.6)	304	Concord, CA	(15.9)	378	Fairfield, CA	(27.7)
232	San Bernardino, CA	(9.7)	304	Richmond, CA	(15.9)	379	Oxnard, CA	(28.3)
233	Hollywood, FL	(9.8)	306	Whittier, CA	(16.0)	380	Fargo, ND	(28.8)
233	Lee's Summit, MO	(9.8)	307	Livermore, CA	(16.1)	381	Menifee, CA	(29.5)
233	Memphis, TN	(9.8)	308	Burbank, CA	(16.2)	382	Canton Twnshp, MI	(29.8)
233	Visalia, CA	(9.8)	309	Sacramento, CA	(16.4)	383	Lake Forest, CA	(31.2)
237	Tempe, AZ	(9.9)	310	Indio, CA	(16.5)	384	Tustin, CA	(31.7)
238	Irving, TX	(10.0)	310	Tyler, TX	(16.5)	385	Citrus Heights, CA	(31.8)
239	Lakewood, CO	(10.1)	312	Reno, NV	(16.6)	386	Virginia Beach, VA	(31.9)
239	Medford, OR	(10.1)	313	Albany, NY	(16.8)	387	St. Petersburg, FL	(32.7)
241	Rochester, NY	(10.2)	313	Chesapeake, VA	(16.8)	388	Concord, NC	(32.9)
242	Somerville, MA	(10.4)	315	Grand Prairie, TX	(17.1)	389	Avondale, AZ	(33.2)
243	Bloomington, IL	(10.5)	315	Orem, UT	(17.1)	389	Brownsville, TX	(33.2)
243	Midland, TX	(10.5)	317	Shreveport, LA	(17.2)	391	Fishers, IN	(33.3)
245	Beaumont, TX	(10.6)	318	Lancaster, CA	(17.3)	392	Redwood City, CA	(33.7)
246	New Haven, CT	(10.7)	318	Rochester, MN	(17.3)	393	Albany, GA	(33.9)
246	Worcester, MA	(10.7)	320	Carrollton, TX	(17.4)	394	League City, TX	(34.0)
248	Gilbert, AZ	(10.8)	320	Denton, TX	(17.4)	395	San Marcos, CA	(34.5)
249	Garden Grove, CA	(10.9)	320	New Bedford, MA	(17.4)	396	San Mateo, CA	(34.6)
250	Green Bay, WI	(11.0)	323	Bethlehem, PA	(17.5)	397	Renton, WA	(35.9)
250	Huntington Beach, CA	(11.0)	324	Sparks, NV	(17.7)	398	Largo, FL	(36.6)
250	San Leandro, CA	(11.0)	325	Hampton, VA	(17.8)	399	Johns Creek, GA	(39.3)
253	Gresham, OR	(11.1)	326	Wilmington, NC	(18.1)	400	Brick Twnshp, NJ	(40.4)
254	Lawton, OK	(11.2)	327	Miramar, FL	(18.5)	401	Reading, PA	(41.0)
255	Decatur, IL	(11.3)	328	Stockton, CA	(18.6)	402	Roswell, GA	(41.2)
255	Melbourne, FL	(11.3)	329	Alhambra, CA	(18.8)	403	Lowell, MA	(41.7)
257	Chandler, AZ	(11.4)	330	Norfolk, VA	(18.9)	404	Escondido, CA	(42.2)
258	Cincinnati, OH	(11.6)	331	Gainesville, FL	(19.0)	405	Mission, TX	(42.8)
258	Durham, NC	(11.6)	332	Elgin, IL	(19.1)	406	Newport Beach, CA	(43.3)
258	El Paso, TX	(11.6)	333	El Monte, CA	(19.3)	407	Round Rock, TX	(44.4)
261	Cambridge, MA	(11.8)	333	Thousand Oaks, CA	(19.3)	408	College Station, TX	(45.1)
261	Cranston, RI	(11.8)	333	Tracy, CA	(19.3)	409	Laredo, TX	(48.5)
263	Hawthorne, CA	(11.9)	336	Corona, CA	(19.4)	410	McAllen, TX	(54.8)
264	West Palm Beach, FL	(12.0)	337	Baldwin Park, CA	(19.5)	411	Colonie, NY	(58.6)
265	Garland, TX	(12.1)	337	O'Fallon, MO	(19.5)	412	Sugar Land, TX	(61.2)
266	Arlington, TX	(12.2)	339	Lakeland, FL	(19.7)	413	Lakewood Twnshp, NJ	(63.0)
266	St. Paul, MN	(12.2)	339	Mission Viejo, CA	(19.7)	NA	Baton Rouge, LA**	NA
268	Vallejo, CA	(12.3)	339	Pomona, CA	(19.7)	NA	Billings, MT**	NA
269	St. Louis, MO	(12.4)	342	Palmdale, CA	(20.1)	NA	Birmingham, AL**	NA
270	Arlington Heights, IL	(12.5)	342	Tucson, AZ	(20.1)	NA	Brooklyn Park, MN**	NA
270	Warwick, RI	(12.5)	344	Inglewood, CA	(20.2)	NA	Buffalo, NY**	NA
272	Newport News, VA	(12.7)	344	Meridian, ID	(20.2)	NA	Champaign, IL**	NA
273	Grand Rapids, MI	(12.8)	346	Charlotte, NC	(20.4)	NA	Cicero, IL**	NA
274	Buena Park, CA	(12.9)	347	Lakewood, CA	(21.0)	NA	Clifton, NJ**	NA
275	Lewisville, TX	(13.1)	348	Dearborn, MI	(21.3)	NA	Davenport, IA**	NA
275	Sunnyvale, CA	(13.1)	348	Syracuse, NY	(21.3)	NA	Duluth, MN**	NA
275	Washington, DC	(13.1)	350	Farmington Hills, MI	(22.0)	NA	Gary, IN**	NA
278	Elk Grove, CA	(13.2)	351	Athens-Clarke, GA	(22.1)	NA	Hillsboro, OR**	NA
279	Vista, CA	(13.4)	351	Bellevue, WA	(22.1)	NA	Hoover, AL**	NA
280	Livonia, MI	(13.8)	351	Daly City, CA	(22.1)	NA	Huntsville, AL**	NA
280	Peoria, AZ	(13.8)	351	Wichita Falls, TX	(22.1)	NA	Indianapolis, IN**	NA
282	McKinney, TX	(13.9)	355	Danbury, CT	(22.3)	NA	Kansas City, MO**	NA
283	Santa Rosa, CA	(14.0)	356	Nampa, ID	(22.7)	NA	Lexington, KY**	NA
284	Torrance, CA	(14.2)	357	Tampa, FL	(22.8)	NA	Mobile, AL**	NA
285	Fremont, CA	(14.3)	358	Everett, WA	(23.1)	NA	Montgomery, AL**	NA
285	Santa Barbara, CA	(14.3)	358	Pasadena, CA	(23.1)	NA	Naperville, IL**	NA
287	Riverside, CA	(14.4)	360	Frisco, TX	(23.4)	NA	Pueblo, CO**	NA
288	Columbus, OH	(14.5)	361	Clearwater, FL	(23.9)	NA	Sterling Heights, MI**	NA
288	Vacaville, CA	(14.5)	362	Simi Valley, CA	(24.2)	NA	Thornton, CO**	NA
			363	Waco, TX	(24.5)	NA	Tuscaloosa, AL**	NA

Source: CQ Press using reported data from the F.B.I. "Crime in the United States 2011"
*Motor vehicle theft includes the theft or attempted theft of a self-propelled vehicle. Excludes motorboats, construction equipment, airplanes, and farming equipment. **Not available.

Alpha Order - City
80. Percent Change in Motor Vehicle Theft Rate: 2007 to 2011
National Percent Change = 37.1% Decrease*

RANK	CITY	% CHANGE	RANK	CITY	% CHANGE	RANK	CITY	% CHANGE
252	Abilene, TX	(43.5)	96	Cheektowaga, NY	(24.8)	236	Fort Wayne, IN	(42.3)
117	Akron, OH	(29.8)	156	Chesapeake, VA	(34.1)	75	Fort Worth, TX	(19.4)
265	Albany, GA	(44.6)	13	Chicago, IL	9.2	288	Fremont, CA	(46.7)
140	Albany, NY	(32.5)	37	Chico, CA	(9.9)	10	Fresno, CA	12.1
300	Albuquerque, NM	(47.9)	106	Chino Hills, CA	(27.8)	8	Frisco, TX	17.4
18	Alexandria, VA	0.8	211	Chino, CA	(39.2)	131	Fullerton, CA	(31.6)
238	Alhambra, CA	(42.4)	393	Chula Vista, CA	(67.3)	245	Gainesville, FL	(42.8)
102	Allentown, PA	(26.7)	NA	Cicero, IL**	NA	182	Garden Grove, CA	(36.4)
4	Allen, TX	27.1	109	Cincinnati, OH	(28.6)	47	Garland, TX	(13.3)
328	Amarillo, TX	(51.8)	NA	Citrus Heights, CA**	NA	12	Gary, IN	11.2
41	Amherst, NY	(10.7)	314	Clarkstown, NY	(48.8)	399	Gilbert, AZ	(68.9)
49	Anaheim, CA	(13.6)	241	Clarksville, TN	(42.5)	286	Glendale, AZ	(46.5)
332	Anchorage, AK	(52.4)	350	Clearwater, FL	(55.1)	178	Glendale, CA	(36.3)
213	Ann Arbor, MI	(39.4)	146	Cleveland, OH	(33.1)	207	Grand Prairie, TX	(38.8)
19	Antioch, CA	0.3	35	Clifton, NJ	(8.9)	252	Grand Rapids, MI	(43.5)
NA	Arlington Heights, IL**	NA	189	Clinton Twnshp, MI	(36.8)	2	Greece, NY	33.5
168	Arlington, TX	(35.4)	3	Clovis, CA	30.7	258	Greeley, CO	(43.9)
89	Arvada, CO	(22.9)	336	College Station, TX	(52.9)	297	Green Bay, WI	(47.5)
152	Asheville, NC	(33.5)	390	Colonie, NY	(66.2)	268	Gresham, OR	(45.1)
152	Athens-Clarke, GA	(33.5)	127	Colorado Springs, CO	(30.6)	173	Hamilton Twnshp, NJ	(35.9)
40	Atlanta, GA	(10.6)	248	Columbia, MO	(43.3)	48	Hammond, IN	(13.4)
336	Aurora, CO	(52.9)	234	Columbus, GA	(41.9)	251	Hampton, VA	(43.4)
352	Aurora, IL	(55.5)	279	Columbus, OH	(45.8)	286	Hartford, CT	(46.5)
173	Austin, TX	(35.9)	98	Compton, CA	(25.2)	150	Hawthorne, CA	(33.4)
NA	Avondale, AZ**	NA	306	Concord, CA	(48.0)	190	Hayward, CA	(36.9)
70	Bakersfield, CA	(18.6)	349	Concord, NC	(55.0)	91	Hemet, CA	(23.2)
229	Baldwin Park, CA	(41.1)	107	Coral Springs, FL	(28.1)	396	Henderson, NV	(67.9)
107	Baltimore, MD	(28.1)	319	Corona, CA	(49.6)	29	Hesperia, CA	(5.4)
358	Baton Rouge, LA	(58.2)	300	Corpus Christi, TX	(47.9)	291	Hialeah, FL	(46.8)
264	Beaumont, TX	(44.5)	159	Costa Mesa, CA	(34.3)	281	High Point, NC	(46.1)
185	Beaverton, OR	(36.6)	103	Cranston, RI	(27.0)	364	Hillsboro, OR	(58.6)
392	Bellevue, WA	(66.3)	230	Dallas, TX	(41.3)	220	Hollywood, FL	(40.1)
198	Bellflower, CA	(37.9)	219	Daly City, CA	(40.0)	NA	Hoover, AL**	NA
317	Bellingham, WA	(49.1)	353	Danbury, CT	(55.7)	176	Houston, TX	(36.1)
383	Bend, OR	(63.9)	NA	Davenport, IA**	NA	205	Huntington Beach, CA	(38.4)
256	Berkeley, CA	(43.8)	164	Davie, FL	(34.8)	NA	Huntsville, AL**	NA
165	Bethlehem, PA	(34.9)	355	Dayton, OH	(56.2)	196	Independence, MO	(37.5)
NA	Billings, MT**	NA	316	Dearborn, MI	(49.0)	161	Indianapolis, IN	(34.5)
NA	Birmingham, AL**	NA	NA	Decatur, IL**	NA	134	Indio, CA	(31.8)
NA	Bloomington, IL**	NA	81	Deerfield Beach, FL	(21.3)	197	Inglewood, CA	(37.6)
56	Bloomington, IN	(15.2)	144	Denton, TX	(32.9)	309	Irvine, CA	(48.5)
343	Bloomington, MN	(53.6)	158	Denver, CO	(34.2)	282	Irving, TX	(46.2)
135	Boca Raton, FL	(31.9)	100	Des Moines, IA	(26.3)	381	Jacksonville, FL	(63.1)
356	Boise, ID	(56.6)	122	Detroit, MI	(30.0)	32	Jackson, MS	(7.3)
292	Boston, MA	(47.1)	23	Downey, CA	(3.0)	131	Jersey City, NJ	(31.6)
5	Boulder, CO	19.7	115	Duluth, MN	(29.4)	NA	Johns Creek, GA**	NA
343	Brick Twnshp, NJ	(53.6)	NA	Durham, NC**	NA	19	Joliet, IL	0.3
51	Bridgeport, CT	(13.9)	307	Edinburg, TX	(48.1)	207	Kansas City, KS	(38.8)
63	Brockton, MA	(16.6)	33	Edison Twnshp, NJ	(7.4)	NA	Kansas City, MO**	NA
50	Broken Arrow, OK	(13.7)	172	Edmond, OK	(35.8)	42	Kennewick, WA	(11.1)
372	Brooklyn Park, MN	(61.6)	401	El Cajon, CA	(69.2)	309	Kenosha, WI	(48.5)
388	Brownsville, TX	(64.7)	65	El Monte, CA	(17.2)	122	Kent, WA	(30.0)
222	Bryan, TX	(40.3)	351	El Paso, TX	(55.3)	248	Killeen, TX	(43.3)
171	Buena Park, CA	(35.7)	376	Elgin, IL	(62.2)	212	Knoxville, TN	(39.3)
NA	Buffalo, NY**	NA	27	Elizabeth, NJ	(4.0)	339	Lafayette, LA	(53.2)
288	Burbank, CA	(46.7)	292	Elk Grove, CA	(47.1)	266	Lake Forest, CA	(44.9)
194	Cambridge, MA	(37.2)	241	Erie, PA	(42.5)	236	Lakeland, FL	(42.3)
119	Camden, NJ	(29.9)	359	Escondido, CA	(58.3)	404	Lakewood Twnshp, NJ	(80.7)
170	Canton Twnshp, MI	(35.6)	309	Eugene, OR	(48.5)	224	Lakewood, CA	(40.5)
377	Cape Coral, FL	(62.3)	92	Evansville, IN	(23.7)	277	Lakewood, CO	(45.7)
329	Carlsbad, CA	(52.0)	342	Everett, WA	(53.5)	359	Lancaster, CA	(58.3)
260	Carmel, IN	(44.0)	308	Fairfield, CA	(48.3)	143	Lansing, MI	(32.7)
90	Carrollton, TX	(23.0)	NA	Fall River, MA**	NA	402	Laredo, TX	(71.0)
22	Carson, CA	(2.5)	273	Fargo, ND	(45.5)	329	Largo, FL	(52.0)
203	Cary, NC	(38.3)	192	Farmington Hills, MI	(37.1)	39	Las Cruces, NM	(10.2)
201	Cedar Rapids, IA	(38.0)	135	Fayetteville, NC	(31.9)	374	Las Vegas, NV	(62.1)
296	Centennial, CO	(47.3)	386	Fishers, IN	(64.5)	21	Lawrence, KS	0.0
NA	Champaign, IL**	NA	60	Flint, MI	(16.1)	1	Lawrence, MA	130.6
359	Chandler, AZ	(58.3)	213	Fontana, CA	(39.4)	138	Lawton, OK	(32.3)
271	Charleston, SC	(45.2)	327	Fort Collins, CO	(51.7)	226	League City, TX	(40.8)
394	Charlotte, NC	(67.6)	85	Fort Lauderdale, FL	(22.1)	347	Lee's Summit, MO	(54.8)
114	Chattanooga, TN	(29.2)	210	Fort Smith, AR	(39.0)	16	Lewisville, TX	4.4

Alpha Order - City (continued)

RANK	CITY	% CHANGE	RANK	CITY	% CHANGE	RANK	CITY	% CHANGE
NA	Lexington, KY**	NA	119	Overland Park, KS	(29.9)	14	Sioux City, IA	5.6
77	Lincoln, NE	(19.7)	202	Oxnard, CA	(38.1)	28	Sioux Falls, SD	(5.1)
67	Little Rock, AR	(18.2)	127	Palm Bay, FL	(30.6)	314	Somerville, MA	(48.8)
97	Livermore, CA	(25.0)	262	Palmdale, CA	(44.3)	137	South Bend, IN	(32.0)
82	Livonia, MI	(21.5)	217	Pasadena, CA	(39.8)	43	South Gate, CA	(11.2)
83	Long Beach, CA	(21.6)	62	Pasadena, TX	(16.5)	299	Sparks, NV	(47.8)
NA	Longmont, CO**	NA	9	Paterson, NJ	16.6	15	Spokane Valley, WA	5.0
268	Longview, TX	(45.1)	173	Pearland, TX	(35.9)	66	Spokane, WA	(17.5)
146	Los Angeles, CA	(33.1)	131	Pembroke Pines, FL	(31.6)	222	Springfield, IL	(40.3)
149	Louisville, KY	(33.3)	368	Peoria, AZ	(60.4)	177	Springfield, MA	(36.2)
323	Lowell, MA	(51.0)	227	Peoria, IL	(41.0)	23	Springfield, MO	(3.0)
16	Lubbock, TX	4.4	192	Philadelphia, PA	(37.1)	51	Stamford, CT	(13.9)
277	Lynchburg, VA	(45.7)	373	Phoenix, AZ	(61.9)	NA	Sterling Heights, MI**	NA
55	Lynn, MA	(15.0)	398	Pittsburgh, PA	(68.4)	224	Stockton, CA	(40.5)
167	Macon, GA	(35.1)	36	Plano, TX	(9.6)	26	St. Joseph, MO	(3.9)
163	Madison, WI	(34.7)	72	Plantation, FL	(18.7)	233	St. Louis, MO	(41.7)
NA	Manchester, NH**	NA	45	Pomona, CA	(13.0)	60	St. Paul, MN	(16.1)
396	McAllen, TX	(67.9)	274	Pompano Beach, FL	(45.6)	382	St. Petersburg, FL	(63.4)
125	McKinney, TX	(30.5)	92	Port St. Lucie, FL	(23.7)	68	Suffolk, VA	(18.5)
104	Medford, OR	(27.2)	203	Portland, OR	(38.3)	390	Sugar Land, TX	(66.2)
357	Melbourne, FL	(57.5)	34	Portsmouth, VA	(7.7)	238	Sunnyvale, CA	(42.4)
247	Memphis, TN	(43.2)	384	Provo, UT	(64.0)	187	Sunrise, FL	(36.7)
NA	Menifee, CA**	NA	NA	Pueblo, CO**	NA	380	Surprise, AZ	(62.6)
140	Merced, CA	(32.5)	25	Quincy, MA	(3.6)	294	Syracuse, NY	(47.2)
374	Meridian, ID	(62.1)	300	Racine, WI	(47.9)	198	Tacoma, WA	(37.9)
394	Mesa, AZ	(67.6)	80	Raleigh, NC	(21.1)	300	Tallahassee, FL	(47.9)
45	Mesquite, TX	(13.0)	30	Ramapo, NY	(5.6)	402	Tampa, FL	(71.0)
152	Miami Beach, FL	(33.5)	129	Rancho Cucamon., CA	(31.4)	322	Temecula, CA	(50.8)
254	Miami Gardens, FL	(43.6)	348	Reading, PA	(54.9)	385	Tempe, AZ	(64.1)
115	Miami, FL	(29.4)	5	Redding, CA	19.7	NA	Thornton, CO**	NA
221	Midland, TX	(40.2)	246	Redwood City, CA	(43.1)	294	Thousand Oaks, CA	(47.2)
256	Milwaukee, WI	(43.8)	272	Reno, NV	(45.4)	76	Toledo, OH	(19.5)
282	Minneapolis, MN	(46.2)	288	Renton, WA	(46.7)	168	Toms River Twnshp, NJ	(35.4)
332	Miramar, FL	(52.4)	207	Rialto, CA	(38.8)	79	Topeka, KS	(20.5)
367	Mission Viejo, CA	(60.1)	59	Richardson, TX	(16.0)	183	Torrance, CA	(36.5)
266	Mission, TX	(44.9)	238	Richmond, CA	(42.4)	190	Tracy, CA	(36.9)
NA	Mobile, AL**	NA	150	Richmond, VA	(33.4)	11	Trenton, NJ	11.8
111	Modesto, CA	(29.0)	369	Rio Rancho, NM	(60.5)	57	Troy, MI	(15.7)
NA	Montgomery, AL**	NA	144	Riverside, CA	(32.9)	365	Tucson, AZ	(59.7)
101	Moreno Valley, CA	(26.4)	94	Roanoke, VA	(24.5)	178	Tulsa, OK	(36.3)
112	Murfreesboro, TN	(29.1)	325	Rochester, MN	(51.6)	NA	Tuscaloosa, AL**	NA
371	Murrieta, CA	(60.8)	363	Rochester, NY	(58.5)	300	Tustin, CA	(47.9)
379	Nampa, ID	(62.5)	98	Rockford, IL	(25.2)	7	Tyler, TX	17.7
178	Napa, CA	(36.3)	319	Roseville, CA	(49.6)	139	Upper Darby Twnshp, PA	(32.4)
231	Naperville, IL	(41.5)	365	Roswell, GA	(59.7)	268	Vacaville, CA	(45.1)
NA	Nashua, NH**	NA	124	Round Rock, TX	(30.2)	105	Vallejo, CA	(27.4)
213	Nashville, TN	(39.4)	285	Sacramento, CA	(46.4)	44	Vancouver, WA	(12.4)
58	New Bedford, MA	(15.9)	334	Salem, OR	(52.6)	274	Ventura, CA	(45.6)
NA	New Haven, CT**	NA	334	Salinas, CA	(52.6)	156	Victorville, CA	(34.1)
318	New Orleans, LA	(49.4)	117	Salt Lake City, UT	(29.8)	94	Virginia Beach, VA	(24.5)
31	New Rochelle, NY	(6.1)	261	San Angelo, TX	(44.1)	148	Visalia, CA	(33.2)
110	New York, NY	(28.8)	54	San Antonio, TX	(14.8)	194	Vista, CA	(37.2)
53	Newark, NJ	(14.6)	218	San Bernardino, CA	(39.9)	386	Waco, TX	(64.5)
325	Newport Beach, CA	(51.6)	346	San Diego, CA	(54.7)	NA	Warren, MI**	NA
313	Newport News, VA	(48.6)	178	San Francisco, CA	(36.3)	NA	Warwick, RI**	NA
213	Newton, MA	(39.4)	84	San Jose, CA	(22.0)	254	Washington, DC	(43.6)
112	Norfolk, VA	(29.1)	359	San Leandro, CA	(58.3)	87	Waterbury, CT	(22.2)
321	Norman, OK	(49.8)	338	San Marcos, CA	(53.1)	155	West Covina, CA	(33.7)
331	North Charleston, SC	(52.1)	235	San Mateo, CA	(42.2)	198	West Jordan, UT	(37.9)
73	Norwalk, CA	(18.8)	324	Sandy Springs, GA	(51.2)	377	West Palm Beach, FL	(62.3)
68	Norwalk, CT	(18.5)	85	Sandy, UT	(22.1)	206	West Valley, UT	(38.6)
185	Oakland, CA	(36.6)	183	Santa Ana, CA	(36.5)	37	Westland, MI	(9.9)
284	Oceanside, CA	(46.3)	297	Santa Barbara, CA	(47.5)	88	Westminster, CA	(22.7)
227	Odessa, TX	(41.0)	162	Santa Clara, CA	(34.6)	166	Westminster, CO	(35.0)
187	O'Fallon, MO	(36.7)	280	Santa Clarita, CA	(46.0)	231	Whittier, CA	(41.5)
309	Ogden, UT	(48.5)	341	Santa Maria, CA	(53.3)	354	Wichita Falls, TX	(56.0)
70	Oklahoma City, OK	(18.6)	258	Santa Monica, CA	(43.9)	64	Wichita, KS	(17.1)
NA	Olathe, KS**	NA	140	Santa Rosa, CA	(32.5)	241	Wilmington, NC	(42.5)
74	Omaha, NE	(19.3)	241	Savannah, GA	(42.5)	NA	Winston-Salem, NC**	NA
129	Ontario, CA	(31.4)	389	Scottsdale, AZ	(65.1)	300	Woodbridge Twnshp, NJ	(47.9)
339	Orange, CA	(53.2)	125	Scranton, PA	(30.5)	248	Worcester, MA	(43.3)
159	Orem, UT	(34.3)	262	Seattle, WA	(44.3)	119	Yakima, WA	(29.9)
274	Orlando, FL	(45.6)	369	Shreveport, LA	(60.5)	78	Yonkers, NY	(20.2)
			345	Simi Valley, CA	(53.9)	399	Yuma, AZ	(68.9)

Source: CQ Press using reported data from the F.B.I. "Crime in the United States 2011"
*Motor vehicle theft includes the theft or attempted theft of a self-propelled vehicle. Excludes motorboats, construction equipment, airplanes, and farming equipment.   **Not available.

Rank Order - City

80. Percent Change in Motor Vehicle Theft Rate: 2007 to 2011 (continued)
National Percent Change = 37.1% Decrease*

RANK	CITY	% CHANGE	RANK	CITY	% CHANGE	RANK	CITY	% CHANGE
1	Lawrence, MA	130.6	73	Norwalk, CA	(18.8)	144	Riverside, CA	(32.9)
2	Greece, NY	33.5	74	Omaha, NE	(19.3)	146	Cleveland, OH	(33.1)
3	Clovis, CA	30.7	75	Fort Worth, TX	(19.4)	146	Los Angeles, CA	(33.1)
4	Allen, TX	27.1	76	Toledo, OH	(19.5)	148	Visalia, CA	(33.2)
5	Boulder, CO	19.7	77	Lincoln, NE	(19.7)	149	Louisville, KY	(33.3)
5	Redding, CA	19.7	78	Yonkers, NY	(20.2)	150	Hawthorne, CA	(33.4)
7	Tyler, TX	17.7	79	Topeka, KS	(20.5)	150	Richmond, VA	(33.4)
8	Frisco, TX	17.4	80	Raleigh, NC	(21.1)	152	Asheville, NC	(33.5)
9	Paterson, NJ	16.6	81	Deerfield Beach, FL	(21.3)	152	Athens-Clarke, GA	(33.5)
10	Fresno, CA	12.1	82	Livonia, MI	(21.5)	152	Miami Beach, FL	(33.5)
11	Trenton, NJ	11.8	83	Long Beach, CA	(21.6)	155	West Covina, CA	(33.7)
12	Gary, IN	11.2	84	San Jose, CA	(22.0)	156	Chesapeake, VA	(34.1)
13	Chicago, IL	9.2	85	Fort Lauderdale, FL	(22.1)	156	Victorville, CA	(34.1)
14	Sioux City, IA	5.6	85	Sandy, UT	(22.1)	158	Denver, CO	(34.2)
15	Spokane Valley, WA	5.0	87	Waterbury, CT	(22.2)	159	Costa Mesa, CA	(34.3)
16	Lewisville, TX	4.4	88	Westminster, CA	(22.7)	159	Orem, UT	(34.3)
16	Lubbock, TX	4.4	89	Arvada, CO	(22.9)	161	Indianapolis, IN	(34.5)
18	Alexandria, VA	0.8	90	Carrollton, TX	(23.0)	162	Santa Clara, CA	(34.6)
19	Antioch, CA	0.3	91	Hemet, CA	(23.2)	163	Madison, WI	(34.7)
19	Joliet, IL	0.3	92	Evansville, IN	(23.7)	164	Davie, FL	(34.8)
21	Lawrence, KS	0.0	92	Port St. Lucie, FL	(23.7)	165	Bethlehem, PA	(34.9)
22	Carson, CA	(2.5)	94	Roanoke, VA	(24.5)	166	Westminster, CO	(35.0)
23	Downey, CA	(3.0)	94	Virginia Beach, VA	(24.5)	167	Macon, GA	(35.1)
23	Springfield, MO	(3.0)	96	Cheektowaga, NY	(24.8)	168	Arlington, TX	(35.4)
25	Quincy, MA	(3.6)	97	Livermore, CA	(25.0)	168	Toms River Twnshp, NJ	(35.4)
26	St. Joseph, MO	(3.9)	98	Compton, CA	(25.2)	170	Canton Twnshp, MI	(35.6)
27	Elizabeth, NJ	(4.0)	98	Rockford, IL	(25.2)	171	Buena Park, CA	(35.7)
28	Sioux Falls, SD	(5.1)	100	Des Moines, IA	(26.3)	172	Edmond, OK	(35.8)
29	Hesperia, CA	(5.4)	101	Moreno Valley, CA	(26.4)	173	Austin, TX	(35.9)
30	Ramapo, NY	(5.6)	102	Allentown, PA	(26.7)	173	Hamilton Twnshp, NJ	(35.9)
31	New Rochelle, NY	(6.1)	103	Cranston, RI	(27.0)	173	Pearland, TX	(35.9)
32	Jackson, MS	(7.3)	104	Medford, OR	(27.2)	176	Houston, TX	(36.1)
33	Edison Twnshp, NJ	(7.4)	105	Vallejo, CA	(27.4)	177	Springfield, MA	(36.2)
34	Portsmouth, VA	(7.7)	106	Chino Hills, CA	(27.8)	178	Glendale, CA	(36.3)
35	Clifton, NJ	(8.9)	107	Baltimore, MD	(28.1)	178	Napa, CA	(36.3)
36	Plano, TX	(9.6)	107	Coral Springs, FL	(28.1)	178	San Francisco, CA	(36.3)
37	Chico, CA	(9.9)	109	Cincinnati, OH	(28.6)	178	Tulsa, OK	(36.3)
37	Westland, MI	(9.9)	110	New York, NY	(28.8)	182	Garden Grove, CA	(36.4)
39	Las Cruces, NM	(10.2)	111	Modesto, CA	(29.0)	183	Santa Ana, CA	(36.5)
40	Atlanta, GA	(10.6)	112	Murfreesboro, TN	(29.1)	183	Torrance, CA	(36.5)
41	Amherst, NY	(10.7)	112	Norfolk, VA	(29.1)	185	Beaverton, OR	(36.6)
42	Kennewick, WA	(11.1)	114	Chattanooga, TN	(29.2)	185	Oakland, CA	(36.6)
43	South Gate, CA	(11.2)	115	Duluth, MN	(29.4)	187	O'Fallon, MO	(36.7)
44	Vancouver, WA	(12.4)	115	Miami, FL	(29.4)	187	Sunrise, FL	(36.7)
45	Mesquite, TX	(13.0)	117	Akron, OH	(29.8)	189	Clinton Twnshp, MI	(36.8)
45	Pomona, CA	(13.0)	117	Salt Lake City, UT	(29.8)	190	Hayward, CA	(36.9)
47	Garland, TX	(13.3)	119	Camden, NJ	(29.9)	190	Tracy, CA	(36.9)
48	Hammond, IN	(13.4)	119	Overland Park, KS	(29.9)	192	Farmington Hills, MI	(37.1)
49	Anaheim, CA	(13.6)	119	Yakima, WA	(29.9)	192	Philadelphia, PA	(37.1)
50	Broken Arrow, OK	(13.7)	122	Detroit, MI	(30.0)	194	Cambridge, MA	(37.2)
51	Bridgeport, CT	(13.9)	122	Kent, WA	(30.0)	194	Vista, CA	(37.2)
51	Stamford, CT	(13.9)	124	Round Rock, TX	(30.2)	196	Independence, MO	(37.5)
53	Newark, NJ	(14.6)	125	McKinney, TX	(30.5)	197	Inglewood, CA	(37.6)
54	San Antonio, TX	(14.8)	125	Scranton, PA	(30.5)	198	Bellflower, CA	(37.9)
55	Lynn, MA	(15.0)	127	Colorado Springs, CO	(30.6)	198	Tacoma, WA	(37.9)
56	Bloomington, IN	(15.2)	127	Palm Bay, FL	(30.6)	198	West Jordan, UT	(37.9)
57	Troy, MI	(15.7)	129	Ontario, CA	(31.4)	201	Cedar Rapids, IA	(38.0)
58	New Bedford, MA	(15.9)	129	Rancho Cucamon., CA	(31.4)	202	Oxnard, CA	(38.1)
59	Richardson, TX	(16.0)	131	Fullerton, CA	(31.6)	203	Cary, NC	(38.3)
60	Flint, MI	(16.1)	131	Jersey City, NJ	(31.6)	203	Portland, OR	(38.3)
60	St. Paul, MN	(16.1)	131	Pembroke Pines, FL	(31.6)	205	Huntington Beach, CA	(38.4)
62	Pasadena, TX	(16.5)	134	Indio, CA	(31.8)	206	West Valley, UT	(38.6)
63	Brockton, MA	(16.6)	135	Boca Raton, FL	(31.9)	207	Grand Prairie, TX	(38.8)
64	Wichita, KS	(17.1)	135	Fayetteville, NC	(31.9)	207	Kansas City, KS	(38.8)
65	El Monte, CA	(17.2)	137	South Bend, IN	(32.0)	207	Rialto, CA	(38.8)
66	Spokane, WA	(17.5)	138	Lawton, OK	(32.3)	210	Fort Smith, AR	(39.0)
67	Little Rock, AR	(18.2)	139	Upper Darby Twnshp, PA	(32.4)	211	Chino, CA	(39.2)
68	Norwalk, CT	(18.5)	140	Albany, NY	(32.5)	212	Knoxville, TN	(39.3)
68	Suffolk, VA	(18.5)	140	Merced, CA	(32.5)	213	Ann Arbor, MI	(39.4)
70	Bakersfield, CA	(18.6)	140	Santa Rosa, CA	(32.5)	213	Fontana, CA	(39.4)
70	Oklahoma City, OK	(18.6)	143	Lansing, MI	(32.7)	213	Nashville, TN	(39.4)
72	Plantation, FL	(18.7)	144	Denton, TX	(32.9)	213	Newton, MA	(39.4)

322 Cities

Rank Order - City (continued)

RANK	CITY	% CHANGE	RANK	CITY	% CHANGE	RANK	CITY	% CHANGE
217	Pasadena, CA	(39.8)	288	Renton, WA	(46.7)	364	Hillsboro, OR	(58.6)
218	San Bernardino, CA	(39.9)	291	Hialeah, FL	(46.8)	365	Roswell, GA	(59.7)
219	Daly City, CA	(40.0)	292	Boston, MA	(47.1)	365	Tucson, AZ	(59.7)
220	Hollywood, FL	(40.1)	292	Elk Grove, CA	(47.1)	367	Mission Viejo, CA	(60.1)
221	Midland, TX	(40.2)	294	Syracuse, NY	(47.2)	368	Peoria, AZ	(60.4)
222	Bryan, TX	(40.3)	294	Thousand Oaks, CA	(47.2)	369	Rio Rancho, NM	(60.5)
222	Springfield, IL	(40.3)	296	Centennial, CO	(47.3)	369	Shreveport, LA	(60.5)
224	Lakewood, CA	(40.5)	297	Green Bay, WI	(47.5)	371	Murrieta, CA	(60.8)
224	Stockton, CA	(40.5)	297	Santa Barbara, CA	(47.5)	372	Brooklyn Park, MN	(61.6)
226	League City, TX	(40.8)	299	Sparks, NV	(47.8)	373	Phoenix, AZ	(61.9)
227	Odessa, TX	(41.0)	300	Albuquerque, NM	(47.9)	374	Las Vegas, NV	(62.1)
227	Peoria, IL	(41.0)	300	Corpus Christi, TX	(47.9)	374	Meridian, ID	(62.1)
229	Baldwin Park, CA	(41.1)	300	Racine, WI	(47.9)	376	Elgin, IL	(62.2)
230	Dallas, TX	(41.3)	300	Tallahassee, FL	(47.9)	377	Cape Coral, FL	(62.3)
231	Naperville, IL	(41.5)	300	Tustin, CA	(47.9)	377	West Palm Beach, FL	(62.3)
231	Whittier, CA	(41.5)	300	Woodbridge Twnshp, NJ	(47.9)	379	Nampa, ID	(62.5)
233	St. Louis, MO	(41.7)	306	Concord, CA	(48.0)	380	Surprise, AZ	(62.6)
234	Columbus, GA	(41.9)	307	Edinburg, TX	(48.1)	381	Jacksonville, FL	(63.1)
235	San Mateo, CA	(42.2)	308	Fairfield, CA	(48.3)	382	St. Petersburg, FL	(63.4)
236	Fort Wayne, IN	(42.3)	309	Eugene, OR	(48.5)	383	Bend, OR	(63.9)
236	Lakeland, FL	(42.3)	309	Irvine, CA	(48.5)	384	Provo, UT	(64.0)
238	Alhambra, CA	(42.4)	309	Kenosha, WI	(48.5)	385	Tempe, AZ	(64.1)
238	Richmond, CA	(42.4)	309	Ogden, UT	(48.5)	386	Fishers, IN	(64.5)
238	Sunnyvale, CA	(42.4)	313	Newport News, VA	(48.6)	386	Waco, TX	(64.5)
241	Clarksville, TN	(42.5)	314	Clarkstown, NY	(48.8)	388	Brownsville, TX	(64.7)
241	Erie, PA	(42.5)	314	Somerville, MA	(48.8)	389	Scottsdale, AZ	(65.1)
241	Savannah, GA	(42.5)	316	Dearborn, MI	(49.0)	390	Colonie, NY	(66.2)
241	Wilmington, NC	(42.5)	317	Bellingham, WA	(49.1)	390	Sugar Land, TX	(66.2)
245	Gainesville, FL	(42.8)	318	New Orleans, LA	(49.4)	392	Bellevue, WA	(66.3)
246	Redwood City, CA	(43.1)	319	Corona, CA	(49.6)	393	Chula Vista, CA	(67.3)
247	Memphis, TN	(43.2)	319	Roseville, CA	(49.6)	394	Charlotte, NC	(67.6)
248	Columbia, MO	(43.3)	321	Norman, OK	(49.8)	394	Mesa, AZ	(67.6)
248	Killeen, TX	(43.3)	322	Temecula, CA	(50.8)	396	Henderson, NV	(67.9)
248	Worcester, MA	(43.3)	323	Lowell, MA	(51.0)	396	McAllen, TX	(67.9)
251	Hampton, VA	(43.4)	324	Sandy Springs, GA	(51.2)	398	Pittsburgh, PA	(68.4)
252	Abilene, TX	(43.5)	325	Newport Beach, CA	(51.6)	399	Gilbert, AZ	(68.9)
252	Grand Rapids, MI	(43.5)	325	Rochester, MN	(51.6)	399	Yuma, AZ	(68.9)
254	Miami Gardens, FL	(43.6)	327	Fort Collins, CO	(51.7)	401	El Cajon, CA	(69.2)
254	Washington, DC	(43.6)	328	Amarillo, TX	(51.8)	402	Laredo, TX	(71.0)
256	Berkeley, CA	(43.8)	329	Carlsbad, CA	(52.0)	402	Tampa, FL	(71.0)
256	Milwaukee, WI	(43.8)	329	Largo, FL	(52.0)	404	Lakewood Twnshp, NJ	(80.7)
258	Greeley, CO	(43.9)	331	North Charleston, SC	(52.1)	NA	Arlington Heights, IL**	NA
258	Santa Monica, CA	(43.9)	332	Anchorage, AK	(52.4)	NA	Avondale, AZ**	NA
260	Carmel, IN	(44.0)	332	Miramar, FL	(52.4)	NA	Billings, MT**	NA
261	San Angelo, TX	(44.1)	334	Salem, OR	(52.6)	NA	Birmingham, AL**	NA
262	Palmdale, CA	(44.3)	334	Salinas, CA	(52.6)	NA	Bloomington, IL**	NA
262	Seattle, WA	(44.3)	336	Aurora, CO	(52.9)	NA	Buffalo, NY**	NA
264	Beaumont, TX	(44.5)	336	College Station, TX	(52.9)	NA	Champaign, IL**	NA
265	Albany, GA	(44.6)	338	San Marcos, CA	(53.1)	NA	Cicero, IL**	NA
266	Lake Forest, CA	(44.9)	339	Lafayette, LA	(53.2)	NA	Citrus Heights, CA**	NA
266	Mission, TX	(44.9)	339	Orange, CA	(53.2)	NA	Davenport, IA**	NA
268	Gresham, OR	(45.1)	341	Santa Maria, CA	(53.3)	NA	Decatur, IL**	NA
268	Longview, TX	(45.1)	342	Everett, WA	(53.5)	NA	Durham, NC**	NA
268	Vacaville, CA	(45.1)	343	Bloomington, MN	(53.6)	NA	Fall River, MA**	NA
271	Charleston, SC	(45.2)	343	Brick Twnshp, NJ	(53.6)	NA	Hoover, AL**	NA
272	Reno, NV	(45.4)	345	Simi Valley, CA	(53.9)	NA	Huntsville, AL**	NA
273	Fargo, ND	(45.5)	346	San Diego, CA	(54.7)	NA	Johns Creek, GA**	NA
274	Orlando, FL	(45.6)	347	Lee's Summit, MO	(54.8)	NA	Kansas City, MO**	NA
274	Pompano Beach, FL	(45.6)	348	Reading, PA	(54.9)	NA	Lexington, KY**	NA
274	Ventura, CA	(45.6)	349	Concord, NC	(55.0)	NA	Longmont, CO**	NA
277	Lakewood, CO	(45.7)	350	Clearwater, FL	(55.1)	NA	Manchester, NH**	NA
277	Lynchburg, VA	(45.7)	351	El Paso, TX	(55.3)	NA	Menifee, CA**	NA
279	Columbus, OH	(45.8)	352	Aurora, IL	(55.5)	NA	Mobile, AL**	NA
280	Santa Clarita, CA	(46.0)	353	Danbury, CT	(55.7)	NA	Montgomery, AL**	NA
281	High Point, NC	(46.1)	354	Wichita Falls, TX	(56.0)	NA	Nashua, NH**	NA
282	Irving, TX	(46.2)	355	Dayton, OH	(56.2)	NA	New Haven, CT**	NA
282	Minneapolis, MN	(46.2)	356	Boise, ID	(56.6)	NA	Olathe, KS**	NA
284	Oceanside, CA	(46.3)	357	Melbourne, FL	(57.5)	NA	Pueblo, CO**	NA
285	Sacramento, CA	(46.4)	358	Baton Rouge, LA	(58.2)	NA	Sterling Heights, MI**	NA
286	Glendale, AZ	(46.5)	359	Chandler, AZ	(58.3)	NA	Thornton, CO**	NA
286	Hartford, CT	(46.5)	359	Escondido, CA	(58.3)	NA	Tuscaloosa, AL**	NA
288	Burbank, CA	(46.7)	359	Lancaster, CA	(58.3)	NA	Warren, MI**	NA
288	Fremont, CA	(46.7)	359	San Leandro, CA	(58.3)	NA	Warwick, RI**	NA
			363	Rochester, NY	(58.5)	NA	Winston-Salem, NC**	NA

Source: CQ Press using reported data from the F.B.I. "Crime in the United States 2011"
*Motor vehicle theft includes the theft or attempted theft of a self-propelled vehicle. Excludes motorboats, construction equipment, airplanes, and farming equipment. **Not available.

Alpha Order - City

81. Police Officers in 2011
National Total = 698,460 Officers*

RANK	CITY	OFFICERS
226	Abilene, TX	181
91	Akron, OH	410
241	Albany, GA	169
125	Albany, NY	312
38	Albuquerque, NM	1,027
130	Alexandria, VA	300
396	Alhambra, CA	84
202	Allentown, PA	197
353	Allen, TX	108
123	Amarillo, TX	320
277	Amherst, NY	153
101	Anaheim, CA	374
97	Anchorage, AK	390
336	Ann Arbor, MI	118
378	Antioch, CA	96
353	Arlington Heights, IL	108
63	Arlington, TX	640
275	Arvada, CO	155
200	Asheville, NC	198
167	Athens-Clarke, GA	231
20	Atlanta, GA	1,693
64	Aurora, CO	638
138	Aurora, IL	285
22	Austin, TX	1,644
356	Avondale, AZ	107
110	Bakersfield, CA	347
404	Baldwin Park, CA	70
9	Baltimore, MD	2,931
60	Baton Rouge, LA	647
158	Beaumont, TX	247
300	Beaverton, OR	137
233	Bellevue, WA	173
NA	Bellflower, CA**	NA
350	Bellingham, WA	109
389	Bend, OR	88
248	Berkeley, CA	165
263	Bethlehem, PA	158
294	Billings, MT	140
44	Birmingham, AL	877
321	Bloomington, IL	125
375	Bloomington, IN	97
347	Bloomington, MN	112
206	Boca Raton, FL	191
132	Boise, ID	292
15	Boston, MA	2,156
241	Boulder, CO	169
316	Brick Twnshp, NJ	127
87	Bridgeport, CT	421
230	Brockton, MA	177
318	Broken Arrow, OK	126
362	Brooklyn Park, MN	105
160	Brownsville, TX	241
309	Bryan, TX	132
398	Buena Park, CA	83
55	Buffalo, NY	736
272	Burbank, CA	156
147	Cambridge, MA	269
148	Camden, NJ	265
398	Canton Twnshp, MI	83
182	Cape Coral, FL	214
356	Carlsbad, CA	107
349	Carmel, IN	110
277	Carrollton, TX	153
NA	Carson, CA**	NA
233	Cary, NC	173
190	Cedar Rapids, IA	204
334	Centennial, CO	119
334	Champaign, IL	119
124	Chandler, AZ	319
95	Charleston, SC	396
19	Charlotte, NC	1,726
102	Chattanooga, TN	370

RANK	CITY	OFFICERS
321	Cheektowaga, NY	125
109	Chesapeake, VA	354
2	Chicago, IL	12,092
379	Chico, CA	95
NA	Chino Hills, CA**	NA
363	Chino, CA	102
178	Chula Vista, CA	219
NA	Cicero, IL**	NA
37	Cincinnati, OH	1,038
394	Citrus Heights, CA	85
253	Clarkstown, NY	163
150	Clarksville, TN	262
170	Clearwater, FL	229
25	Cleveland, OH	1,451
293	Clifton, NJ	141
388	Clinton Twnshp, MI	89
370	Clovis, CA	99
340	College Station, TX	117
356	Colonie, NY	107
65	Colorado Springs, CO	622
261	Columbia, MO	159
79	Columbus, GA	464
18	Columbus, OH	1,805
NA	Compton, CA**	NA
284	Concord, CA	149
276	Concord, NC	154
197	Coral Springs, FL	199
261	Corona, CA	159
85	Corpus Christi, TX	428
306	Costa Mesa, CA	134
298	Cranston, RI	138
7	Dallas, TX	3,511
350	Daly City, CA	109
288	Danbury, CT	145
245	Davenport, IA	167
243	Davie, FL	168
112	Dayton, OH	342
215	Dearborn, MI	186
263	Decatur, IL	158
NA	Deerfield Beach, FL**	NA
281	Denton, TX	150
26	Denver, CO	1,420
106	Des Moines, IA	360
10	Detroit, MI	2,760
345	Downey, CA	114
291	Duluth, MN	143
78	Durham, NC	476
323	Edinburg, TX	124
230	Edison Twnshp, NJ	177
361	Edmond, OK	106
336	El Cajon, CA	118
331	El Monte, CA	121
36	El Paso, TX	1,057
228	Elgin, IL	179
125	Elizabeth, NJ	312
315	Elk Grove, CA	128
236	Erie, PA	172
270	Escondido, CA	157
218	Eugene, OR	185
140	Evansville, IN	282
209	Everett, WA	190
345	Fairfield, CA	114
203	Fall River, MA	196
289	Fargo, ND	144
368	Farmington Hills, MI	100
104	Fayetteville, NC	366
384	Fishers, IN	91
332	Flint, MI	120
226	Fontana, CA	181
228	Fort Collins, CO	179
75	Fort Lauderdale, FL	505
246	Fort Smith, AR	166

RANK	CITY	OFFICERS
80	Fort Wayne, IN	456
24	Fort Worth, TX	1,509
246	Fremont, CA	166
50	Fresno, CA	751
294	Frisco, TX	140
292	Fullerton, CA	142
132	Gainesville, FL	292
272	Garden Grove, CA	156
121	Garland, TX	322
NA	Gary, IN**	NA
177	Gilbert, AZ	220
93	Glendale, AZ	401
165	Glendale, CA	237
180	Grand Prairie, TX	215
128	Grand Rapids, MI	305
372	Greece, NY	98
294	Greeley, CO	140
215	Green Bay, WI	186
348	Gresham, OR	111
239	Hamilton Twnshp, NJ	170
186	Hammond, IN	210
141	Hampton, VA	277
83	Hartford, CT	440
380	Hawthorne, CA	94
215	Hayward, CA	186
408	Hemet, CA	60
114	Henderson, NV	336
NA	Hesperia, CA**	NA
119	Hialeah, FL	329
185	High Point, NC	211
332	Hillsboro, OR	120
128	Hollywood, FL	305
263	Hoover, AL	158
5	Houston, TX	5,294
190	Huntington Beach, CA	204
96	Huntsville, AL	395
203	Independence, MO	196
23	Indianapolis, IN	1,614
406	Indio, CA	65
223	Inglewood, CA	183
200	Irvine, CA	198
114	Irving, TX	336
21	Jacksonville, FL	1,645
84	Jackson, MS	439
47	Jersey City, NJ	806
407	Johns Creek, GA	61
156	Joliet, IL	251
NA	Kansas City, KS**	NA
27	Kansas City, MO	1,387
391	Kennewick, WA	87
197	Kenosha, WI	199
310	Kent, WA	131
172	Killeen, TX	227
98	Knoxville, TN	387
153	Lafayette, LA	257
NA	Lake Forest, CA**	NA
182	Lakeland, FL	214
341	Lakewood Twnshp, NJ	116
NA	Lakewood, CA**	NA
145	Lakewood, CO	270
NA	Lancaster, CA**	NA
214	Lansing, MI	188
86	Laredo, TX	425
302	Largo, FL	136
223	Las Cruces, NM	183
11	Las Vegas, NV	2,644
NA	Lawrence, KS**	NA
336	Lawrence, MA	118
236	Lawton, OK	172
363	League City, TX	102
316	Lee's Summit, MO	127
302	Lewisville, TX	136

Alpha Order - City (continued)

RANK	CITY	OFFICERS
74	Lexington, KY	522
120	Lincoln, NE	327
75	Little Rock, AR	505
398	Livermore, CA	83
323	Livonia, MI	124
46	Long Beach, CA	847
300	Longmont, CO	137
263	Longview, TX	158
3	Los Angeles, CA	9,860
32	Louisville, KY	1,233
174	Lowell, MA	226
99	Lubbock, TX	378
258	Lynchburg, VA	160
232	Lynn, MA	175
136	Macon, GA	289
82	Madison, WI	447
188	Manchester, NH	207
145	McAllen, TX	270
277	McKinney, TX	153
368	Medford, OR	100
253	Melbourne, FL	163
12	Memphis, TN	2,454
NA	Menifee, CA**	NA
394	Merced, CA	85
396	Meridian, ID	84
51	Mesa, AZ	750
171	Mesquite, TX	228
105	Miami Beach, FL	361
196	Miami Gardens, FL	200
35	Miami, FL	1,061
236	Midland, TX	172
16	Milwaukee, WI	1,862
45	Minneapolis, MN	852
197	Miramar, FL	199
NA	Mission Viejo, CA**	NA
294	Mission, TX	140
71	Mobile, AL	561
179	Modesto, CA	217
73	Montgomery, AL	530
NA	Moreno Valley, CA**	NA
175	Murfreesboro, TN	225
393	Murrieta, CA	86
341	Nampa, ID	116
404	Napa, CA	70
250	Naperville, IL	164
243	Nashua, NH	168
30	Nashville, TN	1,315
157	New Bedford, MA	249
107	New Haven, CT	359
29	New Orleans, LA	1,349
263	New Rochelle, NY	158
1	New York, NY	34,542
34	Newark, NJ	1,095
310	Newport Beach, CA	131
94	Newport News, VA	398
298	Newton, MA	138
57	Norfolk, VA	721
248	Norman, OK	165
113	North Charleston, SC	337
NA	Norwalk, CA**	NA
250	Norwalk, CT	164
60	Oakland, CA	647
193	Oceanside, CA	203
289	Odessa, TX	144
356	O'Fallon, MO	107
304	Ogden, UT	135
39	Oklahoma City, OK	1,020
253	Olathe, KS	163
48	Omaha, NE	778
176	Ontario, CA	224
263	Orange, CA	158
389	Orem, UT	88
58	Orlando, FL	702

RANK	CITY	OFFICERS
162	Overland Park, KS	240
166	Oxnard, CA	235
257	Palm Bay, FL	161
NA	Palmdale, CA**	NA
167	Pasadena, CA	231
151	Pasadena, TX	260
108	Paterson, NJ	357
306	Pearland, TX	134
172	Pembroke Pines, FL	227
223	Peoria, AZ	183
184	Peoria, IL	213
4	Philadelphia, PA	6,625
8	Phoenix, AZ	3,079
43	Pittsburgh, PA	880
114	Plano, TX	336
233	Plantation, FL	173
286	Pomona, CA	148
NA	Pompano Beach, FL**	NA
189	Port St. Lucie, FL	205
40	Portland, OR	956
159	Portsmouth, VA	242
370	Provo, UT	99
187	Pueblo, CO	209
221	Quincy, MA	184
195	Racine, WI	202
52	Raleigh, NC	746
353	Ramapo, NY	108
NA	Rancho Cucamon., CA**	NA
272	Reading, PA	156
372	Redding, CA	98
391	Redwood City, CA	87
137	Reno, NV	288
329	Renton, WA	122
372	Rialto, CA	98
280	Richardson, TX	152
206	Richmond, CA	191
56	Richmond, VA	727
325	Rio Rancho, NM	123
103	Riverside, CA	367
154	Roanoke, VA	256
314	Rochester, MN	130
54	Rochester, NY	738
149	Rockford, IL	264
336	Roseville, CA	118
NA	Roswell, GA**	NA
NA	Round Rock, TX**	NA
59	Sacramento, CA	678
206	Salem, OR	191
287	Salinas, CA	146
89	Salt Lake City, UT	414
253	San Angelo, TX	163
13	San Antonio, TX	2,324
131	San Bernardino, CA	296
17	San Diego, CA	1,834
14	San Francisco, CA	2,210
33	San Jose, CA	1,103
384	San Leandro, CA	91
NA	San Marcos, CA**	NA
363	San Mateo, CA	102
325	Sandy Springs, GA	123
356	Sandy, UT	107
114	Santa Ana, CA	336
306	Santa Barbara, CA	134
310	Santa Clara, CA	131
NA	Santa Clarita, CA**	NA
363	Santa Maria, CA	102
190	Santa Monica, CA	204
250	Santa Rosa, CA	164
70	Savannah, GA	563
92	Scottsdale, AZ	406
281	Scranton, PA	150
31	Seattle, WA	1,305
67	Shreveport, LA	616
350	Simi Valley, CA	109

RANK	CITY	OFFICERS
325	Sioux City, IA	123
169	Sioux Falls, SD	230
318	Somerville, MA	126
152	South Bend, IN	258
402	South Gate, CA	80
NA	Sparks, NV**	NA
375	Spokane Valley, WA	97
142	Spokane, WA	275
162	Springfield, IL	240
80	Springfield, MA	456
125	Springfield, MO	312
143	Stamford, CT	274
270	Sterling Heights, MI	157
122	Stockton, CA	321
344	St. Joseph, MO	115
28	St. Louis, MO	1,363
68	St. Paul, MN	596
72	St. Petersburg, FL	533
218	Suffolk, VA	185
284	Sugar Land, TX	149
193	Sunnyvale, CA	203
239	Sunrise, FL	170
325	Surprise, AZ	123
77	Syracuse, NY	494
99	Tacoma, WA	378
111	Tallahassee, FL	346
42	Tampa, FL	948
NA	Temecula, CA**	NA
114	Tempe, AZ	336
263	Thornton, CO	158
NA	Thousand Oaks, CA**	NA
90	Toledo, OH	413
281	Toms River Twnshp, NJ	150
134	Topeka, KS	290
180	Torrance, CA	215
398	Tracy, CA	83
164	Trenton, NJ	238
363	Troy, MI	102
41	Tucson, AZ	949
53	Tulsa, OK	745
139	Tuscaloosa, AL	284
382	Tustin, CA	92
209	Tyler, TX	190
318	Upper Darby Twnshp, PA	126
387	Vacaville, CA	90
384	Vallejo, CA	91
221	Vancouver, WA	184
329	Ventura, CA	122
NA	Victorville, CA**	NA
49	Virginia Beach, VA	776
304	Visalia, CA	135
NA	Vista, CA**	NA
160	Waco, TX	241
209	Warren, MI	190
258	Warwick, RI	160
6	Washington, DC	3,818
134	Waterbury, CT	290
375	West Covina, CA	97
380	West Jordan, UT	94
144	West Palm Beach, FL	271
212	West Valley, UT	189
403	Westland, MI	77
382	Westminster, CA	92
218	Westminster, CO	185
341	Whittier, CA	116
212	Wichita Falls, TX	189
62	Wichita, KS	646
154	Wilmington, NC	256
69	Winston-Salem, NC	585
205	Woodbridge Twnshp, NJ	192
88	Worcester, MA	420
310	Yakima, WA	131
66	Yonkers, NY	619
258	Yuma, AZ	160

Source: Reported data from the F.B.I. "Crime in the United States 2011"
*Sworn officers only, does not include civilian employees.
**Not available

81. Police Officers in 2011 (continued)
National Total = 698,460 Officers*

Rank Order - City

RANK	CITY	OFFICERS
1	New York, NY	34,542
2	Chicago, IL	12,092
3	Los Angeles, CA	9,860
4	Philadelphia, PA	6,625
5	Houston, TX	5,294
6	Washington, DC	3,818
7	Dallas, TX	3,511
8	Phoenix, AZ	3,079
9	Baltimore, MD	2,931
10	Detroit, MI	2,760
11	Las Vegas, NV	2,644
12	Memphis, TN	2,454
13	San Antonio, TX	2,324
14	San Francisco, CA	2,210
15	Boston, MA	2,156
16	Milwaukee, WI	1,862
17	San Diego, CA	1,834
18	Columbus, OH	1,805
19	Charlotte, NC	1,726
20	Atlanta, GA	1,693
21	Jacksonville, FL	1,645
22	Austin, TX	1,644
23	Indianapolis, IN	1,614
24	Fort Worth, TX	1,509
25	Cleveland, OH	1,451
26	Denver, CO	1,420
27	Kansas City, MO	1,387
28	St. Louis, MO	1,363
29	New Orleans, LA	1,349
30	Nashville, TN	1,315
31	Seattle, WA	1,305
32	Louisville, KY	1,233
33	San Jose, CA	1,103
34	Newark, NJ	1,095
35	Miami, FL	1,061
36	El Paso, TX	1,057
37	Cincinnati, OH	1,038
38	Albuquerque, NM	1,027
39	Oklahoma City, OK	1,020
40	Portland, OR	956
41	Tucson, AZ	949
42	Tampa, FL	948
43	Pittsburgh, PA	880
44	Birmingham, AL	877
45	Minneapolis, MN	852
46	Long Beach, CA	847
47	Jersey City, NJ	806
48	Omaha, NE	778
49	Virginia Beach, VA	776
50	Fresno, CA	751
51	Mesa, AZ	750
52	Raleigh, NC	746
53	Tulsa, OK	745
54	Rochester, NY	738
55	Buffalo, NY	736
56	Richmond, VA	727
57	Norfolk, VA	721
58	Orlando, FL	702
59	Sacramento, CA	678
60	Baton Rouge, LA	647
60	Oakland, CA	647
62	Wichita, KS	646
63	Arlington, TX	640
64	Aurora, CO	638
65	Colorado Springs, CO	622
66	Yonkers, NY	619
67	Shreveport, LA	616
68	St. Paul, MN	596
69	Winston-Salem, NC	585
70	Savannah, GA	563
71	Mobile, AL	561
72	St. Petersburg, FL	533
73	Montgomery, AL	530
74	Lexington, KY	522
75	Fort Lauderdale, FL	505
75	Little Rock, AR	505
77	Syracuse, NY	494
78	Durham, NC	476
79	Columbus, GA	464
80	Fort Wayne, IN	456
80	Springfield, MA	456
82	Madison, WI	447
83	Hartford, CT	440
84	Jackson, MS	439
85	Corpus Christi, TX	428
86	Laredo, TX	425
87	Bridgeport, CT	421
88	Worcester, MA	420
89	Salt Lake City, UT	414
90	Toledo, OH	413
91	Akron, OH	410
92	Scottsdale, AZ	406
93	Glendale, AZ	401
94	Newport News, VA	398
95	Charleston, SC	396
96	Huntsville, AL	395
97	Anchorage, AK	390
98	Knoxville, TN	387
99	Lubbock, TX	378
99	Tacoma, WA	378
101	Anaheim, CA	374
102	Chattanooga, TN	370
103	Riverside, CA	367
104	Fayetteville, NC	366
105	Miami Beach, FL	361
106	Des Moines, IA	360
107	New Haven, CT	359
108	Paterson, NJ	357
109	Chesapeake, VA	354
110	Bakersfield, CA	347
111	Tallahassee, FL	346
112	Dayton, OH	342
113	North Charleston, SC	337
114	Henderson, NV	336
114	Irving, TX	336
114	Plano, TX	336
114	Santa Ana, CA	336
114	Tempe, AZ	336
119	Hialeah, FL	329
120	Lincoln, NE	327
121	Garland, TX	322
122	Stockton, CA	321
123	Amarillo, TX	320
124	Chandler, AZ	319
125	Albany, NY	312
125	Elizabeth, NJ	312
125	Springfield, MO	312
128	Grand Rapids, MI	305
128	Hollywood, FL	305
130	Alexandria, VA	300
131	San Bernardino, CA	296
132	Boise, ID	292
132	Gainesville, FL	292
134	Topeka, KS	290
134	Waterbury, CT	290
136	Macon, GA	289
137	Reno, NV	288
138	Aurora, IL	285
139	Tuscaloosa, AL	284
140	Evansville, IN	282
141	Hampton, VA	277
142	Spokane, WA	275
143	Stamford, CT	274
144	West Palm Beach, FL	271
145	Lakewood, CO	270
145	McAllen, TX	270
147	Cambridge, MA	269
148	Camden, NJ	265
149	Rockford, IL	264
150	Clarksville, TN	262
151	Pasadena, TX	260
152	South Bend, IN	258
153	Lafayette, LA	257
154	Roanoke, VA	256
154	Wilmington, NC	256
156	Joliet, IL	251
157	New Bedford, MA	249
158	Beaumont, TX	247
159	Portsmouth, VA	242
160	Brownsville, TX	241
160	Waco, TX	241
162	Overland Park, KS	240
162	Springfield, IL	240
164	Trenton, NJ	238
165	Glendale, CA	237
166	Oxnard, CA	235
167	Athens-Clarke, GA	231
167	Pasadena, CA	231
169	Sioux Falls, SD	230
170	Clearwater, FL	229
171	Mesquite, TX	228
172	Killeen, TX	227
172	Pembroke Pines, FL	227
174	Lowell, MA	226
175	Murfreesboro, TN	225
176	Ontario, CA	224
177	Gilbert, AZ	220
178	Chula Vista, CA	219
179	Modesto, CA	217
180	Grand Prairie, TX	215
180	Torrance, CA	215
182	Cape Coral, FL	214
182	Lakeland, FL	214
184	Peoria, IL	213
185	High Point, NC	211
186	Hammond, IN	210
187	Pueblo, CO	209
188	Manchester, NH	207
189	Port St. Lucie, FL	205
190	Cedar Rapids, IA	204
190	Huntington Beach, CA	204
190	Santa Monica, CA	204
193	Oceanside, CA	203
193	Sunnyvale, CA	203
195	Racine, WI	202
196	Miami Gardens, FL	200
197	Coral Springs, FL	199
197	Kenosha, WI	199
197	Miramar, FL	199
200	Asheville, NC	198
200	Irvine, CA	198
202	Allentown, PA	197
203	Fall River, MA	196
203	Independence, MO	196
205	Woodbridge Twnshp, NJ	192
206	Boca Raton, FL	191
206	Richmond, CA	191
206	Salem, OR	191
209	Everett, WA	190
209	Tyler, TX	190
209	Warren, MI	190
212	West Valley, UT	189
212	Wichita Falls, TX	189
214	Lansing, MI	188
215	Dearborn, MI	186
215	Green Bay, WI	186

Rank Order - City (continued)

RANK	CITY	OFFICERS
215	Hayward, CA	186
218	Eugene, OR	185
218	Suffolk, VA	185
218	Westminster, CO	185
221	Quincy, MA	184
221	Vancouver, WA	184
223	Inglewood, CA	183
223	Las Cruces, NM	183
223	Peoria, AZ	183
226	Abilene, TX	181
226	Fontana, CA	181
228	Elgin, IL	179
228	Fort Collins, CO	179
230	Brockton, MA	177
230	Edison Twnshp, NJ	177
232	Lynn, MA	175
233	Bellevue, WA	173
233	Cary, NC	173
233	Plantation, FL	173
236	Erie, PA	172
236	Lawton, OK	172
236	Midland, TX	172
239	Hamilton Twnshp, NJ	170
239	Sunrise, FL	170
241	Albany, GA	169
241	Boulder, CO	169
243	Davie, FL	168
243	Nashua, NH	168
245	Davenport, IA	167
246	Fort Smith, AR	166
246	Fremont, CA	166
248	Berkeley, CA	165
248	Norman, OK	165
250	Naperville, IL	164
250	Norwalk, CT	164
250	Santa Rosa, CA	164
253	Clarkstown, NY	163
253	Melbourne, FL	163
253	Olathe, KS	163
253	San Angelo, TX	163
257	Palm Bay, FL	161
258	Lynchburg, VA	160
258	Warwick, RI	160
258	Yuma, AZ	160
261	Columbia, MO	159
261	Corona, CA	159
263	Bethlehem, PA	158
263	Decatur, IL	158
263	Hoover, AL	158
263	Longview, TX	158
263	New Rochelle, NY	158
263	Orange, CA	158
263	Thornton, CO	158
270	Escondido, CA	157
270	Sterling Heights, MI	157
272	Burbank, CA	156
272	Garden Grove, CA	156
272	Reading, PA	156
275	Arvada, CO	155
276	Concord, NC	154
277	Amherst, NY	153
277	Carrollton, TX	153
277	McKinney, TX	153
280	Richardson, TX	152
281	Denton, TX	150
281	Scranton, PA	150
281	Toms River Twnshp, NJ	150
284	Concord, CA	149
284	Sugar Land, TX	149
286	Pomona, CA	148
287	Salinas, CA	146
288	Danbury, CT	145
289	Fargo, ND	144
289	Odessa, TX	144
291	Duluth, MN	143
292	Fullerton, CA	142
293	Clifton, NJ	141
294	Billings, MT	140
294	Frisco, TX	140
294	Greeley, CO	140
294	Mission, TX	140
298	Cranston, RI	138
298	Newton, MA	138
300	Beaverton, OR	137
300	Longmont, CO	137
302	Largo, FL	136
302	Lewisville, TX	136
304	Ogden, UT	135
304	Visalia, CA	135
306	Costa Mesa, CA	134
306	Pearland, TX	134
306	Santa Barbara, CA	134
309	Bryan, TX	132
310	Kent, WA	131
310	Newport Beach, CA	131
310	Santa Clara, CA	131
310	Yakima, WA	131
314	Rochester, MN	130
315	Elk Grove, CA	128
316	Brick Twnshp, NJ	127
316	Lee's Summit, MO	127
318	Broken Arrow, OK	126
318	Somerville, MA	126
318	Upper Darby Twnshp, PA	126
321	Bloomington, IL	125
321	Cheektowaga, NY	125
323	Edinburg, TX	124
323	Livonia, MI	124
325	Rio Rancho, NM	123
325	Sandy Springs, GA	123
325	Sioux City, IA	123
325	Surprise, AZ	123
329	Renton, WA	122
329	Ventura, CA	122
331	El Monte, CA	121
332	Flint, MI	120
332	Hillsboro, OR	120
334	Centennial, CO	119
334	Champaign, IL	119
336	Ann Arbor, MI	118
336	El Cajon, CA	118
336	Lawrence, MA	118
336	Roseville, CA	118
340	College Station, TX	117
341	Lakewood Twnshp, NJ	116
341	Nampa, ID	116
341	Whittier, CA	116
344	St. Joseph, MO	115
345	Downey, CA	114
345	Fairfield, CA	114
347	Bloomington, MN	112
348	Gresham, OR	111
349	Carmel, IN	110
350	Bellingham, WA	109
350	Daly City, CA	109
350	Simi Valley, CA	109
353	Allen, TX	108
353	Arlington Heights, IL	108
353	Ramapo, NY	108
356	Avondale, AZ	107
356	Carlsbad, CA	107
356	Colonie, NY	107
356	O'Fallon, MO	107
356	Sandy, UT	107
361	Edmond, OK	106
362	Brooklyn Park, MN	105
363	Chino, CA	102
363	League City, TX	102
363	San Mateo, CA	102
363	Santa Maria, CA	102
363	Troy, MI	102
368	Farmington Hills, MI	100
368	Medford, OR	100
370	Clovis, CA	99
370	Provo, UT	99
372	Greece, NY	98
372	Redding, CA	98
372	Rialto, CA	98
375	Bloomington, IN	97
375	Spokane Valley, WA	97
375	West Covina, CA	97
378	Antioch, CA	96
379	Chico, CA	95
380	Hawthorne, CA	94
380	West Jordan, UT	94
382	Tustin, CA	92
382	Westminster, CA	92
384	Fishers, IN	91
384	San Leandro, CA	91
384	Vallejo, CA	91
387	Vacaville, CA	90
388	Clinton Twnshp, MI	89
389	Bend, OR	88
389	Orem, UT	88
391	Kennewick, WA	87
391	Redwood City, CA	87
393	Murrieta, CA	86
394	Citrus Heights, CA	85
394	Merced, CA	85
396	Alhambra, CA	84
396	Meridian, ID	84
398	Buena Park, CA	83
398	Canton Twnshp, MI	83
398	Livermore, CA	83
398	Tracy, CA	83
402	South Gate, CA	80
403	Westland, MI	77
404	Baldwin Park, CA	70
404	Napa, CA	70
406	Indio, CA	65
407	Johns Creek, GA	61
408	Hemet, CA	60
NA	Bellflower, CA**	NA
NA	Carson, CA**	NA
NA	Chino Hills, CA**	NA
NA	Cicero, IL**	NA
NA	Compton, CA**	NA
NA	Deerfield Beach, FL**	NA
NA	Gary, IN**	NA
NA	Hesperia, CA**	NA
NA	Kansas City, KS**	NA
NA	Lake Forest, CA**	NA
NA	Lakewood, CA**	NA
NA	Lancaster, CA**	NA
NA	Lawrence, KS**	NA
NA	Menifee, CA**	NA
NA	Mission Viejo, CA**	NA
NA	Moreno Valley, CA**	NA
NA	Norwalk, CA**	NA
NA	Palmdale, CA**	NA
NA	Pompano Beach, FL**	NA
NA	Rancho Cucamon., CA**	NA
NA	Roswell, GA**	NA
NA	Round Rock, TX**	NA
NA	San Marcos, CA**	NA
NA	Santa Clarita, CA**	NA
NA	Sparks, NV**	NA
NA	Temecula, CA**	NA
NA	Thousand Oaks, CA**	NA
NA	Victorville, CA**	NA
NA	Vista, CA**	NA

Source: Reported data from the F.B.I. "Crime in the United States 2011"
*Sworn officers only, does not include civilian employees.
**Not available

Alpha Order - City

82. Rate of Police Officers in 2011
National Rate = 238 Officers per 100,000 Population*

RANK	CITY	RATE
229	Abilene, TX	151
103	Akron, OH	206
87	Albany, GA	215
25	Albany, NY	317
148	Albuquerque, NM	186
92	Alexandria, VA	212
376	Alhambra, CA	100
199	Allentown, PA	166
302	Allen, TX	126
204	Amarillo, TX	164
288	Amherst, NY	130
345	Anaheim, CA	110
286	Anchorage, AK	131
360	Ann Arbor, MI	104
387	Antioch, CA	93
251	Arlington Heights, IL	143
180	Arlington, TX	172
251	Arvada, CO	143
68	Asheville, NC	234
120	Athens-Clarke, GA	197
9	Atlanta, GA	398
128	Aurora, CO	193
246	Aurora, IL	144
109	Austin, TX	204
268	Avondale, AZ	138
378	Bakersfield, CA	99
388	Baldwin Park, CA	92
2	Baltimore, MD	468
40	Baton Rouge, LA	279
109	Beaumont, TX	204
229	Beaverton, OR	151
262	Bellevue, WA	139
NA	Bellflower, CA**	NA
281	Bellingham, WA	133
337	Bend, OR	114
244	Berkeley, CA	145
97	Bethlehem, PA	210
281	Billings, MT	133
7	Birmingham, AL	411
208	Bloomington, IL	163
318	Bloomington, IN	120
277	Bloomington, MN	134
75	Boca Raton, FL	223
259	Boise, ID	140
19	Boston, MA	347
183	Boulder, CO	171
191	Brick Twnshp, NJ	169
35	Bridgeport, CT	291
144	Brockton, MA	188
302	Broken Arrow, OK	126
271	Brooklyn Park, MN	137
275	Brownsville, TX	135
188	Bryan, TX	170
367	Buena Park, CA	102
39	Buffalo, NY	280
234	Burbank, CA	149
55	Cambridge, MA	254
21	Camden, NJ	341
388	Canton Twnshp, MI	92
271	Cape Coral, FL	137
376	Carlsbad, CA	100
268	Carmel, IN	138
302	Carrollton, TX	126
NA	Carson, CA**	NA
302	Cary, NC	126
212	Cedar Rapids, IA	161
327	Centennial, CO	117
241	Champaign, IL	146
281	Chandler, AZ	133
23	Charleston, SC	326
79	Charlotte, NC	219
79	Chattanooga, TN	219
219	Cheektowaga, NY	158
221	Chesapeake, VA	157
3	Chicago, IL	447
347	Chico, CA	109
NA	Chino Hills, CA**	NA
292	Chino, CA	129
397	Chula Vista, CA	89
NA	Cicero, IL**	NA
17	Cincinnati, OH	349
371	Citrus Heights, CA	101
103	Clarkstown, NY	206
123	Clarksville, TN	195
97	Clearwater, FL	210
14	Cleveland, OH	365
195	Clifton, NJ	167
388	Clinton Twnshp, MI	92
367	Clovis, CA	102
311	College Station, TX	122
271	Colonie, NY	137
239	Colorado Springs, CO	147
241	Columbia, MO	146
64	Columbus, GA	241
72	Columbus, OH	229
NA	Compton, CA**	NA
315	Concord, CA	121
132	Concord, NC	192
209	Coral Springs, FL	162
365	Corona, CA	103
271	Corpus Christi, TX	137
318	Costa Mesa, CA	120
180	Cranston, RI	172
37	Dallas, TX	287
351	Daly City, CA	107
164	Danbury, CT	179
195	Davenport, IA	167
161	Davie, FL	180
64	Dayton, OH	241
140	Dearborn, MI	190
101	Decatur, IL	207
NA	Deerfield Beach, FL**	NA
288	Denton, TX	130
69	Denver, CO	233
170	Des Moines, IA	176
12	Detroit, MI	387
371	Downey, CA	101
204	Duluth, MN	164
103	Durham, NC	206
219	Edinburg, TX	158
170	Edison Twnshp, NJ	176
292	Edmond, OK	129
327	El Cajon, CA	117
359	El Monte, CA	105
218	El Paso, TX	159
200	Elgin, IL	165
60	Elizabeth, NJ	249
403	Elk Grove, CA	83
192	Erie, PA	168
349	Escondido, CA	108
327	Eugene, OR	117
66	Evansville, IN	239
156	Everett, WA	182
351	Fairfield, CA	107
79	Fall River, MA	219
277	Fargo, ND	134
302	Farmington Hills, MI	126
161	Fayetteville, NC	180
326	Fishers, IN	118
327	Flint, MI	117
393	Fontana, CA	91
311	Fort Collins, CO	122
31	Fort Lauderdale, FL	301
137	Fort Smith, AR	191
164	Fort Wayne, IN	179
116	Fort Worth, TX	199
407	Fremont, CA	77
231	Fresno, CA	150
327	Frisco, TX	117
360	Fullerton, CA	104
70	Gainesville, FL	232
394	Garden Grove, CA	90
262	Garland, TX	139
NA	Gary, IN**	NA
360	Gilbert, AZ	104
176	Glendale, AZ	174
311	Glendale, CA	122
318	Grand Prairie, TX	120
209	Grand Rapids, MI	162
367	Greece, NY	102
236	Greeley, CO	148
166	Green Bay, WI	178
360	Gresham, OR	104
132	Hamilton Twnshp, NJ	192
51	Hammond, IN	258
116	Hampton, VA	199
15	Hartford, CT	352
345	Hawthorne, CA	110
297	Hayward, CA	128
408	Hemet, CA	75
292	Henderson, NV	129
NA	Hesperia, CA**	NA
246	Hialeah, FL	144
114	High Point, NC	200
288	Hillsboro, OR	130
90	Hollywood, FL	214
128	Hoover, AL	193
62	Houston, TX	247
355	Huntington Beach, CA	106
82	Huntsville, AL	218
195	Independence, MO	167
125	Indianapolis, IN	194
401	Indio, CA	84
200	Inglewood, CA	165
388	Irvine, CA	92
225	Irving, TX	152
120	Jacksonville, FL	197
57	Jackson, MS	252
24	Jersey City, NJ	324
405	Johns Creek, GA	78
188	Joliet, IL	170
NA	Kansas City, KS**	NA
31	Kansas City, MO	301
334	Kennewick, WA	116
114	Kenosha, WI	200
259	Kent, WA	140
176	Killeen, TX	174
90	Knoxville, TN	214
93	Lafayette, LA	211
NA	Lake Forest, CA**	NA
85	Lakeland, FL	217
308	Lakewood Twnshp, NJ	125
NA	Lakewood, CA**	NA
148	Lakewood, CO	186
NA	Lancaster, CA**	NA
200	Lansing, MI	165
170	Laredo, TX	176
179	Largo, FL	173
150	Las Cruces, NM	185
159	Las Vegas, NV	181
NA	Lawrence, KS**	NA
223	Lawrence, MA	154
170	Lawton, OK	176
318	League City, TX	120
262	Lee's Summit, MO	139
259	Lewisville, TX	140

328 Cities

Alpha Order - City (continued)

RANK	CITY	RATE
174	Lexington, KY	175
308	Lincoln, NE	125
50	Little Rock, AR	259
371	Livermore, CA	101
297	Livonia, MI	128
159	Long Beach, CA	181
222	Longmont, CO	156
132	Longview, TX	192
52	Los Angeles, CA	257
150	Louisville, KY	185
93	Lowell, MA	211
212	Lubbock, TX	161
100	Lynchburg, VA	209
128	Lynn, MA	193
27	Macon, GA	312
137	Madison, WI	191
141	Manchester, NH	189
109	McAllen, TX	204
337	McKinney, TX	114
284	Medford, OR	132
93	Melbourne, FL	211
13	Memphis, TN	376
NA	Menifee, CA**	NA
355	Merced, CA	106
343	Meridian, ID	111
192	Mesa, AZ	168
216	Mesquite, TX	160
8	Miami Beach, FL	406
154	Miami Gardens, FL	184
46	Miami, FL	262
225	Midland, TX	152
27	Milwaukee, WI	312
78	Minneapolis, MN	221
212	Miramar, FL	161
NA	Mission Viejo, CA**	NA
166	Mission, TX	178
75	Mobile, AL	223
351	Modesto, CA	107
53	Montgomery, AL	256
NA	Moreno Valley, CA**	NA
107	Murfreesboro, TN	205
404	Murrieta, CA	82
257	Nampa, ID	141
394	Napa, CA	90
335	Naperville, IL	115
125	Nashua, NH	194
87	Nashville, TN	215
49	New Bedford, MA	260
43	New Haven, CT	276
11	New Orleans, LA	389
109	New Rochelle, NY	204
6	New York, NY	421
10	Newark, NJ	394
225	Newport Beach, CA	152
82	Newport News, VA	218
212	Newton, MA	161
34	Norfolk, VA	293
239	Norman, OK	147
20	North Charleston, SC	342
NA	Norwalk, CA**	NA
137	Norwalk, CT	191
204	Oakland, CA	164
318	Oceanside, CA	120
257	Odessa, TX	141
277	O'Fallon, MO	134
216	Ogden, UT	160
176	Oklahoma City, OK	174
292	Olathe, KS	129
141	Omaha, NE	189
275	Ontario, CA	135
337	Orange, CA	114
380	Orem, UT	98
35	Orlando, FL	291

RANK	CITY	RATE
268	Overland Park, KS	138
327	Oxnard, CA	117
223	Palm Bay, FL	154
NA	Palmdale, CA**	NA
195	Pasadena, CA	167
183	Pasadena, TX	171
63	Paterson, NJ	243
246	Pearland, TX	144
244	Pembroke Pines, FL	145
327	Peoria, AZ	117
150	Peoria, IL	185
4	Philadelphia, PA	433
97	Phoenix, AZ	210
38	Pittsburgh, PA	285
300	Plano, TX	127
113	Plantation, FL	201
380	Pomona, CA	98
NA	Pompano Beach, FL**	NA
310	Port St. Lucie, FL	123
209	Portland, OR	162
59	Portsmouth, VA	250
400	Provo, UT	86
128	Pueblo, CO	193
119	Quincy, MA	198
54	Racine, WI	255
156	Raleigh, NC	182
297	Ramapo, NY	128
NA	Rancho Cucamon., CA**	NA
168	Reading, PA	177
349	Redding, CA	108
341	Redwood City, CA	112
300	Reno, NV	127
284	Renton, WA	132
380	Rialto, CA	98
231	Richardson, TX	150
156	Richmond, CA	182
15	Richmond, VA	352
262	Rio Rancho, NM	139
325	Riverside, CA	119
48	Roanoke, VA	261
315	Rochester, MN	121
17	Rochester, NY	349
180	Rockford, IL	172
380	Roseville, CA	98
NA	Roswell, GA**	NA
NA	Round Rock, TX**	NA
246	Sacramento, CA	144
311	Salem, OR	122
385	Salinas, CA	96
82	Salt Lake City, UT	218
183	San Angelo, TX	171
183	San Antonio, TX	171
262	San Bernardino, CA	139
262	San Diego, CA	139
44	San Francisco, CA	271
335	San Jose, CA	115
355	San Leandro, CA	106
NA	San Marcos, CA**	NA
360	San Mateo, CA	104
292	Sandy Springs, GA	129
318	Sandy, UT	120
367	Santa Ana, CA	102
231	Santa Barbara, CA	150
343	Santa Clara, CA	111
NA	Santa Clarita, CA**	NA
371	Santa Maria, CA	101
74	Santa Monica, CA	225
384	Santa Rosa, CA	97
60	Savannah, GA	249
154	Scottsdale, AZ	184
120	Scranton, PA	197
93	Seattle, WA	211
30	Shreveport, LA	306
399	Simi Valley, CA	87

RANK	CITY	RATE
236	Sioux City, IA	148
236	Sioux Falls, SD	148
200	Somerville, MA	165
55	South Bend, IN	254
401	South Gate, CA	84
NA	Sparks, NV**	NA
355	Spokane Valley, WA	106
288	Spokane, WA	130
103	Springfield, IL	206
33	Springfield, MA	296
123	Springfield, MO	195
75	Stamford, CT	223
315	Sterling Heights, MI	121
347	Stockton, CA	109
234	St. Joseph, MO	149
5	St. Louis, MO	425
101	St. Paul, MN	207
87	St. Petersburg, FL	215
86	Suffolk, VA	216
150	Sugar Land, TX	185
251	Sunnyvale, CA	143
116	Sunrise, FL	199
365	Surprise, AZ	103
22	Syracuse, NY	339
144	Tacoma, WA	188
144	Tallahassee, FL	188
40	Tampa, FL	279
NA	Temecula, CA**	NA
107	Tempe, AZ	205
286	Thornton, CO	131
NA	Thousand Oaks, CA**	NA
246	Toledo, OH	144
204	Toms River Twnshp, NJ	164
73	Topeka, KS	226
241	Torrance, CA	146
378	Tracy, CA	99
40	Trenton, NJ	279
302	Troy, MI	126
161	Tucson, AZ	180
144	Tulsa, OK	188
27	Tuscaloosa, AL	312
318	Tustin, CA	120
132	Tyler, TX	192
225	Upper Darby Twnshp, PA	152
385	Vacaville, CA	96
405	Vallejo, CA	78
341	Vancouver, WA	112
340	Ventura, CA	113
NA	Victorville, CA**	NA
174	Virginia Beach, VA	175
351	Visalia, CA	107
NA	Vista, CA**	NA
141	Waco, TX	189
255	Warren, MI	142
125	Warwick, RI	194
1	Washington, DC	618
46	Waterbury, CT	262
394	West Covina, CA	90
397	West Jordan, UT	89
45	West Palm Beach, FL	268
251	West Valley, UT	143
388	Westland, MI	92
371	Westminster, CA	101
183	Westminster, CO	171
277	Whittier, CA	134
168	Wichita Falls, TX	177
192	Wichita, KS	168
67	Wilmington, NC	237
57	Winston-Salem, NC	252
132	Woodbridge Twnshp, NJ	192
71	Worcester, MA	231
255	Yakima, WA	142
26	Yonkers, NY	314
188	Yuma, AZ	170

Source: CQ Press using reported data from the F.B.I. "Crime in the United States 2011"
*Sworn officers only, does not include civilian employees.
**Not available

82. Rate of Police Officers in 2011 (continued)
National Rate = 238 Officers per 100,000 Population*

Rank Order - City

RANK	CITY	RATE	RANK	CITY	RATE	RANK	CITY	RATE
1	Washington, DC	618	73	Topeka, KS	226	144	Tacoma, WA	188
2	Baltimore, MD	468	74	Santa Monica, CA	225	144	Tallahassee, FL	188
3	Chicago, IL	447	75	Boca Raton, FL	223	144	Tulsa, OK	188
4	Philadelphia, PA	433	75	Mobile, AL	223	148	Albuquerque, NM	186
5	St. Louis, MO	425	75	Stamford, CT	223	148	Lakewood, CO	186
6	New York, NY	421	78	Minneapolis, MN	221	150	Las Cruces, NM	185
7	Birmingham, AL	411	79	Charlotte, NC	219	150	Louisville, KY	185
8	Miami Beach, FL	406	79	Chattanooga, TN	219	150	Peoria, IL	185
9	Atlanta, GA	398	79	Fall River, MA	219	150	Sugar Land, TX	185
10	Newark, NJ	394	82	Huntsville, AL	218	154	Miami Gardens, FL	184
11	New Orleans, LA	389	82	Newport News, VA	218	154	Scottsdale, AZ	184
12	Detroit, MI	387	82	Salt Lake City, UT	218	156	Everett, WA	182
13	Memphis, TN	376	85	Lakeland, FL	217	156	Raleigh, NC	182
14	Cleveland, OH	365	86	Suffolk, VA	216	156	Richmond, CA	182
15	Hartford, CT	352	87	Albany, GA	215	159	Las Vegas, NV	181
15	Richmond, VA	352	87	Nashville, TN	215	159	Long Beach, CA	181
17	Cincinnati, OH	349	87	St. Petersburg, FL	215	161	Davie, FL	180
17	Rochester, NY	349	90	Hollywood, FL	214	161	Fayetteville, NC	180
19	Boston, MA	347	90	Knoxville, TN	214	161	Tucson, AZ	180
20	North Charleston, SC	342	92	Alexandria, VA	212	164	Danbury, CT	179
21	Camden, NJ	341	93	Lafayette, LA	211	164	Fort Wayne, IN	179
22	Syracuse, NY	339	93	Lowell, MA	211	166	Green Bay, WI	178
23	Charleston, SC	326	93	Melbourne, FL	211	166	Mission, TX	178
24	Jersey City, NJ	324	93	Seattle, WA	211	168	Reading, PA	177
25	Albany, NY	317	97	Bethlehem, PA	210	168	Wichita Falls, TX	177
26	Yonkers, NY	314	97	Clearwater, FL	210	170	Des Moines, IA	176
27	Macon, GA	312	97	Phoenix, AZ	210	170	Edison Twnshp, NJ	176
27	Milwaukee, WI	312	100	Lynchburg, VA	209	170	Laredo, TX	176
27	Tuscaloosa, AL	312	101	Decatur, IL	207	170	Lawton, OK	176
30	Shreveport, LA	306	101	St. Paul, MN	207	174	Lexington, KY	175
31	Fort Lauderdale, FL	301	103	Akron, OH	206	174	Virginia Beach, VA	175
31	Kansas City, MO	301	103	Clarkstown, NY	206	176	Glendale, AZ	174
33	Springfield, MA	296	103	Durham, NC	206	176	Killeen, TX	174
34	Norfolk, VA	293	103	Springfield, IL	206	176	Oklahoma City, OK	174
35	Bridgeport, CT	291	107	Murfreesboro, TN	205	179	Largo, FL	173
35	Orlando, FL	291	107	Tempe, AZ	205	180	Arlington, TX	172
37	Dallas, TX	287	109	Austin, TX	204	180	Cranston, RI	172
38	Pittsburgh, PA	285	109	Beaumont, TX	204	180	Rockford, IL	172
39	Buffalo, NY	280	109	McAllen, TX	204	183	Boulder, CO	171
40	Baton Rouge, LA	279	109	New Rochelle, NY	204	183	Pasadena, TX	171
40	Tampa, FL	279	113	Plantation, FL	201	183	San Angelo, TX	171
40	Trenton, NJ	279	114	High Point, NC	200	183	San Antonio, TX	171
43	New Haven, CT	276	114	Kenosha, WI	200	183	Westminster, CO	171
44	San Francisco, CA	271	116	Fort Worth, TX	199	188	Bryan, TX	170
45	West Palm Beach, FL	268	116	Hampton, VA	199	188	Joliet, IL	170
46	Miami, FL	262	116	Sunrise, FL	199	188	Yuma, AZ	170
46	Waterbury, CT	262	119	Quincy, MA	198	191	Brick Twnshp, NJ	169
48	Roanoke, VA	261	120	Athens-Clarke, GA	197	192	Erie, PA	168
49	New Bedford, MA	260	120	Jacksonville, FL	197	192	Mesa, AZ	168
50	Little Rock, AR	259	120	Scranton, PA	197	192	Wichita, KS	168
51	Hammond, IN	258	123	Clarksville, TN	195	195	Clifton, NJ	167
52	Los Angeles, CA	257	123	Springfield, MO	195	195	Davenport, IA	167
53	Montgomery, AL	256	125	Indianapolis, IN	194	195	Independence, MO	167
54	Racine, WI	255	125	Nashua, NH	194	195	Pasadena, CA	167
55	Cambridge, MA	254	125	Warwick, RI	194	199	Allentown, PA	166
55	South Bend, IN	254	128	Aurora, CO	193	200	Elgin, IL	165
57	Jackson, MS	252	128	Hoover, AL	193	200	Inglewood, CA	165
57	Winston-Salem, NC	252	128	Lynn, MA	193	200	Lansing, MI	165
59	Portsmouth, VA	250	128	Pueblo, CO	193	200	Somerville, MA	165
60	Elizabeth, NJ	249	132	Concord, NC	192	204	Amarillo, TX	164
60	Savannah, GA	249	132	Hamilton Twnshp, NJ	192	204	Duluth, MN	164
62	Houston, TX	247	132	Longview, TX	192	204	Oakland, CA	164
63	Paterson, NJ	243	132	Tyler, TX	192	204	Toms River Twnshp, NJ	164
64	Columbus, GA	241	132	Woodbridge Twnshp, NJ	192	208	Bloomington, IL	163
64	Dayton, OH	241	137	Fort Smith, AR	191	209	Coral Springs, FL	162
66	Evansville, IN	239	137	Madison, WI	191	209	Grand Rapids, MI	162
67	Wilmington, NC	237	137	Norwalk, CT	191	209	Portland, OR	162
68	Asheville, NC	234	140	Dearborn, MI	190	212	Cedar Rapids, IA	161
69	Denver, CO	233	141	Manchester, NH	189	212	Lubbock, TX	161
70	Gainesville, FL	232	141	Omaha, NE	189	212	Miramar, FL	161
71	Worcester, MA	231	141	Waco, TX	189	212	Newton, MA	161
72	Columbus, OH	229	144	Brockton, MA	188	216	Mesquite, TX	160

Rank Order - City (continued)

RANK	CITY	RATE	RANK	CITY	RATE	RANK	CITY	RATE
216	Ogden, UT	160	288	Hillsboro, OR	130	360	San Mateo, CA	104
218	El Paso, TX	159	288	Spokane, WA	130	365	Corona, CA	103
219	Cheektowaga, NY	158	292	Chino, CA	129	365	Surprise, AZ	103
219	Edinburg, TX	158	292	Edmond, OK	129	367	Buena Park, CA	102
221	Chesapeake, VA	157	292	Henderson, NV	129	367	Clovis, CA	102
222	Longmont, CO	156	292	Olathe, KS	129	367	Greece, NY	102
223	Lawrence, MA	154	292	Sandy Springs, GA	129	367	Santa Ana, CA	102
223	Palm Bay, FL	154	297	Hayward, CA	128	371	Citrus Heights, CA	101
225	Irving, TX	152	297	Livonia, MI	128	371	Downey, CA	101
225	Midland, TX	152	297	Ramapo, NY	128	371	Livermore, CA	101
225	Newport Beach, CA	152	300	Plano, TX	127	371	Santa Maria, CA	101
225	Upper Darby Twnshp, PA	152	300	Reno, NV	127	371	Westminster, CA	101
229	Abilene, TX	151	302	Allen, TX	126	376	Alhambra, CA	100
229	Beaverton, OR	151	302	Broken Arrow, OK	126	376	Carlsbad, CA	100
231	Fresno, CA	150	302	Carrollton, TX	126	378	Bakersfield, CA	99
231	Richardson, TX	150	302	Cary, NC	126	378	Tracy, CA	99
231	Santa Barbara, CA	150	302	Farmington Hills, MI	126	380	Orem, UT	98
234	Burbank, CA	149	302	Troy, MI	126	380	Pomona, CA	98
234	St. Joseph, MO	149	308	Lakewood Twnshp, NJ	125	380	Rialto, CA	98
236	Greeley, CO	148	308	Lincoln, NE	125	380	Roseville, CA	98
236	Sioux City, IA	148	310	Port St. Lucie, FL	123	384	Santa Rosa, CA	97
236	Sioux Falls, SD	148	311	College Station, TX	122	385	Salinas, CA	96
239	Colorado Springs, CO	147	311	Fort Collins, CO	122	385	Vacaville, CA	96
239	Norman, OK	147	311	Glendale, CA	122	387	Antioch, CA	93
241	Champaign, IL	146	311	Salem, OR	122	388	Baldwin Park, CA	92
241	Columbia, MO	146	315	Concord, CA	121	388	Canton Twnshp, MI	92
241	Torrance, CA	146	315	Rochester, MN	121	388	Clinton Twnshp, MI	92
244	Berkeley, CA	145	315	Sterling Heights, MI	121	388	Irvine, CA	92
244	Pembroke Pines, FL	145	318	Bloomington, IN	120	388	Westland, MI	92
246	Aurora, IL	144	318	Costa Mesa, CA	120	393	Fontana, CA	91
246	Hialeah, FL	144	318	Grand Prairie, TX	120	394	Garden Grove, CA	90
246	Pearland, TX	144	318	League City, TX	120	394	Napa, CA	90
246	Sacramento, CA	144	318	Oceanside, CA	120	394	West Covina, CA	90
246	Toledo, OH	144	318	Sandy, UT	120	397	Chula Vista, CA	89
251	Arlington Heights, IL	143	318	Tustin, CA	120	397	West Jordan, UT	89
251	Arvada, CO	143	325	Riverside, CA	119	399	Simi Valley, CA	87
251	Sunnyvale, CA	143	326	Fishers, IN	118	400	Provo, UT	86
251	West Valley, UT	143	327	Centennial, CO	117	401	Indio, CA	84
255	Warren, MI	142	327	El Cajon, CA	117	401	South Gate, CA	84
255	Yakima, WA	142	327	Eugene, OR	117	403	Elk Grove, CA	83
257	Nampa, ID	141	327	Flint, MI	117	404	Murrieta, CA	82
257	Odessa, TX	141	327	Frisco, TX	117	405	Johns Creek, GA	78
259	Boise, ID	140	327	Oxnard, CA	117	405	Vallejo, CA	78
259	Kent, WA	140	327	Peoria, AZ	117	407	Fremont, CA	77
259	Lewisville, TX	140	334	Kennewick, WA	116	408	Hemet, CA	75
262	Bellevue, WA	139	335	Naperville, IL	115	NA	Bellflower, CA**	NA
262	Garland, TX	139	335	San Jose, CA	115	NA	Carson, CA**	NA
262	Lee's Summit, MO	139	337	Bend, OR	114	NA	Chino Hills, CA**	NA
262	Rio Rancho, NM	139	337	McKinney, TX	114	NA	Cicero, IL**	NA
262	San Bernardino, CA	139	337	Orange, CA	114	NA	Compton, CA**	NA
262	San Diego, CA	139	340	Ventura, CA	113	NA	Deerfield Beach, FL**	NA
268	Avondale, AZ	138	341	Redwood City, CA	112	NA	Gary, IN**	NA
268	Carmel, IN	138	341	Vancouver, WA	112	NA	Hesperia, CA**	NA
268	Overland Park, KS	138	343	Meridian, ID	111	NA	Kansas City, KS**	NA
271	Brooklyn Park, MN	137	343	Santa Clara, CA	111	NA	Lake Forest, CA**	NA
271	Cape Coral, FL	137	345	Anaheim, CA	110	NA	Lakewood, CA**	NA
271	Colonie, NY	137	345	Hawthorne, CA	110	NA	Lancaster, CA**	NA
271	Corpus Christi, TX	137	347	Chico, CA	109	NA	Lawrence, KS**	NA
275	Brownsville, TX	135	347	Stockton, CA	109	NA	Menifee, CA**	NA
275	Ontario, CA	135	349	Escondido, CA	108	NA	Mission Viejo, CA**	NA
277	Bloomington, MN	134	349	Redding, CA	108	NA	Moreno Valley, CA**	NA
277	Fargo, ND	134	351	Daly City, CA	107	NA	Norwalk, CA**	NA
277	O'Fallon, MO	134	351	Fairfield, CA	107	NA	Palmdale, CA**	NA
277	Whittier, CA	134	351	Modesto, CA	107	NA	Pompano Beach, FL**	NA
281	Bellingham, WA	133	351	Visalia, CA	107	NA	Rancho Cucamon., CA**	NA
281	Billings, MT	133	355	Huntington Beach, CA	106	NA	Roswell, GA**	NA
281	Chandler, AZ	133	355	Merced, CA	106	NA	Round Rock, TX**	NA
284	Medford, OR	132	355	San Leandro, CA	106	NA	San Marcos, CA**	NA
284	Renton, WA	132	355	Spokane Valley, WA	106	NA	Santa Clarita, CA**	NA
286	Anchorage, AK	131	359	El Monte, CA	105	NA	Sparks, NV**	NA
286	Thornton, CO	131	360	Ann Arbor, MI	104	NA	Temecula, CA**	NA
288	Amherst, NY	130	360	Fullerton, CA	104	NA	Thousand Oaks, CA**	NA
288	Denton, TX	130	360	Gilbert, AZ	104	NA	Victorville, CA**	NA
			360	Gresham, OR	104	NA	Vista, CA**	NA

Source: CQ Press using reported data from the F.B.I. "Crime in the United States 2011"
*Sworn officers only, does not include civilian employees.
**Not available

Cities 331

Alpha Order - City

83. Percent Change in Rate of Police Officers: 2010 to 2011
National Percent Change = 1.7% Decrease*

RANK	CITY	% CHANGE	RANK	CITY	% CHANGE	RANK	CITY	% CHANGE
228	Abilene, TX	(3.2)	247	Cheektowaga, NY	(3.7)	112	Fort Wayne, IN	0.6
281	Akron, OH	(5.1)	226	Chesapeake, VA	(3.1)	168	Fort Worth, TX	(1.5)
363	Albany, GA	(11.2)	97	Chicago, IL	1.1	368	Fremont, CA	(11.5)
358	Albany, NY	(10.2)	240	Chico, CA	(3.5)	341	Fresno, CA	(8.5)
246	Albuquerque, NM	(3.6)	NA	Chino Hills, CA**	NA	176	Frisco, TX	(1.7)
40	Alexandria, VA	5.0	24	Chino, CA	6.6	292	Fullerton, CA	(5.5)
99	Alhambra, CA	1.0	361	Chula Vista, CA	(11.0)	256	Gainesville, FL	(4.1)
345	Allentown, PA	(8.8)	NA	Cicero, IL**	NA	316	Garden Grove, CA	(7.2)
40	Allen, TX	5.0	26	Cincinnati, OH	6.4	275	Garland, TX	(4.8)
95	Amarillo, TX	1.2	184	Citrus Heights, CA	(1.9)	NA	Gary, IN**	NA
353	Amherst, NY	(9.7)	158	Clarkstown, NY	(1.0)	37	Gilbert, AZ	5.1
262	Anaheim, CA	(4.3)	88	Clarksville, TN	1.6	44	Glendale, AZ	4.8
75	Anchorage, AK	2.3	266	Clearwater, FL	(4.5)	289	Glendale, CA	(5.4)
305	Ann Arbor, MI	(6.3)	137	Cleveland, OH	(0.3)	275	Grand Prairie, TX	(4.8)
345	Antioch, CA	(8.8)	363	Clifton, NJ	(11.2)	163	Grand Rapids, MI	(1.2)
284	Arlington Heights, IL	(5.3)	355	Clinton Twnshp, MI	(9.8)	184	Greece, NY	(1.9)
42	Arlington, TX	4.9	48	Clovis, CA	4.1	230	Greeley, CO	(3.3)
91	Arvada, CO	1.4	252	College Station, TX	(3.9)	120	Green Bay, WI	0.0
306	Asheville, NC	(6.4)	153	Colonie, NY	(0.7)	392	Gresham, OR	(16.8)
203	Athens-Clarke, GA	(2.5)	282	Colorado Springs, CO	(5.2)	120	Hamilton Twnshp, NJ	0.0
1	Atlanta, GA	32.7	270	Columbia, MO	(4.6)	206	Hammond, IN	(2.6)
220	Aurora, CO	(3.0)	318	Columbus, GA	(7.3)	99	Hampton, VA	1.0
380	Aurora, IL	(13.3)	NA	Columbus, OH**	NA	194	Hartford, CT	(2.2)
99	Austin, TX	1.0	NA	Compton, CA**	NA	240	Hawthorne, CA	(3.5)
109	Avondale, AZ	0.7	106	Concord, CA	0.8	316	Hayward, CA	(7.2)
295	Bakersfield, CA	(5.7)	384	Concord, NC	(14.7)	391	Hemet, CA	(16.7)
161	Baldwin Park, CA	(1.1)	69	Coral Springs, FL	2.5	168	Henderson, NV	(1.5)
97	Baltimore, MD	1.1	334	Corona, CA	(8.0)	NA	Hesperia, CA**	NA
381	Baton Rouge, LA	(13.4)	370	Corpus Christi, TX	(11.6)	338	Hialeah, FL	(8.3)
365	Beaumont, TX	(11.3)	355	Costa Mesa, CA	(9.8)	190	High Point, NC	(2.0)
32	Beaverton, OR	5.6	120	Cranston, RI	0.0	196	Hillsboro, OR	(2.3)
61	Bellevue, WA	3.0	78	Dallas, TX	2.1	228	Hollywood, FL	(3.2)
NA	Bellflower, CA**	NA	103	Daly City, CA	0.9	289	Hoover, AL	(5.4)
194	Bellingham, WA	(2.2)	262	Danbury, CT	(4.3)	37	Houston, TX	5.1
67	Bend, OR	2.7	69	Davenport, IA	2.5	266	Huntington Beach, CA	(4.5)
379	Berkeley, CA	(13.2)	54	Davie, FL	3.4	29	Huntsville, AL	5.8
213	Bethlehem, PA	(2.8)	254	Dayton, OH	(4.0)	147	Independence, MO	(0.6)
32	Billings, MT	5.6	396	Dearborn, MI	(18.8)	220	Indianapolis, IN	(3.0)
9	Birmingham, AL	10.8	166	Decatur, IL	(1.4)	16	Indio, CA	7.7
49	Bloomington, IL	3.8	NA	Deerfield Beach, FL**	NA	180	Inglewood, CA	(1.8)
292	Bloomington, IN	(5.5)	11	Denton, TX	10.2	120	Irvine, CA	0.0
120	Bloomington, MN	0.0	247	Denver, CO	(3.7)	318	Irving, TX	(7.3)
91	Boca Raton, FL	1.4	280	Des Moines, IA	(4.9)	325	Jacksonville, FL	(7.5)
213	Boise, ID	(2.8)	2	Detroit, MI	20.6	196	Jackson, MS	(2.3)
22	Boston, MA	6.8	337	Downey, CA	(8.2)	271	Jersey City, NJ	(4.7)
81	Boulder, CO	1.8	256	Duluth, MN	(4.1)	398	Johns Creek, GA	(22.0)
19	Brick Twnshp, NJ	7.6	141	Durham, NC	(0.5)	196	Joliet, IL	(2.3)
137	Bridgeport, CT	(0.3)	93	Edinburg, TX	1.3	NA	Kansas City, KS**	NA
174	Brockton, MA	(1.6)	230	Edison Twnshp, NJ	(3.3)	54	Kansas City, MO	3.4
73	Broken Arrow, OK	2.4	247	Edmond, OK	(3.7)	344	Kennewick, WA	(8.7)
259	Brooklyn Park, MN	(4.2)	331	El Cajon, CA	(7.9)	141	Kenosha, WI	(0.5)
89	Brownsville, TX	1.5	99	El Monte, CA	1.0	341	Kent, WA	(8.5)
217	Bryan, TX	(2.9)	336	El Paso, TX	(8.1)	61	Killeen, TX	3.0
353	Buena Park, CA	(9.7)	147	Elgin, IL	(0.6)	180	Knoxville, TN	(1.8)
236	Buffalo, NY	(3.4)	328	Elizabeth, NJ	(7.8)	299	Lafayette, LA	(5.8)
53	Burbank, CA	3.5	240	Elk Grove, CA	(3.5)	NA	Lake Forest, CA**	NA
57	Cambridge, MA	3.3	95	Erie, PA	1.2	196	Lakeland, FL	(2.3)
401	Camden, NJ	(26.3)	284	Escondido, CA	(5.3)	403	Lakewood Twnshp, NJ	(28.6)
382	Canton Twnshp, MI	(14.0)	230	Eugene, OR	(3.3)	NA	Lakewood, CA**	NA
240	Cape Coral, FL	(3.5)	139	Evansville, IN	(0.4)	314	Lakewood, CO	(7.0)
338	Carlsbad, CA	(8.3)	304	Everett, WA	(6.2)	NA	Lancaster, CA**	NA
322	Carmel, IN	(7.4)	180	Fairfield, CA	(1.8)	394	Lansing, MI	(17.9)
73	Carrollton, TX	2.4	240	Fall River, MA	(3.5)	230	Laredo, TX	(3.3)
NA	Carson, CA**	NA	313	Fargo, ND	(6.9)	334	Largo, FL	(8.0)
16	Cary, NC	7.7	309	Farmington Hills, MI	(6.7)	21	Las Cruces, NM	6.9
69	Cedar Rapids, IA	2.5	75	Fayetteville, NC	2.3	271	Las Vegas, NV	(4.7)
176	Centennial, CO	(1.7)	275	Fishers, IN	(4.8)	NA	Lawrence, KS**	NA
252	Champaign, IL	(3.9)	230	Flint, MI	(3.3)	147	Lawrence, MA	(0.6)
106	Chandler, AZ	0.8	282	Fontana, CA	(5.2)	161	Lawton, OK	(1.1)
251	Charleston, SC	(3.8)	85	Fort Collins, CO	1.7	362	League City, TX	(11.1)
65	Charlotte, NC	2.8	7	Fort Lauderdale, FL	11.1	331	Lee's Summit, MO	(7.9)
311	Chattanooga, TN	(6.8)	115	Fort Smith, AR	0.5	3	Lewisville, TX	13.8

Alpha Order - City (continued)

RANK	CITY	% CHANGE
230	Lexington, KY	(3.3)
120	Lincoln, NE	0.0
275	Little Rock, AR	(4.8)
158	Livermore, CA	(1.0)
395	Livonia, MI	(18.5)
295	Long Beach, CA	(5.7)
93	Longmont, CO	1.3
289	Longview, TX	(5.4)
120	Los Angeles, CA	0.0
206	Louisville, KY	(2.6)
184	Lowell, MA	(1.9)
259	Lubbock, TX	(4.2)
120	Lynchburg, VA	0.0
240	Lynn, MA	(3.5)
203	Macon, GA	(2.5)
67	Madison, WI	2.7
192	Manchester, NH	(2.1)
89	McAllen, TX	1.5
81	McKinney, TX	1.8
295	Medford, OR	(5.7)
196	Melbourne, FL	(2.3)
14	Memphis, TN	8.4
NA	Menifee, CA**	NA
383	Merced, CA	(14.5)
81	Meridian, ID	1.8
180	Mesa, AZ	(1.8)
284	Mesquite, TX	(5.3)
136	Miami Beach, FL	(0.2)
85	Miami Gardens, FL	1.7
36	Miami, FL	5.2
184	Midland, TX	(1.9)
203	Milwaukee, WI	(2.5)
226	Minneapolis, MN	(3.1)
284	Miramar, FL	(5.3)
NA	Mission Viejo, CA**	NA
NA	Mission, TX**	NA
12	Mobile, AL	8.8
328	Modesto, CA	(7.8)
59	Montgomery, AL	3.2
NA	Moreno Valley, CA**	NA
79	Murfreesboro, TN	2.0
120	Murrieta, CA	0.0
166	Nampa, ID	(1.4)
54	Napa, CA	3.4
259	Naperville, IL	(4.2)
141	Nashua, NH	(0.5)
63	Nashville, TN	2.9
328	New Bedford, MA	(7.8)
400	New Haven, CT	(23.8)
271	New Orleans, LA	(4.7)
386	New Rochelle, NY	(15.7)
109	New York, NY	0.7
385	Newark, NJ	(15.6)
349	Newport Beach, CA	(9.0)
57	Newport News, VA	3.3
220	Newton, MA	(3.0)
352	Norfolk, VA	(9.6)
65	Norman, OK	2.8
15	North Charleston, SC	7.9
NA	Norwalk, CA**	NA
318	Norwalk, CT	(7.3)
147	Oakland, CA	(0.6)
120	Oceanside, CA	0.0
388	Odessa, TX	(16.1)
75	O'Fallon, MO	2.3
147	Ogden, UT	(0.6)
176	Oklahoma City, OK	(1.7)
106	Olathe, KS	0.8
6	Omaha, NE	11.2
49	Ontario, CA	3.8
155	Orange, CA	(0.9)
47	Orem, UT	4.3
210	Orlando, FL	(2.7)
NA	Overland Park, KS**	NA
306	Oxnard, CA	(6.4)
120	Palm Bay, FL	0.0
NA	Palmdale, CA**	NA
112	Pasadena, CA	0.6
302	Pasadena, TX	(6.0)
402	Paterson, NJ	(28.5)
109	Pearland, TX	0.7
326	Pembroke Pines, FL	(7.6)
103	Peoria, AZ	0.9
206	Peoria, IL	(2.6)
119	Philadelphia, PA	0.2
63	Phoenix, AZ	2.9
118	Pittsburgh, PA	0.4
23	Plano, TX	6.7
168	Plantation, FL	(1.5)
220	Pomona, CA	(3.0)
NA	Pompano Beach, FL**	NA
201	Port St. Lucie, FL	(2.4)
271	Portland, OR	(4.7)
35	Portsmouth, VA	5.5
5	Provo, UT	11.7
141	Pueblo, CO	(0.5)
262	Quincy, MA	(4.3)
42	Racine, WI	4.9
141	Raleigh, NC	(0.5)
371	Ramapo, NY	(11.7)
NA	Rancho Cucamon., CA**	NA
388	Reading, PA	(16.1)
303	Redding, CA	(6.1)
322	Redwood City, CA	(7.4)
376	Reno, NV	(12.4)
404	Renton, WA	(32.0)
371	Rialto, CA	(11.7)
13	Richardson, TX	8.7
120	Richmond, CA	0.0
147	Richmond, VA	(0.6)
4	Rio Rancho, NM	13.0
154	Riverside, CA	(0.8)
168	Roanoke, VA	(1.5)
254	Rochester, MN	(4.0)
331	Rochester, NY	(7.9)
213	Rockford, IL	(2.8)
158	Roseville, CA	(1.0)
NA	Roswell, GA**	NA
NA	Round Rock, TX**	NA
190	Sacramento, CA	(2.0)
326	Salem, OR	(7.6)
374	Salinas, CA	(11.9)
345	Salt Lake City, UT	(8.8)
32	San Angelo, TX	5.6
52	San Antonio, TX	3.6
378	San Bernardino, CA	(13.1)
192	San Diego, CA	(2.1)
168	San Francisco, CA	(1.5)
368	San Jose, CA	(11.5)
266	San Leandro, CA	(4.5)
NA	San Marcos, CA**	NA
345	San Mateo, CA	(8.8)
390	Sandy Springs, GA	(16.2)
85	Sandy, UT	1.7
184	Santa Ana, CA	(1.9)
164	Santa Barbara, CA	(1.3)
338	Santa Clara, CA	(8.3)
NA	Santa Clarita, CA**	NA
387	Santa Maria, CA	(15.8)
220	Santa Monica, CA	(3.0)
341	Santa Rosa, CA	(8.5)
351	Savannah, GA	(9.5)
120	Scottsdale, AZ	0.0
295	Scranton, PA	(5.7)
213	Seattle, WA	(2.8)
256	Shreveport, LA	(4.1)
322	Simi Valley, CA	(7.4)
206	Sioux City, IA	(2.6)
25	Sioux Falls, SD	6.5
69	Somerville, MA	2.5
79	South Bend, IN	2.0
236	South Gate, CA	(3.4)
NA	Sparks, NV**	NA
358	Spokane Valley, WA	(10.2)
350	Spokane, WA	(9.1)
247	Springfield, IL	(3.7)
46	Springfield, MA	4.6
16	Springfield, MO	7.7
155	Stamford, CT	(0.9)
292	Sterling Heights, MI	(5.5)
311	Stockton, CA	(6.8)
164	St. Joseph, MO	(1.3)
10	St. Louis, MO	10.7
184	St. Paul, MN	(1.9)
210	St. Petersburg, FL	(2.7)
115	Suffolk, VA	0.5
31	Sugar Land, TX	5.7
357	Sunnyvale, CA	(10.1)
45	Sunrise, FL	4.7
399	Surprise, AZ	(23.1)
266	Syracuse, NY	(4.5)
141	Tacoma, WA	(0.5)
308	Tallahassee, FL	(6.5)
81	Tampa, FL	1.8
NA	Temecula, CA**	NA
37	Tempe, AZ	5.1
168	Thornton, CO	(1.5)
NA	Thousand Oaks, CA**	NA
397	Toledo, OH	(19.6)
20	Toms River Twnshp, NJ	7.2
103	Topeka, KS	0.9
299	Torrance, CA	(5.8)
275	Tracy, CA	(4.8)
405	Trenton, NJ	(34.5)
393	Troy, MI	(17.1)
210	Tucson, AZ	(2.7)
115	Tulsa, OK	0.5
29	Tuscaloosa, AL	5.8
201	Tustin, CA	(2.4)
59	Tyler, TX	3.2
265	Upper Darby Twnshp, PA	(4.4)
377	Vacaville, CA	(12.7)
120	Vallejo, CA	0.0
120	Vancouver, WA	0.0
236	Ventura, CA	(3.4)
NA	Victorville, CA**	NA
176	Virginia Beach, VA	(1.7)
155	Visalia, CA	(0.9)
NA	Vista, CA**	NA
174	Waco, TX	(1.6)
375	Warren, MI	(12.3)
51	Warwick, RI	3.7
299	Washington, DC	(5.8)
139	Waterbury, CT	(0.4)
373	West Covina, CA	(11.8)
284	West Jordan, UT	(5.3)
217	West Palm Beach, FL	(2.9)
315	West Valley, UT	(7.1)
360	Westland, MI	(10.7)
217	Westminster, CA	(2.9)
27	Westminster, CO	6.2
365	Whittier, CA	(11.3)
318	Wichita Falls, TX	(7.3)
112	Wichita, KS	0.6
309	Wilmington, NC	(6.7)
8	Winston-Salem, NC	11.0
220	Woodbridge Twnshp, NJ	(3.0)
120	Worcester, MA	0.0
365	Yakima, WA	(11.3)
28	Yonkers, NY	6.1
236	Yuma, AZ	(3.4)

Source: CQ Press using reported data from the F.B.I. "Crime in the United States 2011"
*Sworn officers only, does not include civilian employees.
**Not available

Rank Order - City

83. Percent Change in Rate of Police Officers: 2010 to 2011 (continued)
National Percent Change = 1.7% Decrease*

RANK	CITY	% CHANGE	RANK	CITY	% CHANGE	RANK	CITY	% CHANGE
1	Atlanta, GA	32.7	73	Broken Arrow, OK	2.4	141	Raleigh, NC	(0.5)
2	Detroit, MI	20.6	73	Carrollton, TX	2.4	141	Tacoma, WA	(0.5)
3	Lewisville, TX	13.8	75	Anchorage, AK	2.3	147	Elgin, IL	(0.6)
4	Rio Rancho, NM	13.0	75	Fayetteville, NC	2.3	147	Independence, MO	(0.6)
5	Provo, UT	11.7	75	O'Fallon, MO	2.3	147	Lawrence, MA	(0.6)
6	Omaha, NE	11.2	78	Dallas, TX	2.1	147	Oakland, CA	(0.6)
7	Fort Lauderdale, FL	11.1	79	Murfreesboro, TN	2.0	147	Ogden, UT	(0.6)
8	Winston-Salem, NC	11.0	79	South Bend, IN	2.0	147	Richmond, VA	(0.6)
9	Birmingham, AL	10.8	81	Boulder, CO	1.8	153	Colonie, NY	(0.7)
10	St. Louis, MO	10.7	81	McKinney, TX	1.8	154	Riverside, CA	(0.8)
11	Denton, TX	10.2	81	Meridian, ID	1.8	155	Orange, CA	(0.9)
12	Mobile, AL	8.8	81	Tampa, FL	1.8	155	Stamford, CT	(0.9)
13	Richardson, TX	8.7	85	Fort Collins, CO	1.7	155	Visalia, CA	(0.9)
14	Memphis, TN	8.4	85	Miami Gardens, FL	1.7	158	Clarkstown, NY	(1.0)
15	North Charleston, SC	7.9	85	Sandy, UT	1.7	158	Livermore, CA	(1.0)
16	Cary, NC	7.7	88	Clarksville, TN	1.6	158	Roseville, CA	(1.0)
16	Indio, CA	7.7	89	Brownsville, TX	1.5	161	Baldwin Park, CA	(1.1)
16	Springfield, MO	7.7	89	McAllen, TX	1.5	161	Lawton, OK	(1.1)
19	Brick Twnshp, NJ	7.6	91	Arvada, CO	1.4	163	Grand Rapids, MI	(1.2)
20	Toms River Twnshp, NJ	7.2	91	Boca Raton, FL	1.4	164	Santa Barbara, CA	(1.3)
21	Las Cruces, NM	6.9	93	Edinburg, TX	1.3	164	St. Joseph, MO	(1.3)
22	Boston, MA	6.8	93	Longmont, CO	1.3	166	Decatur, IL	(1.4)
23	Plano, TX	6.7	95	Amarillo, TX	1.2	166	Nampa, ID	(1.4)
24	Chino, CA	6.6	95	Erie, PA	1.2	168	Fort Worth, TX	(1.5)
25	Sioux Falls, SD	6.5	97	Baltimore, MD	1.1	168	Henderson, NV	(1.5)
26	Cincinnati, OH	6.4	97	Chicago, IL	1.1	168	Plantation, FL	(1.5)
27	Westminster, CO	6.2	99	Alhambra, CA	1.0	168	Roanoke, VA	(1.5)
28	Yonkers, NY	6.1	99	Austin, TX	1.0	168	San Francisco, CA	(1.5)
29	Huntsville, AL	5.8	99	El Monte, CA	1.0	168	Thornton, CO	(1.5)
29	Tuscaloosa, AL	5.8	99	Hampton, VA	1.0	174	Brockton, MA	(1.6)
31	Sugar Land, TX	5.7	103	Daly City, CA	0.9	174	Waco, TX	(1.6)
32	Beaverton, OR	5.6	103	Peoria, AZ	0.9	176	Centennial, CO	(1.7)
32	Billings, MT	5.6	103	Topeka, KS	0.9	176	Frisco, TX	(1.7)
32	San Angelo, TX	5.6	106	Chandler, AZ	0.8	176	Oklahoma City, OK	(1.7)
35	Portsmouth, VA	5.5	106	Concord, CA	0.8	176	Virginia Beach, VA	(1.7)
36	Miami, FL	5.2	106	Olathe, KS	0.8	180	Fairfield, CA	(1.8)
37	Gilbert, AZ	5.1	109	Avondale, AZ	0.7	180	Inglewood, CA	(1.8)
37	Houston, TX	5.1	109	New York, NY	0.7	180	Knoxville, TN	(1.8)
37	Tempe, AZ	5.1	109	Pearland, TX	0.7	180	Mesa, AZ	(1.8)
40	Alexandria, VA	5.0	112	Fort Wayne, IN	0.6	184	Citrus Heights, CA	(1.9)
40	Allen, TX	5.0	112	Pasadena, CA	0.6	184	Greece, NY	(1.9)
42	Arlington, TX	4.9	112	Wichita, KS	0.6	184	Lowell, MA	(1.9)
42	Racine, WI	4.9	115	Fort Smith, AR	0.5	184	Midland, TX	(1.9)
44	Glendale, AZ	4.8	115	Suffolk, VA	0.5	184	Santa Ana, CA	(1.9)
45	Sunrise, FL	4.7	115	Tulsa, OK	0.5	184	St. Paul, MN	(1.9)
46	Springfield, MA	4.6	118	Pittsburgh, PA	0.4	190	High Point, NC	(2.0)
47	Orem, UT	4.3	119	Philadelphia, PA	0.2	190	Sacramento, CA	(2.0)
48	Clovis, CA	4.1	120	Bloomington, MN	0.0	192	Manchester, NH	(2.1)
49	Bloomington, IL	3.8	120	Cranston, RI	0.0	192	San Diego, CA	(2.1)
49	Ontario, CA	3.8	120	Green Bay, WI	0.0	194	Bellingham, WA	(2.2)
51	Warwick, RI	3.7	120	Hamilton Twnshp, NJ	0.0	194	Hartford, CT	(2.2)
52	San Antonio, TX	3.6	120	Irvine, CA	0.0	196	Hillsboro, OR	(2.3)
53	Burbank, CA	3.5	120	Lincoln, NE	0.0	196	Jackson, MS	(2.3)
54	Davie, FL	3.4	120	Los Angeles, CA	0.0	196	Joliet, IL	(2.3)
54	Kansas City, MO	3.4	120	Lynchburg, VA	0.0	196	Lakeland, FL	(2.3)
54	Napa, CA	3.4	120	Murrieta, CA	0.0	196	Melbourne, FL	(2.3)
57	Cambridge, MA	3.3	120	Oceanside, CA	0.0	201	Port St. Lucie, FL	(2.4)
57	Newport News, VA	3.3	120	Palm Bay, FL	0.0	201	Tustin, CA	(2.4)
59	Montgomery, AL	3.2	120	Richmond, CA	0.0	203	Athens-Clarke, GA	(2.5)
59	Tyler, TX	3.2	120	Scottsdale, AZ	0.0	203	Macon, GA	(2.5)
61	Bellevue, WA	3.0	120	Vallejo, CA	0.0	203	Milwaukee, WI	(2.5)
61	Killeen, TX	3.0	120	Vancouver, WA	0.0	206	Hammond, IN	(2.6)
63	Nashville, TN	2.9	120	Worcester, MA	0.0	206	Louisville, KY	(2.6)
63	Phoenix, AZ	2.9	136	Miami Beach, FL	(0.2)	206	Peoria, IL	(2.6)
65	Charlotte, NC	2.8	137	Bridgeport, CT	(0.3)	206	Sioux City, IA	(2.6)
65	Norman, OK	2.8	137	Cleveland, OH	(0.3)	210	Orlando, FL	(2.7)
67	Bend, OR	2.7	139	Evansville, IN	(0.4)	210	St. Petersburg, FL	(2.7)
67	Madison, WI	2.7	139	Waterbury, CT	(0.4)	210	Tucson, AZ	(2.7)
69	Cedar Rapids, IA	2.5	141	Durham, NC	(0.5)	213	Bethlehem, PA	(2.8)
69	Coral Springs, FL	2.5	141	Kenosha, WI	(0.5)	213	Boise, ID	(2.8)
69	Davenport, IA	2.5	141	Nashua, NH	(0.5)	213	Rockford, IL	(2.8)
69	Somerville, MA	2.5	141	Pueblo, CO	(0.5)	213	Seattle, WA	(2.8)

Rank Order - City (continued)

RANK	CITY	% CHANGE
217	Bryan, TX	(2.9)
217	West Palm Beach, FL	(2.9)
217	Westminster, CA	(2.9)
220	Aurora, CO	(3.0)
220	Indianapolis, IN	(3.0)
220	Newton, MA	(3.0)
220	Pomona, CA	(3.0)
220	Santa Monica, CA	(3.0)
220	Woodbridge Twnshp, NJ	(3.0)
226	Chesapeake, VA	(3.1)
226	Minneapolis, MN	(3.1)
228	Abilene, TX	(3.2)
228	Hollywood, FL	(3.2)
230	Edison Twnshp, NJ	(3.3)
230	Eugene, OR	(3.3)
230	Flint, MI	(3.3)
230	Greeley, CO	(3.3)
230	Laredo, TX	(3.3)
230	Lexington, KY	(3.3)
236	Buffalo, NY	(3.4)
236	South Gate, CA	(3.4)
236	Ventura, CA	(3.4)
236	Yuma, AZ	(3.4)
240	Cape Coral, FL	(3.5)
240	Chico, CA	(3.5)
240	Elk Grove, CA	(3.5)
240	Fall River, MA	(3.5)
240	Hawthorne, CA	(3.5)
240	Lynn, MA	(3.5)
246	Albuquerque, NM	(3.6)
247	Cheektowaga, NY	(3.7)
247	Denver, CO	(3.7)
247	Edmond, OK	(3.7)
247	Springfield, IL	(3.7)
251	Charleston, SC	(3.8)
252	Champaign, IL	(3.9)
252	College Station, TX	(3.9)
254	Dayton, OH	(4.0)
254	Rochester, MN	(4.0)
256	Duluth, MN	(4.1)
256	Gainesville, FL	(4.1)
256	Shreveport, LA	(4.1)
259	Brooklyn Park, MN	(4.2)
259	Lubbock, TX	(4.2)
259	Naperville, IL	(4.2)
262	Anaheim, CA	(4.3)
262	Danbury, CT	(4.3)
262	Quincy, MA	(4.3)
265	Upper Darby Twnshp, PA	(4.4)
266	Clearwater, FL	(4.5)
266	Huntington Beach, CA	(4.5)
266	San Leandro, CA	(4.5)
266	Syracuse, NY	(4.5)
270	Columbia, MO	(4.6)
271	Jersey City, NJ	(4.7)
271	Las Vegas, NV	(4.7)
271	New Orleans, LA	(4.7)
271	Portland, OR	(4.7)
275	Fishers, IN	(4.8)
275	Garland, TX	(4.8)
275	Grand Prairie, TX	(4.8)
275	Little Rock, AR	(4.8)
275	Tracy, CA	(4.8)
280	Des Moines, IA	(4.9)
281	Akron, OH	(5.1)
282	Colorado Springs, CO	(5.2)
282	Fontana, CA	(5.2)
284	Arlington Heights, IL	(5.3)
284	Escondido, CA	(5.3)
284	Mesquite, TX	(5.3)
284	Miramar, FL	(5.3)
284	West Jordan, UT	(5.3)
289	Glendale, CA	(5.4)
289	Hoover, AL	(5.4)
289	Longview, TX	(5.4)
292	Bloomington, IN	(5.5)
292	Fullerton, CA	(5.5)
292	Sterling Heights, MI	(5.5)
295	Bakersfield, CA	(5.7)
295	Long Beach, CA	(5.7)
295	Medford, OR	(5.7)
295	Scranton, PA	(5.7)
299	Lafayette, LA	(5.8)
299	Torrance, CA	(5.8)
299	Washington, DC	(5.8)
302	Pasadena, TX	(6.0)
303	Redding, CA	(6.1)
304	Everett, WA	(6.2)
305	Ann Arbor, MI	(6.3)
306	Asheville, NC	(6.4)
306	Oxnard, CA	(6.4)
308	Tallahassee, FL	(6.5)
309	Farmington Hills, MI	(6.7)
309	Wilmington, NC	(6.7)
311	Chattanooga, TN	(6.8)
311	Stockton, CA	(6.8)
313	Fargo, ND	(6.9)
314	Lakewood, CO	(7.0)
315	West Valley, UT	(7.1)
316	Garden Grove, CA	(7.2)
316	Hayward, CA	(7.2)
318	Columbus, GA	(7.3)
318	Irving, TX	(7.3)
318	Norwalk, CT	(7.3)
318	Wichita Falls, TX	(7.3)
322	Carmel, IN	(7.4)
322	Redwood City, CA	(7.4)
322	Simi Valley, CA	(7.4)
325	Jacksonville, FL	(7.5)
326	Pembroke Pines, FL	(7.6)
326	Salem, OR	(7.6)
328	Elizabeth, NJ	(7.8)
328	Modesto, CA	(7.8)
328	New Bedford, MA	(7.8)
331	El Cajon, CA	(7.9)
331	Lee's Summit, MO	(7.9)
331	Rochester, NY	(7.9)
334	Corona, CA	(8.0)
334	Largo, FL	(8.0)
336	El Paso, TX	(8.1)
337	Downey, CA	(8.2)
338	Carlsbad, CA	(8.3)
338	Hialeah, FL	(8.3)
338	Santa Clara, CA	(8.3)
341	Fresno, CA	(8.5)
341	Kent, WA	(8.5)
341	Santa Rosa, CA	(8.5)
344	Kennewick, WA	(8.7)
345	Allentown, PA	(8.8)
345	Antioch, CA	(8.8)
345	Salt Lake City, UT	(8.8)
345	San Mateo, CA	(8.8)
349	Newport Beach, CA	(9.0)
350	Spokane, WA	(9.1)
351	Savannah, GA	(9.5)
352	Norfolk, VA	(9.6)
353	Amherst, NY	(9.7)
353	Buena Park, CA	(9.7)
355	Clinton Twnshp, MI	(9.8)
355	Costa Mesa, CA	(9.8)
357	Sunnyvale, CA	(10.1)
358	Albany, NY	(10.2)
358	Spokane Valley, WA	(10.2)
360	Westland, MI	(10.7)
361	Chula Vista, CA	(11.0)
362	League City, TX	(11.1)
363	Albany, GA	(11.2)
363	Clifton, NJ	(11.2)
365	Beaumont, TX	(11.3)
365	Whittier, CA	(11.3)
365	Yakima, WA	(11.3)
368	Fremont, CA	(11.5)
368	San Jose, CA	(11.5)
370	Corpus Christi, TX	(11.6)
371	Ramapo, NY	(11.7)
371	Rialto, CA	(11.7)
373	West Covina, CA	(11.8)
374	Salinas, CA	(11.9)
375	Warren, MI	(12.3)
376	Reno, NV	(12.4)
377	Vacaville, CA	(12.7)
378	San Bernardino, CA	(13.1)
379	Berkeley, CA	(13.2)
380	Aurora, IL	(13.3)
381	Baton Rouge, LA	(13.4)
382	Canton Twnshp, MI	(14.0)
383	Merced, CA	(14.5)
384	Concord, NC	(14.7)
385	Newark, NJ	(15.6)
386	New Rochelle, NY	(15.7)
387	Santa Maria, CA	(15.8)
388	Odessa, TX	(16.1)
388	Reading, PA	(16.1)
390	Sandy Springs, GA	(16.2)
391	Hemet, CA	(16.7)
392	Gresham, OR	(16.8)
393	Troy, MI	(17.1)
394	Lansing, MI	(17.9)
395	Livonia, MI	(18.5)
396	Dearborn, MI	(18.8)
397	Toledo, OH	(19.6)
398	Johns Creek, GA	(22.0)
399	Surprise, AZ	(23.1)
400	New Haven, CT	(23.8)
401	Camden, NJ	(26.3)
402	Paterson, NJ	(28.5)
403	Lakewood Twnshp, NJ	(28.6)
404	Renton, WA	(32.0)
405	Trenton, NJ	(34.5)
NA	Bellflower, CA**	NA
NA	Carson, CA**	NA
NA	Chino Hills, CA**	NA
NA	Cicero, IL**	NA
NA	Columbus, OH**	NA
NA	Compton, CA**	NA
NA	Deerfield Beach, FL**	NA
NA	Gary, IN**	NA
NA	Hesperia, CA**	NA
NA	Kansas City, KS**	NA
NA	Lake Forest, CA**	NA
NA	Lakewood, CA**	NA
NA	Lancaster, CA**	NA
NA	Lawrence, KS**	NA
NA	Menifee, CA**	NA
NA	Mission Viejo, CA**	NA
NA	Mission, TX**	NA
NA	Moreno Valley, CA**	NA
NA	Norwalk, CA**	NA
NA	Overland Park, KS**	NA
NA	Palmdale, CA**	NA
NA	Pompano Beach, FL**	NA
NA	Rancho Cucamon., CA**	NA
NA	Roswell, GA**	NA
NA	Round Rock, TX**	NA
NA	San Marcos, CA**	NA
NA	Santa Clarita, CA**	NA
NA	Sparks, NV**	NA
NA	Temecula, CA**	NA
NA	Thousand Oaks, CA**	NA
NA	Victorville, CA**	NA
NA	Vista, CA**	NA

Source: CQ Press using reported data from the F.B.I. "Crime in the United States 2011"
*Sworn officers only, does not include civilian employees.
**Not available

Alpha Order - City

84. Percent Change in Rate of Police Officers: 2007 to 2011
National Percent Change = 2.9% Decrease*

RANK	CITY	% CHANGE	RANK	CITY	% CHANGE	RANK	CITY	% CHANGE
33	Abilene, TX	6.3	106	Cheektowaga, NY	(1.2)	134	Fort Wayne, IN	(2.7)
275	Akron, OH	(9.3)	199	Chesapeake, VA	(5.4)	210	Fort Worth, TX	(5.7)
310	Albany, GA	(11.9)	244	Chicago, IL	(7.6)	372	Fremont, CA	(18.1)
294	Albany, NY	(11.0)	365	Chico, CA	(16.8)	325	Fresno, CA	(13.3)
141	Albuquerque, NM	(3.1)	NA	Chino Hills, CA**	NA	311	Frisco, TX	(12.0)
255	Alexandria, VA	(8.2)	39	Chino, CA	4.9	319	Fullerton, CA	(12.6)
57	Alhambra, CA	3.1	391	Chula Vista, CA	(23.9)	184	Gainesville, FL	(4.5)
198	Allentown, PA	(5.1)	NA	Cicero, IL**	NA	271	Garden Grove, CA	(9.1)
91	Allen, TX	0.0	43	Cincinnati, OH	4.8	190	Garland, TX	(4.8)
79	Amarillo, TX	1.2	NA	Citrus Heights, CA**	NA	NA	Gary, IN**	NA
103	Amherst, NY	(0.8)	160	Clarkstown, NY	(3.7)	136	Gilbert, AZ	(2.8)
290	Anaheim, CA	(10.6)	167	Clarksville, TN	(3.9)	8	Glendale, AZ	17.6
69	Anchorage, AK	2.3	313	Clearwater, FL	(12.1)	217	Glendale, CA	(6.2)
384	Ann Arbor, MI	(21.8)	137	Cleveland, OH	(2.9)	333	Grand Prairie, TX	(14.3)
380	Antioch, CA	(19.8)	358	Clifton, NJ	(16.1)	126	Grand Rapids, MI	(2.4)
187	Arlington Heights, IL	(4.7)	362	Clinton Twnshp, MI	(16.4)	81	Greece, NY	1.0
15	Arlington, TX	9.6	323	Clovis, CA	(12.8)	241	Greeley, CO	(7.5)
100	Arvada, CO	(0.7)	350	College Station, TX	(15.3)	105	Green Bay, WI	(1.1)
348	Asheville, NC	(15.2)	109	Colonie, NY	(1.4)	341	Gresham, OR	(14.8)
110	Athens-Clarke, GA	(1.5)	369	Colorado Springs, CO	(17.9)	196	Hamilton Twnshp, NJ	(5.0)
10	Atlanta, GA	16.4	167	Columbia, MO	(3.9)	179	Hammond, IN	(4.4)
130	Aurora, CO	(2.5)	6	Columbus, GA	20.5	65	Hampton, VA	2.6
320	Aurora, IL	(12.7)	NA	Columbus, OH**	NA	31	Hartford, CT	6.7
58	Austin, TX	3.0	NA	Compton, CA**	NA	116	Hawthorne, CA	(1.8)
7	Avondale, AZ	19.0	171	Concord, CA	(4.0)	236	Hayward, CA	(7.2)
241	Bakersfield, CA	(7.5)	355	Concord, NC	(15.8)	400	Hemet, CA	(35.9)
216	Baldwin Park, CA	(6.1)	19	Coral Springs, FL	8.7	262	Henderson, NV	(8.5)
110	Baltimore, MD	(1.5)	320	Corona, CA	(12.7)	NA	Hesperia, CA**	NA
84	Baton Rouge, LA	0.7	NA	Corpus Christi, TX**	NA	333	Hialeah, FL	(14.3)
209	Beaumont, TX	(5.6)	375	Costa Mesa, CA	(18.9)	258	High Point, NC	(8.3)
23	Beaverton, OR	7.9	214	Cranston, RI	(6.0)	66	Hillsboro, OR	2.4
155	Bellevue, WA	(3.5)	13	Dallas, TX	10.8	116	Hollywood, FL	(1.8)
NA	Bellflower, CA**	NA	116	Daly City, CA	(1.8)	327	Hoover, AL	(13.5)
258	Bellingham, WA	(8.3)	147	Danbury, CT	(3.2)	14	Houston, TX	9.8
131	Bend, OR	(2.6)	73	Davenport, IA	1.8	199	Huntington Beach, CA	(5.4)
320	Berkeley, CA	(12.7)	177	Davie, FL	(4.3)	179	Huntsville, AL	(4.4)
77	Bethlehem, PA	1.4	171	Dayton, OH	(4.0)	291	Independence, MO	(10.7)
82	Billings, MT	0.8	255	Dearborn, MI	(8.2)	155	Indianapolis, IN	(3.5)
5	Birmingham, AL	20.9	126	Decatur, IL	(2.4)	376	Indio, CA	(19.2)
174	Bloomington, IL	(4.1)	NA	Deerfield Beach, FL**	NA	91	Inglewood, CA	0.0
171	Bloomington, IN	(4.0)	138	Denton, TX	(3.0)	29	Irvine, CA	7.0
244	Bloomington, MN	(7.6)	333	Denver, CO	(14.3)	217	Irving, TX	(6.2)
27	Boca Raton, FL	7.2	297	Des Moines, IA	(11.1)	179	Jacksonville, FL	(4.4)
271	Boise, ID	(9.1)	15	Detroit, MI	9.6	54	Jackson, MS	3.3
199	Boston, MA	(5.4)	49	Downey, CA	4.1	329	Jersey City, NJ	(13.6)
224	Boulder, CO	(6.6)	155	Duluth, MN	(3.5)	NA	Johns Creek, GA**	NA
73	Brick Twnshp, NJ	1.8	252	Durham, NC	(8.0)	361	Joliet, IL	(16.3)
206	Bridgeport, CT	(5.5)	99	Edinburg, TX	(0.6)	NA	Kansas City, KS**	NA
250	Brockton, MA	(7.8)	324	Edison Twnshp, NJ	(12.9)	179	Kansas City, MO	(4.4)
239	Broken Arrow, OK	(7.4)	326	Edmond, OK	(13.4)	357	Kennewick, WA	(15.9)
29	Brooklyn Park, MN	7.0	388	El Cajon, CA	(23.0)	45	Kenosha, WI	4.7
52	Brownsville, TX	3.8	330	El Monte, CA	(13.9)	226	Kent, WA	(6.7)
196	Bryan, TX	(5.0)	303	El Paso, TX	(11.7)	260	Killeen, TX	(8.4)
313	Buena Park, CA	(12.1)	285	Elgin, IL	(10.3)	59	Knoxville, TN	2.9
21	Buffalo, NY	8.1	286	Elizabeth, NJ	(10.4)	28	Lafayette, LA	7.1
77	Burbank, CA	1.4	226	Elk Grove, CA	(6.7)	NA	Lake Forest, CA**	NA
120	Cambridge, MA	(1.9)	66	Erie, PA	2.4	344	Lakeland, FL	(14.9)
398	Camden, NJ	(34.3)	315	Escondido, CA	(12.2)	397	Lakewood Twnshp, NJ	(33.9)
147	Canton Twnshp, MI	(3.2)	152	Eugene, OR	(3.3)	NA	Lakewood, CA**	NA
344	Cape Coral, FL	(14.9)	112	Evansville, IN	(1.6)	327	Lakewood, CO	(13.5)
350	Carlsbad, CA	(15.3)	254	Everett, WA	(8.1)	NA	Lancaster, CA**	NA
300	Carmel, IN	(11.5)	292	Fairfield, CA	(10.8)	385	Lansing, MI	(22.2)
214	Carrollton, TX	(6.0)	371	Fall River, MA	(18.0)	221	Laredo, TX	(6.4)
NA	Carson, CA**	NA	232	Fargo, ND	(6.9)	267	Largo, FL	(8.9)
163	Cary, NC	(3.8)	364	Farmington Hills, MI	(16.6)	141	Las Cruces, NM	(3.1)
25	Cedar Rapids, IA	7.3	315	Fayetteville, NC	(12.2)	392	Las Vegas, NV	(24.6)
193	Centennial, CO	(4.9)	220	Fishers, IN	(6.3)	NA	Lawrence, KS**	NA
286	Champaign, IL	(10.4)	404	Flint, MI	(48.0)	395	Lawrence, MA	(28.0)
32	Chandler, AZ	6.4	346	Fontana, CA	(15.0)	199	Lawton, OK	(5.4)
138	Charleston, SC	(3.0)	103	Fort Collins, CO	(0.8)	234	League City, TX	(7.0)
35	Charlotte, NC	5.8	3	Fort Lauderdale, FL	23.4	84	Lee's Summit, MO	0.7
378	Chattanooga, TN	(19.5)	87	Fort Smith, AR	0.5	91	Lewisville, TX	0.0

336 Cities

Alpha Order - City (continued)

RANK	CITY	% CHANGE
339	Lexington, KY	(14.6)
112	Lincoln, NE	(1.6)
271	Little Rock, AR	(9.1)
268	Livermore, CA	(9.0)
355	Livonia, MI	(15.8)
303	Long Beach, CA	(11.7)
141	Longmont, CO	(3.1)
264	Longview, TX	(8.6)
46	Los Angeles, CA	4.5
121	Louisville, KY	(2.1)
199	Lowell, MA	(5.4)
211	Lubbock, TX	(5.8)
199	Lynchburg, VA	(5.4)
236	Lynn, MA	(7.2)
38	Macon, GA	5.1
39	Madison, WI	4.9
141	Manchester, NH	(3.1)
87	McAllen, TX	0.5
278	McKinney, TX	(9.5)
247	Medford, OR	(7.7)
174	Melbourne, FL	(4.1)
4	Memphis, TN	22.5
NA	Menifee, CA**	NA
386	Merced, CA	(22.6)
73	Meridian, ID	1.8
255	Mesa, AZ	(8.2)
190	Mesquite, TX	(4.8)
152	Miami Beach, FL	(3.3)
2	Miami Gardens, FL	25.2
79	Miami, FL	1.2
131	Midland, TX	(2.6)
247	Milwaukee, WI	(7.7)
141	Minneapolis, MN	(3.1)
25	Miramar, FL	7.3
NA	Mission Viejo, CA**	NA
69	Mission, TX	2.3
24	Mobile, AL	7.7
368	Modesto, CA	(17.7)
9	Montgomery, AL	17.4
NA	Moreno Valley, CA**	NA
34	Murfreesboro, TN	6.2
126	Murrieta, CA	(2.4)
284	Nampa, ID	(10.2)
123	Napa, CA	(2.2)
300	Naperville, IL	(11.5)
47	Nashua, NH	4.3
147	Nashville, TN	(3.2)
350	New Bedford, MA	(15.3)
367	New Haven, CT	(17.1)
403	New Orleans, LA	(39.4)
372	New Rochelle, NY	(18.1)
125	New York, NY	(2.3)
282	Newark, NJ	(10.0)
353	Newport Beach, CA	(15.6)
116	Newport News, VA	(1.8)
318	Newton, MA	(12.5)
221	Norfolk, VA	(6.4)
12	Norman, OK	14.8
51	North Charleston, SC	4.0
NA	Norwalk, CA**	NA
184	Norwalk, CT	(4.5)
281	Oakland, CA	(9.9)
91	Oceanside, CA	0.0
224	Odessa, TX	(6.6)
123	O'Fallon, MO	(2.2)
159	Ogden, UT	(3.6)
251	Oklahoma City, OK	(7.9)
223	Olathe, KS	(6.5)
22	Omaha, NE	8.0
69	Ontario, CA	2.3
176	Orange, CA	(4.2)
72	Orem, UT	2.1
302	Orlando, FL	(11.6)

RANK	CITY	% CHANGE
239	Overland Park, KS	(7.4)
193	Oxnard, CA	(4.9)
206	Palm Bay, FL	(5.5)
NA	Palmdale, CA**	NA
106	Pasadena, CA	(1.2)
114	Pasadena, TX	(1.7)
394	Paterson, NJ	(27.2)
84	Pearland, TX	0.7
276	Pembroke Pines, FL	(9.4)
76	Peoria, AZ	1.7
347	Peoria, IL	(15.1)
241	Philadelphia, PA	(7.5)
59	Phoenix, AZ	2.9
43	Pittsburgh, PA	4.8
163	Plano, TX	(3.8)
177	Plantation, FL	(4.3)
382	Pomona, CA	(21.6)
NA	Pompano Beach, FL**	NA
383	Port St. Lucie, FL	(21.7)
311	Portland, OR	(12.0)
54	Portsmouth, VA	3.3
39	Provo, UT	4.9
47	Pueblo, CO	4.3
266	Quincy, MA	(8.8)
56	Racine, WI	3.2
244	Raleigh, NC	(7.6)
369	Ramapo, NY	(17.9)
NA	Rancho Cucamon., CA**	NA
396	Reading, PA	(30.3)
353	Redding, CA	(15.6)
338	Redwood City, CA	(14.5)
393	Reno, NV	(24.9)
378	Renton, WA	(19.5)
226	Rialto, CA	(6.7)
39	Richardson, TX	4.9
11	Richmond, CA	15.9
163	Richmond, VA	(3.8)
331	Rio Rancho, NM	(14.2)
298	Riverside, CA	(11.2)
199	Roanoke, VA	(5.4)
217	Rochester, MN	(6.2)
114	Rochester, NY	(1.7)
307	Rockford, IL	(11.8)
341	Roseville, CA	(14.8)
NA	Roswell, GA**	NA
NA	Round Rock, TX**	NA
235	Sacramento, CA	(7.1)
167	Salem, OR	(3.9)
381	Salinas, CA	(20.0)
260	Salt Lake City, UT	(8.4)
15	San Angelo, TX	9.6
36	San Antonio, TX	5.6
348	San Bernardino, CA	(15.2)
274	San Diego, CA	(9.2)
341	San Francisco, CA	(14.8)
387	San Jose, CA	(22.8)
276	San Leandro, CA	(9.4)
NA	San Marcos, CA**	NA
365	San Mateo, CA	(16.8)
91	Sandy Springs, GA	0.0
126	Sandy, UT	(2.4)
187	Santa Ana, CA	(4.7)
147	Santa Barbara, CA	(3.2)
298	Santa Clara, CA	(11.2)
NA	Santa Clarita, CA**	NA
337	Santa Maria, CA	(14.4)
187	Santa Monica, CA	(4.7)
307	Santa Rosa, CA	(11.8)
89	Savannah, GA	0.4
91	Scottsdale, AZ	0.0
190	Scranton, PA	(4.8)
147	Seattle, WA	(3.2)
62	Shreveport, LA	2.7
340	Simi Valley, CA	(14.7)

RANK	CITY	% CHANGE
131	Sioux City, IA	(2.6)
100	Sioux Falls, SD	(0.7)
155	Somerville, MA	(3.5)
89	South Bend, IN	0.4
265	South Gate, CA	(8.7)
NA	Sparks, NV**	NA
303	Spokane Valley, WA	(11.7)
262	Spokane, WA	(8.5)
280	Springfield, IL	(9.6)
100	Springfield, MA	(0.7)
211	Springfield, MO	(5.8)
268	Stamford, CT	(9.0)
206	Sterling Heights, MI	(5.5)
360	Stockton, CA	(16.2)
252	St. Joseph, MO	(8.0)
18	St. Louis, MO	9.5
231	St. Paul, MN	(6.8)
20	St. Petersburg, FL	8.6
52	Suffolk, VA	3.8
1	Sugar Land, TX	28.5
362	Sunnyvale, CA	(16.4)
37	Sunrise, FL	5.3
160	Surprise, AZ	(3.7)
141	Syracuse, NY	(3.1)
62	Tacoma, WA	2.7
358	Tallahassee, FL	(16.1)
184	Tampa, FL	(4.5)
NA	Temecula, CA**	NA
49	Tempe, AZ	4.1
82	Thornton, CO	0.8
NA	Thousand Oaks, CA**	NA
401	Toledo, OH	(36.3)
138	Toms River Twnshp, NJ	(3.0)
98	Topeka, KS	(0.4)
294	Torrance, CA	(11.0)
167	Tracy, CA	(3.9)
399	Trenton, NJ	(35.3)
390	Troy, MI	(23.6)
293	Tucson, AZ	(10.9)
331	Tulsa, OK	(14.2)
108	Tuscaloosa, AL	(1.3)
286	Tustin, CA	(10.4)
62	Tyler, TX	2.7
179	Upper Darby Twnshp, PA	(4.4)
377	Vacaville, CA	(19.3)
402	Vallejo, CA	(37.1)
286	Vancouver, WA	(10.4)
303	Ventura, CA	(11.7)
NA	Victorville, CA**	NA
193	Virginia Beach, VA	(4.9)
134	Visalia, CA	(2.7)
NA	Vista, CA**	NA
121	Waco, TX	(2.1)
374	Warren, MI	(18.4)
226	Warwick, RI	(6.7)
232	Washington, DC	(6.9)
211	Waterbury, CT	(5.8)
333	West Covina, CA	(14.3)
283	West Jordan, UT	(10.1)
294	West Palm Beach, FL	(11.0)
59	West Valley, UT	2.9
389	Westland, MI	(23.3)
238	Westminster, CA	(7.3)
66	Westminster, CO	2.4
307	Whittier, CA	(11.8)
163	Wichita Falls, TX	(3.8)
226	Wichita, KS	(6.7)
278	Wilmington, NC	(9.5)
91	Winston-Salem, NC	0.0
247	Woodbridge Twnshp, NJ	(7.7)
315	Worcester, MA	(12.2)
268	Yakima, WA	(9.0)
160	Yonkers, NY	(3.7)
154	Yuma, AZ	(3.4)

Source: CQ Press using reported data from the F.B.I. "Crime in the United States 2011"
*Sworn officers only, does not include civilian employees.
**Not available

Rank Order - City

84. Percent Change in Rate of Police Officers: 2007 to 2011 (continued)
National Percent Change = 2.9% Decrease*

RANK	CITY	% CHANGE	RANK	CITY	% CHANGE	RANK	CITY	% CHANGE
1	Sugar Land, TX	28.5	73	Brick Twnshp, NJ	1.8	141	Minneapolis, MN	(3.1)
2	Miami Gardens, FL	25.2	73	Davenport, IA	1.8	141	Syracuse, NY	(3.1)
3	Fort Lauderdale, FL	23.4	73	Meridian, ID	1.8	147	Canton Twnshp, MI	(3.2)
4	Memphis, TN	22.5	76	Peoria, AZ	1.7	147	Danbury, CT	(3.2)
5	Birmingham, AL	20.9	77	Bethlehem, PA	1.4	147	Nashville, TN	(3.2)
6	Columbus, GA	20.5	77	Burbank, CA	1.4	147	Santa Barbara, CA	(3.2)
7	Avondale, AZ	19.0	79	Amarillo, TX	1.2	147	Seattle, WA	(3.2)
8	Glendale, AZ	17.6	79	Miami, FL	1.2	152	Eugene, OR	(3.3)
9	Montgomery, AL	17.4	81	Greece, NY	1.0	152	Miami Beach, FL	(3.3)
10	Atlanta, GA	16.4	82	Billings, MT	0.8	154	Yuma, AZ	(3.4)
11	Richmond, CA	15.9	82	Thornton, CO	0.8	155	Bellevue, WA	(3.5)
12	Norman, OK	14.8	84	Baton Rouge, LA	0.7	155	Duluth, MN	(3.5)
13	Dallas, TX	10.8	84	Lee's Summit, MO	0.7	155	Indianapolis, IN	(3.5)
14	Houston, TX	9.8	84	Pearland, TX	0.7	155	Somerville, MA	(3.5)
15	Arlington, TX	9.6	87	Fort Smith, AR	0.5	159	Ogden, UT	(3.6)
15	Detroit, MI	9.6	87	McAllen, TX	0.5	160	Clarkstown, NY	(3.7)
15	San Angelo, TX	9.6	89	Savannah, GA	0.4	160	Surprise, AZ	(3.7)
18	St. Louis, MO	9.5	89	South Bend, IN	0.4	160	Yonkers, NY	(3.7)
19	Coral Springs, FL	8.7	91	Allen, TX	0.0	163	Cary, NC	(3.8)
20	St. Petersburg, FL	8.6	91	Inglewood, CA	0.0	163	Plano, TX	(3.8)
21	Buffalo, NY	8.1	91	Lewisville, TX	0.0	163	Richmond, VA	(3.8)
22	Omaha, NE	8.0	91	Oceanside, CA	0.0	163	Wichita Falls, TX	(3.8)
23	Beaverton, OR	7.9	91	Sandy Springs, GA	0.0	167	Clarksville, TN	(3.9)
24	Mobile, AL	7.7	91	Scottsdale, AZ	0.0	167	Columbia, MO	(3.9)
25	Cedar Rapids, IA	7.3	91	Winston-Salem, NC	0.0	167	Salem, OR	(3.9)
25	Miramar, FL	7.3	98	Topeka, KS	(0.4)	167	Tracy, CA	(3.9)
27	Boca Raton, FL	7.2	99	Edinburg, TX	(0.6)	171	Bloomington, IN	(4.0)
28	Lafayette, LA	7.1	100	Arvada, CO	(0.7)	171	Concord, CA	(4.0)
29	Brooklyn Park, MN	7.0	100	Sioux Falls, SD	(0.7)	171	Dayton, OH	(4.0)
29	Irvine, CA	7.0	100	Springfield, MA	(0.7)	174	Bloomington, IL	(4.1)
31	Hartford, CT	6.7	103	Amherst, NY	(0.8)	174	Melbourne, FL	(4.1)
32	Chandler, AZ	6.4	103	Fort Collins, CO	(0.8)	176	Orange, CA	(4.2)
33	Abilene, TX	6.3	105	Green Bay, WI	(1.1)	177	Davie, FL	(4.3)
34	Murfreesboro, TN	6.2	106	Cheektowaga, NY	(1.2)	177	Plantation, FL	(4.3)
35	Charlotte, NC	5.8	106	Pasadena, CA	(1.2)	179	Hammond, IN	(4.4)
36	San Antonio, TX	5.6	108	Tuscaloosa, AL	(1.3)	179	Huntsville, AL	(4.4)
37	Sunrise, FL	5.3	109	Colonie, NY	(1.4)	179	Jacksonville, FL	(4.4)
38	Macon, GA	5.1	110	Athens-Clarke, GA	(1.5)	179	Kansas City, MO	(4.4)
39	Chino, CA	4.9	110	Baltimore, MD	(1.5)	179	Upper Darby Twnshp, PA	(4.4)
39	Madison, WI	4.9	112	Evansville, IN	(1.6)	184	Gainesville, FL	(4.5)
39	Provo, UT	4.9	112	Lincoln, NE	(1.6)	184	Norwalk, CT	(4.5)
39	Richardson, TX	4.9	114	Pasadena, TX	(1.7)	184	Tampa, FL	(4.5)
43	Cincinnati, OH	4.8	114	Rochester, NY	(1.7)	187	Arlington Heights, IL	(4.7)
43	Pittsburgh, PA	4.8	116	Daly City, CA	(1.8)	187	Santa Ana, CA	(4.7)
45	Kenosha, WI	4.7	116	Hawthorne, CA	(1.8)	187	Santa Monica, CA	(4.7)
46	Los Angeles, CA	4.5	116	Hollywood, FL	(1.8)	190	Garland, TX	(4.8)
47	Nashua, NH	4.3	116	Newport News, VA	(1.8)	190	Mesquite, TX	(4.8)
47	Pueblo, CO	4.3	120	Cambridge, MA	(1.9)	190	Scranton, PA	(4.8)
49	Downey, CA	4.1	121	Louisville, KY	(2.1)	193	Centennial, CO	(4.9)
49	Tempe, AZ	4.1	121	Waco, TX	(2.1)	193	Oxnard, CA	(4.9)
51	North Charleston, SC	4.0	123	Napa, CA	(2.2)	193	Virginia Beach, VA	(4.9)
52	Brownsville, TX	3.8	123	O'Fallon, MO	(2.2)	196	Bryan, TX	(5.0)
52	Suffolk, VA	3.8	125	New York, NY	(2.3)	196	Hamilton Twnshp, NJ	(5.0)
54	Jackson, MS	3.3	126	Decatur, IL	(2.4)	198	Allentown, PA	(5.1)
54	Portsmouth, VA	3.3	126	Grand Rapids, MI	(2.4)	199	Boston, MA	(5.4)
56	Racine, WI	3.2	126	Murrieta, CA	(2.4)	199	Chesapeake, VA	(5.4)
57	Alhambra, CA	3.1	126	Sandy, UT	(2.4)	199	Huntington Beach, CA	(5.4)
58	Austin, TX	3.0	130	Aurora, CO	(2.5)	199	Lawton, OK	(5.4)
59	Knoxville, TN	2.9	131	Bend, OR	(2.6)	199	Lowell, MA	(5.4)
59	Phoenix, AZ	2.9	131	Midland, TX	(2.6)	199	Lynchburg, VA	(5.4)
59	West Valley, UT	2.9	131	Sioux City, IA	(2.6)	199	Roanoke, VA	(5.4)
62	Shreveport, LA	2.7	134	Fort Wayne, IN	(2.7)	206	Bridgeport, CT	(5.5)
62	Tacoma, WA	2.7	134	Visalia, CA	(2.7)	206	Palm Bay, FL	(5.5)
62	Tyler, TX	2.7	136	Gilbert, AZ	(2.8)	206	Sterling Heights, MI	(5.5)
65	Hampton, VA	2.6	137	Cleveland, OH	(2.9)	209	Beaumont, TX	(5.6)
66	Erie, PA	2.4	138	Charleston, SC	(3.0)	210	Fort Worth, TX	(5.7)
66	Hillsboro, OR	2.4	138	Denton, TX	(3.0)	211	Lubbock, TX	(5.8)
66	Westminster, CO	2.4	138	Toms River Twnshp, NJ	(3.0)	211	Springfield, MO	(5.8)
69	Anchorage, AK	2.3	141	Albuquerque, NM	(3.1)	211	Waterbury, CT	(5.8)
69	Mission, TX	2.3	141	Las Cruces, NM	(3.1)	214	Carrollton, TX	(6.0)
69	Ontario, CA	2.3	141	Longmont, CO	(3.1)	214	Cranston, RI	(6.0)
72	Orem, UT	2.1	141	Manchester, NH	(3.1)	216	Baldwin Park, CA	(6.1)

338 Cities

Rank Order - City (continued)

RANK	CITY	% CHANGE
217	Glendale, CA	(6.2)
217	Irving, TX	(6.2)
217	Rochester, MN	(6.2)
220	Fishers, IN	(6.3)
221	Laredo, TX	(6.4)
221	Norfolk, VA	(6.4)
223	Olathe, KS	(6.5)
224	Boulder, CO	(6.6)
224	Odessa, TX	(6.6)
226	Elk Grove, CA	(6.7)
226	Kent, WA	(6.7)
226	Rialto, CA	(6.7)
226	Warwick, RI	(6.7)
226	Wichita, KS	(6.7)
231	St. Paul, MN	(6.8)
232	Fargo, ND	(6.9)
232	Washington, DC	(6.9)
234	League City, TX	(7.0)
235	Sacramento, CA	(7.1)
236	Hayward, CA	(7.2)
236	Lynn, MA	(7.2)
238	Westminster, CA	(7.3)
239	Broken Arrow, OK	(7.4)
239	Overland Park, KS	(7.4)
241	Bakersfield, CA	(7.5)
241	Greeley, CO	(7.5)
241	Philadelphia, PA	(7.5)
244	Bloomington, MN	(7.6)
244	Chicago, IL	(7.6)
244	Raleigh, NC	(7.6)
247	Medford, OR	(7.7)
247	Milwaukee, WI	(7.7)
247	Woodbridge Twnshp, NJ	(7.7)
250	Brockton, MA	(7.8)
251	Oklahoma City, OK	(7.9)
252	Durham, NC	(8.0)
252	St. Joseph, MO	(8.0)
254	Everett, WA	(8.1)
255	Alexandria, VA	(8.2)
255	Dearborn, MI	(8.2)
255	Mesa, AZ	(8.2)
258	Bellingham, WA	(8.3)
258	High Point, NC	(8.3)
260	Killeen, TX	(8.4)
260	Salt Lake City, UT	(8.4)
262	Henderson, NV	(8.5)
262	Spokane, WA	(8.5)
264	Longview, TX	(8.6)
265	South Gate, CA	(8.7)
266	Quincy, MA	(8.8)
267	Largo, FL	(8.9)
268	Livermore, CA	(9.0)
268	Stamford, CT	(9.0)
268	Yakima, WA	(9.0)
271	Boise, ID	(9.1)
271	Garden Grove, CA	(9.1)
271	Little Rock, AR	(9.1)
274	San Diego, CA	(9.2)
275	Akron, OH	(9.3)
276	Pembroke Pines, FL	(9.4)
276	San Leandro, CA	(9.4)
278	McKinney, TX	(9.5)
278	Wilmington, NC	(9.5)
280	Springfield, IL	(9.6)
281	Oakland, CA	(9.9)
282	Newark, NJ	(10.0)
283	West Jordan, UT	(10.1)
284	Nampa, ID	(10.2)
285	Elgin, IL	(10.3)
286	Champaign, IL	(10.4)
286	Elizabeth, NJ	(10.4)
286	Tustin, CA	(10.4)
286	Vancouver, WA	(10.4)

RANK	CITY	% CHANGE
290	Anaheim, CA	(10.6)
291	Independence, MO	(10.7)
292	Fairfield, CA	(10.8)
293	Tucson, AZ	(10.9)
294	Albany, NY	(11.0)
294	Torrance, CA	(11.0)
294	West Palm Beach, FL	(11.0)
297	Des Moines, IA	(11.1)
298	Riverside, CA	(11.2)
298	Santa Clara, CA	(11.2)
300	Carmel, IN	(11.5)
300	Naperville, IL	(11.5)
302	Orlando, FL	(11.6)
303	El Paso, TX	(11.7)
303	Long Beach, CA	(11.7)
303	Spokane Valley, WA	(11.7)
303	Ventura, CA	(11.7)
307	Rockford, IL	(11.8)
307	Santa Rosa, CA	(11.8)
307	Whittier, CA	(11.8)
310	Albany, GA	(11.9)
311	Frisco, TX	(12.0)
311	Portland, OR	(12.0)
313	Buena Park, CA	(12.1)
313	Clearwater, FL	(12.1)
315	Escondido, CA	(12.2)
315	Fayetteville, NC	(12.2)
315	Worcester, MA	(12.2)
318	Newton, MA	(12.5)
319	Fullerton, CA	(12.6)
320	Aurora, IL	(12.7)
320	Berkeley, CA	(12.7)
320	Corona, CA	(12.7)
323	Clovis, CA	(12.8)
324	Edison Twnshp, NJ	(12.9)
325	Fresno, CA	(13.3)
326	Edmond, OK	(13.4)
327	Hoover, AL	(13.5)
327	Lakewood, CO	(13.5)
329	Jersey City, NJ	(13.6)
330	El Monte, CA	(13.9)
331	Rio Rancho, NM	(14.2)
331	Tulsa, OK	(14.2)
333	Denver, CO	(14.3)
333	Grand Prairie, TX	(14.3)
333	Hialeah, FL	(14.3)
333	West Covina, CA	(14.3)
337	Santa Maria, CA	(14.4)
338	Redwood City, CA	(14.5)
339	Lexington, KY	(14.6)
340	Simi Valley, CA	(14.7)
341	Gresham, OR	(14.8)
341	Roseville, CA	(14.8)
341	San Francisco, CA	(14.8)
344	Cape Coral, FL	(14.9)
344	Lakeland, FL	(14.9)
346	Fontana, CA	(15.0)
347	Peoria, IL	(15.1)
348	Asheville, NC	(15.2)
348	San Bernardino, CA	(15.2)
350	Carlsbad, CA	(15.3)
350	College Station, TX	(15.3)
350	New Bedford, MA	(15.3)
353	Newport Beach, CA	(15.6)
353	Redding, CA	(15.6)
355	Concord, NC	(15.8)
355	Livonia, MI	(15.8)
357	Kennewick, WA	(15.9)
358	Clifton, NJ	(16.1)
358	Tallahassee, FL	(16.1)
360	Stockton, CA	(16.2)
361	Joliet, IL	(16.3)
362	Clinton Twnshp, MI	(16.4)
362	Sunnyvale, CA	(16.4)

RANK	CITY	% CHANGE
364	Farmington Hills, MI	(16.6)
365	Chico, CA	(16.8)
365	San Mateo, CA	(16.8)
367	New Haven, CT	(17.1)
368	Modesto, CA	(17.7)
369	Colorado Springs, CO	(17.9)
369	Ramapo, NY	(17.9)
371	Fall River, MA	(18.0)
372	Fremont, CA	(18.1)
372	New Rochelle, NY	(18.1)
374	Warren, MI	(18.4)
375	Costa Mesa, CA	(18.9)
376	Indio, CA	(19.2)
377	Vacaville, CA	(19.3)
378	Chattanooga, TN	(19.5)
378	Renton, WA	(19.5)
380	Antioch, CA	(19.8)
381	Salinas, CA	(20.0)
382	Pomona, CA	(21.6)
383	Port St. Lucie, FL	(21.7)
384	Ann Arbor, MI	(21.8)
385	Lansing, MI	(22.2)
386	Merced, CA	(22.6)
387	San Jose, CA	(22.8)
388	El Cajon, CA	(23.0)
389	Westland, MI	(23.3)
390	Troy, MI	(23.6)
391	Chula Vista, CA	(23.9)
392	Las Vegas, NV	(24.6)
393	Reno, NV	(24.9)
394	Paterson, NJ	(27.2)
395	Lawrence, MA	(28.0)
396	Reading, PA	(30.3)
397	Lakewood Twnshp, NJ	(33.9)
398	Camden, NJ	(34.3)
399	Trenton, NJ	(35.3)
400	Hemet, CA	(35.9)
401	Toledo, OH	(36.3)
402	Vallejo, CA	(37.1)
403	New Orleans, LA	(39.4)
404	Flint, MI	(48.0)
NA	Bellflower, CA**	NA
NA	Carson, CA**	NA
NA	Chino Hills, CA**	NA
NA	Cicero, IL**	NA
NA	Citrus Heights, CA**	NA
NA	Columbus, OH**	NA
NA	Compton, CA**	NA
NA	Corpus Christi, TX**	NA
NA	Deerfield Beach, FL**	NA
NA	Gary, IN**	NA
NA	Hesperia, CA**	NA
NA	Johns Creek, GA**	NA
NA	Kansas City, KS**	NA
NA	Lake Forest, CA**	NA
NA	Lakewood, CA**	NA
NA	Lancaster, CA**	NA
NA	Lawrence, KS**	NA
NA	Menifee, CA**	NA
NA	Mission Viejo, CA**	NA
NA	Moreno Valley, CA**	NA
NA	Norwalk, CA**	NA
NA	Palmdale, CA**	NA
NA	Pompano Beach, FL**	NA
NA	Rancho Cucamon., CA**	NA
NA	Roswell, GA**	NA
NA	Round Rock, TX**	NA
NA	San Marcos, CA**	NA
NA	Santa Clarita, CA**	NA
NA	Sparks, NV**	NA
NA	Temecula, CA**	NA
NA	Thousand Oaks, CA**	NA
NA	Victorville, CA**	NA
NA	Vista, CA**	NA

Source: CQ Press using reported data from the F.B.I. "Crime in the United States 2011"
*Sworn officers only, does not include civilian employees.
**Not available

III. Metropolitan and City Populations

Metropolitan Population in 2011 342
Metropolitan Population in 2010 346
Metropolitan Population in 2007 350

City Population in 2011 354
City Population in 2010 358
City Population in 2007 362

Please note the following for Tables 85 through 87:

- All listings are for Metropolitan Statistical Areas (M.S.A.s) except for those ending with "M.D."
- Listings with "M.D." are Metropolitan Divisions, which are smaller parts of eleven large M.S.A.s. These eleven M.S.A.s further divided into M.D.s are identified using "(greater)" following the metropolitan area name.
- For example, the "Dallas (greater)" M.S.A. includes the two M.D.s of Dallas-Plano-Irving and Fort Worth-Arlington. The data for the M.D.s are included in the data for the overall M.S.A.
- The name of a M.S.A. or M.D. is subject to change based on the changing proportional size of the largest cities included within it. Percent changes are calculated in this book if the MSA or M.D. has not substantially changed, despite the changes in name. In the tables in this book, some M.S.A. and M.D. names are abbreviated to preserve space.

Please note the following for Tables 88 through 90:

- All listings are for cities of 75,000 or more in population that reported data to the F.B.I. for 2011.

Alpha Order - Metro Area

85. Metropolitan Population in 2011
National Total = 311,591,917*

RANK	METROPOLITAN AREA	POP	RANK	METROPOLITAN AREA	POP	RANK	METROPOLITAN AREA	POP
252	Abilene, TX	168,729	176	Charleston, WV	304,676	52	Fort Lauderdale, FL M.D.	1,771,889
99	Akron, OH	703,715	51	Charlotte-Gastonia, NC-SC	1,780,095	177	Fort Smith, AR-OK	301,142
79	Albany-Schenectady-Troy, NY	874,629	226	Charlottesville, VA	203,966	144	Fort Wayne, IN	418,383
264	Albany, GA	159,379	120	Chattanooga, TN-GA	533,526	38	Fort Worth-Arlington, TX M.D.	2,180,968
78	Albuquerque, NM	897,005	356	Cheyenne, WY	92,473	76	Fresno, CA	941,388
265	Alexandria, LA	155,330	5	Chicago (greater), IL-IN-WI	9,491,301	342	Gadsden, AL	104,933
85	Allentown, PA-NJ	823,807	6	Chicago-Joilet-Naperville, IL M.D.	7,906,889	191	Gainesville, FL	267,877
309	Altoona, PA	127,494	213	Chico, CA	222,586	240	Gainesville, GA	182,050
201	Amarillo, TX	255,139	42	Cincinnati-Middletown, OH-KY-IN	2,134,687	96	Gary, IN M.D.	711,687
358	Ames, IA	90,011	186	Clarksville, TN-KY	276,234	304	Glens Falls, NY	129,502
172	Anchorage, AK	310,965	43	Cleveland-Elyria-Mentor, OH	2,078,757	315	Goldsboro, NC	124,178
236	Anderson, SC	189,305	323	Cleveland, TN	116,833	347	Grand Forks, ND-MN	99,832
166	Ann Arbor, MI	344,531	209	College Station-Bryan, TX	233,472	277	Grand Junction, CO	149,279
319	Anniston-Oxford, AL	119,143	104	Colorado Springs, CO	656,862	92	Grand Rapids-Wyoming, MI	773,576
212	Appleton, WI	226,649	246	Columbia, MO	173,414	361	Great Falls, MT	82,049
136	Asheville, NC	430,246	180	Columbus, GA-AL	298,305	197	Greeley, CO	257,229
233	Athens-Clarke County, GA	195,076	364	Columbus, IN	77,186	173	Green Bay, WI	307,576
12	Atlanta, GA	5,338,234	48	Columbus, OH	1,837,882	106	Greenville, SC	644,406
187	Atlantic City, NJ	275,463	134	Corpus Christi, TX	437,195	204	Gulfport-Biloxi, MS	249,760
287	Auburn, AL	140,922	360	Corvallis, OR	86,490	190	Hagerstown-Martinsburg, MD-WV	270,693
114	Augusta, GA-SC	563,924	239	Crestview-Fort Walton Beach, FL	183,286	266	Hanford-Corcoran, CA	154,780
54	Austin-Round Rock, TX	1,752,404	343	Cumberland, MD-WV	104,047	116	Harrisburg-Carlisle, PA	551,228
82	Bakersfield, CA	849,502	7	Dallas (greater), TX	6,505,848	311	Harrisonburg, VA	126,724
28	Baltimore-Towson, MD	2,736,186	16	Dallas-Plano-Irving, TX M.D.	4,324,880	73	Hartford, CT	1,022,173
271	Bangor, ME	153,903	284	Dalton, GA	144,100	159	Hickory, NC	370,132
216	Barnstable Town, MA	217,204	362	Danville, IL	81,871	363	Hinesville, GA	78,942
88	Baton Rouge, LA	809,822	338	Danville, VA	107,834	193	Holland-Grand Haven, MI	263,602
296	Battle Creek, MI	136,043	154	Davenport, IA-IL	381,200	353	Hot Springs, AR	96,750
339	Bay City, MI	107,690	83	Dayton, OH	842,118	222	Houma, LA	210,082
152	Beaumont-Port Arthur, TX	396,925	267	Decatur, AL	154,569	8	Houston, TX	6,071,933
225	Bellingham, WA	204,296	334	Decatur, IL	111,101	142	Huntsville, AL	419,602
263	Bend, OR	159,412	125	Deltona-Daytona Beach, FL	501,334	301	Idaho Falls, ID	131,886
66	Bethesda-Frederick, MD M.D.	1,216,589	31	Denver-Aurora, CO	2,587,784	53	Indianapolis, IN	1,765,211
262	Billings, MT	159,454	111	Des Moines-West Des Moines, IA	572,618	272	Iowa City, IA	153,385
203	Binghamton, NY	252,857	17	Detroit (greater), MI	4,293,012	59	Jacksonville, FL	1,363,935
71	Birmingham-Hoover, AL	1,133,475	49	Detroit-Livonia-Dearborn, MI M.D.	1,819,213	241	Jacksonville, NC	180,026
335	Bismarck, ND	110,613	280	Dothan, AL	146,340	118	Jackson, MS	541,099
255	Blacksburg, VA	164,905	256	Dover, DE	163,973	325	Jackson, TN	116,467
250	Bloomington-Normal, IL	170,082	355	Dubuque, IA	94,143	261	Janesville, WI	161,030
234	Bloomington, IN	193,698	183	Duluth, MN-WI	281,781	276	Jefferson City, MO	150,351
109	Boise City-Nampa, ID	623,381	124	Durham-Chapel Hill, NC	510,752	229	Johnson City, TN	200,508
13	Boston (greater), MA-NH	4,578,146	259	Eau Claire, WI	161,853	283	Johnstown, PA	144,137
46	Boston-Quincy, MA M.D.	1,899,298	35	Edison, NJ M.D.	2,348,037	317	Jonesboro, AR	121,942
179	Boulder, CO	299,698	244	El Centro, CA	176,580	245	Joplin, MO	176,156
310	Bowling Green, KY	126,823	86	El Paso, TX	817,494	330	Kankakee-Bradley, IL	113,791
202	Bremerton-Silverdale, WA	255,073	318	Elizabethtown, KY	120,563	44	Kansas City, MO-KS	2,045,034
77	Bridgeport-Stamford, CT	901,031	359	Elmira, NY	89,229	196	Kennewick-Pasco-Richland, WA	257,314
147	Brownsville-Harlingen, TX	414,768	184	Erie, PA	281,461	148	Killeen-Temple-Fort Hood, TX	413,828
329	Brunswick, GA	113,849	163	Eugene-Springfield, OR	355,459	170	Kingsport, TN-VA	312,618
70	Buffalo-Niagara Falls, NY	1,140,613	162	Evansville, IN-KY	360,616	238	Kingston, NY	183,313
273	Burlington, NC	153,047	368	Fairbanks, AK	34,243	98	Knoxville, TN	704,327
58	Cambridge-Newton, MA M.D.	1,512,246	219	Fargo, ND-MN	211,760	348	Kokomo, IN	99,192
65	Camden, NJ M.D.	1,254,841	302	Farmington, NM	131,499	298	La Crosse, WI-MN	134,312
150	Canton, OH	404,718	158	Fayetteville, NC	371,029	228	Lafayette, IN	202,820
107	Cape Coral-Fort Myers, FL	627,187	295	Flagstaff, AZ	136,324	185	Lafayette, LA	276,242
354	Cape Girardeau, MO-IL	96,620	140	Flint, MI	425,469	80	Lake Co.-Kenosha Co., IL-WI M.D.	872,725
367	Carson City, NV	55,740	278	Florence-Muscle Shoals, AL	147,845	227	Lake Havasu City-Kingman, AZ	203,020
366	Casper, WY	76,057	223	Florence, SC	207,960	110	Lakeland, FL	610,301
194	Cedar Rapids, IA	259,291	345	Fond du Lac, WI	102,076	121	Lancaster, PA	521,101
210	Champaign-Urbana, IL	232,588	175	Fort Collins-Loveland, CO	304,849	130	Lansing-East Lansing, MI	463,686

Note: All listings are for Metropolitan Statistical Areas (M.S.A.s) except for those ending with "M.D." Listings with "M.D." are Metropolitan Divisions which are smaller parts of eleven large M.S.A.s. See explanatory note at beginning of metropolitan area section.

Alpha Order - Metro Area (continued)

RANK	METROPOLITAN AREA	POP
200	Laredo, TX	255,571
220	Las Cruces, NM	211,575
45	Las Vegas-Paradise, NV	1,967,721
333	Lawrence, KS	111,530
313	Lawton, OK	125,426
299	Lebanon, PA	133,994
340	Lewiston-Auburn, ME	107,688
129	Lexington-Fayette, KY	475,361
341	Lima, OH	106,409
174	Lincoln, NE	304,853
97	Little Rock, AR	705,050
308	Logan, UT-ID	127,757
215	Longview, TX	218,879
344	Longview, WA	104,017
4	Los Angeles County, CA M.D.	9,934,033
2	Los Angeles (greater), CA	12,979,653
62	Louisville, KY-IN	1,291,986
181	Lubbock, TX	290,884
199	Lynchburg, VA	255,651
208	Macon, GA	235,351
274	Madera, CA	152,639
112	Madison, WI	571,071
151	Manchester-Nashua, NH	401,245
306	Manhattan, KS	127,888
351	Mankato-North Mankato, MN	97,487
314	Mansfield, OH	124,566
91	McAllen-Edinburg-Mission, TX	791,072
224	Medford, OR	205,369
61	Memphis, TN-MS-AR	1,326,648
195	Merced, CA	258,800
11	Miami (greater), FL	5,640,473
32	Miami-Dade County, FL M.D.	2,530,459
332	Michigan City-La Porte, IN	112,036
290	Midland, TX	139,752
57	Milwaukee, WI	1,562,687
22	Minneapolis-St. Paul, MN-WI	3,304,725
336	Missoula, MT	110,269
146	Mobile, AL	414,980
122	Modesto, CA	520,501
243	Monroe, LA	178,055
275	Monroe, MI	151,906
156	Montgomery, AL	376,339
294	Morristown, TN	137,840
320	Mount Vernon-Anacortes, WA	118,735
321	Muncie, IN	118,272
248	Muskegon-Norton Shores, MI	172,058
189	Myrtle Beach, SC	272,427
293	Napa, CA	138,089
168	Naples-Marco Island, FL	325,902
56	Nashville-Davidson, TN	1,604,276
25	Nassau-Suffolk, NY M.D.	2,845,615
87	New Haven-Milford, CT	810,372
67	New Orleans, LA	1,178,445
1	New York (greater), NY-NJ-PA	18,974,419
3	New York-W. Plains NY-NJ M.D.	11,625,900
41	Newark-Union, NJ-PA M.D.	2,154,867
95	North Port-Bradenton-Sarasota, FL	711,852
279	Norwich-New London, CT	146,560
30	Oakland-Fremont, CA M.D.	2,589,383
167	Ocala, FL	335,813
349	Ocean City, NJ	97,589
288	Odessa, TX	140,016
115	Ogden-Clearfield, UT	557,743
64	Oklahoma City, OK	1,266,404
198	Olympia, WA	256,222
81	Omaha-Council Bluffs, NE-IA	872,617
40	Orlando, FL	2,163,500
254	Oshkosh-Neenah, WI	167,722
327	Owensboro, KY	115,545
84	Oxnard-Thousand Oaks, CA	832,997
117	Palm Bay-Melbourne, FL	550,781
352	Palm Coast, FL	97,000
249	Panama City-Lynn Haven, FL	171,153
257	Pascagoula, MS	162,859
93	Peabody, MA M.D.	747,688
131	Pensacola, FL	455,110
155	Peoria, IL	380,327
9	Philadelphia (greater) PA-NJ-MD-DE	5,988,988
20	Philadelphia, PA M.D.	4,021,780
19	Phoenix-Mesa-Scottsdale, AZ	4,252,245
346	Pine Bluff, AR	101,017
34	Pittsburgh, PA	2,363,799
300	Pittsfield, MA	132,019
357	Pocatello, ID	91,658
137	Port St. Lucie, FL	429,887
36	Portland-Vancouver, OR-WA	2,251,909
123	Portland, ME	514,030
102	Poughkeepsie, NY	673,314
218	Prescott, AZ	214,020
119	Provo-Orem, UT	536,977
260	Pueblo, CO	161,834
258	Punta Gorda, FL	162,158
232	Racine, WI	196,259
69	Raleigh-Cary, NC	1,144,826
305	Rapid City, SD	127,919
149	Reading, PA	412,754
242	Redding, CA	179,306
138	Reno-Sparks, NV	429,004
63	Richmond, VA	1,273,282
18	Riverside-San Bernardino, CA	4,274,518
171	Roanoke, VA	312,395
237	Rochester, MN	187,446
72	Rochester, NY	1,059,061
165	Rockford, IL	350,483
143	Rockingham County, NH M.D.	418,914
270	Rocky Mount, NC	154,324
350	Rome, GA	97,585
39	Sacramento, CA	2,174,392
230	Saginaw, MI	200,018
153	Salem, OR	394,898
141	Salinas, CA	419,936
312	Salisbury, MD	126,390
68	Salt Lake City, UT	1,145,892
328	San Angelo, TX	114,176
37	San Antonio, TX	2,187,591
23	San Diego, CA	3,131,701
15	San Francisco (greater), CA	4,386,357
50	San Francisco-S. Mateo, CA M.D.	1,796,974
47	San Jose, CA	1,858,506
188	San Luis Obispo, CA	272,807
365	Sandusky, OH	77,135
24	Santa Ana-Anaheim, CA M.D.	3,045,620
139	Santa Barbara-Santa Maria, CA	428,878
192	Santa Cruz-Watsonville, CA	265,467
281	Santa Fe, NM	145,783
126	Santa Rosa-Petaluma, CA	489,566
164	Savannah, GA	352,188
113	Scranton--Wilkes-Barre, PA	565,428
21	Seattle (greater), WA	3,493,774
29	Seattle-Bellevue-Everett, WA M.D.	2,686,073
289	Sebastian-Vero Beach, FL	139,909
326	Sheboygan, WI	116,010
316	Sherman-Denison, TX	123,421
282	Sioux City, IA-NE-SD	144,528
211	Sioux Falls, SD	231,036
169	South Bend-Mishawaka, IN-MI	320,549
182	Spartanburg, SC	287,618
128	Spokane, WA	478,614
221	Springfield, IL	210,802
100	Springfield, MA	697,165
133	Springfield, MO	438,299
291	Springfield, OH	138,434
269	State College, PA	154,481
101	Stockton, CA	693,362
235	St. Cloud, MN	190,553
307	St. Joseph, MO-KS	127,813
26	St. Louis, MO-IL	2,824,159
337	Sumter, SC	108,707
103	Syracuse, NY	665,555
89	Tacoma, WA M.D.	807,701
157	Tallahassee, FL	372,419
27	Tampa-St Petersburg, FL	2,821,174
247	Terre Haute, IN	173,306
292	Texarkana, TX-Texarkana, AR	138,304
105	Toledo, OH	651,905
207	Topeka, KS	235,354
160	Trenton-Ewing, NJ	367,733
74	Tucson, AZ	994,140
75	Tulsa, OK	947,512
214	Tuscaloosa, AL	220,518
217	Tyler, TX	214,127
178	Utica-Rome, NY	300,743
286	Valdosta, GA	141,426
145	Vallejo-Fairfield, CA	418,203
322	Victoria, TX	117,812
55	Virginia Beach-Norfolk, VA-NC	1,691,669
132	Visalia-Porterville, CA	447,377
206	Waco, TX	239,849
285	Warner Robins, GA	141,742
33	Warren-Farmington Hills, MI M.D.	2,473,799
10	Washington (greater) DC-VA-MD-WV	5,651,690
14	Washington, DC-VA-MD-WV M.D.	4,435,101
253	Waterloo-Cedar Falls, IA	168,698
297	Wausau, WI	134,647
331	Wenatchee, WA	112,624
60	West Palm Beach, FL M.D.	1,338,125
268	Wichita Falls, TX	154,490
108	Wichita, KS	627,017
324	Williamsport, PA	116,481
94	Wilmington, DE-MD-NJ M.D.	712,367
161	Wilmington, NC	366,909
303	Winchester, VA-WV	129,751
127	Winston-Salem, NC	483,775
90	Worcester, MA	803,419
205	Yakima, WA	247,047
135	York-Hanover, PA	436,359
251	Yuba City, CA	168,854
231	Yuma, AZ	198,522

Source: Reported data from the F.B.I. "Crime in the United States 2011"
*Estimates as of July 2011 based on U.S. Bureau of the Census figures.

85. Metropolitan Population in 2011 (continued)
National Total = 311,591,917*

Rank Order - Metro Area

RANK	METROPOLITAN AREA	POP
1	New York (greater), NY-NJ-PA	18,974,419
2	Los Angeles (greater), CA	12,979,653
3	New York-W. Plains NY-NJ M.D.	11,625,900
4	Los Angeles County, CA M.D.	9,934,033
5	Chicago (greater), IL-IN-WI	9,491,301
6	Chicago-Joilet-Naperville, IL M.D.	7,906,889
7	Dallas (greater), TX	6,505,848
8	Houston, TX	6,071,933
9	Philadelphia (greater) PA-NJ-MD-DE	5,988,988
10	Washington (greater) DC-VA-MD-WV	5,651,690
11	Miami (greater), FL	5,640,473
12	Atlanta, GA	5,338,234
13	Boston (greater), MA-NH	4,578,146
14	Washington, DC-VA-MD-WV M.D.	4,435,101
15	San Francisco (greater), CA	4,386,357
16	Dallas-Plano-Irving, TX M.D.	4,324,880
17	Detroit (greater), MI	4,293,012
18	Riverside-San Bernardino, CA	4,274,518
19	Phoenix-Mesa-Scottsdale, AZ	4,252,245
20	Philadelphia, PA M.D.	4,021,780
21	Seattle (greater), WA	3,493,774
22	Minneapolis-St. Paul, MN-WI	3,304,725
23	San Diego, CA	3,131,701
24	Santa Ana-Anaheim, CA M.D.	3,045,620
25	Nassau-Suffolk, NY M.D.	2,845,615
26	St. Louis, MO-IL	2,824,159
27	Tampa-St Petersburg, FL	2,821,174
28	Baltimore-Towson, MD	2,736,186
29	Seattle-Bellevue-Everett, WA M.D.	2,686,073
30	Oakland-Fremont, CA M.D.	2,589,383
31	Denver-Aurora, CO	2,587,784
32	Miami-Dade County, FL M.D.	2,530,459
33	Warren-Farmington Hills, MI M.D.	2,473,799
34	Pittsburgh, PA	2,363,799
35	Edison, NJ M.D.	2,348,037
36	Portland-Vancouver, OR-WA	2,251,909
37	San Antonio, TX	2,187,591
38	Fort Worth-Arlington, TX M.D.	2,180,968
39	Sacramento, CA	2,174,392
40	Orlando, FL	2,163,500
41	Newark-Union, NJ-PA M.D.	2,154,867
42	Cincinnati-Middletown, OH-KY-IN	2,134,687
43	Cleveland-Elyria-Mentor, OH	2,078,757
44	Kansas City, MO-KS	2,045,034
45	Las Vegas-Paradise, NV	1,967,721
46	Boston-Quincy, MA M.D.	1,899,298
47	San Jose, CA	1,858,506
48	Columbus, OH	1,837,882
49	Detroit-Livonia-Dearborn, MI M.D.	1,819,213
50	San Francisco-S. Mateo, CA M.D.	1,796,974
51	Charlotte-Gastonia, NC-SC	1,780,095
52	Fort Lauderdale, FL M.D.	1,771,889
53	Indianapolis, IN	1,765,211
54	Austin-Round Rock, TX	1,752,404
55	Virginia Beach-Norfolk, VA-NC	1,691,669
56	Nashville-Davidson, TN	1,604,276
57	Milwaukee, WI	1,562,687
58	Cambridge-Newton, MA M.D.	1,512,246
59	Jacksonville, FL	1,363,935
60	West Palm Beach, FL M.D.	1,338,125
61	Memphis, TN-MS-AR	1,326,648
62	Louisville, KY-IN	1,291,986
63	Richmond, VA	1,273,282
64	Oklahoma City, OK	1,266,404
65	Camden, NJ M.D.	1,254,841
66	Bethesda-Frederick, MD M.D.	1,216,589
67	New Orleans, LA	1,178,445
68	Salt Lake City, UT	1,145,892
69	Raleigh-Cary, NC	1,144,826
70	Buffalo-Niagara Falls, NY	1,140,613
71	Birmingham-Hoover, AL	1,133,475
72	Rochester, NY	1,059,061
73	Hartford, CT	1,022,173
74	Tucson, AZ	994,140
75	Tulsa, OK	947,512
76	Fresno, CA	941,388
77	Bridgeport-Stamford, CT	901,031
78	Albuquerque, NM	897,005
79	Albany-Schenectady-Troy, NY	874,629
80	Lake Co.-Kenosha Co., IL-WI M.D.	872,725
81	Omaha-Council Bluffs, NE-IA	872,617
82	Bakersfield, CA	849,502
83	Dayton, OH	842,118
84	Oxnard-Thousand Oaks, CA	832,997
85	Allentown, PA-NJ	823,807
86	El Paso, TX	817,494
87	New Haven-Milford, CT	810,372
88	Baton Rouge, LA	809,822
89	Tacoma, WA M.D.	807,701
90	Worcester, MA	803,419
91	McAllen-Edinburg-Mission, TX	791,072
92	Grand Rapids-Wyoming, MI	773,576
93	Peabody, MA M.D.	747,688
94	Wilmington, DE-MD-NJ M.D.	712,367
95	North Port-Bradenton-Sarasota, FL	711,852
96	Gary, IN M.D.	711,687
97	Little Rock, AR	705,050
98	Knoxville, TN	704,327
99	Akron, OH	703,715
100	Springfield, MA	697,165
101	Stockton, CA	693,362
102	Poughkeepsie, NY	673,314
103	Syracuse, NY	665,555
104	Colorado Springs, CO	656,862
105	Toledo, OH	651,905
106	Greenville, SC	644,406
107	Cape Coral-Fort Myers, FL	627,187
108	Wichita, KS	627,017
109	Boise City-Nampa, ID	623,381
110	Lakeland, FL	610,301
111	Des Moines-West Des Moines, IA	572,618
112	Madison, WI	571,071
113	Scranton--Wilkes-Barre, PA	565,428
114	Augusta, GA-SC	563,924
115	Ogden-Clearfield, UT	557,743
116	Harrisburg-Carlisle, PA	551,228
117	Palm Bay-Melbourne, FL	550,781
118	Jackson, MS	541,099
119	Provo-Orem, UT	536,977
120	Chattanooga, TN-GA	533,526
121	Lancaster, PA	521,101
122	Modesto, CA	520,501
123	Portland, ME	514,030
124	Durham-Chapel Hill, NC	510,752
125	Deltona-Daytona Beach, FL	501,334
126	Santa Rosa-Petaluma, CA	489,566
127	Winston-Salem, NC	483,775
128	Spokane, WA	478,614
129	Lexington-Fayette, KY	475,361
130	Lansing-East Lansing, MI	463,686
131	Pensacola, FL	455,110
132	Visalia-Porterville, CA	447,377
133	Springfield, MO	438,299
134	Corpus Christi, TX	437,195
135	York-Hanover, PA	436,359
136	Asheville, NC	430,246
137	Port St. Lucie, FL	429,887
138	Reno-Sparks, NV	429,004
139	Santa Barbara-Santa Maria, CA	428,878
140	Flint, MI	425,469
141	Salinas, CA	419,936
142	Huntsville, AL	419,602
143	Rockingham County, NH M.D.	418,914
144	Fort Wayne, IN	418,383
145	Vallejo-Fairfield, CA	418,203
146	Mobile, AL	414,980
147	Brownsville-Harlingen, TX	414,768
148	Killeen-Temple-Fort Hood, TX	413,828
149	Reading, PA	412,754
150	Canton, OH	404,718
151	Manchester-Nashua, NH	401,245
152	Beaumont-Port Arthur, TX	396,925
153	Salem, OR	394,898
154	Davenport, IA-IL	381,200
155	Peoria, IL	380,327
156	Montgomery, AL	376,339
157	Tallahassee, FL	372,419
158	Fayetteville, NC	371,029
159	Hickory, NC	370,132
160	Trenton-Ewing, NJ	367,733
161	Wilmington, NC	366,909
162	Evansville, IN-KY	360,616
163	Eugene-Springfield, OR	355,459
164	Savannah, GA	352,188
165	Rockford, IL	350,483
166	Ann Arbor, MI	344,531
167	Ocala, FL	335,813
168	Naples-Marco Island, FL	325,902
169	South Bend-Mishawaka, IN-MI	320,549
170	Kingsport, TN-VA	312,618
171	Roanoke, VA	312,395
172	Anchorage, AK	310,965
173	Green Bay, WI	307,576
174	Lincoln, NE	304,853
175	Fort Collins-Loveland, CO	304,849
176	Charleston, WV	304,676
177	Fort Smith, AR-OK	301,142
178	Utica-Rome, NY	300,743
179	Boulder, CO	299,698
180	Columbus, GA-AL	298,305

Note: All listings are for Metropolitan Statistical Areas (M.S.A.s) except for those ending with "M.D." Listings with "M.D." are Metropolitan Divisions which are smaller parts of eleven large M.S.A.s. See explanatory note at beginning of metropolitan area section.

Rank Order - Metro Area (continued)

RANK	METROPOLITAN AREA	POP	RANK	METROPOLITAN AREA	POP	RANK	METROPOLITAN AREA	POP
181	Lubbock, TX	290,884	244	El Centro, CA	176,580	307	St. Joseph, MO-KS	127,813
182	Spartanburg, SC	287,618	245	Joplin, MO	176,156	308	Logan, UT-ID	127,757
183	Duluth, MN-WI	281,781	246	Columbia, MO	173,414	309	Altoona, PA	127,494
184	Erie, PA	281,461	247	Terre Haute, IN	173,306	310	Bowling Green, KY	126,823
185	Lafayette, LA	276,242	248	Muskegon-Norton Shores, MI	172,058	311	Harrisonburg, VA	126,724
186	Clarksville, TN-KY	276,234	249	Panama City-Lynn Haven, FL	171,153	312	Salisbury, MD	126,390
187	Atlantic City, NJ	275,463	250	Bloomington-Normal, IL	170,082	313	Lawton, OK	125,426
188	San Luis Obispo, CA	272,807	251	Yuba City, CA	168,854	314	Mansfield, OH	124,566
189	Myrtle Beach, SC	272,427	252	Abilene, TX	168,729	315	Goldsboro, NC	124,178
190	Hagerstown-Martinsburg, MD-WV	270,693	253	Waterloo-Cedar Falls, IA	168,698	316	Sherman-Denison, TX	123,421
191	Gainesville, FL	267,877	254	Oshkosh-Neenah, WI	167,722	317	Jonesboro, AR	121,942
192	Santa Cruz-Watsonville, CA	265,467	255	Blacksburg, VA	164,905	318	Elizabethtown, KY	120,563
193	Holland-Grand Haven, MI	263,602	256	Dover, DE	163,973	319	Anniston-Oxford, AL	119,143
194	Cedar Rapids, IA	259,291	257	Pascagoula, MS	162,859	320	Mount Vernon-Anacortes, WA	118,735
195	Merced, CA	258,800	258	Punta Gorda, FL	162,158	321	Muncie, IN	118,272
196	Kennewick-Pasco-Richland, WA	257,314	259	Eau Claire, WI	161,853	322	Victoria, TX	117,812
197	Greeley, CO	257,229	260	Pueblo, CO	161,834	323	Cleveland, TN	116,833
198	Olympia, WA	256,222	261	Janesville, WI	161,030	324	Williamsport, PA	116,481
199	Lynchburg, VA	255,651	262	Billings, MT	159,454	325	Jackson, TN	116,467
200	Laredo, TX	255,571	263	Bend, OR	159,412	326	Sheboygan, WI	116,010
201	Amarillo, TX	255,139	264	Albany, GA	159,379	327	Owensboro, KY	115,545
202	Bremerton-Silverdale, WA	255,073	265	Alexandria, LA	155,330	328	San Angelo, TX	114,176
203	Binghamton, NY	252,857	266	Hanford-Corcoran, CA	154,780	329	Brunswick, GA	113,849
204	Gulfport-Biloxi, MS	249,760	267	Decatur, AL	154,569	330	Kankakee-Bradley, IL	113,791
205	Yakima, WA	247,047	268	Wichita Falls, TX	154,490	331	Wenatchee, WA	112,624
206	Waco, TX	239,849	269	State College, PA	154,481	332	Michigan City-La Porte, IN	112,036
207	Topeka, KS	235,354	270	Rocky Mount, NC	154,324	333	Lawrence, KS	111,530
208	Macon, GA	235,351	271	Bangor, ME	153,903	334	Decatur, IL	111,101
209	College Station-Bryan, TX	233,472	272	Iowa City, IA	153,385	335	Bismarck, ND	110,613
210	Champaign-Urbana, IL	232,588	273	Burlington, NC	153,047	336	Missoula, MT	110,269
211	Sioux Falls, SD	231,036	274	Madera, CA	152,639	337	Sumter, SC	108,707
212	Appleton, WI	226,649	275	Monroe, MI	151,906	338	Danville, VA	107,834
213	Chico, CA	222,586	276	Jefferson City, MO	150,351	339	Bay City, MI	107,690
214	Tuscaloosa, AL	220,518	277	Grand Junction, CO	149,279	340	Lewiston-Auburn, ME	107,688
215	Longview, TX	218,879	278	Florence-Muscle Shoals, AL	147,845	341	Lima, OH	106,409
216	Barnstable Town, MA	217,204	279	Norwich-New London, CT	146,560	342	Gadsden, AL	104,933
217	Tyler, TX	214,127	280	Dothan, AL	146,340	343	Cumberland, MD-WV	104,047
218	Prescott, AZ	214,020	281	Santa Fe, NM	145,783	344	Longview, WA	104,017
219	Fargo, ND-MN	211,760	282	Sioux City, IA-NE-SD	144,528	345	Fond du Lac, WI	102,076
220	Las Cruces, NM	211,575	283	Johnstown, PA	144,137	346	Pine Bluff, AR	101,017
221	Springfield, IL	210,802	284	Dalton, GA	144,100	347	Grand Forks, ND-MN	99,832
222	Houma, LA	210,082	285	Warner Robins, GA	141,742	348	Kokomo, IN	99,192
223	Florence, SC	207,960	286	Valdosta, GA	141,426	349	Ocean City, NJ	97,589
224	Medford, OR	205,369	287	Auburn, AL	140,922	350	Rome, GA	97,585
225	Bellingham, WA	204,296	288	Odessa, TX	140,016	351	Mankato-North Mankato, MN	97,487
226	Charlottesville, VA	203,966	289	Sebastian-Vero Beach, FL	139,909	352	Palm Coast, FL	97,000
227	Lake Havasu City-Kingman, AZ	203,020	290	Midland, TX	139,752	353	Hot Springs, AR	96,750
228	Lafayette, IN	202,820	291	Springfield, OH	138,434	354	Cape Girardeau, MO-IL	96,620
229	Johnson City, TN	200,508	292	Texarkana, TX-Texarkana, AR	138,304	355	Dubuque, IA	94,143
230	Saginaw, MI	200,018	293	Napa, CA	138,089	356	Cheyenne, WY	92,473
231	Yuma, AZ	198,522	294	Morristown, TN	137,840	357	Pocatello, ID	91,658
232	Racine, WI	196,259	295	Flagstaff, AZ	136,324	358	Ames, IA	90,011
233	Athens-Clarke County, GA	195,076	296	Battle Creek, MI	136,043	359	Elmira, NY	89,229
234	Bloomington, IN	193,698	297	Wausau, WI	134,647	360	Corvallis, OR	86,490
235	St. Cloud, MN	190,553	298	La Crosse, WI-MN	134,312	361	Great Falls, MT	82,049
236	Anderson, SC	189,305	299	Lebanon, PA	133,994	362	Danville, IL	81,871
237	Rochester, MN	187,446	300	Pittsfield, MA	132,019	363	Hinesville, GA	78,942
238	Kingston, NY	183,313	301	Idaho Falls, ID	131,886	364	Columbus, IN	77,186
239	Crestview-Fort Walton Beach, FL	183,286	302	Farmington, NM	131,499	365	Sandusky, OH	77,135
240	Gainesville, GA	182,050	303	Winchester, VA-WV	129,751	366	Casper, WY	76,057
241	Jacksonville, NC	180,026	304	Glens Falls, NY	129,502	367	Carson City, NV	55,740
242	Redding, CA	179,306	305	Rapid City, SD	127,919	368	Fairbanks, AK	34,243
243	Monroe, LA	178,055	306	Manhattan, KS	127,888			

Source: Reported data from the F.B.I. "Crime in the United States 2011"
*Estimates as of July 2011 based on U.S. Bureau of the Census figures.

Alpha Order - Metro Area

86. Metropolitan Population in 2010
National Total = 309,330,219*

RANK	METROPOLITAN AREA	POP	RANK	METROPOLITAN AREA	POP	RANK	METROPOLITAN AREA	POP
244	Abilene, TX	159,566	NA	Charleston, WV**	NA	48	Fort Lauderdale, FL M.D.	1,779,016
88	Akron, OH	698,613	NA	Charlotte-Gastonia, NC-SC**	NA	167	Fort Smith, AR-OK	296,159
74	Albany-Schenectady-Troy, NY	851,078	215	Charlottesville, VA	199,881	129	Fort Wayne, IN	418,216
243	Albany, GA	160,950	111	Chattanooga, TN-GA	523,569	36	Fort Worth-Arlington, TX M.D.	2,159,206
72	Albuquerque, NM	884,210	335	Cheyenne, WY	91,857	70	Fresno, CA	926,736
250	Alexandria, LA	155,654	NA	Chicago (greater), IL-IN-WI**	NA	318	Gadsden, AL	104,600
76	Allentown, PA-NJ	828,068	NA	Chicago-Joilet-Naperville, IL M.D.**	NA	180	Gainesville, FL	263,388
287	Altoona, PA	126,459	200	Chico, CA	222,130	225	Gainesville, GA	186,894
189	Amarillo, TX	247,721	34	Cincinnati-Middletown, OH-KY-IN	2,185,076	NA	Gary, IN M.D.**	NA
337	Ames, IA	88,803	176	Clarksville, TN-KY	271,954	282	Glens Falls, NY	127,776
160	Anchorage, AK	313,181	41	Cleveland-Elyria-Mentor, OH	2,081,340	307	Goldsboro, NC	113,929
224	Anderson, SC	187,031	305	Cleveland, TN	114,041	326	Grand Forks, ND-MN	99,717
155	Ann Arbor, MI	346,839	203	College Station-Bryan, TX	214,518	260	Grand Junction, CO	147,126
302	Anniston-Oxford, AL	115,376	97	Colorado Springs, CO	626,259	82	Grand Rapids-Wyoming, MI	774,621
199	Appleton, WI	224,034	235	Columbia, MO	167,279	339	Great Falls, MT	82,913
130	Asheville, NC	417,415	170	Columbus, GA-AL	286,528	183	Greeley, CO	259,483
221	Athens-Clarke County, GA	188,596	343	Columbus, IN	76,785	161	Green Bay, WI	307,162
10	Atlanta, GA	5,432,336	46	Columbus, OH	1,817,671	95	Greenville, SC	648,658
174	Atlantic City, NJ	275,382	133	Corpus Christi, TX	416,086	195	Gulfport-Biloxi, MS	238,426
NA	Auburn, AL**	NA	340	Corvallis, OR	82,256	175	Hagerstown-Martinsburg, MD-WV	273,944
110	Augusta, GA-SC	531,786	228	Crestview-Fort Walton Beach, FL	179,091	256	Hanford-Corcoran, CA	150,689
49	Austin-Round Rock, TX	1,752,518	323	Cumberland, MD-WV	100,405	107	Harrisburg-Carlisle, PA	542,444
77	Bakersfield, CA	822,752	5	Dallas (greater), TX	6,574,246	295	Harrisonburg, VA	121,985
26	Baltimore-Towson, MD	2,720,381	12	Dallas-Plano-Irving, TX M.D.	4,415,040	66	Hartford, CT	1,023,921
257	Bangor, ME	150,537	280	Dalton, GA	131,302	149	Hickory, NC	367,927
201	Barnstable Town, MA	218,615	341	Danville, IL	78,867	345	Hinesville, GA	72,276
NA	Baton Rouge, LA**	NA	317	Danville, VA	105,798	181	Holland-Grand Haven, MI	261,957
273	Battle Creek, MI	134,169	144	Davenport, IA-IL	378,802	327	Hot Springs, AR	99,611
316	Bay City, MI	106,214	75	Dayton, OH	831,823	210	Houma, LA	204,653
145	Beaumont-Port Arthur, TX	376,711	251	Decatur, AL	153,306	7	Houston, TX	5,978,213
211	Bellingham, WA	203,393	315	Decatur, IL	106,467	131	Huntsville, AL	416,848
238	Bend, OR	162,019	116	Deltona-Daytona Beach, FL	500,849	281	Idaho Falls, ID	128,311
61	Bethesda-Frederick, MD M.D.	1,219,883	28	Denver-Aurora, CO	2,555,601	NA	Indianapolis, IN**	NA
246	Billings, MT	157,205	103	Des Moines-West Des Moines, IA	577,321	249	Iowa City, IA	155,935
192	Binghamton, NY	241,233	13	Detroit (greater), MI	4,359,587	54	Jacksonville, FL	1,350,025
NA	Birmingham-Hoover, AL**	NA	44	Detroit-Livonia-Dearborn, MI M.D.	1,895,974	NA	Jacksonville, NC**	NA
310	Bismarck, ND	111,613	264	Dothan, AL	145,215	106	Jackson, MS	546,069
241	Blacksburg, VA	161,019	239	Dover, DE	161,556	306	Jackson, TN	113,975
234	Bloomington-Normal, IL	167,701	331	Dubuque, IA	94,362	242	Janesville, WI	161,013
223	Bloomington, IN	187,290	173	Duluth, MN-WI	276,508	259	Jefferson City, MO	147,169
99	Boise City-Nampa, ID	619,814	115	Durham-Chapel Hill, NC	509,834	217	Johnson City, TN	198,527
11	Boston (greater), MA-NH	4,558,433	240	Eau Claire, WI	161,272	265	Johnstown, PA	143,909
43	Boston-Quincy, MA M.D.	1,908,436	32	Edison, NJ M.D.	2,366,214	296	Jonesboro, AR	121,519
165	Boulder, CO	302,365	232	El Centro, CA	169,405	230	Joplin, MO	174,867
293	Bowling Green, KY	122,243	84	El Paso, TX	756,304	NA	Kankakee-Bradley, IL**	NA
193	Bremerton-Silverdale, WA	240,976	308	Elizabethtown, KY	113,924	40	Kansas City, MO-KS	2,089,752
71	Bridgeport-Stamford, CT	895,941	338	Elmira, NY	87,073	186	Kennewick-Pasco-Richland, WA	251,139
141	Brownsville-Harlingen, TX	401,641	171	Erie, PA	281,637	143	Killeen-Temple-Fort Hood, TX	383,261
322	Brunswick, GA	101,534	NA	Eugene-Springfield, OR**	NA	162	Kingsport, TN-VA	306,196
65	Buffalo-Niagara Falls, NY	1,106,808	153	Evansville, IN-KY	353,847	227	Kingston, NY	179,764
252	Burlington, NC	152,475	347	Fairbanks, AK	38,307	87	Knoxville, TN	706,304
53	Cambridge-Newton, MA M.D.	1,492,762	206	Fargo, ND-MN	208,388	328	Kokomo, IN	98,871
57	Camden, NJ M.D.	1,268,710	286	Farmington, NM	126,955	276	La Crosse, WI-MN	133,588
139	Canton, OH	407,101	152	Fayetteville, NC	363,142	216	Lafayette, IN	198,921
100	Cape Coral-Fort Myers, FL	603,092	289	Flagstaff, AZ	125,838	179	Lafayette, LA	266,765
334	Cape Girardeau, MO-IL	93,412	128	Flint, MI	419,008	NA	Lake Co.-Kenosha Co., IL-WI M.D.**	NA
346	Carson City, NV	55,119	NA	Florence-Muscle Shoals, AL**	NA	NA	Lake Havasu City-Kingman, AZ**	NA
342	Casper, WY	77,252	213	Florence, SC	201,596	101	Lakeland, FL	593,733
182	Cedar Rapids, IA	260,733	324	Fond du Lac, WI	100,387	114	Lancaster, PA	514,044
NA	Champaign-Urbana, IL**	NA	166	Fort Collins-Loveland, CO	298,883	122	Lansing-East Lansing, MI	450,078

Note: All listings are for Metropolitan Statistical Areas (M.S.A.s) except for those ending with "M.D." Listings with "M.D." are Metropolitan Divisions which are smaller parts of eleven large M.S.A.s. See explanatory note at beginning of metropolitan area section.

Alpha Order - Metro Area (continued)

RANK	METROPOLITAN AREA	POP
190	Laredo, TX	245,929
204	Las Cruces, NM	212,820
42	Las Vegas-Paradise, NV	1,951,609
299	Lawrence, KS	118,966
304	Lawton, OK	114,290
279	Lebanon, PA	132,213
314	Lewiston-Auburn, ME	107,282
118	Lexington-Fayette, KY	477,150
320	Lima, OH	103,688
163	Lincoln, NE	304,589
90	Little Rock, AR	693,930
284	Logan, UT-ID	127,228
207	Longview, TX	207,545
321	Longview, WA	102,585
4	Los Angeles County, CA M.D.	9,870,891
2	Los Angeles (greater), CA	12,912,749
58	Louisville, KY-IN	1,268,689
172	Lubbock, TX	278,595
187	Lynchburg, VA	250,323
198	Macon, GA	224,947
255	Madera, CA	151,283
102	Madison, WI	577,374
140	Manchester-Nashua, NH	403,165
290	Manhattan, KS	125,477
332	Mankato-North Mankato, MN	94,016
292	Mansfield, OH	123,762
83	McAllen-Edinburg-Mission, TX	758,016
214	Medford, OR	201,375
55	Memphis, TN-MS-AR	1,313,722
188	Merced, CA	248,716
8	Miami (greater), FL	5,597,226
30	Miami-Dade County, FL M.D.	2,523,928
311	Michigan City-La Porte, IN	111,553
275	Midland, TX	133,704
52	Milwaukee, WI	1,566,270
20	Minneapolis-St. Paul, MN-WI	3,302,492
NA	Missoula, MT**	NA
132	Mobile, AL	416,582
113	Modesto, CA	516,479
229	Monroe, LA	175,187
253	Monroe, MI	151,998
147	Montgomery, AL	371,821
268	Morristown, TN	138,774
297	Mount Vernon-Anacortes, WA	120,890
303	Muncie, IN	115,258
231	Muskegon-Norton Shores, MI	172,745
177	Myrtle Beach, SC	271,797
272	Napa, CA	135,593
158	Naples-Marco Island, FL	325,568
51	Nashville-Davidson, TN	1,608,441
23	Nassau-Suffolk, NY M.D.	2,855,486
79	New Haven-Milford, CT	806,354
62	New Orleans, LA	1,201,385
1	New York (greater), NY-NJ-PA	19,042,526
3	New York-W. Plains NY-NJ M.D.	11,678,308
37	Newark-Union, NJ-PA M.D.	2,142,518
89	North Port-Bradenton-Sarasota, FL	697,913
266	Norwich-New London, CT	141,679
29	Oakland-Fremont, CA M.D.	2,544,121
157	Ocala, FL	336,017
330	Ocean City, NJ	96,094
271	Odessa, TX	135,675
109	Ogden-Clearfield, UT	536,184

RANK	METROPOLITAN AREA	POP
60	Oklahoma City, OK	1,254,299
185	Olympia, WA	254,900
73	Omaha-Council Bluffs, NE-IA	867,616
38	Orlando, FL	2,130,297
NA	Oshkosh-Neenah, WI**	NA
309	Owensboro, KY	113,908
78	Oxnard-Thousand Oaks, CA	807,132
108	Palm Bay-Melbourne, FL	542,130
329	Palm Coast, FL	97,199
237	Panama City-Lynn Haven, FL	166,372
248	Pascagoula, MS	156,225
85	Peabody, MA M.D.	736,478
121	Pensacola, FL	459,393
146	Peoria, IL	372,866
6	Philadelphia (greater) PA-NJ-MD-DE	6,027,122
18	Philadelphia, PA M.D.	4,049,258
17	Phoenix-Mesa-Scottsdale, AZ	4,229,275
325	Pine Bluff, AR	100,121
33	Pittsburgh, PA	2,359,460
283	Pittsfield, MA	127,393
336	Pocatello, ID	90,644
134	Port St. Lucie, FL	415,985
NA	Portland-Vancouver, OR-WA**	NA
112	Portland, ME	521,947
93	Poughkeepsie, NY	675,016
205	Prescott, AZ	209,023
104	Provo-Orem, UT	560,264
247	Pueblo, CO	156,522
245	Punta Gorda, FL	158,377
212	Racine, WI	201,891
63	Raleigh-Cary, NC	1,165,131
291	Rapid City, SD	125,249
135	Reading, PA	412,575
226	Redding, CA	182,780
126	Reno-Sparks, NV	425,023
59	Richmond, VA	1,257,811
16	Riverside-San Bernardino, CA	4,239,406
164	Roanoke, VA	302,738
222	Rochester, MN	187,922
67	Rochester, NY	1,023,376
154	Rockford, IL	353,502
127	Rockingham County, NH M.D.	420,757
261	Rocky Mount, NC	147,080
333	Rome, GA	93,639
35	Sacramento, CA	2,161,081
218	Saginaw, MI	197,310
142	Salem, OR	397,398
136	Salinas, CA	410,773
294	Salisbury, MD	121,993
64	Salt Lake City, UT	1,113,915
313	San Angelo, TX	110,207
39	San Antonio, TX	2,104,901
21	San Diego, CA	3,075,127
15	San Francisco (greater), CA	4,333,063
47	San Francisco-S. Mateo, CA M.D.	1,788,942
45	San Jose, CA	1,848,534
178	San Luis Obispo, CA	268,735
344	Sandusky, OH	76,515
22	Santa Ana-Anaheim, CA M.D.	3,041,858
138	Santa Barbara-Santa Maria, CA	407,452
184	Santa Cruz-Watsonville, CA	256,048
254	Santa Fe, NM	151,535
119	Santa Rosa-Petaluma, CA	472,897

RANK	METROPOLITAN AREA	POP
156	Savannah, GA	337,256
105	Scranton--Wilkes-Barre, PA	551,176
19	Seattle (greater), WA	3,434,812
27	Seattle-Bellevue-Everett, WA M.D.	2,630,578
270	Sebastian-Vero Beach, FL	137,445
NA	Sheboygan, WI**	NA
298	Sherman-Denison, TX	120,587
263	Sioux City, IA-NE-SD	145,711
191	Sioux Falls, SD	242,527
159	South Bend-Mishawaka, IN-MI	318,113
168	Spartanburg, SC	290,534
120	Spokane, WA	472,494
209	Springfield, IL	206,661
91	Springfield, MA	693,388
125	Springfield, MO	434,773
267	Springfield, OH	138,838
258	State College, PA	148,015
92	Stockton, CA	686,072
219	St. Cloud, MN	191,426
288	St. Joseph, MO-KS	126,176
24	St. Louis, MO-IL	2,822,879
319	Sumter, SC	104,569
96	Syracuse, NY	638,467
80	Tacoma, WA M.D.	804,234
150	Tallahassee, FL	363,918
25	Tampa-St Petersburg, FL	2,783,954
NA	Terre Haute, IN**	NA
269	Texarkana, TX-Texarkana, AR	138,018
94	Toledo, OH	671,876
197	Topeka, KS	233,079
148	Trenton-Ewing, NJ	370,040
68	Tucson, AZ	988,683
69	Tulsa, OK	946,096
202	Tuscaloosa, AL	214,600
208	Tyler, TX	207,175
169	Utica-Rome, NY	289,389
277	Valdosta, GA	133,042
137	Vallejo-Fairfield, CA	407,939
301	Victoria, TX	115,411
50	Virginia Beach-Norfolk, VA-NC	1,690,968
124	Visalia-Porterville, CA	435,945
196	Waco, TX	234,649
274	Warner Robins, GA	133,908
31	Warren-Farmington Hills, MI M.D.	2,463,613
9	Washington (greater) DC-VA-MD-WV	5,573,842
14	Washington, DC-VA-MD-WV M.D.	4,353,959
236	Waterloo-Cedar Falls, IA	166,624
278	Wausau, WI	132,256
312	Wenatchee, WA	110,709
56	West Palm Beach, FL M.D.	1,294,282
262	Wichita Falls, TX	146,544
98	Wichita, KS	621,313
300	Williamsport, PA	117,110
86	Wilmington, DE-MD-NJ M.D.	709,154
151	Wilmington, NC	363,901
285	Winchester, VA-WV	127,037
117	Winston-Salem, NC	491,903
81	Worcester, MA	800,461
194	Yakima, WA	239,998
123	York-Hanover, PA	436,009
233	Yuba City, CA	168,270
220	Yuma, AZ	190,887

Source: Reported data from the F.B.I. "Crime in the United States 2011"
*Estimates as of July 2010 based on U.S. Bureau of the Census figures.
**Not available (comparable metro area not included in 2010 crime statistics).

Rank Order - Metro Area

86. Metropolitan Population in 2010 (continued)
National Total = 309,330,219*

RANK	METROPOLITAN AREA	POP
1	New York (greater), NY-NJ-PA	19,042,526
2	Los Angeles (greater), CA	12,912,749
3	New York-W. Plains NY-NJ M.D.	11,678,308
4	Los Angeles County, CA M.D.	9,870,891
5	Dallas (greater), TX	6,574,246
6	Philadelphia (greater) PA-NJ-MD-DE	6,027,122
7	Houston, TX	5,978,213
8	Miami (greater), FL	5,597,226
9	Washington (greater) DC-VA-MD-WV	5,573,842
10	Atlanta, GA	5,432,336
11	Boston (greater), MA-NH	4,558,433
12	Dallas-Plano-Irving, TX M.D.	4,415,040
13	Detroit (greater), MI	4,359,587
14	Washington, DC-VA-MD-WV M.D.	4,353,959
15	San Francisco (greater), CA	4,333,063
16	Riverside-San Bernardino, CA	4,239,406
17	Phoenix-Mesa-Scottsdale, AZ	4,229,275
18	Philadelphia, PA M.D.	4,049,258
19	Seattle (greater), WA	3,434,812
20	Minneapolis-St. Paul, MN-WI	3,302,492
21	San Diego, CA	3,075,127
22	Santa Ana-Anaheim, CA M.D.	3,041,858
23	Nassau-Suffolk, NY M.D.	2,855,486
24	St. Louis, MO-IL	2,822,879
25	Tampa-St Petersburg, FL	2,783,954
26	Baltimore-Towson, MD	2,720,381
27	Seattle-Bellevue-Everett, WA M.D.	2,630,578
28	Denver-Aurora, CO	2,555,601
29	Oakland-Fremont, CA M.D.	2,544,121
30	Miami-Dade County, FL M.D.	2,523,928
31	Warren-Farmington Hills, MI M.D.	2,463,613
32	Edison, NJ M.D.	2,366,214
33	Pittsburgh, PA	2,359,460
34	Cincinnati-Middletown, OH-KY-IN	2,185,076
35	Sacramento, CA	2,161,081
36	Fort Worth-Arlington, TX M.D.	2,159,206
37	Newark-Union, NJ-PA M.D.	2,142,518
38	Orlando, FL	2,130,297
39	San Antonio, TX	2,104,901
40	Kansas City, MO-KS	2,089,752
41	Cleveland-Elyria-Mentor, OH	2,081,340
42	Las Vegas-Paradise, NV	1,951,609
43	Boston-Quincy, MA M.D.	1,908,436
44	Detroit-Livonia-Dearborn, MI M.D.	1,895,974
45	San Jose, CA	1,848,534
46	Columbus, OH	1,817,671
47	San Francisco-S. Mateo, CA M.D.	1,788,942
48	Fort Lauderdale, FL M.D.	1,779,016
49	Austin-Round Rock, TX	1,752,518
50	Virginia Beach-Norfolk, VA-NC	1,690,968
51	Nashville-Davidson, TN	1,608,441
52	Milwaukee, WI	1,566,270
53	Cambridge-Newton, MA M.D.	1,492,762
54	Jacksonville, FL	1,350,025
55	Memphis, TN-MS-AR	1,313,722
56	West Palm Beach, FL M.D.	1,294,282
57	Camden, NJ M.D.	1,268,710
58	Louisville, KY-IN	1,268,689
59	Richmond, VA	1,257,811
60	Oklahoma City, OK	1,254,299
61	Bethesda-Frederick, MD M.D.	1,219,883
62	New Orleans, LA	1,201,385
63	Raleigh-Cary, NC	1,165,131
64	Salt Lake City, UT	1,113,915
65	Buffalo-Niagara Falls, NY	1,106,808
66	Hartford, CT	1,023,921
67	Rochester, NY	1,023,376
68	Tucson, AZ	988,683
69	Tulsa, OK	946,096
70	Fresno, CA	926,736
71	Bridgeport-Stamford, CT	895,941
72	Albuquerque, NM	884,210
73	Omaha-Council Bluffs, NE-IA	867,616
74	Albany-Schenectady-Troy, NY	851,078
75	Dayton, OH	831,823
76	Allentown, PA-NJ	828,068
77	Bakersfield, CA	822,752
78	Oxnard-Thousand Oaks, CA	807,132
79	New Haven-Milford, CT	806,354
80	Tacoma, WA M.D.	804,234
81	Worcester, MA	800,461
82	Grand Rapids-Wyoming, MI	774,621
83	McAllen-Edinburg-Mission, TX	758,016
84	El Paso, TX	756,304
85	Peabody, MA M.D.	736,478
86	Wilmington, DE-MD-NJ M.D.	709,154
87	Knoxville, TN	706,304
88	Akron, OH	698,613
89	North Port-Bradenton-Sarasota, FL	697,913
90	Little Rock, AR	693,930
91	Springfield, MA	693,388
92	Stockton, CA	686,072
93	Poughkeepsie, NY	675,016
94	Toledo, OH	671,876
95	Greenville, SC	648,658
96	Syracuse, NY	638,467
97	Colorado Springs, CO	626,259
98	Wichita, KS	621,313
99	Boise City-Nampa, ID	619,814
100	Cape Coral-Fort Myers, FL	603,092
101	Lakeland, FL	593,733
102	Madison, WI	577,374
103	Des Moines-West Des Moines, IA	577,321
104	Provo-Orem, UT	560,264
105	Scranton--Wilkes-Barre, PA	551,176
106	Jackson, MS	546,069
107	Harrisburg-Carlisle, PA	542,444
108	Palm Bay-Melbourne, FL	542,130
109	Ogden-Clearfield, UT	536,184
110	Augusta, GA-SC	531,786
111	Chattanooga, TN-GA	523,569
112	Portland, ME	521,947
113	Modesto, CA	516,479
114	Lancaster, PA	514,044
115	Durham-Chapel Hill, NC	509,834
116	Deltona-Daytona Beach, FL	500,849
117	Winston-Salem, NC	491,903
118	Lexington-Fayette, KY	477,150
119	Santa Rosa-Petaluma, CA	472,897
120	Spokane, WA	472,494
121	Pensacola, FL	459,393
122	Lansing-East Lansing, MI	450,078
123	York-Hanover, PA	436,009
124	Visalia-Porterville, CA	435,945
125	Springfield, MO	434,773
126	Reno-Sparks, NV	425,023
127	Rockingham County, NH M.D.	420,757
128	Flint, MI	419,008
129	Fort Wayne, IN	418,216
130	Asheville, NC	417,415
131	Huntsville, AL	416,848
132	Mobile, AL	416,582
133	Corpus Christi, TX	416,086
134	Port St. Lucie, FL	415,985
135	Reading, PA	412,575
136	Salinas, CA	410,773
137	Vallejo-Fairfield, CA	407,939
138	Santa Barbara-Santa Maria, CA	407,452
139	Canton, OH	407,101
140	Manchester-Nashua, NH	403,165
141	Brownsville-Harlingen, TX	401,641
142	Salem, OR	397,398
143	Killeen-Temple-Fort Hood, TX	383,261
144	Davenport, IA-IL	378,802
145	Beaumont-Port Arthur, TX	376,711
146	Peoria, IL	372,866
147	Montgomery, AL	371,821
148	Trenton-Ewing, NJ	370,040
149	Hickory, NC	367,927
150	Tallahassee, FL	363,918
151	Wilmington, NC	363,901
152	Fayetteville, NC	363,142
153	Evansville, IN-KY	353,847
154	Rockford, IL	353,502
155	Ann Arbor, MI	346,839
156	Savannah, GA	337,256
157	Ocala, FL	336,017
158	Naples-Marco Island, FL	325,568
159	South Bend-Mishawaka, IN-MI	318,113
160	Anchorage, AK	313,181
161	Green Bay, WI	307,162
162	Kingsport, TN-VA	306,196
163	Lincoln, NE	304,589
164	Roanoke, VA	302,738
165	Boulder, CO	302,365
166	Fort Collins-Loveland, CO	298,883
167	Fort Smith, AR-OK	296,159
168	Spartanburg, SC	290,534
169	Utica-Rome, NY	289,389
170	Columbus, GA-AL	286,528
171	Erie, PA	281,637
172	Lubbock, TX	278,595
173	Duluth, MN-WI	276,508
174	Atlantic City, NJ	275,382
175	Hagerstown-Martinsburg, MD-WV	273,944
176	Clarksville, TN-KY	271,954
177	Myrtle Beach, SC	271,797
178	San Luis Obispo, CA	268,735
179	Lafayette, LA	266,765
180	Gainesville, FL	263,388

Note: All listings are for Metropolitan Statistical Areas (M.S.A.s) except for those ending with "M.D." Listings with "M.D." are Metropolitan Divisions which are smaller parts of eleven large M.S.A.s. See explanatory note at beginning of metropolitan area section.

Rank Order - Metro Area (continued)

RANK	METROPOLITAN AREA	POP	RANK	METROPOLITAN AREA	POP	RANK	METROPOLITAN AREA	POP
181	Holland-Grand Haven, MI	261,957	244	Abilene, TX	159,566	307	Goldsboro, NC	113,929
182	Cedar Rapids, IA	260,733	245	Punta Gorda, FL	158,377	308	Elizabethtown, KY	113,924
183	Greeley, CO	259,483	246	Billings, MT	157,205	309	Owensboro, KY	113,908
184	Santa Cruz-Watsonville, CA	256,048	247	Pueblo, CO	156,522	310	Bismarck, ND	111,613
185	Olympia, WA	254,900	248	Pascagoula, MS	156,225	311	Michigan City-La Porte, IN	111,553
186	Kennewick-Pasco-Richland, WA	251,139	249	Iowa City, IA	155,935	312	Wenatchee, WA	110,709
187	Lynchburg, VA	250,323	250	Alexandria, LA	155,654	313	San Angelo, TX	110,207
188	Merced, CA	248,716	251	Decatur, AL	153,306	314	Lewiston-Auburn, ME	107,282
189	Amarillo, TX	247,721	252	Burlington, NC	152,475	315	Decatur, IL	106,467
190	Laredo, TX	245,929	253	Monroe, MI	151,998	316	Bay City, MI	106,214
191	Sioux Falls, SD	242,527	254	Santa Fe, NM	151,535	317	Danville, VA	105,798
192	Binghamton, NY	241,233	255	Madera, CA	151,283	318	Gadsden, AL	104,600
193	Bremerton-Silverdale, WA	240,976	256	Hanford-Corcoran, CA	150,689	319	Sumter, SC	104,569
194	Yakima, WA	239,998	257	Bangor, ME	150,537	320	Lima, OH	103,688
195	Gulfport-Biloxi, MS	238,426	258	State College, PA	148,015	321	Longview, WA	102,585
196	Waco, TX	234,649	259	Jefferson City, MO	147,169	322	Brunswick, GA	101,534
197	Topeka, KS	233,079	260	Grand Junction, CO	147,126	323	Cumberland, MD-WV	100,405
198	Macon, GA	224,947	261	Rocky Mount, NC	147,080	324	Fond du Lac, WI	100,387
199	Appleton, WI	224,034	262	Wichita Falls, TX	146,544	325	Pine Bluff, AR	100,121
200	Chico, CA	222,130	263	Sioux City, IA-NE-SD	145,711	326	Grand Forks, ND-MN	99,717
201	Barnstable Town, MA	218,615	264	Dothan, AL	145,215	327	Hot Springs, AR	99,611
202	Tuscaloosa, AL	214,600	265	Johnstown, PA	143,909	328	Kokomo, IN	98,871
203	College Station-Bryan, TX	214,518	266	Norwich-New London, CT	141,679	329	Palm Coast, FL	97,199
204	Las Cruces, NM	212,820	267	Springfield, OH	138,838	330	Ocean City, NJ	96,094
205	Prescott, AZ	209,023	268	Morristown, TN	138,774	331	Dubuque, IA	94,362
206	Fargo, ND-MN	208,388	269	Texarkana, TX-Texarkana, AR	138,018	332	Mankato-North Mankato, MN	94,016
207	Longview, TX	207,545	270	Sebastian-Vero Beach, FL	137,445	333	Rome, GA	93,639
208	Tyler, TX	207,175	271	Odessa, TX	135,675	334	Cape Girardeau, MO-IL	93,412
209	Springfield, IL	206,661	272	Napa, CA	135,593	335	Cheyenne, WY	91,857
210	Houma, LA	204,653	273	Battle Creek, MI	134,169	336	Pocatello, ID	90,644
211	Bellingham, WA	203,393	274	Warner Robins, GA	133,908	337	Ames, IA	88,803
212	Racine, WI	201,891	275	Midland, TX	133,704	338	Elmira, NY	87,073
213	Florence, SC	201,596	276	La Crosse, WI-MN	133,588	339	Great Falls, MT	82,913
214	Medford, OR	201,375	277	Valdosta, GA	133,042	340	Corvallis, OR	82,256
215	Charlottesville, VA	199,881	278	Wausau, WI	132,256	341	Danville, IL	78,867
216	Lafayette, IN	198,921	279	Lebanon, PA	132,213	342	Casper, WY	77,252
217	Johnson City, TN	198,527	280	Dalton, GA	131,302	343	Columbus, IN	76,785
218	Saginaw, MI	197,310	281	Idaho Falls, ID	128,311	344	Sandusky, OH	76,515
219	St. Cloud, MN	191,426	282	Glens Falls, NY	127,776	345	Hinesville, GA	72,276
220	Yuma, AZ	190,887	283	Pittsfield, MA	127,393	346	Carson City, NV	55,119
221	Athens-Clarke County, GA	188,596	284	Logan, UT-ID	127,228	347	Fairbanks, AK	38,307
222	Rochester, MN	187,922	285	Winchester, VA-WV	127,037	NA	Auburn, AL**	NA
223	Bloomington, IN	187,290	286	Farmington, NM	126,955	NA	Baton Rouge, LA**	NA
224	Anderson, SC	187,031	287	Altoona, PA	126,459	NA	Birmingham-Hoover, AL**	NA
225	Gainesville, GA	186,894	288	St. Joseph, MO-KS	126,176	NA	Champaign-Urbana, IL**	NA
226	Redding, CA	182,780	289	Flagstaff, AZ	125,838	NA	Charleston, WV**	NA
227	Kingston, NY	179,764	290	Manhattan, KS	125,477	NA	Charlotte-Gastonia, NC-SC**	NA
228	Crestview-Fort Walton Beach, FL	179,091	291	Rapid City, SD	125,249	NA	Chicago (greater), IL-IN-WI**	NA
229	Monroe, LA	175,187	292	Mansfield, OH	123,762	NA	Chicago-Joilet-Naperville, IL M.D.**	NA
230	Joplin, MO	174,867	293	Bowling Green, KY	122,243	NA	Eugene-Springfield, OR**	NA
231	Muskegon-Norton Shores, MI	172,745	294	Salisbury, MD	121,993	NA	Florence-Muscle Shoals, AL**	NA
232	El Centro, CA	169,405	295	Harrisonburg, VA	121,985	NA	Gary, IN M.D.**	NA
233	Yuba City, CA	168,270	296	Jonesboro, AR	121,519	NA	Indianapolis, IN**	NA
234	Bloomington-Normal, IL	167,701	297	Mount Vernon-Anacortes, WA	120,890	NA	Jacksonville, NC**	NA
235	Columbia, MO	167,279	298	Sherman-Denison, TX	120,587	NA	Kankakee-Bradley, IL**	NA
236	Waterloo-Cedar Falls, IA	166,624	299	Lawrence, KS	118,966	NA	Lake Co.-Kenosha Co., IL-WI M.D.**	NA
237	Panama City-Lynn Haven, FL	166,372	300	Williamsport, PA	117,110	NA	Lake Havasu City-Kingman, AZ**	NA
238	Bend, OR	162,019	301	Victoria, TX	115,411	NA	Missoula, MT**	NA
239	Dover, DE	161,556	302	Anniston-Oxford, AL	115,376	NA	Oshkosh-Neenah, WI**	NA
240	Eau Claire, WI	161,272	303	Muncie, IN	115,258	NA	Portland-Vancouver, OR-WA**	NA
241	Blacksburg, VA	161,019	304	Lawton, OK	114,290	NA	Sheboygan, WI**	NA
242	Janesville, WI	161,013	305	Cleveland, TN	114,041	NA	Terre Haute, IN**	NA
243	Albany, GA	160,950	306	Jackson, TN	113,975			

Source: Reported data from the F.B.I. "Crime in the United States 2011"
*Estimates as of July 2010 based on U.S. Bureau of the Census figures.
**Not available (comparable metro area not included in 2010 crime statistics).

Alpha Order - Metro Area

87. Metropolitan Population in 2007
National Total = 301,621,157*

RANK	METROPOLITAN AREA	POP
232	Abilene, TX	157,713
89	Akron, OH	699,760
75	Albany-Schenectady-Troy, NY	852,141
225	Albany, GA	164,983
78	Albuquerque, NM	827,275
244	Alexandria, LA	150,253
79	Allentown, PA-NJ	805,542
278	Altoona, PA	125,800
180	Amarillo, TX	243,547
326	Ames, IA	80,075
157	Anchorage, AK	303,996
217	Anderson, SC	181,370
148	Ann Arbor, MI	345,430
NA	Anniston-Oxford, AL**	NA
192	Appleton, WI	220,208
133	Asheville, NC	405,975
212	Athens-Clarke County, GA	188,310
10	Atlanta, GA	5,276,703
169	Atlantic City, NJ	270,417
273	Auburn, AL	127,500
109	Augusta, GA-SC	528,421
52	Austin-Round Rock, TX	1,553,472
81	Bakersfield, CA	792,216
26	Baltimore-Towson, MD	2,652,974
249	Bangor, ME	146,242
191	Barnstable Town, MA	225,323
85	Baton Rouge, LA	770,283
260	Battle Creek, MI	137,388
303	Bay City, MI	107,654
141	Beaumont-Port Arthur, TX	378,783
211	Bellingham, WA	188,708
238	Bend, OR	154,723
63	Bethesda-Frederick, MD M.D.	1,158,220
243	Billings, MT	150,563
178	Binghamton, NY	246,237
65	Birmingham-Hoover, AL	1,108,901
311	Bismarck, ND	102,688
241	Blacksburg, VA	151,219
NA	Bloomington-Normal, IL**	NA
220	Bloomington, IN	179,055
102	Boise City-Nampa, ID	586,066
11	Boston (greater), MA-NH	4,460,277
43	Boston-Quincy, MA M.D.	1,839,638
NA	Boulder, CO**	NA
290	Bowling Green, KY	114,815
182	Bremerton-Silverdale, WA	241,780
74	Bridgeport-Stamford, CT	884,290
138	Brownsville-Harlingen, TX	395,428
312	Brunswick, GA	101,687
64	Buffalo-Niagara Falls, NY	1,129,953
251	Burlington, NC	145,711
55	Cambridge-Newton, MA M.D.	1,466,454
59	Camden, NJ M.D.	1,244,124
NA	Canton, OH**	NA
101	Cape Coral-Fort Myers, FL	587,220
NA	Cape Girardeau, MO-IL**	NA
333	Carson City, NV	55,713
332	Casper, WY	71,604
173	Cedar Rapids, IA	250,807
NA	Champaign-Urbana, IL**	NA

RANK	METROPOLITAN AREA	POP
158	Charleston, WV	303,537
51	Charlotte-Gastonia, NC-SC	1,635,133
208	Charlottesville, VA	192,228
114	Chattanooga, TN-GA	503,472
325	Cheyenne, WY	86,692
NA	Chicago (greater), IL-IN-WI**	NA
NA	Chicago-Joilet-Naperville, IL M.D.**	NA
194	Chico, CA	215,992
36	Cincinnati-Middletown, OH-KY-IN	2,115,244
179	Clarksville, TN-KY	244,105
37	Cleveland-Elyria-Mentor, OH	2,104,225
299	Cleveland, TN	111,450
207	College Station-Bryan, TX	193,097
99	Colorado Springs, CO	613,181
233	Columbia, MO	157,307
163	Columbus, GA-AL	290,106
330	Columbus, IN	74,805
47	Columbus, OH	1,737,831
126	Corpus Christi, TX	417,469
328	Corvallis, OR	79,314
219	Crestview-Fort Walton Beach, FL	180,091
316	Cumberland, MD-WV	98,759
5	Dallas (greater), TX	6,132,121
17	Dallas-Plano-Irving, TX M.D.	4,107,704
261	Dalton, GA	136,405
NA	Danville, IL**	NA
305	Danville, VA	106,432
NA	Davenport, IA-IL**	NA
76	Dayton, OH	835,430
245	Decatur, AL	150,246
NA	Decatur, IL**	NA
115	Deltona-Daytona Beach, FL	500,013
30	Denver-Aurora, CO	2,464,178
106	Des Moines-West Des Moines, IA	541,394
12	Detroit (greater), MI	4,451,481
42	Detroit-Livonia-Dearborn, MI M.D.	1,951,186
258	Dothan, AL	139,475
242	Dover, DE	150,986
321	Dubuque, IA	92,749
168	Duluth, MN-WI	274,026
NA	Durham-Chapel Hill, NC**	NA
234	Eau Claire, WI	156,492
33	Edison, NJ M.D.	2,298,551
229	El Centro, CA	161,766
86	El Paso, TX	744,171
298	Elizabethtown, KY	111,690
323	Elmira, NY	88,057
166	Erie, PA	278,948
149	Eugene-Springfield, OR	340,482
146	Evansville, IN-KY	351,489
334	Fairbanks, AK	33,156
210	Fargo, ND-MN	189,580
272	Farmington, NM	128,294
147	Fayetteville, NC	345,641
275	Flagstaff, AZ	126,419
122	Flint, MI	440,751
NA	Florence-Muscle Shoals, AL**	NA
199	Florence, SC	201,529
315	Fond du Lac, WI	99,825
165	Fort Collins-Loveland, CO	282,097

RANK	METROPOLITAN AREA	POP
45	Fort Lauderdale, FL M.D.	1,795,143
162	Fort Smith, AR-OK	291,717
130	Fort Wayne, IN	410,350
39	Fort Worth-Arlington, TX M.D.	2,024,417
73	Fresno, CA	898,391
NA	Gadsden, AL**	NA
181	Gainesville, FL	243,506
221	Gainesville, GA	178,408
NA	Gary, IN M.D.**	NA
270	Glens Falls, NY	129,840
289	Goldsboro, NC	115,119
318	Grand Forks, ND-MN	96,813
259	Grand Junction, CO	137,907
84	Grand Rapids-Wyoming, MI	774,927
327	Great Falls, MT	79,880
175	Greeley, CO	247,806
159	Green Bay, WI	302,277
98	Greenville, SC	613,703
NA	Gulfport-Biloxi, MS**	NA
NA	Hagerstown-Martinsburg, MD-WV**	NA
248	Hanford-Corcoran, CA	147,510
110	Harrisburg-Carlisle, PA	526,335
296	Harrisonburg, VA	113,967
70	Hartford, CT	1,006,947
143	Hickory, NC	365,896
331	Hinesville, GA	74,369
NA	Holland-Grand Haven, MI**	NA
319	Hot Springs, AR	96,271
198	Houma, LA	203,401
7	Houston, TX	5,664,249
140	Huntsville, AL	382,202
283	Idaho Falls, ID	119,795
48	Indianapolis, IN	1,687,197
257	Iowa City, IA	140,650
57	Jacksonville, FL	1,290,776
240	Jacksonville, NC	152,338
108	Jackson, MS	532,981
297	Jackson, TN	113,807
231	Janesville, WI	160,629
252	Jefferson City, MO	145,564
206	Johnson City, TN	194,592
250	Johnstown, PA	145,844
293	Jonesboro, AR	114,222
224	Joplin, MO	170,012
NA	Kankakee-Bradley, IL**	NA
NA	Kansas City, MO-KS**	NA
187	Kennewick-Pasco-Richland, WA	231,368
145	Killeen-Temple-Fort Hood, TX	354,141
156	Kingsport, TN-VA	305,118
215	Kingston, NY	182,932
93	Knoxville, TN	682,242
314	Kokomo, IN	100,734
269	La Crosse, WI-MN	129,892
213	Lafayette, IN	186,687
172	Lafayette, LA	255,453
NA	Lake Co.-Kenosha Co., IL-WI M.D.**	NA
202	Lake Havasu City-Kingman, AZ	199,339
103	Lakeland, FL	568,435
117	Lancaster, PA	496,516
119	Lansing-East Lansing, MI	452,907

Note: All listings are for Metropolitan Statistical Areas (M.S.A.s) except for those ending with "M.D." Listings with "M.D." are Metropolitan Divisions which are smaller parts of eleven large M.S.A.s. See explanatory note at beginning of metropolitan area section.

350 Metropolitan and City Populations

Alpha Order - Metro Area (continued)

RANK	METROPOLITAN AREA	POP
185	Laredo, TX	237,170
205	Las Cruces, NM	196,085
44	Las Vegas-Paradise, NV	1,834,533
295	Lawrence, KS	114,212
301	Lawton, OK	109,016
274	Lebanon, PA	127,496
304	Lewiston-Auburn, ME	107,169
121	Lexington-Fayette, KY	441,674
308	Lima, OH	105,114
164	Lincoln, NE	286,039
95	Little Rock, AR	659,776
294	Logan, UT-ID	114,216
197	Longview, TX	204,652
313	Longview, WA	100,916
4	Los Angeles County, CA M.D.	9,929,814
2	Los Angeles (greater), CA	12,929,875
60	Louisville, KY-IN	1,233,503
170	Lubbock, TX	262,990
183	Lynchburg, VA	240,526
188	Macon, GA	230,317
246	Madera, CA	148,765
104	Madison, WI	550,623
NA	Manchester-Nashua, NH**	NA
NA	Manhattan, KS**	NA
NA	Mankato-North Mankato, MN**	NA
276	Mansfield, OH	126,412
88	McAllen-Edinburg-Mission, TX	720,595
201	Medford, OR	199,631
56	Memphis, TN-MS-AR	1,295,670
174	Merced, CA	249,018
8	Miami (greater), FL	5,480,920
31	Miami-Dade County, FL M.D.	2,401,971
300	Michigan City-La Porte, IN	110,465
279	Midland, TX	125,645
53	Milwaukee, WI	1,516,093
20	Minneapolis-St. Paul, MN-WI	3,202,517
310	Missoula, MT	102,898
134	Mobile, AL	405,259
111	Modesto, CA	517,721
223	Monroe, LA	172,092
236	Monroe, MI	155,523
144	Montgomery, AL	364,491
262	Morristown, TN	135,710
286	Mount Vernon-Anacortes, WA	117,546
292	Muncie, IN	114,292
222	Muskegon-Norton Shores, MI	175,119
176	Myrtle Beach, SC	247,229
264	Napa, CA	133,808
154	Naples-Marco Island, FL	321,589
54	Nashville-Davidson, TN	1,492,983
24	Nassau-Suffolk, NY M.D.	2,792,682
NA	New Haven-Milford, CT**	NA
69	New Orleans, LA	1,026,639
1	New York (greater), NY-NJ-PA	18,796,306
3	New York-W. Plains NY-NJ M.D.	11,559,878
35	Newark-Union, NJ-PA M.D.	2,145,195
NA	North Port-Bradenton-Sarasota, FL**	NA
NA	Norwich-New London, CT**	NA
29	Oakland-Fremont, CA M.D.	2,474,091
153	Ocala, FL	322,272
317	Ocean City, NJ	97,291
271	Odessa, TX	128,400
112	Ogden-Clearfield, UT	514,786
62	Oklahoma City, OK	1,189,823
184	Olympia, WA	238,675
77	Omaha-Council Bluffs, NE-IA	829,460
40	Orlando, FL	2,020,346
230	Oshkosh-Neenah, WI	161,620
NA	Owensboro, KY**	NA
80	Oxnard-Thousand Oaks, CA	799,872
107	Palm Bay-Melbourne, FL	538,226
322	Palm Coast, FL	88,451
226	Panama City-Lynn Haven, FL	164,360
239	Pascagoula, MS	153,177
87	Peabody, MA M.D.	737,494
123	Pensacola, FL	440,445
NA	Peoria, IL**	NA
6	Philadelphia (greater) PA-NJ-MD-DE	5,821,531
18	Philadelphia, PA M.D.	3,880,695
14	Phoenix-Mesa-Scottsdale, AZ	4,170,448
309	Pine Bluff, AR	103,240
32	Pittsburgh, PA	2,356,481
267	Pittsfield, MA	130,630
324	Pocatello, ID	87,209
136	Port St. Lucie, FL	400,314
34	Portland-Vancouver, OR-WA	2,171,073
113	Portland, ME	513,311
94	Poughkeepsie, NY	676,768
195	Prescott, AZ	214,698
116	Provo-Orem, UT	498,516
235	Pueblo, CO	155,852
237	Punta Gorda, FL	154,910
203	Racine, WI	197,757
67	Raleigh-Cary, NC	1,033,679
281	Rapid City, SD	121,126
135	Reading, PA	404,031
218	Redding, CA	180,982
131	Reno-Sparks, NV	408,488
61	Richmond, VA	1,205,749
16	Riverside-San Bernardino, CA	4,115,406
161	Roanoke, VA	295,368
216	Rochester, MN	181,608
68	Rochester, NY	1,032,143
NA	Rockford, IL**	NA
127	Rockingham County, NH M.D.	416,691
247	Rocky Mount, NC	148,194
320	Rome, GA	95,960
38	Sacramento, CA	2,091,363
196	Saginaw, MI	204,943
139	Salem, OR	390,689
132	Salinas, CA	408,059
285	Salisbury, MD	117,891
66	Salt Lake City, UT	1,101,656
306	San Angelo, TX	105,706
41	San Antonio, TX	1,975,770
22	San Diego, CA	2,935,792
15	San Francisco (greater), CA	4,154,508
49	San Francisco-S. Mateo, CA M.D.	1,680,417
46	San Jose, CA	1,780,107
171	San Luis Obispo, CA	256,373
329	Sandusky, OH	77,695
21	Santa Ana-Anaheim, CA M.D.	3,000,062
137	Santa Barbara-Santa Maria, CA	397,342
177	Santa Cruz-Watsonville, CA	246,931
NA	Santa Fe, NM**	NA
118	Santa Rosa-Petaluma, CA	464,218
152	Savannah, GA	324,109
105	Scranton--Wilkes-Barre, PA	548,161
19	Seattle (greater), WA	3,294,592
27	Seattle-Bellevue-Everett, WA M.D.	2,518,369
265	Sebastian-Vero Beach, FL	131,526
288	Sheboygan, WI	115,407
284	Sherman-Denison, TX	119,528
254	Sioux City, IA-NE-SD	143,514
193	Sioux Falls, SD	219,627
155	South Bend-Mishawaka, IN-MI	317,804
167	Spartanburg, SC	276,109
120	Spokane, WA	450,805
NA	Springfield, IL**	NA
91	Springfield, MA	687,220
128	Springfield, MO	412,378
256	Springfield, OH	141,098
255	State College, PA	141,328
92	Stockton, CA	684,406
214	St. Cloud, MN	184,856
280	St. Joseph, MO-KS	121,979
23	St. Louis, MO-IL	2,810,914
307	Sumter, SC	105,369
97	Syracuse, NY	648,191
83	Tacoma, WA M.D.	776,223
151	Tallahassee, FL	335,945
25	Tampa-St Petersburg, FL	2,720,592
NA	Terre Haute, IN**	NA
263	Texarkana, TX-Texarkana, AR	135,211
96	Toledo, OH	651,165
189	Topeka, KS	229,580
142	Trenton-Ewing, NJ	365,977
71	Tucson, AZ	963,028
72	Tulsa, OK	908,036
200	Tuscaloosa, AL	199,823
204	Tyler, TX	197,461
160	Utica-Rome, NY	296,125
277	Valdosta, GA	126,232
129	Vallejo-Fairfield, CA	410,623
291	Victoria, TX	114,391
50	Virginia Beach-Norfolk, VA-NC	1,656,896
124	Visalia-Porterville, CA	424,464
190	Waco, TX	227,882
268	Warner Robins, GA	130,014
28	Warren-Farmington Hills, MI M.D.	2,500,295
9	Washington (greater) DC-VA-MD-WV	5,348,654
13	Washington, DC-VA-MD-WV M.D.	4,190,434
228	Waterloo-Cedar Falls, IA	161,918
266	Wausau, WI	131,265
302	Wenatchee, WA	107,897
58	West Palm Beach, FL M.D.	1,283,806
253	Wichita Falls, TX	144,648
100	Wichita, KS	594,974
287	Williamsport, PA	117,037
90	Wilmington, DE-MD-NJ M.D.	696,712
150	Wilmington, NC	337,011
282	Winchester, VA-WV	120,991
NA	Winston-Salem, NC**	NA
82	Worcester, MA	790,004
186	Yakima, WA	234,592
125	York-Hanover, PA	420,251
227	Yuba City, CA	164,006
209	Yuma, AZ	192,098

Source: Reported data from the F.B.I. "Crime in the United States 2011"
*Estimates as of July 2007 based on U.S. Bureau of the Census figures.
**Not available (comparable metro area not included in 2007 crime statistics).

Rank Order - Metro Area

87. Metropolitan Population in 2007 (continued)
National Total = 301,621,157*

RANK	METROPOLITAN AREA	POP
1	New York (greater), NY-NJ-PA	18,796,306
2	Los Angeles (greater), CA	12,929,875
3	New York-W. Plains NY-NJ M.D.	11,559,878
4	Los Angeles County, CA M.D.	9,929,814
5	Dallas (greater), TX	6,132,121
6	Philadelphia (greater) PA-NJ-MD-DE	5,821,531
7	Houston, TX	5,664,249
8	Miami (greater), FL	5,480,920
9	Washington (greater) DC-VA-MD-WV	5,348,654
10	Atlanta, GA	5,276,703
11	Boston (greater), MA-NH	4,460,277
12	Detroit (greater), MI	4,451,481
13	Washington, DC-VA-MD-WV M.D.	4,190,434
14	Phoenix-Mesa-Scottsdale, AZ	4,170,448
15	San Francisco (greater), CA	4,154,508
16	Riverside-San Bernardino, CA	4,115,406
17	Dallas-Plano-Irving, TX M.D.	4,107,704
18	Philadelphia, PA M.D.	3,880,695
19	Seattle (greater), WA	3,294,592
20	Minneapolis-St. Paul, MN-WI	3,202,517
21	Santa Ana-Anaheim, CA M.D.	3,000,062
22	San Diego, CA	2,935,792
23	St. Louis, MO-IL	2,810,914
24	Nassau-Suffolk, NY M.D.	2,792,682
25	Tampa-St Petersburg, FL	2,720,592
26	Baltimore-Towson, MD	2,652,974
27	Seattle-Bellevue-Everett, WA M.D.	2,518,369
28	Warren-Farmington Hills, MI M.D.	2,500,295
29	Oakland-Fremont, CA M.D.	2,474,091
30	Denver-Aurora, CO	2,464,178
31	Miami-Dade County, FL M.D.	2,401,971
32	Pittsburgh, PA	2,356,481
33	Edison, NJ M.D.	2,298,551
34	Portland-Vancouver, OR-WA	2,171,073
35	Newark-Union, NJ-PA M.D.	2,145,195
36	Cincinnati-Middletown, OH-KY-IN	2,115,244
37	Cleveland-Elyria-Mentor, OH	2,104,225
38	Sacramento, CA	2,091,363
39	Fort Worth-Arlington, TX M.D.	2,024,417
40	Orlando, FL	2,020,346
41	San Antonio, TX	1,975,770
42	Detroit-Livonia-Dearborn, MI M.D.	1,951,186
43	Boston-Quincy, MA M.D.	1,839,638
44	Las Vegas-Paradise, NV	1,834,533
45	Fort Lauderdale, FL M.D.	1,795,143
46	San Jose, CA	1,780,107
47	Columbus, OH	1,737,831
48	Indianapolis, IN	1,687,197
49	San Francisco-S. Mateo, CA M.D.	1,680,417
50	Virginia Beach-Norfolk, VA-NC	1,656,896
51	Charlotte-Gastonia, NC-SC	1,635,133
52	Austin-Round Rock, TX	1,553,472
53	Milwaukee, WI	1,516,093
54	Nashville-Davidson, TN	1,492,983
55	Cambridge-Newton, MA M.D.	1,466,454
56	Memphis, TN-MS-AR	1,295,670
57	Jacksonville, FL	1,290,776
58	West Palm Beach, FL M.D.	1,283,806
59	Camden, NJ M.D.	1,244,124
60	Louisville, KY-IN	1,233,503
61	Richmond, VA	1,205,749
62	Oklahoma City, OK	1,189,823
63	Bethesda-Frederick, MD M.D.	1,158,220
64	Buffalo-Niagara Falls, NY	1,129,953
65	Birmingham-Hoover, AL	1,108,901
66	Salt Lake City, UT	1,101,656
67	Raleigh-Cary, NC	1,033,679
68	Rochester, NY	1,032,143
69	New Orleans, LA	1,026,639
70	Hartford, CT	1,006,947
71	Tucson, AZ	963,028
72	Tulsa, OK	908,036
73	Fresno, CA	898,391
74	Bridgeport-Stamford, CT	884,290
75	Albany-Schenectady-Troy, NY	852,141
76	Dayton, OH	835,430
77	Omaha-Council Bluffs, NE-IA	829,460
78	Albuquerque, NM	827,275
79	Allentown, PA-NJ	805,542
80	Oxnard-Thousand Oaks, CA	799,872
81	Bakersfield, CA	792,216
82	Worcester, MA	790,004
83	Tacoma, WA M.D.	776,223
84	Grand Rapids-Wyoming, MI	774,927
85	Baton Rouge, LA	770,283
86	El Paso, TX	744,171
87	Peabody, MA M.D.	737,494
88	McAllen-Edinburg-Mission, TX	720,595
89	Akron, OH	699,760
90	Wilmington, DE-MD-NJ M.D.	696,712
91	Springfield, MA	687,220
92	Stockton, CA	684,406
93	Knoxville, TN	682,242
94	Poughkeepsie, NY	676,768
95	Little Rock, AR	659,776
96	Toledo, OH	651,165
97	Syracuse, NY	648,191
98	Greenville, SC	613,703
99	Colorado Springs, CO	613,181
100	Wichita, KS	594,974
101	Cape Coral-Fort Myers, FL	587,220
102	Boise City-Nampa, ID	586,066
103	Lakeland, FL	568,435
104	Madison, WI	550,623
105	Scranton--Wilkes-Barre, PA	548,161
106	Des Moines-West Des Moines, IA	541,394
107	Palm Bay-Melbourne, FL	538,226
108	Jackson, MS	532,981
109	Augusta, GA-SC	528,421
110	Harrisburg-Carlisle, PA	526,335
111	Modesto, CA	517,721
112	Ogden-Clearfield, UT	514,786
113	Portland, ME	513,311
114	Chattanooga, TN-GA	503,472
115	Deltona-Daytona Beach, FL	500,013
116	Provo-Orem, UT	498,516
117	Lancaster, PA	496,516
118	Santa Rosa-Petaluma, CA	464,218
119	Lansing-East Lansing, MI	452,907
120	Spokane, WA	450,805
121	Lexington-Fayette, KY	441,674
122	Flint, MI	440,751
123	Pensacola, FL	440,445
124	Visalia-Porterville, CA	424,464
125	York-Hanover, PA	420,251
126	Corpus Christi, TX	417,469
127	Rockingham County, NH M.D.	416,691
128	Springfield, MO	412,378
129	Vallejo-Fairfield, CA	410,623
130	Fort Wayne, IN	410,350
131	Reno-Sparks, NV	408,488
132	Salinas, CA	408,059
133	Asheville, NC	405,975
134	Mobile, AL	405,259
135	Reading, PA	404,031
136	Port St. Lucie, FL	400,314
137	Santa Barbara-Santa Maria, CA	397,342
138	Brownsville-Harlingen, TX	395,428
139	Salem, OR	390,689
140	Huntsville, AL	382,202
141	Beaumont-Port Arthur, TX	378,783
142	Trenton-Ewing, NJ	365,977
143	Hickory, NC	365,896
144	Montgomery, AL	364,491
145	Killeen-Temple-Fort Hood, TX	354,141
146	Evansville, IN-KY	351,489
147	Fayetteville, NC	345,641
148	Ann Arbor, MI	345,430
149	Eugene-Springfield, OR	340,482
150	Wilmington, NC	337,011
151	Tallahassee, FL	335,945
152	Savannah, GA	324,109
153	Ocala, FL	322,272
154	Naples-Marco Island, FL	321,589
155	South Bend-Mishawaka, IN-MI	317,804
156	Kingsport, TN-VA	305,118
157	Anchorage, AK	303,996
158	Charleston, WV	303,537
159	Green Bay, WI	302,277
160	Utica-Rome, NY	296,125
161	Roanoke, VA	295,368
162	Fort Smith, AR-OK	291,717
163	Columbus, GA-AL	290,106
164	Lincoln, NE	286,039
165	Fort Collins-Loveland, CO	282,097
166	Erie, PA	278,948
167	Spartanburg, SC	276,109
168	Duluth, MN-WI	274,026
169	Atlantic City, NJ	270,417
170	Lubbock, TX	262,990
171	San Luis Obispo, CA	256,373
172	Lafayette, LA	255,453
173	Cedar Rapids, IA	250,807
174	Merced, CA	249,018
175	Greeley, CO	247,806
176	Myrtle Beach, SC	247,229
177	Santa Cruz-Watsonville, CA	246,931
178	Binghamton, NY	246,237
179	Clarksville, TN-KY	244,105
180	Amarillo, TX	243,547

Note: All listings are for Metropolitan Statistical Areas (M.S.A.s) except for those ending with "M.D." Listings with "M.D." are Metropolitan Divisions which are smaller parts of eleven large M.S.A.s. See explanatory note at beginning of metropolitan area section.

Rank Order - Metro Area (continued)

RANK	METROPOLITAN AREA	POP	RANK	METROPOLITAN AREA	POP	RANK	METROPOLITAN AREA	POP
181	Gainesville, FL	243,506	244	Alexandria, LA	150,253	307	Sumter, SC	105,369
182	Bremerton-Silverdale, WA	241,780	245	Decatur, AL	150,246	308	Lima, OH	105,114
183	Lynchburg, VA	240,526	246	Madera, CA	148,765	309	Pine Bluff, AR	103,240
184	Olympia, WA	238,675	247	Rocky Mount, NC	148,194	310	Missoula, MT	102,898
185	Laredo, TX	237,170	248	Hanford-Corcoran, CA	147,510	311	Bismarck, ND	102,688
186	Yakima, WA	234,592	249	Bangor, ME	146,242	312	Brunswick, GA	101,687
187	Kennewick-Pasco-Richland, WA	231,368	250	Johnstown, PA	145,844	313	Longview, WA	100,916
188	Macon, GA	230,317	251	Burlington, NC	145,711	314	Kokomo, IN	100,734
189	Topeka, KS	229,580	252	Jefferson City, MO	145,564	315	Fond du Lac, WI	99,825
190	Waco, TX	227,882	253	Wichita Falls, TX	144,648	316	Cumberland, MD-WV	98,759
191	Barnstable Town, MA	225,323	254	Sioux City, IA-NE-SD	143,514	317	Ocean City, NJ	97,291
192	Appleton, WI	220,208	255	State College, PA	141,328	318	Grand Forks, ND-MN	96,813
193	Sioux Falls, SD	219,627	256	Springfield, OH	141,098	319	Hot Springs, AR	96,271
194	Chico, CA	215,992	257	Iowa City, IA	140,650	320	Rome, GA	95,960
195	Prescott, AZ	214,698	258	Dothan, AL	139,475	321	Dubuque, IA	92,749
196	Saginaw, MI	204,943	259	Grand Junction, CO	137,907	322	Palm Coast, FL	88,451
197	Longview, TX	204,652	260	Battle Creek, MI	137,388	323	Elmira, NY	88,057
198	Houma, LA	203,401	261	Dalton, GA	136,405	324	Pocatello, ID	87,209
199	Florence, SC	201,529	262	Morristown, TN	135,710	325	Cheyenne, WY	86,692
200	Tuscaloosa, AL	199,823	263	Texarkana, TX-Texarkana, AR	135,211	326	Ames, IA	80,075
201	Medford, OR	199,631	264	Napa, CA	133,808	327	Great Falls, MT	79,880
202	Lake Havasu City-Kingman, AZ	199,339	265	Sebastian-Vero Beach, FL	131,526	328	Corvallis, OR	79,314
203	Racine, WI	197,757	266	Wausau, WI	131,265	329	Sandusky, OH	77,695
204	Tyler, TX	197,461	267	Pittsfield, MA	130,630	330	Columbus, IN	74,805
205	Las Cruces, NM	196,085	268	Warner Robins, GA	130,014	331	Hinesville, GA	74,369
206	Johnson City, TN	194,592	269	La Crosse, WI-MN	129,892	332	Casper, WY	71,604
207	College Station-Bryan, TX	193,097	270	Glens Falls, NY	129,840	333	Carson City, NV	55,713
208	Charlottesville, VA	192,228	271	Odessa, TX	128,400	334	Fairbanks, AK	33,156
209	Yuma, AZ	192,098	272	Farmington, NM	128,294	NA	Anniston-Oxford, AL**	NA
210	Fargo, ND-MN	189,580	273	Auburn, AL	127,500	NA	Bloomington-Normal, IL**	NA
211	Bellingham, WA	188,708	274	Lebanon, PA	127,496	NA	Boulder, CO**	NA
212	Athens-Clarke County, GA	188,310	275	Flagstaff, AZ	126,419	NA	Canton, OH**	NA
213	Lafayette, IN	186,687	276	Mansfield, OH	126,412	NA	Cape Girardeau, MO-IL**	NA
214	St. Cloud, MN	184,856	277	Valdosta, GA	126,232	NA	Champaign-Urbana, IL**	NA
215	Kingston, NY	182,932	278	Altoona, PA	125,800	NA	Chicago (greater), IL-IN-WI**	NA
216	Rochester, MN	181,608	279	Midland, TX	125,645	NA	Chicago-Joilet-Naperville, IL M.D.**	NA
217	Anderson, SC	181,370	280	St. Joseph, MO-KS	121,979	NA	Danville, IL**	NA
218	Redding, CA	180,982	281	Rapid City, SD	121,126	NA	Davenport, IA-IL**	NA
219	Crestview-Fort Walton Beach, FL	180,091	282	Winchester, VA-WV	120,991	NA	Decatur, IL**	NA
220	Bloomington, IN	179,055	283	Idaho Falls, ID	119,795	NA	Durham-Chapel Hill, NC**	NA
221	Gainesville, GA	178,408	284	Sherman-Denison, TX	119,528	NA	Florence-Muscle Shoals, AL**	NA
222	Muskegon-Norton Shores, MI	175,119	285	Salisbury, MD	117,891	NA	Gadsden, AL**	NA
223	Monroe, LA	172,092	286	Mount Vernon-Anacortes, WA	117,546	NA	Gary, IN M.D.**	NA
224	Joplin, MO	170,012	287	Williamsport, PA	117,037	NA	Gulfport-Biloxi, MS**	NA
225	Albany, GA	164,983	288	Sheboygan, WI	115,407	NA	Hagerstown-Martinsburg, MD-WV**	NA
226	Panama City-Lynn Haven, FL	164,360	289	Goldsboro, NC	115,119	NA	Holland-Grand Haven, MI**	NA
227	Yuba City, CA	164,006	290	Bowling Green, KY	114,815	NA	Kankakee-Bradley, IL**	NA
228	Waterloo-Cedar Falls, IA	161,918	291	Victoria, TX	114,391	NA	Kansas City, MO-KS**	NA
229	El Centro, CA	161,766	292	Muncie, IN	114,292	NA	Lake Co.-Kenosha Co., IL-WI M.D.**	NA
230	Oshkosh-Neenah, WI	161,620	293	Jonesboro, AR	114,222	NA	Manchester-Nashua, NH**	NA
231	Janesville, WI	160,629	294	Logan, UT-ID	114,216	NA	Manhattan, KS**	NA
232	Abilene, TX	157,713	295	Lawrence, KS	114,212	NA	Mankato-North Mankato, MN**	NA
233	Columbia, MO	157,307	296	Harrisonburg, VA	113,967	NA	New Haven-Milford, CT**	NA
234	Eau Claire, WI	156,492	297	Jackson, TN	113,807	NA	North Port-Bradenton-Sarasota, FL**	NA
235	Pueblo, CO	155,852	298	Elizabethtown, KY	111,690	NA	Norwich-New London, CT**	NA
236	Monroe, MI	155,523	299	Cleveland, TN	111,450	NA	Owensboro, KY**	NA
237	Punta Gorda, FL	154,910	300	Michigan City-La Porte, IN	110,465	NA	Peoria, IL**	NA
238	Bend, OR	154,723	301	Lawton, OK	109,016	NA	Rockford, IL**	NA
239	Pascagoula, MS	153,177	302	Wenatchee, WA	107,897	NA	Santa Fe, NM**	NA
240	Jacksonville, NC	152,338	303	Bay City, MI	107,654	NA	Springfield, IL**	NA
241	Blacksburg, VA	151,219	304	Lewiston-Auburn, ME	107,169	NA	Terre Haute, IN**	NA
242	Dover, DE	150,986	305	Danville, VA	106,432	NA	Winston-Salem, NC**	NA
243	Billings, MT	150,563	306	San Angelo, TX	105,706			

Source: Reported data from the F.B.I. "Crime in the United States 2011"
*Estimates as of July 2007 based on U.S. Bureau of the Census figures.
**Not available (comparable metro area not included in 2007 crime statistics).

Alpha Order - City

88. City Population in 2011
National Total = 311,591,917*

RANK	CITY	POP
208	Abilene, TX	119,526
110	Akron, OH	199,256
404	Albany, GA	78,454
289	Albany, NY	98,296
32	Albuquerque, NM	551,961
172	Alexandria, VA	141,638
368	Alhambra, CA	84,066
211	Allentown, PA	118,408
351	Allen, TX	86,019
116	Amarillo, TX	194,708
214	Amherst, NY	117,610
54	Anaheim, CA	340,218
63	Anchorage, AK	296,955
226	Ann Arbor, MI	113,848
263	Antioch, CA	103,575
434	Arlington Heights, IL	75,327
50	Arlington, TX	373,128
240	Arvada, CO	108,287
362	Asheville, NC	84,450
218	Athens-Clarke, GA	117,114
40	Atlanta, GA	425,533
55	Aurora, CO	330,740
111	Aurora, IL	198,495
15	Austin, TX	807,022
416	Avondale, AZ	77,317
51	Bakersfield, CA	351,568
428	Baldwin Park, CA	76,276
23	Baltimore, MD	626,848
85	Baton Rouge, LA	231,592
206	Beaumont, TX	120,785
330	Beaverton, OR	90,759
197	Bellevue, WA	124,283
413	Bellflower, CA	77,517
377	Bellingham, WA	82,154
414	Bend, OR	77,455
225	Berkeley, CA	113,903
436	Bethlehem, PA	75,221
256	Billings, MT	105,095
96	Birmingham, AL	213,258
422	Bloomington, IL	76,841
387	Bloomington, IN	80,816
371	Bloomington, MN	83,533
357	Boca Raton, FL	85,542
101	Boise, ID	207,945
24	Boston, MA	621,359
283	Boulder, CO	99,081
435	Brick Twnshp, NJ	75,322
167	Bridgeport, CT	144,496
309	Brockton, MA	94,380
281	Broken Arrow, OK	99,908
425	Brooklyn Park, MN	76,366
128	Brownsville, TX	178,706
409	Bryan, TX	77,804
381	Buena Park, CA	81,477
69	Buffalo, NY	262,484
261	Burbank, CA	104,555
253	Cambridge, MA	105,803
412	Camden, NJ	77,604
332	Canton Twnshp, MI	90,105
146	Cape Coral, FL	156,408
251	Carlsbad, CA	106,566
395	Carmel, IN	79,596
203	Carrollton, TX	121,603
316	Carson, CA	92,792
177	Cary, NC	136,949
190	Cedar Rapids, IA	126,988
266	Centennial, CO	102,125
382	Champaign, IL	81,299
80	Chandler, AZ	239,466
204	Charleston, SC	121,481
16	Charlotte, NC	789,478
134	Chattanooga, TN	169,187
399	Cheektowaga, NY	79,194
91	Chesapeake, VA	224,864
3	Chicago, IL	2,703,713
344	Chico, CA	87,200
433	Chino Hills, CA	75,678
400	Chino, CA	78,900
76	Chula Vista, CA	246,783
367	Cicero, IL	84,144
62	Cincinnati, OH	297,160
366	Citrus Heights, CA	84,280
397	Clarkstown, NY	79,221
179	Clarksville, TN	134,128
235	Clearwater, FL	109,153
45	Cleveland, OH	397,106
365	Clifton, NJ	84,416
297	Clinton Twnshp, MI	96,723
296	Clovis, CA	96,755
300	College Station, TX	95,832
407	Colonie, NY	77,950
41	Colorado Springs, CO	423,680
236	Columbia, MO	108,894
118	Columbus, GA	192,385
17	Columbus, OH	787,609
293	Compton, CA	97,589
199	Concord, CA	123,502
391	Concord, NC	80,069
201	Coral Springs, FL	122,746
152	Corona, CA	154,165
58	Corpus Christi, TX	311,637
230	Costa Mesa, CA	111,253
390	Cranston, RI	80,290
10	Dallas, TX	1,223,021
265	Daly City, CA	102,312
384	Danbury, CT	81,043
279	Davenport, IA	100,207
312	Davie, FL	93,246
173	Dayton, OH	141,631
291	Dearborn, MI	98,079
426	Decatur, IL	76,351
430	Deerfield Beach, FL	76,040
220	Denton, TX	115,769
28	Denver, CO	610,612
104	Des Moines, IA	204,498
19	Detroit, MI	713,239
228	Downey, CA	113,086
345	Duluth, MN	86,931
86	Durham, NC	231,225
401	Edinburg, TX	78,722
278	Edison Twnshp, NJ	100,300
376	Edmond, OK	82,276
276	El Cajon, CA	100,647
222	El Monte, CA	114,809
21	El Paso, TX	662,780
238	Elgin, IL	108,514
195	Elizabeth, NJ	125,386
150	Elk Grove, CA	154,814
267	Erie, PA	102,111
165	Escondido, CA	145,603
144	Eugene, OR	157,848
212	Evansville, IN	118,029
259	Everett, WA	104,635
252	Fairfield, CA	106,559
336	Fall River, MA	89,399
246	Fargo, ND	107,329
393	Farmington Hills, MI	79,680
106	Fayetteville, NC	203,107
417	Fishers, IN	77,186
264	Flint, MI	102,357
112	Fontana, CA	198,374
162	Fort Collins, CO	146,494
136	Fort Lauderdale, FL	167,777
346	Fort Smith, AR	86,861
72	Fort Wayne, IN	254,987
18	Fort Worth, TX	756,803
94	Fremont, CA	216,606
34	Fresno, CA	500,480
209	Frisco, TX	119,451
178	Fullerton, CA	136,750
192	Gainesville, FL	126,049
132	Garden Grove, CA	172,892
84	Garland, TX	231,650
388	Gary, IN	80,704
100	Gilbert, AZ	211,404
87	Glendale, AZ	229,931
117	Glendale, CA	193,973
127	Grand Prairie, TX	179,087
121	Grand Rapids, MI	187,898
299	Greece, NY	96,527
306	Greeley, CO	94,507
262	Green Bay, WI	104,510
250	Gresham, OR	106,718
339	Hamilton Twnshp, NJ	88,760
383	Hammond, IN	81,243
174	Hampton, VA	139,078
196	Hartford, CT	125,006
359	Hawthorne, CA	85,284
163	Hayward, CA	145,881
396	Hemet, CA	79,582
71	Henderson, NV	259,902
323	Hesperia, CA	91,233
88	Hialeah, FL	227,731
255	High Point, NC	105,695
317	Hillsboro, OR	92,586
169	Hollywood, FL	142,686
379	Hoover, AL	82,012
4	Houston, TX	2,143,628
119	Huntington Beach, CA	192,226
125	Huntsville, AL	180,972
217	Independence, MO	117,255
13	Indianapolis, IN	833,024
420	Indio, CA	76,930
231	Inglewood, CA	110,962
95	Irvine, CA	214,872
92	Irving, TX	220,841
12	Jacksonville, FL	834,429
131	Jackson, MS	174,170
74	Jersey City, NJ	248,423
410	Johns Creek, GA	77,738
158	Joliet, IL	147,877
160	Kansas City, KS	146,712
37	Kansas City, MO	461,458
437	Kennewick, WA	75,077
282	Kenosha, WI	99,650
310	Kent, WA	93,861
184	Killeen, TX	130,613
126	Knoxville, TN	180,488
202	Lafayette, LA	121,726
406	Lake Forest, CA	78,172
285	Lakeland, FL	98,750
314	Lakewood Twnshp, NJ	93,152
385	Lakewood, CA	80,989
166	Lakewood, CO	145,470
143	Lancaster, CA	158,474
224	Lansing, MI	114,211
79	Laredo, TX	241,059
402	Largo, FL	78,706
286	Las Cruces, NM	98,710
7	Las Vegas, NV	1,458,474
342	Lawrence, KS	88,200
421	Lawrence, MA	76,843
292	Lawton, OK	97,904
358	League City, TX	85,318
321	Lee's Summit, MO	91,696
294	Lewisville, TX	97,295

354   Metropolitan and City Populations

Alpha Order - City (continued)

RANK	CITY	POP
61	Lexington, KY	297,847
70	Lincoln, NE	260,685
115	Little Rock, AR	194,988
380	Livermore, CA	81,920
295	Livonia, MI	96,869
36	Long Beach, CA	467,691
343	Longmont, CO	87,773
378	Longview, TX	82,148
2	Los Angeles, CA	3,837,207
20	Louisville, KY	665,152
247	Lowell, MA	107,167
81	Lubbock, TX	234,404
423	Lynchburg, VA	76,471
328	Lynn, MA	90,880
318	Macon, GA	92,554
82	Madison, WI	234,225
234	Manchester, NH	109,708
182	McAllen, TX	132,610
181	McKinney, TX	133,876
432	Medford, OR	75,704
418	Melbourne, FL	77,105
22	Memphis, TN	652,725
405	Menifee, CA	78,430
392	Merced, CA	79,886
431	Meridian, ID	75,922
38	Mesa, AZ	445,256
168	Mesquite, TX	142,766
338	Miami Beach, FL	88,975
237	Miami Gardens, FL	108,628
44	Miami, FL	404,901
227	Midland, TX	113,486
29	Milwaukee, WI	597,426
48	Minneapolis, MN	385,531
198	Miramar, FL	123,704
307	Mission Viejo, CA	94,402
403	Mission, TX	78,679
73	Mobile, AL	251,869
105	Modesto, CA	203,530
102	Montgomery, AL	206,754
114	Moreno Valley, CA	195,638
233	Murfreesboro, TN	109,736
258	Murrieta, CA	104,682
375	Nampa, ID	82,459
408	Napa, CA	77,819
170	Naperville, IL	142,280
347	Nashua, NH	86,607
27	Nashville, TN	612,789
301	New Bedford, MA	95,649
185	New Haven, CT	130,019
52	New Orleans, LA	346,974
415	New Rochelle, NY	77,408
1	New York, NY	8,211,875
67	Newark, NJ	278,064
349	Newport Beach, CA	86,187
123	Newport News, VA	182,878
354	Newton, MA	85,665
77	Norfolk, VA	245,704
229	Norman, OK	112,112
287	North Charleston, SC	98,606
248	Norwalk, CA	106,790
353	Norwalk, CT	85,761
47	Oakland, CA	395,317
135	Oceanside, CA	169,050
268	Odessa, TX	102,043
394	O'Fallon, MO	79,617
364	Ogden, UT	84,423
31	Oklahoma City, OK	586,208
191	Olathe, KS	126,671
42	Omaha, NE	412,608
139	Ontario, CA	165,851
176	Orange, CA	138,020
333	Orem, UT	90,033
78	Orlando, FL	241,548
130	Overland Park, KS	174,473
109	Oxnard, CA	200,225
260	Palm Bay, FL	104,596
151	Palmdale, CA	154,546
175	Pasadena, CA	138,734
156	Pasadena, TX	152,179
161	Paterson, NJ	146,685
313	Pearland, TX	93,172
145	Pembroke Pines, FL	156,859
148	Peoria, AZ	156,246
221	Peoria, IL	115,353
5	Philadelphia, PA	1,530,873
6	Phoenix, AZ	1,466,097
59	Pittsburgh, PA	308,609
68	Plano, TX	265,309
350	Plantation, FL	86,113
157	Pomona, CA	150,810
274	Pompano Beach, FL	101,206
138	Port St. Lucie, FL	166,846
30	Portland, OR	589,991
298	Portsmouth, VA	96,676
223	Provo, UT	114,659
239	Pueblo, CO	108,452
315	Quincy, MA	92,834
398	Racine, WI	79,204
43	Raleigh, NC	409,014
363	Ramapo, NY	84,431
137	Rancho Cucamon., CA	167,212
341	Reading, PA	88,363
326	Redding, CA	90,917
411	Redwood City, CA	77,718
89	Reno, NV	227,120
320	Renton, WA	92,354
277	Rialto, CA	100,337
271	Richardson, TX	101,311
257	Richmond, CA	104,920
103	Richmond, VA	206,654
340	Rio Rancho, NM	88,500
60	Riverside, CA	307,443
290	Roanoke, VA	98,191
244	Rochester, MN	107,593
99	Rochester, NY	211,511
154	Rockford, IL	153,331
207	Roseville, CA	120,184
334	Roswell, GA	89,509
269	Round Rock, TX	101,989
35	Sacramento, CA	471,972
147	Salem, OR	156,283
155	Salinas, CA	152,210
120	Salt Lake City, UT	190,038
303	San Angelo, TX	95,161
8	San Antonio, TX	1,355,339
97	San Bernardino, CA	212,392
9	San Diego, CA	1,316,919
14	San Francisco, CA	814,701
11	San Jose, CA	957,062
352	San Leandro, CA	85,949
361	San Marcos, CA	84,766
288	San Mateo, CA	98,350
304	Sandy Springs, GA	95,089
337	Sandy, UT	89,149
56	Santa Ana, CA	328,343
335	Santa Barbara, CA	89,449
213	Santa Clara, CA	117,837
129	Santa Clarita, CA	178,393
275	Santa Maria, CA	100,723
329	Santa Monica, CA	90,791
133	Santa Rosa, CA	169,788
90	Savannah, GA	226,422
93	Scottsdale, AZ	220,462
427	Scranton, PA	76,332
25	Seattle, WA	618,209
108	Shreveport, LA	201,134
194	Simi Valley, CA	125,698
372	Sioux City, IA	83,117
149	Sioux Falls, SD	155,760
429	Somerville, MA	76,216
270	South Bend, IN	101,685
302	South Gate, CA	95,506
325	Sparks, NV	91,025
324	Spokane Valley, WA	91,163
98	Spokane, WA	212,194
219	Springfield, IL	116,600
153	Springfield, MA	153,993
142	Springfield, MO	160,078
200	Stamford, CT	122,870
186	Sterling Heights, MI	129,601
64	Stockton, CA	295,136
419	St. Joseph, MO	77,059
57	St. Louis, MO	320,454
65	St. Paul, MN	287,665
75	St. Petersburg, FL	248,105
355	Suffolk, VA	85,595
389	Sugar Land, TX	80,475
171	Sunnyvale, CA	141,728
356	Sunrise, FL	85,590
210	Surprise, AZ	119,181
164	Syracuse, NY	145,822
107	Tacoma, WA	201,510
122	Tallahassee, FL	183,848
53	Tampa, FL	340,284
273	Temecula, CA	101,274
141	Tempe, AZ	164,008
205	Thornton, CO	120,841
188	Thousand Oaks, CA	128,172
66	Toledo, OH	287,418
322	Toms River Twnshp, NJ	91,543
187	Topeka, KS	128,283
159	Torrance, CA	147,148
370	Tracy, CA	83,897
360	Trenton, NJ	85,196
386	Troy, MI	80,919
33	Tucson, AZ	527,479
46	Tulsa, OK	396,101
327	Tuscaloosa, AL	90,903
424	Tustin, CA	76,428
284	Tyler, TX	98,939
373	Upper Darby Twnshp, PA	83,059
311	Vacaville, CA	93,515
215	Vallejo, CA	117,305
140	Vancouver, WA	164,329
243	Ventura, CA	107,684
216	Victorville, CA	117,266
39	Virginia Beach, VA	443,226
193	Visalia, CA	125,905
305	Vista, CA	94,937
189	Waco, TX	127,431
180	Warren, MI	133,955
374	Warwick, RI	82,572
26	Washington, DC	617,996
232	Waterbury, CT	110,570
245	West Covina, CA	107,345
254	West Jordan, UT	105,713
272	West Palm Beach, FL	101,281
183	West Valley, UT	131,979
369	Westland, MI	84,031
331	Westminster, CA	90,756
241	Westminster, CO	107,962
348	Whittier, CA	86,334
249	Wichita Falls, TX	106,753
49	Wichita, KS	384,796
242	Wilmington, NC	107,826
83	Winston-Salem, NC	232,529
280	Woodbridge Twnshp, NJ	99,915
124	Worcester, MA	182,145
319	Yakima, WA	92,496
113	Yonkers, NY	196,857
308	Yuma, AZ	94,381

Source: Reported data from the F.B.I. "Crime in the United States 2011"
*Estimates as of July 2011 based on U.S. Bureau of the Census figures. Charlotte, Honolulu, Indianapolis, Las Vegas, Louisville, Mobile, and Savannah include areas under their police department but outside the city limits. All populations are for area covered by police department.

Rank Order - City

88. City Population in 2011 (continued)
National Total = 311,591,917*

RANK	CITY	POP
1	New York, NY	8,211,875
2	Los Angeles, CA	3,837,207
3	Chicago, IL	2,703,713
4	Houston, TX	2,143,628
5	Philadelphia, PA	1,530,873
6	Phoenix, AZ	1,466,097
7	Las Vegas, NV	1,458,474
8	San Antonio, TX	1,355,339
9	San Diego, CA	1,316,919
10	Dallas, TX	1,223,021
11	San Jose, CA	957,062
12	Jacksonville, FL	834,429
13	Indianapolis, IN	833,024
14	San Francisco, CA	814,701
15	Austin, TX	807,022
16	Charlotte, NC	789,478
17	Columbus, OH	787,609
18	Fort Worth, TX	756,803
19	Detroit, MI	713,239
20	Louisville, KY	665,152
21	El Paso, TX	662,780
22	Memphis, TN	652,725
23	Baltimore, MD	626,848
24	Boston, MA	621,359
25	Seattle, WA	618,209
26	Washington, DC	617,996
27	Nashville, TN	612,789
28	Denver, CO	610,612
29	Milwaukee, WI	597,426
30	Portland, OR	589,991
31	Oklahoma City, OK	586,208
32	Albuquerque, NM	551,961
33	Tucson, AZ	527,479
34	Fresno, CA	500,480
35	Sacramento, CA	471,972
36	Long Beach, CA	467,691
37	Kansas City, MO	461,458
38	Mesa, AZ	445,256
39	Virginia Beach, VA	443,226
40	Atlanta, GA	425,533
41	Colorado Springs, CO	423,680
42	Omaha, NE	412,608
43	Raleigh, NC	409,014
44	Miami, FL	404,901
45	Cleveland, OH	397,106
46	Tulsa, OK	396,101
47	Oakland, CA	395,317
48	Minneapolis, MN	385,531
49	Wichita, KS	384,796
50	Arlington, TX	373,128
51	Bakersfield, CA	351,568
52	New Orleans, LA	346,974
53	Tampa, FL	340,284
54	Anaheim, CA	340,218
55	Aurora, CO	330,740
56	Santa Ana, CA	328,343
57	St. Louis, MO	320,454
58	Corpus Christi, TX	311,637
59	Pittsburgh, PA	308,609
60	Riverside, CA	307,443
61	Lexington, KY	297,847
62	Cincinnati, OH	297,160
63	Anchorage, AK	296,955
64	Stockton, CA	295,136
65	St. Paul, MN	287,665
66	Toledo, OH	287,418
67	Newark, NJ	278,064
68	Plano, TX	265,309
69	Buffalo, NY	262,484
70	Lincoln, NE	260,685
71	Henderson, NV	259,902
72	Fort Wayne, IN	254,987
73	Mobile, AL	251,869
74	Jersey City, NJ	248,423
75	St. Petersburg, FL	248,105
76	Chula Vista, CA	246,783
77	Norfolk, VA	245,704
78	Orlando, FL	241,548
79	Laredo, TX	241,059
80	Chandler, AZ	239,466
81	Lubbock, TX	234,404
82	Madison, WI	234,225
83	Winston-Salem, NC	232,529
84	Garland, TX	231,650
85	Baton Rouge, LA	231,592
86	Durham, NC	231,225
87	Glendale, AZ	229,931
88	Hialeah, FL	227,731
89	Reno, NV	227,120
90	Savannah, GA	226,422
91	Chesapeake, VA	224,864
92	Irving, TX	220,841
93	Scottsdale, AZ	220,462
94	Fremont, CA	216,606
95	Irvine, CA	214,872
96	Birmingham, AL	213,258
97	San Bernardino, CA	212,392
98	Spokane, WA	212,194
99	Rochester, NY	211,511
100	Gilbert, AZ	211,404
101	Boise, ID	207,945
102	Montgomery, AL	206,754
103	Richmond, VA	206,654
104	Des Moines, IA	204,498
105	Modesto, CA	203,530
106	Fayetteville, NC	203,107
107	Tacoma, WA	201,510
108	Shreveport, LA	201,134
109	Oxnard, CA	200,225
110	Akron, OH	199,256
111	Aurora, IL	198,495
112	Fontana, CA	198,374
113	Yonkers, NY	196,857
114	Moreno Valley, CA	195,638
115	Little Rock, AR	194,988
116	Amarillo, TX	194,708
117	Glendale, CA	193,973
118	Columbus, GA	192,385
119	Huntington Beach, CA	192,226
120	Salt Lake City, UT	190,038
121	Grand Rapids, MI	187,898
122	Tallahassee, FL	183,848
123	Newport News, VA	182,878
124	Worcester, MA	182,145
125	Huntsville, AL	180,972
126	Knoxville, TN	180,488
127	Grand Prairie, TX	179,087
128	Brownsville, TX	178,706
129	Santa Clarita, CA	178,393
130	Overland Park, KS	174,473
131	Jackson, MS	174,170
132	Garden Grove, CA	172,892
133	Santa Rosa, CA	169,788
134	Chattanooga, TN	169,187
135	Oceanside, CA	169,050
136	Fort Lauderdale, FL	167,777
137	Rancho Cucamon., CA	167,212
138	Port St. Lucie, FL	166,846
139	Ontario, CA	165,851
140	Vancouver, WA	164,329
141	Tempe, AZ	164,008
142	Springfield, MO	160,078
143	Lancaster, CA	158,474
144	Eugene, OR	157,848
145	Pembroke Pines, FL	156,859
146	Cape Coral, FL	156,408
147	Salem, OR	156,283
148	Peoria, AZ	156,246
149	Sioux Falls, SD	155,760
150	Elk Grove, CA	154,814
151	Palmdale, CA	154,546
152	Corona, CA	154,165
153	Springfield, MA	153,993
154	Rockford, IL	153,331
155	Salinas, CA	152,210
156	Pasadena, TX	152,179
157	Pomona, CA	150,810
158	Joliet, IL	147,877
159	Torrance, CA	147,148
160	Kansas City, KS	146,712
161	Paterson, NJ	146,685
162	Fort Collins, CO	146,494
163	Hayward, CA	145,881
164	Syracuse, NY	145,822
165	Escondido, CA	145,603
166	Lakewood, CO	145,470
167	Bridgeport, CT	144,496
168	Mesquite, TX	142,766
169	Hollywood, FL	142,686
170	Naperville, IL	142,280
171	Sunnyvale, CA	141,728
172	Alexandria, VA	141,638
173	Dayton, OH	141,631
174	Hampton, VA	139,078
175	Pasadena, CA	138,734
176	Orange, CA	138,020
177	Cary, NC	136,949
178	Fullerton, CA	136,750
179	Clarksville, TN	134,128
180	Warren, MI	133,955
181	McKinney, TX	133,876
182	McAllen, TX	132,610
183	West Valley, UT	131,979
184	Killeen, TX	130,613
185	New Haven, CT	130,019
186	Sterling Heights, MI	129,601
187	Topeka, KS	128,283
188	Thousand Oaks, CA	128,172
189	Waco, TX	127,431
190	Cedar Rapids, IA	126,988
191	Olathe, KS	126,671
192	Gainesville, FL	126,049
193	Visalia, CA	125,905
194	Simi Valley, CA	125,698
195	Elizabeth, NJ	125,386
196	Hartford, CT	125,006
197	Bellevue, WA	124,283
198	Miramar, FL	123,704
199	Concord, CA	123,502
200	Stamford, CT	122,870
201	Coral Springs, FL	122,746
202	Lafayette, LA	121,726
203	Carrollton, TX	121,603
204	Charleston, SC	121,481
205	Thornton, CO	120,841
206	Beaumont, TX	120,785
207	Roseville, CA	120,184
208	Abilene, TX	119,526
209	Frisco, TX	119,451
210	Surprise, AZ	119,181
211	Allentown, PA	118,408
212	Evansville, IN	118,029
213	Santa Clara, CA	117,837
214	Amherst, NY	117,610
215	Vallejo, CA	117,305
216	Victorville, CA	117,266

Rank Order - City (continued)

RANK	CITY	POP
217	Independence, MO	117,255
218	Athens-Clarke, GA	117,114
219	Springfield, IL	116,600
220	Denton, TX	115,769
221	Peoria, IL	115,353
222	El Monte, CA	114,809
223	Provo, UT	114,659
224	Lansing, MI	114,211
225	Berkeley, CA	113,903
226	Ann Arbor, MI	113,848
227	Midland, TX	113,486
228	Downey, CA	113,086
229	Norman, OK	112,112
230	Costa Mesa, CA	111,253
231	Inglewood, CA	110,962
232	Waterbury, CT	110,570
233	Murfreesboro, TN	109,736
234	Manchester, NH	109,708
235	Clearwater, FL	109,153
236	Columbia, MO	108,894
237	Miami Gardens, FL	108,628
238	Elgin, IL	108,514
239	Pueblo, CO	108,452
240	Arvada, CO	108,287
241	Westminster, CO	107,962
242	Wilmington, NC	107,826
243	Ventura, CA	107,684
244	Rochester, MN	107,593
245	West Covina, CA	107,345
246	Fargo, ND	107,329
247	Lowell, MA	107,167
248	Norwalk, CA	106,790
249	Wichita Falls, TX	106,753
250	Gresham, OR	106,718
251	Carlsbad, CA	106,566
252	Fairfield, CA	106,559
253	Cambridge, MA	105,803
254	West Jordan, UT	105,713
255	High Point, NC	105,695
256	Billings, MT	105,095
257	Richmond, CA	104,920
258	Murrieta, CA	104,682
259	Everett, WA	104,635
260	Palm Bay, FL	104,596
261	Burbank, CA	104,555
262	Green Bay, WI	104,510
263	Antioch, CA	103,575
264	Flint, MI	102,357
265	Daly City, CA	102,312
266	Centennial, CO	102,125
267	Erie, PA	102,111
268	Odessa, TX	102,043
269	Round Rock, TX	101,989
270	South Bend, IN	101,685
271	Richardson, TX	101,311
272	West Palm Beach, FL	101,281
273	Temecula, CA	101,274
274	Pompano Beach, FL	101,206
275	Santa Maria, CA	100,723
276	El Cajon, CA	100,647
277	Rialto, CA	100,337
278	Edison Twnshp, NJ	100,300
279	Davenport, IA	100,207
280	Woodbridge Twnshp, NJ	99,915
281	Broken Arrow, OK	99,908
282	Kenosha, WI	99,650
283	Boulder, CO	99,081
284	Tyler, TX	98,939
285	Lakeland, FL	98,750
286	Las Cruces, NM	98,710
287	North Charleston, SC	98,606
288	San Mateo, CA	98,350
289	Albany, NY	98,296
290	Roanoke, VA	98,191
291	Dearborn, MI	98,079
292	Lawton, OK	97,904
293	Compton, CA	97,589
294	Lewisville, TX	97,295
295	Livonia, MI	96,869
296	Clovis, CA	96,755
297	Clinton Twnshp, MI	96,723
298	Portsmouth, VA	96,676
299	Greece, NY	96,527
300	College Station, TX	95,832
301	New Bedford, MA	95,649
302	South Gate, CA	95,506
303	San Angelo, TX	95,161
304	Sandy Springs, GA	95,089
305	Vista, CA	94,937
306	Greeley, CO	94,507
307	Mission Viejo, CA	94,402
308	Yuma, AZ	94,381
309	Brockton, MA	94,380
310	Kent, WA	93,861
311	Vacaville, CA	93,515
312	Davie, FL	93,246
313	Pearland, TX	93,172
314	Lakewood Twnshp, NJ	93,152
315	Quincy, MA	92,834
316	Carson, CA	92,792
317	Hillsboro, OR	92,586
318	Macon, GA	92,554
319	Yakima, WA	92,496
320	Renton, WA	92,354
321	Lee's Summit, MO	91,696
322	Toms River Twnshp, NJ	91,543
323	Hesperia, CA	91,233
324	Spokane Valley, WA	91,163
325	Sparks, NV	91,025
326	Redding, CA	90,917
327	Tuscaloosa, AL	90,903
328	Lynn, MA	90,880
329	Santa Monica, CA	90,791
330	Beaverton, OR	90,759
331	Westminster, CA	90,756
332	Canton Twnshp, MI	90,105
333	Orem, UT	90,033
334	Roswell, GA	89,509
335	Santa Barbara, CA	89,449
336	Fall River, MA	89,399
337	Sandy, UT	89,149
338	Miami Beach, FL	88,975
339	Hamilton Twnshp, NJ	88,760
340	Rio Rancho, NM	88,500
341	Reading, PA	88,363
342	Lawrence, KS	88,200
343	Longmont, CO	87,773
344	Chico, CA	87,200
345	Duluth, MN	86,931
346	Fort Smith, AR	86,861
347	Nashua, NH	86,607
348	Whittier, CA	86,334
349	Newport Beach, CA	86,187
350	Plantation, FL	86,113
351	Allen, TX	86,019
352	San Leandro, CA	85,949
353	Norwalk, CT	85,761
354	Newton, MA	85,665
355	Suffolk, VA	85,595
356	Sunrise, FL	85,590
357	Boca Raton, FL	85,542
358	League City, TX	85,318
359	Hawthorne, CA	85,284
360	Trenton, NJ	85,196
361	San Marcos, CA	84,766
362	Asheville, NC	84,450
363	Ramapo, NY	84,431
364	Ogden, UT	84,423
365	Clifton, NJ	84,416
366	Citrus Heights, CA	84,280
367	Cicero, IL	84,144
368	Alhambra, CA	84,066
369	Westland, MI	84,031
370	Tracy, CA	83,897
371	Bloomington, MN	83,533
372	Sioux City, IA	83,117
373	Upper Darby Twnshp, PA	83,059
374	Warwick, RI	82,572
375	Nampa, ID	82,459
376	Edmond, OK	82,276
377	Bellingham, WA	82,154
378	Longview, TX	82,148
379	Hoover, AL	82,012
380	Livermore, CA	81,920
381	Buena Park, CA	81,477
382	Champaign, IL	81,299
383	Hammond, IN	81,243
384	Danbury, CT	81,043
385	Lakewood, CA	80,989
386	Troy, MI	80,919
387	Bloomington, IN	80,816
388	Gary, IN	80,704
389	Sugar Land, TX	80,475
390	Cranston, RI	80,290
391	Concord, NC	80,069
392	Merced, CA	79,886
393	Farmington Hills, MI	79,680
394	O'Fallon, MO	79,617
395	Carmel, IN	79,596
396	Hemet, CA	79,582
397	Clarkstown, NY	79,221
398	Racine, WI	79,204
399	Cheektowaga, NY	79,194
400	Chino, CA	78,900
401	Edinburg, TX	78,722
402	Largo, FL	78,706
403	Mission, TX	78,679
404	Albany, GA	78,454
405	Menifee, CA	78,430
406	Lake Forest, CA	78,172
407	Colonie, NY	77,950
408	Napa, CA	77,819
409	Bryan, TX	77,804
410	Johns Creek, GA	77,738
411	Redwood City, CA	77,718
412	Camden, NJ	77,604
413	Bellflower, CA	77,517
414	Bend, OR	77,455
415	New Rochelle, NY	77,408
416	Avondale, AZ	77,317
417	Fishers, IN	77,186
418	Melbourne, FL	77,105
419	St. Joseph, MO	77,059
420	Indio, CA	76,930
421	Lawrence, MA	76,843
422	Bloomington, IL	76,841
423	Lynchburg, VA	76,471
424	Tustin, CA	76,428
425	Brooklyn Park, MN	76,366
426	Decatur, IL	76,351
427	Scranton, PA	76,332
428	Baldwin Park, CA	76,276
429	Somerville, MA	76,216
430	Deerfield Beach, FL	76,040
431	Meridian, ID	75,922
432	Medford, OR	75,704
433	Chino Hills, CA	75,678
434	Arlington Heights, IL	75,327
435	Brick Twnshp, NJ	75,322
436	Bethlehem, PA	75,221
437	Kennewick, WA	75,077

Source: Reported data from the F.B.I. "Crime in the United States 2011"

*Estimates as of July 2011 based on U.S. Bureau of the Census figures. Charlotte, Honolulu, Indianapolis, Las Vegas, Louisville, Mobile, and Savannah include areas under their police department but outside the city limits. All populations are for area covered by police department.

Alpha Order - City

89. City Population in 2010
National Total = 309,330,219*

RANK	CITY	POP
210	Abilene, TX	116,938
100	Akron, OH	205,760
418	Albany, GA	73,034
304	Albany, NY	92,713
32	Albuquerque, NM	545,389
151	Alexandria, VA	152,801
347	Alhambra, CA	84,987
233	Allentown, PA	108,473
323	Allen, TX	89,459
118	Amarillo, TX	190,393
231	Amherst, NY	109,138
55	Anaheim, CA	338,492
64	Anchorage, AK	290,334
222	Ann Arbor, MI	111,745
266	Antioch, CA	102,125
425	Arlington Heights, IL	72,061
49	Arlington, TX	383,715
240	Arvada, CO	107,227
396	Asheville, NC	77,067
219	Athens-Clarke, GA	112,851
33	Atlanta, GA	536,472
58	Aurora, CO	323,483
130	Aurora, IL	174,255
17	Austin, TX	796,310
364	Avondale, AZ	82,580
56	Bakersfield, CA	333,458
394	Baldwin Park, CA	77,127
22	Baltimore, MD	639,929
88	Baton Rouge, LA	226,001
228	Beaumont, TX	109,430
297	Beaverton, OR	93,993
184	Bellevue, WA	127,735
NA	Bellflower, CA**	NA
374	Bellingham, WA	81,139
381	Bend, OR	79,556
260	Berkeley, CA	102,700
415	Bethlehem, PA	73,634
237	Billings, MT	108,039
83	Birmingham, AL	231,009
413	Bloomington, IL	74,304
424	Bloomington, IN	72,286
362	Bloomington, MN	82,715
336	Boca Raton, FL	86,707
98	Boise, ID	205,902
21	Boston, MA	644,064
279	Boulder, CO	99,255
380	Brick Twnshp, NJ	79,569
172	Bridgeport, CT	138,810
307	Brockton, MA	92,383
285	Broken Arrow, OK	97,581
423	Brooklyn Park, MN	72,682
125	Brownsville, TX	180,040
405	Bryan, TX	75,350
378	Buena Park, CA	79,929
69	Buffalo, NY	265,128
257	Burbank, CA	103,304
235	Cambridge, MA	108,356
382	Camden, NJ	79,081
377	Canton Twnshp, MI	80,039
142	Cape Coral, FL	160,432
272	Carlsbad, CA	100,461
427	Carmel, IN	71,647
182	Carrollton, TX	130,862
306	Carson, CA	92,409
168	Cary, NC	141,461
183	Cedar Rapids, IA	129,605
282	Centennial, CO	98,902
375	Champaign, IL	80,489
77	Chandler, AZ	241,826
207	Charleston, SC	117,551
16	Charlotte, NC	797,733
135	Chattanooga, TN	172,460
397	Cheektowaga, NY	76,671
89	Chesapeake, VA	225,627
3	Chicago, IL	2,833,649
344	Chico, CA	85,630
NA	Chino Hills, CA**	NA
353	Chino, CA	84,170
86	Chula Vista, CA	229,060
384	Cicero, IL	78,746
57	Cincinnati, OH	332,365
350	Citrus Heights, CA	84,476
387	Clarkstown, NY	78,365
188	Clarksville, TN	126,548
242	Clearwater, FL	105,647
43	Cleveland, OH	426,042
385	Clifton, NJ	78,632
292	Clinton Twnshp, MI	95,167
289	Clovis, CA	95,901
327	College Station, TX	88,416
395	Colonie, NY	77,078
46	Colorado Springs, CO	397,886
255	Columbia, MO	103,417
122	Columbus, GA	184,576
18	Columbus, OH	772,974
299	Compton, CA	93,916
200	Concord, CA	122,119
430	Concord, NC	68,461
186	Coral Springs, FL	127,113
149	Corona, CA	153,311
65	Corpus Christi, TX	287,559
225	Costa Mesa, CA	110,424
376	Cranston, RI	80,125
10	Dallas, TX	1,306,775
267	Daly City, CA	101,939
373	Danbury, CT	81,242
262	Davenport, IA	102,628
305	Davie, FL	92,661
153	Dayton, OH	152,319
363	Dearborn, MI	82,612
409	Decatur, IL	74,857
406	Deerfield Beach, FL	75,195
185	Denton, TX	127,251
27	Denver, CO	607,051
106	Des Moines, IA	202,564
12	Detroit, MI	899,447
241	Downey, CA	106,992
351	Duluth, MN	84,249
81	Durham, NC	233,790
408	Edinburg, TX	75,091
273	Edison Twnshp, NJ	100,395
360	Edmond, OK	83,337
296	El Cajon, CA	94,311
201	El Monte, CA	121,884
24	El Paso, TX	624,322
239	Elgin, IL	107,731
189	Elizabeth, NJ	126,494
167	Elk Grove, CA	142,330
251	Erie, PA	104,077
169	Escondido, CA	140,662
150	Eugene, OR	153,269
212	Evansville, IN	116,541
278	Everett, WA	99,387
249	Fairfield, CA	104,202
319	Fall River, MA	89,741
275	Fargo, ND	99,694
391	Farmington Hills, MI	77,646
96	Fayetteville, NC	208,263
401	Fishers, IN	75,734
229	Flint, MI	109,245
116	Fontana, CA	192,595
173	Fort Collins, CO	138,689
120	Fort Lauderdale, FL	186,170
340	Fort Smith, AR	86,096
72	Fort Wayne, IN	257,009
19	Fort Worth, TX	746,433
101	Fremont, CA	205,477
35	Fresno, CA	484,734
216	Frisco, TX	113,686
180	Fullerton, CA	133,139
211	Gainesville, FL	116,880
139	Garden Grove, CA	166,287
91	Garland, TX	221,921
NA	Gary, IN**	NA
94	Gilbert, AZ	215,215
74	Glendale, AZ	245,387
112	Glendale, CA	196,877
138	Grand Prairie, TX	166,866
117	Grand Rapids, MI	191,566
309	Greece, NY	92,282
301	Greeley, CO	92,804
269	Green Bay, WI	101,320
263	Gresham, OR	102,540
314	Hamilton Twnshp, NJ	91,439
398	Hammond, IN	76,216
160	Hampton, VA	144,545
192	Hartford, CT	125,626
354	Hawthorne, CA	83,849
161	Hayward, CA	144,509
417	Hemet, CA	73,111
70	Henderson, NV	264,280
326	Hesperia, CA	88,876
92	Hialeah, FL	217,995
244	High Point, NC	105,278
286	Hillsboro, OR	97,423
166	Hollywood, FL	142,793
411	Hoover, AL	74,687
4	Houston, TX	2,280,859
114	Huntington Beach, CA	193,545
123	Huntsville, AL	183,357
203	Independence, MO	121,141
13	Indianapolis, IN	825,072
320	Indio, CA	89,621
221	Inglewood, CA	112,100
93	Irvine, CA	217,193
97	Irving, TX	206,308
14	Jacksonville, FL	822,414
131	Jackson, MS	174,153
75	Jersey City, NJ	244,201
432	Johns Creek, GA	59,893
154	Joliet, IL	150,723
164	Kansas City, KS	143,867
36	Kansas City, MO	483,191
429	Kennewick, WA	68,501
281	Kenosha, WI	98,961
343	Kent, WA	85,768
199	Killeen, TX	122,557
121	Knoxville, TN	185,554
213	Lafayette, LA	115,378
400	Lake Forest, CA	75,780
295	Lakeland, FL	94,569
421	Lakewood Twnshp, NJ	72,960
389	Lakewood, CA	77,901
171	Lakewood, CO	139,615
155	Lancaster, CA	148,632
220	Lansing, MI	112,254
84	Laredo, TX	230,674
419	Largo, FL	73,019
287	Las Cruces, NM	97,065
7	Las Vegas, NV	1,416,401
298	Lawrence, KS	93,945
428	Lawrence, MA	69,679
312	Lawton, OK	92,025
410	League City, TX	74,776
333	Lee's Summit, MO	87,707
238	Lewisville, TX	107,968

358 Metropolitan and City Populations

Alpha Order - City (continued)

RANK	CITY	POP
62	Lexington, KY	300,069
71	Lincoln, NE	259,672
115	Little Rock, AR	192,922
368	Livermore, CA	81,769
335	Livonia, MI	87,434
39	Long Beach, CA	462,267
325	Longmont, CO	88,913
388	Longview, TX	78,319
2	Los Angeles, CA	3,841,707
23	Louisville, KY	637,428
258	Lowell, MA	103,065
87	Lubbock, TX	227,867
407	Lynchburg, VA	75,137
338	Lynn, MA	86,340
324	Macon, GA	89,125
79	Madison, WI	238,224
236	Manchester, NH	108,101
177	McAllen, TX	134,623
174	McKinney, TX	138,306
416	Medford, OR	73,525
390	Melbourne, FL	77,861
20	Memphis, TN	673,650
NA	Menifee, CA**	NA
392	Merced, CA	77,484
422	Meridian, ID	72,688
40	Mesa, AZ	452,725
179	Mesquite, TX	133,964
329	Miami Beach, FL	87,990
226	Miami Gardens, FL	110,130
41	Miami, FL	440,482
227	Midland, TX	109,791
28	Milwaukee, WI	605,921
48	Minneapolis, MN	385,704
217	Miramar, FL	113,385
294	Mission Viejo, CA	94,679
NA	Mission, TX**	NA
73	Mobile, AL	255,178
103	Modesto, CA	203,890
102	Montgomery, AL	203,966
111	Moreno Valley, CA	197,294
230	Murfreesboro, TN	109,199
248	Murrieta, CA	104,343
352	Nampa, ID	84,179
404	Napa, CA	75,482
165	Naperville, IL	143,657
337	Nashua, NH	86,523
26	Nashville, TN	616,366
321	New Bedford, MA	89,613
195	New Haven, CT	124,856
51	New Orleans, LA	356,317
414	New Rochelle, NY	73,648
1	New York, NY	8,336,002
67	Newark, NJ	280,379
366	Newport Beach, CA	81,882
113	Newport News, VA	195,225
355	Newton, MA	83,781
80	Norfolk, VA	234,100
223	Norman, OK	111,534
277	North Charleston, SC	99,447
265	Norwalk, CA	102,221
348	Norwalk, CT	84,944
45	Oakland, CA	409,723
132	Oceanside, CA	173,901
268	Odessa, TX	101,580
367	O'Fallon, MO	81,851
371	Ogden, UT	81,431
30	Oklahoma City, OK	571,865
191	Olathe, KS	126,090
38	Omaha, NE	464,628
134	Ontario, CA	172,814
175	Orange, CA	137,606
300	Orem, UT	93,580
78	Orlando, FL	240,222

RANK	CITY	POP
126	Overland Park, KS	178,669
119	Oxnard, CA	189,051
256	Palm Bay, FL	103,350
157	Palmdale, CA	146,819
162	Pasadena, CA	144,496
159	Pasadena, TX	145,713
158	Paterson, NJ	146,356
313	Pearland, TX	91,679
156	Pembroke Pines, FL	147,343
143	Peoria, AZ	158,184
214	Peoria, IL	114,557
5	Philadelphia, PA	1,558,378
6	Phoenix, AZ	1,544,427
60	Pittsburgh, PA	312,737
68	Plano, TX	278,244
346	Plantation, FL	85,000
152	Pomona, CA	152,673
259	Pompano Beach, FL	102,749
140	Port St. Lucie, FL	163,089
31	Portland, OR	564,392
276	Portsmouth, VA	99,576
206	Provo, UT	117,734
253	Pueblo, CO	103,612
317	Quincy, MA	90,304
365	Racine, WI	82,059
44	Raleigh, NC	419,700
393	Ramapo, NY	77,482
128	Rancho Cucamon., CA	176,686
372	Reading, PA	81,370
316	Redding, CA	91,414
412	Redwood City, CA	74,355
90	Reno, NV	222,242
431	Renton, WA	62,968
280	Rialto, CA	99,232
252	Richardson, TX	104,051
254	Richmond, CA	103,442
99	Richmond, VA	205,883
334	Rio Rancho, NM	87,608
61	Riverside, CA	301,859
293	Roanoke, VA	94,795
245	Rochester, MN	105,027
104	Rochester, NY	203,802
146	Rockford, IL	156,180
205	Roseville, CA	119,755
345	Roswell, GA	85,461
224	Round Rock, TX	111,099
37	Sacramento, CA	472,469
147	Salem, OR	155,820
163	Salinas, CA	144,242
127	Salt Lake City, UT	177,873
310	San Angelo, TX	92,234
8	San Antonio, TX	1,392,198
110	San Bernardino, CA	199,214
9	San Diego, CA	1,313,433
15	San Francisco, CA	818,594
11	San Jose, CA	970,252
386	San Leandro, CA	78,447
356	San Marcos, CA	83,671
303	San Mateo, CA	92,724
361	Sandy Springs, GA	82,898
291	Sandy, UT	95,173
54	Santa Ana, CA	340,240
341	Santa Barbara, CA	85,967
218	Santa Clara, CA	112,917
136	Santa Clarita, CA	170,458
331	Santa Maria, CA	87,803
330	Santa Monica, CA	87,817
144	Santa Rosa, CA	158,182
95	Savannah, GA	210,744
85	Scottsdale, AZ	230,496
426	Scranton, PA	71,920
25	Seattle, WA	620,195
107	Shreveport, LA	199,900
202	Simi Valley, CA	121,755

RANK	CITY	POP
358	Sioux City, IA	83,494
141	Sioux Falls, SD	160,679
403	Somerville, MA	75,585
250	South Bend, IN	104,182
288	South Gate, CA	96,182
315	Sparks, NV	91,433
332	Spokane Valley, WA	87,780
105	Spokane, WA	203,272
208	Springfield, IL	117,383
148	Springfield, MA	154,314
145	Springfield, MO	157,110
198	Stamford, CT	122,933
190	Sterling Heights, MI	126,291
63	Stockton, CA	292,047
399	St. Joseph, MO	75,922
52	St. Louis, MO	355,151
66	St. Paul, MN	281,166
76	St. Petersburg, FL	243,666
339	Suffolk, VA	86,226
359	Sugar Land, TX	83,368
178	Sunnyvale, CA	134,073
318	Sunrise, FL	90,016
308	Surprise, AZ	92,294
176	Syracuse, NY	136,284
108	Tacoma, WA	199,595
129	Tallahassee, FL	174,516
53	Tampa, FL	347,830
264	Temecula, CA	102,474
133	Tempe, AZ	173,004
204	Thornton, CO	119,989
196	Thousand Oaks, CA	124,042
59	Toledo, OH	315,647
284	Toms River Twnshp, NJ	98,282
193	Topeka, KS	125,306
170	Torrance, CA	140,411
369	Tracy, CA	81,712
357	Trenton, NJ	83,552
379	Troy, MI	79,794
34	Tucson, AZ	527,107
47	Tulsa, OK	393,412
290	Tuscaloosa, AL	95,570
420	Tustin, CA	72,982
274	Tyler, TX	100,125
383	Upper Darby Twnshp, PA	79,046
311	Vacaville, CA	92,177
215	Vallejo, CA	114,258
137	Vancouver, WA	167,264
247	Ventura, CA	104,661
209	Victorville, CA	117,057
42	Virginia Beach, VA	435,873
194	Visalia, CA	125,036
302	Vista, CA	92,765
187	Waco, TX	127,039
181	Warren, MI	132,266
349	Warwick, RI	84,568
29	Washington, DC	601,723
232	Waterbury, CT	108,489
243	West Covina, CA	105,395
246	West Jordan, UT	104,783
270	West Palm Beach, FL	101,267
197	West Valley, UT	123,089
402	Westland, MI	75,726
322	Westminster, CA	89,604
234	Westminster, CO	108,383
370	Whittier, CA	81,611
271	Wichita Falls, TX	100,716
50	Wichita, KS	376,880
261	Wilmington, NC	102,649
82	Winston-Salem, NC	232,928
283	Woodbridge Twnshp, NJ	98,576
124	Worcester, MA	181,908
342	Yakima, WA	85,802
109	Yonkers, NY	199,296
328	Yuma, AZ	88,291

Source: Reported data from the F.B.I. "Crime in the United States 2011"
*Estimates as of July 2010 based on U.S. Bureau of the Census figures. Charlotte, Honolulu, Indianapolis, Las Vegas, Louisville, Mobile, and Savannah include areas under their police department but outside the city limits. All populations are for area covered by police department.

Metropolitan and City Populations

Rank Order - City

89. City Population in 2010 (continued)
National Total = 309,330,219*

RANK	CITY	POP
1	New York, NY	8,336,002
2	Los Angeles, CA	3,841,707
3	Chicago, IL	2,833,649
4	Houston, TX	2,280,859
5	Philadelphia, PA	1,558,378
6	Phoenix, AZ	1,544,427
7	Las Vegas, NV	1,416,401
8	San Antonio, TX	1,392,198
9	San Diego, CA	1,313,433
10	Dallas, TX	1,306,775
11	San Jose, CA	970,252
12	Detroit, MI	899,447
13	Indianapolis, IN	825,072
14	Jacksonville, FL	822,414
15	San Francisco, CA	818,594
16	Charlotte, NC	797,733
17	Austin, TX	796,310
18	Columbus, OH	772,974
19	Fort Worth, TX	746,433
20	Memphis, TN	673,650
21	Boston, MA	644,064
22	Baltimore, MD	639,929
23	Louisville, KY	637,428
24	El Paso, TX	624,322
25	Seattle, WA	620,195
26	Nashville, TN	616,366
27	Denver, CO	607,051
28	Milwaukee, WI	605,921
29	Washington, DC	601,723
30	Oklahoma City, OK	571,865
31	Portland, OR	564,392
32	Albuquerque, NM	545,389
33	Atlanta, GA	536,472
34	Tucson, AZ	527,107
35	Fresno, CA	484,734
36	Kansas City, MO	483,191
37	Sacramento, CA	472,469
38	Omaha, NE	464,628
39	Long Beach, CA	462,267
40	Mesa, AZ	452,725
41	Miami, FL	440,482
42	Virginia Beach, VA	435,873
43	Cleveland, OH	426,042
44	Raleigh, NC	419,700
45	Oakland, CA	409,723
46	Colorado Springs, CO	397,886
47	Tulsa, OK	393,412
48	Minneapolis, MN	385,704
49	Arlington, TX	383,715
50	Wichita, KS	376,880
51	New Orleans, LA	356,317
52	St. Louis, MO	355,151
53	Tampa, FL	347,830
54	Santa Ana, CA	340,240
55	Anaheim, CA	338,492
56	Bakersfield, CA	333,458
57	Cincinnati, OH	332,365
58	Aurora, CO	323,483
59	Toledo, OH	315,647
60	Pittsburgh, PA	312,737
61	Riverside, CA	301,859
62	Lexington, KY	300,069
63	Stockton, CA	292,047
64	Anchorage, AK	290,334
65	Corpus Christi, TX	287,559
66	St. Paul, MN	281,166
67	Newark, NJ	280,379
68	Plano, TX	278,244
69	Buffalo, NY	265,128
70	Henderson, NV	264,280
71	Lincoln, NE	259,672
72	Fort Wayne, IN	257,009
73	Mobile, AL	255,178
74	Glendale, AZ	245,387
75	Jersey City, NJ	244,201
76	St. Petersburg, FL	243,666
77	Chandler, AZ	241,826
78	Orlando, FL	240,222
79	Madison, WI	238,224
80	Norfolk, VA	234,100
81	Durham, NC	233,790
82	Winston-Salem, NC	232,928
83	Birmingham, AL	231,009
84	Laredo, TX	230,674
85	Scottsdale, AZ	230,496
86	Chula Vista, CA	229,060
87	Lubbock, TX	227,867
88	Baton Rouge, LA	226,001
89	Chesapeake, VA	225,627
90	Reno, NV	222,242
91	Garland, TX	221,921
92	Hialeah, FL	217,995
93	Irvine, CA	217,193
94	Gilbert, AZ	215,215
95	Savannah, GA	210,744
96	Fayetteville, NC	208,263
97	Irving, TX	206,308
98	Boise, ID	205,902
99	Richmond, VA	205,883
100	Akron, OH	205,760
101	Fremont, CA	205,477
102	Montgomery, AL	203,966
103	Modesto, CA	203,890
104	Rochester, NY	203,802
105	Spokane, WA	203,272
106	Des Moines, IA	202,564
107	Shreveport, LA	199,900
108	Tacoma, WA	199,595
109	Yonkers, NY	199,296
110	San Bernardino, CA	199,214
111	Moreno Valley, CA	197,294
112	Glendale, CA	196,877
113	Newport News, VA	195,225
114	Huntington Beach, CA	193,545
115	Little Rock, AR	192,922
116	Fontana, CA	192,595
117	Grand Rapids, MI	191,566
118	Amarillo, TX	190,393
119	Oxnard, CA	189,051
120	Fort Lauderdale, FL	186,170
121	Knoxville, TN	185,554
122	Columbus, GA	184,576
123	Huntsville, AL	183,357
124	Worcester, MA	181,908
125	Brownsville, TX	180,040
126	Overland Park, KS	178,669
127	Salt Lake City, UT	177,873
128	Rancho Cucamon., CA	176,686
129	Tallahassee, FL	174,516
130	Aurora, IL	174,255
131	Jackson, MS	174,153
132	Oceanside, CA	173,901
133	Tempe, AZ	173,004
134	Ontario, CA	172,814
135	Chattanooga, TN	172,460
136	Santa Clarita, CA	170,458
137	Vancouver, WA	167,264
138	Grand Prairie, TX	166,866
139	Garden Grove, CA	166,287
140	Port St. Lucie, FL	163,089
141	Sioux Falls, SD	160,679
142	Cape Coral, FL	160,432
143	Peoria, AZ	158,184
144	Santa Rosa, CA	158,182
145	Springfield, MO	157,110
146	Rockford, IL	156,180
147	Salem, OR	155,820
148	Springfield, MA	154,314
149	Corona, CA	153,311
150	Eugene, OR	153,269
151	Alexandria, VA	152,801
152	Pomona, CA	152,673
153	Dayton, OH	152,319
154	Joliet, IL	150,723
155	Lancaster, CA	148,632
156	Pembroke Pines, FL	147,343
157	Palmdale, CA	146,819
158	Paterson, NJ	146,356
159	Pasadena, TX	145,713
160	Hampton, VA	144,545
161	Hayward, CA	144,509
162	Pasadena, CA	144,496
163	Salinas, CA	144,242
164	Kansas City, KS	143,867
165	Naperville, IL	143,657
166	Hollywood, FL	142,793
167	Elk Grove, CA	142,330
168	Cary, NC	141,461
169	Escondido, CA	140,662
170	Torrance, CA	140,411
171	Lakewood, CO	139,615
172	Bridgeport, CT	138,810
173	Fort Collins, CO	138,689
174	McKinney, TX	138,306
175	Orange, CA	137,606
176	Syracuse, NY	136,284
177	McAllen, TX	134,623
178	Sunnyvale, CA	134,073
179	Mesquite, TX	133,964
180	Fullerton, CA	133,139
181	Warren, MI	132,266
182	Carrollton, TX	130,862
183	Cedar Rapids, IA	129,605
184	Bellevue, WA	127,735
185	Denton, TX	127,251
186	Coral Springs, FL	127,113
187	Waco, TX	127,039
188	Clarksville, TN	126,548
189	Elizabeth, NJ	126,494
190	Sterling Heights, MI	126,291
191	Olathe, KS	126,090
192	Hartford, CT	125,626
193	Topeka, KS	125,306
194	Visalia, CA	125,036
195	New Haven, CT	124,856
196	Thousand Oaks, CA	124,042
197	West Valley, UT	123,089
198	Stamford, CT	122,933
199	Killeen, TX	122,557
200	Concord, CA	122,119
201	El Monte, CA	121,884
202	Simi Valley, CA	121,755
203	Independence, MO	121,141
204	Thornton, CO	119,989
205	Roseville, CA	119,755
206	Provo, UT	117,734
207	Charleston, SC	117,551
208	Springfield, IL	117,383
209	Victorville, CA	117,057
210	Abilene, TX	116,938
211	Gainesville, FL	116,880
212	Evansville, IN	116,541
213	Lafayette, LA	115,378
214	Peoria, IL	114,557
215	Vallejo, CA	114,258
216	Frisco, TX	113,686

Rank Order - City (continued)

RANK	CITY	POP
217	Miramar, FL	113,385
218	Santa Clara, CA	112,917
219	Athens-Clarke, GA	112,851
220	Lansing, MI	112,254
221	Inglewood, CA	112,100
222	Ann Arbor, MI	111,745
223	Norman, OK	111,534
224	Round Rock, TX	111,099
225	Costa Mesa, CA	110,424
226	Miami Gardens, FL	110,130
227	Midland, TX	109,791
228	Beaumont, TX	109,430
229	Flint, MI	109,245
230	Murfreesboro, TN	109,199
231	Amherst, NY	109,138
232	Waterbury, CT	108,489
233	Allentown, PA	108,473
234	Westminster, CO	108,383
235	Cambridge, MA	108,356
236	Manchester, NH	108,101
237	Billings, MT	108,039
238	Lewisville, TX	107,968
239	Elgin, IL	107,731
240	Arvada, CO	107,227
241	Downey, CA	106,992
242	Clearwater, FL	105,647
243	West Covina, CA	105,395
244	High Point, NC	105,278
245	Rochester, MN	105,027
246	West Jordan, UT	104,783
247	Ventura, CA	104,661
248	Murrieta, CA	104,343
249	Fairfield, CA	104,202
250	South Bend, IN	104,182
251	Erie, PA	104,077
252	Richardson, TX	104,051
253	Pueblo, CO	103,612
254	Richmond, CA	103,442
255	Columbia, MO	103,417
256	Palm Bay, FL	103,350
257	Burbank, CA	103,304
258	Lowell, MA	103,065
259	Pompano Beach, FL	102,749
260	Berkeley, CA	102,700
261	Wilmington, NC	102,649
262	Davenport, IA	102,628
263	Gresham, OR	102,540
264	Temecula, CA	102,474
265	Norwalk, CA	102,221
266	Antioch, CA	102,125
267	Daly City, CA	101,939
268	Odessa, TX	101,580
269	Green Bay, WI	101,320
270	West Palm Beach, FL	101,267
271	Wichita Falls, TX	100,716
272	Carlsbad, CA	100,461
273	Edison Twnshp, NJ	100,395
274	Tyler, TX	100,125
275	Fargo, ND	99,694
276	Portsmouth, VA	99,576
277	North Charleston, SC	99,447
278	Everett, WA	99,387
279	Boulder, CO	99,255
280	Rialto, CA	99,232
281	Kenosha, WI	98,961
282	Centennial, CO	98,902
283	Woodbridge Twnshp, NJ	98,576
284	Toms River Twnshp, NJ	98,282
285	Broken Arrow, OK	97,581
286	Hillsboro, OR	97,423
287	Las Cruces, NM	97,065
288	South Gate, CA	96,182
289	Clovis, CA	95,901
290	Tuscaloosa, AL	95,570
291	Sandy, UT	95,173
292	Clinton Twnshp, MI	95,167
293	Roanoke, VA	94,795
294	Mission Viejo, CA	94,679
295	Lakeland, FL	94,569
296	El Cajon, CA	94,311
297	Beaverton, OR	93,993
298	Lawrence, KS	93,945
299	Compton, CA	93,916
300	Orem, UT	93,580
301	Greeley, CO	92,804
302	Vista, CA	92,765
303	San Mateo, CA	92,724
304	Albany, NY	92,713
305	Davie, FL	92,661
306	Carson, CA	92,409
307	Brockton, MA	92,383
308	Surprise, AZ	92,294
309	Greece, NY	92,282
310	San Angelo, TX	92,234
311	Vacaville, CA	92,177
312	Lawton, OK	92,025
313	Pearland, TX	91,679
314	Hamilton Twnshp, NJ	91,439
315	Sparks, NV	91,433
316	Redding, CA	91,414
317	Quincy, MA	90,304
318	Sunrise, FL	90,016
319	Fall River, MA	89,741
320	Indio, CA	89,621
321	New Bedford, MA	89,613
322	Westminster, CA	89,604
323	Allen, TX	89,459
324	Macon, GA	89,125
325	Longmont, CO	88,913
326	Hesperia, CA	88,876
327	College Station, TX	88,416
328	Yuma, AZ	88,291
329	Miami Beach, FL	87,990
330	Santa Monica, CA	87,817
331	Santa Maria, CA	87,803
332	Spokane Valley, WA	87,780
333	Lee's Summit, MO	87,707
334	Rio Rancho, NM	87,608
335	Livonia, MI	87,434
336	Boca Raton, FL	86,707
337	Nashua, NH	86,523
338	Lynn, MA	86,340
339	Suffolk, VA	86,226
340	Fort Smith, AR	86,096
341	Santa Barbara, CA	85,967
342	Yakima, WA	85,802
343	Kent, WA	85,768
344	Chico, CA	85,630
345	Roswell, GA	85,461
346	Plantation, FL	85,000
347	Alhambra, CA	84,987
348	Norwalk, CT	84,944
349	Warwick, RI	84,568
350	Citrus Heights, CA	84,476
351	Duluth, MN	84,249
352	Nampa, ID	84,179
353	Chino, CA	84,170
354	Hawthorne, CA	83,849
355	Newton, MA	83,781
356	San Marcos, CA	83,671
357	Trenton, NJ	83,552
358	Sioux City, IA	83,494
359	Sugar Land, TX	83,368
360	Edmond, OK	83,337
361	Sandy Springs, GA	82,898
362	Bloomington, MN	82,715
363	Dearborn, MI	82,612
364	Avondale, AZ	82,580
365	Racine, WI	82,059
366	Newport Beach, CA	81,882
367	O'Fallon, MO	81,851
368	Livermore, CA	81,769
369	Tracy, CA	81,712
370	Whittier, CA	81,611
371	Ogden, UT	81,431
372	Reading, PA	81,370
373	Danbury, CT	81,242
374	Bellingham, WA	81,139
375	Champaign, IL	80,489
376	Cranston, RI	80,125
377	Canton Twnshp, MI	80,039
378	Buena Park, CA	79,929
379	Troy, MI	79,794
380	Brick Twnshp, NJ	79,569
381	Bend, OR	79,556
382	Camden, NJ	79,081
383	Upper Darby Twnshp, PA	79,046
384	Cicero, IL	78,746
385	Clifton, NJ	78,632
386	San Leandro, CA	78,447
387	Clarkstown, NY	78,365
388	Longview, TX	78,319
389	Lakewood, CA	77,901
390	Melbourne, FL	77,861
391	Farmington Hills, MI	77,646
392	Merced, CA	77,484
393	Ramapo, NY	77,482
394	Baldwin Park, CA	77,127
395	Colonie, NY	77,078
396	Asheville, NC	77,067
397	Cheektowaga, NY	76,671
398	Hammond, IN	76,216
399	St. Joseph, MO	75,922
400	Lake Forest, CA	75,780
401	Fishers, IN	75,734
402	Westland, MI	75,726
403	Somerville, MA	75,585
404	Napa, CA	75,482
405	Bryan, TX	75,350
406	Deerfield Beach, FL	75,195
407	Lynchburg, VA	75,137
408	Edinburg, TX	75,091
409	Decatur, IL	74,857
410	League City, TX	74,776
411	Hoover, AL	74,687
412	Redwood City, CA	74,355
413	Bloomington, IL	74,304
414	New Rochelle, NY	73,648
415	Bethlehem, PA	73,634
416	Medford, OR	73,525
417	Hemet, CA	73,111
418	Albany, GA	73,034
419	Largo, FL	73,019
420	Tustin, CA	72,982
421	Lakewood Twnshp, NJ	72,960
422	Meridian, ID	72,688
423	Brooklyn Park, MN	72,682
424	Bloomington, IN	72,286
425	Arlington Heights, IL	72,061
426	Scranton, PA	71,920
427	Carmel, IN	71,647
428	Lawrence, MA	69,679
429	Kennewick, WA	68,501
430	Concord, NC	68,461
431	Renton, WA	62,968
432	Johns Creek, GA	59,893
NA	Bellflower, CA**	NA
NA	Chino Hills, CA**	NA
NA	Gary, IN**	NA
NA	Menifee, CA**	NA
NA	Mission, TX**	NA

Source: Reported data from the F.B.I. "Crime in the United States 2011"
*Estimates as of July 2010 based on U.S. Bureau of the Census figures. Charlotte, Honolulu, Indianapolis, Las Vegas, Louisville, Mobile, and Savannah include areas under their police department but outside the city limits. All populations are for area covered by police department.

Alpha Order - City

90. City Population in 2007
National Total = 301,621,157*

RANK	CITY	POP
205	Abilene, TX	114,644
92	Akron, OH	208,701
399	Albany, GA	75,137
290	Albany, NY	93,916
33	Albuquerque, NM	513,124
170	Alexandria, VA	137,812
326	Alhambra, CA	87,729
228	Allentown, PA	107,397
380	Allen, TX	78,630
116	Amarillo, TX	187,234
216	Amherst, NY	111,622
54	Anaheim, CA	335,133
63	Anchorage, AK	284,142
215	Ann Arbor, MI	113,011
246	Antioch, CA	101,973
406	Arlington Heights, IL	73,802
47	Arlington, TX	372,073
233	Arvada, CO	105,197
412	Asheville, NC	72,907
212	Athens-Clarke, GA	113,389
34	Atlanta, GA	497,290
58	Aurora, CO	307,621
128	Aurora, IL	174,724
18	Austin, TX	716,817
353	Avondale, AZ	83,487
56	Bakersfield, CA	318,743
378	Baldwin Park, CA	78,943
21	Baltimore, MD	624,237
78	Baton Rouge, LA	228,446
223	Beaumont, TX	109,345
305	Beaverton, OR	91,184
195	Bellevue, WA	118,984
401	Bellflower, CA	74,544
396	Bellingham, WA	76,290
398	Bend, OR	75,185
248	Berkeley, CA	101,343
411	Bethlehem, PA	72,908
249	Billings, MT	101,342
80	Birmingham, AL	227,686
417	Bloomington, IL	71,770
424	Bloomington, IN	68,918
367	Bloomington, MN	80,218
330	Boca Raton, FL	86,868
103	Boise, ID	199,104
24	Boston, MA	591,855
306	Boulder, CO	91,047
383	Brick Twnshp, NJ	77,886
171	Bridgeport, CT	137,655
289	Brockton, MA	94,180
317	Broken Arrow, OK	89,463
419	Brooklyn Park, MN	70,112
123	Brownsville, TX	177,090
427	Bryan, TX	67,484
371	Buena Park, CA	79,890
65	Buffalo, NY	273,832
236	Burbank, CA	104,871
252	Cambridge, MA	101,161
377	Camden, NJ	78,967
323	Canton Twnshp, MI	88,126
138	Cape Coral, FL	159,936
285	Carlsbad, CA	95,056
433	Carmel, IN	62,037
188	Carrollton, TX	123,324
288	Carson, CA	94,359
207	Cary, NC	114,221
184	Cedar Rapids, IA	124,730
270	Centennial, CO	97,746
404	Champaign, IL	74,167
71	Chandler, AZ	250,868
222	Charleston, SC	109,382
17	Charlotte, NC	733,291
143	Chattanooga, TN	155,043

RANK	CITY	POP
375	Cheektowaga, NY	79,164
83	Chesapeake, VA	223,093
3	Chicago, IL	2,824,434
403	Chico, CA	74,288
391	Chino Hills, CA	76,484
363	Chino, CA	80,699
86	Chula Vista, CA	218,718
359	Cicero, IL	81,311
55	Cincinnati, OH	332,388
NA	Citrus Heights, CA**	NA
379	Clarkstown, NY	78,909
206	Clarksville, TN	114,582
227	Clearwater, FL	107,501
40	Cleveland, OH	439,888
374	Clifton, NJ	79,253
275	Clinton Twnshp, MI	96,948
295	Clovis, CA	92,592
400	College Station, TX	74,997
388	Colonie, NY	77,550
46	Colorado Springs, CO	374,112
283	Columbia, MO	95,595
114	Columbus, GA	188,944
15	Columbus, OH	735,981
280	Compton, CA	95,990
191	Concord, CA	122,202
431	Concord, NC	63,284
177	Coral Springs, FL	131,307
147	Corona, CA	153,518
62	Corpus Christi, TX	286,428
219	Costa Mesa, CA	109,835
362	Cranston, RI	80,724
10	Dallas, TX	1,239,104
255	Daly City, CA	100,632
370	Danbury, CT	79,893
258	Davenport, IA	99,631
328	Davie, FL	87,007
141	Dayton, OH	155,526
298	Dearborn, MI	91,748
393	Decatur, IL	76,383
392	Deerfield Beach, FL	76,469
210	Denton, TX	113,936
27	Denver, CO	573,387
110	Des Moines, IA	192,948
12	Detroit, MI	860,971
220	Downey, CA	109,642
345	Duluth, MN	83,932
91	Durham, NC	211,873
421	Edinburg, TX	69,708
260	Edison Twnshp, NJ	99,082
384	Edmond, OK	77,879
304	El Cajon, CA	91,302
186	El Monte, CA	124,182
23	El Paso, TX	616,029
243	Elgin, IL	102,960
182	Elizabeth, NJ	125,621
169	Elk Grove, CA	138,103
247	Erie, PA	101,812
175	Escondido, CA	133,429
153	Eugene, OR	147,458
204	Evansville, IN	114,985
262	Everett, WA	98,845
231	Fairfield, CA	106,098
301	Fall River, MA	91,413
314	Fargo, ND	89,998
372	Farmington Hills, MI	79,475
133	Fayetteville, NC	167,157
429	Fishers, IN	66,099
201	Flint, MI	116,024
124	Fontana, CA	176,490
178	Fort Collins, CO	130,935
115	Fort Lauderdale, FL	187,995
348	Fort Smith, AR	83,860

RANK	CITY	POP
73	Fort Wayne, IN	248,423
19	Fort Worth, TX	670,693
99	Fremont, CA	201,318
36	Fresno, CA	472,170
310	Frisco, TX	90,674
174	Fullerton, CA	133,855
225	Gainesville, FL	108,289
135	Garden Grove, CA	166,414
87	Garland, TX	218,236
273	Gary, IN	97,048
96	Gilbert, AZ	206,681
72	Glendale, AZ	250,444
101	Glendale, CA	200,049
139	Grand Prairie, TX	157,913
111	Grand Rapids, MI	192,376
294	Greece, NY	93,123
309	Greeley, CO	90,707
257	Green Bay, WI	100,010
268	Gresham, OR	98,089
312	Hamilton Twnshp, NJ	90,158
387	Hammond, IN	77,662
161	Hampton, VA	144,490
185	Hartford, CT	124,558
337	Hawthorne, CA	85,609
166	Hayward, CA	140,603
416	Hemet, CA	71,825
70	Henderson, NV	251,270
332	Hesperia, CA	86,750
88	Hialeah, FL	215,853
259	High Point, NC	99,297
311	Hillsboro, OR	90,439
155	Hollywood, FL	146,673
422	Hoover, AL	69,527
4	Houston, TX	2,169,544
109	Huntington Beach, CA	195,067
131	Huntsville, AL	169,391
224	Independence, MO	108,879
14	Indianapolis, IN	797,268
358	Indio, CA	81,909
203	Inglewood, CA	115,223
98	Irvine, CA	201,872
108	Irving, TX	196,676
13	Jacksonville, FL	797,350
127	Jackson, MS	175,525
76	Jersey City, NJ	240,718
NA	Johns Creek, GA**	NA
151	Joliet, IL	148,484
163	Kansas City, KS	143,371
39	Kansas City, MO	447,725
432	Kennewick, WA	63,147
274	Kenosha, WI	96,996
346	Kent, WA	83,929
239	Killeen, TX	104,188
119	Knoxville, TN	183,319
208	Lafayette, LA	114,212
395	Lake Forest, CA	76,359
307	Lakeland, FL	91,009
423	Lakewood Twnshp, NJ	69,298
368	Lakewood, CA	80,138
168	Lakewood, CO	139,407
162	Lancaster, CA	144,210
211	Lansing, MI	113,643
84	Laredo, TX	221,253
407	Largo, FL	73,789
324	Las Cruces, NM	87,958
7	Las Vegas, NV	1,341,156
313	Lawrence, KS	90,044
418	Lawrence, MA	70,462
331	Lawton, OK	86,864
425	League City, TX	68,743
351	Lee's Summit, MO	83,558
272	Lewisville, TX	97,184

Alpha Order - City (continued)

RANK	CITY	POP
66	Lexington, KY	272,815
75	Lincoln, NE	243,243
118	Little Rock, AR	184,594
366	Livermore, CA	80,253
279	Livonia, MI	96,261
35	Long Beach, CA	473,959
342	Longmont, CO	84,278
389	Longview, TX	77,003
2	Los Angeles, CA	3,870,487
22	Louisville, KY	624,030
244	Lowell, MA	102,918
90	Lubbock, TX	213,988
426	Lynchburg, VA	67,932
325	Lynn, MA	87,817
292	Macon, GA	93,205
81	Madison, WI	225,370
218	Manchester, NH	109,873
180	McAllen, TX	129,455
196	McKinney, TX	118,113
415	Medford, OR	71,969
386	Melbourne, FL	77,678
20	Memphis, TN	669,264
NA	Menifee, CA**	NA
381	Merced, CA	78,186
430	Meridian, ID	64,294
38	Mesa, AZ	454,576
176	Mesquite, TX	132,399
333	Miami Beach, FL	86,742
264	Miami Gardens, FL	98,762
43	Miami, FL	410,252
242	Midland, TX	103,118
28	Milwaukee, WI	572,938
48	Minneapolis, MN	371,240
209	Miramar, FL	114,029
284	Mission Viejo, CA	95,095
428	Mission, TX	66,216
69	Mobile, AL	253,842
94	Modesto, CA	208,067
97	Montgomery, AL	202,062
113	Moreno Valley, CA	190,248
278	Murfreesboro, TN	96,264
269	Murrieta, CA	98,051
364	Nampa, ID	80,397
397	Napa, CA	75,266
160	Naperville, IL	144,933
327	Nashua, NH	87,217
29	Nashville, TN	564,169
296	New Bedford, MA	92,373
187	New Haven, CT	124,034
85	New Orleans, LA	220,614
408	New Rochelle, NY	73,603
1	New York, NY	8,220,196
64	Newark, NJ	280,158
365	Newport Beach, CA	80,377
122	Newport News, VA	177,550
356	Newton, MA	82,731
79	Norfolk, VA	227,903
241	Norman, OK	103,721
321	North Charleston, SC	88,431
232	Norwalk, CA	105,330
340	Norwalk, CT	84,343
44	Oakland, CA	396,541
134	Oceanside, CA	166,424
281	Odessa, TX	95,839
390	O'Fallon, MO	76,542
382	Ogden, UT	78,160
30	Oklahoma City, OK	542,199
197	Olathe, KS	117,973
42	Omaha, NE	431,810
126	Ontario, CA	175,537
172	Orange, CA	135,818
297	Orem, UT	91,816
82	Orlando, FL	224,417

RANK	CITY	POP
132	Overland Park, KS	169,224
117	Oxnard, CA	186,367
254	Palm Bay, FL	100,666
165	Palmdale, CA	142,122
156	Pasadena, CA	145,553
158	Pasadena, TX	145,235
152	Paterson, NJ	148,049
410	Pearland, TX	73,190
148	Pembroke Pines, FL	151,817
154	Peoria, AZ	147,223
214	Peoria, IL	113,137
6	Philadelphia, PA	1,435,533
5	Phoenix, AZ	1,541,698
57	Pittsburgh, PA	312,179
68	Plano, TX	259,771
334	Plantation, FL	86,346
142	Pomona, CA	155,161
234	Pompano Beach, FL	104,989
146	Port St. Lucie, FL	154,036
31	Portland, OR	538,133
251	Portsmouth, VA	101,284
202	Provo, UT	115,264
240	Pueblo, CO	103,958
302	Quincy, MA	91,382
373	Racine, WI	79,285
49	Raleigh, NC	367,120
394	Ramapo, NY	76,371
121	Rancho Cucamon., CA	177,683
360	Reading, PA	81,168
303	Redding, CA	91,328
409	Redwood City, CA	73,435
89	Reno, NV	214,197
434	Renton, WA	59,656
256	Rialto, CA	100,451
253	Richardson, TX	100,933
245	Richmond, CA	102,471
112	Richmond, VA	191,785
402	Rio Rancho, NM	74,542
59	Riverside, CA	299,312
308	Roanoke, VA	90,894
267	Rochester, MN	98,287
95	Rochester, NY	206,686
140	Rockford, IL	155,713
217	Roseville, CA	111,497
318	Roswell, GA	88,879
271	Round Rock, TX	97,727
37	Sacramento, CA	460,546
145	Salem, OR	154,484
157	Salinas, CA	145,251
120	Salt Lake City, UT	178,449
322	San Angelo, TX	88,285
8	San Antonio, TX	1,316,882
100	San Bernardino, CA	200,810
9	San Diego, CA	1,261,196
16	San Francisco, CA	733,799
11	San Jose, CA	934,553
385	San Leandro, CA	77,785
369	San Marcos, CA	80,050
300	San Mateo, CA	91,441
335	Sandy Springs, GA	85,830
286	Sandy, UT	94,975
52	Santa Ana, CA	340,223
338	Santa Barbara, CA	85,142
221	Santa Clara, CA	109,420
130	Santa Clarita, CA	170,429
336	Santa Maria, CA	85,782
320	Santa Monica, CA	88,584
144	Santa Rosa, CA	154,953
93	Savannah, GA	208,116
77	Scottsdale, AZ	235,243
413	Scranton, PA	72,444
26	Seattle, WA	585,118
102	Shreveport, LA	199,811
189	Simi Valley, CA	122,677

RANK	CITY	POP
355	Sioux City, IA	82,942
159	Sioux Falls, SD	144,985
405	Somerville, MA	74,156
238	South Bend, IN	104,437
266	South Gate, CA	98,701
329	Sparks, NV	86,884
347	Spokane Valley, WA	83,928
105	Spokane, WA	198,272
198	Springfield, IL	117,185
149	Springfield, MA	151,074
150	Springfield, MO	150,488
194	Stamford, CT	119,510
181	Sterling Heights, MI	128,555
60	Stockton, CA	297,170
414	St. Joseph, MO	72,424
51	St. Louis, MO	348,197
67	St. Paul, MN	271,662
74	St. Petersburg, FL	248,069
350	Suffolk, VA	83,631
357	Sugar Land, TX	82,402
179	Sunnyvale, CA	130,326
299	Sunrise, FL	91,480
261	Surprise, AZ	98,965
167	Syracuse, NY	139,880
107	Tacoma, WA	196,909
137	Tallahassee, FL	159,943
53	Tampa, FL	337,220
291	Temecula, CA	93,665
129	Tempe, AZ	171,320
213	Thornton, CO	113,289
183	Thousand Oaks, CA	125,196
61	Toledo, OH	296,403
287	Toms River Twnshp, NJ	94,469
192	Topeka, KS	121,885
164	Torrance, CA	142,970
343	Tracy, CA	84,151
352	Trenton, NJ	83,551
361	Troy, MI	81,130
32	Tucson, AZ	523,299
45	Tulsa, OK	381,469
349	Tuscaloosa, AL	83,811
420	Tustin, CA	69,945
282	Tyler, TX	95,596
376	Upper Darby Twnshp, PA	79,020
293	Vacaville, CA	93,167
200	Vallejo, CA	116,763
136	Vancouver, WA	161,092
237	Ventura, CA	104,523
235	Victorville, CA	104,872
41	Virginia Beach, VA	435,943
199	Visalia, CA	116,766
315	Vista, CA	89,851
190	Waco, TX	122,514
173	Warren, MI	134,081
339	Warwick, RI	85,139
25	Washington, DC	588,292
229	Waterbury, CT	107,241
226	West Covina, CA	108,097
277	West Jordan, UT	96,681
250	West Palm Beach, FL	101,322
193	West Valley, UT	121,447
341	Westland, MI	84,293
316	Westminster, CA	89,700
230	Westminster, CO	106,383
344	Whittier, CA	84,038
265	Wichita Falls, TX	98,717
50	Wichita, KS	358,294
276	Wilmington, NC	96,913
104	Winston-Salem, NC	198,316
263	Woodbridge Twnshp, NJ	98,769
125	Worcester, MA	175,825
354	Yakima, WA	82,951
106	Yonkers, NY	198,071
319	Yuma, AZ	88,874

Source: Reported data from the F.B.I. "Crime in the United States 2011"
*Estimates as of July 2007 based on U.S. Bureau of the Census figures. Charlotte, Honolulu, Indianapolis, Las Vegas, Louisville, Mobile, and Savannah include areas under their police department but outside the city limits. All populations are for area covered by police department.

90. City Population in 2007 (continued)
National Total = 301,621,157*

RANK	CITY	POP
1	New York, NY	8,220,196
2	Los Angeles, CA	3,870,487
3	Chicago, IL	2,824,434
4	Houston, TX	2,169,544
5	Phoenix, AZ	1,541,698
6	Philadelphia, PA	1,435,533
7	Las Vegas, NV	1,341,156
8	San Antonio, TX	1,316,882
9	San Diego, CA	1,261,196
10	Dallas, TX	1,239,104
11	San Jose, CA	934,553
12	Detroit, MI	860,971
13	Jacksonville, FL	797,350
14	Indianapolis, IN	797,268
15	Columbus, OH	735,981
16	San Francisco, CA	733,799
17	Charlotte, NC	733,291
18	Austin, TX	716,817
19	Fort Worth, TX	670,693
20	Memphis, TN	669,264
21	Baltimore, MD	624,237
22	Louisville, KY	624,030
23	El Paso, TX	616,029
24	Boston, MA	591,855
25	Washington, DC	588,292
26	Seattle, WA	585,118
27	Denver, CO	573,387
28	Milwaukee, WI	572,938
29	Nashville, TN	564,169
30	Oklahoma City, OK	542,199
31	Portland, OR	538,133
32	Tucson, AZ	523,299
33	Albuquerque, NM	513,124
34	Atlanta, GA	497,290
35	Long Beach, CA	473,959
36	Fresno, CA	472,170
37	Sacramento, CA	460,546
38	Mesa, AZ	454,576
39	Kansas City, MO	447,725
40	Cleveland, OH	439,888
41	Virginia Beach, VA	435,943
42	Omaha, NE	431,810
43	Miami, FL	410,252
44	Oakland, CA	396,541
45	Tulsa, OK	381,469
46	Colorado Springs, CO	374,112
47	Arlington, TX	372,073
48	Minneapolis, MN	371,240
49	Raleigh, NC	367,120
50	Wichita, KS	358,294
51	St. Louis, MO	348,197
52	Santa Ana, CA	340,223
53	Tampa, FL	337,220
54	Anaheim, CA	335,133
55	Cincinnati, OH	332,388
56	Bakersfield, CA	318,743
57	Pittsburgh, PA	312,179
58	Aurora, CO	307,621
59	Riverside, CA	299,312
60	Stockton, CA	297,170
61	Toledo, OH	296,403
62	Corpus Christi, TX	286,428
63	Anchorage, AK	284,142
64	Newark, NJ	280,158
65	Buffalo, NY	273,832
66	Lexington, KY	272,815
67	St. Paul, MN	271,662
68	Plano, TX	259,771
69	Mobile, AL	253,842
70	Henderson, NV	251,270
71	Chandler, AZ	250,868
72	Glendale, AZ	250,444
73	Fort Wayne, IN	248,423
74	St. Petersburg, FL	248,069
75	Lincoln, NE	243,243
76	Jersey City, NJ	240,718
77	Scottsdale, AZ	235,243
78	Baton Rouge, LA	228,446
79	Norfolk, VA	227,903
80	Birmingham, AL	227,686
81	Madison, WI	225,370
82	Orlando, FL	224,417
83	Chesapeake, VA	223,093
84	Laredo, TX	221,253
85	New Orleans, LA	220,614
86	Chula Vista, CA	218,718
87	Garland, TX	218,236
88	Hialeah, FL	215,853
89	Reno, NV	214,197
90	Lubbock, TX	213,988
91	Durham, NC	211,873
92	Akron, OH	208,701
93	Savannah, GA	208,116
94	Modesto, CA	208,067
95	Rochester, NY	206,686
96	Gilbert, AZ	206,681
97	Montgomery, AL	202,062
98	Irvine, CA	201,872
99	Fremont, CA	201,318
100	San Bernardino, CA	200,810
101	Glendale, CA	200,049
102	Shreveport, LA	199,811
103	Boise, ID	199,104
104	Winston-Salem, NC	198,316
105	Spokane, WA	198,272
106	Yonkers, NY	198,071
107	Tacoma, WA	196,909
108	Irving, TX	196,676
109	Huntington Beach, CA	195,067
110	Des Moines, IA	192,948
111	Grand Rapids, MI	192,376
112	Richmond, VA	191,785
113	Moreno Valley, CA	190,248
114	Columbus, GA	188,944
115	Fort Lauderdale, FL	187,995
116	Amarillo, TX	187,234
117	Oxnard, CA	186,367
118	Little Rock, AR	184,594
119	Knoxville, TN	183,319
120	Salt Lake City, UT	178,449
121	Rancho Cucamon., CA	177,683
122	Newport News, VA	177,550
123	Brownsville, TX	177,090
124	Fontana, CA	176,490
125	Worcester, MA	175,825
126	Ontario, CA	175,537
127	Jackson, MS	175,525
128	Aurora, IL	174,724
129	Tempe, AZ	171,320
130	Santa Clarita, CA	170,429
131	Huntsville, AL	169,391
132	Overland Park, KS	169,224
133	Fayetteville, NC	167,157
134	Oceanside, CA	166,424
135	Garden Grove, CA	166,414
136	Vancouver, WA	161,092
137	Tallahassee, FL	159,943
138	Cape Coral, FL	159,936
139	Grand Prairie, TX	157,913
140	Rockford, IL	155,713
141	Dayton, OH	155,526
142	Pomona, CA	155,161
143	Chattanooga, TN	155,043
144	Santa Rosa, CA	154,953
145	Salem, OR	154,484
146	Port St. Lucie, FL	154,036
147	Corona, CA	153,518
148	Pembroke Pines, FL	151,817
149	Springfield, MA	151,074
150	Springfield, MO	150,488
151	Joliet, IL	148,484
152	Paterson, NJ	148,049
153	Eugene, OR	147,458
154	Peoria, AZ	147,223
155	Hollywood, FL	146,673
156	Pasadena, CA	145,553
157	Salinas, CA	145,251
158	Pasadena, TX	145,235
159	Sioux Falls, SD	144,985
160	Naperville, IL	144,933
161	Hampton, VA	144,490
162	Lancaster, CA	144,210
163	Kansas City, KS	143,371
164	Torrance, CA	142,970
165	Palmdale, CA	142,122
166	Hayward, CA	140,603
167	Syracuse, NY	139,880
168	Lakewood, CO	139,407
169	Elk Grove, CA	138,103
170	Alexandria, VA	137,812
171	Bridgeport, CT	137,655
172	Orange, CA	135,818
173	Warren, MI	134,081
174	Fullerton, CA	133,855
175	Escondido, CA	133,429
176	Mesquite, TX	132,399
177	Coral Springs, FL	131,307
178	Fort Collins, CO	130,935
179	Sunnyvale, CA	130,326
180	McAllen, TX	129,455
181	Sterling Heights, MI	128,555
182	Elizabeth, NJ	125,621
183	Thousand Oaks, CA	125,196
184	Cedar Rapids, IA	124,730
185	Hartford, CT	124,558
186	El Monte, CA	124,182
187	New Haven, CT	124,034
188	Carrollton, TX	123,324
189	Simi Valley, CA	122,677
190	Waco, TX	122,514
191	Concord, CA	122,202
192	Topeka, KS	121,885
193	West Valley, UT	121,447
194	Stamford, CT	119,510
195	Bellevue, WA	118,984
196	McKinney, TX	118,113
197	Olathe, KS	117,973
198	Springfield, IL	117,185
199	Visalia, CA	116,766
200	Vallejo, CA	116,763
201	Flint, MI	116,024
202	Provo, UT	115,264
203	Inglewood, CA	115,223
204	Evansville, IN	114,985
205	Abilene, TX	114,644
206	Clarksville, TN	114,582
207	Cary, NC	114,221
208	Lafayette, LA	114,212
209	Miramar, FL	114,029
210	Denton, TX	113,936
211	Lansing, MI	113,643
212	Athens-Clarke, GA	113,389
213	Thornton, CO	113,289
214	Peoria, IL	113,137
215	Ann Arbor, MI	113,011
216	Amherst, NY	111,622

Rank Order - City (continued)

RANK	CITY	POP
217	Roseville, CA	111,497
218	Manchester, NH	109,873
219	Costa Mesa, CA	109,835
220	Downey, CA	109,642
221	Santa Clara, CA	109,420
222	Charleston, SC	109,382
223	Beaumont, TX	109,345
224	Independence, MO	108,879
225	Gainesville, FL	108,289
226	West Covina, CA	108,097
227	Clearwater, FL	107,501
228	Allentown, PA	107,397
229	Waterbury, CT	107,241
230	Westminster, CO	106,383
231	Fairfield, CA	106,098
232	Norwalk, CA	105,330
233	Arvada, CO	105,197
234	Pompano Beach, FL	104,989
235	Victorville, CA	104,872
236	Burbank, CA	104,871
237	Ventura, CA	104,523
238	South Bend, IN	104,437
239	Killeen, TX	104,188
240	Pueblo, CO	103,958
241	Norman, OK	103,721
242	Midland, TX	103,118
243	Elgin, IL	102,960
244	Lowell, MA	102,918
245	Richmond, CA	102,471
246	Antioch, CA	101,973
247	Erie, PA	101,812
248	Berkeley, CA	101,343
249	Billings, MT	101,342
250	West Palm Beach, FL	101,322
251	Portsmouth, VA	101,284
252	Cambridge, MA	101,161
253	Richardson, TX	100,933
254	Palm Bay, FL	100,666
255	Daly City, CA	100,632
256	Rialto, CA	100,451
257	Green Bay, WI	100,010
258	Davenport, IA	99,631
259	High Point, NC	99,297
260	Edison Twnshp, NJ	99,082
261	Surprise, AZ	98,965
262	Everett, WA	98,845
263	Woodbridge Twnshp, NJ	98,769
264	Miami Gardens, FL	98,762
265	Wichita Falls, TX	98,717
266	South Gate, CA	98,701
267	Rochester, MN	98,287
268	Gresham, OR	98,089
269	Murrieta, CA	98,051
270	Centennial, CO	97,746
271	Round Rock, TX	97,727
272	Lewisville, TX	97,184
273	Gary, IN	97,048
274	Kenosha, WI	96,996
275	Clinton Twnshp, MI	96,948
276	Wilmington, NC	96,913
277	West Jordan, UT	96,681
278	Murfreesboro, TN	96,264
279	Livonia, MI	96,261
280	Compton, CA	95,990
281	Odessa, TX	95,839
282	Tyler, TX	95,596
283	Columbia, MO	95,595
284	Mission Viejo, CA	95,095
285	Carlsbad, CA	95,056
286	Sandy, UT	94,975
287	Toms River Twnshp, NJ	94,469
288	Carson, CA	94,359
289	Brockton, MA	94,180
290	Albany, NY	93,916
291	Temecula, CA	93,665
292	Macon, GA	93,205
293	Vacaville, CA	93,167
294	Greece, NY	93,123
295	Clovis, CA	92,592
296	New Bedford, MA	92,373
297	Orem, UT	91,816
298	Dearborn, MI	91,748
299	Sunrise, FL	91,480
300	San Mateo, CA	91,441
301	Fall River, MA	91,413
302	Quincy, MA	91,382
303	Redding, CA	91,328
304	El Cajon, CA	91,302
305	Beaverton, OR	91,184
306	Boulder, CO	91,047
307	Lakeland, FL	91,009
308	Roanoke, VA	90,894
309	Greeley, CO	90,707
310	Frisco, TX	90,674
311	Hillsboro, OR	90,439
312	Hamilton Twnshp, NJ	90,158
313	Lawrence, KS	90,044
314	Fargo, ND	89,998
315	Vista, CA	89,851
316	Westminster, CA	89,700
317	Broken Arrow, OK	89,463
318	Roswell, GA	88,879
319	Yuma, AZ	88,874
320	Santa Monica, CA	88,584
321	North Charleston, SC	88,431
322	San Angelo, TX	88,285
323	Canton Twnshp, MI	88,126
324	Las Cruces, NM	87,958
325	Lynn, MA	87,817
326	Alhambra, CA	87,729
327	Nashua, NH	87,217
328	Davie, FL	87,007
329	Sparks, NV	86,884
330	Boca Raton, FL	86,868
331	Lawton, OK	86,864
332	Hesperia, CA	86,750
333	Miami Beach, FL	86,742
334	Plantation, FL	86,346
335	Sandy Springs, GA	85,830
336	Santa Maria, CA	85,782
337	Hawthorne, CA	85,609
338	Santa Barbara, CA	85,142
339	Warwick, RI	85,139
340	Norwalk, CT	84,343
341	Westland, MI	84,293
342	Longmont, CO	84,278
343	Tracy, CA	84,151
344	Whittier, CA	84,038
345	Duluth, MN	83,932
346	Kent, WA	83,929
347	Spokane Valley, WA	83,928
348	Fort Smith, AR	83,860
349	Tuscaloosa, AL	83,811
350	Suffolk, VA	83,631
351	Lee's Summit, MO	83,558
352	Trenton, NJ	83,551
353	Avondale, AZ	83,487
354	Yakima, WA	82,951
355	Sioux City, IA	82,942
356	Newton, MA	82,731
357	Sugar Land, TX	82,402
358	Indio, CA	81,909
359	Cicero, IL	81,311
360	Reading, PA	81,168
361	Troy, MI	81,130
362	Cranston, RI	80,724
363	Chino, CA	80,699
364	Nampa, ID	80,397
365	Newport Beach, CA	80,377
366	Livermore, CA	80,253
367	Bloomington, MN	80,218
368	Lakewood, CA	80,138
369	San Marcos, CA	80,050
370	Danbury, CT	79,893
371	Buena Park, CA	79,890
372	Farmington Hills, MI	79,475
373	Racine, WI	79,285
374	Clifton, NJ	79,253
375	Cheektowaga, NY	79,164
376	Upper Darby Twnshp, PA	79,020
377	Camden, NJ	78,967
378	Baldwin Park, CA	78,943
379	Clarkstown, NY	78,909
380	Allen, TX	78,630
381	Merced, CA	78,186
382	Ogden, UT	78,160
383	Brick Twnshp, NJ	77,886
384	Edmond, OK	77,879
385	San Leandro, CA	77,785
386	Melbourne, FL	77,678
387	Hammond, IN	77,662
388	Colonie, NY	77,550
389	Longview, TX	77,003
390	O'Fallon, MO	76,542
391	Chino Hills, CA	76,484
392	Deerfield Beach, FL	76,469
393	Decatur, IL	76,383
394	Ramapo, NY	76,371
395	Lake Forest, CA	76,359
396	Bellingham, WA	76,290
397	Napa, CA	75,266
398	Bend, OR	75,185
399	Albany, GA	75,137
400	College Station, TX	74,997
401	Bellflower, CA	74,544
402	Rio Rancho, NM	74,542
403	Chico, CA	74,288
404	Champaign, IL	74,167
405	Somerville, MA	74,156
406	Arlington Heights, IL	73,802
407	Largo, FL	73,789
408	New Rochelle, NY	73,603
409	Redwood City, CA	73,435
410	Pearland, TX	73,190
411	Bethlehem, PA	72,908
412	Asheville, NC	72,907
413	Scranton, PA	72,444
414	St. Joseph, MO	72,424
415	Medford, OR	71,969
416	Hemet, CA	71,825
417	Bloomington, IL	71,770
418	Lawrence, MA	70,462
419	Brooklyn Park, MN	70,112
420	Tustin, CA	69,945
421	Edinburg, TX	69,708
422	Hoover, AL	69,527
423	Lakewood Twnshp, NJ	69,298
424	Bloomington, IN	68,918
425	League City, TX	68,743
426	Lynchburg, VA	67,932
427	Bryan, TX	67,484
428	Mission, TX	66,216
429	Fishers, IN	66,099
430	Meridian, ID	64,294
431	Concord, NC	63,284
432	Kennewick, WA	63,147
433	Carmel, IN	62,037
434	Renton, WA	59,656
NA	Citrus Heights, CA**	NA
NA	Johns Creek, GA**	NA
NA	Menifee, CA**	NA

Source: Reported data from the F.B.I. "Crime in the United States 2011"
*Estimates as of July 2007 based on U.S. Bureau of the Census figures. Charlotte, Honolulu, Indianapolis, Las Vegas, Louisville, Mobile, and Savannah include areas under their police department but outside the city limits. All populations are for area covered by police department.

Appendix

Descriptions of Metropolitan Areas in 2011............ 368
County Index: 2011............................. 375
National Crime Trends: 1992 to 2011................ 382

National, Metropolitan, and City Crime Statistics
    Summary: 2011 388

DESCRIPTIONS OF METROPOLITAN AREAS IN 2011

Note: The name of a Metropolitan Statistical Area (M.S.A.) and Metropolitan Division (M.D.) is subject to change based on the changing proportional size of the largest cities included within them. Percent changes are calculated in this book if the M.S.A. or M.D. has not substantially changed, despite the changes in name. In the tables in this book, some M.S.A. and M.D. names are abbreviated to preserve space.

Abilene, TX includes Callahan, Jones and Taylor counties

Akron, OH includes Portage and Summit counties

Albany, GA includes Baker, Dougherty, Lee, Terrell and Worth counties

Albany-Schenectady-Troy, NY includes Albany, Rensselaer, Saratoga, Schenectady and Schoharie counties

Albuquerque, NM includes Bernalillo, Sandoval, Torrance and Valencia counties

Alexandria, LA includes Grant and Rapides parishes

Allentown-Bethlehem-Easton, PA-NJ includes Warren, NJ, Carbon, PA, Lehigh, PA and Northampton, PA counties

Altoona, PA includes Blair County

Amarillo, TX includes Armstrong, Carson, Potter and Randall counties

Ames, IA includes Story County

Anchorage, AK includes Anchorage Municipality and Matanuska-Susitna Borough

Anderson, IN includes Madison County

Anderson, SC includes Anderson County

Ann Arbor, MI includes Washtenaw County

Anniston-Oxford, AL includes Calhoun County

Appleton, WI includes Calumet and Outagamie counties

Asheville, NC includes Buncombe, Haywood, Henderson and Madison counties

Athens-Clarke County, GA includes, Clarke, Madison, Oconee and Oglethorpe counties

Atlanta-Sandy Springs-Marietta, GA includes Barrow, Bartow, Butts, Carroll, Cherokee, Clayton, Cobb, Coweta, Dawson, DeKalb, Douglas, Fayette, Forsyth, Fulton, Gwinnett, Haralson, Heard, Henry, Jasper, Lamar, Meriwether, Newton, Paulding, Pickens, Pike, Rockdale, Spalding and Walton counties

Atlantic City, NJ includes Atlantic County

Auburn-Opelika, AL includes Lee County

Augusta-Richmond, GA-SC includes Burke, GA, Columbia, GA, McDuffie, GA, Richmond, GA and Aiken, SC and Edgefield, SC counties

Austin-Round Rock, TX includes Bastrop, Caldwell, Hays, Travis and Williamson counties

Bakersfield, CA includes Kern County

Baltimore-Towson, MD includes Anne Arundel, Baltimore, Carroll, Harford, Howard and Queen Anne's counties and Baltimore city

Bangor, ME includes Penobscot County

Barnstable Town, MA includes Barnstable County

Baton Rouge, LA includes Ascension, East Baton Rouge, East Feliciana, Iberville, Livingston, Pointe Coupee, St. Helena, West Baton Rouge and West Feliciana parishes

Battle Creek, MI includes Calhoun County

Bay City, MI includes Bay County

Beaumont-Port Arthur, TX includes Hardin, Jefferson and Orange counties

Bellingham, WA includes Whatcom County

Bend, OR includes Deschutes County

Bethesda, MD see Washington, DC

Billings, MT includes Carbon and Yellowstone counties

Binghamton, NY includes Broome and Tioga counties

Birmingham-Hoover, AL includes Bibb, Blount, Chilton, Jefferson, St. Clair, Shelby and Walker counties

Bismarck, ND includes Burleigh and Morton counties

Blacksburg-Christiansburg-Radford, VA includes Giles, Montgomery and Pulaski counties and Radford city

Bloomington, IN includes Greene, Monroe and Owen counties

Bloomington-Normal, IL includes McLean County

Boise City-Nampa, ID includes Ada, Boise, Canyon, Gem and Owyhee counties

Boston-Cambridge-Quincy, MA-NH includes:
- Boston-Quincy, MA Metropolitan Division includes Norfolk, Plymouth, and Suffolk counties
- Cambridge-Newton-Framingham, MA Metropolitan Division includes Middlesex County
- Peabody Metropolitan Division, MA includes Essex County
- Rockingham County-Strafford County Metropolitan Division includes Rockingham and Strafford counties

Boulder, CO includes Boulder County

Bowling Green, KY includes Edmonson and Warren counties

Bremerton-Silverdale, WA includes Kitsap County

Bridgeport-Stamford-Norwalk, CT includes Fairfield County

Brownsville-Harlingen, TX includes Cameron County

Brunswick, GA includes Brantley, Glynn and McIntosh counties

Buffalo-Niagara Falls, NY includes Erie and Niagara counties

Burlington, NC includes Alamance County

DESCRIPTIONS OF METROPOLITAN AREAS IN 2011 (continued)

Burlington-South Burlington, VT includes Chittenden, Franklin and Grand Isle counties

Cambridge, MA see Boston, MA

Camden, NJ see Philadelphia, PA

Canton-Massillon, OH includes Carroll and Stark counties

Cape Coral-Fort Myers, FL includes Lee County

Cape Girardeau-Jackson, MO-IL includes Alexander County, IL and Bollinger and Cape Girardeau Counties, MO

Carson City, NV includes Carson City

Casper, WY includes Natrona County

Cedar Rapids, IA includes Benton, Jones and Linn counties

Champaign-Urbana, IL includes Champaign, Ford and Piatt counties

Charleston, WV includes Boone, Clay, Kanawha, Lincoln and Putnam counties

Charleston-North Charleston-Summerville, SC includes Berkeley, Charleston and Dorchester counties

Charlotte-Gastonia-Concord, NC-SC includes Anson, Cabarrus, Gaston, Mecklenburg, Union and York, SC counties

Charlottesville, VA includes Albemarle, Fluvanna, Greene and Nelson counties and Charlottesville city

Chattanooga, TN-GA includes Catoosa, GA, Dade, GA, Walker, GA, Hamilton, TN, Marion, TN and Sequatchie, TN counties

Cheyenne, WY includes Laramie County

Chicago-Joliet-Naperville, IL-IN-WI includes:
- Chicago-Joliet-Naperville, IL Metropolitan Division includes Cook, DeKalb, DuPage, Grundy, Kane, Kendall, McHenry and Will counties,
- Gary, IN Metropolitan Division includes Jasper, Lake, Newton and Porter counties, and
- Lake County-Kenosha County, IL-WI Metropolitan Division includes Lake, IL and Kenosha, WI counties

Chico, CA includes Butte County

Cincinnati-Middletown, OH-KY-IN includes Dearborn, IN, Franklin, IN, Ohio, IN, Boone KY, Bracken KY, Campbell, KY, Gallatin, KY, Grant, KY, Kenton, KY, Pendleton, KY, Brown, OH, Butler, OH, Clermont, OH, Hamilton, OH and Warren, OH counties

Clarksville, TN-KY includes Christian, KY, Trigg, KY, Montgomery, TN and Stewart, TN counties

Cleveland, TN includes Bradley and Polk counties

Cleveland-Elyria-Mentor, OH includes Cuyahoga, Geauga, Lake, Lorain and Medina counties

Coeur d'Alene, ID includes Kootenai County

College Station-Bryan, TX includes Brazos, Burleson and Robertson counties

Colorado Springs, CO includes El Paso and Teller counties

Columbia, MO includes Boone and Howard counties

Columbia, SC includes Calhoun, Fairfield, Kershaw, Lexington, Richland and Saluda counties

Columbus, GA-AL includes Russell, AL, Chattahoochee, GA, Harris, GA, Marion, GA and Muscogee, GA counties

Columbus, IN includes Bartholomew County

Columbus, OH includes Delaware, Fairfield, Franklin, Licking, Madison, Morrow, Pickaway and Union counties

Corpus Christi, TX includes Aransas, Nueces and San Patricio counties

Corvallis, OR includes Benton County

Crestview-Fort Walton Beach, FL includes Okaloosa County

Cumberland, MD-WV includes Allegany, MD and Mineral, WV counties

Dallas-Fort Worth-Arlington, TX includes:
- Dallas-Plano-Irving, TX Metropolitan Division includes Collin, Dallas, Delta, Denton, Ellis, Hunt, Kaufman and Rockwall counties and
- Fort Worth-Arlington, TX Metropolitan Division includes Johnson, Parker, Tarrant and Wise counties

Dalton, GA includes Murray and Whitfield counties

Danville, IL includes Vermilion County

Danville, VA includes Pittsylvania County and Danville city

Davenport-Moline-Rock Island, IA-IL includes Henry, IL, Mercer, IL, Rock Island, IL and Scott, IA counties

Dayton, OH includes Greene, Miami, Montgomery and Preble counties

Decatur, AL includes Lawrence and Morgan counties

Decatur, IL includes Macon County

Deltona-Daytona Beach-Ormond Beach, FL includes Volusia County

Denver-Aurora, CO includes Adams, Arapahoe, Broomfield, Clear Creek, Denver, Douglas, Elbert, Gilpin, Jefferson and Park counties

Des Moines-West Des Moines, IA includes Dallas, Guthrie, Madison, Polk and Warren counties

Detroit-Warren-Livonia, MI includes:
- Detroit-Livonia-Dearborn, MI Metropolitan Division includes Wayne County and
- Warren-Farmington Hills-Troy, MI Metropolitan Division includes Lapeer, Livingston, Macomb, Oakland and St. Clair counties

Dothan, AL includes Geneva, Henry and Houston counties

Dover, DE includes Kent County

Dubuque, IA includes Dubuque County

Duluth, MN-WI includes Carlton, MN, St. Louis, MN and Douglas, WI counties

DESCRIPTIONS OF METROPOLITAN AREAS IN 2011 (continued)

Durham-Chapel Hill, NC includes Chatham, Durham, Orange and Person counties

Eau Claire, WI includes Chippewa and Eau Claire counties

Edison, NJ see New York, NY

El Centro, CA includes Imperial County

Elizabethtown, KY includes Hardin and Larue counties

Elkhart-Goshen, IN includes Elkhart County

Elmira, NY includes Chemung County

El Paso, TX includes El Paso County

Erie, PA includes Erie County

Essex County, MA see Boston, MA

Eugene-Springfield, OR includes Lane County

Evansville, IN-KY includes Gibson, IN, Posey, IN, Vanderburgh, IN, Warrick, IN, Henderson, KY and Webster, KY counties

Fairbanks, AK includes Fairbanks North Star Borough

Fargo, ND-MN includes Clay, MN and Cass, ND counties

Farmington, NM includes San Juan County

Fayetteville, NC includes Cumberland and Hoke counties

Fayetteville-Springdale-Rogers, AR-MO includes Benton, AR, Madison, AR, Washington, AR and McDonald, MO counties

Flagstaff, AZ includes Coconino County

Flint, MI includes Genesee County

Florence, SC includes Darlington and Florence counties

Florence-Muscle Shoals, AL includes Colbert and Lauderdale counties

Fond du Lac, WI includes Fond du Lac County

Fort Collins-Loveland, CO includes Larimer County

Fort Lauderdale, FL see Miami, FL

Fort Smith, AR-OK includes Crawford, AR, Franklin, AR, Sebastian, AR, Le Flore, OK and Sequoyah, OK counties

Fort Wayne, IN includes Allen, Wells and Whitley counties

Fort Worth, TX see Dallas, TX

Fresno, CA includes Fresno County

Gadsden, AL includes Etowah County

Gainesville, FL includes Alachua and Gilchrist counties

Gainesville, GA includes Hall County

Glens Falls, NY includes Warren and Washington counties

Goldsboro, NC includes Wayne County

Grand Forks, ND-MN includes Polk, MN and Grand Forks, ND counties

Grand Junction, CO includes Mesa County

Grand Rapids-Wyoming, MI includes Barry, Ionia, Kent and Newaygo counties

Great Falls, MT includes Cascade County

Greeley, CO includes Weld County

Green Bay, WI includes Brown, Kewaunee and Oconto counties

Greensboro-High Point, NC includes Guilford, Randolph and Rockingham counties

Greenville, NC includes Greene and Pitt counties

Greenville, SC includes Greenville, Laurens and Pickens counties

Gulfport-Biloxi, MS includes Hancock, Harrison and Stone counties

Hagerstown-Martinsburg, MD-WV includes Washington, MD, Berkeley, WV and Morgan, WV counties

Hanford-Corcoran, CA includes Kings County

Harrisburg-Carlisle, PA includes Cumberland, Dauphin and Perry counties

Harrisonburg, VA includes Rockingham County and Harrisonburg city

Hartford-West Hartford-East Hartford, CT includes Hartford, Middlesex and Tolland counties

Hattiesburg, MS includes Forrest, Lamar and Perry counties

Hickory-Lenoir-Morganton, NC includes Alexander, Burke, Caldwell and Catawba counties

Hinesville-Fort Stewart, GA includes Liberty and Long counties

Holland-Grand Haven, MI includes Ottawa County

Honolulu, HI includes Honolulu County

Hot Springs, AR includes Garland County

Houma-Bayou Cane-Thibodaux, LA includes Lafourche and Terrebonne parishes

Houston-Baytown-Sugar Land, TX includes Austin, Brazoria, Chambers, Fort Bend, Galveston, Harris, Liberty, Montgomery, San Jacinto and Waller counties

Huntington-Ashland, WV-KY-OH includes Boyd, KY, Greenup, KY, Lawrence, OH, Cabell, WV and Wayne, WV counties

Huntsville, AL includes Limestone and Madison counties

Idaho Falls, ID includes Bonneville and Jefferson counties

Indianapolis, IN includes Boone, Brown, Hamilton, Hancock, Hendricks, Johnson, Marion, Morgan, Putnam and Shelby counties

Iowa City, IA includes Johnson and Washington counties

Ithaca, NY includes Tompkins County

Jackson, MI includes Jackson County

Jackson, MS includes Copiah, Hinds, Madison, Rankin and Simpson counties

DESCRIPTIONS OF METROPOLITAN AREAS IN 2011 (continued)

Jackson, TN includes Chester and Madison counties

Jacksonville, FL includes Baker, Clay, Duval, Nassau and St. Johns counties

Jacksonville, NC includes Onslow County

Janesville, WI includes Rock County

Jefferson City, MO includes Callaway, Cole, Moniteau and Osage counties

Johnson City, TN includes Carter, Unicoi and Washington counties

Johnstown, PA includes Cambria County

Jonesboro, AR includes Craighead and Poinsett counties

Joplin, MO includes Jasper and Newton counties

Kalamazoo-Portage, MI includes Kalamazoo and Van Buren counties

Kankakee-Bradley, IL includes Kankakee County

Kansas City, MO-KS includes Franklin, KS, Johnson, KS, Leavenworth, KS, Linn, KS, Miami, KS, Wyandotte, KS, Bates, MO, Caldwell, MO, Cass, MO, Clay, MO, Clinton, MO, Jackson, MO, Lafayette, MO, Platte, MO and Ray, MO counties

Kennewick-Pasco-Richland, WA includes Benton and Franklin counties

Killeen-Temple-Fort Hood, TX includes Bell, Coryell and Lampasas counties

Kingsport-Bristol-Bristol, TN-VA includes Hawkins, TN, Sullivan, TN, Scott, VA, and Washington, VA counties and Bristol city, VA

Kingston, NY includes Ulster County

Knoxville, TN includes Anderson, Blount, Knox, Loudon and Union counties

Kokomo, IN includes Howard and Tipton counties

La Crosse, WI-MN includes Houston, MN and La Crosse, WI counties

Lafayette, IN includes Benton, Carroll and Tippecanoe counties

Lafayette, LA includes Lafayette and St. Martin parishes

Lake Charles, LA includes Calcasieu and Cameron parishes

Lake Havasu City-Kingman, AZ includes Mohave County

Lakeland, FL includes Polk County

Lancaster, PA includes Lancaster County

Lansing-East Lansing, MI includes Clinton, Eaton and Ingham counties

Laredo, TX includes Webb County

Las Cruces, NM includes Dona Ana County

Las Vegas-Paradise, NV includes Clark County

Lawrence, KS includes Douglas County

Lawton, OK includes Comanche County

Lebanon, PA includes Lebanon County

Lewiston, ID-WA includes Nez Perce, ID and Asotin, WA counties

Lewiston-Auburn, ME includes Androscoggin County

Lexington-Fayette, KY includes Bourbon, Clark, Fayette, Jessamine, Scott and Woodford counties

Lima, OH includes Allen County

Lincoln, NE includes Lancaster and Seward counties

Little Rock-North Little Rock, AR includes Faulkner, Grant, Lonoke, Perry, Pulaski and Saline counties

Logan, UT-ID includes Franklin, ID and Cache, UT counties

Longview, TX includes Gregg, Rusk and Upshur counties

Longview, WA includes Cowlitz County

Los Angeles-Long Beach-Santa Ana, CA includes:
- Los Angeles-Long Beach-Glendale, CA Metropolitan Division includes Los Angeles County and
- Santa Ana-Anaheim-Irvine, CA Metropolitan Division includes Orange County

Louisville, KY-IN includes Clark, IN, Floyd, IN, Harrison, IN, Washington, IN, Bullitt, KY, Henry, KY, Jefferson, KY, Meade, KY, Nelson, KY, Oldham, KY, Shelby, KY, Spencer, KY and Trimble, KY counties

Lubbock, TX includes Crosby and Lubbock counties

Lynchburg, VA includes Amherst, Appomattox, Bedford and Campbell counties and Bedford and Lynchburg cities

Macon, GA includes Bibb, Crawford, Jones, Monroe and Twiggs counties

Madera, CA includes Madera County

Madison, WI includes Columbia, Dane and Iowa counties

Manchester-Nashua, NH includes Hillsborough County

Manhattan, KS includes Geary, Pottawatomie, and Riley Counties

Mankato-North Mankato, MN includes Blue Earth and Nicollet Counties

Mansfield, OH includes Richland County

McAllen-Edinburg-Mission, TX includes Hidalgo County

Medford, OR includes Jackson County

Memphis, TN-MS-AR includes Crittenden, AR, DeSoto, MS, Marshall, MS, Tate, MS, Tunica, MS, Fayette, TN, Shelby, TN and Tipton, TN counties

Merced, CA includes Merced County

Miami-Fort Lauderdale-Miami Beach, FL includes:
- Fort Lauderdale-Pompano Beach-Deerfield Beach, FL Metropolitan Division includes Broward County,
- Miami-Miami Beach-Kendall, FL Metropolitan Division includes Miami-Dade County and
- West Palm Beach-Boca Raton-Boynton Beach, FL Metropolitan Division includes Palm Beach County

DESCRIPTIONS OF METROPOLITAN AREAS IN 2011 (continued)

Michigan City-La Porte, IN includes LaPorte County

Midland, TX includes Midland County

Milwaukee-Waukesha-West Allis, WI includes Milwaukee, Ozaukee, Washington and Waukesha counties

Minneapolis-St. Paul-Bloomington, MN-WI includes Anoka, MN, Carver, MN, Chisago, MN, Dakota, MN, Hennepin, MN, Isanti, MN, Ramsey, MN, Scott, MN, Sherburne, MN, Washington, MN, Wright, MN, Pierce, WI and St. Croix, WI counties

Missoula, MT includes Missoula County

Mobile, AL includes Mobile County

Modesto, CA includes Stanislaus County

Monroe, LA includes Ouachita and Union parishes

Monroe, MI includes Monroe County

Montgomery, AL includes Autauga, Elmore, Lowndes and Montgomery counties

Morgantown, WV includes Monongalia and Preston counties

Morristown, TN includes Grainger, Hamblen and Jefferson counties

Mount Vernon-Anacortes, WA includes Skagit County

Muncie, IN includes Delaware County

Muskegon-Norton Shores, MI includes Muskegon County

Myrtle Beach-Conway-North Myrtle Beach, SC includes Horry County

Napa, CA includes Napa County

Naples-Marco Island, FL includes Collier County

Nashville-Davidson-Murfreesboro, TN includes Cannon, Cheatham, Davidson, Dickson, Hickman, Macon, Robertson, Rutherford, Smith, Sumner, Trousdale, Williamson and Wilson counties

Nassau, NY see New York, NY

New Haven-Milford, CT includes New Haven County

New Orleans-Metairie-Kenner, LA includes Jefferson, Orleans, Plaquemines, St. Bernard, St. Charles, St. John the Baptist and St. Tammany parishes

New York-Northern New Jersey-Long Island, NY-NJ-PA includes:
- Edison, NJ, Metropolitan Division includes Middlesex, Monmouth, Ocean and Somerset counties,
- Nassau-Suffolk, NY Metropolitan Division includes Nassau and Suffolk counties,
- New York-White Plains-Wayne, NY-NJ Metropolitan Division includes Bergen, NJ, Hudson, NJ, Passaic, NJ, Bronx, NY, Kings, NY, New York, NY, Putnam, NY, Queens, NY, Richmond, NY, Rockland, NY and Westchester, NY counties and
- Newark-Union, NJ-PA Metropolitan Division includes Essex, NJ, Hunterdon, NJ, Morris, NJ Sussex, NJ, Union, NJ and Pike, PA counties

Niles-Benton Harbor, MI includes Berrien County

North Port-Bradenton-Sarasota, FL includes Manatee and Sarasota counties

Norwich-New London, CT includes New London County

Oakland, CA see San Francisco, CA

Ocala, FL includes Marion County

Ocean City, NJ includes Cape May County

Odessa, TX includes Ector County

Ogden-Clearfield, UT includes Davis, Morgan and Weber counties

Oklahoma City, OK includes Canadian, Cleveland, Grady, Lincoln, Logan, McClain and Oklahoma counties

Olympia, WA includes Thurston County

Omaha-Council Bluffs, NE-IA includes Harrison, IA, Mills, IA, Pottawattamie, IA, Cass, NE, Douglas, NE, Sarpy, NE, Saunders, NE and Washington, NE counties

Orlando, FL includes Lake, Orange, Osceola and Seminole counties

Oshkosh-Neenah, WI includes Winnebago County

Owensboro, KY includes Daviess, Hancock and McLean counties

Oxnard-Thousand Oaks-Ventura, CA includes Ventura County

Palm Bay-Melbourne-Titusville, FL includes Brevard County

Palm Coast, FL includes Flagler County

Panama City-Lynn Haven, FL includes Bay County

Parkersburg-Marietta-Vienna, WV-OH includes Washington, OH, Pleasants, WV, Wirt, WV and Wood, WV counties

Pascagoula, MS includes George and Jackson counties

Peabody, MA see Boston, MA

Pensacola-Ferry Pass-Brent, FL includes Escambia and Santa Rosa counties

Peoria, IL includes Marshall, Peoria, Stark, Tazewell and Woodford counties

Philadelphia-Camden-Wilmington, PA-NJ-DE-MD includes:
- Camden, NJ Metropolitan Division includes Burlington, Camden, and Gloucester counties,
- Philadelphia, PA Metropolitan Division includes Bucks, Chester, Delaware, Montgomery and Philadelphia counties and
- Wilmington, DE-MD-NJ Metropolitan Division includes New Castle, DE, Cecil, MD and Salem, NJ counties

Phoenix-Mesa-Scottsdale, AZ includes Maricopa and Pinal counties

Pine Bluff, AR includes Cleveland, Jefferson and Lincoln counties

Pittsburgh, PA includes Allegheny, Armstrong, Beaver, Butler, Fayette, Washington and Westmoreland counties

Pittsfield, MA includes Berkshire County

Pocatello, ID includes Bannock and Power counties

DESCRIPTIONS OF METROPOLITAN AREAS IN 2011 (continued)

Portland-South Portland-Biddeford, ME includes Cumberland, Sagadahoc and York counties

Portland-Vancouver-Beaverton, OR-WA includes Clackamas, Columbia, OR, Multnomah, OR, Washington, OR, Yamhill, OR, Clark, WA and Skamania, WA counties

Port St. Lucie, FL includes Martin and St. Lucie counties

Poughkeepsie-Newburgh-Middletown, NY includes Dutchess and Orange counties

Prescott, AZ includes Yavapai County

Providence-New Bedford-Fall River, RI-MA includes Bristol, MA, Bristol, RI, Kent, RI, Newport, RI, Providence, RI and Washington, RI counties

Provo-Orem, UT includes Juab and Utah counties

Pueblo, CO includes Pueblo County

Punta Gorda, FL includes Charlotte County

Racine, WI includes Racine County

Raleigh-Cary, NC includes Franklin, Johnston and Wake counties

Rapid City, SD includes Meade and Pennington counties

Reading, PA includes Berks County

Redding, CA includes Shasta County

Reno-Sparks, NV includes Storey and Washoe counties

Richmond, VA includes Amelia, Caroline, Charles city, Chesterfield, Cumberland, Dinwiddie, Goochland, Hanover, Henrico, King and Queen, King William, Louisa, New, Kent, Powhatan, Prince George and Sussex counties and Colonial Heights, Hopewell, Petersburg and Richmond cities

Riverside-San Bernardino-Ontario, CA includes Riverside and San Bernardino counties

Roanoke, VA includes Botetourt, Craig, Franklin and Roanoke counties and Roanoke and Salem cities

Rochester, MN includes Dodge, Olmsted and Wabasha counties

Rochester, NY includes Livingston, Monroe, Ontario, Orleans and Wayne counties

Rockford, IL includes Boone and Winnebago counties

Rockingham County, NH see Boston, MA

Rocky Mount, NC includes Edgecombe and Nash counties

Rome, GA includes Floyd County

Sacramento-Arden-Arcade-Roseville, CA includes El Dorado, Placer, Sacramento and Yolo counties

Saginaw-Saginaw Township North, MI includes Saginaw County

St. Cloud, MN includes Benton and Stearns counties

St. George, UT includes Washington County

St. Joseph, MO-KS includes Doniphan, KS, Andrew, MO, Buchanan, MO and DeKalb, MO counties

St. Louis, MO-IL includes, Bond, IL, Calhoun, IL, Clinton, IL, Jersey, IL, Macoupin, IL, Madison, IL, Monroe, IL, St. Clair, IL, Crawford, MO (pt.), Franklin, MO, Jefferson, MO, Lincoln, MO, St. Charles, MO, St. Louis, MO, Warren, MO and Washington, MO counties and St. Louis city, MO

Salem, OR includes Marion and Polk counties

Salinas, CA includes Monterey County

Salisbury, MD includes Somerset and Wicomico counties

Salt Lake City, UT includes Salt Lake, Summit and Tooele counties

San Angelo, TX includes Irion and Tom Green counties

San Antonio, TX includes Atascosa, Bandera, Bexar, Comal, Guadalupe, Kendall, Medina and Wilson counties

San Diego-Carlsbad-San Marcos, CA includes San Diego County

Sandusky, OH includes Erie County

San Francisco-Oakland-Fremont, CA includes:
- Oakland-Fremont-Hayward, CA Metropolitan Division includes Alameda and Contra Costa counties and
- San Francisco-San Mateo-Redwood City, CA Metropolitan Division includes Marin, San Francisco and San Mateo counties

San Jose-Sunnyvale-Santa Clara, CA includes San Benito and Santa Clara counties

San Luis Obispo-Paso Robles, CA includes San Luis Obispo County

Santa Ana, CA see Los Angeles, CA

Santa Barbara-Santa Maria-Goleta, CA includes Santa Barbara County

Santa Cruz-Watsonville, CA includes Santa Cruz County

Santa Fe, NM includes Santa Fe County

Santa Rosa-Petaluma, CA includes Sonoma County

Savannah, GA includes Bryan, Chatham and Effingham counties

Scranton--Wilkes-Barre, PA includes Lackawanna, Luzerne, Wyoming counties

Seattle-Tacoma-Bellevue, WA includes:
- Seattle-Bellevue-Everett, WA Metropolitan Division includes King and Snohomish counties and
- Tacoma, WA Metropolitan Division includes Pierce County

Sebastian-Vero Beach, FL includes Indian River County

Sheboygan, WI includes Sheboygan County

Sherman-Denison, TX includes Grayson County

Shreveport-Bossier City, LA includes Bossier, Caddo and De Soto parishes

DESCRIPTIONS OF METROPOLITAN AREAS IN 2011 (continued)

Sioux City, IA-NE-SD includes Woodbury, IA, Dakota, NE, Dixon, NE and Union, SD counties

Sioux Falls, SD includes Lincoln, McCook, Minnehaha and Turner counties

South Bend-Mishawaka, IN-MI includes St. Joseph, IN and Cass, MI counties

Spartanburg, SC includes Spartanburg County

Spokane, WA includes Spokane County

Springfield, IL includes Menard and Sangamon counties

Springfield, MA includes Franklin, Hampden and Hampshire counties

Springfield, MO includes Christian, Dallas, Greene, Polk and Webster counties

Springfield, OH includes Clark County

State College, PA includes Centre County

Steubenville-Weirton, OH-WV includes includes Jefferson, OH, Brooke, WV and Hancock, WV counties

Stockton, CA includes San Joaquin County

Sumter, SC includes Sumter County

Syracuse, NY includes Madison, Onondaga and Oswego counties

Tacoma, WA see Seattle, WA

Tallahassee, FL includes Gadsden, Jefferson, Leon and Wakulla counties

Tampa-St. Petersburg-Clearwater, FL includes Hernando, Hillsborough, Pasco and Pinellas counties

Terre Haute, IN includes Clay, Sullivan, Vermillion and Vigo counties

Texarkana, TX-Texarkana, AR includes Miller, AR and Bowie, TX counties

Toledo, OH includes Fulton, Lucas, Ottawa and Wood counties

Topeka, KS includes Jackson, Jefferson, Osage, Shawnee and Wabaunsee counties

Trenton-Ewing, NJ includes Mercer County

Tucson, AZ includes Pima County

Tulsa, OK includes Creek, Okmulgee, Osage, Pawnee, Rogers, Tulsa and Wagoner counties

Tuscaloosa, AL includes Greene, Hale and Tuscaloosa counties

Tyler, TX includes Smith County

Utica-Rome, NY includes Herkimer and Oneida counties

Valdosta, GA includes Brooks, Echols, Lanier and Lowndes counties

Vallejo-Fairfield, CA includes Solano County

Victoria, TX includes Calhoun, Goliad and Victoria counties

Vineland-Millville-Bridgeton, NJ includes Cumberland County

Virginia Beach-Norfolk-Newport News, VA-NC includes Currituck, NC, Gloucester, VA, Isle of Wight, VA, James city, VA, Mathews, VA, Surry, VA and York, VA counties and Chesapeake, VA, Hampton, VA, Newport News, VA, Norfolk, VA, Poquoson, VA, Portsmouth, VA, Suffolk, VA, Virginia Beach, VA and Williamsburg, VA cities

Visalia-Porterville, CA includes Tulare County

Waco, TX includes McLennan County

Warner Robins, GA includes Houston County

Warren, MI see Detroit, MI

Washington-Arlington-Alexandria, DC-VA-MD-WV includes:
- Bethesda-Frederick-Gaithersburg, MD Metropolitan Division includes Frederick and Montgomery counties,
- Washington-Arlington-Alexandria, DC-VA-MD-WV Metropolitan Division includes District of Columbia, DC and Calvert, MD, Charles, MD, Prince George's, MD, Arlington, VA, Clarke, VA, Fairfax, VA, Fauquier, VA, Loudoun, VA, Prince William, VA, Spotsylvania, VA, Stafford, VA and Warren, VA counties and

Alexandria, VA, Fairfax, VA, Falls Church, VA, Fredericksburg, VA, Manassas, VA and Manassas Park, VA cities and Jefferson WV County

Waterloo-Cedar Falls, IA includes Black Hawk, Bremer and Grundy counties

Wausau, WI includes Marathon County

Wenatchee, WA includes Chelan and Douglas counties

West Palm Beach, FL see Miami, FL

Wheeling, WV-OH includes Belmont, OH, Marshall, WV and Ohio, WV

Wichita, KS includes Butler, Harvey, Sedgwick and Sumner counties

Wichita Falls, TX includes Archer, Clay and Wichita counties

Williamsport, PA includes Lycoming County

Wilmington, DE see Philadelphia, PA

Wilmington, NC includes Brunswick, New Hanover and Pender counties

Winchester, VA-WV includes Frederick, VA County, Winchester city, VA and Hampshire, WV County

Winston-Salem, NC includes Davie, Forsyth, Stokes and Yadkin counties

Worcester, MA includes Worcester County

Yakima, WA includes Yakima County

York-Hanover, PA includes York County

Youngstown-Warren-Boardman, OH-PA includes Mahoning, OH, Trumbull, OH and Mercer, PA counties

Yuba City, CA includes Sutter and Yuba counties

Yuma, AZ includes Yuma County

COUNTY INDEX: 2011

COUNTY:	IS IN METROPOLITAN:	COUNTY:	IS IN METROPOLITAN:
Adams, CO	Denver-Aurora, CO	Boise, ID	Boise City-Nampa, ID
Ada, ID	Boise City-Nampa, ID	Bollinger, MO	Cape Girardeau-Jackson, MO-IL
Aiken, SC	Augusta-Richmond County, GA-SC	Bond, IL	St. Louis, MO-IL
Alachua, FL	Gainesville, FL	Bonneville, ID	Idaho Falls, ID
Alamance, NC	Burlington, NC	Boone, IL	Rockford, IL
Alameda, CA	San Francisco-Oakland-Fremont, CA	Boone, IN	Indianapolis, IN
Albany, NY	Albany-Schenectady-Troy, NY	Boone, KY	Cincinnati-Middletown, OH-KY-IN
Albemarle, VA	Charlottesville, VA	Boone, MO	Columbia, MO
Alexander, NC	Hickory-Lenoir-Morganton, NC	Boone, WV	Charleston, WV
Alexander, IL	Cape Girardeau-Jackson, MO-IL	Bossier, LA	Shreveport-Bossier City, LA
Alexandria city, VA	Washington, DC-VA-MD-WV	Botetourt, VA	Roanoke, VA
Allegany, MD	Cumberland, MD-WV	Boulder, CO	Boulder, CO
Allegheny, PA	Pittsburgh, PA	Bourbon, KY	Lexington-Fayette, KY
Allen, IN	Fort Wayne, IN	Bowie, TX	Texarkana, TX-Texarkana, AR
Allen, OH	Lima, OH	Boyd, KY	Huntington-Ashland, WV-KY-OH
Amelia, VA	Richmond, VA	Bracken, KY	Cincinnati-Middletown, OH-KY-IN
Amherst, VA	Lynchburg, VA	Bradley, TN	Cleveland, TN
Anchorage city, AK	Anchorage, AK	Brantley, GA	Brunswick, GA
Anderson, SC	Anderson, SC	Brazoria, TX	Houston-Baytown-Sugar Land, TX
Anderson, TN	Knoxville, TN	Brazos, TX	College Station-Bryan, TX
Andrew, MO	St. Joseph, MO-KS	Bremer, IA	Waterloo-Cedar Falls, IA
Androscoggin, ME	Lewiston-Auburn, ME	Brevard, FL	Palm Bay-Melbourne-Titusville, FL
Anne Arundel, MD	Baltimore-Towson, MD	Bristol city, VA	Kingsport-Bristol-Bristol, TN-VA
Anoka, MN	Minneapolis-St. Paul-Bloomington, MN-WI	Bristol, MA	Providence-New Bedford-Fall River, RI-MA
Anson, NC	Charlotte-Gastonia-Concord, NC-SC	Bristol, RI	Providence-New Bedford-Fall River, RI-MA
Appomattox, VA	Lynchburg, VA	Bronx, NY	New York, NY-NJ-PA
Aransas, TX	Corpus Christi, TX	Brooke, WV	Steubenville-Weirton, OH-WV
Arapahoe, CO	Denver-Aurora, CO	Brooks, GA	Valdosta, GA
Archer, TX	Wichita Falls, TX	Broome, NY	Binghamton, NY
Arlington, VA	Washington, DC-VA-MD-WV	Broomfield, CO	Denver-Aurora, CO
Armstrong, PA	Pittsburgh, PA	Broward, FL	Miami-Fort Lauderdale-Miami Beach, FL
Armstrong, TX	Amarillo, TX	Brown, IN	Indianapolis, IN
Ascension, LA	Baton Rouge, LA	Brown, OH	Cincinnati-Middletown, OH-KY-IN
Asotin, WA	Lewiston, ID-WA	Brown, WI	Green Bay, WI
Atascosa, TX	San Antonio, TX	Brunswick, NC	Wilmington, NC
Atlantic, NJ	Atlantic City, NJ	Bryan, GA	Savannah, GA
Austin, TX	Houston-Baytown-Sugar Land, TX	Buchanan, MO	St. Joseph, MO-KS
Autauga, AL	Montgomery, AL	Bucks, PA	Philadelphia, PA-NJ-DE-MD
Baker, FL	Jacksonville, FL	Bullitt, KY	Louisville, KY-IN
Baker, GA	Albany, GA	Buncombe, NC	Asheville, NC
Baltimore city, MD	Baltimore-Towson, MD	Burke, GA	Augusta-Richmond County, GA-SC
Baltimore, MD	Baltimore-Towson, MD	Burke, NC	Hickory-Lenoir-Morganton, NC
Bandera, TX	San Antonio, TX	Burleigh, ND	Bismarck, ND
Bannock, ID	Pocatello, ID	Burleson, TX	College Station-Bryan, TX
Barnstable, MA	Barnstable Town, MA	Burlington, NJ	Philadelphia, PA-NJ-DE-MD
Barrow, GA	Atlanta-Sandy Springs-Marietta, GA	Butler, KS	Wichita, KS
Barry, MI	Grand Rapids-Wyoming, MI	Butler, OH	Cincinnati-Middletown, OH-KY-IN
Bartholomew, IN	Columbus, IN	Butler, PA	Pittsburgh, PA
Bartow, GA	Atlanta-Sandy Springs-Marietta, GA	Butte, CA	Chico, CA
Bastrop, TX	Austin-Round Rock, TX	Butts, GA	Atlanta-Sandy Springs-Marietta, GA
Bates, MO	Kansas City, MO-KS	Cabarrus, NC	Charlotte-Gastonia-Concord, NC-SC
Bay, FL	Panama City-Lynn Haven, FL	Cabell, WV	Huntington-Ashland, WV-KY-OH
Bay, MI	Bay City, MI	Cache, UT	Logan, UT-ID
Beaver, PA	Pittsburgh, PA	Caddo, LA	Shreveport-Bossier City, LA
Bedford city, VA	Lynchburg, VA	Calcasieu, LA	Lake Charles, LA
Bedford, VA	Lynchburg, VA	Caldwell, MO	Kansas City, MO-KS
Bell, TX	Killeen-Temple-Fort Hood, TX	Caldwell, NC	Hickory-Lenoir-Morganton, NC
Belmont, OH	Wheeling, WV-OH	Caldwell, TX	Austin-Round Rock, TX
Benton, AR	Fayetteville-Springdale-Rogers, AR-MO	Calhoun, AL	Anniston-Oxford, AL
Benton, IA	Cedar Rapids, IA	Calhoun, IL	St. Louis, MO-IL
Benton, IN	Lafayette, IN	Calhoun, MI	Battle Creek, MI
Benton, MN	St. Cloud, MN	Calhoun, SC	Columbia, SC
Benton, OR	Corvallis, OR	Calhoun, TX	Victoria, TX
Benton, WA	Kennewick-Pasco-Richland, WA	Callahan, TX	Abilene, TX
Bergen, NJ	New York, NY-NJ-PA	Callaway, MO	Jefferson City, MO
Berkeley, SC	Charleston-North Charleston-Summerville, SC	Calumet, WI	Appleton, WI
Berkeley, WV	Hagerstown-Martinsburg, MD-WV	Calvert, MD	Washington, DC-VA-MD-WV
Berkshire, MA	Pittsfield, MA	Cambria, PA	Johnstown, PA
Berks, PA	Reading, PA	Camden, NJ	Philadelphia, PA-NJ-DE-MD
Bernalillo, NM	Albuquerque, NM	Cameron, LA	Lake Charles, LA
Berrien, MI	Niles-Benton Harbor, MI	Cameron, TX	Brownsville-Harlingen, TX
Bexar, TX	San Antonio, TX	Campbell, KY	Cincinnati-Middletown, OH-KY-IN
Bibb, AL	Birmingham-Hoover, AL	Campbell, VA	Lynchburg, VA
Bibb, GA	Macon, GA	Canadian, OK	Oklahoma City, OK
Black Hawk, IA	Waterloo-Cedar Falls, IA	Cannon, TN	Nashville-Davidson--Murfreesboro, TN
Blair, PA	Altoona, PA	Canyon, ID	Boise City-Nampa, ID
Blue Earth, MN	Mankato-North Mankato, MN	Cape May, NJ	Ocean City, NJ
Blount, AL	Birmingham-Hoover, AL	Cape Girardeau, MO	Cape Girardeau-Jackson, MO-IL
Blount, TN	Knoxville, TN	Carbon, MT	Billings, MT

COUNTY INDEX: 2011 (continued)

COUNTY:	IS IN METROPOLITAN:	COUNTY:	IS IN METROPOLITAN:
Carbon, PA	Allentown-Bethlehem-Easton, PA-NJ	Cook, IL	Chicago-Joliet-Naperville, IL-IN-WI
Carlton, MN	Duluth, MN-WI	Copiah, MS	Jackson, MS
Caroline, VA	Richmond, VA	Coryell, TX	Killeen-Temple-Fort Hood, TX
Carroll, GA	Atlanta-Sandy Springs-Marietta, GA	Coweta, GA	Atlanta-Sandy Springs-Marietta, GA
Carroll, IN	Lafayette, IN	Cowlitz, WA	Longview, WA
Carroll, MD	Baltimore-Towson, MD	Craighead, AR	Jonesboro, AR
Carroll, OH	Canton-Massillon, OH	Craig, VA	Roanoke, VA
Carson City, NV	Carson City, NV	Crawford, AR	Fort Smith, AR-OK
Carson, TX	Amarillo, TX	Crawford, GA	Macon, GA
Carter, TN	Johnson City, TN	Creek, OK	Tulsa, OK
Carver, MN	Minneapolis-St. Paul-Bloomington, MN-WI	Crittenden, AR	Memphis, TN-MS-AR
Cascade, MT	Great Falls, MT	Crosby, TX	Lubbock, TX
Cass, MI	South Bend-Mishawaka, IN-MI	Cumberland, ME	Portland-South Portland-Biddeford, ME
Cass, MO	Kansas City, MO-KS	Cumberland, NC	Fayetteville, NC
Cass, ND	Fargo, ND-MN	Cumberland, NJ	Vineland-Millville-Bridgeton, NJ
Cass, NE	Omaha-Council Bluffs, NE-IA	Cumberland, PA	Harrisburg-Carlisle, PA
Catawba, NC	Hickory-Lenoir-Morganton, NC	Cumberland, VA	Richmond, VA
Catoosa, GA	Chattanooga, TN-GA	Currituck, NC	Virginia Beach-Norfolk, VA-NC
Cecil, MD	Philadelphia, PA-NJ-DE-MD	Cuyahoga, OH	Cleveland-Elyria-Mentor, OH
Centre, PA	State College, PA	Dade, GA	Chattanooga, TN-GA
Chambers, TX	Houston-Baytown-Sugar Land, TX	Dakota, MN	Minneapolis-St. Paul-Bloomington, MN-WI
Champaign, IL	Champaign-Urbana, IL	Dakota, NE	Sioux City, IA-NE-SD
Charles City, VA	Richmond, VA	Dallas, IA	Des Moines-West Des Moines, IA
Charleston, SC	Charleston-North Charleston-Summerville, SC	Dallas, MO	Springfield, MO
Charles, MD	Washington, DC-VA-MD-WV	Dallas, TX	Dallas-Fort Worth-Arlington, TX
Charlottesville city, VA	Charlottesville, VA	Dane, WI	Madison, WI
Charlotte, FL	Punta Gorda, FL	Danville city, VA	Danville, VA
Chatham, GA	Savannah, GA	Darlington, SC	Florence, SC
Chatham, NC	Durham-Chapel Hill, NC	Dauphin, PA	Harrisburg-Carlisle, PA
Chattahoochee, GA	Columbus, GA-AL	Davidson, TN	Nashville-Davidson--Murfreesboro, TN
Cheatham, TN	Nashville-Davidson--Murfreesboro, TN	Daviess, KY	Owensboro, KY
Chelan, WA	Wenatchee, WA	Davie, NC	Winston-Salem, NC
Chemung, NY	Elmira, NY	Davis, UT	Ogden-Clearfield, UT
Cherokee, GA	Atlanta-Sandy Springs-Marietta, GA	Dawson, GA	Atlanta-Sandy Springs-Marietta, GA
Chesapeake city, VA	Virginia Beach-Norfolk, VA-NC	De Soto, LA	Shreveport-Bossier City, LA
Chesterfield, VA	Richmond, VA	Dearborn, IN	Cincinnati-Middletown, OH-KY-IN
Chester, PA	Philadelphia, PA-NJ-DE-MD	DeKalb, GA	Atlanta-Sandy Springs-Marietta, GA
Chester, TN	Jackson, TN	DeKalb, IL	Chicago-Joliet-Naperville, IL-IN-WI
Chilton, AL	Birmingham-Hoover, AL	DeKalb, MO	St. Joseph, MO-KS
Chippewa, WI	Eau Claire, WI	Delaware, IN	Muncie, IN
Chisago, MN	Minneapolis-St. Paul-Bloomington, MN-WI	Delaware, OH	Columbus, OH
Chittenden, VT	Burlington-South Burlington, VT	Delaware, PA	Philadelphia, PA-NJ-DE-MD
Christian, KY	Clarksville, TN-KY	Delta, TX	Dallas-Fort Worth-Arlington, TX
Christian, MO	Springfield, MO	Denton, TX	Dallas-Fort Worth-Arlington, TX
Clackamas, OR	Portland-Vancouver-Beaverton, OR-WA	Denver, CO	Denver-Aurora, CO
Clarke, GA	Athens-Clarke County, GA	Deschutes, OR	Bend, OR
Clarke, VA	Washington, DC-VA-MD-WV	DeSoto, MS	Memphis, TN-MS-AR
Clark, IN	Louisville, KY-IN	Dickson, TN	Nashville-Davidson--Murfreesboro, TN
Clark, KY	Lexington-Fayette, KY	Dinwiddie, VA	Richmond, VA
Clark, NV	Las Vegas-Paradise, NV	District of Columbia, DC	Washington, DC-VA-MD-WV
Clark, OH	Springfield, OH	Dixon, NE	Sioux City, IA-NE-SD
Clark, WA	Portland-Vancouver-Beaverton, OR-WA	Dodge, MN	Rochester, MN
Clayton, GA	Atlanta-Sandy Springs-Marietta, GA	Dona Ana, NM	Las Cruces, NM
Clay, FL	Jacksonville, FL	Doniphan, KS	St. Joseph, MO-KS
Clay, IN	Terre Haute, IN	Dorchester, SC	Charleston-North Charleston-Summerville, SC
Clay, MN	Fargo, ND-MN	Dougherty, GA	Albany, GA
Clay, MO	Kansas City, MO-KS	Douglas, CO	Denver-Aurora, CO
Clay, TX	Wichita Falls, TX	Douglas, GA	Atlanta-Sandy Springs-Marietta, GA
Clay, WV	Charleston, WV	Douglas, KS	Lawrence, KS
Clear Creek, CO	Denver-Aurora, CO	Douglas, NE	Omaha-Council Bluffs, NE-IA
Clermont, OH	Cincinnati-Middletown, OH-KY-IN	Douglas, WA	Wenatchee, WA
Cleveland, AR	Pine Bluff, AR	Douglas, WI	Duluth, MN-WI
Cleveland, OK	Oklahoma City, OK	Dubuque, IA	Dubuque, IA
Clinton, IL	St. Louis, MO-IL	DuPage, IL	Chicago-Joliet-Naperville, IL-IN-WI
Clinton, MI	Lansing-East Lansing, MI	Durham, NC	Durham-Chapel Hill, NC
Clinton, MO	Kansas City, MO-KS	Dutchess, NY	Poughkeepsie-Newburgh-Middletown, NY
Cobb, GA	Atlanta-Sandy Springs-Marietta, GA	Duval, FL	Jacksonville, FL
Coconino, AZ	Flagstaff, AZ	East Baton Rouge, LA	Baton Rouge, LA
Colbert, AL	Florence-Muscle Shoals, AL	East Feliciana, LA	Baton Rouge, LA
Cole, MO	Jefferson City, MO	Eaton, MI	Lansing-East Lansing, MI
Collier, FL	Naples-Marco Island, FL	Eau Claire, WI	Eau Claire, WI
Collin, TX	Dallas-Fort Worth-Arlington, TX	Echols, GA	Valdosta, GA
Colonial Heights city, VA	Richmond, VA	Ector, TX	Odessa, TX
Columbia, GA	Augusta-Richmond County, GA-SC	Edgecombe, NC	Rocky Mount, NC
Columbia, OR	Portland-Vancouver-Beaverton, OR-WA	Edgefield, SC	Augusta-Richmond County, GA-SC
Columbia, WI	Madison, WI	Edmonson, KY	Bowling Green, KY
Comal, TX	San Antonio, TX	Effingham, GA	Savannah, GA
Comanche, OK	Lawton, OK	El Dorado, CA	Sacramento--Arden-Arcade--Roseville, CA
Contra Costa, CA	San Francisco-Oakland-Fremont, CA	El Paso, CO	Colorado Springs, CO

COUNTY INDEX: 2011 (continued)

COUNTY:	IS IN METROPOLITAN:	COUNTY:	IS IN METROPOLITAN:
El Paso, TX	El Paso, TX	Grant, LA	Alexandria, LA
Elbert, CO	Denver-Aurora, CO	Grayson, TX	Sherman-Denison, TX
Elkhart, IN	Elkhart-Goshen, IN	Greene, AL	Tuscaloosa, AL
Ellis, TX	Dallas-Fort Worth-Arlington, TX	Greene, IN	Bloomington, IN
Elmore, AL	Montgomery, AL	Greene, MO	Springfield, MO
Erie, NY	Buffalo-Niagara Falls, NY	Greene, NC	Greenville, NC
Erie, OH	Sandusky, OH	Greene, OH	Dayton, OH
Erie, PA	Erie, PA	Greene, VA	Charlottesville, VA
Escambia, FL	Pensacola-Ferry Pass-Brent, FL	Greenup, KY	Huntington-Ashland, WV-KY-OH
Essex, MA	Boston-Cambridge-Quincy, MA-NH	Greenville, SC	Greenville, SC
Essex, NJ	New York, NY-NJ-PA	Gregg, TX	Longview, TX
Etowah, AL	Gadsden, AL	Grundy, IA	Waterloo-Cedar Falls, IA
Fairbanks North Star, AK	Fairbanks, AK	Grundy, IL	Chicago-Joliet-Naperville, IL-IN-WI
Fairfax city, VA	Washington, DC-VA-MD-WV	Guadalupe, TX	San Antonio, TX
Fairfax, VA	Washington, DC-VA-MD-WV	Guilford, NC	Greensboro-High Point, NC
Fairfield, CT	Bridgeport-Stamford-Norwalk, CT	Guthrie, IA	Des Moines-West Des Moines, IA
Fairfield, OH	Columbus, OH	Gwinnett, GA	Atlanta-Sandy Springs-Marietta, GA
Fairfield, SC	Columbia, SC	Hale, AL	Tuscaloosa, AL
Falls Church city, VA	Washington, DC-VA-MD-WV	Hall, GA	Gainesville, GA
Faulkner, AR	Little Rock-North Little Rock, AR	Hamblen, TN	Morristown, TN
Fauquier, VA	Washington, DC-VA-MD-WV	Hamilton, IN	Indianapolis, IN
Fayette, GA	Atlanta-Sandy Springs-Marietta, GA	Hamilton, OH	Cincinnati-Middletown, OH-KY-IN
Fayette, KY	Lexington-Fayette, KY	Hamilton, TN	Chattanooga, TN-GA
Fayette, PA	Pittsburgh, PA	Hampden, MA	Springfield, MA
Fayette, TN	Memphis, TN-MS-AR	Hampshire, MA	Springfield, MA
Flagler, FL	Palm Coast, FL	Hampshire, WV	Winchester, VA-WV
Florence, SC	Florence, SC	Hampton city, VA	Virginia Beach-Norfolk, VA-NC
Floyd, GA	Rome, GA	Hancock, IN	Indianapolis, IN
Floyd, IN	Louisville, KY-IN	Hancock, KY	Owensboro, KY
Fluvanna, VA	Charlottesville, VA	Hancock, MS	Gulfport-Biloxi, MS
Fond du Lac, WI	Fond du Lac, WI	Hancock, WV	Steubenville-Weirton, OH-WV
Ford, IL	Champaign-Urbana, IL	Hanover, VA	Richmond, VA
Forrest, MS	Hattiesburg, MS	Haralson, GA	Atlanta-Sandy Springs-Marietta, GA
Forsyth, GA	Atlanta-Sandy Springs-Marietta, GA	Hardin, KY	Elizabethtown, KY
Forsyth, NC	Winston-Salem, NC	Hardin, TX	Beaumont-Port Arthur, TX
Fort Bend, TX	Houston-Baytown-Sugar Land, TX	Harford, MD	Baltimore-Towson, MD
Franklin, AR	Fort Smith, AR-OK	Harrisonburg city, VA	Harrisonburg, VA
Franklin, ID	Logan, UT-ID	Harrison, IA	Omaha-Council Bluffs, NE-IA
Franklin, IN	Cincinnati-Middletown, OH-KY-IN	Harrison, IN	Louisville, KY-IN
Franklin, KS	Kansas City, MO-KS	Harrison, MS	Gulfport-Biloxi, MS
Franklin, MA	Springfield, MA	Harris, GA	Columbus, GA-AL
Franklin, MO	St. Louis, MO-IL	Harris, TX	Houston-Baytown-Sugar Land, TX
Franklin, NC	Raleigh-Cary, NC	Hartford, CT	Hartford-West Hartford-East Hartford, CT
Franklin, OH	Columbus, OH	Harvey, KS	Wichita, KS
Franklin, VA	Roanoke, VA	Hawkins, TN	Kingsport-Bristol-Bristol, TN-VA
Franklin, VT	Burlington-South Burlington, VT	Hays, TX	Austin-Round Rock, TX
Franklin, WA	Kennewick-Pasco-Richland, WA	Haywood, NC	Asheville, NC
Fredericksburg city, VA	Washington, DC-VA-MD-WV	Heard, GA	Atlanta-Sandy Springs-Marietta, GA
Frederick, MD	Washington, DC-VA-MD-WV	Henderson, KY	Evansville, IN-KY
Frederick, VA	Winchester, VA-WV	Henderson, NC	Asheville, NC
Fresno, CA	Fresno, CA	Hendricks, IN	Indianapolis, IN
Fulton, GA	Atlanta-Sandy Springs-Marietta, GA	Hennepin, MN	Minneapolis-St. Paul-Bloomington, MN-WI
Fulton, OH	Toledo, OH	Henrico, VA	Richmond, VA
Gadsden, FL	Tallahassee, FL	Henry, AL	Dothan, AL
Gallatin, KY	Cincinnati-Middletown, OH-KY-IN	Henry, GA	Atlanta-Sandy Springs-Marietta, GA
Galveston, TX	Houston-Baytown-Sugar Land, TX	Henry, IL	Davenport-Moline-Rock Island, IA-IL
Garland, AR	Hot Springs, AR	Henry, KY	Louisville, KY-IN
Gaston, NC	Charlotte-Gastonia-Concord, NC-SC	Herkimer, NY	Utica-Rome, NY
Geary, KS	Manhattan, KS	Hernando, FL	Tampa-St. Petersburg-Clearwater, FL
Geauga, OH	Cleveland-Elyria-Mentor, OH	Hickman, TN	Nashville-Davidson--Murfreesboro, TN
Gem, ID	Boise City-Nampa, ID	Hidalgo, TX	McAllen-Edinburg-Mission, TX
Genesee, MI	Flint, MI	Hillsborough, FL	Tampa-St. Petersburg-Clearwater, FL
Geneva, AL	Dothan, AL	Hillsborough, NH	Manchester-Nashua, NH
George, MS	Pascagoula, MS	Hinds, MS	Jackson, MS
Gibson, IN	Evansville, IN-KY	Hoke, NC	Fayetteville, NC
Gilchrist, FL	Gainesville, FL	Honolulu, HI	Honolulu, HI
Giles, VA	Blacksburg-Christiansburg-Radford, VA	Hopewell city, VA	Richmond, VA
Gilpin, CO	Denver-Aurora, CO	Horry, SC	Myrtle Beach-Conway, SC
Gloucester, NJ	Philadelphia, PA-NJ-DE-MD	Houston, AL	Dothan, AL
Gloucester, VA	Virginia Beach-Norfolk, VA-NC	Houston, GA	Warner Robins, GA
Glynn, GA	Brunswick, GA	Houston, MN	La Crosse, WI-MN
Goliad, TX	Victoria, TX	Howard, IN	Kokomo, IN
Goochland, VA	Richmond, VA	Howard, MD	Baltimore-Towson, MD
Grady, OK	Oklahoma City, OK	Howard, MO	Columbia, MO
Grainger, TN	Morristown, TN	Hudson, NJ	New York, NY-NJ-PA
Grand Forks, ND	Grand Forks, ND-MN	Hunterdon, NJ	New York, NY-NJ-PA
Grand Isle, VT	Burlington-South Burlington, VT	Hunt, TX	Dallas-Fort Worth-Arlington, TX
Grant, AR	Little Rock-North Little Rock, AR	Iberville, LA	Baton Rouge, LA
Grant, KY	Cincinnati-Middletown, OH-KY-IN	Imperial, CA	El Centro, CA

COUNTY INDEX: 2011 (continued)

COUNTY:	IS IN METROPOLITAN:	COUNTY:	IS IN METROPOLITAN:
Indian River, FL	Sebastian-Vero Beach, FL	Lapeer, MI	Detroit-Warren-Livonia, MI
Ingham, MI	Lansing-East Lansing, MI	LaPorte, IN	Michigan City-La Porte, IN
Ionia, MI	Grand Rapids-Wyoming, MI	Laramie, WY	Cheyenne, WY
Iowa, WI	Madison, WI	Larimer, CO	Fort Collins-Loveland, CO
Irion, TX	San Angelo, TX	Larue, KY	Elizabethtown, KY
Isanti, MN	Minneapolis-St. Paul-Bloomington, MN-WI	Lauderdale, AL	Florence-Muscle Shoals, AL
Isle of Wight, VA	Virginia Beach-Norfolk, VA-NC	Laurens, SC	Greenville, SC
Jackson, KS	Topeka, KS	Lawrence, AL	Decatur, AL
Jackson, MI	Jackson, MI	Lawrence, OH	Huntington-Ashland, WV-KY-OH
Jackson, MO	Kansas City, MO-KS	Le Flore, OK	Fort Smith, AR-OK
Jackson, MS	Pascagoula, MS	Leavenworth, KS	Kansas City, MO-KS
Jackson, OR	Medford, OR	Lebanon, PA	Lebanon, PA
James City, VA	Virginia Beach-Norfolk, VA-NC	Lee, AL	Auburn-Opelika, AL
Jasper, GA	Atlanta-Sandy Springs-Marietta, GA	Lee, FL	Cape Coral-Fort Myers, FL
Jasper, IN	Chicago-Joliet-Naperville, IL-IN-WI	Lee, GA	Albany, GA
Jasper, MO	Joplin, MO	Lehigh, PA	Allentown-Bethlehem-Easton, PA-NJ
Jefferson, AL	Birmingham-Hoover, AL	Leon, FL	Tallahassee, FL
Jefferson, AR	Pine Bluff, AR	Lexington, SC	Columbia, SC
Jefferson, CO	Denver-Aurora, CO	Liberty, GA	Hinesville-Fort Stewart, GA
Jefferson, FL	Tallahassee, FL	Liberty, TX	Houston-Baytown-Sugar Land, TX
Jefferson, ID	Idaho Falls, ID	Licking, OH	Columbus, OH
Jefferson, KS	Topeka, KS	Limestone, AL	Huntsville, AL
Jefferson, KY	Louisville, KY-IN	Lincoln, AR	Pine Bluff, AR
Jefferson, LA	New Orleans-Metairie-Kenner, LA	Lincoln, MO	St. Louis, MO-IL
Jefferson, MO	St. Louis, MO-IL	Lincoln, OK	Oklahoma City, OK
Jefferson, OH	Steubenville-Weirton, OH-WV	Lincoln, SD	Sioux Falls, SD
Jefferson, TN	Morristown, TN	Lincoln, WV	Charleston, WV
Jefferson, TX	Beaumont-Port Arthur, TX	Linn, IA	Cedar Rapids, IA
Jefferson, WV	Washington, DC-VA-MD-WV	Linn, KS	Kansas City, MO-KS
Jersey, IL	St. Louis, MO-IL	Livingston, LA	Baton Rouge, LA
Jessamine, KY	Lexington-Fayette, KY	Livingston, MI	Detroit-Warren-Livonia, MI
Johnson, IA	Iowa City, IA	Livingston, NY	Rochester, NY
Johnson, IN	Indianapolis, IN	Logan, OK	Oklahoma City, OK
Johnson, KS	Kansas City, MO-KS	Long, GA	Hinesville-Fort Stewart, GA
Johnson, TX	Dallas-Fort Worth-Arlington, TX	Lonoke, AR	Little Rock-North Little Rock, AR
Johnston, NC	Raleigh-Cary, NC	Lorain, OH	Cleveland-Elyria-Mentor, OH
Jones, GA	Macon, GA	Los Angeles, CA	Los Angeles-Long Beach-Santa Ana, CA
Jones, IA	Cedar Rapids, IA	Loudon, TN	Knoxville, TN
Jones, TX	Abilene, TX	Loudoun, VA	Washington, DC-VA-MD-WV
Juab, UT	Provo-Orem, UT	Louisa, VA	Richmond, VA
Kalamazoo, MI	Kalamazoo-Portage, MI	Lowndes, AL	Montgomery, AL
Kanawha, WV	Charleston, WV	Lowndes, GA	Valdosta, GA
Kane, IL	Chicago-Joliet-Naperville, IL-IN-WI	Lubbock, TX	Lubbock, TX
Kankakee, IL	Kankakee-Bradley, IL	Lucas, OH	Toledo, OH
Kaufman, TX	Dallas-Fort Worth-Arlington, TX	Luzerne, PA	Scranton--Wilkes-Barre, PA
Kendall, IL	Chicago-Joliet-Naperville, IL-IN-WI	Lycoming, PA	Williamsport, PA
Kendall, TX	San Antonio, TX	Lynchburg city, VA	Lynchburg, VA
Kenosha, WI	Chicago-Joliet-Naperville, IL-IN-WI	Macomb, MI	Detroit-Warren-Livonia, MI
Kenton, KY	Cincinnati-Middletown, OH-KY-IN	Macon, IL	Decatur, IL
Kent, DE	Dover, DE	Macon, TN	Nashville-Davidson--Murfreesboro, TN
Kent, MI	Grand Rapids-Wyoming, MI	Macoupin, IL	St. Louis, MO-IL
Kent, RI	Providence-New Bedford-Fall River, RI-MA	Madera, CA	Madera, CA
Kern, CA	Bakersfield, CA	Madison, AL	Huntsville, AL
Kershaw, SC	Columbia, SC	Madison, AR	Fayetteville-Springdale-Rogers, AR-MO
Kewaunee, WI	Green Bay, WI	Madison, GA	Athens-Clarke County, GA
King and Queen, VA	Richmond, VA	Madison, IA	Des Moines-West Des Moines, IA
King William, VA	Richmond, VA	Madison, IL	St. Louis, MO-IL
Kings, CA	Hanford-Corcoran, CA	Madison, IN	Anderson, IN
Kings, NY	New York, NY-NJ-PA	Madison, MS	Jackson, MS
King, WA	Seattle-Tacoma-Bellevue, WA	Madison, NC	Asheville, NC
Kitsap, WA	Bremerton-Silverdale, WA	Madison, NY	Syracuse, NY
Knox, TN	Knoxville, TN	Madison, OH	Columbus, OH
Kootenai, ID	Coeur d'Alene, ID	Madison, TN	Jackson, TN
La Crosse, WI	La Crosse, WI-MN	Mahoning, OH	Youngstown-Warren-Boardman, OH-PA
Lackawanna, PA	Scranton--Wilkes-Barre, PA	Manassas city, VA	Washington, DC-VA-MD-WV
Lafayette, LA	Lafayette, LA	Manassas Park city, VA	Washington, DC-VA-MD-WV
Lafayette, MO	Kansas City, MO-KS	Manatee, FL	North Port-Bradenton-Sarasota, FL
Lafourche, LA	Houma-Bayou Cane-Thibodaux, LA	Marathon, WI	Wausau, WI
Lake, FL	Orlando, FL	Maricopa, AZ	Phoenix-Mesa-Scottsdale, AZ
Lake, IL	Chicago-Joliet-Naperville, IL-IN-WI	Marin, CA	San Francisco-Oakland-Fremont, CA
Lake, IN	Chicago-Joliet-Naperville, IL-IN-WI	Marion, FL	Ocala, FL
Lake, OH	Cleveland-Elyria-Mentor, OH	Marion, GA	Columbus, GA-AL
Lamar, GA	Atlanta-Sandy Springs-Marietta, GA	Marion, IN	Indianapolis, IN
Lamar, MS	Hattiesburg, MS	Marion, OR	Salem, OR
Lampasas, TX	Killeen-Temple-Fort Hood, TX	Marion, TN	Chattanooga, TN-GA
Lancaster, NE	Lincoln, NE	Marshall, IL	Peoria, IL
Lancaster, PA	Lancaster, PA	Marshall, MS	Memphis, TN-MS-AR
Lane, OR	Eugene-Springfield, OR	Marshall, WV	Wheeling, WV-OH
Lanier, GA	Valdosta, GA	Martin, FL	Port St. Lucie, FL

COUNTY INDEX: 2011 (continued)

COUNTY:	IS IN METROPOLITAN:	COUNTY:	IS IN METROPOLITAN:
Matanuska-Susitna, AK	Anchorage, AK	Newport News city, VA	Virginia Beach-Norfolk, VA-NC
Mathews, VA	Virginia Beach-Norfolk, VA-NC	Newport, RI	Providence-New Bedford-Fall River, RI-MA
McClain, OK	Oklahoma City, OK	Newton, GA	Atlanta-Sandy Springs-Marietta, GA
McCook, SD	Sioux Falls, SD	Newton, IN	Chicago-Joliet-Naperville, IL-IN-WI
McDonald, MO	Fayetteville-Springdale-Rogers, AR-MO	Newton, MO	Joplin, MO
McDuffie, GA	Augusta-Richmond County, GA-SC	Nez Perce, ID	Lewiston, ID-WA
McHenry, IL	Chicago-Joliet-Naperville, IL-IN-WI	Niagara, NY	Buffalo-Niagara Falls, NY
McIntosh, GA	Brunswick, GA	Nicollet, MN	Mankato-North Mankato, MN
McLean, IL	Bloomington-Normal, IL	Norfolk city, VA	Virginia Beach-Norfolk, VA-NC
McLean, KY	Owensboro, KY	Norfolk, MA	Boston-Cambridge-Quincy, MA-NH
McLennan, TX	Waco, TX	Northampton, PA	Allentown-Bethlehem-Easton, PA-NJ
Meade, KY	Louisville, KY-IN	Nueces, TX	Corpus Christi, TX
Meade, SD	Rapid City, SD	Oakland, MI	Detroit-Warren-Livonia, MI
Mecklenburg, NC	Charlotte-Gastonia-Concord, NC-SC	Ocean, NJ	New York, NY-NJ-PA
Medina, OH	Cleveland-Elyria-Mentor, OH	Oconee, GA	Athens-Clarke County, GA
Medina, TX	San Antonio, TX	Oconto, WI	Green Bay, WI
Menard, IL	Springfield, IL	Oglethorpe, GA	Athens-Clarke County, GA
Merced, CA	Merced, CA	Ohio, IN	Cincinnati-Middletown, OH-KY-IN
Mercer, IL	Davenport-Moline-Rock Island, IA-IL	Ohio, WV	Wheeling, WV-OH
Mercer, NJ	Trenton-Ewing, NJ	Okaloosa, FL	Crestview-Fort Walton Beach, FL
Mercer, PA	Youngstown-Warren-Boardman, OH-PA	Oklahoma, OK	Oklahoma City, OK
Meriwether, GA	Atlanta-Sandy Springs-Marietta, GA	Okmulgee, OK	Tulsa, OK
Mesa, CO	Grand Junction, CO	Oldham, KY	Louisville, KY-IN
Miami-Dade, FL	Miami-Fort Lauderdale-Miami Beach, FL	Olmsted, MN	Rochester, MN
Miami, KS	Kansas City, MO-KS	Oneida, NY	Utica-Rome, NY
Miami, OH	Dayton, OH	Onondaga, NY	Syracuse, NY
Middlesex, CT	Hartford-West Hartford-East Hartford, CT	Onslow, NC	Jacksonville, NC
Middlesex, MA	Boston-Cambridge-Quincy, MA-NH	Ontario, NY	Rochester, NY
Middlesex, NJ	New York, NY-NJ-PA	Orange, CA	Los Angeles-Long Beach-Santa Ana, CA
Midland, TX	Midland, TX	Orange, FL	Orlando, FL
Miller, AR	Texarkana, TX-Texarkana, AR	Orange, NC	Durham-Chapel Hill, NC
Mills, IA	Omaha-Council Bluffs, NE-IA	Orange, NY	Poughkeepsie-Newburgh-Middletown, NY
Milwaukee, WI	Milwaukee-Waukesha-West Allis, WI	Orange, TX	Beaumont-Port Arthur, TX
Mineral, WV	Cumberland, MD-WV	Orleans, LA	New Orleans-Metairie-Kenner, LA
Minnehaha, SD	Sioux Falls, SD	Orleans, NY	Rochester, NY
Missoula, MT	Missoula, MT	Osage, KS	Topeka, KS
Mobile, AL	Mobile, AL	Osage, MO	Jefferson City, MO
Mohave, AZ	Lake Havasu City-Kingman, AZ	Osage, OK	Tulsa, OK
Moniteau, MO	Jefferson City, MO	Osceola, FL	Orlando, FL
Monmouth, NJ	New York, NY-NJ-PA	Oswego, NY	Syracuse, NY
Monongalia, WV	Morgantown, WV	Ottawa, MI	Holland-Grand Haven, MI
Monroe, GA	Macon, GA	Ottawa, OH	Toledo, OH
Monroe, IL	St. Louis, MO-IL	Ouachita, LA	Monroe, LA
Monroe, IN	Bloomington, IN	Outagamie, WI	Appleton, WI
Monroe, MI	Monroe, MI	Owen, IN	Bloomington, IN
Monroe, NY	Rochester, NY	Owyhee, ID	Boise City-Nampa, ID
Monterey, CA	Salinas, CA	Ozaukee, WI	Milwaukee-Waukesha-West Allis, WI
Montgomery, AL	Montgomery, AL	Palm Beach, FL	Miami-Fort Lauderdale-Miami Beach, FL
Montgomery, MD	Washington, DC-VA-MD-WV	Parker, TX	Dallas-Fort Worth-Arlington, TX
Montgomery, OH	Dayton, OH	Park, CO	Denver-Aurora, CO
Montgomery, PA	Philadelphia, PA-NJ-DE-MD	Pasco, FL	Tampa-St. Petersburg-Clearwater, FL
Montgomery, TN	Clarksville, TN-KY	Passaic, NJ	New York, NY-NJ-PA
Montgomery, TX	Houston-Baytown-Sugar Land, TX	Paulding, GA	Atlanta-Sandy Springs-Marietta, GA
Montgomery, VA	Blacksburg-Christiansburg-Radford, VA	Pawnee, OK	Tulsa, OK
Morgan, AL	Decatur, AL	Pender, NC	Wilmington, NC
Morgan, IN	Indianapolis, IN	Pendleton, KY	Cincinnati-Middletown, OH-KY-IN
Morgan, UT	Ogden-Clearfield, UT	Pennington, SD	Rapid City, SD
Morgan, WV	Hagerstown-Martinsburg, MD-WV	Penobscot, ME	Bangor, ME
Morris, NJ	New York, NY-NJ-PA	Peoria, IL	Peoria, IL
Morrow, OH	Columbus, OH	Perry, AR	Little Rock-North Little Rock, AR
Morton, ND	Bismarck, ND	Perry, MS	Hattiesburg, MS
Multnomah, OR	Portland-Vancouver-Beaverton, OR-WA	Perry, PA	Harrisburg-Carlisle, PA
Murray, GA	Dalton, GA	Person, NC	Durham-Chapel Hill, NC
Muscogee, GA	Columbus, GA-AL	Petersburg city, VA	Richmond, VA
Muskegon, MI	Muskegon-Norton Shores, MI	Philadelphia, PA	Philadelphia, PA-NJ-DE-MD
Napa, CA	Napa, CA	Piatt, IL	Champaign-Urbana, IL
Nash, NC	Rocky Mount, NC	Pickaway, OH	Columbus, OH
Nassau, FL	Jacksonville, FL	Pickens, GA	Atlanta-Sandy Springs-Marietta, GA
Nassau, NY	New York, NY-NJ-PA	Pickens, SC	Greenville, SC
Natrona, WY	Casper, WY	Pierce, WA	Seattle-Tacoma-Bellevue, WA
Nelson, KY	Louisville, KY-IN	Pierce, WI	Minneapolis-St. Paul-Bloomington, MN-WI
Nelson, VA	Charlottesville, VA	Pike, GA	Atlanta-Sandy Springs-Marietta, GA
New Castle, DE	Philadelphia, PA-NJ-DE-MD	Pike, PA	New York, NY-NJ-PA
New Hanover, NC	Wilmington, NC	Pima, AZ	Tucson, AZ
New Haven, CT	New Haven-Milford, CT	Pinal, AZ	Phoenix-Mesa-Scottsdale, AZ
New Kent, VA	Richmond, VA	Pinellas, FL	Tampa-St. Petersburg-Clearwater, FL
New London, CT	Norwich-New London, CT	Pittsylvania, VA	Danville, VA
New York, NY	New York, NY-NJ-PA	Pitt, NC	Greenville, NC
Newaygo, MI	Grand Rapids-Wyoming, MI	Placer, CA	Sacramento--Arden-Arcade--Roseville, CA

COUNTY INDEX: 2011 (continued)

COUNTY:	IS IN METROPOLITAN:	COUNTY:	IS IN METROPOLITAN:
Plaquemines, LA	New Orleans-Metairie-Kenner, LA	San Francisco, CA	San Francisco-Oakland-Fremont, CA
Platte, MO	Kansas City, MO-KS	San Jacinto, TX	Houston-Baytown-Sugar Land, TX
Pleasants, WV	Parkersburg-Marietta-Vienna, WV-OH	San Joaquin, CA	Stockton, CA
Plymouth, MA	Boston-Cambridge-Quincy, MA-NH	San Juan, NM	Farmington, NM
Poinsett, AR	Jonesboro, AR	San Luis Obispo, CA	San Luis Obispo-Paso Robles, CA
Pointe Coupee, LA	Baton Rouge, LA	San Mateo, CA	San Francisco-Oakland-Fremont, CA
Polk, FL	Lakeland, FL	San Patricio, TX	Corpus Christi, TX
Polk, IA	Des Moines-West Des Moines, IA	Sandoval, NM	Albuquerque, NM
Polk, MN	Grand Forks, ND-MN	Sangamon, IL	Springfield, IL
Polk, MO	Springfield, MO	Santa Barbara, CA	Santa Barbara-Santa Maria-Goleta, CA
Polk, OR	Salem, OR	Santa Clara, CA	San Jose-Sunnyvale-Santa Clara, CA
Polk, TN	Cleveland, TN	Santa Cruz, CA	Santa Cruz-Watsonville, CA
Poquoson city, VA	Virginia Beach-Norfolk, VA-NC	Santa Fe, NM	Santa Fe, NM
Portage, OH	Akron, OH	Santa Rosa, FL	Pensacola-Ferry Pass-Brent, FL
Porter, IN	Chicago-Joliet-Naperville, IL-IN-WI	Sarasota, FL	North Port-Bradenton-Sarasota, FL
Portsmouth city, VA	Virginia Beach-Norfolk, VA-NC	Saratoga, NY	Albany-Schenectady-Troy, NY
Posey, IN	Evansville, IN-KY	Sarpy, NE	Omaha-Council Bluffs, NE-IA
Pottawattamie, IA	Omaha-Council Bluffs, NE-IA	Saunders, NE	Omaha-Council Bluffs, NE-IA
Pottawattamie, KS	Manhattan, KS	Schenectady, NY	Albany-Schenectady-Troy, NY
Potter, TX	Amarillo, TX	Schoharie, NY	Albany-Schenectady-Troy, NY
Power, ID	Pocatello, ID	Scott, IA	Davenport-Moline-Rock Island, IA-IL
Powhatan, VA	Richmond, VA	Scott, KY	Lexington-Fayette, KY
Preble, OH	Dayton, OH	Scott, MN	Minneapolis-St. Paul-Bloomington, MN-WI
Preston, WV	Morgantown, WV	Scott, VA	Kingsport-Bristol-Bristol, TN-VA
Prince George's, MD	Washington, DC-VA-MD-WV	Sebastian, AR	Fort Smith, AR-OK
Prince George, VA	Richmond, VA	Sedgwick, KS	Wichita, KS
Prince William, VA	Washington, DC-VA-MD-WV	Seminole, FL	Orlando, FL
Providence, RI	Providence-New Bedford-Fall River, RI-MA	Sequatchie, TN	Chattanooga, TN-GA
Pueblo, CO	Pueblo, CO	Sequoyah, OK	Fort Smith, AR-OK
Pulaski, AR	Little Rock-North Little Rock, AR	Seward, NE	Lincoln, NE
Pulaski, VA	Blacksburg-Christiansburg-Radford, VA	Shasta, CA	Redding, CA
Putnam, IN	Indianapolis, IN	Shawnee, KS	Topeka, KS
Putnam, NY	New York, NY-NJ-PA	Sheboygan, WI	Sheboygan, WI
Putnam, WV	Charleston, WV	Shelby, AL	Birmingham-Hoover, AL
Queen Anne's, MD	Baltimore-Towson, MD	Shelby, IN	Indianapolis, IN
Queens, NY	New York, NY-NJ-PA	Shelby, KY	Louisville, KY-IN
Racine, WI	Racine, WI	Shelby, TN	Memphis, TN-MS-AR
Radford city, VA	Blacksburg-Christiansburg-Radford, VA	Sherburne, MN	Minneapolis-St. Paul-Bloomington, MN-WI
Ramsey, MN	Minneapolis-St. Paul-Bloomington, MN-WI	Simpson, MS	Jackson, MS
Randall, TX	Amarillo, TX	Skagit, WA	Mount Vernon-Anacortes, WA
Randolph, NC	Greensboro-High Point, NC	Skamania, WA	Portland-Vancouver-Beaverton, OR-WA
Rankin, MS	Jackson, MS	Smith, TN	Nashville-Davidson--Murfreesboro, TN
Rapides, LA	Alexandria, LA	Smith, TX	Tyler, TX
Ray, MO	Kansas City, MO-KS	Snohomish, WA	Seattle-Tacoma-Bellevue, WA
Rensselaer, NY	Albany-Schenectady-Troy, NY	Solano, CA	Vallejo-Fairfield, CA
Richland, OH	Mansfield, OH	Somerset, MD	Salisbury, MD
Richland, SC	Columbia, SC	Somerset, NJ	New York, NY-NJ-PA
Richmond city, VA	Richmond, VA	Sonoma, CA	Santa Rosa-Petaluma, CA
Richmond, GA	Augusta-Richmond County, GA-SC	Spalding, GA	Atlanta-Sandy Springs-Marietta, GA
Richmond, NY	New York, NY-NJ-PA	Spartanburg, SC	Spartanburg, SC
Riley, KS	Manhattan, KS	Spencer, KY	Louisville, KY-IN
Riverside, CA	Riverside-San Bernardino-Ontario, CA	Spokane, WA	Spokane, WA
Roanoke city, VA	Roanoke, VA	Spotsylvania, VA	Washington, DC-VA-MD-WV
Roanoke, VA	Roanoke, VA	Stafford, VA	Washington, DC-VA-MD-WV
Robertson, TN	Nashville-Davidson--Murfreesboro, TN	Stanislaus, CA	Modesto, CA
Robertson, TX	College Station-Bryan, TX	Stark, IL	Peoria, IL
Rock Island, IL	Davenport-Moline-Rock Island, IA-IL	Stark, OH	Canton-Massillon, OH
Rockdale, GA	Atlanta-Sandy Springs-Marietta, GA	Stearns, MN	St. Cloud, MN
Rockingham, NC	Greensboro-High Point, NC	Stewart, TN	Clarksville, TN-KY
Rockingham, NH	Boston-Cambridge-Quincy, MA-NH	Stokes, NC	Winston-Salem, NC
Rockingham, VA	Harrisonburg, VA	Stone, MS	Gulfport-Biloxi, MS
Rockland, NY	New York, NY-NJ-PA	Storey, NV	Reno-Sparks, NV
Rockwall, TX	Dallas-Fort Worth-Arlington, TX	Story, IA	Ames, IA
Rock, WI	Janesville, WI	Strafford, NH	Boston-Cambridge-Quincy, MA-NH
Rogers, OK	Tulsa, OK	St. Bernard, LA	New Orleans-Metairie-Kenner, LA
Rusk, TX	Longview, TX	St. Charles, LA	New Orleans-Metairie-Kenner, LA
Russell, AL	Columbus, GA-AL	St. Charles, MO	St. Louis, MO-IL
Rutherford, TN	Nashville-Davidson--Murfreesboro, TN	St. Clair, AL	Birmingham-Hoover, AL
Sacramento, CA	Sacramento--Arden-Arcade--Roseville, CA	St. Clair, IL	St. Louis, MO-IL
Sagadahoc, ME	Portland-South Portland-Biddeford, ME	St. Clair, MI	Detroit-Warren-Livonia, MI
Saginaw, MI	Saginaw-Saginaw Township North, MI	St. Croix, WI	Minneapolis-St. Paul-Bloomington, MN-WI
Salem city, VA	Roanoke, VA	St. Helena, LA	Baton Rouge, LA
Salem, NJ	Philadelphia, PA-NJ-DE-MD	St. John the Baptist, LA	New Orleans-Metairie-Kenner, LA
Saline, AR	Little Rock-North Little Rock, AR	St. Johns, FL	Jacksonville, FL
Salt Lake, UT	Salt Lake City, UT	St. Joseph, IN	South Bend-Mishawaka, IN-MI
Saluda, SC	Columbia, SC	St. Louis city, MO	St. Louis, MO-IL
San Benito, CA	San Jose-Sunnyvale-Santa Clara, CA	St. Louis, MN	Duluth, MN-WI
San Bernardino, CA	Riverside-San Bernardino-Ontario, CA	St. Louis, MO	St. Louis, MO-IL
San Diego, CA	San Diego-Carlsbad-San Marcos, CA	St. Lucie, FL	Port St. Lucie, FL

COUNTY INDEX: 2011 (continued)

COUNTY:	IS IN METROPOLITAN:	COUNTY:	IS IN METROPOLITAN:
St. Martin, LA	Lafayette, LA	Warren, VA	Washington, DC-VA-MD-WV
St. Tammany, LA	New Orleans-Metairie-Kenner, LA	Warrick, IN	Evansville, IN-KY
Suffolk city, VA	Virginia Beach-Norfolk, VA-NC	Washington, AR	Fayetteville-Springdale-Rogers, AR-MO
Suffolk, MA	Boston-Cambridge-Quincy, MA-NH	Washington, IA	Iowa City, IA
Suffolk, NY	New York, NY-NJ-PA	Washington, IN	Louisville, KY-IN
Sullivan, IN	Terre Haute, IN	Washington, MD	Hagerstown-Martinsburg, MD-WV
Sullivan, TN	Kingsport-Bristol-Bristol, TN-VA	Washington, MN	Minneapolis-St. Paul-Bloomington, MN-WI
Summit, OH	Akron, OH	Washington, MO	St. Louis, MO-IL
Summit, UT	Salt Lake City, UT	Washington, NE	Omaha-Council Bluffs, NE-IA
Sumner, KS	Wichita, KS	Washington, NY	Glens Falls, NY
Sumner, TN	Nashville-Davidson--Murfreesboro, TN	Washington, OH	Parkersburg-Marietta-Vienna, WV-OH
Sumter, SC	Sumter, SC	Washington, OR	Portland-Vancouver-Beaverton, OR-WA
Surry, VA	Virginia Beach-Norfolk, VA-NC	Washington, PA	Pittsburgh, PA
Sussex, NJ	New York, NY-NJ-PA	Washington, RI	Providence-New Bedford-Fall River, RI-MA
Sussex, VA	Richmond, VA	Washington, TN	Johnson City, TN
Sutter, CA	Yuba City, CA	Washington, UT	St. George, UT
Tarrant, TX	Dallas-Fort Worth-Arlington, TX	Washington, VA	Kingsport-Bristol-Bristol, TN-VA
Tate, MS	Memphis, TN-MS-AR	Washington, WI	Milwaukee-Waukesha-West Allis, WI
Taylor, TX	Abilene, TX	Washoe, NV	Reno-Sparks, NV
Tazewell, IL	Peoria, IL	Washtenaw, MI	Ann Arbor, MI
Teller, CO	Colorado Springs, CO	Waukesha, WI	Milwaukee-Waukesha-West Allis, WI
Terrebonne, LA	Houma-Bayou Cane-Thibodaux, LA	Wayne, MI	Detroit-Warren-Livonia, MI
Terrell, GA	Albany, GA	Wayne, NC	Goldsboro, NC
Thurston, WA	Olympia, WA	Wayne, NY	Rochester, NY
Tioga, NY	Binghamton, NY	Wayne, WV	Huntington-Ashland, WV-KY-OH
Tippecanoe, IN	Lafayette, IN	Webb, TX	Laredo, TX
Tipton, IN	Kokomo, IN	Weber, UT	Ogden-Clearfield, UT
Tipton, TN	Memphis, TN-MS-AR	Webster, KY	Evansville, IN-KY
Tolland, CT	Hartford-West Hartford-East Hartford, CT	Webster, MO	Springfield, MO
Tom Green, TX	San Angelo, TX	Weld, CO	Greeley, CO
Tompkins, NY	Ithaca, NY	Wells, IN	Fort Wayne, IN
Tooele, UT	Salt Lake City, UT	West Baton Rouge, LA	Baton Rouge, LA
Torrance, NM	Albuquerque, NM	West Feliciana, LA	Baton Rouge, LA
Travis, TX	Austin-Round Rock, TX	Westchester, NY	New York, NY-NJ-PA
Trigg, KY	Clarksville, TN-KY	Westmoreland, PA	Pittsburgh, PA
Trimble, KY	Louisville, KY-IN	Whatcom, WA	Bellingham, WA
Trousdale, TN	Nashville-Davidson--Murfreesboro, TN	Whitfield, GA	Dalton, GA
Trumbull, OH	Youngstown-Warren-Boardman, OH-PA	Whitley, IN	Fort Wayne, IN
Tulare, CA	Visalia-Porterville, CA	Wichita, TX	Wichita Falls, TX
Tulsa, OK	Tulsa, OK	Wicomico, MD	Salisbury, MD
Tunica, MS	Memphis, TN-MS-AR	Williamsburg city, VA	Virginia Beach-Norfolk, VA-NC
Turner, SD	Sioux Falls, SD	Williamson, TN	Nashville-Davidson--Murfreesboro, TN
Tuscaloosa, AL	Tuscaloosa, AL	Williamson, TX	Austin-Round Rock, TX
Twiggs, GA	Macon, GA	Will, IL	Chicago-Joliet-Naperville, IL-IN-WI
Ulster, NY	Kingston, NY	Wilson, TN	Nashville-Davidson--Murfreesboro, TN
Unicoi, TN	Johnson City, TN	Wilson, TX	San Antonio, TX
Union, LA	Monroe, LA	Winchester city, VA	Winchester, VA-WV
Union, NC	Charlotte-Gastonia-Concord, NC-SC	Winnebago, IL	Rockford, IL
Union, NJ	New York, NY-NJ-PA	Winnebago, WI	Oshkosh-Neenah, WI
Union, OH	Columbus, OH	Wirt, WV	Parkersburg-Marietta-Vienna, WV-OH
Union, SD	Sioux City, IA-NE-SD	Wise, TX	Dallas-Fort Worth-Arlington, TX
Union, TN	Knoxville, TN	Woodbury, IA	Sioux City, IA-NE-SD
Upshur, TX	Longview, TX	Woodford, IL	Peoria, IL
Utah, UT	Provo-Orem, UT	Woodford, KY	Lexington-Fayette, KY
Valencia, NM	Albuquerque, NM	Wood, OH	Toledo, OH
Van Buren, MI	Kalamazoo-Portage, MI	Wood, WV	Parkersburg-Marietta-Vienna, WV-OH
Vanderburgh, IN	Evansville, IN-KY	Worcester, MA	Worcester, MA
Ventura, CA	Oxnard-Thousand Oaks-Ventura, CA	Worth, GA	Albany, GA
Vermilion, IL	Danville, IL	Wright, MN	Minneapolis-St. Paul-Bloomington, MN-WI
Vermillion, IN	Terre Haute, IN	Wyandotte, KS	Kansas City, MO-KS
Victoria, TX	Victoria, TX	Wyoming, PA	Scranton--Wilkes-Barre, PA
Vigo, IN	Terre Haute, IN	Yadkin, NC	Winston-Salem, NC
Virginia Beach city, VA	Virginia Beach-Norfolk, VA-NC	Yakima, WA	Yakima, WA
Volusia, FL	Deltona-Daytona Beach-Ormond Beach, FL	Yamhill, OR	Portland-Vancouver-Beaverton, OR-WA
Wabasha, MN	Rochester, MN	Yavapai, AZ	Prescott, AZ
Wabaunsee, KS	Topeka, KS	Yellowstone, MT	Billings, MT
Wagoner, OK	Tulsa, OK	Yolo, CA	Sacramento--Arden-Arcade--Roseville, CA
Wake, NC	Raleigh-Cary, NC	York, ME	Portland-South Portland-Biddeford, ME
Wakulla, FL	Tallahassee, FL	York, PA	York-Hanover, PA
Walker, AL	Birmingham-Hoover, AL	York, SC	Charlotte-Gastonia-Concord, NC-SC
Walker, GA	Chattanooga, TN-GA	York, VA	Virginia Beach-Norfolk, VA-NC
Waller, TX	Houston-Baytown-Sugar Land, TX	Yuba, CA	Yuba City, CA
Walton, GA	Atlanta-Sandy Springs-Marietta, GA	Yuma, AZ	Yuma, AZ
Warren, IA	Des Moines-West Des Moines, IA		
Warren, KY	Bowling Green, KY		
Warren, MO	St. Louis, MO-IL		
Warren, NJ	Allentown-Bethlehem-Easton, PA-NJ		
Warren, NY	Glens Falls, NY		
Warren, OH	Cincinnati-Middletown, OH-KY-IN		

National Crime Trends: 1992 to 2011

In the 20 years from 1992 to 2011, crime rates in the United States fell significantly. The total crime rate dropped 41.8%: from 5,661.3 crimes per 100,000 population in 1992 to a rate of 3,295.0 in 2011. Violent crime rates also decreased, falling 49.0% from 1992 to 2011. In addition, property crime rates dropped 40.7%.

Among individual crime categories, each recorded declines from 1992 to 2011. The nation's motor vehicle theft rate posted the largest decrease, falling 63.6% from 1992 to 2011. The smallest decline was in the larceny-theft rate, which dropped 36.3% during that same 20-year time frame.

The table below shows rates for each category of crime for every year since 1992. Trends for each individual crime are shown in graphs on the following pages. Violent crimes are murder, rape, robbery, and aggravated assault. Property crimes consist of burglary, larceny-theft, and motor vehicle theft. The total crime rate is simply the sum of the seven specific crimes and was calculated by the editors. All rates are crimes per 100,000 population for the year shown.

Year	Crime	Violent Crime	Property Crime	Murder	Rape	Robbery	Assault	Burglary	Larceny-Theft	Motor Vehicle Theft
1992	5,661.40	757.7	4,903.70	9.3	42.8	263.7	441.9	1,168.40	3,103.60	631.6
1993	5,487.10	747.1	4,740.00	9.5	41.1	256	440.5	1,099.70	3,033.90	606.3
1994	5,373.80	713.6	4,660.20	9	39.3	237.8	427.6	1,042.10	3,026.90	591.3
1995	5,275.00	684.5	4,590.50	8.2	37.1	220.9	418.3	987	3,043.20	560.3
1996	5,087.60	636.6	4,451.00	7.4	36.3	201.9	391	945	2,980.30	525.7
1997	4,927.30	611	4,316.30	6.8	35.9	186.2	382.1	918.8	2,891.80	505.7
1998	4,620.10	567.6	4,052.50	6.3	34.5	165.5	361.4	863.2	2,729.50	459.9
1999	4,266.60	523	3,743.60	5.7	32.8	150.1	334.3	770.4	2,550.70	422.5
2000	4,124.80	506.5	3,618.30	5.5	32	145	324	728.8	2,477.30	412.2
2001	4,162.60	504.5	3,658.10	5.6	31.8	148.5	318.6	741.8	2,485.70	430.5
2002	4,125.00	494.4	3,630.60	5.6	33.1	146.1	309.5	747	2,450.70	432.9
2003	4,067.00	475.8	3,591.20	5.7	32.3	142.5	295.4	741	2,416.50	433.7
2004	3,977.30	463.2	3,514.10	5.5	32.4	136.7	288.6	730.3	2,362.30	421.5
2005	3,900.50	469	3,431.50	5.6	31.8	140.8	290.8	726.9	2,287.80	416.8
2006	3,825.90	479.3	3,346.60	5.8	31.6	150	292	733.1	2,213.20	400.2
2007	3,748.20	471.8	3,276.40	5.7	30.6	148.3	287.2	726.1	2,185.40	364.9
2008	3,673.20	458.6	3,214.60	5.4	29.8	145.9	277.5	733	2,166.10	315.4
2009	3,473.20	431.9	3,041.30	5	29.1	133.1	264.7	717.7	2,064.50	259.2
2010	3,350.40	404.5	2,945.90	4.8	27.7	119.3	252.8	701	2,005.80	239.1
2011	3,295.00	386.3	2,908.70	4.7	26.8	113.7	241.1	702.2	1,976.90	229.6

Source: Reported data from the F.B.I.
"Crime in the United States 2011" (Uniform Crime Reports, October 29, 2012)

Crime Rate per 100,000 Population: 1992 to 2011

Violent Crime Rate per 100,000 Population: 1992 to 2011

Source: Reported data from the F.B.I.
"Crime in the United States 2011" (Uniform Crime Reports, October 29, 2012)

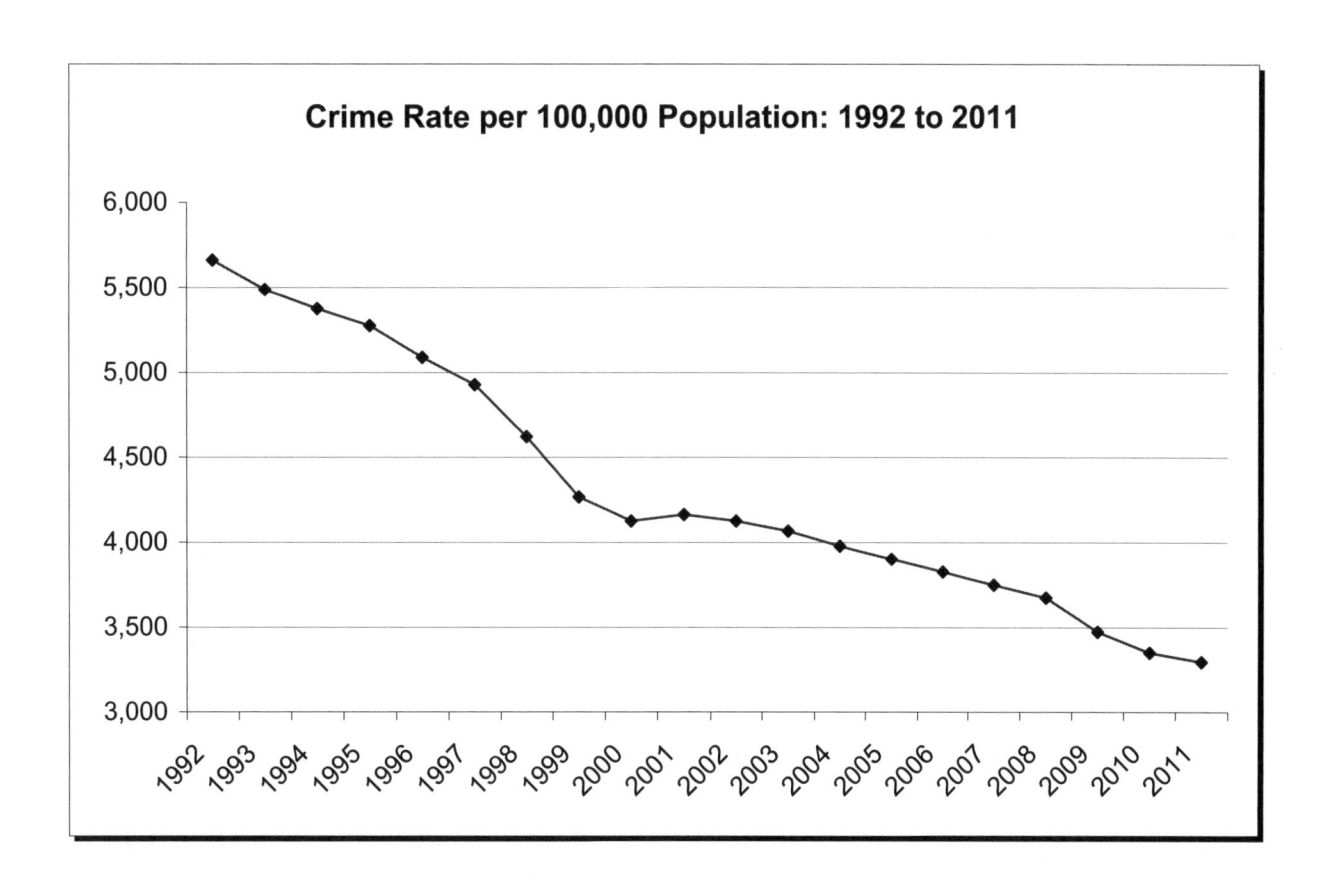

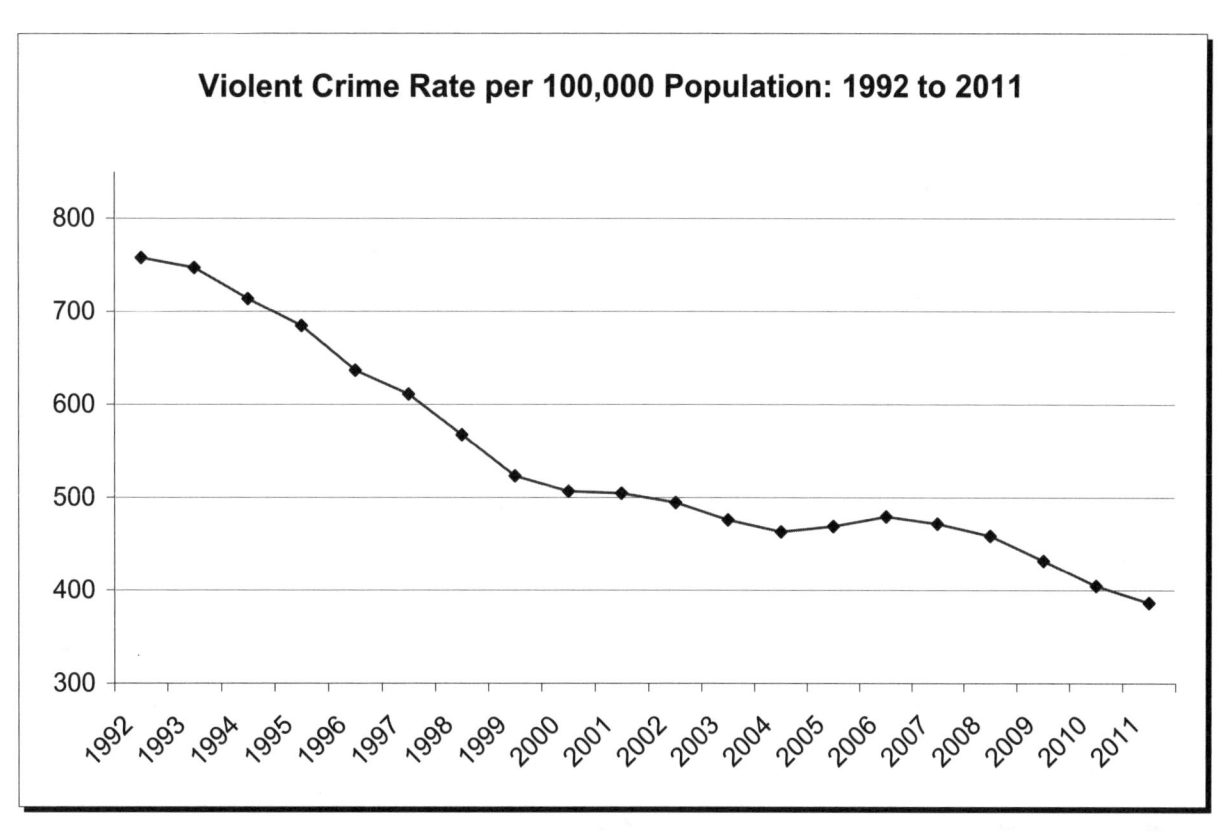

Murder Rate per 100,000 Population: 1992 to 2011

Rape Rate per 100,000 Population: 1992 to 2011

Source: Reported data from the F.B.I.
"Crime in the United States 2011" (Uniform Crime Reports, October 29, 2012)

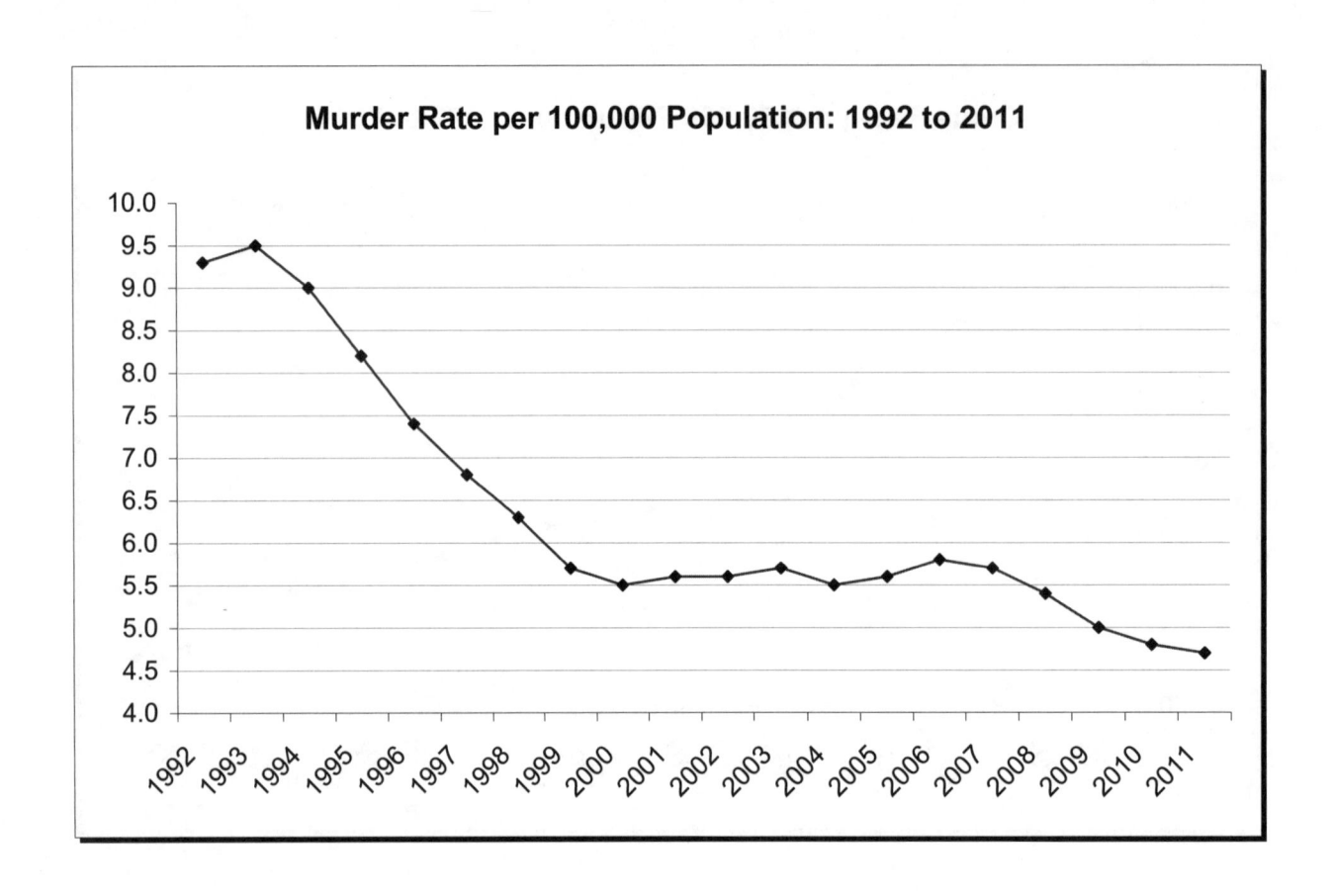

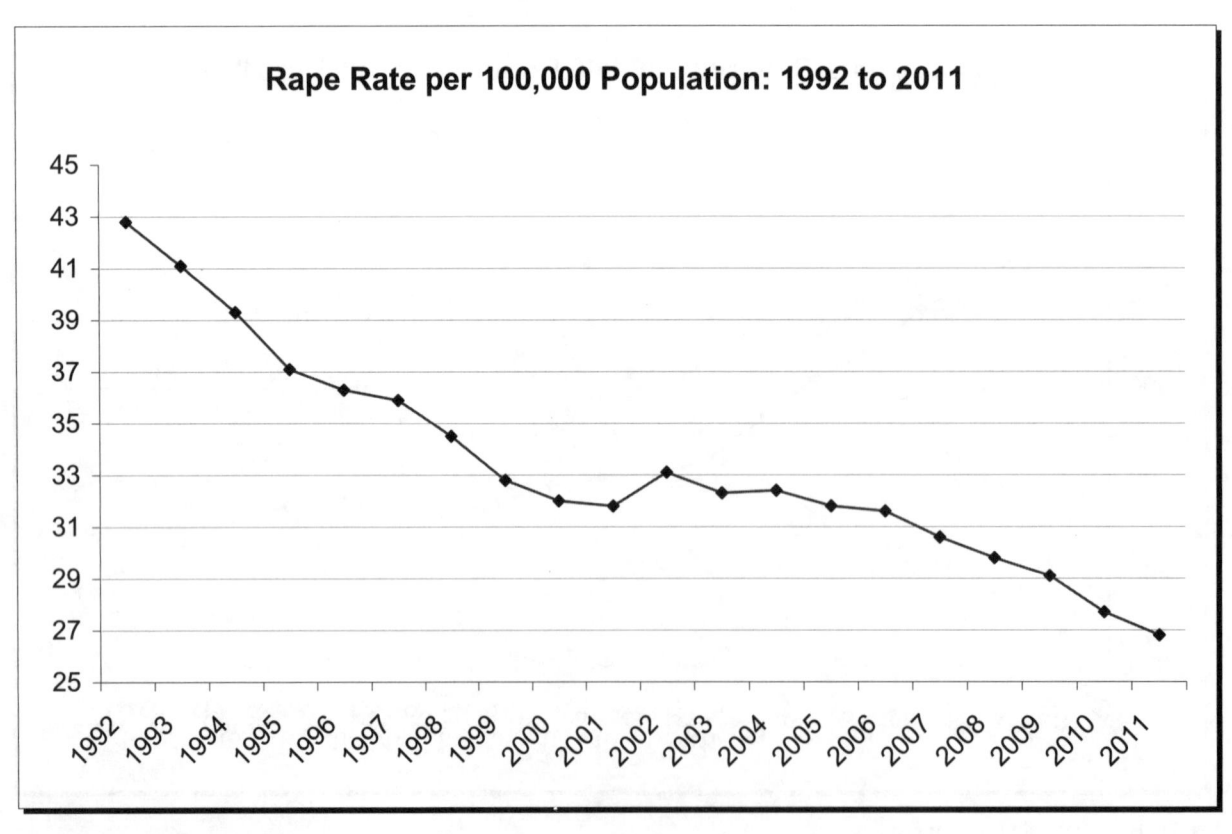

Robbery Rate per 100,000 Population: 1992 to 2011

Aggravated Assault Rate per 100,000 Population: 1992 to 2011

Source: Reported data from the F.B.I.
"Crime in the United States 2011" (Uniform Crime Reports, October 29, 2012)

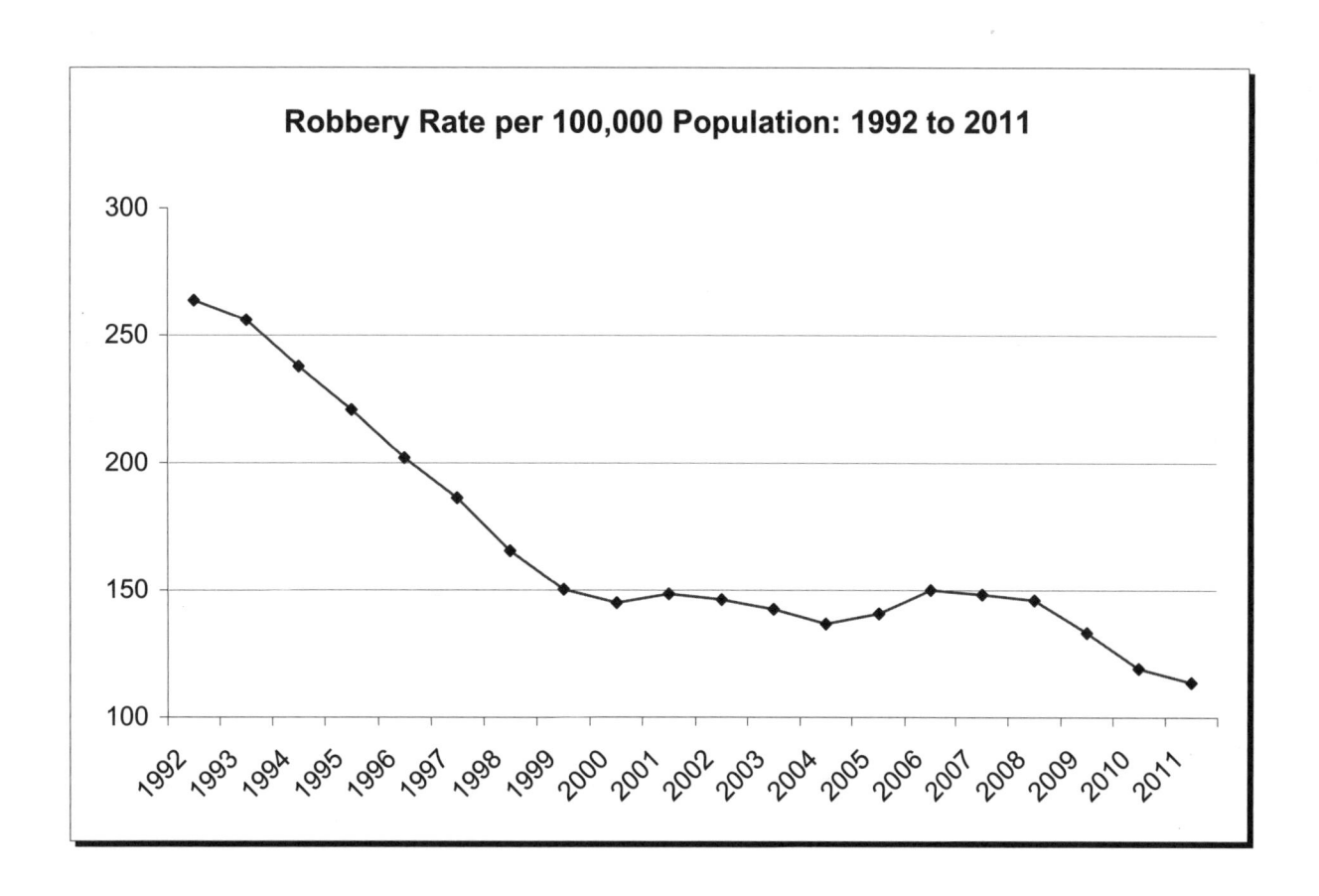

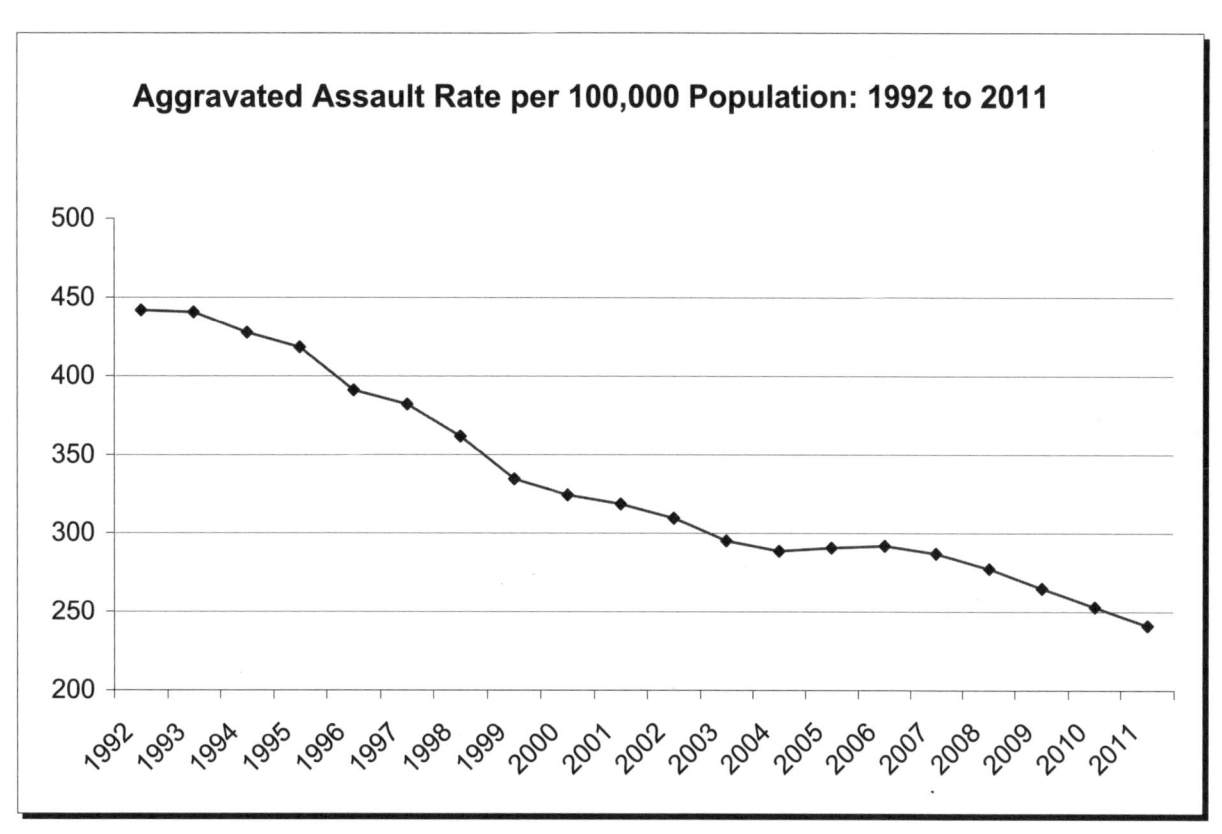

Property Crime Rate per 100,000 Population: 1992 to 2011

Burglary Rate per 100,000 Population: 1992 to 2011

Source: Reported data from the F.B.I.
"Crime in the United States 2011" (Uniform Crime Reports, October 29, 2012)

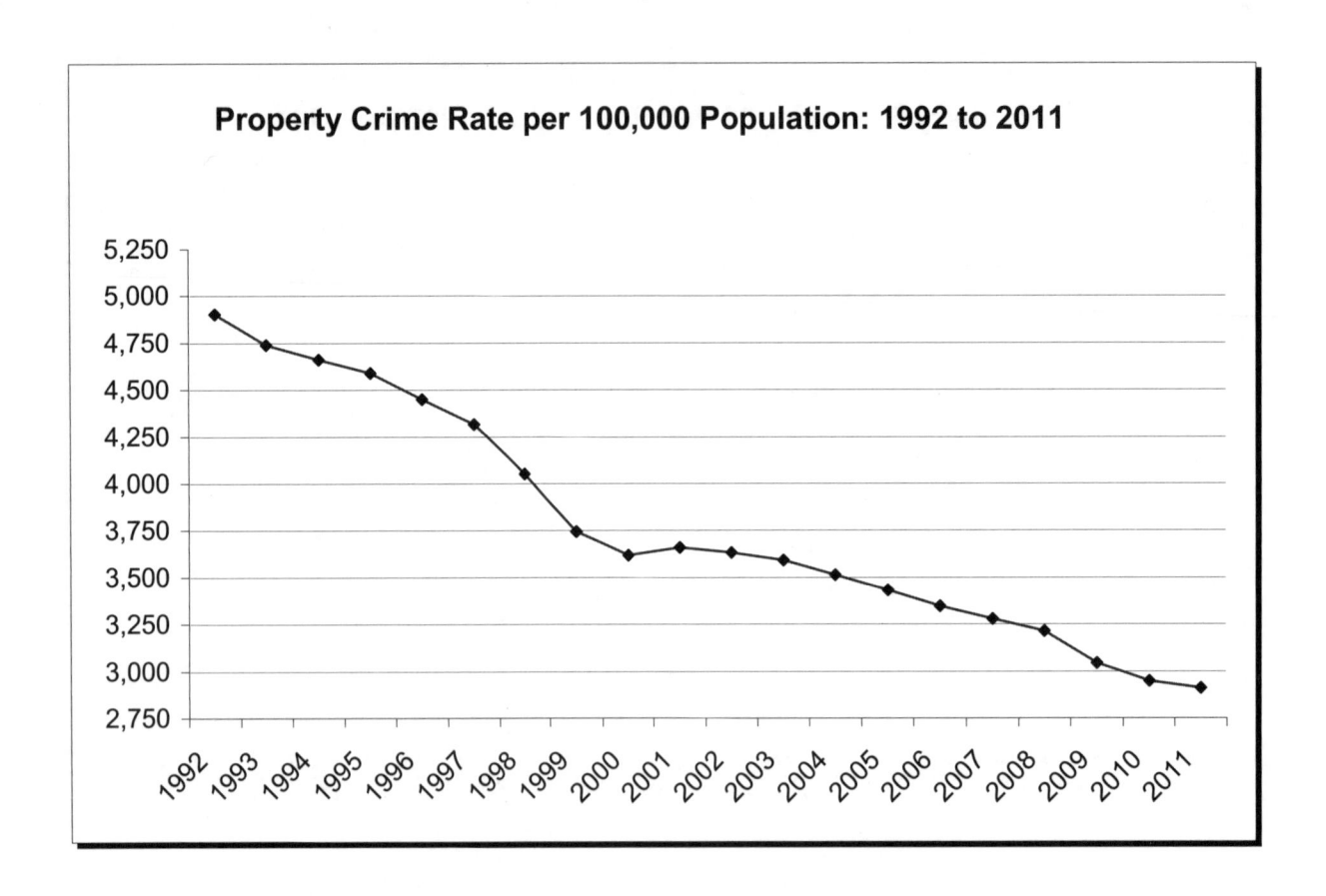

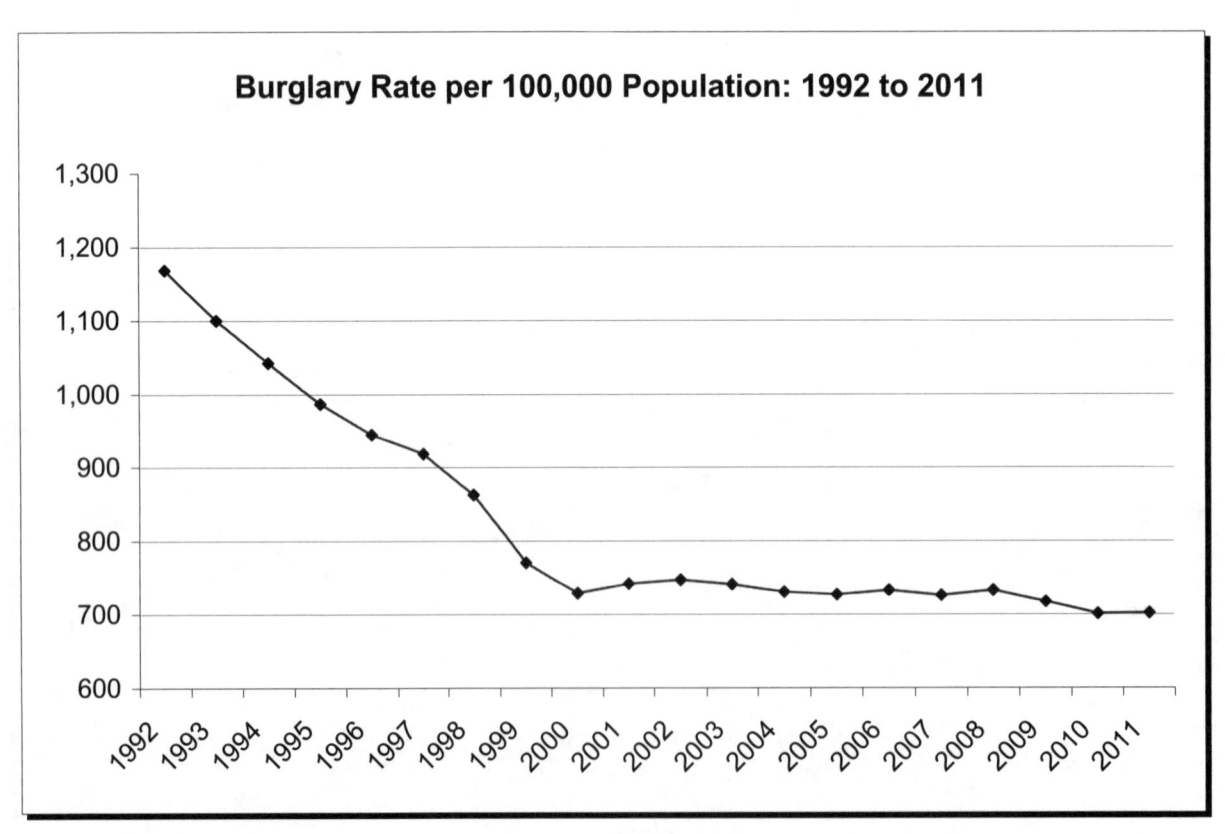

Larceny-Theft Rate per 100,000 Population: 1992 to 2011

Motor Vehicle Theft Rate per 100,000 Population: 1992 to 2011

Source: Reported data from the F.B.I.
"Crime in the United States 2011" (Uniform Crime Reports, October 29, 2012)

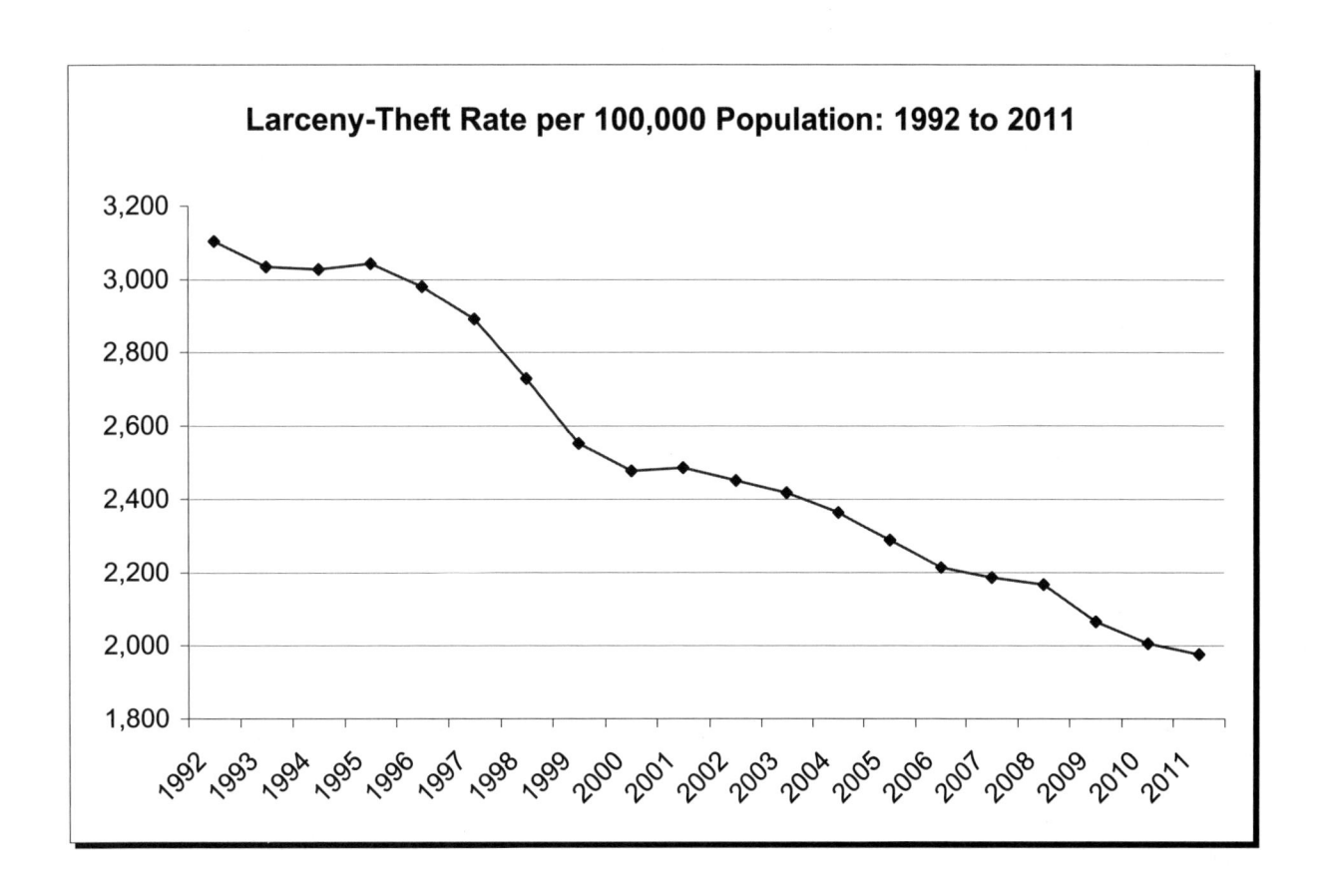

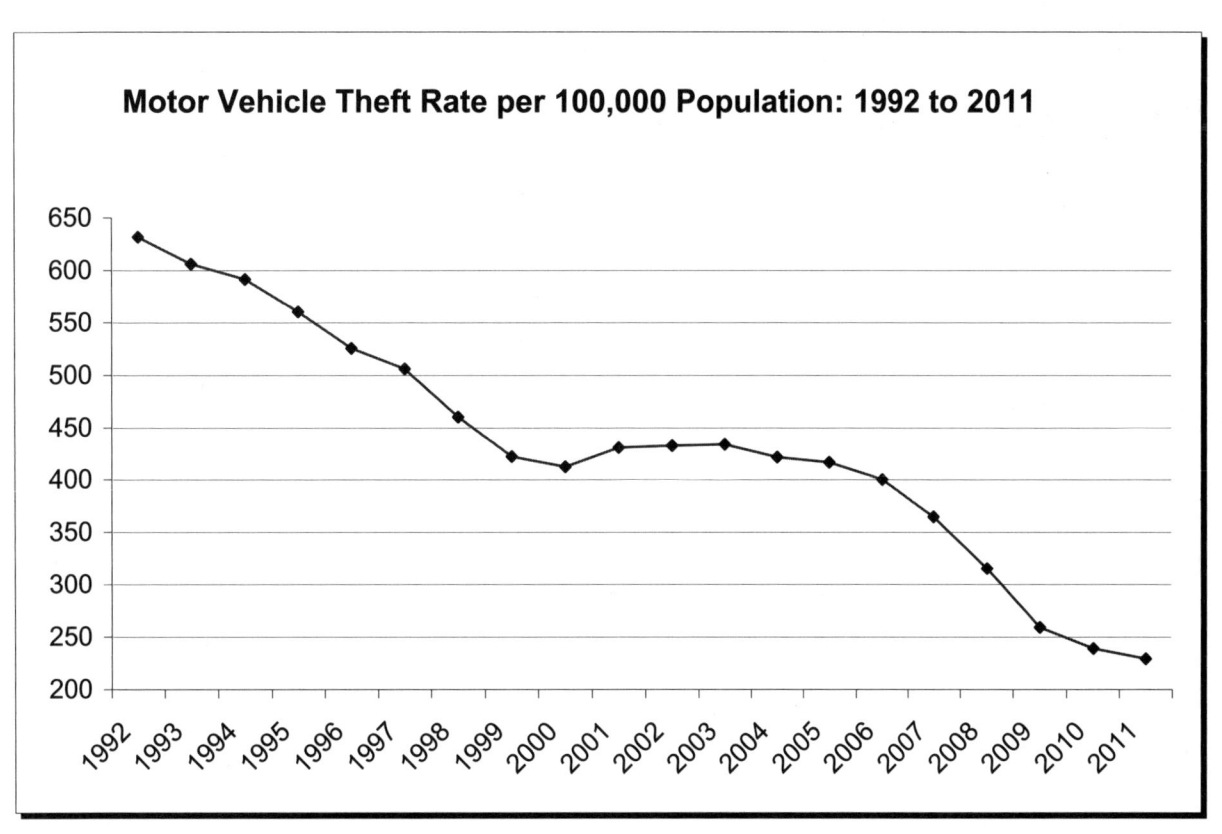

NATIONAL, METROPOLITAN, AND CITY CRIME STATISTICS SUMMARY: 2011

	NATIONAL	METRO*	CITY*
Population 2011	311,591,917	258,465,216	86,449,588
Police (Sworn Officers)	698,460		205,103
Rate of Police Officers (per 100,000 Population)	238		239
Crimes in 2011	10,266,737	8,981,219	3,845,229
Crime Rate in 2011 (per 100,000 Population)	3,295.0	3,474.8	4,447.9
Percent Change in Crime Rate: 2010 to 2011	(1.7)	0.0	(0.2)
Percent Change in Crime Rate: 2007 to 2011	(12.1)	(11.4)	(14.5)
Violent Crimes in 2011	1,203,564	1,107,026	568,964
Violent Crime Rate in 2011 (per 100,000 Population)	386.3	428.3	658.1
Percent Change in Violent Crime Rate: 2010 to 2011	(4.5)	0.0	(1.5)
Percent Change in Violent Crime Rate: 2007 to 2011	(18.1)	(15.0)	(18.3)
Murders in 2011	14,612	13,050	7,439
Murder Rate in 2011 (per 100,000 Population)	4.7	5.0	8.6
Percent Change in Murder Rate: 2010 to 2011	(1.5)	0.0	1.2
Percent Change in Murder Rate: 2007 to 2011	(17.4)	(18.0)	(18.9)
Rapes in 2011	83,425	69,746	28,047
Rape Rate in 2011 (per 100,000 Population)	26.8	27.0	32.4
Percent Change in Rape Rate: 2010 to 2011	(3.2)	0.0	0.9
Percent Change in Rape Rate: 2007 to 2011	(12.4)	(9.7)	(8.5)
Robberies in 2011	354,396	351,558	213,206
Robbery Rate in 2011 (per 100,000 Population)	113.7	136.0	246.6
Percent Change in Robbery Rate: 2010 to 2011	(4.7)	0.0	(1.2)
Percent Change in Robbery Rate: 2007 to 2011	(23.3)	(20.2)	(23.4)
Aggravated Assaults in 2011	751,131	672,672	320,272
Aggravated Assault Rate in 2011 (per 100,000 Population)	241.1	260.3	370.5
Percent Change in Aggravated Assault Rate: 2010 to 2011	(4.6)	0.0	(1.9)
Percent Change in Aggravated Assault Rate: 2007 to 2011	(16.1)	(12.5)	(15.4)
Property Crimes in 2011	9,063,173	7,874,193	3,276,265
Property Crime Rate in 2011 (per 100,000 Population)	2,908.7	3,046.5	3,789.8
Percent Change in Property Crime Rate: 2010 to 2011	(1.3)	0.0	0.0
Percent Change in Property Crime Rate: 2007 to 2011	(11.2)	(10.8)	(13.8)
Burglaries in 2011	2,188,005	1,826,166	786,504
Burglary Rate in 2011 (per 100,000 Population)	702.2	706.5	909.8
Percent Change in Burglary Rate: 2010 to 2011	0.2	0.0	1.9
Percent Change in Burglary Rate: 2007 to 2011	(3.3)	(4.6)	(3.9)
Larceny-Thefts in 2011	6,159,795	5,369,510	2,134,209
Larceny-Theft Rate in 2011 (per 100,000 Population)	1,976.9	2,077.5	2,468.7
Percent Change in Larceny-Theft Rate: 2010 to 2011	(1.4)	0.0	(0.4)
Percent Change in Larceny-Theft Rate: 2007 to 2011	(9.5)	(8.5)	(11.3)
Motor Vehicle Thefts in 2011	715,373	678,517	355,552
Motor Vehicle Theft Rate in 2011 (per 100,000 Population)	229.6	262.5	411.3
Percent Change in Motor Vehicle Theft Rate: 2010 to 2011	(4.0)	0.0	(1.5)
Percent Change in Motor Vehicle Theft Rate: 2007 to 2011	(37.1)	(35.4)	(38.2)

Source: CQ Press using reported data from the F.B.I.
"Crime in the United States 2011" (Uniform Crime Reports, October 29, 2012)
*Metro includes population and crime for all metropolitan statistical areas. City statistics are for cities of 100,000 or more in population.